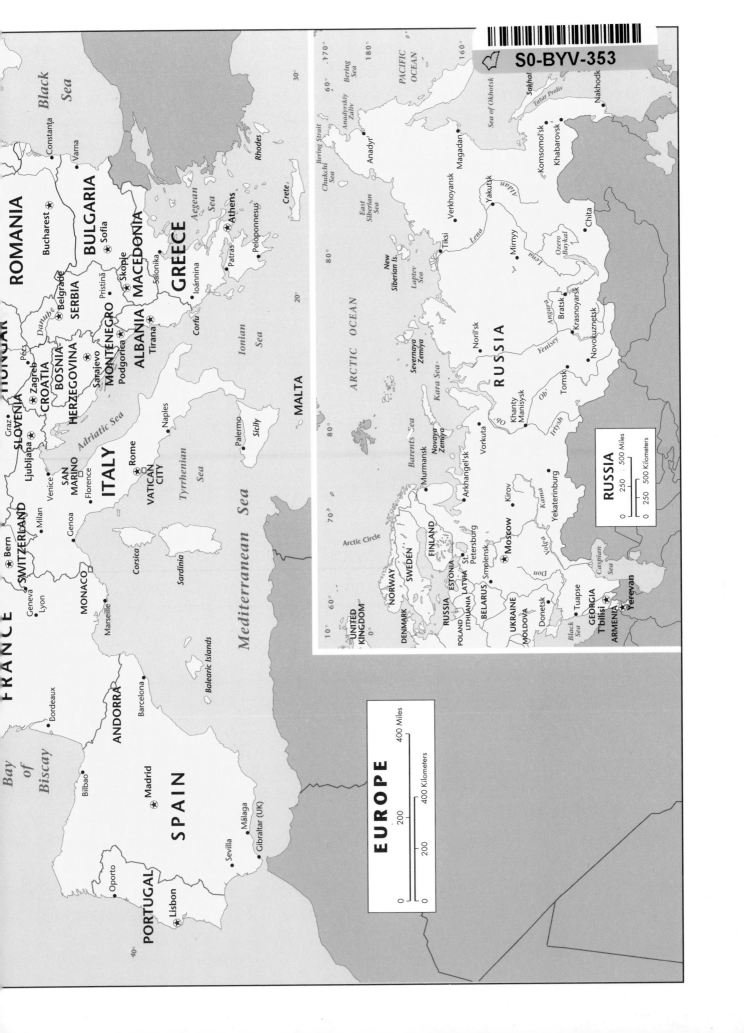

WORLDMARK
ENCYCLOPEDIA OF THE NATIONS

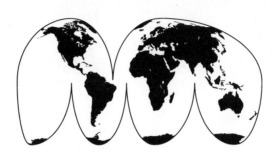

EUROPE

ISSN 1531-1635

WORLDMARK
ENCYCLOPEDIA OF THE NATIONS, TWELFTH EDITION

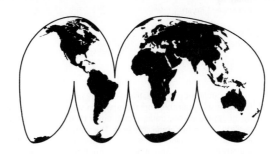

Volume 5
EUROPE

THOMSON
™
GALE

Detroit • New York • San Francisco • New Haven, Conn. • Waterville, Maine • London

THOMSON
GALE

Worldmark Encyclopedia of the Nations, Twelfth Edition
Timothy L. Gall and Jeneen M. Hobby, Editors

Project Editor
Mary Rose Bonk

Editorial
Jennifer Greve,
Kimberly Lewis,
Kate Potthoff

Imaging
Christine O'Bryan

Product Design
Pamela Galbreath

Manufacturing
Rita Wimberly

ISBN 1-4144-1089-1 (set)
ISBN 1-4144-1090-5 (v.1)
ISBN 1-4144-1091-3 (v.2)
ISBN 1-4144-1092-1 (v.3)
ISBN 1-4144-1093-X (v.4)
ISBN 1-4144-1094-8 (v.5)
ISSN 1531-1635 (set)

This title is also available as an e-book
ISBN 1-4144-1113-8
Contact your Gale sales representative for ordering information.

Printed in the United States of America
10 9 8 7 6 5 4 3

CONTENTS

For Conversion Tables, Abbreviations and Acronyms, Glossaries, World Tables, notes to previous editions, and other supplementary materials, see Volume 1.

READER'S GUIDE

GENERAL NOTE: The Twelfth Edition of *Worldmark Encyclopedia of the Nations* (WEN) is comprised of five volumes. Volume 1 is dedicated to the United Nations and its related agencies. Volumes 2 through 5, "Africa," "Americas," "Asia and Oceania," and "Europe," contain entries on the countries of the world.

Reflecting the ever-changing status of the world geopolitical situation, the Twelfth Edition includes entries for 194 countries, one more than the previous edition. This reflects the 2006 decision of Montenegro to dissolve its relationship with Serbia to become an independent nation in its own right. Seven entries describe dependencies. This edition no longer includes volume 6, which was entitled *World Leaders.*

Some notable changes in previous editions include the Eleventh Edition's inclusion of an entry on East Timor, coverage of the aftermath of the terrorist attacks of 11 September 2001, and the expansion of the European Union and the North Atlantic Treaty Organization (NATO). Changes in the Tenth Edition included recording of the change in status for Macau; as of December 1999 Macau came under Chinese authority, and thus Macau was incorporated into the China entry (previously it was described under Portuguese Asian Dependency). Similarly, the entry for United Kingdom Asian Dependency (Hong Kong) was eliminated with the Ninth Edition; as of 1997 Hong Kong came under Chinese authority and, like Macau, is described in that country's entry. Also with the Tenth Edition, the introduction of the euro as currency in the nations of the European Union was noted. The Eighth Edition of this encyclopedia (1995) reported on the dramatic changes in the world in the early 1990s, including the dissolution of the USSR, Czechoslovakia, and Yugoslavia; the unification of Germany; the unification of Yemen; and the independence of Eritrea. These changes resulted in twenty-five new country articles. Whereas the First Edition of the *Worldmark Encyclopedia of the Nations,* in one volume, contained 119 articles, the present Twelfth Edition now contains 201.

In compiling data for incorporation into the *Worldmark Encyclopedia of the Nations,* substantial efforts were made to enlist the assistance of the government of every nation in the world, as well as of all pertinent UN agencies, who cooperated by supplying data and by revising and updating materials relevant to their sphere of interest. Material received from official sources was reviewed and critically assessed by the editors as part of the process of incorporation. Materials and publications of the UN family and of intergovernmental and nongovernmental organizations throughout the world provided a major fund of geographic, demographic, economic, and social data.

In compiling historical, economic, and political data, primary materials generated by governments and international agencies were supplemented by data gathered from numerous other sources including newspapers (most notably *The European,* the *Financial Times,* the *New York Times,* and the *Wall Street Journal*); periodicals (most notably *Current History, Elections Today, The Economist,* the *Far Eastern Economic Review, Foreign Affairs,* and *World Press Review*); and thousands of World Wide Web sites hosted by government agencies and embassies.

The reader's attention is directed to the Glossary of Special Terms for explanations of key terms and concepts essential to a fuller understanding of the text.

COUNTRY NAMES: Country names are reported (as appropriate) in three forms: the short-form name (generally conformed to the U.S. Central Intelligence Agency's *World Factbook 2006*), as commonly used in the text; the English version of the official name (generally conformed to the United Nations list of country names); and the official name in the national language(s). When necessary, textual usages of some short-form names have been rectified, usually through the substitution of an acronym for the official name, in order to strike a better balance between official usages and universal terminology. Thus the following short-form names have been adopted throughout (except in historical context to preserve accuracy): DROC (Democratic Republic of the Congo—known as Zaire prior to the Ninth Edition); ROC (Republic of the Congo); FRG (Federal Republic of Germany); North Korea: DPRK (Democratic People's Republic of Korea); and South Korea: ROK (Republic of Korea). In addition, Vietnam has replaced Viet Nam to reflect common usage.

MAPS: Spellings on the individual country maps reflect national usages and recognized transliteration practice. To clarify national boundaries and landforms, dark shading has been applied to waters, and lighter shading to lands not within that nation's jurisdiction. Cross-hatching has been used to designate certain disputed areas. Rivers that run dry during certain times of the year are indicated by dashed instead of solid lines.

FLAGS AND NATIONAL EMBLEMS: All depictions of flags, flag designations, and national emblems have been reviewed and, where necessary, corrected or changed to reflect their official usage as of 2006. In general, the term "national flag" denotes the civil flag of the nation.

CURRENCY: In most cases, currency conversion factors cited in the Twelfth Edition are as of the first quarter of 2006.

WEIGHTS AND MEASURES: The general world trend toward adoption of the metric system is acknowledged through the use of metric units and their nonmetric (customary or imperial) equivalents throughout the text. The two exceptions to this practice involve territorial sea limits, which are reported in nautical miles, and various production data, for which (unless otherwise stated) units of measure reflect the system in use by the country in question. All tons are metric tons (again, unless otherwise indicated), reflecting the practice of the UN in its statistical reporting.

HOLIDAYS: Except where noted, all holidays listed are official public holidays, on which government offices are closed that would normally be open. Transliterations of names of Muslim holidays have been standardized. For a fuller discussion on these points, and for a description of religious holidays and their origins and meanings, see the Glossary of Religious Holidays in this volume.

GEOGRAPHIC INFORMATION: To update the sections on Location, Size, and Extent; Topography, Climate, Flora and Fauna, and Environment, the following print publications (and their publishers) were used: *Geo-Data: The World Geographical Encyclopedia* (Gale Group), *World Development Indicators 2005* (The World Bank), and *World Resources* (Oxford University Press). Additional data was acquired from these websites: Library of Congress, *Country Studies: Country Profiles* (http://lcweb2.loc.gov/frd/cs/profiles.html); *Ramsar Convention on Wetlands* (http://www.ramsar.org); *UNESCO World Heritage Centre* (http://www.whc.unesco.org); *United Nations Environment Programme* (http://www.unep.org); *Weather Channel: Averages and Records* (http://www.weather.com/common/home/climatology.html); *World Conservation Union: Species Survival Commission* (http://www.iucn.org/themes/ssc); *World Factbook 2006* (https://www.cia.gov/cia/publications/factbook).

POPULATION DATA: Data for the four rubrics describing population (Population, Migration, Ethnic Groups, Languages) were compiled from numerous publications of the U.S. Department of State, the World Bank, the United Nations, and the Organization for Economic Co-Operation and Development (OECD), specifically its publication *Trends in International Migration*. Also consulted were *The State of the World's Refugees* (Oxford University Press) and *International Committee of the Red Cross Annual Report* (International Committee of the Red Cross)

RELIGIONS: Data for this section were compiled in large part from the *2005 International Religious Freedom Report* released by the Bureau of Democracy, Human Rights, and Labor, U.S. Department of State. This is an annual report to Congress compiled in compliance with Section 102(b) of the International Religious Freedom Act (IRFA) of 1998. The *2005 Report* covers the period from 1 July 2004 to 30 June 2005 and includes the work of hundreds of State Department, Foreign Service, and other U.S. government employees. The authors gathered information throughout this period from a variety of sources, including government and religious officials, nongovernmental organizations, journalists, human rights monitors, religious groups, and academics.

TRANSPORTATION: Sources consulted for updated information on transportation include publications of the American Automobile Manufacturers Association, the International Road Transport Union, specifically its publication *World Transport Data,* and the *World Factbook 2006.*

HISTORY: In writing the History rubric, a variety of news and background information sources on each country were used. Full country profiles—including information on the history, economy, political institutions, and foreign relations on most nations of the world—are provided by the U.S. Library of Congress and by the U.S. Department of State; similar formats are published by the *BBC News International* version and *The Economist*'s Country Briefings feature. In consulting news sources for up-to-date information on events, only reported facts (not editorials) were used. The *New York Times* and the *Washington Post* are more comprehensive than the *Wall Street Journal*, whose focus is placed on financial and business news. While the website of the United Nations was used extensively in compiling Volume 1 "United Nations," of the *Worldmark Encyclopedia of the Nations,* its coverage of such problems as politics in the Middle East and global terrorism pertained to and supported the updating of history rubrics of a number of countries. Other organizations that publish journals or studies on global current events, foreign policy, international relations, and human rights include Amnesty International; Human Rights Watch; *Foreign Affairs*, published by the Council on Foreign Relations; and *Great Decisions*, published by the Foreign Policy Association. In addition, the official websites of each nation were consulted critically for information that could be gleaned from a state's view of its own history and place in the world.

GOVERNMENT: The Government rubric is constructed by outlining the institutions of government as they were formed throughout a nation's modern history, up to those existing under the present constitution. *Countries of the World and Their Leaders Yearbook 2006* (Thomson Gale) outlines the form of government and provides information on political conditions.

The U.S. Library of Congress and the U.S. Department of State chronicle constitutional changes and also provide information on the form of government. Electionworld and the *World Factbook 2006* provide information on officeholders in place at the time of publication. The *BBC News International* "Country Profiles" cover current leaders and their political parties, and *The Economist* is comprehensive in its coverage of political structures and political forces in place and at work in the nations it profiles. The official government websites of individual nations were also consulted.

POLITICAL PARTIES: *Countries of the World and Their Leaders Yearbook 2006* not only lists the political parties present in each nation, but provides additional information on the political parties in its "History" and "Government and Political Conditions" sections. *The Economist* also has sections in its country briefings labeled "political structure" and "political forces," which describe the political climate of each nation the magazine profiles. In addition, *The Economist* provides a brief history of the nation, which often includes the history of political parties. Editors reviewed the profiles of selected nations prepared by the U.S. Library of Congress, which include comprehensive coverage of politics and political parties. The *World Factbook 2006* was consulted for a list of political parties, and often, their leaders. The website, Electionworld.org, describes the major political parties and their leaders, and also lists minor and defunct parties. Political Resources on the Net, a website, compiles links to a variety of sites useful to the researcher with a critical eye.

LOCAL GOVERNMENT: *Countries of the World and Their Leaders Yearbook 2006* lists the administrative subdivisions in each nation of the world; as does the U.S. State Department in its *Background Notes,* and the U.S. Central Intelligence Agency in its *World Factbook 2006.* *The Economist* was consulted for a description of regional legislatures. The U.S. Library of Congress "Country Profiles" briefings describe administrative divisions and provincial and local government.

JUDICIAL SYSTEM: *Countries of the World and Their Leaders Yearbook 2006, Background Notes,* and the *World Factbook 2006* all provided basic information on each nation's judicial system. *The Economist* was consulted for a description of the legal systems of each nation it profiles. The U.S. Library of Congress "Country Profiles" briefings provided more in-depth detail about judicial power and structure in the nations it profiles. Jurist, a web-based legal news and real-time legal research service based out of the University of Pittsburgh School of Law in Pittsburgh, Pennsylvania, was consulted as well for concise information on each nation it profiles.

ARMED FORCES: Statistical data on armed forces was compiled from the *World Factbook 2006,* *The Military Balance* (The International Institute for Strategic Studies), the *SIPRI Yearbook* (Stockholm International Peace Research Institute), and other print and online sources including *Current World Nuclear Arsenals* maintained by the Center for Defense Information.

INTERNATIONAL COOPERATION: This section was updated using data provided by news agencies and the following websites: *World Factbook 2006* (https://www.cia.gov/cia/publications/factbook) and *Background Notes* (http://www.state.gov/r/pa/ei/bgn).

ECONOMY: In addition to numerous official online sources, data on the economies of the world were compiled from the most recent editions of the following U.S. government publications: *National Trade Estimate on Foreign Trade Barriers, Country Commercial Guides,* and *Economic Policy and Trade Practices.* *The Economist* was consulted for detailed information on economic structures and select indicators in its "Country Profiles" archive; it also included economic and political forecasts for the nations it profiled. The U.S. Library of Congress "Country Profiles" provided a brief historical overview of the economies of the countries it profiled, in addition to detailing the current state of various sectors of those economies. *The Index of Economic Freedom* (Heritage Foundation) was also consulted for its measurement of independent variables into broad factors of economic freedom.

INCOME: Statistics on national income were obtained from sources published by the United Nations, The World Bank, and the U.S. Central Intelligence Agency (CIA). CIA figures are for gross domestic product (GDP), defined as the value of all final goods and services produced within a nation in a given year. In most cases, CIA figures are given in purchasing power parity terms.

LABOR: Labor statistics were compiled from *World Employment* and *Yearbook of Labour Statistics* (International Labour Office—ILO) and the ILO's website *Child Labor Statistics by Country* (http://www.ilo.org/public/english/standards/ipec/simpoc/countries.htm); the World Bank publication *World Development Indicators 2004;* and the U.S. State Department's *Human Rights Reports 2005.*

AGRICULTURE, FISHING AND FORESTRY: In addition to government sources, statistical data for these sections was compiled from the following yearbooks published by the Food and Agriculture Organization of the United Nations: *Trade; Fishery Statistics: Commodities; Fisheries; Production; Agriculture;* and *Forest Products.*

MINING: Data on mining and minerals production came from various online sources and from statistics compiled by the Minerals Information office of the U.S. Geological Survey, U.S. Department of the Interior, including Volume III of the *Minerals Yearbook.* This volume of the *Minerals Yearbook* is published both electronically on the Internet and in various print formats available from the U.S. Government Printing Office Superintendent of Documents. The *Yearbook* provides an annual review of mineral production and trade and of mineral-related government and industry developments in more than 175 countries.

ENERGY AND POWER: Key sources consulted include *Country Analysis Briefs* (U.S. Energy Information Administration, U.S. Department of Energy), *Key World Energy Statistics* (International Energy Agency), and *World Development Indicators* (The World Bank).

INDUSTRY : The primary source material for the Industry rubric was the U.S. State Department's *Country Commercial Guides,* which provide a comprehensive look at countries' commercial environments, using economic, political, and market analysis. *Background Notes* were consulted for the information on the industrial history and climate of each country profiled. Also useful was information contained in the "Country Profiles" published by the U.S. Library of Congress. The *World Factbook 2006* provides a list of key economic indicators. *The Economist* and, to a lesser extent, *BBC News* were useful in providing background material for the Industry rubric.

SCIENCE AND TECHNOLOGY: The following print sources were consulted: *The Nature Yearbook of Science and Technology* (Palgrave Macmillan Publishers Ltd.); *NIRA's World Directory of Think Tanks* (National Institute for Research Advancement); in addition, the following websites were accessed: *International Science and Technology Activity* (maintained by Industry Canada, Government of Canada); *Economics Departments, Institutes, and Research Centers in the World* (maintained by the Department of Economics, University of Connecticut); *Science and Technology Statistics* (maintained by UNESCO Institute for Statistics); *World Development Indicators* (maintained by The World Bank); and *Annual Statistics* (patent and trademark information, maintained by the World Intellectual Property Organization).

DOMESTIC TRADE: Source material for the Domestic Trade rubric came from the U.S. State Department's *Country Commercial Guides, Background Notes,* and the United Nations publication, *International Trade Statistics Yearbook.* Also used was information contained in the "Country Profiles" published by the U.S. Library of Congress. *The Economist* and, to a lesser extent, the *BBC* were consulted in providing background material for the Domestic Trade rubric. The World Bank's service "Doing Business" database and the U.S. Commercial Service's "Buy USA" website were consulted for information on conducting business in a nation, which included business hours and business regulations. Finally, most nations' government websites provided information on domestic trade.

FOREIGN TRADE: Sources consulted included *2005 International Trade Statistics Yearbook* (Department of Economic and Social Affairs, Statistics Division, United Nations) and *Direction of Trade Statistics* (Real Sector Division, IMF Statistics Department, International Monetary Fund). The U.S. Department of State's *Country Commercial Guides* and *Background Notes* were also used. *The Economist* and the *World Factbook 2006* were consulted in listing import and export partners and key products traded. Various UN bodies—such as UNCTAD and UNESCO—provided up-to-date trade statistics.

BALANCE OF PAYMENTS: Balance of payments tables were computed from the International Monetary Fund's *Balance of Payments Statistics Yearbook.* In some cases, totals are provided even though not all components of those totals have been reported by the government of the country. Accordingly, in some instances numbers in the columns may not add to the total. Supplementing the IMF's *Balance of Payments Statistics Yearbook* were *The Economist's* "Country Briefings," the *World Factbook 2006,* and information taken from the U.S. State Department, in particular, the *Country Commercial Guides.* "Country Profiles" from the U.S. Library of Congress were also used. Also consulted was the United Nations publication *National Accounts Statistics: Main Aggregates and Detailed Tables.*

BANKING AND SECURITIES: Statistical data on securities listings and market activity was compiled in part from *Emerging Stock Markets Factbook, 2005* (Standard and Poor's) as well as from the websites *Country*

Forecasts (www.countrywatch.com) and *International Banking Statistics* (www.bis.org/statistics/bankstats.htm). Various websites specific to the individual countries of the world were also consulted.

INSURANCE: Primary sources for information on insurance include the online resources of the Insurance Information Institute, Rowbotham and Co. LLP., PricewaterhouseCoopers, the Swiss Reinsurance-Company, and J. Zakhour & Co., as well as numerous national websites dealing with insurance.

PUBLIC FINANCE: In addition to official government websites, analytical reports from the U.S. Department of Commerce, and news reports, the following publications were consulted for standardized statistical data: *World Factbook 2006, International Financial Statistics Yearbook, 2002* (International Monetary Fund), and *Government Finance Statistics Yearbook, 2002* (International Monetary Fund).

TAXATION: Information on Taxation was compiled from country data sheets published by international accounting firms (Deloitte and Ernst & Young). Addition information was obtained from the U.S. Commerce Department and the government websites of the countries of the world.

CUSTOMS AND DUTIES: Information on Customs and Duties was compiled from country data sheets published by the accounting firms of Deloitte and Ernst & Young. Additional information was obtained from the U.S. Commerce Department, the World Trade Organization and the government website of the countries of the world.

FOREIGN INVESTMENT: Source material for the Foreign Investment rubric included the U.S. State Department's *Country Commercial Guides*, which provided a comprehensive analysis of the foreign direct investment environments of the countries of the world, as did the World Bank publication, *A Better Investment Climate for Everyone*. The International Monetary Fund's publications *International Financial Statistics Yearbook* and *Balance of Payments Statistics Yearbook*, and the U.S. State Department's *Background Notes* were consulted for the information on foreign direct investment. Also used was information contained in the "Country Profiles" published by the U.S. Library of Congress. *The Economist* was consulted in providing basic FDI figures and other relevant data.

ECONOMIC DEVELOPMENT: Source material for the Economic Development rubric included the U.S. State Department's *Country Commercial Guides* and *Background Notes*. *The Economist* was consulted for economic and political forecasts for selected nations. The U.S. Library of Congress "Country Profiles" provided a brief historical overview of the economies of the countries profiled, in addition to detailing the current state of various sectors of those economies. The *Index of Economic Freedom* was also consulted for its broad description of economic freedom and development. Information on foreign aid was taken from the print publications and websites of the International Monetary Fund, World Bank, and the United States Agency for International Development (USAID).

SOCIAL DEVELOPMENT: Publications consulted in the preparation of this rubric include *2005 Country Reports on Human Rights Practice* (http://www.state.gov/g/drl/rls/hrrpt/2005/index.htm), *International Save the Children Alliance Annual Report 2004* (Cambridge House), *The State of the World's Children* (Oxford University Press), and the *World Development Report* (Oxford University Press). Additional information was obtained from country-specific websites and general news publications.

HEALTH: Statistical sources consulted include *Country Health Briefing Papers* (a series of reports produced by IHSD Limited and DFID Health Systems Resource Centre for the United Kingdom Department for International Development); *Health Care Systems in Transition* (European Observatory on Health Care Systems, World Health Organization Regional Office for Europe); *Health in the Americas*, Volume II (Pan American Health Organization, World Health Organization) as well as numerous websites on the individual nations of the world. In addition, country-specific health profiles published by the World Health Organization and the World Bank were consulted.

HOUSING: The latest government population and housing census information available was used for each country through access of official government websites. Also of use was the World Bank publication *World Development Indicators 2005*. Topics accessed on the World Bank's website included *Countries and Regions, Urban Development*, and *Housing and Land*. Other websites consulted included Habitat for Humanity (http://www.habitat.org), United Nations Human Settlements Programme (http://unhabitat.org) and the U.S. Agency for International Development (USAID—http://www.usaid.gov). USAID topics accessed included *Locations* and *Urban Programs*).

EDUCATION: Data on Education was obtained from various UNESCO publications including *World Education Report, Global Education Digest, Education for All Global Monitoring Report 2005,* and the UNESCO *Statistical Yearbook*. Also consulted was *EdStats* compiled by the World Bank (http://devdata.worldbank.org/edstats/), the *World Factbook 2006* (https://www.cia.gov/cia/publications/factbook), the UNESCO website's *Country and Regional Profiles* (http://www.uis.unesco.org/profiles/), and *World Data on Education* (International Bureau of Education).

LIBRARIES AND MUSEUMS: Some information concerning libraries and museums was accessed through official government websites of various countries when links were available to tourism, education, and/or cultural ministries or departments. In addition, the following websites were consulted: American Library Association (http://www.ala.org); International Federation of Library Associations and Institutions (http://www.ifla.org); Museums of the World (http://www.museum.com); and United Nations Educational, Scientific, and Cultural Organization (http://www.unesco.org).

MEDIA: Primary sources for this section include the annual *Editor & Publisher* publication *International Year Book*, online data provided by UNESCO, and the media sections of the "Country Profiles" featured on the website of *BBC News*. The UNESCO profiles provide key statistics and indicators on education, science and technology, and culture and communication. In addition, government and other websites related to the countries of the world were consulted. Additional sources consulted include the publications *World Development Indicators 2005* (World Bank), *World Media Handbook* (United Nations), *World Factbook 2006*, and *2005 Country Reports on Human Rights Practices*.

ORGANIZATIONS: Lists of member countries were obtained through the official websites of a variety of prominent international organizations and associations, such as the International Federation of Red Cross and Red Crescent Societies, Amnesty International, Kiwanis International, the World Alliance of YMCAs, the World Organization of the Scout Movement, etc. *Associations Unlimited* (Thomson Gale) was also consulted.

TOURISM, TRAVEL, AND RECREATION: Statistical sources consulted include *Yearbook of Tourism Statistics* and *Compendium of Tourism Statistics*, both published by the World Tourism Organization. Tourism websites of the individual countries were also consulted, as well as the United Nations publication *Schedule of Daily Substinence Allowance Rates* and the U.S. Department of State per diem travel allowances published online at www.state.gov/r/pa/ei/bgn.

FAMOUS PERSONS: Entries are based on information available through March 2006. Where a person noted in one country is known to have been born in another, the country (or, in some cases, city) of birth follows the personal name in parentheses.

DEPENDENCIES: Source material for the Dependencies rubric was taken from *Background Notes* and from the website of the United Nations. The Library of Congress's "Country Profiles" archive provided up-to-date information on dependencies. *The Economist* and the website of *BBC News* were also consulted, as was *Countries of the World and Their Leaders Yearbook 2006*.

BIBLIOGRAPHY: Bibliographical listings at the end of country articles are provided as a guide to further reading on the country in question and are not intended as a comprehensive listing of references used in research for the article. Effort was made to provide a broad sampling of works on major subjects and topics as covered by the article; the bibliographies provide, wherever possible, introductory and general works for use by students and general readers, as well as classical studies, recent contributions, and other works regarded as seminal by area specialists. The country article bibliographies were supplemented with information obtained from a search conducted in July 2006. An extensive bibliography listing key references related to the facts in this encyclopedia follows. However, it is not a complete listing since many fact sheets, brochures, World Wide Websites, and other informational materials were not included due to space limitations.

PRINT PUBLICATIONS CONSULTED

African Development Indicators. Washington, D.C.: The World Bank, 1996.

Asia and the Pacific...A Tax Tour, Chicago: Arthur Anderson & Co., 1986.

Balance of Payments Statistics Yearbook. Washington, D.C.: International Monetary Fund, 2004.

A Better Investment Climate for Everyone. Washington, D.C.: World Bank, 2005.

BP Statistical Review of World Energy. London: BP Exploration Operating Company Ltd, June 2005.

Caribbean Basin...a Tax Tour, Chicago: Arthur Anderson & Co., 1985.

Central Intelligence Agency. *World Factbook 2006.* Washington, D.C.: U.S. Government Printing Office, 2006.

Compendium of Tourism Statistics (1999–2003), Madrid: World Tourism Organization, 2005.

Direction of Trade Statistics. Washington, D.C.: International Monetary Fund, quarterly.

Editor & Publisher International Yearbook, New York: Editor & Publisher, 2005.

Ellicott, Karen. *Countries of the World and Their Leaders Yearbook 2006.* Farmington Hills: Thomson Gale, 2005.

Emerging Stock Markets Factbook 2000. Washington, D.C.: International Finance Corporation, 2002.

Entering the 21st Century: World Development Report 1999/2000. New York: Oxford University Press, 2000.

Food and Agriculture Organization of the United Nations. *FAO Statistical Yearbook.* New York: United Nations, 2004.

————. *FAO Yearbook: Fishery Statistics.* New York: United Nations, 2002.

————. *FAO Yearbook: Forest Products.* New York: United Nations, 1999.

————. *FAO Yearbook: Production.* New York: United Nations, 1995.

————. *FAO Yearbook: Trade.* New York: United Nations, 1999.

Global Development Finance. Washington, D.C.: The World Bank, 2005.

Global Education Digest. Montreal: UNESCO Publishing, 2005.

Government Finance Statistics Yearbook. Washington, D.C.: International Monetary Fund, 2002.

Handbook of International Trade and Developmental Statistics. New York: United Nations, 1995.

Handbook of Statistics. New York: United Nations, 2005.

Health in the Americas. Washington, D.C.: World Health Organization, 2002.

Historical Statistics 1960-1993. Paris: Organization for Economic Co-Operation and Development, 1995.

Insurance in the Arab World: Facts and Figures. Beirut: J. Zakhour & Co., undated.

International Committee of the Red Cross. *ICRC Annual Report 2005.* Geneva: ICRC Publications, 2006.

International Financial Statistics Yearbook. Washington, D.C.: International Monetary Fund, 2004.

International Institute for Strategic Studies. *The Military Balance 2003/2004.* London: Oxford University Press, 2004.

International Save the Children Alliance Annual Report 2004, London: Cambridge House, 2005.

International Trade Statistics Yearbook. New York: United Nations, 2003.

Insurance in the Arab World: Facts and Figures. Beirut: J. Zakhour & Co., undated.

The International Insurance Fact Book, New York: Insurance Information Institute, 2005.

Key World Energy Statistics. Paris: International Energy Agency, 2005.

Little Data Book. Washington, D.C.: The World Bank, 2000.

Making Decisions on Public Health: A Review of Eight Countries. Geneva: World Health Organization, 2004.

McCoy, John F., ed. *Geo-Data: The World Geographical Encyclopedia, 3rd ed.* Farmington Hills, MI: Gale Group, 2003.

McDevitt, Thomas M. *World Population Profile.* Washington, D.C.: U.S. Government Printing Office, 1996.

National Accounts for OECD Countries, Main Aggregates, Volume I, 1993–2004. Paris: Organization for Economic Cooperation and Development, 2006.

National Accounts Statistics: Main Aggregates and Detailed Tables. New York: United Nations, 1993.

Nuclear Power Reactors in the World. Vienna: International Atomic Energy Agency, 1996.

Organization for Economic Co-operation and Development (OECD). *Economies at a Glance.* Paris: OECD, 1996.

————. *Revenue Statistics of OECD Member Countries 1965–1992.* Paris: OECD, 1993.

Population and Vital Statistics Report, January 2006. New York: United Nations, 2006.

Schedule of Daily Subsistence Allowance Rates. New York: United Nations, 1999.

Science & Engineering Indicators 1996. Washington, D.C.: National Science Foundation, 1996.

Sivard, Ruth Leger. *World Military and Social Expenditures.* Washington, D.C.: World Priorities, Inc., 1996.

Sources and Methods: Labour Statistics. Geneva: International Labour Office, 1996.

The State of the World's Children 1996. New York: Oxford University Press, 1996.

The State of the World's Refugees: The Challenge of Protection. New York: Penguin Books, 1993.

The State of the World's Refugees: In Search of Solutions. New York: Oxford University Press, 1995.

Stockholm International Peace Research Institute. *SIPRI Yearbook 2005: Armaments, Disarmament and International Security.* London: Oxford University Press, 2005.

Supplement to the 2002 Government Finance Statistics Yearbook, Washington, D.C.: International Monetary Fund, 2002.

Tax Guide to the Americas, Chicago: Arthur Anderson & Co., 1991.

Tourism Market Trends: Africa, Madrid: World Tourism Organization, 1999.

Tourism Market Trends: Americas, Madrid: World Tourism Organization, 1999.

Tourism Market Trends: East Asia & the Pacific, Madrid: World Tourism Organization, 1999.

Tourism Market Trends: Europe, Madrid: World Tourism Organization, 1999.

Tourism Market Trends: Middle East, Madrid: World Tourism Organization, 1999.

Tourism Market Trends: South Asia, Madrid: World Tourism Organization, 1999.

Trends in International Migration 2004. Paris: Organization for Economic Co-Operation and Development, 2005.

UNESCO. *Statistical Yearbook.* Lanham, Md.: UNESCO Publishing and Bernan Press, 1999.

U.S. Agency for International Development, Bureau for Management, Office of Budget. *U.S. Overseas Loans and Grants and Assistance from International Organizations (The Greenbook).* Washington, D.C.: U.S. Government Printing Office, 2004.

U.S. Department of the Interior, U.S. Geological Survey. *Mineral Industries of Africa and the Middle East.* Washington, D.C.: U.S. Government Printing Office, 2003.

———. *Mineral Industries of Asia and the Pacific.* Washington, D.C.: U.S. Government Printing Office, 2002.

———. *Mineral Industries of Europe and Central Eurasia.* Washington, D.C.: U.S. Government Printing Office, 2002.

———. *Mineral Industries of Latin America and Canada.* Washington, D.C.: U.S. Government Printing Office, 2003.

———. *Minerals Yearbook, Vol. III, International.* Washington, D.C.: U.S. Government Printing Office, 2003.

Working Time Laws: A Global Perspective. Geneva: International Labour Office, 2005.

World Bank Atlas. Washington, D.C.: The World Bank, 2004.

World Data on Education. Paris: International Bureau of Education, 2000.

World Development Indicators 2005. Washington D.C.: The World Bank, 2005.

World Development Report 1990: Poverty. New York: Oxford University Press, 1990.

World Development Report 1995: Workers in an Integrating World. New York: Oxford University Press, 1995.

World Development Report 1996: From Plan to Market. New York: Oxford University Press, 1996.

World Development Report 2003: Sustainable Development in a Dynamic World. Washington, D.C.: World Bank, 2003.

World Development Report 2006: Equity and Development. Washington, D.C.: World Bank, 2005.

World Education Report. Paris: UNESCO Publishing, 1998.

World Employment. Geneva: International Labour Office, 1995.

The World Health Report: Make Every Mother and Child Count. Geneva: World Health Organization, 2005.

World Health Statistics 2006. Geneva: World Health Organization, 2006.

World Insurance in 2002: High Premium Growth in Non-Life Insurance. Zurich: Swiss Reinsurance Company, 2002.

World Media Handbook. New York: United Nations, 1992–94.

World Migration Report. New York: United Nations, 2000.

World Motor Vehicle Data. Washington, D.C.: American Automobile Manufacturers Association, 1997.

World Population Projections to 2150. New York: United Nations, 1998.

World Population Prospects: 2004. New York: United Nations, 2005.

World Resources Institute; United Nations Environment Programme; United Nations Development Programme; World Bank. *World Resources 1998–99.* New York: Oxford University Press, 1998.

World Transport Data, Geneva: International Road Transport Union, 1985.

World Urbanization Prospects. New York: United Nations, 2004.

Worldwide Corporate Tax Guide. New York: Ernst & Young, 2005.

Yearbook of Labour Statistics 2005. Geneva: International Labour Office, 2005.

Yearbook of Tourism Statistics (1999–2003), Madrid: World Tourism Organization, 2005.

WEBSITES CONSULTED

In the course of preparing this twelfth edition hundreds of websites were consulted including the official website of each country of the world and those of various non-governmental organizations worldwide. Of special significance are the websites listed below. These sites were accessed in 2005 and 2006 for information relevant to the rubrics listed above.

American Library Association. http://www.ala.org

Amnesty International. http://www.amnesty.org/.

Asia Insurance Review. http://www.asiainsurancereview.com/home.asp

BBC News. *Country Profiles.* http://news.bbc.co.uk/2/hi/country_profiles/default.stm

Central Intelligence Agency. *The World Factbook, 2006.* http://www.cia.gov/cia/publications/factbook/index.html

Council on Foreign Relations. http://www.foreignaffairs.org/.

Country Forecasts. http://www.countrywatch.com

Country Overviews. http://www.developmentgateway.org.

The Economist. http://www.economist.com/countries/index.cfm.

Electionworld. http://www.electionworld.org.

Energy Information Administration. *Country Analysis Briefs, 2005.* http://www.eia.doe.gov/emeu/cabs/

Foreign Policy Association. http://www.fpa.org/.

Growth Competitiveness Index Rankings. http://www.weforum.org.

Habitat for Humanity. http://www.habitat.org

Human Rights Library. http:// www1.umn.edu

Human Rights Watch. http://www.hrw.org/.

Index of Economic Freedom. http://www.heritage.org.

Insurance Information Institute. *International Insurance Factbook 2005.* http://www.internationalinsurance.org/international/toc/

International Banking Statistics. http://www.bis.org/statistics/bankstats.htm

International Federation of Library Associations and Institutions. http://www.ifla.org

International Labour Organization, Bureau of Statistics. http://www.ilo.org/public/english/bureau/stat/index.htm

International Monetary Fund. http://www.imf.org/.

International Research Services. Insurance Services Network, Inc. *Country Profiles.* http://www.isn-inc.com/countries/

Jurist World Law. http://jurist.law.pitt.edu/world/index.htm.

Latin Business Chronicle. http://www.latinbusinesschronicle.com.

Minerals Information Office, U.S. Geological Survey, U.S. Department of the Interior. http://minerals.usgs.gov/minerals/pubs/country/

Museums of the World. http://www.museum.com

New York Times. http://www.nytimes.com/pages/world/index.html.

Patent Applications by Country. http://www.wipo.int/ipstats/en/statistics/patents/.

Permanent Missions to the United Nations. http://www.asiasource.org.

Political Resources on the Net. http://www.politicalresources.net.

PricewaterhouseCoopers. *European Insurance Digest March 2005.* http://www.pwc.com/extweb/pwcpublications.nsf/docid/e48ebe381887a5c885256fac004d16b5

Ramsar Convention on Wetlands. http://www.ramsar.org.

Rowbotham and Co. LLP. *Country Profiles.* http://www.rowbotham.com/countrypage.htm

TradePort. http://www.tradeport.org.

United Nations. http://www.un.org/.

United Nations Conference on Trade and Development (UNCTAD). *UNCTAD Global Surveys: Foreign Direct Investment Prospects Promising for 2005-2008.* http://www.unctad.org.

United Nations Educational, Scientific, and Cultural Organization (UNESCO). http://www.unesco.org.

———. *Education for All Global Monitoring Report 2005.* http://www.efareport.unesco.org/

———. Statistics on Research and Development. http://www.uis.unesco.org.

———. World Heritage Centre. http://www.whc.unesco.org.

United Nations Environment Programme. http://www.unep.org.

United Nations Food and Agricultural Organization. Country Proflies. http://www.fao.org/countryprofiles/inventory.asp?lang=en.

United Nations Human Settlements Programme (UN-HABITAT). http://unhabitat.org.

United Nations Statistics Division. http://unstats.un.org/unsd/default.htm.

U.S. Agency for International Development. http://www.usaid.gov.

U.S. Commercial Service. http://www.buyusa.gov/home/.

U.S. Department of State. *Background Notes.* http://www.state.gov/r/pa/ei/bgn.

———. *Country Commercial Guides.* http://www.state.gov/e/eb/rls/rpts/ccg/.

———. *International Religious Freedom Report 2005.* http://www.state.gov/g/drl/rls/irf/2005/index.htm.

———. *Human Rights Reports, 2005.* http//www.state.gov/g/drl/rls/hrrpt/2005

———. *Refugee Magazine 2004 Year in Review.* http://www.unhcr.ch.

———. *2005 Country Reports on Human Rights Practices*. http://www.state.gov/g/drl/rls/hrrpt/2005/index. htm.

U.S. Library of Congress. http://lcweb2.loc.gov/frd/cs/profiles.html

The Wall Street Journal. http://online.wsj.com/public/us.

The Washington Post. http://www.washpost.com/index.shtml.

The Weather Channel. "Averages and Records." http://www.weather.com/common/home/climatology.html

The World Bank. http://worldbank.org.

———. *Doing Business* database. http://www.doingbusiness.org.

———. *EdStats*. http://devdata.worldbank.org/edstats/td61pop.asp?define=pre

The World Conservation Union: Species Survival Commission. http://www.iucn.org/themes/ssc.

World Development Indicators, Country Overviews. http://www.developmentgateway.org

World Health Organization. Country Immunization Profile. http://www.nt.who.int/immunization_monitoring/en/globalsummary/countryprofileselect.cfm.

World Population Prospects (by country). http://esa.un.org/unpp/p2k0data.asp.

World Investment Report (UN). www.unctad.org.

GUIDE TO COUNTRY ARTICLES

All information contained within a country article is uniformly keyed by means of small superior numerals to the left of the subject headings. A heading such as "Population," for example, carries the same key numeral (6) in every article. Thus, to find information about the population of Albania, consult the table of contents for the page number where the Albania article begins and look for section 6 thereunder. Introductory matter for each nation includes coat of arms, capital, flag (descriptions given from hoist to fly or from top to bottom), anthem, monetary unit, weights and measures, holidays, and time zone.

SECTION HEADINGS IN NUMERICAL ORDER

1	Location, size, and extent	27	Energy and power
2	Topography	28	Industry
3	Climate	29	Science and technology
4	Flora and fauna	30	Domestic trade
5	Environment	31	Foreign trade
6	Population	32	Balance of payments
7	Migration	33	Banking and securities
8	Ethnic groups	34	Insurance
9	Languages	35	Public finance
10	Religions	36	Taxation
11	Transportation	37	Customs and duties
12	History	38	Foreign investment
13	Government	39	Economic development
14	Political parties	40	Social development
15	Local government	41	Health
16	Judicial system	42	Housing
17	Armed forces	43	Education
18	International cooperation	44	Libraries and museums
19	Economy	45	Media
20	Income	46	Organizations
21	Labor	47	Tourism, travel, and recreation
22	Agriculture	48	Famous persons
23	Animal husbandry	49	Dependencies
24	Fishing	50	Bibliography
25	Forestry		
26	Mining		

SECTION HEADINGS IN ALPHABETICAL ORDER

Agriculture	22	Income	20
Animal husbandry	23	Industry	28
Armed forces	17	Insurance	34
Balance of payments	32	International cooperation	18
Banking and securities	33	Judical system	16
Bibliography	50	Labor	21
Climate	3	Languages	9
Customs and duties	37	Libraries and museums	44
Dependencies	49	Local government	15
Domestic trade	30	Location, size, and extent	1
Economic development	39	Media	45
Economy	19	Migration	7
Education	43	Mining	26
Energy and power	27	Organizations	46
Environment	5	Political parties	14
Ethnic groups	8	Population	6
Famous persons	48	Public finance	35
Fishing	24	Religions	10
Flora and fauna	4	Science and technology	29
Foreign investment	38	Social development	40
Foreign trade	31	Taxation	36
Forestry	25	Topography	2
Government	13	Tourism, travel, and recreation	47
Health	41	Transportation	11
History	12		
Housing	42		

FREQUENTLY USED ABBREVIATIONS AND ACRONYMS

AD—Anno Domini
AM—before noon
b.—born
BC—Before Christ
c—Celsius
c.—circa (about)
cm—centimeter(s)
Co.—company
Corp.—corporation
cu ft—cubic foot, feet
cu m—cubic meter(s)
d.—died
E—east
e—evening
e.g.—exempli gratia (for example)
ed.—edition, editor
est.—estimated
et al.—et alii (and others)
etc.—et cetera (and so on)
F—Fahrenheit

fl.—flourished
FRG—Federal Republic of Germany
ft—foot, feet
ft³—cubic foot, feet
GATT—General Agreement on Tariffs and Trade
GDP—gross domestic products
gm—gram
GMT—Greenwich Mean Time
GNP—gross national product
GRT—gross registered tons
ha—hectares
i.e.—id est (that is)
in—inch(es)
kg—kilogram(s)
km—kilometer(s)
kw—kilowatt(s)
kwh—kilowatt-hour(s)
lb—pound(s)
m—meter(s); morning

m³—cubic meter(s)
mi—mile(s)
Mt.—mount
Mw—megawatt(s)
N—north
n.d.—no date
NA—not available
oz—ounce(s)
PM—after noon
r.—reigned

rev. ed.—revised edition
s—south
sq—square
St.—saint
UK—United Kingdom
UN—United Nations
US—United States
USSR—Union of Soviet Socialist Republics
w—west

A fiscal split year is indicated by a stroke (e.g. 1998/99).
For acronyms of UN agencies and their intergovernmental organizations, as well as other abbreviations used in text, see the United Nations volume.
A dollar sign ($) stands for US$ unless otherwise indicated.
Note that 1 billion = 1,000 million.

ALBANIA

Republic of Albania
Republika é Shqipërisë

CAPITAL: Tiranë

FLAG: The flag consists of a red background at the center of which is a black double-headed eagle.

ANTHEM: *Hymni i Flamúrit (Anthem of the Flag)* begins "Rreth flamúrit të për bashkuar" ("The flag that united us in the struggle").

MONETARY UNIT: The lek (L) of 100 qindarka is a convertible paper currency. There are coins of 5, 10, 20, 50 qindarka, and 1 lek, and notes of 1, 3, 5, 10, 25, 50, 100, and 500 leks. L1 = $0.00970 (or $1 = L103.07) as of 2005.

WEIGHTS AND MEASURES: The metric system is the legal standard.

HOLIDAYS: New Year's Day, 1 January; International Women's Day, 8 March; Independence Day, 28 November; Christmas Day, 25 December. Movable Islamic and Christian religious holidays include Small Bayram, Catholic Easter, Orthodox Easter, Great Bayram.

TIME: 1 PM = noon GMT.

¹LOCATION, SIZE, AND EXTENT

Albania is situated on the west coast of the Balkan Peninsula opposite the "heel" of the Italian "boot," from which it is separated on the sw and w by the Strait of Otranto and the Adriatic Sea. It is bordered on the N and E by Serbia and Montenegro and Macedonia, and on the SE by Greece, with a total boundary length of 720 km (447 mi). Comparatively, Albania is slightly smaller than the state of Maryland, with a total area of 28,748 sq km (11,100 sq mi) and extends 340 km (211 mi) N–S and 148 km (92 mi) E–W. Albania's capital city, Tiranë, is located in the west central part of the country.

²TOPOGRAPHY

Albania is predominantly mountainous, with 70% of the territory at elevations of more than 300 m (1,000 ft). The rest of the country consists of a coastal lowland and the lower reaches of river valleys opening onto the coastal plain. The Albanian mountains, representing a southern continuation of the Dinaric system, rise abruptly from the plains and are especially rugged along the country's borders. The highest peak, Mt. Korabit (2,753 m/9,033 ft) lies in eastern Albania on the Macedonian border. The most important rivers—the Drin, the Buna, the Mat, the Shkumbin, the Seman, and the Vijosë—empty into the Adriatic. Albania shares Lake Scutari (Skadarsko Jezero) with Serbia and Montenegro, Lake Ohrid (Ohridsko Jezero) with Macedonia, and Lake Prespë (Prespansko Jezero) with Macedonia and Greece.

³CLIMATE

Albania has a variety of climatic conditions, being situated in the transition zone between the typical Mediterranean climate in the west and the moderate continental in the east. The average annual temperature is 15°C (59°F). Rainy winters (with frequent cyclones) and dry, hot summers are typical of the coastal plain. Summer rainfall is more frequent and winters colder in the mountainous interior. Annual precipitation ranges from about 100 cm (40 in) on the coast to more than 250 cm (100 in) in the mountains.

⁴FLORA AND FAUNA

The mountainous topography produces a variety of flora and fauna. The dry lowlands are occupied by a bush-shrub association known as maquis, in which hairy, leathery leaves reduce transpiration to a minimum. There are some woods in the low-lying regions, but larger forests of oak, beech, and other deciduous species begin at 910 m (2,986 ft). Black pines and other conifers are found at higher elevations in the northern part of the country. There are few wild animals, even in the mountains, but wild birds still abound in the lowland forests.

⁵ENVIRONMENT

Deforestation remains Albania's principal environmental problem, despite government reforestation programs. Forest and woodland account for about 38% of the country's land use. Soil erosion is also a cause for concern, as is pollution of the water by industrial and domestic effluents. While Albania has a comparatively small amount of renewable water resources at 26.7 cu km, 99% of its urban population and 95% of its rural population have access to pure water.

Albania produced 2.9 million metric tons of carbon dioxide emissions in 2000.

As of 2003, about 3.8% of Albania's lands were protected by environmental laws. As of 2002, there were over 3,000 higher plant species (flowering plants only), 68 mammal species, and 193 species of birds. According to a 2006 report issued by the International Union for Conservation of Nature and Natural Resources (IUCN), threatened species included 1 type of mammals, 9 species of birds, 4 types of reptiles, 2 species of amphibian, and 17 species of fish. Endangered species include the Atlantic sturgeon, Mediterranean monk seal, and the hawksbill turtle.

6 POPULATION

The population of Albania in 2005 was estimated by the United Nations (UN) at 3,170,000, which placed it at number 131 in population among the 193 nations of the world. In 2005, approximately 8% of the population was over 65 years of age, with another 27% of the population under 15 years of age. There were 98 males for every 100 females in the country. According to the UN, the annual population rate of change for 2005–10 was expected to be 0.9%, a rate the government viewed as satisfactory. The projected population for the year 2025 was 3,509,000. The population density was 110 per sq km (286 per sq mi).

The UN estimated that 42% of the population lived in urban areas in 2005, and that urban areas were growing at an annual rate of 2.03%. The capital city, Tiranë, had a population of 367,000 in that year. Other important towns and their estimated populations include Durrës, 113,900; Elbasan, 97,000; Shkodër, 90,000; and Vlorë, 85,000.

The population increase in Albania has been exceptionally rapid by European standards. The birthrate, despite a decline from over 40 births per 1,000 of population in the 1950s to 19 in 2000, remains among the highest in Europe. The high birthrate is partially attributed to the ban on birth control during the communist era; as of 2006, the use of birth control remains low, with only 15.3% of married women reported to use contraceptives. Another contributing factor to the population growth is the increase in life expectancy to an average of 74 years of age.

7 MIGRATION

In the 19th century, Albanians emigrated to other Balkan countries (Romania, Bulgaria, Turkey, Greece), and to Egypt and Russia. During the first decades of the 20th century, emigration—for economic reasons—was primarily to the United States (largely to Massachusetts), Argentina, Australia, and France. Emigration following World War II occurred on a very limited scale, mainly for political reasons. Between 1945 and 1990, Albania remained virtually isolated from the rest of Europe. In the early 1990s, about two million Albanians lived in Serbia and Montenegro (formerly Yugoslavia).

In 1997, rebel fighting and an Italian-led multinational force of 6,000 foreign peacekeeping troops prevented thousands of Albanians from fleeing into Greece or Italy. After the 1999 peace of Kosovo, government control of migration flows was absent. By 2004, approximately 25% of the total population, or over 35% of the labor force, emigrated. Of the approximately 900,000 emigrants, most reside in Greece (600,000), Italy (200,000), Western European countries, the United States, and Canada. Since the 1990s, migration has been five times higher than the average migration flow in developing countries. Included in this flow was a significant "brain drain" of scholars that became a "brain waste" as they became underemployed in their country of destination. Albania's net migration rate, estimated in 2005, was -4.8 migrants per 1,000 population. Remittances from Albanians working abroad amounted to $780 million in 2003.

During the NATO air strikes of 1999, Albania hosted 465,000 refugees from Kosovo. Adoption of the Kosovo Peace Plan on 10 June 1999 prompted the return of an estimated 432,500 refugees to Kosovo from Albania. At the end of 2003, there were around 300 refugees in the country, mainly Albanians from Kosovo and the Former Yugoslav Republic of Macedonia, as well as citizens from Iraq and Turkish Kurds. By the end of 2004 Albania's refugee population had declined to just 51.

Between 1992–2003 approximately 6,000 foreigners entered Albania as migrant workers employed mainly in construction, trade, service, and education sectors. Around three-fourths of them came from Turkey, China, Egypt, other Arab and Islamic countries, and European Union (EU) countries.

8 ETHNIC GROUPS

Generally regarded as descendants of the ancient Illyrians, the Albanians make up about 95% of the population. Ethnic Greeks comprise as much as 3% of the populace. Other groups, including Roma, Vlachs, Bulgarians, Macedonians, and Serbs, make up the remaining 2%. The Albanians themselves fall into two major groups: the Ghegs in the north and the Tosks in the south, divided by the Shkumbin River. The Greeks are located primarily in the south.

9 LANGUAGES

Albanian (Shqip), an independent member of the Indo-European family of languages derived from both ancient Illyrian and ancient Thracian, has been greatly modified by Latin, Slavonic, Greek, and Turkish influences. It was not until 1908 that a common Latin alphabet was established for Albanian. In addition to letters of the English alphabet, Albanian uses the diacritics ç (representing the sound of *ch* in *church*) and ë (the sound of *i* in *dirt*). Other unusual letter values are c (the sound of *ts* in *gets*), x (the sound of *ds* in *woods*), xh (the sound of *j* in *jaw*), j (the sound of *y* in *yet*), q (the sound of *ky* in *stockyard*), and y (the sound of the German *ü*). There are two distinct dialects—Gheg, spoken in the north, and Tosk, spoken in the south. During the period between World Wars I and II, Gheg was officially favored as standard Albanian; after World War II, because the principal leaders of the regime were southerners, the Tosk dialect became the standard and is currently the official language. Greek is spoken by a minority in the southeast border area. Vlach, Romani, and other Slavic dialects are also spoken by minority groups.

10 RELIGIONS

In 1990 and 1991, official opposition to religious activities came to an end, and churches and mosques that had been closed under the communist regime were selectively allowed to reopen. Albania is now a self-proclaimed secular state; however, the 1998 constitution calls for freedom of religion. It is estimated that 30–40% of the population actively practice a religion.

Historically, Islam has been the most prominent religion of Albania. In the total population, the percentage of Muslims remains stable at roughly 65–70%, including Sunni Islam and members of the Bektashi school (Shia Sufism). Since 1925, Albania has been considered the world center of the Bektashi school. The Bektashi school represents about 25% of the nation's Muslims. About 20–25% of the population are members of the Orthodox Autocephalous Church of Albania (Albanian Orthodox) and about 10% are Roman Catholic. There are several small Protestant groups.

Geographically, most Muslims are found in the center of the country, with a few groups to the south. Citizens in the south are mainly Orthodox while northerners are generally Catholic. The Greek minority in the south is Orthodox. The four main groups of Sunnis, Bektashis, Orthodox, and Catholics have maintained a heightened degree of social recognition and status due to their historical presence within the country. The State Committee on Cults regulates relations between the government and religious organizations and keeps statistics on groups that contact the Committee for assistance. Registration or licensing is not required for religious organizations.

11 TRANSPORTATION

Many roads are unsuitable for motor transport; bicycles and donkeys are common. There had been virtually no private cars in the country, but they have become more common since the opening of the borders. In 2002, there were 18,000 km (11,185 mi) of roads, of which 7,020 km (4,359 mi) were paved. One of the many recent infrastructural projects was the construction of a 241 km (150 mi) four-lane highway linking Durrës with Greece, via Pogradec and Kapshtica.

Railroad construction began in 1947, and lines in 2001 had a total length of 447 km (228 mi) of standard gauge track. Narrow gauge rail includes the Durrës-Tiranë, Durrës-Elbasan, Ballsh Rrogozhinë, Vorë-Shkodër, and Selenicë-Vlorë lines. In 1979, Albania signed an agreement with the former Yugoslavia to construct a rail link between Shkodër and Titograd; the link was opened to international freight traffic in September 1986.

Albania's rivers are not navigable, but there is some local shipping on lakes Shkodër, Ohrid, and Prespë. Coastwise vessels link the ports of Durrës, Vlorë, Sarandë, and Shëngjin. Durrës is the principal port for foreign trade. The merchant fleet of Albania in 2005 consisted of 25 vessels of 1,000 GRT or over, all cargo ships, totaling about 40,878 GRT. A freight ferry service between Durrës and Trieste was inaugurated in 1983.

In 2004, there were an estimated 11 airports, three of which had paved runways, and one heliport (as of 2005). Flights from Tiranë's international airport connect the Albanian capital with Athens, Belgrade, and Switzerland (the latter route opened in June 1986). In 2003, a total of 159,300 passengers were carried on scheduled domestic and international airline flights.

12 HISTORY

Origins and the Middle Ages

The Albanians are considered descendants of ancient Illyrian or Thracian tribes of Indo-European origin that may have come to the Balkan Peninsula even before the Greeks. Although several Greek colonies were established along the coast, the hinterland remained independent. An Illyrian kingdom was formed in the 3rd century BC, and even after it was conquered by Rome in 167 BC, some mountain tribes were never subdued. Among them were the Albani or Albanoi, whose city Albanopolis was mentioned in the 2nd century BC by Ptolemy in his Geography. Later, while nominally under Byzantine rule, Albania was raided by Slav invaders in the 6th century and was annexed to Bulgaria in the 9th century. Temporary inroads were made by Venice, which established coastal colonies, and by the Normans, who seized Durrës in 1082-

85. Albanian expansion took place under the Angevin kings of Naples in the 13th century, and again under the Serbs in the 14th century. Short-lived independent principalities flourished during the second half of the 14th century.

From the Ottomans to Independence

Turkish advances, which began in 1388, were resisted from 1443 to 1468 by Gjerj Kastrioti, better known as Scanderbeg, the Albanian national hero, but by 1479 the Turks attained complete control of the area. Over the succeeding centuries, Islam spread throughout most of the country. Turkish rule continued through the 19th century, which saw an intensification of nationalistic feeling, often erupting into open rebellion. In November 1912, during the First Balkan War, the National Assembly convened in Vlorë under the chairmanship of Ismail Kemali and proclaimed Albania's independence. The proclamation was supported by Austria-Hungary but opposed by Russia, Serbia, Greece, and Turkey. At a conference in London in 1913, Albania's national boundaries were established—they have remained virtually unchanged since that time—and the nation was placed under the tutelage of the great powers. Albania then became a principal battleground during World War I. By the time the war ended, portions of Albania were under Italian, French, and Yugoslav control.

Albania again asserted its independence in 1920, and a provisional government was established, as the Italians and French withdrew. Following a period of unstable parliamentary government (1921–24), Ahmet Zogu, the chief of the Mat district, seized power with Yugoslav support. He proclaimed Albania a republic in 1925, with himself as president, and a kingdom in 1928, with himself as King Zog I. A series of concessions to Italy made Albania a virtual Italian protectorate, and after Zog was forced into exile in April 1939, Italy occupied Albania, uniting it with the Italian crown. During World War II, Communist-led guerrillas under Enver Hoxha resisted Italian and German forces. The Congress of Permeti (24 May 1944) formed Albania's provisional government, naming Hoxha as premier; the congress banned the return of former King Zog, and called for a constituent assembly to meet after the complete liberation of the country. In November 1944, the Hoxha government was established in Tiranë.

Under Communist Rule

The constitution of 1946 declared Albania a people's republic. Early close relations with Yugoslavia were abruptly severed when the Soviet-Yugoslav break occurred in 1948. Partly because of fundamental differences with Yugoslavia, whose borders included about 1.7 million Albanians, and partly because of ideological divergences, Albanian-Soviet relations worsened at the 22nd Communist Party Congress, and the USSR severed diplomatic relations with Albania in December 1961 and evacuated its naval and submarine bases at Vlorë.

Relations with Communist countries other than China worsened during the 1960s, as Albania ceased to participate in the activities of the Warsaw Treaty Organization by September 1968 following the Soviet invasion of Czechoslovakia. With Yugoslavia, however, there were signs of rapprochement; an Albanian-Yugoslav trade pact was signed in 1970, and trade between the two nations consequently flourished. Gestures were also made to improve relations with Albania's other neighbor, Greece.

Albania's relations with China, its ally and supporter since 1961, seemed to cool somewhat after 1971. China's détente with the United States ran counter to Albania's policy of opposition to the USSR and the United States. China's assistance to Albania ceased when the United States denounced the overthrow of China's "Gang of Four" in October of 1976.

On 28 December 1976, Albania adopted a new constitution that formally established Marxism-Leninism as the dominant ideology and proclaimed the principle of self-reliance. The following year, Albania broke off most of its links with China and accused it of "social imperialist" policies, and in 1978 trade relations were also suspended. In 1983, however, Albania received a Chinese delegation to discuss the resumption of trade relations. Meanwhile, relations with Yugoslavia worsened following the riots by ethnic Albanians in Yugoslavia's Kosovo province in March 1981; Yugoslavia charged that Albania had instigated the protests, and Albania accused Yugoslavia of ethnic discrimination. (Nevertheless, as of 1987 Yugoslavia was Albania's main trading partner, and Albania's first rail connection with the outside world, the Shköder-Titograd link, was opened in 1986.)

Internally, Albania seemed to be locked in bitter political conflict as the 1980s began. Prime Minister Mehmet Shehu, relieved of his defense portfolio in April 1980, died in December 1981, an alleged suicide. A year later, Hoxha charged that Shehu had been working for the US, Soviet, and Yugoslav secret services and that Shehu even had orders from Yugoslavia to kill him. Western and Yugoslav press accounts speculated that Shehu had favored an opening to the West and had been executed in the course of a power struggle. Throughout 1981–83, an extensive purge of those even remotely connected with Shehu was conducted. This was in keeping with previous purges in the 1950s of those sympathizing with Yugoslavia, in the 1960s of pro-Soviet officials, and in the late 1970s of pro-West and pro-China policymakers. On 25 September 1982, according to Albanian reports, a group of armed Albanian exiles landed on the coast and was promptly liquidated. Hoxha alleged that they had been sent by Yugoslavia.

Hoxha died on 11 April 1985 and was succeeded as first secretary of the Workers Party by Ramiz Alia, who had been chairman of the presidium of the People's Assembly since 1982.

In the mid-1980s, Albania took steps to end its isolation. In 1987, it established diplomatic relations with Canada, Spain, Bolivia, and the Federal Republic of Germany. In August 1987, Albania signed a treaty with Greece formally ending the state of war that had existed between the two countries since World War II.

Democracy and a Free-Market Economy

As unrest spread in the late 1980s through Central and Eastern Europe in opposition to long-lasting Communist dictatorships, economic hardships in Albania grew ever deeper. Albania's political leadership had to open up more diplomatic and trade relationships with Western nations as the only available source of potential assistance. At the same time, internal unrest and a search for alternative democratic political solutions led by 1990 to mass protests and calls for the government's resignation. Thousands of Albanians wanted to emigrate in spite of imposed restrictions and became refugees housed in foreign embassies waiting for ships to take them abroad, particularly to Italy. President Ramiz Alia initiated the process for reestablishing diplomatic relations with

the United States, discontinued since the 1939 annexation of Albania by Italy. Restrictions on travel abroad were eased and religious practices allowed for the first time since their prohibition in 1944.

President Berisha and his Democratic Party pushed hard for radical reforms to create a market economy and democratic institutions internally, while bringing Albania back into the international mainstream after half a century of isolation. By the end of 1993 barriers to foreign trade had been removed, the Albanian lek made fully convertible, inflation brought under control, the serious productivity decrease halted, and an anticorruption drive mounted. The privatization of the economy had been successfully initiated, particularly in the agricultural sector, with 90% of land distributed to private farmers. Most subsidies were ended except to large industrial enterprises, which still wait for foreign investments that are not yet coming to the unstable Balkan area. The Communist Party government still intended to maintain both its control and its socialist system while allowing for some democracy. But it was not to be, and by December 1990 the opposition Democratic Party was formed. On 7 February 1991, some 8,000 students went on strike in Tiranë demanding economic changes and the government's resignation. In the face of persistent unrest, President Alia scheduled multiparty elections for 31 March 1991. Even with the Communist Party still in control, the Democratic Party managed to win 75 of the 250 People's Assembly seats (mostly in urban areas) with 160 seats won by the Communist Party. Ramiz Alia was reelected president and a still all-Communist Council of Ministers was appointed under Prime Minister Fatos Nano. By June 1991, continuous unrest forced Alia to agree to a first coalition government between its Communist (renamed Socialist) Party and the new Democratic Party. The latter withdrew from the coalition government in December 1991 charging the majority Socialists with preventing any reforms. President Alia then called for new general elections on 22 March 1992, which gave the Democratic Party a majority of seats (92 of 140). Sali Berisha was elected president with Alexsander Meksi his prime minister. Under Berisha, Alia and Nano were arrested and tried for corruption and abuse of power. They were sentenced to long prison terms, but were released within a few years of their convictions.

In foreign relations, Albania, under Berisha's leadership, tried to balance the internal pressure to assist both the repressed Albanian majority in the Kosovo region of Serbia towards its independence, and the sizable Albanian minority in Macedonia to obtain human and political rights. Albania's Western trade partners realized its internal economic and humanitarian needs and have been generous with their assistance that, between mid-1991 and 1993, has amounted to $1 billion, mostly from European Union countries led by Italy. The United States and Albania also developed very close relations. Albania requested membership in NATO and, even though rejected, continued its cooperation with NATO. Because of its own border problems with Greece, Albania supported the independence of Macedonia and was one of the first nations to recognize Macedonia in spite of Greece's refusal to do so. Albania, a majority (70%) Muslim country, joined the Organization of the Islamic Conference mainly to gain some economic support. Albania also hosted Pope John Paul II's visit in April 1993, having established diplomatic relations with the Vatican in September 1991, and intensified its traditional good relationship with Italy, whose annexation of Albania in 1939 is by now only a faint memory.

In 1994, the border disputes that have occurred since the creation of Albania flared into violence as Greek and Albanian border guards fought against each other in sporadic clashes. Greece expelled over 1,500 Albanians working in Greece without permits.

Albania's borders also became critical in 1994 as smugglers attempted to evade the embargo imposed on Serbia in consequence of its participation in the war in Bosnia. Fuel was shipped into Albania through the ports of Durrës and Vlorë and then taken by tanker truck inland where it was transported via Lake Shkodër into Montenegro and then into Serbia. Because the oil was legitimately imported into the country it was subjected to import duties, which provided in excess of $22 million in tax-revenue for the Albanian government in 1994.

Domestically, Albania began to see the beginning fruits of its painful transition to a market economy as consumer goods and cafe-filled boulevards began to appear for the first time in post-Communist Albania. While wages remained low in comparison with other European countries, living standards were still higher than they had been under Hoxha's Stalinistic economics.

But Albania's efforts to integrate itself into modern Europe suffered a setback when a new constitution, strongly supported by President Sali Berisha, was rejected by voters in November 1994. It would have created a stronger executive and, as a prerequisite for entry into the Council of Europe, would have made Albania a signatory to international human rights treaties. Albania eventually did win acceptance to the Council of Europe in July 1995.

While Albania's parliamentary election in May 1996 returned President Berisha to power, the election was marred by reports of widespread electoral fraud committed by Berisha's Democratic Party and its allies. International observers in Albania to monitor the election confirmed these reports. While the United States and the Organization for Cooperation and Security in Europe expressed private concern over the election tampering, they did not publicly demand that new elections be held. For days after the election, police used truncheons and tear gas to disperse crowds protesting the election fraud and jailed major opposition leaders. In October of 1996 the Democratic Party again won a landslide victory in local elections, but the party was again charged by international observers and opposition parties with massive electoral fraud.

Perhaps the best indicator that the Democratic Party was not as popular as elections indicated came in response to the collapse of several "pyramid schemes" in late 1996 and early 1997, in which at least one-third of the population had invested approximately $800 million by late 1996. Not only were these schemes a dubious investment value, but they had retarded the development of the legitimate Albanian economy by draining money away from legitimate investments, as even banks offering 16% annual interest had trouble attracting new deposits.

Rightly or wrongly, most Albanians identified the government with the pyramid schemes. It was widely believed that the government had used funds provided by the schemes to finance its campaign and that government ministers were involved with starting and running the schemes. The government's own belated actions in reaction to the pyramid schemes, freezing their assets and arresting fund managers, only further infuriated investors because

LOCATION: 39°38′ to 42°39′ N; 19°16′ to 21°4′ E. BOUNDARY LENGTHS: Yugoslavia, 287 kilometers (178 miles); Macedonia, 151 kilometers (94 miles); Greece, 282 kilometers (175 miles); coastline, 362 kilometers (225 miles). TERRITORIAL SEA LIMIT: 15 miles.

it reduced the already slim chances of seeing a return of any of their capital.

Anger over the collapse of the funds initiated the violence that followed throughout the winter and spring, releasing pent-up frustration that quickly spun out of government control and into anarchy. Protests in Tiranë in January 1997 calling for the resignation of the government were peaceful, but in provincial areas

Albanians began destroying anything associated with the government and the Democratic Party, including courthouses, police stations, municipal buildings, and property belonging to state-owned industries. Violence was particularly serious in the southern port city of Vlorë, home to many of Albania's smugglers and drug operators who invested heavily in the schemes. Government officials and soldiers were expelled from most of southern Albania, as citizens (mostly gangsters and smugglers armed with weapons from government stockpiles and even with MIG aircraft from a captured military base) took control of the area.

The government attempted to stop the protests by cracking down on opposition groups and protesters. Curfews were imposed, as well as restrictions on the right of assembly and the press. Major opposition leaders were secretly arrested and imprisoned and the offices of the nation's major opposition newspaper were torched by plain-clothes security officers. A military force dispatched to return the south to government control was unable to dislodge the rebel hold on Vlorë.

At the appearance of government impotence in the south, order broke down throughout Albania, and the looting went completely beyond control. Not only were food and goods looted from government and industrial facilities (as well as weapons from government armories), but university libraries and cherished cultural monuments were destroyed by rampaging crowds.

President Berisha eventually accepted the creation of a coalition government with the aim of restoring order and ending the widespread prevailing anarchy. At Berisha's request a "voluntary militia" was created, and Tiranë returned to government control. However, it soon became apparent that the militia was composed mostly of members of the secret police (which Berisha had promised to dissolve) and Berisha loyalists, creating great mistrust among the opposition members of his cabinet.

As the violence came closer to the Albanian capital, there were calls for an international peacekeeping force to restore order. In April, a 6,000-member peacekeeping force led by French and Italian troops was deployed to patrol the countryside and restore order so the country could hold new elections. While the deployment of these troops put an end to the violence that had rocked Albania for over three months and had cost almost 150 lives, the massive looting and destruction left the country in tatters, and the pillaging of government armories meant that nearly every household had an automatic machine gun.

The identification of the Democrats with the corruption of the pyramid schemes hurt them badly in the July 1997 election, and the Socialist Party and its allies won an overwhelming victory. Nano, who had regained control of the Socialist Party after his release from prison, became prime minister. President Berisha resigned, and the Assembly elected Rexhep Mejdani, of the Democratic Party, as his successor. In November 1998, many of the principles embodied in the country's 1991 interim constitution were given permanent status when a new, Western-style constitution defining Albania as a democratic republic was approved in a nationwide referendum.

Albania was thrust into the international spotlight by the Kosovo crisis in the spring of 1999 as approximately 440,000 Kosovar Albanian refuges fled over the border to escape persecution at the hands of the Serbs after NATO began launching air strikes against Yugoslav military targets in March. Albania served as an outpost for NATO troops. The influx of refugees further strained Albania's weak economy, and millions of dollars' worth of aid was pledged by the World Bank, the European Union, and other sources. By the fall, most of the refugees had returned to their homes, but Albania's struggle with poverty, crime, and corruption continued.

In October 1999, Socialist Prime Minister Pandeli Majko, appointed a year earlier, was ousted after losing favor with senior party leaders; he was replaced by another young, Western-leaning politician, Ilir Meta. Meta immediately moved to modernize the economy, privatize business, fight crime, and reform the judiciary and tax systems. In January 2001, Albania and Yugoslavia re-established diplomatic relations that had been severed during the Kosovo crisis.

Fighting between ethnic Macedonians and ethnic Albanian rebels—largely from the former Kosovo Liberation Army (UCK)—in the northwest region of Macedonia around the town of Tetovo intensified in March 2001 (it had begun in 2000). Fears in Macedonia of the creation of a "Greater Albania," including Kosovo and parts of Macedonia, were fueled by the separatist movement. On 13 August, the Ohrid Framework Agreement was signed by the Macedonian government and ethnic Albanian representatives, granting greater recognition of ethnic Albanian rights in exchange for the rebels' pledge to turn over weapons to the NATO peacekeeping force.

General elections were held in June 2001 and were won by the Socialist Party once again, taking over half of the 140 parliamentary seats. In the elections, the Union for Victory, a coalition of five political parties, came in second. As of September, a coalition government was in place. Meta listed European integration and an end to energy shortages as his priorities. But by December, the Socialist Party was plagued by a rift between Meta and party chairman Nano, after Nano accused Meta's government of corruption and incompetence and demanded that the cabinet be restructured. On 29 January 2002, Meta resigned after failing to resolve the split in the party. Pandeli Majko became the country's new prime minister, but feuding in the Socialist Party leadership continued. In June, parliament elected former Defense Minister Alfred Moisiu as president, replacing Mejdani. His election came after days of political infighting, during which Nano and Berisha were barred from running. In the end, both Nano and Berisha backed Moisiu as the sole consensus candidate for the position. And in August, Nano became prime minister for the fourth time after the Socialist Party decided to merge the roles of prime minister and party chairman.

In November 2002, NATO announced that of 10 countries aspiring to join the organization, 7 would accede in 2004, leaving Albania, Macedonia, and Croatia to wait until a later round of expansion. In January 2003, Albania and Macedonia agreed to intensify bilateral cooperation, especially in the economic sphere, so as to prepare their way to NATO and EU membership. Also that month, the EU and Albania began Stabilization and Association Agreement talks, seen as the first step toward EU membership.

In the spring of 2004, the failure of Nano's government to bring about economic and social improvements for the everyday Albanian led to opposition staged demonstrations in Tiranë asking for his resignation. However, general elections were held, as scheduled, in the summer of the next year. The Democratic Party of Albania (PD) emerged victorious taking 55 out of 140 seats, while its allies took 18 seats. In spite of having this slim majority in the People's Assembly, the prime minister could not be nominated for another two months due to political wrangling and accusations of rigged elections. Finally, on 3 September 2005, Sali Berisha was nominated as prime minister by president Moisiu. Berisha assured the people he had learned from his past mistakes and pledged to reduce corruption and taxation, improve the economic and social environment, and make progress towards EU and NATO integration.

13 GOVERNMENT

Under the 1976 constitution, Albania was a socialist republic. Legislative authority was vested in the unicameral People's Assembly, elected every four years from a single list of candidates. In elections held 2 February 1987, 250 deputies were elected by 1,830,653 voters, with no votes cast against and one vote invalid. Voter participation was allegedly 100%. Suffrage was extended to men and women from the age of 18 and was compulsory. The 1976 constitution specified that "the rights of citizens are indivisible from the fulfillment of their duties and cannot be exercised in opposition to the socialist order."

Through most of the 1990s, Albania's government was based on the 29 April 1991 Law on Constitutional Provisions that established the principle of separation of powers, the protection of private property and human rights, a multiparty parliament, and a president of the republic with broad powers. After defeating a proposed constitutional measure in 1994, Albanian voters approved a new constitution in November 1998 giving the Albanian government a shape more like those of Western nations. Many provisions of the 1991 interim constitution were made permanent in the new document, which guaranteed a number of basic rights, including religious freedom, property rights, and human rights for ethnic minorities. After being cut to 140 members in 1992, the unicameral People's Assembly was expanded to 155 in 1997; it was subsequently reduced to 140 once again. Of these members, 100 are directly elected and 40 are elected by proportional representation. The president is elected by the People's Assembly for a five-year term, and the prime minister is appointed by the president. A Council of Ministers is nominated by the prime minister and approved by the president.

Alfred Spiro Moisiu, of the Socialist Party, was elected to a five-year term as president by the People's Assembly in June 2002. Sali Berisha, who served as president between 1992 and 1997, was appointed to the prime minister post by Moisiu, after his party—the Democratic Party of Albania—won the general elections in July 2005.

14 POLITICAL PARTIES

Before the 1990s, the only political party was the Communist Party, which was founded in 1941 and has been known officially as the Workers Party (Partija e Punes) since 1948. As of November 1986, it had about 147,000 members, as compared with 45,382 in 1948. The Albanian Democratic Front was the party's major subsidiary organization; other subsidiary groups included the Union of Albanian Working Youth and the Women's Union of Albania.

Under the 1976 constitution, the first secretary of the Workers Party was commander-in-chief of the armed forces. The constitution described the Workers Party as the "sole directing political power in state and society."

The primary political parties include the Democrats (led by Sali Berisha), a Western-style conservative party; the Democratic Alliance, a breakaway group of Democrats still largely allied with them; the Socialists (led by Fatos Nano), composed largely of former Communist Party members; and the Social Democrats, a Western-style progressive party largely allied with the socialists.

Although in the early years of post-Communist Albania there were genuine ideological differences between the parties, such distinctions have now blurred. Even the Socialist Party, composed largely of former Communists, has called for budget cuts and an IMF-backed austerity program. As of the election of 4 July 2005, seats in the unicameral National Assembly were distributed as follows: the Democratic Party of Albania (PD), 55; the Socialist Party (PS), 40; the Republican Party (PR), 11; the Social Democratic Party (PSD), 7; the Socialist Movement for Integration (LSI), 5; and other, 22.

15 LOCAL GOVERNMENT

Albania is divided into 12 regions (qarqe), 36 districts (rrethe), including the city of Tiranë (or Tirana), 65 cities and towns, and 309 communes (as of 2002). All subdivisions are governed by people's councils. The councils direct economic, social, cultural, and administrative activity in their jurisdictional areas and appoint executive committees to administer day-to-day activities.

International observers deemed local elections held in 2000 to have achieved a certain level of democracy, but identified irregularities that need to be addressed in reforms in the Albanian electoral code. The third round of local elections held on 12 October 2003 did not address these irregularities. Several international organizations noted that international standards for democratic elections have not been met. Partial run-offs were held in November and December, following a boycott by the Democratic Party commissioners. The distribution of votes at the local level was as follows: the Socialist Party of Albania (PS), 34.6%; the Democratic Party (PD), 32.2%; the Social Democratic Party (PSD), 5.3%; the Republican Party (PR), 3.3%; and the Agrarian Environmental Party (PAA), 3.2%.

16 JUDICIAL SYSTEM

The judicial system includes district courts, six courts of appeal and a supreme court, or Court of Cassation. The district courts are trial level courts from which appeal can be taken to a court of appeals and then to the Court of Cassation. At each of the three levels, the courts are divided into civil, criminal, and military chambers. Justices of the Supreme Court serve for seven years.

There is also a Constitutional Court (also known as the High Court) with jurisdiction to resolve questions of constitutional interpretation that arise during the course of any case on appeal. In a 1993 decision, the Constitutional Court invalidated a law that would have disbarred lawyers who were active during the Communist era, and ordered the lawyers reinstated. Justices of the Constitutional Court serve a maximum of nine years.

Parliament appoints the seven members of the Court of Cassation and five of the nine judges on the Constitutional Court, with the rest appointed by the president. A Supreme Judicial Council appoints all other judges. In 1992, the Supreme Judicial Council began to remove judges who had served under the former Communist regime.

Although the constitution provides for an independent judiciary, the system is plagued by a lack of resources and trained staff, and is subject to political pressure, intimidation, and corruption.

[17] ARMED FORCES

As of 2005, the Albanian armed forces were in the midst of a major restructuring to be completed by 2010. The new army was to consist of five divisions and a commando brigade of three battalions. In 2005, Army personnel numbered more than 16,000 and were armed with 373 main battle tanks, 123 armored personnel carriers, and 1,197 artillery pieces. The Navy had an estimated 2,000 active personnel and was equipped with 20 patrol/coastal vessels, 4 mine warfare and 2 logistical/support vessels. The Albanian Air Force totaled 3,500 active members and had 26 combat capable aircraft, including 15 fighters and 11 fighter ground attack aircraft. The 2005 defense budget totaled $116 million.

[18] INTERNATIONAL COOPERATION

Albania, a United Nations member since 14 December 1955, belongs to numerous specialized agencies, such as FAO, IAEA, IFAD, ILO, UNESCO, WHO, WIPO, ICAO, WMO, the World Bank, IFC, IMF, and the WTO (2000). Albania was originally a member of the Council for Mutual Economic Assistance (CEMA) and the Warsaw Pact, but in 1968 it formally announced its withdrawal from both (it had ended participation in CMEA in 1961). The country is a part of the Central European Initiative, the Agency for the French-Speaking Community (ACCT), and one of 12 members of the Black Sea Cooperation Zone. Albania is part of the Council of Europe, the Euro-Atlantic Partnership Council, the International Confederation of Free Trade Unions and the World Federation of Trade Unions, the Islamic Development Bank, and the Organization of the Islamic Conference (OIC).

In November 2002, NATO announced that Albania would have to wait until a later round of expansion to join. As of 2003, Albania had applied for membership in the European Union, although it was not among the 13 candidate countries from eastern and southern Europe being considered for the next round of accession. However, in January 2003, Albania and the European Union began Stabilization and Association Agreement talks, which were regarded as the possible first steps toward EU membership.

Albania joined the OSCE 19 June 1991. The country also participates in the Organization for the Prohibition of Chemical Weapons, the NATO Partnership for Peace, and the Adriatic Charter (2003). In May 2003, Albania and the United States signed a treaty on the Prevention of Proliferation of Weapons of Mass Destruction and the Promotion of Defense and Military Relations. Albania was one of four nations to contribute troops to the combat phase of Operation Enduring Freedom (2004), a US initiative in Iraq.

In cooperation on environmental issues, Albania participates in the Basel Convention (hazardous waste), the Convention on Biological Diversity, Ramsar, the Montréal Protocol (ozone layer protection), and the UN Conventions of the Law of the Seas Climate Change, and Desertification.

[19] ECONOMY

Albania has always been an underdeveloped country. Before World War II, there were only a few small-scale industrial plants and only a few of the larger towns had electricity. Subsoil resources were potentially rich, but only coal, bitumen, and oil were extracted—by Italian companies. Transportation was poorly developed. Stockbreeding contributed about half of the agricultural output; by 1938, tilled area represented only 23% of the agricultural land. Forests were exploited and reforestation neglected.

After the war, the Communist regime pursued an industrialization program with a centrally planned economy. Development projects received priority, especially mining, industry, power, and transportation. Consumer goods, agriculture, livestock, and housing were relatively neglected. By 1950, Albania had its first standard-gauge railways, a textile combine, a hydroelectric power plant, a tobacco fermentation plant, and a sugar refinery. Mineral extraction, especially of oil, chrome ore (the main export product), and iron-nickel, was increased. Land cultivated under crops or orchards expanded by over 70% from the 1950s to the 1980s. Although collectivized, farmland was again privatized in 1992 and distributed to peasants. But despite significant progress, living standards in Albania were still among the lowest in Europe. When central planning was abandoned, there was no mechanism to take its place, and GDP fell 45% during 1990–92. It rose by at least 5% in 1995, however. After prices were freed, the inflation rate shot up to 226% in 1992, but dropped to 86% in 1993. Consumer prices and unemployment mounted rapidly in 1994.

More trouble followed in 1997 with the countrywide collapse of financial pyramid schemes. The resulting chaos left the government paralyzed, and over 1,500 Albanians died in the ensuing violence that swept the country before an international peacekeeping force restored order. More economic hardship struck Albania in 1999 as the country received 450,000 Kosovar refugees. Western aid helped the Albanians manage the influx.

As Albania entered the 21st century, its economy had begun to improve. Inflation remained low, the economy was expanding at a rate of approximately 7% a year, and foreign direct investment was growing. Economic growth came largely from the transportation, service, and construction sectors. The state was privatizing industries, and as of 2002, nearly all land in Albania was privately owned. However, the country's transition to a free-market economy did not come without difficulties. Unemployment remained high, and the economy remained based on agriculture (around 50%). Crime and corruption were problems, as were governmental bureaucratic hurdles that hamper business activity. The country's infrastructure was still outmoded and in disrepair, and in dire need of funding. Severe energy shortages caused blackouts and were responsible for small businesses failing; in 2003, the country was increasing its imports of electricity.

In 2001, Albania joined Bosnia and Herzegovina, Bulgaria, Croatia, the former Yugoslav Republic of Macedonia, Romania, and Serbia and Montenegro (Yugoslavia) in creating a Balkan free trade zone. Tariffs on selected goods were to be eliminated under the agreement. In September 2000, Albania joined the World Trade Organization, signaling its commitment to the process of economic reform.

By 2003, and 2004, Albania would register some of the highest rates of growth in Europe (around 6%), with a nominal GDP of

$7.83 billion in 2004. Most of this growth was fueled by an expansion in the services, construction, and transport sectors, as well as by remittances from abroad (a common growth generator in developing countries, especially those that border developed economies), domestic demand, and private investment. The inflation rate in 2004 was 3.2%, the foreign currency reserves rose to $1.244 billion, while its fiscal deficit declined to 4.9%.

The EU remains Albania's main trading partner, with Italy and Greece taking the lion's share. Although exports have been growing steadily, they have been outpaced by the increase of imports. Thus, in 2004 exports totaled $ .6 billion, while imports marked $2.2 billion. Albania's main exports are textiles, footwear, mineral products, and metals; its imports include agricultural products, metals and minerals, and machinery.

Albania has enjoyed a relatively stable environment in the early years of the 21st century, its economic growth has been steady and strong (the GDP is projected to grow in 2005 by 6%), and its moves towards a functional market economy have been courageous. However, the country is still one of the poorest in Europe and remains subject to political instability and economic downside risks, such as shortages of the electricity supply and possible delays in the privatization of large enterprises.

20 INCOME

The US Central Intelligence Agency (CIA) reports that in 2005 Albania's gross domestic product (GDP) was estimated at $18.1 billion. However, Albania has a large gray economy that may be as large as 50% of official GDP. The CIA defines GDP as the value of all final goods and services produced within a nation in a given year and computed on the basis of purchasing power parity (PPP) rather than value as measured on the basis of the rate of exchange based on current dollars. The per capita GDP was estimated at $4,900. The annual growth rate of GDP was estimated at 6%. The average inflation rate in 2005 was 2.5%. It was estimated that agriculture accounted for 23.6% of GDP, industry 20.5%, and services 55.9%.

According to the World Bank, in 2003 remittances from citizens working abroad totaled $889 million or about $281 per capita and accounted for approximately 15.6% of GDP. Foreign aid receipts amounted to $342 million or about $108 per capita and accounted for approximately 5.4% of the gross national income (GNI).

The World Bank reports that in 2003 household consumption in Albania totaled $3.89 billion or about $1,229 per capita based on a GDP of $5.7 billion, measured in current dollars rather than PPP. Household consumption includes expenditures of individuals, households, and nongovernmental organizations on goods and services, excluding purchases of dwellings. It was estimated that for the period 1990 to 2003 household consumption grew at an average annual rate of 5.5%. In 2001 it was estimated that approximately 62% of household consumption was spent on food, 13% on fuel, 3% on health care, and 10% on education. It was estimated that in 2004 about 25% of the population had incomes below the poverty line.

21 LABOR

The labor force numbered an estimated 1.09 million in 2004, excluding 352,000 emigrant workers. For that same year, agricultural workers accounted for an estimated 58% of the country's labor force, with those in the private nonagricultural sector accounting for 20% and those in the public sector accounting for 23%. In 2004, Albania's unemployment rate was officially put at 14.4%, however the actual unemployment rate may be in excess of 30%. When communism was abandoned in favor of a free-market economy in 1991, a transitional dislocation of workers and resources took place, resulting in an estimated unemployment rate of 40% in 1992. In 2001, the unemployment rate remained high, up to an estimated 30%.

In 1991, workers were granted the legal right to create independent trade unions. The Independent Confederation of Trade Unions of Albania (BSPSH) was formed as the umbrella organization for several smaller unions. The rival Confederation of Unions, closely tied to the Socialist Party, operates mostly as a continuation of the state-sponsored federation of the Communist era.

As of 2005, all citizens had the right to organize and bargain collectively, except the military and civilian employees of the military. About 20% of the workforce was unionized, but that number is shrinking. Generally, labor unions in Albania operate from a weak position, and those unions that represent employees in the public sector usually negotiate directly with the government. In addition, little privatization has occurred outside the retail and agricultural sectors and few private employees are unionized.

The minimum work age is 14, with restrictions placed on employment of those under 18 years old. Children between 14 and 16 years old may work part-time. Although the labor code sets the maximum workweek at 40 hours, the actual workweek for many is six days/week. There is no legal minimum wage rate for workers in the private sector, although government workers, 18 years of age and older, were paid a minimum wage of about $118/month in 2005, which does not provide a decent living wage for a family.

The enforcement of occupational health and safety standards and regulations is the responsibility of the Ministry of Labor and Equal Opportunities. However, what regulations and standards that do exist are generally not enforced. In addition, the law provides no remedies for workers who leave the workplace because of hazardous conditions. The enforcement of the labor code is severely limited by the Albanian government's lack of funding.

22 AGRICULTURE

In 2004, about 58% of the economically active population was engaged in agriculture, compared with 85% before World War II (1939–45). Although Albania's mountainous terrain limits the amount of land available for agriculture, the cultivated and arable area was about 21% of the total (578,000 hectares/1,428,000 acres) in 2000. Nearly two-thirds of the population is rural, and agriculture provided 25% of value-added GDP in 2003.

The first collective farm was created in 1946, but collectivization did not move forward on a large scale until 1955. By early 1962, 1,263 collectives included about 2,000 villages and covered almost 80% of the cultivated area. Consolidation reduced the collectives to 1,064 by December 1964. State farms, meanwhile, had expanded and by 1960 they accounted for about 12% of the cultivated area. By 1964, only 10% of the cultivated area was privately farmed, and by 1973, 100% of the agricultural land was reported as socialized, either in collective or state farms. Collective farm consolidations and mergers reduced their number to 420 in April 1983, including "advanced type" cooperatives. The cooperatives accounted for 74% of total agricultural production. By the mid-1980s, the number of collective farmers was about 800,000.

After the government abandoned central planning, the economy collapsed from the void. The decline saw the agricultural sector shrink by 21% in 1991, but agricultural production rebounded in 1992 in response to the privatization of cooperative farms and the elimination of fixed pricing. The number of tractors increased from 359 in 1950 to 4,500 in 1960 and to 12,500 in 1991; 7,915 were in service in 2002. In 2002, irrigation systems covered 59% of the cropland. Artificial fertilizers supplied to farms rose from 8,000 tons of active substance in 1960 to 99,900 tons in 1978. However, fertilizer use fell from 145 kg per hectare in 1983 to about 5 kg per hectare in 2002.

Wheat is the principal crop; corn, oats, sorghum, and potatoes are also important. Greater emphasis is being placed on the production of cash crops—cotton, tobacco, rice, sugar beets, vegetables, sunflowers, and fruits and nuts. FAO estimates of crop output in 2004 (in tons) included wheat, 300,000; corn, 200,000; sugar beets, 40,000; vegetables and melons, 679,100; potatoes, 175,000; grapes, 80,000; oats, 15,000; and oranges, 2,200.

23 ANIMAL HUSBANDRY

The major problem of Albanian animal husbandry has been a shortage of fodder. As a result, livestock numbers remained virtually constant or increased very slowly in the postwar decades. When central planning was abandoned, uncertain monetary and credit policies caused inflation to soar, which eroded export earnings. Albania, which had been a net exporter of food products, became heavily dependent on food aid. Sheep, originally the most important livestock, numbered 1.84 million in 1946 and 1.8 million in 2004. Additional estimated numbers of livestock for 2004 included poultry, 4,300,000; goats, 1,030,000; cattle, 700,000; hogs, 109,000; and horses, 65,000. Estimates of livestock products in 2004 include 900,000 tons of cows' milk, 70,000 tons of sheep's milk, 65,000 tons of goats' milk, 39,000 tons of beef and veal, 8,500 tons of pork, 12,000 tons of mutton and lamb, and 25,800 tons of eggs.

24 FISHING

Fishing is an important occupation along the Adriatic coast. In 1958, a development program for inland fisheries was begun, and the results were improved exploitation and conservation as well as increased fish reserves and catches. Annual fish production was estimated at 3,560 tons in 2003 of which 65% came from marine fishing. Exports of fish products amounted to almost $13.5 million in 2003.

25 FORESTRY

Forests cover 1 million hectares (2.5 million acres), or about 36% of the total land area. As a result of exploitation, erosion, and neglect, about 70% of the forested area consists of little more than shoots and wild shrubs, and exploitation of the remaining accessible forests exceeds optimum annual limits. Roundwood production in 2003 totaled 296,000 cu m, with about 56% used for firewood. Between 1971 and 1978, 65,310 hectares (161,380 acres) were forested, compared with a total of 61,900 hectares (153,000 acres) for 1961–70.

26 MINING

After the abandonment of central planning in 1992, Albania's mineral industry was marginal, with technical difficulties contributing to the decline. Nearly half a century of self-imposed isolation during the Communist era crippled the industry with a shortage of capital, aging and inadequate machinery, over staffing, and environmental damage. In 1995, the government adopted a law to privatize the mineral industry, and administrative preparations for privatization began in 1996.

Mineral deposits traditionally associated with Albania included chromite, copper ore, and nickeliferous iron ore. From the late 1970s through 1990, Albania was the principal chromite-producing country in Europe; the country often ranked second in the world in exports and third in production. In this period, exports of chromite, ferrochromium, and petroleum refinery products constituted the country's chief sources of foreign exchange. For much of the 1990s, the chromite mining and processing industry paralleled the country's moribund economy.

In 2003, chromite production was 220,000 metric tons, down from 300,000 in 1996. The most important chromite mines were at Katjel, Mëmlisht, and Bulqize, in the upper reaches of the Drin River. A chromium-ore enrichment plant was put into operation at Bulqize in 1972. In the 1980s, chromite production amounted to more than one million metric tons per year.

In 2000, the government awarded Hayri Ogelman Madencilik, of Turkey, a long-term concession to upgrade and operate the Kalimash mining and beneficiation complex, and to develop mines at the Perollajt and Vllahane deposits in the northeastern part of the country.

Copper ore concentrate production was 8,691 metric tons in 1999, the last year for which there is any data, according to the US Geological Survey. Copper was mined at Pukë and Rrubig, where the ore was concentrated and smelted. The deposits near Kukës were the richest in Albania.

Production of bauxite in 2002 totaled 71,312 metric tons and was estimated at 229,317 metric tons for 2003. Bauxite deposits were found mostly in central Albania, east of Tiranë, as well as in the northern alpine region, near the border with Serbia. Bauxite reserves were estimated at 12 million tons, with the largest deposit at Daijti. Because of a lack of domestic refining capacity, bauxite was exported.

Albania was one of the few countries producing natural asphalt, mined at Selenicë. All production of asphalt and bitumen in 2002 totaled 4,200 metric tons.

27 ENERGY AND POWER

Albania has both thermal and hydroelectric power stations to generate electricity, but the latter are more significant and have the greater potential. Total power production increased from 85 million kWh in 1955 to 578 million kWh in 1967, and to 4.9 billion kWh in 1985. In 2004, electricity generation was 5.68 billion kWh. In 2002, 13% came from fossil fuels, 87% from hydropower, and none from other sources. In the same year, consumption of electricity totaled 5.286 billion kWh, with total capacity at 1.671 million kW. Rural electrification was achieved in 1970.

The 24,000-kW Shkopet plant and the 27,000-kW Bistricë plant became operational in 1962. A 100,000-kW thermal plant at Fier went into operation in 1968, and the Mao Zedong hydroelectric plant was completed in 1971. The "Light of the Party" hydroelectric plant on the Drin River, with a total installed capacity of 500,000 kW, began operations in 1978. The seventh five-year plan (1981–85) provided for construction of a hydropower station at Koman, also on the Drin, with a capacity of 600,000 kW; the first two turbines were installed there by early 1986.

Petroleum production has become significant. Crude oil output rose from 108,000 tons in 1938 to 870,000 tons in 1967, and 3,500,000 tons in 1985. In 2002, production totaled 6,360 barrels per day. Oil refineries are located at Ballsh, Stalin, Fier, and Çerrik. Albania also produced 1.77 billion cu ft of natural gas in 2002. Sizable coal deposits were discovered near Tiranë in 1969.

28 INDUSTRY

Before World War II, industry was confined to a cement plant at Shkodër and to small-scale flour-milling, food-processing, cigarette-making, and fellmongery (processing animal hides). In 1937–39, industry's contribution to the GNP was only 10%, by far the lowest in Eastern Europe. There was virtually no export of industrial products. After the war, the government emphasized industrial development, primarily development projects. Gross industrial output increased annually by 20% during 1951–60, by 12% during 1961–70, by 9% during 1971–80, by 5% during 1981–85, and by 3% during 1986–90. The socialized sector accounted for over 95% of gross output by the late 1950s and 100% by the 1970s. The industrial labor force, which virtually tripled between 1946 and 1960, continued to increase rapidly during the 1960s and, in 1994, 15% of all wage and salary earners were employed in industry (including mining).

Industrial production fell 44% in 1992 and 10% in 1993, but by 1995 industrial productivity was growing at a rate of 6%. Privatization was proceeding slowly, with joint state-private ventures planned or sale of state enterprises at auction. In 1994, over one-half of the nonfarm workforce was employed by the state. As of 2002, the industrial sector accounted for 27% of GDP. Major industries include food processing, textiles and clothing, lumber, oil, cement, chemicals, and basic metals. Albania has two oil refineries, with a capacity of 26,000 barrels per day in 2002. In 2001, the government privatized a brewery, distillery, dairy, and pharmaceutical company, and planned to sell the Savings Bank of Albania and INSIG, the state-owned insurance company. The construction sector showed potential for growth in 2002–03, as the country had a housing deficit and existing housing is old and in poor condition.

While the importance of agriculture in Albania's economy has decreased, other sectors (such as services, transport, and construction) have benefited from investment in 2004. The telecommunications industry in particular has grown substantially due to significant inflow of capital from two new mobile companies. Tourism, the only sector to register a net positive trade balance, has the prospective of becoming one of Albania's main growth engines. Another sector that has good future prospects is mining—due in part to increases in the price of raw materials. In addition to these developments, there are plans for a 1600-acre Energy Park at Vlora. This park is supposed to respond to Albania's energy shortages by means of large foreign direct investments. To date, 80% of Albania's GDP is generated by the private sector.

29 SCIENCE AND TECHNOLOGY

The main scientific organization, the Academy of Sciences (founded in 1972 and located in Tiranë), has a scientific library and numerous attached research institutes dealing with various aspects of agriculture, fisheries, and veterinary science; medicine; natural sciences (biology, computer science and applied mathematics, energetics, nuclear physics, hydrometeorology, seismology, and geology) and technology (oil and gas geology and technology, industrial projects studies and design hydraulics, metallurgy, mining, roads and railways, chemistry mechanics, minerals, building technology); and the food industry. The Geologists' Association of Albania, founded in 1989, has 450 members (as of 1997).

The University of Tiranë, founded in 1957, has faculties in natural science, medicine, and mechanics and electronics. Its Natural Science Museum has exhibits relating to zoology, botany, and geology. Luigi Gurakugi University of Shkodër, founded in 1991 and based on the former Higher Pedagogical Institute founded in 1957, has a faculty in natural sciences. The Agricultural University of Tiranë, founded in 1971, has faculties in agronomy, veterinary science, and forestry. In 1987–97, science and engineering students accounted for 19% of college and university employment. The Fan S. Noli University in Korçë was founded in 1971 as the Higher Agricultural Institute and renamed in 1992. The Centre for Scientific and Technical Information and Documentation in Tiranë was founded in 1981.

In 2002, high technology exports amounted to $2 million, some 1% of the country's manufactured exports in that year.

30 DOMESTIC TRADE

Wholesale trade became a state monopoly in 1946. Initially, private retail trade played an important role, but by 1970 trade was fully socialized. By December 1990, retail units had been privatized again. All price controls were eliminated except on a few consumer items and monopoly-controlled products.

Shops in Albania are generally small, but department stores and a few larger supermarkets with limited stocks have been established in Tiranë, Durrës, Korcë, and other larger cities. Consumer cooperatives conduct trade in the rural areas. Albania has a small, but growing, advertising sector.

Albanian business hours are Monday through Friday from 8 AM to 6 PM. Shop hours are Mondays and Tuesdays, 7 AM to 2 PM and 5 to 8 PM, and other weekdays, 7 AM to 2 PM. Many shops are open seven days a week, since there is no legislation regulating shop hours. Before 1 January 1959, all sales were for cash. Since then, date limited consumer credit was sanctioned, but most transactions are still in cash.

31 FOREIGN TRADE

Before World War II, about 50% of the exports consisted of the entire production of chrome ore and crude oil and some timber; the balance consisted of agricultural goods and fish. Good grains, sugar, and coffee made up about 20% of the imports; textiles, about 24%; and paper, machinery, chemicals, leather, metals, and

Principal Trading Partners – Albania (2003)

(In millions of US dollars)

Country	Exports	Imports	Balance
World	447.1	1,863.8	-1,416.7
Italy-San Marino-Holy See	334.8	623.8	-289.0
Greece	57.4	373.5	-316.1
Germany	15.3	105.4	-90.1
Serbia and Montenegro	10.5	10.3	0.2
Austria	5.5	30.1	-24.6
Turkey	3.7	122.3	-118.6
Macedonia	3.0	5.5	-2.5
Russia	2.3	52.7	-50.4
United States	2.3	18.6	-16.3
France-Monaco	2.1	20.3	-18.2

(…) data not available or not significant.

SOURCE: *2003 International Trade Statistics Yearbook,* New York: United Nations, 2004.

Balance of Payments – Albania (2003)

(In millions of US dollars)

Current Account		-406.8
Balance on goods	-1,336.3	
Imports	-1,783.5	
Exports	447.2	
Balance on services	-82.9	
Balance on income	170.4	
Current transfers	841.9	
Capital Account		157.0
Financial Account		200.6
Direct investment abroad	…	
Direct investment in Albania	178.0	
Portfolio investment assets	-22.5	
Portfolio investment liabilities	…	
Financial derivatives	…	
Other investment assets	-71.6	
Other investment liabilities	116.7	
Net Errors and Omissions		147.4
Reserves and Related Items		-98.1

(…) data not available or not significant.

SOURCE: *Balance of Payment Statistics Yearbook 2004,* Washington, DC: International Monetary Fund, 2004.

oil products, about 53%. As the value of imports almost tripled that of exports, the deficit was met largely by Italian loans. Italy received two-thirds of Albanian exports and supplied Albania with up to half its imports. Under the Communist government, foreign trade became a state monopoly. The volume of turnover increased substantially and the structure and orientation changed radically.

As of the year 2000, Albania was running a trade deficit of $814 million (US dollars), a considerable increase since the 1990s. The expansion in imports was largely due to increased domestic demand for foreign goods, as well as increased demand for electronics. Between 1950 and 1967, trade volume increased six fold, to L1,043 million in 1967. Total trade volume (imports plus exports) rose 49% between 1966 and 1970. In 1960, trade with the socialist states accounted for about 90% of total trade; the Soviet share of this was half. Political and economic differences between Albania and the USSR resulted in suspension of aid to and trade with Albania. In 1961, 54% of total foreign trade was with the USSR and 7% with China; by 1964, trade with the former had ceased entirely, while trade with China had risen to 55%. After the Albanian-Chinese split in the late 1970s, economic contacts with China ceased. Talks aimed at renewing trade between the two nations were held in 1983, resulting in trade agreements worth about $5–7 million.

In 2000, Albania exported leather products, apparel, footwear components, tobacco products, and metal ores. The production of chromium ore, formerly an integral part of the Albanian export schedule, has plummeted in recent years. Imports in 2000 included raw materials, machinery, transportation equipment, fuel, minerals, metals, and foodstuffs. Albania exported its goods primarily to Italy, Greece, and Germany. The chief sources of Albania's imports were Italy, Greece, Germany, Turkey, Bulgaria, and the Former Yugoslav Republic of Macedonia.

32 BALANCE OF PAYMENTS

The US Central Intelligence Agency (CIA) reports that in 2002 the purchasing power parity of Albania's exports was $340 million while imports totaled $1.5 billion resulting in a trade deficit of $1.16 billion.

The International Monetary Fund (IMF) reports that in 2001 Albania had exports of goods totaling $305 million and imports

totaling $1.33 billion. The services credit totaled $534 million and debit $444 million. The IMF attributes the fall in exports in recent years to a decline in industrial production. Recent increases in imports were due to increased domestic demand for imported goods, in addition to large increases in electricity imports. Remittances from abroad have improved Albania's balance of payments.

33 BANKING AND SECURITIES

The Communist regime nationalized all banking and financial institutions in 1945 and established the Bank of the Albanian State (now simply the Bank of Albania), which became the bank of issue. The bank also controlled foreign transactions, helped prepare financial plans for the economy, accepted savings deposits, financed economic activities, and performed other banking functions. An agricultural bank was created in 1970 to provide credit facilities for agricultural cooperatives.

On 10 August 1949, the Directorate of Savings was established to grant loans and to accept savings deposits in branches throughout the country; the system has grown steadily ever since.

When the Soviet Union collapsed in 1991, Albania decided to develop a market economy. The banking system changed to meet the demands of a free-market economy. However, in October 1996, the Islamic Conference's financing arm, the Islamic Development Bank, made a $12 million loan to Albania. The logic of the government's Islamic focus is unclear.

The government's position has been weakened considerably as a result of the collapse of four of the country's major pyramid investment schemes, leading to anarchic, nationwide demonstrations by furious investors. In January of 1997, a 20,000-strong crowd marched on Skanderberg Square, where it demanded that the government guarantee all deposits in the companies. Notable pyramid investment companies included VEFA, Kamberi, Populli, Xhaferri, Gervnasi, Gjallica, and Sudja.

The informal financial market has absorbed millions of dollars of savings and remittances in recent years (estimates run as high as $1 billion), at the expense of the country's inefficient and uncompetitive banking sector. The pyramid investment schemes attracted hundreds of thousands of depositors—local estimates put participation in the companies at about 75% of all households—by guaranteeing to pay high interest rates on cash deposits within a short period of time.

Much of the blame for crisis rested with the government, whose policy towards the companies was not simply cavalier but actively encouraging. It did not pay attention to requests made by the central bank governor to regulate the pyramid schemes more tightly.

The privatization of the three state-owned commercial banks has long been advocated by the International Monetary Fund and the World Bank. The government has privatized the Rural Commercial Bank and the National Commercial Bank, and is working towards privatizing the Savings Bank of Albania, which holds nearly 80% of all Albanian bank deposits. The International Monetary Fund reports that in 2001, currency and demand deposits—an aggregate commonly known as M1—were equal to $997 million. In that same year, M2—an aggregate equal to M1 plus savings deposits, small time deposits, and money market mutual funds—was $2.7 billion. The discount rate, the interest rate at which the central bank lends to financial institutions in the short term, was 10.82%.

34 INSURANCE

Insurance was nationalized by the Communist government after World War II. Under the jurisdiction of the Ministry of Finance, the program is administered by the Institute for Insurance, created in 1950. Half the profits are earmarked for the state budget, the other half for a reserve fund. In 1990, income from social insurance contributions totaled L967 million. Total expenditures—for temporary disability, pregnancy, childbirth, rest home stay, and pensions—were L1,440 million. In 2002, Albania's parliament passed a law to privatize the insurance agency, hoping to create a competitive industry.

35 PUBLIC FINANCE

Albania began its transition from a centrally planned economy to a market driven economy in 1992, after GDP had collapsed by over 50% in 1989. The government elected in 1992 set in motion a series of aggressive economic reforms to light the path towards a market economy. Among the reforms were price and exchange regime liberalization, fiscal consolidation, monetary restraint, and a rigid income policy. Stalling progress in 1997 was followed by a resumption of growth the next year.

The US Central Intelligence Agency (CIA) estimated that in 2005 Albania's central government took in revenues of approximately $1.9 billion and had expenditures of $2.3 billion. Revenues minus expenditures totaled approximately -$417 million. Total external debt was $1.41 billion.

The International Monetary Fund (IMF) reported that in 2002, the most recent year for which it had data, general government revenues were L153,197 million and expenditures were L187,109 million. The value of revenues was US$1,093 million and expenditures US$1,335 million, based on a market exchange rate for 2002 of US$1 = L140.15 as reported by the IMF. Government outlays by

Public Finance – Albania (2002)		
(In millions of leks, general government figures)		
Revenue and Grants	**153,197**	**100.0%**
Tax revenue	103,162	67.3%
Social contributions	24,920	16.3%
Grants	4,119	2.7%
Other revenue	20,996	13.7%
Expenditures	**187,109**	**100.0%**
General public services	48,983	26.2%
Defense	7,537	4.0%
Public order and safety	11,944	6.4%
Economic affairs	28,080	15.0%
Environmental protection	...	...
Housing and community amenities	9,021	4.8%
Health	13,719	7.3%
Recreational, culture, and religion	2,609	1.4%
Education	19,034	10.2%
Social protection	46,183	24.7%

(…) data not available or not significant.

SOURCE: *Government Finance Statistics Yearbook 2004*, Washington, DC: International Monetary Fund, 2004.

function were as follows: general public services, 26.2%; defense, 4.0%; public order and safety, 6.4%; economic affairs, 15.0%; housing and community amenities, 4.8%; health, 7.3%; recreation, culture, and religion, 1.4%; education, 10.2%; and social protection, 24.7%.

36 TAXATION

As of 1999, personal income is taxed in six brackets, from 5–30%, with 5% starting at an income of about $86/month, and the 30% rate, plus a flat fee of about $45, applied to incomes over about $1,030/month. The corporate income tax rate is 25%, applied equally to both domestic and on income earned in Albania by foreign-owned companies. Tax preferences previously accorded foreign investors—a four-year tax holiday, and up to a 60% reduction on income from reinvested profits—were removed for future foreign investors on the advice of the IMF and World Bank. There is property tax on agricultural land and buildings. Indirect taxes include a value-added tax (VAT) applied to businesses with annual turnover exceeding five million lek (about $43,000), small business taxes, and excise taxes on tobacco, alcohol, soft drinks, coffee, gasoline products, perfumes, and deodorants. The VAT rate is 20%. Small businesses with annual turnover of less than two million lek a year pay a yearly lump sum ranging from 15,000 lek to 100,000 lek. Businesses with turnover in the range of two million lek to five million lek pay a 4% of turnover tax. Exports are exempt from both excise and VAT. Financial transactions are exempt from VAT, and liquefied gas is exempt from excise.

37 CUSTOMS AND DUTIES

Under the jurisdiction of the Ministry of Trade, the general directorate of customs and duties administers customs regulations. With certain exemptions, all goods are subject to duties ranging from 5–10%, depending on product type. Having become a member of the World Trade Organization in September 2000, Albania is working with Bulgaria, Croatia, Macedonia, Romania, and Serbia and Montenegro to create a regional free trade zone.

38 FOREIGN INVESTMENT

Prior to 1990, no foreign capital was invested in postwar Albania, but various communist states aided the Albanian industrialization program, supplying credit, machinery and equipment, and technicians. Prior to 1961, assistance by Soviet-bloc technicians in geologic surveys, construction, and operation of factories was vital to Albanian economic growth. Following the Soviet suspension of credits, withdrawal of technicians, and elimination of trade, China increased its activity in all these areas. In 1978, China terminated all its economic and military cooperation with Albania and the following year Albania was for the first time without any foreign assistance. In the 1980s, some economic assistance was provided by the FRG.

After the fall of communism, foreign investment was encouraged and 149 joint ventures were agreed upon. A $10 million Coca-Cola bottling plant set up in 1994 outside of Tiranë (directly employing about 100 people), the European Bank for Reconstruction and Development, and a local Albanian company were early ventures. In 1995, Albania concluded a bilateral investment treaty with the United States. At the end of 1995, foreign investment was projected to rise to about $600 million, with about one-half of that coming from Italy. However, the prospects for foreign investment dropped sharply in 1997 in the wake of the violence and property destruction that followed the collapse of the pyramid schemes in which many Albanians had sunk their savings. The violent removal of the Prime Minister in 1998 and the influx of Kosovar refugees in 1999 were added deterrents to foreign investment. From 1997 to 1999, foreign direct investment in Albania averaged only $44.57 million, but in 2000 the rate of inflow tripled to $143 million and then in 2001 to $181 million. The rate of investment decreased slightly in subsequent years, but rose again in 2004, reaching $300 million.

In 2003, the UN Development Program assisted the Albanian government in setting up the Investment Promotion Agency (ANIH) that replaces the Economic Development Agency. Previously, the government had put few restrictions on foreign investment, but had offered no tax or financial incentives beyond national treatment. There are initiatives aimed at attracting foreign investment, but as of now they remain unimplemented or in the planning stage.

While the climate for investors has definitely improved over the past years, there are still a number of inconsistencies that make the investment process rather cumbersome. Thus, the physical and financial infrastructure still requires considerable development, there are frequent shortages of power and water in certain areas, corruption remains a major concern, and the rule of law (especially in questions regarding property ownership) is not as strong as it should be. In 2005, Albania had one of the lowest rates of foreign investment in Europe.

39 ECONOMIC DEVELOPMENT

Albania formerly had a state-controlled, centrally planned economy, with emphasis on industrial development and socialized agriculture. Under Workers Party directives, short-term and long-range plans were formulated by the Economic Planning Commission, a government agency. By the mid-1980s, the economy was virtually under complete state control; enterprises were either directly owned by the state or managed through cooperatives.

From 1951, Albanian economic development was directed by five-year plans, most of which stressed heavy industry. A sweeping economic reform program was announced in 1992. It called for widespread private ownership of farmland, state-owned companies and housing, and the removal of trade restrictions and price controls. Yet after nearly a decade of post-Communist rule, Albania remains by far the poorest country in Europe. For much of the 1990s, economic reforms were stifled by rampant corruption. Only after the collapse of pyramid investment schemes did the situation begin to improve. Nevertheless, Albania relies heavily on foreign aid and seeks to secure more funding for infrastructure improvements.

Economic development in the early 2000s was stimulated by the construction and service industries: the lack of housing under communism led to a demand for new housing construction, and the development of tourism in Albania's seaside resorts has fueled the service sector. The country is undergoing an economic restructuring program with the International Monetary Fund (IMF) and World Bank. A three-year Poverty Reduction and Growth Facility program with the IMF was negotiated in 2002, in the amount of some $38 million. In 2003, Albania entered into negotiations with the European Union (EU) for a Stabilization and Association Agreement.

By 2005, Albania was still one of Europe's poorest countries. Although the economy has registered significant growth rates in the past years, it is lagging behind its neighbors. Unemployment is rampant at 15% (with other estimates placing it at 25%); half of the population is engaged in agriculture, while a fifth is said to be working abroad; the export rate is growing but is still too small; imports are growing at a fast pace and are coming mainly from Italy and Greece—money for those imports are provided through foreign aid and from the money sent home by Albanians working abroad.

40 SOCIAL DEVELOPMENT

In 1947, the first law providing benefits for disability, old age, survivors, and retirement was introduced. Current pension law sets retirement age at 60 for males and 55 for females, with 35 years of contributions. Mothers with six or more children are eligible at age 50, with 30 years of contributions. The amount of the pension is up to 75% of average net wages during 3 of the last 10 years of employment. Disability pensions provide as much as twice the basic pension or 80% of the last average wage. Employers' contributions are 26% of payroll. Additional sums are provided by employees and by the state budget.

Unemployment benefits introduced in 1993 require at least one year's contributions, and a willingness to undergo training to be eligible. The employer, at 6% of payroll, makes contributions. A flat rate for benefits allows for a minimum standard of living. A program of Family Allowances fully funded by the government was introduced in 1992. Maternity and sickness benefits are also provided, and were last updated in 2003. In 1996/7 the pyramid saving scheme scandal wiped out about 60% of private savings. The scandal coupled with the influx and maintenance of Kosovo refugees, undermined public confidence and trust in the government's ability to deliver public services. Corruption remains another major barrier. Social assistance and social welfare systems are in need of fundamental reform.

Albania's constitution prohibits discrimination based on sex. Roughly half of the labor force is comprised of women. The Labor Code incorporates the principle of equal pay for equal work. Women remain underrepresented in higher positions and often are underemployed. Women have equal access to higher education, many obtaining professional positions in the medical and legal fields. However, discrimination in the workplace continues. Abuse, trafficking, and violence against women and children remain significant problems. Albania is a source country for women and children trafficked for the purposes of sexual exploitation. Domestic violence and sexual harassment are prevalent, and are largely unreported. In 2004, in some regions of the country, women are still considered chattel.

Religious tolerance is prevalent, and the constitution provides for coexistence between ethnic groups. The Office of National Minorities was established to monitor Albania's minority issues. Nevertheless, societal discrimination against Roma, the Egyptian community, and homosexuals persists. Blood feuds, or violent rival factions, contribute to an atmosphere of fear in some areas.

[41] HEALTH

Health care facilities in the 1990s were substandard and much of their equipment obsolete. In 1992 Albania had 16 hospitals, with 14,000 beds. In 1996, hospital beds declined to 9,600. In 2004, there were an estimated 139 physicians and 404 nurses per 100,000 people. There is a medical school in Tiranë (part of the Enver Hoxha University) and some Albanians receive medical training abroad. Tertiary care, available mostly in Tiranë, includes a teaching hospital, an obstetric and gynecological facility, a facility for treating respiratory diseases, and a military hospital. Albania's health care system was strained by the admission of as many as 500,000 Albanian refugees from Kosovo in the spring of 1999.

The general improvement of health conditions in the country is reflected in the lower mortality rate, down to an estimated 6.49 deaths per 1,000 in 2000, as compared with 17.8 per 1,000 in 1938. In 2005, average life expectancy was estimated at 77.24 years, compared to 38 years at the end of World War II. Albania's infant mortality rate, estimated at 21.52 per 1,000 live births in 2005, has also declined over the years since the high rate of 151 per 1,000 live births in 1960. Albania had high immunization rates for children up to one year old: tuberculosis at 94%; diphtheria, pertussis, and tetanus, 99%; measles, 95%; and polio, 99.5%. As of 2002 the number of people living with HIV/AIDS was estimated at less than 100. The leading causes of death are cardiovascular disease, trauma, cancer, and respiratory disease.

[42] HOUSING

During World II, about 61,000 buildings of all types were destroyed, including 35,400 dwellings. Housing was generally primitive in rural areas and poor elsewhere. After the war, housing continued to be a problem for a variety of reasons: primary emphasis on industrial construction, shortages of materials and skilled labor, and lack of or inadequate assistance for private building. Moreover, the increase of urban population worsened an already desperate situation. Consequently, new housing construction was

concentrated in Tiranë, Vlorë, Elbasan, Shkodër, Durrës, and Korçë, as well as in other industrial and mining sites.

According to the results of a 2001 census, there are about 520,936 residential buildings in the country containing about 785,000 dwellings. Most of the existing stock (29%) was built 1961–80. About 27% of all units were built before 1945. Only about 120,000 (15%) units were built 1991–2001. About 30% of all dwelling spaces (over 50% of urban units) are block flats that were constructed and owned by the government during the Communist era. (Most public housing was privatized during the period from 1992–93.) In 2001, there were 253 dwelling units per 1,000 people and an average of 1 household of about 4.46 people lived in each occupied dwelling. About 13% of all dwellings were vacant in 2001.

A 1998 Household Living Condition survey indicated that about 74% of rural households did not have an indoor toilet and 54% did not have access to running water. In comparison, 18% of urban households were without an indoor toilet and 5% lacked running water. The survey also indicated that about 95% of all units were owned by an occupant. The most common form of housing construction is a concrete frame filled with brick or block in-fill. Tiranë is the largest urban settlement and the site of 17% of the country's housing units (over 134,000 units in 2001).

[43] EDUCATION

The adult literacy rate for 2004 was estimated at about 98.7%, with 99.2% for males and 98.3% for females. Public expenditures on education were estimated at 2.6% of GDP in 2003.

Preschool training for children ages three through six is common but not obligatory. The basic educational program lasts for eight years (ages 6 to 14) and is divided into two cycles of four years each. In 2003, the average enrollment for primary school was about 95%. The pupil to teacher ratio for primary school was at about 21:1 in 2003. Secondary education consists of a four-year program. Vocational programs of three to five years are also open to students who have passed their basic educational requirements. Enrollment in secondary school was at about 77% in 2003. The academic year runs from October to June. The educational system is regulated through the Ministry of Education and Science.

Institutes of higher learning include two agricultural schools, one institute for fine arts, one institute of physical culture, and three teacher-training institutes. In 1957, the Institute of Sciences was elevated to university rank, and Tiranë State University became the first and only institution of university status in Albania. It was later renamed Enver Hoxha University of Tiranë. In 1971, two more universities were founded—Universiteti I Koree and Universiteti Bujguesor I Tiranes. In 1991, the University of Shkodër was established. Approximately 16% of the adult population was enrolled in tertiary education programs in 2003.

[44] LIBRARIES AND MUSEUMS

The largest library in Albania is the National Library in Tiranë (1922) with over one million volumes. The University of Tiranë library has 700,000 volumes. Tiranë also has several university libraries with specialized collections, including the Higher Agricultural Institute Library (126,000 volumes) and the Fine Arts Institute Library (40,000 volumes). Albania's Public Assembly maintains a library of 41,000 volumes, also in Tiranë. Public libraries exist in many communities with notable ones in Elbasan

(284,000 volumes), Shkodër (250,000 volumes), Durrës (180,000 volumes), and Korçë (139,000 volumes). The Albanian Library Association (ALA), the nation's first and only national association for libraries and librarians, was established in 1993.

The principal museums are the Museum of Archaeology, the Fine Arts Gallery, the Museum of the Struggle for National Liberation, the Natural Science Museum, and the National Historical Museum, all located in Tiranë. There are some 30 provincial museums, among them the Berat Museum, known for its collection of historic documents; the Museum of Architecture in Berat; the Onufri Iconographic Museum, located in Berat's main castle and housing a distinguished collection of medieval icons; the Museum of Education in Elbasan; the Museum of Albanian Medieval Art in Korge; and the Shkodër Museum in Shkodër, a historical museum tracing Albanian culture to the Neolithic Age. The cities of Berat and Gjirokastër, the first dating from antiquity and the second from the Middle Ages, have been designated "museum-cities."

45 MEDIA

In 2003, there were an estimated 83 mainline telephones for every 1,000 people; about 98,500 people were on a waiting list for mainline phone service installation. The same year, there were approximately 358 mobile phones in use for every 1,000 people.

Radio and TV broadcasting is governed by the National Council of Radio and Television (NCRT), a seven-member bipartisan body elected by the Parliament. There are at least 17 radio stations (13 AM and 4 FM). As of 2005, there were three television broadcast stations. The Albanian Radio and Television (RTSh) was the sole public broadcaster in 2004. About 30% of the station's budget comes from the government and the station tends to devote most of its coverage to government concerns. Television was introduced in 1961, color broadcasts in 1981. About 80% of the population rely on television as a primary source of news and information. In 2003, there were an estimated 260 radios and 318 television sets for every 1,000 people.

There are several daily newspapers published in Tiranë. In 2002 the four major ones were *Koha Jone* (Our Time, circulation 400,000); *Zërii Popullit* (People's Voice—circulation 105,000), published by the Socialist Party; *Rlindia Demokratike* (The Democratic Revival—circulation 50,000), published by the Democratic Party; and *Bashkimi Kombetar* (circulation 30,000), published by the Democratic Front. There are about 200 publications overall, including daily and weekly newspapers, magazines, newsletters, and pamphlets. At least 18 papers and magazines were published in Greek, with primary distribution throughout the south. *Albanian Newspaper* (circulation 30,000) is published in Italian and *Albanian Daily News* is a daily paper published in English. Agjensia Telegrafike Shqiptare (Albanian Telegraphic Agency) is the official news agency.

Though the law protects freedom of speech and press, nearly all news stories are designed to suit the publisher's political and economic interests. The Albanian Telegraphic Agency is the primary news service.

In 2004, the country had about 455 Internet hosts. In 2003, there were 11.7 personal computers for every 1,000 people and 10 of every 1,000 people had access to the Internet.

46 ORGANIZATIONS

Trade unions in Albania were prohibited until 1991. Before 1991 the official trade unions of the country were responsible for promoting the production goals of the country's Communist government. In 1991, independent trade unions were established to promote the rights of workers. The Union of Independent Trade Unions is the most important umbrella trade organization. Other trade unions operate in the defense, agriculture, food processing, and mining sectors of the economy. The Chamber of Commerce of the republic of Albania promotes the economic and business activities of the country in world markets. Other chambers of commerce are located in Shkodei, Durrës, and Gjirokastër. The Foreign Investors Association promotes foreign investment within the country. The Albanian Consumers Association is based in Tiranë. There are a number of national professional medical organizations, such as the Albanian Medical Association and the Albanian Dental Association. The Organic Agriculture Association was established in 1997 and Tiranë is the site of the Regional Environmental Center for Central and Eastern Europe.

The Open Society Foundation for Albania is a nonprofit organization established in 1992 to encourage the process of the democratization of Albanian society. It is sponsored in part by the SOROS Foundation Network, a fund established by American philanthropist George Soros.

There are a number of youth organizations in the country. The Albanian International Youth Committee (AIYC) serves as the major nongovernmental youth platform that encompasses several different youth and student organizations. It is supported by the Albanian Youth Federation (AYF) and seeks to represent the views of organized Albanian youth. A youth scouting movement (Beslidhja Skaut Albania) is active in the country. The World Organization of Scouting opened a national chapter in Albania (Beslidhja Skaut Albania) in 2005. There are also organizations of the YMCA/YWCA.

The Red Cross and the Red Cross Youth have active chapters in the country. There are also chapters of the Lions Club and Kiwanis International.

47 TOURISM, TRAVEL, AND RECREATION

Albania was once the most inaccessible country in Eastern Europe, with tight entry regulations keeping most Western visitors out. In the early 1980s, persons explicitly forbidden to visit the country were US citizens, Soviet citizens, and full-bearded men. However, since the advent of democracy, Albania has slowly become accessible to the outside world. Tourists from the United States, New Zealand, Australia, and members of the European Union and the EFTA no longer have a visa requirement. Upon arrival a three-month entry level visa is issued, which can be extended. Citizens of other countries must obtain a visa prior to arrival from the nearest Albanian embassy. In promoting travel to Albania, the official tourist agency cites the Adriatic beaches, especially at Durrës, Vlorë, and Sarandë, and the picturesque lakes. The most popular sports are football (soccer), gymnastics, volleyball, and basketball.

In 2003, there were 557,210 visitor arrivals; tourists spent a total of $537 million. Hotel rooms numbered 4,161. The average length of stay was about three nights.

In 2004, the US Department of State estimated the daily cost of staying in Tiranë at $205. Other areas were estimated at $106 per day.

48 FAMOUS ALBANIANS

Much Albanian popular lore is based on the exploits of the national hero Gjergj Kastrioti (known as Scanderbeg, 1405–68), who led his people against the Turks.

Ahmet Bey Zogu (1895–1961), shepherd, military commander, minister of the interior, and premier, was elected first president of the new republic in 1925; in 1928, when Albania became a kingdom, he ascended the throne as Zog I. After Italian forces occupied Albania in April 1939, he fled the country, dying in exile in southern France. Two major political leaders were Enver Hoxha (1908–85), postwar Albania's first premier, minister of foreign affairs, and defense minister; and Mahmet Shehu (1913–81), who replaced Hoxha as premier in 1954, when Hoxha became first secretary of the Workers Party's Central Committee.

Albania's written literature of a nationalist character first developed among Italo-Albanians in Calabria in the mid-19th century and among the Albanian intellectuals in Constantinople in the second half of the 19th century. Naim Erashëri (1846–1900), Albania's national poet, belonged to the Constantinople group. His most highly regarded works are *Bagëti e Bujqësi (Cattle and Land), Histori e Skenderbeut (History of Scanderbeg),* and a collection of short poems, *Lulet e Verës (Spring Flowers).* Kostandin Kristoforidhi (K. Nelko, 1827–95) translated the Old and New Testaments into Albanian and compiled a standard Albanian-Greek dictionary. Faik Konitza (1875–1942), prewar Albanian minister to Washington, edited a literary review, *Albania,* which became the focal publication of Albanian writers living abroad. Gjergj Fishta (1871–1940), a Franciscan friar who was active in the nationalist movement, wrote a long epic poem, *Lahuta e Malcís (The Lute of the Mountains),* which is regarded as a masterpiece of Albanian literature. Bishop Fan Stylian Noli (1882–1965), a political leader in the early 1920s, was Albania's foremost translator of Shakespeare, Ibsen, Cervantes, and other world classics. Lasgush Poradeci (1899–1987) was a highly regarded lyric poet. Ismail Kadare (b.1926), winner of the Booker International Prize and candidate for the Nobel Prize in Literature, takes as his subjects contemporary Albanian society, the communist regime, and Albanian old traditions (*kanun*). Kadare's works include *Gjenerali i Ushtrisë së Vdekur (The General of the Dead Army)* and *Pallati i ëndrrave (The Palace of Dreams).*

49 DEPENDENCIES

Albania has no territories or colonies.

50 BIBLIOGRAPHY

Destani, Beytullah (ed.). *Albania and Kosovo: Political and Ethnic Boundaries, 1867–1946.* New York: Archive Editions, 1999.

Elsie, Robert. *Albanian Literature: A Short History.* London, Eng.: I. B. Tauris, 2005.

———. *Historical Dictionary of Albania.* Lanham, Md.: Scarecrow, 2004.

Frucht, Richard (ed.). *Eastern Europe: An Introduction to the People, Lands, and Culture.* Santa Barbara, Calif.: ABC-CLIO, 2005.

Green, Sarah F. *Notes from the Balkans: Locating Marginality and Ambiguity on the Greek-Albanian Border.* Princeton, N.J.: Princeton University Press, 2005.

Hall, Derek R. *Albania and the Albanians.* New York: St. Martin's Press, 1994.

Hoshi, Iraj, Ewa Balcerowicz, and Leszek Balcerowicz (eds.). *Barriers to Entry and Growth of New Firms in Early Transition: A Comparative Study of Poland, Hungary, Czech Republic, Albania, and Lithuania.* Boston: Kluwer Academic Publishers, 2003.

King, Russell, Nicola Mai, and Stephanie Schwandner-Sievers (eds.). *The New Albanian Migration.* Portland, Ore.: Sussex Academic Press, 2005.

Marx, Trish. *One Boy from Kosovo.* New York: HarperCollins, 2002.

ANDORRA

Principality of Andorra
Principat d'Andorra

CAPITAL: Andorra la Vella

FLAG: The national flag is a tricolor of blue, yellow, and red vertical stripes. On the state flag (shown here) the yellow stripe bears the coat of arms.

ANTHEM: The *Himne Andorra* begins "El gran Carlemany mon pare" ("Great Charlemagne my father").

MONETARY UNIT: Andorra has no currency of its own; the euro, adopted by both Spain and France, is used. There are coins of 1, 5, 10, 20, and 50 cents and 1 euro and 2 euros. There are notes of 5, 10, 20, 50, 100, 200, and 500 euros. €1 = $1.25475 (or $1 = €0.79697) as of 2005.

WEIGHTS AND MEASURES: The metric system and some old local standards are used.

HOLIDAYS: New Year's Day, 1 January; National Festival, 8 September; Christmas, 25 December. Movable religious holidays include Good Friday and Easter Monday.

TIME: 1 PM = noon GMT.

¹LOCATION, SIZE, AND EXTENT

Landlocked Andorra lies in southwestern Europe on the southern slopes of the Pyrénées Mountains between the French departments of Ariège and Pyrénées-Orientales to the N and the Spanish provinces of Gerona and Lérida to the S, with a total boundary length of 120.3 km (74.6 mi).

Andorra is about 2.5 times the size of Washington, D.C., with a total area of 468 sq km (180 sq mi), extending 30.1 km (18.7 mi) E–W and 25.4 km (15.8 mi) N–S.

Andorra's capital city, Andorra la Vella, is located in the southwestern part of the country.

²TOPOGRAPHY

Andorra is situated in a single drainage basin, but its main stream, the Riu Valira, has two distinct branches and six open basins; hence the term "Valleys" (Les Valls) was traditionally employed as part of the name of the principality. The section of the river flowing through El Serrat by way of Ordino and La Massánan is the Valira del Nord, while that flowing through Canillo, Encamp, and Les Escaldes is the Valira d'Orient. Most of the country is rough and mountainous, and there is little level surface. All the valleys are at least 900 m (3,000 ft) high, and the mean altitude is over 1,800 m (6,000 ft). There are lofty peaks, of which the highest is Coma Pedrosa (2,946 m/9,665 ft).

³CLIMATE

Because of its high elevation, Andorra has severe winters. The northern valleys are completely snowed up for several months. Most rain falls in April and October. Humidity is very low. Summers are warm or mild, depending on the altitude. There are considerable variations between maximum day and night temperatures.

⁴FLORA AND FAUNA

The plant and animal life is similar to that found in the neighboring areas of France and Spain. Chestnut and walnut trees grow only in the area around Sant Julía de Lòria, the lowest village. Elsewhere, evergreen oaks still are common. Higher regions and many valleys have pines, firs, and various forms of subalpine and alpine plant life. At the highest altitudes there are no trees, but grass is plentiful during the summer. There are carnations, violets, bellflowers, and daisies, as well as blackberries, wild strawberries, and moss. Bears, wolves, foxes, martens, Pyrenean chamois, rabbits, hares, eagles, vultures, wild ducks, and geese may be found in isolated areas. The mountain streams contain trout, brochet, and crayfish.

⁵ENVIRONMENT

Andorra was once heavily forested. One explanation for the name of the country is that it came from the Moorish word *aldarra*, meaning "place thick with trees." Andorra's mountainous environment attracts 12 million tourists each year. In recent decades, however, the forested area has been decreasing steadily. Overgrazing of mountain meadows by sheep, with consequent soil erosion, is another environmental problem. According to a 2006 report issued by the International Union for Conservation of Nature and Natural Resources (IUCN), threatened species included 1 type of mammal: the common otter. The Apollo butterfly and the lesser horseshoe bat are vulnerable species.

⁶POPULATION

The population of Andorra in 2005 was estimated by the United Nations (UN) at 74,000, which placed it at number 183 in population among the 193 nations of the world. In 2005, approximately 13% of the population was over 65 years of age, with another 15% of the population under 15 years of age. According to the UN, the annual population rate of change for 2005–10 was expected to be 0.7%, a rate the government viewed as satisfactory. The projected population for the year 2025 was 81,000. The population density was 164 per sq km (426 per sq mi).

The UN estimated that 92% of the population lived in urban areas in 2005, and that urban areas were growing at an annual rate of 2.35%. The capital city, Andorra la Vella, had a population of 21,000 in that year. Other leading towns are Les Escaldes, Sant Julía de Lòria, Encamp, and La Massánan.

The population is concentrated in the seven urbanized valleys that form Andorra's political districts.

7 MIGRATION

Immigration consists mainly of Spanish, Portuguese, and French nationals who intend to work in Andorra; these groups make up some 70% of the population. Spanish nationals account for the largest group of foreign residents, comprising approximately 43% of the population in 1999. There is also a small but rapidly growing group of African immigrants, especially from North Africa, working mostly in agriculture and construction. Immigrant workers are supposed to hold temporary work authorization permits, which are valid only as long as the job exists for which the permit was obtained. However, more than 4,000 immigrants did not have work permits in 1999, due to the fact that the quota for immigration is not as high as the number of workers needed in the country. In 2005, the net migration rate was estimated as 6.53 migrants per 1,000 population. In 2004, approximately 63% of the population was not born in Andorra. The government views the migration levels as satisfactory.

8 ETHNIC GROUPS

Native Andorrans made up only about 33% of the total population in 1998; they are of Catalan stock. About 43% of the population was Spanish, 11% were Portuguese, and about 7% were French. About 6% are from other groups.

9 LANGUAGES

The official language is Catalan. French, Portuguese, and Castilian are also spoken.

10 RELIGIONS

Traditionally, over 90% of all Andorrans are Roman Catholic. Though it is not an official state religion, the constitution acknowledges a special relationship with the Roman Catholic Church, offering some special privileges to that group. The Muslim community is primarily made up of North African immigrants. Other Christian denominations include the Anglican Church, Jehovah's Witnesses, the Reunification Church, the New Apostolic Church, and the Church of Jesus Christ of Latter-day Saints. There is a small community of Hindus.

11 TRANSPORTATION

A north-south highway links Andorra la Vella with the Spanish and French borders. Secondary roads and trails also cross the border but are sometimes closed in winter because of deep snows. There were 269 km (167 mi) of roads in 2001, of which 198 km (123 mi) were paved. As of 1995 there were 40,127 motor vehicles, of which 35,941 were passenger cars and 4,186 were trucks, taxis, and buses.

Buses, the principal means of mass transit, provide regular service to Seo de Urgel and Barcelona in Spain, and to Perpignan in France. Among several cable cars, the most important operates between Encamp and Engolasters Lake. Vehicles from neighboring countries transport most merchandise.

Andorra does not have railways or commercial airports, but the airport at Seo de Urgel is only 20 km (12.5 mi) from Andorra la Vella. The nearest international airports are at Barcelona, Spain, located 215 km (134 mi) from Andorra, and at Toulouse, France, 165 km (103 mi) away. There is daily bus service from the Barcelona and Toulouse airports to Andorra.

12 HISTORY

According to one tradition, Charlemagne gave the region the name Andorra for its supposed likeness to the biblical town of Endor. Tradition also asserts that Charlemagne granted the Andorran people a charter in return for their help in fighting the Moors, and that Charlemagne's son Louis I, king of France, confirmed the charter.

It is generally agreed that Charles the Bald, the son of Louis, appointed the count of Urgel (now Seo de Urgel) overlord of Andorra and gave him the right to collect the imperial tribute. The bishop of Urgel, however, also claimed Andorra as part of the endowment of his cathedral. In 1226, the lords of the countship of Foix, in present-day south-central France, by marriage became heirs to the counts of Urgel. The quarrels between the Spanish bishop and the French counts over rights in Andorra led in 1278 to their adoption of a paréage, a feudal institution recognizing equal rights of two lords to a seigniorage.

In 1505, Germaine of Foix married Ferdinand V of Castile, thereby bringing the lordship of Andorra under Spanish rule. On taking over the kingdom in 1519, Emperor Charles V granted the lordship of Les Valls, as it was then known, to Germaine of Foix's line in perpetuity. Henry III of Navarre, who was also count of Foix, in 1589 ascended the French throne as Henry IV, and by an edict of 1607 established the head of the French state, along with the bishop of Urgel, as co-princes of Andorra.

In 1793, the French revolutionary government refused the traditional Andorran tribute as smacking of feudalism and renounced its suzerainty, despite the wish of the Andorrans to enjoy French protection and avoid being under exclusively Spanish influence.

Andorra remained neutral in the Napoleonic wars with Spain. Napoleon restored the co-principality in 1806 after the Andorrans petitioned him to do so. French title to the principality subsequently passed from the kings to the president of France.

Long an impoverished land having little contact with any nations other than adjoining France and Spain, Andorra after World War II achieved considerable prosperity through a developing tourist industry. This development, abetted by improvements in transport and communications, has tended to break down Andorra's isolation and to bring Andorrans into the mainstream of European history. Public demands for democratic reforms led to the extension of the franchise to women in the 1970s and to the creation of new and more fully autonomous organs of government in the early 1980s.

Andorra formally became a parliamentary democracy in May 1993 following approval of a new constitution by a popular referendum in March 1993. The new constitution retained the French and Spanish co-princes although with reduced, and narrowly defined, powers. Civil rights were greatly expanded including the legalization of political parties and trade unions, and provision was made for an independent judiciary. Andorra entered into a customs union with the European Communities (now the EU) in 1991 and was admitted to the UN on 28 July 1993. The country has been seeking ways to improve its export potential and increase its economic ties with its European neighbors. The financial services sector of the economy is highly important, given Andorra's status as a tax haven and its banking secrecy laws.

¹³GOVERNMENT

The governmental system of Andorra is unique. The constitution adopted in 1993 retained the French and Spanish co-princes but reduced their powers. The co-princes are the president of France and the bishop of Urgel, Spain. The co-princes are represented in Andorra by permanent delegates and veguers. Both the delegates and veguers reside in Andorra and acquire Andorran nationality ex officio, but they are not typically native Andorrans.

Legislation is enacted by the General Council, consisting of 28 members (14 members chosen from the national constituency and 14 representing the 7 parishes), elected for a four-year term since December 1981.

As of 2005, the president of the General Council was Marc Forné Molné. The General Council designates as its head a first syndic (*syndic procureur général*) and a second syndic for the conduct of administration; upon election to their four-year terms, these syndics cease to be members of the council.

The right to vote, which at one time was limited to third-generation Andorran males of 25 years of age or over, by 1981 had been extended to include all native Andorrans of Andorran parentage (at age 21) and first-generation Andorrans of foreign parentage (at age 28). In October 1985, the voting age was lowered to 18 years. In October 1992, the suffrage was broadened to include spouses of Andorran citizens and long-term residents.

¹⁴POLITICAL PARTIES

Prior to 1993, political parties were illegal in Andorra, though the Democratic Party of Andorra (formed in 1979) was tolerated. There have been two main factions in organized political life—conservatives and liberals. However, in the 2001 elections, three parties with distinct political tenets competed: the conservative Liberal Party of Andorra (PLA), the left-of-center Social Democratic Party (PS), and the Andorran Democratic Center Party (CDA).

The general election of December 1993, in which five parties gained representation, was the first under Andorra's new constitution. The results of the general election held April 2005 were as follows: the Liberal Party of Andorra (PLA), 14 seats; the Social Democratic Party (PS), 12; and the Andorran Democratic Center Party (CDA) 2.

¹⁵LOCAL GOVERNMENT

Andorra is divided into seven parishes or districts: Andorra la Vella, Canillo, Encamp, La Massána, Escaldes-Engordany, Ordino,

LOCATION: 42°25′ to 42°40′ N; 1°25′E. BOUNDARY LENGTHS: France, 60 kilometers (37.3 miles); Spain, 65 kilometers (40.4 miles).

and Sant Juliá de Lòria. Eligible voters in each of the districts elect members of its parish council (*comú*).

Parish councils administer local affairs. Each council generally consists of 8 to 14 members elected by universal suffrage for four-year terms at the same time as general councilors. Councils elect a senior consul and a junior consul.

¹⁶JUDICIAL SYSTEM

The 1993 constitution guarantees an independent judiciary and the judiciary has in fact been independent. A Superior Council of Justice oversees and administers the judicial system. The Superior Council of Justice has five members. One member each is appointed by the two co-princes, the head of government, the president of the General Council, and members of the lower courts. Members of the judiciary are appointed for six-year terms. The judicial process is fair and efficient.

The new constitution also calls for respect for the promotion of liberty, equality, justice, tolerance, defense of human rights, dignity of the person, and privacy, and guarantees against arbitrary arrest and detention.

Under the current system, civil cases in the first instance are heard by four judges (*batlles*). Appeals are heard in the Court of

Appeal. Final appeals in civil cases are brought before the Supreme Court of Andorra at Perpignan, France, or the Ecclesiastical Court of the Bishop of Seu d'Urgell, Spain.

Criminal cases are heard in Andorra la Vella by the Tribunal des Cortes, consisting of the veguers, and the judge of appeal, two judges, and two members of the General Council. Few criminal trials are held, and the principality's jail is used only for persons awaiting sentencing. Sentenced criminals have the choice of French or Spanish jails. The courts apply the customary law of Andorra, supplementing it where necessary with Roman law and customary Catalan law. Traditional laws are compiled in the Manual Digest of 1748 and the Politar of 1763; legal standards are found in the Instructions to Bailiffs of 1740.

[17] ARMED FORCES

Andorra has no defense force, and the police force is small. The sole military expenses are for ammunition used in salutes at official ceremonies, the lone responsibility of Andorra's small army. France and Spain are pledged to defend Andorra.

[18] INTERNATIONAL COOPERATION

Andorra was admitted to the United Nations on 28 July 1993. It participates in the ECE, ICAO, ITU, UNESCO, UNCCD, IC-CROM, WHO, WIPO, WToO, and is an observer at the WTO. It is also a member of the Council of Europe, the ICCt, and Interpol. Andorra joined the OSCE on 25 April 1996. As of 1991, Andorra has had a special agreement with the European Union. Andorra is part of the Organization for the Prohibition of Chemical Weapons. In cooperation on environmental issues, Andorra is part of the Basel Convention.

[19] ECONOMY

The Andorran economy is primarily based on trade and tourism, with the traffic between France and Spain providing most of the revenue. Andorra is attractive for shoppers from France and Spain because of low taxes. However, Andorra's comparative advantage has recently eroded as the economies of France and Spain have been opened up, providing broader availability of goods and lower tariffs. Approximately 10 million tourists visit Andorra each year, drawn by Andorra's summer and winter resorts.

The Andorran banking system is of significant importance as a tax haven for foreign financial transactions and investments.

Prior to the creation of the European Union there was an active trade in consumer goods, which were duty-free in Andorra. With the creation of the EU, Andorran manufactured goods remain tariff free, but Andorran agricultural products are subject to EU tariffs. The production of agricultural goods is limited, though, as only 2% of the land is arable. Most food has to be imported.

[20] INCOME

The US Central Intelligence Agency (CIA) reports that in 2005 Andorra's gross domestic product (GDP) was estimated at $1.9 billion. The CIA defines GDP as the value of all final goods and services produced within a nation in a given year and computed on the basis of purchasing power parity (PPP) rather than value as measured on the basis of the rate of exchange based on current dollars. The per capita GDP was estimated at $26,800. The annual growth rate of GDP was estimated at 2%. The average inflation rate in 2004 was 4.3%.

[21] LABOR

Total employment as of 2001 was estimated at 33,000. As of 2000, an estimated 1% were employed in the agricultural sector, with 21% employed in industry and 78% in the services sector. There is virtually no unemployment in Andorra.

Under the constitution passed in 1993, workers were granted the right to form and maintain trade union associations without prejudice, but implementation has not been provided. Associations must register with the government, and in 2002, there were 600 such associations. However, no unions existed as of that year. The right to strike is not covered under the law, nor does it specifically cover collective bargaining. With no business regulation or registration requirements, smuggling goods between France and Spain is a leading source of informal employment.

There are government-mandated health and safety standards, which are regularly enforced with routine inspections. There is a government-set minimum wage, which was $7.20 per hour in 2005. The minimum working age is 18, with some exceptions allowing 16- and 17-year-olds to work. The workweek is limited to 40 hours, with an additional 66 hours per month of overtime allowed.

[22] AGRICULTURE

Because of Andorra's mountainous character, only about 2% of the land is suitable for crops. However, until the tourism sector in Andorra experienced an upsurge, agriculture had been the mainstay of the economy. Hay, tobacco, and vegetables must be irrigated; cereals, mainly rye and barley, are dry-cropped. Most of the cropped land is devoted to hay production for animal feed. Since there is insufficient sunlight on northward-facing slopes and the lands in shadow are too cold for most crops, some southward-facing fields high in the mountains must be used even though they are a considerable distance from the farmers' homes.

Tobacco, the most distinctive Andorran crop, is grown on the best lands. Andorran tobacco is usually mixed with eastern tobaccos, because of its strong quality. Other farm products include cereals, potatoes, and garden vegetables. Grapes are used mainly for raisins and for the making of anisette. The lack of modern methods on Andorra's family farms is causing the agricultural sector to decrease in importance. Most food is now imported.

[23] ANIMAL HUSBANDRY

For many centuries, until eclipsed by tourism and other service industries, sheep raising was the basis of Andorra's economy. Andorran mules are still greatly prized. Cattle, sheep, and goats are raised both in the valleys and in some of the higher areas. Cattle are raised mainly for their meat, and there are few dairy cows. When the cattle move upward in the spring, entire families move to temporary villages in the mountains to herd, mow, and plant. Large droves of sheep and goats from France and Spain feed in Andorra in the summer, and the Spanish-owned animals in particular are looked after by Andorran shepherds. On their way back to their native land, many of the animals are sold at annual fairs; the Spanish fairs are usually held in Andorra in September and the French in November. Andorra's own animal fairs are also held in the fall.

Livestock includes an estimated 9,000 sheep, 1,100 cattle, and 200 horses. Meat production has increased in recent years, but imports account for about 90% of total meat consumption. The milk produced is sufficient for domestic consumption, and some milk has been exported to Spain.

24 FISHING

The streams are full of trout and other freshwater fish, but Andorra imports most fish for domestic consumption from Spain.

25 FORESTRY

About 10,000 hectares (24,700 acres), or 22% of the total land area, is forested. Fuel wood may be freely gathered by anyone, but it may not be bought or sold. Wood needed for building purposes is cut in rotation from a different district each year. For centuries logs have been shipped to Spain. Most reforestation is in pines.

26 MINING

For hundreds of years, Andorran forges were famous in northern Spain. There are still iron ore deposits in the valley of Ordino and in many of the mountain areas, but access to them is difficult. In addition to iron, small amounts of lead are still mined, and alum and building stones are extracted. The sulfurous waters of Les Escaldes are used in washing wool.

27 ENERGY AND POWER

The largest hydroelectric plant, at Encamp, has a capacity of 26.5 MW and provides about 40% of Andorra's electric power needs, with most of the remainder being imported from Spain. The total installed capacity in 1991 was 35,000 kW. Energy production in 1992 totaled 140 million kWh.

There are four gas companies, with Andor Gas supplying propane and the others butane.

28 INDUSTRY

Manufacturing accounted for approximately 5% of GDP in 2004. Andorra produces cigars, cigarettes, textiles, leather, building materials, and furniture, both for local use and for export. Woolen blankets and scarves are made at Les Escaldes.

Many enterprises produce frozen foods, pastry, and other commodities. There are distilleries for the production of anisette, vermouth, liqueurs, and brandy.

Several firms manufacture woolen goods. There are a number of construction companies, the largest producing building materials from iron.

29 SCIENCE AND TECHNOLOGY

Students wishing to pursue scientific and technical careers usually receive their training abroad. The Andorra Scientific Society in Andorra la Vella was founded in 1983. The National Motor Car Museum in Encamp, founded in 1988, exhibits cars, motorbikes, and bicycles dating from 1898 to 1950.

30 DOMESTIC TRADE

Andorra la Vella has many stores where commodities of all kinds and origins may be purchased. The larger villages have small general stores. The French, Spanish, and Andorran animal fairs that take place at Andorra la Vella, Encamp, Ordino, and elsewhere are attended by most Andorrans and by many French and Spanish farmers.

There is a high level of competition between the large department stores and the small shops. There are some 600 retail establishments in the country, of which the department and jewelry stores are the most numerous, followed by food and clothing outlets. Trade in consumer goods is very active, particularly with French and Spanish shoppers who are attracted by the lower tax rates on purchases. Handicrafts, cigars, cigarettes, and furniture are major products manufactured for both domestic and export markets.

There are over 270 hotels and 400 restaurants catering to the thriving tourist trade.

31 FOREIGN TRADE

Owing to the large traffic of unaccounted goods across Andorra's borders, official statistics do not reflect the true volume of transactions. Of recorded trade, close to half is with Spain and over one-quarter with France. The majority of imports consist of consumer goods sold to visitors. Reported imports exceed recorded exports by some 26:1.

A customs union with the EC (now the EU) took effect in 1991, allowing industrial goods to pass between Andorra and EC members under a uniform customs tariff. The EU's external tariffs are to be applied by Andorra to its trade with non-EU members.

32 BALANCE OF PAYMENTS

Most goods have to be imported, and there is a structural trade deficit. Owing to the large traffic of unaccounted goods across Andorra's borders, official statistics do not reflect the true volume of transactions.

Principal Trading Partners – Andorra (2002)

(In millions of US dollars)

Country	Exports	Imports	Balance
World	63.2	1,198.1	-1,134.9
Spain	33.6	599.5	-565.9
France-Monaco	18.6	293.8	-275.2
Germany	6.0	61.4	-55.4
Norway	0.8	...	0.8
United States	0.6	15.5	-14.9
Italy-San Marino-Holy See	0.4	38.4	-38.0
Netherlands	0.4	11.7	-11.3
Switzerland-Liechtenstein	0.3	18.9	-18.6
United Arab Emirates	0.3	...	0.3
Portugal	0.2	3.6	-3.4

(…) data not available or not significant.

SOURCE: *2003 International Trade Statistics Yearbook*, New York: United Nations, 2004.

33 BANKING AND SECURITIES

An unofficial Convention of Banks and Bankers periodically attends to financial affairs. The banking system attracts foreign financial transactions and investments because there are no direct taxes in Andorra.

There were six private banks in 1997: Banc Internácional d'Andorra, Banca Mora, Banca Privada d'Andorra, Credit Andorra, Banc Agricol i Comercial d'Andora, and Banca Reig. About half of all deposits are made in pesetas, with one-fourth in francs and the balance in other currencies.

There is no stock exchange, and therefore, stocks and bonds are not traded in Andorra.

34 INSURANCE

The principal firm is the Andorra Insurance Co., established in 1951, which provides coverage that includes life, fire, accident, and plate glass. There are several other insurance companies, including Assegurances Bercia, Assegurances GAN, Assegurances Generali France, Assegurances Generals, Assegurances la Catalana, Assegurances La Equitativa, Assegurances Layetana, Assegurances Lepanto, Assegurances Riba, Assegurances Royal Insurance, Assegurances Santamaria Cosan, Assegurances Schweiz, Atlantis Compañía d'Assegurances, CMA, Commercial Union Assegurances, Compañía Andorrana d'Assegurances, Financera d'Assegurances, Generali, Grup Assegurador Catalana Occident, Multinacional Aseguradora, Patrimoine Assegurances, Santamaria Cosan Assegurances, Unio I Aliança de Previsio, and Zürich Delegacio.

35 PUBLIC FINANCE

The US Central Intelligence Agency (CIA) estimated that in 1997 Andorra's central government took in revenues of approximately $385 million and had expenditures of $342 million. Revenues minus expenditures totaled approximately $43 million.

36 TAXATION

There is no income tax on the individual or corporate level. Employees pay social security taxes at rates of 5-9%; employers pay 13%. As of October 1991, a value-added tax had been enacted and was expected to impose charges of 1-7% on the production and import of goods. Also scheduled for implementation under the 1992 budget law were a registration tax on certain activities, to provide 8.6% of government revenues, and a tax on electricity consumption and telephone services to contribute 1.6% of state revenues.

37 CUSTOMS AND DUTIES

Andorra is a member of the EU Customs Union and generally abides by the EU trade regime. However, its agricultural exports are treated as of non-EU origin and, therefore, are subject to ordinary tariffs.

38 FOREIGN INVESTMENT

Andorra has no formal investment incentive programs, other than offering some financial support for the development of tourist facilities. Andorran banks attract foreign depositors and investors, in part due to the lack of taxes but also due to Andorra's bank secrecy laws. As such, this has long made Andorra a tax haven and a refuge for smugglers. In 2004, however, Andorra was obliged to accept the EU's Savings Tax Directive, and as of July 2005, imposes a withholding tax of 15% on return of savings paid to citizens of EU member states, of which 75% is remitted onwards to the states concerned. In 2001, a Department for the Prevention of Money Laundering was established, which is authorized to carry out unannounced inspections and hands information to the public prosecutor's office or to the government.

39 ECONOMIC DEVELOPMENT

Government policy is to encourage local industries and to promote private investment. In addition to handicrafts, manufacturing includes cigars, cigarettes, and furniture. Tourism accounts for 80% of gross domestic product (GDP), and the banking sector significantly contributes to the economy.

In 2002, Andorra adopted the EU's common currency, the euro. In 2004, Andorra signed a series of accords with the EU in the fields of economic, social, and cultural cooperation.

40 SOCIAL DEVELOPMENT

There is a social welfare system that was first introduced in 1966. Programs include old-age, disability, and survivors' pensions, health and maternity coverage, and workers' compensation.

There is no legal discrimination against women, although they have only enjoyed full suffrage since 1970 and play only a very minimal role in the country's government. Women's rights advocates have reported that pregnant women frequently lose their jobs. On average, women earn 25% less than men. In 2004, violence against women declined, but there was an increase in child abuse. Children's welfare is promoted by the government.

The constitution prohibits discrimination on the basis of birth, race, sex, origin, religion, or any other personal or social condition. Foreign nationals, primarily from Spain, France, Portugal, and the United Kingdom, account for over 40% of the population. While accorded the same rights and freedoms as citizens, foreigners lack access to some of the social benefits provided by law. Recent legislation has improved living conditions for immigrant workers, but many still have only temporary work permits and face deportation if they lose their jobs.

The rights of freedom of speech, press, peaceful assembly, religion, and movement are provided by the constitution and are respected in practice.

41 HEALTH

Infant mortality was estimated at 4.05 per 1,000 births in 2005. Life expectancy for that year was estimated at 83.5 years, the highest in the world. The 1999 birth rate was 10.27 and the overall mortality rate was 5.5 per 1,000 people. In the same year the fertility rate was 1.25. In 2004, Andorra had 259.4 physicians, 302.4 nurses, 1.8 midwives, and 62 dentists per 100,000 people.

42 HOUSING

Most Andorran houses are made of stone. Since the flat land is used for farm crops, the rural houses are frequently backed against the mountainsides. The high villages (*cortals*) are situated on a line between the highest fields and the lowest limits of high-level pastures. Isolated houses (*bordes*) are found at higher elevations. Many families maintain temporary dwellings in the highest pasture areas. All residents have access to safe water and sanitation systems.

⁴³EDUCATION

By law, students must attend school between the ages of 6 and 16. There are essentially three coexisting school systems in the country: French, Spanish, and Andorran. The French government partially subsidizes education in Andorra's French-language schools; schools in the southern section, near Spain, are supported by the church. The local language, Catalan, has been introduced at a school under the control of the Roman Catholic Church. About 50% of Andorran children attend French primary schools, and the rest attend Spanish or Andorran school. In general, Andorran schools follow the Spanish curriculum, and their diplomas are recognized by Spain. Primary school enrollment in 2003 was estimated at about 89%; 88% for boys and 90% for girls. The same year, secondary school enrollment was about 71%; 69% for boys and 74% for girls. The pupil to teacher ratio for primary school was at about 12:1 in 2003; the ratio was about 7:1 for secondary classes.

The University of Andorra was established in July 1997. It has a small enrollment and mostly offers long-distance courses through universities in Spain and France. The majority of secondary graduates who continue their education attend schools in France or Spain. In 2003, about 8% of eligible adult students were enrolled in tertiary programs. Virtually the entire adult population is literate. Andorra also has a nursing school and a school of computer science.

⁴⁴LIBRARIES AND MUSEUMS

The National Library and National Archives founded in 1974 and 1975 respectively are located in Andorra la Vella; the library holds over 45,000 volumes. Small museums reflect a variety of interests. The Museu Nacional de l'Automòbil (National Automobile Museum) is located in Encamp. Museu Postal (Postal Museum) is in Ordino. Also in Ordino is the Nikolaï Siadristy Museum—Museum of Miniatures, the first permanent museum of the artist Siadristy's miniatures.

⁴⁵MEDIA

Automatic telephone service was begun in 1967. In 2001, there were 35,000 mainline and 23,500 mobile cellular phones in use. Postal and telegraph services are handled by the Spanish and French administrations; a telex system was installed in 1970.

ORTA (public) and Radio Valira, are radio broadcast stations operated by Andorrans and supervised by the General Council. Andorrans also receive broadcasts from Spain and France. As of 1998, there were 15 FM radios stations. Andorra does not have its own television stations; television transmission is provided through technical accords with the Spanish and French government networks. In 1997 there were 16,000 radios and 27,000 television sets in use throughout the country.

The two main daily papers are the independent publications of *Diari D'Andorra* (*Andorra Daily*—2002 circulation 3,000) and *El Peridico de Andorra*. *Poble Andorra* is a major weekly publication with a circulation of about 3,000. Other newspapers, with smaller circulations, are the dailies *Independent* and *Informacions Diari,* and the weeklies *Correu Andorra* and *Informacions.* French and Spanish newspapers are also widely available.

As of 2001, there were an estimated 24,500 Internet users. In 2004, there were about 4,144 Internet hosts in the country.

The Andorran constitution ensures freedom of speech and press, and the government is said to respect these rights in practice.

⁴⁶ORGANIZATIONS

There are about 10 human rights associations in the country, the most active being the Association of Immigrants in Andorra (AIA), which defends the rights of foreign residents. The Association of Andorran Women (AAW) focuses on women's rights.

The Andorra Chamber of Commerce, Industry and Services works to support commercial and economic growth in Andorra by promoting commercial and industrial instruction; collaborating with the educational government in the administration of practical training for companies; coordinating trade fairs, exhibitions, and conventions; and supporting research programs. There are networking and educational associations representing a variety of professions, such as the Andorran Medical Association, the Andorran College of Dentists, the Andorran Bar Association, and the Andorran College of Engineers.

The Youth Council of Andorra (Area de Jovent), founded in 1988, serves as a nongovernmental platform for major youth and student organizations. The General Union of Andorran Students (Agrupacio General dels Estudiants d'Andorra (AGEA), founded in 1990, is a union of university students. Other youth NGOs include: the Andorran Red Cross Youth, Andorran Catholic Student Movement, and youth associations of Andorran Kiwanis, Lions and Rotary clubs. Andorra also sponsors an organization of the Special Olympics and a few national sports organizations, including groups for squash and sailing.

There are national chapters of the Red Cross Society, Caritas, and UNICEF.

⁴⁷TOURISM, TRAVEL, AND RECREATION

Tourism has brought considerable prosperity to Andorra and now constitutes the principal source of income. Visitors, mostly from France and Spain, come to Andorra each summer to attend the fairs and festivals, to buy consumer items at lower prices than are obtainable in the neighboring countries, and to enjoy the pleasant weather and beautiful scenery. There is skiing at Pas de la Casa and Soldeu in winter.

Shrines and festivals are both key attractions to tourists. Romanesque churches and old houses of interest are located in Ordino, Encamp, Sant Julía de Lória, Les Escaldes, Santa Coloma, and other villages. The best known is the shrine of Our Lady of Meritxell, Andorra's patroness, between Canillo and Encamp.

Pilgrims come from France and Spain to pay homage on 8 September, the festival day of Andorra's patroness. Each of the larger villages has its own festival during which the *sardana*, Andorra's national dance, is performed.

There is an International Jazz Festival at Escaldes-Engordany in July and the International Music Festival of Ordino in September.

In 2003, about 3,138,000 tourists visited Andorra, of whom 72% came from Spain, a 3% decline from 2002. Visitors need a valid passport to enter Andorra. No visa is required.

In 2003, the US Department of State estimated the daily cost of a stay in Andorra at $226.

⁴⁸FAMOUS ANDORRANS

There are no internationally famous Andorrans.

⁴⁹DEPENDENCIES

Andorra has no territories or colonies.

⁵⁰BIBLIOGRAPHY

Cameron, Peter. *Andorra*. New York: Farrar, Straus and Giroux, 1997.

De Cugnac, Pascal. *Pyrenees and Gascony: Including Andorra*. London: Hachette UK, 2000.

Taylor, Barry. *Andorra*. Oxford, England, and Santa Barbara, Calif.: Clio Press, 1993.

United Nations Conference on Trade and Development. *Handbook of International Trade and Development Statistics*. New York: United Nations, 1993.

World Bank. *World Tables 1994*. Baltimore and London, England: Johns Hopkins University Press, 1994.

ARMENIA

Republic of Armenia

Hayastani Hanrapetut 'Yun

CAPITAL: Yerevan

FLAG: Three horizontal bands of red (top), blue, and gold.

ANTHEM: *Mer Hayrenik.*

MONETARY UNIT: The dram (introduced 22 November 1993) is a paper currency in denominations of 10, 25, 50, 100, 200, and 500 drams. The dram (D) replaced the Armenian ruble and the Russian ruble (R). Currently D1 =$0.00225 (or $1 = D445) as of 2005.

WEIGHTS AND MEASURES: The metric system is in force.

HOLIDAYS: New Year's Day, 1–2 January; Christmas, 6 January; Day of Remembrance of the Victims of the Genocide, 24 April; Peace Day, 9 May; Anniversary of Declaration of First Armenian Republic (1918), 28 May; Public Holiday, 21 September; Day of Remembrance of the Victims of the Earthquake, 7 December; New Year's Eve, 31 December.

TIME: 4 PM = noon GMT.

¹LOCATION, SIZE, AND EXTENT

Armenia is a landlocked nation located in southeastern Europe/southwestern Asia. Comparatively, the area occupied by Armenia is slightly smaller than the state of Maryland with a total area of 29,800 sq km (11,506 sq mi). Armenia shares boundaries with Georgia on the N, Azerbaijan on the E and S, Iran on the S, and Turkey on the W and has a total boundary length of 1,254 km (778 mi). Armenia's capital city, Yerevan, is located in the west-central portion of the country on the Hrazdan River.

²TOPOGRAPHY

The topography of Armenia features the high Armenian Plateau and three primary mountain ranges, the Lesser Caucasus Mountains in the north, the Vardenis Range in central Armenia, and the Zangezur Range in the southeast. There is little forest land and a few fast flowing rivers. The Aras River Valley contains good soil. Mount Aragats, an extinct volcano in the plateau region, is the highest point in Armenia at 13,425 ft (4,095 m). The nation occasionally suffers from severe earthquakes. In December 1988, a massive earthquake struck near the city of Kumayri, killing over 25,000 people.

³CLIMATE

Armenia's climate ranges from subtropical to alpine-like in the mountains. The mean temperature in midsummer is 25°C (77°F). In midwinter, the mean temperature is 0°C (32°F). Rainfall is infrequent. The capital city receives 33 cm of rain annually (13 in), though more rainfall occurs in the mountains.

⁴FLORA AND FAUNA

Armenia is located in what geographers call the Aral Caspian Lowland. The country has broad sandy deserts and low grassy plateaus. The region is home to European bison, snow leopards, cheetahs, and porcupines.

⁵ENVIRONMENT

In 2000, Armenia's chief environmental problems resulted from natural disasters, pollution, and warfare. A strong earthquake in 1988 resulted in 55,000 casualties. Radiation from the meltdown of the nuclear reactor facility at Chernobyl in the former Soviet Union also polluted the environment. The nation's soil has also been polluted by chemicals including DDT and the Hrazdan and Ares rivers have also been polluted. The war between Armenia and Azerbaijan has strained the country's economy, limiting the resources that can be devoted to environmental preservation. It has also led to an energy blockade that has caused deforestation as trees are cut for firewood. Yet another environmental hazard is the restarting of the Metsamor nuclear power plant, which has been brought online without the safety systems recommended by the IAEA.

From 1990–1995, deforestation occurred at an average annual rate of 2.69%. However, some reforestation projects have been initiated. As of 2003, 7.6% of the total land area in Armenia is protected, including two sites protected as Ramsar wetlands: Lake Sevan and Lake Arpi. As of 2002, 11 of the nation's 84 species of mammal were threatened, as were 4 species of bird and 1 higher plant species. Endangered species include the Barbel sturgeon, Dahl's jird, and the field adder.

⁶POPULATION

The population of Armenia in 2005 was estimated by the United Nations (UN) at 3,033,000, which placed it at number 133 in population among the 193 nations of the world. In 2005, approximately 11% of the population was over 65 years of age, with another 22% of the population under 15 years of age. There were 87 males for every 100 females in the country. According to the UN, the annual population rate of change for 2005–10 was expected to be 0.3%; this low rate, attributed to a decline in fertility rates and migration, was considered too low by the government. The projected population for the year 2025 was 3,258,000. The population density was 102 per sq km (264 per sq mi).

The UN estimated that 65% of the population lived in urban areas in 2005, and that population in urban areas was changing at an annual rate of -0.43%. The capital city, Yerevan, had a population of 1,079,000 in that year. Other urban centers and their estimated populations include Kumayri (206,600) and Kirovakan (170,200). Most of the cities and towns are located along the river valleys in the north and west.

7 MIGRATION

Independent Armenia is only a portion of historic Armenia, which at its greatest extent also included lands now in Turkey, Iran, and Azerbaijan. There are Armenian communities in these countries and also in Russia, Georgia, Lebanon, Syria, and the United States. Between 1988 and 1993 around 360,000 ethnic Armenians arrived in Armenia from Azerbaijan as a result of the conflict over the disputed territory of Nagorno-Karabakh. In 1995 a citizenship law, which included special provisions making naturalization much easier for refugees from Azerbaijan, was enacted. By the end of January 2004, the number of refugees from Azerbaijan obtaining Armenian citizenship topped 65,000. One of the largest naturalizations of refugees in recent decades, United Nations High Commissioner for Refugees (UNHCR) supported the process with financial and material assistance. In 2003, there were 50,000 internally displaced persons (IDP) within the country. The UNHCR reported that at the end of 2004 there were 235,235 refugees in Armenia and 68 asylum seekers, of which over 50,000 refugees were assisted by UNHCR. From 1998 to 2003, except for 2000, remittance flows to Armenia grew by 20% per year.

Armenia has a net migration rate of -6.1 migrants per 1,000 population as of 2005. The government views both the immigration and emigration levels as too high.

8 ETHNIC GROUPS

A 2004 report indicates that Armenians comprise an estimated 98% of the population. Minority groups include the Azeri, Russians, Ukrainians, Belarussians, Jews, Assyrians, Georgians, Greeks, and Yezidi Kurds. As of 1993, most of the Azeris had emigrated from Armenia.

9 LANGUAGES

Armenian is spoken by about 97% of the population. Armenian belongs to an independent branch of the Indo-European linguistic family. It is a highly inflective language, with a complicated system of declensions. It is agglutinative, rich in consonants, and has no grammatical gender. The vocabulary includes many Persian loan words. There are two main dialects: East Armenian, the official language of Armenia, and West, or Turkish, Armenian. The alphabet, patterned after Persian and Greek letters, has 38 characters. Armenian literature dates from the early 5th century AD. Yezidi is

spoken by about 1% of the population; Russian and other various languages are spoken by the remaining 2%.

10 RELIGIONS

In 2005, about 90% of the population were nominally members of the Armenian Apostolic Church. Catholic churches, both Roman and Mekhitaris (Armenian Uniate), had an estimated 180,000 adherents. The next largest group was the Yezidi, a Kurdish ethnic and religious group that practice a mixture of beliefs from Islam, Zoroastrianism, and animism; they had an estimated 30,000 to 40,000 members. Other Christian denominations include Pentecostals, Greek Orthodox, Jehovah's Witnesses, the Armenian Evangelical Church, Baptists, Seventh-Day Adventists, the Church of Jesus Christ of the Latter-day Saints (Mormons). Most Jews, Muslims, and Baha'is are located in Yerevan.

Armenia became a Christian country in the 4th century AD. In 1991, the Law on Freedom of Conscience established the separation of church and state but granted the Armenian Apostolic Church status as the national church. All religious denominations and organizations outside of the Armenian Apostolic Church must be registered in order to operate. Those that are not registered are prohibited from publishing newspapers or magazines, sponsoring television or radio broadcasts, and renting meeting space. In 1997 amendments tightened registration requirements by raising the minimum number of adult members to qualify for registration from 50 to 200. The laws also indicate that a petitioning organization must adhere to a doctrine that is based on "historically recognized Holy Scriptures." Registration and monitoring of religious groups was originally under the jurisdiction of a government-based Council of Religious Affairs. In 2002 the president abolished the council and announced that a new office, under the prime minister, would handle matters of religion. The National Minorities and Religious Affairs Department was also established by the government.

The Armenian Apostolic Church is a member of the World Council of Churches.

11 TRANSPORTATION

As of 2004, there were 825 km (513 mi) of 1.520-m (broad) gauge railroad, not including industrial lines. An estimated 828 km (515 mi) are electrified. Supplies that arrive from Turkey by rail must be reloaded, due to a difference in rail gauges. Goods that cross Georgia or Azerbaijan are subject to travel delay from strikes and blockages and may be interdicted.

As of 2003, the highway system included 7,633 km (4,748 mi) of roads, all of which are paved. Of that total, 1,561 km (971 mi) are expressways.

There were an estimated 16 airports as of 2004, 11 of which had paved runways (as of 2005). The Zvartnots airport at Yerevan is fairly well maintained and receives scheduled flights from Moscow, Paris, New York, London, Amsterdam, Athens, Beirut, Dubai (UAE), Frankfurt, Istanbul, Prague, Tehrān, Vienna, Zürich, and Sofia. In 2003, 367,000 passengers were carried on scheduled domestic and international flights.

Cargo shipments to landlocked Armenia are routed through ports in Georgia and Turkey.

¹²HISTORY

Armenian territories were first united into an empire under Tigranes the Great (95–55 BC), whose extensive lands included parts of Syria and Iraq. Defeated by the Roman general Pompey, Armenia became a client state of the Roman Empire. Rome and Sasanian Persia partitioned Armenia, and after them Byzantium and the Ummayed and Abbasid caliphates controlled parts of Armenia. Armenia adopted Christianity at the beginning of the 4th century AD. The Seljuk Turks invaded Armenia in the 11th century, followed by Genghis Khan and Timur, leading to mass emigrations. Persia and Ottoman Turkey divided Armenia into eastern and western portions in the 16th–18th centuries. Russia took over Persia's holdings in 1828, and during the latter part of the 19th century both Russia and Turkey carried out harsh repression against nationalist activities among Armenians under their sway, leading to many deaths and mass emigrations. During World War I, Ottoman Turkey carried out forced resettlement and other harsh policies against Armenians, which Armenians term their national genocide. The historical experience remains a contentious issue in Armenian-Turkish relations.

After the Bolshevik revolution in Russia in 1917, Armenia declared independence in May 1918. Armenia's population of 750,000 included as many as 300,000 who had survived flight from Turkey, and the heavy burden of independence among hostile neighbors (it clashed with Turkey, Georgia, and Azerbaijan) and an inhospitable climate may have led to as many as 150,000 deaths from famine and disease. Although the August 1920 Treaty of Sevres accorded international recognition of Armenian independence, the Russian Red Army conquered Armenia in November 1920. In 1922, Armenia was named part of a Transcaucasian Soviet Federated Socialist Republic, which encompassed lands now in Armenia, Azerbaijan, and Georgia, but it became a separate union republic in 1936. During the 1920s, Moscow drew internal borders in the Caucasus, which resulted in Nagorno-Karabakh (NK), then a mostly ethnic Armenian region, being incorporated into Azerbaijan, separated from the rest of Soviet Armenia by a few miles of Azerbaijani territory. NK was given the status of an "autonomous republic."

Following a February 1988 call by the Nagorno-Karabakh (NK) legislature for unification with Armenia, the Armenian Supreme Soviet in December 1989 declared that NK, a largely ethnically Armenian-populated enclave within Azerbaijan, was part of Armenia. It also proclaimed Armenia's sovereignty over its land and resources. A popular referendum on independence was held in Armenia on 21 September 1991, in which 94% of the eligible population reportedly participated and which was approved by 99%. The Armenian legislature declared Armenia's independence two days later. Armenia received worldwide diplomatic recognition upon the collapse of the Soviet Union in December 1991.

Beginning in 1988, conflict engulfed NK, with Azerbaijan resisting the secession or independence of its enclave. Casualties were estimated at over 5,000. Emigration of 350,000 Armenians residing in Azerbaijan and over one million Azerbaijani residing in Armenia or NK followed pogroms in both states and conflict in NK and surrounding areas. In December 1991, a referendum in NK (boycotted by local Azerbaijani) approved NK's independence and a Supreme Soviet was elected, which on 6 January 1992, declared NK's independence and futilely appealed for world rec-

LOCATION: 40°0′ N to 45°0′ E BOUNDARY LENGTHS: Total boundary lengths, 1,254 kilometers (780 miles); Azerbaijan (east), 566 kilometers (352 miles); Azerbaijan (south), 221 kilometers (137 miles); Georgia, 164 kilometers (102 miles); Iran, 35 kilometers (22 miles); Turkey, 268 kilometers (167 miles).

ognition. In 1993, Armenian forces gained control over NK and surrounding areas, occupying over 20% of Azerbaijani territory, which they continued to hold despite an Azerbaijani offensive in 1993–1994 that reportedly cost 6,000 Azeri casualties. A cease-fire has held fitfully since May 1994, but talks on a political settlement remain inconclusive. In the six-year period of conflict from 1988 to 1994, more than 35,000 people were killed and nearly one million have been left homeless.

In November 1989, Levon Ter-Petrosyan became a leader of the Armenian National Movement (ANM), which grew out of the Karabakh Committee to push for Armenia's independence, and its chairman in March 1990. ANM and other nationalist deputies cooperated to elect him chairman of the Armenian Supreme Soviet in August 1990, inflicting a serious blow on the Armenian Communist Party. Following Armenia's declaration of independence, presidential elections were held on 16 October 1991. Ter-Petrosyan was supported by the ANM, winning 83% of the vote against six other candidates, including internationally famous dissident Paruir Hairikian of the Association for National Self-Determination and Sos Sarkisyan of the Armenian Revolutionary Federation (ARF; called Dashnaktsutyun in Armenian, meaning "federation"). Ter-Petrosyan was sworn into office on 11 November 1991, for a five-year term. His suspension of the activities of Armenian Revolutionary Federation party in December 1994 and a trial of its leaders raised concerns among some observers about possible setbacks to democratization.

Elections to Armenia's unicameral 190-member National Assembly (legislature) were held in June 1995, at the same time as a referendum in which Armenian voters adopted the country's first post-Communist new constitution. International observers reported many campaign and voting irregularities. Observers from the Organization for Security and Cooperation in Europe (OSCE) judged the elections "free but not fair," in part because the main opposition party, the ARF, was banned from participation, the government dominated campaigning, the CEC appeared heavily pro-government in its decisions, and security officers constituted a chilling presence in many voting places. Voting irregularities reported on election day by the international observers included the violation of secret voting and pressure in voting places to cast a ballot for certain parties or candidates. In all, the Republic Bloc and other pro-government parties won 166 out of 190 seats, while the opposition won only 18 and independents four (two seats were undecided).

Ter-Petrosyan won reelection as president on 22 September 1996, by garnering 51.75% of the vote, a far smaller majority than in 1991, barely avoiding runoff balloting. Ter-Petrosyan's main opponent in the presidential race was Vazgen Manukian, head of the National Democratic Union (NDU) party. He garnered 41.3% of the presidential vote. Manukian had worked closely with Ter-Petrosyan in the Karabakh Committee. Following the presidential election, followers of Manukian's electoral coalition demonstrated against what they and many international observers termed irregular voting procedures. On 25 September 1996, tens of thousands of protesters stormed the legislative building in Yerevan and assaulted the legislative speaker and deputy speaker, both belonging to the ANM. The crowd was dispersed by police with few injuries or deaths.

In March 1997, in an attempt to garner greater public support for his regime, Ter-Petrosyan appointed a highly popular war hero of the NK conflict, Robert Kocharian, to the post of prime minister of Armenia. Ter-Petrosyan and others viewed Kocharian as having the leadership abilities necessary to help revive the slumping economy and to increase tax collection. In accepting the prime ministership, Kocharian resigned as president of NK.

Ter-Petrosyan announced in September 1997 that he had accepted an Organization for Security and Cooperation in Europe (OSCE) peace plan as a basis for resolving the NK conflict that would require "compromises" from Armenia. The two-stage plan called for NK Armenians to withdraw from most territories they had occupied outside of NK and for international peacekeepers to be deployed, followed by discussion of NK's status. The announcement brought open criticism from Kocharian and other Armenian and NK officials. On 1 February 1998, Yerkrapah, a legislative faction and militia group composed of veterans of the NK conflict, and headed by the country's defense minister, called for

Ter-Petrosyan to resign. Many members of Ter-Petrosyan's ANM legislative faction defected, leading to the resignation of the parliamentary speaker. Heated debate in the legislature culminated with Ter-Petrosyan's resignation on 3 February 1998. Ter-Petrosyan denounced the "bodies of power" for demanding his resignation, referring obliquely to Kocharian, Defense Minister Vazgen Sarkisyan, and Minister of the Interior and National Security Serzh Sarkisyan. Although the constitution called for the legislative speaker to assume the duties of acting president pending an election, the resignation of the speaker caused these duties to devolve upon Prime Minister Kocharian. A special presidential election was scheduled for 16 March 1998.

Twelve candidates succeeded in registering for the March presidential election. The main contenders were Kocharian, Vazgen Manukyan (who had run against Ter-Petrosyan in 1996 and was head of the National Democratic Union), and Karen Demirchyan (head of the Armenian Communist Party from 1974 to 1988). Since none of the candidates won the required "50% plus one" of the 1.46 million votes cast (in a 64% turnout), a runoff election was held on 30 March. In the runoff, acting President and Prime Minister Kocharian received 59.5% of 1.57 million votes cast (in a 68.5% turnout). The OSCE concluded that "this election showed improvement in some respects over the 1996 election," but did "not meet OSCE standards to which Armenia has committed itself." Observers alleged ballot box stuffing, discrepancies in vote counting, and fraud perpetrated by local authorities that inflated the number of votes for Kocharian. Nevertheless, he was inaugurated on 9 April 1998. The legislature selected Demirchyan as its speaker on 10 June.

On 27 October 1999, gunmen entered the legislature and opened fire on deputies and officials, killing Prime Minister Vazgen Sarkisyan and Speaker Karen Demirchyan, two deputy speakers, and four others. The purported leader of the gunmen claimed they were targeting the prime minister and were launching a coup to "restore democracy" and end poverty, and took dozens hostage. President Robert Kocharian rushed to the legislature and helped negotiate the release of the hostages, promising the gunmen a fair trial. The killings appeared the product of personal and clan grievances. Abiding by the constitution, the legislature met on 2 November and appointed Armen Khachatryan (a member of the majority Unity bloc) as speaker, and Kocharian named Sarkisyan's brother Aram the new prime minister the next day, seeking to preserve political balances. Political infighting intensified. The military prosecutor investigating the assassinations detained a presidential aide, appearing to implicate Kocharian in the assassinations. The Unity and Stability factions in the legislature also threatened to impeach Kocharian in April 2000. Seeking to counter challenges to his power, Kocharian in May 2000 fired his prime minister and defense minister. In October 2001, on the second anniversary of the shootings in parliament, thousands of protesters staged demonstrations in Yerevan to demand Kocharian's resignation. In December 2003, six individuals were sentenced to life imprisonment for their roles in the 1999 assassinations. The death penalty in Armenia had been abolished that August. Protests against Kocharian's presidency continued in 2004, despite his reelection in 2003.

Although Armenia has the highest economic growth rate of any country in the former Soviet Union, more than 50% of the population lives in poverty. Unemployment and emigration remain problems, and Armenia is under a trade blockade from Turkey and Azerbaijan over the dispute in Nagorno-Karabakh—goods are transported only through Georgia. However, US and European companies interested in tapping oil and gas reserves in the Caspian Sea have been planning the construction of a pipeline through the Caucasus to Turkey. In September 2001, Russian President Vladimir Putin visited Armenia, the first Russian president to do so since independence. Armenia and Russia negotiated a 10-year economic cooperation package, and an agreement was reached on expanding a Russian military base in Armenia.

Presidential elections were held on 19 February 2003, with no candidate receiving 50% of the votes; a runoff election was scheduled for 5 March. Kocharian took 48.3% of the first-round vote, with Stepan Demirchyan—son of Karen Demirchyan, the former parliamentary speaker assassinated in 1999—taking 27.4% of the vote. Artashes Geghamian came in third with 16.9%. The opposition called the election fraudulent and said it would not recognize the vote, and observers from the Organization for Security and Cooperation in Europe (OSCE) declared the election "flawed." Stuffing of ballot boxes allegedly took place, although many ballots were cast in transparent boxes, in an attempt to have a fair vote. Also, Kocharian received five times as much television coverage as all of his opponents combined. In the run-off election held on 5 March, Kocharian was reelected president with 67.5% of the vote; Demirchyan received 32.5%.

13 GOVERNMENT

Armenia adopted its post-Soviet constitution by public referendum on 5 July 1995 by 68% of the voters. A commission headed by Ter-Petrosyan had drawn up the draft constitution. It provides for a strong presidential system of government with a weak legislative system, granting the president power to appoint and remove the prime minister, judges, and prosecutors. It also gives him liberal grounds for dissolving the legislature, declaring martial law, and limiting human rights by declaring a state of emergency. The president serves a five-year term. The prime minister is nominated by the president and is subject to legislative approval. The prime minister with presidential and legislative approval appoints the Cabinet of Ministers. The unicameral National Assembly has 131 members, who serve four-year terms; 75 members are elected by party list, and 56 by direct vote.

14 POLITICAL PARTIES

Armenia held elections to a new single-chamber 131-seat legislature on 30 May 1999, with 75 deputies elected by party list and 56 elected by direct vote. Twenty-one parties and blocs fielded candidates on the party list vote, but only six passed a 5% vote hurdle. The Unity bloc garnered 42% of over two million votes cast, gaining 29 seats, followed by the Communist Party of Armenia with about 12% of the vote. In constituency balloting, the Unity Bloc (which included the country's two largest parties, the People's Party and the Republican Party) garnered the most seats (35), followed by nonparty-affiliated candidates (29). Other major parties that received at least 7% of the party list vote in the 1999 legislative race include the National Democratic Union, Armenian Revolutionary Federation-Dashnaktsutyun, Law-Governed Country Party, Communist Party of Armenia, the Armenian Pan-National

Movement, Law and Unity bloc, and the Mission Party. The other registered parties included both those newly created for the legislative race and more traditional parties. They were the Mighty Motherland, Homeland bloc, Ramkavar Azatakan Party (Liberal Democratic Party), Freedom Party, Democratic Party of Armenia, Union of Socialist Forces and Intelligentsia bloc, Union of Communist and Socialist Parties, Youth Party of Armenia, Decent Future, National State Party, Free Hayk Mission Party, Shamiram Party, and ONS+ bloc (the National Self-Determination and Homeland-Diaspora).

Legislative elections were held on 25 May 2003. The Republican Party won 23.5% of the vote (23 seats) for deputies elected by party list, followed by Justice Bloc, 13.6% (14 seats); Rule of Law, 12.3% (12 seats); ARF (Dashnak), 11.4% (11 seats); National Unity, 8.8% (9 seats); United Labor Party, 5.7% (6 seats). However, seats by party change frequently as deputies switch parties or declare themselves independent.

15 LOCAL GOVERNMENT

The regional governmental structure is closely modeled after the national structure. The president appoints governors to Armenia's 11 provinces (marzer), including the mayor of the capital of Yerevan, which has the status of a marz. Each province has both executive and legislative bodies that control the provincial budget and businesses within the region. Regional governments do not have authority to pass laws independent of national legislation. Marzer are divided into rural and urban communities (hamainkner), and Yerevan is divided into 12 districts. The communities and Yerevan districts are governed by community chiefs and legislative bodies called councils of elders (avakani). In the cities, community chiefs hold the title of mayor. In 1997 a law on self-government was passed calling for decentralization in some areas and some fiscal independence for local governments. Elections for mayors, community chiefs, and local councils in 654 constituencies were held 20 October 2002, with a 46% voter turnout rate (an increase of close to 20% from the turnout in 1999). Local elections are held every three years. There were fewer complaints of electoral irregularities than in previous elections. The ruling Republican Party fielded the most candidates, and 18 other parties, in addition to independents, participated. The Law-Governed Country Party came in second, and the Armenian Revolutionary Federation was third. Local elections were held once again in October 2005, and voters decided not to return many incumbents to office.

16 JUDICIAL SYSTEM

The constitution provides for an independent judiciary, but in practice courts are vulnerable to pressure from the government, though legal reforms are resulting in some changes. The court system consists of district courts of first instance, an Appeals Court, and a Court of Cassation. Judges for the local courts of first instance and the Court of Appeals began operating under a new judicial system in January 1999. Judges were selected for their posts based on examinations and interviews by the Minister of Justice, approval of a list of nominees by the Council of Justice, and approval by the president. Unless they are removed for malfeasance, they serve for life. About one-half of Soviet-era judges have been replaced. Prosecutors and defense attorneys also began retraining and recertification. A military bureaucracy continues to follow Soviet-era practices.

A Constitutional Court has the power to review the constitutionality of legislation, approves international agreements, and settles electoral disputes. Its effectiveness is limited. It only accepts cases referred by the president, two-thirds of the members of the legislature, or election-related cases brought by candidates in legislative or presidential races. The president appoints four of the nine judges of the Constitutional Court.

The constitution establishes a Council of Justice, headed by the president and including the prosecutor general, the minister of justice, and 14 other members appointed by the president. The Council appoints and disciplines judges in courts of first instance and the Court of Appeals. A Council of Court Chairs has been created to reduce the power of the Ministry of Justice and increase the independence of the judicial system. It is responsible for financial and budgetary issues involving the courts, and consists of 21 senior judges.

A criminal procedure code entered into force in January 1999 specifies that a suspect may be detained for no more than 12 months pending trial, has the right to an attorney, right to a public trial and to confront witnesses, and the right to appeal.

[17]ARMED FORCES

The active armed forces numbered 48,160 in 2005. There were 45,000 personnel in the Army, organized into five corps that would include a mix of motorized and standard rifle regiments, armored and other support units. Equipment in 2005 included 110 main battle tanks, 104 armored infantry fighting vehicles, 140 armored personnel carriers, and 229 artillery pieces. The Air and Defense Aviation Forces numbered 3,160 personnel with 16 combat capable aircraft (one fighter and 15 fighter ground attack aircraft) and 12 attack helicopters. Paramilitary forces numbered 1,000 and were made up of border troops and Ministry of Internal Affairs personnel. The military budget in 2005 totaled $135 million.

[18]INTERNATIONAL COOPERATION

Armenia was admitted to the United Nations on 2 March 1992. The country serves as a member of several specialized agencies within the United Nations, such as FAO, IAEA, ICAO, IDA, IFC, IFAD, ILO, IMF, UNCTAD, UNESCO, UNIDO, WIPO, and WHO. Armenia is a member of the CIS and the Council of Europe. The country was admitted to the OSCE on 30 January 1992 and serves as an observer in the OAS. It became a full member of the WTO on 5 February 2003. Armenia is one of 12 members of the Black Sea Economic Cooperation Zone, which was established in 1992. It is also a part of the Euro-Atlantic Partnership Council and the EBRD. Armenia is a member of the Organization for the Prohibition of Chemical Weapons and the NATO Partnership for Peace. The country ratified the Conventional Armed Forces in Europe (CFE) Treaty in July 1992. The Armenia government supports the cause of the ethnic Armenian secessionists in the Nagorno-Karabakh region of Azerbaijan. The OSCE is serving as a mediator in what has been a sometimes violent struggle.

In environmental cooperation, Armenia is part of the Basel Convention, the Conventions on Biological Diversity and Long Range Transboundary Air Pollution, Ramsar, the Kyoto Protocol, the Montréal Protocol, the Nuclear Test Ban Treaty, and the UN Conventions on the Law of the Sea, Climate Change, and Desertification.

[19]ECONOMY

As part of the Soviet Union, the Armenian economy featured large-scale agro-industrial enterprises and a substantial industrial sector that supplied machine tools, textiles, and other manufactured goods to other parts of the USSR in exchange for raw materials. Trade with its neighbors, on which resource-poor Armenia relies heavily, was jeopardized by the outbreak of conflict over the Nagorno-Karabakh enclave in 1988, and by political instability in Georgia and Azerbaijan. Also, in December 1988, a severe earthquake did considerable damage to Armenia's productive capacity, aggravating its regional trade deficit. The physical damage had not been repaired when the economy suffered the implosion that accompanied the breakup of the Soviet Union in 1991.

With independence, as real GDP fell 60% from 1992–93, small-scale agriculture came to dominate in place of the former agro-industrial complexes, with crops of grain, sugar beets, potatoes, and other vegetables, as well as grapes and other fruit. Growth was not registered until 1994, at 5%, when, in July, a cease-fire was signed by Armenia, Azerbaijan and Nagorno-Karabakh, and, in December, the government embarked on a comprehensive IMF-monitored program of macroeconomic stabilization and structural reform. By 1996, growth was in double digits and inflation in single digits, although set-backs, which began in late 1996, reduced real GDP growth to 3% in 1997, while inflation surged to 27%. In 1998, real growth reached 7.3% while inflation fell to a single digit 8.7%, despite the negative impacts of the Russian financial crisis and a continuing Azerbaijan-led economic blockade over the unresolved Nagorno-Karabakh issue.

Growth in the first nine months of 1999 was at an annual rate of 6%, but this was reduced to 3% for the year in the disruptions following the hostage-takings and assassinations of the prime minister and parliamentary speaker in October, a stated motive for which was the large proportion of Armenians living in poverty (at 55% in 2001 by CIA estimates). Inflation was held to 0.7% in the crisis, due to policy changes that have continued to keep inflation at a low level. Moderate GDP growth of 6% was achieved in 2000 while prices, as measured by the consumer price index, actually declined an estimated 0.8%.

In 2001, targeted real growth under the IMF-guided program was 6% but actual growth was about 10% (CIA est.) as the effects of economic reforms, the privatization of small and medium-sized enterprises, and increased foreign investment began to impact performance. IMF and CIA estimates for 2002 were for real growth between 12.5% and 12.9%, with stable price levels. Barring major disruptions (only too likely as the war in Iraq, launched 19 March 2003, added another source of instability to the region), Armenia was expected to attain its pre-independence level of per-capita income by 2005. Growth sectors include telecommunications, assembly of electric and electronic appliances, agriculture and food processing, energy generation and distribution, construction, coal and gold mining, and international air communications.

The IMF-sponsored economic liberalization program encouraged remarkable GDP growth rates: 13.9% in 2003, 10.1% in 2004, and a predicted 8.0% in 2005. Rising investment levels, exports, and real incomes also contributed to this growth. Inflation, tamed in 2002, was on the rise in 2003 and 2004, at 4.7% and 7.0% respectively. For the most part however, the government has done a good job of keeping the inflation in check, and stabilizing the local currency. Despite encouraging economic figures though, unemployment remains fairly high (at around 14%) and poverty is a critical issue that needs to be dealt with immediately.

20 INCOME

The US Central Intelligence Agency (CIA) reports that in 2005 Armenia's gross domestic product (GDP) was estimated at $15.3 billion. The CIA defines GDP as the value of all final goods and services produced within a nation in a given year and computed on the basis of purchasing power parity (PPP) rather than value as measured on the basis of the rate of exchange based on current dollars. The per capita GDP was estimated at $5,100. The annual growth rate of GDP was estimated at 8%. The average inflation rate in 2005 was 2.4%. It was estimated that agriculture accounted for 24.9% of GDP, industry 34.6%, and services 40.5%.

According to the World Bank, in 2003 remittances from citizens working abroad totaled $168 million or about $55 per capita and accounted for approximately 6.0% of GDP. Foreign aid receipts amounted to $247 million or about $81 per capita and accounted for approximately 8.5% of the gross national income (GNI).

The World Bank reports that in 2003 household consumption in Armenia totaled $2.35 billion or about $768 per capita based on a GDP of $2.8 billion, measured in current dollars rather than PPP. Household consumption includes expenditures of individuals, households, and nongovernmental organizations on goods and services, excluding purchases of dwellings. It was estimated that for the period 1990 to 2003 household consumption grew at an average annual rate of 1.8%. In 2001 it was estimated that approximately 52% of household consumption was spent on food, 18% on fuel, 3% on health care, and 15% on education. It was estimated that in 2003 about 43% of the population had incomes below the poverty line.

21 LABOR

As of 2004, Armenia's labor force numbered 1.2 million. In 2002, an estimated 25% were involved in industry, 45% in agriculture, and 30% in services. The unemployment rate was estimated at 30% in 2003.

Legislation passed in 1992 guarantees workers the right to bargain and organize collectively. An independent labor federation was created in 1997. However, organized labor remained weak as of 2005, because of high unemployment and a slow economy. Collective bargaining does not occur because most large employers are still under state control. Labor disputes are generally settled in economic or regular courts of law. According to the Confederation of Labor Unions (CLU) an estimated 290,000 workers belonged to 25 labor unions in 2005.

Armenians are guaranteed a monthly minimum wage which was set at around $26.00 as of 2005. The standard legal workweek was 40 hours, with mandatory overtime and rest periods. Children under the age of 16 are prohibited by law from full-time labor, although children at age 14 can be employed if permission is given by the child's parents and from the labor union. Due to the dire economic situation, none of these legal standards are relevant. Although the government is required to promulgate mini-

mum occupational health and safety standards, as of end 2005, such standards have yet to be implemented. In addition, a lack of government resources and general worker insecurity prevent any effective enforcement of the nation's labor laws.

22 AGRICULTURE

Before the collapse of the Soviet Union, about 16% of Armenia's land was cultivated. As of 2002, there were an estimated 560,000 hectares (1,384,000 acres) of arable cropland (20% of the total land area), of which 65,000 hectares (160,600 acres) were planted with permanent crops. Agriculture engaged about 45% of the economically active population in 2003. That year, agricultural production was 13% higher than what it had been during 1999–2001.

Production for 2004 included tomatoes, 222,047 tons; potatoes, 575,942 tons; wheat, 296,000 tons; and grapes, 148,892 tons. In 2002, there were some 18,300 tractors and 4,000 harvester-threshers in service.

23 ANIMAL HUSBANDRY

Over one-fifth of the total land area is permanent pastureland. In 2004, the livestock population included: sheep, 580,000; cattle, 565,800; pigs, 85,300; goats, 48,300; and horses, 12,500. There were also some 3.6 million chickens. In 2004, some 54,000 tons of meat were produced, including 33,400 tons of beef and veal, 7,200 tons of mutton and lamb, 4,300 tons of poultry, and 8,500 tons of pork. In 2004, 535,800 tons of milk, 31,500 tons of eggs, 4,500 tons of cheese, and 1,200 tons of greasy wool were also produced. Meat, milk, and butter are the chief agricultural imports.

24 FISHING

Fishing is limited to the Arpa River and Lake Sevan. Commercial fishing is not a significant part of the economy. The total catch in 2003 was 1,633 tons. Trout and carp are the principal species.

25 FORESTRY

Forests cover an estimated 12.4% of Armenia. Soviet mismanagement, the 1988 earthquake, hostilities with Azerbaijan, and fuel shortages have impaired development. Available timber is used for firewood during the harsh winters. Imports of forestry products totaled $12.2 million in 2003.

26 MINING

Mineral resources in Armenia are concentrated in the southern region, where several operating copper and molybdenum mines were located. Armenia had been mining one-third of the former Soviet Union's (FSU) output of molybdenum (2,073 metric tons in 2002, down from 3,100 metric tons in 2000). Copper mines were located at Kapan, Kadzharan, Agarak, Shamlugh, and Akht'ala; the latter two were not in operation in 2002. Kadzharan and Agarak also had molybdenum mines. Despite relative proximity to rail and port facilities that supplied European markets, the mineral sector's ability to compete on the world market was inhibited by infrastructure problems. Armenia's production of perlite has been estimated at a steady 35,000 metric tons annually, from 1998 through 2002.

In 2002, Armenia produced industrial minerals such as clays, diatomite, dimension stone, limestone (12.5 million short tons), salt (30,300 metric tons), and semiprecious stones. It mined copper (16,641 metric tons of copper concentrate), copper-zinc, and native gold deposits. The Zod and Megradzor gold mines ceased operations in 1997. The government hoped to revive the gold industry through the recovery of gold tailings at the Cuarat gold mill. Significant by-product constituents in the nonferrous ores in 2002 included barite, gold (estimated at 3,200 kg), lead, rhenium, selenium, silver (5,500 kg), tellurium, and zinc.

Armenia's exports of mineral products in 2002 accounted for around 70% of its total exports by value. In that year, total exports were valued at $507.2 million.

27 ENERGY AND POWER

With only negligible reserves of oil, natural gas, and coal, and with no production, Armenia is heavily reliant on foreign imports. Following the breakup of the Soviet Union, oil consumption has declined from 48,400 barrels per day in 1992 to 38,630 barrels per day in 2002. Natural gas consumption in 2002 was 38.49 billion cu ft. Total electrical consumption in 2002 was 4.446 billion kWh.

Net electricity generation in 2002 totaled 5.215 billion kWh, primarily from the reopened Medzamor nuclear plant at Yerevan (815,000 kW capacity), the Hrazdan (near Akhta) oil/natural gas plant (1,110,000 kW capacity), the Yerevan heat/power plant (550,000 kW capacity), and the Sevan-Hrazdan hydroelectric plant and smaller plants (925,000 kW capacity). Of total electricity generated in 2002, some 31% came from hydroelectric plants, 40% from nuclear power, and 29% from thermal power. Total capacity in 2002 was 3.341 million kW. The Medzama plant, reopened in 1995, increased electricity generation by 40% and has enabled electricity to be supplied around the clock for the first time in years. However, the Armenian government has promised to decommission the plant by 2004 to save money on maintenance if enough alternative power sources can be found by that time. As of 2002 three major and 38 smaller hydroelectric projects were planned, at a total cost of $300 million, with backing by the World Bank.

As of 1999, the domestic distribution grid for electric power was scheduled for restructuring and privatization, with assistance from the World Bank and the US Agency for International Development (USAID). A December 1988 earthquake disrupted the Yerevan nuclear power plant, creating almost total dependence on imported oil and natural gas for power. When ethnic hostilities with Azerbaijan again resurfaced in 1992, Azerbaijan discontinued service of its pipeline to Armenia (with natural gas from Turkmenistan). The only other supply routes passed either through Turkey (which was sympathetic to Azerbaijan) or through Georgia (which was dealing with its own civil chaos). Since the 1994 ceasefire with Azerbaijan, the revival of energy supplies has helped start the recovery of Armenia's economy. If Armenia and Azerbaijan ever resolve their disputes, the transit of oil and gas from the Caspian Sea region abroad will become possible.

28 INDUSTRY

Before the earthquake in 1988, Armenia exported trucks, tires, electronics, and instruments to other republics. A number of these plants were destroyed by the earthquake. Armenia was also a major producer of chemical products, some 59% of which were exported to other republics. Armenia has the highest number of

specialists with higher education and second highest number of scientists of all the former Soviet republics. Since the collapse of the Soviet Union, industrial production has been severely disrupted by political instability and shortages of power. Much of Armenia's industry is idle or operating at a fraction of its capacity.

Economic blockades by Turkey and Azerbaijan as part of the continuing dispute over Nagorno-Karabakh have cut Armenia off from an old direct gas pipeline from Azerbaijan, as well as precluded it from participation in any of the east–west pipelines being built in the post-Soviet era. The alternative Armenia has pursued is a gas pipeline from Iran delivering Turkmenistan gas (to avoid sanctions on customers of Iran, which were renewed by the US Congress in August 2001). Intergovernmental agreements on the project were signed in 1992 and 1995. In December 1997 the Korpezehe-Kurt-Kwi pipeline feeding Turkmen natural gas directly into the Iranian system was opened. In December 2001 agreement was reached on a route that bypassed the Azeri exclave of Nakhichevan, running from Kadzharan to the southern border at Megri. Work on the Armenian section of the Iran-Armenian gas pipeline was to have begun in 2002 but was delayed until 2003 by disputes over the price Iran was intending to charge.

Light industry dominates Armenia's industrial sector and is striking for its diversity. The leading industries in 2002 included metal-cutting machine tools, forging-pressing machines, electric motors, tires, knitted wear, hosiery, shoes, silk fabric, chemicals, trucks, instruments, microelectronics, gem cutting (in 2002, 53 diamond-polishing companies exported $150 million worth of diamonds), jewelry manufacture (up 200% in 2002), software development, food processing, and brandy. Most of the country's small and medium-sized enterprises have been privatized, spurring the recovery of industrial growth.

Progress has been slower with larger industries often due to the lack of viable bidders. About 70% of the larger operations had been privatized by 1998, the year Armenia passed legislation for the sale of the country's electricity transmission and distribution networks, retaining government control over power generation. To support the privatization, the European Bank for Reconstruction and Development (EBRD) bought a 20% share in each of Armenia's four distribution companies in an agreement preserving the government's right to buy back the shares should the agreement be abrogated. In 2002, after two failed offerings, management of the electricity distribution network was won by Daewoo Engineering. In 2001, Armenia reached a debt-to-equity agreement with Russia to exchange the debt it owed Russia—at almost $100 million and requiring about $20 million a year to service, the largest and only nonconcessional part of Armenia's external debt—for five nonperforming state-run enterprises. The centerpiece was the Hrazdan Thermal Power Plant, valued at about $100 million, but also including the "Mars" Electronics Factory established in 1986 for making robots, and three research institutes. Under the debt for property agreement the Russian government will turn the operations over to private entrepreneurs.

Armenia has the highest number of cooperatives (per capita) in the Commonwealth of Independent States. By CIA estimates for 2000, industry accounted for 32% of GDP, but employed about 42% of the labor force. In 2002, with 12.5% overall GDP growth, industry grew 16%, including a 42% growth in construction. The country is projecting growth along with partnership opportunities in areas such as power generation, aviation, construction, electronics, apparel, tourism, food processing, industrial property acquisition, banking, and other areas.

In 2004, industry accounted for 36.1% of the overall GDP; agriculture made up 22.9% of the economy, while services came in first with 41.1%. What is remarkable though, is the fact that only about 25% of the working population was employed by the industry, whereas around 45% worked in agriculture. This indicates a high productivity rate in the industrial sector, and a low one in agriculture. The industrial production growth rate was, at 15%, higher than the GDP growth rate, indicating that industry is the main engine of the Armenian economy. Particularly metallurgy, energy, and machine building managed to attract new investment and helped boost the industrial sector output.

29 SCIENCE AND TECHNOLOGY

The Armenian National Academy of Sciences, founded in 1943 and headquartered in Yerevan, has departments of physical, mathematical, and technological sciences; and natural sciences; and 32 research institutes in fields such as agriculture; biological, mathematical, physical, and earth sciences; and technology. Yerevan State University (founded in 1919) has faculties of mechanics, mathematics, physics, radiophysics, chemistry, biology, geology, geography, and mathematical cybernetics and automatic analysis. Also in Yerevan are the State Engineering University of Armenia (founded in 1930), the Yerevan State Medical University (founded in 1922), the Yerevan Zootechnical and Veterinary Institute (founded in 1929), and the Armenian Scientific and Technical Library. In 1987–97, science and engineering students accounted for 29% of college and university enrollments.

As of 2002, there were 1,606 researchers and 147 technicians per million people, actively engaged in research and development (R&D). Spending on R&D accounted for $24.25 million, or 0.25% of GDP in 2002. Of that amount, government accounted for 55.2% of R&D spending, while foreign sources accounted for 11.2%. The remainder was undistributed. In 2002, high technology exports totaled $3 million, 2% of the country's manufactured exports.

30 DOMESTIC TRADE

As of 1999, there were about 23,128 wholesale and retail companies registered in Armenia, accounting for over 54% of the total registered businesses. The main retail center is in Yerevan. A majority of retail establishments are small food and specialty item shops. Many of these work with wholesalers and sell items on a consignment basis. There are also large open markets in Yerevan and other cities offering a wide variety of food, clothing, housewares, and electronics.

Beginning in 1996, the government launched a major privatization drive. By 1999, over 80% of small businesses and over 60% of medium and large corporations were in private hands. Nearly all farmland is privately owned. Seasonal open-air food markets are also popular. Some of these markets still engage in bartering.

31 FOREIGN TRADE

Armenia's main trading partners are Belgium, Russia, the United States, Iran, Switzerland, Israel, Georgia, the United Kingdom, the UAE, and the EU. Exports include gold and diamonds, aluminum, transport equipment, electrical equipment, and scrap metal. Im-

Principal Trading Partners – Armenia (2003)

(In millions of US dollars)

Country	Exports	Imports	Balance
World	667.9	1,211.8	-543.9
Israel	142.3	123.4	18.9
Belgium	123.8	129.1	-5.3
Russia	96.0	196.1	-100.1
United States	54.9	99.1	-44.2
Germany	43.6	35.4	8.2
United Kingdom	39.8	56.5	-16.7
Switzerland-Liechtenstein	31.6	42.1	-10.5
Netherlands	21.8	10.8	11.0
Iran	21.4	63.5	-42.1
Italy-San Marino-Holy See	18.8	38.1	-19.3

(…) data not available or not significant.

SOURCE: *2003 International Trade Statistics Yearbook*, New York: United Nations, 2004.

ports include grain and other foods, fuel and energy. Inter-republic trade has suffered as a result of border hostilities, particularly the ongoing conflict over the Armenian enclave of Nagorno-Karabakh in Azerbaijan, which may prevent the proposed Caspian Sea oil pipeline from passing through Armenia. As of 2003, recent talks between the leaders of Armenia and Azerbaijan represented a positive step toward resolving the dispute.

Due to its delicate geographic placement, Armenia scores modest foreign trade figures. In 2004, exports totaled only $850 million (FOB—Free on Board), while imports climbed to $1.3 billion (FOB). Main export commodities were precious or semiprecious stones and metals (accounting for 42.5% of total exports), base metals (19.5%), mineral products (11.7%), prepared foodstuffs (9.7%). Principal imports included precious or semiprecious stones and metals (22.5%), mineral products (16.2%), machinery and equipment (10.1%), and prepared foodstuffs (7.0%). These last figures indicate that while Armenia has a vibrant industry, it is not exploiting it to its fullest potential. Existing trade barriers probably hinder the export of manufactured goods, so it has to resort to trading mainly natural resources.

32 BALANCE OF PAYMENTS

Although the government is working to reduce Armenia's large trade deficits by improving export performance, the conflict over the Armenian enclave of Nagorno-Karabakh in Azerbaijan continues to weaken the economy by disrupting normal trade and supply links. Armenia receives large amounts of humanitarian assistance.

The US Central Intelligence Agency (CIA) reported that in 2001 the purchasing power parity of Armenia's exports was $338.5 million while imports totaled $868.6 million resulting in a trade deficit of $530.1 million.

The International Monetary Fund (IMF) reported that in 2001 Armenia had exports of goods totaling $353 million and imports totaling $773 million. The services credit totaled $187 million and debit $204 million.

Exports of goods and services continued to grow in the following years, reaching $696 million in 2003, and $738 million in 2004. Imports followed a similar path, totaling $1.1 billion in

Balance of Payments – Armenia (2003)

(In millions of US dollars)

Current Account		**-190.6**
Balance on goods	-434.1	
Imports	-1,130.2	
Exports	696.1	
Balance on services	-68.3	
Balance on income	93.4	
Current transfers	218.5	
Capital Account		**89.9**
Financial Account		**174.8**
Direct investment abroad	-0.4	
Direct investment in Armenia	120.9	
Portfolio investment assets	0.1	
Portfolio investment liabilities	0.2	
Financial derivatives	...	
Other investment assets	-63.6	
Other investment liabilities	117.6	
Net Errors and Omissions		**-1.7**
Reserves and Related Items		**-72.4**

(…) data not available or not significant.

SOURCE: *Balance of Payment Statistics Yearbook 2004,* Washington, DC: International Monetary Fund, 2004.

2003, and $1.2 billion in 2004. The resource balance was consequently negative in both years, at around -$400 million. The current account balance was also negative, dropping to -$190 million in 2003, and recuperating to -$161 million in 2004. Reserves of foreign exchange and gold reached $555 million in 2004, covering almost six months of imports.

33 BANKING AND SECURITIES

The Central Bank of Armenia is charged with regulating the money supply, circulating currency, and regulating the commercial banks of the country. Commercial banks in Armenia include the Ardshinbank, Armagrobank, Armeconombank, Armimplexbank, Arminvestbank, Bank Armcommunication, Bank "Capital," Bank "Haykap," Central Bank of Armenia, Commercial Bank "Ardana," Commercial Bank Anelik, "Gladzor" Joint Stock Commercial Bank, Masis Commercial Bank, and the State Specialized Savings Bank of the Republic of Armenia. Leading foreign banks include: Mellat Bank (Iran) and Midland Armenia (UK).

The IMF has been concerned about the direction of policy taken by the National Bank of Armenia and the slow pace of financial reform. Armenia's financial sector is overbanked and beset with nonperforming credits, mainly to large state enterprises. Armenia has been a model reforming country among the former Soviet republics, and multilateral creditors are worried that public pressure may now force the government to loosen monetary and fiscal policies.

It was revealed in January 1997 that the central bank's credits to finance the government's budget gap has surpassed their $100 million limit in the first 10 months of 1996. The bank has been forced to intervene in the domestic markets, selling foreign exchange reserves to maintain the stability of the dram. The dram has lost some 14% in value since September 1996, when it stood at D412:$1. By the end of June1997 the rate had gone down to almost D500:$1. The International Monetary Fund reports that in 2001,

currency and demand deposits—an aggregate commonly known as M1—were equal to $141.6 million. In that same year, M2—an aggregate equal to M1 plus savings deposits, small time deposits, and money market mutual funds—was $310.3 million. The discount rate, the interest rate at which the central bank lends to financial institutions in the short term, was 19.4%.

There are three stock exchanges in Armenia the largest of which is the Yerevan Stock Exchange which listed 91 companies in 1999 and had total capitalization of $17 million. The next largest is the "Adamand" Yerevan Commodity and Stock Exchange which listed 45 companies.

34 INSURANCE

Insurance is largely controlled by government organizations inherited from the Soviet system, although private insurance companies are not unknown.

35 PUBLIC FINANCE

In 1994, the government began a three-year effort to privatize the national industries. Loans from the IMF, World Bank, EBRD, and other financial institutions and foreign countries aimed at eliminating the government's budget deficit. However, by 1996, external public debt exceeded $353 million with annual debt service payments exceeding $55 million. Loans to Armenia since 1993 total over $800 million.

The US Central Intelligence Agency (CIA) estimated that in 2005 Armenia's central government took in revenues of approximately $786.1 million and had expenditures of $930.7 million. Revenues minus expenditures totaled approximately -$144.6 million. Total external debt was $1.868 billion.

The International Monetary Fund (IMF) reported that in 2002, the most recent year for which it had data, central government revenues were D338,463 million. The value of revenues was us$590 million, based on an exchange rate for 2002 of us$1 = D573.35 as reported by the IMF.

Public Finance – Armenia (2002)

(In millions of drams, central government figures)

Revenue and Grants	**338,463**	**100.0%**
Tax revenue	227,447	67.2%
Social contributions	44,711	13.2%
Grants	50,480	14.9%
Other revenue	15,826	4.7%
Expenditures	...	...
General public services	...	...
Defense	...	...
Public order and safety	...	...
Economic affairs	...	...
Environmental protection	...	...
Housing and community amenities	...	...
Health	...	...
Recreational, culture, and religion	...	...
Education	...	...
Social protection	...	...

(…) data not available or not significant.

SOURCE: *Government Finance Statistics Yearbook 2004,* Washington, DC: International Monetary Fund, 2004.

^{36}TAXATION

Armenia's complex tax system was revised in 1997 and again in 2001. The top corporate profit tax rate was lowered from 30% to 20%. As of 1 July 2001 a single rate was applied to all taxable profits, defined as the difference between revenues and the sum of wages, amortization payments, raw and intermediate purchases, social security contributions, insurance fees, and interest expenses. Newly formed enterprises are exempt from taxes for the first two years, but there is no provision for carrying forward losses.

Individual income taxes are withheld by enterprises and are paid to the Ministry of Finance monthly. The personal income tax has been reduced from three bands to two: 10% for monthly taxable income up to D80,000 ($144) and 20% plus a payment of D8,000 ($14.40) for taxable income between D120,000 and D320,000 ($1,892) for monthly taxable income above D80,000. Armenians also pay taxes to social security and pension funds. In 1992, Armenia introduced a value-added tax, which stood at 20% in 2003. Excise taxes are applied to diesel fuel, oil, spirits, wine and beer at various rates. There are also land taxes and property taxes. Achieving a higher level of tax collection has been an important part of Armenia's economic reform programs. The fiscal deficit was projected at 2.4% of GDP for 2003.

^{37}CUSTOMS AND DUTIES

All exports are duty-free. Minor customs duties (up to 10%) are imposed on certain imports. Imports of machinery and equipment for use in manufacturing by enterprises with foreign investment are exempt from all customs duties.

^{38}FOREIGN INVESTMENT

Armenia's investment climate is regulated by the bilateral investment treaty (BIT) signed with the United States on 23 September 1992 and by the law on foreign investment adopted by Armenia on 31 July 1994. Armenia has also concluded BITs on investment and investment protection with 15 other countries: Georgia, Turkmenistan, Kyrgyzstan, Ukraine, Iran, Egypt, Romania, Cyprus, Greece, France, Germany, Canada, Argentina, China, and Vietnam. Its investment policy is geared to attract foreign investment, with foreign investors accorded national treatment and any sector open to investment. As of 2003, under the law of profit tax, two-year tax holidays are accorded foreign investors whose equity investment in a resident company is at least 500 million drams, or a little less than one million dollars. There are no limits on the repatriation of profits, or on the import and export of hard currency, so long as the currency is imported or earned in Armenia. Otherwise there is a $10,000 limit on the export of cash.

In late 1997, the government initiated the privatization of 11 of the larger state owned enterprises (SOEs), including the energy sector. It was not until 2002, however, that a suitable and willing foreign investor, Daewoo Engineering, was found to manage privatized electricity distribution. Operations at the Zvartnots International Airport have also been successfully leased. The 2001 debt-for-equity swap with Russia, whereby five unproductive SOEs (Hrazdan Thermal Power Plant, the "Mars" Electronics Factory established in 1986 to build robots, and three research labs) were exchanged for the cancellation of Armenia's debt with Russia (about $100 million of nonconcessional lending that was costing

almost $20 million/year to service) promised to increase Russian private investment in Armenia as the Russian government passed the assets on to private investors.

From 1998–2000 annual inflow of foreign direct investment (FDI) ranged from $120 million to $230 million, though it fell to $75.9 million in 2001 in the wake of the global contraction of foreign investment following the 11 September 2001 terrorist attacks on the US World Trade Center. In 2002, FDI increased 12% to about $85 million. A large share of FDI comes from the Armenian diaspora in the United States, Russia, Iran, France, Greece, the United Kingdom, Germany, and Syria. Since 1998, the Lincy Foundation of Armenian American Kirk Kirkorian has made available about $165 million to support small and medium enterprise (SME) development (offering concessional loans for businesses that are at least 51% Armenian owned), assistance for tourism development ($20 million in 2000), and infrastructure repair ($60 million in 2002 and $80 million in 2003). Armenia's accession to the World Trade Organization in 2000 has helped improve the investment climate as a consequence of meeting the WTO's strictures for membership.

The flow of foreign capital into Armenia continued to grow steadily, reaching $155 million in 2003, and $300 million in 2004. The main FDI sources have been Russia, the United States, Greece, France, and Germany. Unfortunately, only a small part of the capital inflows were geared towards green field investments. At the end of 2003, the accumulated stock of FDI amounted to 32% of the GDP.

^{39}ECONOMIC DEVELOPMENT

Development planning in Armenia has been aimed at counteracting the effects of three devastating blows to its economy: the earthquake of 1988; open warfare and economic blockade over Nagorno-Karabakh; and the combination of hyperinflation and industrial collapse following its separation from the Soviet Union. The government has been aggressive in launching economic reform, beginning with its privatization of agricultural land in 1991, which boosted crop output 30% and resulted in a 15% increase in agricultural production. In December 1994, Armenia embarked on a series of ambitious programs of economic reform guided by the International Monetary Fund (IMF) that have resulted in nine years of positive growth rates. On its present course, Armenia will achieve its pre-independence level of per capita income by 2005. By 1997, privatization of most small industry, as well as an estimated 70% of larger enterprises, was complete. Progress has been slower with larger state-owned enterprises (SOEs), not least because the government has had difficulty finding bidders at its cash sales auctions. In 1997, the ministries controlling the SOEs were merged, and their functions changed from direct control to general supervision and special support. The Ministry of Industry and the Ministry of Trade, and certain parts of the Ministry of Economy and the Ministry of Privatization and Foreign Investment were also merged in order to streamline the bureaucracy.

In late 1997, 11 large enterprises were offered for sale and in 1998 the parliament passed a law allowing for the sale of the state electricity transmission and distribution networks. Viable bidders were not immediately forthcoming and on 5 December 2000, as a means of supporting the privatization program, the European Bank of Reconstruction and Development (EBRD) agreed to take

20% shares in each of Armenia's four electricity distribution companies, with provision for the Armenian government's right to buy back the shares if the agreements were abrogated. The privatization process of the distribution networks stalled in 2001 and 2002 as twice the government failed to attract any final bids. To make the offer more attractive, the government merged the four distribution companies into one closed-end joint stock company, Electricity Networks of Armenia, and on 31 October 2002, 100% of the shares were acquired by the English company, Midland Resources Holding, Ltd. Midland in turn contracted with Daewoo International of South Korea to manage the newly privatized company. By 2002, only a small fraction of a total 100 larger SOEs had been privatized, according to the US Agency for International Development (USAID).

The republic has substantial deposits of gold, copper, zinc, bauxite, and other minerals, which could be developed with Western capital. The government is currently exploring alternative trade routes, and seeking export orders from the West to aid production and earn foreign exchange. Much of Armenia's industry remains idle or operating at low capacity utilization in large part because of the country's political isolation from oil and gas supplies.

Armenia's determination to create a market-oriented economy and democratic society has engaged (in addition to the IMF) the World Bank and EBRD as well as other financial institutions and foreign countries. Nevertheless, Armenia continues to remain economically isolated in comparison with its Caucasian neighbors.

The Armenian economy is expected to grow strongly in the coming years, based on increased domestic consumption, which in turn is fueled by higher wages and remittances from abroad. In addition, further investments are expected to come in the country as a result of economic restructuring and trade-oriented policies. Armenia boasts a highly educated work force, a diverse and dynamic industrial base, and a strategic geographic location. However, as long as the Nagorno-Karabakh conflict will not be resolved, the economy will find it hard to reach its fullest potential.

40 SOCIAL DEVELOPMENT

Pension and disability benefit systems were first introduced in 1956 and 1964. More recent legislation was passed in 2002 and implemented in 2003. Retirement is set at age 63 for men and age 59.5 for women, although earlier retirement is allowed for those engaged in hazardous work. The cost is covered by employee, employer, and government contributions. Work injury legislation provides 100% of average monthly earnings for temporary disability and a proportion of wages up to a maximum of 100% for permanent disability, depending on the extent of incapacity. Unemployment, sickness, and maternity benefits and family allowances are also provided under Armenian law.

Women in Armenia largely occupy traditional roles despite an employment law that formally prohibits discrimination based on sex. Women do not receive the same professional opportunities as men and often work in low-level jobs. In 2004 women earned approximately 40% less than men. Societal attitudes do not view sexual harassment in the workplace worthy of legal action. Violence against women and domestic violence is widespread and underreported. According to a recent survey, 45% of women were subject to psychological abuse, and 25% of women were physically abused. Most women do not report domestic abuse due to fear of reprisal and embarrassment.

The constitution protects the freedom of assembly and the freedom of religion. The government allows minorities, such as the Russians, Jews, Kurds, Yezids, Georgians, Greeks, and Assyrians, the right to preserve their cultural practices, the law allows them to study in their native language. Discrimination is prohibited on the basis of race, sex, religion, language disability, or social status. Human rights abuses appear to be widespread. Prison conditions fail to meet international standards and accusations of police brutality are not uncommon.

41 HEALTH

The infant mortality rate was 23.28 per 1,000 live births in 2005, an increase over the previous five years. The estimated maternal mortality rate was 35 per 100,000 live births as of 1999. Life expectancy in 2005 averaged 71.55 years. There were 7,000 war-related deaths from 1989 to 1992; the death rate was estimated at 10 per 1,000 people in 2002. The incidence of tuberculosis was 58 per 100,000 people. Immunization rates declined as of 1994 due to war and earthquakes but have begun to recover. In 1999, the immunization rates were as follows for a child under the age of one: tuberculosis, 72%; polio, 95%; and measles, 92%. In the same year, the estimated immunization rate for DPT was 91%. In 2000 the total fertility rate was 1.3 births per woman and the maternal mortality rate was an estimated 35 per 100,000 live births.

As of 2004, there were an estimated 352 physicians and 473 nurses per 100,000 people and the country spent an estimated 7.8% of its GDP on health care. In this former republic of the Soviet Union, health care has undergone rapid changes in the last few years. The break from the Soviet Union has meant a disruption of the system that once provided member states with equipment, supplies, and drugs. Out-of-pocket payments by individual are now required for most health care services. However, the health care delivery itself is still largely organized as it was during the Soviet era, with regional clinics and walk-in centers delivering most primary health care services.

The incidence of heart disease is high compared to other moderately developed countries. There is nearly a 50% chance of dying of heart disease after age 65 for both women and men. The HIV/AIDS prevalence was 0.10 per 100 adults in 2003. As of 2004, there were approximately 2,600 people living with HIV/AIDS in the country. There were an estimated 200 deaths from AIDS in 2003.

42 HOUSING

Housing throughout Armenia has been somewhat scarce for the past two decades due to a number of factors, including a history of state control, a devastating earthquake in 1988, and civil conflicts. Since the 1993 passage of a law on privatization for previously state and public-owned housing, about 96% of apartments were privatized and transferred to ownership by the existing tenants.

A large number of buildings are neglected and in serious disrepair and utilities are limited and expensive. The total number of housing units in 2001 was at about 750,719. Nearly 59% were multi-unit dwellings, most of which are in urban areas. About 25% of all multi-unit homes were built before 1960; another 52% were built between 1960 and 1980. Only about 85% of the population have access to improved water supplies. Only 9% have central heating. About 50% of the population rely on wood burning stoves as a primary heating source.

Overcrowding and homelessness is a great concern, particularly among the population of refugees and displaced persons. In 2001, about 11% of all households lived in one-room homes. In 2001, it was estimated that about 40,000 families (5% of all households) had no permanent shelter. Nearly 40% of these people lived in temporary shelters called *domics* within the earthquake zone. Another 40,000 families were on waiting lists for new permanent housing because of overcrowding. About 1,200 new housing units were completed in 2001. The same year, there were about 29,000 unfinished housing units (4,487 buildings). Most of these were started in the late 1980s and early 1990s within the earthquake zone, and were simply left incomplete because of lack of funds and materials.

43 EDUCATION

Education is compulsory between the ages of 7 and 14 years and is free at both the primary and secondary levels. The system is broken into three levels. Primary school lasts for three years, followed by intermediate school, which lasts for five years. This is followed by two years of general secondary education. Primary school enrollment in 2003 was estimated at about 94%; 95% for boys and 93% for girls. The same year, secondary school enrollment was about 83%; 82% for boys and 85% for girls. The pupil to teacher ratio for primary school was at about 17:1 in 2003; the ratio for secondary school was about 10:1.

Since the early 1990s, increasing emphasis has been placed on Armenian history and culture. The school year runs from September to July. Instruction is available in Armenian and Russian. The education system is coordinated through the Ministry of Education and Science and the Council of Rectors of Higher Educational Establishments. About 3.2% of the GDP was given to education in 2003.

The adult literacy rate for 2004 was estimated at about 99%, with a fairly even rate between men and women. There are two universities in Yerevan: the Yerevan State University (founded in 1919) and the State Engineering University of Armenia. Seven other educational institutions are located in the capital. There are several other institutes of higher education throughout the country. About 25% of all age-eligible students were enrolled in tertiary education programs in 2003.

44 LIBRARIES AND MUSEUMS

There are two branches of the National Library, with the main branch in Yerevan comprising 6.2 million volumes as of 2002. The main library of the Armenian Academy of Sciences in Yerevan has 4.4 million volumes. The Armenian Academy of Sciences and the universities each have research libraries. The Armenian Library Association was established in 1995.

Yerevan's museums include the National Gallery of Arts; the Yerevan Children's Picture Gallery, a unique collection of children's art from Armenia and around the world; the Museum of Modern Art; the House Museum of Ovanes Tumanjan, Armenia's most renowned poet; and the Museum of Ancient Manuscripts. There are also museums devoted to the composer Aram Khachaturian (including his piano) and the filmmaker Sergei Paradjanov, Armenia's most famous sons. The Genocide Memorial and Museum at Tsitsernakaberd is in Yerevan. The Matenadaran Manuscript Museum, also in Yerevan, was established to preserve the ancient written culture of the region.

45 MEDIA

In 2003, there were an estimated 148 mainline telephones for every 1,000 people; about 60,800 people were on a waiting list for telephone service installation. The same year, there were approximately 30 mobile phones in use for every 1,000 people. Communications are the responsibility of the Ministry of Posts and Telecommunications and are operated by Armental, a 90% Greek-owned company. Yerevan is linked to the Trans-Asia-Europe fiber-optic cable through Iran. Communications links to other former Soviet republics are by land line or microwave, and to other countries by satellite and through Moscow.

A majority of citizens rely on radio and television as a primary source of news and information. Armenian and Russian radio and television stations broadcast throughout the country. In 2004, there were over 20 radio stations and over 40 television broadcasters, most of which were privately owned and operated. In 2003, there were an estimated 264 radios and 229 television sets for every 1,000 people. Though cable television service is available, only about 1.2 of every 1,000 people are subscribers. In 2003, there were 15.8 personal computers for every 1,000 people and 37 of every 1,000 people had access to the Internet. There were four secure Internet servers available in 2004.

The three largest newspapers as of 2002 were *Golos Armenii* (*The Voice of Armenia*, circulation 20,000), *Hayastani Hanrapetutyun* (a joint publication of the parliament and the newspaper's staff), and *Respublika Armenia*, (the Russian-language version of *Hayastani Hanrapetutyun*). According to the Yerevan Press Club, the total newspaper circulation in the country in 2004 was 60,000, an increase of 20,000 from 2003. There were about 27 newspapers available in the capital.

Armenia's constitution provides for freedom of expression, and is said to generally uphold freedom of speech and press. However, journalists seem to adhere to an unspoken rule of self-censorship, particularly when reporting on political issues, since they traditionally depend on the government for funding and access to facilities. The government has, it is noted, begun to shed itself of the state publishing apparatus, and it has dissolved the Ministry of Information.

46 ORGANIZATIONS

Important political movements in Armenia include the Armenian National Movement and the National Self-Determination Association. Armenian trade unions belong to the umbrella organization Council of Armenia Trade Unions. The Chamber of Commerce and Industry of the Republic of Armenia promotes the economic and business activities of the country in world markets.

The National Academy of Sciences of Armenia encourages the public interest in science and seeks to ensure availability and effectiveness of science education programs. The Armenian Physical Society serves a similar role. The group also works with various research programs. The Independent Media Center promotes the freedom and accuracy of press and other media. The Armenian Medical Association promotes research and education in the field; there are also several professional associations for specialized fields of medicine.

There are a number of national sporting organizations, including the Athletic Federation of the Republic of Armenia, the Armenian National Paralympic Committee, and other groups sponsoring football (soccer), baseball, skiing, and the Special Olympics. The National Youth Council of the Republic of Armenia coordinates youth organizations through the support of the Ministry of Culture, Sports, and Youth. An affiliate of the United Nations of Youth (UNOY), a foundation based in the Netherlands, was established in Armenia in 1994. Other youth groups include the Aragast Youth Club and the Armenian Euro Club Unipax. There are active chapters of the Girl Guides and Girls Scouts; the World Organization of Scouting is represented by the Armenian National Scout Movement. The Armenian Junior Chamber is a national leadership development organization. The YMCA is also present.

Organizations representing the rights and role of women in society include the League of Armenian Women, the Union of the Protection of Women's, Children and Family Rights, and the Women's Alliance. There is a national chapter of the Red Cross Society, World Vision, and Habitat for Humanity. The Armenian Relief Society supports local community health development programming.

47 TOURISM, TRAVEL, AND RECREATION

Although there is a shortage of resources, Armenia has been investing in new hotels to increase tourism. Outdoor activities and scenery seem to be the primary attractions. Lake Sevan, the world's largest mountain lake, is a popular summer tourist spot. The Tsakhador ski resort is open year round for skiing in the winter and hiking and picnicking the rest of the year. Mt. Ararat, the traditional site of the landing of Noah's Ark, is located along the border with Turkey. Yerevan, Armenia's capital, also boasts theaters; the casinos in Argavand are popular with tourists and Albanian citizens.

In 2003, there were about 206,000 visitor arrivals, as compared to 45,000 in 2000. Tourist receipts totaled $90 million in 2003.

In 2002, the US Department of State estimated the daily cost of staying in Yerevan at $184.

48 FAMOUS ARMENIANS

Levon Ter-Petrosyan was president of Armenia from 1991 until 1998. Gagik G. Haroutunian has been prime minister, vice president, and chairman of the Council of Ministers since November 1991. Gregory Nare Katzi, who lived in the 10th century, was Armenia's first great poet. Nineteenth-century novelists include Hakob Maliq-Hakobian (1835?–1888) whose pen name is "Raffi" and the playwright Gabriel Sundukian (1825–1912). G. I. Gurdjieff (1872?–1949) was a Greek-Armenian mystic and teacher. Soviet aircraft designer Artem Mikuyan (1905–70) served as head of the MiG design bureau. Arshile Gorky (1904–48) was an Armenian-American abstract expressionist painter.

49 DEPENDENCIES

Armenia has no territories or colonies.

50 BIBLIOGRAPHY

Abrahamian, Levon and Nancy Sweezy (eds.). *Armenian Folk Arts, Culture, and Identity.* Bloomington: Indiana University Press, 2001.

Adalian, Rouben Paul. *Historical Dictionary of Armenia.* Lanham, Md.: Scarecrow Press, 2002.

De Waal, Thomas. *Black Garden: Armenia and Azerbaijan Through Peace and War.* New York: New York University Press, 2003.

Karanian, Matthew. *Edge of Time: Traveling in Armenia and Karabagh.* 2nd ed. Washington, D.C.: Stone Garden Productions, 2002.

Kohut, David R. *Historical Dictionary of the "Dirty Wars."* Lanham, Md.: Scarecrow Press, 2003.

Libaridian, Gerard J. *Modern Armenia: People, Nation, State.* New Brunswick, N.J.: Transaction Publishers, 2004.

Seddon, David (ed.). *A Political and Economic Dictionary of the Middle East.* Philadelphia: Routledge/Taylor and Francis, 2004.

Suny, Ronald Grigor. *Looking Toward Ararat: Armenia in Modern History.* Bloomington: Indiana University Press, 1993.

Transcaucasia, Nationalism and Social Change: Essays in the History of Armenia, Azerbaijan, and Georgia. Ann Arbor: University of Michigan Press, 1996.

Walker, Christopher J. *Armenia: the Survival of a Nation,* Rev. 2nd ed. New York: St. Martin's Press, 1990.

World Bank. *Public Expenditure Review of Armenia.* Washington, D.C.: World Bank, 2003.

AUSTRIA

Republic of Austria
Republik Österreich

CAPITAL: Vienna (Wien)

FLAG: The flag consists of a white horizontal stripe between two red stripes.

ANTHEM: *Land der Berge, Land am Ströme (Land of Mountains, Land on the River)*.

MONETARY UNIT: The euro replaced the schilling as the national currency in 2002. The euro is divided into 100 cents. There are coins in denominations of 1, 2, 5, 10, 20, and 50 cents and 1 euro and 2 euros. There are notes of 5, 10, 20, 50, 100, 200, and 500 euros. €1 = $1.25475 (or $1 = €0.79697) as of 2005.

WEIGHTS AND MEASURES: The metric system is in use.

HOLIDAYS: New Year's Day, 1 January; Epiphany, 6 January; May Day, 1 May; Assumption, 15 August; National Day, 26 October; All Saints' Day, 1 November; Immaculate Conception, 8 December; Christmas, 25 December; St. Stephen's Day, 26 December. Movable religious holidays include Easter Monday, Ascension, Whitmonday, and Corpus Christi. In addition, there are provincial holidays.

TIME: 1 PM = noon GMT.

---

¹LOCATION, SIZE, AND EXTENT

Austria, with an area of 83,858 sq km (32,378 sq mi), is a landlocked country in Central Europe, extending 573 km (356 mi) E–W and 294 km (183 mi) N–S. Comparatively, Austria is slightly smaller than the state of Maine. Bounded on the N by Germany and the Czech Republic, on the E by Hungary, on the S by Slovenia and Italy, and on the W by Liechtenstein and Switzerland, Austria has a total boundary length of 2,562 km (1,588 mi).

While not making any territorial claims, Austria oversees the treatment of German speakers in the South Tyrol (now part of the autonomous province of Trentino-Alto Adige), which was ceded to Italy under the Treaty of St.-Germain-en-Laye in 1919.

Austria's capital city, Vienna, is located in the northeastern part of the country.

²TOPOGRAPHY

Most of western and central Austria is mountainous, and much of the flatter area to the east is hilly, but a series of passes and valleys permits travel within the country and has made Austria an important bridge between various sections of Europe. The principal topographic regions are the Alps, constituting 62.8% of Austria's land area; the Alpine and Carpathian foothills (11.3%); the Pannonian lowlands of the east (11.3%); the granite and gneiss highlands of the Bohemian Massif (10.1%); and the Vienna Basin (4.4%).

The highest point of the Austrian Alps is the Grossglockner, 3,797 m (12,457 ft). The Danube (Donau) River, fully navigable along its 350-km (217-mi) course through northeastern Austria, is the chief waterway, and several important streams—the Inn, Enns, Drava (Drau), and Mur—are tributaries to it. Included within Austria are many Alpine lakes, most of the Neusiedler See (the lowest point in Austria, 115 m/377 ft above sea level), and part of Lake Constance (Bodensee).

³CLIMATE

Climatic conditions depend on location and altitude. Temperatures range from an average of about -7 to -1°C (20 to 30°F) in winter to about 18 to 24°C (65 to 75°F) in July. Rainfall ranges from more than 102 cm (50 in) annually in the western mountains to less than 66 cm (26 in) in the driest region, near Vienna.

⁴FLORA AND FAUNA

Plants and animals are those typical of Central Europe. Austria is one of Europe's most heavily wooded countries, with 47% of its area under forests. Deciduous trees (particularly beech, birch, and oak) and conifers (fir) cover the mountains up to about 1,200 m (4,000 ft); above that point fir predominates and then gives way to larch and stone pine. There is a large variety of wildlife. Although chamois are now rare, deer, hare, fox, badger, marten, Alpine chough, grouse, marmot, partridge, and pheasant are still plentiful. The birds of the reed beds around the Neusiedler See include purple heron, spoonbill, and avocet. The ibex, once threatened, has begun breeding again. Hunting is strictly regulated.

⁵ENVIRONMENT

The Ministry of Health and Environmental Protection, established in 1972, is responsible for the coordination at the national level of all environmental protection efforts, addressing its efforts toward problems including waste disposal, pollution, noise, sulfur dioxide, and carbon monoxide levels, as well as emissions by the iron, steel, and ceramics industries. A toxic waste law enacted in 1984 established strict regulations for the collection, transport, and disposal of dangerous substances. The Austrian government has imposed strict regulations on gas emissions, which helped to reduce sulphur dioxide by two-thirds over an eight-year period beginning in 1980. In 1992 Austria was among the 50 countries with the highest level of industrial carbon dioxide emissions, producing 56.6 million metric tons of emissions, or 7.29 m tons per capita. In 1996, the level rose to 59.3 million metric tons. In 2000, the total was 60.8 million metric tons.

Austrians continue to fight the problem of acid rain which has damaged 25% of the country's forests. In general, environmental legislation is based on the "polluter pays" principle. The water resources fund of the Ministry for Buildings and Technology distributed more than s20 billion for canalization and waste-water purification plants between 1959 and the early 1980s; the Danube and the Mur have been the special focus of efforts to improve water quality.

Endangered species include Freya's damselfly and the dusky large blue butterfly. As of 2002, there were at least 83 species of mammals, 230 breeding and wintering bird species, and over 3,000 species of plants. According to a 2006 report issued by the International Union for Conservation of Nature and Natural Resources (IUCN), threatened species included 5 types of mammals, 8 species of birds, 7 species of fish, 22 types of mollusks, 22 other invertebrates, and 3 species of plants. Endangered species include Freya's damselfly, slender-billed curlew, bald ibis, Danube salmon, and the European mink. About 33% of the total land area is protected, including19 Ramsar wetland sites.

6 POPULATION

The population of Austria in 2005 was estimated by the United Nations (UN) at 8,151,000, which placed it at number 92 in population among the 193 nations of the world. In 2005, approximately 15% of the population was over 65 years of age, with another 16% of the population under 15 years of age. There were 96 males for every 100 females in the country. According to the UN, the annual population rate of change for 2005–10 was expected to be 0.1%, a rate the government viewed as too low. The projected population for the year 2025 was 8,396,000. The population density was 97 per sq km (252 per sq mi).

The UN estimated that 54% of the population lived in urban areas in 2005, and that urban areas were growing at an annual rate of just 0.08%. The capital city, Vienna (Wien), had a population of 2,179,000 in that year. Other large cities and their estimated populations include Graz, 237,810; Linz, 188,968; Salzburg, 145,000; and Innsbruck, 140,000.

7 MIGRATION

Every Austrian has the constitutional right to migrate. For several years after the end of World War II (1945), fairly large numbers of Austrians emigrated, mostly to Australia, Canada, and the United States, but as the economy recovered from war damage, emigration became insignificant. Austria retains the principle of the right of asylum, and the benefits of Austrian social legislation are granted to refugees and displaced persons. Between 1945 and 1983, 1,942,782 refugees from more than 30 countries came to Austria, of whom about 590,000 became Austrian citizens (including some 302,000 German-speaking expatriates from Czechoslovakia, Romania, and Yugoslavia). Following the political upheavals in Hungary in 1956, Czechoslovakia in 1968, and Poland in 1981, Austria received large numbers of refugees from these countries: 180,432 Hungarians, about 100,000 Czechs and Slovaks, and 33,142 Poles. Between 1968 and 1986, 261,857 Jewish emigrants from the Soviet

Union passed through Austria, about one-third of them going to Israel and the rest to other countries, primarily the United States. Of Austrians living abroad, some 186,900 were residents of Germany in 1991. Estimated as of 2005, Austria had a net migration rate of 1.97 migrants per 1,000 population.

In 2003 of Austria's roughly eight million inhabitants, 9.4% were foreign residents, with about two-thirds of them coming from the successor states of the former Yugoslavia, Germany, and Turkey. Between 1985 and 2001, over 254,000 foreigners were naturalized. Austria's proportion of foreign-born residents in 2001 was even higher than that of the United States, reaching a level of 12.5%.

By the end of 2004 there were 38,262 asylum seekers and 18,319 refugees in Austria. The majority of those seeking asylum were from the Russian Federation, Serbia and Montenegro, Moldova, India, Turkey, China, and Pakistan. Approximately 16% of the asylum seekers were from the Russian Federation alone. Citizenship legislation has been changed to allow foreign spouses to become citizens only after five years of marriage to the same Austrian spouse.

In 2003, the foreign labor force was 11.8% of the total labor force. Turkish workers traditionally have had the highest unemployment rate of all foreign worker groups.

8 ETHNIC GROUPS

Austrians are a people of mixed Dinaric, Nordic, Alpine, and East Baltic origin. In a 2001 census, about 91.1% of respondents were Austrian. Minority groups include Croatians, Slovenes, Slovaks, Romas, Czechs, Serbs, Bosniaks, and Hungarians. These make up about 4% of the population. Turks make up about 1.6% of the population and Germans constitute less than 1%.

9 LANGUAGES

The official national language is German and nearly 99% of the inhabitants speak it as their mother tongue. People in Vorarlberg Province speak German with an Alemannic accent, similar to that in Switzerland. Slovene is the official language in Carinthia and both Croatian and Hungarian are official languages in Burgenland. In other provinces, Austrians speak various Bavarian dialects. There are also small groups of Czech, Slovak, and Polish speakers in Vienna.

10 RELIGIONS

As of 2001, about 74% of the people were Roman Catholic, but reports indicate that only about 17% of all Roman Catholics were active participants in formal religious service. About 4.7% of the population belonged to the Lutheran and Presbyterian churches (Evangelical Church, Augsburg and Helvetic Confessions). Muslims accounted for about 4.2% of the population. The Jewish community stood at about 0.1% of the population; and Eastern Orthodox (Russian, Greek, Serbian, Romanian, Bulgarian) at 2.2%. Other Christian churches had accounted for about 0.9% of the population. These include the Armenian Apostolic Church, the New Apostolic Church, the Syrian Orthodox Church, the Church of Jesus Christ of Latter-day Saints, and the Methodist Church of Austria, among others. The Church of Scientology reportedly had somewhere between 5,000 and 6,000 members and the Unification Church had about 700 members. Other small groups within the country, which are termed as "sects" by the government,

LOCATION: 46°22′ to 49°1′ N; 9°22′ to 17°10′ E BOUNDARY LENGTHS: Germany, 784 kilometers (487 miles); Czech Republic, 362 kilometers (225 miles); Slovakia, 91 kilometers (57 miles); Hungary, 366 kilometers (227 miles); Slovenia, 330 kilometers (205 miles); Italy, 430 kilometers (267 miles); Liechtenstein, 37 kilometers (23 miles); Switzerland, 164 kilometers (102 miles).

include: Hare Krishna, the Divine Light Mission, Eckankar, the Osho movement, Sai Baba, Sahaja Yoga, Fiat Lux and the Center for Experimental Society Formation. About 12% of respondents claimed to be atheists and 2% indicated no religious affiliation at all.

The constitution provides for freedom of religion and this right is generally respected in practice. The government is secular, but many Roman Catholic holidays are celebrated as public holidays. Religious organizations are divided into three legal categories under the 1874 Law on Recognition of Churches and the 1998 Law on the Status of Religious Confessional Communities, and each division offers a different level of rights. Those divisions are: officially recognized religious societies, religious confessional communities, and associations. There were 13 officially recognized religious societies in 1998. The Ecumenical Council of Austrian Churches provides an interfaith forum for discussions on a variety of issues. Pro Oriente, an international organization of Catholic and Orthodox churches, also holds an active chapter in the country.

11 TRANSPORTATION

Austria has a dense transportation network. The Federal Railway Administration controls some 90% of Austria's 6,021 km (3,745 mi) of railways in 2004, which is made up of standard and narrow gauge track. Of the 5,565 km (3,461 mi) of standard-gauge track, 3,859 km (2,400 mi) are electrified, while 146 km (91 mi) of the 456 km (284 mi) of narrow-gauge track are electrified.

In 2003, paved highways totaled 133,718 km (83,172 mi) and included 1,677 km (1,043 mi) of expressways. In 2003, there were 4,054,308 passenger cars, and 335,318 commercial vehicles in use.

Austria has 358 km (223 mi) of inland waterways, over 80% of which are navigable by engine-powered vessels. Most of Austria's overseas trade passes through the Italian port of Trieste; the rest is shipped from German ports. In 2005, the oceangoing merchant fleet of Austria consisted of 8 ships of 1,000 GRT or over, with a capacity of 29,624 GRT.

In 2004, there were an estimated 55 airports in Austria. As of 2005, a total of 24 had paved runways, and there was also one heliport. Of the six major airports in Austria—Schwechat (near Vienna), Graz, Innsbruck, Klagenfurt, Linz, and Salzburg—Schwechat is by far the most important. In 2003, Austrian air carriers provided flights for 6.903 million passengers and carried 431,000 freight ton km.

¹²HISTORY

Human settlements have existed in what is now Austria since prehistoric times. In 14 BC, the region, already overrun by various tribes, including the Celts, was conquered by the Romans, who divided it among the provinces of Noricum, Pannonia, and Illyria. The Romans founded several towns that survive today: Vindobona (Vienna), Juvavum (Salzburg), Valdidena (Innsbruck), and Brigantium (Bregenz). After the fall of the Roman Empire, Austria became (about AD 800) a border province of Charlemagne's empire until the 10th century, when it was joined to the Holy Roman Empire as Österreich ("Kingdom of the East").

From the late 13th to the early 20th century, the history of Austria is tied to that of the Habsburg family. In 1282, Rudolf von Habsburg (Rudolf I, newly elected German emperor) gave Austria (Upper and Lower Austria, Carinthia, Styria, and Carniola) to his sons, Albrecht and Rudolf, thus inaugurating the male Habsburg succession that would continue unbroken until 1740. The highest point of Habsburg rule came in the 1500s when Emperor Maximilian I (r.1493–1519) arranged a marriage between his son and the daughter of King Ferdinand and Queen Isabella of Spain. Maximilian's grandson became King Charles I of Spain in 1516 and, three years later, was elected Holy Roman emperor, as Charles V. Until Charles gave up his throne in 1556, he ruled over Austria, Spain, the Netherlands, and much of Italy, as well as over large possessions in the Americas. Charles gave Austria to his brother Ferdinand, who had already been elected king of Hungary and Bohemia in 1526; the Habsburgs maintained their reign over Austria, Bohemia, and Hungary until 1918.

When the last Habsburg king of Spain died in 1700, France as well as Austria laid claim to the throne. The dispute between the continental powers erupted into the War of the Spanish Succession (1701–14) and drew in other European countries in alliance with the respective claimants. At the end of the war, Austria was given control of the Spanish Netherlands (Belgium), Naples, Milan, and Sardinia. (It later lost Naples, together with Sicily, in the War of the Polish Succession, 1733–35.) In 1740, after the death of Charles VI, several German princes refused to acknowledge his daughter and only child, Maria Theresa, as the legitimate ruler of Austria, thus provoking the War of the Austrian Succession (1740–48). Maria Theresa lost Silesia to Prussia but held on to her throne, from which she proceeded to institute a series of major internal reforms as ruler of Austria, Hungary, and Bohemia. After 1765, she ruled jointly with her son, Holy Roman Emperor Joseph II (r.1765–90). Following his mother's death in 1780, Joseph, an enlightened despot, sought to abolish serfdom and introduce religious freedom, but he succeeded only in creating considerable unrest. Despite the political turmoil, Austria's cultural life flourished during this period, which spanned the careers of the composers Haydn and Mozart.

During the French Revolutionary and Napoleonic wars, Austria suffered a further diminution of territory. In 1797, it gave up Belgium and Milan to France, receiving Venice, however, in recompense. In 1805, Austria lost Venice, as well as the Tyrol and part of Dalmatia, to Napoleon. Some restitution was made by the Congress of Vienna (1814–15), convened after Napoleon's defeat; it awarded Lombardy, Venetia, and Istria and restored all of Dalmatia to Austria, but it denied the Habsburgs the return of former possessions in Baden and the Netherlands.

From 1815 to 1848, Austria, under the ministry of Prince Klemens von Metternich, dominated European politics as the leading power of both the German Confederation and the Holy Alliance (Austria, Russia, and Prussia). Unchallenged abroad, the reactionary Metternich achieved peace at home through ruthless suppression of all liberal or nationalist movements among the people in the Habsburg Empire. In 1848, however, revolutions broke out in Hungary and Bohemia and in Vienna itself; Metternich resigned and fled to London. Although the revolutions were crushed, Emperor Ferdinand I abdicated in December. He was succeeded by his 18-year-old nephew, Franz Josef I, who was destined to occupy the Austrian throne for 68 years, until his death in 1916. During his reign, Austria attempted to set up a strong central government that would unify all the Habsburg possessions under its leadership. But nationalist tensions persisted, exacerbated by outside interference. In 1859, in a war over Habsburg-controlled Lombardy, French and Sardinian troops defeated the Austrians, ending Austrian preeminence in Italian politics; and in 1866, Prussia forced Austria out of the political affairs of Germany after the Seven Weeks' War. In 1867, Hungarian nationalists, taking advantage of Austria's weakened state, compelled Franz Josef to sign an agreement giving Hungary equal rights with Austria. In the ensuing Dual Monarchy, the Austrian Empire and the Kingdom of Hungary were united under one ruler. Each country had its own national government, but both shared responsibility for foreign affairs, defense, and finance. Self-government for the empire's Magyar (Hungarian) population was balanced by continued suppression of the Slavs.

On 28 June 1914, at Sarajevo, Serbian patriots, members of the Slavic movement, assassinated Archduke Francis Ferdinand, nephew of the emperor and heir to the Austrian throne. Their act set off World War I, in which Austria-Hungary was joined by Germany (an ally since 1879), Italy (a member, with the first two, of the Triple Alliance of 1882), and Turkey. They became known as the Central Powers. In 1915, Italy defected to the side of the Allies—France, Russia, the United Kingdom, and (from 1917) the United States. After the defeat of the Central Powers and the collapse of their empires in 1918, Austria, now reduced to its German-speaking sections, was proclaimed a republic. The Treaty of St.-Germain-en-Laye (1919) fixed the borders of the new state and forbade it any kind of political or economic union with Germany without League of Nations approval.

During the next decade, Austria was plagued by inflation, food shortages, unemployment, financial scandals, and, as a consequence, growing political unrest. The country's two major political groupings, the Christian Socialist Party and the Social Democratic Party, were almost equal in strength, with their own private paramilitary movements. A small Austrian Nazi party, advocating union with Germany, constituted a third group. In March 1933, Chancellor Engelbert Dollfuss, leader of the Christian Socialists, dissolved the Austrian parliament, suspended the democratic constitution of 1920, and ruled by decree, hoping to control the unrest. In February 1934, civil strife erupted; government forces broke up the opposition Social Democratic Party, executing or imprisoning many persons. Dollfuss thereupon established an authoritarian corporate state along Fascist lines. On 25 July, the Nazis, emboldened by Adolf Hitler's rise in Germany, assassinated Dollfuss in an abortive coup. Kurt von Schuschnigg, who had served under

Dollfuss as minister of justice and education, then became chancellor. For the next four years, Schuschnigg struggled to keep Austria independent amid growing German pressure for annexation (*Anschluss*). On 11 March 1938, however, German troops entered the country, and two days later Austria was proclaimed a part of the German Reich. In 1939, Austria, now known as Ostmark, entered World War II as part of the Axis alliance.

Allied troops entered Austria in April 1945, and the country was divided into US, British, French, and Soviet zones of occupation. Declaring the 1920 constitution in force, the occupying powers permitted Austrians to set up a provisional government but limited Austrian sovereignty under an agreement of 1946. Austria made effective use of foreign economic aid during the early postwar years. The United States and the United Kingdom supplied $379 million worth of goods between 1945 and 1948; another $110 million was provided by private organizations; and Marshall Plan aid amounted to $962 million. Inflation was checked by the early 1950s, and for most of the remainder of that decade the economy sustained one of the world's highest growth rates.

On 15 May 1955, after more than eight years of negotiations, representatives of Austria and the four powers signed, at Vienna, the Austrian State Treaty, reestablishing an independent and democratic Austria, and in October all occupation forces withdrew from the country. Under the treaty, Austria agreed to become permanently neutral. As a neutral nation, Austria has remained outside the political and military alliances into which postwar Europe is divided. Economically, however, it has developed close links with Western Europe, joining EFTA in 1960 and concluding free-trade agreements with the EEC (now the EU) in 1972. Because of its location, Austria served as an entrepôt between the Western trade blocs and the CMEA, with which it also had trade relations. Austria was twice the site of US-USSR summit meetings. In June 1961, President John F. Kennedy and Premier Nikita S. Khrushchev conferred in Vienna, and in June 1979, presidents Jimmy Carter and Leonid I. Brezhnev signed a strategic arms limitation agreement in the Austrian capital. Austria joined the EU in 1995 and European economic and monetary union in 1999.

On 8 July 1986, following elections in May and June, former UN Secretary-General Kurt Waldheim was sworn in as president of Austria. During the presidential campaign, Waldheim was accused of having belonged to Nazi organizations during World War II and of having taken part in war crimes while stationed in Greece and Yugoslavia with the German army from 1942 to 1945; he denied the charges. After his inauguration, diplomats of many nations made a point of avoiding public contact with the new president, and on 27 April 1987, the US Justice Department barred him from entering the United States. To the dismay of many leaders, Pope John Paul II granted Waldheim an audience at the Vatican on 25 June.

Waldheim declined to run for a second term, and in July 1992, Thomas Klestil was elected federal president and he was reelected on 19 April 1998. Relations with Israel, which had been strained under Waldheim's presidency, returned to normal.

The growing strength of Austria's Freedom Party, headed by Jörg Haider, is evidence of a turn to the right in Austrian politics. Although the party did not capture the votes it wanted to in the 17 December 1995 legislative elections, in the elections for European Parliament on 14 October 1996 the aggressively nationalist, anti-

immigrant, anti-European Freedom Party took 28% of the vote, 2% behind the Social Democrats. The People's Party and Social Democrats remained together in a coalition throughout the 1990s and prepared Austria for entry into the European economic and monetary union. Cautious reforms took place, and the administration privatized state-owned enterprises, brought down inflation to less than 1% in 1998, and reduced the budget deficit to 2%. Average growth rates between 1997 and 2000 were over 2%. Unemployment fell to 4% in 2000. However, the global economic downturn that began in 2001 caused Austria's economy to suffer; coupled with costs resulting from severe flooding in August 2002, Austria's budget deficit increased sharply. In 2004–05 the economy rebounded: GDP growth was once again at 2%, allowing Austria to retain its position among the top European economies.

The Freedom Party scored a triumph in the general election of October 1999, coming in second behind the Social Democrats with 27% of the vote. After the traditional coalition of Social Democrats and the conservative People's Party failed to reach agreement on the next government in early 2000, the leader of the People's Party, Wolfgang Schüssel, turned to Haider and the Freedom Party to form a new administration. President Klestil had no choice but to accept the new coalition agreement. Its installation on 3 February 2000 provoked widespread protests both within Austria and from other members of the European Union. The EU partners decided to boycott Austria in all official meetings, a decision that caused a severe crisis in the EU itself. Haider resigned as party chairman in April 2000 although he remained governor of Carinthia. His withdrawal from federal politics did not soften the views of the EU, which imposed diplomatic sanctions on Austria. (They were lifted in September 2000.) A power struggle within the Freedom Party between Haider and Austria's Vice-Chancellor and Freedom Party chair Susanne Riess-Passer in September 2002 resulted in Riess-Passer's resignation, along with that of two Freedom Party ministers. The People's Party/Freedom Party coalition government collapsed, and new elections were called for 24 November 2002. In those elections, Schüssel's People's Party made wide gains; the Freedom Party suffered a major defeat. It dropped to 10% of the vote, down from its 2000 showing of 27%. Despite these results, and after failed negotiations with the Social Democrats and Greens, Schüssel formed a coalition government with the Freedom Party, which was sworn in on 1 April 2003. Schüssel subsequently moved closer to the right, notably on asylum and immigration issues (in October 2003, his government introduced a package of asylum legislation which are seen as the most restrictive in Europe). In April 2005, the Freedom Party split when Haider left to form the Alliance for Austria's Future. Members of both groups remain in government.

After the new government took office in 2003, it launched a series of austerity measures designed to save the government €8 billion. Early retirement was to be cancelled, cuts were planned in public services and the health care system was to be reformed, and, most controversially, drastic cuts were proposed in the nation's pension system. As a result, approximately 500,000 Austrians took part in nationwide strikes in May 2003, the largest in 50 years.

In January 2001, the Austrian government and several Austrian companies agreed to provide $360 million to a general settlement fund to compensate Jews who had their property and assets seized by the Nazis during World War II. Each victim of Nazi persecution was to receive $7,000. Austria also created a social fund to pay pensions to survivors no longer living in the country, in the amount of $100 million.

Following the 11 September 2001 terrorist attacks on the United States, Austria passed a Security and Defense Doctrine, representing a shift in Austria's longstanding policy of neutrality. Although Austria will not participate in military alliances requiring mutual defense commitments, the country is gradually moving towards closer integration with European security structures, which would allow for participation in the EU rapid reaction force and NATO's Partnership for Peace program. Austria contributed peacekeeping forces to the former Yugoslavia, and supported NATO strikes on Serbia during the Kosovo conflict. Austria contributed 60 soldiers to the international military protection force in Afghanistan following the US-led military campaign there.

In April 2004, Heinz Fischer was elected president. In May 2005, the Austrian parliament ratified the EU constitution. However, the rejection of that constitution by the French and Dutch in referenda held later in May and June 2005 doomed the plan for further European union indefinitely. Concerns about immigration, poor economies, EU expansion, and loss of national identity are some of the reasons French and Dutch voters gave for rejecting the constitution.

13 GOVERNMENT

The second Austrian republic was established on 19 December 1945. According to the constitution of 1920, as amended in 1929, Austria is a federal republic with a democratically elected parliament. The president, elected by popular vote for a six-year term, appoints a federal chancellor (*Bundeskanzler*), usually the leader of the largest party in parliament, for a term not exceeding that of parliament (four years); upon the chancellor's proposal, the president nominates ministers (who should not serve in parliament at the same time) to head the administrative departments of government. The ministers make up the cabinet, which formulates and directs national policy. Cabinet ministers serve out their terms subject to the confidence of a parliamentary majority. The president is limited to two terms of office.

The parliament, known as the Federal Assembly (*Bundesversammlung*), consists of the National Council (*Nationalrat*) and Federal Council (*Bundesrat*). The Bundesrat has 62 members, elected by the country's unicameral provincial legislatures (*Landtage*) in proportion to the population of each province. The Nationalrat has 183 members (prior to 1970, 165 members), elected directly in nine election districts for four-year terms by secret ballot on the basis of proportional representation. All citizens 25 years of age or older are eligible to serve in parliament; all citizens 18 years of age or older may vote. Voting is compulsory for presidential elections. The electoral law was amended in February 1990 to extend the franchise to Austrians living permanently or temporarily abroad. All legislation originates in the Nationalrat; the Bundesrat exercises only a suspensory veto.

14 POLITICAL PARTIES

The restoration of the republic in 1945 revived political activity in Austria. In general elections that November, the Austrian People's Party (Österreichische Volkspartei—ÖVP), successor to the prewar Christian Socialists, emerged as the strongest party, with the reborn Socialist Party of Austria (Sozialistische Partei Österreichs—SPÖ) trailing slightly. The ÖVP and SPÖ, controlling 161 of the 165 seats in the Nationalrat, formed a coalition government and worked closely with the Allies to construct an independent and democratic Austria. This coalition held until after the elections of 1966, when the ÖVP, with a majority of 11 seats, formed a one-party government headed by Chancellor Josef Klaus. In 1970, the SPÖ won a plurality in the Nationalrat and was able to put together a minority Socialist government under its leader, Bruno Kreisky. Kreisky remained in power until 1983—longer than any other non-Communist European head of government. The Socialist Party was renamed the Social Democratic Party in 1991, and began to advocate free-market oriented policies. It has also supported Austria's entry into the EC (now EU).

The ÖVP, also referred to as Austria's Christian Democratic Party, favors free enterprise, competition, and the reduction of class differences. Organized into three constituencies—businessmen, farmers, and employees—it advocates provincial rights and strongly supports the Catholic Church. The SPÖ, also known as the Social Democratic Party, advocates moderate reforms through democratic processes. It favored continued nationalization of key industries, economic planning, and widespread social welfare benefits. It is closely allied with the Austrian Trade Union Federation and its constituent unions. The economic policy differences between the two parties diminished in the 1990s as both recognized the need to introduce structural reforms and bring down budget deficits. Their main disagreements are on the pace of change, rather than on the need to introduce reforms.

A third political group, the Union of Independents (Verband der Unabhängigen—VdU), appeared in 1949. Strongly antisocialist, with anticlerical, pan-German elements, it challenged the coalition in the elections of that year, winning 16 seats. By the mid-1950s, however, the VdU, consistently denied a voice in government by the two major parties, had begun to disintegrate. In 1955, it was reorganized, under new leadership, as the Freedom Party of Austria (Freiheitliche Partei Österreichs—FPÖ). In 1970, with six seats in the Nationalrat, the FPÖ was accepted as a negotiating partner by the SPÖ. The party favors individual initiative over collective security. By the turn of the 21st century, under the leadership of Jörg Haider, the FPÖ was an extreme nationalist, anti-immigrant, anti-European party. In June 1992, FPÖ dissidents founded the Free Democratic Party. In 2005, Haider split from the FPÖ to form the Alliance for the Future of Austria (BZÖ).

The Communist Party of Austria (Kommunistische Partei Österreichs—KPÖ) has declined steadily in strength since the end of World War II. It has had no parliamentary representation, for example, since 1959, when it lost the three seats won in 1956. The KPÖ was the first party in the Nationalrat to propose, in 1953, that Austria become a neutral nation.

In the elections of 24 April 1983, dominated by economic issues, the SPÖ (with 47.8% of the vote) won 90 seats, down from 95 in 1979; the ÖVP (with 43.21%) 81; and the FPÖ (with 4.97%) 12. The KPÖ polled 0.66% of the vote but won no seats. Two new environmentalist groups, the United Greens of Austria (Vereinten Grünen Österreichs) and the Alternative List–Austria (Alternative Liste Österreichs), likewise failed to gain representation in the Nationalrat, although they collectively polled more than 3%

of the total vote. In May, Kreisky, having failed to win a clear majority, resigned. He was succeeded as party leader and chancellor by Fred Sinowatz, who proceeded to form a coalition government with the FPÖ.

Following the election of Kurt Waldheim to the presidency in June 1986, Sinowatz resigned and was succeeded by Franz Vranitzky, a former finance minister. The SPÖ-FPÖ coalition broke down in September 1986. Following parliamentary elections on 23 November 1986, a new government was sworn in on 21 January 1987, with Vranitzky from the SPÖ as chancellor and Alois Mock, FPÖ chairman, as vice-chancellor and prime minister.

In the general election of 7 October 1990, the "grand coalition" continued. The 183 seats in the Nationalrat were distributed as follows: SPÖ (80), ÖVP (60), FPÖ (33), and the Green Alternative (10). It also governed after the 1995 elections.

The 1999 elections finally brought change and was a watershed event. In the legislative election held on 3 October 1999, the 183 seats in the Nationalrat were distributed as follows: SPÖ (65), ÖVP (52), FPÖ (52), Greens (14), and Liberal Forum (0). Compared to the 1995 elections, the SPÖ lost 6 seats, the Liberal Forum lost all of its 10 seats and had no representation in the new National Assembly, the ÖVP retained more or less its share of the vote, while the Greens went from 9 to 14 seats and the FPÖ went from 40 seats to 52 seats and became, together, with the People's Party, the second-largest bloc in parliament. The leader of the ÖVP, Wolfgang Schüssel, formed a coalition with the FPÖ, and became chancellor.

Following the 24 November 2002 elections, party strength in the Nationalrat was distributed as follows: ÖVP, 42.3% (79 seats); SPÖ, 36.5% (69 seats); FPÖ, 10% (18 seats); the Greens, 9.5% (17 seats); the Liberal Forum, 1% (no seats); and the KPÖ, 0.6% (no seats). Schüssel remained chancellor, and formed a government with the FPÖ, as he was unable to persuade the SPÖ and the Greens to join in a coalition with the ÖVP. As of 2005, a coalition government comprising the ÖVP and Jörg Haider's Alliance for the Future of Austria, which split from the FPÖ that April, was ruling the country.

In the presidential election held on 25 April 2004, Heinz Fischer of the SPÖ was elected president with 52.4% of the vote, defeating Benita Ferrero-Waldner of the ÖVP (47.6% of the vote). Fischer succeeded Thomas Klestil, who had served as president since 1992.

15 LOCAL GOVERNMENT

Austria is divided into nine provinces (Länder): Vienna (Wien), Lower Austria (Niederösterreich), Upper Austria (Oberösterreich), Styria (Steiermark), Carinthia (Kärnten), Tyrol (Tirol), Salzburg, Burgenland, and Vorarlberg. The relationship between the provinces and the central government is defined by the constitution. Most administrative, legislative, and judicial authority—including taxation, welfare, and police—is granted to the central government. The Länder, which enjoy all residual powers, act as executors of federal authority.

Each province has its own unicameral legislature, elected on the basis of proportional representation. All legislation must be submitted through the provincial governor (Landeshauptmann) to the competent federal ministry for concurrence. If such concurrence is not obtained, the provincial legislature can reinstate the bill by majority vote. In case of prolonged conflict between the federal authorities and the provincial legislatures, the Constitutional Court may be appealed to for settlement.

The provincial governor, elected by the provincial legislature (Landtag), is assisted by a cabinet (Landesrat) consisting of ministries analogous to those at the federal level. Each province is divided into several administrative districts (Bezirke), each of which is under a district commissioner (Bezirkshauptmann). Local self-government is vested in popularly elected communal councils which, in turn, elect various local officers, including the mayor (Bürgermeister) and his deputies. There are some 2,300 communities in Austria, as well as 15 cities that have independent charters and fall directly under provincial authority rather than that of the districts. Vienna is both a municipality and a province.

16 JUDICIAL SYSTEM

Austria in 2005 had 140 local courts (Bezirksgerichte) with civil jurisdiction. There were also 20 provincial and district courts (Landesgerichte and Kreisgerichte) with civil and criminal jurisdiction and four higher provincial courts (Oberlandesgerichte) with criminal jurisdiction, located in Vienna, Graz, Innsbruck, and Linz. The Supreme Court (Oberster Gerichtshof), in Vienna, acts as the final appellate court for criminal and civil cases. The Constitutional Court (Verfassungsgerichtshof) has supreme jurisdiction over constitutional and civil rights issues. The Administrative Court (Verwaltungsgerichtshof) ensures the legal functioning of public administration. A central auditing authority controls financial administration. Judges are appointed by the federal government and cannot be removed or transferred. Trial by jury was reintroduced in 1951. There is no capital punishment.

The judiciary is independent of the other branches. Judges are appointed for life and can only be removed for specific reasons established by law and only after formal court action has been taken.

Before the mid 1990s, the law allowed for detention of suspects for 48 hours without judicial review and up to two years of detention during the course of a criminal investigation. Amendments to the law in 1994 required more stringent judicial review of pretrial and investigative detention. Criminal defendants are afforded a presumption of innocence, public trials, and jury trial for major offenses, as well as a number of other procedural rights.

17 ARMED FORCES

As of 2005, Austria's active armed forces totaled 39,900 personnel plus another 9,500 civilians. In addition, another 60,000 reservists undergo refresher training annually. The Army is the largest service in terms of manpower, with 33,200 personnel in 2005. Equipment included 114 main battle tanks, 220 light tanks, 637 armored personnel carriers, and 684 artillery pieces. Austria's Air Force in 2005 had 6,700 active personnel, which operated 40 combat capable aircraft, which included 12 fighters. There were also 17 transport and 44 training aircraft. The 2005 defense budget totaled $2.29 billion. Austrian armed forces in 2005 were deployed to 12 countries or regions under UN, NATO or European Union command.

18 INTERNATIONAL COOPERATION

The Federal Constitutional Law on the Neutrality of Austria, adopted on 26 October 1955, bound the nation to neutrality and banned it from joining any military alliances or permitting the establishment of foreign military bases on its territory. However, since 1995, the country has been rethinking this position on neutrality. In December 2001, Austria adopted a Security and Defense Doctrine; although Austria will not participate in military alliances requiring mutual defense commitments, the country is gradually moving toward greater integration with European security arrangements, which would allow for participation in the EU rapid reaction force and NATO's Partnership for Peace program.

Austria became a member of the UN on 14 December 1955. It is a member of ECE and all the nonregional specialized agencies, such as FAO, IFC, ILO, WHO, and the World Bank. The country became a member of the WTO 1 January 1995 and of the OSCE on 30 January 1992. Vienna has served an important role as a meeting place and headquarters site for a variety of international activities. The headquarters of OPEC, IAEA, UNIDO, and the International Institute for Applied Systems Analysis are located in Vienna. Austria belongs to the Council of Europe, the OECD, the Paris Club, the European Space Agency, and the European Union. Austria's interest in the Third World is exemplified by membership in the Asian and Inter-American development banks and by its permanent observer status with the OAS.

Austria is part of the Australia Group, the Zangger Committee, and the Organization for the Prohibition of Chemical Weapons. Austrian troops have been part of UN peacekeeping forces in Kosovo (est. 1999), Western Sahara (est. 1991), Ethiopia and Eritrea (est. 2000), Georgia (est. 1993), and Cyprus (est. 1964).

In environmental cooperation, the country is part of the Antarctic Treaty; the Basel Convention; Conventions on Biological Diversity, Whaling, and Air Pollution; Ramsar; CITES; the International Tropical Timber Agreements; the Kyoto Protocol; the Montréal Protocol; MARPOL; and the Nuclear Test Ban Treaty.

19 ECONOMY

Liberalization inspired by the EU and greater acceptance of the values of competition have transformed Austria's economy since the 1980s. Previously, the state maintained a strong presence in the Austrian economy, but in the 21st century private enterprise increasingly takes on a primary position. Basic industries, including mineral production, heavy industry, rail and water transport, and utilities, were nationalized during 1946–47 and in 1970 were reorganized under a state-owned holding company, the Austrian Industrial Administration (Österreichische Industrieverwaltungs-Aktiengesellschaft—ÖIAG). In 1986, the ÖIAG was renamed the Österreichische Industrieholding AG, and a process of restructuring and privatization took place that traversed the 1990s and early 2000s. German companies in particular took advantage of the privatization of Austrian firms.

Austria's period of unparalleled prosperity lasted from the 1950s through the early 1970s; the economy was characterized by a high rate of growth, modest price increases, and a favorable climate in industrial relations. By 1975, Austrian industry, the single most important sector of the economy, had more than quadrupled in value over 1945. But the general economic slowdown that followed the oil price hike of late 1973 affected Austria as it did other European countries. During 1978–81, annual real growth averaged 2.6%, about standard for the OECD countries, but there was no real growth in 1981 and only 1.1% growth in 1982, as Austria endured its most prolonged recession since World War II. The following years saw an improvement. Between 1984 and 1991, annual real GDP growth averaged 2.8%. In 1992, it was 1.7%. Following the mild recession in 1993, Austria's economy—driven by strong exports, investment, and private consumption—expanded an average of 2% throughout the 1990s. GDP growth stood at 2.4% in 2004, and dropped to an estimated 1.7% in 2005. GDP growth was forecast at 1.8% for 2006, and to accelerate to 2.1% for 2007. Despite the impact of high oil prices projected for 2006, inflation was expected to ease over the 2006–07 period. The inflation rate (at consumer prices) stood at 1.8% in 2004.

Due in large measure to a global economic downturn and resulting low domestic demand, in 2002 Austria was experiencing its worst slowdown in over a decade. However, in 2001, Austria balanced its budget for the first time in 30 years, in part due to an increase in taxes. (The only countries with higher tax burdens than Austria are Denmark, Finland, and Sweden.) However, the conservative government led by the Austrian People's Party that came into power in November 2002 gave less priority to maintaining a balanced budget, and by 2003, the budget deficit was -1.1%, and was expected to rise to -2% in 2006, with a modest improvement in 2007. Austria's ratio of government debt to GDP remained high among European countries in the early 2000s, at over 65%. Austria benefited from its proximity to the faster-growing economies of Central and Eastern Europe in the early 2000s, but was negatively impacted by the low growth in Germany, its largest trading partner. Severe flooding in Central Europe during August 2002 resulted in extra budget outlays for flood damage. The unemployment rate stood at 4.5% in 2004. Austria profits from a high productivity rate. It has also met with success in privatizing most of its large manufacturing firms. Austria in the early 2000s invested in high-growth industries such as telecommunications, biotechnology, medical and pharmaceutical research, and electronics.

20 INCOME

The US Central Intelligence Agency (CIA) reports that in 2005 Austria's gross domestic product (GDP) was estimated at $269.4 billion. The CIA defines GDP as the value of all final goods and services produced within a nation in a given year and computed on the basis of purchasing power parity (PPP) rather than value as measured on the basis of the rate of exchange based on current dollars. The per capita GDP was estimated at $32,000. The annual growth rate of GDP was estimated at 1.9%. The average inflation rate in 2005 was 2.3%. It was estimated that agriculture accounted for 2.3% of GDP, industry 30.8%, and services 66.9%.

According to the World Bank, in 2003 remittances from citizens working abroad totaled $2.294 billion or about $284 per capita and accounted for approximately 0.9% of GDP.

The World Bank reports that in 2003 household consumption in Austria totaled $144.16 billion or about $17,819 per capita based on a GDP of $253.1 billion, measured in current dollars rather than PPP. Household consumption includes expenditures of individuals, households, and nongovernmental organizations on goods and services, excluding purchases of dwellings. It was estimated that for the period 1990 to 2003 household consumption grew at an average annual rate of 2.3%. It was estimated that in 1999 about 3.9% of the population had incomes below the poverty line.

21 LABOR

In 2005, the labor force was estimated at 3.49 million workers. As of 2005, an estimated 70% of the workforce was engaged in the services sector, 27% in industry, and 3% in agriculture. Foreign laborers, mainly from the former Yugoslavia and Turkey, constitute a significant part of the total workforce. The unemployment rate has risen slightly in recent years, from 3.6% in 1994 to 4.8% in 2002. As of 2005, Austria's unemployment rate was estimated at 5.1%.

Workers were organized into the 13 trade unions affiliated in the Austrian Trade Union Federation (Österreichische Gewerkschaftsbund—ÖGB), accounting for an estimated 47% of the nation's workforce, as of 2005. This confederation negotiates collective bargaining agreements with the Federal Economic Chamber (Bundeskammer der gewerblichen Wirtschaft) representing employers. Although the right to strike is recognized, strikes are rarely used due to cooperation between labor and management. Collective bargaining is prevalent. Disputes over wages, working hours, working conditions, and vacations are settled by a labor court or an arbitration board.

The workweek is set at a maximum of 40 hours, although most Austrian workers put in 38–38.5 hours per week. A 50% differential is generally paid for overtime on weekdays, 100% on Sundays and holidays. In addition, it is required that an employee be given at least 11 hours off between workdays. There is no national minimum wage. Most employees are covered by collective bargaining agreements, which set wages by industry. However, the unofficial accepted minimum is $14,880 to $17,360 per year which provides a family with a decent standard of living. The minimum legal age for employment is 15 years, and this is effectively enforced.

22 AGRICULTURE

Although small, the agricultural sector is highly diversified and efficient. Most production is oriented toward local consumption.

Of Austria's total area, about 18% was arable in 2002; meadows and pasturelands constituted another 24%. The best cropland is in the east, which has the most level terrain. Farms are almost exclusively family-owned. Most holdings are small or medium-sized and, in many cases, scattered. As of 2003, agriculture employed 4.5% of the labor force. In 2003, agriculture (together with forestry) contributed 2.3% to Austria's total GDP.

The use of farm machinery has been increasing steadily; 330,000 tractors were in operation in 2002, up from 78,748 in 1957. Austria today uses less land and manpower and produces more food than it did before World War II (1939–45). Better seeding and more intensive and efficient application of fertilizers have helped raise farm yields and have enhanced self-sufficiency in foodstuffs. Agriculture is highly protected by the government; overproduction, especially evidenced by recurring grain surpluses, requires a hefty subsidy to be paid by the government in order to sell abroad at market prices. Nevertheless, the Austrian government has been able to maintain farm income, although Austria has some of the highest food costs in Europe.

Chief crops, in terms of sown area and yield, are wheat, rye, oats, barley, potatoes, and sugar beets. Austria is near self-sufficiency in wheat, oats, rye, fruits, vegetables, sugar, and a number of other items. Major crop yields in 2004 included (in tons) sugar beets, 2,935,000; barley, 1,007,000; wheat, 1,719,000; potatoes, 693,000; rye, 213,000; and oats, 139,000. Vineyards yielded 351,000 tons of grapes crushed for wine.

23 ANIMAL HUSBANDRY

Dairy and livestock breeding, traditionally the major agricultural activities, account for about three-fifths of gross agricultural income.

Milk, butter, cheese, and meat are excellent, and Austria is self-sufficient in dairy products and in most meats. In 2004, livestock included 3,245,000 hogs, 2,052,000 head of cattle, 325,000 sheep, 85,000 horses, and 11,600,000 million poultry. Meat and poultry production in 2004 totaled 996,000 tons. During 2004, Austrian dairy farms produced 3,559,000 tons of milk, 169,000 tons of cheese, and 32,000 tons of butter. In 2004, some 88,700 tons of eggs were produced, which satisfied over 90% of domestic demand. By specializing in quality strains of cattle, hogs, and horses, Austrian breeders have gained wide international recognition. Livestock products, primarily milk, account for about 35% of agricultural exports.

24 FISHING

Fishing is not important commercially, and fish do not constitute a large part of the Austrian diet. Commercial catches consist mainly of carp and trout. The total catch in 2003 was 2,605 tons. Aquacultural production in 2003 was 2,233 tons, mostly rainbow trout. A sizable segment of the population engages in sport fishing.

25 FORESTRY

Austria has the second-largest percentage of forest in the European Union. About 47% of Austria's total area is forested, mostly in the foothills and mountains. Styria, in the southeast, is 60% covered with forests, while Burgenland in the east has only 32% forest coverage. About two-thirds of the trees are coniferous, primarily spruce; beech is the most important broadleaf type.

Over-cutting during World War II (1939–45) and in the postwar period resulted in a decline in timber production from 9.5 million cu m (335 million cu ft) in 1936 to a low of about 7.1 million cu m (251 million cu ft). From 1950 to 2003, sawn lumber output rose from 4,000 cu m (141,000 cu ft) to 10.5 million cu m (370.7 million cu ft). Competition reduced the number of sawmills from 5,100 in 1950 to 1,400 in 2003, with about 10,000 employees. Bark beetle infestations adversely affected production in the mid-1990s. Total roundwood yield was 17.1 million cu m (602 million cu ft) in 2003. In 2004, about 7.8 million cu m (247 million cu ft) of softwood lumber logs were produced. To prevent over cutting, export restrictions have been introduced, and reforestation on both public and private land is compulsory. Exports of raw timber and cork are supplemented by exports of such forestry products as paper, cardboard boxes, prefabricated houses, toys, matches, turpentine, and volatile oils. Austria is the world's fourth-largest softwood lumber exporter, with shipments valued at €1.28 billion in 2003.

26 MINING

After a period of postwar expansion, mineral production has stagnated in recent decades, and metals mining continues to decline, because of high operating costs, increased foreign competition, low ore grades, and environmental problems. All the metal mines in the country were closed, except an iron ore operation at Erzberg (producing 1.8 million tons of iron ore and concentrate in 2000) and a tungsten operation at Mittersill, which was the West's largest underground tungsten mine. Most of the growth in the mineral resources area was in the production of industrial minerals, the area in which future mining activities will most likely be concentrated, mostly for domestic consumption.

Austria produces 2.5% of the world's graphite, ranking 10th in the world, and is one of the world's largest sources of high-grade graphite. In 2000, estimated output was 12,000 metric tons, down from 30,000 metric tons in 1996. The country produces 1.6% of the world's talc, ranking ninth, with a reported output in 2003 of 137,596 tons of crude talc and soapstone. The country's only producer of talc, Luzenac Naintsch AG, operated three mines, in the Styria region, and produced a range of talc, chloritic talc, dolomite talc, and chlorite-mica-quartz ores.

Output of other minerals in 2003 output in metric tons, include: limestone and marble, 24,477,000 metric tons; dolomite, 6,079,000 metric tons, for the domestic cement industry, along with calcite and limestone; gypsum and anhydrite, 1,004,000 metric tons; brine salt, 3,422,000 cubic meters (salt mines are owned by the government, with plans to privatize the operations); tungsten, 1,400 tons; pumice (trass), 4,000 tons; and crude kaolin, 100,000 metric tons. Gold production in 2003 was 25 kg. Crude magnesite production was reported at 767,000 metric tons in 2003.

Lignite production has been declining since 1963. In 2003, lignite production totaled 1,152,000 metric tons. Production of bituminous coal declined steadily after World War II, and in 1968 ceased altogether.

27 ENERGY AND POWER

Austria is one of the foremost producers of hydroelectric power in Europe. The most important power facilities are publicly owned; 50% of the shares of the large private producers are owned by provincial governments.

In 2000, net electricity generation was 58.8 billion kWh, of which 28.5% came from fossil fuels, 68.6% from hydropower, none from nuclear energy, and the remainder from other sources. In the same year, consumption of electricity totaled 54.8 million kWh. Total installed capacity at the beginning of 2001 was 14.2 million kW. In 2000 petroleum accounted for 39% of energy consumption, natural gas 20%, coal 10%, nuclear energy 0%, and hydroelectric power 31%. During the winter, when there is less flowing water for hydroelectric power, domestic electricity demands must be supplemented by imports from neighboring countries.

Oil, first produced in 1863, is found both in Upper Austria, near Wolfsegg am Hausruck, and in Lower Austria, in the vicinity of Vienna. After reaching a peak of about 3,700,000 tons in 1955, oil production gradually declined to 22,000 barrels per day in 2000. Natural gas production was 1.698 billion cu m (60 billion cu ft)

in 1998, far short of domestic needs; consumption amounted to 6.862 billion cu m (242 billion cu ft) in that year.

28 INDUSTRY

Industrial output has increased vastly since the beginning of World War II and contributed 30.8% of the GDP in 2004. The industrial production growth rate in 2004 was 3.3%. In 1946, the federal parliament nationalized basic industries. Major parts of the electric and electronics, chemical, iron and steel, and machinery industries remained state controlled until the 1990s, when the Austrian government embarked upon a privatization program. As of 2005, the steel, aluminum, and petroleum industries were majority-owned by private shareholders. Other privatizations in the early 2000s were the Austrian tobacco company, the Vienna airport company, Telekom Austria, Voest-Alpine Steel, and Boehler Uddeholm, an important tool and specialty steel manufacturer.

Iron and steel production greatly expanded its output after 1937. A total of 155,403 automobiles were manufactured in 2001 and 24,988 heavy trucks were produced in 2000. The sale of automotive parts and equipment was a $3 billion industry in 2004, albeit a decline from $3.35 billion in 2003 and $3.87 billion in 2002.

Traditionally, the most important sectors of the textile industry have been embroidery, spinning, weaving, and knitting. However, foreign competition cut into the Austrian textile industry. Following the expiration of the World Trade Organization's longstanding system of textile quotas at the beginning of 2005, the EU signed an agreement with China in June 2005, imposing new quotas on 10 categories of textile goods, limiting growth in those categories to between 8% and 12.5% a year. The agreement runs until 2007, and was designed to give European textile manufacturers time to adjust to a world of unfettered competition. Nevertheless, barely a month after the EU-China agreement was signed, China reached its quotas for sweaters, followed soon after by blouses, bras, T-shirts, and flax yarn. Tens of millions of garments piled up in warehouses and customs checkpoints, which affected both retailers and consumers.

The chemical industry, which was relatively unimportant before World War II, now ranks second in value of production, behind the mechanical and steel industry. Other leading industries, in terms of production value and employment, are electrical and electronic machinery and equipment, pulp and paper, ceramics, and especially foodstuffs and allied products. Austria has always been famous for its skilled craftsmen, such as glassblowers, goldsmiths, jewelers, lacemakers, potters, stonecutters, and wood-carvers.

The country is taking steps to change its image from one in which traditional "rust belt" industries such as steel and heavy engineering dominate. In 2005, the electronics, biotechnology, and medical and pharmaceutical sectors were high growth industries.

29 SCIENCE AND TECHNOLOGY

Numerous research institutes in Austria play an important role in conducting and coordinating advanced agricultural, medical, scientific, and technical research. The Austrian Research Council supports and coordinates scientific research. The major learned society is the Austrian Academy of Sciences (founded in 1847 and headquartered in Vienna). The Austrian Science Foundation (founded in 1967) and the Austrian Industrial Research Fund together form the Austrian Research Council, which supports and coordinates scientific, applied, and industrial research and development and advises federal and state governments on scientific matters. The Natural History Museum and the Trade and Industrial Museum of Technology, both in Vienna and founded in 1748 and 1907, respectively, each have large libraries.

Austria has 11 universities offering training in basic and applied sciences and 13 federal colleges of technology. In 2004, provisional data showed Austrian spending on research and development (R&D) as totaling €5.273 billion, of which 41.5% came from business, 36.7% from the government and 21.5% from foreign sources. In 1987–97, science and engineering students accounted for 29% of college and university enrollments. In 2002, of all bachelor's degrees awarded, 26.5% were in the sciences (natural, mathematics and computers, and engineering). As of 1998 (the latest year for which data was available), there were 2,346 researchers and 993 technicians per million people, that were actively engaged in R&D. In 2002, high-tech exports were valued at $8.433 billion and accounted for 15% of all manufactured exports.

30 DOMESTIC TRADE

Vienna is the commercial, banking, and industrial center. Railroad lines passing through it connect Austria with all neighboring countries. Vienna is also the major, but not the only, distribution center; every large provincial city is the hub of marketing and distribution for the surrounding area. Most items are sold in privately owned general or special stores, but consumer cooperatives are also active. Though small specialty shops have accounted for about 90% of retail establishments, larger outlets and shopping malls are becoming popular. For instance, close to the small village of Parndorf, Burgenland, 40 minutes outside of Vienna, there is a designer outlet featuring more than 90 department stores and specialty shops selling over 350 international brands. Although modeled after the American shopping mall, the McArthur Glen Designer Outlet resembles an Austrian baroque village.

By law, most Austrian shops may be open no more than 66 hours per week. Legal shopping hours are from 6 AM to 7:30 PM Monday through Friday, and 6 AM to 5 PM on Saturdays. However, normal business hours are from 8 or 9 AM to 6 PM, Mondays through Fridays. Saturday shopping hours are normally 8 or 9 AM to 12 or 1 PM. Banks usually stay open from 8 AM to 12:30 PM and from 1:30 to 3 PM (5:30 PM on Thursday) on the weekdays. Retail establishments are governed by stricter rules than in the United States. Sunday hours are generally not permitted.

Advertising is displayed in newspapers, periodicals, and trade journals, and on posters on public conveyances, public stands, and billboards. Considerable advertising is done in cinemas. International fairs are held every spring and autumn in Vienna, and specialized fairs are held regularly in Dornbirn, Graz, Innsbruck, Klagenfurt, Ried im Innkreis, and Wels.

31 FOREIGN TRADE

Austria depends heavily on foreign trade. During the Cold War, the government consistently maintained strong ties with the West while being careful to preserve the country's neutrality. In 1972, Austria achieved association with the EEC without encountering much Soviet opposition. Austria formerly had long-term bilateral trade agreements with CMEA nations, and played an important role as a mediator in East–West trade dealings. It applied

Principal Trading Partners – Austria (2003)			
(In millions of US dollars)			
Country	Exports	Imports	Balance
World	89,216.3	91,516.5	-2,300.2
Germany	28,370.2	37,502.2	-9,132.0
Italy-San Marino-Holy See	8,007.6	6,426.8	1,580.8
Switzerland-Liechtenstein	4,937.1	3,860.3	1,076.8
United States	4,621.2	3,533.0	1,088.2
France-Monaco	3,968.6	3,554.3	414.3
United Kingdom	3,939.6	2,092.0	1,847.6
Hungary	3,588.6	2,967.5	621.1
Czech Republic	2,725.8	2,973.3	-247.5
Spain	2,281.8	1,587.9	693.9
Netherlands	1,844.2	2,742.6	-898.4

(…) data not available or not significant.

SOURCE: *2003 International Trade Statistics Yearbook*, New York: United Nations, 2004.

for membership in 1989, ushering a new era in relations with the countries of Central and Eastern Europe. Austria became a member of the EU in 1995, and a member of the EMU in 1999; euro notes and coins were introduced in place of the Austrian schilling in 2002.

Austria's commodity trade pattern has changed significantly since the 1930s. Because of its increasing self-sufficiency in agricultural production, expansion in output of certain basic industries, and development of new industries, Austria is no longer as dependent as in pre-World War II years on imports of food and raw materials.

The rise in industrial capacity has resulted in an extensive rise in export volume, with finished and semifinished goods accounting for well over 80% of the total export value. The major industry and export commodity in Austria is the automobile and its components, made up of plates and sheets of iron or steel, internal combustion engines and piston parts, motor vehicle parts and accessories, and complete passenger motor cars. These exports comprise a large portion of Austria's exports, while machinery and paper products continue to be important commodities. Medicinal and pharmaceutical product exports are increasing, but are still low compared to those of the automobile industry.

Approximately 71% of Austria's trade is with EU nations. Although Germany, Italy, and the United States remain Austria's main trading partners, expanding trade with the new EU members of Central and Eastern Europe that joined the EU in May 2004 represent a sizeable element of Austrian economic activity.

In 2004, exports totaled an estimated $102.7 billion, and the total value of imports was estimated at $101.2 billion, for a trade surplus of $1.5 billion.

32 BALANCE OF PAYMENTS

Revenues in 2004 were estimated at $142.5 billion; expenditures were estimated at $146.4 billion. Austria's current account balance in 2004 was estimated at -$3.283 billion.

33 BANKING AND SECURITIES

The Austrian National Bank (Österreichische Nationalbank), originally opened on 2 January 1923 but taken over by the Ger-

Balance of Payments – Austria (2003)

(In millions of US dollars)

Current Account		**-1,363.0**
Balance on goods		1,140.0
Imports	-88,479.0	
Exports	89,619.0	
Balance on services		1,662.0
Balance on income		-1,836.0
Current transfers		-2,330.0
Capital Account		**-12.0**
Financial Account		**-457.0**
Direct investment abroad		-7,061.0
Direct investment in Austria		7,276.0
Portfolio investment assets		-18,414.0
Portfolio investment liabilities		22,992.0
Financial derivatives		-744.0
Other investment assets		-15,117.0
Other investment liabilities		10,610.0
Net Errors and Omissions		**-203.0**
Reserves and Related Items		**2,036.0**

(…) data not available or not significant.

SOURCE: *Balance of Payment Statistics Yearbook 2004,* Washington, DC: International Monetary Fund, 2004.

man Reichsbank in 1938, was reestablished on 3 July 1945. The bank is a corporation with capital shares fixed by law at s150 million; 50% of the shares are, by law, owned by the government. The central bank and the bank of issue, it preserves the domestic purchasing power of the Austrian currency and its value in terms of stable foreign currencies, and controls external transactions affecting the balance of payments. It also sets reserve requirements for credit institutions.

The Austrian banking system also includes joint-stock banks, banking houses, and private banks, as well as postal savings banks, private savings banks, mortgage banks, building societies, and specialized cooperative credit institutions. The most important credit institutions are the joint-stock commercial banks, the two largest of which, the Creditanstalt-Bankverein and the Österreichische Länderbank, were nationalized in 1946; shares representing 40% of the nominal capital of the two were sold to the public in 1957.

On 12 January 1997, the coalition partners, after long and intensive negotiations, agreed to sell Credit and staff-Bankverein to the indirectly state-owned Bank Austria, which is dominated by the senior coalition party, the Social Democratic Party (SPO). The sale created a financial and industrial giant in Austria, which holds about one-quarter of the assets of all financial institutions.

The International Monetary Fund reports that in 2001, currency and demand deposits—an aggregate commonly known as M1—were equal to $52.9 billion. In that same year, M2—an aggregate equal to M1 plus savings deposits, small time deposits, and money market mutual funds—was $171.2 billion.

A special decree of Empress Maria Theresa (1 August 1771) provided for the establishment of a stock exchange in Vienna. From the mid-19th century to the beginning of World War I, it was the main capital market of middle and eastern Europe, and from 1918 to 1938, it had continuous international importance as an equity market for the newly founded nations originating from the former monarchy. The exchange also deals in five Austrian and sev-

en foreign investment certificates. The Austrian Traded Index has grown steadily in the past few years, growing 8.71% in 2002, and averaging a growth rate of 10.15% in the past five years. Market capitalization as of December 2004 stood at $85.815 billion, with the index up 57.4% at 2,431.4 from the previous year. There were 99 companies listed on the Wiener Borse AG in 2004.

34 INSURANCE

Insurance in Austria is regulated by the Ministry of Finance under legislation effective 1 January 1979. Motor-vehicle third-party liability, aviation accident and third-party liability, workers' compensation, product liability, professional indemnity for certain professions, and nuclear-risk liability coverage are compulsory. Armed sportsmen, accountants, pipeline operators, and notaries are also required to carry liability insurance. In 2003, the value of all direct premiums written totaled $14.996 billion, of which nonlife premiums accounted for the largest portion at $8.410 billion. The nation's top nonlife insurer for 2003 was Allianz Elementar with gross nonlife written premiums of $983.5 million. Austria's top life insurer that same year was Sparkassen-Vericherung, with gross life written premiums of$857.5 million.

35 PUBLIC FINANCE

The government's proposed annual budget is submitted to the Nationalrat before the beginning of each calendar year (which coincides with the fiscal year). Within certain limits, the Finance Minister can subsequently permit the maximum expenditure levels to be exceeded, but any other excess spending must receive the approval of the Nationalrat in the form of a supplementary appropriations bill or an amendment to the budgetary legislation. Annual expenditures, which in the early 1960s rose markedly owing to increases in defense expenditures, social services, federal operations, and capital expenditures, were less expansionary in 1965–70. During the 1970s, the annual budget again began to rise, expenditures increasing at a faster rate than revenues, but by

Public Finance – Austria (2002)

(In millions of euros, central government figures)

Revenue and Grants	**85,652**	**100.0%**
Tax revenue	45,783	53.5%
Social contributions	33,848	39.5%
Grants	365	0.4%
Other revenue	5,657	6.6%
Expenditures	**87,934**	**100.0%**
General public services	13,710	15.6%
Defense	1,911	2.2%
Public order and safety	2,683	3.1%
Economic affairs	5,653	6.4%
Environmental protection	230	0.3%
Housing and community amenities	1,007	1.1%
Health	11,403	13.0%
Recreational, culture, and religion	651	0.7%
Education	9,005	10.2%
Social protection	41,681	47.4%

(…) data not available or not significant.

SOURCE: *Government Finance Statistics Yearbook 2004,* Washington, DC: International Monetary Fund, 2004.

the mid-1980s, both expenditures and revenues were increasing at about the same rate. As a result of a mini-recession in 1993, the budget deficit widened to 4.7% of GDP in 1994. The increase in the budget deficit was mainly due to the government's decision to let automatic stabilizers work, when it became apparent that business activity was slowing down. Rising budget deficits present an economic challenge to the government. Despite these problems, Austria managed to meet the criteria necessary to join the European Monetary Union (EMU) in 1999.

The US Central Intelligence Agency (CIA) estimated that in 2005 Austria's central government took in revenues of approximately $148.6 billion and had expenditures of $154.5 billion. Revenues minus expenditures totaled approximately -$5.9 billion. Public debt in 2005 amounted to 64.5% of GDP. Total external debt was $510.6 billion.

The International Monetary Fund (IMF) reported that in 2002, the most recent year for which it had data, central government revenues were €85,652 million and expenditures were €87,934 million. The value of revenues was us$80,606 million and expenditures us$82,537 million, based on an exchange rate for 2002 of us$1 = €1.0626 as reported by the IMF. Government outlays by function were as follows: general public services, 15.6%; defense, 2.2%; public order and safety, 3.1%; economic affairs, 6.4%; environmental protection, 0.3%; housing and community amenities, 1.1%; health, 13.0%; recreation, culture, and religion, 0.7%; education, 10.2%; and social protection, 47.4%.

36 TAXATION

The income tax for individuals in 2005 was progressively set up to 50% on a four-bracket progressive schedule: 21% (on taxable income from €3,640 to €7,270; 31% (€7,270 to €21,800); 41% (€21,800 to 50,870); and 50% above €51,000. Married people are taxed separately. Payroll withholding tax is in effect.

Taxes are levied on corporations (25% on distributed and undistributed profits), trade income, real estate, inheritance, dividends, gifts, and several miscellaneous services and properties. A value-added tax was introduced 1 January 1973 at a basic rate of 16%. The standard rate in 2005 was 20%. A reduced rate of 10% applied to basic foodstuffs, agricultural products, rents, tourism, and entertainment; banking transactions are exempt and exports are untaxed. There was also an augmented rate of 32% on automobiles, airplanes, and ships.

Capital gains and dividend income are taxed at 25% and are withheld at the source. There is no wealth tax. In accordance with EU guidelines, tax exemptions and reductions are included in incentive packages for investment in economically depressed and underdeveloped areas along Austria's eastern border.

37 CUSTOMS AND DUTIES

Austria is committed to a program of progressive trade liberalization. As a member of the European Union, non-EU imports are covered by the EU's common tariff policy, the TARIC (integrated tariff). For most manufactured goods, this tariff results in the addition of a 3.5% duty. Import quotas affect other imports such as raw materials or parts. In addition, imports are levied an import

value-added tax, which is 20% for everything except food products, for which it is 10%.

Import licenses are required for a variety of products, including agricultural produce and products, tobacco and tobacco products, salt, war materials, and poisons. An automatic licensing procedure is applied to certain products. Free-trade zones are located at Graz, Linz, Bad Hall, and Vienna.

38 FOREIGN INVESTMENT

Between 1948 and 1954, an estimated $4 billion was invested in the Austrian economy. Austria raised foreign capital largely through loans rather than as direct investment. Many post-World War II projects were financed by US aid; US grants and loans in the postwar period totaled about $1.3 billion before they began to taper off in 1952. To stimulate domestic and foreign investment, especially in underdeveloped areas of Austria, two specialized investment credit institutions were founded in the late 1950s.

The Austrian government welcomes productive foreign investment, offering a wide range of assistance and incentives at all levels ranging from indirect tax incentives to direct investment grants. Until 2006, 41% of Austria's land area is eligible for support under various EU structural reform programs. In 2005, Austria lowered its corporate tax from 34% to25%, making the investment climate more agreeable to foreign companies. Of particular interest are investments in industries that are seeking to create new employment in high technology, promoting capital-intensive industries linked with research activities, improving productivity, replacing imports, increasing exports, and are environmentally "friendly." Austria has strict environmental laws, rejects nuclear energy, and has tight restrictions on biotech products. Full foreign ownership is permitted, except in nationalized sectors, and such enterprises have the same rights and obligations as domestic companies.

Austria has sizeable investments in the countries of Central and Eastern Europe, and continues to move low-tech and labor-intensive production to those regions. Austria has the potential to attract EU firms seeking convenient access to developing markets in Central and Eastern Europe and the Balkans.

Following record inflows in 2000 and 2001 and a significant drop in 2002, foreign direct investment rebounded in 2003 to $8.1 billion, equal to 2.9% of GDP, the third highest ever. New FDI in the first half of 2004 amounted to $2.1 billion. This raised the value of FDI stock in Austria to $62 billion by mid-2004. New Austrian direct investment abroad reached $7.7 billion in 2003, equal to 2.7% of GDP. In the first half of 2004, the amount was $3.1 billion. This raised the value of Austrian direct investment stock abroad to $61.5 billion by mid-2004.

39 ECONOMIC DEVELOPMENT

The federal government held a majority share in two of the three largest commercial banks and all or most of the nation's electricity, coal and metal mining, and iron and steel production, as well as part of Austria's chemical, electrical, machine, and vehicle industries. The republic's share in the nationalized industries was handed over on 1 January 1970 to the Austrian Industrial Administration Co. (Österreichische Industrieverwaltungs-Aktiengesellschaft—ÖIAG), of which the government was the sole shareholder. The ÖIAG, in line with the government's industrialization program, regrouped the nationalized industries into six sectors:

iron and steel; nonferrous metals; shipbuilding and engineering; electrical engineering; oil and chemicals; and coal. This was later regrouped into five sections: steel; metals; machinery and turnkey operations; electronics, petroleum, petrochemicals and plastics; and chemicals, pharmaceuticals, and fertilizers.

The nationalized establishments operated according to free-enterprise principles and did not receive tax concessions. Private investors were subsequently allowed to buy shares in them. The government, however, maintained voting control in these transactions. The legislation providing for ÖIAG's reorganization of the iron and steel industry included codetermination provisions granting employees the right to fill one-third of the seats on the board of directors. The postal, telephone, and telegraph services and radio and television transmission were state monopolies, as was the trade in tobacco, alcohol, salt, and explosives.

During the 1970s, the government placed new emphasis on centralized economic planning. Key elements in the new policy were the planning of public investment, selective promotion of private sector investment, coordinated expansion of the energy sector and state-owned industry, and assistance for the structural improvement of agriculture. Special emphasis was given to the reform of the handicrafts industry.

In 1986, the ÖIAG was renamed the Österreichische Industrieholding AG, and a process of restructuring and privatization took place in 1993. In 1996, the post and telecommunications monopoly was privatized, and other companies were split up and taken over by foreign, and especially German, companies. The agricultural sector has gone through substantial reform through the EU's common agricultural policy. Computer software and services, telecommunications, advertising, and Internet services are growing commercial enterprises.

In the 21st century, Austria needs to emphasize its knowledge-based sectors of the economy, continue to deregulate the service sector, and encourage greater participation in the labor market of its aging population. The aging phenomenon, together with already high health and pension costs, poses problems in tax and welfare policies.

40 SOCIAL DEVELOPMENT

Austria has one of the most advanced and comprehensive systems of social legislation in the world. The General Social Insurance Bill of 1955 unified all social security legislation and greatly increased the scope of benefits and number of insured. All wage and salary earners must carry sickness, disability, accident, old age, and unemployment insurance, with varying contribution levels by employer and employee for each type of insurance. Health insurance is available to industrial and agricultural workers, federal and professional employees, and members of various other occupational groups. For those without insurance or adequate means, treatment is paid for by public welfare funds.

Unemployment benefits mostly range from 40–50% of previous normal earnings. After three years' service, regular benefits are paid up to between 20 and 30 weeks; thereafter, for an indefinite period, a worker, subject to a means test, may receive emergency relief amounting to 92–95% of the regular benefit. Work injury laws were first enacted in 1887. Citizens are eligible for old age pensions after age 65 (men) and age 60 (women) if they have 35

years of contributions paid or credited. In 2004 the age for retirement began increasing by one month per quarter.

Employers must contribute 4.5% of payroll earnings to a family allowance fund. Family allowances are paid monthly, depending on the number of dependent children, with the amount doubled for any child who is severely handicapped. The state provides school lunches for more than 100,000 children annually. In addition, it administers the organization of children's holiday programs and provides for the care of crippled children, for whom there is a state training school. The state also grants a special birth allowance and a payment for newlyweds setting up their first home; unmarried people establishing a common household may apply for tax remission. The government provides maternity benefits, takes care of destitute old people, and provides for war victims and disabled veterans. Administration of social insurance is carried out in the provinces by autonomous bodies in which both employers and employees are represented. Payment is also made to victims of political persecution during the Nazi era and to victims of violent crime.

Women make up an increasing percentage of the work force. Austrian women earn 79% as much as men. While the number of women in government is low in relation to the overall population, there are female members of parliament, cabinet ministers, state secretaries, town councilors, and mayors. The law proscribes sexual harassment in the workplace, and the government generally enforces these laws. It is believed that violence against women is a widespread problem, and cases generally remain unreported. The government provides shelters and hotlines for victims. Children's rights are fully protected by law.

The constitution provides for the freedoms of religion and assembly, and the government respects these rights. A growing problem is right-wing extremism and the emergence of neo-Nazi groups. Racial violence against ethnic minorities in Austria is evident. In 2005, Austria adopted an Equal Treatment Bill to combat racism and discrimination.

41 HEALTH

Austria's federal government formulates health policy directive and public hygiene standards are high. The country spent an estimated 8.2% of GDP on health care annually as of 1999 and, in recent years, has expanded its public health facilities. Virtually every Austrian has benefits of health insurance. In principle, anyone is entitled to use the facilities provided by Austria's health service. The costs are borne by the social insurance plan or, in cases of hardship, by the social welfare program.

As of 2004, there were an estimated 324 physicians and 589 nurses per 100,000 people. Life expectancy in 2005 was 78.92 years. The infant mortality rate for that year was 4.66 per 1,000 live births that year. In 1999, 6% of births were low weight. Improvement has been made in lowering the under-age-five mortality rate from 43 children per 1,000 in 1960 to 5 per 1,000 in 2004. An estimated 90% of married women (ages 15–49) used contraceptives.

As of 1999, Austria immunized its one-year-old children as follows: diphtheria, pertussis, and tetanus (90%) and measles (90%). The overall death rate in 2002 was 10 per 1,000 people, and in 1999 there were 16 cases of tuberculosis per 100,000 people. The HIV/AIDS prevalence was 0.30 per 100 adults in 2003. As of 2004, there were approximately 10,000 people living with HIV/AIDS in the country. There were an estimated 100 deaths from AIDS in 2003. Vienna's medical school and research institutes are world famous; spas (with thermal springs), health resorts, and sanatoriums are popular among Austrians as well as foreigners.

42 HOUSING

During the First Republic (1919–38), Vienna and several other Austrian municipalities supported a progressive housing policy and built model apartment houses for workers. From the end of World War II until 1967, 157,386 small homes were built under the Federal Accommodation Fund, and 75,663 damaged homes were repaired under the Housing Reconstruction Fund. A system of subsidies for public housing has since been decentralized, and control turned over to local authorities. The Housing Improvement Act of 1969 provided for state support for modernization of outdated housing.

In 2003, there were an estimated 3,863,262 dwellings in the nation. About 74% of all dwellings were privately owned. As of 1990, 25% of Austria's housing stock had been built before 1919; 19% between 1971 and 1980; 18% between 1961 and 1970; 15% between 1945 and 1960; 13% after 1981; and 10% between 1919 and 1944. About 53,000 new dwellings were completed in 2000 and 41,914 were built in 2002.

43 EDUCATION

The Austrian educational system has its roots in the medieval monastic schools that flourished toward the end of the 11th century. The present state education system goes back to the school reforms introduced by Maria Theresa in 1774. In 1869, the Imperial Education Law unified the entire system of compulsory education.

In 1962, Austria's education system was completely reorganized under a comprehensive education law, and compulsory education was extended from eight to nine years. Since 1975, all schools are coeducational and education at state schools is free of charge. Primary education lasts for four years. After primary school, pupils may either attend a general secondary school (*Hauptschule*), which is organized into two four-year courses of study (lower and upper secondary), or an academic secondary school, which also covers an eight-year program. Financial support is provided for postsecondary schooling. Secondary age students may also choose a five-year vocational program. Those who complete their studies at secondary or higher vocational school are qualified to attend the universities. Disabled students either attend special schools or are mainstreamed into regular classrooms. The primary language of instruction is German. The school year runs from October to June.

In 2001, about 84% of children ages three to five attended preschool programs. Primary school enrollment in 2003 was estimated at about 90% of age-eligible students; 89% for boys and 91% for girls. The same year, secondary school enrollment was about 89%, with equal percentages of boys and girls. The pupil to teacher ratio for primary school was at about 13:1 in 2003; the ratio for secondary school was about 11:1.

Austria maintains a vigorous adult education system. Almost all adult education bodies owe their existence to private initiative. The Ministry of Education, under the auspices of the Development Planning for a Cooperative System of Adult Education in Austria, has joined private bodies in setting up projects for en-

hancing the quality of adult education programs. As of 2003, public expenditure on education was estimated at 5.7% of GDP.

As of 2002, the adult literacy rate was estimated at 98%. There are 12 university-level institutions and six fine-art colleges offering 430 subjects and about 600 possible degrees. There are several other institutes of higher education throughout the country. In 2003, about 49% of the tertiary age population were enrolled in some type of higher education program.

44 LIBRARIES AND MUSEUMS

Austria is rich in availability of large library collections and is filled with strong, unique collections. The largest and most important of Austria's 2,400 libraries is the Austrian National Library, which contains more than 2.6 million books and over 3 million nonbook materials. It includes nine special collections: manuscripts and autographs, incunabula (old and precious prints), maps and globes, music, papyri, portrait and picture archives, Austrian literature archives, pamphlets and posters, and a theater collection. The National Library serves as a center for the training of professional librarians, prepares the Austrian national bibliography, and provides a reference service for Austrian libraries. The largest university libraries are the University of Vienna (5.5 million volumes), Graz University (3 million), and Innsbruck University (1.4 million). There are at least 12 prominent scientific libraries in the country, primarily associated with universities. Austria also has several hundred private libraries, such as the renowned libraries in the monasteries at Melk and Admont. The Austrian Institute of Economic Research in Vienna maintains an internationally renowned research library and electronic databases on international economic trends and forecasts.

The Haus-, Hof-, and Staatsarchiv, founded in Vienna in 1749, was combined in 1945 with the Allgemeine Verwaltungsarchiv to form the Austrian State Archives. The Archives' collection ranks as one of the most important in the world, with more than 100,000 manuscripts and documents, some dating as far back as the year 816. Most notable are the state documents of the Holy Roman Empire—including those of the Imperial Court Council (from 1555), the Imperial Court Chancellery (from 1495), and the Mainz Imperial Chancellery (from 1300); documents of the subsequent Austrian State Chancellery; and those of the Austro-Hungarian Foreign Ministry.

There are over 700 museums in Austria, including art museums, archaeology and history museums, science and technology museums, and regional museums. There are eight recognized historical sites in the country. The most important museums had their origins in the private collections of the House of Habsburg. The Museum of Fine Arts (Kunsthistorisches Museum) in Vienna (1871) contains a vast collection of Flemish, Italian, and German paintings by old masters. It also houses distinguished collections of Egyptian and Oriental objects, classical art, sculpture and applied art, tapestries, coins, and old musical instruments. The Albertina Museum houses the world's largest graphic art collection, including the most extensive collection in existence of the works of Albrecht Dürer. The Secular Treasury (Schatzkammer) houses the jewels and insignia of the Holy Roman Empire and of all the Austrian emperors. The numerous collections formerly in the possession of the imperial court have in large part been brought together for display in the Natural History Museum, the Museum of Fine Arts, and the Hofburg (Innsbruck). Vienna's Schönbrunn Palace contains a collection of imperial coaches from the Habsburg court. The Austrian Gallery in Belvedere Castle (Vienna), formerly the summer palace of Prince Eugene of Savoy, houses unique examples of medieval Austrian art as well as works of 19th- and 20th-century Austrian artists. The Museum of Modern Art was opened in Vienna's Palais Liechtenstein in 1979; incorporated into it was the Museum of the 20th Century, founded in 1962. Also of interest is Vienna's Lipizzaner Museum, featuring the city's famous white horses, and a museum of Sigmund Freud's apartment and office.

There are also other castles, manor houses, monasteries, and convents, many of which date from the Middle Ages and which are of interest for their architecture as well as for their contents. Important scientific collections are housed in the Natural History Museum, the Museums of Anthropology and Folklore, and the Technical Museum, all in Vienna; the Joanneum, in Graz; the Ferdinandeum, in Innsbruck; the Carolino Augusteum and the House of Nature, in Salzburg; and the Folk Museum, in Hallstatt, Upper Austria, which contains local prehistoric discoveries dating from the 4th and 3rd centuries BC. Salzburg has two historical museums dedicated to Mozart—the house where he was born and another house in which he lived. In Vienna, there is a museum dedicated to Sigmund Freud.

The Jewish Museum Vienna contains a memorial to Austrian victims of the Holocaust and a 40,000-volume research library on the history of the Jews in Austria and Vienna. There is also a Holocaust memorial at the site of the Maunthausen concentration camp.

45 MEDIA

The Austrian Post and Telegraph Administration operates all telephone, telegraph, teletype, and postal services. In 2003, there were an estimated 481 mainline telephones for every 1,000 people. The same year, there were approximately 879 mobile phones in use for every 1,000 people.

Oesterreichischer Rundfunk (ORF) is the primary public broadcasting company in Austria. The first national commercial television license was granted to ATV in 2000. Commercial radio stations began in the 1990s. As of 2001, there were a total of about 2 AM and 65 FM radio stations in the country and 10 television stations. In 2003, there were an estimated 763 radios and 637 television sets for every 1,000 people. Nearly 157 of every 1,000 people held subscriptions to cable television. The same year, there were 369.3 personal computers for every 1,000 people and 462 of every 1,000 people had access to the Internet. There were 1,586 secure servers in the country in 2004.

As of 2005, Austria had 15 national and regional daily newspapers. Vienna accounts for about half of total readership. The two most widely read papers are the tabloids *Kronen Zeitung* (circulation 850,000 in 2005) and *Der Kurier* (circulation 172,000 in 2005). Other leading dailies (with 2005 circulation figures unless noted) include *Kleine Zeitung* (171,405 in 2004), *Oberösterreichische Nachrichten* (in Linz, 123,000 in 2002), *Salzburger Nachrichten* (126,000), *Tiroler-Tageszeitung* (in Innsbruck, 103,600 in 2002), and *Die Presse* (76,000), and *Der Standard* (71,000). *Neue Zeit*, published in Graz, is a major daily for the Social Democrat party with a circulation of about 66,100 in 2002. The leading periodicals include the weeklies *Wochenpresse—Wirtschaftswoche* and *Profil* and the monthly *Trend* which had a circulation of 95,000 in 1995.

Freedom of the press is constitutionally guaranteed and there is no state censorship; the Austrian Press Council is largely concerned with self-regulatory controls and the effective application of a code of ethics. The Austrian Press Agency is independent of the government and operates on a nonprofit basis; most major newspapers share in its financing.

46 ORGANIZATIONS

The Federal Economic Chamber, including representatives of commerce, industry, trade, and transport, has official representatives in most counties. Every province has an economic chamber organized in the same way as the federal chamber. District chambers of agriculture are combined into provincial chambers, which are further consolidated in a national confederation. Provincial chambers of labor are combined in a national chamber. Austria has a committee on the International Chamber of Commerce.

The Federation of Austrian Industrialists, with an organizational membership of almost 5,000, is subdivided into departments for trade, industry, finance, social policies, and communications, with sections for press relations and organization. There are associations of bankers, insurance companies, and publishers, as well as other commercial and professional groups.

Austria has a large number of scholarly associations, as well as several groups dedicated to the support and promotion of various arts and sciences. The latter include the Association for Sciences and Politics, the Austrian Academy of Sciences, the Austrian Association of Music, the Austrian Physical Society, the Austrian P.E.N. Center, and the Austrian Science Fund. Filling a specialty niche, Vienna is home to the International Confederation of Accordionists and the International Gustav Mahler Society.

The Austrian Medical Chamber is a notable institution for the promotion of health education, research, and policy making. There are numerous associations representing a wide variety of specialized medical fields and promoting research for the treatment and prevention of particular diseases and conditions.

The Austrian Sports Federation represents over three million athletes in the country in promoting education and competition in a wide variety of sports. There are numerous association for particular sports, including Frisbee, football (soccer), baseball, golf, ice hockey, tennis, and badminton. There is an Austrian Paralympic Committee, an Olympic Committee, and a Special Olympics committee.

The Austrian Union of Students (AUS), the national university student coordinating body, is incorporated under Austrian federal public law to serve as a legal representative body for Austrian university students through Federal Ministries responsible for higher education and through the National Parliament. The secretariat of the National Unions of Students of Europe (ESIB) is housed within the AUS. Other youth organizations, representing a variety of concerns and interests, include the Austrian Socialist Youth Organization, Young Austrian People's Party, Union of Liberal Youth, Communist Youth of Austria, Austrian Catholic Youth Group, Cartel Association of Austrian Catholic Student Unions, Protestant Youth Welfare Organization, Protestant Student Community, Austrian Trade Union Youth Organization, Austrian Friends of Nature Youth Organization, Junior Chamber Austria, and Austrian Alpine Youth Organization. Scouting organizations are also present for both boys and girls.

Organizations of Greenpeace, The Red Cross, and Amnesty International are also present. There are active chapters of Lions Clubs and Kiwanis International.

47TOURISM, TRAVEL, AND RECREATION

Austria ranks high among European tourist countries. It has a year-round tourist season: in winter, tourists come to the famous skiing resorts and attend outstanding musical events in Vienna; in summer, visitors are attracted by scenery, sports, and cultural festivals, notably in Vienna and Salzburg. Of the 4,000 communities in Austria, nearly half are considered tourist centers.

Tourist attractions in the capital include 15 state theaters and the Vienna State Opera (which also houses the Vienna Philharmonic); the Vienna Boys' Choir; St. Stephen's Cathedral; the Schönbrunn and Belvedere palaces; and the Spanish Riding Academy, with its famous Lippizaner stallions. Just beyond the city boundary are the Vienna Woods, with their picturesque wine taverns.

About 40 or 50 towns and villages qualify as major resorts for Alpine skiing, and Innsbruck has been the site of two Winter Olympics, in 1964 and 1976. Mountaineering is another Austrian specialty, with Austrian climbers having scaled high peaks all over the world. Austrians have frequently taken titles in world canoeing championships. Football (soccer) is a very popular sport. Austria also puts on a number of prominent annual events for cyclists. Probably the most challenging tour on the amateurs' program is the "Tour d'Autriche," which has been held every year since 1949. This race through Austria's mountains covers a total distance of almost 1,500 kilometers. Motor racing, motorcycle racing and speedway racing are also extremely popular sports in Austria.

Foreign tourist traffic is the leading single source of foreign exchange, and tourism is a major contributor to the Austrian economy. An estimated 13,748,371 foreign visitors arrived in Austria in 2003. Receipts from tourism amounted to $16 billion. That year there were 282,614 rooms in hotels, inns, and pensions with 631,085 beds and a 36% occupancy rate. The average length of stay was four nights.

Visitors entering Austria for a short stay need only a valid passport if from the United States or the European Union countries, but an Austrian visa is required for visits exceeding three months.

In 2005, the US Department of State estimated the daily cost of staying in Austria at $255 to $276.

48FAMOUS AUSTRIANS

Political Figures

Monarchs who played a leading role in Austrian and world history include Rudolf I of Habsburg (1218–91), founder of the Habsburg dynasty and Holy Roman emperor from 1273; Maria Theresa (1717–80), who succeeded to the Habsburg dominions by means of the Pragmatic Sanction of 1740; her son Joseph II (1741–90), the "benevolent despot" who became Holy Roman emperor in 1765; Franz Josef (1830–1916), emperor of Austria at the outbreak of World War I; and his brother Maximilian (Ferdinand Maximilian Josef, 1832–1867), who became emperor of Mexico

in 1864, ruling on behalf of Emperor Napoleon III of France, and was deposed and executed. Prince Klemens Wenzel Nepomuk Lothar von Metternich (1773–1859), Austrian foreign minister from 1809 to 1848, was the architect of the European balance of power established at the Congress of Vienna in 1815. Adolf Hitler (1889–1945), born in Braunau, was dictator of Germany from 1933 until his death. Leading Austrian statesmen since World War II are Bruno Kreisky (1911–1990), Socialist Party chairman and chancellor of Austria from 1970 to 1983; and Kurt Waldheim (b.1918), Austrian diplomat and foreign minister, who was UN secretary-general from 1971 to 1981 and was elected to the presidency in June 1986.

Artists, Writers, and Scientists

Austria has produced many excellent artists, writers, and scientists but is probably most famous for its outstanding composers. Beginning in the 18th century and for 200 years, Vienna was the center of European musical culture. Among its great masters were Franz Joseph Haydn (1732–1809), Wolfgang Amadeus Mozart (1756–91), Franz Schubert (1797–1828), Anton Bruckner (1824–96), Gustav Mahler (1860–1911), Hugo Wolf (1860–1903), Arnold Schönberg (1874–1951), Anton von Webern (1883–1945), and Alban Berg (1885–1935). Although born in northwestern Germany, Ludwig van Beethoven (1770–1827) and Johannes Brahms (1833–97) settled in Vienna and spent the rest of their lives there. Composers of light music, typical of Austria, are Johann Strauss, Sr. (1804–49), Johann Strauss, Jr. (1825–99), Dalmatian-born Franz von Suppé (Francesco Ezechiele Ermenegildo Cavaliere Suppe-Demelli, 1819–95), Hungarian-born Franz Lehár (1870–1948), and Oskar Straus (1870–1954). Outstanding musicians are the conductors Clemens Krauss (1893–1954), Karl Böhm (1894–1981), and Herbert von Karajan (1908–89); the pianists Artur Schnabel (1882–1951) and Alfred Brendel (b.1931); and the violinist Fritz Kreisler (1875–1962).

Leading dramatists and poets include Franz Grillparzer (1791–1872), Nikolaus Lenau (1802–50), Ludwig Anzengruber (1839–81), and Hugo von Hofmannsthal (1874–1929). Novelists and short-story writers of interest are Adalbert Stifter (1805–68), Marie von Ebner-Eschenbach (1830–1916), Arthur Schnitzler (1862–1931), Hermann Bahr (1863–1934), Stefan Zweig (1881–1942), Robert Musil (1880–1942), Hermann Broch (1886–1952), Yakov Lind (b.1927), Peter Handke (b.1942), and Elfriede Jelinek (b.1946), who won the 2004 Nobel Prize in Literature. Although born in Czechoslovakia, the satiric polemicist Karl Kraus (1874–1936), the poet Rainer Maria Rilke (1875–1926), the novelist and short-story writer Franz Kafka (1883–1924), and the poet and novelist Franz Werfel (1890–1946) are usually identified with Austrian literary life. Film directors of Austrian birth include Max Reinhardt (Maximilian Goldman, 1873–1943), Erich von Stroheim (Erich Oswald Stroheim, 1885–1957), Fritz Lang (1890–1976), Josef von Sternberg (1894–1969), Otto Preminger (1905–86), and Billy Wilder (1906–2002). Internationally known performers born in Austria include Lotte Lenya (Karoline Blamauer, 1900–81) and Maximilian Schell (b.1930).

Architects and Artists

Two great architects of the Baroque period were Johann Bernhard Fischer von Erlach (1656–1723) and Johann Lucas von Hildebrandt (1668–1745). Three prominent 20th-century painters were

Gustav Klimt (1862–1918), Oskar Kokoschka (1886–1980), and Egon Schiele (1890–1918).

Physicians

Psychoanalysis was founded in Vienna by Sigmund Freud (1856–1939) and extended by his Austrian colleagues Alfred Adler (1870–1937), Otto Rank (1884–1939), Theodor Reik (1888–1969), and Wilhelm Reich (1897–1957). Eugen Böhm-Bawerk (1851–1914) and Joseph Alois Schumpeter (1883–1950) were outstanding economists. A renowned geneticist was Gregor Johann Mendel (1822–84). Christian Johann Doppler (1803–53), a physicist and mathematician, described the wave phenomenon known today as the Doppler shift. Lise Meitner (1878–1968) was the physicist who first identified nuclear fission. Austrian Nobel Prize winners in physics are Erwin Schrödinger (1887–1961), in 1933; Victor Franz Hess (1883–1964), authority on cosmic radiation, in 1936; and atomic theorist Wolfgang Pauli (1900–1958), discoverer of the exclusion principle, in 1945. Winners of the Nobel Prize in chemistry are Fritz Pregl (1869–1930), who developed microanalysis, in 1923; Richard Zsigmondy (1865–1929), inventor of the ultramicroscope, in 1925; biochemist Richard Kuhn (1900–1967), a pioneer in vitamin research, in 1938; and biochemist Max Ferdinand Perutz (1914–2002) for research in blood chemistry, in 1962. Winners of the Nobel Prize in physiology or medicine are otologist Robert Bárány (1876–1936), in 1914; psychiatrist Julius Wagner-Jauregg (1857–1940), for developing a treatment for general paresis, in 1927; Karl Landsteiner (1868–1943), discoverer of blood groups, in 1930; German-born pharmacologist Otto Loewi (1873–1961), for his study of nerve impulse transmission, in 1936; Carl Ferdinand Cori (1896–1984) and his wife, Gerti Theresa Radnitz Cori (1896–1957), whose work with enzymes led to new ways of fighting diabetes, in 1947; and Konrad Lorenz (1903–1989), discoverer of the "imprinting" process of learning, in 1973. In 1974, Friedrich August von Hayek (1899–1992), a noted monetary theorist, was awarded the Nobel Prize in economics.

Humanitarians

The Nobel Peace Prize was awarded to Baroness Berta Kinsky von Suttner (b.Prague, 1843–1914), founder of the Austrian Society of Peace Lovers and author of *Lay Down Your Arms!*, in 1905; and to Alfred Hermann Fried (1864–1921), a prolific publicist for the cause of international peace, in 1911. One of the most influential philosophers of the contemporary age was Ludwig Josef Johann Wittgenstein (1889–1951). Rudolf Steiner (1861–1925), the founder of anthroposophy, was an Austrian. Theodor Herzl (b.Budapest, 1860–1904), founder of the Zionist movement, was an early advocate of the establishment of a Jewish state in Palestine. Simon Wiesenthal (b.Poland, 1908–2005), a Nazi concentra-

tion-camp survivor, searched for Nazi war criminals around the world.

Athletes

Austrians have excelled in international Alpine skiing competition. In 1956, Toni Sailer (b.1935) won all three Olympic gold medals in men's Alpine skiing events. Annemarie Moser-Pröll (b.1953) retired in 1980 after winning a record six women's World Cups, a record 62 World Cup races in all, and the 1980 women's downhill skiing Olympic championship. Franz Klammer (b.1953), who won the 1976 men's downhill Olympic title, excited spectators with his aggressive style. Arnold Schwarzenegger (b.1947) was once the foremost bodybuilder in the world and became a successful Hollywood actor and governor of California.

[49] DEPENDENCIES

Austria has no territories or colonies.

[50] BIBLIOGRAPHY

Ake, Anne. *Austria*. San Diego: Lucent Books, 2001.

Annesley, Claire (ed.). *A Political and Economic Dictionary of Western Europe*. Philadelphia: Routledge/Taylor and Francis, 2005.

Austria. Singapore: APA Publications, 2001.

Austrian Women in the Nineteenth and Twentieth Centuries. Providence, R.I.: Berghahn Books, 1996.

Bisanz-Prakken, Marian. *Rembrandt and His Time: Masterworks from the Albertina, Vienna*. New York: Hudson Hills Press, 2005.

Brook-Shepherd, Gordon. *The Austrians: A Thousand Year Odyssey*. London: Harper Collins, 1996.

Healy, Maureen. *Vienna and the Fall of the Habsburg Empire: Total War and Everyday Life in World War I*. New York: Cambridge University Press, 2004.

International Smoking Statistics: A Collection of Historical Data from 30 Economically Developed Countries. New York: Oxford University Press, 2002.

MacHardy, Karin Jutta. *War, Religion and Court Patronage in Habsburg Austria: The Social and Cultural Dimensions of Political Interaction, 1521–1622*. New York: Palgrave, 2002.

Roman, Eric. *Austria-Hungary and the Successor States: A Reference Guide from the Renaissance to the Present*. New York: Facts On File, 2003.

Wessels, Wolfgang, Andreas Maurer, and Jürgan Mittag (eds.). *Fifteen into One?: the European Union and Its Member States*. New York: Palgrave, 2003.

BELARUS

Republic of Belarus
Respublika Belarus

CAPITAL: Minsk

FLAG: Two horizontal bands of red (top) and green, with the red band twice as wide as the green. At the hoist is a vertical band showing a traditional Belarussian ornamental pattern.

ANTHEM: *Maladaya Belarus.*

MONETARY UNIT: The Belarus ruble (BR) circulates along with the Russian ruble (R). The government has a varying exchange rate for trade between Belarus and Russia. BR1 = $0.00047 (or $1 = BR2,140) as of 2005.

WEIGHTS AND MEASURES: The metric system is in force.

HOLIDAYS: New Year's Day, 1 January; Orthodox Christmas, 7 January; International Women's Day, 8 March; Labor Day, 1 May; Victory Day, 9 May; Independence Day, 27 July; Day of Commemoration, 2 November; Christmas, 25 December.

TIME: 2 PM = noon GMT.

¹LOCATION, SIZE, AND EXTENT

Belarus is a landlocked nation located in eastern Europe, between Poland and Russia. Comparatively the area occupied by Belarus is slightly smaller than the state of Kansas, with a total area of 207,600 sq km (80,154 sq mi). Belarus shares boundaries with Latvia on the N, Russia on the N and E, Ukraine on the S, Poland on the SW, and Lithuania on the NW. The boundary length of Belarus totals 3,098 km (1,925 mi).

The capital city of Belarus, Minsk, is located near the center of the country.

²TOPOGRAPHY

The topography of Belarus is generally flat and contains much marshland. The Belarussian Ridge (Belorusskya Gryda) stretches across the center of the country from the southwest to the northeast. The highest elevation is at Dzerzhinskaya Gora, 346 m (1,135 ft).

³CLIMATE

The country's climate is transitional between continental and maritime. July's mean temperature is 19°C (67°F). January's mean temperature is -5°C (23°F). Rainfall averages between 57 cm (22.5 in) and 61 cm (26.5 in) annually.

⁴FLORA AND FAUNA

About 45% of the country is forest land. Pine trees are found throughout the north, but spruce, alder, ash, birch, and oak trees are also common. Some of the mammals in the forest include deer, brown bears, rabbits, and squirrels. The southern region is a swampy expanse. The marshes are home to ducks, frogs, turtles, archons, and muskrats.

⁵ENVIRONMENT

As part of the legacy of the former Soviet Union, Belarus's main environmental problems are chemical and nuclear pollution. Belarus was the republic most affected by the accident at the Chernobyl nuclear power plant in April 1986. Northerly winds prevailed at the time of the accident; therefore, most of the fallout occurred over farmland in the southeastern section of the country (primarily in the Gomel and Mogilev oblasts). Most experts estimate that 25–30% of Belarus's farmland was irradiated and should not be used for agricultural production or to collect wild berries and mushrooms, although it continues to be used for these and other purposes. Belarus has 88 UNESCO World Heritage Sites, including the Bialowieza Forest. There are seven Ramsar wetland sites. In 2003, about 6.3% of the total land area was protected.

In addition, Belarus has significant air and water pollution from industrial sources. The most common pollutants are formaldehyde, carbon emissions, and petroleum-related chemicals. In 1992, Belarus was among the world's top 50 nations in industrial emissions of carbon dioxide, producing 102 million metric tons, or 9.89 metric tons per capita. In 1996, the total fell to 61.7 million metric tons. The soils also contain unsafe levels of lead, zinc, copper, and the agricultural chemical DDT. All urban and rural dwellers have access to safe drinking water.

As of 2002, Belarus had over 2,000 species of plants, 74 mammal species, and 194 bird species. According to a 2006 report issued by the International Union for Conservation of Nature and Natural Resources (IUCN), threatened species included 6 types of mammals, 4 species of birds, and 8 other invertebrates. Endangered species include the European bison and the European mink.

⁶POPULATION

The population of Belarus in 2005 was estimated by the United Nations (UN) at 9,776,000, which placed it at number 81 in population among the 193 nations of the world. In 2005, approximately 14% of the population was over 65 years of age, with another 16% of the population under 15 years of age. There were 88 males for every 100 females in the country. According to the UN, the annual population rate of change for 2005–10 was expected to be -0.6%, a rate, viewed by the government as too low, that reflects low fertility rates and high mortality rates, especially among adult men. The projected population for the year 2025 was 9,399,000. The population density was 47 per sq km (122 per sq mi).

The UN estimated that 72% of the population lived in urban areas in 2005, and that urban areas were growing at an annual rate of 0.09%. The capital city, Minsk, had a population of 1,705,000 in that year. The estimated population of other major cities included Homyel, 481,000; Mahilyow, 374,000; Hrodna, 317,366; and Brest (formerly Brest-Litovsk), 290,000.

Almost 25% of the population of Belarus was killed during World War II, and combined with the fatalities of the Soviet-era purges, the postwar population was one-third smaller than it had been in 1930. It was not until the 1970s that the population returned to prewar levels.

7 MIGRATION

With the breakup of the Soviet Union in 1991, some two million Belarussians were among the various nationality groups who found themselves living outside their autonomous regions or native republics. Most of the Belarussians who have returned to Belarus fled other former Soviet republics because of fighting or ethnic tensions. From 1989 to 1995, 3,000 Belarussians returned from Azerbaijan and 3,000 Belarussians returned from Kyrgyzstan. From 1991 to 1995, 16,000 Belarussians returned from Kazakhstan and 10,000 Belarussians returned from Tajikistan. In 1999 Belarus had 131,200 internally displaced persons from the ecological effects of the accident at the Chernobyl nuclear power plant, and 160,000 "returnees" (ethnic Belarussians who had returned to Belarus from other former republics).

A defining characteristics of migration between former Soviet republics is its irregular or transient quality and the existence of "shuttle" migrants. Some 2005 estimates suggest that there are 10 million irregular migrants in the region. The estimated net migration rate for Belarus in 2005 was 2.42 per 1000 population. The government views the immigration level as too high.

As of 2004, Belarus had an estimated 8,200 asylum seekers officially registered with the United Nations High Commissioner for Refugees (UNHCR). In 2004, about 2,100 Belarussians made asylum claims, the majority in Sweden.

8 ETHNIC GROUPS

In 2005, an estimated 81.2% of the total population was Belarussian. Russians made up about 11.4% of the populace; Poles, Ukrainians, and other groups combined to make up about 7.4% of the population.

9 LANGUAGES

Belarussian belongs to the eastern group of Slavic languages and is very similar to Russian. It did not become a separate language until the 15th century, when it was the official language of the grand duchy of Lithuania. It is written in the Cyrillic alphabet but has two letters not in Russian and a number of distinctive sounds. The vocabulary has borrowings from Polish, Lithuanian, German, Latin, and Turkic. Russian and other languages are also spoken.

10 RELIGIONS

As of 2005, the State Committee on Religious and National Affairs estimated that approximately 80% of the population were Belarussian Orthodox. About 15–20% were Roman Catholics. Between 50,0000 and 90,000 people were Jewish. Other minority religions included the Greek Rite Catholic Church, the Belarus Autocephalous Orthodox Church, Seventh-Day Adventists, Calvinism, Lutheranism, Jehovah's Witnesses, the Apostolic Christian Church, and Islam.

Since the 1994 elections, the country's first president, Alyaksandr Lukashenka, who claims to be an "Orthodox atheist," has maintained a policy of favoring the Belarussian Orthodox Church (a branch of the Russian Orthodox Church) as the country's chief religion. A 2003 Concordat between the government and the Belarussian Orthodox Church (BOC) more firmly established the special relationship between the government and the BOC. The BOC works closely with the government in developing and implementing political policies, including those related to such departments as the ministries of education, defense, health, and labor. The president grants the Orthodox Church special financial aid that is not given to other denominations and has declared the preservation and development of Orthodox Christianity a "moral necessity."

The government's State Committee on Religious and National Affairs (SCRNA), established in 1997, categorizes religions and may deny any faith it designates as "nontraditional" permission to register. The traditional faiths are the BOC, the Roman Catholic Church, Orthodox Judaism, Sunni Islam, and Evangelical Lutheranism. In 2002, Lukashenka passed a new law on religion that prohibits all religious groups from importing or distributing religious materials without prior approval from the government. The new law prevents foreigners from leading any religious organizations and prohibits those organizations from establishing clerical training schools within the country. The new law also set a more complex registration system and prohibits the operations of any unregistered group.

11 TRANSPORTATION

About 5,512 km (3,417 mi) of broad and standard gauge railways traverse Belarus, connecting it to Russia, Ukraine, Lithuania, Poland, and Latvia, as of 2004. Of that total, broad gauge accounts for 5,497 km (3,419 mi). Of the 93,055 km (57,880 mi) of highways in 2003, all were hard-surfaced. As of 2003, there were 1,557,800 passenger cars and 25,400 commercial vehicles registered for use.

The European Bank for Reconstruction and Development (EBRD) initiated a study of railways and roads in 1993 to help determine location advantages for future development in Belarus. The focus of the EBRD study also included the development of the trucking industry.

Because Belarus is landlocked, there are no ports or merchant fleet. Although, there are, as of 2003, some 2,500 km (1,555 mi) of navigable canals and rivers, but whose use is limited by their location near the country's perimeter, and by shallowness. In 1995, Belarus claimed to have retained 5% of the merchant fleet of the former Soviet Union. As of 2004, there were an estimated 133 airports in the country. As of 2005, a total of 44 had paved runways and there is also a single heliport. In 2003, scheduled airline traffic carried about 234,000 domestic and international passengers.

12 HISTORY

The Belarussians are the descendants of Slavic tribes that migrated into the region in the 9th century. They trace their distinct identity from the 13th century when the Mongols conquered Russia and parts of Ukraine. During this period, Belarus managed to maintain its identity as part of the Grand Duchy of Lithuania. The union of the Grand Duchy with the Polish Kingdom in 1569, resulting in the emergence of the Polish-Lithuanian Commonwealth (Rzeczpospolita), put the territory of Belarus under Polish rule. As a result of the partitions of Rzeczpospolita in 1772, 1793, and 1795 by Imperial Russia, Austria, and Prussia, Belarus fell to the Russian Empire.

In March 1918, at the time of the Soviet-German Treaty of Brest-Litovsk in which Moscow agreed to relinquish claim to a substantial amount of territory captured by Germany in exchange for peace, the Belarussian National Republic was formed with German military assistance. However, after the German government collapsed in November 1918 and German forces were withdrawn from the region, Bolshevik troops moved in and set up the Belarussian Soviet Socialist Republic in January 1919. In 1922 the Belarus SSR became one of 15 socialist republics to form the Union of Soviet Socialist Republics. Two years later, Belarus's borders were enlarged at the expense of Russia and Ukraine. Later, parts of eastern Poland were annexed to Belarus by Stalin under the 1939 Molotov-Ribbentrop pact. However, Belarus was devastated by World War II.

During the decades of Soviet rule, Belarus underwent intense Russification, and its leaders generally complied with Soviet policy. However, after extensive nuclear contamination by the 1986 Chernobyl accident in neighboring Ukraine, Belarussian nationalists, acting from exile in Lithuania, organized the Belarussian People's Front. The nationalist upsurge of the period was intensified by the discovery of mass graves from the Stalinist purges of the 1930s at Kuroplaty and other locations. Although the Belarussian leadership still supported keeping the Soviet Union intact, Belarus's parliament declared Belarus a sovereign state within the USSR in July 1990. Shortly after the abortive August 1991 coup attempt against Mikhail Gorbachev, Belarus declared its independence on 26 August 1991.

Belarus's first president, Alyaksandr Lukashenko, was elected in July 1994, the same year the country adopted its first post-Communist constitution. Lukashenko has halted economic and political reform, and silenced or even jailed his critics using internal security forces. At the end of 1996, Belarus sent the last of its nuclear missiles back to Russia. Also in November 1996, Lukashenko won a plebiscite to expand his power as president, although most observers agreed that the election was not fair. On 28 November 1996, Lukashenko signed into law a new constitution containing provisions that gave him almost total control of all branches of government and extended his term by two years to 2001. A new bicameral National Assembly replaced the old Parliament. During 1996, Lukashenko suspended the registration of new enterprises, stopped privatization, and spurned World Bank assistance. Under the new constitution, the president has the right to hire and

LOCATION: 53°53′ N; 28°0′ E BOUNDARY LENGTHS: Total boundary lengths, 3,098 kilometers (1,925 miles); Latvia 141 kilometers (88 miles); Lithuania 502 kilometers (312 miles); Poland, 605 kilometers (376 miles); Russia 959 kilometers (596 miles); Ukraine, 891 kilometers (554 miles).

fire the heads of the Constitutional Court and the Central Bank, and he also has the right to dissolve parliament and veto its decisions. Most members of the international community criticized the plebiscite expanding Lukashenko's power, and do not recognize the 1996 constitution or the bicameral legislature that it established.

The constitutional changes implemented by the president sparked strong protests, including public demonstrations and opposition by the Constitutional Court and members of parliament, some of whom attempted to form their own assembly. However, all dissent was effectively suppressed, and Lukashenko remained in power. After boycotting the April 1999 local elections, his political opponents held an alternative presidential election in July. This was followed by a new crackdown that forced opposition leader Semyon Sharetsky into exile. From exile Sharetsky proclaimed himself the nation's legitimate ruler, but his action had little effect on the actual state of political affairs in the country. Another prominent political dissident, Voctor Gonchar, was reported missing in September 1999.

In April 1997, Lukashenko and Russia's President Yeltsin signed an initial charter for economic union that included a plan to adopt a common currency. However, over the following two years, implementation of the integration plan moved slowly, and in September 1999, Belarus took steps to peg the country's currency to the euro. Nevertheless, at the end of year, Belarus and Russia reaffirmed their intentions of forming an economic alliance. The leaders of both countries signed a new treaty in December 1999, and it was approved by both parliaments. In April 2000 Russia's new president, Vladimir Putin, reconfirmed his country's commitment to strengthening ties with Belarus.

Parliamentary elections held in 2001 were criticized by election observers as being neither free nor fair. Lukashenko and his administration manipulated the election process to make sure a minimum of opposition candidates were elected to parliament. Turnout in 13 constituencies was so low that a repeat of the voting was necessary (it was held in March 2001). On 9 September 2001, Lukashenko was reelected president in what Organization for Security and Cooperation in Europe (OSCE) observers described as undemocratic elections. Lukashenko won 75.6% of the vote, with opposition candidate Vladimir Goncharik winning 15.4% and Liberal Democratic Party leader Syargey Gaydukevich winning 2.5%. The government reported 83.9% of eligible voters participated in the election.

In June 2002, Russian president Vladimir Putin refused to follow the path to integration that Belarus had proposed for the two nations, saying it would lead to the recreation of "something along the lines of the Soviet Union." While Lukashenko pledged not to relinquish Belarus's sovereignty in the union with Russia, Putin put forth a proposal for the "ultimate unification" of both countries. Putin envisioned a federation based on the Russian constitution, with the Russian ruble as the state's sole currency and the election of a president in 2004. A constitution for the union was approved in March 2003. In April 2003, the speaker of the Russian Duma indicated Armenia, Ukraine, and Moldova might be probable candidates for joining the Belarus-Russian union. Although Lukashenko's relations with Moscow continued to improve (Russia endorsed the 2001 elections and the 2004 referendum), as of 2006, little progress had been made in solving some of the problems related to the organization and structure of the Belarus-Russian union.

European policy has not been coherent or proactive in facing the human right violations in Belarus. In November 2002, 14 EU states imposed a travel ban on Lukashenko and several of his government ministers as a way of protesting Belarus's poor human rights record. However, Lukashenko continued to eliminate political opponents, attack independent press, and expand his powers. In February 2003, Lukashenko pledged support for Iraq in the prelude to war that began on 19 March, led by a US and UK coalition, to project an image of a strong and independent leader.

Among European countries Poland has been playing the most active role in promoting democratic changes and market transformation in Belarus, and supporting the country's national revival. However, the Polish government has not developed a strong or consistent policy of dealing with Lukashenko. The Belarussian Union of Poles (ZPB), an organization representing the 400,000 ethnic Poles living in Belarus, had its headquarters raided by police in July 2005, after Lukashenko accused the organization of

plotting his overthrow. Poland recalled its ambassador after the incident, and relations between the two countries were strained as of early 2006.

On 16 December 2005 presidential elections were announced for 19 March 2006.

[13]GOVERNMENT

In May 1993, a draft constitution was presented to the 12th session of parliament, which adopted 88 of the new constitution's 153 articles.

Until mid-1994, Belarus was the only former Soviet republic not to have a president. The chairman of the Supreme Soviet was considered the chief of state, but power remained in the hands of the Council of Ministers headed by a prime minister.

On 19 July 1994, elections for president were held in Belarus. Alyaksandr Lukashenko received 80.1% of the vote. He was elected on a platform of clearing out the ruling Communist establishment. Lukashenko, however, is not a democrat but a Communist populist, who appears to have no plans for implementing political or economic reform.

He has been cited by Human Rights Watch for numerous violations and, by Western standards, rules as a dictator.

In November 1996, Lukashenko won a plebiscite to expand his powers. He signed a new constitution into law giving the president power to dissolve parliament and authorized the formation of a new bicameral National Assembly with a 64-member upper house, the Council of the Republic, and a 110-member lower house, the House of Representatives. All legislators serve four-year terms. The president's term was also extended until 2001, the year when he was reelected. The October 2004 referendum, criticized by Western observers as fraudulent, revised the constitution to eliminate presidential term limits. Consequently, Lukashenko was eligible to run for a third term in September 2006. Parliamentary elections held at the same time resulted in the election of only pro-Lukashenko candidates, with many opposition candidates disqualified on technicalities.

[14]POLITICAL PARTIES

The Communist Party was declared illegal after the abortive August 1991 coup attempt, but was relegalized in February 1993. With two other pro-Communist parties it merged into the People's Movement of Belarus in May 1993. On the whole, political parties have not gathered the momentum evident in other former Soviet republics. None of the parties has had a large public following.

The parties with the greatest representation in the 260-member unicameral Supreme Council elected in 1995 were the Communist Party (42 seats) and the Agrarian Party (33). Following the elections in October 2004, which were widely criticized internationally, all the seats were won by pro-Lukashenko candidates. The Supreme Council was disbanded under the terms of the 1996 constitution and replaced with a bicameral legislature, for which the first elections were held in January 1997.

The primary pro-government party is the Belarussian Popular Patriotic Union, which supports President Lukashenko and the proposed union with Russia. Other pro-government parties include the Agrarian Party (AP), the Belarussian Communist Party (KPB), the Liberal Democratic Party of Belarus, and the Social-Sports Party. The primary opposition party is the Belarussian

Popular Front, whose chairman, Zyanon Paznyak, was in exile in the United States and whose other leaders were jailed at various times. The Popular Front was one of three parties that organized the alternative presidential elections held in 1999 to protest the extension of President Lukashenko's term to 2001. Other opposition parties are the Belarussian Social-Democrat Party Narodnaya Gromada (BSDP NG), the Belarussian Social-Democratic party Hromada, the United Civic party (UCP), the Party of Communists Belarussian (PKB), and the Women's Party "Nadezhda". The opposition Belarussian Party of Labor was liquidated in August 2004, but remains active.

15 LOCAL GOVERNMENT

Belarus is divided into six provinces (oblasts) and one municipality. The oblasts are roughly parallel to counties in the United States. Each has a capital city, and the name of the oblast is typically derived from the name of this city. The names of the six oblasts are Brestskaya, Homyel'skaya, Hrodzyenskaya, Mahilyowskaya, Minskaya, and Vitsyebskaya. The municipality is Horad Minsk. Local Councils of Deputies are elected for four-year terms. A 1994 decree gave the president the right to appoint and dismiss senior local officials. The constitutional modifications passed in 1996 give the president increased powers over local government, including the power of nullifying rulings by local councils.

16 JUDICIAL SYSTEM

The courts system consists of district courts, regional courts, and the Supreme Court. Higher courts serve as appellate courts but also serve as courts of first instance. There are also economic courts, and a Supreme Economic Court. Trials are generally public unless closed on grounds of national security. Litigants have a right to counsel and, in cases of need, to appointment of counsel at state expense.

The president appoints all district level and military judges. The 1996 constitution gives the president the power to appoint 6 of the 12 members of the Constitutional Court, including the chief justice. The Council of the Republic appoints the other remaining 6 members of the Constitutional Court. The judiciary is not independent and is under the influence of the executive. Legislation concerning independence of the judiciary was passed in 1995, but the laws have not been implemented. The Constitutional Court was established in 1994, and adjudicates serious constitutional issues, but it has no power to enforce its decisions. Prosecutors are responsible to the Procurator General who is appointed by the Council of the Republic according to the 1996 constitution. The offices of prosecutors consist of district offices, regional, and republic level offices.

17 ARMED FORCES

The active armed forces of Belarus numbered 72,940 in 2005. The reserves consisted of 289,500 individuals who had military service within the last five years. The nation's military is organized into three services: an army; an air force; and an air defense force. The Army numbered 29,600 active personnel, and was supported by 1,586 main battle tanks, 1,588 armored infantry fighting vehicles, 916 armored personnel carriers, and 1,499 artillery pieces. The Air Force and Air Defense Force numbered a combined 18,170 active personnel. The Air Force had 210 combat capable aircraft, including 50 attack helicopters. The Air Defense Force operated 175 surface-to-air missile batteries. Belarus also had a paramilitary force of 110,000 personnel, which included 12,000 border guards, an 87,000-man militia, and 11,000 Ministry of Interior Troops. The militia and the border guards are also under the command of the Interior Ministry. In 2005 the defense budget totaled $251 million.

18 INTERNATIONAL COOPERATION

Belarus was admitted to the United Nations on 22 October 1945 and serves on several specialized agencies, such as IAEA, IMF, UNCTAD, UNESCO, UNIDO, WHO, and the World Bank. It is an observer in the WTO. Belarus joined the OSCE on 30 January 1992. The country is part of the Commonwealth of Independent Nations (CIS) and the Central European Initiative. In 2000, Belarus, Kazakhstan, Russia, Kyrgyzstan, and Tajikistan established the Eurasian Economic Community.

The country has signed the Nuclear Nonproliferation Treaty and has formal diplomatic ties with many nations. It is a member of the Nuclear Suppliers Group (London Group) and the Nonaligned Movement. The country is also a member of the NATO Partnership for Peace. The United States recognized Belarus's sovereignty 25 December 1991. US diplomatic relations with Belarus were established two days later. Belarus has unresolved boundary disputes with Ukraine and Latvia.

In environmental cooperation, Belarus is part of the Basel Convention, the Conventions on Biological Diversity and Air Pollution, Ramsar, CITES, the London Convention, the Montréal Protocol, MARPOL, and the UN Conventions on Climate Change and Desertification.

19 ECONOMY

Belarus's economy has been geared toward industrial production, mostly in machinery and metallurgy with a significant military component, although trade and services account for an increasing share of economic activity. Forestry and agriculture, notably potatoes, grain, peat, and cattle, are also important. Belarus's economy is closely integrated with those of Eastern Europe and the other republics of the former Soviet Union, and the breakup of the Soviet Union was highly disruptive to it. The demand for military products was cut sharply, and supplies of imported energy and raw materials were curtailed.

Despite repeated calls by the IMF for economic reform in Belarus, the Lukashenko government remains committed to maintaining state control over most industries. Lukashenko's administration has also come under severe criticism for its monetary policies. Western analysts accuse the Belarussian government of printing more money to subsidize higher salaries, thereby fueling inflation.

In 1997, Belarus and Russia signed a treaty of union, to provide for close cooperation in foreign affairs and military and economic policies, including freedom of movement for citizens, property ownership, and participation in local elections. Each country will retain its sovereignty, independence, territorial integrity, and other aspects of statehood however. A constitution for the union was approved in 2003.

The business climate remains poor in Belarus: as of 2000, production had increased, but products were uncompetitive on the world market and many were placed in warehouses for storage. Losses from state-owned businesses are largely written off, which prevents those businesses from going bankrupt and keeps unemployment artificially low. Because Lukashenko controls all governmental power, there are no checks and balances or legal provisions for regulating business matters. However, as of 2003, Belarus had six free economic zones, which have attracted foreign investment, especially from Poland, Russia, and Germany, with the United States as the sixth-largest investor.

Economic expansion has been strong over the past years, with a boost of the GDP growth rate from 7.1% in 2003, to 11.0% in 2004; in 2005, the rate is expected to return to the 2003 level. This expansion was fueled by strong domestic demand, as a result of an increase in real wages, and due to a better and more stable macroeconomic situation. Inflation has been fairly high, but decreasing—in 2004 it was 18.1%, and by 2005 it was expected to dwindle further to 13.0%. Unemployment is very low at 2%, but a large number of the working force is believed to be underemployed.

Despite having an economy that seems to be doing well on paper, most international analysts agree that as long as Lukashenko will continue to favor the obsolete industrial base, and as long as he will continue to pump subsidies into the agricultural sector (the peasants and the blue collar workers are his main constituency), Belarus will not achieve healthy and sustainable economic growth.

20 INCOME

The US Central Intelligence Agency (CIA) reports that in 2005 Belarus's gross domestic product (GDP) was estimated at $77.8 billion. The CIA defines GDP as the value of all final goods and services produced within a nation in a given year and computed on the basis of purchasing power parity (PPP) rather than value as measured on the basis of the rate of exchange based on current dollars. The per capita GDP was estimated at $7,600. The annual growth rate of GDP was estimated at 7.8%. The average inflation rate in 2005 was 11.5%. It was estimated that agriculture accounted for 9.3% of GDP, industry 31.6%, and services 59.1% in 2005.

According to the World Bank, in 2003 remittances from citizens working abroad totaled $162 million or about $16 per capita and accounted for approximately 0.9% of GDP. Foreign aid receipts amounted to $32 million or about $3 per capita and accounted for approximately 0.2% of the gross national income (GNI).

The World Bank reports that in 2003 household consumption in Belarus totaled $10.42 billion or about $1,055 per capita based on a GDP of $17.6 billion, measured in current dollars rather than PPP. Household consumption includes expenditures of individuals, households, and nongovernmental organizations on goods and services, excluding purchases of dwellings. It was estimated that for the period 1990 to 2003 household consumption grew at an average annual rate of 3.0%. In 2001 it was estimated that approximately 36% of household consumption was spent on food, 15% on fuel, 7% on health care, and 10% on education. It was estimated that in 2003 about 27.1% of the population had incomes below the poverty line.

21 LABOR

The labor force as of end 2003 numbered 4.305 million workers. Of that total in that same year, an estimated 14% were engaged in agriculture, 51.3% in services, and 34.7% in industry. In 2004, the number of registered unemployed was officially put at 2%, but there was a large segment of the working population that was underemployed.

Although the constitution provides for the right of workers to form and join independent unions, these rights are not respected in practice. Union activity is discouraged, and almost impossible to conduct in most of the state-owned larger industries. Strikes are legally permitted but tight control by the regime over public demonstrations makes it difficult to strike or hold public rallies. The government has harassed and arrested union leaders, and broken up union-sponsored activities. In addition, workers who are fired for union or political activity are not required to be re-hired by their employers.

Forced or compulsory labor by adults or children is prohibited. The statutory minimum employment age is 16, although a child of 14 can be employed if the parent or legal guardian gives written consent. In addition, minors under the age of 18 cannot work at hazardous jobs, or those which will adversely affect his or her education. Also they cannot work overtime on government holidays, or on the weekend. The workweek was set at 40 hours, with a 24-hour rest period per week. Safety and health standards in the workplace are often ignored. As of 2005, the minimum wage was us$55 a month, which does not provide a decent standard of living. However, average real wages were officially reported (as of end 2005) at around us$250 per month, although many receive additional income from the underground economy.

22 AGRICULTURE

Belarus had about 5,570,000 hectares (14,159,000 acres) of arable land (27.6% of the total) in 2002. Agriculture engaged about 14% of the economically active population in 2003 and accounted for 9.3% of GDP in 2005. Production levels (in 1,000 tons) for 2004 include: potatoes, 9,900; sugar beets, 3,088; barley, 2,070; rye, 1,480; wheat, 1,025; and oats, 765. In 2002, 64,200 and 13,800 tractors and combines, respectively, were in service.

23 ANIMAL HUSBANDRY

About 15% of the total land area is devoted to pastureland. In 2004, there were some 3,924,000 cattle, 3,287,000 pigs, 63,000 sheep, and 24,000,000 chickens. Of the 639,500 tons of meat produced in 2004, beef and veal accounted for 35%; poultry, 14%; pork, 50%, and other meats, 1%. Belarus produces more dairy products than any other former Soviet republic except Russia, with 5.2 million tons of milk, 77,400 tons of butter and ghee, and 80,800 tons of cheese produced in 2004. That year, egg production amounted to 163,300 tons; honey, 3,100 tons.

24 FISHING

As a landlocked nation, fishing is confined to the system of rivers (Pripyat, Byarezina, Nyoman, Zach Dvina, Sozh, Dnieper) that cross Belarus. The total catch in 2003 was 12,318 tons, with aquaculture accounting for 44% of that amount.

25 FORESTRY

About 45% of the total land area was covered by forests in 2000. Radioactive contamination of some forestland from the 1986 Chernobyl disaster has severely restricted output. In 2003, Belarus produced 7.5 million cu m (265 million cu ft) of roundwood, of which 1,518,000 cu m (53.6 million cu ft) were exported for a value of $35.7 million.

26 MINING

Potash was the one significant mineral resource possessed by Belarus, which ranked second in world output in 2000. During the 1980s, Belarus produced 5 million tons per year (calculated based on potassium oxide content), about 50% of the former Soviet Union's output. After the breakup of the Soviet Union, production fell to 1.95 million tons by 1993. A program was then undertaken to raise the quality of potash to world standards to increase exports. Total production in 2002 was 3.8 million tons, down from 4.55 million tons in 1999. Potash was mined in the Salihorsk region, by the Belaruskaliy production association. Accumulated waste from the industry has raised environmental concerns. Two plants produced 2.17 million tons of cement in 2002.

27 ENERGY AND POWER

Domestic electricity is produced by four thermal plants. Belarus also imports electricity generated by nuclear and hydroelectric plants. In 2004, a total of 30 billion kWh was generated, of which 24.841 billion kWh came from thermal sources and 0.028 billion kWh from hydropower. In the same year, consumption of electricity totaled 28.015 billion kWh. Total capacity in 2002 was 7.838 million kW.

Only a small portion of Belarus's energy requirement is met by local production. Belarus has been producing oil since 1964 and had 37 operational fields in 1995. As of 2002 Belarus had oil reserves estimated at 198 million barrels, but there was a lack of foreign investment to fund exploration. In 2002, around 36,500 barrels of oil were produced per day, along with a nominal amount of peat and natural gas. Peat is found throughout the country and is processed by 37 fuel briquetting plants. Natural gas production in 2002 totaled 6.71 billion cu ft. There are two major oil refineries: Mazyr and Navapolatsk. Although oil consumption has been cut roughly in half since the early 1990s, Belarus was still obliged to import 75% of its oil from Russia as of 2002. In December 2002, Belarus sold its 11% stake in Slavneft, a joint Belarus and Russian state-run oil company, to Russia.

Belarus is an important transit route for Russian oil and natural gas exports to Eastern Europe, via pipelines that can carry up to 1,030,000 barrels per day of oil and 22.7 billion cu m (800 billion cu ft) per year of natural gas. Roughly half of Russia's net oil exports travel through Belarus, and a trade agreement between the two countries exempts Russia from paying export duties on this oil. In March 1993, Poland and Russia entered into an agreement to build a 2,500-mile natural gas pipeline from Russia's northern Yamal Peninsula, through Belarus and Poland, to Germany. When completed by 2010, the planned capacity of the new pipeline will be more than 56.6 billion cu m (2 trillion cu ft) per year. To maintain stable supplies of oil and natural gas, Belarus has entered into a joint project with Russia, sponsored by the European Bank for Reconstruction and Development (EBRD), to develop 60 million tons of oil from idle wells in Russia's Tymen region in exchange for guaranteed Russian oil supplies.

28 INDUSTRY

Belarus's industrial base is relatively well-developed and diversified compared to other newly independent states. Industry accounted for 31.6% of GDP in 2005. Belarus's main industries are engineering, machine tools, agricultural equipment, fertilizer, chemicals, defense-related products, prefabricated construction materials, motor vehicles, motorcycles, textiles, threads, and some consumer products, such as refrigerators, watches, televisions, and radios. The types of motor vehicles produced are off-highway dump trucks with up to 110-metric-ton load capacity, tractors, earth movers for construction and mining, and 25-metric-ton trucks for use in roadless and tundra areas.

While there had been an increase in industrial production as of 2002, a high volume of unsold industrial goods remain stocked in warehouses, due to high overhead costs that make Belarussian products uncompetitive on the world market. Belarus has taken few steps to privatize state-owned industries: it was estimated that around 10% of all Belarussian enterprises were privatized as of 2000.

By 2004, the participation of industry in the overall economic output had decreased to 36.4%, while its share in the labor fell to 34.7%; agriculture made up 11% of the GDP, and employed 14% of the labor force; services came in first with 52.6%, and 51.3% respectively. The industrial production growth was less than half of the GDP growth rate, at 4%, but it recovered in the first nine months of 2005 (10%), and was well above the same rate in Russia and Ukraine (4% and 3.2% respectively).

29 SCIENCE AND TECHNOLOGY

The Academy of Sciences of Belarus, founded in 1929 and headquartered in Minsk, has departments of physics, mathematics, and informatics; physical and engineering problems of machine building and energetics; chemical and geological sciences, biological sciences, and medical-biological sciences; it also operates numerous research institutes.

The Belarussian State University, founded in 1921 at Minsk, has faculties of applied mathematics, biology, chemistry, geography, mechanics and mathematics, physics, and radiophysics and electronics. The Belarussian State Technological University, founded in 1930 at Minsk, has faculties of chemistry technology and engineering, forestry, and organic substances technology. In 1987–97, science and engineering students accounted for 48% of college and university enrollment.

The Belarussian State Scientific and Technical Library, located in Minsk, had more than 1.2 million volumes as of 1996. In 2002, total research and development (R&D) expenditures in Belarus amounted to $348.3 million, or 0.6% of GDP, of which 63.4% came from the government, 24.4% from business, 10.1% from foreign sources, and 2.2% from higher education. In that year, 1,870 researchers and 207 technicians per million people were actively engaged in R&D. In 2002, high technology exports totaled $212 million, or 4% of manufactured exports.

30 DOMESTIC TRADE

In 1992, retail prices rose more than 1,000%. The same year a parallel national currency (called the ruble) was introduced and declared the only legal tender for purchasing goods such as food, alcohol, and tobacco. In 1998, the inflation rate was 182%. Though the government had initiated some capitalist reforms from 1991 to 1994, President Alexander Lukashenko (elected 1994) has significantly slowed efforts toward privatization through a program of "market socialism." The government has administrative control of prices and currency exchange rates and has also reestablished certain management rights over private enterprises. As of early 2003, nearly 80% of industry was state-owned. Independent banks had also been renationalized.

31 FOREIGN TRADE

Before the collapse of the Soviet Union, Belarus exported about 40% of its industrial output to other Soviet republics and imported 90% of its primary energy and 70% of its raw materials from them. Belarus has remained exceedingly dependant on Russia for economic support; a proposed EU-style partnership between the two nations threatens its economic independence.

In 2000, Belarus exported machinery and transport equipment, chemicals, petroleum products, and manufactured goods. Imports included fuel, natural gas, industrial raw materials, textiles, and sugar. Belarus's major trading partners are Russia, Ukraine, Poland, and Germany. Imports and exports grew at an annual pace of over 61% in 1995.

Unlike Russia, Belarus did not manage to maintain a positive resource balance in 2004—while exports grew to $11.5 billion (FOB—Free on Board), they were surpassed by imports, at $13.6 billion. Russia continued to dominate Belarus's trade, receiving 47% of its exports, and sending 68.2% of its imports. Other important trading partners included the United Kingdom, Germany, the Netherlands, and Poland.

32 BALANCE OF PAYMENTS

The US Central Intelligence Agency (CIA) reported that in 2001 the purchasing power parity of Belarus's exports was $7.5 billion, while imports totaled $8.1 billion, resulting in a trade deficit of $600 million.

The International Monetary Fund (IMF) reported that in 2001 Belarus had exports of goods totaling $7.26 billion and imports

Balance of Payments – Belarus (2001)		
(In millions of US dollars)		
Current Account		-285.2
Balance on goods	-806.9	
Imports	-8,063.1	
Exports	7,256.2	
Balance on services	410.4	
Balance on income	-42.8	
Current transfers	154.1	
Capital Account		56.3
Financial Account		247.1
Direct investment abroad	-0.3	
Direct investment in Belarus	95.8	
Portfolio investment assets	10.5	
Portfolio investment liabilities	-45.4	
Financial derivatives	...	
Other investment assets	-139.2	
Other investment liabilities	325.7	
Net Errors and Omissions		-99.6
Reserves and Related Items		81.4

(…) data not available or not significant.

SOURCE: *Balance of Payment Statistics Yearbook 2004*, Washington, DC: International Monetary Fund, 2004.

totaling $8.06 billion. The services credit totaled $1.01 billion and debit $603 million.

Unlike any other country in the region, Belarus recently witnessed a trade recoil, with exports of goods and services decreasing from $11.6 billion in 2003, to $9.9 billion in 2004; imports went down from $12.3 billion in 2003, to $10.3 billion in 2004. The resource balance was consequently negative, but not alarming— -$678 million in 2003, and -$441 million in 2004. The current account balance followed a similar path, improving from -$505 million in 2003, to -$271 million in 2004. Total reserves (including gold) were insignificant at $432 million, covering less than a month of imports in 2004.

33 BANKING AND SECURITIES

The National Bank of Belarus is the central bank of Belarus, charged with regulating the money supply, circulating currency, and regulating the commercial banks of the country. The currency unit is the ruble. There are no current figures on the level of foreign currency reserves, but it is widely assumed that these have dwindled to perilously low levels because of the need for the National Bank of Belarus to maintain the local currency at its overvalued exchange rate on the Minsk Interbank Currency Exchange (MICE). The central bank has also had to turn to the street market to replenish reserves; in August, 1996, it bought $25 million, paying effectively 10% more than it would have through MICE. Under Belarus's "currency corridor," the Belarussian ruble cannot fall below BR615,000: $1 at its twice-weekly auctions at the MICE. The street market accounts for 70–80% of foreign exchange trading. The International Monetary Fund reports that in 2001, currency and demand deposits—an aggregate commonly known as M1—were equal to $640.0 million. In that same year, M2—an aggregate equal to M1 plus savings deposits, small time deposits, and money market mutual funds—was $1.8 billion. The discount

Principal Trading Partners – Belarus (2003)			
(In millions of US dollars)			
Country	Exports	Imports	Balance
World	9,945.6	11,558.0	-1,612.4
Russia	4,879.9	7,601.9	-2,722.0
United Kingdom	938.3	79.3	859.0
Poland	434.2	348.5	85.7
Germany	421.2	820.7	-399.5
Netherlands	413.8	93.4	320.4
Latvia	344.3	44.3	300.0
Ukraine	343.5	362.1	-18.6
Lithuania	265.0	154.2	110.8
China	162.3	71.8	90.5
Italy-San Marino-Holy See	135.3	284.0	-148.7

(…) data not available or not significant.

SOURCE: *2003 International Trade Statistics Yearbook*, New York: United Nations, 2004.

rate, the interest rate at which the central bank lends to financial institutions in the short term, was 48%.

34 INSURANCE

No recent information about the insurance industry in Belarus is available.

35 PUBLIC FINANCE

Because it was formerly a part of the Soviet Union, Belarus has a well-established industrial base, but the transition from a centrally planned economy to a free market economy has not been easy. Privatization, although in progress, has been happening slowly, and foreign investment is discouraged by the "hostile" business climate.

The US Central Intelligence Agency (CIA) estimated that in 2005 Belarus's central government took in revenues of approximately $5.9 billion and had expenditures of $6.3 billion. Revenues minus expenditures totaled approximately -$440 million. Total external debt was $4.662 billion.

The International Monetary Fund (IMF) reported that in 2002, the most recent year for which it had data, central government revenues were BR6,960.4 billion and expenditures were BR7,089 billion. The value of revenues was US$4 million and expenditures US$4 million, based on an official exchange rate for 2002 of US$1 = BR1,790.917 as reported by the IMF. Government outlays by function were as follows: general public services, 20.9%; defense, 4.6%; public order and safety, 4.4%; economic affairs, 13.0%; health, 3.6%; recreation, culture, and religion, 1.4%; education, 4.1%; and social protection, 47.9%.

36 TAXATION

Belarus imposes a wide array of taxes on business and citizens. In 2005, the corporate income tax for resident companies was 24% and 30% for insurance companies and banks. Securities transactions are taxed at 40%. Companies with profits of over 5,000 times

Public Finance – Belarus (2002)

(In billions of rubels, central government figures)

Revenue and Grants	**6,960.4**	**100.0%**
Tax revenue	3,711.9	53.3%
Social contributions	2,845.6	40.9%
Grants	16.1	0.2%
Other revenue	386.8	5.6%
Expenditures	**7,089**	**100.0%**
General public services	1,484.8	20.9%
Defense	323.6	4.6%
Public order and safety	311.8	4.4%
Economic affairs	924.8	13.0%
Environmental protection	...	...
Housing and community amenities	1.3	0.0%
Health	253.4	3.6%
Recreational, culture, and religion	101.4	1.4%
Education	293.5	4.1%
Social protection	3,394.3	47.9%

(...) data not available or not significant.

SOURCE: *Government Finance Statistics Yearbook 2004*, Washington, DC: International Monetary Fund, 2004.

the minimum wage are taxed an additional 15% under certain conditions. Joint ventures in which foreign participation is more than 30% are eligible for a three-year tax holiday.

The main indirect tax is the country's value-added tax (VAT) with a standard rate of 18%. A reduced rate of 10% is placed upon certain foodstuffs, agricultural products, repair services, hairdressers, and laundries. Other consumption taxes include a 3% turnover tax and excise taxes ranging from 10–75%. There are also taxes on the use of natural resources, including the Chernobyl nuclear plant. Individual income is taxed according to a progressive schedule of rates ranging from 12% (up from 4.7%) to 30%. There is a 64.8% employer payroll tax for social security and employment taxes. There are also direct taxes on property and land.

37 CUSTOMS AND DUTIES

A 1995 customs union with Russia allows goods to flow between the two countries duty-free. However, the union required Belarus to conform its customs rates to those of Russia, resulting in a tariff increase from 5–10% to 20–40%. In 1995, Belarus also introduced a 20% import VAT (value-added tax) to be paid at the border on all incoming goods, except certain raw material used by local manufacturers.

38 FOREIGN INVESTMENT

The European Bank for Reconstruction and Development (EBRD) financed several major infrastructure improvement and commercial projects. The World Bank was financing construction and telecommunication projects, but these were discontinued in 1996 by President Lukashenko. At the end of the decade, President Lukashenko's steadfast refusal to implement market reforms continued to keep foreign investment levels low. In May 2002, however, the government announced a new program aimed at raising the share of foreign investment in GDP from 19% to 26–28%, with most investments coming from Russia. Several state-owned enterprises (SOEs), including oil refineries and chemical plants, were to be transformed into joint stock companies in preparation of selling 49.9% in blocks of 10%. Many restrictions are still tied to foreign investments and in June 2003, President Lukashenko announced that he had turned down proposals from foreign investors amounting to $10 billion because of unacceptable terms. The president stated that the government's goal was at least $1 billion in foreign direct investment (FDI) in 2003.

FDI inflow for Belarus reached $444 million in 1999, up from $352 million in 1997 and $203 million in 1998. However, the inflow was reduced to a trickle in 2000 ($90 million) and 2001 ($169 million). During the decade 1993 to 2003, according to the Belarus government, foreign investment totaled $4 billion, $1.7 billion in FDI and $2.5 billion in credits guaranteed by the government. All but a small proportion of foreign investment has come from Russia. Other sources include the Netherlands, Germany, and the United States (McDonald's, Coca Cola, and Ford). However, McDonald's and Coca Cola have both had problems with the government and the Ford plant is closed.

Investments have regained strength in 2004, but they were still relatively low to the GDP. What is worse, though, is the fact that only a small percentage of investments come from outside the country—due to a relatively inauspicious business climate and continued state control of major national companies. For the most part, investments are fueled by a high domestic demand (such as financing of new housing), and only a small part went to productive assets.

³⁹ECONOMIC DEVELOPMENT

In the summer of 1995, the Belarussian president announced the policy of "market socialism," after a period of economic liberalization and privatization that had taken place from 1991–94. The government still controls key market sectors as the private sector only makes up 20% of the economy. Most of the heavy industry in Belarus remains state-owned. Belarus offers easy credit to spur economic growth, but this comes at the price of high inflation. To combat spiraling wages and prices, President Lukashenko imposed price controls. These policies have driven away foreign investment and left Belarus economically isolated.

Bad harvests in 1998 and 1999 and continued trade deficits worsened the climate of economic development. The government resorted to inflationary monetary policies, including the printing of money, to pay salaries and pensions. In 2000, the government tightened its monetary policies, but in 2002, the International Monetary Fund (IMF) criticized Belarus for its economic performance, and refused to resume loans to the country. (IMF loans were last offered in 1995.) The balance of payments situation remained weak from 2001–03, as the ruble rose against the US dollar and the Russian ruble. The current account deficit was $279 million or 2% of gross domestic product (GDP) in 2003. There were plans in 2003 for monetary and currency union with Russia, which would require substantial macroeconomic reforms on the part of Belarus.

The country's good economic performance is expected to falter in the coming years due to the concerted effect of a series of factors. First of all, oil prices (which have boosted export returns) are expected to level off soon. An appreciation of the currency will work as a disincentive for exporters, while the growth of wages cannot exceed the growth in productivity for too long. Also, Belarus's most important trade partner, Russia, will probably curtail imports, as it is itself in an economically difficult position.

⁴⁰SOCIAL DEVELOPMENT

Old age, disability, and survivors are protected by a social insurance system updated in 1999. Sickness, maternity, work injury, family allowance, and unemployment benefits are covered by the system. Employers contribute between 10–35% of payroll depending on the type of company. The government covers the cost of social pensions and subsidies as needed. Retirement is set at age 60 for men and age 55 for women. Workers' compensation laws were first instituted in 1939. Family allowances are available for families with one or more children.

The human rights record of Belarus has worsened in recent years, after President Lukashenka amended the constitution to extend his stay in office and handpick members of parliament. Reports of police brutality are widespread and prison conditions are poor. Arbitrary arrests and detention have been reported, as well as incidents of severe hazing in the military. As of 2004, political opponents and protests are met with a violent government response. The government abridges freedom of the press, speech, assembly, religion, and movement. Religious freedom and equality is provided for in the constitution, but religions other than Rus-

sian Orthodox are discriminated against. There were a number of right wing and skinhead groups active in 2004.

Domestic abuse and violence against women continued to be a significant problem in 2004. Although laws against rape exist, most women do not report the crime due to fear that the police will blame the victim. Spousal rape is not viewed as a crime. While there are no legal restrictions on women's participation in public life, social barriers are considerable, and women commonly experience discrimination when it comes to job opportunities. The law mandates equal pay for equal work, but few women reach senior management or government positions. Trafficking in women remains a serious problem.

⁴¹HEALTH

The basic framework of the health care system has remained the same since the breakup of the Soviet Union. Health care is administered through a network of hospitals, polyclinics, tertiary care centers, and walk-in clinics. As of 2004, there were an estimated 450 physicians, 1,234 nurses, 44 dentists, and 31 pharmacists per 100,000 people. In addition to hospitals and medical personnel, the medical infrastructure comprises pharmacies and other retail outlets from which people and institutions acquire medicines and other basic medical supplies. Health care expenditures were an estimated 5.6% of GDP.

The incident with the most wide-ranging effects on the health of the Belarussian population was the accident at the Chernobyl nuclear power plant in April 1986. An estimated 2.2 million Belarussians were directly affected by radioactive fallout. As a result of the disaster, the population is constantly subject to increased amounts of background radiation that weakens the immune systems of individuals in contaminated areas; many are said to suffer from "Chernobyl AIDS."

The 1999 birthrate was 10 per 1,000 inhabitants, with 101,317 births. Life expectancy in 2005 was 68.72 years. In 1997, children one year of age were immunized at the following rates: tuberculosis, 98%; diphtheria, pertussis, and tetanus, 97%; polio, 98%; and measles, 98%. The infant mortality rate in 2005 was 13.37 per 1,000 live births. Maternal mortality was estimated at 28 per 100,000 live births in 1998. In 1999, there were 80 deaths from tuberculosis per 100,000 people.

The HIV/AIDS prevalence was 0.30 per 100 adults in 2003. As of 2004, there were approximately 15,000 people living with HIV/AIDS in the country. There were an estimated 1,000 deaths from AIDS in 2003.

The National AIDS Center was established in 1990.

⁴²HOUSING

The lack of adequate, affordable housing continues to be a problem for Belarus, but certain advances have been made. After the 1986 Chernobyl nuclear plant disaster, the government was forced to seal off 485 human settlement areas, displacing about 135,000 people. Over 65,000 apartments and homes have since been built to house these people. Since 1992, the government has been reforming housing laws to secure the constitutional right of citizens to acquire, build, reconstruct, or lease housing facilities.

In 1999, about 97% of the population were living in what was defined as conventional dwellings (primarily detached houses, separate or shared apartments or flats, and hostels). About 56%

were living in separate flats. About 31% were in detached houses. Those living in flats had the greatest access to improved utilities, such as central heating, central piped hot water, and flush toilets. Nationwide, only about 68% of the population had flush toilets in the home (1999), and only 71% had piped water. About 26.5% of the total population were using stove heating. About 66% of the housing stock had been built in the period 1961–90.

43 EDUCATION

Education is compulsory for children between the ages of 6 and 15. The primary school program covers four years of study and the basic education covers five years. General secondary programs are offered at gymnasiums (general studies), lyceums (affiliated with universities), and colleges (vocational studies); general secondary studies courses cover an additional two years. Students also have an option of attending a four-year technical school (technicum) or a three-year trade school instead of the general programs.

Primary school enrollment in 2003 was estimated at about 94% of age-eligible students. The same year, secondary school enrollment was about 85% of age-eligible students. The student-to-teacher ratio for primary school was at about 16:1 in 2003. The ratio for secondary school was about 9:1. It is estimated that about 98.7% of all students complete their primary education. The academic year runs from September to July.

Education at public higher education institutes is free for students who pass the entrance competition. In 2005, there were 44 public higher education institutions, including 25 universities, 9 academies, 4 institutes, 5 colleges, and 1 technical school. There were also 13 private higher education institutions. Total enrollment at these institutions was about 545,800. The largest public institute is the Belarussian State University, which is located in Minsk and was founded in 1921. The adult literacy rate for 2004 was estimated at about 99.8%, with equal rates for men and women.

The official languages of education are Belarussian, which is written in the Cyrillic script, and Russian. The government is now putting more emphasis on replacing Russian with Belarussian. The Ministry of Education and the National Institute for Higher Education are the primary administrative bodies. As of 2003, public expenditure on education was estimated at 6% of GDP.

44 LIBRARIES AND MUSEUMS

As of 2002, the National Library in Minsk held 7.6 million volumes. The country also had an extensive public library system. Universities with significant library holdings include the Belarussian State Polytechnic Academy (over two million volumes), Belarussian State University (1.7 million volumes), and the Minsk Teacher Training Institute (1.2 million volumes). The presidential library holds 1.5 million volumes, and the Gomel Regional Library has 1.3 million volumes.

The country records 14,392 monuments and historic sites. The State Art Museum in Minsk houses the country's largest collection of fine arts. The Belarussian State Museum of the Great Patriotic War (World War II) in Minsk houses artifacts and memorials of the country's great travails during the war. There is a historical and archaeological museum in Grodno and a natural history museum in Belovezskaja Pusca.

45 MEDIA

The Ministry of Telecommunications controls all telecommunications through Beltelcom. In 2003, there were an estimated 311 mainline telephones for every 1,000 people; about 292,800 people were on a waiting list for telephone service installation. The same year, there were approximately 113 mobile phones in use for every 1,000 people.

The government operates the only nationwide television and radio stations; however, there are several local stations. Some Russian, Polish, and Lithuanian stations are received in various parts of the country, but the government has blocked certain programming and has removed some channels from local cable access. In 2003, there were an estimated 199 radios and 362 television sets for every 1,000 people. About 77.2 of every 1,000 people were cable subscribers. In 2003, 141 of every 1,000 people had access to the Internet. There were four secure Internet servers in the country in 2004. All ISPs are controlled by the state.

The most widely read newspapers (with 2002 circulation figures) are *Sovetskaya Belorussiya* (*Soviet Belorussia*, 330,000); *Narodnaya Hazeta* (*People's Newspaper*, 259,597); *Respublika* (*Republic*, 130,000); *Vechernii Minsk* (*Evening Minsk*, 111,000); *Svaboda* (90,000); *Zvyazda* (*Star*, 90,000); and *Belorusskaya Niva* (*Belarussian Cornfield*, 80,000).

Most of the higher circulation papers are controlled by the state in some way. Though freedom of the press is granted in the 1996 constitution, the government continues to restrict this right through a virtual monopoly over forms of mass communication and its desire to limit media criticism of its actions. It controls the editorial content and policy of the largest circulation daily newspapers and of radio and television broadcasts and places severe restrictions on the editorial content of independent publications or broadcasts. Local radio and television stations are pressured to refrain from reporting on national issues. Government authorities reserve the right to ban and censor publications presenting critical reports on national issues. In 2004, the government suspended publication of 25 privately-owned newspapers.

46 ORGANIZATIONS

Belarus's important business and commercial organizations include the Chamber of Commerce and Industry of the Republic of Belarus. Important agricultural and industrial organizations include the Belarussian Peasants' Union, the Union of Entrepreneurs and Farmers, and the Union of Small Ventures. There are number of professional associations, particularly for members of medical professions.

The National Academy of Sciences and the Belarussian Physical Society promote public interest and education in science. The Belarussian Think Tanks is a public policy center involved in developing and promoting ideas to create democracy, market economy, and respect for human rights in Belarus.

Political interest youth organizations include the Belarussian Patriotic Youth Union and the Youth Front of Belarus (est. 1993). The Belarus Youth Information Center (YIC) was founded in 1994 to encourage and support youth involvement in science, culture, and education. The Belarussian Students Association is an affiliate member of the National Union of Students in Europe (ESIB). There is an organization of Girl Guides in the country, YMCA/YWCA, and a Junior Chamber Belarus. Several sports associations are active, representing such pastimes as baseball and softball, track and field, badminton, tennis, and air sports. The country sponsors a National Olympic Committee, a Paralympic Committee, and a Special Olympics chapter.

The International Association for Volunteer Effort serves to promote and provide a network for voluntary service organizations, including Lions Club International, which is active in the country. There is also a League of Youth Voluntary Service. There are active chapters of the Red Cross, Caritas and UNICEF.

47 TOURISM, TRAVEL, AND RECREATION

Scenery, architecture, and cultural museums and memorials are primary attractions in Belarus. The Belavaezhskaja Puscha Nature Reserve features a variety of wildlife and a nature museum. The city of Hrodna is home to the baroque Farny Cathedral, the Renaissance Bernadine church and monastery, and the History of Religion Museum, which is part of a renovated 18th-century palace. There are also two castles in the area, both housing museums. A valid passport and visa are required of all visitors. An HIV test is required for visits longer than 90 days.

In 2003, there were 63,779 tourist arrivals in Belarus, up from 61,033 in 2000. Tourism receipts totaled $339 million.

In 2005, the US Department of State estimated the cost of staying in Minsk at $187 per day.

48 FAMOUS BELARUSSIANS

Frantsky Sharyna, who lived in the first quarter of the 16th century, translated the Bible into Belarussian. Symeon of Polatsk was a 17th-century poet who wrote in Belarussian. Naksim Bahdanovich was an important 19th-century poet. Modern writers include Uladzimir Dubouka (1900–1976) and Yazep Pushcha, both poets. Kuzma Chorny and Kandrat Krapiva (1896–1991) were writers of fiction during the outpouring of Belarussian poetry and literature during the 1920s. Famous modern composers from Belarus included Dzmitry Lukas, Ryhor Pukst, and Yauhen Hlebau (1929–2000).

49 DEPENDENCIES

Belarus has no territories or colonies.

50 BIBLIOGRAPHY

Aleksievich, Svetlana. Keth Gessen (trans.). *Voices from Chernobyl*. Normal, Ill.: Dalkey Archive, 2005.

Brawer, Moshe. *Atlas of Russia and the Independent Republics*. New York: Simon and Schuster, 1994.

Dean, Martin. *Collaboration in the Holocaust: Crimes of the Local Police in Belorussia and Ukraine, 1941–44*. New York: St. Martin's Press, 2000.

Korosteleva, Elena, Colin W. Lawson, and Rosalind J. Marsh (eds.). *Contemporary Belarus: Between Democracy and Dictatorship*. London, Eng.: RoutledgeCurzon, 2003.

Mandel, David. *Labour after Communism: Auto Workers and Their Unions in Russia, Ukraine, and Belarus*. New York: Black Rose Books, 2004.

McElrath, Karen (ed.). *HIV and AIDS: A Global View*. Westport, Conn.: Greenwood Press, 2002.

White, Stephen, Elena Korosteleva, and John Löwenhardt (eds.). *Postcommunist Belarus*. Lanham, Md.: Rowman and Littlefield, 2004.

BELGIUM

Kingdom of Belgium
Dutch: Koninkrijk België;
French: Royaume de Belgique

CAPITAL: Brussels (Brussel, Bruxelles)

FLAG: The flag, adopted in 1831, is a tricolor of black, yellow, and red vertical stripes.

ANTHEM: *La Brabançonne (The Song of Brabant),* named after the Duchy of Brabant.

MONETARY UNIT: The euro replaced the Belgian franc in 2002. The euro is divided into 100 cents. There are coins in denominations of 1, 2, 5, 10, 20, and 50 cents and 1 euro; and 2 euros. There are notes of 5, 10, 20, 50, 100, 200, and 500 euros. €1 = $1.25475 (or $1 = €0.79697) as of 2005.

WEIGHTS AND MEASURES: The metric system is the legal standard.

HOLIDAYS: New Year's Day, 1 January; Labor Day, 1 May; Independence Day, 21 July; Assumption Day, 15 August; All Saints' Day, 1 November; Armistice Day, 11 November; Dynasty Day, 15 November; and Christmas, 25 December. Movable religious holidays are Easter Monday, Ascension, and Whitmonday.

TIME: 1 PM = noon GMT.

¹LOCATION, SIZE, AND EXTENT

Situated in northwestern Europe, Belgium has an area of 30,510 sq km (11,780 sq mi) and extends 280 km (174 mi) SE–NW and 222 km (137 mi) NE–SW. Comparatively, the area occupied by Belgium is about the same size as the state of Maryland. Belgium borders on the Netherlands to the N, Germany and Luxembourg to the E, France to the S and SW, and the North Sea to the NW, with a total boundary length of 1,385 km (859 mi).

Belgium's capital city, Brussels, is located in the north-central part of the country.

²TOPOGRAPHY

The coastal region, extending about 16–48 km (10–30 mi) inland, consists of sand dunes, flat pasture land, and polders (land reclaimed from the sea and protected by dikes), and attains a maximum of 15 m (50 ft) above sea level. Eastward, this region gradually gives way to a gently rolling central plain, whose many fertile valleys are irrigated by an extensive network of canals and waterways. Altitudes in this region are about 60–180 m (200–600 ft). The Ardennes, a heavily wooded plateau, is located in southeast Belgium and continues into France. It has an average altitude of about 460 m (1,500 ft) and reaches a maximum of 694 m (2,277 ft) at the Signal de Botrange, the country's highest point. Chief rivers are the Schelde (Scheldt, Escaut) and the Meuse (Maas), both of which rise in France, flow through Belgium, pass through the Netherlands, and empty into the North Sea.

³CLIMATE

In the coastal region, the climate is mild and humid. There are marked temperature changes farther inland. In the high southeasterly districts, hot summers alternate with very cold winters.

Except in the highlands, rainfall is seldom heavy. The average annual temperature is 8°C (46°F); in Brussels, the mean temperature is 10°C (50°F), ranging from 3°C (37°F) in January to 18°C (64°F) in July. Average annual rainfall is between 70 and 100 cm (28 to 40 in).

⁴FLORA AND FAUNA

The digitalis, wild arum, hyacinth, strawberry, goldenrod, lily of the valley, and other plants common to temperate zones grow in abundance. Beech and oak are the predominant trees. Among mammals still found in Belgium are the boar, fox, badger, squirrel, weasel, marten, and hedgehog. The many varieties of aquatic life include pike, carp, trout, eel, barbel, perch, smelt, chub, roach, bream, shad, sole, mussels, crayfish, and shrimp.

⁵ENVIRONMENT

About 520 sq km (200 sq mi) of reclaimed coastal land is protected from the sea by concrete dikes. As of 2000, Belgium's most significant environmental problems were air, land, and water pollution due to the heavy concentration of industrial facilities in the country. The sources of pollution range from nuclear radiation to mercury from industry and pesticides from agricultural activity. The country's water supply is threatened by hazardous levels of heavy metals, mercury, and phosphorous. It has a renewable water supply of 12 cu km. Pollution of rivers and canals was considered the worst in Europe as of 1970, when strict water-protection laws were enacted.

Air pollution reaches dangerous levels due to high concentrations of lead and hydrocarbons. Belgium is also among the 50 nations that emit the highest levels of carbon dioxide from industrial sources. In 1996 its emission level was 106 million metric tons. Belgium's problems with air pollution have also affected neighboring countries by contributing to the conditions which cause acid rain.

The Ministry of Public Health and Environment is Belgium's principal environmental agency, and there is also a Secretary of State for Public Health and Environment. The Belgian government has created several environmental policies to eliminate the country's pollution problems: the 1990–95 plan on Mature Development, an Environmental Policy Plan, and the Waste Plan.

According to a 2006 report issued by the International Union for Conservation of Nature and Natural Resources (IUCN), threatened species included 9 types of mammals, 10 species of birds, 6 species of fish, 4 types of mollusks, and 7 other invertebrates. The Mediterranean mouflon, the Atlantic sturgeon, and the black right whale are listed as endangered. There are nine Ramsar wetland sites within the country.

6 POPULATION

The population of Belgium in 2005 was estimated by the United Nations (UN) at 10,458,000, which placed it at number 77 in population among the 193 nations of the world. In 2005, approximately 17% of the population was over 65 years of age, with another 17% of the population under 15 years of age. There were 96 males for every 100 females in the country. According to the UN, the annual population rate of change for 2005–10 was expected to be 0.1%, a rate the government viewed as satisfactory. The projected population for the year 2025 was 10,809,000. The population density was 342 per sq km (887 per sq mi).

The UN estimated that 97% of the population lived in urban areas in 2005, and that urban areas were growing at an annual rate of 0.16%. The capital city, Brussels (Brussel, Bruxelles), had a population of 998,000 in that year. Other major urban areas are located within 100 km (60 mi) of Brussels. The largest cities and their estimated populations include Antwerp (Antwerpen, Anvers), 952,600; Gent (Ghent, Gand), 230,951; Charleroi, 206,779; Liège (Luik), 196,825; Brugge (Bruges), 117,172; and Namur (Namen), 106,213.

The government has conducted a census every 10 years since 1848. Since 1984 the registration of births and deaths has been delegated to the Flemish and Walloon language communities. Belgium's population has distinctive language and ethnic divisions. The Ardennes region in the south is the least densely populated region.

7 MIGRATION

At the end of 2001, 862,000 persons of foreign nationality were living in Belgium. About 65% were those of other EU countries, primarily Italy, France, the Netherlands, and Spain. There were also a considerable number of Moroccans and Turks living in Belgium that year. In 2003 the foreign labor force in Belgium was 7.6%, and the foreign population was 8.3%. The net migration rate of Belgium was 1.23 migrants per 1,000 population as estimated for 2005.

As of 2004, Belgium hosted approximately 13,500 refugees. In 2004 there were 22,863 asylum applications, mostly from Russia, the Democratic Republic of the Congo, and Iran.

8 ETHNIC GROUPS

Two thousand years ago the population of Belgium, as mentioned by Julius Caesar in his book on the Gallic wars, was of Celtic stock. This population was displaced or lost its identity, however, during the great invasions that brought down the Roman Empire. The Salian Franks, who settled there during the 4th century AD, are considered the ancestors of Belgium's present population. The origin of the language frontier in Belgium has never been satisfactorily explained. In the indigenous population, the ratio of Flemings (Dutch speakers) to Walloons (French speakers) is about 5 to 3. In 2004, the Flemings constituted about 58% of the total population; Walloons accounted for 31.7%. The remaining 11% was comprised of those with mixed ancestry or other groups.

9 LANGUAGES

According to a 1970 constitutional revision, there are three official languages in Belgium—French, Dutch (also called Flemish), and German. Dutch is the language of the four provinces of Antwerp, Limburg, East Flanders (Oost-Vlaanderen), and West Flanders (West-Vlaanderen), which form the northern half of the country. French is the language of the four southern Walloon provinces of Hainaut, Liège, Luxembourg, and Namur. The central province of Brabant is divided into three districts—one French-speaking (Nivelles, Nijvel), one Dutch-speaking (Leuven, Louvain), and one bilingual (composed of the 19 boroughs of the capital city, Brussels). The majority of people in the Brussels metropolitan area are French-speaking. According to 2005 estimates, 60% of the total population speak Dutch (Flemish), 40% speak French, less than 1% speak German, and 11% are legally bilingual in Dutch and French.

The relationship between the two major language groups has been tense at times. For many years, French was the only official language. A series of laws enacted in the 1930s established equality between the two languages. Dutch became the language of administration, the schools, and the courts in the Flemish region (Flanders), while French continued to be the language of Wallonia. The use of German is regulated in the same way in the German-speaking municipalities in the province of Liège. As a rule, French is studied in all secondary schools in the Flemish region, while Dutch is a required secondary-school subject in Wallonia.

In 1963, a set of laws created four linguistic regions (with bilingual status for Brussels), a decision incorporated into the constitution in 1970. Subsequent legislation in 1971–74 provided for cultural autonomy, regional economic power, and linguistic equality in the central government. Disagreement over the future status of bilingual Brussels intensified during the late 1970s. In 1980, after a political crisis, the Flemish and Walloon regions were given greater autonomy, but the issue of Brussels, a predominantly French-speaking territory surrounded by a Dutch-speaking region, remained intractable and was deferred.

10 RELIGIONS

According to a 2001 Survey and Study of Religion conducted by universities within the country, about 47% of the population were nominally Roman Catholic. However, other sources have reported that Roman Catholics account for as high as 75% of the popula-

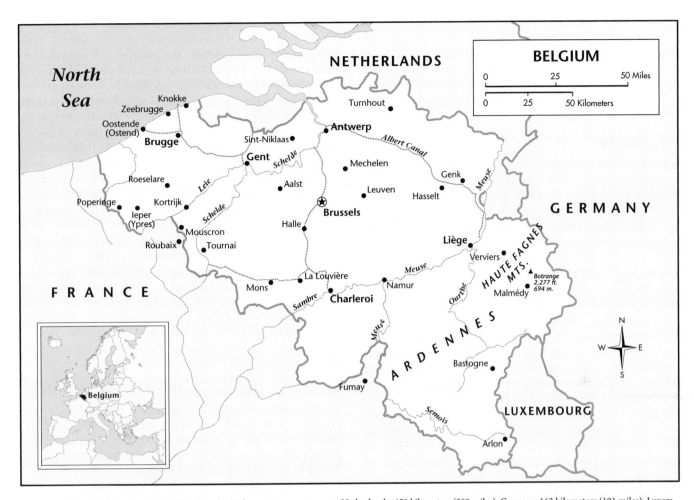

LOCATION: 49°29′52″ to 51°30′21″ N; 2°32′48″ to 6°25′38″ E. BOUNDARY LENGTHS: Netherlands, 450 kilometers (280 miles); Germany, 162 kilometers (101 miles); Luxembourg, 148 kilometers (92 miles); France, 620 kilometers (385 miles); North Sea, 66 kilometers (41 miles). TERRITORIAL SEA LIMIT: 12 miles.

tion. The Roman Catholic Church estimates that of its total Belgian membership, only about 10–15% are active participants.

Based on the Survey and Study of Religion, the Muslim population numbered about 364,000, most of whom were Sunni. Protestants numbered between 125,000 and 140,000. Greek and Russian Orthodox adherents numbered about 70,000. The Jewish community was approximately 45,000 to 55,000 and Anglicans numbered approximately 10,800. The largest unrecognized religions included the Jehovah's Witnesses, with 27,000 members, and the Church of Jesus Christ of Latter-day Saints (Mormons), with about 3,000 members. About 350,000 people belong to laics, the government's term for nonconfessional philosophical organizations. Estimates indicate that up to 15% of the population do not practice any religion at all. About 7.4% claim to follow the tenets of nonconfessional philosophical organizations (laic).

The constitution provides for freedom of religion and this right is generally respected in practice. The government gives "recognized" status to Roman Catholicism, Protestantism, Judaism, Anglicanism, Islam, and Orthodox Christianity. These groups are allowed to receive some funding from the government. Laic groups are also considered as a recognized religion. Some social discrimination has been reported by Jews, Muslims, and members of "unrecognized" groups.

11 TRANSPORTATION

In 2004, the densest railway network in the world comprised 3,521 km (2,190 mi) of track operated by the government-controlled Belgian National Railway Co., of which 2,927 km (1,821 mi) was electrified. In addition, Belgium has a regional railway network of 27,950 km (17,367 mi). The road network in 2003 comprised 149,757 km (89,417 mi) of highways, of which 117,110 km (72,842 mi) were paved, including 1,747 km (1,087 mi) of expressways. All major European highways pass through Belgium. In 2003, Belgium had 4,793,271 passenger cars and 661,948 commercial vehicles registered for use.

Inland waterways comprise 2,043 km (1,270 mi) of rivers and canals, and are linked with those of France, Germany, and the Netherlands. In 2003, a total of 1,570 km (976 mi) of these waterways are in regular commercial use. The chief port, Antwerp (one of the world's busiest ports), on the Scheldt River, about 84 km (52 mi) from the sea, handles three-fourths of the country's foreign cargo. Other leading ports are Gent and Zeebrugge. Liège is the third-largest inland river port in Western Europe, after Duisburg, Germany, and Paris. In 2005 the Belgian merchant fleet was comprised of 53 vessels, with a total of 1,146,301 GRT. The fleet numbered 101 ships (2.2 million GRT) in 2002, but offshore registry programs and so-called "flags of convenience" have enticed ship owners into foreign registry.

In 2004, there were an estimated 43 airports. As of 2005 a total of 25 had paved runways, and there was also a single heliport. The Belgian national airline, Sabena, formed in 1923, is the third-oldest international airline. Brussels National Airport, an important international terminus, is served by more than 30 major airlines. In 2003, a total of 2.904 million passengers flew on scheduled domestic and international flights.

12 HISTORY

Belgium is named after the Belgae, a Celtic people whose territory was conquered in 57 BC by Julius Caesar and was organized by him as Gallia Belgica. In 15 BC, Augustus made Gallia Belgica (which at that time included much of present-day France) a province of the Roman Empire. In the 5th century AD, it was overrun by the Franks, and in the 8th century, it became part of the empire of Charlemagne. But this empire soon fell apart, and in the 10th century there emerged several feudal units that later would become provinces of Belgium. These included the counties of Flanders, Hainaut, and Namur, the duchy of Brabant, and the prince-bishopric of Liège. During the three following centuries, trade flourished in the towns of the county of Flanders. Antwerp, Bruges, Ypres (Ieper), and Ghent in particular became very prosperous. In the 15th century, most of the territory that currently forms Belgium, the Netherlands, and Luxembourg—formerly called the Low Countries and now called the Benelux countries—came under the rule of the dukes of Burgundy as the result of a shrewd policy of intermarriage. Through the marriage of Mary of Burgundy with Archduke Maximilian of Austria, those same provinces, then collectively known as the Netherlands, became part of the Habsburg Empire in the early 1500s. When Maximilian's grandson Emperor Charles V divided his empire, the Netherlands was united with Spain (1555) under Philip II, who dedicated himself to the repression of Protestantism. His policies resulted in a revolt led by the Protestants.

Thus began a long war, which, after a 12-year truce (1609–21), became intermingled with the Thirty Years' War. Under the Treaty of Westphalia (1648), which ended the Thirty Years' War, independence was granted to the northern Protestant provinces. The southern half remained Roman Catholic and under Spanish rule. By this time, the southern Low Countries (the territory now known as Belgium) had become embroiled in Franco-Spanish power politics. Belgium was invaded on several occasions, and part of its territory was lost to France.

Under the Peace of Utrecht (1713), which concluded the War of the Spanish Succession, Belgium became part of the Austrian Empire. The country was occupied by the French during the War of the Austrian Succession (1744) but was restored to Austria by the Treaty of Aix-la-Chapelle (1748). Belgium entered a period of recovery and material progress under Maria Theresa and her son Joseph II. The latter's administrative reforms created widespread discontent, however, which culminated in the Révolution Brabançonne of 1789. Leopold II, successor to Joseph II, defeated the Belgians and reoccupied the country, but his regime won little popular support. In 1792, the French army invaded the Belgian provinces, which were formally ceded to France by the Treaty of Campo Formio (1797). This French regime was defeated by the anti-Napoleonic coalition at Waterloo in 1815.

Belgium was united with the Netherlands by the Congress of Vienna in 1815. This action caused widespread discontent, culminating in a series of uprisings. The Dutch were compelled to retreat, and on 4 October 1830, Belgium was declared independent by a provisional government. The powers of the Congress of Vienna met again at London in June 1831 and accepted the separation of Belgium and the Netherlands. However, William I, king of the United Netherlands, refused to recognize the validity of this action. On 2 August 1831, he invaded Belgium, but the Dutch force was repulsed by a French army. In 1839, he was forced to accept the Treaty of the XXIV Articles, by which Belgian independence was formally recognized. The European powers guaranteed Belgium's status as "an independent and perpetually neutral state."

In 1831, the Belgian Parliament had chosen Prince Leopold of Saxe-Coburg-Gotha as ruler of the new kingdom, which was already in the process of industrialization. In 1865, Leopold I was succeeded by Leopold II (r.1865–1909), who financed exploration and settlement in the Congo River Basin of Africa, thereby laying the foundations of Belgium's colonial empire. Leopold's nephew, Albert I, came to the throne in 1909. At the outbreak of World War I, German troops invaded Belgium (4 August 1914). The Belgian army offered fierce resistance, but by the end of November 1914, the only Belgian towns not occupied by the Germans were Nieuport (Nieuwpoort), Furnes (Veurne), and Ypres. Belgium, on the side of the Allies, continued to struggle to liberate the kingdom. Ypres, in particular, was the scene of fierce fighting: nearly 100,000 men lost their lives at a battle near there in April and May 1915 (during which the Germans used chlorine gas), and at least 300,000 Allied troops lost their lives in this region during an offensive that lasted from late July to mid-November 1917.

Under the Treaty of Versailles (1919), Germany ceded to Belgium the German-speaking districts of Eupen, Malmédy, St. Vith, and Moresnet. The country made a remarkable recovery from the war, and by 1923, manufacturing industries were nearly back to normal. After a heated controversy with Germany over reparations payments, Belgium joined France in the occupation of the Ruhr in 1923. In 1934, Leopold III succeeded Albert.

Belgium was again attacked on 10 May 1940, when, without warning, the German air force bombed Belgian airports, railroad stations, and communications centers, and Belgian soil was invaded. Antwerp fell on 18 May and Namur on 23 May. By the end of the month, British, French, and Belgian forces were trapped in northwestern Belgium. King Leopold III surrendered unconditionally on 28 May and was taken prisoner of war. The Belgian government-in-exile, in London, continued the war on the side of the Allies. With the country's liberation from the Germans by the Allies and the well-organized Belgian underground, the Belgian government returned to Brussels in September 1944. During the Allied landings in Normandy, King Leopold III had been deported to Germany. In his absence, his brother Prince Charles was designated by parliament as regent of the kingdom.

The country was economically better off after World War II than after World War I. However, a tense political situation resulted from the split that had developed during the war years between Leopold III and the exiled government in London, which had repudiated the king's surrender. After his liberation by the US 7th Army, the king chose to reside in Switzerland. On 12 March 1950, 57.7% of the Belgian electorate declared itself in favor of allowing Leopold III to return as sovereign. The general elections of 4 June 1950 gave an absolute majority to the Christian Social Party, which favored his return, and on 22 July 1950, Leopold came back from exile. But the Socialists and Liberals continued to oppose his resumption of royal prerogatives, and strikes, riots, and demonstrations ensued. On 1 August 1950, Leopold agreed to abdicate, and on 17 July 1951, one day after Leopold actually gave up his throne, his son Baudouin I was formally proclaimed king.

In 1960, the Belgian Congo (now the Democratic Republic of the Congo), a major vestige of Belgium's colonial empire, became independent. The event was followed by two years of brutal civil war, involving mercenaries from Belgium and other countries. Another Belgian territory in Africa, Ruanda-Urundi, became independent as the two states of Rwanda and Burundi in 1962.

Belgium was transferred into a federal state in July 1993. The country is divided into three regions (Flanders, Wallonia, and Brussels) and three linguistic communities (Flemish, French, and German). Voters directly elect members to the regional parliaments. The French-speaking branch of the Socialist party dominates Wallonia while the Dutch-speaking faction of the Christian Democratic Party governs Flanders. As a participant in the Marshall Plan, a member of NATO, and a leader in the movement for European integration, Belgium shared fully in the European prosperity of the first three postwar decades. Domestic political conflict during this period centered on the unequal distribution of wealth and power between Flemings and Walloons. The Flemings generally contended that they were not given equal opportunity with the Walloons in government and business and that the Dutch language was regarded as inferior to French. The Walloons, in turn, complained of their minority status and the economic neglect of their region and feared being outnumbered by the rapidly growing Flemish population. In response to these conflicts, and after a series of cabinet crises, a revised constitution adopted in 1970 created the framework for complete regional autonomy in economic and cultural spheres. In July 1974, legislation provided for the granting of autonomy to Flanders, Wallonia, and Brussels upon a two-thirds vote in parliament. However, the necessary consensus could not be realized. In 1977, a Christian Social–Socialist coalition proposed to establish a federal administration representing the three regions, but could not obtain parliamentary approval for the proposal. In 1980, however, following several acts of violence as a result of the dispute, parliament allowed the establishment in stages of regional executive and legislative bodies for Flanders and Wallonia, with administrative control over cultural affairs, public health, roads, and urban projects.

Labor unrest and political violence has erupted in the past. In 1982, as a result of an industrial recession, worsened by rising petroleum prices and debt servicing costs, the government imposed an austerity program; an intensification of the austerity program, announced in May 1986, aimed to cut public sector spending, restrain wages, and simplify the taxation system. Vigorous trade-union protests have taken place to protest the freezing of wages and cuts in social security payments. Belgium has one of the largest national debts in Western Europe. Since 1995, however, unions have gone along with pay freezes to restore profitability and improve labor market performance.

A riot in May 1985, at a soccer match between English and Italian clubs, caused the death of 39 spectators and precipitated a po-litical crisis. The government coalition collapsed over charges of inefficient policing, and a general election returned the Christian Social–Liberal alliance to power in November 1985. This in turn accelerated terrorist attacks on public places as well as NATO facilities, responsibility for which was claimed by an extreme left-wing group, Cellules Combattantes Communistes (CCC). Security was tightened in 1986. Linguistic disputes between the French- and Dutch-speaking sections have continued to break out. Extremist parties have sought to capitalize on anti-immigrant feeling among the general population. The Flemish Blok (now Flemish Interest) has been the third-largest party in Flanders and openly advocates an independent Flanders in order to get rid of French-speakers and foreigners.

Economic performance was buoyant from 1996, with growth rates averaging close to 3%; however, with the global economic downturn of the beginning of the 21st century, Belgium's growth rates have lowered. Belgium joined the European economic and monetary union in January 1999 with no problems. Actual unemployment was around 12% as of 2004 but was closer to 20% if elderly unemployed people and people in special government-sponsored programs were included.

Parliamentary elections were held on 18 May 2003, and the Flemish Liberals and Democrats (VLD) finished first in the Flemish elections, defeating the Socialists and Christian Democrats, and the far-right Vlaams Blok. In Wallonia, the Socialists came in first. In both elections, the Greens suffered. Prime Minister Guy Verhofstadt, in office since 1999, formed a center-left coalition of Liberals and Socialists after the May elections. Under Verhofstadt's leadership, Belgium legalized euthanasia and the use of marijuana, and approved gay marriages.

Under Belgium's "universal jurisdiction" law, enacted in 1993, Belgian courts can hear cases involving war crimes and crimes against humanity even if the crimes were not committed in Belgium and did not involve Belgian citizens. Amendments to the law in April 2003 made it harder to bring a case where neither victim, plaintiff, nor accused were Belgian. Israeli Prime Minister Ariel Sharon and former US president George H. W. Bush were charged with war crimes under the law, relating to the 1982 Sabra and Shatila massacres in Lebanon, and the bombing of a civilian shelter in the 1991 Gulf War, respectively. Due to pressure from the United States, Belgian courts now may try only cases which involve charges against Belgian citizens or people resident in Belgium.

The European Union was divided over the use of military force by the United States and UK in the months leading up to the war in Iraq that began on 19 March 2003. Belgium stood with France and Germany in opposing a military response to the crisis.

In 2004, the far-right Vlaams Blok increased its share of the vote in regional and European elections. However, the Belgian High Court ruled that the party was racist and stripped it of the right to state funding and access to television. The party was subsequently reorganized under a new name, the Vlaams Belang, or Flemish Interest.

In May 2005, the government survived a confidence vote, enabling it to put to rest a dispute over the voting rights of French speakers in Dutch-speaking areas around Brussels. This came after months of negotiations over the issue, which sparked demonstrations and riots and brought the government to the brink of collapse.

[13] GOVERNMENT

Belgium is a hereditary monarchy governed under the constitution of 1831. This document has been frequently amended in recent years to grant recognition and autonomy to the Dutch- and French-speaking communities. Executive power is vested in the king, who appoints and removes ministers, civil servants, judges, and officers. In June 1991, parliament approved a constitutional amendment to allow female members of the royal family to succeed to the throne. The monarch, however, would continue to be known as king regardless of gender.

With approval of parliament, the king has the power to declare war and conclude treaties; he is commander-in-chief of the armed forces. According to the constitution, the king's rights include conferring titles of nobility, granting pardons, and administering the coinage of money. However, none of the king's acts becomes effective unless countersigned by a minister, who assumes responsibility for such acts before parliament. Therefore, the king must choose ministers who represent the majority in parliament. Each ministry is created in response to necessity, and there is no fixed number of ministers.

Legislative power is vested in the king and in the two-chamber parliament. The Chamber of Representatives has 150 members, who are elected for a four-year term through a system of proportional representation. The Senate has 71 members, with 40 directly elected and 31 indirectly elected or co-opted for a four-year term. All persons 18 years of age and older are entitled to vote in parliamentary elections, and those who fail to vote are subject to fines. In time of emergency, the king may convoke extraordinary sessions. The government and both chambers may introduce legislation, and both chambers have equal rights. When a bill is introduced, a committee examines it and appoints a rapporteur, who reports on it before the full assembly. The king may dissolve the chambers either simultaneously or separately, but an election must be provided for within 40 days and a session of the new parliament must meet within two months.

In accordance with the constitutional reform of 1980, there are three communities: the Dutch-, the French-, and the German-speaking communities. They have, in a wholly autonomous manner, responsibility for cultural affairs, education, and for matters concerning the individual. There are also three regions (Flanders, Wallonia, and Brussels), which are responsible for the regional aspects of a broad range of concerns, including the economy, energy, public works and housing, employment, and environmental policy. The institutions of the communities and regions are based on the same principles as those of the national political structure: each entity has a "regional parliament" (the council), whose decisions are implemented by a "regional government" (the executive). The council and the executive are directly elected and can only be brought down by a vote of no confidence.

On 14 July 1993, parliament approved a constitutional revision creating a federal state.

[14] POLITICAL PARTIES

Political parties in Belgium are organized along ethnolinguistic lines, with each group in Flanders having its Walloon counterpart. The three major political alliances are the Christian Social parties, which have consisted of the Parti Social Chrétien (PSC) and the Christelijke Volkspartij (CVP); the Socialist parties, the Parti Socialiste (PS) and Socialistische Partij (SP); and the Liberal parties, Parti Réformateur et Liberal (PRL) and Flemish Liberal Democrats (VLD). The People's Union (Volksunie, or VU) was the Flemish nationalistic party, while the French-speaking Democratic Front (Front Démocratique des Francophones—FDF) affirms the rights of the French-speaking population of Brussels. The Flemish Interest (Vlaams Belang—VB) is separatist and antiforeigner while the much smaller far-right National Front (Front Nationale—FN) is openly racist and xenophobic. In 2001, the CVP was renamed the Christian Democratic and Flemish Party (CD and V); the SP was renamed the Social Progressive Alternative Party, or SPA; and the VU split into two parts—the conservative wing established the New Flemish Alliance (NVA), and the left-liberal wing became the Spirit Party. Groen! (formerly AGALEV) is the Flemish Green Party, and ECOLO represents francophone Greens. In 2002, the PSC was renamed the Democratic Humanistic Center (CDH), and the PRL, FDF, and the MCC or Movement of Citizens for Change (created in 1998 by a former leader of the francophone Christian Democrats), formed a new alliance called the Reform Movement (MR). Although these changes in parties' names and new groupings have taken place in the last few years, the Belgian political landscape has not been seriously reorganized.

Following the 13 June 1999 election, party strength in the Chamber of Representatives was as follows: CVP, 14.1% (22 seats); PS, 10.1% (19 seats); SP, 9.6% (14 seats); VLD, 14.31% (23 seats); PRL, 10.1% (18 seats); PSC, 5.9% (10 seats); VB, 9.9% (15 seats); VU, 5.6% (8 seats); ECOLO, 7.3% (11 seats); AGALEV, 7.0% (9 seats); FN 1.5% (1 seat) (150 total seats).

The 1999 election ended the political career of Prime Minister Jean-Luc Dehaene, the Flemish Christian Democrat who led a center-left coalition of francophone and Flemish socialists and his francophone Christian Democratic Party throughout the 1990s. Six parties (French-speaking and Dutch-speaking branches of the Liberal, Socialist, and Green parties) reached a core agreement only three weeks after the election on forming a "blue-red-green" coalition government. It was Belgium's first government in 40 years not to include the Christian Democrats, the first to include the Greens, and the first since 1884 to be led by a Liberal prime minister (Guy Verhofstadt).

The presence of the Greens means a commitment to a progressive withdrawal from nuclear energy, starting with gradual decommissioning of nuclear power stations more than 40 years old. However, the Greens were dealt a setback in the 2003 elections. In the 18 May 2003 elections, the party strength was distributed as follows: VLD, 15.4% (25 seats); SP.A-Spirit, 14.9% (23 seats); CD and V, 13.2% (21 seats); PS, 13% (25 seats); VB, 11.6% (18 seats); MR, 11.4% (24 seats); CDH, 5.5% (8 seats); N-VA, 3.1% (1 seat); ECOLO, 3.1% (4 seats); AGALEV, 2.5%, no seats; FN, 2%, (1 seat), and Vivant (Alive), a human rights party, took 1.2% of the vote but secured no seats. Verhofstadt formed a center-left coalition government.

[15] LOCAL GOVERNMENT

Belgium is divided into 10 provinces: Antwerp, East Flanders, West Flanders, and Limburg in the north, Hainaut, Liège, Luxembourg, and Namur in the south, Flemish Brabant, and Walloon Brabant. Each of the provinces has a council of 50 to 90 members elected for four-year terms by direct suffrage and empowered to legislate in matters of local concern. A governor, appointed by the king, is the highest executive officer in each province.

There are 482 communes. Each municipality has a town council elected for a six-year term. The council elects an executive body called the board of aldermen. The head of the municipality is the burgomaster, who is appointed by the sovereign upon nomination by the town council. Recently, the number of municipalities has been greatly reduced through consolidation.

In 1971, Brussels was established as a separate bilingual area, presided over by a proportionally elected metropolitan council. Linguistic parity was stipulated for the council's executive committee.

16 JUDICIAL SYSTEM

Belgian law is modeled on the French legal system. The judiciary is an independent branch of government on an equal footing with the legislative and the executive branches. Minor offenses are dealt with by justices of the peace and police tribunals. More serious offenses and civil lawsuits are brought before district courts of first instance. Other district courts are commerce and labor tribunals. Verdicts rendered by these courts may be appealed before five regional courts of appeal or the five regional labor courts in Antwerp, Brussels, Gent, Mons, and Liège. All offenses punishable by prison sentences of more than five years must be dealt with by the 11 courts of assize (one for each province and the city of Brussels), the only jury courts in Belgium. The highest courts are five civil and criminal courts of appeal and the supreme Court of Cassation. The latter's function is to verify that the law has been properly applied and interpreted. The constitutionality of legislation is the province of the Council of State, an advisory legal group.

When an error of procedure is found, the decision of the lower court is overruled and the case must be tried again. The death penalty was abolished for all crimes in Belgium in 1996.

A system of military tribunals, including appellate courts, handles both military and common-law offenses involving military personnel. The government is considering narrowing the jurisdiction of these courts to military offenses. All military tribunals consist of four officers and a civilian judge.

Detainees must be brought before a judge within 24 hours of arrest. Although there are provisions for bail, it is rarely granted. Defendants have right to be present, to have counsel, to confront witnesses, to present evidence, and to appeal.

17 ARMED FORCES

Belgium's active armed forces in 2005 numbered 36,900, with 18,650 reservists. In terms of personnel, the army is the largest, with 24,800 active members (4,200 reservists), followed by the air force with 6,350 active members (1,600 reservists), and the navy with 2,450 active personnel (1,200 reservists). Belgium also has an 1,800 active member medical service (850 reservists) and a Joint Service force of 1,500 active members (2,200 reservists). The army is equipped with 52 main battle tanks, 104 armored infantry fighting vehicles, 223 armored personnel carriers, and 132 artillery pieces (48 self-propelled). The air force operated 90 combat aircraft, in addition to 36 transports, two early warning/electronic intelligence aircraft, and 49 helicopters. The navy operates a pair of guided missile frigates in addition to one patrol vessel, and

six mine warfare/counter measures/hunter ships and nine logistics and support vessels. In 2005 Belgium spent $3.35 billion on defense.

18 INTERNATIONAL COOPERATION

Belgium is a charter member of the UN, having joined on 27 December 1945, and participates in ECE and all the nonregional specialized agencies. Paul-Henri Spaak of Belgium served as the UN General Assembly's first president (1946–47); from 1957 to 1961, he also served as the secretary-general of NATO, of which Belgium is also a member. The country has been partnered with Luxembourg in the Belgium-Luxembourg Economic Union (BLEU) since 1922. In 1958, Belgium signed a treaty forming the Benelux (Belgium-Netherlands-Luxembourg) Economic Union, following a 10-year period in which a customs union of the three countries was in effect. Belgium is also a member of the Asian Development Bank, Council of Europe, the European Union, the European Investment Bank, the Paris Club (G-10), G-9, the Western European Union, and OECD. It is also is a permanent observer of the OAS and a member of the OSCE (1973) and the WTO (1995).

Brussels, the seat of EU institutions, has become an important regional center for Western Europe. In 1967, the Supreme Headquarters Allied Powers Europe (SHAPE) was transferred from Rocquencourt, near Paris, to a site near Mons. On 16 October 1967, the NATO Council's headquarters were moved from Paris to Brussels. Belgium is a member of the Permanent Court of Arbitration.

Belgium is part of the Organization for the Prohibition of Chemical Weapons, Nuclear Suppliers Group (London Group), the Australia Group, the Nuclear Energy Agency, the European Space Agency, the Zangger Committee, and the European Organization for Nuclear Research. The country has offered support for UN efforts in Kosovo (est. 1999), India and Pakistan (est. 1949), Burundi (est. 2004), and the DROC (est. 1999).

In environmental cooperation, Belgium is part of the Antarctic Treaty, the Basel Convention, the Conventions on Biological Diversity and Air Pollution, Ramsar, CITES, the London Convention, the International Tropical Timber Agreements, the Kyoto Protocol, the Montréal Protocol, MARPOL, the Nuclear Test Ban Treaty, and UN Conventions on the Law of the Sea, Climate Change, and Desertification.

19 ECONOMY

In relation to its size and population, Belgium is among the most highly industrialized countries in Europe. Poor in natural resources, it imports raw materials in great quantity and processes them largely for export. Exports equal around 80% of GDP, and about three-quarters of Belgium's foreign trade is with other EU countries.

With the exception of Luxembourg and Ireland, Belgium is the most open economy in the EU as measured by the value of exports and imports relative to GDP, and one of the most open in the world. Belgium's economy is highly integrated with that of its three main neighbors—Germany, France, and the Netherlands.

For a century and a half, Belgium maintained its status as an industrial country, not only by virtue of its geographical position and transport facilities but also because of its ability for most of this period to shape production to meet the changing requirements of world commerce. Since the 1950s, the Belgian parliament enacted economic expansion laws to enable long-established industries to modernize obsolete plant equipment. Belgium's highly developed transportation systems are closely linked with those of its neighbors. Its chief port, Antwerp, is one of the world's busiest. Belgium has a highly skilled and productive workforce, and the economy is diversified. By 2004, the service sector accounted for approximately 73% of GDP, followed by industry (25.7%) and agriculture (1.3%).

Real growth averaged 5.4% annually during 1967–73 but, like that of other OECD countries, slumped to 2.5% during 1973–80, and 0.7% during 1981–85. It averaged 2.6% during 1984–91 and was 2.3% in 1995. In 1993, Belgium's recession was the most severe in the EU after Germany's. By 1998, real growth stood at 2.8%. Real GDP growth in 2003 was 1.1% due to the global economic downturn existing in 2001–03. Growth picked up in 2004, to 2.7%, but was expected to slow to 1.3% in 2005, due to the impact of high oil prices on Belgium and its export markets. A slight recovery was forecast for 2006 (1.7%) and 2007 (2%). Average inflation was forecast at 2.7% in 2005, 2.5% in 2006, and 2.1% in 2007. The government will need to keep the budget from falling into deficit; budget surpluses will be needed until around 2030 to provide for the costs of an aging population. The 2006 budget was expected to be in balance for the seventh year in a row.

In 1993, when Belgium became a federal state with three distinct regions (Flanders, Wallonia, and Brussels), substantial economic powers were given to each region, such as jurisdiction over industrial development, research, trade promotion, and environmental regulation. Belgium has been seen as a "laboratory state," in that its federal system might stand as a precursor to a more unified EU based on regional divisions.

In 2004 Belgium had the fourth-highest standard of living in the world. However, being a highly taxed and indebted country, some businesses have stated Belgium stifles private enterprise.

20 INCOME

The US Central Intelligence Agency (CIA) reports that in 2005 Belgium's gross domestic product (GDP) was estimated at $329.3 billion. The CIA defines GDP as the value of all final goods and services produced within a nation in a given year and computed on the basis of purchasing power parity (PPP) rather than value as measured on the basis of the rate of exchange based on current dollars. The per capita GDP was estimated at $31,800. The annual growth rate of GDP was estimated at 1.5%. The average inflation rate in 2005 was 2.7%. It was estimated that agriculture accounted for 1% of GDP, industry 24%, and services 74.9% in 2004.

According to the World Bank, in 2003 remittances from citizens working abroad totaled $3.933 billion or about $378 per capita and accounted for approximately 1.3% of GDP.

The World Bank reports that in 2003 household consumption in Belgium totaled $165.38 billion or about $15,902 per capita based on a GDP of $301.9 billion, measured in current dollars rather than PPP. Household consumption includes expenditures of individuals, households, and nongovernmental organizations on goods and services, excluding purchases of dwellings. It was estimated that for the period 1990 to 2003 household consumption grew at an average annual rate of 1.8%. In 2001 it was estimated that approximately 17% of household consumption was spent on food, 8% on fuel, 3% on health care, and 1% on education. It was estimated that in 1989 about 4% of the population had incomes below the poverty line.

21 LABOR

As of 2005, the Belgian workforce was estimated at 4.77 million people. In 2003, it was estimated that the service industry employed 74.2% of workers, while 24.5% were employed in industry, and 1.3% in agriculture. The overall unemployment rate climbed to 12% in 1998, but fell to 7.2% by 2002. In 2005, unemployment had risen slightly to an estimated 7.6%.

The law provides workers with the right to associate freely and workers fully exercise their right to organize and join unions. Approximately 63% of the country's workforce (employed and unemployed) are union members. Workers have a broad right to strike except in "essential" industries including the military. A single collective bargaining agreement, negotiated every other year, covers about 2.4 million private sector workers. This gives unions considerable control over economic policy. In addition, unions also freely exercise the right to strike.

Belgium has a five-day, 38-hour workweek. Overtime pay is time-and-a-half on Mondays through Saturdays, with double-time paid on Sundays. Overtime is limited to 11 hours daily and up to 50 hours weekly. In addition, an 11-hour rest period is required between two work periods. Children under the age of 15 years are prohibited from working. Those between the ages of 15 and 18 may engage in part-time work-study programs, or work during school vacations. Child labor laws and standards are strictly enforced. In 2005, the national minimum wage was $1,492 per month, in addition to extensive social benefits. This minimum wage provides a decent standard of living for workers and their families.

22 AGRICULTURE

Agriculture's role in the economy continues to decrease. In 2003, about 1.3% of the employed population worked on farms, compared with 3.7% in 1973. Agriculture's share in the GNP fell from 3.8% in 1973 to about 1.5% in 2002. Many marginal farms have disappeared; the remaining farms are small but intensively cultivated. Average farm size grew from 6.17 hectares (15.2 acres) in 1959 to 26.88 hectares (66.4 acres) in 2005, when there were 51,540 farms (down from 269,060 in 1959). About 80% of the country's food needs are covered domestically. The richest farm areas are in Flanders and Brabant. About 1.4 million hectares (3.4 million acres), or 45% of Belgium's total area, are under cultivation. Over half the land cultivated is used for pastureland or green fodder; one-quarter is used for the production of cereals. Total production of grains in 2004 was around 2.5 million tons, of which wheat accounted for about 65%; corn, 22%; barley, 10%; and spelt, triticale, oats, rye, and other grains, 8%.

Government price policy encourages increased production of wheat and barley with decreasing production of rye and oats. Increased emphasis is being placed on horticulture, and nearly all fruits found in temperate climates are grown in Belgium. Chief among these are apples, pears, and cherries. Producers of tomatoes and apples were obliged to refrain from marketing part of their 1992 harvests in order to hold up prices. Tomato production in 2004 totaled 250,000 tons, about 1% of European production.

Belgium imports considerable quantities of bread and feed grains, fodder concentrates, and fruits. Its only agricultural exports are processed foods and a few specialty items such as endive, chicory, flower bulbs, sugar, and chocolates. In 2004, agricultural products amounted to 8.6% of exports; there was an agricultural trade surplus of $3.2 billion that year. Imports from other EU countries account for 85% of agricultural imports.

23 ANIMAL HUSBANDRY

Livestock raising is the most important single sector of Belgian agriculture, accounting for over 60% of agricultural production. In 2004 there were about 2.7 million head of cattle, 6.4 million hogs, 151,000 sheep, and 33,000 horses. Belgian farmers breed some of the finest draft horses in the world, including the famous Percherons.

The country is self-sufficient in butter, milk, meat, and eggs. Some cheese is imported, mainly from the Netherlands. Milk production amounted to 3.35 million tons in 2004.

24 FISHING

The chief fishing ports are Zeebrugge and Ostend (Oostende, Ostende), from which a fleet of 156 boats (with a combined 23,262 GRT) sail the North Atlantic from the North Sea to Iceland. The total catch in 2003 was 27,800 tons, whose exports were valued at $762.4 million. Principal species caught that year were plaice, sole, turbot, and cod.

25 FORESTRY

Forests cover 21% of the area of Belgium. Commercial production of timber is limited; roundwood production in 2003 was estimated at 4.76 million cu m (168 million cu ft). Most common trees are beech and oak, but considerable plantings of conifers have been made in recent years. Belgium serves as a large transshipment center for temperate hardwood logs, softwood lumber, and softwood plywood. Large quantities of timber for the woodworking industry are typically imported from the Democratic Republic of the Congo. The total output of Belgium's wood processing and furniture industry in 2004 was €5.65 billion, with furniture accounting for 52%; wood panels, 22%; and construction, packing, and other wood products, 26%.

The total value of exports of forest products in 2003 was $4.7 billion, with imports of $3.9 billion. Belgium's wood processing industry consists of over 2,000 enterprises, 65% of which are furniture manufacturers, typically with fewer than five employees.

26 MINING

Belgium's only remaining active mining operations in 2003 were for the production of sand and gravel and the quarrying of some stone, including specialty marbles and the Belgian blue-gray limestone called "petit granite." An important producer of marble for more than 2,000 years, Belgium was recognized for the diversity and quality of its dimension stone. All the marble quarries are in Wallonia, and red, black, and gray are the principal color ranges of the marble. The country was an important producer of such industrial materials as carbonates, including limestone, dolomite, silica sand, whiting, and sodium sulfate.

The mineral-processing industry was a significant contributor to the Belgian economy. The refining of copper, zinc, and minor metals, and the production of steel (all from imported materials), were the most developed mineral industries in Belgium. The country possessed Europe's largest electrolytic copper and zinc refineries, and one of the continent's largest lead refineries. In addition, Belgium retained its position as the world's diamond capital. Estimated production figures for 2003, in metric tons, included: secondary copper, 125,000 and primary zinc, 230,000. Hydraulic cement output in 2003 totaled 8 million tons, with lime and deadburned dolomite at 1.7 million tons. Quarried Belgian bluestone, or petit granite, totaled 1.2 million cu m in 2003. Petite granite, which is actually a dark blue–gray crinoidal limestone, was one of the most important facing stones the country produces.

Belgium was once a major producer of coal, as the Belgian coal mining industry dates back to the 12th century. Coal was mined in the Sambre-Meuse Valley; the last mines closed in 1992. Metallic mining was in its heyday from 1850 to 1870, after which mining activity decreased until the last iron ore operations at Musson and Halanzy were closed in 1978. Belgium has no economically exploitable reserves of metal ores.

27 ENERGY AND POWER

In 1998 there were about 120 power stations operating in Belgium; capacity as of 2002 was 14.223 million kW. Electricity generated in that year totaled 76.516 billion kWh, of which 44.992 billion kWh was from nuclear sources and 29.535 kWh came from fossil fuels. In 1981, only 25% of the nation's power was from nuclear sources. By 2002, that figure had risen to 40%, or 5.738 million kW. Hydroelectric generation in 2002 totaled 0.356 billion kWh, while geothermal and other sources accounted for 1.633 kWh. Electricity consumption in the same year was 78.760 billion kWh. The principal sources of primary energy for conventional power production are low-grade coal and by-products of the oil industry. Belgium is heavily dependent on imports of crude oil, but it exports refined oil products. Power rates in Belgium are regulated through a voluntary agreement between labor, industry, and private power interests. In 2000, total energy consumption was 2.8 quadrillion Btu, of which 45% came from petroleum, 23% from natural gas, 12% from coal, 17% from nuclear energy, and the remainder from hydroelectric and other renewable sources.

28 INDUSTRY

Industry, highly developed in Belgium, is devoted mainly to the processing of imported raw materials into semifinished and finished products, most of which are then exported. Industry accounted for 24% of GDP in 2004. Steel production is the single most important sector of industry, with Belgium ranking high among world producers of iron and steel. However, it must import all its iron ore, which comes principally from Brazil, West Africa, and Venezuela. About four-fifths of Belgium's steel products and more than three-quarters of its crude steel output are exported. In recent years, Belgian industry has been hampered by high labor costs, aging plant facilities, and a shrinking market for its products. Nevertheless, industrial production rose by nearly 11% between 1987 and 1991, as a result of falling energy costs (after 1985) and financial costs, and only a moderate rise in wage costs. Industrial production continued to rise in the late 1990s; 1997 registered a 4% growth rate, while it slowed to 3.1% in 1998. The industrial growth rate in 2000 was 5.3%; it was -0.5% in 2001, due to the global economic downturn, and rebounded to an estimated 3.5% in 2004.

Production of crude steel declined from 16.2 million tons in 1974 to 11.3 million tons in 1991, while the output of finished steel dropped from 12.2 million tons to 8.98 million tons. In 2004, Belgium's total crude steel production was 11.7 million metric tons. Belgium as a steel-producing country ranked 18th in the world in 2004, and was the 5th largest steel exporting country in the world. The industry employs some 19,500 people. By 1981, 60% of all Belgian steel production and 80% of all Wallonian steel (concentrated in Charleroi and Liège) came under the control of a single company, the government-owned Cockerill-Sambre. Government subsidies for this firm ended (in conformity with EC policy) in 1985. In 1998, French-owned Usinor agreed to take over Cockerill-Sambre, the last major steel making enterprise in Wallonia. As a result of this and other mergers, the Belgian steel industry is now dominated by one multinational company, Arcelor, based in Luxembourg. Arcelor, which was created in 2001, is the largest steel company in the world and is a merger of Usinor, Arbed, and Arcelia.

Belgium also produces significant amounts of crude copper, crude zinc, and crude lead. The bulk of metal manufactures consists of heavy machinery, structural steelwork, and industrial equipment. The railroad equipment industry supplies one of the most extensive railroad systems in Europe. An important shipbuilding industry is centered in Temse, south of Antwerp. Belgian engineering and construction firms have built steel plants, chemical works, power stations, port facilities, and office buildings throughout the world.

Belgium's automotive industry has always been one of the strongest components of its economy. Belgium is a world leader in the car assembly industry; with nearly 95% of its output designed for export, Belgium has the highest per capita production in the world. Belgium's local automotive production in 2003 was estimated at $23.5 billion.

The textile industry, dating from the Middle Ages, produces cottons, woolens, linens, and synthetic fibers. With the exception of flax, all raw materials are imported. Centers of the textile industry are Bruges, Brussels, Verviers, Gent, Courtrai (Kortrijk), and Malines (Mechelen). Carpets are made in large quantities at Saint-Nicolas (Sint-Niklaas). Brussels and Bruges are noted for fine linen and lace. Foreign competition has cut into the Belgian textile industry, however. Following the expiration of the World Trade Organization's longstanding system of textile quotas at the beginning of 2005, the EU signed an agreement with China in June 2005 imposing new quotas on 10 categories of textile goods, limiting growth in those categories to between 8% and 12.5% a year. The agreement runs until 2007, and was designed to give European textile manufacturers time to adjust to a world of unfettered competition. Nevertheless, barely a month after the EU-China agreement was signed, China reached its quotas for sweaters, followed soon after by blouses, bras, T-shirts, and flax yarn. Tens of millions of garments piled up in warehouses and customs checkpoints, which affected both retailers and consumers.

The chemical industry manufactures a wide range of products, from heavy chemicals and explosives to pharmaceuticals and photographic supplies. The diamond-cutting industry in Antwerp supplies most of the United States's industrial diamond requirements. Eighty percent of all rough diamonds are handled in Antwerp, and 50% of all polished diamonds pass through Antwerp. The Antwerp World Diamond Center is concentrated in a two-square-mile area, comprising more than 1,500 diamond companies and four diamond bourses. Those working in the Belgian diamond industry are increasingly being pressured to refrain from buying "conflict diamonds" from Africa, whose proceeds have fueled civil wars in a number of African countries, including Sierra Leone, the Democratic Republic of the Congo, and Angola. Belgium has one of the largest glass industries in the world. Val St. Lambert is especially known for its fine crystal glassware. Belgian refineries (chiefly in Antwerp) turn out oil products.

29 SCIENCE AND TECHNOLOGY

The Royal Academy of Sciences, Letters, and Fine Arts, founded in Brussels in 1772, and since divided into French and Flemish counterparts, has sections for mathematics, physical sciences, and the natural sciences. There are, in addition, many specialized societies for the study of medicine, biology, zoology, anthropology, astronomy, chemistry, mathematics, geology, and engineering. The National Scientific Research Fund (inaugurated in 1928), in Brussels, promotes scientific research by providing subsidies and grants to scientists and students. The Royal Institute of Natural Sciences (founded in 1846), also in Brussels, provides general scientific services in the areas of biology, mineralogy, paleontology, and zoology. In 1987–97, science and engineering students accounted for 41% of college and university enrollment. In 2004 total research and development (R&D) expenditures provisionally amounted to €6.712 billion. As of 2001 (the latest year for which there is complete data) there were 1,462 technicians and 3,134 researchers per million people actively engaged in R&D. In that same year, 64.3% of R&D expenditures came from business, with 21.4% from the government, and 11.8% from foreign sources. In 2002, high technology exports totaled $15.736 billion or 11% of manufactured exports.

Among the nation's distinguished scientific institutions are the Center for the Study of Nuclear Energy in Mol (founded in 1952); the National Botanical Garden of Belgium in Meise (founded in 1870); the Royal Observatory of Belgium in Brussels (founded in 1826); the Institute of Chemical Research in Tervuren (founded in 1928); the Royal Meteorological Institute in Brussels (reorganized in 1913); the Von Karman Institute for Fluid Dynamics in Rhode-St-Genese (founded in 1956) and supported by NATO; and the Institute of Spatial Aeronomy in Brussels (founded in 1964). Belgium has 18 universities and colleges offering degrees in basic and applied sciences.

30 DOMESTIC TRADE

Brussels is the main center for commerce and for the distribution of manufactured goods. Other important centers include Antwerp, Liège, and Ghent. Most large wholesale firms engage in import and export. Customary terms of sale are payment within 30–90 days after delivery, depending upon the commodity and the credit rating of the purchaser.

In 1994, the government began privatization efforts of several public sector corporations, including banks and airlines. The domestic market is relatively small. Instead, the economy relies heavily on trade as various industries have capitalized on the country's prime central European location, which serves as a regional transit and distribution center. The country also serves as a vital test market for many European goods and franchises.

Business hours are mainly from 8 or 9 AM to 5 or 6 PM, Monday through Friday, with an hour for lunch. Banks are open from 9 AM to between 3:30 and 5 PM, Monday–Friday. Retail stores are generally open from 9 AM to 6 PM, Monday through Saturday; some may close for lunch. Larger stores and shopping centers stay open until 9 PM on Fridays. Important international trade fairs are held annually in Brussels and Ghent. Advertising techniques are well developed, and the chief media are the press, radio, and television.

31 FOREIGN TRADE

Foreign trade plays a greater role in the Belgian economy than in any other EU country except Luxembourg. Exports constituted around 80% of GDP in the early 2000s. Belgium's chief exports are iron and steel (semifinished and manufactured), chemicals, textiles, machinery, road vehicles and parts, nonferrous metals, diamonds, and foodstuffs. Its imports are general manufactures, foodstuffs, diamonds, metals and metal ores, petroleum and petroleum products, chemicals, clothing, machinery, electrical equipment, and motor vehicles. In 1921, Belgium partnered with Luxembourg in the Belgium-Luxembourg Economic Union (BLEU).

In 2004, 77.4% of Belgium's exports and 74% of its imports were traded with EU countries. Belgium's leading markets in 2004 were Germany (17.5% of total exports), France (17.4%), the Netherlands (12.9%), the United Kingdom (8.6%), and Italy (5.4%). Belgium's leading suppliers in 2004 were the Netherlands (19.9% of all imports), Germany (16.6%), France (13.7%), the United Kingdom (7.8%), and the United States (5.6%).

32 BALANCE OF PAYMENTS

Belgium ran deficits on current accounts each year from 1976 through 1984. Trade deficits, incurred consistently in the late 1970s and early 1980s, were only partly counterbalanced by invisible exports, such as tourism and services, and capital transfers. Belgium in the early 2000s had a high current account surplus—$14.3 billion in 2003, and averaging 4.2% of GDP from 2000–04. The current account surplus in 2004 was estimated at $11.4 billion.

Belgium in the early 2000s was attempting to meet the EU's Maastricht target of a cumulative public debt of not more than 60% of GDP. However, the public debt only fell below 100% of GDP at the end of 2003, for the first time in nearly 30 years. Public debt stood at 96.2% of GDP in 2004.

The total value of exports in 2003 was estimated at $189.2 billion. Imports were estimated at $173 billion, for a trade surplus of $16.2 billion.

33 BANKING AND SECURITIES

The National Bank of Belgium (Banque Nationale de Belgique-BNB, founded in 1850), the sole bank of issue, originally was a joint-stock institution. The Belgian government took over 50% of its shares in 1948. Its directors are appointed by the government, but the bank retains a large degree of autonomy. In Belgium, most regulatory powers are vested in the Banking Commission, an autonomous administrative body that monitors compliance of all banks with national banking laws. In order to restrain inflation and maintain monetary stability, the BNB varied its official discount rate from 2.75% in 1953 to a peak of 8.75% in December 1974; by 1978, the rate was reduced to 6%, but it rose steadily to a high of 15% in 1981 before declining to 11.5% at the end of 1982 and 9.75% by December 1985. By 1993 the discount rate was 5.25%. At the time of its abolition on December 15, 1998, the discount rate was 2.75%.

By law, the name "bank" in Belgium may be used only by institutions engaged mainly in deposit bank activities and short-term operations. Commercial banks are not authorized to invest long-term capital in industrial or business enterprises. The largest commercial bank, the General Banking Society, came into being in 1965 through a merger of three large banks. The National Society for Industrial Credit provides medium-term loans to in-

Principal Trading Partners – Belgium (2003)

(In millions of US dollars)

Country	Exports	Imports	Balance
World	255,300.6	235,365.9	19,934.7
Germany	49,863.2	41,378.0	8,485.2
France-Monaco	44,204.9	31,200.1	13,004.8
Netherlands	29,854.6	39,035.7	-9,181.1
United Kingdom	23,459.0	17,784.9	5,674.1
United States	16,786.9	13,837.6	2,949.3
Italy-San Marino-Holy See	13,853.3	7,879.5	5,973.8
Spain	10,122.7	4,774.8	5,347.9
Areas nes	4,757.0	...	4,757.0
India	4,350.9	1,998.6	2,352.3
Sweden	3,594.9	5,152.1	-1,557.2

(...) data not available or not significant.

SOURCE: *2003 International Trade Statistics Yearbook*, New York: United Nations, 2004.

Balance of Payments – Belgium (2003)

(In millions of US dollars)

Current Account		**11,623.0**
Balance on goods	9,532.0	
Imports	-193,767.0	
Exports	203,299.0	
Balance on services	1,919.0	
Balance on income	6,830.0	
Current transfers	-6,658.0	
Capital Account		**-968.0**
Financial Account		**726.0**
Direct investment abroad	-23,302.0	
Direct investment in Belgium	33,768.0	
Portfolio investment assets	-3,190.0	
Portfolio investment liabilities	5,739.0	
Financial derivatives	-3,848.0	
Other investment assets	-80,013.0	
Other investment liabilities	71,572.0	
Net Errors and Omissions		**-13,104.0**
Reserves and Related Items		**1,723.0**

(...) data not available or not significant.

SOURCE: *Balance of Payment Statistics Yearbook 2004*, Washington, DC: International Monetary Fund, 2004.

dustrial firms and exporters. Other institutions supply credit to small business and to farmers. The leading savings institute is the General Savings and Retirement Fund, which operates mainly through post office branches. The International Monetary Fund reports that in 2001, currency and demand deposits—an aggregate commonly known as M1—were equal to $63.1 billion. In that same year, M2—an aggregate equal to M1 plus savings deposits, small time deposits, and money market mutual funds—was $241.7 billion.

The Bourse in Belgium is a very old institution. As early as the 13th century, merchants from the main commercial centers, particularly Genoa and Venice, used to gather in front of the house of the Van der Bourse family in Brugge, which was then the prosperous trading center of the low countries. The word "Bourse" is often considered to have originated in Brugge.

The Brussels Stock Exchange was founded in 1801 after Napoleon, then Consul of the Republic, issued a decree of the 13th Messidor in the 9th Year that "There shall be an exchange in Brussels, in the Department of the Dyle." The law of 30 December 1867, completely abolished the provisions then in force controlling the profession of broker, the organization of the exchanges and the operations transacted there. After the crisis of 1929 through 1933, a commission was created to assure investors of greater security. The Commercial Code of 1935 still controls the organization of the stock exchange in large measure. Since the law of 4 December 1990, the Société de la Bourse de valeirs mobiliéres de Bruxelles (SBVMB) is organized under the form of a cooperative society. There is also an exchange in Antwerp. Market capitalization as of December 2004 stood at $818.520 billion, with the local BEL 20 Index up 30.7% from the previous year at 2,932.6.

The exchanges deal in national, provincial, and municipal government bonds, government lottery bonds, and company shares. The issuance of shares and bonds to the public is subject to the control of the Banking Commission in Brussels. There are also a number of special industrial exchanges; the most prominent one is the Diamond Exchange in Antwerp.

34 INSURANCE

Insurance transactions are regulated by the Insurance Control Office of the Ministry of Economic Affairs. Compulsory classes of insurance in Belgium are workers' compensation, automobile liability, and inland marine liabilities. Life and disability insurance needs are to a large extent met by Belgium's extensive social security system. Compulsory insurance includes third-party automobile liability, workers' compensation, "no fault" liability for property owners with free access to property, hunter's liability, and nuclear liability for power facilities.

In 1996 and 1997, a general pattern of mergers and acquisitions among European union insurers formed, as companies sought to strategically take advantage of the single market in insurance, which became effective in July 1994. Many insurance companies throughout the European Union (EU) are considered too small to operate effectively on an international scale, to meet the challenge of *bancassurance*, or to invest sufficiently in the new technology needed to survive in the increasingly competitive industry. In 2003, the value of direct premiums written totaled $33.814 billion, of which $21.004 billion was accounted for by life insurance premiums. The country's top life insurer that year was ETHIAS Life,

Public Finance – Belgium (2002)		
(In millions of euros, central government figures)		
Revenue and Grants	**112,364**	**100.0%**
Tax revenue	69,460	61.8%
Social contributions	39,976	35.6%
Grants	408	0.4%
Other revenue	2,521	2.2%
Expenditures	**112,249**	**100.0%**
General public services	42,466	37.8%
Defense	3,233	2.9%
Public order and safety	2,568	2.3%
Economic affairs	4,859	4.3%
Environmental protection	66	0.1%
Housing and community amenities	...	...
Health	16,748	14.9%
Recreational, culture, and religion	274	0.2%
Education	2,975	2.7%
Social protection	39,060	34.8%
(…) data not available or not significant.		

SOURCE: *Government Finance Statistics Yearbook 2004*, Washington, DC: International Monetary Fund, 2004.

with gross life premiums written of $3,458.8 million. The top nonlife insurer was Axa Belgium, with gross written nonlife premiums (including healthcare) of $1,265.1 million in 2003.

35 PUBLIC FINANCE

The government's budgetary year coincides with the calendar year. In the final months of the year, the minister of finance places before Parliament a budget containing estimated revenues and expenditures for the following year, and a finance law authorizing the collection of taxes is passed before 1 January. Inasmuch as expenditure budgets generally are not all passed by then, "provisional twelfths" enable the government to meet expenditures month by month, until all expenditure budgets are passed. Current expenditures, supposedly covered by the usual revenues (including all tax and other government receipts), relate to the normal functioning of government services and to pension and public debt charges. Capital expenditures consist mainly of public projects and are normally covered by borrowings. Improvements in fiscal and external balances in the early 1990s and a slowdown in external debt growth enables the Belgian government to easily obtain loans on the local credit market. As a member of the G-10 group of leading financial nations, Belgium actively participates in the IMF, World Bank, and the Paris Club. Belgium is a leading donor nation, and it closely follows development and debt issues, particularly with respect to the DROC and other African nations.

The US Central Intelligence Agency (CIA) estimated that in 2005 Belgium's central government took in revenues of approximately $180.4 billion and had expenditures of $180.5 billion. Revenues minus expenditures totaled approximately -$100 million. Public debt in 2005 amounted to 93.6% of GDP. Total external debt was $980.1 billion.

Government outlays by function were as follows: general public services, 37.8%; defense, 2.9%; public order and safety, 2.3%; economic affairs, 4.3%; environmental protection, 0.1%; health,

14.9%; recreation, culture, and religion, 0.2%; education, 2.7%; and social protection, 34.8%.

36 TAXATION

The most important direct tax is the income tax. Since enactment of the tax law of 20 November 1962, this tax has been levied on the total amount of each taxpayer's income from all sources. As of 2005, the top individual income tax rate is 50%, excluding local taxes. Local taxes are levied at rates varying from 4–10%. Taxes are not paid in one lump sum, but rather by a series of prepayments on the various sources of income. There is a withholding tax on salaries that is turned over directly to the revenue officer. Self-employed persons send a prepayment to the revenue officer during the first half of July. Banks and stockbrokers who offer dividends must first deduct a prepayment of 25%. Taxes on real estate are based on the assessed rental value.

The general corporate income tax, which is levied on all distributed profits, was lowered from 48% to 45% in 1982, to 43% in 1987, to 38% in 1993, and stands at 33% as of 2005. Nondistributed profits are taxed at progressive rates ranging from 28–41%. In some instances, local government bodies are entitled to impose additional levies. Numerous tax exemptions are granted to promote investments in Belgium.

In 1971, a value-added tax system was introduced, replacing sales and excise taxes. A general rate of 21% was applied as of 1996 to industrial goods, with a reduced rate of 6% applying to basic necessities and an interim rate of 12% to certain other products, such as social housing and agricultural products.

37 CUSTOMS AND DUTIES

Customs duties are levied at the time of importation and are generally ad valorem. Belgium applies the EU common external tariff (CET) to goods imported from non-EU countries. There is a single duty system (the CET) among all EU members for products coming from non-EU members. Theoretically, no customs duties apply for goods imported into Belgium from EU countries. Value-added taxes are levied on the importation of foodstuffs, tobacco, alcohol, beer, mineral water, and fuel oils. There are no export duties.

38 FOREIGN INVESTMENT

Foreign investment in Belgium generally takes the form of establishing subsidiaries of foreign firms in the country. Belgium is the economic as well as the political center of Europe. The Belgian government actively promotes foreign investment. In recent years, the government has given special encouragement to industries that will create new skills and increase export earnings. The government grants equal treatment under the law, as well as special tax inducements and assistance, to foreign firms that establish enterprises in the country. There is no regulation prescribing the proportion of foreign to domestic capital that may be invested in an enterprise. The foreign investor can repatriate all capital profits and long-term credit is available. Local authorities sometimes offer special assistance and concessions to new foreign enterprises in their area. Since the start of EU's single market, most, but not all,

trade and investment rules have been implemented by Belgium in order to be in line with other EU member nations.

The corporation tax rate was reduced in 2003 to 33.99% (24.98% for small companies). Over time, the Belgian government intends to reduce the corporate tax rate to 30%. The standard rate of value-added tax (VAT) is 21%. Overall, Belgium has strong competitive advantages, such as an excellent transportation infrastructure, high-quality industrial sites, and a skilled and productive workforce.

As of 2005, some of Belgium's leading sectors for US foreign investment were automotive parts and service equipment, biotechnology, computer services and software, consumer goods, electric power systems and services, environmental technologies, plastic materials and resins, telecommunication services and equipment, textile fabrics, and travel and tourism services.

Between 2001 and 2005, Belgium was expected to attract an annual average of $30.2 billion in foreign direct investment. With 3.4% of total world FDI, Belgium ranks seventh. Countries with large investments in Belgium include the United States, Germany, United Kingdom, Netherlands, France, and Switzerland. In 2004, foreign direct investment outflows from the 25 EU countries fell by some 25%, while inflows coming from the rest of the world fell by more than 50%. These falls were strongly influenced by investment flows with the United States. With inflows higher than outflows by €4 billion, Belgium was the EU's largest net recipient of FDI from outside the EU. Belgium was the fourth highest recipient of FDI from within the EU in 2004, at €19 billion, behind the United Kingdom, Luxembourg, and France. In all, Belgium's intra-EU outflows totaled €16.6 billion, and intra-EU inflows totaled €18.9 billion. Extra-EU outflows totaled €4.4 billion, and extra-EU inflows totaled €8.8 billion. Belgian investment abroad is substantial in the fields of transport (particularly in Latin American countries), nonferrous metals, metalworking, and photographic materials.

Belgium has well-developed capital markets to accommodate foreign finance and portfolio investment. More than half its banking activities involve foreign countries. The world's first stock market was opened in Antwerp in the 14th century. At the end of 2000, the Brussels Stock Market merged with the Paris and Amsterdam bourses (and later Lisbon) to form the Euronext stock exchange. Euronext forms the largest (in volume) multinational stock and derivatives exchange in Europe. In 1996, the European Association of Securities Dealers Automated Quotation (EASDAQ) Exchange opened in Belgium, modeled on the NASDAQ electronic exchange, dedicated to young dynamic "dot.com" start-ups. In April 2001, NASDAQ bought majority ownership and renamed it NASDAQ-Europe.

39 ECONOMIC DEVELOPMENT

Belgian economic policy is based upon the encouragement of private enterprise, with very little government intervention in the economy. Also, as a country heavily dependent upon foreign trade, Belgium has traditionally favored the freest exchange of goods, without tariffs or other limitations. Restrictions on free enterprise and free trade have always been due to external pressure and abnormal circumstances, as in time of war or economic decline.

To meet increased competition in world markets and to furnish relief for areas of the country suffering from chronic unemployment, the government has taken measures to promote the modernization of plants and the creation of new industries. Organizations have been established to provide financial aid and advice, marketing and scientific research, studies on methods of increasing productivity, and nuclear research for economic utilization. Government policy aims at helping industry to hold costs down and to engage in greater production of finished (rather than semi-finished) goods. Results have been mixed, with greater success in chemicals and light manufacturing than in the critical iron and steel industry.

In 1993, the government modified its policy of forbidding more than 49% private ownership in government banks, insurance companies, and the national telecommunications company. In 2000, the government enacted tax reform, reducing corporate, trade, and income taxes. The tax cuts planned through 2006, although improving work and investment incentives, will have to be countered by reduced government spending to compensate for the lost revenue. The telecommunications sector has been liberalized, as have the gas and energy markets.

Belgium successfully attained a budget deficit of less than 3% by the end of 1997, as stipulated by the EU. Due to a strict control of spending, the government has managed to balance the budget in recent years; the 2006 budget foresees balance for the seventh year in a row, but is based on optimistic growth and revenue assumptions. A main economic policy priority has for many years been the reduction of the large public debt, which fell below 100% of GDP at the end of 2003, for the first time in nearly 30 years. With Belgium's employment rate one of the lowest in the EU, the government has created a target of increasing employment by 200,000 by 2007.

40 SOCIAL DEVELOPMENT

Belgium has a social insurance system covering all workers dating back to 1900 for old age and 1944 for disability. The current law was last updated in 2001, and the age to receive full retirement benefits will be increasing to age 65 by 2009. The law provides for disability and survivorship benefits as well. Sickness and maternity benefits were originally established in 1894 with mutual benefits societies. There is work accident and occupational disease coverage for all employed persons. Family allowances cover all workers, with special systems for civil servants and the self-employed.

The Belgian government has taken an active stance to protect and promote the rights of women and children. Domestic violence is a problem and in 2004 the government initiated a national plan to increase awareness. Belgium's equal opportunity law includes a sexual harassment provision, giving women a stronger legal basis for complaints. Child protection laws are comprehensive, and governmental programs for child welfare are amply funded. The government also attempts to integrate women at all levels of decision-making and women play an important role in both the public and private sectors.

Legislation prohibits discrimination based on race, ethnicity or nationality, and penalizes incitement of hate and discrimination. The constitution provides for the freedom of religion. Although minority rights are well protected in Belgium, extreme-right political parties with xenophobic beliefs have gained ground in recent years. In 2004, there were several attacks on Jews and Muslims.

41 HEALTH

Every city or town in Belgium has a public assistance committee (elected by the city or town council), which is in charge of health and hospital services in its community. These committees organize clinics and visiting nurse services, run public hospitals, and pay for relief patients in private hospitals. There is a national health insurance plan, membership of which covers practically the whole population. A number of private hospitals are run by local communities or mutual aid societies attached to religious organizations. A school health program includes annual medical examinations for all school children. Private and public mental institutions include observation centers, asylums, and colonies where mental patients live in groups and enjoy a limited amount of liberty.

A number of health organizations, begun by private initiative and run under their own charters, now enjoy semiofficial status and receive government subsidies. Among them are the Belgian Red Cross, the National Tuberculosis Society, the League for Mental Hygiene, and the National Children's Fund. The last of these, working through its own facilities and through cooperating agencies, provides prenatal and postnatal consultation clinics for mothers, a visiting nurse service, and other health services. Health expenditures were estimated at 8.8% of total GDP.

Roughly 60% of Belgium's hospitals are privately operated, non-profit institutions. As of 2004, there were an estimated 418 physicians, 1074 nurses, 70 dentists, and 145 pharmacists per 100,000 people. Nearly 100% of the Belgium population has access to health services. In 1999, the country immunized one-year-old children as follows: diphtheria, pertussis, and tetanus, 96%, and measles, 83%. The infant mortality rate in 2005 was 5 per 1,000 live births, one of the lowest in the world. Average life expectancy for that year was 79 years. The HIV/AIDS prevalence was 0.20 per 100 adults in 2003. As of 2004, there were approximately 10,000 people living with HIV/AIDS in the country. There were an estimated 100 deaths from AIDS in 2003.

42 HOUSING

Belgium no longer has a housing shortage. In the mid-1970s, an average of over 60,000 new dwellings were built every year; by the early 1980s, however, the government sought by reducing the value-added tax on residential construction to revitalize the depressed housing market. Public funds have been made available in increasing amounts to support the construction of low-cost housing, with low-interest mortgages granted by the General Savings and Retirement Fund.

The 2001 census reports a total of 4,248,502 private, occupied dwellings in the country. About 82% of the population live in single-family homes. About 14% are apartment dwellers. The average household size is 2.4 persons. About 68% of all units are occupied by owners or crowners.

43 EDUCATION

Education is free and compulsory for children between the ages of 6 and 18. Belgium has two complete school systems operating side by side. One is organized by the state or by local authorities and is known as the official school system. The other, the private school system, is largely Roman Catholic. For a long time, the rivalry between the public and private systems and the question of subsidies to private schools were the main issues in Belgian politics. The controversy was settled in 1958, and both systems are presently financed with government funds along more or less identical lines.

Within the public system, there are also some variations in programming between the French community and the Flemish community. In both, the primary (elementary) school covers six years of study. In the French system, secondary school is divided into three levels, with each level lasting two years. Following this course of study, a student may choose to continue in a one-year program for professional development, technical training, or preparation for university studies. There are also programs for artistic development. In the Flemish system, secondary students may choose between four educational tracks: general, technical, artistic, or vocational. Each track covers a six-year course of study. Most children between the ages of three and five attend some type of preschool program. The academic year runs from September to July.

Primary school enrollment in 2003 was estimated at about 100% of age-eligible students. The same year, secondary school enrollment was about 97% of age-eligible students. The student-to-teacher ratio for primary school was at about 12:1 in 2003.

Higher education centers on the eight main universities: the state universities of Ghent, Liège, Antwerp, and Mons; the two branches of the Free University of Brussels, which in 1970 became separate private institutions, one Dutch (Vrije Universiteit Brussel) and the other French (Université Libre de Bruxelles); the Catholic University of Brussels; and the Catholic University of Louvain, which also split in 1970 into the Katholicke Universiteit Leuven (Dutch) and the Université Catholique de Louvain (French). Total enrollment in tertiary education programs for 2001 was at about 367,000. In 2003, about 61% of the tertiary age population were enrolled in some type of higher education program. The adult literacy rate is estimated at about 98%.

As of 2003, public expenditure on education was estimated at 6.3% of GDP.

44 LIBRARIES AND MUSEUMS

There are large libraries, general and specialized, in the principal cities. Brussels has the kingdom's main reference collections, including the Royal Library (founded in 1837), with about four million volumes, as well as the Library of Parliament (1835) with 600,000 volumes, the Library of the Royal Institute of Natural Sciences (681,000 volumes), and the General Archives of the Kingdom, founded in 1794, with 350,000 documents from the 11th to the 20th centuries. Antwerp is the seat of the Archives and the Museum of Flemish Culture, which has an open library of 55,000 volumes. The university libraries of Louvain (1.2 million volumes), Gent (three million volumes), and Liège (1.7 million volumes) date back to 1425, 1797, and 1817, respectively. The library of the Free University of Brussels (1846) has 1.8 million volumes. Also in Brussels is the library of Commission of the European Communities. In addition, there are several hundred private, special, and business libraries, especially in Antwerp and Brussels, including Antwerp's International Peace Information Service (1981) with 25,000 volumes related to disarmament, and the library of the Center for American Studies in Brussels, with 30,000 volumes dealing with American civilization.

Belgium's 200 or more museums, many of them with art and historical treasures dating back to the Middle Ages and earlier, are found in cities and towns throughout the country. Among Antwerp's outstanding institutions are the Open-Air Museum of Sculpture in Middelheim Park, displaying works by Rodin, Maillol, Marini, Moore, and others; the Rubens House, containing 17th-century furnishings and paintings by Peter Paul Rubens; and the Folk Art Museum (1907) featuring popular music and crafts unique to Flemish Culture and mythology. Brussels' museums include the Royal Museum of Fine Arts (founded 1795), which has medieval, Renaissance, and modern collections; Royal Museum of Central Africa (1897), which has rich collections of African arts and crafts, natural history, ethnography, and prehistory; the Royal Museum of Art and History (1835), with its special collections of Chinese porcelain and furniture, Flemish tapestries, and of 18th- and 19th-century applied and decorative art; and the Museum of Modern Art, featuring 20th-century paintings, sculptures, and drawings. Museums in Bruges, Liège, Gent, Malines, and Verviers have important general or local collections.

45 MEDIA

International and domestic telegraph and telephone service, operated by a government agency, is well developed. In 2003, there were an estimated 489 mainline telephones for every 1,000 people. The same year, there were approximately 793 mobile phones in use for every 1,000 people.

National radio and television service is organized into Dutch and French branches. Commercial broadcasting is permitted, hence costs are defrayed through annual license fees on radio and television receivers. There are two national public stations, one broadcasting in French, the other in Dutch. In addition, there are at least two Dutch-language, one French-language, and one German language commercial stations. In 2003, there were an estimated 793 radios and 541 television sets for every 1,000 people. About 377.7 of every 1,000 people are cable subscribers. Also in 2003, there were 318.1 personal computers for every 1,000 people and 386 of every 1,000 people had access to the Internet. There were 946 secure Internet servers in the country in 2004.

The Belgian press has full freedom of expression as guaranteed by the constitution of 1831. There are some restrictions on the press regarding slander, libel, and the advocating of racial or ethnic hate, violence, or discrimination. Newspapers are published in French and Dutch, and generally reflect the views of one of the major parties. Agence Belga is the official news agency.

The major daily newspapers published in French, with their 2002 circulations and political affiliation, include *Le Soir* (Independent), 178,500; *La Lanterne* (Socialist), 129,800; *La Libre Belgique* (Catholic-Independent), 80,000; and *La Nouvelle Gazette* (Liberal), 94,600. Dutch language papers include *De Standaard* (Flemish-Catholic), 372,000; *De Gazet van Antwerpen* (Christian Democrat), 148,000; and *Het Volk/Nieuwe Gids* (Catholic-Labor), 143,300. The Flemish language paper *Het Laatste Nieuws* (Independent) had a 2002 daily circulation of 308,808. About 500 weeklies appear in Belgium, most of them in French or Dutch and a few in German or English. Their overall weekly circulation is estimated to exceed 6.5 million copies.

46 ORGANIZATIONS

Among Belgium's numerous learned societies are the Royal Academy of Sciences, Letters, and Fine Arts and the Royal Academy of Medicine; in addition, there are the Royal Academy of French Language and Literature and the Royal Academy of Dutch Language and Literature. There is a cultural council for each of the three official languages. Architects, painters, and sculptors are organized in the Association of Professional Artists of Belgium.

Business and industry are organized in the Belgium Business Federation (1885), the Chambers of Commerce, and the American Chamber of Commerce in Brussels, as well as on the basis of industrial sectors and in local bodies. Among the latter, the Flemish and Walloon economic councils and the nine provincial economic councils are the most important. The ACP Business Forum, the Association of European Chambers of Commerce and Industry, and the International Confederation of Free Trade Unions meet in Brussels. There are a vast number of national professional, trade, and industry associations for a wide variety of occupations and professions.

The many sports societies include the Royal Belgian Athletic League, the Jockey Club Royal de Belgique, and soccer, cycling, archery, homing pigeon, tennis, hunting, boating, camping, and riding clubs. Youth organizations include four branches of the World Organization of Scouting and an organization of Girl Guides.

Veterans' and disabled veterans' associations, voluntary associations to combat the major diseases, and philanthropic societies are all active in Belgium.

There are active chapters of the Red Cross, UNICEF, CARE International, Greenpeace, Caritas, and Amnesty International.

47TOURISM, TRAVEL, AND RECREATION

Belgium has three major tourist regions: the seacoast, the old Flemish cities, and the Ardennes Forest in the southeast. Ostend is the largest North Sea resort; others are Blankenberge and Knokke. Among Flemish cities, Brugge, Gent, and Ypres stand out, while Antwerp also has many sightseeing attractions, including the busy port, exhibitions of the diamond industry, and the Antwerp Zoo, an oasis of green in the city center. Brussels, home of the European Community headquarters, is a modern city whose most famous landmark is the Grand Place. The capital is the site of the Palais des Beaux-Arts, with its varied concert and dance programs, and of the Théâtre Royal de la Monnaie, home of the internationally famous Ballet of the 20th Century. St. Michael's Cathedral and Notre Dame du Sablon are the city's best-known churches. The Erasmus House in the suburb of Anderlecht and the Royal Palace and Gardens at nearby Laeken are popular tourist centers. Louvain possesses an architecturally splendid city hall and a renowned university. Malines, seat of the Belgian primate, has a handsome cathedral. Liège, in the eastern industrial heartland, boasts one of the finest Renaissance buildings, the palace of its prince-bishops. Tournai is famous for its Romanesque cathedral. Spa, in the Ardennes, is one of Europe's oldest resorts and gave its name to mineral spring resorts in general. Namur, Dinant, and Huy have impressive fortresses overlooking one of the most important strategic crossroads in Western Europe, the Meuse Valley.

All travelers are required to have a valid passport; visas are issued for stays of up to 30 days. No visa is required for citizens of the United States or Canada.

There were 5.2 million visitor arrivals in 2003, when receipts from tourism amounted to $8.7 billion. In that year, Belgium had 63,220 hotel rooms and 16,368 beds.

In 2005, the US Department of State estimated the daily cost of staying in Belgium at between $161 and $320.

48FAMOUS BELGIANS

Belgium has produced many famous figures in the arts. In the 15th century, one of the great periods of European painting culminated in the work of Jan van Eyck (1390?–1441) and Hans Memling (1430?–94). They were followed by Hugo van der Goes (1440?–82), and Pieter Brueghel the Elder (1525?–69), the ancestor of a long line of painters. Generally considered the greatest of Flemish painters are Peter Paul Rubens (1577–1640) and Anthony Van Dyck (1599–1641). In the 19th century, Henri Evenepoel (1872–99) continued this tradition. The 20th century boasts such names as James Ensor (1860–1949), Paul Delvaux (1897–1994), and René Magritte (1898–1967). Modern Belgian architecture was represented by Victor Horta (1861–1947) and Henry van de Velde (1863–1957).

Belgium made substantial contributions to the development of music through the works of such outstanding 15th- and 16th-century composers as Johannes Ockeghem (1430?–95), Josquin des Prés (1450?–1521), Heinrich Isaac (1450?–1517), Adrian Willaert (1480?–1562), Nicolas Gombert (1490?–1556), Cipriano de Rore (1516–65), Philippe de Monte (1521–1603), and Roland de Lassus (known originally as Roland de Latre and later called Orlando di Lasso, 1532–94), the "Prince of Music." Later Belgian composers of renown include François-Joseph Gossec (1734–1829), Peter Van Maldere (1729–68), André Ernest Modeste Grétry (1741–1813), César Franck (1822–90), and Joseph Jongen (1873–1953). Among famous interpreters are the violinists Eugène Ysaye (1858–1931) and Arthur Grumiaux (1921–86). André Cluytens (1905–67) was the conductor of the National Orchestra of Belgium. Maurice Béjart (Maurice Berger, b.1927), an internationally famous choreographer, was the director of the Ballet of the 20th Century from 1959 until 1999.

Outstanding Belgian names in French historical literature are Jean Froissart (1333?–1405?) and Philippe de Commynes (1447?–1511?), whereas early Dutch literature boasts the mystical writing of Jan van Ruysbroeck (1293–1381). The 19th century was marked by such important writers as Charles de Coster (1827–79), Camille Lemonnier (1844–1913), Georges Eeckhoud (1854–1927), and Emile Verhaeren (1855–1916) in French; and by Hendrik Conscience (1812–83) and Guido Gezelle (1830–99) in Flemish. Among contemporary authors writing in French, Michel de Ghelderode (1898–1962), Suzanne Lilar (1901–1992), Georges Simenon (1903–1989), and Françoise Mallet-Joris (b.1930) have been translated into English. Translations of Belgian authors writing in Dutch include works by Johan Daisne (1912–78) and Hugo Claus (b.1929).

Eight Belgians have won the Nobel Prize in various fields. The poet and playwright Maurice Maeterlinck (1862–1949), whose symbolist dramas have been performed in many countries, received the prize for literature in 1911. Jules Bordet (1870–1961) received the physiology or medicine award in 1919 for his contributions to immunology. The same award went to Corneille J. F. Heymans (1892–1968) in 1938 and was shared by Albert Claude (1898–1983) and Christian de Duve (b.1917) in 1974. Russian-born Ilya Prigogine (1917–2003) won the chemistry prize in 1977. Three Belgians have won the Nobel Peace Prize: Auguste Beernaert (1829–1912) in 1909, Henri Lafontaine (1854–1943) in 1913, and Father Dominique Pire (1910–69) in 1958.

Belgium's chief of state since 1951 had been King Baudouin I (1930–93), the son of Leopold III (1901–83), who reigned from 1934 until his abdication in 1951. Baudouin was succeeded by his younger brother Albert II (b.1934) in 1993.

⁴⁹DEPENDENCIES

Belgium has no territories or colonies.

⁵⁰BIBLIOGRAPHY

Annesley, Claire (ed.). *A Political and Economic Dictionary of Western Europe*. Philadelphia: Routledge/Taylor and Francis, 2005.

Coppieters, Bruno and Michel Huysseune, (eds.). *Secession, History and the Social Sciences*. Brussels, Belgium: VUB Brussels University Press, 2002.

De Vries, André. *Brussels: A Cultural and Literary History*. New York: Interlink Books, 2003.

Fitzmaurice, John. *The Politics of Belgium: A Unique Feudalism*. London: Hurst, 1996.

Gagnon, Alain-G. and James Tully, (eds.). *Multinational Democracies*. New York: Cambridge University Press, 2001.

International Smoking Statistics: A Collection of Historical Data from 30 Economically Developed Countries. New York: Oxford University Press, 2002.

MacDonald, Mandy. *Belgium: A Quick Guide to Culture and Etiquette*. Portland, Ore.: Graphic Arts Books, 2005.

Murray, James M. *Bruges, Cradle of Capitalism, 1280–1390*. New York: Cambridge University Press, 2005.

OECD. *Belgium-Luxembourg*. OECD Economic Surveys. Paris (annual).

Warmbrunn, Werner. *The German Occupation of Belgium: 1940–1944*, New York: P. Lang., 1993.

Wee, Herman van der. *The Low Countries in Early Modern Times*. Brookfield, Vt.: Variorum, 1993.

Wessels, Wolfgang, Andreas Maurer, and Jürgan Mittag (eds.). *Fifteen into One?: the European Union and Its Member States*. New York: Palgrave, 2003.

BOSNIA AND HERZEGOVINA

Republic of Bosnia and Herzegovina
Republika Bosnia i Herzegovina

CAPITAL: Sarajevo

FLAG: Introduced in early 1998, the flag consists of a yellow triangle on a royal blue field, with a row of white stars running diagonally along the triangle's edge. The yellow triangle represents the country's three main ethnic groups, while the royal blue field and stars symbolize a possible future inclusion in the Council of Europe.

ANTHEM: *Zemljo Tisucljetna (Thousand-Year-Old Land).*

MONETARY UNIT: 1 convertible marka (KM) = 100 convertible pfenniga. KM1 = $0.00699 ($1 = KM143) as of 2005.

WEIGHTS AND MEASURES: The metric system is the legal standard.

HOLIDAYS: New Year's Day, 1–2 January; Labor Days, 1–2 May; 27 July; 25 November.

TIME: 1 PM = noon GMT.

---

¹LOCATION, SIZE, AND EXTENT

Bosnia and Herzegovina is located in southeastern Europe on the Balkan Peninsula, between Croatia and Serbia and Montenegro. Comparatively, Bosnia and Herzegovina is slightly smaller than the state of West Virginia, with a total area of 51,129 sq km (19,741 sq mi). Bosnia and Herzegovina shares boundaries with Croatia on the N, W, and S, Serbia and Montenegro on the E, and the Adriatic Sea on the S, with a total boundary length of 1,459 km (906 mi). Bosnia and Herzegovina's capital city, Sarajevo, is located near the center of the country.

²TOPOGRAPHY

The topography of Bosnia and Herzegovina features hills, mountains, and valleys. Approximately 50% of the land is forested. The country has three main geographic zones: high plains and plateaus along the northern border with Croatia, low mountains in the center, and the higher Dinaric Alps which cover the rest of the country. Approximately 10% of the land in Bosnia and Herzegovina is arable. Bosnia and Herzegovina's natural resources include coal, iron, bauxite, manganese, timber, wood products, copper, chromium, lead, and zinc. Bosnia and Herzegovina is subject to frequent and destructive earthquakes.

³CLIMATE

The climate features hot summers and cold winters. In higher elevations of the country, summers tend to be short and cold while winters tend to be long and severe. Along the coast, winters tend to be short and rainy. In July, the mean temperature is 22.5°C (72.5°F). January's mean temperature is 0°C (32°F). Annual rainfall averages roughly 62.5 cm (24.6 in).

⁴FLORA AND FAUNA

The region's climate has given Bosnia and Herzegovina a wealth of diverse flora and fauna. Ferns, flowers, mosses, and common trees populate the landscape. Beech forests are found throughout the mountains, with spruce found at some higher altitudes. Wild animals include deer, brown bears, rabbits, fox, and wild boars.

⁵ENVIRONMENT

Metallurgical plants contribute to air pollution. Ongoing interethnic civil strife has seriously damaged the country's infrastructure and led to water shortages. Urban landfill sites are limited. As of 2000, about 44.4% of the total land area is forested. Deforestation was not a significant problem. In 2003, only 0.5% of the total land area was protected. Hutovo Blato is a Ramsar wetland site. The Sutjeska National Park in the south covers an area of about 17,500 hectares (43,250 acres).

As of 2002, there were at least 72 species of mammals and 205 species of birds. According to a 2006 report issued by the International Union for Conservation of Nature and Natural Resources (IUCN), threatened species included 8 types of mammals, 8 species of birds, 1 type of reptile, 1 species of amphibian, 11 species of fish, 10 other invertebrates, and 1 species of plant. Endangered species include the slender-billed curlew, Danube salmon, and the field adder.

⁶POPULATION

The population of Bosnia and Herzegovina in 2005 was estimated by the United Nations (UN) at 3,840,000, which placed it at number 125 in population among the 193 nations of the world. In 2005, approximately 12% of the population was over 65 years of age, with another 18% of the population under 15 years of age. There were 94 males for every 100 females in the country. According to the UN, the annual population growth rate for 2005–10 was expected to be 0.1%, a rate the government viewed as too low. The government is concerned about high numbers of working-age people leaving the country and problems with reproductive health care practices. (An estimated 30% of all pregnancies end in abortion.) The projected population for the year 2025 was 3,677,000. The population density was 75 per sq km (195 per sq mi).

The UN estimated that 43% of the population lived in urban areas in 2005, and that urban areas were growing at an annual rate of 1.45%. The capital city, Sarajevo, had a population of 579,000 in that year.

Civil strife greatly reduced the population through war, genocide, and emigration. When the Dayton Peace Agreement was signed in 1996, there were an estimated two million Bosnian refugees and displaced persons. That year, there were an estimated 25,000 more deaths than births, creating a population decrease of 1%. By 2006 the population was no longer declining, but massive emigration continued to be a concern for the country's economic future.

7 MIGRATION

Many people living in Bosnia and Herzegovina fled the war that followed independence. In other countries, their numbers were lumped together with other refugees from "Yugoslavia" or "former Yugoslavia." As of 1999, more than 330,000 Bosnian refugees were still in need of a permanent home. An estimated 110,000 Bosnian refugees and 30,000 displaced people returned to their homes from outside and within Bosnia in 1998. Only some 41,000 minority returns occurred in 1998, and some 3,000 in 1999. In 2003, there were 330,000 internally displaced persons (IDP) within the country.

In 2005, the net migration rate was estimated as .3 migrants per 1,000 population. Worker remittances in 2003 totaled $870 million. The government views the emigration level as unsatisfactory.

8 ETHNIC GROUPS

In 2002, about 48.3% of the people were Bosniak (Muslim) and 34% were Serbs. Croats made up about 15.4% of the populace.

9 LANGUAGES

Croatian, Serbian, and Bosnian are all spoken.

10 RELIGIONS

Throughout its history, ethnicity and religion have served as flash points for conflict and changes in government. Ethnic groups tend to be closely linked with distinct religious affiliations; however, the rate of active religious participation is considered to be low. The Bosniaks are generally Muslim. As such, nearly 40% of the population is Muslim. The Serbs are generally Serbian Orthodox, a faith practiced by about 31% of the population. Most of the Serbian Orthodox live in the Republika Srpska. The Croats are primarily Roman Catholic, a faith practiced by about 15% of the population. Protestants account for about 4% of the population. Missionary groups include Seventh-Day Adventists, Jehovah's Witnesses, Methodists, the Church of Jesus Christ of Latter-day Saints (Mormons), and Krishna Consciousness. There is a small Jewish community.

The constitution provides for freedom of religion and this right is generally respected in practice. In 2004, the state passed a Law on Religious Freedom which provides for greater freedom of religion and governs the legal licensing of religious groups.

11 TRANSPORTATION

Bosnia and Herzegovina's railway system, as of 2004, consisted of 1,021 km (634 mi) of standard gauge track, of which 795 km (494 mi) had been electrified. In 2002, there were 21,846 km (13,575 mi) of highways, of which 14,020 km (8,712 mi) were paved.

Ports include those at Bosanska Gradiska, Bosanski Brod, Bosanski Samac, and Brčko. All are inland waterway ports on the Sava. However, none are fully operational. Large sections of the Sava are blocked by downed bridges, silt and debris. There is no merchant marine.

In 2004 there were an estimated 27 airports. Of these in 2005, eight had paved runways and there were also five heliports. In 2003, about 73,000 passengers were carried on scheduled flights.

12 HISTORY

Origins

Bosnia and Herzegovina occupies the area between historical Croatia-Slavonia to the north, Dalmatia to the south, and Serbia and Montenegro to the east/southeast. Populated in ancient times by Thracians, Illyrians, Celts, with Greek colonies since 400 BC, the area was taken over by the Romans around 168 BC. However, it took the Romans some one hundred and fifty years to gain control of the entire area, which they called Dalmatia Province. The most difficult aspect of their occupation was getting past the coastal cities to build roads to rich mining sites in the interior, which still maintained its native, Illyrian character in resistance to pressures to Romanize. Eventually, many Romanized Illyrians became important leaders in the Roman armies and administration and some even became emperors. The division of the Roman Empire into the western and eastern halves in AD 395 found Bosnia as the frontier land of the western half, since the dividing line ran south from Sirmium on the Sava river along the Drina River to Skadar Lake by the Adriatic coast.

Slavic tribes have been raiding and settling in the Balkan area in large numbers since the 5th century AD, moving in slowly from their original lands east of the Carpathian Mountains. These early Slavic settlers were joined in the 7th century AD by Croatian and Serbian tribes invited by Byzantine Emperor Heraclius to help him fight the Avars. The area of Bosnia and Herzegovina became the meeting ground of Croats (western area) and Serbs (eastern area). As medieval Bulgarians, Croatians, and Serbians developed their first states, Bosnia became a battleground among them and the Byzantine Empire. Christianization of the area was completed by the 9th century, when most of the Bosnian area came under the influence of Rome and Croats became Catholic, while most Serbs fell under the influence of the Byzantine Empire and became Eastern Orthodox.

The Bosnian area between the 9th and 11th centuries was essentially under Croatian influence when not conquered by Bulgarians, Serbs, or Byzantium. After Hungary and Croatia effected their royal union in AD 1102, Hungary took over Bosnia and the Dalmatian cities in 1136. Bosnia was then ruled by Croatian "Bans" under joint Hungarian-Croatian sovereignty. When the soldiers supplied by Ban Borić (r.1150–1167) to the Hungarian Army were defeated by Byzantium in 1167 at Zemun, Bosnia came under Byzantine rule. Hungary renewed its claim to Bosnia in 1185, during Ban Kulin's reign (1180–1204), which was marked by his independence from Hungary, partly due to the inaccessibility of its mountainous terrain.

Geography itself was an incentive to the local autonomy of Bosnia's individual regions of Podrina, Central Bosnia, Lower Bosnia, and Hum (today's Herzegovina). Each region had its own local hereditary nobility and customs, and was divided into districts (*Župas*). The typical Bosnian family of this period had possession of its land without dependence on a feudal relationship to prince or king, as was the case in much of Europe. Bosnia was nominally Catholic under the jurisdiction of the Archbishop of Dubrovnik, who would consecrate a Bishop of Bosnia, usually from local Bosnian priests. These Bosnian Catholics used a Slavic liturgy and a modified Cyrillic alphabet called "Bosaniča" and had no knowledge of Latin. The region of Hum, on the other hand, was settled by Serbs in the interior, was mixed Orthodox and Catholic in the coastal area and mostly ruled by princes of the Serbian dynasty (Nemanja) until 1326.

The Catholic Church in Bosnia was isolated from the coastal areas and had developed its own Slavic liturgy and practices. These customs were suspect to the Latin hierarchy in both Hungary and the coastal cities. Ignorance of the language and customs of simple people and poor communications generated rumors and accusations of heresy against the Bosnian Church and Ban Kulin, its supposed protector. Kulin called a Church Council in 1203 at Bolino Polje that declared its loyalty to the Pope and renounced errors in its practices. Reports of heresy in Bosnia persisted, possibly fanned by Hungary, and caused visits by Papal legates in the 1220s. By 1225 the Pope was calling on the Hungarians to launch a crusade against the Bosnia heretics. In 1233, the native Bishop of Bosnia was removed and a German Dominican appointed to replace him. In spite of Ban Ninoslav's (1233–1250) renunciation of the "heresy," the Hungarians undertook a crusade in 1235–41, accompanied by Dominicans who were already erecting a cathedral in Vrhbosna (today's Sarajevo) in 1238. The Hungarians used the crusade to take control of most of Bosnia, but had to retreat in 1241 because of the Tartars' attack on Hungary. This allowed the Bosnians to regain their independence and in 1248 the Pope sent a neutral team (a Franciscan and a Bishop from the coastal town of Senj) to investigate the situation but no report is extant.

The Hungarians insisted that the Bosnian Church, which they suspected of practicing dualist, Manichaeic beliefs tied to the Bogomils of Bulgaria and the French Cathars, be subjected to the Archbishop of Kalocsa in Hungary, who it was thought would intervene to end these heretical practices. In 1252, the Pope obliged. However, no Bishop was sent to Bosnia itself—only to Djakovo in Slavonia—so this act had no impact on the Bosnian Church. The crusades against the Bosnian Church caused a deep animosity towards the Hungarians that in the long run weakened Bosnian's determination to resist the invasion of the Islamic Turks. Thus the Bosnian Church that professed to be loyal to Catholicism, even though it continued in its practice of ascetic and rather primitive rituals by its Catholic monastic order, was pushed into separation from Rome.

Around 1288, Stjepan Kotroman became Ban of the Northern Bosnia area. In his quest to consolidate all of Bosnia under his rule, though, he was challenged by the Šubić family of Croatia, who had taken over Western Bosnia. Paul I Šubić then expanded his family's area of control, becoming Ban of Bosnia and later, in 1305, Ban of All Bosnia. However, the power of the Šubić family declined in subsequent years, and Kotroman's son Stjepan Kotromanić was able to take control of Central Bosnia by 1318, serving as a vassal of the Croatian Ban of Bosnia, Mladen Šubić. Kotromanić then allied himself with Charles Robert, King of Hungary, to defeat Mladen Šubić, helping Kotromanić to consolidate his control over Bosnia, the Neretva River Delta, and over Hum, which he took in 1326 but lost in 1350 to Dušan the Great of Serbia. In recognition of the role the Hungarians had played in his consolidation of power in Bosnia, Ban Kotromanić gave his daughter Elizabeth into marriage to King Louis of Hungary in 1353, the year of his death.

Raised in the Orthodox faith, Kotromanić was converted to Catholicism by Franciscan fathers, an order he had allowed into Bosnia in 1342. The Franciscans concentrated their efforts at conversion on the members of the Bosnian Church (or Bogomili) and, by 1385, had built some 35 monasteries, four in Bosnia itself. Since most Franciscans were Italian and did not know the Slavic language, their effectiveness was not as great as it could have been and it was concentrated in the towns where numerous non-Bosnians had settled to ply their trades. During this period silver and other mines were opened which were administered by the townspeople of Dubrovnik. This influx of commerce helped in the development of prosperous towns in key locations and customs duties from increased trade enriched Bosnian nobles. A whole new class of native craftsmen developed in towns where foreign colonies also prospered and interacted with the native population, thus raising Bosnia's overall cultural level.

Kotromanić's heir was his nephew Tvrtko (r.1353–91) who would become the greatest ruler of Bosnia. Tvrtko could not command the loyalty of the nobles at first, however, and he soon lost the western part of Hum (1357) to Hungary as the dowry promised to King Louis of Hungary when he married Elizabeth, Kotromanić's daughter. But by 1363, Tvrtko had grown powerful enough to repel Hungarian attacks into Northern Bosnia. In 1366 Tvrtko fled to the Hungarian Court, having been unable to repress a revolt by his own nobles, and with Hungarian help regained his lands in 1367. In 1373 he obtained the upper Drina and Lim Rivers region. In 1377 he was crowned King of Bosnia and Serbia (his grandmother was a Nemanja) at the Mileševo monastery where Saint Sava, the founder of the Serbian Orthodox Church, was buried. Between 1378 and 1385, Tvrtko also gained control of the coastal territory of Trebinje and Konavli near Dubrovnik, along with the port city of Kotor. In 1389, Tvrtko sent his troops to support the Serbian armies of Prince Lazar and Vuk Branković at the legendary Battle of Kosovo Polje. The battle itself was a draw but it exhausted the Serbs' capability to resist the further Turkish invasions. The Turks retreated, having suffered the death of Sultan Murad I, assassinated by a Serbian military leader, and Tvrtko's commander at Kosovo claimed victory. Having sent such a message to Italy, Tvrtko was hailed as a savior of Christendom. He had made a first step towards a possible unification of Bosnia and Serbian lands, but the Turks, and then his own death in 1391, made it impossible.

Bosnia did not disintegrate after Tvrtko's death, but was held together through a Council of the key nobles. The Council elected weak kings to maintain their own power and privileges. Tvrtko had no legitimate descendants so his cousin Dabiša (r.1391–95) was elected, followed by his widow Helen of Hum (r.1395–98), and then Stjepan Ostoja (r.1398–1404), opposed by Tvrtko II (r.1404–09), probably Tvrtko I's illegitimate son. Between 1404 and 1443, Bosnia witnessed civil wars between factions of the nobles taking opposite sides in the Hungarian wars of succession. Thus Stjepan Ostoja was returned to the throne from 1409 to 1418, followed by Stjepan Ostojić (r.1418–21), then Tvrtko II again (r.1421–43). During this period the Turks participated in Bosnian affairs as paid mercenaries, through their own raids, and by taking sides in the struggles for the Bosnian throne. The Turks supported Tvrtko II, who managed to rule for over 20 years by recognizing the sovereignty of both the Hungarians and Turks, and playing one against the other. After the Turks' conquest of Serbia in 1439 made them direct neighbors of Bosnia along the Drina River, Turkish raids into Bosnia increased. The Ottomans assumed a key role in internal Bosnian affairs and became the mediator for Bosnian nobles' quarrels. The Bosnian nobles and their Council clung to their opposition to a centralized royal authority, even though it could have mounted a stronger defense against Hungarians and Turks. Thus Bosnia grew ever weaker with the skillful maneuvering of the Turks. Twenty years after Tvrtko II's death, in 1443, the Turks conquered an exhausted Bosnia with a surprise campaign.

Herzegovina (named after the ruler of Hum, Stefan Vukčić who called himself Herzeg/Duke) was occupied by the Turks gradually by 1482, and the two regions were subject to the Ottoman Empire for the next 400 years until the 1878 takeover by Austria.

Under Ottoman Rule

The mass conversion of Bosnian Christians to Islam, a rather unique phenomenon in European history, is explained by two schools of thought. The traditional view recognizes the existence of a strong Bogomil heresy of dualism and social protest. These Bosnian Christians, having been persecuted by both Catholic and Orthodox Churches and rulers, welcomed the Ottomans and easily converted in order to preserve their land holdings. In doing so, they became trusted Ottoman soldiers and administrators. The other school of thought denies the existence of a strong and influential Bogomil heresy, but defines the Bosnian Christian church as a nativistic, anti-Hungarian, loosely organized religion with a Catholic theological background and simple, peasant-based practices supported by its monastic order. The rulers/kings of Bosnia were Catholic (with the single exception of Ostoja) and very tolerant of the Orthodox and so-called Bosnian religions. However, these religious organizations had very few priests and monks, and therefore were not very strong. The Bosnian Church was practically eliminated in 1459 through conversions to official Catholicism, or the forced exile of its leadership. Thus, by the time of the Turkish conquest, the Bosnian Church had ceased to exist and the allure of privileged status under the Ottomans was too strong for many to resist.

Bosnia and Herzegovina was ruled by a Pasha or Vizier appointed by the Sultan and assisted by a Chancellor, supreme justice, and treasurer, each heading his own bureaucracy, both central and spread into eight districts (*Sandžaks*). Justice was administered by a *khadi* who was both prosecutor and judge using the Koran for legal guidance, thus favoring Muslim subjects. Catholics, who were outside the established Orthodox and Jewish communities represented by the Greek Orthodox Patriarch and Chief Rabbi in Constantinople, were particularly exposed to arbitrary persecutions. In spite of all this, communities of followers of the Orthodox (Serbian) Church and Catholic (Croatian) Church survived into the late 19th century when in 1878 Austria obtained the authority to occupy Bosnia and Herzegovina, putting an end to four centuries of Ottoman rule. The Ottomans introduced in Bosnia and Herzegovina their administration, property concepts, and customs. The adherents to Islam were the ruling class, regardless of their national or ethnic backgrounds. Christian peasants practically became serfs to Muslim landlords while in the towns civil and military administrators had control over an increasingly Muslim population. Large numbers of Bosnians fled the Turkish takeover and settled in Venetian-occupied coastal areas where many continued the fight against the Turks as "Uskoki" raiders. Others emigrated north or west into Slavonia and Croatia and were organized as lifetime soldiers along military regions (*Krajina*) in exchange for freemen status, land, and other privileges. On the Bosnian side, Christians were not required to enter military service, but the so-called "blood tax" took a heavy toll by turning boys forcibly into Muslim Janissaries—professional soldiers converted to Islam who would generally forget their origins and become oppressors of the Sultan's subjects. Girls were sent to harems. Taxation became more and more oppressive, leading to revolts by the Christian peasantry that elicited bloody repressions.

Under Austro-Hungarian Rule

Historically both Croats and Serbs have competed for control over Bosnia. The Croats, who had included Bosnia in their medieval kingdom, could not effectively continue their rule once joined with the more powerful Hungarians in their royal union. The Serbs, on the other hand, were assisted by Hungary in their expansion at the expense of the Byzantine Empire. Later, they also received Hungarian support in their resistance to Turkish inroads and therefore could not invest their energies in Bosnia, in their view a "Hungarian" territory. Thus Bosnia was able to assert its own autonomy and individuality, but did not evolve into a separate nation. With the Austrian occupation, however, a new period began marked by a search for a Bosnian identity, supported by Austria who had an interest in countering the national unification ambitions of both Croats and Serbs.

The population of Bosnia and Herzegovina was divided into three major religious-ethnic groups: Croatian Catholics, Serbian Orthodox, and Bosnian Muslims. With the disappearance of the Bosnian Church just before the Ottoman occupation in 1463, most Bosnians were Croatian and Catholic, with a Serbian Orthodox population concentrated in Eastern Herzegovina and along the Drina River frontier with Serbia. The Serbs were mostly peasants, many of whom became serfs to Muslim landlords. Their priests, who were generally poorly educated, lived as peasants among them. Serbian urban dwellers, insignificant in number at first, grew to be an important factor by the late Ottoman period and developed their own churches and schools in the 19th century. Crafts and commerce were the main occupations of the new Serbian middle class.

Croats were also mostly peasants and, like the Serbs, became serfs to Muslim landlords. Members of the Franciscan order lived among the peasants, even though they also had built several monasteries in urban centers. There was almost no Croat middle class

LOCATION: 44°17′ N; 17°30′ E. BOUNDARY LENGTHS: Total land boundary lengths, 1,459 kilometers (905 miles); Croatia, 932 kilometers (578 miles); Yugoslavia, 527 kilometers (327 miles); total coastline, 20 kilometers (12 miles).

at the start of the Austrian period and the Catholic clergy was generally its advocate.

The Muslim group consisted of three social subgroups: the elites, the peasants, and urban lower classes. Most Muslims were peasants, but they were free peasants with a standard of living not better than that of the Christian serf-peasants. The Muslim hodžas (priests) lived among the peasants as peasants themselves. The second subgroup consisted of merchants, craftsmen, and artisans and were mostly concentrated in towns. Together with the urban lower classes, these two groups made up the Muslim majorities in most towns by 1878. The members of the Muslim elites were mostly religious functionaries, landowners, and commercial entrepreneurs, all favored by Islamic laws and traditions. Following the 1878 occupation, Austria recognized the right of Turkish functionaries to keep their posts, the right of Muslims to be in communication with their religious leaders in the Ottoman Empire, the right of Turkish currency to circulate in Bosnia, and also promised to respect all traditions and customs of the Bosnian Muslims. The Austrian approach to the administration of Bosnia and Herzegovina was close to the British colonial model that retained the existing elites and cultural individuality while gradually introducing Western administrative and education models.

Bosnia and Herzegovina was divided by the Turks into six administrative regions that were confirmed by Austria: Sarajevo, Travnik, Bihać, Donja Tuzla, Banja Luka, and Mostar (Herzegovina). Each was headed by a regional supervisor. Participation in cultural and religious organizations was encouraged, while engaging in politics was prohibited. The Austrians promoted a policy of equality between Christians and Muslims, banned organizations of an open political purpose, and prohibited the use of national names (Serb and Croat) for public institutions. At the same time, educational institutions designed to promote loyalty to Bosnia (and Austria) as such were encouraged. Censorship and other means were used to insulate Bosnians from the influence of their Croatian and Serbian co-nationals across the borders. By terminating the earlier Muslim secular/religious unity, many administrative and judicial functions were no longer carried out by the Muslim elites, but were instead presided over by the Austrian bureaucracy and judiciary, though a separate Muslim judiciary was continued. The Muslim landowners lost some privileges but were able to retain their land and the system of serfdom was allowed to continue.

A widespread and important institution supporting Muslim cultural life was the Vakif (Vakuf in Serbian/Croatian). The Vakuf was a revenue-producing property set up and administered as a family foundation for the support of specified causes. Once set up, a Vakuf could not be sold, bequeathed, or divided and was exempt from normal taxes. In 1878 it was estimated that one-fourth to one-third of usable land in Bosnia was tied to Vakufs. The administration of Vakufs was lax and open to much manipulation and abuse. The Austrian administration was able to establish effective controls over the Vakuf system by 1894 through a centralized commission and the involvement of prominent Muslims in the administration of Vakuf revenues in support of Islamic institutions.

The continuation of serfdom by the Austrian authorities was a deep disappointment for the peasants that were eagerly expecting emancipation. Abuses led to peasant revolts until the Austrians introduced cash payments of the tithe (one-tenth of harvest due to the state) and the appraising of harvest value as basis for payment in kind (one-third) to the landlord. A land-registry system was instituted in 1884, and landowners that could not prove legal ownership lost title to some properties. This policy generated wide discontent among Muslim landowners. Another cause of frequent disorders were cases of religious conversions. Under Muslim law, a Muslim convert to another faith was to be executed (this penalty was later eased to banishment). The Austrian policy of confessional equality required a freedom of religious conversion without any penalty and a conversion statute was issued in 1891.

The general aim of the Austrian administration was to guide the development of a coequal confessional society that would focus its efforts on cultural and economic progress without political and national assertiveness. Benjamin von Kallay, the first Austrian Chief Administrator for Bosnia and Herzegovina wanted to avoid anything that could lead to the creation of a separate Muslim nation in Bosnia. On the other hand, he was determined to insulate Bosnians from external developments in the South Slavic areas. Such a position was unrealistic, however, since all of the main groups—Serbs, Croats, and Muslims—identified themselves with their own national/religious groups in the neighboring areas and had developed intense cultural/political relationships with them. Serbs looked at Serbia's successes and hoped for unification with their motherland. Croats followed closely the Croatian-Hungarian tensions and hoped likewise for their unification. The Muslim community, meanwhile, struggled for its own cultural/religious autonomy within a Bosnia that still recognized the Ottoman Sultan's sovereignty and looked to him for assistance.

The unilateral annexation of Bosnia and Herzegovina to Austria in 1908 exacerbated Austria's relations with Serbia (and almost caused a war) and with the Hungarian half of the Hapsburg Crown that opposed the enlargement of the Slavic population of Austria-Hungary. Serbia's victories in the Balkan wars added fuel to the "Yugoslav" movement among the South Slavs of Austria, including Bosnia and Herzegovina. Here the Austrian administration countered the growing "Yugoslav" assertiveness with a "divide and rule" initiative of developing a separate "Bosnian" national consciousness which they hoped would tie together Serbs, Croats, and Muslims. All nationalist movements use elements of history to develop their own mythology to unite their members. Thus, the medieval Bosnian kingdom was the basis for development of a Bosnian national consciousness. It was opposed by most Serbs and Croats, who awaited unification with Serbia or Croatia, but gave some sense of security to the more isolated Muslim Bosnian community. Already by the beginning of the 20th century, separate ethnic organizations and related political associations had to be allowed. The 1908 annexation led to the promulgation of a constitution, legal recognition of political parties, and a Bosnian Parliament in 1910. The internal political liberalization then allowed the Austrian administration to concentrate on the repression of student radicals, internal and external terrorists, and other such perceived threats to their rule.

The Muslim community was split internally, with a leadership dominated by landowners and weakened by the forced emigration to Turkey of its top leaders. It finally came together in 1906 and formed the Muslim National Organization (Muslimanska Narodna Organizacija) as its political party, with the blessing of its émigré leaders in Istanbul. Intense negotiations with the Austrian administration produced agreements on religious and cultural autonomy as well as landowners' rights. The latter were a preeminent concern, and landowners were able to preserve their ownership rights based on Ottoman law and the peasants' payments of compulsory dues. The religious autonomy of the Muslim faith was assured by having the nominees for the top offices confirmed by the Sultan's religious head upon request by the Austrian Embassy in Istanbul. The same process was also used in matters of religious dogma and law.

Cultural autonomy for Muslims was affirmed through the streamlining of the preexisting vakuf system into local, regional, and central assemblies responsible for the operation of the vakufs and the related educational system. Overall, the Muslims of Bosnia had achieved their objectives: preserving their large landholdings with peasants still in a quasi-serfdom condition; assuring their cultural autonomy; and retaining access to the Sultan, head of a foreign country, in matters of their religious hierarchies. Politically, the Muslim National Organization participated in the first parliament as part of the majority supportive of the Austrian government.

Serbs and Croats had also formed political organizations, the nature of which reflected Bosnia's peculiar ethnic and socio-political conditions. The Serbian National Organization (Srpska Narodna Organizacija) was founded in 1907 as a coalition of three factions. The Croatian National Community (Hrvatska Narodna Zajednica) was formed in 1908 by liberal Croat intellectuals, followed in 1910 by the Croatian Catholic Association (Hrvatska Katolička Udruga). A cross-ethnic Social Democratic party, formed in 1909, failed to win any seats in the Parliament. A Muslim Progressive Party, formed in 1908, found hardly any support even after changing its name to the Muslim Independent Party. The Muslims were more conservative and were opposed to the agrarian reform demanded by the Serbs and Croats, who each continued to favor an association or unification with their respective "Mother Country." Croats asserted the Croatian character of Bosnia based on its Croatian past, while Serbs just as adamantly claimed its Serbian character and supported Serbia's "Greater Serbia" policies.

Given the demographics of Bosnia and Herzegovina (1910 census: Serbian Orthodox, 43%; Croat Catholics, 23%; Muslims, 32%) each side needed the support of the Muslims who, though pressured to declare themselves Serbs or Croats, very seldom would do so and would rather keep their own separate identity. Up until the Balkan wars, Muslims and Serbs would support one another hoping for some kind of political autonomy. Croats advocated unification with Croatia and a trialist reorganization of the Hapsburg Monarchy, giving the united South Slavs a coequal status with Austrians and Hungarians. Any cooperation by the Muslims was predicated on support for the continuation of serfdom. This stance prevented cooperation with the Croatian Catholic Association, which insisted on agrarian reform and the termination of serfdom.

With the Serbian victories and Ottoman defeat in the Balkan wars, Serbs became more assertive and Croats more willing to cooperate with them in the growing enthusiasm generated by the idea of "Yugoslavism." A parliamentary majority of Serbs and Croats could have effected the liberation of the peasants in 1913 but the Hungarians opposed it. The assassination of Archduke Ferdinand on 28 June 1914, and World War I, combined to make the issue moot when the Parliament was adjourned. The assassination of the Archduke was apparently the work of members of the "Young Bosnia" students association supported (unofficially) by Serbia through its extremist conspiratorial associations, the "Black Hand" and the "Serbian National Defense." The Austrian ultimatum to Serbia was extremely harsh but Serbia met all the conditions that did not violate its sovereignty. Austria nevertheless declared war and immediately attacked Serbia. The Serbian community of Bosnia and Herzegovina was subjected to a regime of terror and indiscriminate executions by the Austrian authorities. Serbian leaders were subjected to trials, court martial proceedings, and infamous concentrations camps where internees died of epidemics and starvation.

First (Royal) Yugoslavia

Throughout World War I, Bosnians fought in Austrian units, particularly on the Italian front until Austria's surrender. The Bosnian National Council decided to unite with the Kingdom of Serbia, as Vojvodina did and the Montenegrin assembly did on 24 November 1918. On 27 November 1918 the delegation from the Zagreb-based National Council of the Slovenes, Croats, and Serbs also requested unification with Serbia of the Slovene, Croat, and Serbian lands of Austria-Hungary. Following the Declaration of Union on 1 December 1918, a provisional government was set made up of representatives of Serbia and the National Council, with other groups added later. A provisional Assembly was also convened consisting of members of the Serbian Parliament, nominees from the National Council and other regional Assemblies such as Bosnia and Herzegovina and Vojvodina. In November 1920 a Constituent Assembly was elected and functioned as both the legislature and constitutional convention. Bosnian Serbs supported the Serbian Agrarian Party, while two Muslim parties, the National Muslim Organization from Bosnia and Herzegovina and the Džemijet Party of the Kosovo and Macedonia Muslims had seats in the assembly. Croats, on the other hand, joined the mainstream parties of Croatia.

By joining the Kingdom of Serbs, Croats, and Slovenes in 1918, Bosnia and Herzegovina ceased to exist as a distinct political/historical unit, particularly since the heads of local governments were appointed by and directly accountable to the central government in Belgrade. After 10 years of a tumultuous parliamentary history culminating in the assassination of Croatian deputies, King Alexander dissolved parliament and disbanded all political parties, establishing a royal dictatorship in 1929. He then reorganized the country into a "Yugoslavia" made up of nine administrative regions (banovine) named after rivers. What once was Bosnia and Herzegovina was split among four of the new units (Vrbaska, Drinska, Primorska, and Zetska). Serb and Croat peasants were finally freed from their feudal obligations to Muslim landlords through the agrarian reforms decreed in 1919 and slowly implemented over the next 20 years. Except for Bosnia and Herzegovina and Dalmatia, land held by ex-enemies (Austrians, Hungarians, Turks) were expropriated without compensation and redistributed to the peasants—1.75 million of them plus 2.8 million dependents. As a result, the average size of agricultural holdings fell to 15 acres, causing inefficiencies and very low yields per acre. Peasants were forced to borrow even to buy food and necessities. They fell deeply in debt, both to local shopkeepers who charged 100–200% interest and to banks that charged exorbitant rates up to 50%. In comparison, peasant cooperatives in Slovenia used single digit interest rates.

Politically, the Muslim Organization, as a small party, allied itself mostly with the Slovene People's Party and either the Serbian Democratic or Radical parties in order to participate in a series of governments before the 1929 royal dictatorship was implemented. The Muslim Organization's main goals were to obtain the best possible compensation for land expropriated from Bosnia's Muslim landowners and to preserve the Muslims' cultural identity. In 1932, Muslim leaders joined the Croats, Slovenes, and some Liberal Serbs in issuing the Zagreb manifesto calling for an end to the King's dictatorship and for democratization and regional autonomies. For this the centralist regime interned and imprisoned several of the leaders and instituted wider repressions. Following the assassination of King Alexander in 1934 in Marseille, France, the Croat Peasants Party was joined by the Muslims, Serbian Agrarians, and Serbian Democrats in opposition to the Centralists, winning 38% of the votes in spite of the government's intimidating tactics. With the opposition refusing to take part in the parliament, a new government was formed by the Serbian Radicals with the inclusion of the Muslims and the Slovene People's Party.

This new coalition government lasted until 1939, but was never able to resolve the "Croatian" autonomy issue. In addition, while under the leadership of Milan Stojadinović, Yugoslavia's foreign policy moved the country closer to Italy and Germany. Meanwhile a growing consensus had developed that the "Croatian" question had to be solved, particularly in view of the aggressive ambitions of Yugoslavia's neighbors. Thus, the Regent Prince Paul and Dr. Vladimir Maček, leader of the Croatian Peasant Party, worked with the Minister of Social Policy, Dragiša Cvetković, on an agreement establishing a Croatian Banovina made up of the historical regions of Croatia-Slavonia and Dalmatia along with parts of Vojvodina, Srem, and Bosnia. The president of the senate, Monsignor Anton Korošec (also leader of the Slovene People's Party), engineered the resignation of five ministers, two Slovenes, two Muslim, and Dragiša Cvetković. Regent Paul then called on Cvetković to form a new government. Dr. Maček became vice-premier and Ivan Subašić was named Ban of the autonomous Croatian Banovina, which was given its own Sabor (parliament). The Croatian parties considered this development as a positive first phase towards their goal of an independent Croatia that would incorporate all of Bosnia and Herzegovina. The Serbian centralists, on the other hand, saw this phase as a threat to their own designs of incorporating Bosnia and Herzegovina (and Serb populated areas of Croatia) into a "Greater Serbia" unit of Yugoslavia. Thus, on the eve of World War II, the stage was set for a direct confrontation between the independent minded Croatians and centralistic Serbs. The Muslims of Bosnia were caught in their crossfire.

World War II

Germany, Italy, and their allies Hungary, Romania, and Bulgaria, attacked Yugoslavia on 6 April 1941 and divided the country among themselves. The Croatian terrorist Ustaša organization collaborated with the aggressors and was allowed to proclaim an Independent State of Croatia on 10 April 1941. This new state incorporated the old Croatian Banovina in addition to all of Bosnia and Herzegovina. Of its total population of 6.3 million, one-third were Serbian and 750,000 were Muslim. Once entrenched in power, the Ustaša troops began implementing their plan for "cleansing" their Greater Croatia of the Serbian population by the use of terror, mass deportations, and genocidal massacres later condemned by the Nürnberg Court.

The Serbian population responded in kind with its Cetnik formations and by joining the Partisan resistance movement led by Josip Broz-Tito, head of the Yugoslav Communist Party. Bosnia and Herzegovina suffered terrible losses in several German-led offensives against Bosnian resistance, and in the internecine civil war among Communist-dominated Partisans, nationalist Cetniks (mostly Serbs), and Croatian Ustaše and home guard units. The Muslim population in particular was caught in the middle be-

tween the Ustaše and the Serbian Cetniks. The Ustaše considered the Muslims of Croatian origin and expected them to collaborate with the Ustaša regime. The Serbian Cetniks, on the other hand, viewed most Muslims as the hated Turks and Ustaša collaborators, and therefore engaged in slaughters of Muslims, particularly in Eastern Bosnia around the cities of Foča and Goražde.

The political programs of the Cetniks and Partisans were a reflection of the old centralist (Serbian) hegemony and the Federalist positions of the prewar opposition parties. Thus the Partisan resistance, though aiming at a revolutionary power grab, offered a federated Yugoslavia made up of individual republics for each national group—Serbs, Croats, Slovenes, newly recognized Macedonians and Montenegrins. To avoid a battle over a Serbian-Croatian border issue, Bosnia and Herzegovina was resurrected as a buffer area between Serbia and Croatia. It would also allow (again) for the cultural autonomy of the Muslim population. The Allied and Soviet support the Partisans received enabled them to prevail, and they organized Socialist Yugoslavia as a Federative People's Republic with Bosnia and Herzegovina as one of the constituent republics approximately within the boundaries of the former Austrian province.

When Soviet armies entered Yugoslavia from Romania and Bulgaria in the fall of 1944—Marshal Tito with them—military units and civilians that had opposed the partisans had no choice but retreat to Austria or Italy to save themselves. Among them were the Cetnik units of Draža Mihajlović, and "home guards" from Serbia, Croatia, and Slovenia that had been under German control but were pro-Allies in their convictions and hopes. Also in retreat were the units of the Croatian Ustaša that had collaborated with Italy and Germany in order to achieve (and control) an "independent" greater Croatia, and in the process had committed terrible and large-scale massacres of Serbs, Jews, Gypsies, and others who opposed them. Of course, Serbs and Partisans counteracted and a fratricidal civil war raged over Yugoslavia, pitting Croats against Serbs, Communists against Nationalists. These skirmishes not only wasted countless lives, they used up the energy and property that could have been used instead against the occupiers. After the end of the war, the Communist-led forces took control of all of Yugoslavia and instituted a violent dictatorship that committed systematic crimes and human rights violations on an unexpectedly large scale. Thousands upon thousands of their former opponents were returned from Austria by British military authorities only to be tortured and massacred by Partisan executioners.

Second (Communist) Yugoslavia

Such was the background for the formation of the second Yugoslavia as a Federative People's Republic of five nations—Slovenes, Croats, Serbs, Macedonians, and Montenegrins—and Bosnia and Herzegovina as a buffer area with its mix of Serb, Muslim, and Croat populations. The problem of large Hungarian and Muslim Albanian populations in Serbia was solved by creating the autonomous region of Vojvodina (Hungarian minority) and Kosovo (Muslim Albanian majority) to assure their political and cultural development. Tito attempted a balancing act to satisfy most of the nationality issues that were carried over unresolved from the first Yugoslavia, but failed to satisfy anyone.

Compared to pre-1941 Yugoslavia where Serbs enjoyed their controlling role, the numerically stronger Serbs in the new Yugoslavia had "lost" the Macedonian area they considered "Southern Serbia"; they had lost the opportunity to incorporate Montenegro into Serbia; they had lost direct control over the Hungarian minority in Vojvodina and Muslim Albanians of Kosovo (viewed as the cradle of the Serbian nation since the Middle Ages); they could not longer incorporate into Serbia the large Serbian populated areas of Bosnia; and they had not obtained an autonomous region for the large minority Serbian population within the Croatian Republic. The Croats, while gaining back from Hungary the Medjumurje area and from Italy the cities of Rijeka (Fiume), Zadar (Zara), some Dalmatian islands, and the Istrian Peninsula, had "lost" the Srem area to Serbia and Bosnia and Herzegovina, which had been part of the World War II "independent" Croatian state under the Ustaša leadership. In addition, the Croats were confronted with a deeply resentful Serbian minority that became ever more pervasive in public administrative and security positions. The Slovenes had obtained back from Hungary the Prekmurje enclave and from Italy most of the Slovenian lands taken over by Italy following World War I (Julian Region and Northern Istria). Italy retained control over the "Venetian Slovenia" area, the Gorizia area, and the port city of Trieste. (Trieste was initially part of the UN protected "Free Territory of Trieste," split in 1954 between Italy and Yugoslavia, with Trieste itself given to Italy.) Nor were the Slovenian claims to the southern Carinthia area of Austria satisfied. The "loss" of Trieste was a bitter pill for the Slovenes and many blamed it on the fact that Tito's Yugoslavia was, initially, Stalin's advance threat to Western Europe, thus making Western Europe and the United States more supportive of Italy.

The official position of the Marxist Yugoslav regime was that national rivalries and conflicting interests would gradually diminish through their sublimation into a new Socialist order. Without capitalism, nationalism was supposed to wither away. Therefore, in the name of their "unity and brotherhood" motto, any "nationalistic" expression of concern was prohibited and repressed by the dictatorial and centralized regime of the "League of Yugoslav Communists" acting through the "Socialist Alliance" as its mass front organization. As a constituent Republic of the Federal Yugoslavia, Bosnia and Herzegovina shared in the history of the second experiment in "Yugoslavism."

After a short postwar "coalition" government period, the elections of 11 November 1945, boycotted by the noncommunist "coalition" parties, gave the Communist-led People's Front 90% of the vote. A Constituent Assembly met on November 29 and abolished the monarchy, establishing the Federative People's Republic of Yugoslavia. In January 1946, a new constitution was adopted, based on the 1936 Soviet constitution. The Stalin-engineered expulsion of Yugoslavia from the Soviet-dominated Cominform Group in 1948 was actually a blessing for Yugoslavia after its leadership was able to survive Stalin's pressures. Survival had to be justified, both practically and in theory, by developing a "road to Socialism" based on Yugoslavia's own circumstances. This new "road map" evolved rather quickly in response to some of Stalin's accusations and Yugoslavia's need to perform a balancing act between the NATO alliance and the Soviet bloc. Having taken over all power after World War II, the Communist dictatorship under Tito pushed the nationalization of the economy through a policy of forced industrialization, to be supported by the collectivization of agriculture.

The agricultural reform of 1945–46 (limited private ownership of a maximum of 35 hectares (85 acres) and a limited free market after the initial forced delivery of quotas to the state at very low prices) had to be abandoned because of the strong passive, but at times active, resistance by the peasants. The actual collectivization efforts were initiated in 1949 using welfare benefits and lower taxes as incentives along with direct coercion. But collectivization had to be abandoned by 1958 simply because its inefficiency and low productivity could not support the concentrated effort of industrial development.

By the 1950s, Yugoslavia had initiated the development of its internal trademark: self-management of enterprises through workers councils and local decision-making as the road to Marx's "withering away of the state." Following the failure of the first five-year plan (1947–51), the second five-year plan (1957–61) was completed in four years by relying on the well-established self-management system. Economic targets were set from the local to the republic level and then coordinated by a Federal Planning Institute to meet an overall national economic strategy. This system supported a period of very rapid industrial growth in the 1950s. But a high consumption rate encouraged a volume of imports, largely financed by foreign loans, far in excess of exports. In addition, inefficient and low-productivity industries were kept in place through public subsidies, cheap credit, and other artificial protective measures that led to a serious crisis by 1961.

Reforms were necessary and, by 1965, "market socialism" was introduced with laws that abolished most price controls and halved import duties while withdrawing export subsidies. After necessary amounts were left with the earning enterprise, the rest of the earned foreign currencies were deposited with the national bank and used by the state, other enterprises, or were used to assist less developed areas. Councils were given more decision-making power on investing their earnings. They also tended to vote for higher salaries in order to meet steep increases in the cost of living. Unemployment grew rapidly even though "political factories" were still subsidized. The government thus relaxed its restrictions to allow labor migration particularly to West Germany where workers were needed for its thriving economy. Foreign investment was encouraged up to 49% in joint enterprises, and barriers to the movement of people and exchange of ideas were largely removed. The role of trade unions continued to be one of transmission of instructions from government to workers, allocation of perks along with the education/training of workers, monitoring legislation, and overall protection of the self-management system. Strikes were legally neither allowed nor forbidden but—until the 1958 miners strike in Trbovlje, Slovenia—were not publicly acknowledged and were suppressed. After 1958, strikes were tolerated as an indication of problems to be resolved. Unions, however, did not initiate strikes but were expected to convince workers to go back to work.

Having survived its expulsion from the Cominform in 1948 and Stalin's attempts to take control, Yugoslavia began to develop a foreign policy independent of the Soviet Union. By mid-1949 Yugoslavia ceased its support of the Greek Communists in their civil war against the then Royalist government of Greece. In October 1949, Yugoslavia was elected to one of the nonpermanent seats on the UN Security Council and openly condemned North Korea's aggression toward South Korea. Following the "rapprochement" opening with the Soviet Union initiated by Nikita Khrushchev and his 1956 denunciation of Stalin, Tito intensified his work on developing the movement of nonaligned "third world" nations. This would become Yugoslavia's external trademark, in cooperation with Nehru of India, Nasser of Egypt, and others. With the September 1961 Belgrade summit conference of nonaligned nations, Tito became the recognized leader of the movement. The nonaligned position served Tito's Yugoslavia well by allowing Tito to draw on economic and political support from the Western powers while neutralizing any aggressiveness from the Soviet bloc. While Tito had acquiesced, reluctantly, to the 1956 Soviet invasion of Hungary for fear of chaos and its liberalizing impact on Yugoslavia, he condemned the Soviet invasion of Dubček's Czechoslovakia in 1968, as did Romania's Ceausescu, both fearing their countries might be the next in line for "corrective" action by the Red Army and the Warsaw Pact. Just before his death on 4 May 1980, Tito also condemned the Soviet invasion of Afghanistan. Yugoslavia actively participated in the 1975 Helsinki Conference and agreements and the first 1977–78 review conference that took place in Belgrade, even though Yugoslavia's one-party communist regime perpetrated and condoned numerous human rights violations. Overall, in the 1970s and 1980s, Yugoslavia maintained fairly good relations with its neighboring states by playing down or solving pending disputes—such as the Trieste issue with Italy in 1975—and by developing cooperative projects and increased trade.

Ravaged by the war, occupation, resistance, and civil war losses and preoccupied with carrying out the elimination of all actual and potential opposition, the Communist government faced the double task of building its Socialist economy while rebuilding the country. As an integral part of the Yugoslav federation, Bosnia and Herzegovina was, naturally, impacted by Yugoslavia's internal and external political developments. The main problems facing communist Yugoslavia and Bosnia and Herzegovina were essentially the same as the unresolved ones under Royalist Yugoslavia. As the "Royal Yugoslavism" had failed in its assimilative efforts, so did the "Socialist Yugoslavism" fail to overcome the forces of nationalism. Bosnia and Herzegovina differs from the other republics because its area has been the meeting ground of Serbian and Croatian nationalist claims, with the Muslims as a third party, pulled to both sides. Centuries of coexistence of the three major national groups had made Bosnia and Herzegovina into a territorial maze where no boundaries could be drawn to clearly separate Serbs, Croats, and Muslims without resorting to violence and forced movements of people. The inability to negotiate a peaceful partition of Bosnia and Herzegovina between Serbia and Croatia doomed the first interwar Yugoslavia to failure. The Socialist experiment with "Yugoslavism" in post-World War II Yugoslavia was particularly relevant to the situation in Bosnia and Herzegovina where the increasing incidence of intermarriage, particularly between Serbs and Croats, caused the introduction of the "Yugoslav" category with the 1961 census. By 1981 the "Yugoslav" category was selected by 1.2 million citizens (5.4% of the total population), a large increase over the 273,077 number in 1971. Muslims, not impacted much by intermarriage, have also been recognized since 1971 as a separate "people" and numbered two million in 1981 in Yugoslavia. The 1991 census showed the population of Bosnia and Herzegovina consisting mainly of Muslims (43.7%),

Serbs (31.4%), and Croats (17.3%) with 6% "Yugoslavs" out of a total population of 4,364,000.

Bosnia as a political unit has existed since at least 1150. Headed by a Ban in the Croatian tradition, Bosnia lasted for over 300 years with an increasing degree of independence from Hungary through King Tvrtko I and his successors until the occupation by the Ottoman Turks in 1463 (1482 for Herzegovina). Bosnia and Herzegovina was then ruled by the Turks for 415 years until 1878, and by Austria-Hungary for 40 years until 1918. Bosnia and Herzegovina ceased to be a separate political unit only for the 27 years of the first Yugoslavia (1918–1945) and became again a separate unit for 47 years as one of the republics of the Federal Socialist Republic of Yugoslavia until 1992. Yet, in spite of an 800-year history of common development, the Serbs, Croats, and Muslims of Bosnia and Herzegovina never assimilated into a single nation. Bosnia was initially settled by Croats who became Catholic and then by Orthodox Serbs escaping from the Turks. Under the Turks, large numbers converted to Islam and, in spite of a common language, their religious and cultural differences kept the Serbs, Croats, and Muslims apart through history so that Bosnia and Herzegovina has been more a geographic-political notion than a unified nation.

Consequently, while the resurgent nationalism was galvanizing Croatia into an intensifying confrontation with Serbia, the Bosnian leadership had to keep an internal balance by joining one or the other side depending on its own interests. Bosnia and Herzegovina was torn between the two opposing "liberal" and "conservative/centralist" coalitions. In terms of widening civil and political liberties, Bosnia and Herzegovina usually supported in most cases the liberal group. Its own economic needs as a less developed area, however, pulled it into the conservative coalition with Serbia in order to keep the source of development funds flowing to itself, Montenegro, Macedonia, and Serbia (for the Kosovo region). Also, the "Yugoslav" framework was for Bosnia and Herzegovina an assurance against its possible, and very likely bloody, partitioning between Serbia and Croatia.

The liberal group, centered in Slovenia and Croatia, grew stronger on the basis of the deepening resentment against forced subsidizing of less-developed areas of the federation and buildup of the Yugoslav army. Finally, the increased political and economic autonomy enjoyed by the Republics after the 1974 constitution and particularly following Tito's death in 1980, assisted in turning Tito's motto of "unity and brotherhood" into "freedom and democracy" to be achieved through either a confederated rearrangement of Yugoslavia or by complete independence of the Republics. The debate over the reforms of the 1960s had led to a closer scrutiny—not only of the economic system, but also of the decision-making process at the republic and federal levels, particularly the investment of funds to less developed areas that Slovenia and Croatia felt were very poorly managed, if not squandered. Other issues of direct impact on Bosnia and Herzegovina fueled acrimony between individual nations, such as the 1967 Declaration in Zagreb claiming a Croatian linguistic and literary tradition separate from the Serbian one, thus undermining the validity of the "Serbo-Croatian" language. Also, Kosovo Albanians and Montenegrins, along with Slovenes and Croats, began to assert their national rights as superior to their rights as Yugoslav nationals.

The Eighth Congress of the League of Communists of Yugoslavia (LCY) in December 1964 acknowledged that ethnic prejudice and antagonisms existed in socialist Yugoslavia. The Congress went on record against the position that Yugoslavia's nations had become obsolete and were disintegrating into a socialist "Yugoslavism." Thus the republics, based on individual nations, became bastions of a strong Federalism that advocated the devolution and decentralization of authority from the federal to the republic level. "Yugoslav Socialist Patriotism" was at times defined as a deep feeling for one's own national identity within the socialist self-management of Yugoslavia.

Economic reforms were the other focus of the Eighth LCY Congress led by Croatia and Slovenia, with emphasis on efficiencies and local economic development decisions with profit criteria as their basis. The liberal bloc (Slovenia, Croatia, Macedonia, Vojvodina) prevailed over the conservative group and the reforms of 1965 did away with central investment planning and political factories. The positions of the two blocks hardened into a national-liberal coalition that viewed the conservative, centralist group led by Serbia as the Greater Serbian attempt at majority domination.

To the conservative centralists the devolution of power to the republic level meant the subordination of the broad "Yugoslav" and "Socialist" interests to the narrower "nationalist" interest of republic national majorities. With the Croat League of Communists taking the liberal position in 1970, nationalism was rehabilitated as long as it didn't slide into chauvinism. Thus the "Croatian Spring" bloomed and impacted all the other republics of Yugoslavia. Meanwhile, as the result of a series of 1967–68 constitutional amendments that limited federal power in favor of the republics and autonomous provinces, the federal government was seen by liberals more as an inter-republican problem-solving mechanism bordering on a confederacy. A network of inter-republican committees established by mid-1971 proved to be very efficient at resolving a large number of difficult issues in a short time. The coalition of liberals and nationalists in Croatia generated sharp condemnation in Serbia, where its own brand of nationalism grew stronger, but as part of a conservative-centralist alliance. Thus the liberal/federalist versus conservative/centralist opposition became entangled in the rising nationalism within each opposing bloc. The devolution of power in economic decision-making spearheaded by the Slovenes assisted in the "federalization" of the League of Communists of Yugoslavia. This resulted in a league of quasi-sovereign republican parties. Under strong prodding from the Croats, the party agreed in 1970 to the principle of unanimity for decision making that, in practice, meant a veto power for each republic. However, the concentration of economic resources in Serbian hands continued with Belgrade banks controlling half of total credits and some 80% of foreign credits. This was also combined with the fear of Serbian political and cultural domination. The Croats were particularly sensitive regarding language, alarmed by the use of the Serbian version of Serbo-Croatian as the norm with the Croatian version as a deviation. The language controversy thus exacerbated the economic and political tensions, leading to easily inflamed ethnic confrontations.

Particularly difficult was the situation in Croatia and Serbia because of issues relating to their ethnic minorities—Serbian in Croatia and Hungarian/Albanian in Serbia. Serbs in Croatia sided with the Croat conservatives and sought a constitutional amendment guaranteeing their own national identity and rights and, in the process, they challenged the "sovereignty" of the Croatian nation and state, as well as its right to self-determination, including the right to secession. The conservatives won and the amendment declared that "the Socialist Republic of Croatia (was) the national state of the Croatian nation, the state of the Serbian nation in Croatia, and the state of the nationalities inhabiting it."

Meanwhile Slovenia, not burdened by large minorities, developed a similar liberal and nationalist direction along with Croatia. This fostered an incipient separatist sentiment opposed by both the liberal and conservative party wings. Led by Stane Kavčić, head of the Slovenian government, the liberal wing gained as much political local latitude from the federal level as possible during "Slovenian Spring" of the early 1970s. By the summer of 1971, the Serbian party leadership was pressuring President Tito to put an end to the "dangerous" development of Croatian nationalism. While Tito wavered because of his support for the balancing system of autonomous republic units, the situation quickly reached critical proportions also in terms of the direct interests of Bosnia and Herzegovina. Croat nationalists, complaining about discrimination against Croats in Bosnia and Herzegovina, demanded the incorporation of Western Herzegovina into Croatia. Serbia countered by claiming Southeastern Herzegovina for itself. Croats also advanced many economic and political claims: to a larger share of their foreign currency earnings, to the issuance of their own currency, to establishment of their own national bank to negotiate foreign loans, to the printing of Croatian postage stamps, to a Croatian army and to recognition of the Croatian Sabor (Assembly) as the highest Croatian political body and, finally, to Croatian secession and complete independence.

Confronted with such intensive agitation, the liberal Croatian party leadership could not back down and did not try to restrain the public demands nor the widespread university students' strike of November 1971. This situation caused the loss of support from the liberal party wings of Slovenia and even Macedonia. At this point Tito intervened, condemned the Croatian liberal leadership on 1 December 1971 and supported the conservative wing. The liberal leadership group resigned on 12 December 1971. When Croatian students demonstrated and demanded an independent Croatia, the Yugoslav army was ready to move in if necessary. A wholesale purge of the party liberals followed, with tens of thousands expelled from the party. Key functionaries lost their positions, while several thousands were imprisoned (including Franjo Tudjman who later became president in independent Croatia). Leading Croatian nationalist organizations and their publications were closed. On 8 May 1972 the Croatian party also expelled its liberal wing leaders and the purge of nationalists continued through 1973 in Croatia, as well as in Slovenia and Macedonia. However, the issues and sentiments raised during the "Slovene and Croat Springs" of 1969–71 did not disappear. Tito and the conservatives were forced to satisfy nominally some demands and the 1974 constitution was an attempt to resolve the strained inter-republican relations as each republic pursued its own interests over and above a conceivable overall "Yugoslav" interest.

Beginning in 1986, work began on amendments to the 1974 constitution. They created a furor, particularly in Slovenia. Opposition was strongest to the amendments that proposed creation of a unified legal system, central control of transportation and communication, centralizing the economy into a unified market, and granting more control to Serbia over its autonomous provinces of Kosovo and Vojvodina. These changes were seen as being accomplished at the expense of the individual republics. A recentralization of the League of Communists was also recommended but opposed by liberal/nationalist groups.

By 1989, the relations between Slovenia and Serbia reached a crisis point, especially following the Serbian assumption of control in the Kosovo and Vojvodina provinces (as well as in Montenegro). Serbian President Milošević's tactics were extremely distasteful to the Slovenians and the use of force against the Albanian population of the Kosovo province worried the Slovenes (and Croats) about the possible use of force by Serbia against Slovenia itself. The tensions with Serbia convinced the Slovenian leadership of the need to take protective measures and, in September 1989, draft amendments to the constitution of Slovenia were published. These included the right to secession, the sole right of the Slovenian legislature to introduce martial law and to control the deployment of armed forces in Slovenia.

A last attempt at salvaging Yugoslavia was to be made as the extraordinary Congress of the League of Communists of Yugoslavia convened in January 1990 to review proposed reforms such as free multiparty elections and freedom of speech. The Slovenian delegation attempted to broaden the spectrum of reforms but was rebuffed and walked out on 23 January 1990, pulling out of the Yugoslav League. The Slovenian Communists then renamed their party the Party for Democratic Renewal. On 10 April 1990 the first free elections since before World War II were held in Slovenia. A coalition of six newly formed democratic parties, called Demos, won 55% of the votes, with the remainder going to the Party for Democratic Renewal, the former Communists, 17%; the Socialist Party, 5%; and the Liberal Democratic Party (heir to the Slovenia Youth Organization), 15%. The Demos coalition organized the first freely elected Slovenian government of the post-Communist era with Dr. Lojze Peterle as the prime minister.

Milan Kučan, former head of the League of Communists of Slovenia, was elected president with 54% of the vote. His election was seen as recognition of his efforts to effect a bloodless transfer of power from a monopoly by the Communist party to a free multiparty system and his standing up to the recentralizing attempts by Serbia.

All of these developments had also a deep impact on Bosnia and Herzegovina. When the Antifascist Council of the National Liberation of Yugoslavia (AVNOJ) proclaimed the federal principle on 29 November 1943, Bosnia and Herzegovina was included as one of the constituent republics of post-World War II Yugoslavia. Muslims were not considered a "nation" yet. Serbs claimed that Muslims were Islamized Serbs, and Croats claimed that Muslims were descendants of the Croatian Bosnian Church that had converted to Islam. The Muslims themselves, meanwhile, claimed their own separate identity and were recognized as equal to Serbs and Croats.

The sense of Muslim identity grew stronger and incorporated demands for Muslim institutions parallel to the Serbian and Croatian ones. Muslims sought to define themselves as the only "true" Bosnians and thus a call to define Bosnia and Herzegovina as a "Muslim" Republic. Muslim activist groups multiplied during the 1970s and 1980s.

Since the 1970s and into the late 1980s the Muslims' self-assertiveness as an ethnic community grew ever stronger and was viewed as a balancing element between Serbs and Croats. As the winds of change away from communism swept the western republics of Slovenia and Croatia in 1989 and 1990, Bosnia and Herzegovina also was preparing for multiparty elections to be held on 18 November 1990. Meanwhile, across Bosnia and Herzegovina's borders with Croatia, the Serbian population was clamoring for its own cultural and political autonomy. Serbs perceived threats from the Croatian Democratic Union, the winner in the April 1990 elections in Croatia.

By July 1990, a Bosnia and Herzegovina branch of the Croatia-based Serbian Democratic Party had become very active in the 18 Bosnian communes with Serbian majorities adjacent to the Croatia Krajina (border area). By the fall of 1990, the program of the Serbian Democratic Party in Croatia had advanced a plan to include the Bosnian Serbs into a joint Krajina state, which would have a federal arrangement with Serbia proper. This arrangement, it was hoped, would undercut any thoughts of a confederation of Slovenia, Croatia, and Bosnia and Herzegovina. Such a confederation, however, was favored by the Party of Democratic Action (Muslim) and the Croatian Democratic Union. In spite of their differences in long-term goals, the three nationalist parties were committed to the continuation of Bosnia and Herzegovina and to the termination of Communist rule. On 1 August 1990, Bosnia and Herzegovina declared itself a "sovereign and democratic state." The former Communist Party became the Party of Democratic Change, while Yugoslavia's Prime Minister Marković formed the Alliance of Reform Forces that advocated his economic reforms. The Muslim Party, Serbian Party, and Croatian Democratic Union then formed a coalition government with Alija Izetbegović of the Muslim Party as President of Bosnia and Herzegovina.

Independence and War

Meanwhile, Slovenia and Croatia had published a joint proposal in October 1990 for a confederation of Yugoslavia as a last attempt at a negotiated solution, but to no avail. The Slovenian legislature also adopted a draft constitution in October proclaiming that "Slovenia will become an independent state." On 23 December 1990, a plebiscite was held on Slovenia's "disassociation" from Yugoslavia if a confederation solution could not be negotiated within a six-month period. An overwhelming majority of voters approved the secession provision. Slovenia declared its independence on 25 June 1991. On 27 June 1991, the Yugoslav Army tried to seize control of Slovenia and its borders with Italy, Austria, and Hungary under the pretext that it was its constitutional duty to assure the integrity of Socialist Yugoslavia. The Yugoslav Army units were surprised by the resistance they encountered from the Slovenian "territorial guards" which surrounded Yugoslav Army tank units, isolated them, and engaged in close combat, mostly along border checkpoints. These battles ended in most cases with Yugoslav units surrendering to the Slovenian forces. The war in Slovenia was ended in 10 days due to the intervention of the European Community; a cease-fire was declared, which gave time to the Yugoslav Army to retreat from Slovenia by the end of October 1991.

The coalition government of Bosnia and Herzegovina had a very difficult time maintaining the spirit of ethnic cooperation won in its elections, while the situation in Slovenia and Croatia was moving to the point of no return with their declaration of independence of 25 June 1991 and the wars that followed. Particularly worrisome were the clashes in Croatia between Serbian paramilitary forces and Croatian police and the intervention of the Yugoslav Army in order to "keep the peace." Another element that worried the Bosnian government was the concentration of Yugoslav Army units in Bosnia and Herzegovina following their retreat first from Slovenia and then from Croatia. In October 1991, the Serbian Democratic Party held a plebiscite in the two-thirds of Bosnian territory under Serbian control and announced the establishment of a Serbian Republic inside Bosnia and Herzegovina.

In December 1991, the Bosnian Parliament passed a Declaration of Sovereignty and President Izetbegović submitted to the European Community an application for international recognition of Bosnia and Herzegovina as an independent nation. A referendum on independence was held on 29 February 1992. With the Serbs abstaining in opposition to the secession from Yugoslavia, Muslims and Croats approved an independent Bosnia and Herzegovina by a vote of 99.7%. In reaction to the referendum, Serbs proceeded to prepare for war in close cooperation with the Yugoslav army.

On 1 March 1992 in Sarajevo a Serbian wedding party was fired upon. This was the spark that ignited armed confrontations in Sarajevo and other areas of Bosnia and Herzegovina. The Bosnian Serbs by late March of 1992, formally established their own "Serbian Republic of Bosnia and Herzegovina." The international recognition of Bosnia and Herzegovina by the European Community and the United States (along with the recognition of Slovenia and Croatia) was issued on 6 April 1992. This action was viewed as another affront to the Serbs, and gave more impetus to Serbian determination to oppose the further splitting of Yugoslavia that would cause the final separation of Serbs in Croatia and Bosnia and Herzegovina from Serbia proper. The bond among the Serbs of Croatia and Bosnia with the Serbian government controlled by Slobodan Milošević, and with the Yugoslav Army was firmly cemented. The decision of Serbia, along with the Serbs of Bosnia and Croatia, to take advantage of Yugoslavia's demise and try to unite Serbian territories in Croatia and Bosnia and Herzegovina with Serbia proper precipitated the wars in Croatia first and then in Bosnia and Herzegovina. Desperate acts by Serbs engaged in "ethnic cleansing" (torching, and systematic rape and executions in imitation of the World War II Ustaša tactics) revolted the whole world and elicited retaliation by the initially allied Croats and Muslims.

War spread in Bosnia in mid-1992 with the relentless bombardment of Sarajevo by Serbs and the brutal use of "ethnic cleansing," primarily by Serbs intent on freeing the areas along the Drina River of Muslim inhabitants. Croats and Muslims retaliated in kind, if not in degree, while Serbs took over control of some 70% of the country and used concentration camps and raping of women as systematic terror tactics to achieve their "cleansing" goals. Croats kept control of western Herzegovina, while their Muslim allies tried to resist Serbian attacks on mostly Muslim cities and towns full of refugees exposed to shelling and starvation while the world watched in horror. The European Community, the United States, the UN, and NATO coordinated peacekeeping efforts, dangerous air deliveries to Sarajevo, airdrops of food and medicinal supplies to keep the people of Sarajevo from dying of starvation and sicknesses.

The various plans proposing the division of Bosnia and Herzegovina into three ethnic cantons were not acceptable to the winning Serbian side. The cantonization plans were also a partial cause for the breakdown of the Muslim-Croatian alliance when the two sides began fighting over areas of mixed Croat and Muslim populations. One such area was the city of Mostar in Herzegovina, where the Croats had established the Croatian union of "Herzeg-Bosnia," later named the state of Herzeg-Bosnia. Finally, under the threat of air strikes from NATO, the Serbs agreed to stop the shelling of Sarajevo and hand over (or remove) their heavy artillery by February 1994, so Sarajevo could get a respite from its bloody siege of several years. A truce was implemented by mid-February 1994 and was barely holding while continuing negotiations were taking place that, on US initiative, brought Croats and Muslims back together on a confederation plan accepted by the two sides and signed in Washington on 18 March 1994.

In July 1994, the EC, the United States, and Russia agreed on a partition plan giving the Croat-Muslim side 51% of the land, with 49% offered to the Bosnian Serbs who, holding 70%, would need to give up a large area under their control. As of the end of July 1994, the Bosnian Serbs' parliament had rejected the plan and had resumed occasional sniping and mortar shelling of Sarajevo, shooting at UN peacekeepers and supply airplanes, and blocking of the single access road to Sarajevo. After almost two-and-a-half years of war, destruction, and terrible suffering imposed on the people of Bosnia and Herzegovina, the efforts of the international community and its very cumbersome decision-making process had brought Bosnia and Herzegovina back to the partitioning plan originally agreed on at a Lisbon meeting in February 1992. In the fall of 1994, President Milošević of Serbia had closed the borders between Serbia and Bosnia and Herzegovina in order to stop any further assistance to the "Republika Srpska" that he himself helped establish. President Milošević agreed to "extricate" Serbia from its direct support for the Bosnian Serbs in the hope that a compromise partitioning plan that would allow each side to "confederate" with Croatia and Serbia respectively and would offer both sides the opportunity to turn their energies to positive efforts of physical and psychological reconstruction.

The quest to create a "Greater Serbia" continued into July 1995, when Bosnian Serbs overran the UN protected areas of Srebrenica and Zepa, extending their territory near the Croatian border. Over 8,000 Bosnian Muslim men and boys were summarily executed at Srebrenica. In retaliation, NATO forces initiated air raids on Bosnian Serb positions on 30 August 1995. Two weeks later, Bosnian Serb forces began lifting their siege on Sarajevo, and agreed to enter into negotiations on the future of Bosnia. Pressured by air strikes and diplomacy, Serb leaders joined authorities from Croatia and Bosnia in Dayton, Ohio, for US-sponsored peace talks.

The Dayton Accords

After three years of war, the General Framework Agreement for Peace in Bosnia and Herzegovina was completed on 21 November 1995 in Dayton, Ohio. Signed in Paris in mid-December, the agreement called for 60,000 NATO peacekeepers to oversee the disarming process. The agreement, known as the Dayton Accords, provided for the continuity of Bosnia and Herzegovina as a single state with two constituent entities: the Federation of Bosnia and Herzegovina (FBH) and the Republika Srpska (RS). The FBH occupies the 51% of the territory with a Bosniak (Muslim) and Croat majority, while the RS occupies the remaining 49% with a Bosnian Serb majority. Following the signing of the Dayton Accords, the UN economic sanctions against the Federal Republic of Yugoslavia and the Bosnian Serb party were suspended, and the arms embargo was lifted (except for heavy weapons). During 1996, the NATO-led Implementation Force assisted with the military aspects of the Dayton Accords to provide stability in order to facilitate civilian reconstruction and the return of refugees and displaced persons. Elections were scheduled and conducted on 11 September 1996.

In March 1996, the International Criminal Tribunal for the former Yugoslavia filed its first charges against Serbian soldiers accused of committing atrocities in Bosnia. Among those cited were Serb generals Djordje Djukic and Ratko Mladic, and the former Bosnian Serb leader Radovan Karadzic. In May 1997, the tribunal completed its first trial with a conviction of a Bosnian Serb police officer for murdering two Muslim policemen and the torture of Muslim civilians.

Casualty estimates from the war vary from as low as 25,000 to over 250,000 persons. Some three million people became refugees or internally displaced persons. About 320,000 Bosnians had taken refuge in Germany during the war. However, the refugees returned to find a significant housing shortage and massive unemployment. Moreover, the goals of the Dayton Accords to encourage the rebuilding of multi-ethnic communities have not been realized. Bosnian Serb and Bosnian Croat leaders continued to reinforce ethnic partitions and resisted cooperation with Bosniaks to carry out the peace agreement.

Despite the Dayton Accords, outbreaks of violence persisted. The legacy of centuries of confrontations by the Austro-Hungarian, Russian, and Turkish Empires in the Balkans continued to haunt the area and a rekindling of the conflict was almost inevitable. In June 1998 NATO peacekeeping forces decided to extend their stay until a more stable peace was achieved. General elections held in 1998 were relatively quiet, but tensions in the Kosovo region increased as Yugoslav forces attacked Kosovar rebels. In March 1999 NATO jets downed two Yugoslav MiG fighters, allegedly thwarting an attempted attack on peacekeeping forces. Fighting between Serbs and ethnic Albanians in Kosovo raged as NATO aircraft bombed the area. Russia attempted to pass a resolution in the UN Security Council to forbid further bombing runs by NATO warplanes, but failed. Violent conflicts dissipated through the next year, as the International Court of Justice furthered reparations for crimes, and Yugoslavia agreed to a peace plan on 3 June 1999.

Bosnia and Croatia signed a border agreement in July 1999. The strategically located city of Brčko—previously Serb-ruled, and a main site of contention between the country's factions—received a Muslim-Croat/Serb coalition government in March 1999 from the Hague International Court of Justice. Officials from the Serb Republic were disturbed because this portion of land was the one territorial link between the western and eastern portions of the Republic. In 1999, NATO began reducing the 25-nation peacekeeping force by one-third over a period of six months. Mass gravesites continued to be unearthed in northeastern Bosnia, near Sarajevo and in Srebrenica as numerous war criminals were arrested and brought to trial at the Hague.

Municipal elections were held in March 2000, and general elections took place that November. The November elections resulted in a win for the Serbian nationalist Serb Democratic Party (SDS), formerly lead by Karadzic, in the Republika Srpska; the Croatian nationalist HDZ party won among ethnic Croat voters; but the reformist Social Democratic Party narrowly beat the Bosnian Muslim nationalist Party of Democratic Action (SDA) party in certain areas of the Federation. In May 2001, Bosnian Serbs used force to break up ceremonies marking the rebuilding of two destroyed mosques in Banja Luka and Trebinje.

Parliamentary, presidential, and municipal elections were held in October 2002, and nationalists strengthened their positions. The work of the International Criminal Tribunal for the former Yugoslavia at The Hague continued. In 2001, former Bosnian Serb President Biljana Plavsic surrendered to the tribunal, but pleaded not guilty to charges of genocide; however, in October 2002, she changed her plea to one of guilty of crimes against humanity, and was sentenced to 11 years in prison. In early 2001, a verdict against three Bosnian Serbs found guilty of torturing and raping Bosnian Muslim women marked the first time the tribunal called rape a crime against humanity. Later that year the tribunal found Bosnian Serb general Radislav Krstic guilty of genocide for his role in the massacre at Srebrenica; he was sentenced to 46 years in prison.

In May 1999, former Yugoslav President Milošević was indicted by the tribunal for war crimes committed in Kosovo; he was subsequently indicted for crimes committed in Bosnia and Herzegovina and Croatia, including charges of genocide carried out in Bosnia and Herzegovina from 1992–95. His trial began in February 2002. In December 2004, the NATO-led Stabilization Force in Bosnia and Herzegovina (SFOR), whose goal was to deter renewed hostilities, concluded its mission. Peacekeeping operations were taken up by the European Union Force in Bosnia and Herzegovina (EUFOR). In June 2005, a Bosnian armed unit with members from all three main ethnic groups left for Iraq, to support the US-led coalition at war there.

¹³ GOVERNMENT

Several proposals contributed to the current system of government, which was outlined through the Dayton Accords of 1995. The February 1992 Lisbon proposal first suggested the partitioning of Bosnia and Herzegovina into "ethnic cantons," but was rejected by the Muslim side. The Vance-Owen proposal of early January 1993 dividing Bosnia and Herzegovina, still a unified state, into nine "ethnic majority" provinces with Sarajevo as a central weak government district was accepted by Croats and Muslims on 7 January 1993 and ratified on 20 January 1993 by the Bosnian Serbs' Parliament with a 55-to-15 vote in spite of deep misgivings. However, two key events delayed the necessary detailed implementation discussions: Croat forces' attacks on Muslims in Bosnia and Herzegovina and on Serbs in Croatia, and the new administration of US President Bill Clinton, from whom the Bosnian Muslims hoped to obtain stronger support, even military intervention. Thus by mid-March 1993, only the Croats had agreed to the three essential points of the Vance-Owen proposal, namely the Constitutional Principles (10 provinces), the Military Arrangements, and the detailed map of the 10 provinces. On 25 March 1993 the Bosnian Muslims agreed to all the terms, but the Bosnian Serb legislature on 2 April 1993 rejected the revised 10-province map and the Vance-Owen plan was scuttled.

The Owen-Stoltenberg plan was based on a June 1993 proposal in Geneva by Presidents Tudjman and Milošević about partitioning Bosnia and Herzegovina into three ethnic-based "states." Owen-Stoltenberg announced the new plan in August 1993 indicating that the three ethnic states were realistically based on the acceptance of Serbian and Croatian territorial "conquests." At the same time the Croat Bosnian "parliament" announced the establishment of the "State of Herzeg-Bosnia" and the Croatian Democratic Alliance withdrew its members from the Bosnian Parliament. The Bosnian Parliament then rejected the Owen-Stoltenberg Plan while seeking further negotiations on the Muslim state's territory and clarifications on the international status of Bosnia and Herzegovina.

The next plan, developed with the more proactive participation of the United States and bringing together again the Croats and Muslims into a federation of their own, was signed in Washington on 18 March 1994 following the Sarajevo cease-fire of 17 March. On 31 March 1994 the Bosnian assembly in Sarajevo approved the new constitutional provisions establishing a Federation of Muslims and Croats with the presidency to alternate between Croats and Muslims. The Geneva contact group (United States, United Kingdom, France, Germany, Russia) agreed on a new partition plan in July 1994 that divided Bosnia and Herzegovina: 51% to the joint Muslim-Croat federation and 49% to the Serbs.

Under the Dayton Accords, a constitution for Bosnia and Herzegovina was established that recognized a single state with two constituent entities. The Federation of Bosnia and Herzegovina (FBH) incorporated the 51% of the country with a Bosnian Muslim and Bosnian Croat majority, while the Republika Srpska (RS) occupied the 49% of the country with a Bosnian Serb majority. The constitution specified a central government with a bicameral legislature, a three-member presidency comprised of a member of each major ethnic group, a council of ministers, a constitutional court, and a central bank. The bicameral Parliamentary Assembly consists of a House of Peoples, with 15 delegates, and the House of Representatives, with 42 members. In each house, two-thirds of the representatives are from the Federation of Bosnia and Herzegovina and one-third from the Republika Srpska.

As a result of the Dayton Accords, Bosnia and Herzegovina is administered in a supervisory role by a High Representative chosen by the UN Security Council. As of 2005, that representative was Paddy Ashdown.

Elections for central and federation-level canton offices were conducted on 14 September 1996 as specified by the Dayton Accords. Alija Izetbegović, Momcilo Krajisnik, and Kresimir Zubak were elected to the presidency representing respectively the Bosniaks (Muslims), Serbs, and Croats. Izetbegović was named Chair in accordance with the new constitution. Krajisnik, later accused of joining Karadzic in siphoning off million of dollars in potential tax revenue through gasoline and cigarette monopolies, boycotted the council after one meeting, paralyzing the government.

Izetbegović was reelected to the Muslim seat of the joint presidency in the September 1998 elections; Ante Jelavic won the Croat seat; and Zivko Radisic, the Serb seat. An eight-month chairper-

sonship rotates among the three joint presidents. Elections were held in 2002. Sulejman Tihić won the Muslim seat; Dragan Cović, the Croat seat; and Mirko Sarović, the Serb seat. In April 2003, Sarović resigned following a report by Western intelligence agencies regarding an affair involving illegal military exports to Iraq and allegations of spying on international officials. He was replaced by Borislav Paravac. In March 2005, High Representative Paddy Ashdown removed Dragan Cović from the presidency, who faced corruption charges. He was replaced by Ivo Miro Jović.

The FBH government has a president and a bicameral parliament (House of Representatives and House of Peoples). The RS government has a president and a unicameral legislature (National Assembly). As a result of a 2002 constitutional reform process, an RS Council of Peoples was established in the RS National Assembly. In 2003, High Representative Paddy Ashdown abolished the Supreme Defense Council of the RS, and altered the constitutions of the RS and FBH, removing all reference to statehood from both.

14 POLITICAL PARTIES

Three main political parties wield significant political power at all levels of government. The Serb Democratic Party (SDS) dominates the Republika Srpska, the Party of Democratic Action (SDA) is the main Bosniak (Muslim) nationalist party, and the Croatian Democratic Union of Bosnia and Herzegovina (HDZ) represents Croat areas. However, a reformist party, the Social Democratic Party (SDP) in the FBH is gaining in popularity. Other parties include: Party for Bosnia and Herzegovina (SBIH); Civic Democratic Party (GDS); Croatian Peasants' Party of BIH (HSS); Croat Christian Democratic Union of Bosnia and Herzegovina (HKDU); Croat Party of Rights (HSP); Independent Social Democratic Party (SNSD); Liberal Bosniak Organization (LBO); Liberal Party (LS); Muslim-Bosniak Organization (MBO); Republican Party of Bosnia and Herzegovina (RP); Serb Civic Council (SGV); Socialist Party of Republika Srpska (SPRS); Serb Radical Party (SRS); Democratic Socialist Party (DSP); Social Democrats of Bosnia Herzegovina; Party for Democratic Progress (PDP); National Democratic Union (DNZ); Social Democratic Union (SDU): Serb National Alliance (SNS); and the Coalition for a United and Democratic BIH (coalition of SDA, SBIH, LS, and GDS). Parliamentary elections were held on 5 October 2002, and seats in the House of Representatives were distributed as follows: SDA, 10 seats; the SBiH, 6 seats; the SDS, 5 seats; HDZ, 5 seats; the SDP, 4 seats; the SNSD, 3 seats; the PDP, 2 seats; and 6 other parties took 1 seat each.

15 LOCAL GOVERNMENT

Bosnia and Herzegovina is divided into the Federation of Bosnia and Herzegovina (FBH) and the Republika Srpska (RS). The FBH is further divided into 10 cantons: Goražde, Livno, Middle Bosnia, Neretva, Posavina, Sarajevo, Tuzla Podrinje, Una Sana, West Herzegovina, and Zenica Doboj. There are also municipal governments. Brčko district, in northeastern Bosnia, is an administrative unit under the sovereignty of Bosnia and Herzegovina; it is not part of either the RS or the FBH, and the district remains under international supervision.

16JUDICIAL SYSTEM

The 1995 Dayton Accords established a constitution including a Constitutional Court composed of nine members. The Constitutional Court's original jurisdiction lies in deciding any constitutional dispute that arises between the FBH and the RS or between Bosnia and Herzegovina and one or both of the FBH and the RS. The Court also has appellate jurisdiction within the territory of Bosnia and Herzegovina. The constitution provides for an independent judiciary, although it is subject to influence by nationalist elements, political parties, and the executive branch. Original court jurisdiction exists in both municipal and cantonal courts (10 in the FBH); the RS has 5 municipal courts and district courts. Appeals in the FBH are taken to the Federation Supreme Court, and in the RS to the RS Supreme Court. The constitution provides for open and public trials. The legal system is based on civil law system.

17ARMED FORCES

As of 2005, the armed forces of Bosnia and Herzegovina (BiH) consisted of 24,672 active personnel, of which the army is the largest service with 16,400. However, the country is composed of two political entities: the Muslim and Croat-based Federation of Bosnia and Herzegovina and the Serb-based Republika Srpska. As a result, the country's armed forces, as well as its equipment, are divided between the two entities. In December 2003, the Bosnian parliament passed a law that established a chain of command that went from the State Presidency to the Ministry of Defense, then to the Joint Staff, then to a joint Operational Command, and from there, down to the armed forces of each entity. In 2005, the Federation Army (excluding 40,000 reservists) had 16,400 active personnel, supported by 188 main battle tanks, 35 armored infantry fighting vehicles, 129 armored personnel carriers, and more than 946 artillery pieces. The Army of the Republika Srpska had 8,200 active personnel and 20,000 reservists. Equipment included 137 main battle tanks, 74 armored infantry fighting vehicles, 74 armored personnel carriers, and 500 artillery pieces. The (Serb) air wing includes 14 combat capable aircraft, of which there are 13 fighter ground attack aircraft. Under the Dayton Peace Accord (1995) and the Common Defence Policy (2001) the armed forces are being reduced. Defense spending in 2005 totaled $143 million.

18INTERNATIONAL COOPERATION

Bosnia and Herzegovina was admitted to the United Nations on 22 May 1992 and serves in several specialized agencies, such as the FAO, IAEA, UNESCO, UNIDO, and WHO. The country is an observer in the WTO. Bosnia and Herzegovina joined the OSCE on 30 April 1992. The country is also a member of G-77, the Council of Europe, the Southeast Europe Cooperation Initiative (SECI), and the Central European Initiative. Bosnia and Herzegovina is an observer in the OAS and the OIC. The country is part of the Nonaligned Movement and has supported UN efforts in Ethiopia and Eritrea (est. 2000) and the DROC (est. 1999). Diplomatic relations with Croatia, Albania, and Serbia and Montenegro have

been stable since the signing of Dayton Accords (1995). In environmental cooperation, Bosnia and Herzegovina is part of the Basel Convention, the Convention on Long-Range Transboundary Air Pollution, Ramsar, the Montréal Protocol, the Nuclear Test Ban Treaty, and the UN Convention son the Law of the Sea and Climate Change.

19ECONOMY

Before the war, Bosnia and Herzegovina ranked next to Macedonia as the poorest republic of the former Yugoslav SFR. Although industry accounted for over 50% of GDP, Bosnia and Herzegovina was primarily agricultural. Farms were small and inefficient, thus necessitating food imports. Industry was greatly overstaffed, with Bosnia and Herzegovina accounting for much of the former Yugoslav SFR's metallic ore and coal production. Timber production and textiles also were important.

The destructive impact of the war on the economy led to a 75% drop in GDP. Since the Dayton Accords of 1995, trade increased in Croat areas, and significant growth began in Muslim areas. Reconstruction programs initiated by the international community financed the construction of infrastructure and provided loans to the manufacturing sector. External aid amounted to $5 billion between 1995–99. This aid caused growth rates to increase to 30%, but as of 2003, that rate had stabilized to around 6%. Actual GDP growth by that year had reached half its prewar level.

Privatization has been slow and Western financial organizations are increasing calls for reform in this area, especially in telecommunications and energy. (The private sector accounts for only 35% of the economy.) Foreign direct investment remains low, due in part to corruption and many layers of bureaucracy. Tax reform is needed, as is reform of the banking industry and the financial services sector. In 2002, the government adopted a poverty reduction strategy designed to create more jobs and increase exports. As foreign aid declines in coming years, Bosnia and Herzegovina will need to increase exports to generate hard currency revenues. Some progress was made in this area in 2001 with exports of clothing, furniture, and leather goods.

The economic rate of recovery has been spectacular and encouraging in subsequent years. Thus, the GDP growth rate improved from 5.6% in 2002, to 7.0% in 2003, and 8.3% in 2004; it was expected to grow even further, at 9.5%, in 2005. Unemployment, similar to most former Yugoslav republics, save Slovenia, remains a major problem. In 2004, the unemployment rate was 44%, although many of the officially jobless are thought to be working within the grey economy. Inflation has decreased to insignificant levels (0.8% in 2004), and it may pose a problem to the country's export sector.

20INCOME

The US Central Intelligence Agency (CIA) reports that in 2005 Bosnia and Herzegovina's gross domestic product (GDP) was estimated at $28.3 billion. Bosnia has a large informal sector that could also be as much as 50% of official GDP. The CIA defines GDP as the value of all final goods and services produced within a nation in a given year and computed on the basis of purchasing power parity (PPP) rather than value as measured on the basis of the rate of exchange based on current dollars. The per capita GDP was estimated at $6,800. The annual growth rate of GDP was estimated at 5.2%. The average inflation rate in 2005 was 1.4%. It was estimated that agriculture accounted for 14.2% of GDP, industry 30.8%, and services 55%.

According to the World Bank, in 2003 remittances from citizens working abroad totaled $1.178 billion or about $307 per capita and accounted for approximately 16.9% of GDP. Foreign aid receipts amounted to about $130 per capita.

The World Bank reports that in 2003 household consumption in Bosnia and Herzegovina totaled $6.4 billion or about $1,670 per capita based on a GDP of $7.0 billion, measured in current dollars rather than PPP. Household consumption includes expenditures of individuals, households, and nongovernmental organizations on goods and services, excluding purchases of dwellings.

It was estimated that in 2004 about 25% of the population had incomes below the poverty line.

21 LABOR

The labor force in 2002 numbered 1.026 million. As of end 2004, the official unemployment rate stood at an estimated 45.5%. However, the actual unemployment rate may be between 25% and 30%, due to the so-called "gray economy." There is no data available as to the occupational breakdown of the Bosnian work force.

All workers are legally entitled to form or join unions and to strike, but labor activity is limited due to high unemployment rates and economic hardship. Unions are highly politicized and are formed along ethnic lines. Strikes were used frequently in 2001 as a form of protest against arrears in salaries and overdue wages.

The minimum employment age in the Bosnian-Croat Federation and the Republika Srpska entities is 15. However, many younger children often assist with family agricultural work and minors between the ages of 15 and 18, in order to work, must provide a valid health certificate. As of 2005, the minimum wage was $193 per month in the Federation and $51 in Republika Srpska. The legal workweek in both entities is 40 hours, although seasonal workers may work up to 60 hours per week. Laws in both entities require a 30-minute rest period during the work day. Safety and health regulations are generally ignored due to the economic devastation of war.

22 AGRICULTURE

About 21.3% (1,030,000 hectares/2,545,000 acres) of the total area was considered arable land in 2002. About 4% of the economically active population was engaged in agriculture in 2003. During the disintegration of Yugoslavia, civil fighting in the major agricultural areas often interrupted harvests and caused considerable loss of field crops. Principal crops harvested in 2004 included (in 1,000 tons): corn, 800; wheat, 250; potatoes, 350; fruit, 157; oats, 55; and rye, 12.

23 ANIMAL HUSBANDRY

There are some 1.2 million hectares (three million acres) of permanent pastureland, representing about 23.5% of the total land area. Because of the breakup of Yugoslavia and subsequent civil war, the livestock population fell significantly during the 1990s. In 2004, the livestock inventory included (in 1,000s): sheep, 670; cattle, 440; pigs, 300; horses, 18; and chickens, 4,700.

Production of meat fell from 158,000 tons in 1990 to 24,000 tons in 1999, and amounted to 32,300 tons in 2004. In 2004, milk production was 460,000 tons; egg production was 15,100 tons during that time.

24 FISHING

With no ports on its 20 km (12 mi) of Adriatic coastline, marine fishing is not commercially significant. Inland fishing occurs on the Sava, Una, and Drina Rivers. The total catch in 2003 was 8,635 tons, 77% from inland waters.

25 FORESTRY

About 2.7 million hectares (6.7 million acres) are forested, accounting for nearly 53% of the total land area. Much of the output is used for fuel. In 2003, forest product imports totaled $24 million; exports, $65.3 million.

26 MINING

Bosnia and Herzegovina's mineral resources include iron ore, lead, zinc, manganese, and bauxite. Iron ore production was centered in Varescaron, Jablanica, Ljubija, and Radovan; lead and zinc ore was mined at Olovo, Varescaron, and Srebrenica; manganese ore operations were centered at Bosanska Krupa; bauxite deposits were worked at Vlasenica, Zvornik, and Banja Luka; substantial nickel deposits had been worked near Visegrad; and substantial nickel deposits had been worked near Visegrad. Energoinvest operated a lead-zinc mine at Srebrenica, a manganese mine at Buzim, bauxite mines in many locations, alumina plants at Birac-Zvornik and Mostar, an aluminum smelter at Mostar, and a petroleum refinery at Bosanski Brod. Before the civil war, Bosnia and Herzegovina was a major center for metallurgical industries in the former Yugoslavia and a major producer of bauxite, alumina, and aluminum. Mineral production in 2003 were, in metric tons: iron ore, 126,929; bauxite, 229,317; lead, (none reported for 2003); zinc, (none reported for 2003); salt, 84,000; crude gypsum, 77,500; ceramic clay, 35,861; and ornamental stone, 35,800 sq m. Other nonfuel mineral resources included asbestos, barite, bentonite, kaolin, lime, magnesite, ammonia nitrogen, glass sand, sand and gravel, soda ash, caustic soda, and crushed and brown stone. Capacity utilization in industrial minerals mining has fallen and modernization and privatization were essential for long-term viability.

27 ENERGY AND POWER

As of 2002, total electrical capacity was 3.950 million kW. Generation for that year amounted to 10.401 billion kWh, of which 5.215 billion kWh was hydroelectric and 5.186 billion kWh were produced by conventional thermal plants. Electrical generation was irregular during the civil conflict of the early to mid-1990s. Total electricity consumption in 2000 was 2.6 billion kWh. In 2002, consumption had risen to 8.559 billion kWh.

Brown coal and lignite mines are located around Tuzla. Coal production is consumed primarily by the country's thermal electric power stations. A petroleum refinery at Bosanski Brod reportedly had an annual capacity of 100 million tons in 1995, and depends entirely on imports; however, the refinery was extensively damaged in April 1993 during local fighting.

28 INDUSTRY

Mining and mining-related activities make up the bulk of Bosnia and Herzegovina's industry. Steel production, vehicle assembly, textiles, tobacco products, wooden furniture, and domestic appliances are also important industries. Industrial capacity, largely damaged or shut down in 1995 because of the civil war, has increased. In 1998, industrial production grew an estimated 35%. Nevertheless, this figure remains lower than the pre-1992 rate, and in 2001, output stood only about half its prewar level. In the Republika Srpska, the Serb Democratic Party controls every significant production facility, government department, and state institution. Privatization began in 1999, but as of 2001, only 7 of 138 strategic enterprises had been sold. Large gains were made in the export of clothing, furniture, and leather goods in 2001. The construction sector in 2002 held promise for growth, as projects to improve infrastructure were underway.

Industrial production growth in 2004 was outpaced by the GDP growth rate, reaching only 5.5%, as opposed to 8.3%. This is an indicator that industry was outperformed by the services sector, which contributed 55% to the overall GDP; industry came in second with a 30.8% share in the GDP composition; agriculture contributed 14.2%. The industrial output growth seemed to recover in 2005, with strong performances by the manufacturing and mining sectors.

29 SCIENCE AND TECHNOLOGY

Scientific and engineering education is provided at the universities of Sarajevo, Banja Luka, and Tuzla (founded in 1948, 1975, and 1976, respectively). The Institute for Thermal and Nuclear Technology, founded in 1961, is located in Sarajevo. Leading professional groups include the Society of Mathematicians, Physicists and Astronomers, the Union of Engineers and Technicians, and the Medical Society of Bosnia and Herzegovina, all headquartered in Sarajevo.

30 DOMESTIC TRADE

Bosnia and Herzegovina is still struggling with efforts to move from socialism to private sector, market-led capitalism. Commerce has been severely restricted by the ongoing interethnic civil strife. In the Bosnian Serb area, senior police commanders and officials in the governing Serb Democratic Party have a monopoly on cigarette and gasoline sales. Retail establishments tend to be very small with limited inventories; however, some large shopping centers are gaining ground. Direct marketing and sales are also gaining in popularity. Installment plans and financing, even for very low cost items, is common, since credit is not widely available or accepted.

Though postwar reconstruction is nearly complete, as of 2002, the country's economy still depended heavily on foreign aid. With the establishment of the Central Bank and currency board in 1997, inflation has since been brought under control; however, unemployment is still high, at about 40% in 2002. As of 2002, the private sector only accounts for about 35% of the economy.

31 FOREIGN TRADE

Due to the UN trade embargo, international trade with Bosnia and Herzegovina was limited during the civil war. In 2000, exports amounted to nearly $1 billion, up from less than $400 million in 1998. Clothing, furniture, and leather goods led this upswing in export revenues. Exports went mainly to Italy, Yugoslavia, and Switzerland. Imports in 2000 totaled $3.6 billion, with Croatia, It-

Principal Trading Partners – Bosnia and Herzegovina (2003)			
(In millions of US dollars)			
Country	**Exports**	**Imports**	**Balance**
World	1,027.5	3,311.9	-2,284.4
Croatia	208.2	642.6	-434.4
Germany	191.7	476.0	-284.3
Italy-San Marino-Holy See	144.5	354.4	-209.9
Switzerland-Liechtenstein	124.6	68.3	56.3
Slovenia	109.1	347.5	-238.4
Serbia and Montenegro	92.3	64.4	27.9
Austria	40.8	150.3	-109.5
France-Monaco	10.6	66.5	-55.9
Luxembourg	10.2	...	10.2
Macedonia	9.4	13.5	-4.1

(…) data not available or not significant.

SOURCE: *2003 International Trade Statistics Yearbook*, New York: United Nations, 2004.

aly, and Slovenia supplying 21%, 16%, and 14% of the total value, respectively.

Before the war, manufactured goods accounted for 31% of exports; machinery and transport equipment, 20.8%; raw materials, 18%; other manufactured products, 17.3%; chemicals, 9.4%; fuel and lubricants, 1.2%; and food and live animals, 1.2%. Fuels and lubricants made up 32% of annual imports before the war; machinery and transport equipment, 23.3%; other manufactured items, 21.3%; chemicals, 10%; raw materials, 6.7%; food and live animals, 5.5%; and beverages and tobacco, 1.9%.

Exports totaled $1.7 billion (FOB—Free on Board) in 2004, and mainly went to Italy (22.3%), Croatia (21.1%), Germany (20.8%), Austria (7.4%), Slovenia (7.1%), and Hungary (4.8%). Base metals topped the list of exports, with 24.9% of total exports; followed by wood and wood products (15.2%); mineral products (11.8%); and chemicals (7.5%). Imports were more than three times as high as exports, at $5.2 billion, and mainly came from Croatia (23.8%), Slovenia (15.8%), Germany (14.8%), Italy (11.4%), Austria (6.6%), and Hungary (6.1%). The most import import commodities were machinery (15.5%), mineral products (12.7%), foodstuffs (11.7%), and chemicals (9.4%).

32 BALANCE OF PAYMENTS

The US Central Intelligence Agency (CIA) reported that in 2001 the purchasing power parity of Bosnia and Herzegovina's exports was $1.1 billion while imports totaled $3.1 billion resulting in a trade deficit of $2 billion. The International Monetary Fund (IMF) reported that in 2001 Bosnia and Herzegovina had exports of goods totaling $1.17 billion and imports totaling $3.92 billion. The services credit totaled $288 million and debit $228 million. Although Bosnia and Herzegovina runs large trade deficits, due to low domestic production, the gap between imports and exports in the early 2000s was narrowing steadily. Export growth in 2001 was fueled by duty-free access of Bosnian exports to the EU.

Exports of goods and services totaled $2.1 billion (FOB—Free on Board) in 2004, up from $1.5 billion in 2003. Imports grew from $5.6 billion in 2003, to $6.7 billion in 2004. The resource balance was on a negative upsurge, growing from -$4.1 billion in 2003, to a whopping -$4.6 billion in 2004. A similar trend was registered for the current account balance, which deteriorated from

```
┌─────────────────────────────────────────────────────┐
│ Balance of Payments – Bosnia and Herzegovina (2003)   │
│                                                         │
│ (In millions of US dollars)                             │
│                                                         │
│ Current Account                              -2,096.0   │
│   Balance on goods             -3,927.9                 │
│     Imports          -5,425.9                           │
│     Exports           1,498.0                           │
│   Balance on services             190.7                 │
│   Balance on income               242.7                 │
│   Current transfers             1,398.6                 │
│ Capital Account                                478.8    │
│ Financial Account                              931.9    │
│   Direct investment abroad          ...                 │
│   Direct investment in Bosnia and Herzegovina   381.8   │
│   Portfolio investment assets       ...                 │
│   Portfolio investment liabilities  ...                 │
│   Financial derivatives             ...                 │
│   Other investment assets         135.9                 │
│   Other investment liabilities    414.2                 │
│ Net Errors and Omissions                       414.9    │
│ Reserves and Related Items                     270.4    │
│                                                         │
│ (…) data not available or not significant.              │
│                                                         │
│ SOURCE: Balance of Payment Statistics Yearbook 2004,    │
│ Washington, DC: International Monetary Fund, 2004.      │
└─────────────────────────────────────────────────────┘
```

-$1.7 billion in 2003, to -$1.9 billion in 2004. The national reserves (including gold) were $1.8 billion in 2003, covering approximately 4 months of imports; in 2004, they grew to $2.4 billion.

33 BANKING AND SECURITIES

The central bank of Bosnia and Herzegovina is the National Bank of Bosnia and Herzegovina. In June 1992 Yugoslavia's central bank refused to issue Yugoslavian dinars in Bosnia and Herzegovina. Commercial banks in the country include Privredna Banka Sarajevo, Hrvatsk A Banka d.d. Mostar, and Investiciono-Komercijalua Banka d.d. Zenica.

In 1996, Croatian dinars were used in Croat-held areas for currency, presumably to be replaced by new Croatian kuna. Old and new Serbian dinars were used in Serb-held areas. Hard currencies, such as the deutschmark, supplanted local currencies in areas held by the Bosnian government. In April 1997 the presidential council agreed on a single currency, the konvertibilni marka (KM), for both the Muslim/Croat and Bosnian Serb parts of the country.

Bank privatization is problematic, but improving. Some of the state-owned banks targeted for privatization were actually privatized during the war. Many are considered insolvent, but in 2001, individual bank deposits in Federation banks were up 178%. The International Monetary Fund reports that in 2001, currency and demand deposits—an aggregate commonly known as M1—were equal to $1.3 billion. In that same year, M2—an aggregate equal to M1 plus savings deposits, small time deposits, and money market mutual funds—was $2.2 billion.

34 INSURANCE

No recent information is available.

35 PUBLIC FINANCE

The US Central Intelligence Agency (CIA) estimated that in 2005 Bosnia and Herzegovina's central government took in revenues of approximately $4.3 billion and had expenditures of $4.4 billion.

Revenues minus expenditures totaled approximately -$28 million. Total external debt was $3.1 billion.

36 TAXATION

Current information is unavailable due to civil unrest.

37 CUSTOMS AND DUTIES

Bosnia has signed free trade agreements with Croatia, Serbia and Montenegro, and Slovenia. Tariff rates for imports from other countries are zero, 5% or 10%, depending on the good, with consumption and luxury goods generally receiving the higher rates.

38 FOREIGN INVESTMENT

Private investment plummeted during the civil war, when UN sanctions were in force. The conclusion of the Dayton Peace Accords in 1995 brought positive changes in the investment climate. In May 1998, a law on foreign direct investment (FDI) was passed and in June 1998, a law on privatization. While privatization of small and medium enterprises made good progress, the state of larger strategic firms has progressed more slowly. As of spring 2002, only 7 of 138 large state-owned enterprises had been sold and only 35% of the economy had been privatized. The largest foreign sale was the Zenica Steel Mill, which became the BH Steel Company in a joint venture with Kuwait Consulting and Investment Company (KCIC) in which both sides put up $60 million (KCIC paid $12 million in 1999 and took over $48 million of debt).

In 1997, only $1 million of FDI flowed into Bosnia and Herzegovina, but this jumped to $54.6 million in 1998 and then to $148.8 million in 1999. A decline occurred in 2001 to $131.5 million (when riots broke out in two Republika Srpska towns over the rebuilding of mosques), but the numbers recovered to $164 million. The overwhelming majority of foreign investment into Bosnia and Herzegovina comes from aid groups and international financial institutions.

From 1994 to 2002, over half (55.5%) of FDI was in manufacturing, thanks primarily to the BH Steel Company venture. Banking has received 16.5% (mainly from Dubai, Austria, and Croatia); services, 6.8%; trade, 6.2%; transport, 0.9%; and tourism, 0.7%.

Previous years have seen Bosnia and Herzegovina take on major changes in an attempt to attract foreign investors. A liberal State Foreign Investment Policy Law, a common currency, and a more streamlined trade and customs policy were some of the most noteworthy attempts to increase capital inflows. However, these efforts failed to bring about the desired result—an indicator that more changes of the legal framework and business environment have to be undertaken. Foreign investments totaled around $1.9 billion in 2003. In the first nine months of 2004, $367 million in FDI came into the country, with 60% of these inflows going to the banking sector.

39 ECONOMIC DEVELOPMENT

Following the 1995 peace agreement, economic assistance was expected to lay the groundwork for a revival of the economy. The actual distribution of assistance to particular entities or areas was tied to the government's compliance with the Dayton Accords. Into 2005, privatization and reconstruction were ongoing. The absence of a single market in Bosnia and Herzegovina is an obstacle to economic development, as is the lack of legal certainty and a high degree of bureaucratization. A central bank was established in 1997, and a new currency launched in 1998. Successful debt negotiations have been held with the London Club and the Paris Club.

In 2004, Bosnia and Herzegovina scored an important increase in economic output, but the GDP was still below prewar levels. Apart from a series of systemic and political problems, the country has to fight rampant unemployment, a large underground economy, and an inflation level that was not helping the already low export levels. However, one of Bosnia's long-term goals is EU integration. A series of planned privatizations and restructurings in the energy, transportation, telecommunication, and construction sectors were expected to jump-start the economy and create a circle of cumulative causations that will attract future investments in the future.

40 SOCIAL DEVELOPMENT

Social welfare systems have been in crisis since the wars of the 1990s. International efforts are in place to shift from humanitarian aid to a sustainable social welfare system. There is also an effort to reformulate disability pensions.

Although gender discrimination is proscribed by the 2003 Law on Gender Equality, the extent of legal and social discrimination against women varies by region. Women in urban areas pursue professional careers in such areas as law, medicine, and academia, while their rural counterparts are often relegated to the margins of public life. Violence against women remains underreported and there are accounts of police inaction in domestic situations. It was estimated in 2004 that over 25% of families experiences domestic violence. The problem is more significant in rural areas, and is exacerbated by poverty and alcoholism. Trafficking of women remains a major problem in the region.

All sides were guilty of human rights atrocities in the war and its aftermath. By 1995, it was estimated that up to two-thirds of the country's prewar population have become refugees or displaced persons. Women were targeted for cruel treatment during the war, and Serb forces systematically used rape as a tool to accelerate ethnic cleansing. The worst single incident of genocide in Europe since World War II occurred in the Bosnian "safe haven" of Srebrenica in 1995. Over 7,000 men and boys were massacred at Srebrenica. As of 2005, many if not most of the perpetrators of these vicious acts remain unpunished.

Human rights abuses have continued in the political entities established by the 1995 Dayton Peace Accords. Discrimination and harassment of minority ethnic groups remain a huge problem in all regions. There are widespread reports of police brutality and corruption, and prison standards are poor. However, human rights groups are able to operate without government restrictions.

41 HEALTH

There were over 200,000 war-related deaths in the 1990s (120,000 in 1992 alone) and many Bosnians were permanently disabled. Besides causing hundreds of thousands of deaths and injuries, the Bosnian war destroyed much of the health care infrastructure. Many hospitals were destroyed and infant mortality rates increased.

In 2005, the average life expectancy was 78 years. The infant mortality rate was 11 deaths per 1,000 live births in that year. In 2002 the birth rate was estimated at 13 per 1,000 people and the death rate was 8 per 1,000. In 1999, an estimated 83% of children under one had a measles vaccination and 90% of children were immunized for diphtheria. In 1999, there were 87 cases of tuberculosis per 100,000 people.

Salaries for health care providers are low, and medical equipment is outdated. As of 2004, there were an estimated 134 physicians, 411 nurses, 16 dentists, and 9 pharmacists per 100,000 people. Primary care is provided through health centers (*dom zdravlyas*) and outpatient branches called *ambulantas*. As of 1999 there were 87 *dom zdravlyas* in the Bosnian Federation, staffed by general practitioners and nurses, providing primary care, preventive care, health education, and rehabilitation. Among the secondary and tertiary care facilities in the Republika Srpska is one in Banja Luka that has 1,327 beds and one in Sarajevo with 776 beds. The country has five medical schools. Health expenditure was estimated at 8% of GDP.

The HIV/AIDS prevalence was 0.10 per 100 adults in 2003. As of 2004, there were approximately 900 people living with HIV/AIDS in the country. There were an estimated 100 deaths from AIDS in 2003.

42 HOUSING

There is a chronic housing shortage in Bosnia and Herzegovina, since a majority of all homes, and even a few entire towns, were destroyed during the civil war in the period 1992–1995. Over two million people were forced from their homes during that time and about 65% of the housing stock was destroyed or seriously damaged. Since 1998, over 100,000 housing units have been repaired in some way, but many existing homes are still in serious need of repair and utilities are not always available. With the help of international assistance programs, only about half of the nation's refugees and displaced residents were able to return to their homes by 2001.

43 EDUCATION

Before the Bosnian war of the early 1990s, the area covered by present-day Bosnia and Herzegovina had 641 primary and 243 secondary schools. By 1996, these totals had been reduced to 270 primary and 141 secondary schools. There were fewer than 200,000 primary pupils, taught by 8,000 teachers, and 65,500 secondary students, with 4,100 teachers.

Education at the elementary level is free and compulsory for students between the ages of 6 and 15. At the secondary level, children have the option to take up general education (gymnasium), vocational, or technical. General secondary lasts for four years and qualifies the students for university education. In 2001 the government began a modernization program for primary and secondary education, covering curriculum, special needs education, in-service teacher training, and other areas. The academic year runs from October to July. The languages of instructions are Croatian and Serbian. Education is administered by the Ministry of Education, Science, Culture and Sports. Each of the country's 10 cantons also has its own education ministry.

There are four main universities: the University of Banja Luka (founded in 1975); the University of Mostar (founded in 1977); the University of Tuzla (founded in 1976); and the University of Sarajevo (founded in 1949), which offers programs in the social sciences, humanities, sciences, medicine, law, and engineering. Several other academies have been founded throughout the country since 1993. The adult literacy rate for 2004 was estimated at about 95.6%, with 98.4% for males and 91.1% for females.

44 LIBRARIES AND MUSEUMS

Numerous historic sites have been damaged by war, including the National and University Library of Bosnia and Herzegovina, which sustained major damage and a large loss of materials in a 1992 bombing. Outside groups, such as UNESCO, have since been working to rebuild the National Library. In Banja Luka, there is an important university and public library founded in 1936, and holding 226,000 volumes with an impressive collection of Eastern manuscripts. The University of Sarajevo also housed an impressive library, but it was badly damaged during the civil war. The National Museum of Bosnia and Herzegovina has a library with 162,000 volumes.

Prior to the 1992 war, Sarajevo was a major cultural center in the Balkans. It still hosts nearly a dozen museums, including the Museum of the Old Orthodox Church, the Museum of Young Bosnia, the State Museum, and the Museum of the City of Sarajevo, as well as Bosnia's National Museum. In the provinces are the Museum of the National Struggle for Liberation in Jajce and the Museum of Herzegovina in Mostar.

45 MEDIA

In general, the telephone and telegraph network is in need of modernization and expansion. Service in many urban centers is said to be below the level of other former Yugoslav republics. In 2003, there were an estimated 245 mainline telephones for every 1,000 people. The same year, there were approximately 274 mobile phones in use for every 1,000 people.

There are over 200 commercial radio and television stations, but the most influential stations are those operated by the Public Broadcasting Service of Bosnia-Herzegovina and Serb Republic Radio-TV. In 2003, there were an estimated 243 radios for every 1,000 people. The number of television sets in use was unavailable in the same survey. Also in 2003, about 26 of every 1,000 people reported having access to the Internet. There were 15 secure Internet servers in the country in 2004.

In Sarajevo, the daily newspaper *Oslobodjenje* (*Liberation*) managed to publish continuously throughout the siege of that city despite power and phone line outages, newsprint shortages, and direct attacks on its offices. Founded in 1943 as a Nazi resistance publication, *Oslobodjenje*, which is published in Serbo-Croatian, had a circulation of 56,000 in 2002. In 1993, two of its editors received international recognition from the *World Press Review*.

The constitution signed in Dayton, Ohio, on 21 November 1995, provides for freedom of speech and the press. However, the extreme ethnic segregation in various regions is reported to put the media in each area under considerable regional restrictions. The development of independent media is beginning to be implemented, through the sponsorship of private organizations, cultural societies, and political parties, along with Western aid organizations.

46 ORGANIZATIONS

The Bosnia and Herzegovina Chamber of Commerce promotes trade and commerce in world markets. There are some professional associations, particularly those representing medical professionals in specialized fields.

There are over a dozen learned societies in Bosnia and Herzegovina. Research institutions in the country are concentrated in the areas of nuclear technology, meteorology, historical monument preservation, and language.

Youth organizations include the Student Union of Bosnia and Herzegovina and the Council of Scout Associations. There are a number of sports associations, including those dedicated to such favorite pastimes as tennis, skating, and handball. There is also an active committee of the Special Olympics.

There is a national chapter of UNICEF and the Red Cross Society. Volunteer service organizations, such as the Lions Clubs International, are also present.

47 TOURISM, TRAVEL, AND RECREATION

Civil war has limited the development of a tourism industry in Bosnia and Herzegovina. Sarajevo, the capital city, is growing as a tourist attraction. The city was the site of the 1984 Winter Olympics. In 2003, there were about 165,000 tourist arrivals. Tourist receipts totaled $258 million.

According to the US Department of State, the cost of staying in Sarajevo in 2005 was about $172 per day.

48 FAMOUS BOSNIANS AND HERZEGOVINIANS

Dr. Alija Izetbegović (1925–2003) was the president of Bosnia and Herzegovina from 1991–96, and was a member of the three-man presidency from 1996–2000 until he stepped down due to ill heath. Dzemd Bijedic (1917–1977) was a leader of Yugoslavia from 1971 until 1977, when he was killed in a plane crash. The 1914 assassination of the Austrian Archduke Franz Ferdinand in Sarajevo led to WW I.

49 DEPENDENCIES

Bosnia and Herzegovina has no territories or colonies.

50 BIBLIOGRAPHY

Allen, Beverly. *Rape Warfare: The Hidden Genocide in Bosnia-Herzegovina and Croatia*. Minneapolis: University of Minnesota Press, 1996.

Andjelic, Neven. *Bosnia-Herzegovina: The End of a Legacy*. London: Frank Cass, 2003.

Bose, Sumantra. *Bosnia after Dayton: Nationalist Partition and International Intervention*. New York: Oxford University Press, 2002.

Cousens, Elizabeth M. *Toward Peace in Bosnia: Implementing the Dayton Accords*. Boulder, Colo.: Lynne Rienner, 2001.

Cuvalo, Ante. *Historical Dictionary of Bosnia and Herzegovina*. Lanham, Md.: Scarecrow, 1997.

Doubt, Keith. *Sociology after Bosnia and Kosovo: Recovering Justice*. Lanham, Md.: Rowman and Littlefield, 2000.

Filipovic, Zlata. *Zlata's Diary: A Child's Life in Sarajevo*. New York: Viking, 1994.

Frucht, Richard (ed.). *Eastern Europe: An Introduction to the People, Lands, and Culture.* Santa Barbara, Calif.: ABC-CLIO, 2005.

Jones, Lynne. *Then They Started Shooting: Growing Up in Wartime Bosnia.* Cambridge, Mass.: Harvard University Press, 2004.

King, David C. *Bosnia and Herzegovina.* New York: Marshall Cavendish Benchmark, 2005.

Lovrenovic, Ivan. *Bosnia: A Cultural History.* New York: New York University Press, 2001.

Mahmutcehajic, Rusmir. *Bosnia the Good: Tolerance and Tradition.* New York: Central European University Press, 2000.

McElrath, Karen (ed.). *HIV and AIDS: A Global View.* Westport, Conn.: Greenwood Press, 2002.

Pinson, Mark (ed.) *The Muslims of Bosnia-Herzegovina: Their Historic Development from the Middle Ages to the Dissolution of Yugoslavia.* 2nd ed., Cambridge, Mass.: Harvard University Press, 1996.

Pejanovic, Mirko. *Through Bosnian Eyes: The Political Memoir of a Bosnian Serb.* West Lafayette, Ind.: Purdue University Press, 2004.

Sacco, Joe. *War's End: Profiles from Bosnia, 1995–1996.* Montréal: Drawn and Quarterly, 2005.

Schuman, Michael. *Bosnia and Herzegovina.* New York: Facts On File, 2004.

Terry, Sara. *Aftermath: Bosnia's Long Road to Peace.* New York: Channel Photographics, 2005.

Velikonja, Mitja. *Religious Separation and Political Intolerance in Bosnia-Herzegovina.* College Station, Tex.: Texas A and M University Press, 2003.

Yugoslavia, the Former and Future: Reflections by Scholars from the Region. Washington, D.C.: Brookings Institution, 1995.

BULGARIA

Republic of Bulgaria
Republika Bulgariya

CAPITAL: Sofia (Sofiya)

FLAG: The flag is a tricolor of white, green, and red horizontal stripes.

ANTHEM: *Bulgariya mila, zemya na geroi (Dear Bulgaria, Land of Heroes).*

MONETARY UNIT: The lev (LV) of 100 stotinki has coins of 1, 2, 5, 10, 20, and 50 stotinki and 1 and 2 leva, and notes of 1, 2, 5, 10, 20, 50, and 100 leva. LV1 = $0.64103 (or $1 = LV1.56) as of 2005.

WEIGHTS AND MEASURES: The metric system is the legal standard.

HOLIDAYS: New Year's Day, 1 January; Labor Days, 1–2 May; Education and Culture Day, 24 May; Christmas, 24–25 December.

TIME: 2 PM=noon GMT.

¹LOCATION, SIZE, AND EXTENT

Part of the Balkan Peninsula, Bulgaria has an area of 110,910 sq km (42,822 sq mi), and extends 330 km (205 mi) N–S and 520 km (323 mi) E–W. Comparatively, the area occupied by Bulgaria is slightly larger than the state of Tennessee. Bulgaria is bounded on the N by Romania, on the E by the Black Sea, on the SE by Turkey, on the S by Greece, and on the W by Macedonia and Serbia, with a total boundary length of 1,808 km (1,123 mi).

Bulgaria's capital city, Sofia, is located in the west central part of the country.

²TOPOGRAPHY

Bulgaria consists of a number of roughly parallel east–west zones. They are the Danubian tableland in the north, the Balkan Mountains (Stara Planina) in the center, and the Thracian Plain, drained by the Maritsa River, in the south. The Rhodope, Rila, and Pirin mountains lie in the southwestern part of the country. The average elevation is 480 m (1,575 ft), and the highest point, in the Rila Mountains, is the Musala, at 2,925 m (9,596 ft). The Danube (Dunav), Bulgaria's only navigable river, forms most of the northern boundary with Romania. Located along the Eurasian Tectonic Plate, the country does experience some low-level magnitude earthquakes.

³CLIMATE

Bulgaria lies along the southern margins of the continental climate of Central and Eastern Europe. Regional climatic differences occur in the Danubian tableland, exposed to cold winter winds from the north, and the Thracian Plain, which has a modified Mediterranean climate and is protected by the Balkan Mountains against the northern frosts. January temperatures are between 0° and 2°C (32–36°F) in the lowlands but colder in the mountains; July temperatures average about 22° to 24°C (72–75°F). Precipitation is fairly regularly distributed throughout the year and amounts to an average of 64 cm (25 in).

⁴FLORA AND FAUNA

As of 2002, there were at least 81 species of mammals, 248 species of birds, and over 3,500 species of plants in the country. In the northeast lies the typical steppe grassland zone of the Dobrudja, merging into the wooded steppe of the Danubian tableland. Most trees in this area have been cut down to make room for cultivated land. The Balkan Mountains are covered by broadleaf forests at lower altitudes and by needle-leaf conifers at higher elevations. The vegetation of the Thracian Plain is a mixture of the middle-latitude forest of the north and Mediterranean flora. Deforestation has reduced the amount of wildlife, which includes bears, foxes, squirrels, elks, wildcats, and rodents of various types. Fish resources in the Black Sea are not extensive.

⁵ENVIRONMENT

Bulgaria's air pollution problem results from the combined influence of industry and transportation. In the mid-1990s, Bulgaria was among the 50 countries with the highest industrial emissions of carbon dioxide, producing 54.3 million metric tons, or 6.08 metric tons per capita. In 1996, the total was 55.2 million metric tons. Industrial pollutants, especially from metallurgical plants, are responsible for damage to 115 sq mi of land in Bulgaria. Bulgaria's rivers and the Black Sea are seriously affected by industrial and chemical pollutants, raw sewage, heavy metals, and detergents. However, nearly 100% of the population have access to safe drinking water.

Twenty-five percent of Bulgaria's forests have been significantly damaged by airborne pollutants. In 2000, about 33.4% of the total land area was forested. Only 4.5% of the country's total land area is protected, including the Pirin National Park and the Srebarna Nature Reserve, which are both natural UNESCO World Heritage Sites. There are 10 Ramsar wetland sites.

According to a 2006 report issued by the International Union for Conservation of Nature and Natural Resources (IUCN), threatened species included 12 types of mammals, 11 species of birds, 2 types of reptiles, 10 species of fish, and 11 other invertebrates. Endangered species in Bulgaria include the Rosalia long-horn, Atlantic sturgeon, and slender-billed curlew.

6 POPULATION

The population of Bulgaria in 2005 was estimated by the United Nations (UN) at 7,741,000, which placed it at number 94 in population among the 193 nations of the world. In 2005, approximately 17% of the population was over 65 years of age, with another 14% of the population under 15 years of age. There were 94 males for every 100 females in the country. According to the UN, the annual population rate of change for 2005–10 was expected to be -0.5%, a rate the government viewed as too low. With one of the lowest fertility rates in the world, Bulgaria has experience population declines since 1990. The projected population for the year 2025 was 6,565,000. The population density was 70 per sq km (181 per sq mi).

The UN estimated that 70% of the population lived in urban areas in 2005, and that urban areas were declining in population at an annual rate of -0.31%. The capital city, Sofia (Sofiya), had a population of 1,076,000 in that year. Other large cities include Plovdiv, 715,904; Varna, 320,668; Burgas, 259,985; Ruse, 266,213; and Stara Zagora, 167,708.

7 MIGRATION

Emigration between 1948 and 1951 consisted mainly of Jews going to Israel and Turks going to Turkey. A high of 99,477 (of whom 98,341 were Turks) was reached in 1951. Most of the emigrants since the 1950s have been Turks bound for Turkey or other Balkan countries. A total of 313,894 emigrated to Turkey in 1989 because of government persecution. More than 100,000 had returned to Bulgaria by February 1990. Meanwhile, about 150,000 ethnic Bulgarians also emigrated. In 1991 about three million Bulgarians were living abroad. Of those emigrating 85% were under age 30.

According to *Migration News*, due to low fertility and emigration, Bulgaria's population is shrinking faster than any other nation in Europe. The majority of those leaving Bulgaria are moving to Germany, Spain, the Netherlands, and North America. The net migration rate, estimated for 2005, was -4.3 migrants per 1,000 population. Once the European Union (EU) lifted visa requirements for Bulgarians in 2001, Bulgarians illegally migrated to Western countries. Between April 2001 and October 2002, about 6,561 Bulgarians were arrested and expelled from EU counties, the United States, and Canada. The number of illegal foreigners in Bulgaria is low. Due to the high unemployment rate (12% in 2004), there are serious restrictions on foreign workers.

As of 2004, there were 4,684 refugees and about 920 registered asylum seekers in Bulgaria. Most of the refugees and asylum seekers were from Afghanistan, Iraq, Serbia, Montenegro, and Armenia.

8 ETHNIC GROUPS

In 2001, Bulgarians accounted for an estimated 83.9% of the total population. The Turks, who constituted about 9.4% of the total, are settled mainly in the southern Dobrudja and in the eastern Rhodope Mountains. Romas account for about 4.7% of the popu-

lation. Other groups, including Macedonians, Armenians, Tatars, and Circassians, make up the remaining 2% of the populace.

Macedonians live mainly in the Pirin region of southwestern Bulgaria. Romanian-speaking Vlachs live in the towns and countryside of northwestern Bulgaria. Greek-speaking Karakatchans are nomadic mountain shepherds of Romanian origin. The Gagauzi of northeastern Bulgaria are a Turkish-speaking group of Christian Orthodox religion. Bulgaria's cities have small minorities of Russians, Jews, Armenians, Tatars, and Greeks.

9 LANGUAGES

Bulgarian is classified as a Slavic language of the southern group, which also includes Macedonian, Serbo-Croatian, and Slovenian. Old Bulgarian, also known as Old Church Slavonic, was the first Slavic language fixed in writing (9th century). For this purpose, two Bulgarian monks, Cyril and Methodius, created a new alphabet, based partly on the Greek, that became known as the Cyrillic alphabet. Both the grammar and the vocabulary of modern Bulgarian show Turkish, Greek, Romanian, and Albanian influences.

According to a 2001 census, 84.5% of the population speak Bulgarian, 9.6% speak Turkish, 4.1% speak Roma, and 1.8% speak other languages or did not specify a primary language.

10 RELIGIONS

According to a 2004 report, about 82.6% of the population belonged at least nominally to the Bulgarian (Eastern) Orthodox Church. There were also an estimated 12.2% who were Muslims. Other religious groups include Roman Catholics, Jews, Uniate Catholics, Protestants, and Gregorian-Armenians.

After seizing power in 1946, the Communist regime, whose aim was eventually to establish an atheistic society, sought during the ensuing period to replace all religious rites and rituals with civil ceremonies. The new constitution of 1991 guaranteed freedom of religion to all, but named the Bulgarian Orthodox Church as a "traditional" religion of state. Under a 2002 Confessions Act, all religious groups except for the Bulgarian Orthodox Church must register with the Sofia Municipal Court in order to offer public worship. The registration process tends to be long and selective.

11 TRANSPORTATION

The Bulgarian Railway Company (BDZ) oversees Bulgaria's railway system. Railroads are still the basic means of freight transportation in Bulgaria. Of the 4,294 km (2,671 mi) of railroad lines in use in 2004, about 94% were standard gauge. A total of 245 km (152 mi) of narrow gauge right of way accounted for the remainder.

In 2003, roadways extended for 102,016 km (63,453 mi), of which 93,855 km (58,378 mi) were paved, including 328 km (204 mi) of expressways. Road transportation has grown steadily in recent years. Bulgaria has many highway projects underway, including portions of the Trans-European Motorway (TEM), a route connecting Budapest with Athens via Vidin and Sofia and with Istanbul via eastern Bulgaria. As of 2003, there were 2,309,300 passenger cars and 337,200 commercial vehicles registered for use.

Water transportation is also significant. As of 2005, Bulgaria's maritime fleet was comprised of 64 ships with a total capacity of 757,972 GRT, as compared with 97,800 GRT in 1961. The major seaports are Burgas and Varna. Principal river ports are Ruse,

BULGARIA

0   25   50 Miles

0   25   50 Kilometers

R O M A N I A

⊛ Bucharest

Zaječar   • Vidin
• Craiova
Silistra   Constanța •

Dunav (Danube)   *Dunărea*

Lom   Kozloduy   Alexandria •   • **Ruse**

Beleňe •   **Razgrad**   Dobrich •

Ogosta   • Mikhaylovgrad   *Yantra*

Iskur   • Pleven

SERBIA   Vratsa •   Veliko   Türgovishte •   • Shumen   **Varna**
Tŭrnovo •   *Kamchiya*

B A L K A N   *Osum*   Gabrovo •   M O U N T A I N S   *Black Sea*

Kremikovtsi •   *Stryama*   Sliven •
⊛ **Sofia**   Kazanlŭk •

Pernik •   Panagyurishte •   *Tundzha*   **Burgas**

Priboj •   Yambol •

Struma   ▲ Musala   Stara   Elkhovo •
9,596 ft.   Zagora •
2925 m.   Pazardzhik •   **Plovdiv**   *Maritsa*

Blagoevgrad •   Asenovgrad •   Svilengrad •

R H O D O P E   **TURKEY**

MACEDONIA   *Mesta*

Strumica •   Smolyan •   *Arda*   Kŭrdzhali •
Rudozem •   M T S .
Madan •

G R E E C E   Bulgaria

Alexandroupolis •

Thessaloníki •   *Aegean Sea*

LOCATION: 41°14′ to 44°13′ N; 22°22′ to 28°37′ E. BOUNDARY LENGTHS: Romania, 608 kilometers (378 miles); Black Sea, 354 kilometers (220 miles); Turkey, 240 kilometers (149 miles); Greece, 494 kilometers (307 miles); Macedonia, 148 kilometers (92 miles); Serbia, 318 kilometers (198 miles). TERRITORIAL SEA LIMIT: 12 miles.

Lom, and Vidin. In addition, the country as of 2004 had 470 km of navigable internal waterways.

In 2004 there were an estimated 213 airports. As of 2005 a total of 128 had paved runways, and there was also a single heliport. Sofia's Vrazhdebna Airport is the major air center, but there are also international airports at Varna and Burgas, as well as seven domestic airports. Initially a joint Soviet-Bulgarian concern, Bulgarian Airlines (BALKAN) passed into Bulgarian hands in 1954. Civilian airlines in Bulgaria carried about 75,000 passengers on scheduled domestic and international airline flights in 2003.

12 HISTORY

Ancient Thrace and Moesia, the areas that modern Bulgaria occupies, were settled in the 6th century AD by Southern Slavs migrating from the area north of the Carpathian Mountains (mod-

ern-day Ukraine and Romania). The Thracian tribes, which had populated that territory since the middle of the 2nd century BC, were displaced or conquered. In the 7th century AD, the Bulgars, a Central Asian Turkic tribe, crossed the Danube River to settle permanently in the Balkans. In alliance with the overpowered Slavs, the Bulgars formed the Bulgarian state, which was recognized by the Byzantine Empire in 681 AD. The name and initial political framework of the new state were taken from the Bulgars, but the language and the culture remained predominantly Slavic.

In the late 9th century, Bulgaria became an arena for political and cultural rivalry between the Byzantine Empire centered in Constantinople and the Roman Empire. The Bulgarians adopted Christianity from the Byzantine Empire and embraced the Cyrillic alphabet, named for St. Cyril. As a result, the integration of the disparate tribes into a Bulgarian people was more or less complete by the end of the 9th century.

The early Bulgarian state reached its territorial and cultural height under Simeon I (r.893–927). In 1018, Bulgaria, which had struggled to assert itself against Constantinople since its foundation, fell under Byzantine dominance. The country rose again as a major Balkan power in the 12th and 13th centuries, especially under Ivan Asen II (r.1218–41) whose rule extended over nearly the whole Balkan Peninsula except the Greek islands. However, by the end of the 14th century, Bulgaria was overrun by the Ottoman Turks, who ruled the country for nearly five centuries.

The Ottoman rule was often oppressive and sought to assimilate Bulgarian Christianity, culture, and language. Rebellions were frequent but sporadic and unorganized. However, in the early 19th century, under the influence of Western ideas such as liberalism and nationalism, a well-organized national liberation movement emerged. Its efforts culminated in the April uprising of 1876, which was brutally crushed. Russia, a rival of the Ottoman Empire at the time, insisted on a peaceful solution to the Bulgarian question. When diplomacy failed, Russia declared war on Turkey. The Bulgarian state was restored in the aftermath of the Russian-Turkish War of 1877–1878.

Apprehensive of the existence of a big Bulgarian state under Russian influence, the Congress of Berlin (June–July 1878) divided the Bulgarian territories into three parts. Northern Bulgaria was given the status of an independent principality under Turkish suzerainty, with its capital at Sofia. Southern Bulgaria (then known as Eastern Rumelia) remained under Turkish rule as an autonomous province. Lastly, ethnic Bulgarians in the regions of Macedonia and Thrace were unconditionally returned to the Ottoman Empire. The decisions of the Congress triggered first the Kresna–Razlog uprising (1878–1879), which sought to unify the Principality of Bulgaria and Eastern Rumelia; and the Ilinden–Preobrazhenie Uprising (1903), which demanded the liberation of Macedonia. Neither rebellion was immediately successful.

In 1879 the First Grand National Assembly adopted the first Constitution of Bulgaria and elected the German prince Alexander Battenberg as the prince of Bulgaria. In 1885, the continuing unrest in Eastern Rumelia culminated in a military coup, which annexed the province to Bulgaria. Stefan Stambolov, premier from 1887 to 1894, consolidated the country's administration and economy. In 1908 Bulgaria declared itself a kingdom completely independent of Turkey.

Striving to unite "all Bulgarians," the country took part in the First Balkan War (October 1912–May 1913) and fought with the anti-Turkish coalition (Greece, Serbia, and Montenegro) against the Ottomans. Bulgaria gained most of Thrace including a long-desired outlet to the Aegean Sea. But as a result of a dispute over Macedonia, Bulgaria became pitted against Greece and Serbia. Turkey joined the Greece-Serbia coalition in the hope of winning back some of its territories. Romania also sided against Bulgaria in the Second Balkan War (June–July 1913), and Bulgaria was defeated. As a result, Bulgaria lost southern Dobrudja to Romania, a large part of Macedonia to Serbia, western Thrace to Greece and southeastern Thrace to Turkey. Having sided with the Central Powers in World War I in an attempt to recoup its losses, Bulgaria also lost its outlet to the Aegean Sea and additional parts of Mace-

donia and Dobrudja through the Treaty of Neuilly (27 November 1919).

At the end of World War I, Bulgarian ruler Tsar Ferdinand of Saxe-Coburg-Gotha abdicated in favor of his son, Boris III, who ruled Bulgaria until his death in 1943. After an early period of stability and initial progressive reform under the leadership of Premier Alexander Stamboliski (assassinated in 1923 after agreeing to recognize Yugoslav sovereignty in Macedonia), growing political rivalries allowed Tsar Boris to establish a military government in 1934 and then to personally assume dictatorial powers in 1935.

When World War II broke out, Bulgaria moved toward an alliance with Germany in the hope of recovering lost territories. In 1940, Romania was forced to return southern Dobrudja, and during the war, Bulgaria occupied Macedonia and western Thrace. By 1943, some 20,000 Jews were deported but protests from political and clerical leaders stopped further cooperation, thus saving all of the remaining 50,000 Jews in the country. Bulgaria did, however, actively deport Jews in all areas it conquered.

After Tsar Boris's sudden death in 1943, a cabinet, which was in most respects a German puppet, assumed power. Coordinated mainly by Communists, resistance to the Germans and the authoritarian Bulgarian regime was widespread by 1943. In September 1944, Soviet troops entered the country. At that time, the Bulgarian government withdrew from the occupied territories, severed relations with Germany, and intended to sign an armistice with the Western Allies. But Moscow declared war on Bulgaria and proceeded with the occupation of the country. A coalition government—the Fatherland Front (Otechestven Front)—was established, which, with the assistance of the Soviet army, came under the domination of the Communist Party. Subsequently, anti-Communist political activists were purged.

A plebiscite in September 1946 replaced the monarchy with the People's Republic of Bulgaria and the Communists openly took power. The 1947 peace treaty formally ending Bulgaria's role in World War II allowed the nation to keep southern Dobrudja but limited the size of its armed forces.

Shortly after coming to power, the Bulgarian Communist Party fell under increasing pressure from Moscow to demonstrate its loyalty by stepping up the "socialist transformation" in the country. The Bulgarian leadership moved to ascertain its effective monopoly on political power by eliminating political opposition in the country and "nationalist" elements within the party and to emulate the Soviet economic experience through the introduction of a planned economy. A new constitution in 1947 instituted the nationalization of industry, banking, and public utilities and the collectivization of agriculture. Centralized planning was introduced for the development of the national economy through a series of five-year plans, which stressed the expansion of heavy industry at the expense of agriculture and light industry. Subsequently, Bulgaria joined the Warsaw Pact and CMEA, thus placing itself firmly within the Soviet bloc.

Under Todor Zhivkov, first secretary of the Communist Party since 1954 and president since 1971, the Bulgarian government remained unquestionably loyal to the Soviet Union. This continued even after Soviet leader Joseph Stalin's death in 1953. While some freedom of expression was gradually restored, labor camps closed, and persecution of the Christian church ended, upheavals like those in Poland and Hungary in 1956 or in Czechoslovakia in 1968 were not allowed in Bulgaria. Still, a cultural "thaw" took place in the late 1970s under the leadership of Zhivkov's daughter, Lyudmila Zhivkova. To further strengthen support for the regime, the party leadership devoted enormous resources to the celebration of the national past and culture. However, the period of the so-called "revival process" (with two peaks in 1972–1974 and 1984–1985) was marked by a campaign to assimilate members of Bulgaria's Turkish minority by forcing them to take Slavic names, prohibiting them from speaking Turkish in public, and subjecting them to other forms of harassment; more than 300,000 Bulgarian Turks crossed the border into Turkey to escape persecution.

The Communist regime drew its legitimacy by preserving the strong egalitarian and statist political traditions in the country. Additionally, the relatively good economic performance and impressive set of social policy achievements generated a considerable level of popular support. The developmental rise in mechanization, technical sophistication, and productivity was remarkable especially given the lack of natural resources and energy endowment and the very low initial material and cultural levels. However, despite these accomplishments, Bulgaria remained one of the countries with the lowest living standards in both Western and Eastern Europe. Moreover, the many and generous social policies were secured at the expense of economic efficiency.

Thus the radical changes introduced in the Soviet Union by Mikhail Gorbachev were welcomed and readily replicated in Bulgaria. A program of far-reaching political and economic changes was announced in July 1987, including an administrative overhaul meant to reduce the number of Communist Party functionaries by as much as two-thirds, the introduction of self-management for individual enterprises, and liberalization of rules for joint ventures with foreign investors. Economic and political restructuring throughout the Soviet Bloc empowered reformist elements within the Bulgarian Communist Party, which were growing increasingly restive under Zhivkov.

Although Zhivkov was never a despot in the Stalinist mold, by the early 1980s his regime was growing increasingly corrupt, autocratic, and erratic. The long-time ruler resisted attempts to change and moved into a pattern of direct confrontation with reformists, led by his foreign minister, Petar Mladenov. Mladenov, who had close ties to Gorbachev, wanted to change Bulgaria's image, which had been tarnished by Zhivkov's intensifying efforts to "assimilate" the country's ethnic Turks. Finally, in November 1989, Mladenov, backed by other reformists within the party, was able to take advantage of an international environmental conference convened in Sofia to press for Zhivkov's resignation. Mladenov was also successful in winning support from Defense Minister Dobri Dzhurov, thus leaving Zhivkov without resort to the military. Zhivkov had no choice but to resign.

Mladenov had intended to reform the Communist Party, not remove it from power. However, demonstrations on ecological issues in the streets of Sofia in November 1989 soon broadened into a general campaign for political reform. However, as the newly emergent opposition groups signaled their entry into the political arena by organizing the Union of Democratic Forces (UDF), the Communist leaders invited opposition leaders to roundtable negotiations meant to provide the elite with a safe channel against the anticipated popular backlash against communism. A new democratic constitution was negotiated and multiparty elections held in June 1990.

In something of a surprise, the Socialists led by Mladenov received nearly 53% of the 1990 vote, while the UDF got only about a third; the rest of the votes went to the Movement for Rights and Freedoms (MRF), which had emerged to represent the interests of the country's one million ethnic Turks. Popular hostility to Mladenov forced him to resign about a month after the election. Since the Socialists remained generally in charge of the government, there was little tangible progress with economic reform, and Bulgaria's economy, left in poor condition by Zhivkov, continued to decline. In addition, a great deal of effort was devoted to the attempt to prosecute Zhivkov and his prominent cronies for malfeasance, incompetence, and other failings. Zhivkov fought back vigorously, exposing the sins of former colleagues who had remained in power.

Although convictions were eventually obtained (in 1992, with additional charges brought in 1993), the exercise served to undermine public sympathy for the Socialists. That opened the way for the National Assembly to appoint the leader of the UDF and famous dissident, Zhelyu Zhelev, as a president. Moreover, the first Socialist government, led by Prime Minister Andrei Lukanov, a Mladenov ally, collapsed after a few months of its coming to power; in December 1990, the replacement government of Dimitar Popov, an unaffiliated technocrat, outlined an ambitious program of economic reform.

The National Assembly passed a new constitution in July 1991, making Bulgaria the first of the Eastern Bloc countries to adopt a new basic law. Among other things, this document called for new parliamentary elections to be held in October 1991. The UDF received 34%, the Socialists, 33%, and the MRF, 8%. The UDF adamantly refused to cooperate with the former Communists, instead taking the MRF as their coalition partner. Filip Dimitrov of the UDF led Bulgaria's first non-Communist government since World War II; however, most of his ministers were chosen for technical expertise rather than party affiliation and 60% of them were drawn from outside the National Assembly. In January 1992, there were direct presidential elections. Zhelev received 45% of the votes while his Socialist opponent, Velko Vulkanov, received 30%.

Dimitrov undertook an ambitious program of economic and political transformation: he invested his administration in returning property confiscated by the Communists and in the privatization of industry by issuing shares in government enterprises to all citizens. However, Bulgaria's economy continued to deteriorate and unemployment continued to grow as uncompetitive industries failed, exposing strains within the ruling coalition. In late 1992 the Dimitrov government was replaced by a minority coalition of the Socialists, the MRF, and some defecting UDF deputies. Widely seen only as a caretaker prime minister, Lyuben Berov defied predictions, remaining in power for more than 15 months.

The UDF was unrelenting in its hostility to Berov, accusing Berov of trying to "re-communize" Bulgaria; they submitted as many as six votes of no-confidence in a single year. This increasing political deadlock and the continued deterioration of Bulgaria's economy led to new parliamentary elections in 1994.

Pledging to defend ordinary citizens against the excesses of the free market, the Bulgarian Socialist Party and its two nominal coalition partners won an absolute majority in the 1994 elections.

The BSP government, headed by Zhan Videnov, failed to move forward with economic reforms and by the end of 1996, Bulgaria had become the poorest country in Europe with average wages at only $30 a month. In the November 1996 presidential elections, Petar Stoyanov of the UDF was elected president by a wide margin over Socialist party candidate Ivan Marazov.

Fueled by a slow pace of structural reforms, rampant corruption, and a failure to establish market discipline, Bulgaria's problems culminated in a severe economic crisis in 1996–1997. Without a stable government and with their economy in free fall, Bulgarians demonstrated in the capital for new parliamentary elections. After a few months of chaos and hyperinflation, a major foreign exchange crisis, and the collapse of the banking sector, Bulgaria adopted a Currency Board Arrangement with the International Monetary Fund in July 1997. A conservative fiscal policy and a significant acceleration of structural reforms have underpinned the Currency Board Arrangement.

The elections held in April 1997 were won by a four-party alliance, United Democratic Forces (UtDF), anchored by the UDF. The new prime minister Ivan Kostov quickly instituted economic reforms, passed a tough budget, and clamped down on crime and corruption. The economy began to stabilize and popular discontent began to subside. New IMF loans were approved, and the government embarked on a campaign to attract foreign investment and speed up privatization. The battle against entrenched political corruption continued through 1999 and 2000 and included the dismissal of top government officials. The government increasingly embraced the West, declaring its interest in NATO membership and allowing access to its airspace during the NATO bombing of Serbia in the spring of 1999.

In 1999 Bulgaria also started the accession negotiations to become a member of the European Union (EU). Despite much economic and political progress achieved by the Kostov cabinet, the citizenry was nevertheless disillusion with the party's corruption and its inability to address the high unemployment in the country.

In April 2001, Simeon Saxe-Coburg-Gotha, the exiled son of Tsar Boris, established a political party, the National Movement for Simeon II (NMS2), pledging to fight corruption, to improve Bulgaria's chances for EU membership, and to better the economy (through deregulation, privatization, and investment). Saxe-Coburg-Gotha was accused (both by the left and the right) of being an opportunist and a populist without competence and political experience, but he claimed his party's intent was not to restore the monarchy but to move ahead with reforms. And as the elections came closer, Saxe-Coburg-Gotha's popularity kept growing. His NMS2 party won 120 of 240 parliament seats in the 2001 elections. Having failed to win an absolute majority, the NMS2 signed a coalition agreement with the Movement for Rights and Freedoms. Saxe-Coburg-Gotha's cabinet included two MRF and two BSP ministers.

However, only 100 days after Saxe-Coburg-Gotha came to power, workers (including miners, power engineers, health professionals, transport, construction, railway and metal workers, and teachers) took to the streets of Sofia to protest the lack of progress in improving the economy and their living standards.

Saxe-Coburg-Gotha pursued a strongly pro-Western course. Bulgaria sent a nearly 500-strong stabilization force patrol to Iraq.

In November 2002, NATO officially invited Bulgaria to join the organization in 2004. Also in 2002, the EU announced that Bulgaria was not ready to become a member in 2004, but was expected to join the EU in 2007. In Luxembourg on 25 April 2005, the Treaty of Accession of Republic of Bulgaria to the European Union was signed. At the time, support for Bulgaria's integration in the EU was about 65%.

Four years after Saxe-Coburg-Gotha came to power, the government reported significant economic growth (5.3 %) but corruption and organized crime continued to plague the country, and high unemployment, low standard of living, and increasing inequality continue to face Bulgarians. Moreover, for the first time in Bulgaria's post-Communist history, ethnic tensions escalated into riots between the Bulgarian and Roma communities in several Bulgarian cities, including Sofia. Hopes for better social protection, disillusionment with Saxe-Coburg-Gotha's policies, and heightened ethnic tensions were all reflected in the results of the 25 June 2005 parliamentary elections. The Coalition for Bulgaria (CfB) won the elections but failed to muster majority. The NMS2 came second but received only half of the votes it got in the 2001 elections. The right was in disarray, as the conservative votes were divided among three parties. Lastly, the rising support for the MRF, the third-largest parliamentary group, was paralleled by the emergence of an ultranationalist coalition, Attack Coalition (ATAKA). After the elections, ATAKA was largely marginalized by other parties and soon began to crumble as its representatives began to defect.

In the political maneuvering that followed the elections, the Socialist bid for forming a government was immediately supported by the MRF but was blocked by the NMS2. The stumbling blocks in the negotiations process seem to be the distribution of key posts and the head of the future cabinet. As negotiations dragged on, the EU urged a rapid resolution of the situation so the country could continue implementing the reforms required for accession in 2007. Ending weeks of postelection deadlock, the new Bulgarian government formally took office on 17 August, after parliament approved the nominations of Prime Minister Sergey Stanishev of the Bulgarian Socialist Party and his 17 cabinet members. The new cabinet was finally elected following a coalition deal among the three leading parties—the BSP, the NMS2, and the MRF—that jointly control 169 out of 240 seats in the legislature.

Prime Minister Stanishev maintained that EU membership was his government's top priority and pledged to make up for lost time. He also promised to intensify the campaign against corruption and organized crime and confirmed that the 400 remaining Bulgarian troops deployed in Iraq will be withdrawn before the end of 2006.

13 GOVERNMENT

The Bulgarian constitution of July 1991 provides for a multiparty presidential–parliamentary form of republican government, in which all the citizens of the Republic of Bulgaria take part with the right to vote. The document provides clear distinctions among the legislative, executive, and judicial branches of government.

The Council of Ministers is the main executive body, headed by the prime minister. The Council of Ministers conducts the internal and foreign policy of the state, secures public order and national security, and exercises control over the public administration and the military forces. The president, who is chief of state, is popularly elected to a five-year term, and may serve a maximum of two terms. The president serves as commander-in-chief of the armed forces and appoints and dismisses their senior command. Among the president's duties is also setting the date for national referenda, scheduling parliamentary elections and naming of the prime minister, who must be confirmed by the National Assembly. Together with the prime minister or the respective minister, the president countersigns decrees to promulgate newly adopted laws. The emerging tradition is that the president sets the overall direction of policy, while the prime minister and his cabinet, presently 14 people, are responsible for day-to-day implementation.

The legislative branch of government is the National Assembly, with 240 members elected to four-year terms. Deputies are elected on a proportional voting basis in a mixed proportional/majoritarian system of elections, in which parties must receive at least 4% of the total national vote in order to receive seats. The largest parliamentary group constructs the cabinet. A simple majority is required to approve the Council of Ministers and to adopt regular legal acts. Amendments to the constitution, however, require approval by a three-quarters majority. Members of parliament represent not only their electoral regions but also the whole nation. The National Assembly elects temporary and permanent commissions, where parliamentarians participate. Members of the National Assembly, as well as member of the Council of Ministers, have the right to introduce draft laws, but only the Council of Ministers develop draft laws on the state budget.

14 POLITICAL PARTIES

Bulgaria did not develop the welter (confusing array) of political parties that most of the other post-Communist societies enjoyed—or suffered.

The Bulgarian Socialist Party (BSP) is the successor of the former Bulgarian Communist Party and combines various leftist factions. Some are of social democratic orientation while others remain attached to communism. The 1989 internal coup left the party with strong public support—53% of the vote in the 1991 elections. In 1994 the socialists won a majority in the parliamentary elections for the second time after the fall of state socialism but fell out of favor after two years of particularly disastrous economic policies, which had reduced their popular support to 10% by the end of 1996. The reputation of the BSP is still tied to its inability to deal with the problems of 1996 in the minds of the populace. The BSP remained in opposition after the 1997, 2001, and 2005 elections. In 2000, the socialists remaining in the BSP also made a significant break with the past by changing their former negative attitude towards NATO membership (without however cooling down support for good relations with Russia). In December 2001, Sergey Stanishev was elected as the new party leader with a mission to not only redefine and reform the BSP but also to rejuvenate it by trying to attract younger supporters. In addition, BSP became a full member of the Socialist International. In its campaign for the 2005 parliamentary elections, the party chose to focus on the neglected social rights of the Bulgarian citizens.

The Union of Democratic Forces (UDF) was created in the final days of the Communist regime (1989) as a platform movement uniting 15 different formerly dissident political groups. When the UDF came to power in 1992, the divisions between these factions

weakened the government, which lost a vote of confidence in parliament in 1994. Under the leadership of Ivan Kostov in early 1997, the UDF was transformed into a single party with liberal ideology. During the 1996–1997 political and parliamentary crisis, the UDF dominated the a conservative coalition, United Democratic Forces (UtDF), which became the main opposition force to the Bulgarian Socialist Party and won a majority in the 1997 parliamentary elections. Kostov stepped down after the party lost in the 2001 parliamentary elections and was succeeded by his former foreign minister Nadezhda Mikhailova in June 2002. However, despite the party losing the 2003 local elections, Mihailova was reelected as UDF chairwoman.

In February 2004, Ivan Kostov, together with about 2,000 party members (among them 29 members of parliament), left the party. In May 2004, the group around Kostov established a new right-wing party named Democrats for Strong Bulgaria (DSB), which vows to work for a country with strong democracy, capable state institutions, and wealthy society. The party won about 6% of the vote in the 2005 elections.

The Union of Free Democrats (UFD) is one of the smaller rightist parties in Bulgaria. It was founded by Stefan Sofiyanski in December 2001 as a split-off of the Union of Democratic Forces. The party's main goals are economic prosperity, political stability, and integration in the EU and NATO.

The Movement for Rights and Freedoms (MRF) primarily represents the interests of Bulgaria's large Turkish minority (about 10% of the population), which was harshly repressed during the Zhivkov years. In economic issues the MRF advocates neoliberal policies. Even though the party did not participate in Dimitrov's cabinet, the MRF initially supported the UDF and later was the pivot on which the Berov cabinet hinged; then, however, the party switched to being an informal coalition partner of the Socialists. Nevertheless, it supported the UtDF government during its tenure in office. For the 2001 parliamentary elections the MRF formed a coalition with two small parties and got in power together with the NMS2. Yet, nationalist antipathy among many Bulgarians towards the country's large Turkish minority makes the MRF an unpopular coalition partner for most political parties. In fact in 1991 the MRF was accused of "being an ethnic party" and has proven a costly partner in the majority of post-1989 governments.

While ethnic Turks have been represented in parliament since 1990, parties have included very few members of the Roma national minority. Still, compared with Roma in Slovakia and Romania for example, Bulgarian Roma are relatively successful in exercising influence on the government through the formation of an umbrella coalition. Nonetheless, Roma efforts are hampered by corruption and the lack of focused agendas among Roma organizations. Discrimination, unwillingness of mainstream political parties to encourage Roma participation, and the lack of political engagement within the Roma community itself are all obstacles to the political inclusion of the Roma.

The National Movement Simeon II (NMS2) is a coalition of the unregistered movement Simeon II and two registered parties—Bulgarian Party of Women (led by Vessela Draganova-Dencheva) and the Movement for National Revival (headed by Tosho Peikov). Registered as a party in April 2002, it was founded by Simeon Saxe-Coburg-Gotha, the exiled son of Tsar Boris. Simeon Saxe-Coburg-Gotha's advisors and top ministers were young Bulgarian emigrants who, having built careers abroad mostly in Western finance, returned to their homeland to affect economic change. The NMS2 proposed to bring about change to Bulgaria's economic and political outlook "within 800 days." Thousands of Bulgarians hastened to join the NMS2 in what many saw as a protest against those who ruled Bulgaria since the collapse of communism. In the 2001 elections, the NMS2 took the lead in forming a new government but the popularity of the party quickly declined. The movement places NATO and EU integration high on the political agenda. After the 2005 elections, the party received only half of the seats it had in the previous assembly.

In the 25 June 2005 parliamentary elections, the Coalition for Bulgaria (dominated by the Bulgarian Socialist Party) was backed by 31.1% of votes and received a total of 83 seats in the 240-seat Assembly. The National Movement Simeon II (NMS2) garnered 19.9%, and 53 seats. The Movement for Rights and Freedoms (MRF) ranked third with 12.7% and 33 seats. The surprise in the 2005 elections, the nationalist coalition ATAKA received 8.2% and 17 seats. The United Democratic Forces (UDF), which was supported by 7.7% of the voters, received 20 seats, whereas the other rightist party Democrats for Strong Bulgaria (DSB) won 6.5% and 17 seats. Lastly, the Bulgarian People's Union (BPU), a coalition of the Union of Free Democrats (SSD) and the Agrarian Party of Anastasia Mozer (BZNS), won 5.2% and 13 seats.

15 LOCAL GOVERNMENT

Bulgaria is divided into 262 municipalities (obshtini). The municipality is the main administrative territorial unit for local government and is governed by a mayor and an elected municipal council. Municipal councils determine the policy of every municipality, including economic development, environmental, and educational policies, as well as cultural activities. Mayors are in charge of the whole executive activity of their municipality, of keeping the public order, and of organizing distribution of the municipal budget.

Bulgaria is also divided into 28 provinces (oblasti), which are larger administrative territorial units through which the government decentralizes its policies. The Council of Ministers appoints the regional governor for each province.

In preparation for EU accession, six planning regions were created in 1999 to fulfill the requirements for receiving cohesion funds. However, as of mid-2006, those regions existed on paper only.

16 JUDICIAL SYSTEM

Bulgaria has an independent judicial system. The 1991 constitution provides for regional courts, district courts, a Supreme Court of Cassation, which rules on decisions by the lower courts, and a Supreme Administrative Court, which rules on the legality of actions by institutions of government. A Constitutional Court is responsible for judicial review of legislation and for resolving issues of competency of the other branches of government as well as impeachments and election law. Judges are appointed by the Supreme Judicial Council, which organizes and administers the judiciary. The Constitutional Court has 12 judges appointed to a nine-year term by the National Assembly, the president, and judicial authorities.

Military courts handle cases involving military personnel and national security issues. Under the 1991 constitution, the judicia-ry is independent of the legislative and executive branches. The trials are public. Criminal defendants have the right to confront witnesses, the right to counsel, and the right to know the charges against them to prepare their defense. The constitution prohibits arbitrary interference with privacy, home, or correspondence.

Bulgaria accepts compulsory jurisdiction of the International Court of Justice.

17 ARMED FORCES

As of 2005, the armed forces of Bulgaria consisted of 51,000 active personnel with reserves numbering 303,000. For that year, the army numbered 25,000 active members, while the navy had 4,370 active personnel and the air force 13,100 active members. The army that year had 1,474 main battle tanks, 18 reconnaissance vehicles, 214 armored infantry fighting vehicles, 1,643 armored personnel carriers, and 1,774 artillery pieces. The navy's major units consisted of one tactical submarine, one frigate, seven corvettes, 16 patrol/coastal vessels, and 20 mine warfare ships. The air force had 137 combat capable aircraft, including 35 fighters and 94 fighter ground attack aircraft. There were also a 34,000-member paramilitary force that included 12,000 border guards, 4,000 security police, and 18,000 railway and construction troops. Bulgaria participated in six missions abroad, including Afghanistan and Iraq. The defense budget for 2005 totaled $630 million.

18 INTERNATIONAL COOPERATION

Bulgaria joined the United Nations on 14 December 1955 and participates in the ECE and all the nonregional specialized agencies. It belongs to the WTO (1996) and is a candidate for membership in the European Union. The nation also belongs to NATO (2004), the Council of Europe, the Central European Initiative, G-9, the Central European Free Trade Agreement (CEFTA), and the OSCE, and has observer status in the OAS. Bulgaria is part of the Australia Group, the Zangger Committee, the European Organization for Nuclear Research (CERN), and the Nuclear Suppliers Group (London Group). It is a guest in the Nonaligned Movement. In environmental cooperation, Bulgaria is part of the Antarctic Treaty, the Basel Convention, Conventions on Biological Diversity and Air Pollution, Ramsar, CITES, the Kyoto Protocol, the Montréal Protocol, MARPOL, the Nuclear Test Ban Treaty, and the UN Conventions on the Law of the Sea, Climate Change, and Desertification.

19 ECONOMY

Before World War II, Bulgaria was an agricultural country, consisting mainly of small peasant farms; farming provided a livelihood for about 80% of the population. After the war, the Communist regime initiated an industrialization program. By 1947, a sizable portion of the economy was nationalized, and collectivization of agriculture followed during the 1950s. Until 1990, the country had a centrally planned economy, along Soviet lines, and its sequence of five-year economic plans, beginning in 1949, emphasized industrial production. In 1956, according to official Bulgarian statistics, industry contributed 36.5% of national income, and agriculture and forestry, 32.9%; in 1992, the respective contributions were 42.5% and 12%.

Although Bulgaria has brown coal and lignite, iron ore, copper lead, zinc, and manganese, it lacks other important natural resources and must export in order to pay for needed commodities. Because it relied on the USSR and other CMEA countries for essential imports and as the major market for its exports, and lacks foreign exchange, the Bulgarian economy was greatly influenced by the breakup of the Soviet bloc and the switch to hard-currency foreign trade. In the 1970s, the economic growth rate was quite high (6.8% annually), but the pace of growth slowed in the 1980s, mainly because of energy shortages. The average annual growth rate was only 2% in that decade.

With the disintegration of Soviet-bloc trade and payments arrangements, GDP declined by about 10% in 1990, 13% in 1991, 8% in 1992, and an estimated 4% in 1993. Meanwhile, Bulgaria began an economic reform program supported by the World Bank and IMF. But the economy remained largely state controlled, although there was progress in privatizing many smaller enterprises. The private sector accounted for only about 20% of GDP in 1993 and 45% in 1996. Efforts at economic reform stalled in 1994 as the Socialist government again failed to privatize state-owned industries and institute structural reforms aimed at creating a market economy. The economy was further plagued by wide-scale corruption among businessmen from the former Communist Party who stripped state enterprises of their assets and transferred the funds out of the country. By 1997, the Bulgarian economy was at the brink of collapse with inflation at 300%, the banking system in chaos, and the government on the verge of bankruptcy. Bulgaria became the poorest country in Europe with average monthly wages of $30 a month.

Angry with the governing Socialists, tens of thousands of Bulgarians demonstrated in the capital calling for early elections. In April of 1997 a new government took power and instituted structural reforms designed to bring order to the economy. The government of Prime Minister Ivan Kostov quickly moved to implement market reforms. While operating under the direction of an IMF currency board, Bulgaria pegged the lev to the deutschmark (and now also to the euro), and reduced inflation to 1%. In 1997, the private sector accounted for 65% of GDP. This milestone marked the first time in the post-Communist era that the private sector outperformed the public sector in production. In addition to structural reforms, the Kostov government also moved to combat corruption by becoming the first non-OECD country to ratify the anti-bribery convention.

As of 2003, industry increasingly was being privatized, and agriculture was almost completely privatized. Bulgaria started accession talks with the EU in 2000, but was not one of 10 new countries formally invited to join the body in December 2002. If Bulgaria completes its accession requirements, it is expected to join the EU in 2007, along with Romania. Bulgaria's laws are being harmonized with EU laws, and customs barriers between them are breaking down. By the end of 1999, more than 50% of Bulgaria's exports went to EU nations.

Following the 2001 elections that brought Simeon Saxe-Coburg-Gotha to office as prime minister, the stock market soared 100%, but the government in 2002 was unable to live up to its pledge to improve living standards. Foreign direct investment rose modestly in 2002, and although economic growth slowed that year from its 5.8% high in 2000, it was higher than that of many other European countries. Tourism was strong in 2002, and although the weather was poor that year, Bulgaria's agricultural sector performed well. Taxes were lowered, and there is a zero percent capital gains tax on stock market investments.

Bulgaria's overall economic performance has been positive in the last couple of years. In 2004, the GDP grew by 5.7%, and was expected to expand by 6% in 2005, and 4.5% in 2006. This growth was fueled by an increase in domestic demand (encouraged by higher real wages and remittances from abroad), a more dynamic job market, and bank credits. Inflation was rather high in 2004, peaking at 6.2%, but was expected to regress to 4% in 2005. At 12%, unemployment was on a downward path in 2004, and was expected to drop even further by 2006, to 10%. This was the result of a more dynamic private job market, and government policies geared towards unemployment reduction. Corruption, however, remains a stumbling block to Bulgaria's economic success, and a challenge that has to be addressed before the 2007 EU accession deadline.

²⁰INCOME

The US Central Intelligence Agency (CIA) reports that in 2005 Bulgaria's gross domestic product (GDP) was estimated at $67.0 billion. The CIA defines GDP as the value of all final goods and services produced within a nation in a given year and computed on the basis of purchasing power parity (PPP) rather than value as measured on the basis of the rate of exchange based on current dollars. The per capita GDP was estimated at $9,000. The annual growth rate of GDP was estimated at 5.4%. The average inflation rate in 2005 was 4.5%. It was estimated that agriculture accounted for 9.3% of GDP, industry 30.4%, and services 60.3% in 2005.

According to the World Bank, in 2003 remittances from citizens working abroad totaled $67 million or about $9 per capita and accounted for approximately 0.3% of GDP. Foreign aid receipts amounted to $414 million or about $53 per capita and accounted for approximately 2.1% of the gross national income (GNI).

The World Bank reports that in 2003 household consumption in Bulgaria totaled $13.72 billion or about $1,754 per capita based on a GDP of $19.9 billion, measured in current dollars rather than PPP. Household consumption includes expenditures of individuals, households, and nongovernmental organizations on goods and services, excluding purchases of dwellings. It was estimated that for the period 1990 to 2003 household consumption grew at an average annual rate of -0.4%. In 2001 it was estimated that approximately 30% of household consumption was spent on food, 17% on fuel, 8% on health care, and 11% on education. It was estimated that in 2002 about 13.4% of the population had incomes below the poverty line.

²¹LABOR

In 2005, Bulgaria's workforce totaled an estimated 3.34 million. As of third quarter 2004, an estimated 11% of workers were in agriculture, with 32.7% in industry and the remaining 56.3% in the service sector. Unemployment was estimated at 11.5% in 2005.

The constitution guarantees the right of all to form or join trade unions of their own choosing. The labor code recognizes the right to strike when all other means of conflict resolution have been exhausted. Essential employees, mainly military and law enforcement personnel, are forbidden to strike and political strikes are prohibited as well. Although the law forbids discrimination against union members and union organizing activities, there are reports of union members and organizers being harassed, demoted, dismissed or relocated. There are also reports that some newly hired workers are being forced to sign "yellow dog" contracts, namely agreements that they would not join a union or help organize one. About 18% of Bulgaria's workforce is unionized, although that percentage has been decreasing.

Minimum age for employment is 16 years, with 18 years the minimum for hazardous work. In the formal sector these regulations are generally observed, but in certain industries, family operations, and illegal businesses, children are exploited. The law establishes a standard workweek of 40 hours with at least one 24-hour rest period per week. Overtime rates of no less than 150% during weekdays, 175% during weekends, and 200% during official holidays are mandated by law. The minimum wage was about $94 per month as of 2005, but is inadequate to support a worker and a family with a decent standard of living. Minimum health and safety standards exist and are effectively enforced in the public sector, but not effectively enforced in the largely unregulated and often informal private sector.

22 AGRICULTURE

In 2002, the total arable land area covered 3,583,000 hectares (8,834,000 acres). The average annual agricultural growth rate was -2.1% for 1980–90 and -0.4% for 1990–2000. By 2000, agricultural output was only two-thirds of what it was in 1990. However, during 2002–04, crop production averaged 2.9% higher than during 1999–2001. In 2005, agriculture accounted for 9.3% of GDP. In 2004, agriculture (including fishing and forestry) engaged about 11% of the economically active population.

Collectivized agriculture became the norm under the Communist government after 1958. In March 1991, the government adopted a land law which restored ownership rights to former owners of expropriated land. These owners were to receive 20–30 hectares (49–74 acres) each of land approximating the type and location of the former holdings, regardless of whether or not the owner cultivates that land. After February 1991, full price liberalization for producers and consumers was to occur. However, the agricultural sector was still shrinking due to the lack of progress in the implementation of privatization and property restitution. A grain crisis developed when Bulgaria exported a million tons of wheat in 1995. Currency depreciations, increased taxes, and lack of funds exacerbated the disintegration of the agricultural sector in the mid-1990s.

The principal grain-growing areas are the Danube tableland and southern Dobrudja. The production of major crops in 2004 (in thousands of tons) was wheat, 3,961; corn, 2,123; barley, 1,181; sunflower seeds, 1,079; and rapeseed, 22.

Bulgaria is a major supplier of grapes, apples, and tomatoes to Europe and the former Soviet Union. Potatoes and paprika are also important crops. Production in 2004 included (in thousands of tons): grapes, 400; apples, 30; tomatoes, 400; and potatoes, 574. About 60,000 tons of tobacco were also produced that year.

Machinery available to agriculture has increased significantly. Tractors rose from 25,800 units in 1960 to 53,800 units in 1985, before falling to 32,100 in 2002; combines increased from 7,000 to 16,000 in 1985, but by 2002 numbered only 9,000 in use. About 16% of the cultivated area is irrigated.

23 ANIMAL HUSBANDRY

Meadows and pastures make up about 18% of the total land area. Bulgaria had 2,100,000 sheep, 18,000,000 chickens, 1,000,000 hogs, 750,000 goats, 668,000 cattle, 200,000 donkeys, and 150,000 horses in 2004. Meat production (in carcass weight) in 2004 amounted to 479,000 tons. In the same year, the country produced 1,590,000 million tons of milk and 92,000 tons of eggs.

24 FISHING

Fishing resources in the Black Sea are less than abundant. Before 1960, the annual catch was slightly above 5,000 tons. Fishing output reached a high of 167,100 tons in 1976, then fell to 115,607 tons in 1982. Prior to 1989, Bulgaria used to produce about 20,000 tons of fish from freshwater aquaculture. The fish farms and fish processing industries went through major restructuring and privatization during the 1990s. Only after 2000 did the fish industry register some growth. In 2003, the total catch was 16,498 tons, about 80% from inland waters. Fishing vessels are based at the ports of Varna and Burgas. The most popular river fish is sturgeon. Due to environmental limitations, the government sets an annual sturgeon quota; for 2003 it was 22 tons. The beluga caviar quota set that year was 1,720 kg (3,780 lb).

25 FORESTRY

Forests cover 3,700,000 hectares (9,143,000 acres), or 33.4% of Bulgaria's territory. About 80% of the total forest area is wooded forest land. Forests are about 34% coniferous and 66% deciduous, and mainly occupy regions of higher altitudes. Over half of the forests in Bulgaria are situated on slopes of over 20°, making harvesting and reforestation very difficult. The principal lumbering areas are the Rila and western Rhodope Mountains in the southwest and the northern slopes of the Balkan Mountains in the center. Forestry and the forest industry contribute about 2% to the GDP.

Intensive exploitation and neglect before and during World War II (1939–45) and even more intensive exploitation following the war contributed to the deterioration of the forests. So during 1945–65, 860,000 hectares (2,125,000 acres) were reforested; the 20-year plan (1961–80) called for the planting of 1.4 million hectares (3.5 million acres). During the 1980s, annual reforestation averaged 50,000 hectares (123,500 acres). Despite the intensive harvesting during 1950–73 (which exceeded the government's Forest Management Plan—FMP), the total timber volume has increased from 165 million cu m (5.8 billion cu ft) in 1934 to 404 million cu m (14 billion cu ft) in 1995. The FMP decreased the amount of timber permitted to be cut from 6.8 million cu m (240 million cu ft) in 1955 to 6.2 million cu m (219 million cu ft) of roundwood in 1995 because fewer large trees are available. Roundwood production has decreased from 8.6 million cu m (304 million cu ft) in 1960 to 4.8 million cu m (522 million cu ft) in 2003. Forestry exports in 2003 totaled $139.3 million. Bulgaria exports logs to Turkey, Greece, Italy, and Macedonia; veneer to Greece and Syria; and particleboard to Greece, Macedonia, and Egypt. The main problems prohibiting greater roundwood production are diseases, drying of trees, and pests. Acid rain and heavy metals have not hurt the local forests. In 1998, the government began a forestry restitution and privatization program covering 3.6 million hectares (8.9 million acres). The average annual reforestation rate was 0.6% during 1990–2000.

26 MINING

Bulgaria was an important regional producer of nonferrous metal ores and concentrates, and was mostly self-sufficient in mineral requirements. Mining and metalworking in the region was well documented by Roman times, when Bulgaria and Romania, known respectively as Thrace and Dacia, were important sources of base and precious metals. Small quantities of bismuth, chromite, copper, gold, iron, lead, magnesite, manganese, molybdenum, palladium, platinum, silver, tellurium, tin, uranium, and zinc were mined, as well as the industrial minerals anhydrite, asbestos fiber, barite, bentonite, common clays, refractory clays, dolomite, feldspar, fluorspar, gypsum, kaolin, industrial lime, limestone, nitrogen (in ammonia), perlite, pyrites, salt (all types), sand and gravel, silica (quartz sand), calcined sodium carbonate, dimension stone, sulfur (content of pyrite), sulfuric acid, and crushed stone. Most of the copper deposits were within a roughly 50 km-wide (30 mi) swath from Burgas in the east, to the former Yugoslavia in the west, and almost all was produced by two enterprises, Asarel-Medet, at Panagurishte, and Elatzite-Med, at Srednogorie; copper was also mined at Burgas and Malko Turnovo. Lead and zinc were mined chiefly in the Rhodope Mountains, at Madan and Rudozem. Production outputs for 2003 were: gold, 2,142 kg; gross copper, 26,415,000 tons; barite ore (run of mine), 637,000 metric tons; limestone and dolomite, 11,000,000 tons; industrial lime, 2,902,000 tons; and silica, 610,000 tons. Manganese ore production was zero in 1999 and 2000, but totaled 1,516 metric tons in 2001 and 4 metric tons each in 2002 and 2003.

In 1998, the National Program for Sustainable Development of Mining in Bulgaria was drafted and approved, and the Underground Resources Act was enacted. The latter, which aimed to promote private enterprise and foreign investment, stipulated that underground mineral wealth was the property of the state, and provided for claims by domestic and foreign companies for the development and operation of mineral deposits for up to 35 years with potential 15-year extensions. Improved economic performance at the end of the 1990s, the significant shift away from economic uncertainties during the transition from central economic planning, improving political stability in the Balkans, and greater investor confidence in the legal underpinnings of the growing privatization process combined to contribute to the $1 billion net foreign investment in 2000, one-third more than in 1999.

27 ENERGY AND POWER

Bulgaria has only modest reserves of oil and natural gas, but somewhat larger recoverable reserves of coal. But it is nuclear power that allows Bulgaria to be an exporter of electricity.

In 2002 Bulgaria's output of electrical power was estimated at between 40.9 and 43.1 billion kWh, of which: around 43% came from fossil fuels; 5% from hydropower; 49% from nuclear energy; and the remainder from geothermal and other sources. In the same year, consumption of electricity is estimated at 31.797 billion kWh to 32.7 billion kWh. Total installed capacity is estimated at about 11.8 GW in 2002, of which: hydropower accounts for 1.672 million kW; nuclear for 3.782 million kW; and thermal for 6.326 million kW.

As previously noted, Bulgaria's nuclear power generating capability accounts for a major portion of the country's electrical power output, as well as allowing Bulgaria to be a power exporter. That capability is based upon its Kozloduy facility, which has six reactors, of which only four are working. In 2002, Bulgaria exported 8.335 billion kWh of electricity. In 2001, it earned $150 million from exports of electric power to Serbia and Montenegro, Kosovo, Greece, Turkey, and Macedonia.

Bulgaria is heavily reliant on petroleum product imports. The country's proven oil reserves, as of 1 January 2005, were estimated at 15 million barrels, with production and consumption estimated in 2004 at 1,000 barrels per day and 86,000 barrels per day, respectively. Exploration for oil and natural gas is primarily centered in the Black Sea and in the northern part of the country. Bulgaria's sole refinery is located at Burgas, the country's main port. In 2002, refinery output was put at 123,140 barrels per day, but according to an Energy Information Administration analysis brief, updated as of March 2005, actual refining capacity was estimated at 115,000 barrels per day.

Bulgaria's consumption of natural gas far exceeds its proven reserves and production, and it must rely on imports to meet almost its entire natural gas needs. As of 1 January 2005, Bulgaria's proven reserves of natural gas were estimated at 0.2 trillion cu f. Output in 2002 was estimated at only 0.1 billion cu ft. Imports and consumption were both estimated at 174 billion cu ft. for that same year

Coal is the most important mineral fuel, with lignite accounting for nearly 90% and brown coal for around 10%. Bulgaria was estimated in 2002 to have recoverable coal reserves of 2,988 million short tons. Production, consumption and imports of coal are estimated at: 28.4 million short tons; 32.4 million short tons; and 4.0 million short tons, respectively

28 INDUSTRY

Before World War II, Bulgarian industry, construction, mining, and handicrafts contributed only 17% to the net national income and accounted for only 8% of employment. Handicrafts in 1939 contributed almost half the net industrial output, followed by textiles and food processing. In the postwar period, the Communist regime nationalized industry and, through economic planning, emphasized a heavy industrialization program that resulted in a substantial increase in the metalworking and chemical industries. Between 1950 and 1960, the annual rate of growth of output in industry (including mining and power production) was 14.8%, according to the official index of gross output. Official statistics indicate that industrial output grew by 1,100% between 1956 and 1980, with the production of capital goods increasing by 1,500% and the production of consumer goods by 658%. Industrial output increased by 9.1% annually during 1971–75, 6% during 1976–80, 6.8% during 1980–85, and 2.7% during 1985–90. Ferrous metallurgy was given special emphasis in the 1960s, machine-building and chemicals in the 1970s and early 1980s, and high technology in the mid-1980s.

Even before the collapse of communism, industrial and agricultural production fell annually until 1997 and 1998, respectively, when the Kostov reforms took effect. Although traditional industries remain the foundation of the industrial sector, Bulgaria expects high-technology production to post gains in the future as high-tech companies establish operation there.

Industry accounted for 29% of GDP in 2001. The privatization of Bulgaria's industries was largely complete as of 2002, with the exception of a few large companies, such as Bulgartabac. The construction sector should realize strong growth due to the need to undertake major infrastructure projects. Growth in 2003 was expected in light industry, including electronics, textiles, and food processing.

In 2004, industry accounted for 30.1% of the GDP (and 32.7% of the labor force); agriculture made up 11.5% of the GDP (and 11% of the labor force), while services came in first with a 58.4% representation in the economic output, and 56.3% of the workforce.

Primary industries included electricity, gas and water, food, beverages and tobacco, machinery and equipment, base metals, chemical products, coke, refined petroleum, and nuclear fuel. Bulgaria also produces electrical components and computers. The industrial production growth rate reached 5.2% in 2004.

29 SCIENCE AND TECHNOLOGY

In 1996, Bulgaria had 25 agricultural, medical, scientific, and technological learned societies and 117 research institutes. The Bulgarian Academy of Sciences (founded in 1869) is the main research organization. The Academy of Medicine (founded in 1972) has five higher medical institutes. Total expenditures on research and development (R&D) in 2002 totaled $278.313 million or 0.5% of GDP. Of that amount, 69.8% came from the government, while 24.8% came from business. Higher education and nonprofit sources each accounted for 0.2% in 2002. The remainder came from foreign sources. In that same year there were 1,158 researchers and 466 technicians per million people, actively engaged in R&D. High technology exports in 2002 totaled $85 million, accounting for 3% of the country's manufactured exports. A large-scale program of scientific and technological cooperation of CMEA countries was adopted at the end of 1985.

Bulgaria has 18 universities and colleges offering degrees in basic and applied sciences. In Sofia are the National Natural History Museum (founded in 1889) and the National Polytechnical Museum (founded in 1968). In 1987–97, science and engineering students accounted for 27% of university enrollment.

30 DOMESTIC TRADE

Private shops and small supermarkets are open in many cities and local farmer's markets are still active. A few warehouse stores have opened in Sofia. The government has remained committed to privatization efforts. By the end of 1999, 71% of state-owned assets had been privatized. Bulgaria has also attracted a number of foreign investors, including US companies such as American Standard, McDonald's, Kraft Foods, and Hilton International. However, Germany is the top foreign investor.

Newspapers and magazines are the important means of advertising to the population at large. Radio advertisements are permitted for half an hour each day.

Offices are open from 8:30 AM to 12:30 PM and from 1:30 to 5:30 PM, Monday through Friday. Normal banking hours are 8 AM to 12 noon, Monday–Friday, and 8 to 11 AM on Saturday.

Principal Trading Partners – Bulgaria (2003)			
(In millions of US dollars)			
Country	Exports	Imports	Balance
World	7,540.2	10,901.1	-3,360.9
Italy-San Marino-Holy See	1,057.5	1,114.7	-57.2
Germany	812.1	1,555.1	-743.0
Greece	781.8	725.0	56.8
Turkey	690.0	667.4	22.6
Belgium	457.7	149.7	308.0
France-Monaco	382.5	614.5	-232.0
Area nes	352.3	100.1	252.2
United States	337.0	279.3	57.7
Serbia and Montenegro	249.0	…	249.0
Romania	230.0	262.2	-32.2

(…) data not available or not significant.

SOURCE: *2003 International Trade Statistics Yearbook,* New York: United Nations, 2004.

31 FOREIGN TRADE

The principal imports were crude oil, natural gas, diesel fuel, fuel oil, coal, textiles, and machinery and equipment.

Geographic distribution of trade has changed radically twice: since World War II and the collapse of the Soviet bloc. Whereas before the war Bulgaria traded mainly with the countries of Western and Central Europe, after the war, trade shifted almost entirely to the countries of the Communist bloc. In 1991, 49.8% of all exports still went to the former USSR and 43.2% of all imports still came from the former USSR.

By the mid-1990s, weak demand in the former Soviet bloc markets led to an increase in exports to European Union countries which now take about 56% of Bulgaria's exports. Other important export areas include Central and Eastern European, and other OECD countries. Principal export markets in 2004 included Italy (with 13.1% of all exports), Germany (11.6%), Turkey (9.3%), Belgium (6.1%), Greece (5.6%), US (5.3%), and France (4.9%). The main import partners were Germany (with 15.1% of all imports), Italy (10.2%), Russia (7.9%), Greece (7.5%), Turkey (6.9%), and France (4.4%). Exports totaled $9.1 billion (FOB—Free on Board) in 2004; imports grew to $12.2 billion (FOB); the trade deficit was $3.1 billion.

32 BALANCE OF PAYMENTS

During the postwar industrialization program, Bulgaria had a trade imbalance, made up largely by credits, particularly from the former USSR. From 1952 to 1958, the country had visible export surpluses, but another industrialization drive resulted in a trade imbalance during 1959–61, and there were persistent imbalances during the latter part of the 1960s. In the early 1970s, export surpluses were reported for most years; there were also small surpluses in 1979, 1980, and 1984. With the collapse of COMECON trade, Bulgaria began exporting agricultural products and light manufactured products in exchange for consumer goods. During the first nine months of 1992, Bulgaria recorded its first surplus in many years. Failure of the government to institute economic reforms, however, led to severe economic hardship and trade deficits of $1.4 billion in 1993 and $1.6 billion in 1994. In 1994, the

Balance of Payments – Bulgaria (2003)

(In millions of US dollars)

Current Account		**-1,675.8**
Balance on goods		-2,478.0
Imports	-9,922.8	
Exports	7,444.8	
Balance on services		599.6
Balance on income		-489.1
Current transfers		691.7
Capital Account		**-0.2**
Financial Account		**2,058.1**
Direct investment abroad		-21.8
Direct investment in Bulgaria		1,419.4
Portfolio investment assets		-72.0
Portfolio investment liabilities		-130.0
Financial derivatives		-1.1
Other investment assets		147.5
Other investment liabilities		716.1
Net Errors and Omissions		**349.9**
Reserves and Related Items		**-732.0**

(…) data not available or not significant.

SOURCE: *Balance of Payment Statistics Yearbook 2004,* Washington, DC: International Monetary Fund, 2004.

deficit was partially financed by almost $1.1 billion in aid from other countries and international financial institutions. In 2000, the current account deficit was financed by $1 billion in foreign direct investment and additional funding from international financial institutions.

The US Central Intelligence Agency (CIA) reported that in 2002 the purchasing power parity of Bulgaria's exports was $5.3 billion while imports totaled $6.9 billion resulting in a trade deficit of $1.6 billion.

The International Monetary Fund (IMF) reported that in 2001 Bulgaria had exports of goods totaling $5.11 billion and imports totaling $6.7 billion. The services credit totaled $2.42 billion and debit $1.88 billion. By 2004, the exports of goods and services grew to $14 billion, while the imports totaled $16.5 billion. The resulting resource balance was thus -$2.5 billion, while the current account balance hit -$1.8 billion. Bulgaria's total reserves (including gold) amounted to $9.2 billion in 2004.

33 BANKING AND SECURITIES

All banks were nationalized in 1947 in accord with Soviet banking policies. Until 1969, the Bulgarian National Bank (BNB) was the chief banking institution handling deposits of state and local governments and national enterprises. It was the bank of issue and was authorized to credit enterprises with funds for facilities and activities not covered by the capital investment plan. In 1969 it was renamed the Bulgarian Central Bank and remained the bank of issue. Two new banks—the Industrial Bank and the Agricultural and Trade Bank—assumed the functions of providing credit for industry and for agriculture and individuals, respectively. In 1968, the Bulgarian Foreign Trade Bank was established as a joint-stock company. The State Savings Bank was the chief savings institution.

In 1996, the Bulgarian National Bank, lacking reserves, virtually gave up attempts to stabilize the exchange rate and contain infla-

tion. However, the outlines of future economic policy under a new government appear to be decided, given that all parties agreed that a currency board was the linchpin of economic stabilization. The IMF opened negotiations with the caretaker government on the introduction of a currency board, which it made a condition of further funding. When Bulgaria achieved independence in 1991, a two-tier banking system was formed. The Bulgarian National Bank became the country's central bank. The country has a state savings bank with 491 branches. There are about 80 commercial banks in Bulgaria. Some of the commercial banks are cross-border banks that are involved in the foreign exchange market. Some of the banks licensed for cross-border foreign exchange include: Agricultural and Co-operative Bank (1987), Balkenbank (1987), Biochim Commercial Bank (1987), Bulgarian Post-Office Bank, Economic Bank (1991), Hemus Commercial Bank, and the Bank for Economic Enterprise (December 1991).

In a related move that was also seen as a step towards the restrictive regime of a currency board, the central bank announced in late January of 1997 that it would no longer be fixing a base interest rate. Instead, the BNB would set an indicative rate defined by the interest on short-term government bonds. Banks themselves would be able to set their own rates according to market principles, without interference from the central bank. In 2001, the exchange rate to the dollar was 2.1847 leva. The International Monetary Fund reports that in 2001, currency and demand deposits—an aggregate commonly known as M1—were equal to $2.2 billion. In that same year, M2—an aggregate equal to M1 plus savings deposits, small time deposits, and money market mutual funds—was $5.5 billion. The money market rate, the rate at which financial institutions lend to one another in the short term, was 3.74%.

The First Bulgarian Stock Exchange was established in Sofia on 8 November, 1991 as a joint stock company with capital of Lv10,000,000 divided into 10,000 shares of Lv1,000 each. Designated as SOFIX, it is managed by a Board of Directors and by a Chief Executive. The exchange currently trades mainly in unlisted securities. As of 2004, there were 332 companies listed on the SOFIX. Market capitalization as of December 2004 stood at $2.804 billion, with the SOFIX Index up 37.6% from the previous year at 625.3.

34 INSURANCE

Private insurance companies were nationalized in 1947 and absorbed into the State Insurance Institute. Property insurance and life insurance are compulsory for collective farms and voluntary for cooperatives, social organizations, and the population in general. Insurance policies and premiums have increased steadily for both. Third-party automobile liability and workers' compensation are also compulsory insurances. The Insurance Regulatory body is the Ministry of Finance. Since March of 1998, foreigners have been permitted to own a Bulgarian insurer. In 2003, total direct premiums written totaled $387 million, of which nonlife premiums accounted for $343 million. Bulgaria's top nonlife insurer was Bulstrad, with $58.9 million of gross nonlife premiums written in

2003. That same year, DZI was the country's top life insurer with $18.1 million of gross life premiums written.

35 PUBLIC FINANCE

An annual budget for all levels of government, becoming effective on 1 January, is voted by the National Assembly, after having been prepared by the Ministry of Finance. The disintegration of the Communist system in November 1989 and the subsequent collapse of the Soviet trade bloc caused severe economic disruption, pushing the government's budget deficit to 8.5% of GDP in 1990 (not including interest payments on commercial foreign debt). However, by the late 90s the country was seeing unprecedented growth (5.8% in 2000), due to aggressive market reforms put in place by the government during the prior decade.

The US Central Intelligence Agency (CIA) estimated that in 2005 Bulgaria's central government took in revenues of approximately $1.1 trillion and had expenditures of $1 trillion. Revenues minus expenditures totaled approximately $0.1 trillion. Public debt in 2005 amounted to 32.4% of GDP. Total external debt was $15.46 billion.

The International Monetary Fund (IMF) reported that in 2003, the most recent year for which it had data, central government revenues were Lv12,484 million and expenditures were Lv12,417 million. The value of revenues was us$7,092 million and expenditures us$7,054 million, based on an exchange rate for 2003 of us$1 = Lv1.7604 as reported by the IMF. Government outlays by function were as follows: general public services, 17.1%; defense, 6.6%; public order and safety, 7.6%; economic affairs, 11.9%; housing and community amenities, 0.7%; health, 11.9%; recreation, culture, and religion, 1.6%; education, 5.2%; and social protection, 37.3%.

36 TAXATION

Bulgaria revised much of its tax system in 1996. One of the changes states that foreign persons receiving remuneration as lecturers and consultants, royalties, license payments, and remuneration for technical services, are charged with a 32% tax at the time of payment. The personal income tax is progressively rated up to 24%. As of 1 January 2005, the standard corporate or profit tax rate is 15%. A withholding tax of 7% is assessed on dividends. Employers are required to contribute 37% of employees' gross salaries for social security insurance while the employees contribute an additional 2%. The value-added tax covers all goods, services and imports at a standard rate of 20%. However, exemptions include insurance and financial services, the transfer of or the renting of land, and educational and health related services. Other taxes include a property tax at a rate of 2–4%.

37 CUSTOMS AND DUTIES

Most imports are subject only to declaration and registration. However, special licenses are required for imports of tobacco, alcoholic beverages, oils, military hardware, radioactive materials, jewelry, precious metals, pharmaceutical items, and narcotics. The Ministry of Foreign Trade supervises the collection of customs duties. The amount collected is not published.

Goods arriving from foreign points to be unloaded in Bulgaria must have customs manifests and other shipping documents as specified by law. Customs duties are paid ad valorem at a rate of

Public Finance – Bulgaria (2003)		
(In millions of leva, central government figures)		
Revenue and Grants	**12,484**	**100.0%**
Tax revenue	6,527	52.3%
Social contributions	3,654	29.3%
Grants	306	2.5%
Other revenue	1,997	16.0%
Expenditures	**12,417**	**100.0%**
General public services	2,127	17.1%
Defense	815	6.6%
Public order and safety	949	7.6%
Economic affairs	1,477	11.9%
Environmental protection	...	...
Housing and community amenities	87	0.7%
Health	1,479	11.9%
Recreational, culture, and religion	195	1.6%
Education	651	5.2%
Social protection	4,637	37.3%

(…) data not available or not significant.

SOURCE: *Government Finance Statistics Yearbook 2004,* Washington, DC: International Monetary Fund, 2004.

5–40% on industrial products and 5–70% on agricultural products. Goods from EU nations receive preferential tariff rates. Duty must be paid on all goods except those specifically exempt, such as many foods products, farm machinery, toiletries, fertilizer and pesticide, mining equipment, and medical and dental supplies. In August 1987, the national assembly adopted a law to establish tariff-free zones to attract foreign investment beginning in January 1988. Taxes on imports include a value-added tax of 20%, a 0.5% customs clearance fee, and a 3% import surcharge.

38 FOREIGN INVESTMENT

Bulgaria has realized the need to attract foreign investment and has one of the most liberal foreign investment laws in the region. The 1997 Foreign Investment Law set up the Foreign Investment Agency (FIA) to administer the regime. In 1999, currency laws were liberalized to conform with IMF Article VIII obligations. Foreign investors can enter into joint ventures, start new (greenfield) ventures, purchase companies in Bulgaria's privatization process, or acquire portfolio shares. The law governing privatizations is the 1992 Law on the Transformation and Privatization of State and Municipal Enterprises. In November 2000, amendments were made to enhance the transparency and efficiency of the privatization process and to bring it under parliamentary control, but domestic political turmoil and austerity under an IMF stand-by program combined with the external economic slowdown to bring foreign investment in privatization to a low of less than $20 million in 2001. By 2000, about 78% of the state enterprises slated for privatization had been sold off with foreign investors participating mainly through direct cash purchases. The government encourages the use of Brady bonds (debt-for-equity swaps) in payment instruments. Bulgarian bad debt bonds (zunks) can be purchased on the local market at a 30–35% discount on the face value and are accepted at a 40% premium in privatization sales.

Under legislation from 1987 and since revised, Bulgaria has six free zones where companies with foreign participation can receive equal or preferential treatment. The most profitable free zone is the one at Plovdin. Others are on the Danube (at Ruse and Vidin), near the Turkish border (at Svilengrad), near the Serbia border (Dragomen), and on the Black Sea (at Burgas, which has the most advanced warehousing and transshipment facilities).

In 1992, foreign direct investment (FDI) was $34.4 million, mostly from Austria and Hungary. In 1993, FDI jumped to $102.4 million, $22 million from privatization and over half ($56 million) from Germany. By 1997, FDI inflow had risen to $636.2 million. Most ($421.4 million) came from privatization sales and the largest source was Belgium ($264 million). In 1998, the effects of the Russian financial crisis helped produce the first postindependence decline to $620 million; $155.8 million was from privatization and Cyprus was the largest source ($109 million), mainly from Stambouli Enterprises. In 1999, FDI inflow recovered to $818 million, with $226.7 million coming from privatization sales and with Germany, Cyprus, and Russia each the source of over $100 million FDI. FDI inflow peaked in 2000 at $1 billion, with $366 million from privatization. The largest sources were Italy ($339.7 million) and Greece ($241million). The global economic slowdown beginning in 2001 reduced FDI inflow to $812.9 million in 2001 and to an estimated $478.7 million in 2002. Contributions from privatization reached a low of $19.2 million, recovering to an estimated $135.6 million in 2002. In 2001, Greece ($240.2 million) and Italy ($146.5 million) were the sources of the largest investments, and in 2002, the only FDI inflow over $100 million was from Austria ($137.7 million). A main source of disinvestments was Korea (Daewoo and Hyundai), with negative flows of -$9.2 million in 2001 and -$41.3 million in 2002.

From 1992 to 2002, total FDI inflow was $5.14 billion, $1.58 billion from privatization sales. Sources include at least 25 countries, with the top five being Greece (12.4%), Germany (12.2%), Italy (10.5%), Belgium (9.4%), and Austria (8.7%). The sectors receiving the most net FDI 1998 to 2002 were banks and other financial activities (23.5%); trade and repair services (14.1%); telecommunications (9.1%); petroleum, chemicals, rubber and plastics (7.2%); and mineral products including cement and glass (6.8%). In 2004, FDI reached a record high of $2.5 billion (the equivalent of 9.2% of the GDP), and was expected to remain high in 2005 at around $2.1 billion. The main source of FDI has been the EU, with around 67% of total investments.

Capital markets are small and underdeveloped in Bulgaria. The new Bulgaria Stock Exchange opened in 1998 with 998 companies and a total market valuation of $992 million. In December 2001, there were 399 listed companies with a market capitalization of $505 million. However, Bulgaria offers a favorable investment climate, boasting strong economic growth, political stability, a well educated workforce and competitive costs. It is a good springboard to other markets in Europe and the Middle East, and as EU accession candidate in 2007 it can serve as an entry point to otherwise well protected markets.

³⁹ECONOMIC DEVELOPMENT

Until 1990 when the post-Communist government began a program of privatization, the economy was almost entirely nationalized or cooperatively owned and operated on the basis of state plans. These were designed to expand the economy as a whole, with emphasis on the growth of heavy industry (fuels, metals, ma-

chinery, chemicals) and on the development of export goods. In 1971, productive enterprises were grouped into more than 60 state concerns responsible for almost all nonagricultural production.

Bulgaria's first five-year plan (1949–53) emphasized capital investment in industry. The period was marked by a slow pace in agricultural production (owing largely to collectivization and small investment), an inadequate supply of consumer goods, and a poor livestock output. The 1953–57 plan provided for a decrease in industrial investment, with a resultant improvement in agriculture, housing, and living conditions. The food-processing industry, important for export, began to receive greater attention in 1958, as did textiles and clothing. The lagging rate of growth during the early 1960s was due mainly to poor agricultural output and to a slower industrial pace. The third five-year plan (1958–62), with its "big leap forward" (1959–60), was claimed to have reached its goals by the end of 1960, but definite shortcomings remained. The fourth plan (1961–65) devoted 70% of total investment to industry, while agriculture received only 6.5%. Investments directed by the fifth plan (1966–70) adhered essentially to precedent, with some shift toward agriculture, and this trend continued under the sixth plan (1971–75). Of total investment during 1971–73, over 40% went to industry and 15% to agriculture. The 1976–80 plan resulted in a 35% increase in industrial output and a 20% increase in agricultural output. The overall growth rate began to slow down in the late 1970s, and the 1981–85 plan reflected the concept of a more gradual economic growth. Under the 1986–90 plan, it was projected that national income would grow by 22–25%, industrial output by 25–30%, and agricultural production by 10–12%. Priority was to be given to the development of high technology.

In the 1990s, the post-Communist government began a program to reform of the nation's economy. It rescheduled the foreign debt, abolished price controls, and became a member of the International Monetary Fund (IMF) and IBRD. The reforms, however, were not embraced by the Socialist government that took power in 1994 and by 1996 the economy was in a tailspin. The government led by Prime Minister Ivan Kostov that took power in 1997 laid the financial groundwork for a market economy by selling off state firms, strengthening the currency (lev), and doing away with price controls, state subsidies, monopolies, and trade restrictions. As a result of its successful stabilization of the lev and inflation, Bulgaria is viewed favorably by investors and is a candidate for membership in the European Union (EU). Membership in that body was expected for 2007 if accession requirements are met, including progress on privatization.

The government of Prime Minister Simeon Saxe-Coburg-Gotha, which came to power in 2001, took steps to reduce taxes, rein in corruption, and encourage foreign investment. Bulgaria nevertheless suffers from high unemployment and low standards of living. A $337 million stand-by arrangement with the IMF, approved in February 2002, expired in February 2004. The government, while pledging to the IMF that it would adhere to sound macroeconomic policies (including controlling spending, strengthening tax administration, curbing inflation, balancing the budget, and strengthening the country's external financing position), stated the improvement of Bulgarians' living standards was central to the country's economic development.

Although Bulgaria has registered some of the highest GDP growth rates in Europe, the real income of the population (and subsequently their living standards) have failed to develop as quickly. Policy makers in Bulgaria are therefore looking to match the macroeconomic boom with similar improvements at the population level, particularly in terms of lower unemployment and more job opportunities. The national elections from June 2005 were followed by political turmoil, none of the parties being able to gain a clear majority. Eventually, the socialist party managed to form a government around Prime Minister Sergei Stanishev and promised to continue economic reforms and market restructuring. Together with Romania, Bulgaria is seeking to meet the EU accession date of 2007. Corruption remains the main point of contention for both countries, and is an issue that needs to be addressed promptly in the coming period.

40 SOCIAL DEVELOPMENT

The code for compulsory social insurance was revised in 2000. It provides for dual coverage by a social insurance system and mandatory private insurance. The program covers all employees, self-employed persons, farmers, artists, and craftsman. Old age benefits begin at age 61 and 6 months for men and 56 and 6 months for women; these will be increased incrementally until 2009 when retirement age will be 63 for men and 60 for women. Survivors' and disability pensions are also provided, as well as work injury and unemployment benefits. Maternity benefits amount to 90% of earnings for 135 days. The government provides family allowance benefits based on the age and number of children.

Although women have equal rights under the constitution, they have not had the same employment opportunities as men. Although many women attend university, they have a higher rate of unemployment, and are likely to work in low paid jobs. Violence against women remains a serious problem, and domestic violence is considered a family problem and not a criminal matter. The government provides no shelter or counseling for women. There exists societal stigma against rape victims, and no laws prohibit sexual harassment. Trafficking in women remains a huge problem.

A significant problem of discrimination against the Roma minority continued in 2004. Although freedom of speech is provided for by the constitution, the government maintains influence over the media and libel is a criminal offense. The government and public have limited tolerance for religious freedom.

41 HEALTH

The Ministry of Health is the controlling and policy-making agency for the health system in Bulgaria. An estimated 4% of GDP went to health expenditure. The Bulgarian government passed a bill restoring the right of the private sector to practice medicine and permitting the establishment of private pharmacies, dentists, and opticians. Bulgarian citizens resident in the country still have use of the free national health service. Bulgaria is in the process of restructuring its health care system from one based on command and control to one founded on pluralism. Medical care has never been well funded, but the shift from a centrally planned to a private enterprise system has left the medical sector in disarray. Doctors continue to receive low wages and operate inadequate and outdated machinery and patients on the whole receive minimal health services. In 1993, the World Bank assessed the country's problems and recommended numerous changes and improvements. The Ministry of Health sought funding for 19–21 addi-

tional health centers and the rehabilitation of 67 secondary centers served by 283 emergency medical teams. Utilization of health care services, including hospitalization, outpatient treatment, and preventive care, declined throughout the 1990s.

Bulgaria has 98 municipal hospitals with an average of 227 beds apiece, and 32 general district hospitals with an average of 874 beds. In addition there were 12 university hospitals in Sofia. As of 2004, there were an estimated 338 physicians, 443 nurses, 81 dentists, and 16 pharmacists per 100,000 people. Mortality in 2000 was 13 per 1,000, compared with 8.1 in 1960.

Stroke mortality is among the highest in Europe and circulatory diseases account for more than half of all deaths. Smoking is on the increase; alcohol consumption is high; physical activity is low; and obesity is common. Bulgarians have a high intake of fats, sugars, and salt. One out of eight people has high blood pressure. Improved maternal and child care lowered infant mortality from 108.2 per 1,000 in 1951 to 13 per 1,000 in 2000. However, by 2005 the infant mortality rate increased to an estimated 20.55 per 1,000 live births. In 1999, there were 46 cases of tuberculosis per 100,000 people despite high immunizations for this disease. In the same year Bulgaria immunized children up to one year old as follows: diphtheria, pertussis, and tetanus, 96%, and measles, 96%. An estimated 76% of married women (ages 15 to 49) used contraception. The fertility rate has deceased from 2.2 per woman in 1960 to 1.3 per woman in 2000. Bulgaria's maternal mortality rate is below the average for countries of medium human development. Approximately 99% of the population had access to safe drinking water. Life expectancy in 2005 was 72 years on average.

The HIV/AIDS prevalence was 0.10 per 100 adults in 2003. As of 2004, there were approximately 346 people living with HIV/AIDS in the country. There were an estimated 100 deaths from AIDS in 2003.

42 HOUSING

There are two main types of housing environments in the country: street district and housing complexes. Most of the street district housing was built before World War II and consists of private lots built to follow a street regulation plan. Beginning in the 1950s, housing complexes were built on public property, though the homes themselves are privately owned. Over 120 complexes have been built in the last 50 years, with a large number of prefab homes. Capital investment for housing construction during the period 1976–80 amounted to Lv3.5 billion. At the end of 1985 there were 3,092,000 dwelling units in the country, 24% more than in 1975; by 1991, this figure had risen to 3,406,000. In 2004 there were an estimated 3,704,798 dwellings; about 477 per 1,000 population. The average number of people per household was 2.09. About 11% of all housing stock are one-room dwellings; about 65% are two- or three-room units. About 63% of all dwellings are in urban areas.

Although housing construction during the period 1976–85 averaged about 60,000 units per year, the housing shortage continues, especially in the larger cities, because of the influx into urban areas of new workers and because of the emphasis placed on capital construction. In 1975, to curb urban growth, the government instituted tight restrictions on new permits for residences in major cities. In December 1982, the Communist Party decreed that, in order to halt the growth of Sofia, a number of enterprises in the capital would be closed or moved elsewhere.

43 EDUCATION

Education is free and compulsory for eight years between the ages of 7 and 19. Primary education is divided into two stages of four years in each stage. Secondary students then choose either a general studies or vocational training program, each of which lasts for four years. The Academic year runs from September to June. The language of instruction is Bulgarian.

In 2001, about 70% of children between the ages of three and five were enrolled in some type of preschool program. Primary school enrollment in 2003 was estimated at about 90% of age-eligible students. The same year, secondary school enrollment was about 87% of age-eligible students. It is estimated that about 97% of all students complete their primary education. The student-to-teacher ratio for primary school was at about 17:1 in 2003; the ratio for secondary school was about 12:1.

There are over 30 higher education institutions, including four universities. The most important is the University of Sofia, founded in 1888. The others include the University of Plovdiv (founded 1961), the University of Veliko Tarnovo (founded 1971), and the American University in Bulgaria (founded 1991). All higher level institutions had a total of 262,757 students and 26,303 teaching staff in 1997. In 2003, about 39% of the tertiary age population were enrolled in some type of higher education program. The adult literacy rate for 2004 was estimated at about 98%, with fairly even rates for men and women.

As of 2003, public expenditure on education was estimated at 3.6% of GDP.

44 LIBRARIES AND MUSEUMS

The St. Cyril and St. Methodius National Library, established in 1878 in Sofia, is the largest in Bulgaria (2.52 million volumes); since 1964, the Elin Pelin Bulgarian Bibliographic Institute has been attached to it. Other important libraries are the Central Library of the Scientific Information Center (with 740,000 volumes), the Bulgarian Academy of Sciences library (1.74 million volumes), the Sofia University Library (1,500,000 volumes), and the Ivan Vazov National Library in Plovdiv (with 1,300,000 volumes). The Pencho Slaveykov Public library in Varna has over 800,000 volumes. The Union of Librarians and Information Services Officers was established in Bulgaria in 1990.

Bulgaria has some 200 museums, of which the most important include the National Archaeological Museum (attached to the Academy of Sciences) and the National Art Gallery (with a collection of national and foreign art), both in Sofia. Other museums are devoted to history, science, and the revolutionary movement, and include the Bojana Church Museum in Sofia, the Museum of Wood Carvings and Mural Painting in Trjauna, with an important collection of artifacts from the Bulgarian National Revival Period in the 18th and 19th centuries, and the Open-Air Museum of Ethnography in Gabrovo.

45 MEDIA

Telecommunications systems are owned and operated by the state. In 2003, there were an estimated 380 mainline telephones for every 1,000 people; about 114,600 people were on a waiting list for telephone service installation. The same year, there were approximately 466 mobile phones in use for every 1,000 people.

In Spring 2000, the government awarded a license for the first privately owned television station with nationwide coverage to the Balkan News Corporation; in 2003, Nova TV became the second national commercial station. All other national television stations are state-owned, though there are a number of privately operated regional stations. In 2003, there were an estimated 543 radios for every 1,000 people; the number of television sets was not available in the same survey. It is estimated that about 133 of every 1,000 people subscribe to cable television services. In 2003, there were 51.9 personal computers for every 1,000 people and 206 of every 1,000 people had access to the Internet. There were 46 secure Internet servers in the country in 2004.

The principal Sofia papers, with their publishers and estimated daily circulations (2002), are: *24 Chasa*, Vest Publishing House, 330,000; *Bulgarska Armiya*, Ministry of Defense, 30,000; *Demokratsiya*, Union of Democratic Forces, 45,000; *Duma*, Socialist Party, 130,000; *Trud*, Confederation of Independent Trade Unions, 200,000; *Zemedelsko Zname*, Agrarian People's Union, 178,000; and *Zemya*, Socialist Party, 53,000.

The constitution of Bulgaria ensures freedom of speech and of the press, and the government is said to generally respect these rights. National television and radio broadcasting remain under supervision of the Council for Electronic Media and the Communications Regulation Commission.

46 ORGANIZATIONS

Bulgaria's important economic organizations include the Bulgarian Chamber of Commerce and Industry (1985) and organizations dedicated to promoting Bulgaria's exports in world markets. There are trade unions representing a wide variety of vocations. The Confederation of Independent Trade Unions of Bulgaria was founded in 1901 and taken over by the Communists after World War II. In 1990, it became an independent organization. It has about 75 member federations and four association members. There are professional and trade organizations representing a variety of fields.

The Bulgarian Medical Association serves as a national organization promoting high standards of healthcare, advancement in medical research, and the free dissemination of health information. There are also several similar medical organizations dedicated to promoting research and education concerning specific conditions and diseases.

There are several associations promoting a wide range of sports and leisure activities, including bobsledding, badminton, baseball, chess, yoga, and amateur radio. The National Federation of Sports in Schools was established in 1993 to promote and coordinate sport activities through the schools. There are national branches of the Olympic Committee, the Special Olympics, and the Paralympic Committee.

The Bulgaria Academy of Science promotes scientific study and advancement, conducts research projects, and maintains a museum. The Institute of Art Studies is cosponsored by the Academy of Science as an organization dedicated to promoting Bulgarian art and culture.

Since 1990, a number of youth organizations have developed throughout the country. The Bulgarian Democratic Youth, with about 90,000 members, became the successor to the Dimitrov Young Communist League. The group serves to advance civic enterprise and control and promote a social environment for enterprising youth. Student groups include the Federation of Independent Student Associations, the Bulgarian Association of University Women, the Independent Student Trade Union, and the Student League of Beliko Turnovo. There is an Organization of Bulgarian Scouts and active branches of YMCA/YWCA.

There are national chapters of the Red Cross Society, UNICEF, Habitat for Humanity, and Caritas.

⁴⁷TOURISM, TRAVEL, AND RECREATION

Bulgaria is rich in mineral waters and has numerous tourist spas. Visitors are attracted to the Black Sea resorts and the archaeological monuments. There are three national parks—Pirin, Rila, and Central Balkan—all rich in historic sites and self-regulating ecosystems. Lying between the slopes of the Balkan and the Sredna Gora mountain range is the Valley of Roses. Foreign visitors to Bulgaria must have a passport. Visas are not required for stays of up to 30 days.

In 2003, about 6.2 million tourists visited Bulgaria, a 12% increase from 2002. In that same year, tourist receipts totaled $2.1 billion. There were 143,960 beds available in hotels and other establishments, with an occupancy rate of 34%. Visitors stayed in Bulgaria an average of four nights.

In 2004, the US Department of State estimated the cost of staying in Sofia at $221 per day. In smaller towns the daily costs were approximately $87.

⁴⁸FAMOUS BULGARIANS

The founders of modern Bulgarian literature, writing before the end of Turkish rule, were Georgi Rakovski (1821–67), Petko Slaveikov (1827–95), Lyuben Karavelov (1835–79), and Kristo Botev (1848–76), who was one of Bulgaria's greatest poets. The most significant writer after the liberation of 1878 was Ivan Vazov (1850–1921), whose *Under the Yoke* gives an impressive picture of the struggle against the Turks. Pentcho Slaveikov (1866–1912), the son of Petko, infused Bulgarian literature with philosophical content and subject matter of universal appeal; his epic poem *A Song of Blood* recalls an insurrection suppressed by the Turks in 1876. In the period between the two world wars, Nikolai Liliyev (1885–1960) and Todor Trayanov (1882–1945) were leaders of a symbolist school of poetry. Elin Pelin (1878–1949) and Iordan Iovkov (1884–1939) wrote popular short stories on regional themes. More recent writers and poets include Nikola Vaptzarov, Christo Shirvenski, Dimiter Dimov, Orlin Vassilev, and Georgi Karaslavov. Elias Canetti (1905–94), Bulgarian born but lived from 1938 until his death in the United Kingdom, received the Nobel Prize for literature in 1981. Tzvetan Todorov (b.1939), is a Bulgarian philosopher and literary theorist living in France; he is the author of *The Conquest of America* (1982). Ivan Mrkvicka (1856–1938), a

distinguished Czech painter who took up residence in Bulgaria, founded the Academy of Fine Arts in Sofia.

A prominent Bulgarian statesman was Alexander Stamboliski (1879–1923), Peasant Party leader who was premier and virtual dictator of Bulgaria from 1920 until his assassination. The best known modern Bulgarian, Georgi Dimitrov (1882–1949), was falsely charged in 1933 with burning the Reichstag building in Berlin; he became general secretary of the Comintern until its dissolution and prime minister of Bulgaria in 1946. Traicho Kostov (1897–1949), an early revolutionary leader, was a principal architect of Bulgaria's postwar economic expansion. Caught up in the Tito-Stalin rift, he was expelled from the Politburo and executed in December 1949. Todor Zhivkov (1911–1998) was first secretary of the Bulgarian Communist Party between 1954 and 1989, the longest tenure of any Warsaw Pact leader. His was marked by ardent and steadfast support of Soviet policies and ideological positions. Zhivkov's daughter Lyudmila Zhivkova (1942–81), a Politburo member since 1979, was regarded by Western observers as second only to her father in power and influence. Zhivkov was replaced by Dimitar Popov as premier of a coalition government headed by the Socialist Party (formerly the Communist Party). Simeon II (b.1937) was the last tsar of Bulgaria from 1943–46, and was prime minister from 2001–05. He is also known as Simeon of Saxe-Coburg-Gotha.

⁴⁹DEPENDENCIES

Bulgaria has no territories or colonies.

⁵⁰BIBLIOGRAPHY

Anguelov, Zlatko. *Communism and the Remorse of an Innocent Victimizer.* College Station, Tex.: Texas A&M University Press, 2002.

Detrez, Raymond. *Historical Dictionary of Bulgaria.* 2nd ed. Lanham, Md.: Scarecrow, 2006.

Dimitrov, Georgi. *The Diary of Georgi Dimitrov, 1933–1949.* New Haven: Yale University Press, 2003.

The Fragility of Goodness: Why Bulgaria's Jews Survived the Holocaust: A Collection of Texts. Princeton, N.J.: Princeton University Press, 2001.

Frucht, Richard (ed.). *Eastern Europe: An Introduction to the People, Lands, and Culture.* Santa Barbara, Calif.: ABC-CLIO, 2005.

International Smoking Statistics: A Collection of Historical Data from 30 Economically Developed Countries. New York: Oxford University Press, 2002.

McElrath, Karen (ed.). *HIV and AIDS: A Global View.* Westport, Conn.: Greenwood Press, 2002.

Otfinoski, Steven. *Bulgaria.* 2nd ed. New York: Facts On File, 2004.

Petkov, Petko. *The United States and Bulgaria in World War I.* Boulder, Colo.: East European Monographs, 1991.

CROATIA

Republic of Croatia
Republika Hrvatska

CAPITAL: Zagreb

FLAG: Red, white, and blue horizontal bands with the Croatian coat of arms (red and white checkered).

ANTHEM: *Lijepa Nasa Domovina.*

MONETARY UNIT: The Croatian kuna (HRK was introduced in 1994, consisting of 100 lipa. HRK1 = $0.16892 (or $1 = HRK5.92) as of 2005.

WEIGHTS AND MEASURES: The metric system is the legal standard.

HOLIDAYS: New Year's Day, 1 January; Epiphany, 6 January; Labor Day, 1 May; Republic Day, 30 May; National Holiday, 22 June; Assumption, 15 August; Christmas, 25–26 December.

TIME: 7 PM = noon GMT.

¹LOCATION, SIZE, AND EXTENT

Croatia is located in southeastern Europe. Comparatively, the area occupied by Croatia is slightly smaller than the state of West Virginia with a total area of 56,542 sq km (21,831 sq mi). Croatia shares boundaries with Slovenia on the w, Hungary on the N, Serbia on the E, Bosnia and Herzegovina on the s and E, and the Adriatic Sea on the w, and has a total boundary length of 8,020 km (4.983 mi), including 5,835 km (3,626 mi) of coastline. Croatia's capital city, Zagreb, is located in the northern part of the country. Croatia's territory includes 1,185 nearby islands in the Adriatic Sea, of which only 66 are inhabited.

²TOPOGRAPHY

The topography of Croatia is geographically diverse, with flat plains along the Hungarian border, as well as low mountains and highlands near the Adriatic coast. The country is generally divided into three main geographic zones: the Pannonian and Peri-Pannonian Plains in the east and northwest, the central hills and mountains, and the Adriatic coast. Approximately 24% of Croatia's land is arable. Croatia's natural resources include: oil, some coal, bauxite, low-grade iron ore, calcium, natural asphalt, silica, mica, clays, and salt. Croatia's natural environment experiences effects from frequent earthquakes, air pollution from metallurgical plants, coastal pollution from industrial and domestic waste, and forest damage.

³CLIMATE

Croatia's climate in the lowlands features hot, dry summers and cold winters. In Zagreb, the average annual temperature is 12°C (53°F) with average highs of 2°C (35°F) in January and 27°C (80°F) in July. In the mountains, summers are cool and winters cold and snowy. Along the coast, the climate is Mediterranean with mild winters and dry summers. In Split, the average annual temperature is 17°C (62°F). Annual average precipitation is about 94 cm (37 in).

⁴FLORA AND FAUNA

The region's climate has given Croatia a wealth of diverse flora and fauna. Ferns, flowers, mosses, and common trees populate the landscape. Along the Adriatic Sea there are subtropical plants. Native animals include deer, brown bears, rabbits, fox, and wild boars. As of 2002, there were at least 76 species of mammals, 224 species of birds, and over 4,200 species of plants throughout the country.

⁵ENVIRONMENT

Air pollution (from metallurgical plant emissions) and deforestation are inland environmental problems. In 1996 industrial carbon dioxide emissions totaled 17.5 million metric tons. In 2000, total emissions were at 19.6 million metric tons. Coastal water systems have been damaged by industrial and domestic waste. All of Croatia's urban dwellers have access to safe drinking water. Environmental management is becoming more decentralized, thereby empowering city and municipal administrations to determine environmental policy. Croatia's 195 protected areas cover 421,000 hectares (1,040,000 acres), or 7.5% of the country's natural areas. The Plitvice Lakes National Park is a natural UNESCO World Heritage Site. There are four Ramsar wetland sites. In 2000, about 31% of the total land area was forested.

According to a 2006 report issued by the International Union for Conservation of Nature and Natural Resources (IUCN), threatened species included 7 types of mammals, 9 species of birds, 1 type of reptiles, 2 species of amphibians, 27 species of fish, and 11 species of invertebrates. Endangered species include the Atlantic sturgeon, slender-billed curlew, and the Mediterranean monk seal.

⁶POPULATION

The population of Croatia in 2005 was estimated by the United Nations (UN) at 4,438,000, which placed it at number 117 in population among the 193 nations of the world. In 2005, approximately

16% of the population was over 65 years of age, with another 17% of the population under 15 years of age. There were 93 males for every 100 females in the country. According to the UN, the annual population rate of change for 2005–10 was expected to be -0.3%, a rate the government viewed as too low. The projected population for the year 2025 was 4,318,000. The population density was 78 per sq km (203 per sq mi).

The UN estimated that 56% of the population lived in urban areas in 2005, and that urban areas were growing at an annual rate of 0.50%. The capital city, Zagreb, is by far the largest city in the country. It had a population of 688,000 in 2005. Other cities and their estimated populations include Split, 265,000; Rijeka, 206,000; and Osijek, 165,000.

7 MIGRATION

In the early 1990s, some 160,000 people living in Croatia fled to neighboring countries to escape ethnic conflict, with another 120,000 fleeing to countries abroad. Total returns to Croatia as of February 2000 numbered over 112,000, including 36,000 Croatian Serbs who repatriated from Serbia and Montenegro. Also, nearly 74,000 internally displaced people had returned to their homes within Croatia. In February 2000, an estimated 250,000 Croatian Serb refugees were still registered in Serbia and Montenegro and Bosnia and Herzegovina. Of these, more than 25,000 had applied for return under the government's Return Programme. The total number of migrants living in Croatia in 2000 was 425,000. In 2004, the United Nations High Commissioner for Refugees (UN-HCR) was assisting some 23,744 people in Croatia: 3,663 refugees, 7,468 returnees, and over 12,500 internally displaced people. In addition, there were 852 voluntary repatriations to Bosnia and Herzegovina and 6,616 to Serbia and Montenegro. In 2004, an estimated 200 Croatians sought asylum in Ireland and Sweden. The net migration rate in 2005 was estimated at 1.58 migrants per 1,000 population. The government views the emigration level as too high.

8 ETHNIC GROUPS

As of the 2001 census, Croats make up about 89.6% of the population and Serbs account for 4.5%. The remainder include Bosniaks, Hungarians, Slovenians, Czechs, and Roma.

9 LANGUAGES

Serbo-Croatian is the native language and is used by 96% of the populace. Since 1991, Croats have insisted that their tongue (now called Croat) is distinctive. The spoken language is basically the same, but Serbs use the Cyrillic alphabet and Croats the Roman alphabet. The Croatian alphabet has the special consonants č, ć, š, ž, dj, dž, and nj, representing sounds provided by the Cyrillic alphabet. The remaining 4% of the population speak various other languages, including Italian, Hungarian, Czech, Slovak, and German.

10 RELIGIONS

Christianity was introduced into the area in the 7th century. Under the Yugoslav Socialist Republic, churches—Roman Catholic in particular—experienced repression by the state. This moderated in 1966, when an agreement with the Vatican recognized a religious role for the clergy. The latest estimates recorded a Roman Catholic population of 85%, with 6% Orthodox Christians, and 1% Muslims. Less than 1% were Jewish and about 4% belong to other faiths, including the Church of Jesus Christ of Latter-day Saints, Jehovah's Witnesses, Greek Catholic, Pentecostal, Hare Krishna, Baptist, Seventh-Day Adventist, and the Church of Christ. About 2% of the population are atheists. The Orthodox are primarily Serbs; other minority religions can be found mostly in urban areas. No formal restrictions are placed on religious groups, and all are free to conduct public services and run social and charitable institutions.

The constitution provides for freedom of conscience and religion and this right is generally respected in practice. Though there is no official state religion, the Roman Catholic Church, the Serbian Orthodox Church, the Islamic community, and several smaller Christian denominations have signed agreements with the government through which they qualify for state support. A 2003 Regulation on Forms and Maintaining Records of Religious Communities in Croatia requires all religious organizations to register with the government in order to receive legal status under the Law on Religious Communities.

11 TRANSPORTATION

Croatia's railroads consist of two main routes. An east–west route originating in Serbia nearly parallels the Sava before reaching Zagreb and continuing on to Slovenia and Hungary. The north–south route connects the coastal cities of Split and Rijeka to Zagreb. Another railway connects Dubrovnik to Bosnia and Herzegovina. As of 2004, there were 2,726 km (1,694 mi) of standard gauge railroad line. However, some parts remain inoperative or out of use due to territorial disputes. Highways totaled 28,588 km (17,782 mi) in 2003, of which 24,186 km (15,044 mi) were paved roads, including 583 km (363 mi) of expressways. As of 2003, there were 1,293,400 passenger cars and 143,100 commercial vehicles registered for use.

Rijeka, Split, and Kardeljevo (Ploce) are the main seaports along the Adriatic. There are 785 km (488 mi) of perennially navigable inland waters. Vukovar, Osijek, Sisak, and Vinkovci are the principal inland ports. In 2005, Croatia had 73 ships of at least 1,000 GRT, for a total capacity of 750,579 GRT.

Croatia had an estimated 68 airports in 2004. As of 2005 a total of 23 had paved runways, and there was one heliport. Principal airports include Dubrovnik, Split, and Pleso at Zagreb. In 2003, about 1.267 million passengers were carried on scheduled domestic and international flights.

12 HISTORY

Origins through the Middle Ages

Slavic tribes penetrated slowly but persistently into the Balkan area beginning in the 5th century. Their migration, and that of the Serbians, occurred upon the invitation of the Byzantine emperor Heraclius I (r. 610–641) in 626, to repel the destructive inroads of the Avars. A coalition of Byzantine and Croat forces succeeded in forcing the Avars out of Dalmatia first, and then from the remainder of Illirycum and the lands between the Drava and Sava rivers. The Croats settled on the lands that they had freed from the Av-

LOCATION: 45°10′ N 15°30′ E. BOUNDARY LENGTHS: Total boundary lengths, 2,197 kilometers (1,365 miles); Serbia, 241 kilometers (165 miles); Bosnia and Herzegovina, 932 kilometers (579 miles); Slovenia, 670 kilometers (416 miles); Hungary, 329 kilometers (204 miles); Montenegro, 25 kilometers. COASTLINE: 5,790 kilometers (3,598 miles); mainland coastline, 1,778 kilometers (1,105 miles); islands coastline, 4,012 kilometers (2,493 miles).

ars and established their own organized units that included indigenous Slavic tribes.

By the year 1000, Venice, having defeated the Croatian fleet, controlled the entire Adriatic coast. The coastal cities, while welcoming the Italian cultural influence of Venice, feared potential Venetian domination over their trading interests with the enormous Balkan hinterland. Thus Dubrovnik (formerly called Ragusa), with its growing fleet, preferred to remain tied to the more distant Byzantine Empire.

Zvonimir, son-in-law of the Hungarian king Bela I, was crowned king of Croatia in 1075. Zvonimir died around 1089 without an

heir, leaving his widow with the throne, but the nobles opposed her rule because of her Hungarian ancestry. The king of Hungary intervened to protect his sister's interests (and his own) by occupying Pannonian Croatia. The area was recovered in 1095 by Peter Svacic from Knin (1093–97). Peter, the last independent king of Croatia, was killed in battle in 1096 by King Koloman of Hungary, who then conquered Croatia. After concluding a nonaggression pact with Venice, which had retained control of the coastal islands and cities, the Croats rebelled and drove the Hungarian forces back to the Drava River frontier between Croatia and Hungary.

Royal Union with Hungary

In 1102, Koloman regrouped and attacked Croatia. He stopped at the Drava River, however, where he invited the nobles representing the 12 Croatian tribes to a conference. They worked out the so-called Pacta Conventa, an agreement on a personal royal union between Hungary and Croatia (including Slavonia and Dalmatia). The overall administration of the state would be by a "ban" (viceroy) appointed by the king, while regional and local administration were to stay in the hands of the Croatian nobles. This legal arrangement, with some practical modifications, remained the basis of the Hungarian-Croatian personal royal union and relationship until 1918.

Internal warfare among Croatia's nobility weakened its overall ability to resist attack from Venice. In 1377, Tvrtko (1353–1390) proclaimed himself king of the Serbs, Bosnia, and the Croatian coast. Venice was defeated in 1385, and was forced to surrender all rights to the coastal cities all the way to Durazzo in today's Albania. Dubrovnik also gained its independence from Venice, recognizing the sovereignty of the Hungarian-Croatian king.

Defense against the Turks

By the mid-15th century the threat from both the Turks and Venice was growing more ominous, leading King Sigismund to establish three military defense regions in 1432. As these defensive regions were further developed, they attracted new, mostly Serbian, settlers/fighters who became the strong Serbian minority population in Croatia. The Ottoman threat brought about the appointment of Vladislav Jagiellon, the king of Poland, as king of Hungary and Croatia in 1440. Vladislav was succeeded in 1445 by Ladislas, son of Albert of Hapsburg, and therefore king of both Austria and Hungary/Croatia. Since Ladislas was a minor, John Hunyadi, a brilliant general, was appointed regent. Hunyadi had to protect the throne from the counts of Celje, who, in 1453, also claimed the title of ban of Croatia. Ulrich, one of the counts of Celje, fell victim to Hunyadi's assassins at the defense of Belgrade from the Turks in 1456. This murder was avenged by King Ladislas V, who had Hunyadi executed in 1456.

After 1520, the Turks began effective rule over some Croatian territory. In 1522, the Croatian nobility asked Austrian archduke Ferdinand of the Hapsburgs to help defend Croatia against the Turks, but by 1526, the Turks had conquered Eastern Slavonia and had advanced north into Hungary. On 29 August 1526, in a massive battle at Mohacs, the Turks defeated the Hungarian and Croatian forces, killing King Louis. By 1528, the Ottomans held the southern part of Croatia, and by 1541 had conquered Budapest. Dubrovnik, on the other hand, had accepted the Ottoman suzerainty in 1483, keeping its autonomy through its extensive trade with the Turkish empire. Most coastal towns were under the protection of Venice, with its good trade relations with the Turks.

In 1526, after King Louis's death at Mohacs, Ferdinand of Hapsburg was elected king of Hungary and Croatia. The Hapsburg rulers began to encroach on the rights of Croats by turning the throne from a traditionally elected position into a hereditary one, and by allocating Croatian lands as fiefs to their supporters, turning the Croatian peasants from free men into serfs.

King Ferdinand III (r.1637–1657) consolidated Hungary and Croatia under Hapsburg rule. Under Ferdinand's son, Leopold I (who in 1658 had also become the German emperor), the status of Hungary and Croatia continued to deteriorate. All power was centralized in the hands of the king/emperor and his court. Leopold tried to emulate the absolutist model practiced by Louis XIV of France. The Turkish offensives of 1663 were successfully repelled by the Croatian brothers Nicholas and Peter Zrinski. Following the defeat of the Turks at Saint Gotthard in western Hungary in 1664, Leopold I unilaterally concluded a 20-year peace treaty with the Turks based essentially on the prewar situation.

The Peace of Vasvar proved to the Hungarians and Croats that the Hapsburg court was not interested in fighting the Turks for Hungary and Croatia. This situation led to a conspiracy by the Zrinski brothers and key Hungarian nobles against the Hapsburg Court. But the Turks warned the Hapsburgs of the conspiracy, and Peter Zrinski and his coconspirator Francis Frankopan were executed on 30 April 1671 (Nicholas Zrinski had died in 1664). Leopold I suspended for 10 years the office of the Croatian ban.

The last king of the male Hapsburg line was Charles III (r.1711–1740). In 1722, during his reign the Hungarian parliament agreed to extend the Hapsburg hereditary right to its female line (Charles had no son), something already agreed to by the Croatian parliament in 1712. At the same time the Hungarians obtained a legal guarantee on the indivisibility of the realm of the Crown of Saint Stephen, which included Croatia. Charles was thus followed by his daughter Maria Teresa (r.1740–1780) who, by decree, divided Croatia into regions headed by her appointees. Joseph II, her son, emancipated the serfs, tried to improve education, tried to impose the German language as a unifying force, closed monasteries in an attempt to control the Roman Catholic Church, and decreed religious toleration. In the 1788 war against the Turks, Joseph II suffered a devastating defeat; he died two years later.

Leopold II, Joseph II's brother, succeeded him, and recognized Hungary and Croatia as kingdoms with separate constitutions. Hungarian replaced Latin as the official language of the Hungarian parliament. Hungarians then began trying to establish the Hungarian language in Croatia, Slavonia, and Dalmatia, thus initiating a hundred-year struggle of the Croats to preserve their identity.

Napoleon and the Spring of Nations

With the peace treaty of Campoformio ending the war against Napoleon in 1797, Austria obtained the territories of the Venice Republic, including the Adriatic coast as far as Kotor. In 1806, Napoleon seized Dubrovnik, and in 1809 he obtained control of Slovenian and Croatian territories and created his Illyrian Provinces. The French regime levied heavy taxes and conscription into Napoleon's armies. With Napoleon's defeat, all of Dalmatia reverted back to direct Austrian administration until the end of World War I in 1918.

In 1825, Francis I called the Hungarian parliament into session and the Hungarians resumed their pressure to introduce the Hungarian language into Croatian schools. Ljudevit Gaj became the leader of the movement calling for the reassertion of the independent Kingdom of Croatia and advocated the introduction of "Illyrian" (Croatian) as the official language to replace Latin. A member of the Illyrian movement, Count Janko Draškovic, also promoted the idea of reorganizing the Hapsburg lands into a federation of political units with coequal rights. The Croatian parliament then nullified the previous agreement on using Hungarian, and made Croatian the official language of parliament. In 1840, the Croatian

Sabor voted for the introduction of Croatian as the language of instruction in all Croatian schools and at the Zagreb Academy.

The struggle over the Croatian language and national identity brought about the establishment of the first political parties in Croatia. The Croatian-Hungarian Party supported a continued Croat-Hungarian commonwealth. The Illyrian Party advocated an independent kingdom of Croatia comprising all the Croatian lands including Bosnia and Herzegovina. The Austrian government banned the term "Illyrian" and the name of the Illyrian party of Ljudevit Gaj and Draskovic was changed to the National Party.

At the next session of the Hungarian parliament in 1843, the Croatian delegation walked out when not permitted to use Latin instead of Hungarian. The Croatian National Party submitted to the emperor its demands to reestablish an independent government of Croatia, elevate the Zagreb Academy to university status, and raise the Zagreb bishopric to the archbishopric rank. The lines were thus drawn between the Hungarian and Croatian nationalists. This situation came to a head in 1848 when great unrest and revolts developed in Austria and Hungary.

Autonomy or Independence

Francis Joseph I (r.1848–1916) ascended to the Hapsburg throne on 2 December 1848 and ruled for a long time, favoring the Hungarians against the Croats. Croatian parties had split between the pro-Hungarian union and those advocating Croatian independence based on ancient state rights. The latter evolved into the "Yugoslav" (South Slavic Unity) movement led by Bishop Josip Juraj Strossmayer and the "Pravaši" movement for total Croatian independence led by Ante Starcevic. Austria and Hungary resolved their problems by agreeing on the "dual monarchy" concept. The Hungarian half of the dual monarchy consisted of Hungary, Transylvania, Croatia, Slavonia, and Dalmatia. A ban would be appointed by the emperor-king of Hungary upon the recommendation of the Hungarian premier, who would usually nominate a Hungarian noble. Croatia-Slavonia-Dalmatia was recognized as a nation with its own territory, the Croatian language was allowed, and it was granted political autonomy in internal affairs. But in reality, the Hungarians dominated the political and economic life of Croatia.

Yugoslavism

In the 1870s, Ivan Mazuranic was appointed ban of Croatia. He implemented general administrative reform and a modern system of education. The Sabor instituted a supreme court and a complete judicial system. The 1878 Congress of Berlin allowed Austria's military occupation and administration of Bosnia and Herzegovina and the Sandzak area (lost by the Turks after their defeat by Russia in 1877). The Croatian Sabor then requested the annexation of those areas, but Austria and Hungary refused. Croatia and Serbia were deeply disappointed, and Serbia began supporting terrorist activities against the Austrians. In 1881, the military region was joined to Croatia, thus increasing the size of its Serbian Orthodox population. This offered the Hungarian ban Khuen Hedervary the opportunity to play Serbs against Croats in order to prevent their joint front. The relations between Croats and Serbs continued to deteriorate.

By 1893, there was a united Croatian opposition that called for equality with Hungary, the unification of all Croatian lands, and which invited the Slovenes to join Croatia in the formation of a new state within the framework of the Hapsburg monarchy. This united opposition took the name of Croatian Party of Right ("Stranka Prava"). National unification, however, had strong opposition from powerful forces: the Hungarians with their Great Hungary Drive; the Serbs, who wanted to annex Bosnia and Herzegovina into Serbia; the Italians, claiming Istria, Rijeka, and Dalmatia; and the Austrians, and their Pan-Germanic partners.

Croats and Serbs formed a Croat-Serbian coalition, winning a simple majority in the 1908 Croatian parliamentary elections, followed by the Party of Right and the Peasant Party, led by the brothers Anthony and Stephen Radic. Also in 1908, the direct annexation of Bosnia and Herzegovina by Austria took place. The Party of Right and the Peasant Party supported the annexation, hoping that the next step would be Bosnia and Herzegovina's incorporation into a unified Croatia. Serbia, conversely, was enraged by the annexation. Assassination attempts increased and led to the assassination of Archduke Ferdinand and his wife in Sarajevo on 28 June 1914. These tragedies followed the Serbian victories and territorial expansion in the wake of the 1912 and 1913 Balkan wars.

The idea of a separate state uniting the South Slavic nations ("Yugoslavism") grew stronger during World War I (1918–18). An emigré "Yugoslav Committee" was formed and worked for the unification of the South Slavs with the Kingdom of Serbia. In 1917, an agreement was reached on the formation of a "Kingdom of Serbs, Croats, and Slovenes" upon the defeat of Austro-Hungary.

Royal Yugoslavia

The unification of Croatia and the new "Kingdom of Serbs, Croats, and Slovenes" on 1 December 1918 was flawed by the inability to work out an acceptable compromise between the Serbs and Croat-Slovenes. The National Council for all Slavs of former Austro-Hungary was formed on 12 October 1918 in Zagreb (Croatia) and was chaired by Monsignor Anton Korosec, head of the Slovenian People's Party. On 29 October 1918, the National Council proclaimed the formation of a new, separate state of Slovenes, Croats, and Serbs of the former Austro-Hungary. The Zagreb Council intended to negotiate a federal type of union between the new state and the Kingdom of Serbia that would preserve the respective national autonomies of the Slovenes, Croats, and Serbs. Monsignor Korosec had negotiated a similar agreement in principle with Serbian prime minister Nikola Pašic in Geneva, but the Serbian government reneged on it. While Korosec was detained in Geneva, a delegation of the National Council went to Belgrade and submitted to Serbia a declaration expressing the will to unite with the Kingdom of Serbia, and Serbia readily agreed. On 1 December 1918, Prince Alexander of Serbia declared the unification of the "Kingdom of Serbs, Croats, and Slovenes."

The provisional assembly convened in 1918, with the addition to the Serbian parliament of representatives from the other south Slavic historical regions, while the Croatian Sabor was deprived of its authority. The elections to the Constituent Assembly were held on 28 November 1920 but the 50-member delegation of the Croatian Republican Peasant Party refused to participate. The new Vidovdan Constitution was adopted on 28 June 1921 by a "simple majority" vote of 223 to 35, with 111 abstentions in the absence of the Croatian delegation with 50 votes.

The period between 1921 and 1929 saw a sequence of 23 governments, a parliament without both the Croatian delegation's 50 votes and the Communist Party's 58 votes (it continued its work underground). This situation assured control to the Serbian majority, but it was not possible to govern the new country effectively without the participation of the Croats, the second-largest nation.

Finally, in 1925, Prime Minister Pašic invited Stjepan Radic, head of the Croatian Peasant Party, to form a government with him. However, not much was accomplished and Pašic died just a few years later. On 20 June 1928 Radic was shot in parliament by a Serbian deputy and died the next month. Riots broke out as a result of his assassination.

Dr. Vlatko Macek, the new Croatian Peasant Party leader, declared that "there is no longer a constitution, but only king and people." A coalition government under Prime Minister Monsignor Anton Korošec, head of the Slovene People's Party, lasted only until December 1928. King Alexander dissolved the parliament on 6 January 1929, abolished the 1921 constitution, and established his own personal dictatorship as a temporary arrangement.

At first, most people accepted King Alexander's dictatorship as a necessity, which gave the country an opportunity to focus on building its economy from the foundation of postwar reconstruction. Royal decrees established penalties of death or 20 years in prison for terrorism, sedition, or Communist activities. All elected local councils and traditional political parties were dissolved. Freedom of the press was severely constrained and government permission was required for any kind of association. All power was centralized and exercised by the king through a council of ministers accountable only to him.

On 3 October 1929, the country was renamed the Kingdom of Yugoslavia, and the territorial regions (banovinas) were named after rivers to emphasize the king's opposition to national names. One of the consequences of the dictatorship and its harsh measures against political opposition and cultural nationalism was the emigration of some political opponents, among them some of the top leadership of the Croatian Peasant Party and the leader of the Ustaša movement, Ante Pavelic.

The new constitution, initiated by King Alexander on 3 September 1931, was in theory a return to civil liberties and freedoms of association, assembly, and expression. But in reality, all such freedoms were limited by the king's decrees that remained in force. Parliament was to consist of two houses with a council of ministers still accountable directly to the king. The Croatian opposition grew stronger, and in the winter of 1932, their Zagreb Manifesto called for the removal of Serbian hegemony, and for popular sovereignty. In reaction, the regime interned or imprisoned political opponents. Croatia was seething with rebellion, and the three-year prison sentence for opposition leader Macek would have sparked an open revolt, were it not for the danger of Fascist Italy's intervention.

The worldwide economic depression hit Yugoslavia hard in 1932. Opposition continued to grow to the king's dictatorship, which had not proffered any solutions to the so-called Croatian question. In late 1934, the king planned to release Macek from prison, reintroduce a real parliamentary system, and try to reach some compromise between Serbs and Croats. Unfortunately, King Alexander was assassinated in Marseille on 9 October 1934 by agents of the Ustaša group, which was trained in terrorism in Hungary with Mussolini's support. Prince Paul, King Alexander's cousin, headed the interim government, releasing Macek and other political leaders, but otherwise continuing the royal dictatorship. On 5 May 1935, the elections for a new parliament were so shamefully improper that a boycott of parliament began. Prince Paul consulted with Macek, and a new government of reconstruction was formed by Milan Stojadinovic. The new government initiated serious discussions with Macek on a limited autonomous Croatian entity that would be empowered on all matters except the armed forces, foreign affairs, state finance, customs, foreign trade, posts, and telegraphs.

Since 1937, the thorniest issue discussed had been the make-up of the federal units. Serbs wanted to unite with Macedonia, Vojvodina, and Montenegro. Croatia wanted Dalmatia and a part of Vojvodina. Slovenia was recognized as a separate unit, but Bosnia and Herzegovina posed a real problem, with both Croats and Serbs claiming ownership over a land that contained a substantial minority of Bosnian Muslims. Meanwhile, intense trade relations with Germany and friendlier relations with Italy were bringing Yugoslavia closer to those countries. Adolph Hitler's annexation of Austria and Czechoslovakia in 1938 made it imperative that Yugoslavia resolve its internal problem before Hitler and Mussolini attempted to destabilize and conquer Yugoslavia.

Stojadinovic resigned, and Prince Paul appointed Dragiša Cvetkovic as prime minister, charging him with the task of reaching a formal agreement with the Croatian opposition. The agreement was concluded on 26 August 1939. Macek became the new vice-premier, a territorial region of Croatia was established that included Dalmatia and western Herzegovina, and the traditional Sabor of Croatia was revived. But autonomy for Croatia was not received well by most of Serbia. Concerned with the status of Serbs in Croatia, Serbia was anxious to incorporate most of Bosnia and Herzegovina. Even less satisfied was the extreme Croatian nationalist Ustaša movement, whose goal was an independent greater Croatia inclusive of Bosnia and Herzegovina. For the Ustaša, this goal was to be achieved by any means and at any cost, including violence and support from foreign powers. Tensions between the extremes of the failed Yugoslavia had seemingly reached the boiling point.

World War II

Meanwhile, the clouds of World War II had gathered with Italy's takeover of Albania and its war with Greece, and Hitler's agreement with Stalin followed by his attack on Poland in the fall of 1939, resulting in its partitioning. Hungary, Romania, and Bulgaria had joined the Axis powers and England and France had entered the war against Germany and Italy. With the fall of France in 1940, Hitler decided to assist Mussolini in his war with Greece through Bulgaria, and therefore needed Yugoslavia to join the Axis so Germany would be assured of ample food and raw materials.

The Yugoslav Government had limited choices—either accept the possibility of immediate attack by Germany, or join the Axis, with Hitler's assurance that no German troops would pass through Yugoslavia towards Greece. The regent was aware of Yugoslavia's weak defense capabilities and the inability of the Allies to assist Yugoslavia against the Axis powers, despite security agreements with Britain and France. Yugoslavia signed a treaty with Hitler on 26 March 1941 and on 27 March a coup d'etat by Serbian military officers forced the regent to abdicate. The military declared Prince Peter the new king, and formed a government with General Dušan Simovic as premier and Macek as vice-premier. The new government tried to temporize and placate Hitler, who was enraged by the deep anti-German feeling of the Yugoslav people who shouted in demonstrations, "Bolje rat nego pact" (Better war than the pact). Feeling betrayed, Hitler unleashed the German fury on Yugoslavia on 6 April 1941 by bombing Belgrade and other centers without any warning or formal declaration of war.

The war was over in 11 days, with the surrender signed by the Yugoslav Army Command while the Yugoslav government (with young King Peter II) fled the country for allied territory and settled in London. Yugoslavia was partitioned among Germany, Italy, Hungary, Bulgaria, and Italian-occupied Albania, while Montenegro, under Italian occupation, was to be restored as a separate kingdom. Croatia was set up as an independent kingdom with an Italian prince to be crowned Tomislav II. Ante Pavelic was installed by the Italians and Germans as head of independent Croatia (after Macek had declined Hitler's offer). Croatia was forced to cede part of Dalmatia, with most of its islands and the Boka Kotorska area, to Italy. In exchange, Croatia was given Bosnia and Herzegovina and the Srijem region up to Belgrade.

On 10 April 1941, the "resurrection of our independent State of Croatia" was proclaimed in Zagreb by Slavko Kvaternik for Ante Pavelic, who was still in Italy with some 600 of his Ustaše. With Pavelic's arrival in Zagreb five days later, the Ustaša regime was established, with new laws that expressed the basic Ustaša tenets of a purely Croatian state viewed as the bulwark of Western civilization against the Byzantine Serbs. Slavko Kvaternik explained how a pure Croatia would be built—by forcing one-third of the Serbs to leave Croatia, one-third to convert to Catholicism, and one-third to be exterminated. Soon Ustaša bands initiated a bloody orgy of mass murders of Serbs unfortunate enough not to have converted or left Croatia on time. The enormity of such criminal behavior shocked even the conscience of German commanders, but Pavelic had Hitler's personal support for such actions which resulted in the loss of lives of hundreds of thousands of Serbs in Croatia and Bosnia and Herzegovina. In addition, the Ustaša regime organized extermination camps, the most notorious one at Jasenovac where Serbs, Jews, Gypsies, and other opponents were massacred in large numbers. The Serbs reacted by forming their own resistance groups ("Cetniks") or by joining with the Communist-led partisan resistance, and thus struck back at the Ustaša in a terrible fratricidal war encouraged by the Germans and Italians.

The Ustaša regime organized its armed forces into the Domobrani, its Ustaša shock troops, and the local gendarmerie. Its attempt at organizing the Croatian people in the fascist mode failed, however. Most Croats remained faithful to the Croatian Peasant Party Democratic principles, or joined the Partisan movement led by Josip Broz-Tito that offered a federal political program. With respect to Bosnia and Herzegovina, the Ustaša regime never attained real control. The continuous fighting generated by Cetniks and Partisans fighting one another while being pursued by the Ustaša, the Germans, and the Italians made it impossible for the Ustaša to dominate. Most Croats rejected (and deeply resented) the trappings of an imported Fascist mystique and the abuse of their Catholic faith as a cover or justification for the systematic slaughter of their Serbian neighbors.

By the spring of 1942, the Ustaša regime began to retreat from its policy and practice of extermination of Serbs. But the terrible harm was done, and one consequence was the deep split between the Serbian members and their Croatian colleagues within the cabinet of the Yugoslav government-in-exile. The Serbs held the entire Croatian nation accountable for the Ustaša massacres, and reneged on the 1939 agreement establishing the Croatian Banovina as the basis for a federative reorganization in a postwar Yugoslavia. This discord made the Yugoslav government-in-exile incapable of offering any kind of leadership to the people in occupied Yugoslavia. The fortunes of war and diplomacy favored the Communist Partisans—after Italy's surrender in September 1943, it handed over to the Partisans armaments and supplies from some 10 Italian divisions. More and more Croats left their homeguard, and even some Ustaša units, to join the Partisans. Some Ustaša leaders, on the other hand, conspired against Pavelic in order to negotiate with the allies for recognition of the "independent" state of Croatia. But they were caught and executed in the summer of 1944.

With the entry of Soviet armies into Yugoslav territory in October 1944, the Communist Partisans swept over Yugoslavia in pursuit of the retreating German forces. Pavelic and his followers, along with the Croatian homeguard units, moved north to Austria at the beginning of May 1945 to escape from the Partisan forces and their retaliation. The Partisans took over Croatia, launching terrible retaliation in the form of summary executions, people's court sentences, and large scale massacres, carried out in secret, of entire homeguard and other Ustaša units.

Communist Yugoslavia

Such was the background for the formation of the second Yugoslavia led by Tito as a Federative People's Republic of five nations—Slovenia, Croatia, Serbia, Macedonia, Montenegro—with Bosnia and Herzegovina as a buffer area with its mix of Serbs, Muslims, and Croats. The problem of large Hungarian and Muslim Albanian populations in Serbia was solved by creating the autonomous regions of Vojvodina (Hungarian minority) and Kosovo (Muslim Albanian majority) that assured their political and cultural development. Tito attempted a balancing act to satisfy most of the nationality issues that were still unresolved from the first Yugoslavia, and decades of ethnic and religious conflict.

In pre-1941 Yugoslavia, Serbs had enjoyed a controlling role. After 1945 the numerically stronger Serbs had lost the Macedonian area they considered Southern Serbia, lost the opportunity to incorporate Montenegro into Serbia, and had lost direct control over both the Hungarian minority in Vojvodina and Muslim Albanians of Kosovo, which had been viewed as the cradle of the Serbian nation since the Middle Ages. They could no longer incorporate into Serbia the large Serbian-populated areas of Bosnia, and had not obtained an autonomous region for the large minority of Serbian population within the Croatian Republic. The Croats—while gaining back from Hungary the Medjumurje area and from Italy the cities of Rijeka (Fiume), Zadar (Zara), some Dalmatian islands, and the Istrian Peninsula—had lost the Srijem area to Serbia, and Bosnia and Herzegovina. In addition, the Croats were confronted with a deeply resentful Serbian population that became ever more pervasive in public administrative and security positions.

The official position of the Marxist Yugoslav regime was that national rivalries and conflicting interests would gradually diminish through their sublimation into a new Socialist order. Without capitalism, nationalism was supposed to wither away. Therefore, in the name of unity and brotherhood, nationalistic expression of concern was prohibited, and repressed by the dictatorial and centralized regime of the League of Yugoslav Communists acting through the Socialist Alliance as its mass front organization. After a short postwar coalition government, the elections of 11 November 1945, boycotted by the non-communist coalition parties, gave the communist People's Front 90% of the votes. A constituent assembly met on 29 November, abolished the monarchy, and established the Federative People's Republic of Yugoslavia. In January 1946, a new constitution was adopted, based on the 1936 Soviet constitution.

The Communist Party of Yugoslavia took over total control of the country and instituted a regime of terror through its secret police. To destroy the bourgeoisie, property was confiscated, and the intelligentsia were declared "enemies of the people," to be executed or imprisoned. Large enterprises were nationalized, and forced-labor camps were formed. The church and religion were persecuted, properties confiscated, religious instruction and organizations banned, and education used for Communist indoctrination. The media was forced into complete service to the totalitarian regime, and education was denied to "enemies of the people."

The expulsion of Yugoslavia from the Soviet-dominated Cominform Group in 1948, engineered by Soviet leader Joseph Stalin, was actually a blessing for Yugoslavia. Yugoslavia's "road to Socialism" evolved quickly in response to Stalin's pressures and Yugoslavia's need to perform a balancing act between the North Atlantic Treaty Organization (NATO) and the Soviet bloc. Tito also pushed the nationalization of the economy through a policy of forced industrialization supported by the collectivization of agriculture.

By the 1950s, Yugoslavia had initiated the development of what would become its internal trademark: self-management of enterprises through workers' councils and local decision-making as the road to Marx's "withering away of the state." Following the failure of the first five-year plan (1947–51), the second five-year plan (1957–61) was completed in four years by relying on the well-established self-management system. Economic targets were set from the local to the republic level and then coordinated by a federal planning institute to meet an overall national economic strategy. This system supported a period of very rapid industrial growth in the 1950s. But a high consumption rate encouraged a volume of imports financed by foreign loans that exceeded exports. In addition, inefficient and low productivity industries were kept in place through public subsidies, cheap credit, and other artificial protective measures, leading to a serious crisis by 1961. Reforms were necessary and, by 1965, market socialism was introduced with laws that abolished most price controls and halved import duties while withdrawing export subsidies. The agricultural reform of 1945–46 limited private ownership to a maximum of 35 hectares (85 acres). The limited free market (after the initial forced delivery of quotas to the state at very low prices) had to be abandoned because of resistance by the peasants. The actual collectivization efforts were initiated in 1949 using welfare benefits and lower taxes as incentives, along with direct coercion. But collectivization had to be abandoned by 1958 simply because its inefficiency and low productivity could not support the concentrated effort of industrial development.

The government relaxed its restrictions to allow labor migration, particularly large from Croatia to West Germany, where workers were needed for its thriving economy. Foreign investment was encouraged (up to 49%) in joint enterprises, and barriers to the movement of people and exchange of ideas were largely removed. The role of trade unions continued to include transmission of instructions from government to workers, allocation of perks, the education/training of workers, monitoring of legislation, and overall protection of the self-management system. Strikes were legally allowed, but the 1958 miners' strike in Trbovlje, Slovenia, was not publicly acknowledged and was suppressed. After 1958, strikes were tolerated as an indication of problems to be resolved.

After the split from the Cominform, Yugoslavia began also to develop a foreign policy independent of the Soviet Union. By mid-1949, Yugoslavia ceased its support of the Greek Communists in their civil war against the then-Royalist government of Greece. In October 1949, Yugoslavia was elected to one of the nonpermanent seats on the UN Security Council and openly condemned Communist-supported North Korea's aggression towards South Korea. Following Nikita Khrushchev's 1956 denunciation of Stalin, Tito intensified his work on developing the movement of nonaligned "third world" nations. This would become Yugoslavia's external trademark, in cooperation with Nehru of India, Nasser of Egypt, and others. With the September 1961 Belgrade summit conference of nonaligned nations, Tito became the recognized leader of the movement. The nonaligned position served Tito's Yugoslavia well by allowing Tito to draw on economic and political support from the Western powers while neutralizing aggressive behavior from the Soviet bloc.

While Tito had acquiesced, reluctantly, to the 1956 Soviet invasion of Hungary for fear of political chaos and its liberalizing impact on Yugoslavia, he condemned the Soviet invasion of Dubcek's Czechoslovakia in 1968, as did Romania's Ceausescu, both fearing their countries might be the next in line for "corrective" action by the Red Army and the Warsaw Pact. Just before his death on 4 May 1980, Tito also condemned the Soviet invasion of Afghanistan. Yugoslavia actively participated in the 1975 Helsinki Conference and Agreements, and the first 1977–78 review conference that took place in Belgrade, even though Yugoslavia's one-party Communist regime perpetrated and condoned numerous human rights violations.

The debates of the 1960s led to a closer scrutiny of the Communist experiment. The 1967 Declaration in Zagreb, claiming a Croatian linguistic and literary tradition separate from the Serbian one, undermined the validity of the "Serb-Croatian" language and a unified Yugoslavian linguistic heritage. Also, Kosovo Albanians and Montenegrins, along with Slovenes and Croats, began to assert their national rights as superior to the right of the Yugoslavian federation. The eighth congress of the League of Communists of Yugoslavia (LCY) in December 1964 acknowledged that ethnic prejudice and antagonism existed in socialist Yugoslavia, and that Yugoslavia's nations were disintegrating into a socialist Yugoslavism. Thus the republic, based on individual nations, became an advocate of a strong federalism that devolved and decentralized authority from the federal to the republic level. Yugoslav Socialist Patriotism was defined as a feeling for both national identity and for the overall socialist self-management framework of Yugoslavia, despite the signs of a deeply divided country.

As the Royal Yugoslavism had failed in its assimilative efforts, so did the Socialist Yugoslavism fail to overcome the forces of nationalism. In the case of Croatia, there were several key factors sustaining the attraction to its national identity: more than a thousand years of its historical development, the carefully nurtured tradition of Croatian statehood, a location bridging central Europe and the Balkan area, an identification with Western European civilization, and the Catholic religion with the traditional role of Catholic priests (even under the persecutions by the Communist regime). In addition, Croatia had a well-developed and productive economy with a standard of living superior to most other areas of the Yugoslav Federation other than Slovenia. This generated a growing resentment against the forced subsidizing by Croatia and Slovenia of less developed areas, and for the buildup of the Yugoslav Army. Finally, the increased political and economic autonomy enjoyed by the Republic of Croatia after the 1974 constitution and particularly following Tito's death in 1980, added impetus to the growing Croatian nationalism.

Croatian Spring

The liberal bloc (Slovenia, Croatia, Macedonia, Vojvodina) prevailed over the conservative group, and the reforms of 1965 did away with central investment planning and political factories. The positions of the two blocs hardened into a national-liberal coalition that viewed the conservative, centrist group led by Serbia as the Greater Serbian attempt at majority domination. The devolution of power in economic decision making, spearheaded by the Slovenes, assisted in the federalization of the League of Communists of Yugoslavia as a league of quasi-sovereign republican parties. Under strong prodding from the Croats, the party agreed in 1970 to the principle of unanimity for decision making. In practice, this meant each republic had veto power. However, the concentration of economic resources in Serbian hands continued, with Belgrade banks controlling half of total credits and some 80% of foreign credits. Fear of Serbian political and cultural domination continued, particularly with respect to Croatian language sensitivities aroused by the use of the Serbian version of Serbo-Croatian as the norm, with the Croatian version as a deviation.

The language controversy thus exacerbated the economic and political tensions between Serbs and Croats, spilling easily into ethnic confrontations. To the conservative centrists the devolution of power to the republic level meant the subordination of the broad Yugoslav and Socialist interests to the narrow nationalist interest of national majorities. With the Croat League of Communists taking the liberal position in 1970, nationalism was rehabilitated. Thus the "Croatian Spring" bloomed and impacted all the other republics of Yugoslavia. Meanwhile, through a series of constitutional amendments in 1967–68 that limited federal power in favor of republics and autonomous provinces, the federal government came to be viewed by liberals as an inter-republican problem-solving mechanism bordering on a confederalist arrangement. A network of inter-republican committees established by mid-1971 proved to be very efficient, resolving a large number of difficult issues in a short time. The coalition of liberals and nationalists in Croatia, however, also generated sharp condemnation in Serbia, where its own brand of nationalism grew stronger, but as part of a conservative-centrist alliance. Thus, the liberal/federalist versus conservative/centrist conflict became entangled in the rising nationalism within each opposing bloc.

Particularly difficult were the situations in Croatia and Serbia because of their minorities issues. Serbs in Croatia sided with the Croat conservatives and sought a constitutional amendment guaranteeing their own national identity and rights. In the process, the Serbs challenged the sovereignty of the Croatian nation. The conservatives prevailed, and the amendment declared that "the Socialist Republic of Croatia (was) the national state of the Croatian nation, the state of the Serbian nation in Croatia, and the state of the nationalities inhabiting it."

Meanwhile, Slovenia, not burdened by large minorities, developed in a liberal and nationalist direction. This fostered an incipient separatist sentiment opposed by both the liberal and conservative party wings. Led by Stane Kavcic, head of the Slovenian Government, the liberal wing gained as much political local latitude from the federal level as possible during the "Slovenian Spring" of the early 1970s. By the summer of 1971, the Serbian Party leadership was pressuring President Tito to put an end to what was in their view the dangerous development of Croatian nationalism. While Tito wavered because of his support for the balancing system of autonomous republic units, the situation quickly reached critical proportions. Croat nationalists, complaining about discrimination against Croats in Bosnia and Herzegovina, demanded the incorporation of western Herzegovina into Croatia. Serbia countered by claiming southeastern Herzegovina for itself. Croats also advanced demands for a larger share of their foreign currency earnings, the issuance of their own currency, their own national bank that would directly negotiate foreign loans, the printing of Croatian postage stamps, to a Croatian Army, to recognition of the Croatian Sabor as the highest Croatian political body and, finally, to Croatian secession and complete independence.

Confronted with such intensive agitation, the liberal Croatian Party leadership could not back down and did not restrain the public demands nor the widespread university students' strike of November 1971. This situation caused the loss of support from the liberal party wings of Slovenia and even Macedonia. Tito intervened, condemning the Croatian liberal leadership on 1 December 1971, while supporting the conservative wing. The liberal leadership group resigned on 12 December 1971. When Croatian students demonstrated and demanded an independent Croatia, the Yugoslav Army was ready to move in if necessary. A wholesale purge of the party liberals followed with tens of thousands expelled. Key functionaries lost their positions, several thousands were imprisoned (including Franjo Tudjman who later became president of independent Croatia), and leading Croatian nationalist organizations and their publications were closed. On 8 May 1972 the Croatian Party also expelled its liberal wing leaders and the purge of nationalists continued through 1973.

However, the issues and sentiments raised during the "Slovene and Croat Springs" of 1969–71 did not disappear. Tito and the conservatives were forced to satisfy nominally some demands, and the 1974 Constitution was an attempt to resolve the strained inter-republican relations as each republic pursued its own interests over and above any conceivable overall Yugoslav interest. The repression of liberal-nationalist Croats was accompanied by the growing influence of the Serbian element in the Croatian Party (24% in 1980) and police force (majority). This influence contributed to the ongoing persecution and imprisonments of Croatian nationalists into the 1980s. Tito's widespread purges of the "Croatian Spring" movement's leadership and participants in 1971 had repressed the reawakened Croatian nationalism, but could not eliminate it. Croatian elites had realized the disadvantages of the Croatian situation and expressed it in 1970–71 through the only channel then available—the Communist Party of Croatia and its liberal wing. With the purges, this wing became officially silent in order to survive, but remained active under the surface, hoping for its turn. This came with the 1974 constitution and its devolution of power to the republic level, and was helped along by the growing role of the Catholic church in Croatia. The Catholic church, as the only openly organized opposition force in the country, became the outspoken defender of Croatian nationalism. As a result, Catholic leaders and priests were subjected to persecution and furious attacks by the government.

Yugoslavia—a House Divided

After Tito's death in 1980, relations between the Croatian majority and the Serbian minority became strained. Tito had set up a rotating presidency in which the leaders of each of the six republics and two autonomous regions of Serbia would have the Yugoslavian presidency for one year at a time. Unfortunately, the Serbian president that first held the office was not recognized by the Croats. Demands for autonomy by the half million Serbs in Croatia were brushed aside by the Croats, who pointed out the absence of such autonomy for Croats in Vojvodina and Bosnia and Herzegovina. Thus the conservatives' control of the League of Communist of Croatia between 1972 and 1987 could not prevent the resurfacing of the Croat question, which led in a few years to Croatia's disassociation from Yugoslavia and to war.

As the Communist parties of the various republics kept losing in membership and control, the clamoring for multiparty elections became irresistible. The first such elections were held on 8 April 1990 in Slovenia where a coalition of non-Communist parties (Demos) won, and formed the first non-Communist Government since 1945. In Croatia, the Croatian Democratic Union (HDZ) under the leadership of Dr. Franjo Tudjman, had worked illegally since 1989 and had developed an effective network of offices throughout Croatia and in Vojvodina and Bosnia and Herzegovina. The HDZ had also established its branches abroad from where, particularly in the United States, it received substantial financial support. Thus, in the elections of late April-early May 1990 the Croatian Democratic Union was able to obtain an overwhelming victory with 205 of 356 seats won and a majority in each of the three chambers of the Croatian Assembly. In the most important Socio-Political Chamber, Dr. Tudjman's party won 54 of the 80 seats, with the Communists and their allies obtaining only 26 seats. On 30 May 1990, Dr. Tudjman was elected president of Croatia with 281 of 331 votes and Stjepan Mesic became prime minister. Krajina Serbs voted either for the former Communists or for their new Serbian Democratic Party (SNS) led by Jovan Raškovic. The Serbian Democratic Party gained five delegates to the parliament and became the main voice of the Serbs in Croatia.

The overwhelming victory of Dr. Tudjman's party made the Serbs very uncomfortable. Their traditional desire for closer political ties to Serbia proper, the prospect of losing their overrepresentation (and jobs) in the Croatian Republic's administration, and fear of the repetition of the World War II Ustaša-directed persecutions and massacres of Serbs made them an easy and eager audience for Slobodan Milošević's policy and tactics of unifying all Serbian lands to Serbia proper. Tensions between Croats and Serbs increased when Tudjman proposed constitutional amendments in June 1990 defining Croatia as the Sovereign State of the Croats and other nations and national minorities without specifically mentioning the Serbs of Croatia. The Serbs feared they would be left unprotected in an independent Croatia and therefore strongly supported Milošević's centralist policies. This fear, and the anti-Croatian propaganda from Belgrade that claimed the revival of the Ustaša, and called upon Serbs to defend themselves, caused Jovan Raškovic to reject the invitation from Tudjman to join the new government as its deputy prime minister. Instead, Raškovic ended the participation in legislative activities of the five Serbian Democratic Party deputies. At the end of August 1990, a new Serbian National Council adopted a "Declaration on the Sovereignty and Autonomy of the Serbian People" implying the need for cultural autonomy for the Serbs if Croatia were to remain a member of the Yugoslav Federation, but claiming political autonomy for the Serbs if Croatia were to secede from the Yugoslav Federation. A referendum held on 18 August 1990 by Serbs in Croatia gave unanimous support to their "Declaration on Sovereignty" as the foundation for the further development of their Knin Republic—as their council of Serbian-majority communes was called, from the name of the Dalmatian city of Knin where it was based.

The Tudjman government refrained from taking any action against the Knin Republic in order to avoid any reason for interference by the Yugoslav Army. But Tudjman made very clear that territorial autonomy for the Serbs was out of the question. When in December 1990 Croatia proclaimed its sovereignty and promulgated its new constitution, the Serbs of Croatia established a "Serbian Autonomous Region," immediately invalidated by the constitutional court of Croatia. Then in February 1991, Croatia and Slovenia declared invalid all federal laws regarding the two republics. On 28 February, the Krajina Serbs declared their autonomy in response to Croatia's call for disassociation from the Yugoslav Federation. Violence spread in many places with clashes between the Serbian paramilitary and special Croatian police units with Yugoslav Army units ordered to intervene. The Yugoslav Army was also used in Serbia in March 1991 to aid Serbian authorities against large Serbian opposition demonstrations in Belgrade. The sight of Yugoslav tanks in the streets of Belgrade, with two dead and some 90 wounded, signaled the decision of the Yugoslav Army to defend Yugoslavia's borders and oppose interethnic clashes that could lead to a civil war. Clearly the Serbian leadership and the Yugoslav Army top command (mostly Serbian) had cemented their alliance, with the goal of preserving Yugoslavia as a centralized state through pressuring Slovenia and Croatia into disarming their territorial defense units and by threatening forceful intervention in case of their refusal. But Slovenia and Croatia continued to buy arms for their defense forces, and to proclaim their intentions to gain independence.

At the end of March 1991, there were again bloody armed clashes between the Krajina Serbs and Croatian police, and again the Yugoslav Army intervened around the Plitvice National Park, an area the Serbs wanted to join to their Knin Republic. For President Tudjman this Serbian action was the last straw—Croatia had been patient for eight months, but could wait no longer. The overall determination of Serbia to maintain a unitary Yugoslavia hardened, as did the determination of Slovenia and Croatia to attain their full independence. This caused the Yugoslav Army leadership to support Serbia and Slobodan Milošević, who had made his position clear by the spring of 1991 on the potential unilateral separation of Slovenia, Croatia, and Bosnia and Herzegovina. Since there was no substantial Serbian population in Slovenia, its disassociation did not present a real problem for Milošević. However, separation by Croatia and Bosnia and Herzegovina would necessitate border revisions in order to allow for lands with Serbian populations to be joined to Serbia.

Independence

A last effort to avoid Yugoslavia's disintegration was made by Bosnia and Herzegovina and Macedonia with their 3 June 1991 compromise proposal to form a Community of Yugoslav Republics whereby national defense, foreign policy, and a common market would be administered centrally while all other areas—other than armed forces and diplomatic representation—would fall into the jurisdiction of the member states. But it was already too late. Serbia opposed the federal nature of the proposal and this left an opening for the establishment of separate armed forces. In addition, Milošević and the Yugoslav Army had already committed to the support of the Serbs' revolt in Croatia. In any case, both Milošević and Tudjman were past the state of salvaging Yugoslavia. They met in Split on 12 June 1991 to discuss how to divide Bosnia and Herzegovina into ethnic cantons.

The federal government of Yugoslavia ceased to exist when its last president (Stjepan Mesic, Croatia's future president) and prime minister (Ante Markovic), both Croatian, resigned on 5 December 1991. Both Croatia and Slovenia reaffirmed their decision to disassociate from federal Yugoslavia after a three-month moratorium, in the Brioni Declaration of 7 July 1991. The European Community held a conference on Yugoslavia, chaired by Lord Carrington, where a series of unsuccessful cease-fires was negotiated for Croatia. The conference also attempted to negotiate new arrangements based on the premise that the Yugoslav Federation no longer existed, a position strongly rejected by Serbia, who viewed with great suspicion Germany's support for the independence of Slovenia and Croatia. Germany granted recognition to Slovenia and Croatia on 18 December 1991, while other European community members and the United States followed suit. The European community continued its efforts to stop the killing and destruction in Croatia, along with the UN special envoy, Cyrus Vance, who was able to conclude a peace accord on 3 January 1992 calling for a major UN peacekeeping force in Croatia. Part of the accord was also an agreement by the Serbian side to hand over to the UN units their heavy weapons and to allow the return to their homes of thousands of refugees. The international community stood firmly in support of the preservation of Yugoslavia. The United States and the European community had indicated that they would refuse to recognize the independence of Slovenia and Croatia if they unilaterally seceded. At the same time, Slovenia and Croatia defined their separation as a disassociation by sovereign nations, and declared their independence on 25 June 1991. Milošević was prepared to let Slovenia go, but Croatia still held around 600,000 ethnic Serbs. Milošević knew that a military

attack on a member republic would deal a mortal blow to both the idea and the reality of a "Yugoslavia" in any form. Thus, following the Yugoslav Army's attack on Slovenia on 27 June 1991, Milošević used the Yugoslav Army and its superior capabilities toward the goal of establishing the Serbian autonomous region of Krajina in Croatia. Increased fighting from July 1991 caused the tremendous destruction of entire cities (for example, Vukovar) and large-scale damage to medieval Dubrovnik. Croatia had been arming since 1990 with the financial aid of émigrés, and thus withstood fighting over a seven-month period, suffering some 10,000 deaths, 30,000 wounded, over 14,000 missing and lost to the Krajina Serbs (and to the Yugoslav Army). Croatia also lost about one-third of its territory—from Slavonia to the west and around the border with Bosnia and south to northern Dalmatia.

By late 1992, rebel Serbs controlled about one-third of Croatia's territory. In 1993, the Krajina Serbs voted to integrate with Serbs in Bosnia and Serbia. Although the Croatian government and the Krajina Serbs agreed to a cease-fire in March 1994, further talks disintegrated. This portion of land was strategically important to Croatia because it held the land routes to the Dalmatian coast (supporting the once-thriving tourist industry), the country's petroleum resources, and the access route from Zagreb into Slavonia. Also in 1994, the Croatian government agreed to give up its plan to partition Bosnia with Serbia. In return for US political support (which included military training and equipment), Croatia began cooperating with the Bosnian Muslims and recognized the sovereignty of Bosnia and Herzegovina.

In May 1995, the Croatian Army—in a mission it called "Operation Storm"—quickly occupied western Slavonia, and by August 1995, the Krajina region was under Croatian control. International reaction to the military mission was mild, and was largely judged as vindication for earlier Serb aggression. An estimated 200,000 Serbs fled from the region their ancestors had occupied for 200 years. Before the Croatian Army could move into eastern Slavonia, the government halted the mission, upon insistence by the United States. The cessation of the Croatian military campaign before it reached eastern Slavonia probably prevented a future round of revenge killings.

Eastern Slavonia was then put under UN control, with a force of about 5,500 military and police peacekeepers. With the signing of a basic agreement between the Croatian government and the Eastern Slavonia Serbs at the Dayton Peace Accords in Dayton, Ohio, in 1995, the UN had the support to establish the UN Transitional Administration for Eastern Slavonia (UNTAES) on 15 January 1996. The UNTAES established a Transitional Police Force, in which Serb and Croat police forces jointly administered the region, in order to prepare the area for reversion to Croatian control in July 1997. On 15 January 1998, any Serbs remaining in eastern Slavonia became Croatian citizens. Also, the Serbs that fled Croatia for fear of persecution were invited back into the country on 26 June 1998, when the Croatian parliament adopted the Croatian government's Return Program.

The 1997 elections that supported the reigning President Tudjman and his HDZ party were considered "fundamentally flawed." The tight grip that Tudjman kept on the Croatian nation through control of the media, police, and judicial system were considered not only undemocratic, but unconstitutional. In 1999, President Tudjman announced that "National issues are more important than democracy," alienating many Croatians and concerning international observers. Tudjman cooperated with some requests of the International Criminal Tribunal for the Former Yugoslavia (ICTY), but refused to comply with others, especially the insistence on field investigations into the military operations of the 1990s. The ruling party agreed in 1999 to hold new parliamentary elections in January 2000, but these were scheduled too late for Tudjman to organize his resistance. He died on 10 December 1999, and Speaker of Parliament Vlatko Pavletic assumed interim power. On 18 February 2000, Stjepan Mesic was elected president of Croatia, signaling a new era in Croatian history that promised to be more European and more peaceful. In February 2005, Mesic was elected for a second term, with 66% of the vote, over his main contender—Jadranka Kosor.

The parliamentary elections held in early 2000 resulted in an end to the rule of the HDZ party, which won only 46 of 151 seats in the House of Representatives; Social Democratic Party (SDP) leader Ivica Racan led a center-left coalition government as prime minister. Constitutional reforms later that year reduced the powers exercised by the president, and replaced the semi-presidential system of government with a parliamentary one. In 2001, parliament approved a constitutional amendment abolishing its upper house, the House of Counties. The HDZ branded the government's move as politically motivated, as it controlled the upper house, and had been able to delay reform-minded legislation.

In November 2003, the parliamentary elections were won by the HDZ, which took 66 out of 152 seats in the House of Representatives. The SDP got only 34 seats, while other parties, and representatives, had to settle for 10 seats or less. Ivo Sanader, the leader of HDZ, was invited by president Mesic to form a government. Subsequently, the parliament gave its consent, and Sanader was appointed prime minister with 88 votes in favor. Sanader promised his party underwent major changes since the death of Tudjman, and pledged to uphold democracy and the rule of law. He is a strong supporter of EU and NATO membership.

In September 2001, the ICTY indicted Milošević for war crimes and crimes against humanity committed in the war in Croatia. He went on trial in The Hague in February 2002. However, in September 2002, under pressure from nationalists, the Croatian government declined to turn over to the Hague tribunal former Army chief-of-staff Janko Bobetko, indicted for war crimes. In March 2003, former Maj. Gen. Mirko Norac was sentenced in a Croatian court to 12 years in prison for orchestrating the killings of Serb civilians in 1991. He was the most senior Croatian Army officer to be convicted for war crimes in a Croatian court. Norac had given himself up to Croatian authorities in March 2001 on the understanding that he would not be extradited to the ICTY.

In February 2003, Croatia submitted its application for membership to the EU; it concluded its Stabilization and Association Agreement (SAA) with the EU in May 2001. In October 2005, the EU gave Croatia the green light for the continuation of accession talks although some of its deemed war criminals were still at large. Croatia is also an aspirant for NATO membership.

13 GOVERNMENT

Croatia is a democratic republic with a president and parliamentary system of government. The parliament of Croatia, formed on 30 May 1990, adopted a new constitution on 22 December 1990. The executive authority is held by the president, elected for five years, and a government cabinet headed by the prime minister. Constitutional reforms in 2000 significantly reduced the powers exercised by the president. However, the president remains the supreme commander of the armed forces, and participates in foreign and national security policy decision-making. The constitutional court assures legality. In October 2005, the president was Stjepan Mesic, and the prime minister was Ivo Sanader.

In March 2001, amendments to the constitution abolished the upper house of parliament (House of Counties) in what had been a bicameral legislature (also including the lower house, or House of Representatives). The unicameral parliament, known as the Sabor (Assembly), has up to 160 members elected for four-year terms. In 2005 there were 140 domestic representatives, 8 representatives for the minorities, and 4 Diaspora representatives.

The threshold that parties must cross for representation in parliament is 5% of the turnout in each of the 10 electoral districts. Croatian citizens that live outside the country's borders are counted in a distinct electoral unit, and their votes are weight directly against the number of domestic votes to determine the number of parliamentary seats the Diaspora will receive. (To vote, one must be 18 or older, or 16 if employed.) The prime minister is nominated by the president, in line with the balance of power in the Assembly. Domestic policy-making is the responsibility of parliament.

14 POLITICAL PARTIES

In the presidential elections of May 1997, Tudjman, founder of the Christian Democratic Union (HDZ) in 1988, won a second term as president of Croatia, with 61.2% of the vote. International monitors, however, condemned the elections as seriously biased in favor of the incumbent. Zdravko Tomac of the socialist Social Democrat Party won 21.1% of the vote, and Vlado Gotovac of the moderate Social Liberal Party received 17.7%. After the death of Tudjman at the end of 1999, presidential elections were held in January and February 2000. Thirteen candidates successfully registered for the election. Stjepan Mesic of the Croatian People's Party (HNS), supported by the Croatian Peasant Party (HSS)/Istrian Democratic Sabor (IDS)/LS liberal coalition, defeated rival Drazen Budiša of the Social Democratic Party (SDP)/Croatian Social Liberal Party (HSLS) coalition, 41.1% to 27.7% in the first round, with Croatian Democratic Union (HDZ) candidate Mate Granic gaining 22.5% of the vote, and 56% to 44% in the second round of the ballot. Mesic won in 17 out of 21 counties. Voter turnout in round one was 63% and 61% in round two. Mesic was voted in, for a second term, in 2005. He had the support of eight political parties and defeated his main contender—Jadranka Kosor—in the second round of the elections, with 66% of the popular vote.

In the parliamentary elections held 23 November 2003, HDZ garnered 66 seats in the House of the Representatives; the SDP won 34; the HSS and HNS both won 10; the HSP (the Croatian Party of Rights) won 8; the IDS won 4; Libra, HSU (the Croatian Party of Pensioners), and SDSS (Independent Democratic Serb Party), all won 3; while 11 seats went to others. The HDZ formed a minority government coalition with DC (Democratic Center), HSLS, HSU, and SDSS. The leader of HDZ, Ivo Sanader, became the new prime minister.

15 LOCAL GOVERNMENT

Local government in Croatia consists of municipalities that are grouped into 20 counties and 1 city. Citizens are guaranteed the right to local self-government with competencies to decide on matters, needs, and interest of local relevance. Counties consist of areas determined by history, transportation, and other economic factors. The 20 counties are: Zagreb, Kradina-Zagorje, Sisacko-Moslavacka, Karlovac, Varazdin, Koprivnica-Krizevci, Bjelovar-Bilogora, Hrvatsko Primorje-Gorski Kotar, Lika-Senj, Virovitica-Podravina, Pozega-Slavonija, Slavonski Brod-Posavina, Zadar-Knin, Osijek-Baranja, Šibenik, Vukovar-Srijem, Dalmatia-Split, Istria, Dubrovnik-Neretva, Medjimurje; and the City of Zagreb.

The mayor of Zagreb is elected by the city assembly and is approved by the president. In the local elections of 2001, tens of thousands of candidates contested 566 councils and assemblies at the municipal, town, county, and Zagreb City levels. (There are approximately 440 municipalities and 120 towns in Croatia). A total of 3.8 million voters were registered for the elections. The local election results roughly mirrored those of the parliamentary elections of 2000. However, in the May 2005 local elections voter turn out was estimated to be lower than 35%, with the SDP prevailing in the bigger cities—Zagreb, Split, and Rijeka. HDZ's popularity decreased dramatically since the parliamentary elections in 2003—the party garnered only about 16% of the local vote, mostly in rural areas and small towns.

16 JUDICIAL SYSTEM

The judicial system is comprised of municipal and county courts, a Supreme Court, an Administrative Court, and a Constitutional Court. A High Judicial Council (made up of 11 members serving eight-year terms) appoints judges and public prosecutors. The judicial system, supervised by the justice and administration ministry, remains subject to ethnic bias and political influence, especially at the local level. Judges are prohibited constitutionally from being members of any political party.

A commercial court system handles all commercial and contractual disputes. The Supreme Court judges are appointed for an eight-year term by the Judicial Council. The Constitutional Court has 13 judges (11 prior to March 2001) who are also elected in the same manner. The military court system was abolished in November 1996. The constitution prohibits the arbitrary interference with privacy, family, home or correspondence, but these freedoms are not always protected by the government.

17 ARMED FORCES

The armed forces of Croatia are restricted by the Dayton Peace Accords. In 2005 the number of active armed forces personnel totaled 20,800 with 108,200 reservists. The Army had 14,050 active personnel, followed by the Navy with 2,500 and the Air Force with 2,300. The Army had 291 main battle tanks, 104 armored infantry fighting vehicles, 53 armored personnel carriers, and 1,452 artillery pieces. The Navy's principal units included one tactical submarine, two corvettes, five patrol/coastal vessels, five amphibious landing craft, and seventeen logistics/support vessels. The Air Force had 27 combat capable aircraft, including 20 fighters and 9 attack helicopters. Croatia also had a paramilitary force of 10,000 armed police. Croatia as of 2005 was involved in 12 foreign countries or regions as part of NATO and UN military and peacekeeping missions. Croatia's military budget in 2005 was $626 million.

18 INTERNATIONAL COOPERATION

Croatia was admitted to the United Nations on 22 May 1992; it is part of the ECE and serves on several specialized agencies, such as the FAO IAEA, ICAO, IMF, UNESCO, UNIDO, WHO, and the World Bank. The nation was admitted to the WTO on 30 November 2000. Croatia is a member of the OSCE, the Council of Europe, the Central European Initiative, Euro-Atlantic Partnership Council, and the European Bank for Reconstruction and Development. The nation is a candidate for membership in the European Union. Croatia participates in the NATO Partnership for Peace and the Adriatic Charter, and sits as an observer in the OAS.

Croatia is an observer in the Nonaligned Movement and is part of the Organization for the Prohibition of Chemical Weapons The UN sent peacekeeping troops to Croatia in the spring of 1992 to mediate an ongoing civil war in the region. In environmental cooperation, Croatia is part of the Basel Convention, Conventions on Biological Diversity and Air Pollution, Ramsar, CITES, the London Convention, the Montréal Protocol, MARPOL, the Nuclear Test Ban Treaty, and the UN Conventions on the Law of the Sea, Climate Change and Desertification.

19 ECONOMY

Before the dissolution of the Yugoslav SFR, Croatia was its second-most prosperous and industrialized area (after Slovenia). Per capita output in Croatia was comparable to that of Portugal and about 33% above the Yugoslav average. Croatia's economic problems were largely inherited from a legacy of Communist mismanagement and a bloated foreign debt. More recently, fighting caused massive infrastructure and industrial damage to bridges, power lines, factories, buildings, and houses. Croatia's economy also had to grapple with a large population of refugees and internally displaced persons. As a result of the war and loss in output capacity, GDP fell by more than 40%.

Yet while the economy has stabilized in recent years, Croatia continues to suffer from structural problems. Under the late President Franjo Tudjman, the Croatian government regularly bailed out failing banks and businesses, regardless of their survivability. This practice needs to be stopped and industry restructured if Croatia is to progress on the path of market reforms. Although unemployment remains high and the country has a growing trade deficit, Croatia in the early 2000s experienced a growth in tourism and an increase in remittances and investment from expatriate Croats. Many small and medium-sized businesses have been privatized, and even larger state-owned industries were in the process of being restructured in 2002, such as shipbuilding. In October 2001, the government signed a Stabilization and Association Agreement with the EU, which moves the country in the direction of integration with the EU. Croatia joined the WTO in 2000. Major growth sectors are energy, tourism, construction, transportation, and telecommunications.

In 2002, the GDP growth rate reached a peak at 5.2%, falling in subsequent years at 4.3% (2003), and 3.7% (2004); for 2005, it was expected to fall even further at 3.1%. The inflation has dropped substantially since 2000, and has stabilized at around 2%. Unemployment, although on a downward path, remained a problem in 2004, at 18.7%. Despite recent moderate economic performance, Croatia's prospects for the future appeared positive. In January 2005, presidential elections were held, and the coalition government started negotiations for EU entry, with the expected accession date being set for 2009 or 2010. A number of privatizations were to be completed by that date, and the government was to prove that Croatia stood as a politically stable and trustworthy country.

20 INCOME

The US Central Intelligence Agency (CIA) reports that in 2005 Croatia's gross domestic product (GDP) was estimated at $53.3 billion. The CIA defines GDP as the value of all final goods and services produced within a nation in a given year and computed on the basis of purchasing power parity (PPP) rather than value as measured on the basis of the rate of exchange based on current dollars. The per capita GDP was estimated at $11,600. The annual growth rate of GDP was estimated at 3.2%. The average inflation rate in 2002 was 3.2%. It was estimated that agriculture accounted for 7% of GDP, industry 32.8%, and services 62.2% in 2005.

According to the World Bank, in 2003 remittances from citizens working abroad totaled $1.069 billion or about $241 per capita and accounted for approximately 3.7% of GDP. Foreign aid receipts amounted to $121 million or about $27 per capita and accounted for approximately 0.4% of the gross national income (GNI).

The World Bank reports that in 2003 household consumption in Croatia totaled $16.91 billion or about $3,805 per capita based on a GDP of $28.8 billion, measured in current dollars rather than PPP. Household consumption includes expenditures of individuals, households, and nongovernmental organizations on goods and services, excluding purchases of dwellings. It was estimated that for the period 1990 to 2003 household consumption grew at an average annual rate of 3.4%. In 2001 it was estimated that approximately 24% of household consumption was spent on food, 18% on fuel, 4% on health care, and 3% on education. It was estimated that in 2003 about 11% of the population had incomes below the poverty line.

21 LABOR

In 2005, there were an estimated 1.7 million persons in Croatia's labor force. As of 2004, employment by sector was as follows: industry 32.8%; agriculture, 2.7%; and 64.5% in the services sector. In 2004, the official unemployment rate was placed at 18.7%. However, labor force surveys indicated that unemployment was at an estimated 14%.

All workers, except the military and police, may form and join unions of their own choosing without prior authorization. Generally, unions were independent of political parties and of the government. About 64% of the workforce was unionized in 2005. The right to strike and bargain collectively is protected by law, although there are restrictions and limitations. Nonpayment of wages continues to be a serious problem.

National minimum wage standards are in place, but are insufficient in providing a worker and family with a decent living standard. The minimum wage was set at $308 per month as of 2005. In 2002 the standard workweek was shortened from 42 to 40 hours. Workers are also entitled to a 30-minute break every day, one day off every seven days, and a minimum of eighteen days paid vacation per year. The minimum working age is 15 and this is generally enforced. In addition, workers under the age of 18 are prohibited from working overtime, at night or under hazardous conditions. There are also occupational safety and health standards, but these are not routinely respected.

22 AGRICULTURE

An estimated 1,588,000 hectares (3,924,000 acres), or 28.4% of total land, was arable in 2002. About 2.7% of the economically active population was engaged in agriculture in 2004; in 2005 it accounted for about 7% of GDP.

The civil war reduced agricultural output in the years immediately following the breakup of the Yugoslav SFR. Production of 2004 major crops included (in thousands of tons): wheat, 840; corn, 2,200; sugar beets, 1,000; grapes, 350; apples, 58; and plums, 30. Total production of cereals fell from 3,179,000 tons in 1997 to 2,355,000 in 2004. Plums are used in the production of slivovitz, a type of plum brandy.

23 ANIMAL HUSBANDRY

About 28% of the total land area consists of pastures. In 2004, there were 1,489,000 pigs, 466,000 cattle, 721,000 sheep, 93,000 goats, 10,000 horses, and 10,235,000 chickens. That year, 140,686 tons of meat were produced, including 70,000 tons of pork, 35,500 tons of poultry, 23,000 tons of beef, and 1,800 tons of mutton. Milk production in 2004 totaled 768,500 tons; eggs, 45,700 tons; and cheese, 23,935 tons. Cattle breeding accounts for about 50% of agriculture's contribution to the GDP.

24 FISHING

With a mainland coastline of 1,778 km (1,105 mi) and island coastlines totaling 4,012 km (2,493 mi) on the Adriatic, Croatia is suited to the development of marine fishing. However, Croatia lacks adequate fishing vessels as well as the infrastructure to transport and process seafood. The total catch in 2003 was 19,946 tons, of which 98% was from marine waters. Sardine is the principal saltwater species caught; carp is the most common freshwater species. Croatia's annual catch has declined steadily due to overfishing for a variety of species. However, fish farming has resulted in an overproduction of freshwater species and a decline in prices. Aquaculture produced 7,605 tons of fish in 2003.

25 FORESTRY

About 32% of the total area was forest or woodland in 2000. Croatia supplies small but good quality oak and beech; the wood industry has traditionally been oriented to the Italian market (accounting for over 35% of exports), and suffered damages during the civil war. Total roundwood production in 2003 was 3.8 million cu m (136 million cu ft), with exports of 560,000 cu m (19.8 million cu ft). Croatian exports of hardwood lumber typically consist of 50% beech, 30% oak, and 6% ash. Panels and veneer are also exported and Croatia is starting to increase the output of value-added products such as veneer sheets, plywood, and particle board. Total exports of wood products amounted to $274.9 million in 2003. The forestry sector along with the whole of Croatian industry is also attempting to produce in accordance with European standards and develop standardized contracts.

26 MINING

Aside from petroleum, the chief minerals industry, Croatia produced small quantities of ferrous and nonferrous metals and industrial minerals, mainly for domestic needs. In 2003, the mining and quarrying sector saw production increase by about 15% from 2002. Cement output in 2003 was up 8% from 2002. The production of clays, lime, nitrogen, pumice, stone, and sand and gravel satisfied most of Croatia's demand for construction materials; the importance of industrial minerals was expected to grow with continued postwar reconstruction. Mineral production in 2003 included cement, 3.654 million tons; salt, processed at Pag Island, 31,281 metric tons; bentonite, 13,568 metric tons; crude gypsum, 166,000 metric tons; and quartz, quartzite, and glass sand, 237,141 metric tons. Bauxite production dropped to zero in 2003, from 1,500 tons in 1996. Prior to the breakup of Yugoslavia, Croatia was the federation's chief producer of natural gas and petroleum, and a leading producer of iron and steel. The minerals sector was heavily hurt by the 1991–92 war, which damaged facilities, affected the market for raw materials, and disrupted normal commercial activities; the outlook remained captive to political and social stabilization in the region.

27 ENERGY AND POWER

Croatia's electric power generating capacity totaled 3.595 million kW in 2002, of which 2.076 million kW was hydroelectric and 1.519 kW conventional thermal sources. Although for that same year, a total of 11.755 billion kWh was produced, of which 6.443 billion kWh came from conventional thermal fuel sources and 5.311 billion kWh came from hydropower, consumption of electricity outstripped output, at 14.453 billion kWh, thus requiring Croatia to import 3.927 billion kWh in that year.

As of 1 January 2004, Croatia had proven oil reserves of 75 million barrels. In 2002 estimated oil production totaled 22,000 barrels per day. As with electricity, Croatia's demand for oil outstripped its output in that year. Consumption that year totaled an estimated 91,000 barrels daily, thus forcing Croatia to rely on imports to make up the difference. Imports in 2002 were estimated at 69,000 barrels per day.

Croatia, as of 1 January 2004, had proven natural gas reserves totaling 0.87 trillion cu ft. In 2001 production of natural gas was estimated at 62 billion cu ft, while consumption came to 100 billion cu ft. As a result, Croatia imported an estimated 38 billion cu ft of natural gas in 2001.

Although Croatia has recoverable coal reserves in 2001 of 43 million short tons, there was no known production. Thus to meet its need for coal, all the coal consumed in 2001, 0.88 million short tons, was imported.

28 INDUSTRY

Light industry, especially for the production of consumer goods, was more advanced in Croatia than in the other republics of the former Yugoslav SFR. Croatia's main manufacturing industries include chemicals and plastics, machine tools, fabricated metal products, electronics, pig iron and rolled steel products, aluminum processing, paper and wood products (including furniture), building materials (including cement), textiles, shipbuilding, petroleum and petroleum refining, and food processing and beverages.

The collapse of Yugoslavia and the hostilities following Croatia's declaration of independence in 1991 damaged industrial production. Manufacturing employed about 335,000 people in 1995. The textile and clothing industry accounted for about 11% of total industrial output in 1995; the food industry, 17%. Industrial production increased 3.7% in 1998 and accounted for 24% of GDP. Industrial production increased to 33% of GDP in 2002. There is a need for reconstruction of basic infrastructure and housing, which should provide increased activity in the construction sector. The government was pursuing privatization of state-owned enterprises; the sale of INA, the national oil and gas company (which was expected to be completed by 2002) was finalized in 2003.

Although industry is an important part of the Croatian economy, in 2004 it performed sub par—the industrial production growth rate was only 2.7%, as compared to the 3.7% GDP growth rate. Still, it made 30.8% of the Croatian economy, and employed 32.8% of the labor force; agriculture participated with 7% to the overall GDP, and employed 2.7% of the working people; services came in first with 62.2% and 64.5% respectively. Croatia has to increase the privatization pace of state-owned companies if it is to accede to the EU by 2009/2010.

29 SCIENCE AND TECHNOLOGY

The Croatian Academy of Sciences and Arts (founded in 1866 and headquartered in Zagreb) has sections devoted to mathematical sciences and physics, natural sciences, and medical sciences. The country also had, as of 1996, 13 medical, scientific, and technical research institutes. The Museum of Natural Sciences (founded in 1924) is located in Split and the Croatian Natural History Museum (founded in 1846) and the Technical Museum (founded in 1954) are in Zagreb. The universities of Zagreb (founded in 1669), Osijek (founded in 1975), Rijeka (founded in 1973), and Split (founded in 1974) offer degrees in basic and applied science. In 1987–97, science and engineering students accounted for 30% of university enrollment.

As of 2002, Croatia had 1,920 researchers and 444 technicians per million people engaged in research and development (R&D). In 2002, Croatian R&D expenditures totaled $519.726 million, or 1.14% of GDP. High technology exports that year were valued at $432 million, accounting for 12% of the country's manufactured exports. R&D spending for the year 2000 (the latest year for which there is spending breakdown data) came mostly from the government, accounting for 54.2% of R&D spending. Business accounted for 44.2%, with foreign sources accounting for the rest.

30 DOMESTIC TRADE

Domestic trade occurs mainly between urban industry and rural agriculture. Civil strife and economic recessions in the past decade have severely weakened the domestic economy. The government has looked toward foreign investments to boost the economy. Privatization and anticorruption programs are likely to attract such foreign investments. A boost in the tourism industry has also aided the economy. As of 2002, about 58% of the GDP was contributed by the services sector.

Normal working hours for public offices are 8:30 AM to 5:00 PM, Monday through Friday. Banks are typically open from 7:00 AM to 7:00 PM, Monday through Friday, and from 7:00 AM until noon on Saturdays. During the week, shops are open from 7:00 AM to 8:00 PM, and from 7:00 AM until 3:00 PM on Saturdays. Summer holidays may translate into closed businesses during the months of July and August.

31 FOREIGN TRADE

Ships are Croatia's major export (13.6% of exports), while other commodities fall close behind, including refined petroleum products (8.1%), polymers (2.9%), men's outerwear (3.4%), and women's outerwear (2.6%). Croatia's diverse export market also includes various chemicals, foodstuff, and raw materials.

In 2004, exports reached $7.8 billion (FOB—Free on Board), but were more than doubled by imports at $16.7 billion (FOB). Croatia mainly exports transport equipment, textiles, chemicals, foodstuffs, and fuels, and its most important export partners are Italy (which received 23% of Croatia's total exports), Bosnia and Herzegovina (13.4%), Germany (11.4%), Austria (9.6%), and Slovenia (7.6%). The most important import commodities were machinery, transport and electrical equipment, chemicals, fuels and lubricants, and foodstuffs, and they mainly came from Italy (17.1%), Germany (15.5%), Russia (7.3%), Slovenia (7.1%), Austria (6.9%), and France (4.4%).

32 BALANCE OF PAYMENTS

Before the civil war, Croatia led the Yugoslav SFR in worker remittances, as thousands of Croats held factory jobs in Germany and elsewhere. In order to provide a framework for economic recovery, the government organized the Ministry for Reconstruction, which plans to rebuild war-damaged regions and infrastructure for tourism, which could bring in much needed foreign currency. Croatia had almost no foreign exchange reserves in 1991, but by the beginning of 1996 the National Bank of Croatia reported $1,386 million in foreign exchange reserves.

Croatia's balance of payments situation has been helped by tourism receipts, but its strong export sectors registered declines in the early 2000s. In 2000, Croatia's main exports were ships and boats, petroleum products, and textiles and apparel. The textiles and apparel sectors were faced with competition from low-wage countries, and in wood product exports, Croatian producers compete with lower-priced Southeast Asian products. Croatian farmers state they are unable to compete with subsidized farm products in the EU. The food processing and chemical industries have been losing their markets due to their inability to produce competitively priced goods of high quality.

The US Central Intelligence Agency (CIA) reported that in 2002 the purchasing power parity of Croatia's exports was $5.1 billion while imports totaled $9.7 billion resulting in a trade deficit of $4.6 billion.

The International Monetary Fund (IMF) reported that in 2001 Croatia had exports of goods totaling $4.75 billion and imports totaling $8.76 billion. The services credit totaled $4.87 billion and debit $1.94 billion.

Exports of goods and services totaled $17.8 billion in 2004, up from $14.9 billion in 2003. Imports grew from $17.2 billion in 2003, to $20.2 billion in 2004. The resource balance was relatively stable over this time period, slightly depreciating from -$2.3 billion in 2003, to -$2.4 billion in 2004. A reverse trend was registered for the current account balance, which improved from -$2.1 billion in 2003, to -$1.6 billion in 2004. The national reserves (including gold) were $8.2 billion in 2003, covering less than 6 months of imports; by 2004, they increased to $8.8 billion.

33 BANKING AND SECURITIES

The National Bank of Croatia was founded in 1992. It has the responsibility of issuing currency and regulating the commercial banking sector. The Croatian dinar was issued 23 December 1991, and was replaced in 1994 by the kuna.

Principal Trading Partners – Croatia (2003)

(In millions of US dollars)

Country	Exports	Imports	Balance
World	6,164.2	14,153.3	-7,989.1
Italy-San Marino-Holy See	1,629.5	2,573.7	-944.2
Bosnia-Herzegovina	892.3	230.7	661.6
Germany	733.0	2,205.3	-1,472.3
Slovenia	510.9	1,048.4	-537.5
Austria	479.5	936.1	-456.6
Serbia and Montenegro	191.0	85.8	105.2
France-Monaco	174.7	748.6	-573.9
United States	164.0	366.6	-202.6
Liberia	100.3	...	100.3
Malta	93.1	...	93.1

(...) data not available or not significant.

SOURCE: *2003 International Trade Statistics Yearbook,* New York: United Nations, 2004.

Balance of Payments – Croatia (2003)

(In millions of US dollars)

Current Account		**-2,098.6**
Balance on goods		-7,921.0
Imports	-14,206.3	
Exports	6,285.2	
Balance on services		5,641.5
Balance on income		-1,212.9
Current transfers		1,393.7
Capital Account		**83.6**
Financial Account		**4,612.9**
Direct investment abroad		-80.5
Direct investment in Croatia		1,955.9
Portfolio investment assets		155.1
Portfolio investment liabilities		854.4
Financial derivatives		...
Other investment assets		-2,520.6
Other investment liabilities		4,248.7
Net Errors and Omissions		**-1,206.4**
Reserves and Related Items		**-1,391.6**

(...) data not available or not significant.

SOURCE: *Balance of Payment Statistics Yearbook 2004,* Washington, DC: International Monetary Fund, 2004.

Commercial banks in Croatia include: Dalmatinska Banka, Zadar (1957), Dubrovačka Banka, Dubrovnik (1990), Slavonska Banka, Samobor (1873), Istarska Banka, Pula, and Osijek (1990). As of February 1996 Croatia had 57 banks. In 1995, Raiffeisenbank Austria d.d. Zagreb began operating in Croatia as the first bank with 100% foreign capital.

Bad lending practices, whereby banks willingly lend to local companies regardless of creditworthiness, has plagued the Croatian banking sector. Many Croatian banks remained in crisis into 2000. Since independence, a total of 15 Croatian banks have gone bankrupt.

The Croatian Bank for Reconstruction and Development (HBOR) was established in 1992 as a 100% government-owned institution, with the tasks of financing reconstruction and development and promoting exports through credits and credit guarantees. The International Monetary Fund reports that in 2001, currency and demand deposits—an aggregate commonly known as M1—were equal to $2.8 billion. In that same year, M2—an aggregate equal to M1 plus savings deposits, small time deposits, and money market mutual funds—was $12.7 billion. The money market rate, the rate at which financial institutions lend to one another in the short term, was 3.9%. The discount rate, the interest rate at which the central bank lends to financial institutions in the short term, was 5.9%.

The Zagreb Stock Exchange (ZSE) started operations in 1991. However, out of the entire portfolio of the Croatian Privatization Fund only 2% was privatized through the exchange. The introduction of the new Privatization Act in 1996 was expected to increase the role of the stock exchange, as was the adoption of an Investment Funds Act and a Securities Act. The Securities Law regulates the public offer of securities, legal entities who are authorized to conduct business with securities, securities transactions, prohibitions regarding businesses with securities, and the protection of investors. As of 2004, a total of 145 companies were listed on the ZSE, which had a capitalization of $10.959 billion. In 2004, the CROBEX rose 32.1% to 1,565.8.

34 INSURANCE

The Insurance Companies Supervision Directorate grants approvals for insurance companies' operations and supervises the operations of insurance companies doing business in Croatia. Insurance companies may be established by domestic or foreign entities and may be formed as a joint-stock, mutual, private, or public company. Pension funds (divided between employees, self-employed and independent farmers) controlled substantial financial assets in Croatia as of 1997. In 2003, direct premiums written totaled $905 million, of which nonlife premiums accounted for $704 million. In 2002, the country's top nonlife insurer was Croatia, with $304.2 million in gross nonlife premiums written. The top life insurer, that same year was Grawe, with $33 million in gross life premiums written.

35 PUBLIC FINANCE

The fiscal year follows the calendar year. The IMF and World Bank have granted Croatia $192 million and $100 million, respectively, to repair economic imbalances from war and to curb hyperinflation. The EBRD has approved financial support totaling $230 million for infrastructure, telecommunications, and energy

Public Finance – Croatia (2001)		
(In millions of kunas, central government figures)		
Revenue and Grants	**65,484**	**100.0%**
Tax revenue	40,492	61.8%
Social contributions	21,778	33.3%
Grants	...	...
Other revenue	3,214	4.9%
Expenditures	**73,796**	**100.0%**
General public services	6,969	9.4%
Defense	3,894	5.3%
Public order and safety	4,137	5.6%
Economic affairs	6,001	8.1%
Environmental protection	...	...
Housing and community amenities	2,549	3.5%
Health	11,815	16.0%
Recreational, culture, and religion	925	1.3%
Education	5,896	8.0%
Social protection	31,610	42.8%

(…) data not available or not significant.

SOURCE: *Government Finance Statistics Yearbook 2004*, Washington, DC: International Monetary Fund, 2004.

projects which otherwise would be unobtainable by the Croatian government.

The US Central Intelligence Agency (CIA) estimated that in 2005 Croatia's central government took in revenues of approximately $17.6 billion and had expenditures of $19.3 billion. Revenues minus expenditures totaled approximately -$1.6 billion. Public debt in 2005 amounted to 52.1% of GDP. Total external debt was $29.28 billion.

The International Monetary Fund (IMF) reported that in 2001, the most recent year for which it had data, central government revenues were HrK65,484 million and expenditures were HrK73,796 million. The value of revenues was us$7,852 million and expenditures us$8,848 million, based on an exchange rate for 2001 of us$1 = HrK8.340 as reported by the IMF. Government outlays by function were as follows: general public services, 9.4%; defense, 5.3%; public order and safety, 5.6%; economic affairs, 8.1%; housing and community amenities, 3.5%; health, 16.0%; recreation, culture, and religion, 1.3%; education, 8.0%; and social protection, 42.8%.

36 TAXATION

In December 2000 the government adopted a package of tax laws including the General Tax Law, the Law on Tax Advising, the Law on Corporate Profit Tax, and the Income Tax Law. In general, the new laws reduced some rates, but widened the tax base. The corporate profits tax was reduced from 35% to 20%. Reduced corporate tax rates of 5%, 10% and 15% are available for companies locating in "special care areas" (62 municipalities and towns deemed to be undeveloped) and in the Vukovar area. The corporate tax rate is also reduced for larger new investments: 7% for investments of at least HrK10 million (about $1.56 million); 3% for investments of at least HrK20 million (about $3.12 million); and 0% on investments over HrK60 million (about $9.3 million). Companies operating in one of Croatia's 12 free trade zones (FTZs) pay half the standard corporate tax rate (10%) or 0% if their investment is more that HrK1 million (about $156,000). There is no separate foreign investment law in Croatia, so branches of foreign companies are taxed the same as domestic companies, though only on profits made in Croatia. There is also a municipal firm tax of up to HRK2,000 (about $312).

Changes to the Personal Income Tax (PIT) Law, effective 1 January 2003, increased the number of PIT tax brackets from four to five (counting the personal allowance tax free amount), increasing slightly the bands for the lower rates, but introducing a new highest rate of 45%. The new rates were 0% up to about $2,609 a year (using $1 = HRK6.9); 15% for the next increment of income up to $5,217 a year; 25% on the next increment to $11,740 a year; 35% on the next increment to $39,364 a year; and 45% on income above $36,522 a year. Croatians are taxed on their worldwide income while foreigners pay only on income realized in Croatia. Deductions from taxable income are allowed for medical and housing expenses. There is a 15% withholding tax on dividend, interest and royalty income. Local surcharges on state income taxes range from up to 10% in small municipalities to up to 30% in Zagreb. The inheritance and gift tax is 5%, and there is a 5% real property transaction tax. Property taxes are assessed locally.

The employee's contribution to social security is 20%. By the pension reform legislation effective as of 1 January 2002, 15% goes to the national pension fund and 5% to new private pension funds. The new pension system is mandatory for workers under 40 as of 1 January 2002, and optional for workers 40 to 50 years old. Workers over 50 continue to contribute all 20% to the national pension fund. As of January 2003, the cap on social security contributions by an employee was set at $54,620 per year. The employers' contributions to social security, amounting to 17.2%, go for health and unemployment insurance: 15% for general health insurance, 0.5% for work-related accident insurance, and 1.7% for unemployment insurance.

The main indirect taxes in Croatia are the value-added tax (VAT), with a flat rate of 22%, and excise taxes. Specified goods and services, such as those from banks and insurance companies, are exempt from the VAT (0% rate). Slot machines are taxed at about $14.50 per month, while winnings from games of chance are subject to the 22% VAT. Per-unit excise taxes are assessed on petroleum products, tobacco, beer, alcoholic drinks, coffee, and nonalcoholic drinks. Luxury goods carry a 30% excise. Producers and importers of vehicles (cars, motorbikes, boats and airplanes) pay excise taxes, while buyers of used vehicles pay a sales tax. Auto insurance premiums are taxed at 15%, for liability insurance, and 10%, for comprehensive insurance. There are local consumption taxes on alcoholic drinks up to 3%.

37 CUSTOMS AND DUTIES

The Customs Law, Law on Customs Tariffs, and Law on Customs Services were implemented in 1991. Croatia adopted all of the international tariffs and protection agreements ratified by the former Yugoslav SFR that did not contravene Croatia's constitution. The customs system was considerably changed in 1996 with a new customs law that harmonized the system with that of the European Union. In 2000, customs laws were revamped yet again to allow the government to change tariff rates annually. Customs duties range mainly from 0–18%. The average tariff for industrial goods is 5% and for agricultural goods 27%. In 1996, goods such as raw materials, semifinished goods, spare parts, supplies used for repairing war damage, and the household possessions of returning Croatian refugees were exempted from customs duty and subject only to an administrative charge of 1%. The Customs Tariff lists all the goods specified and grouped into a system of 11 sections and 97 chapters with remarks on each chapter to simplify the customs declaration procedure.

Croatia has free trade agreements with Bosnia and Herzegovina, Hungary, Macedonia, and Slovenia, and has an Association Agreement with the European Union.

38 FOREIGN INVESTMENT

Attracting foreign investment is a key goal of the comprehensive strategy for long-term development, "Croatia in the 21st Century," adopted 21 June 2001 with an aim of becoming a fully integrated member of the European Union. The day before, the bilateral investment treaty (BIT) with the United States entered into force. Croatia does not have a separate foreign investment law, so foreign firms generally receive national treatment under the 1995 Company Law. The Law on Free Trade Zones (FTZs) was adopted in June 1996. Companies making infrastructure investments of at least $125,000 are eligible for a five-year tax holiday, while others (except those in retail trade, which are excluded from FTZs) pay half Croatia's corporate income tax rate (10% instead of 20%). Exported goods are fully exempt from custom duties and taxes. The government has designated 12 FTZ locations. The Croatian constitution states that rights acquired through capital investments cannot be withdrawn by law or any legal act and it also insures free repatriation of profits and capital upon disinvestment.

From 1993 to 2000, total foreign investment in Croatia totaled $4.68 billion, about 24% from the United States and 24% from Germany. Most foreign direct investment (FDI) has come through the privatization of government-owned assets and most has been directed to trade, services, banking, and telecommunications, rather than industry. The inflow of FDI was $0.55 billion in 1997, $1 billion in 1998, and peaked at $1.6 billion in 1999, due largely to the sale of 35% of the state telecommunications company, Hrvatske Telekomunikacye (HT), to Deutsche Telekom (DT) for $830 million. In 2000, FDI inflow fell back to $1.1 billion, then recovered to almost $1.5 billion in 2001 due to the sale of another 16% of HT to DT for $422 million, giving DT a 51% majority ownership. In 2002, FDI fell back to $900 million.

In foreign portfolio investment, as of 31 December 2001, US investors held $734 million of Croatia securities, $255 million in equity shares in Croatian companies, and $479 million in long-term debt securities. Outward investment by Croatian firms from 1993 through the first quarter of 2001 totaled $413 million, 39% going to Poland and 28% to Bosnia and Herzegovina.

The total stock of FDI that entered into Croatia between 1993 and 2003 was $10.1 billion, averaging around $1 billion per year. In the first three quarters of 2004, $877 million was invested in Croatia, which appeared to be down significantly over 2003, when total FDI amounted to $1.7 billion. Most of these investments went to telecommunications (20.9%), banking (19.6%), pharmaceuticals (11.3%), and petroleum production (7.8%). The largest investors were Austria (with 25.7% of total foreign capital inflows), Germany (20.7%), and the United States (14.7%).

Croatia's performance in terms of FDI inflow has been average if compared to other countries in Central and Eastern Europe. Most foreign capital was used for acquiring state-owned enterprises (or shares in those), and less was used for greenfield investments. The situation was expected to change in future years though, as the political system in the country has become more stable, and the government was gearing up for the EU accession.

39 ECONOMIC DEVELOPMENT

In October 1993, the government adopted an ambitious three-phase program intended to stabilize the economy through fiscal stabilization, currency reform, and accelerated privatization. The plan, however, relies upon cooperation with international financial organizations.

Economic development has been closely tied with privatization. By 1995, the process of ownership transformation had been fully completed by 2,554 companies. There were 221 companies that had the two Croatian Pension Funds and Croatian Privatization Funds (CPF) as majority owners, and 1,225 companies having the same funds as minority owners. The CPF is legally obliged to offer the shares of its portfolio for sale at auction, and as a rule sells its shares through the Zagreb Stock Exchange. Continued liberalization is expected by the reformist government of Ivica Racan, who aimed in 2003 to speed Croatia's anticipated membership in the European Union. The national insurance, oil, and gas companies were planned to be privatized during 2002–03. Croatia is a member of the IMF, IBRD, and EBRD (as one of the Yugoslav SFR's successor states). Upon the outbreak of conflict in Yugoslavia, the United States suspended all benefits to Yugoslavia under the General System of Preferences, but benefits under this program were subsequently extended on 11 September 1992 to all the former Yugoslav SFR republics except Serbia and Montenegro. Despite the economic adversity, foreign investors have been keen to identify business opportunities in Croatia's relatively stable economy.

In February 2003, Croatia negotiated a 14-month, $146-million Stand-By Arrangement with the IMF to support the government's economic and financial program. Strong domestic demand and business and government investment contributed to a 5% real gross domestic product (GDP) growth in the first nine months of 2002, compared to 3.8% in 2001. The government deficit declined in 2002, and inflation fell. The currency remained stable as well. The public debt rose, however, to 57.5% of GDP at the end of 2002, up from 55% at the end of 2001. This general economic success was due in part to a good tourist season, and a large highway construction program, in addition to increased private consumption and rising investment.

Croatia's economic performance was weaker in 2003 and 2004, partly due to a relatively unattractive investment climate. Croatia has failed to attract major greenfield investments which would have renewed its economic base, and would have created more dynamism in the market. Red tape, corruption, and problems posed by domestic companies, have also kept a lot of investors away. Nonetheless, the country boasts an educated workforce, a stable government, equality under the law, and the prospects of joining both the EU and NATO—all factors that make it a very attractive market, with great future potential.

40 SOCIAL DEVELOPMENT

The effects of the 1991 war, the great refugee burden, the disruptions of the Bosnian war, the absence of significant international aid, and other factors combined to strain the country's social fabric and economy. In 1993, the average standard of living stood at less than 50% of its level before 1991. Over 400,000 Croats were displaced by the war and its aftermath.

Croatia's first pension laws date back to 1922, with most recent changes in 2003. The law provides for a dual system of a social system and mandatory private insurance. Health and maternity benefits, workers' compensation, unemployment coverage, and family allowances are also provided. Retirement is set at age 63 for men and age 58 for women.

Women hold lower paying positions in the work force than men even though gender discrimination is prohibited by law. Also, women are more likely to be unemployed. Rape and spousal rape are grossly underreported, and there are only four women's shelters. Domestic abuse rose considerably in 2004, with 50% more cases registered. The weak economic situation, the aftermath and uncertainty from the war, and alcohol abuse are considered aggravating factors.

The constitution states that all persons shall enjoy all rights and freedoms, regardless of race, color, sex, language, religions, political opinion, national origin, property, birth, education or social status. However, ethnic tensions continue. Muslims and Serbs in Croatia face considerable discrimination. Arbitrary detention and torture, abuse of detainees, and other human rights violations continue. The Roma population also suffers discrimination.

41 HEALTH

Croatia is in the process of improving health care since the war years in the 1990s. Life expectancy in 2005 was 74.45 and infant mortality rate per 1,000 live births was 6.84. The overall mortality rate was 11 per 1,000 people.

Croatia had 84 hospitals in 1997, including both general and tertiary care facilities. The country is known for its spas, where patients receive preventive and rehabilitative care that makes use of spring water and other natural resources, as well as such treatments as massage. As of 2004, there were an estimated 237 physicians, 499 nurses, 68 dentists, 50 pharmacists, and 34 midwives per 100,000 people. Approximately 95% of the population had access to safe drinking water and 100% had adequate sanitation.

Immunization rates for children under the age of one were as follows: tuberculosis, 98%; diphtheria, pertussis, and tetanus, 92%; measles, 93%; and polio, 92%. In 1999, the incidence of tuberculosis was 61 per 100,000 people.

The HIV/AIDS prevalence was 0.10 per 100 adults in 2003. As of 2004, there were approximately 200 people living with HIV/AIDS in the country. There were an estimated 10 deaths from AIDS in 2003.

42 HOUSING

After years of war, the country is just beginning the process of rebuilding not only homes for the thousands who were displaced by the conflict, but industries, businesses, and civic buildings as well. As of the mid-1990s, nearly 800,000 displaced persons and refugees from Bosnia and occupied Croat territories were in Croatia, of whom approximately 640,000 have found temporary housing with families in Croatia. By 1997, thousands of refugees (mostly from Eastern Slavonia) still remained housed in coastal hotels.

According to the 2001 census, there were a total of 1,877,126 dwellings in the nation; about 1,660,649 dwellings were for permanent residents. Most dwellings had between two to four rooms. About 70,817 dwellings had been built since 1996. There were about 1,455,116 households representing 4,272,590 people. Most households had between two to four members.

As of 2001, the government has implemented a Welfare Supported Housing Construction Program to assist low-income families unable to purchase apartments.

43 EDUCATION

Education at the elementary level is free and compulsory for children between the ages of 6 and 15 years. Primary education covers an eight-year course of study. Secondary education covers a four-year course of study in one of three tracks: grammar schools, technical and vocational schools, and art schools. The academic year runs from October to June. The primary language of instruction is Croatian.

In 2001, about 38% of children between the ages of three and six were enrolled in some type of preschool program. Primary school enrollment in 2003 was estimated at about 89% of age-eligible students. The same year, secondary school enrollment was about 87% of age-eligible students. It is estimated that about 95.5% of all students complete their primary education. The student-to-teacher ratio for primary school was at about 18:1 in 2003. The ratio for secondary school was about 11:1.

In higher education, there are five universities: University of Osijek (founded in 1975), University of Rijeka (founded in 1973), University of Split (founded in 1974), University of Zadar, and University of Zagreb (founded in 1669). There are also 7 polytechnic schools and 17 professional schools. In 2003, about 39% of the tertiary age population were enrolled in some type of higher education program. The adult literacy rate for 2004 was estimated at about 98.1%, with 99.3% for men and 97.1% for women.

As of 2003, public expenditure on education was estimated at 4.5% of GDP, or 10% of total government expenditures.

44 LIBRARIES AND MUSEUMS

The National and University Library of Croatia in Zagreb (founded in 1606) had 2.5 million volumes in 2002. The Zagreb public library holds close to 300,000 volumes. In 1995, the country reported having 232 public libraries with a combined collection of 4.6 million volumes. The Information and Documentation Centre and Library of the Institute for International Relations is also in Zagreb, with holdings that include books, periodicals and journals, and official documents from various countries and in a variety of languages. The Croatia Library Association was founded in 1940.

Major museums in Zagreb include the Historical Museum of Croatia, Strossmeyer's Gallery of Old Masters, and the Gallery of Modern Art. Other major cultural centers include Split, which houses the Museum of Croatian Medieval Archeology, and Dubrovnik, with the Natural Sciences Museum among others. In all, the country boasts over 100 museums.

45 MEDIA

In 2003, there were an estimated 417 mainline telephones for every 1,000 people. The same year, there were approximately 584 mobile phones in use for every 1,000 people.

Government controlled Croatian Radio-Television (Hrvatska Radiotelevizija) has charge of all broadcasting. In 1999, Croatian Radio ran 16 AM and 98 FM stations with 5 shortwave options. In 1995, there were 36 television stations. It has been estimated that 80% of the population relies on the government-sponsored television news program, *Dnevnik*, for national news. Independent local stations can only cover about 65% of the country's territory. In 2003, there were an estimated 330 radios for every 1,000 people; the number of televisions was not available in the same survey. In 2003, there were 173.8 personal computers for every 1,000 people and 232 of every 1,000 people had access to the Internet. There were 146 secure Internet servers in the country in 2004.

In 1995, there were nine daily newspapers with a combined circulation of over 400 million, and 563 nondailies (including over 60 weeklies); there were about 400 periodicals. As of 2002, the major dailies included *Vecernji List* (circulation 200,000), published in Zagreb, and *Novi List* (60,000), published in Rijeka, as well as the sports daily *Sportske Novosti* (55,000), published in Zagreb. In 1994, there were some 2,600 book titles published.

In October 1996, a comprehensive Law on Public Information was passed in Parliament with general support from all parties to regulate the media. In general, government influence on media through state ownership of most print and electronic media outlets restricts constitutionally-provided freedoms of speech and press.

46 ORGANIZATIONS

In 1852, the Chamber of Commerce and Crafts was first organized in Zagreb. In 1990, the Croatian Chamber of the Economy (CCE) was established as the authentic representative of the Croatian economy. The CCE consists of 20 county chambers and promotes trade and commerce in world markets along with the Association of Independent Businesses and the Zagreb Trade Fair.

Since 1994, over 30 professional organizations have been founded in the CCE. A number of organizations promoting research and education in various medical and scientific fields have also formed, including the Croatia Medical Association. The Rudjer Boskovic Institute is a national organization that conducts research and educational programs for the natural sciences. The Croatian Academy of Sciences and Arts has been active since 1861. The Croatian Physical Society formed in 1990.

There are many sports associations throughout the country, including the general Croatian Athletic Federation and a chapter of the Special Olympics. Youth organizations include the umbrella organization of the Croatian National Youth Council (NSMH), the Croatian Club for the United Nations (CCUN), and the Junior Chamber of Croatia (JCC), as well as scouting programs. Among many national women's organizations are the Croatian Association of University Women the Women's Infoteka, and Be Active, Be Emancipated (BABE).

There are national chapters of the Red Cross Society and Amnesty International.

47 TOURISM, TRAVEL, AND RECREATION

Tourist attractions include visits to Dubrovnik and Split to enjoy the climate, scenery, and excellent swimming from April to October. Beautiful historic churches and ancient palaces can be found in the major cities. The many nudist camps and casinos are also popular attractions.

Approximately 3,086,506 foreign visitors arrived in Croatia in 2003. That year the average length of stay was five nights. There were 77,113 hotel rooms with 193,538 beds and a 27% occupancy rate. Tourism expenditure receipts totaled $6.5 billion.

In 2003, the US Department of State estimated the daily cost of staying in Zagreb at $220.

48 FAMOUS CROATS

Dr. Franjo Tudjman was president of Croatia from May 1990 until his death in 1999. Stjepan Mesić (b.1934) has been president since 2000. Nikica Valentić, Ivica Račan, and Ivo Sanader have all served as prime minister in recent years. Two Nobel prize winners have come from Croatia, both chemists: Lavoslav Ružička (1887–1976) and Vladimir Prelog (1906–98).

Josip Broz-Tito (1892–1980) was the leader of Communist Yugoslavia for many years after World War II. In 1948, he led his country away from the Communist bloc formed by the Soviet Union. Tito served in the Red Army during the Russian Civil War and led the Yugoslav resistance movement during World War II.

There are several internationally known figures in literature and the arts: Ivan Gundulic (1589–1638) wrote about the Italian influences in Croatia in *Dubravka*. Count Ivo Vojnović (1857–1929) is best known for *A Trilogy of Dubrovnik*. Miroslav Krleya (1857–1981) captured the concerns of prerevolutionary Yugoslavia in his trilogy of the Glembay family (1928–32) and in novels like *Return of Philip Latinovicz* (1932) and *Banners* (1963).

Double-agent Duško Popov (1912–1981), who worked during World War II, was the model for Ian Fleming's James Bond. The wartime figure, Andrija Artukovic (1899–1988), known as "Butcher of the Balkans" for his activities in support of Germany, is from Croatia. Religious leader Franjo Seper (1884–1981) was born in Croatia, as was inventor Nikola Tesla (1856–1943). Musician Artur Radzinski (1894–1958) became conductor of the New York Philharmonic in 1943 and of the Chicago Symphony in 1947. Zinka Kumc Milanov (1906–1989) was a dramatic opera soprano with the New York Metropolitan Opera in the 1950s and 1960s. Mathilde Mallinger (1847–1920) was a famous Croatian soprano who performed with Berlin Opera from 1869–1882.

49 DEPENDENCIES

Croatia has no territories or colonies.

50 BIBLIOGRAPHY

Ceriani, Conatella. *Croatia*. New York: DK Publishing, 2003.

Frucht, Richard (ed.). *Eastern Europe: An Introduction to the People, Lands, and Culture*. Santa Barbara, Calif.: ABC-CLIO, 2005.

Glenny, Michael. *The Fall of Yugoslavia: The Third Balkan War*. New York: Penguin, 1992.

Malovic, Stjepan. *The People, Press, and Politics of Croatia*. Westport, Conn.: Praeger, 2001.

McElrath, Karen (ed.). *HIV and AIDS: A Global View*. Westport, Conn.: Greenwood Press, 2002.

Stallaerts, Robert. *Historical Dictionary of the Republic of Croatia*. Lanham, Md.: Scarecrow, 2003.

Terterov, Marat and Visnja Bojanic, (eds.). *Doing Business with Croatia*. 2nd ed. Sterling, Va.: Kogan Page, 2004.

CZECH REPUBLIC

Czech Republic
Ceskaá Republika

CAPITAL: Prague (Praha)

FLAG: The national flag consists of a white stripe over a red stripe, with a blue triangle extending from hoist to midpoint.

ANTHEM: *Kde domov můj (Where Is My Native Land).*

MONETARY UNIT: The koruna (Kc) is a paper currency of 100 haléru, which replaced the Czechoslovak koruna (Kcs) on 8 February 1993. There are coins of 1, 5, 10, 20, and 50 heller and of 1, 2, 5, 10, 20, and 50 koruny, and notes of 10, 20, 50, 100, 200, 500, 1,000, 2,000, and 5,000 koruny. Kc1 = $0.04216 (or $1 = Kc23.72) as of 2005.

WEIGHTS AND MEASURES: The metric system is the legal standard.

HOLIDAYS: New Year's Day, 1 January; Labor Day, 1 May; Anniversary of Liberation, 9 May; Day of the Apostles, St. Cyril and St. Methodius, 6 July; Christmas, 25 December; St. Stephen's Day, 26 December. Easter Monday is a movable holiday.

TIME: 1 PM = noon GMT.

¹LOCATION, SIZE, AND EXTENT

The Czech Republic is a strategically located landlocked country in Eastern Europe. It sits astride some of the oldest and most significant land routes in Europe. Comparatively, the Czech Republic is slightly smaller than the state of South Carolina with a total area of 78,866 sq km (30,450 sq mi). It shares boundaries with Poland (on the NE), Slovakia (on the SE), Austria (on the S), and Germany (on the W and NW) and has a total boundary length of 1,881 km (1,169 mi). The capital city of the Czech Republic, Prague, is located in the north central part of the country.

²TOPOGRAPHY

The topography of the Czech Republic consists of two main regions. Bohemia in the west is comprised of rolling plains, hills, and plateaus surrounded by low mountains. Moravia in the east is very hilly. The country's highest point is Mt. Snezka at 1,602 m (5,256 ft) in the Krkonose Mountains along the north central border with Poland. The Elbe River is the nation's longest with a distance of 1,165 km (724 mi); located in the northwest, it runs north into Germany.

³CLIMATE

The Czech Republic has a Central European moderate and transitional climate, with variations resulting from the topography of the country. The climate is temperate with cool summers, and cold, cloudy, and humid winters. The average temperature in Prague ranges from about -1°C (30°F) in January to 19°C (66°F) in July. A generally moderate oceanic climate prevails in the Czech lands. Rainfall distribution is greatly influenced by westerly winds, and its variation is closely correlated to relief. Over three-fifths of the rain falls during the spring and summer, which is advantageous for agriculture. The precipitation range is from 50 cm (20 in) to more than 127 cm (50 in); rainfall is below 58 cm (23 in) in western Bohemia and southern Moravia.

⁴FLORA AND FAUNA

Plants and animals are Central European in character. Almost 70% of the forest is mixed or deciduous. Some original steppe grassland areas are still found in Moravia, but most of these lowlands are cultivated. Mammals commonly found in the Czech Republic include the fox, hare, hart, rabbit, and wild pig. A variety of birds inhabit the lowlands and valleys. Fish such as carp, pike, and trout appear in numerous rivers and ponds. As of 2002, there were at least 81 species of mammals, 205 species of birds, and over 1,900 species of plants throughout the country.

⁵ENVIRONMENT

The Czech Republic suffers from air, water, and land pollution caused by industry, mining, and agriculture. Lung cancer is prevalent in areas with the highest air pollution levels. In the mid-1990s, the nation had the world's highest industrial carbon dioxide emissions, totaling 135.6 million metric tons per year, a per capita level of 13.04 metric tons. However, in 2000, total carbon dioxide emissions had decreased to about 118.8 million metric tons. Like the Slovak Republic, the Czech Republic has had its air contaminated by sulfur dioxide emissions resulting largely from the use of lignite as an energy source in the former Czechoslovakia, which had the highest level of sulfur dioxide emissions in Europe, and instituted a program to reduce pollution in the late 1980s. Western nations have offered $1 billion to spur environmental reforms, but the pressure to continue economic growth has postponed the push for environmental action.

The Czech Republic has a total of about 13 cu km of freshwater resources, of which 2% is used for farming and 57% is used for industry. Both urban and rural dwellers have access to safe drinking water. Airborne emissions in the form of acid rain, combined with air pollution from Poland and the former GDR, have destroyed much of the forest in the northern part of the former Czechoslovakia. Land erosion caused by agricultural and mining practices is also a significant problem.

In 2000, about 34% of the total land area was forested. In 2003, about 16.1% of the total land area was protected by the government. There are 11 Ramsar wetland sites in the country.

According to a 2006 report issued by the International Union for Conservation of Nature and Natural Resources (IUCN), threatened species included 6 types of mammals, 9 species of birds, 7 species of fish, 2 types of mollusks, 17 species of other invertebrates, and 4 species of plants. Endangered species include the Atlantic sturgeon, slender-billed curlew, and Spengler's freshwater mussel.

6 POPULATION

The population of Czech Republic in 2005 was estimated by the United Nations (UN) at 10,212,000, which placed it at number 78 in population among the 193 nations of the world. In 2005, approximately 14% of the population was over 65 years of age, with another 15% of the population under 15 years of age. There were 95 males for every 100 females in the country. According to the UN, the annual population rate of change for 2005–10 was expected to be -0.1%, a rate the government viewed as too low. The country has one of the lowest fertility rates in the world. The projected population for the year 2025 was 10,217,000. The population density was 129 per sq km (335 per sq mi), with the most densely populated areas in North Bohemia, Central Bohemia, and in Moravia.

The UN estimated that 77% of the population lived in urban areas in 2005, and that urban areas were growing at an annual rate of 0.05%—essentially a standstill. The capital city, Prague (Praha), had a population of 1,170,000 in that year. Other major cities and their estimated populations include Brno, 400,000; Ostrava, 331,448; and Plzen (Pilsen), 175,049.

7 MIGRATION

After World War II, nearly 2.5 million ethnic Germans were expelled from the Sudeten region, which was part of Czechoslovakia and Poland. The emigration wave from Czechoslovakia after the Communist takeover in February 1948 included some 60,000 people; another 100,000 persons left the country after the invasion of the Warsaw Pact countries in August 1968. Emigration slowed during the 1970s to about 5,000 annually, but during the 1980s, some 10,000 people (according to Western estimates) were leaving each year. *Migration News* reported that in mid-2004 legal foreign workers numbered 170,000, mainly Slovaks (72,000), Ukrainians (39,400), and Vietnamese (21,400). This was an strong increase from 20,000 legal foreign workers 10 years earlier. *Migration Information* estimated the illegal migrant population as ranging from 300,000 to 340,000.

The Czech Republic encountered its first refugee influx in 1990. From 1990–2000 there were more than 22,000 applicants. In 2004 there were 1,144 refugees. In 2004, 1,119 people sought asylum. The net migration rate for 2005 was estimated as .97 migrants per 1,000 population. In 2000 there were 236,000 migrants living in the Czech Republic. The government views both the immigration and emigration levels as too high.

8 ETHNIC GROUPS

Between 1945 and 1948, the deportation of the Sudeten Germans altered the ethnic structure of the Czech lands. Since the late 1940s, most of the remaining Germans have either assimilated or emigrated to the West. In 2001, Czechs constituted 90.4% of the total population, Moravians accounted for 3.7%, and Slovaks made up 1.9%. Other ethnic groups include Germans, Roma, and Poles.

9 LANGUAGES

Czech, which belongs to the Slavic language group, is the major and official language. In addition to the letters of the English alphabet, the Czech language has both vowels and consonants with acute accents (indicating length) and háčeks: á, é, í, ó, ú, č, dč, ě, ň, ř, š, ť, ž, as well as ů (the circle also indicates length). In Czech, q, w, and x are found only in foreign words. There are numerous dialects. Many older Czechs speak German; many younger people speak Russian and English. Slovak is also spoken.

10 RELIGIONS

Though the country has a strong tradition of Christianity, the Communist rule of 1948 to 1989 greatly repressed religious practice so that many citizens do not claim membership in any religious organizations. In 2001, only about 38% of the population claimed to believe in God. About 52% claimed to be atheist. Only about 5% of the population are practicing Roman Catholics, while about 1% are practicing Protestants. The Islam community has about 20,000–30,000 members while the Jewish community has only a few thousand people.

The constitution provides for religious freedom, and the government reportedly respects this right in practice. Religious affairs are handled by the Department of Churches at the Ministry of Culture. In 2002 the Religious Freedom and the Position of Churches and Religious Associations established a tiered registration system for religious organizations. There is no requirement to register; however, officially registered groups are granted certain legal rights and various subsidies from the government.

11 TRANSPORTATION

There are some 9,543 km (5,936 mi) of standard and narrow gauge railroads in the Czech Republic, connecting Prague with Plzen, Kutná Hora, and Brno, as of 2004. Of that total, 9,421 km (5,860 mi) are standard gauge. The Czech Republic had 127,672 km (79,412 mi), of roadway in 2002, all of which were paved, including 518 km (322 mi) of expressways. In 2003, there were 3,706,012 passenger cars and 445,000 commercial vehicles registered for use. As a landlocked nation, the Czech Republic relies on coastal outlets in Poland, Croatia, Slovenia, and Germany for international commerce by sea. As of 2004, there were 664 km of navigable inland waterways, on the Elbe, Vltava, and Oder rivers. The principal river ports are Prague on the Vltava and Děčin on the Elbe. In 2004 there were an estimated 120 airports. As of 2005, a total of 44 had paved runways, and there were also two heliports. Principal airports include Turany at Brno, Mosnov at Ostrava, and Ruzyne at Prague. Ruzyne is the nation's primary commercial airlink. In

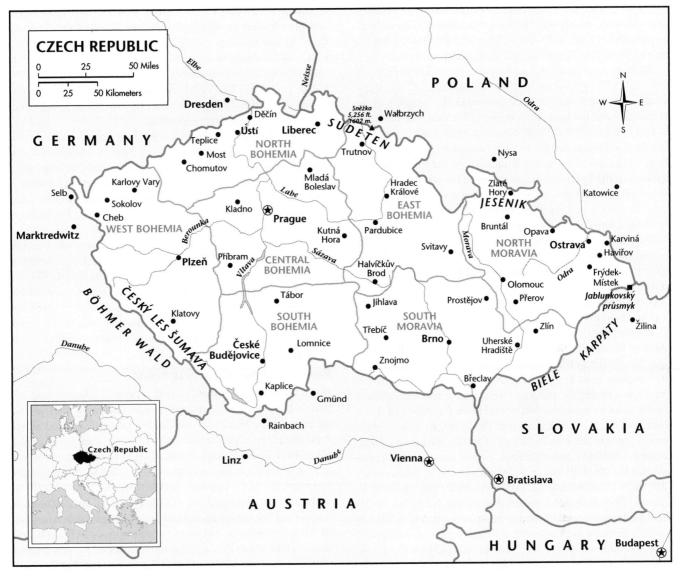

CZECH REPUBLIC

0 25 50 Miles

0 25 50 Kilometers

POLAND

Sněžka 5,256 ft. 1,602 m.

Dresden

Děčín

Teplice

Ústí

Liberec

SUDETEN

Wałbrzych

Most

NORTH BOHEMIA

Trutnov

Nysa

Chomutov

GERMANY

Mladá Boleslav

Hradec Králové

Zlaté Hory

Katowice

Karlovy Vary

Kladno

EAST BOHEMIA

JESENÍK

Selb

Prague

Kutná Hora

Pardubice

Bruntál

Opava

Ostrava

Karviná

Sokolov

WEST BOHEMIA

Svitavy

NORTH MORAVIA

Havířov

Cheb

Marktredwitz

Plzeň

Příbram

CENTRAL BOHEMIA

Halvíčkův Brod

Olomouc

Přerov

Frýdek-Místek

Jablunkovský průsmyk

Klatovy

Tábor

Jihlava

Prostějov

SOUTH BOHEMIA

Lomnice

Třebíč

SOUTH MORAVIA

Zlín

Žilina

ČESKÝ LES ŠUMAVA

Brno

Uherské Hradiště

BÖHMER WALD

České Budějovice

Znojmo

Břeclav

BIELE

KARPATY

Danube

Kaplice

Gmünd

SLOVAKIA

Rainbach

Czech Republic

Linz

Danube

Vienna

AUSTRIA

Bratislava

HUNGARY Budapest

LOCATION: 49°26′ to 51°3′ N; 12°6′ to 18°54′ E. BOUNDARY LENGTHS: Poland, 658 kilometers (409 miles); Slovakia, 214 kilometers (133 miles); Austria, 362 kilometers (225 miles); Germany, 646 kilometers (401 miles).

all, Czech airports in 2003 performed 36 million freight ton-km of service. In that same year, domestic and international flights carried 3.392 million passengers.

With the separation of Czechoslovakia, the new Czech Republic has rapidly replaced its former Eastern European trading partners with Western ones (primarily Germany and the rest of the EU). This shift in the direction of transportation of goods into and out of the Czech Republic has overloaded the current infrastructure of roads, airports, and railroads. In 1993, the government targeted several goals to develop the transportation network, including: the development of priority connections between Prague and Vienna, Berlin, Warsaw, Nuremberg, Munich, and Linz; the construction of 264 km (164 mi) of new highways over the next 8–10 years for improved trucking links; expansion of the Prague Ruzyne airport; connection to Western Europe's high-speed rail system; and the acquisition of better rolling stock.

Most goods are shipped by truck. Currently, underdeveloped railroads and waterways often cannot accommodate intermodal

transport. As of 2001, a $3.5 billion project was underway to modernize the rail system.

12 HISTORY

The first recorded inhabitants of the territory of the present-day Czech Republic were the Celtic Boii tribe, who settled there about 50 BC. They were displaced in the early modern era by German tribes (Marcomanni, Quidi) and later by Slavs, who pushed in from the east during the so-called Migration of the Peoples. The new settlers kept the Roman version of the name Boii for that region, Boiohaemum, which later became Bohemia. The first unified state in the region was that of a Frankish merchant named Samo, who protected his lands from the Avar empire in Hungary and the Franks of the West, reigning until his death in 658. This mercantile city-state lasted until the 9th century, when it grew into the Moravian Empire. The fidelity of this new empire had strategic importance to both the Eastern and the Western Church, who sent missionaries to convert the Moravian people. Beginning in 863, two

Orthodox monks, Cyril and Methodius, succeeded in converting large numbers of people to the Byzantine church (introducing a Slavic alphabet named "Cyrillic" after one of the monks), but Roman Catholic missionaries gained the majority of converts.

The Moravian Empire was destroyed at the end of the 9th century (903–907) by invading Magyars (Hungarians), who incorporated the eastern lands into their own, while the Kingdom of Bohemia inherited the lands and peoples of the west. The Premyslid Dynasty took control of the Bohemian kingdom, allying with the Germans to prevent further Magyar expansion. In the year 1085, Prince Vratislave was the first Bohemian prince to receive royal status from the Byzantine Empire, gaining his title by supporting Henry IV against Pope Gregory VII. A century later, in 1212, Premysl Otakar I was given the Golden Bull of Sicily, proclaiming Bohemia a kingdom in its own right, and the Bohemian princes the hereditary rulers of that land. During the 13th century, the powers gained by the Premyslid Dynasty through the German alliance waned as this relationship brought the substantial migration of Germans into Bohemia and Moravia. The next line to rule Bohemia, starting with John of Luxembourg (1310–1346), came to power before a time of great social and religious strife. Charles IV of Luxembourg was not only King of Bohemia (1346–1378), but Holy Roman Emperor as well, ushering in the Czech "Golden Age," but his ties to the Roman Catholic Church would later tear the Kingdom apart. In 1348 he founded the Charles University in Prague, one of the first learning institutions to operate outside of the Church's monasteries, which nourished the minds of Bohemian intellectuals. As the citizens of Prague began to learn of the intransigence of the Roman Catholic Church, Wenceslas IV, successor to Charles IV, experienced a series of economic and political crisis (1378–1419) that escalated with The Great Schism of the Church. Bohemia became a center of passionate opposition to the Catholic Church, and to German domination, led by Jan Hus in the Hussite movement. Burned at the stake for heresy in 1415 by German Emperor Sigismund, Hus became a national martyr and hero, and the country was in open rebellion (1420–1436). During this time, Sigismund conducted six crusades in Bohemia to end the revolution, until he finally succeeded in 1434. By 1436, tired of fighting, both sides signed the Compacts of Basle. These documents allowed the Hussite denomination, and became the model of religious tolerance, which did not last for long. In 1462 Hungary extended its control over Bohemia, ruling through the Jagellon Dynasty until 1526, when Ferdinand of Hapsburg was elected to the Crown of St. Wenceslas, making Bohemia the property of the House of Hapsburg.

The Czechs were predominantly Protestant, while their new rulers were bent on introducing the Roman Catholic faith to Bohemia, exacerbating civil tensions. Although Protestants were able to secure certain civil rights, and the freedom to worship, peace was fragile. In 1618 two Protestant churches were closed, leading Protestants to throw two royal governors out of the windows of Prague Castle, an act known as the "Defenestration of Prague." At the same time, 27 Protestant nobles were executed by the Habsburgs. In the Thirty Years' War, which followed, the Czechs deposed their Catholic king, replacing him with Frederick of the Palatinate, a Protestant. The Protestant forces of the Bohemian Estates were defeated by the Catholic Emperor in 1620, at the Battle of White Mountain, and the Catholics again took the throne. This represented a disaster for the Czechs, who had their lands seized and their leaders executed, while nearly 30,000 of their number fled. The war ended in 1648 with the Peace of Westphalia, which sanctioned the large-scale immigration of Germans, resulting in the gradual Germanification of Czech territory. Under Empress Maria-Theresa (1740–1780) Bohemia became part of Austria, and the most industrialized part of the Austrian Empire, but Czech culture and language were suppressed.

Political tranquility was ended by the riots, which broke out across Europe in 1848. On 11 March 1848, a demonstration in Prague demanded freedom of the press, equality of language, a parliament to represent Czech interests, and an end to serfdom. A Pan-Slavic Congress was convened in Prague in June of the same year, under Francis Palacky, a Bohemian historian. The Austrian authorities responded by imposing a military dictatorship, which struggled to restrain a steadily rising tide of nationalist aspirations. When World War I began, thousands of Czech soldiers surrendered to the Russians, rather than fight for the Austro-Hungarians. They were transformed into the Czech Legion, which fought for the Russians until the Russian Revolution of 1917. Although Austria retained nominal control of Bohemia until the war's end, a separate Czech National Council began functioning in Paris as early as 1916.

Formation of the Czechoslovak Republic

It was the members of that Council, especially Eduard Benes and Tomas Masaryk, who were instrumental in gaining international support for the formation of an independent Czech and Slovak state at war's end. The Czechoslovak Republic, established 28 October 1918 under President Tomas Masaryk, was a contentious mix of at least five nationalities—Czechs, the so-called Sudeten Germans, Slovaks, Moravians, and Ruthenians—who created one of the 10 most developed countries in the world, during the interwar period. All these nationalities were granted significant rights of self-determination, but many groups wished for full independence, and some of the Sudeten Germans hoped for reunification with Germany. In 1938 Adolph Hitler demanded that the Sudeten German area, which was the most heavily industrialized part of the country, be ceded to Germany. A conference consisting of Germany, Italy, France, and Great Britain, was convened, without Czechoslovakian representation. Ignoring the mutual assistance pacts, which Czechoslovakia had signed with both France and the USSR, this conference agreed on 30 September 1938 that Germany could occupy the Sudetenland. On 15 March 1939, Hitler took the remainder of the Czech lands, beginning an occupation that lasted until 9 May 1945.

Many prominent Czechs managed to escape the Germans, including Eduard Benes, the president, who established Provisional Government in London, in 1940, and Klement Gottwald, the communist leader, who took refuge in Moscow. In 1945, negotiations between Benes, Gottwald, and Josef Stalin established the basis for a postwar government, which was formed in the Slovak city of Kosice in April 1945 and moved to Prague the following month.

The government was drawn entirely from the National Front, an alliance of parties oriented toward Soviet Russia, with whom Czechoslovakia now had a common border, after the USSR incorporated Ruthenia. Although deferring to the communists, the National Front government managed to run Czechoslovakia as a democracy until 1948. The communists had been the largest vote getter in the 1946 elections, but it seemed likely that they might lose in 1948. Rather than risk the election, they organized a putsch, with Soviet backing, forcing President Benes to accept a government headed by Gottwald. Benes resigned in June 1948, leaving the presidency open for Gottwald, while A. Zapotocky became prime minister. In a repeat of Czech history, Jan Masaryk, foreign minister at the time, and son of T. Masaryk, was thrown from a window during the coup, a "defenestration" which was reported as a suicide.

Once Czechoslovakia became a People's Republic, and a faithful ally of the Soviet Union, a wave of purges and arrests rolled over the country (1949–1954). In 1952 a number of high officials, including Foreign Minister V. Clementis and R. Slansky, head of the Czech Communist Party, were hanged for "Tito-ism" (after the Yugoslavian president who had been dismissed from the Cominform) and "national deviation."

After an unsuccessful Army coup on his behalf, Novotny resigned, in March 1968, and Czechoslovakia embarked on a radical liberalization, which Dubček termed "socialism with a human face." The leaders of the other eastern bloc nations and the Soviet leaders viewed these developments with alarm. Delegations went back and forth from Moscow during the "Prague Spring" of 1968, warning of "counterrevolution." By July the neighbors' alarm had grown; at a July meeting in Warsaw they issued a warning to Czechoslovakia against leaving the socialist camp. Although Dubček himself traveled to Moscow twice, in July and early August, to reassure Soviet party leader Brezhnev of the country's fidelity, the Soviets remained unconvinced.

On the night of 20–21 August 1968, military units from all the Warsaw Pact nations, save Romania, invaded Czechoslovakia, to "save it from counterrevolution." Dubček and other officials were arrested, and the country was placed under Soviet control. Repeated efforts to find local officials willing to act as Soviet puppets failed, so on 31 December 1968 the country was made a federal state, comprised of the Czech Socialist Republic and the Slovak Socialist Republic. In April Gustav Husak, once a reformer, but now viewing harmony with the USSR as the highest priority, was named head of the Czech Communist Party. A purge of liberals followed, and in May 1970 a new Soviet-Czechoslovak friendship treaty was signed; in June Dubček was expelled from the party.

Between 1970 and 1975 nearly one-third of the party was dismissed, as Husak consolidated power, reestablishing the priority of the federal government over its constituent parts and, in May 1975, reuniting the titles of party head and republic president. Civil rights groups formed within the country; including a group of several hundred in 1977 that published a manifesto called "Charter 77," protesting the suppression of human rights in Czechoslovakia. These groups did not seriously impinge upon Husak's power, but his successors had difficulty suppressing the liberalization movement.

Once again, it was revolution in the USSR which set off political change in Czechoslovakia. Husak ignored Soviet leader Mikhail Gorbachev's calls for *perestroika* and *glasnost* until 1987, when Husak reluctantly endorsed the general concept of Party reform, but delayed implementation until 1991. Aging and in ill health, Husak announced his retirement in December 1987, declaring that Milos

Jakes would take his post. Jakes had been a lifelong compromiser and accommodator who was unable to control dissenting factions within his party, which were now using the radical changes in the Soviet Union as weapons against one another.

Even greater pressure came in early autumn 1989, when the West German Embassy in Prague began to accept East German refugees who were trying to go west. Increasingly the East German government was being forced to accede to popular demand for change, which in turn emboldened Czech citizens to make similar demands. On 17 November 1989, a group of about 3,000 youths gathered in Prague's Wenceslas Square, demanding free elections. On Jakes's orders, they were attacked and beaten by security forces; igniting a swell of public indignation, expressed in 10 days of nonstop meetings and demonstrations. This "Velvet Revolution" ended on 24 November, when Jakes and all his government resigned. Novotny resigned his presidency soon after. Although Alexander Dubček was put forward as a possible replacement, he was rejected because he was Slovak. The choice fell instead on Vaclav Havel, a playwright and dissident, and founder of the Charter 77 group, who was named president on 29 December 1989.

Dismantling of the apparatus of a Soviet-style state began immediately, but economic change came more slowly, in part because elections were not scheduled until June 1990. In the interim, the old struggle between Czechs and Slovaks resulted in the country being renamed the Czech and Slovak Federal Republic. In the June elections the vote went overwhelmingly to Civic Forum and its Slovak partner, and economic transformation was begun, although there were continued tensions between those who wished a rapid move to a market economy and those who wanted to find some "third way" between socialism and capitalism. Equally contentious was the sentiment for separation by Slovakia, the pressure for which continued to build through 1991 and 1992. In the June 1992 elections the split between the two parts of the country became obvious, as Czechs voted overwhelmingly for the reform and anticommunist candidates of Vaclav Klaus' Civic Democratic Party (ODS), while Slovaks voted for V. Meciar and his Movement for Democratic Slovakia, a leftist and nationalist party. Legislative attempts to strengthen the federative structure, at the expense of the legislatures of the two constituent republics, failed, and the republics increasingly began to behave as though they were already separate so that, for example, by the end of 1992, 25.2% of Czech industry was been privatized, as opposed to only 5.3% of Slovak industry. The prime ministers of the two republics eventually agreed to separate, in the so-called "velvet divorce," which took effect 1 January 1993.

Havel (who did not subscribe to any party in the interest of political tranquility) was reconfirmed as president by a vote of the Czech parliament on 26 January 1993. Klaus was successful in fostering growth in the newly formed Czech Republic, emerging from close 1996 elections with another term as prime minister, but after the first glow of liberation, major cracks in the system became visible. Milos Zeman of the Social Democratic Party (CSSD) challenged Klaus' policies, during and after the 1996 elections, especially those relating to economic growth (which was slowing). The year 1996 also saw the first elections for the 81-member Senate, the upper body of parliament, which reflected a major split in the attitude of Czech voters. Governmental democracy and a newly liberated economy had not brought about the immediate transformation that Czech citizens wanted to see, and they ended up blaming the ODS party for their woes. This, and charges of corruption in the ODS party, brought about the triumph of the opposition. In the 1998 elections, the majority of votes went to the Social Democratic Party, in a platform that stressed economic regulation and the socialist approach to government. Milos Zeman was appointed as the prime minister by President Vaclav Havel on 17 July 1998. Havel had been reelected president the previous January for another five-year term.

In March 1999, the Czech Republic became a member of NATO. In January 2001, the largest street demonstrations since the overthrow of Communism were held to protest the appointment of Jiri Hodac as the head of public service television. He was seen as a political appointee and was accused of compromising editorial independence. Hodac resigned following the protests. In April, Vladimir Spidla became leader of the Social Democrats; he was more left-wing than Zeman, and was dismissive of ODS leader Vaclav Klaus. When in the June 2002 elections the Social Democrats gained the largest number of seats in the Chamber of Deputies, Spidla became prime minister. Spidla formed a government with the Coalition, composed of the Christian-Democratic Union/Czechoslovak People's Party, and the Freedom Union (Koalice), holding 101 seats in the 200-seat Chamber (70 seats for the CSSD, and 31 for the Coalition). The ODS came in second with 58 seats, and the Communists, in their best showing since the Velvet Revolution, came in third with 41 seats.

In August 2002, Central Europe was plagued by torrential rain, and Prague suffered its worst flooding in 200 years. The city's historic district was spared, but towns and villages across the country were devastated.

The Czech Republic was one of 10 new countries to be formally invited to join the EU in December 2002, and its accession was completed in 2004. Issues to be resolved by the countries include adoption of the euro, migration, and agriculture, among others.

Havel stepped down as president in February 2003, after his second five-year term expired. Havel's rival and former prime minister, Vaclav Klaus, was elected president by a slim majority of 142 votes in the 281-member parliament after two inconclusive elections and three rounds of balloting on 28 February. Although when he left the presidency opinions about his legacy were mixed in the Czech Republic, on the international scene Havel remains eternally popular for being a voice for democracy.

In the 2004 European Parliament elections the CSSD garnered only 8.8% of the votes, signaling that the party's popularity among voters was on a downward spiral. As a consequence, in July 2004, the Socialists decided to sack the prime minister, Vladimir Spidla, and replace him with the minister of interior, Stanislav Gross.

Gross, who was an engine-driver trainee for the state railway company before the Velvet Revolution, became a Social Democrat in 1992 and quickly worked his way up the party ranks. He was only 35 when he replaced Spidla—Europe's youngest prime minister. His reign was short-lived though. Plagued by scandals and corruption and faced with the dissolution of his own government, Gross resigned only nine months after his appointment. Jiri Paroubek, the regional development minister in Gross's government, was appointed as the new Czech prime minister on 25 April 2005. He faced the difficult task of cutting public spending in prepa-

ration for the eurozone membership while improving his party's popularity among voters in anticipation of the 2006 elections.

13 GOVERNMENT

The Czech Republic has a democratic government, based on a bicameral parliamentary democracy and the free association of political parties. Human and civil rights are guaranteed by the Bill of Fundamental Rights and Freedoms, a part of the constitution. The constitution of the Czech Republic was adopted by the Czech legislature in December 1992. It mandates a parliament; a Senate with 81 members who are elected for six-year terms, and a Chamber of Deputies or lower house of 200 members who are elected for four-year terms. Every two years, one third of the Senate's seats come up for reelection. The first Senatorial elections were held in November 1996. The last Senatorial elections were held in November 2004 with the next being scheduled for November 2006. The Chamber of Deputies was first seated by popular vote in 1992. The last elections took place in June 2002 with the next scheduled for June 2006. A resolution by parliament is passed by a clear majority, while a constitutional bill or an international treaty must be passed by at least a 60% majority. All citizens over the age of 18 can vote.

The head of the executive branch is the president, who is elected by parliament for a five-year term, and may serve two terms successively. The president is the supreme commander of the armed forces and has the power to veto bills passed by parliament under certain conditions. The last successful presidential election was held on 28 February 2003 and named Vaclav Klaus as president. This election came after Vaclav Havel stepped down from office on 2 February 2003 after earlier elections held 15 and 24 January 2003 were inconclusive. The next presidential elections were scheduled for January 2008. The prime minister, or premier, comes from the majority party, or a coalition, and is appointed by the president. The president appoints the ministers of the government on the recommendation of the prime minister.

14 POLITICAL PARTIES

Before 1996, the strongest political party in the republic was the Civic Democratic Party (ODS), headed by former prime minister Vaclav Klaus, a right-wing conservative party supporting democracy and a liberal economy. Supporters of the ODS are, in general, highly educated business people who come from Prague or other major cities. The ODS right-wing coalition with the Civic Democratic Alliance (ODA), Christian Democratic Union, and Christian Democratic Party, lost its majority in Parliament by two seats in the 1996 elections. Klaus and his coalition governed in the minority with the blessing of the opposition Social Democrats (CSSD), a socialist left-wing party that focuses on economic reform/growth in a planned economy. Supporters of the CSSD are mainly blue-collar laborers from industrial areas.

In December 1997, the ODS coalition (ODS, Christian Democratic Union/Czechoslovak People's Party or KDU-CSL, and ODA) was forced to resign due to the collapse of the union, government scandals, and a worsening economy. A temporary government was formed in January 1998, led by Mr. Tošovsk, which was given the task to prepare the country for new elections. These were held in June 1998, where the Czech Social Democratic Party gained the majority of votes (32.3%). After negotiating with the ODS, which gained 27.74% of the votes, the CSSD formed a minority government, creating the first left-oriented party since Communist rule.

In the 1998 elections, the CSSD gained 74 seats in the Chamber of Deputies and 25 seats in the Senate, while the ODS gained 63 seats in the lower house and 29 in the Senate. The Christian Democratic Union-Czechoslovak People's Party (KDU-CSL, Catholic-conservative) took 20 seats in the Chamber and 13 in the Senate, and the Freedom Union (US, break-off party from the ODS) won 19 seats in the lower house and 3 in the Senate. Voters who became disillusioned with the bad policies of the ODS coalition took a significant number of seats away from the party, and gave them to the Freedom Union. The Communist Party won 24 seats in the Chamber of Deputies and 2 seats in the Senate.

President Havel, who was reelected on 26 January 1993, did not subscribe to any political party in the interest of political tranquility. He appointed Milos Zeman of the majority Social Democratic Party as prime minister on 17 July 1998.

In the 2002 elections, the CSSD gained 70 seats in the Chamber of Deputies and 11 seats in the Senate. The ODS took 58 seats in the Chamber and 26 in the Senate, and the Coalition, a grouping of the KDU-CSL and the Freedom Union (US), won 31 seats in the Chamber and 31 seats in the Senate. The Communist Party, in its strongest showing since the end of Communist rule, took 41 seats in the lower house and 3 seats in the Senate. The CSSD formed a majority government (101 seats) in the Chamber of Deputies with the Coalition. Vladimir Spidla of the CSSD became prime minister; following disastrous results in the 2004 European Parliament elections, he was replaced with Stanislav Gross—the former minister of interior. Accusations of corruption, and threats from the Christian Democrats to leave the coalition, forced Gross to resign after only nine months in office. On 25 April 2005 he was replaced with Jiri Paroubek, his former regional development minister.

Vaclav Klaus of the ODS was inaugurated president on 7 March 2003, after parliament voted him into office in February, after many rounds of voting. Next parliamentary elections were scheduled for June 2006.

15 LOCAL GOVERNMENT

The Czech Republic is divided into 6,000 municipalities for local administration, 13 self-governing regions, popularly elected for a four-year period of office, and the capital city of Prague, with a mayor and city council elected for four-year terms. Under Communist rule, Czechoslovakia's government was so centralized that little to no local government existed. Such institutions have become more common since the formation of the 1992 constitution and democratic rule.

16 JUDICIAL SYSTEM

Under the 1992 constitution, the judiciary has been completely reorganized to provide for a system of courts, which includes a Supreme Court; a supreme administrative court; high, regional, and district courts; and a constitutional court. The Supreme Court, which is situated in Brno, is the highest appellate court and has national jurisdiction. The High Courts, with seats in Prague and Olomouc, represent the second instance in the judicial system. The District Courts deal with proceedings in the first instance and are situated in the capital towns of the administrative districts.

The 15-member constitutional court created in 1993 rules on the constitutionality of legislation. Constitutional court judges are appointed by the president, subject to Senate approval, for 10-year terms.

Military courts were abolished in 1993 and their functions transferred to the civil court system. The new judiciary is independent from the executive and legislative branches and appears to be impartial in its application of the law. Criminal defendants are entitled to fair and open public trials. They have the right to have counsel and enjoy a presumption of innocence.

17 ARMED FORCES

The Czech Republic had 22,272 active personnel in 2005. The Army numbered 16,663 active members with 298 main battle tanks. The Air Force had 5,609 active personnel, with 40 combat capable aircraft. The Czech Republic also had a 5,600 member paramilitary force made up of 4,000 border guards and 1,600 internal security personnel. The Czech Republic provided support to NATO, UN and peacekeeping missions in nine countries in Asia, Europe and Africa. Military spending in 2005 amounted to $2.19 billion.

The Košice Agreement of 1945 provided for military organization, equipment, and training to be modeled after those of the former USSR. Czechoslovakia was a signatory to the Warsaw Pact of 14 May 1955, which provided for military cooperation with the USSR and other Soviet-bloc countries and for a joint command with headquarters in Moscow.

18 INTERNATIONAL COOPERATION

Czechoslovakia was a charter member of the Untied Nations, admitted on 24 October 1945. The Czech Republic became a member of the UN on 8 January 1993; it is part of the ECE and serves on several specialized agencies, such as the IFC, IMF, WHO, the World Bank, and UNESCO. The Czech Republic was admitted to NATO on 12 March 1999 and became a member of the European Union on 1 May 2004. It is also a member of the OECD, the OSCE, the Central European Initiative, the Council of Europe, and the European Bank for Reconstruction and Development. The country is an observer in the OAS and an affiliate member of the Western European Union.

The nation is part of the European Organization for Nuclear Research (CERN), the Nuclear Suppliers Group (London Group), and the Nuclear Energy Agency. It is also a part of the Australia Group and the Zangger Committee. In environmental cooperation, the Czech Republic is part of the Antarctic Treaty, Basel Convention, Conventions on Biological Diversity and Air Pollution, Ramsar, CITES, the Kyoto Protocol, the Montréal Protocol, MARPOL, the Nuclear Test Ban Treaty, and the UN Conventions on the Law of the Sea, Climate Change, and Desertification.

19 ECONOMY

Before World War II, Bohemia and Moravia were among the most agriculturally and industrially developed areas in Europe. In 1993, the Czech Republic emerged from 40 years of centralized economic planning in the Communist era (including the more balanced economic development of the 1960s) with a more prosperous and less debt-ridden economy than most other post-Communist countries. It enjoys an extensive industrial sector strong in both heavy and precision engineering, self-sufficiency in a variety of agricultural crops as well as an exportable surplus of meat, extensive timber resources, and adequate coal and lignite to supply two-thirds of its total energy needs.

After recovering from a recession following the 1993 separation from Slovakia, the republic enjoyed GDP growth of 4.8% in 1995. GDP growth of up to 5.5% was forecast for 1996 and 1997. Unemployment also stabilized at less than 3% through 1996. The annual rate of inflation dropped from 20% in 1993 to 9% in 1996. The thriving economy of the mid-1990s depended upon loans easily secured from state-owned banks to newly privatized companies that did not have effective managers. This method of fueling the economy collapsed in a 1997 currency crisis which caused the economy to go into a three-year recession. Following this collapse, the government rescued and privatized the four largest banks in the Czech Republic, which stabilized the banking sector, now largely foreign-owned. The banks had begun to lend again by 2001.

As of 2001, the country was receiving the highest level of foreign direct investment per capita in Central Europe, and 40% of industrial production was coming from foreign-owned companies. This high level of investment drove the value of the koruna up in 2001, which, coupled with a downturn in the global economy, put a damper on industry. The steel and engineering industries were struggling in the early 2000s, but growth in information technology and electronics diversified the economy. The telecommunications, energy, gas, and petrochemical sectors were due to be privatized by 2002.

Severe flooding in Central Europe in August 2002 negatively impacted the Czech economy. The tourism sector was especially affected.

The country was formally invited to join the EU in December 2002, and it will need to keep its budget deficit below the 3% of GDP mandated by the EU for entering into European economic and monetary union (it was 5.3% in 2002). The deficit is balanced against the influx of revenue from privatization, however, which reached 11.3% of GDP in 2002. Accession to the EU was completed in 2004.

The relatively slow pace of growth from 2001 and 2002 was replaced with moderately high growth rates of the GDP in 2003 and 2004: 3.7% and 4.0% respectively; in 2005 the economy was expected to strengthen even further, with a real GDP growth of 4.3%. This moderate growth is the sign of a maturing economy that is trying to embed the market in a stable system. Inflation remained fairly stable, hovering around 3%. The unemployment rate fluctuated between 9% and 10%.

The Czech Republic remains one of the strongest economies in Central and Eastern Europe. The main growth engines are exports, foreign and domestic investment, and tourism. The state-owned telecommunications company—Cesky Telecom—was to be privatized in 2005, which together with improvements in the financial sector, and better management of EU funds was supposed to strengthen the economy on the short term. Car manufacturing (the Czech Republic is part of the so-called "Detroit of Europe" region), and tourism are two of the country's strongest industries.

20 INCOME

The US Central Intelligence Agency (CIA) reports that in 2005 Czech Republic's gross domestic product (GDP) was estimated at $184.9 billion. The CIA defines GDP as the value of all final goods and services produced within a nation in a given year and computed on the basis of purchasing power parity (PPP) rather than value as measured on the basis of the rate of exchange based on current dollars. The per capita GDP was estimated at $18,100. The annual growth rate of GDP was estimated at 4.6%. The average inflation rate in 2005 was 2%. It was estimated that agriculture accounted for 3.4% of GDP, industry 39.3%, and services 57.3% in 2004.

According to the World Bank, in 2003 remittances from citizens working abroad totaled $500 million or about $49 per capita and accounted for approximately 0.6% of GDP. Foreign aid receipts amounted to $263 million or about $26 per capita and accounted for approximately 0.3% of the gross national income (GNI).

The World Bank reports that in 2003 household consumption in Czech Republic totaled $45.59 billion or about $4,470 per capita based on a GDP of $90.4 billion, measured in current dollars rather than PPP. Household consumption includes expenditures of individuals, households, and nongovernmental organizations on goods and services, excluding purchases of dwellings. It was estimated that for the period 1990 to 2003 household consumption grew at an average annual rate of 2.8%. In 2001 it was estimated that approximately 24% of household consumption was spent on food, 14% on fuel, 5% on health care, and 12% on education.

21 LABOR

As of 2005, the labor force was estimated at 5.27 million. Among wage earners in 2002, an estimated 4% were engaged in agriculture; 38% in industry; and 58% in services. The estimated unemployment rate in 2005 was 9.1%.

The right to form and join unions is protected by law. As of 2005, about 20% of the Czech labor force was unionized, although union membership was on the decline. The major labor confederation is the Czech-Moravian Chamber of Trade Unions. Workers are freely allowed to organize and engage in collective bargaining. Striking is also allowed, but only after mediation efforts fail. However, workers in certain critical sectors cannot strike and are limited only to mediation. Collective bargaining is usually conducted on a company-by-company basis between unions and employers.

In 2005, the standard workweek was 40 hours, with at least two days of rest. There is also a mandatory 30-minute rest period during the eight-hour day. Overtime is limited to eight hours per week and is subject to employee consent. The minimum working age is 15 years with some exceptions allowing legal employment to 14-year-old workers. There are strict standards for all workers under the age of 18, and these standards are routinely enforced. Occupational health and safety standards are prescribed and effectively enforced except in some industries still awaiting privatization. As of 2005, the minimum wage was $287 per month and is considered to provide a decent standard of living for a worker and a family.

22 AGRICULTURE

Agriculture is a small but important sector of the economy which has steadily declined since the "Velvet Revolution" of 1989. In 2003, cultivated areas accounted for 43% of the total land area. Agriculture contributed 3.4% to GDP in 2004.

The principal crops are grains (wheat, rye, barley, oats, and corn), which support the Czech Republic's dozens of small breweries. Production in 2004 included wheat, 5,042,000 tons; barley, 2,330,000 tons; rye, 313,000 tons; oats, 227,000 tons; and corn, 552,000 tons. At 166 liters (44 gallons) per person, the Czech Republic is the world's highest per capita beer-consuming nation. There is a long tradition of brewing in the Czech Republic; some of the world's oldest brands were invented there. After Germany, the Czech Republic is Europe's largest producer of hops; production in 2004 was 6,311 tons. Other important crops include oilseeds, sugar beets, potatoes, and apples.

Agriculture lags behind other sectors in the restoration of private properties seized after 1948. As of 1993, agricultural subsidies were restricted to the formation of new farms, and the production of wheat, dairy products, and meat. Over the long term, the government estimates that over 250,000 agricultural workers will need to find employment in other sectors and that arable land in use will decrease by 9%.

23 ANIMAL HUSBANDRY

Hogs, cattle, and poultry are the main income-producers in the livestock sector. In 2004 there were an estimated 1,428,000 head of cattle and 3,126,000 hogs. The number of chickens that year reached an estimated 14.2 million; sheep, 115,900; goats, 11,900; and horses, 24,000.

Meat, poultry, and dairy production have been oriented toward quantity rather than quality. In 2004, meat production totaled 759,254 tons, with pork accounting for 52%.

24 FISHING

Fishing is a relatively unimportant source of domestic food supply. Production is derived mostly from pond cultivation and, to a lesser extent, from rivers. The total catch in 2003 was 5,127 tons, all from inland waters. Aquacultural production amounted to 19,670 tons that year.

25 FORESTRY

The Forest Code (1852) of the Austro-Hungarian Empire was incorporated into the laws of the former Czechoslovakia and governed forest conservation until World War II (1939–45). Most forests were privately owned, and during the world wars, they were excessively exploited. The Czech Republic had an estimated 2,632,000 hectares (6,504,000 acres) of forestland in 2000, accounting for 34% of the total land area. As of 2003, forest ownership was 62% state, 21% private, and 15% municipal. Total roundwood production in 2003 was 14.5 million cu m (512 million cu ft), with exports of 2.5 million cu m (88 million cu ft). Since the Czech government began property restitution, the need for wood products has far outstripped domestic supply, especially for furniture and construction materials.

26 MINING

The mining and processing sector's share of GDP in 2002 was 1.2%, down from 3.7% in 1993. Mining and processing of industrial minerals and the production of construction materials continued to be of regional and domestic importance. Economic resources of most metals have been depleted. As of end 2000 only gold-bearing and tin-tungsten ores were among the exceptions. All the raw materials consumed by the country's steel industry were imported, including iron ore and concentrate, manganese ore, copper, and unwrought lead and zinc. Lead and zinc have not been mined for about seven years, and the number of registered lead deposits declined from 17 in 1998 to nine in 2002, none of which were being worked. The country's eight iron ore deposits were no longer worked. In 2002: kaolin production was 3.65 million metric tons, down from 5.543 million tons in 2001; common sand and gravel, 12.464 million cu m, up from 12.1 million cu m in 2001; foundry sand, 676,000 tons, compared to 771,000 tons in 2001; glass sand, 853,000 tons, compared to 974,000 tons in 2001; dimension stone, 285 million cu m, down from 300 million cu m in 2001; limestone and calcareous stones, 10.186 million tons; building stone, 10.6 million cu m; hydrated lime and quicklime, 1.12 million tons; feldspar, 401,000 metric tons, up from 373,000 metric tons in 2001; diatomite, 28,000 metric tons, down from 83,000 metric tons in 2001; and graphite, 16,000 metric tons, down from 17,000 metric tons in 2001. Output of crude gypsum and anhydrite went from 24,000 metric tons in 2001 to 108,000 metric tons in 2002. The Czech Republic also produced arsenic, hydraulic cement, bentonite, dolomite, crude gemstones and pyrope-bearing rock, illite, iron ore, nitrogen, quartz, salt, basalt (for casting), silver, sodium compounds, sulfuric acid, talc, uranium, wollastonite, and zeolites.

27 ENERGY AND POWER

The Czech Republic has only small proven reserves of oil and natural gas, but relatively abundant recoverable reserves of coal.

The electricity production market in the Czech Republic is dominated by Ceske Energeticke Zavody (CEZ), which is majority owned by the state. In 2003, CEZ provided 74% of the country's power, with the remaining 26% of the nation's power provided by 8 regional power companies, of which CEZ holds a majority stake in 5.

In 2002, the Czech Republic had 15.298 million kW of electrical generating capacity. This included conventional thermal at 11.537 million kW; nuclear at 2.760 million kW; hydroelectric at 1.000 million kW; and geothermal/other at 0.001 million kW. For that same year, electricity generation was estimated at 71.8 billion kWh, of which 50.835 billion kWh came from conventional thermal sources; 17.801 billion kWh from nuclear sources; 2.467 billion kWh from hydropower; and 0.655 billion kWh from geothermal/other sources. Electricity consumption in 2002 was estimated at 55 billion kWh. Exports of electricity for 2002 totaled 20.900 billion kWh, with imports for that year at 9.502 billion kWh.

The Czech Republic has two operational nuclear power plants: Dukovany; and Temelin, the latter located 37 miles from the Austrian border. Temelin initially went online in December 2000, with a second reactor placed on trial operation 8 April 2003. The following month, both Temelin reactors became fully operational. Both plants are operated by CEZ and generated 42% of the company's power, accounting for 30% of its installed generating capacity in 2003. In 2002, nuclear power accounted for almost 25% of the electric power produced by the Czech Republic. Nuclear power is an important part of the Czech.

The Czech Republic's crude oil reserves are limited, totaling an estimated 15 million barrels as of 1 January 2004. Oil production in 2003 came to an estimated 13,200 barrels per day, with preliminary figures showing a consumption rate for all oil products of 186,000 barrels per day for that year. According to British Petroleum, oil product consumption totaled 202,000 barrels per day for 2004. As a result, the Czech Republic is heavily dependent upon imported oil. In 2002, total crude and refined oil product imports totaled 191,410 barrels per day While much of the Czech Republic's oil imports come from Russia, the country has been able to tap other sources via the Ingolstadt-Kralupy nad Vltavou-Litvinov (ILK) pipeline, which permits crude oil to be transported from Trieste by way of the Trans-Alpine pipeline. The ILK pipeline is operated by Mero CR.

As with oil, the Czech Republic has only limited reserves of natural gas. In 2002, consumption and production of natural gas was estimated at 337 billion cu ft, and 5.4 billion cu ft, respectively. Imports for that year came to 343.76 billion cu ft. Estimated natural gas reserves have been placed at 0.14 trillion cubic ft, as of 1 January 2004.

The Czech Republic, between 1993 and 2002, has seen its demand for coal fall 23%. In spite of this, coal remains an important source of energy. In 2002, coal accounted for 43% of the nation's primary energy demand. Estimated recoverable coal reserves in the Czech Republic amounted to 6,259 million short tons in 2001. Coal production and consumption of all types in 2002, was estimated at 70.4 million short tons and 65 million short tons, respectively.

28 INDUSTRY

Before World War II, Czechoslovakia favored traditional export-oriented light industries, including food processing. Concentration on the production of capital goods since the war has been at the expense of consumer goods and foodstuffs, although there have been increases in the metalworking industry and in the production of glass, wood products, paper, textiles, clothing, shoes, and leather goods. Some of these and other consumer goods—such as the world-famous pilsner beer, ham, and sugar—had figured prominently in the pre-World War II export trade, but machinery was predominant under the Communist regime.

The extent of Czechoslovakian industry still ranks both the Czech and Slovak republics among the world's most industrialized countries. A final wave of privatization begun in 1995 has resulted in an 80% private stake in industry, although the government maintains some control over steel, telecommunications, transport, and energy industries. However, in 2001, the energy utility CEZ was due to be privatized. Industry accounted for 40.7% of GDP and 38% of employment through 1995. However, while industrial wages continued to grow through 1996, output fell 3.5%, forcing the government to implement new austerity measures to spur renewed growth. Nevertheless, industry, which accounted for over 40% of the economy, registered a 4.7% decline in 1998. The recession, which continued into 1999, brought disillusionment to many Czechs who had emerged from the 1989 "Velvet Revolution" as the most prosperous citizens of the former East Bloc. The European recession, which began on the heels of the economic downturn in the United States beginning in 2001, further exacerbated the struggling Czech economy. Industry accounted for 41% of GDP in 2001, and employed 35% of the work force. Although the relative contribution of industry to the economy had begun to decline in 2002, the industrial base remained diversified.

Major industries in the Czech Republic include fuels, ferrous metallurgy, machinery and equipment, coal, motor vehicles, glass,

and armaments. The country is particularly strong in engineering. The Czech Republic in 2001 was receiving the highest foreign direct investment in the region, which was devoted to restructuring industrial companies. Forty percent of industrial production in 2001 came from companies with foreign capital, up from 15% in 1997. The Czech Republic produced 465,268 automobiles in 2001, up 2% from 2000. Skoda Auto, now owned by Volkswagen, is a successful Czech enterprise.

In 2004, the industrial sector contributed 39.3% to the overall GDP, and employed 38% of the total labor force; agriculture was not a big contributor to the GDP—only 3.4%, and employed only 4% of the working population; services came in first with 57.3% and 58% respectively. The industrial production growth rate was slightly higher than the GDP growth rate, reaching 4.7% in 2004. Car manufacturing remains the main industrial driving force, and is followed by metallurgy, machinery and equipment, glass, and armaments.

29 SCIENCE AND TECHNOLOGY

The Czech Academy of Science has divisions of life and chemical sciences, mathematics, and physical and earth sciences, and 43 attached medical, scientific, and technical research institutes. In addition, there are 28 specialized agricultural, medical, scientific, and technical learned societies. There are technology museums in Brno, Mladá Boleslav, and Prague, and the latter also has a natural history museum. The Czech Republic has 13 universities offering degrees in medicine, natural sciences, mathematics, engineering, and agriculture. In 1987–97, science and engineering students accounted for 28% of university enrollment. In 2002, a total of 30.2% of all bachelor's degrees awarded were science degrees (natural sciences, mathematics and computers, and engineering).

In 2003, total expenditures for research and development (R&D) amounted to Kc32,246.6 million, of which 51.5% came from business, 41.8% came from government sources, 2.2% came from higher education, and 4.6% came from foreign sources. In 2002 (the latest year for which this data was available) there were 1,467 researchers and 792 technicians per million people actively engaged in R&D. High technology exports in 2002 totaled $4.494 billion, accounting for 14% of manufactured exports that year.

30 DOMESTIC TRADE

In the Communist period, marketing and distribution, including price-fixing, were controlled by the federal government; administration on the lower levels was handled by the national committees. Cooperative farms sold the bulk of their produce to the state at fixed prices, but marginal quantities of surplus items were sold directly to consumers through so-called free farmers' markets. Starting in 1958, the government operated a program of installment buying for certain durable consumer goods, with state savings banks granting special credits.

The "Velvet Revolution" of 1989 brought rapid privatization program on an innovative voucher system. Each citizen was given an opportunity to purchase a book of vouchers to be used in exchange for shares in state-owned businesses. As a result, more than 20,000 shops, restaurants, and workshops in both the Czech and Slovak republics were transferred to private owners by public auction in a wave of "small" privatization, and through distribution of ownership shares. Under communism, nearly 97% of businesses were state-owned. Today, about 80% of the economy is wholly or partially in private hands.

The commercial center of the country is Prague. Though there are numerous small shops throughout the city, American and European style supermarkets and department stores are developing and providing stiff competition. Shopping malls have also begun to develop. Though most transactions are still in cash, credit cards are gaining a wider acceptance within major cities. Direct marketing, particularly through catalog sales, has become more popular, particularly in areas outside of the major cities.

Businesses generally adhere to a standard 40-hour workweek, though many may close early on Fridays. Most businesses do not keep weekend hours.

31 FOREIGN TRADE

Czechoslovak foreign trade has traditionally involved the import of raw materials, oil and gas, and semi-manufactured products and the export of semifinished products and consumer and capital goods. In 1989, trade with former Eastern bloc nations accounted for 56% of Czechoslovakia's total foreign trade; by the end of 1992 their share had more than halved to 27%.

The Czech Republic engages in the export of numerous manufactured goods that are used in the production of automobiles, furniture, and electrical appliances. The manufacturing of metals, including iron and steel plates and sheets, and base metal bring in 5.7% of export dues. The road vehicle industry results in 15.6% of exports. Other export commodities include textiles (4.3%), glassware (which the country is famous for producing—1.6%), furniture (2.7%), and electrical machinery (2.9%). A majority of these products are exported to Germany.

Total exports grew to $66.5 billion (FOB—Free on Board) in 2004. Machinery and transport equipment made up the bulk of total export at 52%, and were followed by raw materials and fuels (9%), and chemicals (5%). The main destination points were Germany (where 36.1% of total exports went), Slovakia (8.4%), Austria (6%), Poland (5.3%), the United Kingdom (4.7%), France (4.7%), Italy (4.3%), and the Netherlands (4.3%). Imports totaled. $68.2 billion, and came mainly from Germany (31.8%), Slovakia (5.4%), Italy (5.3%), China (5.2%), Poland (4.8%), France (4.8%), and Russia (4.1%). The main import commodities included machinery and transport equipment (46%), raw materials and fuels (15%), and chemicals (10%).

32 BALANCE OF PAYMENTS

The current account balance in 2001 improved from 2000, when it stood at approximately $3.5 billion, or 4.8% of GDP, due to a narrowing trade gap. Strong inflows of foreign direct investment have led to surpluses in the financial account, which easily cover the current account deficit.

The US Central Intelligence Agency (CIA) reported that in 2001 the purchasing power parity of the Czech Republic's exports was $38 billion while imports totaled $41.7 billion resulting in a trade deficit of $3.7 billion.

The International Monetary Fund (IMF) reported that in 2001 the Czech Republic had exports of goods totaling $33.4 billion and imports totaling $36.5 billion. The services credit totaled $7.09 billion and debit $5.6 billion.

Exports of good and services grew faster than imports in 2004, jumping at $76.6 billion (from $56.5 in 2003); imports expanded from $58.5 to $77 billion. Thus, while the resource balance was -$2 billion in 2003, by 2004 it improved to -$400 million. The current account balance remained fairly stable, reaching -$5.6 billion in 2004. The country's total reserves (including gold) grew to $28.5 billion in the same year, covering almost five months of imports.

33 BANKING AND SECURITIES

The Czech National Bank (CNB) is the country's central bank, charged with issuing currency and regulating the state's commercial banking sector. Since mid-1996 domestic credit and M2 growth have fallen sharply. Growth in M2 stood at 7.8% at the end of December 1996, well below the central bank's 13-17% growth

Principal Trading Partners – Czech Republic (2003)

(In millions of US dollars)

Country	Exports	Imports	Balance
World	48,720.4	51,239.3	-2,518.9
Germany	18,025.6	16,685.3	1,340.3
Slovakia	3,884.0	2,656.8	1,227.2
Austira	3,042.8	2,196.9	845.9
United Kingdom	22,621.5	1,389.4	21,232.1
Poland	2,336.4	2,129.9	206.5
France-Monaco	2,304.0	2,525.4	-221.4
Italy-San Marino-Holy See	2,165.3	2,725.7	-560.4
Netherlands	2,010.3	1,122.1	888.2
United States	1,189.4	1,594.2	-404.8
Hungary	1,110.6	1,042.7	67.9

(…) data not available or not significant.

SOURCE: *2003 International Trade Statistics Yearbook,* New York: United Nations, 2004.

Balance of Payments – Czech Republic (2003)

(In millions of US dollars)

Current Account		**-5,661.0**
Balance on goods		-2,505.0
Imports	-51,242.0	
Exports	48,736.0	
Balance on services		559.0
Balance on income		-4,166.0
Current transfers		540.0
Capital Account		**-3.0**
Financial Account		**5,855.0**
Direct investment abroad		-242.0
Direct investment in Czech Republic		2,514.0
Portfolio investment assets		-3,006.0
Portfolio investment liabilities		1,753.0
Financial derivatives		143.0
Other investment assets		2,279.0
Other investment liabilities		2,414.0
Net Errors and Omissions		**251.0**
Reserves and Related Items		**-442.0**

(…) data not available or not significant.

SOURCE: *Balance of Payment Statistics Yearbook 2004,* Washington, DC: International Monetary Fund, 2004.

target for 1996 and in the middle of its 8–12% target range for 1997.

In the mid-1990s, there were 36 commercial and savings banks in the Czech Republic. The state had one state financial bank, 21 Czech joint-stock companies, 6 partly owned foreign banks, and 7 foreign banks. The new Czech Export Bank commenced operations in late 1996. The International Monetary Fund reports that in 2001, currency and demand deposits—an aggregate commonly known as M1—were equal to $15.3 billion. In that same year, M2—an aggregate equal to M1 plus savings deposits, small time deposits, and money market mutual funds—was $42.3 billion. The money market rate, the rate at which financial institutions lend to one another in the short term, was 4.69%. The discount rate, the interest rate at which the central bank lends to financial institutions in the short term, was 4.75%.

The origins of the first exchange in Prague go back to the 1850s when foreign exchange and securities were the principal trading products. An exchange trading securities and commodities was established in 1871. The volumes traded at the exchange fluctuated considerably and in 1938 official trading was suspended. After World War II the operation of the Prague Exchange was not restored and in 1952 the Exchange was officially abolished. In 1990 eight banks became members of the Preparatory Committee on Stock Exchange Foundation. In 1992 this institution transformed itself into a stock exchange. The Prague Stock Exchange has been trading debt securities (mostly government and bank issues) since April 1993. Volume in mid-1993 was Kc18 million, of which two-thirds were listed issues. Leading Czech banks include: Ceská sporitelna (Czech Savings Bank), Investicní a poštovní banka (Investment and Postal Bank), Komercní banka (Commercial Bank), and the Ceskoslovenská obchodní banka (Czechoslovak Commercial Bank). As of 2004, a total of 554 companies were listed on the Prague Stock Exchange. Total capitalization that year totaled $30.863 billion. In 2004, the PX 50 rose 56.6% from the previous year to 1,032.0,

---

Public Finance – Czech Republic (2003)

(In billions of koruny, central government figures)

Revenue and Grants	**852.04**	**100.0%**
Tax revenue	416.1	48.8%
Social contributions	387.25	45.4%
Grants	12.4	1.5%
Other revenue	36.29	4.3%
Expenditures	**979.81**	**100.0%**
General public services	121.63	12.4%
Defense	46.04	4.7%
Public order and safety	56.04	5.7%
Economic affairs	135.03	13.8%
Environmental protection	12.57	1.3%
Housing and community amenities	24.62	2.5%
Health	162.17	16.6%
Recreational, culture, and religion	9.54	1.0%
Education	92.52	9.4%
Social protection	319.66	32.6%

(...) data not available or not significant.

SOURCE: *Government Finance Statistics Yearbook 2004,* Washington, DC: International Monetary Fund, 2004.

---

34 INSURANCE

The pre-World War II insurance companies and institutions of the former Czechoslovakia were reorganized after 1945 and merged, nationalized, and centralized. Since 1952, the insurance industry has been administered by the State Insurance Office, under the jurisdiction of the Ministry of Finance. Two enterprises conducted insurance activities, the Czech and the Slovak Insurance Enterprises of the State.

Property insurance and car insurance are used by more than 80% of the population in the Czech Republic. By 2001, the Czech Republic's state insurance enterprise, Ceska Pojistovna, had been joined by nearly two dozen other firms, including branches of foreign companies. Most offer standard life and health insurance, as well as property coverage and commercial insurance. Third-party auto insurance, workers' compensation, employer's liability and liability for lawyers, auditors, architects, civil engineers, airlines and hunters are compulsory. By law however, Ceska Pojistovna must write the automobile liability cover, and it maintains control of the market. As of 2003, the value of all direct premiums written totaled $3.714 billion, of which nonlife premiums accounted for $2.290 billion. Ceska pojistovna was the country top nonlife and life insurer in that same year, with gross nonlife and life premiums written totaling $835.9 million and $618.4 million, respectively.

By 1997, proposals to switch the country's pay-as-you-go pension system into one incorporating mandatory private savings and voluntary pension insurance were developed. The introduction of such a scheme drew sharp criticism from the opposition and met with skepticism from the CNB, which has indicated that the quality of capital market regulation would have to improve considerably before pension funds of the kind proposed could be built up.

35 PUBLIC FINANCE

In the early 1990s, it was estimated that about 97% of businesses were under state control. By 2003, the nonprivate sector accounted for less than 20% of business ownership. In fact, the Czech Republic's economy advanced so quickly out of communism that the country was admitted to the EU in 2004.

The US Central Intelligence Agency (CIA) estimated that in 2005 Czech Republic's central government took in revenues of approximately $48.1 billion and had expenditures of $53 billion. Revenues minus expenditures totaled approximately -$4.8 billion. Public debt in 2005 amounted to 33.1% of GDP. Total external debt was $43.2 billion.

The International Monetary Fund (IMF) reported that in 2003, the most recent year for which it had data, central government revenues were Kc852.04 billion and expenditures were Kc979.81 billion. The value of revenues was us$30 million and expenditures us$34 million, based on an official exchange rate for 2003 of us$1 = Kc28.209 as reported by the IMF. Government outlays by function were as follows: general public services, 12.4%; defense, 4.7%; public order and safety, 5.7%; economic affairs, 13.8%; environmental protection, 1.3%; housing and community amenities, 2.5%; health, 16.6%; recreation, culture, and religion, 1.0%; education, 9.4%; and social protection, 32.6%.

36 TAXATION

As of 1 January 2006, the standard corporate income tax rate in the Czech Republic is 24%. Dividends are subject to a withholding tax of 15% and are not included in taxable income. If 25% of the shares have been held for two years, a participation exemption applies. Personal income tax is progressive with four brackets and a top rate of 32% (15% up to yearly income of about $4,000, 20% on income between $4,000 and $8,000, 25% on income between $8,000 and $12,000, and 32% on income above $12,000, with additional lump sums of $600, $1400, and $2400, respectively, paid at the 20%, 25%, and 32% levels). Payroll taxes of 47.5% (35% paid by the employer and 12.5% paid by the employee) cover pension insurance, sickness insurance, and employment insurance. There is a real estate transfer tax of 3%; gift taxes of 1–40%; and inheritance taxes of 0.5–20%. Withholding taxes are applied to income of nonresidents: 15% on income from dividends and interest; and 25% on income from royalties and operating licenses. The Czech Republic has bilateral tax treaties (BITs) with about 65 countries. In the BITs withholding rates are generally lower.

The main indirect tax is a system of value-added taxes (VATs) which replaced turnover taxes as of 1 January 1993. There are three VAT rates: 19% on most goods and some services; 5% on basic foodstuffs, minerals, pharmaceuticals, medical equipment, paper products, books, newspapers, and public transport services; and 0% on exports.

37 CUSTOMS AND DUTIES

On 1 January 1993, Czechoslovakia divided into two independent states, the Czech Republic and the Slovak Republic. Both states maintain a customs union that continues most of the same trade policies of the former Czechoslovakia. All imports into the Czech Republic, except those from the Slovak Republic, are subject to an ad valorem rate of up to 80%, but with an average of 4.6%. There is also a value-added tax (VAT) of 19% for everything except necessities, such as food and pharmaceuticals, for which it is 5%. Preferential treatment is granted to developing countries. The Czech Republic has trade agreements with Bulgaria, Hungary, Poland, Romania, Slovakia, and Slovenia, which comprise the Central European Free Trade Agreement (CEFTA).

38 FOREIGN INVESTMENT

Moody's Investors Service gave the Czech Republic the first investment-grade A rating to be awarded to a former Soviet bloc country. As of 2001, foreign direct investment (FDI) stock per capita in the Czech Republic was $2,432, the highest among the Eastern European transitional economies. FDI has served Czech economic development in providing capital and managerial expertise for restructuring its enterprises. National treatment is the general rule, with screening of foreign investment proposals required only in banking, insurance and defense industries. A competitive exchange rate and low wages have been conducive to foreign investment, but in 1998 a six-point incentive package approved by the Czech government helped ratchet annual FDI inflows to about double previous levels. Incentives—tax breaks up to 10 years, duty-free imports, rent reductions, benefits for job creation, training grants, and incentives for reinvestments and expansions—are available for investments above $10 million, or above $5 million

in regions where unemployment is over 25%. The Czech Republic has also authorized nine commercial or industrial custom-free zones that operate according to the same rules as those in the European Union. By 2002, the government had negotiated bilateral investment treaties (BITs) with 66 countries, the BIT with the United States in force since 1992.

From 1993 to 2001, the Czech Republic attracted $26.76 billion cumulative FDI inflow, of which 27.6% has come from the Netherlands, 26% from Germany, 10.2% from Austria, 8.6% from France, 6.2% from the United States, 4.1% from Belgium, 3.8% from Switzerland, 3.1% from the United Kingdom, 1.9% from Denmark, and 8.5% from other counties. Annual FDI inflow jumped from about $880 million in 1993 to 2.5 billion in 1995 due to the first foreign investment in the state-owned telecommunications system and German investment in the automotive industry. In 1997, FDI inflow had fallen back to $1.3 billion, but in 1998, with the introduction of incentives for foreign investment, FDI inflow rose to $3.7 billion and then spiked to $6.3 billion in 1999. For 2000 and 2001, annual FDI was just below $5 billion, and in 2002, reached a record $7.5 billion. By economic sector, the principal destinations for FDI flows into the Czech Republic from 1990 to 2000 have been financial intermediation (18%), wholesale trade (15%), nonmetallic mineral products manufacture (7.5%), and motor vehicle manufacture (6.5%). Other significant areas have been food and beverages, energy, and retail sales. In 2000, direct investment outflow from the Czech Republic totaled $726 million, 37.7% to Slovenia, 25.6% to Poland, and 15.9% to Russia.

In 2002, the inflow of capital from abroad reached $9.3 billion—the second-largest FDI per capita in Central and Easter Europe, after Slovenia. The total stock of foreign investment was $41.1 billion in 1993–2003, growing by almost $14 billion between 2002 and 2003, and averaging $4.1 billion annually. Germany and the Netherlands were the main investors, with $11.3 billion (31%) and $9.6 billion (26.0%) respectively. They were followed by the United States and Austria, with $3.6 billion (10.1%) each, France with $2.2 billion (6%), and the United Kingdom with $1.9 billion (5.2%). Overall, the Czech Republic has received more FDI per capita than any other country in Central and Eastern Europe, most of it going towards manufacturing, financial services, hotels and restaurants, and transportation and telecommunications.

39 ECONOMIC DEVELOPMENT

Post-communist economic recovery has been implemented by development of the private sector, particularly in the trade and services areas, increased exports to industrialized nations, control of inflation, and achievement of a positive trade balance. The most promising growth sectors are those involving advanced technology, environmental protection, biotechnology, and, generally, high value-added production. At the end of 1996, approximately 80% of the Czech Republic's large companies had been privatized, most via voucher privatization, through which nearly six million Czechs bought vouchers exchangeable for shares in companies that were to be privatized. By 1997, however, the recovery had petered out and the Czech Republic plunged into a recession which lasted through 1999. Most analysts blamed the downturn on an incomplete restructuring.

In 2002, the nonprivate sector accounted for only 20% of business; however, the state has retained minority shares in many heavy industrial enterprises, and many large firms were placed under the control of state-owned banks due to voucher privatization. (Bank privatization was in the completion stages in 2003.) The EU contributed significant resources to prepare the country for accession, including speeding administrative, regulatory, and judicial reform; accession to the EU was completed in 2004. The government is faced with high unemployment; a need for industrial restructuring; transformation of the housing sector; reform of the pension and healthcare systems; and a solution to environmental problems. The decline in industry's contribution to the economy has led to factory closings and job losses. Real gross domestic product (GDP) growth increased to 2.2% in the first quarter of 2003, despite the global economic recession and in part due to high household consumption.

By 2004 the GDP growth rate reached 4.0%, and its increase was attributed to significant inflows of foreign capital and growing consumer demand. High investment rates have managed to expand productivity, and helped create new jobs and increase real wages. Inflation remained fairly low over this time period, strengthening the national currency, but at the same time undermining the export sector. As part of the EU, the Czech Republic can tap into a large market, and its maturing economy allows it to compete with countries from Western Europe.

40 SOCIAL DEVELOPMENT

Social welfare programs in the former Czechoslovakia dated back to the Austro-Hungarian Empire. Work injury laws were first introduced in 1887 and sickness benefits in 1888. During the First Republic (1918–39), social insurance was improved and extended. After World War II, new social legislation made sickness, accident, disability, and old age insurance compulsory. The trade unions administered health insurance and family allowances. The government's Bureau of Pension Insurance administered the pension insurance program, which was funded by the government and employers. In 1960, social welfare committees were established within the regional and district national committees to exercise closer control.

Current programs include old age pensions, disability, survivor benefits, sickness and maternity, work injury, unemployment, and family allowances. Employers are required to contribute 21.5% of payroll, while employees contribute 6.5% to the pensions program. The retirement age has been gradually increasing.

In recent years, women have played an increasingly greater role in Czech society and now account for about half of the labor force. Although the principle of equal pay for equal work is generally followed, women hold a disproportionate share of lower-paying positions. The unemployment rate for women is greater than for men, and only a small number of women hold senior positions in the work force. Rape and domestic violence is underreported, although societal attitudes are slowly improving to help victims seek assistance from authorities. In 2004, the Criminal Code was amended to recognize domestic violence as a distinct crime. Crisis centers exist to help victims of sexual abuse and violence. Sexual harassment is prohibited by law. Trafficking in women and children is evident.

The Roma minority, officially estimated to number 150,000–175,000, face discrimination in housing, employment, and often are subject to harassment. Racially motivated crime is on the increase, as is skinhead activity. Religious freedom is generally tolerated. The Czech Republic's human rights record is fairly good, although judicial backlogs result in extended pretrial detention in some cases and sporadic police violence has been reported.

41 HEALTH

The Czech health care system combines compulsory universal health insurance with mixed public and private care. Health insurance is funded by individuals, employers, and the government. A number of physicians have private practices and maintain contracts with the insurance system for reimbursement of their services. As of 2004, there were an estimated 342 physicians, 946 nurses, 65 dentists, 51 pharmacists, and 48 midwives per 100,000 people. Health care expenditure was estimated at 7.2% of GDP.

Health activities are directed by the Ministry of Health through the National Health Service. Factories and offices have health services, ranging from first-aid facilities in small enterprises to hospitals in the largest. All school children receive medical attention, including inoculations, X-rays, and annual examinations. In 1999, children up to one year of age were immunized for the following diseases: diphtheria, pertussis, and tetanus, 98%; and measles, 95%.

Special attention has been devoted to preventive medicine, with campaigns waged against tuberculosis, venereal diseases, cancer, poliomyelitis, diphtheria, and mental disturbances. Diseases of the circulatory system are the leading cause of death. Free guidance and care given to women and children have resulted in a low infant mortality rate of 3.93 per 1,000 live births in 2005, one of the lowest in the world. The total fertility rate in the same year was 1.2. The maternal mortality rate in 1998 was low at 14 maternal deaths per 100,000 live births. Average life expectancy in 2005 was 76.02 years. The HIV/AIDS prevalence was 0.10 per 100 adults in 2003. As of 2004, there were approximately 2,500 people living with HIV/AIDS in the country. There were 10 reported deaths from AIDS in 2003.

42 HOUSING

Currently, the lack of affordable housing, which inhibits labor mobility, is a major factor slowing economic growth in the Czech Republic. Problems include lack of financing, shortages of materials and labor, and a poorly developed infrastructure. In the mid-1990s the government drafted a new housing policy which, among other things, would lift existing restrictive legal provisions barring occupants from buying and reselling flats and differentiate rents according to quality and location of flats.

According to the 2001 census, there were about 4,366,293 dwelling units within the country with about 87% permanently occupied. About 1,969,568 dwellings are houses. There is an average of 2.69 people per household.

43 EDUCATION

Education is under state control and free, up to and including the university level. Nine years of education are compulsory. There is a general primary school program that lasts for nine years. However, after the fifth year, some students may choose to enter more specialized programs that will include their secondary education studies as well. Secondary programs include general academic studies (gymnasium), vocational studies, technical programs, or art studies (music and drama). The academic year runs from September to June. The primary languages of instruction are Czech, German, and English.

In 2001, about 95% of children between the ages of three and five were enrolled in some type of preschool program. Primary school enrollment in 2003 was estimated at about 87% of age-eligible students. The same year, secondary school enrollment was about 90% of age-eligible students. Most students complete their primary education. The student-to-teacher ratio for primary school was at about 17:1 in 2003; the ratio for secondary school was about 11:1.

Universities in the current Czech Republic include the world-famous Charles University at Prague (founded 1348); Palacky University at Olomouc (1576; reestablished 1946); and J. E. Purkyne University at Brno (1919; reestablished 1945). In 2003, about 36% of the tertiary age population were enrolled in some type of higher education program. The adult literacy rate is estimated at about 99%.

As of 2003, public expenditure on education was estimated at 4.4% of GDP, or 9.6% of total government expenditures.

44 LIBRARIES AND MUSEUMS

The National Library of the Czech Republic (six million volumes in 2005) in Prague is the result of a 1958 amalgamation of six Prague libraries, including the venerable University Library, founded in 1348. It holds a valuable expensive collection of Mozart's papers and manuscripts. Other collections of significance are the university libraries at Brno and Olomouc. The State Research Library, including all six of its branches, holds more than six million volumes. In 1997, the Czech Republic had 6,245 public libraries with 53.7 million volumes and 1.4 million registered users. The Jirí Mahen Library in Brno, established in 1921, is the largest municipal library in the region of Moravia; the library holds about 800,000 books and operates a system of 35 branch locations. The Association of Library and Information Professionals of the Czech Republic had about 1,200 members in 2005.

Castles, mansions, churches, and other buildings of historical interest are public property. Many serve as museums and galleries. The largest museum in the country is the world-famous National Museum in Prague. The National Gallery, also in Prague, contains outstanding collections of medieval art and 17th-century and 18th-century Dutch paintings. Other Prague museums of note include the Jewish Museum, the Antonin Dvorak Museum (celebrating the life of the Czech composer, 1841–1904), and the Museum of Toys, holding the world's second-largest exposition of toys. Other outstanding museums and galleries are located in Brno and Plzen. The Prague Botanical Gardens are among the finest in Europe.

45 MEDIA

In 2003, there were an estimated 360 mainline telephones for every 1,000 people; about 27,300 people were on a waiting list for telephone service installation. The same year, there were approximately 965 mobile phones in use for every 1,000 people.

In 2000, there were 31 AM and 304 FM radio stations and 150 television stations. In 2003, there were an estimated 803 radios and 538 television sets for every 1,000 people. About 94.4 of every 1,000 people were cable subscribers. In 2003, there were 177.4 personal computers for every 1,000 people and 308 of every 1,000 people had access to the Internet. There were 316 secure Internet servers in the country in 2004.

Major newspapers, their publishers (where applicable), and estimated 2002 circulation totals are: *Blesk*, 420,000; *Hospodarske Noviny*, 130,000; *Mladá Fronta*, Socialist Union of Youth, 350,000; *Moravskoslezsky Den*, 130,000; *Obansky Denikof*, 109,000; *Práce*, Revolutionary Trade Union Movement, 220,600; *Rudé Právo*, Communist Party, 350,000; *Svobodné Slovo*, Socialist Party, 230,000; *Svoboda*, 100,000; and *Vecernik Praha*, 130,000.

Formerly, the Communist Party and the government controlled all publishing. Formal censorship, via the government's Office for Press and Information, was lifted for three months during the Prague Spring of 1968, but prevailed after that time until the late 1980s. As of 1999, the government was said to fully uphold the legally provided freedoms of free speech and a free press.

46 ORGANIZATIONS

The most important umbrella labor organization is the Czech and Slovak Confederation of Trade Unions, an organization that promotes democracy. The World Federation of Trade Unions has an office in Prague. Confederation of Industry of the Czech Republic (est. 1990) is also in Prague. Professional societies representing a wide variety of careers are also active. Important political associations include the Czech Democratic Left Movements and the Civic Movement. The Center for Democracy and Free Enterprise (est. 1991) promotes development of democratic institutions and a free market economy.

The Academy of Sciences of the Czech Republic was founded in 1993 to support and encourage research and educational institutions involved in the fields of natural and technical sciences, social sciences, and humanities.

Youth organizations include the Czech Association of Scouts and Guides (CASG), YMCA and YWCA, and chapters of The Red Cross Youth. There are many sports associations in the country, some of which are affiliated with international organizations as well. National women's organizations include the Gender Studies Center in Prague and the Czech Union of Women.

Multinational organizations based in Prague include the International Association for Vehicle Systems Dynamics and the International Union of Speleology. There are national chapters of Amnesty International and the Red Cross.

47 TOURISM, TRAVEL, AND RECREATION

Prague, which survived World War II relatively intact, has numerous palaces and churches from the Renaissance and Baroque periods. There are many attractive mountain resorts, especially in northern Bohemia. The mineral spas in Prague are popular as well as the historic monuments. Football (soccer), ice hockey, skiing, canoeing, swimming, and tennis are among the favorite sports. A passport is required for all foreign nationals, whether temporary visitors or transit passengers. Visas are not required for stays of up to 90 days.

There were 94,984,476 tourist arrivals in 2003. Hotel rooms numbered 97,282, with 225,288 beds and an occupancy rate of 35%. Tourist receipts amounted to $4 billion, and the average stay was three nights.

In 2004, the US Department of State estimated the cost of staying in Prague at $306 per day.

⁴⁸FAMOUS CZECHS

The founder of modern Czechoslovakia was Tomáš Garrigue Masaryk (1850–1937), a philosopher-statesman born of a Slovak father and a Czech mother. Eduard Beneš (1884–1948), cofounder with Masaryk of the Czechoslovak Republic, was foreign minister, premier, and president of the republic (1935–38 and 1940–48). Jan Masaryk (1886–1948), son of Tomáš G. Masaryk, was foreign minister of the government-in-exile and, until his mysterious death, of the reconstituted republic. Klement Gottwald (1896–1953) became a leader of the Czechoslovak Communist Party in 1929 and was the president of the republic from 1948 to 1953; Antonín Zápotock (1884–1957), a trade union leader, was president from 1953 to 1957. Alexander Dubček (1921–92) was secretary of the Czechoslovak Communist Party and principal leader of the 1968 reform movement that ended with Soviet intervention. Gen. Ludvík Svoboda (1895–1979) was president of the republic from 1968 to 1975. Gustáv Husák (1913–91) was general secretary of the Communist Party from 1969 to 1987; he became president of the republic in 1975. Parliamentary elections at the end of 1989 saw the rise of the playwright Vaclav Havel (b.1936) to power. The Czech and Slovak republics decided to split in 1992. Havel was elected first president of the Czech Republic in parliamentary elections. Vaclav Klaus (b.1941) was elected the second president of the Czech Republic in 2003.

Perhaps the two most famous Czechs are the religious reformer John Huss (Jan Hus, 1371–1415) and the theologian, educator, and philosopher John Amos Comenius (Jan Amos Komensk, 1592–1670), an early advocate of universal education. *The History of the Czech People* by František Palack (1798–1876) inspired Czech nationalism. Karel Havliček (1821–56) was a leading political journalist, while Alois Jirásek (1851–1930) is known for his historical novels. The most famous woman literary figure is Božena Němcová (1820–62), whose *Babička (The Grandmother)*, depicting country life, is widely read to this day. A poet of renown, Jaroslav Vrchlick (1853–1912) wrote voluminous poetry and translations. *The Good Soldier Schweik* by Jaroslav Hašek (1883–1923) is a renowned satire on militarism. Karel Capek (1890–1938), brilliant novelist, journalist, and playwright, is well known for his play *R.U.R.* (in which he coined the word *robot*). Jan Patočka (1907–77) was one of the most influential Central European philosophers of the 20th century. Bedřich Smetana (1824–84), Antonín Dvořák (1841–1904), Leoš Janáček (1854–1928), and Bohuslav Martinu (1890–1959) are world-famous composers. The leading modern sculptor, Jan Stursa (1880–1925), is best known for his often-reproduced *The Wounded*.

Prominent 20th-century Czech personalities in culture and the arts include the writers Vladislav Vančura (1891–1942) and Ladislav Fuks (1923–94), the painter Jan Zrzav (1890–1977), and the Czech filmmakers Jirí Trnka (1912–69) and Karel Ze-

man (1910–89). Leaders of the "new wave" of Czechoslovak cinema in the 1960s were Ján Kadár (1918–79) and Miloš Forman (b.1932), both expatriates after 1968. Josef Koudelka (b.1938) is a Czech photographer who resides in France. The best-known political dissidents in the 1970s and 1980s were the playwrights Pavel Kohout (b.1928) and Václav Havel (b.1936), and the sociologist Rudolf Battek (b.1924). The novelist Milan Kundera (b.1929), who has lived in France since 1975, is the best-known contemporary Czech writer. Czechs have become top world tennis players: Martina Navrátilová (b.1956), expatriate since 1975, Ivan Lendl (b.1960), Hana Mandlíková (b.1962), Jana Novotná (b.1968), and Martina Hingis (b.1980) have thrilled audiences with their skills on the courts.

There have been only two Czechoslovak Nobel Prize winners: in chemistry in 1959, Jaroslav Heyrovsk (1890–1967), who devised an electrochemical method of analysis; and in literature in 1984, the poet Jaroslav Seifert (1901–86).

⁴⁹DEPENDENCIES

The Czech Republic has no territories or colonies.

⁵⁰BIBLIOGRAPHY

Andreyev, Catherine. *Russia Abroad: Prague and the Russian Diaspora, 1918–1938*. New Haven, Ct.: Yale University Press, 2004.

Appel, Hilary. *A New Capitalist Order: Privatization and Ideology in Russia and Eastern Europe*. Pittsburgh, Pa.: University of Pittsburgh Press, 2004.

Boehm, Barbara Drake and Jiri Fajt (eds.). *Prague: The Crown of Bohemia, 1347–1437*. New York: Metropolitan Museum of Art, 2005.

Bradley, J. F. N. *Czechoslovakia's Velvet Revolution: A Political Analysis*. New York: Columbia University Press, 1992.

———. *Politics in Czechoslovakia, 1945–1990*. New York: Columbia University Press, 1991.

Burton, Richard D. E. *Prague: A Cultural and Literary History*. New York: Interlink Books, 2003.

Cottey, Andrew. *East-Central Europe After the Cold War: Poland, the Czech Republic, Slovakia and Hungary in Search of Security*. Houndmills, England: Macmillan Press, 1995.

Eckhart, Karl, et al (eds.) *Social, Economic and Cultural Aspects in the Dynamic Changing Process of Old Industrial Regions: Ruhr District (Germany), Upper Silesia (Poland), Ostrava Region (Czech Republic)*. Piscataway, N.J.: Transaction Publishers, 2003

Frucht, Richard (ed.). *Eastern Europe: An Introduction to the People, Lands, and Culture*. Santa Barbara, Calif.: ABC-CLIO, 2005.

Holy, Ladislav. *The Little Czech and the Great Czech Nation: National Identity and the Post-Communist Transformation of Society*. Cambridge: Cambridge University Press, 1996.

Hoshi, Iraj, Ewa Balcerowicz, Leszek Balcerowicz (eds.). *Barriers to Entry and Growth of New Firms in Early Transition: A Comparative Study of Poland, Hungary, Czech Republic, Albania, and Lithuania*. Boston: Kluwer Academic Publishers, 2003.

International Smoking Statistics: A Collection of Historical Data from 30 Economically Developed Countries. New York: Oxford University Press, 2002.

Kriseova, Eda. *Vaclav Havel: the Authorized Biography*. New York: St. Martin's Press, 1993.

Lawson, George. *Negotiated Revolutions: The Czech Republic, South Africa and Chile*. Burlington, Vt.: Ashgate, 2005.

McElrath, Karen (ed.). *HIV and AIDS: A Global View*. Westport, Conn.: Greenwood Press, 2002.

Otfinoski, Steven. *The Czech Republic*. 2nd ed. New York: Facts On File, 2004.

Reuvid, Jonathan, (eds.). *Doing Business with the Czech Republic*. London: Kogan Page, 2002.

Shawcross, William. *Dubček*. New York: Simon and Schuster, 1990.

———. *Dubček: Dubček and Czechoslovakia, 1968–1990*. London: Hogarth, 1990.

Vogt, Henri. *Between Utopia and Disillusionment: A Narrative of the Political Transformation in Eastern Europe*. New York: Berghahn Books, 2004.

DENMARK

Kingdom of Denmark
Kongeriget Danmark

CAPITAL: Copenhagen (København)

FLAG: The Danish national flag, known as the Dannebrog, is one of the oldest national flags in the world, although the concept of a national flag did not develop until the late 18th century when the Dannebrog was already half a millennium old. The design shows a white cross on a field of red.

ANTHEM: There are two national anthems—*Kong Kristian stod ved hojen mast (King Christian Stood by the Lofty Mast)* and *Der er et yndigt land (There Is a Lovely Land).*

MONETARY UNIT: The krone (Kr) of 100 øre is a commercially convertible paper currency with one basic official exchange rate. There are coins of 25 and 50 øre, and 1, 5, 10, and 20 kroner, and notes of 50, 100, 500, and 1,000 kroner. Kr1 = $0.16863 (or $1 = Kr5.93) as of 2005.

WEIGHTS AND MEASURES: The metric system is the legal standard, but some local units are used for special purposes.

HOLIDAYS: New Year's Day, 1 January; Constitution Day, 5 June; Christmas Day, 25 December; Boxing Day, 26 December. Movable religious holidays include Holy Thursday, Good Friday, Easter Monday, Prayer Day (4th Friday after Easter), Ascension, and Whitmonday.

TIME: 1 PM = noon GMT.

¹LOCATION, SIZE, AND EXTENT

Situated in southern Scandinavia, the Kingdom of Denmark consists of Denmark proper, the Faroe Islands, and Greenland. Denmark proper, comprising the peninsula of Jutland (Jylland) and 406 islands (97 of them inhabited), has an area of 43,094 sq km (16,638 sq mi) and extends about 402 km (250 mi) N–S and 354 km (220 mi) E–W. Comparatively, the area occupied by Denmark is slightly less than twice the size of the state of Massachusetts. The Jutland Peninsula accounts for 29,767 sq km (11,493 sq mi) of the total land area, while the islands have a combined area of 13,317 sq km (5,142 sq mi). Except for the southern boundary with Germany, the country is surrounded by water—Skagerrak on the N, Kattegat, Øresund, and Baltic Sea on the E, and the North Sea on the W. Denmark's total boundary length is 7,382 km (4,587 mi), of which only 68 km (42 mi) is the land boundary with Germany.

Bornholm, one of Denmark's main islands, is situated in the Baltic Sea, less than 160 km (100 mi) due E of Denmark and about 40 km (25 mi) from southern Sweden. It has an area of 588 sq km (227 sq mi) and at its widest point is 40 km (25 mi) across.

Denmark's capital city, Copenhagen, is located on the eastern edge of the country on the island of Sjaelland.

²TOPOGRAPHY

The average altitude of Denmark is about 30 m (98 ft), and the highest point, Yding Skovhoj in southeastern Jutland, is only 173 m (568 ft). In parts of Jutland, along the southern coast of the island of Lolland, and in a few other areas, the coast is protected by dikes. All of Denmark proper (except for the extreme southeast of the island of Bornholm, which is rocky) consists of a glacial de-posit over a chalk base. The surface comprises small hills, moors, ridges, hilly islands, raised sea bottoms, and, on the west coast, downs and marshes. There are many small rivers and inland seas. Good natural harbors are provided by the many fjords and bays.

³CLIMATE

Denmark has a temperate climate, the mildness of which is largely conditioned by the generally westerly winds and by the fact that the country is virtually encircled by water. There is little fluctuation between day and night temperatures, but sudden changes in wind direction cause considerable day-to-day temperature changes. The mean temperature in February, the coldest month, is 0°C (32°F), and in July, the warmest, 17°C (63°F). Rain falls fairly evenly throughout the year, the annual average amounting to approximately 61 cm (24 in).

⁴FLORA AND FAUNA

Plants and animals are those common to middle Europe. There are many species of ferns, flower, fungi, and mosses; common trees include spruce and beech. Few wild or large animals remain. Birds, however, are abundant; many species breed in Denmark and migrate to warmer countries during the autumn and winter. Fish and insects are plentiful. As of 2002, there were at least 43 species of mammals, 196 species of birds, and over 1,400 species of plants throughout the country.

⁵ENVIRONMENT

Denmark's most basic environmental legislation is the Environmental Protection Act of 1974, which entrusts the Ministry of the Environment, in conjunction with local authorities, with antipollution responsibilities. The basic principle is that the polluter must pay the cost of adapting facilities to environmental requirements; installations built before 1974, however, are eligible for government subsidies to cover the cost of meeting environmental standards.

Land and water pollution are two of Denmark's most significant environmental problems although much of Denmark's household and industrial waste is recycled. In the mid-1990s, Denmark averaged 447.3 thousand tons of solid waste per year. Animal wastes are responsible for polluting both drinking and surface water. Nitrogen and phosphorus pollution threaten the quality of North Sea waters. A special treatment plant at Nyborg, on the island of Fyn, handles dangerous chemical and oil wastes. The nation has about 6 cu km of renewable water resources with 43% of annual withdrawals used for farming and 27% for industrial purposes.

Remaining environmental problems include air pollution, especially from automobile emissions; excessive noise, notably in the major cities; and the pollution of rivers, lakes, and open sea by raw sewage. In the early 1990s Denmark ranked among 50 nations with the heaviest industrial carbon dioxide emissions. In 1996, emissions totaled 56.5 million metric tons per year. In 2000, the emissions total dropped to 44.6 million metric tons.

As of 2003, Denmark had at least 220 protected sites, with an area of over 1.3 million hectares, or about 34% of the total land area. The Ilulissat Icefjord is a natural UNESCO World Heritage Site; there are 38 Ramsar wetland sites. According to a 2006 report issued by the International Union for Conservation of Nature and Natural Resources (IUCN), threatened species included 4 types of mammals, 10 species of birds, 7 species of fish, 1 type of mollusk, 10 species of other invertebrates, and 3 species of plants. Endangered species include the coalfish whale, blue whale, loggerhead, leatherback turtle, and Atlantic sturgeon.

6 POPULATION

The population of Denmark in 2005 was estimated by the United Nations (UN) at 5,418,000, which placed it at number 108 in population among the 193 nations of the world. In 2005, approximately 15% of the population was over 65 years of age, with another 19% of the population under 15 years of age. There were 98 males for every 100 females in the country. According to the UN, the annual population rate of change for 2005–10 was expected to be 0.2%, a rate the government viewed as satisfactory. The projected population for the year 2025 was 5,527,000. The population density was 126 per sq km (326 per sq mi).

The UN estimated that 72% of the population lived in urban areas in 2005, and that urban areas were growing at an annual rate of 0.28%. The capital city, København (Copenhagen), had a population of 1,066,000 in that year. Other large towns are Aarhus (Århus), 291,258; Odense, 184,308; Aalborg (Ålborg), 162,521; Esbjerg, 82,314; and Randers, 62,252.

7 MIGRATION

Emigration is limited, owing mainly to the relatively high standard of living in Denmark. There are 500 refugees accepted every year by Denmark for resettlement. These refugees are those who need an alternative place to their first country of asylum, usually for protection-related reasons. An Integration Act took effect 1 January 1999. Under this act, most foreign nationals, including

refugees, must participate in a three-year integration program, during which their social assistance is reduced. In 2004 Denmark received 65,310 refugees. The main countries of origin for these refugees were Bosnia and Herzegovina (25,395), Iraq (11,831), and Afghanistan (6,369). Also in 2004, Denmark received 3,235 asylum applications; of these, about 15% were given permission to stay. The countries of origin for asylum seekers were Bosnia and Herzegovina, Iraq, Palestine, Russia, Serbia and Montenegro, Somalia, and Iran.

In April 1999 the government enacted a plan ("Lex Kosovo") to provide temporary protection for evacuees from Macedonia. (These were Kosovars who had already sought asylum in Denmark but whose cases were pending or had been rejected.) Under this plan, all were granted temporary protection for a renewable six-month period. As of August 1999, 2,823 people had been evacuated from Macedonia to Denmark.

In 2005 the net migration rate was estimated as 2.53 migrants per 1,000 population.

8 ETHNIC GROUPS

The population of Denmark proper is of indigenous northern European stock, and the Danes are among the most homogeneous peoples of Europe. The population is comprised of Scandinavian, Inuit (Eskimo), and Faeroese peoples. There is also a small German minority in southern Jutland and small communities of Turks, Iranians, and Somalis.

9 LANGUAGES

Danish is the universal language. In addition to the letters of the English alphabet, it has the letters ae, ø, and å. A spelling reform of 1948 replaced aa by å, but English transliteration usually retains the aa. There are many dialects, but they are gradually being supplanted by standard Danish. Modern Danish has departed further from the ancient Nordic language of the Viking period than have Icelandic, Norwegian, and Swedish (to which Danish is closely related), and there is a substantial admixture of German and English words. Danish may be distinguished from the other Scandinavian languages by its change of k, p, and t to g, b, and d, in certain situations and by its use of the glottal stop. Faeroese and Greenlandic (an Eskimo dialect) are also used. Many Danes have a speaking knowledge of English and German, and many more are capable of understanding these languages.

10 RELIGIONS

About 84.3% of the people are nominally members of the official state religion, the Evangelical Lutheran Church, which is supported by the state and headed by the sovereign. Only about 3% of these Evangelical Lutherans are active members. Muslims are the next largest group with about 3% of the population. Protestants and Roman Catholics together make up another 3% of the population. Christian denominations represented in the country include Baptists, Jehovah's Witnesses, Methodists, Seventh-Day Adventists, The Church of Jesus Christ of Latter-day Saints (Mormons), Anglicans, and Russian Orthodox. Copenhagen is the site of the European headquarters for the Church of Scientology, which is not officially recognized as a religion by the state. There are about 7,000 Jews in the country. An indigenous religion known as Forn

LOCATION: 54°33′31″ to 57°44′55″ N; 8°4′36″ to 15°11′59″ E. BOUNDARY LENGTHS: Germany, 68 kilometers (42 miles); total coastline, 7,314 kilometers (4,545 miles).
TERRITORIAL SEA LIMIT: 3 miles.

Sidr was officially recognized in 2003; followers worship the old Norse gods. About 5.4% of the population claim no religious affiliation and 1.5% claim to be atheists.

Religious freedom is provided by the constitution and this right is generally respected in practice. As the official church of state, the Evangelical Lutheran Church is the only church which receives state funding. A number of other religious groups have complained that this system is unfair and contrary to religious equality. In 1999 an independent four-member council appointed by the government published guidelines and principles for official approval of religious organizations. The guidelines establish clear requirements that religious organizations must fulfill, including providing a full written text of the religion's central traditions, descriptions of its rituals, an organizational structure accessible for public control and approval, and constitutionally elected representatives who can be held responsible by authorities. The guidelines also forbid organizations to "teach or perform actions inconsistent with public morality or order." Official approval offers tax-exempt status to the organization and marriages within approved churches are automatically recognized by the state.

11 TRANSPORTATION

Transportation is highly developed in Denmark. The road system is well engineered and adequately maintained. Among the most important bridges are the Storstrom Bridge linking the islands of Sjaelland and Falster, and the Little Belt Bridge linking Fyn and Jutland. A new train and auto link joins Sjaell and Fyn (18 km/11 mi); a new series of bridges connecting Denmark to Sweden—spanning 4.9 mi across the Oresund Strait and costing Kr13.9 billion—opened in July 2000. The link reduces transit time between the two countries to 15 minutes for cars and trucks and less than 10 minutes for high-speed trains. Cars travel on the upper tier and trains on the lower. As of 2002, Denmark had 71,474 km (44,414 mi) of roadways, all of which were paved, including 880 km (547 mi) of expressways. In 2003, Denmark had 1,894,649 passenger cars and 428,949 commercial vehicles registered for use.

The railway system had a total of 2,628 km (1,635 mi) of standard gauge railroad in 2004, of which 595 km (370 mi) was electrified.

The Danish merchant fleet as of 2005 was composed of 287 ships of at least 1,000 GRT, for a total of 6,952,473 GRT. The majority of these vessels belonged to the Danish International Registry, an offshore registry program allowing foreign-owned vessels to sail under the Danish flag. Denmark, which pioneered the use of motor-driven ships, has many excellent and well-equipped harbors, of which Copenhagen is the most important. Denmark also had 417 km of navigable inland waterways, as of 2001.

There were an estimated 97 airports in 2004, of which 28 had paved runways as of 2005. Kastrup Airport near Copenhagen is a center of international air traffic. Domestic traffic is handled by Danish Airlines in conjunction with SAS, a joint Danish, Norwegian, and Swedish enterprise. In 2003, about 5.886 million passengers were carried on scheduled domestic and international airline flights.

12 HISTORY

Although there is evidence of agricultural settlement as early as 4000 BC and of bronze weaponry and jewelry by 1800 BC, Denmark's early history is little known. Tribesmen calling themselves Danes arrived from Sweden around AD 500, and Danish sailors later took part in the Viking raids, especially in those against England. Harald Bluetooth (d.985), first Christian king of Denmark, conquered Norway, and his son Sweyn conquered England. During the reign of Canute II (1017–35), Denmark, Norway, and England were united, but in 1042, with the death of Canute's son, Hardecanute, the union with England came to an end, and Norway seceded. During the next three centuries, however, Danish hegemony was reestablished over Sweden and Norway, and in the reign of Margrethe (1387–1412) there was a union of the Danish, Norwegian, and Swedish crowns. In 1523, the Scandinavian union was dissolved, but Norway remained united with Denmark until 1814.

The Reformation was established in Denmark during the reign of Christian III (1534–59). A series of wars with Sweden during the 17th and early 18th centuries resulted in the loss of Danish territory. Meanwhile, under Frederik III (r.1648–70) and Christian

V (r.1670–99), absolute monarchy was established and strengthened; it remained in force until 1849. Freedom of the press and improved judicial administration, introduced by Count Johann von Struensee, adviser (1770–72) to Christian VII, were abrogated after his fall from favor. Having allied itself with Napoleon, Denmark was deprived of Norway by the terms of the Peace of Kiel (1814), which united Norway with Sweden; and as a result of the Prusso-Danish wars of 1848–49 and 1864, Denmark lost its southern provinces of Slesvig, Holstein, and Lauenburg. Thereafter, the Danes concentrated on internal affairs, instituting important economic changes (in particular, specialization in dairy production) that transformed the country from a nation of poor peasants into one of prosperous smallholders. Denmark remained neutral in World War I, and after a plebiscite in 1920, North Slesvig was reincorporated into Denmark.

Disregarding the German-Danish nonaggression pact of 1939, Hitler invaded Denmark in April 1940, and the German occupation lasted until 1945. At first, the Danish government continued to function, protecting as long as it could the nation's Jewish minority and other refugees (some 7,200 Jews eventually escaped to neutral Sweden). However, when a resistance movement developed, sabotaging factories, railroads, and other installations, the Danish government resigned in August 1943 rather than carry out the German demand for the death sentence against the saboteurs. Thereafter, Denmark was governed by Germany directly, and conflict with the resistance intensified.

After the war, Denmark became a charter member of the UN and of NATO. In 1952, it joined with the other Scandinavian nations to form the Nordic Council, a parliamentary body. Having joined EFTA in 1960, Denmark left that association for the EEC in 1973. Meanwhile, during the 1950s and 1960s, agricultural and manufacturing production rose considerably, a high level of employment was maintained, and foreign trade terms were liberalized. However, the expense of maintaining Denmark's highly developed social security system, growing trade deficits (due partly to huge increases in the price of imported oil), persistent inflation, and rising unemployment posed political as well as economic problems for Denmark in the 1970s and 1980s, as one fragile coalition government succeeded another.

Economic performance was strong after the mid-1990s. Annual growth of GDP was 3% between 1994 and 1998 although the rate dropped to 1.6% in 1999. (It was projected to be 2.3% in 2005–06.) Thanks to strong growth, unemployment fell from 12.2% in 1994 to 6% in 1999. In March 2000, the buoyant economic outlook prompted Prime Minister Poul Nyrup Rasmussen to announce a referendum on Economic and Monetary Union to take place on 28 September 2000; it was rejected by 53.2% of the electorate. Voters narrowly rejected the Maastricht Treaty on European Union in 1992, but later approved it in 1993 after modifications were made in Denmark's favor. One of the special agreements was that Denmark could opt not to join EMU. For all practical purposes, however, Danish monetary policy has closely followed that of the European Central Bank and the Danish crown shadows the euro (the European single currency).

As with other European countries, Denmark in the 21st century sees illegal immigration as a major problem. The issue was a deciding one in the 20 November 2001 elections, with the right-wing xenophobic Danish People's Party (founded in 1995) gaining 12%

of the vote and 22 seats to become the third-largest party in parliament. The new government composed of the Liberal Party and the Conservative Party formed by Prime Minister Anders Fogh Rasmussen depended upon the Danish People's Party for legislative support. In June 2002, parliament passed a series of laws restricting the rights of immigrants, including the abolition of the right to asylum on humanitarian grounds, and cuts of 30–40% in the social benefits available to refugees during their first seven years of residency. In February 2005, Fogh Rasmussen won a second term as prime minister as his Liberal Party again formed a coalition with the Conservative Party. Rasmussen became the first Danish Liberal leader to win a second consecutive term. The Danish People's Party, although not part of the governing coalition, strengthened its presence in parliament by two seats.

13 GOVERNMENT

Denmark is a constitutional monarchy. Legislative power is vested jointly in the crown and a unicameral parliament (Folketing), executive power in the sovereign—who exercises it through his or her ministers—and judicial power in the courts. The revised constitution of 1953 provides that powers constitutionally vested in Danish authorities by legislation may be transferred to international authorities established, by agreement with other states, for the promotion of international law and cooperation.

The sovereign must belong to the Lutheran Church. The crown is hereditary in the royal house of Lyksborg, which ascended the throne in 1863. On the death of a king, the throne descends to his son or daughter, a son taking precedence.

Executive powers belong to the crown, which enjoys personal integrity and is not responsible for acts of government. These powers are exercised by the cabinet, consisting of a prime minister and a variable number of ministers, who generally are members of the political party or coalition commanding a legislative majority. No minister may remain in office after the Folketing has passed a vote of no confidence in him or her.

The single-chamber Folketing, which has been in existence since 1953, is elected every four years (more frequently, if necessary) by direct and secret ballot by Danish subjects 18 years of age and older. Under the 1953 constitution there are 179 members, two of whom are elected in the Faroe Islands and two in Greenland. Of the remaining 175 members, 135 are elected by proportional representation in 17 constituencies, and 40 supplementary seats are divided among the parties in proportion to the total votes cast.

A parliamentary commission, acting as the representative both of the Folketing and of the nation, superintends civil and military government administration.

14 POLITICAL PARTIES

Until 1849, the Danish form of government was autocratic. The constitution of 1849 abolished privileges, established civil liberties, and laid down the framework of popular government through a bicameral parliament elected by all men over 30. In 1866, however, the National Liberal Party, composed largely of the urban middle class, succeeded in obtaining a majority for a constitution in which the upper chamber (Landsting) was to be elected by privileged franchise, the great landowners gaining a dominant position. This proved the starting point of a political struggle that divided Denmark until 1901. Formally, it concerned the struggle of the directly elected chamber, the Folketing, against the privileged Landsting, but in reality it was the struggle of the Left Party (made up largely of farmers, but after 1870 also of workers) to break the monopoly of political influence by the Right Party (consisting of the landowning aristocracy and the upper middle class). Meanwhile, the workers established trade unions, their political demands finding expression in the Social Democratic Party. In 1901, Christian IX called on the Left to form a government, and thereafter it was the accepted practice that the government should reflect the majority in the Folketing.

In 1905, the Left Party split. Its radical wing, which seceded, became a center party, the Social Liberals, and sought to collaborate with the Social Democrats. In 1913, these two parties together obtained a majority in the Folketing, and a Social Liberal government led Denmark through World War I. A new constitution adopted in 1915 provided for proportional representation and gave the vote to all citizens, male and female, 25 years of age and older (changed in 1978 to 18 years). In an attempt to obtain a broader popular base, the old Right Party adopted the name Conservative People's Party, and thenceforth this party and the Moderate Liberals (the old Left Party), the Social Liberals, and the Social Democrats formed the solid core of Danish politics. The Social Democrats briefly formed governments in 1924 and in 1929, in association with the Social Liberals.

During the German occupation (1940–45), a coalition government was formed by the main political parties, but increasing Danish popular resistance to the Germans led the Nazis to take over executive powers. From 1945 to 1957, Denmark was governed by minority governments, influence fluctuating between the Social Democrats on the one hand and the Moderate Liberals and Conservatives on the other, depending on which of the two groups the Social Liberals supported. In 1953, a new constitution abolished the Landsting and introduced a single-chamber system in which parliamentarianism is expressly laid down.

Aims of the Social Democratic Party are to nationalize monopolies, redistribute personal incomes by taxation and other measures, partition farm properties to form independent smallholdings, and raise working-class living standards through full employment. It supports the principle of mutual aid, as practiced in a combination of social welfare and widespread public insurance schemes. The Conservative Party advocates an economic policy based on the rights of private property and private enterprise and is firmly opposed to nationalization and restrictions, though it is in favor of industrial protection. It calls for a national contributory pensions scheme that would encourage personal initiative and savings. The major parties support the UN and NATO and favor inter-Scandinavian cooperation.

Issues in the 1970s focused less on international matters than on policies affecting Denmark's economy. The general elections of December 1973 resulted in heavy losses for all the established parties represented in the Folketing and successes for several new parties, notably the center-left Democratic Center Party and the "Poujadist" Progress Party led by Mogens Glistrup, an income tax expert who reputedly became a millionaire by avoiding taxes and providing others with advice on tax avoidance. The Progress Party, established early in 1973, advocated the gradual abolition of income tax and the dissolution of over 90% of the civil service.

The Social Democrats, who had been in power, lost significantly in this election, and their chairman, Anker Jørgensen, resigned as prime minister. In mid-December, Poul Hartling was sworn in as prime minister, with a Liberal Democratic cabinet. The 22 Liberal members in the Folketing made up the smallest base for any government since parliamentary democracy was established in Denmark.

When it became clear in December 1974 that the Folketing would not approve the drastic anti-inflation program the Hartling government had announced, general elections were again called for. In the January 1975 balloting, the Liberals almost doubled their representation in the Folketing. However, because most of the other non-Socialist parties had lost support and because three of the four left-wing parties simultaneously gained parliamentary seats, the preelection lack of majority persisted, and Hartling resigned at the end of the month. After several attempts at a coalition by Hartling and Anker Jørgensen, the latter's alignment of Social Democrats and other Socialist-oriented minority parties finally succeeded in forming a new government. Jørgensen remained prime minister through general elections in 1977, 1979, and 1981. In September 1982, however, dissension over Jørgensen's plan to increase taxes in order to create new jobs, boost aid to farmers, and reduce the budget deficit led the government to resign. A four-party coalition led by Poul Schlüter, the first Conservative prime minister since 1901, then took power as a minority government, controlling only 66 seats out of 179. After the defeat of his 1984 budget, Schlüter called for new elections, which were held in January 1984 and increased the number of seats controlled by the coalition to 79. Following elections in September 1987, however, the number of seats held by the coalition fell to 70.

The 1994 election brought to power a three-party coalition of Social Democrats, Center Democrats, and Radical Liberals (they commanded a total of 76 seats in the 179-seat parliament). The 1994 election produced significant difficulties for the political right. The Conservatives were usually the major right-wing force with a legacy of heading governments but it saw its representation drop to 28 seats from 31 while the Liberal Party increased its share of the vote from 15.8% to 23.3% and thereby became the largest opposition party. The center-left coalition survived the departure of the Center Democrats in 1996, which rejected Prime Minister Poul Nyrup Rasmussen's decision to seek support for the 1997 budget from the far left. The fragile two-party coalition stumbled from one crisis to another in 1997 and the 1998 election promised to bring a Liberal-Conservative cabinet back to power. In February 1998, the Social Democrats recovered in opinion polls and Nyrup Rasmussen called a snap election.

The election results were as follows: Social Democrats 35.9% (65 seats), Radical Liberals 3.9% (7 seats), Center Democrats 4.3% (8 seats), Christian People's Party 2.5% (4 seats), Socialist People's Party 7.6% (13), Unity Party 2.7% (5 seats), Liberals 23% (43), Conservatives 8.9% (17), Progress Party 2.4% (4), and Danish People Party 7.4% (13 seats). Following the 1998 election, the Social Democratic and Radical Liberal coalition remained intact with Nyrup Rasmussen as prime minister. The Conservatives suffered a dramatic defeat and saw their share of the vote drop from 15% to 8.9%. The two far right parties—the Danish People's Party and the Progress Party—recorded the biggest gains by taking votes from the mainstream right-wing parties. In March 2000, Nyrup

Rasmussen reshuffled his cabinet to breathe new life into government and to respond to the pressures coming from the Danish People's Party, which accused the government of being soft on immigration. Campaigning on a platform "Denmark for the Danes," the People's Party attracted a large number of sympathizers.

The issue of immigration remained primary in the early elections called for by Nyrup Rasmussen on 20 November 2001. Nyrup Rasmussen's Social Democrats suffered a major defeat, gaining only 29.1% of the vote and 52 seats. Center-right parties gained their largest majority since 1926. The Liberal Party (31.3% of the vote and 56 seats) and the Conservative People's Party (9.1% and 16 seats) formed a minority government headed by Anders Fogh Rasmussen (no relation to Poul Nyrup Rasmussen) that depended upon the anti-immigrant Danish People's Party (12% and 22 seats) for legislative support. Other parties represented in the Folketing following the 2001 elections were as follows: Socialist People's Party, 6.4% (12 seats); Radical Left, 5.2% (9 seats); Unity List— the Red Greens, 2.4% (4 seats); Christian People's Party, 2.3% (4 seats); and the 2 representatives each from the Faroe Islands and Greenland.

Elections for the Folketing were next held on 8 February 2005. The percentage of the vote gained by each party and distribution of seats was as follows: Liberal Party, 29% (52 seats); Social Democrats, 25.9% (47 seats); Danish People's Party, 13.2% (24 seats); Conservative Party, 10.3% (18 seats); Social Liberal Party, 9.2% (17 seats); Socialist People's Party 6% (11 seats); Unity List, 3.4% (6 seats); and the two representatives each from the Faroe Islands and Greenland. Anders Fogh Rasmussen led a Liberal-Conservative coalition for a second consecutive term as prime minister. After the election, Fogh Rasmussen pledged to continue a "fair and firm immigration policy."

15 LOCAL GOVERNMENT

A major reform of local government structure took effect on 1 April 1970. Copenhagen, Fredericksberg, and the regional municipality of Bornholm enjoy dual status as both local and county authorities. The previous distinction between boroughs and urban and rural districts was abolished, and the number of counties was reduced from 25 to 14 (the number in 2005 stood at 13). The primary local units (municipalities), reduced from 1,400 to 275 (271 as of 2005), are governed by an elected council (kommunalbestyrelse) composed of 9 to 31 members who, in turn, elect a mayor (borgmester) who is vested with executive authority. Each county is governed by an elected county council (amtsiåd), which elects its own chairman, or county mayor (amstborgmester). County councils look after local matters, such as road building and maintenance, health and hospital services, and general education.

A major restructuring of local government was planned for 2007. The government's proposal was for the counties to be replaced by five regions, and for a reduction of the municipalities to 98. The new municipalities were to take over most of the responsibilities of the former counties. Most of the new municipalities were expected to have populations exceeding 20,000 people.

The Faroe Islands and Greenland enjoy home rule, with Denmark retaining responsibility for foreign affairs, defense, and monetary matters. Representatives of the Faroe Islands announced plans to organize a referendum on independence from Denmark by fall 2000. The government's response was to threaten to cut off all aid to the Faroese if they opted for independence. The referendum planned for May 2001 was cancelled.

16 JUDICIAL SYSTEM

As a rule, cases in the first instance come before one of 82 county courts. Certain major cases, however, come under one of the two High Courts (Landsrettes), in Copenhagen and Viborg, in the first instance; otherwise these courts function as courts of appeal. The High Courts generally sit in chambers of three judges. In jury trials (only applicable in cases involving serious crimes) three High Court judges sit with 12 jurors. The Supreme Court (Hojesteret) is made up of a president and 18 other judges, sitting in two chambers, each having at least five judges; it serves solely as a court of appeal for cases coming from the High Courts. Special courts include the Maritime and Commercial Court. An Ombudsman elected by and responsible to parliament investigates citizen complaints against the government or its ministers.

The judiciary is fully independent of the executive and legislative branches. Judges are appointed by the monarch on recommendation of the Minister of Justice and serve life terms. They may be dismissed only for negligence or for criminal acts. Denmark accepts compulsory jurisdiction of the International Court of Justice with reservations.

17 ARMED FORCES

Since 1849 Danish military defense has been based on compulsory national service. All young men must register at the age of 18 and are subject to 9–12 months' service. Voluntary military service is popular because of educational benefits. Total active armed forces numbered 21,180 in 2005, including 680 Joint Service personnel. The Army consisted of 12,500 active members, with the Navy at 3,800, and the Air Force at 4,200. There were also 129,700 members in the reserves which included about 59,300 in the volunteer home guard. The Danish Army had 231 main battle tanks, 310 armored personnel carriers, and 860 artillery pieces (176 are towed). Denmark's navy operated three guided missile corvettes in addition to 67 patrol/coastal and six minewarfare vessels. The Danish Air Force operates 62 combat capable aircraft. Danish forces participated in NATO, UN, and European Union missions in 13 countries/regions around the globe, including support for Operation Enduring Freedom. Military expenditures for 2005 amounted to $3.17 billion.

18 INTERNATIONAL COOPERATION

Denmark became a charter member of the United Nations on 24 October 1945 and belongs to ECE and several nonregional specialized agencies. In association with WHO, Denmark has supported UN relief work by supplying medical personnel to assist developing countries. The European regional office of WHO is in Copenhagen. The country is a member of the WTO. Denmark participates actively in multilateral technical aid programs, and the Danish Council for Technical Cooperation provides additional aid to developing countries in Asia and Africa. The nation also assists the African Development Bank and the Asian Development Bank. Denmark is a member of NATO and of various inter-European organizations including the Council of Europe, the European Investment Bank, G-9, the Paris Club, and the OECD.

Denmark is a member of the European Union and an observer in the OAS.

As a member of the Nordic Council, Denmark cooperates with other northern countries—Finland, Iceland, Norway, and Sweden—in social welfare and health insurance legislation and in freeing its frontiers of passport control for residents of other Scandinavian countries. The nation also participates in the regional Council of the Baltic Sea States and the Barents Council. Denmark has observer status in the Western European Union.

Denmark belongs to the Australia Group, the Zangger Committee, the Nuclear Suppliers Group (London Group), the European Organization for Nuclear Research (CERN), and the Nuclear Energy Agency. In environmental cooperation, Denmark is part of the Antarctic Treaty; the Basel Convention; Conventions on Biological Diversity, Whaling, and Air Pollution; Ramsar; CITES; the London Convention; International Tropical Timber Agreements; the Kyoto Protocol; the Montréal Protocol; MARPOL; the Nuclear Test Ban Treaty; and the UN Conventions on the Law of the Sea, Climate Change and Desertification.

19 ECONOMY

Denmark was traditionally an agricultural country. After the end of World War II, manufacturing gained rapidly in importance and now contributes 25.5% of national income, compared with 2.2% for agriculture. As of 2004, the service sector accounted for over 72.3% of GDP. Important service sectors are communications and information technologies, management consulting, and tourism. Shipping remains the most important service sector in Denmark: Denmark has always been a prominent maritime nation, and since much Danish shipping operates entirely in foreign waters, it contributes considerably to the nation's economy. Denmark also has important investments abroad.

Danish living standards and purchasing power are among the highest in the world, but the domestic market is limited by the small population, and most important industries must seek foreign markets in order to expand. Natural resources are limited, and therefore Denmark must export in order to pay for the raw materials, feeds, fertilizers, and fuels that must be imported. Integration into the EU's common agricultural policy has considerably improved Danish terms of trade by providing higher prices.

Productivity increased greatly in the postwar period. In agriculture the volume index for production rose steadily, while the agricultural labor force decreased. Similarly, improved techniques and mechanization in industry enabled production to increase, despite a percentage decline in the number of persons employed. In the 21st century, high-tech agriculture is a mark of Denmark's thoroughly modern market economy. As well, up-to-date small-scale and corporate industry, extensive government welfare measures, a stable currency, and a high dependence upon foreign trade all contribute to Denmark's prosperity.

From 1961 to 1971, the average annual rate of price increases in Denmark was 6.1%; in 1972, it was 6.6%; in 1973, 9.3%; and in 1974, partly because of rising oil costs, 15.2%. Throughout the remainder of the 1970s and through 1982, inflation remained in the 9–12% bracket. It then dropped from 6.9% in 1983 to 1.3% in 1993. By 1995, it had increased to 3.3% but in 1998 was down again to 1.8%. The inflation rate averaged 2% over the 2001–05 period.

Economic activity slackened during the 1970s, with GDP growth at 2.3% a year, down from a rate of about 4.5% during 1960–70. Growth remained moderate during the 1980s, averaging 2% a year. The GDP grew by 2.2% in 1990, but only at 1% in 1991, 1.2% in 1992, and 1.1% in 1993. In 1994, growth began to rebound, with GDP growing by 3.1%; in 1998 growth was 2.6%. In 2001, GDP growth was only 0.9%, down from 3% in 2000, largely due to the global economic slowdown and poor domestic demand. GDP growth recovered in 2004, helped by income tax cuts, and was forecast to remain solid in 2005–06. GDP growth was estimated at 2.9% in 2005, falling gradually to 2.6% in 2006 and 2.1% in 2007. This rapid economic expansion is being driven by strong household demand for goods and services, as well as healthy investment growth.

Recessions in 1974–75 and 1980–81 spurred a substantial rise in unemployment. From a rate of 0.9% in 1973, unemployment reached 12.3% in 1993. By 1995, it had decreased to 10.2%, still quite high compared to the United States, but about the same as other EU countries. By 1998, however, it fell to an estimated 6.5%. The unemployment rate stood at 6% in 2003 and 6.2% in 2004, among the lowest of EU countries.

Throughout the 1970s and through most of the next six years, Denmark's trade balance was in chronic deficit, but a surplus was registered in 1987 and continued through 1997. Denmark's vulnerability to the Asian and Russian financial crises in the late 1990s resulted in a balance of payments deficit in 1998. As of 2005, the current account had been in surplus since 1998. The current account balance as a percentage of GDP over the 2001–05 period was 2.8%.

Although Denmark easily met all of the criteria for membership in the European economic and monetary union (EMU), it opted to stay out of the euro zone. Denmark participates in the exchange-rate mechanism (ERM 2), which pegs the Danish krone to the euro. A referendum to ratify the EU constitutional treaty had been postponed indefinitely as of December 2005.

The government was likely to continue an expansionary fiscal policy in 2006, and the general government budget surplus was forecast to narrow. The Danish government lowered income and corporate taxes in 2004. Government debt remains high, at 47.4% of GDP in 2003, albeit down from the 2000–02 period.

20 INCOME

The US Central Intelligence Agency (CIA) reports that in 2005 Denmark's gross domestic product (GDP) was estimated at $182.1 billion. The CIA defines GDP as the value of all final goods and services produced within a nation in a given year and computed on the basis of purchasing power parity (PPP) rather than value as measured on the basis of the rate of exchange based on current dollars. The per capita GDP was estimated at $33,500. The annual growth rate of GDP was estimated at 2.2%. The average inflation rate in 2005 was 1.9%. It was estimated that agriculture accounted for 2.2% of GDP, industry 24%, and services 73.8%.

According to the World Bank, in 2003 remittances from citizens working abroad totaled $941 million or about $175 per capita and accounted for approximately 0.4% of GDP. Foreign aid receipts amounted about $8 per capita.

The World Bank reports that in 2003 household consumption in Denmark totaled $100.33 billion or about $18,624 per capita based on a GDP of $211.9 billion, measured in current dollars rather than PPP. Household consumption includes expenditures of individuals, households, and nongovernmental organizations on goods and services, excluding purchases of dwellings. It was estimated that for the period 1990 to 2003 household consumption grew at an average annual rate of 1.7%. In 2001 it was estimated that approximately 16% of household consumption was spent on food, 11% on fuel, 3% on health care, and 17% on education.

21 LABOR

In 2005, Denmark's labor force was estimated at 2.9 million. Of those employed in 2002, an estimated 79% were in the services sector, 17% in industry, and 4% in agriculture. The Danish unemployment rate in 2005 was estimated at 5.7%. The 1982–90 period brought a 1.3% decline in agricultural employment, a slight decrease in employment in manufacturing, and a large increase in employment in services, especially government services (education, social welfare, etc.). With the aim of holding down unemployment, the government offers the option of early retirement, apprenticeship and trainee programs, and special job offerings for the long-term unemployed.

As of 2005, an estimated 78% of all wage-earners were organized into trade unions. These unions are independent of the government or political parties. Most unions are limited to particular trades. Most workers are entitled to strike and that option is exercised often. Collective bargaining is practiced widely. Military personnel and the police are also allowed to form and join a union.

Although there is no nationally mandated minimum wage rate, the average net wage (including pension benefits) for adult workers was $29 per hour in 2004, which was sufficient to provide a decent standard of living for a family. The typical private sector workweek, as set by contract, not law, was 37 hours in 2005. Overtime is not compulsory. The minimum age for full-time work is 15 years, although children as young as 13 can work part-time, although there are limits imposed as to the tasks they can perform and the hours worked. Health and safety standards are set by law and cover school-age children in the workplace.

22 AGRICULTURE

About 54% of the land in 2002 was cultivated, most of it for feed and root crops. In 2003, agriculture engaged 3.4% of the labor force. Although agriculture is of great significance to the Danish economy, its relative importance declined from 19% of the GDP in 1961 to 2.1% in 2003.

The majority of farms are small and medium-sized; about 63% are smaller than 50 hectares (124 acres). In 2004, there were 45,624 Danish farms. Thousands of smallholdings have been established since 1899 under special legislation empowering the state to provide the land by partitioning public lands, by expropriation, and by breaking up large private estates. In the more newly established holdings, the farmer owns only the buildings (for which the state advances loans), the land being owned by the state and the smallholder paying an annual rent fixed under the land-tax assessment. Comparatively few new holdings have been established since 1951.

Grain growing and root-crop production are the traditional agricultural pursuits, but considerable progress has been made in recent decades in apple growing and the production of field, forage, flower, and industrial seeds. Although the soil is not particularly fertile and holdings are kept deliberately small, intensive mechanization and widespread use of fertilizers and concentrated feeds result in high yields and excellent quality. In 2002 there were 123,000 tractors and 97,000 harvester-threshers.

The crop yields of major crops for 2004 were (in thousands of tons): barley, 3,590; wheat, 4,759; rye, 146; sugar beets, 2,829; rapeseed (canola), 469; and corn for fodder, 4,381.

Agricultural exports supplied 17.2% of the value of Danish exports in 2004. Farm products provide materials for industrial processing, and a significant share of industry supplies the needs of domestic agriculture.

The Danish government devotes particular effort to maintaining the volume, price, quality, and diversity of agricultural products, but internal regulation is largely left to private initiative or exercised through private organizations, notably the cooperatives.

23 ANIMAL HUSBANDRY

Denmark is generally regarded as the world's outstanding example of intensive animal husbandry. It maintains a uniformly high standard of operations, combining highly skilled labor, scientific experimentation and research, modern installations and machinery, and versatility in farm management and marketing. The excellent cooperative system guarantees the quality of every product of its members. Meat, dairy products, and eggs contribute a most important share of Danish exports. There is a close relationship between cost of feed and export prices.

The livestock population in 2004 included 1,646,000 head of cattle (including 563,000 dairy cows), 13,233,000 hogs, 141,000 sheep, 39,000 horses, and 16,136,000 chickens. Mink, fox, polecat, finnraccoon, and chinchilla are raised for their pelts. In 2004, 12.6 million pelts were processed, valued at Kr2.7 billion.

The value of exported meat and animal products in 2004 amounted to $4.6 billion, consisting primarily of live pigs and pork, cheese, and canned meat. Production in 2004 included 4,569,000 tons of milk, 46,700 tons of butter, and 335,500 tons of cheese. In addition, egg production was 81,000 tons in 2004. Some 50% of all eggs consumed domestically are produced by alternative methods, a phrase that generally refers to layers raised organically or in free-range. The government's goal is for all eggs to ultimately be produced by noncaged layers. Organic milk is also a growing market. Organically produced feed's share of the domestic market is also increasing.

24 FISHING

The country's long coastline, conveniently situated on rich fishing waters, provides Denmark with excellent fishing grounds. Fishing is an important source of domestic food supply, and both fresh and processed fish are important exports. During 1990–95, the government financially supported fleet reduction in order to alleviate structural problems in the industry, and 605 vessels left the fleet during those years. At the beginning of 2005, there were 2,180 Danish fishing vessels, with a combined 95,685 GRT. The catch is composed mainly of herring and sprat, cod, mackerel, plaice, salmon, and whiting; but sole and other flatfish, tuna, and other varieties are also caught. In 2004, total Danish landings were 984,037 tons.

Denmark is one of the world's leading seafood exporters. In 2003, fish exports were valued at $3.2 billion, up 17% from 2000.

25 FORESTRY

A law of 1805 placing all forestland under reservation stated that "where there is now high forest there must always be high forest." Various measures were adopted to maintain forest growth. Later revisions of the law compelled all woodland owners to replant when trees are felled and to give adequate attention to drainage, weeding out of inferior species, and road maintenance. As a result, forests, which occupied only 5% of Denmark's land area and were actually in danger of extinction at the beginning of the 19th century, now make up 10% of the land and are in excellent condition. The total forest area in 2000 was 486,000 hectares (1,200,000 acres). Spruce and beech are the most important varieties. The government would like to increase forest area to 800,000 hectares (1,977,000 acres), nearly 20% of Denmark's total area, during the next 80 years.

Roundwood harvested in 2003 amounted to 1.8 million cu m (64 million cu ft), of which about 75% came from conifers and 25% came from broadleaf species. Denmark is a large importer of softwood lumber, especially from the other Scandinavian countries, and is a large particleboard consumer. Total Danish wood trade in 2003 amounted to $2.3 billion, consisting of imports of $1.9 billion and exports totaling $391.5 million. Pine logs account for about 60% of the total value of imported wood, much of it used by the furniture industry. Danish furniture exports in 2004 amounted to more than $2.5 billion.

On 3 December 1999, the first hurricane ever recorded in Denmark destroyed large tracts of its forested areas. Estimated loss of trees amounted to 150% of Denmark's normal annual timber harvest.

26 MINING

Denmark's industrialized market economy depended on imported raw materials, its mineral resources were mainly fossil fuels in the North Sea, and the nonfuel minerals industry included mining and quarrying of chalk, clays, diatomite, limestone (agricultural and industrial), and sand and gravel (onshore and offshore). The industrial minerals sector was particularly active. There were some 90 pits in Denmark from which clay was mined; this material was used primarily by the cement, brick making, and ceramic tile industries. The production of sand, gravel, and crushed stone has become more important in recent years, not only in meeting domestic demand, but also as an export to Germany and other Scandinavian countries. Kaolin, found on the island of Bornholm, was used mostly for coarse earthenware, furnace linings, and as filler for paper; production was 2,500 metric tons in 2004, unchanged from 2000. There were important limestone, chalk, and marl deposits in Jutland. Chalk production totaled 1,950,000 tons in 2004. Limonite (bog ore) was extracted for gas purification and pig iron production. Large deposits of salt were discovered in Jutland in 1966; in 2004, 610,000 metric tons were mined. The country also produced fire clay, extracted moler, lime (hydrated and quicklime), nitrogen, peat, crude phosphates, dimension stone (mostly granite), and sulfur. According to the constitution, sub-surface resources belonged to the nation, and concessions to exploit them required parliamentary approval.

27ENERGY AND POWER

Denmark's energy sector is marked by negligible sources of waterpower, and no nuclear power plants. However, the country has significant oil and natural gas reserves located in the North Sea, and it is also turning to wind power as an important source of electrical power generation.

In 2002, Denmark's electrical generating capacity totaled 12.746 million kW. Of that total, conventionally fueled capacity accounted for 10.049 million kW. Geothermal/other fuel based capacity was next at 2.868 million kW and hydropower based capacity at 0.011 million kW. In that same year, Denmark generated 36.367 billion kWh of electric power, of which thermal fuel powered generation accounted for 29.319 billion kWh, followed by geothermal/other powered generation at 29.319 billion kWh, and hydropower generation at 0.032 billion kWh. Imports of electrical power in 2002 totaled 8.900 billion kWh, with exports for that year at 11.100 billion kWh. The Danish electrical generating sector is marked by its use of alternative or geothermal/other power sources, most notably, wind-driven generation. Although 80% of the nation's electric power was generated by fossil fuels, slightly more than 19% was generated by alternative sources. According to a report by BusinessWeek online, dated 30 April 2001, around 13% of Denmark's electric power is wind generated, and the country has become a leader in the manufacturing of wind powered generating equipment.

Denmark's position flanking the North Sea has given the nation a share of the significant oil and natural gas reserves that have been discovered there. As of 1 January 2002, Denmark had proven oil reserves of 1.23 billion barrels. By the end of 2004, according to British Petroleum (BP), Denmark's proven oil reserves rose to 1.3 billion barrels. In 2002, Denmark produced an average of 370,760 barrels per day of crude oil. In 2004, that total rose to an average of 394,000 barrels per day, according to BP. In addition, between 1999, and 2005, a number of new fields have begun to produce, boosting the country's crude oil output. However, starting in 1997, Denmark's oil consumption has steadily fallen, according to BP. In that year the consumption of all oil products dropped to 229,000 barrels per day, from 235,000 barrels per day in 1996. In 2003, total oil product consumption fell to 193,000 barrels per day, and in 2004 fell 1.8% to 189,000 barrels per day.

Denmark has proven reserves of natural gas, as of end 2004, of 0.09 trillion cu m, and output has steadily risen over the previous three decades. According to BP, in 2002, Denmark produced 8.4 billion cu m of natural gas. In 2004, output rose to 9.4 billion cu m.

Denmark has no proven coal reserves and must therefore import all the coal it consumes. In 2002, imports of hard black coal totaled 6,946,000 tons.

28INDUSTRY

Manufacturing greatly expanded after the end of World War II and now accounts for a greater share of national income than does agriculture. In 2004, manufacturing (including mining and utilities) accounted for 25.5% of the GDP, employing approximately 17% of the total working population. In the important food and drink industry, which tends to be relatively stable, the pattern differs for various branches, but meat packing has developed remarkably. The chemical, metalworking, and pharmaceutical industries have made notable progress. Handicrafts remain important, and Danish stone, clay, glass, wood, and silver products are world famous. Other important industries include: iron, steel, machinery and transportation equipment, textiles and clothing, electronics, construction, furniture, shipbuilding and refurbishment, and windmills.

In the world market, Danish manufacturers, having a limited supply of domestic raw materials, a relatively small home market, and a naturally advantageous geographic position, have concentrated on the production of high-quality specialized items rather than those dependent on mass production. For example, Denmark became the world's largest supplier of insulin, the raw materials for which come from livestock intestines; the Danish company Novo Nordisk is the world leader in insulin and diabetes care. Denmark by the early 2000s produced some 20–25% of the world's hearing aids.

Machinery, by far the most important industrial export, includes cement-making machinery, dairy machinery, diesel engines, electric motors, machine tools, and refrigeration equipment. Other important exports include meat and meat products (especially pork and pork products—Denmark is the world's largest exporter of pork), fish, dairy products, chemicals, furniture, ships, and windmills.

29SCIENCE AND TECHNOLOGY

The Ministry of Research is the central administrative unit for research policy. Among advisory bodies to it are the Danish Council for Research Policy, the Danish Natural Science Research Council, the Danish Medical Research Council, the Danish Agricultural and Veterinary Research Council, the Danish Technical Research Council, and the Danish Committee for Scientific and Technical Information and Documentation. The chief learned societies are the Royal Danish Academy of Science and Letters (founded in 1742) and the Danish Academy of Technical Sciences (founded in 1937). Denmark also has 29 specialized learned societies in the fields of agricultural and veterinary science, medicine, natural sciences, and technology. Among the principal public research institutions are the universities Aalborg, Aarhus, Copenhagen, Odense, and Roskilde; the Royal Veterinary and Agricultural University at Frederiksberg; the Technological University of Denmark near Copenhagen; the National Hospital in Copenhagen; the Risø National Laboratory near Roskilde; the Danish Institute for Fisheries and Marine Research at Charlottenlund; and the Danish Meteorological Institute at Copenhagen. In 1987–97, science and engineering students accounted for 25% of university enrollment. In 2002, a total of 10.6% of all bachelor's degrees awarded were for the sciences (natural sciences, mathematics and computers, and engineering). Many of the world's preeminent theoretical nuclear physicists have worked at the Niels Bohr Institute for Astronomy, Physics, and Geophysics of Copenhagen University. Copenhagen has museums of geology and zoology and botanical gardens.

Research and development (R&D) expenditures in 2002 totaled $4,178.639 million or 2.51% of GDP. For that same year, there were 3,153 technicians and 4,822 researchers per million people actively engaged in R&D. In 2001, business provided 61.5% of all funding for R&D activities, followed by government at 28%, foreign sources at 7.8% and higher education at 2.6%. Total R&D spending that year came to $3,877.477 million, or 2.40% of GDP. In 2002, high-tech exports were valued at $8.089 billion and accounted for 22% of manufactured exports.

30 DOMESTIC TRADE

Large units are becoming more common in wholesale as well as retail trade, ordering directly from local manufacturers and foreign suppliers. Retail operations now include purchasing organizations, various types of chains, cooperatives, self-service stores, supermarkets, and department stores. Chain stores are gaining dominance in the nonfood retail goods market. The food retail sector is dominated by Dansk Supermarked, Coop Danmark, and about 30 other independent food import establishments. A 25% value-added tax applies to most goods and services.

Danish retail trade is marked by keen competition between independent retailers, manufacturers' chains, and consumer cooperatives. About 30% of all Danish retail establishments are in the greater Copenhagen area, and these account for almost 40% of all retail sales.

Business opening hours vary between 8 and 9 AM; closing is between 5:30 and 7 PM for stores and 4 to 4:30 PM for offices. Early closing (1 PM) on Saturdays is now standard. Banking hours are from 9:30 AM to 4 PM, Monday through Friday; also, 4 to 6 PM on Thursday.

General, trade, and technical periodicals are important media, and direct-mail, television, and film advertising are used extensively. The most important trade exhibition, the International Fair, takes place every spring in Copenhagen.

31 FOREIGN TRADE

The Danish economy depends heavily on foreign trade. Denmark is a net exporter of food and energy. Raw materials for use in production used to account for more than half the value of imports, but have seen a considerable decline in recent years. Farm products traditionally comprised the bulk of total Danish exports, but since 1961, industrial exports have greatly exceeded agricultural exports in value. In 2003, industrial products accounted for 81%

of Denmark's total commodity exports by value (of which machinery and instruments covered 35%); agricultural and fishing exports accounted for 10% (of which pork and pork products covered 48%—Denmark is the world's largest exporter of pork). Raw materials and semi-manufactures accounted for 43% of imports, consumer goods 29%, capital equipment 14%, transport equipment 7%, fuels 5%, and other imports 2%.

Denmark's trading partners in 2003 (according to percent of total trade in goods) included Germany (21%), Sweden (13%), the United Kingdom (8%), the United States (5%), Norway (5%), Japan (2%), and eastern European countries (5%).

To curb domestic demand, the government introduced several fiscal restraint measures in 1986, resulting in a decline in imports. Such measures and a tight-money policy have curbed inflation and made Danish exports more competitive, leading to trade surpluses in the late 1980s, 1990s, and early 2000s. In 2004, total exports were $75.6 billion and imports were $67.2 billion, for a trade surplus of $8.4 billion.

A great producer of food, Denmark's commodity exports include meat, fresh fish, and cheese, each of which command a substantial percentage of the world's food exports in their categories. The country also exports fine furniture and medicaments.

32 BALANCE OF PAYMENTS

The decline in Denmark's trade balance since the end of World War II resulted in a serious deterioration in the balance-of-payments position, particularly after 1960. In the late 1960s, the course of Denmark's international economic activity paralleled trends in continental Europe, with high trade and capital flow levels being accompanied by a deteriorating current-account position; this condition continued into the early 1970s. The Danish government had hoped that Denmark's entry into the EC would reduce the country's persistent deficit and bring the balance on current account into a more favorable position, but this was not

---

Principal Trading Partners – Denmark (2003)

(In millions of US dollars)

Country	Exports	Imports	Balance
World	64,614.0	56,230.5	8,383.5
Germany	11,182.1	12,904.9	-1,722.8
Sweden	7,875.0	7,206.2	668.8
United Kingdom	5,066.4	3,921.3	1,145.1
Areas nes	4,978.6	398.9	4,579.7
United States	3,688.4	1,823.0	1,865.4
Norway	3,652.2	2,533.9	1,118.3
France-Monaco	2,907.6	2,717.5	190.1
Netherlands	2,880.3	3,884.6	-1,004.3
Finland	1,994.5	1,301.3	693.2
Italy-San Marino-Holy See	1,942.3	2,300.7	-358.4

(…) data not available or not significant.

SOURCE: *2003 International Trade Statistics Yearbook*, New York: United Nations, 2004.

Balance of Payments – Denmark (2003)

(In millions of US dollars)

Current Account		**6,139.0**
Balance on goods	10,142.0	
Imports	-55,060.0	
Exports	65,202.0	
Balance on services	3,811.0	
Balance on income	-3,981.0	
Current transfers	-3,833.0	
Capital Account		**-45.0**
Financial Account		**-4,495.0**
Direct investment abroad	-1,314.0	
Direct investment in Denmark	2,908.0	
Portfolio investment assets	-21,938.0	
Portfolio investment liabilities	6,012.0	
Financial derivatives	-12.0	
Other investment assets	-9,983.0	
Other investment liabilities	19,832.0	
Net Errors and Omissions		**3,075.0**
Reserves and Related Items		**-4,674.0**

(…) data not available or not significant.

SOURCE: *Balance of Payment Statistics Yearbook 2004*, Washington, DC: International Monetary Fund, 2004.

the case in the late 1970s. Although current account deficits were reduced somewhat in 1980–81, thanks to the devaluation of the krone and the restrictive income and fiscal policies implemented in 1979–80, the deficit again increased in 1982 and by 1985 was at the highest level since 1979.

In 1990, after a century of deficits, the balance of payments showed a surplus of $1.3 billion, and rose to $4.7 billion in 1993. In 1994 the surplus dropped to $2.7 billion, but by 2002 it stood at $8.4 billion. The surplus has allowed Denmark to begin repaying its large foreign debt, which peaked in 1988 at $44 billion, or 40% of GDP. (External debt stood at $21.7 billion in 2000.) Net interest payments on debt continue to be a burden, accounting for about 10% of goods and services export earnings.

As of 2005, except for one year—1998—Denmark had had comfortable current account surpluses for 15 years. The current account surplus stood at $6.5 billion in 2004.

33 BANKING AND SECURITIES

By an act of 7 April 1936, the Danish National Bank, the bank of issue since 1818, was converted from an independent to an official government corporation. Its head office is in Copenhagen, and it has branches in provincial towns. The Nationalbank performs all the usual functions of a central bank, and it holds almost all the nation's foreign exchange reserves. Commercial banks provide short-term money to business and individuals, almost always in the form of overdraft credits, which are generally renewable.

Danish banks, hit particularly hard by the Nordic banking crisis of 1991–93, have rebounded. By the end of the decade, they had rebounded completely. Their recovery was bolstered in large part by continuing capital gains in securities markets. In mid-2003, there were 187 commercial and savings banks, eight mortgage credit institutions, 30 investment companies, 138 nonlife insurance companies, and 94 life assurance companies and multi-employer pension funds.

Credit and mortgage societies are active in Denmark. In 1982, index-linked real estate loans were introduced, initially carrying nominal interest rates of 2.5% per year, with balance and installments adjusted yearly according to variations in the consumer price index and wage indexes. In the mid-1990s, the lending rate was about 12%. The International Monetary Fund reports that in 1999, currency and demand deposits—an aggregate commonly known as M1—were equal to $54.7 billion. In that same year, M2—an aggregate equal to M1 plus savings deposits, small time deposits, and money market mutual funds—was $97.5 billion. The money market rate, the rate at which financial institutions lend to one another in the short term, was 3.37%. The discount rate, the interest rate at which the central bank lends to financial institutions in the short term, was 3%.

The stock exchange (or Bourse) in Copenhagen was built during 1619-30 by Christian IV. He subsequently sold it to a Copenhagen merchant, but it reverted to the crown and in 1857 was finally sold by Frederik VII to the Merchants' Guild. Although it is the oldest building in the world built as an exchange and still used as one, the nature of the business transacted in it has greatly changed. Originally a commodity exchange equipped with booths and storage rooms, the Bourse is now almost exclusively a stock exchange. In 1970, the Stock Exchange was placed under the jurisdiction of the Ministry of Commerce with a governing committee

of 11 members. Only a few bond issues are made by manufacturing firms each year. In 1980, Denmark took the initial step toward becoming the first country to convert the issuing of stock, share, and bond certificates into a computer account registration system. As of 2004, a total of 178 companies were listed on the Copenhagen Stock Exchange, which had a total capitalization of $151.342 billion. In that same year, the KFX Copehagen rose 0.7% from the previous year to 286.7.

34 INSURANCE

The Danish insurance industry is regulated by the Danish Supervisory Authority of Financial Affairs. Danish companies do most stock insurance business. Some government-owned insurance companies sell automobile, fire, and life insurance and handle the government's war-risk insurance program. In Denmark, third-party auto insurance, workers' compensation, nuclear power station insurance, hunter's liability, dog liability, third-party aircraft liability and mortgaged property insurance are compulsory. The two primary pieces of legislation affecting the insurance industry are the Insurance Companies Act and the Insurance Contracts Act. The first contains regulations for establishing and operating insurance companies and describes the public supervision of the insurance business. The second governs relations between insurance companies, policy holders, and claimants. In 2003, the value of all direct premiums written totaled $16.737 billion, with life premiums accounting for the largest portion at $10.944 billion. Denmark's top nonlife insurer that same year was Tryg Skade, with gross nonlife premiums written of $1,177.9 million. Danica Pension was the country's top life insurer in 2003 with gross life premiums written of $1.772.4.

35 PUBLIC FINANCE

The finance bill is presented to the Folketing yearly; the fiscal year follows the calendar year. As a general rule, the budget is prepared on the "net" principle, the difference between receipts and expen-

---

Public Finance – Denmark (2003)

(In millions of kroner, central government figures)

Revenue and Grants	**532,687**	**100.0%**
Tax revenue	420,202	78.9%
Social contributions	29,548	5.5%
Grants	7,716	1.4%
Other revenue	75,221	14.1%
Expenditures	**504,284**	**100.0%**
General public services	137,385	27.2%
Defense	23,218	4.6%
Public order and safety	13,265	2.6%
Economic affairs	34,347	6.8%
Environmental protection	...	...
Housing and community amenities	8,257	1.6%
Health	4,484	0.9%
Recreational, culture, and religion	11,417	2.3%
Education	63,669	12.6%
Social protection	208,242	41.3%

(...) data not available or not significant.

SOURCE: *Government Finance Statistics Yearbook 2004,* Washington, DC: International Monetary Fund, 2004.

ditures—surplus or deficit—of public undertakings being posted to the revenue accounts. By far the largest amounts of public expenditure are for social security, health, education and research, unemployment insurance, pensions, allowances, and rent subsidies. Under a new tax reform plan, agreed upon by the government and the Danish People's Party in March 2003, Danish citizens received tax relief in 2004, although at a lesser rate than originally was hoped. Denmark has yet to accept the euro as its currency, although it meets all the criteria set forth by the European Monetary Union to do so. The 1993 Finance Act serves as an example of how revenue is only to a limited degree spent on the public sector's own operational and initial expenditure, but mainly repaid to citizens. Out of the Kr340 billion the government had at its disposal in 1993, 46% was to be sent back to individual citizens as income transfers. In addition, the government transferred 12% of the budget to municipalities in the form of block grants, which also will largely end up as transfer payments to individuals.

The US Central Intelligence Agency (CIA) estimated that in 2005 Denmark's central government took in revenues of approximately $148.8 billion and had expenditures of $142.6 billion. Revenues minus expenditures totaled approximately $6.2 billion. Public debt in 2005 amounted to 40.4% of GDP. Total external debt was $352.9 billion.

The International Monetary Fund (IMF) reported that in 2003, the most recent year for which it had data, central government revenues were Kr532,687 million and expenditures were Kr504,284 million. The value of revenues was us$80,857 million and expenditures us$76,546 million, based on a market exchange rate for 2003 of us$1 = Kr6.588 as reported by the IMF. Government outlays by function were as follows: general public services, 27.2%; defense, 4.6%; public order and safety, 2.6%; economic affairs, 6.8%; housing and community amenities, 1.6%; health, 0.9%; recreation, culture, and religion, 2.3%; education, 12.6%; and social protection, 41.3%.

36 TAXATION

Denmark's taxes are among the highest in the world. Danish residents are liable for tax on global income and net wealth. Nonresidents are liable only for tax on certain types of income from Danish sources.

The corporate income tax in Denmark is 30%, which must be prepaid during the income tax year to avoid a surcharge. Capital gains are also taxed at the 30% rate.

Personal income tax is collected at state, county and local levels. A tax ceiling ensures that combined income taxes do not exceed 59% of income. Income tax rates are progressive: 39% on income up to €22,118; 45% on income between €22,118 and €36,025; and 60% on income above €36,025. Several kinds of deductions or reductions can be applied to taxable income. Dividends are taxed at 28% up to the amount of personal allowance, after which the rate goes to 43%. Royalties are subject to a 30% tax rate. There is also a voluntary church tax with an average rate of 0.8%. The social security contribution from employee earnings is 9%, 8% for unemployment insurance and 1% for special pension scheme savings. The voluntary church tax and social security contributions do not count toward the 59% tax ceiling. Tax is withheld at the source. Foreign researchers and key employers may qualify for a gross tax

of 25% on their salary instead of paying regular income tax. They are still liable for 9% social security contributions.

Denmark's main indirect tax in the value-added tax (VAT) first introduced in March 1967 with a standard rate of 10%. The current standard rate of 25% was introduced in January 1992. Daily newspapers and a few other goods and services are exempt from the VAT.

37 CUSTOMS AND DUTIES

Denmark—a consistent advocate of free and fair conditions of international trade—had until recently the lowest tariff rate in Europe. However, owing to shortages of foreign currency, Denmark did impose quantitative restrictions on imports, and as late as 1959 about 64% of Danish industrial production was so protected. On joining the European Free Trade Association (EFTA) on 8 May 1960, Denmark began eliminating tariff rates and quantitative restrictions on industrial products from other EFTA countries. By 1 January 1970, those that remained were abolished. On 1 January 1973, Denmark ended its membership in EFTA and became a member of the European Community, which not only represents a free trade area but also seeks to integrate the economies of its member states.

Denmark adheres to provisions of GATT on import licensing requirements although certain industrial products must meet Danish and EC technical standards. Denmark converted to the Harmonized System of import duties on 1 January 1988. Most products from European countries are duty-free. Duty rates for manufactured goods range from 5–14% of CIF value, and a 25% VAT is applied to imported, as well as domestic, products. Basic necessities and foodstuffs are given a 0% rate. Agricultural products are governed by the Common Agricultural Policy (CAP), a system of variable levies, instead of duties.

38 FOREIGN INVESTMENT

Denmark is a rich, modern society with state-of-the art infrastructure and distribution system. A highly-skilled labor force and a northern location in Europe make it attractive to foreign investors wishing to have access to markets in Scandinavia, the Baltics, and other northern European destinations. Denmark is a firm advocate of liberal trade and investment policies and actively courts foreign investment.

Foreign investors are treated on an equal footing with Danish investors; investment capital and profits may be freely repatriated. After the late 1950s, Denmark attracted a moderate amount of foreign investment. In 1998, however, annual FDI inflows jumped from $2.8 billion to $7.7 billion and then soared to $32.3 billion in 2000. In terms of success in attracting FDI, Denmark went from the 62nd ranked country (out of 140 countries studied) on UNCTAD's Inward FDI Performance Index for the period 1988 to 1990 to the 12th ranked country for the period 1998–2000. Denmark's ranking in terms of potential for inward FDI increased from 10th place in the world to 8th place. In the economic slowdown of 2001 and in decline in FDI inflows that followed the 11 September 2001 terrorist attacks in the United States, annual FDI inflow fell to about $14 billion in 2001 and to an estimated $7.7 billion in 2002.

The total stock of FDI in Denmark increased by 79% from 1998–2003, and corresponded to approximately 25% of GDP in

2003 (at $54 billion). Danish investment abroad amounted to 27% of GDP. The corporate tax is relatively low by EU-15 standards, at 28%. There is no additional local tax, franchise, or net wealth tax. The corporate tax is paid after deductions for expenses.

The largest foreign investors in Denmark are the United States, Sweden, and the United Kingdom. The main sources of FDI stock in Denmark in 2003 were the United States (28%), Sweden (20%), the United Kingdom (10%), Norway (9%), and Germany (4%). The main destinations of Danish investment abroad in 2003 were the United Kingdom (12%), Norway (10%), Sweden (9%), the United States (6%), and Germany (6%).

39 ECONOMIC DEVELOPMENT

For many years, Danish governments followed a full-employment policy and relied chiefly on promotion of private enterprise to achieve this end. Beginning in the late 1970s, however, the government increased its intervention in the economy, in response to rising unemployment, inflation, and budget deficits. Inflation has been curbed and budget deficits reduced. This bolstered the currency from devaluation, but at the cost of restraining growth, and unemployment continued to rise.

Government influence on private enterprise through the exercise of import and export licensing has diminished in recent years. The discount policy of the National Bank is of major importance to the business community. Control of cartels and monopolies is flexible. The government has in recent years sold part or whole interest in many business entities, including the national telecommunications company TDC, Copenhagen airports, and the government's computer services company, Datacentralen. Most of the country's power stations are owned and operated by local governments and municipalities.

Capital incentives are available to assist new industries, mainly in the less-developed areas of Denmark. Municipalities also provide infrastructure, industrial parks, or inexpensive land. Under a 1967 provision, the Regional Development Committee (composed of representatives of a number of special-interest organizations and central and local authorities) can grant state guarantees or state loans for the establishment of enterprises in less developed districts.

In 1978, Denmark reached the UN target for official development assistance (ODA) in the mid-1970s: 0.7% of GNP. It reached 0.96% of GNP in 1991, second only to Norway, and 1.01% in 2001, when it led the world in ODA. In 2004, Denmark set aside 0.84% of its GNP for ODA, third highest behind Norway and Luxembourg. Denmark's official assistance to developing countries amounted to $2 billion in 2004.

Unemployment was at a 25-year low in 2002, and the economy weathered the global economic recession fairly well. (Unemployment was also low in 2004, at 6.2%.) The government ran fiscal surpluses in order to prepare for the costs of an aging population. Nevertheless, state spending to total economic activity remains one of the highest in the world. Small and medium-sized businesses characterize the private sector, with companies with less than 50 employees accounting for approximately half of total employment, and only 12% of the workforce work in firms with more than 500 employees. Women are highly represented in the labor force.

The government was likely to continue an expansionary fiscal policy in 2006, and the general government budget surplus was forecast to narrow. The Danish government lowered income and corporate taxes in 2004, and announced in 2005 that it was working on simplifying the rules governing the taxation of dividends. Government debt remains high, but the public budget was in surplus in 2005.

40 SOCIAL DEVELOPMENT

Denmark was one of the first countries in the world to establish efficient social services with the introduction of relief for the sick, unemployed, and aged. Old age benefits date back to 1891. Social welfare programs include health insurance, health and hospital services, insurance for occupational injuries, unemployment insurance and employment exchange services, old age and disability pensions, rehabilitation and nursing homes, family welfare subsidies, general public welfare, and payments for military accidents. Maternity benefits are payable up to 52 weeks. In 2004 the retirement age increased to 69 years for residents.

According to the constitution, any incapacitated person living in Denmark has a right to public relief. Benefits such as maintenance allowances for the children of single supporters, day care, and others, involve neither repayment nor any other conditions; some others are regarded as loans to be repaid when possible. Family allowances are paid to families with incomes below a certain threshold; rent subsidies require a means test. Denmark has a dual system of universal medical benefits for all residents and cash sickness benefits for employees. All Danish citizens over 67 years of age may draw old age pensions. Disability pensions, equal in amount to old age pensions plus special supplements, are paid to persons with a stipulated degree of disablement.

Women make up roughly half of the work force. Laws guarantee equal pay for equal work, and women have and use legal recourse if they feel discriminated against. Spousal rape and spousal abuse are criminal offenses. There are crisis centers that counsel and shelter victims of domestic violence. Children's rights are well protected.

The constitution provides for freedom of the press and speech, assembly and association, and for religious freedom, and generally respects these rights. Discrimination based on sex, creed, race, or ethnicity is prohibited by law.

41 HEALTH

Denmark's health care system has retained the same basic structure since the early 1970s. The administration of hospitals and personnel is dealt with by the Ministry of the Interior, while primary care facilities, health insurance, and community care are the responsibility of the Ministry of Social Affairs. Anyone can go to a physician for no fee and the public health system entitles each Dane to his/her own doctor. Expert medical/surgical aid is available, with a qualified nursing staff. Costs are borne by public authorities, but high taxes contribute to these costs. As of 2004, there were an estimated 366 physicians and 972 nurses per 100,000 people. In addition, there were 90 dentists, 49 pharmacists, and 25 midwives per 100,000 people.

The total fertility rate in 2000 was 1.7, while the maternal mortality rate was 10 per 100,000 live births. Approximately 63% of married women (ages 15 to 49) used contraception. Cardiovascular diseases and cancer were the leading causes of death. Denmark's cancer rates were the highest in the European Union. The HIV/AIDS prevalence was 0.20 per 100 adults in 2003. As of 2004, there were approximately 5,000 people living with HIV/AIDS in the country. There were an estimated 100 deaths from AIDS in 2003.

Danish citizens may choose between two systems of primary health care: medical care provided free of charge by a doctor whom the individual chooses for a year and by those specialists to whom the doctor refers the patient; or complete freedom of choice of any physician or specialist at any time, with state reimbursement of about two-thirds of the cost for medical bills paid directly by the patient. Most Danes opt for the former. All patients receive subsidies on pharmaceuticals and vital drugs; everyone must pay a share of dental bills. Health care expenditure was estimated at 8.4% of GDP.

Responsibility for the public hospital service rests with county authorities. Counties form public hospital regions, each of which is allotted one or two larger hospitals with specialists and two to four smaller hospitals where medical treatment is practically free. State-appointed medical health officers, responsible to the National Board of Health, are employed to advise local governments on health matters. Public health authorities have waged large-scale campaigns against tuberculosis, venereal diseases, diphtheria, and poliomyelitis. The free guidance and assistance given to mothers of newborn children by public health nurses have resulted in a low infant mortality rate of 4.56 per 1,000 live births (2005). Medical treatment is free up to school age, when free school medical inspections begin. As of 2001, children up to one year of age were vaccinated against diphtheria, pertussis, and tetanus (99%) and measles (92%). In 2005, life expectancy at birth was 77.62 years. The overall death rate was 11 per 1,000 people.

42 HOUSING

In recent decades, especially since the passage of the Housing Subsidy Act of 1956, considerable government support has been given to housing. For large families building their own homes, government loans have been provided on exceptionally favorable terms, and special rent rebates have been granted to large families occupying apartments in buildings erected by social building societies or in buildings built with government loans since 1950. Subject to certain conditions, housing rebates have been granted to pensioners and invalids. An annual grant is made to reduce householders' maintenance expenses. This extensive support helped to reduce the wartime and immediate postwar housing shortage.

In 2005, there were 2,633,886 dwellings in the nation; 94% were occupied. About 38% were detached, single-family homes; another 35% were detached, multi-family homes and 12% were terraced or linked dwellings. Of the occupied dwellings, about 51% were owner occupied. About 26% of all dwellings consist of five rooms and a kitchen; only about 48,892 dwellings do not have a kitchen at all. During the period 1991–2004, less than 20,000 new homes were built each year. About 17,778 new dwellings were built in 2004, mostly by private builders. Approximately 231,906 dwellings were built before 1900. About 40% of the housing stock was built 1950–79.

43 EDUCATION

Primary, secondary, and most university and other higher education are free. Preschools are operated by private persons or organizations with some government financial aid. Education has been compulsory since 1814; currently, it is compulsory for nine years, for children ages 7 to 16. The Danish primary school system, known as the Folkeskole, covers the nine required years and many opt for an additional 10th year. English is included in the curriculum from the fifth grade. After basic schooling, two-thirds of the pupils apply for practical training in a trade or commerce at special schools. The remaining one-third enroll in secondary schools, which finish after three years with student examination and pave the way for higher education at universities. Municipal authorities, with some financial aid from the central government, have been responsible for providing schools for these children.

In 2001, about 90% of children between the ages of three and six were enrolled in some type of preschool program. Primary school enrollment in 2003 was estimated at about 100% of age-eligible students. The same year, secondary school enrollment was about 96% of age-eligible students. Most students complete their primary education. The student-to-teacher ratio for primary school was at about 10:1 in 2000; the ratio for secondary school was also about 10:1.

Adult education exists side by side with the regular school system. Founded as early as 1844, the folk high schools are voluntary, self-governing high schools imparting general adult education. In addition, there are hundreds of schools for higher instruction of pupils without previous special training. There are 12 universities, including the University of Copenhagen (founded in 1479), the University of Aarhus (founded as a college in 1928 and established as a university in 1933), the University of Odense (opened in 1966), and the University Center at Roskilde (founded in 1970). Attached to the various faculties are institutes, laboratories, and clinics devoted primarily to research, but also offering advanced instruction. There are about 100 specialized colleges with professional programs. Many specialized schools and academies of university rank provide instruction in various technical and artistic fields. All these institutions are independent in their internal administration. In 2003, about 67% of the tertiary age population were enrolled in some type of higher education program. The adult literacy rate for has been estimated at nearly 100%.

As of 2003, public expenditure on education was estimated at 8.5% of GDP, or 15.4% of total government expenditures.

44 LIBRARIES AND MUSEUMS

Denmark's national library, the Royal Library in Copenhagen, founded by Frederik III in 1653, is the largest in Scandinavia, with over 4.6 million volumes. The manuscript department of the Royal Library holds an extensive collection of the manuscripts and correspondence of Hans Christian Andersen and the Søren Kierkegaard Archives (manuscripts and personal papers). The National Museum of Photography (over 25,000 pieces) and the Museum of Danish Cartoon Art are also housed at the Royal Library. Three other large libraries are the University Library in Copenhagen, Copenhagen Public Libraries, and the State Library at Aarhus. The Regional Library of Northern Jutland includes a central library, 17 branch locations and 3 mobile units. As of 2002, there were 250 free public libraries throughout the country with 892 points of service. That year, the public libraries had a total of more than 31.4 million volumes. The Danish Library Association was founded in 1905. The Danish Union of Librarians had about 5,500 members in 2005.

Among the largest museums are the National Museum (with rare ethnologic and archaeological collections), the Glyptotek (with a large collection of ancient and modern sculpture), the State Art Museum (containing the main collection of Danish paintings as well as other Scandinavian artists), the Thorvaldsen Museum, the Hirshsprung Collection, and the Rosenborg Palace, all in Copenhagen, and the National Historical Museum in Frederiksborg Castle, at Hillerod. Among the newer facilities is the Amalienborg Museum in Copenhagen, which opened in 1994 and houses treasures of the royal family. The National Museum of Science and Technology in Elsinore includes the Teknisk Museum (Museum of Technology) and the Trafikmuseum (Transport Museum); the Kommunikationsmuseum (Museum of Communications) in Aalborg is an extension of the Teknisk Museum.

45 MEDIA

Although the government telephone service owns and operates long-distance lines and gives some local service, the bulk of local telephone service is operated by private companies under government concession with government participation. In 2003, there were an estimated 669 mainline telephones for every 1,000 people. The same year, there were approximately 883 mobile phones in use for every 1,000 people. Telegraph services are owned and operated by the government.

The radio broadcasting services are operated by the Danish State Radio System, on long, medium, and short waves. Television broadcasting hours are mainly devoted to current and cultural affairs and to programs for children and young people. There is no commercial advertising on radio or television; owners of sets pay an annual license fee. As of 1998 there were 2 AM and 355 FM radio stations and 26 television stations. In 2003, there were an estimated 1,400 radios and 859 television sets for every 1,000 people. About 236.7 of every 1,000 people are cable subscribers. In 2003, there were 576.8 personal computers for every 1,000 people and 513 of every 1,000 people had access to the Internet. There were 1,724 secure Internet servers in the country in 2004.

The largest daily newspapers (with their political orientation and 2002 circulation totals) are *Ekstra Bladet* (independent/social-liberal, 159,500), *Politiken* (independent/social-liberal, 153,500), *Berlingske Tidende* (independent/conservative, 160,100), *B.T.* (independent/conservative, 144,900), *Aarhus Stiftstidende* (independent, 176,400), *Vendsyssel Tidende* (independent, 114,000), *Aalborg Stiftstidende* (independent, 72,700), and *Fyens Stiftstidende* (independent, 66,400).

Complete freedom of expression, including that in print and electronic media, is guaranteed under the constitution. The media in Denmark are largely independently operated and are free from government interference.

46 ORGANIZATIONS

Nearly every Danish farmer is a member of at least one agricultural organization and of one or more producer cooperatives. The oldest agricultural organization, the Royal Agricultural Society of Denmark, was established in 1769, but most of the other organizations have been founded since 1850. They promote agricultural education and technical and economic development. Local societies have formed provincial federations, which in turn have combined into two national organizations, the Federation of Danish Agricultural Societies and the Federation of Danish Smallholders Societies. The Cooperative Movement of Denmark comprises three groups: agricultural cooperatives, retail cooperatives, and urban cooperatives. Owners of estates and large farms belong to separate organizations specializing in the affairs of larger agricultural units. Most consumers' cooperative societies belong to the Danish Cooperative Wholesale Society, which makes bulk purchases for member societies and also manufactures various products.

The Federation of Danish Industries and the Industrialists' Association in Copenhagen represent industrial undertakings and trade associations, safeguard and promote the interests of industry, and deal with trade questions of an economic nature. The Danish Confederation of Trade Unions has also been influential. The Council of Handicrafts represents various crafts, trades, and industries, and gives subsidies to technical and trade schools. The leading organizations of the wholesale trade are the Copenhagen Chamber of Commerce and the Provincial Chamber of Commerce. There are also active professional societies representing a broad range of career fields.

The scholarly and cultural organization of the Royal Danish Academy of Sciences and Letters was founded in 1742. A wide variety of organizations exist to promote research and education in medical and scientific fields, such as Danish Academy of Technical Sciences, the Danish Dental Association, the Danish Medical Society, and the Danish Cancer Society. The Danish Council of Ethics is appointed by the government to conduct research and offer legislative recommendations on bioethical issues.

A number of national and regional cultural organizations are active, as are associations representing popular sports and recreational activities. The Danish Athletic Federation represents about 30,000 athletes nationwide. The Danish Youth Council is an umbrella organization representing about 62 youth organizations with a combined membership of over one million youth. Youth organizations include the Conservative Youth of Denmark, Danish 4-H Youth, Danish Socialist Democratic, Faroe Islands Youth Council, Greenland Youth Council (SORLAK), scouting programs, and YMCA/YWCA.

Denmark has active chapters of The Red Cross, CARE, Caritas, Greenpeace, UNICEF, and Amnesty International.

47 TOURISM, TRAVEL, AND RECREATION

Dozens of castles, palaces, mansions, and manor houses, including the castle at Elsinore (Helsingør)—site of Shakespeare's *Hamlet*—are open to the public. Tivoli Gardens, the world-famous amusement park, built in 1843 in the center of Copenhagen, is open from May through mid-September. Copenhagen is an important jazz center and holds a jazz festival in July. The Royal Danish Ballet, of international reputation, performs in Copenhagen's Royal Theater, which also presents opera and drama. Greenland, the world's largest island, is part of the Kingdom of Denmark and attracts tourists to its mountains, dog sledges, and midnight sun.

A valid passport is required of all visitors except for Scandinavian nationals. Visas are not required for stays of up to 90 days.

Approximately 1,294,477 tourists visited Denmark in 2003. There were 41,729 hotel rooms with 106,080 beds and an occupancy rate of 35% in that year.

In 2005, the US Department of State estimated the cost of staying in Copenhagen at $288 per day.

48 FAMOUS DANES

Denmark's greatest classic writer and the founder of Danish literature is Ludvig Holberg (1684–1754), historian, philologist, philosopher, critic, and playwright, whose brilliant satiric comedies are internationally famous. Another important dramatist and poet is Adam Gottlob Oehlenschlaeger (1779–1850). The two most celebrated 19th-century Danish writers are Hans Christian Andersen (1805–75), whose fairy tales are read and loved all over the world, and the influential philosopher and religious thinker Søren Kierkegaard (1813–55). Nikolaj Frederik Severin Grundtvig (1783–1872), noted theologian and poet, was renowned for his founding of folk high schools, which brought practical education to the countryside. The leading European literary critic of his time was Georg Morris Brandes (Cohen, 1842–1927), whose *Main Currents in 19th-Century European Literature* exerted an influence on two generations of readers. Leading novelists include Jens Peter Jacobsen (1847–85); Martin Anderson Nexø (1869–1954), author of *Pelle the Conquerer* (1906–10) and *Ditte* (1917–21); and Johannes Vilhelm Jensen (1873–1950), who was awarded the Nobel Prize for literature in 1944 for his series of novels. Karl Adolph Gjellerup (1857–1919) and Henrik Pontoppidan (1857–1943) shared the Nobel Prize for literature in 1917. Isak Dinesen (Karen Blixen, 1885–1962) achieved renown for her volumes of gothic tales and narratives of life in Africa. Jeppe Aaksjaer (1866–1930), poet and novelist, is called the Danish Robert Burns. A great film artist is Carl Dreyer (1889–1968), known for directing *The Passion of Joan of Arc, Day of Wrath,* and *Ordet.* Famous Danish musicians include the composers Niels Gade (1817–90) and Carl Nielsen (1865–1931), the tenors Lauritz Melchior (1890–1973) and Aksel Schiøtz (1906–75), and the soprano Povla Frijsh (d.1960). Notable dancers and choreographers include August Bournonville (1805–79), originator of the Danish ballet style; Erik Bruhn (1928–86), who was known for his classical technique and was director of ballet at the Royal Swedish Opera House and of the National Ballet of Canada; and Fleming Ole Flindt (b.1936), who has directed the Royal Danish Ballet since 1965. The sculptor Bertel Thorvaldsen (1770–1844) is the artist of widest influence. Jørn Utzon (b.1918) is an architect best known for his design of the Sydney Opera House.

Notable scientists include the astronomers Tycho Brahe (1546–1601) and Ole Rømer (1644–1710); the philologists Ramus Christian Rask (1787–1832) and Otto Jespersen (1860–1943); the physicist Hans Christian Ørsted (1777–1851), discoverer of electromagnetism; Nobel Prize winners for physics Niels Bohr (1885–1962) in 1922 and his son Aage Niels Bohr (b.1922) and Benjamin Mottelson (b.1926) in 1975; Niels Rybert Finsen (b.Faroe Islands, 1860–1904), August Krogh (1874–1949), Johannes A. G. Fibiger (1867–1928), and Henrik C. P. Dam (1895–1976), Nobel Prize-winning physicians and physiologists in 1903, 1920, 1926, and 1944, respectively. Jens Christian Skou (b.1918) shared the Nobel prize in chemistry in 1997. Frederik Bajer (1837–1922) was awarded the Nobel Prize for peace in 1908. Knud Johan Victor Rasmussen (1879–1933), explorer and anthropologist born in Greenland, was an authority on Eskimo ethnology.

Queen Margrethe II (b.1940) became sovereign in 1972.

49 DEPENDENCIES

Faroe Islands

The Faroe Islands (Faerøerne in Danish and Føroyar in the Faroese language), whose name stems from the Scandinavian word for sheep (får), are situated in the Atlantic Ocean, due N of Scotland, between 61°20′ and 62°24′N and 6°15′ and 7°41′W. The 18 islands, 17 of which are inhabited, cover an area of 1,399 sq km (540 sq mi). Among the larger islands are Streymoy (Strømø) with an area of 373 sq km (144 sq mi), Eysturoy (Østerø) with 286 sq km (110 sq mi), Vágar (Vaagø) with 178 sq km (69 sq mi), Suduroy (Syderø) with 166 sq km (64 sq mi), and Sandoy (Sandø) with 112 sq km (43 sq mi). The maximum length of the Faroe Islands is 112 km (70 mi) N–S and the maximum width is 79 km (49 mi) NE–SW. The total coastline measures 1,117 km (694 mi).

The estimated population in July 2002 was 46,011. Most Faroese are descended from the Vikings, who settled on the islands in the 9th century. The Faroes have been connected politically with Denmark since the 14th century. During World War II (1939–45), they were occupied by the British, and in this period important political differences emerged. The Faroese People's party advocated independence for the islands; the Unionists preferred to maintain the status quo; and the Faroese Social Democrats wanted home rule. After the war, it was agreed to establish home rule under Danish sovereignty, and since 23 March 1948, the central Danish government has been concerned only with matters of common interest, such as foreign policy and foreign-currency exchange. The Faroes have their own flag, levy their own taxes, and issue their own postage stamps and banknotes. The Faroese language, revived in the 19th century and akin to Icelandic, is used in schools, with Danish taught as a first foreign language.

The Faroese parliament, or Logting, dates back to Viking times and may be Europe's oldest legislative assembly. Members are elected by popular vote on a proportional basis from 7 constituencies to the 32-member Logting; representation has been fairly evenly divided among the four major parties. After the April 2002 election, the Union Party had 8 seats; Republican Party, 8; Social Democrats, 7; People's Party 7. The Independence Party and the Center Party had one seat each. The islands elect two representatives to the Folketing (Danish parliament).

In keeping with the islands' name, sheep raising was long the chief activity, but in recent years the fishing industry has grown rapidly. The total fish catch was nearly 360,000 metric tons in 1996; fisheries exports generated 94% of the territory's $471 million in exports in 1999. Principal varieties of fish caught are cod, herring, and haddock; almost the entire catch is exported. Exports go mainly to Denmark (32%), the United Kingdom (21%), France (9%), Germany (7%), Iceland (5%), and the United States (5%). Imports valued at $469 million in 1999, come mainly from Denmark (28%), Norway (26%), Germany (7%), Sweden (5%), and Iceland (4%). Agriculture is limited to the cultivation of root vegetables, potatoes, and barley, and contributed 27% to the gross domestic product (GDP) in 1999.

The economy is regulated by an agreement with Denmark whereby the central government facilitates the marketing of Faroese fisheries products and guarantees to some extent an adequate supply of foreign currency.

Greenland

Greenland (Grønland in Danish, Kalaallit Nunaat in Greenlandic) is the largest island in the world. Extending from 59°46' to 83°39' N and from 11°39' to 73°8'w, Greenland has a total area of 2,166,086 sq km (836,330 sq mi). The greatest N–S distance is about 2,670 km (1,660 mi), and E–w about 1,290 km (800 mi). Greenland is bounded on the N by the Arctic Ocean, on the E by the Greenland Sea, on the SE by the Denmark Strait (separating it from Iceland), on the S by the Atlantic Ocean, and on the W by Baffin Bay and Davis Strait. The coastline measures 44,087 km (27,394 mi). The ice-free strip along the coast, rarely exceeding 80 km (50 mi) in width, is only 410,449 sq km (158,475 sq mi) in area. The rest of the area, covered with ice measuring at least 2,100 m (7,000 ft) thick in some places, amounts to 1,755,637 sq km (677,855 sq mi). Greenland has a typically arctic climate, but there is considerable variation between localities, and temperature changes in any one locality are apt to be sudden. Rainfall increases from north to south, ranging from about 25 to 114 cm (10–45 in). Land transport is very difficult, owing to the ice and rugged terrain, and most local travel must be done by water. SAS operates flights on the Scandinavia-US route via Greenland, and tourists are being attracted by Greenland's imposing scenery.

The population, grouped in a number of scattered settlements of varying sizes, was estimated at 56,376 in 2002, down from 58,203 in 1996. Greenlanders are predominantly Eskimos, with some admixture of Europeans. The Greenlandic language, an Eskimo-Aleut dialect, is in official use. Most native Greenlanders were engaged in hunting and fishing, but a steadily increasing number are now engaged in administration and in private enterprises. The Europeans chiefly follow such pursuits as administration, skilled services, and mining.

The Vikings reached Greenland as early as the 10th century. By the time Europeans rediscovered the island, however, Norse culture had died out and Greenland belonged to the Eskimos. Danish colonization began in the 18th century, when the whale trade flourished off Greenland's western shore. In 1933, the Permanent Court of Arbitration at The Hague definitively established Danish jurisdiction over all Greenland. Up to 1953, the island was a colony; at that time it became an integral part of Denmark. Greenland held that status until 1979, when it became self-governing after a referendum in which 70% of the population favored home rule. The 31 members in the Landsting (parliament) are elected by popular vote on the basis of proportional representation. In the election held November 2001, the left-wing Siumut Party won 10 seats; Inuit Ataqatigiit, 8; the right-wing Atassut Party, 7; the Demokratiit, 5; and the Katusseqatigiit, 1. Greenland elects two representatives to the Folketing; following the December 2002 election, the representatives were from the Siumut and Inuit Ataqatigiit parties.

Fishing, hunting (mainly seal, and to a lesser extent fox), and mining are the principal occupations. Greenland's total fish catch in 1994 was 112,576 tons, and fisheries exports were valued at $267 million. Agriculture is not possible in most of Greenland, but some few vegetables are grown in the south, usually under glass.

At Ivigtut, on the southwest coast, a deposit of cryolite has long been worked by a Danish government-owned corporation, but reserves are believed to be nearing depletion. The government has a controlling interest in the lead-zinc mine at Mestersvig, on the east coast. Production began in 1956 and has continued sporadically. Low-grade coal mined at Disko Islands, midway on the west coast, is used for local fuel needs. Mining activities ceased in 1990 but exploration activity has revealed the potential for economic exploitation of antimony, barite, beryllium, chromite, coal, colombium, copper, cryolite, diamond, gold, graphite, ilmenite, iron, lead, molybdenum, nickel, platinum-group metals, rare earths, tantalum, thorium, tungsten, uranium, zinc, and zirconium. Fish and fish products make up the bulk of exports. Raw materials are administered jointly by a Denmark-Greenland commission. Underground resources remain in principle the property of Denmark, but the Landsting has veto power over matters having to do with mineral development.

A US Air Force base is situated at Thule, in the far north along the west coast, only 14° from the North Pole; Greenland also forms part of an early-warning radar network. An international meteorological service, administered by Denmark, serves transatlantic flights. In 1960, a 1,500-kW atomic reactor was set up in northern Greenland to supply electric power to a new US scientific base built on the icecap, 225 km (140 mi) inland from Thule.

50 BIBLIOGRAPHY

Annesley, Claire (ed.). *A Political and Economic Dictionary of Western Europe.* Philadelphia: Routledge/Taylor and Francis, 2005.

Decent Work in Denmark: Employment, Social Efficiency and Economic Security. Geneva, Switz.: International Labour Office, 2003.

International Smoking Statistics: A Collection of Historical Data from 30 Economically Developed Countries. New York: Oxford University Press, 2002.

Kinze, Carl Christian. *Marine Mammals of the North Atlantic.* Princeton, N.J.: Princeton University Press, 2002.

Miller, Kenneth E. *Friends and Rivals: Coalition Politics in Denmark, 1901–1995.* Lanham, Md.: University Press of America, 1996.

Pasqualetti, Martin J., Paul Gipe, Robert W. Righter, (eds.). *Wind Power in View: Energy Landscapes in a Crowded World.* San Diego: Academic Press, 2002.

Wessels, Wolfgang, Andreas Maurer, and Jürgan Mittag (eds.). *Fifteen into One?: the European Union and Its Member States.* New York: Palgrave, 2003.

ESTONIA

Republic of Estonia
Eesti Vabariik

CAPITAL: Tallinn

FLAG: Three equal horizontal bands of blue (top), black, and white.

ANTHEM: *Mu isamaa, mu õnn ja rõõm (My Native Land, My Pride and Joy).*

MONETARY UNIT: The Estonian kroon (EEK) was introduced in August 1992, replacing the Russian ruble. EEK1 = $0.08032 (or $1 = EEK12.45) as of 2005.

WEIGHTS AND MEASURES: The metric system is in force.

HOLIDAYS: New Year's Day, 1 January; Independence Day, 24 February; Labor Day, 1 May; Victory Day, anniversary of the Battle of Vonnu in 1919, 23 June; Midsummer Day, 24 June; Christmas, 25–26 December. A movable religious holiday is Good Friday, the Friday before Easter.

TIME: 2 PM = noon GMT.

¹LOCATION, SIZE, AND EXTENT

Estonia is located in northeastern Europe, bordering the Baltic Sea, between Sweden and Russia. Comparatively, the area occupied by Estonia is slightly smaller than the states of New Hampshire and Vermont combined, with a total area of 45,226 sq km (17,462 sq mi). Estonia shares boundaries with the Baltic Sea on the N and W, Russia on the E, and Latvia on the S. Estonia's land boundaries total 633 km (392 mi). Its coastline is 3,794 km (2,352 mi). Estonia's capital city, Tallinn, is located in the northern part of the coast.

²TOPOGRAPHY

The topography of Estonia consists mainly of marshy lowlands with a hilly region in the southeast. Over a third of the country is forest. The highest point is Suur Munamagi, located in the Haanja Uplands of the south, with an altitude of 318 m (1,043 ft). The lowest point is at sea level (Baltic Sea).

The country has more than 1,000 natural and artificial lakes. The largest lake is Lake Peipus, located along the border with Russia. The shared lake has a total area of 3,555 sq km (1,386 sq mi). The Pärnu is the longest river with a length of 144 km (89 mi). The Narva and Ema are also chief rivers.

³CLIMATE

The proximity of the Baltic Sea influences the coastal climate. At the most western point, Vilsandi Saar, the mean temperature is 6°C (42.8°F). At the country's most eastern points, the mean temperature is between 4.2 and 4.5°C (36 to 40°F). Rainfall averages 50 cm (20 in) on the coast. Inland, rainfall averages 70 cm (28 in). Rainfall is heaviest during the summer and lightest in the spring.

⁴FLORA AND FAUNA

Calcareous soil and a relatively mild climate permit rich flora and fauna in western Estonia. Native plants number over 1,600 species. The abundance of woodland and plant species provides a suitable habitat for elk, deer, wild boar, wolf, lynx, bear, and otter. As of 2002, there were at least 65 species of mammals and 205 species of birds.

⁵ENVIRONMENT

Air, water, and land pollution rank among Estonia's most significant environmental challenges. The combination of 300,000 tons of dust from the burning of oil shale by power plants in the northeast part of the country and airborne pollutants from industrial centers in Poland and Germany poses a significant hazard to Estonia's air quality.

Estonia's water resources have been affected by agricultural and industrial pollutants, including petroleum products, which have also contaminated the nation's soil. Some rivers and lakes within the country have been found to contain toxic sediments in excess of 10 times the accepted level for safety.

The nation's land pollution problems are aggravated by the 15 million tons of pollutants that are added yearly to the existing 250 million tons of pollutants. In 1994, 24,000 acres of the country's total land area were affected. Radiation levels from the nuclear accident at Chernobyl exceed currently accepted safety levels.

In 2003, about 11.8% of the total land area was protected, including 11 Ramsar Wetlands of International importance. According to a 2006 report issued by the International Union for Conservation of Nature and Natural Resources (IUCN), threatened species included four types of mammals, three species of birds, one species of fish, and four species of invertebrates. The European mink and the Atlantic sturgeon are among those listed as endangered.

⁶POPULATION

The population of Estonia in 2005 was estimated by the United Nations (UN) at 1,345,000, which placed it at number 147 in population among the 193 nations of the world. In 2005, approximately 16% of the population was over 65 years of age, with another 16% of the population under 15 years of age. There were 85 males for every 100 females in the country. According to the UN, the annual population rate of change for 2005–10 was expected to be -0.3%, a rate the government viewed as too low. The decline in population was due to an extremely low birth rate (1.7 births per woman). The projected population for the year 2025 was 1,171,000. The population density was 30 per sq km (77 per sq mi), with the northern portion of the country being the most densely populated.

The UN estimated that 69% of the population lived in urban areas in 2005, and that population in urban areas was declining at an annual rate of -0.90%. The capital city, Tallinn, had a population of 391,000 in that year. Other cities and their populations were Tartu, 101,297; Narva, 85,000; Kohtla-Järve, 72,000; and Pärnu, 55,000.

7 MIGRATION

Newly independent in 1918, Estonia was occupied and annexed in 1940 by the Soviet Union. It was occupied by German troops the following year. When the Soviet army returned in 1944, more than 60,000 Estonians fled to Sweden and Germany. Other Estonians were sent to Soviet labor camps. Many Russians migrated to Estonia under Soviet rule. Some left after Estonia became independent again.

After the breakup of the Soviet Union in 1991, Estonia suffered from waves of transit migration. As of 1999, ethnic Estonians represent only 65% of the total population of Estonia. Russians, Ukrainians, and Belarussians represent nearly 33%, and other groups comprise the remaining 2%. Only 70% of inhabitants are citizens of Estonia, mainly the ethnic Estonians and about 100,000 Russians. Some 90,000 Russians with permanent residence in Estonia are citizens of Russia. These large ethnic minorities live segregated from ethnic Estonians and tend not to understand the Estonian language. The total number of migrants living in Estonia in 2000 was 365,000, approximately one-quarter of the population. In 2004 a population of 150,536 stateless people existed in Estonia. In 2003 remittances to Estonia were $9.1 million. In 2005 the net migration rate was estimated as -3.18 migrants per 1,000 population. The government views the migration levels as satisfactory.

8 ETHNIC GROUPS

According to a 2000 census, Estonians make up about 67.9% of the population, Russians 25.6%, Ukrainians 2.1%, Belarussians 1.3%, Finns 0.9%, and others 2.2%. Non-Estonians were found chiefly in the northeastern industrial towns, while rural areas were over 80% Estonian.

9 LANGUAGES

Estonian is a member of the Finno-Ugric linguistic family. It is closely related to Finnish and distantly related to Hungarian. Standard Estonian is based on the North Estonian dialect. Most of the sounds can be pronounced as either short, long, or extra long. Changing the duration of a sound in a word can alter the grammatical function of the word or change its meaning completely. The language is highly agglutinative, and there are no less than 14 cases of noun declension. Most borrowed words are from German. The alphabet is Roman. The first text written in Estonian dates from 1525. Estonian is the official language and is spoken by

about 67.3% of the population; however, Russian (29.7%), Ukrainian, English, Finnish, and other languages are also used.

10 RELIGIONS

Christianity was introduced into Estonia in the 11th century. During the Reformation it converted largely to Lutheranism, although political events in the 18th and 19th century occasioned a strong Russian Orthodox presence. Independence from the Soviet Union, achieved in 1991, relieved the pressure under which religious groups had labored since 1940.

In 2005 there were an estimated 165 congregations of the Estonian Evangelical Lutheran Church with about 180,000 members. There were also about 59 congregations of the Estonian Apostolic Orthodox Church (20,000 members) and 30 congregations of the Estonian Orthodox Church (150,000 members). While Lutherans and Orthodox constitute the majority, there are smaller communities of Baptists, Methodists, Roman Catholics, Methodist, Jehovah's Witnesses, Pentecostals, and other Christian denominations. The Church of Jesus Christ of Latter-day Saints (Mormons) has a significant number of missionaries in the country. There are also Jewish, Muslim, and Buddhist communities; however, each of these minority faiths has less than 6,000 followers. About 70,000 people in the country claimed to be atheists.

The constitution provides for freedom of religion and this right is generally respected in practice. All religious organizations must register with the Religious Affairs Department of the Ministry of Interior Affairs. Basic Christian ecumenical religious instruction is available in public schools as an elective. Certain Christian holidays are observed as national holidays.

11 TRANSPORTATION

Estonia in 2004 had a total of 958 km (596 mi) of broad gauge railroad track, all common carrier railway lines, not including industrial lines, of which 132 km (82 mi) was electrified. Tallinn, Haapsalu, Pärnu, Tartu, and Narva are provided rail access to Russia, Latvia, and the Baltic Sea. In order to overcome problems in rolling stock shortages and load fluctuations, a second line of tracks is being laid along the Tallinn-Narva route.

Highways in 2003 totaled 56,849 km (35,360 mi), of which 13,303 km (8,274 mi) are paved, including 99 km (62 mi) of expressways. Motor vehicles dominate domestic freight transportation, carrying nearly 75% of all dispatched goods.

The Baltic Sea (with the Gulf of Finland and Gulf of Riga) provides Estonia with its primary access to international markets. The principal maritime ports are Tallinn and Pärnu. The merchant fleet had 43 vessels of at least 1,000 GRT for a total capacity of 212,998 GRT in 2005. Sea transportation has increased especially since the completion of Tallinn's new harbor and the acquisition of high capacity vessels. Ships carry grain from North America and also serve West African cargo routes. In 1990, a ferry service opened between Tallinn and Stockholm. During one of these commutes in September 1994, the ferry *Estonia* sank off the coast of Finland, resulting in about 900 deaths. The tragedy brought international attention to the safety design of roll-on/roll-off ferries in use worldwide. As of 2003, Estonia had some 500 km (311 mi) of navigable internal waterways.

There were an estimated 29 airports in 2004, of which 12 had paved runways, and one heliport (as of 2005). The principal airport at Tallinn has direct air links to Helsinki and Stockholm. Estonian Air is the principal international airline. In 2003, about 395,000 passengers were carried on scheduled domestic and international airline flights.

¹²HISTORY

What is now Estonia was ruled in turn by the Danes, the Germans, and the Swedes from the Middle Ages until the 18th century. Russia annexed the region in 1721. During the 19th century, an Estonian nationalist movement arose which by the early 20th century sought independence.

After the 1917 Bolshevik Revolution and the advance of German troops into Russia, Estonia declared independence on 24 February 1918. But after the German surrender to the Western powers in November 1918, Russian troops attempted to move back into Estonia. The Estonians, however, pushed out the Soviet forces by April 1919, and the following year Soviet Russia recognized the Republic of Estonia.

The Nazi-Soviet Pact of 1939 assigned Estonia to the Soviet sphere of influence. The Red Army invaded in June 1940 and "admitted" the Estonian Soviet Socialist Republic into the USSR in August 1940. However, Hitler's forces invaded the USSR in June 1941 and took control of Estonia shortly thereafter. The German Army retreated in 1944, and Soviet forces once again occupied Estonia.

Taking advantage of the relatively greater freedom allowed under Mikhail Gorbachev in the late 1980s, an Estonian nationalist movement, the Popular Front, was launched in 1987. Estonia declared its independence from Moscow on 20 August 1991. A new constitution was adopted on 28 June 1992.

With much fanfare, the last Russian tanks and 2,000 troops were removed from Estonia on 17 August 1994, ending 50 years of military presence in Estonia. Russia also announced it would begin dismantling two nuclear reactors within Estonia. Estonia demanded the return of more than 750 sq mi of land that Russia considered part of its territory, but that belonged to Estonia before World War II. When Estonia renewed its claim to those lands, the Russian government began constructing 680 border posts, many of which are guarded by armed soldiers and linked by fences.

One of the worst maritime disasters since World War II occurred on 28 September 1994, when the ferry *Estonia*, en route from Tallinn to Sweden, sank off the coast of Finland, killing about 900 people. Investigators reported that locks on the huge front cargo door of the ferry failed during a storm, letting in a flood of water that caused the ship to sink in only a few minutes.

The 1995 parliamentary vote reflected dissatisfaction among rural inhabitants and pensioners and signaled a change from the vigorous free-market reforms that dominated Estonia's transition from Soviet rule. The results of the election, however, didn't significantly alter Estonia's commitment to a balanced budget, a stable currency, or a good foreign investment climate. Following the March 1995 elections, Tiit Vähi was approved as prime minister, but he and his cabinet resigned in October 1995 amidst a scandal within the administration that involved telephone tapping and the clandestine sales of weapons. President Lennart Meri later appointed a new government, which reinstated Vähi as prime minister. In September 1996 Meri won a second presidential term, al-

LOCATION: 57°30′ to 59°40′ N; 21°50′ to 28°10′ E. BOUNDARY LENGTHS: Latvia, 339 kilometers (211 miles); Russia, 294 kilometers (183 miles); total coastline, 3,794 kilometers (2,358 miles).

though the election was turned over to an electoral college after no candidate won the required two-thirds majority in parliamentary balloting in August. Following a no-confidence vote in February 1997, Prime Minister Vähi resigned and was replaced by Mart Siimann, who formed a minority government.

Reformers once again won control of Estonia's parliament in the March 1999 general elections, in which a coalition of center-right parties gained a slim majority, wining 53 out of 101 seats. (However, the left-leaning Center Party won 28 seats, the highest number for a single party.) Mart Laar was named prime minister. The new government was expected to emphasize political reforms as much as economic ones, focusing on the elimination of corruption and inefficiency in the civil service, courts, and police.

Since it gained its independence in 1991, Estonia's foreign policy focused on integration with Western Europe, with the specific long-range goals of EU and NATO membership. One of these goals received a boost in 1998 when Estonia was invited by the European Union to begin negotiations toward membership. In December 2002, the EU formally invited Estonia, one of 10 new candidate countries, to join the body as of May 2004. A referendum on Estonia's entry into the EU was held on 14 September 2003, and on 1 May 2004 Estonia became a member of the EU. In November 2002, Estonia was one of seven Central and East European countries to be invited to join NATO, with accession taking place on 29 March 2004. Internally, Estonia still faces the challenge of integrating its minority population of ethnic Russians fully into the nation's public life.

In September 2001 Arnold Rüütel was elected president, succeeding Meri, who was barred by the constitution from seeking a third consecutive term. Rüütel's victory was seen as a reaction to popular dissatisfaction with the government and growing economic problems in small towns and rural areas, among other reasons. However, because none of the presidential candidates received the required two-thirds vote in parliament after three rounds of voting, an electoral college, composed of all members of parliament and 266 local government representatives, elected the president. In January 2002, Laar resigned as prime minister and Siim Kallas took his place. The next presidential election was to take place fall 2006.

Parliamentary elections held on 2 March 2003 resulted in the formation of a coalition government made up of the center-right Res Publica, the right-leaning Reform Party, and the rural party People's Union. Thirty-six-year-old Juhan Parts became prime minister on 10 April. On 24 March 2005, Parts resigned, and President Arnold Rüütel asked Reform Party chairman Andrus Ansip to form a new government. Ansip became prime minister on 12 April, representing the Reform Party, the Center Party, and the People's Union. The next parliamentary elections were scheduled for March 2007.

As of 2005, Estonia had the most advanced information infrastructure of any country in the former Communist Eastern bloc. Around 700,000 of Estonia's approximately 1.4 million people bank online, up from zero in 1997. Citizens use the Internet to access state services and to conduct any number of business transactions, and many people who never owned a landline telephone now rely on wireless phones.

After nearly 10 years of negotiations, in May 2005 Russia and Estonia signed a treaty delimiting their border. In June, the Estonian parliament ratified the border treaty, but introduced an amendment referring to the Soviet occupation, despite warnings from Russia not to do so. Russia reacted by withdrawing from the treaty.

13 GOVERNMENT

Estonia adopted a new post-Soviet constitution on 28 June 1992. It declares Estonia a parliamentary democracy with a unicameral parliament. The parliament (Riigikogu) has 101 seats. Members of parliament serve four-year terms. The president (who is elected for a five-year term), prime minister and the cabinet make up the executive branch of government. The president is the head of state while the prime minister is the head of government. Both the parliament and the president are elected by direct universal suffrage of citizens 18 years or older.

14 POLITICAL PARTIES

The Independent Communist Party of Estonia split from the Communist Party of the Soviet Union in January 1991. The Pro Patria Party, the Estonian Social Democratic Party, the Christian-Democratic Union of Estonia, the Estonian National Independence Party, and Estonian Green Movement were among the many parties that emerged in recent years. The Popular Front of Estonia, founded in 1988 to unite pro-independence forces, has lost much of its influence and role since the attainment of independence. The non-Estonian, mainly Russian, interests are represented by the Inter-Movement of the Working People of Estonia and the Union of

Work Collectives, both founded in 1988. In addition, a Russian Democratic Movement has emerged that specifically represents the Russian-speaking population of Estonia.

In the parliamentary elections of March 1995, the Coalition Party and Rural Union (made up of four parties: Coalition Party, Country People's Party, Farmer's Assembly, and Pensioners' and Families' League) won 41 seats; Reform Party-Liberals, 19; Center Party, 16; Pro Patria, 8; Our Home is Estonia, 6; Moderates (consisting of the Social Democratic Party and Rural Center Party), 2; and Right-Wingers, 5.

The Pro Patria and the Estonian National Independence Party, which had allied themselves in the 1995 election, joined forces at the end of that year to form the Fatherland Union. In the March 1999 elections, the Fatherland Union and two other parties formed a broader coalition that won a narrow majority in parliament, garnering a total of 53 parliamentary seats (Fatherland Union, 18; Estonian Reform Party, 18; Moderates, 17). However, the party winning the single largest number of seats was the Estonian Center Party, with 28. The remaining seats were distributed as follows: the Estonian Coalition Party, 7; the Estonian Rural People's Union, 7; and the United People's Party, 6.

In the 2 March 2003 elections, the Center Party and Res Publica, a new political party, each won 28 seats in the Riigikogu; the Reform Party took 19 seats; the People's Union won 13; the Fatherland Union took 7 seats; and the Moderates won 6. The Res Publica, Reform, and People's Union parties formed a coalition government, securing 60 of 101 seats in parliament. The next parliamentary elections were to be held March 2007.

15 LOCAL GOVERNMENT

Estonia's major administrative divisions are 15 counties (*maakond*). The counties are further subdivided into municipalities—rural communes (*vald*) and urban municipalities (*linn*). Since October 2005, there were 227 municipalities in Estonia, 34 of them urban and 193 of them rural.

While only citizens are allowed to vote in Estonia's national elections, residents of Estonia, including noncitizens, are allowed to vote in local elections. Noncitizens, however, cannot be candidates in local (or national) elections. Office-holders serve three-year terms. The last local elections were held on 16 October 2005. In the 2005 local elections, some 800,000 Estonians, or 80% of the eligible electorate, had access to a new e-voting system via the Internet, the largest run by any European country. In the end, only 1% of voters cast their vote online.

16 JUDICIAL SYSTEM

The 1992 constitution established a court system consisting of three levels of courts: (1) rural, city, and administrative courts, (2) circuit courts of appeal, and (3) the National Court. The National Court engages in constitutional review of legislation. At the rural and city courts, the decisions are made by a majority vote with a judge and two lay members. There are 2 city courts, 14 county courts, and 4 administrative courts in Estonia (20 courts of first instance). There are three circuit courts of appeal, at Tallinn and Tartu, and the Viru circuit court located in the city of Jõhvi. The National Court has 19 judges.

The constitution provides for an independent judiciary and the judiciary is independent in practice. The Chief Justice of the National Court, nominated by the president and confirmed by the Riigikogu, nominates National Court judges, whose nominations need to be confirmed by the Riigikogu. The Chief Justice of the National Court also nominates the lower court judges who are then appointed by the president. Judges are appointed for life. The 1992 interim criminal code abolishes a number of political and economic crimes under the former Soviet Criminal Code. A new criminal procedural code was adopted in 1994.

The constitution provides for a presumption of innocence, access to prosecution evidence, confrontation and cross-examination of witnesses, and public trials.

[17]ARMED FORCES

Active armed forces numbered 4,934 in 2005, with some 24,000 reservists. The Army maintained four defense regions with 3,429 soldiers. The Navy numbered 331 active members and the Air Force had 195 active personnel. The Estonian Border Guard numbered 2,600 and also served as the coast guard. The estimated defense expenditure in 2005 was $207 million. As of 2005, Estonian forces were deployed in Afghanistan, Bosnia, Iraq, Serbia and Montenegro, and as United Nations observers in the Middle East.

[18]INTERNATIONAL COOPERATION

Estonia was admitted to the United Nations (UN) on 17 February 1991 and belongs to several specialized UN agencies, such as the FAO, IAEA, World Bank, ICAO, ILO, IMF, IMO, UNESCO, and the WHO. The country is also a member of the OSCE, the European Bank for Reconstruction and Development, the Council of the Baltic Sea States, the Council of Europe, the European Investment Bank, and NATO. Estonia joined the WTO in 1999 and the European Union in 2004. It has observer status in the OAS and is an affiliate member of the Western European Union.

Estonia belongs to the Australia Group and the Nuclear Suppliers Group (London Group). In environmental cooperation, Estonia is part of the Antarctic Treaty, the Basel Convention, Conventions on Biological Diversity and Air Pollution, Ramsar, CITES, the Kyoto Protocol, the Montréal Protocol, MARPOL, and the UN Convention on Climate Change.

[19]ECONOMY

Estonia has one of the strongest economies among the former Soviet republics. Its mineral resources include 60% of former Soviet oil shale deposits, as well as phosphates. Light manufacturing dominates industry, with major sectors that include textiles, furniture, and electronics. Agriculture is based mainly on rearing livestock, but dairy farming is also significant. Estonia is self-sufficient in electrical power.

The economy started to revive after the 1992 monetary reform, reintroducing the preoccupation quasi-convertible Estonian kroon. Estonia's economy quickly became one of the strongest post-Communist economies in eastern Europe as successive governments remained committed to the implementation of market reforms. Growth continued until 1998, when Estonia underwent its first post-Soviet economic downturn. GDP growth slowed to 4% in 1998 and declined to -1.1% in 1999. The economy began to improve the following year.

Estonia's economic progress is linked to its liberal foreign trade regime (there are few tariffs or nontariff barriers), effective bank-

ruptcy legislation, and swift privatization. State subsidies were in the process of being abolished in the early 2000s, and all of these measures helped to stabilize and restructure the economy. As a result, Estonia received high levels of foreign direct investment. Although the global economy was in a downturn in the early 2000s, Estonia was able to maintain GDP growth rates of around 5%, higher than many other European countries. Major growth sectors include information technology, transportation, and construction services. Estonia was formally invited to join the EU in December 2002, and was finally accepted in May 2004. The country became a member of the WTO in 1999.

The GDP growth rate in 2004 was 6.2%, up from 5.1% in 2003; in 2005, the economy was expected to expand by 6.0%. The inflation rate has been fluctuating, but, at 3.0% in 2004, it was well under control and did not pose any problems to the economy. Unemployment was, at 9.6%, fairly high, although on a downward trend (in 2000 the unemployment rate was 13.6%); in 2005, unemployment was expected to drop further to 9.2%. Electronics and telecommunications are two of the main growth sectors, but Estonia is strongly dependent on the economic performance of three of its main trade partners: Finland, Sweden, and Germany.

[20]INCOME

The US Central Intelligence Agency (CIA) reports that in 2005 Estonia's gross domestic product (GDP) was estimated at $21.8 billion. The CIA defines GDP as the value of all final goods and services produced within a nation in a given year and computed on the basis of purchasing power parity (PPP) rather than value as measured on the basis of the rate of exchange based on current dollars. The per capita GDP was estimated at $16,400. The annual growth rate of GDP was estimated at 7.1%. The average inflation rate in 2005 was 4%. It was estimated that agriculture accounted for 4.1% of GDP, industry 29.1%, and services 66.8%.

According to the World Bank, in 2003 remittances from citizens working abroad totaled $40 million or about $30 per capita and accounted for approximately 0.4% of GDP. Foreign aid receipts amounted to $85 million or about $62 per capita and accounted for approximately 1.0% of the gross national income (GNI).

The World Bank reports that in 2003 household consumption in Estonia totaled $5.14 billion or about $3,800 per capita based on a GDP of $9.1 billion, measured in current dollars rather than PPP. Household consumption includes expenditures of individuals, households, and nongovernmental organizations on goods and services, excluding purchases of dwellings. It was estimated that for the period 1990 to 2003 household consumption grew at an average annual rate of 2.5%. In 2001 it was estimated that approximately 41% of household consumption was spent on food, 24% on fuel, 8% on health care, and 4% on education. It was estimated that in 1995 about 8.9% of the population had incomes below the poverty line.

[21]LABOR

In 2005, Estonia's workforce was estimated at 670,000. As of 2003, agriculture accounted for 6.2% of the workforce, with 32.5% engaged in industry, and 61.3% in the services sector. Unemployment was estimated at 9.2% in 2005.

The Estonian constitution guarantees the right to form and freely join a union or employee association. The Central Organization of Estonian Trade Unions (EAKL) was founded in 1990 as a voluntary and culturally Estonian organization to replace the Estonian branch of the Soviet labor confederation. In 2002, the EAKL claimed 58,000 members. A rival union, the Organization of Employee Unions, split off from the EAKL in 1993, and claimed about 40,000 members in 2001. In 2005, about 10% of the Estonian workforce was unionized. Workers had the right to strike, and of collective bargaining, both of which were freely practiced. About 15% of Estonia's workforce were covered under collective bargaining agreements as of 2005.

The statutory minimum employment age is 18, although children aged 15 to 17 years may work with parental permission. Children between the ages of 13 and 15 can also work, but in addition to parental or guardian approval, they must also have the approval of a labor inspector. Minors under the age of 18 are also prohibited from performing dangerous and hazardous work. The number of hours minors can work and when they can work are also limited. The standard workweek is legally set at 40 hours with a mandatory 24-hour rest period. The monthly minimum wage was about $218 in 2005, with around 94% of the nation's workforce earning more than the minimum rate.

22 AGRICULTURE

In 2003, agricultural lands covered 561,000 hectares (1,386,000 acres), or 13.2% of Estonia's land area. During the Soviet period, forced collectivization reduced the share of labor in agriculture from 50% to less than 20%. By 2003, however, there were 36,859 private farms, with an average size of 21.6 hectares (53.4 acres). Agriculture accounted for 15.1% of GDP in 1991 and 4% in 2003.

Principal crops in 2004 included potatoes, 170,900 tons; barley, 289,500 tons; wheat, 184,700 tons; rye, 19,700 tons; and oats, 75,200 tons. In 2004 agricultural products accounted for 5.1% of exports and 8.4% of imports; the agricultural trade deficit was $430.8 million that year.

23 ANIMAL HUSBANDRY

Over 10% of the total land area is meadow or pastureland. In 2005, there were 340,100 pigs, 249,000 head of cattle, 38,800 sheep, and 2,162,000 chickens. Meat production is well developed and provides a surplus for export. In 2005, 15,300 tons of beef, 40,000 tons of pork, and 15,000 tons of poultry were produced. That year, Estonia's dairy cows produced 650,000 tons of milk. Cattle breeding was the main activity during the Soviet era, and production quotas were set extremely high, which required massive imports of feed. Pork production has risen in recent years to offset the decline in the total cattle herd. The wool clip in 2005 was 80 tons.

24 FISHING

Estonia's Baltic and Atlantic catch is marketed in the former Soviet Union, in spite of its own need for quality fish products. The fishing industry is seen as an important way to acquire access to the world market, but scarcity of raw materials currently limits its development. The total catch in 2003 was 80,580 tons. The total value of fisheries exports increased from $79.7 million in 2000 to $142.1 million in 2003. The two major species of the 2003 catch were Atlantic herring and European sprat, each of which accounted for 37%.

25 FORESTRY

The government estimated that some 45% of the land area was covered by forests and woodlands in 1999. The production of wood and wood products is the second-largest industry after textiles; two cellulose plants (at Tallinn and Kehra) use local raw material, but have caused significant environmental problems. There is also a fiberboard processing plant (for furniture making) at Püssi. Roundwood production amounted to 10.2 million cu m (360 million cu ft) in 2004; when exports of 3.4 million cu m (120 million cu ft) of roundwood were valued at $131.3 million. Total forestry exports in 2003 amounted to $533.3 million; imports, $205.7 million.

26 MINING

Oil shale was the primary mineral of importance. The country also produced cement, clays, nitrogen, peat, sand and gravel, and industrial silica sand. Production figures for 2003 were: clays for brick, 134,900,000 cu m, down from 149,000,000 cu m in 2002; clays for cement, 27.3 million cu m, up from 19.0 million cu m in 2002; and sand and gravel, 4.470 million cu m. Phosphate quarrying at the Maardu deposit ceased because of environmental concerns.

27 ENERGY AND POWER

Estonia gets most of its energy from oil shale, found in abundance in the northeastern region of the country. Oil shale is burned to produce electricity and accounts for approximately 6,000 barrels per day of oil production in 2004. With domestic consumption in that year totaling 60,000 barrels per day, Estonia had to import the difference primarily from Russia. There are no natural gas reserves in Estonia, which relies on imports from Russia. Natural gas consumption in 2004 stood at 50 billion cu ft, with imports accounting for all of it.

Estonia is however, a net exporter of electricity, sending its surplus power to parts of northwest Russia and to Latvia. In 2004, a total of 8.9 billion kWh was generated, most of it from Estonia's oil shale-fired plants at Narva. Domestic consumption of electricity for that year totaled 6.4 billion kWh, with generating capacity put at 3.3 GW. Surplus electricity from the two plants is exported to Latvia and the Russian Federation.

28 INDUSTRY

Estonian industrial production focuses on shipbuilding, electric motors, furniture, clothing, textiles, paper, shoes, and apparel. Extractive industries include oil shale, phosphate, and cement production. According to the US Central Intelligence Agency, industry accounted for 29% of GDP in 2001. In 1991, 26.6% of industrial output was accounted for by the food industry, 25.9% by light industry, 12.7% by machine-building and metalworks, 10.3% by the timber industry, and 8.5% by chemicals. The textile mills of Kreenholmi Manufacturer in Narva and Bălți Manufacturer in Tallinn are the country's largest industrial enterprises. Construction was slated to be a principal growth sector in 2002.

Between 1990 and 1995, industrial output shrank by an average of 14.9% per year, but most of the decline occurred in the years immediately after independence; by 1994, industrial production was on the rise. In 1995, value added by industry accounted for 28% of GDP and has remained stable since.

The industrial production growth rate was 5% in 2000, lower than the GDP growth rate (7.8%), and an indication of an under-performing industrial sector. In 2004, industry had a 28.9% share in the GDP; agriculture made up a small part of the economy (4.1%), while services was the best performing sector, with a 67% share in the GDP. Current industries include engineering, electronics, wood and wood products, textiles, information technology, and telecommunications.

29 SCIENCE AND TECHNOLOGY

The Academy of Sciences, founded in 1938, has divisions of astronomy and physics, informatics and technical sciences, and biology, geology, and chemistry, and research institutes devoted to biology, ecology, experimental biology, zoology and botany, environmental biology, marine sciences, astrophysics and atmospheric physics, chemical physics and biophysics, chemistry, geology, physics, computer research and design, cybernetics, and energy. Other research institutes in the country are devoted to preventive medicine and oil shale research. Tallinn Technical University (founded in 1918) offers science and engineering degrees. The University of Tartu, founded in 1632, has faculties of biology and geography, mathematics, medicine, and physics and chemistry, as well as an institute of general and molecular pathology. Estonian Agricultural University was founded in 1951. In 1987–97, science and engineering students accounted for 27% of university enrollment.

In 2002, expenditures for research and development (R&D) totaled $134.267 million, or 0.81% of GDP. Of that total, 53.8% came from government sources, while business provided 29.2%, followed by foreign sources at 14.4%, higher education at 2.4% and private nonprofit institutions at 0.2%. In that same year Estonia had 2,253 researchers and 386 technicians per million people that were actively engaged in R&D. In 2002 high technology exports by Estonia totaled $375 million, accounting for 12% of manufactured exports.

30 DOMESTIC TRADE

Before the collapse of the Soviet Union, Estonia's domestic trade was underdeveloped by international standards. Most trading companies were owned either by the state or by cooperatives. In recent years, many shops have been privatized or municipalized, new private shops established, and the assortment of goods widened. By 1992, there were 4,026 shops in Estonia.

Open-air markets control a large segment of domestic food sales. Market prices are usually lower than those in grocery stores, making it difficult for them to compete. Retail sales of food products amounted to $441 million in 1995.

31 FOREIGN TRADE

During the Soviet era, Estonia's foreign trade was characterized by large net imports, 80–85% of which came from other Soviet republics, which were also the destination of 95% of Estonian exports. Beginning in 1992, the value of exports began to surpass that of imports, and the share of trade with other former Soviet

Principal Trading Partners – Estonia (2003)			
(In millions of US dollars)			
Country	Exports	Imports	Balance
World	5,622.5	7,966.6	-2,344.1
Finland	1,231.1	1,264.5	-33.4
Sweden	700.8	610.2	90.6
Russia	643.2	811.1	-167.9
Germany	469.8	881.9	-412.1
Latvia	417.6	191.1	226.5
Lithuania	226.6	228.0	-1.4
Ukraine	200.5	340.2	-139.7
United Kingdom	199.8	177.5	22.3
Denmark	179.3	157.1	22.2
Norway	170.4	83.9	86.5

(…) data not available or not significant.

SOURCE: *2003 International Trade Statistics Yearbook,* New York: United Nations, 2004.

republics diminished. In 2000, Estonia's exports totaled $3.8 billion, 69% of which went to EU nations.

The most important export industry in Estonia is electronics (24.5%). Cork, wood, and their manufactures account for the second-largest consolidated group of commodity exports (11.9%). Other important exports include apparel (5.3%), textiles (4.4%), and furniture (3.8%).

In 2004, exports reached $5.7 billion (FOB—Free on Board), while imports grew to $7.3 billion (FOB). The bulk of exports went to Finland (23.1%), Sweden (15.3%), Germany (8.4%), Latvia (7.9%), Russia (5.7%), and Lithuania (4.4%). Imports included machinery and equipment (33.5%), chemical products (11.6%), textiles (10.3%), foodstuffs (9.4%), and transportation equipment (8.9%), and mainly came from Finland (22.1%), Germany (12.9%), Sweden (9.7%), Russia (9.2%), Lithuania (5.3%), and Latvia (4.7%).

32 BALANCE OF PAYMENTS

Since independence, Estonia has dismantled a Soviet-era system of trade barriers and tariffs to become one of the world's most free-trading nations. In the early 1990s, exports to the West quadrupled, helping to generate a strong surplus in the current account. By the late 1990s and early 2000s, however, the balance of trade on goods became generally negative. Services and capital inflows produced income in the form of foreign direct investment, which remained strong.

The US Central Intelligence Agency (CIA) reported that in 2002 the purchasing power parity of Estonia's exports was $3.4 billion while imports totaled $4.4 billion resulting in a trade deficit of -$1 billion.

The International Monetary Fund (IMF) reported that in 2001 Estonia had exports of goods totaling $3.34 billion and imports totaling $4.13 billion. The services credit totaled $1.64 billion and debit $1.07 billion.

Exports of goods reached $6.0 billion in 2004, and were expected to grow to $7.6 billion in 2005. Imports were expected to reach $9.3 billion in 2005, up from $7.9 billion in 2004. The resource balance was consequently negative, reaching -$1.9 billion in 2004, and -$1.7 billion in 2005. The current account balance was also

Balance of Payments – Estonia (2003)

(In millions of US dollars)

Current Account		**-1,199.2**
Balance on goods		-1,579.5
Imports	-6,183.0	
Exports	4,603.4	
Balance on services		850.7
Balance on income		-576.7
Current transfers		106.3
Capital Account		**39.7**
Financial Account		**1,337.4**
Direct investment abroad		-148.2
Direct investment in Estonia		890.8
Portfolio investment assets		-394.3
Portfolio investment liabilities		558.2
Financial derivatives		-1.8
Other investment assets		-127.3
Other investment liabilities		560.0
Net Errors and Omissions		**-8.6**
Reserves and Related Items		**-169.4**

(…) data not available or not significant.

SOURCE: *Balance of Payment Statistics Yearbook 2004*, Washington, DC: International Monetary Fund, 2004.

negative, at -$1.4 billion in 2004, and an expected -$1.5 billion in 2005. Foreign exchange reserves (excluding gold) grew to $1.8 billion in 2004, covering less than three months of imports.

33 BANKING AND SECURITIES

All links with the Soviet budget and financial system were severed in 1991, and today Estonia has the strongest and most advanced banking system in the Baltic States. In January 1990 the Bank of Estonia was created, which merged two years later with the Estonian branch of Gosbank (the Soviet State Bank) to form the country's new central bank. In December 1988 the authorities established the first Estonian commercial bank, the Tartu Commercial Bank, and by September 1991 there were 20 commercial banks responsible for 27% of total credit extended by banks. The commercial banks include the Bank of Tallinn (1990), Estonian Commercial Bank of Industry (1991), Cand Bank of Estonia (1990), and South Estonian Development Bank. Savings banks include the Estonian Savings Bank, a bank with 432 branches.

Like those of other Eastern European countries, Estonia's banking sector has suffered from an excessive number of banks: there were 43 by the end of 1992. Consolidations took place in 1993, with the banks being merged in Eesti Uhispank (Estonian Unified Bank). As of 2001 there were 7 licensed commercial banks in Estonia. The merger agreement between the Union Bank of Estonia and the North Estonian Bank was signed in January 1997. With combined assets of EEK4.97 billion ($414 million), the merger pushed Union Bank of Estonia (the name of the new entity) from third to second place in terms of assets. Hansabank remained Estonia's largest bank, especially after its merger with Hoiupank (Saving Bank). In 1999, SwedBank bid successfully for a majority interest in Hansabank.

Since independence, Estonia's banks have played a major role in fostering a climate of economic stability. In 1997, they took the initiative in tightening credit in the wake of the Asian finan-

cial crisis. This action, which resulted in a rise in interest rates, checked fears of a too-rapid economic expansion, which would bring about inflation. The International Monetary Fund reports that in 2001, currency and demand deposits—an aggregate commonly known as M1—were equal to $1.4 billion. In that same year, M2—an aggregate equal to M1 plus savings deposits, small time deposits, and money market mutual funds—was $2.3 billion. The money market rate, the rate at which financial institutions lend to one another in the short term, was 4.92%.

There are two stock exchanges in Estonia: the Estonian Stock Exchange and the Tallinn Stock Exchange, inaugurated in May 1996. As of 2004, there were 13 companies listed on the Tallinn Stock Exchange, which had a capitalization that year of $6.203 billion. The TALSE rose 57.1% in 2004 from the previous year to 448.8.

34 INSURANCE

Since Estonia regained its independence, it has sought to develop a system of health insurance involving the decentralization of medical care. Third-party automobile liability insurance is compulsory.

35 PUBLIC FINANCE

The new government exercises fiscal responsibility characterized by a strictly balanced budget. No transfers or preferential credits are given to public enterprises, and governmental borrowing from the central bank is forbidden. In January 1996 Estonia instituted a centralized treasury system for managing the government's budget.

The US Central Intelligence Agency (CIA) estimated that in 2005 Estonia's central government took in revenues of approximately $5.1 billion and had expenditures of $5 billion. Revenues minus expenditures totaled approximately $109 million. Public debt in 2005 amounted to 3.8% of GDP. Total external debt was $10.09 billion.

Public Finance – Estonia (2001)

(In millions of krooni, central government figures)

Revenue and Grants	**29,896**	**100.0%**
Tax revenue	16,128	53.9%
Social contributions	10,471	35.0%
Grants	624	2.1%
Other revenue	2,673	8.9%
Expenditures	**29,237**	**100.0%**
General public services	5,681	19.4%
Defense	1,450	5.0%
Public order and safety	2,095	7.2%
Economic affairs	2,766	9.5%
Environmental protection	…	…
Housing and community amenities	…	…
Health	4,763	16.3%
Recreational, culture, and religion	1,157	4.0%
Education	2,137	7.3%
Social protection	9,188	31.4%

(…) data not available or not significant.

SOURCE: *Government Finance Statistics Yearbook 2004*, Washington, DC: International Monetary Fund, 2004.

The International Monetary Fund (IMF) reported that in 2001, the most recent year for which it had data, central government revenues were EEK29,896 million and expenditures were EEK29,237 million. The value of revenues was US$1,710 million and expenditures US$1,673 million, based on an exchange rate for 2001 of US$1 = EEK17.478 as reported by the IMF. Government outlays by function were as follows: general public services, 19.4%; defense, 5.0%; public order and safety, 7.2%; economic affairs, 9.5%; health, 16.3%; recreation, culture, and religion, 4.0%; education, 7.3%; and social protection, 31.4%.

36TAXATION

Estonia does not tax the income of resident or permanently established nonresident companies. Instead, they are subject only to a tax on distributions (dividends, fringe benefits, gifts, profit distributions, and those payments not related to the payer's business) to resident legal entities, resident and nonresident persons, and nonresident companies. In 2006, those subject are taxed at 22%. A further reduction to 20% is slated to take effect in 2007. Interest payments are subject to a 24% withholding tax that is paid to resident persons, and on that portion of interest paid to nonresident persons or companies that is over the market interest rate. Royalty payments made to nonresident firms and persons, are subject to a 15% withholding tax. Resident persons and companies are subject to a higher, 24% withholding rate. Generally, capital gains received by resident persons and companies are taxed as income. For companies, the gains are taxed as part of the distribution, when it is made. Individuals do not pay a capital gains tax on the sale of their primary residence.

Personal income taxes, in 2006, are assessed at the same flat rate of 22% as corporate profits. Some school fees, living allowances, and interest on loans for the purchase of residential housing are deductible from taxable income. A withholding tax of 22% is imposed on dividends paid to nonresidents that hold less than 20% of the share capital in the paying company. However, Estonia has double tax treaties with at least 22 countries in which withholding taxes are eliminated or substantially reduced. A new Law on Social Tax came into effect in January 1999. The rate of social tax is 33% payable by employers and self-employed individuals. There are relatively few allowable deductions from taxable income in the Estonian tax code. The annual land tax varies from 0.1–2.5% of assessed value.

Main indirect tax is a value-added tax (VAT) set at a with a standard rate of 18% by a new Law on VAT passed in July 2001 and effective in January 2002. Reduced rates of 0% and 5% apply to some goods and services, including a 0% rate on exported goods and a specific list of exported services. Excise duties are levied on tobacco, alcoholic beverages, motor fuel, motor oil, and fuel oil (but not liquefied or compresses gas), motor vehicles, and packages (imposed to encourage recycling of package material). There is a gambling tax, and a customs processing fee on each customs declaration submitted. Rights of recording are taxed at 0.4%. Local governments have the authority to impose taxes and municipal taxes range from 1–2%.

37CUSTOMS AND DUTIES

Estonia has a liberal trade regime, with few tariff or nontariff barriers. Among the few items that have tariffs placed on them are agricultural goods produced in countries that are not among Estonia's preferred trading partners. There is also a value-added tax (VAT) levied ad valorem on everything except a few select commodities, including medicines and medical equipment, funeral equipment, and goods for nonprofit purposes.

38FOREIGN INVESTMENT

Estonia has successfully attracted a large number of joint ventures with Western companies, benefiting from a well-developed service sector and links with Scandinavian countries. The foreign investment act passed by the Supreme Council in September 1991 offers tax relief to foreign investors. Property brought into Estonia by foreign investors as an initial capital investment is exempt from customs duties, but is subject to value-added tax. A foreign investor is legally entitled to repatriate profits after paying income tax.

In 1998, foreign direct investment (FDI) inflows peaked at $580.6, up from $266.7 million in 1997. FDI inflow averaged $346 million in 1999 and 2000, but increased to $538 million in 2001. Estonia's share of world FDI flows from 1998 to 2000 were 2.3 times its share of world GDP, making it 16th among the 140 countries ranked on FDI performance by UNCTAD.

Industry accounts for 46% of the total foreign investment, primarily in the pulp and paper, transportation, and services sectors. Wholesale and retail trade accounts for 27% of foreign investment; transport, 14%. Estonian agribusiness is an area of growing interest to foreign investors.

During the past decade, Estonia has been one of the best performing Central and Eastern European countries in terms of foreign investments attracted. Numerous foreign companies have considered Estonia to be an attractive market, and today companies partly or wholly owned by foreign nationals make up one-third of the country's GDP, and over 50% of its exports. In 2004, total capital inflows rose to $850 million, with Sweden and Finland being the largest investors.

39ECONOMIC DEVELOPMENT

After passing an ownership act in June 1990, the government began a privatization program at the beginning of 1991. Most of the nearly 500 state-owned companies have since passed into new hands. The Estonian Privatization Agency (EPA) was established to oversee major privatization programs. In late 1995, EPA announced privatization plans for Estonian Railways, Estonian Energy, Estonian Oil Shale, Estonian Telekom, and Tallinn Ports. Estonian Gas, Estonian Tobacco, and Estonian Air were privatized in 1996. As of 2002, only the port and the main power plants remained state-controlled.

Estonia has excellent intellectual property laws, has enacted modern bankruptcy legislation, and has seen the emergence of well-managed privately held banks. The constitution mandates a balanced budget, and the climate for foreign investment is positive. In 2003, the economy was vulnerable, and the size of the current account deficit was a particular concern. The government was urged by the International Monetary Fund (IMF) to pursue a fiscal surplus policy, to prepare for membership in the European Union (EU). The country joined the World Trade Organization (WTO) in 1999 and the EU in 2004.

The economy expanded at healthy rates in the first half of 2005, and is expected to continue the trend for a couple of more years.

This growth was fueled by increased private consumption and fixed investment. The export sector has been another sector that has registered high growth rates, and it is predicted to out-perform the import sector in coming years.

40 SOCIAL DEVELOPMENT

Social security programs were originally introduced in 1924. After independence from the Soviet Union, new social insurance systems were introduced. The current law was implemented in 2003. Pension systems are funded by contributions from employers and the government. Retirement is set at age 63 for men and 59 for women, and is set to increase to age 63 for both men and women. Other social welfare programs include worker's compensation, unemployment assistance, survivorship payments, maternity and sickness benefits, and family allowances. There is a family allowance for all children under 17 years of age.

Women constitute slightly more than half the work force, and in theory are entitled to equal pay. Although women on average achieve higher educational levels than men, their average pay was lower. Sexual harassment is not officially reported. Domestic violence is a widespread problem and is grossly underreported; spousal abuse is not a criminal offense. Public attention is focused increasingly on the welfare of children in the wake of family crises caused by economic dislocation. Educational issues were aggressively addressed in 2004.

Ethnic Russians sometimes face discrimination in housing and employment. Estonian language requirements make it difficult for many of them to find public sector employment. Citizenship has not automatically been extended to ethnic Russians living in Estonia, and a significant proportion of the population remain noncitizens. Discrimination based on race, sex, nationality, or religion is illegal under the constitution. Prison conditions remain poor, and police brutality is commonly reported.

41 HEALTH

A major reform of the primary care system was implemented in 1998, making family practitioners independent contractors with combined private and public-financed payment. In 2000, there was an estimated fertility rate of 1.2. The maternal mortality rate was 50 maternal deaths per 100,000 live births as of 1998. In 2005, the infant mortality rate was an estimated 7.87 per 1,000 and the overall death rate as of 2002 was 13.4 per 1,000 people. Life expectancy in 2005 averaged 71.77 years. In 1999, Estonia immunized children up to one year old against diphtheria, pertussis, and tetanus, 95%; and measles, 92%.

The number of hospitals in Estonia decreased significantly during the 1990s, with the number of available beds cut by one-third between 1991 and 1995. As of 1998, there were 78 hospitals, with a total of 10,509 beds. As of 2004, there were an estimated 316 physicians and 629 nurses per 100,000 people. The country's only medical school is the Tartu University Medical Faculty.

The HIV/AIDS prevalence was 1.10 per 100 adults in 2003. As of 2004, there were approximately 7,800 people living with HIV/AIDS in the country. There were an estimated 200 deaths from AIDS in 2003.

42 HOUSING

According to 2000 census figures, the total number of dwellings in the country was at about 628,615. Of these 617,399 were described as conventional dwellings; 424,769 were apartments and 171,086 were single-family, detached dwellings. About 85% of all conventional dwellings were owned by private citizens residing in Estonia. About 3.8% of all conventional dwellings are owned by housing associations. Only about 3.7% of all conventional dwellings were built in 1991 or later; 59% of the housing stock was built during the period 1961–1990. The housing costs of low-income families are subsidized.

43 EDUCATION

Prior to the 1990s, the Soviet system of education was followed. This was modified after Estonia's separation from the USSR. Primary education (basic school) covers nine years. This is followed by a general secondary school (gymnasium) or a vocational school, both of which cover a three-year program. Students in vocational schools may choose to continue in an advanced program of another three years. The academic year runs from September through June. The primary languages of instruction are Estonian, Russian, and English.

In 2001, most children between the ages of three and six were enrolled in some type of preschool program. Primary school enrollment in 2003 was estimated at about 95% of age-eligible students. The same year, secondary school enrollment was about 88% of age-eligible students. Most students complete their primary education. The student-to-teacher ratio for primary school was at about 14:1 in 2003; the ratio for secondary school was about 10:1.

There are two well-known universities: the University of Tartu, founded in 1632, and the Talliva Technical University, founded in 1936, which mainly offers engineering courses. In 2003, about 66% of the tertiary age population were enrolled in some type of higher education program; with 50% for men and 83% for women. The adult literacy rate for 2004 was estimated at about 99.8%.

As of 2003, public expenditure on education was estimated at 5.7% of GDP.

44 LIBRARIES AND MUSEUMS

The National Library of Estonia in Tallinn, founded in 1918, contains over 3.2 million volumes. Other important libraries located in Tallinn include the Estonian Technical Library (11.8 million volumes) and the Estonian Academic Library (2.2 million). The Tartu State University Library is the largest academic library with 3.7 million volumes. In 2004, there were 564 public libraries in the country, along with 512 school libraries and 75 research and special libraries.

The Estonian History Museum in Tallinn was established in 1864. It contains 230,000 exhibits that follow the history of the region's people from ancient times to the present. The Estonian National Museum in Tartu, established in 1909, features exhibits about the living conditions of Estonians. Also in Tallinn is the Art Museum of Estonia, the Estonian Open Air Museum, the Estonian Theater and Music Museum, and the Tallinn City Museum. Tartu University houses a Museum of Classical Antiquities.

⁴⁵MEDIA

Though the telecommunications system has had recent improvements in the form of foreign investment through business ventures, there are still thousands of residents on waiting lists for service lines, with the average wait for service at about 1.4 years in 2000. In 2003, there were an estimated 341 mainline telephones for every 1,000 people; about 4,500 people were on a waiting list for telephone service installation. The same year, there were approximately 777 mobile phones in use for every 1,000 people.

Estonian Radio began regular broadcasting in 1926. In 1937, the highest radio tower in Europe (196.7m) was built in Türi. In the 1970s, Estonian Radio was the first in the former Soviet Union to carry advertising. Estonian television began broadcasting in 1955, and started color broadcasts in 1972. It broadcasts on four channels in Estonian and Russian. As of 2001, there were 98 FM radio stations and 3 television stations. In 2003, there were an estimated 1,136 radios and 507 television sets for every 1,000 people. About 117 of every 1,000 people are cable subscribers. Also in 2003, there were 440.4 personal computers for every 1,000 people and 444 of every 1,000 people had access to the Internet. There were 113 secure Internet servers in the country in 2004.

Journalism was subject to varying degrees of censorship from the Russian occupation in 1940 until the late 1980s. The most popular daily newspapers (with 2002 circulation figures) are *Noorte Haal* (*The Voice of Youth*, 150,000), *Postimees* (*Postman*, 59,200), *Paevaleht* (*The Daily Paper*, 40,000), and *Rahva Haal* (*The Voice of the People*, 175,000). The most widely read weeklies (with 1995 circulation figures) are the *Maaleht* (Country News, 50,000) and the *Eesti Ekspress* (Estonian Express, 55,000).

Estonia has an active publishing industry, although it faced economic difficulties in the early 1990s. The ISBN code has been used in Estonia since 1988. There were 2,291,000 book titles published in 1994.

The government is said to respect constitutional provisions for free expression. Foreign publications are widely available and private print and broadcast media operate freely.

⁴⁶ORGANIZATIONS

The Chamber of Commerce and Industry of the Republic of Estonia promotes trade and commerce with its neighbors. Also, there is a chamber of commerce in Tartu. Professional societies and trade unions have developed for a number of careers.

Research and educational organizations include the Estonian Academy of Sciences and the Estonian Medical Association. There are also several associations dedicated to research and education for specific fields of medicine and particular diseases and conditions.

The Estonian Institute, established in 1989, promotes the appreciation of Estonian culture abroad. Ars Baltica is a multination group based in Vilnius that promotes appreciation for regional arts and culture.

Most student organizations belong to the umbrella organizations of the Federation of Estonian Student Unions or the Federation of Estonian Universities. Other youth organizations include the Estonian Green Movement, YMCA/YWCA, Junior Chamber, the Estonian Scout Associations, and the Girl Guides. In 1989

Estonian sports were reorganized and the Soviets reduced their control of Estonia's sports system. In the same year the National Olympic Committee was restored. Other sports associations have since formed, including groups for wind surfing, yachting, Frisbee, and football (soccer). The Estonian Association of University Women promotes educational and professional opportunities for women.

The Estonian Institute for Human Rights monitors actions concerning civil rights and offers legal aid and information to the public. Volunteer service organizations, such as the Lions Clubs and Kiwanis International, are also present. There is a national chapter of the Red Cross Society.

⁴⁷TOURISM, TRAVEL, AND RECREATION

Visitors are drawn to the country's scenic landscapes, Hanseatic architecture, music and dance festivals, regattas, and beach resorts. The ancient town of Tallinn, noted for its architectural preservation, is a major tourist attraction and is linked by regular ferries to Helsinki and Stockholm.

There were 3,377,837 foreign arrivals in Estonia in 2003, almost 61% of whom came from Northern Europe. Tourist receipts totaled $886 million. The 12,445 hotel rooms with 27,487 beds had an occupancy rate of 47%. The average length of stay was two nights.

In 2005, the US Department of State estimated the daily expenses in Tallinn at $210.

⁴⁸FAMOUS ESTONIANS

Lennart Meri (b.1929), writer, filmmaker, and historian, became president of Estonia in 1992 and won a second term in 1996. He left office in 2001, and was succeeded by Arnold Rüütel (b.1928). Writer Friedrich Reinhold Kreutzwald (1803–1882) wrote the epic *Kalevipoeg* (Son of Kalev), which was published by the Estonian Learned Society in 1857–61 and marked the beginning of Estonian national literature.

The revolution of 1905 forced many Estonian writers to flee the country. In 1906 a stable government was established in Estonia and a literary movement took hold, Birth of Young Estonia. The movement was led by poet Gustav Suits (1883–1956). He fled to Finland in 1910 but returned after the Russian Revolution of 1917. Later, Suits became a professor of literature at Tartu University. His fellow writers and poets between the revolution of 1917 and 1940 included Friedbert Tuglas (1886–1971) and Marie Under (1883–1980). Writers who fled abroad during World War II include Karl Rumor (1886–1971) and Arthur Adson (1889–1977). Estonian writers banned or exiled during the Soviet period include the playwright Hugo Raudsepp (1883–1952). American Architect Louis Kahn (1901?–1974) was born in Estonia.

⁴⁹DEPENDENCIES

Estonia has no territories or colonies.

⁵⁰BIBLIOGRAPHY

Frucht, Richard (ed.). *Eastern Europe: An Introduction to the People, Lands, and Culture.* Santa Barbara, Calif.: ABC-CLIO, 2005.

Kasekamp, Andres. *The Radical Right in Interwar Estonia*. New York: St. Martin's Press, 2000.

McElrath, Karen (ed.). *HIV and AIDS: A Global View*. Westport, Conn.: Greenwood Press, 2002.

Miljan, Toivo. *Historical Dictionary of Estonia*. Lanham, Md.: Scarecrow, 2004.

Raun, Toivo U. *Estonia and the Estonians*. Stanford, Calif.: Hoover Institution Press, 2001.

Terterov, Marat (ed.). *Doing Business with Estonia*. Sterling, Va.: Kogan Page, 2004.

Vogt, Henri. *Between Utopia and Disillusionment: A Narrative of the Political Transformation in Eastern Europe*. New York: Berghahn Books, 2004.

FINLAND

Republic of Finland
Suomen Tasavalta

CAPITAL: Helsinki

FLAG: The civil flag contains an ultramarine cross with an extended right horizontal on a white background.

ANTHEM: *Maammelaulu* (in Swedish, *Vårt land; Our Land).*

MONETARY UNIT: The euro replaced the markkaa as the official currency in 2002. The euro is divided into 100 cents. There are coins in denominations of 1, 2, 5, 10, 20, and 50 cents and 1 euro and 2 euros. There are notes of 5, 10, 20, 50, 100, 200, and 500 euros. €1 = $1.25475 (or $1 = €0.79697) as of 2005.

WEIGHTS AND MEASURES: The metric system is the legal standard.

HOLIDAYS: New Year's Day, 1 January; May Day, 1 May; Independence Day, 6 December; Christmas, 25–26 December. Movable holidays include Good Friday, Easter Monday, Whitsun, and Midsummer Day (late June). Epiphany, Ascension, and All Saints' Day are adjusted to fall always on Saturdays.

TIME: 2 PM = noon GMT.

¹LOCATION, SIZE, AND EXTENT

Part of Fenno-Scandia (the Scandinavian Peninsula, Finland, Karelia, and the Kola Peninsula), Finland has an area of 337,030 sq km (130,128 sq mi), of which 31,560 sq km (12,185 sq mi) is inland water. Comparatively, the area occupied by Finland is slightly smaller than the state of Montana. Its length, one-third of which lies above the Arctic Circle, is 1,160 km (721 mi) N–S; its width is 540 km (336 mi) E–W.

Finland borders on Russia to the E, the Gulf of Finland to the SE, the Baltic Sea to the SW, the Gulf of Bothnia and Sweden to the W, and Norway to the NW and N, with a total land boundary of 2,628 km (1,629 mi) and a coastline of about 1,126 km (698 mi, excluding islands and coastal indentations).

Finland's capital, Helsinki, is located on the country's southern coast.

²TOPOGRAPHY

Southern and western Finland consists of a coastal plain with a severely indented coastline and thousands of small islands stretching out to the Åland Islands. Central Finland is an extensive lake plateau with a majority of the country's 60,000 lakes; 24.5% of the area of Mikkelin Province is water.

Northern Finland is densely forested upland. The highest elevations are in the Norwegian border areas; northwest of Enontekiö rises Haltia, a mountain 1,328 m (4,357 ft) above sea level. Extensive, interconnected lake and river systems provide important natural waterways.

³CLIMATE

Because of the warming influence of the Gulf Stream and the prevailing wind patterns, Finland's climate is comparatively mild for the high latitude. During the winter, the average temperature ranges from -14°C to -3°C (7–27°F), while summer mean temperatures range from 13–18°C (55–65°F). Snow cover lasts from about 90 days in the Åland Islands to 250 days in Enontekiö. Average annual precipitation (including both rain and snow) ranges from 40 cm (16 in) in northern Finland to 71 cm (28 in) in southern Finland.

⁴FLORA AND FAUNA

Forests, chiefly pine, spruce, and birch, are economically the most significant flora. There are more than 1,100 native species of higher plants; flora is richest in southern Finland and the Åland Islands. Of 22,700 species of fauna, more than 75% are insects. At least 60 species of mammals are native to Finland. Fur-bearing animals (otter, marten, ermine) are declining in number, while elk, fox, and beaver have increased. Of some 248 species of breeding birds, the best known is the cuckoo, the harbinger of spring. Of some 66 species of freshwater fish, 33 have some economic importance; in fresh waters, the perch, walleyed pike, great northern pike, and others are plentiful. Salmon remains the favorite of fly rod enthusiasts.

⁵ENVIRONMENT

Finland's main environmental issues are air and water pollution, and the preservation of its wildlife. Finland's principal environmental agency is the Ministry of the Environment, established in 1983. Beginning in 1987, environmental protection boards were established for every community with more than 3,000 inhabitants. To preserve the shoreline profile, 30–50% of the shores suitable for recreational use may not be built on. Industrial pollutants from within the country and surrounding countries affect the purity of both the nation's air and water supplies. In 1996 carbon dioxide emissions from industrial sources totaled 59.1 million metric tons. However, the total dropped to about 53.4 million metric tons in 2000. Acid rain from high concentrations of sulfur in the air has damaged the nation's lakes. The nation has 107 cu km of renewable water resources with 85% used for industry and 12% used in domestic and urban areas. In 1993, the Finnish Council of State introduced new approaches to the control of water pollution. Lead-free gasoline was introduced in 1985.

Care is taken to protect the flora and fauna of the forests, which are of recreational as well as economic importance. Closed hunting seasons, nature protection areas, and other game-management measures are applied to preserve threatened animal species. As of 2003, about 9.3% of Finland's total land area was protected. According to a 2006 report issued by the International Union for Conservation of Nature and Natural Resources (IUCN), threatened species included 3 types of mammals, 10 species of birds, 1 species of fish, 1 type of mollusk, and 1 species of plant. Endangered species include the Siberian sturgeon, European mink, and the Saimaa ringed seal.

6 POPULATION

The population of Finland in 2005 was estimated by the United Nations (UN) at 5,246,000, which placed it at number 110 in population among the 193 nations of the world. In 2005, approximately 16% of the population was over 65 years of age, with another 18% of the population under 15 years of age. There were 96 males for every 100 females in the country. According to the UN, the annual population rate of change for 2005–10 was expected to be 0.2%, a rate the government viewed as satisfactory. The projected population for the year 2025 was 5,427,000. The population density was 15 per sq km (40 per sq mi). Population distribution is uneven, however, with the density generally increasing from northern and inland regions to the southwestern region.

The UN estimated that 62% of the population lived in urban areas in 2005, and that urban areas were growing at an annual rate of 0.24%. The capital city, Helsinki, had a population of 1,075,000 in that year. Other large cities and their estimated populations include Espoo, 229,443; Tampere, 206,097; Vantaa, 185,429; and Turku, 175,059. Rovaniemi, with a population of 58,500, is considered the capital of Finnish Lapland.

7 MIGRATION

From 1866 to 1930, a total of 361,020 Finns emigrated, mostly to the United States and, after the US restriction of immigration, to Canada. After World War II, about 250,000 to 300,000 Finns permanently emigrated to Sweden. This migration ended by the 1980s because of a stronger Finnish economy.

More than 400,000 people fled the Soviet occupation of the Karelia region during World War II. There was also a heavy migration from rural areas, particularly the east and northeast, to the urban, industrialized south, especially between 1960 and 1975. By 1980, 90% of all Finns lived in the southernmost 41% of Finland.

From 1990 to 2000, the number of foreign citizens in Finland increased from 21,000 to 100,000. In April 1990, it was declared that all Finns living within the former Soviet Union, many known as Ingrians, could be considered return migrants to Finland. As of 2003, 25,000 Ingrians had returned to Finland, with approximately the same number awaiting entry interviews. Finland's

long-standing ethnic minorities include Swedes, Sami (indigenous population), Jews, Romani or Gypsies, Tartars, and Russians. However, by 2004 its foreign born population represented over 168 nations. Most of these foreign born were from the former Soviet Union, former Yugoslavia, Sweden, Iraq, Somalia, Turkey, the United States, China, Vietnam, Thailand, and returning Finns. The estimated net migration rate in 2005 was 0.89 migrants per 1,000 population.

During the latter half of the 1990s, Finland received an average of 700–900 asylum seekers per year. Approximately 60% of applicants were granted a residence permit. By July 1999, more than 1,000 Slovak Romas applied for asylum, prompting the Finnish government to implement a temporary four-month visa plan for Slovak citizens. By August 1999, some 993 people had been evacuated from Macedonia to Finland; the evacuees were granted temporary protection. As of 2004, Finland had 11,325 refugees and asylum seekers.

Finland accepts 500 refugees each year for those who need an alternative to their first country of asylum.

8 ETHNIC GROUPS

The Finns are thought to be descended from Germanic stock and from tribes that originally inhabited west-central Russia. Excluding the Swedish-speaking minority, there are only two very small non-Finnish ethnic groups: Lapps and Gypsies. Finns constitute about 93.4% of the total population, Swedes make up 5.7%, Russians account for 0.4%, Estonians for 0.2%, Roma for 0.2%, and Sami (Lapps) for 0.1%. Several societies have been established to foster the preservation of the Lappish language and culture.

9 LANGUAGES

From the early Middle Ages to 1809, Finland was part of the Kingdom of Sweden, and its official language was Swedish. Finnish did not become an official language until 1863. In 2003, 92% of the population was primarily Finnish-speaking and 5.6% was primarily Swedish-speaking. Swedish-speaking Finns make up more than 95% of the population of the Åland Islands and Swedish-speaking majorities are also found in parts of Uudenmaan, Turun-Porin, and Vaasan provinces. Swedish, the second legal language, is given constitutional safeguards. Only a minority of individuals have another language as their mother tongue, principally Lapp, Russian, English, or German. Finnish belongs to the Finno-Ugric language group and is closely related to Estonian; more distantly to the Komi, Mari, and Udmurt languages spoken among those peoples living in Russia; and remotely to Hungarian.

10 RELIGIONS

Both the Evangelical Lutheran Church and the Orthodox Church are considered state churches. As of 2004, about 84.1% of the inhabitants belong to the Evangelical Lutheran Church. Reports indicate, however, that only between 2–10% of Lutherans attend services on a regular basis. Approximately 1% of the inhabitants, largely evacuees from the Karelian Isthmus, are members of the Orthodox Church in Finland. Another 1% belong to the Pentecostal Church. Other religious bodies include the Free Church, Jehovah's Witnesses, Adventists, Roman Catholics, Methodists, Mormons, Baptists, Swedish Lutherans, and Jews. There are about

20,000 Muslims in the country. About 10% of the population claim no religious affiliation.

Freedom of religion has been guaranteed since 1923. As a state church, the Evangelical Lutheran Church has an elected Church Assembly that makes legislative proposals to the parliament, which can be approved or rejected, but not altered. The Orthodox Church has three dioceses, in Helsinki, Karelia, and Oulu, and owes allegiance to the Ecumenical Patriarch of Constantinople. Citizens who belong to one of these state churches pay a church tax as part of their income tax. For members, the church handles state registrar duties, such as record keeping for births, deaths and marriages. There is a registration service available for members of other faiths. Religious groups must register with the government in order to qualify for tax relief.

11 TRANSPORTATION

In 2004 there were an estimated 78,168 km (48,620 mi) of roads, of which 50,616 km (31,483 mi) were paved, including 653 km (406 mi) of expressways. In 2003 registered motor vehicles included 2,259,383 passenger cars and 334,009 commercial vehicles.

There were 5,851 km (3,639 mi) of broad gauge railway lines in operation in 2004, of which 99% were operated by the Finnish State Railways, and some 2,400 km (1493 mi) were electrified. In 2005, there were 94 ships in Finland's merchant fleet of 1,000 GRT or more, totaling 1,152,175. Import traffic is concentrated at Naantali, Helsinki, Kotka, and Turku, while the ports of Kotka, Hamina, Kemi, Oulu, and Rauma handle most exports. Icebreakers are used to maintain shipping lanes during winter months. More than 900 people were killed in September 1994 when the ferry *Estonia* sank in rough seas off the Finnish coast while sailing from Estonia to Sweden. In 2004 there were 7,842 km (4,877 mi) of navigable inland waterways, of which includes the 3,577 km (2,224 mi) Saimaa Canal System, of which the southern part was leased from Russia.

Airports numbered 148 in 2004, of which 76 had paved runways as of 2005. Helsinki-Vantaa is the principal airport, located at Helsinki. State-run Finnair is engaged in civil air transport over domestic and international routes. In 1962, Finnair took over Kar-Air, the second-largest air carrier in Finland. In 2003, around 6.184 million passengers were carried on scheduled domestic and international airline flights.

12 HISTORY

Finland, a province and a grand duchy of the Swedish kingdom from the 1150s to 1809 and an autonomous grand duchy of Russia from 1809 until the Russian Revolution in 1917, has been an independent republic since 1917. Ancestors of present-day Finns—hunters, trappers, agriculturists—came to Finland by way of the Baltic regions during the first centuries AD, spreading slowly from south and west to east and north. Swedish control over Finnish territory was established gradually beginning in the 12th century in a number of religious crusades. By 1293, Swedish rule had extended as far east as Karelia (Karjala), with colonization by Swedes in the southwest and along the Gulf of Bothnia. As early as 1362, Finland as an eastern province of Sweden received the right to send representatives to the election of the Swedish king. On the basis of the Swedish constitution, Finland's four estates—nobles, clergy, burghers and peasant farmers—were also entitled to send representa-

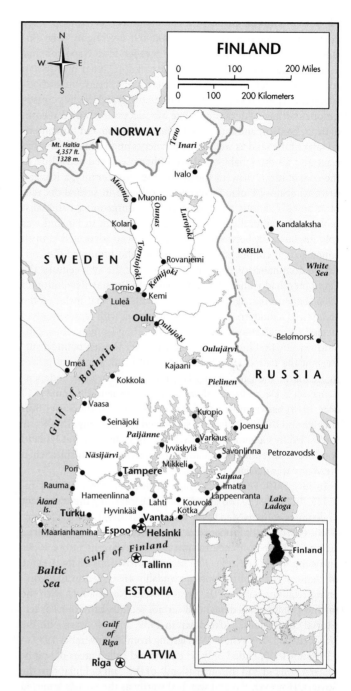

LOCATION: 59°30′10″ to 70°5′30″ N; 19°7′3″ to 31°35′20″ E. BOUNDARY LENGTHS: Russia, 1,313 kilometers (820 miles); Sweden, 586 kilometers (364 miles); Norway, 729 kilometers (445 miles); total coastline, 1,126 kilometers (694 miles). TERRITORIAL SEA LIMIT: 4 miles.

tives to the Diet in Stockholm. As a result of over six centuries of Swedish rule, Finnish political institutions and processes (marked by growing constitutionalism and self-government), economic life, and social order developed largely along Swedish lines. Swedish colonization in Finland was concentrated in the southern and western regions of Finland.

When Sweden was a great power in European politics in the 17th century, Finland and the Finns bore a heavy military burden. Finland was a battleground between the Swedes and Russia, whose encroachments on southeastern Sweden were persistent as Swedish power declined in the 18th century. After Sweden's military defeat in the Napoleonic wars of 1808–09, sovereignty over Finland was transferred to Russia from Sweden after Napoleon and Tsar Alexander I concluded the Peace of Tilsit. Under the Russian rule of Alexander I, Finland was granted a privileged autonomous status that enabled Finland to continue the grand duchy's constitutional heritage. Alexander I, like his successors, took a solemn oath to "confirm and ratify the Lutheran religion and fundamental laws of the land as well as the privileges and rights which each class and all the inhabitants have hitherto enjoyed according to the constitution." Toward the end of the 19th century, a Russian drive to destroy Finland's autonomy ushered in several decades of strained relations and galvanized the burgeoning nationalist movement. Culturally, the nationalist movement in Finland was split linguistically between the Fennomen who advocated Finnish language and culture and the Svecomen who promoted the continued dominance of Swedish. By the end of the 19th century, the Fennomen had gained the upper hand. In Russia's Revolution of 1905, Finland managed to extract concessions that included the creation of a modern, unicameral parliament with representatives elected through universal suffrage, including women. Thus, Finland was the first European country to offer women political suffrage at the national level. After the Bolshevik seizure of power in Russia in the late fall of 1917, Finland declared its independence on 6 December. A short civil war ensued (28 January–10 May 1918) between the Red faction supported by the Soviet Bolsheviks and the White faction supported by Germany. The White forces, led by General Mannerheim, were victorious, but Finland was forced to reorient its alliances toward the western allies when Germany was defeated in WWI.

In July 1919, Finland became a democratic parliamentary republic. In the nearly two decades of peace following the settlement of disputes with Sweden (over the Åland Islands) and the former USSR (East Karelia) there were noteworthy economic and social advances. Despite its neutral pro-Scandinavianism in the 1930s and support for the collective security provisions of the League of Nations, the country was unavoidably entangled in the worsening relations between the great powers. Negotiations with the former USSR, which demanded certain security provisions or territorial concessions, broke down in 1939, and two wars with the USSR ensued. The Winter War, lasting from 30 November 1939 to 13 March 1940, ended only when Finland ceded areas of southeastern Finland and the outer islands of the Gulf of Finland to the Soviets. However, Finland watched warily as the Soviets annexed the independent Baltic states of Estonia, Latvia, and Lithuania. After appeals to western allies went unfulfilled, Finland turned toward Germany for protection, and when Germany attacked the USSR on 26 June 1941, Finland entered the war on the German side. During the early part of the Continuation War, which lasted from 26 June 1941 to 19 September 1944, the Finns pushed the Soviets back to the old frontier lines and held that position for nearly three years. In 1944, a Russian counterattack forced Finland to ask for peace. The armistice terms of 1944, later confirmed by the Paris Peace Treaty of 10 February 1947, provided for cession of territory and payment of reparations to the Soviets and required Finland to expel the German troops on its soil; this resulted in German-Finnish hostilities from October 1944 to April 1945. Under the 1947 peace treaty Finland ceded some 12% of its

territory to the USSR, imprisoned several prominent politicians, reduced its armed forces, and undertook to pay heavy economic reparations. A Soviet naval base was established only 25 km from Helsinki. A separate Treaty of Friendship, Cooperation, and Mutual Assistance, concluded in 1948 under heavy Soviet pressure, obligated Finland to resist attacks on itself or the USSR and in effect precluded Finland from undertaking any significant foreign policy initiative without the Kremlin's approval.

Finland's postwar policy, based on the Paasikivi Line named for the president that formulated the policy, has been termed dismissively as "Finlandization." It is true that Finland maintained a scrupulous and cautious policy of neutrality in foreign affairs. However, after 1955, when the Soviets withdrew from their Finnish base, Finland became an increasingly active member of the United Nations and the Nordic Council, as well as various western economic organizations. Despite Soviet pressure, the Finnish Communist Party steadily declined in influence. Finland's standing was further enhanced by the signing of the 1975 Helsinki treaty, which called for pan-European cooperation in security, economic, political, and human rights matters. The dominant figure of postwar politics was Urho Kekkonen, the Agrarian (later Center) Party leader who held the presidency from 1956 to 1981, when he resigned because of ill health. The cornerstone of his policy was maintenance of a center-left coalition (including the Communists), good relations with the former USSR, and a foreign policy of "active neutrality."

Despite the negative connotations, "Finlandization" was something of a success. Unlike the Baltic states, Finland maintained sovereign independence and even managed to prosper in the post-WWII environment. Postwar political stability allowed a striking economic expansion and transformation in Finland. In 1950, nearly 70% of Finns worked on the land; now that figure is about 8%. Kekkonen's long rule ended in a resignation owing to ill health and the Social Democratic leader Mauno Koivisto, then prime minister, became acting president in October 1981. Koivisto was elected president in his own right in January 1982 and reelected in 1988.

Koivisto's tenure as president ended in 1994. In the presidential elections of February 1994 when voters for the first time directly elected the president, Martti Ahtisaari, former UN mediator and of the Finnish Social Democratic Party, defeated Elisabeth Rehn (defense minister) of the Swedish People's Party in a runoff election. Ahtisaari chose not to run for reelection in 2000, and in that contest no fewer than five candidates for the presidency were women. On 6 February 2000, Finns elected their first female president, Tarja Halonen, the Social Democratic foreign minister in the Lipponen government, who won 51.6% of the vote in a runoff electoral contest with Esko Aho, leader of the Center Party.

Finland faced a deep recession brought about in part by the collapse of the Soviet market that accounted for 20% of Finnish exports. During 1991–94, the recession pushed unemployment up to nearly 20%. The collapse of the Soviet Union and the dissolution of the FCMA Treaty by mutual agreement of Finland and the USSR prompted Finland to reassess its relationship with Europe. In March 1994, Finland completed negotiations for membership in the EU. Finland's relationship with the EU was a major issue of political debate even within the governing coalition. Following a referendum held in October 1994 with 57% approval, Finland formally joined the EU at the beginning of 1995. Finland also joined the European economic and monetary union in 1999, and adopted the euro as its currency in 2002.

Beyond Finlandization: Finland and the European Union

While a relative newcomer to European politics, Finland entered the political limelight as it took over the six-month rotating presidency of the European Union in the second half of 1999. The priorities of the Finnish presidency included a number of pressing issues: preparing for institutional reform necessary prior to enlargement of the Union; increasing the transparency of the functioning of EU institutions; boosting employment and deepening the social dimension of European cooperation; environmental responsibility; and finally, in the area of foreign policy, the Finns championed the "Northern Dimension" which would extend a number of cooperative schemes to include the EU and non-EU countries along the Baltic, including increased ties with northwestern Russia. Though highly touted, this last initiative foundered as Europe continued to be preoccupied with ongoing NATO efforts in Kosovo. At the presidency's concluding summit (December 1999) of the European Council in Helsinki, the Finns could nonetheless point to a number of successes under their presidency. The groundwork for opening accession negotiations with six more applicant countries from Eastern Europe and recognizing Turkey's applicant status were approved by the 15 heads of state. In addition, the European Council approved the establishment of a rapid reaction force outside the structure of NATO, which would allow Europe to have an independent capacity to react in areas in which NATO was not engaged. This was an important accomplishment for Finland, whose neutral status makes participation in NATO actions problematic. However, in recent years, Finland has considered NATO membership; its military policy calls for increased cooperation with and participation in NATO and EU-led operations, including NATO's "Partnership for Peace" program. But the majority of Finns oppose NATO membership.

The issue of Finland's support for the US-led war in Iraq that began on 19 March 2003 was a deciding factor in the 16 March parliamentary elections. Opposition leader Anneli Jäätteenmäki accused sitting Prime Minister Paavo Lipponen of moving Finland too close to the US position on the use of military force to disarm Iraq, and her party went on to win the elections, albeit by a slim majority. Finland donated €1.6 million for humanitarian aid in Iraq. In June 2003, Prime Minister Jäätteenmäki resigned amid accusations that she used leaked confidential information on Iraq to help her party win the March elections. The secret information was based on talks between Lipponen and US President George W. Bush in the run-up to the Iraq war. Jäätteenmäki was accused of lying to parliament over her use of the classified documents, which she had requested and obtained during her election campaign. Jäätteenmäki was replaced as prime minister by Matti Vanhanen. Jäätteenmäki was acquitted in March 2004 of inciting an aide to Lipponen to leak the documents.

In May and June 2005, workers in the paper industry—which accounts for one-quarter of total Finnish export earnings—went on a seven-week strike over the issues of holiday pay and working hours. The paper industry workers wanted better pay and shorter working hours during the Christmas and midsummer holiday seasons. A lockout instituted by paper mill employers resulted in the closure of mills around the country. In July, unions and employers gave backing to a new three-year work and pay package.

Presidential elections were held on 15 January 2006. President Tarja Halonen came out ahead, with 46.3% of the vote, and Sauli Niinistö came in second with 24.1% of the vote. Since no candidate received a majority of the vote, a runoff election was held on 29 January. Results were Halonen, 51.8%, and Niinistö, 48.2% of the votes cast.

13 GOVERNMENT

Finland's republican constitution combines a parliamentary system with a strong presidency. Legislative powers are vested in the Eduskunta (parliament), a unicameral body established in 1906. Members of parliament are elected for four-year terms by proportional representation from 15 multi-member electoral districts under universal suffrage at age 18. Finland was the first country in Europe to grant suffrage to women in national elections (1906). After the 2003 elections nine parties were represented, but the five largest (and traditional) parties shared 181 seats. The 1994 presidential election was the first direct presidential vote since the country gained independence in 1917. Previously voters selected slates of electors who then chose the president. Currently the president is elected directly in a two-stage vote. If no candidate gets a majority in the first round, a second round is held between the two candidates with the largest first round totals. The president is elected for a six-year term.

Finland's political system traditionally has been more like the French than most other European parliamentary democracies because of the division of executive power between the president and the prime minister. The president is the constitutionally designated head of state that appoints the cabinet, serves as commander-in-chief of the armed forces and, until recently, had primary responsibility for foreign policy. Traditionally, Finnish presidents have been responsible for foreign policy and remained neutral on domestic issues. During the Cold War, Finnish presidents had a special role in reassuring the USSR of Finnish good intentions. The president previously had the power to dissolve the legislature and order new elections, initiate legislation, and issue decrees. The president could veto legislation by not signing a bill, but if the Eduskunta after a general election passed it again without amendment, it became law.

On 1 March 2000, a new Finnish constitution entered into force. The new constitution increases the power of the parliament in relation to the government (cabinet) and increases the power of the government in relation to the president. The power of the Finnish presidency has been circumscribed in rather dramatic fashion while the power of the prime minister has increased. In the past, the Finnish president had the right to intervene in the formation of the government and to dissolve a recalcitrant government. Under the new constitution, the president only formally appoints the prime minister and is bound by the decisions derived from negotiations among the parliamentary groups. Party leaders with the most seats in parliament select the prime minister, in a complex bargaining process. The president appoints other ministers on the recommendation of the prime minister. The president may accept the resignation of a government or minister only in the event of a vote of no confidence by the parliament. In addition, under the new constitution, the government is more responsible to the parliament. For instance, the government must submit its program to parliament immediately after being appointed so that the parliament may take a vote of confidence in the government. Foreign and security policy have become shared responsibilities between the president and the government, with the prime minister and foreign minister taking an active role in formulating a consensus approach to Finnish foreign policy. The government, not the president, now has responsibility over issues related to EU affairs, given the impact of much European law on domestic legislation. The parliament has created a "Grand Committee" to scrutinize EU matters and to ensure parliament's influence on EU decision-making.

Since 1945 no single party has ever held an absolute parliamentary majority, so all cabinet or governmental decisions involve coalitions. The cabinet is composed of the heads of government ministries and has as its primary responsibility the preparation of governmental budgets and legislation and the administration of public policies. The prime minister and cabinet serve only so long as they enjoy the support of a working majority in parliament, and there have been frequent changes of government.

Women are fairly well represented in both the executive and legislative branches of government in Finland. Women hold 37% of the seats in the 200-member Eduskunta and there were 8 women among the 18 cabinet members after the 2003 elections. Women have held top leadership positions, including defense minister (Elisabeth Rehn) and foreign minister (Tarja Halonen) and speaker of parliament. In February 2000, Finns elected Tarja Halonen their first female president. Anneli Jäätteenmäki was named prime minister following elections in March 2003. Halonen was reelected president in 2006.

14 POLITICAL PARTIES

Four major partisan groupings have dominated political life in Finland, although none commands a majority position among the electorate. The Finnish Social Democratic Party (Suomen Sosialidemokraattinen Puolue—SDP) was organized in 1899 but did not become a significant political force until 1907, following the modernization of the country's parliamentary structure. Swedish-speaking Socialists have their own league within the SDP. The party's program is moderate, and its emphasis on the partial nationalization of the economy has in recent decades given way to support for improvement of the condition of wage earners through legislation. The SDP has generally worked closely with the trade union movement and has been a vigorous opponent of communism.

The Center Party (Keskusrapuolue—KESK; until October 1965, the Agrarian League—Maalaisliitto) was organized in 1906. While initially a smallholders' party, it won some support from middle and large landowners but virtually none from nonagricultural elements. In an effort to gain a larger following in urban areas, the party changed its name and revised its program in 1965. In February 1959, an Agrarian League splinter party, the Finnish Small Farmers' Party, was formed; in August 1966, it took the name Finnish Rural Party (Suomen Maaseudun Puolue—SMP). The Liberal People's Party (Liberaalinen Kansanpuolue—LKP) was formed in December 1965 as a result of the merger of the Finnish People's Party and the Liberal League; in 1982, the LKP merged with the KESK.

The National Coalition Party (Kansallinen Kokoomus—KOK), also known as the Conservative Party, was established in 1918 as the successor to the conservative Old Finnish Party. Its program, described as "conservative middle-class," has traditionally emphasized the importance of private property, the established church, and the defense of the state.

The Finnish Christian League (Suomen Kristillinen Liitto—SKL), founded in 1958, was formed to counter the increasing trend toward secularization and is usually found on the political right with the KOK.

The Swedish People's Party (Svenska Folkpartiet—SFP), organized in 1906 as the successor to the Swedish Party, has stressed its bourgeois orientation and the need for protecting the common interests of Finland's Swedish-speaking population.

The Finnish People's Democratic League (Suomen Kansan Demokraattinen Liitto—SKDL) represents the extreme left. Emerging in 1944, and illegal before then, the SKDL was a union of the Finnish Communist Party (organized in 1918) and the Socialist Unity Party. The SKDL had urged close relations with the former USSR and the Communist bloc, but it later moderated its demands for the establishment of a "people's democracy" in Finland. In 1986, a minority group within the SKDL was expelled; for the 1987 elections, it established a front called the Democratic Alternative (DEVA). Following the collapse of the Soviet Union, the SKDL in May 1990 merged with other left parties to form the Left Alliance (Vasemmistoliitto—VL).

The Greens, an environmentalist alliance, won four seats in the Eduskunta in 1987, although they were not formally organized as a political party.

From the end of World War II until 1987, Finland was ruled by a changing center-left coalition of parties that included the SDP, KESK, SKDL, LKP, SFP, and SMP. The government formed on 30 April 1987 included seven members of the KOK, including the prime minister, Harri Holkeri; eight from the SDP; two from the SFP; and one from the SMP. Conservative gains in the 1987 election put non-Socialists in their strongest position in parliament in 50 years. Following the general election of March 1991, the Center Party led by Esko Aho emerged as the largest single party in parliament. A new four-party, center-right coalition was formed composed of the Center Party, the National Coalition Party, the Swedish People's Party, and the Finnish Christian League.

The victory by the SDP in the 1995 parliamentary elections ended the reign of the right-center coalition that held control during four years of economic stagnation. The SDP's leader, Paavo Lipponen, became Finland's new prime minister in April 1995. Lipponen fashioned a "rainbow coalition" following the March 1995 elections that included the following: the Social Democratic Party (with Lipponen as prime minister), the National Coalition Party, the Left Alliance, the Swedish People's Party, and the Green League. In opposition were the Center Party, the Finnish Christian League, the Young Finns, the Ecology Party, the True Finns, and the Åland Island's Party representative.

The parliamentary election in 1999 reflected a mixture of discontent and continuity. A cooling economy (caused by Russia's economic collapse in 1998), the opposition's plans for radical tax cuts, and controversy about EU policies dominated the campaign. Opposition leader (and former prime minister) Aho promised radical tax and economic policy changes. He could govern only if he succeeded in prying the Conservatives out of Lipponen's coalition. SDP party scandals over privatization of the telecommunications sector and other issues threatened the otherwise impressive performance of the rainbow coalition that many thought would not survive the full parliamentary term.

The outcome of the 1999 elections was a setback for the Social Democrats, whose share of the votes declined from 28.3% in 1995 to 22.9% in 1999. The SDP parliamentary delegation declined from 63 to 51. The Conservatives advanced from 17.9% of the vote in 1995 (and 39 seats) to 21% in 1999 (and 46 seats). The three smaller coalition parties continued to share 42 seats among them. The opposition Centrists advanced modestly from 19.9 to 22.4% of the vote (gaining four seats for a total of 48). The SDP remained the largest parliamentary group, and Lipponen retained the right to renew his coalition, making it the longest-serving government in Finnish history.

The elections of 2003 were colored by disagreements between Lipponen's Social Democrats and the Center Party led by Anneli Jäätteenmäki. Jäätteenmäki accused Lipponen of closely aligning Finland with the US position on forcibly disarming Saddam Hussein's regime in Iraq. Jäätteenmäki's criticisms were popular with voters, and the Center Party emerged with 24.7% of the vote to take 55 seats in the Eduskunta. The representation of the other parties in parliament in 2003 was as follows: SDP, 22.9% (53 seats); KOK, 18.5% (40 seats); the Left Alliance, 9.9% (19 seats); the Greens, 8%, (14 seats); the Christian Democrats, 5.3% (7 seats); the People's Party, 4.6% (8 seats); the agrarian True Finns Party, 1.6% (3 seats); and the representative from the Åland Island's Party held one seat. Jäätteenmäki formed a coalition government with the Social Democratic Party and the Swedish People's Party. She later resigned in June as a result of accusations that she misused confidential government documents regarding talks between Lipponen and President George W. Bush over the run-up to the Iraq war. Jäätteenmäki in 2004 was acquitted of charges she incited an aide to Lipponen to leak the documents.

15 LOCAL GOVERNMENT

There is an ancient and flourishing tradition of local self-government extending back to the 14th century. The present law on local government was enacted in 1976. There are six provinces (*lääni*), each headed by a governor appointed by the president. One of them, Ahvenanmaa (Åland Islands), has long enjoyed special status, including its own elected provincial council, and a statute effective 1 January 1952 enlarged the scope of its autonomy. The other provinces are directly responsible to the central government.

Below the provincial level, the local government units in 2005 included 432 municipalities. The number of municipalities has fluctuated over the years, but the trend has been downwards. (In 1955, there were 547 municipalities.) Each local government unit is self-governing and has a popularly chosen council. Local elections are held every four years; being partisan in nature, they are regarded as political barometers. The councilors are unsalaried. Local administration is carried out under the supervision of council committees, but professional, full-time managers usually run day-to-day affairs. The functions of local government include education, social welfare, health, culture, utilities, and collection of local taxes.

16 JUDICIAL SYSTEM

There are three levels of courts: local, appellate, and supreme. The municipal courts of the first instance are staffed in each case by a magistrate and two councilors. Each of the six appellate courts is headed by a president and staffed by appellate judges. In certain criminal cases these courts have original jurisdiction. The final court of appeal, the Supreme Court (Korkeinoikeus), sits in Helsinki. There are also the Supreme Administrative Court, a number of provincial administrative courts, and some special tribunals. The administration of justice is under the supervision of a chancellor of justice and a parliamentary ombudsman.

The judiciary is independent from the executive and legislative branches. Supreme Court judges are appointed to permanent positions by the president and are independent of political control. Retirement is mandatory at age 70.

Like most other Nordic judicial systems, Finland's constitution calls for a Parliamentary Ombudsman. The Ombudsman is an independent official from the legal field, who is elected by the parliament and charged with "overseeing the courts of law, other public authorities and public servants in the performance of their official duties as well as public employees and other persons in the exercise of public functions...In discharging his or her duties, the Parliamentary Ombudsman shall also oversee the implementation of Constitutional rights and international human rights." The Ombudsman and Deputy Ombudsman investigate complaints by citizens regarding the public authorities, conduct investigations, and may intervene in matters of his or her own initiative. This important institution assists citizens in navigating the often Byzantine bureaucratic maze of the social welfare state and provides greater accountability and transparency in the enormous Finnish public sector.

17 ARMED FORCES

Total armed forces in Finland numbered 28,300 active personnel in 2005, with reserves totaling 237,000. The Army had 20,500 personnel, while the Navy had 5,000, and the Air Force 2,800. The Army's equipment included 226 main battle tanks, 263 armored infantry fighting vehicles, 614 armored personnel carriers, and 1,446 artillery pieces. Major naval units included 11 patrol/coastal vessels, 19 mine warfare ships, six amphibious landing craft, and 35 logistical/support vessels. The Air Force had 63 combat capable aircraft, consisting of fighter ground attack aircraft. The Air Force also operated one antisubmarine warfare aircraft and 22 transports. Finland's paramilitary frontier guard numbered 3,100. The defense budget in 2005 totaled $2.7 billion. Finland's armed forces also provided observers and troops to nine different UN and NATO operations in 2005.

18 INTERNATIONAL COOPERATION

Finland has been a UN member since 14 December 1955; it participates in several UN specialized agencies, such as the FAO, World Bank, IAEA, ILO, UNESCO, UNIDO, and the WHO. Finland is also a member of the OECD, the WTO, G-9, and the Paris Club. The country joined the European Union in 1995. In addition, Finland plays a role in the African Development Bank and Asian Development Bank, and is involved in a number of bilateral projects, primarily in African countries. The nation holds observer status in the Western European Union and the OAS.

Officially neutral, Finland seeks to maintain friendly relations with both the United States and Russia, its powerful eastern neighbor. Finland has hosted many major meetings and conferences, including rounds I, III, V, and VII of the Strategic Arms Limitation Talks (SALT) between the United States and USSR (1969–72). In November 1972, the multilateral consultations on the Conference on Security and Cooperation in Europe (CSCE, now the OSCE) began in Helsinki. These initial consultations were followed by the first phase of CSCE at the foreign ministerial level and then by the third phase at the highest political level, culminating with the signing of the Final Act in Helsinki on 1 August 1975. Foreign ministers of the United States, Canada, and 33 other European countries met in Helsinki on 30 July 1985 to commemorate the 10th anniversary of the signing of the Final Act.

Finland has a close relationship with the other Scandinavian (Nordic) countries. The main forum of cooperation is the Nordic Council, established in 1952; Finland joined in 1955. A common labor market was established in 1954, granting citizens of member states the right to stay and work in any other Scandinavian country without restrictions. Finland also belongs to the Council of the Baltic Sea States (est. in 1992).

Finland is part of the Australia Group, the Nuclear Suppliers Group (London Group), the European Organization for Nuclear Research (CERN), the Nuclear Energy Agency, the Zangger Committee, and the Organization for the Prohibition of Chemical Weapons. In environmental cooperation, Finland is part of the Antarctic Treaty; the Basel Convention; Conventions on Biological Diversity, Whaling, and Air Pollution; Ramsar; CITES; the London Convention; International Tropical Timber Agreements; the Kyoto Protocol; the Montréal Protocol; MARPOL; the Nuclear Test Ban Treaty; and the UN Conventions on the Law of the Sea, Climate Change and Desertification.

19 ECONOMY

At the end of World War II, Finland's economy was in desperate straits. About 10% of the country's productive capacity had been lost to the former USSR, and over 400,000 evacuees had to be absorbed. Between 1944 and 1952, Finland was burdened with reparation payments to the USSR, rising inflation, and a large population growth. However, the GDP reached the prewar level by 1947, and since then the economy has shown consistent growth.

Handicapped by relatively poor soil, a severe northern climate, and lack of coal, oil, and most other mineral resources necessary for the development of heavy industry, the Finns have nonetheless been able to build a productive and diversified economy. This was made possible by unrivaled supplies of forests (Finland's "green gold") and waterpower resources ("white gold"), as well as by the Finnish disposition toward hard work, frugality, and ingenuity. Agriculture, long the traditional calling of the large majority of Finns, has been undergoing continuous improvement, with growing specialization in dairying and cattle breeding. The industries engaged in producing timber, wood products, paper, and pulp are highly developed, and these commodities continue to make up a significant proportion of the country's exports. After World War II, and partly in response to the demands of reparations payments, a metals industry was developed, its most important sectors being

foundries and machine shops, shipyards, and engineering works. The 1990s saw Finland develop one of the world's leading high tech economies. Dependent on foreign sources for a considerable portion of its raw materials, fuels, and machinery, and on exports as a source of revenue, the Finnish economy is very sensitive to changes at the international level.

The annual growth of GDP averaged 4.3% between 1986 and 1989, after which it was hard hit by the collapse of the former USSR, formerly Finland's chief trading partner. For 40 years, Finland and the USSR had conducted trade on a barter basis, a practice that ended in 1991. GDP was flat in 1990, fell by 7.1% in 1991, a further 4% in 1992, and 3.6% in 1993.

The regional economic recovery in Europe during 1994 helped Finland's economy to turn around. By early 1995, the economy began to show signs of strong growth—GDP had grown 4.5% by the end of that year, and by 2000, it had reached 6.1%. In October 1996 Finland agreed to join the European currency grid, which limits currency fluctuations to 15% up or down, and proclaimed its determination to join European economic and monetary union (EMU); it joined the EMU in 1999. Thus far, it is the only Nordic EU member to join, as Denmark and Sweden decided to opt out of the EMU.

The success of the Finnish economy in the late 1990s was largely due to the country's success in the high tech sector. Finland has one of the highest rates in the world for per capita Internet connections and mobile phone ownership; in 2002, 75% of Finns owned a mobile phone. Chief among Finnish companies is Nokia, the world's leading producer of mobile phones.

In 2001, the global economy was in a downturn, and Finland's economy was duly affected. Demand for Finnish exports declined, and industrial production shrank for the first time in 10 years. In 2001, Finland's GDP growth was among the lowest of the euro zone, at 0.7%, and unemployment remained above the euro zone average (9%). However, the service sector (accounting for over 60% of GDP) remained strong. In 2004, the government cut taxes and tempered inflation in order to prod private consumption and promote GDP growth. GDP growth was estimated at 1.6% in 2005, and was forecast to accelerate to 2.5% in 2006 and 2.7% in 2007, still well below the growth rates seen in the latter part of the 1990s. The inflation rate was expected to be 1.3% in 2005, rising to 1.8% in 2006 and 2% in 2007. The unemployment rate was estimated at 8.9% in 2004, above the EU average, but the government estimated the unemployment rate would drop to 8.5% in 2005. A relatively inflexible labor market and high employer-paid social security taxes hamper growth in employment.

20 INCOME

The US Central Intelligence Agency (CIA) reports that in 2005 Finland's gross domestic product (GDP) was estimated at $158.4 billion. The CIA defines GDP as the value of all final goods and services produced within a nation in a given year and computed on the basis of purchasing power parity (PPP) rather than value as measured on the basis of the rate of exchange based on current dollars. The per capita GDP was estimated at $30,300. The annual growth rate of GDP was estimated at 1.7%. The average inflation rate in 2005 was 1.2%. It was estimated that agriculture accounted for 3.1% of GDP, industry 30.4%, and services 66.5%.

According to the World Bank, in 2003 remittances from citizens working abroad totaled $642 million or about $123 per capita and accounted for approximately 0.4% of GDP.

The World Bank reports that in 2003 household consumption in Finland totaled $84.55 billion or about $16,223 per capita based on a GDP of $161.9 billion, measured in current dollars rather than PPP. Household consumption includes expenditures of individuals, households, and nongovernmental organizations on goods and services, excluding purchases of dwellings. It was estimated that for the period 1990 to 2003 household consumption grew at an average annual rate of 2.1%. In 2001 it was estimated that approximately 17% of household consumption was spent on food, 10% on fuel, 4% on health care, and 15% on education.

21 LABOR

The Finnish labor force numbered an estimated 2.61 million in 2005. Of these workers, 32% were engaged in public services, 22% in industry, 14% in commerce, 10% in finance, insurance, and business service, 8% in agriculture and forestry, 8% in transport and communications, and 6% in construction. From the mid-1960s to the mid-1970s, the rate of unemployment fluctuated between 1.5% and 4% of the total workforce. Since then, however, the unemployment rate has crept upward, reaching 8.5% in 2002. In 2005, the unemployment had fallen slightly to an estimated 7.9%.

The law provides for the right to form and join unions. As of 2005, about 79% of workers were members of a trade union. These unions are not regulated by the government or political parties. Labor relations are generally regulated by collective agreements among employers, employees and the government. Workers have the right to strike, but such actions are considered legal only if an employment contract is not in effect and that the strike is being carried out pursuant of new contract negotiations. Strikes that may involve the national security are put before an official dispute board that can make nonbinding recommendations to the cabinet as to the strike's duration.

Child labor regulations are strictly enforced by the labor ministry. Minors under the age of 16 cannot work at night or more than six hours per day. In addition there are occupational health and safety restrictions applied to child labor. The law does not mandate minimum wages, as it is established by industry in collective bargaining negotiations for each sector of the workforce. The workweek is legally set at 40 hours with five days of work and premium pay for overtime, which is limited to 250 hours annually and 138 hours in any four-month period. Health and safety standards are effectively enforced.

22 AGRICULTURE

Finnish farming is characterized by the relatively small proportion of arable land under cultivation, the large proportion of forestland, the small-sized landholdings, the close association of farming with forestry and stock raising, and the generally adverse climatic and soil conditions. Farming is concentrated in southwestern Finland; elsewhere, cultivation is set within the frame of the forest. In 2004, there were 70,983 farms. The average farm had about 31 hectares (78 acres) of arable land. Small-sized farms were encouraged by

a series of land reforms beginning with the Lex Kallio of 1922. The Land Use Act of 1958 sought to improve the conditions of existing farms by increasing the land area, amalgamating nonviable farms, and introducing new land-use patterns. The agricultural labor force was 5.5% of the economically active population in 2000. In 2003, agriculture contributed 5% to GDP.

The principal crops in 2004 (in tons) were barley, 1,725,000; oats, 1,002,000; sugar beets, 1,064,000; potatoes, 619,000; and wheat, 782,000. A total of 2,243,000 hectares (5,542,000 acres) were classified as arable in 2004.

23 ANIMAL HUSBANDRY

Livestock production contributes about 70% of total agricultural income. Livestock in 2004 included cattle, 969,000 head; hogs, 1,365,000; sheep, 109,000; and horses, 61,000. There were 3,981,000 poultry that same year. Some 201,000 reindeer are used by the Lapps as draft animals and for meat.

In recent years, Finland has attained exportable surpluses in some dairy, pork, and eggs. Production in 2004 included pork, 198,000 tons; beef, 93,000 tons; eggs, 58,000 tons; butter, 58,000 tons; and cheese, 93,000 tons. Milk production in 2004 was estimated at 2.3 billion liters.

24 FISHING

At the beginning of 2004, the Finnish fishing fleet consisted of 3,798 vessels, with an average vessel capacity of 5 GRT. The total catch in 2003 was 135,295 tons and exports of fishery commodities totaled $13 million. The most important catch is Atlantic herring, with 64,020 tons caught in 2003. Other important species are rainbow trout, perch, pike, salmon, and cod. In 2005, salmon and herring caught in the Gulf of Bothnia and Gulf of Finland were found to contain higher levels of dioxins potentially harmful to human health.

25 FORESTRY

Forestry in Finland has been controlled since the 17th century. Since 1928, the government has emphasized a policy of sustainable yields, with production reflecting timber growth. Forest land covered 26.3 million hectares (65 million acres), or over 85% of the total land area, in 2003. The total growing stock is around 2.0 billion cu m (71 billion cu ft), and the annual increment is estimated at 83 million cu m (2.9 billion cu ft). The most important varieties are pine (47% of the total growing stock), spruce (34%), birch (15%), aspen, and alder. About 61% of the productive woodland is privately owned (in 440,000 holdings); 24% is owned by the state; the remainder is owned by companies, communes, and religious bodies. There are 170 major sawmills in Finland with a combined output of 13.5 million cu m (477 million cu ft) in 2004. Numerous small sawmills serve local markets.

In 2004, the roundwood harvest was estimated at 53.8 million cu m (1.9 billion cu ft), of which 13.5 million cu m (477 million cu ft) were processed as sawnwood, 25 million cu m (883 million cu ft) as wood pulp, and 4.5 million cu m (159 million cu ft) as firewood. Finland ranks fourth in Europe (after Sweden, Germany, and Russia) as a producer of sawn softwood. Over 70% of annual Finnish forestry output is exported, including over 90% of all printing paper and 50% of all particleboard produced. Over 60% of forestry product exports are sent elsewhere in Europe; Finland supplies Europe with about 10% of its demand. In 2004, exports of forestry products were valued at nearly $11 billion, or about 25% of total exports.

In 1999, Finland launched its National Forest Program 2010. The goal of the program is to raise industrial roundwood production to 63–68 million cu m (2.2–2.4 billion cu ft) while adhering to ecosystem management principles. The Finnish Forest Research Institute estimates that roundwood harvesting can rise to 74 million cu m per year and still sustain the growing stock.

26 MINING

For the metals industry, a key sector of its industrialized market economy, Finland depended on imports of raw materials, especially crude oil, iron ore, nickel matte, petroleum products, and zinc concentrate. Copper refining and metals production constituted a major mineral industry, with most output destined for export. Outokumpu Oyj was the third-largest zinc metal producer in Europe (15% share of the market and 5% share of world zinc production). In 2004, Finland mined chromite, copper, nickel, zinc, feldspar, lime, nitrogen, phosphate rock, pyrite, sodium sulfate, limestone and dolomite, quartz silica sand, sulfur, talc, and wollastonite. The Kemi mine, on the Gulf of Bothnia near the Swedish border, was the only chromium mine in Scandinavia and one of the largest in the world, with estimated reserves of 150 million tons and an annual capacity of one million tons. Mine output of zinc in 2004 was 69,333 metric tons, down from 70,652 metric tons in 2003; feldspar, 57,149 metric tons, up from 48,353 metric tons in 2003; chromite (gross weight of ore, concentrate, and foundry sand), 550,000 metric tons, up from 549,000 metric tons in 2003 and copper (mine output), 15,500 metric tons, up from 14,900 in 2003. Exploration activities were focused largely on diamond, gold, and base metals deposits (sulfide zinc, zinc, copper, chalcopyrite, pyrite, sphalerite, and platinum-group metals, or PGM). Finland also had capacities to mine mica, phophate-apatite, quartz, and quartzite, and to mine and produce 8 million tons per year of apatite.

Mineral reserves were declining, and many were expected to be exhausted soon, as a result of extensive mining over the past 400 years. Although Finland had scarce mineral resources, it was influential in the global mining industry as a world leader in mining technology, ore processing, and metallurgy. With the acquisition of the metallurgical businesses of Lurgi Metallurgie AG of Germany, Outokumpu Technology became the world's leading supplier of copper and zinc plants, a major supplier of aluminum technologies, and the key supplier of innovative technologies for the ferrous metals and ferroalloy industries. Government involvement in the mineral industry was considerably higher in Finland than elsewhere in the EU. State-owned companies such as Finnminers Group, Kemira Oyj, Outokumpu, and Rautaruukki Oy dominated the domestic minerals industry, while institutions such as the State Geological Research Institute and the State Technological Research Center were active in exploration and research.

27 ENERGY AND POWER

Finland relies upon imports to meet its fossil fuel needs. In 2002, imports of crude oil and refined petroleum products averaged 315,460 barrels per day, with consumption at 215,790 barrels per day. Exports of the difference averaged 115,220 barrels per day.

Imports and consumption of dry natural gas came to 160.01 billion cu ft, and 159.94 billion cu ft, respectively in 2002.

Finland's electric power generating capacity in 2002 stood at 16.475 million kW, of which the bulk, 10.898 million kW, was dedicated to conventional thermal generation. Hydropower capacity, nuclear and geothermal/other came to 2.895 million kW, 2.640 million kW and 0.042 million kW, respectively in 2002. Total electricity production for that year amounted to 71.303 billion kWh, of which conventional thermal sources totaled 29,770 billion kWh. Hydroelectric, nuclear and geothermal/other sources produced: 10.668 billion kWh; 21.180 billion kWh; and 9.685 billion kWh. Consumption of electricity was 78.312 billion kWh in 2002. Finland has four nuclear power plants, two 465-MW reactors at the Loviisa plant and two 735-MW reactors at the Tvo facility. Most of Finland's waterpower resources are located along the Oulu and Kemi rivers.

28 INDUSTRY

Since the end of World War II, industrial progress has been noteworthy. Contributing factors include the forced stimulus of reparation payments, large quantities of available electric power, increased mining operations, growing mechanization of agriculture and forestry, development of transportation and communications, and steady foreign demand for Finnish exports. In terms of value of production and size of labor force, the electronics and electrical industry is, as of 2005, the most important, displacing the metals industry. Also highly significant are the food, pulp and paper, machinery, chemical, and shipbuilding industries. The most important industrial regions center around Helsinki, Tampere, Turku, Lappeenranta, Lahti, Jyväskylä, and the valleys of the Kymi and Kokemäki rivers, and coastal towns like Kotka, Rauma, and Pori. The state no longer owns a majority of the outstanding stock in most industrial companies.

The growth in Finnish industry, from 25.8% of GDP in 1990 to 28.4% by 2000 and 30.2% in 2004, is atypical for developed countries, where the services sector has tended to increase more than industry. In 2004, industry employed 22% of the labor force. Finland is a world leader in the making of cellular telephone handsets, paper machinery, medical devices, and instruments for environmental measurements. Nokia, the largest company in the country, produces the most mobile telephones in the world (it is, however, nearly 90% foreign-owned, especially by American pension foundations). Biotechnology is an increasingly important sector, with strength in pharmaceuticals, biomaterials, diagnostics, and industrial enzymes. Finland's biotechnology industry ranked sixth in Europe in 2005. The software industry is one of Finland's most promising industrial sectors; currently, there are more than 3,000 software companies in Finland, many of them start-ups or in early growth stages. The electrical engineering industry's roots go back to the late 19th century: the company founded by Gottfried Strömberg, who built generators and electric motors, is now a profitable arm of the Asea Brown Boveri Group. Finnish companies such as Instru, Vaisala, and Neles (now part of Metso) have succeeded in areas such as industrial automation and medical and meteorological technology. Metso, formed from Valmet and Tampella, is today the world's leading producer of paper machines. Although certain fashion (Luhta and Marimekko) and footwear (Palmroth) design companies are important, the previously strong "heavy" textile industry—making cotton, woolen, and other fabrics—has virtually disappeared due to foreign competition.

29 SCIENCE AND TECHNOLOGY

Scientific research is carried out at state research institutes, private research centers, and institutions of higher learning. The Technology Development Center, established in 1983 under the Ministry of Trade and Industry, oversees technological research and coordinates international research activities. The Academy of Finland (founded in 1947), a central governmental organ for research administration, reports directly to the Ministry of Education. It promotes scientific research and develops national science policy by maintaining research fellowships, sponsoring projects, and publishing reports. Finland has 13 universities offering courses in basic and applied sciences. The University of Helsinki operates a natural history museum that has zoological, botanical, and geological components. The principal learned societies, all in Helsinki, are the Federation of Finnish Scientific Societies (founded in 1899), the Finnish Academy of Science and Letters (founded in 1908), and the Finnish Society of Sciences and Letters (founded in 1838); preeminent in technological development is the Finnish Technical Research Center (founded in 1942) at Espoo.

In 1987–97, science and engineering students accounted for 39% of university enrollment. In 2002, science degrees (natural sciences, mathematics and computers, and engineering) accounted for 32.2% of all bachelor's degrees awarded.

In 2002, expenditures on research and development (R&D) amounted to $4.7 billion or 3.46% of GDP. Business enterprises, including those in which the central or local government owns major shares, financed 69.5% of the nation's research, followed by government at 26.1%, with foreign sources and higher education accounting for 3.1% and 0.2%, respectively. High technology exports in 2002 totaled $9.139 billion, or 24% of the country's manufactured exports. In that same year, there were 7,431 researchers (excluding technicians) per million people actively engaged in research and experimental development.

30 DOMESTIC TRADE

Domestic trade is carried on through the customary wholesale and retail channels. Kesko is Finland's largest retailer. The S-Group consists of cooperative societies and SOK with their subsidiaries. The S-Group's largest retail area is the grocery trade. Valio, a dairy company, is the leading food business company in terms of net turnover.

Office hours are from 8 AM to 5 PM, Mondays through Fridays, with lunch lasting from one to two hours. Government offices are open from 8 AM to 4 PM. Stores and shops are open from 9 AM to 6 PM, Monday through Friday, and 9 AM to 3 PM on Saturday, but department stores and shopping malls stay open until 8 PM on weekdays and until 4 PM on Saturday.

Advertising is found on television, radio, the Internet, and in traditional print sources. There are two public and two commercial television stations in Finland. In 2005, Finland became the first European country to issue a license for commercial television service for mobile phones. By 2005, there were 83 commercial radio stations in Finland with almost 300 frequencies around the country; commercial radio in Finland got its start in 1985. Finland

Principal Trading Partners – Finland (2003)			
(In millions of US dollars)			
Country	Exports	Imports	Balance
World	52,503.3	41,572.5	10,930.8
Germany	6,027.7	6,130.5	-102.8
Sweden	5,087.0	4,543.7	543.3
United States	4,148.6	1,931.3	2,217.3
United Kingdom	4,140.1	2,184.1	1,956.0
Russia	3,861.6	4,915.0	-1,053.4
Netherlands	2,339.2	1,633.3	705.9
Italy-San Marino-Holy See	2,017.8	1,556.3	461.5
Areas nes	1,549.4	322.3	1,227.1
China	1,432.1	1,774.0	-341.9
Spain	1,391.8	682.4	709.4

(…) data not available or not significant.

SOURCE: *2003 International Trade Statistics Yearbook*, New York: United Nations, 2004.

recently rescinded a ban on alcohol advertising, but maintains a ban on tobacco advertising.

31 FOREIGN TRADE

Exports of goods and services contribute 33% of the country's GDP. Exports in 2004 totaled $61.04 billion, and imports totaled $45.17 billion, for a trade surplus of $15.87 billion. The EU is by far Finland's largest trading partner. In 2003, 53% of all exports went to the EU, and 55% of all Finnish imports originated from the EU. Although Germany—Finland's largest EU trading partner in 2004—is within the euro zone, its other two main EU trading partners, the United Kingdom and Sweden, are outside it. Therefore, in 2003, only 32.8% of exports went to the euro area, and only 34.5% of imports originated there. Finland's leading markets in 2004 were Sweden (11.1% of all exports), Germany (10.7%), Russia (8.9%), the United Kingdom (7%), and the United States (6.4%). Leading suppliers in 2004 were Germany (14.6% of all imports), Russia (13.1%), Sweden (10.9%), China (4.6%), and France (4.5%).

32 BALANCE OF PAYMENTS

Finnish households and businesses became more cautious in spending, due to the deep recession in the early 1990s and the slowdown in the global economy that began in 2001. Nonetheless, the financial health of Finnish companies improved in the late 1990s and into the 2000s.

The trade surplus in 2004 stood at $15.87 billion. The current account surplus stood at $11.39 billion in 2004. The current account surplus averaged 6.2% of GDP from 2000–04. Public debt was estimated at 46.8% of GDP in 2004.

33 BANKING AND SECURITIES

The central bank is the Bank of Finland—the fourth-oldest in Europe—established in 1811 with headquarters in Helsinki and seven branch offices. Possessing extensive autonomy though subject to parliamentary supervision, and endowed with extensive monetary and fiscal powers, the Bank is administered by a six-member board of management appointed by the president of the republic.

Balance of Payments – Finland (2003)

(In millions of US dollars)

Current Account		**9,295.0**
Balance on goods		13,390.0
Imports	-39,097.0	
Exports	52,487.0	
Balance on services		-1,968.0
Balance on income		-1,115.0
Current transfers		-1,013.0
Capital Account		**108.0**
Financial Account		**-6,329.0**
Direct investment abroad		7,538.0
Direct investment in Finland		2,899.0
Portfolio investment assets		-9,872.0
Portfolio investment liabilities		8,943.0
Financial derivatives		1,716.0
Other investment assets		-16,164.0
Other investment liabilities		-1,389.0
Net Errors and Omissions		**-3,582.0**
Reserves and Related Items		**507.0**

(…) data not available or not significant.

SOURCE: *Balance of Payment Statistics Yearbook 2004*, Washington, DC: International Monetary Fund, 2004.

It has an exclusive monopoly over the issuance of notes. Completing its preparations for Economic and Monetary Union (EMU), on 17 January 1997 the government submitted to the Eduskunta a proposal for a new Act of the Bank of Finland. The main purpose of the act was to prepare the Bank of Finland institutionally for Stage 3 of EMU by providing for its independence ahead of the move to a single currency, in line with the requirements set out in the Maastricht treaty.

As of 1999, leading deposit banks in Finland included: Nordea (Merita Nordbanken, the result of a merger between Merita and Swedish Nordbanken, Danish Unidanmark, and Norwegian

Public Finance – Finland (2002)

(In millions of euros, central government figures)

Revenue and Grants	**56,864**	**100.0%**
Tax revenue	32,996	58.0%
Social contributions	17,252	30.3%
Grants	750	1.3%
Other revenue	5,866	10.3%
Expenditures	**50,390**	**100.0%**
General public services	6,384	12.7%
Defense	2,024	4.0%
Public order and safety	1,578	3.1%
Economic affairs	5,220	10.4%
Environmental protection	267	0.5%
Housing and community amenities	359	0.7%
Health	4,147	8.2%
Recreational, culture, and religion	579	1.1%
Education	6,292	12.5%
Social protection	23,800	47.2%

(…) data not available or not significant.

SOURCE: *Government Finance Statistics Yearbook 2004*, Washington, DC: International Monetary Fund, 2004.

Christiania Bank); OKO Bank (the Cooperative Bank Group, the first bank in the world to offer online banking transaction services, in 1996); and the Sampo Group (the result of a merger between Sampo Insurance Company and the Leonia bank group). Eight major commercial banks and 40 savings banks serve the country. Six foreign banks have branches in Finland.

In 1996 the markka stayed firm against the German mark. In the fourth quarter of 1996 Finland's three-month money-market rate, the Helibor, fell by nearly 40 basis points, from 3.48% to just 3.09%. The fall resulted in further convergence with German money-market rates. The International Monetary Fund reports that in 2001, currency and demand deposits—an aggregate commonly known as M1—were equal to $37.3 billion. In that same year, M2—an aggregate equal to M1 plus savings deposits, small time deposits, and money market mutual funds—was $59.8 billion. The money market rate, the rate at which financial institutions lend to one another in the short term, was 4.26%.

An exchange at Helsinki (established in 1912) is authorized to deal in stocks. As of 2004, there were 134 companies listed on the Helsinki Stock Exchange (HEX), which had a market capitalization of $183.765 billion in that same year. In 2004, the HEX 25 rose 19.6% from the previous year to 1,831.0.

34 INSURANCE

Insurance in Finland is highly developed and diversified. There are 56 Finnish insurance companies, 16 of them engaged in life insurance. Workers' compensation, hunter's liability, workers' pension, nuclear liability, ship owners' and employers' liability, and automobile third-party insurance are compulsory. Other forms of insurance include fire, burglary, water damage, maritime, funeral, livestock, fidelity guarantee, and credit.

In 2003, direct premiums written totaled $14.123 billion, of which life insurance accounted for $11.065 billion. The country's top nonlife insurer that same year was If Vahinkovakuutus, with $962.2 million in gross nonlife premiums written. Nordea was the country's leading life insurer that year with $1,040.7 million of life premiums written.

35 PUBLIC FINANCE

Budget estimates are prepared by the Ministry of Finance and submitted to the legislature. They are referred to the finance committee and subsequently reported back to the full body. Supplementary budgets are usual. Finland's budget balance continued its sharp deterioration in 1992, as the deep recession resulted in decreased tax revenues and increased social expenditures. Extensive government support for the fragile banking system and increased interest expenditures were also responsible. The rest of the 1990s, however, proved much more auspicious for the fast-growing Finnish economy. GDP grew 5.6% in 2000, fueled by a booming electronics industry.

The US Central Intelligence Agency (CIA) estimated that in 2005 Finland's central government took in revenues of approximately $99.6 billion and had expenditures of $97.1 billion. Revenues minus expenditures totaled approximately $2.4 billion. Public debt in 2005 amounted to 42% of GDP. Total external debt was $211.7 billion.

The International Monetary Fund (IMF) reported that in 2002, the most recent year for which it had data, central government revenues were €56,864 million and expenditures were €50,390 million. The value of revenues was us$53,514 million and expenditures us$47,415 million, based on an exchange rate for 2002 of us$1 = €1.0626 as reported by the IMF. Government outlays by function were as follows: general public services, 12.7%; defense, 4.0%; public order and safety, 3.1%; economic affairs, 10.4%; environmental protection, 0.5%; housing and community amenities, 0.7%; health, 8.2%; recreation, culture, and religion, 1.1%; education, 12.5%; and social protection, 47.2%.

36 TAXATION

As of 1 January 2005 the standard corporate income tax rate was 26%, which is also the capital gains tax rate. Branches of foreign companies are taxed equally. The Lutheran Church and the Orthodox Church receive a share of the corporate tax. Withholding taxes, reduced or eliminated through double taxation treaties which Finland has with about 60 countries, are otherwise 28% on dividends, and on income from royalties. Interest paid to resident persons received from debentures, bonds, and bank deposits are subject to a 28% withholding tax. Generally, nonresidents are exempt from this tax. Dividends paid from one resident company to another resident company are also exempt.

Personal income taxes are assessed in a progressive schedule up to 33.5% on taxable income over €56,900. Local income taxes vary from 16–21% of income, depending upon the taxing municipality. Also at the municipal level is a religious tax with proportional rates ranging from 1–2.25% of taxable income. Other direct taxes include a wealth tax, a tax on the transfer of property assets (4.1%), and a tax on transfers of movable assets (1.6%). The amount of national, local, wealth, and health insurance taxes are limited to no more than 60% of taxable income.

Main indirect tax is a value-added tax (VAT) with a standard rate of 22%. A reduced rate of 17% is charged on basic foodstuffs and animal feed. Medicines, books, public transportation, hotel services, and cultural events at subject to an 8% VAT. Exports, the sale or rental of immovable property, insurance, healthcare, educational and financial/bank services are exempt.

37 CUSTOMS AND DUTIES

Finland, as a member of the European Union, allows imports from EU and EFTA countries to enter duty-free. Finland is also a part of the European Economic Area, an agreement that eliminates trade barriers in Europe. Because it is a member of the European Union, Finland complies with trade agreements the EU has made with non-EU countries. Customs duties are levied based on the goods' CIF value (cost, insurance, and freight) at the time and place of importation.

38 FOREIGN INVESTMENT

Finland is favorably disposed toward foreign investment and there is in general no ban on wholly foreign-owned enterprises. Regulations have been liberalized over the years and are generously interpreted. Certain acquisitions of large Finnish companies may require follow-up clearance from the Ministry of Trade and Industry, the purpose of which is to protect "essential national interests." The Aland Islands are an exception to these open investment practices: based on international agreements dating from 1921, property ownership and the right to conduct business are limited to only those individuals with right of domicile in the Aland Islands.

The government started to privatize fully state-owned companies in the early 1990s. By 2005, however, the state, on the global and competitive markets, had switched its role to a risk investor in new, promising, and innovative high-technology companies.

By international standards, the amount of direct investment in Finland had in the past been relatively modest. From 1988 to 1990 its share of world foreign direct investment (FDI) was only half of its share of world GDP. In terms of overall attractiveness as a foreign investment destination, Finland was ranked sixth out of the 140 countries in UNCTAD's study of inward FDI potential. In the 1990s, this potential became more fully realized as foreign investments increased steadily. In the period 1998 to 2000, Finland's share of (FDI) flows grew to be almost twice its share of world GDP. It has continued to be ranked highly in overall attractiveness for foreign investment in the early 2000s. In 2005, Finland was ranked by Transparency International as the second least corrupt country in the world, tied with New Zealand and just behind Iceland.

Annual FDI inflow stood at over $12 billion in 1998, up from $2.1 billion in 1997. FDI inflow fell to $4.6 billion in 1999, but increased to $8.8 billion in 2000. In the global slowdown of 2001, FDI inflow to Finland fell to $3.6 billion. Most investment comes from Sweden, the United Kingdom, the United States, Germany, and France. Finnish investment abroad is in the form of long-term export credits and direct investment by private companies. In 2003, there was a net inflow of investment to Finland, in the amount of €5.2 billion. At the end of 2003, the book value of the stock of outward direct investment was €60.3 billion, and the book value of the stock of inward direct investment was €36.6 billion.

The corporate tax rate stood at 26% in 2005 (down from 29%), and the tax rate on capital gains was 28%. The net wealth tax was to be abolished as of 1 January 2006. The Finnish labor force is highly skilled and well educated, which makes for an attractive investment climate.

39 ECONOMIC DEVELOPMENT

Over a decade after the end of the Cold War, Finland has entered a new phase in its economic development. After a three-year recession in which the Finnish economy reeled from the collapse of the Soviet market in the early 1990s, Finland rebounded by shifting its economic sights westward. The successful development of high tech industries has placed Finland in the forefront of the communications boom. This factor, combined with European Union (EU) membership in 1995, radically altered Finland's economic significance.

Economic activity is spread between the north and the south of the country, particularly in the information and communications technology sector. Oulu in northern Finland is a technology center, for example, as is the Helsinki region in the south. Agricultural activity is concentrated in the southern part of Finland, although reindeer husbandry is focused in the far north.

Finland's educational system is one of the best among OECD countries, and its highly developed welfare state allowed the country to convert easily to the euro. Early retirement has depressed the labor supply, however, and the population is aging rapidly. This could lower potential economic growth in the future. Pension reform was enacted in 2002. The main domestic issue for Finland in 2005 remained improving the labor market, both by reducing the unemployment rate, and by increasing participation in employment. Recent tax cuts have been intended to stimulate the labor market and to keep public finances on a sound footing. Finland must further its integration with the EU and develop better relations with Baltic-rim countries, particularly Russia. Finland remains vital as a transshipment channel to Russian markets, especially in the northern regions.

Finland has put relatively more funds into research and development than most other western countries, as demonstrated by the success of the electronics and other high-tech industries.

40 SOCIAL DEVELOPMENT

Social welfare legislation in Finland is patterned largely on Scandinavian models. The system has evolved gradually in response to social needs. Major benefits include employees' accident insurance, old age and disability pensions, unemployment insurance, sickness insurance, compensation for war invalids, and family and child allowances. The first laws were implemented in 1927, with the most recent update in 2003. Family allowance payments are based on number of children and marital status of the parents. There are also birth grants, and child home care allowances for parents who stay home to care for a child under age three. A universal pension system currently covers all Finnish citizens who have lived in the country for at least three years and foreign nationals with at least five years' residence. Payments begin at age 65.

Women have a high level of education and hold a large number of elective political posts. Finland has a comprehensive equal rights law. However, women seldom hold high-paying management positions in the private sector, and it was estimated in 2004 that women earn on average only 82 cents for every dollar that a male earns. Although there is violence against women, the government takes actions to combat it. There are strict criminal penalties for violence against women, and there are many shelters and programs to assist victims. The relatively high level of domestic violence seems to be due to the high rate of alcoholism.

Indigenous Sami (Lapps) receive government subsidies, which enable them to maintain their traditional reindeer herding lifestyle. Minorities' rights and culture are traditionally protected by law. However, increasing hostility toward immigrants in recent years prompted the passage of a new law designed to facilitate the integration of immigrants into Finnish society and the granting of political asylum.

41 HEALTH

In Finland, the local authorities are responsible for the majority of health services. The entire population is covered by health insurance, which includes compensation for lost earnings and treatment cost. This program is run by the Social Insurance Institution and is supplemented by private services. In 1991, a new Private Health Care Act took effect to enhance the quality of services provided.

In 2004, there were an estimated 311 physicians per 100,000 people. In addition, Finland had approximately 2,171 nurses per 100,000 people, the largest per capita number of nurses in the world. There were also an estimated 91 dentists, 149 pharmacists, and 77 midwives per 100,000 people. Health care, safe water, and sanitation are available to 100% of the population. An estimated 6.8% of the GDP went to health expenditures.

Approximately 80% of married women (ages 15 to 49) were using contraceptives. The fertility rate was 1.7 children per woman throughout her childbearing years. Children were vaccinated against the following diseases: diphtheria, pertussis, and tetanus, 100%; polio, 99%; and measles, 98%.

The infant mortality rate in 2005 was 3.57 per 1,000, one of the world's lowest. Heart disease among men is high relative to other European countries and diseases of the circulatory system cause about half of all deaths in the country, with cancer being the second leading cause of death. The likelihood of dying after age 65 from heart disease was 366 per 1000 men and 351 per 1000 women. Life expectancy in 2005 was 78.35 years.

While female health is good by international standards, male mortality in the over-25 age bracket is much higher in Finland than in most industrial countries. The main reason for the excessive male death rate is cardiovascular disease. Tobacco consumption decreased from 1.7 kg (3.7 lbs) in 1984–86 to 1.5 kg (3.3 lbs) a year per adult in 1995. The HIV/AIDS prevalence was 0.10 per 100 adults in 2003. As of 2004, there were approximately 1,500 people living with HIV/AIDS in the country. There were an estimated 100 deaths from AIDS in 2003.

In 1994, Finland became the first country to eradicate indigenous cases of measles, German measles, and mumps. The diseases have disappeared except for a small number of cases brought in from abroad.

42 HOUSING

At the end of World War II, Finland faced a critical housing shortage. About 14,000 dwellings had been severely damaged during the war and only a modest amount of new housing was built from 1939 to 1944. Some 112,000 dwellings were lost to the ceded territories, and homes had to be found for the displaced persons. Government participation was inevitable in this situation. Two measures passed in the late 1940s, the Land Acquisition Act and the Arava Law, made large-scale credit available on reasonable terms. In the period 1949–59, a total of 334,000 dwellings were built, including 141,900 supported by the Land Acquisition Act and 89,400 supported by the Arava Law.

The migration into urban centers that continued throughout the 1950s and 1960s resulted in a constant urban housing shortage even after the war losses had been replaced. During the period 1960–65, the number of new dwellings averaged about 37,000 annually. To stimulate housing construction, the government passed the Housing Act in 1966 providing for increased government support. As a result of this Act, the number of new dwellings supported by government loans rose rapidly. In the period 1966–74, a total of 466,900 dwellings were completed, of which 214,700 were supported by government loans.

From 1974 through 1985, another 558,000 new units were added to the housing stock. In 1991, 51,803 new dwellings were completed, down from 65,397 in 1990. The total number of dwellings in 2000 was 2,512,442. In 2003, the total number of dwelling units was about 2,604,000. About 57.6% of all units were owner occupied. About 53.9% of all households are in single-family residences; 40% of all households are in single-family detached dwellings. Overcrowding, which is defined as more than one person per room (excluding the kitchen), affects about 20% of the population.

43 EDUCATION

The public school system unites the primary school and lower secondary school into a compulsory nine-year comprehensive school, with a six-year lower level and a three-year upper level. Instruction is uniform at the lower level. At the upper one, there are both required and elective courses. The upper secondary school (gymnasium) and vocational schools continue with three-year programs.

In 2001, about 55% of children between the ages of three and six were enrolled in some type of preschool program. Primary school enrollment in 2003 was estimated at about 100% of age-eligible students. The same year, secondary school enrollment was about 95% of age-eligible students. Nearly all students complete their primary education. The student-to-teacher ratio for primary school was at about 16:1 in 2003.

People's high schools and workers' academies are evidence of the widespread interest in popular or adult education. Although they are owned by private foundations or organizations, these ventures also receive state subsidies. Higher education falls into three categories: universities and institutions of university status; people's high schools or colleges; and workers' academies. Entrance to the universities is through annual matriculation examinations. There are 20 universities and 20 polytechnical schools. All of the universities are owned and operate by the state. The polytechnic schools are co-funded by state and local governments. Among the best known institutes are the University of Helsinki (founded 1640), Turku University (founded 1922), the Helsinki School of Economics, and the University of Tampere. University study is free of charge. In 2003, about 88% of the tertiary age population were enrolled in some type of higher education program; 80% for men and 96% for women. The adult literacy rate for 2000 was estimated at 100%.

As of 2003, public expenditure on education was estimated at 6.4% of GDP, or 12.7% of total government expenditures.

44 LIBRARIES AND MUSEUMS

The largest library in Finland is the Helsinki University Library, with 2.6 million volumes in 2002; it acts both as the general library of the university and as the national library. Next in size are the Helsinki City Library (a regional library with 1.76 million volumes) and the libraries at Turku University (1.9 million) and Åbo Academy (1.7 million). There are about 400 research and university libraries in Finland, most of which are small. There are 19 regional libraries in the country. The Espoo City Library is one such regional library; it sponsors 14 branch locations, 2 institutional locations, and 2 mobile units.

The number of museums has grown rapidly since World War II. There are over 200 museums and 19,100 monuments and historic sites throughout the country. Many museums, which are accessible only from May to September, are open-air, depicting local or rural history. Among the better-known museums are the National, Mannerheim, and Municipal museums and the Ateneum Art Museum in Helsinki; the Turku Art Museum and Provincial Museum; the Runeberg Museum at Porvoo; and the outdoor museums at Helsinki and Turku.

45 MEDIA

Telephone lines are both state and privately owned, but long-distance service is a state monopoly. In 2003, there were an estimated 492 mainline telephones for every 1,000 people. The same year, there were approximately 910 mobile phones in use for every 1,000 people.

Broadcasting is run by Oy Yleisradio Ab, a joint-stock company of which the government owns over 90%, and MTV, a commercial company. Regular television transmission began in 1958. As of 1999 there were 6 AM and 105 FM radio stations and 120 television stations. In 2003, there were an estimated 1,624 radios and 679 television sets for every 1,000 people. The same year, there were 441.7 personal computers for every 1,000 people and 534 of every 1,000 people had access to the Internet. There were 1,283 secure Internet servers in the country in 2004.

In 2001, there were about 256 newspapers, with 56 dailies. Major newspapers, with their political affiliation and daily circulation in 2002, are *Helsingen Sanomat* (in Helsinki), independent, 472,600; *Ilta-Sanomat* (Helsinki), independent, 218,100; *Aamulehti* (Tampere), conservative, 132,900; *Turun Sanomat* (Turku), independent, 113,400; *Iltalehti* (Helsinki), 101,980; *Kaleva* (Oulu), independent, 83,800; *Kauppalehti* (Helsinki), 80,000; *Keskisuomalainen* (Jyväskylä), Center Party, 79,200; *Hufvudstadbladet* (Helsinki, Swedish), independent, 59,200; *Satakunnan Kansa* (Pori), conservative, 58,000; and *Kansan Uutiset* (Helsinki), Finn. People's Democratic League, 42,400. The leading weekly journals in 1995 were *Seura* (circulation 276,000) and *Apu* (254,000).

The broadcast and print media enjoy independence and support from the government, which abides by legally provided free speech and press.

46 ORGANIZATIONS

The cooperative movement is highly developed. Cooperatives have developed extensive educational and informational programs, including a lively cooperative press and many training schools. They are divided into three major groups. Pellervo-Seura is the Central Organization of Farmers' Cooperatives. It provides educational and advisory services to its 800 member organizations. All the agricultural cooperative central organizations are members of Pellervo: the Cooperative Dairy Association, Meat Producers' Central Federation, Central Cooperative Egg Export Association, a wholesalers' cooperative for farm inputs and products, and the forest products cooperative. The Kulutusosuuskuntien Keskusliitto (KK) Cooperative Organizations, the so-called progressive cooperatives, include the KK (educational union of KK cooperatives), OTK (general wholesalers for KK cooperatives), and insurance associations. The FSA Cooperative Organizations are the Swedish-speaking cooperatives. Among their members are the FSA (general union of the Swedish-Finnish cooperatives), Labor (cooperative purchasing wholesalers), Åland Central Cooperative (a central cooperative for cooperative dairies on the Åland Islands), cooperative marketing associations for eggs and dairy products, and the Central Fish Cooperative.

Occupational and trade associations are numerous. In the agricultural sector the most influential is the Central Union of Agricultural Producers, a nonpolitical farmers' trade union. The Federation of Agricultural Societies concentrates on advisory and educational functions. Important in industry and commerce are the Confederation of Finnish Industries, Central Federation of Handicrafts and Small Industry, Central Board of Finnish Wholesalers' and Retailers' Associations, and the Finnish Foreign Trade Association. Professional associations are available for a wide variety of fields. The Central Chamber of Commerce of Finland has its headquarters in Helsinki.

Cultural and philanthropic organizations are also numerous; among the most influential are the Finnish Academy, the Finnish Cultural Fund, and the Wihuri Foundation. Other national cultural organizations include the Fine Arts Association of Finland and the Finnish Society of Sciences and Letters. There are also associations for a variety of hobbyists.

The Finnish Medical Association promotes research and education on health issues and works to establish common policies and standards in healthcare. There are also several associations dedicated to research and education for specific fields of medicine and particular diseases and conditions, such as the Finnish Heart Association and the Finnish Diabetes Association.

National youth organizations exist for a variety of interests, including Finnish 4-H Federation, Finnish Union of Students, Guides and Scouts of Finland, the Youth League of the Coalition Party, and chapters of YMCA/YWCA. Some youth organizations are linked to political parties, such as the Youth League of the Coalition Party. The National Council of Women of Finland is an umbrella organization for women's rights groups throughout the country. The Finnish White Ribbon Union works with groups dedicated to helping women and youth who are victims of drug and alcohol addictions.

The Finnish League for Human Rights is based in Helsinki. At the level of international cooperation are such organizations as the Norden societies and the League for the United Nations. The Red Cross, Amnesty International, and Greenpeace also have active chapters.

47 TOURISM, TRAVEL, AND RECREATION

Finland offers natural beauty and tranquility in forest cottages and on the tens of thousands of islands that dot the 60,000 lakes and the Baltic Sea. Winter offers cultural events and cross-country skiing; winter festivals feature sled and skating competitions, ice castles, and crafts. Finland is the original home of the sauna, a national tradition. Popular sports include skiing, cycling, fishing, golfing, running, rowing, and wrestling. A valid passport is required. Visits of over 90 days require a tourist/business visa.

In 2003, approximately 4,527,000 foreign visitors arrived in Finland, of whom 35% came from Russia. There were 55,767 hotel rooms with 120,051 beds, and an occupancy rate of 46%. Tourist expenditure receipts totaled $2.6 billion.

In 2005, the US Department of State estimated the daily cost of staying in Helsinki at $304. Other areas averaged $310 per day.

48 FAMOUS FINNS

Great Finnish literary figures include Elias Lönnrot (1802–84), compiler of the national epic, the *Kalevala;* Johan Ludwig Runeberg (1804–77), the most important of the 19th-century Finnish-Swedish writers, known for his *Elk Hunters* and *Songs of Ensign*

Stål; Aleksis Kivi (1834–72), the founder of modern Finnish-language literature and author of *The Seven Brothers;* Juhani Aho (1861–1921), master of Finnish prose; Eino Leino (1878–1926), perhaps the greatest lyric poet to write in Finnish; Frans Eemil Sillanpää (1888–1964), a Nobel Prize winner (1939), known to English-language audiences through his *Meek Heritage* and *The Maid Silja;* Toivo Pekkanen (1902–57), whose novels portray the impact of industrialization on Finnish life; Mika Waltari (1908–79), member of the Finnish Academy; Väinö Linna (1920–92), a Scandinavian Literature Prize winner (1963) and author of *The Unknown Soldier* (1954); and the antiwar novelist and playwright Veijo Meri (b.1928).

Finnish architects who are well known abroad include Eliel Saarinen (1873–1950) and his son Eero Saarinen (1910–61), whose career was chiefly in the United States; Alvar Aalto (1898–1976); Viljo Revell (1910–64); and Aarne Ervi (1910–77). Leading sculptors were Wäinö Aaltonen (1894–1966) and Eila Hiltunen (1922–2003); Laila Pullinen (b.1933) is also famous. Five representative painters are Helena Schjerfbeck (1852–1946), Albert Edelfelt (1854–1905), Akseli Gallen-Kalléla (1865–1931), Pekka Halonen (1865–1933), and Tyko Sallinen (1879–1955). Arts and crafts hold an important place in Finnish culture: leading figures are Tapio Wirkkala (1915–85) and Timo Sarpaneva (b.1926). Finnish music has been dominated by Jean Sibelius (1865–1957). Also notable are the composer of art songs Yrjö Kilpinen (1892–1957), the composer of operas and symphonies Aulis Sallinen (b.1935), and opera and concert bass Martti Talvela (1935–89).

Scientists of international repute are A. I. Wirtanen (1895–1973), Nobel Prize winner for chemistry in 1945; Rolf Nevanlinna (1895–1980), mathematician; Pentti Eskola (1883–1964), geologist; V. A. Heiskanen (1895–1971), professor of geodesy; Aimo Kaarlo Cajander (1879–1943), botanist and silviculturist; Edward Westermarck (1862–1939), ethnographer and sociologist; and Yrjö Väisälä (1891–1971), astronomer. Ragnar Arthur Granit (1900–1991) shared the Nobel Prize in physiology or medicine in 1967. Linus Torvalds (b.1969) is a software engineer best known for initiating the development of Linux.

Outstanding athletes include Hannes Kolehmainen (1890–1966) and Paavo Nurmi (1897–1973), who between them won 14 Olympic medals in track. Another distance runner, Lasse Viren (b.1949), won gold medals in both the 1972 and 1976 games. Other Olympic gold medalists include skier Janne Lahtela (b.1974) and Nordic combined athlete Samppa Lajunen (b.1979).

Major political figures of the 19th century were Johan Wilhelm Snellman (1806–81) and Yrjö Sakari Yrjö-Koskinen (1830–1903). Inseparably linked with the history of independent Finland is Marshal Carl Gustaf Emil Mannerheim (1867–1951), and with the recent postwar period President Juho Kusti Paasikivi (1870–1956). Sakari Tuomioja (1911–64) was prominent in UN affairs. President Urho Kekkonen (1900–86) was instrumental in preserving Finland's neutrality. Mauno Henrik Koivisto (b.1923) served as president from 1982 until 1994. Martti Oiva Kalevi Ahtisaari (b.1937), a former president (1994–2000) and UN diplomat, is noted for his international peace work. Tarja Kaarina Halonen (b.1943) became Finland's first woman president in 2000. She was reelected in 2006.

49 DEPENDENCIES

Finland possesses no territories or colonies.

50 BIBLIOGRAPHY

Annesley, Claire (ed.). *A Political and Economic Dictionary of Western Europe*. Philadelphia: Routledge/Taylor and Francis, 2005.

Bako, Elemer. *Finland and the Finns: A Selective Bibliography*. Washington, D.C.: Library of Congress, 1993.

Dun and Bradstreet's Export Guide to Finland. Parsippany, N.J.: Dun and Bradstreet, 1999.

International Smoking Statistics: A Collection of Historical Data from 30 Economically Developed Countries. New York: Oxford University Press, 2002.

Jussila, Osmo. *From Grand Duchy to Modern State: A Political History of Finland since 1809*. London, Eng.: Hurst, 1999.

Maude, George. *Historical Dictionary of Finland*. Lanham, Md.: Scarecrow, 1995.

Nordstrom, Byron J. *Scandinavia since 1500*. Minneapolis: University of Minnesota Press, 2000.

Salminen, Esko. *The Silenced Media: The Propaganda War between Russia and the West in Northern Europe*. New York: St. Martin's Press, 1999.

Siikala, Anna-Leena (ed.). *Myth and Mentality: Studies in Folklore and Popular Thought*. Helsinki: Finnish Literature Society, 2002.

FRANCE

French Republic
République Française

CAPITAL: Paris

FLAG: The national flag is a tricolor of blue, white, and red vertical stripes.

ANTHEM: *La Marseillaise.*

MONETARY UNIT: The euro replaced the franc as the official currency in 2002. The euro is divided into 100 cents. There are coins in denominations of 1, 2, 5, 10, 20, and 50 cents and 1 euro and 2 euros. There are notes of 5, 10, 20, 50, 100, 200, and 500 euros. €1 = $1.25475 (or $1 = €0.79697) as of 2005.

WEIGHTS AND MEASURES: The metric system is the legal standard.

HOLIDAYS: New Year's Day, 1 January; Labor Day, 1 May; World War II Armistice Day, 8 May; Bastille Day, 14 July; Assumption, 15 August; All Saints' Day, 1 November; World War I Armistice Day, 11 November; Christmas, 25 December. Movable holidays include Easter Monday, Ascension, and Pentecost Monday.

TIME: 1 PM = noon GMT.

¹LOCATION, SIZE, AND EXTENT

Situated in Western Europe, France is the second-largest country on the continent, with an area (including the island of Corsica) of 547,030 sq km (211,209 sq mi). Comparatively, the area occupied by France is slightly less than twice the size of the state of Colorado. It extends 962 km (598 mi) N–S and 950 km (590 mi) E–W. France is bounded on the N by the North Sea and Belgium, on the NE by Luxembourg and Germany, on the E by Switzerland and Italy, on the S by the Mediterranean Sea, on the SW by Andorra and Spain, on the W by the Bay of Biscay and the Atlantic Ocean, and on the NW by the English Channel, with a total boundary length of 6,316 km (3,925 mi), of which 3,427 km (2,130 mi) is coastline.

France's capital city, Paris, is located in the north central part of the country.

²TOPOGRAPHY

France topographically is one of the most varied countries of Europe, with elevations ranging from 2 m (7 ft) below sea level at Rhône River delta to the highest peak of the continent, Mont Blanc (4,807 m/15,771 ft), on the border with Italy. Much of the country is ringed with mountains. In the northeast is the Ardennes Plateau, which extends into Belgium and Luxembourg; to the east are the Vosges, the high Alps, and the Jura Mountains; and along the Spanish border are the Pyrenees, much like the Alps in ruggedness and height.

The core of France is the Paris Basin, connected in the southwest with the lowland of Aquitaine. Low hills cover much of Brittany and Normandy. The old, worn-down upland of the Massif Central, topped by extinct volcanoes, occupies the south-central area. The valley of the Rhône (813 km/505 mi), with that of its tributary the Saône (480 km/298 mi), provides an excellent passageway from the Paris Basin and eastern France to the Mediterranean.

There are three other main river systems: the Seine (776 km/482 mi), draining into the English Channel; the Loire (1,020 km/634 mi), which flows through central France to the Atlantic; and the Garonne (575 km/357 mi), which flows across southern France to the Atlantic.

³CLIMATE

Three types of climate may be found within France: oceanic, continental, and Mediterranean. The oceanic climate, prevailing in the western parts of the country, is one of small temperature range, ample rainfall, cool summers, and cool but seldom very cold winters. The continental (transition) type of climate, found over much of eastern and central France, adjoining its long common boundary with west-central Europe, is characterized by warmer summers and colder winters than areas farther west; rainfall is ample, and winters tend to be snowy, especially in the higher areas. The Mediterranean climate, widespread throughout the south of France (except in the mountainous southwest), is one of cool winters, hot summers, and limited rainfall. The mean temperature is about 11°C (53° F) at Paris and 15°C (59° F) at Nice. In central and southern France, annual rainfall is light to moderate, ranging from about 68 cm (27 in) at Paris to 100 cm (39 in) at Bordeaux. Rainfall is heavy in Brittany, the northern coastal areas, and the mountainous areas, where it reaches more than 112 cm (44 in).

⁴FLORA AND FAUNA

France's flora and fauna are as varied as its range of topography and climate. It has forests of oak and beech in the north and center, as well as pine, birch, poplar, and willow. The Massif Central has chestnut and beech; the subalpine zone, juniper and dwarf pine. In the south are pine forests and various oaks. Eucalyptus (imported from Australia) and dwarf pines abound in Provence. Toward the Mediterranean are olive trees, vines, and mulberry and fig trees, as well as laurel, wild herbs, and the low scrub known as maquis (from which the French resistance movement in World War II took its name).

The Pyrenees and the Alps are the home of the brown bear, chamois, marmot, and alpine hare. In the forests are polecat and marten, wild boar, and various deer. Hedgehog and shrew are common, as are fox, weasel, bat, squirrel, badger, rabbit, mouse, otter, and beaver. The birds of France are largely migratory; warblers, thrushes, magpies, owls, buzzards, and gulls are common. There are storks in Alsace and elsewhere, eagles and falcons in the mountains, pheasants and partridge in the south. Flamingos, terns, buntings, herons, and egrets are found in the Mediterranean zone. The rivers hold eels, pike, perch, carp, roach, salmon, and trout; lobster and crayfish are found in the Mediterranean.

As of 2002, there were at least 93 species of mammals, 283 species of birds, and over 4,600 species of plants throughout the country.

5 ENVIRONMENT

The Ministry for the Environment is the principal environmental agency. France's basic law for the protection of water resources dates from 1964. The mid-1970s brought passage of laws governing air pollution, waste disposal, and chemicals. In general, environmental laws embody the "polluter pays" principle, although some of the charges imposed—for example, an aircraft landing fee—have little effect on the reduction of the pollutant (i.e., aircraft noise).

Water pollution is a serious problem in France due to the accumulation of industrial contaminants, agricultural nitrates, and waste from the nation's cities. As of 1994, 20% of France's forests were damaged due to acid rain and other contaminants. France has 179 cu km of renewable water resources with 72% used for industrial purposes and 10% used for farming.

Air pollution is a significant environmental problem in France, which had the world's 11th-highest level of industrial carbon dioxide emissions in 1992, totaling 362 million metric tons, a per capita level of 6.34 metric tons. The total level of carbon dioxide emissions in 2000 was about the same at 362.4 million metric tons. Official statistics reflect substantial progress in reducing airborne emissions in major cities: the amount of sulfur dioxide in Paris decreased from 122 micrograms per cu m of air in 1971 to 54 micrograms in 1985. An attempt to ban the dumping of toxic wastes entirely and to develop the technology for neutralizing them proved less successful, however, and the licensing of approved dump sites was authorized in the early 1980s.

In 2003, 13.3% of France's total land area was protected; these areas include both national and regional parks, as well as 8 biosphere reserves, 2 UNESCO World Heritage Sites, and 15 Ramsar Wetlands of International Importance. According to a 2006 report issued by the International Union for Conservation of Nature and Natural Resources (IUCN), threatened species included 16 types of mammals, 15 species of birds, 3 types of reptiles, 3 species of amphibians, 16 species of fish, 34 types of mollusks, 31 species of other invertebrates, and 2 species of plants. Endangered or extinct species in France include the Corsican swallowtail, the gray wolf, the false ringlet butterfly, the Pyrenean desman, and the Baltic sturgeon. It has been estimated that 25% of all species known to have appeared in France were extinct, endangered, or in sub-

stantial regression. Extinct species include Perrin's cave beetle and the Sardinian pika.

6 POPULATION

The population of France in 2005 was estimated by the United Nations (UN) at 60,742,000, which placed it at number 21 in population among the 193 nations of the world. In 2005, approximately 16% of the population was over 65 years of age, with another 19% of the population under 15 years of age. There were 95 males for every 100 females in the country. According to the UN, the annual population rate of change for 2005–10 was expected to be 0.4%, a rate the government viewed as too low. The projected population for the year 2025 was 63,377,000. The population density was 110 per sq km (285 per sq mi), with much of the population concentrated in the north and southeast areas of the country.

The UN estimated that 76% of the population lived in urban areas in 2005, and that urban areas were growing at an annual rate of 0.67%. The capital city, Paris, had a population of 9,794,000 in that year. The next largest cities and their estimated populations include Lyon, 1,408,000; Marseille, 1,384,000; and Lille, 1,031,000. Other major urban centers include Toulouse, Nice, Strasbourg, Nantes, Bordeaux, Montpellier, Rennes, Saint-Étienne, and Le Havre.

7 MIGRATION

A new law on immigration and asylum was passed by parliament in May 1998. The law included amendments to include the French constitution's provision to protect "those fighting for freedom" and those threatened with inhuman and degrading treatment in their country of origin. France hosted some 6,300 Kosovar Albanians who arrived in 1999 under the UNHCR/IOM Humanitarian Evacuation Programme. In 2004, a total of 110,321 asylum applications were submitted to France, mostly from Asia, Africa, and Europe. In the same year, recognition of refugee status was granted to some 14% of asylum seekers. Refugees enjoy all the rights of regular immigrants. In 2004 France harbored 139,852 refugees, mainly Sri Lankans, Vietnamese, Turks, Cambodians, Congolese, and Serbians.

Populations of concern to the United Nations High Commissioner for Refugees (UNHCR) in France numbered 151,452. In 2005 it was estimated that illegal foreigners numbered 200,000–400,000. According to *Migration News*, France deported 11,000 illegals in 2003, 16,000 in 2004, and an expected 23,000 in 2005. Minorities are not recognized in France. They are expected to connect with "the Indivisible Republic," entitled in the French constitution. Nevertheless, in Paris environs between April and August 2005, rioting and fires killed immigrants. Police evacuated rundown buildings where asylum seekers and irregular foreigners lived in crowded conditions.

Remittances to France in 2002 were $761 million. In 2005, the net migration rate was estimated as 0.66 migrants per 1,000 population.

8 ETHNIC GROUPS

The French are generally derived from three basic European ethnic stocks: Celtic, Latin, and Teutonic (Frankish). There are also small groups of Flemings, Catalans, Germans, Armenians, Roma, Russians, Poles, and others. The largest resident alien groups are

Algerians, Portuguese, Moroccans, Italians, Spaniards, Tunisians, and Turks.

9 LANGUAGES

Not only is French the national language of France, but it also has official status (often with other languages) throughout much of the former French colonial empire, including about two dozen nations in Africa. In all, it is estimated that more than 300 million people have French as their official language or mother tongue. Moreover, French is the sole official language at the ICJ and UPU, and shares official status in most international organizations. Other languages spoken within France itself include Breton (akin to Welsh) in Brittany; a German dialect in Alsace and Lorraine; Flemish in northeastern France; Spanish, Catalan, and Basque in the southwest; Provençal in the southeast, and an Italian dialect on the island of Corsica.

10 RELIGIONS

According to 2005 estimates, about 83–88% of the population are nominally Roman Catholic, but church officials claim that only about 8% are practicing members of the church. About 2% are Protestant, mostly Calvinist or Lutheran. Muslims (mostly North African workers) make up about 7–8%. Jews and Bahais each made up about 1%. There are about 250,000 Jehovah's Witnesses and between 80,000 and 100,000 Orthodox Christians. Christian Scientists, Mormons, and Scientologists are also represented. About 6% of the population have no religious affiliation.

The French Jewish community is one of the largest in the world, along with those in the United States, Israel, and the successor states of the former USSR; more than half are immigrants from North Africa. The 600,000 members are divided between Reform, Conservative, and Orthodox groups. Jews have enjoyed full rights of citizenship in France since 1791, and the emancipation of Central European Jewry was accomplished, to a large extent, by the armies of Napoleon Bonaparte. Anti-Semitism became a flaming issue during the Dreyfus affair in the late 1890s; in the 1980s, principal French synagogues were under police guard because of a wave of attacks by international terrorists.

The constitution provides for freedom of religion, and the government reportedly respects this right in practice. Church and state have been legally separate since 1905. Registration for religious groups is not required, but most groups choose to do so in order to gain tax-exempt status. The 2001 About-Picard Law allows for the dissolution of groups that endanger the physical or psychological well-being of individuals, promote illegal medical practices, violate the freedom of others, or commit fraud. Groups which advocate religious interests in dialogue with the government include the Council of Bishops (Catholic), the Protestant Federation of France, the General Consistory of Jews of France, and the French Council of the Muslim Faith. The Interministerial Monitoring Mission Against Sectarian Abuses monitors the activities of religious sects or cults that are considered to be a possible threat to society or may be acting in violation of the law.

11 TRANSPORTATION

France has one of the most highly developed transportation systems in Europe. Its outstanding characteristic has long been the degree to which it is centralized at Paris—plateaus and plains offering easy access radiate from the city in all directions, and rivers with broad valleys converge on it from all sides. In 2003, the French road network totaled 891,290 km (554,438 mi), all of which was paved, and included about 10,390 km (6,462 mi) of national highways. In 2003 there were 29,560,000 passenger cars and 6,068,000 commercial vehicles in use.

All French railroads were nationalized in 1938 and are part of the national rail network Société Nationale des Chemins-de-Fer Français, 51% of whose shares are controlled by the government. As of 2004 there were 29,519 km (18,361 mi) of standard and narrow gauge railway track in operation, of which about 14,481 km (9,007 mi) were electrified. Standard gauge track accounted for nearly the entire system, with narrow gauge right of way accounting for only 167 km (104 mi). Le Train à Grande Vitesse (TGV), the fastest train in the world, averaging 250 km (155 mi) per hour over most of its run, entered service between Paris and Lyon in 1981. TGV service between Paris and Lausanne became fully operational in 1985. The TGV set another world speed record on 18 May 1990 with a registered speed of 515.2 km/h (320.2 mph). The Paris subway (métro), begun in the early 1900s but extensively modernized, and the city's regional express railways cover a distance of 472 km (293 mi). The métro has over one million passengers a day. Parisian bus lines carry about 800,000 passengers daily. Other cities with subways are Marseille, Lille, and Lyon, with construction underway in Toulouse.

Two high-speed rail tunnels under the English Channel link Calais and Folkestone, England (near Dover). The 50-km (31-mi) project by Eurotunnel, a British-French consortium, was completed in 1993. From these terminals, people can drive their cars and trucks onto trains, which can make the underground trek in about 30 minutes. Rail lines that run through the tunnel include Le Shuttle, which provides both freight and passenger service, and Eurostar, a high-speed passenger-only line. In November 1996 a truck aboard a Le Shuttle train caught fire in the tunnel, causing extensive damage but no loss of life. Service was partially restored within weeks of the incident and full repairs were completed by the following May.

France, especially in its northern and northeastern regions, is well provided with navigable rivers and connecting canals, and inland water transportation is of major importance. As of 2000, there were about 8,500 km (5,287 mi) of navigable waterways, of which 1,686 km (1,048 mi) was accessible to craft of 3,000 metric tons. The French merchant marine, as of 2005, had a total of 56 ships with 1,000 GRT or over, and a total capacity of 703,639 GRT. Kerguelen, an archipelago in the French Antarctic Territory, offers an offshore registry program which is less regulatory than official French registry. The leading ports are Marseille, Le Havre, Dunkerque, Rouen, Bordeaux, and Cherbourg. Other important ports include Boulogne, Brest, Fos-Sur-Mer, Sete, and Toulon. More than half of freight traffic to and from French ports is carried by French ships.

In 2004 there were an estimated 478 airports in France. In 2005, a total of 288 had paved runways, and there were also three heliports. France's national airline, Air France, is government subsidized. It operates regularly scheduled flights to all parts of the world. The Concorde, jointly developed by France and the United Kingdom at a cost of more than £1 billion, entered regular transatlantic service in 1976. Both British Airways and Air France ceased operations of Concorde passenger flights in 2003.

There are two major private airlines: the Union des Transports Aériens, which provides service to Africa and the South Pacific, and Air Inter, which operates within metropolitan France. The two international airports of Paris, Charles de Gaulle and Orly, both located in Paris, lead all others in France in both passenger and freight traffic. In 2003, about 47.259 million passengers were carried on scheduled domestic and international air flights.

12 HISTORY

Cave paintings and engravings, the most famous of them at Lascaux, near Montignac in the southwest, attest to human habitation in France as early as 30,000 years ago. Relics from the period between 4000 and 1800 BC include some 4,500 dolmens (structures consisting of two vertical stones capped by a horizontal stone), nearly 1,000 of them in Brittany alone, and more than 6,000 menhirs (single vertical stones), measuring 1.5–21.3 m (5–70 ft) in height and weighing up to 350 tons. There may already have been 2–3 million people in France when Phoenician and Greek colonists founded cities on the southern coast around 600 BC.

Detailed knowledge of French history begins with the conquest of the region (58–51 BC) by Julius Caesar. The country was largely inhabited by Celtic tribes known to the Romans as Gauls. Under Roman rule the Gallic provinces were among the most prosperous and civilized of the empire. Roman roads, traces of which still may be seen, traversed the land. Numerous cities were founded. Latin superseded the Celtic dialects. Christianity spread rapidly in Roman Gaul after its introduction there in the 1st century, and by the time the empire began to disintegrate a few hundred years later, the Gauls were a thoroughly Romanized and Christianized people. Early in the 5th century, Teutonic tribes invaded the region from Germany, the Visigoths settling in the southwest, the Burgundians along the Rhône River Valley, and the Franks (from whom the French take their name) in the north. The Germanic invaders probably never constituted more than a dominant minority of the population.

The first leader to make himself king of all the Franks was Clovis (466–511), who began his reign in 481, routing the last forces of the Roman governors of the province in 486. Clovis claimed that he would be baptized a Christian in the event of his victory against the Visigoths, which was said to have guaranteed the battle. Clovis regained the southwest from the Visigoths, was baptized in 496, and made himself master of western Germany, but after his death the kingdom disintegrated and its population declined under the Merovingian dynasty. In 732, Charles Martel was able to rally the eastern Franks to inflict a decisive defeat on the Saracens—Muslim invaders who already controlled the Iberian Peninsula—between Poitiers and Tours. He spawned the Carolingian family, as well as his grandson, Charlemagne (r.768–814), who was the greatest of the early Frankish rulers. Ruling "by the sword and the cross," he gave the kingdom an efficient administration, created an excellent legal system, and encouraged the revival of learning, piety, and the arts. He added to the territories under his rule through wide conquests, eventually reigning over an area corresponding to present-day France, the FRG, the Low Countries, and northern Italy. On Christmas Day in the year 800, he was crowned emperor of the West and ruler of the 1st Holy Roman Empire by the pope in Rome.

After the death of Charlemagne, the vast Carolingian Empire broke up during a century of feuding, the title of emperor passing to German rulers in the east. The territory of what is now France was invaded anew, this time by pagan tribes from Scandinavia and the north, and the region that later became known as Normandy was ceded to the Northmen in 911 by Charles III ("the Simple," r.898–923). At the end of the century, Hugh Capet (r.987–996) founded the line of French kings that, including its collateral branches, was to rule the country for the next 800 years. Feudalism was by now a well-established system. The French kings were the dukes and feudal overlords of the Île de France, centered on Paris and extending roughly three days' march around the city. At first, their feudal overlordship over the other provinces of France was almost entirely nominal. Some of the largest of these, like the Duchy of Brittany, were practically independent kingdoms. The Duchy of Normandy grew in power when William II, duke of Normandy, engaged in the Norman Conquest of England (1066–70) and became king as William I ("the Conqueror"), introducing the French language and culture to England. The powers of the French monarchy were gradually extended in the course of the 11th and early 12th centuries, particularly by Louis VI, who died in 1137. The power of his son Louis VII (r.1137–80) was challenged by Henry of Anjou, who, upon his accession to the English throne as Henry II in 1154, was feudal master of a greater part of the territory of France, including Normandy, Brittany, Anjou, and Aquitaine. Henry's sons, Richard and John, were unable to hold these far-flung territories against the vigorous assaults of Louis's son Philip Augustus (r.1180–1223). By 1215, Philip had not only reestablished the French crown's control over the former Angevin holdings in the north and west but also had firmly consolidated the crown's power in Languedoc and Toulouse. Philip's grandson Louis IX (St. Louis), in a long reign (1226–70), firmly established the strength of the monarchy through his vigorous administration of the royal powers. The reign of Louis's grandson Philip IV ("the Fair," 1285–1314) marks the apogee of French royal power in the medieval period. He quarreled with the papacy over fiscal control of the French clergy and other aspects of sovereignty. His emissaries arrested Pope Boniface VIII and after his death removed the seat of the papacy to Avignon, where the popes resided under French dominance (the so-called Babylonian Captivity) until 1377.

It is estimated that between 1348 and 1400 the population dropped from 16 million to 11 million, mainly from a series of epidemics, beginning with the Black Death (bubonic plague) of 1348–50. In 1415, Henry V of England; taking advantage of civil war between the Gascons and Armagnacs, and the growing insanity of Charles VI; launched a new invasion of France and won a decisive victory at Agincourt. Charles VI (r.1380–1422) was compelled under the Treaty of Troyes (1420) to marry his daughter Catherine to Henry and to declare the latter and his descendants heirs to the French crown. Upon Henry's death in 1422, his infant son Henry VI was crowned king of both France and England, but in the same year, Charles's son, the dauphin of France, reasserted his claim, formally assumed the royal title, and slowly began the reconquest.

LOCATION: 42°20′ to 51°5′ N; 4°47′ W to 8°15′ E. BOUNDARY LENGTHS: Belgium, 620 kilometers (387 miles); Luxembourg, 73 kilometers (45 miles); Germany, 451 kilometers (280 miles); Switzerland, 573 kilometers (358 miles); Italy, 488 kilometers (305 miles); Andorra, 60 kilometers (37 miles); Spain, 623 kilometers (389 miles); total coastline (including islands), 3,427 kilometers (2,125 miles). TERRITORIAL SEA LIMIT: 12 miles.

Philip the Fair was succeeded by three sons, who reigned briefly and who left no direct male heirs, ending the Capetian dynasty. In 1328, his nephew Philip VI (in accordance with the so-called Salic Law, under which succession could pass through a male line only) mounted the throne as the first of the Valois kings. The new king's title to the throne was challenged by Edward III of England, whose mother was the daughter of Philip the Fair. In 1337, Edward as-serted a formal claim to the French crown, shortly thereafter quar-tering the lilies of France on his shield. The struggle that lasted from 1337 to 1453 over these rival claims is known as the Hun-dred Years' War. Actually it consisted of a series of shorter wars and skirmishes punctuated by periods of truce. Edward won a no-table victory at Crécy in 1346, in a battle that showed the superi-ority of English ground troops and longbows against the French knights in armor. In 1356, the French royal forces were routed by the Prince of Wales at Poitiers, where the French king, John II, was taken prisoner. By terms of the Treaty of Brétigny (1360), the kingdom of France was dismembered, the southwest being formally ceded to the king of England. Under Charles V (r.1364–80), also called "Charles the Wise," however, the great French soldier Bertrand du Guesclin, through a tenaciously conducted series of skirmishes, succeeded in driving the English from all French territory except Calais and the Bordeaux region.

1422–1789

The first part of the Hundred Years' War was essentially a dynastic rather than a national struggle. The English armies themselves were commanded by French-speaking nobles and a French-speaking king. Although the legitimate succession to the French crown was the ostensible issue throughout the war, the emerging forces of modern nationalism came into play with the campaign launched by Henry V, whose everyday language was English and who, after Agincourt, became an English national hero. France owed no small measure of its eventual success to the sentiment of nationalism that was arising throughout the country and that found its personification in the figure of Joan of Arc. Early in 1429, this young woman of surprising military genius, confident that she had a divinely inspired mission to save France, gained the confidence of the dauphin. She succeeded in raising the siege of Orléans and had the dauphin crowned Charles VII at Reims. Joan fell into English hands and at Rouen in 1431 was burned at the stake as a heretic, but the French armies continued to advance. Paris was retaken in 1436, and Rouen in 1453; by 1461, when Charles died, the English had been driven from all French territory except Calais, which was recaptured in 1558.

Louis XI (r.1461–83), with the support of the commercial towns, which regarded the king as their natural ally, set France on a course that eventually destroyed the power of the great feudal lords. His most formidable antagonist, Charles the Bold, duke of Burgundy, who ruled virtually as an independent monarch, commanded for many years far more resources than the king of France himself. But after the duke was defeated and killed in a battle against the Swiss in 1477, Louis was able to reunite Burgundy with France. When Louis's son Charles VIII united Brittany, the last remaining quasi-independent province, with the royal domain by his marriage to Anne of Brittany, the consolidation of the kingdom under one rule was complete.

Under Charles VIII (r.1483–98) and Louis XII (r.1498–1515), France embarked on a series of Italian wars, which were continued under Francis I (r.1515–47) and Henry II (r.1547–59). These wars developed into the first phase of a protracted imperialistic struggle between France and the house of Habsburg. Although the Italian wars ended in a French defeat, they served to introduce the artistic and cultural influences of the Italian Renaissance into France on a large scale. Meanwhile, as the Reformation gained an increasing following in France, a bitter enmity developed between the great families that had espoused the Protestant or Huguenot cause and those that had remained Catholic. The policy of the French monarchy was in general to suppress Protestantism at home while supporting it abroad as a counterpoise to Habsburg power. Under the last of the Valois kings, Charles IX (r.1560–74) and Henry III (r.1574–89), a series of eight fierce civil wars devastated France,

called The Wars of Religion. Paris remained a stronghold of Catholicism, and on 23–24 August 1572, a militia led by the Duke of Guise slaughtered thousands of Protestants in the Massacre of St. Bartholomew. The Protestant Henry of Navarre was spared because of his royal status and eventually, on the death of Henry III, he acceded to the throne, beginning the Bourbon dynasty. Unable to capture Paris by force, Henry embraced Catholicism in 1593 and entered the city peacefully the following year. In 1598, he signed the Edict of Nantes, which guaranteed religious freedom to the Huguenots. With the aid of his minister Sully, Henry succeeded in restoring prosperity to France.

Assassinated in 1610 by a Catholic fanatic after 19 attempts on his life, Henry IV was succeeded by his young son Louis XIII, with the queen mother, Marie de Médicis, acting as regent in the early years of his reign. Later, the affairs of state were directed almost exclusively by Cardinal Richelieu, the king's minister. Richelieu followed a systematic policy that entailed enhancing the crown's absolute rule at home and combating the power of the Habsburgs abroad. In pursuit of the first of these objectives, Richelieu destroyed the political power of the Protestants by strictly monitoring the press and French language through the Academie Francaise; in pursuit of the second he led France in 1635 into the Thirty Years' War, then raging in Germany, on the side of the Protestants and against the Austrians and the Spanish. Richelieu died in 1642, and Louis XIII died a few months later. His successor, Louis XIV, was five years old, and during the regency of his mother, Anne of Austria, France's policy was largely guided by her adviser Cardinal Mazarin. The generalship of the prince de Condé and the vicomte de Turenne brought France striking victories. The Peace of Westphalia (1648), which ended the Thirty Years' War, and the Peace of the Pyrenees (1659) marked the end of Habsburg hegemony and established France as the dominant power on the European continent. The last attempt of the French nobles in the Paris Parliament to rise against the crown, called the Fronde (1648–53), was successfully repressed by Mazarin even though the movement had the support of Condé and Turenne.

The active reign of Louis XIV began in 1661, the year of Mazarin's death, and lasted until his own death in 1715. Louis XIV had served in the French army against Spain before his accession, and married the daughter of the King of Spain in order to bring peace to the region, despite his love for Mazarin's niece. Assisted by his able ministers Colbert and Louvois, he completed Mazarin's work of domestic centralization and transformed the French state into an absolute monarchy based on the so-called divine right of kings. Industry and commerce were encouraged by mercantilist policies, and great overseas empires were carved out in India, Canada, and Louisiana. By transforming the nobles into perennial courtiers, financially dependent on the crown, the king clipped their wings. Lavish display marked the early period of his reign, when the great palace at Versailles was built, beginning the era of French Classicism.

The reign of Louis XIV marked the high point in the prestige of the French monarchy. It was a golden age for French culture as well, and French fashions and manners set the standard for all Europe. Nevertheless, the Sun King, as he was styled, left the country in a weaker position than he had found it. In 1672, he invaded the Protestant Netherlands with his cousin Charles I of England, defeating Spain and the Holy Roman Empire as well in 1678. In

1685, he revoked the Edict of Nantes, and an estimated 200,000 Huguenots fled the country to escape persecution. Whole provinces were depopulated, and the economy was severely affected by the loss of many skilled and industrious workers. Louis undertook a long series of foreign wars, culminating in the War of the Spanish Succession (1701–14), in which England, the Netherlands, and most of the German states were arrayed against France, Spain, Bavaria, Portugal, and Savoy. In the end, little territory was lost, but the military primacy of the country was broken and its economic strength seriously sapped.

The reign of Louis XV (1715–74) and that of his successor, Louis XVI (1774–93), which was terminated by the French Revolution, showed the same lavish display of royal power and elegance that had been inaugurated by the Sun King. At the same time, the economic crisis that Louis XIV left as his legacy continued to grow more serious. A series of foreign wars cost France its Indian and Canadian colonies and bankrupted the country, including the French and Indian War (1755–1760). Meanwhile, the locus of the economic power in the kingdom had shifted to the hands of the upper bourgeoisie in the Enlightenment, who resented the almost wholly unproductive ruling class that espoused Classicism. The intellectual currents of the so-called Age of Reason were basically opposed to the old order. Voltaire attacked the Church and the principle of absolutism alike; Diderot advocated scientific materialism; Jean-Jacques Rousseau preached popular sovereignty. The writer changed from a royal servant into a revolutionary force.

1789–1900

In 1789, faced with an unmanageable public debt, Louis XVI convened, for the first time since the reign of Louis XIII, the States-General, the national legislative body, to consider certain fiscal reforms. The representatives of the third estate, the Commons, met separately on 17 June and proclaimed themselves the National Assembly. This action, strictly speaking, marked the beginning of the French Revolution, although the act that best symbolized the power of the revolution was the storming of the Bastille, a royal prison, by a Paris mob on 14 July—an event still commemorated as a national holiday. With the support of the mob, which forced the king, his wife Marie Antoinette, and his family from the palace at Versailles into virtual imprisonment in the Tuilerie in Paris; the Assembly was able to force Louis to accept a new constitution including The Declaration of the Rights of Man and the Citizen, providing for a limited monarchy, the secularization of the state, and the seizure of Church lands. War with Austria, which wished to intervene to restore the status quo ante in France, broke out in 1792. The Assembly's successor, the National Convention, elected in September 1792, proclaimed the First French Republic. Louis XVI was convicted of treason and executed. The radical group of Jacobins under Maximilien Robespierre's leadership exercised strict control through committees of public welfare and a revolutionary tribunal. The Jacobins attempted to remake France in the image of an egalitarian republic. Their excesses led to a Reign of Terror (1793–94), carried out indiscriminately against royalists and such moderate republican groups as the Girondins. Manifold opposition to the Jacobins and specifically to Robespierre combined to end their reign in the summer of 1794. In 1795, a new constitution of moderate character was introduced, and executive power was vested in a Directory of five men. The Directory,

weakened by inefficient administration and military reverses, fell in turn in 1799, when the military hero Napoleon Bonaparte engineered a coup and established the Consulate. Ruling autocratically as the first consul, Bonaparte established domestic stability and decisively defeated the Austrian-British coalition arrayed against France. In 1804, he had himself proclaimed emperor as Napoleon I and, until his downfall in 1814, he ruled France in that capacity.

Capitalizing on the newly awakened patriotic nationalism of France, Napoleon led his imperial armies to a striking series of victories over the dynastic powers of Europe. By 1808, he was the master of all Europe west of Russia with the exception of the British Isles. That year, however, the revolt in Spain—upon whose throne Napoleon had placed his brother Joseph—began to tax French military reserves. Napoleon's ill-fated attempt to conquer Russia in 1812 was followed by the consolidation of a powerful alliance against him, consisting of Russia, Prussia, Britain, and Sweden. The allies defeated Napoleon at Leipzig in 1813 and captured Paris in the spring of 1814. Napoleon was exiled to the island of Elba, just off the northwest coast of Italy, and Louis XVIII, a brother of Louis XVI, was placed on the French throne. In March 1815, Napoleon escaped from Elba, rallied France behind him, and reentered Paris in triumph behind the fleeing Louis XVIII. He was, however, finally and utterly crushed by the British and Prussian forces at Waterloo (18 June 1815) and spent the remaining years of his life as a British prisoner of war on the island of St. Helena in the South Atlantic.

After the final fall of Napoleon, Louis XVIII ruled as a moderate and peaceful monarch until 1824, when he was succeeded by his brother Charles X, an ultra royalist. Charles attempted to restore the absolute powers of the monarchy and the supremacy of the Catholic Church. In 1830, he was ousted after a three-day revolution in which the upper bourgeoisie allied itself with the forces of the left. Louis Philippe of the house of Orléans was placed on the throne as "citizen-king," with the understanding that he would be ruled by the desires of the rising industrial plutocracy. In 1848, his regime was overthrown in the name of the Second Republic. Four years later, however, its first president, Louis Napoleon, the nephew of Napoleon I, engineered a coup and had himself proclaimed emperor under the title Napoleon III. The Second Empire, as the period 1852–71 is known, was characterized by colonial expansion and great material prosperity. The emperor's aggressive foreign policy eventually led to the Franco-Prussian War (1870–71), which ended in a crushing defeat for France and the downfall of Napoleon III. France was stripped of the border provinces of Alsace and Lorraine (which once belonged to the Holy Roman Empire) and was forced to agree to an enormous indemnity. A provisional government proclaimed a republic on 4 September 1870 and took over the responsibility for law and order until a National Assembly was elected in February 1871. Angered at the rapid capitulation to Prussia by the provisionals and the conservative National Assembly, the national guard and radical elements of Paris seized the city in March and set up the Commune. During the "Bloody Week" of 21–28 May, the Commune was savagely dispatched by government troops.

Democratic government finally triumphed in France under the Third Republic, whose constitution was adopted in 1875. Royalist sentiment had been strong, but the factions backing different branches of the royal house had been unable to agree on a candidate for the throne. The Third Republic confirmed freedom of speech, the press, and association. It enforced complete separation of church and state. Social legislation guaranteeing the rights of trade unions was passed, and elections were held on the basis of universal manhood suffrage. The Third Republic, however, was characterized by an extremely weak executive. A long succession of cabinets was placed in power and shortly thereafter removed from office by the all-powerful lower house of the national legislature. Nevertheless, the republic was strong enough to weather an attempt on the part of the highly popular Gen. Georges Boulanger to overthrow the regime in the late 1880s, as well as the bitter dispute between the left-wing and right-wing parties occasioned by the trumped-up arrest and long imprisonment of Capt. Alfred Dreyfus, a scandal in which Dreyfus's being Jewish was as much an issue as the treason he had allegedly committed. The eventual vindication of Dreyfus went hand in hand with the decisive defeat of the monarchists and the emergence of a progressive governing coalition, with Socialist representation.

The 20th Century

During World War I (1914–18), the forces of France, the United Kingdom, Russia, and, from 1917, the United States were locked in a protracted struggle with those of Germany, Austria-Hungary, and Turkey. Although France, under the leadership of Georges Clemenceau, could claim a major share in the final Allied victory, it was in many respects a Pyrrhic victory for France. Almost all the bitter fighting in the west was conducted on French soil, and among the Allies French casualties—including nearly 1,400,000 war dead—were second only to those sustained by Russia. The heavily industrialized provinces of Alsace and Lorraine were restored to France under the Treaty of Versailles (1919), and Germany was ordered to pay heavy war reparations. Nevertheless, the French economy, plagued by recurrent crises, was unable to achieve great prosperity in the 1920s, and the worldwide economic depression of the 1930s (exacerbated in France by the cessation of German reparations payments) was accompanied in France by inflation, widespread unemployment, and profound social unrest. Right- and extreme left-wing elements caused major disturbances on 6 February 1934. In 1936, the left-wing parties carried the parliamentary elections and installed a so-called Popular Front government under a Socialist, Léon Blum. Blum nationalized certain war industries, carried out agricultural reforms, and made the 40-hour week mandatory in industry. Increasing conservative opposition forced the Popular Front government from power, however, and in the face of the growing menace of Adolf Hitler's Germany, the leftists accepted the conservative government of Édouard Daladier in 1938. In a futile attempt to secure peace, Daladier acquiesced in British Prime Minister Neville Chamberlain's policy of appeasement toward Hitler. Hitler was not to be appeased, however, and when Germany invaded Poland in September 1939, France joined the United Kingdom in declaring war on Germany.

On 10 May 1940, the Germans launched a great invasion of the west through the Low Countries and the heavily wooded and sparsely defended Ardennes region. In less than a month, German forces outflanked the French Maginot Line fortifications and routed the French armies between the Belgian frontier and Paris. Marshal Pétain, the aged hero of World War I, hastily formed a government and sued for peace. With the exception of a triangu-

lar zone with its northern apex near Vichy, all France was placed under the direct occupation of the Germans. The Vichy regime ended the Third Republic and proclaimed a constitution based on the slogan "labor, family, fatherland," as opposed to the traditional republican "liberty, equality, fraternity." While the Vichy government did its best to accommodate itself to the German victory, French resistance gathered overseas around Gen. Charles de Gaulle, a brilliant career officer who had escaped to London on 18 June 1940 to declare that France had "lost a battle, not the war." De Gaulle organized the Provisional French National Committee, and this committee of the Free French later exercised all the powers of a wartime government in the French territories where resistance to the Germans continued. The Free French forces took part in the fighting that followed the Allied invasion of North Africa in 1942, and in 1943 a provisional French government was established at Algiers. Regular French units and resistance fighters alike fought in the 1944 campaign that drove the Germans from France, and shortly after the liberation of Paris, de Gaulle's provisional government moved from Algiers to the capital. It was officially recognized by the United States, the United Kingdom, and the former USSR in October 1944.

France's postwar vicissitudes have been political rather than economic. De Gaulle resigned as head of the government early in 1946 over the issue of executive powers, and in spite of his efforts the Fourth Republic, under a constitution that came into effect in December 1946, was launched with most of the weaknesses of the Third Republic. Almost all powers were concentrated in the hands of the National Assembly, the lower house of Parliament, and there were numerous warring political parties.

Although the people of metropolitan France overwhelmingly approved de Gaulle's program for eventual Algerian independence, some French army officers and units attempted to overthrow the government by terrorism, which de Gaulle suppressed by temporarily assuming emergency powers. Peace negotiations were successfully concluded with Algerian rebel leaders, and Algeria gained independence on 1 July 1962. By then, nearly all of France's former African territories had attained independence. France has continued to provide economic assistance, and its ties with most of the former colonies have remained close. Almost continuous fighting overseas in French colonies, first in Indochina, which was lost in 1954, and later in Algeria, the scene of a nationalist rebellion among the Muslims, placed a heavy burden on France and led, especially after the Suez expedition of 1956, to disillusionment on the part of elements in the French army, which felt that its work was being undermined by a series of vacillating parliamentary governments. In May 1958, extremists among the French settlers in Algeria, acting with a group of army officers, seized control of Algiers. Sympathetic movements in Corsica and in metropolitan France raised the specter of a right-wing coup. The government found itself powerless to deal with the situation, and on 1 June, Gen. de Gaulle, regarded as the only leader capable of rallying the nation, was installed as premier. He ended the threat peaceably, and in the fall of 1958, he submitted to a national referendum a new constitution providing for a strong presidency; the constitution won overwhelming approval. Elections held in November swept candidates pledged to support de Gaulle into office, and in December 1958, he was officially named the first president of the Fifth Republic.

During the mid-1960s, de Gaulle sought to distance France from the Anglo-American alliance. France developed its own atomic weapons and withdrew its forces from the NATO command; in addition, de Gaulle steadfastly opposed the admission of the United Kingdom to the EEC, of which France had been a founding member in 1957. The Treaty of Rome in 1957 created the original European Economic Community that consisted of Germany, Belgium, France, Italy and The Netherlands, and formed EURATOM, which created an open forum for scientific exchange and nuclear arms regulation on the continent.

The political stability of the mid-1960s ended in the spring of 1968, with student riots and a month-long general strike that severely weakened the Gaullist regime. In April 1969, Gen. de Gaulle resigned following a defeat, by national referendum, of a Gaullist plan to reorganize the Senate and regional government. In June, Georges Pompidou, a former premier in de Gaulle's government, was elected the second president of the Fifth Republic. Between 1969 and 1973, the Gaullist grip on the French populace continued to weaken, at the end of which time de Gaulle was forced to accept the United Kingdom, Ireland and Denmark into the EC, and to work within the economic constraints of the "Snake Mechanism" which, starting in 1972, linked EC currencies. In 1974, after President Pompidou died in office, an Independent Republican, Valéry Giscard d'Estaing, narrowly won a national runoff election (with Gaullist help) and became the third president of the Fifth Republic. Giscard strengthened relations with the United States but continued to ply a middle course between the superpowers in world affairs. The European Currency Unit (ECU) was born in 1979 from the economic stresses of the 1970s, leading eventually to the introduction of the common currency, the euro, in 2002.

Although Giscard's center-right coalition held firm in the March 1978 legislative elections, a Socialist, François Mitterrand, was elected president in May 1981, and the Socialists captured a parliamentary majority in June. Mitterrand launched a program of economic reforms, including the nationalization of many industrial companies and most major banks. However, three devaluations of the franc, high unemployment, and rising inflation led to the announcement of an austerity program in March 1983. In foreign policy, Mitterrand took an activist stance, opposing the US attempt in 1982 to halt construction of a natural gas pipeline between the former USSR and Western Europe, committing French troops to a peacekeeping force in Lebanon, and aiding the Chadian government against domestic insurgents and their Libyan backers.

In July 1984, Mitterrand accepted the resignation of Prime Minister Pierre Mauroy and named Laurent Fabius to replace him, signaling his intention to stress economic austerity and modernization of industry. In foreign affairs, the government attempted some retrenchment during 1984, withdrawing peacekeeping troops from Lebanon and announcing a "total and simultaneous" withdrawal of French and Libyan troops from Chad. However, Libyan troops did not actually withdraw as envisioned, and fighting there prompted a return of French troops in 1986. A major scandal was the disclosure in 1985 that French agents were responsible for the destruction in New Zealand, with the loss of a life, of a ship owned by an environmentalist group protesting French nuclear tests in the South Pacific.

In March 1986 elections, the Socialists lost their majority in the National Assembly, and Mitterrand had to appoint a conservative prime minister, Jacques Chirac, to head a new center-right cabinet. This unprecedented "cohabitation" between a Socialist president and a conservative government led to legislative conflict, as Chirac, with backing from the National Assembly, successfully instituted a program, opposed by Mitterrand, to denationalize 65 state-owned companies. Chirac encountered less success late in 1986 as he sought to deal with a wave of terrorist violence in Paris. In 1988, Chirac challenged Mitterand for the presidency, but in the May runoff election, Mitterand won a commanding 54% of the vote and a second seven-year term. Chirac then resigned, and Mitterand formed a minority Socialist government.

Economic and social problems as well as government scandals strained relations between the Socialist Mitterrand, the Conservative PM Eduard Balladur in the second cohabitation, and a center-right government. Unemployment remained high and new legislation increased police powers to combat illegal immigration. Several prominent politicians were the subject of corruption charges and in 1993 legal proceedings were instituted against former primer minister, Laurent Fabius, related to an HIV-infected blood scandal. A prominent Socialist prime minister, Pierre Beregovoy, committed suicide in May 1993 over media allegations of financial improprieties.

In May 1995, Jacques Chirac was elected president, winning 52.64% of the popular vote, compared to 47.36% for socialist Lionel Jospin, and Alain Juppé was appointed prime minister. The National Assembly had elected an RPR-Gaullist majority in 1993, setting the country firmly in the grips of the type of conservatism that had been ousting socialist and Social Democrats in much of Western Europe during the mid-to-late 1980s. Chirac immediately set about instituting austerity measures to rein in government spending in the hope of meeting certain rigid monetary guidelines so that France would be ready to join the European Monetary Union (EMU) in 1999. The EMU would create a single European currency, the "euro," to replace member countries' individual currencies. The idea of a monetary union had never been widely popular in France and the Maastricht Treaty, which set down conditions for EMU membership passed by only a slim margin.

Many of Chirac's attempts to reduce public spending and limit—or even erode—France's welfare state met with stern resistance. With the signing of the Amsterdam Treaty of 1997, Chirac sensed the need for a reaffirmation of his commitment to meet austerity measures for EMU membership. Chirac dissolved the National Assembly, calling for parliamentary elections in 1997, one year earlier than constitutionally mandated. In doing so, the French president believed he would demonstrate that the majority of the population believed in responsible cutbacks in government spending and anti-inflammatory monetary policy, despite the adverse effects they might have on the country's already quite high inflation. In May and June of 1997, elections were held and Chirac's plan badly backfired with the Socialists winning a commanding majority, along with the Communists. After the elections, a demoralized Chirac appointed Socialist leader Lionel Jospin prime minister, beginning the third cohabitation government. Jospin, a halfhearted supporter of monetary union, called for a program of increased government spending to create 700,000 jobs, a reduction in the work week from 39 to 35 hours, and made a broad pledge to protect the welfare state. The euro was successfully launched in 1999, and the currency was circulated in January 2002.

Presidential elections were held on 21 April and 5 May 2002. In the first round, Chirac won 19.9% of the vote, National Front leader Jean-Marie Le Pen came in second with 16.9%, and Prime Minister Jospin finished third with 16.2% of the vote. The strong showing by Le Pen sent shock waves throughout France and Europe, as his extreme right-wing, anti-immigrant, xenophobic party demonstrated its popularity. Jospin announced he was retiring from politics; for the first time since 1969 the Socialists did not have a candidate in a presidential runoff, marking a major defeat for the French left.

In the second round of voting, Chirac overwhelmingly defeated Le Pen, taking 82.2% of the vote to Le Pen's 17.8%. It was the largest majority since direct presidential elections were first introduced, and was preceded by a major popular campaign against Le Pen. Chirac named centrist Jean-Pierre Raffarin to be prime minister. In elections for the National Assembly held in June 2002, the center-right coalition Union for the Presidential Majority (consisting of Chirac's Rally for the Republic and the Liberal Democracy party and created on the wake of the first round on the ashes of the short-lived *Union en Mouvement*) won a landslide victory, taking 33.7% of the vote and 357 of 577 seats in parliament. The Socialist Party finished second with 24.1% and 140 seats. Le Pen's National Front failed to win a single seat.

Jean-Pierre Raffarin started out by governing through ordinances, and eventually obtained a majority from his party that was large enough to carry him through the legislative elections. His political line exhibited a peculiar communicative style and enforced reforms with unflagging certainty – his adversaries would term this style "neo-liberalism." In 2003 alone, he led policies to reform the retirement system and to regionalize most administrative offices that were centralized in Paris, despite strong social unrest and demonstrations—In the summer of 2003, civil servants went on strike against the reform of the retirement benefits system and part-time workers in entertainment went on strike, demanding higher salaries and improved benefits. Raffarin's popularity rate began to plummet; this, combined with the sharp electoral defeat sustained at the regional elections, was blamed on his social policies. As a consequence, the prime minister dissolved the government, and handpicked Jean-Louis Borloo as minister of social affairs. However, the prime minister had to handle both the former's social agenda—sustaining rent-controlled housing, backed up by President Chirac—and Sarkozy's extremely conservative managing of the finances. Jean-Pierre Raffarin then faced even more criticism especially from Dominique de Villepin.

Raffarin's term of office came to a brisk end after the "no" vote to the referendum held on 29 May 2005, on whether to adopt the project of the European Constitutional Treaty. He offered to resign on 31 May 2005, and was immediately replaced by Dominique de Villepin.

Dominique de Villepin had been named minister of foreign affairs in 2002, upon the reelection of President Chirac. In 2002–03, France was confronted with a major foreign policy dilemma. Throughout 2002, the United States and United Kingdom were committing troops to the Persian Gulf region, positioning themselves against Iraq and accusing its leader, Saddam Hussein, of possessing weapons of mass destruction. In the event that Iraq

would not disarm itself of any weapons of mass destruction it might possess, it was evident that the United States and United Kingdom might use those troops to force a regime change in Iraq. The UN Security Council unanimously passed Resolution 1441 on 8 November 2002, calling upon Iraq to disarm itself of chemical, biological, and nuclear weapons or weapons capabilities, to allow the immediate return of UN and International Atomic Energy Agency (IAEA) weapons inspectors, and to comply with all previous UN resolutions regarding the country since the end of the Gulf War in 1991. The United States and United Kingdom indicated that if Iraq would not comply with the resolution, "serious consequences" might result, meaning military action. The other three permanent members of the Security Council, France, Russia, and China, expressed their reservations with that position. France was the most vocal opponent of war, and threatened to use its veto power in the Security Council if another Security Council resolution authorizing the use of force was called for. The United States and United Kingdom abandoned diplomatic efforts at conflict resolution in March 2003, and on 19 March, the coalition went to war in Iraq. Once coalition forces defeated Iraq and plans for reconstruction of the country were being discussed in April, France stressed the need for a strong role to be played by the UN in a postwar Iraq.

On 31 May 2005, Dominique de Villepin was chosen by President Chirac to become prime minister. In his inaugural speech, he gave himself 100 days to earn the trust of the French people and to give France its confidence back. He was increasingly perceived as a potential presidential candidate, an opinion reinforced by his acting as head of state during the cabinet meeting held on 7 September 2005 and for the 60th session of the UN General Assembly held on 14–15 September 2005 while President Chirac suffered from a cerebral vascular complication.

The eruption of rioting in many parts of France in fall 2005 posed the most serious challenge to government authority since the student riots that took place in Paris in 1968. The government imposed a state of emergency. Thousands of vehicles were set on fire in nearly 300 towns; more than 1,500 people had been arrested by mid-November 2005, when the violence began to subside. Areas with large African and Arab communities were most affected (France has Europe's largest Muslim population and over half the country's prison population is Muslim), where anger among many immigrant families over unemployment and discrimination has long been simmering. France's youth unemployment rate in 2005 was 23%, one of Europe's worst, and in "sensitive urban zones," youth unemployment reached 40%. The unrest caused politicians to rethink their social and economic policies.

13 GOVERNMENT

Under the constitution of the Fifth Republic (1958), as subsequently amended, the president of the republic is elected for a five-year term (changed from a seven-year term following a referendum on 24 September 2000) by direct universal suffrage. If no candidate receives an absolute majority of the votes cast, a runoff election is held between the two candidates having received the most votes. If the presidency falls vacant, the president of the Senate assumes the office until a new election can be held within 20–35 days. The president appoints the prime minister and, on the prime minister's recommendation, the other members of the cabinet. The president has the power to dissolve the National Assembly, in which event new elections must be held in 20–40 days. When the national sovereignty is gravely menaced, the president is empowered to take special measures after consultation with the premier and other appropriate officials. The National Assembly, however, may not be dissolved during the exercise of exceptional powers. The president promulgates laws approved by the legislature, has the right of pardon, and is commander of the armed forces.

The bicameral parliament consists of two houses, the National Assembly and the Senate. Under a system enacted in 1986, the National Assembly is composed of 577 deputies, each representing an electoral district. If no candidate receives a clear majority, there is a runoff among those receiving at least 12.5% of the vote; a plurality then suffices for election. All citizens aged 18 or over are eligible to vote.

The deputies' term of office, unless the Assembly is dissolved, is five years. The Senate consisted, as of 2003, of 321 members indirectly elected to nine-year terms, one-third being chosen every three years. Of the total, 296 represented metropolitan France, 13, overseas departments and territories, and 12, French citizens residing abroad; all are chosen by electoral colleges. In addition, European elections are held to choose 87 French deputies out of 626 in the European Parliament every five years, with proportional representation.

To become law, a measure must be passed by parliament. Parliament also has the right to develop in detail and amplify the list of matters on which it may legislate by passing an organic law to that effect. Regular parliamentary sessions occur once a year, lasting nine months each (amended in 1995 from two shorter sessions a year). A special session may be called by the prime minister or at the request of a majority of the National Assembly. Bills, which may be initiated by the executive, are introduced in either house, except finance bills, which must be introduced in the Assembly. These proceedings are open to the public, aired on television, and reported.

The prime minister and the cabinet formulate national policy and execute the laws. No one may serve concurrently as a member of parliament and a member of the executive. Under certain circumstances, an absolute majority in the National Assembly may force the executive to resign by voting a motion of censure. Under the new law of 1993, members of the government are liable for actions performed in office deemed to be crimes or misdemeanors, and tried by the Court of Justice.

14 POLITICAL PARTIES

French political life has long been ruled both by considerations of political theory and by the demands of political expediency. Traditional issues such as the separation of church and state help to distinguish between right and left, but otherwise the lines separating all but the extremist political parties are difficult to draw. One result of this has been the proliferation of political parties; another, the assumption by political parties of labels that seldom indicate any clear-cut platform or policy.

Broadly, since the late 1950s, French politics has been dominated by four political groups: the Gaullists, an independent center-right coalition, the Socialists, and the Communists. After the parliamentary elections of 23 and 30 November 1958, the first to

be held under the constitution of the Fifth Republic, the largest single group in the Assembly was the Union for the New Republic (UNR), which stood for the policies of Gen. de Gaulle, elected president of the republic for a seven-year term in 1958. Independents of the right were the second-largest group, and the Christian Socialists (Mouvement Républicain Populaire) and several leftist groups followed. Only 16 members were elected by the center groups and only 10 were Communists.

In the November 1962 elections, the Gaullist UNR scored an unparalleled victory, polling 40.5% of the total votes cast. As a result of the elections, several old parliamentary groups disappeared, and new groups emerged: the Democratic Center (Centre Démocratique) with 55 seats; the Democratic Rally (Rassemblement Démocratique), 38 seats; and the Independent Republicans (Républicains Indépendants—RI), 33 seats. The UNR and the Democratic Workers Union (Union Démocratique du Travail—UDT), left-wing Gaullists, agreed to a full merger of their parties and together controlled 219 seats.

In the first presidential elections held by direct universal suffrage in December 1965, President de Gaulle was reelected on the second ballot with 55.2% of the total vote. In the March 1967 general elections, the UNR-UDT gained 246 seats against 116 for the Socialists and 73 for the Communists. Following nationwide strikes and civil disturbances by workers and students in the spring of 1968, new parliamentary elections were held in June, in which de Gaulle's supporters won a sweeping victory.

The Union for the Defense of the Republic (Union pour la Défense de la République—UDR) emerged as the new official Gaullist organization. Political movements of the center joined to form the Progress and Modern Democracy group (Centre-PDM), while Socialists and the democratic left united under the Federation of the Left. Of the 487 Assembly seats, the UDR won 292 seats; RI, 61; Federation of the Left, 57; Communists, 34; Centre-PDM, 33; and independents, 10.

On 28 April 1969, following the defeat in a national referendum of a Gaullist plan to reorganize the Senate and regional government, President de Gaulle resigned. He was succeeded by former premier Georges Pompidou, a staunch Gaullist, who won 58% of the vote in elections held on 15 June 1969. During the Pompidou administration, Gaullist control was weakened by an alliance between the Communist and Socialist parties. In March 1973 elections, the Gaullist UDR lost 109 seats, falling to 183 of the 490 seats at stake. The Communists and Socialists increased their representation to 72 and 103, respectively. The remaining seats were won by the RI (55) and by centrists, reformists, and unaffiliated candidates (77).

On 2 April 1974, President Pompidou died. In elections held on 5 May, Gaullist candidate and former premier Jacques Chaban-Delmas was defeated, receiving only 15% of the votes cast. The leader of the leftist coalition, François Mitterrand, received over 11 million votes, and Valéry Giscard d'Estaing, the leader of the RI, over 8 million. However, as neither had won a majority, a runoff election was held on 19 May. Giscard, with the help of Gaullist votes, defeated Mitterrand by a margin of 50.7% to 49.3%. Jacques Chirac of the UDR was made premier, with a cabinet made up mainly of RI and UDR members.

A new Gaullist party, the Rally for the Republic (Rassemblement pour la République—RPR), founded by Chirac in 1976, received 26.1% of the vote in the second round of the 1978 legislative elections, winning 154 seats in the National Assembly. That year, the centrist parties had formed the Union for French Democracy (Union pour la Démocratie Française—UDF). The federation, which included the Republican Party (Parti Républicain), the successor to the RI, won 23.2% of the vote in the second round of balloting, giving the centrist coalition 124 seats in the National Assembly. The Socialists and Communists, who ran on a common platform as the Union of the Left, together won 199 seats (Socialists 113, Communists 86) and 46.9% of the vote. Independents, with the remaining 3.8%, controlled 14 seats, for a total of 491.

In the presidential elections of 26 April and 10 May 1981, Mitterrand received 25.8% of the vote on the first ballot (behind Giscard's 28.3%) and 51.8% on the second ballot, to become France's first Socialist president since the 1930s. Within weeks, Mitterrand called new legislative elections: that June, the Socialists and their allies won 49.2% of the vote and 285 seats, the RPR 22.4% and 88 seats, the UDF 18.6% and 63 seats, the Communists 7% and 44 seats; independents won the remaining 2.8% and 11 seats. In return for concessions on various political matters, four Communists received cabinet portfolios, none relating directly to foreign affairs or national security. The sweeping victory of the left was, however, eroded in March 1983 when Socialist and Communist officeholders lost their seats in about 30 cities in municipal balloting. Meanwhile, the Communists had become disaffected by government policies and did not seek appointments in the cabinet named when a new Socialist prime minister, Laurent Fabius, was appointed in July 1984.

The National Assembly elections held in March 1993 represented a major defeat for the Socialist Party and their allies. The RPR and UDF won 247 and 213 seats, respectively, while the Socialists were reduced to 67 seats. The Communists also suffered losses, securing only 24 seats. Minor parties and independents won 26 seats. In cantonal elections held in March 1985, the candidates of the left won less than 40% of the vote, while candidates on the right increased their share by 10–15%. The Socialists lost 155 of the 579 Socialist seats that were at stake. As a result, the Socialists introduced a new system of proportional voting aimed at reducing their losses in the forthcoming general election of 16 March 1986. The Socialists and their allies nevertheless won only 33% of the vote and 216 seats out of 577 in the expanded National Assembly. The RPR, the UDF, and their allies received 45% of the vote and 291 seats. The Communists, suffering a historic defeat, split the remaining 70 seats evenly with the far-right National Front, which won representation for the first time. The Socialists remained the largest single party, but the coalition led by the RPR and UDF had a majority; on that basis, Mitterrand appointed RPR leader Chirac as prime minister, heading a center-right government. Following his defeat by Mitterrand in the May 1988 presidential election, Chirac resigned and a minority Socialist government was formed.

In 1995, Jacques Chirac was elected president, defeating Socialist Lionel Jospin. In 1997, one year before they were scheduled, Chirac called for new parliamentary elections, hoping to achieve a mandate to inaugurate his policy of fiscal austerity. Instead, the Gaullists suffered a stunning defeat by the Socialists and Communists, leading to the appointment of Jospin as prime minister. In those elections, held 25 May and 1 June 1997, the Gaullists saw their parliamentary presence decline from 464 seats to 249; the

Socialists (and related splinter groups) went from 75 seats to 273; the Communists from 24 to 38; the Greens from no seats to 8; and the far-right National Front maintained its single seat.

The first round of presidential elections were held on 21 April 2002, with Jospin coming in third behind National Front leader Jean-Marie Le Pen and Jacques Chirac in the first round. Two days after these results, on 23 April 2002, the Union en Mouvement (Union in Motion—UEM) was dissolved and replaced by the Union pour la majorité présidentielle (Union for Presidential Majority—UMP) in order to create a major public support behind Chirac in his second round face-off with Le Pen. In May 2002, Jacques Chirac defeated Jean-Marie Le Pen in the second round, taking 82.2% of the vote to Le Pen's 17.8%.

In the National Assembly elections held in June 2002, Chirac's UMP (RPR united with the Liberal Democracy party, formerly the Republican Party) won an overwhelming majority of seats, taking 357 to the Socialists' 140. The National Front failed to win a single seat; the UDF held 29 seats and the Communists took 21. The Greens held only three seats.

On 17 November 2002, the UMP changed its name to Union pour un Mouvement Populaire (Union for a Popular Movement), keeping the same acronym but modifying the out-of-date appellation.

Its first test occurred in March 2004, during the cantonal and regional elections. While suffering a devastating loss, it managed, through alliances, to secure a relative majority of the votes.

Its second test was the European elections, also held in 2004. The UMP won only 17% of the votes, while the Socialist Party earned 29% and the UDF (composed of members that refused to join in the UMP) reached 12%. The UDF's relative success was largely caused by the attractive alternative that it offered voters that were unhappy with the government's take on social and European issues.

The relative slump of the right can also be explained by the rise of popularity of the National Front and the unpopularity generated by the Raffarin governments.

15 LOCAL GOVERNMENT

In 1972, parliament approved a code of regional reforms that had been rejected when proposed previously by President de Gaulle in 1969. Under this law, the 96 departments of metropolitan France were grouped into 22 regions. Regional councils composed of local deputies, senators, and delegates were formed and prefects appointed; in addition, regional economic and social committees, made up of labor and management representatives, were created. This system was superseded by the decentralization law of 2 March 1982, providing for the transfer of administrative and financial authority from the prefect to the general council, which elects its own president; the national government's representative in the department is appointed by the cabinet. The 1982 law likewise replaced the system of regional prefects with regional councils, elected by universal direct suffrage, and, for each region, an economic and social committee that serves in an advisory role; the national government's representative in each region, named by the cabinet, exercises administrative powers. The first regional assembly to be elected was that of Corsica in August 1982; the first direct assembly elections in all 22 regions were held in March 1986.

Each of the 96 departments (and four overseas: Martinique, Guadeloupe, Reunion and French Guiana) is further subdivided for administrative purposes into *arrondissements*, cantons, and communes (municipalities). The basic unit of local government is the commune, governed by a municipal council and presided over by a mayor. A commune may be an Alpine village with no more than a dozen inhabitants, or it may be a large city, such as Lyon or Marseille. The majority, however, are small. In 1990, only 235 communes out of 36,551 had more than 30,000 inhabitants; 84% of all communes had fewer than 1,500 inhabitants, and 43% had fewer than 300. (As of 2002, France had 36,763 communes). Most recently the trend has been for the smallest communes to merge and create larger urban communities, or to come together as communal syndicates to share responsibilities. Municipal councilors are elected by universal suffrage for six-year terms. Each council elects a mayor who also serves as a representative of the central government. Several communes are grouped into a canton, and cantons are grouped into arrondissements, which have little administrative significance. As of 1 January 2005, France had 36,779 communes (214 of them overseas).

16 JUDICIAL SYSTEM

There are two types of lower judicial courts in France, the civil courts (471 tribunaux d'instance and 181 tribunaux de grande instance in 1985, including overseas departments) and the criminal courts (tribunaux de police for petty offenses such as parking violations, tribunaux correctionnels for criminal misdemeanors). The function of the civil courts is to judge conflicts arising between persons; the function of the criminal courts is to judge minor infractions (*contraventions*) and graver offenses (*délits*) against the law. The most serious crimes, for which the penalties may range to life imprisonment, are tried in assize courts (*cours d'assises*); these do not sit regularly but are called into session when necessary. They are presided over by judges from the appeals courts. In addition, there are special commercial courts (*tribunaux de commerce*), composed of judges elected among themselves by tradesmen and manufacturers, to decide commercial cases; conciliation boards (*conseils de prud'hommes*), made up of employees and employers, to decide their disputes; and professional courts with disciplinary powers within the professions. Special administrative courts (*tribunaux administratifs*) deal with disputes between individuals and government agencies. The highest administrative court is the Council of State (*Conseil d'État*).

From the lower civil and criminal courts alike, appeals may be taken to appeals courts (*cours d'Appel*), of which there were 27 in 2003. Judgments of the appeals courts and the courts of assize are final, except that appeals on the interpretation of the law or points of procedure may be taken to the highest of the judicial courts, the Court of Cassation in Paris. If it finds that either the letter or spirit of the law has been misapplied, it may annual a judgment and return a case for retrial by the lower courts. The High Court of Justice (*Haute Cour de Justice*), consisting of judges and members of parliament, is convened to pass judgment on the president and cabinet members if a formal accusation of treason or criminal behavior has been voted by an absolute majority of both the National Assembly and the Senate. The death penalty was abolished in 1981.

The Conseil Constitutionnel, created by the 1958 constitution, is now the only French forum available for constitutional review of legislation. Challenges to legislation may be raised by the president of the republic, the prime minister, the president of the Senate, the president of the National Assembly, 60 senators, or 60 deputies of the National Assembly during the period between passage and promulgation (signature of president). Once promulgated, French legislation is not subject to judicial review.

The French judiciary is fully independent from the executive and legislative branches. The judiciary is subject to European Union mandates, which guide national law. This has been the case in the Court of Cassation since 1975, in the Council of State since 1989, and now even in the civil courts.

17 ARMED FORCES

In 2005 there were 254,895 active personnel in the French armed services. An additional 104,275 served in the Gendarmerie Nationale, which is heavily armed. Reserves totaled 21,650 from all services. In 2005 the military budget was $41.6 billion.

France's strategic nuclear forces in 2005 had 4,041 active personnel, of which 2,200 were Navy personnel, 1,800 Air Force, and 41 Gendarmarie Nationale. Equipment included four SSBNs, 24 Navy and 60 Air Combat Command fighter/ground attack aircraft. The French have the third-largest nuclear arsenal in the world with a suspected total of 482 weapons. The Army in 2005 numbered 133,500 military and 28,500 civilian personnel. Included were 7,700 members of the Foreign Legion, a 14,700 member marine force and an estimated 2,700 Special Operations Forces, as part of the French Army. Equipment included 926 main battle tanks, 1,809 reconnaissance vehicles, 601 armored infantry fighting vehicles, 4,413 armored personnel carriers, and 787 artillery pieces (105 towed).

The French Navy numbered 46,195 active personnel and 10,265 civilians in 2005. For that year, the Navy was equipped with 10 modern submarines (4 SSBNs and 6 SSNs), 34 principal surface combatants (including one CVN and one CVH or helicopter carrier), and 85 other ships for mine warfare, amphibious operations, and logistics and support. France had 6,443 naval aviation personnel. There were also 2,050 naval marines, including 500 commandos. The Navy also provided coast guard services and fishery protection. The French Air Force numbered 65,400 active members, plus 5,700 civilians, and operated 295 combat capable aircraft.

France maintains substantial forces abroad in a number of countries, current and former possessions, and protectorates. These forces are supported by aircraft and naval ships in the Indian and Pacific oceans, and in the Carribean. France has substantial garrisons in Antilles-Guyana, New Caledonia, Réunion Island, and Polynesia, and it provides military missions and combat formations to several African nations. Troops are also deployed on peacekeeping missions in several different regions and countries.

18 INTERNATIONAL COOPERATION

France is a charter member of the United Nations, having joined on 24 October 1945, and actively cooperates in ECE, ECLAC, ESCAP, and most of the nonregional specialized agencies; it is one of the five permanent members of the Security Council. France joined the WTO in 1995. France is also a founding member of the European Union. Although France still belongs to NATO, in 1966 the nation withdrew its personnel from the two integrated NATO commands—Supreme Headquarters Allied Powers Europe (SHAPE) and Allied Forces Central Europe (AFCENT). In December 1995, the country announced an intention to increase participation in the NATO military wing once again. France is a member of the Asian Development Bank, the African development Bank, the Central African States Development Bank (BDEAC), European Bank for Reconstruction and Development, Council of Europe, OAS (as a permanent observer), OECD, OSCE, G-5, G-7, G-8, the Association of Caribbean States (ACS), and the Paris Club.

Since 2003, France has supported four UN Security Council (UNSC) resolutions on Iraq. The country serves as a commissioner on the UN Monitoring, Verification, and Inspection Commission and has also offered support to UN missions in Kosovo (est. 1999), Lebanon (1978), the Western Sahara (1991), Ethiopia and Eritrea (2000), Liberia (2003), the DROC (1999), and Haiti (2004).

France belongs to the Australia Group, the Nuclear Suppliers Group (London Group), the Nuclear Energy Agency, the Zangger Committee, the Organization for the Prohibition of Chemical Weapons, and the European Organization for Nuclear Research (CERN). In environmental cooperation, France is part of the Antarctic Treaty; the Basel Convention; Conventions on Biological Diversity, Whaling, and Air Pollution; Ramsar; CITES; the London Convention; International Tropical Timber Agreements; the Kyoto Protocol; the Montréal Protocol; MARPOL; and the UN Conventions on the Law of the Sea, Climate Change and Desertification.

[19]ECONOMY

France is one of the most richly endowed countries of Europe. The favorable climate, extensive areas of rich soil, and long-established tradition of skilled agriculture have created ideal conditions for a thriving farm economy. Agriculture and the agro-food industries account for a larger share of economic activity than in many other west European nations. Large deposits of iron ore, a well-integrated network of power plants, important domestic reserves of natural gas, good transport, and high standards of industrial workmanship have made the French industrial complex one of the most modern in Europe.

After World War II, France's economy was stronger than it had been in the period between the two world wars. But on the debit side were the extremely high costs of France's colonial campaigns in Indochina and North Africa; the periodic lack of confidence of French investors in the nation's economy, resulting in the large-scale flight of funds; and the successive devaluations of the franc.

Through most of the 1960s and early 1970s, the French economy expanded steadily, with GDP more than doubling between 1959 and 1967. However, the international oil crisis of 1974 led to a sharp rise in import costs; the resulting inflation eroded real growth to about 3% annually between 1977 and 1979. Further oil price increases in 1979–80 marked the beginning of a prolonged recession, with high inflation, high unemployment, balance-of-payments deficits, declining private investment, and shortages in foreign exchange reserves. However, GDP grew by an annual average of 2.5% between 1984 and 1991. During the early 1990s,

GDP expanded by an average 2%, a modest rate. By the late 1990s, however, the economy began to record higher growth rates. In 1998 the French economy grew by 3.3% in real terms. Unemployment, however, remained high at 11.5%. To combat this, the Socialist-led coalition of Lionel Jospin enacted legislation cutting the work week to 35 hours in 2000. This measure, along with other incentives, resulted in unemployment falling under 10% as over 400,000 new jobs were created in the first half of 2000. In 2002, GDP growth was low (1%), due to the global economic slowdown and a decline in investment. However, France's exports increased at a greater rate than imports, fueling the economy. France in 2002 fell from being the world's fourth-largest industrialized economy to fifth, being replaced by the United Kingdom. In 2004, France had a $1.737 trillion economy, in purchasing power parity terms. In 2004, real GDP growth was 1.9%. In 2005, real GDP growth was expected to slow to 1.4%, before picking up to 1.6% in 2006 and 2.2% in 2007.

France and the United States are the world's top two exporting countries in defense products, agricultural goods, and services. Taxes remain the highest in the G-8 industrialized countries, and the tax structure is seen as a hindrance to business activity. The fastest-growing sectors of the economy have been telecommunications, aerospace, consulting services, meat and milk products, public works, insurance and financial services, and recreation, culture, and sports. Although the government has privatized many large companies, banks, and insurers, it still controls large sectors of the economy, including energy, transportation, and the defense industry.

The French social model, characterized by heavy state involvement in the economy, a tax on wealth, and generous benefits for workers, has proved to be a strong disincentive to growth and job creation. Unemployment, at 9.8% in September 2005, is double that in the United Kingdom. The pension system and rising healthcare costs strain public finances. Attempts to liberalize the economy have met strong resistance from labor unions and the left. Pension reforms proposed by the government of Jean-Pierre Raffarin in early 2003 were met by huge protests and strikes in France. Discontent with the economy played a large role in France's rejection of the EU constitution in May 2005. Dominique de Villepin, who became prime minister after the EU vote, promised to focus on unemployment and was in the process of engineering the sale of parts of Gaz de France and Electricité de France (the world's largest generator of nuclear power) to help compensate for state deficits. Violent unrest in hundreds of towns erupted in the fall of 2005, triggered by frustration over high unemployment among urban youth. Politicians were faced with the challenge to craft social and economic policies to address the underlying causes of the rioting, which was centered in communities with large African and Arab populations, where youth unemployment reportedly approached 40% (and stood at 25% in the country overall).

[20]INCOME

The US Central Intelligence Agency (CIA) reports that in 2005 France's gross domestic product (GDP) was estimated at $1.8 trillion. The CIA defines GDP as the value of all final goods and services produced within a nation in a given year and computed on the basis of purchasing power parity (PPP) rather than value as measured on the basis of the rate of exchange based on current dollars. The per capita GDP was estimated at $29,900. The annual growth rate of GDP was estimated at 1.5%. The average inflation rate in 2005 was 1.9%. It was estimated that agriculture accounted for 2.5% of GDP, industry 21.4%, and services 76.1%.

According to the World Bank, in 2003 remittances from citizens working abroad totaled $11.418 billion or about $191 per capita and accounted for approximately 0.6% of GDP.

The World Bank reports that in 2003 household consumption in France totaled $976.15 billion or about $16,324 per capita based on a GDP of $1.8 trillion, measured in current dollars rather than PPP. Household consumption includes expenditures of individuals, households, and nongovernmental organizations on goods and services, excluding purchases of dwellings. It was estimated that for the period 1990 to 2003 household consumption grew at an average annual rate of 1.6%. In 2001 it was estimated that approximately 22% of household consumption was spent on food, 9% on fuel, 3% on health care, and 8% on education. It was estimated that in 2000 about 6.5% of the population had incomes below the poverty line.

21 LABOR

In 2005, the French workforce was estimated at 27.72 million. In 1999 (the latest year for which data was available), 71.5% of the workforce was employed in the services sector, with industry accounting for 24.4%, and 4.1% in agriculture. As of 2005, the unemployment rate was estimated at 10%, although overall youth unemployment was much higher (25%), with unemployment among urban youth approaching 40%.

Although only about 7% of the workforce was unionized as of 2005, trade unions have significant influence in the country. Workers freely exercise their right to strike unless it is prohibited due to public safety. Many unions are members of international labor organizations. Collective bargaining is prevalent. It is illegal to discriminate against union activity.

The government determines the minimum hourly rate, which was the equivalent of $9.64 as of 2005. This amount provides a decent standard of living for a family. The standard legal workweek is set at 35 hours with restrictions on overtime. Children under age 16 are not permitted to work, and there are restrictions pertaining to employment of those under 18. Child labor laws are strictly enforced. The labor code and other laws provide for work, safety, and health standards.

22 AGRICULTURE

Agriculture remains a vital sector of the French economy, even though it engages only about 3.3% of the labor force and contributes about 3% of the GDP. Since the early 1970s, the agricultural labor force has diminished by about 60%. In 2003, France's full-time farm labor force of 592,550 was still the second-highest in the EU. France, whose farms export more agricultural food products than any other EU nation (accounting for 19% of the EU's total agricultural output in 2003), is the only country in Europe to be completely self-sufficient in basic food production; moreover, the high quality of the nation's agricultural products contributes to the excellence of its famous cuisine. France is one of the leaders in Europe in the value of agricultural exports—chiefly wheat, sugar, wine, and beef. Tropical commodities, cotton, tobacco, and vegetable oils are among the chief agricultural imports.

As of 2003 36% of France's area was arable. About 11.8 million hectares (29.1 million acres) of the usable farm area is under annual crops, with another 228,000 hectares (563,000 acres) in permanent crops. There were 735,000 farms in France in 1995, of which only 454,000 were managed by full-time farmers. Since the 1950s, the number of farms has declined and the size of individual holdings has increased. By 1983 there were about 1.13 million farms, as compared to 2.3 million in 1955, and the average farm size was about 26 hectares (64 acres). Average farm size had grown to around 50 hectares (124 acres) in 2000. Because French law provides for equal rights of inheritance, traditionally much of the farmland came to be split up into small, scattered fragments. One of the major aims of postwar plans for rural improvement has been the consolidation of these through reallotment. Such consolidation also fosters the growth of mechanization. In 2003 there were 1,264,000 tractors (fourth in the world after the United States, Japan, and Italy) compared with 100,000 in 1948, and 1,327,900 in 1974.

Of the total productive agricultural area, about 61% is under cultivation, 35% is pasture, and 4% vineyards. The most productive farms are in northern France, but specialized areas, such as the vegetable farms of Brittany, the great commercial vineyards of the Languedoc, Burgundy, and Bordeaux districts, and the flower gardens, olive groves, and orchards of Provence, also contribute heavily to the farm economy.

Among agricultural products, cereals (wheat, barley, oats, corn, and sorghum), industrial crops (sugar beets, flax), root crops (potatoes), and wine are by far the most important. In 2004, the wheat crop totaled 39,704,000 tons and barley, 11,040,000 tons. Other totals (in tons) included oats, 598,000; corn, 16,391,000; sugar beets, 30,554,000; rapeseed, 3,969,000 tons; and sunflower seed, 1,467,000 tons. Wine production in 2004 totaled 557 million liters from 7,542,000 tons of grapes. There is large-scale production of fruits, chiefly apples, pears, peaches, and cherries.

23 ANIMAL HUSBANDRY

Output of animal products in 2003 was valued at nearly €23.7 billion, the highest in the EU. In 2005, farm animals included 19.3 million head of cattle, 15 million swine, 10.2 million sheep and goats, and 355,000 horses. Poultry and rabbits are raised in large numbers, both for farm families and for city markets. Percheron draft horses are raised in northern France, range cattle in the central highlands and the flatlands west of the Rhône, and goats and sheep in the hills of the south. Meat production in 2005 included 1,529,000 tons of beef and veal, 2,257,000 tons of pork, 1,971,000 tons of poultry, and 123,000 tons of mutton. Meat exports in 2004 were valued at over $3.3 billion.

Dairy farming flourishes in the rich grasslands of Normandy. Total cows' milk production in 2005 was 25,282,000 tons. France produces some 300 kinds of cheese; in 2005, production totaled about 1,824,000 tons. Butter and egg production were 426,000 and 1,245,000 tons, respectively. Dairy and egg exports generated $5 billion in 2005.

²⁴FISHING

France's 4,716 km (2,930 mi) of coastline, dotted with numerous small harbors, has long supported a flourishing coastal and high-seas fishing industry. Total fish production in 2003 amounted to 874,397 tons (valued at €1,686 million) with the fresh wild catch accounting for 44%; the frozen wild catch, 27%; and aquaculture, 28%. French aquaculture consists mainly of oyster and mussel production; most of the facilities are located along the English Channel and the Atlantic coasts. Aquaculture yielded 246,919 tons in 2003, valued at €542 million.

Herring, skate, whiting, sole, mackerel, tuna, sardines, lobsters, and mussels make up the principal seafood catch, along with cod, mostly from the fishing banks off northern North America, where French fishing vessels have sailed for centuries. Production of canned seafood products in 2003 totaled 80,501 tons, mostly tuna, mackerel, and sardines.

In 2004, France's trade deficit for seafood products was 604,050 tons, valued at over €2.1 billion. The United Kingdom and Norway are France's leading seafood suppliers.

²⁵FORESTRY

Forestry production in France has been encouraged by the government since the 16th century, when wood was a strategic resource in building warships. Although much of the original forest cover was cut in the course of centuries, strict forest management practices and sizable reforestation projects during the last 100 years have restored French forests considerably. Since 1947, the government has subsidized the afforestation and replanting of 2.1 million hectares (5.2 million acres) of forestland along with thousands of miles of wood transport roads. The reforestation project in the Landes region of southwestern France has been particularly successful. During 1990–2000, the forested area increased by an annual average of 0.4%. About 66% of the forestland is covered with oak, beech, and poplar and 34% with resinous trees. There were some 16 million hectares (39.5 million acres) of forest in 2001, amounting to 29% of France's total area. This makes France the third most forested country in the EU, behind Sweden and Finland. The forestry and wood products sector employed 257,000 persons in 35,000 companies in 2000. In 2004, the gross value added by France's forestry industry was €2.9 billion.

Production of roundwood in 2004 was 34.6 million cu m (1.22 billion cu ft), and was supplemented with imports. Hardwood log production reached 6.5 million cu m (229 million cu ft) that year, while plywood panel production amounted to 500,000 cu m (17.6 million cu ft). Softwood log production totaled 13 million cu m (459 million cu ft) in 2004. Trade in forestry products in 2003 amounted to $8.1 billion in imports and $6.3 billion in exports.

In December 1999, a hurricane hit France and damaged an estimated 50 million cu m (1.8 billion cu ft) of trees, with 31 million cu m (1.1 billion cu ft) in public forests.

²⁶MINING

France was a major European mineral producer, despite significant declines in the production of traditional minerals in recent years. France was among the leading producers of coal, was Europe's only producer of andalusite, and counted iron among its top export commodities in 2002. France was also self-sufficient in salt,

potash, fluorspar, and talc. Talc de Luzenac, a subsidiary of Rio Tinto, was the leading producer of talc in the world. In addition, France had sizable deposits of antimony, bauxite, magnesium, pyrites, tungsten, and certain radioactive minerals. One of the world's most developed economies, France had to make considerable changes in the structure of its industries, particularly those mineral industries controlled by the state. Prior to 2000, the state's heavy economic and political involvement was a main element of national mineral policy. Cessation of government subsidies to unprofitable operations, cheaper foreign sources, and depletion of mineral reserves have greatly affected the industry, particularly bauxite, coal, iron ore, lead, uranium, and zinc. The government has made efforts to promote the private sector, to proceed with a program of privatization, and to reduce the dependence of state-owned companies on subsidies. To encourage exploration, the government in 1995 passed a law expediting the granting of surveying and mining licenses.

Production figures for 2003 were: agricultural and industrial limestone, 12,000 metric tons; hydraulic cement, 20 million tons; salt (rock, refined brine, marine, and in solution), 6.673 million tons; crude gypsum and anhydrite, 3.5 million tons (France was one of Europe's largest producers of gypsum, with two-thirds coming from the Paris Basin); marketable kaolin and kaolinitic clay, 323,000 tons; crude feldspar, 671,000 tons; marketable fluorspar, 89,000 tons; barite, 81,000 metric tons, up slightly from 80,000 metric tons in 2003; kyanite, andalusite, and related materials, 65,000 tons; mica, 10,000 metric tons; and crude and powdered talc (significant to the European market), 645,000 metric tons. In 2003 France also produced copper; gold; silver; powder tungsten; uranium; elemental bromine; refractory clays; diatomite; lime; nitrogen; mineral, natural, and iron oxide pigments; Thomas slag phosphates; pozzolan and lapilli; and soda ash and sodium sulfate. No iron ore was produced in 2003; the iron ore basin, stretching from Lorraine northward, used to produce more than 50 million tons per year, but its high phosphorus and low iron content limited its desirability. Terres Rouges Mine, the last to operate in Lorraine, closed in 1998. France ceased producing bauxite (named after Les Baux, in southern France) in 1993. Mining of lead and zinc has completely ceased.

²⁷ENERGY AND POWER

France's energy and power sector is marked by modest reserves of oil, natural gas and coal, and a heavy reliance upon nuclear energy to meet its energy needs.

As of 1 January 2005, France had estimated proven oil reserves of 0.1 billion barrels, with the bulk of its oil production in the Paris and Aquitaine Basins. In 2001, crude oil production was 28,000 barrels per day, but declined to 23,300 barrels per day in 2004. Total oil product output, including refinery gain, came to an estimated 76,600 barrels per day, of which 30% was crude oil. In 2004, domestic demand for oil came to an estimated 1,976.900 barrels per day, making France the world's 10th-largest consumer of oil. As a result of the disparity between consumption and production, France has had to import crude oil. In 2004, net imports of crude oil came to 1.96 million barrels per day.

Like its oil resources, France's coal and natural gas reserves are very limited. As of 1 January 2005, the country had an estimated 500 billion cu ft of proven natural gas reserves. Production and consumption of natural gas in 2003 totaled an estimated 100 billion cu ft and 1,554.5 billion cu ft, respectively.

France's recoverable coal reserves, production, and consumption in 2003 were estimated at 16.5 million short tons; 1.9 million short tons; and 21.4 million short tons, respectively. In April 2004, France closed its last operating coal mine and has since relied on coal imports to meet its demand for coal.

During the 1950s France became increasingly dependent on outside sources for petroleum. Although petroleum and natural gas continued to be produced in France itself (as they are today), the nation came to rely almost entirely on imports from oil fields of the Middle East, putting a heavy strain on the country's foreign exchange reserves. Discoveries of large supplies of natural gas and petroleum in the Sahara Desert changed the outlook radically; in 1967 France was able to meet almost half its fuel needs from countries within the franc zone. Petroleum production from the Saharan fields rose spectacularly from 8.7 million tons in 1960 to 53 million tons in 1970. Although France lost title to the Saharan deposits after Algerian independence, arrangements were made with the Algerian government to keep up the flow of oil to France.

Developments in the 1970s exposed the limitations of this strategy. Algeria took controlling interest in French oil company subsidiaries in 1971. The oil shocks of the mid- and late 1970s drove France's fuel and energy imports up; in 1975, fuel imports accounted for 22.9% of all imports. In response, France began an energy conservation program, but oil consumption continued to increase between 1973 and 1980, when fuel imports made up 26.6% of total imports. Mergers involving France's top oil companies in 1999 and 2000 created the fourth-largest oil company in the world, TotalFinaElf.

France's electric power sector is marked by a heavy reliance upon nuclear power. France has become the world's leading producer of nuclear power per capita, with the world's second-greatest nuclear power capacity (exceeded only by the United States). Nuclear power accounts for 78.5% of the electric power generated in France, followed by hydroelectric at 11.5% and conventional thermal at 9.3%. In 2003, France had an installed generating capacity estimated at 112 GW, with production and consumption estimated at 536.9 billion kWh and 433.3 billion kWh, respectively. All electric power generation and distribution is controlled by the state-owned monopoly, Electricite de France (EdF). However, France has slowly begun to deregulate its electricity sector and to privatize EdF. France is also Europe's second-largest power market, exceeded only by Germany.

28 INDUSTRY

Industry has expanded considerably since World War II, with particularly significant progress in the electronics, transport, processing, and construction industries. France is the world's fourth-leading industrial power, after the United States, Japan, and Germany (although France was surpassed by the United Kingdom in 2002 as the world's fourth-largest economy). Manufacturing accounted for almost 80% of total exports of goods and services in 2005, and exports represent about 27% of French GDP.

In 2004, the industrial sector accounted for 24.3% of GDP. Manufacturing, including construction and engineering, accounts for 29% of all jobs, 40% of investments, and almost 80% of exports. The state has long played an active role in French industry, but government involvement was greatly accelerated by a series of nationalization measures enacted by the Socialists in 1982. By 1983, about one-third of French industry—3,500 companies in all—was under state control. However, there was some privatization during 1986–88, later resumed in 1993, with 21 state-owned industries, banks, and insurance companies scheduled to be sold. Although substantial progress had been made in privatization in the early 2000s, the government still held a majority stake in such industries as aeronautics, defense, automobiles, energy, and telecommunications. In July 2005, the government partially privatized Gaz de France, and in October gave the go-ahead for the partial privatization of Electricité de France.

Although France's industrial output has quadrupled since 1950, by 2005 nearly 1.5 million jobs had been lost since the 1980s. This shrinkage reflects not only steadily rising productivity, but also the major restructuring of industry due to globalization and the instability of oil markets. In this respect, French industry has seen a rapid concentration of its firms and a sharp rise in direct investment abroad. As of 2005, French companies controlled some 15,800 subsidiaries outside France, employing 2.5 million people. On the other hand, 2,860 companies controlled by foreign capital are responsible for 28% of France's output, 24% of jobs, and 30% of the manufacturing sector. France is the third-largest destination of inward investment in the world, after the United States and the United Kingdom, above all in the fields of information technology, pharmaceuticals, machine tools, and precision instruments.

The steel industry has suffered because of international competition and a general shift away from steel to aluminum and plastics. The French aluminum industry is dominated by a factory in Dunkirk owned by Pechiney, which was privatized at the end of 1995.

The French automotive industry ranks third in world exports. The two leading companies are PSA (which controls the Peugeot and Citroen brands) and Renault, the latter state-owned. The domestic market, however, has fallen prey to foreign competitors, especially from Germany and Japan, forcing the French auto makers to make greater use of robots, lay off workers, and open plants abroad.

The French aircraft industry, not primarily a mass producer, specializes in sophisticated design and experimental development. Some of its models, such as the Caravelle and the Mirage IV, have been used in over 50 countries. Aérospatiale became a state company after World War II. Airbus, based in Toulouse and formed in 1970 following an agreement between Aérospatiale and Deutsche Aerospace (Germany), is the world's largest manufacturer of commercial aircraft. Airbus was incorporated in 2001 under French law as a simplified joint stock company. The Airbus A380 will seat 555 passengers and be the world's largest commercial passenger jet when it enters service in 2006.

The chemical industry, although not as strong as its rivals in Germany and the United States, ranks fourth in the world. The pharmaceuticals, perfume, and cosmetics industry is highly significant. France is the world's largest exporter of perfumes.

The textile industry is also important: France is the world's fourth-largest exporter of women's clothing. However, foreign competition has cut into the French textile industry. Following the expiration of the World Trade Organization's longstanding system of textile quotas at the beginning of 2005, the EU signed an agreement with China in June 2005 imposing new quotas on 10 categories of textile goods, limiting growth in those categories to between 8% and 12.5% a year. The agreement runs until 2007, and was designed to give European textile manufacturers time to adjust to a world of unfettered competition. Nevertheless, barely a month after the EU-China agreement was signed, China reached its quotas for sweaters, followed soon after by blouses, bras, T-shirts, and flax yarn. Tens of millions of garments piled up in warehouses and customs checkpoints, which affected both retailers and consumers.

Agribusiness is an increasingly important industry, supplying France's vast number of restaurants and hotels. The food processing industry is a major force in the French economy. Cooperative ventures are particularly important to the food industry. France is the world's second-largest wine producer after Italy. It is the world's second-largest exporter of cheeses.

The great concentrations of French industry are in and around Paris, in the coal basin of northern France, in Alsace and Lorraine, and around Lyon and Clermont-Ferrand. French industry, in general, is strong on inventiveness and inclined toward small-scale production of high-quality items. The French government offers subsidies and easy credit to firms undertaking relocation, reconversion, or plant modernization.

29 SCIENCE AND TECHNOLOGY

French inventors played a pivotal role in the development of photography and the internal combustion engine. To French ingenuity the world also owes the first mechanical adding machine (1642), the parachute (1783), the electric generator (1832), the refrigerator (1858), and the neon lamp (1910). French industry has pioneered in the development of high-speed transportation systems, notably the supersonic Concorde and the TGV high-speed train, and French subway companies have built or provided equipment for mass-transit systems in Montréal, Mexico City, Río de Janeiro, and other cities.

France is a leading exporter of nuclear technology and has developed the first commercial vitrification plant for the disposal of radioactive wastes by integrating them in special glass and then encasing the glass in stainless steel containers for burial. In 1965, France was the third nation, after the USSR and the United States, to launch its own space satellite. The French no longer launch their own satellites, however, preferring instead to contribute to the European Space Agency.

The Académie des Sciences, founded by Louis XIV in 1666, consists of eight sections: mathematics, physics, mechanics, astronomy, chemistry, cellular and molecular biology, animal and plant biology, and human biology and medical sciences. The Centre National de la Recherche Scientifique (CNRS), founded in 1939, controls more than 1,370 laboratories and research centers. In 1996, the CNRS employed 19,391 researchers and engineers and 7,263 technicians and administrative staff. In addition, there are well over 100 other scientific and technological academies, learned societies, and research institutes. France has a large number of universities and colleges that offer courses in basic and applied sciences. The Palais de la Découverte in Paris (founded in 1937) is a scientific center for the popularization of science. It has departments of mathematics, astronomy, physics, chemistry, biology, medicine, and earth sciences, and includes a planetarium

and cinema. A similar Parisian facility is the Cité des Sciences et de l'Industrie (founded in 1986). The city also has the Musée National des Techniques (founded in 1794) and the Musée de l'Air et de l'Espace (founded in 1919).

In 1987–97, science and engineering students accounted for 37% of university enrollment. In 2002, of all bachelor's degrees awarded, 27.1% were for the sciences (natural, mathematics and computers, and engineering).

In 2002, France's total research and development (R&D) expenditures amounted to $36,357.186 billion or 2.27% of GDP, of which business provided 52.1%, followed by the government at 38.4%, foreign sources at 8%, and higher education at 0.7%. In that same year, high-tech exports were valued at $52.58.2 billion and accounted for 21% of manufactured exports. R&D personnel in 2002 numbered 3,134 scientists and engineers per million people.

30 DOMESTIC TRADE

The heart of French commerce, both domestic and foreign, is Paris. One-third of the country's commercial establishments are in the capital, and in many fields Parisian control is complete. The major provincial cities act as regional trade centers. The principal ports are Marseille, for trade with North Africa and with the Mediterranean and the Middle East; Bordeaux, for trade with West Africa and much of South America; and Le Havre, for trade with North America and northern Europe. Dunkerque and Rouen are important industrial ports.

The trend away from traditional small retailers is seen as a threat to tradition and, in some areas of the country, government assistance is offered to small retailers. Even so, larger retail outlets and hypermarkets have gained ground. Mail order sales and specialty chain stores have also grown. In 1999, metropolitan France had about 30,000 wholesale enterprises. In 2000, there were 5,863 supermarkets. In 2002, there were about 107 department stores. Among the 50 largest commercial companies in France are the department stores Au Printemps and Galeries Lafayette. A value-added tax (VAT) of 19.6% applies to most goods and services.

Business hours are customarily on weekdays from 9 AM to noon and from 2 to 6 PM. Normal banking hours are 9 AM to 4:30 PM, Monday–Friday. Most banks are closed on Saturdays; to serve a particular city or larger district, one bank will usually open Saturday mornings from 9 AM to noon. Store hours are generally from 10 AM to 7 PM, Monday–Saturday. Most businesses close for three or four weeks in August.

Advertising in newspapers and magazines and by outdoor signs is widespread. A limited amount of advertising is permitted on radio and television. Trade fairs are held regularly in Paris and other large cities.

31 FOREIGN TRADE

Leading French exports, by major categories, are capital goods (machinery, heavy electrical equipment, transport equipment, and aircraft), consumer goods (automobiles, textiles, and leather), and semifinished products (mainly chemicals, iron, and steel). Major imports are fuels, machinery and equipment, chemicals and paper goods, and consumer goods.

The French trade balance was favorable in 1961 for the first time since 1927, but after 1961 imports rose at a higher rate than exports. Trade deficits generally increased until the 1990s. From 1977 to 1985, the trade deficit nearly tripled. Among factors held responsible were heavy domestic demand for consumer products not widely produced in France, narrowness of the range of major exports, and a concentration on markets not ripe for expansion of exports from France, notably the EU and OPEC countries. In the following years a growing change in the trade balance developed, and the deficit narrowed appreciably in 1992. By 1995, France had a trade surplus of $34 billion. By 2004, however, France once again had a trade deficit, of $7.9 billion. In all, France is the world's fourth-largest exporter of goods and the third-largest provider of services. France is the largest producer and exporter of farm products in Europe. Total trade for 2004 amounted to $858.2 billion, over 40% of GDP.

Garnering the highest revenues of export commodities from France are transport machinery, including automobiles, vehicle parts, and aircraft. French wine, perfumes, and cosmetics represent about a quarter each of the world market in their respective categories.

Trade with EU countries accounted for 61% of all French trade in 2004. In 2004, France's leading markets were Germany (15% of total exports), Spain (10.4%), the United Kingdom (9.4%), and Italy (9.3%). Leading suppliers were Germany (17.4% of all imports), Italy (9%), Belgium-Luxembourg (7.8%), and Spain (7.4%).

³²BALANCE OF PAYMENTS

Between 1945 and 1958, France had a constant deficit in its balance of payments. The deficit was financed by foreign loans and by US aid under the Marshall Plan, which totaled more than $4.5 billion. A 1958 currency reform devalued the franc by 17.5%, reduced quota restrictions on imports, and allowed for repatriation of capital; these measures, combined with increased tourist trade and greater spending by US armed forces in the franc zone, improved France's payments position. With payments surpluses during most of the 1960s, gold and currency reserve holdings rose to $6.9 billion by the end of 1967. However, a massive deficit in 1968 led to another devaluation of the franc in 1969, and by 31 December 1969, gold and reserve holdings had dropped to $3.8 billion. After surpluses in 1970–72 raised international reserves to over $10 billion, price increases for oil and other raw materials resulted in substantial negative balances on current accounts in 1973 and 1974; because of this, France required massive infusions of short-term capital to meet its payments obligations.

Huge surpluses on the services account led to positive payments balances during 1977–80, when reserves rose by nearly $9.7 billion. After that, France's trade position deteriorated sharply. Foreign exchange reserves fell from $27.8 billion as of March 1981 to $14.1 billion by March 1983. To meet its payments obligation, France had to secure a $4 billion standby credit from international banks as well as loans from Saudi Arabia and the EC. During the mid-1980s, the trade deficit generally moderated; the current accounts balance recovered in 1985 from the heavy deficits of the past.

In 1992, the merchandise trade account recorded a surplus after having recorded a significant deficit of 1990. Trade in industrial goods (including military equipment) and a surplus in the manufacturing sector (the first since 1986) were responsible for the boost in exports. Economic growth rose throughout 1994 due to exports to English-speaking countries and a strong economy in Europe. Exports of both goods and services significantly contributed to GDP growth in 1995 with exports of goods totaling $270.4 billion and imports totaling $259.2 billion, resulting in a trade balance on goods of $11.2 billion. Exports of services totaled $97.8 billion while imports totaled $78.5 billion, resulting in a balance on services of $19.2 billion.

Although France in recent years has run consistent trade and current account surpluses, the country's trade balance showed a deficit in 2001, the first since 1991. It turned around in 2002. The value of merchandise exports in 2004 totaled $421.1 billion, while imports totaled $429.1 billion, resulting in a trade deficit of $7.9 billion. Total trade for 2004 amounted to $858.2 billion, over 40% of GDP. France for several years had posted surpluses on the services and investment income balances. Nevertheless, the current account recorded a deficit of $4.8 billion, or 2% of GDP in 2004.

³³BANKING AND SECURITIES

The Banque de France, founded in 1800, came completely under government control in 1945. It is the bank of issue, sets discount rates and maximum discounts for each bank, regulates public and private finance, and is the Treasury depository. In 1945, a provisional government headed by Gen. de Gaulle also nationalized France's four largest commercial banks, and the state thus came to control 55% of all deposits. The four banks were Crédit Lyonnais, the Société Générale, the Banque Nationale pour le Commerce et l'Industrie, and the Comptoir National d'Escompte de Paris. In 1966, the Banque Nationale and the Comptoir merged and formed the Banque Nationale de Paris (BNP).

In 1982, Socialist president François Mitterrand nationalized 39 banks, bringing the state's control over deposits to 90%. Among leading banks nationalized in 1982 was the Crédit Commercial de France, but this bank and Société Générale were privatized in 1987 by the Chirac government.

Balance of Payments – France (2003)

(In billions of US dollars)

Current Account		4.4
Balance on goods		1.0
Imports	-360.8	
Exports	361.9	
Balance on services		14.9
Balance on income		7.6
Current transfers		-19.2
Capital Account		-8.2
Financial Account		-0.7
Direct investment abroad		-57.4
Direct investment in France		47.8
Portfolio investment assets		-147.5
Portfolio investment liabilities		136.2
Financial derivatives		-7.1
Other investment assets		-20.0
Other investment liabilities		47.4
Net Errors and Omissions		5.8
Reserves and Related Items		-1.3

(…) data not available or not significant.

SOURCE: *Balance of Payment Statistics Yearbook 2004*, Washington, DC: International Monetary Fund, 2004.

France's (and Europe's) biggest bank is a curiosity. Crédit Agricole, founded at the end of the 19th century, was for most of its life a federation of rurally based mutual credit organizations. It has preserved its rural base and plays the leading role in providing farmers with state-subsidized loans. After 1982 it was allowed to pursue a policy of diversification, so that farmers eventually accounted for only 15% of its customers. In 1995 Crédit Agricole was listed as the eighth-biggest bank in the world, being preceded by six Japanese banks and HSBC Holdings.

In 1999, BNP and rival Société Générale attempted to take over another private bank, Paribas. Concurrently, BNP was waging a takeover bid for Société Générale itself. Ultimately, BNP won outright control of Paribas, but only 36.8% of the shares of Société Générale.

La Poste, the postal service, which in France is an independent public entity, also offers financial services and held about 10% of the market in 2002. By virtue of the Banking Act of January 1984, the main regulatory authority for the banking sector is the Commission Bancaire. It is presided over by the governor of the Banque de France. The International Monetary Fund reports that in 2001, currency and demand deposits—an aggregate commonly known as M1—were equal to $300.4 billion. In that same year, M2—an aggregate equal to M1 plus savings deposits, small time deposits, and money market mutual funds—was $896.5 billion.

Public issues of stocks and bonds may be floated by corporations or by limited partnerships with shares. Publicly held companies that wish their stock to be traded on the exchange must receive prior authorization from the Stock Exchange Commission within the Ministry of Finance. In January 1962, the two principal Paris stock exchanges were merged. The six provincial exchanges specialize in shares of medium-size and small firms in their respective regions. In 2004, a total of 701 companies were listed on EURONEXT Paris. Total market capitalization in that same year came to $1,857.235 billion. In 2004, the CAC 40 index was up 7.4% from the previous year to 3,821.2.

Measured by stock market capitalization, the Paris Bourse is the third-largest in Europe after London and Frankfurt. The Lyon Bourse is the most active provincial stock exchange. MATIF (marché à terme des instruments financiers), the financial futures exchange, was opened in Paris in 1986 and has proved a success. The Société des Bourses Françaises (SBF), the operator of the French stock market, has been determinedly pursuing a policy of reform and modernization, and it expects to benefit from the liberalization of financial services brought about by the EU's Investment Services Directive (ISD). French legislation, providing for the liberalization of financial services, transposed the directive into national law.

34 INSURANCE

Insurance is supervised by the government directorate of insurance, while reinsurance is regulated by the Ministry of Commerce. In 1946, a total of 32 major insurance companies were nationalized, and a central reinsurance institute was organized. All private insurance companies are required to place a portion of their reinsurance with the central reinsurance institute. In France, workers' compensation, tenants' property damage, third-party automobile,

hunter's liability insurance, and professional indemnity for some professions are among those insurance lines that are compulsory.

However, as of 1996, the insurance sector was being shifted completely into private hands. Union des Assurances de Paris (UAP), which is France's largest insurance group, was privatized in 1994. The combining of insurance services with retail banking has become fashionable in recent years, hence the neologism *bancassurance*. Partners in this practice are UAP and BNP. Another development has been to forge alliances across the Rhine in Germany. Since July 1994, insurers registered in other European Union (EU) countries have been able to write risks in France under the EU Non-Life Directive.

In 2003, the value of direct premiums written totaled $163.679 billion, of which life premiums totaled $105.436 billion. In 2002, Groupama GAN was France's leading nonlife insurer, with $7.5 billion of nonlife premiums written. CNP was the leading life insurer, that same year, with $15.3 billion in written life premiums.

35 PUBLIC FINANCE

The fiscal year runs from 1 January to 31 December. Deficits have been commonplace, but in recent years, efforts have been made to cut back on the growth of taxes and government spending and, since 1986, to remove major state enterprises from the expense of government ownership. Deficit reduction became a top priority of the government when France committed to the European Monetary Union (EMU). Maastricht Treaty targets for the EMU required France to reduce the government's budget deficit to 3% of GDP by 1997. The government still maintains a fairly tight hold on myriad enterprises, ranging from energy to financial services to industry; government spending accounted for 52% of GDP in 2001.

The US Central Intelligence Agency (CIA) estimated that in 2005 France's central government took in revenues of approximately $1.06 trillion and had expenditures of $1.1 trillion. Revenues minus expenditures totaled approximately -$84 billion. Pub-

Public Finance – France (2002)

(In billions of euros, central government figures)

Revenue and Grants	**674.87**	**100.0%**
Tax revenue	351.19	52.0%
Social contributions	277.86	41.2%
Grants	4.36	0.6%
Other revenue	41.46	6.1%
Expenditures	**727.39**	...
General public services	110.77	15.2%
Defense	37.51	5.2%
Public order and safety	12.29	1.7%
Economic affairs	67.27	9.2%
Environmental protection	1.47	0.2%
Housing and community amenities	6.04	0.8%
Health	...	...
Recreational, culture, and religion	5.41	0.7%
Education	70.97	9.8%
Social protection	...	...

(...) data not available or not significant.

SOURCE: *Government Finance Statistics Yearbook 2004*, Washington, DC: International Monetary Fund, 2004.

lic debt in 2005 amounted to 66.5% of GDP. Total external debt was $2.826 trillion.

The International Monetary Fund (IMF) reported that in 2002, the most recent year for which it had data, central government revenues were €674.87 billion and expenditures were €727.39 billion. The value of revenues was us$635 million and expenditures us$292 million, based on a market exchange rate for 2002 of us$1 = €1.0626 as reported by the IMF. Government outlays by function were as follows: general public services, 15.2%; defense, 5.2%; public order and safety, 1.7%; economic affairs, 9.2%; environmental protection, 0.2%; housing and community amenities, 0.8%; recreation, culture, and religion, 0.7%; and education, 9.8%.

36 TAXATION

As with most industrialized democratic systems, France's tax system is complex and nuanced, though also subject to recent movements to reductions and simplifications. The basic corporate income tax rate for filings in 2006 was 33.33%, with a social surcharge of 3.3% that is applied when the global corporate income tax charge is over €763,000. A 1.5% surcharge for 2005 was abolished for fiscal years ending on or after 1 January 2006. Long-term capital gains by firms were taxed at a basic rate of 15%, plus surcharges. However, starting in 2006, the tax rate on long-term gains from qualified shareholdings received by companies will drop to 8%. Short-term capital gains are taxed according to the progressive individual income tax schedule. The main local tax is the business tax, charged on 84% of a value derived from the rental value of the premises, 16% of the value fixed assets, and 18% of annual payroll, and at rates set by local authorities each year. The business tax (taxe professionelle) varies significantly from place to place, with a range of 0–4%.

Individual income tax in France is assessed in accordance with a progressive schedule of statutory rates up to 48.09%. However, French tax law contains many provisions for exemptions and targeted reductions from taxable income, so that the actual income tax paid is highly individualized. Taxable capital gains for individuals include the sale of immovable property, securities and land (excluding bonds or the individual's primary residence). Gains that exceed the annual exemption are subject to a 27% tax rate. Past the fifth year, the capital gain is reduced by 10% per each year of ownership. Exempt are capital gains on the sale of the principal residence. If the sale of securities exceeds €15,000, the gains are taxed at a 27% rate.

The main indirect tax is the value-added tax (VAT) first introduced in January 1968. The standard rate in 2005 was 19.6%, with a 5.5% on most foodstuffs and agricultural products, medicines, hotel rooms, books, water and newspapers. A 2.1% rate applies to certain medicines that are reimbursed by the social security system. Nonindustrial businesses that do not pay the VAT on consumption (banks, insurance companies, the medical sector, associations, nonprofit organizations, etc.) pay a wage tax to cover social levies assessed according to a progressive schedule. Generally, social security contributions by employers range from range from approximately 35–45%, with the employee responsible for 18–23%. Inheritance taxes (succession duties) range from 5–60%, as do gift (donations) taxes. There is also a patrimonial tax of 3% on the fair market value of property owned in France, although foreign companies whose French financial assets are more than

50% are exempt. Also, foreign property holders may be exempt according to the terms of a bilateral tax treaty with France. (France is party to a numerous bilateral tax treaties with provisions that can greatly reduce tax liabilities for foreign investors.) Local taxes include a property tax, charged to owners of land and buildings, and a housing tax, charged to occupants of residential premises, assessed according to the rental value of the property. The social security system is operated separately from the general tax system, financed by contributions levied on earned income in accordance with four regimes: a general regime covering 80% of French citizens, a regime for agricultural workers, a special regime for civil servants and railway workers, and a regime for the self-employed. Tax levies have been used, however, to shore up the finances in the social security system.

37 CUSTOMS AND DUTIES

Virtually all import duties are on an ad valorem CIF (cost, insurance, and freight) value basis. Minimum tariff rates apply to imports from countries that extend corresponding advantages to France. General rates, fixed at three times the minimum, are levied on imports from other countries. France adheres to the EU's common external tariff for imports. Most raw materials enter duty-free, while most manufactured goods have a tariff of 5–17%. The recession of the early 1980s gave rise to calls for protectionist measures (e.g., against Japanese electronic equipment), but the socialist government remained ostensibly committed to free trade principles. Observers noted, however, that cumbersome customs clearance procedures were being used to slow the entry of certain Japanese imports, notably videotape recorders, to protect French firms. There is a standard 19.6% VAT on most imports, with a reduced rate of 5.5% for basic necessities.

38 FOREIGN INVESTMENT

Investment regulations are simple, and a range of financial incentives for foreign investors is available. France's skilled and productive labor force; central location in Europe, with its free movement of people, services capital, and goods; good infrastructure; and technology-oriented society all attract foreign investors. However, extensive economic regulation and taxation, high social costs, and a complex labor environment are all challenges for the investor.

All direct investments in France require advance notification of—and in some cases approval by—the Treasury Department. Investments from other EU countries cannot be refused, but the department may specify whether the investment is to be financed from French or foreign sources. High taxes dampen the investment climate: the standard rate of corporation tax in 2005 was 33.3%. In 2000, the standard rate of value-added tax (VAT) was cut from 20.6% to 19.6%.

Foreign direct investment (FDI) in France climbed from $6.5 billion in 1973 to over $150 billion in 1997. The book value of total FDI stock in France in 2003 was $349 billion.

The annual inflow of FDI rose to almost $31 billion in 1998, up from $23 billion in 1997. From 1999 to 2002, annual FDI inflows averaged $47.7 billion. In 2002, FDI inflow was $48.2 billion, and in 2003 it was $52 billion. The major investors are the United States, the United Kingdom, the Netherlands, Germany, and Belgium. In 2003, the outflow of investment totaled $63 billion.

France invests most heavily in the United Kingdom, the United States, Germany, and Switzerland.

39 ECONOMIC DEVELOPMENT

Since World War II (1939–45), France has implemented a series of economic plans, introduced to direct the postwar recovery period but later expanded to provide for generally increasing governmental direction of the economy. The first postwar modernization and equipment plan (1947–53) was designed to get the machinery of production going again; the basic economic sectors—coal, steel, cement, farm machinery, and transportation—were chosen for major expansion, and productivity greatly exceeded the target goals. The second plan (1954–57) was extended to cover all productive activities, especially agriculture, the processing industries, housing construction, and expansion of overseas production. The third plan (1958–61) sought, in conditions of monetary stability and balanced foreign payments, to achieve a major economic expansion, increasing national production by 20% in four years. After the successful devaluation of 1958 and an improvement in the overall financial and political situation, growth rates of 6.3% and 5% were achieved in 1960 and 1961, respectively. The fourth plan (1962–65) called for an annual rate of growth of between 5% and 6% and an increase of 23% in private consumption; the fifth plan (1966–70), for a 5% annual expansion of production, a 25% increase in private consumption, and the maintenance of full financial stability and full employment; and the sixth plan (1971–75), for an annual gross domestic product (GDP) growth rate of between 5.8% and 6% and growth of about 7.5% in industrial production. The sixth plan also called for increases of 31% in private consumption, 34% in output, and 45% in social security expenditure.

The seventh plan (1976–80) called for equalization of the balance of payments, especially through a reduction of dependency on external sources of energy and raw materials; a lessening of social tensions in France by a significant reduction in inequalities of income and job hierarchies; and acceleration of the process of decentralization and deconcentration on the national level in favor of the newly formed regions. Because of the negative impact of the world oil crisis in the mid-1970s, the targets of the seventh plan were abandoned in 1978, and the government concentrated on helping the most depressed sectors and controlling inflation.

In October 1980, the cabinet approved the eighth plan (1981–85). It called for development of advanced technology and for reduction of oil in overall energy consumption. After the Socialists came to power, this plan was set aside, and an interim plan for 1982–84 was announced. It aimed at 3% GDP growth and reductions in unemployment and inflation. When these goals were not met and France's international payments position reached a critical stage, the government in March 1983 announced austerity measures, including new taxes on gasoline, liquor, and tobacco, a "forced loan" equivalent to 10% of annual taxable income from most taxpayers, and restrictions on the amount of money French tourists could spend abroad. A ninth plan, established for the years 1984–88, called for reducing inflation, improving the trade balance, increasing spending on research and development, and reducing dependence on imported fuels to not more than 50% of total energy by 1990. The 10th plan, for 1989–92, gave as its central objective increasing employment. The main emphasis was on

education and training, and improved competitiveness through increased spending on research and development.

France adopted legislation for a 35-hour work week in 1998 that became effective in 2000. The object was to create jobs. Pension reform was being legislated in 2003, amid much popular protest. France's demography is changing, with the active population beginning to decline in 2007—this is due to reduce annual per capita GDP growth. Spending on health care increased in the early 2000s. The general government financial deficit exceeded the EU limit of 3% of GDP in 2004.

By the mid-1990s, and in line with European Union (EU) policy, French economic policy took a turn away from state dominance and moved toward liberalization. Large shares of utilities and telecommunications were privatized. Moreover, austerity came to the fore in budgetary planning as the government moved to meet the criteria for Economic and Monetary Union (EMU). France adopted the euro as its currency in 1999, and discontinued the franc in favor of euro bills and coins in 2002. Public debt, however, was estimated at 67.7% of GDP in 2004, among the highest of the G-8 nations. Despite privatization efforts, the state in the early 2000s still owned large shares in corporations in such sectors as banking, energy, automobiles, transportation, and telecommunications.

Economic policy challenges for France in 2006 included reducing the budget deficit and making inroads into the rate of unemployment, which remains high even by EU standards. This requires reforming the tax and benefits system, as well as public administration and the legal framework for the labor market, but social resistance to such reforms is high.

Concerned about its stake in the EU Common Agricultural Policy (France is the largest beneficiary of the policy), in October 2005, France called a meeting of EU foreign ministers and demanded that the negotiating authority of the European Trade Commissioner be restricted. The commissioner, Peter Mandelson, emerged from that meeting in a stronger position and insisted that France had no power to block his proposals. That November, France threatened to veto any deal brokered by Mandelson that would go too far in reducing EU farm subsidies and tariffs.

In 2005, Prime Minister Dominique de Villepin was at odds with his political rival and interior minister Nicolas Sarkozy over the pace of economic reforms. De Villepin advocated gradual reforms, while Sarkozy called for a "rupture" with the past.

French loans to its former African territories totaled CFA Fr50 billion by November 1972, when President Pompidou announced that France would cancel the entire amount (including all accrued interest) to lighten these countries' debt burdens. In 1993, France spent $7.9 billion on international aid, $6.3 billion in 1997, and $5.4 billion in 2002.

40 SOCIAL DEVELOPMENT

France has a highly developed social welfare system. The social security fund is financed by contributions from both employers and employees, calculated on percentages of wages and salaries, and is partially subsidized by the government. Old age insurance guarantees payment of a pension when the insured reaches age 60. Disability insurance pays a pension to compensate for the loss of earnings and costs of care. Unemployment insurance is provided for all workers. Workers' medical benefits are paid directly for all necessary care. Maternity benefits are payable for six weeks before and 10 weeks after the expected date of childbirth for the first and second child. There is a universal system of family allowances for all residents, including a birth grant, income supplements for reduced work, and child care benefits.

Equal pay for equal work is mandated by law, although this is not always the case in practice. Men continue to earn more than women and unemployment rates are higher for women than for men. Sexual harassment is illegal in the workplace and is generally effectively enforced. In 2004 legislation was passed creating a High Authority to Fight Discrimination and Promote Equality. Rape and spousal abuse laws are strictly enforced and the penalties are severe. Shelters, counseling, and hotlines are available to victims of sexual abuse and violence.

Religious freedom is provided for by the constitution. However, large Arab/Muslim, African, and Jewish communities have been subject to harassment and prejudice. Extremist anti-immigrant groups have increasingly been involved in racial attacks. Discrimination on the basis of race, sex, disability, language, religion, or social status is prohibited.

41 HEALTH

Under the French system of health care, both public and private health care providers operate through centralized funding. Patients have the option of seeing a private doctor on a fee basis or going to a state-operated facility. Nearly all private doctors are affiliated with the social security system and the patients' expenses are reimbursed in part. Many have private health insurance to cover the difference. During the 1980s, there was a trend away from inpatient and toward outpatient care, with a growing number of patients receiving care at home. Cost containment initiatives were raised in the 1980s and early 1990s to increase patient contributions and establish global budgets for public hospitals. In 1991, new reforms to strengthen the public sector were initiated. The social security system subsidizes approximately 75% of all health care costs. Pharmaceutical consumption in France is among the highest of all OECD member countries (exceeded only by Japan and the United States). In 1992, the French government imposed a price-fixing mechanism on drugs.

France's birth rate was estimated at 11.9 per 1000 in 2002. Approximately 79% of France's married women (ages 15 to 49) used contraception. The total fertility rate in 2000 was 1.9 children per woman during her childbearing years.

As of 2004, there were an estimated 329 physicians, 667 nurses, 68 dentists, and 101 pharmacists per 100,000 people. Life expectancy in 2005 averaged 79.6. The infant mortality rate was 4.26 per 1,000 live births that year. The overall death rate was an estimated 9.1 per 1,000 people as of 2002. Tobacco and alcohol consumption continue to be health concerns in France.

Efforts to immunize children up to one year old include: diphtheria, pertussis, and tetanus, polio, and measles. The HIV/AIDS prevalence was 0.40 per 100 adults in 2003. As of 2004, there were approximately 120,000 people living with HIV/AIDS in the country. There were an estimated 1,000 deaths from AIDS in 2003.

42 HOUSING

In 2004, there were 30.3 million dwellings nationwide. About 25.4 million, or 84%, were primary residences, 2.9 million were second homes, and about 1.8 million, or 6.1%, were vacant. About 58%

of all dwellings are detached homes. The number of people per household was about 2.3. Over 2.9 million residential buildings were built in 1990 or later.

After World War II, in which 4.2 million dwellings were destroyed and one million damaged, the government took steps to provide inexpensive public housing. Annual construction rose steadily through the 1950s and 1960s; in 1970–75, housing construction of all types increased by an annual average of more than 6%. In 1975, the total number of new dwellings completed was 514,300. Construction slowed thereafter, and by 1996 the number had declined to 236,270.

In accordance with a law of 1953, industrial and commercial firms employing 10 or more wage earners must invest 1% of their total payroll in housing projects for their employees. These funds can finance either public or private low-cost housing. Concerns must undertake construction of low-cost projects either on their own responsibility or through a building concern to which they supply capital. Special housing allowances are provided for families who must spend an inordinately large share of their income on rent or mortgages.

43 EDUCATION

The supreme authority over national education in France is the Ministry of Education. Education is compulsory for children from the age of 6 to 16 and is free in all state primary and secondary schools. Higher education is not free, but academic fees are low, and more than half of the students are excused from payment.

Since the end of 1959, private institutions have been authorized to receive state aid and to ask to be integrated into the public education system. In 2003, about 15% of elementary-school children and 25% of secondary-level students attended private schools, the majority of which are Roman Catholic. In Brittany, most children attend Catholic schools. Freedom of education is guaranteed by law, but the state exercises certain controls over private educational institutions, nearly all of which follow the uniform curriculum prescribed by the Ministry of Education.

Primary school covers five years of study. There are two levels of secondary instruction. The first, the collège, is compulsory; after four years of schooling are successfully completed, the student receives a national diploma (brevet des collèges). Those who wish to pursue further studies enter either the two-year lycée d'enseignement professionel or the three-year lycée d'enseignement général et technologique. The former prepares students for a certificate of vocational competence, the latter for the baccalauréat, which is a prerequisite for higher education. Choice of a lycée depends on aptitude test results. The academic year runs from September to June. The primary language of instruction is French.

In 2001, nearly all children between the ages of three and five were enrolled in some type of preschool program. Primary school enrollment in 2003 was estimated at about 99% of age-eligible students. The same year, secondary school enrollment was about 94% of age-eligible students. It is estimated that about 98% of all students complete their primary education. The student-to-teacher ratio for primary school was at about 19:1 in 2003; the ratio for secondary school was about 12:1.

There are about 70 public universities within 26 académies, which now act as administrative units. Before the subdivision of these 26 units, the oldest and most important included Aix-Marseille (founded in 1409), Besançon (1691), Bordeaux (1441), Caen (1432), Dijon (1722), Grenoble (1339), Lille (1562), Montpellier (1180, reinstituted 1289), Nancy-Metz (1572), Paris (1150), Poitiers (1432), Rennes (1735, founded at Nantes 1461), Strasbourg (1538), and Toulouse (1229). The old University of Paris, also referred to as the Sorbonne, was the oldest in France and one of the leading institutions of higher learning in the world; it is now divided into 13 units, only a few of which are at the ancient Left Bank site. There are Catholic universities at Argers, Lille, Lyon, and Toulouse.

Besides the universities and specialized schools (such as École Normale Supérieure, which prepares teachers for secondary and postsecondary positions), higher educational institutions include the prestigious Grandes Écoles, which include the École Nationale d'Administration, École Normale Supérieure, Conservatoire National des Arts et Métiers, and École Polytechnique. Entrance is by competitive examination. Advanced-level research organizations include the Collège de France, École Pratique des Hautes Études, and École des Hautes Études en Sciences Sociales. In 2003, about 56% of the tertiary age population were enrolled in some type of higher education program; with 49% for men and 63% for women. The adult literacy rate has been estimated at about 98%.

As of 2003, public expenditure on education was estimated at 5.6% of GDP, or 11.4% of total government expenditures.

⁴⁴LIBRARIES AND MUSEUMS

Paris, the leader in all intellectual pursuits in France, has the largest concentration of libraries and museums. The Bibliothèque Nationale, founded in Paris in 1480, is one of the world's great research libraries, with a collection of over 10.4 million books, as well as millions of manuscripts, prints, maps, periodicals, and other items of importance (including 11 million stamps and photographs). The libraries of the 13-unit University of Paris system have collective holdings of more than six million volumes, and each major institution of higher learning has an important library of its own. The national archives are located in the Hôtel Rohan Soubise in Paris. There are dozens of libraries and historic sites dedicated to specific French writers and artists, including the Maison de Balzac in Paris, the Musée Calvin in Noyon, the Musée Matisse in Nice, the Musée Rodin in Meydon (there is also a National Museum of Rodin in Paris), and the Musée Picasso in Paris. Most provincial cities have municipal libraries and museums of varying sizes.

There are more than 1,000 museums in France. The Louvre, which underwent an extensive renovation and addition in the 1980s, including the construction of its now-famous glass pyramid, contains one of the largest and most important art collections in the world, covering all phases of the fine arts from all times and regions. The Cluny Museum specializes in the arts and crafts of the Middle Ages. The Museum of Man is a major research center as well. The Centre National d'Art et de Culture Georges Pompidou opened in 1977 on the Beaubourg Plateau (Les Halles). Primarily a museum specializing in contemporary art, it also houses several libraries (including the public library of Paris), children's workshops, music rooms, and conference halls. The Musée d'Orsay, a major new museum housing impressionist and postimpressionist paintings and many other works set in historical context, opened to the public in December 1986 in a former train station. Many of the 19th-century and 20th-century paintings in the Musée d'Orsay

had previously been housed in the Musée du Jeu de Paume. Many of the great churches, cathedrals, castles, and châteaus of France are national monuments.

⁴⁵MEDIA

Postal, telephone, and telegraph systems are operated by the government under the direction of the Ministry of Post, Telegraph, and Telephones. In 2003, there were an estimated 566 mainline telephones for every 1,000 people. The same year, there were approximately 696 mobile phones in use for every 1,000 people.

The government-controlled Office de Radiodiffusion-Télévision Française was replaced in January 1975 by seven independent state-financed companies. A law of July 1982 allowed greater independence to production and programming organizations. Under deregulation, many private radio stations have been established. Of the three state-owned television channels, TF-1, the oldest and largest, was privatized in 1987; a fourth, private channel for paying subscribers was started in 1984. Contracts were awarded in 1987 to private consortiums for fifth and sixth channels. As of 1999 there were 41 AM and 800 FM radio stations (many of the FM stations were repeaters) and 310 TV stations. In 2003, there were an estimated 950 radios and 632 television sets for every 1,000 people. about 57.5 of every 1,000 people are cable subscribers. Also in 2003, there were 347.1 personal computers for every 1,000 people and 366 of every 1,000 people had access to the Internet. There were 3,855 secure Internet servers in the country in 2004.

Traditionally, the French press falls into two categories. The *presse d'information,* with newspapers with the largest circulation, emphasizes news; the *presse d'opinion,* usually of higher prestige in literary and political circles but of much lower daily circulation, presents views on political, economic, and literary matters. In 2002, there were over 100 dailies in the country. Some of the important regional papers rival the Parisian dailies in influence and circulation.

Leading national newspapers (with their organizational affiliation and 2005 circulation totals unless noted) are: *Le Figaro* (moderate conservative, 326,800), *Le Monde* (independent, elite, 324,400), *International Herald Tribune* (English-language, 210,000 in 2002), *Liberation* (135,600), *L'Humanité* (Communist, 49,500), and *La Croix* (Catholic, 98,200 in 2002). Some leading regional dailies include *Ouest-France* (in Rennes, mass-appeal, 761,100 in 2005), *La Voix du Nord* (in Lille, conservative, 356,903 in 2004), *Sud-Ouest* (in Bordeaux, independent, 359,300 in 2002), *Nice-Matin* (in Nice, radical independent, 243,800 in 2002), *Les Dernieres Nouvelles D'Alsace* (in Strasbourg, 215,460 in 2004), *La Dépêche du Midi* (in Toulouse, radical, 218,214 in 2004), and *Le Telegramme* (in Morlaix, 199.710 in 2004). *L'Express* and *Le Point* are popular news weeklies.

The Agence France-Presse is the most important French news service. It has autonomous status, but the government is represented on its board of directors. There are some 14,000 periodicals, of which the most widely read is the illustrated Paris-Match, with a weekly circulation (in 1995) of 868,370. Several magazines for women also enjoy wide popularity, including *Elle,* (1995 circulation 360,000). Also for women are magazines publishing novels in serial form. The most popular political weeklies are *L'Express* (left-wing), with a circulation of about 419,000; the satirical *Le Canard Enchaîné* (left-wing), circulation 500,000; *Le Nouvel Obser-*

vateur (left-wing), circulation 399,470; and the news-magazine *Le Point* (independent), circulation 280,770. Filmmaking is a major industry, subsidized by the state.

The law provides for free expression including those of speech and press, and these rights are supported by the government.

46 ORGANIZATIONS

The Confédération Générale d'Agriculture, originating in its present form in the resistance movement of World War II, has become the principal voice for farmers. The Société des Agriculteurs de France is considered the organization of landowners. Agricultural cooperatives, both producers' and consumers', are popular. There are also more than 44 large industrial trade organizations. Chambers of commerce function in the larger cities and towns. The International Chamber of Commerce has its headquarters in Paris, the national capital.

There are professional associations covering a wide variety of fields. The Association Medicale Francaise is a networking association for physicians that also promotes research and education on health issues and works to establish common policies and standards in healthcare. There are also several associations dedicated to research and education for specific fields of medicine and particular diseases and conditions. The World Medical Association has an office in Ferney-Voltaire.

The Institute of France (founded in 1795) consists of the famous French Academy (Académie Française), the Academy of Sciences, the Academy of Humanities, the Academy of Fine Arts, and the Academy of Moral Sciences and Politics. There are many scientific, artistic, technical, and scholarly societies at both national and local levels. The multinational organization of European Academy of Arts, Sciences and Humanities is based in Paris. The United Nations Educational, Scientific and Cultural Organization (UNESCO) has an office in Paris as does the European Space Agency.

There are also many associations and organizations dedicated to various sports and leisure time activities. Youth organizations are numerous and range from sports groups, to volunteer and service organizations, religious and political organizations. Some groups with international ties include Junior Chamber, YMCA/YWCA, and the Guides and Scouts of France. Volunteer service organizations, such as the Lions Clubs and Kiwanis International, are also present. The Red Cross, the Society of St. Vincent de Paul, CARE, UNICEF, and Greenpeace have national chapters.

47 TOURISM, TRAVEL, AND RECREATION

France has countless tourist attractions, ranging from the museums and monuments of Paris to beaches on the Riviera and ski slopes in the Alps. Haute cuisine, hearty regional specialties, and an extraordinary array of fine wines attract gourmets the world over; the area between the Rhone River and the Pyrenees contains the largest single tract of vineyards in the world. In 1992 Euro Disneyland, 20 miles east of Paris, opened to great fanfare but was plagued by the European recession, a strong French franc, bad weather, and difficulty marketing itself to the French.

The most popular French sport is soccer (commonly called "le foot"). The men's soccer team won the World Cup in 1998. Other favorite sports are skiing, tennis, water sports, and bicycling. Between 1896 and 1984, France won 137 gold, 156 silver, and 158 bronze medals in the Olympic Games. Paris hosted the Summer Olympics in 1900 and 1924; the Winter Olympics took place at Chamonix in 1924, Grenoble in 1968, and Albertville in 1992. Le Mans is the site of a world-class auto race.

Tourists need a valid passport to enter France. A visa is not necessary for tourist/business stays of up to 90 days.

France is one of the world's top tourist destinations. In 2003, there were approximately 75,048,000 visitors, of whom 51% came from Western Europe. The 603,279 hotel rooms with 1,206,558 beds had an occupancy rate of 58%. The average length of stay that same year was two nights.

In 2005, the US Department of State estimated the daily expenses of staying in Paris at $418. Elsewhere in France, expenses ranged from $187 to $374 per day.

48 FAMOUS FRENCH

Principal figures of early French history include Clovis I (466?–511), the first important monarch of the Merovingian line, who sought to unite the Franks; Charles Martel ("the Hammer," 689?–741), leader of the Franks against the Saracens in 732; his grandson Charlemagne (742–814), the greatest of the Carolingians, crowned emperor of the West on 25 December 800; and William II, Duke of Normandy (1027–87), later William I of England ("the Conqueror," r.1066–87). Important roles in theology and church history were played by St. Martin of Tours (b.Pannonia, 316?–97), bishop of Tours and founder of the monastery of Marmoutier, now considered the patron saint of France; the philosopher Pierre Abélard (1079–1142), traditionally regarded as a founder of the University of Paris but equally famous for his tragic romantic involvement with his pupil Héloïse (d.1164); and St. Bernard of Clairvaux (1090?–1153), leader of the Cistercian monastic order, preacher (1146) of the Second Crusade (1147–49), and guiding spirit of the Knights Templars. The first great writer of Arthurian romances was Chrétien de Troyes (fl.1150?).

The exploits of famous 14th-century Frenchmen were recorded by the chronicler Jean Froissart (1333?–1401). Early warrior-heroes of renown were Bertrand du Guesclin (1320–80) and Pierre du Terrail, seigneur de Bayard (1474?–1524). Joan of Arc (Jeanne d'Arc, 1412–31) was the first to have a vision of France as a single nation; she died a martyr and became a saint and a national heroine. Guillaume de Machaut (1300?–1377) was a key literary and musical figure. François Villon (1431–63?) was first in the line of great French poets. Jacques Coeur (1395–1456) was the greatest financier of his time. Masters of the Burgundian school of composers were Guillaume Dufay (1400?–1474), Gilles Binchois (1400?–1467), Jan Ockeghem (1430?–95), and Josquin des Prez (1450?–1521). Jean Fouquet (1415?–80) and Jean Clouet (1485–1541) were among the finest painters of the period. The flag of France was first planted in the New World by Jacques Cartier (1491–1557), who was followed by the founder of New France in Canada, Samuel de Champlain (1567–1635).

The era of Louis XIV ("le Roi Soleil," or "the Sun King," 1638–1715) was in many respects the golden age of France. Great soldiers—Henri de La Tour d'Auvergne, vicomte de Turenne (1611–75), François Michel Le Tellier, marquis de Louvois (1639–91), and Louis II de Bourbon, prince de Condé, called the Grand Condé (1621–86)—led French armies to conquests on many battlefields. Great statesmen, such as the cardinals Armand Jean du Plessis, duc de Richelieu (1585–1642), and Jules Mazarin (1602–

61), managed French diplomacy and created the French Academy. Great administrators, such as Maximilien de Bethune, duc de Sully (1560–1641), and Jean-Baptiste Colbert (1619–83), established financial policies. Noted explorers in the New World were Jacques Marquette (1637–75), Robert Cavalier, Sieur de La Salle (1643–87), and Louis Jolliet (1645–1700). Jean-Baptiste Lully (1632–87), Marc-Antoine Charpentier (1634–1704), and François Couperin (1668–1733) were the leading composers. Nicolas Poussin (1594–1665), Claude Lorrain (1600–1682), and Philippe de Champaigne (1602–74) were the outstanding painters. In literature, the great sermons and moralizing writings of Jacques Bénigne Bossuet, bishop of Meaux (1627–1704), and François Fénelon (1651–1715); the dramas of Pierre Corneille (1606–84), Molière (Jean-Baptiste Poquelin, 1622–73), and Jean Racine (1639–99); the poetry of Jean de La Fontaine (1621–95) and Nicolas Boileau-Despréaux (1636–1711); the maxims of François, duc de La Rochefoucauld (1613–80), and Jean de La Bruyère (1645–96); the fairy tales of Charles Perrault (1628–1703); the satirical fantasies of Savinien de Cyrano de Bergerac (1619–55); and the witty letters of Madame de Sévigné (1626–96) made this a great age for France. Two leading French philosophers and mathematicians of the period, René Descartes (1596–1650) and Blaise Pascal (1623–62), left their mark on the whole of European thought. Pierre Gassendi (1592–1655) was a philosopher and physicist; Pierre de Fermat (1601–55) was a noted mathematician. Modern French literature began during the 16th century, with François Rabelais (1490?–1553), Joachim du Bellay (1522–60), Pierre de Ronsard (1525–85), and Michel de Montaigne (1533–92). Ambroise Paré (1510–90) was the first surgeon, and Jacques Cujas (1522–90) the first of the great French jurists. Among other figures in the great controversy between Catholics and Protestants, Claude, duc de Guise (1496–1550), and Queen Catherine de Médicis (Caterina de'Medici, b.Florence, 1519–89) should be mentioned on the Catholic side, and Admiral Gaspard de Coligny (1519–72), a brilliant military leader, on the Protestant side. Two famous kings were Francis I (1494–1547) and Henry IV (Henry of Navarre, 1553–1610); the latter proclaimed the Edict of Nantes in 1598, granting religious freedom to his Protestant subjects. The poetic prophecies of the astrologer Nostradamus (Michel de Notredame, 1503–66) are still widely read today.

1700–1900

During the 18th century, France again was in the vanguard in many fields. Étienne François, duc de Choiseul (1719–85), and Anne Robert Jacques Turgot (1727–81) were among the leading statesmen of the monarchy. Charles Louis de Secondat, baron de La Brède et de Montesquieu (1689–1755), and Jean-Jacques Rousseau (b.Switzerland, 1712–78) left their mark on philosophy. Denis Diderot (1713–84) and Jean Le Rond d'Alembert (1717–83) created the Great Encyclopedia (*Encyclopédie ou Dictionnaire Raisonné des Sciences, des Artes et des Métiers*). Baron Paul Henri Thiery d'Holbach (1723–89) was another philosopher. Jeanne Antoinette Poisson Le Normant d'Etoiles, marquise de Pompadour (1721–64), is best known among the women who influenced royal decisions during the reign of Louis XV (1710–74). French explorers carried the flag of France around the world, among them Louis Antoine de Bougainville (1729–1811) and Jean La Pérouse (1741–88). French art was dominated by the painters Antoine Watteau (1684–1721), Jean-Baptiste Chardin (1699–1779), François

Boucher (1703–70), and Jean Honoré Fragonard (1732–1806) and by the sculptor Jean Houdon (1741–1828). Jean-Philippe Rameau (1683–1764) was the foremost composer. French science was advanced by Georges Louis Leclerc, Comte de Buffon (1707–88), zoologist and founder of the Paris Museum, and Antoine Laurent Lavoisier (1743–94), the great chemist. In literature, the towering figure of Voltaire (François Marie Arouet, 1694–1778) and the brilliant dramatist Pierre Beaumarchais (1732–99) stand beside the greatest writer on gastronomy, Anthelme Brillat-Savarin (1755–1826).

The rule of Louis XVI (1754–93) and his queen, Marie Antoinette (1755–93), and the social order they represented, ended with the French Revolution. Outstanding figures of the Revolution included Jean-Paul Marat (1743–93), Honoré Gabriel Riquetti, comte de Mirabeau (1749–91), Maximilien Marie Isidore Robespierre (1758–94), and Georges Jacques Danton (1759–94). Napoleon Bonaparte (1769–1821) rose to prominence as a military leader in the Revolution and subsequently became emperor of France. Marie Joseph Paul Yves Roch Gilbert du Motier, marquis de Lafayette (1757–1834), was a brilliant figure in French as well as in American affairs. This was also the period of the eminent painter Jacques Louis David (1748–1825) and of the famed woman of letters Madame Germaine de Staël (Anne Louise Germaine Necker, baronne de Staël-Holstein, 1766–1817).

During the 19th century, French science, literature, and arts all but dominated the European scene. Among the leading figures were Louis Jacques Mendé Daguerre (1789–1851), inventor of photography, and Claude Bernard (1813–78), the great physiologist. Other pioneers of science included Jean-Baptiste Lamarck (1744–1829) and Georges Cuvier (1769–1832) in zoology and paleontology, Pierre Laplace (1749–1827) in geology, André Marie Ampère (1775–1836), Dominique François Arago (1786–1853), and Jean Bernard Léon Foucault (1819–68) in physics, Joseph Louis Gay-Lussac (1778–1850) in chemistry, Camille Flammarion (1842–1925) in astronomy, and Louis Pasteur (1822–95) in chemistry and bacteriology. Louis Braille (1809–52) invented the method of writing books for the blind that bears his name. Auguste (Isidore Auguste Marie François Xavier) Comte (1798–1857) was an influential philosopher. Literary figures included the poets Alphonse Marie Louis de Lamartine (1790–1869), Alfred de Vigny (1797–1863), Alfred de Musset (1810–57), Charles Baudelaire (1821–67), Stéphane Mallarmé (1842–98), Paul Verlaine (1844–96), and Arthur Rimbaud (1854–91); the fiction writers François René Chateaubriand (1768–1848), Stendhal (Marie Henri Beyle, 1783–1842), Honoré de Balzac (1799–1850), Victor Marie Hugo (1802–85), Alexandre Dumas the elder (1802–70) and his son, Alexandre Dumas the younger (1824–95), Prosper Merimée (1803–70), George Sand (Amandine Aurore Lucie Dupin, baronne Dudevant, 1804–76), Théophile Gautier (1811–72), Gustave Flaubert (1821–80), the Goncourt brothers (Edmond, 1822–96, and Jules, 1830–70), Jules Verne (1828–1905), Alphonse Daudet (1840–97), Emile Zola (1840–1902), and Guy de Maupassant (1850–93); and the historians and critics François Guizot (1787–1874), Jules Michelet (1798–1874), Charles Augustin Sainte-Beuve (1804–69), Alexis de Tocqueville (1805–59), Ernest Renan (1823–92), and Hippolyte Adolphe Taine (1828–93). Charles Maurice de Talleyrand (1754–1838), Joseph Fouché (1763–1820), Adolphe Thiers (1797–1877), and Léon Gambetta (1838–82) were leading statesmen. Louis Hector Berlioz (1803–69) was the greatest figure in 19th-century French music. Other figures were Charles François Gounod (1818–93), composer of *Faust*, Belgian-born César Auguste Franck (1822–90), and Charles Camille Saint-Saëns (1835–1921). Georges Bizet (1838–75) is renowned for his opera *Carmen*, and Jacques Lévy Offenbach (1819–80) for his immensely popular operettas.

In painting, the 19th century produced Jean August Dominique Ingres (1780–1867), Ferdinand Victor Eugène Delacroix (1789–1863), Jean-Baptiste Camille Corot (1796–1875), Honoré Daumier (1808–79), and Gustave Courbet (1819–77), and the impressionists and postimpressionists Camille Pissarro (1830–1903), Édouard Manet (1832–83), Hilaire Germain Edgar Degas (1834–1917), Paul Cézanne (1839–1906), Claude Monet (1840–1926), Pierre Auguste Renoir (1841–1919), Berthe Morisot (1841–1895), Paul Gauguin (1848–1903), Georges Seurat (1859–91), and Henri de Toulouse-Lautrec (1864–1901). Auguste Rodin (1840–1917) was the foremost sculptor; Frédéric Auguste Bartholdi (1834–1904) created the Statue of Liberty. The actresses Rachel (Elisa Félix, 1821–58) and Sarah Bernhardt (Rosine Bernard, 1844–1923) dominated French theater.

The Twentieth and Twenty-First Centuries

In 20th-century political and military affairs, important parts were played by Georges Clemenceau (1841–1929), Ferdinand Foch (1851–1929), Henri Philippe Pétain (1856–1951), Raymond Poincaré (1860–1934), Léon Blum (1872–1950), Jean Monnet (1888–1979), Charles de Gaulle (1890–1970), Pierre Mendès-France (1907–82), François Maurice Marie Mitterrand (1916–96), and Valéry Giscard d'Estaing (b.1926). Winners of the Nobel Peace Prize include Frédéric Passy (1822–1912) in 1901, Benjamin Constant (1852–1924) in 1909, Léon Victor Auguste Bourgeois (1851–1925) in 1920, Aristide Briand (1862–1932) in 1926, Ferdinand Buisson (1841–1932) in 1927, Léon Jouhaux (1879–1954) in 1951, and René Cassin (1887–1976) in 1968. Albert Schweitzer (1875–1965), musician, philosopher, physician, and humanist, a native of Alsace, received the Nobel Peace Prize in 1952.

Famous scientists include the mathematician Jules Henri Poincaré (1854–1912); the physicist Antoine Henri Becquerel (1852–1908), a Nobel laureate in physics in 1903; chemist and physicist Pierre Curie (1859–1906); his wife, Polish-born Marie Sklodowska Curie (1867–1934), who shared the 1903 Nobel Prize for physics with her husband and Becquerel and won a Nobel Prize again, for chemistry, in 1911; their daughter Irène Joliot-Curie (1897–1956) and her husband, Frédéric Joliot-Curie (Jean-Frédéric Joliot, 1900–1958), who shared the Nobel Prize for chemistry in 1935; Jean-Baptiste Perrin (1870–1942), Nobel Prize winner for physics in 1926; the physiologist Alexis Carrel (1873–1944); and Louis de Broglie (1892–1987), who won the Nobel Prize for physics in 1929. Other Nobel Prize winners for physics include Charles Édouard Guillaume (1861–1938) in 1920, Alfred Kastler (1902–84) in 1966, Louis Eugène Néel (1904–2000) in 1970, Pierre-Gilles de Gennes (b.1932) in 1991, and Georges Charpak (b.1924) in 1992; for chemistry, Henri Moissan (1852–1907) in 1906, Victor Grignard (1871–1935) in 1912, Paul Sabatier (1854–1941) in 1912, and Yves Chauvin (b.1930) in 2005. Also, in physiology or medicine: in 1907, Charles Louis Alphonse Laveran (1845–1922); in 1913, Charles Robert Richet (1850–1935); in 1928, Charles Jules

Henri Nicolle (1866–1936); in 1965, François Jacob (b.1920), André Lwoff (1902–94), and Jacques Monod (1910–76); and in 1980, Jean-Baptiste Gabriel Dausset (b.1916).

The philosopher Henri Bergson (1859–1941) received the 1927 Nobel Prize for literature. Émile Durkheim (1858–1917) was a founder of modern sociology. Pierre Teilhard de Chardin (1881–1955), a Jesuit, was both a prominent paleontologist and an influential theologian. Claude Lévi-Strauss (b.Belgium, 1908) is a noted anthropologist, Pierre Bourdieu (1930–2002) was an important sociologist, and Fernand Braudel (1902–85) was an important historian. Twentieth-century philosophers included: Louis Althusser (1918–1990), Raymond Aron (1905–1983), Gaston Bachelard (1884–1962), Georges Bataille (1897–1962), Jean Baudrillard (b.1929), Gilles Deleuze (1925–1995), Jacques Derrida (1930–2004), Michel Foucault (1926–1984), Pierre-Félix Guattari (1930–1992), Philippe Lacoue-Labarthe (b.1940), Henri Lefebvre (1901–1991), Emmanuel Lévinas (1906–1995), Jean-François Lyotard (1924–1998), Maurice Merleau-Ponty (1908–1961), and Paul Ricoeur (1913–2005).

Honored writers include Sully-Prudhomme (René François Armand, 1839–1907), winner of the first Nobel Prize for literature in 1901; Frédéric Mistral (1830–1914), Nobel Prize winner in 1904; Edmond Rostand (1868–1918); Anatole France (Jacques Anatole Thibaut, 1844–1924), Nobel Prize winner in 1921; Romain Rolland (1866–1944), Nobel Prize winner in 1915; André Paul Guillaume Gide (1869–1951), a 1947 nobel laureate; Marcel Proust (1871–1922); Paul Valéry (1871–1945); Colette (Sidonie Gabrielle Claudine Colette, 1873–1954); Roger Martin du Gard (1881–1958), Nobel Prize winner in 1937; Jean Giraudoux (1882–1944); François Mauriac (1885–1970), 1952 Nobel Prize winner; Jean Cocteau (1889–1963); Louis Aragon (1897–1982); André Malraux (1901–76); Anaïs Nin (1903–1977); Jean-Paul Sartre (1905–80), who was awarded the 1964 Nobel Prize but declined it; Simone Lucie Ernestine Marie Bertrand de Beauvoir (1908–86); Simone Weil (1909–43); Jean Genet (1910–86); Jean Anouilh (1910–87); Albert Camus (1913–60), Nobel Prize winner in 1957; Claude Simon (1913–2005), a 1985 Nobel laureate; Marguerite Duras (1914–96); Roland Barthes (1915–80); and Georges Perec (1936–1982). Antoine de Saint-Exupéry (1900–1944) was a French writer and aviator. Romanian-born Eugene Ionesco (1912–94) and Irish-born Samuel Beckett (1906–89) spent their working lives in France. Significant composers include Gabriel Urbain Fauré (1845–1924), Claude Achille Debussy (1862–1918), Erik Satie (1866–1925), Albert Roussel (1869–1937), Maurice Ravel (1875–1937), Francis Poulenc (1899–1963), Olivier Messiaen (1908–92), Darius Milhaud (1892–1974), and composer-conductor Pierre Boulez (b.1925). The sculptor Aristide Maillol (1861–1944) and the painters/artists Henri Matisse (1869–1954), Georges Rouault (1871–1958), Georges Braque (1882–1963), Spanish-born Pablo Picasso (1881–1974), Russian-born Marc Chagall (1887–1985), Marcel Duchamp (1887–1968), Fernand Léger (1881–1955), and Jean Dubuffet (1901–85) are world famous.

Of international renown are actor-singers Maurice Chevalier (1888–1972), Yves Montand (Ivo Livi, 1921–91), and Charles Aznavour (b.1924); actor-director Jacques Tati (Jacques Tatischeff, 1907–82); actors Charles Boyer (1899–1978), Jean-Louis Xavier Trintignant (b.1930), Jean-Paul Belmondo (b.1933), and Gérard Depardieu (b.1948); actresses Simone Signoret (Simone Kamin-

244   France

er, 1921–85), Jeanne Moreau (b.1928), Leslie Caron (b.1931), Brigitte Bardot (b.1934), Catherine Deneuve (b.1943), Isabelle Huppert (b.1953), Isabelle Adjani (b.1955), Juliette Binoche (b.1964), Julie Delpy (b.1969), and Audrey Tautou (b.1978); singer Edith Piaf (1915–63); master of mime Marcel Marceau (b.1923); and directors Georges Méliès (1861–1938), Abel Gance (1889–1981), Jean Renoir (1894–1979), Robert Bresson (1901–99), René Clément (1913–96), Eric Rohmer (Jean-Marie Maurice Scherer, b.1920), Alain Resnais (b.1922), Jean-Luc Godard (b.1930), Louis Malle (1932–95), and François Truffaut (1932–84). One of the most recognizable Frenchmen in the world was oceanographer Jacques-Yves Cousteau (1910–97), who popularized undersea exploration with popular documentary films and books.

⁴⁹DEPENDENCIES

French overseas departments include French Guiana, Guadeloupe, Martinique, and Saint-Pierre and Miquelon (described in the *Americas* volume under French American Dependencies) and Réunion (in the *Africa* volume under French African Dependencies). French overseas territories and collectivities include French Polynesia, French Southern and Antarctic Territories, New Caledonia, and Wallis and Futuna (see French Asian Dependencies in the *Asia* volume), and Mayotte (in the *Africa* volume). The inhabitants of French overseas departments and territories are French citizens, enjoy universal suffrage, and send elected representatives to the French parliament.

⁵⁰BIBLIOGRAPHY

Annesley, Claire (ed.). *A Political and Economic Dictionary of Western Europe*. Philadelphia: Routledge/Taylor and Francis, 2005.

Cogan, Charles. *French Negotiating Behavior: Dealing with La Grande Nation*. Washington, D.C.: United States Institute of Peace Press, 2003.

Cook, Malcolm (ed.). *French Culture Since 1945*. New York: Longman, 1993.

France: From the Cold War to the New World Order. New York: St. Martin's Press, 1996.

Gildea, Robert. *France Since 1945*. Oxford: Oxford University Press, 1996.

Gough, Hugh and John Horne. *De Gaulle and Twentieth-century France*. New York: Edward Arnold, 1994.

Graham, Bruce Desmond. *Choice and Democratic Order: the French Socialist Party, 1937–1950*. New York: Cambridge University Press, 1994.

Hewitt, Nicholas (ed.). *The Cambridge Companion to Modern French Culture*. New York: Cambridge University Press, 2003.

Illustrated Guide to France. New York: W.W. Norton, 2003.

International Smoking Statistics: A Collection of Historical Data from 30 Economically Developed Countries. New York: Oxford University Press, 2002.

Jones, Colin. *The Cambridge Illustrated History of France*. Cambridge: Cambridge University Press, 1994.

Kelly, Michael (ed.). *French Culture and Society: The Essentials*. New York: Oxford University Press, 2001.

Noiriel, Gérard. *The French Melting Pot: Immigration, Citizenship, and National Identity*. Minneapolis: University of Minnesota Press, 1996.

Northcutt, Wayne. *Mitterrand: A Political Biography*. New York: Holmes and Meier, 1992.

———. *The Regions of France: A Reference Guide to History and Culture*. Westport, Conn.: Greenwood Press, 1996.

Planhol, Xavier de. *An Historical Geography of France*. Cambridge: Cambridge University Press, 1994.

Raymond, Gino. *Historical Dictionary of France*. Lanham, Md.: Scarecrow, 1998.

Young, Robert J. *France and the Origins of the Second World War*. Basingstoke: Macmillan, 1996.

Wessels, Wolfgang, Andreas Maurer, and Jürgan Mittag (eds.). *Fifteen into One?: the European Union and Its Member States*. New York: Palgrave, 2003.

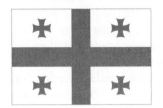

GEORGIA

Republic of Georgia
Sakartveld Respublika

CAPITAL: T'bilisi (Tbilisi)

FLAG: White rectangle, in its central portion a red cross connecting all four sides of the flag; in each of the four corners is a small red bolnur-katskhuri cross; the five-cross flag appears to date back to the 14th century.

ANTHEM: *National Anthem of the Republic of Georgia.*

MONETARY UNIT: The lari (L) was issued in 1995 to replace government coupons that were introduced in 1993. L1 = $0.54945 (or $1 = L1.82) as of 2005.

WEIGHTS AND MEASURES: The metric system is in force.

HOLIDAYS: New Year's Day, 1–2 January; Christmas, 7 January; Independence Day, 26 May; St. George's Day, 22 November.

TIME: 3 PM = noon GMT.

---

¹LOCATION, SIZE, AND EXTENT

Georgia is located in southeastern Europe, bordering the Black Sea, between Turkey and Russia. Comparatively, the area occupied by Georgia is slightly smaller than the state of South Carolina, with a total area of 69,700 sq km (26,911 sq mi). Georgia shares boundaries with Russia on the N and E, Azerbaijan on the E and s, Armenia and Turkey on the s, and the Black Sea on the w. Georgia's land boundary totals 1,461 km (906 mi). Its coastline is 310 km (192 mi). Its capital city, T'bilisi, is located in the southeastern part of the country.

²TOPOGRAPHY

The topography of Georgia is mainly mountainous, with the great Caucasus Mountains in the north and lesser Caucasus Mountains in the south. The highest point in the nation is Mount Shkhara at a height of 5,201 m (17,064 ft) in the Greater Caucasus. The Kolkhida Lowland opens to the Black Sea in the west and the Kura River basin lies in the east. The Kura River is the nation's longest river with a length of 1,514 km (941 mi). Good soils occur in the river valley flood plains and in the foothills of the Kolkhida Lowland.

³CLIMATE

Georgia's climate along the Black Sea coast is similar to that along the Mediterranean, warm, humid, and almost subtropical. Farther inland the climate is continental, with warm summers and cold winters. July's mean temperature is 23°C (73.8°F). The mean temperature in January is -3°C (27.3°F). The annual rainfall in Georgia is 51 cm (20 in). In the mountains it is much cooler, with snow and ice all year in altitudes above 3,600 m (12,000 ft).

⁴FLORA AND FAUNA

The country's land is composed of gently rolling plains. The Caucasus Mountains in Georgia begin a series of high mountains in Central Asia. The subtropical zone of the Black Sea coast of the Caucasus Mountains has a distinctive vegetation: woods of black alder, oak, elm, and beech with a profusion of lianas and an admixture of evergreens. Mountain goats, Caucasian goats, Caucasian antelope, European wild boar, porcupine, and the leopard inhabit the Caucasus, and reptiles and amphibious creatures abound. As of 2002, there were at least 107 species of mammals, 208 species of birds, and over 4,300 species of plants throughout the country.

⁵ENVIRONMENT

Georgia suffers from pollution of its air, water, and soil. Air pollution is especially heavy in Rust'avi. In 1996, Georgia's industrial carbon dioxide emissions totaled 2.9 million metric tons; in 2000, the total was at 6.2 million metric tons. The Mtkvari River and the Black Sea are both heavily polluted. Pesticides from agricultural areas have significantly contaminated the soil.

In 2003, 2.3% of Georgia's total land area was protected. There are two Ramsar wetland sites: one in central Kolkheti and the other at the Ispani II marshes. According to a 2006 report issued by the International Union for Conservation of Nature and Natural Resources (IUCN), threatened species included 11 types of mammals, 8 species of birds, 7 types of reptiles, 1 species of amphibian, 6 species of fish, and 10 species of invertebrates. Species on the endangered list include Atlantic sturgeon, slender-billed curlew, Mediterranean monk seals, Darevsky's viper, and the Armenian birch mouse.

⁶POPULATION

The population of Georgia in 2005 was estimated by the United Nations (UN) at 4,501,000, which placed it at number 116 in population among the 193 nations of the world. In 2005, approximately 13% of the population was over 65 years of age, with another 19% of the population under 15 years of age. There were 90 males for every 100 females in the country. According to the UN, the annual population growth rate for 2005–10 was stagnant at 0.0%, a rate the government viewed as too low. The projected population for the year 2025 was 4,178,000. The population density was 64 per sq km (167 per sq mi), with the majority of the population living near the Black Sea or in the river valleys.

The UN estimated that 52% of the population lived in urban areas in 2005, and that urban areas were growing at an annual rate of -0.88%. The capital city, T'bilisi (Tbilisi), had a population of 1,064,000 in that year. Other cities and their estimated populations include Kútáisi, 268,800, and Rustavi, 181,400.

7 MIGRATION

With independence in 1991 came three secessionist movements in three autonomous areas and conflicts in two of them. The conflict in South Ossetia in 1991, followed by the conflict in Abkhazia in 1992 and 1993, resulted in the mass displacement of ethnic Georgians, Ossetians, and Abkhaz, as well as other ethnic minorities. As many as 200,000 Georgians may have fled the fighting in Abkhazia in 1993. By December 1996, Georgia had 280,000 internally displaced persons. In February of 1997, a voluntary repatriation plan was agreed upon for persons to return to South Ossetia. Hostilities resumed in Gali in May 1998, displacing some 40,000 residents. Georgia's first census in 2002 detailed 4,961 stateless and 8,058 foreign citizens.

By year end 2004 there remained 237,069 internally displaced persons, mainly in urban areas, 29.6% in T'bilisi and 46.4% in Samegrelo-Zemo Svaneti region. Repatriation of Meskhetian Turks began in 2003 and was planned to continue until 2011. Transit migration, trafficked migrants (primarily women from other former Soviet states), migrants from Asia and Africa, and irregular migrants were of increasing concern in 2004 as Georgia looked to membership in the European Union (EU). In addition, in that same year there were 2,559 refugees, mainly Chechen/Kist from the Pankisi Gorge, and 11 asylum seekers.

Georgian emigration during the 1990s was estimated between 300,000 to more than 1.5 million. In 2004, some 8,934 Georgians sought asylum in over 18 countries, mainly Austria, France, Slovakia, and Sweden. In 2005, the net migration rate was estimated as -4.62 migrants per 1,000 population, a significant change from -9.2 per 1,000 in 1990. The government views the migration levels as too high.

8 ETHNIC GROUPS

According to the 2002 census, 83.3% of the population are Georgian. The leading minorities are Azeris with 6.5%, Armenians with 5.7%, Russians with 1.5%, and others (including Ossetians and Abkhaz) with 2.5%.

9 LANGUAGES

Georgian is the official language and is spoken by about 71% of the population. Georgian is a South Caucasian language called Kartveli by its speakers. There is no article and a single declension with six cases. The alphabet is a phonetic one with 33 symbols. The literature dates from the 5th century AD.

Russian is spoken by 9% of the population, Armenian by 7%, Azeri by 6%, and various other languages are spoken by the remaining 7%. Abkhaz is the official language in Abkhazia.

10 RELIGIONS

In the 4th century AD Christianity briefly enjoyed the status of official religion, but successive conquests by Mongols, Turks, and Persians left Georgia with a complex and unsettled ethnic and religious heritage. According to the 2002 census, over 70% of the population are nominally Georgian Orthodox. About 13% are members of other Orthodox groups, including Russian, Armenian, and Greek. A small number of ethnic Russians belong to dissident Orthodox groups such as the Molokani, Staroveriy (Old Believers) and the Dukhoboriy. About 9.9% of the population are Muslims, most of whom are ethnic Azeris, Georgian Muslims of Ajara, and ethnic Chechen Kists. Less than 1% of the population are Roman Catholics. Smaller Christian denominations include Baptists, Seventh-Day Adventists, Pentecostals, Jehovah's Witnesses, the Armenian Apostolic Church, and the New Apostolic Church. There are also small numbers of Bahai's and Hare Krishnas. There are about 8,000 Jews in the country.

In 2002, the parliament ratified a concordat with the Georgian Orthodox Church (GOC) granting them special recognition; however, the constitution has established a separation of church and state and freedom of religion. Some non-Orthodox groups have complained of the privileged status granted to the GOC. For instance, the GOC is allowed to review public school textbooks and to make suggestions on content. Registration of religious organizations is not required, but many do so in order to gain the legal status necessary to rent office or worship space and import written materials.

11 TRANSPORTATION

Railroads in Georgia as of 2004, consisted of 1,612 km (1,003 mi) of broad and narrow gauge lines, all of which were electrified. Nearly all of the country's railways were broad gauge, accounting for 1,575 km (980 mi), with narrow gauge lines making up only 37 km (23 mi). Railways serve primarily as connections to the Black Sea for inland cities like T'bilisi, Chiat'ura, Jvari, and Tkvarcheli. Highways in 2003 totaled an estimated 20,247 km (12,594 mi), of which 7,973 km (4,959 mi) were paved. The maritime fleet of 175 ships (of 1,000 GRT or over) had a capacity of 855,908 GRT in 2005. Batumi and Poti are the principal Black Sea ports. As of 2004, Georgia had an estimated 30 airports, 19 of which had paved runways, and three heliports (as of 2005). Its only international airport is T'bilisi which is capable of handling 1,000–1,200 passengers per hour. In 2003 there were about 2,000 aircraft departures, and around 124,000 passengers carried on scheduled domestic and international airline flights.

12 HISTORY

Georgia has existed as a state on a sporadic basis since classical times. The first Georgian state can be traced to the 4th century BC. Throughout its history Georgia has been conquered by the Romans, Iranians, the Arabs, the Turks, the Mongols and the Hordes of Tamerlane. Georgia did enjoy independence for short periods of time from the 6th to the 12th centuries AD. The Mongols invaded and conquered Georgia by 1236. Later the Ottoman and Persian empires competed for control of the region. Western Georgia be-

LOCATION: 42°0′ N; 44°0′ E. BOUNDARY LENGTHS: Total boundary lengths, 1,461 kilometers (908 miles): Armenia, 164 kilometers (102 miles); Azerbaijan, 322 kilometers (200 miles); Russia, 723 kilometers (450 miles); Turkey, 252 kilometers (157 miles); total coastline, 310 kilometers (193 miles).

came a Russian protectorate in 1783. All of Georgia was absorbed directly in the Russian empire during the 19th century.

During the tumult of the Russian revolution, Georgia declared its independence on 26 May 1918. Twenty-two countries recognized this new state, including Soviet Russia. Nonetheless, the Soviet Red Army invaded in February 1921 and Georgia's brief independence came to an end.

Many Georgians fell victim in the late 1920s and 1930s to Soviet collectivization, crash industrialization, and Stalin's purges (despite his Georgian-Ossetian ethnic origins). Nationalist riots were brutally suppressed in 1924 and 1956, and nationalist mass demonstrations occurred in 1978 and 1988. In April 1989, many Georgian demonstrators were murdered, some with shovels, by Soviet military and police forces during a peaceful protest against perceived Russian support for Abkhaz autonomy demands.

Georgia's first multiparty legislative elections, held in October 1990, resulted in a victory for the party coalition Round Table-Free Georgia, headed by academic and dissident Zviad Gamsakhurdia. He was subsequently selected by the deputies to serve as chairman of the legislature. Following a March 1991 referendum, a formal declaration of independence was unanimously ap-

proved by the legislature on April 9. Gamsakhurdia was popularly elected as president in May, but still faced opposition from, among others, parties belonging to the National Congress, a national liberation body formed in October 1990. The Mkhedrioni paramilitary group, led by Jaba Ioseliani, was allied with the National Congress. During 1991, Gamsakhurdia's erratic attempts to remake Georgian society and politics caused the head of the National Guard, Tengiz Kitovani, to also join the opposition. The National Guard and Mkhedrioni spearheaded a general assault to overthrow Gamsakhurdia in December 1991, forcing him to flee the country in early January 1992.

A military council formed by Ioseliani, Kitovani, and others assumed power, suspending the Soviet-era constitution (and replacing it with one from 1921), dissolving the legislature, and declaring emergency rule. Former Georgian leader Eduard Shevardnadze (the Communist Party boss of Georgia from 1972 to 1985) was invited in early March 1992 to head a provisional government. He formed a civilian State Council to rule until elections could be held, and was elected head of its four-member presidium. During legislative elections in October 1992, he was elected speaker in an uncontested race. The new legislature granted Shevardnadze wide-ranging powers as head of state pending completion of a new constitution. In May 1993, Shevardnadze moved to consolidate his power by securing the resignations of Kitovani and Ioseliani from government posts. Gamsakhurdia returned from exile in September 1993 to the western Georgian region of Mingrelia and led a revolt to unseat Shevardnadze. Pro-Shevardnadze forces, assisted by the Russian military, were able to put down the revolt by early November 1993. Gamsakhurdia's death was reported in early January 1994. In further moves by Shevardnadze to consolidate power, Kitovani was arrested in January 1995 for planning an illegal paramilitary attack on Abkhazia, and he neutralized Ioseliani's Mkhedrioni.

Several of Georgia's ethnic minorities stepped up their dissident and separatist actions in the late 1980s and early 1990s. South Ossetians in 1989 called for their territory to be joined with North Ossetia in Russia, or for independence. Repressive efforts by former Georgian president Gamsakhurdia triggered conflict in 1990, reportedly leading to about 1,500 deaths and 50,000 displaced persons, mostly ethnic Georgians. In June 1992, Russian president Boris Yeltsin brokered a cease-fire, and a predominantly Russian military "peacekeeping" force numbering about 500 was stationed in South Ossetia. A coordinating commission on settlement of the Georgian-Ossetian conflict, composed of OSCE, Russian, Georgian, and North and South Ossetian emissaries, meets regularly, but rapprochement remains elusive. The November 1999 OSCE Summit Declaration urged Georgia and South Ossetia to agree on resettling displaced persons and called for international aid for the region. In his state of the nation speech on 9 February 2000, Shevardnadze praised the Russian peacekeepers and successes in reconciliation between ethnic Ossetians and Georgians.

Georgia's southern Ajaria region is to a large extent self-governing, under conditions resembling a police state. Ajaria's authorities claim that regional laws take precedence over national laws, and Shevardnadze has had to undertake extensive negotiations to establish national law in the region.

The Abkhaz conflict has resulted in about 10,000 deaths and over 200,000 refugees and displaced persons, mostly ethnic Georgians. In July 1992, the Abkhaz Supreme Soviet declared its effective independence from Georgia. This prompted Georgian national guardsmen to attack Abkhazia. In October 1992, the UN Security Council (UNSC) approved the first UN observer mission to a NIS state, termed UNOMIG, to help reach a settlement. In September 1993, Russian and North Caucasian "volunteer" troops that reportedly made up the bulk of Abkhaz separatist forces broke a cease-fire and quickly routed Georgian forces. Abkhaz-Georgian talks leading to a cease-fire were held under UN auspices, with the participation of Russia and the OSCE. In April 1994, the two sides signed framework accords on a political settlement and on the return of refugees and displaced persons. A Quadripartite Commission was set up to discuss repatriation, composed of Abkhaz and Georgian representatives and emissaries from Russia and the UN High Commissioner for Refugees. The next month, a cease-fire was signed by Georgia and Abkhazia, providing for Russian troops (acting as Commonwealth of Independent States or CIS peacekeepers) to be deployed in a security zone along the Enguri River, which divides Abkhazia from the rest of Georgia. The Russian Defense Ministry in 1999 reported the deployment of about 1,700 peacekeepers.

A major point of contention between the two sides is Georgia's demand that displaced persons be allowed to return to Abkhazia, after which an agreement on broad autonomy for Abkhazia may be negotiated. The Abkhazians have insisted upon recognition of their "equal status" with Georgia as a precondition to large-scale repatriation. The CIS in 1997–1998 endorsed Shevardnadze's call for creating a special Abkhaz-Georgian administration, with UN and OSCE participation, to first seek peace in Abkhazia's Gali area, and to expand the security zone and give Russian peacekeepers police powers. Abkhazia refused to countenance changing the peacekeeping mandate. Although Shevardnadze has criticized the failures of the Russian peacekeepers, in February 2000 he stated that he saw no alternative to their presence, since no other international forces have come forward.

After a hiatus of two years, UN-sponsored peace talks were reconvened in mid-1997. In late 1997, the sides agreed to set up a Coordinating Council to discuss cease-fire maintenance and refugee, economic, and humanitarian issues. Coordinating Council talks and those of the Quadripartite Commission have been supplemented by direct discussions between an envoy from Vladislav Ardzinba, whom Abkhazian separatists have elected as their president, and the Georgian State Secretary. Abkhaz forces in mid-1998 reportedly expelled 30,000–40,000 ethnic Georgians who resided in the Gali area. In June 1999 in Istanbul, the two sides agreed to resume contacts they had cut off the year before, and a working group agreed to implement the separation of warring forces.

In November 1995, Eduard Shevardnadze was elected to the re-created post of president, receiving 74.32% of the vote in a six-person race, and a new parliament was selected. International observers termed the elections generally free and fair nationwide except in the region of Ajaria.

Seven candidates were registered to run in Georgia's 9 April 2000 presidential election. The major challengers to Shevardnadze were Jumbar Patiashvili, former first secretary of the Georgian Communist Party (who ran in the 1995 presidential race), and Aslan Abashidze, chairman of the Ajarian Supreme Council. Both challengers were leaders of the Revival Bloc that contested the 1999 legislative races. Abashidze did not actively campaign and withdrew from the race one day before the vote, alleging an unfair contest. Other speculation was that he withdrew in return for concessions from Shevardnadze on local power and finances. Voting did not take place in Abkhazia or South Ossetia. The Georgian Central Election Commission (CEC) reported that Shevardnadze received 80% of 1.87 million votes and Patiashvili received 17% (less than he received in 1995). The 150 OSCE monitors reported on April 10 that the election did not meet OSCE standards, though "fundamental freedoms were generally respected during the election campaign and candidates were able to express their views." They stressed that the government aided the incumbent, state media were biased, vote counting and tabulation procedures lacked uniformity and, at times, transparency, ballot box stuffing had taken place, and some voting protocols reportedly had been tampered with.

In March 2001, officials from Georgia and Abkhazia signed an accord stating they would not use force against one another. However, meetings between the two sides were cancelled later in the year due to continuing hostilities and hostage incidents. On 8 October 2001, a UNOMIG helicopter was shot down over Abkhazia, and all nine people on board were killed. As of February 2003, those responsible for the downing had not been identified. In August 2002, Georgia and Abkhazia failed to come to an agreement on the withdrawal of Abkhaz fighters from the Kodori Gorge, the only enclave controlled by Georgia in Abkhazia. Georgia was concerned that Russians were supporting the Abkhaz fighters. In January 2003, UN Secretary-General Kofi Annan declared little progress had been made on talks to determine the future status of Abkhazia, and that the mandate for UNOMIG should be extended another six months, until 31 July 2003.

Upon coming into his second term in office, Shevardnadze claimed he would fight corruption and low living standards, undertake market reforms, and protect the territorial integrity of Georgia. Georgia desired NATO membership, and on 22 November 2002, Shevardnadze formally requested that Georgia be invited into the alliance. Russia did not immediately react to the announcement. In 1999, the OSCE demanded that Russia remove all of its troops from Georgia. In 2001, Russia vacated the Gudauta and Vaziani bases and the Marneuli military airfield, but did not agree to a time frame for a departure from the Akhalkalaki and Batumi military bases. One sore spot in Georgian-Russian relations remains the situation in Chechnya. Russian officials have accused Georgia of aiding Chechen rebels, especially in the Pankisi Gorge region of Georgia. Russia regards the armed conflict in Chechnya as a part of the international campaign against terrorism, and has demanded Georgia cooperate in combating Chechens in the region. In September 2002, Russia warned Georgia that it would take military action if Georgia failed to deal with Chechen rebels in the Pankisi Gorge. The United States, since 11 September 2001, has claimed that members of the al-Qaeda organization are operating in the Pankisi Gorge, and has enlisted Georgia's support in undertaking antiterror operations there. In April and May 2002, US Special Forces arrived in Georgia to train and equip troops for counterterrorist operations. On 8 February 2003, Russia claimed that terrorists recently arrested in Great Britain and France had trained in the Pankisi Gorge, and used laboratories built there to produce the poisonous toxin ricin that can be used as an agent in chemical warfare.

The end of 2003 brought with it drastic changes for Georgians. The parliamentary elections that were held on 2 November 2003 were criticized by national and international organizations as being grossly rigged. Mikhail Saakashvili, who received a law degree from Columbia University and worked in the United States for a short while, denounced the election results and urged the population of Georgia to nonviolent civil disobedience against the authorities. People responded to Saakashvili's call and mounted protests in T'bilisi (the so-called "Rose Revolution"), crying for fair elections. (The "Rose Revolution" inspired similar movements in other parts of the world, most notably in Ukraine where the "Orange Revolution" brought about long awaited change.) President Shevardnadze eventually bowed down under the pressure, and on 23 November 2003 resigned from his post, leaving parliamentary speaker Nino Burjanadze in charge until fresh presidential elections could be staged. This move was followed by a decision of the Supreme Court to annul the parliamentary elections results.

On 4 January 2004, Saakashvili emerged victorious in the presidential elections—he received support from all the opposition parties and garnered a 96.3% of the votes. His party, the National Movement-Democratic Front, subsequently won 67.6% of the votes (and 135 out of 150 party list seats in parliament) in the rerun of the parliamentary elections; the Rightist Opposition got 7.6% (15 seats), while other parties received less than 7%. The new prime minister was Zurab Noghaideli.

This victory, however, came in a context where Georgia was very politically, socially, and economically unstable. Aslan Abashidze, the leader of the Ajarian Autonomous Republic in western Georgia, accused Saakashvili of planning to invade Ajaria and declared a state of emergency and the mobilization of armed forces. He failed to attract support from Russia though, and intense criticism from several foreign governments and international organizations forced him to resign in May 2004 and leave for Moscow. These events were followed by tensions in the other two problematic regions—South Ossetia and Abkhazia. Parliamentary elections in South Ossetia in May 2004, and troubled presidential elections in Abkhazia in October 2004, were not recognized by the government in T'bilisi. A proposal on autonomy for South Ossetia presented by Saakashvili was consequently refused by the South Ossetian leaders who asked for full independence.

In May 2005, George W. Bush became the first US president to visit Georgia. That same month, the Baku-T'bilisi-Ceyhan pipeline was officially opened, with US secretary of energy Samuel Bodman joining the presidents of Kazakhstan, Azerbaijan, Georgia, and Turkey at the opening ceremony. A year later, oil began flowing through the pipeline.

13 GOVERNMENT

Until 1995, Georgia was governed according to a constitution dating back to 1921. Shevardnadze, though, pushed for the adoption of a new constitution giving the president added powers. A new constitution was approved by the legislature in August 1995. It reestablishes a strong presidency, though affirming a balance of executive and legislative powers more equitable than those in most other new constitutions approved by former Soviet republics. The president is elected for a five-year term. The constitution establishes a unicameral, 235-member legislature elected by single-mandate constituencies (85 seats) and party lists (150 seats). Legislators serve four-year terms. Government ministers are responsible to the president, who is assisted by a state minister. Shevardnadze in December 1999 decreed enhanced powers for the state minister "equal to those of a prime minister." The speaker's only constitutional powers are to sign bills and serve as acting president in case the president is indisposed or dies. The legislature agreed that federal provisions would be added to the constitution after Georgia's territorial integrity has been assured. The breakaway regions of South Ossetia and Abkhazia are currently not under the control of the central government, and Ajaria is at least partly self-governing.

Voting for the new legislature took place on 5 November 1995, simultaneous with the presidential race. Only three of the 54 parties running received at least 5% of the party list vote required to win seats, though other parties won representation through constituency races; they have formed eight legislative factions. The elections were judged "consistent with democratic norms" by international observers.

Legislative elections were held in the spring of 2004. Voting was by party lists (150 seats) and single-member constituencies (73 seats; 12 sitting members representing separatist Abkhaz districts were allowed to retain their seats). Fifteen parties and blocs were registered but only two parties received at least 7% of the vote needed to gain party list seats (the new minimum was approved in July 1999). The National Movement-Democratic Front won 135 seats; the Rightist Opposition won 15.

¹⁴POLITICAL PARTIES

Major political parties that won representation in the legislature elected in 1999, based on their share of the party list voting, included Shevardnadze's Georgian Citizens' Union (gaining 891,000 of 2.1 million party list votes cast), Ajarian leader Abashidze's pro-government Revival Union (537,000 votes), and Industry Will Save Georgia (151,000 votes). The Georgian Labor Party just failed to gain enough votes to win party list seats (141,000 votes). Other parties that gained more than 1% of the party list vote included the opposition National Democratic Party (NDP; it won the second-largest number of such seats in 1995), the People's Party, and the United Communist Party. Most of the minor political parties and groups characterized themselves as opposed to the government.

In November 2003, former President Eduard Shevardnadze resigned from office in a bloodless "Rose Revolution" following protests against his rule and what were seen to be fraudulent parliamentary elections. The election results were later annulled. Presidential elections were held on 4 January 2004, and Mikhail Saakashvili was elected president. His party, the National Movement-Democratic Front, won 135 seats out of the 150 that are on the party lists; the Rightist Opposition won the other 15.

¹⁵LOCAL GOVERNMENT

Georgia's administrative subdivisions include the Abkhazian and Ajarian Autonomous Republics. The Georgian Supreme Soviet stripped South Ossetia of its autonomous status in late 1990, following its demands to secede and become a part of Russia. Abkhazia and South Ossetia consider themselves self-ruling, and Ajaria has substantial effective autonomy. There are 53 districts (*rayons*) and 11 cities, whose governors or mayors are appointed by the president. Local assembly (*sakrebulo*) elections were held for the first time under the new constitution in November 1998. Thirteen parties participated in the voting for more than 150,000 candidates for 10,000 municipal and district (*rayon*) assemblies or councils. In small towns and villages of fewer than 2,000 voters, 654 majoritarian elections were held, while elsewhere 377 proportional elections by party lists took place. The Citizen's Union Party won the largest number of seats, followed by the Revival bloc, the National Democratic Party, and the Labor Party, though 12 of the 13 parties won some seats. Inadequate funding and the absence of legislation limited the functions of the new locally elected governments. Opposition parties accused the government and the ruling Citizens' Union Party of retaining the effective power to appoint the mayors of the largest cities and the regional leaders. There remains considerable contention between the central government and the Autonomous Ajarian Republic over the scope of local powers.

Local elections were held on 2 June 2002, and 4774 *sakrebulo* seats in regional Georgia were decided, along with 49 seats in T'bilisi. Independents won 2,749 of the regional seats, with the New Right Party taking 544 seats; Industry Will Save Georgia taking 478 seats; and the Revival Party/21st Century Bloc taking 195

seats. The Citizens' Union of Georgia won only 69 seats in a major defeat, faring poorly in both T'bilisi and the regions. This was attributed to a split between the two main factions of the party prior to the elections, both of which strove for the right to campaign as the CUG. The conservative faction won the right to campaign as the CUG in the week prior to the elections, and the reformist faction campaigned as the Christian Conservative Party.

¹⁶JUDICIAL SYSTEM

Before 1995, Georgia's legal system retained traces of the pre-Soviet era, the Soviet period, the Gamsakhurdia presidency, and the State Council period. Courts included district courts, a T'bilisi city court, a supreme court in each of the two autonomous republics, and at the highest level the Supreme Court of the Republic.

The 1995 constitution provides for an independent judiciary. However, the judiciary is subject to some executive pressure and pressure from extensive family and clan networks. The Law on Common Courts, passed in 1997, establishes a three-tier court system. District courts hear petty criminal and civil cases. Regional courts of appeal have original and appellate jurisdiction. They try major criminal and civil cases, review cases, and can remand cases to the lower court for retrial. The Supreme Court was envisioned as the highest appellate court, but it also hears some capital cases and appeals from the Central Electoral Commission.

A constitutional court was set up in September 1996. It arbitrates constitutional disputes between the branches of government and rules on individual claims of human rights abuses.

Administration of the court system was transferred from the Justice Ministry to a Council of Justice in 1997, to increase the independence of the courts from budgetary and other influence. The council consists of four members from each of the three branches of government.

The constitution provides for the rights to presumption of innocence, to have a public trial, to legal counsel, and to refuse to make a statement in the absence of counsel. A criminal procedures code was approved in November 1997, and a new criminal code was passed in June 1999. The criminal procedures code aimed at reducing the dominant power of prosecutors over arrests and investigations. Under the new procedures, judges issue warrants for arrest and detention orders, and detentions must follow correct legal procedures, including informing detainees of their rights, allowing visits by family members and lawyers, and treating detainees without brutality. In mid-1999, however, some of the liberal strictures on defendants' rights were reversed at the insistence of the prosecutors, who continue to have a major influence over the courts.

Under the Law on Common Courts, Georgia has launched a system of testing judges on basic legal principles; many of those who have taken the test have failed. Georgia's accession to the Council of Europe in April 1999 led to new legislation taking jurisdiction over the prison system away from the Interior (police) Ministry and giving it to the Ministry of Justice.

¹⁷ARMED FORCES

Georgia had a total of 11,320 active personnel in its armed forces as of 2005, supported by 1,578 reservists in the National Guard. The Army was the largest force in terms of manpower, with 7,042 active personnel. The Navy and the Air Force each had 1,350 active members. The Army had 86 main battle tanks, 89 armored infantry fighting vehicles, 91 armored personnel carriers, and 109 artillery pieces. Major naval units included 11 patrol/coastal vessels and six amphibious landing craft. The Air Force had seven combat capable aircraft that included six fighter ground attack aircraft, plus another used in a training capacity. The service also operated three attack helicopters. Paramiltary troops numbered 11,700, including 6,300 Ministry of Interior troops and 5,400 border guards. Georgian armed forces were deployed to Iraq in a peacekeeping support role, and under NATO in Serbia and Montenegro. There are also troops from 25 countries in Georgia acting as observers and in a peacekeeping role. The nation's defense budget in 2005 totaled $44 million.

18 INTERNATIONAL COOPERATION

Georgia was admitted to the United Nations on 21 July 1992. The country is a member of several UN specialized agencies, such as the FAO, IAEA, ICAO, IFAD, ILO, IMF, UNCTAD, UNESCO, UNIDO, WHO, and the World Bank. Georgia joined the Commonwealth of Independent State (CIS) in 1993 and became a member of the WTO in 2000. The nation also belongs to the OSCE, the Council of Europe, the Black Sea Economic Cooperation Zone, the Euro-Atlantic Partnership Council, and the European Bank for Reconstruction and Development. Georgia has observer status in the OAS and is part of the NATO Partnership for Peace. In 2001, Georgia, Uzbekistan, Ukraine, Azerbaijan, and Moldova formed a social and economic development union known as GUAAM. Uzbekistan withdrew from the partnership in 2005.

In 1993, a UN Observer Mission (UNOMIG) was established in Georgia to monitor cease-fire agreements between the State of Georgia and the region of Abkhazia and to support ongoing CIS peacekeeping forces in that region. About 23 countries offer support for UNOMIG.

In environmental cooperation, Georgia is part of the Basel Convention, Conventions on Biological Diversity and Air Pollution, Ramsar, CITES, the Kyoto Protocol, the Montréal Protocol, MARPOL, and the UN Conventions on the Law of the Sea, Climate Change and Desertification.

19 ECONOMY

Over a decade after its emergence from the Soviet Union as an independent state, Georgia's economy has not fully recovered from the hyperinflation and economic collapse that by 1994 had reduced its GDP to 20% of its 1990 levels. In 2002 its GDP levels were still only at 40% of what they were in the 1980s. Continued civil strife and unresolved separatist struggles with Abkhazia and South Ossetia have combined with pervasive corruption, tax evasion, and a "shadow economy" larger than the legitimate one to stifle the country's economic progress. Shortfalls in revenues have caused the government to turn to external as well as domestic financing to cover chronic budget deficits. Foreign borrowing has in turn led to balance of payments problems and resort to IMF facilities. Georgia has entered into three programs with the IMF since independence. A short standby arrangement, June 1995 to February 1996, was followed on expiration by a multi-year program under the Extended Structural Adjustment Facility (ESAF), which was in effect to 13 August 1999 when the IMF withdrew due to the failure of Georgia to meet budgetary targets. In January 2001, a revised program with more realistic targets was approved under the Poverty Reduction and Growth Facility (PRGF). In March 2001, having an IMF-supervised program underway, Georgia was able to reach an agreement with the Paris Club for rescheduling some of its sovereign debt owed to Paris Club members. From May to October 2001, the IMF again suspended disbursements to Georgia because of its failure to meet the program's conditionals. The 2001 PRGF program was scheduled to expire in January 2004; the government sought and was awarded a new three-year PRGF in June 2004.

Georgia's mild climate makes it an important agricultural producer, raising a growing range of subtropical crops (including tea, tobacco, citrus fruits, and flowers) in the coastal region and exporting them to the northern republics in return for manufactured goods. Georgia supplied almost all of the former Soviet Union's citrus fruits and tea, and much of its grape crop.

In 1996, the government embarked on a program for the privatization of land holdings. The country also has deposits of manganese, coal, iron ore, and lead, plus a skilled, educated work force. There were several oil refineries operating at the Black Sea port of Batumi. Since low points in 1994 and 1995, there has been sustained growth, although not in all sectors, and inflation has been brought substantially under control. Inflation fell from 163% (consumer prices) in 1995 to 39% in 1996 and 7% in 1997. The growth in GDP reached double digits, 11.2% (1996) and 10.6% (1997), stimulated in part by work on the Baku-Supsa pipeline (opened in April 1999). Since 1998, however, GDP growth slowed to about 3% a year due a combination of the effect of economic crises in Russia and Turkey (which together supply 40% of Georgia's imports and buy over 40% of its exports), an influx of refugees since 1999 from neighboring war-torn Chechnya, severe droughts affecting Georgia's agricultural output in 1998 and 2000, and, from 2001, the global economic slowdown. In 1998, overall GDP growth slowed to 3%, as agricultural production dropped 10% and industrial production dropped 2%. Growth remained at only 3% in 1999. GDP growth was even lower (2%) in 2000, despite 11% growth in industrial production, due to a recurrence of drought which caused agricultural production to fall 15% in one year.

In 2001, agriculture recovered somewhat, growing 6%, but industrial production fell back 5%, reflecting in part an 11% decrease in exports to countries outside the CIS. Exports to CIS countries, by contrast, rose 23% in 2000 and 9% in 2001. Georgia official statistics report that the GDP grew overall by 4.5% in 2001, while the US CIA estimated growth at 8.4%. Inflation, which spurted to 19% in 1999, fell to moderate levels of between 4% and 5% in 2000 and 2001.

In 2002, the economy was hampered by the necessity of importing over 90% of the petroleum products consumed due to the shutting down of its only two remaining refineries. The larger 106,000-barrels-per-day refinery at Batumi was closed for modernization and expansion under an agreement with Japan's Mitsui Corp. A small 4,000 barrels-per-day refinery, built in 1998 and idle for much of 2001, was closed permanently in 2002 by its operation company, CanArgo, in favor of a plan to replace it with a larger 30,100-barrels-per-day facility. Georgia's future economic prospects were thought to have improved greatly in December 2002 however, with the announcement of an agreement on the Georgia portion of the Baku-T'bilisi-Ceyhan (BTC) pipe-line, which opened in May 2005. In addition to the BTC project, which is to pipe oil from the Caspian Sea to the Turkish port of Ceyhan on the Mediterranean to supply Western European markets, Georgia and Turkey concluded another agreement to build a railway from T'bilisi to Kars, Turkey. The railway would transport oil to Turkish refineries. Plans also exist to develop Georgia into a transit center for natural gas.

The economy experienced an explosive expansion in 2003, with a GDP growth rate of 11.1%. The economy cooled down in 2004, growing by 6.2%, but was expected to pick up again in 2005, with a projected growth rate of around 8.0%. The inflation rate was stable, fluctuating between 4% and 6%. As such, inflation did not pose a problem to the overall economy, although it was expected to rise in 2005 to 8.5%. The "Rose Revolution" in 2003 brought hope that the economy would take a turn for the better by emulating a Western development pattern. The Baku-T'bilisi-Ceyhan oil pipe lines and the Baku-T'bilisi-Erzerum gas pipe lines have brought much needed investment into the country and helped alleviate the chronic unemployment. However, Georgia's energy sector was still dependent on imports from Russia as of 2005, and its market needed heavy restructuring before it could reach functional economy status.

20 INCOME

The US Central Intelligence Agency (CIA) reports that in 2005 Georgia's gross domestic product (GDP) was estimated at $16.1 billion. The CIA defines GDP as the value of all final goods and services produced within a nation in a given year and computed on the basis of purchasing power parity (PPP) rather than value as measured on the basis of the rate of exchange based on current dollars. The per capita GDP was estimated at $3,400. The annual growth rate of GDP was estimated at 10%. The average inflation rate in 2005 was 8%. It was estimated that agriculture accounted for 16% of GDP, industry 26.8%, and services 57.2%.

According to the World Bank, in 2003 remittances from citizens working abroad totaled $246 million or about $54 per capita and accounted for approximately 6.2% of GDP. Foreign aid receipts amounted to $220 million or about $43 per capita and accounted for approximately 5.5% of the gross national income (GNI).

The World Bank reports that in 2003 household consumption in Georgia totaled $3.12 billion or about $684 per capita based on a GDP of $4.0 billion, measured in current dollars rather than PPP. Household consumption includes expenditures of individuals, households, and nongovernmental organizations on goods and services, excluding purchases of dwellings. It was estimated that for the period 1990 to 2003 household consumption grew at an average annual rate of 4.5%. In 2001 it was estimated that approximately 33% of household consumption was spent on food, 13% on fuel, 2% on health care, and 4% on education. It was estimated that in 2001 about 54% of the population had incomes below the poverty line.

21 LABOR

The labor force was estimated at 2.1 million in 2001 (the latest year for which data was available). Agriculture provided work to 40% of the labor force, with another 40% engaged in services and

the remaining 20% in industry. The estimated unemployment rate was 17% in 2001.

Employees have the right to form or join unions freely. A confederation of independent trade unions has emerged with the abandonment of the old centralized Soviet trade unions. Georgia's main trade union is the Amalgamated Trade Unions of Georgia. Workers are permitted to engage in collective bargaining, but this practice is not extensive.

The minimum employment age is 16 except in unusual circumstances, and this minimum employment age is generally respected. The government sets public-sector salaries dependent on the pay grade of the employee. The lowest such wage was $10.80 per month in 2002. There is no state prescribed minimum wage for the private sector. In general, wages and salaries do not provide a decent standard of living for a family. The legal standard workweek is 41 hours with a 24-hour rest period weekly.

22 AGRICULTURE

About 15% of Georgia's total land area was considered arable in 2003. Since independence in April 1991, Georgian agriculture has become much more associated with the private sector; 99% of agricultural land is now privately held. In 2003, agriculture accounted for an estimated 20% of GDP.

During the Soviet era, Georgia produced almost the entire citrus and tea crop and most of the grape crop for the entire Soviet Union. In 2004, production levels (in thousands of tons) included corn, 410; wheat, 186; barley, 61; tea, 24; vegetables and melons, 490; and grapes, 180.

23 ANIMAL HUSBANDRY

Meadows and pastures account for about 30% of the Georgian land area. In 2005, the livestock population included cattle, 1,250,000; sheep, 689,000; pigs, 484,000; buffaloes, 35,000; horses, 44,000; and chickens, 9,100,000. Beef production in 2005 totaled some 51,000 tons; pork, 35,000 tons; and chicken, 15,000 tons. About 781,000 tons of milk were produced in 2005, as were 31,500 tons of eggs.

In mid-1993, a ban was placed on the export of dairy products (including milk), cattle and poultry, meat and meat products, and leather. Georgia does not produce enough meat and dairy products to satisfy domestic demand. Meat imports in 2004 exceeded $19.7 million.

24 FISHING

The Black Sea and Kura River are the main sources of the domestic catch. The total catch in 2003 was about 3,361 tons, with marine fishing accounting for 97%. Anchovies made up 67% of the total catch in 2003. Commercial fishing is not a significant contributor to the economy.

25 FORESTRY

About 44% of Georgia is covered with forests or woodlands, but the mountainous terrain inhibits forestry production. Timber production is primarily for domestic use; exports of forestry products amounted to only $17.9 million in 2003.

26MINING

Georgia had significant mineral deposits, but the future of the industry depended on a more secure climate for investment, through greater political and economic stability. Manganese was the country's foremost mineral commodity in the Soviet era, producing 5 million tons in the mid-1980s; production has since fallen precipitously, reaching 59,100 metric tons in 2000, but had increased to an estimated 80,000 metric tons in 2002. Manganese came from the Chiat'ura basin; reserves of high-grade ore were almost depleted.

The Madneuli region was a major site of barite, copper, lead-zinc, gold, and silver mining. Lead and zinc were mined at the Kvaisi deposit, and arsenic was mined from the Lukhumi and Tsansa deposits. In 1995, the Georgian State Geology Committee, Gruzgeologiya, stated that Georgia had gold reserves of 250 tons and silver reserves of 1,500 tons, with another 250 tons of prospective gold reserves.

In 1996, Georgia permitted foreign firms to manage metallurgical enterprises. The Zestafoni ferroalloy plant was signed over to the Russian-Georgian Bank for Reconstruction and Development in conjunction with a US partner, North Atlantic Research, to be managed for a period of 10 years.

Mine output of copper was 8,000 metric tons in 2002. In that same year, gold output was estimated at 2,000 kg, and for silver, an estimated 33,000 kg. Also produced in 2002 were mine lead, barite, bentonite, mine zinc, and cement.

27ENERGY AND POWER

Georgia must rely on imports for most of its energy needs. Its limited oil reserves were placed at about 30 million barrels in 2003. The country produced 2,000 barrels per day in 2004, much less than the 42,200 barrels of oil it consumed each day that same year. However, oil exploration is actively being carried out both on land and along the Black Sea coast. Most of the oil comes primarily from Azerbaijan, and Russia. Natural gas reserves in 2003 were placed at 0.3 trillion cu ft, with production and consumption at 0.6 billion cu ft and at 35.3 billion cu ft, respectively in that year.

Georgia has two oil refineries, a 106,000-barrel-per-day (bpd) facility at Batumi and a smaller refinery at Sartichala. Georgia plans on utilizing its Black Sea ports to become a significant transshipment point for oil produced by Azerbaijan (and the other republics of central Asia). On 8 March 1996, Georgia and Azerbaijan signed a 30-year agreement to pump a portion of the oil produced in the Azeri waters of the Caspian Sea to the Georgian port of Suspa. From there, the oil will be shipped across the Black Sea to western markets via Turkey. The pipeline along this route became operational in April 1999 following substantial upgrades. Additionally, improved ties with Iran will reduce dependence on energy imports from Russia, from which Georgia is trying to distance itself economically.

Deteriorating plants and equipment prevent Georgia's power sector from operating at full capacity, and power outages are common in many areas of the country. As with its imports of natural gas, Georgia is in arrears in paying for the electricity it has been obliged to import from Armenia, Azerbaijan, and Russia. The country has substantial untapped hydroelectric potential, however, and is planning to build two new hydroelectric plants on the Rioni River and a third, the 40-MW Minadze station, on the Kura River. In 2003, electricity production amounted to 6.7 billion kWh. In 2002, hydropower accounted for 83% of the electricity produced and 16.6% was from fossil fuel. Installed capacity in 2003 was 4.4 GW, with consumption at 6.8 billion kWh for that year. The two major power plants are a thermal plant at T'bilisi (with a capacity of 1,280,000 kW) and the Enguri hydroelectric plant (with a 1,325,000 kW capacity). Consumption of electricity in 2000 totaled 7.9 billion kWh.

Georgia is one of the 12 former Soviet republics to found the Intergovernmental Council on Oil and Gas (ICOG), which stresses international cooperation in the oil and natural gas industry and will entitle members to receive Russian energy resources in exchange for investment in Russia's oil and natural gas industries.

28INDUSTRY

Heavy industry, based on the country's mineral resources, predominates, and includes metallurgy, construction materials, and machine building. Light industry includes food processing, beverage production, consumer durables, garments, and oil-processing. Hyperinflation in 1994 together with continuing political unrest severely affected industrial production. By 1995, industrial output of state enterprises was one-fifth of the 1990 level.

In 1996, although industrial production rose 6% for the year, less than 20% of the country's industries were operating, most at less than 15% of capacity. In 1997 another improvement of 7% was recorded, but in 1998, due mainly to the financial crisis in Russia, industrial production fell 2%. By the end of 1998, the privatization of small businesses was largely completed, with over 12,860 becoming privately owned. Among the large state enterprises, about 1,200 had been changed into joint stock companies, 910 of which have since been privatized.

Despite a model legal framework for the privatization of its enterprises, industry in Georgia had only been 15.2% privatized as of 2002, with the construction industry at about 18.5%, mainly because of a lack of buyers. The least privatized sector is energy, where, according to a recent USAID assessment, the infrastructure borders on catastrophic failure.

Growth in industrial production returned in 1999 and 2000, at 7% and 11%, respectively, but in 2001, there was a decline of 5%, due, externally, to declining export demand in non-CIS countries, and, internally, to the shutdown of most of Georgia's refinery production. Before independence, Georgia had several refineries, but by 2001, it had only two: one at the Black Sea port of Batumi with a 106,000 b/d capacity, and the other, a small 4,000 b/d refinery built in 1998 near CanArgo's Ninotsminda oil field called the Georgian-American Oil Refinery (GAOR).

In 2001, the GAOR operated only between July and September, and at less than 50% capacity. In September 2001, CanArgo shut it down, announcing plans to build a $200 million refinery in its place that would have a 30,100 b/d capacity. In 2002, the Batumi refinery was also closed, undergoing a $250 million upgrade and expansion directed by the Mitsui Corporation. As a result, Georgia has been obliged to import over 90% of its petroleum products.

Mitsui has undertaken the work without Georgian government guarantees of its investment. The lack of such guarantees caused two other Japanese companies, Marubeni and JGC, to drop out of the project. Georgia's most promising industrial development came in December 2002, when agreement was announced for the construction of Georgia's part of the Baku-T'bilisi-Ceyhan (BTC) pipeline; the pipeline was officially opened on 25 May 2005.

Industry accounted for 26.8% of overall economic output in 2005, and it was the sector with the smallest representation in the working population; agriculture and services were by far the largest employers (both with an approximate equal representation in the labor force—40%), although they achieved different productivity levels—agriculture accounted for 16% of the GDP, while services came in first with 57.2%. Current important industries include steel, aircraft, machine tools, electrical appliances, mining (manganese and copper), chemicals, wood products, and wine.

29 SCIENCE AND TECHNOLOGY

The Georgian Academy of Sciences has departments of mathematics and physics, earth sciences, applied mechanics, machine building, and control processes, chemistry and chemical technology, agricultural science problems, biology, and physiology and experimental medicine. Georgia has 44 research institutes, many attached to the academy, conducting research concerning agriculture, fisheries, and veterinary science; and medicine, natural sciences, and technology. The academy's Sukhumi Botanical Garden is maintained at Chavchavadze. The Scientific and Technical Library of Georgia, with more than 10 million volumes in 1996, is located in T'bilisi. Eight colleges and universities offer degrees in basic and applied sciences. In 1987–97, science and engineering students accounted for 39% of university enrollment.

In 2002, research and development spending totaled $33.702 million, or 0.29% of GDP. As of that same year, high technology exports totaled $41 million, or 38% of all manufactured exports. As of 2002, there were 2,317 researchers and 241 technicians per million people actively engaged in R&D.

30 DOMESTIC TRADE

The war in Abkhazia severely disrupted domestic trade in 1993 and hyperinflation in 1994 led to widespread fighting in the nation and catastrophic economic decline. Economic conditions began to improve by the mid-1990s following the influx of foreign aid. Agriculture continues to be a primary basis for the domestic economy. The fastest growing segment of the economy, however, is in services, which accounted for about 55% of the GDP in 2002. Small privately owned shops are still more prevalent than supermarkets or larger retail establishments. Business hours are generally from 9 AM to 6 PM, Monday through Friday.

31 FOREIGN TRADE

Traditionally Georgia has been heavily dependent on Russia for power, bridges, roads, and other economic essentials. In return, Georgia sends Russia fruit, wine, and other agricultural products. Georgia's current government, however, is pursuing closer links with the EU and Turkey.

In 2005, exports reached $1.4 billion (FOB—Free on Board), while imports grew to $2.5 billion (FOB). The bulk of exports went to Turkey (18.3%), Turkmenistan (17.8%), Russia (16.2%), Arme-

---

Principal Trading Partners – Georgia (2003)

(In millions of US dollars)

Country	Exports	Imports	Balance
World	475.5	1,135.4	-659.9
Russia	84.0	155.3	-71.3
Turkey	82.4	112.1	-29.7
Turkmenistan	58.4	9.9	48.5
Armenia	41.1	12.0	29.1
Switzerland-Liechtenstein	33.3	14.5	18.8
Ukraine	30.2	80.3	-50.1
United Kingdom	27.9	145.6	-117.7
Azerbaijan	16.6	93.8	-77.2
United States	15.4	90.8	-75.4
Netherlands	9.9	22.3	-12.4

(…) data not available or not significant.

SOURCE: *2003 International Trade Statistics Yearbook*, New York: United Nations, 2004.

---

nia (8.4%), the United Kingdom (4.9%), and Azerbaijan (3.9%). Principal exports were ferro alloys, copper and gold, ferrous waste and scrap, iron and steel, wine, and mineral water. Imports included oil, gas, electricity, tubes and pipes, and automotives, and mainly came from Russia (14%), Turkey (11%), the United Kingdom (9.3%), Azerbaijan (8.5%), Germany (8.2%), the Ukraine (7.7%), and the United States (6%).

32 BALANCE OF PAYMENTS

Georgia's high level of imports, until 2000, was largely due to its capital account surplus, stemming from the inflows of investments, loans, and grants, rather than from weak export performance. Georgia's capital account subsequently fell into deficit.

The US Central Intelligence Agency (CIA) reported that in 2002 the purchasing power parity of Georgia's exports was $515 million

---

Balance of Payments – Georgia (2003)

(In millions of US dollars)

Current Account		-397.1
Balance on goods	-636.0	
Imports	-1,466.6	
Exports	830.6	
Balance on services	52.5	
Balance on income	34.3	
Current transfers	152.0	
Capital Account		19.9
Financial Account		323.0
Direct investment abroad	-3.8	
Direct investment in Georgia	337.9	
Portfolio investment assets	…	
Portfolio investment liabilities	…	
Financial derivatives	…	
Other investment assets	-6.1	
Other investment liabilities	-5.0	
Net Errors and Omissions		6.6
Reserves and Related Items		47.7

(…) data not available or not significant.

SOURCE: *Balance of Payment Statistics Yearbook 2004*, Washington, DC: International Monetary Fund, 2004.

while imports totaled $750 million resulting in a trade deficit of $235 million.

The International Monetary Fund (IMF) reported that in 2000 Georgia had exports of goods totaling $459 million and imports totaling $971 million. The services credit totaled $206 million and debit $216 million.

Exports of goods and services reached $1.1 billion in 2004, down from $1.3 billion in 2003. Imports decreased from $1.9 billion in 2003, to $1.8 billion in 2004. The resource balance was consequently negative in both years, reaching -$583 million in 2003 and -$637 million in 2004. The current account balance was also negative, decreasing from -$391 million in 2003, to -$430 million in 2004. Foreign exchange reserves (including gold) decreased to $187 million in 2004, barely covering a month of imports.

33 BANKING AND SECURITIES

The National Bank of Georgia (NBG), the state's central bank, was founded in 1991. The NBG has the functions of a central bank, namely issuing currency, managing the exchange rate, controlling monetary and credit aggregates, and regulating the activities of the banking sector.

In September 1995 Georgia introduced a new currency, the lari (l), to replace its interim currency, the coupon, at the rate of l1 = coupon1,000,000. The coupon had been introduced in May 1993 after the collapse of the ruble zone in response to a severe cash shortage in the republic. The coupon experienced one of the steepest devaluations of any currencies in the former Soviet Union, plummeting from around coupon1,000 = $1 shortly after its introduction to coupon1,550,000=$1 by December 1994. The coupon was scarcely used by the private sector, where the majority of transactions were carried out in dollars and rubles.

The government has since had more success with the lari. The new currency was introduced at l1.3 = $1, and given the dramatic success in reducing inflation, by the end of November 1996 it had appreciated slightly to trade around l1.28 = $1. However, by 2001, it had lost some value, trading at l2.07 = $1.

At the time of independence there were, in addition to the NBG, five specialized commercial banks, about 200 small domestic commercial banks, and the former Georgian branches of the Soviet Savings Bank and Vneshekonombank. During 1993 and 1994, a large number of small banks were set up, peaking at 227 by mid-1994. Several of these have since collapsed, leaving creditors bankrupt. In December 1994, the central bank stripped 28 commercial banks of their licenses on the ground that they had insufficient funds. In June 1995, the head of the central bank, Nodar Javakhishvili, moved to further stiffen capital requirements and stripped 22 more banks of the licenses. This was followed in July and August with similar measures that resulted in 58 additional banks losing their licenses. Also during 1995 was the merger of three state banks (Eximbank, Industrial Bank, and the Savings Bank) into the United Georgian Bank. State-owned banks accounted for some 75% of banking sector assets.

The first foreign bank, the Georgian-US bank, was opened in T'bilisi in early 1994. In September 1996 a joint investment bank began its operations with its founding capital contributed by the United Georgian Bank, the Commercial Bank of Greece, and the European Bank for Reconstruction and Development (EBRD). Emlak Bankasi, a Turkish bank, and the Caucasus Development

Bank, based in Azerbaijan, currently maintain offices in T'bilisi. In 1997, the EBRD announced that it is to lend $5 million to Absolute Bank, a US-Georgian joint venture, with 60% US ownership. The bank has $3 million in assets, making it one of the largest Georgian banks in terms of capital.

Other commercial banks include the Agricultural Bank (1991), the Bank of Industry and Construction (1991), Housing Bank of Georgia (1991), and the State Savings Bank (1989).

The International Monetary Fund reports that in 2001, currency and demand deposits—an aggregate commonly known as M1—were equal to $190.2 million. In that same year, M2—an aggregate equal to M1 plus savings deposits, small time deposits, and money market mutual funds—was $356.0 million. The money market rate, the rate at which financial institutions lend to one another in the short term, was 17.5%.

The Caucasian Exchange, a stock exchange, opened recently in Georgia.

34 INSURANCE

Georgia's insurance system is largely inherited from government-controlled Soviet institutions. The civil war impairs growth of the insurance sector.

35 PUBLIC FINANCE

Georgia has been notorious for mismanaging its budget. In 1999, the IMF put one of its programs in the country on hold because Georgia could not meet the conditional budgetary targets the IMF set forth. A more realistic budget in the second half of 2000 paved the way for a new IMF program beginning in January 2001. Georgia's progress towards those new budgetary goals has been uneven, but it has remained on track.

The US Central Intelligence Agency (CIA) estimated that in 2005 Georgia's central government took in revenues of approximately $872.5 billion and had expenditures of $1 billion. Revenues minus expenditures totaled approximately $871.4 billion. Total external debt was $1.9 billion.

The International Monetary Fund (IMF) reported that in 2003, the most recent year for which it had data, central government revenues were l933.3 million and expenditures were l1,009.8 million. The value of revenues was us$435 million and expenditures us$471 million, based on an exchange rate for 2003 of us$1 = l2.1457 as reported by the IMF. Government outlays by function were as follows: general public services, 34.1%; defense, 6.0%; public order and safety, 10.7%; economic affairs, 8.8%; housing and community amenities, 0.6%; health, 1.0%; recreation, culture, and religion, 2.5%; education, 4.1%; and social protection, 32.4%.

36 TAXATION

As of 2004, Georgia has a standard corporate profits tax of 20%. Capital gains are considered part of taxable profits and are taxed at the corporate rate. Taxes on dividends, interest, and management fees are withheld at the source at a rate of 10%. Foreign entities not permanently established pay a withholding tax of 10% on dividends, interest, and royalty payments. There is also a withholding tax of 4% on insurance premiums and payments for international telecommunications and transportation services. A 1% tax on property of enterprises (TPE) is charged foreign companies that have permanent establishments in Georgia. There is also a per-

Public Finance – Georgia (2003)

(In millions of lari, central government figures)

Revenue and Grants	**933.3**	**100.0%**
Tax revenue	602.3	64.5%
Social contributions	222.7	23.9%
Grants	48.4	5.2%
Other revenue	59.9	6.4%
Expenditures	**1,009.8**	**100.0%**
General public services	344.1	34.1%
Defense	60.4	6.0%
Public order and safety	107.6	10.7%
Economic affairs	88.5	8.8%
Environmental protection	...	...
Housing and community amenities	5.6	0.6%
Health	10.3	1.0%
Recreational, culture, and religion	25	2.5%
Education	41	4.1%
Social protection	327.3	32.4%

(…) data not available or not significant.

SOURCE: *Government Finance Statistics Yearbook 2004*, Washington, DC: International Monetary Fund, 2004.

sonal income tax, paid by resident and nonresident individuals, which has four brackets, the first one being a negative income tax of 12% up to an income of l200 (about $93). For l201–350 (about $165), the tax is l24 ($11) plus 15%. For l351–600 ($286), the tax is l46.5 ($22) plus 17%. Above l600, the tax is l98 ($42) plus 20%. Social charges are deducted from employees' salaries: 15% for the health protection fund and 1% for the social security fund. Employers' contributions are 3% for the health protection fund, 27% for social security, and 1% for unemployment. There is also a value-added tax (VAT) of 20% (reduced from 28%), in addition to various excise taxes, ranging from 10–90%

Georgia has one of the worst rates of tax compliance in the world. Chronic shortfalls in revenue collection means that the state must turn to external financing and loans from the National Bank of Georgia to make up for budget deficits. External borrowing to cover budget shortfalls have been the primary reason Georgia has had to turn to the IMF and the Paris Club for stand-by credit agreements and rescheduling of sovereign debt. The high rate of tax evasion puts legitimate business at a competitive disadvantage with a large "shadow economy," estimated officially to constitute 40–60% of the economy, but generally believed, according to the US State Department, to be much higher. Estimates of underpaying of taxes by enterprises have been close to 80%.

37 CUSTOMS AND DUTIES

Georgia has an open trade regime, with most commodities carrying tariffs of either 5% or 12%, although automobiles have considerably higher rates. Some goods, such as grains, humanitarian goods, and aviation fuel, are exempt from carrying customs tariffs. Imported goods are also subject to a value-added tax (VAT) of 20% and an excise tax of 5–100% is levied on luxury goods.

38 FOREIGN INVESTMENT

Georgia was one of the first former Soviet republics to adopt market reforms on foreign investment. However, political instability has hampered efforts to attract capital from abroad. Oil and gas pipeline projects and expanded privatization sales promised to reverse this trend. By the mid-1990s both GDP and total foreign investment began to grow steadily. In September 1998 the decision was made to make all future economic regulations in full conformity with the norms of the European Community. Legislation in 2000 extended the scope of the privatization program, created a capital market, and provided for the registration of enterprise and agricultural land, all conducive to improving Georgia's investment climate. Also in 2000, the currency appeared to have stabilized. The main hindrances to foreign investment flows are not the legal framework but pervasive corruption and arbitrary and biased administration.

Annual foreign direct investment (FDI) inflow swelled to $242 million in 1997 and $265.3 million in 1998 mainly due to work on the Baku-Supsa pipeline and on the Supsa terminal. FDI flows fell to an annual average of $124.3 million 1999 to 2001. Total FDI stock from 1990 to 2000 was an estimated $672 million. The United States has been the leading source of foreign investment, accounting for about 22%.

Investment levels have, as expected, soared in recent years. Mainly due to work on the Baku-Tibilisi-Ceyhan pipeline and the Shah Deniz gas pipeline, FDI levels have grown from $163 million in 2002, to $336 million in 2003, and $490 million in 2004. Preliminary data for 2005 shows that inflows of capital have reached $284 million in the first half of the year. An encouraging fact is the winding down of the effects of the pipeline projects, and the increase in foreign investments as a result of privatizations done by the government.

39 ECONOMIC DEVELOPMENT

In late 1992, the government inaugurated its Medium-Term Program of Macroeconomic Stabilization and Systemic Change focusing on price and trade liberalization, budget constraints for public enterprises, and privatization. As part of a small enterprise privatization program, the first auction of small-scale assets was held in T'bilisi in March 1993. Practically all housing has been privatized, as well as a high percentage of agricultural land. Privatization was progressing as of 2003, and the government was developing the legal framework necessary for a good climate of investment. Nevertheless, due to a lack of enough foreign direct investment in 2003, the transportation and communication infrastructure remains in poor condition.

In spite of these reforms, political instability continues to hamper Georgian economic development. Although the Baku-T'bilisi-Ceyhan oil pipeline brings much needed foreign investment, most observers feel that the fate of the Georgian economy hinges on the ultimate fate of the Caucasus.

Corruption hampers economic development, and has undermined the credibility of the government's economic reforms. The size of the shadow economy is also a concern. The Paris Club rescheduled Georgian debt in 2001. That year, Georgia negotiated a three-year $144 million Poverty Reduction and Growth Facility (PRGF) Arrangement with the IMF, which was due to expire in 2004. The IMF encouraged the country to implement tax reform, to improve revenue collection, strengthen the banking system, and to combat corruption and smuggling.

The construction of the Baku-T'bilisi-Ceyhan oil pipe lines and the Baku-T'bilisi-Erzerum gas pipe lines have been extremely beneficial for the economy of Georgia. The economy has registered impressive growth rates (11.1% in 2003, and 8% in 2005), unemployment has been alleviated, and the privatization of several national enterprises has been made easier as a result. A strong industrial sector, together with higher productivity rates in the agricultural sectors, will ensure that the impressive economic expansion will continue at similar rates for at least another couple of years. The government needs to speed up reforms however, and ensure a proper economic restructuring by developing and diversifying its manufacturing and export bases.

40 SOCIAL DEVELOPMENT

All employees are eligible for old age benefits, which are funded primarily by employers, who contribute 31% of payroll. Disability and death are not covered. A special social pension exists for the aged and disabled who do not qualify for the employee pension system as determined by need. Paid maternity leave is provided for up to eight weeks, although it is reported that employers frequently withhold benefits. Temporary disability is only payable if the employer is responsible for the injury, although unemployment and permanent disability benefits are provided. Medical services are provided to needy residents by government health officials. Family allowances, initiated in 2002, provide for all needy residents, and is funded by the government.

Women remain predominantly in low-skilled, low-paying jobs, regardless of qualifications. Female participation in politics has been discouraged, and women rarely fill leadership positions in the private sector. Discrimination and harassment in the workplace are common. Violence against women is a serious problem and there are virtually no mechanisms to assist victims. Societal bias discourages the reporting of domestic abuse or sexual violence. In 2004, kidnapping of women for marriage still occurred.

Human rights abuses by the police and security forces continue, often to obtain confessions or extract money. Prison conditions are inhumane and life threatening, and corruption is endemic in the judicial and law enforcement systems. There is some discrimination against ethnic minorities.

41 HEALTH

Since 1995 there have been wide-ranging reforms to the centralized system of health care inherited from the former Soviet Union. Staffed by a disproportionate number of specialists, and supporting a relatively high number of hospital beds, the system proved too costly and inefficient to maintain. In the period immediately following independence, financial shortages led to delayed payment, or even nonpayment, of medical staff salaries; a virtual halt to investment in new medical equipment and buildings; and the emergence of a black market in pharmaceuticals. Changes in health care policy since 1995 include introduction of a health insurance system and an end to free health care outside a basic package of health benefits, as well as new systems of provider payment. The network of rural and urban primary care centers is still largely a holdover from the Soviet era, but the payment structure for services has changed. Health care expenditure was estimated at 2.8% of GDP.

In 2004, there were an estimated 391 physicians, 372 nurses, 29 midwives, and 30 dentists per 100,000 people. Immunization rates for the country in 1997 were as follows: children up to one year old were vaccinated against tuberculosis, 76%; diphtheria, pertussis, and tetanus, 92%; polio, 98%; and measles, 95%.

Life expectancy in 2005 was an average of 75.88 years and the infant mortality rate was 18.59 per 1,000 live births. The total fertility rate has decreased from 2.9 children per woman of childbearing years in 1960 to 1.1 in 2000. The under-five mortality rate was 59 per 1,000 live births. The maternal mortality rate was much lower than the average in Eastern Europe. In 1995 there were 22 maternal deaths per 100,000 live births. The estimated overall mortality rate as of 2002 was 14.6 per 1,000 people. There were approximately 2,000 civil war-related deaths in 1992. A diphtheria epidemic has spread through the former Soviet Union. In most affected countries, the incidence rate of reported diphtheria has increased two- to tenfold every year.

The HIV/AIDS prevalence was 0.10 per 100 adults in 2003. As of 2004, there were approximately 3,000 people living with HIV/AIDS in the country. There were an estimated 200 deaths from AIDS in 2003.

42 HOUSING

Before independence, most urban housing was regulated by the government while most rural housing was privately owned. Beginning in the mid 1990s, legislation towards privatization led to the legalization of an open real estate market. Unfortunately, the need for adequate housing is far greater than current supplies. In 1989, there were 152,033 people registered and waiting for adequate housing. Overcrowding became a problem as extended families stayed together in one household simply because of the lack of alternative housing. Natural disasters have caused trouble for an already problematic housing situation. Mudslides are common in some areas. In 1987, a mudslide destroyed 210 homes and seriously damaged 850 more. In 1991, an earthquake destroyed 46,000 homes. Civil unrest has caused a great deal of homelessness as well. As of 2001, there were about 300,000 displaced persons throughout the country.

During 1995 a total of 55,423 sq m of dwelling was built in the republic, but this represented only a 4.4% increase in new dwelling area since 1987. Building costs are high, with the price of one square meter often between $500 and $1,000. At the 2002 census, there were 1,243,158 private households, with the average size of household at 3.5 persons.

In western Georgia, a typical older home is wooden, raised off the ground slightly in areas where flooding or very damp ground is problematic. In the drier climate of eastern Georgia, stone (later brick) houses with flat roofs were constructed along roads. In urban regions, two-story brick or cement block homes are not uncommon.

43 EDUCATION

Georgia's educational system was based on the Soviet model until the late 1980s, when there was a de-emphasis of Soviet educational themes in favor of Georgian history and language. Georgian students are taught in a number of languages, including Georgian,

Russian, Armenian, Azerbaijani, Abkhazian, and Ossetian. Education is compulsory for nine years, beginning at age seven. Elementary school covers six years of study. This is followed by either seven years of general secondary school or six years of technical school. The academic year runs from September to June.

In 2001, about 41% of children between the ages of three and five were enrolled in some type of preschool program. Primary school enrollment in 2003 was estimated at about 89% of age-eligible students. The same year, secondary school enrollment was about 78% of age-eligible students. It is estimated that about 82% of all students complete their primary education. The student-to-teacher ratio for primary school was at about 16:1 in 2000; the ratio for secondary school was about 8:1.

There are 24 state institutions of higher learning in the country and 73 private accredited institutions. These include the Iran Dzhavakhiladze University of T'bilisi, Georgian Technical University, Abkhazian State University, and State University of Batumi. In 2003, about 38% of the tertiary age population were enrolled in some type of higher education program. The adult literacy rate has been estimated at about 99%.

As of 2003, public expenditure on education was estimated at 2.2% of GDP, or 11.8% of total government expenditures.

44 LIBRARIES AND MUSEUMS

The National Library in T'bilisi holds over six million volumes, while the Georgian State Public Library has eight million. The largest library in the country, however, is the Scientific and Technological Library of Georgia, which contains 10.1 million volumes. There are dozens of private libraries held by various scientific, cultural, and religious organizations and extensive university library holdings. Chief among the latter are T'bilisi State University (three million volumes), the Polytechnic University in T'bilisi (1.14 million volumes), and the Pedagogical Institute in T'bilisi (336,000 volumes).

Most of the country's cultural institutions are in T'bilisi, including the State Art Museum, the Museum of Fine Arts, the State Museum of Georgia, the T'bilisi Museum of History and Ethnography, and the Georgian State Museum of Oriental Art. There are local or specialty museums in Gori, Suchumi, and Kútáisi.

45 MEDIA

Georgia has international telecommunications links via landline to other former Soviet republics and Turkey. There is also a low capacity satellite earth station and connections via Moscow. In 2003, there were an estimated 133 mainline telephones for every 1,000 people; about 138,800 people were on a waiting list for telephone service installation. The same year, there were approximately 107 mobile phones in use for every 1,000 people.

In 2004, there were 54 independent television stations in the country, but only three provided national service. Though independently operated, most stations rely on some amount of support from the national or regional governments. There are at least 10 radio stations in operation, most of which are privately owned. Primary news agencies include the state operated Sakinform, and the privately held Prime-News, Iprinda, and Kavkasia-Press. In 2003, there were an estimated 568 radios and 357 television sets

for every 1,000 people. About 12.4 of every 1,000 people were cable subscribers. Also in 2003, there were 31.6 personal computers for every 1,000 people and 31 of every 1,000 people had access to the Internet. There were 11 secure Internet servers in the country in 2004.

In 2001, there were about 200 independent newspapers throughout the country. The most widely read was *Sakartvelos Respublika*, with a 1995 circulation of 40,000. In T'bilisi, the major daily is *Vestnik Gruzzi* (*Georgian Herald*). There are also several general and special interest periodicals available.

The constitution and a 1991 press law provide for a free press, but in practice the government is said to restrict some press rights. Libel laws, as well as pressure from business and society leaders and government authorities, inhibit hard core investigative reporting.

46 ORGANIZATIONS

Georgia's Chamber of Commerce and Industry promotes trade and commerce with its fellow members of the CIS. The country belongs to the International Chamber of Commerce as well. Union organizations in Georgia include the Confederation of Independent Trade Unions, an umbrella organization. Important political organizations include the all-Georgian Mecrab Kostava Society and the Paramilitary group Mkhredrioni.

The Georgian Academy of Sciences, promoting research and education in all branches of science, was established in 1941. The Georgian Medical Association serves as a physician networking organization while also promoting research and education on health issues and working to establish common policies and standards in healthcare There are also associations dedicated to research and education for specific fields of medicine and particular diseases and conditions, such as Georgian Association of Cardiology.

Youth organizations include the National Youth Council of Georgia (through the Department of Youth and Sport), the United Nations of Youth: Georgia, YMCA/YWCA, and scouting programs. There are also several sports associations promoting amateur competition in such pastimes as baseball, track and field, badminton, and figure skating.

Volunteer service organizations, such as the Lions Clubs and Kiwanis International, are also present. There are national chapters of the Red Cross Society and Caritas.

47 TOURISM, TRAVEL, AND RECREATION

Bounded by the Black Sea and the Caucasus Mountains, Georgia has been known for its lucrative tourist industry, but tourism declined after independence due to political and economic turmoil. Mtskheta, the ancient capital, is home to the Svetitskhoveli Cathedral, an 11th-century edifice that is the spiritual center of the Georgian Orthodox Church, and a major tourist attraction. The present-day capital, T'bilisi, is over 1,000 years old and offers historic citadels, cathedrals, and castles, as well as warm springs and dramatic mountain views. In 2002, approximately 298,469 tourists visited Georgia. There were 3,712 hotel rooms with 8,250 beds and an occupancy rate of 71%.

In 2005, the US Department of State estimated the average daily expenses for T'bilisi at $245. Other areas ranged from $96 to $128 per day.

⁴⁸FAMOUS GEORGIANS

Eduard A. Shevardnadze (b.1928), a key figure in the Soviet government, was president of Georgia from 1992 until 2003, when he resigned in the midst of mounting criticism following disputed elections, known as the "Rose Revolution." Mikhail Saakashvili (b.1967) was elected president in January 2004. Joseph Stalin (1879–1953), a key figure in the Soviet period, was born in Gori, Georgia. The medieval poet Shota Rustaveli, who was from Georgia, wrote the masterpiece *Knight in the Tiger's Skin*. Nineteenth-century poets include Ilia Chavchavadze (1837–1907), Akaki Tsereteli (1840–1915), and Vazha Pshwda. Writers of that century include Titsian Tabidze (1895–1937), Giorgi Leonidze, and Irakli Abashidze. Painters include Niko Pirosmanashvili (1862–1918), and Irikli Toidze. Composers include Zakhari Paliashvili (1871–1933) and Meliton Balanchivadze (1862–1937).

⁴⁹DEPENDENCIES

Georgia has no territories or colonies.

⁵⁰BIBLIOGRAPHY

Giannakos, S.A. (ed.). *Ethnic Conflict: Religion, Identity, and Politics*. Athens: Ohio University Press, 2002.

Nationalism and History: The Politics of Nation Building in Post-Soviet Armenia, Azerbaijan and Georgia. Toronto, Canada: University of Toronto Centre for Russian and East European Studies, 1994.

Streissguth, Thomas. *The Transcaucasus*. San Diego, Calif.: Lucent Books, 2001.

Transcaucasia, Nationalism and Social Change: Essays in the History of Armenia, Azerbaijan, and Georgia. Ann Arbor: University of Michigan Press, 1996.

GERMANY

Federal Republic of Germany
Bundesrepublik Deutschland

CAPITAL: Berlin

FLAG: The flag is a tricolor of black, red, and gold horizontal stripes—the flag of the German (Weimar) Republic from 1919 until 1933.

ANTHEM: *Einigkeit und Recht und Freiheit (Unity and Justice and Liberty).*

MONETARY UNIT: The euro replaced the deutsche mark as the official currency in 2002. The euro is divided into 100 cents. There are coins in denominations of 1, 2, 5, 10, 20, and 50 cents and 1 euro and 2 euros. There are notes of 5, 10, 20, 50, 100, 200, and 500 euros. €1 = $1.25475 (or $1 = €0.79697) as of 2005.

WEIGHTS AND MEASURES: The metric system is the legal standard.

HOLIDAYS: New Year's Day, 1 January; Labor Day, 1 May; German Unity Day, 3 October; Repentance Day, Wednesday before the 3rd Sunday in November (except Bavaria); Christmas, 25–26 December. Movable religious holidays include Good Friday, Easter Monday, Ascension, and Whitmonday. In addition, the movable Carnival/Rose Monday holiday and various provincial holidays also are celebrated.

TIME: 1 PM = noon GMT.

¹LOCATION, SIZE, AND EXTENT

Germany is located in western Europe, bordering the North Sea between France and Poland. Germany is slightly smaller than the state of Montana, with a total area of 357,021 km sq (137,847 mi sq). Germany shares boundaries with Denmark and the Baltic Sea on the N, Poland and the Czech Republic to the E, Austria to the SE, Switzerland to the S, France to the SW, Luxembourg, Belgium, and the Netherlands to the W, and the North Sea to the NW. Germany's boundary length totals 6,010 km (3,734 mi), of which 2,389 km (1,484 mi) is coastline. Germany's capital city, Berlin, is located in the northeastern part of the country.

²TOPOGRAPHY

The topography of Germany is varied. The area along the Baltic coast is sandy, with dunes and small hills. Adjacent to the coast are forested ridges and numerous lakes of the Mecklenburg lake plateau. Around Berlin, the relief is less hilly. The southern limit of the lowland area is formed by a wide zone of fertile loess, reaching from Magdeburg to the highlands in the South. These highlands include the Harz Mountains; the densely wooded Thuringian Forest and the Erzgebirge (Ore Mountains), where the Fichtelberg rises to 1,214 m (3,983 ft). In the northeast, the wide German lowland—characterized by sandy North Sea shores, heath and moor (in the south), and highest altitudes of about 300 m (1,000 ft)—rises slowly to the central Germany uplands. These low, eroded mountains (1,070–1,520 m/3,500–5,000 ft) extend from the Rhine to the former border of East Germany.

In the west are a wide rift valley and a narrow gorge carved by the Rhine River. A group of plateaus and low mountains, averaging 460 m (1,500 ft) in altitude and including the Black Forest and Odenwald Mountains (highest peak, the Feldberg, 1,493 m/4,898 ft), form the greater part of southern Germany. They merge grad-

ually with the highest walls of the Bavarian Alps (2,440–2,740 m/8,000–9,000 ft), which form the boundary between Germany, Switzerland, and Austria; the Zugspitze (2,962 m/9,718 ft), on the Austrian border, is the highest point in Germany.

The only major lake is Lake Constance (Bodensee; within Germany, 305 sq km/118 sq mi), which is shared with Switzerland and Austria. Except in the extreme south, all of Germany is drained by rivers that empty into the North Sea. The Rhine, with its two main tributaries, the Mosel and the Main, dominates the western areas; farther east are the Ems, the Weser, the Elbe, and the Oder. These rivers have estuaries that are important for the ports located there. In the south, the Danube flows from west to east. The East Frisian Islands are off the northwest coast; the North Frisian Islands lie along the coast of Schleswig. The small island of Helgoland is opposite the mouth of the Elbe River.

³CLIMATE

The climate is temperate; rapid changes in temperature are rare. Average temperatures in January, the coldest month of the year, range from 1.5°C (35°F) in the lowlands to -6°C (21°F) in the mountains. July is the warmest month of the year, with average temperatures between 18°C (64°F) in low-lying areas to 20°C (68°F) in the sheltered valleys of the south. The upper valley of the Rhine has an extremely mild climate. Upper Bavaria experiences a warm alpine wind (Föhn) from the south. The Harz Mountains form their own climatic zone, with cool summers, cold wind, and heavy snowfalls in winter.

Precipitation occurs throughout the year: in the northern lowlands, from 51 to 71 cm (20–28 in); in the central uplands, from 69 to 152 cm (27–60 in); in the Bavarian Alps, to more than 200 cm (80 in). The higher mountains are snow covered from at least January to March.

⁴FLORA AND FAUNA

Plants and animals are those generally common to middle Europe. Beeches, oaks, and other deciduous trees constitute one-third of the forests; conifers are increasing as a result of reforestation. Spruce and fir trees predominate in the upper mountains, while pine and larch are found in sandy soil. There are many species of ferns, flowers, fungi, and mosses. Fish abound in the rivers and the North Sea. Wild animals include deer, wild boar, mouflon, fox, badger, hare, and small numbers of beaver. Various migratory birds cross Germany in the spring and autumn. As of 2002, there were at least 76 species of mammals, 247 species of birds, and over 2,600 species of plants throughout the country.

⁵ENVIRONMENT

Industrialization has taken its toll on Germany's environment, including that of the former GDR, which, according to a 1985 UNESCO report, had the worst air, water, and ground pollution in Europe. Since 1976, the Petrol Lead Concentration Act has limited the lead content of gasoline; for control of other automotive pollutants, the government looked toward stricter enforcement of existing laws and to technological improvements in engine design. The Federal Emission Protection Act of 1974, based on the "polluter pays" principle, established emissions standards for industry, agriculture and forestry operations, and public utilities. Nevertheless, by 1994, 50% of Germany's forests had been damaged by acid rain.

Germany has 107 cu km of renewable water resources, of which 86% are used for industrial purposes. Water pollution is evident in virtually every major river of the FRG, and the Baltic Sea is heavily polluted by industrial wastes and raw sewage from the rivers of eastern Germany. In the 1980s, the Rhine, from which some 10 million Germans and Dutch draw their drinking water, was 20 times as polluted as in 1949. Between November 1986 and January 1987 alone, 30 tons of mercury, 900 lb of pesticides, 540 tons of nitrogen fertilizers, and 10 tons of benzene compound were discharged into the river. The Effluency Levies Act, effective January 1978, requires anyone who discharges effluents into waterways to pay a fee reckoned in accordance with the quantity and severity of the pollutant; the proceeds of this act are allocated for the building of water treatment plants and for research on water treatment technology and reduced-effluent production techniques.

Significant sources of air pollution include emissions from coal-burning utility plants and exhaust emissions from vehicles using leaded fuels. In 1996 industrial carbon dioxide emissions totaled 861 million metric tons. However, the total carbon dioxide emissions in 2000 was down to 785.5 metric tons. The nation has set maximum levels for biocides in the soil, to protect food supplies. Under the nation's basic waste disposal law of 1972, some 50,000 unauthorized dump sites have been closed down and 5,000 regulated sites established; provisions governing toxic wastes were added in 1976. Germany's principal environmental agency is the Ministry of Environment, Nature Conservation and Reactor Safety, created in June 1986.

In 1970, the first German national park, with an area of 13,100 hectares (32,370 acres), was opened in the Bavarian forest, and in 1978 a second national park (21,000 hectares/52,000 acres) was opened near Berchtesgaden. The third national park, in Schleswig-Holstein (285,000 hectares/704,250 acres), opened in 1985, and a fourth, in Niedersachsen (240,000 hectares/593,000 acres), opened in 1986. The Messel Pit Fossil Site became a natural UNESCO World Heritage Site in 1995. There are also 32 Ramsar wetland sites. As of 2003, 32.6% of Germany's total land area is protected. According to a 2006 report issued by the International Union for Conservation of Nature and Natural Resources (IUCN), threatened species included 9 types of mammals, 14 species of birds, 12 species of fish, 9 types of mollusks, 22 species of other invertebrates, and 12 species of plants. Endangered species include Freya's damselfly, Atlantic sturgeon, slender-billed curlew, and the bald ibis. Species believed to be extinct include the Bavarian pine vole, Tobias' caddisfly, the wild horse, and the false ringlet butterfly.

⁶POPULATION

The population of Germany in 2005 was estimated by the United Nations (UN) at 82,490,000, which placed it at number 14 in population among the 193 nations of the world. In 2005, approximately 18% of the population was over 65 years of age, with another 15% of the population under 15 years of age. There were 95 males for every 100 females in the country.

Because of a low birthrate, an aging population, and emigration, Germany's population generally declined from the mid-1970s until around 1990. A heavy influx of immigrants in the 1990s more than compensated for the slight population loss due to more deaths than births. Although the annual growth rate in the 1980s was only 0.1%, immigration in the 1990s led to an annual growth rate in that decade of 0.8%. With immigration slowing, according to the UN, the annual population rate of change for 2005–10 was expected to be -0.1%, a rate the government viewed as too low.

The projected population for the year 2025 was 82,017,000. The population density was 231 per sq km (598 per sq mi).

The UN estimated that 88% of the population lived in urban areas in 2005, and that urban areas were growing at an annual rate of 0.19%. The capital city, Berlin, had a population of 3,327,000 in that year. Other large urban areas are: the Rhein-Main urban agglomerate, which includes Darmstadt, Frankfurt, Offenbach and Wiesbaden, 3,721,000; the Rhein-Neckar urban agglomerate which includes, Ludwigshafen am Rhein, Heidelberg, Mannheim, Frankenthal, Neustadt an der Weinstrasse and Speyer 1,625,000; the Rhein-Ruhr Middle urban agglomerate, which includes, Düsseldorf, Mönchengladbach, Remscheid, Solingen and Wuppertal 3,325,000; the Rhein-North urban agglomerate which includes, Duisburg, Essen, Krefeld, Mühlheim an der Ruhr, Oberhausen, Bottrop, Gelsenkirchen, Bochum, Dortmund, Hagen, Hamm and Herne 6,566,000; the Rhein-South urban agglomerate which includes Bonn, Cologne (Köln) and Leverkusen 3,084,000; the Saarland urban agglomerate which includes Neunkirchen, Saarbrücken and Saarlouis 896,000; Hamburg, 2,686,000; Stuttgart, 2,705,000; Munich (München), 2,318,000; Hanover (Hannover), 1,296,000; Bielefeld, 1,312,000; Nurenberg (Nürnberg), 1,206,000; Aachen, 1,073,000; Karlsruhe, 990,000; Saarland, 896,000; and Bremen, 889,000.

⁷MIGRATION

From 1946 to 1968, 475,505 Germans emigrated to the United States, 262,807 to Canada, and 99,530 to Australia and Oceania.

GERMANY

LOCATION: 47°16′ to 55°4′ N; 5°52′ to 15°2′ E. BOUNDARY LENGTHS: Denmark, 68 kilometers (42 miles); Poland, 456 kilometers (285 miles); Czech Republic, 646 kilometers (403 miles); Austria, 784 kilometers (487 miles); Switzerland, 334 kilometers (208 miles); France, 451 kilometers (281 miles); Luxembourg, 138 kilometers (86 miles); Belgium, 167 kilometers (104 miles); Netherlands, 577 kilometers (358 miles); total coastline, 2,389 kilometers (1,480 miles). TERRITORIAL SEA LIMIT: 12 miles.

During the same period, however, millions of people of German origin and/or speech migrated to West Germany from eastern Europe, notably from the former Czechoslovakia and East Germany. Migration from East Germany to West Germany reached a climax just before the erection of the frontier wall in Berlin on 13 August 1961. It is estimated that about 4 million people—many of them skilled workers and professionals—crossed from East Germany to West Germany during the 40-year existence of East Germany. Immigration of ethnic Germans from Poland continued to be heavy after 1968, totaling about 800,000 between 1970 and 1989.

According to German law, persons who are not ethnic Germans are foreigners (except for the few granted citizenship) even if they were born and have spent their entire lives in Germany. Conversely, ethnic Germans are not foreigners even if emigrating from birthplaces and homes in eastern Europe.

From 1992 until 1996, 560,000 ethnic Germans (out of a total of 1.1 million in 1989) had left Central Asia for Germany. These returning ethnic Germans were formerly deported by Soviet leader Joseph Stalin during World War II as they were living in the Volga region and other parts of the former Soviet Union.

Some 350,000 Bosnians were granted temporary protection in Germany in the early 1990s. Repatriation plans began for the Bosnians in October 1996, when 30,000 Bosnians repatriated voluntarily. During 1998, approximately 83,000 people returned to Bosnia under the Government-Assisted Return Programme (GARP). Another 2,021 were returned forcibly. By 1999, more than 250,000 Bosnians had returned to their homeland.

Under the UNHCR/IOM Humanitarian Evacuation Programme, 14,689 people had been evacuated from Macedonia to Germany as of 1999. The evacuees, as well as Kosovars who had already sought asylum in Germany but whose cases were still pending or already rejected, were granted temporary protection, renewable every three months. As of 20 August 1999, 4,147 evacuees had returned to their homeland. In 2005 Germany returned 51,000 Kosovars, including 34,000 Roma to the UN-administered province.

Germany remains the third-largest asylum country in Europe, receiving 876,622 refugees in 2004. The main countries of origin were Serbia and Montenegro, Turkey, Iraq, Ukraine, Afghanistan, Russia, and Iran. Of these refugees 86,151—mainly from Serbia and Montenegro, Turkey, Iraq, Russia, Iran, India, and Pakistan—sought asylum. In 2005 slow job growth in Germany caused many young Germans to migrate abroad for jobs, inspiring the term "reverse foreign worker."

The 2004 estimate of worker remittances received by Germany was $6 billion. However, it was also estimated that in that same year Germany was the source of $10 billion in remittances. The 2005 estimate of Germany's net migration rate was 2.18 migrants per 1,000 population.

8 ETHNIC GROUPS

Until the late 1950s, the population was 99% German; the Danes in Schleswig-Holstein were the sole national minority. The influx of foreigners as "guest workers" beginning in the late 1950s led to an upsurge in the number of permanent foreign residents. Germans account for about 91.5% of the total population. About 2.4% of the population are Turkish. Other minority groups include Italians, Greeks, Poles, Russians, Serbo-Croatians, and Spanish. Even persons born and reared in Germany are considered foreigners unless they are ethnically German or naturalized. The Roma (Sinti) were recognized as "national minorities" in 1995.

9 LANGUAGES

German is the official language, and although dialectical variations are considerable, High German is standard. Low German, spoken along the North and Baltic Sea coasts and in the offshore islands, is in some respects as close to Dutch as it is to standard German. Sorbian (also known as Wendish or Lusatian) is a Slavic language spoken by the Sorbian minority. Under the GDR it was taught in schools in their settlement area. There was a daily newspaper in

Sorbian and a publishing house for Sorbian literature. Many of Germany's sizable foreign-born population still speak their native languages, and there are numerous Turkish-speaking school children. Romani is spoken by the nation's small Roma population; the language has no written form and the Roma generally restrict the use of the language to within their own community.

In 1996, new rules were established reforming German orthography. Designed to eliminate the last vestiges of Gothic spelling, the rules, among other things, eliminated hyphens, restored some umlauts, and replaced the ß character. Confusion ensued when newly published dictionaries differed in their spellings of many words.

10 RELIGIONS

According to a 2004 report, the Evangelical Church, a federation of several church bodies including Lutheran, Uniate, and Reformed Protestant Churches, has about 27 million members, accounting for 33% of the population. Church officials report that only about 4% of members attend services on a regular basis. The Catholic Church also has 27.2 million members, or 33.4% of the population, with only about 17.5% of members active. Muslims make up approximately 3.4–3.9% of the populace with 3.1 to 3.5 million practitioners. Orthodox churches claim 1.1 million members, or 1.3% of the people. The Greek Orthodox Church is the largest division, followed by Romanian, Serbian, Russian (Moscow Patriarchate and Orthodox), Syrian, and Armenian Apostolic. Other Christian churches have about one million members, or 1.2% of the population. The largest of these are the New Apostolic Church (430,000 members), Jehovah's Witnesses (165,000 members), Baptists (87,000 members), and Methodists (66,000 members). Smaller groups include the Church of Jesus Christ of Latterday Saints (Mormons), Seventh-Day Adventists, the Apostolate of Jesus Christ, Mennonites, Quakers, and the Salvation Army.

About 87,500 members of Jewish congregations live in Germany, making up 0.1% of the populace. There were also small numbers of Unification Church members, Scientologists, Hare Krishnas, members of the Johannish Church, Buddhists, the International Grail Movement, Ananda Marga, and Sri Chinmoy. Approximately 21.8 million people, or 26.6% of the population, belonged to smaller religious organizations or had no religious affiliation at all.

Freedom of religion is guaranteed, and although there is no official state religion, churches can receive financial support from the government.

11 TRANSPORTATION

Although the German transportation network was heavily damaged during World War II, the system is now one of the best developed in Europe (although much of the infrastructure in the former East Germany needs significant improvement). Because of the country's central location, almost all continental surface traffic has to cross its terrain. In 2004, the railroad system consisted of 46,142 km (28,700 mi) of operational standard and narrow gauge track. Of that total, standard gauge lines accounted for 45,928 km (28,567 mi), of which 20,084 km (12,492 mi) was electrified. Narrow gauge lines accounted for 238 km (148 mi), of which only 16 km (10 mi) was electrified. The greater part of Germany's rail system is operated by the government-owned Federal Railways System.

Highways and roads in 2003 totaled 231,581 km (144,043 mi), all of which were paved. As of 2003, there were 45,022,926 passenger cars and 3,541,193 commercial vehicles in use.

The total length of regularly used navigable inland waterways and canals was 7,300 km (4,540 mi) in 2004. Canals link the Elbe with the Ems, the Ems with the Dortmund, and the Baltic with the North Sea. The most important inland waterway consists of the Rhine and its tributaries, which carry more freight than any other European waterway. The Kiel Canal is an important connection between the Baltic Sea and North Sea. Major ports and harbors include Berlin, Bonn, Brake, Bremen, Bremerhaven, Cologne, Dresden, Duisburg, Emden, Hamburg, Karlsruhe, Kiel, Lubeck, Magdeburg, Mannheim, Rostock, and Stuttgart. In 2005, the FRG had a merchant fleet comprised of 332 ships of 1,000 GRT or more with a combined capacity of 5,721,495 GRT.

Germany had an estimated 550 airports in 2004. As of 2005, a total of 332 had paved runways, and there were also 33 heliports. Major airports include Schonefeld, Tegel, and Tempelhof at Berlin, Halle at Leipzig, Osnabruck at Munster, as well as those at Bremen, Dresden, Frankfurt, Düsseldorf, Hamburg, Hanover, Cologne-Bonn, Stuttgart, Nurenberg, and Munich. Lufthansa, organized in 1955, is the major air carrier; its route network includes both North and South America, the Near and Far East (including Australia), Africa, and Europe. In 2003, about 72.693 million passengers were carried on scheduled domestic and international airline flights, and 7,298 million freight ton-km of service was performed

12 HISTORY

Hunting and gathering peoples roamed the land now known as Germany for thousands of years before the first farmers appeared in the sixth millennium BC. By the time these Indo-Europeans made contact with the Romans late in the 2nd century BC, the Teutons of the north had driven most of the Celts westward across the Rhine. During the succeeding centuries, Germanic tribes such as the Alemanni, Burgundians, Franks, Lombards, Vandals, Ostrogoths, and Visigoths gradually developed in the territory between the Rhine estuary in the west, the Elbe River in the east, and northern Italy in the south. Some of these peoples, whom the Romans called barbarians (from the Latin *barbari,* meaning "foreigners"), overran Italy and helped destroy the Roman Empire; others settled in Britain, France, and Spain. The area on either side of the Rhine was contested until Charlemagne, king of the Franks (r.768–814), extended his domain to include most of Germany as far as the Elbe; he was crowned emperor at Rome in 800. Charlemagne's empire was eventually divided among his three grandsons, and the German sector itself was divided in the latter part of the 9th century.

Otto I, greatest of a new Saxon dynasty, united Germany and Italy and was crowned first Holy Roman emperor in 962. The strength of the rising Holy Roman Empire was undercut, however, by the two-pronged involvement in Italy and in Eastern Europe. Successive generations of Germanic emperors and of various ducal families engaged in constant struggles within Germany as well as with the papacy, and dispersed their energies in many ventures beyond the confines of the empire. Frederick I (Barbarossa,

r.1152–90), of the Hohenstaufen family, overcame the last of the powerful duchies in 1180. His grandson Frederick II (r.1212–50), the most brilliant of medieval emperors, reigned from Sicily and took little interest in German affairs. Four years after his death, the empire broke up temporarily, and there followed a 19-year interregnum. In 1273, Rudolf of Habsburg was elected emperor, but neither he nor any of his immediate successors could weld the empire into a manageable unit.

The Holy Roman Empire's loose and cumbersome framework suffered from lack of strong national authority at the very time when powerful kingdoms were developing in England, France, and Spain. In the ensuing period, the Holy Roman emperors tended to ally themselves against the nobility and with the prosperous German cities and with such potent confederations of towns as the Hanseatic and Swabian leagues. During the 15th century and part of the 16th, Germany was prosperous: commerce and banking flourished, and great works of art were produced. However, the already weak structure of the empire was further undermined by a great religious schism, the Reformation, which began with Martin Luther in 1517 and ended in the ruinous Thirty Years' War (1618–48), which directly and indirectly (through disease and famine) may have taken the lives of up to two million people. Thereafter, Germany remained fragmented in more than 300 principalities, bishoprics, and free cities. In the 18th century, Prussia rose to first rank among the German states, especially through the military brilliance of Frederick II ("the Great," r.1740–86).

During the French Revolution and the Napoleonic wars, German nationalism asserted itself for the first time since the Reformation. Although frustrated in the post-Napoleonic era, the nationalist and liberal movements were not eradicated, and they triumphed briefly in the Frankfurt parliament of 1848. Thereafter, a number of its leaders supported the conservative but dynamic Prussian chancellor, Otto von Bismarck. After a series of successful wars with Denmark (1864), Austria (the Seven Weeks' War, 1866), and France (the Franco-Prussian War, 1870–71), Bismarck brought about the union of German states (excluding Austria) into the Second Empire, proclaimed in 1871.

Germany quickly became the strongest military, industrial, and economic power on the Continent and joined other great powers in overseas expansion. While Bismarck governed as chancellor, further wars were avoided and an elaborate system of alliances with other European powers was created. With the advent of Wilhelm II as German emperor (r.1888–1918), the delicate international equilibrium was repeatedly disturbed in a series of crises that culminated in 1914 in the outbreak of World War I. Despite initial successes, the German armies—leagued with Austria-Hungary and Turkey against the United Kingdom, France, Russia, and eventually the United States—were defeated in 1918. As a consequence of the war, in which some 1,600,000 Germans died, the victorious Allies through the Treaty of Versailles (1919) stripped Germany of its colonies and of the territories won in the Franco-Prussian War, demanded the nation's almost complete disarmament, and imposed stringent reparations requirements. Germany became a republic, governed under the liberal Weimar constitution. The serious economic and social dislocations caused by the military defeat and by the subsequent economic depression, however, brought Adolf Hitler and the National Socialist (Nazi) Party to power in 1933. Hitler converted the republic into a dictatorship, consolidated Germany's position at home and abroad, and began a military expansion that by 1939 had brought a great part of Europe under German control, either by military occupation or by alliance, leading to World War II.

Germany signed a military alliance with Italy on 22 May 1939 and a nonaggression pact with the former USSR on 23 August. Hitler's army then invaded Poland on 1 September, and France and Britain declared war on Germany two days later. France surrendered on 22 June 1940; the British continued to fight. On 10 December 1941, Germany declared war on the United States, three days after the attack on Pearl Harbor by its ally Japan. Hitler's troops were engaged on three major fronts—the eastern front (USSR), the North African front, and the western front (France). Hitler relied heavily on air power and bombed Britain continuously during 1941–42. But by 1943, German forces were on the defensive everywhere, thus marking the beginning of the end of the Nazi offensive thrusts. Finally, on 7 May 1945, after Hitler had committed suicide, the Allies received Germany's unconditional surrender. It is estimated that more than 35 million persons were killed during World War II. Of this number, at least 11 million were civilians. Among them were nearly 6 million Jews, mostly eastern Europeans, killed in a deliberate extermination by the Nazi regime known as the Holocaust; there were also about 5 million non-Jewish victims, including Gypsies, homosexuals, political dissidents, and the physically and mentally handicapped.

From Division to Reunification

After the surrender in 1945, Germany was divided into four occupation zones, controlled respectively by the former USSR, the United States, the United Kingdom, and France. Berlin was likewise divided, and from April 1948 through May 1949 the USSR sought unsuccessfully to blockade the city's western sectors; not until the quadripartite agreement of 1971 was unimpeded access of the FRG to West Berlin firmly established. In 1949, pending a final peace settlement, Germany was divided into the Federal Republic of Germany, or West Germany, consisting of the former United Kingdom, French, and US zones of occupation, and the German Democratic Republic, or East Germany, consisting of the former Soviet zone of occupation. Territories in the east (including East Prussia), which were in German hands prior to 1939, were taken over by Poland and the former USSR.

The FRG's first chancellor (1949–63), Konrad Adenauer, the leader of the Christian Democratic Union (CDU), followed a policy of "peace through strength." During his administration, the FRG joined NATO in 1955 and became a founding member of the EC in 1957. That same year, the Saar territory, politically autonomous under the Versailles Treaty but economically tied to France after 1947, became a German state after a free election and an agreement between France and the FRG. A treaty of cooperation between those two nations, signed on 22 January 1963, provided for coordination of their policies in foreign affairs, defense, information, and cultural affairs. The cost of this program of cooperation with the West was further alienation from the GDR and abandonment, for the foreseeable future, of the goal of German reunification. Many citizens, including a significant number of skilled and highly educated persons, had been covertly emigrating through Berlin in the West, and on 13 August 1961, East Berlin was sealed off from West Berlin by a wall of concrete and barbed wire. The Western Allies declared that they accepted neither the legality nor the potential practical consequences of the partition and reaffirmed their determination to ensure free access and the continuation of a free and viable Berlin.

On 16 October 1963, Adenauer resigned and was succeeded by former Finance Minister Ludwig Erhard, who is generally credited with stimulating the FRG's extraordinary postwar economic development—the so-called economic miracle. Kurt George Kiesinger of the CDU formed a new coalition government on 17 November 1966 with Willy Brandt, leader of the Social Democratic Party, as a vice-chancellor. Three years later, Brandt became chancellor, and the CDU became an opposition party for the first time. One of Brandt's boldest steps was the development of an "Eastern policy" (Ostpolitik), which sought improved relations with the Socialist bloc and resulted, initially, in the establishment of diplomatic ties with Romania and the former Yugoslavia. On 7 December 1970, the FRG signed a treaty with Poland reaffirming the existing western Polish boundary of the Oder and western Neisse rivers and establishing a pact of friendship and cooperation between the two nations. That August, the FRG had concluded a nonaggression treaty with the former USSR; a 10-year economic agreement was signed on 19 May 1973. Throughout the late 1960s and early 1970s, tensions over the Berlin division in particular and between the two Germanys generally eased markedly, as did, in consequence, the intensity of pressures from both Allied and Soviet sides over the issue of reunification. In an effort to normalize inter-German relations, FRG Chancellor Willy Brandt and GDR Chairman Willi Stoph exchanged visits in March and May 1970, the first such meetings since the states were established. A basic treaty between the two Germanys was reached on 21 December 1972 and ratified by the Bundestag on 17 May 1973; under the treaty, the FRG recognized the sovereignty and territorial integrity of the GDR, and the two nations agreed to cooperate culturally and economically. Two years later, the GDR and FRG agreed on the establishment of permanent representative missions in each others' capitals. Relations with Czechoslovakia were normalized by a treaty initialed 20 June 1973. The early 1970s brought an upsurge of terrorism on German soil, including the killing by Palestinians of Israeli athletes at the 1972 Summer Olympics in Munich. The terrorist wave, which also enlisted a number of German radicals, continued into the mid-1970s but declined thereafter.

Brandt remained chancellor until 6 May 1974, when he resigned after his personal aide, Günter Guillaume, was arrested as a spy for the GDR. Helmut Schmidt, Brandt's finance minister, was elected chancellor by the Bundestag on 16 May. Under Schmidt's pragmatic leadership, the FRG continued its efforts to normalize relations with Eastern Europe, while also emphasizing economic and political cooperation with its West European allies and with the United States. Schmidt remained chancellor until the fall of 1982, when his governing coalition collapsed in a political party dispute. General elections in March 1983 resulted in a victory for the CDU, whose leader, Helmut Kohl, retained the chancellorship he had assumed on an interim basis the previous October. In January 1987 elections, Kohl was again returned to power, as the CDU and its coalition allies won 54% of the seats in the Bundestag.

The exodus of East Germans through Hungary in the summer of 1989 as well as mass demonstrations in several East German cities, especially Leipzig, led to the collapse of the German Democratic Republic in the fall of 1989. Chancellor Kohl outlined a 10-point plan for peaceful reunification, including continued membership in NATO and free elections in March 1990. Following these elections, the two Germanys peacefully evolved into a single state. Four-power control ended in 1991 and, by the end of 1994, all former Soviet forces left the country, although British, French, and American forces remained for an interim period. Berlin became the new capital of Germany, although the shift from Bonn to Berlin took place over several years.

Unification has been accompanied by disillusionment and dissatisfaction with politics and the economy. A falling GDP and rising unemployment have raised concerns that the costs of unification were underestimated. By 1997, the German government had given more than $600 billion to eastern Germany through business subsidies, special tax breaks, and support payment for individuals, while private companies invested $500 million more. Even so, the eastern German economy was fundamentally bankrupt with unemployment at about 20%. Some analysts predict that convergence of the two economies will not be complete for another 10 to 20 years. In the meantime, the financial drain imposed on Bonn by the east threatened to imperil Germany's other convergence project, European economic unification. However, Germany and 11 other EU countries introduced a common European currency, the euro, in January 2002.

By October 1996, Chancellor Helmut Kohl had been in office for 14 years, becoming the longest-serving postwar German chancellor. In 1998, German voters decided it was time for a change. In the September parliamentary elections, Kohl's CDU (Christian Democratic) coalition was defeated by the SPD, and Gerhard Schröder became the first Social Democrat in 18 years to serve as Germany's chancellor. The following month, Schröder formed a center-left coalition with the Green Party. The new coalition inaugurated "Future Program 2000" to tackle the country's economic woes and in June 1999 pushed through the most extensive reform package in German history, which included major cuts in state spending as well as tax cuts. In April 1999, the German government was transferred from Bonn back to its prewar seat in Berlin, where the Bundestag moved into the renovated (and renamed) building formerly known as the Reichstag.

In July 1999 Johannes Rau became the first Social Democrat to be elected president of Germany in 30 years. However, continuing dissatisfaction with the nation's budget deficit and other problems resulted in a disappointing showing for the Social Democrats in local elections in September 1999.

In July 2000 government negotiators reached an agreement on the payment of compensation to persons subjected to forced and slave labor under the Nazi regime. A total of DM10 billion was to be paid out under the auspices of a specially created foundation. Official figures showed that racist attacks increased by 40% in 2000, a worrying trend.

In June 2001, the government and representatives from the nuclear industry signed an agreement to phase out nuclear energy over the next 20 years.

Following the 11 September 2001 terrorist attacks on New York and Washington, D.C., Germany agreed to deploy 4,000 troops to the US-led campaign in Afghanistan directed to oust the Taliban regime and al-Qaeda forces. It was Germany's largest deployment outside Europe since World War II, and in November, Schröder survived a parliamentary confidence vote following his decision to deploy the troops.

Parliamentary elections were held on 22 September 2002. Schröder, unable to campaign on a strong economy, staked out a foreign policy position that ran counter to that of the United States. Throughout 2002, the United States and the United Kingdom were committing troops to the Persian Gulf region, and, in the event that Iraq would not disarm itself of any weapons of mass destruction it might possess, it was evident that the United States and the United Kingdom might use those troops to force a regime change in Iraq. Schröder announced Germany unconditionally would not support a war in Iraq, and that Germany was in favor of a peaceful settlement to the conflict. Edmund Stoiber of the CDU was Schröder's opponent in the September elections, and the race between them was exceedingly close. Stoiber took a more nuanced position on the question of Iraq, and accused Schröder of damaging German-American relations. Stoiber was more popular with voters on matters of fighting unemployment (9.8% nationwide), and improving a sluggish economy. The SPD and CDU/CSU each won 38.5% of the vote, but the SPD emerged with 251 to 248 seats in the Bundestag (due to a peculiarity in the German voting system which awards extra seats to a party if it wins more constituency seats than it is entitled to under the party vote), and in coalition with the 55 seats won by the Green Party, formed a government with Schröder remaining chancellor.

The UN Security Council unanimously passed Resolution 1441 on 8 November 2002, calling upon Iraq to disarm itself of chemical, biological, and nuclear weapons or weapons capabilities, to allow the immediate return of UN and International Atomic Energy Agency (IAEA) weapons inspectors, and to comply with all UN resolutions regarding the country since the end of the Gulf War in 1991. The United States and the United Kingdom indicated that if Iraq would not comply with the resolution, "serious consequences" might result, meaning military action. The other three permanent members of the Security Council, France, Russia, and China, expressed their reservations with that position. Germany became a two-year (nonveto bearing) member of the Security Council in January 2003, and aligned itself with France, the most vocal opponent of war. The United States and the United Kingdom abandoned diplomatic efforts at conflict resolution in March, and on 19 March, the coalition went to war in Iraq. Once coalition forces defeated Iraq and plans for reconstruction of the country were being discussed in April, Germany stressed the need for a strong role to be played by the UN in a postwar Iraq.

Although Schröder was popular for his position toward Iraq, he became increasingly criticized for the economic underperformance of Germany. Major challenges included the growing level of unemployment, high level of state deficit, and the slow economic growth. During Schröder's second term, Germany became the world's largest exporter of goods, surpassing the United States.

The high unemployment level became quite astonishing, because Germany's low unemployment rate was at one point the envy of the industrial world. In the year 2000, Germany's unemployment rate exceeded 8%. By the end of 2002 over four million people were unemployed in Germany. The unemployment level in 2004 climbed to an even higher mark. The situation got worse in early 2005, when Germany's Federal Labor Agency announced that on January 2005 more than five million Germans were unemployed, which was the highest number since 1932, when the economic devastation of the Great Depression brought the Weimar Republic to an end. The important unemployment level during the first three month of 2005 triggered a negative reaction, even from those who supported the government. Critics complained that the Social Democrat-Green administration of Chancellor Gerhard Schröder was not doing enough.

In addition to the high rate of unemployment Germany also experienced growing state deficit, which meant that it spent more than it earned. In the early 1990s Germany pressured the EU to change its rules, such that no EU member state's deficit could be more then 3% of its GDP, but Germany in 2002 was in fact breaking this rule with a GDP of 3.75%. Furthermore, Wirtschafts–und Währungspolitik Bulletin and Federal Statistics Office reported that in 2004 Germany's budget deficit remained at 3.7% of its gross domestic product, which means that it exceeded the European Union's rules for the third year in a row.

Germany has struggled to produce GDP growth of even 1% a year. In comparison to the other Western European countries, from 1995 to 2003 the Western European economies, averaged together, grew by 18.1%, but in Germany it experienced growth of only 10.2%. Although, the Federal Statistics Office in Wiesbaden reported that in May 2005 the German economy experienced some improvement by expanding at the greatest pace since 2001, slightly rebounding from a contraction. Unfortunately, consumer spending, the biggest part of the economy, has not increased for some time.

To deal with the economic challenges in 2003 Gerhard Schröder launched a major reform package called "Agenda 2010." Agenda 2010 was Schröder's plan to reform Germany's declining economy and restore Germany's competitiveness in the world market. This policy aimed to reform health, education, labor training, social security, family welfare, unemployment benefits, and pensions. Agenda 2010s priority was labor-market reform. Neither these reforms nor reduced taxation did much to improve the slow economic growth or lower the unemployment that had reached especially great proportions since the Great Depression.

Following the protests on 1 January 2005 the government's controversial reform of unemployment benefits, also called "Hartz IV" reform, came into effect. Under this reform, those who have been unemployed for over a year would qualify for a flat-rate benefit, only if they could prove that they were actively looking for work. Schröder's inability to deal with the weak economy was thought to have contributed to his loss of the chancellery in the 2005 elections to Angela Merkel (CDU/CSU). A very tense election race followed by an alliance between the two opposing parties; the CDU/CSU and the SDP became known as the Grand Coalition. On 10 October 2005 Merkel officially became the chancellor of Germany.

Merkel defined the main goal of her government as reducing unemployment, and improving GDP growth. It was her goal to improve the German economy by pursuing a mix of reforms including cutting public spending, lowering corporate tax rates, accelerating labor-market, and pushing through other reforms begun by Merkel's predecessor. She also intended to increase value-added tax, social insurance contributions, and the top rate of income tax.

During her first few months in office, Angela Merkel attained an 85% approval rating. During the third quarter of 2005, the economy posted a 0.6% increase over the previous year's period and it was forecasted that Germany's GDP would grow by 1.6–1.8% in 2006. Although Germany's unemployment rate was still at 11.3%, it had been gradually decreasing since mid-2005.

Angela Merkel presided over a fragile coalition government consisting of her conservative Christian Democratic Union (CDU) party, the conservative Christian Social Union (CSU), and the left-leaning Social Democratic Party (SDP). Consequently, to push any reforms or programs through, she would have to be able to work together with the Social-Democrats.

In the field of foreign policy, Angela Merkel acknowledged the importance of Franco-German relations. She intended to maintain Germany's strong ties with France; however, not as exclusively as they used to be. Merkel was interested in working with the new EU member states and repairing relations with the United States. During Merkel's term it was thought that Germany might become less involved with Russia due to her criticism of the Russian president, Putin's, policies in Chechnya and human rights abuses. Germany would continue to support Turkey in its desire to become a European Union member state and to support Iraq from outside. The next chancellery election was scheduled for November 2009.

13 GOVERNMENT

Germany is a federal republic founded in 1949. Germany's Basic Law (Grundgesetz) or its constitution, was promulgated on 23 May 1949. On 3 October 1990, the Federal Republic of Germany and the German Democratic Republic were unified in accordance with Article 23 of the Basic Law, under which the FRG is governed. German governmental structure consists of three branches: the executive branch represented by a president (titular chief of state) and a chancellor (executive head of government), a legislative branch composed of a bicameral parliament, and a judicial branch represented by the independent Federal Constitutional Court. The federal government exercises complete sovereignty and may be amended by a two-thirds vote of the legislature.

The federal chancellor and his or her cabinet ministers and the federal president compose a federal executive branch. This branch is situated at the center of the German political system, where the chancellor is the head of federal government and an elected president performs the largely ceremonial functions of proposing the chancellor to the Bundestag, promulgating laws, formally appointing and dismissing judges and federal civil servants, and receiving foreign ambassadors. The president is elected for a five-year term by a federal convention composed of members of the Bundestag and an equal number of delegates elected by the provincial legislatures.

Every four years, after national elections and seating of the newly elected Bundestag (parliament) members, the federal president nominates a chancellor candidate to that parliamentary body and the chancellor is elected by majority vote in the Bundestag. Since a chancellor can only be elected by a coalition possessing a majority of the seats in parliament, each individual chancellor belongs to a particular party and represents the ideologies of that party. The Bundestag cannot remove the chancellor simply with a vote of no-confidence. The Basic Law allows only for a "constructive" vote of no-confidence; that is, the Bundestag can remove a chancellor only when it simultaneously agrees on a successor.

The chancellor's authority is drawn from the provisions of the Basic Law and from his or her status as leader of the party (or coalition of parties) holding a majority of seats in the Bundestag. The chancellor has powers of patronage and agenda-setting circumscribed by coalition government. Thus, the chancellor outlines federal policy and declares guidelines for cabinet ministers. Any formal policy guidelines issued by the chancellor are legally binding directives and must be implemented by the cabinet ministers. Guideline power allows the chancellor to interfere in any policy issue and to determine the government's approach to the problem.

Ministers are appointed and dismissed by the federal president with chancellor's approval; no Bundestag approval is needed. By and large, the chancellor and ministers are accountable to the Bundestag.

The bicameral legislature (the federal parliament) consists of a federal council (Bundesrat) and a federal diet (Bundestag).

The Bundestag is the principal legislative chamber in the parliament. Members of the Bundestag are the only federal officials directly elected by the public. The Bundestag had 497 voting deputies in 1987; 22 nonvoting deputies represented West Berlin. Following unification, Bundestag membership was raised to 662 deputies; as of September 2005 it stood at 614. Elections are held every four years (or earlier if a government falls from power). Candidates must be at least 18 years of age. Bundestag members are elected for four-year terms by universal, free, and secret ballot, and may be reelected. The most important organizational structures within the Bundestag are parliamentary groups (Fraktionen), which are formed by each political party represented in the chamber. Among other things, the Bundestag may introduce federal bills. However, it usually responds to federal bills introduced by the federal government or by the federal council.

The Bundesrat is the body that represents the interests of the states (Länder) within this federal structure. It consists of 69 representatives appointed by the provincial governments according to the population of each province. Each state has three to six votes depending on population and is required to vote as a block. The federal council participates in the Federation's policy-making and thus acts as a counterweight to the federal diet (Bundestag). It also serves as a link between the federation and the federal states' delegations representing the governments of the states. It can reject any federal bill and it has an absolute veto power over any federal legislation that has an impact on the states.

Disagreements between the two chambers are handled by a conciliating committee.

14 POLITICAL PARTIES

The "five percent clause," under which parties represented in the Bundestag must obtain at least 5% of the total votes cast by the electorate, has prevented the development of parliamentary splinter groups. In order to become a leading force in the parliament, parties have to win the local elections and become a majority by building coalitions. The coalition that receives the most votes respectively has the most votes in the parliament. Since party elections happen on the regional level, consistency of the parliament depends on the outcome of the Länder's elections.

The chancellor of Germany always belongs to the coalition of the parties that received the largest number of seats in the Bundestag. The chancellor seemingly could push his reforms by counting on the support of his coalition. However, coalitions do not agree on everything and often are fragmented. In addition, there is some fragmentation within each party. Additionally, after the German unification, there has been noticeable discrepancy between east and west because Western and Eastern Germany had different patterns of party developments.

Looking back, only three parties gained representation in the Bundestag following the elections of September 1965. The Christian Democratic Union (Christlich-Demokratische Union—CDU) and its Bavarian affiliate, the Christian Social Union (Christlich-Soziale Union—CSU), with 245 seats, remained the strongest group, as it had been since the first Bundestag was elected in 1949. The Social Democratic Party (Sozialdemokratische Partei Deutschlands—SPD) increased its seats to 202 and remained the major opposition party. The Free Democratic Party (Freie Demokratische Partei—FDP), winning 49 seats, joined with the CDU and the CSU to form the "small coalition" government of Chancellor Ludwig Erhard.

The coalition government was dissolved in October 1966, following a budgetary disagreement between the CDU/CSU and the FDP. In November 1966, the CDU/CSU joined with the SPD to form a new coalition government, but following the general elections of September 1969, the SPD and FDP formed a coalition government with a combined strength of 254 seats. The elections of November 1972 resulted in a coalition composed of the SPD's 230 seats and the FDP's 42, over the CDU/CSU's 224 seats. Following the resignation of SPD leader Willy Brandt, Helmut Schmidt (SPD) was elected chancellor by the Bundestag in May 1974 by a 267–255 vote. The SPD/FDP coalition retained its majorities in the elections of 1976 (SPD 214, FDP 39) and 1980 (SPD 218, FDP 53).

In the general election of 25 January 1987, the results were as follows: CDU/CSU, 44.3% (223 seats); FDP, 9.1% (46 seats); SPD, 37% (186 seats); and the Greens, 8.3% (42 seats). The first all-Germany elections were held 2 December 1990. The results were as follows: CDU/CSU, 43.8% (319 seats); SPD, 33.5% (239 seats); FDP, 11.0% (79 seats); and Greens, 1.2% (8). The Party of Democratic Socialism (PDS), successor to the SED (Communist party), won 2.4% of the vote and 17 seats. East German parties were allowed to win seats if they received at least 5% of the vote in East Germany. After the breakup of the coalition in 1982, however, the CDU/CSU swept to victory in the voting of March 1983, winning 244 seats and 48.8% of the vote, compared with 226 seats (44.5%) in 1980 and 243 seats (48.6%) in 1976. The swing party, the FDP, took 34 seats (6.9%) and joined the CDU/CSU in a coalition behind Chancellor Helmut Kohl. The SPD polled 38.2% (down from 42.9% in 1980) and captured 193 seats, for a drop of 25.

The CDU and CSU emphasize Christian precepts but are not denominational parties. They favor free enterprise and are supported by small business, professional groups, farmers, and Christian-oriented labor unions. In foreign policy, the CDU/CSU alliance supports European integration and the strengthening of NATO.

The SPD is the oldest and best organized of all German parties. In recent decades it has modified its traditional Marxist program and made an appeal not only to industrial workers but also to farmers, youth, professional people, and the petty bourgeoisie. Its revised Godesberg Program (1959) envisages a mixed economy, support for European integration and NATO, public owner-ship of key industries, a strong defense force, and recognition of religious values.

The FDP is a more heterogeneous organization, consisting of both classical liberals and strongly nationalistic groups. The party is supported mainly by business interests and Protestant groups. It rejects socialism or state capitalism in principle. The Greens (Die Grünen) constitute a coalition of environmentalists and antinu-clear activists; in 1983, they became the first left-wing opposition party to gain a parliamentary foothold since the Communists won 15 seats in 1949. In 1990, in cooperation with Alliance 90, a loose left-wing coalition, the Greens were able to clear the 5% hurdle and win Bundestag seats.

The October 1994 elections saw a weakening of the Free Demo-cratic and Christian Democratic coalition and a strengthening of the Social Democrats and the Greens. The Christian Democrats won 41.5% of the vote and the Free Democrats 6.9%. This gave the governing coalition 341 seats in parliament and a majority of only 10 seats as compared to its previous 134-seat edge. The combined opposition alliance took 48.1% of the vote (331 seats): the Social Democrats took 36.4%; the Greens, 7.3%; and the former Com-munists in eastern Germany (now called the Party of Democratic Socialism), 4.4%.

Kohl's CDU-CSU coalition was weakened further in the Sep-tember 1998 parliamentary elections, winning only 245 seats (35.1%), compared with 298 for the SDP (40.9%). Seats won by other parties were as follows: Greens, 47; Free Democrats, 44; and Party of Democratic Socialism, 35. Following the election, Ger-many's new chancellor Gerhard Schröder formed a center-left co-alition government with the Green Party.

Elections held in September 2002 saw both the SPD and the CDU-CSU coalition each win 38.5% of the vote; however, the SPD came away with 251 seats to 248 for the CDU-CSU. The SPD re-newed its coalition with the Greens, who took 8.5% of the vote and 55 seats, and Schröder remained chancellor. The Free Demo-crats took 7.4% of the vote and 47 seats, and the PDS won 4.3% of the vote and held 2 seats in the Bundestag. On 23 May 2004, Horst Koehler was elected president with the next election scheduled for May 2009.

In the November 2005 elections, Gerhard Schröder (SPD/Greens coalition) lost the chancellery office to Angela Merkel (CDU/CSU-FDP coalition). It was the first time in German his-tory that one of the two larger parties has nominated a woman for this position. The election campaign turned into a tense race of Merkel running against Schröder. Election polls fluctuated as well as did the predictions of the election results. Polls showed that right before the election day, at least a quarter of German voters were still undecided.

Germany held the elections on 18 September 2005, except in a constituency in Dresden that held the elections on 2 October. Un-surprisingly, both candidates came close with the Christian Dem-ocrats receiving only 1% more votes and four more seats than the SPD. Exit polls showed that neither coalition group had won a majority of seats in the federal diet (Bundestag), and both parties lost seats compared to 2002. The SPD/Green coalition fell from 306 seats (in a house of 603) to 273 seats (in a house of 614). At the same time the CDU/CSU-FDP coalition fell from 295 seats to 286 seats. In the final distribution of seats in the federal diet, CDU

got 180 seats, CSU received 46 seats, FDP gained 61 seats, SPD got 222 seats, the Greens remained with 51 seats, and the recently formed left-wing Left Party (or PDS/WASG alliance) climbed up to 54 seats. The next parliamentary elections were to be held Sep-tember 2009.

Neither of the coalitions (SPD-Greens and CDU/CSU-FDP) could achieve a majority of vote in the federal diet (Kandzler-mehrheit) that is required to elect a chancellor. Both chancellors claimed a victory, but to make it functional, they had to negotiate with all of the parties to form an appropriate winning coalition. On 10 October, a round of negotiations ended with the Grand Co-alition between the CDU/CSU and the SPD. Angela Merkel offi-cially became chancellor on the condition that 16 seats in the new cabinet would be equally split up between the CDU/CSU and the SPD and with the SPD controlling 8 out of the 14 ministries, in-cluding the ministries of foreign affairs and finance.

15 LOCAL GOVERNMENT

The Basic Law guarantees local self-government, and the states (Länder) are granted all powers not specifically reserved to the federal government. The Federal Republic consists of 13 Länder, and 3 free states (Freistaaten); Baden-Wuerttemberg, Bayern (Fre-istaat), Berlin, Brandenburg, Bremen, Hamburg, Hessen, Meck-lenburg-Vorpommern, Niedersachsen, Nordrhein-Westfalen, Rheinland-Pfalz, Saarland, Sachsen(Freistaat), Sachsen-Anhalt, Schleswig-Holstein, and Thueringen (Freistaat).

Länder each have ministerial governments and legislatures. They have primary responsibility for the maintenance of law and order; jurisdiction over their own finances, taxes, and administra-tion; and supreme authority in education and other cultural activi-ties. Through the Bundesrat, the Länder have considerable influ-ence in federal legislation and can prevent the central government from imposing radical reforms.

Communes (Gemeinden) are the basic units of local govern-ment, apart from the municipalities, and have the right to regulate such local matters as those involving schools, building, cultural affairs, and welfare. Halfway between the Länder and the com-munes are the counties (Landkreise), which have autonomy in such matters as road building, transportation, and hospitals. They are administered by a Landrat, the chief official, and a Kreistag (country legislature).

16 JUDICIAL SYSTEM

Cases of the first instance are tried by local or Landkreis courts and the superior courts in each of the Länder. The Federal Court of Justice in Karlsruhe, the court of last resort in regular civil and criminal cases, consists of members appointed by a committee that includes federal and Land ministers and several Bundestag members. A court of appeal and the several Land and Landkreis courts are subordinate to the Karlsruhe tribunal. Special courts handle administrative, labor, financial, and social welfare matters. The Federal Constitutional Court, the highest court in the land, has competence to decide problems concerning the Basic Law and to test the constitutionality of laws. The court has 16 members: one 8-member panel elected by a committee of the Bundestag, the other by the Bundesrat.

The judiciary is independent of the legislative and judicial branches and remains free from interference or intimidation. The

Basic Law provides for the rights to a fair trial and prohibits arbitrary interference with privacy, family, home and correspondence. The government authorities generally respect these prohibitions.

17 ARMED FORCES

The unification of Germany in 1991 brought the amalgamation of the People's Army of the German Democratic Republic and the Bundeswehr of the Federal Republic—on the Bundeswehr's terms, modified by political guidance. Essentially, West Germany abolished the East German Ministry of Defense and officer corps, but kept much of the GDR's Russian equipment and a few of its career officers and noncommissioned specialists. The Bundeswehr occupied East German military installations and found many of them beyond repair for training and suitable housing. The Bundeswehr moved eastward with all deliberate speed, especially since six Russian divisions and a tactical air force still remained in German installations. (With dependents these dispossessed Russians numbered almost 500,000). Meanwhile, Germany's NATO allies still maintained an integrated ground and air forces of almost 250,000 troops in western Germany, although this force shrank with the departure of the Canadian and Belgian forces, and the reduction of the American and British contingents in the 1990s.

The German active armed forces in 2005 numbered 284,500, supported by 358,650 reserves. Active Army personnel numbered 191,350. The German Army has large amounts of equipment including 2,398 main battle tanks, 409 reconnaissance vehicles, 2,067 armored infantry fighting vehicles, 3,123 armored personnel carriers, and 1,682 artillery pieces. In addition, the Germans have abundant air defense weapons, helicopters, engineering equipment, and sophisticated antitank weapons.

The German Navy has 20,700 active memebers, including 3,700 naval aviation personnel. The Navy operates 13 tactical submarines and 14 major surface combat vessels (all frigates), 14 patrol and coast combatants, and 23 mine warfare ships.

The German Air Force numbered 51,400 active personnel in 2005. It is structured into the Air Force Command and Transport Command. Equipment for the air force includes 417 combat capable aircraft and 96 transport aircraft of all types.

In 2005 Germany's defense budget totaled $30.2 billion. German armed forces are actively involved in peacekeeping and UN missions abroad. Germany has troops in France and Poland, and trains with the United States military.

18 INTERNATIONAL COOPERATION

The Federal Republic of Germany became a full member of the United Nations on 18 September 1973; it belongs to several non-regional specialized UN agencies. It is also an active participant in the Council of Europe, the European Union, NATO, OECD, OSCE, the Asian Development Bank, the African Development Bank, the Council of the Baltic Sea States, the Euro-Atlantic Partnership Council, the Caribbean Development Bank, G-5, G-7, G-8, and the Paris Club (G-10). Germany is a permanent observer of the OAS and a nonregional member of the West African Development Bank. The country is a member of the WTO.

Germany has supported UN operations and missions in Kosovo (1999), Ethiopia and Eritrea (2000), Sierra Leone (1999), and Georgia (1993). Germany is part of the Australia Group, the Zangger Committee, the Nuclear Suppliers Group (London Group), the Nuclear Energy Agency, the Organization for the Prohibition of Chemical Weapons, and the European Organization for Nuclear Research (CERN).

In environmental cooperation, Germany is part of the Antarctic Treaty; the Basel Convention; Conventions on Biological Diversity, Whaling, and Air Pollution; Ramsar; CITES; the London Convention; International Tropical Timber Agreements; the Kyoto Protocol; the Montréal Protocol; MARPOL; the Nuclear Test Ban Treaty; and the UN Conventions on the Law of the Sea, Climate Change and Desertification.

19 ECONOMY

Germany, with a GDP of $2.83 trillion (at market exchange rate) and $2.43 trillion (purchasing power parity—PPP) in 2005, has the world's third-largest economy in exchange-rate terms and the fifth-largest economy measured by PPP. It is the largest economy in Europe. More than in most other advanced economies, manufacturing remains at the heart of the German economy, although the share of overall industrial output (excluding construction) in GDP declined from 26.9% in 1992 to 22.6% in 2002. As of 2005, the steelmaking sector in the Ruhr region had declined significantly, and agriculture had become a sector of only marginal importance for the economy as a whole.

Before unification in 1990, GNP in West Germany increased at an annual average rate of 7% between 1950 and 1960 and 5.4% between 1960 and 1970. This rate slowed to 3.1% between 1970 and 1980 and 2.3% between 1980 and 1990. However, the unification of Germany in October 1990 proved a heavy economic burden on the west. In 1992, the former East Germany accounted for only 8% of GDP. Transfer payments and subsidies for the east resulted in a large public deficit. Alarmed at the potential for inflation, the Bundesbank pursued a tight monetary policy. This boosted the value of the mark and had a recessionary effect on the European economy. The unemployment rate in 1993 was 7.3% in the west, but 15.8% in the east because so many antiquated, inefficient enterprises were unable to compete in a market economy. These factors led to the recession of 1992–93 with growth in the GDP dropping to 1.1%. The economy recovered in 1994, posting a growth rate of 2.9%, but declined to 1.9% in 1995 and 1% in 1996.

Strong exports in 1997 were expected to bring the growth rate back to 3.5% with sustained growth projected at 4–4.5% for 1998–2000. Such hopes failed to materialize, as the real growth rate for 1998 was 2.7%. The costs of reunification saddled the country with $300 billion in debt, forcing western Germans to pay a 7.5% "solidarity" surtax for reconstructing the eastern section. Even with the infusion of cash, the eastern sector was essentially bankrupt in the late 1990s with 25% unemployment and worker output at 50% of its western counterpart. However, high unemployment did not result in a drop in the hourly wage rate. High labor costs also plague the west where workers average a 38-hour work week and enjoy six weeks of vacation per year. To remain competitive, German companies cut staff and relocated manufacturing jobs to lower-wage countries.

The coalition government of Social Democrats and Greens elected in 1998 pledged to combat Germany's economic sluggishness through a reform program dubbed "Future Program 2000." This program included budget cuts, tax reforms, and a major reform of the pension system. The government also tried to coordinate better labor-management cooperation in its effort to implement its reforms. This coalition government was returned to power in 2002, and Chancellor Gerhard Schröder called on citizens to "renew Germany" by pulling together during difficult economic times. Germany, on the brink of recession, saw a drop in the government's popularity. Schröder threatened to resign in 2003 if his reform package, called "Agenda 2010," was not passed by 2004. This program included a relaxation of job protections, reductions in unemployment and health care benefits, and an easing of the rules on collective bargaining. Indeed, the Social Democrats' traditional support from unions was compromised by the proposed reforms, including, as in France, pension reform: strikes broke out in Germany, France, Austria, and Italy in 2003 due to opposition to cuts in old-age benefits. Neither the reforms of "Agenda 2010" nor reduced taxation did much to improve consumer confidence for Germany's industrial workers, who were unemployed in large numbers. The unemployment rate in Germany stood at 10.6% in 2004, and at 12.4% for the first quarter of 2005.

As a result of elections held in September 2005, a "grand coalition" of the Christian Democratic Union (CDU) and the Social Democratic Party (SDP), headed by Chancellor Angela Merkel, was faced with the task of implementing further economic reforms. Reforming business taxes was one item on the policy agenda. The federal corporation tax rate is 25%, with local taxes pushing the total tax burden on companies up to 38%.

GDP growth was predicted to be a weak 0.9% in 2005, and 1.1% in 2006, with consumer prices rising by 1.9% in 2005 and 1.8% in 2006. Germany was expected to be forced to meet the EU's 3% budget-deficit ceiling by 2007. In 2005, a deficit of 3.7% of GDP was forecast, 3.4% in 2006, and 3.1% in 2007.

20 INCOME

The US Central Intelligence Agency (CIA) reports that in 2005 Germany's gross domestic product (GDP) was estimated at $2.4 trillion. The CIA defines GDP as the value of all final goods and services produced within a nation in a given year and computed on the basis of purchasing power parity (PPP) rather than value as measured on the basis of the rate of exchange based on current dollars. The per capita GDP was estimated at $29,700. The annual growth rate of GDP was estimated at 0.8%. The average inflation rate in 2005 was 2%. It was estimated that agriculture accounted for 1.1% of GDP, industry 28.6%, and services 70.3%.

According to the World Bank, in 2003 remittances from citizens working abroad totaled $5.693 billion or about $69 per capita and accounted for approximately 0.2% of GDP.

The World Bank reports that in 2003 household consumption in Germany totaled $1.408 trillion or about $17,069 per capita based on a GDP of $2.4 trillion, measured in current dollars rather than PPP. Household consumption includes expenditures of individuals, households, and nongovernmental organizations on goods and services, excluding purchases of dwellings. It was estimated that for the period 1990 to 2003 household consumption grew at an average annual rate of 1.5%. In 2001 it was estimated that approximately 14% of household consumption was spent on food, 7% on fuel, 2% on health care, and 10% on education.

21 LABOR

Germany's labor force in 2005 was estimated at 43.32 million workers. Employment by sector in 2003 was as follows: industry 31.9%; agriculture 2.5%; services 65.5%; other occupations 0.1%. Unemployment was estimated at 11.6% in 2005.

The right to organize and to join trade unions is guaranteed by law. As of 2005, about 28% of the eligible labor force was unionized. In 1991, the western trade unions successfully expanded eastward, where they created western structures in the new states, totally dominating overall development so that no GDR trade union survived reunification. Disputes concerning the interpretation of labor agreements are settled before special labor courts. Wages and working conditions in virtually all commercial and industrial establishments are governed by collective bargaining agreements between employers' associations and trade unions. Germany in 2005 did not have an administratively or legislated minimum wage rate.

As of 2005, children under the age of 15 were generally prohibited from employment, and these child labor laws were strictly enforced. Minors 13 and 14 years of age were permitted to work on a farm up to three per day, or deliver newspapers up to two hours per day. Although the average workweek ranges from 36 to 39 hours, the law allows a maximum workweek of 48 hours. Also mandated are a 25% premium for overtime; paid holidays and vacations (15 workdays annually, minimum, and 18 days for employees over 35 years of age); and a 10% premium for night work. However, under various collective bargaining agreements, most workers are entitled to an even greater wage premium for overtime work and even more vacation time than legally required (six weeks per year is typical). About 74% of Germany's labor force in 2005 was covered by a collective bargaining agreement, which partly explains the relatively high wages in the absence of a minimum wage law, and why working time and vacation provisions exceed legal requirements. Health and safety standards are stringently regulated.

22 AGRICULTURE

Although 34% of the total area of Germany is devoted to crop production, production falls far short of satisfying industrial and consumer demand. Agriculture accounted for only 1% of GDP in 2003. The total amount of arable land in 2003 came to 12,040,000 hectares (29,750,000 acres). In 2003, the average size of Germany's 420,697 farms was about 40 hectares (100 acres).

Article 15 of the 1990 Treaty (for monetary, economic and social union) arranged for transitional price supports for GDR farmers until an integration within the EU agricultural market could occur. Before reunification, agriculture had engaged about 6.1% and 3% of the economically active populations of the former GDR and old FRG, respectively. Agriculture engaged 2.5% of Germany's population in 2002. The former GDR Länder contribute significantly to German agricultural production. The chief crops in order of yield in 2004 were sugar beets, 27,159,000 tons; wheat, 25,427,000 tons; barley, 12,933,000 tons; and potatoes, 13,044,000 tons. Apples and pears as well as cherries and peaches are significant fruit crops. In 2003, apple production was the smallest since 1995 from bad pollination and forest damage. Viticulture is important in the southwest, and Germany is a renowned producer of wines for world consumption; 105 million liters of wine were produced in 2004. Germany is the world's second-largest importer of agricultural products (after the United States), with nearly $50.8 billion in 2004.

23 ANIMAL HUSBANDRY

The government regulates the marketing of livestock, meat, and some dairy products; it also controls the distribution of livestock for slaughter and meat. Livestock in 2005 included 13,257,000 head of cattle (including five million milk cows), and 26,235,000 hogs, 2,138,000 sheep, 520,000 horses, 112,000,000 chickens, and 8,000,000 turkeys. Milk production amounted to 27.6 million tons in 2005; cheese, 2,074,000 tons; and butter, 444,000 tons. Meat production in 2005 included 4.5 million tons of pork, 1.1 million tons of beef, 1 million tons of poultry, and 54,000 tons of lamb, mutton, and goat. In 2002, of the 2.8 million cattle tested for BSE ("mad cow" disease), 0.003% were confirmed positive. Some 798,000 tons of eggs were produced in 2005. Germany is the leading meat, milk, and honey producer of Europe.

24 FISHING

The importance of the fishing industry has declined in recent years. At the beginning of 2004, the German fishing fleet consisted of 2,281 vessels with 66,008 GRT. In 2004, there were 88 fishery companies employing 9,004 people. The total catch in 2004 amounted to 288,000 tons, of which 125,000 tons came from domestic ports. The main fishing areas are the North Sea, the Baltic Sea, and the waters off Greenland. Overfishing is a serious environmental problem. The government subsidizes capacity reduction and modernization measures. The fish varieties accounting for the greatest volume are herring, mackerel, cod, and sardines. Aquaculture consists mostly of pond-raised trout and carp. Imports of fish products totaled 774,095 tons in 2004 (valued at $2.63 billion), while exports amounted to 370,508 tons (valued at $1.14 billion). Norway and Denmark together supply 40% of Germany's fish and seafood imports. Germany is the fourth-largest fish processing country in the EU (after the United Kingdom, France, and Spain). Processed fish production amounted to 474,428 tons in 2004, valued at $1.91 billion.

25 FORESTRY

Total forest area amounted in 2000 to over 10.7 million hectares (26.5 million acres), about 31% of the total land area. Reforestation has resulted in a 6% increase in the forest area since the end of World War II (1939–45). Deciduous species (such as beech, oak, ash, maple, and alder) originally covered about two-thirds of the area, and conifers were only predominant in higher elevations. Today, hardwood trees comprise only one-third of the forests. Principal softwood species include silver fir, pine, spruce, and Douglas fir, which was introduced from the northwest United States late in the 19th century. The most thickly wooded of the federal Länder are Hessen and Rhineland-Pfalz. A total of 54 million cu m (1.9 billion cu ft) of timber was cut in 2005. The wood products industry consists of about 185,000 companies employing more than 1.3 million people, larger than the German automotive industry. Almost half of the raw timber is used by sawmills for lumber production. The German sawmilling industry consists of about 2,500 sawmills producing around 17 million cu m (600 mil-

lion cu ft) of softwood lumber and 1.2 million cu m (42.4 million cu ft) of hardwood lumber. Total trade in forest products during 2004 included $14.8 billion in imports and $6.3 billion in exports. Output of paper and paperboard totaled 20.4 million tons in 2004, highest in Europe. High domestic labor costs compel Germany to import substantial quantities of value-added products such as veneers and panels.

26 MINING

Germany's export-oriented economy was the largest in Europe. Approximately one-third of Germany's gross domestic product (GDP) depended upon exports. Germany was also a major processing nation, relying on imports of raw materials for the metals processing industry and the manufacture of industrial mineral products. The country was a leader in the mining equipment manufacturing sector, and was among the largest and most technologically advanced producers of iron, coal, and cement. Although the underground mining sector has steadily declined, certain minerals remained important domestically and worldwide. In 2003, Germany was the world's largest lignite producer, the world's third-largest producer of potash, a leading producer of kaolin in Western Europe, a major European producer of crude gypsum, and self-sufficient in feldspar and salt. The only metal mineral still mined in Germany was uranium.

Except for the very large lignite and potash operations, most of the producing and processing facilities in operation were small. The restructuring and privatization of facilities in the former German Democratic Republic (GDR) continued in 2003, including of the mineral-resource industries. Production figures for 2003 were, in million tons: potash, 3.563; kaolin, 3.5; marketable gypsum and anhydrite, 1.748, down from 1.761 in 2001; feldspar, 0.5; industrial dolomite and limestone, 106, up from 76 in 2001; and marketable salt (evaporated, rock, and other), 16.3, up from 15.6 in 2001. In 2003, Germany also produced barite; bromine; chalk; clays (bentonite, ceramic, fire, fuller's earth, brick); diatomite; fluorspar; graphite; lime; quicklime; dead-burned dolomite; nitrogen; phosphate materials, including Thomas slag; mineral and natural pigments; pumice; dimension stone; quartz; quartzite; slate; building sand; gravel; terrazzo splits; foundry sand; industrial glass sand; talc; and steatite. In terms of overseas developments, Süd-Chemie AG was the largest bentonite producer in Europe. Between 140 and 160 small- to medium-sized clay mines were in operation; about one-half of the high-quality refractory and ceramic clays produced were from the Rhineland-Palatinate area. No iron ore was mined in 1999 and 2000; demand was met by imports of 47 million tons.

27 ENERGY AND POWER

Germany is the greatest consumer of electric power in Europe. In 2003, total installed capacity was estimated at 119.8 GW. Total production of electric power in that year amounted to an estimated 558.1 billion kWh, of which 63% was produced in conventional thermal plants (mainly fueled by hard coal), 28% in nuclear installations, and 6% from other renewable sources. As of November 2005, there were 17 nuclear plants, and as of 2003, Germany ranked fourth internationally in nuclear power generation. In 2001, the German government and its utility companies signed an agreement to gradually phase out nuclear power over the coming decades due to environmental concerns.

Proven natural gas reserves were estimated at 9.9 trillion cu ft, as of 1 January 2005. Domestic production in 2003 accounted for slightly more than 24% of the natural gas consumed in 2003. In that year, domestic demand for natural gas was put at an estimated 3.3 trillion cu ft, while domestic production that year was estimated at 0.8 trillion cu ft. Major natural gas suppliers to Germany are Russia, the Netherlands, and Norway. In 2000 production began at Germany's first offshore gas field in the North Sea. It is expected to produce 3.3 billion cu m (116 billion cu ft) of gas per day for 16 years. Production of oil was estimated at 169,300 barrels per day in 2005, of which 38% was crude oil. Local production is not sufficient to cover consumption, which totaled an estimated 2.6 million barrels per day in 2005.

Germany has extensive coal reserves. In 2003, recoverable reserves of coal totaled an estimated 7,428.5 million short tons, with consumption and production estimated at 273 million short tons and 229.1 million short tons, respectively, for that same year. Germany's hard coal (anthracite and bituminous) deposits lie deep underground and are difficult to mine economically. As a result, hard coal extraction is subsidized by the government, which for 2005, plans to spend $3.5 billion for subsidies. However, by 2012, coal subsidies are slated to fall to $2.3 billion, the result of a pact with the coal industry reached in 1997. Brown coal, or lignite, however, is easier to obtain and does not require subsidies from the government. It also accounts for the vast bulk of German coal output. In 2003, of the 273.0 million short tons of coal produced, brown coal accounted for 86% of production, with 13% for bituminous and 1% for anthracite. The lignite industry, which is centered in the eastern part of the country, was drastically changed as a result of unification and the introduction of the strict environmental and safety laws of the pre-1991 FRG.

Germany is also looking at renewable energy sources. Under the Renewable Energy Sources Act, Germany is looking to have 12.5% of its energy supplied by renewable sources by 2010, and 20% by 2020. During the 1990s, more than 5,000 electricity-generating windmills were installed in Germany, mostly along the North Sea coast, and wind power is expected to supply 3.5% of electricity by 2010. As of November 2005, Germany had 14,600 MW of installed wind power capacity and 390 MW of installed solar voltaic capacity.

28 INDUSTRY

Germany is the world's third-largest industrial power, behind the United States and Japan. The major industrial concentrations of western Germany are the Ruhr-Westphalia complex; the Upper Rhine Valley, Bremen and Hamburg, notable for shipbuilding; the southern region, with such cities as Munich and Augsburg; and the central region, with such industrial cities as Salzgitter, Kassel, Hanover, and Braunschweig. In the east, most of the leading industries are located in the Berlin region or in such cities as Dresden, Leipzig, Dessau, Halle, Cottbus, and Chemnitz.

The main industrial sectors in the former GDR were electrical engineering and electronics, chemicals, glass, and ceramics. The optical and precision industries were important producers of export items. Following unification, wages in the east were allowed to reach levels far exceeding productivity. As a result, many facto-

ries closed and industrial production plunged by two-thirds before stabilizing.

German industry has been struggling with high labor costs, stiff international competition, and high business taxes. Large industrial concerns like Daimler-Benz have spun off unprofitable companies, cut staff, and are looking for ways to boost productivity. Policies such as these have led to a loss of some two million industrial jobs since 1991. Other companies, like the electronics giant Siemens, have moved plants abroad in search for lower labor costs and to secure positions in developing economies like China and Thailand.

Despite the costs of restructuring the former GDR, Germany had some of the largest and most successful companies in the world as of late 2005, from automobiles to advanced electronics, steel, chemicals, machinery, shipbuilding, and textiles. German industrial products are known for their high quality and reliability. Nevertheless, the global recession that began in 2001 negatively affected German industry, with 45,000 insolvencies in 2002, including Holzmann, the large construction company. The construction industry, which experienced a post-reunification boom in the early 1990s, experienced an 8% drop in orders at the beginning of 2002. Although German industry (excluding construction) as a percentage of GDP declined from 26.9% in 1992 to 22.6% in 2002, manufacturing in 2005 remained at the heart of the German economy.

29 SCIENCE AND TECHNOLOGY

The reunification of East and West Germany has created great opportunities for the entire population but has also placed great strains on the nation. Perhaps nowhere is this more evident than in science, engineering and technical education, and vocational training. Germany maintains an excellent science and technology educational system and vocational training in many fields. About 140,000 science and engineering students graduated per year in the last years of the 20th century. Still, the challenge of incorporating the former German Democratic Republic (GDR) into a complete and modern German nation is daunting. Public and university research facilities in the former East Germany are old and poorly maintained, and science and engineering students have been found to be poorly trained and equipped to work in more modern West German institutions and companies. It is believed that the German government will need to completely rebuild the science and technology infrastructure in the former GDR before it can compare with more modern German facilities.

The German national science and technology budget is applied to many areas of science and technology, and leading fields include traditional areas of German strength, like chemical, automotive and telecommunications research and development. Current policy emphasizes the application of science and technology to enhance Germany's economic and competitive standing, while protecting the nation's health and the environment. Support for science and technology also occurs at other levels. There are independent laboratories, comprised of both the national laboratories and private research institutes like the Max Planck and Fraunhofer Societies. In addition, German industry supports many important types of research and development, and the German states, or Länder, provide still more resources for scientific research. The Ministry for Science and Technology (BMFT), an organization without parallel in the United States, both coordinates and sets priorities for the entire national science and technology program. Finally, Germany's participation in the European Union also has a significant science and technology component—Germany provides funding, scientists, and laboratories for broad European research and development. In 2003 total research and development (R&D) expenditures in Germany amounted to $56,592.7 billion, or 2.64% of GDP. Of that total, 65.5% came from the business sector, followed by the government at 31.6%, the foreign sector at 2.3%, and by higher education at 0.4%.

In 2002, there were 3,222 scientists and engineers and 1,435 technicians per million people that were actively engaged in R&D. High-tech exports that same year were valued at $86.861 billion, accounting for 17% of manufactured exports.

Germany has numerous universities and colleges offering courses in basic and applied sciences. In 1987–97, science and engineering students accounted for 47% of university enrollment. In 2002, of all bachelor's degrees awarded, 30.2% were in the sciences (natural, mathematics and computers, and engineering).

The Natural History Museum in Berlin (founded in 1889) has geological, paleontological, mineralogical, zoological, and botanical components. The country has numerous specialized learned societies concerned with agriculture and veterinary science, medicine, the natural sciences, and technology.

30 DOMESTIC TRADE

Wholesalers, retailers, mail-order houses, door-to-door salespersons, department stores, consumer cooperatives, and factory stores all engage in distribution. There are about 630,000 commercial enterprises in Germany, with over than 760,000 local units. Nearly 5 million people are employed in domestic trade, which has a yearly turnover of over €1 trillion.

Chain stores are common, with the top 10 German retail organizations accounting for almost 80% of total German retail turnover. Convenience shops are a fast growing market outlet in Germany.

The economy is generally described as a "social market economy." The state continues to own some major sections of the economy and provides subsidies for the growth and development of some sectors. However, free enterprise and competition are encouraged. Privatization of public utilities has resulted in greater competition and lower prices. The economy as a whole is primarily export oriented, with nearly one-third of national product exported.

Usual business hours for retail stores are from 9 AM to 6 or 6:30 PM on weekdays and from 9 AM to 4 PM on Saturday. Retail stores are not open on Sundays or holidays unless they have a special limited permit allowing them to be open. Twenty-four-hour shopping is available only at certain gas stations and at other sites related to travel. Wholesale houses and industrial plants usually have a half day (noon closing) on Saturday. Banks are open Monday–Friday from 8:30 AM to 1 PM and from 2:30 PM to 4 PM (5:30 PM on Thursday).

31 FOREIGN TRADE

Germany is one of the world's great trading nations. In 2003 and 2004 it was the largest exporter in the world. In 2004, Germany's exports amounted to $909.7 billion, compared with the United

Principal Trading Partners – Germany (2003)

(In millions of US dollars)

Country	Exports	Imports	Balance
World	748,531.3	601,761.0	146,770.3
France-Monaco	78,002.5	54,904.7	23,097.8
United States	68,614.2	42,098.1	26,516.1
United Kingdom	61,340.5	35,356.2	25,984.3
Italy-San Marino-Holy See	53,914.0	37,926.5	15,987.5
Netherlands	44,117.2	46,495.2	-2,378.0
Austria	38,872.0	23,437.7	15,434.3
Belgium	37,109.9	28,711.2	8,398.7
Spain	36,266.2	18,393.2	17,873.0
Switzerland-Liechtenstein	28,571.8	21,011.6	7,560.2
China	20,401.4	28,259.7	-7,858.3

(…) data not available or not significant.

SOURCE: *2003 International Trade Statistics Yearbook*, New York: United Nations, 2004.

States' $811.1 billion. German imports stood at $717.9 billion, resulting in a trade surplus of $191.8 billion in 2004.

Manufactured products are the leading exports. Germany supplies a large portion of the world with automobiles and car parts. Germany's motor vehicle exports made up 18.4% of its total exports in 2004. Diverse machinery exports, including nonelectrical and electrical parts, also account for a large percentage of the world's exports in those commodities (and 14% of Germany's total exports in 2004). Chemical products, telecommunications technology, in addition to devices for electricity production and distribution, are the next leading exports. The leading markets for Germany's goods in 2004, in order of importance, were France, the United States, the United Kingdom, Italy, and the Netherlands.

In 2004, Germany's major imports were chemical products (11% of total imports), motor vehicles (10.3%), petroleum and natural gas (6.8%), machinery (6.7%), and computers and related products (4.8%). Germany's leading suppliers in 2004, in order of importance, were France, the Netherlands, the United States, Italy, and the United Kingdom.

32 BALANCE OF PAYMENTS

After experiencing deficits during 1979–81, Germany's current accounts balance rebounded to a surplus of about DM9.9 billion in 1982 and then kept rising to DM76.5 billion in 1986, primarily because of falling prices for crude oil and other imports, combined with appreciation of the deutsche mark relative to other European currencies. By 1989, Germany's current account surplus was nearly 5% of GNP. With reunification, however, this changed immediately. Imports rushed in as former-GDR residents sought newly available consumer goods, and exports fell as goods and services were diverted to the east. As a result, Germany recorded current account deficits since 1991, created in part because of the substantial foreign borrowing undertaken to finance the cost of unification. Even so, large current account surpluses from the 1970s and 1980s helped Germany to maintain its position as the world's second-largest creditor with net foreign assets estimated at $185 billion in 1995. From 1990 to 1996, however, Germany's share of world exports dropped from 12% to 9.8% due in large part to high

Public Finance – Germany (2003)		
(In billions of euros, central government figures)		
Revenue and Grants	**653.46**	**100.0%**
Tax revenue	245.87	37.6%
Social contributions	378.34	57.9%
Grants	10.54	1.6%
Other revenue	18.71	2.9%
Expenditures	**698.61**	**100.0%**
General public services	95.55	13.7%
Defense	25.47	3.6%
Public order and safety	3.0	0.4%
Economic affairs	46.59	6.7%
Environmental protection	0.37	0.1%
Housing and community amenities	6.19	0.9%
Health	134.55	19.3%
Recreational, culture, and religion	0.83	0.1%
Education	3.09	0.4%
Social protection	382.97	54.8%

(…) data not available or not significant.

SOURCE: *Government Finance Statistics Yearbook 2004*, Washington, DC: International Monetary Fund, 2004.

labor costs which were making it hard for Germany to compete in the global economy. Germany in 2001 ranked second behind the United States in numbers of both exports and imports, and ran a current account surplus. By 2004, it was the world's leading exporter, and had a current account surplus estimated at $73.59 billion.

33 BANKING AND SECURITIES

The central banking system of Germany consists of the German Federal Bank (Deutsche Bundesbank), currently located in Frankfurt am Main (but which is expected to move to Berlin, the capital), one bank for each of the Länder (Landeszentralbanken), and one in Berlin, which are the main offices for the Federal Bank. Although the Federal Bank is an independent institution, the federal government holds the bank's capital and appoints the presidents as well as the board of directors; the Central Bank Council acts as overseer. All German banks are subject to supervision by the German Federal Banking Supervisory Authority (Bundesaufsichtsamt für das Kreditwesen) in Berlin.

The Federal Bank is the sole bank of issue. Until the advent of the euro in 1999 it set interest and discount rates. These functions are now the domain of the European Central Bank (ECB). However, the Federal Bank maintains a leading role in domestic banking. The largest commercial banks are the Deutsche Bank, Dresdner Bank, and Commerzbank. In 1997 Germany had 232 commercial banks, including the "big three," 56 subsidiaries or branches of foreign banks, and 80 private banks. There are also 13 central giro institutions. In addition, there are 657 savings banks and 18 credit institutions with special functions, including the Kreditanstalt für Wiederaufbau (Reconstruction Loan Corporation), which is the channel for official aid to developing countries. In all, there were over 45,000 bank offices in 2002. The German financial system includes just under 2,700 small industrial and agricultural credit cooperatives and allied institutions, in addition to four central institutions; 33 private and public mortgage banks that obtain funds from the sale of bonds; the postal check and postal savings system; and 34 building societies. In April 2000, a proposed merger between two of the "big three," Deutsche Bank and Dresdner Bank, collapsed. The deal would have reduced operating costs by relieving both banks of their branch networks.

After the Bundesbank just missed its target range for M3 growth for 1996 of 4% to 7%, it decided on a two-year target for monetary supply growth to cover the 1997-98 period leading up to the planned hand-over of responsibility to the ECB on 1 January 1999.

In 1996 Moody's Investments Service capped an extremely poor year for Deutsche Bank by reducing its triple A rating to Aa1. This reflects the fact that elite banks are finding it harder to retain the triple A rating as banking becomes internationally more competitive. Deutsche Bank announced that it hoped to shed 1,300 employees through attrition by 2000.

The International Monetary Fund reports that in 2001, currency and demand deposits—an aggregate commonly known as M1—were equal to $544.8 billion. In that same year, M2—an aggregate equal to M1 plus savings deposits, small time deposits, and money market mutual funds—was $1,849.3 billion. The money market rate, the rate at which financial institutions lend to one another in the short term, was 4.37%.

Under the constitution, the governments of the Länder regulate the operations of stock exchanges and produce exchanges. Eight stock exchanges operate in Berlin, Bremen, Düsseldorf, Frankfurt, Hamburg, Hannover, Munich, and Stuttgart. Germany has several other independent exchanges for agricultural items. There are no restrictions on foreign investments in any securities quoted on the German stock exchanges. However, a foreign (or domestic) business investor that acquires more than 25% of the issued capital of a German quoted company must inform the company of this fact. The most notable recent banking legislation is the January 2002 elimination of the capital gains tax on holdings sold by one corporation to another. In 2004, a total of 660 companies were listed on the Deutsche Borse AG. Market capitalization in 2004 totaled 41,194.517 billion. The DAX in 2004 rose 7.3% from the previous year to 4,256.1.

34 INSURANCE

In 2003, the value of direct premiums written totaled $170.811 billion, of which nonlife premiums accounted for $94.073 billion. Germany's top nonlife insurer in that same year was Allianz Versicherungswirtschafe with gross nonlife premiums written of $9,071.1 million. The country's leading life insurer that year was Allianz Leben, with $11,554.2 billion in life insurance premiums written. Worker's compensation, third party automobile liability, legal liability for drug companies, airlines, hunters, auditors, tax advisors, security firms, architects, lawyers, nuclear power station operators, and accident and health insurance are compulsory. The insurance sector is highly regulated and, despite the opening of the European Union (EU) market, it will be difficult for foreign companies to win the confidence of potential German customers.

35 PUBLIC FINANCE

The 1967 Law for the Promotion of Economic Stability and Growth requires the federal and state governments to orient their budgets to the main economic policy objectives of price stability, high employment, balanced foreign trade, and steady commensurate growth. The Financial Planning Council, formed in 1968, coordinates the federal government, states, municipalities, and the Bundesbank in setting public budgets. Income, corporate turnover, mineral oil, and trade taxes account for more than 80% of all tax revenue, with the federal government controlling just under half of it. Since the 1960s, social insurance provisions have accounted for the largest share of federal expenditures. Germany's reunification in 1990 raised special problems with regard to economic and financial assimilation. The Unification Treaty provided that the new states should be incorporated in the financial system established by the Basic Law as much as possible from the onset. Therefore, since 1991, the new states have basically been subject to the same regulations with regard to budgetary management and tax distribution as the western states. A "German Unity Fund" was initiated to provide financial support for the new states (and their municipalities); it is jointly financed by the western states, with most of the money being raised in the capital market.

The US Central Intelligence Agency (CIA) estimated that in 2005 Germany's central government took in revenues of approximately $1.2 trillion and had expenditures of $1.3 trillion. Revenues minus expenditures totaled approximately -$113 billion. Public debt in 2005 amounted to 68.1% of GDP. Total external debt was $3.626 trillion.

The International Monetary Fund (IMF) reported that in 2003, the most recent year for which it had data, central government revenues were €653.46 billion and expenditures were €698.61 billion. The value of revenues was us$738 million and expenditures us$788 million, based on a market exchange rate for 2003 of us$1 = €.8860 as reported by the IMF. Government outlays by function were as follows: general public services, 13.7%; defense, 3.6%; public order and safety, 0.4%; economic affairs, 6.7%; environmental protection, 0.1%; housing and community amenities,

0.9%; health, 19.3%; recreation, culture, and religion, 0.1%; education, 0.4%; and social protection, 54.8%.

36 TAXATION

In 2000, the German tax system underwent a major reform featuring a dramatic reduction in taxes on business (from a corporate income tax rate of 40% to 25%, and the elimination altogether of a 53% tax on investment profits), as well as a scheduled reduction in the top income tax rate to 42% by 2005 from 56% in the 1980s, and 53% in 2000. As of 2005, Germany's corporate income tax rate was 25%, plus a 5.5% surcharge. There is also a 5% basic trade tax, although rates in the main cities range from 20–25%. A nonresident corporation, whose headquarters and management are outside of Germany, does not have to pay the surcharge. Business related capital gains are taxed as income, with a 95% exemption on gains from the sale of most shareholdings by companies for tax years ending after 31 December 2003. Business activities are also subject to municipal trade taxes of 12–20.5%, depending upon the municipality.

As of 2005, Germany's progressive individual income tax had a top rate of 42%, plus a 5.5% surcharge. Although self-employed persons are subject to the country's trade tax, the tax can be credited against a person's individual income tax. In 2005 the progressive schedule of income tax rates saw an increase in the 0%, tax-free base to €7,665, with decreases in other brackets. However, the threshold for the highest tax rate decreased from €55,008 in 2002 to €52,293 in 2003 to €52,152 in 2005. Rates and exemptions depend on the number of children, age, and marital status of taxpayer. Individuals also pay an 8–9% church tax, although non-churchgoers, and members of the Orthodox or Anglican Churches are exempt from paying any church tax. Other direct taxes include an inheritance and gift tax, a net worth tax, and a 2% real estate transfer tax.

The main indirect tax in Germany is a value-added tax (VAT) introduced in 1968 with a standard rate of 10%. By 2003, the standard rate had risen to 16%. A reduced rate of 7% applies to some basic foodstuffs, water supplies, medical care and dentistry, medical equipment for disabled persons, books, newspapers and periodicals, some shows, social housing, agricultural inputs, social services, and public transportation. Items exempt from the VAT include admissions to cultural events, building land, supplies for new buildings, TV licenses, telephones and faxes, basic medical and dental care, the use of sports facilities, and some waste disposal services. Exports are also zero-rated.

37 CUSTOMS AND DUTIES

Germany is a member of the European Union and thus has a common import customs tariff and complies with trade agreements put in place by the EU. Germany is also a contracting party to the Harmonized System Convention. In regard to trade with non-EU countries, most raw materials enter duty-free, while most manufactured goods are subject to varying rates between 5% and 8%. Germany levies a 15% value-added tax on industrial goods.

38 FOREIGN INVESTMENT

All foreign investment must be reported to the German Federal Bank (Bundesbank), but there are no restrictions on the repatriation of capital or profits. Until the 1998 deregulation of Deutsche

---

Balance of Payments – Germany (2003)

(In billions of US dollars)

Current Account		54.9
Balance on goods	151.7	
Imports	-601.4	
Exports	753.1	
Balance on services	-50.4	
Balance on income	-13.9	
Current transfers	-32.5	
Capital Account		0.4
Financial Account		-79.7
Direct investment abroad	-1.5	
Direct investment in Germany	11.3	
Portfolio investment assets	-37.6	
Portfolio investment liabilities	103.5	
Financial derivatives	-0.7	
Other investment assets	-170.3	
Other investment liabilities	15.7	
Net Errors and Omissions		23.8
Reserves and Related Items		0.7

(…) data not available or not significant.

SOURCE: *Balance of Payment Statistics Yearbook 2004*, Washington, DC: International Monetary Fund, 2004.

Telekom, telecommunications remained closed to foreign investment. There is no special treatment for foreign investors. As of 2005, incentives for investment in the former GDR deemed to be desirable included accelerated depreciation, loans at below-market interest rates, and cash investment grants and subsidies. Still applicable in all of Germany as of 2005 were cash grants; tax incentives such as capital reserve allowances and special depreciation allowances; investment grants; and credit programs, including low-interest loans. Foreign firms may also participate in government and/or subsidized research and development programs.

Although few formal barriers exist, high labor costs have discouraged foreign companies from setting up manufacturing plants in Germany. Nevertheless, the German government and industry enthusiastically encourage foreign investment in Germany. German law provides foreign investors national treatment.

There are eight free ports in Germany operated under EU Community law. These duty-free zones within the ports are open to both domestic and foreign entities.

Across the 10-year period 1991 to 2001, total foreign direct investment (FDI) totaled $393 billion, the third highest total in the world. Half of this came in 2000, when FDI inflow reached over $195 billion. Annual FDI inflow had been $12 billion in 1997, rising to $24.5 billion in 1998, to $54.7 billion in 1999. With the bursting of the dot.com bubble in 2001, FDI inflow to Germany fell to about $21.1 billion in 2001 and was estimated at $36.2 billion in 2002.

According to the Bundesbank, FDI in Germany in 2003 (the latest figures available) had fallen to $12.9 billion, about two-thirds less than the 2002 high. In GDP terms, 2003 flows of FDI represented 0.6% of Germany's GDP, while the total stock of FDI in 2003 equaled 26.1% of GDP.

FDI outflows from Germany peaked at almost $106.5 billion in 1999. FDI outflows were about $36.9 billion in 2001 and $8.7 billion in 2002. German flows of direct investment abroad plunged to $2.6 billion in 2003.

39 ECONOMIC DEVELOPMENT

Germany describes its economy as a "social market economy." Outside of transportation, communications, and certain utilities, the government has remained on the sidelines of entrepreneurship. Beginning in 1998, and in line with EU regulations, the German government began deregulating these fields as well. It has, nevertheless, upheld its role as social arbiter and economic adviser. Overall economic priorities are set by the federal and Land governments pursuant to the 1967 Stability and Growth Act, which demands stability of prices, a high level of employment, steady growth, and equilibrium in foreign trade. In addition to the state, the independent German Federal Bank (Bundesbank), trade unions, and employers' associations bear responsibility for the nation's economic health. With the advent of the euro in 1999, much of the Federal Bank's authority in monetary matters was transferred to the European Central Bank (ECB). In the international arena, Germany has acted as a leader of European economic integration.

Government price and currency policies have been stable and effective. Less successful have been wage-price policies, which have been unable to control a continued upward movement. Inflationary pressures have increased and combined with a general leveling off in productivity and growth. Attempts to neutralize competition by agreements between competitors and mergers are controlled by the Law Against Restraints of Competition (Cartel Act), passed in 1957 and strengthened since then. The law is administered by the Federal Cartel Office, located in Bonn.

Unemployment remained at an average 9% in the early 2000s; it was twice as high in eastern Germany as in western Germany. As of the first quarter of 2005, the unemployment rate stood at 12.4%. Although much effort has been expended to integrate the former East German economy with the West's (infrastructure has improved drastically and a market economy has been introduced), progress in causing the two economies to converge slowed in the late 1990s and early 2000s. Annual transfers from West to East amounted to approximately $70 billion in 2005. Germany had the weakest GDP growth in the EU from 1994–2003, when Germany's economy was moribund.

The aging population, combined with high unemployment, has pushed social security outlays to a level exceeding contributions from workers. Corporate restructuring and growing capital markets are setting the foundations allowing Germany to thrive globally and to lead the process of European economic integration, particularly if labor-market rigidities are addressed. However, in the short run, rising expenditures and lowered revenues have raised the budget deficit above the EU's 3% debt limit.

40 SOCIAL DEVELOPMENT

The social security system of the FRG remained in place following unification with the German Democratic Republic. However, the GDR system continued to apply on an interim basis within the former GDR territory. The two systems were merged effective 2 January 1992. The social insurance system provides for sickness and maternity, workers' compensation, disability, unemployment, and old age; the program is financed by compulsory employee and employer contributions. Old age pensions begin at age 65 after five years of contribution. Worker's medical coverage is comprehensive, including dental care. Unemployment coverage includes all workers, trainees, apprentices, and at-home workers in varying degrees. The government funds a family allowance to parents with one or more children.

Equal pay for equal work is mandated by law, but women continue to earn less than men. Women continue to be underrepresented in managerial positions. Sexual harassment of women in the workplace is recognized and addressed. Although violence against women exists, the law and government provides protection. Victims of violence can receive police protection, legal help, shelter and counseling. Children's rights are strongly protected.

Freedom of religion is guaranteed by the Basic Law in Germany, although there have been reports of some discrimination against minority religions. Extremist right-wing groups continue to commit violent acts against immigrants and Jews although the government is committed to preventing such acts. The Basic Law also provides for the freedom of association, assembly, and expression.

41 HEALTH

Health insurance in Germany is available to everyone. Benefits are broad and nationally uniform, with only minor variations among plans. They include free choice of doctors; unlimited physician visits; preventive checkups; total freedom from out-of-pocket payments for physician services; unlimited acute hospital care (with a nominal co-payment); prescription drug coverage (with a minimal co-payment); comprehensive dental benefits (with a 25–30% co-payment); vision and hearing exams, glasses, aids, prostheses, etc.; inpatient and psychiatric care (and outpatient psychiatric visits); monthly home care allowances; maternity benefits; disability payments; and rehabilitation and/or occupational therapy. Health care expenditure was estimated at 10.5% of GDP. Expenditures on health are among the highest in the world.

In 2004, there were approximately 362 physicians, 951 nurses, 78 dentists, and 58 pharmacists per 100,000 people. There were about 2,260 hospitals in Germany, with about 572,000 beds. A gradual deinstitutionalization of people with chronic mental illness has taken place, with the number of hospital beds declining from 150,000 in the former West Germany in 1976 to a total of 69,000 in Germany as a whole as of 1995. Germany immunized 85% of children up to one year old against diphtheria, pertussis, and tetanus.

Average life expectancy was 78.65 years in 2005. Infant mortality was 4.16 per 1,000 live births in the same year, one of the lowest in the world. As of 2002, the birth rate was estimated at 8.9 per 1,000 live births and the overall death rate at 10.4 per 1,000 people. Contraceptive use is high. Nearly 75% of married women 15–49 used some form of birth control. The total fertility rate in 2000 was 1.4 children per woman throughout her childbearing years. The maternal mortality rate was low at 8 deaths per 100,000 live births.

The HIV/AIDS prevalence was 0.10 per 100 adults in 2003. As of 2004, there were approximately 43,000 people living with HIV/AIDS in the country. There were an estimated 1,000 deaths from AIDS in 2003.

Tobacco consumption has decreased significantly from 2.4 kg (5.3 lbs) in 1984 to 2.1 kg (4.6 lbs) a year per adult in 1995. The heart disease average in Germany was higher than the European average.

42 HOUSING

Nearly 2.8 million of the country's 12 million dwellings were destroyed or made uninhabitable as a result of World War II. In the early 1950s, there were 10 million dwellings available for 17 million households. From 1949 to 1978, over 18 million housing units were built, a construction rate of over 500,000 a year; since then, new construction has slowed, averaging 357,000 new units annually during the period 1980–85. Over 4.2 million housing units were built in 1991 or later (excluding residential homes).

Over half of the population live in residential buildings of three or more dwelling units. Nearly 98% of all dwelling units are in such multi-unit residential buildings; of these, about 42.6% are owner occupied. About 69% of the dwelling units in residential buildings have central heating systems. Gas and oil are the most common energy sources. In 2002, there was a total of about 38,957,100 dwelling units nationwide; only 254,900 were residential homes. The average number of persons per household is 2.2.

43 EDUCATION

Most schools and kindergartens are the responsibility of the states, not of the federal government. Therefore, though the overall struc-

ture is basically the same, it is difficult for a pupil to transfer from one school to another. German teachers are civil servants. They are required to have a teaching degree and are paid according to a uniform salary scale. Attendance at all public schools and universities is free.

Children start school after their sixth birthday and are required to attend on a full-time basis for nine or ten years, depending on the state of residence. After four years of primary or elementary school (*Grundschule*), students choose from three types of secondary school. The best pupils go to a gymnasium, which prepares them for the university matriculation examination, or *abitur*. A second option is the *realschule*, leading to technical job training and middle-management employment. The third type is the *hauptschule*, or general school.

However, a network of correspondence courses has developed, geared for those who wish to continue their studies while working. In Germany, vocational training is the rule. On-the-job training in an authorized company is combined with instruction in a vocational school. Vocational training is concluded by taking a theoretical and practical examination before a Board of the Chamber, and those who pass are given a certificate. This system of vocational training has clearly reduced youth unemployment.

In 2001, nearly all children between the ages of three and five were enrolled in some type of preschool program. Primary school enrollment has been estimated at about 84% of age-eligible students. In 2003, secondary school enrollment was about 88% of age-eligible students. Nearly all students complete their primary education. The student-to-teacher ratio for primary school was at about 14:1 in 2003; the ratio for secondary school was also about 14:1.

Higher education is represented by three types of institutions: universities (*technische universitäten*), colleges of art and music, and universities of applied sciences (*fachhochscchulen*). There are also several *fachschulen*, which offer continuing vocational training for adults. In 2003, about 51% of the tertiary age population were enrolled in some type of higher education program. The adult literacy rate has been estimated at about 99%.

As of 2003, public expenditure on education was estimated at 4.8% of GDP, or 9.5% of total government expenditures.

44 LIBRARIES AND MUSEUMS

Germany had no national library until 1913, when the German Library (7.2 million volumes in 2002) in Leipzig brought together an extensive collection literature of the German language under one roof. The library also contains 3.9 million volumes of works written in exile by German authors during the Nazi era. In 1990 a further consolidation of German libraries was completed with the establishment of the German Library in Frankfurt, which had 18 million volumes in 2002. Other prominent libraries are the Bavarian State Library in Munich (7.6 million books) and the Prussian Cultural Property State Library (10 million books) in Berlin. The Herzog-August Library in Wolfenbüttel (848,000 volumes) has archives of 12,000 handwritten medieval books. One of the most important collections of German literature is at the Central Library of German Classics in Weimar. The Berlin Central and Regional Library, the public library network for the area, contains over 3.1 million print and electronic sources. The German Library for the Blind in Leipzig was founded in 1894. It serves as a publishing house and production center for Braille texts and audio books, as well as a public lending library containing 40,000 book titles and 5,000 titles of sheet music in Braille.

Germany has more than 4,500 state, municipal, association, private, residential, castle, palace, and church and cathedral treasures museums, which annually attract over 100 million visitors. Berlin has the Egyptian and Pergaman Museums, the Painting Gallery of Old Masters, and the National Gallery of Modern Art. The Jewish Museum opened in Berlin in 2001 offering exhibits on the history and culture of the Jewish people in the region. The Germanic National Museum in Nüremberg has the largest collection on the history of German art and culture from antiquity to the 20th century. The German Museum in Munich is one of the most well known natural sciences and technology museums in Europe. The Pinakothek Moderne, opened in 2003, houses a huge modern art collection in Munich. In addition, there are hundreds of smaller museums, ethnological and archaeological institutions, scientific collections, and art galleries.

The Bach Archive in Leipzig contains a museum, research institute, and library dedicated to the life and work of the composer J.S. Bach, who once served as the city's music director. Beethoven Haus in Bonn and the Richard Wagner Museum Haus in Bayreuth honor two more famous German composers. Museums on the life and work of Goethe are located in Frankfurt (birthplace) and Weimer. Lutherhaus in Wittenberg serves as a historical museum for both the life and work of Martin Luther and the Protestant Reformation that he ignited.

45 MEDIA

Since reunification, postal services have been under the jurisdiction of the Deutsche Bundespost Postdienst and telecommunications under Deutsche Bundespost Telekom. Intensive capital investments since reunification have rapidly modernized and integrated most of the obsolete telephone network of the former GDR. In 2003, there were an estimated 657 mainline telephones for every 1,000 people. The same year, there were approximately 785 mobile phones in use for every 1,000 people.

There are 11 regional broadcasting corporations, including Zweites Deutsches Fernsehen, which operates Channel Two nationally. In 1999 there were 77 AM, 1,621 FM, and 373 television stations. In 2003, there were an estimated 570 radios and 675 television sets for every 1,000 people. About 250.8 of every 1,000 people were cable subscribers. Also in 2003, there were 484.7 personal computers for every 1,000 people and 473 of every 1,000 people had access to the Internet. There were 13,847 secure Internet servers in the country in 2004.

There are about 305 national, regional, and local newspapers in Germany, as well as a large number of other periodicals. Of the newspapers sold on the street, the *Bild* has the largest circulation at about 3.8 million in 2005. The *Berliner Zeitung*, founded in 1945 but completely redesigned in 1997, is a nationally prominent daily with a circulation on 2005 of about 180,000. Other influential daily national newspapers (with 2005 circulation rates unless noted) are: the *Express* (Cologne, 468,800 in 2004), *Rheinische Post* (Duesseldorf, 443,100 in 2004), the *Sachsische Zeitung* (Dresden, 416,800 in 2004), the *Frankfurter Allgemeine Zeitung* (Frankfurt, 377,000), *Die Welt* (244,000 in 2004), *Frankfurter Rundschau*

(167,000), *Suddeutsche Zeitung* (Munich, 437,000), *Der Tagesspiegel* (135,000), and *Die Tageszeitung* (59,000).

Over 20,000 periodicals are published in Germany. The best-known internationally is the news magazine *Der Spiegel* which is modeled after the American *Time* magazine. The German Press Agency, owned by German newspaper publishers and publishers' organizations, furnishes domestic and international news. There are hundreds of small press agencies and services.

The Basic Law provides for free press rights, and the government mostly supports these rights in practice, though propaganda of Nazi and certain other proscribed groups is illegal, as are statements endorsing Nazism.

46 ORGANIZATIONS

The Federation of German Industries, the Confederation of German Employers' Associations, the Federation of German Wholesale and Foreign Traders, and the Association of German Chambers of Commerce represent business in the FRG. There are about 14 regional associations of chambers of business and industry located in the largest cities; many maintain branch offices in smaller cities. The chambers are organized into provincial associations and are headed by the Permanent Conference of German Industry and Trade. The cooperative movement is well developed. Consumer cooperatives are represented in the International Cooperative Alliance by the Central Association of German Cooperatives, founded in 1949; it also represents credit cooperatives. The central association of agricultural cooperatives, the German Raiffeisen Society, is located in Wiesbaden. The Association of German Peasants is the largest society of farmers. There is also a Central Association of German Artisan Industries. The private Association of Consumers operates more than 150 local advisory centers. Professional societies and associations are numerous and represent a wide variety of occupations and fields of study.

Civil action groups (Bürgerinitiativen) have proliferated in recent years. August 13 Working Committee serves in part as a human rights awareness organization. Deutscher Frauenring serves as an umbrella organization for national women's groups. The Red Cross is active. There are national chapters of Habitat for Humanity, CARE and Caritas.

The German Academy of Arts in Berlin and the Academy of Fine Arts in Dresden are well-known arts organizations. There is a network of seven academies of science in Germany. The UNESCO Institute for Education has an office in Hamburg. A few cultural and learned associations particular to Germany include the International Gottfried Wilhelm Leibniz Society, the International Heinrich Schutz Society, and the International Hegel Gesellschaft Society. There are numerous organizations dedicated to research and education in scientific fields, particularly those relating to medicine.

There are about 80 youth associations, most of which belong to the Federal Youth Ring. The scouting movement is highly active and political parties sponsor groups associated in the Ring of Political Youth. In total there are about 90 national youth organizations and youth associations. Many of them are part of the umbrella organization known as the German Federal Youth Association.

There are thousands of groups and associations sponsoring various arts and cultural activities and special organizations for various hobbies and sports. The German Sports Confederation serves as an umbrella organization for over 88,000 sports clubs nationwide. There are also many patriotic and religious organizations in the country.

47 TOURISM, TRAVEL, AND RECREATION

Germany is famous for its beautiful scenery, particularly the Alps in the south and the river valleys of the Rhine, Main, and Danube; the landscape is dotted with castles and medieval villages. Theater, opera, and orchestral music abound in the major cities. The area that was formerly the German Democratic Republic offers a number of Baltic beach resorts and scenic Rügen Island. Residents of the United States and Canada need only a valid passport to enter Germany for a period of no more than three months; citizens of other countries need a visa. All border formalities for residents of other European Community countries were abandoned with the lifting of trade barriers in 1993.

Facilities for camping, cycling, skiing, and mountaineering are abundant. Football (soccer) is the favorite sport; Germany hosted and won the World Cup competition in 1974, and was scheduled to host in 2006. Tennis has become more popular since Boris Becker won the Wimbledon Championship in 1985; German Steffi Graf was inducted into the International Tennis Hall of Fame in 2004. The Olympic Games were held in Berlin in 1936, during the Hitler years, and in Munich in 1972.

Approximately 16,357,037 tourists visited Germany in 2003, almost 34% of whom came from Western Europe. There were 892,302 hotel rooms with about 1.6 million beds and an occupancy rate of 33%. The average length of stay was two nights. Tourism receipts totaled $31.6 billion that year.

In 2005, the US Department of State estimated the daily expenses in Munich at $350; in Cologne, $323; and in Berlin, $353.

48 FAMOUS GERMANS

The roster of famous Germans is long in most fields of endeavor. The name of Johann Gutenberg (1400?–1468?), who is generally regarded in the Western world as the inventor of movable precision-cast metal type, and therefore as the father of modern book printing, might well head the list of notable Germans. Martin Luther (1483–1546), founder of the Reformation, still exerts profound influence on German religion, society, music, and language.

The earliest major names in German literature were the poets Wolfram von Eschenbach (1170?–1220?), Gottfried von Strassburg (d.1210?), and Sebastian Brant (1457?–1521). Hans Sachs (1494–1576) wrote thousands of plays, poems, stories, and songs. Hans Jakob Christoffel von Grimmelshausen (1620?–76) created a famous picaresque novel, *Simplicissimus*. The flowering of German literature began with such renowned 18th-century poets and dramatists as Friedrich Gottlieb Klopstock (1724–1803), Gotthold Ephraim Lessing (1729–81), Christoph Martin Wieland (1733–1813), and Johann Gottfried von Herder (1744–1803), and culminated with the greatest German poet, Johann Wolfgang von Goethe (1749–1832), and the greatest German dramatist, Johann Christoph Friedrich von Schiller (1759–1805). Leaders of the Romantic movement included Jean Paul (Jean Paul Friedrich Richter, 1763–1825), August Wilhelm von Schlegel (1767–1845), Novalis (Friedrich von Hardenberg, 1772–1801), Ludwig Tieck (1773–1853), E. T. A. (Ernst Theodor Wilhelm—the A stood for

Amadeus, the middle name of Mozart) Hoffmann (1776–1822), and Heinrich Wilhelm von Kleist (1777–1811). The brothers Jakob Grimm (1785–1863) and Wilhelm Grimm (1786–1859) are world-famous for their collections of folk tales and myths. Heinrich Heine (1797–1856), many of whose poems have become folksongs, is generally regarded as the greatest German poet after Goethe. Other significant poets are Friedrich Hölderlin (1770–1843), Friedrich Rückert (1788–1866), Eduard Mörike (1804–75), Stefan Georg (1868–1933), and Rainer Maria Rilke (1875–1926). Playwrights of distinction include Friedrich Hebbel (1813–63), Georg Büchner (1813–37), Georg Kaiser (1878–1945), Ernst Toller (1893–1939), and Bertolt Brecht (1898–1957). Two leading novelists of the 19th century were Gustav Freytag (1816–95) and Theodor Storm (1817–88). Germany's 20th-century novelists include Ernst Wiechert (1887–1950), Anna Seghers (Netty Reiling, 1900–1983), and Nobel Prize winners Gerhart Johann Robert Hauptmann (1862–1946), Thomas Mann (1875–1955), Nelly Sachs (1891–1970), and Heinrich Böll (1917–86). Other major writers of the 20th and 21st centuries include German-born Erich Maria Remarque (1898–1970), Günter Grass (b.1927), Christa Wolf (b.1929), and Peter Handke (b.1942).

Leading filmmakers include G. W. (Georg Wilhelm) Pabst (b.Czechoslovakia, 1885–1967), F. W. (Friedrich Wilhelm Plumpe) Murnau (1888–1931), Fritz Lang (b.Austria, 1890–1976), German-born Ernst Lubitsch (1892–1947), Max Ophüls (Oppenheimer, 1902–57), Leni (Helene Bertha Amalie) Riefenstahl (1902–2003), Volker Schlöndorff (b.1939), Werner Herzog (b.1942), Rainer Werner Fassbinder (1946–82), Wim Wenders (b.1945), and Doris Dörrie (b.1955). Outstanding performers include Emil Jannings (Theodor Friedrich Emil Janenz, b.Switzerland, 1886–1950), Marlene Dietrich (1901–1992), and Klaus Kinski (Claus Günther Nakszynski, 1926–91).

The two giants of German church music were Heinrich Schütz (1585–1672) and, preeminently, Johann Sebastian Bach (1685–1750). Significant composers of the 18th century were German-born Georg Friedrich Handel (1685–1759), Carl Philipp Emanuel Bach (1714–88), and Christoph Willibald von Gluck (1714–87). The classical period and music in general were dominated by the titanic figure of Ludwig von Beethoven (1770–1827). Romanticism in music was ushered in by Carl Maria von Weber (1786–1826), among others. Outstanding composers of the 19th century were Felix Mendelssohn-Bartholdy (1809–47), Robert Schumann (1810–56), Richard Wagner (1813–83), and Johannes Brahms (1833–97). Major figures of the 20th and 21st centuries are Richard Strauss (1864–1949), Paul Hindemith (1895–1963), Carl Orff (1895–1982), German-born Kurt Weill (1900–50), Hans Werner Henze (b.1926), and Karlheinz Stockhausen (b.1928). Important symphonic conductors included Otto Klemperer (1885–1973), Wilhelm Furtwängler (1886–1954), Karl Böhm (1894–1981), and Eugen Jochum (1902–87). Among Germany's outstanding musical performers are singers Elisabeth Schwarzkopf (b.1915) and Dietrich Fischer-Dieskau (b.1925), and pianists Walter Gieseking (1895–1956) and Wilhelm Kempff (1895–91).

Veit Stoss (1440?–1533) was one of the greatest German sculptors and woodcarvers of the 15th century; another was Tilman Riemenschneider (1460?–1531). Outstanding painters, engravers, and makers of woodcuts were Martin Schongauer (1445?–91), Matthias Grünewald (1460?–1528?), Hans Holbein the Elder (1465?–

1524), Lucas Cranach (1472–1553), Hans Holbein the Younger (1497?–1543), and above all, Albrecht Dürer (1471–1528). More recent artists of renown are the painters Emil Nolde (1867–1956), Franz Marc (1880–1916), Max Beckmann (1884–1950), the US-born Lyonel Feininger (1871–1956), Otto Dix (1891–1969), Max Ernst (1891–1976), and Horst Antes (b.1936); the painter and cartoonist George Grosz (1893–1959); the sculptors Ernst Barlach (1870–1938) and Wilhelm Lehmbruck (1881–1919); the painter-etcher-sculptor Käthe Kollwitz (1867–1945); the Dadaist Hannah Höch (1889–1978); the painter-sculptor-installation artist Joseph Beuys (1921–1986); the painter and sculptor Anselm Kiefer (b.1945); and the architects Walter Gropius (1883–1969), leader of the Bauhaus School of Design, Ludwig Mies van der Rohe (1886–1969), Erich Mendelsohn (1887–1953), Gottfried Böhm (b.1920), and Helmut Jahn (b.1940).

Scholars and Leaders

German influence on Western thought can be traced back at least as far as the 13th century, to the great scholastic philosopher, naturalist, and theologian Albertus Magnus (Albert von Bollstädt, d.1280) and the mystic philosopher Meister Eckhart (1260?–1327?). Philipp Melanchthon (Schwartzerd, 1497–1560) was a scholar and religious reformer. Gottfried Wilhelm von Leibniz (1646–1716) was an outstanding philosopher, theologian, mathematician, and natural scientist. The next two centuries were dominated by the ideas of Immanuel Kant (1724–1804), Moses Mendelssohn (1729–86), Johann Gottlieb Fichte (1762–1814), Friedrich Ernst Daniel Schleiermacher (1768–1834), Georg Wilhelm Friedrich Hegel (1770–1831), Friedrich Wilhelm Joseph von Schelling (1775–1854), Arthur Schopenhauer (1788–1860), Ludwig Andreas Feuerbach (1804–72), Karl Marx (1818–83), Friedrich Engels (1820–95), and Friedrich Wilhelm Nietzsche (1844–1900). In the 20th century, Edmund Husserl (1859–1938), Oswald Spengler (1880–1936), Karl Jaspers (1883–1969), Martin Heidegger (1889–1976), and Hans-Georg Gadamer (1900–2002) are highly regarded. Figures of the Frankfurt School of social and political philosophy include Theodor Adorno (1903–1969), Max Horkheimer (1895–1973), Walter Benjamin (1892–1940), Herbert Marcuse (1898–1979), and Jürgen Habermas (b.1929). Political theorist Hannah Arendt (1906–1975) is also highly regarded, as is Carl Schmitt (1888–1985). One of the founders of modern Biblical scholarship was Julius Wellhausen (1844–1918). Franz Rosenzweig (1886–1929) was one of the most influential modern Jewish religious thinkers, as was Gershom Scholem (1897–1982).

Among the most famous German scientists are Johann Rudolf Glauber (1694–1768), Justus von Liebig (1803–73), Robert Wilhelm Bunsen (1811–99), and Nobel Prize winners Hermann Emil Fischer (1852–1919), Adolf von Baeyer (1835–1917), Eduard Buchner (1860–1917), Wilhelm Ostwald (1853–1932), Otto Wallach (1847–1931), Richard Martin Willstätter (1872–1942), Fritz Haber (1868–1934), Walther Nernst (b.Poland, 1864–1941), Heinrich Otto Wieland (1877–1957), Adolf Otto Reinhold Windaus (1876–1959), Carl Bosch (1874–1940), Friedrich Bergius (1884–1949), Otto Hahn (1879–1968), Hans Fischer (1881–1945), Friedrich Bergius (1884–1949), Georg Wittig (1897–1987), Adolf Butenandt (1903–1995), Otto Diels (1876–1954), Kurt Alder (1902–58), Hermann Staudinger (1881–1965), Karl Ziegler (1898–1973), Manfred Eigen (b.1927), Ernst Otto Fischer (b.1918), Johann Deisenhofer

(b.1943), Robert Huber (b.1937), and Hartmut Michel (b.1948) in chemistry; Karl Friedrich Gauss (1777–1855), Georg Simon Ohm (1787–1854), Hermann Ludwig Ferdinand von Helmholtz (1821–94), Heinrich Rudolf Hertz (1857–1894), and Nobel Prize winners Wilhelm Konrad Röntgen (1845–1923), Max Karl Ernst Ludwig Planck (1858–1947), Albert Einstein (1879–1955), Gustav Ludwig Hertz (1887–1975), Werner Heisenberg (1901–76), Walter Bothe (1891–1957), Carl-Friedrich von Weizsäcker (b.1912), Rudolf Mössbauer (b.1929), Hans Bethe (1906–2005), Klaus von Klitzing (b.1943), Ernst Ruska (1906–1988), Gerd Binnig (b.1947), Johannes Georg Bednorz (b.1950), Hans Georg Dehmelt (b.Germany, 1922), Wolfgang Paul (1913–1993), Wolfgang Ketterle (b.1957), and Theodor Wolfgang Hänsch (b.1941) in physics; Rudolf Virchow (1821–1902), August von Wassermann (1866–1925), and Nobel Prize winners Robert Koch (1843–1910), Paul Ehrlich (1854–1915), Emil von Behring (1854–1917), Otto H. Warburg (1883–1970), Konrad Lorenz (Austria, 1903–89), Konrad Emil Bloch (1912–2000), Feodor Felix Konrad Lynen (1911–1979), Max Delbrück (b.Germany 1906–1981), Sir Bernard Katz (b.Germany 1911–2003), Georges Jean Franz Köhler (1946–1995), Erwin Neher (b.1944), Bert Sakmann (b.1942), Christiane Nüsslein-Volhard (b.1942), and Günter Blobel (b.1936), in physiology or medicine; earth scientists Alexander von Humboldt (1769–1859) and Karl Ernst Richter (1795–1863); and mathematician Georg Friedrich Bernhard Riemann (1826–66). Notable among German inventors and engineers are Gabriel Daniel Fahrenheit (1686–1736), developer of the thermometer; Gottlieb Daimler (1834–1900), Rudolf Diesel (b.Paris, 1858–1913), and Felix Wankel (1902–88), developers of the internal combustion engine; airship builder Count Ferdinand von Zeppelin (1838–1917); and rocketry pioneer Wernher von Braun (1912–77). Leading social scientists, in addition to Marx and Engels, were the historians Leopold von Ranke (1795–1886) and Theodor Mommsen (1817–1903), Nobel Prize winner in literature; the political economist Georg Friedrich List (1789–1846); the sociologists Georg Simmel (1858–1918) and Max Weber (1864–1920); and the German-born anthropologist Franz Boas (1858–1942). Johann Joachim Winckelmann (1717–68) founded the scientific study of classical art and archaeology. Heinrich Schliemann (1822–90) uncovered the remains of ancient Troy, Mycenae, and Tiryns; Wilhelm Dörpfeld (1853–1940) continued his work.

Outstanding figures in German political history are the Holy Roman emperors Otto I (the Great, 912–973), Frederick I (Barbarossa, 1123–90), Frederick II (1194–1250), and Spanish-born Charles V (1500–58); Frederick William (1620–88), the "great elector" of Brandenburg; his great-grandson Frederick II (the Great, 1712–86), regarded as the most brilliant soldier and statesman of his age; Otto Eduard Leopold von Bismarck (1815–98), the Prussian statesman who made German unity possible; Austrian-born Adolf Hitler (1889–1945), founder of Nazism and dictator of Germany (1933–45); and Konrad Adenauer (1876–1967), FRG chancellor (1948–63). Walter Ernst Karl Ulbricht (1893–1973), chairman of the Council of State (1960–73), and leader of the SED from 1950 to 1971, was the dominant political figure in the GDR until his death in 1973. Erich Honecker (1912–94) became first secretary of the SED in 1971 and was chairman of the Council of State and SED general secretary from 1976 until the FRG and GDR merged in 1990. Willi Stoph (1914–1999), a member of the Politburo since 1953, served as chairman of the Council of Ministers in 1964–73 and again from 1976 on. Willy Brandt (1913–1992), FRG chancellor (1969–74) won the Nobel Peace Prize for his policy of Ostpolitik. Other Nobel Peace Prize winners were Ludwig Quidde (1858–1941), Gustav Stresemann (1878–1929), Carl von Ossietzky (1889–1938), and Albert Schweitzer (1875–1965).

Baron Friedrich Wilhelm Ludolf Gerhard Augustin von Steuben (1730–94) was a general in the American Revolution. Karl von Clausewitz (1780–1831) is one of the great names connected with the science of war. Important military leaders were Hellmuth von Moltke (1800–1891); Gen. Paul von Hindenburg (1847–1934), who also served as president of the German Reich (1925–34); and Gen. Erwin Rommel (1891–1944).

Pope Benedict XVI (b.Joseph Alois Ratzinger, 1927) became the 265th pope in 2005. He is the ninth German pope, the last being the Dutch-German Adrian VI (1522–1523).

⁴⁹DEPENDENCIES

Germany has no territories or colonies.

⁵⁰BIBLIOGRAPHY

Annesley, Claire (ed.). *A Political and Economic Dictionary of Western Europe*. Philadelphia: Routledge/Taylor and Francis, 2005.

Berg-Schlosser, Dirk and Ralf Rytlewski (eds.). *Political Culture in Germany*. New York: St. Martin's Press, 1993.

Briel, Holger (ed.). *German Culture and Society: The Essential Glossary*. London: Arnold, 2002.

Bullock, Alan Louis Charles. *Hitler and Stalin: Parallel Lives*. London: Harper-Collins, 1991.

Eckhart, Karl, et al. (eds.). *Social, Economic and Cultural Aspects in the Dynamic Changing Process of Old Industrial Regions: Ruhr District (Germany), Upper Silesia (Poland), Ostrava Region (Czech Republic)*. Piscataway, N.J.: Transaction Publishers, 2003.

Gortemaker, Manfred. *Unifying Germany, 1989–1990*. New York: St. Martin's Press, 1994.

Hiden, John. *Republican and Fascist Germany: Themes and Variations in the History of Weimar and the Third Reich, 1918–45*. New York: Longman, 1996.

International Smoking Statistics: A Collection of Historical Data from 30 Economically Developed Countries. New York: Oxford University Press, 2002.

Mitcham, Samuel W. *Retreat to the Reich: The German Defeat in France, 1944*. Westport, Conn.: Praeger, 2000.

Sarkar, Saral K. *Green-alternative Politics in West Germany*. New York: United Nations University Press, 1993.

Shirer, William L. *The Rise and Fall of the Third Reich*. New York: Simon and Schuster, 1960.

Summers, Randal W., and Allan M. Hoffman (ed.). *Domestic Violence: A Global View*. Westport, Conn.: Greenwood Press, 2002.

Tipton, Frank B. *A History of Modern Germany Since 1815*. Berkeley: University of California Press, 2003.

Verhey, Jeffrey. *The Spirit of 1914: Militarism, Myth and Mobilization in Germany*. New York: Cambridge University Press, 2000.

Vogt, Henri. *Between Utopia and Disillusionment: A Narrative of the Political Transformation in Eastern Europe*. New York: Berghahn Books, 2004.

Wessels, Wolfgang, Andreas Maurer, and Jürgan Mittag (eds.). *Fifteen into One?: the European Union and Its Member States*. New York: Palgrave, 2003.

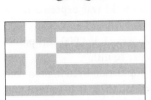

GREECE

Hellenic Republic
Elliniki Dhimokratia

CAPITAL: Athens (Athínai)

FLAG: The national flag consists of nine equal horizontal stripes of royal blue alternating with white and a white cross on a royal-blue square canton.

ANTHEM: *Ethnikos Hymnos (National Hymn),* beginning "Se gnorizo apo tin kopsi" ("I recognize you by the keenness of your sword").

MONETARY UNIT: The euro replaced the drachma as official currency in 2002. The euro is divided into 100 cents. There are coins in denominations of 1, 2, 5, 10, 20, and 50 cents and 1 euro and 2 euros. There are notes of 5, 10, 20, 50, 100, 200, and 500 euros. €1 = $1.25475 (or $1 = €0.79697) as of 2005.

WEIGHTS AND MEASURES: The metric system is the legal standard.

HOLIDAYS: New Year's Day, 1 January; Epiphany, 6 January; Independence Day, 25 March; Labor Day, 1 May; Assumption, 15 August; National Day (anniversary of successful resistance to Italian attack in 1940), 28 October; Christmas, 25 December; Boxing Day, 26 December. Movable religious holidays include Shrove Monday, Good Friday, and Easter Monday.

TIME: 2 PM = noon GMT.

¹LOCATION, SIZE, AND EXTENT

Greece is the southernmost country in the Balkan Peninsula, with a total area of 131,940 sq km (50,942 sq mi); about a fifth of the area is composed of more than 1,400 islands in the Ionian and Aegean seas. Comparatively, the area occupied by Greece is slightly smaller than the state of Alabama. Continental Greece has a length of 940 km (584 mi) N–S and a width of 772 km (480 mi) E–W. It is bounded on the N by Macedonia and Bulgaria, on the NE by Turkey, on the E by the Aegean Sea, on the S by the Mediterranean Sea, on the SW and W by the Ionian Sea, and on the NW by Albania, with a total land boundary length of 1,228 km (763 mi) and a coastline of 13,676 km (8,498 mi). The capital city of Greece, Athens, is located along the country's southern coast.

²TOPOGRAPHY

About four-fifths of Greece is mountainous, including most of the islands. The most important range is the Pindus, which runs down the center of the peninsula from north to south at about 2,650 m (8,700 ft) in average elevation. Mt. Olympus (Ólimbos; 2,917 m/9,570 ft) is the highest peak and was the legendary home of the ancient gods.

Greece has four recognizable geographic regions. The Pindus range divides northern Greece into damp, mountainous, and isolated Epirus (Ipiros) in the west and the sunny, dry plains and lesser mountain ranges of the east. This eastern region comprises the plains of Thessaly (Thessalía) and the "new provinces" of Macedonia (Makedonia) and Thrace (Thraki)—"new" because they became part of Greece after the Balkan wars in 1912–13. Central Greece is the southeastern finger of the mainland that cradled the city-states of ancient Greece and comprises such classical provinces as Attica (Atikí), Boeotia (Voiotia), Doris, Phocis,

and Locris. Southern Greece consists of the mountainous, four-fingered Peloponnesus (Pelopónnisos), separated from the mainland by the Gulf of Corinth (Korinthiakós Kólpos). Islands of the Aegean comprise the numerous Cyclades (Kikládes); the Dodecanese (Dhodhekánisos), including Rhodes (Ródhos); and the two large islands of Crete (Kríti) and Euboea (Évvoia).

Greek rivers are not navigable. Many dry up in the summer and become rushing mountain torrents in the spring. The longest river is the Maritsa, which runs along the northeast border a distance of 480 km (300 mi).

Greece is located above the convergence of the Eurasian and the African Tectonic Plates, a situation which causes frequent earthquakes and tremors. While many quakes are low magnitude tremors with minimal damage and injury, stronger quakes are not entirely uncommon. On 14 August 2003, a 6.3 magnitude earthquake occurred in western Greece causing injuries to about 50 people and damaging roads and buildings.

³CLIMATE

The climate in southern Greece and on the islands is Mediterranean, with hot, dry summers and cool, wet winters. Winters are severe in the northern mountain regions. The summer heat is moderated by mountain and sea breezes. Precipitation is heaviest in the north and in the mountains. Average annual rainfall varies from 50 to 121 cm (20–48 in) in the north and from 38 to 81 cm (15–32 in) in the south. The mean temperature of Athens is 17°c (63°F), ranging from a low of 2°c (36° F) in the winter to a high of 37°c (99°F) in the summer.

⁴FLORA AND FAUNA

Of the 4,992 species of higher plants recorded in Greece, about 742 are endemic to the country. Many pharmaceutical plants and other rare plants and flowers considered botanical treasures flourish in Greece. Vegetation varies according to altitude. From sea level to 460 m (1,500 ft), oranges, olives, dates, almonds, pomegranates, figs, grapes, tobacco, cotton, and rice abound. From 460 to 1,070 m (1,500–3,500 ft) are forests of oak, chestnut, and pine. Above 1,070 m (3,500 ft), beech and fir are most common.

Fauna are not plentiful, but bear, wildcat, jackal, fox, and chamois still exist in many sparsely populated areas. The wild goat (agrimi), which has disappeared from the rest of Europe, still lives in parts of Greece and on the island of Crete. There are about 95 species of mammal throughout the country. Migratory and native birds abound and there are more than 250 species of marine life. Natural sponges are a main export item.

5 ENVIRONMENT

Among Greece's principal environmental problems are industrial smog and automobile exhaust fumes in metropolitan Athens. Over half of all industry is located in the greater Athens area. From June to August 1982, the air pollution became so oppressive that the government closed down 87 industries, ordered 19 others to cut production, and banned traffic from the city center. In July 1984, the smog again reached the danger point, and 73 factories were ordered to cut production and cars were banned from the city. In January 1988, the number of taxis in the center of Athens was halved, and private cars were banned from the city's three main thoroughfares. The smog regularly sends hundreds of Greeks to the hospital with respiratory and heart complaints. Greece is among the 50 nations with the world's highest levels of industrial carbon dioxide. In 1992, it ranked 37th, with emissions totaling 73.8 million metric tons, a per capita level of 7.25. In 1996, the total rose to 80.6 million metric tons.

Water pollution is a significant problem due to industrial pollutants, agricultural chemicals such as fertilizers and pesticides, and sewage. The Gulf of Saronikos is one of the most polluted areas because 50% of Greece's industrial facilities are located there. Greece has 58 cu km of renewable water resources with 81% used for farming and 3% used for industrial purposes.

Greece's pollution problems are the result of almost complete disregard for environmental protection measures during the rapid industrial growth of the 1970s, compounded by unbalanced development and rapid, unregulated urban growth. Government policies have emphasized rational use of natural resources, balanced regional development, protection of the environment, and increased public participation in environmental matters. Four environmental and planning services were consolidated under the Ministry for Physical Planning, Housing, and the Environment.

In 2003, about 3.6% of the total land area was protected by the state. Meteora and Mount Athos are UNESCO World Heritage Sites. There are 10 Ramsar wetland sites in the country. According to a 2006 report issued by the International Union for Conservation of Nature and Natural Resources (IUCN), threatened species included 11 types of mammals, 14 species of birds, 6 types of reptiles, 4 species of amphibians, 27 species of fish, 1 type of mollusk, 10 species of other invertebrates, and 2 species of plants. Endangered species include the Mediterranean monk seal, the hawksbill turtle, Atlantic sturgeon, and the large copper butterfly.

6 POPULATION

The population of Greece in 2005 was estimated by the United Nations (UN) at 11,100,000, which placed it at number 74 in population among the 193 nations of the world. In 2005, approximately 18% of the population was over 65 years of age, with another 15% of the population under 15 years of age. There were 98 males for every 100 females in the country. According to the UN, the annual population rate of change for 2005–10 was expected to be stagnant at 0.0%, a rate the government viewed as too low. The projected population for the year 2025 was 11,394,000. The population density was 84 per sq km (218 per sq mi).

The UN estimated that 60% of the population lived in urban areas in 2005, and that urban areas were growing at an annual rate of 0.58%. The capital city, Athens (Athínai), had a population of 3,215,000 in that year. Another major urban area is Thessaloniki with a metropolitan population of 824,000.

7 MIGRATION

Under League of Nations supervision in 1923, more than one million Greek residents of Asia Minor were repatriated, and some 800,000 Turks left Greece. During the German occupation (1941–44) and the civil war (1944–49), there was a general movement of people from the islands, the Peloponnesus, and the northern border regions into the urban areas, especially the Athens metropolitan area, including Piraiévs. Between 1955 and 1971 about 1,500,000 peasants left their farms—about 600,000 going to the cities, the rest abroad. According to the 1981 census, 813,490 Greeks had migrated since 1975 to urban areas, and 165,770 had moved to rural areas. The growth rate of the Athens, Thessaloniki, Pátrai, Iráklion, and Vólos metropolitan areas during 1971–81 far exceeded the population growth rate for the nation as a whole.

Many Greeks leave the country for economic reasons. In the years after World War II, the number of annual emigrants has varied from a high of 117,167 (in 1965) to a low of 20,330 (in 1975). The net outflow of Greek workers during the 1960s was 450,000; during the 1970s, however, there was a net inflow of 300,000. This mainly reflected declining need for foreign labor in western Europe.

In 1974, when the Greek military government collapsed, about 60,000 political refugees were living overseas; by the beginning of 1983, about half had been repatriated, the remainder being, for the most part, Communists who had fled to Soviet-bloc countries after the civil war of 1944–49. After the fall of Communism in 1989 slightly more than half of the migrants to Greece were Albanians, followed by other influxes from nearby countries. In 2002 Greece received $1.18 billion in remittances.

In 2004, Greece received 7,375 applications for asylum, as compared to 4,367 in 1997. Most of them were from Iraq, Afghanistan, Georgia, Algeria, and Iran. In that same year Greece had a population of 2,489 refugees and another 3,459 persons of concern (primarily Iraqi Christians) according to the United Nations High Commissioner for Refugees (UNHCR). According to *Migration News*, in 2005 Greece had 900,000 to 1.2 million immigrants, including 400,000 in irregular status. In August 2005 Greece passed a new immigration law allowing for foreigners legally living in the country in 2004 to become permanent residents in 2006. However, the ethnic Greek Albanians and about 500,000 unauthorized foreigners were excluded from this policy change.

In 2005, the net migration rate was estimated as 2.18 migrants per 1,000 population.

8 ETHNIC GROUPS

About 98% of the population is Greek. Minority groups include Turks, Macedonian Slavs, Albanians, Armenians, Bulgarians, Jews, and Vlachs. Though a number of citizens identify themselves as Pomaks, Romas, Macedonians, Slavomacedonians, Roma, and Arvanites, the government does not officially acknowledge these groups as minorities. Though some citizens describe themselves as Turks or Turkish, use of the term is prohibited in titles of organizations or associations. The Greeks also object to use of the term Macedonian by the Slavic speaking inhabitants of that region.

9 LANGUAGES

Modern Greek, the official language, is the first language of about 99% of the population. English, learned mostly outside the school system, and French are widely spoken. Turkish and other minority languages, such as Albanian, Pomakic, Kutzovalachian, and Armenian, also are spoken. The vernacular and the language of popular literature are called dimotiki (demotic). The official language dialect—katharevousa—generally used by the state, the press, and universities, employs classical terms and forms. In 1976, the government began to upgrade the status of dimotiki in education and government. The liturgical language is akin to classical Greek.

10 RELIGIONS

The government does not keep statistics on membership in religious groups; however, it is estimated that about 97% of the population are nominally members of the Greek Orthodox Church. Official estimates place the number of Muslims at about 98,000 people, with most living in Thrace. Jehovah's Witnesses and the Roman Catholic Church each have about 50,000 members. There are about 30,000 Protestants and 5,000 Jews. There are small congregations of the Church of Jesus Christ of Latter-day Saints (Mormons), the Church of Scientology, and the Anglican church. There is a very small Baha'i community.

Under the constitution, the Eastern Orthodox Church of Christ (Greek Orthodox) is the "prevailing" religion of Greece; the church is self-governing under the ecumenical patriarch resident in Istanbul, Turkey, and is protected by the government, which pays the salaries of the Orthodox clergy. The Orthodox Church is also allowed a significant influence in economic and political policies. The constitution prohibits proselytizing. The Orthodox Church, Judaism, and Islam are considered to be "legal persons of public law," a designation of preferred legal status that makes it easier for these groups to own property and gain legal representation in court. Religious groups must obtain a house of prayer permit through the Ministry of Education and Religion in order to open a public place of worship. Approval for a permit is based in part on the opinion of the local Orthodox bishop.

11 TRANSPORTATION

Greek transportation was completely reconstructed and greatly expanded after World War II. The length of roads in 2002 was 117,000 km (72,704 mi), of which 107,406 km (66,742 mi) were paved. Toll highways connect Athens with Lamía and Pátrai. In 2003 there were 5,024,600 motor vehicles, including 3,885,908 passenger cars and 1,138,692 commercial vehicles in use.

The Hellenic State Railways, a government organ, operates the railroads, which in 2004 had a total length of 2,571 km (1,597 mi), that which consisted of standard, narrow and dual gauge lines. Standard gauge lines made up the bulk of the nation's railway system, at 1,565 km (973 mi), of which 764 km (475 mi) was electrified. Narrow gauge lines accounted for 983 km (611 mi), with dual gauge trackage amounting to 23 km (14 mi). The agency also operates a network of subsidiary bus lines connecting major cities. The privately owned Hellenic Electric Railways operates a high-speed shuttle service between Piraiévs and Athens.

Principal ports are Elevsís, Thessaloniki, Vólos, Piraiévs, Iráklion, and Thíra. In 2005 the Greek merchant fleet had 861 ships (down from 2,893 in 1982) of 1,000 GRT or over, for a total of 30,186,624 GRT. In addition, Greek shipowners had many other ships sailing under Cypriot, Lebanese, Liberian, Panamanian or other foreign registries. The Greek fleet was hard hit by the international shipping slump of the 1980s. The inland waterway system consists of three coastal canals and three inland rivers, for a total of 80 navigable km (50 mi).

Greece had an estimated 80 airports in 2004. As of 2005, a total of 67 had paved runways, and there were also eight heliports. Athens' main airport connects the capital by regular flights to major cities in Europe, the Middle East, and North America. The new Athens airport at Spata opened March 2001. Olympic Airways, nationalized in 1975, operates a large internal domestic network as well as international flights. In 2003, about 7.519 million passengers were carried on domestic and international flights. Also during 2003, Greek aircraft performed 63 million freight ton-km of service.

12 HISTORY

Civilization in Greece first arose on Crete in the 3rd millennium BC, probably as a result of immigration from Asia Minor (now Turkey). The Minoan civilization (c.3000–c.1100 BC), named after the legendary King Minos (which may have been a title rather than a name), was centered in the capital of Knossos, where it became known as Helladic (c.2700–c.1100 BC). During the 2nd millennium BC, Greece was conquered by Indo-European invaders: first the Achaeans, then the Aeolians and Ionians, and finally the Dorians. The Greeks, who called themselves Hellenes after a tribe in Thessaly (they were called Greeks by the Romans after another tribe in northwestern Greece), adapted the native culture to their own peasant village traditions and developed the characteristic form of ancient Greek political organization, the city-state (polis). The resulting Mycenaean civilization (c.1600–c.1100 BC), named after the dominant city-state of Mycenae, constituted the latter period of the Helladic civilization.

The Mycenaeans, who were rivals of the Minoans, destroyed Knossos about 1400 BC and, according to legend, the city of Troy in Asia Minor about 1200 BC. The Minoan and Mycenaean civilizations both came to a relatively abrupt end about 1100 BC, possibly as a result of the Dorian invasion, but the foundations had already been laid for what was to become the basis of Western civilization. It was the Greeks who first tried democratic government; produced the world's first outstanding dramatists, poets, historians, philosophers, and orators; and made the first scientific study of medicine, zoology, botany, physics, geometry, and the social sciences.

In the 1st millennium BC, overpopulation forced the Greeks to emigrate and to colonize areas from Spain to Asia Minor. The Greeks derived their alphabet from the Phoenicians during the 8th century BC. By the 6th century BC, the two dominant *polises* (city-states) were Athens and Sparta. The 5th century BC, recognized as the golden age of Athenian culture, brought the defeat of the Persians by the Athenians in the Persian Wars (490–479 BC) and the defeat of Athens and its allies by Sparta and its allies in the Peloponnesian War (431–404 BC). The territory that is present-day Greece was under Spartan rule.

The inability of Greeks to unite politically led to the annexation of their territories by Philip II of Macedon in 338 BC and by his son Alexander the Great. Through Alexander's ambition for world empire and his admiration of Greek learning, Greek civilization was spread to all his conquered lands. The death of Alexander in 323 BC, the breakup of his empire, and the lack of national feeling among the Greeks prepared the way for their conquest by Rome at the close of the Macedonian Wars in 146 BC.

Greece was made a Roman province, but Athens remained a center of learning. To speak the Greek language was to speak the language of culture, commerce, art, and politics. Greeks were widely influential in Rome, in the Egyptian city of Alexandria, and elsewhere. For this reason, the period between the death of Alexander and the beginning of the Roman Empire is known as the Hellenistic period.

When the Roman Empire was officially divided in AD 395, Greece, by this time Christianized, became part of the Eastern Roman Empire, eventually known as the Byzantine Empire (so named from Byzantium, the former name of Constantinople, its capital). The Byzantine Empire lasted for more than a thousand years. During this period, Greek civilization continued to contribute to Byzantine art and culture.

The formal schism between Eastern Orthodox Christianity and Roman Catholicism came in 1054, when Pope Leo IX and Patriarch Michael Cerularius excommunicated each other. The continuity of Byzantine rule was broken by the fall of Constantinople in the Fourth Crusade in 1204. Under the Latin Empire of the East, which lasted until 1261, Greece was divided into feudal fiefs, with the Duchy of Athens passing successively under French, Spanish, and Florentine rulers.

The Ottoman Turks, who conquered Constantinople in 1453 and the Greek peninsula by the end of the decade, gave the Greeks a large degree of local autonomy. Communal affairs were controlled by the Orthodox Church, and Greek merchants ranged throughout the world on their business ventures, but Greece itself was poverty-stricken. Following an unsuccessful attempt to overthrow the Turks in 1770—an uprising aided by Russia, as part of Catherine the Great's plan to replace Muslim with Orthodox Christian rule throughout the Near East—the Greeks, led by the archbishop of Patras, proclaimed a war of independence against the Turks on 25 March 1821. The revolution, which aroused much sympathy in Europe, succeeded only after Britain, France, and Russia decided to aid the Greeks in 1827. These three nations recognized Greek independence through the London Protocol of 1830, and the Ottomans accepted the terms later in the year.

The same three powers also found a king for Greece in the person of Otto I of Bavaria. During his reign (1832–1844), Otto I faced a series of foreign and domestic problems. In March 1844, Otto's administration was pressured to draft a constitution to establish a new government. Under this document, the leader would reign as a constitutional monarch and the legislature would be elected by all property-holding males over the age of 25. Otto managed to hold onto power for another decade, until the outbreak of the Crimean War (1854–1856). Otto sent troops to occupy Ottoman territory with the pretense of protecting Christians in the Balkans, but the European powers sided against him. Otto, humiliated, was forced to give up his "Christian Cause" in the Balkans. He abdicated in 1862.

Next Prince William George of Denmark, who ruled as King George I, took control of Greece until his assassination in 1913. During and after his rule, Greece gradually added islands and neighboring territories with Greek-speaking populations, including the Ionian Islands, ceded by the British in 1864; Thessaly, seized from Turkey in 1881; Macedonia, Crete, and some Aegean islands in 1913; and the Dodecanese Islands and Rhodes, ceded by Italy in 1947.

The first half of the 20th century for Greece was a period of wars and rivalries with Turkey; of republican rule under the Cretan patriot Eleutherios Venizelos; of occupation by Italy and Germany during World War II (in World War I, Greece had been neutral for three years and had then sided with the Allies); and of a five-year civil war (1944–49) between the government and the Communist-supported National Liberation Front, in which US aid under the Truman Doctrine played a significant role in defeating the insurgency. In September 1946, the Greeks voted back to the throne the twice-exiled George II (grandson of George I), who was succeeded upon his death in April 1947 by his brother Paul I. A new constitution took effect in 1952, the same year Greece joined NATO. For much of the decade, Greece backed demands by Greek Cypriots for *enosis*, or the union of Cyprus with Greece, but in 1959, the Greek, Turkish, and Cypriot governments agreed on a formula for an independent Cyprus, which became a reality in 1960.

King Paul died on 6 March 1964 and was succeeded by his son Constantine. Meanwhile, a parliamentary crisis was brewing, as rightist and leftist elements struggled for control of the army, and the government sought to purge the military of political influence. On 21 April 1967, a right wing military junta staged a successful coup d'etat. Leftists were rounded up, press censorship was imposed, and political liberties were suspended. After an unsuccessful countercoup on 13 December 1967, King Constantine and the royal family fled to exile in Italy. Lt. Gen. George Zoetakis was named regent to act for the king, and Col. George Papadopoulos was made premier. A constitutional reform was approved by 92% of the voters in a plebiscite held under martial law on 29 September 1968. Under the new constitution, individual rights were held to be subordinate to the interests of the state, many powers of the king and legislature were transferred to the ruling junta, and the army was granted extended powers as overseer of civil order. The constitution outlawed membership in the Communist Party. US military aid to Greece, suspended after the 1967 coup, was restored by President Richard M. Nixon in September 1970.

Following an abortive naval mutiny in 1973, Greece was declared a republic by the surviving junta. Papadopoulos became

GREECE

0 25 50 75 100 Miles

0 25 50 75 100 Kilometers

BULGARIA

Black Sea

MACEDONIA

RHODOPE MTS.

Ohridsko Jezero

Prespansko Jezero

ALBANIA

Serrai   Dráma   Xánthi   Souflíon

Flórina   Kavála

Borovë   ÓROS   Giannitsá   Kilkís   Alexandroúpolis

GRÁMMOS   Struma   Axiós   Marmara Denizi

Libohovë   Véroia   Kozáni   Thessaloníki   Thásos

Katateríni   Chalkidhikí   Çanakkale

Samothráki

Áthos

Peninsula   6,670 ft.

2033 m.

Aliakman   Óros Ólimbos   Thermaïkós   Koufós   Límnos

9,570 ft.   Kólpos   Myrina   Lésvos   Burhaniye

Kérkyra   Ioánnina   2917 m.   Sklíthron   Samos

Corfu   Trikala   Lárisa   Vólos   Vrissá

Paxoí   Párga   Akhelóös   Áno Vasiliká   Pélagos   TURKEY

Árta   Halus   Skópelos

Prévaza   Timfristós   Lamía   Strofyliá   Skíros   Chíos

Levkás   7,595 ft.   Mólos   ÉVVOIA   Izmir

Pálairos   2315 m.   Agrínion   Thebes   Khalkís   Ákra Kafirévs

Kefallinía   Itháki   Lúmní   Delphi   Ákra Araxos   Mégara   Andros   Sámos

Trikonís   Athens   Ikaría

Chionáta   Pátrai   Korinthiakós   Peiraiéfs   SPORADES

PELOPONNESUS   Kólpos   Mýkonos

Zákinthos   Kórinthos   Náfplion   Tínos   Kos

Olympia   Árgos   Galatás   KYKLÁDES   Páros   Náxos

Katákolon   Alfiós   Trípolis   Ydra   Ródhos

Líkaion Óros   Spetsopoúla   DODEKANISOS   Ródhos

Filiatrá   4,662 ft.   Spárti   Mílos

Kalámai   1421 m.   Molái   Apolakkiá

Pylos   Schíza   Neápolis   Karpathos

Messiniakós   Lakonikós

Kólpos   Kólpos   Mitáta   Kíthira

Ákra Tainaron

Sea of Crete

Ákra Voúxa

Chaniá   Pánormos

Kámbos   Elyrus   Iráklion   Ákra Sídheros

Ákra Kriós   CRETE   Cnossus   Karpathos

MEDITERRANEAN   Chóra   Myrtos   Zákros

SEA   Sfakion   Ákra Lithinon

Gávdos

Ionian Sea

Greece

LOCATION: 34°48′2″ to 41°45′1″ N; 19°22′41″ to 29°38′39″ E. BOUNDARY LENGTHS: Macedonia, 228 kilometers (142 miles); Bulgaria, 494 kilometers (308 miles); Turkey, 206 kilometers (128 miles); Albania, 282 kilometers (176 miles); total coastline, 13,676 kilometers (8,496 miles). TERRITORIAL SEA LIMIT: 6 miles.

president, only to be overthrown by a group of officers following the bloody repression of a student uprising. The complicity of the junta in a conspiracy by Greek army officers on Cyprus against the government of Archbishop Makarios precipitated the final fall from power of Greece's military rulers in July 1974, when the Turkish army intervened in Cyprus and overwhelmed the island's Greek contingent. Constantine Karamanlis, a former prime min-

ister and moderate, returned from exile to form a civilian government that effectively ended eight years of dictatorial rule.

General elections were held on 17 November 1974, the first since 1964, marking the recovery of democratic rule. In a referendum held on 8 December 1974, 69% of the electorate voted to end the monarchy and declare Greece a parliamentary republic. On 7 June 1975, a democratic constitution was adopted by the new legislature, although 86 of the 300 members boycotted the session. Karamanlis became Greece's first prime minister under the new system, and on 19 June 1975, parliament elected Konstantinos Tsatsos as president.

Prime Minister Karamanlis, who had withdrawn Greece from NATO's military structure in 1974 to protest Turkey's invasion of Cyprus, resumed military cooperation with NATO in the fall of 1980 (a few months after he was elected president of Greece) and brought his nation into the European Community (EC) effective 1 January 1981. With the victory of the Pan-Hellenic Socialist Movement (Panellinio Socialistikou Kinema—PASOK) in the elections of October 1981, Greece installed its first Socialist government. The new prime minister, Andreas Papandreou—the son of former prime minister George Papandreou and a man accused by rightists in 1967 of complicity in an abortive leftist military plot—had campaigned on a promise to take Greece out of the EC (although his government did not do so). In November 1982, he refused to allow Greek participation in NATO military exercises in the Aegean, which were then canceled. In January 1983, the government declared a general amnesty for the Communist exiles of the 1944–49 civil war.

In mid-1982, in an attempt to deal with the deepening economic crisis, the government created a ministry of national economy, which embraced industrial and commercial affairs. The proposed "radical socialization" of the economy, however, provoked widespread opposition, which limited it to the introduction of worker participation in supervisory councils; state control was imposed only on the pharmaceutical industry (in 1982). Of Greece's largest enterprises, only the Heracles Cement Co. was nationalized (in 1983). Relations with labor were strained as the government sought to balance worker demands that wages be indexed to inflation with the growing need for austerity; in late 1986, the government imposed a two-year wage freeze, which provoked widespread strikes and demonstrations.

In 1985, Prime Minister Papandreou unexpectedly withdrew his support for President Karamanlis's bid for a second five-year term and announced amendments to the constitution that would transfer powers from the president to the legislature and prime minister. Karamanlis resigned and Papandreou proceeded with his proposed changes, calling an election in June and winning a mandate to follow through with them (parliament's approval was given in March 1986). Subsequently, however, the government began to lose power; the opposition made substantial gains in the 1986 local elections, and a 1987 scandal associated with Papandreou further weakened the government. In January 1988, Papandreou met with Turkish premier Turgut Ozal in Switzerland; they agreed to work toward solving the problems between the two countries.

Two rounds of parliamentary elections were held in 1989; neither was conclusive. After the June vote, the center-conservative New Democracy (ND) party, with 146 of 300 seats, formed a government with left wing parties and concentrated on investigating scandals of the Papandreou government, including those of the former prime minister himself. That government resigned in the fall, and new elections were held in November. The ND and PASOK both improved their totals and an all-party coalition was formed to address economic reform. That government, however,

also failed. In April 1990 elections, the ND emerged victorious to lead the government.

In the balloting of 10 October 1993, PASOK won 171 seats to 110 for the ND and Papandreou was again elected prime minister, despite repeated scandals of both personal and political nature. In 1995, parliament appointed Konstandinos Stephanopoulos president. Voters appeared dissatisfied with ND's economic reforms while PASOK won support for its hard-line foreign policy demanding that the former Yugoslav Republic of Macedonia change its name. Many Greeks believe the name of the newly independent state implies territorial designs on the northern Greek region, which once formed part of historic Macedonia. In 1995, Papandreou became ill and was not able to adequately perform his duties. In January 1996, PASOK named Costas Simitis prime minister. In June of that year, Papandreou died at 77, ending the tumultuous political career of postwar Greece's most important—and controversial—politician.

In 1996, Simitis, facing strong resistance to austerity measures from labor and farmers, called on the president to dissolve parliament and hold early elections. Simitis had vowed not to call for a dissolution, but faced with mounting opposition to his austerity measures—taken to prepare the Greek economy for European monetary union in 1999—felt he needed a reinforced mandate. The election, held on 22 September 1996, returned PASOK and Simitis to power, giving them, in fact, a commanding majority in parliament.

The next four years were highlighted by continued Greek-Turkish tension, and Simitis's push for Greek entry into the monetary union. Relations with Turkey reached a new low in early 1999 when Turkey's most-wanted man, Kurdish terrorist leader Abdullah Ocalan, was captured by the Turkish secret services in Nairobi, Kenya. Ocalan had sought refuge in the Greek embassy and was seized while en route to the airport, apparently on the way to an asylum-granting country in Africa. Ocalan's capture led to subsequent Turkish charges that the Greek state sponsored international terrorism.

The outbreak of a war in Kosovo little over a month later also placed Greece in an awkward diplomatic position. Although the overwhelming majority of the Greek public opposed the war, the Simitis government maintained its ties to NATO and offered logistical—although not combat—support to its allies. Nevertheless, the widespread anti-Western backlash remained for some months. Rioting greeted US president Bill Clinton when he visited Greece in November 1999.

Unexpectedly, relations with Turkey began to significantly improve in August 1999 following a devastating earthquake in Turkey that killed over 20,000 Turkish citizens. Greece was among the first countries to offer aid to its traditional foe. When a smaller earthquake struck Greece the following month, Turkey reciprocated the Greek gesture. In the aftermath of the tragedies, Greece and Turkey continued a dialogue that resulted in the signing of cooperation accords in the areas of commerce and the fight against terrorism. In addition, Greece supported the decision of the December 1999 European Union (EU) summit in Helsinki to place Turkey as a candidate for EU membership, which also contributed to improving relations between Greece and Turkey. When the EU in late 2002 announced Turkey would not be one of 10 new candidate countries invited to join the body as of 2004, Greece pressed the EU to set a date for the start of accession talks. Greece itself entered the euro zone on 1 January 2002.

Relations between the two countries also warmed due to co-operation on a project to build a natural gas pipeline connecting them; the pipeline was scheduled to be in operation by November 2006.

Negotiations between the Greek and Turkish leaders in Cyprus were held in early 2003 to see if they could agree on a plan to unify the island prior to Cyprus signing an EU accession treaty on 16 April. The talks failed, and the internationally recognized Greek government of Cyprus signed the accession treaty. However, later that month, Turkish-Cypriot leader Rauf Denktash opened the borders of northern Cyprus to Greeks, and by 15 May 2003, about 250,000 Greek Cypriots and 70,000 Turkish Cypriots—40% of the island's combined population—had visited each other's side.

Approximately 90% of Greece's population was opposed to the US-led war in Iraq that began on 19 March 2003. Prime Minister Costas Simitis indicated that by waging war, the United States and United Kingdom were undermining the EU. Yet he gave the coalition permission to use of Greece's airspace in launching strikes against Iraq.

Greece's international standing received a boost when the country hosted the 2004 Summer Olympics.

In February 2005, parliament elected Karolos Papoulias president by a vote of 279 out of 300 votes; he took office on 12 March 2005.

13 GOVERNMENT

Before the 1967 coup, executive power was vested in the crown but was exercised by a Council of Ministers appointed by the king and headed by a premier. The 1975 constitution abolished the 146-year-old Greek monarchy and created the office of president as head of state. If a majority in parliament fails to agree on the selection of a president, the office is filled in a general election. The president, who is limited to two five-year terms, appoints the prime minister, who is head of government and requires the confidence of parliament to remain in power. (The constitution was amended in 1986 to reduce the power of the president, limiting his right to dissolve parliament on his own initiative and depriving him of the right to dismiss the prime minister, veto legislation, or proclaim a state of emergency; basically, these powers were transferred to parliament.) The prime minister selects a cabinet from among the members of parliament.

Legislative power is vested in a parliament (Vouli), a unicameral body of 300 deputies elected by direct, universal, secret ballot for maximum four-year terms. A proportional electoral system makes it possible for a party with a minority of the popular vote to have a parliamentary majority. In the 1974 elections, voting was made compulsory for all persons aged 21–70 residing within 200 km (124 mi) of their constituencies. Suffrage is now universal and compulsory at age 18.

14 POLITICAL PARTIES

After World War II, political parties in Greece centered more on leaders than platforms. The Greek Rally, founded and led by Field Marshal Alexander Papagos, won control of the government in the 1951 elections. About 10% of the vote was received by the Union of the Democratic Left, a left wing party founded in 1951 as

a substitute for the Communist Party, outlawed since 1947. When Papagos died in October 1955, Constantine Karamanlis formed a new party called the National Radical Union, which won the elections of 1956, 1958, and 1961 and held power until 1963, when Karamanlis resigned and the newly formed Center Union, comprising a coalition of liberals and progressives and led by George Papandreou, subsequently won a narrow plurality, with Papandreou becoming prime minister. In elections held in February 1964, the Center Union won 174 out of 300 seats; however, King Constantine dismissed Papandreou in July 1965, and Stephanos Stephanopoulos formed a new government. This government, too, was short-lived. Political conflict came to a head when Panayotis Kanellopoulos, leader of the National Radical Union, who had been appointed premier of a caretaker government, set new elections for 28 May 1967. On 21 April, however, a military coup resulted in the cancellation of elections and suppression of political parties, which lasted until 1974.

On 28 September 1974, following his return from exile, Karamanlis formed the New Democracy Party (Nea Dimokratia—ND), advocating a middle course between left and right and promoting closer ties with Western Europe. The Center Union–New Forces (EKND), renamed the Union of the Democratic Center (EDHK) in 1976, rallied liberal factions of the former Center Union and announced a line that generally paralleled ND policies. The EDHK disintegrated following the 1981 elections. Other groups to emerge, most of them led by former opponents of the junta, included the Pan-Hellenic Socialist Movement (Panellinio Socialistiko Kinema—PASOK), led by Andreas Papandreou; the United Left (UL), which brought together elements of the Union of the Democratic Left and the Communist Party to oppose the upcoming elections; and the National Democratic Union (NDU), which represented an amalgam of various elements, including some royalists and right wing activists. Also in 1974, the Communist Party (Kommounistiko Komma Ellados—KKE) was made legal for the first time since 1947; the party later split into two factions, the pro-Soviet KKE-Exterior and the Eurocommunist wing, called the KKE-Interior. In May 1986, the KKE-Interior changed its name to the New Hellenic Left Party.

In the general elections held on 17 November 1974, the ND won an overwhelming majority in parliament, with the EKND forming the major opposition. The ND was again the winner in 1977, although its parliamentary majority dropped from 220 to 172. After parliament elected Karamanlis president in 1980, George Rallis succeeded him as prime minister. In the elections of 18 October 1981, Papandreou's PASOK won 48% of the popular vote and commanded a clear parliamentary majority. Although PASOK won again in the election of 2 June 1985, its share of the total votes cast fell to 45.8%.

In the elections of 10 October 1993, PASOK had about the same percentage (46.9%) and a majority of 171 seats. The ND followed with 110 seats and an offshoot party, Political Spring, had 10 seats. The Communists gained 9 places.

In the parliamentary elections of 22 September 1996, PASOK retained its majority, but lost 9 seats. ND emerged with 108 seats; the KKE, 11; Coalition of the Left and Progress, 10; and the Democratic and Social Movement Parties, 9. The Political Spring lost all its seats in the election, gaining only 2.95% of the popular vote.

PASOK continued its dominance of the post-1974 era with yet another victory at the polls on 9 April 2000. In a close election PASOK won 158 seats (43.8% of the vote), ND earned 125 seats (42.7%), the KKE held steady at 11 (5.5%), while the Coalition of the Left and Progress saw its share of the seats drop to 6 (3.2%). The Democratic Social Movement failed to clear the 3% hurdle needed for representation and Political Spring once again failed to win any seats.

Following the 7 March 2004 elections, ND increased its seats in parliament to 165 (45.5%), while PASOK's number declined to 117 (40.6%). The KKK gained one seat, winning 12 (5.9%), with the Coalition of the Left and Progress (Synaspismos) holding steady at 6 seats (3.3%).

15 LOCAL GOVERNMENT

The 1975 constitution restored the large measure of local self-government initially provided for in the constitution of 1952 and re-emphasized the principle of decentralization, although local units must depend on the central government for funding. Under the military regime of 1967–74, local units had been closely controlled by the central authorities.

Greece is divided into 13 regional governments (*periferiarchis*), which are subdivided into 51 prefectures or nomarchies (*nomoi*), in addition to the autonomous administration of Mt. Áthos (Aghion Oros) in Macedonia. Each prefecture is governed by a prefect *(nomoi)* who is elected. There are also 272 municipalities or *demoi* (cities of more than 10,000 inhabitants), administered by mayors; communes (with 300 to 10,000 inhabitants), each run by a president and a community council; and localities.

The rocky promontory of Mt. Áthos, southeast of Salonika, is occupied by 20 monasteries, of which 17 are Greek, one Russian, one Serbian, and one Bulgarian. Mt. Áthos is governed by a 4-member council and a 20-member assembly (1 representative from each monastery). The special status of Mt. Áthos was first formalized in the 1952 constitution.

16 JUDICIAL SYSTEM

The 1975 constitution (Syntagma) has been revised twice, in 1985 and in 2001. The constitution provides for an independent judiciary.

The constitution designates the Supreme Court (Areios Pagos) as the highest court of appeal. It consists of both penal and civil sections. A Council of State does not hear cases but decides on administrative disputes, administrative violations of laws, and revision of disciplinary procedures affecting civil servants. The Comptrollers Council decides cases of a fiscal nature. The 1975 constitution also established a Special Supreme Tribunal as a final arbiter in disputes arising over general elections and referenda, in addition to exercising review of the constitutionality of laws. Other elements of the judicial system include justices of the peace, magistrates' courts, courts of first instance, courts of appeal, and various administrative courts. Judges of the Supreme Court, the courts of appeal, and the courts of first instance are appointed for life on the recommendation of the Ministry of Justice. The president has the constitutional right, with certain exceptions, to commute and reduce sentences.

17 ARMED FORCES

In 2005 Greece's active armed forces totaled 163,850 members and were supported by some 325,000 reservists. As of that year, there were 110,000 active personnel in the Army, 19,250 in the Navy, and 23,000 in the Air Force. The Greek field army has a large and varied combined arms structure, with units manned at three different levels of readiness: 85% are fully ready; 65% are ready within 24 hours; and 20% are ready within 48 hours. The 1,150 troops serving on Cyprus include 1 mechanized brigade. The Army operates 1,723 main battle tanks, 175 reconnaissance vehicles, 501 armored infantry fighting vehicles, 1,640 armored personnel carriers, and 4,660 artillery pieces. The Navy had 13 tactical submarines, 18 frigates, 4 corvettes, 36 patrol and coastal combatants, and 13 mine warfare vessels, as well as various amphibious and support vessels. The Navy's aviation arm is focused on antisubmarine warfare and search and rescue. The Air Force operated 283 combat capable aircraft in addition to 120 fixed and rotary wing transport aircraft. The paramilitary consisted of 4,000 coast guard and customs officers. Greek military personnel provided support to UN peacekeeping missions in seven countries or regions around the world. In 2005, the defense budget totaled $4.46 billion. The United States has one major naval base on Greek soil and several smaller installations.

18 INTERNATIONAL COOPERATION

Greece is a charter member of the United Nations (UN), having joined on 25 October 1945, and participates in ECE and several nonregional specialized agencies. Greece was admitted to NATO in 1951 but suspended its military participation (1974–80) because of the Cyprus conflict. It belongs to the Council of Europe, the OECD, OSCE, WTO, G-6, the European Bank for Reconstruction and Development, the Black Sea Economic Cooperation Zone, and the Western European Union. Greece is also a permanent observer at the OAS. The country became a full member of the European Union as of 1 January 1981.

In August 1987, Greece and Albania signed a pact ending the state of war that had existed between them since World War II (1939–45). The Greek government continues to be in dispute with the neighboring Republic of Macedonia over the name of the latter. In 1995, Greece agreed to recognize the country as the Former Yugoslav Republic of Macedonia. Greece and Turkey have unresolved boundary disputes in the Aegean Sea and tension between the two countries has grown in connection with the Greek-Turkish disputes in the nation of Cyprus. Greece has supported UN operations and missions in Kosovo (est. 1999), Western Sahara (est. 1991), Ethiopia and Eritrea (est. 2000), and Georgia (est. 1993). Greece has guest status in the Nonaligned Movement.

Greece belongs to the Australia group, the Zangger Committee, the Nuclear energy Agency, the Nuclear Suppliers Group (London Group), and the European Organization for Nuclear Research (CERN). In environmental cooperation, Greece is part of the Antarctic Treaty, the Basel Convention, Conventions on Biological Diversity and Air Pollution, Ramsar, CITES, the London Convention, International Tropical Timber Agreements, the Kyoto Protocol, the Montréal Protocol, MARPOL, the Nuclear Test Ban Treaty, and the UN Conventions on the Law of the Sea, Climate Change and Desertification.

¹⁹ECONOMY

The Greek economy suffers from a paucity of exploitable natural resources and a low level of industrial development relative to the rest of Western Europe. By 1992, it had fallen behind Portugal to become the poorest European Community (now European Union—EU) member; with the entrance into the EU of 10 primarily Eastern European nations in 2004, that was no longer the case. In 2004, agriculture (with forestry and fishing) generated about 7% of GDP but employed about 12% of the labor force. Agricultural exports include tobacco, cotton, wheat, raisins, currants, fresh fruits, tomato products, olive oil, and olives. In 2004, industry and construction accounted for about 22% of GDP and 20% of the labor force. Wholesale and retail trade and other services provided some 71% of GDP, employing 68% of the labor force.

Next to food processing, textile manufacturing used to be the most important industry, but chemicals and metals and machinery have outstripped it in recent years. Paper products has been a fast-growing industry since 1980. Greece has stimulated foreign investments in the development of its mineral resources by constitutionally providing guarantees for capital and profits. The government has encouraged tourism, which has developed into a major source of revenue (15% of GDP in 2004). Greece continues to play a dominant role in the international shipping industry.

During the late 1950s and 1960s, the government took steps to reclaim land, develop new farms, increase credits and investments for agriculture, protect agricultural prices, and improve the agricultural product and utilize it to the best advantage; however, the country still depends on many imports to meet its food needs. Industrial output contributed substantially to the rapid increase in national income after 1960, and manufacturing and service industries were the fastest-growing sectors in the 1970s. In the 1980s, however, the economy retracted sharply because of the worldwide recession and growth in real terms was sluggish. In the best year of the decade, 1988, GDP grew by 4.9%. In 1993, GDP dropped by 0.5%, but rebounded in 1995 by 2.0%. Inflation, which neared 20% in 1991, had been lowered to 8.1% in 1995, lower than the many European Union (EU) countries that struggled mightily with inflation in the mid-1990s. As Greece pursued an economic austerity program aimed at meeting the criteria for European economic and monetary union (EMU), inflation continued to fall, reaching less than 4% at the end of 1998. Greece entered into the EMU in 2001.

As of 2006, Greece had failed to meet the EU's Growth and Stability Pact budget deficit criteria of 3% of GDP since 2000. Greece is a recipient of EU aid, amounting to 3.3% of annual GDP. The country's public debt burden is a major drag on economic growth and prosperity, at 112% of GDP in 2004. Unemployment remained high at 10% in 2004 and the country was in need of introducing social insurance reform. Greece has a large public sector (some 40% of GDP), but is implementing privatization policies. Per capita GDP is about 70% of the leading euro-zone economies. Public and private investment was strong in 2003, in preparation for the 2004 Olympic Games that were held in Athens; the Greek economy grew at a rate of approximately 4% in 2003 and 2004. Spending on the Olympic Games contributed to an estimated general government deficit of 6.6% of GDP in 2004; however, the deficit was forecast to fall substantially in 2005–07, although it was projected to remain above the 3% of GDP limit established by the EU's Growth and Stability Pact. GDP growth was expected to slow from 4.2% in 2004 to 3.4% in 2005, 3.1% in 2006, and 2.9% in 2007. Inflation was likely to rise from 3% in 2004 to 3.8% in 2005, driven by indirect tax rises and high international oil prices, before easing again to 3.3% in 2006 and 2.8% in 2007.

²⁰INCOME

The US Central Intelligence Agency (CIA) reports that in 2005 Greece's gross domestic product (GDP) was estimated at $242.8 billion. The CIA defines GDP as the value of all final goods and services produced within a nation in a given year and computed on the basis of purchasing power parity (PPP) rather than value as measured on the basis of the rate of exchange based on current dollars. The per capita GDP was estimated at $22,800. The annual growth rate of GDP was estimated at 3.3%. The average inflation rate in 2005 was 3.8%. It was estimated that agriculture accounted for 6.2% of GDP, industry 22.1%, and services 71.7%.

According to the World Bank, in 2003 remittances from citizens working abroad totaled $1.564 billion or about $142 per capita and accounted for approximately 0.9% of GDP.

The World Bank reports that in 2003 household consumption in Greece totaled $114.60 billion or about $10,418 per capita based on a GDP of $172.2 billion, measured in current dollars rather than PPP. Household consumption includes expenditures of individuals, households, and nongovernmental organizations on goods and services, excluding purchases of dwellings. It was estimated that for the period 1990 to 2003 household consumption grew at an average annual rate of 2.4%.

²¹LABOR

In 2005, Greece's labor force was estimated at 4.72 million people. In 2004, it was estimated that agriculture accounted for 12% of the labor force, followed by industry at 20% and the services sector at 68%. Unemployment was estimated at 10.8% in 2005.

In 2005, about 26% of salaried, nonagricultural employees belonged to unions. Altogether, there were over 4,000 trade unions. Unions were organized on a territorial rather than a plant basis: all workers of a certain trade in a town usually belong to one union. On a nationwide scale, union members of the same trade or profession form a federation; the General Confederation of Greek Workers (GSEE) is the central core of the private sector union movement. Government plays an important role in labor-management relations. Collective bargaining and the right to strike are protected by law, although workers must give notice of an intent to strike (4 days for public utilities, 24 hours in the private sector). Because of a history of compulsory arbitration as a means to resolve labor disputes, unions successfully lobbied for new legislation, passed in 1992, which restricted the use of compulsory arbitration in favor of mediation procedures.

As of 2005, the maximum legal workweek is 40 hours in the private sector and 37.5 hours in the public sector. The minimum monthly salary negotiated by the GSEE for that same year was around $35 per day or $779 per month. This amount provided a decent standard of living for a family. Annual vacations (of up to a month) with pay are provided by law. In general, employment of children under the age of 15 in the industrial sector was prohibited. The minimum age for children employed in cinemas, theaters and family businesses was 12. Industrial health and safety standards are set by law and regularly enforced.

22AGRICULTURE

Agriculture in Greece suffers not only from natural limitations, such as poor soils and droughts, but also from soil erosion, lack of fertilizers, and insufficient capital investment. The total farm labor force in 2003 was 129,900 full-time and nearly 1.4 million part-time workers.

About 30% of the land area is cultivable, and it supports over half of the population. Of the land under cultivation in 2003, about 72% was planted in seasonal crops, and 28% in orchards and vineyards. About 38% of the agricultural land was irrigated in 2003. Although agriculture accounts for 17% of the work force, its role in the economy is declining; in 2003 agriculture accounted for 7% of GDP, down from 25% in the 1950s.

In recent decades, Greek agriculture has been characterized by an increasing diversification of fruit crops for export. Agricultural production of principal crops in 2004 was estimated as follows (in thousands of tons): sugar beets, 2,300; corn, 2,300; olives, 2,130; tomatoes, 1,800; wheat, 1,800; peaches and nectarines, 955; oranges, 903; cotton, 359; apples, 288; barley, 220; and tobacco, 127.

Progress has been made toward modernization in machinery and cultivation techniques. Agricultural products, including processed foods, beverages, and tobacco, make up one-third of total exports. To expand agricultural production and encourage farm prosperity, the government exempts agricultural income from most taxes, extends liberal farm credits, and subsidizes agriculture. It also operates a service by which individual growers or cooperatives may hire heavy farm equipment at low prices, encourages the development of industries that use farm products, provides educational programs, and has sought to halt the trend toward ever-smaller farm holdings. There were 255,000 tractors, 5,150 harvester-threshers, and 13,450 milking machines in use in 2003.

23ANIMAL HUSBANDRY

In 2005 there were 9,000,000 sheep, 5,400,000 goats, 1,000,000 hogs, 600,000 head of cattle, 68,000 donkeys, 29,000 horses, 28,000 mules, and 28,000,000 chickens. Although production of milk, meat, and cheese has risen greatly since the end of World War II (1939–45), Greece still must import substantial quantities of evaporated and condensed milk, cheese, cattle, sheep, hides, and meat. Estimated meat production in 2005 included 134,000 tons of poultry, 134,000 tons of pork, 124,000 tons of mutton and goat meat, and 75,000 tons of beef and veal. Livestock products in 2005 included (in thousands of tons) cow's milk, 780; sheep milk, 700; goat milk, 495; cheese, 246; eggs, 105; honey, 15; and butter, 4. Recent modernization in machinery has especially helped poultry and hog operations. Exports of dairy and egg products were valued at $216.4 million in 2004 (mostly going to European Union nations).

24FISHING

The fishing industry has expanded and been modernized in recent years. In 2002, the Greek fishing fleet consisted of 19,504 vessels with 97,579 GRT, and there were 33,992 people employed in small scale fisheries. The total fish catch was 197,596 tons in 2003.

A total of $317.2 million of fish and fish products were exported that year. In the north of Greece, freshwater fisheries have been restocked and developed, but the inland catch only accounted for 3% of total volume in 2003.

Sponge fishing, formerly an important undertaking in the Dodecanese and other regions, decreased in volume from 135.5 tons of sponges in 1955 to 2.5 tons in 2003.

25FORESTRY

Forests cover about 28% of the total area. Much of the forest area was destroyed during the 1940s, but the government's reforestation program planted more than 100 million trees during the 1970s and 1980s. Pine, fir, and oak are the most common trees, and resin and turpentine are the principal products. In 2004, 1,672,000 cu m (59,022,000 cu ft) of roundwood were harvested, including 1.073 million cu m (37.88 million cu ft) of firewood. Sawn wood production in 2004 totaled 196,000 cu m (6,911,000 cu ft), and wood-based panels, 770,000 cu m (27.2 million cu ft). Production of timber is insufficient to meet the domestic demand, and many forestry products are imported. Total trade in forestry products in 2003 amounted to $929 million imports and $112.4 million in exports.

26MINING

The minerals industry, consisting of the mining, industrial minerals, and metal processing sectors, was a small but important part of the national economy. Greece, the only Balkan country in the European Union (EU), was the union's largest producer of bauxite, magnesium, nickel, and perlite, and was second to the United States in bentonite production (from Milos Island). Chromite (from Tsingeli Mines, near Volos) and zinc (from Kassandra Mines, in Olympias and Stratoni) were other important commodities. Greek marble, produced in all parts of the country, continued to play a leading role in the international dimension stone market because of its versatility and many colors (ash, black, brown, green, pink, red, and multicolored). With the exception of bauxite, Greece's mines operated far below their productive capacity. A relatively small industrial base, lack of adequate investment, and distance from EU markets, have restricted the export potential of the country. The emerging Balkan markets could offer opportunities for growth. About 50% of the country's mineral production was exported. Northern Greece was thought to contain a significant amount of exploitable mineral resources, and most new activities were directed toward gold.

Production in 2003 of bauxite was 2.418 million metric tons, compared to 2,468,865 metric tons in 2002. Nickel (content of ferronickel) output in 2003 was estimated at 18,000 metric tons, while crude perlite production in that year was estimated at 850,000 metric tons, up from 838,997 metric tons in 2002. Other types of magnesite produced were dead-burned, caustic-calcined, and crude huntite/hydromagnesite, which had unique flame-retardant properties. Grecian Magnesite S.A., with its open-pit mine at Yerakini, was a leading magnesite producer in the western world. Also produced in 2003 were alumina, lead, manganese, silver, barite, cement, kaolin, feldspar, gypsum (from Crete), anhydrite, nitrogen, pozzolan (Santorin earth, from Milos), pumice (from Yali), salt, silica, sodium compounds, dolomite, marble, flysch, quartz, sulfur, zeolite, and crude construction materials. No asbestos was produced in 2003. Other mineral deposits of commercial importance were antimony, gold (placer dredger), asbestos, emery, ceramic clay, talc, and limestone. Industrial processing of mineral ores was very limited until the 1960s and 1970s, when facilities for refining nickeliferous iron ore and bauxite were developed.

27 ENERGY AND POWER

Coal and oil are imported to supply power for the many small generating plants spread over the country. Before World War II, the Athens-Piraiévs Electricity Co. operated the only modern plant in Greece, which ran on imported coal. In 1950, the government-organized Public Power Corp. was established to construct and operate electricity generating plants and power transmission and distribution lines; by 1955, it had erected four major power plants. In 1965, the first two units of the Kremasta hydroelectric station were opened; by 2001, installed capacity totaled 10.2 million kW. Production of electricity increased from 8,991 million kWh in 1970 to 50,400 million kWh in 2000, of which 91.5% was provided by thermal power, 6.6% by hydroelectric stations, and the rest by other sources. It has been estimated that 15% of Greece's energy needs can be supplied by wind power by 2010, and there are wind farms on Crete, Andors, and a number of other Greek islands. As of 2002, solar water heaters were used in 20% of Greek homes.

As of 2003, 63% of Greece's total energy consumption came from oil. Greece has actively explored offshore oil resources. A field off Thásos in the northern Aegean began operations in July 1981. Total production, however, fell from 25,000 to 6,000 barrels per day between 1986 and 1998. In 2004, oil production totaled an estimated 6,411 barrels per day, of which crude oil accounted for 2,836 barrels per day, from reserves estimated at 7 million barrels, as of 1 January 2005. Consumption in 2004 totaled an estimated 429,000 barrels per day, making Greece strongly reliant on imported oil, mostly from Russia, Libya, OPEC, the Persian Gulf, and Egypt. Natural gas production in 2003 totaled an estimated 1.0 billion cu ft, compared with an estimated consumption of 86 billion cu ft for that same year. Two-thirds of Greece's imports of natural gas come from Russia, with the remainder from Algeria. Greece's only substantial fossil fuel resource is brown coal, or lignite. Its lignite reserves totaled an estimated 4,299 million short tons in 2003, with production and consumption estimated at 75.3 million short tons and 76 million short tons, respectively for that same year.

28 INDUSTRY

Manufacturing, which now ranks ahead of agriculture as an income earner, has increased rapidly owing to a vigorous policy of industrialization. However, Greek industry must rely on imports for its raw materials, machinery, parts, and fuel. Greece has only a rudimentary iron and steel industry and does not manufacture basic transport equipment, such as cars and trucks. Industry is concentrated in the Athens area.

Chief industries in 2006 were food, beverages and tobacco; metals and metals manufactures; machinery and electrical goods; chemicals; textiles; and nonmetallic minerals. Although the government controls certain basic industries, such as electric power and petroleum refining, most industry is privately owned. The portion of government-controlled industries is declining as the state has divested itself of substantial control over key hold-

ings such as Olympic Airways and the telecommunications company, OTE. There is substantial room for investment in tourism infrastructure.

The industrial sector accounted for 22% of GDP in 2004, and it grew by 4.1% that year. High technology equipment is a growth sector, as are the production of electrical machinery, office machinery and computers, defense products, building products and equipment, medical equipment, environmental engineering products and services, and certain agricultural products.

29 SCIENCE AND TECHNOLOGY

The Academy of Athens, founded in 1926, oversees the activities of research institutes in astronomy and applied mathematics and in atmospheric physics and climatology. Greece has five other scientific research institutes. Specialized scientific learned societies include the Association of Greek Chemists, founded in 1924, and the Greek Mathematical Society, founded in 1918, both headquartered in Athens. Advanced scientific and technical training is provided at nine colleges and universities. The University of Athens has maintained a zoological museum since 1858. In the early 1980s, the government established a Ministry of Research and Technology to foster scientific and technological development.

In the period 1987–97, science and engineering students accounted for 26% of university enrollment. In 2001, Greece had 1,357 scientists and engineers per million people who were engaged in research and development (R&D). In that same year, total spending on R&D amounted to 1,226.070 million, or 0.65% of GDP. The government sector accounted for the largest portion of R&D spending in 2001 at 46.6%, followed by the business sector at 33.1%. Foreign sources accounted for 18.4%, with higher education accounting for 2%. In 2002, high technology exports by Greece totaled $524 million, or 10% of the country's manufactured exports.

30 DOMESTIC TRADE

Industry and trade are centered on about 20 seaports throughout the country. Athens, Piraeus, and Thessaloniki are the principal commercial cities; importers and exporters have offices in these cities and branches in other centers. There are about 300,000 wholesale and retail trading establishments in the country.

In general, small shops specialize in particular lines of merchandise, but there are a growing number of department stores. Most people buy in the small shops and in the markets. Usual private sector business hours are from 8 or 9 AM to 5 PM Monday through Friday. Banking hours are from 8:30 AM to 2 PM Monday through Friday. Stores are open from 9 AM to 6 PM, Monday through Saturday, but some have longer evening hours. Businesses are often closed for extended vacations throughout July and August, reopening in September after the annual trade fair.

Advertising is used widely in the towns and cities, and several advertising agencies are active in Athens and Thessaloniki. The most common media are television, newspapers, radio, films, billboards, neon signs, and window displays. The principal annual trade fair is the International Fair of Thessaloniki, held in September.

Principal Trading Partners – Greece (2003)

(In millions of US dollars)

Country	Exports	Imports	Balance
World	13,671.4	44,856.5	-31,185.1
Germany	1,757.3	5,654.0	-3,896.7
Italy-San Marino-Holy See	1,470.3	5,625.0	-4,154.7
United Kingdom	999.6	1,856.3	-856.7
United States	878.3	2,264.6	-1,386.3
Bulgaria	834.1	419.5	414.6
Cyprus	642.8	...	642.8
France-Monaco	581.7	3,004.2	-2,422.5
Turkey	532.5	881.6	-349.1
Spain	501.9	1,633.9	-1,132.0
Macedonia	364.4	...	364.4

(…) data not available or not significant.

SOURCE: *2003 International Trade Statistics Yearbook*, New York: United Nations, 2004.

31 FOREIGN TRADE

Garments and cotton have traditionally provided Greece with the most exports, followed by petroleum products; fruit, nuts, and vegetable oils; and tobacco. Tobacco exports from Greece are substantial on the world commodities export market. In 2004, the major exports were machinery (19.3% of all exports), food (17.1%), and transportation (13.7%, not including services). The major imports in 2004 were machinery (20.7% of all imports), chemicals and plastics (14.2%), and food (13.7%). Trade is the second-largest services sub-sector, after property management. The transportation and communications sector has grown in importance following the liberalization of the telecommunications market, while the financial services sector also increased in the mid-2000s. Greece's leading markets in 2004 were Germany (12.6% of all exports), Italy (10.5%), the United Kingdom (7%), and France (4.2%). Leading suppliers included Germany (12.3% of all imports), Italy (12%), France (6.5%), and the Netherlands (5.1%).

32 BALANCE OF PAYMENTS

Because it imports more than twice the value of its exports, Greece has registered chronic annual deficits in its balance of payments. The major contributors to Greece's foreign exchange earnings are tourism, shipping services, and remittances from Greek workers abroad. Greece's relatively small industrial base and lack of substantial investment since the mid-1990s limited the country's export potential. Greece's productive base expanded in 1999 and 2000, however, in part due to a thriving stock exchange, and low interest rates. A devaluation of the drachma in 1998 and Greece's inclusion in the euro zone in 1999 restored Greek competitiveness. Merchandise exports amounted to $15.7 billion in 2004 and imports to $47.4 billion, while the current-account deficit was $13 billion. The current-account balance averaged -6.7% from 2001–05.

33 BANKING AND SECURITIES

The government-controlled Bank of Greece (founded in 1927) is the central bank and the bank of issue; it also engages in other banking activities, although the European Central Bank is in charge of monetary policy. There are 33 Greek commercial banks, which are dominated by two massive, state-controlled banking groups, the National Bank and the Commercial Bank. Nineteen of the commercial banks are foreign, including three American banks. The two leading private banks are Alpha Credit and Ergo, which ranked third and fifth, respectively, in 1997 in the Greek banking industry in terms of assets. Banks still must redeposit 70% of all their foreign exchange deposits with the Bank of Greece at the going interest rate plus a small commission. In 1999, as part of a general privatization program, the government began selling shares in the National Bank of Greece and Ionian Bank was sold outright and taken over by Alpha Credit.

The Currency Committee, composed of five cabinet ministers, controls the eight specialized credit institutions: the Agricultural Bank, National Investment Bank, National Investment Bank for Industrial Development, Hellenic Industrial Development Bank, National Mortgage Bank, Mortgage Bank, Postal Savings Bank, and Consignments and Loans Fund. The money supply in 2001, as measured by M1, was 24.7 billion euros. The International Monetary Fund reports that in 2001, currency and demand deposits—an aggregate commonly known as M1—were equal to $22.2 billion. In that same year, M2—an aggregate equal to M1 plus savings deposits, small time deposits, and money market mutual funds—was $129.6 billion.

The Athens Stock Exchange (Chrimatisterion) was founded by royal decree in 1876. In 1967, significant reforms were instituted, including more stringent listing requirements, bringing about a rapid increase in the number of listed securities. New legislation was introduced in 1988 to expand and liberalize its activities. The rule changes provided for the establishment of brokerage companies, thus breaking the traditional closed shop of individual brokers. In 1997 there were 53 brokerage houses and just 6 private brokers. Computerized trading was implemented in 1992 and there has since been a rapid evolution of the market. The aim is

Balance of Payments – Greece (2003)

(In millions of US dollars)

Current Account		**-11,225.0**
Balance on goods		-25,606.0
Imports	-38,184.0	
Exports	12,578.0	
Balance on services		13,033.0
Balance on income		-2,924.0
Current transfers		4,272.0
Capital Account		**1,411.0**
Financial Account		**6,168.0**
Direct investment abroad		-9.0
Direct investment in Greece		717.0
Portfolio investment assets		-9,807.0
Portfolio investment liabilities		23,456.0
Financial derivatives		111.0
Other investment assets		-4,413.0
Other investment liabilities		-3,887.0
Net Errors and Omissions		**-1,076.0**
Reserves and Related Items		**4,722.0**

(…) data not available or not significant.

SOURCE: *Balance of Payment Statistics Yearbook 2004*, Washington, DC: International Monetary Fund, 2004.

to secure total dematerialization of shares and to allow brokers to screen-trade from their offices. A satellite trading floor was established in Thessaloniki in 1995. In 1996, Greek law was harmonized with the European Union financial services directive, and banks may now be directly represented on the floor of the exchange instead of having to establish subsidiary brokerage houses. The late 1990s witnessed a boom on the exchange. In 1998, the index rose 85%, while the first five months of 1999 saw a further jump of 43.7%. However, this expansion did not continue into the new millennium. Between 2002 and 2003, the index lost 33.1% of its value. As of 2004, a total of 340 companies were listed on the Athens Stock Exchange (ASE), which had a market capitalization of $125.242 billion that year. In 2004, the ASE rose 23.1% from the previous year to 2,786.2.

34 INSURANCE

Most of Greece's large insurance companies are partly or wholly owned by banks. In addition, insurers are required to join several unions, trade groups, and insurance pools. Brokers in Greece also must be accepted by the Ministry of Trade. In Greece, the social security scheme and third-party automobile liability insurance are compulsory. In 2003, the direct premiums written were valued at $3.668 billion, of which nonlife premiums accounted for $2.040 billion. Ethniki was the country's largest nonlife and life insurer in 2003, with total gross earned non life premiums (including personal accident and inwards reinsurance) and gross written life insurance premiums valued at $361.2 million and $258.3 million respectively.

Insurance companies have begun to develop private pension schemes and corporate pension schemes. However, most occupational pension funds remain under state control because they are part financed by state-enacted levies. Insurance companies have also been responsible for the recent explosion in unit trusts (mutual funds), from two in 1989 to 152 in December 1995, when there were more than D2 trillion (7.8% of GDP) under management.

35 PUBLIC FINANCE

The state budget includes ordinary revenues and expenditures and a special investment budget administered by the Ministry of Coordination. The public sector, which employs 15% of the workforce, has many more civil servants than required for a country the size of Greece. Public payrolls, liberal social security benefits, and loss-generating state owned companies have all contributed to a government deficit. Recent austerity measures implemented to meet the criteria for European Monetary Union membership significantly lowered the budget shortfall.

The US Central Intelligence Agency (CIA) estimated that in 2005 Greece's central government took in revenues of approximately $94.1 billion and had expenditures of $103.4 billion. Revenues minus expenditures totaled approximately -$9.2 billion. Public debt in 2005 amounted to 108.9% of GDP. Total external debt was $75.1 billion.

36 TAXATION

The corporate income tax rate in Greece in 2005 was 32%. The profits of general partnerships (OE) and limited partnerships (EE) were taxed at 25%. A discount of 2.5% was given to companies that settled their corporate tax liability in full when they filed their

Public Finance – Greece (2000)		
(In millions of euros, central government figures)		
Revenue and Grants	**57,882**	**100.0%**
Tax revenue	31,682	54.7%
Social contributions	16,648	28.8%
Grants	1,351	2.3%
Other revenue	8,201	14.2%
Expenditures	**59,244**	**100.0%**
General public services	...	...
Defense	...	...
Public order and safety	...	...
Economic affairs	...	...
Environmental protection	...	...
Housing and community amenities	...	...
Health	...	...
Recreational, culture, and religion	...	...
Education	...	...
Social protection	...	...

(...) data not available or not significant.

SOURCE: *Government Finance Statistics Yearbook 2004*, Washington, DC: International Monetary Fund, 2004.

tax returns. A surcharge is applied to gross rental income, but the surcharge is not to exceed the primary corporate tax. Capital gains were taxed at rates between 20% and 35%. Dividends paid to the corporate or individual shareholder are not taxed. Interest paid to Greek legal entities is 20% and 35% to foreign legal entities that do not have a permanent establishment in Greece.

The progressive personal income tax schedule for 2005 has a top rate of 40%. Various deductions or tax credits can be applied to taxable income for medical and hospitalization expenses; social security taxes; interest payments on home loans; and donations to charitable organizations, with special deductions for families whose income is derived primarily from their own work on agricultural enterprises. The withholding tax is 15% on interest income from banks and 10% on interest income derived from treasury bills and corporate bands. There is a 20% tax on royalty payments, but these are often reduced or eliminated in bilateral double tax prevention treaties, of which Greece has concluded more than 35. Gift and inheritance taxes, property taxes on large estates having a certain value, real estate transfer taxes, and taxes on urban property and rural property are also levied.

The main indirect tax in Greece is its value-added tax (VAT) introduced in January 1987. The standard VAT rate in 2005 was 19%. There were also three reduced rates—0% on domestic transportation, lawyers and land registrar fees; 4.5% on books and newspapers; and 9% on foodstuffs, agricultural products and medical materials. Excise duties are charged on tobacco, alcohol, gasoline, and automobiles.

37 CUSTOMS AND DUTIES

The import tariff protects domestic products and provides a source of government revenue. Many Greek industries are not yet large enough or sufficiently modern to compete in price with foreign products, either in markets abroad or in Greece itself. As a full member of the European Union (EU) since 1981, Greece eliminated its remaining tariffs and quotas on imports from EU nations by 1986 and aligned its own tariffs on imports from other countries with those of EU members. Greek exports to EU countries are tariff-free. Imports from non-EU countries are subject to the EU's common customs tariff. Most raw materials enter duty-free, while manufactured goods have rates between 5% and 7%. Textiles, electronics, and some food products have higher rates. Motor vehicles, yachts, and motorcycles are subject to special duties. In addition, Greece imposes an 8–19% value-added tax and special consumption taxes on alcohol and tobacco.

38 FOREIGN INVESTMENT

The government encourages foreign capital investment and protects foreign investors against compulsory appropriation of their assets in Greece. Incentives include reduced tax rates and increased depreciation rates.

Total direct foreign investment (FDI) was estimated at $3.78 billion in 1995. From 1995 to 1997, FDI inflow averaged about $1 billion a year. In the wake of the Russian financial crisis of 1998, FDI inflow fell to $700 million in 1998 and to $567 million in 1999. FDI inflow in 2000 reached over $1 billion and grew to a record $1.56 billion in 2001. In 2002, FDI inflow fell nearly 90% to $50.3 million. For the period 1999 to 2002, FDI inflow averaged about $833 million.

Outward FDI flow was $542 million in 1999, over $2 billion in 2000, and $611 million in 2001. Outward FDI increased to $655.3 million in 2002. For the period 1999 to 2002, average outward FDI from Greece was $993.3 billion.

From 2001–05, FDI inflows averaged 0.6% of GDP. The corporate tax rate was being cut from 35% to 32% on income earned in 2005, to 29% on income earned in 2006, and to 25% on income earned in 2007. Value-added tax (VAT) is levied at 19%, 8%, and 4.5%. Although there is no official estimate of total foreign investment in Greece, as of 2002 the total stock of FDI was estimated at $6 billion, or approximately 4.3% of GDP. Greece's investment abroad is directed primarily to the Balkans. Greek direct investment in the Balkans was estimated at $3.6 billion in 2002.

39 ECONOMIC DEVELOPMENT

Until the mid-1970s, Greek governments devoted themselves principally to expanding agricultural and industrial production, controlling prices and inflation, improving state finances, developing natural resources, and creating basic industries. In 1975, the Karamanlis government undertook a series of austerity measures designed to curb inflation and redress the balance-of-payments deficit. A new energy program included plans for stepped-up exploitation of oil and lignite reserves, along with uranium exploration in northern Greece. Increased efforts at import substitution were to be undertaken in all sectors. On 7 March 1975, in an effort to strengthen confidence in the national currency, the government announced that the value of the drachma would no longer be quoted in terms of a fixed link with the US dollar, but would be based on daily averages taken from the currencies of Greece's main trade partners.

The Socialist government that took office in 1981 promised more equal distribution of income and wealth through "democratic planning" and measures to control inflation and increase productivity. It imposed controls on prices and credit and began to restructure public corporations. But the government was cautious in introducing what it called "social control in certain key sectors" of the economy, and it ordered detailed studies to be made first. Its development policies emphasized balanced regional growth and technological modernization, especially in agriculture. The conservative government that came to power in 1990 adopted a 1991–93 "adjustment program" that called for reduction of price and wage increases and a reduction in the public-sector deficit from 13% to 3% of GDP. Twenty-eight industrial companies were to be privatized.

The chief goal of the Simitis government was admission to the European Monetary Union (EMU). As a consequence, his government instituted an austerity program aimed to tackle chronically high inflation, unemployment, and a bloated public sector. By 1998–99, these policies showed significant progress. Greece gained admission to the EMU in 2001, and adopted the euro as its new currency in 2002. The Greek economy was growing at rates above European Union (EU) averages from 2002–05; however, unemployment and inflation rates were still higher than in most euro-area countries. In 2004, Greece's general government debt stood at approximately 112% of GDP. Greece benefits from EU aid, equal to about 3.3% of GDP.

Privatization of state-owned enterprises has moved at a relatively slow pace, especially in the telecommunications, banking, aerospace, and energy sectors. In 2003, preparations for the 2004 Olympics drove investment, but spending on the Olympic Games contributed to a general government deficit of 6.6% of GDP in 2004. With the aid of EU grants, Greece will need to update its infrastructure, especially in the northern regions and on the islands. Improvements in road, rail, harbor, and airport links financed through the EU's Community Support Framework (CSF) programs have contributed to economic decentralization.

40 SOCIAL DEVELOPMENT

The Social Insurance Foundation, the national social security system, is supported by contributions from employees, employers and the government. It provides for old age, disability and survivorship. Work injury and unemployment benefits are also provided. Sickness and maternity benefits have been in place since 1922. Current benefits include medical care, hospitalization, medicine, maternity care, dental coverage, appliances, and transportation. Payments also include birth and funeral grants.

Although the law mandates equal pay for equal work, according to statistics in 2004 women's pay amounted to 75.5% of men's pay. Domestic violence and rape remains underreported, and the number of prosecutions and convictions is low. Women are beginning to enter traditionally male-oriented careers such as law and medicine, but only make up 42.5% of the work force. Sexual harassment is specifically prohibited by law.

Occasional human rights abuses, involving residents, illegal aliens and persons in custody, have been reported. Government measures to improve prison conditions continue. The constitution prohibits discrimination on the basis of nationality, race, language, religion, or political beliefs. In practice the government does not always protect these rights.

41 HEALTH

Since World War II, the government has broadened health services by building new hospitals and providing more clinics and medical personnel. Total health care expenditure was estimated at 8.4% of GDP. As of 2004, there were an estimated 410 physicians per 100,000 people. There are severe air quality problems in Athens. Pulmonary tuberculosis, dysentery, and malaria, which were once endemic, have been controlled. The incidence of typhoid, which was formerly of epidemic proportions, dropped to only 149 cases in 1985 following the application of US aid to improve sanitary conditions in more than 700 villages. At present, 100% of the population has access to safe water. In 2005, the infant mortality rate was 5.53 per 1,000 live births. The total fertility rate in 1980 (2.2) has dropped to 1.3 as of 2000. The birthrate was an estimated 9.8 per 1,000 people. The sharp birth rate decline since World War II has been attributed to the legalization of abortion. In 2005, life expectancy averaged 79.09 years. As of 2002, the overall mortality rate was estimated at 9.8 per 1,000 people.

The HIV/AIDS prevalence was 0.10 per 100 adults in 2003. As of 2004, there were approximately 600 people living with HIV/AIDS in the country. There were an estimated 200 deaths from AIDS in 2003.

42 HOUSING

Construction of new dwellings (including repairs and extensions) reached 88,477 units in 1985 and rose to 120,240 in 1990. Most new construction is in Athens or Thessaloniki, indicating the emphasis on urban development. Considerable amounts of private investment have been spent on the construction of apartment houses in urban areas. In 2001, the total number of dwelling units was 5,476,162. About 47.9% of all dwelling units are owner occupied. About 40% of all dwellings are single household homes.

43 EDUCATION

Education is free and compulsory for nine years beginning at age six, and primary education lasts for six years. Secondary education is comprised of two steps: first three years, followed by an additional three years of college preparation. At the upper secondary levels, students may choose to attend a three-year vocational school. The central and local governments pay the cost of state schools, and private schools are state-regulated. The academic year runs from September to June. Greek is the primary language of instruction.

In 2001, about 68% of children between the ages of four and five were enrolled in some type of preschool program. Primary school enrollment in 2003 was estimated at about 99% of age-eligible students. The same year, secondary school enrollment was about 86% of age-eligible students. Nearly all students complete their primary education. The student-to-teacher ratio for primary school was at about 12:1 in 2003; the ratio for secondary school was about 9:1.

In July 1982, the Socialist government initiated a program to democratize the higher-education system; a law was approved that diminished the power of individual professors by establishing American-style departments with integrated faculties. Junior faculty members and representatives of the student body were granted a role in academic decision-making. The legislation also curbed university autonomy by establishing the National University Council to advise the government on higher-education planning, and the Academy of Letters and Sciences to set and implement university standards.

Greece has six major universities: Athens, Salonika, Thrace, Ioánnina, Crete, and Pátrai—together with the National Technical University of Athens, the new University of the Aegean, and the Technical University of Crete, plus seven special institutions of higher education. There are several technological educational institutions, which offer nondegree programs of higher education. Private universities are constitutionally banned. In 2003, about 74% of the tertiary age population were enrolled in some type of higher education program. The adult literacy rate for 2004 was estimated at about 91%, with 94% for men and 88.3% for women.

As of 2003, public expenditure on education was estimated at 4% of GDP, or 7% of total government expenditures.

44 LIBRARIES AND MUSEUMS

The National Library traces its origins to 1828, when it was established on the island of Aíyina; the library was moved to its present site in Athens in 1903 and today has more than 2.5 million volumes. Both the National Library and the Library of Parliament (1.5 million volumes) act as legal depositories for Greek publications and are open to the public. Public libraries are located mainly in provincial capitals, and there are regional libraries with bookmobile services for rural areas.

Besides the libraries attached to the universities and other educational institutions, there are several specialized research libraries located in Athens. Outstanding special collections can be found at the Democritus Nuclear Research Center (91,000 volumes), the Center of Planning and Economic Research (30,000 volumes), the Athens Center of Ekistics (30,000 volumes), and the Gennadius Library (80,000 volumes), which houses a large collection on modern Greek history. Being at the crossroads of different civilizations and an important European country, there are several libraries attached to various cultural and ethnic studies centers. Notable among these are the libraries of the Institute for Balkan Studies in Thessaloniki, the British Council, the Society for Byzantine Studies in Athens, and the Center for Asia Minor Studies in Athens.

Most museums are devoted to antiquities and archaeology. One of the richest collections of Greek sculpture and antiquities is found at the National Archaeological Museum in Athens, which is also home to the Byzantine and Christian Museum, Benaki Museum, and Kanellopoulos Museum. The most impressive archaeological remains, of course, are the great temples and palaces at Athens (particularly the Parthenon and the Stoa of Attalos), Corinth, Salonika, Delphi, Olympia, Mycenae, the island of Delos, and Knossos, on Crete. There are also notable museums dedicated to the work of other cultures, including the Byzantine Museum and the Jewish Museum, both in Athens. Among the newer facilities are the Hellenic Children's Museum (1987), the Museum of Greek Popular Musical Instruments (1991), the Museum of Delphic Celebrations of Angelos and Eva Sikelianou (1991), the Nikolaos Parantinos Museum of Sculpture (1991), and the Maria Callas Museum (2003) all located in Athens.

45 MEDIA

The Greek Telecommunications Authority operates domestic telegraph and telephone communications. In 2003, there were an estimated 454 mainline telephones for every 1,000 people; about 1,700 people were on a waiting list for telephone service installation. The same year, there were approximately 902 mobile phones in use for every 1,000 people.

Radio Athens broadcasts are carried by provincial relay stations located in various parts of the country; other stations are operated by the Greek armed forces and by the Hellenic National Radio and Television Institute. There are numerous independent radio and television stations. In 2003, there were an estimated 466 radios and 519 television sets for every 1,000 people. The same year, there were 81.7 personal computers for every 1,000 people and 150 of every 1,000 people had access to the Internet. There were 290 secure Internet servers in the country in 2004.

In 2002, there were over 150 daily papers throughout the country. The largest Athens dailies (with estimated 2002 circulation rates) are *To Vima* (250,000), *Eleftheros Typos* (167,186), *Ta Nea* (135,000), *Ethnos* (84,700), *Apogevmatini* (72,900), and *Avriani* (51,300).

The constitution provides for freedom of speech and press, and with a few exceptions the government is said to respect these rights. On matters involving the politically sensitive subject of the recognition of certain ethnic minorities, it is reported that the government is restrictive. The constitution also allows for seizure of publications that insult the president, offend religious beliefs, contain obscene articles, advocate violent overthrow of the political system, or disclose military and defense information. However, such action is very rare.

46 ORGANIZATIONS

Most of the larger cities and towns have associations of commerce, industry, handicrafts, and finance. There are some consumers' and producers' cooperatives; chambers of commerce and industry function in Athens, Piraiévs, and Salonika. There are professional and trade organizations for a variety of occupations and industries, such as the Association of Greek Honey Processors and Exporters, the Greek Association of Industries and Processors of Olive Oil, and the Pan-Hellenic Association of Meat-Processing Industries. The Federation of Greek Industries draws together many of these business and manufacturing organizations.

The Academy of Athens serves to promote public interest in science and works to improve availability and effectiveness in science education programs. Artists, writers, musicians, educators, and journalists are organized into professional associations. Scholarly societies include those devoted to archaeology, anthropology, geography, history, political science, and sociology. Several professional associations also promote research and education in their field.

National youth organizations in Greece include the Greek Democratic Socialist Youth, Girl Guides and Girl Scouts of Greece, the Association of Boy Scouts, YMCA/YWCA, the Greek Youth Federation, the Radical Left Youth, and the Student and Scientist Christian Association of Greece. There are several sports organization in Greece, including the historical societies of the Hellenic Federation of Ancient Olympic Games and the International Society of Olympic Historians. The World Chess Federation is based in Athens.

There are national chapters of the Red Cross Society, Caritas, and Amnesty International.

47 TOURISM, TRAVEL, AND RECREATION

Principal tourist sites, in addition to the world-famous Parthenon and Acropolis in Athens, include Mt. Olympus (the home of the gods in ancient mythology), the site of the ancient oracle at Delphi, the Agora at Corinth, the natural spring at the rock of the Acropolis, and the Minoan ruins on Crete. Operas, concerts, ballet performances, and ancient Greek dramas are presented at the Athens Festival each year from July to September; during July and August, Greek classics also are performed in the open-air theater at Epidaurus, 40 km (25 mi) east of Árgos. Popular sports include swimming at the many beaches, sailing, water-skiing, fishing, golf, and mountain climbing.

The Greek government encourages tourists and facilitates their entry and accommodation. A passport is needed for admission; residents of the United States, Australia, Canada, and 37 other countries do not require a visa for a stay of up to 90 days.

About 14,180,000 tourists visited Greece in 2002. There were 330,970 hotel rooms in 2003 with 628,170 beds. The average length of stay that same year was seven nights.

In 2005, the US Department of State estimated the cost of staying in Athens at $294 per day. Elsewhere in the country, daily expenses ranged from $53 to $296.

48 FAMOUS GREEKS

The origins of Western literature and of the main branches of Western learning may be traced to the era of Greek greatness that began before 700 BC with the epics of Homer (possibly born in Asia Minor), the *Iliad* and the *Odyssey.* Hesiod (fl.700 BC), the first didactic poet, put into epic verse his descriptions of pastoral life, including practical advice on farming, and allegorical myths. The poets Alcaeus (620?–580? BC), Sappho (612?–580? BC), Anacreon (582?–485? BC), and Bacchylides (fl.5th cent. BC) wrote of love, war, and death in lyrics of great feeling and beauty. Pindar (522?–438? BC) celebrated the Panhellenic athletic festivals in vivid odes. The fables of the slave Aesop (b.Asia Minor, 620?–560? BC) have been famous for more than 2,500 years. Three of the world's greatest dramatists were Aeschylus (525–456 BC), author of the *Oresteia* trilogy; Sophocles (496?–406? BC), author of the Theban plays; and Euripides (485?–406? BC), author of *Medea, The Trojan Women,* and *The Bacchae.* Aristophanes (450?–385? BC), the greatest author of comedies, satirized the mores of his day in a series of brilliant plays. Three great historians were Herodotus (b.Asia Minor, 484?–420? BC), regarded as the father of history, known for *The Persian Wars;* Thucydides (460?–400? BC), who generally avoided myth and legend and applied greater standards of historical accuracy in his *History of the Peloponnesian War;* and Xenophon (428?–354? BC), best known for his account of the Greek retreat from Persia, the *Anabasis.* Outstanding literary figures of the Hellenistic period were Menander (342–290? BC), the chief representative of a newer type of comedy; the poets Callimachus (b.Libya, 305?–240? BC), Theocritus (b.Italy, 310?–250? BC), and Apollonius Rhodius (fl.3d cent. BC), author of the *Argonautica;* and Polybius (200?–118? BC), who wrote a detailed history of the Mediterranean world. Noteworthy in the Roman period were Strabo (b.Asia Minor, 64? BC–AD 24?), a writer on geography; Plutarch (AD 46?–120?), the father of biography, whose *Parallel Lives* of famous Greeks and Romans is a chief source of information about great figures of antiquity; Pausanias (b.Asia Minor, fl. AD 150), a travel writer; and Lucian (AD 120?–180?), a satirist.

The leading philosophers of the period preceding Greece's golden age were Thales (b.Asia Minor, 625?–547? BC), Pythagoras (570?–500? BC), Heraclitus (b.Asia Minor, 540?–480? BC), Protagoras (485?–410? BC), and Democritus (460?–370? BC). Socrates (469?–399 BC) investigated ethics and politics. His greatest pupil, Plato (429?–347 BC), used Socrates' question-and-answer method of investigating philosophical problems in his famous dialogues. Plato's pupil Aristotle (384–322 BC) established the rules of deductive reasoning but also used observation and inductive reasoning, applying himself to the systematic study of almost every form of human endeavor. Outstanding in the Hellenistic period were Epicurus (341?–270 BC), the philosopher of moderation; Zeno (b.Cyprus, 335?–263? BC), the founder of Stoicism; and Diogenes (b.Asia Minor, 412?–323 BC), the famous Cynic. The oath of Hippocrates (460?–377 BC), the father of medicine, is still recited by newly graduating physicians. Euclid (fl.300 BC) evolved the system of geometry that bears his name. Archimedes (287?–212 BC) discovered the principles of mechanics and hydrostatics. Eratosthenes (275?–194? BC) calculated the earth's circumference with remarkable accuracy, and Hipparchus (190?–125? BC) founded scientific astronomy. Galen (AD 129?–199?) was an outstanding physician of ancient times.

The sculptor Phidias (490?–430? BC) created the statue of Athena and the figure of Zeus in the temple at Olympia and supervised the construction and decoration of the Parthenon. Another renowned sculptor was Praxiteles (390?–330? BC).

The legal reforms of Solon (638?–559? BC) served as the basis of Athenian democracy. The Athenian general Miltiades (554?–489? BC) led the victory over the Persians at Marathon in 490 BC, and Themistocles (528?–460? BC) was chiefly responsible for the victory at Salamis 10 years later. Pericles (495?–429? BC), the virtual ruler of Athens for more than 25 years, added to the political power of that city, inaugurated the construction of the Parthenon and other noteworthy buildings, and encouraged the arts of sculpture and painting. With the decline of Athens, first Sparta and then Thebes, under the great military tactician Epaminondas (418?–362 BC), gained the ascendancy; but soon thereafter, two military geniuses, Philip II of Macedon (382–336 BC) and his son Alexander the Great (356–323 BC), gained control over all of Greece and formed a vast empire stretching as far east as India. It was against Philip that Demosthenes (384–322 BC), the greatest Greek orator, directed his diatribes, the *Philippics*.

The most renowned Greek painter during the Renaissance was El Greco (Domenikos Theotokopoulos, 1541–1614), born in Crete, whose major works, painted in Spain, have influenced many 20th-century artists. An outstanding modern literary figure is Nikos Kazantzakis (1883–1957), a novelist and poet who composed a vast sequel to Homer's *Odyssey*. Leading modern poets are Kostes Palamas (1859–1943), Georgios Drosines (1859–1951), and Constantine Cavafy (1868–1933), as well as George Seferis (Seferiades, 1900–72), and Odysseus Elytis (Alepoudhelis, 1911–96), winners of the Nobel Prize for literature in 1963 and 1979, respectively. The

work of social theorist Cornelius Castoriadis (1922–97) is known for its multidisciplinary breadth. Musicians of stature are the composers Nikos Skalkottas (1904–49), Iannis Xenakis (b.Romania, 1922–2001), and Mikis Theodorakis (b.1925); the conductor Dmitri Mitropoulos (1896–1960); and the soprano Maria Callas (Calogeropoulos, b.United States, 1923–77). Filmmakers who have won international acclaim are Greek-Americans John Cassavetes (1929–89) and Elia Kazan (1909–2003), and Greeks Michael Cacoyannis (b.1922) and Constantin Costa-Gavras (b.1933). Actresses of note are Katina Paxinou (1900–73); Melina Mercouri (1925–94), who was appointed minister of culture and science in the Socialist cabinet in 1981; and Irene Papas (Lelekou, b.1926).

Outstanding Greek public figures in the 20th century include Cretan-born Eleutherios Venizelos (1864–1936), prominent statesman of the interwar period; Ioannis Metaxas (1871–1941), dictator from 1936 until his death; Constantine Karamanlis (1907–98), prime minister (1955–63, 1974–80) and president (1980–85) of Greece; George Papandreou (1888–1968), head of the Center Union Party and prime minister (1963–65); and his son Andreas Papandreou (1919–96), the PASOK leader who became prime minister in 1981. Costas Simitis (b.1936) was leader of PASOK and prime minister from 1996–2004. He was succeeded by Kóstas Karamanlís (b.1956).

49 DEPENDENCIES

Greece has no territories or colonies.

50 BIBLIOGRAPHY

Brown, John Pairman. *Ancient Israel and Ancient Greece: Religion, Politics, and Culture*. Minneapolis: Fortress Press, 2003.

Bryant, Joseph M. *Moral Codes and Social Structure in Ancient Greece: A Sociology of Greek Ethics from Homer to the Epicureans and Stoics*. Albany, N.Y.: State University of New York Press, 1996.

Camp, John M. *The World of the Ancient Greeks*. London: Thames and Hudson, 2002.

Cosmopoulos, Michael B. (ed.). *The Parthenon and Its Sculptures*. New York: Cambridge University Press, 2004.

Frucht, Richard (ed.). *Eastern Europe: An Introduction to the People, Lands, and Culture*. Santa Barbara, Calif.: ABC-CLIO, 2005.

Green, Sarah F. *Notes from the Balkans: Locating Marginality and Ambiguity on the Greek-Albanian Border*. Princeton, N.J.: Princeton University Press, 2005.

Greene, Ellen (ed.). *Women Poets in Ancient Greece and Rome*. Norman: University of Oklahoma Press, 2005.

Halkias, Alexandra. *The Empty Cradle of Democracy: Sex, Abortion, and Nationalism in Modern Greece*. Durham: Duke University Press, 2004.

Hazel, John. *Who's Who in the Greek World*. New York: Routledge, 2000.

International Smoking Statistics: A Collection of Historical Data from 30 Economically Developed Countries. New York: Oxford University Press, 2002.

Lawrence, A.W. *Greek Architecture*. New Haven, Conn.: Yale University Press, 1996.

Legg, Kenneth R. *Modern Greece: A Civilization on the Periphery*. Boulder, Colo.: Westview Press, 1997.

Morris, Ian. *The Greeks: History, Culture, and Society*. Upper Saddle River, N.J.: Pearson Prentice Hall, 2006.

Sheehan, Sean. *Illustrated Encyclopedia of Ancient Greece*. Los Angeles, Calif.: The J. Paul Getty Museum, 2002.

Speake, Graham (ed.) *Encyclopedia of Greece and the Hellenic Tradition*. Chicago: Fitzroy Dearborn, 2000.

Wessels, Wolfgang, Andreas Maurer, and Jürgan Mittag (eds.). *Fifteen into One?: the European Union and Its Member States*. New York: Palgrave, 2003.

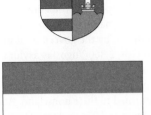

HUNGARY

Republic of Hungary
Magyar Népköztársaság

CAPITAL: Budapest

FLAG: The national flag, adopted in 1957, is a tricolor of red, white, and green horizontal stripes.

ANTHEM: *Isten áldd meg a magyart (God Bless the Hungarians).*

MONETARY UNIT: The forint (Ft) of 100 fillérs is a paper currency with flexible rates of exchange. There are coins of 10, 20, and 50 fillérs and 1, 2, 5, 10, 20, 100, and 200 forints, and notes of 50, 100, 500, 1,000, and 5,000 forints. Ft1 = $0.00508 (or $1 = Ft196.83) as of 2005.

WEIGHTS AND MEASURES: The metric system is the legal standard.

HOLIDAYS: New Year's Day, 1 January; Anniversary of 1848 uprising against Austrian rule, 15 March; Labor Day, 1 May; Constitution Day, 20 August; Day of the Proclamation of the Republic, 23 October; Christmas, 25–26 December. Easter Monday is a movable holiday.

TIME: 1 PM = noon GMT.

¹LOCATION, SIZE, AND EXTENT

Hungary is a landlocked country in the Carpathian Basin of Central Europe, with an area of 93,030 sq km (35,919 sq mi), extending 268 km (167 mi) N–S and 528 km (328 mi) E–W. Comparatively, the area occupied by Hungary is slightly smaller than the state of Indiana. It is bounded on the N by Slovakia, on the NE by the Ukraine, on the E by Romania, on the s by Serbia and Croatia, on the sw by Slovenia, and on the w by Austria, with a total boundary length of 2,171 km (1,349 mi). Hungary's capital city, Budapest, is located in the north central part of the country.

²TOPOGRAPHY

About 84% of Hungary is below 200 m (656 ft) in altitude, its lowest point, at the Tisza River, being 78 m (256 ft) above sea level and the highest being Mt. Kékes (1,014 m/3,327 ft) in the Mátra Mountains, northeast of Budapest. The country has four chief geographic regions: Transdanubia (Dunántúl), the Great Plain (Alföld), the Little Plain (Kisalföld), and the Northern Mountains. Hungary's river valleys and its highest mountains are in the northeast. Generally, the soil is fertile. The chief rivers are the Danube (Duna) and Tisza. The largest lake is Balaton, which has an area of 601 sq km (232 sq mi).

³CLIMATE

Hungary lies at the meeting point of three climatic zones: the continental, Mediterranean, and oceanic. Yearly temperatures vary from a minimum of -14°C (7°F) to a maximum of 36°C (97°F). The mean temperature in January is -4°C to 0°C (25° to 32°F) and in July, 18° to 23°C (64° to 73°F). Rainfall varies, but the annual average is approximately 63 cm (25 in)—more in the west and less in the east—with maximum rainfall during the summer months. Severe droughts often occur in the summers.

⁴FLORA AND FAUNA

Plants and animals are those common to Central Europe. Oak is the predominant deciduous tree; various conifers are located in the mountains. Among the abundant wildlife are deer, boar, hare, and mouflon. The Great Plain is a breeding ground and a migration center for a variety of birds. Fish are plentiful in rivers and lakes. As of 2002, there were at least 83 species of mammals, 208 species of birds, and over 2,200 species of plants throughout the country.

⁵ENVIRONMENT

Chemical pollution of the air and water is extensive, but resources to combat pollution are scarce: a 1996 government study estimated that US$350 million were needed to combat pollution, but only US$7 million were allocated for this purpose. According to the study, air pollution affects 179 areas of the country, soil pollution affects 54 areas, and water pollution affects 32. Hungary is also one of 50 nations that lead the world in industrial carbon dioxide emissions, with a 1992 total of 59.9 million metric tons, a per capita level of 5.72 metric tons. However, the total carbon dioxide emissions dropped to 54.2 million metric tons in 2000. Hungary has 6 cu km of renewable water resources, with 55% used for industrial purposes and 36% used for farming activity. Hungary's principal environmental agency is the National Council for Environment and Nature Conservation, under the auspices of the Council of Ministers.

Geothermal aquifers lie below most of Hungary. The water brought from these to the earth's surface ranges in temperature from 40°C (104°F) to 70°C (158°F). In the southwest, geothermal aquifers have produced water at 140°C (284°F). Some of these waters are cooled and used for drinking water, but many aquifers are used to heat greenhouses.

In 2003, about 7% of the total land area was protected. According to a 2006 report issued by the International Union for Conservation of Nature and Natural Resources (IUCN), threatened species included 7 types of mammals, 9 species of birds, 1 type of reptile, 8 species of fish, 1 type of mollusk, 24 species of other invertebrates, and 1 species of plant. Endangered species included the longicorn, the alcon large blue butterfly, the dusky large blue butterfly, and the Mediterranean mouflon.

⁶POPULATION

The population of Hungary in 2005 was estimated by the United Nations (UN) at 10,086,000, which placed it at number 79 in population among the 193 nations of the world. In 2005, approximately 16% of the population was over 65 years of age, with another 16% of the population under 15 years of age. There were 91 males for every 100 females in the country. According to the UN, the population for 2005–10 was expected to decline annually by -0.4%, a rate the government viewed as too low. The fertility rate, which had been declining since the 1990s, reached just 1.5 births per woman in 2005. The projected population for the year 2025 was 9,588,000. The population density was 108 per sq km (281 per sq mi).

Since the early 1950s, there has been a fundamental shift of the population from rural to urban areas. The UN estimated that 65% of the population lived in urban areas in 2005. The urban growth rate has substantially slowed in recent years, with the UN estimating annual growth in urban areas at just 0.14% as of 2005. The capital city, Budapest, had a population of 1,708,000 in that year. Other urban areas include: Debrecen, 217,706; Miskolc, 211,000; Szeged, 178,878; Pécs, 172,177; Nyíregyháza, 115,643; Székesfehérvár, 111,478; and Kecskemét, 107,267.

⁷MIGRATION

Sizable migration during the two world wars resulted from military operations, territorial changes, and population transfers. Peacetime emigration in the decades before World War I was heavy (about 1,400,000 between 1899 and 1913). Emigration of non-Magyars was prompted by the repressive policy of Magyarization; groups also left because of economic pressures, the majority going to the United States and Canada. In the interwar period, migration was negligible, but after 1947 many thousands left, despite restrictions on emigration. As a result of the October 1956 uprising, approximately 250,000 persons fled Hungary. The largest numbers ultimately emigrated to the United States, Canada, the United Kingdom, Germany, France, Switzerland, and Australia. Emigration totaled 42,700 between 1981 and 1989. By the 1990s, emigration was virtually nonexistent; only 778 persons left in 1991, according to official statistics.

Between 1990 and 2003, some 115,000 immigrants acquired Hungarian citizenship, granted almost exclusively to ethnic Hungarians from neighboring countries. At the end of 2000, 3% of Hungary's population (294,000) were foreign-born, resulting from international migration, and as a consequence of historic events such as border changes or citizenship agreements. According to *Migration Information Source*, from 1990 to 2003, the border guards recorded 152,000 cases of foreigners attempting to enter illegally, and 80,000 efforts to leave Hungary illegally. These activities indicate Hungary's transit role in illegal migration.

Since 1960, net migration from the villages to the cities has decreased, from about 52,000 that year to 20,814 in 1986. Since 1989, Hungary has received nearly 155,000 refugees, with major influxes from Romania in 1988–89 and the former Yugoslavia in 1991–92. About 5,400 asylum seekers have been recognized as refugees since 1989. In the 1990s Hungary provided temporary protection for over 32,000 Bosnians. Most of these refugees resettled to another country or repatriated. The Temporary Protection status of some 480 Bosnian refugees, who remained in Hungary in the latter part of the 1990s, was withdrawn by the government in mid-1999. As a result of the Kosovo crisis, 2,800 Yugoslav asylum seekers arrived in Hungary, including 1,000 Kosovo Albanians. The organized voluntary repatriation of refugees began in August 1999, when the first 185 Kosovars returned to their homeland. At the end of 2004 there were 7,708 refugees and 354 asylum seekers in Hungary. Asylum seekers were from Georgia and Turkey. In 2004, 832 Hungarians applied for asylum in Canada.

As a member of the European Union (EU) since 1 May 2004, Hungary's migration and illegal migration border controls have tightened. According to *Migration Information Source*, as of 2002 some 115,000 foreign citizens with a valid long-term permit (i.e., good for at least one year) or permanent residence permit resided in Hungary; 43% were Romanian citizens, 11% Yugoslavians, 8% Ukrainians, and most of these were ethnic Hungarians, and 6% were Chinese. This population amounted to 1.13% of Hungary's total population. These changing waves of labor migration are also characterized by a new form of labor migration within the EU, termed "walk-over-the-border for employment," where workers seeking higher wages travel from one country to a neighboring one, such as from Slovakia to Hungary.

In 2005, the net migration rate was estimated as 0.86 migrants per 1,000 population.

⁸ETHNIC GROUPS

Ethnically, Hungary is essentially a homogeneous state of Magyar extraction. The 2001 census indicates that Hungarians constitute about 92.3% of the total population. Roma account for about 1.9%. Ethnic Germans make up about 0.7% of the population. There are also small groups of Croats, Poles, Ukrainians, Greeks, Serbs, Slovenes, Armenians, Ruthenians, Bulgarians, Slovaks, and Romanians.

⁹LANGUAGES

Hungarian, also known as Magyar, is the universal language. In addition to the letters of the English alphabet, it has the following letters and combinations: *á, é, í, ó, ö, ő, ú, ü, cs, dz, dzs, gy, ly, ny, sz, ty, zs*. Written in Latin characters, Hungarian (Magyar) belongs to the Finno-Ugric family, a branch of the Ural-Altaic language group. Hungarian (Magyar) is also characterized by an admixture of Turkish, Slavic, German, Latin, and French words. In addition to their native language, many Hungarians speak English, German, French, or (since World War II) Russian. In 2002, 98.2% of the population spoke Hungarian; 1.8% spoke various other languages.

¹⁰RELIGIONS

According to a 2001 census, approximately 55% of the people are nominally Roman Catholic, 15% are members of the Reformed Church, 3% of the population are Lutheran, and less than 1% are Jewish. About 3% of the population describe themselves as

LOCATION: 45°48′ to 48°35′ N; 16°5′ to 22°58′ E. BOUNDARY LENGTHS: Slovakia, 515 kilometers (320 miles); Ukraine, 103 kilometers (64 miles); Romania, 443 kilometers (275 miles); Serbia, 151 kilometers (94 miles); Croatia, 329 kilometers (204 miles); Slovenia, 102 kilometers (63 miles); Austria, 366 kilometers (227 miles).

Greek Catholics. About 15% of the population claim no religious affiliation.

About one million Jews lived in Hungary before World War II and an estimated 600,000 were deported in 1944 to concentration camps. According to estimates from the World Jewish Restitution Organization, there are between 70,000 and 110,000 Jews currently residing in Hungary. There are also seven Buddhist and five Orthodox denominations. There are three Islamic communities.

A 1990 Law on the Freedom of Conscience provides for separation of church and state and safeguards the liberty of conscience of all citizens and the freedom of religious worship. However, the state does grant financial support to religious denominations for religious practice, educational work, and maintenance of public collections. To promote further support of religious institutions, between 1997–99 the government signed separate agreements with the country's four largest churches (the Roman Catholic, Jewish, Lutheran, and Calvinist churches) and two smaller groups (Hungarian Baptist and Budai Serb Orthodox). The government also provides funds each year for the revitalization of churches based on annual negotiations between the Ministry of Cultural Heritage and the Ministry of Finance.

11 TRANSPORTATION

Transportation facilities have improved steadily since the 1960s. Budapest is the transportation center. In 2002, roads totaled 159,568 km (99,251 mi), of which some 70,050 km (43,571 mi) were paved, including 527 km (328 mi) of expressways. In 2003, Hungary had 2,777,219 passenger cars and 394,988 commercial vehicles registered for use.

As of 2004, Hungary had 7,937 km (4,937 mi) of broad, standard and narrow gauge railroad lines. Of that total, standard gauge lines accounted for the largest portion at 7,682 km (4,778 mi), followed by narrow gauge lines at 219 km (136 mi) and broad gauge lines at 36 km (22 mi). Most freight is carried by trucks; railway transport is of lesser importance. The railroad and bus networks are state owned.

Permanently navigable waterways totaled 1,622 km (1,009 mi) in 2004, of which most were on the Danube and Tisza rivers. In addition to the government shipping enterprises—which operate the best and largest ships and handle the bulk of water traffic—the Shipping Cooperative, an association of small operators, continues to function. In 1999, the latest year for which data was available), the merchant marine fleet consisted of 2 cargo ships with a total capacity of 12,949 GRT.

Hungary had an estimated 44 airports in 2004. As of 2005 a total of 19 had paved runways, and there were also five heliports. Ferihegy Airport in Budapest is the most important center for domestic and international flights. All domestic traffic is handled by the Hungarian Air Transportation Enterprise (Magyar Légiközlekedési Vallalat—MALÉV). In 2003, about 2.369 million passengers were carried on scheduled domestic and international airline flights.

12 HISTORY

Ancient human footprints, tools, and a skull found at Vértesszóllós date the earliest occupants of present Hungary at a period from 250,000 to 500,000 years ago. Close to that site, at Tata, objects used for aesthetic or ceremonial purposes have been discovered, among the earliest such finds made anywhere in the world.

Celtic tribes settled in Hungary before the Romans came to occupy the western part of the country, which they called Pannonia and which the Roman Emperor Augustus conquered in 9 BC. Invasions by the Huns, the Goths, and later the Langobards had little lasting effect, but the two subsequent migrations of the Avars (who ruled for 250 years and, like the Huns, established a khanate in the Hungarian plain) left a more lasting impression.

The Magyars (Hungarians) migrated from the plains south and west of the Ural Mountains and invaded the Carpathian Basin under the leadership of Árpád in AD 896. For half a century they ranged far and wide, until their defeat by Otto the Great, king of Germany and Holy Roman emperor, near Augsburg in 955. They were converted to Christianity under King Stephen I (r.1001–1038), who was canonized in 1083. The Holy Crown of St. Stephen became the national symbol, and a constitution was gradually developed. The Magna Carta of Hungary, known as the Golden Bull of 1222, gave the nation a basic framework of national liberties to which every subsequent Hungarian monarch had to swear fidelity. Hungary was invaded at various times during the medieval period; the Mongols succeeded in devastating the country in 1241–42.

Medieval Hungary achieved its greatest heights under the Angevin rulers Charles Robert and Louis the Great (r.1342–82), when Hungarian mines yielded five times as much gold as those of any other European state. Sigismund of Luxembourg, king of Hungary, became Holy Roman emperor in 1410, largely on the strength of this national treasure. During the 15th century, however, Turkish armies began to threaten Hungary. The Balkan principalities to the south and southeast of Hungary developed as buffer states, but they did not long delay the advance of the Turks; nor could the victories of János Hunyadi, brilliant as they were, ultimately stem the Turkish tide. With the Turks temporarily at bay, the Hungarian renaissance flourished during the reign of Hunyadi's son, Matthias Corvinus (1458–90), but his successors in the 16th century overexploited the gold mines, brutally suppressed a peasant revolt, and allowed the Magyar army to deteriorate. Hungary's golden age ended with the rout by the Turks at Mohács in 1526.

Thereafter, warring factions split Hungary, but power was gradually consolidated by the Habsburg kings of Austria. With the defeat of the Turks at Vienna in 1683, Turkish power waned and that of the Habsburgs became stronger. The Hungarians mounted many unsuccessful uprisings against the Habsburgs, the most important insurrectionist leaders being the Báthorys, Bocskai, Bethlen, and the Rákóczys. In 1713, however, the Hungarian Diet accepted the Pragmatic Sanction, which in guaranteeing the continuing integrity of Habsburg territories, bound Hungary to Austria.

During the first half of the 19th century, in the aftermath of the French Revolution and the Napoleonic wars, Hungary experienced an upsurge of Magyar nationalism, accompanied by a burst of literary creativity. The inability of a liberal reform movement to establish a constitutional monarchy led to the revolt of 1848, directed by Lajos Kossuth and Ferenc Deák, which established a short-lived Hungarian republic. Although Hungarian autonomy was abolished as a result of intervention by Austrian and Russian armies, Austria, weakened by its war with Prussia, was obliged to give in to Magyar national aspirations. The Compromise (Ausgleich) of 1867 established a dual monarchy of Austria and Hungary and permitted a degree of self-government for the Magyars.

After World War I, in which Austria-Hungary was defeated, the dual monarchy collapsed, and a democratic republic was established under Count Mihály Károlyi. This was supplanted in March 1919 by a Communist regime led by Béla Kun, but Romanian troops invaded Hungary and helped suppress it. In 1920, Hungary became a kingdom without a king; for the next 25 years, Adm. Miklós von Nagybánya Horthy served as regent. The Treaty of Trianon in 1920 formally freed the non-Magyar nationalities from Hungarian rule but also left significant numbers of Magyars in Romania and elsewhere beyond Hungary's borders. The fundamental policy of interwar Hungary was to recover the "lost" territories, and in the hope of achieving that end, Hungary formed alliances with the Axis powers and sided with them during World War II. Hungary temporarily regained territories from Czechoslovakia, Romania, and Yugoslavia. In March 1944, the German army occupied Hungary, but Soviet troops invaded the country later that year and liberated it by April 1945.

In 1946, a republican constitution was promulgated, and a coalition government (with Communist participation) was established. Under the terms of the peace treaty of 1947, Hungary was forced to give up all territories acquired after 1937. The Hungarian Workers (Communist) Party seized power in 1948 and adopted a constitution (on the Soviet model) in 1949. Hungarian foreign trade was oriented toward the Soviet bloc, industry was nationalized and greatly expanded, and collectivization of land was pressed. Resentment of continued Soviet influence over Hungarian affairs was one element in the popular uprising of October 1956, which after a few days' success—during which Hungary briefly withdrew from the Warsaw Treaty Organization—was summarily put down by Soviet military force. Many people fled the country, and many others were executed. From that time on, Hungary was a firm ally of the USSR. In 1968, the New Economic Mechanism was introduced in order to make the economy more competitive and open to market forces; reform measures beginning in 1979 further encouraged private enterprise. The movement toward relaxation of tensions in Europe in the 1970s was reflected in the improvement of Hungary's relations with Western countries, including the reestablishment of diplomatic relations with the FRG in 1973. A US-Hungarian war-claims agreement was signed that year, and on 6 January 1978 the United States returned the Hungarian coronation regalia.

The New Economic Mechanism that had been instituted in 1968 was largely abandoned, at Soviet and Comecon insistence, a decade later. This compounded the blows suffered by Hungary's economy during the energy crisis of the late 1970s, leading to a ballooning of the country's foreign indebtedness. By the late 1980s the country owed $18 billion, the highest per capita indebtedness in Europe.

This indebtedness was the primary engine of political change. The necessity of introducing fiscal austerity was "sweetened" by the appointment of reform-minded Károly Grosz as prime minister in 1987. Faced with continued high inflation, the government took the step the following year of forcing János Kádár out entirely, giving control of the party to Grosz. In 1989 Grosz and his supporters went even further, changing the party's name to Hungarian Socialist Party, and dismantling their nation's section of the Iron Curtain. The action that had the most far-reaching consequences, however, came in October 1989 when the state constitution was amended so as to create a multiparty political system.

Although Hungarians had been able to choose among multiple candidates for some legislative seats since as early as 1983, the foundations of a true multiparty system had been laid in 1987–88, when large numbers of discussion groups and special interest associations began to flourish. Many of these, such as the Network of Free Initiatives, the Bajscy-Zsilinszky Society, the Hungarian Democratic Forum, and the Alliance of Free Democrats, soon became true political parties. In addition, parties that had existed before the 1949 imposition of Communist rule, such as the People's Party, the Hungarian Independence Party, and the Social Democrats, began to reactivate themselves.

All of these groups, or the parties they had spawned, competed in the 1990 general election, the first major free election to be held in more than four decades. No party gained an absolute majority of seats, so a coalition government was formed, composed of the Democratic Forum, Smallholders' Party, and Christian Democrats, with Forum leader Jozsef Antall as prime minister. Arpad Goncz, of the Free Democrats, was selected as president. An important indicator of Hungary's intentions came in June 1989, when the remains of Imre Nagy, hanged for his part in the events of 1956, were reentered with public honors; politicians and other public figures used the occasion to press further distance from Communism and the removal of Soviet troops. Another sign of public sentiment was the first commemoration in 40 years of the anniversary of the Revolution of 1848.

Under Antall Hungary pursued a vigorous program of economic transformation, with the goal of transferring 30–35% of state assets to private control by the end of 1993. Hungary's liberal investment laws and comparatively well-developed industrial infrastructure permitted the nation to become an early leader in attracting Western investors. However, there were large blocs in society, and within the Democratic Forum itself, that found the pace of transition too slow, particularly since the government did not keep to its own time schedule.

In addition to its economic demands, this radical-right contingent also has a strongly nationalist, or even xenophobic, agenda, which has tended to polarize Hungarian national politics. Approximately 10% of the Hungarian population is non-Hungarian, including large populations of Jews and Roma (Gypsies). There are also large Hungarian populations in neighboring states, particularly in Romania, all of whom had been declared dual citizens of Hungary in 1988. The appeal to "Hungarian-ness" has been touted fairly frequently, widening preexisting tensions within the dominant Democratic Forum party, and weakening their coalition in parliament. The Smallholders Party withdrew from the coalition in 1992, and in 1993 other elements were threatening to do the same.

The Democratic Forum's loss of popularity was vividly exposed in the parliamentary elections of May 1994, when the party, led by acting head Sandor Leszak, lost almost one-third of the seats it had controlled. In that election voters turned overwhelmingly to the Hungarian Socialist Party, giving the former Communist party an absolute majority of 54%. Voter turnout in the two-tier election was as high as 70%, leaving little doubt that Hungarian voters had repudiated the Democratic Forum and its programs of forced transition to a market economy.

Hungary's international indebtedness remained very high—the country ran a $936 million trade deficit for the first two months of 1994 alone—obligating new prime minister Gyula Horn to continue most of the same economic reform programs which the Socialists' predecessors had begun. There was concern, however, that the Socialists' absolute majority could lead to a reversal of some of the important democratic gains of the recent past. Those concerns sharpened in July 1994, when Prime Minister Horn unilaterally appointed new heads for the state-owned radio and television, who immediately dismissed or suspended a number of conservative journalists.

On 8 January 1994 Hungary formally accepted the offer of a compromise on NATO membership. The offer involved a new defense partnership between Eastern Europe and NATO. By July 1997, NATO agreed to grant Hungary full membership (along with Poland and the Czech Republic) in the organization in 1999. In order to help them qualify to join NATO and the EU, Hungary and Romania signed a treaty on 16 September 1996 ending a centuries-old dispute between the two neighbors. The agreement ended five years of negotiations over the status of Romania's 1.6 million ethnic Hungarians. On 12 March 1999, Hungary, Poland, and the Czech Republic were formally admitted to NATO, becoming the first former Warsaw Pact nations to join the alliance.

Despite improvements in the economy, the position of the Socialists was undermined by dissatisfaction among those negatively affected by privatization and austerity measures, as well as by financial scandals in 1997. The Socialist government was toppled in national elections held in May 1998, and a new center-right coalition government was formed in July by Viktor Orbán, leader of the victorious Federation of Young Democrats-Hungarian Civic Party (Fidesz).

In 1997 Hungary was invited to begin negotiations leading to membership in the European Union. It was formally invited to join the body in 2002 at the EU summit in Copenhagen. It was accepted as a full member on 1 January 2004. In 2000, parliament elected Ferenc Madl as president.

Under Victor Orbán, Hungary experienced increasing prosperity, but also increasing social division. Fidesz is a strong supporter of ethnic Hungarians in neighboring countries. Indeed, parliament in June 2001 passed a controversial law entitling Hungarians living in Romania, Slovakia, Ukraine, Serbia, Croatia, and Slovenia to a special identity document allowing them to temporarily work, study, and claim health care in Hungary. In June 2003 the law was amended by the parliament, with a majority of the Hungarian population agreeing with it. However, the referendum held in December 2004, in conjunction with this law, was invalidated due to low turnout.

Orbán's party was challenged in the April 2002 general elections by the Socialist Party, which chose Péter Medgyessy as its candidate for prime minister. Although Medgyessy characterized his party as patriotic, he stressed it was less extreme than Fidesz, and supported diversity as well as traditional values of fairness and social justice.

The 2002 campaign was divisive, and saw nationalists come out in force in favor of Fidesz. Although it won the largest bloc of seats in the National Assembly in the second round of voting (aligned with the Hungarian Democratic Forum), it was the Socialists in concert with the Alliance of Free Democrats that formed a coalition government with Medgyessy as prime minister.

In June 2002, allegations surfaced that Medgyessy had worked as a counterintelligence officer in the secret service under the Communist regime in the late 1970s and early 1980s. Medgyessy claimed he never collaborated with Moscow's KGB, but instead sought out Soviet spies attempting to disrupt Hungary's efforts to join the IMF. Upon his admission, his popularity soared.

In the summer of 2004, internal problems within his own party, as well as growing opposition from the coalition partners—the Alliance of Free Democrats, led Medgyessy to resign. He was replaced with Ferenc Gyurcsany, the former sports minister and one of the government's most popular figures. Gyurcsany received 453 votes, while his main contender—Peter Kiss—got 166.

The new prime minister promised to strengthen the coalition, boost economic growth, and improve living conditions for Hungarians. However, strict budget controls (many imposed by the EU), and unfulfilled election promises dramatically decreased the popular support for his government, and party. In the 2004 European Parliament elections, the Young Democrats (the main opposition party) led the pack, and predictions for the 2006 national parliamentary elections showed Socialists as garnering only 20% of the votes.

In June 2005, opposition-backed Laszlo Solyom was elected as the new president of Hungary. He garnered 185 votes, in the third round of elections, followed closely by the Socialist's nominee—Katalin Szili—with 182 votes.

13 GOVERNMENT

Hungary's present constitution remains based upon the 1949 Soviet-style constitution, with major revisions made in 1972 and 1988. The 1988 revisions mandated the end of the Communist Party's monopoly on power, removed the word People's from the name of the state, and created the post of president to replace the earlier Presidential Council.

The present system is a unitary multiparty republic, with a parliamentary government. There is one legislative house (the National Assembly), with 386 members who are elected to four-year terms. The head of state is the president, who is elected by the parliament, for a five-year term. In 2005, Laszlo Solyom—a university professor and former president of the Constitutional Court—was elected president by a simple majority of the legislative vote. The next presidential elections were scheduled for June 2010.

The head of the government is the prime minister, leader of the largest party seated in the parliament. The prime minister is elected by the National Assembly on the recommendation of the president. In the Antall government important ministerial and other posts were split among representatives of various parties. As of 2005, the prime minister was Ferenc Gyurcsany, a wealthy businessman and popular political figure. Gyurcsany replaced Péter Medgyessy in 2004, following dissentions within the ruling coalition.

14 POLITICAL PARTIES

Following the general elections of April 2002, four political parties were represented in the 386-member National Assembly, split into two coalitions. This situation raised fears that Hungary was drifting into a two-party state, divided by ideology and personalities, instead of reflecting other interests not represented in government.

The predominant party is the Hungarian Socialist Party (MSZP), whose government was toppled in 1998, but returned to power in 2002, receiving 42.05% of the popular vote and garnering 178 seats in the National Assembly. The MSZP is the Hungarian Communist Party renamed and, to a certain extent, reoriented. The party's platform indicates strong support for the market economy system, albeit with a wide net of social services. It supports diversity in Hungarian society, as opposed to the center-right's more populist, nationalistic party Fidesz.

The leading opposition party was the Federation of Young Democrats-Hungarian Civic Party (also known as Fidesz), which held 164 seats. The party's leader, Viktor Orbán, was named prime minister in 1998; he was out of office in 2002 when the Socialists came to power. Originally known as the Federation of Young Democrats, the party was formed on an anti-Communist platform by student activists and young professionals in 1988. During the 1990s, it evolved into a mainstream center-right party and was renamed in 1995.

The Alliance of Free Democrats (SzDSz), which holds 20 seats, is the coalition partner of the MSZP. This party was a liberal opposition party during the Antall government, with positions strongly in favor of closer integration with Europe, cooperation with Hungary's neighbors, and support for alien Hungarians. In economic terms their platform is very similar to that of the MSZP, which was the basis of their agreement to enter into a coalition. However, their alliance had frequent disputes that in result undermined their political strength.

The Hungarian Democratic Forum (MDF), which has been reduced to 24 seats, is a party of strong support for the ethnic minorities within Hungary. It is currently aligned with Fidesz. The Hungarian Justice and Life Party (MIEP) first gained parliamentary representation in 1998, winning 14 seats, and was founded by Istvan Csurka, who was expelled from the MDF for his nationalist and anti-Semitic sentiments. The party is populist in orientation, seeking to elevate "Hungarian values." It won 4.4% of the vote in 2002 but held no seats. The next legislative elections were scheduled for April 2006.

The Independent Smallholders' Party (FKgP), which held 48 seats in the 1998 government but no seats in the government formed in 2002, is a center-right party that seeks to ensure Hungarian interests in the context of European integration. It draws particular support from rural districts and among farmers.

Other parties include the centrist Center Party and the communist Worker's Party. Hungary also has a noticeable "skinhead" movement, which has provoked fights and other disturbances, especially with Gypsies.

15 LOCAL GOVERNMENT

Hungary is divided administratively into 19 counties, 20 urban counties, and the capital city of Budapest also has county status. At the local and regional level, legislative authority is vested in county, town, borough, and town precinct councils whose members are directly elected for four-year terms. Members of the county councils are elected by members of the lower-level councils. Hungary also has provisions for minority self-government, which is not based territorially, because minorities live dispersed throughout the country. Municipality councils must seek the approval of minority self-governments for matters affecting minority education and culture, among others.

16 JUDICIAL SYSTEM

Cases in the first instance usually come before provincial city courts or Budapest district courts. Appeals can be submitted to county courts or the Budapest Metropolitan Court. The Supreme Court is basically a court of appeal, although it may also hear important cases in the first instance. As of 2003, a new intermediate court of appeal was to be established between county courts and the Supreme Court, designed to alleviate the backlog of court cases.

The president of the Supreme Court is elected by the National Assembly. A National Judicial Council nominates judicial appointees other than those of the Constitutional Court. The state's punitive power is represented by the public prosecutor. Peter Polt was appointed as prosecutor general in 2000.

The Constitutional Court reviews the constitutionality of laws and statutes as well as compliance of these laws with international treaties the government has ratified. The 11 members of the Constitutional Court are elected by parliament for nine-year terms with a two-thirds majority; their mandates may be renewed in theory, but as of 2002, this had not happened in practice.

17 ARMED FORCES

In 2005, Hungary had a total of 32,300 active personnel in its armed forces, including an army of 23,950 and an air force of 7,500 personnel. The Hungarian Army operates 238 main battle tanks, 178 armored infantry fighting vehicles, 458 armored personnel carriers, and over 573 artillery pieces. The Air Force operates 14 combat capable aircraft, as well as 12 attack helicopters and 17 support aircraft. All major equipment is of Soviet design. There is a small Army maritime wing with 60 personnel operating three river craft to patrol the Danube River. Paramilitary forces, consisting of frontier and border guards, under the direction of the Ministry of the Interior, number about 12,000. There are about 44,000 military reservists. The defense budget was estimated at $1.43 bil-

lion in 2005. Hungary provides UN observers and peacekeepers to eight regions or countries.

18 INTERNATIONAL COOPERATION

Hungary has been a member of the United Nations since 14 December 1955 and participates in ECE and most of the nonregional specialized agencies except the IFAD. Hungary became a member of the OECD in 1996, a NATO member in 1999, and a member of the European Union in 2004. Hungary is also a member of the WTO, the Council of Europe, G-9, and the OSCE. The nation has observer status in the OAS and is a member affiliate of the Western European Union.

Hungary is part of the Australia Group, the Zangger Committee, the Nuclear Suppliers Group, the Organization for the Prohibition of Chemical Weapons, the European Organization for Nuclear Research (CERN), and the Nuclear Energy Agency. In environmental cooperation, Hungary is part of the Antarctic Treaty, the Basel Convention, Conventions on Biological Diversity and Air Pollution, Ramsar, CITES, the London Convention, International Tropical Timber Agreements, the Kyoto Protocol, the Montréal Protocol, MARPOL, the Nuclear Test Ban Treaty, and the UN Conventions on the Law of the Sea, Climate Change, and Desertification.

19 ECONOMY

Before World War II, industrial growth was slow because adequate capital was lacking. Since 1949, however, industry has expanded rapidly, and it now contributes a larger share than agriculture to the national income. The government has no capital investments abroad, but it participates in limited economic activities in developing countries. Substantial industrial growth continued through the 1960s and mid-1970s, but output in the socialized sector declined during 1979–80, and growth was sluggish in the 1980s.

After the fall of Communism in 1989, Hungary began a painful transition to a market economy. Between 1990 and 1992, GDP dropped by about 20%. Freed to reach their own level, consumer prices rose 162% between 1989 and 1993. The rate of unemployment was 12.2% at the end of 1992. By late 1998, private-sector output was over 85% of the GDP.

By 1994, Hungary was in an economic slump unknown since the reforms toward capitalism began. Export earnings were down, inflation was on the rise, and Hungary's gross debt rose to about $31.6 billion in mid-1995 (the highest per capita foreign debt in Europe). The IMF directed the government to curb social spending, but restricting social welfare during a period of high unemployment was unpopular with voters. The government began a stabilization plan in March 1995 designed to decrease the budget deficit by FT170 billion (3–4% of the GDP) and to decrease the current account deficit to $2.5 billion from the record high of $4 billion in 1994. The government cut expenditures, increased its revenues, devalued the forint by 9%, introduced a crawling peg exchange rate policy, added an 8% surcharge on imports, and called for wage controls at state-owned companies. As a result of the program, inflation and GDP growth rose. In addition, the black market economy was estimated to be as much as 30% of GDP.

In the years since its implementation, the stabilization program has borne fruit. By 1999, the IMF assistance had been repaid. The Hungarian economy exhibited strong growth rates with

GDP increases of 4.6% and 5.1% in 1997 and 1998, respectively. Although a hard winter and the Kosovo conflict appeared to hamper Hungarian efforts to match the prior years' growth rate levels, the economy performed well in 2000, led by an increase in foreign direct investment. Since then, manufacturing output and productivity increased, and export industries did well, although increases in wages and a rapid appreciation of the forint in 2002 moderated export growth. The global economic downturn that began in 2001 had an impact on the Hungarian economy, as GDP rose by 3.3% in the first half of 2002, down from 6.6% in the first half of 2000. Although this growth rate was higher than most European nations in 2002, it was below the rate needed for Hungary to reach the wealth levels of EU countries.

Due to government efforts at privatization, over 80% of the economy was privately owned by 2001, and Hungary stands as a model for countries undergoing market reforms. In December 2002, Hungary was formally invited to join the EU; it was accepted as a full member in May 2004 as one of the most advanced of the 10 candidate countries slated for accession.

As an EU member, Hungary maintained its position as one of the most dynamic and strong economies in Central and Eastern Europe. Its position within the European Union, and the fact that it is still comparatively cheaper to do business there than in other Western European countries, makes Hungary a prime target for investments. However, Hungary is being challenged by some of its neighbors that have managed to maintain lower labor costs, and a more attractive tax system. Already some of the investments in the country have moved further east, to countries like Romania and Ukraine, and some of the bids for new investments have been lost for the same reasons.

Although the GDP growth was slower in 2002 and 2003 (3.3% and 2.9% respectively), it recuperated lost ground in 2004, with a 4% increase, and is expected to exceed 4% in 2005. Inflation decreased to 7% in 2004, and unemployment was only 5.9% in the same time period. However, in order to catch up with the developed economies in the EU, Hungary should register (according to the IMF specialists) annual growth rates of 5–5.25%. This means that further investments have to be attracted to generate funds for the state. Consequently, the governments planned to sell Budapest Airport and Antenna Hungaria in 2005. Attracting additional foreign investments is increasingly difficult though, as the country has to fight with rather high budget deficits (5.9% in 2004), and with increased competition from its neighbors.

20 INCOME

The US Central Intelligence Agency (CIA) reports that in 2005 Hungary's gross domestic product (GDP) was estimated at $159.0 billion. The CIA defines GDP as the value of all final goods and services produced within a nation in a given year and computed on the basis of purchasing power parity (PPP) rather than value as measured on the basis of the rate of exchange based on current dollars. The per capita GDP was estimated at $15,900. The annual growth rate of GDP was estimated at 3.7%. The average inflation rate in 2005 was 3.7%. It was estimated that agriculture accounted for 3.9% of GDP, industry 30.9%, and services 65.3%.

According to the World Bank, in 2003 remittances from citizens working abroad totaled $295 million or about $29 per capita and accounted for approximately 0.4% of GDP. Foreign aid receipts amounted to $248 million or about $25 per capita and accounted for approximately 0.3% of the gross national income (GNI).

The World Bank reports that in 2003 household consumption in Hungary totaled $56.30 billion or about $5,574 per capita based on a GDP of $82.8 billion, measured in current dollars rather than PPP. Household consumption includes expenditures of individuals, households, and nongovernmental organizations on goods and services, excluding purchases of dwellings. It was estimated that for the period 1990 to 2003 household consumption grew at an average annual rate of 1.6%. In 2001 it was estimated that approximately 25% of household consumption was spent on food, 17% on fuel, 6% on health care, and 20% on education. It was estimated that in 1997 about 17.3% of the population had incomes below the poverty line.

21 LABOR

Hungary's workforce in 2005 was estimated at 4.18 million. In 2003, agriculture accounted for 5.5% of the labor force, with 33.7% in manufacturing, and 60.7% in the services sector. In 2005, the estimated unemployment rate stood at 7.1%.

Before World War II, trade unions had not developed substantially; their combined membership was only about 100,000, principally craftsmen. After the war, the government reduced the number of the traditional craft unions, organized them along industrial lines, and placed them under Communist Party control. The Central Council of Hungarian Trade Unions (SZOT) held a monopoly over labor interests for over 40 years. Since wages, benefits, and other aspects of employment were state-controlled, the SZOT acted as a social service agency, but was dissolved in 1990 with the shift away from centralization to democracy. The National Federation of Trade Unions is its successor, with 735,000 members in 1999. There are now several other large labor organizations in Hungary, including the Democratic League of Independent Trade Unions, with some 100,000 members, and the Federation of Workers' Councils, with 56,000 members. Labor disputes are usually resolved by conciliation boards; appeal may be made to courts. Since 1991, most unions have been hesitant to strike, preferring instead to act as a buffer between workers and the negative side effects of economic reform. Collective bargaining is permitted but is not widespread.

The eight-hour day, adopted in several industries before World War II, is now widespread. The five-day week is typical, but many Hungarians have second or third jobs. The law prohibits employment for children under the age of 15 and closely regulates child labor. The minimum wage in 2002 was $140 per month which was not sufficient to provide a decent lifestyle for a family. Most workers earn more than this amount. Health and safety conditions in the workplace do not meet international standards, and regulations are not enforced due to limited resources.

22 AGRICULTURE

In 2003, 52% of the land (4,820,000 hectares/11,910,000 acres) was arable. More than half of Hungary's area lies in the Great Plain; although the soil is fertile, most of the region lacks adequate rainfall and is prone to droughts, requiring extensive irrigation. In 2003, some 230,000 hectares (568,000 acres) of land were irrigated. In 2003, agriculture contributed 4% to GDP.

Before World War II (1939–45), Hungary was a country of large landed estates and landless and land-poor peasants. In the land reform of 1945, about 35% of the land area was distributed, 1.9 million hectares (4.7 million acres) among 640,000 families and 1.3 million hectares (3.2 million acres) in state farms. In 1949, the government adopted a policy of collectivization based on the Soviet kolkhoz, and by the end of 1952, 5,110 collectives, many forcibly organized, controlled 22.6% of total arable land. Peasant resentment led to a policy change in 1953, and many collectives were dissolved, but the regime returned to its previous policy in 1955. As a result of the 1956 uprising, collectives were again dissolved; but a new collectivization drive begun in 1959 was essentially completed by 1961. Meanwhile, the proportion of the economically active population employed in agriculture decreased steadily. In 1949, agricultural employees accounted for 55.1% of the total labor force; in 2003, agriculture accounted for 10.7% of the engaged labor force and gross agricultural output was valued at over €1.95 billion. In 2004, Hungary had an agricultural trade surplus of $1.3 billion.

Hungary has achieved self-sufficiency in temperate zone crops, and exports about one-third of all produce, especially fruit and preserved vegetables. The traditional agricultural crops have been cereals, with wheat, corn (maize), and rye grown on more than half the total sown area. In recent years, considerable progress has been made in industrial crops, especially oilseeds and sugar beets. Fruit production (especially for preserves) and viticulture are also significant; the wine output in 2004 was estimated at 48 million liters. That year, over 650,000 tons of grapes were produced on 93,000 hectares (230,000 acres).

The principal field crops harvested in 2004 included (in tons): corn, 8,317,000; wheat, 6,020,000; sugar beets, 3,130,000; potatoes, 767,000; rye, 125,000.

23 ANIMAL HUSBANDRY

Although animal husbandry is second only to cereal cultivation in agricultural production, the number and quality of animals are much lower than in neighboring countries. An inadequate supply of fodder is one of the chief deficiencies. In 2005 there were 4,059,000 hogs, 1,397,000 sheep, 723,000 head of cattle, and 68,000 horses; poultry numbered 32,800,000. The 2005 output of livestock products was 1,034,000 tons (live weight) of meat, 2,043,000 tons of milk, and 5,000 tons of wool; egg production was 180,200 tons.

24 FISHING

Fishing was unimportant before World War II (1939–45), but production has increased in recent years. The best fishing areas are the Danube and Tisza rivers, Lake Balaton, and various artificial ponds. The catch is composed mainly of carp, catfish, eel, and perch. The 2003 catch was 18,406 tons, 64% from aquaculture. Hungary imports around $15–20 million in seafood annually to meet demand.

25 FORESTRY

Forests totaled 1,840,000 hectares (4,547,000 acres), or 19.9% of Hungary's total land area, in 2000. The forest consists of the fol-lowing main species: oak, 23%; black locust, 20%; pine and fir, 15%; Austrian and turkey oak, 11%; poplars, 9%; beech, 6%; hornbeam (blue beech), 6%; and others, 10%. Because of the relatively small forest area and the high rate of exploitation, Hungary traditionally has had to import timber. During the 1960s, a systematic reforestation program began. Reforestation affected about 440,000 hectares (1,087,000 acres) during 1960–68 but only about 65,000 hectares (161,000 acres) in 1970–74 and 64,322 hectares (158,942 acres) during 1975–81. From 1990–2000, some 136,000 hectares (336,000 acres) were annually reforested.

Roundwood production has remained stagnant in recent years, at 5,660,000 cu m (200 million cu ft) in 2004. Less than 12% of the production is softwood; Hungary's wood imports consist mostly of softwood, while exports are based on hardwood products. Production of wood products in 2004 (in thousands of cu m) included: sawn wood, 204; wood-based panels, 638; paper and paperboard, 579; and pulpwood, 653.

Privatization of agricultural land, including forests, finished in 1996. According to estimates from the Ministry of Agriculture's Forestry Office, 55% of forests were under state control, 44.5% were owned by private individuals, and 0.5% belonged to municipalities.

26 MINING

In 2002, Hungary produced modest amounts of fossil fuels and industrial minerals, cement and coal being the dominant components of industrial minerals and metals. Although the country had significant output of alumina and bauxite, the output of primary aluminum was modest, due to limited domestic energy sources. Construction aggregates and cement continued to play an important role in Hungary's economy, especially in view of the modernization process necessary for the country's infrastructure, for which planned highway construction through 2008 would be an important element. Mineral reserves were small and generally inadequate.

Bauxite mining and refining to alumina, as well as manganese mining, remained the only metal mining and processing operations in Hungary in 2002. Production of bauxite, found in various parts of western Hungary, was 720,000 tons in 2002, compared with 1 million tons in 2001. Total resources of bauxite were estimated to be 23 million metric tons, with commercial reserves at 16 million metric tons. Bakony Bauxitbany Kft. constituted Hungary's bauxite mining industry in 2002. Hungary also produced 40,000 metric tons of manganese ore concentrate (gross weight) in 2002, up from 338,000 metric tons in 2001, and 250,000 tons of gypsum and anhydrite in 2002. A total of 500,000 tons of calcined lime were also produced that same year. In addition, Hungary produced alumina (calcined basis), bentonite, common clays, diatomite, kaolin, nitrogen, perlite, sand (common, foundry, and glass) and gravel, dimension stone, dolomite, limestone, sulfuric acid, and talc. Although Hungary no longer mined copper, past surveys of the deep-lying Recsk copper ore body, in the Matra mountains, discovered 172–175 million tons of copper ore at a grade of 1.12% copper and about 20 million tons of polymetallic ore at a grade of 4.22% lead and 0.92% zinc as well as smaller quantities of gold, molybdenum, and silver. After failing to attract foreign investment, the exploration shaft and adit at Recsk was closed, the equipment removed, and the facilities flooded in 1999.

Exploration for gold in the Recsk region continued in 2000, as 35 million tons of gold-bearing enargite copper ore was delineated with a grade of 1.47 grams per ton of gold.

²⁷ENERGY AND POWER

Hungary has modest reserves of oil, natural gas, and coal. In addition, the country's electric power sector relies upon nuclear power to provide a sizable portion of its electric power needs.

In 2002, Hungary's electric power generating capacity stood at 8.393 million kW, of which conventional thermal plants accounted for: 6.478 million kW; nuclear 1.866 million kW; hydropower 0.048 million kW; and geothermal/other 0.001 million kW. Electric output in 2002 came to 34.061 billion kWh, of which: conventional thermal sources accounted for 20.548 billion kWh; nuclear 13.255 billion kWh; hydropower 0.192 billion kWh; and geothermal/other 0.066 billion kWh. Electric power consumption in 2002 totaled 35.977 billion kWh. Imports and exports of electric power that year came to 12.6 billion kWh and 8.3 billion kWh, respectively. By the end of 1963, all villages were connected with electric power. Hungary's sole nuclear power plant, at Pécs, consists of four second-generation, Soviet-designed, VVER-440/213 reactors, which began production in 1982. As of 2002, modernization was planned to extend the operating life of the reactors by 20 years. The normal lifespan of the four units would end between 2012 and 2017. However, if the continuous operation of the power plant is to be maintained, the needed modernization would have to start in 2007.

Hungary's reserves of crude oil and natural gas are estimated, as of 1 January 2004, at 102.5 million barrels and 1.2 trillion cu ft, respectively. Refining capacity for that same date is estimated at 161,000 barrels per day. Coal reserves in 2001, were estimated at 1,209 million short tons. In 2003, Hungary's total oil production was estimated at 45,700 barrels per day, with natural gas and coal output estimated in 2002 at 110 billion cu ft and 14.2 million short tons, respectively. Consumption of oil, natural gas and coal outstrips domestic production. Demand for oil in 2003 was estimated at 137,000 barrels per day, while natural gas and coal consumption in 2002 were estimated at 473 billion cu ft and 15 million short tons, respectively. However, the consumption of coal has declined. Between 1993 and 2003, Hungary's demand for coal fell 21%. Brown coal, or lignite, accounted for all domestic coal output in 2002. Uranium, discovered in 1953 near Pécs, is expected to supply its nuclear station until 2020.

²⁸INDUSTRY

Hungary is poor in the natural resources essential for heavy industry and relies strongly on imported raw materials. Industry, only partially developed before World War II, has expanded rapidly since 1948 and provides the bulk of exports. Industrial plants were nationalized by 1949, and the socialized sector accounted for about 98.5% of gross production in 1985.

Hungary has concentrated on developing steel, machine tools, buses, diesel engines and locomotives, television sets, radios, electric light bulbs and fluorescent lamps, telecommunications equipment, refrigerators, washing machines, medical apparatus and other precision engineering equipment, pharmaceuticals, and petrochemical products. Textile and leather production has decreased in relative importance since World War II, while chemi-

cals grew to become the leading industry in the early 1990s. Food processing, formerly the leading industry, provides a significant portion of exports; meat, poultry, grain, and wine are common export items.

In 1993, industrial production was only two-thirds of the 1985 level. In 1997, industrial output increased in the manufacture of road vehicles, consumer electronics, insulated cables, office equipment and computers, steel products, aluminum metallurgy, household chemical products and cosmetics, rubber and plastic products, and paper and pulp production. In 1992, Suzuki and Opel began producing automobiles in Hungary, the first produced there since before World War II. Suzuki increased annual output at the Magyar Suzuki Corporation from 29,000 to 50,000 units starting in the 1995 fiscal year. Since 1990, Hungary has developed industrial strength in the automotive field as well as an expanding automotive sourcing industry in plastics and electronics. In 2001, Hungary produced 144,313 automobiles, a 5% increase over 2000. In 2000, it produced 1,621 heavy trucks, a 24% increase over 1999. In 2000, close to 14% of total Hungarian industrial output was accounted for by the vehicle manufacturing industry.

The growth in manufacturing output and productivity in the early 2000s has been supported by a considerable amount of foreign investment. Successive Hungarian governments have pursued privatization policies and policies to restructure industry, so that by 2002, 80% of the economy was privately owned. High-tech equipment (computers, telecommunication equipment, and household appliances) showed the strongest industrial growth in 2001. Industries targeted for growth in 2003 were the automotive industry, the general industrial and machine tool industry, and the information technology industry. Housing construction was another growth sector in 2002.

In 2004, the share of the industrial output in the GDP was 31.4%, while its representation in the labor force was 27.1%. Agriculture contributed 3.3% to the GDP, while occupying 6.2% of the labor force; services came in first with a 65.3% share in the economy, and a 66.7% representation in the labor force. The industrial production growth rate was 9.6% in 2004, and most of this growth occurred in industries like motor vehicles, chemicals (especially pharmaceuticals), textiles, processed foods, construction materials, metallurgy and mining.

²⁹SCIENCE AND TECHNOLOGY

In 2002, there were 486 technicians and 1,473 researchers per million people that were actively engaged in research and development (R&D). Total expenditures on R&D during that year amounted to $1.374 million, or 1.01% of GDP. Of that total, the government sector accounted for the majority of spending at 58.6%, followed by business at 29.7%, foreign investors at 10.4%, and higher education at 0.3%. Undistributed funds accounted for the remainder. High-tech exports in 2002 were valued at $7.364 billion and accounted for 25% of manufactured exports.

Among major scientific organizations are the Hungarian Academy of Sciences (founded in 1825), the Association for Dissemination of Sciences (founded in 1841), and the Federation of Technical and Scientific Societies (founded in 1948), with 32 agricultural, medical, scientific, and technical member societies. In 1996, Hungary had 45 research institutes concerned with agriculture and veterinary science, medicine, natural sciences, and technology. There are 25 universities and colleges offering courses in basic and applied science. In 1987–97, science and engineering students accounted for 32% of university enrollment. In 2002, science degrees (natural sciences, mathematics and computers, and engineering) accounted for 11.9% of all bachelor's degrees awarded.

In addition to the National Museum of Science and Technology, Budapest has museums devoted to transport, electrical engineering, agriculture, natural history, and foundries.

30 DOMESTIC TRADE

Budapest is the business and trade center of the country, though most production facilities lie elsewhere. Over the past few years, the retail and wholesale sector has grown along Western standards. Throughout most of the country, small, family-owned and operated retail establishments predominate. However, in Budapest supermarkets, department stores, and indoor shopping malls have grown rapidly.

The Polus Center, the first American-style shopping mall in Central Europe, opened on the outskirts of Budapest in November 1996. West End City Center, the largest mall complex in Central Europe, was opened in Budapest in 1999. As of 2002, there were about 400 franchise operations nationwide. Several foreign chains are present. Retail purchases are still primarily cash based, though some banks are beginning to issue credit cards. A 12% value-added tax (VAT) applies to food, books, hotel accommodations and utilities. A 25% VAT applies to most other good and services. Additional excise taxes (ranging from 10–35%) apply to some products, such as gold, coffee, wine, and automobiles.

New regulations passed in January 1997 concerning trade in food products and the operation of retail outlets focus on the reduction of black market activity, consumer protection, and harmonization with EU law. Nevertheless, the underground economy remained at around 30% in 1999.

Business hours extend from 9 or 10 AM to 4 or 5 PM for offices and general stores and to 3 or 4 PM for banks. Early closing (between noon and 1 PM) on Saturdays is widespread; Sunday closing is general. Food stores open between 6 and 8 AM and close between 7 and 9 PM weekdays; a few remain open on Sundays.

Principal Trading Partners – Hungary (2003)

(In millions of US dollars)

Country	Exports	Imports	Balance
World	43,007.8	46,675.0	-3,667.2
Germany	14,572.2	11,672.2	2,900.0
Austria	3,475.3	2,981.3	494.0
Italy-San Marino-Holy See	2,484.7	3,362.9	-878.2
France-Monaco	2,467.9	2,285.4	182.5
United Kingdom	1,966.8	1,291.7	675.1
Netherlands	1,764.6	1,024.0	740.6
Sweden	1,396.7	558.7	838.0
United States	1,339.4	1,528.2	-188.8
Spain	1,173.6	918.6	255.0
Romania	1,100.0	598.2	501.8

(…) data not available or not significant.

SOURCE: *2003 International Trade Statistics Yearbook,* New York: United Nations, 2004.

Newspapers and general, trade, and technical magazines are used for advertising; there is also broadcast and outdoor advertising. A major industrial fair, held since 1906, takes place every spring and autumn in Budapest.

31 FOREIGN TRADE

Hungary imports raw materials and semifinished products and exports finished products. Within that general framework, however, the structure, volume, and direction of Hungarian foreign trade have changed perceptibly in recent years. The total trade volume expanded from HUF18.344 million (foreign exchange) in 1959 to HUF2.657 billion in 1994. In 2000, exports were estimated at $28.1 billion (up from $12.9 billion in 1995), while imports were estimated to be $32.1 billion (up from $15.4 billion in 1995).

The majority of Hungary's export market is concentrated in the manufacturing industry, including electrical machinery, motor vehicle parts, polymers, petroleum refining, telecommunications equipment, and aluminum. Manufactured goods make up 82% of all exports. Other important exports include apparel (4.4%), polymers (2.2%), and meat (2.1%).

In 2004, Hungary's exports reached $54.6 billion (FOB—Free on Board), while its imports (FOB) grew to $58.7 billion; the trade deficit was $4.1 billion. The most important export partners were Germany (where 31.4% of Hungary's exports went), Austria (6.8%), France (5.7%), Italy (5.6%), and the United Kingdom (5.1%). The bulk of exports were made up of machinery and equipment (61.1%), and other manufactures (28.7%); other export commodities included food products (6.5%), raw materials (2%), fuels and electricity (1.6%). Imports came mainly from Germany (29.2%), Austria (8.3%), Russia (5.7%), Italy (5.5%), the Netherlands (4.9%), China (4.8%), and France (4.7%). The main import commodities included machinery and equipment (51.6%), other manufactures (35.7%), fuels and electricity (7.7%), food products (3.1%), and raw materials (2.0%).

32 BALANCE OF PAYMENTS

Having scrapped central planning, the Hungarian government is engaged in stabilizing the economy and taming inflation. In 1992, exports had grown by 7.4%, but recession in export markets, western European protectionism, an appreciating forint, bankruptcies of firms producing one-third of exports, and drought caused Hungarian trade to slow down. In 1994, Hungary had a current account deficit of $4 billion, but it shrank to $2.5 billion in 1995, and to a further $1 billion in 2001. Export markets were weak in 2003, and were not expected to rebound until mid-2004. Strong private consumption growth was sustaining the growth of the economy in 2003, but the current account deficit was forecast at 5.4% of GDP in 2003/04.

The US Central Intelligence Agency (CIA) reported that in 2002 the purchasing power parity of Hungary's exports was $31.4 billion while imports totaled $33.9 billion resulting in a trade deficit of $2.5 billion.

The International Monetary Fund (IMF) reported that in 2001 Hungary had exports of goods totaling $28.1 billion and imports totaling $30.1 billion. The services credit totaled $7.71 billion and debit $5.55 billion.

By 2004, the exports of goods and services expanded to $65.3 billion, while imports reached $68.3 billion; this resulted in a

Balance of Payments – Hungary (2003)

(In millions of US dollars)

Current Account		**-7,364.0**
Balance on goods	-3,365.0	
Imports	-46,594.0	
Exports	43,229.0	
Balance on services	-197.0	
Balance on income	-4,455.0	
Current transfers	653.0	
Capital Account		**-77.0**
Financial Account		**7,311.0**
Direct investment abroad	-1,598.0	
Direct investment in Hungary	2,506.0	
Portfolio investment assets	35.0	
Portfolio investment liabilities	2,900.0	
Financial derivatives	36.0	
Other investment assets	-2,606.0	
Other investment liabilities	6,309.0	
Net Errors and Omissions		**466.0**
Reserves and Related Items		**-336.0**

(…) data not available or not significant.

SOURCE: *Balance of Payment Statistics Yearbook 2004*, Washington, DC: International Monetary Fund, 2004.

negative resource balance of $3 billion. Also, the current account deficit worsened, growing from -$7.2 billion in 2003, to -$8.8 billion in 2004. The reserves of foreign exchange and gold grew from $11.5 in 2003 to $14.8 in 2004, covering less than four months of imports. Hungary is a major recipient of aid from the EU—for 2004–06 it had $4.2 billion available in structural adjustment and cohesion funds. The external aid is dwarfed however by the external debt, which grew from $47.4 billion in 2003 to $61.3 billion in 2004.

33 BANKING AND SECURITIES

Banking was nationalized in 1948, when the National Bank of Hungary was installed as the bank of issue, with a monopoly on credit and foreign exchange operations.

Following the 1987 reform of the banking system, the National Bank retained its central position as a bank of issue and its foreign exchange monopoly, but its credit functions were transferred to commercial banks. Three new commercial banks were established: the Hungarian Credit Bank, the Commercial and Credit Bank, and the Budapest Bank. Two other commercial banks, both founded in the 1950s, are the Hungarian Foreign Trade Bank and the General Banking and Trust Co. These six banks serve the financial needs of enterprises and government operations. The main bank for the general public is the National Savings Bank; in 1987 there were also 262 savings cooperatives. The Central Corporation of Banking Companies handles state property, performs international property transactions for individuals, and deals with the liquidation of bankrupt companies. The State Development Institution manages and controls development projects. In 1987 there were also three banks with foreign participation: the Central European International Bank (66% of shares held by six foreign companies), Citibank Budapest (80% owned by Citibank New York), and Unibank (45% owned by three foreign companies). In 1991 there were 10 government owned commercial banks, 16 joint-

stock owned commercial banks, 5 government owned specialized financial institutions, one offshore bank, and 260 savings cooperatives. By 1997, Hungary had over 30 commercial banks, about 10 specialized financial institutions, and 260 savings cooperatives. By 1998, around 75% of all banks had been privatized and 70% of these shares had foreign owners. Upon joining the OECD in 1996, Hungary ceased its ban on the establishment of foreign branches, effective January 1998.

The International Monetary Fund reports that in 2001, currency and demand deposits—an aggregate commonly known as M1—were equal to $9.7 billion. In that same year, M2—an aggregate equal to M1 plus savings deposits, small time deposits, and money market mutual funds—was $24.3 billion. The discount rate, the interest rate at which the central bank lends to financial institutions in the short term, was 9.8%.

In Budapest, an authentic commodity and stock exchange functioned from 1867 until 1948, when it was closed down as the country transformed into a centralized socialist economy. The reorganization of the Hungarian securities market, after a pause of some 40 years, started at the beginning of the 1980s. The Exchange was founded eventually on 21 June 1990. The bull market on the Budapest Stock Exchange (BUX) continued during the final quarter of 1996. The BUX index closed 1996 at 4,125, up 170% compared with end-1995. The increase was the second strongest in the world, following the Venezuela market. By 7 February 1997, the BUX index had reached 5,657. By mid-2000, the index stood at over 8,800, but as of mid-2003, it had dropped to just over 8,000 amid the global recession. However, by the end of 2004, the BUX had recovered, rising 57.2% that year to close at 14,742.6. In 2004, a total of 47 companies were listed on the BUX, which had a market capitalization of $28.711 billion.

34 INSURANCE

Before World War II, 49 private insurance companies—25 domestic and 24 foreign—conducted business activities in Hungary. All insurance was nationalized in 1949 and placed under the State Insurance Institute, a government monopoly. A new institution, Hungária Insurance Co., was founded in 1986. As of 1997, the regulatory authority was the Insurance Supervisor (allami Biztositasfeluegyelet). Compulsory insurance in Hungary includes third-party auto liability, workers' compensation, and liability for aircraft, watercraft, and several professions. In 2003, the value of direct premiums written totaled $2.454 billion, of which nonlife premiums made up the largest portion at $1.473 billion. Allianz Hungaria was the country's leading nonlife insurer, with gross written nonlife premiums of $621.8 million for 2003. ING was Hungary's top life insurer in 2003, with gross written life premiums totaling $280.1 million.

35 PUBLIC FINANCE

In recent years, the government has presented its budget bill to the National Assembly sometime during the first several months of the year, but the budget itself becomes effective on 1 January, when the fiscal year begins. It is prepared by the Ministry of Finance. Although Hungary had one of the most liberal economic regimes of the former Eastern bloc countries, its economy still suffered the growing pains of any country trying to come out of com-

Public Finance – Hungary (2002)

(In billions of forint, central government figures)

Revenue and Grants	**6,338.1**	**100.0%**
Tax revenue	3,656.6	57.7%
Social contributions	2,159.1	34.1%
Grants	23.4	0.4%
Other revenue	499	7.9%
Expenditures	**7,781.6**	**100.0%**
General public services	2,188	28.1%
Defense	231.5	3.0%
Public order and safety	333	4.3%
Economic affairs	1,599.3	20.6%
Environmental protection	40.4	0.5%
Housing and community amenities	33.8	0.4%
Health	453.3	5.8%
Recreational, culture, and religion	141	1.8%
Education	407.4	5.2%
Social protection	2,353.8	30.2%

(…) data not available or not significant.

SOURCE: *Government Finance Statistics Yearbook 2004*, Washington, DC: International Monetary Fund, 2004.

munism and privatize its industries. The last few years, however, Hungary has enjoyed a remarkable expansion, averaging annual GDP growth of 4.5% between 1996 and 2002. Inflation in that period dropped from 28% to 7%, and unemployment fell to 6%, less than most EU countries. Eighty percent of GDP is now produced by privately owned companies. Still, Hungary's foreign debts remain large, putting a damper on the economy's otherwise spectacular performance.

The US Central Intelligence Agency (CIA) estimated that in 2005 Hungary's central government took in revenues of approximately $51.4 billion and had expenditures of $58.3 billion. Revenues minus expenditures totaled approximately -$6.9 billion. Public debt in 2005 amounted to 60.9% of GDP. Total external debt was $76.23 billion.

The International Monetary Fund (IMF) reported that in 2002, the most recent year for which it had data, central government revenues were Ft6,338.1 billion and expenditures were Ft7,781.6 billion. The value of revenues was us$25 million and expenditures us$30 million, based on an exchange rate for 2002 of us$1 = Ft257.887 as reported by the IMF. Government outlays by function were as follows: general public services, 28.1%; defense, 3.0%; public order and safety, 4.3%; economic affairs, 20.6%; environmental protection, 0.5%; housing and community amenities, 0.4%; health, 5.8%; recreation, culture, and religion, 1.8%; education, 5.2%; and social protection, 30.2%.

36TAXATION

As of 2006, Hungary's corporate tax rate is 16%. Capital gains are also taxed at the 16% rate. However, only 50% of capital gains generated from stock transactions are subject to the tax. Capital gains from the sale of business assets are treated as business income. The withholding tax on dividends paid to foreign companies is 20% unless recipients reinvest them in Hungarian companies. Dividends paid to individuals are subject to a 25% withholding tax, and dividends that are in excess of 30% of the return on equity are

subject to a 35% rate. However, most tax treaties with Hungary reduce the withholding tax to between 5% and 15%.

The progressive personal income tax schedule in Hungary has a top rate of 38%. Individuals receiving capital gains on immovable property or the sale of securities are subject to a 25% tax. Individuals also can take allowances against the taxes they owe in the form of tax deductions or tax credits. The main deduction from taxable income is 20% of annual income up to a certain maximum. The disabled are given an extra deduction. There are also partial deductions allowed for school fees, interest paid for the purchase of a house, and for donations to charity. Inheritance and gift taxes range from 11–15%. There is a 2–6% tax on the transfer of housing, and a 10% tax on the transfer of large estates. Local authorities may levy individual income and corporate taxes.

The major indirect tax in Hungary is the value-added tax (VAT). The normal VAT rate is 25%, with a reduced rate of 15% for items of social value, food and other staple items. A 5% VAT applies to certain medical materials and supplies, and to textbooks. Housing leases, health and education services, and financial services are exempt from the VAT. Other taxes include a stamp tax and a consumption tax imposed on cars, jewelry, gasoline, alcohol, cigarettes, and cosmetics at rates between 10% and 200%.

37CUSTOMS AND DUTIES

Under Hungary's liberalized import policies, 93% of all imports do not require licenses. Under World Trade Organization (WTO) rules, import licenses on certain products from WTO states are no longer required. Under the same regulations, duties for countries with most-favored-nation status stood at around 8% in 2002, but could be over 100% for selected commodities.

38FOREIGN INVESTMENT

Even before the repudiation of communism, Hungary sought to enter joint ventures with Western countries. By the end of 1996, Hungary had attracted $15 billion in foreign direct investment. Since 1989, Hungary has attracted nearly one-third of all foreign direct investment in Central Europe and Eastern Europe. In 1995–96, the government adopted a stringent economic reform program of liberalization and privatization, and by 2002, the private sector, which had been 20% of the economy in 1989, was about 80%. Hungary has five free trade zones in which corporations are treated as foreign and are exempt from custom duties and taxes.

In the period 1988 to 1990, Hungary's share of world FDI inward flows was five and a half times its share in world GDP, the sixth-largest ratio in the world. Annual foreign direct investment (FDI) inflows into Hungary reached a peak in 1995 at about $4.5 billion, from which point they declined steadily until 2001, when there was an upswing to $2.4 billion from $1.6 billion in 2000. In 2002, FDI inflow fell to less than $1.5 billion. The average FDI inflow from 1998 to 2001 was about $2 billion a year. For the period 1998 to 2000, Hungary's share of FDI inflows was about equal to its share of world GDP. Total FDI stock, from 1989 to 2002, is estimated at about $34 billion.

The largest single source of foreign investment has been the United States, followed by Germany, the Netherlands, Austria, the United Kingdom, and France.

Of foreign capital invested in Hungary through 2000, 50% has been in manufacturing, 15% in telecommunications, 13% in energy, 6% in banking and finance, and 10% in other areas. FDI out-flows from Hungary have averaged about $400,000 per year and as of 2001, foreign stock held by Hungarians totaled $2.2 billion.

The flow of foreign investment reached peak levels in 2003 and 2004, with €2.3 billion and €2.5 billion respectively. The Hungarian Ministry of Economics and Transportation estimated that by 2004 the total stock of FDI exceeded €42 billion, with the United States and Germany taking the lion's share of this total. The same agency expects the flow of FDI to grow to €3–3.5 billion in 2005. Most of the investments went to manufacturing (46%); real estate (12%); trade and repair (11%); finance (10%); transport, telecommunications, storage and post (10%); and the energy sector (5%). By 2003, the biggest investors in Hungary were: Deutsche Telekom A.G., Germany (with cumulative investments exceeding $1.7 billion); Audi A.G., Germany ($1.4 billion); General Electric, US ($1.1 billion); Telenor ASA, Norway ($1 billion); and, Vodafone, Netherlands ($850 million).

39 ECONOMIC DEVELOPMENT

During the first 20 years after World War II, Hungary had the following economic plans: the three-year plan (1947–49) for economic reconstruction; the first five-year plan (1950–54) which aimed at rapid and forced industrialization and which was slightly modified in 1951 and by the "new course" policy of 1953; the one-year plan of 1955; the second five-year plan (1956–60), designed to further industrialization but discarded as a result of the October 1956 uprising; the three-year plan (1958–60), which also emphasized industrialization, although it allocated greater investment for housing and certain consumer goods; and the new second five-year plan (1961–65), which provided for a 50% increase in industrial production. These were followed by the third five-year plan (1966–70); the fourth five-year plan (1971–75), with greater emphasis on modernization of industrial plants producing for export and housing construction; the fifth five-year plan (1976–80), which called for amelioration of the gap in living standards between the peasantry and the working class; the sixth five-year plan (1981–85), emphasizing investment in export industries and energy conservation and seeking to curb domestic demand; and the seventh five-year plan (1986–90), which projected growth of 15–17% in NMP, 13–16% in industrial production, and 12–14% in agriculture.

Far-reaching economic reforms, called the New Economic Mechanism (NEM), were introduced on 1 January 1968. In order to create a competitive consumers' market, some prices were no longer fixed administratively, but were to be determined by market forces. Central planning was restricted to essential materials, and managers of state enterprises were expected to plan and carry out all the tasks necessary to ensure profitable production. In the early years of the NEM, the growth rate of industrial output surpassed target figures; national income rose substantially, surpassing any previous planning periods; and productivity increased significantly in all sectors of the national economy. However, following the huge oil price increases of 1973–74, the government returned to more interventionist policies in an attempt to protect Hungary's economy from external forces. Beginning in 1979, the government introduced a program of price reform, aimed at aligning domestic with world prices; changes in wage setting, intended to encourage productivity; and decentralization of industry, in-cluding the breakup of certain large enterprises and the creation of small-scale private ones, especially in services. New measures introduced in 1985 and 1986 included the lifting of government subsidies for retail prices (which led to sharp price increases) and the imposition of management reform, including the election of managers in 80% of all enterprises. The 1991–95 economic program aimed to fully integrate Hungary into the world economy on a competitive basis. The program's main features were to accelerate privatization, control inflation, and institute measures to prepare the way for the convertibility of the forint.

Reforms slowed in 1993 and 1994, and the privatization of state firms stopped. However, privatization accelerated in 1995 as the result of new laws passed in May of that year, which made the process simpler and allowed for the rapid privatization of small firms. Some large utilities were privatized in 1995; the first wave of the electricity and gas company privatization totaled $3.2 billion, primarily from German, Italian, and French interests. Budapest Bank, one of the country's largest banks, was sold to GE Capital Services. Hungary is now one of the few countries in Eastern Europe to have privatized major portions of its telecommunications and energy sectors. In 1995, the government received $4.5 billion in privatization proceeds. From the mid-1990s, a massive amount of foreign investment flowed into the country. (It stood at just under $23.5 billion by the end of 2001, which was equivalent to about 46% of GDP.)

In 1994, the Development Assistance Committee of the OECD distributed $68.3 million in aid to Hungary. Net concession flows from multilateral institutions that year amounted to $132 million. With the adoption of an International Monetary Fund (IMF)-backed stabilization program in 1995, Hungary exhibited consistent GDP annual growth of 4% in the late 1990s. Moreover, Hungary has repaid its entire debt to the IMF, and was formally invited to join the EU in 2002, and finally accepted in 2004, together with nine other countries.

The private sector now produces 80% of GDP. The economy was suffering from the effects of currency appreciation in 2003, and from rises in wages in 2001–02. Hungary's markets in 2003 were weak, given the dismal state of the global economy. (Exports in 2001 reached the equivalent of some 60% of GDP, up from 30.6% in 1991.) The current account deficit reached 5.9% of GDP for in 2004.

The Hungarian economy improved as it joined the EU, but the rate of improvement was deemed unsatisfactory. The GDP growth rate was 4% in 2004, but IMF specialists consider that the economy needs to grow by 5–5.25% annually if Hungary is to catch up with Western Europe in the timeline that it set for itself. The Hungarian policy makers are trying to attract additional investments in the country as a way of fostering additional growth. This task is made difficult however by increasing competition from neighboring countries, and the need to implement a leaner and more flexible tax system.

40 SOCIAL DEVELOPMENT

A national social insurance system was relatively well advanced before World War II for the nonagricultural population. A 1972 decree of the Council of Ministers extended this system to cover virtually the entire population, including craftsmen; by 1974, 99% of the population enjoyed the benefits of social insurance. Coverage includes relief for sickness, accidents, unemployment, and old age and incapacity, and provides maternity allowances for working women, allowances for children, and payment of funeral expenses. Men can collect old age pensions at the age of 62 after 20 years of employment. As of 2005, women collect at age 60, and will meet the same standards as men by 2009. The social insurance system also provides for disability and survivorship benefits. Medical care is provided directly to the insured through the public health service.

Women have the same legal rights as men, including inheritance and property rights. They hold a large number of the positions in teaching, medicine, and the judiciary, but generally earn less than men. Women are underrepresented in senior positions in both the private and public sectors. Sexual harassment in the workplace is commonplace, and it is not prohibited by law. Spousal abuse is a huge problem; approximately 20% of women were victimized in 2004. Sexual abuse, rape, and domestic violence are underreported due to cultural prejudice.

Minority rights are protected by law, allowing for the creation of minority local government bodies for limited self-rule. The law also preserves ethnic language rights and encourages minorities to preserve their cultural traditions. Despite these efforts, the Roma minority continues to face discrimination and prejudice. There were also reports of excessive police force in certain cases, as well as pretrial detention.

41 HEALTH

The Ministry of Health administers the state health service, with the counties and districts forming hospital regions. By the end of 1974, 99% of the population was covered by social insurance and enjoyed free medical services; those few not insured pay for medical and hospital care. Limited private medical practice is permitted. In 1992, the Ministry of Welfare proposed a compulsory health care scheme based on the German system, to be administered by the National Health Security Directorate. After the termination of socialism in 1989, the Hungarian health system was largely unchanged. About 5% of clinics were privatized and health care was available to nearly all of Hungary's people. Health expenditures comprised an estimated 6.8% of the gross domestic product.

As of 2004, there were an estimated 316 physicians, 852 nurses, and 46 dentists per 100,000 people. Hungary's birthrate was estimated at 9 per 1,000 people. Contraceptives were used by an estimated 73% of married women. Average life expectancy was 72.40 years in 2005. Free professional assistance given to insured pregnant women and to the mothers of newborn children, maternity leave and grants, and improved hygienic conditions helped lower the infant mortality rate to 8.57 per 1,000 live births in 2005. As of 2000, the total fertility rate was 1.3 per woman during her childbearing years.

The country faces severe problems in maintaining an acceptable level of health care for its population. The UN considers its death rate unacceptable (13 per 1,000 in 1999). The heart disease occurrence is below the average for wealthier countries. The likelihood of death after age 65 from heart disease was 283 (male) and 283 (female) per 1,000 people during 1990–1993. The number of cardiovascular deaths in 1994 was 74,182 people. Arteriosclerosis is a major cause of death (100 per 100,000 people). Contribut-

ing factors include the incidence of cardiovascular disease, which is directly related to stress through pressures of work, together with smoking and dietary factors. Hungary has one of the highest smoking rates in Europe. In 1990, there were 40 reported cases of tuberculosis per 100,000 people. Virtually all children up to one year old were vaccinated against tuberculosis, diphtheria, pertussis, and tetanus, polio and measles.

Compulsory testing for HIV has been widespread since 1988 in Hungary's attempt to stop the spread of AIDS. Hungary has resisted pressure from international agencies to switch from compulsory to voluntary testing. The HIV/AIDS prevalence was 0.10 per 100 adults in 2003. As of 2004, there were approximately 2,800 people living with HIV/AIDS in the country. There were an estimated 100 deaths from AIDS in 2003.

42 HOUSING

The construction rate for new dwellings has been greater in smaller cities and towns than in Budapest, where as of 1980, 17.3% of all housing units were built before 1900 and 56.3% before 1945. About 20,320 new dwellings were completed in 2000; about 31,511 dwellings were completed or under construction in 2001. According to national statistics, in 2005 there were about 4,127,743 dwelling units nationwide. About 84% were owner occupied. Only about 130,208 units were owned by municipal governments. Most homes have an average of four rooms. It has been estimated that about 1.2 million people are affected by overcrowding.

Low-income residents and other private builders generally rely on the labor of family and friends, buying the essential materials little by little; they may apply for loans if necessary to complete the dwelling.

43 EDUCATION

Before education was nationalized in 1948, most schools were operated by religious bodies, especially the Roman Catholic Church. The educational system is under the control of the Ministry of Education and is supervised by the local councils, which receive financial assistance from the central government. As of 2003, public expenditure on education was estimated at 5.5% of GDP, or 14.1% of total government expenditures.

Education is free for 12 years of study and compulsory for 10 years. The state also pays the bulk of costs for higher education. Primary school covers eight years of study. Secondary schools are divided into academic schools (*gimnázium*) and vocational schools (*szakközépiskola*). Programs at academic schools run from four to six years. Vocational school programs generally cover four years of study. In addition to its regular primary education, Hungary has over 100 primary schools with special music programs based on the pedagogy of the 20th-century composer Zoltan Kodály; at these "music primary schools," music receives as much emphasis as all other subjects. The academic year runs from September to June.

In 2001, about 80% of children between the ages of three and six were enrolled in some type of preschool program. Primary school enrollment in 2003 was estimated at about 91% of age-eligible students. The same year, secondary school enrollment was about 94% of age-eligible students. Most students complete their primary education. The student-to-teacher ratio for primary school was at about 9.6:1 in 2003; the ratio for secondary school was about 11:1.

Hungary has about 77 institutions of higher education, including 25 universities and 47 colleges. Adult education expanded after World War II, especially through workers' schools and correspondence courses. Although there are university fees, many students are exempt from payment or pay reduced fees. In 2003, about 51% of the tertiary age population were enrolled in some type of higher education program. The adult literacy rate for 2004 was estimated at about 99%.

⁴⁴LIBRARIES AND MUSEUMS

Hungary's National Archives were established in 1756; among its treasures are some 100,000 items from the period prior to the Turkish occupation (1526). Hungary's National Széchényi Library is the largest and most significant in the country. Founded in Budapest in 1802, it has more than 2.5 million books and periodicals and more than 4.5 million manuscripts, maps, prints, and microfilms. Other important libraries are the Lóránd Eötvös University Library (1.5 million volumes) and the Library of the Hungarian Academy of Sciences (2.1 million volumes), both in Budapest; and the Central Library of the Lajos Kossuth University in Debrecen (1.27 million volumes). There are numerous local and regional public libraries.

There were over 500 museums (about 70 in Budapest) and many zoological and botanical gardens. One of the largest institutions is the Hungarian National Museum, which displays relics of prehistoric times as well as artifacts reflecting the history of Hungary from the Magyar conquest through 1849, including the Hungarian coronation regalia. A branch of the National Museum is the Hungarian Natural History Museum. Other museums, all in Budapest, include the Ethnographical Museum, the Museum of History, the Hungarian National Gallery, and the Museum of Fine Arts. Many castles and monasteries throughout the country have been converted to museums. There is also a Bela Bartok Museum, a Chinese Museum, a House of Terror museum (2002), and a Franz Lizst Memorial Museum and Research Center, all in Budapest.

⁴⁵MEDIA

Budapest is the principal communications center. Although telecommunication services in Hungary were long underdeveloped, services improved significantly during the 1990s, and investment in value-added services, such as the Internet and VSAT, grew. In 2003, there were an estimated 349 mainline telephones for every 1,000 people; about 28,000 people were on a waiting list for telephone service installation. The same year, there were approximately 769 mobile phones in use for every 1,000 people.

In 2004, there were two state-owned public service television stations and two national commercial television stations. The same year, there were one public service radio and two national commercial radio stations. There are some smaller regional stations. In 2003, there were an estimated 690 radios and 475 television sets for every 1,000 people. About 190.7 of every 1,000 people were cable subscribers. Also in 2003, there were 108.4 personal computers for every 1,000 people and 232 of every 1,000 people had access to the Internet. There were 210 secure Internet servers in the country in 2004.

Budapest has always been Hungary's publishing center. The largest dailies (with affiliations and 2002 circulation rates as available) are *Népszabadság* (Hungarian Socialist Workers' Party, 316,000), *Népszava* (Hungarian Trade Unions, 120,000), *Mai Nap* (100,000), *Kurir* (80,000), *Magyar Hírlap* (Budapest Party Committee and Metropolitan Council, 75,000), *Expressz* (75,000), and *Magyar Nemzet* (Patriotic People's Front, 70,000).

The constitution of Hungary provides for free speech and a free press, and the government is said generally to respect these rights. Although previously all means of communication had been government property, 1995 saw the beginning of the privatization process, with aims to put most print and broadcast media in private hands.

⁴⁶ORGANIZATIONS

There is a Chamber of Commerce in Budapest. The International Labour Organization has a subregional office in Budapest. Hungary is a member of the International Chamber of Commerce. Trade and professional associations exist representing a variety of occupations, including the steel and automotive workers, journalists, teachers, librarians, engineers, architects, and various medical professionals. There is a Confederation of Professional Unions based in Budapest.

Organizations promoting research and study of various medical and scientific fields also exist. Some of these are member organizations of the Federation of Hungarian Medical Societies and/or the Hungarian Academy of Sciences. A cultural organization particular to Hungary is the International Kodaly Society; named for the music composer, scholar, and teacher, this organization promotes appreciate and study of music, particularly for youth. The multinational scientific organization of the International Measurement Confederation is based in Budapest.

Notable national youth organizations include the Federation of Young Democrats of Hungary, the Goncol Environmental Youth Alliance, the National Union of Hungarian Students, and Young Musicians of Hungary. The Hungarian Scout Association is also active, as are various chapters of the YMCA/YWCA. There are several sports associations promoting amateur competition in such pastimes as tennis, badminton, skating, and baseball. There is a national chapter of the Paralympic Committee. National women's organizations include the Association of Hungarian Women and the National Council of Hungarian Women.

Volunteer service organizations, such as the Lions Clubs and International, are also present. The Red Cross, Caritas, and Amnesty International have active chapters in the country.

⁴⁷TOURISM, TRAVEL, AND RECREATION

Among Hungary's diverse tourist attractions are Turkish and Roman ruins, medieval towns and castles, more than 500 thermal springs (some with resort facilities), and Lake Balaton, the largest freshwater lake in Europe. Budapest is a major tourist attraction and cultural capital, with 2 opera houses, over 200 monuments and museums, and several annual arts festivals.

Popular sports include handball, football (soccer), tennis, and volleyball. The Budapest Grand Prix, the only Formula-1 motor race in Eastern Europe, was inaugurated in August 1986. A valid passport is required of all foreign visitors. Citizens of the United

States and Canada are not required to have a visa for stays of up to 90 days.

Hungary had 31,412,483 visitors in 2003, about 48% of whom came from Central and Eastern Europe. There were 64,091 hotel rooms with 158,634 beds and an occupancy rate of 38%. The average length of stay was three nights. Tourist expenditure receipts totaled $3.4 billion.

In 2004, the US Department of State estimated the daily expenses for staying in Budapest at $218. Other areas were much lower at $93 per day.

⁴⁸FAMOUS HUNGARIANS

The foundations for modern Hungarian literature begin with the movement known as the Period of Linguistic Reform, whose leaders were the versatile writer Ferenc Kazinczy (1759–1831) and Ferencz Kölcsey (1790–1838), lyric poet and literary critic. Among the outstanding literary figures was Dániel Berzsenyi (1772–1836) of the Latin School. Károly Kisfaludy (1788–1830) founded the Hungarian national drama. Mihaly Vörösmarty (1800–55), a fine poet, related the Magyar victories under Árpád in his *Flight of Zalán*. He was followed by Hungary's greatest lyric poet, Sándor Petöfi (1823–49), a national hero who stirred the Magyars in their struggle against the Habsburgs in 1848 with his *Arise Hungarians*. Another revolutionary hero was Lajos Kossuth (1802–94), orator and political author. János Arany (1817–82), epic poet and translator, influenced future generations, as did Mór Jókai (1825–1904), Hungary's greatest novelist. The outstanding dramatist Imre Madách (1823–64) is known for his *Tragedy of Man*. Endre Ady (1877–1919) was a harbinger of modern poetry and Western ideas; Attila József (1905–1937) is another well-known poet. Lyric poets of the contemporary era include László Nagy (1925–78), János Pilinszky (1921–81), and Ferenc Juhász (b.1928). Gyula Illyés (1902–83), a poet, novelist, and dramatist, was one of the outstanding figures of 20th-century Hungarian literature. Ferenc Molnár (1878–1952) is known for his plays *Liliom, The Swan,* and *The Guardsman*. György Lukács (1885–1971) was an outstanding Marxist writer and literary critic. Hungarian-born Arthur Koestler (1905–83), a former radical, was a well-known anti-Communist novelist and writer. Imre Kertész (b.1929) is a Jewish-Hungarian author, Holocaust concentration camp survivor, and winner of the Nobel Prize in literature in 2002.

János Fadrusz (1858–1903) and József Somogyi (1916–93) are among Hungary's best-known sculptors. The outstanding Hungarian painter Mihály Munkácsy (1844–1900) is best known for his *Christ before Pilate*. Victor Vasarely (1908–97), a world-famous painter of "op art," was born in Budapest and settled in France in 1930. Miklós Ybl (1814–91) was a leading architect; and Gyula Halasz (1899–1984), better known as Brassai, was a well-known photographer. The Hungarian-born Joseph Pulitzer (1847–1911) was a noted journalist and publisher in the United States. Hungarian musicians include the composers Franz (Ferenc) Liszt (1811–86), Ernst (Ernö) von Dohnányi (1877–1960), Béla Bartók (1881–1945), Zoltán Kodály (1882–1967), and György Ligeti (b.1923); violinists Jeno Hubay (1858–1937) and Joseph Szigeti (1892–1973); cellist János Starker (b.1924); and pianists Lili Kraus (1903–86) and Erwin Nyiregyhazi (1903–87). Renowned Hungarian-born conductors who became famous abroad include Fritz Reiner (1888–1963), George Széll (1897–1970), Eugene Ormándy (1899–1985), Antal Doráti (1906–88), and Ferenc Fricsay (1914–63). Miklós Jancsó (b.1921) is a distinguished film director, and Vilmos Zsigmond (b.1930) a noted cinematographer; Béla Lugosi (Blasko, 1882–1956) and Peter Lorre (Laszlo Loewenstein, 1904–64) were famous actors.

Notable scientists include Lóránd Eötvös (1848–1919), inventor of torsion balance; Ányos Jedlik (1800–95), known for his research on dynamos; and the psychoanalyst Sándor Ferenczi (1873–1933). Ignaz Philipp Semmelweis (1818–65) pioneered in the use of antiseptic methods in obstetrics. Béla Schick (1877–1967) invented the skin test to determine susceptibility to diphtheria.

Hungarian-born Nobel Prize winners are Róbert Bárány (1876–1936) in 1914, Albert Szent-Györgyi (1893–1986) in 1937, and Georg von Békésy (1899–1972) in 1961 in physiology or medicine, Georg de Hevesy (1885–1966) in 1944 in chemistry, and Dénés Gábor (1900–79) in 1971 for physics. Budapest-born scientists who contributed to atomic research in the United States were Leó Szilárd (1898–1964), Eugene Paul Wigner (1902–95), John von Neumann (1903–57), and Edward Teller (1908–2003). Theodore van Karman (Todor Kármán, 1881–1963) is the father of aerodynamics. Paul Erdős (1913–1996) was an important mathematician, as was John von Neumann (Neumann János, 1903–1957). Eugene Paul Wigner (1902–1995), physicist and mathematician, received the 1963 Nobel Prize in physics. George Andrew Olah (b.1927 as György Oláh), a Hungarian-American chemist, won the Nobel Prize in chemistry in 1994.

Imre Nagy (1895?–1958) served as prime minister from 1953 to 1955, but was removed from office because of his criticism of Soviet policy; the uprising of October 1956 briefly brought Nagy back to the premiership. Arrested after the Soviet military intervention, Nagy was tried and executed in 1958. János Kádár (1912–89), first secretary of the HSWP since 1956, initially aligned himself with Nagy but subsequently headed the government established after Soviet troops rolled in. Kádár, who held the premiership from late 1956 to 1958 and again from 1961 to 1965, was the preeminent political leader in Hungary until his removal in May 1988. Gyula Horn (b.1932), a former communist, was named prime minister in 1994. He served in that post until 1998, when he was succeeded by Viktor Orbán (b.1963), who was prime minister between 1998 and 2002. Péter Medgyessy (b.1942) served as prime minister from 2002 until 2004, not completing his term. Ferenc Gyurcsány (b.1961) succeeded him.

George Soros (b.1930), philanthropist, was born in Budapest.

⁴⁹DEPENDENCIES

Hungary has no territories or colonies.

⁵⁰BIBLIOGRAPHY

Frucht, Richard (ed.). *Eastern Europe: An Introduction to the People, Lands, and Culture.* Santa Barbara, Calif.: ABC-CLIO, 2005.

Hankiss, Elemer. *East European Alternatives.* New York: Oxford University Press, 1990.

Hill, Raymond. *Hungary.* 2nd ed. New York: Facts On File, 2004.

Hoensch, Jorg K. *A History of Modern Hungary, 1867–1994.* 2nd ed. New York: Longman, 1996.

Horvath, Michael J. *Hungarian Civilization: A Short History.* College Park, Md.: University of Maryland, 2000.

Hoshi, Iraj, Ewa Balcerowicz, and Leszek Balcerowicz (eds.). *Barriers to Entry and Growth of New Firms in Early Transition: A Comparative Study of Poland, Hungary, Czech Republic, Albania, and Lithuania*. Boston: Kluwer Academic Publishers, 2003.

International Smoking Statistics: A Collection of Historical Data from 30 Economically Developed Countries. New York: Oxford University Press, 2002.

Kun, Joseph C. *Hungarian Foreign Policy: The Experience of a New Democracy*. Westport, Conn.: Praeger, 1993.

Litván, György (ed.). *The Hungarian Revolution of 1956: Reform, Revolt, and Repression, 1953–1956*. English version edited and translated by János M. Bak and Lyman H. Legters. New York: Longman, 1996.

McElrath, Karen (ed.). *HIV and AIDS: A Global View*. Westport, Conn.: Greenwood Press, 2002.

Roman, Eric. *Austria-Hungary and the Successor States: A Reference Guide from the Renaissance to the Present*. New York: Facts On File, 2003.

Rose-Ackerman, Susan. *From Elections to Democracy: Building Accountable Government in Hungary and Poland*. New York: Cambridge University Press, 2005.

Szekely, Istvan P. and David M. G. Newberry (eds.). *Hungary: an Economy in Transition*. Cambridge: Cambridge University Press, 1993.

ICELAND

Republic of Iceland
Lveldi Ísland

CAPITAL: Reykjavík

FLAG: The national flag, introduced in 1916, consists of a red cross (with an extended right horizontal), bordered in white, on a blue field.

ANTHEM: *O Guð; vors lands (O God of Our Land).*

MONETARY UNIT: The new króna (к), introduced 1 January 1981 and equivalent to 100 old krónur, is a paper currency of 100 aurar. There are coins of 5, 10, and 50 aurar and 1, 10 and 50 krónur, and notes of 10, 50, 100, 500, 1,000 and 5,000 krónur. к1 = $0.01571 (or $1 = к63.65) as of 2005.

WEIGHTS AND MEASURES: The metric system is used.

HOLIDAYS: New Year's Day, 1 January; Labor Day, 1 May; National Holiday, 17 June; Bank Holiday, August; Christmas, 25–26 December. Movable religious holidays include Holy Thursday, Good Friday, Easter Monday, Ascension, and Whitmonday. Half-holidays are observed on Christmas Eve, 24 December, and New Year's Eve, 31 December.

TIME: GMT.

¹LOCATION, SIZE, AND EXTENT

Iceland, the westernmost country of Europe, is an island in the North Atlantic Ocean, just below the Arctic Circle and a little more than 322 km (200 mi) E of Greenland, 1,038 km (645 mi) W of Norway, and 837 km (520 mi) NW of Scotland. It has an area of 103,000 sq km (39,769 sq mi), extending 490 km (304 mi) E–W and 312 km (194 mi) N–S. Comparatively, the area occupied by Iceland is slightly smaller than the state of Kentucky. The total length of coastline is about 4,988 km (3,099 mi). The republic includes many smaller islands, of which the chief are the Westman Islands (Vestmannaeyjar) off the southern coast.

Iceland's capital city, Reykjavík, is located on the country's southwest coast.

²TOPOGRAPHY

Iceland consists mainly of a central volcanic plateau, with elevations from about 700 to 800 m (2,297–2,625 ft), ringed by mountains, the highest of which is Hvannadalshnúkur (2,119 m/6,952 ft), in the Örfajökull glacier. Lava fields cover almost 11% of the country, and glaciers almost 12%. Among the many active volcanoes there is an average of about one eruption every five years. The largest glacier in Europe, Vatnajökull (about 8,400 sq km/3,200 sq mi), is in southeast Iceland. There are also many lakes, snowfields, hot springs, and geysers (the word "geyser" itself is of Icelandic origin).

The longest river is the Thjórsá (about 230 km/143 mi) in southern Iceland. Most rivers are short and none are navigable, but because of swift currents and waterfalls, Iceland's rivers have important waterpower potential. There are strips of low arable land along the southwest coast and in the valleys. Good natural harbors are provided by fjords on the north, east, and west coasts.

³CLIMATE

Despite Iceland's northern latitude, its climate is fairly mild because of the Gulf Stream, part of which almost encircles the island. There are no extreme temperature variations between seasons, but frequent weather changes are usual, particularly in the south, which experiences many storms and heavy precipitation. Temperatures at Reykjavík range from an average of 11°C (52°F) in July to -1°C (30°F) in January, with an annual mean of about 5°C (41°F). Humidity is high, and there is much fog in the east. Annual rainfall in the north ranges from 30 to 70 cm (12–28 in); in the south, 127–203 cm (50–80 in); and in the mountains, up to 457 cm (180 in). Winters are long and fairly mild, summers short and cool. Summer days are long and nights short; in winter, days are short and nights long.

⁴FLORA AND FAUNA

Although there are a few small trees (ash, aspen, birch, and willow), the chief forms of vegetation are grass, mosses, and small shrubs (heather, willow, dwarf birch). Some 340 different species of flowers have been listed, but most of these are sparse.

The fox, the chief indigenous animal, is common. Wild reindeer, introduced in the 18th century and once abundant, were almost exterminated and therefore have been protected in recent years; they are found chiefly in the northeastern highlands. The waters around Iceland abound in whales, many types of seals, and many kinds of fish. Dolphin, grampus, porpoise, and rorqual are numerous. Cod, haddock, and herring are particularly abundant, but there are also sole, shark, halibut, redfish, saithe, and other fish. Salmon abound in many rivers and trout in rivers and lakes. There are about 88 species of breeding birds; most are aquatic. The chief resident birds are eiderduck (raised commercially for their down) and ptarmigan. Other characteristic indigenous birds are swan, eagle, falcon, and gannet, all rare now and protected. Iceland has no reptiles or frogs and very little insect life.

5ENVIRONMENT

Because of Iceland's sparing use of hydrocarbon fuels, its air is cleaner than that of most industrialized nations. However, its water supply is polluted by excessive use of fertilizers (current estimates put Iceland's yearly usage of fertilizers at 2,500 lbs per acre). Population increases in the cities also contribute to water pollution. Iceland has 170 cu km of renewable water resources with 6% used for industrial purposes. Industrial carbon dioxide emissions totaled 2.1 million metric tons per year in 1996. Protected lands, which account for 9.5% of Iceland's total land area, include four national parks, with a total area of 619,300 hectares (1,530,315 acres) and 27 nature reserves, covering 256,861 hectares (634,714 acres). Principal environmental responsibility is vested in the Ministry of Social Affairs.

According to a 2006 report issued by the International Union for Conservation of Nature and Natural Resources (IUCN), threatened species included 7 types of mammals and 8 species of fish. Endangered species include the leatherback turtle and four species of whales. The great auk has become extinct.

6POPULATION

The population of Iceland in 2005 was estimated by the United Nations (UN) at 295,000, which placed it at number 168 in population among the 193 nations of the world. In 2005, approximately 12% of the population was over 65 years of age, with another 23% of the population under 15 years of age. There were 100 males for every 100 females in the country. According to the UN, the annual population rate of change for 2005–10 was expected to be 0.8%, a rate the government viewed as satisfactory. The projected population for the year 2025 was 335,000. Iceland is one of the least densely populated countries in the world, with an overall population density of 3 per sq km (7 per sq mi). The interior of the country is largely uninhabited.

The UN estimated that 94% of the population lived in urban areas in 2005, and that urban areas were growing at an annual rate of 0.71%. The capital city, Reykjavík, had a population of 184,000 (more than half the nation's population) in that year. The next largest towns and their estimated populations are Kópavogur (25,291), south of Reykjavík; Hafnarfjördur (21,300), about 10 km (6 mi) from Reykjavík; and Akureyri (16,475), on the north coast.

7MIGRATION

Little immigration has occurred since the original settlement in the 9th and 10th centuries. In the last quarter of the 19th century, because of unfavorable economic conditions, about 12,000 residents of Iceland emigrated to Canada and the United States. After 1900, net emigration decreased substantially.

As of 1997, just 375 refugees had arrived in Iceland since 1956. During the Kosovo crisis, Iceland offered to take up to 100 refugees under the UNHCR/IOM Humanitarian Evacuation Programme. A total of 70 people were actually evacuated to Iceland, 16 of whom returned to Kosovo by 1999. There were 16,000 migrants living in Iceland in 2000. In 2004 Iceland had 239 refugees, and 19 asylum seekers. In 2005 the net migration rate was estimated as 2.06 migrants per 1,000 population. The government views the migration levels as satisfactory.

8ETHNIC GROUPS

The population is almost entirely Icelandic, many of whom descended from the Norse and Celtic settlers who came in the late 9th and early 10th centuries.

9LANGUAGES

Icelandic, the national language, derives from the Old Norse language that was spoken throughout Scandinavia at the time of settlement. It has changed little through the centuries, partly because of the country's isolation and partly because of the people's familiarity with the classical language, as preserved in early historical and literary writings. There is comparatively little difference between the old language and the modern, or between the written language and the spoken. To this day, Icelanders are able to read the great 13th-century sagas without special study.

10RELIGIONS

The Church, the national church, is endowed by the state, but there is complete freedom for all faiths, without discrimination. All of Iceland constitutes a single diocese of the national church, headed by a bishop with his seat at Reykjavík; there are 281 parishes. As of 2004, about 86% of the population were nominally members of this established church, though it is believed that most do not practice actively. A 2003 Gallup poll indicated that 43% of Lutherans did not attend church at all and only 10% said that they attend church one or more times a month. About 4.3% of the population belong to one of three Lutheran Free Churches: the Reykjavík Free Church, the Hafnarfjordur Free Church, or the Reykjavík Independent Church. Another 4.4% (about 13,025 people) belong to one of 21 different denominations that are registered and recognized by the state. The largest of these groups is the Roman Catholic Church (5,582 members); the smallest is the First Baptist Church (10 members). Seventh-Day Adventists, Jehovah's Witnesses, Buddhists, Baha'is, Muslims, and Jews are also represented by small congregations.

11TRANSPORTATION

There are no railways or navigable inland waters. All important towns and districts can be reached by bus and truck via interurban roads. In 2004, Iceland's roadway system totaled 13,004 km (8,088 mi), of which only 4,331 km (2,694 mi) were paved or were surfaced with oiled gravel. Registered passenger cars in 2003 numbered 161,721 and there were 27,977 commercial vehicles.

In 2005, Iceland's merchant marine fleet consisted of three ships of 1,000 GRT or more, with a total capacity of 4,341 GRT. In addition, there are about 1,000 civilian vessels, mostly small fishing craft. Most of the import and export trade is handled in Reykjavík. Akureyri, on the north coast, is the largest port serving the outlying areas.

Iceland had an estimated 98 airports in 2004, of which 5 had paved runways as of 2005. The principal airport is Keflavik at Reykjavík. In the 1950s, Icelandic Airlines was the first transatlantic airline to offer fares drastically lower than those of the major carriers. Icelandair, formed by a merger of Icelandic Airlines and Iceland Air in the early 1970s, operates domestic routes as well

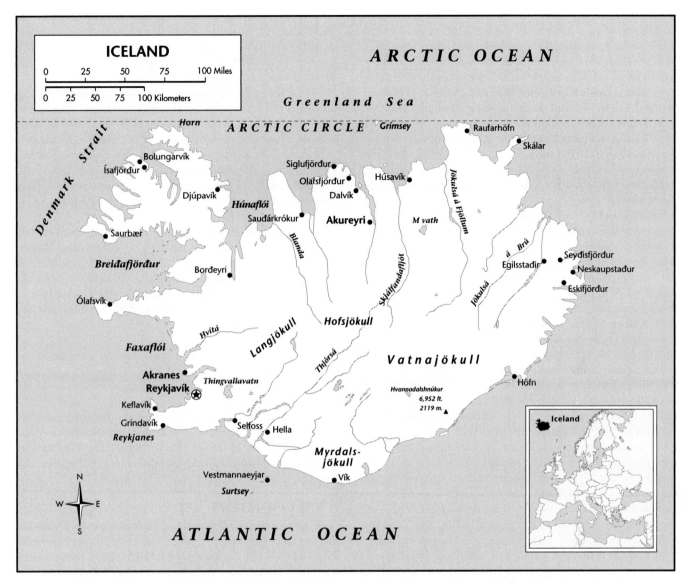

ICELAND

| 0 | 25 | 50 | 75 | 100 Miles |
| 0 | 25 | 50 | 75 | 100 Kilometers |

ARCTIC OCEAN

Greenland Sea

ARCTIC CIRCLE

Horn
Grímsey
Raufarhöfn
Skálar
Bolungarvík
Ísafjörður
Djúpavík
Siglufjörður
Ólafsfjörður
Húsavík
Dalvík
Húnaflói
Saurbær
Sauðárkrókur
Akureyri
M vath
Jökulsá á Fjöllum
Breiðafjörður
Borðeyri
Blanda
á Brú
Seyðisfjörður
Egilsstaðir
Neskaupstaður
Ólafsvík
Skjálfandafljót
Jökulsá
Eskifjörður
Hvítá
Langjökull
Hofsjökull
Faxaflói
Vatnajökull
Akranes
Thingvallavatn
Reykjavík
Thjórsá
Hvannadalshnúkur
6,952 ft.
2119 m.
Höfn
Keflavík
Grindavík
Selfoss
Hella
Reykjanes
Myrdals-
jökull
Vestmannaeyjar
Vík
Surtsey

Denmark Strait

ATLANTIC OCEAN

N W E S

Iceland

LOCATION: 63°19′ to 67°7′5″ N; 13°16′7″ to 24°32′3″ W. BOUNDARY LENGTHS: Total coastline, 4,970 kilometers (3,090 miles). TERRITORIAL SEA LIMIT: 12 miles.

as international flights to the United Kingdom, Scandinavia, and Germany, and transatlantic flights with stopovers at Reykjavík. In 2001 (the latest year for which data was available), 1,357,900 passengers were carried on scheduled domestic and international flights.

12 HISTORY

Iceland's first known settler, Ingólfur Arnarson, sailed from his native Norway to Iceland and settled at what is now Reykjavík in 874. During the late 9th and early 10th centuries, the island was settled by other Norwegians fleeing the oppressive rule of their king and by smaller groups of Scottish and Irish emigrants. In 930, a central legislative and judicial assembly, the Althing, was established, and a uniform code of laws for the entire country was compiled. Christianity was introduced in 1000, but the memory of the old pagan religion was preserved in 12th and 13th-century Icelandic literature. Many of the early settlers were great seafarers and continued their westward voyages of discovery and exploration from Iceland. Most famous of these were Eric the Red (Eiríkur

Thorvaldsson), who discovered and settled in Greenland in 982, and his son Leif Ericsson (Leifur Eiríksson), who around the year 1000 discovered the North American continent, which he called Vinland ("wineland") because of the grapes he found there. Icelanders acknowledged the sovereignty of Haakon IV of Norway in a treaty of 1262, which established a purely personal union, ending the independent republic or commonwealth in Iceland. When all the Scandinavian countries came under the rule of Denmark at the end of the 14th century, Iceland became a Danish dominion. Lutheranism was introduced in the 1540s. Exclusive trading rights with Iceland were given in 1602 to a private Danish trading company. Danes had a complete monopoly of trade with Iceland until 1786, when trade was opened to all subjects of the kings of Denmark, including Icelanders.

The last decades of the 18th century were a period of economic ruin for Iceland, compounded by poor harvests, epidemics, and volcanic eruptions (notably that of 1783, the worst in Iceland's history); the population dwindled to 38,000 by 1800, less than half the number in the period of independence. In that year, the king abolished the Althing, long since reduced in power. Within a few decades, however, a nationalist movement had attained considerable strength, winning the reestablishment of the Althing (but only as an advisory body) in 1843, followed by the opening of trade with all countries in 1854. After a long constitutional struggle—led by a national hero, Jón Sigurðsson, who was both statesman and scholar—limited home rule was granted in 1874, and almost complete home rule in 1903. By agreement with Denmark in 1918, Iceland was declared a free and independent state, but personal union with the Danish crown was retained. The Danish king continued to function as king of Iceland, and Denmark conducted Iceland's foreign affairs; but Iceland had the right to terminate this union after 25 years.

Cut off from Denmark during World War II by the German occupation of that country, Iceland established diplomatic relations with the United Kingdom and the United States. British forces took over the protection of the island in 1940 and were replaced the following year by US troops that remained in Iceland until early 1947. In a referendum held in May 1944, more than 97% of those participating voted to end the union with the king of Denmark and, on 17 June 1944, Iceland became an independent republic. In 1946, it was admitted to UN membership. Three years later, Iceland became a party to the Atlantic Pact (NATO), and a bilateral defense agreement was signed in 1951 providing for a US military presence. In March 1970, Iceland joined EFTA, and a tariff agreement was ratified with the EC in February 1973. To protect its fishing industry, Iceland unilaterally extended its fishing zone in 1958, and again in 1972 and 1975, provoking conflict with the United Kingdom and other countries. Casualties resulted from the most serious outbreak of the "cod war" with the United Kingdom in late 1975 and in February 1976. An agreement ended the conflict in June 1976 and relations with the United Kingdom improved. Disputes over fisheries resources have also arisen with the Norwegians periodically, though both Norway and Iceland are united in their opposition to the international ban on whaling.

In 1985, the parliament unanimously voted to declare Iceland a nuclear-free zone, banning any deployment of nuclear weapons. Reykjavík was the scene of the October 1986 summit meeting between US president Ronald Reagan and Soviet leader Mikhail Gorbachev on arms control and nuclear disarmament.

Depressed world fish prices weakened the economy in the early 1990s, resulting in a no-growth GDP and higher unemployment. A number of factors have combined to reinvigorate the Icelandic economy. The government launched an austerity program to trim the Icelandic welfare state which included measures such as increasing the retirement age from 65 to 67 years of age (with future increases to age 70 envisioned). Icelanders are also being asked to pay for a greater portion of social services out of their own pockets. Demand in Europe and the United States for Icelandic fish has rebounded and fish exports account for 70% of exports and 50% of foreign earnings. Liberalization of many sectors of the economy such as telecoms and banking, required under the EEA (European Economic Area) agreement with the European Union in exchange for greater access to the EU market, has reduced public expenditures and positively affected governmental finances. By 1999, Iceland had experienced four years of more than 5% GDP growth, and purchasing power was increasing at four times the OECD average. Unemployment had dropped to 2%, and Iceland has dealt with its labor shortage by initiating labor immigration from the Philippines. The economic boom years from 1996–2001 slowed in 2002, and Iceland experienced a mild recession with a GDP growth rate of -0.5%. Growth of GDP increased from 2003–05, however, nearing 6% by 2005.

Iceland was in the international headlines at the end of 1998 for altogether different reasons. In December 1998, the Icelandic parliament agreed after two full revisions of the legislation to create a health database of medical records of all Icelanders for use by a private company seeking to decode the human genome. Iceland's isolated, homogeneous population is a boon to medical researchers seeking to decode the genetic sequences of many hereditary diseases, but the lack of informed consent by individuals in the legislation became a heated political issue.

A public opinion poll taken in June 2002 indicated a 50–50 split between supporters and opponents of EU membership. However, conservative Independence Party leader and Prime Minister Davíð Oddsson remained resolutely opposed to EU membership, stating in 2002 that Iceland's affairs should not be dictated by conditions in "Paris or Berlin." Oddsson in 2005, however, indicated in a speech that a policy change was not ruled out depending upon how the EU evolved.

Iceland rejoined the International Whaling Commission in 2002 with reservations. It declared it would engage in whaling for scientific purposes, and resume commercial whaling of Minke and Fin whales after 2006.

President Ólafur Ragnar Grímsson was reelected president in June 2004. In September of that year, Prime Minister Davíð Oddsson switched positions with Foreign Minister Halldór Ásgrímmson. Oddsson had held the position of prime minister for a record 13 years.

13 GOVERNMENT

Iceland is an independent republic. Executive power is vested in the president and the government, legislative power in the president and the legislative assembly (Althing). The president is elected by universal suffrage for a four-year term. Effective executive power is exercised by a prime minister enjoying the confidence of the Althing: the prime minister is appointed by the president, and the prime minister in turn selects a cabinet composed of ministers responsible to the Althing for their acts. The president must sign all legislation before it becomes law.

All citizens who have reached the age of 18 may vote, provided they have resided in Iceland for the five years immediately preceding an election. In 2003, 87.5% of Icelanders eligible to vote in the parliamentary elections did so. By a system of proportional representation, voters elect the 63 members of the unicameral (since 1991) Althing from eight constituencies at a general election held every four years, but sooner if the governing coalition loses its ability to command a legislative majority. Because of the widely varying populations of the constituencies (Reykjavík constitutes one-third of the nation's population), each constituency has a minimum of five seats, and more populous regions have more. Three-quarters of the seats in any constituency are divided by the parties according to proportional representation of that region, while the final quarter of the seats in each constituency are apportioned according to the national vote tally to ensure national proportional representation. Any citizen qualified to vote is eligible to run for a seat in the Althing. When any amendment to the constitution is voted, the Althing is dissolved and new elections are held; if the new Althing accepts the proposed amendment, it becomes law when ratified by the president.

The institution of the Althing has parliamentary immunity and its members swear allegiance to the constitution. Government ministers are normally members of the Althing and enjoy full parliamentary privileges. The constitution and the rules of procedure of the Althing specify the rights and duties of parliamentarians, and the legislative year of the Althing begins on 1 October. The legislative agenda of the Althing is divided among 12 standing committees. At the first meeting following the inauguration ceremony, the president of the Althing is elected. In addition to acting as the chief executive of Althing, the president sits on the five-person presidium along with the four vice presidents. The presidium is responsible for the organization of parliamentary activities. Sessions of the Althing are normally held four days a week.

14 POLITICAL PARTIES

No one major party in recent years has been able to command a majority of the electorate, and coalition governments have been the rule. Principal parties include the Independence Party (Sjálfstoeðisflokkurinn) (IP), a conservative grouping; the Progressive Party (Framsóknarflokkurinn) (PP), an agrarian, left-center party; the Progressive Alliance (Althýðubandalag) (PA), a formerly Communist-oriented party, now a far-left party; and the Social Democratic People's Party (Althýðuflokkurinn) (SDP), a center-left group. An Independence Party splinter group, the Citizens' Party (CP), lost its parliamentary representation by securing no seats. Iceland is unique among the Nordic states (which lead the OECD countries on all indicators of gender equality) in that it is the only one to have a women's party, which has gained a foothold in parliament. In 1995, the Icelandic Women's Alliance, a political party devoted to feminist issues, gained three seats in the Althing.

Of these parties, the Independence Party dates back to 1929, and the Progressive and Social Democratic People's (formerly Labor) parties to 1916; all three have been the source of various splinter groups. The People's Alliance became a distinct political party in 1970; it grew out of an alliance among Communist-oriented elements in the Social Democratic People's Party and other groups, and in effect replaced the earlier People's Union–Socialist Party (Sameiningarflokkur althyðu-Sósíalistaflokkurinn).

It was the issue of NATO and the US military presence that in March 1956 broke up an early alliance between Progressives and Independents, and the elections that year led to a new coalition of the Progressive, Labor, and People's Union–Socialist parties, all of which opposed the US military base on Iceland. (After the Hungarian uprising of October 1956, however, the Progressive and Labor parties reversed their stand.) That government fell because of Communist opposition to a proposed wage freeze, and after elections in October 1959, a government formed by the Independence and Labor parties came into office. This coalition endured for some time. But after the loss of four seats in the June 1971 general elections, a new government, composed of the Progressive Party, the People's Alliance, and the Liberal and Left Alliance (a party established in 1969 on a platform opposing Iceland's participation in NATO and its defense agreement with the United States) came

into power under Prime Minister Olafur Jóhannesson. Then, on 29 August 1974, after gains by the Independence Party in June elections, a coalition of Independents and Progressives was sworn in under Geir Hallgrímsson of the Independence Party.

Two short-lived coalition governments followed. The first, a leftist coalition including the Social Democrats, People's Alliance, and Progressive Party, led by Olafur Jóhannesson, was dissolved when the Social Democrats left the coalition in October 1979. Following an election that December, a second coalition was eventually formed from members of the Independence Party, the People's Alliance, and the Progressives, with Gunnar Thoroddsen, deputy chairman of the Independence Party, as prime minister. After three unsuccessful attempts by party leaders to form a governing coalition following the April 1983 elections, Vigdís Finnbogadóttir—who in August 1981 had been elected president, becoming the first woman to become democratically elected head of state—threatened to request the formation of a government of civil servants. Eventually, Progressive leader Steingrímur Hermannsson formed and headed a coalition of the Independence and Progressive parties. Following the 1987 elections, Thorsteinn Pálsson of the Independence Party replaced Hermannsson as prime minister.

The general election of April 1991 resulted in a new center-right coalition led by Davíð Oddsson of the Independence Party and members of the Social Democratic People's Party. Vigdís Finnbogadóttir was reelected unopposed for a fourth four-year term in June 1992. The left-right coalition of the IP and SDP was dissolved after the elections of April 1995 when Oddsson formed a new coalition government composed of the Independence Party and the Progressive Party, chaired by Halldór Ásgrímsson, minister for foreign affairs and external trade. This coalition remained in power after the 1999 elections in which the Independence Party increased its share of the popular vote while the Progressives polled more poorly. Two new parties gained representation in the Althing in 1999, the environmental Left-Green Party (Vinstrihreyfing-Grnt framboð) and the Liberal Party (Frjáslyndi Flokkurin). Of all 63 parliamentarians, 41 were men and 22 were women. In the presidential elections of 29 June 1996, Vigdís Finnbogadóttir chose not to run and Dr. Ólafur Ragnar Grímsson won with 41.4% of the vote. In 2000, Grímsson was reappointed president, unopposed, to a second four-year term. Grímsson faced two opponents in the 2004 presidential election, but beat them soundly (with 85.6% of the vote).

In the 10 May 2003 elections for the Althing, the Independence Party secured 33.7% of the vote and 22 seats in parliament. The opposition Social Democratic Alliance (which now includes the People's Alliance, Social Democratic Party, and Women's List) won 31% of the vote and took 20 seats. The Progressive Party won 17.7% of the vote and 12 seats, and entered into a coalition with the Independence Party. Therefore, the Independence/Progressive coalition held a slim majority of 34 seats in parliament, compared with the 43 it held after the 1999 elections. The Left-Green Alliance secured 8.8% of the vote and 5 seats, and the Liberal Party won 7.4% and held 4 seats. Following the election, Prime Minister Oddsson stated that in 2004, Minister of Foreign Affairs Halldór Ásgrímsson would become prime minister in a new government. He held true to his pledge, and Ásgrímsson became prime minister on 15 September 2004.

¹⁵LOCAL GOVERNMENT

Iceland is divided into eight regions (*landshluta*), 23 counties (*sýslur*), and 23 independent towns (*kaupstaðir*). A magistrate or sheriff (*sýslumaðour*) administers each county. Within the counties are 101 municipalities (as of 2004), each governed by a council: town councils are elected by proportional representation, rural councils by simple majority. The local government units supervise tax collections, police administration, local finances, employment, and other local affairs.

¹⁶JUDICIAL SYSTEM

District courts are courts of first instance. There are eight district courts in Iceland, which have jurisdiction in both civil and criminal cases. Appeals are heard by the Supreme Court, consisting of nine justices (all appointed for life by the president), who elect one of their number as chief justice for a two-year term. There are special courts for maritime cases, labor disputes, and other types of cases.

The courts are free from political control. Although the Ministry of Justice administers the lower courts, the Supreme Court oversees independent and fair application of the law.

A recent reform project transferred all judicial authority for criminal and civil cases from local officials (chiefs of police) to newly established district courts. This complete separation of judicial and executive power in regional jurisdictions was completed in 1992. Iceland did not accept compulsory ICJ jurisdiction.

¹⁷ARMED FORCES

Iceland is the only NATO member with no military force of its own, although the government does maintain a 130-member coast guard with three patrol and one logistical/support vessels. US forces (1,658 personnel), along with Dutch forces, are stationed in Iceland.

¹⁸INTERNATIONAL COOPERATION

Iceland became a member of the United Nations on 19 November 1946 and belongs to ECE and most of the nonregional specialized agencies, such as FAO, UNESCO, ILO, IFC, IFAD, the World Bank, and WHO. It belongs to the Council of Europe, the WTO, European Bank for Reconstruction and Development, the Euro-Atlantic Partnership Council, EFTA, NATO, the OECD, and the OSCE. The country is an associate member of the Western European Union. Iceland hold membership in the Council of the Baltic Sea States, the Nordic Council, the Nordic Investment Bank, the Arctic Council, and Barents Euro-Arctic Council. In 2001, the government established the Icelandic Crisis Response Unit (ICRU), which is designed to expand national support for cooperation in peacekeeping initiatives through the United Nations.

Iceland belongs to the Australia Group, the Nuclear Energy Agency, and the Organization for the Prohibition of Chemical Weapons. In environmental cooperation, Iceland is part of the Basel Convention, Conventions on Biological Diversity and Air Pollution, Ramsar, CITES, the London Convention, the Kyoto Protocol, the Montréal Protocol, MARPOL, the Nuclear Test Ban Treaty, and the UN Conventions on the Law of the Sea, Climate Change and Desertification.

¹⁹ECONOMY

Iceland's economy, once primarily agricultural, is now based overwhelmingly on fishing. Crop raising plays a small role, since most of the land is unsuitable for cultivation and the growing season is short. Sheep raising and dairying are the chief agricultural activities, with horse breeding also substantial. Iceland is generally self-sufficient in meat, eggs, and dairy products, but sugar and cereal products must be imported. Since Iceland has almost no known mineral resources and has had no concentrations of population until recent decades, industry is small-scale and local, depends heavily on imported raw and semi-manufactured materials, and cannot compete favorably with foreign industry, especially with imports from low-income countries.

Although the economy is based on private ownership and operates mainly on a free-enterprise basis, public enterprises account for a sizable share of GDP (about 30% in the mid-1990s). The cooperative movement is important in rural trade, and the national and local governments own some productive facilities in certain fields requiring large amounts of capital not available from private sources. The economy developed rapidly after World War II, with a rate of capital investment so high at times as to strain available resources. GNP growth fell from 9% in 1977 to -3% in 1983 but recovered to 9% in 1987. After that, it averaged -0.4% through 1993. From 1992–2001 the economy grew impressively. GDP per capita reached one of the highest levels among OECD countries. This performance was largely due to market liberalization, privatization, and other factors that spurred entrepreneurship and investment.

For a time, inflation ran rampant, rising from 30 to 45% in the late 1970s to nearly 50% annually during 1981–85. It then moderated, dropping to only 3.7% in 1991 and 1.7% in 1998; it rose again to 9.4% at the beginning of 2002. Unemployment, traditionally low, was 2% in 1999 and 3.2% in 2002.

After 2001, the overheated economy slowed. The government tightened monetary policy and exercised fiscal restraint to reduce domestic demand. The króna went through a period of devaluation and inflation rose. However, the weak currency resulted in a surge in exports, which was also helped by increased production. Aluminum exports were up 22% in 2002. Iceland is in the process of reducing its dependence upon fishing, and the aluminum industry is one sector that is contributing to the diversification of the economy; in addition, the government is taking advantage of Iceland's inexpensive and abundant supply of geothermal energy. Iceland was in a mild recession in 2002, but the economy was expected to recover by 2003 or 2004.

The GDP growth in 2004 was 5.2%, up from 4.2% in 2003; in 2005, the economy was expected to expand by 5.9%. The inflation rate has been fluctuating, but at 3.2% in 2004, it was well under control and did not pose any problems to the economy. A similar trend was registered by the unemployment rate, which reached 3.2% in 2004, and was expected to decrease to 2.1% in 2005. The government of Iceland continues to oppose EU membership for fear of losing control of the fishing industry, which is one of the country's main economic engines.

20 INCOME

The US Central Intelligence Agency (CIA) reports that in 2005 Iceland's gross domestic product (GDP) was estimated at $10.3 billion. The CIA defines GDP as the value of all final goods and services produced within a nation in a given year and computed on the basis of purchasing power parity (PPP) rather than value as measured on the basis of the rate of exchange based on current dollars. The per capita GDP was estimated at $34,600. The annual growth rate of GDP was estimated at 5.9%. The average inflation rate in 2005 was 4.1%. It was estimated that agriculture accounted for 11.8% of GDP, industry 22.3%, and services 65.9%.

Approximately 16% of household consumption was spent on food, 8% on fuel, 3% on health care, and 10% on education.

21 LABOR

The labor force was estimated at 160,000 in 2005. In 2003, agriculture, fishing or fish processing accounted for 10.3% of the workforce, with 18.3% in manufacturing, and 71.4% in the services sector. In 2005 the estimated unemployment rate was 2.1%.

As of 2002, about 85% of workers are union members. Principal unions are the Icelandic Federation of Labor (associated with the ICFTU) and the Municipal and Government Employees' Association. Labor disputes are settled by direct negotiations or by special courts, however strikes are permitted. Collective bargaining is used to negotiate pay, hours, and other conditions.

The customary workweek is 40 hours. Workers are entitled to overtime pay in excess of eight hours per day. There is no legal minimum wage, but wages are negotiated through collective bargaining. Even the lowest paid workers earn sufficient wages to provide a decent standard of living. Child labor standards are stringent and strictly enforced.

22 AGRICULTURE

About 78% of Iceland is agriculturally unproductive, and only about 1% of the land area is actually used for cultivation. Of this amount, 99% is used to cultivate hay and other fodder crops, with the remaining 1% used for potato and fodder root production. There were about 4,000 full-time farmers in the 1990s, with about 75% living on their own land; some holdings have been in the same family for centuries. In the 19th century and earlier, agriculture was the chief occupation, but by 1930, fewer than 36% of the people devoted their energies to farming, and the proportion has continued to fall. Hay is the principal crop; other crops are potatoes, turnips, oats, and garden vegetables. In hot-spring areas, vegetables, flowers and even tropical fruits are cultivated for domestic consumption in greenhouses heated with hot water from the springs. Besides hay and other fodder crops, about 7,500 tons of potatoes were produced in 2004. There are agricultural institutions in Borgarfjörður, Hjaltadalur, Hvanneyri, and Reykir; between 15–20% of all farmers have finished an agricultural degree program.

23 ANIMAL HUSBANDRY

Sheep raising is extensive, and mutton and lamb are primary meat products. Sheep are permitted to find their own grazing pasture during the warmer months and are rounded up toward the middle of September and put in shed for the winter. Cattle are raised mainly for dairying, and their number has been rising steadily; beef production is negligible. Sheep in 2005 numbered an estimated 454,000; cattle, 64,000 head; horses, 72,000; and poultry, 190,000. Estimated livestock production in 2005 included milk, 112,000 tons; mutton and lamb, 8,500 tons; and eggs, 2,600 tons. Iceland is self-sufficient in meat, dairy products, and eggs.

Icelandic farm animals are directly descended from the sheep, cattle, goats, pigs, poultry, dogs, cats, and especially horses (which were an invaluable means of travel) brought by 10th century Scandinavian settlers. In sparsely populated areas, such as the western fjords and on the east coast, farming is chiefly limited to raising sheep, although sheep farming exists in all areas of the country. Milk is produced mostly in the south and north. Except for poultry, egg, and pig production, farms are small in acreage and usually family-run. About 2,000 farmers are engaged in full-time sheep farming, and 1,000 more in mixed farming. There are also about 1,800 dairy farms in operation; Icelanders consume on average 175 liters (46.2 gal) of milk per capita per year, one of the highest amounts in the world. Cheese consumption is fourth highest, after France, Germany, and Italy. Horse-breeding is also a growing branch of animal husbandry in Iceland, as the popularity of the Iceland horse (which has five gaits) grows at home and abroad.

Animal farming is a highly mechanized industry carried out by well-educated farmers; nearly one fifth of all farmers matriculate at one of three agricultural colleges in Iceland.

24 FISHING

Accounting for about 9% of Iceland's employment, fishing and fish processing provide the primary source of foreign exchange. Exports of fish products were valued at $1.5 billion in 2003. Icelanders consume more fish per capita annually (over 91.5 kg/201 lb live weight equivalent) than any other people in Europe. Cod is caught during the first five months of the year off the southwest coast. Herring are taken off the north and northeast coasts from June to September and off the southwest from September to December. In 2005, the fish catch was 1,984,349 tons (12th in the world), up from 1,502,445 tons in 1990. The 2003 catch included 680,291 tons of capelin, 501,494 tons of blue whiting, 250,039 tons of Atlantic herring, 206,670 tons of Atlantic cod, 60,402 tons of haddock, and 57,940 tons of pollock.

The fishing fleet as of 2004 consisted of 70 stern trawlers totaling 86,048 GRT and 869 other decked fishing vessels of 101,031 GRT. Most fishing vessels are now equipped with telecommunications devices, computers, and automated equipment. Through the early 1980s, about 250 whales a year were caught off the coast, providing lucrative export products. Although Iceland had agreed to phase out whaling in order to comply with the 1982 ban by the International Whaling Commission, in 1987 it announced its intention to take 100 whales a year for scientific purposes. The FAO reported that Iceland took 39 whales in 2003.

Abundant quantities of pure water and geothermal heat give Iceland an advantage over other nations in fish farming. Aquaculture is being developed to offset lean years in the natural fish catch, and to produce more expensive and profitable species of fish.

[25] FORESTRY

There are no forests of commercial value, and the existing trees (ash, birch, aspen, and willow) are small; only about 1% of the total land area is considered forested. The originally extensive birch forests were cut down for firewood and to clear land for grazing sheep. In recent years, the remaining woods have been protected and reforestation has begun. Imports of forestry products amounted to about $76.4 million in 2004.

[26] MINING

Diatomite was a leading export commodity in 2004, and ferrosilicon production and geothermal power were Iceland's major mineral industries. Diatomite production, from Lake Myvatn, was estimated at 28,000 metric tons in 2004. Iceland also produced hydraulic cement, nitrogen, pumice, salt, scoria, sand (basaltic, calcareous, and shell), sand and gravel, and crushed stone (basaltic and rhyolite); these minerals were used by local industries. Among Iceland's other mineral resources, spar and sulfur deposits, once mined, were no longer worked extensively. Peat was common, but little used and sulfur and lignite were being processed experimentally, the former with the use of subterranean steam. The country's aluminum plant and ferrosilicon plant relied on imported raw materials and inexpensive hydroelectric and geothermal energy. Ferrosilicon production in 2004 totaled an estimated 118,000 metric tons in 2004.

[27] ENERGY AND POWER

Iceland has no known reserves of oil, natural gas or coal. Thus, the country is entirely reliant upon imports to meet its demand for fossil fuels. However, the country does rely upon hydroelectric power and geothermal/other sources to generate electric power and to provide heat.

In 2002, refined oil imports were reported at 15,760 barrels per day, while demand was reported at 18,050 barrels per day. Coal imports and consumption for 2002, were each placed at 161,000 short tons There were no imports of natural gas in 2002.

Hydroelectric power is the main source of electric power for Iceland, followed by geothermal and conventional thermal sources, respectively. In 2002, electric power generating capacity totaled 1.460 million kW, with hydropower accounting for 1.109 million kW, geothermal at 0.202 million kW, and conventional thermal at 0.149 million kW. Electric energy output in 2002 was 8.277 billion kWh, with hydroelectric output accounting for 83%, alternative sources for 16%, and conventional thermal fuels at less than 1%. Electric power demand in 2002 totaled 7.698 billion kWh. Peat, formerly an important source of heat on the farms, has been virtually abandoned.

Hot springs are used for heating greenhouses in which vegetables, fruit, and flowers are raised, and for heating public buildings. Since 1943, most of Reykjavík has been heated by water from hot springs at Reykir, some 160 km (100 mi) from the city. About 85% of the population lives in homes heated with geothermal power. In recent years, however, a significant decline in flow from geothermal drill holes has raised concern that this energy resource may not be so boundless as was once thought.

[28] INDUSTRY

Fish processing is the most important industry. Facilities for freezing, salting, sun-curing, and reducing to oil or fish meal are flexible enough to allow shifting from one process to another in accordance with demand. By-products include fish meal and cod-liver oil.

Although Iceland's industry is focused on fish processing, the country in the 21st century needs to diversify its economy, as fish stocks are declining. (Nevertheless, fishing accounted for 12% of GDP in 2001 and 40% of total exports.) The manufacturing of energy-intensive industries, particularly aluminum, are rising. The ISAL aluminum smelter has expanded its capacity, and in 2002, construction of another aluminum smelter was underway. Production exports rose 22% in 2001. Other projects included the construction of a magnesium plant and the enlargement of the ferro alloy plant. Other industry is small-scale and designed to meet local needs. Chief manufactures include fishing equipment, electric stoves and cookers, paints, clothing, soaps, candles, cosmetics, dairy products, confectionery, and beer. Clothing factories are situated in Reykjavík and Akureyri. Icelandic ammonium nitrate needs are more than met by a fertilizer plant at Gufunes with an annual production capacity of 60,000 tons. A cement factory in Akranes with a capacity of 115,000 tons per year supplies most domestic cement requirements; total production in the mid-1990s amounted to 83,100 tons per year. Production of aluminum rose from 40,000 tons in 1970 to 99,300 tons per year in the same period. A ferro-silicon smelter, which began production in 1979, produced some 66,000 tons per year and a diatomite processing plant produced 25,000 tons.

In 2004, the industry had a 9.6% share in the GDP and employed 18.3% of the labor force; agriculture made up 11.2% of the economy, and together with fishing and fish processing employed 10.3% of the work force; services was by far the largest economic sector, with a 79.2% share in the GDP, and a 71.4% representation in the work force. The industrial production growth rate was 8.8% in 2004, higher than the GDP growth rate, which indicates that industry is currently a growth engine in Iceland.

[29] SCIENCE AND TECHNOLOGY

The Icelandic Research Council coordinates science policy and advises the government on scientific matters. It has five research institutes devoted to marine science, technology, agriculture, the fish industry, and the construction and building industries. Other research institutes and learned societies include the Surtsey Research Society, the Icelandic Meteorological Office, the Association of Chartered Engineers in Iceland, the Agricultural Society of Iceland, the Iceland Glaciological Society, the Icelandic Natural History Society, and the Icelandic Society of Sciences, all located at Reykjavík.

The Icelandic Council of Science, an independent agency under the Ministry of Culture and Education, aims to stimulate and encourage scientific research. The University of Iceland has faculties of medicine, engineering, dentistry, and science. Two agricultural colleges are located in Hólum i Hjaltadal and Hvanneyri. The Icelandic College of Engineering and Technology is located at Reykjavík. In 1987–97, science and engineering students accounted for 41% of university enrollment. In 2002, of all bachelor's degrees awarded, 17.2% were in the sciences (natural, mathematics and computers, and engineering).

In 2001, there were 6,592 researchers and 2,082 technicians per million people that were actively engaged in research and development (R&D). For that same year, R&D expenditures totaled $262.371 million, or 3.08% of GDP. Of that amount, business accounted for the largest slice at 46.2%, followed by the government sector at 34%, with foreign sources and higher education accounting for 18.3% and 1.6%, respectively.

30 DOMESTIC TRADE

Foreign firms do not have branches in Iceland. Their business is conducted by Icelandic agents. Imports are handled by these agents, by wholesale or retail importers, or by the Federation of Iceland Cooperative Societies, and distribution is through private channels. Most advertising is translated and disseminated directly by agents. Foreign trade fairs are held from time to time.

Of the wholesale enterprises, 80–90% are concentrated in Reykjavík; more than half the retail establishments are likewise in the capital. Much trade is handled by cooperative societies, most of which are joined in the Federation of Iceland Cooperative Societies. A sales tax of 14% applies to most food items and books. A 24.5% tax applies to most other goods and services.

Business hours are from 9 AM to 6 PM on weekdays, and from 9 or 10 AM to noon on Saturdays. Banking hours are from 9:15 AM to 4 PM, Monday–Friday, with an additional hour from 5 to 6 PM on Thursday.

31 FOREIGN TRADE

The fishing industry of Iceland supports most of its commodity export market (60%). It supplies the world export market with 10.5% of its salted, dried, or smoked fish, second only to Norway in volume. Other important exports include aluminum (19%), animal feed (6.3%), iron (2.6%), diatomite, and ferrosilicon.

In 2004, exports reached $2.9 billion (FOB—Free on Board), while imports grew to $3.3 billion (FOB). The bulk of exports went to the United Kingdom (19.1%), Germany (17.2%), the Netherlands (11.5%), the United States (9.8%), Spain (6.8%), and Den-

Principal Trading Partners – Iceland (2003)

(In millions of US dollars)

Country	Exports	Imports	Balance
World	2,380.6	2,826.5	-445.9
United Kingdom	417.1	210.1	207.0
Germany	415.0	333.9	81.1
Netherlands	266.8	174.3	92.5
United States	225.0	210.9	14.1
Spain	150.5	51.4	99.1
Denmark	121.5	227.0	-105.5
Norway	106.4	195.9	-89.5
France-Monaco	96.3	90.4	5.9
Portugal	90.2	13.3	76.9
Japan	77.1	107.9	-30.8

(…) data not available or not significant.

SOURCE: 2003 International Trade Statistics Yearbook, New York: United Nations, 2004.

Balance of Payments – Iceland (2003)

(In millions of US dollars)

Current Account		-572.0
Balance on goods	-210.0	
Imports	-2,596.0	
Exports	2,386.0	
Balance on services	-105.0	
Balance on income	-242.0	
Current transfers	-16.0	
Capital Account		-5.0
Financial Account		758.0
Direct investment abroad	-169.0	
Direct investment in Iceland	147.0	
Portfolio investment assets	-593.0	
Portfolio investment liabilities	3,696.0	
Financial derivatives	…	
Other investment assets	-1,978.0	
Other investment liabilities	-345.0	
Net Errors and Omissions		126.0
Reserves and Related Items		-307.0

(…) data not available or not significant.

SOURCE: Balance of Payment Statistics Yearbook 2004, Washington, DC: International Monetary Fund, 2004.

mark (4.6%). Imports included machinery and equipment, petroleum products, foodstuffs, and textiles, and mainly came from Germany (12.3%), the United States (9.9%), Norway (9.7%), Denmark (7.9%), the United Kingdom (7.2%), Sweden (6.7%), and the Netherlands (6%).

32 BALANCE OF PAYMENTS

The difference between imports and exports since World War II has been met by drawing from large wartime reserves, by Marshall Plan aid, and, since 1953, by income from US defense spending at Keflavík, the NATO airbase. Widely fluctuating current account deficits, attributable mainly to the trade imbalance, averaged more than 6.5% of GNP during 1971–75. During the next four years, although still largely negative, the current account balance improved; from 1980 through 1985, however, Iceland's current accounts position again deteriorated, this time because of large deficits in services.

Iceland suffered a prolonged recession during 1987–93 due to cuts in fish catch quotas necessitated in part by overfishing. Again, there was a significant deterioration in the balance of payments, especially on the current account and merchandise trade balances. In 1994 the economy recovered with the help of a 6.3% growth in exports, due to a better than expected performance in the fishing sector. The external current account balance was positive for the first time since 1986. Iceland experienced successful economic performance in the 1990s but fell into recession in 2001, which negatively impacted the current account deficit.

The US Central Intelligence Agency (CIA) reported that in 2002 the purchasing power parity of Iceland's exports was $2 billion while imports also totaled $2 billion.

The International Monetary Fund (IMF) reported that in 2000 Iceland had exports of goods totaling $1.9 billion and imports totaling $2.38 billion. The services credit totaled $1.05 billion and debit $1.16 billion.

Exports of goods reached $2.9 billion in 2004, and were expected to grow to $3.2 billion in 2005. Imports were expected to reach $4.6 billion in 2005, up from $3.4 billion in 2004. The resource balance was consequently negative, reaching -$0.4 billion in 2004, and -$0.6 billion in 2005. The current account balance was also negative, at -$1.0 billion in 2004, and an expected -$2.1 billion in 2005. Foreign exchange reserves (including gold) grew to $935 million in 2004, covering less than four months of imports.

33 BANKING AND SECURITIES

In March 1961, the Central Bank of Iceland was founded to issue notes and assume other central bank functions previously exercised by the National Bank of Iceland, a wholly state-owned bank established in 1885. Other banks are the Agricultural Bank, a state bank founded in 1929; the Fisheries Bank, a private joint-stock bank founded in 1930, with most of its shares held by the government; the Industrial Bank, a joint-stock bank established in 1953, with part of the shares owned by the government; the Iceland Bank of Commerce, founded in 1961; the Cooperative Bank of Iceland, founded in 1963; and the People's Bank, founded in 1971. All banks have main offices in Reykjavík, and some have branches in other towns. Savings banks are distributed throughout the country.

In 1955, Iceland took the first step toward indexation of financial assets. The Economic Management Act of 1979 established a system of full indexation of savings and credit, most provisions of which were gradually implemented over the next two years. Most deposits are now indexed, and legislation that took effect in November 1986 gave banks increased power to determine their interest rate.

In 1990 the number of commercial banks in Iceland were reduced from seven to four. A number of banks were forced to merge into the Islandbanki because of financial trouble. In 1997 there were four commercial banks, two of which, the Landsbanki and Bunadar banki, are still state-owned. The country's two other banks, Islandsbanki and Sparisjodabanki, are privately-owned.

The whole basis on which the financial system is supervised and regulated, however, has been transformed by Iceland's accession to the European Economic Area (EEA) in 1994. Under the agreement, Iceland has been required to implement into national law the common minimum standards for the supervision of financial institutions—banks, insurance companies, and securities firms—developed at EU level.

Since 15 June 1973, the market rate of the Icelandic króna has been floating vis-à-vis other currencies. A currency reform that took effect on 1 January 1981 introduced a new króna equivalent to 100 old krónur. The money supply, as measured by M2, totaled к135,353 million in 1995. The International Monetary Fund reports that in 1998, currency and demand deposits—an aggregate commonly known as M1—were equal to $820.5 million. In that same year, M2—an aggregate equal to M1 plus savings deposits, small time deposits, and money market mutual funds—was $3.2 billion. The money market rate, the rate at which financial institutions lend to one another in the short term, was 8.12%. The discount rate, the interest rate at which the central bank lends to financial institutions in the short term, was 8.5%.

The Securities Exchange of Iceland (SEI) was established in 1985 on the basis of rules set by the Central Bank. A new Act on the Icelandic Stock Exchange was passed in February 1993, granting a monopoly to the exchange. As of 2004, a total of 34 companies were listed on the stock exchange, which had a market capitalization that year of $17.629 billion. In 2004, the ICEX-15 rose 58.9% from the previous year to 3,359.6.

34 INSURANCE

There are many mutual insurance societies in addition to the national health and social insurance scheme. Almost all direct insurance is written by domestic companies that conduct business in the various kinds of property and life insurance. Automobile liability insurance and homeowners' coverage against fire, floods, earthquakes, and volcanic eruptions are compulsory. The Ministry of Insurance Affairs is the principal supervisory body. In 2003, direct premiums written totaled $345 million, of which nonlife premiums accounted for $314 million. In 2002, Sjova Almennar was Iceland's top nonlife and life insurer, with gross written nonlife premiums (for nonlife and life insurers) and life premiums of $112.7 million and $14.4 million, respectively.

35 PUBLIC FINANCE

Since 1984, Iceland's budget has shown a deficit averaging nearly 2% of GDP, raising its net indebtedness relative to GDP to almost 30% in 1994. Government attempts to balance the budget were frustrated by the economic downturn during 1987–93 and by fiscal concessions to expedite wage settlements. Consequently, the deficit has been larger than expected, reaching 34% of GDP in 1999.

The US Central Intelligence Agency (CIA) estimated that in 2005 Iceland's central government took in revenues of approximately $6.9 billion and had expenditures of $6.7 billion. Revenues minus expenditures totaled approximately $234 million. Public debt in 2005 amounted to 34% of GDP. Total external debt was $3.073 billion.

Public Finance – Iceland (2002)

(In millions of kronur, central government figures)

Revenue and Grants	**259,012**	**100.0%**
Tax revenue	197,026	76.1%
Social contributions	23,904	9.2%
Grants	...	...
Other revenue	38,081	14.7%
Expenditures	**262,231**	**100.0%**
General public services	48,434	18.5%
Defense	...	...
Public order and safety	12,881	4.9%
Economic affairs	41,198	15.7%
Environmental protection	...	...
Housing and community amenities	2,383	0.9%
Health	68,812	26.2%
Recreational, culture, and religion	8,227	3.1%
Education	26,106	10.0%
Social protection	54,190	20.7%

(...) data not available or not significant.

SOURCE: *Government Finance Statistics Yearbook 2004*, Washington, DC: International Monetary Fund, 2004.

The International Monetary Fund (IMF) reported that in 2002, the most recent year for which it had data, central government revenues were к259,012 million and expenditures were к262,231 million. The value of revenues was us$2,826 million and expenditures us$2,861 million, based on an exchange rate for 2002 of us$1 = к91.662 as reported by the IMF. Government outlays by function were as follows: general public services, 18.5%; public order and safety, 4.9%; economic affairs, 15.7%; housing and community amenities, 0.9%; health, 26.2%; recreation, culture, and religion, 3.1%; education, 10.0%; and social protection, 20.7%.

36 TAXATION

Recent tax reforms in Iceland have produced a steady drop in corporate income tax rates throughout the 1990s and, since 1995, decreased marginal rates and increased thresholds for personal income tax. The corporate income tax rate, at 50% in 1989, was decreased from 30% in 2001 to 18% in 2002. The income tax on partnerships, was decreased from 38% in 2001 to 26% in 2002. Since March 1999, Iceland has also offered an offshore corporate tax rate of 5% to international trading companies (ITCs) that exclusively trade in goods and services outside of Iceland. Capital gains are taxed as ordinary income at 18%, although gains may be offset by extraordinary depreciation. Dividends paid to nonresident companies are subject to a 15% tax rate, while dividends paid to nonresident persons are subject to a 10% tax rate.

The personal income tax schedule in Iceland consists of a tax free allowance (about $10,457 in 2002 increased to $10,785 in 2003); a total tax rate that is the sum of the central government's general rate (25.75% in 2002 and 2003) and the municipal tax rate (12.8% in 2002 and 2003) giving a total tax rate of 38.55%; and a central government surtax (7% in 2002 reduced to 5% in 2003) which is applied to income above a certain threshold ($51,404 in 2002 and $52,818 in 2003) creating a three-bracket structure with maximum tax rate of 45.54% in 2002 decreased to 43.54% in 2003. Seamen are allowed special a special tax reduction amounting to about $9.40 a day in 2003. The social security tax, paid by the employer, is 5.73%. Since 1999, reductions in social security taxes (0.2% in 1999 and 0.4% as of May 2000) have been offered to employers in exchange for their contribution to supplementary employee pension premiums. In 2003 the wealth tax rate, applied to assets above about $61,000, was halved from 1.2% to 0.6% and a 0.25% surtax on net wealth above approximately $81,800 was abolished largely because of increases in real property values following an assessment review by the Valuation Office in 2002. Inheritance and gift taxes range from 11–15%. There is a 2–6% tax on the transfer of housing, and a 10% tax on the transfer of large estates. Local authorities may levy individual income and corporate taxes.

The major indirect tax is Iceland's value-added tax (VAT) with a normal rate of 24.5% on domestic goods and services. There is a reduced rate of 14% applied to most foodstuffs, books, newspapers and periodicals, subscriptions to radio and the TV, hotels, electricity, geothermal heating. Exempted from VAT are exports of goods and services, as well as services connected with imports and exports. Other categories for exemption include health services, social services, education, libraries, the arts, sports, passenger transport, postal services, rental of property, insurance, and banking.

37 CUSTOMS AND DUTIES

Over 90% of imports are not subject to import restrictions or duties other than the same value-added tax applied to domestically produced goods. Special excise taxes are levied on sugar and some sugar products, potatoes, and motor vehicles. Agricultural products remain the most heavily taxed. In March 1970, Iceland acquired full membership in EFTA. On 28 February 1973, Iceland ratified a trade agreement with the European Community (later named the European Union) leading to the elimination of tariffs on industrial goods. A law authorizing the establishment of free trade zones went into effect in 1992. Iceland's trade regime underwent considerable liberalization in the 1990s with accession to the European Economic Area (EEA) in 1993, and the Uruguay Round in 1994.

Current duty rates generally range from 0–30% ad valorem and the average weighted tariff is 3.6%. Some goods enter duty-free, such as meat, fish, and dairy products.

38 FOREIGN INVESTMENT

Icelanders have been reluctant to permit substantial foreign investment; nearly all such investment is limited to participation in joint ventures in which Icelandic interests hold a majority share. There is only one wholly foreign-owned industrial facility in the country, a Swiss aluminum-processing facility. Two others, a ferro-silicon and a diatomite plant, have foreign equity participation. From the beginning of 1993, Icelanders have been free to invest abroad.

For the period 1988 to 1990, Iceland's share in world foreign direct investment (FDI) inflow was only 30% of its share in world GDP. For the period 1998 to 2000, its share of world FDI inflows was 40% of its share of world GDP, a marginal improvement. Except for a fall to $66 million in 1998, yearly FDI inflows to Iceland have in the range of $146 million (2001) to $158 million (2000).

Energy-intensive industrial activities is one of the main areas for foreign investments, due to the inexpensive energy resources available in Iceland. The national telephone company was expected to be privatized by the end of 2005, and the government has started discussing about opening part of the fishing industry to limited foreign investment. Biomedical and genetic research are two areas with future potential for investments.

39 ECONOMIC DEVELOPMENT

The national government and some local governments are involved in trawler fishing, herring processing, merchant shipping, electric power facilities, and certain other industries. To a considerable degree, the central government supervises the export-import trade and the fishing and fish-processing industries. It may set uniform prices of export commodities and may shift export and import trade to specific countries as balance-of-payments considerations require. It channels investment funds into fields it considers desirable.

The government supports farmers in the rebuilding or enlarging of their homes, livestock sheds, and barns, and assists them in the purchase of machinery. Equipped with crawler tractors and excavators, a government agency helps farmers enlarge cultivated areas and break, drain, and level new lands for the establishment of homesteads. Thousands of new acres have thus been brought under cultivation.

The government fixes prices of essential foods and other basic consumption items and subsidizes them, both to limit prices for the consumer and to maintain farm incomes. It also fixes mark-ups that manufacturers, wholesalers, retailers, and importers may place on a wide variety of products.

In the early 1990s, the government concentrated on maintaining the value of the króna by bringing down inflation, even at the cost of economic growth. Wage gains were restricted. In late 1992, plans were made public for a Fisheries Development Fund that would buy and scrap unneeded vessels and thereby promote efficiency. The Fund would also be used to help firms establish joint ventures abroad and buy fishing rights. Plans were also under way to sell several state-owned companies, with the money used for research and development and reducing the deficit. Entry into the European Economic Area (EEA) in 1994 and the Uruguay Round brought increased trade liberalization and foreign investment. The country experienced rapid economic growth during the late 1990s, but high domestic spending led to a widening current account deficit that peaked at 10% of GDP in 2000.

The economy went into recession in 2001, and inflation rose. The government tightened monetary and fiscal policy that brought inflation down, but GDP growth remained negative in 2002. The government adopted a floating exchange rate for the króna in March 2001. Gross external debt amounted to 130% of GDP at the end of 2002. The government is looking to diversify exports, which is expected to stabilize the economy.

More than 70% of export revenues are contributed by the fishing industry, which makes the Icelandic economy susceptible to declining fish stocks and fluctuations in world prices for fish and fish products. To better equip for the future, Iceland has started diversifying its economic base, and branched out into software production, biotechnology, and financial services. At the same time, it has started expanding its manufacturing and tourism sectors. The current economic growth is expected to be sustained until 2007, and will have private consumption as its prime engine.

40 SOCIAL DEVELOPMENT

There is a universal pension covering all residents and a mandatory occupational pension covering all employees and self-employed persons. Universal pensions covering all residents are paid by employer and government contributions, while the cost of employment pensions is shared by employees and employers. Benefits include old age, disability, and survivorship pensions. Sickness and maternity benefits are available to all residents. The first laws covering sickness and maternity were instituted in 1936. Medical benefits cover all residents.

The number of women in the work force is high, partially due to a comprehensive subsidized day care program. In 2004 more than 75% of women were actively engaged in the work force. Equal pay for equal work is required by law although men continue to earn more than women. The government takes serious measures to protect women against violence and sexual abuse, though many cases remain unreported.

The constitution provides for the freedom of speech and press, assembly and association, and religion. These rights are generally respected by the government. There is very little discrimination based on race, gender, religion, disability, language, or social status.

41 HEALTH

The Director of Public Health is responsible for all health matters. Iceland had an estimated 347 physicians, 893 nurses, 77 midwives, 120 dentists, and 85 pharmacists per 100,000 people in 2004. In the 1990s there were an estimated 53 hospitals, with 3,985 beds. Two-thirds of the beds were in nursing and senior living homes, with the remaining one-third in hospitals. Public expenditures on health were among the highest in industrialized countries at 19.3% of the gross domestic product.

As of 2002, Iceland had estimated birth and death rates of, respectively, 14.4 and 6.9 per 1,000 people. Life expectancy was estimated at 80.19 years, among the highest in the world. Infant mortality in 2005 was estimated at 3.31 per 1,000 live births, one of the lowest in the world. The total fertility rate was two children per woman during her childbearing years. The incidence of tuberculosis, once widespread, has been greatly reduced. Leprosy, also common in earlier times, has been virtually eliminated, with no new cases reported in recent decades. Approximately 99% of Iceland's children were immunized against measles. The HIV/AIDS prevalence was 0.20 per 100 adults in 2003. As of 2004, there were approximately 220 people living with HIV/AIDS in the country. There were an estimated 100 deaths from AIDS in 2003.

The major causes of death were circulatory system diseases, cerebrovascular disease, malignant neoplasms (cancers), and diseases of the respiratory system.

42 HOUSING

In 2003, there were about 111,157 dwellings in the nation; about 383 dwellings for every 1,000 inhabitants. About 53% of all dwellings were one- or two-family houses; 45% were apartments. About 37% of all dwellings had five or more rooms and a kitchen. Most rural buildings were at one time made of turf, then of wood, and most recently of stone and concrete. In the towns, turf houses long ago gave way to wooden ones, but for some decades most new housing has been concrete. Virtually all dwellings have electricity, piped water, and central heating.

43 EDUCATION

Education is compulsory for 10 years of basic education (ages 6 to 16). Students may then choose to attend a general or technical secondary school, each offering four-year programs. Specialized vocational schools are also available to secondary students, including a commercial high school, a school of navigation, two schools of agriculture, and a health professions school. In some remote rural areas, a system of "alternate teaching" is in effect. This allows children to study intensively for a week or two at a boarding school, then return home for the same period of time. The academic year runs from September to May.

Most children between the ages of three and five are enrolled in some type of preschool program. Primary school enrollment in 2003 was estimated at about 100% of age-eligible students. The same year, secondary school enrollment was about 86% of age-eligible students. Nearly all students complete their primary education. The student-to-teacher ratio for primary school was at about 11:1 in 2003; the ratio for secondary school was about 13:1.

There are at least eight *háskóli;* a term that refers to both traditional universities and other institutions of higher education that do not have research programs. The University of Iceland in Reykjavík, founded in 1911, has faculties of law and economics, theology, medicine and dentistry, philosophy (art and humanities), and engineering. Tuition is free; only nominal registration and examination fees must be paid. In 2003, about 63% of the tertiary age population were enrolled in some type of higher education program; with 45% for men and 81% for women. The adult literacy rate has been estimated at about 99.9%.

As of 2003, public expenditure on education was estimated at 7.6% of GDP.

44 LIBRARIES AND MUSEUMS

The National and University Library in Reykjavík (founded in 1818; 900,000 items) serves as a national library as well as a public lending library. Other leading libraries, in the Reykjavík include the City Library of Reykjavík, which sponsors seven branch location and bookmobile, and the National Archives, which contains a collection of documents covering 800 years of Icelandic history. In 2000, there were about 106 public libraries in the country.

The important museums, also all in Reykjavík, are the Icelandic National Museum (founded in 1863), the Natural History Museum (1889), and a museum devoted to the sculptures and paintings of Einar Jónsson. The Arni Magnusson Institute contains Iceland literature and documents that were somewhat recently returned to the Icelandic government after being held by Denmark for centuries. Also in the capital are the National Gallery of Iceland, the Living Art Museum, and the Sigurjón Ólaffson Museum, among others. The Kopavogur Art Museum contains exhibits primarily on modern and contemporary art. A Salt Fish Museum opened in Grindavik in 2002 to commemorate the country's fishing industry.

45 MEDIA

Radio and radiotelephone communications are maintained with Europe and America and an underwater telegraph cable connects Iceland with Europe. The telephone, telegraph, and radio systems are publicly owned and administered. In 2003, there were 190,700 mainline phones and 279,100 mobile phones in use throughout the country.

The government-owned Icelandic National Broadcasting Service (RUV) provides the primary national radio and television broadcasts. There are, however, several smaller private stations. As of 1999 there were 5 AM and 147 FM radio stations and 14 television stations. In 1997 there were 260,000 radios and 98,000 television sets throughout the country. In 2003, there were about 195,000 Internet subscribers nationwide served by about 122,175 Internet hosts.

There are five daily newspapers, four of which are published in Reykjavík. With their political orientation and average daily circulation in 2002, they were: *Morgunblaid,* Independence Party, 53,000; *DV Dagblaid,* 44,000; *Tíminn,* Progressive Party, 14,000; *Althydublaid,* 4,000; and *Dagur-Tíminn* (Akureyri), Progressive Party. Icelandreview.com is an English-language news site. Nondaily newspapers are published in Reykjavík and other towns. Various popular and scholarly periodicals are published in Reykjavík.

The law prohibits the production, showing, distribution, and/or sale of violent movies, which are defined as containing scenes depicting the mistreatment or the brutal killing of men or animals. The Motion Picture Review Committee, which includes six members, is appointed by the Minister of Education and Culture to review all movies before they are shown. The committee also rates the films based on their suitability for children. By their evaluation, the committee may ban a film or require edits before its release.

The constitution provides for freedom of speech and press, and the government is said to respect these rights in practice.

46 ORGANIZATIONS

The Iceland Chamber of Commerce and the Confederation of Icelandic Employers are based in Reykjavík. Organizations representing laborers, businesses, and industries include the Farmers Association of Iceland, the Federation of Icelandic Industries, and the Federation of Icelandic Trade.

There are professional associations representing a wide variety of fields, such as the Icelandic Teachers Union and the Icelandic Nurses' Association. Many of these promote research and education in particular fields, such as the Icelandic Medical Association. There are several other associations dedicated to research and education for specific fields of medicine and particular diseases and conditions, such as the Icelandic Heart Association.

Notable national youth organizations include the Federation of Young Progressives, Independence Party Youth Organization, National Council of Icelandic Youth, National Union of Icelandic Students, Social Democratic Youth Federation, Youth Movement of the People's Alliance, YMCA/YWCA, and The Icelandic Boy and Girl Scouts Association. There are several sports associations in the country representing such pastimes as football (soccer), badminton, squash, mountain biking, skiing, skating, and track and field.

Learned societies include the Icelandic Archaeological Society, the Icelandic Historical Society, the Icelandic Literary Society, the Music Society, the Icelandic Natural History Society, and the Agricultural Association. There are also the Icelandic Artists' Association, the Iceland Association of Pictorial Artists, the Icelandic Actors' Association, the Icelandic Musicians' Association, the Icelandic Composers' Society, the Icelandic Architects' Association, and the Icelandic Writers' Association. Among other cultural organizations are the Icelandic-American Society, the Danish Society, the Danish-Icelandic Society, the Anglo-Icelandic Society, the Alliance Française, the Nordic Society, and the Union of Women's Societies.

The Salvation Army, Caritas, Amnesty International, and the Red Cross all have active chapters within the country. Volunteer service organizations, such as the Lions Clubs and Kiwanis International, are also present.

47 TOURISM, TRAVEL, AND RECREATION

Iceland offers such diverse and unusual natural attractions as active volcanoes, glaciers, and hot springs. Among popular participatory sports are swimming (possible year-round in geothermal pools), salmon fishing, pony trekking, bird-watching, skiing, river rafting, and golf. Tourists may arrange to stay in modern hotels, guest houses, on farms, or in youth hostels.

Citizens of the Scandinavian countries do not require a passport when visiting Iceland. All other visitors need valid passports and visas, except residents of some 60 countries (including the United States, Australia, and Canada). Visas are good for up to three months. A certificate of vaccination against yellow fever is required if traveling from an infected country.

In 2003, there were 569,194 tourist arrivals, almost an 11% increase from 2002. There were 7,330 hotel rooms with 14,948 beds and an occupancy rate of 42%.

In 2005, the US Department of State estimated the daily cost of traveling in Reykjavík from May through September at $442, and $352 the rest of the year. The cost of a stay in Keflavik-Grindavik was estimated at $367 per day.

48 FAMOUS ICELANDERS

Famous early Icelanders were Eric the Red (Eiríkur Thorvaldsson), who discovered and colonized Greenland in 982, and his son Leif Ericsson (Leifur Eiríksson, b.970), who introduced Christianity to Greenland and discovered the North American continent (c.1000). Two famous patriots and statesmen were Bishop Jón Arason (1484–1550), who led the fight for liberty against the power of the Danish king, and Jón Sigurðsson (1811–79), Iceland's national hero, champion of the fight for independence. Vigdís Finnbogadottír (b.1930) served four consecutive terms as president from 1980 to 1996, becoming the first female elected to the presidency of any republic.

Prominent writers were Ari Thorgilsson (1067–1148), father of Icelandic historical writing; Snorri Sturluson (1178–1241), author of the famous *Prose Edda*, a collection of Norse myths; and Hallgrímur Pétursson (1614–74), author of Iceland's beloved Passion Hymns. Leading poets include Bjarni Thorarensen (1786–1841) and Jónas Hallgrímsson (1807–45), pioneers of the Romantic movement in Iceland; Matthías Jochumsson (1835–1920), author of Iceland's national anthem; Thorsteinn Erlingsson (1858–1914), lyricist; Einar Hjörleifsson Kvaran (1859–1939), a pioneer of realism in Icelandic literature and an outstanding short-story writer; Einar Benediktsson (1864–1940), ranked as one of the greatest modern Icelandic poets; Jóhann Sigurjónsson (1880–1919), who lived much of his life in Denmark and wrote many plays based on Icelandic history and legend, as well as poetry; and the novelist Halldór Kiljan Laxness (1902–98), who received the Nobel Prize for literature in 1955.

Niels Ryberg Finsen (1860–1904), a physician who pioneered in the field of light (ray) therapy, received the Nobel Prize for medicine in 1903. Stefán Stefánsson (1863–1921) was the pioneer Icelandic botanist. Helgi Pjeturss (1872–1949), geologist and philosopher, was an authority on the Ice Age and the geology of Iceland. Einar Jónsson (1874–1954), Iceland's greatest sculptor, is represented in European and American museums.

Singer, songwriter, and composer Björk (b.1965), formerly the lead singer of the Icelandic band The Sugarcubes, works in a variety of musical genres. The former world chess champion Bobby Fischer (b.1943) became an Icelandic citizen in 2005. Russian pianist and composer Vladimir Ashkenazy (b.1937) has been a citizen since 1972.

49 DEPENDENCIES

Iceland has no territories or colonies.

50 BIBLIOGRAPHY

Durrenberger, E. Paul. *The Dynamics of Medieval Iceland: Political Economy and Literature*. Iowa City: University of Iowa Press, 1992.

Images of Contemporary Iceland: Everyday Lives and Global Contexts. Iowa City: University of Iowa Press, 1996.

International Smoking Statistics: A Collection of Historical Data from 30 Economically Developed Countries. New York: Oxford University Press, 2002.

Jochens, Jenny. *Women in Old Norse Society*. Ithaca, N.Y.: Cornell University Press, 1995.

Karlsson, Gunnar. *The History of Iceland*. Minneapolis: University of Minnesota Press, 2000.

Magnusson, Magnus. *The Icelandic Sagas*. London: Folio Society, 2002.

Ross, Margaret Clunies (ed.). *Old Icelandic Literature and Society*. New York: Cambridge University Press, 2000.

Sullivan, Paul. *Waking Up in Iceland*. London, Eng.: Sanctuary, 2003.

Tulinius, Torfi H. *The Matter of the North: The Rise of Literary Fiction in Thirteenth-Century Iceland*. Odense, Denmark: Odense University Press, 2002.

IRELAND

Éire

CAPITAL: Dublin (Baile Átha Cliath)

FLAG: The national flag is a tricolor of green, white, and orange vertical stripes.

ANTHEM: *Amhrán na bhFiann (The Soldier's Song).*

MONETARY UNIT: The euro replaced the Irish punt as the official currency in 2002. The euro is divided into 100 cents. There are coins in denominations of 1, 2, 5, 10, 20, and 50 cents and 1 euro and 2 euros. There are notes of 5, 10, 20, 50, 100, 200, and 500 euros. €1 = $1.25475 (or $1 = €0.79697) as of 2005.

WEIGHTS AND MEASURES: Since 1988, Ireland has largely converted from the British system of weights and measures to the metric system.

HOLIDAYS: New Year's Day, 1 January; St. Patrick's Day, 17 March; Bank Holidays, 1st Monday in June, 1st Monday in August, and last Monday in October; Christmas Day, 25 December; St. Stephen's Day, 26 December. Movable religious holidays include Good Friday and Easter Monday.

TIME: GMT.

¹LOCATION, SIZE, AND EXTENT

An island in the eastern part of the North Atlantic directly west of the United Kingdom, on the continental shelf of Europe, Ireland covers an area of 70,280 sq km (27,135 sq mi). Comparatively, the area occupied by Ireland is slightly larger than the state of West Virginia. The island's length is 486 km (302 mi) N–S, and its width is 275 km (171 mi) E–W. The Irish Republic is bounded on the N by the North Channel, which separates it from Scotland; on the NE by Northern Ireland; and on the E and SE by the Irish Sea and St. George's Channel, which separate it from England and Wales. To the W, from north to south, the coast is washed by the Atlantic Ocean.

Ireland's capital city, Dublin, is located on the Irish Sea coast.

²TOPOGRAPHY

Ireland is a limestone plateau rimmed by coastal highlands of varying geological structure. The central plain area, characterized by many lakes, bogs, and scattered low ridges, averages about 90 m (300 ft) above sea level. Principal mountain ranges include the Wicklow Mountains in the east and Macgillycuddy's Reeks in the southwest. The highest peaks are Carrantuohill (1,041 m/3,414 ft) and Mt. Brandon (953 m/3,127 ft), near Killarney, and, 64 km (40 mi) south of Dublin, Lugnaquillia (926 m/3,039 ft).

The coastline, 1,448 km (900 mi) long, is heavily indented along the south and west coasts where the ranges of Donegal, Mayo, and Munster end in bold headlands and rocky islands, forming long, narrow fjordlike inlets or wide-mouthed bays. On the southern coast, drowned river channels have created deep natural harbors. The east coast has few good harbors.

Most important of the many rivers is the Shannon, which rises in the mountains along the Ulster border and drains the central plain as it flows 370 km (230 mi) to the Atlantic, into which it empties through a wide estuary nearly 110 km (70 mi) long. Other important rivers are the Boyne, Suir, Liffey, Slaney, Barrow, Blackwater, Lee, and Nore.

³CLIMATE

Ireland has an equable climate, because the prevailing west and southwest winds have crossed long stretches of the North Atlantic Ocean, which is warmer in winter and cooler in summer than the continental land masses. The mean annual temperature is 10°C (50°F), and average monthly temperatures range from a mild 4°C (39°F) in January to 16°C (61°F) in July. Average yearly rainfall ranges from less than 76 cm (30 in) in places near Dublin to more than 254 cm (100 in) in some mountainous regions. The sunniest area is the extreme southeast, with an annual average of 1,700 hours of bright sunshine. Winds are strongest near the west coast, where the average speed is about 26 km/hr (16 mph).

⁴FLORA AND FAUNA

Since Ireland was completely covered by ice sheets during the most recent Ice Age, all existing native plant and animal life originated from the natural migration of species, chiefly from other parts of Europe and especially from Britain. Early sea inundation of the land bridge connecting Ireland and Britain prevented further migration after 6000 BC. Although many species have subsequently been introduced, Ireland has a much narrower range of flora and fauna than Britain. Forest is the natural dominant vegetation, but the total forest area is now only 9.6% of the total area, and most of that remains because of the state afforestation program. The natural forest cover was chiefly mixed sessile oak woodland with ash, wych elm, birch, and yew. Pine was dominant on poorer soils, with rowan and birch. Beech and lime are notable natural absentees that thrive when introduced.

The fauna of Ireland is basically similar to that of Britain, but there are some notable gaps. Among those absent are weasel, polecat, wildcat, most shrews, moles, water voles, roe deer, snakes, and common toads. There are also fewer bird and insect species. Some introduced animals, such as the rabbit and brown rat, have been very successful. Ireland has some species not native to Britain, such as the spotted slug and certain species of wood lice. Ireland's isolation has made it notably free from plant and animal diseases. Among the common domestic animals, Ireland is particularly noted for its fine horses, dogs, and cattle. The Connemara pony, Irish wolfhound, Kerry blue terrier, and several types of cattle and sheep are recognized as distinct breeds.

As of 2002, there were at least 25 species of mammals, 143 species of birds, and over 900 species of plants throughout the country.

5 ENVIRONMENT

Ireland enjoys the benefits of a climate in which calms are rare and the winds are sufficiently strong to disperse atmospheric pollution. Nevertheless, industry is a significant source of pollution. In 1996, carbon dioxide emissions from industrial sources totaled 34.9 million metric tons. In 2002, the total of carbon dioxide emissions was at 42.2 million metric tons. Water pollution is also a problem, especially pollution of lakes from agricultural runoff. The nation has 49 cu km of renewable water resources.

Principal responsibility for environmental protection is vested in the Department of the Environment. The Department of Fisheries and Forestry, the Department of Agriculture, and the Office of Public Works also deal with environmental affairs. Local authorities, acting under the supervision of the Department of the Environment, are responsible for water supply, sewage disposal, and other environmental matters.

In 2003, about 1.7% of the total land area was protected, including 45 Ramsar wetland sites. According to a 2006 report issued by the International Union for Conservation of Nature and Natural Resources (IUCN), threatened species included four types of mammals, eight species of birds, six species of fish, one type of mollusk, two species of other invertebrates, and one species of plant. Threatened species include the Baltic sturgeon, Kerry slug, and Marsh snail. The great auk has become extinct.

6 POPULATION

The population of Ireland in 2005 was estimated by the United Nations (UN) at 4,125,000, which placed it at number 122 in population among the 193 nations of the world. In 2005, approximately 11% of the population was over 65 years of age, with another 21% of the population under 15 years of age. There were 99 males for every 100 females in the country. According to the UN, the annual population rate of change for 2005–10 was expected to be 0.8%, a rate the government viewed as satisfactory. The projected population for the year 2025 was 4,530,000. The population density was 59 per sq km (152 per sq mi).

The UN estimated that 60% of the population lived in urban areas in 2005, and that urban areas were growing at an annual rate of 1.37%. The capital city, Dublin (Baile Átha Cliath), had a population of 1,015,000 in that year. The other largest urban centers (and their estimated populations) were Cork (193,400), Limerick 84,900), Galway (65,832), and Waterford (44,594).

7 MIGRATION

The great famine in the late 1840s inaugurated the wave of Irish emigrants to the United States, Canada, Argentina, and other countries: 100,000 in 1846, 200,000 per year from 1847 to 1850, and 250,000 in 1851. Since then, emigration has been a traditional feature of Irish life, although it has been considerably reduced since World War II. The net emigration figure decreased from 212,000 for 1956–61 to 80,605 for 1961–66 and 53,906 for 1966–71. During 1971–81, Ireland recorded a net gain from immigration of 103,889. As of November 1995, more than 150,000 people had left Ireland in the previous 10 years, unemployment being the main reason. The top two destinations were the United Kingdom and the United States.

During the 1990s there was a considerable rise in the number of asylum seekers, from 39 applications in 1992 to 4,630 in 1998. The main countries of origin were Nigeria, Romania, the Democratic Republic of the Congo, Libya, and Algeria. Also, during the Kosovo crisis in 1999, Ireland took in 1,033 Kosovar Albanians who were evacuated from Macedonia under the UNHCR/IOM Humanitarian Evacuation Programme. In 2004 Ireland had 7,201 refugees and 3,696 asylum seekers. Asylum seekers are primarily from Nigeria and the Democratic Republic of the Congo and six other countries.

In 2005, the net migration rate was estimated as 4.93 migrants per 1,000 population, up from -1.31 in 1999.

8 ETHNIC GROUPS

Within historic times, Ireland has been inhabited by Celts, Norsemen, French Normans, and English. Through the centuries, the racial strains represented by these groups have been so intermingled that no purely ethnic divisions remain. The Travellers are group of about 25,000 indigenous nomadic people who consider themselves to be a distinct ethnic minority.

9 LANGUAGES

Two languages are spoken, English and Irish (Gaelic). During the long centuries of British control, Irish fell into disuse except in parts of western Ireland. Since the establishment of the Irish Free State in 1922, the government has sought to reestablish Irish as a spoken language throughout the country. It is taught as a compulsory subject in schools and all government publications, street signs, and post office notices are printed in both Irish and English. English, however, remains the language in common use. Only in a few areas (the Gaeltacht), mostly along the western seaboard, is Irish in everyday use. In 1995, a national survey found that only 5% of Irish people frequently used the Irish language and only 2% considered it their native tongue. About 30% of the population, however, claims some proficiency in Gaelic.

10 RELIGIONS

According to the 2002 census, about 88.4% of the population were nominally Roman Catholic. The next largest organization was the Church of Ireland (Anglican), with a membership of about 2.9%

of the population. About 0.52% of the population were Presbyterian, 0.25% were Methodist, 0.49 were Muslim, and less than 0.1% were Jewish. There are small communities Jehovah's Witnesses. For ecclesiastical purposes, the Republic of Ireland and Northern Ireland (UK) constitute a single entity. Both Roman Catholics and Episcopalian churches have administrative seats at Armagh in Northern Ireland. The Presbyterian Church has its headquarters in Belfast. The constitutional right to freedom of religion is generally respected in practice.

11 TRANSPORTATION

The Irish Transport System (Córas Iompair Éireann-CIE), a state-sponsored entity, provides a nationwide coordinated road and rail system of public transport for goods and passengers. It is also responsible for maintaining the canals, although they are no longer used for commercial transport. Ireland's railroads, like those of many other European countries, have become increasingly unprofitable because of competition from road transport facilities. There were 3,312 km (2,056 mi) of track in 2004, all of it broad gauge. CIE receives an annual government subsidy.

A network of good main roads extends throughout the country, and improved country roads lead to smaller towns and villages. Ninety-six percent of all inland passenger transport and 90% of inland freight are conveyed by road. Bus routes connect all the major population centers and numerous moderate-sized towns. In 2002, there were 95,736 km (59,548 mi) of roads, of which all were surfaced. In 2003 there were 1,520,000 passenger cars and 272,000 commercial vehicles in use.

In 2005, Ireland's merchant fleet consisted of 39 vessels of 1,000 GRT or more. The state-supported shipping firm, the British and Irish Steam Packet Co. (the B and I Line), is largely engaged in cross-channel travel between Ireland and the United Kingdom, providing passenger and car ferry services as well as containerized freight services, both port to port and door to door. The Irish Continental Line operates services to France, linking Rosslare with Le Havre and Cherbourg; it also runs a summer service between Cork and Le Havre. Brittany Ferries operates a weekly service between Cork and Roscoff. Other shipping concerns operate regular passenger and freight services to the United Kingdom and freight services to the Continent. There are deepwater ports at Cork and Dublin and 10 secondary ports. Dublin is the main port. As of 2004, Ireland had 753 km (468 mi) of navigable inland waterways, but which were accessible only by pleasure craft.

In 2004 there were an estimated 36 airports, of which 15 had paved runways as of 2005. Aer Lingus (Irish International Airlines), the Irish national airline, operates services between Ireland, the United Kingdom, and continental Europe as well as transatlantic flights. Many foreign airlines operate scheduled transatlantic passenger and air freight services through the duty-free port at Shannon, and most transatlantic airlines make nonscheduled stops there; foreign airlines also operate services between Ireland, the United Kingdom, and continental Europe. The three state airports at Dublin, Shannon, and Cork are managed by Aer Rianta on behalf of the Ministry for Transport and Power. A domestic airline, Aer Arann Teo, connects Galway with the Aran Islands

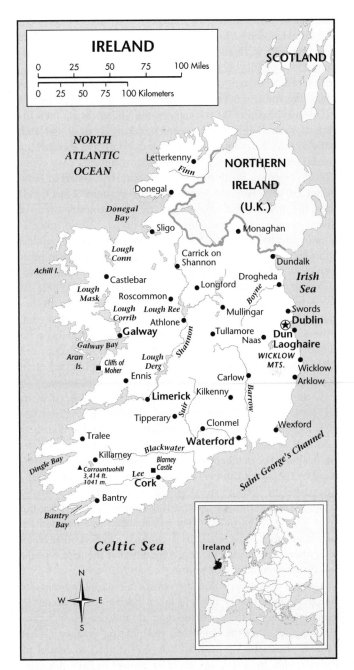

LOCATION: 63°19′ to 67°7′5″ N; 13°16′7″ to 24°32′3″ W. BOUNDARY LENGTHS: total coastline, 4,970 kilometers (3,090 miles). TERRITORIAL SEA LIMIT: 12 miles.

and Dublin. In 2003, about 28.864 million passengers were carried on scheduled domestic and international airline flights.

12 HISTORY

The pre-Christian era in Ireland is known chiefly through legend, although there is archaeological evidence of habitation during the Stone and Bronze ages. In about the 4th century BC, the tall, red-haired Celts from Gaul or Galicia arrived, bringing with them the Iron Age. They subdued the Picts in the north and the Érainn tribe in the south, then settled down to establish a Gaelic civilization, absorbing many of the traditions of the previous inhabitants. By the 3rd century AD, the Gaels had established five permanent kingdoms—Ulster, Connacht, Leinster, Meath (North Leinster), and Munster—with a high king, whose title was often little more than honorary, at Tara. After St. Patrick's arrival in AD 432, Christian Ireland rapidly became a center of Latin and Gaelic learning. Irish monasteries drew not only the pious but also the intellectuals of the day, and sent out missionaries to many parts of Europe.

Toward the end of the 8th century, the Vikings began their invasions, destroying monasteries and wreaking havoc on the land, but also intermarrying, adopting Irish customs, and establishing coastal settlements from which have grown Ireland's chief cities. Viking power was finally broken at the Battle of Clontarf in 1014. About 150 years later, the Anglo- Norman invasions began. Gradually, the invaders gained control of the whole country. Many of them intermarried, adopted the Irish language, customs, and traditions, and became more Irish than the Gaels. But the political attachment to the English crown instituted by the Norman invasion caused almost 800 years of strife, as successive English monarchs sought to subdue Gaels and Norman-Irish alike. Wholesale confiscations of land and large plantations of English colonists began under Mary I (Mary Tudor) and continued under Elizabeth I, Cromwell, and William III. Treatment of the Irish reached a brutal climax in the 18th century with the Penal Laws, which deprived Catholics and Dissenters (the majority of the population) of all legal rights.

By the end of the 18th century, many of the English colonists had come to regard themselves as Irish and, like the English colonists in America, resented the domination of London and their own lack of power to rule themselves. In 1783, they forced the establishment of an independent Irish parliament, but it was abolished by the Act of Union (1800), which gave Ireland direct representation in Westminster. Catholic emancipation was finally achieved in 1829 through the efforts of Daniel O'Connell, but the great famine of the 1840s, when millions died or emigrated for lack of potatoes while landlords continued to export other crops to England, emphasized the tragic condition of the Irish peasant and the great need for land reform.

A series of uprisings and the growth of various movements aimed at home rule or outright independence led gradually to many reforms, but the desire for complete independence continued to grow. After the bloodshed and political maneuvers that followed the Easter Uprising of 1916 and the proclamation of an Irish Republic by Irish members of Parliament in 1919, the Anglo-Irish Treaty was signed in 1921, establishing an Irish Free State with dominion status in the British Commonwealth. Violent opposition to dominion status and to a separate government in Protestant-dominated Northern Ireland precipitated a civil war lasting almost a year. The Free State was officially proclaimed and a new constitution adopted in 1922, but sentiment in favor of a reunified Irish Republic remained strong, represented at its extreme by the terrorist activities of the Irish Republican Army (IRA). Powerful at first, the IRA lost much of its popularity after Éamon de Valera, a disillusioned supporter, took over the government in 1932. During the civil violence that disrupted Northern Ireland from the late 1960s on, the Irish government attempted to curb the "provisional wing" of the IRA, a terrorist organization that used Ireland as a base for attacks in the north. Beginning in 1976, the government assumed emergency powers to cope with IRA activities, but the terrorist acts continued, most notably the assassination on 27 August 1979 of the British Earl Mountbatten.

The Irish government continued to favor union with Northern Ireland, but only by peaceful means. In November 1985, with the aim of promoting peace in Northern Ireland, Ireland and the United Kingdom ratified a treaty enabling Ireland to play a role in various aspects of Northern Ireland's affairs. On 10 April 1998 the Irish Republic jointly signed a peace agreement with the United Kingdom to resolve the Northern Ireland crisis. Ireland pledged to amend articles 2 and 3 of the Irish Constitution, which lay claim to the territory of the North, in return for the United Kingdom promising to amend the Government of Ireland Act. On 22 May 1998, 94.4% of the electorate voted in a referendum to drop Ireland's claim to Northern Ireland. A year after the agreement, several key provisions of the Good Friday Agreement had been implemented. The peace process has since then witnessed long moments of gloom in spite of the ongoing involvements of the British and Irish prime ministers to resolve the situation in Northern Ireland. One of the largest obstacles was the disarmament of the IRA and the reservations on the part of the Ulster Unionists to share power with Sinn Feìn, the political arm of the IRA. Finally, in May 2000, the IRA proposed that outside observers be shown the contents of arms dumps and reinspect them at regular intervals to ensure that weaponry had not been removed and was back in circulation. The Ulster Unionists agreed to power-sharing arrangements and to endorse devolution of Northern Ireland. Decommissioning of the IRA did not progress in early 2001, however, and David Trimble, the first minister of the power-sharing government, resigned in July 2001. Sinn Feìn's offices at Stormont, the Northern Ireland Assembly, were raided by the police in October 2002, due to spying allegations. On 14 October 2002, devolution was suspended and direct rule from London returned to Northern Ireland. Elections planned for the assembly in May 2003 were indefinitely postponed by British Prime Minister Tony Blair, due to a lack of evidence of peaceful intentions on the part of the IRA. Talks aimed at restoring devolved government in 2004 failed due to the continued IRA possession of illegal arms and its refusal to disband and pull out of illegal activities. Progress did not look eminent as of January 2005, when some IRA members were brutally murdered and the provisional government seemed to make attempts to protect those responsible for the murders from prosecution.

The years since the proclamation of the Irish Free State have witnessed important changes in governmental structure and international relations. In 1937, under a new constitution, the governor-general was replaced by an elected president, and the name of the country was officially changed to Ireland (Éire in Irish). In 1948, Ireland voted itself out of the Commonwealth of Nations, and on 18 April 1949, it declared itself a republic. Ireland was admitted to the UN in 1955 and became a member of the EC in 1973. Ireland, unlike the United Kingdom, joined the European economic and monetary union in 1999 without problem, and adopted the euro as its currency. However, Irish voters in June 2001 rejected the Treaty of Nice, which allowed for the enlargement of the EU. The other 14 members of the EU all approved the treaty by parliamentary vote, but Ireland's adoption required amending the constitution, which stipulated a popular vote. Voter turnout was low (34.8%), and when the treaty was put to Irish voters once again in October 2002, the government conducted a massive education campaign to bring voters to the polls. This time, voter turnout was 48.5%, and 63% of voters in the October referendum approved the Nice Treaty. Ten new EU candidate countries joined the body on 1 May 2004.

Ireland has also benefited from progressive leadership. Mary Robinson, an international lawyer, activist, and Catholic, was elected president in November 1990. She became the first woman to hold that office. In 1974, while serving in the Irish legislature, she shocked her fellow country people by calling for legal sale of contraceptives. Her victory came at a period in Irish history dominated by controversy over the major issues of the first half of the 1990s: unemployment, women's rights, abortion, divorce, and homosexuality. Robinson promoted legislation that enabled women to serve on juries and gave 18-year-olds the right to vote. In 1997, Mary McAleese, who lived in Northern Ireland, became the first British subject to be elected president of the Irish Republic until 2004. In March 2002, Irish voters rejected a referendum proposal that would further restrict abortion laws. The vote was 50.4% against the proposal and 49.6% in favor. The vote was a setback to Prime Minister Bertie Ahern. However, Ahern's Fianna Fáil party overwhelmingly defeated the opposition Fine Gael party in the May 2002 elections.

In June 2004, local and European elections were held. In October 2004, McAleese won a second seven-year term as President; however, this was in light of the fact that opposing parties didn't nominate alternative candidates. She will not be eligible for another reelection in the October 2011 elections. Senate elections were scheduled to occur in July 2007, and the House of Representatives were scheduled to be held one month prior, in May 2007.

13 GOVERNMENT

Constitutionally, Ireland is a parliamentary democracy. Under the constitution of 1937, as amended, legislative power is vested in the Oireachtas (national parliament), which consists of the president and two houses—Dáil Éireann (house of representatives) and Seanad Éireann (senate)—and sits in Dublin, the capital city. The president is elected by popular vote for seven years. Members of the Dáil, who are also elected by popular suffrage, using the single transferable vote, represent constituencies determined by law and serve five-year terms. These constituencies, none of which may return fewer than three members, must be revised at least once every 12 years, and the ratio between the number of members to be elected for each constituency and its population as ascertained at the last census must be the same, as far as practicable, throughout the country. Since 1981, there have been 166 seats in the Dáil.

The Seanad consists of 60 members: 49 elected from five panels of candidates representing (a) industry and commerce, (b) agricultural and allied interests and fisheries, (c) labor, (d) cultural and educational interests, and (e) public administration and social services; 6 elected by the universities; and 11 nominated by the taoiseach (prime minister). Elections for the Seanad must be held within 90 days of the dissolution of the Dáil; the electorate consists of members of the outgoing Seanad, members of the incoming Dáil, members of county councils, and county borough authorities. The taoiseach is assisted by a *tánaiste* (deputy prime minister) and at least six but not more than 14 other ministers. The constitution provides for popular referendums on certain bills

of national importance passed by the Oireachtas. Suffrage is universal at age 18.

The chief of state is the president, who is elected by universal suffrage to serve a seven-year term and may be reelected only once. The presidency is traditionally a figurehead role with limited powers. The president appoints a cabinet based upon a nomination from the prime minister and approval from the house of representatives. As of 2005, Mary McAleese held the presidential office. The head of government is the prime minister, who is nominated by the house of representatives and appointed by the president. As of 2005 Bertie Ahern was prime minister and had occupied the position since 26 June 1997.

A number of amendments having to do with European integration, Northern Ireland, abortion, and divorce have been added to the 1937 constitution, which may only be altered by referendum. A recent referendum in 2004 ended in a 4-to-1 vote that native-born children could not be granted automatic citizenship.

14 POLITICAL PARTIES

The major political parties are the Fianna Fáil, the Fine Gael, Labour, and the Progressive Democrats. Because the members of the Dáil are elected by a proportional representation system, smaller parties have also at times won representation in the Oireachtas. In 1986, Sinn Feìn, the political arm of the Provisional IRA, ended its 65-year boycott of the Dáil and registered as a political party winning one seat in the Dáil in the 6 June 1997 elections.

Fianna Fáil, the Republican Party, was founded by Éamon de Valera. It is the largest party since 1932 and has participated in government during 55 of the past 73 years, as of 2004. When the Anglo-Irish Treaty of 1921 was signed, de Valera violently opposed the dominion status accepted by a close vote of the Dáil. Until 1927, when the government threatened to annul their election if they did not fulfill their mandates, de Valera and his followers boycotted the Dáil and refused to take an oath of allegiance to the English crown. In 1932, however, de Valera became prime minister, a position he held continuously until 1947 and intermittently until 1959, when he became president for the first of two terms. From 1932 to 1973, when it lost its majority to a Fine Gael–Labour coalition, Fianna Fáil was in power for all but six years.

Fine Gael is the present name for the traditionally center-right party (of the Christian democratic type) and is second-largest party in Ireland. It grew out of the policies of Arthur Griffith, first president of the Irish Free State, and Michael Collins, first minister for finance and commander-in-chief of the army. W. T. Cosgrave, their successor, accepted the conditions of the 1921 treaty as the best then obtainable and worked out the details of the partition boundary and dominion status. This party held power from the first general election of 1922 until 1932. Since 1948, as the principal opponent of Fianna Fáil, it has provided leadership for several coalition governments. The policies of Fine Gael traditionally have been far more moderate than those of Fianna Fáil, although it was an interparty coalition government dominated by Fine Gael and Labour that voted Ireland out of the Commonwealth in 1948.

The Labour party incorporated the Democratic Left into its party in 1998, but still failed to increase its seats in the 2002 election (it is much smaller than Fine Gael). The party moved toward the center under the leadership of Pat Rabitte.

In 1985, a group of parliamentarians broke away from Fianna Fáil because of the autocratic leadership of Charles Haughey. They formed the Progressive Democrats (PDs) party, which supported liberal economic orthodoxy in the 1980s. It joined in a coalition with Fianna Fáil in 1997 and has been influential in economic policy making.

In the 2002 elections, two smaller parties increased their seat holdings. Sinn Fein, the political wing of the IRA, added four seats to the one it had won in the Dáil in 1997. The Green Party increased its holdings from two to six seats. It opposed European integration and participation in European security structures.

In the general elections of 24 November 1982 (the third general election to be held within a year and a half), Fianna Fáil won 75 seats, Fine Gael 70, and the Labour Party 16. Two members of the Workers' Party and three independents were also elected. Garret FitzGerald was elected taoiseach (1983-1987), heading a Fine Gael-Labour coalition. It was the second time in a year that he had replaced Charles J. Haughey of the Fianna Fáil in that office. In December 1979, Haughey had replaced Jack Lynch as head of his party and become prime minister. The 1987 elections saw Fianna Fáil raise its representation, despite a drop in its proportion of the vote compared to the 1982 elections. Fine Gael and Labour lost seats, while the Progressive Democrats and Workers' Party (which increased its representation from two to four seats) increased their seat holding. In a bitter contest, Charles Haughey was elected taoiseach (1987-1991) and formed a minority Fianna Fáil government. Albert Reynolds was taoiseach (prime minister) from 1991 to 1994.

An early general election in 1992 saw the two largest parties—Fianna Fáil and Fine Gael—lose seats to the Labour Party. Albert Reynolds of Fianna Fáil was reelected taoiseach of the Fianna Fáil-Labour Coalition. From 1994 to 1997, John Bruton, of the Fianna Gael-Labour-Democratic Left was prime minister. However, a center-right alliance led by Bertie Ahern of Fianna Fáil defeated Prime Minister Bruton's three-party left-of-center coalition in the 6 June 1997 general election. Although Bruton's own party, Fine Gael, increased its share of the vote, its coalition partners, the Labour Party and the Democratic Left, both lost seats. Fianna Fáil won 77 seats outright, 6 shy of the 83 required for a majority. Other parties winning seats were Labor (17), Democratic Left (4), Progressive Democrats (4), Greens (2), Sinn Fein (1), Socialists (1), and Independents (6).

Fianna Fáil joined with the Progressive Democrats and Independents to form a new government with Bertie Ahern as taoiseach (prime minister). In 1999, the Labour Party and the Democratic Left merged and the new party is called the Labour Party. The electoral significance of this realignment of the left is not yet clear, but the merger provides the Irish electorate with a more viable social democratic alternative to the governing coalition.

Bertie Ahern remained prime minister after Fianna Fáil won 41.5% of the vote on 16 May 2002, capturing 81 seats in the Dáil. Fine Gael won 22.5% of the vote and 31 seats, its worst defeat in 70 years. The Labour Party took 10.8% of the vote and 21 seats. Other parties winning seats were the Progressive Democrats (8), the Greens (6), Sinn Feìn (5), the Socialist Party (1), and Independents (13). The next presidential election was scheduled for October 2011 and the next legislative elections were scheduled for 2007.

15 LOCAL GOVERNMENT

The provinces of Ulster, Munster, Leinster, and Connacht no longer serve as political divisions, but each is divided into a number of counties that do. Prior to the passage of the new Local Government Act of 2001 and its implementation in 2002, Ireland was divided into 29 county councils, 5 boroughs, 5 boroughs governed by municipal corporations, 49 urban district councils, and 26 boards of town commissioners. Under the new system, the county councils remain the same, but the corporations no longer exist. The cities of Dublin, Cork, Limerick, Waterford, and Galway are city councils, while Drogheda, Wexford, Kilkenny, Sligo, and Clonmel are the five borough councils. The urban district councils and town commissions are now one and the same and known as town councils, of which there are 75.

Local authorities' principal functions include planning and development, housing, roads, and sanitary and environmental services. Health services, which were administered by local authorities up to 1971, are now administered by regional health boards, although the local authorities still continue to pay part of the cost. Expenditures are financed by a local tax on the occupation of property (rates), by grants and subsidies from the central government, and by charges made for certain services. Capital expenditure is financed mainly by borrowing from the Local Loans Fund, operated by the central government, and from banking and insurance institutions.

16 JUDICIAL SYSTEM

Responsibility for law enforcement is in the hands of a commissioner, responsible to the Department of Justice, who controls an unarmed police force known as the civil guard (Garda Síochána). Justice is administered by a Supreme Court, a High Court with full original jurisdiction, eight circuit courts, and 23 district courts with local and limited jurisdiction. Judges are appointed by the president, on the advice of the prime minister and cabinet.

Individual liberties are protected by the 1937 constitution and by Supreme Court decisions. The constitution provides for the creation of "special courts" to handle cases which cannot be adequately managed by the ordinary court system. The Offenses Against the State Act formally established a special court to hear cases involving political violence by terrorist groups. In such cases, in order to prevent intimidation, the panel of judges sits in place of a jury.

The judiciary is independent and provides a fair, efficient judicial process based upon the English common law system. Judicial precedent makes it a vital check on the power of the executive in Ireland. It can declare laws unconstitutional before and after they have been enacted, as well. Typically, however, the relationship between the judiciary and the other two branches of government has been untroubled by conflict.

The Supreme Court has affirmed that the inviolability of personal privacy and home must be respected in law and practice. This is fully respected by the government. Revelations about corruption by leading politicians forced the government to set up an independent tribunal. It investigated payments to politicians, especially to the former prime minister Charles Haughey, who was a recipient of large sums of money from businessmen for his personal use.

A former judge, Hugh O'Flaherty, was forced to resign from the Supreme Court over his handling of a dangerous driving case in 1999. His case provoked much public outrage after it was discovered that the government quickly boosted his annual pension prior to his resignation.

17 ARMED FORCES

The Irish army and its reserves, along with the country's air corps, and navy, constitute a small but well-trained nucleus that can be enlarged in a time of emergency. In 2005, the active defense force numbered 10,460, with reserves numbering 14,875. The army had 8,500 active personnel equipped with 14 Scorpion light tanks, 33 reconnaissance vehicles, 42 armored personnel carriers, and 537 artillery pieces. Navy personnel totaled 1,100 in 2005. Major naval units included eight patrol/coastal vessels. The air corps consisted of 860 personnel, outfitted with two maritime patrol and three transport aircraft. The navy also operated two assault and 11 utility helicopters. Ireland provided support to UN, NATO and European Union peacekeeping or military operations in 10 countries or regions. The defense budget in 2005 was $959 million.

18 INTERNATIONAL COOPERATION

Ireland, which became a member of the United Nations on 14 December 1955, belongs to ECE and several nonregional specialized agencies, such as the FAO, UNESCO, UNHCR, IFC, the World Bank, and WHO. On 1 January 1973, Ireland became a member of the European Union. The country is also a member of the WTO, the European Bank for Reconstruction and Development, the Paris Club, the Euro-Atlantic Partnership Council, and the OSCE. Ireland is a founding member of OECD and the Council of Europe. The country also participates as an observer in the OAS and the Western European Union.

Irish troops have served in UN operations and missions in the Congo (est. 1999), Cyprus (est. 1964), Kosovo (est. 1999), Lebanon (est. 1978), Liberia (est. 2003), and Côte d'Ivoire (est. 2004), among others. Ireland is a guest of the Nonaligned Movement, It is also a part of the Australia Group, the Zangger Committee, the Nuclear Suppliers Group (London Group), the Organization for the Prohibition of Chemical Weapons, and the Nuclear Energy Agency. In environmental cooperation, Ireland is part of the Basel Convention; Conventions on Biological Diversity, Whaling, and Air Pollution; Ramsar; the London Convention; International Tropical Timber Agreements; the Kyoto Protocol; the Montréal Protocol; MARPOL; the Nuclear Test Ban Treaty; and the UN Conventions on the Law of the Sea, Climate Change and Desertification.

19 ECONOMY

Until the 1950s, Ireland had a predominantly agricultural economy, with agriculture making the largest contribution to the GNP. However, liberal trade policies and the drive for industrialization stimulated economic expansion. In 1958, agriculture accounted for 21% of the GNP, industry 23.5%, and other sectors 55.5%. By 2002, however, agriculture accounted for only 5% of the total, industry 46%, and services 49%.

Ireland's economy was initially slower in developing than the economies of other West European countries. The government carried on a comprehensive public investment program, particularly in housing, public welfare, communications, transportation, new industries, and electric power. Growth rose quickly in the 1960s and, since then, the government has tried to stimulate output, particularly of goods for the export market. Thus, manufactured exports grew from £78.4 million in 1967 to £11,510 million in 1992.

In the 1970s Ireland began to approach the income of the rest of Western Europe until it lost fiscal control in the latter part of the 1970s due to the oil crisis. During the early 1980s, Ireland suffered considerably from the worldwide recession, experiencing double-digit inflation and high unemployment. The economy continued to lag through 1986, but the GNP grew 30% between 1987 and 1992, and continued at a yearly pace of about 7.5% until 1996 when it was expected to slow to about 5.25%. However, the Irish economy grew faster than any other in the European Union during the so-called "Celtic Tiger" years of the second half of the 1990s, when growth rates were in double digits. The good economic performance was mainly due to strong consumer and investor confidence and strong export opportunities.

Ireland suffered from the global economic slowdown that began in 2001, however, and the average annual growth 2000–04 was 6.1%. Though Ireland started out the decade with a growth rate of 6.2%, it dropped to 4.4% in 2003 and had not regained even a percentage point as of 2005.

Although substantially lower than in 1986 when it topped 18%, unemployment remained high until 1998, when it dropped to 7.7%. The estimated unemployment rate in 2005 was 4.2%. The inflation rate stood at 2.4% in 1998 and was 2% in 2003 and 3% in 2004. Inflation was steadily falling, from a rate of 4.9% in 2000 to 2.2% in 2004.

Ireland has depended on substantial financial assistance from the European Union designed to raise the per capita gross national product to the EU average. Almost $11 billion was allocated for the period 1993–99 from the EU's Structural and Cohesion Funds. During the 1990s, living standards rose from 56% to 87% of the EU average.

In the latter half of the 1990s, the economic situation greatly improved and Ireland recorded growth rates of 7% 1996–2000. Unemployment fell from 16% in 1993 to 5% in 2000. Due to the global economic downturn that began in 2001, however, even Ireland's booming economy slowed. Services, pharmaceuticals, and information technology are important sectors of the economy in the 21st century.

20 INCOME

The US Central Intelligence Agency (CIA) reports that in 2005 Ireland's gross domestic product (GDP) was estimated at $136.9 billion. The CIA defines GDP as the value of all final goods and services produced within a nation in a given year and computed on the basis of purchasing power parity (PPP) rather than value as measured on the basis of the rate of exchange based on current dollars. The per capita GDP was estimated at $34,100. The annual growth rate of GDP was estimated at 4.9%. The average inflation rate in 2005 was 2.7%. It was estimated that agriculture accounted for 5% of GDP, industry 46%, and services 49%.

According to the World Bank, in 2003 remittances from citizens working abroad totaled $337 million or about $84 per capita and accounted for approximately 0.2% of GDP.

The World Bank reports that in 2003 household consumption in Ireland totaled $54.84 billion or about $13,730 per capita based on a GDP of $153.7 billion, measured in current dollars rather than PPP. Household consumption includes expenditures of individuals, households, and nongovernmental organizations on goods and services, excluding purchases of dwellings. It was estimated that for the period 1990 to 2003 household consumption grew at an average annual rate of 5.6%. In 2001 it was estimated that approximately 21% of household consumption was spent on food, 10% on fuel, 4% on health care, and 7% on education. It was estimated that in 1997 about 10% of the population had incomes below the poverty line.

21 LABOR

In 2005, Ireland's workforce was estimated at 2.03 million. Of those employed in 2003, an estimated 6.4% were in agriculture, 27.8% in industry, and 65.4% in services. The estimated unemployment rate in 2005 was 4.2%.

The right to join a union is protected by law, and as of 2002, about 31% of the labor force were union members. The Irish Congress of Trade Unions (ICTU) represents 64 unions and is independent of political parties and the government. The right to strike, except for police and military personnel, is exercised in both the public and private sectors. Employers are legally prohibited from discriminating against those who participate in union activity. Collective bargaining is used to determine wages and other conditions of employment.

Children under age 16 are legally prohibited from engaging in regular, full-time work. Under certain restrictions, some part-time or educational work may be given to 14- and 15-year-olds. Violations of child labor laws are not common. The standard workweek is 39 hours, and the legal limit on industrial work is nine hours per day and 48 hours per week. A national minimum wage of $5.45 went into effect in 2001.

22 AGRICULTURE

About 1,184,000 hectares (2,926,000 acres), or 17.2% of the total area, were devoted to growing crops in 2003. About 6% of the agricultural acreage is used for growing cereals, 1.5% for growing root and green crops, and the balance for pasture and hay. Thus most of the farmland is used to support livestock, the leading source of Ireland's exports. Most farms are small, although there has been a trend toward consolidation. Agriculture accounts for about 10% of Irish employment. In 2003, there were 135,250 agricultural holdings, with a farm labor force of 104,540 full-time and 140,980 part-time workers. Principal crops (with their estimated 2004 production) include barley, 1,159,000 tons; sugar beets, 1,500,000 tons; wheat, 849,000 tons; potatoes, 500,000 tons; and oats, 134,000 tons.

Over half of agricultural production, by value, is exported. The benefits of the EU's Common Agricultural Policy, which provides secure markets and improved prices for most major agricultural products, account in part for the increase of Ireland's agricultural income from £314 million in 1972 (before Ireland's accession) to £1,919.9 million in 1995. The estimated value of crop output was €1.3 billion in 2005.

The government operates a comprehensive network of services within the framework of the Common Agricultural Policy, includ-ing educational and advisory services to farmers. Under a farm modernization scheme, capital assistance is provided to farmers for land development, improvement of farm buildings, and other projects, with part of the cost borne by the EU. In 1974, pursuant to an European Community directive, incentives were made available to farmers wishing to retire and make their lands available, by lease or sale, for the land reform program.

23 ANIMAL HUSBANDRY

With some 90% of Ireland's agricultural land devoted to pasture and hay, the main activity of the farming community is the production of grazing animals and other livestock, which account for about 53% of agricultural exports. In 2005, total livestock output was valued at €2.17 billion, with cattle and milk each accounting for around 40%. During 2002–04, livestock output was down 4.5% from 1999–2001.

The estimated livestock population in 2005 was 7,000,000 head of cattle (including 1.1 million dairy cows), 1,757,000 pigs, and 12,700,000 poultry. In 2005, butter production was estimated at 142,000 tons, cheese 118,750 tons, and wool (greasy) 12,000 tons. Milk production in 2005 was 5,500,000 tons.

Since livestock is a major element in the country's economy, the government is particularly concerned with improving methods of operation and increasing output. A campaign for eradication of bovine tuberculosis was completed in 1965, and programs are under way for eradication of bovine brucellosis, warble fly, and sheep scab.

24 FISHING

Salmon, eels, trout, pike, perch, and other freshwater fish are found in the rivers and lakes; sea angling is good along the entire coast; and deep-sea fishing is done from the south and west coasts. The fishing industry has made considerable progress as a result of government measures to improve credit facilities for the purchase of fishing boats and the development of harbors; establishment of training programs for fishermen; increased emphasis on market development and research; establishment of hatcheries; and promotion of sport fishing as an attraction for tourists. The Irish fishing fleet consisted of 1,376 vessels with a capacity of 77,888 gross tons in 2002.

Leading varieties of saltwater fish are mackerel, herring, cod, whiting, plaice, ray, skate, and haddock. Lobsters, crawfish, and Dublin Bay prawns are also important. In 2003, the value of fish exports was $453.5 million, up 32% from 2000. Aquaculture accounted for 19% of the volume. The total fish production in 2003 was 364,861 tons. Mackerel, herring, and blue whiting accounted for 24% of the volume that year.

25 FORESTRY

Once well forested, Ireland was stripped of timber in the 17th and 18th centuries by absentee landlords, who made no attempt to reforest the denuded land, and later by the steady conversion of natural forest into farms and grazing lands. In an effort to restore part of the woodland areas, a state forestry program was inaugurated in 1903; since then, over 350,000 hectares (865,000 acres) have been planted. More than half the planting is carried out in the western counties. In 2000, about 9.6% of Ireland was forested; about 95% of the trees planted are coniferous. The aim of the forestry program is to eliminate a large part of timber imports—a major drain on the balance of payments—and to produce a surplus of natural and processed timber for export. Roundwood removals totaled 2.5 million cu m (88 million cu ft) in 2004.

26 MINING

Ireland was a leading European Union (EU) producer of lead and zinc in 2003, and an important producer of lead, alumina, and peat. Mineral production in 2003 included zinc, 419,014 kg, compared to 252,700 kg in 2002; mined lead, 50,339,000 tons, compared to 32,486,000 tons in 2002; and an estimated 1.2 million metric tons of alumina. Other commercially exploited minerals were silver, hydraulic cement, clays for cement production, fire clay, granite, slate, marble, rock sand, silica rock, gypsum, lime, limestone, sand and gravel, shales, dolomite, diatomite, building stone, and aggregate building materials.

Zinc production centered on three zinc-lead mines, the Lisheen (a joint venture of Anglo American PLC and Ivernia West PLC), the Galmoy (Arcon International Resources PLC), and the Tara (Outokumpu Oyj), three of Europe's most modern mines. Outokumpu announced that because of low zinc prices, it was closing the Tara Mine (at Navan, County Meath), the largest lead-zinc field in Europe, and putting it on care and maintenance; the Tara came into production in the late 1970s. The Galmoy Mine was producing 650,000 tons per year of ore at target grades of 11.3% zinc and 1% lead, and the Lisheen Mine, which mined its first ore in 1999 and began commercial production in 2001, initially planned to produce 160,000 tons per year of zinc concentrate, to be increased to 330,000 tons per year of zinc concentrate and 40,000 tons per year of lead in concentrate at full production; both were on the Rathdowney Trend mineralized belt, southwest of Dublin. Cambridge Mineral Resources PLC continued diamond and sapphire exploration work, identifying numerous diamond indicator minerals and recovering significant quantities of ruby and sapphire. Gold was discovered in County Mayo in 1989, with an estimated 498,000 tons of ore at 1.5 grams per ton of gold. There was a marked increase in mining exploration beginning in the early 1960s, resulting in Ireland becoming a significant source of base metals.

27 ENERGY AND POWER

Ireland's energy and power sector is marked by a lack of any oil reserves, thus making it totally dependent upon imports. However, the country has modest natural gas reserves, and a small refining capacity.

In 2002, Ireland's imports of crude and refined petroleum products averaged 211,230 barrels per day. Domestic refinery production for that year averaged 65,230 barrels per day. Demand for refined oil products averaged 180,440 barrels per day.

Ireland's proven reserves of natural gas were estimated as of 1 January 2002 at 9.911 billion cu m. Output in 2001 was estimated at 815 million cu m, with demand and imports estimated at 4.199 billion cu m and 3.384 billion cu m, respectively, for that year.

Ireland's electric power generating sector is primarily based upon the use of conventional fossil fuels to provide electric power. Total generating capacity in 2002 stood at 4.435 million kW, of which conventional thermal capacity accounted for 4.049 million kW, followed by hydropower at 0.236 million kW and geothermal/ other at 0.150 million kW. Total power production in 2002 was 22.876 billion kWh, of which 94% was from fossil fuels, mostly thermal coal and oil stations, 3.9% from hydropower, and the rest from geothermal/other sources.

Ireland's Coal production consists of high-ash semibituminous from the Connaught Field, and is used for electricity production. In 2002, Ireland imported 3,148,000 short tons of coal, of which 3,090,000 short tons consisted of hard coal, and 58,000 short tons of lignite.

28 INDUSTRY

Since the establishment of the Irish Free State, successive governments encouraged industrialization by granting tariff protection and promoting diversification. Following the launching of the First Program for Economic Expansion by the government in 1958, considerable progress was made in developing this sector of the economy, in which foreign industrialists played a significant role. The Industrial Development Authority (IDA) administers a scheme of incentives to attract foreign investment. In addition, several government agencies offer facilities for consulting on research and development, marketing, exporting, and other management matters.

Official policy favors private enterprises. Where private capital and interest were lacking, the state created firms to operate essential services and to stimulate further industrial development, notably in the fields of sugar, peat, electricity, steel, fertilizers, industrial alcohol, and transportation. Although efforts have been made to encourage decentralization, about half of all industrial establishments and personnel are concentrated in Dublin and Cork.

Industry grew by an average annual rate of more than 5% from 1968 to 1981, and peaked at 12% in 1984 before subsiding to an annual rate of about 4%. The greatest growth was in high technology industries, like electronics and pharmaceuticals, where labor productivity also was growing substantially, thus limiting increases in the number of jobs. The most important products of manufacturing, by gross output, are food, metal, and engineering goods, chemicals and chemical products, beverages and tobacco, nonmetallic minerals, and paper and printing. The making of glass and crystal are also important industries. Industrial production continued to grow into the late 1990s, the "Celtic Tiger" years, posting a 15.8% growth in 1998.

Industry employed 28% of the labor force in 2000, and accounted for 36% of GDP in 2001. The value of industry output in 2000 was 12.3% higher than in 1999. Computer and pharmaceutical enterprises, largely owned by foreign companies, were responsible for high manufacturing output in 2000. Although there is no formal governmental privatization plan, the government planned to privatize the state-owned natural gas distributor (Bord Gas), the state-owned airline (Aer Lingus), and the state-owned electricity distributor (ESB) as of 2002.

Ireland was shifting attention away from industry and towards services. Activity was quickened by preferential corporation tax rates for manufacturers and manufactures were decreasing relative to services and agriculture. Yet, in 2004 the industrial production growth rate was 7%.

29 SCIENCE AND TECHNOLOGY

The major organizations doing scientific research in Ireland are the Agricultural Institute (established in 1958) and the Institute for Industrial Research and Standards (1946). The Dublin Institute of Advanced Studies, established by the state in 1940, includes a School of Theoretical Physics and a School of Cosmic Physics. The Royal Irish Academy, founded in 1785 and headquartered in Dublin, promotes study in science and the humanities and is the principal vehicle for Ireland's participation in international scientific unions. It has sections for mathematical and physical sciences and for biology and the environment.

The Royal Dublin Society (founded in 1731) promotes the advancement of agriculture, industry, science, and art. Ireland has 13 other specialized learned societies concerned with agriculture, medicine, science, and technology. Major scientific facilities include the Dinsink Observatory (founded in 1785) and the National Botanic Gardens (founded in 1795), both in Dublin.

Most scientific research is funded by the government; the government advisory and coordinating body on scientific matters is the National Board for Science and Technology. Medical research is supported by the Medical Research Council and Medico-Social Research Board. Veterinary and cereals research is promoted by the Department of Agriculture. The Department of Fisheries and Forestry and the Department of Industry and Energy have developed their own research programs. The UNESCO prize in science was awarded in 1981 for the development of clofazimines, a leprosy drug produced by the Medical Research Council of Ireland with aid from the Development Cooperation Division of the Department of Foreign Affairs.

Research and development (R&D) expenditures in 2001 (the latest year for which data was available) totaled $1.427 million, or 1.14% of GDP. Of that amount, 67.2% came from the business sector, with 25.2% coming from the government. Foreign sources accounted for 6%, while higher education provided 1.7%. As of 2002, there were some 2,471 researchers per one million people that were actively engaged in R&D. In that same year, high-tech exports were valued at $31.642 billion and accounted for 41% of manufactured exports. Ireland has 21 universities and colleges that offer courses in basic and applied science. In 1987–97, science and engineering students accounted for 31% of university enrollment. In 2002, a total of 29.3% of all bachelor's degrees awarded were in the sciences (natural, mathematics and computers, and engineering).

30 DOMESTIC TRADE

Dublin is the financial and commercial center, the distribution point for most imported goods, and the port through which most of the country's agricultural products are shipped to Britain and the Continent. Cork, the second-largest manufacturing city and close to the transatlantic port of Cobh, is also important, as is Limerick, with its proximity to Shannon International Airport. Other important local marketing centers are Galway, Drogheda, Dundalk, Sligo, and Waterford.

The trend in retail establishments was changing from small shops owned and operated by individuals, to larger department stores, outlets, and chain stores operated by management companies. As of 2002, there were about 52,000 retail and 2,500 wholesale outlets across the country. There were about 9,000 retail food outlets. A 21% value-added tax applies to most goods and services.

Principal Trading Partners – Ireland (2003)

(In millions of US dollars)

Country	Exports	Imports	Balance
World	93,037.3	53,781.6	39,255.7
United States	19,161.5	8,368.6	10,792.9
United Kingdom	16,835.7	16,611.1	224.6
Belgium	11,668.8	840.6	10,828.2
Germany	7,708.2	3,892.7	3,815.5
France-Monaco	5,689.6	2,116.5	3,573.1
Netherlands	4,773.8	1,898.3	2,875.5
Italy-San Marino-Holy See	4,233.5	1,203.9	3,029.6
Switzerland-Liechtenstein	3,014.8	552.2	2,462.6
Spain	2,654.8	743.2	1,911.6
Japan	2,415.6	2,591.6	-176.0

(…) data not available or not significant.

SOURCE: *2003 International Trade Statistics Yearbook,* New York: United Nations, 2004.

Office business hours are usually 9 or 9:30 AM to 5:30 PM. Shops are generally open from 9 AM to 6 PM, although most supermarkets are open until 9 PM on Thursday and Friday. In general, banking hours are 10 AM to 12:30 PM and 1:30 to 4 PM, Monday through Friday, and 3 to 5 PM on Thursday. Most offices are closed on Saturday, and shops close on either Wednesday or Saturday afternoon. Businesses may close for extended periods during the months of July and August.

31 FOREIGN TRADE

Ireland began opening to free trade in the 1960s. It is now one of the most open and largest exporting markets (on a per capital level). Growth was heavily encouraged by the export sectors in the 1990s and the average annual export volume growth was near an annual rate of 20% between 1996 and 2000.

Computers and office products have become some of Ireland's most profitable export products (28%). The country also manufactures musical instruments (5.2%), making 12.7% of the world's exports. Other export items include chemicals like nitrogen compounds (10.9%), electronic circuitry (5.2%), and medicines (4.9%).

As of 2003, the United States absorbed 20.5% of Ireland's exports, the United Kingdom 18.1%, Belgium 12.6%, Germany 8.3%, France 6.1%, Netherlands 5.1%, and Italy 4.6%. Import partners include the United Kingdom (34.8% of imports), the United States (15.6%), Germany (8.1%), and the Netherlands (4.1%). Imported commodities include data processing equipment, machinery and equipment, chemicals, petroleum and petroleum products, textiles, and clothing.

32 BALANCE OF PAYMENTS

The volume of Irish exports increased dramatically 1995–2000, registering an average annual growth of 16.9%; the rate of import growth over the same period was only slightly lower at 16.6%. The year 2000 was the first since 1991 that the current account was not in surplus. The reduction of the balance of payments surplus in the early 2000s suggested that the level of Irish imports was increasing due to increased demand for luxury items and services, rather than from a decline in exports. The US Central Intelligence Agency (CIA) reported that in 2002 the purchasing power parity of Ireland's exports was $85.3 billion while imports totaled

Balance of Payments – Ireland (2003)

(In millions of US dollars)

Current Account		**-2,105.0**
Balance on goods	37,807.0	
Imports	-51,763.0	
Exports	89,570.0	
Balance on services	-14,306.0	
Balance on income	-26,142.0	
Current transfers	536.0	
Capital Account		**442.0**
Financial Account		**951.0**
Direct investment abroad	-3,528.0	
Direct investment in Ireland	26,599.0	
Portfolio investment assets	-161,319.0	
Portfolio investment liabilities	106,389.0	
Financial derivatives	-2,355.0	
Other investment assets	-48,864.0	
Other investment liabilities	84,028.0	
Net Errors and Omissions		**-1,178.0**
Reserves and Related Items		**1,890.0**

(…) data not available or not significant.

SOURCE: *Balance of Payment Statistics Yearbook 2004,* Washington, DC: International Monetary Fund, 2004.

$48.3 billion resulting in a trade surplus of $37 billion. Irish export growth during those years, in fact, consistently surpassed EU growth. However, the slowdown in the global economy and the slower than predicted growth in the euro area was expected to negatively impact Irish exports.

33 BANKING AND SECURITIES

In 1979, Ireland joined the European Monetary System, thus severing the 150-year-old tie with the British pound. The Central Bank of Ireland, established in 1942, is both the monetary authority and the bank of issue. Its role quickly expanded considerably, particularly in monetary policy. Commercial deposits with the Central Bank have strongly increased since 1964, when legislation first permitted it to pay interest on deposits held for purposes other than settlement of clearing balances. Since July 1969, the Central Bank has accepted short-term deposits from various institutions, including commercial and merchant banks. With the advent of the European Monetary Union (EMU) in 1999, authority over monetary policy shifted to the European Central Bank.

The commercial banking sector is dominated by two main Irish-owned groups, the Bank of Ireland Group and the Allied Irish Banks Group. Successive governments have indicated that they would like to see a third banking force (possibly involving a strategic alliance with a foreign bank). Other major banks include the National Irish Bank, a member of the National Australia Bank, and Ulster Bank, a member of the National Westminster Bank Group. The International Monetary Fund reports that in 2001, currency and demand deposits—an aggregate commonly known as M1—were equal to $21.1 billion. In that same year, M2—an aggregate equal to M1 plus savings deposits, small time deposits, and money market mutual funds—was $94.1 billion. The money market rate, the rate at which financial institutions lend to one another in the short term, was 3.31%.

A number of other commercial, merchant, and industrial banks also operate. Additionally, Ireland's post office operates the Post

Office Savings Banks and Trustee Savings Banks. The Irish stock exchange has its trading floor in Dublin. All stockbrokers in Ireland are members of this exchange. The Irish Stock Exchange is small by international standards, with a total of 76 domestic companies listed at the end of 2001. Total market capitalization at the end of 2001 was (21.8 billion for the government securities market, making it one of the EU's smallest stock markets, however fast-growing.

The Stock Exchange Act came into effect on 4 December 1995, and separated the Dublin Stock Exchange from the London Stock Exchange. Since that date, the Dublin Stock Exchange has been regulated by the Central Bank of Ireland. As of 2004, there were a total of 53 companies listed on the Irish Stock Exchange, which had a market capitalization of $114.085 billion. In 2004, the ISEQ index rose 26% from the previous year to 6,197.8.

34 INSURANCE

Insurance firms must be licensed by the Insurance Division of the Ministry of Industry, Trade, Commerce, and Tourism. The regulatory body is the Irish Brokers' Association. The Insurance Acts of 1936 and 1989 outline the monitoring of insurers, brokers, and agents.

In Ireland, workers' compensation, third-party automobile, bodily injury, and property damage liability are compulsory. In 1997, shareholders of Irish Life, Ireland's largest life assurance company, unanimously approved the company's £100 million ($163 million) takeover of an Illinois life assurance company, Guarantee Reserve. In 2003, the value of direct premiums written totaled $17.328 billion, of which life premiums accounted for $9.037 billion. Hibernian General in 2003 was Ireland's top nonlife insurer, with net written nonlife premiums (less reinsurance) of $992.2 million, while Irish Life was the nation's leading life insurer with gross written life premiums of $2.362 million.

Public Finance – Ireland (1997)

(In millions of pounds, central government figures)

Revenue and Grants	**17,762**	**100.0%**
Tax revenue	13,990	78.8%
Social contributions	2,172	12.2%
Grants	925	5.2%
Other revenue	675	3.8%
Expenditures	**17,432**	**100.0%**
General public services	3,810	21.9%
Defense	506	2.9%
Public order and safety	…	…
Economic affairs	2,907	16.7%
Environmental protection	…	…
Housing and community amenities	366	2.1%
Health	2,835	16.3%
Recreational, culture, and religion	119	0.7%
Education	2,368	13.6%
Social protection	4,521	25.9%

(…) data not available or not significant.

SOURCE: *Government Finance Statistics Yearbook 2004,* Washington, DC: International Monetary Fund, 2004.

35 PUBLIC FINANCE

Ireland's fiscal year follows the calendar year. Expenditures of local authorities are principally for health, roads, housing, and social welfare.

The US Central Intelligence Agency (CIA) estimated that in 2005 Ireland's central government took in revenues of approximately $70.4 billion and had expenditures of $69.4 billion. Revenues minus expenditures totaled approximately $1 billion. Public debt in 2005 amounted to 27.5% of GDP. Total external debt was $1.049 trillion.

Government outlays by function were as follows: general public services, 21.9%; defense, 2.9%; economic affairs, 16.7%; housing and community amenities, 2.1%; health, 16.3%; recreation, culture, and religion, 0.7%; education, 13.6%; and social protection, 25.9%.

36 TAXATION

To stimulate economic expansion and encourage investment in Irish industry, particularly in the area of industrial exports, tax adjustments have been made to give relief to export profits, expenditures for mineral development, shipping, plant and machinery, new industrial buildings, and investments in Irish securities. As of 1 January 2003, with Ireland's accession to the EU, the government had mostly completed the transition of the tax regime from an incentive regime to a low, single-tax regime with 12.5% as the country's rate for most corporate profits. Passive income, including that from interest, royalties, and dividends, is taxed at 20%. Capital gains are also taxed at 20%. As of 2005, Ireland was party to double-taxation agreements with 42 countries the terms of which provide for the reduction or elimination of many capital income tax rates and related withholding taxes. The incentive 10% corporation tax rate, applied to industrial manufacturing, to projects licensed to operate in the Shannon Airport area, and to various service operations, was still in effect in 2003, but, in an agreement with the European Commission, was scheduled to be phased out by 2010.

Ireland has a progressive personal income tax with a top rate of 42% on incomes above €29,400 for single taxpayers. Married taxpayers are subject to a higher income threshold level. For those over 65 years old, tax exemptions amounted to €15,000 per person. Deductions were available for mortgage payments and pension contributions. Since 1969, the government has encouraged artists and writers to live in Ireland by exempting from income tax their earnings from their works of art. Royalties and other income from patent rights are also tax-exempt. The gift and inheritance taxes are based upon the relationship of the beneficiary to the donor. Between a parent and child, the tax-free threshold in 2003 was €441,200; for any other lineal descendent, the tax-free threshold was one-tenth this amount, or €44,120; and for any other person, one-twentieth, or €22,060. Land taxes are assessed at variable rates by local governments, and there is a buildings transfer tax based on the price of the transfer.

The major indirect tax is Ireland's value-added tax (VAT) instituted 1 January 1972 with a standard rate of 16.37% plus a number of reduced, intermediate, and increased rates. As of 1 March 2002, the standard rate was increased to 21% from 20%, and the reduced rate of 12.5% increased to 13.5% as of 1 January 2003. The re-

duced rate applies to domestic fuel and power, newspapers, hotels and new housing. Ireland also has an extensive list of goods and services to which a 0% VAT rate is applied including, books and pamphlets, gold for the Central Bank, basic foodstuffs and beverages, agricultural supplies, medicines and medical equipment, and, more unusually, children's clothing and footwear, and wax candles. A 4.8% rate applies to livestock by unregistered farmers. Excise duties are charged on tobacco products, alcohol, fuel, and motor vehicles. Per unit and/or annual stamp taxes are assessed on checks, credit cards, ATM cards, and Laser cards.

37 CUSTOMS AND DUTIES

From the time of the establishment of the Irish Free State, government policy was to encourage development of domestic industry by maintaining protective tariffs and quotas on commodities that would compete with Irish-made products. Following Ireland's admission to the European Community (now the European Union), the country's tariff schedule was greatly revised. The schedule vis-à-vis third-world countries and the United States was gradually aligned with EC tariffs and customs duties between Ireland and the EC were phased down to zero by July 1977. Duty rates on manufactured goods from non-EU countries range from 5–8%, while most raw materials enter duty-free. Certain goods still require import licenses and tariffs are based on the Harmonized System. The Shannon Free Trade Zone, the oldest official free trade area in the world, is located at the Shannon International Airport.

38 FOREIGN INVESTMENT

The Irish government has successfully attracted FDI (foreign direct investment) over the years with various policies and preferential tax rates. To stimulate economic expansion, the Industrial Development Authority encourages and facilitates investment by foreign interests, particularly in the development of industries with export potential. Special concessions include nonrepayable grants to help establish industries in underdeveloped areas and tax relief on export profits. Freedom to take out profits is unimpaired. Engineering goods, computers, electronic products, electrical equipment, pharmaceuticals and chemicals, textiles, foodstuffs, leisure products, and metal and plastic products are among the items produced. Much of the new investment occurred after Ireland became a member of the European Union.

Annual foreign direct investment (FDI) inflows into Ireland increased steadily through the 1990s. In the period 1988 to 1990, Ireland's share of world FDI inflows was only 70% of its share of world GDP, but for the period 1998 to 2000, Ireland's share of FDI inflows was over five times its share of world GDP. In 1998, annual FDI inflow reached $11 billion, up from $2.7 billion in 1997, and then jumped to almost $15 billion in 1999. FDI inflows to Ireland peaked in 2000, at over $24 billion, mainly from high-tech computer and pharmaceutical companies. FDI inflow dropped sharply to $9.8 billion in 2001 with the global economic slowdown.

Leading sources of foreign investors, in terms of percent of foreign companies invested in Ireland, have been the United States (43%), the United Kingdom (13%), Germany (13%), other European countries (22%), Japan (4%), and others (5%). As of 2000, the primary destinations of foreign investment were, in order, manufacturing, finance, and other services.

39 ECONOMIC DEVELOPMENT

Government policies are premised on private enterprise as a predominant factor in the economy. Specific economic programs adopted in recent decades have attempted to increase efficiency in agriculture and industry, stimulate new export industries, create employment opportunities for labor leaving the agricultural sector, and reduce unemployment and net emigration. In pursuit of these objectives, the government provides aids to industry through the Industrial Development Authority (IDA), the Industrial Credit Co., and other agencies. Tax concessions, information, and advisory services are also provided.

The IDA seeks to attract foreign investment by offering a 10% maximum corporation tax rate for manufacturing and certain service industries, generous tax-free grants for staff training, ready-built factories on modern industrial estates, accelerated depreciation, export-risk guarantee programs, and other financial inducements. IDA also administers industrial estates at Waterford and Galway. The Shannon Free Airport Development Co., another government-sponsored entity, administers an industrial estate on the fringes of Shannon Airport, a location that benefits from proximity to the airport's duty-free facilities. A third entity, Udaras Na Gaeltachia, promotes investment and development in western areas where Irish is the predominant language. As of 1986 there were some 900 foreign-owned plants in Ireland.

Price control legislation was introduced under the Prices Act of 1958, amended in 1965 and 1972. In general, manufacturers, service industries, and professions are required to obtain permission from the Ministry of Commerce and Trade for any increase. Price changes are monitored by a National Prices Commission, established in 1971. The economic plan for 1983–1987, called The Way Forward, aimed at improving the cost-competitiveness of the economy by cutting government expenditures and restraining the growth of public service pay, among other measures. The 1987–1990 Program for National Recovery is generally credited with creating the conditions to bring government spending and the national debt under control. The 1991–1993 Program for Economic and Social Progress was to further reduce the national debt and budget deficit and to establish a schedule of wage increases.

A 1994–1999 national development plan called for investment of £20 billion and aimed to achieve an average annual GDP growth rate of 3.5%. The government hoped to create 200,000 jobs through this plan, with funding by the state, the EU, and the private sector. Half of the money was earmarked for industry, transport, training, and energy.

At the end of the 1990s, Ireland boasted the fastest growing economy in the EU with a 9.5% GDP real growth rate in 1998. Total expenditures on imports and exports in 2000 were equivalent to 175% of GDP, far ahead of the EU average, which made Ireland's economy one of the most open in the world. Ireland became known as the "Celtic Tiger," to compare with the formerly fast-growing economies of East Asia prior to the Asian financial crisis of 1997. In 2000, the economy grew by 11.5%, the highest growth rate ever recorded in an OECD member country. Wage inequality grew, however, and spending on infrastructure failed to keep pace with social or industrial demands. Corporate taxes were as low as 12.5% in some circumstances in the early 2000s. Economic growth decelerated rapidly in 2001, to 6%. Inflation fell as did housing prices, but they rose again in 2002. Tax increases were expected in 2003 and 2004, and the government was facing pressures to cut spending. GDP growth was 4.4% in 2003 and 4.5% in 2004.

40 SOCIAL DEVELOPMENT

A social insurance program exists for all employees and self-employed persons, and for all residents with limited means. The system is financed through employee contributions, employer contributions, and government subsidies. Benefits are available for old age, sickness, disability, survivorship, maternity, work injury, unemployment, and adoptive services. There are also funds available for those leaving the workforce to care for one in need of full time assistance. The system also provides bereavement and a widowed parent's grant. The universal medical care system provides medical services to all residents. The workmen's compensation act was first initiated in 1897. Parents with one or more children are entitled to a family allowance.

The predominance of the Roman Catholic Church has had a significant impact on social legislation. Divorce was made legal only in 1995. Contraceptives, the sale of which had been entirely prohibited, became available to married couples by prescription in the early 1980s. In 1985, the need for a prescription was abolished, and the minimum age for marriage was raised from 14 to 18 for girls and from 16 to 18 for boys. Abortion remains illegal.

Domestic abuse and spousal violence remain serious problems, although improvements were seen in 2004. The government funds victim support centers, and there are active women's rights groups to address these issues. The law prohibits gender discrimination in the workplace, but inequalities persist regarding promotion and pay. The government addresses the issue of child abuse, and funds systems to promote child welfare.

The government attempts to curb discrimination against foreign workers and the ethnic community known as "Travellers." There have been reports of racially motivated incidents including violence and intimidation. In general, the government respects the human rights of its citizens.

41 HEALTH

Health services are provided by regional boards under the administration and control of the Department of Health. A comprehensive health service, with free hospitalization, treatment, and medication, is provided for low-income groups. The middle-income population is entitled to free maternity, hospital, and specialist services, and a free diagnostic and preventive service is available to all persons suffering from specified infectious diseases. Insurance against hospital and certain other medical expenses is available under a voluntary plan introduced in 1957.

Since World War II, many new regional and county hospitals and tuberculosis sanatoriums have been built. As of 2004, there were an estimated 237 physicians, 51 dentists, and 83 pharmacists per 100,000 population. In addition, there were more than 1662 nurses per 100,000 people, the third most per capita in the world.

While deaths from cancer, particularly lung cancer, and heart disease are rising, those from many other causes have been decreasing rapidly. Infant mortality has been reduced from 50.3 per 1,000 live births in 1948 to 5.39 in 2005. Tuberculosis, long a major cause of adult deaths, declined from 3,700 cases in 1947 to only 15 per 100,000 in 2000. Average life expectancy at birth in 2005 was 77.56 years. The general mortality rate was an estimated 8 per 1,000 people as of 2002. The major causes of death were heart and circulatory disease, cancer, and ischemic heart disease. Heart disease rates were higher than average for highly industrialized countries.

The HIV/AIDS prevalence was 0.10 per 100 adults in 2003. As of 2004, there were approximately 2,800 people living with HIV/AIDS in the country. There were an estimated 100 deaths from AIDS in 2003.

42 HOUSING

The aim of public housing policy is to ensure, so far as possible, that every family can obtain decent housing at a price or rent it can afford. Government subsidies are given to encourage home ownership, and local authorities provide housing for those unable to house themselves adequately. Housing legislation has encouraged private construction through grants and loans. Projected and existing housing needs are assessed regularly by local authorities, and their reports are the basis for local building programs, which are integrated with national programs and reconciled with available public resources.

According to the 2002 census, there were about 1,279,617 dwellings available in permanent housing units. Of these, about 74% were owner occupied. The number of households was listed as 1,287,958, with 43.7% of all households living in single-family detached homes. The average number of persons per household was 2.95.

43 EDUCATION

Ten years of education are compulsory. Primary school covers eight years of education, with most students entering at age four. This is followed by a three-year junior secondary school and a two-year senior secondary program. Some schools offer a transition year program between the junior and senior levels. This transition year is meant to be a time of independent study for the student, when he or she focuses on special interests, while still under the guidance of instructors, in order make a decision concerning the direction of their future studies. At the senior level, students may choose to attend a vocational school instead of a general studies school. While private, religious-based secondary schools were once the norm, there are now many multi-denominational, public schools available at all levels. Coeducational programs have also grown substantially in recent years. The academic year runs from September to June. The primary languages of instruction are Irish and English.

Primary school enrollment in 2003 was estimated at about 96% of age-eligible students. The same year, secondary school enrollment was about 83% of age-eligible students; 80% for boys and 87% for girls. It is estimated that nearly all students complete their primary education. The student-to-teacher ratio for primary school was at about 19:1 in 2003.

Ireland has two main universities: the University of Dublin (Trinity College) and the National University of Ireland, which consists of three constituent colleges in Dublin, Galway, and Cork. St. Patrick's College, Maynooth, is a recognized college of the National University. Universities are self-governing, but each receives an annual state grant, as well as supplementary grants for capital outlays. There are also various colleges of education, home eco-

nomics, technology, and the arts. In 2003, about 52% of the tertiary age population were enrolled in some type of higher education program. The adult literacy rate has been estimated at about 98%.

As of 2003, public expenditure on education was estimated at 4.3% of GDP, or 13.5% of total government expenditures.

44 LIBRARIES AND MUSEUMS

Trinity College Library, which dates from 1591 and counts among its many treasures the Book of Kells and the Book of Durrow, two of the most beautiful illuminated manuscripts from the pre-Viking period, is the oldest and largest library in Ireland, with a stock of 4.1 million volumes. The Chester Beatty Library, noted for one of the world's finest collections of Oriental manuscripts and miniatures, is also in Dublin. The National Library of Ireland, which also serves as a lending library, was founded in 1877 and houses over one million books, with special collections including works on or by Jonathan Swift and W. B. Yeats. The National Photographic Archive of over 600,000 photographs is also housed in the National Library. The University College Dublin library has more than one million volumes. The Dublin City Public Library system has about 31 branches and service points and holdings of over 1.5 million items.

Dublin, the center of cultural life in Ireland, has several museums and a number of libraries. The National Museum contains collections on Irish antiquities, folk life, fine arts, natural history, zoology, and geology. The National Gallery houses valuable paintings representing the various European schools from the 13th century to the present. The National Portrait Gallery provides a visual survey of Irish historical personalities over the past three centuries. The Municipal Gallery of Modern Art has a fine collection of works by recent and contemporary artists. There is a Heraldic Museum in Dublin Castle; the National Botanic Gardens are at Glasnevin; and the Zoological Gardens are in Phoenix Park. There is a James Joyce Museum in Dublin housing personal memorabilia of the great writer, including signed manuscripts. Yeats Tower in Gort displays memorabilia of W. B. Yeats. The Dublin Writers' Museum opened in 1991.

Public libraries and small museums, devoted mostly to local historical exhibits, are found in Cork, Limerick, Waterford, Galway, and other cities.

45 MEDIA

In 2003, there were an estimated 491 mainline telephones for every 1,000 people. The same year, there were approximately 880 mobile phones in use for every 1,000 people.

An autonomous public corporation, Radio Telefís Éireann (RTE), is the Irish national broadcasting organization. Ireland's second radio service, Raidio na Gaeltachta, an Irish language broadcast, was launched by RTE in 1972; it broadcasts VHF from County Galway. In 2004, there were an additional 49 independent radio stations. RTE operates three television networks and there is one independent television station. In 2003, there were an estimated 695 radios and 694 television sets for every 1,000 people. About 134 of every 1,000 people were cable subscribers. Also in 2003, there were 420.8 personal computers for every 1,000 people and 317 of every 1,000 people had access to the Internet. There were 1,245 secure Internet servers in the country in 2004.

In 2001, there were eight independent national newspapers, as well as many local newspapers. There were three major independent current affairs magazines along with hundreds of special interest magazines. Ireland's major newspapers, with political orientation and estimated 2002 circulation, are: *Sunday Independent*, Fine Gael, 310,500; *Sunday World*, independent, 229,000; *Irish Independent*, Fine Gael, 168,200; *Irish Times*, independent, 119,200; *Irish Examiner* (in Cork), 63,600; and *Cork Evening Echo*, Fine Gael, 28,800. Waterford, Limerick, Galway, and many other smaller cities and towns have their own newspapers, most of them weeklies. The Censorship of Publication Board has the right to censor or ban publication of books and periodicals. In 2003, the Board censored nine magazines for containing pornographic materials.

The constitution provides for free speech and a free press; however, government bodies may decree without public hearing or justification any material unfit for distribution on moral grounds. The Office of Film Censor, which rates films and videos before they can be distributed, can ban or require edits of movies which contain content considered to be "indecent, obscene, or blasphemous," or which expresses principles "contrary to public morality." In 2001, 26 videos were banned, primarily for violent or pornographic content. In 2004, one video was banned.

46 ORGANIZATIONS

The Chambers of Commerce of Ireland in Dublin is the umbrella organization for regional chambers. The Irish Congress of Trade Unions is also based in Dublin. There are trade unions and professional associations representing a wide variety of occupations. The Consumers Association of Ireland is active in advocating consumer information services.

The oldest and best known of the learned societies are the Royal Dublin Society, founded in 1731, and the Royal Irish Academy, founded in 1785. The Royal Irish Academy of Music was added in 1856, the Irish Society of Arts and Commerce in 1911, the Irish Academy of Letters in 1932, and the Arts Council of Ireland in 1951. Many organizations exist for research and study in medicine and science, including the Royal Academy of Medicine in Ireland.

National youth organizations include the Church of Ireland Youth Council, Comhchairdeas (the Irish Workcamp Movement), Confederation of Peace Corps, Federation of Irish Scout Associations, Irish Girl Guides, Girls' Brigade Ireland, Junior Chamber, Student Christian Movement of Ireland, Voluntary Service International, Workers Party Youth, Young Fine Gael, and chapters of YMCA/YWCA. The Irish Sports Council serves as an umbrella organization for numerous athletic organizations both on amateur and professional levels.

Civil rights organizations include the Irish Council for Civil Liberties and the National Women's Council of Ireland. Several organizations are available to represent those with disabilities. International organizations with chapters in Ireland include the Red Cross, Habitat for Humanity, and Amnesty International.

47 TOURISM, TRAVEL, AND RECREATION

Among Ireland's numerous ancient and prehistoric sights are a restored Bronze Age lake dwelling (*crannog*) near Quin in County Clare, burial mounds at Newgrange and Knowth along the Boyne, and the palace at the Hill of Tara, the seat of government up to the Middle Ages. Numerous castles may be visited, including Blarney Castle in County Cork, where visitors kiss the famous Blarney Stone. Some, such as Bunratty Castle and Knappogue Castle, County Clare, and Dungaire Castle, County Galway, offer medieval-style banquets, and some rent rooms to tourists.

Among Dublin's tourist attractions are the Trinity College Library, with its 8th-century illuminated Book of Kells; Phoenix Park, the largest enclosed park in Western Europe and home of the Dublin Zoo; and literary landmarks associated with such writers as William Butler Yeats, James Joyce, Jonathan Swift, and Oscar Wilde. Dublin has long been noted for its theaters, foremost among them the Abbey Theatre, Ireland's national theater, which was founded in 1904 by Yeats and Lady Gregory. Dublin was the European Community's Cultural Capital of Europe for 1991, during which time the National Gallery, Civic Museum, and Municipal Gallery were all refurbished and several new museums opened, including the Irish Museum of Modern Art.

Traditional musical events are held frequently, one of the best known being the All-Ireland Fleadh at Ennis in County Clare. Numerous parades, concerts, and other festivities occur on and around the St. Patrick's Day holiday of 17 March. Ireland has numerous golf courses, some of worldwide reputation. Fishing, sailing, horseback riding, hunting, horse racing, and greyhound racing are other popular sports. The traditional sports of Gaelic football, hurling, and camogie (the women's version of hurling) were revived in the 19th century and have become increasingly popular. The All-Ireland Hurling Final and the All-Ireland Football Final are held in September.

A passport is required of all visitors. Visas are not required for stays of up to 90 days, although an onward/return ticket may be needed.

Income from tourism and travel contributes significantly to the economy. Approximately 6,774,000 tourists visited Ireland in 2003, about 61% of whom came from the United Kingdom. That same year tourism receipts totaled $5.2 billion. There were 62,807 hotel rooms in 2002, with a 59% occupancy rate.

According to the US Department of State in 2005, the daily cost of staying in Dublin was $403; in Cork, $292.

48 FAMOUS IRISH

A list of famous Irish must begin with St. Patrick (c.385–461), who, though not born in Ireland, represents Ireland to the rest of the world. Among the "saints and scholars" of the 6th to the 8th centuries were St. Columba (521–97), missionary to Scotland; St. Columban (540?–616), who founded monasteries in France and Italy; and Johannes Scotus Erigena (810?–80), a major Neoplatonic philosopher.

For the thousand years after the Viking invasions, the famous names belong to warriors and politicians: Brian Boru (962?–1014), who temporarily united the kings of Ireland and defeated the Vikings; Hugh O'Neill (1547?–1616), Owen Roe O'Neill (1590?–1649), and Patrick Sarsfield (d. 1693), national heroes of the 17th century; and Henry Grattan (1746–1820), Wolf Tone (1763–98), Edward Fitzgerald (1763–98), Robert Emmet (1778–1803), Daniel O'Connell (1775–1847), Michael Davitt (1846–1906), Charles Stewart Parnell (1846–91), Arthur Griffith (1872–1922), Patrick Henry Pearse (1879–1916), and Éamon de Valera (b.US, 1882–

1975), who, with many others, fought Ireland's political battles. The politician and statesman Seán MacBride (1904-88) won the Nobel Peace Prize in 1974.

Irishmen who have made outstanding contributions to science and scholarship include Robert Boyle (1627–91), the physicist who defined Boyle's law relating to pressure and volume of gas; Sir William Rowan Hamilton (1805–65), astronomer and mathematician, who developed the theory of quaternions; George Berkeley (1685–1753), philosopher and clergyman; Edward Hincks (1792–1866), discoverer of the Sumerian language; and John Bagnell Bury (1861–1927), classical scholar. The nuclear physicist Ernest T. S. Walton (1903–95) won the Nobel Prize for physics in 1951.

Painters of note include Sir William Orpen (1878–1931), John Butler Yeats (1839–1922), his son Jack Butler Yeats (1871–1957), and Mainie Jellet (1897–1944). Irish musicians include the pianist and composer John Field (1782–1837), the opera composer Michael William Balfe (1808–70), the tenor John McCormack (1884–1945), and the flutist James Galway (b.Belfast, 1939).

After the Restoration, many brilliant satirists in English literature were born in Ireland, among them Jonathan Swift (1667–1745), dean of St. Patrick's Cathedral in Dublin and creator of *Gulliver's Travels;* Oliver Goldsmith (1730?–74); Richard Brinsley Sheridan (1751–1816); Oscar Fingal O'Flahertie Wills Wilde (1854–1900); and George Bernard Shaw (1856–1950).

Thomas Moore (1779–1852) and James Clarence Mangan (1803–49) wrote patriotic airs, hymns, and love lyrics, while Maria Edgeworth (1767–1849) wrote novels on Irish themes. Half a century later the great literary revival led by Nobel Prize-winning poet-dramatist William Butler Yeats (1865–1939), another son of John Butler Yeats, produced a succession of famous playwrights, poets, novelists, and short-story writers: the dramatists Lady Augusta (Persse) Gregory (1859?–1932), John Millington Synge (1871–1909), Sean O'Casey (1884–1964), and Lennox Robinson (1886–1958); the poets AE (George William Russell, 1867–1935), Oliver St. John Gogarty (1878–1957), Pádraic Colum (1881–1972), James Stephens (1882–1950); Austin Clarke (1890–1974), Thomas Kinsella (b.1928), and Seamus Heaney (b.1939), who won the 1995 Nobel Prize in literature; the novelists and short-story writers George Moore (1852–1932), Edward John Moreton Drax Plunkett, 18th baron of Dunsany (1878–1957), Liam O'Flaherty (1896–1984), Seán O'Faoláin (1900–91), Frank O'Connor (Michael O'Donovan, 1903–66), and Flann O'Brien (Brian O'Nolan, 1911–66). Two outstanding authors of novels and plays whose experimental styles have had worldwide influence are James Augustine Joyce (1882–1941), the author of *Ulysses,* and Samuel Beckett (1906–89), recipient of the 1969 Nobel Prize for literature.

The Abbey Theatre, which was the backbone of the literary revival, also produced many outstanding dramatic performers, such as Dudley Digges (1879–1947), Sara Allgood (1883–1950), Arthur Sinclair (1883–1951), Maire O'Neill (Mrs. Arthur Sinclair, 1887–1952), Barry Fitzgerald (William Shields, 1888–1961), and Siobhan McKenna (1923–1986). For many years Douglas Hyde (1860–1949), first president of Ireland (1938–45), spurred on the Irish-speaking theater as playwright, producer, and actor.

In addition to the genres of Irish folk and dance music, contemporary Irish popular and rock music has gained international attention. Van Morrison (b.1945), is a singer and songwriter from Belfast whose career began in the 1960s and was going strong in the 2000s. Enya (b.1961), is Ireland's best-selling solo musician. The Irish rock band U-2 is led by Bono (b.1960): Bono has also spearheaded efforts to raise money for famine relief in Ethiopia, to fight world poverty, to campaign for third-world debt relief, and to raise world consciousness to the plight of Africa, including the spread of HIV/AIDS on the continent.

⁴⁹ DEPENDENCIES

Ireland has no territories or colonies.

⁵⁰ BIBLIOGRAPHY

Aughey, Arthur. *The Politics of Northern Ireland: Beyond the Belfast Agreement.* New York: Routledge, 2005.

Gibbons, Luke, Richard Kearney, and Willa Murphy (eds.). *Encyclopedia of Contemporary Irish Culture.* London: Routledge, 2002.

Hachey, Thomas E. *The Irish Experience: A Concise History.* Armonk, N.Y.: M. E. Sharpe, 1996.

Harkness, D. W. *Ireland in the Twentieth Century: Divided Island.* Hampshire, England: Macmillan Press, 1996.

International Smoking Statistics: A Collection of Historical Data from 30 Economically Developed Countries. New York: Oxford University Press, 2002.

Maillot, Agnes. *The New Sinn Fé´in: Irish Republicanism in the Twenty-First Century.* New York: Routledge, 2004.

McElrath, Karen (ed.). *HIV and AIDS: A Global View.* Westport, Conn.: Greenwood Press, 2002.

O'Dowd, Mary. *A History of Women in Ireland, 1500–1800.* New York: Pearson Longman, 2005.

Roy, James Charles. *The Fields of Athenry: A Journey through Irish History,* Boulder, Colo.: Westview Press, 2001.

Turner, Michael Edward. *After the Famine: Irish Agriculture, 1850-1914.* Cambridge, UK: Cambridge University Press, 1996.

Wessels, Wolfgang, Andreas Maurer, and Jürgan Mittag (eds.). *Fifteen into One?: the European Union and Its Member States.* New York: Palgrave, 2003.

Whelan, Kevin. *The Tree of Liberty: Radicalism, Catholicism, and the Construction of Irish Identity, 1760-1830.* Cork, Ireland: Cork University Press in association with Field Day, 1996.

ITALY

Italian Republic
Repubblica Italiana

CAPITAL: Rome (Roma)

FLAG: The national flag is a tricolor of green, white, and red vertical stripes.

ANTHEM: *Fratelli d'Italia (Brothers of Italy).*

MONETARY UNIT: The euro replaced the lira as the official currency in 2002. The euro is divided into 100 cents. There are coins in denominations of 1, 2, 5, 10, 20, and 50 cents and 1 euro and 2 euros. There are notes of 5, 10, 20, 50, 100, 200, and 500 euros. €1 = $1.25475 (or $1 = €0.79697) as of 2005.

WEIGHTS AND MEASURES: The metric system is the legal standard.

HOLIDAYS: New Year's Day, 1 January; Epiphany, 6 January; Liberation Day, 25 April; Labor Day, 1 May; Assumption, 15 August; All Saints' Day, 1 November; National Unity Day, 5 November; Immaculate Conception, 8 December; Christmas, 25 December; St. Stephen's Day, 26 December. Easter Monday is a movable holiday. In addition, each town has a holiday on its Saint's Day.

TIME: 1 PM = noon GMT.

¹LOCATION, SIZE, AND EXTENT

Situated in southern Europe, the Italian Republic, including the major islands of Sicily (Sicilia) and Sardinia (Sardegna), covers a land area of 301,230 sq km (116,306 sq mi). Comparatively, the area occupied by Italy is slightly larger than the state of Arizona. The boot-shaped Italian mainland extends into the Mediterranean Sea with a length of 1,185 km (736 mi) SE–NW and a width of 381 km (237 mi) NE–SW. It is bordered on the N by Switzerland and Austria, on the NE by Slovenia, on the E by the Adriatic and Ionian seas, on the W by the Tyrrhenian and Ligurian seas, and on the NW by France, with a total land boundary length of 1,932 km (1,200 mi) and a coastline of 7,600 km (4,712 mi).

Situated off the toe of the Italian boot, Sicily has a surface area of 25,708 sq km (9,926 sq mi). Sardinia, which is about 320 km (200 mi) NW of Sicily, covers an area of some 24,090 sq km (9,300 sq mi). Within the frontiers of Italy are the sovereign Republic of San Marino, with an area of 61.2 sq km (23.6 sq mi), and the sovereign state of Vatican City, which covers 44 hectares (108.7 acres).

The long-disputed problem of Trieste, a 518 sq km (200 sq mi) area situated at the head of the Adriatic Sea, between Italy and Yugoslavia, was resolved in 1954, when Italy assumed the administration of Zone A, the city and harbor of Trieste, and Yugoslavia of Zone B, the rural hinterlands of the Istrian Peninsula. A treaty of October 1975 made the partition permanent.

Italy's capital city, Rome, is located in the west-central part of the country.

²TOPOGRAPHY

Except for the fertile Po River Valley in the north and the narrow coastal belts farther south, Italy's mainland is generally mountainous, with considerable seismic activity. During Roman times, the city of Pompeii, near present-day Naples (Napoli), was devastated first by an earthquake in AD 63 and then by the famed eruption of Mt. Vesuvius (1,277 m/4,190 ft) in AD 79. In the last century, a 7.2 magnitude earthquake in the Calabrian-Sicilian region occurred in December 1908 that leveled the cities of Reggio di Calabria and Messina and left about 100,000 dead. A quake in the south on 23 November 1980 (and subsequent aftershocks) claimed at least 4,500 lives.

The Alpine mountain area in the north along the French and Swiss borders includes three famous lakes—Como, Maggiore, and Garda—and gives rise to six small rivers that flow southward into the Po. Italy's highest peaks are found in the northwest in the Savoy Alps, the Pennines, and the Graian chain. They include Mont Blanc (4,807 m/15,771 ft), on the French border; Monte Rosa (Dufourspitze, 4,634 m/15,203 ft) and the Matterhorn (Monte Cervino, 4,478 m/14,692 ft), on the Swiss border; and Gran Paradiso (4,061 m/13,323 ft). Marmolada (3,342 m/10,965 ft), in northeast Italy, is the highest peak in the Dolomites.

At the foot of the Alps, the Po River, the only large river in Italy, flows from west to east, draining plains covering about 17% of Italy's total area and forming the agricultural and industrial heartland. The Apennines, the rugged backbone of peninsular Italy, rise to form the southern border of the Po Plain. Numerous streams and a few small rivers, including the Arno and the Tiber (Tevere), flow from the Apennines to the west coast. The highest peak on the peninsula is Corvo Grande (2,912 m/9,554 ft). Vesuvius is the only active volcano on the European mainland.

While altitudes are lower in southern Italy, the Calabrian coast is still rugged. Among the narrow, fertile coastal plains, the Plain of Foggia in northern Apulia, which starts along the Adriatic, and the more extensive lowland areas near Naples, Rome, and Livorno (Leghorn) are the most important. The mountainous western coastline forms natural harbors at Naples, Livorno, La Spezia, Genoa (Genova), and Savona, and the low Adriatic coast permits natural ports at Venice (Venezia), Bari, Brindisi, and Taranto.

Sicily, separated from the mainland by the narrow Strait of Messina, has the Madonie Mountains, a continuation of the Apennines, and the Plain of Catania, the largest plain on the island. Mount Etna (3,369 m/11,053 ft) is an isolated and active volcano in the northeast.

Sardinia, in the Tyrrhenian Sea, is generally mountainous and culminates in the peak of Gennargentu (1,834 m/6,017 ft). The largest and most fertile plains are the Campidano in the south and the Ozieri in the north. The principal bay is Porto Torres in the Gulf of Asinara.

³CLIMATE

Climate varies with elevation and region. Generally, however, Italy is included between the annual isotherms of 11°c and 19°c (52°F and 66°F). The coldest period occurs in December and January, the hottest in July and August. In the Po Plain, the average annual temperature is about 13°c (55°F); in Sicily, about 18°c (64°F); and in the coastal lowlands, about 14°c (57°F). The climate of the Po Valley and the Alps is characterized by cold winters, warm summers, and considerable rain, falling mostly in spring and autumn, with snow accumulating heavily in the mountains. The climate of the peninsula and of the islands is Mediterranean, with cool, rainy winters and hot, dry summers. Mean annual rainfall varies from about 50 cm (20 in) per year, on the southeast coast and in Sicily and Sardinia, to over 200 cm (80 in), in the Alps and on some westerly slopes of the Apennines. Frosts are rare in the sheltered western coastal areas, but severe winters are common in the Apennine and Alpine uplands.

⁴FLORA AND FAUNA

Plants and animals vary with area and altitude. Mountain flora is found above 1,980 m (6,500 ft) in the Alps and above 2,290 m (7,500 ft) in the Apennines. The highest forest belt consists of conifers; beech, oak, and chestnut trees grow on lower mountain slopes. Poplar and willow thrive in the Po Plain. On the peninsula and on the larger islands, Mediterranean vegetation predominates: evergreens, holm oak, cork, juniper, bramble, laurel, myrtle, and dwarf palm.

Although larger mammals are scarce, chamois, ibex, and roe deer are found in the Alps, and bears, chamois, and otters inhabit the Apennines. Ravens and swallows are characteristic birds of Italy. Abundant marine life inhabits the surrounding seas.

As of 2002, there were at least 90 species of mammals, 250 species of birds, and over 5,900 species of plants throughout the country.

⁵ENVIRONMENT

Italy has been slow to confront its environmental problems. Central government agencies concerned with the environment are the Ministry for Ecology (established in 1983), the Ministry of Culture and Environmental Quality, the National Council for Research, and the Ministry for Coordination of Scientific and Technological Research. Localities also have responsibility for environmental protection, but most of the burden of planning and enforcement falls on regional authorities. The principal antipollution statute is Law No. 319 of 1976 (the Merli Law), which controls the dis-

posal of organic and chemical wastes; enforcement, however, has proved difficult.

Air pollution is a significant problem in Italy. United Nations sources estimate that carbon monoxide emissions increased by 12% in the period between 1985 and 1989. In the 1990s Italy had the world's 10th highest level of industrial carbon dioxide emissions, which totaled 407.7 million metric tons per year, a per capita level of 7.03 metric tons. In 2000, the total of carbon dioxide emissions was at 428.2 million metric tons.

Water pollution is another important environmental issue in Italy. The nation's rivers and coasts have been polluted by industrial and agricultural contaminants and its lakes contaminated by acid rain. In 2001 the nation had 160 cu km of renewable water resources with 53% used in farming activity and 33% used for industrial purposes. Facilities for the treatment and disposal of industrial wastes are inadequate.

In July 1976, the city of Seveso, north of Milan (Milano), gained international attention after an explosion at a small Swiss-owned chemical plant released a cloud of debris contaminated by a toxic by-product, dioxin. More than 1,000 residents were evacuated, and pregnant women were advised to have abortions.

The long-term threat posed by flooding, pollution, erosion, and sinkage to the island city of Venice was highlighted by a disastrous flood in November 1966, which damaged priceless art treasures and manuscripts in Florence (Firenze). The digging of artesian wells in the nearby mainland cities of Mestre and Marghera so lowered the water table that the Venetian islands sank at many times the normal annual rate of 4 mm (0.16 in) a year between 1900 and 1975; with the wells capped as a protective measure, Venice's normal sinkage rate was restored. As of the mid-1980s, however, little effort had been made to control the number and speed of powerboats on the Grand Canal (the churning of whose waters causes buildings to erode), nor had the national government begun to implement a master plan for Venice approved in principle three years earlier. Rome has implemented a project designed, in part, to protect the Roman Forum and other ancient monuments from the vibration and pollution of motor vehicles.

In 2003, only about 7.9% of the total land area was protected. According to a 2006 report issued by the International Union for Conservation of Nature and Natural Resources (IUCN), threatened species included 12 types of mammals, 15 species of birds, 4 types of reptiles, 5 species of amphibians, 17 species of fish, 16 types of mollusks, 42 species of other invertebrates, and 3 species of plants. Threatened species include the Sicilian fir, the black vulture, the spotted eagle, the wild goat, the great white shark, and the red-breasted goose. The Sardinian pika is extinct.

⁶POPULATION

The population of Italy in 2005 was estimated by the United Nations (UN) at 58,742,000, which placed it at number 23 in population among the 193 nations of the world. In 2005, approximately 19% of the population was over 65 years of age, with another 14% of the population under 15 years of age. There were 94 males for every 100 females in the country. According to the UN, the annual population rate of change for 2005–10 was expected to be stagnant at 0.0%, a rate the government viewed as too low. The projected population for the year 2025 was 57,630,000. The population den-

ITALY

LOCATION: 47°05′ to 36°38′N; 6°37′ to 18°31′ E. BOUNDARY LENGTHS: Switzerland, 744 kilometers (462 miles); Austria, 430 kilometers (267 miles); Slovenia, 209 kilometers (130 miles); total coastline including islands of Sicily and Sardinia, 7,458 kilometers (4,634 miles); France, 514 kilometers (320 miles). TERRITORIAL SEA LIMIT: 12 miles.

sity was 195 per sq km (505 per sq mi), with the Po Valley being one of the most densely populated areas of the country.

The UN estimated that 90% of the population lived in urban areas in 2005, and that population in urban areas was declining at an annual rate of -0.04%. The capital city, Rome (Roma), had a population of 2,665,000 in that year. Other major cities and their estimated populations include Milan, 4,007,000; Naples, 2,905,000; Turin (Torino), 1,182,000; Genoa, 803,000; Florence, 778,000; Palermo, 721,164; and Bologna, 369,955.

⁷MIGRATION

Emigration, which traditionally provided relief from overpopulation and unemployment, now represents only a fraction of the millions of Italians who emigrated during the two decades prior to 1914. From 1900 to 1914, 16 of every 1,000 Italians left their homeland each year; by the late 1970s, that proportion had declined to about 1.5 per 1,000. Of the 65,647 Italians who emigrated in 1989, some 26,098 went to Germany; 16,347 to Switzerland; 5,277 to France; 4,076 to the United States; and 23,849 to other countries. Immigration in 1989 totaled approximately 81,201 people, of whom West Germans accounted for 13,198. In 1990, 781,100 immigrants lived in Italy. This figure did not include some 600,000 who were believed to be illegal immigrants.

The overall impetus to emigrate has been greatly reduced by economic expansion within Italy itself and by the shrinking job market in other countries, especially Germany. Nevertheless, Germany had 560,100 Italian residents at the end of 1991, and France had 253,679 in 1990. Particularly significant in the first two decades after World War II was the considerable migration from the rural south to the industrial north, but by the mid-1980s, this flow had become insignificant.

In 1998, Italy received a total of 7,112 asylum applications, an increase of over 380% over the 1,858 applications lodged in 1997. The main countries of origin were Serbia and Montenegro, Iraq, and Turkey. Refugee status was granted in 29.6% of decisions on the applications made in 1998. Italy also hosted 5,816 people who arrived in 1999 from Macedonia under the UNHCR/IOM Humanitarian Evacuation Programme. However, in 2004 there were no asylum seekers in Italy, but 15,604 refugees and 886 stateless persons of concern to United Nations High Commissioner for Refugees (UNHCR). In 2005, the net migration rate was estimated as 2.07 migrants per 1,000 population.

8 ETHNIC GROUPS

Italy has been the home of various peoples: Lombards and Goths in the north; Greeks, Saracens, and Spaniards in Sicily and the south; Latins in and around Rome; and Etruscans and others in central Italy. For centuries, however, Italy has enjoyed a high degree of ethnic homogeneity. The chief minority groups are the German-speaking people in the Alto Adige (South Tyrol) region and the Slavs of the Trieste area.

9 LANGUAGES

Italian, the official language, is spoken by the vast majority of people. While each region has its own dialect, Tuscan, the dialect of Tuscany, is the standard dialect for Italian. French is spoken in parts of Piedmonte and in Valle d'Aosta, where it is the second official language; Slovene is spoken in the Trieste-Gorizia area. German is widely used in Bolzano Province, or South Tyrol (part of the Trentino-Alto Adige region), which was ceded by Austria in 1919; under agreements reached between Italy and Austria in 1946 and 1969, the latter oversees the treatment of these German-speakers, who continue to call for greater linguistic and cultural autonomy.

10 RELIGIONS

Roman Catholicism, affirmed as the state religion under the Lateran Treaty of 1929, lost that distinction under a concordat with the Vatican ratified in 1985. However, the Catholic Church continues to hold a privileged status with the state. An estimated 87% of native-born Italian citizens claim to be members of the Roman Catholic faith; however, only about 20% are active participants. Jehovah's Witnesses form the second-largest denomination among native-born Italian citizens, with about 400,000 adherents. However, if immigrants are counted, the second-largest religion is Islam, with an estimated one million followers. About 100,000 people are Scientologists, 60,000 are Buddhists, 30,000

are Waldensians (a Calvinist sect), 30,000 are Jewish, and 20,000 are Mormons. The Orthodox and Protestant churches have small communities. Hinduism and Bahaism are also represented. About 14% of the population claim to be atheists or agnostics.

11 TRANSPORTATION

Italy's highway system, one of the world's best, in 2002 totaled 479,688 km (298,366 mi), all of which were paved, and included 6,620 km (4,117 mi) of expressways. These expressways carry heavy traffic along such routes as Milan-Como-Varese, Venice-Padua, Naples-Salerno, and Milan-Bologna-Florence-Rome-Naples. A major highway runs through the Mont Blanc Tunnel, connecting France and Italy. In 2003, there were an estimated 34,310,446 passenger cars and 4,166,033 commercial vehicles.

In 2004, Italy maintained a total of 19,319 km (12,016 mi) of standard and narrow gauge rail lines. Of that total, standard gauge accounts for 18,001 km (11,196 mi) of which 11,333 km (7,049 mi) are electrified, while 280 km (174 mi) of narrow gauge lines are electrified. The government owns and operates 80% of the rail system, the Italian State Railway (Ferrovie dello Stato-FS), including the principal lines. Connections with French railways are made at Ventimiglia, Tenda, and Mont Cenis; with the Swiss, through the Simplon and St. Gotthard passes; with the Austrian, at the Brenner Pass and Tarvisio; and with the Slovenian, through Gorizia.

The navigable inland waterway system, totaling about 2,400 km (1,490 mi), is mainly in the north and consists of the Po River, the Italian lakes, and the network of Venetian and Po River Valley canals. There is regular train-ferry and automobile-ferry service between Messina and other Sicilian ports. Freight and passengers are carried by ship from Palermo to Naples. Sardinia and the smaller islands are served by regular shipping. Regular passenger service is provided by hydrofoil between Calabria and Sicily, and between Naples, Ischia, and Capri.

As of 2005, Italy had 565 merchant vessels of 1,000 GRT or more, totaling 8,970,017 GRT. Genoa and Savona on the northwest coast and Venice on the Adriatic handle the major share of traffic to and from the northern industrial centers. Naples, second only to Genoa, is the principal port for central and southern Italy, while Livorno is the natural outlet for Florence, Bologna, and Perugia. Messina, Palermo, and Catania are the chief Sicilian ports, and Cagliari handles most Sardinian exports.

In 2004 there were an estimated 134 airports. As of 2005, a total of 98 had paved runways, and there were also three heliports. Italy's one national airline, Alitalia, which is almost entirely government-owned, maintains an extensive domestic and international network of air routes. Rome's Fiumicino and Milan's Malpensa and Linate are among the most important airports, being served by nearly every major international air carrier. In 2003, Italian civil aviation performed a total of 1,359 million freight ton-km and carried about 34.953 million passengers on scheduled domestic and international airline flights.

12 HISTORY

The Italian patrimony, based on Roman antecedents—with a tradition that extends over 2,500 years—is the oldest in Europe, next to Greece's. The Ligurians, Sabines, and Umbrians were among the earliest-known inhabitants of Italy, but in the 9th century BC they were largely displaced in central Italy by the Etruscans, a seafaring people, probably from Asia Minor. Shortly thereafter there followed conquests in Sicily and southern Italy by the Phoenicians and the Greeks. By 650 BC, Italy was divided into ethnic areas: the Umbrians in the north, the Ligurians in the northwest, the Latins and Etruscans in the central regions, and the Greeks and Phoenicians in the south and Sicily. The Etruscan civilization, a great maritime, commercial, and artistic culture, reached its peak about the 7th century, but by 509 BC, when the Romans overthrew their Etruscan monarchs, its control in Italy was on the wane. By 350 BC, after a series of wars with both Greeks and Etruscans, the Latins, with Rome as their capital, gained the ascendancy, and by 272 BC, they managed to unite the entire Italian peninsula.

This period of unification was followed by one of conquest in the Mediterranean, beginning with the First Punic War against Carthage (264–241 BC). In the course of the century-long struggle against Carthage, the Romans conquered Sicily, Sardinia, and Corsica. Finally, in 146 BC, at the conclusion of the Third Punic War, with Carthage completely destroyed and its inhabitants enslaved, Rome became the dominant power in the Mediterranean. From its inception, Rome was a republican city-state, but four famous civil conflicts destroyed the republic: Sulla against Marius and his son (88–82 BC), Julius Caesar against Pompey (49–45 BC), Brutus and Cassius against Mark Antony and Octavian (43 BC), and Mark Antony against Octavian. Octavian, the final victor (31 BC), was accorded the title of Augustus ("exalted") by the Senate and thereby became the first Roman emperor. Under imperial rule, Rome undertook a series of conquests that brought Roman law, Roman administration, and Pax Romana ("Roman peace") to an area extending from the Atlantic to the Rhine, to the British Isles, to the Iberian Peninsula and large parts of North Africa, and to the Middle East as far as the Euphrates.

After two centuries of successful rule, in the 3rd century AD, Rome was threatened by internal discord and menaced by Germanic and Asian invaders, commonly called barbarians (from the Latin word *barbari*, "foreigners"). Emperor Diocletian's administrative division of the empire into two parts in 285 provided only temporary relief; it became permanent in 395. In 313, Emperor Constantine accepted Christianity, and churches thereafter rose throughout the empire. However, he also moved his capital from Rome to Constantinople, greatly reducing the importance of the former. From the 4th to the 5th century, the Western Roman Empire disintegrated under the blows of barbarian invasions, finally falling in 476, and the unity of Italy came to an end. For a time, Italy was protected by the Byzantine (Eastern Roman) Empire, but a continuing conflict between the bishop of Rome, or pope, and the Byzantine emperor culminated in a schism during the first half of the 8th century.

After the fall of the Roman Empire and the reorganization of the peninsula, from the 6th to the 13th century, Italy suffered a variety of invaders and rulers: the Lombards in the 6th century, the Franks in the 8th century, the Saracens in the 9th, and the Germans in the 10th. The German emperors (of the Holy Roman Empire), the popes, and the rising Italian city-states vied for power from the 10th to the 14th century, and Italy was divided into several, often hostile, territories: in the south, the Kingdom of Naples, under Norman and Angevin rule; in the central area, the Papal States; and in the north, a welter of large and small city-states, such as Venice, Milan, Florence, and Bologna.

By the 13th century, the city-states had emerged as centers of commerce and of the arts and sciences. Venice, in particular, had become a major maritime power, and the city-states as a group acted as a conduit for goods and learning from the Byzantine and Islamic empires. In this capacity, they provided great impetus to the developing Renaissance, which between the 13th and 16th centuries led to an unparalleled flourishing of the arts, literature, music, and science. However, the emergence of Portugal and Spain as great seagoing nations at the end of the 15th century undercut Italian prosperity. After the Italian Wars (1494–1559), in which France tried unsuccessfully to extend its influence in Italy, Spain emerged as the dominant force in the region. Venice, Milan, and other city-states retained at least some of their former greatness during this period, as did Savoy-Piedmont, protected by the Alps and well defended by its vigorous rulers.

Economic hardship, waves of the plague, and religious unrest tormented the region throughout the 17th century and into the 18th. The French Revolution was brought to the Italian peninsula by Napoleon, and the concepts of nationalism and liberalism infiltrated everywhere. Short-lived republics and even a Kingdom of Italy (under Napoleon's stepson Eugene) were formed. But reaction set in with the Congress of Vienna (1815), and many of the old rulers and systems were restored under Austrian domination. The concept of nationalism continued strong, however, and sporadic outbreaks led by such inveterate reformers as Giuseppe Mazzini occurred in several parts of the peninsula down to 1848–49. This Risorgimento ("resurgence") movement was brought to a successful conclusion under the able guidance of Count Camillo Cavour, prime minister of Piedmont. Cavour managed to unite most of Italy under the headship of Victor Emmanuel II of the house of Savoy, and on 17 March 1861, the Kingdom of Italy was proclaimed with Victor Emmanuel II as king. Giuseppe Garibaldi, the popular republican hero of Italy, contributed much to this achievement and to the subsequent incorporation of the Papal States under the Italian monarch. Italian troops occupied Rome in 1870, and in July 1871, it formally became the capital of the kingdom. Pope Pius IX, a longtime rival of Italian kings, considered himself a "prisoner" of the Vatican and refused to cooperate with the royal administration.

The 20th Century

The new monarchy aspired to great-power status but was severely handicapped by domestic social and economic conditions, particularly in the south. Political and social reforms introduced by Premier Giovanni Giolitti in the first decade of the 20th century improved Italy's status among Western powers but failed to overcome such basic problems as poverty and illiteracy. Giolitti resigned in March 1914 and was succeeded by Antonia Salandra. During World War I, Italy, previously an ally of the Central Powers, declared itself neutral in 1914 and a year later, in April 1915, joined the British and French in exchange for advantages offered by the secret Treaty of London. At the Versailles Peace Conference, Italy, which had suffered heavy losses on the Alpine front and felt slighted by its Western allies, failed to obtain all of the territories that it claimed.

This disappointment, coupled with the severe economic depression of the postwar period, created great social unrest and led eventually to the rise of Benito Mussolini, who, after leading his Fascist followers in a mass march on Rome, became premier in 1922. He established a Fascist dictatorship, a corporate state, which scored early successes in social welfare, employment, and transportation; in 1929, he negotiated the Lateran Treaties, under which the Holy See became sovereign within the newly constituted Vatican City State and Roman Catholicism was reaffirmed as Italy's official religion (the latter provision was abolished in 1984). The military conquest of Ethiopia (1935–36) added to Italy's colonial strength and exposed the inability of the League of Nations to punish aggression or keep the peace.

Italy joined Germany in World War II, but defeats in Greece and North Africa and the Allied invasion of Sicily toppled Mussolini's regime on 25 July 1943. Soon Italy was divided into two warring zones, one controlled by the Allies in the south and the other (including Rome) held by the Germans, who had quickly moved in, rescued Mussolini, and established him as head of the puppet "Italian Social Republic." When German power collapsed, Mussolini was captured and executed by Italian partisans.

The conclusion of the war left Italy poverty-stricken and politically disunited. In 1946, Italy became a republic by plebiscite; in the following year, a new constitution was drafted, which went into effect in 1948. Under the peace treaty of 10 February 1947, Italy was required to pay $360 million in reparations to the USSR, Yugoslavia, Greece, Ethiopia, and Albania. By this time, the Italian economy, initially disorganized by Mussolini's dream of national self-sufficiency and later physically devastated by the war, was in a state of near collapse. By the early 1950s, however, with foreign assistance (including $1,516.7 million from the United States under the Marshall Plan), Italy managed to restore its economy to the prewar level. From this point, the Italian economy experienced unprecedented development through the 1960s and 1970s.

Politically, postwar Italy has been marked by a pattern of accelerating instability, with 48 different coalition governments through 15 March 1988. In May 1981, the coalition of Prime Minister Arnaldo Forlani was brought down after it was learned that many government officials, including three cabinet ministers, were members of a secret Masonic lodge, Propaganda Due (P-2), that had reportedly been involved in illegal right-wing activities. Left-wing terrorism, notably by the Red Brigades (Brigate Rosse), also plagued Italy in the 1970s and early 1980s. In January 1983, 23 Red Brigade members were sentenced to life imprisonment in connection with the kidnapping and murder of Prime Minister Aldo Moro in 1978; another 36 members received sentences of varying lengths for other crimes, including 11 murders and 11 attempted murders, committed between 1976 and 1980. By the mid-1980s, the Mafia actively engaged in extortion, government corruption, and violent crime, as well as a central role in global heroin trafficking.

By 1986, however, internal security had improved. A major effort against organized crime was under way in the mid-1980s; over 1,000 suspects were tried and the majority convicted in trials that took place in Naples beginning in February 1985 and in Sicily beginning in February 1986.

Revelations of corruption and scandals involving senior politicians, members of the government administration, and business leaders rocked Italy in the early 1990s. Hundreds of politicians, party leaders, and industrialists were either under arrest or under investigation. The scandals discredited the major parties that had governed Italy since 1948, and the instability gave impetus to new reformist groups.

In August 1993, Italy made significant changes in its electoral system. Three-fourths of the seats in both the Chamber and the Senate would be filled by simple majority voting. The remainder would be allocated by proportional representation to those parties securing at least 4% of the vote. The first elections under the new system in March 1994 resulted in a simplification of electoral alliances and brought a center-right government to power. Silvio Berlusconi, founder of the "Go Italy" (Forza Italia) movement, emerged as prime minister. Berlusconi, a successful Italian businessman, was a newcomer to Italian politics. He was supported by the Alliance for Freedom coalition, which had received over 42% of the vote and 366 seats.

Berlusconi's government, however, became victim to charges of government corruption and on 22 December 1994 he was forced to resign in the face of a revolt by the Northern League, one of the parties in his ruling coalition. Three weeks after Berlusconi's resignation, his treasury minister, Lamberto Dini was named prime minister. He formed a government of technocrats and set about to enact fiscal and electoral reforms. Pragmatism and a lack of viable alternatives kept him in power until supporters of his main political rival, Silvio Berlusconi, presented a motion that he step down. When Dini learned that two splinter groups in his center-left coalition (the Greens and the Communist Refounding party) would not vote in his favor, he resigned on 11 January 1996 rather than face a no-confidence vote.

The elections, held on 21 April 1996, saw a center-left coalition, dominated by the former communists (DS), take control of the country for the first time in 50 years. Romano Prodi, an economics professor with little political experience, was chosen to serve as prime minister on 16 May. His coalition government collapsed after it failed to win a vote of no-confidence over the budget. President Oscar Luigi Scalfaro asked Massimo D'Alema, the leader of the DS and of the largest party in the Olive Tree, to form a new administration. His cabinet retained the same members from the left and center as before. This government also continued to pursue fiscal consolidation to join European economic and monetary union in 1999. Prodi left for Brussels to take up the presidency of the European Commission in May 1999. D'Alema reshuffled his cabinet in 1999 but it finally fell in April 2000. The immediate cause was the dismal performance in regional elections. The center-left won 7 out of 15 regions while the right, under the leadership of Silvio Berlusconi, took 8 regions.

The coalition of 12 discordant political blocs backed the Treasury Minister, Giuliano Amato, to become the new prime minister (appointed by President Carlo Azeglio Ciampi, in office since May 1999). Prior to the fall of the D'Alema administration, the government had scheduled an important referendum to scrap the last remaining vestiges of direct proportional representation in the electoral system. Only one-third of the electorate bothered to vote on 21 May 2000, not enough to validate the referendum outcome.

Berlusconi's House of Liberties coalition, led by Go Italy, secured 368 seats in the Chamber of Deputies in the May 2001 parliamentary elections, to the Olive Tree coalition's 242 seats. (The House of Liberties coalition also won a majority in the Senate.) After becoming Italy's 59th postwar prime minister, Berlusconi faced long-standing charges of criminal wrongdoing, including bribery; he became the first sitting Italian prime minister to appear at his own trial. It was not until December 2004 that Berlusconi was cleared of all charges.

Italy offered the use of its airspace and military bases to the US-led coalition in its war with Iraq, which began on 19 March 2003, although Italy did not send troops to the region and did not allow coalition forces to launch a direct attack on Iraq from Italy. Some 75% of Italians opposed the use of military force against the Saddam Hussein regime, but Berlusconi adopted a position of solidarity with the US-led coalition.

13 GOVERNMENT

In a plebiscite on 2 June 1946, the Italian people voted (12,700,000 to 10,700,000) to end the constitutional monarchy, which had existed since 1861, and establish a republic. At the same time, a constituent assembly was elected, which proceeded to draft and approve a new constitution; it came into force on 2 January 1948. Under this constitution, as amended, the head of the Italian Republic is the president, who is elected for a seven-year term by an electoral college consisting of both houses of parliament and 58 regional representatives. Elections for a new president must be held 30 days before the end of the presidential term. Presidential powers and duties include nomination of the prime minister (referred to as president of the Council of Ministers) who, in turn, chooses a Council of Ministers (cabinet) with the approval of the president; the power to dissolve parliament, except during the last six months of the presidential term of office; representation of the state on important occasions; ratification of treaties after parliamentary authorization; and the power to grant pardons and commute penalties. Although the constitution limits presidential powers, a strong president can play an important political as well as ceremonial role.

Legislative power is vested in the bicameral parliament, consisting of the Chamber of Deputies and the Senate. Members of the 630-seat lower house, the Chamber of Deputies, must be at least 25 years old and are elected for five-year terms. The 315 elective members of the Senate must be at least 40 years old and are elected for five-year terms. Former presidents of the republic are automatically life senators, and the president may also appoint as life senators persons who have performed meritorious service. Citizens must be at least 25 years of age to vote for senators; otherwise, those over the age of 18 may vote in all other elections.

In August 1993, Italy made significant changes in its electoral system. Three-fourths of the seats in both the Chamber and the Senate would be filled by simple majority voting. The remainder would be allocated by proportional representation to those parties securing at least 4% of the vote. The first elections under the new system in March 1994 resulted in a simplification of electoral alliances and brought a center-right government to power. Silvio Berlusconi, founder of the "Go Italy" (Forza Italia) movement, emerged as prime minister.

The constitution gives the people the right to hold referenda to abrogate laws passed by the parliament; a referendum requires at least 500,000 signatures. Four referenda had been held by 1987 (against the legalization of divorce in 1974, against increased police powers and state financing of the political parties in 1978, and against government cuts in wage indexation in 1985), and in all of them, the voters approved the parliamentary decisions.

In May 1999, Carlo Azeglio Ciampi was elected by the parliament as president of the Republic of Italy.

On 21 May 2000, Italian voters were asked to decide on electoral reform by increasing the number of lower house seats filled on the basis of a nonproportional system to 100%, effectively scrapping the last remaining element of pure proportional representation. The referendum needed to secure a quorum of 50% of the electorate to gain validity. The final turnout of 32% was much lower than expected and was an alarming sign of voter fatigue and popular disaffection.

On 13 May 2001, Silvio Berlusconi was again elected as head of state, this time as the leader of the five-party "Freedom House" political coalition of Forza Italia, the National Alliance, the Northern League, the Christian Democratic Center, and the United Christian Democrats. Although this coalition government was the longest running in Italy's postwar history, after a low showing in regional elections, Berlusconi was forced to resign and form a new government in April 2005. Italy's 60th government since liberation was formed on 23 April 2005.

14 POLITICAL PARTIES

Italy has a complex system of political alignments in which the parties, their congresses, and their leaders often appear to wield more power than parliament or the other constitutional branches of government.

Basic party policy is decided at the party congresses—generally held every second year—which are attended by locally elected party leaders. At the same time, the national party leadership is selected.

The most important political party traditionally had been the Christian Democratic Party (Partito Democrazia Cristiana—DC), which stood about midway in the political spectrum. In the 1983 national elections, the DC commanded 32.9% of the vote and won 225 seats in the Chamber of Deputies, down from 38.3% and 262 seats in 1979; in 1987, however, its electoral strength increased again, to 34.3% and 234 seats. From 1948 until 1981, the prime minister of Italy was consistently drawn from the ranks of the DC, whose religious and anti-class base constitutes both its strength and its weakness. Its relationship with the Church gave it added strength but also opened it to criticism, as did its popular association with the Mafia. In 1992, massive investigations uncovered widespread corruption, leading to many arrests and resignations of senior government officials. As a result of these scandals and corruption charges, the DC disbanded in 1994.

To the right and the left of the DC stood a wide range of parties, the most prominent of which was the Italian Communist Party (Partito Comunista Italiano—PCI), the largest Communist party in Western Europe at the time. The PCI had been second in power and influence only to the DC, but in the 1980s, its electoral base declined, despite the fact that it effectively severed its ties with both the former USSR and Marxism-Leninism.

Of all the parties of the mid to late 20th century, the most powerful were, in addition to the DC and PCI, were Italian Socialist Party (Partito Socialista Italiano—PSI), the Italian Socialist Democratic Party (Partito Socialista Democratico Italiano—PSDI), the Italiant Republican Party (Partito Repubblicano Italiano—PRI), the Italian Liberal Party (Partito Liberale Italiano—PLI), the Radical Party (Partito Radicale), the Italian Social Movement, (Movimento Sociale Italiano—MSI), the Proletarian Democracy (Democrazia Proletaria—DP), and the enviornmentalist Greens party. However, the 1990s saw the demise, creation, and restructuring of many Italian political parties. As of 2005, only the PRI and the Greens parties exist. Partly due to the end of the Cold War, in part due to the Mafia crackdown in the 1990s, and primarily due to the related corruption scandals that involved most of the major parties, the overhaul of the political party system was so significant that, although there has been little actual constitutional change, the post-1992 period is often referred to as the "Second Republic."

With the rise in political parties, government functioning was dominated by coalition party formations. The April 1996 election saw a resurgence of the left as the Olive Tree coalition, anchored by former communists calling themselves the Party of the Democratic Left (PDS), gained 284 seats in the 630-seat Chamber of Deputies and 157 seats in the 315-seat Senate. The Refounded Communists won 35 seats in the Chamber of Deputies, the separatist Northern League 59, the center-right Freedom Alliance 246, and others 6. The elections of April 1992 failed to resolve Italy's political and economic problems. The election of March 1994 under new voting rules resulted in the following distribution of seats in the Chamber (lower house): Alliance for Freedom, 42.9% (Forza Italia, Northern League, National Alliance—366 seats); Progressive Alliance, 32.2% (Democratic Party of the Left, Communist Refounding, Democratic Alliance, Greens, Reformers—213 seats); and Pact for Italy, 15.7% (Popular Party, others—46 seats).

The domination of the center-left came to an end in the May 2001 election when Berlusconi's right-leaning coalition, Freedom House (formerly the House of Liberties), was comprised of his Forza Italia (Go Italy) party; the National Alliance, Northern League, Christian-Democratic Center Party; United Christian Democrats; and the New Italian Socialist Party. This coalition won 368 seats in the Chamber of Deputies, and 177 in the Senate. The Olive Tree coalition—composed of the Democrats of the Left, the Daisy Alliance (including the Italian Popular Party, Italian Renewal, Union of Democrats for Europe, and the Democrats), the Sunflower Alliance (including the Greens and the Italian Democratic Socialists), and the Italian Communist Party—came in second with 242 seats in the lower house (128 in the Senate). The Communist Refounding took 11 seats in the Chamber of Deputies, and the Olive-Southern Tyrols People's Party of German speakers secured 5 seats in the lower house.

15 LOCAL GOVERNMENT

Under the terms of the 1948 constitution, Italy is divided into 20 regions. Five of these regions (Sicily, Sardinia, Trentino–Alto Adige, Friuli–Venezia Giulia, and the Valle d'Aosta) have been granted semiautonomous status, although the powers of self-government delegated from Rome have not been sufficient to satisfy the militant separatists, especially in Alto Adige. Legislation passed in 1968 granted the remaining 15 regions an even more limited degree of autonomy. All the regions elect a regional council. The councils and president are elected by universal franchise under a proportional system analogous to that of the parliament at Rome.

The regions are subdivided into a total of 94 provinces, which elect their own council and president, and each region is in turn subdivided into communes—townships, cities, and towns—that constitute the basic units of local administration. Communes are governed by councils elected by universal suffrage for a four-year term. The council elects a mayor and a board of aldermen to administer the commune. A commissioner in each region represents the federal government.

16 JUDICIAL SYSTEM

Minor legal matters may be brought before conciliators, while civil cases and lesser criminal cases are tried before judges called *pretori*. There are 159 tribunals, each with jurisdiction over its own district; 90 assize courts, where cases are heard by juries; and 26 assize courts of appeal. The Court of Cassation in Rome acts as the last instance of appeal in all cases except those involving constitutional matters, which are brought before the special Constitutional Court (consisting of 15 judges). For many years, the number of civil and criminal cases has been increasing more rapidly than the judicial resources to deal with them.

The Italian legal system is based on Roman law, although much is also derived from the French Napoleonic model. The law assuring criminal defendants a fair and public trial is largely observed in practice. The 1989 amendments to the criminal procedure law both streamlined the process and provide for a more adversarial (as opposed to inquisitorial) system along the American model.

By law the judiciary is autonomous and independent of the executive branch. In practice, there has been a perception that magistrates were subject to political pressures and that political bias of individual magistrates could affect outcomes. Since the start of "clean hands" investigations of the government, including the judiciary, in 1992 for kickbacks and corruption, magistrates have taken steps to distance themselves from political parties and other pressure groups.

17 ARMED FORCES

Since 1949 Italy, as a member of NATO, has maintained large and balanced modern forces. The total strength in 2005 was 191,875 active personnel, with reserves numbering 56,500. Army personnel numbered 112,000, and whose equipment included 320 main battle tanks, 300 reconnaissance vehicles, 122 armored infantry fighting vehicles, 2,036 armored personnel carriers, 14 amphibious assault vehicles, and 1,562 artillery pieces. Navy personnel in 2005 totaled 33,100, including 2,000 Marines. Major Italian naval vessels included 1 aircraft carrier, 2 destroyers, 12 frigates, 8 corvettes, 14 patrol/coastal vessels, 13 mine warfare ships, 3 amphibious ships, and 94 logistics/support vessels. The navy also operated six tactical submarines. The air force had a total strength of 44,743 personnel with 199 combat capable aircraft, in addition to various electronic warfare, antiair defense, transport and training aircraft. In 2005, Italy also had a paramilitary force of 254,300 active personnel, of which 111,367 were Carabinieri. Italian armed forces were deployed among 19 countries or regions in various peacekeeping, training or active military missions. Italy's military budget for 2005 was $17.2 billion.

18 INTERNATIONAL COOPERATION

Italy has been a member of the United Nations since 14 December 1955 and participates in the ECE and several UN nonregional specialized agencies, such as FAO, UNESCO, UNIDO, UNHCR, IFC, WHO, and the World Bank. It is a member of the Council of Europe, the European Union, NATO, and the OECD. Italy held the EU presidency from July to December 2003. Italy also participates in the Asian, African, Caribbean, European, and the Inter-American development banks, and is a part of G-7, G-8, and G-10. The country holds observer status in the Black Sea Economic Cooperation Zone, the OAS, and the Latin American Integration Association (LAIA).

Italy is a guest in the Nonaligned Movement. The country has supplied troops for UN operations and missions in Kosovo (est. 1999), Lebanon (est. 1978), India and Pakistan (est. 1949), and Ethiopia and Eritrea (est. 2000), among others. Italy belongs to the Australia Group, the Zangger Committee, the Nuclear Suppliers Group (London Group), the Nuclear Energy Agency, the Organization for the Prohibition of Chemical Weapons, and the European Organization for Nuclear Research (CERN).

In environmental cooperation, Italy is part of the Antarctic Treaty; the Basel Convention; Conventions on Biological Diversity, Whaling, and Air Pollution; Ramsar; CITES; the London Convention; International Tropical Timber Agreements; the Kyoto Protocol; the Montréal Protocol; MARPOL; the Nuclear Test Ban Treaty; and the UN Conventions on the Law of the Sea, Climate Change and Desertification.

19 ECONOMY

As the Italian economy, the world's sixth-largest, has expanded since the 1950s, its structure has changed markedly. Agriculture, which in 1953 contributed 25% of the GNP and employed 35% of the labor force, contributed in 1968 only 11% of the GNP and employed only 22% of the active labor force—despite continued increases in the value of agricultural production. Agriculture's contribution to the GDP further declined to 8.4% in 1974, 5% in 2001, and 2.3% in 2004. Conversely, the importance of industry has increased dramatically. Industrial output almost tripled between 1953 and 1968 and generally showed steady growth during the 1970s; in 2004, industry (including fuel, power, and construction) contributed 28.8% to the GDP. Precision machinery and motor vehicles have led the growth in manufacturing, and Italy has generally been a leader in European industrial design and fashion. Services in 2004 accounted for 68.9% of the economy. However, apart from tourism and design, Italy is not internationally competitive in most service sectors.

Despite this economic achievement, a number of basic problems remain. Natural resources are limited, landholdings often are poor and invariably too small, industrial enterprises are of minimal size and productivity, and industrial growth has not been translated into general prosperity. The rise in petroleum prices during the mid-1970s found Italy especially vulnerable, since the country is almost totally dependent on energy imports. In addition, because economic activity is centered predominately in the north, Italians

living in the northern part of the country enjoy a substantially higher standard of living than those living in the south.

Partly because of increased energy costs, inflation increased from an annual rate of about 5% in the early 1970s to an annual average of 16.6% during 1975–81, well above the OECD average. Inflation was brought down to 14.6% in 1983 and to between 4 and 6% during most of the 1990s. In 1997 it was reduced to under 2%, its lowest level in 30 years. The inflation rate was estimated at 2.3% in 2004.

From 1981 through 1983, Italy endured a period of recession, with rising budget deficits, interest rates above 20%, virtually no real GDP growth, and an unemployment rate approaching 10%. Unemployment hovered around the 10 to 12% range for most of the 1990s and at 9% into the 2000s. Between 1985 and 1995, GDP growth averaged 1.9% a year. It was quite low in 2003, at 0.7%. The GDP growth rate stood at an estimated 1.3% in 2004, and was flat in 2005. Economic growth was expected to pick up to a still disappointing 1–1.2% in 2006–07.

Italy's large public debt, public sector deficit, low productivity growth, and burdensome and complex tax system, are generally blamed for the poor state of the economy. A rigid labor market and generous pension system are also seen as responsible for a sluggish economy. The Silvio Berlusconi administration by 2002 had abolished an inheritance tax, a move which was popular among affluent Italians. The 2005 budget included substantial tax cuts and a reduction in the number of tax rates from five to four. The corporate tax rate was reduced from 36% to 33% in 2004. Berlusconi also attempted to loosen labor laws to increase temporary work contracts and to ease hiring and firing practices. The government in the early 2000s was geared toward implementing spending cuts to spur consumer spending and corporate research and development. Pension reform, called a "financial time bomb" by economists, was proposed by the government and resulted in strikes in parts of Italy in mid-2003. Italy spends a massive 14% of GDP on pensions. In 2004, Italy raised the minimum age for state pensions from 57 to 60, but only beginning in 2008.

One of Italy's strengths is the thriving state of its small firms, which are often family owned. In 2003, the average number of workers per enterprise was just over four, the second-lowest figure in the EU. These small businesses are able to succeed in niche markets. However, the high proportion of small businesses has meant that Italy spends less on research and development than other European countries: in 2003, Italian spending on R&D as a share of GDP was barely half of the EU average. This causes Italy to experience a loss of competitiveness, and sluggish growth. In 2004, the economy grew by less than the euro-area average for the eighth time in nine years. Many Italian firms are still in traditional manufacturing areas that should have been abandoned when competition from Southeast Asia and China grew in the 1990s.

Italians spend more than other Europeans on clothes and shoes, and are second only to Spaniards in spending in bars, restaurants, and hotels. Because many Italians rent their living spaces, expenditure on housing is low.

20 INCOME

The US Central Intelligence Agency (CIA) reports that in 2005 Italy's gross domestic product (GDP) was estimated at $1.6 trillion. The CIA defines GDP as the value of all final goods and services produced within a nation in a given year and computed on the basis of purchasing power parity (PPP) rather than value as measured on the basis of the rate of exchange based on current dollars. The per capita GDP was estimated at $28,300. The annual growth rate of GDP was estimated at 0%. The average inflation rate in 2005 was 1.9%. It was estimated that agriculture accounted for 2.1% of GDP, industry 28.8%, and services 69.1%.

According to the World Bank, in 2003 remittances from citizens working abroad totaled $2.137 billion or about $37 per capita and accounted for approximately 0.1% of GDP.

The World Bank reports that in 2003 household consumption in Italy totaled $887.34 billion or about $15,405 per capita based on a GDP of $1.5 trillion, measured in current dollars rather than PPP. Household consumption includes expenditures of individuals, households, and nongovernmental organizations on goods and services, excluding purchases of dwellings. It was estimated that for the period 1990 to 2003 household consumption grew at an average annual rate of 1.6%. In 2001 it was estimated that approximately 23% of household consumption was spent on food, 12% on fuel, 3% on health care, and 17% on education.

21 LABOR

Italy's labor force in 2005 was estimated at 24.49 million. In 2003 the occupational breakdown had 4.9% in agriculture, 32.2% in industry, 62.8% in the services sector, and 0.1% in undefined occupations. The estimated unemployment rate in 2005 was 7.9%.

The law provides the right to form and join unions, and many workers exercise this right. According to union claims, between 35% and 40% of the nation's workforce was unionized as of 2005. About 35% of the labor force was covered by collective bargaining agreements, which also included nonunion employees. The right to strike is constitutionally protected, and workers engage in collective bargaining. Employers may not discriminate against those engaged in union activity.

As of 2005, the legal workweek was set at 40 hours, with overtime not to exceed two hours per day or an average of 12 hours per week. However, in the industrial sector, maximum overtime was set at no more than 80 hours per quarter and 250 hours annually, unless limited by a collective bargaining agreement. Minimum wages in Italy are not set by law, but through collective labor contracts, which establish wages and salaries in every major field. In most industries these minimum rates offered a worker and family a decent standard of living. Labor contracts may also call for additional compulsory bonuses, and basic wages and salaries are adjusted quarterly to compensate for increases in the cost of living. With some limited exceptions, children under age 15 are prohibited by law from employment.

22 AGRICULTURE

Of Italy's total land area of 29.4 million hectares (72.6 million acres), 10.7 million hectares (26.4 million acres), or 36.4% of the land, were under annual or permanent crops in 2003. Small, individually owned farms predominate, with the majority three hectares (7.4 acres) or less. In 2001, about 5% (1.4 million persons) of the economically active population was in the agricultural sector.

Despite government efforts, the agricultural sector has shown little growth in recent decades. The imports of agricultural products increased from $19.6 billion in 1987 to $31.6 billion in 2004.

Italy has to import about half of its meat. The land is well suited for raising fruits and vegetables, both early and late crops, and these are the principal agricultural exports. Although yields per hectare in sugar beets, tomatoes, and other vegetable crops have increased significantly, both plantings and production of wheat declined between 1974 and 1981. Thus, although Italy remains a major cereal-producing country, wheat must be imported. The government controls the supply of domestic wheat and the import of foreign wheat.

Production of major agricultural products in 2004 (in thousands of tons) included sugar beets, 10,100; wheat, 8,628; corn, 10,983; tomatoes, 7,497; oranges, 2,064; potatoes, 1,809; apples, 2,069; barley, 1,167; and rice, 1,496. In 2004, Italy produced 8,692,000 tons of grapes, and 4,531,000 tons of olives, and 879,000 tons of olive oil. In 2003, Italy had 1,680,000 tractors (third in the world) and 37,500 harvester-threshers.

23 ANIMAL HUSBANDRY

Some 4,377,000 hectares (10,816,000 acres) are meadows and pastures. Both a growing need for fodder and insufficient domestic production compel Italy to import large amounts of corn. In 2005, the country had 6,314,000 head of cattle, 9,272,000 hogs, 8,020,000 sheep, 1,985,000 goats, 300,000 horses, and an estimated 100 million chickens. That year, total meat production from hogs, cattle, sheep, and goats was 4,099,000 tons. Of the meat produced, 38% was pork, 29% was beef, 24% was poultry, 2% was mutton, and 7% was from other sources. Meat production falls short of domestic requirements, and about half of all meat consumed must be imported. Although Italy produced 10.5 million tons of cow milk in 2005, dairy farming remains comparatively undeveloped. Both dairy and beef cattle are raised mainly in the north. The value of animal output in 2003 exceeded €14.3 billion, third highest in the EU after France and Germany.

24 FISHING

Italy's geography provides abundant access to marine fishing. Peninsular Italy and the islands of Sicily and Sardinia together have over 8,000 km (4,900 mi) of coastline and over 800 landing ports equipped for fishing boats. There are also 1,500 sq km (580 sq mi) of lagoons and 1,700 sq km (650 sq mi) of marine ponds. Although coastal and deep-sea fishing in the Mediterranean engage over 50,000 fishermen, the fishing industry is unable to meet domestic needs. As of 2003 there were 15,915 Italian fishing vessels with a fishing capacity (gross tonnage) of 178,334 tons. Since the extension of the 200-mile limit zones and the consequent drop in the total catch, Italy's fishing industry has declined because their deep-sea vessels were not suited to Mediterranean fishing. Also, about 1,700 vessels (10% of the fleet) went out of service during 2000–02 as a result of EU-funded policies for the reduction of fishing in the Mediterranean. The total catch in 2003 was 314,807 tons, 98% from marine fishing, with a value of about €1.4 billion. Anchovies, sardines, hake, mullets, and swordfish together accounted for 44% of the volume in 2003. In 2003, Italy produced 89,000 tons of canned tuna and 20,000 tons of canned anchovies. The majority of the Italian fish harvest (up to 50%) is not officially recorded but sold directly to restaurants, wholesalers, and fishmongers. Anchovy, rainbow trout, sardine, and European hake are the main finfish species caught. Sponges and coral are also commercially important. The main commercial fishing ports are Mazara del Vallo, Palermo, San Benedetto del Tronto, Chioggia-Venezia, and Genoa.

There are over a thousand intensive production fish farms that belong to the Italian Fish Farming Association, with 60% located in northern Italy. Total Italian aquaculture production in 2003 was 244,000 tons, valued at €250 million.

25 FORESTRY

The major portion of the 10 million hectares (24.7 million acres) of forest is in the Alpine areas of northern Italy; few extensive forests grow in central or southern Italy or on the islands. Italy has more softwood than hardwood growth and extensive coppice (thicket and small shrub) stands. The overall forest structure consists of 42% coppice stands, 26% softwoods, and 25% hardwood high stands. The only species that are commercially important are chestnut, beech, oak, and poplar. Chestnut and beech stands account for 31% of the hardwood forest and for over 40% of Italian wood production; oak comprises 8% of wood production. Poplar is the only species grown using managed forestry practices. Poplar plantations account for only 1% of the total forest area but for 50% of domestic wood output. Forest resources are stable and meet about 19% of annual demand. Italian wood output in 2003 consisted of 9 million cu m (318 million cu ft). Approximately 90% of Italian forest product exports consist of wooden furniture, semifinished wood products, and other finished wood products. The Italian furniture industry accounted for 37,987 firms with 229,054 employees in 2002, with an industry turnover of almost €22.8 billion. The diversity in species composition, ownership patterns, topographic constraints, and conflicting resource management strategies have all contributed to limiting the productivity of Italian forest resources. Italy is a major importer of hardwood and softwood lumber, since its rugged terrain and disjointed forestland restrict domestic production. In 2002, the Italian wood and wood product sectors employed 412,815 workers in 87,906 companies with a total turnover of about $36 billion. Some 80% of the raw materials used for manufacturing furnished wooden products are imported. Imports of forest products in 2004 were valued at $9.5 billion, while exports totaled $4.3 billion.

26 MINING

Although Italy was relatively poor in mineral resources, it was, nevertheless, a major producer of feldspar, pumice and related materials, as well as of crude steel, cement (second-largest in the EU), and a leading producer of dimension stone and marble. The country also continued to supply a significant portion of its own need for some minerals. Industrial mineral production in 2003, including construction materials, was the most important sector of the economy. Italy has been a significant processor of imported raw materials, and a significant consumer and exporter of mineral and metal semi-manufactured and finished products.

Production totals for the leading minerals in 2003 were: feldspar, estimated at 2,500 metric tons; barite, estimated at 30,000 metric tons, unchanged from 1999; fluorspar (acid-grade and metallurgical-grade), estimated at 45,000 tons; hydraulic cement, estimated at 40 million tons; pumice and pumiceous lapilli, estimated at 600,000 tons (from Lipari Island, off the northern coast of Sicily); and pozzolan, estimated at 4 million tons (from Lipa-

ri). Alumina production (calcined basis) in 2003 was estimated at 925,000 metric tons. In addition, Italy produced antimony oxides, gold (from Sardinia), mine lead, mine manganese, bromine, crude clays (including bentonite, refractory, fuller's earth, kaolin, and kaolinitic earth), diatomite, gypsum, lime, nitrogen, perlite, mineral pigments, salt (marine, rock, and brine), sand and gravel (including volcanic and silica sands), soda ash, sodium sulfate, stone (alabaster, dolomite, granite, limestone, marble, marl, quartz, quartzite, sandstone, serpentine, and slate), sulfur, and talc and related materials.

Marble and travertine quarrying from the famous mines in the Massa and Carrara areas was still significant. Marble was quarried at hundreds of locations from the Alps to Sicily. The most important white-marble-producing area was in the Apuan Alps, near Carrara, and accounted for one-third of the country's 100,000 tons of white marble. Important colored-marble-producing areas included the Lazio region, Lombardy, the Po Valley, Puglia, Sicily, Venice, and Verona-Vincenza. Reserves of several types were considered to be unlimited; half of the country's output was in block form and half was exported.

27 ENERGY AND POWER

Italy's proven oil and natural gas reserves are each the fourth-largest in the European Union (EU). The country has completely stopped the production of coal. Still, Italy must rely heavily on foreign sources to meet its energy needs.

According to the Oil and Gas Journal, Italy has proven oil reserves estimated at 622 million barrels, as of 1 January 2005. Estimated production in 2004 averaged 147,000 barrels daily, of which crude oil accounted for 104,000 barrels per day, of which about 89% was accounted for by the National Hydrocarbon Agency (Ente Nazionale Idrocarburi), or ENI, Italy's largest oil and natural gas company of which the Italian government holds a controlling 35% stake. However, domestic demand far outstrips production, with consumption in 2004 estimated at 1.90 million barrels per day. Net imports for that year are estimated at 1.75 million barrels per day. In 2004, the former Soviet Union was Italy's largest supplier at 28%, followed by Libya (24%), Saudi Arabia (13%), and Iran (10%).

More than 70% of ENI's production comes from the Val d'Agri project in the south of Italy, the Villafortuna project in the north, and from the Aquila project off the Adriatic coast in the southeast. Development of the Tempa Rossa field, with an estimated 200 million barrels of oil, is being led by France's Total, and is expected to enter production by 2007 with a peak output of 50,000 barrels per day.

Oil has been partly replaced by natural gas, whose consumption is expected to continue rising in the future, driven largely by the construction of combined-cycle, gas-fired turbines. Italy has proven natural gas reserves of 8.0 trillion cu ft, as of 1 January 2005, according to the Oil and Gas Journal. Natural gas production in 2004, according to Eurostat totaled 440 billion cu ft. Combined with declining field output, Italy's reliance on natural gas imports has increased. In 2004, imported natural gas accounted 84% of the country's demand vs. 59% in 1985, according to Eurostat. Algeria (38%), Russia (32%), and the Netherlands (14%) were Italy's largest natural gas suppliers in 2004.

In 2001, Italy completely closed down its domestic coal production industry, when it shuttered its last production facility. In 2002, coal met only 6.8% of Italy's energy needs. In that year, demand for coal amounted to 21.8 million short tons, of which most was used to provide electricity. In the first half of 2004, South Africa supplied 26% of the coal consumed by Italy, followed by Colombia (12%) and the United States (11%).

Italy's total electric generating capacity was estimated at 69.1 GW in 2002, with thermal accounting for 78% of capacity, hydropower at 19% and other renewable sources at 3%. In 2002, it was estimated that output totaled 262 billion kWh, with consumption totaling an estimated 294 billion kWh, and net imports totaling an estimated 32 billion kWh.

28 INDUSTRY

Characterized both by a few large industrial concerns controlling the greater part of industrial output and by thousands of small shops engaged in artisan-type production, Italian industry expanded rapidly in the postwar period. Industrial production almost tripled between 1955 and 1968 and has generally showed continued growth, although the global recession that began in 2001 slowed industrial production and the economy as a whole. The lack of domestic raw materials and fuels represents a serious drag on industrial expansion. Industry accounted for 28.8% of GDP in 2004, and employed 32% of the labor force. Manufacturing accounts for approximately 90% of total merchandise exports.

Three state-holding companies have played a large role in industry: ENI (National Hydrocarbon Agency), IRI (Industrial Reconstruction Institute), and EFIM (Agency for Participation and Financing of Manufacturing Industry). IRI was the 16th-largest industrial company in the world in 1993, with sales of $50.5 billion; it had shareholdings in over 100 companies (including banks, electronics, engineering, and shipbuilding) and 333,600 employees in 1992. EFIM controlled armaments and metallurgy industries. Debt-ridden EFIM was liquidated, IRI became dismantled through sell-offs, and as of 2005, the state had reduced its stake in ENI and Enel (Ente Nazionale per l'Energia Elettrica), the national electricity company. Major private companies are the Fiat automobile company; the Olivetti company (office computers and telecommunications); the Montedison chemical firm; and the Pirelli rubber company. The bulk of heavy industry is concentrated in the northwest, in the Milan-Turin-Genoa industrial triangle. The government has made concerted efforts to attract industry to the underdeveloped southeast.

With the drive toward greater European integration in full gear, Italy, along with its fellow EU member-states, is liberalizing its economic and commercial legislation. These promise a marked change in the Italian business scene as mergers and foreign investment increase. In early 1999, Olivetti mounted a successful hostile takeover for Telecom Italia.

Italy has become known for niche products, including fashion eye-wear, specialized machine tools, packaging, stylish furniture, kitchen equipment, and other products featuring high design. The "made in Italy" stamp is associated with quality and style. Traditional industries are iron and steel, machinery, chemicals, food processing (including olive oil, wine, and cheese), textiles, clothing, footwear, motor vehicles, and ceramics. The construction industry stands to gain in importance in the early 2000s, as Italy's less-developed regions are slated for infrastructure development.

Foreign competition has cut into the Italian textile industry. Following the expiration of the World Trade Organization's long-standing system of textile quotas at the beginning of 2005, the EU signed an agreement with China in June 2005, imposing new quotas on 10 categories of textile goods, limiting growth in those categories to between 8% and 12.5% a year. The agreement runs until 2007, and was designed to give European textile manufacturers time to adjust to a world of unfettered competition. Nevertheless, barely a month after the EU-China agreement was signed, China reached its quotas for sweaters, followed soon after by blouses, bras, T-shirts, and flax yarn. Tens of millions of garments piled up in warehouses and customs checkpoints, which affected both retailers and consumers.

29 SCIENCE AND TECHNOLOGY

The still-standing aqueducts, bathhouses, and other public works of both ancient republic and empire testify to the engineering and architectural skills of the Romans. The rebirth of science during the Renaissance brought the daring speculations of Leonardo da Vinci (including discoveries in anatomy, meteorology, geology, and hydrology, as well as a series of fascinating though ultimately impractical designs for a "flying machine"), advances in physics and astronomy by Galileo Galilei, and the development of the barometer by Evangelista Torricelli. To later Italian scientists and inventors the world owes the electric battery (1800), the electroplating process (1805), and the radiotelegraph (1895).

In 2001, Italy had 1,156 scientists and engineers per million people engaged in research and development (R&D). In that same year, expenditures on R&D totaled $16.7 trillion or 1.11% of GDP. High technology exports in 2002 totaled $19.730 billion, or 9% of the country's manufactured exports.

The National Research Council (Consiglio Nazionale delle Ricerche—CNR), founded in 1923, is the country's principal research organization. CNR institutes and associated private and university research centers conduct scientific work in mathematics, physics, chemistry, geology, technology, engineering, medicine, biology, and agriculture. Especially noteworthy are the National Institute of Nuclear Physics, in Rome, and the Enrico Fermi Center for Nuclear Studies, in Milan.

Italy has 47 universities offering courses in basic and applied sciences. The Instituto e Museo di Storia della Scienza di Firenzo, founded in 1930, is located in Florence. In 1987–97, science and engineering students accounted for 30% of university enrollment. In 2002, of all bachelor's degrees awarded, 25.8% were in the sciences (natural, mathematics and computers, and engineering)

30 DOMESTIC TRADE

Milan is the principal commercial center, followed by Turin, Genoa, Naples, and Rome. Genoa, the chief port of entry for Milan and Turin, handles about one-third of Italy's trade; Naples is the principal entrepôt for central and southern Italy. Adriatic as well as Middle Eastern trade is carried through Ancona, Bari, and Brindisi. Although small retail units predominate, department stores and supermarkets are playing an increasingly important role. In

2000, Italy ranked second in Europe in franchise business operations with about 562 companies and over 31,400 franchises.

Advertising in all forms is well developed, and the usual mass media (billboards, neon signs, newspapers and magazines, radio, cinema, and television) are used extensively. Market research is handled by over 100 firms.

Usual business hours in northern Italy are from 8:30 AM until 12:30 PM and from 3:30 to 6:30 PM. In central and southern Italy, customary hours are 8:30 AM to 12:45 PM and 4:30 or 5 to 7:30 or 8 PM. Most firms are closed in August. In general, banking hours are 8:30 AM to 1:30 PM and 3 PM to 4 PM, Monday through Friday. Retail establishments are generally closed on Sundays.

31 FOREIGN TRADE

Industrial products, textiles and apparel, shoes, and foodstuffs are Italy's most important exports. However, the textile industry has been hit hard by foreign competition in recent years, especially from China. Fuels, meat, grain products, and various raw materials are among the major imports. Trade deficits were substantial between the end of World War II and 1955, but between 1956 and 1968 the deficit gradually declined, and Italy's trade balance continued in relative equilibrium through 1972. Then, as prices of crude oil and other raw-material imports rose, Italy again began registering growing trade deficits. In 1993, however, a large surplus was recorded because of an export boom that followed the devaluation of the lira in September 1992, and Italy has had a trade surplus ever since. In 2004, the value of exports of goods was $352.2 billion, and imports were $341.3 billion, resulting in a trade surplus of $10.9 billion.

The bulk of manufactured imports come from EU countries and the United States, which are also the leading customers for Italian exports. The big commodity exports from Italy in 2004 included industrial and automobile machinery and parts (40.3%), textiles, clothing, and leather (13.5%), chemicals (9.6%), and metal products (9.5%). The major imports included machinery and transportation equipment (34.5%), chemicals (13.4%), energy minerals (10.3%), and metals and metal products (10.3%). Italy's leading markets in 2004 were Germany (14.1% of all exports), France (12.5%), the United States (8.3%), and the United Kingdom (7.1%). Italy's leading suppliers in 2004 were Germany (18.1% of all imports), France (11.4%), the Netherlands (5.8%), and the United Kingdom (4.8%).

32 BALANCE OF PAYMENTS

Italy did not have serious balance of payments problems after the mid-1970s. Exports soared after 1992, turning Italy's balance of payments positive. The growth in exports was extremely strong in the northeast, where small and medium-sized companies produce high-quality and low-cost products—ranging from industrial machinery to ski boots—for French, German, Japanese, and Indian customers.

Italy had current account surpluses from 1993 to 1999, but in 2000 the country registered a $5.6 billion deficit, after an $8.2 billion surplus in 1999. Italy experienced weak economic growth in the period 2001–05. In 2004, the current account balance showed a deficit estimated at $15.1 billion (0.9% of GDP).

Balance of Payments – Italy (2003)		
(In millions of US dollars)		
Current Account		-21.9
Balance on goods	9.7	
Imports	-283.6	
Exports	293.3	
Balance on services	-1.4	
Balance on income	-22.1	
Current transfers	-8.2	
Capital Account		3.1
Financial Account		19.4
Direct investment abroad	-9.9	
Direct investment in Italy	17.3	
Portfolio investment assets	-58.5	
Portfolio investment liabilities	61.4	
Financial derivatives	-5.4	
Other investment assets	-29.8	
Other investment liabilities	44.3	
Net Errors and Omissions		0.6
Reserves and Related Items		-1.1

(…) data not available or not significant.

SOURCE: *Balance of Payment Statistics Yearbook 2004,* Washington, DC: International Monetary Fund, 2004.

33 BANKING AND SECURITIES

The Banca d'Italia, the central bank, was the sole bank of issue and exercised credit control functions until Italy's accession to the European Central Bank, which now controls monetary policy and the euro, the EU's common currency (excepting the United Kingdom, Denmark, and Sweden). La Banca d'Italia is still responsible for controlling domestic inflation and balance of payments pressures.

In March 1979, Italy became a founder member of the European Monetary System (EMS) and its Exchange Rate Mechanism (ERM). During the first 10 years of its membership, the lira was allowed to diverge by up to 6% against other member currencies before action had to be taken, compared with 2.25% for other ERM currencies. Uncertainty about Italy's ability to meet the convergence targets of the 1992 Treaty for European Union (Merastricht) for inflation, interest rates, and participation to stabilize the rate, the lira was withdrawn from the ERM in September 1992, after which the lira declined to just under DM1:L1,000. At the beginning of 1996 it began to appreciate again, and immediately after the April election it rose to L1,021:DM1. The introduction of the euro in 2002, however, made all that irrelevant.

In 2002, five banks are of nationwide standing: Intesa-Bci, San Paolo-IMI, the Banca di Roma, Unicredito Italiano, and the Banca Nazionale del Lavoro. There are many major international banks with branches in Italy. Among the more important are Chase, Citibank, Bank of America, HSBC, and others. The Istituto Mobiliare Italiano is the leading industrial credit institution; it also administers important government industrial investments. In 1987, the government privatized Mediobanca, another major industrial credit institution.

Two major banks, formally part of the Instituto per la Ricostruzione Industriale (IRI) group, were privatized in 1993–94: Unicredito Italiano (CREDIT) and Banca Commerciale Italiana (COMIT). The privatization of another IRI bank specializing in medium- and long-term lending, the Instituto Mobiliare Italiano (IMI), was completed in 1996.

A new banking law was passed in 1993, to bring Italy into conformity with the EU's Second Banking directive, and to introduce two major innovations which aim to move Italy toward a model of universal banking. It allows banks to hold shares in industrial concerns; and it eliminates the distinction between banks (aziende di credito) and special credit institutions (aziende di credito speciale), thus allowing all banks to perform operations previously limited to specific types of intermediary.

On 30 January 1997, the government drafted legislation to promote restructuring and consolidation in Italy's largely inefficient and highly fragmented banking sector. The bill is the latest in a series of attempts since 1990 to rationalize the sector. However, it comes just as Italy's two biggest banks, CARIPLO and what is now San Paolo-IMI, announced plans to begin privatization by the end of 1997, and other banks in the private sector begin to negotiate strategic alliances, notably between: the private sector bank Ambroveneto and CARIPLO; Cassa di Resparmia di Torino and the Cassa di Risparmio di Verona. Mergers are also changing the face of the Italian banking industry. In early 1999, four of the five largest Italian banks were involved in such deals. Unicredito Italiano and Banca Commerciale Italiana merged to form Eurobanca, while San Paolo-IMI and Banca di Roma also planned to combine their operations. The International Monetary Fund reports that in 2001, currency and demand deposits—an aggregate commonly known as M1—were equal to $458.4 billion. In that same year, M2—an aggregate equal to M1 plus savings deposits, small time deposits, and money market mutual funds—was $628.9 billion. The money market rate, the rate at which financial institutions lend to one another in the short term, was 4.26%.

There are 10 stock exchanges in operation. The most important is that in Milan (established in 1808). The others, in order of importance, are Rome (1812), Turin (1850), Genoa (1855), Bologna (1861), Florence (1859), Naples (1813), Venice (1600), Trieste (1755), and Palermo (1876). Since 1974, the markets have been regulated by the National Commission for Companies and the Stock Exchange.

Radical reforms have been introduced in recent years in order to vitalize the stock market, which is greatly undercapitalized considering the size of the Italian economy. At the end of 1995, the capitalization of the Milan bourse was the equivalent of just 18% of GDP, compared with 32% in France and 122% in the United Kingdom. However, by 2002 market capitalization had increased to 41% of GDP.

In September 1991, stock market intermediation companies (SIM), a new form of stock broking and fund management firm, were introduced to accompany the shift from the open-outcry call auction system to a screen-based continuous auction market, which was completed in July 1994. In order to stimulate the demand for shares, in 1994 shareholders were given the option of paying a 12.5% flat tax rate instead of declaring dividends as part of taxable income. At the beginning of 1996, proposed Services Directive included the privatization of the stock market and the administrative bodies that run it as one of its main objectives.

Despite a certain amount of volatility, the Milan stock exchange index (MIB) has risen by 10.6% on 26 March 1997 since the end of 1996 and daily volume of transactions were up substantially. In early-mid-2000, the MIB index hovered between 31,700–31,800. However, since the onset of the global recession, the index has dropped significantly. From January 2002 to January 2003, the MIB dropped 4.4%, down to 16,208, slightly more than half of its peak value. In 2004, the MIB-30 Index rose 16.9% from the previous year to 31,220. On the Borsa Italiana, a total of 269 companies were listed as of 2004, which had a market capitalization of $789.563 billion.

34 INSURANCE

The insurance industry is government-supervised, and insurers must be authorized to do business. Automobile insurance was made compulsory in 1971, and coverage is also required for aircraft, powerboats, hunters, auditors, yachts, nuclear facilities, and insurance brokers. Among the most important nonlife insurance companies in Italy as of 2003 were Ras, Generali, Sai, and Assitalia. Leading life insurance companies as of 2003 included Alleanza, Creitras, Generali, and Sanpaolo. In 2003, the value of direct premiums written totaled $111.761 billion, with life premiums accounting for $71.694 billion. Italy's top nonlife insurer in 2003 was Fondiaria-SAI, with total written nonlife premiums (including personal accident and healthcare) of $4,272.6 million. In that same year, the country's leading life insurer was Creditras, with gross written life premiums of $5,977.6 million.

The insurance regulatory body is the Instituto per Viglanza sulle Assicurazioni Private di Interesse Collettivo (ISVAP-the Institute for Control of Private Insurance Companies). European Union reporting and other insurance directives are being implemented. A unique and helpful feature of Italian insurance company reports is the inclusion of financial statements of major subsidiary or affiliated companies.

The Italian insurance market was traditionally characterized by a relatively large number of insurers with no one organization dominating the industry, although there were some very large, old insurance organizations which date back to the early 19th century. There are a number of foreign insurance companies operating through subsidiaries in Italy: these are primarily French and German companies. Italy's market indicates moderately low penetration when compared to North America and Northern Europe, especially for life products. In recent years, the volume of life products has increased quite rapidly as the consumer has become aware that the Italian Social Security System benefits will have to be supplemented by individual savings and as insurance awareness has increased through advertising campaigns and the distribution of insurance products through the extensive branch banking system of the country. Foreign influence and industry consolidation in the Italian insurance industry is expected to rise due to the adoption of the euro and the emerging willingness of Italian companies to mount hostile takeover bids. Much of the new merger-mania expected to sweep Italian insurance is projected to come from the banking sector as banks continue to expand their interests in insurance sales.

35 PUBLIC FINANCE

Reflecting both increasing economic activity and the pressures of inflation, the Italian budget has expanded continually since 1950. The Italian economy has traditionally run a high govern-

Public Finance – Italy (2000)

(In billions of euros, central government figures)

Revenue and Grants	444.5	100.0%
Tax revenue	278.47	62.6%
Social contributions	147.51	33.2%
Grants	0.47	0.1%
Other revenue	18.06	4.1%
Expenditures	450.9	100.0%
General public services	...	...
Defense	...	...
Public order and safety	...	...
Economic affairs	...	...
Environmental protection	...	...
Housing and community amenities	...	...
Health	...	...
Recreational, culture, and religion	...	...
Education	...	...
Social protection	...	...

(...) data not available or not significant.

SOURCE: *Government Finance Statistics Yearbook 2004*, Washington, DC: International Monetary Fund, 2004.

ment debt, but in recent years it has been quelled somewhat, despite lackluster growth. In 1995, the debt stood at 124% of GDP, but declined to 110.6% in 2000 and 109.4% in 2001. At that point the Italian government still had a long way to go to get down to the EU-imposed debt-to-GDP ration of 60%. Since 1996, Italy has maintained a primary budget surplus, net of interest payments, and has reduced its deficit in public administration from 1.7% of GDP in 2000 to 1.4% in 2001. However, given the high national debt, the EU remains concerned about Italy's budgetary policies.

The US Central Intelligence Agency (CIA) estimated that in 2005 Italy's central government took in revenues of approximately $785.7 billion and had expenditures of $861.5 billion. Revenues minus expenditures totaled approximately -$75.8 billion. Public debt in 2005 amounted to 107.3% of GDP. Total external debt was $1.682 trillion.

36 TAXATION

The Italian tax system is considered among the most complicated in the world. Since the late 1990s, the government has been using tax cuts to stimulate economic growth. On 1 January 1998 the government introduced the Dual Income Tax (DIT) system designed to encourage investment by taxing income deemed to be derived from the increase in equity capital in a company at a lower rate than the standard corporate income tax rate. In 2003, the corporate income tax rate (IRPEG), at 36% in 2002, was reduced to 34%. As of 2005, the standard corporate rate was 33%, excluding a 4.25% regional tax (IRAP) on productive activities. Capital gains realized by companies are taxable as business income under the IRPEG and IRAP, and capital losses are deductible. Dividends are taxed at 27% with complete withholding ("payment at the source" or PAYE). This rate may be reduced to 12.5% if residents can show that they had a "nonsubstantial participation" in the firm. A 0% rate applies to dividends paid to resident companies. The PAYE rate for dividends paid to branches of companies from other EU countries is 12.5%

The schedule of personal income tax rates was reformed in 2003 to reduce tax rates and to increase the amount covered by the lowest income band. As of 2005, the individual tax rate progressively increases to a top rate of 39%. However, a solidarity contribution of 4% pushes the top rate to 43%. On 25 October 2001 Italy's gift and inheritance taxes were abolished by the Parliament.

Italy's main indirect tax is its value-added tax (VAT) introduced on 1 January 1973 with a standard rate of 12%, replacing a turnover tax on goods and services. Since 10 January 1997 the standard rate has been at 20% and is applicable to most goods and services. A reduced rate of 10% is applied to some foodstuffs, certain fuel supplies, some transport and some housing, consumers, catering services and live animals. A 4% rate is applied to some foodstuffs, books, newspapers and periodicals, agricultural inputs, and medical equipment. Basic medical and dental services, as well as financial and insurance services are exempt from VAT. A 0% rate is applied to supplies of unwrought gold and ferrous and nonferrous metal scrap, and land not suitable for buildings. Other taxes on transactions include stamp taxes, and contract registration tax.

37 CUSTOMS AND DUTIES

Italy's membership in the European Union has greatly influenced its tariff structure. Duties on imports from then-European Community members and their dependencies were gradually reduced following the Rome Pact in 1957 and disappeared by 1969, more than a year ahead of schedule. Duties on goods from Greece, which entered the European Community in 1981, were reduced gradually and eliminated by 1986. Italy's adjustment of its tariff structure to that of the now-European Union also has resulted in a substantial reduction of duties on products imported from areas other than the European Union, including the United States.

Import duties on manufactured goods from non-EU countries range from 5–8%, while raw materials enter mostly duty-free. Other import taxes include a value-added tax (VAT) that ranges from 0–20% depending on the product and excise taxes on alcoholic beverages, tobacco, sugar and petroleum products.

38 FOREIGN INVESTMENT

Because of a lack of domestic venture capital, the government encourages foreign industrial investment through tax concessions on a case-by-case basis. Foreign ownership, however, is limited by law and includes the following regulations: foreign investment can be limited for "reasons essential to the national economy." As a consequence, foreign investment in banks is limited to less than 5% of an institution's capital without government consent. Although privatization is encouraging foreign investment, defense industries remain off limits to non-Italians. However, the extent of the state's direct involvement in the economy has been greatly reduced by the privatization program carried out by successive governments since 1993, encouraged by EU restrictions on state aid to industry and the need to reduce public-sector debt. In an effort to increase confidence of foreign investors in Italy's economic development, the government has enacted legislation providing special incentives, particularly for investments in the south—Sicily, Sardinia, and the peninsula south of Rome. In recent years, and in accordance with EU liberalization, foreign restrictions on foreign investment in Italy have eased. The corporate tax rate was cut from 36% to 33% in 2004.

Annual foreign direct investment (FDI) into Italy was $2.6 billion in 1998, down from $3.7 billion in 1997. Total FDI stock in Italy in 1998 was about $103 billion. Annual FDI inflow jumped to almost $7 billion in 1999 and continued to increase for the next three years: to $13.4 billion in 2000, $14.9 billion in 2001, and $15.2 billion in 2002, an average of $13.7 billion a year. Total FDI stock in Italy reached about $140 billion by 2002. Italy has remained an underachiever, however, in the attraction of FDI. For the period 1988 to 1990, Italy's share of world FDI inflows was 60% of its share of world GDP. For the period 1998 to 2000, Italy's share of world inward FDI had dropped to only 20% of its share of world GDP. About 63% of inward stock in the 1990s had come from EU countries, up from 55% in the 1980s.

In the 1980s, outward FDI had about equaled inward FDI in Italy, but in the 1990s Italy became a net outward investor. From 1999 to 2002, average annual outward FDI from Italy was $18.4 billion. As of 2001, FDI stock held by Italians in foreign countries totaled about $236 billion. Roughly 60% of Italian holdings of outward stock in the 1990s were in EU countries, the same as in the 1980s.

From 2000–04, FDI inflows averaged 1.2% of GDP. In 2004, Italy jumped from 12th to 9th most attractive FDI destination in the world, driven primarily by increased confidence among US and Asian investors, according to the FDI Confidence Index. In 2004, intra-EU-25 FDI inflows to Italy amounted to €10.2 billion; extra-EU-25 inflows amounted to €1.9 billion. That year, outward Italian FDI flows to the EU-25 amounted to €14.2 billion; outward FDI flows from Italy to non-EU-25 countries amounted to €0.5 billion. In all, inward FDI in 2004 totaled €16.8 billion; outward FDI totaled €19.3 billion.

39 ECONOMIC DEVELOPMENT

Under Mussolini, business and labor were grouped into corporations that, in theory at least, jointly determined economic policy. Also, under the Fascist regime, direct government control over the economy was increased through the creation of powerful economic bodies, such as the Institute for Industrial Reconstruction. Although the corporative system disappeared after the fall of Mussolini, the concept of economic planning remained firmly implanted among the large Marxist parties, as well as among Christian Democratic leaders, who—by different means and for different reasons—sought to create a society free from the class warfare associated with a strictly liberal economic system.

Principal government objectives following World War II were reconstruction of the economy; stabilization of the currency; and long-term, large-scale investment aimed at correcting the imbalance of the Italian economy and, in particular, the imbalance between northern and southern Italy. The first and second phases of this policy were accomplished by 1949. Then the government, supported by domestic financial and industrial groups and by foreign aid, principally from the United States, embarked on the third and most important phase, best known as the Vanoni Plan (after former finance minister Ezio Vanoni). Notable in this development effort was the Cassa per il Mezzogiorno, a government agency set up to develop southern Italy and attract private investment to the region. Between 1951 and 1978, government spending on infra-

structure in the south was $11.5 billion; additional low-cost loans totaled $13 billion, and outright grants amounted to $3.2 billion.

Simultaneously, direct government control of the economy increased through such government agencies as ENI (National Hydrocarbon Agency), whose activities expanded rapidly in the postwar era. The nationalization of the electric industry, in order to lay the industrial base for a more highly planned economy, and the creation of the National Economic Planning Board composed of leaders from government, industry, and labor were further indications of the importance attached to the concept of a planned Italian economy.

The combined effects of inflation, increased energy prices, and political instability posed serious economic problems during the 1970s. With Italy mired in recession in the early 1980s, economic policy was directed at reducing the public sector deficit, tightening controls on credit, and maintaining a stable exchange rate, chiefly through a variety of short-term constraints. A period of recovery began in 1983, leading to expanded output and lower inflation but also to expanded unemployment. The economic policy aims in 1987 included the reduction of the public-sector deficit and unemployment. Furthermore, improvement in the external sector (due mainly to the fall of oil prices and depreciation of the dollar) led to liberalization of the foreign exchange market in 1987.

Priorities of the early 1990s were cutting government spending, fighting tax evasion to reduce public debt, and selling off state-owned enterprises. At the end of the decade the results of these policies were mixed. Liberalization provided the impetus for greater foreign investment, while the funds generated from privatization eased the public debt. Italy qualified for the first round of Economic and Monetary Union (EMU) and entered the euro zone in 1999. Tax evasion remains a problem; the underground economy is still estimated at nearly 25% of official GDP. Moreover, the economic disparities between the prosperous north and the impoverished south remain.

The strength of the economy rests on the back of small- and medium-sized family-owned companies, mostly in the north and center of the country. In 2005, the average Italian company employed 4 people, and industrial companies had an average of around 9 employees, compared with an average 15 employees in the EU. In mid-2000, Italy's largest state holding company, Istituto per la Ricostruzione Industriale (IRI), was liquidated.

Italy's public debt in 2004 was estimated at 105.6% of GDP. The EU's mandated debt to GDP ratio is 60%. The budget deficit was forecast to rise from about 3% of GDP in 2004 to 4–4.5% in 2005–06, before falling to just under 4% in 2007. GDP growth remained flat in 2005, but was expected to pick up to a still disappointing 1–1.2% in 2006–07. Reform of the pension system continues to be a controversial policy issue. The focus of economic policy has been on cutting taxes, fighting unemployment, enhancing competitiveness, and reducing both the budget deficit and debt. However, the only areas in which the government had made limited progress by 2005 were in the labor market and the pension system. Balancing fiscal austerity and policies to promote growth pose a major economic policy challenge.

40 SOCIAL DEVELOPMENT

Social welfare legislation in Italy, begun in 1898, was redesigned by law in 1952 and has subsequently been expanded. All workers and their families are covered and receive old-age, disability, and survivor pensions, unemployment and injury benefits, health and maternity coverage. The system is primarily funded by employer contributions, along with employee payments and some government subsidies. Family allowances are paid for primarily by employer contributions, and are determined by the size and income of the family. Conditions for old age pensions have varying conditions. The first maternity coverage was initiated in 1912, and was most recently updated in 2001.

Despite full legal rights under law, women face some social discrimination in Italy. On average, women earn less than men and are underrepresented in management, the professions, and other areas. Sexual abuse and violence remain a problem, although when reported, the authorities prosecute perpetrators and assist victims. Increased public awareness of sexual harassment and violence increased the number of reported abuses in 2004. The government is committed to protecting and promoting children's rights.

Human rights are generally respected in Italy. Lengthy pretrial detentions still occur due to the slow pace of the judicial system, and occasional cases of the mistreatment of prisoners were reported. Discrimination based on race, sex, religion, ethnicity, disability, and language is prohibited by law.

41 HEALTH

A national health plan, begun in 1980, seeks to provide free health care for all citizens, but certain minimum charges remain. It is financed by contributions from salaries, by employers, and by the central government. Patients are still able to choose their own health care providers. Reform implementation in the 1980s and 1990s has been difficult. In 1994, the government announced plans to dismantle public universal insurance. Reforms in 1999 sought to integrate primary care with other health care programs, including home care, social services, and health education. Consistent health reforms are hampered by frequent political changes in administration. Most private hospitals have contracts with the national plan, but health care services are more highly concentrated in the northern regions of Italy. The shortage of medical personnel and hospital facilities in Italy's rural areas remains serious. Closure of a number of underutilized hospitals was planned and the government has been making efforts to curb the state deficit in health expenditures; budgets and estimates are repeatedly more than demand. Health care expenditures were 8.2% of GDP.

As of 2004, Italy had the highest number of physicians per capita at an estimated 606 per 100,000 people. In addition, there were approximately 446 nurses, 59 dentists and 110 pharmacists per 100,000 population. In the same year, Italy had 842 public hospitals and 539 private ones, for a total of approximately 276,000 beds.

The infant mortality rate, 72.1 per 1,000 live births in 1948, decreased to 5.94 per 1,000 by 2005, when average life expectancy was estimated to be 79.68 years. As of 2002, birth and death rates were estimated respectively at 8.9 and 10.1 per 1,000 people. Approximately 78% of married women (ages 15 to 49) were using contraception.

In 1999, immunization rates for children up to one year of age were: diphtheria, pertussis, and tetanus, 95%, and measles, 70%. The major causes of death were circulatory system diseases, cancers, respiratory diseases, and accidents and violence. As of 2004,

there were approximately 140,000 people living with HIV/AIDS in the country. The HIV/AIDS prevalence was 0.50 per 100 adults in 2003. There were an estimated 1,000 deaths from AIDS in 2003.

42 HOUSING

Italy's housing and public building program was a major item in the general program of postwar reconstruction. Between 1940 and 1945, almost 20% of the habitable rooms in the country were destroyed. From June 1945 to June 1953, however, of the 6,407,000 rooms destroyed or severely damaged, 354,100 were rebuilt and 4,441,000 were repaired. Under a special housing program, originally instituted with funds from UNRRA and subsequently financed by employer and employee contributions, a total of 15 million rooms were constructed between 1953 and 1961, alleviating the nation's immediate housing problems.

In the 1980s 59% of all dwellings were owner occupied and 36% were rented. Almost 88% had indoor flush toilets, 99.5% had electricity, 59% had central heating, and 34% were heated by a stove or similar source. In 1999, 156,000 new dwellings were completed.

43 EDUCATION

Education is free and compulsory for eight years (for students age 6 through 15), this includes five years of elementary school and three years of lower secondary school. Next, students may choose to attend a technical school, a vocational school, or one of several academic secondary schools, which offer a choice of specialized programs in classical, scientific, linguistic, and artistic studies. All secondary programs generally cover a five-year course of study.

In 2001, about 98% of children between the ages of three and five were enrolled in some type of preschool program. Primary school enrollment in 2003 was estimated at about 99% of age-eligible students. The same year, secondary school enrollment was about 91% of age-eligible students. The student-to-teacher ratio for primary school was at about 11:1 in 2003.

There are 55 state universities and 23 other universities, colleges, and higher learning institutes, including the University of Bologna (founded in the 11th century), the oldest in Italy, and the University of Rome, which is the country's largest. In 2003, about 57% of the tertiary age population were enrolled in some type of higher education program; with 49% for men and 65% for women. The adult literacy rate for 2003 was estimated at about 98.6%.

As of 2003, public expenditure on education was estimated at 4.7% of GDP, or 10.3% of total government expenditures.

44 LIBRARIES AND MUSEUMS

Italy, with its rich cultural heritage, is one of the world's great storehouses of books and art. Among its many of libraries, the most important are in the national library system, which contains two central libraries, in Florence (5.3 million volumes) and Rome (5 million), and four regional libraries, in Naples (1.8 million volumes), Milan (1 million), Turin (973,000) and Venice (917,000). The existence of two national central libraries, while most nations have one, came about through the history of the country, as Rome was once part of the Papal States and Florence was the first capital of the unified Kingdom of Italy. While both libraries are designated as copyright libraries, Florence now serves as the site designated for conservation and cataloging of Italian publications and the site in Rome catalogs foreign publications acquired by the state libraries. All of the national libraries are public. The Estense Library in Modena holds 425,600 volumes, including illuminated manuscripts from the 14th to 18th centuries. The university libraries in Bologna (1.1 million volumes) and Naples (750,000 volumes) each hold important collections. The Medici-Laurentian and Marucelliana (544,000) libraries in Florence and the Ambrosiana Library in Milan are also important research centers. Italy's public library system has about 84 branches and holds a total of 41 million volumes.

Italy, a world center of culture, history and art, has more than 3,000 museums. Among the more important are the Villa Giulia Museum and the National Gallery in Rome; the National Archeological Museum and the National Museum of San Martino in Naples; the National Museum in Palermo; the Galleria dell'Academia, and Uffizi, Medici, Pitti, Bargello, and St. Mark's Museums in Florence; the National Museum in Cagliari, Sardinia; the Brera Museum in Milan; the Museum of Siena; the Archaeological Museum of Syracuse (Siracusa); the National Museum of Urbino; and the Guggenheim Museum and the Academy and Libreria Sansoviniana in Venice. Venice also has the Jewish Museum, the Diocesan Museum of Sacred Art, a Natural History Museum, an Archeological Museum, and the Museum of Byzantine Icons. The Campidoglio Museum, the Museum of Villa Borghese, and the Palazzo Barberini Museum, all in Rome, each contain important works of art by Italian masters. Naples hosts the Museum of Ethnoprehistory of Castel Dell'ovo and museums of paleontology, mineralogy, anthropology, and astronomy. The National Museum of Science and technology in Milan has an extensive exhibit on Leonardo da Vinci, including models of some of the machines designed by the Renaissance man. A Goethe museum, with manuscripts and illustrations describing Goethe's travels in Italy, opened in 1997 in Rome. Villa Torlonia, Mussolini's home, was renovated in 2001 and opened as a museum.

45 MEDIA

Communication systems in Italy, including telephone, telex, and data services, are generally considered to be modern, well developed, and fully automated. In 2003, there were an estimated 484 mainline telephones for every 1,000 people. The same year, there were approximately 1,018 mobile phones in use for every 1,000 people.

Radiotelevisione Italiana (RAI), a government corporation, broadcasts on three channels. In 2004, there were an additional four national broadcast channels, three of which were operated by Mediaset, a company owned by Prime Minister Berlusconi. A 2004 media law initiated an intent to partially privatize RAI. Advertising appears on RAI television, two of the three RAI radio networks, and on many private stations. In 2003, there were an estimated 878 radios for every 1,000 people. The number of television sets was unavailable in the same survey. Also in 2003, there were 230.7 personal computers for every 1,000 people and 337 of every 1,000 people had access to the Internet. There were 1,994 secure Internet servers in the country in 2004.

As of 2002, there were about 90 daily newspapers in the country, but not all of them had national circulation. The major daily newspapers (with their political orientations and estimated circulations) are: *La Repubblica* (Rome), left-wing, 754,300 in 2004; *Corriere della Sera* (Milan), independent, 582,500 in 2002; *La Stampa*

(Turin), liberal, 536,233 in 2004; *Il Sole-24 Ore* (a financial newspaper from Milan), 397,000 in 2002; *Il Messaggero* (Rome), left of center, 337,157 in 2004; *Il Resto del Carlino* (Bologna), 251,173 in 2004; *Il Giornale* (Milan), independent, 215,000 in 2002; and *L'Unità* (Rome-Milan), Communist, 200,760 in 2002. *Panorama* is the most popular news weekly with a circulation of 545,500 in 2002. The periodical press is becoming increasingly important. Among the most important periodicals are the pictorial weeklies—*Oggi, L'Europeo, Epoca, L'Espresso,* and *Gente. Famiglia Cristiana* is a Catholic weekly periodical with a wide readership.

Italy enjoys a free press, with vigorous expression of all shades of opinion. The majority of papers are published in northern and central Italy, and circulation is highest in these areas. Rome and Milan are the most important publication centers. A considerable number of dailies are owned by the political parties, the Roman Catholic Church, and various economic groups. In general, the journalistic level of the Italian papers is high, and two dailies, Milan's *Corriere della Sera* and Turin's *La Stampa*, enjoy international respect.

The law provides for freedom of speech and the press, and the government is said to respect these rights in practice.

46 ORGANIZATIONS

Italian society abounds with organizations of every description. Many of these are associated with or controlled by political parties, which have their ideological counterparts in labor organizations, agricultural associations, cultural groups, sports clubs, and cooperatives. Among the most important organizations are the National Confederation of Smallholders and the General Confederation of Italian Industry, which strongly influences economic policy. The General Confederation of Agriculture, the General Confederation of Trade, and the General Confederation of Master Craftsmen also are influential. There are chambers of commerce in most major cities. There are labor and trade unions and professional associations representing a wide variety of occupations. A large number of professional organizations are dedicated to research and education in specialized fields of medicine or for particular diseases and conditions.

Catholic Action and the Catholic Association of Italian Workers are the most prominent of the religious organizations. The international religious Order of St. Augustine and the Society of Jesus (Jesuits) are based in Rome.

A number of political and religious organizations sponsor youth chapters. Scouting programs and chapters of the YMCA/ YWCA are also active for youth. Sports associations are plentiful and include such a variety of pastimes as tennis, badminton, tae kwon do, cricket, and football (soccer). National women's organizations include the National Italian Women's Council, the Italian Association for Women in Development, and the Italian Women's Center, based in Rome.

International organizations within the country include Amnesty International, Caritas, and the Red Cross.

47 TOURISM, TRAVEL, AND RECREATION

Among Italy's tourist attractions are the artistic and architectural treasures of Rome and Florence; the thousands of historic churches and galleries in smaller cities; the canals and palaces of Venice; the ruins of ancient Pompeii; the Shroud of Turin, reputed to be the burial cloth of Jesus; and the delicacies of northern Italian cooking, as well as the heartier fare of the south. Tourists are also lured by Italy's many beaches and by excellent Alpine skiing. Italians enjoy a wide variety of sports, including football (soccer), bowling, tennis, track and field, and swimming. Italy won the World Cup in soccer three times, in 1934 (as host), 1938, and 1982. Cortina d'Ampezzo, in the Dolomites, was the site of the 1956 Winter Olympics. Rome hosted the Summer Olympics in 1960. Turin was the host the 2006 Winter Olympics.

A valid passport is necessary to travel to Italy. For stays of up to 90 days a visa is not required. Within eight days all travelers must register with local police and obtain a visitor's permit. Proof of sufficient funds for the visit may also be required.

Tourism, a major industry in Italy, brought in 39,604,118 visitors in 2003. There were 999,722 hotel rooms with 1,969,495 beds and an occupancy rate of 39%. Tourism expenditure receipts totaled $32.5 billion.

In 2005, the US Department of State estimated the daily expenses for staying in Rome at $490; in Florence, $437; in Milan, $442; and in Venice, $341.

⁴⁸FAMOUS ITALIANS

The Italian peninsula has been at the heart of Western cultural development at least since Roman times. Important poets of the Roman republic and empire were Lucretius (Titus Lucretius Carus, 96?–55 BC), Gaius Valerius Catullus (84?–54 BC), Vergil (Publius Vergilius Maro, 70–19 BC), Horace (Quintius Horatius Flaccus, 65–8 BC), and Ovid (Publius Ovidius Naso, 43 BC–AD 18). Also prominent in Latin literature were the orator-rhetorician Marcus Tullius Cicero (106–43 BC); the satirists Gaius Petronius Arbiter (d. AD 66) and Juvenal (Decimus Junius Juvenalis, AD 60?–140?); the prose writers Pliny the Elder (Gaius Plinius Secundus, AD 23–79), his nephew Pliny the Younger (Gaius Plinius Caecilius Secundus, AD 61?–113?), and Lucius Apuleius (AD 124?–170?); and the historians Sallust (Gaius Sallustius Crispus, 86–34 BC), Livy (Titus Livius, 59 BC–AD 17), Cornelius Tacitus (AD 55?–117), and Suetonius (Gaius Suetonius Tranquillus, AD 69?–140). Gaius Julius Caesar (100?–44 BC), renowned as a historian and prose stylist, is even more famous as a military and political leader. The first of the Roman emperors was Octavian (Gaius Octavianus, 63 BC–AD 14), better known by the honorific Augustus. Noteworthy among later emperors are the tyrants Caligula (Gaius Caesar Germanicus, AD 12–41) and Nero (Lucius Domitius Ahenobarbus, AD 37–68), the philosopher-statesman Marcus Aurelius (Marcus Annius Verius, AD 121–180), and Constantine I (the Great; Flavius Valerius Aurelius Constantinus, b. Moesia, 280?–337), who was the first to accept Christianity. No history of the Christian Church during the medieval period would be complete without mention of such men of Italian birth as St. Benedict of Nursia (480?–543?), Pope Gregory I (St. Gregory the Great, 540?–604), St. Francis of Assisi (1182?–1226), and the philosopher-theologians St. Anselm (1033?–1109) and St. Thomas Aquinas (1225–74).

No land has made a greater contribution to the visual arts. In the 13th and 14th centuries there were the sculptors Niccolò Pisano (1220–84) and his son Giovanni (1245–1314); the painters Cimabue (Cenni di Pepo, 1240–1302?), Duccio di Buoninsegna (1255?–1319), and Giotto di Bondone (1276?–1337); and, later in the period, the sculptor Andrea Pisano (1270?–1348). Among the many great artists of the 15th century—the golden age of Florence and Venice—were the architects Filippo Brunelleschi (1377–1446), Lorenzo Ghiberti (1378–1455), and Leone Battista Alberti (1404–72); the sculptors Donatello (Donato di Niccolò di Betto Bardi, 1386?–1466), Luca della Robbia (1400–1482), Desiderio da Settignano (1428–64), and Andrea del Verrocchio (1435–88); and the painters Fra Angelico (Giovanni de Fiesole, 1387–1455), Sassetta (Stefano di Giovanni, 1392–1450?), Uccello (Paolo di Dono, 1397–1475), Masaccio (Tomasso di Giovanni di Simone Guidi, 1401–28?), Fra Filippo Lippi (1406?–69), Piero della Francesca (Pietro de' Franceschi, 1416?–92), Giovanni Bellini (1430?–1516), Andrea Mantegna (1431–1506), Antonio dei Pollaiuolo (1433–98), Luca Signorelli (1441?–1523), Perugino (Pietro Vannucci, 1446–1524), Sandro Botticelli (Alessandro Filipepi, 1447?–1510), Ghirlandaio (Domenico Currado Bigordi, 1449–94), and Vittore Carpaccio (1450–1522).

During the 16th century, the High Renaissance, Rome shared with Florence the leading position in the world of the arts. Major masters included the architects Bramante (Donato d'Agnolo, 1444?–1514) and Andrea Palladio (1508–80); the sculptor Benvenuto Cellini (1500–1571); the painter-designer-inventor Leonardo da Vinci (1452–1519); the painter-sculptor-architect-poet Michelangelo Buonarroti (1475–1564); and the painters Titian (Tiziano Vecelli, 1477–1576), Giorgione da Castelfranco (Giorgio Barbarelli, 1478?–1510), Raphael (Raffaelo Sanzio, 1483–1520), Andrea del Sarto (1486–1531), and Correggio (Antonio Allegri, 1494–1534). Among the great painters of the late Renaissance were Tintoretto (Jacopo Robusti, 1518–94) and Veronese (Paolo Cagliari, 1528–88). Giorgio Vasari (1511–74) was a painter, architect, art historian, and critic.

Among the leading artists of the Baroque period were the sculptor and architect Giovanni Lorenzo Bernini (1598–1680) and the painters Michelangelo Merisi da Caravaggio (1560?–1609), Giovanni Battista Tiepolo (1690–1770), Canaletto (Antonio Canal, 1697–1768), Pietro Longhi (1702–85), and Francesco Guardi (1712–93). Leading figures in modern painting were Umberto Boccioni (1882–1916), Amedeo Modigliani (1884–1920), Giorgio di Chirico (b. Greece, 1888–1978), and Giorgio Morandi (1890–1964). A noted contemporary architect was Pier Luigi Nervi (1891–1979).

Music, an integral part of Italian life, owes many of its forms as well as its language to Italy. The musical staff was either invented or established by Guido d'Arezzo (995?–1050). A leading 14th-century composer was the blind Florentine organist Francesco Landini (1325–97). Leading composers of the High Renaissance and early Baroque periods were Giovanni Pierluigi da Palestrina (1525–94); the madrigalists Luca Marenzio (1533–99) and Carlo Gesualdo, prince of Venosa (1560?–1613); the Venetian organists Andrea Gabrieli (1510?–86) and Giovanni Gabrieli (1557–1612); Claudio Monteverdi (1567–1643), the founder of modern opera; organist-composer Girolamo Frescobaldi (1583–1643); and Giacomo Carissimi (1605–74). Important figures of the later Baroque era were Arcangelo Corelli (1653–1713), Antonio Vivaldi (1678–1743), Alessandro Scarlatti (1660–1725), and his son Domenico Scarlatti (1683–1757). Italian-born Luigi Cherubini (1760–1842) was the central figure of French music in the Napoleonic era, while Antonio Salieri (1750–1825) and Gasparo Spontini (1774–1851) played important roles in the musical life of

Vienna and Berlin, respectively. Composers of the 19th century who made their period the great age of Italian opera were Gioacchino Antonio Rossini (1792–1868), Gaetano Donizetti (1797–1848), Vincenzo Bellini (1801–35), and, above all, Giuseppe Verdi (1831–1901). Niccolò Paganini (1782–1840) was the greatest violinist of his time. More recent operatic composers include Ruggiero Leoncavallo (1853–1919), Giacomo Puccini (1858–1924), and Pietro Mascagni (1863–1945). Renowned operatic singers include Enrico Caruso (1873–1921), Luisa Tetrazzini (1874–1940), Titta Ruffo (1878–1953), Amelita Galli-Curci (1882–1963), Beniamino Gigli (1890–1957), Ezio Pinza (1892–1957), and Luciano Pavarotti (b.1935). Ferruccio Busoni (1866–1924), Ottorino Respighi (1879–1936), Luigi Dallapiccola (1904–75), Luigi Nono (1924–1990), and Luciano Berio (1925–2003) are major 20th-century composers. Arturo Toscanini (1867–1957) is generally regarded as one of the greatest operatic and orchestral conductors of his time; two noted contemporary conductors are Claudio Abbado (b.1933) and Riccardo Muti (b.1941). The foremost makers of stringed instruments were Gasparo da Salò (Bertolotti, 1540–1609) of Brescia, Niccolò Amati (1596–1684), Antonius Stradivarius (Antonio Stradivari, 1644–1737), and Giuseppe Bartolommeo Guarneri (del Gesù, 1687?–1745) of Cremona. Bartolommeo Cristofori (1655–1731) invented the pianoforte.

Italian literature and literary language began with Dante Alighieri (1265–1321), author of *The Divine Comedy*, and subsequently included Petrarch (Francesco Petrarca, 1304–74), Giovanni Boccaccio (1313–75), Lodovico Ariosto (1474–1533), Pietro Aretino (1492–1556), and Torquato Tasso (1544–95). An outstanding writer of the Baroque period was Metastasio (Pietro Trapassi, 1698–1782), and Carlo Goldoni (1707–93) was the most prominent playwright of the 18th century. The time of Italy's rebirth was heralded by the poets Vittorio Alfieri (1749–1803), Ugo Foscolo (1778–1827), and Giacomo Leopardi (1798–1837). Alessandro Manzoni (1785–1873) was the principal Italian novelist of the 19th century, and Francesco de Sanctis (1817–83) the greatest literary critic. Among the Italian literary figures of the late 19th and early 20th centuries, Giosuè Carducci (1835–1907; Nobel Prize winner, 1906), Giovanni Verga (1840–1922), Gabriele d'Annunzio (1863–1938), Luigi Pirandello (1867–1936; Nobel Prize winner, 1934), and Grazia Deledda (1875–1936; Nobel Prize winner, 1926) achieved international renown. Leading writers of the postwar era are Ignazio Silone (Secondo Tranquilli, 1900–78), Alberto Moravia (Pincherle, 1907–1990), Italo Calvino (1923–87), Umberto Eco (b.1932), and the poets Salvatore Quasimodo (1908–68; Nobel Prize winner, 1959) and Eugenio Montale (1896–1981; Nobel Prize winner, 1975). Outstanding film directors are Italian-born Frank Capra (1897–1991), Vittorio de Sica (1902–74), Luchino Visconti (1906–76), Roberto Rossellini (1906–77), Michelangelo Antonioni (b.1912), Federico Fellini (1920–93), Sergio Leone (1929–1989), Pier Paolo Pasolini (1922–75), Franco Zeffirelli (b.1923), Lina Wertmüller (Arcangela Felice Assunta Wertmüller von Elgg, b.1928), and Bernardo Bertolucci (b.1940). Famous film stars include Italian-born Rudolph Valentino (Rodolfo Alfonso Raffaele Pierre Philibert Guglielmi, 1895–1926), Marcello Mastroianni (1924–1996), and Sophia Loren (Scicoloni, b.1934).

In philosophy, exploration, and statesmanship, Italy has produced many world-renowned figures: the traveler Marco Polo (1254?–1324); the statesman and patron of the arts Cosimo de' Medici (1389–1464); the statesman, clergyman, and artistic patron Roderigo Borgia (Lanzol y Borja, b. Spain, 1431?–1503), who became Pope Alexander VI (r.1492–1503); the soldier, statesman, and artistic patron Lorenzo de' Medici, the son of Cosimo (1449–92); the explorer John Cabot (Giovanni Caboto, 1450?–98?); the explorer Christopher Columbus (Cristoforo Colombo or Cristóbal Colón, 1451–1506); the explorer Amerigo Vespucci (1454–1512), after whom the Americas are named; the admiral and statesman Andrea Doria (1468?–1540); Niccolò Machiavelli (1469–1527), author of *The Prince* and the outstanding political theorist of the Renaissance; the statesman and clergyman Cesare Borgia (1475?–1507), the son of Rodrigo; the explorer Sebastian Cabot (1476?–1557), the son of John; Baldassare Castiglione (1478–1529), author of *The Courtier*; the historian Francesco Guicciardini (1483–1540); the explorer Giovanni da Verrazano (1485?–1528?); the philosopher Giordano Bruno (1548?–1600); the political philosopher Giovanni Battista Vico (1668–1744); the noted jurist Cesare Bonesana Beccaria (1735–94); Giuseppe Mazzini (1805–72), the leading spirit of the Risorgimento; Camillo Benso di Cavour (1810–61), its prime statesman; and Giuseppe Garibaldi (1807–82), its foremost soldier and man of action. Notable intellectual and political leaders of more recent times include the Nobel Peace Prize winner in 1907, Ernesto Teodoro Moneta (1833–1918); the sociologist and economist Vilfredo Pareto (1848–1923); the political theorist Gaetano Mosca (1858–1941); the philosopher, critic, and historian Benedetto Croce (1866–1952); the educator Maria Montessori (1870–1952); Benito Mussolini (1883–1945), the founder of Fascism and dictator of Italy from 1922 to 1943; Carlo Sforza (1873–1952) and Alcide De Gasperi (1881–1954), famous latter-day statesmen; and the Communist leaders Antonio Gramsci (1891–1937), Palmiro Togliatti (1893–1964), and Enrico Berlinguer (1922–84).

Italian scientists and mathematicians of note include Leonardo Fibonacci (1180?–1250?), Galileo Galilei (1564–1642), Evangelista Torricelli (1608–47), Francesco Redi (1626?–97), Marcello Malpighi (1628–94), Luigi Galvani (1737–98), Lazzaro Spallanzani (1729–99), Alessandro Volta (1745–1827), Amedeo Avogadro (1776–1856), Stanislao Cannizzaro (1826–1910), Camillo Golgi (1843–1926; Nobel Prize winner, 1906), Guglielmo Marconi (1874–1937; Nobel Prize winner, 1909), Enrico Fermi (1901–54; Nobel Prize winner, 1938), Giulio Natta (1903–79; Nobel Prize winner, 1963), Italian-American Emilio Gino Segrè (1905–1989; Nobel Prize winner, 1959), Daniel Bovet (1907–1992; Nobel Prize winner, 1957), Renato Dulbecco (b.1914; Nobel Prize winner, 1975), Carlo Rubbia (b.1934; Nobel Prize winner, 1984), and Rita Levi-Montalcini (1909-1989; Nobel Prize winner, 1986), and Italian-American Riccardo Giacconi (b.1931; Nobel Prize winner, 2002).

49 DEPENDENCIES

Italy has no territories or colonies.

50 BIBLIOGRAPHY

Andrews, Geoff. *Not a Normal Country: Italy after Berlusconi*. Ann Arbor, Mich.: Pluto Press, 2005.

Baranski, Zygmunt G. and Rebecca J. West (eds.). *The Cambridge Companion to Modern Italian Culture*. New York: Cambridge University Press, 2001.

Ben-Ghiat, Ruth. *Fascist Modernities: Italy, 1922–1945*. Berkeley: University of California Press, 2001.

Duggan, Christopher. *A Concise History of Italy*. New York: Cambridge University Press, 1994.

Findlen, Paula (ed.). *The Italian Renaissance: The Essential Readings*. Malden, Mass.: Blackwell, 2002.

Gardner, Richard N. *Mission Italy: On the Front Lines of the Cold War*. Lanham, Md.: Rowan and Littlefield, 2005.

Ginsborg, Paul. *A History of Contemporary Italy: Society and Politics, 1943–1988*. London: Penguin, 1990.

Hearder, Harry. *Italy: A Short History*. New York: Cambridge University Press, 2001.

International Smoking Statistics: A Collection of Historical Data from 30 Economically Developed Countries. New York: Oxford University Press, 2002.

Moliterno, Gino (ed.). *Encyclopedia of Contemporary Italian Culture*. New York: Routledge, 2000.

Torriglia, Anna Maria. *Broken Time, Fragmented Space: A Cultural Map for Postwar Italy*. Buffalo: University of Toronto Press, 2002.

Wessels, Wolfgang, Andreas Maurer, and Jürgan Mittag (eds.). *Fifteen into One?: the European Union and Its Member States*. New York: Palgrave, 2003.

LATVIA

Republic of Latvia
Latvijas Republika

CAPITAL: Riga

FLAG: The flag consists of a single white horizontal stripe on a maroon field.

ANTHEM: *Dievs, svēti Latviju! (God bless Latvia!).*

MONETARY UNIT: The lat was introduced as the official currency in May 1993; $1 = Ls1.78571 (or $1 = Ls0.56) as of 2005.

WEIGHTS AND MEASURES: The metric system is in force.

HOLIDAYS: New Year's Day, 1 January; Good Friday (movable); Midsummer Festival, 23–24 June; National Day, Proclamation of the Republic, 18 November; Christmas, 25–26 December; New Year's Eve, 31 December.

TIME: 2 PM = noon GMT.

---

¹LOCATION, SIZE, AND EXTENT

Latvia is located in northeastern Europe, bordering the Baltic Sea, between Sweden and Russia. Comparatively, Latvia is slightly larger than the state of West Virginia, with a total area of 64,589 sq km (24,938 sq mi). Latvia shares boundaries with Estonia on the N, Russia on the E, Belarus on the S, Lithuania on the SW, and the Baltic Sea on the W. Latvia's land boundary length totals 1,150 km (713 mi). Its coastline is 531 km (330 mi). Latvia's capital city, Riga, is located near the southern edge of the Gulf of Riga.

²TOPOGRAPHY

The topography of Latvia consists mainly of a central and eastern lowland plains enclosed in areas of uplands consisting of moderate-sized hills. The highest point in the country is Gaizinkalns (312 m/1,024 ft), located near the edge of the Vidzme uplands. The nation's longest river is the Daugava (Dvina); which begins in Russia and passes through both Belarus and Latvia in its course to the Gulf of Riga. The total length of the Daugava is 1,020 km (632 mi).

³CLIMATE

The country's climate is influenced by geographical location and by its closeness to the North Atlantic Ocean. The average temperature in July is between 16.8°C and 17.6°C (62–64°F). In January the average temperature ranges between –2.8°C and 6.6°C (31–44°F). The rainfall in the country is between 56–79 cm (22–31 in).

⁴FLORA AND FAUNA

Half of Latvia's soil is podzolic humus, which covers about one-third of the country's arable land. Woodlands make up about 47% of the country's territory, with one-half of the forests consisting of pines, birch, and firs. About 10% of the total land area is covered in marshes, swamps, or peat bogs. Species native to Latvia are the wild boar, Eurasian beaver, and brown bear. The Baltic Sea coast is home to a significant population of seals. The routes of migratory birds pass along the Black Sea and over the country. As of 2002, there were at least 83 species of mammals, 216 species of birds, and over 1,150 species of plants throughout the country.

⁵ENVIRONMENT

Air and water pollution are among Latvia's most significant environmental concerns and are largely related to a lack of waste treatment facilities. In 2000, the total of carbon dioxide emissions was at 6 million metric tons. Cars and other vehicles account for a majority of the country's air pollution. Acid rain has contributed to the destruction of Latvia's forests. Latvia's water supply is perilously polluted with agricultural chemicals and industrial waste. The Gulf of Riga and the Daugava River are both heavily polluted.

According to a 2006 report issued by the International Union for Conservation of Nature and Natural Resources (IUCN), threatened species included four types of mammals, eight species of birds, three species of fish, and eight species of invertebrates. Threatened species include the black vulture, the asp, the Eurasian beaver, the medicinal leech, the marsh snail, and the Russian desman. In 2003, about 13.4% of the total land area was protected, including six Ramsar wetland sites.

⁶POPULATION

The population of Latvia in 2005 was estimated by the United Nations (UN) at 2,300,000, which placed it at number 138 in population among the 193 nations of the world. In 2005, approximately 16% of the population was over 65 years of age, with another 15% of the population under 15 years of age. There were 84 males for every 100 females in the country. According to the UN, the annual population rate of change for 2005–10 was expected to be -0.5%, a rate the government viewed as too low. The country has had low fertility rates since the mid-1990s. The projected population for the year 2025 was 2,156,000. The population density was 36 per sq km (92 per sq mi).

The UN estimated that 68% of the population lived in urban areas in 2005, and that population in urban areas was declining at an annual rate of -0.99%. The capital city, Riga, had a population of 733,000 in that year, and Daugavpils had an estimated of 124,887. There were 75 urban localities, many located on rivers or coastal areas.

7 MIGRATION

Some 250,000 Latvians fled Soviet occupation during World War II, and others were sent to Soviet labor camps. After the war many Russians moved to Latvia.

With independence in 1991, citizenship issues surrounding the large non-Latvian ethnic population became a problem. Only 55% were ethnic Latvians; 32% were Russians; 3.9% Belarussians; and 9.1% other. Immigration from other former Soviet republics came to 4,590 in 1992. A breakthrough came in 1998 when the Citizenship Law was changed, abolishing the annual quota of naturalizations and entitling children born after independence to automatically acquire Latvian citizenship upon request from their parents. A total of 51,778 persons emigrated when Latvia gained independence in 1991; almost all of them went to Russia, Ukraine, or Belarus.

In 2000 there were 613,000 migrants living in Latvia. This amounts to about 25% of the total population. In 2004 noncitizens in Latvia numbered 452,003, and 173 were stateless, all of concern to the United Nations High Commissioner for Refugees (UNHCR). In 2005, the net migration rate was an estimated -2.25 migrants per 1,000 population, a change from -8.8 per 1,000 in 1990. The government views the immigration level as too high, but the emigration level as satisfactory.

8 ETHNIC GROUPS

According to 2002 estimates, the percentage of ethnic Latvians is about 57.7% of the total population. Russians constitute about 29.6% of the population; Belarussians make up 4.1%; Ukrainians account for 2.7%; Poles for 2.5%; Lithuanians for 1.4%; and others 2%. The Romani population is estimated at about 13,000 to 15,000 people. Nearly half the Russians and Ukrainians lived in Riga, where Russians formed a majority of the population. All residents of pre-1940 Latvia and their descendants are citizens. Naturalization requires 16 years' residence and fluency in Latvian.

9 LANGUAGES

Latvian (also called Lettish), a Baltic language written in the Roman alphabet, is the official language; it is spoken by about 58.2% of the population. It is highly inflected, with seven noun cases and six verb declensions. The stress is always on the first syllable. There are three dialects. The macron is used for long vowels, and there is a hacek for "h." A cedilla adds the y sound. Education is now available in both Latvian and Russian, the latter of which is spoken by about 37.5% of the population. Lithuania and other languages are spoken by about 4.3% of the population.

10 RELIGIONS

After declaring independence from the Soviet Union in 1991, freedom of religion and worship was restored for the first time since 1941. Christianity had arrived in Latvia in the 12th century, and the Reformation made Lutheranism the primary religious persua-

sion after 1530. Currently the three largest faiths are Catholicism, Lutheranism, and Orthodoxy.

In 2004, the Latvian Justice Ministry had registered more than 1,000 religious congregations, including 308 Lutheran, 264 Roman Catholic, 125 Orthodox, 96 Baptist, 67 Old Believer (a breakaway Orthodox sect dating from the 17th century), 50 Seventh-Day Adventist, 15 Muslim, 13 Jehovah's Witnesses, 13 Methodists, 13 Jewish, 11 Hare Krishna, 5 Buddhist, 4 Mormon, and over 100 others. According to church membership rolls submitted to the Justice Ministry, the Lutheran Church has about 556,000 members, the Roman Catholic Church has about 430,405 members, and the Orthodox Churches have about 350,000 members. There are only about 6,000 Jews in the country.

The constitution provides for freedom of religion and this right is generally respected in practice. Though there is no state religion, six religions are recognized by the government as traditional religions: Lutheranism, Roman Catholicism, Orthodoxy, Old Believers, the Baptist Church, and Judaism. All other religions are categorized as "new" religions; these groups have not offered any reports of significant discrimination. Certain Christian holidays are celebrated as national holidays. The New Religions Consultative offers opinions to the government on specific issues. The Ecclesiastical Council offers regular input on issues of common concern.

11 TRANSPORTATION

Latvia's railroad system, as of 2004, consisted of 2,303 km (1,432 mi) of broad and narrow gauge railway that linked the country's port cities with Russia. More than 80% of railway use is for daily commuting. Of the total rail lines in operation, 2,270 km (1,412 mi) was broad gauge, of which 257 km (160 mi) had been electrified. In 2003, there were 69,919 km (43,490 mi) of highways in Latvia, all of which were paved. In that same year, there were 619,081 passengers cars and 125,030 commercial vehicles in use. Maritime ports include Riga, Ventspils, and Liepāja. In 2005, the merchant fleet consisted of 19 ships of 1,000 GRT or more, with a total of 53,153 GRT. Ventspils is the terminus of the 750 km (466 mi) oil pipeline from Polotsk, Belarus. As of 2004, the country also had 300 km (186 mi) of navigable waterways.

In 2004, Latvia had an estimated 50 airports, 23 of which had paved runways as of 2005. The principal airport at Riga has international air links to Helsinki, Stockholm, Copenhagen, and New York, as well as direct flights to Austria, Germany, Israel, Russia, and Belarus. In 2003 about 340,000 passengers were carried on scheduled domestic and international airline flights.

12 HISTORY

Germans, Poles, Swedes, and Russians competed for influence in what is now Latvia from the Middle Ages until the 18th century, when it was incorporated into the Russian Empire. During the 19th century, a Latvian nationalist movement arose which by the early 20th century sought independence. The political chaos in Europe following World War I provided the opportunity for Latvia to break away from Russia's control.

On 18 November 1918, the independent Republic of Latvia was proclaimed. Moscow recognized Latvian independence in the August 1920 Soviet-Latvian treaty, and the new republic joined the League of Nations in 1922. Latvia prospered economically during

LOCATION: 57°0′ N; 25°0′ E. BOUNDARY LENGTHS: Total boundary lengths, 1,150 kilometers (715 miles); Belarus, 141 kilometers (88 miles); Estonia, 339 kilometers (211 miles); Lithuania, 453 kilometers (281 miles); Russia, 217 kilometers (135 miles).

the 1920s, and began to export dairy and grain products to Europe. During the 1930s, as tensions in Europe escalated, the Soviet government allied itself with the United Kingdom and France, which in July 1939 granted the concession that Soviet troops could move into the Baltic States in case an indirect aggression was made by Germany. Sensing that an alliance between the United Kingdom, France, and the USSR would leave Germany politically and militarily surrounded, the Nazi government decided to reach its own agreement with the Soviet government in August 1939. A secret protocol to the 1939 Nazi-Soviet pact assigned Latvia to the Soviet sphere of influence.

Soviet forces invaded Latvia on 17 June 1940, and Latvia was incorporated into the USSR. Thousands of Latvia's military and law enforcement officials were executed; political and social leaders were imprisoned. Latvian civilians were deported en masse to Soviet camps in Siberia; 15,000 alone were expelled on the night of 14 June 1941. The Soviets, however, lost control of Latvia to the Germans in July 1941, shortly after Hitler launched his attack on the USSR. Soviet forces recaptured Latvia in 1944. During the Teheran Conference of November/December 1943 between US

president Franklin D. Roosevelt and the Soviet leader Joseph Stalin, it was agreed that the USSR would maintain control of the Baltic States, and this agreement was confirmed at the Conference of Yalta in February 1945.

Following World War II, forced collectivization of agriculture began another round of deportations in 1949, bringing the total number of postwar deportees to more than 200,000. The Soviet policy of russification sought to replace Latvian language and culture with those of Russia. Freedom of speech, press, and religion was denied. For most of the 50 years of Soviet rule, political dissent was strictly forbidden.

Soviet president Mikhail Gorbachev's policy of *glasnost* and *perestroika* allowed Latvians to voice their long-suppressed desire for national self-determination. In June 1987, an openly anti-Soviet demonstration took place in Riga. In 1988, political activists founded the Latvian National Independence Movement and the Latvian Popular Front (LPF). On 23 August 1989, Latvians, Lithuanians, and Estonians organized a massive demonstration of Baltic solidarity. The LPF united independence forces and gained a majority in the elections for the Latvian Supreme Council in the spring of 1990. On 4 May 1990 provisional independence and a period of transitional rule were proclaimed.

On 21 August 1991—shortly after the failure of a coup against Gorbachev—Latvia proclaimed its full independence. The first postindependence elections for the new Saeima (parliament) were held on 5–6 June 1993. On 30 April 1994, the Latvian and Russian governments signed a series of accords calling for the withdrawal of nearly all Russian armed forces from Latvia by the end of that year. On 12 June 1995, Latvia, Estonia, and Lithuania signed accords with the EU that were to eventually lead to full membership. A second parliamentary election the same year resulted in a legislature that was strongly divided between pro-Western and pro-Russian contingents. At the end of 1995, Andris Shkele, a former government official and businessman, became prime minister, heading a broad-based coalition cabinet. Shkele, who retained his post until 1997, balanced the budget and sped up economic reform, although his leadership style alienated many other politicians.

The Russian economic decline of 1998 decreased the market for Latvian goods and services, seriously hurting its economy and increasing unemployment. In October of the same year, Shkele's People's Party won a plurality of the vote in new parliamentary elections, but the former prime minister's personal unpopularity resulted in the formation of a minority government by a coalition that opted to exclude him. Latvia elected its first female president in June 1999, when Vaira Vike-Freiberga, a Canadian psychology professor of Latvian birth known for promoting Latvian cultural interests internationally, was chosen as her homeland's new head of state. She was inaugurated on 8 July 1999. One of her first acts as president was to veto new legislation that would have required the use of the Latvian language in government and business communications, thus further disenfranchising Latvia's large Russian-speaking minority, whose rights and status remained a problematical issue for the country as the new century began. In May 2002, Latvia changed its election law to omit a clause requiring parliamentary candidates to be speakers of the Latvian language, a provision seen as discriminatory to Russian speakers. The change was seen to improve Latvia's chances for membership in the North Atlantic Treaty Organization.

In November 2002, NATO formally invited Latvia, along with six other countries, to become a member. That December, Latvia also received an invitation to join the European Union (EU). Latvia joined NATO and the EU in the spring of 2004.

General elections were held on 5 October 2002, and a new party, the centrist New Era, topped the polls with 23.9% of the votes, taking 26 of the 100 seats in the Saeima. New Era is led by Einars Repse, the former head of the central bank, who managed the country's economy through difficult post-Soviet years; he oversaw the replacement of the currency, from the Russian ruble to the lat, an event that was seen as heralding Latvia's economic revival. Repse was named prime minister, heading a center-right coalition government formed by New Era, Latvia's First Party, the Alliance of Greens and Farmers, and the For Fatherland and Freedom Party. The For Human Rights in a United Latvia party came in second with 18.9% of the vote and 24 seats. Twenty parties competed for seats in parliament in the election. Repse, who campaigned for lower taxes, a pared-down government, and the elimination of corruption, launched a new office in 2003, an "Anti-Absurdity"

bureau. Dedicated to help ordinary people fight "the arbitrariness of those in power, the laziness of civil servants, and the lack of order in national and local government," it is a sounding board for a variety of public complaints.

Both Repse and President Vike-Freiberga supported the 2003 US-led military campaign against Saddam Hussein's regime in Iraq. Vike-Freiberga emphasized the need to maintain the trans-Atlantic relationship guaranteeing Latvia's security, and the country's opposition to the rule of dictators who challenge the international community.

¹³GOVERNMENT

The 1990 declaration of provisional independence reinstated the 1922 constitution. From 1990 to 1993, Latvia was in a state of transition and authority was held by the Supreme Council. The new Saeima (parliament) consists of a single chamber with 100 deputies. A party must receive at least 5% of the national vote to hold a seat in parliament. Deputies are elected to a term of four years by citizens over the age of 18.

The executive branch of government is made up of the president, prime minister, and the cabinet. The Saeima elects the president for a four-year term. Executive power lies with the prime minister, who heads the Council of Ministers (cabinet). In June 1999, the Saeima elected Vaira Vike-Freiberga to the presidency. He was reelected in 2003 and will remain in office until the next election, scheduled to take place in June 2007.

Only citizens of Latvia at the time of the 1940 Soviet invasion and their descendants were allowed to vote in the 1993 elections. This meant that an estimated 34% of the country's residents (primarily Russians) were ineligible to vote. A citizenship law passed in June 1944 restricted naturalization to fewer than 2,000 resident aliens a year. On 22 July 1994, bowing to domestic and international pressure, the Saeima amended the citizenship law, eliminating the quota system. Applicants need a minimum of five years of continuous residence, basic knowledge of the Latvian language, history, and constitution, and a legal source of income; they must also take an oath of loyalty to Latvia and renounce any other citizenship. Thus the new citizenship law accelerates the naturalization process for the several hundred thousand Russian-speakers living in Latvia.

¹⁴POLITICAL PARTIES

The Latvian Popular Front, established in 1988 to unite pro-independence forces, split apart after independence was achieved, giving way to a number of new parties, many defined by their stance on the status of the country's Russian-speaking population. Following the October 1998 elections the 100 seats in the Saeima were distributed as follows: People's Party, 24; Latvian Way Union, 21; Fatherland and Freedom/Latvian National Conservative Party, 17; Popular Harmony Party, 16; Latvian Social Democratic Alliance, 14; and New Party, 8. There were also other political parties not represented in the Saeima.

Following the October 2002 parliamentary elections, New Era, a new party led by former central bank head Einars Repse, won the most seats in the Saeima (26), followed by the For Human Rights in a United Latvia Party with 24, the People's Party with 21, the Alliance of Greens and Farmers with 12, Latvia's First Party with 10, and the For Fatherland and Freedom Party with 7. Repse was named prime minister, leading a coalition of New Era, Latvia's First Party, the Alliance of Greens and Farmers, and the For Fatherland and Freedom Party. The next parliamentary elections were scheduled to take place in October 2006.

15 LOCAL GOVERNMENT

Latvia's local governmental structure is divided into two levels. On the first tier are cities, parishes (*pagasti*), and newly formed joint municipalities. In addition, there is district government. Citizens who live in the respective territories elect the decision-making bodies of city, parish or joint-municipal governments. These governments delegate representatives to the district governments (counties). As of 2005, there were 7 large municipalities, and 26 administrative counties. The seven large municipalities have dual status as city and regional governments.

16 JUDICIAL SYSTEM

A 1991 constitution, which supplements the reinstated 1922 constitution, provides for a number of basic rights and freedoms. The courts have been reorganized along democratic lines. Regional courts were added in 1995 to hear appeals of lower court decisions. There are now district courts, regional courts, a Supreme Court, and the Constitutional Court.

More serious criminal cases are heard before a panel consisting of a judge and two lay assessors. There is a provision for a 12-member jury in capital cases. The judiciary is independent; however, it suffers from a lack of personnel and training. In 1996, a seven-member Constitutional Court was established with power to hear cases at the request of the president, the cabinet, prosecutors, the Supreme Court, local government, or one-third of parliament members. The Constitutional Court may also rule on the constitutionality of legislation or its conformity with Latvia's international obligations.

17 ARMED FORCES

The Latvian armed forces in 2005 totaled 5,238 active personnel with reserves numbering 11,204. The Army totaled 1,817 active members, followed by the Navy with 685 active personnel and the Air Force with 255 active members. The remaining active manpower was deployed in Administration and Command (1,055), Central Support (782) and 644 among other forces. Army equipment included three main battle tanks, two reconnaissance vehicles, and 124 artillery pieces. The Air Force operated 14 transport and 5 training fixed wing aircraft, and 6 support helicopters. The Navy operated one patrol/coastal vessel, three mine warfare and two logistics/support vessels. Latvia assisted in UN and NATO operations in Bosnia, Serbia-Montenegro, Iraq and Afghanistan. The defense budget for 2005 totaled $278 million.

18 INTERNATIONAL COOPERATION

Latvia was admitted to the United Nations on 17 September 1991 and serves in several specialized agencies, such as UNESCO, FAO, IFC, the World Bank, WHO, and the ILO. The country is a member of the WTO, the Council of Europe, Euro-Atlantic Partnership Council, the European Bank for Reconstruction and Development, the OSCE, and the Council of the Baltic Sea States. Latvia joined the European Union and NATO in 2004. Latvia is an observer in the OAS and a member affiliate of the Western European

Union. In environmental cooperation, Latvia is part of the Basel Convention, Conventions on Biological Diversity and Air Pollution, CITES, the Kyoto Protocol, the Montréal Protocol, MARPOL, and the UN Conventions on the Law of the Sea and Climate Change.

19 ECONOMY

Latvia has a relatively well-developed infrastructure and a diversified industrial base, which accounts for about 26% of GDP. Agriculture constitutes approximately 5% of GDP and centers around the cultivation of potatoes, cereals, fodder, and other crops, as well as dairy farming. The largest sector of the economy is the service sector, with wholesale and retail trade, transportation, financial services, communications, and real estate management the most important industries.

Latvia's GDP fell about 30% in 1992 due to a steep decline in industrial exports to Russia. However, by 1994, GDP rose by 2%. A banking crisis caused by the collapse of Latvia's largest bank (as well as some smaller commercial banks) inhibited economic growth in 1995. Difficulties in revenue collection and inadequate control over governmental spending led to a high budget deficit. As a result, GDP fell by 1.6% in 1995. GDP growth improved markedly during the mid- to late-1990s, but it slowed somewhat in 1999, due to the Russian financial crisis of the previous year. By 2001 it stood at 7.7%. Compared to a 960% inflation rate in 1992, inflation was down to 26.3% in 1994, 16% in 1996, and 4.7% in 1998. Unemployment during the early 2000s remained stable between 7–8%.

Since independence was achieved in 1991, Latvia continued with its privatization program and market reforms in the hope of qualifying for EU accession. By mid-2003, 98% of former state-owned industries had been sold, and the private sector accounted for two-thirds of GDP. Latvia joined the WTO in 1999, and was formally invited to join the EU in December 2002, and was accepted as a full member in May 2004. Latvian governments in the early 2000s implemented strict monetary policies and liberal trade policies, attempted to keep budget deficits low, and tried to provide for a more competitive economic environment. Latvia attracted a large amount of foreign direct investment since 1991; Demark was its largest investor. However, investors who shy away from Latvia often do so because of corruption, organized crime, excessive bureaucracy, and a need for regulatory reform.

GDP growth was very strong in 2004, at 8.5%, jumping from 7.5% in 2003, and 6.4% in 2002; in 2005, the economy is expected to grow by 6.0%. This rapid growth was mainly fueled by high domestic demand, which, in turn, was fueled by higher rates of bank lending. Other factors that contributed to the GDP growth were foreign investments, and a dynamic export market. Inflation has remained fairly stable until 2003, but in 2004 it made a slight jump, reaching 6.2%. Unemployment continued to be a problem, hovering around 8.5%.

20 INCOME

The US Central Intelligence Agency (CIA) reports that in 2005 Latvia's gross domestic product (GDP) was estimated at $29.4 billion. The CIA defines GDP as the value of all final goods and services produced within a nation in a given year and computed on the basis of purchasing power parity (PPP) rather than value as measured on the basis of the rate of exchange based on current dollars. The per capita GDP was estimated at $12,800. The annual growth rate of GDP was estimated at 7.8%. The average inflation rate in 2005 was 5.9%. It was estimated that agriculture accounted for 4.1% of GDP, industry 26%, and services 69.9%.

According to the World Bank, in 2003 remittances from citizens working abroad totaled $171 million or about $74 per capita and accounted for approximately 1.5% of GDP. Foreign aid receipts amounted to $114 million or about $49 per capita and accounted for approximately 1.0% of the gross national income (GNI).

The World Bank reports that in 2003 household consumption in Latvia totaled $6.98 billion or about $3,007 per capita based on a GDP of $11.1 billion, measured in current dollars rather than PPP. Household consumption includes expenditures of individuals, households, and nongovernmental organizations on goods and services, excluding purchases of dwellings. It was estimated that for the period 1990 to 2003 household consumption grew at an average annual rate of 0.3%. In 2001 it was estimated that approximately 30% of household consumption was spent on food, 16% on fuel, 6% on health care, and 23% on education.

21 LABOR

The 2005 labor force was estimated at 1.11 million workers. Unemployment in that year was estimated at 8.8%. As of 2003, the service sector accounted for 59.2% of those employed, with 27% in industry and the remaining 13.8% in agriculture.

Latvian workers have the legal right to form and join labor unions. As of 2002, about 30% of the labor force was unionized. Unions are generally nonpolitical, have the right to strike (with some limits), are free to affiliate internationally, can bargain collectively, and are mostly free of government interference in their negotiations with employers.

The minimum employment age is 15, and the mandatory maximum workweek is set at 40 hours. Latvian labor regulations also provide workers with four weeks of annual vacation and special assistance to working mothers with small children. Certain minimum standards of labor conditions are defined by law, although they are not effectively enforced. The legal minimum wage was $98 per month in 2002.

22 AGRICULTURE

As of 2003, out of a total land area of 6,205,000 hectares (15,333,000 acres), about 30% was crop land. Agriculture accounted for about 5% of GDP and engaged around 12% of the labor force in 2003. Agricultural output declined by an annual average of 7% during 1990–2000.

Privatization of agriculture progressed rapidly after 1991. By the beginning of 1993, over 50,000 private farms had been established, and many agricultural facilities were being privatized. Production of primary crops in 2004 (in thousands of tons) included wheat, 530; barley, 275; rye, 100; potatoes, 628.4; rapeseed, 103.6; and dry beans, 0.5.

23 ANIMAL HUSBANDRY

About 621,000 hectares (1,534,000 acres) of land are meadows and pastures, representing 10% of the total land area. In 2005, there were 371,100 head of cattle, 435,700 pigs, 38,600 sheep, 3,450,000 chickens, and 15,500 horses. In 2005, some 74,650 tons of meat

were produced, 80% of which was beef and pork. Milk and egg production in 2005 totaled 790,500 and 32,045 tons, respectively.

Before World War II (1939–45), Latvia was a prominent dairy producer; in the postwar period, the number of cattle, poultry, and pigs rose steeply. Milk production stabilized in 1995, after four years of decreases in dairy cattle and milk production.

24 FISHING

The total catch in 2003 was 115,180 tons, down from 416,197 tons in 1991. Nearly all the landings are from marine fishing. Principal species include sprat, herring, sardines, cod, and mackerel. In February 2005, the Latvian government banned the retail sale of salmon caught in the Baltic Sea and Gulf of Riga, due to levels of dioxin detected in tested fish. Fish packing is an important industry in Latvia; in 2003, fisheries exports amounted to nearly $131.9 million.

25 FORESTRY

Latvia's forests and woodlands covered 2.9 million hectares (7 million acres), or approximately 47% of the total land area in 2000 (up from 24.7% in 1923). Before World War II (1939–45), the timber and paper industries accounted for 29% of employment; by 1990, the number had fallen to 9%. In 1939, the timber industry contributed 53.5% to total exports; in 1990, wood and paper exports accounted for 2.2% of total exports. The timber cut in 2004 was 12,419,000 cu m (438 million cu ft), with 8% used as fuel wood. Production amounts in 2004 included: sawn wood, 3,920,000 cu m (138 million cu ft); particleboard and plywood, 394,000 cu m (13.9 million cu ft); and paper and paperboard, 38,000 tons. Exports of forest products amounted to over $1 billion in 2003.

Jaako Poyry Consulting AB (Sweden), a subsidiary of Finland's Jaako Poyry Group, has been doing a study for a new pulp plant in Jēkabpils, financed by the Latvian government and the Swedish International Development Authority. The new plant will have a capacity to produce 350,000 tons of bleached softwood per year, and will require an investment of up to $1 billion.

26 MINING

Latvia was dependent on imports for raw materials. Limestone (for cement) and sand and gravel mines were spread throughout the country. Ceramic clays, dolomite, and gypsum also were produced. Peat (taken from 85 deposits, for fuel) covered approximately 10% of Latvia's territory, with the heaviest concentration in the eastern plains. Tonnage production figures for 2003 were: peat, 1,076,142 metric tons, compared with 1,484,970 metric tons in 2002; and sand and gravel, 1,044,959 metric tons, compared with 761,614 metric tons in 2003. 2004 production figures for cement totaled 295,205 metric tons; gypsum, 159,133 metric tons; and limestone 431,590 metric tons.

27 ENERGY AND POWER

Hydroelectric generated power is the source for the bulk of the electric power Latvia produces. In 2002, hydroelectric sources accounted for 63% of the power produced. However, Latvia's heavy reliance upon hydropower, means that in a dry year, the country is estimated to be capable of producing only around 60% of the power it needs. Latvia's power imports come largely from Russia, and other Baltic Sea nations. During 2004, Latvia produced 4.4

billion kWh of electricity, but demand for that year came to 5.5 billion kWh. Latvia's electric power generating capacity in 2004 stood at 2.2 GW.

As of 2004, Latvia has no known reserves of oil or natural gas, and no oil refining capacity. Thus the country must import all required gas and petroleum products, most of which comes from Russia. However, Latvia's territorial waters in the Baltic Sea are thought to contain as many as 300 million barrels of oil. In 2002 Latvia awarded five-year offshore exploration rights to a US-Norwegian joint venture.

In 2004, refined petroleum was consumed at a rate of 47,000 barrels per day, with imports averaging the same amount. Demand for natural gas in 2004 came to 62 billion cu ft, all of which was imported. Although Latvia did have recoverable coal reserves of two million short tons in 2004, there was no production or imports of coal.

28 INDUSTRY

Latvia's industrial base has centered mainly on heavy industries such as chemicals and petrochemicals, metal working, and machine building. Major manufactured items include railway carriages, buses, mopeds, washing machines, radios, electronics, and telephone systems. Since 1995, output of buses has fallen, but there has been an increase in the production of transport vehicles and passenger rail cars. Base chemical production has also declined slightly, as demand for household detergents and fibers has fallen. Other important industries include paper, petrochemicals, mechanical engineering, and communications.

Prior to 1998, the food processing sector provided the largest portion of the country's manufacturing output. Following the 1998 economic crisis in Russia, that sector declined, as Latvia depended upon Russia for exports. As of 2002, however, food processing showed potential for growth. In 2001, industry accounted for 26% of GDP, and employed around 25% of the work force. Although some 50 enterprises are excluded from privatization (including ports, the railway company, and the postal service), only a few large state enterprises had not been privatized as of 2002, including the Latvian Shipping Company (Lasco), and the electricity utility company (Latvenergo). Ninety-eight percent of former state-owned enterprises had been sold as of 2002.

By 2004, the participation of the industry in the overall economic output has decreased to 24.8%, while its share in the labor fell to 25%; agriculture made up 4.4% of the GDP, and employed 15% of the labor force; services came in first with 70.8%, and 60% respectively. The industrial production growth rate equaled the GDP growth rate, at 8.5%, hinting that the services sector grew faster, while the agriculture sector lagged behind.

29 SCIENCE AND TECHNOLOGY

The Latvian Academy of Sciences has divisions of physical and technical sciences and of chemical and biological sciences.

Fifteen research institutes, most attached to the academy, conduct medical, technical, and scientific research. The University of Latvia (founded in 1919) has faculties of physics and mathematics, chemistry, and biology. The Riga Technical University (founded in 1990) has various engineering faculties. Both are in Riga, as are the Latvian Academy of Medicine (founded in 1951), the Riga Aviation University (founded in 1919), and the Stradin Museum

of the History of Medicine. The Latvian University of Agriculture (founded in 1939) is located in Jelgava, and the National Botanical Garden is situated in Salaspils.

In 1987–97, science and engineering students accounted for 23% of university enrollment. In 2002, Latvia had 1,478 scientists and engineers and 282 technicians per million people actively engaged in research and development (R&D). For that same year, Latvia's expenditures on R&D totaled $100.082 million, or 0.46% of GDP, with government providing the largest portion at 42.7%, followed by foreign sources at 35.6%. Business provided the remaining 21.7%. High technology exports in 2002 totaled $51 million, or 4% of all manufactured exports.

30 DOMESTIC TRADE

The traditional, small, privately owned farmer's markets, bakeries, and dairies are still prevalent throughout the country; however, large supermarkets are making their mark in larger cities. Latvia's center of domestic commerce is in Riga. One of the countries first malls opened with major investment from a Finnish department store chain. The most widely demanded domestic services include dressmaking and repair; house construction and repair; and automotive servicing. As of 2002, privatization of previously state-owned companies and industries was nearly complete.

Shops are generally open from 9 or 10 AM to 7 or 8 PM.

31 FOREIGN TRADE

Like most of the former Soviet republics, Latvia's trade was formerly dominated by the other Soviet states, but it has been relatively successful in achieving a wider range of trade partners. Latvia's major commodity exports include wood (29%), iron and steel (6.3%), textile yarn (5.6%), furniture (4.5%), and fish (1%).

In 2004, Latvia's exports reached $3.6 billion (FOB—Free on Board), while imports grew to $6.0 billion (FOB). Most of the exports went to the United Kingdom (which received 12.8% of total exports), Germany (12%), Sweden (10%), Lithuania (9.1%), Estonia (8%), Russia (6.4%), and Denmark (5.4%). Since domestic demand is predicted to grow slowly in the EU area, Latvian exporters will likely re-orient to faster growing markets, such as Estonia and Russia. Imports included machinery and equipment, chemi-

---

Principal Trading Partners – Latvia (2003)

(In millions of US dollars)

Country	Exports	Imports	Balance
World	2,893.7	5,244.0	-2,350.3
United Kingdom	449.9	118.0	331.9
Germany	428.9	842.3	-413.4
Sweden	305.4	328.4	-23.0
Lithuania	237.2	508.1	-270.9
Estonia	190.5	336.5	-146.0
Denmark	173.7	178.9	-5.2
Russia	155.8	455.4	-299.6
Netherlands	93.9	162.5	-68.6
United States	83.8	91.3	-7.5
Finland	77.7	387.5	-309.8

(…) data not available or not significant.

SOURCE: *2003 International Trade Statistics Yearbook,* New York: United Nations, 2004.

```
┌─────────────────────────────────────────────────────────────┐
│ Balance of Payments – Latvia (2003)                          │
│                                                              │
│ (In millions of US dollars)                                  │
│ ───────────────────────────────────────────────────────     │
│                                                              │
│ Current Account                                   -956.0     │
│   Balance on goods                    -1,998.0               │
│     Imports                 -5,169.0                         │
│     Exports                  3,171.0                         │
│   Balance on services                    583.0               │
│   Balance on income                      -59.0               │
│   Current transfers                      518.0               │
│ Capital Account                                     34.0     │
│ Financial Account                                  917.0     │
│   Direct investment abroad               -32.0               │
│   Direct investment in Latvia            359.0               │
│   Portfolio investment assets           -286.0               │
│   Portfolio investment liabilities        62.0               │
│   Financial derivatives                    6.0               │
│   Other investment assets               -666.0               │
│   Other investment liabilities         1,474.0               │
│ Net Errors and Omissions                            85.0     │
│ Reserves and Related Items                         -80.0     │
│                                                              │
│ (…) data not available or not significant.                   │
│                                                              │
│ SOURCE: Balance of Payment Statistics Yearbook 2004, Washington, DC: │
│ International Monetary Fund, 2004.                            │
└─────────────────────────────────────────────────────────────┘
```

cals, fuels, and vehicles, and mainly came from Germany (13.9%), Lithuania (12.2%), Russia (8.7%), Estonia (7%), Finland (6.3%), Sweden (6.1%), Poland (5.4%), and Belarus (4.8%).

32 BALANCE OF PAYMENTS

The US Central Intelligence Agency (CIA) reported that in 2002 the purchasing power parity of Latvia's exports was $2.3 billion while imports totaled $3.9 billion resulting in a trade deficit of $1.6 billion.

The International Monetary Fund (IMF) reported that in 2001 Latvia had exports of goods totaling $2.22 billion and imports of goods totaling $3.57 billion. The services credit totaled $1.19 billion and debit $692 million.

Exports of goods and services continued to grow in the following years, reaching $4.7 billion in 2003, and $5.1 billion in 2004. Imports followed a similar path, totaling $6.1 billion in 2003, and $6.5 billion in 2004. The resource balance was consequently negative in both years, at around -$1.4 billion. The current account balance was also negative, dropping to -$1 billion in 2003, and -$1.2 billion in 2004. External debt was relatively high, at $10.3 billion in 2004, and an expected $10.8 billion in 2005.

33 BANKING AND SECURITIES

In 1991 banking matters were transferred to the Bank of Latvia from Soviet bank officials. Previously, Latvia had its branch of the Soviet State Bank (Gosbank). The central bank had the authority to issue Latvian rubles and regulate the commercial banking sector. There are many banks in Latvia, including the Baltic Transit Bank, Banka Atmoda, Latgale Stocj Commercial Bank, Latvian Credit Bank, Investment Bank of Latvia, and the Latvian Land Bank.

Latvia effectively exited the ruble zone on 20 July 1992. By early 1993 the Bank of Latvia introduced a national currency, the lat.

The lat is now fully convertible for capital and current account purposes.

Latvia's banking sector has proved one of the country's most successful industries and also its most controversial. Riga has developed into an offshore financial center, offering numbered accounts and related services, and drawing in a substantial chunk of flight capital from other former Soviet republics. Owing to fairly liberal banking laws in the early 1990s, a large number of banks (54 as of May 1995) had been established. Subsequently, capital and other requirements have been progressively tightened. For existing banks, the minimum reserve requirements have been raised from Ls100,000 as of 1995 to Ls1.0 million by 31 March 1998. As of April 1995 all banks had to be audited by one of the recognized international accounting firms. The stricter capital regime has led to an inevitable attrition, with 11 banks losing their licenses between 1992 and 1995. Only some 15 banks made profits in 1994 and had adequate reserves. The audits also revealed huge losses at Baltija Bank (Latvia's largest institution, with some 200,000 private depositors), which had been incurred as a result of systematic fraud. Latvian banks suffered heavy losses in 1999 as a result of the Russian financial crisis.

In February 1997, the Bank of Latvia gave its approval to the proposed merger between the Latvian Savings Bank and the United Baltic Bank of Riga. As a result of the merger, the state now owns 75% of shares in the Latvian Savings Bank. The government's plans are to privatize the newly merged entity. Total assets of Latvia's 23 commercial banks were us$5 billion as of June 2001. In recent years, Scandinavian banks have begun acquiring shares in Baltic banks. The International Monetary Fund reports that in 2001, currency and demand deposits—an aggregate commonly known as M1—were equal to $1.4 billion. In that same year, M2—an aggregate equal to M1 plus savings deposits, small time deposits, and money market mutual funds—was $2.5 billion. The money market rate, the rate at which financial institutions lend to one another in the short term, was 5.23%. The discount rate, the interest rate at which the central bank lends to financial institutions in the short term, was 3.5%.

In 1995, the Riga Stock Exchange (RIGSE) listed 17 companies and had a market capitalization of $10 million. As of 2004, a total of 39 companies were listed, with a market capitalization valued at 1.655 billion. In 2004, the RIGSE rose 43.5% from the previous year to 413.6.

34 INSURANCE

All of Latvia's insurers, foreign and domestic, must be licensed by the Superintendent of Insurance. Foreign companies entering the Latvian market will find that licenses are relatively easy to obtain, although each class of insurance offered must be approved by the Superintendent of Insurance. In Latvia, third-party automobile liability insurance is compulsory. In 2003, the value of all direct premiums written totaled $209 million, of which nearly all were accounted for by the nonlife lines, which accounted for $200 million. Latvia's top nonlife insurer in 2003 was Balta, with gross written nonlife premiums of $45.9 million, while Ergo Latvija Dziviba was the country's leading life insurer that year, with gross written life premiums of $5.4 million.

35 PUBLIC FINANCE

Latvia's structural transition out of the planned economy under communism has occurred more or less spontaneously since independence. As of 2002, the thriving private sector accounted for two-thirds of employment and GDP. Privatization is generally considered to be near-finished; although the government still owns a few key companies, most are in private hands, even the utilities, and the government is working to sell off its ownership of what remains in order to satisfy its commitments to the IMF.

The US Central Intelligence Agency (CIA) estimated that in 2005 Latvia's central government took in revenues of approximately $5.6 billion and had expenditures of $5.8 billion. Revenues minus expenditures totaled approximately -$243 million. Public debt in 2005 amounted to 12% of GDP. Total external debt was $13.2 billion.

The International Monetary Fund (IMF) reported that in 2003, the most recent year for which it had data, central government revenues were Ls1,715.5 million and expenditures were Ls1,796.2 million. The value of revenues was us$3,004 million and expenditures us$3,146 million, based on an official exchange rate for 2003 of us$1 = Ls.571 as reported by the IMF. Government outlays by function were as follows: general public services, 19.3%; defense, 4.5%; public order and safety, 8.1%; economic affairs, 11.8%; housing and community amenities, 1.1%; health, 11.2%; recreation, culture, and religion, 2.4%; education, 6.5%; and social protection, 35.0%.

36 TAXATION

In 1995 Latvia replaced its profits tax with 25% business income tax (BIT). Under amendments in 2001, the BIT rate was reduced to 22% for 2002, and to 19% for 2003, and as of 2005, stood at 15% which applies to all businesses. Reduced rates for small-enter-

---

Public Finance – Latvia (2003)

(In millions of lats, central government figures)

Revenue and Grants	**1,715.5**	**100.0%**
Tax revenue	901.4	52.5%
Social contributions	561.9	32.8%
Grants	51.1	3.0%
Other revenue	201.1	11.7%
Expenditures	**1,796.2**	**100.0%**
General public services	347.1	19.3%
Defense	80.3	4.5%
Public order and safety	145.9	8.1%
Economic affairs	211.2	11.8%
Environmental protection	...	...
Housing and community amenities	20.6	1.1%
Health	200.8	11.2%
Recreational, culture, and religion	43.8	2.4%
Education	117.4	6.5%
Social protection	629.1	35.0%

(...) data not available or not significant.

SOURCE: *Government Finance Statistics Yearbook 2004,* Washington, DC: International Monetary Fund, 2004.

---

prises was eliminated in 2004. Branches of foreign companies are taxed at the same rate as Latvian companies, but are eligible for the same deductions and allowances. For companies operating in Latvia, capital gains are included in corporate income and are taxed at the corporate rate. There is a 2% withholding tax for nonresident companies on proceeds from the sale of Latvian real estate. The withholding rate on dividends is either 0% or 10% depending upon whether the payer and receiver meet certain guidelines regarding residency. Withholding taxes on various forms of capital income may be reduced or eliminated according to the terms of bilateral double tax prevention agreements. Shipping companies, cargo or passenger, engaged primarily in international commerce, may choose to be taxed according to a tonnage tax introduced in 2002. There are no local taxes.

As of 1995, Latvians pay personal income tax at a flat rate of 25% of taxable income. Taxable income is determined by lump sum deductions, and specific allowances for social security payments, donations to charity, hospitalization and medical expenses, and some school fees. There is also a property tax and a land tax.

The main indirect tax is Latvia's value-added tax (VAT) with a standard rate of 18% for most goods and services. A reduced rate of 5% is applied to medical (including veterinary) and hotel services, and water and waste collection services. A 0% VAT applies to exports. Exempted from the VAT agricultural services, insurance, rent on dwellings, as well as certain financial services and royalties from copyrights. There are also excise taxes levied on luxury products at rates ranging from 10-100%, customs taxes, and stamp taxes.

37 CUSTOMS AND DUTIES

Latvia imposes a standard 18% VAT on imports. However, certain items qualify for lower rates of 0–9%. Tariff rates depend on both the type of good imported and its origin. Goods from countries with most-favored nation (MFN) status receive lower rates, usually 15% (but up to 45% for agricultural products), while goods from non-MFN countries receive slightly higher rates, usually 20% (but up to 55% for agricultural products).

Latvia has free trade agreements with Sweden, Finland, Norway, Switzerland, and Kyrgyzstan. US products receive MFN status. Latvia has also formed a free trade area with Estonia and Lithuania. In January 1995, a free trade agreement went into effect with the European Union, which reduced tariffs on most industrial products to zero and set a schedule on tariff reductions over a course of five years for certain agricultural products. Latvia joined the World Trade Organization in February 1999.

38 FOREIGN INVESTMENT

In November 1991, a foreign investment act was passed permitting joint ventures in the form of either public or private limited companies. Businesses that are at least 30% foreign-owned receive a two-year tax holiday and a 50% tax abatement for the following two years.

At the end of 1995, foreign direct investment (FDI) in Latvia totaled $521 million, based on registered statutory capital. The largest investors were Denmark (26.1%), Russia (19.4%), the United States (13.5%), Germany (6.4%), the United Kingdom (5.2%), and the Netherlands (4.2%). Finland and Sweden were also significant investors. Industry accounted for only 17% of all foreign investment and there were approximately 5,200 firms with a foreign capital share.

FDI inflow into Latvia reached $521 million in 1997, averaging $400 million a year 1996 to 2000, but fell sharply in the global economic downturn of 2001 to less than $201 million. From 1995 to 2001 Latvia stock of FDI nearly quadrupled, reaching $2.3 billion in 2001. In the period 1988 to 1990, Latvia's share of world FDI inflows was almost five times its share of world GDP, but for the period 1998 to 2000, Latvia's share of FDI inflows was only 60% greater than its share of world GDP.

The leading sources of FDI from 1996 to 2001 were the United States (13%), Germany(11%), and Demark (11%). The primary destinations of foreign investment inflow were trade (22%), finance (16%), and business services, especially real estate (16%). The largest foreign affiliate is the telecommunications company Lattelekom SA of Finland. The largest foreign bank invested is Hansabanka SA of Estonia.

As a new member of the EU, Latvia registered an increased inflow of capital from Western Europe in 2004. This trend is expected to temper down in future years however. Also, the relative share of FDI in capital flows will likely go down, which will put an increased burden on domestic banks. Despite this, Latvia remains an attractive market for investments, and the prospects of joining the euro zone works towards the country's favor.

39 ECONOMIC DEVELOPMENT

The government began introducing economic reforms in 1990 to effect the transition to a market-driven economy. Individual and family-owned businesses, cooperatives, and privately and publicly held companies are now permitted. The privatization process was simplified with a 1994 law that created the Privatization Agency (PA) and the State Property Fund. Distribution of privatization vouchers was completed by March 1995, with certificates valued at Ls2.8 billion distributed to 2.2 million Latvians.

The privatization program focuses on international tenders and public offerings of shares. By mid-1994, 450 state enterprises had been transferred for privatization. The first international tender of 45 enterprises came in November 1994, followed by 80 more in 1995. Large-scale privatization began in 1996 and continued into the beginning of the 21st century, when privatization was almost complete (with the exception of large state utilities).

In 2001, Latvia negotiated a 20-month, $44-million Stand-By Arrangement with the International Monetary Fund (IMF). Real GDP growth was strong in 2001–02, led by investment and consumption. Inflation was low during those years. In 2003, per capita GDP stood around 50% above its level in 1995. Latvia's economy in 2003 was regarded as one of the best of the 10 countries slated for EU admission in 2004. The government was taking steps toward achieving a balanced budget by reducing government spending in 2003.

In anticipation of the 2006 election, the government is seeking to exploit the strong revenue growth and increase public spending. In addition, it plans to sell off its share in the Ventspils oil terminal and thus give an extra boost to the overall economic growth. One of the biggest threats to economic expansion is the, recently, growing inflation rate—which could also affect Latvia's prospect of joining the euro zone in 2008. In an attempt to curb inflation the government will likely cut taxes on diesel fuel, and ask the EU to temporary lift the ban over imports of fuel that do not meet EU standards.

40 SOCIAL DEVELOPMENT

Social insurance provides benefits for old age, disability, and survivorship pensions for employees and self-employed persons. The first laws were enacted in 1922, and most recently were updated in 2001. Pensions are funded by contributions from employees and employers in most sectors. Age requirements for pensions are set at 62 for men and 59.5 for women, but is increasing to meet the same standards for men by 2009. The government funds programs to provide for active military personnel, individuals caring for infants, and spouses of diplomatic staff. Sickness and maternity benefits are provided to employed persons, while medical benefits are provided to all permanent residents. A universal program of family allowances exists, as well as workers' compensation and unemployment programs.

Employment discrimination based on gender is legally banned, although women are barred from certain occupations considered dangerous. In practice, women face unequal treatment in terms of both pay and hiring, including discrimination stemming from the cost of legally mandated childbirth benefits if a woman is hired. Sexual harassment is common in the workplace although prohibited by law. Domestic violence is pervasive. As of 2004 there were no shelters for abused or battered women, and few resources exist for victims of sexual assault.

Latvia's main human rights problem in recent years stems from the large number of minorities who were not granted citizenship after independence. These noncitizens, mainly ethnic Russians, do not have clear travel, property, and residency rights. Instances of excessive use of force by security forces were still reported, and prison conditions remained poor.

41 HEALTH

Primary care is provided at large urban health centers, hospital and walk-in emergency facilities, individual and group private practices, rural clinics staffed by midwives and physicians' assistants, and workplace clinics run by large private employers and the military. Total health care expenditure was estimated at 6.7% of GDP. As of 2004, there were an estimated 291 physicians, 509 nurses, 53 dentists, and 21 nurses per 100,000 people. In the same year, Latvia had 151 hospitals, of which 31 were located in Riga (including all specialized hospitals).

As of 2002, the crude birth rate and overall mortality rate were estimated at 8.3 and 14.7 per 1,000 people respectively. Life expectancy in 2005 was 71.05 years and the infant mortality rate was 9.55 per 1,000 live births. The total fertility rate in 2000 was 1.2 per woman during childbearing years. Immunization rates for one-year-olds were as follows: diphtheria, pertussis, and tetanus, 95%; and measles, 97%. Measles, neonatal tetanus and polio had been almost completely eradicated.

Cardiovascular disease is a major cause of mortality in Latvia, with a rate of nearly 400 per 1,000 people over age 65. The HIV/AIDS prevalence was 0.60 per 100 adults in 2003. As of 2004, there were approximately 7,600 people living with HIV/AIDS in the country. There were an estimated 500 deaths from AIDS in 2003.

42 HOUSING

In the 1990s 165,000 families (one out of five) were registered for new housing. Approximately 200,000 people lived in the 8% of existing housing stock that was in substandard condition. But the government has made some progress in reforms for the housing sector. In 1993, 54% of housing was owned by state and municipalities. In 1999 the majority of property (70%) was privately owned. The government anticipates that by the end of the privatization process about 80% of housing will be private property, while municipalities will maintain only 20% of the housing as low-cost rental or social houses.

At the 2000 census, about 26% of all respondents lived in single-family houses; 68.5% lived in apartments. About 60% of all dwellings were owner occupied. About 52% of the population were living in housing units built in 1970 or earlier. About 43.7% of the population were in dwellings built during the period 1971–95.

Since 1996, the government has signed several agreements with international organizations for funds to improve housing projects. In 2000, the Housing Crediting Program was initiated to promote a new mortgage system.

43 EDUCATION

The modern Latvian educational system is based on the reforms introduced in 1991. Compulsory education lasts for nine years beginning at the age of seven. At this stage, students have a choice between basic vocational school (two or three years), general secondary school (three years), or vocational secondary school (four years, offering a diploma that may fulfill the prerequisite for university studies).

In 2001, about 60% of children between the ages of three and six were enrolled in some type of preschool program. Primary school enrollment in 2003 was estimated at about 86% of age-eligible students. The same year, secondary school enrollment was about 88% of age-eligible students. Nearly all students complete their primary education. The student-to-teacher ratio for primary school was at about 14:1 in 2003.

Entrance examinations are a prerequisite for admission into universities. Higher education is offered by both private and public institutions. The state offers free higher education in some areas of specialized study. Latvia has a total of about 34 state-recognized institutions of higher learning, including two major universities: the University of Latvia and the Riga Technical University. In 2003, about 73% of the tertiary age population were enrolled in some type of higher education program; with 55% for men and 91% for women. The adult literacy rate for 2004 was estimated at about 99.7%.

As of 2003, public expenditure on education was estimated at 5.8% of GDP.

44 LIBRARIES AND MUSEUMS

The National Library in Riga holds about 2.1 million volumes; the main library site was designed by Gunnar Birkerts, who was born in Latvia but has an architectural firm in the United States. The Latvian Academic Library in Riga holds 1.2 million books and the University of Latvia holds about two million; both libraries also include large collections of periodicals. The Riga City Library (Bibliotheca Rigensis), established in 1524, was the first public library in the nation. In 2005, there were about 892 public libraries in the nation, including 7 branches of the Latvian Library for the Blind.

The larger museums are located in Riga, including the State Museum of Fine Arts, the History Museum of Latvia, The Latvian Photography Museum, and the Museum of Foreign Art. Riga also hosts the Museum of Natural History; the Riga Film Museum; the State Museum of Art; the Literature, Theater, and Music Museum; the Latvian Sports Museum, and the Latvian War Museum. In 1990, Bauska Castle was converted into a historic museum. The Bauska Art Museum holds over 8,000 works of art by Russian and Western European artists. With the end of the Soviet era, a number of new museums devoted to Latvian culture and history opened in the 1990s, including museums of architecture, photography, telecommunications, Jewish life in Latvia, and a museum chronicling 50 years of Soviet occupation. There are a local history museums in almost every region.

45 MEDIA

International communications links are via leased connection to the Moscow international gateway switch and the Finnish cellular network. In 2003, there were an estimated 285 mainline telephones for every 1,000 people; about 16,200 people were on a waiting list for telephone service installation. The same year, there were approximately 526 mobile phones in use for every 1,000 people.

The Committee for Television and Radio controls broadcasting. Domestic and international programming in Latvian, Russian, Swedish, English, and German is broadcast by Latvian Radio. In 1998, there were 8 AM and 56 FM stations. Latvian State Television broadcasts on two channels, and there are several independent television stations with daily broadcasts. Cable and satellite services are available, and foreign broadcasts can also be seen. In 2003, there were an estimated 700 radios and 859 television sets for every 1,000 people. About 176.8 of every 1,000 people were cable subscribers. Also in 2003, there were 188 personal computers for every 1,000 people and 404 of every 1,000 people had access to the Internet. There were 80 secure Internet servers in the country in 2004.

Latvia publishes many newspapers, periodicals, and books, in both Latvian and Russian. The most widely read newspapers (with 2002 circulations) are *Diena* (*The Day*, 110,000), *Sovietskaya Latviya* (*Soviet Latvia*, 71,300), *SM Segodna* (a Russian language daily, 65,000), and *Riga Balss* (*The Voice*, 56,800). Foreign language newspapers include the weekly *Baltic Times* in English.

The constitution provides for free speech and a free press, and the government is said to respect these rights in practice. A 1991 Press Law prohibits censorship of the press or other mass media; however, a Law on the Media imposes regulations on the content and language of broadcasts.

46 ORGANIZATIONS

Important economic organizations in Latvia include the Latvian Chamber of Commerce, an organization that promotes trade and commerce with its Baltic neighbors, Europe, and The Russian Federation. There are five business and trade organizations including: the Latvia International Commerce Center, Latvian Small Business Association, and the World Latvian Businessmen's Association. The largest trade union in Latvia is the umbrella organization of the Association of Free Trade Unions, founded in 1990.

The Latvian Academy of Sciences promotes public interest and education for all branches of science. Several medical fields have professional associations. There are also several environmental protection and preservation organizations.

National youth organizations include the Student Council of the University of Latvia, United Nations Student Association of Latvia, YMCA/YWCA of Latvia, Junior Chamber, and the Scout and Guide Central Organization of Latvia. There are a wide variety of sports associations represented in the country. National women's organizations include the Women's National League of Latvia and the Latvian Association of University Women.

There are national chapters of the Red Cross Society and Caritas.

47 TOURISM, TRAVEL, AND RECREATION

With a population of almost one million, Riga is the major tourism center of the Baltic states. Its historic architecture has undergone extensive restoration. The white sand beaches offer sailing and river rafting along with many spas. Latvia boasts 12,310 rivers and 3,000 lakes, which are popular for boating, as well as country castles and medieval towns. Tennis, horseback riding, fishing, hunting, sailing, water sports, and winter sports are available to visitors, as well as a ski marathon in February, the Sport Festival of Riga in May, and the International Riga Marathon in July.

All visitors need passports valid for at least three months after the planned stay. Visas are not required for stays of up to 90 days.

There were 2,469,888 foreign visitors who arrived in Latvia in 2003, an 8% increase from 2002. The 7,618 hotel rooms with 14,983 beds had a 32% occupancy rate. The average length of stay was two nights. Tourist expenditure receipts totaled $271 million.

In 2005, the US Department of State estimated the daily cost of travel in Latvia at $219.

48 FAMOUS LATVIANS

Guntis Ulmanis (b.1939) was president of Latvia from 1993 to 1999. Vaira Vike-Freiberga (b.1937), Latvia's first female president, succeeded him in 1999, and was reelected in 2003. Turis Alumans was Latvia's first poet. He started a school of poetry that produced the poets Krisjanis Barons (1823–1923) and Atis Kronvalds in the 19th century. Romantic literature in the 20th century was symbolized by Janis Rainis's (1865–1929) *Fire and Night*.

49 DEPENDENCIES

Latvia has no territories or colonies.

50 BIBLIOGRAPHY

Dreifelds, Juris. *Latvia in Transition*. New York: Cambridge University Press, 1996.

Eglitis, Daina Stukuls. *Imagining the Nation: History, Modernity, and Revolution in Latvia*. University Park, Pa.: Pennsylvania State University Press, 2002.

Estonia, Latvia, and Lithuania: Country Studies. Washington, D.C.: Department of the Army, 1996.

Frucht, Richard (ed.). *Eastern Europe: An Introduction to the People, Lands, and Culture*. Santa Barbara, Calif.: ABC-CLIO, 2005.

Karklins, Rasma. *Ethnopolitics and Transition to Democracy: the Collapse of the USSR and Latvia*. Baltimore: Johns Hopkins University Press, 1994.

McElrath, Karen (ed.). *HIV and AIDS: A Global View*. Westport, Conn.: Greenwood Press, 2002.

Plakans, Andrejs. *The Latvians: A Short History*. Stanford, Calif.: Hoover Institution Press, Stanford University, 1995.

Shafir, Gershon. *Immigrants and Nationalists: Ethnic Conflict and Accommodation in Catalonia, the Basque Country, Latvia, and Estonia*. Albany: State University of New York, 1995.

Terterov, Marat. *Doing Business with Latvia*. Sterling, Va.: Kogan Page, 2003.

LIECHTENSTEIN

Principality of Liechtenstein
Fürstentum Liechtenstein

CAPITAL: Vaduz

FLAG: The national flag is divided into two horizontal rectangles, blue above red. On the blue rectangle, near the hoist, is the princely crown in gold.

ANTHEM: *Oben am jungen Rhein (On the Banks of the Young Rhine).*

MONETARY UNIT: The Swiss franc (SwFr) of 100 centimes, or rappen, has been in use since February 1921. There are coins of 1, 5, 10, 20, and 50 centimes and 1, 2, and 5 francs, and notes of 10, 20, 50, 100, 500, and 1,000 francs. SwFr1 = $0.80418 (or $1 = SwFr1.2435; as of 2004).

WEIGHTS AND MEASURES: The metric system is the legal standard.

HOLIDAYS: New Year's Day, 1 January; Epiphany, 6 January; Candlemas, 2 February; St. Joseph's Day, 19 March; Labor Day, 1 May; Assumption, 15 August; Nativity of Our Lady, 8 September; All Saints' Day, 1 November; Immaculate Conception, 8 December; Christmas, 25 December; St. Stephen's Day, 26 December. Movable religious holidays include Good Friday, Easter Monday, Ascension, Whitmonday, and Corpus Christi.

TIME: 1 PM = noon GMT.

¹LOCATION, SIZE, AND EXTENT

Liechtenstein, roughly triangular in shape, is a landlocked country situated in the Rhine River Valley. The fourth-smallest country in Europe, it is bordered by the Austrian province of Vorarlberg to the N and E, the Swiss canton of Graubünden to the S, and the Rhine River and the Swiss canton of St. Gallen to the W, with a total boundary length of 76 km (47 mi).

The principality has an area of 160 sq km (62 sq mi) and extends 24.5 km (15.2 mi) N–S and 9.4 km (5.8 mi) E–W. Comparatively, the area occupied by Liechtenstein is about 0.9 times the size of Washington, DC.

Liechtenstein's capital city, Vaduz, is located in the western part of the country.

²TOPOGRAPHY

Liechtenstein is divided into a comparatively narrow area of level land bordering the right bank of the Rhine River and an upland and mountainous region occupying the remainder of the country; the level land occupies about two-fifths of the total surface area. The greatest elevation, Grauspitz (2,599 m/8,527 ft), is in the south, in a spur of the Rhaetian Alps.

³CLIMATE

Climatic conditions in Liechtenstein are less severe than might be expected from its elevated terrain and inland situation; the mitigating factor is a warm south wind called the Föhn. The annual lowland temperature varies between -4.5°C (24°F) in January and 19.9°C (68°F) in July. Late frost and prolonged dry periods are rare. Average annual precipitation is 105 cm (41 in).

⁴FLORA AND FAUNA

The natural plant and animal life of Liechtenstein displays a considerable variety because of the marked differences in altitude. A number of orchid species are able to grow because of the warmth carried by the Föhn. In the higher mountain reaches are such alpine plants as gentian, alpine rose, and edelweiss. Common trees include the red beech, sycamore, maple, alder, larch, and various conifers. Indigenous mammals include the deer, fox, badger, and chamois. Birds, including ravens and eagles, number about 120 species.

⁵ENVIRONMENT

The Nature Conservation Act, adopted in 1933, was the nation's first major piece of environmental legislation; the Water Conservation Act dates from 1957, and air pollution laws were passed in 1973 and 1974. All wastewater is purified before being discharged into the Rhine. According to a 2006 report issued by the International Union for Conservation of Nature and Natural Resources (IUCN), threatened species included two types of mammals, one species of bird, and five species of invertebrates. Threatened species include the great horned owl, the Eurasian beaver, the hermit beetle, and the Apollo butterfly.

⁶POPULATION

The population of Liechtenstein in 2005 was estimated by the United Nations (UN) at 35,000, which placed it at number 187 in population among the 193 nations of the world. In 2005, approximately 11% of the population was over 65 years of age, with another 18% of the population under 15 years of age. According to the UN, the annual population rate of change for 2005–10 was expected to be 0.4%, a rate the government viewed as satisfactory. The projected population for the year 2025 was 40,000. The population density was 219 per sq km (567 per sq mi), with the population heavily concentrated in the Rhine Valley, in which the two largest communities, Vaduz and Schaan, are located.

The UN estimated that 21% of the population lived in urban areas in 2005, and that urban areas were growing at an annual rate of 1.51%. The capital city, Vaduz, had a population of 5,000 in that year.

7 MIGRATION

There were 12,000 foreign residents in Liechtenstein in 2000, comprising approximately one-third of the total population. Moreover, about 6,885 Austrians and Swiss commute to Liechtenstein daily. Several hundred Italian, Greek, and Spanish workers have migrated to the principality on a semipermanent basis. In 1998 and 1999, Liechtenstein accepted a high number of Kosovo Albanian asylum seekers, granting them temporary protection. The number of asylum seekers and people under temporary protection comprised nearly 2% of the overall population of Liechtenstein in 1999. In 2004 there were 149 refugees and 68 asylum seekers. The estimated net migration rate in 2005 was 4.8 migrants per 1,000 population. The government views the migration levels as satisfactory.

8 ETHNIC GROUPS

The indigenous population, accounting for 86% of the total population, is described as being chiefly of Alemannic stock, descendants of the German-speaking tribes that settled between the Main and Danube rivers. Italian, Turkish, and various other groups account for the remaining 14%.

9 LANGUAGES

German is the official language. The population speaks an Alemannic dialect.

10 RELIGIONS

The state religion is Roman Catholicism, to which about 78% of the population adhere; however, absolute freedom of worship prevails. About 0.07% of the population are Protestants and 0.04% are Muslims. The Eastern Orthodox Church has about 254 members. Buddhists, Jehovah's Witnesses, Anglicans, Jews, Baha'is and New Apostolics each have less than 80 members.

11 TRANSPORTATION

The line of the Arlberg express (Paris to Vienna) passes through Liechtenstein at Schaan-Vaduz, extending for 18.5 km (11.5 mi), but few international trains stop. The main center for reaching Liechtenstein is Buchs, Switzerland, about 8 km (5 mi) from Vaduz.

Postal buses are the chief means of public transportation both within the country and to Austria and Switzerland. A tunnel, 740 m (2,428 ft) in length, connects the Samina River Valley with the Rhine River Valley.

In 2002, there were some 250 km (155 mi) of paved roadways. A major highway runs through the principality, linking Austria and Switzerland.

The nearest airport is in Zürich, Switzerland. As of 2004, the country had 28 km (17 mi) of navigable waterways.

12 HISTORY

The territory now occupied by the Principality of Liechtenstein first acquired a political identity with the formation of the sub-country of Lower Rhaetia after the death of Charlemagne in 814. The County of Vaduz was formally established in 1342 and became a direct dependency of the Holy Roman Empire in 1396. The area (to which, in 1434, was added the Lordship of Schellenberg, in the north) was ruled in turn by various families, such as the counts of Montfort, von Brandis, van Sulz, and von Hohenems.

During the Thirty Years' War (1618–48), the area was invaded first by Austrian troops and then, in 1647, by the Swedes. After the von Hohenems line encountered financial difficulty, Prince Johann Adam of Liechtenstein purchased from them first Schellenberg (1699) and then Vaduz (1712). The Liechtenstein family thus added to its vast holdings in Austria and adjoining territories.

The Principality of Liechtenstein as such was created on 23 January 1719 by act of Holy Roman Emperor Charles VI, who made it a direct fief of the crown and confirmed the rule of Prince Anton-Florian, Johann Adam's successor, under the title of Prince von und zu Liechtenstein.

During the Napoleonic wars, Liechtenstein was invaded by both the French and the Russians. Following the Treaty of Pressburg (1805), Liechtenstein joined the Confederation of the Rhine, which made the principality a sovereign state. In 1815, following the downfall of Napoleon, Liechtenstein joined the newly formed Germanic Confederation.

With Prussia's victory over Austria in the Seven Weeks' War (1866), the Confederation was dissolved and the constitutional ties of Liechtenstein to other German states came to an end. In the war, Liechtenstein had furnished Austria-Hungary with 80 soldiers; two years later, the principality disbanded its military force for all time.

From 1852, when the first treaty establishing a customs union was signed, until the end of World War I, Liechtenstein was closely tied economically to Austria. After the war, the collapse of the Austrian currency and economy inclined the principality to seek economic partnership with its other neighbor, Switzerland. A treaty concluded with Switzerland in 1923 provided for a customs union and the use of Swiss currency.

Liechtenstein (like Switzerland) remained neutral in World War II, as it had in World War I. After Germany was defeated in 1945, Nazi sympathizers in Liechtenstein who had supported incorporation of the principality into Hitler's Third Reich were prosecuted and sentenced. The postwar decades have been marked by political stability and outstanding economic growth.

Prince Franz Josef II, who succeeded his granduncle, Franz I, in 1938, was the first reigning monarch actually to reside in Liechtenstein. On 26 August 1984, Franz Josef II handed over executive authority to his eldest son and heir, Crown Prince Hans-Adam. Hans-Adam II has been ruling prince since 13 November 1989, after Franz Josef II died.

Liechtenstein has sought further integration into the world community. The country was admitted to the UN in September 1991. In Europe, Liechtenstein joined EFTA in 1991 and became a member of the European Economic Area (EEA) in 1995.

Disagreements between Prince Hans-Adam II and parliament arose in the latter half of 1999. In September, the prince's assertion that he had the right to dissolve the government at his discretion raised tensions to the point where Hans-Adam threatened to go into exile in Austria. In October, the European Court of Human Rights ruled on a complaint filed by Dr. Herbert Wille, a senior judge whom the prince had refused to re-appoint because of Wille's assertion that the country's Supreme Court rather than its monarch should be the ultimate authority on constitutional issues. The court ruled that in depriving Wille of his judicial position because of his political views, the prince had violated the judge's freedom of speech. Wille was awarded 10,000 Swiss francs in compensation as well as payment of his legal costs.

Sixty-four percent of Liechtenstein's voters approved a new constitution for Liechtenstein in a referendum held in March 2003; Hans-Adam II will be granted near-absolute powers. Turnout was large, with 14,800 of Liechtenstein's 17,000 electorate casting votes. The prince now has the right to dissolve government, control a committee appointing judges, and has veto power over legislation. The constitution also gives the people the power to call a referendum and abolish the monarchy. As a result of the changes, which many observers deemed undemocratic, Prince Hans-Adam II rescinded his pledge to leave the country. On 15 August 2004 Prince Hans-Adam II transferred the official duties of the ruling prince to his son and heir apparent, Alois, who was seen as less confrontational than his father. Prince Hans-Adam II retained the status of Chief of State.

Liechtenstein ranks as one of the world's most prosperous countries with one of the world's highest living standards while its people pay very low taxes. In 1999, the royal family itself was ranked as the wealthiest in all of Europe while Prince Hans-Adam II personally was ranked as Europe's third-wealthiest monarch. However, in 2000 Liechtenstein ranked among the top 15 countries named by an international task force investigating countries whose banking laws make money laundering possible. Liechtenstein took steps in 2001 to make its banking system more transparent, however a 2003 International Monetary Fund report concluded that although the banking sector had updated its banking regulation, there were not enough staff to fully enforce the regulations.

13 GOVERNMENT

Liechtenstein is a constitutional monarchy ruled by the hereditary princes of the house of Liechtenstein. The monarchy is hereditary in the male line. The constitution of 5 October 1921, as amended in 1987, provides for a unicameral parliament (Landtag) of 25 members elected for four years. Election is by universal suffrage at age 18 and is on the basis of proportional representation. Women gained the right to vote in 1984. A new voting system that went into effect as of the 1974 national elections provides nine representatives for the Upper Land district and six representatives for the Lower Land district.

A new constitution was approved in March 2003 that grants the ruling prince extensive powers, including the right to veto legislation and to control the appointment of judges, in addition to the rights guaranteed to him under the former constitution.

The prince can call and dismiss the Landtag. On parliamentary recommendation, he appoints the prime minister, who must be of Liechtenstein birth, and the deputy prime minister for four-year

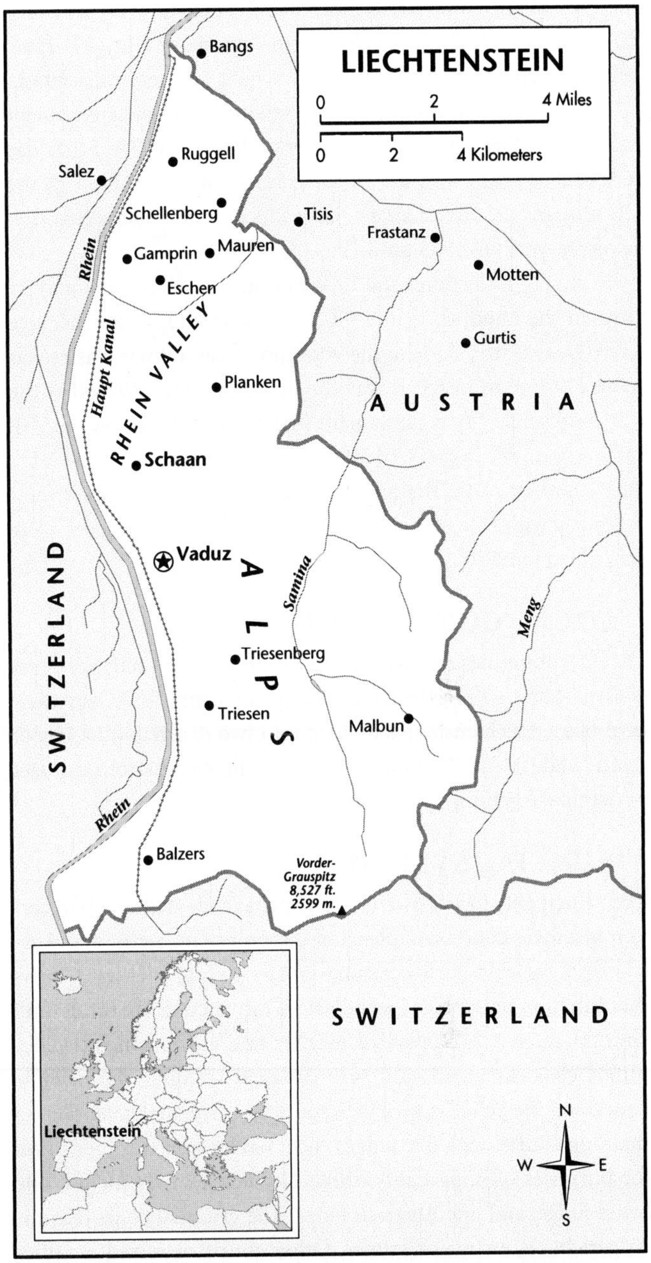

LOCATION: 47°3′ to 47°14′ N; 9°29′ to 9°38′ E. BOUNDARY LENGTHS: Austria, 34.9 kilometers (21.7 miles); Switzerland, 41.1 kilometers (25.5 miles).

terms. It is the regular practice for the prime minister to be of the majority party and the deputy prime minister to be selected from the opposition. The Landtag appoints four councilors for four-year terms to assist in administration. Any group of 1,000 persons or any three communes may propose legislation. Bills passed by the Landtag may be submitted to popular referendum. A law is valid when it receives majority approval by the Landtag and the prince's signed concurrence.

14 POLITICAL PARTIES

The two principal parties are the Fatherland Union (Vaterländische Union—VU) and the Progressive Citizens' Party (Fortschrittliche Bürgerpartei—FBP). In the general elections of 1997, the VU, which has held a majority since 1978, won 13 seats in the Landtag and the FBP 10. Other parties included the Free List (Freie Liste—FL), two seats; and the Liechtenstein Non-party List (Uberparteiliche Liste Liechtensteins—ULL), which was not represented.

The general elections in 1993 resulted in a coalition government headed by Mario Frick of the Fatherland Union (VU). Frick was reelected as prime minister by the Landtag in 1997. Although the VU remains the largest single party, Liechtenstein had a coalition government from 1938 until 1997.

In the 2001 elections, the FBP won 49.9% of the vote and 13 seats in the Landtag, to the VU's 41.1% and 11 seats. The Free List (Greens) won 8.8% of the vote and 1 seat. Otmar Hasler was named prime minister. It was the first time since 1978 that the FBP held a majority in parliament. The 2005 elections saw the FBP retaining power with 48.7% of the vote and 12 seats, to the VU's 38.2% and 10 seats. The minority party Free List increased their following with 13% of the vote and 3 seats. The next elections were scheduled for 2009.

15 LOCAL GOVERNMENT

The 11 communes (gemeinden) are fully independent administrative bodies within the laws of the principality. They levy their own taxes. Liechtenstein is divided into two districts—the Upper Land (Vaduz) and the Lower Land (Schellenberg)—for purposes of national elections.

16 JUDICIAL SYSTEM

The principality has its own civil and penal codes, although in certain instances courts composed of Liechtenstein, Swiss, and Austrian judges have jurisdiction over Liechtenstein cases. Courts that function under sole Liechtenstein jurisdiction are the county court (Landgericht), presided over by one judge, which decides minor civil cases and summary criminal offenses; the juvenile court; and the Schöffengericht, a court for misdemeanors. The remaining courts, with five judges each, have a mixed composition for purposes of impartiality: three Liechtenstein lay judges, one Swiss judge, and one Austrian judge. The criminal court (Kriminalgericht) is for major crimes. Other courts of mixed jurisdiction are the assize court (Schöffengericht-Vergehen), the superior court (Obergericht), and a supreme court (Oberster Gerichtshof). An administrative court of appeal hears appeals from government actions, and the Constitutional Court determines the constitutionality of laws. In June 1986, Liechtenstein adopted a new penal code abolishing the death penalty.

The constitution provides for public trials and judicial appeal. The judiciary is separate from the executive and legislative branches. The 2003 referendum gave the prince the ultimate right to control the appointment of the country's judges.

The constitution provides for freedom of assembly, association and religion. Crime is rare and Switzerland is responsible for Liechtenstein's defense. Liechtenstein retains a restrictive law on the availability of abortion, and is allowable only when the life or health of a woman is threatened.

17 ARMED FORCES

Since 1868, no military forces have been maintained in Liechtenstein, but there is obligatory military service for able-bodied men up to 60 years of age in case of emergency.

18 INTERNATIONAL COOPERATION

Liechtenstein became a member of the United Nations on 18 September 1990; it belongs to the IAEA, ITU, UNCTAD, UPU, and WIPO. Liechtenstein is also a member of the Council of Europe, the European Bank for Reconstruction and Development, EFTA, the OSCE, and the WTO. The principality joined the European Economic Area in 1995. Liechtenstein now has diplomatic relations with nearly 50 countries. In environmental cooperation, the country is part of the Basel Convention, Conventions on Biological Diversity and Air Pollution, Ramsar, CITES, the Kyoto Protocol, the Montréal Protocol, and the UN Conventions on Climate Change and Desertification.

19 ECONOMY

Despite its small size and limited national resources, Liechtenstein is one of the richest countries in the world on a per capita GDP basis. It has developed since the 1940s from a mainly agricultural to an industrialized country and a prosperous center of trade and tourism. Factories produce a wide range of high-technology manufactures, especially precision instruments. Liechtenstein is also a world leader in specialized dental products. Industrial products are manufactured almost exclusively for export.

Special economic advantages enjoyed by very small nations of Europe (e.g., the issuance of new postage stamps, free exchange of currencies, and liberal laws that provide incentives for the establishment of bank deposits and of nominal foreign business headquarters) also play a part in this prosperity.

In 1999 Liechtenstein became the subject of an international investigation into money laundering. Although Liechtenstein subsequently drafted legislation to combat money laundering, the Finance Action Task Force placed the principality on the international "black list" for failing to cooperate with international authorities on the matter.

About 35% of the people employed in Liechtenstein commute from Switzerland and Austria. Liechtenstein remains a well-known tax haven, and a location for holding companies to establish nominal offices; these provide for 30% of state revenues. The country has no central bank and does not print its own currency, but uses the Swiss franc instead. Liechtenstein is engaged in harmonizing its economic policies with those of the EU.

In 1999, its GDP (at purchasing power parity) was $825 million, an 11% improvement over the previous year. In 2002, the unemployment rate for the country's 10,000 domestic workers was 1.3%. More than 19,000 workers commute to Liechtenstein from neighboring countries—Austria, Switzerland, and Germany.

20 INCOME

The US Central Intelligence Agency (CIA) reports that in 2005 Liechtenstein's gross domestic product (GDP) was estimated at $825.0 million. The CIA defines GDP as the value of all final goods and services produced within a nation in a given year and computed on the basis of purchasing power parity (PPP) rather than value as measured on the basis of the rate of exchange based on current dollars. The per capita GDP was estimated at $25,000. The annual growth rate of GDP was estimated at 11%. The average inflation rate in 2001 was 1%.

21 LABOR

As of end 2001 (the latest year for which data was available), there were 29,000 persons in the labor force, including 19,000 foreigners, of whom 13,000 commuted to work from Switzerland, Germany and Austria. As of that date, 1.3% of the workforce were in the agricultural sector, with industry accounting for 47.4% and the services sector 51.3%. Liechtenstein's workforce is highly skilled, but there are not enough native-born workers to meet industry's needs. Unemployment as of September 2002 was 1.3%.

All workers, including foreigners, are entitled to form and join unions. There is one trade union that represents about 13% of the workforce. Strikes are permitted but are not generally used. Most collective bargaining agreements are adapted from ones signed between Swiss workers and employers.

There is no minimum wage, although wages are among the highest in the world. The legal workweek is 45 hours in the industrial sector and 48 hours in nonindustrial firms. The actual workweek is usually 40 to 43 hours. Occupational safety and health standards are set by the government and are rigorously enforced. The minimum working age is 16, but exceptions to this may be made for children wishing to leave school at the age of 14.

22 AGRICULTURE

Liechtenstein has only 912 hectares (2,254 acres) of arable land. Until the end of World War II (1939–45), the economy was primarily focused on agriculture. In the Rhine Valley, the most productive area, the chief vegetables are corn, potatoes, and garden produce. On gradual mountain slopes, a variety of grapes and orchard fruits are grown.

23 ANIMAL HUSBANDRY

Alpine pasture, particularly well suited for cattle grazing, covers over 35% of the total land area.

In 2005, cattle numbered about 6,000; hogs, 3,000; and sheep, 2,900.

24 FISHING

There is no commercial fishing in Liechtenstein. Rivers and brooks are stocked for sport fishing.

25 FORESTRY

The forests of Liechtenstein not only supply wood but also have an important function in preventing erosion, landslides, and floods. Forests cover about 7,000 hectares (17,200 acres).

More than 90% of all forestland is publicly owned; of the 474 hectares (1,171 acres) of private forest, 158 hectares (390 acres) are the property of the prince. The most common trees are spruce, fir, beech, and pine. Roundwood production in 2004 amounted to 22,167 cu m (782,820 cu ft).

26 MINING

There was no mining of commercial importance.

27 ENERGY AND POWER

The first Liechtenstein power station went into operation in 1927; its capacity is now 900 kW. Another station was constructed in 1947–49; it has an installed capacity of 9,600 kW. Total installed capacity in 1989 was 23,000 kW; production amounted to 150 million kWh in 1995. Since domestic production no longer meets local requirements, supplementary energy is imported from Switzerland, especially in winter. In 1995, 92.5% of Liechtenstein's energy requirement was imported from abroad. Consumption of electricity in 2001 was 313.5 million kWh. Imports of electricity in the same year totaled 232.8 million kWh.

28 INDUSTRY

The industry of Liechtenstein, limited by shortages of raw materials, is primarily devoted to small-scale production of precision manufactures. The output includes optical lenses, dental products, high-vacuum pumps, heating equipment, electron microscopes, electronic measuring and control devices, steel bolts, knitting machines, and textiles. Pharmaceuticals, electronics, ceramics, and metal manufacturing are also important. The largest industrial companies in Liechtenstein are Hilti (construction services), Balzers (electro-optical coatings), Hilcona (frozen foods), and Ivoclar-Vivadent (dental medical technology). Liechtenstein's industry is completely geared to exports; industrial exports rose from SwFr196.7 million in 1967 to SwFr3.0 billion in 1996. Around 48% of the labor force is engaged in industry, trade, and construction.

In 1999, industry made up approximately 40% of the overall GDP. By 2004, this share fell to 26.4%. Trade and services are the main contributors to the economy, with a 71.6% share.

29 SCIENCE AND TECHNOLOGY

Like Swiss industry, manufacturing in Liechtenstein entails a high degree of precision and technological sophistication. Balzers, the country's second-largest employer, is known for its leading role in providing equipment and thin film technology for the CD-ROM industry. Liechtenstein itself has no educational institutions offering advanced scientific training. The Liechtensteinische Gesellschaft für Umweltschutz, founded in 1973, is concerned with environmental protection.

30 DOMESTIC TRADE

Liechtenstein and Switzerland are essentially linked in one common economic zone. The domestic economy is largely based on industry and financial services. The primary product industries are electronics, metal manufacturing, and medical precision instruments. About 48% of the work force are foreigners, with 29% commuting from Switzerland and Austria. Vaduz and Schaan, the chief commercial centers, have some specialty shops, but the smaller communities have only general stores. Regular business hours are generally from 8 AM to 6:30 PM. Normal banking hours are from 8:15 AM to noon and from 1:30 PM to 4 or 5 PM, Monday through Friday.

31 FOREIGN TRADE

Goods to and from Liechtenstein pass freely across the frontier with Switzerland, with which Liechtenstein maintains a customs union. Exports in the mid-1990s averaged SwFr2,021,800 per year, as compared with SwFr893,385,000 in 1980. Exports in 1994 were valued at $2.6 billion. Some 40% of exports in 1996 went to EEA countries.

Important exports include precision instruments, ceramics, textiles, and pharmaceuticals. Liechtenstein imports mainly raw materials, light machinery, and processed foods. In the mid-1990s, imports averaged SwFr1,074,600,000 per year.

In 2003, Liechtenstein's exports reached $3.6 billion. Most of these exports went to the EU and Switzerland. The principal export commodities were construction techniques, electronic products, car parts, dental products, and processed agricultural products.

32 BALANCE OF PAYMENTS

The US Central Intelligence Agency (CIA) reported that in 1996 the purchasing power parity of Liechtenstein's exports was $2.47 billion while imports totaled $917.3 million resulting in a trade surplus of $1.5527 billion.

33 BANKING AND SECURITIES

Although there is a national bank, the duties of the central bank are performed by the Swiss National Bank, a consequence of the currency union with Switzerland. Liechtenstein's banks form an important part of the economy, and they have experienced significant growth in the 1990s. An estimated 4% of the work force was employed by the banking sector in the 1990s.

The National Bank of Liechtenstein (Liechtensteinische Landesbank), founded in 1861, is the state bank of issue; in addition, it deals in real estate mortgages and ordinary banking operations. Liechtenstein Global Trust (LGT), the country's biggest financial institution (owned by the royal family), and the Private Trust Bank Corp., founded in 1956, play an important role in the finance and credit spheres of Liechtenstein's economy. Banking is linked with the Swiss banking system, as is securities trading. In 1945, Liechtenstein's banks had a combined balance sheet of SwFr38 million; in 2003, it was SwFr120 billion, an astonishing SwFr3.6 million for every person in the country. Net income from Liechtenstein's banks totaled SwFr232.5 million in 1996, and contributed over 12% to the country's national income in terms of taxes and dividends paid.

Because of Liechtenstein's strict bank secrecy, several thousand foreign businesses are nominally headquartered there. The secrecy laws are, however, waived in the case of criminal intent. There are at present no restrictions on foreign investors' access to financing in Liechtenstein. New laws to combat insider trading and money laundering have recently tightened fiduciary regulations.

34 INSURANCE

Insurance activities in Liechtenstein are variously conducted by the government (old age and survivors' insurance), by private companies under government regulation (e.g., life, accident, health, and fire), and by farmers' associations. In 1996, a new insurance law came into force, focusing on attracting insurance business from abroad, as Liechtenstein is now a member of the European Economic Area.

35 PUBLIC FINANCE

Liechtenstein's economy has experienced more extensive development and industrialization in the past 40 years than any other Western country. In that period, it went from a predominantly agricultural economy to a highly advanced industry-driven economy.

The US Central Intelligence Agency (CIA) estimated that in 1998 Liechtenstein's central government took in revenues of approximately $424.2 million and had expenditures of $414.1 million. Revenues minus expenditures totaled approximately $10.1 million.

36 TAXATION

The main taxes are levied on personal income, business income, and principal. Personal income tax rates are determined by taxable income and taxable wealth. The basic tax rate is 1.2% on income and 0.06% on wealth. However, the communes levy a communal tax of 200%, which brings the combined tax rates to 17.82% on income and 0.89% on wealth. In addition, a surcharge is levied on the basic tax on income and wealth at rates ranging from 5–395%. Thus, the totals of basic tax, communal tax, and surcharges results in the national tax due. Corporations pay income tax at a rate of 7.5–15%. However, if the company's distributed dividends exceed 8% of taxable capital, an increase of 1–5% is added, based upon the dividend distribution percentage, which can push the maximum rate to 20%. Dividends and interest are subject to a 4% withholding tax. Royalty income is not taxed.

Other levies include a capital gains tax on the sale of real estate; death, estate, and gift duties; a motor vehicle registration tax; and a value-added tax (VAT) on goods and services within Liechtenstein and Switzerland at a standard rate of 7.5%.

Firms domiciled in Liechtenstein but conducting no gainful pursuits there benefit from extremely favorable tax arrangements, a prime factor in the establishment of nominal business headquarters. Foreign clients pay 1% per year in capital taxes; and only 0.5% for foundations with taxable assets exceeding SwFr10 million. The communes may impose property and income taxes.

Since joining the European Economic Area in 1995, Liechtenstein has not entered into any agreements covering double taxation, except for Austria.

37 CUSTOMS AND DUTIES

There have been no customs between Switzerland and Liechtenstein since a customs treaty was ratified in 1924. On the Austrian border, Switzerland collects the customs at its own rates. Liechtenstein's part of the duties is calculated on the basis of population and the principality pays an annual indemnification to Switzerland for customs and administration.

38 FOREIGN INVESTMENT

The Prince of Liechtenstein Foundation has established a number of ventures abroad, mainly in the field of investment management and counseling.

Several thousand foreign companies have established offices in Liechtenstein because taxes are very low, banking operates in strict secrecy, and the principality is politically stable. Some industrial establishments are owned and managed by Swiss interests.

39 ECONOMIC DEVELOPMENT

The government generally encourages the increasing diversification of industry and the development of tourism. The principality's low taxes and highly secret banking system are attractive to foreign corporations wanting to safeguard patents and trademarks and to individuals who want to protect their wealth for the future. Thousands of corporations have established nominal headquarters in Liechtenstein. In recent years, the principality is accused of serving as a center for money laundering. In 2002, the International Monetary Fund (IMF) conducted an Offshore Financial Center (OFC) Assessment of Liechtenstein, to evaluate the regulation and monitoring of the country's financial center. The IMF approved of Liechtenstein's efforts to fight money laundering and the financing of international terrorism, and of its planned establishment of an independent supervisory authority.

Research and development is a driving force of Liechtenstein's economic success; in 2000, total research and development spending rose over 20% to around $149 million. Also, the industrial sector is diversified and dynamic, serving mostly niche markets outside the country. The relative attractive tax base keeps some of the more prominent companies (Hilti and Unaxis Balzers) in the country, and the low public spending costs (Liechtenstein has no army, no university, and no major medical clinics) keep the federal budget on a surplus. Export income per capita outweighs that of Germany by more than 10 times.

40 SOCIAL DEVELOPMENT

There is a universal pension system covering all residents, employed persons, and self-employed individuals. It is funded primarily by the government along with contributions from employees and employers. It provides benefits for old age, disability, and survivorship. A social insurance system and universal medical coverage provides sickness and maternity benefits. All residents and persons employed in Liechtenstein are entitled to medical coverage. Work injury and unemployment insurance are provided to all employed persons. There is a family allowance based on number of children and a birth grant provided to all residents and nonresident workers.

Equality for women is protected by law, and several groups monitor and promote women's rights. An equal opportunity law addresses workplace discrimination and sexual harassment. In 2004 the government-sponsored mentoring classes to inspire women to run for seats in parliament. Domestic violence laws have been enacted and are actively implemented. Human rights are fully respected in Liechtenstein.

41 HEALTH

The government regulates the practice of medicine and subsidiary occupations, such as nursing and pharmacy. Life expectancy in 2005 was about 79.55 years. As of 2002, the crude birth rate and overall mortality rate were estimated at, respectively, 11.2 and 6.8 per 1,000 people. The infant mortality rate was an estimated 4.7 per 1,000 births in 2005.

In 2000, Liechtenstein had an estimated 2.5 physicians per 1,000 people. There were approximately 8.3 hospital beds per 1,000 people. A program of preventive medicine, introduced in 1976, provides regular examinations for children up to the age of 10.

42 HOUSING

Houses in the countryside are similar to those found in the mountainous areas of Austria and Switzerland. Liechtenstein does not have a significant housing problem. About 82% of all dwellings have central heating, 89% have a kitchen, 91% have a private bath, 95% have hot water, and 88% have a common sewage system.

43 EDUCATION

Education is based on Roman Catholic principles and is under government supervision. In 1974, the compulsory primary school attendance period was lowered from eight years to five, beginning at age seven. Kindergarten, offered to children ages five to seven, is optional, followed by five compulsory years of primary school. Secondary education is divided into three tracks: *oberschule* (general); *realschule* (which offers vocational and, in some cases, university preparatory education), and *gymnasium* (which provides an eight-year program to prepare students for a university education, with concentrations in either the classics and humanities or economics and mathematics). Liechtenstein also has an evening technical school, a music school, and a children's pedagogic-welfare day school.

While there are no universities in Liechtenstein, gymnasium graduates are may attend universities in Switzerland and Austria and the University of Tubingen in Germany without passing an examination.

44 LIBRARIES AND MUSEUMS

The National Library (founded in 1961) serves as the public, academic, and national library. It is located in Vaduz and has over 200,000 volumes. There are three specialized libraries maintained by private institutes, and a small library attached to a state music school.

The National Museum, located in Vaduz, includes collections from the Prince and the State, containing an important Rubens collection. The Prince Liechtenstein Art Gallery, founded in 1620 and located in Vaduz, is an important cultural institution in Liechtenstein. The museum is housed upstairs in the tourist information office. Also in the capital are a postage museum and a state historical museum. A ski museum opened in Vaduz in 1994, and there are also museums in Schaan, Schellenberg, and Triesenberg.

45 MEDIA

The post office (including telegraph and telephone services) is administered by Switzerland. Liechtenstein, however, issues its own postage stamps. The Swiss dial system extends to the principality.

Direct-dialing is used throughout the country and includes international service. In 2002, there were 19,900 mainline phones and 11,400 mobile phones in use throughout the country. Telegraph service is efficient.

As of 2001, there were one state and one private television station broadcast, along with a private radio station. Residents also receive radio and television broadcasts from neighboring countries. In 1997 there were 21,000 radios and 12,000 television sets in the country. In 2002, there were 20,000 Internet subscribers in the country.

Two daily newspapers are published. The *Liechtensteiner Volksblatt* reflects the political outlook of the Progressive Citizen's Party. It had a circulation of about 8,200 in 2002. *The Liechtensteiner Vaterland* reflects the views of the Fatherland Union. It had a circulation of about 9,580 in the same year. *Liechtensteiner Wochenzeitung*, a weekly, had a circulation of 14,000.

The media is said to enjoy a large degree of autonomy and freedom from interference, owing to an independent press, an effective judiciary, and a democratic political system.

46ORGANIZATIONS

Organizations include the Chamber of Industry and Commerce, the Historical Society of the Principality of Liechtenstein, three concert societies, and various other cultural organizations. There are professional organizations representing several fields and occupations. Kiwanis and Lion's clubs are active in the country. Charitable institutions include the Liechtenstein Caritas Society (founded in 1924) and the Liechtenstein Red Cross Society (1945). Youth organizations include the Scouts and Guides of Liechtenstein. There are also several organizations devoted to sports and leisure activities.

47TOURISM, TRAVEL, AND RECREATION

Attractions include mountaineering and nature walks, the castles of Vaduz and Gutenberg (overlooking Balzers), the ruins of several fortresses, the numerous local brass bands and choirs, as well as the operetta societies of Vaduz and Balzers. The most popular sports are swimming, golf, tennis, hiking, and skiing. The ski resort of Malbun has 12 hotels and 7 ski lifts.

Modern, comfortable buses offer regular service throughout Liechtenstein, connecting with Austria and Switzerland. In Vaduz, the lower country, and the Alpine regions there are hotels and guest houses.

The government actively encourages and supports the tourism industry. In 2003, there were 49,002 visitors, mainly from Luxembourg and Switzerland. Hotel rooms numbered 591 with 1,160 beds and an occupancy rate of 25%. The average length of stay that year was two nights.

48FAMOUS LIECHTENSTEINERS

Joseph Rheinberger (1839–1901), an organist and composer who lived in Munich, was the teacher of many famous composers. Prince John II (r. 1858–1929) was admired for donating some SwFr 75 million to the struggling country after World War I. Prince Franz Josef II (1906–89), whose rule began in 1938, was Europe's longest-reigning sovereign. Liechtenstein's current monarch is Prince Hans Adam II (b.1945), who first was given executive power in 1984 and assumed control in 1989. Prince Alois (b.1968) is regent.

In 1980, Hanni Wenzel (b.1956) and her brother Andreas (b.1958) won the World Cup international skiing championships.

49DEPENDENCIES

Liechtenstein has no territories or colonies.

50BIBLIOGRAPHY

Annesley, Claire (ed.). *A Political and Economic Dictionary of Western Europe*. Philadelphia: Routledge/Taylor and Francis, 2005.

Beattie, David. *Liechtenstein: A Modern History*. New York: I.B. Tauris, 2004.

Duursma, Jorri. *Self-Determination, Statehood, and International Relations of Micro-States: The Cases of Liechtenstein, San Marino, Monaco, Andorra, and the Vatican City*. New York: Cambridge University Press, 1996.

Meier, Regula A. *Liechtenstein*. Santa Barbara, CA: Clio Press. 1993.

LITHUANIA

Republic of Lithuania
Lietuvos Respublika

CAPITAL: Vilnius

FLAG: Three equal horizontal bands of yellow (top), green, and red.

ANTHEM: *Tautiška Giesme (The National Song).*

MONETARY UNIT: The Lithuanian lita (LTL) of 100 cents has replaced the transitional system of coupons (talonas) which had been in force since October 1992, when the Soviet ruble was demonetized. There are coins of 1, 2, 5, 10, 20, and 50 cents and 1, 2, and 5 litas, and notes of 10, 20, 50, and 100 litas; LTL1 = $0.36364 (or $1 = LTL2.75) as of 2005.

WEIGHTS AND MEASURES: The metric system is in force.

HOLIDAYS: New Year's Day, 1 January; Day of the Restoration of the Lithuanian State, 16 February; Good Friday (movable); Anniversary of the Coronation of Grand Duke Mindaugas of Lithuania, 6 July; National Day of Hope and Mourning, 1 November; Christmas, 25–26 December.

TIME: 2 PM = noon GMT.

¹LOCATION, SIZE, AND EXTENT

Lithuania is located in eastern Europe, bordering the Baltic Sea, between Latvia and Poland. Comparatively, it is slightly larger than the state of West Virginia with a total area of 65,200 sq km (25,174 sq mi). Lithuania shares boundaries with Latvia on the N and NE, Belarus on the S and SE, Poland on the SW, Russia-Kaliningrad Oblast on the W, and the Baltic Sea on the NW. Lithuania's land boundary length totals 1,273 km (791 mi). Its coastline is 99 km (62 mi).

Lithuania's capital city, Vilnius, is located in the southeastern part of the country.

²TOPOGRAPHY

The topography of Lithuania features a central lowland terrain with many scattered small lakes and fertile soil. Moderate highlands lie to the east and south, with a few hilly regions in the west. The main hill regions are the Zemaical Uplands of the northwest and the Baltic Highlands of the southeast. The highest point in the country is Juozapine, located in the Baltic Highlands. It has an elevation of 292 meters (958 feet). The lowest point is at sea level (Baltic Sea).

There are about 758 rivers in the country that are longer than 10 kilometers; but very few are navigable. The Neman, which cuts through the center of the country from Belarus to the Baltic Sea, is the longest river, with a length of 936 kilometers (582 miles). There are over 2,500 lakes in the country, most of which are in the eastern central regions. The largest is Lake Druksiai, which is located on the northeast border with Belarus and covers an area of 44.5 square kilometers (17.2 square miles).

³CLIMATE

Lithuania's climate is transitional between maritime and continental. Yearly, the mean temperature is 6.1°C (43°F). The mean temperature in July is 17.1°C (63°F). Rainfall averages from 49 cm (24 in) to 85 cm (33 in) depending on location.

⁴FLORA AND FAUNA

The country is located in the mixed forest zone. The country's vegetation is a mixture of coniferous, broadleaf woodlands, arctic, and steppe species. There are about 68 species of mammals, 203 breeding bird species, 7 reptile species, 13 amphibian species, and about 60 fish species. The country has rabbit, fox, red deer, roe, elk, wild boar, badger, raccoon dog, wolf, lynx, and gallinaceous birds. Roach, ruff, bream, and perch can be found in Lithuania's lakes and streams.

⁵ENVIRONMENT

Lithuania's environmental problems include air pollution, water pollution, and the threat of nuclear contamination. In 2000, the total of carbon dioxide emissions was at 11.9 million metric tons. A UN report on Lithuania stated that air pollution has damaged about 68.4% of the nation's forests. Water pollution results from uncontrolled dumping by industries and the lack of adequate sewage treatment facilities.

After the nuclear accident at Chernobyl that contaminated much of Lithuania with excessive radiation, Lithuanians are concerned about nuclear energy development, especially the use of nuclear power generated by plants of the same kind as the one at Chernobyl.

Lithuania's pollution problems have also affected the nation's wildlife. Although 10% of Lithuania's total land area was protected as of 2003, many of the country's original animal and plant species are now extinct. According to a 2006 report issued by the International Union for Conservation of Nature and Natural Resources (IUCN), threatened species included five types of mammals, four species of birds, three species of fish, and five species of invertebrates. Threatened species include the European bison, the asp, the red wood ant, the marsh snail, and the Russian desman. The wild horse has become extinct.

⁶POPULATION

The population of Lithuania in 2005 was estimated by the United Nations (UN) at 3,415,000, which placed it at number 128 in population among the 193 nations of the world. In 2005, approximately 15% of the population was over 65 years of age, with another 18% of the population under 15 years of age. There were 87 males for every 100 females in the country. According to the UN, the annual population rate of change for 2005–10 was expected to be -0.3%, a rate the government viewed as too low; the population growth rate fell below zero in the mid-1990s. The projected population for the year 2025 was 3,134,000. The population density was 53 per sq km (136 per sq mi).

The UN estimated that 67% of the population lived in urban areas in 2005, but that population in urban areas was declining at an annual rate of -0.49%. The capital city, Vilnius, had a population of 549,000 in that year. Other large cities include Kaunas and Klaipėda.

⁷MIGRATION

Many Lithuanians unable to accept Soviet occupation in 1940 were deported to Siberia. However, Russian immigration to Lithuania was never as heavy as to the other Baltic republics. Lithuania has been used as a transit country to western Europe for many years. Government policy was to return asylum seekers to their homelands or detain them indefinitely. However, a Lithuanian refugee law passed 27 July 1997 established an asylum procedure. The total number of migrants living in Lithuania in 2000 was 339,000. In 2004, there were 9,459 persons of concern to the United Nations High Commissioner for Refugees (UNHCR), 9,028 stateless, 408 refugees, and 28 asylum seekers. Remittances in 2003 were $30.5 million. In 2005, the net migration rate was an estimated -1.71 migrants per 1,000 population. The government views the migration levels as satisfactory.

⁸ETHNIC GROUPS

According to the 2001 census, Lithuanians form about 83.4% of the population. Russians constituted about 6.3%; Poles made up 6.7%; the remaining minority ethnic groups include Belarussians, Ukrainians, Tatars, and Karaites. There are about 3,000 in the Romani community.

⁹LANGUAGES

Lithuanian, the official language, is noted for its purity in retaining ancient Indo-European language forms and has some remarkable similarities with Sanskrit. It is highly inflected, with seven noun cases. Like Latvian, it has rising, falling, and short intonations. Its Roman alphabet has many special symbols, including the hacek, dot, and cedilla. The majority (82%) speak Lithuanian for their first tongue. Polish (5.6%) and Russian (8%) are also widely used.

Minorities have the right to official use of their languages where they form a substantial part of the population.

¹⁰RELIGIONS

The country witnessed extensive suppression of religious activities during the Soviet period. The 2001 census indicated that about 79% of the population were nominally Roman Catholic. The next largest denomination, the Russian Orthodox Church, accounted for about 4.1% of the population. The Old Believers (an Orthodox sect) have about 27,000 members. About 20,000 people are Lutherans, 7,000 are Evangelical Reformed, 4,000 are Jewish, 2,700 are Sunni Muslim, and about 300 are Greek Catholic. About 9.4% of the population claimed no specific religious affiliation.

Lithuania is one of a few countries to have an active community of Karaites. The faith is a branch of Judaism, with tenets based exclusively on a literal interpretation of the Hebrew scriptures. The Karaites have two centers of worship in the country, in Vilnius and Trakia, with a total of about 250 members. The Karaites are considered to be an ethnic community as well. They speak a Turkic-based language and use the Hebrew alphabet.

The constitution allows for freedom of religion, but the government reserves the right to place restrictions on religious organizations with practices that might contradict the constitution or public law. The government recognizes nine groups as "traditional" faiths that are eligible for state assistance: Latin Rite Catholics, Greek Rite Catholics, Evangelical Lutherans, the Evangelical Reformed Church, Orthodox Christians, Old Believers, Jews, Sunni Muslims, and Karaites. Denominations considered "nontraditional" by the government include Jehovah's Witnesses, Baptists, Seventh-Day Adventists, and Pentecostals, as well as about 160 other religious organizations. Certain Christian holidays are celebrated as national holidays.

¹¹TRANSPORTATION

Lithuania's railroad system in 2004 consisted of 1,998 km (1,241 mi) of broad, standard and narrow gauge lines that were used to provide rail access to the Baltic Sea for Vilnius, Kaunas, and other major urban areas. Of that total, broad gauge lines accounted for the bulk at 1,807 km (1,124 mi) of which, 122 km (76 mi) was electrified. Narrow gauge accounted for another 169 km (105 mi), with standard gauge accounting for the remainder.

As of 2003, Lithuania had 78,893 km (49,071 mi) of roadway, of which 21,617 km (13,446 mi) were paved, including 417 km (259 mi) of expressways. In 2004 there were 600 km (373 mi) of perennial navigable waterways. Sea routes link Klaipėda on the Baltic Sea with 200 foreign ports. Kaunas is the principal inland port. In 2005, the merchant fleet consisted of 54 ships (of 1,000 GRT or over) totaling 296,856 GRT. A railway sea ferry from Klaipėda to Mukran (Germany) began in 1986. As of 2004, there were an estimated 102 airports, of which 33 had paved runways as of 2005. Principal airports include Palanga, Vilnius, and Kaunas International at Kaunas, and one commercial airport in Siauliai. Two international airlines serve Lithuania: Lithuanian Airlines and Lietuva. In 2003, about 329,000 passengers were carried on scheduled domestic and international airline flights.

LOCATION: 56°0′ N; 24°0′ E. BOUNDARY LENGTHS: Total boundary lengths, 1,372 kilometers (854 miles); Latvia, 453 kilometers (282 miles); Belarus, 502 kilometers (312 miles); Poland, 91 kilometers (57 miles); Russia, 227 kilometers (141 miles); Baltic Sea coastline, 99 kilometers (62 miles).

12 HISTORY

Lithuanians are a branch of the Balts, whose permanent and lasting settlement of modern day Lithuania dates back to 200 BC, much earlier than most of Europe whose people and cultures were still in flux well into the 5th century AD. Lithuanian, along with Latvian, is thus one of the oldest languages in Europe.

The first Lithuanian state was established by Grand Duke and later King Mindaugas in 1236. Grand Duke Gediminas, who ruled from 1316–41, is credited with founding the capital of Vilnius and the Jagiellionian dynasty, whose members would become figures of power in Lithuania, Poland, and Hungary for the next 200 years.

In the late 14th century Lithuania ruled a vast area covering much of modern day Belarus and Ukraine and stretching to the Black Sea. However, the country was constantly threatened by the German Teutonic Order, which occupied the southern Baltic coast. The power struggle had a religious element, since outside of a brief eight-year period, Lithuania remained devoutly pagan until 1386. That year Grand Duke Jogaila (Polish: *Jagiello*) wed the Polish queen Jadwiga and thereby converted to Christianity the last remaining European pagans. The combined Polish-Lithuanian armies led by Jogaila and his cousin Vytautas (Polish: *Witold*) decisively beat the Teutonic Knights at the battle of Grunwald in 1410.

The marriage of Jogaila to Jadwiga and his ascension to the Polish throne marked the beginning of a political union with Poland, intertwining the histories of the two nations for 400 years. The union was made formal in the 1569 Lublin Agreement, which created a Polish-Lithuanian Commonwealth with an elected monarch chosen by the gentry of both states. Although in principle it was a union of two equals, the Polish influence on the culture and politics of the Commonwealth was stronger, due among other things simply to the larger size and population of the Polish state. Lithuania prospered and developed during the Commonwealth's Golden Age in the 16th century with the founding of the region's first university in Vilnius in 1579 and the development of a distinct Lithuanian baroque artistic style.

The 18th century saw the decline of the Commonwealth and occupation by foreign powers. What is now Lithuania was annexed to the Russian Empire in the final partition in 1795. During the 19th century, a Lithuanian nationalist movement arose leading to uprisings against Russian rule and, in turn, to Russian persecutions including the outlawing of the Lithuanian language.

On 16 February 1918, Lithuania proclaimed its independence after the defeat of both Germany and Russia in World War I. The new Bolshevik government in Moscow attempted to establish Soviet power in Lithuania, but failed. After a series of armed border conflicts between Lithuania, Russia and Poland, in 1920 Moscow recognized Lithuanian independence, but Poland annexed Vilnius, and the Lithuanian capital had to be moved to Kaunas. A secret protocol to the 1939 Nazi-Soviet pact assigned Lithuania to the Soviet sphere of influence. Wishing to avoid conflict, the Lithuanian government allowed Soviet forces to be stationed on its territory. The local government was forced to resign in June 1940. Rigged elections created a parliament which proclaimed Lithuania to be a Soviet Socialist Republic in July 1940. Moscow lost control of Lithuania soon after Germany attacked the USSR in June 1941.

Lithuania suffered heavily at the hands of both powers. While the Nazis succeeded in exterminating most of Lithuania's 240,000 Jews, the Soviets deported tens of thousands of Lithuanians to Siberia. Soviet forces recaptured Lithuania in 1944, although armed resistance against Soviet rule continued for several years after World War II.

Forty-five years of Soviet occupation did not erase the Lithuanian national identity. The first open protests against Soviet rule occurred in 1987 and in 1988. Vytautas Landsbergis established the Sajudis anti-Communist political movement which strove to create an autonomous republic and later an independent state. With the crumbling of the Eastern Bloc and fall of the Berlin Wall in 1989, Soviet pressure eased, and opposition parties were allowed to participate in elections to the Lithuanian Supreme Soviet held on 24 February 1990. Sajudis won a clear majority and Lithuania became the first Soviet republic to proclaim independence on 11 March 1990.

Although Soviet president Mikhail Gorbachev's policy of *glasnost* and *perestroika* had intended to allow a greater voice to Lithuanian self-determination, full Lithuanian independence from the Soviet Union was not what many in the Kremlin had in mind. The August 1991 coup by hardliners in Moscow was accompanied by a crackdown in Vilnius, with Soviet troops storming the TV tower killing 14 civilians and injuring 700. It was not until the failure of the coup and collapse of the Soviet Union that the government in Moscow fully recognized Lithuanian independence.

Since independence, Lithuania has been preoccupied with reforming its economic and political institutions. Privatization has transformed its economy to a market-oriented one. Politically, a thriving press and open democracy have been established. Former Communists won the first postindependence elections in 1992, but conservatives took back the parliament in 1996 elections, in response to growing allegations of government corruption. Presidential elections the following year were surrounded by controversy over the eligibility for office of candidate Valdas Adamkus, who had lived in the United States for over 30 years following World War II. Adamkus was elected in runoff elections in January 1998.

Parliamentary elections were held on 8 October 2000, resulting in a win for former president Algirdas Brazauskas' Social Democratic Coalition, which won 31.1% of the vote, taking 51 of 141 seats in the Seimas. However, a grouping of four smaller parties formed a new centrist government with Rolandas Paksas as prime minister. Presidential elections were held on 22 December 2002, and Adamkus took the lead in the first round of voting, with 35.3% of the vote, to 19.7% for Paksas. In what surprised many experts, Paksas campaigned vigorously for the run-off vote held on 5 January 2003, and won the second round with 54.9% to 45.1% for Adamkus.

Paksas did not serve out his entire term. When he was impeached in April 2004 for having ties with Russian organized crime and participating in influence peddling, the country was temporarily thrown into disarray. In the early election that followed, the Constitutional Court did not allow Paksas to run again despite his continued popularity, especially in rural regions. Adamkus seized the opportunity to return to office and beat Kazimira Prunskiene, the country's first post-Soviet prime minister, who was supported by those loyal to Paksas.

Given the history of Russian domination of Lithuania, it is understandable that Lithuania's primary foreign policy objective has been to improve relations with the West and especially to gain entrance into NATO and the EU. In November 2002, Lithuania was formally invited to join NATO, and became a member in 2004. In May 2004 Lithuania joined the European Union along with nine other ex-Communist states and Malta. Lithuania supported the 2003 US-led military campaign to disarm and remove Saddam Hussein's regime in Iraq.

13 GOVERNMENT

On 25 October 1992, Lithuanian voters approved a new constitution, which called for a 141-member unicameral legislature (Seimas) and a popularly elected president. The constitution requires whoever is elected as president to sever his or her formal party ties. All who were permanent residents of Lithuania in November 1989 have been granted the opportunity to become citizens, irrespective of their ethnic origins. Members of the Seimas are elected for four-year terms, and the president is directly elected for a five-year term. The prime minister is appointed by the president; all others ministers are nominated by the prime minister and appointed by the president. All ministerial appointments must be approved by the Seimas. Suffrage is universal at age 18.

14 POLITICAL PARTIES

The majority party in the Seimas since the 1996 parliamentary elections was the conservative Homeland Union Party, or TS, led by Vytautas Landsbergis, which won 70 out of 141 seats. Overall, 28 parties competed for the 141 parliamentary seats in elections held on 20 October 1996 (first round) and 10 November 1996 (second round). The other party of the right wing, the Christian Democrats, also did well, winning 16 seats, and entered into a coalition government with the TS and the Lithuanian Center Union, which won 13 seats. The Democratic Labor Party (composed mostly of ex-Communists), which had been the majority party in the previous parliament, won only 12 seats. Other parties with parliamentary representation included the Lithuanian Social Democratic Party and the Lithuanian Democratic Party.

The Homeland Union-Conservative coalition suffered in the October 2000 parliamentary elections, capturing only nine seats. Former president Algirdas Brazauskas led four leftist parties in a Social Democratic Coalition, winning 51 of the 141 seats in parliament. However, a coalition ("New Policy") composed of the ideologically diverse Liberal Union (33 seats), New Alliance (28), Center Union (2), Modern Christian Democratic Union (3), and two smaller parties formed a new government, bypassing the Social Democratic Coalition. Rolandas Paksas was named prime minister.

In the elections of October 2004, the Labor Party—a recent political formation led by Russian millionaire Voktor Uspaskich—won 39 seats, Homeland Union 25, the Social Democrats 20, Liberal and Center Union 18, Social Liberals 11, Union of Farmers and New Democracy 10, Liberal Democrats 10, Electoral Action 2, and independents claimed 6 seats.

In the presidential elections held in June 2004, Valdas Adamkus beat Kazimiera Prunskiene with 52.2% of the vote. Adamkus will be in office until the next election that was scheduled for June 2009.

15 LOCAL GOVERNMENT

For administrative purposes, Lithuania's 10 provinces are divided into 44 regions, there are also urban districts, towns, and rural administrative units called *apylinkes*. Each level of local government has its own elected officials.

16 JUDICIAL SYSTEM

After Lithuania broke away from the Soviet Union, its legal system was transformed from that of the old Soviet regime to a democratic model. The system now consists of a Constitutional Court and a Supreme Court, whose members are elected by the Seimas, as well as district and local courts, whose judges are appointed by the president. A Court of Appeals hears appellate cases from the district courts.

A new civil and criminal procedure code and a court reform law were enacted in 1995. The government has reviewed its laws to bring them into accord with the European Convention on Human Rights.

The judiciary is independent.

17 ARMED FORCES

In 2005 the active armed forces of Lithuania totaled 13,510, supported by 8,200 reservists. The Army numbered 11,600 active personnel, followed by the Air Force with 1,200 members and the Navy with 710 active personnel. The country also had a paramilitary force of 14,600, that consisted of 5,000 border guards and a 9,600-member Riflemen Union. There was also a 540-person Coast Guard. Army equipment included three reconnaissance vehicles, 137 armored personnel carriers, and 133 artillery pieces. Naval forces operated 2 frigates, 3 patrol/coastal vessels, 2 mine warfare ships and, 1 logistics/support vessel. The Air Force operated 11 transport and 6 training fixed wing aircraft, in addition to 12 support helicopters. Lithuanian forces served in Afghanistan, Iraq, Bosnia, and Serbia-Montenegro. The defense budget for 2005 was $333 million.

18 INTERNATIONAL COOPERATION

Lithuania was admitted to the United Nations on 17 September 1991; it is a member of several specialized agencies, such as the FAO, IAEA, World Bank, ILO, IMF, UNCTAD, UNESCO, UNIDO, and the WHO. Lithuania is also a member of the WTO, the OSCE, the Council of Europe, the European Bank for Reconstruction and Development, the Euro-Atlantic Partnership Council, and the Council of the Baltic Sea States. It is a member affiliate of the Western European Union. Lithuania joined the European Union and NATO in 2004.

Lithuania has foreign diplomatic missions in 94 countries. The country has offered support to UN missions and operations in Kosovo (est. 1999). It is part of the Australia Group, the Nuclear Suppliers Group (London Group), and the Organization for the Prohibition of Chemical Weapons. In environmental cooperation, Lithuania is part of the Basel Convention, Conventions on Biological Diversity and Air Pollution, Ramsar, CITES, the Kyoto Protocol, the Montréal Protocol, MARPOL, and the UN Conventions on the Law of the Sea and Climate Change.

19 ECONOMY

Until 1940, Lithuania's economy was primarily agricultural, mainly in the form of dairy farms and livestock raising. The main industries are machine building and metalworking, although light industry and food processing are also well developed. Like the other Baltic states, Lithuania has few natural resources, primarily peat and amber.

Due to modernization that occurred during Soviet dominance, Lithuania built up a large, if somewhat inefficient, industrial sector that in 2001 accounted for 32% of the country's economy. The service sector is 61% while agriculture accounts for about 13% of the economy.

In 1992, Lithuania's GDP fell 21.6%. In that year, the government adopted an IMF-directed program aimed at privatizing the economy, controlling inflation, eliminating price controls, and lowering the budget deficit. In June 1993 Lithuania's convertible currency, the litas, was introduced, setting off another round of inflation, while GDP continued to decline, by 16.2% in 1993 and 9.8% in 1994. In 1994, the government entered into a three-year arrangement with the IMF under its Extended Fund Facility (EFF) aimed primarily at bringing inflation under control. 1995 was the first year of positive growth (3.3%) since independence, although unemployment remained high, at 16.4% in 1995. Inflation, which was still in double digits in 1996 (23%), fell to single digits (5.1%) by 1998 and unemployment fell to 6.4%. The economy registered real growth until 1999—4.7% in 1996, 7.3% in 1997 and 5.1% in 1998—but then was overtaken by the effects of the August 1998 financial crisis in Russia, still one of Lithuania's largest trading partners. Real GDP declined 3.9% in 1999 as unemployment jumped to 8.4%. Inflation remained under control, however, at 0.3%.

Growth returned in 2000, with real GDP up 3.3%, but unemployment continued to soar, peaking at 13.2% in March 2001. Growth in 2001 was 5.9%, above expectations, and in the first half of 2002, growth averaged about 5.6%. In February 2002, the government repegged the litas from the US dollar to the euro, at a rate of 3.4528 litas per euro. Inflation was about 1% for the year and by December 2002, unemployment had moderated to 10.9%. About 80% of Lithuanian's enterprises have been privatized since independence, and by 2002 over 25% of its trade was with countries outside the old Soviet bloc. Lithuania acceded to the WTO 31 May 2001 and was admitted to the EU in 2004.

In 2003, the Lithuanian economy was one of the most dynamic in Europe with a GDP growth rate of 9.7%. Prime factors for this economic expansion have been domestic and foreign investments. Rising fuel costs, as well as a shortage of qualified labor, have slowed down this boom by 2004—the GDP growth rate returned to a more modest, but still respectable, 6.7%, and was expected to continue to decline to 5.7% in 2005. Unemployment went down, from 10.3% in 2003 to 6.8% in 2004, and was expected to continue the decrease in 2005, to 5.8%. Inflation has remained negligible over all this time period, hovering at around 1%.

Overall, the economy in Lithuania is on a healthy path, with the private sector contributing to more than 80% of the country's GDP, with significant inflows of foreign capital, and with a dynamic and increasingly efficient local market.

20 INCOME

The US Central Intelligence Agency (CIA) reports that in 2005 Lithuania's gross domestic product (GDP) was estimated at $49.4 billion. The CIA defines GDP as the value of all final goods and services produced within a nation in a given year and computed on the basis of purchasing power parity (PPP) rather than value as measured on the basis of the rate of exchange based on current dollars. The per capita GDP was estimated at $13,700. The annual growth rate of GDP was estimated at 6.4%. The average inflation rate in 2005 was 2.6%. It was estimated that agriculture accounted for 5.7% of GDP, industry 32.4%, and services 62%.

According to the World Bank, in 2003 remittances from citizens working abroad totaled $115 million or about $33 per capita and accounted for approximately 0.6% of GDP. Foreign aid receipts amounted to $372 million or about $108 per capita and accounted for approximately 2.1% of the gross national income (GNI).

The World Bank reports that in 2003 household consumption in Lithuania totaled $11.79 billion or about $3,414 per capita based on a GDP of $18.4 billion, measured in current dollars rather than PPP. Household consumption includes expenditures of individuals, households, and nongovernmental organizations on goods and services, excluding purchases of dwellings. It was estimated that for the period 1990 to 2003 household consumption grew at an average annual rate of 5.4%. In 2001 it was estimated that approximately 33% of household consumption was spent on food, 13% on fuel, 4% on health care, and 27% on education.

21 LABOR

In 2005, Lithuania's labor force was estimated at 1.61 million. As of 2003, the services sector accounted for 54% of the workforce, with industry employing 28.1% and agriculture the remaining 17.9%. The unemployment rate was approximately 5.3% in 2005.

The constitution recognizes the right for workers to form and join trade unions. Approximately 13% of employees are union members. There are four major trade union organizations. The law also provides the right of workers to strike, except those in essential services in the public sector. Collective bargaining is permitted but only utilized on a limited basis.

The legal minimum wage is periodically adjusted by the government for inflation, but these adjustments lag behind the inflation rate. The minimum wage was $107.50 per month as of 2002, but it is not universally enforced. The legal minimum age for employment is 16 years without parental consent, and 14 years with written parental consent. The 40-hour workweek is standard for most workers. The law stipulates occupational health and safety standards, but these are not effectively enforced and many industrial plants are unsafe.

22 AGRICULTURE

Out of Lithuania's 6,268,000 hectares (15,488,000 acres) of land area, 47.6% consisted of cropland and permanent pastures. Privatization in agriculture rapidly advanced after 1991; over 70,000 private farms had been established by 1996. In 2003, there were over 272,000 agricultural holdings. However, due to a lack of financial resources and inefficiency in the crediting system, many of these new farmers are only operating at subsistence levels. Agricultural output decreased by a yearly average of 1.1% during 1990–2000. However, during 2002–04, crop production was up 9.5% from 1999–2001. In 2003, the value of crop output was €669.7 million and agriculture accounted for 7% of GDP.

Crops of importance in 2004 included potatoes, 1,021,000 tons; barley, 970,000 tons; wheat, 1,315,000 tons; rye, 180,000 tons; dry beans, 5,200 tons, vegetables and melons, 379,000 tons; and rapeseed, 204,500 tons.

23 ANIMAL HUSBANDRY

About 8% of the total land area consists of permanent pastureland. Livestock in 2005 included 792,000 head of cattle, 1,074,000 pigs, 8,210,000 chickens, 22,100 sheep, and 63,600 horses. Meat production in 2005 totaled 216,700 tons, of which 28% was beef, 51% was pork, and 21% was chicken. Milk production exceeded 1.7 million tons in 2005, while 50,000 tons of eggs were produced. In 2003, the value of animal and animal product output was €514.9 million.

24 FISHING

Klaipeda's fishing port is the center of the fishing industry. In 2003, the total catch was 159,561 tons, down from 470,251 tons in 1991. Principal species in 2003 included mackerel, sardines, and hairtail. Fisheries exports were valued at $115.1 million in 2003.

There are two aquacultural facilities operating in Lithuania, consisting primarily of carp.

25 FORESTRY

Forests cover about 32% of Lithuania. The forestry, wood products, and paper industries are some of Lithuania's oldest—furniture, matches, and timber products were manufactured in Kaunas and Vilnius in the mid-1800s, and furniture-making prevailed from 1919–40. Currently, chemical timber processing, and the production of furniture, pulp, paper, wood fiber, wood chips, joinery articles, and cardboard, are the main activities of the forestry sector. Intensive timber processing, as well as the recycling of industrial waste are being expanded. The timber cut yielded over 6.1 million cu m (216 million cu ft) of roundwood in 2004. Sawn wood production that year was 1,450,000 cu m (51 million cu ft); paper and paperboard, 99,000 tons. Exports of forest products amounted to $335.7 million in 2004.

26 MINING

Lithuania's production of nonhydrocarbon minerals in 2003 included cement, limestone, nitrogen (from ammonia) and peat. Other industrial minerals produced included clays, and sand and gravel. Lithuania remained dependent on imports for its metals and fuel needs. Peat was extracted in the Siauliai, Ezherelis, Paraistis, and Baltoyi-Boke regions. Mineral production figures in 2003 included: limestone, 944,600 metric tons, down from 984,300 metric tons in 2002; cement, 596,900 metric tons, compared to 605,800 metric tons in 2002; and peat, 366,900 metric tons, down from 513,000 metric tons in 2002. Following complaints from Lithuania's sole producers of cement and quicklime, the government launched antidumping investigations directed against Belarussian products. If the government were to take steps to protect the domestic construction material market, Lithuania could lose its export market in Belarus.

27 ENERGY AND POWER

Lithuania is alone among the three nations that comprise the Baltic States (the other two are Latvia and Estonia) to have any known petroleum reserves. Although it does not have any known reserves of natural gas, it does have a small amount of recoverable coal reserves.

Lithuania had 12 million barrels of proven oil reserves in 2004, but potential onshore and offshore reserves could be much greater. Oil production in 2004 averaged 14,000 barrels per day, with consumption averaging 107,000 barrels per day that same year. As a result, Lithuania imports the bulk of its oil, mostly from Russia. Lithuania is also a net natural gas importer, with consumption of 110 billion cu ft in 2004. Russia's Gazprom is a major source of the country's gas imports.

Lithuania also operates the only petroleum refinery among the Baltic States, the Mazheikiai oil refinery, which has a production capacity of 263,000 barrels per day.

Lithuania has recoverable coal reserves of 4 million short tons, as of 2004. However there is no recorded domestic production or consumption of coal for that year.

In 2004, net electricity generation was 19.8 billion kWh. Consumption in that same year came to 11.6 billion kWh. In 2002, most of Lithuania's electric power came from the Ignalina nuclear plant. Of the 17.121 billion kWh of power generated that year, the Ignalina facility generated 82.6% of the country's power, while only 15% came from conventional thermal plants and the rest from hydroelectric sources. However, as of March 2005, the Lithuanian government was reported to have plans to close down the Ignalina facility in two stages, starting in 2005 and ending in 2009. Total installed generating capacity in 2004 was placed at 5.8 GW.001 was 5.8 million kW.

28 INDUSTRY

Lithuania underwent rapid industrialization during the Soviet era and has significant capacity in machine building and metalworking, as well as the textile and leather industries, and agro-processing (including processed meat, dairy products, and fish). The country's diverse manufacturing base also includes an oil refinery and high-tech minicomputer production. Other industrial products include refrigerators and freezers, electric motors, television sets, metal-cutting machine tools, small ships, furniture, fertilizers, optical equipment, and electronic components. Due to a rapid program of privatization, more than 80% of Lithuania's enterprises are privately owned. Most capital investment has gone into the industrial sector. Major infrastructure projects were planned in 2002, including upgrading the oil refinery, the nuclear power plant, construction of a main highway, and the modernization of sea-port facilities. The industrial sector accounted for about 31% of GDP in 2001.

By 2004, the representation of the industrial sector in the GDP increased to 33.4%, while its representation in the labor force was 30%; agriculture composed 6.1% of the economy, and 20% of the labor force; services came in first with 60.5% and 50% respectively. Industry remained an important growth factor in 2004, registering a 12% increase and outweighing the overall growth rate of the economy.

29 SCIENCE AND TECHNOLOGY

The Lithuanian Academy of Science, founded in 1941, has departments of mathematical, physical, and chemical sciences; biological, medical, and agricultural sciences; and technical sciences. In 1987–97, science and engineering students accounted for 31% of university enrollment. Ten research institutes concerned with medicine, natural sciences, and technology, mostly in Vilnius, and a botanical garden in Kaunas are attached to the academy. Four other institutes conduct research in medicine and forestry. Seven universities and colleges offer degrees in basic and applied sciences.

In 2002, Lithuania had 1,824 scientists and engineers and 430 technicians per one million people engaged in research and development (R&D). In that same year, Lithuania spent $243.617 million, or 0.68% of GDP on R&D. The largest contributor was the government, accounting for 65.1% of expenditures, followed by business at 27.9% and by foreign investors at 7.1%. High technology exports in 2002 totaled $130 million, or 5% of the country's manufactured exports.

30 DOMESTIC TRADE

Vilnius, Klaipėda, and Kaunas each have shopping areas and several markets; many smaller towns have a central market. Several supermarkets have opened within the past few years. There are also a number of newer privately-owned import businesses taking root. As of 2002, manufacturing accounted for about 23% of the GDP and wholesale/retail sales were up to about 15% and 8.4% respectively. For a time, inflation (estimated at 23% in 1996) severely hindered domestic purchasing power. By 1998, however, inflation was down to 5.1% and the 2002 estimate was at 0.8%. A cash economy still prevails, though some major hotels and restaurants have accepted credit cards.

31 FOREIGN TRADE

Lithuania depends heavily on trade, particularly with other republics of the former Soviet Union. In 2000, total imports were valued at $5.5 billion, and exports at $3.8 billion. In the mid-to-late 1990s, Lithuania was trading more with Western nations, and reducing its reliance on trade with former Soviet republics. Trade with the West increased from 15% to 60% between 1990 and 1995, while trade with former Soviet republics fell from 78% in 1990 to 40% in 1995. Since Lithuania's independence in 1990, growing disruptions in trade with Russia and the other former Soviet republics have resulted in a steep decline in import volumes and numerous domestic shortages.

In 2004, exports grew to $8.9 billion (FOB—Free on Board), while imports reached $11 billion. Mineral products make up Lithuania's most beneficial export commodity (23%), followed by textiles and clothing (16%), and machinery and equipment (11%). Other export commodities include chemicals (6%), wood and wood products (5%), and foodstuffs (5%). The most important export partners, in 2004, were Germany (receiving 10.2% of total exports), Latvia (10.2%), Russia (9.3%), France (6.3%), the United Kingdom (5.3%), Sweden (5.1%), Estonia (5%), Poland (4.8%), the Netherlands (4.8%), Denmark (4.8%), the United States (4.7%), and Switzerland (4.6%). The main import commodities were mineral products (21%), machinery and equipment (17%), transport equipment (11%), chemicals (9%), textiles and clothing (9%), and metals (5%); and most of these came from Russia (23.1%), Germany (16.7%), Poland (7.7%), the Netherlands (4.0%), and Latvia (3.8%).

32 BALANCE OF PAYMENTS

The US Central Intelligence Agency (CIA) reported that in 2002 the purchasing power parity of Lithuania's exports was $5.4 billion while imports totaled $6.8 billion resulting in a trade deficit of $1.4 billion.

The International Monetary Fund (IMF) reported that in 1998 Lithuania had exports of goods totaling $4.89 billion and imports totaling $6 billion. The services credit totaled $1.16 billion and debit $700 million.

The exports of goods and services continued to grow in the following years, reaching $9.5 billion in 2003, and $11 billion in 2004. Imports followed a similar path, totaling $10.5 billion in 2003, and $12.4 billion in 2004. The resource balance was consequently negative in both years, at -$1 billion and -$1.4 billion respectively. The current account balance was also negative, dropping to -$1.2 billion in 2003, and -$1.3 billion in 2004. Total reserves (including gold) decreased from $3.5 billion in 2003 to $3 billion in 2004, covering around three months of imports.

33 BANKING AND SECURITIES

Since 1991, Lithuania has reorganized its banking sector numerous times. A myriad of banks emerged after independence, most of them weak. Consequently, consolidations, mergers, and collapses became a regular feature of the country's banking system.

On 3 July 1992 the government adopted a new currency unit, the lita, to replace the ruble. Between 1992 and 1995, six banks lost their licenses and two were merged; as of mid-1996, 16 were either suspended or facing bankruptcy procedures. The first serious crisis centered on Aurasbankas, the eighth-largest bank in the country, and the deposit bank for many ministries. The Bank of Lithuania suspended Aurasbankas's operations in mid-1995 because of liquidity problems caused by bad lending and deposit-

Principal Trading Partners – Lithuania (2003)

(In millions of US dollars)

Country	Exports	Imports	Balance
World	7,162.2	9,803.0	-2,640.8
Switzerland-Liechtenstein	833.3	76.8	756.5
Russia	725.8	2,160.4	-1,434.6
Germany	709.5	1,583.3	-873.8
Latvia	692.1	155.5	536.6
United Kingdom	455.3	325.5	129.8
France-Monaco	363.2	407.3	-44.1
Denmark	338.7	278.6	60.1
Estonia	308.1	135.3	172.8
Sweden	286.9	342.6	-55.7
Netherlands	245.1	248.7	-3.6

(…) data not available or not significant.

SOURCE: *2003 International Trade Statistics Yearbook*, New York: United Nations, 2004.

Balance of Payments – Lithuania (2003)

(In millions of US dollars)

Current Account		-1,278.4
Balance on goods		1,704.2
Imports	-9,362.0	
Exports	7,657.8	
Balance on services		614.4
Balance on income		-482.2
Current transfers		293.7
Capital Account		67.5
Financial Account		1,642.3
Direct investment abroad		-37.2
Direct investment in Lithuania		179.2
Portfolio investment assets		29.8
Portfolio investment liabilities		222.3
Financial derivatives		-28.0
Other investment assets		-100.9
Other investment liabilities		1,377.2
Net Errors and Omissions		181.2
Reserves and Related Items		-612.7

(…) data not available or not significant.

SOURCE: *Balance of Payment Statistics Yearbook 2004*, Washington, DC: International Monetary Fund, 2004.

taking practices. In July 1995, the minimum capital requirement for existing banks was raised from LTL5 million to LTL10 million, the level already established for new banks. By May 1999, only five commercial banks remained. Moreover, foreign investment by Sweden's Swedbank and SE-Banken, helped keep Hansapank-Hoiupank and Uhispank-Tallinna, respectively.

Operations at Lithuania's largest bank, the Joint-Stock Innovation Bank, were suspended on 20 December 1995, and those of the Litimpeks bank, the country's second-largest, two days later. The two were in the process of merging to create the Lithuania United Bank and the fraud was uncovered during pre-merger audits. Due to rumors of a devaluation of the currency, a shortage of foreign exchange throughout the whole banking sector was created.

The International Monetary Fund reports that in 2001, currency and demand deposits—an aggregate commonly known as M1—were equal to $1.7 billion. In that same year, M2—an aggregate equal to M1 plus savings deposits, small time deposits, and money market mutual funds—was $3.2 billion. The money market rate, the rate at which financial institutions lend to one another in the short term, was 3.37%.

The National Stock Exchange, which opened in September 1993, is the most active in the region, with 245 listed companies. Monthly turnover by the end of 1994 had reached LTL20.8 million. The market gains continued into 1999 as the index rose 15%. As of 2004, there were a total of 43 companies listed on the Vilnius Stock Exchange (VILSE), with a market capitalization of $6.463 billion. In 2004, the VILSE Index rose 68.2% from the previous year to 293.4.

In 1997, a key feature of the new economic framework in Lithuania was the pegging of the lita to a currency basket composed of the dollar and the deutschemark. In 1999, the Bank of Lithuania announced its intention to peg the lita to the euro in 2001.

34 INSURANCE

Lithuania's health insurance system is reminiscent of the Soviet era through a state-run system of coverage for all residents. In 2003, the value of all direct insurance premiums written totaled $266 million, of which nonlife premiums accounted for $196 million. Lithuania's top nonlife insurer in 2003 was Lietuvos Draudimas, with gross written nonlife premiums of $64.7 million. As of 2004, Lithuania's leading life insurer was Hansa Gywybes Draudimus, which had gross written life insurance premiums of $32.5 million.

35 PUBLIC FINANCE

Lithuania had, of course, a planned economy under the Soviet regime, and the implementation of collective farming ravaged the agricultural sector for over a decade. It was not until the early 1960s and the introduction of chemicals that crop production recovered to pre-WWII levels. The crop boom that followed as a result of the chemical innovations left many ecological problems. Privatization following independence occurred slowly but steadily, and in 1998 it looked like the economy had survived the growing pains of dismantling the socialist system. However, the August 1998 collapse of the Russian ruble reverted Lithuania's economy back to negative growth and refocused the country's trade toward the West. In 1997, exports to former Soviet nations accounted for

Public Finance – Lithuania (2003)

(In millions of litai, central government figures)

Revenue and Grants	**16,091**	**100.0%**
Tax revenue	9,716	60.4%
Social contributions	4,851	30.1%
Grants	435	2.7%
Other revenue	1,089	6.8%
Expenditures	**17,192**	**100.0%**
General public services	4,345	25.3%
Defense	891	5.2%
Public order and safety	1,088	6.3%
Economic affairs	2,183	12.7%
Environmental protection	96	0.6%
Housing and community amenities	1	<1.0%
Health	2,084	12.1%
Recreational, culture, and religion	289	1.7%
Education	1,238	7.2%
Social protection	4,976	28.9%

(...) data not available or not significant.

SOURCE: *Government Finance Statistics Yearbook 2004*, Washington, DC: International Monetary Fund, 2004.

45% of total exports. By 2002, that number was only 19%, as 71% of exports went to EU member countries and candidates. Privatization was nearly complete as of 2002, except for the energy sector, where energy company privatization was completely on hold and gas company privatization delayed.

The US Central Intelligence Agency (CIA) estimated that in 2005 Lithuania's central government took in revenues of approximately $8.4 billion and had expenditures of $9.1 billion. Revenues minus expenditures totaled approximately -$674 million. Public debt in 2005 amounted to 21.4% of GDP. Total external debt was $10.47 billion.

The International Monetary Fund (IMF) reported that in 2003, the most recent year for which it had data, central government revenues were LTL16,091 million and expenditures were LTL17,192 million. The value of revenues was us$5,257 million and expenditures us$5,585 million, based on an exchange rate for 2003 of us$1 = LTL3.061 as reported by the IMF. Government outlays by function were as follows: general public services, 25.3%; defense, 5.2%; public order and safety, 6.3%; economic affairs, 12.7%; environmental protection, 0.6%; health, 12.1%; recreation, culture, and religion, 1.7%; education, 7.2%; and social protection, 28.9%.

36 TAXATION

Lithuania has one of the most liberal tax regimes in Europe. The corporate income rate as of 2005 was 15%. Small enterprises with gross income of less than €144,810 (LTL500,000) and which have no more than 10 employees are taxed at 13% of profits. Capital gains are considered part of corporate income and are taxed at the corporate rate. Dividends are generally taxed at 15% but if paid to a nonresident company that owns more than 10% of its voting shares (i.e., its parent company), there is no tax. This provision is not applicable to companies operating in Free Economic Zones (FEZs), which offer 80% reduction in the corporate income tax rate for the first five years, and a 50% reduction for an additional five years. The statutory withholding rates are 15% for dividend income and 10% for interest and royalties. Withholding rates on capital income are often reduced to 10% and 5% in bilateral double tax prevention treaties between Lithuania and other countries.

Personal income as of 2005 was taxed at a flat rate of 33%. However, plans by the government call for this rate to be reduced to 30% in 2006, 27% in 2007 and to 24% in 2008. In addition, certain other types of income are subject to a 15% rate. These include income from distributed profits, the sale or rental of property, creative activities and other types of individual activities. Individuals receiving capital gains from either the sale of property or shares are taxed at 15% on the gains. However, capital gains from shares held for more than a year may be exempt if certain conditions are met. If the gains are derived from the sale of immovable property in Lithuania, they are exempt if the property was held for more than three years. Deductions from income for the primary flat tax include a nontaxable minimum which is higher for disabled persons, single parents and other specified groups, plus all social security and social assistance payments, death benefits, court awards, gifts, allowances for insurance payments, charity donations, and most payments to pension accounts. In 2003 a 1.5% real estate tax was introduced. Gifts and inheritances are taxed at 0%, 5% and 10% depending on the amount involved.

The main indirect tax is Lithuania's value-added tax (VAT) enacted 22 December 1993 and most lately revised in 1 July 2002 for application in 2003. The VAT has a standard rate of 18%, applicable to most goods and services, and three reduced rates of 9%, 5% and 0%. The 9% rate is applied to the renovation and construction of buildings financed from certain sources. The 5% rate is applied to certain foodstuffs, newspapers, books, passenger and luggage transport, drugs and medicines, and hotel accommodations. Exports and some export related services, international transport, ships and aircraft, and European Union related trade or supplies are zero-rated. Exempted from the VAT are educational, healthcare, insurance and financial services, the leasing, sale or transfer of immovable property (including dwellings), and social, sports, cultural, radio and television services, if provided by nonprofit organizations. There are also excise duties on ethyl alcohol and alcoholic beverages, tobacco and fuels. However, by the new Law on Excise Duties of 1 July 2002, excise taxes on jewelry, electrical energy, coffee, chocolate, and other food products were abolished, while turnover taxes replaced excises on sugar, luxury cars, liquid cosmetics containing ethyl alcohol, and publications of an erotic and/or violent nature. In 1999, the government introduced a pollution tax on packets to encourage the recycling of packaging material.

37 CUSTOMS AND DUTIES

Most foreign imports, including all raw materials, are duty-free. Exceptions include food products (5–10%), fabrics (10%), electronics (10%), cement (25%), and window glass (50%). The average tariff on consumer products is 15%. Alcoholic beverages are subject to duties ranging from 10% for beer to 100% for some liquor. An 18% VAT is also placed on imports. In 1993, Lithuania, Estonia, and Latvia formed a free trade area, which eliminated customs duties and quotas between the three Baltic States. In ac-

cordance with Lithuania's participation in the European Union, some duties on EU goods have been lowered.

38 FOREIGN INVESTMENT

In May 1991, a foreign investment law was passed permitting majority holdings by nonresidents and guaranteeing the full transfer of profits.

Various tax benefits may be granted to foreign investors depending on the type and size of the investment. When purchasing privatized Lithuanian companies or forming joint ventures, foreign investors are usually expected to provide employment guarantees.

Foreigners from European Union and NATO-member nations may own land, while foreigners from all other nations may not. The provision is aimed primarily at foreigners from former Soviet republics who are the main non-Western investors in Lithuania. Foreigners not eligible to own land may rent it for a period of up to 99 years.

In 1998, foreign direct investment (FDI) inflow into Lithuania reached $925.5 million, up from $354.5 million the year before, due largely to the privatization of Lithuania's telecommunications company. From 1999 to 2001, FDI inflow averaged $437 million a year. In 2002, contrary to worldwide trends of decreasing inward FDI flows, FDI in Lithuania rose 21.9% to $543 million.

On 1 July 2004 total foreign direct investment in Lithuania reached $5.7 billion, with most of it coming from the EU. The largest chunk of this capital inflow went to the following sectors: processing (31.1%), trade (17.9%), transportation and communication (17.1%), and financial mediation (15.7%).

Lithuania continues, despite its small size, to be an attractive location for FDI and a competitive center for product sourcing. It boasts a highly skilled labor force, competitive costs, a stable political and economic environment, a strong currency, and the region's most developed infrastructure.

39 ECONOMIC DEVELOPMENT

In 1990, the Lithuanian government began a comprehensive economic reform program aimed at effecting the transformation to a market-driven economy. Reform measures include price reform, trade reform, and privatization. By mid-1993, 92% of housing and roughly 60% of businesses slated for privatization had been privatized. By 1996, about 36% of state enterprises and about 83% of all state property had been privatized. International aid agencies committed about $765 million of assistance in 1992–95. Most international aid went either to infrastructure construction or loan credits to business. Citing continued progress toward democratic development, in 1999 the United States announced that it was terminating economic assistance to Lithuania. Having established itself as a democratic society with a market economy, Lithuania was invited to join the EU in 2002, and it became a member in 2004.

In 2001, Lithuania negotiated a 19-month, $119-million standby arrangement with the International Monetary Fund (IMF). In 2002, the country's GDP grew at a rapid pace (6–6.7%), unemployment was declining, the inflation rate fell to near zero, and there was a lower-than-expected general government deficit. In 2002, the tax system was aligned with EU requirements, the financial situation of municipalities and the Health Insurance Fund was improved, privatization moved forward and the financial sector was strengthened. The privatization program for 2003 included the sale of a second 34% stake in Lithuania Gas, one or two electricity distribution companies, and four alcohol producers.

In 2003, Lithuania was one of the most dynamic economies in Europe, with a 9.7% growth of the GDP, and it continued strongly through 2004 and 2005. Unemployment was on a downward spiral, and inflation was very stable, fluctuating around the 1% mark. However, income levels still lag behind the rest of the EU, and greenfield investments need to be attracted to counteract the effects of a more expensive future market. An inflow of structural funds from the EU is expected to trigger a short-term economic boom.

40 SOCIAL DEVELOPMENT

A national system of social insurance covers all of Lithuania's residents and was most recently updated in 2003. Old age, sickness, disability, and unemployment benefits are paid on an earnings-related basis, from contributions by both employers and employees. Retirement is set at age 62.5 for men, and age 59 for women, gradually increasing to age 60 by 2006. Family allowance benefits are provided by states and municipalities to families with low incomes. There is a universal system of medical care, and a dual social insurance and social assistance program for maternity and health payments. Unemployment benefits are provided to applicants with at least 24 months of previous contributions and is paid for a period not exceeding six months in a 12-month period.

Legally, men and women have equal status, including equal pay for equal work, although in practice women are underrepresented in managerial and professional positions. Discrimination against women in the workplace persists. Violence against women, especially domestic abuse, is common. It is estimated that 80% of women experience psychological abuse, 35% experience physical abuse, and 17% are victims of sexual abuse. Child abuse is also a serious social problem. Authorities link the upsurge in abuse to alcoholism.

Human rights are generally respected in Lithuania, and human rights organizations are permitted to operate freely and openly. Prolonged detention still occurs in some cases, and poor prison conditions persist. Anti-Semitic incidents increased in 2004.

41 HEALTH

In 2004, Lithuania had approximately 403 physicians, 797 nurses, 71 dentists, and 65 pharmacists per 100,000 people. Most primary care providers are women. In 1994, the Public Health Surveillance Service was established to oversee control of communicable diseases, environmental and occupational health, and some other areas. Total health care expenditure was estimated at 6.3% of GDP.

One-year-old children were immunized as follows: tuberculosis, 97%; diphtheria, pertussis, and tetanus, 96%; polio, 89%; and measles, 94%. The rates were 93% for DPT and 97% for measles. The HIV/AIDS prevalence was 0.10 per 100 adults in 2003. As of 2004, there were approximately 1,300 people living with HIV/AIDS in the country. There were an estimated 200 deaths from AIDS in 2003.

Life expectancy was 73.97 years in 2005. The infant mortality rate for that year was 6.89 per 1,000 live births. The maternal mortality rate was 18 per 100,000 live births. As of 2002, the crude birth rate and overall mortality rate were estimated at, respectively, 8.3 and 14.7 per 1,000 people.

42 HOUSING

In 2001, national statistics indicated that there were about 1,293,029 dwelling units in the country, an average of 356 housing units per 1,000 people. About 32% of all housing units were individual houses; 61% were apartments. About 97% of these units are privately owned. The average living space is about 21.5 square meters per person. About 79% of all conventional dwellings are equipped with piped water, 72% had bath and shower facilities, and 52% had central heating. City governments are being encouraged to take more responsibility for social housing projects. Homeowners associations are being encouraged and new laws are being drafted for residential building associations. The Housing Loan Insurance Company was established in 2000 to provide insurance of loans and to promote housing loans with a low (5%) down payment.

43 EDUCATION

Education is free and compulsory for all children between the ages of 7 and 15 years (for 9 years). While Lithuanian is the most common medium of instruction, children also study Polish, Russian, and Yiddish. Primary school covers four years of study, followed by six years of basic or lower secondary school. Students then move on to either two years of senior secondary school or vocational schools, which offer two- to three-year programs. The academic year runs from September to June.

In 2001, about 55% of children between the ages of three and six were enrolled in some type of preschool program. Primary school enrollment in 2003 was estimated at about 91% of age-eligible students. The same year, secondary school enrollment was about 94% of age-eligible students. Nearly all students complete their primary education. The student-to-teacher ratio for primary school was at about 16:1 in 2003; the ratio for secondary school was about 11:1.

The four main universities are: Kaunas University of Technology (founded in 1950); Vilnius Technical University (founded in 1961); Vilnius University (founded in 1579); and Vytautas Magnus University (founded in 1922). In 2003, about 72% of the tertiary age population were enrolled in some type of higher education program; 56% for men and 88% for women. The adult literacy rate for 2004 was estimated at about 99.6%.

As of 2003, public expenditure on education was estimated at 5.9% of GDP.

44 LIBRARIES AND MUSEUMS

The National Library at Vilnius has about 9.2 million volumes. Founded in 1570, the Vilnius University Library has over 5.3 million volumes. Vilnius also has the Central Library of the Academy of Sciences, with about 3.66 million volumes. There are dozens of other special collections in the country, including libraries maintained by the Union of Lithuanian Writers, the State Institute of Art, and the Institute of Urban Planning. The Institute of Lithuanian Literature and Folklore in Vilnius contains over 240,000 printed items. The Lithuanian Librarians' Association was established in 1931, disbanded under German occupation in 1941, and reorganized in 1989.

The majority of Lithuania's museums are in Vilnius, and these include the Lithuanian Art Museum (1941), the National Museum (1856), the Museum of Lithuanian Religious History, and, founded in 1991 just after gaining independence from the Soviet Union, the Lithuanian State Museum, dedicated to the country's suffering under and resistance to Soviet occupation. The Mikalojus Konstantinas Ciurlionis National Art Museum, named for a famous native composer and painter, is located in Kaunas; special branches of this museum include the Devil's Museum, a collection of artwork depicting devils, and a Ceramics Museum. The Museum of the Center of Europe, an open-air museum displaying large-scale works by European artists, was opened in Vilnius in 1994. There is also a Park of Soviet Sculptures in Druskininkai. The Lithuanian Theater, Music and Film Museum in Vilnius was founded by the Ministry of Culture. There are several other specialized museums, including the Museum of Genocide Victims (Vilnius), Museum of the History of Lithuania Medicine and Pharmacy (Kaunas), Museum of Ancient Beekeeping (Ignalina), and the Museum of Vilnius Sport History. There are several regional museums associated with secondary schools; these contain materials on local arts and history, as well as the history of the school to which the museum is linked.

45 MEDIA

In 2003, there were an estimated 239 mainline telephones for every 1,000 people; about 1,300 people were on a waiting list for telephone service installation. The same year, there were approximately 630 mobile phones in use for every 1,000 people.

Broadcasting is controlled by Lithuanian Television and Radio Broadcasting. Radio Vilnius broadcasts in Lithuanian, Russian, Polish, and English. As of 2001 there were 29 AM and 142 FM radio stations. In 2003, there were an estimated 524 radios and 487 television sets for every 1,000 people. About 76.9 of every 1,000 people were cable subscribers. Also in 2003, there were 109.7 personal computers for every 1,000 people and 202 of every 1,000 people had access to the Internet. There were 47 secure Internet servers in the country in 2004.

The most popular daily newspapers are *Lietuvos Rytas* (*Lithuania's Morning*, in Russian), with a 2002 circulation of 85,000; *Respublika* (55,000); *Lietuvos Aidas* (*The Echo of Lithuania*, 20,000); and *Kauno Diena* (*Kaunas Daily*, 57,000). There are also several periodicals available.

The constitution provides for free speech and a free press, and the government is said to uphold these provisions. Since independence, the independent print media have flourished, producing some 2,000 newspapers and periodicals, and plans for a number of private radio and television stations are underway.

46 ORGANIZATIONS

Important economic organizations include the Association of Chamber of Commerce and Industry, an organization that coordinates the activities of all the chambers of commerce in Lithuania. There are three umbrella trade union organizations in the country: the Lithuania Confederation of Free Trade Unions, the Lithuania Union of Trade Unions, and the Lithuanian Workers' Union. Professional associations exist for a number of fields and occupations.

The Lithuanian Academy of Sciences promotes education and research in a wide variety of scientific fields. The Lithuanian Medical Association promotes research and education on health issues and works to establish common policies and standards in healthcare. There are several other associations dedicated to research and education for specific fields of medicine and particular diseases and conditions, such as the Lithuanian Heart Association.

There are a number of sports associations in the country, representing such pastimes as speed skating, squash, tae kwon do, tennis, badminton, weightlifting, and baseball. There are also branches of the Paralympic Committee. The Council of Lithuanian Youth Organizations helps organize and support a variety of youth groups. Scouting programs and chapters of the YMCA/YWCA are also active for youth. Volunteer service organizations, such as the Lions Clubs and Kiwanis International, are also present. The Red Cross is also active.

47 TOURISM, TRAVEL, AND RECREATION

The capital city of Vilnius has one of the largest historic districts in Eastern Europe, distinguished primarily by its Baroque churches, many of which have been reclaimed since independence by money and missionaries from abroad. Kaunas, Lithuania's second-largest city, offers the tourist old merchants' buildings and museums. The seaside resort towns are active in the summer. The traveler can participate in tennis, fishing, sailing, rowing, and winter sports. Lithuanians have long distinguished themselves at basketball, and have contributed top players to the Soviet teams. Seven Lithuanians have Olympic gold medals, and the national basketball team won a bronze medal in Barcelona in 1992 and again in Sydney in 2000.

All visitors need a valid passport. Visas are not required for nationals of the European Union states, the United States, Canada, Japan, Australia, and some South American countries. Travelers of non-European Union countries must carry proof of medical insurance to cover travel in Lithuania.

About 3.6 million tourists visited Lithuania in 2003. There were 7,694 hotel rooms with 15,142 beds and an occupancy rate of 32%. The average length of stay in Lithuania was two nights. Tourist expenditure receipts totaled $700 million that year.

In 2004, the US Department of State estimated the daily cost of traveling in Lithuania at $205.

48 FAMOUS LITHUANIANS

President Valdas Adamkus (b.1926) was chief of state from 1998–2003, and then beginning again in 2004.

49 DEPENDENCIES

Lithuania has no territories or colonies.

50 BIBLIOGRAPHY

The Baltic States: The National Self-Determination of Estonia, Latvia, and Lithuania. New York: St. Martin's, 1994.

Donskis, Leonidas. *Identity and Freedom: Mapping Nationalism and Social Criticism in Twentieth-Century Lithuania*. New York: Routledge, 2002.

Frucht, Richard (ed.). *Eastern Europe: An Introduction to the People, Lands, and Culture*. Santa Barbara, Calif.: ABC-CLIO, 2005.

Hoshi, Iraj, Ewa Balcerowicz, and Leszek Balcerowicz (eds.). *Barriers to Entry and Growth of New Firms in Early Transition: A Comparative Study of Poland, Hungary, Czech Republic, Albania, and Lithuania*. Boston: Kluwer Academic Publishers, 2003.

Krickus, Richard J. *Showdown: The Lithuanian Rebellion and the Breakup of the Soviet Empire*. Washington, DC.: Brassey's, 1997.

Lieven, Anatol. *The Baltic Revolution: Estonia, Latvia, Lithuania, and the Path to Independence*. New Haven: Yale University Press, 1993.

McElrath, Karen (ed.). *HIV and AIDS: A Global View*. Westport, Conn.: Greenwood Press, 2002.

Otfinoski, Steven. *The Baltic Republics*. New York: Facts On File, 2004.

Petersen, Roger Dale. *Resistance and Rebellion: Lessons from Eastern Europe*. New York: Cambridge University Press, 2001.

Senn, Alfred Erich. *Lithuania Awakening*. Berkeley: University of California Press, 1990.

LUXEMBOURG

Grand Duchy of Luxembourg
[French] *Grand-Duché de Luxembourg;*
[German] *Grossherzogtum Luxemburg*

CAPITAL: Luxembourg

FLAG: The flag is a tricolor of red, white, and blue horizontal stripes.

ANTHEM: *Ons Hémecht (Our Homeland).*

MONETARY UNIT: The Luxembourg franc was replaced by the euro as official currency as of 2002. The euro is divided into 100 cents. There are coins in denominations of 1, 2, 5, 10, 20, and 50 cents and 1 euro and 2 euros. There are notes of 5, 10, 20, 50, 100, 200, and 500 euros. €1 euro = $1.25475 (or $1 = €0.79697) as of 2005.

WEIGHTS AND MEASURES: The metric system is the legal standard.

HOLIDAYS: New Year's Day, 1 January; Labor Day, 1 May; public celebration of the Grand Duke's Birthday, 23 June; Assumption, 15 August; All Saints' Day, 1 November; Christmas, 25–26 December. Movable religious holidays include Shrove Monday, Easter Monday, Ascension, and Pentecost Monday.

TIME: 1 PM = noon GMT.

1 LOCATION, SIZE, AND EXTENT

A landlocked country in Western Europe, Luxembourg has an area of 2,586 sq km (998 sq mi), with a length of 82 km (51 mi) N–S and a width of 57 km (35 mi) E–W. Comparatively, the area occupied by Luxembourg is slightly smaller than the state of Rhode Island. The eastern boundary with Germany is formed by the Our, Sûre (Sauer), and Moselle rivers. Luxembourg is bordered on the S by France and on the W and N by Belgium, with total border length of 359 km (223 mi).

Luxembourg's capital city, Luxembourg, is located in the south central part of the country.

2 TOPOGRAPHY

The country is divided into two distinct geographic regions: the rugged uplands (Oesling) of the Ardennes in the north, where the average elevation is 450 m (1,476 ft) with the highest point, Buurgplaatz, at 559 m (1,834 ft); and the fertile southern lowlands, called Bon Pays (Good Land), with an average altitude of 250 m (820 ft).

The entire area is crisscrossed by deep valleys, with most rivers draining eastward into the Sûre, which in turn flows into the Moselle on the eastern border. The northern region, comprising one-third of the country, is forested and has poor soil.

3 CLIMATE

Luxembourg's climate is temperate and mild. Summers are generally cool, with a mean temperature of about 17°C (63°F); winters are seldom severe, average temperature being about 0°C (32°F). The high peaks of the Ardennes in the north shelter the country from rigorous north winds, and the prevailing northwesterly winds have a cooling effect. Rainfall is plentiful in the extreme southwest; precipitation throughout the country averages about 75 cm (30 in) annually.

4 FLORA AND FAUNA

The principal trees are pine, chestnut, spruce, oak, linden, elm, and beech, along with fruit trees. There are many shrubs, such as blueberry and genista, and ferns; a multitude of lovely flowers; and many vineyards. Only a few wild animal species (deer, roe deer, and wild boar) remain, but birds are plentiful, and many varieties of fish are found in the rivers, including perch, carp, bream, trout, pike, and eel.

5 ENVIRONMENT

The Ministry of the Environment is the main environmental agency. Government statistics indicate considerable improvement in pollution control over the past few decades. Emissions of particles of sulfur dioxide declined substantially from 1972 to 1983. As of 1994, emissions of smoke, sulfur dioxide, nitrogen dioxide, and lead were well within EU acceptable limits. Luxembourg has about 0.2 cu mi of water. Luxembourg has produced an average of about 3.3 tons of particulate emissions and 22 tons of hydrocarbon emissions per year.

Forest reserves have been severely depleted since 1800, when three-fourths of the country was forest; today forest and woodland cover only one-fifth of Luxembourg. During World War II, German requisitions and heavy demands for fuel contributed to this depletion.

According to a 2006 report issued by the International Union for Conservation of Nature and Natural Resources (IUCN), threatened species included three types of mammals, three species of birds, two types of mollusks, and two species of other invertebrates. Threatened species include the spotted eagle, the southern damselfly, and the great snipe.

6 POPULATION

The population of Luxembourg in 2005 was estimated by the United Nations (UN) at 457,000, which placed it at number 163 in population among the 193 nations of the world. In 2005, approximately 14% of the population was over 65 years of age, with another 19% of the population under 15 years of age. There were 97 males for every 100 females in the country. According to the UN, the annual population rate of change for 2005–10 was expected to be 0.4%, a rate the government viewed as too low. The projected population for the year 2025 was 544,000. The population density was 176 per sq km (457 per sq mi).

The UN estimated that 91% of the population lived in urban areas in 2005, and that urban areas were growing at an annual rate of 1.42%. The capital city, Luxembourg, had a population of 77,000 in that year. The chief industrial city is Esch-sur-Alzette, with a population of 28,000. Other urban areas and their estimated populations include Differdange, 19,005; Dudelange, 17,000; and Schifflange, 8,084.

7 MIGRATION

During the 19th century, thousands of Luxembourgers emigrated, chiefly to the United States. In 1870, however, rich deposits of iron ore were uncovered in southern Luxembourg, and during the period of industrialization and prosperity that followed, many persons from neighboring countries migrated to Luxembourg.

Since the adoption of national asylum legislation in April 1996, there has been a significant increase in the number of asylum seekers. In 1997, 431 people applied for asylum. By 1998, 1,709 people applied. Between January and July 1999, as many as 2,404 people submitted asylum applications.

As of 12 August 1999, some 101 people had been evacuated from Macedonia to Luxembourg. Evacuees were given a six-month renewable residence permit, as well as work permits, social assistance, and the right to family reunification. As of 1999, none of the evacuees had returned. Also as of 1999, Luxembourg officials were in the process of adopting a law on temporary protection. In 2004 there were 1,590 refugees and no asylum seekers. The estimated net migration rate in 2005 was 8.86 migrants per 1,000 population.

8 ETHNIC GROUPS

The indigenous inhabitants of Luxembourg consider themselves a distinct nationality, with a specific ethnic character. A strong indication of that character is the national motto, "Mir woelle bleiwe wat mir sin" ("We want to remain what we are"), for despite a history of long foreign domination, Luxembourgers have retained their individuality as a nation. There are also native-born residents of Celtic, French, Belgian, or German ancestry, as well as a substantial immigrant population of Portuguese, Italian, and other Europeans (guest and worker residents).

9 LANGUAGES

Luxembourgers speak Luxembourgian, or Letzeburgesch, the original dialect of the country, as well as French and German. All three are official languages. Letzeburgesch is a Germanic dialect related to the Moselle Frankish language that was once spoken in western Germany. It rarely appears in written form.

Letzeburgesch, French, and German are all languages of instruction in primary schools, while French is the most common language of instruction in secondary schools. Government publications are generally in French. English is also spoken.

10 RELIGIONS

The country is historically Roman Catholic and it is estimated that over 90% of the population are nominally members of this church. The largest Protestant denominations are the Lutheran and Calvinist churches. About 6,000 people are Muslim, about 5,000 are Orthodox Christians (Greek, Serbian, Russian, and Romanian), and about 1,000 are Jewish. There are also small communities of the Baha'is, Mormons, Jehovah's Witnesses and members of the Universal Church. It is believed that the number of atheists is small, but growing.

The constitution provides for freedom of religion and this right is respected in practice. A special Concordat of 1801 allows certain religious groups to receive financial support. For instance, the state pays salaries for Roman Catholic and Greek and Russian Orthodox priests, Jewish rabbis, and pastors of some Protestant denominations. The state also supports some private religious schools. Certain Christian holidays are celebrated as national holidays.

11 TRANSPORTATION

Transportation facilities are excellent. The railways are consolidated into one organization, the *Société Nationale des Chemins de Fers Luxembourgeois* (CFL), with the government of Luxembourg controlling 51% of the stock and the remaining 49% divided between the French and Belgian governments. Railway lines, totaling 274 km (170 mi) in 2004, provide direct links with Belgium via Arlon, with France via Metz and Longwy, and with Germany via Trier. There is through-train service to Paris and various other points in France. In that same year, 242 km (150 mi) of railway were electrified.

In 2002 there were 5,210 km (3,241 mi) of state and local roads, all of which were paved, including 147 km (91 mi) of expressways. Direct roads connect all important towns, and the main arteries are suitable for heavy motor traffic. As of 2003 there were 287,245 cars and 35,904 commercial vehicles in use. In the 1990s, a program was underway to link Luxembourg's highways to those of Belgium, France, and Germany.

The only river available for industrial transport is the Moselle, which for 37 km (23 mi) allows navigation of barges of up to 1,500 tons. In 2005, the merchant fleet comprised 40 ships of 1,000 GRT or more, with a total of 652,454 GRT. There were two airports in 2004, only one of which had a paved runway. There was also a single heliport. The principal airport is Findel, located near the city of Luxembourg. Regular flights to other European cities are operated by Luxair, the national carrier, and by foreign airlines. Luxembourg's largest airline, Cargolux, ranks among Europe's top 10 cargo carriers. Luxembourg and the United States have shared open sky aviation rights since a 1995 agreement. In 2001 (the latest year for which data was available), 885,900 passengers were carried on scheduled airline flights.

12 HISTORY

The land now known as Luxembourg fell under the successive domination of the Celts, the Romans, and the Riparian Franks before its founding as the County of Luxembourg in 963 by Sigefroid, count of the Ardennes, who reconstructed a small ruined fortress called Lucilinburhuc (Little Burg) on the site of the present capital. The area tripled in size during the reign of Countess Ermesinde (1196–1247). John, count of Luxembourg (r. 1309–46) and king of Bohemia, became the national hero; although blind for many years, the inveterate knight-errant laid the foundations for a powerful dynasty before he fell in the Battle of Crécy, in northern France, during the Hundred Years' War. His son Charles (1316–78) was the second of four Luxembourg princes to become Holy Roman emperor. He made Luxembourg a duchy, but under his successors the country was ruined financially.

Luxembourg came under Burgundian rule in 1443 and remained in foreign hands for more than 400 years. Successively it passed to Spain (1506–1714, excepting 1684–97, when it was ruled by France), Austria (1714–95), and France (1795–1815). The Congress of Vienna in 1815 made Luxembourg a grand duchy and allotted it as an independent state to the king of the Netherlands, after ceding to Prussia its territory east of the Moselle, Sûre, and Our. Luxembourg lost more than half its territory to Belgium in 1839, but gained a larger measure of autonomy, although Dutch kings continued to rule as grand dukes. By the Treaty of London in 1867, Luxembourg was declared an independent and neutral state under the protection of the Great Powers, but was required to dismantle its mighty fortress. In 1890, the house of Nassau-Weilbourg, through the Grand Duke Adolphe (r. 1890–1905), became the ruling house of Luxembourg. The country was occupied by German troops in World War I. In 1919, Grand Duchess Charlotte succeeded to the throne, and on 28 September 1919, in a referendum held to decide the country's future, a plurality supported her. In 1921, Luxembourg formed an economic union with Brussels.

The Germans again invaded the country in May 1940, but the grand ducal family and most members of the government escaped to safety. Under the Nazi occupation, the people suffered severely, particularly when their revolt in 1942 protesting compulsory service in the German army was savagely repressed. Luxembourg was liberated by Allied forces in September 1944.

That year, while still in exile, the government agreed to form an economic union with Belgium and the Netherlands; the first phase, the Benelux Customs Union, was effected in 1948. In February 1958, a treaty of economic union, which became effective in 1960, was signed by representatives of the three countries. During the postwar decades, Luxembourg also became an active member of NATO and the EC.

In April 1963, Luxembourg celebrated its 1,000th anniversary as an independent state. On 12 November 1964, Grand Duchess Charlotte abdicated in favor of her son, Jean. The Grand Duke announced on Christmas Day 1999 that he planned to abdicate in favor of his eldest son Prince Henri in September 2000. (Prince Henri took the throne on 7 October 2000.) Jean's reign was marked by continued prosperity, as Luxembourg's economy shifted from dependence on steel to an emphasis on services, notably finance and telecommunications. Luxembourg is now among the world's top 10 financial centers and the financial sector employs approximately 10% of the workforce (20,000 people) and accounts

LOCATION: 49°26′52″ to 50°10′58″ N; 5°44′10″ to 6°31′53″ E. BOUNDARY LENGTHS: Germany, 135 kilometers (84 miles); France, 73 kilometers (45 miles); Belgium, 148 kilometers (92 miles).

for around 22% of national income. There is an industrial sector which initially was dominated by steel but has become increasingly diversified to include chemicals, rubber, and other products. Luxembourg had an incredibly high 2005 GDP per capita of US$58,900.

Different governments have played a key role in the diversification process and the development of a skilled workforce has been an important instrument. Equally important is the country's tax regime. Luxembourg's 0% withholding tax on crossborder savings acts as a magnet for investors. Its favorable tax law is at odds with the rest of the European Union and pressures for European-wide harmonization would diminish the sector's competitive advantage.

The country's growth rate has been among the highest in the European Union and averaged over 4% annually between 1994 and 2000. Luxembourg suffered due to the global economic downturn and the turmoil in international stock markets that began in 2001, as its small, open economy specializes in financial services. Luxembourg joined the Economic and Monetary Union in 1999, and adopted the euro as its currency. Prime Minister Jean-Claude Juncker was considered for the presidency of the European Commission in 2005, however he promised to remain as prime minister if he won the election of 2003, and so stayed on in Luxembourg.

[13] GOVERNMENT

Luxembourg is a constitutional monarchy, governed by the constitution of 1868 as revised in 1919 (when universal suffrage and proportional representation were introduced) and subsequently. The grand ducal crown is hereditary in the house of Nassau-Weilbourg. Legislative power is vested in the Chamber of Deputies, the 60 (prior to 1984, 64 members) members of which are elected for five-year terms. In addition, the Council of State, composed of 21 members appointed for life by the sovereign, acts as a consulting body in legislative, administrative, and judicial matters and has the right of suspensive veto.

Executive power rests jointly in the sovereign, who may initiate legislation, and a prime minister (president of the government), appointed by the monarch, who in turn selects a cabinet. The prime minister, together with the cabinet, must command a majority in the Chamber of Deputies. Voting is compulsory, and eligibility begins at age 18.

[14] POLITICAL PARTIES

Since 1947, shifting coalitions among the three largest parties have governed the country. The Christian Social Party (Parti Chrétien Social—PCS) is a Catholic, promonarchist movement favoring progressive labor legislation and government protection for farmers and small business. Except for the period 1974–79, the PCS has been the dominant partner in all ruling coalitions since World War I. The Socialist Party (Parti Ouvrier Socialiste Luxembourgeois—POSL) supports improvement and extension of the present system of social welfare programs. The third major group, the Democratic Party (Parti Démocratique—PD), favors social reforms and minimal government activity in the economy. Other parties have included the Luxembourg Communist Party (Parti Communiste—PC), which has its main strength with steelworkers in the industrialized south, and the Social Democratic Party (Parti Social-Démocrate Luxembourgeois—PSDL), which split from the POSL in 1971. In addition, the ecologist Green Party has representation in parliament, as does the Action Committee for Democracy and Justice (ADR), a pensioners' party. The Marxist and Reformed Communist Party, known as "The Left," secured one seat in the Chamber of Deputies in 1999.

Following the June 1999 elections, the distribution of seats in the 60-member unicameral Chamber of Deputies was: PCS, 19; POSL, 13; PD, 15; and other groups, 13. The coalition of the PCS and POSL, which had governed for 15 years, was replaced by a coalition of the PCS and PD. Jean-Claude Juncker, leader of PCS, remained as prime minister. Following the June 2004 elections, distribution of seats was: PCS 24, POSL 14, PD 10, Green Party 7, ADR 5. The next elections were scheduled to be held in June 2009.

[15] LOCAL GOVERNMENT

Luxembourg is divided into three districts (Luxembourg, Diekirch, and Grevenmacher) comprising 12 cantons, which in turn make up 118 communes. The districts are headed by commissioners—civil servants who are responsible to the central government. Each commune elects an autonomous communal council headed by a burgomaster; the councils elect government officials at the local level. Local elections are held every six years.

[16] JUDICIAL SYSTEM

The legal system is similar to the French Napoleonic Code, except for the commercial and penal divisions, which are similar to their Belgian counterparts. Minor cases generally come before one of three justices of the peace. On a higher level are the two district courts, one in the city of Luxembourg and the other in Diekirch. The Superior Court of Justice is composed of the Court of Cassation, a Court of Appeal, and a department of public prosecution. The Court of Cassation comprises a bench of five judges, responsible for hearing cases that seek to overturn or set aside decisions given by the various benches of the Court of Appeal. The Court of Appeal consists of nine benches of three judges each, hearing civil, commercial, and criminal cases. Judges are appointed for life terms. New administrative courts began operations in 1997, after a 1995 decision by the European Court of Human Rights that Luxembourg's Council of State could no longer serve as both a legislative advisory body and an administrative court. The death penalty was abolished in 1979. The prosecutor as well as the defendant may appeal verdicts in criminal cases. An appeal results in a completely new judicial procedure with the possibility that a sentence may be increased or decreased.

Trade unions and striking are constitutionally guaranteed and news media is free to report without fear of retribution. There is a minority population of Bosnians who live in Luxembourg who face mild social racism.

Luxembourg is a member of the UN and is the site of the European Court of Justice.

[17] ARMED FORCES

In 1967, Luxembourg abolished conscription and created a volunteer military force that is part of NATO. Responsibility for defense matters is vested in the Ministry of Public Force, which also controls the police and gendarmerie.

In 2005 the armed forces of Luxembourg consisted of the army with 900 active personnel and a gendarmerie of 612. NATO maintains 17 early warning aircraft with Luxembourg registration. Luxembourg maintains 23 personnel in the UN peacekeeping mission in Bosnia. Another nine are in Afghanistan and 26 in Serbia-Montenegro. More than 5,000 American soldiers, including Gen. George S. Patton, are buried at the American Military Cemetery near the capital. Budgeted defense expenditures in 2005 were $264 million.

[18]INTERNATIONAL COOPERATION

Luxembourg is a founding member of the United Nations, having joined the organization on 24 October 1945, and participates in ECE and several nonregional specialized agencies, such as the FAO, IAEA, the World Bank, UNESCO, UNIDO, the ILO, IMF, and the WHO. Since 1921, it has been joined with Belgium in the Belgium-Luxembourg Economic Union (BLEU). It is also a partner with Belgium and the Netherlands in the Benelux Economic Union. Luxembourg is a member of the Council of Europe, the Asian Development Bank, NATO, OECD, OSCE, WTO, the Euro-Atlantic Partnership Council, the European Bank for Reconstruction and Development, the Western European Union, and the European Union. Luxembourg held the EU presidency for the first half of 2005. The country is the home site of the European Court of Justice, the European Court of Auditors, European Investment Bank, and other EU organizations. The Secretariat of the European Parliament is also located in Luxembourg.

Luxembourg belongs to the Australia Group, the Zangger Committee, the Nuclear Energy Agency, and the Nuclear Suppliers Group (London Group). In environmental cooperation, the country is part of the Basel Convention, Conventions on Biological Diversity and Air Pollution, Ramsar, CITES, the London Convention, International Tropical Timber Agreements, the Kyoto Protocol, the Montréal Protocol, MARPOL, the Nuclear Test Ban Treaty, and the UN Conventions on the Law of the Sea, Climate Change, and Desertification.

[19]ECONOMY

In relation to its size and population, Luxembourg is one of the most highly industrialized countries in the world. Its standard of living rivals that of any country in Europe. Steelmaking, traditionally the most important industry, has seen its contribution to GDP decline from 21% in 1974 to 1.8% in 1996. Iron ore, formerly mined in limited quantities, is no longer produced because supplies have been exhausted. The country's lack of industrial fuels makes it completely dependent on imports of coke for steel production. In 2001, Luxembourg's steel producer, ARBED, merged with France's USINOR and Spain's ACERALA to create the world largest steel company, NewCo, in order to increase competitiveness. Other industries—plastics, rubber and chemicals and other light industries—have been successfully developed, and the service industries, most notably banking, have expanded rapidly. Services now contribute 69% to GDP (2000 estimate).

Agriculture is generally small-scale, with livestock and vineyards comprising the most important segment.

The worldwide recession of the early 1980s adversely affected Luxembourg's economy; between 1985 and 1992, however, GDP grew by 32%, or 4% per year. Growth for 1998 was 2.9%. Inflation, as high as 9.4% in 1982, was only 0.3% in 1986 and averaged 3.3% during 1988–92. Average inflation 1999 to 2001 was 2.3%. Total GDP, at $13.9 billion in 1998 (purchasing power parity) had risen over 38% to $19.2 billion by 2001. Per capita income in 2001 was $45,500, one of the highest in the world, with GDP growth reported at 8.3%.

Luxembourg is known for having one the lowest unemployment rates in Europe. The unemployment rate averaged just 1.4% between 1984 and 1991 and was 3% in 1998. In 2001, unemploy-ment was at 2.7%, the range where it remained until registering a slight increase in 2004, to 4.3%.

Economic expansion continued at stately rates (similar to most other Western European countries), reaching 2.5% in 2002, 2.9% in 2003, and 4.5% in 2004; the GDP growth rate for 2005 was expected to be 3.6%. This expansion was mainly fueled by the country's up and coming financial and service oriented (especially media and communications) sectors. The steel sector, while being the subject of major restructurings in the past two decades, remained one of the backbones of the economy. Inflation remained stable at around 2%.

[20]INCOME

The US Central Intelligence Agency (CIA) reports that in 2005 Luxembourg's gross domestic product (GDP) was estimated at $29.4 billion. The CIA defines GDP as the value of all final goods and services produced within a nation in a given year and computed on the basis of purchasing power parity (PPP) rather than value as measured on the basis of the rate of exchange based on current dollars. The per capita GDP was estimated at $62,700. The annual growth rate of GDP was estimated at 3.5%. The average inflation rate in 2005 was 2.6%. It was estimated that agriculture accounted for 0.5% of GDP, industry 16.3%, and services 83.1%.

Approximately 17% of household consumption was spent on food, 9% on fuel, 3% on health care, and 7% on education.

[21]LABOR

In 2005, the labor force was estimated at 200,000, of whom 105,000 were foreign workers crossing the border from France, Belgium and Germany. Of those employed as of 2004, the services sector accounted for an estimated 86%, while 13% were in industry and 1% in agriculture. The estimated unemployment rate was 3.7% in 2005.

Labor relations have been generally peaceful since the 1930s. Foreign investors are attracted by the positive relationship which exists in Luxembourg between employers and the labor force. There is a strong trade union movement. About 50% of the labor force was organized into unions as of 2005. Although independent, the two largest labor organizations are associated with major political parties. Workers may strike only after their dispute is submitted to the National Conciliation Office and all mediation efforts have failed. Collective bargaining is widely practiced.

As of 2005, unskilled workers who are over 18 years of age with no dependents are entitled to a minimum wage of $1,390 per month, while the minimum for skilled workers was $1,475 per month. However, these totals were insufficient to provide a worker and family with a decent living standard. Most workers earned more than the minimum rate. Wage agreements are generally arrived at by industry-wide bargaining between labor and management. The maximum workweek is legally set at 40 hours. Overtime is paid at premium rates. Work on Sunday is restricted. Children under the age of 16 are prohibited from employment except in some special circumstances. The law mandates a safe working environment and this is effectively enforced by the Ministry of Labor.

22 AGRICULTURE

Over 27% of the work force and 50% of the land (126,629 hectares/312,900 acres) are devoted to agriculture and grazing; the majority of agricultural land consists of meadows and pastures. Farms are generally small and highly mechanized, although average farm size has been increasing. While the number of farms of 2 hectares (5 acres) or more fell from 10,570 in 1950 to 2,263 in 2002, the average holding increased from 13.16 to 57.18 hectares (from 32.52 to 141.3 acres) over the same period. Crop production in 2002 included (in tons): corn, 137,721; forage crops, 146,182; bread grains, 79,126; potatoes, 20,105; and pulses, 2,327.

Vineyards including Ehnen, Stadtbredmis, and Bech-Kleinmacher are located in the Moselle River Valley. In 2002/03, wine production totaled 15.39 million liters, consisting of rivaner, elbling, auxerrois, riesling, pinot blanc, and pinot gris. Wine and clover seeds are the important agricultural exports. In addition, millions of rosebushes, a major specialty crop, are exported annually. Chief fruits produced include apples, plums, and cherries.

23 ANIMAL HUSBANDRY

Livestock breeding is relatively important, particularly because of Luxembourg's dairy product exports. In 2005, livestock included 184,172 head of cattle, 75,000 pigs, 7,500 sheep, and 3,100 equines. A total of 48,615 tons of meat, and 272,000 tons of milk were produced in 2005.

24 FISHING

There is some commercial fishing for domestic consumption and much private fishing for sport. The rivers teem with perch, carp, trout, pike, eel, and bream.

25 FORESTRY

About 88,620 hectares (218,980 acres) were covered by forests in 2000, of which 53% was private forest. Forestry production in 2004 included 277,180 cu m (9.8 million cu ft) of roundwood, over 50% from broad-leaved trees. Chief commercial woods are spruce and oak. In 2004, forest product imports exceeded exports by $13.7 million.

26 MINING

In 2003, Luxembourg's mineral sector consisted primarily of raw materials processing, information systems, and mineral trading. Metals produced included crude and semi-manufactured steel, while industrial minerals consisted of hydraulic cement, crude gypsum and anhydrite, and Thomas slag phosphates. The iron and steel industry was the most important mineral industry sector, with steel products as the country's main export commodity. Mining in Luxembourg was represented by small industrial mineral operations that produced material for domestic construction, including cement manufacture. In 2003, Luxembourg produced 2.7 million metric tons of crude steel and 2.8 million metric tons of semi-manufactured steel. Hydraulic cement production in 2003 was estimated at 700,000 metric tons, with crude gypsum and anhydrite output estimated at 400 metric tons in that same year. Production of Thomas slag phosphates (by gross weight) totaled and estimated 475,000 metric tons in 2003. Luxembourg's traditional source of mineral wealth was iron ore, concentrated between Re-

dange and Dudelange. Because of mine depletion, production declined from 2.08 million tons in 1976, to 429,000 in 1981, when the last iron mines were closed.

27 ENERGY AND POWER

Luxembourg imports all the petroleum products, natural gas and coal it requires, since it has no oil, natural gas or coal reserves.

In 2002, imports of petroleum products (all refined) averaged 52,290 barrels per day, while consumption for that year averaged 51,680 barrels per day. Natural gas imports and consumption in 2002 each totaled 42.06 billion cu ft. Coal imports that year consisted of hard coal and totaled 140,000 short tons.

Total electric generating capacity in 2002 was 128 MW, of which nearly 52% used fossil fuels, 31% was hydroelectric, and the remainder geothermal/other. Production of electrical energy in 2002 amounted to 2.526 billion kWh of which 92.2% was from fossil fuels, almost 8% from hydropower, and the rest from other renewable sources. Consumption of electricity in 2002 was 5.787 billion kWh. The steel industry consumes 80% of total industrial energy demand.

28 INDUSTRY

Massive restructuring of the steel industry and continuing diversification of the industrial base characterized the 1980s. Under the ongoing industrial diversification program, more than 80 new firms were launched between 1960 and 1985, providing jobs for 10,332 people. Chemicals, rubber, metal processing, glass, and aluminum became increasingly important, while some other industries, including construction, remained depressed; traditional light industries such as tanneries, glove-making plants, and textile mills were forced either to close down or to greatly reduce their scale of operations.

In 1997, steel was responsible for 29% of all exports. Production of steel was 2,613,000 tons in 1995 (5,462,000 tons in 1970); rolled steel products, 3,709,000 tons (4,252,000 tons in 1970). Luxembourg's blast furnaces and steel mills are located in the Bassin Minier of the southwest. Mergers have given ARBED, a private multinational firm with significant government shareholding, virtually complete control of the steel industry. A merger with France's USINOR and Spain's ACERALIA in 2001 made ARBED the world's largest steel producer; it was renamed "NEWCO" temporarily, and was searching for niche markets for highly specialized steel products.

In recent years, Luxembourg has diversified its industrial production away from steel, producing chemicals, medical products, rubber, tires, glass, and aluminum. The financial sector has compensated for the decline in steel production, and other service-sector growth areas in 2002 were cargo shipping, satellite transmission, and television and radio broadcasting.

In 2004, industry contributed to 16.3% of the GDP, and employed 13% of the labor force. The largest share of the economy went to the services sector, which made up 83.1% of the GDP, and employed 86% of the working force, with some 35% of the people working in Luxembourg representing cross-border labor from France, Belgium, and Germany. The industrial production growth rate, at 2.9%, was slightly smaller than the GDP growth rate, hinting to a more dynamic services sector in 2004.

29 SCIENCE AND TECHNOLOGY

The Grand Ducal Institute, the central learned society, includes medical and scientific sections. The Society of Luxembourg Naturalists, founded in 1890, had 575 members in 1996. Two public research centers conduct research on health and applied science. The University Center of Luxembourg, founded in 1969, has a sciences department. The Higher Institute of Technology, founded in 1979, offers courses in engineering and computing. Sociéte Européenne des Satellites at Betzdorf is the control center for a group of satellites important to Europe's broadcasting industry.

In 2000, Luxembourg had 3,757 researchers and 3,820 technicians engaged in research and development (R&D) per one million people. In that same year, the country spent $420.967 million or 1.71% of GDP on R&D, with the overwhelming majority of the expenditures, 90.7%, coming from business, with government accounting for 7.7% and foreign investors at 1.7%.

30 DOMESTIC TRADE

The commercial code is similar to that of Belgium and trade practices are nearly identical. The city of Luxembourg is the headquarters for the distribution of imported goods within the country and Antwerp in Belgium is the principal port of entry. Consequently, manufacturers' agents and importers maintain offices in one or both of those cities. The commercial laws and solid economic base are highly attractive to foreign investors. About 35% of the workforce is made up of foreign workers, many of whom are commuters from neighboring countries. French, German, and English are the languages of business correspondence. Advertising is extensive, particularly in newspapers and on Radio-Télé-Luxembourg.

Most shops and stores are open 9 AM to 6 PM Monday through Friday. Banking hours are on weekdays, 9 AM to 4:30 PM. Private business hours are usually from 8 AM to 5 PM.

31 FOREIGN TRADE

Luxembourg remains dependent on foreign trade, even though domestic demand has become an increasingly important factor in fueling the economy. The nation's trade position has weakened with the decline of the steel industry: between 1974 and 1981, imports grew by 55% while exports rose only 7%, as the trade balance swung into deficit. Between 1985 and 1992, imports grew by 42% and exports rose only 24%.

Trade with European nations accounted for 88.6% of imports and 88.7% of exports in 2000. With 23% of the total export volume in 2000, Germany was Luxembourg's biggest customer. Luxembourg imported more goods from Belgium (35%) than any other country.

Unlike some of its Western European counterparts, Luxembourg continued to register a trade deficit in recent years. In 2003, exports totaled $13.4 billion (FOB—Free on Board), while imports rose to $16.3 billion (CIF—Cost and Freight). Principal export commodities included machinery and equipment, steel products, chemicals, rubber products, and glass, and mainly went to Germany (which in 2004 received 22.1% of Luxembourg's total exports), France (20.1%), Belgium (10.2%), United Kingdom (8.4%), Italy (7.3%), Spain (5.9%), and the Netherlands (4.3%). Imports included minerals, metals, foodstuffs, and quality consumer goods,

Principal Trading Partners – Luxembourg (2003)			
(In millions of US dollars)			
Country	Exports	Imports	Balance
World	9,986.1	13,639.1	-3,653.0
Germany	2,565.5	3,682.1	-1,116.6
France-Monaco	1,990.2	1,922.0	68.2
Belgium	1,233.4	4,626.8	-3,393.4
United Kingdom	591.4	322.8	268.6
Italy-San Marino-Holy See	584.5	327.6	256.9
Netherlands	457.4	732.0	-274.6
Spain	284.7	113.1	171.6
United States	241.3	288.6	-47.3
Special Categories	182.2	363.1	-180.9
Austria	151.2	135.7	15.5

(...) data not available or not significant.

SOURCE: *2003 International Trade Statistics Yearbook*, New York: United Nations, 2004.

and chiefly came from Belgium (29.8%), Germany (22.6%), China (12.6%), France (12%), and the Netherlands (4.2%).

32 BALANCE OF PAYMENTS

Luxembourg enjoyed a favorable trade balance from 1951 until 1975, when rising energy costs and structural weakness in the steel industry led to deterioration in terms of trade. The overall balance of payments has, however, tended to show a surplus, mainly because of income from banking services. The levels of imports and exports remain relatively stable, with the level of imports fluctuating significantly only when large capital purchases are made in the aviation sector.

The US Central Intelligence Agency (CIA) reported that in 2000 the purchasing power parity of Luxembourg's exports was $7.85

Balance of Payments – Luxembourg (2003)		
(In millions of US dollars)		
Current Account		2,492.0
Balance on goods		-2,463.0
Imports	-13,696.0	
Exports	11,233.0	
Balance on services		8,535.0
Balance on income		-3,025.0
Current transfers		-556.0
Capital Account		-176.0
Financial Account		-1,790.0
Direct investment abroad		-96,428.0
Direct investment in Luxembourg		87,871.0
Portfolio investment assets		-78,423.0
Portfolio investment liabilities		99,152.0
Financial derivatives		6,836.0
Other investment assets		-30,035.0
Other investment liabilities		9,236.0
Net Errors and Omissions		-417.0
Reserves and Related Items		-108.0

(...) data not available or not significant.

SOURCE: *Balance of Payment Statistics Yearbook 2004*, Washington, DC: International Monetary Fund, 2004.

Public Finance – Luxembourg (2003)

(In millions of euros, central government figures)

Revenue and Grants	**10,092**	**100.0%**
Tax revenue	6,386	63.3%
Social contributions	3,000	29.7%
Grants	74	0.7%
Other revenue	633	6.3%
Expenditures	**10,099**	**100.0%**
General public services	1,503	14.9%
Defense	79	0.8%
Public order and safety	242	2.4%
Economic affairs	924	9.1%
Environmental protection	140	1.4%
Housing and community amenities	85	0.8%
Health	1,273	12.6%
Recreational, culture, and religion	278	2.8%
Education	1,012	10.0%
Social protection	4,564	45.2%

(…) data not available or not significant.

SOURCE: *Government Finance Statistics Yearbook 2004*, Washington, DC: International Monetary Fund, 2004.

billion while imports totaled $10.25 billion resulting in a trade deficit of $2.4 billion.

The International Monetary Fund (IMF) reported that in 2001 Luxembourg had exports of goods totaling $9 billion and imports totaling $11.4 billion. The services credit totaled $19.9 billion and debit $13.7 billion.

Exports of goods and services totaled $47 billion in 2004, up from $36 billion in 2003. Imports followed a similar trend, growing from $30 billion in 2003, to $39 billion in 2004. The resource balance was consequently positive, reaching $6 billion in 2003 and $8 billion in 2004. The current account balance improved from $2.2 billion in 2003, to $2.8 billion in 2004. National reserves (including gold) were insignificant at $331 million.

33 BANKING AND SECURITIES

Banking has been gaining in importance since the 1970s and has become the most significant part of the economy; by 1998, banking and insurance employed about 15% of the total workforce. The principal bank and the sole bank of issue is the International Bank of Luxembourg (*Banque Internationale à Luxembourg*), founded in 1856. The Belgium-Luxembourg monetary agreement, as renewed for 10 years in 1991, provided for the establishment of the Luxembourg Monetary Institute to represent the nation at international monetary conferences and institutions. The banking sector has benefited from favorable laws governing holding companies. The European Investment Bank, the European Court of Auditors (both EU institutions), and the European Monetary Fund are headquartered in Luxembourg, as are all of the big six accounting firms. As a financial center, Luxembourg has the advantages of strict banking secrecy, a trained multilingual workforce, and a government that is sympathetic to the sector's needs. These last two factors are proving attractive to the developing cross-border insurance business. In addition, a strict 1992 law aimed at combating money laundering reinforces Luxembourg's reputation as a corrupt-free environment. The financial sector is currently active in three main areas: the Eurobond market, investment funds, and the developing cross-border life insurance market.

Faced with the impossibility of raising the capital for its steel industry alone, Luxembourg has always been open to the financial world. But its current success in the field owes more to legislation in neighboring countries and external economic factors than to any deliberate policy on the part of the government.

The Euro-markets have made Luxembourg the home of Cedel Bank, one of the two international clearing and settlement depositories. In 2001 this group recorded a consolidated gross operating income of 979.5 million euros and a pretax operating profit of 113.4 million euros. In 1999, Cedel and Deutsche Börse Clearing announced a merger. The new company is called Cedel International and will serve as a single European clearing organization.

Luxembourg controls about 90% of Europe's offshore investment funds, making it the fourth-largest world market. The International Monetary Fund reports that in 2001, currency and demand deposits—an aggregate commonly known as M1—were equal to $46.0 billion. In that same year, M2—an aggregate equal to M1 plus savings deposits, small scale time deposits, and money market mutual funds—was $139.4 billion.

The Luxembourg Bourse, founded in 1929 in the city of Luxembourg, primarily handles stocks and bonds issued by domestic companies, although it also lists Belgian securities. The exchange was closed down on 10 May 1940. Dealing resumed but was limited to domestic and German securities. The exchange was again closed down when the country was liberated and did not reopen until October 1945.

34 INSURANCE

Third-party liability insurance is compulsory for all automobile owners, as is insurance for nuclear operators, hunters, hotel operators, boats and aircraft, windsurfers and parachutists. Domestic insurance companies issue both life and nonlife policies. The Third European Life Directive has permitted life companies to operate in any European Union (EU) country while still being controlled by domestic regulations. As of 1996, there were 23 subsidiaries of leading European companies that had been set up in Luxembourg, attracted by the availability of skilled staff and the proximity to major European markets. Direct premiums written in 2003 totaled US$8.232 billion, with US$1.102 billion of the total comprised of nonlife premiums and US$7.130 comprised of life insurance premiums. In that same year, Luxembourg's top nonlife insurer had gross written nonlife premiums (including healthcare) of US$223.2 million, while the country's leading life insurer that same year was le Foyer with gross written life insurance premiums of US$223.2 million.

The *Commissariat aux Assurances* regulates insurance companies in Luxembourg.

35 PUBLIC FINANCE

The budget of the Luxembourg government is presented to the Chamber of Deputies late in each calendar year and becomes effective the following year. Government finances are generally strong, and budgets are usually in surplus.

The US Central Intelligence Agency (CIA) estimated that in 2005 Luxembourg's central government took in revenues of approximately $15.1 billion and had expenditures of $15.8 billion. Revenues minus expenditures totaled approximately -$690 million.

The International Monetary Fund (IMF) reported that in 2003, the most recent year for which it had data, central government revenues were €10,092 million and expenditures were €10,099 million. The value of revenues was us$11,391 million and expenditures us$11,242 million, based on a market exchange rate for 2003 of us$1 = €.8860 as reported by the IMF. Government outlays by function were as follows: general public services, 14.9%; defense, 0.8%; public order and safety, 2.4%; economic affairs, 9.1%; environmental protection, 1.4%; housing and community amenities, 0.8%; health, 12.6%; recreation, culture, and religion, 2.8%; education, 10.0%; and social protection, 45.2%.

36TAXATION

Luxembourg has come under pressure to share information on the interest paid on the hither-to-secret savings accounts maintained by nonresidents. In June 2003, the EU Commissioners issued a directive that would allow Luxembourg (as well as Belgium and Austria) to apply increased withholding taxes in lieu of directly sharing information on the interest tax paid on these accounts. Withholding rates of 15–20% would be applied 2004 to 2007, rising to 25% 2007 to 2009, and to 35% after 2009. The US Bush administration stood opposed to these EU initiatives to deal with tax evasion on the grounds that they would eliminate useful "tax competition."

Luxembourg's corporate income tax (IRC) rates in 2004 ranged from 20–22%. In addition, there is a 4% employment fund surtax. Companies are also subject to municipal taxes that average 7.5%. Taken as a whole, the taxes produce an effective tax rate of 30.38% on profits. Since 2002 the municipal tax was no longer deductible for corporate tax purposes. Capital gains are taxed as ordinary income, although some capital gains are tax-exempt. Dividends paid to nonresidents are subject to 20% withholding unless the payments are to a parent company resident in the EU that owns at least 10% of the subsidiary paying dividends. Subsidiaries of foreign companies are considered resident companies ("capital societies") and are taxed at the same rate.

Personal income in Luxembourg is taxed according to a progressive schedule with a top rate of 38%. There is a 2.5% surtax for the employment fund. Social security taxes are separate for blue- and white-collar employees. Employer social security tax rates (in 2004) for blue- and white-collar employees are 13.01% and 10.76%, respectively. Employee tax rates are 12.90% and 10.65%, respectively. Other taxes include a wealth tax, gift taxes, local real estate taxes, registration taxes, subscription and net worth taxes.

The main indirect tax is Luxembourg's value-added tax (VAT), introduced 1 January 1970 with a standard rate of 8% and a reduced rate of 4%. Revisions as of 10 January 1992 instituted a standard rate of 15% with reduced rates of 3% and 6%, and a "parking" (intermediate) rate of 12% (applied to heating oil, intellectual services, advertising, wine and certain other services). The 3% rate is applied to foodstuffs, newspapers, books, and periodicals, medicines and medical equipment, medical and dental care, and other basic goods and services. The 6% rate is applied to gas and electricity.

37CUSTOMS AND DUTIES

Tariff policies have been traditionally liberal. Luxembourg adheres to the trade regulations of the European Union. Luxembourg levies its own 15% value-added tax on imports if their final destination is Luxembourg. Nontariff barriers exist also in the form of health, safety, and packaging regulations.

38FOREIGN INVESTMENT

Foreign capital investment in Luxembourg has traditionally been small. In recent years, however, US investments have risen substantially, with the value of direct investments in manufacturing alone in excess of $1 billion in 1993. Moderate-sized investments by Luxembourg firms have been made in Germany, France, Belgium, and South American countries. To encourage private investment from abroad, the government grants tax relief for up to 10 years in certain cases. Profits from investment may be transferred out of the country and invested capital may be repatriated with a minimum of regulation. Statistics on Luxembourg's inward and outward foreign investment are calculated and published in conjunction with Belgium's.

Presently, Luxembourg is one of the main actors (in conjunction with the United Kingdom and France) in terms of FDI outflows external to the EU. In 2003, Luxembourg was the EU's second-largest investor outside the boundaries of the union, with capital outflows of $37 billion. At the same time, due to its new role in the financial intermediation sector, Luxembourg has become the biggest recipient of FDI in the EU, with capital inflows reaching around $46 billion (49% of the EU25 total). It was followed at a distance by Ireland, with FDI inflows of $6 billion. Financial intermediation, whose receiving and sending actors almost always reside outside Luxembourg, accounted for 94% of outflows and 98% of inflows.

39ECONOMIC DEVELOPMENT

The keystone of the economic system is free enterprise, and the government has attempted to promote the well-being of private industry by every means short of direct interference. The full-employment policy pursued by every postwar government has produced a high ratio of economically active population to total population. Not only is the population economically active, it is also highly skilled, a fact not overlooked by foreign companies seeking to invest. The government encourages the diversification of industry by tax concessions and other means. Luxembourg's successful economy continues to attract immigrants; the immigrant population comprises over one-third of the Grand Duchy's total.

Banking has become an important sector of the economy, compensating for a decline in the steel industry. Successive governments have taken steps to encourage foreign investment, and investment incentives cover taxes, construction, and plant equipment. Government priorities in 2002 included balancing the budget, keeping spending growth in line with GDP growth, and running a general government surplus. The government was enacting tax cuts in 2002, and increased spending in infrastructure, research and development, education, and pension benefits. Obstacles were removed to part-time employment, more flexible working time arrangements were made, and child care facilities were expanded.

Today, Luxembourg is one of the most developed countries in the world (it actually has the highest income per capita in the world—approximately $55,000), and offers a welcoming and dynamic business environment. Its investment fund sector is second only to the one in Paris, and in 2004 it managed assets of over $1.027 trillion. The country is also home to one of Europe's biggest and most successful media conglomerates—RTL Group. Its location within the heart of Europe, its highly educated labor force, a stable tax system, and low business costs, make it a very attractive market for investors, and a reputable competitor for other developed economies.

40 SOCIAL DEVELOPMENT

An extensive system of social insurance covers virtually all employees and their families. Sickness, maternity, old age, disability, and survivors' benefits are paid, with both employee and employer contributing and the government absorbing part of the cost. Retirement is set at age 65 for both men and women. Birth, maternity, child and education allowances are also provided to all residents. There is a choice for medical service providers. Parental leave and child-rearing allowances are available as well. The government covers the total cost for family allowances. Work injury laws were first instituted in 1902.

Women are well represented in politics and the professions. Although legally entitled to equal pay for equal work, in practice women's salaries are somewhat lower than men's for comparable work. However, the number of women in the workplace increased in 2004. The Ministry for the Promotion of Women is charged with ensuring equal opportunities for women. Violence against women is taken seriously by the authorities, and most abusers are prosecuted. Children's rights are fully protected and the government amply funds systems providing education and health care.

Human rights are fully respected in Luxembourg.

41 HEALTH

Luxembourg has an advanced national health service, supervised by the Ministry of Public Health. Public health facilities are available to physicians and treatment of patients is on a private basis. Hospitals are operated either by the state or by the Roman Catholic Church.

In 2004, there were an estimated 255 physicians, 74 pharmacists, 64 dentists, and 39 midwives per 100,000 people. There were 32 hospitals with 4,438 beds. Public health officials have waged efficient national campaigns against contagious diseases and infant mortality has been reduced from 56.8 per 1,000 live births in 1948 to an estimated 4.81 as of 2005.

It was estimated that 80% of the country's children were immunized against measles. As of 2002, the crude birth rate and overall mortality rate were estimated at, respectively, 12 and 8.8 per 1,000 people. The fertility rate was one of the lowest in the world. The average woman living through her childbearing years had 1.5 children. Average life expectancy was estimated at 78.74 years in 2005. Leading causes of death are circulatory/heart diseases, cancer, road accidents, and suicide. The HIV/AIDS prevalence was 0.20 per 100 adults in 2003. As of 2004, there were approximately 500 people living with HIV/AIDS in the country. There were an estimated 100 deaths from AIDS in 2003.

42 HOUSING

The immediate post-World War II housing shortage created by the considerable war damage has been alleviated by substantial construction of private homes and apartment buildings. The government has helped by making home loans at low interest rates available to buyers. In 1981 there were 128,281 private households in Luxembourg. In 2001, there were about 171,953 private households. About 169,198 households were living in single-family units. Of these, 67% were living in owner-occupied dwellings. Housing satisfaction is one of the highest in the European Union.

43 EDUCATION

School attendance is compulsory between the ages of 6 and 15. Pupils attend primary schools for six years and then enter a general secondary or technical school for a period of up to seven years. The school year runs from October to July. The primary languages of instruction are French and German. In 2001, about 84% of children between the ages of three and five were enrolled in some type of preschool program. Primary school enrollment in 2003 was estimated at about 90% of age-eligible students. The same year, secondary school enrollment was about 80% of age-eligible students; 77% for boys and 83% for girls. It is estimated that about 86.5% of all students complete their primary education. The student-to-teacher ratio for primary school was at about 12:1 in 2003; the ratio for secondary school was about 11:1.

Postsecondary institutions in Luxembourg include the Central University of Luxembourg (founded in 1969), Superior Institute of Technology, and teacher training schools. However, most advanced students attend institutions of higher learning in Belgium and France. In 2003, about 12% of the tertiary age population were enrolled in some type of higher education program. The adult literacy rate for 2002 was estimated at about 100%.

As of 2003, public expenditure on education was estimated at 3.6% of GDP, or 8.5% of total government expenditures.

44 LIBRARIES AND MUSEUMS

The National Library in Luxembourg is the largest in the country, with over 650,000 volumes. Other major libraries belong to the Centre Universitaire (120,000 volumes), the European Community Court of Justice (120,000), the Abbey of St. Maurice at Clervaux (100,000), the Seminary of Luxembourg (110,000), and the European Parliament (150,000). The Grand Ducal Institute maintains a few specialized collections in the city of Luxembourg, as does the government. In Esch-sur-Alzette the public library has close to 66,000 volumes and features a special collection of Luxembourgensia.

The National Museum of History and Art (founded in 1845) exhibits fine arts as well as the history of Luxembourg. The city of Luxembourg also hosts the Museum of Natural History, founded in 1988 and moved to a new building in 1996, the year that the Museum of the History of Luxembourg opened in the same city. The home where the 19th-century French writer Victor Hugo lived as an exile is in Vianden, and there is a museum of wine in Ehren.

45 MEDIA

Direct-dial telephone service is in use throughout the country, and includes efficient international service. In 2002, there were 355,400 mainline phones and 473,000 mobile phones in use nationwide. Telegraph service is also widely available.

Radio-Télé-Luxembourg broadcasts on five radio channels (in Letzeburgesch, French, German, English, and Dutch) and two television channels (Letzeburgesch and French). The powerful commercial network reaches not only the domestic audience but millions of French, Germans, and other Europeans. The country is home to the Societe Europeenne des Satellites, the largest satellite operator in Europe. In 1999 there were 2 AM and 9 FM radio stations and 5 television stations. In 1997, there were 285,000 radios and about 285,000 television sets. In 2002, there were 165,000 Internet subscribers in the country.

As of 2001, there are six daily and two weekly newspapers. The daily press is small in circulation but has high standards. Luxembourg does not have an independent news agency of its own but relies on foreign news agencies for information. The most popular dailies in 2002 were the *Luxemburger Wort* (German and French, circulation 87,777); *Tageblatt* (German and French) (29,469); and *La Républicaine Lorraine* (French) (15,000). The weekly *Telecran* had a 2002 circulation of 45,000.

The law provides for freedom of speech and the press, and the government is said to uphold these provisions in practice.

46 ORGANIZATIONS

The principal agricultural organization is Centrale Paysanne Luxembourgeoise, under which are grouped all producer cooperatives and other farmers' societies. Organizations promoting the interests of industry include federations of artisans, manufacturers, merchants, and winegrowers. The Luxembourg Chamber of Commerce is active in representing local business interests. The Luxembourg Confederation of Christian Trade Unions promotes worker's rights for all.

Several professional associations are active in supporting a wide variety of occupations and fields. The Association of Doctors and Dentists serves as a professional networking organization while also promoting research and education on health issues and working to establish common policies and standards in healthcare. There are several other associations dedicated to research and education for specific fields of medicine and particular diseases and conditions.

The Christian Social Women organization promotes women's rights and encourages political participation. Scouting programs are active for youth. There are also several sports associations active within the country, including the multinational European Table Tennis Union.

Kiwanis and Lions clubs also have programs in the country. International organizations with active chapters include the Red Cross, Amnesty International, UNICEF, and Greenpeace.

47 TOURISM, TRAVEL, AND RECREATION

Picturesque Luxembourg, with approximately 130 castles, has long been a tourist attraction. Among the points of greatest attraction are Vianden; Clervaux, with its castle of the De Lannoi family, forebears of Franklin Delano Roosevelt; the famous abbey of Clervaux; Echternach, an ancient religious center; the Moselle region; and the fortifications of the capital. Popular sports for both residents and visitors include fishing, rowing, swimming, hiking, rock climbing, cycling, and golf. More than 5,000 American soldiers are buried at the American Military Cemetery near the capital, including Gen. George S. Patton.

Visitors from Canada, Australia, the United States, and most of the Western European and South American countries require a passport. No visas are necessary for stays of less than three months. There were 581,450 visitors who arrived in Luxembourg in 2003, many of whom came from Belgium and the Netherlands. Hotel rooms numbered 7,626 with 14,620 beds and an occupancy rate of 25%. The average length of stay that year was two nights. Tourist expenditure receipts totaled $2.9 billion.

In 2005, the US Department of State estimated the daily cost of traveling in Luxembourg at $301.

48 FAMOUS LUXEMBOURGERS

Count Sigefroid founded the nation in 963, and Countess Ermesinde (r.1196–1247) tripled the extent of the country. Other outstanding historical personages are Henry VII of Luxembourg (c.1275–1313), who became Holy Roman emperor in 1308; his son John the Blind (1296–1346), count of Luxembourg (1309–46) and king of Bohemia (1310–46), a national hero; and the latter's son Charles (1316–78), who became Holy Roman emperor as Charles IV (1346–78). Grand duke from 1890 to 1905 was Adolphe (1817–1905), one-time duke of Nassau (1839–66) and the founder of the present dynasty, the house of Nassau-Weilbourg, whose origins go back to 1059.

Joseph Bech (1887–1975), prime minister from 1926 to 1937 and from 1953 to 1958, served as foreign minister for 33 years. Luxembourg-born Robert Schuman (1886–1963), French premier (1947–48) and foreign minister (1948–53), was a key figure in the postwar movement for West European integration. Grand Duchess Charlotte (1896–1985) abdicated in 1964 in favor of her son Grand Duke Jean (b.1921), ruled from 1964–2000. The current ruler is his son Grand Duke Henri (b.1955).

An artist of note was painter Joseph Kutter (1894–1941). Gabriel Lippmann (1845–1921) was awarded the Nobel Prize in physics (1908) for his pioneering work in color photography.

49 DEPENDENCIES

Luxembourg has no territories or colonies.

50 BIBLIOGRAPHY

Annesley, Claire (ed.). *A Political and Economic Dictionary of Western Europe*. Philadelphia: Routledge/Taylor and Francis, 2005.

Clark, Peter. *Luxembourg*. New York: Routledge, 1994.

D and B's Export Guide to Luxembourg. Parsippany, N.J.: Dun and Bradstreet, 1999.

Kelly, Mary, Gianpietro Mazzoleni, and Denis McQuail (eds.). *The Media in Europe*. 3rd ed. Thousand Oaks, Calif.: Sage, 2004.

Newcomer, James. *The Grand Duchy of Luxembourg: The Evolution of Nationhood*. Luxembourg: Editions Emile Borschette, 1995.

Wessels, Wolfgang, Andreas Maurer, and Jürgan Mittag (eds.). *Fifteen into One?: the European Union and Its Member States*. New York: Palgrave, 2003.

MACEDONIA

Former Yugoslav Republic of Macedonia
Republika Makedonija

CAPITAL: Skopje

FLAG: The flag consists of a gold sun with eight rays on a red field.

ANTHEM: *Denec Nad Makedonija (Today over Macedonia)*

MONETARY UNIT: The currency in use is the denar (DEN). Denominations from smallest to largest are fifty deni, one denar, two denari, and five denari. US$1 = DEN0.02044 (or DEN1 = US$48.92; as of 2005), but exchange rates are likely to fluctuate.

WEIGHTS AND MEASURES: The metric system is in effect in Macedonia.

HOLIDAYS: Orthodox Christmas, 7 January; national holiday, 2 August; Day of Referendum, 8 September.

TIME: 1 PM = noon GMT.

¹LOCATION, SIZE, AND EXTENT

Macedonia is a landlocked nation located in southeastern Europe. Macedonia is slightly larger than the state of Vermont with a total area of 25,333 sq km (9,781 sq mi). Macedonia shares boundaries with Serbia to the N, Bulgaria to the E, Greece to the S, and Albania to the W, and has a total boundary length of 766 km (476 mi). Macedonia's capital city, Skopje, is located in the northwestern part of the country.

²TOPOGRAPHY

The topography of Macedonia features a mountainous landscape covered with deep basins and valleys. There are two large lakes, each divided by a frontier line. Approximately 24% of Macedonia's land is arable. Natural resources include chromium, lead, zinc, manganese, tungsten, nickel, low-grade iron ore, asbestos, sulfur, and timber. Located above a thrust fault line of the Eurasian Tectonic Plate, the nation experiences frequent tremors and occasional severe earthquakes. In 1963, 6.0 magnitude quake at Skopje caused the death of about 1,100 people and destroyed much of the city.

³CLIMATE

Macedonia's climate features hot summers and cold winters. Fall tends to be dry in the country. In July the average temperature is between 20 and 23°C (68 and 73°F). The average temperature in January is between -20 and 0°C (-4 and 32°F). Rainfall averages 51 cm (20 in) a year. Snowfalls can be heavy in winter.

⁴FLORA AND FAUNA

The terrain of Macedonia is rather hilly. Between the hills are deep basins and valleys, populated by European bison, fox, rabbits, brown bears, and deer. Pine trees are common in the higher mountain regions while beech and oak cover some of the lower mountain regions. The Macedonian pine is an ancient native species found most prominently on Mount Pelister near the south-

west border. Ducks, turtles, frogs, raccoons, and muskrats inhabit the country's waterways. As of 2002, there were at least 78 species of mammals, 109 species of birds, and over 3,500 species of plants throughout the country.

⁵ENVIRONMENT

Air pollution from metallurgical plants is a problem in Macedonia, as in the other former Yugoslav republics. In 2000, the total of carbon dioxide emissions was at 11.2 million metric tons. All urban dwellers have access to safe drinking water. Earthquakes are a natural hazard. Forest and woodland cover 35% of the nation's land area. As of 2003, approximately 7.1% of Macedonia's total land area was protected, including one World Heritage Site and one Ramsar Wetland of International Importance. According to a 2006 report issued by the International Union for Conservation of Nature and Natural Resources (IUCN), threatened species included nine types of mammals, nine species of birds, two types of reptiles, four species of fish, and five species of invertebrates. Threatened species include the field adder, Apollo butterfly, and noble crayfish. One species of mollusk has become extinct.

⁶POPULATION

The population of Macedonia in 2005 was estimated by the United Nations (UN) at 2,039,000, which placed it at number 139 in population among the 193 nations of the world. In 2005, approximately 11% of the population was over 65 years of age, with another 20% of the population under 15 years of age. There were 100 males for every 100 females in the country. According to the UN, the annual population rate of change for 2005–10 was expected to be 0.4%, a rate the government viewed as satisfactory. The projected population for the year 2025 was 2,120,000. The population density was 79 per sq km (205 per sq mi), with lowland regions being the most populated.

The UN estimated that 59% of the population lived in urban areas in 2005, and that urban areas were growing at an annual rate of

419

0.73%. The capital city, Skopje, had a population of 447,000 in that year. Most towns have fewer than 15,000 residents.

7 MIGRATION

In February 1999, violence in Kosovo forced more than 10,000 refugees to flee to Macedonia. The situation reached an emergency level when hundreds of thousands of refugees were arriving in late March and early April. By early June, the refugee population had grown to some 260,000. Macedonia did not have sufficient resources to cope with an emergency of this magnitude. At the government's request, some third-country asylum nations enacted bilateral evacuation programs, independently of the United Nations High Commissioner for Refugees (UNHCR). Also, a joint UNHCR/IOM Humanitarian Evacuation Programme was established, under which more than 90,000 refugees were evacuated from Macedonia to 29 countries. A Humanitarian Transfer Programme was also organized to set up camps in Albania for 1,300 refugees. The total number of migrants that year was 626,000, including 484,400 refugees.

In 2003 remittances to Macedonia were $148 million. The net migration rate for Macedonia in 2005 was -0.7 migrants per 1,000 population. The government views the migration levels as too high.

8 ETHNIC GROUPS

According to the 2002 census, Macedonians comprise about 64.2% of the population. Another 25.2% are ethnic Albanians, mostly living in the west, particularly the northwest. Other groups include Turks (3.9%), Roma (2.7%), Serbs (1.8%), and others (including Bosniaks and Vlachs, 2.2%).

9 LANGUAGES

Macedonian is a southern Slavic tongue that was not officially recognized until 1944, and is the primary language of 66.5% of the population. Bulgarians claim it is merely a dialect of their own language. As in Bulgarian, there are virtually no declensions and the definite article is suffixed. Also as in Bulgarian—and unlike any other Slavic language—an indefinite article exists as a separate word. It is written in the Cyrillic alphabet, but with two special characters—r and k. Minority languages are officially recognized at the local level. Albanian is spoken by about 25.1% of the population, Turkish by about 3.5%, Roma by 1.9%, Serbian by 1.2%, and various other languages by 1.8%.

10 RELIGIONS

About 66% of the population are nominally Macedonian Orthodox; another 30% are Muslim, 1% are Roman Catholic, and about 3% belong to various other faiths. The other faiths are mostly various Protestant denominations. Islam is commonly practiced among ethnic Albanians living primarily in the western part of the country and in the capital of Skopje. The Roman Catholic community is centered in Skopje, as is a small Jewish community.

Though the constitution allows for religious freedom, the government places some restrictions on religious groups that concern the establishment of houses of worship and the collection of monetary donations. Religious groups are registered under the Law on Religious Communities and Religious Groups.

11 TRANSPORTATION

A railway connects Skopje with Serbia to the north and the Greek port of Salonika to the south. In 2004, rail trackage totaled 699 km (434 mi) of standard gauge track, of which 233 km (144 mi) were electrified. As of 2002, a 56 km (35 mi) extension of the Kumanovo-Beljakovce line to the Bulgarian border at Gyueschevo was under construction. In 2001, there were 8,684 km (5,396 mi) of highways, of which 5,540 km (3,442 mi) were paved, including 133 km (83 mi) of expressways.

As of 2004, there were an estimated 17 airports, including 10 with paved runways (as of 2005). In 2003, about 201,000 passengers were carried on scheduled domestic and international flights.

12 HISTORY

Origin and Middle Ages

Macedonia is an ancient name, historically related to Philip II of Macedon, whose son became Alexander the Great, founder of one of the great empires of the ancient world. As a regional name, Macedonia, the land of the Macedons, has been used since ancient Greek times for the territory extending north of Thessaly and into the Vardar River Valley and between Epirus on the west and Thrace on the east. In Alexander the Great's time, Macedonia extended west to the Adriatic Sea over the area then called Illyris, part of today's Albania. Under the Roman Empire, Macedonia was extended south over Thessaly and Achaia.

Beginning in the 5th century AD Slavic tribes began settling in the Balkan area, and by 700 they controlled most of the Central and Peloponnesian Greek lands. The Slavic conquerors were mostly assimilated into Greek culture except in the northern Greek area of Macedonia proper and the areas of northern Thrace populated by "Bulgarian" Slavs. That is how St. Cyril and Methodius, two Greek brothers and scholars who grew up in the Macedonian city of Salonika, were able to become the "Apostles of the Slavs," having first translated Holy Scriptures in 863 into the common Slavic language they had learned in the Macedonian area.

Through most of the later Middle Ages, Macedonia was an area contested by the Byzantine Empire, with its Greek culture and Orthodox Christianity, the Bulgarian Kingdom, and particularly the 14th century Serbian empire of Dušan the Great. The Bulgarian and Serbian empires contributed to the spread of Christianity through the establishment of the Old Church Slavic liturgy.

After Dušan's death in 1355 his empire collapsed, partly due to the struggle for power among his heirs and partly to the advances of the Ottoman Turks. Following the defeat of the Serbs at the Kosovo Field in 1389, the Turks conquered the Macedonian area over the next half century and kept it under their control until the 1912 Balkan war.

Under Ottoman Rule

The decline of the Ottoman Empire brought about renewed competition over Slavic Macedonia between Bulgaria and Serbia. After the Russo-Turkish war of 1877 ended in a Turkish defeat, Bulgaria, an ally of Russia, was denied the prize of the Treaty of San Stefano (1878) in which Turkey had agreed to an enlarged and autonomous Bulgaria that would have included most of Macedonia. Such an enlarged Bulgaria—with control of the Vardar River

Valley and access to the Aegean Sea—was, however, a violation of a prior Russo-Austrian agreement. The Western powers opposed Russia's penetration into the Mediterranean through the port of Salonika and, at the 1878 Congress of Berlin, forced the "return" of Macedonia and East Rumelia from Bulgaria to Turkey. This action enraged Serbia, which had fought in the war against Turkey, gained its own independence, and hoped to win control of Bosnia and Herzegovina, which had been given over to Austrian control, for itself.

In this situation both Serbia and Bulgaria concentrated their efforts on Macedonia, where Greek influence had been very strong through the Greek Orthodox Church. The Bulgarians obtained their own Orthodox Church in 1870, that extended its influence to the Macedonian area and worked in favor of unification with Bulgaria through intensive educational activities designed to "Bulgarize" the Slavic population. Systematic intimidation was also used, when the Bulgarians sent their terrorist units (komite) into the area. The Serbian side considered Macedonia to be Southern Serbia, with its own dialect but using Serbian as its literary language. Serbian schools predated Bulgarian ones in Macedonia and continued with their work.

While individual instances of Macedonian consciousness and language had appeared by the end of the 18th century, it was in the 1850s that "Macedonists" had declared Macedonia a separate Slavic nation. Macedonian Slavs had developed a preference for their central Macedonian dialect and had begun publishing some writings in it rather than using the Bulgaro-Macedonian version promoted by the Bulgarian Church and government emissaries. Thus, Macedonia, in the second half of the 19th century, while still under the weakening rule of the Turks, had become the object of territorial and cultural claims by its Greek, Serb, and Bulgarian neighbors. The most systematic pressure had come from Bulgaria and had caused large numbers of "Bulgaro-Macedonians" to emigrate to Bulgaria—some 100,000 in the 1890s—mainly to Sophia, where they constituted almost half the city's population and an extremely strong pressure group.

Struggle for Autonomy

More and more Macedonians became convinced that Macedonia should achieve at least an autonomous status under Turkey, if not complete independence. In 1893, a secret organization was formed in Salonika aiming at a revolt against the Turks and the establishment of an autonomous Macedonia. The organization was to be independent of Serbia, Bulgaria, and Greece and was named the Internal Macedonian Revolutionary Organization (IMRO), a group that became Socialist, revolutionary, and terrorist in nature. Much like Ireland's IRA, IMRO spread through Macedonia and became an underground paragovernmental network active up to World War II. A pro-Bulgarian and an independent Macedonian faction soon developed, the first based in Sophia, the second in Salonika. Its strong base in Sophia gave the pro-Bulgarian faction a great advantage and it took control and pushed for an early uprising in order to impress the Western powers into intervening in support of Macedonia.

The large scale uprising took place on 2 August 1903 (Ilinden–"St. Elijah's Day") when the rebels took over the town of Kruševo and proclaimed a Socialist Republic. After initial defeats of the local Turkish forces, the rebels were subdued by massive Ottoman

LOCATION: 41°50′ N; 22°0′ E. BOUNDARY LENGTHS: Total boundary lengths, 748 kilometers (465 miles); Albania, 151 kilometers (94 miles); Bulgaria, 148 kilometers (92 miles); Greece, 228 kilometers (142 miles); Serbia, 221 kilometers (137.3 miles).

attacks using scorched earth tactics and wholesale massacres of the population over a three-month period. Europe and the United States paid attention and forced Turkey into granting reforms to be supervised by international observers. However, the disillusioned IMRO leadership engaged in factional bloody feuds that weakened the IMRO organization and image. This encouraged both Serbs and Greeks in the use of their own armed bands—Serbian Cetniks and Greek Andarte—creating an atmosphere of gang warfare in which Bulgaria, Serbia, and Greece fought each other (instead of the Turks) over a future division of Macedonia. In the meantime, the Young Turks movement had spread among Turkish officers and military uprisings began in Macedonia in 1906. These uprisings spread and Turkish officers demanded a constitutional system. They believed that Turkey could be saved only by Westernizing. In 1908 the Young Turks prevailed, and offered to the IMRO leadership agrarian reforms, regional autonomy, and introduction of the Macedonian language in the schools. However, the Young Turks turned out to be extreme Turkish nationalists bent on the assimilation of other national groups. Their denationalizing efforts caused further rebellions and massacres in the Balkans. Serbia, Greece, Bulgaria, and Montenegro turned for help to the great powers, but to no avail. In 1912 they formed the Balkan League, provisionally agreed on the division of Turkish Balkan territory among themselves, and declared war on Turkey in October 1912 after Turkey refused their request to establish the four autonomous regions of Macedonia—Old Serbia, Epirus, and Albania—already provided for in the 1878 Treaty of Berlin.

Balkan Wars

The quick defeat of the Turks by the Balkan League stunned the European powers, particularly when Bulgarian forces reached the suburbs of Istanbul. Turkey signed a treaty in London on 30 May 1913 giving up all European possessions with the exception of Istanbul. However, when Italy and Austria vetoed a provision granting Serbia access to the Adriatic at Durazzo and Alessio and agreed to form an independent Albania, Serbia demanded a larger part of Macedonia from Bulgaria. Bulgaria refused and attacked both Serbian and Greek forces. This caused the second Balkan War that ended in a month with Bulgaria's defeat by Serbia and Greece with help from Romania, Montenegro, and Turkey. The outcome was the partitioning of Macedonia between Serbia and Greece. Turkey regained the Adrianople area it had lost to Bulgaria. Romania gained a part of Bulgarian Dobrudja while Bulgaria kept a part of Thrace and the Macedonian town of Strumica. Thus Southern Macedonia came under the Hellenizing influence of Greece while most of Macedonia was annexed to Serbia. Both Serbia and Greece denied any Macedonian "nationhood." In Greece, Macedonians were treated as "Slavophone" Greeks while Serbs viewed Macedonia as Southern Serbia and Serbian was made the official language of government and instruction in schools and churches.

First and Second Yugoslavia

After World War I, the IMRO organization became a terrorist group operating out of Bulgaria with a nuisance role against Yugoslavia. In later years, some IMRO members joined the Communist Party and tried to work toward a Balkan Federation where Macedonia would be an autonomous member. Its interest in the dissolution of the first Yugoslavia led IMRO members to join with the Croatian Ustaša in the assassination of King Alexander of Yugoslavia and French Foreign Minister Louis Barthou in Marseille on 9 October 1934. During World War II, Bulgaria, Hitler's ally, occupied the central and eastern parts of Macedonia while Albanians, supported by Italy, annexed western Macedonia along with the Kosovo region. Because of Bulgarian control, resistance was slow to develop in Macedonia; a conflict between the Bulgarian and Yugoslav Communist parties also played a part. By the summer of 1943, however, Tito, the leader of the Yugoslav Partisans, took over control of the Communist Party of Macedonia after winning its agreement to form a separate Macedonian republic as part of a Yugoslav federation. Some 120,000 Macedonian Serbs were forced to emigrate to Serbia because they had opted for Serbian citizenship. Partisan activities against the occupiers increased and, by August 1944, the Macedonian People's Republic was proclaimed with Macedonian as the official language and the goal of unifying all Macedonians was confirmed. But this goal was not achieved. However, the "Pirin" Macedonians in Bulgaria were granted their own cultural development rights in 1947, and then lost them after the Stalin-Tito split in 1948. The Bulgarian claims to Macedonia were revived from time to time after 1948.

On the Greek side, there was no support from the Greek Communist Party for the unification of Macedonian Slavs within Greece with the Yugoslav Macedonians, even though Macedonian Slavs had organized resistance units under Greek command and participated heavily in the postwar Greek Communists' insurrection. With Tito's closing the Yugoslav-Greek frontier in July 1949 and ending his assistance to the pro-Cominform Greek Communists, any chance of territorial gains from Greece had dissipated. On the Yugoslav side, Macedonia became one of the co-equal constituent republics of the Federal Socialist Republic of Yugoslavia under the Communist regime of Marshal Tito. The Macedonian language became one of the official languages of Yugoslavia, along with Slovenian and Serbo-Croatian, and the official language of the Republic of Macedonia where the Albanian and Serbo-Croatian languages were also used. Macedonian was fully developed into the literary language of Macedonians, used as the language of instruction in schools as well as the newly established Macedonian Orthodox Church. A Macedonian University was established in Skopje, the capital city, and all the usual cultural, political, social, and economic institutions were developed within the framework of the Yugoslav Socialist system of self-management. The main goals of autonomy and socialism of the old IMRO organization were fulfilled, with the exception of the unification of the "Pirin" (Bulgarian) and "Greek" Macedonian lands.

All of the republics of the former Federal Socialist Republic of Yugoslavia share a common history between 1945 and 1991, the year of Yugoslavia's dissolution. The World War II Partisan resistance movement, controlled by the Communist Party of Yugoslavia and led by Marshal Tito, won a civil war waged against nationalist groups under foreign occupation, having secured the assistance, and recognition, from both the Western powers and the Soviet Union. Aside from the reconstruction of the country and its economy, the first task facing the new regime was the establishment of its legitimacy and, at the same time, the liquidation of its internal enemies, both actual and potential. The first task was accomplished by the 11 November 1945 elections of a constitutional assembly on the basis of a single candidate list assembled by the People's Front. The list won 90% of the votes cast. The three members of the "coalition" government representing the Royal Yugoslav Government in exile had resigned earlier in frustration and did not run in the elections. The Constitutional Assembly voted against the continuation of the Monarchy and, on 31 January 1946, the new constitution of the Federal People's Republic of Yugoslavia was promulgated. Along with state-building activities, the Yugoslav Communist regime carried out ruthless executions, massacres, and imprisonments to liquidate any potential opposition.

The Tito-Stalin conflict that erupted in 1948 was not a real surprise considering the differences the two had had about Tito's refusal to cooperate with other resistance movements against the occupiers in World War II. The expulsion of Tito from the Cominform group separated Yugoslavia from the Soviet Bloc, caused internal purges of pro-Cominform Yugoslav Communist Party members, and also nudged Yugoslavia into a failed attempt to collectivize its agriculture. Yugoslavia then developed its own brand of Marxist economy based on workers' councils and self-management of enterprises and institutions, and became the leader of the nonaligned group of nations in the international arena. Being more open to Western influences, the Yugoslav Communist regime relaxed somewhat its central controls. This allowed for the development of more liberal wings of Communist parties, particularly in Croatia and Slovenia, which agitated for the devolution of power from the federal to the individual republic level in order to better cope with the increasing differentiation between the more productive republics (Slovenia and Croatia) and the less developed areas. Also, nationalism resurfaced with tensions particularly strong between Serbs and Croats in the Croatian Republic, leading to the repression by Tito of the Croatian and Slovenian "Springs" in 1970–71.

The 1974 constitution shifted much of the decision-making power from the federal to the republics' level, turning the Yugoslav Communist Party into a kind of federation (league) of the republican parties, thus further decentralizing the political process. The autonomous provinces of Vojvodina and Kosovo were also given a quasi-sovereign status as republics, and a collective presidency was designed to take over power upon Tito's death. When Tito died in 1980, the delegates of the six republics and the two autonomous provinces represented the interests of each republic or province in the process of shifting coalitions centered on specific issues. The investment of development funds to assist the less developed areas became the burning issue around which nationalist emotions and tensions grew ever stronger, along with the forceful repression of the Albanian majority in Kosovo.

The economic crisis of the 1980s, with runaway inflation, inability to pay the debt service on over \$20 billion in international loans that had accumulated during Tito's rule, and low productivity in the less-developed areas became too much of a burden for Slovenia and Croatia, leading them to stand up to the centralizing power of the Serbian (and other) Republics. The demand for a reorganization of the Yugoslav Federation into a confederation of sovereign states was strongly opposed by the coalition of Serbia, Montenegro, and the Yugoslav army. The pressure towards political pluralism and a market economy also grew stronger, leading to the formation of non-Communist political parties that, by 1990, were able to win majorities in multiparty elections in Slovenia and then in Croatia, thus putting an end to the era of the Communist Party monopoly of power. The inability of the opposing groups of centralist and confederalist republics to find any common ground led to the dissolution of Yugoslavia through the disassociation of Slovenia, Croatia, Bosnia and Herzegovina, and Macedonia, leaving only Serbia and Montenegro together in a new Federal Republic of Yugoslavia.

The years between 1945 and 1990 offered the Macedonians an opportunity for development in some areas, in addition to their cultural and nation-building efforts, within the framework of a one-party Communist system. For the first time in their history the Macedonians had their own republic and government with a very broad range of responsibilities. Forty-five years was a long enough period to have trained generations for public service responsibilities and the governing of an independent state. In addition, Macedonia derived considerable benefits from the Yugoslav framework in terms of federal support for underdeveloped areas (Bosnia and Herzegovina, Kosovo, Macedonia, Montenegro). Macedonia's share of the special development funds ranged from 26% in 1966 to about 20% in 1985, much of it supplied by Croatia and Slovenia.

In the wake of developments in Slovenia and Croatia, Macedonia held its first multiparty elections in November–December 1990, with the participation of over 20 political parties. Four parties formed a coalition government that left the strongest nationalist party (IMRO) in the opposition. In January 1991 the Macedonian Assembly passed a declaration of sovereignty.

Independence

While early in 1989 Macedonia supported Serbia's Slobodan Milošević in his recentralizing efforts, by 1991, Milošević was viewed as a threat to Macedonia and its leadership took positions closer to the confederal ones of Slovenia and Croatia. A last effort to avoid Yugoslavia's disintegration was made 3 June 1991 through a joint proposal by Macedonia and Bosnia and Herzegovina, offering to form a "community of Yugoslav Republics" with a centrally administered common market, foreign policy, and national defense. However, Serbia opposed the proposal.

On 26 June 1991—one day after Slovenia and Croatia had declared their independence—the Macedonian Assembly debated the issue of secession from Yugoslavia with the IMRO group urging an immediate proclamation of independence. Other parties were more restrained, a position echoed by Macedonian president Kiro Gligorov in his cautious statement that Macedonia would remain faithful to Yugoslavia. Yet by 6 July 1991, the Macedonian Assembly decided in favor of Macedonia's independence if a confederal solution could not be attained.

Thus, when the process of dissolution of Yugoslavia took place in 1990–91, Macedonia refused to join Serbia and Montenegro and opted for independence on 20 November 1991. The unification issue was then raised again, albeit negatively, by the refusal of Greece to recognize the newly independent Macedonia for fear that its very name would incite irredentist designs toward the Slav Macedonians in northern Greece. The issue of recognition became a problem between Greece and its NATO allies in spite of the fact that Macedonia had adopted in 1992 a constitutional amendment forbidding any engagement in territorial expansion or interference in the internal affairs of another country. In April 1993, Macedonia gained membership in the UN, but only under the name of "Former Yugoslav Republic of Macedonia." Greece also voted against Macedonian membership in the Conference on Security and Cooperation in Europe on 1 December 1993. However, on 16 December 1993, the United Kingdom, Germany, Denmark, and the Netherlands had announced the initiation of the recognition process for Macedonia and other countries joined the process, which resulted in recognition of Macedonia by the United States on 8 February 1994. In April 1994 the EU began to take legal action in the European Court of Justice against Greece for refusing to lift a trade blockade against Macedonia that it initiated two months earlier. However, by October 1995, Greece agreed to lift the embargo, in return for concessions from Macedonia that included changing its national flag, which contained an ancient Greek emblem depicting the 16-pointed golden sun of Vergina. The dispute over the name of Macedonia remained, but the agreement defused the threat of violence in the region.

On 3 October 1995, Macedonian president Kiro Gligorov narrowly survived a car-bomb attack that killed his driver. The next day, parliament named its speaker, Stojan Andov, as the interim president after determining that Gligorov was incapable of performing his functions. Gligorov resumed his duties in early 1996. As tensions between majority Albanians and minority Serbs in the neighboring Yugoslav province of Kosovo heated up from 1997 to 1999, fears mounted that full-scale fighting would spread to Macedonia. Ethnic violence erupted in the town of Gostivar in July 1997 after the Macedonian government sent in special military forces to remove the illegal Albanian, Turkish, and Macedonian flags flying outside the town hall. Several thousand protesters, some armed, had gathered and were in a stalemate with police. During the skirmish, police killed three ethnic Albanians and several policemen were shot. The Albanian nationalist Kosovo Liberation Army also claimed attacks against two police stations in Macedonia in December 1997 and January 1998. As the violence mounted the United Nations Security Council voted unanimously on 21 July 1998 to renew the UNPREDEP (United Nations Preventive Deployment Force) mandate another six months and to bolster the contingent with 350 more soldiers.

When full-scale fighting in Kosovo erupted in early 1999 and NATO responded with air strikes against Serbia, Macedonia became the destination for tens of thousands of Kosovar Albanian refugees fleeing from Serbian ethnic cleansing. For a while the situation in Macedonia remained tense as the government, fearful of a spillover of the fighting into its territory, closed its frontiers to refugees. Nonetheless, the presence of NATO forces and pledges of international aid prevented (aside from errant bombs and a couple of cross-border incursions) a spread of the fighting and maintained domestic stability in Macedonia.

However, in 2000, violence on the border with Kosovo increased, putting Macedonian troops in a state of high alert. In February 2001, fighting broke out between government forces and ethnic Albanian rebels, many of who were from the Kosovo Liberation Army, but some were also ethnic Albanians from within Macedonia. The insurrection broke out in the northwest, where rebels took up arms around the town of Tetovo, where ethnic Albanians make up a majority of the population. NATO deployed additional forces along the border with Kosovo to stop the supply of arms to the rebels; however, the buffer zone proved ineffective. As fighting intensified in March, the government closed the border with Kosovo. The UN High Commissioner for Refugees estimated that 22,000 ethnic Albanians had fled the fighting by that time. Fears in Macedonia of the creation of a "Greater Albania," including Kosovo and parts of Macedonia, were fueled by the separatist movement, and mass demonstrations were held in Skopje urging tougher action against the rebels. The violence continued throughout the summer, until August, when the Ohrid Framework Agreement was signed by the government and ethnic Albanian representatives, granting greater recognition of ethnic Albanian rights in exchange for the rebels' pledge to turn over weapons to the NATO peacekeeping force.

In November 2001, parliament amended the constitution to include reforms laid out in the Ohrid Framework Agreement. The constitution recognizes Albanian as an official language, and increases access for ethnic Albanians to pubic-sector jobs, including the police. It also gives ethnic Albanians a voice in parliament, and guarantees their political, religious and cultural rights. In March 2002, parliament granted an amnesty to the former rebels who turned over their weapons to the NATO peacekeepers in August and September 2001. By September 2002, most of the 170,000 people who had fled their homes in advance of the fighting in 2001 had returned.

Parliamentary elections were held on 15 September 2002, which saw a change in leadership from the nationalist VMRO-DPMNE party of Prime Minister Ljubco Georgievski to the moderate Social Democratic League of Macedonia (SDSM)-led "Together for Macedonia" coalition. Branco Crvenkovski became prime minister. At that time Boris Trajkovski was president; he had been elected from the VMRO-DPMNE party in 1999. In the September 2002 elections, former ethnic Albanian rebel-turned-politician Ali Ahmeti saw his Democratic Union for Integration party (DUI) claim victory for the Albanian community, which makes up more than 25% of the Macedonian population. Ahmeti, former political leader of the National Liberation Army (NLA), delayed taking his seat in parliament until December, for fear it would ignite protests among Macedonians who still regarded him as a terrorist. Indeed, in January 2003, the DUI headquarters in Skopje came under assault from machine-gunfire and a grenade, the fourth such attack on DUI offices.

In November 2002, NATO announced that of 10 countries aspiring to join the organization, 7 would accede in 2004, leaving Albania, Macedonia, and Croatia to wait until a later round of expansion. In January 2003, Albania and Macedonia agreed to intensify bilateral cooperation, especially in the economic sphere, so as to prepare their way for NATO and EU membership.

The year 2004 was a rather tumultuous one for Macedonia, and Macedonians. In February, President Trajkovski, who was on his way to a conference in Mostar, Bosnia, died in a plane crash. Two months later, elections were staged to replace him. Branko Crvenkovski, the acting prime minister and the leader of the ruling Social Democratic Union of Macedonia, won the second round of the election, with 62.7% of the vote; his main opponent—Sasko Kedev of the VMRO-DPMNE—got 37.3%. In June 2004, Hari Kostov, the former minister of interior, became prime minister following approval by the parliament. His reign was to be chaotic and short lived though—ethnic protests littered the country as parliament implemented legislation that gave Albanians more autonomy in the areas where they predominated. In November 2004, Kostov resigned and his place was taken by the defense minister, Vlado Buckovski (who also took over the leadership of the Social Democratic Union). In the summer 2005, the parliament passed a law that allowed ethnic Albanians to fly the Albanian flag in the areas where they compose the majority.

13 GOVERNMENT

Macedonia achieved its independence from the former Yugoslavia on 20 November 1991, having adopted its constitution on 17 November 1991. Macedonia's unicameral assembly of 120 seats is called the Sobranje. Eighty-five members are elected in single-seat constituencies, and 35 are elected by proportional representation. The executive branch consists of the president (elected by popular vote for a five-year term) and the Council of Ministers (elected by the majority vote of all the deputies in the Sobranje). The prime minister is elected by the assembly. In November 2001, parliament amended the constitution to include greater recognition of ethnic Albanian political, religious, and cultural rights. In October 2005, the president of Macedonia was Branko Crvenkovski, while Vlado Buckovski—the leader of the Social Democratic Union—occupied the prime minister post.

14 POLITICAL PARTIES

Following the 2002 elections, party representation in the Sobranje (Assembly) was as follows: the Together for Macedonia coalition (composed of 10 parties led by the Social Democratic League of Macedonia and the Liberal Democratic Party—SDSM-LDP), 40.5% (59 seats); Internal Macedonian Revolutionary Organization-Democratic Party for Macedonian Unity (VMRO-DMPNE), 24.4% (34 seats); Democratic Union for Integration (DUI), 11.9% (16 seats); Democratic Party of Albanians (PDS), 5.2% (7 seats); Democratic Prosperity Party (PDP), 2.3% (2 seats); National-Democratic Party (NDP), 2.1% (1 seat); and the Socialist Party of Macedonia (SPM), 2.1% (1 seat). The DUI, PDS, PDP, and NDP are ethnic Albanian parties. The next legislative elections were scheduled to take place in 2006. The last presidential election was held in 2004 and Social-Democrat Branko Crvenkovski won a majority in the second round over his main opponent, VMRO-DPMNE candidate Sasko Kedev. The next presidential elections were scheduled to take place in April 2009.

15 LOCAL GOVERNMENT

Macedonia's 85 municipalities form the structure of local government. (Out of these municipalities, 10 represent the greater Skopje area.) The municipality is the basic self-managed sociopolitical community. Council members are directly elected for four-year terms, as are the mayors of the municipalities. Citizens may form neighborhood (village and suburb) governing bodies. Where the number of members of a particular nationality exceeds 20% of the total number of inhabitants in a municipality, the language and alphabet of that nationality shall be in official use, in addition to Macedonian and the Cyrillic alphabet.

The local elections held in April 2005 went without ethnic tensions, although international observers drew attention to irregularities during all of the three voting rounds. Despite criticism, Prime Minister Buckovski considered the local election process to be a "model" for the future. The ruling Together for Macedonia coalition won 36 mayoral races; the Albanian Democratic Union of Integration (a coalition partner of the former) won 15; the VMRO-DPMNE, 21; the VMRO-People's Party, 3; the Democratic Party of Albanians/Party of Democratic Prosperity, 2; the Macedonian Roma Alliance, 1; the rest of the seven mayoral seats were won by mayors supported by a voter's bloc. Trifun Kostovski won the city of Skopje race over the candidate of the SDSM-led coalition—Risto Penov.

16 JUDICIAL SYSTEM

The judicial system is comprised of three tiers: municipal courts, district courts, and the Supreme Court. A Constitutional Court handles issues of constitutional interpretation, including protection of individual rights. The constitution directs the establishment of a people's ombudsman to defend citizens' fundamental constitutional rights; the office became functional in 1997. An independent Republican Judicial Council appoints judges, who are confirmed by parliament. The Constitutional Court has not yet rendered any decisions in the area of protection of individual rights or liberties. The constitution guarantees the autonomy and independence of the judiciary.

17 ARMED FORCES

In January 1992, the Macedonian Assembly approved the formation of a standing army of 25,000–30,000 troops. However, the actual size of the military was 10,890 active personnel in 2005, of which the army was the largest service with 9,760 active members. The army was equipped with 61 main battle tanks, 51 reconnaissance vehicles, 11 armored infantry fighting vehicles, 207 armored personnel carriers, and 944 artillery pieces. Although there is no data as to the number of reservists, the nation's reserve forces were broken down in 2005 into eight infantry brigades and one (each) artillery, antitank and air defense regiments. The army also operated a maritime patrol arm equipped with five patrol/coastal vessels. The air force had 1,130 active personnel which had four combat capable aircraft made up of four fighter ground attack aircraft. The nation's paramilitary force consisted of a police force numbering 7,600, of which some 5,000 were armed. As of 2005, foreign forces stationed in Macedonia consist of 260 US personnel attached to KFOR 1. The national defense budget in 2005 totaled $129 million.

In March 1997, rioters in neighboring Albania looted government armories, making off with hundreds of thousands of AK-47 assault rifles. Substantial numbers of those weapons were smuggled into Macedonia and sold to ethnic Albanians.

18 INTERNATIONAL COOPERATION

The Former Yugoslav Republic of Macedonia was admitted to the United Nations on 8 April 1993; it is a part of ECE and a member of several nonregional specialized agencies, such as FAO, IAEA, IMF, UNESCO, UNIDO, WHO, and the World Bank. Macedonia is also a member of the Council of Europe, the Euro-Atlantic Partnership Council, the European Bank for Reconstruction and Development, the NATO Partnership for Peace, and the OSCE.

In February 1994 Macedonia's sovereignty was recognized by the United States and EU countries. Greece objected to the use of the name Macedonia by the nation and imposed a trade embargo for this and other issues. Greece and Macedonia signed an interim agreement in 1995 ending the embargo and opening negotiations for diplomatic recognition. Also in 1995, Macedonia ratified the European Convention on Human Rights and accepted the jurisdiction of the European Court of Human Rights. The convention includes several Eastern and Central European nations that see membership as a precursor to possible admission to the European Union in the future.

In environmental cooperation, Macedonia is part of the Basel Convention, Conventions on Biological Diversity and Air Pollution, Ramsar, CITES, the Kyoto Protocol, the Montréal Protocol, and the UN Conventions on the Law of the Sea and Climate Change.

19 ECONOMY

Although the poorest of the six former Yugoslav republics, Macedonia nevertheless can sustain itself in food and energy needs using its own agricultural and coal resources. Due to the scarcity of arable land in the Vardar River Valley and other valleys in the west, expatriate employment in Serbia and Germany has become more common.

In August 1992, because it resented the use of "Macedonia" as the republic's name and feared a hidden ambition to lay claim to the Greek province with the same name, Greece imposed a partial blockade on Macedonia. Greece later imposed a full trade embargo against Macedonia in February 1994. This blockade, combined with the UN sanctions on Serbia and Montenegro, cost the economy an estimated $2 billion by the end of 1994. Macedonia's per capita GNP fell from $1,800 to less than $760 because of the sanctions and the Greek blockade. After threats of legal action by the EU, in October 1995 Greece ceased the embargo and promised not to interfere with Macedonia's commerce.

From 1998 to 2000 real GDP growth averaged a little over 4%, but in 2001, in the wake of rising global tensions and a global economic slowdown, real GDP growth fell 4.5%. Although 2002 saw an end to the contraction, growth was estimated at only 0.3%. Inflation had jumped to 6.1% in 2000, but moderated to 3.7% in 2001, and was projected at only 1% in 2002. Unemployment remains a serious problem. The official estimate for 2002 was almost 32%, with some 70% of 15- to 24-year-olds without work. In 2001, agriculture accounted for about 10% of GDP; industry, 32%; and services, 58%.

In 2004, the GDP growth rate was 5.3%, up from 4.7% in 2003; by 2005 however, it was expected to fall to 5.0%. Inflation decreased to negative values in 2004 (-0.4 %), but overall it tended to hover around 1%. At around 37%, unemployment remains a big problem for the Macedonian economy, although many of the seemingly jobless are thought to hold jobs in the informal sector. The economic growth is expected to remain steady over the next years, and will be fueled by rapid growth in a series of key sectors: transport and telecommunications, trade and financial services. This growth will in turn spur an increase in domestic demand, and a recovery of the industrial sector (especially steel production).

20 INCOME

The US Central Intelligence Agency (CIA) reports that in 2005 Macedonia's gross domestic product (GDP) was estimated at $15.6 billion. The CIA defines GDP as the value of all final goods and services produced within a nation in a given year and computed on the basis of purchasing power parity (PPP) rather than value as measured on the basis of the rate of exchange based on current dollars. The per capita GDP was estimated at $7,400. The annual growth rate of GDP was estimated at 4%. The average inflation rate in 2005 was 1%. It was estimated that agriculture accounted for 11.7% of GDP, industry 32.1%, and services 56.2%.

According to the World Bank, in 2003 remittances from citizens working abroad totaled $171 million or about $8 per capita and accounted for approximately 3.7% of GDP. Foreign aid receipts amounted to $234 million or about $114 per capita and accounted for approximately 5.0% of the gross national income (GNI).

The World Bank reports that in 2003 household consumption in Macedonia totaled $3.46 billion or about $165 per capita based on a GDP of $4.7 billion, measured in current dollars rather than PPP. Household consumption includes expenditures of individuals, households, and nongovernmental organizations on goods and services, excluding purchases of dwellings. It was estimated that for the period 1990 to 2003 household consumption grew at

an average annual rate of 2.1%. In 2001 it was estimated that approximately 33% of household consumption was spent on food, 15% on fuel, 6% on health care, and 9% on education. It was estimated that in 2003 about 30.2% of the population had incomes below the poverty line.

21 LABOR

There were an estimated 855,000 persons in the Macedonian labor force in 2004. As of 2003, 22% were in agriculture, 33.9% in industry, 43.8% in the services sector, with 0.3% in undefined occupations.

The constitution guarantees citizens the right to form labor unions with restrictions on the military, police, and government workers. Approximately 50% of the workforce is organized. The Confederation of Trade Unions of Macedonia (SSSM) is the labor confederation which is the successor to the old Communist Party labor confederation, and is still the government's primary negotiating partner on social issues. Employees have little bargaining power in the weak economic environment. Strikes may be utilized to protect employee interests.

Macedonian law establishes a 40-hour workweek, with a 24-hour rest period (minimum) plus vacation and sick leave. The minimum employment age by law is 15 years, with minors under the age of 18 limited by the number of hours they can work and by the types of work they can perform. The law provides that workplaces must meet minimum occupational health and safety standards but reports indicate that these are not effectively enforced. As of 2005, Macedonia did not have a legal national minimum wage. The average monthly wage that year was about $250, and did not provide a family with a living wage. It was estimated by the government that around 29.6% of the population lived below the poverty line.

22 AGRICULTURE

As of 2003, there were some 612,000 hectares (1,512,000 acres) of arable land, representing 24% of the total land area. Most private farms are very small; 65% of private farmers own at most one hectare (2.7 acres) sometimes scattered in five or six locations.

Wheat production is concentrated in south central Macedonia and in public farms. Corn and barley are produced throughout the country, mostly by the private sector. About 80% of agricultural land is held by the private sector. The remaining 20% is held by state-owned enterprises known as Kombinats. Estimated grain production in 2004 included: wheat, 358,000 tons; barley, 150,000 tons; and corn, 146,000 tons. Rye, rice, and oats are also grown in smaller quantities. Other important crops produced in 2004 included (in 1,000 tons): tomatoes, 117; potatoes, 199; sunflower seeds, 7.4; sugar beets, 52; and walnuts, 3.7. In 2004, 247,600 tons of grapes and 26,000 tons of plums were produced. Tobacco is grown throughout Macedonia and is planted on 4% of the arable land. Production was 21,140 tons in 2004.

23 ANIMAL HUSBANDRY

Meadows and pastures accounted for about 25% of the total land area. Livestock in 2005 consisted of 1,200,000 sheep, 265,000 head of cattle, 200,000 pigs, and 3,000,000 chickens. Cattle numbers have increased slightly since 1992 due mainly to the increase in cows. About 50% of cattle are for the dairy sector. There are about

30 state farms with 250–1,200 cows in the Skopje and Bitola areas. Over 90% of cattle, however, are in private hands, with most farmers rarely having more than three cows because of limited land. Cow milk accounts for 74% of milk production; sheep milk, 26%. The rapidly growing goat sector is also contributing to increasing milk production. The raising of goats was prohibited during the socialist era in order to protect forestry resources. Production in 2005 included (in tons): mutton, 7,500; beef, 10,000; poultry, 4,000; and milk, 263,000.

24 FISHING

Inland fishing occurs on Lake Ohrid, Lake Prespa, and the Vardar River. The total catch in 2003 was 1,648 tons (primarily trout and carp), all from inland fishing. Macedonia has no direct access to the sea for marine fishing.

25 FORESTRY

About 36% of the total area consisted of forests and woodlands in 2000, mostly in the eastern and southern regions. Bitola is the center for the wood products industry. Total roundwood production in 2004 was 812,000 cu m (28.7 million cu ft), with 85% used as firewood.

26 MINING

Macedonia's mining and quarrying sector output, by value, dropped approximately 39% in 2003 from the previous year, although the country's gross domestic product (GDP) that year rose by 3.1% from 2002. Lead-zinc ore was mined at Kamenica and Probistip; copper, at Bucim; and iron ore, at Tajmite, Demir Hisar, and Damjan. Gold, bentonite, diatomite, feldspar, lime, talc, pumice, stone (carbonite and silicate), gypsum, and sand and gravel were also produced in 2003. Most of the industrial minerals produced went mainly to Balkan countries, the EU, and Russia. Production totals in 2003 were: mined lead (by gross weight), 40,000 metric tons, down from 200,000 metric tons in 2002; zinc (refined primary and secondary metal), 15,100 metric tons, down from 38,000 metric tons in 2002; copper (concentrate by gross weight), 15,000 metric tons; silver, 10,000 kg, down from 12,000 kg in 2002; and gold 400 kg, down from 500 kg in 2002. No chromite was produced in 1998, 1999, 2000 or 2003. Nickel output in 2003 totaled 5,600 metric tons, up from 5.100 metric tons in the previous year.

27 ENERGY AND POWER

In 2002, 5.762 billion kWh of electricity were generated, of which 86.7% came from conventional thermal plants and the rest from hydropower. Installed capacity totaled 1,568,000 kW in 2001. Consumption of electricity in 2002 was 6.150 billion kWh.

Macedonia's only domestic mineral fuel is coal. In 2002, the country produced 8,356,000 short tons, all of which was brown coal or lignite. Imports of coal totaled 183,000 short tons. Demand for coal in 2002 came to 8,092,000 short tons.

Macedonia imported an average of 11,540 barrels per day of refined petroleum products, with demand that year averaging 20,160 barrels per day. There were no record imports or production of natural gas in 2002.

28 INDUSTRY

Macedonia's industries are centered around Skopje. Steel and chemical production, along with buses, textiles, food processing, tobacco, furniture, and ceramics are important industries. In 1995, the government began privatizing its 25 largest public industries. Industry accounted for 31% of GDP in 2001. The Kosovo crisis of 1999 severely disrupted the Macedonian economy, as did the ethnic Albanian armed insurgency in Macedonia in 2001.

In 2004, industry made up 26% of the GDP, down from 32.8% in 2003. Services benefited from this loss, growing from a 55.5% participation in the GDP in 2003, to 62.8% in 2004. Agriculture remained relatively stable, at about 11%. The industrial production growth rate in 2004 was consequently 0%, indicating a loss of momentum for the industrial sector. Main industries were resource based and included coal, metallic chromium, lead, zinc, ferronickel, textiles, wood products, tobacco, food processing, buses, and steel. By 2005, industry showed signs of recovery, with the industrial output growth jumping to 8.2% in the first nine months of the year.

29 SCIENCE AND TECHNOLOGY

The Former Yugoslav Republic of Macedonia uses only low levels of technology for its agriculture and mining industries. Oil refining is performed by distillation only.

The Macedonian Academy of Sciences and Arts, founded in 1967 at Skopje, has sections of biological and medical sciences and of mathematical and technical sciences. The country also has an Association of Sciences and Arts, founded in 1960 at Bitola, as well as specialized learned societies concerned with physics, pharmacy, geology, medicine, mathematics and computers, veterinary surgery, engineering, forestry, and agriculture. Macedonia has research institutes dealing with geology, natural history, cotton, animal breeding, tobacco, animal husbandry, and water development.

The University of Skopje (founded in 1949) has faculties of civil engineering, agriculture, veterinary medicine, forestry, medicine, pharmacy, mechanical engineering, electrotechnical engineering, technology and metallurgy, natural and mathematical sciences, stomatology, and geology and mining. In 1987–97, science and engineering students accounted for 47% of university enrollment. The Natural History Museum of Macedonia (founded in 1926) is located in Skopje.

Macedonia in the period 1990–2001, had 387 scientists and engineers and 29 technicians per million people engaged in research and development (R&D). In 2002, Macedonia spent $34.212 million on R&D, or 0.68% of its GDP. Of that amount, government sources accounted for 76.3% of R&D spending, with foreign sources accounting for 8.6%; business accounted for 7.8%; and higher education 7.3%. High technology exports in 2002 totaled $9 million, or 1% of its manufactured exports.

30 DOMESTIC TRADE

The commercial and industrial center of the country is Skopje, with industries that include glass, beer, bricks, and tobacco. Prilep serves as the nation's agricultural center for tobacco and fruit. Kumanovu is an industrial center for canning and tobacco processing and a trading center for cattle, fruit, and liquor. Domestic commerce typically centers around an urban marketplace, where marketing of farm products is carried out. Formal trade of products and commodities through state enterprises has declined since independence. However, private traders do not always offer a consistent and reliable market outlet for producers.

31 FOREIGN TRADE

In 1999, exports amounted to $1.2 billion, of which manufactured goods accounted for an estimated 89%; agriculture, 9%; and mining, 2%. Imports in 1999 totaled $1.8 billion, of which machinery and transport equipment accounted for an estimated 20%; manufactured goods, 16%; food and live animals, 12%; chemicals, 10%; fuels and lubricants, 9%; other manufactured products, 5%; raw materials (excluding fuels), 3%; and beverages and tobacco, 2%.

In 2004, exports totaled $1.6 billion (FOB—Free on Board), while imports grew to $2.7 billion. Macedonia's main export partners were Serbia and Montenegro (which received 31.4% of total exports), Germany (19.9%), Greece (8.9%), Croatia (6.9%), and the United States (4.9%). Imports mainly came from Greece (15.4%), Germany (13.1%), Serbia and Montenegro (10.4%), Slovenia (8.6%), Bulgaria (8.1%), Turkey (6%), and Romania (4.7%).

The structure of the trade has changed dramatically since 1999. Over the course of only five years, Macedonia's export structure changed to: textiles and clothing (which accounted for 32.3% of all exports), iron and steel (24.2%), chemicals (4.8%), petroleum and petroleum products (4.5%), and tobacco (4.4%). Principal imports included: petroleum and petroleum products (10.2%), road vehicles (6.3%), industrial machinery (4.9%), meat and meat preparations (3.0%), and medical and pharmaceutical products.

32 BALANCE OF PAYMENTS

The US Central Intelligence Agency (CIA) reported that in 2002 the purchasing power parity of Macedonia's exports was $1 billion while imports totaled $1.6 billion resulting in a trade deficit of $600 million.

The International Monetary Fund (IMF) reported that in 2001 Macedonia had exports of goods totaling $1.15 billion and imports totaling $1.58 billion. The services credit totaled $234 million and debit $337 million.

Exports of goods and services totaled $1.7 billion in 2004, up from $1.4 billion in 2003. Imports grew from $2.1 billion in 2003, to $2.8 billion in 2004. The resource balance was on a negative upsurge, growing from -$0.7 billion in 2003, to -$1.1 billion in 2004. A similar trend was registered for the current account balance, which deteriorated from -$149 million in 2003, to -$414.8 million in 2004 (or -3.3% of the GDP). The national reserves (excluding gold) were $897 million in 2003, covering approximately five months of imports; in 2004, they grew to $905 million. Macedonia's balance of payment trade deficit was expected to decrease in 2005 as a result of export growth, especially of metals.

33 BANKING AND SECURITIES

In 1992, the National Bank of Macedonia was created to issue currency, conduct monetary polices, and regulate the banking sector of the country.

Commercial banks in Macedonia include the Komercijalna Banka and Scopanska Banka, both in Skopje. The currency unit is the Macedonia denar (DEN) introduced on 10 May 1993, at a rate

of 1:1,000 against the coupon. The central bank also introduced a floating rate for the denar against major currencies. There are no security exchanges in the country.

Under a five-year stabilization program agreed with the IMF, the government is focusing on reducing inflation, overhauling the financial system, and launching structural reforms. Despite the Greek blockade, the program met its fiscal targets in 1994 with the state deficit declining to 2.5% of GDP in 1994. Reform of the state banking system made progress in 1996, although banks are still lending to inefficient state enterprises. Privatization has made some progress with the privatization agency raising $8 million in revenue in 1994 through the sale of four large companies and 14 medium-sized and small companies.

The International Monetary Fund reports that in 2001, currency and demand deposits—an aggregate commonly known as M1—

Principal Trading Partners – Macedonia (2003)

(In millions of US dollars)

Country	Exports	Imports	Balance
World	1,363.3	2,299.9	-936.6
Germany	278.4	303.9	-25.5
Serbia and Montenegro	273.8	212.6	61.2
Greece	179.8	300.2	-120.4
Italy-San Marino-Holy See	95.4	122.6	-27.2
United States	72.8	56.5	16.3
Croatia	66.1	63.5	2.6
France-Monaco	54.7	51.5	3.2
Netherlands	46.8	49.1	-2.3
United Kingdom	35.1	38.6	-3.5
Turkey	32.8	78.8	-46.0

(…) data not available or not significant.

SOURCE: *2003 International Trade Statistics Yearbook*, New York: United Nations, 2004.

Balance of Payments – Macedonia (2003)

(In millions of US dollars)

Current Account		-278.5
Balance on goods		-851.5
Imports	-2,210.5	
Exports	1,359.0	
Balance on services		654.6
Balance on income		-32.4
Current transfers		607.9
Capital Account		-6.7
Financial Account		248.4
Direct investment abroad		-0.3
Direct investment in Macedonia		94.6
Portfolio investment assets		0.3
Portfolio investment liabilities		3.3
Financial derivatives		…
Other investment assets		12.2
Other investment liabilities		138.3
Net Errors and Omissions		90.4
Reserves and Related Items		-53.5

(…) data not available or not significant.

SOURCE: *Balance of Payment Statistics Yearbook 2004*, Washington, DC: International Monetary Fund, 2004.

were equal to $164.1 million. In that same year, M2—an aggregate equal to M1 plus savings deposits, small time deposits, and money market mutual funds—was $887.3 million. The discount rate, the interest rate at which the central bank lends to financial institutions in the short term, was 10.7%.

³⁴INSURANCE

In 1995, the Makedonija Insurance and Reinsurance Company was offering the following types of insurance: property, liability, life, accident, motor, fire, and marine.

³⁵PUBLIC FINANCE

The US Central Intelligence Agency (CIA) estimated that in 2005 Macedonia's central government took in revenues of approximately $2.1 billion and had expenditures of $2.2 billion. Revenues minus expenditures totaled approximately -$84 million. Public debt in 2005 amounted to 32.6% of GDP. Total external debt was $2.207 billion.

³⁶TAXATION

As of 2005, Macedonia had a 15% corporate tax rate, which was also applied to branch operations. Capital gains, interest and royalties are considered income and are taxed at the corporate rate. Dividends paid to resident companies are not considered income, if the dividends were paid out of taxable income. Dividends paid to individuals are taxed at the corporate rate, but are applied to only 50% of the gross dividend amount. Personal income taxes range from 1.28–2.17%. Payroll taxes include a 21.2% rate for the pension fund, a 9.2% rate for the health fund, a 1.6% employment tax, and a 0.5% additional health fund contribution. On 1 April 2000 a value-added tax (VAT) was introduced. As of 2005, the standard VAT rate was 18%. There is also a reduced rate of 5% applied to basic goods and services. Other taxes include excise taxes on petrol, fuel oil, alcoholic beverages, tobacco, and property taxes.

³⁷CUSTOMS AND DUTIES

Macedonia has adopted a duty-free import agreement with Slovenia, Croatia, and Serbia (as of October 1996). Importers pay only a border crossing tax for document handling. Macedonia is also seeking to establish a trade zone with Bulgaria and Albania. Tariffs, as of 2005, ranged from 0–30%, with the average at 10.5%, and were based on the item's cost, insurance and freight (CIF) value. However, products such as beverages, cereals, vegetables and fruit were subject to a 60% rate. The VAT is also applied to imports based on the CIF plus duty value. Corruption in the customs system discourages trade.

³⁸FOREIGN INVESTMENT

Macedonia's isolation, technological disadvantages, and penchant for political instability created a poor climate for potential foreign investors. In 1995, the government began restructuring and privatizing its largest state-owned companies. After 1997, inflows of foreign investment increased substantially.

The country has taken important steps towards attracting new foreign direct investment (FDI), and has created a legislative framework that does not discriminate between domestic investors and their foreign counterparts. In 2004, the Macedonian privatization process was almost complete, with residual shares still being owned by the government in a couple of key industries. By the end of 2005, the government planned to privatize the national electric company—ESM—and sell off its 48% participation in the telephone company.

After hitting a peak in 2001 (with capital in-flows totaling $445 million), when Hungary was the largest source of FDI, the rate of foreign investments slowed down in subsequent years, totaling $82 million in 2002, $98 million in 2003, and $104 million in the first three quarters of 2004. The biggest investing countries in 2004 were Switzerland (with $7.1 million invested), Greece ($6.6 million), and Slovenia ($1 million).

³⁹ECONOMIC DEVELOPMENT

In May 1994, the EBRD established a $10 million facility to guarantee Komercijalna Banka's designated correspondent banks against nonpayment under confirmed letters of credit. By securing credit facilities, the bank's clients are able to stimulate production and increase exports. In 1995, net resource flows from international financial institutions consisted of $43 million from the World Bank, $37 million from the International Monetary Fund (IMF), and $16 million from other institutions.

In 1995, the government began privatizing its largest state-owned industries. A total of 1,200 enterprises were to be privatized, 65% of them classified as small (fewer than 50 employees). The portion of a company's share capital, which is community-owned, is known as social capital; this forms the basis of the privatization process. In theory, social capital is owned by the company's employees. However, there are severe restrictions that make it nontransferable and hence valueless to the individual.

The Kosovo crisis of 1999 placed severe burdens on Macedonia's already-strained economy as an influx of Kosovar refugees flooded across the border and trade routes were disrupted. Fighting between government forces and ethnic Albanian rebels that began in February 2001 further disrupted the economy. Real GDP declined by 4.5% in 2001, and government spending mushroomed. Spending on security raised the general government deficit to 7.2% of GDP, compared with a surplus of 1.8% in 2000.

In 2003, the IMF approved a $28 million standby arrangement for Macedonia, which expired in June 2004. The loan was geared to support the government's economic program for fiscal stability following the 2001 crisis, to promote growth, improve the business climate, and improve living standards for Macedonians.

Although Macedonia's economy has been improving steadily, there still are a number of problems that need to be dealt with. Two of the most important issues are the rampant unemployment and an inflation rate that discourages exports. A 2005 World Bank report that looked at the business climate in 155 countries ranked Macedonia 81st in terms of the ease of conducting commercial operations. The government responded promptly to the results of this report and implemented a package of laws that would make it easier for entrepreneurs or investors to start a business. However, the 2006 business climate still had numerous weak spots that needed to be addressed through a concerted effort by the legislative.

⁴⁰SOCIAL DEVELOPMENT

Macedonia, historically the poorest of the former Yugoslav republics, has suffered further from the imposition of international sanctions against Serbia, the rising tide of refugees, and increasing unemployment. Social care is funded by the government to assist the disabled, elderly, unemployed, and poor. Maternity benefits are available for nine months, and women are guaranteed the right to return to work within two years after childbirth.

Although women have the same legal rights as men, the traditional cultures of both Christian and Muslim communities have limited their advancement in society. There are some professional women but generally women are not represented in the higher levels of professional or public life. Sexual harassment in the workplace is prevalent, especially in the private sector. Widespread violence against women in the home remains unpunished by authorities, and it is extremely rare for criminal charges to be filed against abusive husbands. In 2004 Macedonia submitted its first report to the UN Committee on the Elimination of Discrimination Against Women. Children, like adults, have been victims of internal conflict and ethnic violence. Resources are scarce to fund programs to benefit children.

Ethnic minorities, including Albanians and Turks, complain of widespread discrimination. Restrictive naturalization policies have left many Albanians without Macedonian citizenship, and therefore without voting rights. Abuse by police of prisoners and suspects is widespread, with most cases involving Roma, ethnic Albanians, or Kosovar refugees.

41 HEALTH

Following the breakup of the former Yugoslavia, the availability of health care statistics for Macedonia was hampered by internal hostilities. Separate health care data was slowly emerging from the new independent regions. Physicians in Macedonia are adequately trained, but there is a shortage of pharmaceuticals and medical equipment. Patients who are seriously ill will often go abroad for medical help.

As of 2002, the crude birth rate and overall mortality rate were estimated at, respectively, 13.4 and 7.7 per 1,000 people. There were two births per married woman of childbearing age during 1999. The infant mortality rate has been reduced from 54 per 1,000 live births in 1980 to 10.09 in 2005. The life expectancy at birth for the average Macedonian was 73.73 in 2005

The immunization rates for children under the age of one were as follows: diphtheria, whooping cough and tetanus, 87%; measles, 85%; and tuberculosis, 90%. The HIV/AIDS prevalence was 0.10 per 100 adults in 2003. As of 2004, there were approximately 200 people living with HIV/AIDS in the country. There were an estimated 100 deaths from AIDS in 2003.

42 HOUSING

During the years of the former Yugoslav SFR, there was a chronic shortage of housing in Macedonia and the other republics. Since independence, the ability to find an available apartment or condominium has improved. Federal banks have begun loan programs making it now possible to finance the construction of seasonal homes in the country or by resort areas. In the 1994, there were about 580,342 dwellings supporting about 501,963 households. There was an average of 3.85 people per household. In 2002, there were about 698,143 dwelling units supporting 564,296 households. The average number of people per household was 3.58.

43 EDUCATION

Public education at the primary level is compulsory for eight years, generally for students between the ages of 7 and 15. Elementary school covers these first eight years of study. This is followed by a four-year secondary program of general, technical, vocational, or special (arts) studies.

In 2001, about 28% of children between the ages of three and six were enrolled in some type of preschool program. Primary school enrollment in 2003 was estimated at about 91% of age-eligible students. In 2001, secondary school enrollment was about 81% of age-eligible students. Nearly all students complete their primary education. The student-to-teacher ratio for primary school was at about 20:1 in 2003; the ratio for secondary school was about 16:1.

At the postsecondary level, there are two universities: the Bitola University, which was founded in 1979, and the University of Skopje, founded in 1949. The language of instruction is Macedonian, and there are faculties of law, engineering, medicine, arts, science, physical education, architecture, and agriculture. In 2003, about 27% of the tertiary age population were enrolled in some type of higher education program; 24% of men and 32% of women. The adult literacy rate for 2004 was estimated at about 96.1%, with 98.2% for men and 94.1% for women.

As of 2003, public expenditure on education was estimated at 3.5% of GDP.

44 LIBRARIES AND MUSEUMS

The Kliment Ohridski National and University Library in Skopje (1944) holds over 1.5 million items and is the largest collection in the country. The District of Skopje Public Library has 953,000 volumes.

In Skopje are the Fine Arts Museum, the Museum of Contemporary Art, and the Museum of the City of Skopje. There are also several archaeological and historical museums. The National Museums, specializing in archeology and ethnology, are in Ohrid and Stip, and there is an Islamic Art museum in Bitola. In Strumica is the Institute for Protection of Cultural Monuments, Natural Rarities, and Museum.

45 MEDIA

In 2003, there were an estimated 271 mainline telephones for every 1,000 people. The same year, there were approximately 177 mobile phones in use for every 1,000 people.

Though most media are government owned, an independent television station, A-1, broadcasts from Skopje. Macedonian Radio and Television (MRTV) is the only public broadcaster in the country and has the widest range, reaching about 90% of the population. This government-owned station operates three national TV networks and one satellite network, as well as one radio station. In 2004, there were about 150 local radio and television stations registered in the country. In 2003, there were an estimated 205 radios for every 1,000 people. The number of television sets was unavailable in the same survey. In 2003, there were 100,000 Internet subscribers in the country.

Several daily newspapers are published in Skopje, as well as a number of periodicals. Newspapers in Albanian and a Turkish language paper are available nationally and subsidized by the government, including the Albanian-language *Flaka e Vlazermit*

(*Flame of Brotherhood*) and the Turkish language *Birlik*. In 1994 *Delo,* a new weekly with reportedly nationalistic leanings, began publication. As of 2002, the leading newspapers were *Nova Makedonia* (circulation 25,000) and *Vecer* (29,200).

The constitution forbids censorship and the government is said to respect this in practice. However, the government has restricted certain parts of the media during civil conflicts.

46 ORGANIZATIONS

The Chamber of Economy of Macedonia coordinates trade and commerce with the world.

The Macedonian Academy of Science, founded in 1967, coordinates and finances scientific research conducted in Macedonia. Macedonian Medical Association promotes research and education on health issues and works to establish common policies and standards in healthcare. There are several other associations dedicated to research and education for specific fields of medicine and particular diseases and conditions. There are professional associations representing other fields as well.

There are youth organizations affiliated with major political parties. There is also an active scouting association. The National Student Union of Macedonia is an umbrella organization representing youth groups involved in cultural, educational, and social activities. National women's organizations include Journalism About Women's and Children's Rights and Environment in Macedonia and the Union of Women's Organizations of the Republic of Macedonia.

There are national chapters of the Red Cross Society, Caritas, and Habitat for Humanity.

47 TOURISM, TRAVEL, AND RECREATION

Macedonia has very modest levels of tourist activity. Medieval monasteries and Orthodox churches are primary attractions. Turkish baths and bazaars can also be found. In the winter tourists are attracted to Popova Shapka, one of the most popular ski resorts in Macedonia. The city of Mavrovo, home to the Mavrovo National Park, has over 140 different bird species and over 45 different species of other animals making it attractive to hunters worldwide. The ski resorts, monasteries, and beautiful topography make Mavrovo one of the most visited cities in Macedonia. In 2000, there were about 224,000 tourist arrivals and tourism receipts totaled $37 million. The 6,636 hotel rooms had an occupancy rate of only 15% that year. A valid passport is required for entry into Macedonia. A visa is not required for tourist/business stays of up to 90 days.

In 2005, the US Department of State estimated the daily cost of staying in Macedonia at $230.

48 FAMOUS MACEDONIANS

Kiro Gligorov (b.1917) was president of Macedonia from 1991 to 1999. Boris Trajkovski (1956–2004) was president from 1999 to 2004. Trajovski died in a plane crash and was succeeded by Branko Crvenkovski (b.1962). Mother Teresa (Agnes Gonxha Bojaxhiu, 1910–1997) was from Skopje but left at age 17 to join a convent in Calcutta, India. In 1948, Mother Teresa left the convent to found the Missionaries of Charity. She won the Nobel Peace Prize in 1979.

Phillip II (382 BC–336 BC) was the father of Alexander the Great. During Philip II's reign of 359–336 BC, he established a federal system of Greek States. Macedonian Alexander the Great (356 BC–323 BC) founded an enormous empire that extended from Greece to northern India. Cassandar (353 BC–297 BC) succeeded Alexander the Great, and was king of Macedonia between 316 BC and 297 BC. To consolidate his power, Cassandar murdered Alexander's mother, widow, and son. Philip V (237 BC–179 BC) warred against the Romans and tried to rebuild the kingdom.

49 DEPENDENCIES

Macedonia has no territories or colonies.

50 BIBLIOGRAPHY

Ackermann, Alice. *Making Peace Prevail: Preventing Violent Conflict in Macedonia.* Syracuse, N.Y.: Syracuse University Press, 2000.

Allcock, John B. *Explaining Yugoslavia.* New York: Columbia University Press, 2000.

Civil-Military Relations in the Soviet and Yugoslav Successor States. Boulder, Colo.: Westview Press, 1996.

Danforth, Loring M. *The Macedonian Conflict: Ethnic Nationalism in a Transnational World.* Princeton, N.J.: Princeton University Press, 1995.

Frucht, Richard (ed.). *Eastern Europe: An Introduction to the People, Lands, and Culture.* Santa Barbara, Calif.: ABC-CLIO, 2005.

Generation in Jeopardy: Children in Central and Eastern Europe and the Former Soviet Union. Armonk, N.Y.: M. E. Sharpe, 1999.

Georgieva, Valentina and Sasha Konechni. *Historical Dictionary of the Republic of Macedonia.* Lanham, Md.: Scarecrow, 1998.

Pearson, Brenda. *Putting Peace into Practice: Can Macedonia's New Government Meet the Challenge?* Washington, D.C.: U.S. Institute of Peace, 2002.

Phillips, John. *Macedonia: Warlords and Rebels in the Balkans.* London: I. B. Tauris, 2002.

Poulton, Hugh. *Who Are the Macedonians?* Bloomington, Ind.: Indiana University Press, 1995.

Shea, John. *Macedonia and Greece: The Struggle to Define a New Balkan Nation.* Jefferson, N.C.: McFarland, 1997.

Vacalopoulos, Apostolos E. *Contemporary Ethnological Problems in the Balkans.* Thessaloniki: Society for Macedonian Studies, 1991.

MALTA

The Republic of Malta
Repubblika Ta' Malta

CAPITAL: Valletta

FLAG: The national flag consists of two equal vertical stripes, white at the hoist and red at the fly, with a representation of the Maltese Cross, edged with red, in the canton of the white stripe.

ANTHEM: *L'Innu Malti (The Maltese Hymn).*

MONETARY UNIT: The Maltese lira (LM) consists of 100 cents, with each cent divided into 10 mils. There are coins of 2, 3, and 5 mils and of 1, 2, 5, 10, 25, and 50 cents, and notes of 2, 5, 10, and 20 lira. Gold and silver coins of 1, 2, 4, 5, 10, 20, 25, 50, and 100 lira also are in circulation. ML1 = $2.70270 (or $1 = ML0.37) as of 2005.

WEIGHTS AND MEASURES: The metric system is the legal standard, but some local measures are still in use.

HOLIDAYS: New Year's Day, 1 January; National Day, 31 March; May Day, 1 May; Assumption, 15 August; Republic Day, 13 December; Christmas, 25 December. Movable holidays include Good Friday.

TIME: 1PM = noon GMT.

¹LOCATION, SIZE, AND EXTENT

Malta lies in the central Mediterranean Sea, 93 km (58 mi) south of Sicily and 290 km (180 mi) from the nearest point of the North African mainland. There are three main islands—Malta, Gozo to the NW, and Comino between them—as well as two small uninhabited islands, Cominotto and Filfla. Extending for 45 km (28 mi) SE–NW and 13 km (8 mi) NE–SW, Malta's total area is 316 sq km (122 sq mi)—Malta, 245.7 sq km (94.9 sq mi); Gozo, 67.1 sq km (25.9 sq mi); Comino, 2.8 sq km (1.1 sq mi). Comparatively, the area occupied by Malta is slightly less than twice the size of Washington, DC. The total coastline is 252.81 km (157 mi).

Malta's capital city, Valletta, is located on the east coast of the island of Malta.

²TOPOGRAPHY

The islands of Malta are a rocky formation (chiefly limestone) running from east to northeast, with clefts that form deep harbors, bays, creeks, and rocky coves. The highest point of the nation is Ta'Dmejrek (253 m/803 ft), located on the southwest shore of Malta. Beaches range from rocky to sandy terrain. The northern beach of Ramla Bay is known for its red sands.

³CLIMATE

The climate is typically Mediterranean, with fairly hot, dry summers and rainy, mild winters. The average winter temperature is 9°C (48°F); the average summer temperature, 31°C (88°F). Rainfall occurs mostly between November and January and averages about 56 cm (22 in) per year.

⁴FLORA AND FAUNA

The islands are almost treeless. Vegetation is sparse and stunted. Carob and fig are endemic and the grape, bay, and olive have been cultivated for centuries. There are some rock plants.

The weasel, hedgehog, and bat are native to Malta. White rabbits and mice have been introduced. Many types of turtles, tortoises, and butterflies and several varieties of lizard also are found. Common varieties of Mediterranean fish, as well as the seal and porpoise, inhabit the surrounding waters.

⁵ENVIRONMENT

Malta's most significant environmental problems include inadequate water supply, deforestation, and the preservation of its wildlife. The country's extremely limited fresh water resources have led to increasing dependence on desalination. The nation's agriculture suffers from lack of adequate water for crops due to limited rainfall.

Malta was one of the first countries to ratify the 1976 Barcelona Convention for the protection of the Mediterranean from pollution. Malta's government has made recent efforts to control environmental damage including passage of the Environmental Protection Act of 1991 and the creation of a Ministry for the Environment. The Ministry of Health and Environment belongs to the International Union for the Conservation of Nature and Natural Resources. In cooperation with the World Wildlife Fund, the Ghadira wetland area was made a permanent nature reserve in 1980.

According to a 2006 report issued by the International Union for Conservation of Nature and Natural Resources (IUCN), threatened species included 1 type of mammal, 10 species of birds,

11 species of fish, and 3 types of mollusks. Endangered species include the slender-billed curlew, Mediterranean monk seal, hawksbill turtle, and Atlantic ridley.

6 POPULATION

The population of Malta in 2005 was estimated by the United Nations (UN) at 405,000, which placed it at number 165 in population among the 193 nations of the world. In 2005, approximately 13% of the population was over 65 years of age, with another 18% of the population under 15 years of age. There were 99 males for every 100 females in the country. According to the UN, the annual population rate of change for 2005–10 was expected to be 0.2%, a rate the government viewed as satisfactory. The projected population for the year 2025 was 396,000. The population density was 1,266 per sq km (3,278 per sq mi), which makes it one of the most densely populated countries in the world.

The UN estimated that 91% of the population lived in urban areas in 2005, and that urban areas were growing at an annual rate of 0.56%. The capital city, Valletta, had a population of 83,000 in that year. Other major cities (and their estimated populations) include Birkirkara (25,000), Qormi (19,900), and Sliema (14,000).

7 MIGRATION

High population density and unemployment have led to emigration. Most foreigners living in Malta are British nationals and their dependents. Malta has no national refugee law, and all recognized refugees in Malta are resettled in third countries. Since 1983, Malta has received some 2,400 asylum applications. Of these, 1,860 have been resettled. The total number of migrants in 2000 was 9,000. In 2004 refugees in Malta numbered 1,558. There were 141 asylum seekers in that same year. *Migration News* reported that Malta had allowed asylum seekers to stay up to three years, but recent influxes of boatloads of migrants from Africa resulted in migrants held in detention centers, and Malta's threat in August 2005 to suspend its obligations under the 1951 Geneva refugee convention. In 2005 the net migration rate was 2.06 migrants per 1,000 population. The government views the migration levels as satisfactory. In 2003 remittances to Malta were $633,760.

8 ETHNIC GROUPS

Most Maltese are believed to be descended from the ancient Carthaginians and Phoenicians, but there are strong elements of Italian and other Mediterranean stock. A few thousand people are of Arab, African, or Eastern European origin.

9 LANGUAGES

Maltese, a Semitic language with Romance-language assimilations, is the national language and the language of the courts. Maltese and English are both official languages.

10 RELIGIONS

Roman Catholicism is the official state religion, but there is freedom of worship for all faiths. An estimated 95% of the population is Roman Catholic, with about 63% actively practicing. Most of the Protestants in the country are not Maltese; British retirees and vacationers from other countries tend to form the Protestant population. Jehovah's Witnesses, the Church of Jesus Christ of Latter-day Saints, the Fellowship of Evangelical Churches, and the Bible Baptist Church have active groups on the island. There is one Muslim mosque and one Jewish congregation. Zen Buddhism and the Baha'i Faith are also represented.

11 TRANSPORTATION

Malta has no railways. In 2003, there were 2,254 km (1,402 mi) of roadways, of which 1,973 km (1,227 mi) were paved. Passenger cars in 2003 totaled 200,509, while there were 44,586 commercial vehicles in use that same year. Ferry and hydrofoil services connect Malta and Gozo.

The harbors of Valletta, among the finest in the Mediterranean, are a port of call for many lines connecting northwestern Europe and the Middle and Far East. Roughly 3,000 ships dock at Valletta each year. As of 2005, a total of 1,140 vessels of 1,000 GRT or more totaling 27,208,819 GRT were registered in Malta (a flag of convenience registry with ships from 49 countries). There was one airport in 2004, the principal airport at Luqa. A new terminal is designed to handle 2.2 million passengers per year (or 2,000 at any given moment). The national air carrier is Malta Airlines. In 2001 (the latest year for which data was available), 1,405,200 passengers were carried on scheduled domestic and international airline flights.

12 HISTORY

The strategic importance of the island of Malta was recognized in the time of the Phoenicians, whose occupation of Malta was followed by that of the Greeks, the Carthaginians, and the Romans. The apostle Paul was shipwrecked at Malta in AD 58, and the islanders were converted to Christianity within two years. With the official split of the Roman Empire in 395, Malta was assigned to Byzantium, and in 870 it fell under the domination of the Saracens. In 1090, it was taken by Count Roger of Normandy, and thereafter it was controlled by the rulers of Sicily—Norman and, later, Aragonese. The Emperor Charles V granted it in 1530 to the Knights of St. John, who had been driven from Rhodes by the Turks. The Knights surrendered Malta to Napoleon in 1798. Two years later, the British ousted the French garrison, with the aid of a revolt by the Maltese people. British possession of Malta was confirmed in 1814 by the Treaty of Paris.

During almost the entire 19th century, a British military governor ruled the colony. After World War I, during which the Maltese remained loyal to Britain, discontent and difficulties increased. The 1921 constitution granted a considerable measure of self-government, but political tensions reemerged, and the constitution, after having twice been suspended, was revoked in 1936. A new constitution in 1939 reinstated Malta as a British crown colony. In World War II the Maltese again remained loyal to the United Kingdom, and for gallantry under heavy fire during the German-Italian siege (1940–43), the entire population was awarded the George Cross.

Substantial self-government was restored in 1947. The Maltese, however, carried on negotiations with the United Kingdom for complete self-government, except in matters of defense and foreign affairs. In August 1962, Prime Minister Borg Olivier requested the United Kingdom to grant Malta independence, and Malta became a sovereign and independent nation within the Commonwealth of Nations on 21 September 1964. At the same time, mutual defense and financial agreements were signed with the United Kingdom. Under subsequent accords negotiated between 1970 and 1979, British troops withdrew from Malta, and the NATO naval base on the main island was closed.

On 13 December 1974, Malta formally adopted a republican form of government, and the former governor-general, Sir Anthony Mamo, became the first president. Dom Mintoff, leader of the Malta Labor Party and prime minister from 1971 through 1984, instituted socialist measures and initiated a nonaligned policy in foreign affairs. Although the Labor Party narrowly lost the popular vote in the 1981 elections, it retained its parliamentary majority; to protest the gerrymandering that allegedly made this possible, the opposition Nationalist Party boycotted parliament, and strikes and civil violence ensued. In January 1987, a new law guaranteed that, following future elections, the new government would be formed by the party that won a majority of the popular vote.

On 23 November 1985 Malta became the scene of one of the deadliest hijackings in history, when an Egypt Air flight commandeered by three Palestinian terrorists was forced to land there. In a gun battle, an Egyptian sky marshal on the plane shot and killed the hijackers' leader, and the pilot landed the plane in Malta. After an Israeli and an American passenger were executed, Egyptian commandos set off an explosive charge and rushed the plane, but 57 passengers and another hijacker died in the raid from smoke inhalation, explosive wounds, or gunshots. The surviving hijacker, Omar Mohammed Ali Rezaq, was released from prison by Maltese authorities in 1993 under a general amnesty program. He was later apprehended in Nigeria and extradited to the United States for air piracy, and convicted and sentenced in 1996.

In May 1987, the Nationalist Party won a popular majority but only 31 of 65 seats in parliament. In accordance with the new law, the Nationalists were given four additional seats, for a total of 35 in an expanded 69-seat parliament, and the Nationalist Eddie Fenech Adami became prime minister, replacing the Laborite Carmelo Mifsud Bonnici. The Nationalists were returned to power in February 1992 with a slightly higher majority. Eddie Fenech Adami remained prime minister. Vincent Tabone, president, had been elected in 1989.

Maltese politics have revolved around foreign policy issues, in particular, Malta's relationship with Europe. The Nationalist Party government has been a strong proponent of EU membership. In July 1990, Malta applied for full membership in the European Union. However, after the Labor Party won the 1996 elections, the government's stance shifted towards maintaining neutrality. The Labor government also adopted economic policies, such as raising utility rates, that alienated both the electorate and elements within its own party, which withdrew their support for Prime Minister Alfred Sant. He called new elections three years ahead of schedule, in September 1998, and the Nationalist Party won a majority in a vote seen at least partly as a referendum on the European Union membership question. In March 1999, Guido de Marco of the Nationalist Party was elected president by the House of Representatives. Having regained the post of prime minister, NP leader Fenech Adami moved to reactivate Malta's EU membership application and adopted policies—such as the reimposition of a controversial value-added tax—intended to pave the way for membership approval. Malta was one of 10 new candidate countries formally invited to join the European Union in December 2002. Malta held its referendum on EU membership on 8 March

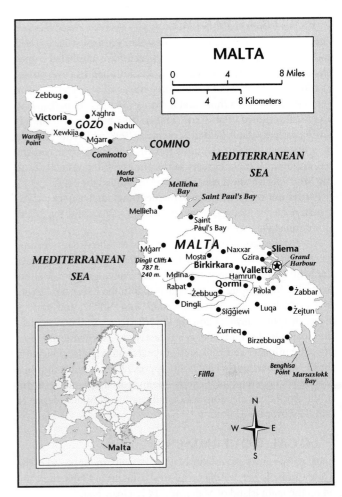

LOCATION: 35°48′ to 36°N; 14°10′30″ to 14°35′ E. TERRITORIAL SEA LIMIT: 12 miles.

2003, with 53.6% voting in favor of joining the body versus 46.4% against. Malta became an official member on 1 May 2004.

Elections were held on 12 April 2003, resulting in a win for the Nationalist Party (35 seats); the Labor Party received 30 seats. The next scheduled elections for the legislature were to take place in April 2008. On 29 March 2004, the House of Representatives elected a new president, Eddie Fenech Adami; Lawrence Gonzi, former deputy prime minister, took over the post of prime minister. The next presidential elections were scheduled to take place in 2009.

¹³GOVERNMENT

The Malta independence constitution came to force on 21 September 1964. Ten years later, Malta became a republic, while remaining within the Commonwealth of Nations. The unicameral parliament, the House of Representatives, consists of 65 members elected for a five-year term by universal adult suffrage (18 years of age and over), under a system of proportional representation. Additional seats may be allocated until a majority of one seat is obtained.

The House elects the head of state, the president of the republic, who holds office for five years. The president appoints the prime minister and, on the latter's advice, the other members of the cabinet. The prime minister, who is the leader of the majority party, is responsible for general direction and control of the government.

[14]POLITICAL PARTIES

There are two major political parties, the Nationalist Party (NP) and the Malta Labor Party (MLP), which have alternated in political power. The Nationalist Party was returned to government in 1987 after 16 years of Labor Party rule, and won reelection in February 1992 with a three-seat majority (34 to 31) in parliament. The MLP regained control in October 1996 but lost it again following early elections held in September 1998, which the NP won by a five-seat margin. Elections held in April 2003 returned the NP to power; it took 35 seats in the House of Representatives to the MLP's 30. The next elections were scheduled for 2008.

Parties not represented in parliament include Democratic Alternative (AD), Malta Democratic Party (PDM), and the Malta Communist Party (PKM).

After the elections of 1996, MLP leader Alfred Sant became prime minister after a narrow upset victory (official results gave the MLP 50.72% of the vote). The MLP campaigned for Maltese neutrality by pledging to stop efforts to join the European Union, to end Malta's associate membership with NATO, and to seek closer ties with Libya. Following the NP victory in the 1998 election, party leader Eddie Fenech Adami was returned to the post of prime minister and took steps to reactivate Malta's application for EU membership. When voters approved EU membership in a March 2003 referendum, Fenech Adami looked upon the NP win in the April 2003 elections as a confirmation of Malta's desire to join the European Union.

[15]LOCAL GOVERNMENT

Local government was established in 1993 with the approval of the Local Councils Act, setting up 68 local councils in Malta; there are 54 on the main island of Malta, and 14 in Gozo.

[16]JUDICIAL SYSTEM

The superior courts consist of a Constitutional Court (with the power to review laws and executive acts), two courts of appeal, the civil court, court of magistrates, criminal court, and special tribunals. The president, on the advice of the prime minister, appoints the chief justice and 16 judges. Retirement is at age 65 for judges and age 60 for magistrates. The judiciary operates in an independent manner. Defendants in criminal cases have the right to counsel of choice. Indigent defendants are afforded court-appointed counsel at public expense.

The constitution guarantees the right to free speech, assembly and association. Trade unions are legal and limits on the right to strike were eased in 2002. However, the law permits compulsory arbitration to be held even if it is requested by only one of the parties involved, this is against the International Labor Organization's principles.

Divorce is illegal on the island and violence against women continues to be a problem. Malta is a member of most international organizations including the UN and the WTO.

[17]ARMED FORCES

The armed forces of Malta numbered 2,237 in 2005 and were divided into three regiments. Malta's defense budget in 2005 totaled $48.5 million. Equipment included eight patrol/coastal vessels, two transport aircraft, and seven utility helicopters. Italy has 49 military personnel stationed in Malta.

[18]INTERNATIONAL COOPERATION

Malta joined the United Nations on 1 December 1964 and participates in ECE and several nonregional specialized agencies, such as the FAO, IAEA, World Bank, ILO, UNESCO, UNIDO, and the WHO. Malta is also a member of the Commonwealth of Nations, the Council of Europe, the European Bank for Reconstruction and Development, the Alliance of Small Island States (AOSIS), and the OSCE. Malta joined the European Union in 2004. The country is an observer affiliate in the Western European Union. Malta is a part of the Nonaligned Movement. The nation also participates in the Nuclear Suppliers Group (London Group) and the Organization for the Prohibition of Chemical Weapons.

In environmental cooperation, Malta is part of the Basel Convention, Conventions on Biological Diversity and Air Pollution, Ramsar, CITES, the London Convention, the Kyoto Protocol, the Montréal Protocol, MARPOL, the Nuclear Test Ban Treaty, and the UN Conventions on the Law of the Sea, Climate Change, and Desertification.

[19]ECONOMY

Malta has few natural resources besides limestone. Agriculture is limited by the rocky nature of the islands, and most food must be imported. Industrial raw materials are lacking and also must be imported. Until 1964, the dominant factor in the economy was the presence of British military forces; with the withdrawal of UK military personnel by 1979, the dockyards were converted to commercial use. Malta's economy now relies on light industry, tourism, and other service industries, in addition to shipbuilding, maintenance, and repairs. The government holds shares in a variety of enterprises, including joint ventures. A stock exchange opened in 1992.

In 2001 GNP per capita (purchasing power parity) was $15,000. That same year, GDP real growth was estimated at 4%. Agriculture contributed 3% to GDP, industry amounted to 23%, while services were 74%. Malta became a full member of the European Union in May 2004.

The country's economic performance in recent years has been anything but spectacular. While in 2002, the GDP registered a modest growth rate of 2.2%, in 2003 it fell to -1.8%, and recuperated to 1.4% in 2004; in 2005, the economy was expected to grow by 1.5%. Inflation has been kept stable at around 2.5%. The unemployment rate was on the rise, growing from 4.7% in 2002, to 5.7% in 2003, and 7.2% in 2004.

[20]INCOME

The US Central Intelligence Agency (CIA) reports that in 2005 Malta's gross domestic product (GDP) was estimated at $7.5 billion. The CIA defines GDP as the value of all final goods and services produced within a nation in a given year and computed on the basis of purchasing power parity (PPP) rather than value as measured on the basis of the rate of exchange based on current dollars. The per capita GDP was estimated at $18,800. The annual growth rate of GDP was estimated at 1.4%. The average inflation rate in 2005 was 2.8%. It was estimated that agriculture accounted for 3% of GDP, industry 23%, and services 74%.

According to the World Bank, in 2003 remittances from citizens working abroad totaled $1 million or about $3 per capita.

21 LABOR

Malta's workforce in 2005 was estimated at 160,000. In 2005 it was estimated that services accounted for 75% of employment, while 22% were engaged in industry and the remaining 3% in agriculture. The unemployment rate in 2005 was estimated at 7.8%.

Labor is highly organized in Malta, and about 63% of Malta's workers were unionized in 2002. As of that year there were 38 registered trade unions. The largest union, the General Worker's Union, although independent, is informally associated with the Labor Party. The General Workers' Union was integrated with the Socialist Labor Party until 1992, when this affiliation was formally ended. Although certain compulsory arbitration and mediation provisions limit the right to strike, workers still enjoy a broad right to strike including antidiscrimination provisions to protect striking workers' employment. Comprehensive collective bargaining is practiced.

The legal minimum working age is 16, and this is effectively enforced by the government. The standard workweek is 40 hours but workers in some trades can work up to 45 hours per week. Occupational safety and health standards are set by law but enforcement is uneven and accidents remain frequent. In 2002, the weekly minimum wage was $112 for adults.

22 AGRICULTURE

Agriculture is carried out in small fields, consisting usually of strips of soil between rocks, and is characterized to a large extent by terracing. The total area under cultivation was about 11,000 hectares (27,200 acres) in 2003. Most farms are small. Wheat, barley, and grapes are the principal crops for domestic consumption, while potatoes, onions, wine, cut flowers, seeds, and fruit are the chief export crops. The total value of agricultural crops exported in 2004 was estimated at $76 million, while agricultural imports amounted to nearly $400.3 million that year.

23 ANIMAL HUSBANDRY

Malta's livestock population in 2005 included 17,900 head of cattle, 73,000 pigs, 14,900 sheep, 5,400 goats, and 1,000,000 poultry. Total meat production in 2005 was 18,838 tons, half of it pork.

24 FISHING

Fishing is primarily for local consumption. In 2003, the total catch was 2,019 tons. Principal species included gilthead seabream, European sea bass, dolphinfish, and bluefin tuna. Exports of fish products were valued at $18.8 million in 2003.

25 FORESTRY

There are no forests on the islands. In 2004, $85 million in forest products were imported.

26 MINING

In 2004, Malta produced 6,000 cu m of salt, obtained in the desalination of sea water; 20 hard limestone quarries yielded 1.2 million cu m of limestone. The country also produced small amounts of cement, fertilizer, lime and plaster. The mining sector accounted for less than 0.5% of GDP, and the broader mineral industry economy depended mainly on trade and the storage of crude oil, refinery products, and other nonfuel mineral commodities for transshipment.

27 ENERGY AND POWER

Malta, with no proven reserves of oil, natural gas, nor any refining capacity, is totally dependent on imported fuel for its energy requirements.

In 2002, imports of petroleum products averaged 17,980 barrels per day, while demand came to 18,050 barrels per day. There were no imports of natural gas or coal in 2002.

Electricity is the main source of power. In 2002, thermal power stations on the main island made up Malta's total installed capacity of 0.570 million kW. Production of electrical energy that year was 1.929 billion kWh, of which 100% was generated from fossil fuels. Consumption of electricity was 1.794 billion kWh. Since 1995, the Maltese government has been exploring offshore areas for crude oil with the help of foreign companies such as Amoco, Royal Dutch Shell, and Nimir of Saudi Arabia.

28 INDUSTRY

Malta's principal industries are shipbuilding, maintenance and repairs, food processing, electronics, footwear, and textiles and clothing. Other products include beverages, tobacco products, lace, metals, rubber products, and plastic goods. Total industrial production amounted to 26% of GDP in 1999, the most recent year for which figures are available. The manufacturing sector grew by 17% from 1995–99. As of 2002, Malta's manufacturing sector was seen to be benefiting from the global economic downturn. Some foreign-owned companies closed operations elsewhere in the world and concentrated a degree of production in Malta, which was considered a competitive location for manufacturing activity. Manufacturing output rose 3% in 2001.

In 2003, industry made up 23% of the overall GDP, and was estimated to employ about the same percentage of the labor force; agriculture represented 3% of the GDP, while services came in first with 74%.

29 SCIENCE AND TECHNOLOGY

Malta's technological development has been confined largely to the shipbuilding and repair industry and the manufacture of electronic computer parts. The University of Malta has faculties of dental surgery, mechanical and electrical engineering, medicine and surgery, and science. In 1988, research and development expenditures amounted to 10,000 lira; 5 technicians and 34 scientists and engineers were engaged in research and development. The

Agrarian Society founded in 1844 is headquartered in Valletta. The Chamber of Architects and Civil Engineers is headquartered in St. Andrews. In 2000 (the latest year for which data was available), Malta spent $5.382 million on research and development.

30 DOMESTIC TRADE

Valletta is the commercial center of Malta. Most large importers prefer to distribute goods through their own shops. Small retail establishments predominate with a few larger supermarkets and outlet stores springing up in the past few years. Billboards, newspapers, radio, and television are the main advertising media.

Shopping hours are from 9 AM to 1 PM and from 3 to 7 PM. Banks are open from 8:30 AM to 2 PM, Monday through Thursday, and from 8:30 AM to 3:30 PM on Friday. Some bank branches are open on Saturdays from 8:30 AM to 12 NOON. Businesses and industries are open on weekdays from 8:30 AM to 5:30 PM and on Saturdays from 8 AM to 1 PM. Most establishments are closed on Sundays and many places have shorter hours during the summer months.

31 FOREIGN TRADE

Because it depends on external sources for much of its food, fuel, raw materials, and manufactured articles, Malta imports considerably more than it exports.

Most of Malta's commodity exports are electronic microcircuits (62%). Other export commodities include clothes (5.9%), refined petroleum products (4.4%), and toys (4.3%).

In 2004, Malta's exports totaled $2.6 billion (FOB—Free on Board), while imports grew to $3.4 billion (FOB). Its main export partners were the United States (which received 15.7% of total exports), France (15.5%), Singapore (14.5%), United Kingdom (11.2%), and Germany (10.8%). Imports included machinery and transport equipment, manufactured and semi-manufactured goods, food, drink, and tobacco, and they mainly came from Italy (25.4%), France (13.1%), United Kingdom (12%), Germany (8.9%), the United States (5.2%), and Singapore (4.1%).

32 BALANCE OF PAYMENTS

Traditionally, Malta has had a large trade deficit because it must import most of its food and raw materials. The expansion of industry and the improvement of living standards in recent years have further increased the deficit, which is made up by other foreign receipts in the form of tourist revenues, transfers, and financial assistance, formerly from the United Kingdom and more recently from Italy and Libya. Malta's outstanding debt stood at close to $2 billion by the end of 1999.

The US Central Intelligence Agency (CIA) reported that in 2001 the purchasing power parity of Malta's exports was $2 billion while imports totaled $2.8 billion resulting in a trade deficit of $800 million.

The International Monetary Fund (IMF) reported that in 2001 Malta had exports of goods totaling $2 billion and imports totaling $2.5 billion. The services credit totaled $1.11 billion and debit $791 million.

Exports of goods and services continued to grow in the following years, reaching $2.5 billion in 2003, and $2.7 billion in 2004. Imports followed a similar path, totaling $3.2 billion in 2003, and $3.6 billion in 2004. The resource balance was consequently neg-

ative in both years, at around -$700 million in 2003 and -$900 million in 2004. The current account balance was on a downward path, dropping to -$274 million in 2003, and -$543 million in 2004. Reserves of foreign exchange and gold reached $2.9 billion in 2004, covering more than nine months of imports.

33 BANKING AND SECURITIES

In June 1968, activities of the Currency Board were transferred to the new Central Bank of Malta. The Central Bank is responsible for the regulation of the banking system, the money supply, the issue of currency, and the administration of exchange control. The Central Bank manages the official external reserves and advises the Minister of Finance regarding the exchange rate of the Maltese lira. The Maltese lira is calculated on the basis of a currency basket, which currently consists of the ECU, pound sterling, and

Principal Trading Partners – Malta (2001)

(In millions of US dollars)

Country	Exports	Imports	Balance
World	1,958.8	2,726.8	-768.0
United States	388.0	315.3	72.7
Germany	255.8	238.9	16.9
Singapore	230.9	182.3	48.6
France-Monaco	182.8	409.3	-226.5
United Kingdom	169.5	273.5	-104.0
Switzerland-Liechtenstein	132.4	37.0	95.4
Bunkers, ship stores	127.5	...	127.5
Italy-San Marino-Holy See	67.4	543.8	-476.4
Belgium	60.9	34.0	26.9
Japan	58.5	58.3	0.2

(…) data not available or not significant.

SOURCE: *2003 International Trade Statistics Yearbook*, New York: United Nations, 2004.

Balance of Payments – Malta (2003)

(In millions of US dollars)

Current Account		**-270.7**
Balance on goods		-689.2
Imports	-3,194.1	
Exports	2,504.9	
Balance on services		435.6
Balance on income		37.3
Current transfers		-54.3
Capital Account		**6.3**
Financial Account		**166.4**
Direct investment abroad		-23.7
Direct investment in Malta		309.5
Portfolio investment assets		-1,545.7
Portfolio investment liabilities		-10.5
Financial derivatives		25.1
Other investment assets		-38.9
Other investment liabilities		1,450.6
Net Errors and Omissions		**241.8**
Reserves and Related Items		**-144.0**

(…) data not available or not significant.

SOURCE: *Balance of Payment Statistics Yearbook 2004*, Washington, DC: International Monetary Fund, 2004.

Public Finance – Malta (2000)

(In millions of liri, central government figures)

Revenue and Grants	**532.77**	**100.0%**
Tax revenue	371.85	69.8%
Social contributions	94.97	17.8%
Grants	9.55	1.8%
Other revenue	56.4	10.6%
Expenditures	**623.77**	**100.0%**
General public services	112.28	18.0%
Defense	10.23	1.6%
Public order and safety	24.15	3.9%
Economic affairs	86.8	13.9%
Environmental protection	1.78	0.3%
Housing and community amenities	15.77	2.5%
Health	71.12	11.4%
Recreational, culture, and religion	9.52	1.5%
Education	72.3	11.6%
Social protection	219.82	35.2%

(…) data not available or not significant.

SOURCE: *Government Finance Statistics Yearbook 2004*, Washington, DC: International Monetary Fund, 2004.

US dollar. Foreign reserves, excluding gold, totaled $1,605 million at the end of 1995. There are four commercial banks—the Bank of Valletta, HSBC Bank Malta, Lombard Bank Malta, and APS Bank—as well as the National Savings Bank.

In November 1995, Midland Bank (United Kingdom) became the first foreign bank to be granted a license to operate in the domestic market. In 1999, Hong Kong and Shanghai Banking Corporation (HSBC) acquired 67.1% of the shares of Mid-Med. The bank was subsequently renamed HSBC Bank Malta and became the largest bank operating on the island. Six international banking institutions are established in Malta: Turkiye Garanti Bankas, First Austrian Bank Malta, First International Merchant Bank, Izola Bank, Bank of Valletta International, and HSBC Bank Malta. Total assets/liabilities of the deposit-money banks stood at LM1.88 billion in 1995, while the assets/liabilities of domestic and international banking institutions amounted to LM155 million and LM407.7 million, respectively.

The International Monetary Fund reports that in 2001, currency and demand deposits—an aggregate commonly known as M1—were equal to $1.4 billion. In that same year, M2—an aggregate equal to M1 plus savings deposits, small time deposits, and money market mutual funds—was $6.1 billion. The discount rate, the interest rate at which the central bank lends to financial institutions in the short term, was 4.25%.

Turnover at the Malta Stock Exchange dropped sharply to LM75.8 million ($70 million) in 2002, a fall of LM93.7 million compared with levels in 2001. Total market capitalization in 2002 was LM1.6 billion. In 1994 the Malta International Business Authority became the Malta Financial Services Center (MFSC), responsible for the regulation and registration of financial services provided in and from Malta.

34 INSURANCE

All customary types of insurance are available. Many foreign insurance companies have representatives in Malta. In 2003, the val-

ue of all direct insurance premiums written totaled $235 million, of which life insurance premiums accounted for $118 million. For that same year, Middlesea Valletta was Malta's top life insurer, with gross written life insurance premiums of $58.4 million.

35 PUBLIC FINANCE

The principal sources of recurrent revenues are income taxes, and customs and excise taxes. Tourism is steadily increasing as an important segment of the economy, although the 11 September terrorist attacks put a damper on it. Malta has developed a fairly high budget deficit in recent years, and fiscal policy has been dedicated to reversing the situation. Public debt grew from 24% of GDP in 1990 to 56% in 1999, but by 2000 it had been brought down to just 6.6% of GDP.

The US Central Intelligence Agency (CIA) estimated that in 2005 Malta's central government took in revenues of approximately $2.5 billion and had expenditures of $2.7 billion. Revenues minus expenditures totaled approximately -$200 million. Total external debt was $130 million.

The International Monetary Fund (IMF) reported that in 2000, the most recent year for which it had data, central government revenues were LM532.77 million and expenditures were LM623.77 million. The value of revenues was us$2,331 million and expenditures us$2,722 million, based on an exchange rate for 2000 of us$1 = LM0.22851 as reported by the IMF. Government outlays by function were as follows: general public services, 18.0%; defense, 1.6%; public order and safety, 3.9%; economic affairs, 13.9%; environmental protection, 0.3%; housing and community amenities, 2.5%; health, 11.4%; recreation, culture, and religion, 1.5%; education, 11.6%; and social protection, 35.2%.

36 TAXATION

In 1999, the ruling Nationalist government announced that it would raise taxes in an effort to bring the budget in line. An integral part of the new package would be measures to combat tax evasion, a phenomena that Finance Minister John Dalli characterized as a "national sport." In 1998, one of the Nationalist's first steps was the reintroduction of the value-added tax (VAT) that the previous Labor government dismantled. As of 2005, the corporate tax rate was a flat 35% and was the only tax imposed on company profits. Generally, capital gains are taxed as income for both companies and individuals. However gains received from securities listed on the Malta Stock Exchange are exempt. Dividends paid out of resident company profits that have already been taxed at the 35% rate are not taxed further at the individual level. However, dividends paid out of untaxed income to a resident are subject to a 15% withholding tax. Dividends paid out of company income that was taxed below the 35% rate are subject to a withholding tax that is the difference between the current and lower rates.

Individual incomes were taxed according to a progressive schedule with 35% as the top rate. Social security taxes totaled 19%, 10% paid by the employer and 9% by the employee. Reduced rates were available under certain circumstances on both corporate and individual income taxes. The main indirect tax was the VAT, set at a standard rate of 18%. There were also stamp taxes.

37 CUSTOMS AND DUTIES

Although traditionally a protectionist state, Malta's nationalist government is moving to dismantle its trade barriers in an effort to prepare for EU accession. Customs are collected mainly in the form of ad valorem duties; there are specific duties on petroleum, spirits, and tobacco. Preferential treatment is accorded to imports from the European Union. There is also a value-added tax (VAT) of 18% on all imports.

38 FOREIGN INVESTMENT

Malta encourages foreign investment through tax holidays, export incentives, investment and accelerated depreciation allowances, reduced taxes on reinvested profits, grants to cover training costs and management services, a generous attitude toward repatriation of profits and capital, and few restrictions on foreign ownership of Maltese firms. No data for the total value of foreign direct investment in Malta is available; the only investment figures that are kept are those collected by the government at the time of the original application for assistance by the companies. SGS Thomson Ltd. (Italy and France), first established in Malta in 1981, had an investment of $266 million in machinery as of 1995.

In 1998, foreign direct investment (FDI) inflows were $267 million, up from $80.8 million in 1997, and then soared to $822 million in 1999. FDI inflows fell to $652 million in 2000 and then to $314 million in 2001. For the period 1998 to 2000, Malta was fifth in the world in terms of success in attracting foreign investment. Malta's share of world FDI flows was 4.6 times its share of world GDP during this period.

Capital inflows totaled $555 million in 2002, and an estimated $333 million in 2003. Most investments came from Germany, the United States, France, the United Kingdom, Italy, and Austria. Foreign companies employ a significant part of the Maltese population.

39 ECONOMIC DEVELOPMENT

The Nationalist government's primary aim was to radically transform Malta's economy in an effort to meet EU standards in time for the next round of enlargement. The elimination of trade barriers, deficit reduction, and more efficient tax collection comprise the most significant elements of the government's EU-harmonization plan. Malta was formally invited to join the European Union in December 2002, and was finally accepted as a full member in May 2004.

Malta's economic growth has fluctuated over the past years, going into the negative in 2001 and 2003. Nonetheless, the economy is projected to grow stronger in the future as a result of higher investments in construction, and due to government efforts to meet fiscal criteria for euro qualification. Also, a slight increase in exports and private consumption are expected to help this trend.

40 SOCIAL DEVELOPMENT

The National Insurance Act of 1956, as amended in 1987, provides benefits for sickness, unemployment, old age, widowhood, disability, and industrial injuries. Coverage includes all residents aged 16 and over, and excludes full time students and unemployed married women. Pensions are funded by contributions from employers, employees, and the government. These benefits are sup-plemented by social assistance under the National Assistance Act of 1956. Legislation establishing family allowances was enacted in 1974, and maternity benefits were mandated in 1981. As of 2004, employers were required to provide 14 weeks of maternity leave with pay set at a flat weekly rate. Work injury laws have been on the books since 1929.

Women make up a growing portion of the labor force due to changing social patterns and economic necessity. However, they are often channeled into traditionally female occupations or work in family-owned businesses, and remain underrepresented at the management level. Working women generally earn less than men. Domestic violence against women remains a problem but is addressed by the government through specialized police units, legal assistance, shelters, and legislation. These efforts paid off with a decrease in domestic violence in 2004. Women have equality in matters of family law, although divorce is not legal.

The law mandates protection of all groups against economic, social, and political discrimination. The government is committed to protecting human rights, and human rights organizations are free to operate in Malta.

41 HEALTH

Free health services are administered by the government run polyclinics. British, Belgian, and other foreign medical personnel work in Malta's hospitals. Infant mortality decreased from 23.3 per 1,000 live births in 1973 to an estimated 3.89 in 2005. Average life expectancy at birth was 78.86 years. As of 2004, there was an estimated 293 physicians, 377 nurses, 40 dentists, and 192 pharmacists per 100,000 people. The HIV/AIDS prevalence was 0.20 per 100 adults in 2003. As of 2004, there were approximately 500 people living with HIV/AIDS in the country. There were an estimated 100 deaths from AIDS in 2003.

42 HOUSING

Malta has the somewhat unusual situation of having a large surplus of housing stock. In 1995, about 23% of the housing stock was vacant, translating into about 35,723 dwellings. About 36% of vacant homes are considered to be second homes in private ownership. In 2003, an estimated 52,000 homes were vacant. Despite the surplus, the government continues to issue an overabundance of housing construction permits. For the period of 1994–2001, the Planning Authority issued about 3,000 permissions for housing development per year. The average increase in households was only about 1,700 per year for the same period.

Many new homes are being built in rural or suburb areas, a move which has been somewhat detrimental to urban areas since residents leaving the cities are often simply abandoning their urban properties. Some of these properties have fallen into disrepair, but many are still considered to be in adequate and good condition. Residential property is seen as a good investment for those who can afford to own their own homes and about 70% of all homes are owner occupied. Unfortunately, those who own a second home are often not willing to offer the property for affordable rental. Which also means that those who cannot afford to own their own home often find it difficult to find an affordable place to rent. The government provides some rental properties for low-income families and have made plans to encourage property owners to open their properties for rental.

43 EDUCATION

Maltese law requires that the teachings of the Roman Catholic Church be included in the public school curriculum, and legislation passed in 1983 requires all schools to provide free education. Education is compulsory for 11 years for children between the ages of 5 and 16 and is free in public schools. Primary school covers six years of study, followed by five years of junior lyceum (lower secondary). Students then have an option of attending a two-year high school or a four-year vocational school. Private independent and church secondary schools may have more specialized curriculums. The academic year runs from October to June.

Most children between the ages of three and four are enrolled in some type of preschool program. Primary school enrollment in 2003 was estimated at about 96% of eligible students. The same year, secondary school enrollment was about 87% of eligible students. It is estimated that nearly all students complete their primary education. The student-to-teacher ratio for primary school was at about 19:1 in 2003; the ratio for secondary school was about 10:1. In 2003, private schools accounted for about 36.5% of primary school enrollment and 27.3% of secondary enrollment.

Institutes of higher education include the University of Malta, the International Maritime Law Institute, and the School of Art. In 2003, about 30% of the tertiary age population were enrolled in some type of higher education program. The adult literacy rate for 2004 was estimated at about 87.9%, with 86.4% for men and 89.2% for women.

As of 2003, public expenditure on education was estimated at 4.6% of GDP.

44 LIBRARIES AND MUSEUMS

The National Library of Malta (founded in 1555) is located in Valetta and held 380,000 volumes in 2002. The National Archives is housed in Rabat. The University of Malta Library (1769) is in Msida and contains over 700,000 volumes. The Malta Public Libraries consist of the main Central Public Library at Floriana, 7 regional libraries and 38 branch libraries. There is also a Gozo Public Library. There are over 50 school libraries throughout Malta.

Valletta is the site of the National Museum of Archaeology, the National Museum of Fine Arts, the Palace Armory, the National War Museum, and the St. John's Museum. The Folk Museum and the Museum of Political History are at Vittoriosa, where the Malta Maritime Museum also opened in 1992. There is an archeological museum located in a Copper Age temple in Mgarr and a museum of Zomon antiquities in Rabat.

45 MEDIA

In 2003, there were 208,300 mainline phones and 290,000 mobile phone in use nationwide.

Malta's government radio service transmits on two channels (one Maltese, one English). The Labor Party and the Nationalist Party both own one radio and one television station. The Catholic Church also sponsors a radio station. There are other private stations as well. Television programs are received primarily from a local service and from Italy. As of 2001 there were 1 AM and 18 FM radio stations and 6 television stations, plus 1 commercial cable network. In 1997, there were 255,000 radios and 280,000 tele-

vision sets throughout the country. In 2002, there were 120,000 Internet users.

The press includes daily and Sunday newspapers, published in both Maltese and English. Leading papers (with estimated 2002 circulations) are *It-Torca* (Maltese, 30,000 daily), *L'Orizzont* (Maltese, 25,000 weekly), the *Times* (English, 23,000 daily), *Il-Mument* (Maltese, 25,000 weekly), and *In-Nazzion Taghna* (Maltese, 20,000 daily).

The constitution provides for freedom of speech and press, and the government is said to respect these rights in practice.

46 ORGANIZATIONS

The Chamber of Commerce is located in Valletta. There are several professional and trade organizations representing a variety of occupations. The largest independent private business organization is the General Retailers and Traders' Union–Malta. The Malta Federation of Industry also has some influence. The Medical Association of Malta represents the interests of doctors and patients. Other professional unions and associations are active on a national level.

The Malta Cultural Institute promotes primarily the arts of music and dance. Sports associations include organizations for such sports as cricket, football (soccer), weightlifting, and badminton. National youth organizations include the Malta Youth Labor Brigade, Nationalist Party Youth Movement, Scout Association of Malta, Student Democrats of Malta, University Student Council of Malta, University Students' Catholic Movement, and the Young Christians. The National Council of Woman of Malta encourages equal opportunity for women in business and education.

Multinational organizations based in Malta include the International Ocean Institute and Greenpeace Mediterranean. There is a national chapter of the Red Cross Society.

47 TOURISM, TRAVEL, AND RECREATION

Tourism, a major industry, has played a large role in developing the Maltese economy since the 1990s. Malta has many scenic and historical attractions, especially in Valletta, plus excellent beaches. Football (soccer) is the national sport; hockey, badminton, darts and rugby are also popular as well as billiards and snooker.

US citizens and most Western Europeans do not require a visa for stays of up to 90 days. In 2003, about 1,127,000 visitors arrived in Malta, of whom 40% came from the United Kingdom. That year there were 41,365 beds available in hotels and other accommodations with a 53% occupancy rate.

In 2005, the US Department of State estimated the daily cost of staying in Malta at $209.

48 FAMOUS MALTESE

The city of Valletta derives its nomenclature from Jehan Parisot de la Vallette (1494–1568), Grand Master of the Knights of St. John, who successfully withstood a great Turkish siege in 1565. Dominic (Dom) Mintoff (b.1916), a founder of Malta's Labour Party, was prime minister during 1955–58 and 1971–84. Agatha Barbara (1923–2002), a former cabinet minister, was elected the first woman president of Malta on 16 February 1982. Edward Fenech-

Adami (b.1934), who served as prime minister from 1987–96 and from 1998–2004, became president in 2004.

49 DEPENDENCIES

Malta has no territories or colonies.

50 BIBLIOGRAPHY

Balbi, Francesco. Trans. by Ernle Bradford. *The Siege of Malta, 1565*. Rochester, N.Y.: Boydell Press, 2005.

Berg, Warren G. *Historical Dictionary of Malta*. Lanham, Jd.: Scarecrow, 1995.

Five Small Open Economics. New York: Oxford University Press, 1993.

Gregory, Desmond. *Malta, Britain, and the European Powers*. Madison: Fairleigh Dickinson University Press, 1996.

Holland, James. *Fortress Malta: An Island under Siege, 1940–1943*. New York: Miramax Books/Hyperion, 2003.

Spooner, Tony. *Supreme Gallantry: Malta's Role in the Allied Victory, 1939–1945*. London: J. Murray, 1996.

Terterov, Marat (ed.). *Doing Business with Malta*. Sterling, Va.: Kogan Page, 2003.

MOLDOVA

Republic of Moldova
Republica Moldoveneasca

CAPITAL: Chişinău

FLAG: Equal vertical bands of blue, yellow, and red; emblem in center of yellow stripe is Roman eagle with shield on its breast.

ANTHEM: n/a

MONETARY UNIT: The leu is a paper currency, replacing the Russian ruble. 1MLD = $0.07962 (or $1 = MLD12.56) as of 2005.

WEIGHTS AND MEASURES: The metric system is in force.

HOLIDAYS: Independence Day, 27 August.

TIME: 2 PM = noon GMT.

¹LOCATION, SIZE, AND EXTENT

Moldova is a landlocked nation located in eastern Europe, between Ukraine and Romania. Comparatively, it is slightly larger than the state of Maryland with a total area of 33,843 sq km (13,067 sq mi). Moldova shares boundaries with Ukraine on the N, E, and S; and Romania on the W. Moldova's border length totals 1,389 km (864 mi).

Its capital city, Chişinău, is located in the south central part of the country.

²TOPOGRAPHY

Moldova consists mostly of a hilly plain that is cut by deep valleys with many rivers and streams. The terrain slopes gradually southward. The Codri Hills run through the center of the country and contain the nation's highest point of Mount Balanesti, at 430 meters (1,410 feet). The lowest point is along the Dniester River, with an elevation of 2 meters (6.6 feet).

The Dniester, along the eastern border, is the longest river with a total length of 1,400 kilometers (870 miles). The second longest river, the Prut, is a major tributary of the Danube. There are no major lakes, but saline marshes are found along the lower reaches of the Prut and in river valleys of southern Moldova.

³CLIMATE

The climate is of the humid continental type. The country is exposed to northerly cold winds in the winter and moderate westerly winds in the summer. The average temperature in July is 20°C (68°F). The average temperature in January is -4°C (24°F). Rainfall averages 58 cm (22.8 in) a year.

⁴FLORA AND FAUNA

Three-fourths of the country's terrain features chernozem (black soil), which supports the natural vegetation of steppe-like grasslands. The central hill country is densely forested. Common trees include oak, maple, linden, hornbeam, and beech. Badgers, polecats, ermines, wild boar, foxes, and hares are common animals.

Larks, blackbirds, and jays are common birds. Carp, bream, trout, and pike populate the lakes and streams. As of 2002, there were at least 68 species of mammals, 175 species of birds, and over 1,700 species of plants throughout the country.

⁵ENVIRONMENT

The natural environment in Moldova suffers from the heavy use of agricultural chemicals (including banned pesticides such as DDT), which have contaminated soil and groundwater. Poor farming methods have caused widespread soil erosion. In 2000, total carbon dioxide emissions was at 6.6 million metric tons. As of 2003, 1.4% of Moldova's total land area is protected. According to a 2006 report issued by the International Union for Conservation of Nature and Natural Resources (IUCN), threatened species included four types of mammals, eight species of birds, one type of reptile, nine species of fish, and five species of invertebrates. Threatened species include the European bison, European souslik, and the great bustard.

⁶POPULATION

The population of Moldova in 2005 was estimated by the United Nations (UN) at 4,206,000, which placed it at number 121 in population among the 193 nations of the world. In 2005, approximately 10% of the population was over 65 years of age, with another 20% of the population under 15 years of age. There were 92 males for every 100 females in the country. According to the UN, the annual population rate of change for 2005–10 was expected to be -0.2%; the rate fell below zero in the mid-1990s. The government is concerned about the low fertility rate and high emigration rate, both of which contribute to the population decline. The projected population for the year 2025 was 3,967,000. The population density was 125 per sq km (323 per sq mi).

The UN estimated that 45% of the population lived in urban areas in 2005, and that urban areas were growing at an annual rate of 0.47%. The capital city, Chişinău, had a population of 662,000 in that year. Tiraspol had an estimated 209,800 people; Bălţi (Beltsy), 207,738; and Tighina, 144,900.

7MIGRATION

There was a net emigration of 6,000 in 1979–88 to other Soviet republics. This grew to 16,300 in 1989 and 29,800 in 1990. Since independence in 1991, Moldova has experienced difficulties. A short but violent civil war in 1992—the Trans-Dniestrian conflict—resulted in the internal displacement of some 51,000 people and the external displacement of some 56,000 refugees, who fled to the Ukraine. There is no central authority in Moldova that registers and determines claims for refugee status. In 2004, there were 57 refugees and 184 asylum seekers. In 2004, some 5,641 Moldovans were refugees in Germany and 4,799 in the United States. Between 2000 and 2004, 900 Moldovans sought asylum in European and non-European countries. However, in 2004 over 6,700 Moldovans sought asylum in European countries, Ireland, and the United Kingdom. In 2005, the net migration rate was an estimated -0.25 migrants per 1,000 population, a significant change from -5.8 per 1,000 in 1990. The government views the immigration level as satisfactory, but the emigration level as too high.

8ETHNIC GROUPS

The most recent estimates indicate that the population is 64.5% Moldovan/Romanian; 13.8% Ukrainian; 13% Russian; 2% Bulgarian; 1.5% Jewish; and 5.2% Gagauz or other. The Gagauz are a Christian Turkic minority that live primarily in the south. The government estimates the number of Roma to be about 11,600; however, nongovernmental organizations have placed the estimated Romani population at anywhere between 20,000 and 200,000.

9LANGUAGES

Moldovan, the official language, is considered a dialect of Romanian rather than a separate language. It is derived from Latin but, unlike the other Romance languages, preserved the neuter gender and a system of three cases. There are a large number of Slavonic-derived words. Under Soviet rule the language was written in the Cyrillic alphabet, but Latin script was restored in 1989. This switch has caused problems, particularly in the separatist Transnistrian region where local authorities have closed schools that were teaching the Latin script.

Russian and Gagauz, a Turkish dialect, are also spoken within the country. Government officials are expected to know both Moldovan and Russian.

10RELIGIONS

Over 90% of the population belong to one of two Orthodox denominations: the Moldovan Orthodox or the Bessarabian Church. About 3.6% of the population belong to the Old Rite Russian Orthodox Church (Old Believers). Other Christian denominations include Roman Catholics, Baptists, Pentecostals, Seventh-Day Adventists, Jehovah's Witnesses, Lutherans, Presbyterians, and Mormons. The Jewish community has about 31,300 members. There are also communities of Muslims and Baha'is. Though there is no state religion, the Moldovan Orthodox Church has a privileged status with the state and the government imposes some restrictions on religious groups that are not officially registered. For instance, unregistered groups are not permitted to build churches.

11TRANSPORTATION

In 2004, Moldova's railroad system consisted of 1,138 km (707 mi) of standard and broad gauge railways, not including industrial lines. Of that total, broad gauge accounted for nearly all of it at 1,124 km (698 mi). As of 2003, Moldova's highway system consisted of 12,730 km (7,910 mi) of roadway, of which 10,973 km (6,818 mi) were paved. As of 2004, Moldova had 424 km (263 mi) of inland waterways. As of 2005, Moldova's merchant fleet consisted of two cargo vessels of 1,000 GRT or more. Access to the sea is through Ukraine or Romania. There were an estimated 23 airports in 2004, six with paved runways, as of 2005. Air transport is provided by Air Moldova International and Moldavian Airlines, both private carriers, and a state company, Air Moldova. In 2003, about 179,000 passengers were carried on domestic and international airline flights.

12HISTORY

The region that is now Moldova (also called Bessarabia) has historically been inhabited by a largely Romanian-speaking population. The region was part of the larger Romanian principality of Moldova in the 18th century, which in turn was under Ottoman suzerainty. In 1812, the region was ceded to the Russian Empire, which ruled until March 1918 when it became part of Romania. Moscow laid the basis for reclaiming Moldova by establishing a small Moldovian Autonomous Soviet Socialist Republic on Ukrainian territory in 1924.

The 1939 Nazi-Soviet pact assigned Moldova to the Soviet sphere of influence. Soviet forces seized Moldova in June 1940. After the Nazi invasion of the USSR, Germany helped Romania to regain Moldova. Romania held it from 1941 until Soviet forces reconquered it in 1944.

Moldova declared its independence from the USSR on 27 August 1991. In December, Mircea Snegur was elected the first president of the new nation. Moldova's new constitution was adopted on 28 July 1994, replacing the old Soviet constitution of 1979. The Agrarian Democratic Party, composed largely of former Communist officials, won a majority of seats in the new parliament elected the same year.

Although independent, Moldova has remained one of the poorest countries in Europe and has confronted internal problems with two breakaway regions, the predominantly Turkish Gagauz region in the southern part of the country, and the largely Russian Transdniestria region east of the Dniester River. Russian forces have remained in the latter region and have supported its Russian population in proclaiming an independent "Transdniestria Republic," with which the Moldovan government was still trying to reach a political settlement as of 2003.

Petru Lucinschi (Independent), former speaker of the parliament, defeated Snegur in a December 1996 presidential runoff election (54% to 46%) and became Moldova's new president early in 1997. The following year, Moldova's Communist Party won a parliamentary majority in legislative elections. By 1999 Lucinschi was seeking to strengthen the nation's presidency in order to overcome an extended stalemate between the executive branch and parliament that was preventing the government from effectively addressing the nation's pressing economic problems. In a referendum, voters approved constitutional changes proposed by Lucinschi, but they were rejected by the parliament.

In July 2000, parliament cancelled the direct election of the president, and he or she is now elected by parliament for a four-year term. Parliament failed to chose a new president by December 2000, and early parliamentary elections were held in February 2001. Communists took 71 of 101 seats, and in April, Vladimir Voronin, head of the Communist Party, became president. Voronin campaigned on a platform of protecting human rights, continuing the process of democratization, and ensuring that citizens had adequate food, employment, and medical care.

In February 2003, Voronin, a native of Transdniester, proposed a new initiative to settle the dispute with Transdniester. He called for a new constitution that would turn Moldova into a loose confederation of two states, and grant the Russian language official status. Both Moldova and Transdniester would have their own governing and legislative bodies, and budgets. Defense, customs, and monetary systems would be common for the federation. However, when in January 2002 plans had been announced to make Russian an official language and compulsory in school, mass protests were held, and ended only when the plans were revoked. As of February 2003, Russia maintained 2,500 troops in Transdniester, although in 1999 it agreed to withdraw all of its troops by 2001. The situation in Transdniester is complicated by fears among the Slavic population of Moldova's unification with Romania. On the other hand, at the beginning of 2003, consultations were taking place on the possible entry of Moldova into a union with Russia and Belarus.

The Communist Party stayed on track with market reforms and the European integration process. Although it is considered to be one of the poorest countries in Europe, and despite an economic base that is fairly fragile, between 2001 and 2004 Moldova registered GDP growth rates of over 6%. Also, the national currency—the Moldovan leu—was been very stable over this time period.

In the March 2005 elections the Communist Party managed to hold on to power by garnering 46.1% of the votes; the Democratic Moldova Bloc got 28.4%, the Christian Democratic Popular party (PPCD) got 9.1%, and other parties got 16.4%. The popularity of the Communist Party was not as big as it was in 2001—they only won 56 parliamentary seats out of the 101 available—but they still managed to vote President Voronin in for a second term.

Moldova's middle-term goal of joining the European Union, and its short term goal of having its citizens travel freely within the Schengen space, were hampered by the raging conflict in the Transdniester region. The European Union stated that Moldova had no immediate prospects for integration.

13 GOVERNMENT

Elections to Moldova's first postindependence parliament were held on 27 February 1994. The parliament consists of a single chamber of 101 seats, and members are elected for four-year terms on the basis of proportional representation. In order to enter the parliament, parties must garner at least 6% of the votes; blocks of two parties need 9%, blocks of three or more parties need 12%, while independent candidates have to poll at least 3%. The votes

LOCATION: 47°0′ N; 29°0′ E. BOUNDARY LENGTHS: Total boundary lengths, 1,389 kilometers (864 miles); Romania, 450 kilometers (280 miles); Ukraine, 939 kilometers (584 miles).

obtained by the parties that did not pass these thresholds are redistributed in favor of the parties that did, according to their overall representation in the Parliament.

Prior to 2000, the president was directly elected. As of July 2000, however, the president is elected by parliament for a four-year term and may serve no more than two consecutive terms. The president nominates the prime minister upon consultation with parliament. The cabinet is selected by the prime minister, subject to approval by parliament.

The July 1994 constitution and the law provide for freedom of speech, press, assembly, and religion; however, the law requires that religious groups register with the government. Peaceful assembly is allowed; however, permits for demonstrations must be approved and political parties and private organizations are required to register with the government.

Reforms approved in 1995 authorized the creation of a court to deal with constitutional issues and a system of appeals courts.

14 POLITICAL PARTIES

Although 26 parties or coalitions of parties participated in the February 1994 elections, only four received more than the 4% of the national vote (then) required to gain seats.

The Agrarian Party had been the largest political group in the parliament with a plurality of 46 seats, following the departure of 10 deputies in 1995. They left to join a new party, the Party of Renewal and Conciliation, headed by then-president Mircea Snegur. The Socialist-Edenstro bloc had 26 seats, while the pro-Romanian parties, the Popular Front and the Peasants and Intellectuals bloc, had 11 and 9 seats, respectively.

Although the Party of Moldovan Communists won the single largest number of parliamentary seats (40) in the elections held on 22 March 1998, they had insufficient support to form a governing coalition and thus remained an opposition party, while the governing coalition consisted of the Democratic Convention of Moldova (26 seats), the Bloc for a Democratic and Prosperous Moldova (24), and the Party of Democratic Forces (11).

Twelve political parties or blocs participated in the parliamentary elections held on 25 February 2001. Three of them gained seats in parliament: the Communist Party, 71; the centrist Braghis Alliance (led by Dumitru Braghis) of the Social-Democratic Alliance of Moldova, 19; and the conservative Christian Democratic Popular Party, 11.

In 2005, 9 parties, 2 alliances, and 12 independent candidates entered the electoral race. The Communist Party (PCRM) won 56 of 101 parliamentary seats, the centrist and pro-Russian Democratic Moldova Block (BMD)—led by Dumitru Braghis and Chișinău mayor Serafim Urechean—won 34, while the rightist and pro-Romanian Christian Democratic Popular Party (PPCD) won 11. Despite their fragile majority, the communists managed to vote former president Vladimir Voronin in for a second term—he received 75 of the 101 parliamentary votes. Vasile Tarlev was the designated prime minister.

15 LOCAL GOVERNMENT

Following administrative reforms, Moldova's 40 districts, or *raions,* have been reorganized into nine counties, one municipality (Chișinău), and two territorial units (Transdniestria and Gagauzia).

The Russian minority on the east bank of the Dniester River have proclaimed their independence as the "Transdniestria Republic," but it has not been recognized by the Moldovan government, which is, however, willing to allow this region a degree of autonomy. The predominantly Turkish Gagauz region has also been granted autonomy.

16 JUDICIAL SYSTEM

There are courts of first instance, an appellate court, a Supreme Court, and a Constitutional Court. The Supreme Court is divided into civil and criminal sections.

The Constitutional Court was created in 1995. A 1995 judicial reform law provided for a system of appeals courts.

There are district courts of the first instance and five regional tribunals. The Higher Appeals Court and the Supreme Court are both in Chișinău. However, as of 2003, there was a backlog of cases at the tribunal and the Higher Appeals Court levels, due to lack of funding.

The Superior Court of Magistrates nominates and the president appoints judges for an initial period of five years. The judges may be reappointed for a subsequent 10 years, and finally, on their third term, they serve until retirement age. The judiciary is more independent now than when it was subject to the Soviet regime. The Constitutional Court made several rulings in 1996 that demonstrated its independence. For example, in April 1996 the Constitutional Court found that the attempted dismissal of Defense Minister Creanga by President Snegur was unconstitutional. The Constitutional Court also overturned a Central Electoral Commission decision to exclude a presidential candidate from competing in the November 1996 election. And in 2000, the Court ruled that legislation requiring political parties to be registered for two years prior to participating in elections was unconstitutional.

Criminal defendants enjoy a presumption of innocence and are afforded a number of due process rights, including a public trial and a right of appeal. In practice, a number of convictions have been overturned on appeal.

In 2004 Moldova was deemed one of the most corrupt nations in the world. While the constitution states that the judiciary is independent, there have been several reports of political interference in the judicial process, and corruption among underpaid judges was believed to be pervasive.

17 ARMED FORCES

In 2005 the active armed forces numbered 6,750 personnel, backed by 66,000 reservists. The Army had 5,710 personnel, with 44 armored infantry fighting vehicles, 266 armored personnel carriers, and 227 artillery pieces. The Air Force had 1,040 active members, with five transport aircraft and eight support helicopters. There is also a paramilitary force that consisted of 2,379 internal troops and 900 riot police, all of which are under the Ministry of Interior. The defense budget for 2005 totaled $9.2 million. Moldova has peacekeeping forces in Sudan, Côte d'Ivoire, and Liberia. Russia has an estimated 1,400 troops stationed in Moldova.

18 INTERNATIONAL COOPERATION

Moldova was admitted to the United Nations on 2 March 1992, and is a member of the ECE and several nonregional specialized agencies, such as the IAEA, ICAO, ILO, IMF, UNCTAD, UNESCO, UNIDO, WHO, and the World Bank. Moldova joined NATO's Partnership for Peace on 16 March 1994. It is also a member of the Council of Europe, the WTO, the Black Sea Economic Cooperation Zone, the Commonwealth of Independent States (CIS), the Euro-Atlantic Partnership Council, the European Bank for Reconstruction and Development, the OSCE, and the NATO Partnership for Peace. In 2001, Georgia, Uzbekistan, Ukraine, Azerbaijan, and Moldova formed a social and economic development union known as GUAAM. Uzbekistan withdrew from the partnership in 2005.

In environmental cooperation, Moldova is part of the Basel Convention, Conventions on Biological Diversity and Air Pollution, CITES, the Kyoto Protocol, the Montréal Protocol, and the UN Conventions on Climate Change and Desertification.

19 ECONOMY

At 51% of GDP in 2000, services comprise the most important sector of Moldova's economy, while agriculture accounted for 28%. The country's wide range of crops provides significant export revenue and employment.

Moldova has no major mineral deposits and must import all of its supplies of coal, oil, and natural gas. Since the breakup of the Soviet Union in 1991, energy shortages have contributed to sharp production declines. Moldova is seeking alternative energy sources and working to develop its own energy supplies including solar power, wind, and geothermal. The country is implementing a national energy conservation program.

In 1998, the Moldovan economy experienced an 8.6% decline due primarily to fallout from the financial crisis in Russia, by far its biggest export market. Continuing financial turmoil in Ukraine and Romania hurt Moldova's exports, which were needed to pay for imports of fuel from these countries. About one-fourth of Moldova's external debt burden, which peaked at 75% of GDP in 2000, is traceable to energy imports from Russia, which has on occasion suspended gas supplies, and from the Ukraine and Romania, both of which have on occasion suspended electricity power to Moldova. Further isolation occurred in 1999 when the IMF halted loans following the refusal of the Moldovan parliament to carry out privatization plans. By year's end, the Moldovan economy had contracted to roughly one-third of its 1989 level, with end of period inflation soaring to 45.8%. In 2000, the contraction was halted with real GDP growth of 2.2%, and in December, the government entered into a three-year arrangement with the IMF under its Poverty Reduction and Growth Facility (PRGF). Although average inflation for 2000 was 31.3%, by the end of the year the rate had moderated to 18.5%. In 2001 and 2002, inflation has been reduced to single digits: 6.4% and 8%, respectively. Real growth was 6.1% in 2001 and peaked at 4.8% in 2002. The external debt burden had eased somewhat to 58% of GDP.

The economy continued to expand in the following years, registering GDP growth rates of 6.3% in 2003, and 7.3% in 2004; the estimates for 2005 place the growth at 6.0%. This increase was encouraged mainly by remittances send by Moldovans working abroad, and by a strong economic performance in Moldova's neighboring countries. However, the prolonged and deep economic recession that preceded this economic expansion put Moldova in a lagging position in comparison with all its neighbors.

Today, Moldova still is one of Europe's poorest economies. The GDP per capita was only $717 in 2004, and the country's production capacity was reduced due to the exodus of working-age Moldovans. The inflation rate was on the rise in 2004, reaching 12.4%, after falling to 5.2% in 2002. The fact that most of its industry is located in secessionist Transnistria and its dependence on trade with neighboring countries makes Moldova extremely vulnerable.

20 INCOME

The US Central Intelligence Agency (CIA) reports that in 2005 Moldova's gross domestic product (GDP) was estimated at $9.4 billion. The CIA defines GDP as the value of all final goods and services produced within a nation in a given year and computed on the basis of purchasing power parity (PPP) rather than value as measured on the basis of the rate of exchange based on current dollars. The per capita GDP was estimated at $2,100. The annual growth rate of GDP was estimated at 6%. The average inflation rate in 2005 was 12%. It was estimated that agriculture accounted for 20.5% of GDP, industry 23.9%, and services 55.6%.

According to the World Bank, in 2003 remittances from citizens working abroad totaled $465 million or about $110 per capita and accounted for approximately 23.5% of GDP. Foreign aid receipts amounted to $117 million or about $28 per capita and accounted for approximately 5.1% of the gross national income (GNI).

The World Bank reports that in 2003 household consumption in Moldova totaled $1.86 billion or about $438 per capita based on a GDP of $2.0 billion, measured in current dollars rather than PPP. Household consumption includes expenditures of individuals, households, and nongovernmental organizations on goods and services, excluding purchases of dwellings. It was estimated that for the period 1990 to 2003 household consumption grew at an average annual rate of 8.7%. In 2001 it was estimated that approximately 31% of household consumption was spent on food, 11% on fuel, 3% on health care, and 15% on education. It was estimated that in 2001 about 80% of the population had incomes below the poverty line.

21 LABOR

Moldova's civilian workforce in 2005 totaled 1.34 million. As of 2003, industry accounted for 16% of the labor force, while 43% were in agriculture, and nearly 41% were in the service sector. The unemployment rate in 2002 was estimated at 8%. Approximately 25% of working age Moldovans are employed outside the country.

The law provides workers with the right of association, including the right to form and join labor unions. The General Federation of Trade Unions of Moldova (GFTU) is the successor to the previously existing Soviet trade union system. Various industrial unions still maintain voluntary membership in the GFTU, and there have been no attempts to form alternate trade union structures. Government workers do not have the right to strike, nor do those in essential services such as health care and energy. Unions in the private sector may strike if two-thirds of their membership assents. Collective bargaining is used to negotiate workers' pay and benefits.

The unrestricted minimum working age is 18, with restrictions as to the number of hours that may be worked for those between 16 and 18 years of age. Children generally do not work except in agriculture on family farms. The labor code stipulates a standard workweek of 40 hours, with at least one day off weekly. In 2002, the monthly minimum wage was $9.00 in the public sector and $12.75 in private firms. The median salary was estimated to be $39 per month.

²²AGRICULTURE

Cropland covers about 65% of the Moldovan land area. Agricultural activities engaged 23% of the labor force in 2000. Agriculture is the most important sector of the Moldovan economy, accounting for 28% of GDP and 60% of exports in 2004. Agricultural output had an average annual decline of 13.7% during 1990–2000. Crop production during 2002–04 was up 7.2% from 1999–2001. In 2000, state-controlled farms accounted for only 1.2% of gross agricultural production, down from 10.2% in 1995. About 14% of all cropland is under irrigation.

Moldovan crops and their 2004 production amounts (in tons) include: sugar beets, 907,000; wheat, 690,000; grapes, 600,000; corn, 1,840,000; sunflowers, 331,000; barley, 260,000; potatoes, 318,000; and soybeans, 35,000.

Wine and tobacco products are important agricultural exports. Wine exports in 2003 were estimated at 20 million liters, accounting for about 3% of world market share. Tobacco production was 10,200 tons in 2004. All tobacco is grown on state farms; the monopoly and lack of buyers has limited privately grown tobacco. Wine and tobacco exports in 2004 were valued at $215.8 million and $8.9 million, respectively, and together accounted for about 23% of exports.

²³ANIMAL HUSBANDRY

About 13% of the total land area consists of pastureland. In 2005, the livestock population included 400,000 head of cattle, 500,000 pigs, 830,000 sheep, 115,000 goats, and 14,000,000 chickens. Pork production amounted to 38,500 tons in 2005, when 23,500 tons of beef were produced. In 2005, 630,000 tons of cow's milk and 43,000 tons of eggs were also produced.

²⁴FISHING

With no direct connection to the Black Sea, fishing is limited to the Dnister River. The total catch in 2003 was 2,981 tons, with carp accounting for 93% of the landings. Commercial fishing is not a significant part of the national economy.

²⁵FORESTRY

Forested areas accounted for about 9.9% of the total land area in 2000. Production is largely domestically consumed; wood and paper product imports in 2004 amounted to $29.2 million.

²⁶MINING

Moldova did not possess significant mineral resources. More than 100 deposits of gypsum, limestone, sand, and stone were exploited. Production totals for 2002 were: gypsum, 32,000 metric tons (estimated); sand and gravel, 300,000 metric tons; lime, 3,500 metric tons; and cement, 300,000 metric tons. Moldova also produced crude steel, peat, oil, and natural gas.

²⁷ENERGY AND POWER

Moldova, as of 1 January 2005, had no proven reserves of oil or natural gas, and as of 2002, no estimated recoverable reserves of coal. As a result, Moldova must rely upon imports of refined oil products and natural gas from Russia, Ukraine, and Belarus to meet its fossil fuel needs.

In 2004 consumption and imports of refined oil each came to an estimated 33,000 barrels per day. In 2002, natural gas consumption and imports each came to an estimated 78 billion cu ft. In 2002, Moldova imported and consumed 200,000 short tons of coal.

Electric power generating capacity has declined since Moldova gained its independence in 1992 due to lack of funds, civil disturbances, and a general economic downturn in the 1990s. Total installed generating capacity in 2002 was estimated at one million kW. Total electricity generation and consumption in 2002 was estimated at 3.9 billion kWh and 4.6 billion kWh, respectively. Conventional thermal fuel sources provided around 78% to 90% of the electric generated, with hydropower providing the remainder.

²⁸INDUSTRY

Moldova's industry, including processed food, is composed of approximately 600 major and mid-sized enterprises and associations. It accounts for 23% of Moldova's GDP.

In 1998 the most prominent industries were: food processing (57%), electric energy (18%), engineering and metal processing (5%); production of construction materials (4%), light industry (5.4%), and forestry, wood processing, pulp and paper (3%). Other industrial products include agricultural machinery, foundry equipment, shoes, hosiery, textiles, washing machines, and refrigerators and freezers.

In the wake of the economic downturn in 1998, Moldova's industrial production declined 11% from the previous year. Growth in industrial output was a component of improved economic performance in 2001, as industrial output registered a 3.1% growth rate that year. This growth expanded to 17% in 2004, but industrial representation in GDP and labor force remained low in 2004, at 24.8% and 14% respectively; agriculture made up 22.4% of the economy, and occupied 40% of the labor force; services came in first with a 52.8% contribution to the GDP, and 46% representation in the labor force. Most of the country's industry is situated in conflict riddled and politically instable Transnistria, which makes any current industrial strategy superfluous.

²⁹SCIENCE AND TECHNOLOGY

The Moldovan Academy of Sciences, founded in 1961, has sections of physico-mathematical sciences, biological and chemical sciences, technical sciences, agricultural sciences, and medical sciences, and 14 research institutes concerned with the natural sciences. Four scientific institutes conduct medical and agricultural research. Moldovan State University, founded in 1945, has faculties of physics, mathematics and cybernetics, chemistry, biology, and soil science. The Technical University of Moldova, founded in 1964, and the Chişinău Medical Institute and State Agricultural University of Moldova, founded in 1932, are located in Chişinău. M.V. Frunze Agricultural Institute is another educational institution in the sciences. In 1987–97, science and engineering students accounted for 52% of university enrollment. In 2002, there were 171 researchers and 201 technicians per million people that were engaged in research and development (R&D). In that same year, high technology exports totaled $8 million, or 4% of manufactured exports. In 1997 (the latest year for which data was available), Moldova spent $47.191 million, or 0.81% of GDP on R&D.

Of that amount, 51.4% came from the business sector, followed by 47.8% from government sources. Higher education and foreign sources accounted for 0.2% and 0.6%, respectively.

30 DOMESTIC TRADE

Chişinău is the main commercial center, with a well-developed system for product distribution. Both national and foreign firms have a strong presence within the retail sector. Since two-thirds of Moldova is rural, local farm markets play an important role in the domestic economy. A great deal of progress had been made in liberalizing and privatizing the economy. With US assistance, nearly all of the nation's farmlands were under private ownership as of 2000. As of January 2003, nearly 2,000 small, medium, and large-sized enterprises had also been transferred to private ownership.

In purchasing power parity terms, per capita gross domestic product (GDP) was $1,900 in 2004, with more than 80% of the population under the poverty line. Most of the household consumption is fueled by remittances sent home by Moldovans working abroad.

31 FOREIGN TRADE

Traditionally, Moldova has maintained a trade surplus with the other Soviet republics and a trade deficit with the rest of the world. However, as of 2005, Moldova's only significant trade surplus is with Russia. Total imports almost double total exports.

A trade agreement between the United States and Moldova providing reciprocal most-favored-nation tariff treatment became effective in 1992. The same year, an overseas Private Investment Corporation agreement, encouraging US private investment by providing direct loans and loan guarantees, was signed. In 1993 a bilateral investment treaty was signed between the United States and Moldova; a general system of preferences status was granted in 1995 as well as the availability of EX-IM bank coverage. Wine tops the list of Moldova's export commodities (24%), followed by apparel (16%). Other exports include tobacco (6.5%), glassware (5.7%), and meat (5.4%). The European Union was Moldova's main trade partner in 2003. Russia and the Ukraine came in second, with a representation of 22.4% and 16.7% in its overall trade respectively.

Principal Trading Partners – Moldova (2003)

(In millions of US dollars)

Country	Exports	Imports	Balance
World	790.3	1,398.6	-608.3
Russia	308.5	182.3	126.2
Romania	90.2	96.9	-6.7
Italy-San Marino-Holy See	82.4	116.6	-34.2
Ukraine	56.2	308.8	-252.6
Germany	56.2	135.3	-79.1
Belarus	41.1	50.6	-9.5
United States	33.6	34.5	-0.9
Austria	11.3	14.6	-3.3
France-Monaco	9.3	35.1	-25.8
Kazakhstan	9.2	48.1	-38.9

(…) data not available or not significant.

SOURCE: *2003 International Trade Statistics Yearbook,* New York: United Nations, 2004.

Balance of Payments – Moldova (2003)

(In millions of US dollars)

Current Account		**-142.3**
Balance on goods	-622.3	
Imports	-1,428.6	
Exports	806.3	
Balance on services	-39.5	
Balance on income	215.0	
Current transfers	304.5	
Capital Account		**-12.8**
Financial Account		**22.6**
Direct investment abroad	-0.1	
Direct investment in Moldova	58.5	
Portfolio investment assets	2.0	
Portfolio investment liabilities	-23.9	
Financial derivatives	…	
Other investment assets	-49.7	
Other investment liabilities	35.8	
Net Errors and Omissions		**89.5**
Reserves and Related Items		**43.0**

(…) data not available or not significant.

SOURCE: *Balance of Payment Statistics Yearbook 2004,* Washington, DC: International Monetary Fund, 2004.

In 2004, exports totaled $1.03 billion (FOB—Free on Board), while imports where almost double that at $1.83 billion (FOB). Russia remains Moldova's main export market, receiving 35.8% of total exports; it is followed by Italy (13.9%), Romania (10%), Germany (7.3%), Ukraine (6.6%), Belarus (6%), and the United States (4.6%). Imports came mainly from the Ukraine (24.6%), Russia (12.2%), Romania (9.3%), Germany (8.5%), and Italy (7.4%). Main import categories were fuel and energy, capital goods, and foods.

32 BALANCE OF PAYMENTS

External debt stood at $1.3 billion in 2002. That year, $168.7 million in debt service payments were due, accounting for over 60% of all budget revenues. The government took the dramatic step of handing 50% of ownership of its gas lines to Russia's Gazprom, one of its largest creditors. In 2000, the IMF had approved a three-year $142 million loan to reduce poverty and promote growth.

The US Central Intelligence Agency (CIA) reported that in 2002 the purchasing power parity of Moldova's exports was $590 million while imports totaled $980 million, resulting in a trade deficit of $390 million.

Exports of goods and services reached $1.2 billion in 2004; imports climbed at $2.0 billion, resulting in a resource balance of -$766 million. The current account balance was -$173 million in 2004, an improvement from the previous year's -$181 deficit. External debt reached $1.4 billion in the same year, and its total reserves (including gold) were $321 million, covering only two months of imports.

33 BANKING AND SECURITIES

Moldova's banking sector will play a key role in the country's transition from a managed economy to a market economy. The banking system was reformed in 1991. The National Bank of Moldova (NBM, the central bank) is charged with implementing monetary policy and issuing currency. State banks include the State Savings Bank, with 1,000 branches, and the Bank for Foreign Economic Exchange. Holdovers from the old Soviet system include three regional banks, which have been changed to joint-stock companies whose shares are owned by state enterprises. There are 20 commercial banks in the country with licenses to perform international transactions. The currency unit is the leu, introduced in late November 1993.

November 1993 was a turning point for Moldova's financial stability. The NBM became a fully independent central bank with its own administrative council, and was no longer required to finance industrial and agricultural funding shortfalls. As the leu was introduced, the NBM started phasing out credit emissions. As of January 1994, the NBM became fully responsible for monetary policy.

The bank has two policy instruments: reserve requirements which were raised progressively throughout 1994, and interest rates. The discount rate reached a peak of 377% in February 1994, and was kept high despite the subsequent dramatic fall in inflation. As of 2001, the money market rate was 11%.

The banking system comprises four former Soviet banks, Agroindbank, Molindconbank, Moldotsbank, and the Savings Bank, as well as 20 commercial banks at the end of 2002. As in many other republics of the former Soviet Union, licensing procedures in the early 1990s were quite lax, with the result that the country is now overbanked, with too many small institutions, and a relatively high level of nonperforming loans (11% of total commercial bank balance sheets as of mid-1996).

Moldova's 15 voucher funds have played an important role in the privatization program. Most citizens have opted to invest their vouchers in the funds rather than directly acquire shares in newly privatized companies.

The International Monetary Fund reports that in 2001, currency and demand deposits—an aggregate commonly known as M1—were equal to $194.3 million. In that same year, M2—an aggregate equal to M1 plus savings deposits, small time deposits, and money market mutual funds—was $377.1 million. The money market rate, the rate at which financial institutions lend to one another in the short term, was 11%.

The Chişinău-based Moldovan Stock Exchange opened for business in June 1995. Trading is electronic and is based on an order-driven system. As of mid-1996, it listed 11 shares. The most actively traded shares are Cupicini Canning Factory and Banea de Economii. As of 1998, there were 15 investment funds and eight trust companies. A commodities exchange is planned. The government began auctioning 91-day treasury bills in 1995 and introduced 730-day treasury bills in 1997.

Foreign currency reserves at the NBM rose by one-third in 1996, from $226.7 million at end-1995 to $304.1 million. This is to be explained by the substantial inflows of funds from multilateral institutions, notably the World Bank and the European Bank for Reconstruction and Development. In December 1996, Moldova made its debut in the international bond market with a $30 million floating rate note issued as a private placement through Merrill Lynch.

34 INSURANCE

The demand for insurance services continues to rise. Forty companies employing 2,800 persons competed for the insurance market in 1998.

35 PUBLIC FINANCE

In 1993, following independence, Moldova undertook a massive privatization program. By January 2003, 80% of all housing units were in private hands, as were nearly all small, medium, and large businesses. Agriculture was privatized ending in 2000 through a US-sponsored program called "Pamint" (land).

The US Central Intelligence Agency (CIA) estimated that in 2005 Moldova's central government took in revenues of approximately $1 billion and had expenditures of $1 billion. Revenues minus expenditures totaled approximately $4 million. Public debt in 2005 amounted to 72.9% of GDP. Total external debt was $1.926 billion.

The International Monetary Fund (IMF) reported that in 2003, the most recent year for which it had data, central government revenues were MLD7,376.8 million and expenditures were MLD6,828.5 million. The value of revenues was us$529 million and expenditures us$487 million, based on an exchange rate for 2003 of us$1 = MLD13.9449 as reported by the IMF. Government outlays by function were as follows: general public services, 33.4%; defense, 1.7%; public order and safety, 7.7%; economic affairs, 3.3%; environmental protection, 0.5%; health, 6.2%; recreation, culture, and religion, 1.5%; education, 9.2%; and social protection, 36.5%.

36 TAXATION

The personal income tax rate ranges from 10–50%. The corporate rate is a standard 18%. Capital gains derived from the sale, exchange or transfer of capital assets are taxed at an effective rate of 9%. Dividends are subject to a 10% withholding tax if paid to nonresidents, and 18% if paid to resident legal entities. Dividends

---

Public Finance – Moldova (2003)

(In millions of lei, central government figures)

Revenue and Grants	**7,376.8**	**100.0%**
Tax revenue	4,052.5	54.9%
Social contributions	1,978.2	26.8%
Grants	...	...
Other revenue	1,346.1	18.2%
Expenditures	**6,828.5**	**100.0%**
General public services	2,279.4	33.4%
Defense	114.7	1.7%
Public order and safety	525.5	7.7%
Economic affairs	227.8	3.3%
Environmental protection	35.3	0.5%
Housing and community amenities	0.8	<1.0%
Health	421.8	6.2%
Recreational, culture, and religion	101.6	1.5%
Education	627	9.2%
Social protection	2,494.6	36.5%

(…) data not available or not significant.

SOURCE: *Government Finance Statistics Yearbook 2004*, Washington, DC: International Monetary Fund, 2004.

received by resident individuals from resident and nonresident companies are considered part of taxable income. Dividends paid to Moldovan citizens by resident firms are exempt from taxation. Payroll taxes are charged at rates of 4.7–30%. Also levied is a 20% value-added tax (VAT). A reduced rate applies to bread, milk and other dairy products. For five years, 2002 to 2007, a number of housing projects will be exempt from VAT.

37 CUSTOMS AND DUTIES

Moldova's foreign trade environment is characterized by extensive export and import tariffs, exhaustive license requirements, and export quotas. Under the provisions of a 2001 budget law, all imports are assessed a 5% tax of their customs cost regardless of their country of origin. Moldova also levies customs tariffs on all imports except those from the former Soviet Union, Romania, the European Union, and a select group of countries with which Moldova has free trade agreements. Excise taxes apply to automobiles (30%), alcoholic beverages (50%), electronics (50%), and cigarettes (70%). Since 1998 most imports are subject to a value-added tax (VAT) that amounts to 20% of the customs value of the goods. Grain and medical supplies may be imported duty-free.

38 FOREIGN INVESTMENT

With the exception of certain state-controlled enterprises, current legislation does not restrict foreign capital participation in Moldovan enterprises. Some foreign equity participation in privatization of government-owned enterprises is also possible. Land under privatized enterprises can now be owned by the enterprise owners. Barriers in Moldova to foreign investment involve the underdeveloped banking, insurance, legal, and trade services.

In 1997 and 1998, average annual foreign direct investment (FDI) inflows into Moldova had reached $77 million, up from about $24 million in 1996. In 1998, the financial crisis in Russia, which accounts for a 30% share of Moldova's inward FDI, helped reduce inflows to $40.6 million for the year, but in 2000 and 2001, record levels of FDI inflows of $143 million and $160 million, respectively, were attained. Total FDI stock has increased 22 times over since independence. The total stock of FDI in Moldova reached $620 million in 2001, equivalent to 36% of GDP and about 82% of gross fixed capital formation (compared to the world average of 22%). Moldova's share of world inflows of FDI from 1998 to 2000, while small in absolute terms, was 1.7 times its share of world GDP. Foreign investment was $110.8 million in 2003, and by 2004 total investments made up 17.1% of the GDP.

Moldova remains a relatively unattractive market for investors due to the ongoing conflict in Transnistria. It has however a significant future potential due to its highly educated population, low wages, and competitive costs.

39 ECONOMIC DEVELOPMENT

In March 1993, the Moldovan government inaugurated the Program of Activity of the Government 1992–95 to make the transition to a market-oriented economy. The first stage focused on stabilization, including price liberalization, and the second stage concentrated on economic recovery and growth, including privatization, agrarian reform, infrastructure development, social protection, and trade reform. However, the government was slow to institute privatization in the agricultural sector. Although the government backed privatization, freed prices and interest rates, and removed export controls, economic growth was difficult. By 1998, Moldova's economy stood at one-third its 1989 level. In large part, this decline is due to unfavorable circumstances: the Transnistrian conflict, the collapse of the Soviet Union, the near-total loss of the grape crop in 1997, and the Russian 1998 financial crisis.

As of 2002, close to 2,000 small, medium, and large enterprises had been privatized, as were 80% of all housing units. Nearly all of Moldova's agricultural land is privatized as well. In 2000, Moldova negotiated a three-year $147 million Poverty Reduction and Growth Facility (PRGF) Arrangement with the International Monetary Fund (IMF), to expire in December 2003. Moldova joined the WTO in 2001. That year, the government adopted laws to combat money laundering and the financing of terrorism. The economy had turned around: spurred by industrial growth and a good harvest in 2001, real gross domestic product (GDP) growth increased by 6%. Nevertheless, Moldova carries a heavy external debt burden, and depends upon international financial support, including from the private sector.

Moldova remains one of Europe's poorest economies, and is highly dependent on agriculture. It has virtually no mineral resources, its industrial base is situated in conflict stricken Transnistria, and it relies on Russia and Romania for most of its energy supply. The World Bank considers Moldova to be a low-income country, and most of the household consumption (and subsequently most of its economic growth) is fueled by remittances from abroad.

40 SOCIAL DEVELOPMENT

A social insurance system provides benefits for old age, disability, and survivorship in addition to worker's compensation for injury and unemployment, and family allowances. Benefits are available to salaried citizens, agricultural workers, the self-employed, and public officials. The government contributes the whole cost of social pensions for those who are excluded from coverage from the national social security system. Medical care is available to all residents. Moldova has comprehensive legislation for the protection of children, including programs for paid maternity leave, a birth grant, and family allowances. Sickness and maternity benefits were first implemented in 1993, and were updated in 2003.

Although women are accorded equal rights under the law, they are underrepresented in government and other leadership positions. Nevertheless, the president of the country's largest bank is a woman, and women constitute a growing percentage of public-sector managers. Several women's organizations participate in political or charitable activities. Domestic violence remains a problem and is rarely prosecuted. In 2004 the government took efforts to increase public awareness of the problem.

The constitution provides for equality under the law regardless of race, sex, disability, religion, or social origin, but discrimination persists. The minority Roma population continues to suffer violence and harassment. Human rights are generally observed and respected, although there were reports of mistreatment of prisoners and detainees. Prison conditions remain harsh.

41 HEALTH

Moldova has been working on developing its own standards for health care. As of 2004, there were an estimated 35 physicians per 100,000 people. Total health care expenditures were 6.4% of GDP.

The birth rate was 14 per 1,000 people and the maternal mortality rate was 34 per 100,000 live births in 2003. Average life expectancy was 65.18 years in 2005. The infant mortality rate for that year was 40.42 per 1,000 live births. The overall death rate was estimated at 12.6 per 1,000 people as of 2002. In 1992, there were approximately 1,000 deaths from ethnic conflict within the country. Nearly the entire urban population (96%), but only 9% of the rural population, had access to sanitation.

Moldova's immunization rates for children up to one year old were: tuberculosis, 99%; diphtheria, pertussis, and tetanus, 97%; polio, 98%; and measles, 99%. Despite immunization rates, epidemic diphtheria has spread throughout the new independent states of the former Soviet Union. The HIV/AIDS prevalence was 0.20 per 100 adults in 2003. As of 2004, there were approximately 5,500 people living with HIV/AIDS in the country. There were an estimated 300 deaths from AIDS in 2003.

42 HOUSING

In 2000, there were about 1.3 million housing units in about 910,000 buildings nationwide. Though the government has encouraged privatization of housing and individual home ownership, most residents, particularly in urban areas, find home ownership to be far too expensive in a poor economy. The existing housing stock is in serious disrepair and overcrowding is an issue. Most structures were built before 1980 and maintenance has been poor. Only about 28.9% of all dwellings have an indoor bathroom; only 31% have access to a sewage system. About 62% of all households use wells as a primary source of water. In 1999, only 2,900 structures were completed. Most new housing is built with brick or stone and concrete frames. The average number of rooms per dwelling is about 2.8.

43 EDUCATION

While Moldova was a part of the Soviet Union, its education system was based on the Soviet pattern, and Russian was the language of instruction. However, after its separation, extensive changes were introduced in the education system. Education is compulsory for 11 years, between the ages of 6 and 17. Primary school covers four years of study. This is followed by five years of general secondary studies. Upper secondary studies may cover two or three years of study, depending on a student's interests. The academic year runs from September to July.

In 2001, about 39% of children between the ages of three and six were enrolled in some type of preschool program. Primary school enrollment in 2003 was estimated at about 79% of age-eligible students. The same year, secondary school enrollment was about 69% of age-eligible students. It is estimated that about 82.5% of all students complete their primary education. The student-to-teacher ratio for primary school was at about 19:1 in 2003; the ratio for secondary school was about 13:1.

The Moldovan State University was founded in 1945 and uses both Moldovan and Russian as languages of instruction. In 2003, about 30% of the tertiary age population were enrolled in some type of higher education program; 26% for men and 34% for women. The adult literacy rate for 2004 was estimated at about 96.2%.

The primary administrative body is the Ministry of Education, Youth and Sports. As of 2003, public expenditure on education was estimated at 4.9% of GDP, or 21.4% of total government expenditures.

44 LIBRARIES AND MUSEUMS

The National Library at Chişinău holds 418,000 volumes. The Scientific and Technical Library of Moldova holds about 600,000 volumes. The country's largest library, at the State University of Moldova, has over 1.82 million volumes, including a valuable rare books collection. The Technical University of Moldova has over 1.04 million volumes. The country had a public library system of over 1,300 branches.

Chişinău is home to several museums, including the National Museum of Fine Arts, the National History Museum, the Museum of Ethnography and Archaeology, and the Alexander Pushkin House and Museum. The Museum of Popular Art is in Ivancea.

45 MEDIA

Telecommunications links are via land line to the Ukraine and through Moscow's switching center to countries beyond the former USSR. In 2003, there were an estimated 219 mainline telephones for every 1,000 people; about 88,000 people were on a waiting list for telephone service installation. Also in 2003, there were approximately 132 mobile phones in use for every 1,000 people.

The state-operated Teleradio-Moldova operates one television and one radio station. Many stations are independent. In 2003, there were about 20 radio stations and 30 television stations in operation. In 2003, there were an estimated 758 radios and 296 television sets for every 1,000 people. About 24.6 of every 1,000 people were cable subscribers. Also in 2003, there were 17.5 personal computers for every 1,000 people and 80 of every 1,000 people had access to the Internet. There were nine secure Internet servers in the country in 2004.

A wide variety of political views and commentaries are expressed through a number of newspapers and periodicals. National and city governments sponsor newspapers, as do political parties, professional organizations, and trade unions. The largest newspapers in 2002 were *Moldova Suverana* (*Sovereign Moldova*, circulation 105,000), *Nezavisimaya Moldova* (*Independent Moldova*, 60,692), and *Viata Satului* (*Life of the Village*, 50,000).

The constitution provides for free speech and a free press, and the government is said to generally respect these rights.

46 ORGANIZATIONS

The Chamber of Commerce and Industry of the Republic of Moldova handles the internal and external economic affairs of the country. The Central Union of Consumers Co-operatives of the Republic of Moldova serves farmers as well as a variety of food producers and retailers. There are trade and professional associations throughout the country as well.

Political associations and organizations in the country include the Union of Council of Labor Collectives (ULC), Ecology Movement of Moldova (EMM), the Christian Democratic League of Women of Moldova, and the Alliance of Working People of Moldova.

The Academy of Sciences of Moldova works to promote public interest and education in scientific fields.

There are several sports associations within the country, including branches of the Special Olympics and the Paralympic Committee. The National Scout Organization of Moldova offers programs for youth.

The NGO Club was formed to assist in the development and consolidation of various organizations, as well as to serve as an informational network between groups. National women's organizations include the Women's Organization of Moldova (est. 1996) and the Gender in Development (GID) Project (est. 1994). International organizations with national chapters include Save the Children, Caritas, and the Red Cross.

47 TOURISM, TRAVEL, AND RECREATION

Picturesque scenery, several casinos, and wineries are the primary attractions of Moldova, including Cricova, the underground wine city. Unfortunately, civil unrest since Moldova's independence has caused a decline in tourism. In 2003, there were 23,598 tourist arrivals and tourism receipts totaled $83 million. There were 2,559 hotel rooms with 4,632 beds and an occupancy rate of 22%. Tourists need a valid passport to enter Moldova. Members and candidates to join the European Union, Canada, Japan, the United States, and many other European countries do not need a visa to enter Moldova for stays of up to 90 days.

In 2004, the US Department of State estimated the daily cost of staying in Moldova at $202.

48 FAMOUS MOLDOVANS

Petru Lucinschi (b.1940) was elected president in 1996, and served until 2001. He succeeded Mircea Snegur (b.1940), the first president of the Republic of Moldova. Vladimir Nicolae Voronin (b.1941) became president in 2001.

49 DEPENDENCIES

Moldova has no territories or colonies.

50 BIBLIOGRAPHY

Brezianu, Andrei. *Historical Dictionary of the Republic of Moldova.* Lanham, Md.: Scarecrow Press, 2000.

Dannreuther, Roland. *European Union Foreign and Security Policy: Towards a Neighbourhood Strategy.* New York: Routledge, 2004.

Dima, Nicholas. *From Moldavia to Moldova: The Soviet-Romanian Territorial Dispute.* 2nd ed. Boulder, Colo.: East European Monographs, 1991.

Dyer, Donald (ed.). *Studies in Moldovan: The History, Culture, Language and Contemporary Politics of the People of Moldova.* Boulder, Colo.: East European Monographs, 1996.

Gribincea, Mihai. *Agricultural Collectivization in Moldavia: Basarabia during Stalinism, 1944–1950.* Boulder, Colo.: East European Monographs, 1996.

King, Charles. *The Moldovans: Romania, Russia, and the Politics of Culture.* Stanford, Calif.: Hoover Institution Press, 2000.

Lobell, Steven E. and Philip Mauceri (eds.). *Ethnic Conflict and International Politics: Explaining Diffusion and Escalation.* New York: Palgrave Macmillan, 2004.

McElrath, Karen (ed.). *HIV and AIDS: A Global View.* Westport, Conn.: Greenwood Press, 2002.

Mitrasca, Marcel. *Moldova: A Romanian Province under Russian Rule: Diplomatic History from the Archives of the Great Powers.* New York: Algora, 2002.

MONACO

Principality of Monaco
Principauté de Monaco

CAPITAL: The seat of government is at Monaco-Ville

FLAG: The national flag consists of a red horizontal stripe above a white horizontal stripe.

ANTHEM: *Hymne Monégasque,* beginning "Principauté Monaco, ma patrie" ("Principality of Monaco, my fatherland").

MONETARY UNIT: The euro replaced the French franc as the official currency in 2002. The euro is divided into 100 cents. There are coins in denominations of 1, 2, 5, 10, 20, and 50 cents and 1 euro and 2 euros. There are notes of 5, 10, 20, 50, 100, 200, and 500 euros. €1 = $1.25475 (or $1 = €0.79697) as of 2005. Monégasque coins also circulate; denominations are 10, 20, and 50 centimes, and 1, 2, 5, 10, and 50 francs. Fr1 = $0.184 (or $1 = Fr5.4) as of March 2006.

WEIGHTS AND MEASURES: The metric system is the legal standard.

HOLIDAYS: New Year's Day, 1 January; St. Dévôte, 27 January; Labor Day, 1 May; Assumption, 15 August; All Saints' Day, 1 November; National Day, 19 November; Immaculate Conception, 8 December; Christmas, 25 December. Movable religious holidays include Easter Monday, Ascension, Pentecost Monday, and Fête-Dieu.

TIME: 1 PM = noon GMT.

¹LOCATION, SIZE, AND EXTENT

The second-smallest country in Europe and the world after the Vatican, Monaco is situated in the southeastern part of the French department of Alpes-Maritimes. The area, including recent reclamation, is 195 hectares (482 acres), or 1.95 sq km (0.75 sq mi). Comparatively, the area occupied by Monaco is about three times the size of the Mall in Washington, DC. The principality's length is 3.18 km (1.98 mi) E–W, and its width is 1.1 km (0.68 mi) N–S. Bounded on the N, NE, SW, and W by France and on the E and SE by the Mediterranean Sea, Monaco has a total border length of 8.5 km (5.3 mi), of which 4.1 km (2.5 mi) is coastline.

²TOPOGRAPHY

There are four main areas (determined more by economic activity than geographic difference): La Condamine, the business district around the port; Monte Carlo, the site of the famous casino, which is at a higher elevation; Monaco-Ville, on a rocky promontory about 60 m (200 ft) above sea level; and Fontvieille, a 22-hectare (54-acre) industrial area of La Condamine that was reclaimed by landfill in the 1960s and 1970s.

³CLIMATE

Winters are mild, with temperatures rarely falling below freezing and with a January average of about 8°C (46°F). Summer heat is tempered by sea breezes; the average maximum in July and August is 26°C (79°F). Rainfall averages about 77 cm (30 in) a year, and some 300 days a year have no precipitation whatsoever.

⁴FLORA AND FAUNA

Palms, aloes, carobs, tamarisks, mimosas, and other Mediterranean trees, shrubs, and flowers are abundant. Monaco does not have a distinctive fauna.

⁵ENVIRONMENT

Monaco is noted for its beautiful natural scenery and mild, sunny climate. The principality has sponsored numerous marine conservation efforts. Its own environment is entirely urban. According to UN reports, Monaco's environmental circumstances are very good. The nation has consistently monitored pollution levels in its air and water to ensure the safety of its citizens. One-fifth of the nation's land area (1.95 sq km) and two marine areas are protected by environmental statutes.

The government has also instituted a system of air pollution control facilities controlled by the Environmental Service. Citizens are encouraged to use public transportation to limit the amount of gas emissions. Similar techniques have been applied to the protection of Monaco's water supply. Noise levels from industry and transportation are also monitored to ensure safe levels.

Monaco also has a sea-farming area which annually produces 800 tons of fish grown in clean water. Monaco is known for its activity in the field of marine sciences. The Oceanographic Museum, formerly directed by Jacques Cousteau, is renowned for its work and exhibits on marine life.

According to a 2006 report issued by the International Union for Conservation of Nature and Natural Resources (IUCN), threatened species included 26 species of marine life. Threatened species included the great white shark, the blue shark, striped dolphin, albacore tuna, and swordfish.

6 POPULATION

The population of Monaco in 2005 was estimated by the United Nations (UN) at 33,000, which placed it at number 188 in population among the 193 nations of the world. In 2005, approximately 22% of the population was over 65 years of age, with another 13% of the population under 15 years of age. According to the UN, the annual population rate of change for 2005–10 was expected to be 0.6%, a rate the government viewed as satisfactory. The projected population for the year 2025 was 44,000. The population density was 16,988 per sq km (44,000 per sq mi), making Monaco the most densely populated nation in the world.

The UN reported that 100% of the population lived in urban areas in 2005. Most of the people in Monaco are resident foreigners.

7 MIGRATION

There is a long waiting list for Monégasque citizenship. A 1992 law allows Monégasque women to confer citizenship on their children. In 2005, the net migration rate was an estimated 7.71 migrants per 1,000 population. In 2000, more than two-thirds of the residents were noncitizens. The government views the migration levels as satisfactory.

8 ETHNIC GROUPS

On the evidence of certain place names, the native Monégasques are said to be of Rhaetian stock; they make up only 16% of the population. The foreign residents are a highly cosmopolitan group: 47% are French; 16% are Italian; and various other groups comprise the remaining 21%.

9 LANGUAGES

French is the official language. English and Italian are also widely spoken. Many inhabitants speak the Monégasque language, which has its origins in the Genoese dialect of Italian and the Provençal language of southern France.

10 RELIGIONS

About 90% of the population adheres to Roman Catholicism, which is the official state religion. Freedom of worship is guaranteed by the constitution. Monaco is also part of the diocese of Gibraltar of the Church of England. There are five Catholic churches and one cathedral in the principality, two Protestant churches, and one Jewish synagogue. Though there are a small number of Muslims, there are no mosques.

11 TRANSPORTATION

French national roads join Monaco to Nice toward the west, and to Menton and the Italian Riviera toward the east. In 2002 there were 50 km (31 mi) of roadways, all of them paved. There is frequent bus service. The principality itself is served by motorbuses and taxicabs. In 1995 there were 17,000 passenger cars and 4,000 commercial vehicles. The southeastern network of the French national railroad system serves Monaco with about 1.7 km (1 mi) of track. Express trains on the Paris-Marseille-Nice-Ventimiglia line pass through the principality. Monaco is only 10 km (6 mi) from the international airport at Nice and is connected with it by bus and by a helicopter shuttle service. In 2001 (the latest year for which data was available), 77,800 passengers were carried on domestic and international airline flights. The harbor provides access by sea.

12 HISTORY

The ruling family of Monaco, the house of Grimaldi, traces its ancestry to Otto Canella (c.1070–1143), who was consul of Genoa in 1133. The family name, Grimaldi, was adapted from the Christian name of Canella's youngest son, Grimaldo. The Genoese built a fort on the site of present-day Monaco in 1215, and the Grimaldi family secured control late in the 13th century. The principality was founded in 1338 by Charles I, during whose reign Menton and Roquebrune were acquired. Claudine became sovereign upon the death of her father, Catalan, in 1457. She ceded her rights to her husband and cousin, Lambert, during whose reign, in 1489, the duke of Savoy recognized the independence of Monaco. The first Monégasque coins were minted in the 16th century. Full recognition of the princely title was obtained by Honoré II in 1641.

The last male in the Grimaldi line, Antoine I, died in 1731. His daughter Louise-Hippolyte in 1715 had married Jacques-François-Léonor de Goyon-Matignon, Count of Thorigny, who adopted the name Grimaldi and assumed the Monégasque throne. France annexed the principality in 1793, but independence was reestablished in 1814. The following year, the Treaty of Stupinigi placed Monaco under the protection of the neighboring kingdom of Sardinia. In 1848, the towns of Roquebrune and Menton, which constituted the eastern extremity of Monaco, successfully rebelled and established themselves as a republic. In 1861, a year after the Sardinian cession of Savoy and Nice to France, Roquebrune and Menton also became part of that nation.

The economic development of Monaco proceeded rapidly with the opening of the railroad in 1868 and of the gambling casino. Since that time, the principality has become world famous as a tourist and recreation center. Gambling, operated by Société des Bains de Mer, a state controlled group, recorded a 30% increase in gambling receipts in 1998. Real estate and retail sales have also registered strong growth in recent years. As of 2005 Monaco has no unemployment and provides jobs for 25,000 Italian and French commuters. More than half of government revenues, however, come from value-added tax. The rate levied by France is also in effect in Monaco. France has the highest VAT in the European Union and has come under pressure to adjust its rate downward in conformity with the rest of the EU. However, Monaco is not an EU member. Light industry and banking have also become important. Monaco joined the United Nations on 28 May 1993. Monaco is the second-smallest independent state in the world, after the Holy See, and is almost entirely urban.

Prince Rainier III, once married to the American actress Grace Kelly, led the country 1949–2005 and is often credited for the country's impressive economic growth. Tourism, banking and other types of financial services augment the economy's former dependence on gambling. Rainier died in early 2005 and in July 2005, Prince Albert II, son of Rainier and Kelly, assumed the throne. The event was somewhat overshadowed by his admission of having a 22-month-old illegitimate child. His illegitimate son will not be able to inherit the throne, although Prince Albert has acknowledged paternity and assumed his financial responsibilities.

¹³GOVERNMENT

Monaco is a constitutional monarchy ruled, until 2002, by the hereditary princes of the Grimaldi line. Prior to constitutional changes made in 2002, if the reigning prince were to die without leaving a male heir, Monaco, according to treaty, would be incorporated into France. Because Prince Rainier III's son Albert was a 43-year-old bachelor in 2002, without male heirs, and his own health was failing, Rainier changed Monaco's constitution to allow one of his two daughters, Caroline or Stephanie, to inherit the throne and preserve the Grimaldi dynasty.

On 7 January 1911, Monaco's first constitution was granted by Prince Albert I. On 29 January 1959, Prince Rainier III temporarily suspended part of the constitution because of a disagreement over the budget with the National Council (Conseil National), and decreed that the functions of that body were to be assumed temporarily by the Council of State (Conseil d'État). In February 1961, the National Council was restored and an economic advisory council established to assist it.

A new constitution was promulgated on 17 December 1962. It provides for a unicameral National Council of 18 (now 24) members elected every five years (now 16 by majority vote and 8 by proportional representation); it shares legislative functions with the prince. Executive operations are conducted in the name of the prince by a minister of state (a French citizen) with the assistance of the Council of Government, consisting of three civil servants who are in charge of finances, public works, and internal affairs, respectively. All are appointed by the prince.

Women were enfranchised for municipal elections in 1945, and participated in elections for the National Council for the first time in February 1963. Until 2003, suffrage was exercised only by true-born Monégasques of 21 and over. Naturalized Monégasques were granted voting rights in 2003 and the voting age was reduced to 18.

¹⁴POLITICAL PARTIES

Monaco does not have political parties as such, but candidates compete on the basis of various lists. Major political groups have been the National and Democratic Union (Union Nationale et Démocratique—UND), founded in 1962; Communist Action (Action Communale—AC); Évolution Communale (EC); and the Movement of Democratic Union (MUD). In the general election of February 1998, the UND took all 18 seats in the National Council. Elections held on 9 February 2003 were the first under a new electoral law establishing 24 seats in the National Council. A unified opposition list, the Union for Monaco, composed of the National Union for the Future of Monaco and the Rally for the Monégasque Family, took 58.5% of the vote and 21 seats, to the UND's 41.5% and 3 seats. The introduction of proportionality voting enabled the UND to obtain its seats. The next election was scheduled for 2008.

¹⁵LOCAL GOVERNMENT

Municipal government is conducted by an elected council (Conseil Communal) of 15 members, headed by a mayor. The council members are elected by universal suffrage for four-year terms, and the mayor is chosen by the Communal Council. The three communes that made up Monaco before 1917—Monaco-Ville,

LOCATION: 43°43′49″ N; 7°25′36″ E. BOUNDARY LENGTHS: France, 5.4 kilometers (3.4 miles); Mediterranean coastline, 7.3 kilometers (4.5 miles). TERRITORIAL SEA LIMIT: 12 miles.

La Condamine, and Monte Carlo—each had its own mayor from 1911 to 1917. Since that date, they have formed a single commune, together with Fontvieille.

Anne Marie Campora became mayor of Monte Carlo in 1991 succeeding Jean-Louis Médecin who had served as mayor since 1971. Georges Marsan was elected mayor of Monte Carlo in 2003.

¹⁶JUDICIAL SYSTEM

A justice of the peace tries petty cases. Other courts are the court of first instance, the court of appeal, the court of revision, and the criminal court. The highest judicial authority is vested in the Supreme Court, established as part of the 1962 constitution, which interprets the constitution and sits as the highest court of appeals. It has five full members and two assistant members, named by the prince on the basis of nominations by the National Council and other government bodies.

The Code Louis, promulgated by Prince Louis I (d.1701) and based on French legal codes, was formally adopted in 1919. Under the 1962 constitution the prince delegates his authority to the judiciary to render justice in his name.

The legal guarantee of a fair and public trial for criminal defendants is respected in practice. Defendants have the right to counsel at public expense if necessary.

The constitution provides for freedom of speech, although the penal code prohibits denunciations of the royal family. The constitution differentiates between the rights of nationals and those of noncitizens; of the estimated 32,000 residents in the principality, only about 7,000 are actual Monégasques.

Monaco is a member of the United Nations and International Criminal Court.

17 ARMED FORCES

France assumed responsibility for the defense of Monaco as part of the Versailles Treaty in 1919. There is no army in the principality. A private guard protects the royal family, and a police force of 390 ensures public safety.

18 INTERNATIONAL COOPERATION

Monaco joined the United Nations on 28 May 1993 and is a member of the ECE and several nonregional specialized agencies, such as the FAO, IAEA, ICAO, IMO, ITU, UNCTAD, UNESCO, WHO, and WIPO. Monaco is also a member of the Council of Europe and the OSCE. The headquarters of the International Hydrographic Bureau (IHB) is located in Monaco.

A treaty providing in detail for mutual administrative assistance between France and Monaco became operative on 14 December 1954. Fiscal relations between the two countries are governed by a convention signed on 18 May 1963. France may station troops in Monaco and make use of Monaco's territorial waters. As a result of a customs union with France and French control of Monaco's foreign policy, the principality operates within the European Union.

In environmental cooperation, Monaco is part of the Basel Convention; Conventions on Biological Diversity, Whaling, and Air Pollution; Ramsar; CITES; the London Convention; the Montréal Protocol; MARPOL; and the UN Conventions on the Law of the Sea, Climate Change, and Desertification.

19 ECONOMY

Monaco depends for its livelihood chiefly on income from tourism, real estate, financial services, and small, high value-added, nonpolluting industry. A substantial part of the principality's revenue from tourist sources comes from the operations of Sea-Bathing Co. (Société des Bains de Mer—SBM), in which the government holds a 69% interest. The SBM operates the gambling casino at Monte Carlo as well as four hotels, 19 restaurants, a cabaret, and the Thermos Margins spa. Its reported profits in 2002 were about $21 million, down from close to $30 million in 2001. The government also retains monopolies in telephone services, postal services and tobacco. A 22-hectare landfill project at Fontvielle increased Monaco's total land area. Land reclamation since Prince Rainier's accession to the throne in 1949 has increased Monaco's territory by 23%.

The principality does not publish statistics on its economy and all estimates are rough. The government's annual income was estimated at $586 million for 1997, about 25% derived from tourism. Monaco also serves as a tax haven for foreign non-French residents. In 2000 the OECD published a list of "uncooperative tax havens" that included Monaco. Two years later, Monaco was still on the list, though 31 other jurisdictions had been removed by promising to take corrective actions.

Estimate data put together by the United Nations Statistic Division shows that the economy of the principality has been expanding modestly. Similar to other countries in Europe, the GDP growth rate was 2.7% in 2001, falling to 1.9% and 1.4% in 2002 and 2003 respectively, and recuperating again in 2004, at 3%. Unemployment in 1998 was estimated to be around 3.1%.

20 INCOME

The US Central Intelligence Agency (CIA) reports that in 2005 Monaco's gross domestic product (GDP) was estimated at $870.0 million. The CIA defines GDP as the value of all final goods and services produced within a nation in a given year and computed on the basis of purchasing power parity (PPP) rather than value as measured on the basis of the rate of exchange based on current dollars. The per capita GDP was estimated at $27,000. The annual growth rate of GDP was estimated at 0.9%. The average inflation rate in 2000 was 1.9%. It was estimated that agriculture accounted for 17% of GDP.

21 LABOR

There is virtually no unemployment in Monaco, as the Prince guarantees all his subjects lifetime employment. The major employer of the working population is the SBM; others work in industry or in service establishments. As of January 1994 (the latest year for which data was available), the labor force totaled 30,540, of which 4,000 worked in the industrial sector, 2,200 in construction, and 1,500 in the financial sector.

Owners and workers are each grouped in syndicates. Less than 10% of the workforce in 2005 was unionized. However, most of these union workers commute from outside the principality. About two-thirds of all employees commute from France and Italy. Unions operate independently of the government and political parties. The rights to strike, organize, and bargain collectively are protected by law, although public government workers may not strike. Labor disruptions are infrequent.

The minimum working age is 16, although special restrictions apply until the age of 18. Employers who violate the minimum age laws can be criminally prosecuted. The standard workweek is 39 hours. The minimum wage is the French minimum plus an additional 5% to adjust for travel costs for commuters. In 2005, this wage was equivalent to $9.60 per hour. This provides a family with a decent standard of living, and most workers earn more than the minimum. Health and safety standards are rigorously enforced.

22 AGRICULTURE

There is no agriculture.

23 ANIMAL HUSBANDRY

There is a dairy industry serving local needs.

24 FISHING

Some fishing is carried on to meet domestic requirements. The annual catch was 3,000 tons in 2003. Monaco actively engages in marine science research, and in marine life preservation. The Oceanographic Institute has been studying the effects of radiation in the ocean since 1961.

25 FORESTRY

There are no forests.

26 MINING

There is no mining.

27 ENERGY AND POWER

Services are provided by the Monégasque Electric Co. and Monégasque Gas Co. In 1991, standby electrical capacity totaled 10,000 kW; power is supplied by France.

28 INDUSTRY

The tourist industry dominates Monaco's economic life, but small-scale industries produce a variety of items for domestic use and for export, contributing 11.6% of business turnover in the mid-1990s. Most industrial plants are located on Fontvieille. About 700 small businesses make pottery and glass objects, paper and cards, jewelry, perfumes, dolls, precision instruments, plastics, chemicals and pharmaceuticals, machine tools, watches, leather items, and radio parts. There are flour mills, dairies, and chocolate and candy plants, as well as textile mills and a small shipyard. The chemicals, pharmaceuticals, and cosmetics industries consisted of 23 companies with 1,000 employees that generated approximately 45% of the total industrial turnover in the 1990s. Due to territorial constraints, Monaco's industries are forced to expand their facilities upward; some industrial buildings rise as high as 13 stories. A new construction project begun in 2001 was extending the pier used by cruise ships in the main harbor.

29 SCIENCE AND TECHNOLOGY

Marine sciences have been the focus of scientific inquiry in the principality for several decades. Prince Albert (1848–1922), who reigned in Monaco during the early 1900s, was well-known internationally for his work as an oceanographer, and he inaugurated the Oceanographic Museum of Monaco at Monaco-Ville in 1910. His interest led to the establishment of a focus on oceanography for scientific pursuits in Monaco. Jacques-Yves Cousteau, a famous oceanographer and activist, was involved with Monaco's activities in marine life research.

In March 1961, in its first research agreement concluded with a member government, the International Atomic Energy Agency, with the government of Monaco and the Oceanographic Institute in Monaco, undertook to research the effects of radioactivity in the sea. The Oceanographic Institute put at the disposal of the project a number of valuable facilities, including marine-biology laboratories, oceanographic vessels, specialized fishing equipment, and a wide variety of electronic and monitoring equipment.

The Scientific Center of Monaco, founded in 1960 at Monte Carlo, conducts pure and applied research in oceanology and the environment. The Museum of Prehistoric Anthropology, founded in 1902 at Monte Carlo, is concerned with prehistory and quaternary geology.

30 DOMESTIC TRADE

Domestic trade practices are similar to those in other towns along the French Riviera. Specialty shops deal primarily in tourist souvenirs. The SBM controls most of the amusement facilities and owns most major hotels, sporting clubs, workshops, a printing press, and various retail shops. In the mid-1990s, commerce represented 21% of the economic turnover in Monaco. There is no personal income tax. Business taxes are low, but still account for about 50% of government income. Tourism and related services account for about 25% of revenues.

Advertising media include magazines, billboards, and motion pictures. General business hours are from 8:30 AM to 12:30 PM and from 2 to 6 PM, Monday–Friday. Banking hours are 9 AM to 12 noon and 2 to 4 PM, Monday–Friday.

31 FOREIGN TRADE

Statistical information is not available. Foreign trade is included in the statistics for France, with which Monaco has a customs union. France also collects the Monegasque trade duties, and serves as the principality's link to the EU market.

In 2003, the US Department of State estimated that Monaco's exports totaled $644 million, while its imports reached $513 million.

32 BALANCE OF PAYMENTS

The economy is driven by such foreign currency-earning activities as banking and tourism. Since separate records are not kept of Monaco's foreign trade transactions, payment statistics are not available.

The United Nations Statistics Division has looked at the data available in France, and came up with some estimates of the exports and imports of goods and services in Monaco. Thus, exports totaled $299 million in 2004, up from $257 million in 2003 and $219 million in 2002. Imports grew from $205 million in 2002, to $246 million in 2003, and $296 million in 2004. Consequently, Monaco has, year to year, managed to keep a positive, although fragile, resource balance. In 2000, it was estimated that the country's external debt was $18 billion—an impressive figure when compared to the size of the principality.

33 BANKING AND SECURITIES

Foreign currency circulates within Monaco under the supervision of the French government. The most important local bank is Crédit Foncier de Monaco, founded in 1922. As of 1994, there were 45 banks operating in Monaco. In 1999, an Monaco's banking industry had approximately 310,000 accounts and employed 1,700 people. The vast majority of customers were nonresidents. Total assets in 1998 were estimated at a little over $44 billion.

There is no securities exchange.

34 INSURANCE

Branches of French insurance companies provide life, fire, accident, and other forms of insurance. They include: CGRM-Compagnie Générale de Réassurance de Monte Carlo; Concorde; Mutuelle de Marseille Assurances Compagnie Générale de Réassurance; and the Shipowners' Mutual Strike Insurance Association (Bermuda)—all located in Monte Carlo.

35 PUBLIC FINANCE

The US Central Intelligence Agency (CIA) estimated that in 1995 Monaco's central government took in revenues of approximately $518 million and had expenditures of $531 million. Revenues minus expenditures totaled approximately -$13 million. Total external debt was $18 billion.

36 TAXATION

There are no personal income taxes. Indirect taxes include the following: a value-added tax of 19.6% (as of 2005); a service tax on compensation received by Monégasque firms for services rendered in Monaco and France; excise taxes on alcoholic beverages; registration fees; and warranty duties on gold, platinum, and silver jewelry. Monaco is treated as part of France for VAT purposes.

There is a tax of up to 33.3% on the profits of businesses that obtain more than 25% of their gross profits from operations outside Monaco. Corporations whose income is derived from royalties, licenses, trademarks, or other industrial or artistic property rights are subject to this tax, whether or not the income arises outside Monaco. Qualifying new companies may be assessed at reduced rates. There are no inheritance or gift taxes between spouses or between parents and children. Between brothers and sisters, the rate is 8%; between uncles or aunts and nephews or nieces, 10%; between other relatives, 13%; and between unrelated persons, 16%.

37 CUSTOMS AND DUTIES

By treaty, France and Monaco form a customs union that treats the Monaco coast as part of France. The French customs service collects the duties on cargoes discharged in Monaco and pays a share to the principality.

Monaco imposes a duty on all exports to places other than France; the levy applies whether the transfer of goods is actual or fictitious.

38 FOREIGN INVESTMENT

Monaco permits foreign businesses to establish their headquarters in its territory; ownership and management must be made a matter of public record. Although both corporations and limited partnerships with shares are allowed, in fact only corporations are in existence. Two persons may form a corporation; the minimum capital must be fully subscribed and at least one-fourth paid up front. Foreign companies may establish subsidiaries in Monaco. Low taxes on company profits are a considerable incentive for locating in Monaco.

39 ECONOMIC DEVELOPMENT

The government strenuously promotes Monaco as a tourist and convention attraction. A government-financed International Convention Center offers large conference rooms, projection equipment, television and radio recording studios, telex communications, and simultaneous translation into five languages.

Two major development and reclamation projects were undertaken under Prince Rainier. These are the major landfill and reclamation project at Fontvieille, and the Monte Carlo Bord de Mer. At Fontvieille, the government financed the reclamation of 220,000 sq m (2,368,000 sq ft) of inundated shore, creating a "platform" for residential construction and new port facilities.

The Monte Carlo seashore scheme, also government-financed, involved the relocation of railroad tracks underground in order to create a man-made beach, with a boardwalk and other tourist attractions. The beach lies between two other land reclamation projects: the Larvotto, a sports complex financed by SBM, and the Portier, an entertainment complex developed by the government.

Near the Larvotto the government has reserved a zone for the construction of residential and tourist accommodations. In the 1980s, Monaco concentrated on the development of business tourism, with the construction of the Monte Carlo Convention Center and the International Conference Center.

40 SOCIAL DEVELOPMENT

The social insurance system provides old age, survivorship and disability pensions. It is funded through employee and employer contributions. Sickness and maternity benefits are available to all employed persons with a special program for the self-employed. Workers and their dependents are reimbursed for medical expenses including primary and specialized care, pharmaceuticals, hospitalization, transportation, dental care and appliances. Employers are required to provide workers' compensation through private insurance plans. Unemployment benefits are provided through the French system. There is also a family allowance, a prenatal allowance and an education grant.

Women have become increasingly visible in public life, and are well represented in the professions. Equal pay for equal work is prevalent, although women are underrepresented in business. Reports of violence against women are rare, and domestic abuse is a criminal offense. Human rights are respected in Monaco.

41 HEALTH

In 2004, Monaco had the third most physicians per capita in the world. There were an estimated 586 physicians per 100,000 people in the country, as well as 1,430 nurses, 107 dentists, and 192 pharmacists per 100,000 people. The entire population has access to safe water and sanitation.

As of 2002, the crude birth rate and overall mortality rate were estimated at, respectively, 9.6 and 12.9 per 1,000 people. In 2005, the infant mortality rate was estimated at 5.43 per 1,000 live births. Life expectancy for that year was 79.57. The immunization rates for children under one year of age were as follows: diphtheria, tetanus, and whooping cough, 99%; polio, 99%; measles, 98%; and tuberculosis, 90%.

AIDS cases, although present, are not considered a major problem.

42 HOUSING

In 2000, there were about 18,396 housing units in the nation. About 31% of the housing stock was built 1915–61; another 26% was built 1968–81. About 21% of the housing stock was built 1982–2000. About 25% of all dwellings are owner occupied. In recent years, the government has stressed the construction of luxury housing. All new construction or alteration of existing buildings requires government approval.

43 EDUCATION

Education is offered in Monaco from the preschool to the secondary and technical levels and is compulsory from age 6 to 16. There are five years of primary school and seven years of secondary school. Attendance is 90%, and virtually all adults are literate. In 2003, approximately 5.1% of total government expenditure was allocated to education.

In 2001, there were about 2,000 students enrolled in primary schools and 3,000 enrolled in secondary schools. The pupil-teacher ratio at the primary level was estimated at 15 to 1 in 2000; the ratio for secondary school was 8 to 1. In 2003, private schools accounted for about 30% of primary school enrollment and 24.7% of secondary enrollment.

The University of Southern Europe was renamed the International University of Monaco in 2002. The university offers degrees in business and business administration. Students may travel abroad for higher education. The adult literacy rate has been estimated at about 99%. In 2003, public expenditure on education was estimated 5.1% of total government expenditures.

44 LIBRARIES AND MUSEUMS

The palace archives include the private collections of the princes of Monaco, as well as a collection of money minted since 1640. The Louis Notari Library in Monaco (1909) has a collection of over 285,000 volumes. There is a Princess Grace Irish Library in Monaco featuring 1,500 pieces of Irish folk music and personal papers of Princess Grace and Prince Rainier.

The Oceanographic Museum in Monaco-Ville, founded in 1910 by Prince Albert I and previously directed by the noted Jacques-Yves Cousteau, contains a library of 50,000 volumes, an aquarium, and displays of rare marine specimens. In addition to the museum, the Oceanographic Institute conducts research in various marine areas, including the effects of radiation on the sea and its life forms.

The Exotic Gardens include thousands of varieties of cacti and tropical plants. The National Museum in Monte Carlo was established 1972. There is a Museum of Prehistoric Anthropology in Monte Carlo and a Wax Museum of the Princes of Monaco. There is a Napoleonic Museum in Monaco-Ville. The Museum of Stamps and Coins opened in 1996 to display the private collection of Prince Rainier.

45 MEDIA

Postal and telegraphic services are operated by France, but Monaco issues its own postage stamps. Local telephone service is controlled by Monaco, while France is responsible for international service. In 2002, there were 33,700 mainline phones and 19,300 mobile phones in use nationwide.

Radio Monte Carlo and Télé Monte Carlo provide radio and television services and have had broadcast programs since 1954. Radio Monte Carlo's home service is broadcast in French. The system also provides overseas service in 12 foreign languages and is majority owner of the Cyprus-based Radio Monte Carlo relay station, a privately funded religious broadcasting service in 35 languages under the name Trans World Radio. As of 1999, Monaco

had 3 AM and 4 FM radio stations and 5 television stations. In 1997, there were 34,000 radios and 25,000 television sets throughout the country. In 2002, there were 16,000 Internet users in the country.

Two dailies in Nice, *Nice-Matin* and *L'Espoir,* publish special editions for Monaco. International publications are readily available. The *Journal de Monaco,* an official publication, appears once a week, and the *Tribune de Monaco* is published biweekly.

Freedom of expression is legally guaranteed. However, there is a Penal Code prohibition on public denunciations of the ruling family. Otherwise, the government is said to uphold free speech and a free press.

46 ORGANIZATIONS

Monaco is the seat of the International Academy of Tourism, which was founded in 1951 by Prince Rainier III. The academy publishes a quarterly, *Revue Technique du Tourisme,* and, in several languages, an international dictionary of tourism.

The International Hydrographic Bureau, which sponsors international conferences in its field, has its headquarters in Monaco. The following international organizations also have their headquarters in Monaco: International Commission for Scientific Exploration of the Mediterranean Sea, International Center for Studies of Human Problems, and the International Commission for Legal-Medical Problems.

National youth organizations include the Association of Scouts and Guides of Monaco, the Princess Stephanie Youth Center, and Catholic Youth of Monaco. There are several sports associations in Monaco; the country is home to the International Association of Athletics Federations.

Other organizations include the Monégasque Red Cross, Caritas, the St. Vincent de Paul Society, the Society of Monégasque Traditions, the Commission for the Monégasque language (established 1985), and the Union of French Interests.

47 TOURISM, TRAVEL, AND RECREATION

Monaco has been famous for attracting wealth and titled tourists since its gambling casino was established at Monte Carlo in 1856. In 2005, gambling accounted for almost 25% of the annual revenue. Among the many attractions are the Louis II Stadium, the many museums and gardens, and the beach. The Monte Carlo opera house was the site of many world premiere performances, including Massenet's *Le Jongleur de Notre Dame* (1902) and *Don Quichotte* (1910), Fauré's *Pénélope* (1913), and Ravel's *L'Enfant et les sortilèges* (1925). It was also the home of Serge Diaghilev's Russian Ballet (founded in 1911), later known as the Ballet Russe de Monte Carlo.

The principality has excellent sports facilities. The Monte Carlo Rally, a world-famous driving championship, ends with a finish line in Monaco.

No restriction is placed on the entrance of French nationals into Monaco. A valid passport is required for citizens of other countries who visit. Visas are not required for tourist/business stays of up to 90 days.

About 235,000 visitors arrived in Monaco in 2003, about 25% of whom came from Italy. Hotel rooms numbered 2,191 in 2002 with an occupancy rate of 63%. The average length of stay that year was three nights.

In 2005, the US Department of State estimated the cost of staying in Monaco at $247 per day.

48 FAMOUS MONEGASQUES

Prince Albert (1848–1922), who reigned from 1889 to 1922, was famous as an oceanographer. In 1956, his great-grandson Rainier III (1923–2005), reigning monarch from 1949–2005, married Grace Patricia Kelly (1929–82), a US motion picture actress, whose death on 14 September 1982 following an automobile accident was mourned throughout Monaco. Their son, Prince Albert (b.1958) became Prince Albert II upon his father's death; Princess Caroline (b.1957) and Princess Stéphanie (b.1965) are the daughters of Rainier III and Grace.

49 DEPENDENCIES

Monaco has no territories or colonies.

50 BIBLIOGRAPHY

Annesley, Claire (ed.). *A Political and Economic Dictionary of Western Europe*. Philadelphia: Routledge/Taylor and Francis, 2005.

Duursma, Jorri. *Self-Determination, Statehood, and International Relations of Micro-States: The Cases of Liechtenstein, San Marino, Monaco, Andorra, and the Vatican City*. New York: Cambridge University Press, 1996.

Taraborrelli, J. Randy. *Once Upon a Time: Behind the Fairy Tale of Princess Grace and Prince Rainier*. New York: Warner Books, 2003.

MONTENEGRO

Republic of Montenegro

CAPITAL: Podgorica

FLAG: The flag, adopted in 2004, is a red banner with a gold border bearing the gold coat of arms of Montenegro.

ANTHEM: *Oj svijetla majska zoro (Oh, Bright Dawn of May)*

MONETARY UNIT: The euro is the official currency. The euro is divided into 100 cents. There are coins in denominations of 1, 2, 5, 10, 20, and 50 cents and 1 euro and 2 euros. There are notes of 5, 10, 20, 50, 100, 200, and 500 euros. As of 26 May 2006, €1=$1.27213 (or $1=€0.785927).

WEIGHTS AND MEASURES: The metric system is in force.

HOLIDAYS: For the union of Serbia and Montenegro: New Year's Day, 1 and 2 January; Orthodox Christmas, 7 January; Orthodox New Year, 13 January; Unification of Serbia, 28 March; Yugoslavia Day, 27 April; Labor Day, 1 May; Victory Day, 9 May; St. Vitus Day, 28 June; Serbian Uprising, 7 July.

TIME: 1 PM = noon GMT.

¹LOCATION, SIZE, AND EXTENT

Montenegro is situated in southeastern Europe along the Adriatic Sea. The total area is 13,812 sq km (5,333 sq mi). Montenegro is bordered on the NW by Bosnia and Herzegovina, on the E by Serbia (the SE border is with the UN-administered province of Kosovo, which is claimed by Serbia), on the S by Albania, and on the SW by the Adriatic Sea and a narrow strip of Croatia; total land boundary length is 614 km (302 mi) and the coastline is 294 km (183 mi). Montenegro's capital is Podgorica, located in the lowland plain region of the south.

²TOPOGRAPHY

The shoreline of southwestern Montenegro is highly elevated, with no offshore islands. The limestone mountains of Rumija, Sutorman, Orjen, and Lovcen separate the narrow strip of land that is the coastline from the inland regions. Of the 294 km (183 mi) of coastline, 52 km (32 mi) are beaches. The largest bay is the Bay of Kotor, which is the world's southernmost fjord. In the limestone area bordering the coastline, plants and animals are scarce, and patches of fertile land can be found in karst depressions and crater-like hollows. Lake Scutari (Skadarsko Jezero) is the largest lake in the country, covering an are of about 400 sq km (150 sq mi). The Zeta plain and Zeta River valley region on which Lake Scutari (Skadarsko) is found is a lowland region. Northern Montenegro is composed of limestone mountains. The highest peak in Montenegro is Mt. Durmitor (Bobotov kuk), at 2,522 m (8,274 ft). Other high peaks are Bjelasica, Komovi, and Visitor. These mountain ranges are rich in pasturelands, forests, and mountain lakes. The Piva, Tara, Moraca, and Cehotina rivers and their tributaries

have carved deep canyons: the Tara Canyon, at a depth of 1,300 m (4,265 ft), is the deepest canyon in Europe.

Located on the Eurasian Tectonic Plate, there are several fault lines running through the country which are seismically active. Earth tremors are fairly common and destructive earthquakes have occurred.

³CLIMATE

The Adriatic climate along the south brings hot and dry summers and relatively cold winters with heavy snowfall inland. Podgorica is the warmest city, with an average July temperature of 26°C (80°F) and an average January temperature of 5°C (41°F). In the mountainous regions, the climate is sub-alpine. Snow on Mt. Durmitor can reach up to 5 m (16 ft). Annual precipitation ranges from 56 to 190 cm (22 to 75 in).

⁴FLORA AND FAUNA

About 80% of the territory is comprised of forests, natural pasturelands, and meadows. There are 2,833 plant species and subspecies, which comprise nearly one quarter of European flora. The animals found in Montenegro include types of hare, pheasant, deer, stag, wild boar, fox, chamois, mouflon, crane, duck, and goose.

⁵ENVIRONMENT

Coastal waters are polluted from sewage outlets, especially in resort areas such as Kotor. Destructive earthquakes are a natural hazard.

According to a 2006 report issued by the International Union for Conservation of Nature and Natural Resources (IUCN), the number of threatened species in the combined union of Serbia and Montenegro included 10 types of mammals, 10 species of birds, 1 type of reptile, 1 species of amphibian, 20 species of fish, 19 species of invertebrates, and 1 species of plants. Threatened species include Atlantic sturgeon, slender-billed curlew, black vultures, asps, bald ibis, several species of shark, the red wood ant, and beluga. At least one type of mollusk has become extinct.

National parks in Montenegro include Durmitor, Lovcen, Biogradska gora, and Lake Skadar. Mt. Durmitor and the old city of Kotor are UNESCO World Heritage sites.

6 POPULATION

The population of Montenegro in 2006 was estimated at 678,000. According to the UN, the annual population rate of change for the combined union of Serbia and Montenegro for 2005–2010 was expected to be 0.2%, due to a low fertility rate and high emigration rate. The population density for Serbia and Montenegro was 105 per sq km (272 per sq mi). The UN estimated that 52% of the population lived in urban areas in 2005, and that urban areas were growing at an annual rate of 0.47%. The estimated population of Podgorica in 2003 was 136,500 for the city proper and around 170,000 for the municipality.

7 MIGRATION

The following information on migration pertains to the union of Serbia and Montenegro, prior to the 2006 independence of Montenegro. During the 1960s and 1970s, many Serbs fled from the Yugoslav Socialist Federal Republic, seeking political and economic freedom. The breakup of the Yugoslav SFR in the early 1990s and the ethnic hostilities that came in its aftermath resulted in enormous migrations to and from its various former republics. During the first half of 1999, the situation of refugees and internally displaced people deteriorated even further. As of 30 June 1999, the United Nations High Commissioner for Refugees (UNHCR) reported 508,000 refugees from Bosnia and Herzegovina and Croatia; 770,000 returnees to Kosovo, as well as 500,000 affected remained; 220,000 Serb, Montenegrin, and Roma internally displaced persons from Kosovo in the rest of former Yugoslavia. The total number of migrants in 2000 was 626,000. By the end of 2004, these numbers were still rising; UNHCR reported a total of 627,476 persons of concern. There were 276,683 refugees, 180,117 Croatians, and over 95,000 from Bosnia and Herzegovina. In addition, in that same year there were 248,154 internally displaced persons, 85,000 local residents at risk, and 8,143 returned refugees (primarily to Croatia), and another 9,456 refugees returning to their place of origin during the year. In 2004, over 204,000 Serbs and Montenegrins were refugees in Germany, the United Kingdom, Sweden, Switzerland, Canada, France, and Australia. Also, in that same year over 29,000 Serbs and Montenegrins sought asylum in 18 countries primarily in Europe, and in the United Kingdom and the United States.

In 2005 the net migration rate was an estimated -1.3 migrants per 1,000 population, down from 3.9 migrants per 1,000 in 1990. The government views the migration levels as too high. Worker remittances in 2003 amounted to $2.7 billion.

8 ETHNIC GROUPS

According to a 2003 census, 43.16% of the population of Montenegro are Montenegrins, 32% Serbs, 7.77% Bosniaks, 5.03% ethnic Albanians, 4% other Muslim Slavs, 1.1% Croatians, 0.42% Roma, and 6.56% other population.

9 LANGUAGES

Serbian is the principal language of the population; Albanian accounts for a small minority. There is some disagreement regarding the Montenegrin dialect of Serbian: some Montenegrins claim it as a separate language.

10 RELIGIONS

The ancestors of the Serbs converted to Christianity in the 9th century and sided with Eastern Orthodoxy after the Great Schism of 1054 that split Christendom between the Eastern and Roman Churches. Islam came to the area from the Ottoman Turks in the 15th century.

About 74% of the total population are Serbian Orthodox; the Montenegrin Orthodox Church also exists but is canonically unrecognized. Muslims account for 17.74% of the population, with smaller numbers of Roman Catholics and Protestants. Protestant denominations include Baptists, Adventists, Reformed Christians, Evangelical Christians, Evangelical Methodists, Jehovah's Witnesses, the Church of Christ, Mormons, and Pentecostals. There is a small Jewish community in the country.

11 TRANSPORTATION

The Belgrade-Bar rail line links Serbia to Montenegro and terminates at the Adriatic Sea. Other major rail lines in Montenegro are Podgorica-Niksic and Podgorica-Skandar (Albania). Rail service is provided by locomotives manufactured in the 1950s and 1960s. The total length of standard-gauge tracks is 250 km (155.35 mi), most of which are electrified.

Two main roads in Montenegro are the Adriatic highway from Igalo to Ulcinj, and the system Petrovac to Podgorica-Kolasin-Bijelo Polje near the Serbian border connecting northern and southern Montenegro. There are 5,227 km (3,248 mi) of roads in Montenegro, of which 1,729 km (1,074.4 mi) are highways and regional roads, while the rest are local.

Important ports are Bar, Kotor, and Zelenika. Montenegro has a fleet of more than 40 ships, with a total carrying capacity of 1,000,000 metric tons. The port of Bar is equipped to handle around 5 million metric tons of cargo per year.

There were five airports in Montenegro in 2004, the major two being Podgorica and Tivat. Montenegro Airlines provides domestic and international service..

12 HISTORY

Montenegro's early history is as part of the medieval development of Serbia, known as Duklja or Zeta, north of Lake Scutari (Skadarsko). The Serbs, one of the large family of Slavic nations, first began settling in the Balkans around the 7th century in the areas now known as Bosnia, Kosovo, and Montenegro, straddling the line that since AD 395 had divided the Eastern and Western halves of the Roman Empire.

Tracing the origins of the Serbs (and Croats) has fueled many debates among historians, but there seems to be a consensus on their Sarmatian (Iranian) origin. Having assimilated into the Slavic tribes, the Serbs migrated with them west into central Europe (White Serbia) in the Saxony area and from there moved to the

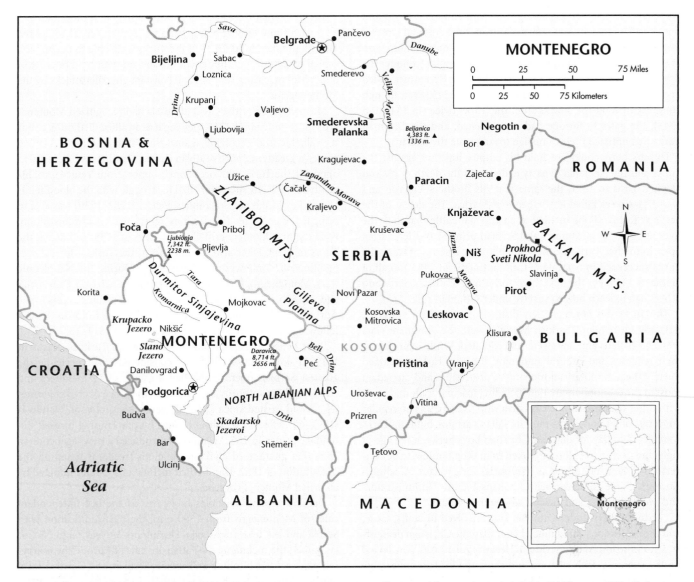

LOCATION: Approximately 41°50′ to 43°35′ N; 18°30′ to 20°30′ E. BOUNDARY LENGTHS: Albania, 172 kilometers (108 miles); Serbia, 203 kilometers (126 miles); Croatia, 25 kilometers (16 miles); Bosnia and Herzegovina, 225 kilometers (140 miles); Adriatic Sea coastline, 199 kilometers, (124 miles).

Balkans around AD 626 upon an invitation by the Byzantine emperor Heraclius to assist him in repelling the Avar and Persian attack on Constantinople. Having settled in the Balkan area the Serbs organized several principalities of their own, made up of a number of clans headed by leaders known as *zupans*. Both the Byzantine Empire and the Bulgars tried to conquer them, but the Serbs were too decentralized to be conquered.

Between the 9th and 12th centuries, several Serbian principalities evolved, among them Raška in the mountainous north of Montenegro and southern Serbia, and Zeta (south Montenegro along the Adriatic coast), whose ruler Mihajlo (Michael) was anointed king by Pope Gregory VII in 1077.

In the late 10th century the Bulgarian khan (leader) Samuilo extended his control over Bosnia, Raška, and Zeta, north to the Sava River, and south over Macedonia. Raška became the area from where the medieval Serbian empire developed. Stephen Nemanja, grand zupan of Raška, fought against the Byzantines in AD 1169, and added Zeta to his domain in 1186. He built several Serbian

monasteries, including Hilandar on Mount Athos. His son, Rastko, became a monk (Sava) and the first Serbian archbishop of the new Serbian Autocephalous Church in 1219. The second son, Stephen, received his crown from Pope Innocent IV in 1202. Stephen developed political alliances that, following his death in 1227, allowed Serbia to resist the pressure from Bulgaria and, internally, keep control over subordinate zupans. Archbishop Sava (later Saint Sava) preferred the Byzantine Church and utilized the Orthodox religion in his nation-building effort. He began by establishing numerous Serbian-Orthodox monasteries around Serbia. He also succeeded in turning Zeta from Catholicism to Serbian Orthodoxy.

The medieval Serbian empire, under Stephen Dušan the Mighty (1331–55) extended from the Aegean Sea to the Danube (Belgrade), along the Adriatic and Ionian coasts from the Neretva River to the Gulf of Corinth and controlled, aside from the central Serbian lands, Macedonia, Thessaly, the Epirus, and Albania. The Serbian Church obtained its own patriarchate, with its center in

Peć. Serbia became an exporting land with abundant crops and minerals. Dušan, who was crowned tsar of "the Serbs and Greeks" in 1346, gave Serbia its first code of laws based on a combination of Serbian customs and Byzantine law. His attempt to conquer the throne of Byzantium failed, however, when the Byzantines called on the advancing Ottoman Turks for help in 1345. Even though Dušan withstood the attacks from the Turks twice (in 1345 and 1349), the gates to Europe had been opened, and the Ottoman Turks had initiated their campaign to subjugate the Balkans.

Dušan's heirs could not hold his empire together against the Turks and the Nemanja dynasty ended with the death of his son Stephen Uroš in 1371, the same year his brothers Vukašin and Ivan Ugleš were killed at the battle of Marica. The defeat of the Serbs at Kosovo Polje in 1389 in an epochal battle that took the lives of both Sultan Murad I and Serbian prince Lazar left Serbia open to further Turkish conquest. Following a series of wars, the Turks succeeded in overtaking Constantinople in 1453 and all of Serbia by 1459. For the next three-and-a-half centuries, Serbs and others had to learn how to survive under Ottoman rule.

The Turks did not make any distinctions based on ethnicity, but only on religion. Turkish Muslims were the dominant class while Christians and Jews were subordinated. While maintaining their religious and cultural autonomy, the non-Turks developed most of the nonmilitary administrative professions and carried on most of the economic activities, including internal trade and trade with other countries of the Christian world. There was no regular conscription of non-Turks into the sultan's armies, but non-Turks were taxed to pay for defense. Christian boys between the age of eight and twenty were forcibly taken from their families to be converted to Islam and trained as "Janissaries" or government administrators. Some these former Christians became administrators and even became grand viziers (advisers) to sultans.

Urban dwellers under Ottoman rule, involved in crafts, trade, and the professions, fared much better than the Christian peasantry, who were forced into serfdom. Heavy regular taxes were levied on the peasants, with corruption making the load so unbearable that the peasants rebelled.

Two distinct cultures lived side by side—Turkish Muslim in cities and towns as administrative centers and Christian Orthodox in the countryside. The numerous Serbian monasteries built around the country since the Nemanja dynasty became the supportive network for Serbian survival. The Serbian Church was subjected after 1459 to the Greek patriarchate for about a century until a Serbian patriarchate emerged again. The Serbian patriarchate covered a large area from north of Ohrid to the Hungarian lands north of the Danube and west through Bosnia.

Montenegro was subjected to continuous fighting for 400 years, from the mid-1400s to the mid-1800s. Living in a very harsh mountain territory, the Montenegrins were natural and fierce fighters, and not even the large Turkish armies could conquer them. Until 1851, Montenegro was ruled by bishops. The bishops' role strengthened the Montenegrins' loyalty to the Orthodox Church and prevented their conversion to Islam, except in the lowlands and coastal areas occupied by the Turks. In 1696, Danilo Petrović Njegoš (1696–1737) was elected Vladika (bishop), and his dynastic family ruled Montenegro until its unification with Serbia into the first Yugoslavia.

The Montenegro area was an almost impregnable mountain fortress with some limited access from the Adriatic coast where the Turks had taken hold. In 1714 the Turks were able to occupy the capital of Cetinje, but they could not sustain their hold because of difficulties in getting supplies and constant guerrilla attacks by the Montenegrins.

Meanwhile, Peter the Great of Russia had recognized Montenegro's independence in 1715, viewing it as an allied Orthodox country valuable in his struggle against the Ottoman Empire. Having gained a greatly supportive ally in Russia, Danilo was successful in opposing the Turks with occasional support from Venice until his death in 1737. His successors had to struggle with the blood feuds among key Montenegrin families. Peter I (1782–1830) was able to bring together the feuding factions, reorganize his administration, issue the first Montenegrin Code of Laws in 1798, and defeat the Turks in 1799. Peter also obtained from the Turks a formal recognition of Montenegro's independence. During the Napoleonic wars, Montenegro, Russia's ally, fought the French over Dubrovnik and, in 1806, occupied the Gulf of Kotor, thus gaining access to the Adriatic sea. But Montenegro had to relinquish Kotor to Austria following the Congress of Vienna decisions in 1814–15.

Peter I died in 1830, having repelled again Turkish attacks in 1819–21 and 1828–29. Peter II, considered by many to be the greatest Serbian poet, established a senate of 12 members and centralized his authority by abolishing the office of civil governor, which had existed since 1516. However, his successor, Danilo II (1851–60), effected a radical change by proclaiming himself hereditary prince in 1852. Danilo II introduced a new legal code in 1855 that guaranteed civil and religious freedoms based on the constitution of 1852. Danilo died in 1860 of a wound inflicted by an exiled Montenegrin rebel.

Danilo's nephew Nicholas took over as the last independent ruler of Montenegro from 1860 until the 1918 unification with Serbia and the first Yugoslavia. During his 58-year reign Nicholas gained the nickname of "Father-in-Law of Europe" by marrying six daughters into Italian, Russian, Serbian, and German royal families. Through a series of wars with Turkey (1862, 1876, 1912, and 1913), Nicholas succeeded in more than doubling Montenegro's territory. Following the 1913 Balkan War, Montenegro and Serbia divided the Sandžak area and became neighbor states, both primarily populated by Serbs. Montenegro also gained access to the Adriatic Sea south of Lake Scutari (Skadar), which was divided in 1913 between Montenegro and the newly formed Albanian state.

Between 1880 and 1912, Montenegro took advantage of an era of relative peace to develop roads, education, agriculture, postal services, and banks, mostly with foreign investment especially from Italy, whose queen was Nicholas's daughter Elena.

The first Montenegrin parliament met in 1905, with 62 elected and 14 *ex officio* members. Following the successful Balkan wars, Serbian-Montenegrin relations grew closer, and by 1914, the two Serbian kingdoms proposed a union in which they would share their armed forces, foreign policy, and customs while maintaining their separate royal dynasties. World War I (1913–18) interrupted this process. Montenegro's poor defense led to Austrian occupation for the better part of the war; thus Montenegro ceased to officially participate in the war.

A Montenegrin Committee for National Union was formed by exiles in Paris who supported the 20 July 1917 Corfu Declaration on the establishment of a Kingdom of Serbs, Croats, and Slovenes. The Montenegrin Committee felt the time had come to unite with the Kingdom of Serbs, Croats, and Slovenes. King Nicholas opposed such a move and was deposed. On 24 November 1918, a resolution was passed in favor of Montenegro's union with the Kingdom of Serbia. Thus, Montenegro became part of the first Yugoslavia on 1 December 1918. Montenegrins participated very actively in political life, mostly supporting the centralist Serbian positions.

During World War II (1939–45), Italy controlled Montenegro and attempted unsuccessfully to revive the old kingdom. In the post-World War II Socialist Federative Yugoslavia, Tito reestablished Montenegro as a separate republic due to strong Montenegrin representation in the circle of his closest collaborators. Most Montenegrins took the side of the Serbian centralists against the liberal elements in the League of Communists and, in the late 1980s and early 1990s, supported Slobodan Milošević. With the demise of Yugoslavia, Montenegro joined Serbia in forming the Federal Republic of Yugoslavia.

On 14 March 2002, under mediation by the European Union (EU), Serbia and Montenegro agreed to form a new federal union, called Serbia and Montenegro. Montenegro's prime minister, Milo Djukanovic, was reluctant to sign the agreement, being the leader of the drive for independence of Montenegro's population of 660,000. However, the union of Serbia and Montenegro came into existence in 2003. The constitution provided for either of the two constituent republics to vote for independence in three years (2006). In February 2005, officials from Montenegro asked their Serbian counterparts for an early secession of the two republics claiming the union was inefficient and squandered money. Serbian Prime Minister Vojislav Kostunica refused the proposal and indicated that European integration and economic development should be the main focus of Serbia and Montenegro.

A referendum on full independence for Montenegro was held on 21 May 2006. To be accepted internationally, a 55% majority was required for a "yes" vote to the question: "Do you want the Republic of Montenegro to be an independent state with full international and legal subjectivity?" The Montenegrin diaspora had the right to vote, with the exception of Montenegrins living in Serbia, who were barred from voting in the referendum. The vote on independence was 55.5% in favor. Voter turnout was 86.3%. A demand by pro-Serbian unionist parties for a recount was rejected. Serb politicians, Orthodox church leaders, and Montenegrins from the mountainous inland regions bordering Serbia opposed secession. However, ethnic Montenegrins and Albanians from the coastal area favored independence. Serbian President Boris Tadic recognized the independence of Montenegro. Serbia became the successor state to the union of Serbia and Montenegro, inheriting its seat in the United Nations (UN) and seats in other international institutions: Montenegro will have to apply for UN and EU membership on its own once it has been granted recognition by other states. Serbia's ambition to join the EU has been hampered by its failure to arrest key war crimes suspects, including Ratko Mladic. Serbia inherits legal claim to the UN-administered province of Kosovo.

Montenegro's independence cuts Serbia off from the sea; therefore, the two nations will need to cooperate on sharing the former union's assets. Montenegrins may be given favorable treatment to use Serbia's hospitals, universities, and other public services. The substantial pro-union minority in Montenegro will also strengthen Serbia's hand in creating a smooth transition to independence. The pro-union bloc in the referendum was led by the Socialist People's Party (SNP), headed by Predrag Bulatovic. National elections were due to be held in autumn 2006.

13 GOVERNMENT

Prior to Montenegro's independence in 2006, a constitutional charter for the state of Serbia and Montenegro was ratified by both parliaments in January 2003, and the constitution for the unified state was approved on 4 February 2003. The constitution allowed the member republics to hold independence referendums in 2006, which Montenegro did. Following the yes vote on independence in mid-2006, Montenegro was engaged in forming a new government.

As a constituent state of the union of Serbia and Montenegro, Montenegro had a republican form of government. Representatives in Montenegro's Assembly (parliament) hold office for four years. The Assembly enacted laws, passed the budget, appointed the president and members of the cabinet, the president and justices of the Constitutional Court, and the judges of all courts of law. The Assembly may pass a vote of no-confidence on the government by a vote of its members.

The president of Montenegro proposes candidates to the Assembly for prime minister, as well as for the president and justices of the Constitutional Court; grants pardons; proposes the holding of referenda; and represents the country at home and abroad.

14 POLITICAL PARTIES

Elections for Montenegro's parliament were held on 21 October 2002. Eleven parties were represented: the Democratic Party of Socialists of Montenegro (DPS), 30 seats; Social Democratic Party of Montenegro (SDP), 5; Civic Party of Montenegro, 1; non-partisans, 2; Socialist People's Party of Montenegro, 19; Serbian People's Party of Montenegro, 6; People's Party of Montenegro, 5; Liberal Alliance of Montenegro, 4; Democratic Union of Albanians, 1; and the Democratic League of Montenegro, 1. The government coalition was comprised of the DPS, SDP, Civic Party, and non-partisans.

On 11 May 2003, Filip Vujanović of the DPS was elected president with 63.3% of the vote. Voter turnout was 48.5%. As of 2006, Milo Dukanović was serving as prime minister.

15 LOCAL GOVERNMENT

Montenegro has 21 municipalities (opština).

16 JUDICIAL SYSTEM

The republic of Montenegro followed the system of separation of powers: the judicial, legislative, and executive branches are independent of one another. The judiciary is autonomous and independent. The Constitutional Court has the power of judicial review. Appointments to the judiciary are for life.

[17]ARMED FORCES

The following information on armed forces pertains to the union of Serbia and Montenegro and was reported prior to June 2006, when Montenegrins approved an independence referendum. Active armed forces numbered approximately 65,300 in 2005, supported by 250,000 reservists. The Army had 55,000 active personnel and was equipped with 962 main battle tanks, 525 armored infantry fighting vehicles, 288 armored personnel carriers and 2,729 artillery pieces. The Navy had 3,800 active personnel, including 900 Marines. Major naval units included eight tactical submarines, three frigates, 31 patrol/coastal vessels, 10 mine warfare ships, 23 amphibious landing craft, and seven logistical/support vessels. The Air Force had 6,500 active members, along with 101 combat capable aircraft, including 39 fighters, 51 fighter ground attack aircraft and 17 armed helicopters. There was also a paramilitary force that consisted of 45,100 personnel, of which an estimated 4,100 made up special police units, 35,000 were Ministry of Interior personnel and an estimated 6,000 were Montenegrin Ministry of Interior Personnel. Sixteen military personnel were stationed in four African countries under UN command. In addition, military contingents from 45 countries were stationed in Serbia and Montenegro as part of the Kosovo Peace Implementation Force. The defense budget in 2005 totaled $706 million.

[18]INTERNATIONAL COOPERATION

The Socialist Federal Republic of Yugoslavia was an original member of the United Nations (1945) until its dissolution and the establishment of Bosnia and Herzegovina, Croatia, Slovenia, the Former Yugoslav Republic of Macedonia, and the Federal Republic of Yugoslavia as new states. The Federal Republic of Yugoslavia was admitted to the United Nations on 1 November 2000. Following the adoption and promulgation of the Constitutional Charter of Serbia and Montenegro on 4 February 2003, the name of the Federal Republic of Yugoslavia was changed to Serbia and Montenegro. Serbia and Montenegro participated in several nonregional specialized UN agencies, such as the FAO, UNESCO, UNHCR, UNIDO, the World Bank, IAEA, and the WHO.

Serbia and Montenegro was a member of the Council of Europe, the Black Sea Economic Cooperation Zone, the European Bank for Reconstruction and Development, and the OSCE. It had observer status in the OAS and the WTO. In environmental cooperation, the country was part of Basel Convention, Ramsar, the London Convention, the Montréal Protocol, and the UN Conventions on the Law of the Sea and Climate Change.

Serbia is recognized as the successor state to the former union of Serbia and Montenegro. Montenegro will have to apply for membership in the UN and other international bodies.

[19]ECONOMY

During the UN economic sanctions that lasted from 1992 to 1995, economic activity in the former Yugoslavia was extremely limited. By 1994, hyperinflation had brought formal economic activity to a virtual halt. By 1996, GDP had fallen to only 50.8% of 1990s total. Industry declined to just 46.6% of 1990s output; agriculture, 94.4%; construction, 37.5%; transportation, 29.3%; trade, 60.6%;

and services, 81.1%. Formal lifting of these sanctions occurred in October 1996. However, the United States sponsored an "Outer Wall" of sanctions, which prevented Yugoslavia from joining international organizations and financial institutions. Taken together, the "Outer Wall," the Kosovo war, and continuing corruption continue to stifle Yugoslav economic development. In October 2000, the coalition government began implementation of stabilization and market-reform measures. Real growth in 2000 was reported as 5%. A donors' conference in June 2001 raised $1.3 billion in pledges for help in infrastructural rebuilding. Real GDP in 2001 was 5.5% and an estimated 4% in 2002.

Economic output was positive, but volatile after 2002, dropping to 2.1% in 2003 and jumping to 8% in 2004; in 2005 the GDP growth rate in Serbia and Montenegro was estimated at 4%.

In Montenegro, inflation fell from 7.5% in 2003 to 5% in 2004. The financial sector showed marked improvement. Economic reforms launched in 2003, driven by the goal of EU integration, had not yet led to markedly higher levels of growth or reduced unemployment by 2006. In 2003, the absolute poverty rate was recorded at 12.2%, with more than a third of the population classified as economically vulnerable.

[20]INCOME

The following information on income pertains to the union of Serbia and Montenegro, prior to Montenegro's independence in 2006. The CIA defines GDP as the value of all final goods and services produced within a nation in a given year and computed on the basis of purchasing power parity (PPP) rather than value as measured on the basis of the rate of exchange based on current dollars. In 2005, the per capita GDP for Serbia and Montenegro was estimated at $2,700. The annual growth rate of GDP was estimated at 5%. It was estimated that agriculture accounted for 16.6% of GDP, industry 25.5%, and services 57.9%.

According to the World Bank, in 2003 remittances from citizens working abroad totaled $1.397 billion or about $172 per capita and accounted for approximately 6.8% of GDP. Foreign aid receipts amounted to $1,317 million or about $163 per capita and accounted for approximately 6.4% of the gross national income (GNI).

The World Bank reports that in 2003 household consumption in Serbia and Montenegro totaled $18.27 billion or about $2,246 per capita based on a GDP of $20.7 billion, measured in current dollars rather than PPP. Household consumption includes expenditures of individuals, households, and nongovernmental organizations on goods and services, excluding purchases of dwellings.

[21]LABOR

The following information on labor pertains to the union of Serbia and Montenegro, prior to Montenegro's independence in 2006. The labor force in Serbia and Montenegro was estimated at 3.22 million in 2005. The unemployment rate in 2005 was estimated at 31.6%, with Kosovo's unemployment at around 50%. There was no data available as to the occupational breakdown of the country's workforce.

With the exception of the military, all workers are entitled to form unions. However, the majority of unions are government-sponsored or affiliated: independent unions are rare. Therefore, unions have not been effective in improving work conditions or wage structure increases. Virtually all of the workers in the formal economy are union members. Strikes are permitted and are utilized especially to collect unpaid wages. Collective bargaining is still at rudimentary level.

The minimum employment age is 16 although younger children frequently work on family farms. As of 2005, there was no national minimum wage rate. On average, the full-time monthly wage in the public sector that year was $181, while the average wage in the private sector was $250. Neither wage rate offered a decent living wage for a family. The official workweek was set at 40 hours, with required rest periods and overtime limited to 20 hours per week or 40 hours per month. Health and safety standards are not a priority due to harsh economic circumstances.

22 AGRICULTURE

In addition to honey and high-quality wines (Vranac, Krstac, among others), Montenegro produces many vegetables (tomatoes, peppers, cucumbers) and fruits (plums, apples, grapes, citrus fruits, and olives). Other crops include blueberries, edible mushrooms, and wild sage.

Serbia and Montenegro had 3,717,000 hectares (9,160,000 acres) of arable land in 2003. Serbia historically accounted for 60% of agricultural production. Vojvodina is the major agricultural region.

In 2000, 20% of the labor force was engaged in agriculture. Between 1991 and 1996, total agricultural production in the former Yugoslavia declined by 10%. During that time, production of farm crops fell by 9%; cereals by 12%. Viticultural production, however, increased by 51%. However, by 1999, total agricultural output was at 92% of the average during 1989–91. During 2002–04, crop production was 10% higher than during 1999–2001.

Agriculture contributed an estimated 17% to GDP in 2002. Major crops produced in 2004 in Serbia and Montenegro included (in thousands of tons): corn, 6,287; wheat, 2,746; sugar beets, 2,643; potatoes, 1,098; and grapes, 490.

23 ANIMAL HUSBANDRY

The following information on animal husbandry pertains to the union of Serbia and Montenegro, prior to Montenegro's independence in 2006. In 2005, the livestock population included 3,550,000 pigs and hogs, 1,796,600 sheep, 1,230,000 head of cattle, 182,000 goats, 40,000 horses, and 17,464,000 poultry. Total meat production that year was 848,240 tons; milk, 1,852,000 tons. Between 1990 and 1999, total livestock production increased by 1.8%, but during 2002–04 it fell by 5.4% from 1999–2001.

24 FISHING

In Serbia and Montenegro, the total catch in 2003 was 3,665 tons, 86% from inland waters. Common carp accounts for much of the inland catch.

25 FORESTRY

Forests and woodlands cover 720,000 ha (1,779,192 acres) in Montenegro, accounting for 54% of the total surface area of the republic. Of this figure, the major part (572,000 ha (1,413,469 acres) is in the northern region of the country. Total roundwood production in Serbia and Montenegro in 2004 was 3,520,000 cu m (124.3 billion cu ft), of which about 75% came from public forests. Sawnwood production amounted to 575,000 cu m (20.3 million cu ft); plywood and particle board, 59,000 cu m (2.1 million cu ft). In 2004, exports of forest products in Serbia and Montenegro amounted to nearly $139.1 million; imports, $352.9 million.

26 MINING

The following information on mining pertains to the union of Serbia and Montenegro prior to Montenegro's independence in 2006. In 2003 industrial production in Serbia and Montenegro fell by 3% compared to 2002, although mining and quarrying operations reported a 1% increase from 2002. Aggregated production from the metals mining sector in 2003 fell by 33% from the previous year, although the output of basic metals increased by 2%. The country also confronted continuing economic sanctions and the loss of control of Kosovo, with its ores and production facilities for nickel, lead, zinc, coal, lignite, ferronickel, and tin-plate. In light of this, Serbia and Montenegro's gross domestic product (GDP) was officially reported to have increased by 3% in 2003. The country had significant capacities to produce refined aluminum, lead, silver, and zinc. In 2003, the output of bauxite fell by about 12% from 2002, although aluminum output remained at around 2002 levels. Although exports of primary aluminum and aluminum alloys in 2002 grew by 18% over 2001, data for 2003 indicated a steep drop in those exports. Mining in Serbia dates back to the Middle Ages, when silver, gold, and lead were extracted. Yugoslavia's bauxite mining, alumina-refining, and aluminum-smelting industries were located primarily in Montenegro, which was accorded favorable treatment by the European Commission.

Mine output of metals in 2003 were: lead ore (gross weight), 183,000 metric tons, down from 733,000 metric tons in 2000 and 284,000 metric tons in 2002; bauxite (gross weight), 540,000 metric tons, down from 612,000 metric tons in 2002 and from 630,000 metric tons in 2000; agglomerate iron ore and concentrate saw no recorded production from 2001 through 2003; and copper ore (gross weight), 5,710,000 tons, down from 12.896,000 tons in 2000 and from 7,968,000 tons in 2002. Production of silver in 2003 totaled 2,028 kg, down from 6,838 kg in 2002. Output of refined gold in 2003 was estimated at 600 kg, down from 900 kg in 2002. In 2003, the country also produced alumina, magnesium, palladium, platinum, and selenium. Among the industrial minerals produced were asbestos, bentonite, ceramic clay, fire clay, feldspar, pumice, lime, magnesite, mica, kaolin, gypsum, quartz sand, salt, nitrogen, caustic soda, sodium sulfate, sand and gravel, and stone.

27 ENERGY AND POWER

According to Montenegrin government sources, three power plants—the Perucica and Piva hydroelectric plants and the Pljevlja thermoelectric plant—produce approximately 3 billion kWh per year. Montenegro has the capacity to produce 2,700,000 metric tons of coal.

28 INDUSTRY

Industry was the primary engine of economic development in Montenegro in the second half of the 20th century. During that period, the growth of the power and energy sector, metallurgy (steel and aluminum), and transportation infrastructure formed the basis for overall economic growth and development. Approximately 90% of Montenegro's industrial products were marketed outside the republic.

By the early 2000s, Montenegro had facilities for producing 400,000 metric tons of crude steel; 1,000,000 metric tons of bauxite; 280,000 metric tons of alumina; 100,000 metric tons of aluminum; and 75,000 metric tons of sea salt.

Industries in Montenegro include metal processing, engineering, wood-processing, textile manufacture, chemicals, leather and footwear, apparel, household appliances, construction, and machinery.

Montenegro processes and finishes agricultural products. The country has fish-processing plants, flour mills, dairies, slaughterhouses, bakeries, breweries, juice factories, fruit processing factories, grape processing plants and wine cellars, medicinal herb processing plants, tobacco and cigarette factories, and confectioners, among other industries.

By 2006, the industrial sector was in poor shape due to the lingering effects of war and isolation in the former Yugoslavia. Montenegro was expected to seek foreign investment to modernize its industries to enable it to become competitive in world markets.

29 SCIENCE AND TECHNOLOGY

Scientific and technological policies are developed and implemented by the Ministry of Education and Science of the Republic of Montenegro. There are 13 registered research institutions in Montenegro and one university (the University of Montenegro, located in Podgorica).

30 DOMESTIC TRADE

Podgorica serves as the economic and commercial center of the country. The domestic economy has been held back for the past few years due to the lack of major privatization reforms and trouble in the general European economy. Hours of business are usually 8 AM to 4 PM, Monday to Friday.

31 FOREIGN TRADE

The following information on foreign trade pertains to the union of Serbia and Montenegro prior to Montenegro's independence in 2006. The UN imposed sanctions on international trade with Yugoslavia in May 1992 and lifted them in December 1995. During the war, when sanctions were in force, dozens of Cypriot companies, set up by senior Serbian officials and businessmen, trafficked millions of dollars in illegal trade.

Trade started to catch up in subsequent years, and in 2004 exports reached $3.2 billion (FOB—Free on Board). In the same year, imports were almost triple, at $9.5 billion (FOB), indicating that the economy in the two republics was in disarray, but that it was trying to redress itself through a renewal of its industrial base. Most of the import commodities included machinery and transport equipment, fuels and lubricants, manufactured goods, chemicals, food and live animals, and raw materials. The imports mainly came from Germany (18.5%), Italy (16.5%), Austria (8.3%), Slovenia (6.7%), Bulgaria (4.7%), and France (4.5%). Exports included manufactured goods, food and live animals, and raw materials, and largely went to Italy (which receive 29% of total

exports), Germany (16.6%), Austria (7%), Greece (6.7%), France (4.9%), and Slovenia (4.1%).

32 BALANCE OF PAYMENTS

Montenegro, both as its own republic and as a constituent republic of Serbia and Montenegro until mid-2006, maintained a relatively high current account deficit. For Serbia and Montenegro, exports of goods and services totaled $5.9 billion in 2004, up from $4.2 billion in 2003. Imports grew from $8.7 billion in 2003, to $12.8 billion in 2004. Consequently, the resource balance was on a negative upsurge, growing from -$4.5 billion in 2003, to -$7.1 billion in 2004. A similar trend was registered for the current account balance, which deteriorated from -$2.0 billion in 2003, to -$3.1 billion in 2004. The national reserves of Serbia and Montenegro (including gold) were $3.6 billion in 2003, covering less than 6 months of imports; by 2004, they increased to $4.3 billion.

33 BANKING AND SECURITIES

Montenegro has its own independent central bank. There were 10 licensed banks in Montenegro in 2005. Montenegro's last bank with direct government majority ownership was being privatized in 2006.

34 INSURANCE

Insurance of public transport passengers, motor vehicle insurance, aircraft insurance, and insurance on bank deposits are compulsory. In 2003, the value of all direct insurance premiums written in Serbia and Montenegro totaled $436 million, of which nonlife premiums accounted for $420 million. In that same year, the top nonlife insurer was Dunav, which had gross written nonlife premiums of $138.6 million, while the country's leading life insurer was Zepter, which had gross written life insurance premiums of $7.1 million.

35 PUBLIC FINANCE

As of mid-2006, Montenegro had voted to become an independent nation; statistics on the new country's revenue and expenditures were not available.

The US Central Intelligence Agency (CIA) estimated that in 2005 Serbia and Montenegro's central government took in revenues of approximately $11.4 billion and had expenditures of $11.1 billion. Revenues minus expenditures totaled approximately $330 million. Public debt in 2005 amounted to 53.1% of GDP. Total external debt was $15.43 billion.

36 TAXATION

Montenegro's top income tax rate is 22%. It has a flat corporate tax rate of 9%.

37 CUSTOMS AND DUTIES

Montenegro has an average customs rate of 3–5%, with a 20% rate applied to seasonal fruits and vegetables. Montenegro applies a 17% value-added tax (VAT) on all products, with water, bread, milk, fat, oil, sugar and medicines exempt. Montenegro imposes excise taxes on certain luxury goods.

Montenegro has only one authorized free trade zone (FTZ) that has yet to become operational.

38 FOREIGN INVESTMENT

Foreign investment was severely restricted during the years of the economic embargo. Since the sanctions were lifted, foreign investors from neighboring countries, Russia, and Asia have expressed an interest in capital investment. The main sectors attracting the interest of foreign investors are metal manufacturing and machinery, infrastructure improvement, agriculture and food processing, and chemicals and pharmaceuticals. Foreign investors may hold majority shares in companies.

In 1997, foreign direct investment (FDI) inflows into the former Yugoslavia reached $740 million, but dried up with the onset of the conflict in Kosovo. FDI inflows averaged $122.5 million in 1998 and 1999, then fell to $25 million in 2000. In 2001, FDI inflow reached $125 million.

In the following years, Serbia and Montenegro undertook an aggressive program of reforms aimed at both reestablishing the area as a major transportation hub, and at attracting foreign investment. These policies seem to have paid off as in 2004, capital inflows jumped to $3.4 billion. While Serbia and Montenegro was considered to be a risky place for doing business, the political and economic climate was steadily improving as of 2005. Montenegro both before and after independence placed a great deal of importance upon attracting new foreign investment; such economic development will help make the case for Montenegro's possible entry into the European Union (EU).

39 ECONOMIC DEVELOPMENT

Officials in general see revitalization of the infrastructure (roads, rail and air transport, telecommunications, and power production) as one step toward economic recovery. Another important aspect of economic reconstruction will be the revival of former export industry, such as agriculture, textiles, furniture, pharmaceuticals, and nonferrous metallic ores.

In 2002, the International Monetary Fund (IMF) approved a three-year $829 million Extended Arrangement to support economic programs in Serbia and Montenegro (which was known as Yugoslavia at the time) 2002–05.

While politically and economically Montenegro is much more stable than in previous years, the economy is still in a quasi-state of disarray, with high unemployment, a large gray market, and a relapsing industrial base. Foreign investors, as well as several international financial institutions (EBRD, IMF, and the World Bank), appreciated recent economic developments in Montenegro as being positive, and in 2004 increased their capital transfers to the region.

The economy is expected to grow moderately in 2006, as a result of a boom in several sectors: trade, financial services and transport and communications. The growth is to be sustained by continued investment in newly privatized companies, by strong local demand, and by an expansion of the services sector. Montenegro has privatized most major industries other than electricity. By 2005, approximately 65% of state-owned companies had been sold off and only 25% of banking assets remained in state or social ownership.

The US Agency for International Development (USAID) remains the primary foreign aid donor in Montenegro. The European Agency for Reconstruction (EAR), Germany, and the United Kingdom have smaller budgets and, like USAID, work in the areas of economic policy reform and enterprise development, among other programs such as civil society, independent media development, and the rule of law. The International Finance Corporation (IFC) focuses on small and medium enterprise development. The World Bank and EBRD focus on economic growth and infrastructure investments. The UN Development Program (UNDP), with funding from EAR, Germany, Canada, and the Netherlands, works in the environment, enterprise development, and civil society development areas. Montenegro has implemented an Economic Reform Agenda.

40 SOCIAL DEVELOPMENT

A social insurance system for Serbia and Montenegro, updated in 2003, provides old age, disability, and survivorship benefits. The pension plan is funded by contributions from both employers and employees. The retirement varies depending on years of insurance; retirement from insured employment is necessary. Montenegro provides its own system for sickness and maternity benefits. Medical services are provided directly to patients through government facilities. Workers' compensation, unemployment benefits, and family allowances are also available. Family allowances vary according to the number of children in the family are adjusted periodically for cost of living changes.

Traditional gender roles keep women from enjoying equal status with men and few occupy positions of leadership in the private sector. However, women are active in human rights and political organizations. High levels of domestic abuse persist and social pressures prevent women from obtaining protection against abusers.

41 HEALTH

The government provides obligatory health care to citizens for preventive, diagnostic, therapeutic, and rehabilitative services. In the union of Serbia and Montenegro, there were approximately 228 health institutions and about 3,000 other clinics, mostly private, in 2005. As of 2004, there were an estimated 20 physicians per 100,000 people.

In 2005 infant mortality in Serbia and Montenegro was reported at 15.53 per 1,000 live births. Overall mortality was 7.4 per 1,000 people in Montenegro. Average life expectancy in 2005 for Serbia and Montenegro was 74.73 years.

The HIV/AIDS prevalence was 0.20 per 100 adults in 2003. As of 2004, there were approximately 10,000 people living with HIV/AIDS in Serbia and Montenegro. There were an estimated 100 deaths from AIDS in 2003.

42 HOUSING

At the beginning of 1996, there were 3,124,000 dwellings in Serbia and Montenegro, with an average of 3.4 persons per dwelling. Housing area at that time averaged 20 sq m (215 sq ft) per person. New housing completions during 1995 totaled 14,337 units, of which 11,847 were in the public sector, and 2,490 were in the private sector. In 2002, Serbia and Montenegro counted about 2,790,411 households with an average of 2.89 people per household.

43 EDUCATION

As of 2005/06, education is compulsory for nine years of primary school. This may be followed by three years of secondary school, with students having the option to attend general, vocational, or art schools. The academic year runs from October to July. In 2001, about 43% of children between the ages of three and six were enrolled in some type of preschool program in the union of Serbia and Montenegro. Primary school enrollment in 2001 was estimated at about 96% of age-eligible students. The same year, secondary school enrollment was about 82% of age-eligible students. It is estimated that about 96% of all students complete their primary education. The student-to-teacher ratio for primary school was at about 20:1 in 2000; the ratio for secondary school was about 14:1. In Montenegro, elementary and secondary schools are managed by school boards, while principals are responsible for day-to-day administration. School boards and principals are appointed by the Ministry of Education and Science for four-year terms. Teachers must have a university degree and pass a professional (state) examination.

Montenegro has one university with 15 faculties. In 2001, it was estimated that about 36% of the tertiary age population were enrolled in tertiary education programs. The adult literacy rate for 2004 was estimated at about 96.4%.

As of 2003, public expenditure on education for the union of Serbia and Montenegro was estimated at 3.3% of GDP.

44 LIBRARIES AND MUSEUMS

The Central National Library of Montenegro has 1.5 million volumes.

Serbia and Montenegro prior to Montenegro's independence had over 2,500 cultural monuments, including about 100 museums and 37 historical archives libraries.

Culturally, Montenegro has been shaped by Mediterranean, middle European, Eastern European, and Asian civilizations. Archaeological treasures include Crvena Stijena (Red Rock), Bioce okapine (shelters) in the Moraca Canyon, and Malisina pecina (cave) and Medena stijena (rock) in the Cehotina Canyon.

Pre-Roman, Roman, Gothic, and Baroque architectural styles may be found. The city of Kotor is a UNESCO World Heritage site. The region of Lake Scutari (Skadarsko) has many monasteries built on goricas (small islands), including Beska, Moracnik, Starcevo, Kom, and Vranjina, along with the fortresses of Zabljak and Lesendro.

Islamic culture is evidenced in the Mosque of Husein-pasha Boljanic in Pljevlja, as well as in residential architecture (such as the Redzepagics' Manor in Plav).

Montenegro has a long literary and printing history, beginning in the 12th century. The town of Cetinje, which features a monastery of Cetinje and museum complex and Biljarda, built by

Njegos as a residence in 1838, is recognized as a cultural capital. Other buildings in Cetinje include King Nikola's Palace, numerous embassies, Prince Heir's Palace, the Zetski dom theater, and the house of parliament.

Montenegro has a rich heritage of theater, film, poetry, prose, and painting.

45 MEDIA

In 2003, there were an estimated 243 mainline telephones for every 1,000 people in Serbia and Montenegro; about 313,500 people were on a waiting list for telephone service installation. The same year, there were approximately 338 mobile phones in use for every 1,000 people.

Television stations included TV Montenegro, a state-funded company that operated two networks and a satellite channel; TV IN; Montenegrin Broadcasting Company (MBC), private; ntv Montena, private; TV Elmag, private; and TV Pink M—Montenegrin offshoot of Belgrade-based network. The following radio stations were operating: Radio Montenegro, a state-funded company that operated two networks; Radio Elmag, private; Antena M, private; and Radio D, private. The news agency MNNews-Mina is private.

The ownership and editorial positions of television and radio stations usually reflects regional politics. In 2004, Serbia and Montenegro had about 297 radios and 282 television sets for every 1,000 people. The same year, there were 27.1 personal computers for every 1,000 people and 79 of every 1,000 people had access to the Internet. There were nine secure Internet servers in the country in 2004.

In 1791, the first Serbian-language newspaper was published in Vienna, Austria. Privately owned newspapers are sometimes critical of the government. The dailies with the largest circulation in Serbia and Montenegro (as of 2002) were *Politika* (*Politics*, 300,000) and *Vecernje Novosti* (*Evening News*, 169,000). Other newspapers that are essentially controlled by the government, included (with 2002 circulation) *Borba* (85,000), *Jedinstvo* (6,090), *Dnevnik* (61,000), and *Pobjeda* (19,400). There are several minority language newspapers.

While the government provides for freedom of speech and of the press, libel suits have been fairly prevalent and some media sources have practiced self-censorship in order to avoid problems with government officials. In Montenegro press freedom is guaranteed and media laws passed in 2002 provide for the transformation of state-funded broadcasting company into a public broadcaster. But some media watchdogs have pointed to ongoing political influence over editorial policies. In 2004, the killing of Dusko Jovanovic, the editor of the opposition daily newspaper Dan, sparked an outcry. Demonstrators accused the authorities of complicity.

Overseas donors and organizations have encouraged the growth of independent media outlets. But commercial operators compete for a small pool of advertising revenue. The market—with dozens of private radio and TV stations—was said to be saturated. The Montenegrin media enjoyed greater freedom than their Serbian counterparts in the last years of Slobodan Milošević's rule. Many private outlets managed to break the former state monopoly.

In Montenegro, the following media were publishing in 2005: Vijesti, private daily; Pobjeda, daily; Dan, daily; Republika, daily; and Monitor, private weekly.

46 ORGANIZATIONS

The Montenegrin P.E.N. Center was founded in 1990. There are several organizations for professional journalists in Serbia and Montenegro, including the Journalists' Federation of Yugoslavia, the Journalists' Association of Serbia, Independent Journalists' Association, and the Association of Private Owners of the Media. National youth organizations include the Union of Socialist Youth of Yugoslavia, Junior Chamber, and the Youth Council of Montenegro. Scouting organizations are also active. The Child Rights Center and Child to Child are national groups working to promote the rights of children and youth. There are a variety of sports associations available promoting amateur competition among athletes of all ages. There are active chapters of the Paralympic Committee, as well as a national Olympic Committee.

There is a national chapter of the Red Cross Society.

47 TOURISM, TRAVEL, AND RECREATION

Rich architecture, museums, galleries, cathedrals, parks, rivers, and the many beaches are just some of the attractions that bring visitors to Montenegro. Montenegro has four national parks; the largest are the Lake of Skadar (Skadarsko) Basin (40,000 hectares/98,800 acres) and Durmitor (39,000 hectares/96,300 acres). Montenegro has two UNESCO natural area and heritage sites: Mt. Durmitor and the old city of Kotor. Popular sports in Montenegro are tennis, football, volleyball, water sports, bocanje (a kind of bowling), skiing, and rafting. The Ministry of Sports of the Montenegrin government was founded in 1993. There are numerous sand and pebble beaches on the Montenegrin coastline. It is one of the warmest and sunniest tourist regions in Europe. Although classified as a Mediterranean country, Montenegro is a mountainous region in which areas of 1,000 m (3,280.8 ft) or higher comprise 60.5% of the nation's territory.

Prior to Montenegro's independence, all visitors needed a valid passport to enter Serbia and Montenegro. Serbia requires an onward/return ticket, sufficient funds for the stay, and a certificate showing funds for health care. Visas are required for all nationals except those of 41 countries including the United State, Australia, and Canada. According to 2005 US Department of State estimates, the cost of staying in the country averaged $157.

In 2003, there were 599,430 visitors to Montenegro (10.7% more than in 2002), of whom 141,787 were foreign tourists. There were 3,976,266 hotel rooms booked (7.8% more than in 2002), of which foreign visitors accounted for 915,738.

48 FAMOUS MONTENEGRINS

Prince Danilo II of Montenegro (r.1851–60) introduced a new legal code in 1855 that guaranteed civil and religious freedoms. King Nikola I Petrović Njegoš (1841–1921) was the only king of Montenegro, reigning as a king from 1910 to 1918 and as a prince from 1860 to 1910. He was also a poet who wrote "Onamo, 'namo," the popular anthem of Montenegro. King Alexander of Yugoslavia (1888–1934) was assassinated in Marseille, France. Prince Paul of Yugoslavia (1893–1976) ruled as a regent for Peter II (1923–70) from 1934 to 1941 and was forced into exile after signing a secret pact with the Nazi government.

Important Montenegrin poets of the 20th century include Risto Ratkovic and Radovan Ziogovic. Important prose writers include Mihailo Lalic, whose realistic novels portray Montenegro's place in World War II. Painters include Petar Lubarda, Milo Milunovic, Dado Djuric, Branko Filipovic-Filo, Vojo Stanic, and Uros Toskovic.

49 DEPENDENCIES

Montenegro has no dependencies or territories.

50 BIBLIOGRAPHY

Bennett, Christopher. *Yugoslavia's Bloody Collapse: Causes, Course and Consequences.* London: Hurst and Company, 1995.

Boehm, Christopher. *Blood Revenge: The Enactment and Management of Conflict in Montenegro and Other Tribal Societies.* Philadelphia: University of Pennsylvania Press, 1987.

Bokovoy, Melissa, Jill A. Irvine, and Carol S. Lilly, (ed.). *State-Society Relations in Yugoslavia, 1945-1992.* New York: St. Martin's, 1997.

Cohen, Lenard J. *Broken Bonds: Yugoslavia's Disintegration and Balkan Politics in Transition.* Boulder, Colo.: Westview, 1995.

Denitch, Bogdan Denis. *Ethnic Nationalism: The Tragic Death of Yugoslavia.* Minneapolis: University of Minnesota Press, 1996.

Dyker, David A., and Ivan Vejvoda, (ed.). *Yugoslavia and After: A Study in Fragmentation, Despair and Rebirth.* New York: Longman, 1996.

Fleming, Thomas. *Montenegro: The Divided Land.* San Francisco: Chronicle Books, 2002.

Frucht, Richard (ed.). *Eastern Europe: An Introduction to the People, Lands, and Culture.* Santa Barbara, Calif.: ABC-CLIO, 2005.

Houston, Marco. *Nikola and Milena, King and Queen of the Black Mountain: The Rise and Fall of Montenegro's Royal Family.* London: Leppi Publications, 2003.

International Smoking Statistics: A Collection of Historical Data from 30 Economically Developed Countries. New York: Oxford University Press, 2002.

Judah, Tim. *The Serbs: History, Myth, and the Destruction of Yugoslavia.* New Haven, Conn.: Yale University Press, 1997.

Klemencic, Matjaz. *The Former Yugoslavia's Diverse Peoples: A Reference Sourcebook.* Oxford, Eng.: ABC-Clio, 2003.

Lampe, John R. *Yugoslavia as History: Twice There Was a Country.* New York: Cambridge University Press, 1996.

Malesevic, Siniša. *Ideology, Legitimacy, and the New State: Yugoslavia, Serbia, and Croatia.* Portland, Ore.: Frank Cass, 2002.

Pavkovic, Aleksandar. *The Fragmentation of Yugoslavia: Nationalism in a Multinational State.* New York: St. Martin's, 1997.

Ramet, Sabrina P. *Balkan Babel: The Disintegration of Yugoslavia from the Death of Tito to Ethnic War*. Boulder, Colo.: Westview, 1996.

Schuman, Michael. *Serbia and Montenegro*. 2nd ed. New York: Facts On File, 2004.

Stevenson, Francis Seymour. *A History of Montenegro*. Boston: Adamant Media Corporation, 2002.

Terterov, Marat (ed.). *Doing Business with Serbia and Montenegro*. Sterling, Va.: Kogan Page, 2004.

Treadway, John D. *The Falcon and the Eagle: Montenegro and Austria-Hungary, 1908-1914*. West Lafayette, Ind: Purdue University Press, 1983.

West, Richard. *Tito: And the Rise and Fall of Yugoslavia*. New York: Carroll and Graf, 1995.

NETHERLANDS

Kingdom of the Netherlands
Koninkrijk der Nederlanden

CAPITAL: Constitutional capital: Amsterdam. Seat of government: The Hague ('S Gravenhage; Den Haag)

FLAG: The national flag, standardized in 1937, is a tricolor of red, white, and blue horizontal stripes.

ANTHEM: *Wilhelmus van Nassouwen (William of Nassau).*

MONETARY UNIT: The guilder was replaced by the euro as official currency as of 2002. The euro is divided into 100 cents. There are coins in denominations of 1, 2, 5, 10, 20, and 50 cents and 1 euro and 2 euros. There are notes of 5, 10, 20, 50, 100, 200, and 500 euros. €1 = $1.25475 (or $1 = €0.79697) as of 2005.

WEIGHTS AND MEASURES: The metric system is the legal standard.

HOLIDAYS: New Year's Day, 1 January; Queen's Day, 30 April; National Liberation Day, 5 May; Christmas, 25–26 December. Movable religious holidays include Good Friday, Holy Saturday, Easter Monday, Ascension, and Whitmonday.

TIME: 1 PM = noon GMT.

¹LOCATION, SIZE, AND EXTENT

Situated in northwestern Europe, the Netherlands has a total area of 41,526 sq km (16,033 sq mi), of which inland water accounts for more than 7,643 sq km (2,951 sq mi). The land area is 33,883 sq km (13,082 sq mi). Comparatively, the area occupied by the Netherlands is slightly less than twice the size of the state of New Jersey. The Netherlands extends 312 km (194 mi) N–S and 264 km (164 mi) E–W. The land area increases slightly each year as a result of continuous land reclamation and drainage. The Netherlands is bounded on the E by Germany on the S by Belgium, and on the W and N by the North Sea, with a total boundary length of 1,478 km (918 mi), of which 451 km (280 mi) is coastline.

The capital city of the Netherlands, Amsterdam, is in the western part of the country.

²TOPOGRAPHY

The country falls into three natural topographical divisions: the dunes, the lowlands or "polders" (low-lying land reclaimed from the sea and from lakes and protected by dikes), and the higher eastern section of the country. About 27% of the land lies below sea level. A long range of sand dunes on the western coast protects the low alluvial land to the east from the high tides of the North Sea, and farther east and southeast are found diluvial sand and gravel soil. The highest point of land, the Vaalserberg, is situated in the extreme south and is 321 m (1,053 ft) above sea level; the lowest point, 7 m (23 ft) below sea level, is Prins Alexanderpolder, an area of reclaimed land situated northeast of Rotterdam. The most extensive polder is that of East Flevoland in the province of Flevoland; it has an area of nearly 55,000 hectares (136,000 acres). Many dikes have been constructed along the lower Rhine and Meuse (Maas) rivers, as well as on a portion of the North Sea coast and along nearly the whole of the coast of the former Zuider Zee (formally called the Ijsselmeer since its enclosure by a dike in

1932). There are many canals in the country, most of which have numerous locks.

³CLIMATE

The Netherlands has a maritime climate, with cool summers and mild winters. The average temperature is 2°C (36°F) in January and 19°C (66°F) in July, with an annual average of about 10°C (50°F). Clouds generally appear every day, and in the winter months fog often abounds, while rainfall occurs frequently. Average annual rainfall is about 76.5 cm (30 in). The mild, damp climate is ideal for dairying and livestock raising, but the limited sunshine restricts the growing of food crops.

⁴FLORA AND FAUNA

Plants and animals that thrive in temperate climates are found in the Netherlands. The most common trees are oak, elm, pine, linden, and beech. The country is famous for its flowers, both cultivated varieties (best known among them the Dutch tulip) and wild flowers such as daisies, buttercups, and the purple heather that blooms on the heaths in September. Birds are those characteristic of Western and Central Europe, with large numbers of seagulls swarming over the coastal areas from time to time. Many kinds of fish abound along the North Sea coast and in the lakes and rivers. Wild or large animals are practically nonexistent. As of 2002, there were at least 55 species of mammals, 192 species of birds, and over 1,200 species of plants throughout the country.

⁵ENVIRONMENT

In recent years, as a result of rapid population and economic growth, the government has placed increased emphasis on preservation of the natural environment. One key concern is the pressure put on the countryside, traditionally the domain of the smallholder, by the demands of modern mechanized agriculture and the needs of a large urban population for recreational areas and waste disposal. To help solve this environmental problem, the government has instituted comprehensive land-use planning by means of a system of zoning that indicates the priorities for land use in each zone. Air and water pollution are significant environmental problems in the Netherlands.

The nation has one of the world's highest levels of industrial carbon dioxide emissions, which totaled 155 million metric tons in 1996. Efforts at controlling air pollution reduced sulphur dioxide emissions between 1980 and 1990 from 490,000 tons to 240,000 tons. In 2000, the total of carbon dioxide emissions was at 138.9 million metric tons. Severe pollution of the country's rivers results from industrial and agricultural pollution, including heavy metals, organic compounds, nitrates, and phosphates.

The Netherlands has about 11 cu km of renewable water resources, of which 61% of the annual withdrawal is used for industrial purposes. Solid waste in the nation's cities has been reported at an average of 7.6 million tons yearly. Aggravating the situation are the prevailing southwesterly winds, which carry the pollutants from coastal industries inland, and the great rivers that carry pollution into the Netherlands from originating countries farther inland.

In 1971, the Ministry of Health and Environment was established; a countrywide system of air pollution monitoring by the National Institute of Public Health has been in place since 1975. Since the mid-1970s, discharges of heavy metals into industrial wastewater and emissions of most major air pollutants from industrial use of fossil fuels have been substantially reduced. Progress has also been recorded in reducing automotive emissions. An excise tax surcharge on gasoline and diesel fuel was imposed for pollution abatement in 1981.

As of 2003, 14.2% of the country's total land area was protected, including 49 Ramsar wetland sites. According to a 2006 report issued by the International Union for Conservation of Nature and Natural Resources (IUCN), threatened species included 9 types of mammals, 11 species of birds, 7 species of fish, 1 type of mollusk, and 6 species of other invertebrates. Endangered species include Atlantic sturgeon, slender-billed curlew, Atlantic ridley, and Spengler's freshwater mussel.

⁶POPULATION

The population of Netherlands in 2005 was estimated by the United Nations (UN) at 16,296,000, which placed it at number 59 in population among the 193 nations of the world. In 2005, approximately 14% of the population was over 65 years of age, with another 19% of the population under 15 years of age. There were 99 males for every 100 females in the country. According to the UN, the annual population rate of change for 2005–10 was expected to be 0.4%, a rate the government viewed as satisfactory. The projected population for the year 2025 was 16,934,000. The population density was 399 per sq km (1,033 per sq mi), with over 45% of the population concentrated in the three most densely populated provinces: Utrecht, North Holland, and South Holland.

The UN estimated that 62% of the population lived in urban areas in 2005, and that urban areas were growing at an annual rate of 1.04%. The constitutional capital, Amsterdam, had a population of 705,000 in that year. The Rotterdam metropolitan area had 1,112,000 inhabitants. Other major cities and their estimated populations include The Hague ('s Gravenhage; Den Haag), which is the seat of government, 472,087; Utrecht, 275,362; Eindhoven,

209,286; Tilburg, 200,251; Groningen, 181,020; and Haarlem, 150,213.

⁷MIGRATION

In the past although the government encouraged emigration to curb overpopulation, more people migrated to the Netherlands than have left the country. Rapid economic growth in the 1960s drew many unskilled laborers from Mediterranean countries, and during the 1970s many people left Suriname for the Netherlands when the former Dutch colony became independent. At first both groups settled mainly in the western region, but after 1970 the pattern of internal migration changed, as increasing numbers left the western provinces to settle in the east and south. The traditional pattern of migration from the countryside to the cities has likewise been altered, and since the 1970s the trend has been largely from the larger cities to small towns and villages. By 2003 it was becoming harder for asylum migrants to find work. In addition, in 2004, employer groups asked for the streamline of admissions for skilled foreigner workers.

In 1990, some 57,344 persons left the Netherlands, of which 36,749 were Dutch nationals. In the same year, 81,264 immigrants arrived in the Netherlands, representing an increase of 24% over 1989. In 2002 the top 10 migrant-sending countries were Turkey, the Netherlands Antilles and Aruba, Morocco, Germany, the United Kingdom, China (excluding Taiwan), Angola, Suriname, and the United States. However, in 2003 for the first time since 1982, there were more emigrants (104,800) than immigrants (104,500). In that same year, the percent of foreign-born broke down as follows: 17.6% from Africa (mainly Morocco); 21.2% from the Americas (mainly from the Netherlands Antilles and South America); 34.3% from Asia (mainly from Indonesia); and 26.1% from Europe (with Germans the largest group). However, the large numbers of migrants from the Antilles has been decreasing, while emigration to these countries has increased. The number of Turks and Moroccans returning to their country of origin has been increasing between 2000 and 2004.

Since the election of a conservative government in 2002, the Dutch integration policy of multiculturalism (where all cultures were considered of equal value and there was no need for foreigners to integrate into Dutch society) was being eroded with new policies requiring immigrants to pass a test of Dutch language and culture. After the death of filmmaker Theo Van Gogh in 2004 at the hands of a Dutch-born man of Moroccan descent, a law was passed that made being a member of a "terrorist" organization a crime. By 2005, new policies included integration exams for foreign residents under age 65 with less than eight years of schooling in the Netherlands. In 2004, about 5.7% of Dutch residents were Muslim. According to *Migration News*, in 2005 Moroccan and Turkish groups created a working group, "Genoeg is genoeg" (Enough is enough), to coordinate a campaign against these hard-hitting immigration and integration policies.

At the beginning of 1996, there were 72,000 recognized refugees and 23,000 applications for asylum. By 1998, as many as 45,217 asylum applications were submitted. In 1999, 4,060 people were evacuated from Macedonia to the Netherlands. Following the trend in the 25 countries of the European Union, the Netherlands in 2004 had the lowest number of asylum seekers since 1988. In 2004, the United Nations High Commissioner for Refugees (UNHCR) had

NETHERLANDS

0   25   50 Miles

0   25   50 Kilometers

East Frisian Islands

Frisian Islands

West

Terschelling

Ameland

Schiermonnikoog

Vlieland

Waddenzee

Emden

Leeuwarden

Princess Margriet Canal

Groningen

Texel

Veendam

Den Helder

Dam with locks

Heerenveen

Assen

IJsselmeer

Emmen

Northeast Polder

Hoogereen

Meppen

Alkmaar

Emlichheim

Noordzee-kanaal

Lelystad

Zwolle

North Sea

Zaanstad

Flevoland Polder

Roalte

Rheine

Haarlem

IJssel

Amsterdam

Enschede

Apeldoorn

Leiden

Amersfoort

The Hague

Utrecht

Hengelo

Delft

Amsterdam-Rijnkanaal

Arnhem

Winterswijk

Rotterdam

Nederrijn

Borken

Lek

Dordrecht

Waal

Nijmegen

Maas

's-Hertogenbosch

GERMANY

Oosterschelde

Wilhelminakanaal

Zuid-Willemskanaal

Breda

Rhein

Middelburg

Tilburg

Westerschelde

Eindhoven

Maas

Düsseldorf

Antwerp

Mönchengladbach

Gent

BELGIUM

Heerlen

Schelde

Maastricht

Aachen

Brussels

Netherlands

Liege

FRANCE

LOCATION: 50°45′ to 53°52′N; 3°21′ to 7°13′ E. BOUNDARY LENGTHS: Germany, 577 kilometers (358 miles); Belgium, 450 kilometers (280 miles); North Sea coastline, 451 kilometers (280 miles). TERRITORIAL SEA LIMIT: 12 miles.

a total of 155,257 persons of concern in the Netherlands: 126,805 refugees and 28,452 asylum seekers. The main countries of origin for refugees were Iraq (28,640), Afghanistan (26,437), Bosnia and Herzegovina (19,943), and Somalia (13,046).

In 2005, the net migration rate was an estimated 2.8 migrants per 1,000 population.

8 ETHNIC GROUPS

The Dutch are an ethnically homogeneous people descended from Frankish, Saxon, and Frisian tribes. Ethnic homogeneity slightly changed as a result of the arrival of some 300,000 repatriates and immigrants from Indonesia, mostly Eurasian, and more than 140,000 from Suriname. The influx of Turks and other workers from the Mediterranean area has further added to the ethnic mix. The most recent estimates indicate that about 80% of the total population are Dutch; the principal minority groups are Turkish, Moroccan, Surinamese, and Antillean.

9LANGUAGES

Dutch and Frisian are the official languages. Frisian, the native language of about 300,000 persons, is closely related to the Anglo-Saxon tongue but has many points in common with Dutch, which belongs to the Germanic language group. There are six Dutch dialects. Many Netherlanders speak and understand English, French, and German, which are taught in secondary schools.

10RELIGIONS

Dutch society is becoming increasingly secular. According to the Social Cultural Planning Bureau, church membership has steadily declined from 76% in 1958 to 41% in 1995. Only about 26% of those claiming a religious affiliation are active in their religious community. According to a 2004 report, an estimated 31% of the population were nominally Roman Catholics, 14% were Dutch Reformed, 6% were Muslim, 6% were Calvinist Reformist, 3% were non-Christian (Hindu, Jewish, or Buddhist); and about 40% were atheist or agnostic.

The Dutch Reformed Church, whose membership has declined by more than 60% since 1950, is the largest Protestant denomination. The Calvinist Reformed Church is the second-largest Protestant group. Other Protestant denominations include Baptist, Lutheran, and Remonstrant. The Jewish community has less than 25,000 members. The Muslim community is primarily of the Sunni branch. Many of them are migrant workers from Morocco and Turkey or immigrants from other countries such as Iraq, Somalia, and Bosnia. There are about 95,000 Hindus, primarily from Suriname. The Hindu based movements of Ramakrishna, Hare Krishna, Sai Baba, and Osho are also represented. About 17,000 people are Buddhist.

11TRANSPORTATION

Merchant shipping has always been of great economic importance to the seagoing Dutch. The Netherlands Maritime Institute is internationally famous, and the Dutch ship-testing station at Wageningen is known for its research in marine engineering. The Dutch merchant marine had 558 ships (of 1,000 GRT or over) totaling 4,796,460 GRT in 2005. Emphasis has been placed on the development of new vessels suitable for container transport and on improving the Dutch tanker fleet. Rotterdam is the Netherlands' chief port and the world's largest. There are also ports and harbors at Amsterdam, Delfzijl, Dordrecht, Eemshaven, Groningen, Haarlem, Ijmuiden, Maastricht, Terneuzen, and Utrecht.

In 2004, there were 5,046 km (3,136 mi) of navigable waterways of which 3,745 km (2,327 mi) are canals and are capable of handling vessels of up to 50 tons.

The railway system in 2004 consisted of 2,808 km (1,744 mi) of standard gauge rail lines, of which 2,061 km (1,280 mi) was electrified. Passenger transport on railways is subsidized as part of the national policy for promoting public transport. Public transport is provided for urban areas by municipal and regional transport companies, and minibus service in rural areas has ensured public transport for all towns with 1,000 residents or more. Also in

2001, there were 116,500 km (72,393 mi) of roadways, of which 104,850 km (65,153 mi) were paved, including 2,235 km (1,389 mi) of expressways. In 2003 there were 7,151,000 passenger cars and 1,080,000 commercial vehicles in use. The state subsidizes the construction of urban and rural cycle paths.

In 2004, there were an estimated 28 airports. In 2005 a total of 20 had paved runways, and there was also one heliport. Principal airports include Schiphol at Amsterdam, Reina Beatrix at Aruba, and Hato at Curacao. The world's first airline from the standpoint of continuous corporate existence and operation is Royal Dutch Airlines (Koninklijke Luchtvaart Maatschappij-KLM), which began regularly scheduled operations in 1920. The Netherlands government owns a large part of the outstanding capital stock. KLM serves some 115 cities in 70 countries. Also in 2003, about 23.455 million passengers were carried on domestic and international flights.

12HISTORY

When, in about 55 BC, Julius Caesar conquered a large part of the lowlands near the mouths of the Rhine and Meuse (Maas) rivers, this region was populated by Celtic and Germanic tribes. To the north of the Rhine delta, several Germanic tribes had settled, among which the Batavi and the Frisians were the most important. The Batavi served with the Roman legions until they rebelled in AD 70, but even after the revolt was quelled, Batavian soldiers fought for Rome. About 300 years later, successive waves of powerful Germanic tribes, such as the Salic or West Franks, invaded this region, called the Low Countries, and gradually pushed the Frisians back to the east coast of the North Sea, except in the extreme northern section of the mainland where Saxons had settled. By the time of Charlemagne (742–814), the Saxons and Frisians had been completely conquered by the West Franks, and the Frankish language had replaced the languages of the Germanic tribes.

Soon after the death of Charlemagne and the disintegration of his realm, several duchies and counties were founded in the Low Countries by local leaders. With the coming of the Middle Ages, Holland (now the North and South Holland provinces) became the most important region and extended its power and territory under Count Floris V (r.1256–96). The ancient bishopric of Utrecht was another important principality. As the Middle Ages drew to a close, individual cities such as Amsterdam, Haarlem, and Groningen rose to eminence, together with the Duchy of Gelderland. In the 15th century, the dukes of Burgundy acquired, by various means, most of the Low Countries. Upon the extinction of the male line of the Burgundian dynasty and the marriage of Mary of Burgundy and Archduke (later Emperor) Maximilian I in 1477, however, the Austrian house of Habsburg fell heir to the lands.

The Habsburgs

Mary's son, Philip of Habsburg, married Joanna of Castile, heiress to the Spanish throne, and their son, Charles, became King Charles I of Spain in 1516 and Holy Roman Emperor Charles V in 1519. In 1547, he decreed the formal union of the Netherlands and Austria, and in 1549, the union of the Netherlands and Spain. By the end of his reign in 1555, he was master of the Low Countries. His son, Philip II, concentrated his efforts on the aggrandizement of Spain. To bring the Low Countries under his direct control, he tried to stamp out the rising force of Protestantism and suppressed the political, economic, and religious liberties long cherished by the population. As a result, both Roman Catholics and Protestants rebelled against him under the leadership of William the Silent, prince of Orange, who by marriage had acquired large properties in the Netherlands.

For 10 years, the 17 provinces comprising the Low Countries united in a common revolt. Much of the area was freed in 1577, with William as the acknowledged ruler, but not even his moderation and statesmanship sufficed to keep the northern and southern provinces united. In 1578, the southern region (now Belgium) began to turn against William. In 1579, the northern provinces concluded the Union of Utrecht, in which the province of Holland was the most prominent. The Union, or United Provinces, carried on the fight against Spain, and William was the soul of the resistance until his death by assassination in 1584. William's son Maurits, governor (stadtholder) of the republic from 1584 to 1624, carried on a successful campaign against Spain, but final recognition of Dutch independence by the Spanish government was not obtained until the end of the Eighty Years' War with the Treaty of Westphalia (1648). Meanwhile, the southern provinces remained loyal to Spain and to the Roman Catholic Church, and were thereafter known as the Spanish Netherlands.

Independence brought mixed success in the 17th century for the United Provinces. Dutch prosperity was nourished by settlements and colonies in the East Indies, India, South Africa, the West Indies, South America, and elsewhere. The government was oligarchic but based on republican and federative principles. The Dutch were noted for their religious freedom, welcoming religious refugees—Spanish and Portuguese Jews, French Huguenots, and English Pilgrims.

While they became a leading commercial and maritime power, controversy over the leadership, and external economic and military threats complicated political and economic stability. Trade and territory disagreements with England resulted in the First Anglo-Dutch War that began in 1652 but ended with the Treaty of Westminster in 1654. The English were quick to attack again, beginning the Second Anglo-Dutch War, which ended with successful Dutch attacks, but also in the loss of colonial possession in North America—of the area that now surrounds New York City— via a trade-off under the 1667 Treaty of Breda.

Arts, sciences, literature, and philosophy flourished alongside trade and banking during the Dutch "golden era." In 1672, however, England declared war on the Republic, igniting the Third Anglo-Dutch War; France, Münster, and Cologne soon followed in their own attack. The new stadtholder William III rose out of what is known as the "Disastrous Year" to triumphantly end the war with England in 1674 and lead a coalition against the aggressive France of Louis XIV. William III (r.1672–1702), great-grandson of William the Silent and grandson of the English King Charles I and his English wife, Mary, were invited by the English Parliament to occupy the British throne in 1688, but they continued to take keen interest in Dutch affairs. The Dutch republic of which William had been governor survived for nearly a century after his death. Its position was continually threatened, however, by intense rivalries among and within the provinces. Four naval wars with Britain from the middle of the 17th century to the end of the 18th also sapped Dutch strength. In 1795, a much-weakened republic was overrun by revolutionary French armies.

After the brief Napoleonic occupation, the great powers of Europe at the Congress of Vienna (1814–15) set up a new kingdom of the Netherlands, composed of the former United Provinces and the former Spanish or Austrian Netherlands, and installed a prince of the house of Orange as King William I. The constitution that was founded in 1814 was last revised in 1983. In 1830, a revolt by the southern provinces resulted in the establishment of the kingdom of Belgium. Thereafter, the much-reduced kingdom was mainly concerned with domestic problems, such as the school conflict over secular versus religious instruction, social problems stemming from the industrialization of the country, and electoral reforms.

In foreign affairs, relations with Belgium were gradually improved after a decade of war and tension following Belgian independence, and Dutch claims to the principality of Luxembourg ended with the death of William III in 1890.

The World Wars to the Present

Foreign policies based on neutrality successfully met their test in World War I. Although the Netherlands mobilized their army, they remained neutral, even as the Germans invaded Belgium and all the surrounding states were at war.

The Netherlands again declared their neutrality when World War II erupted in 1939. Neutrality was preserved until the German World War II war machine overran the country in May 1940. Queen Wilhelmina (r.1890–1948) refused to surrender to the Germans, and instead fled to Britain with other officials of her government. Although Dutch resistance lasted only five days, destruction was widespread; nearly the whole of downtown Rotterdam was wiped out, and the cities of Arnhem and Nijmegen suffered great damage. In addition, Dutch factory equipment was carried away to Germany, bridges and railroads were blown up or removed, cattle were stolen, and part of the land was flooded. The Dutch withstood severe repression until their liberation by Allied forces in May 1945. Wilhelmina abdicated in 1948 and was succeeded by her daughter, Juliana (r.1948–80).

The East Indies, most of which had been under Dutch rule for over 300 years, were invaded by Japanese forces in January 1942. After Japanese troops continued through the territory, the Dutch surrendered in March when Japanese arrived on Java. In 1945, a group of Indonesians proclaimed an independent republic and resisted Dutch reoccupation. After four years of hostilities and following UN intervention, the Netherlands recognized the independence of Indonesia in December 1949. Suriname (formerly Dutch Guiana), controlled by the Netherlands since 1815, became an independent nation on 25 November 1975. This Dutch colonial legacy was the root cause of several violent outbreaks during the late 1970s, as a group of South Moluccans, a few of the 40,000 Moluccans living in the Netherlands, used terrorism on Dutch soil to dramatize their demand for the independence of the South Molucca Islands from Indonesia. The Netherlands Antilles and Aruba continue to be dependent areas.

As for many western countries, the 1960s and 1970s brought extensive cultural and social change. Traditional class and religious lines that had supported separate education and social status were erased, leading to significant change for women's rights, sexuality, economic, and environmental issues.

Reform of the social security system was the major political issue in the 1990s, along with efforts to reduce public spending. Years of administrative tinkering with the social security system has reduced the number of claimants, increased labor force participation, and generated a central government budget surplus of 1% of GDP in 2000. The budget surplus prompted heated cabinet discussions as the Labor Party wished to use the extra money for redistribution while the neo-liberal conservatives hoped to lower tax rates. Buyant growth rates of more than 3% in the period 1996–2001 brought down the official unemployment level to 2.7%. However, the global economic downturn that began in 2001 was one cause of the Netherlands' shrinking economy in late 2002 and early 2003. The government also passed a number of radical social measures that received parliamentary approval in recent years including conditions for administering euthanasia, legalization of prostitution, legalization of gay marriages, and laws banning discrimination.

A founder of the European Coal and Steel Community, the Netherlands became part of the Economic and Monetary Union and strongly supports an independent European central bank, low inflation, and stable currency. It hosted two different intergovernmental conferences of the European Union and chaired the finalization of the Treaty of European Union (Maastricht Treaty) in 1991 and the Amsterdam Treaty in 1997.

In May 2002, Pim Fortuyn, an anti-immigration leader of his own political party, was assassinated by a single gunman. His party, List Pim Fortuyn, came in second in the 15 May 2002 parliamentary elections. The conservative Christian Democrats, led by Jan Peter Balkenende, came in first, and Balkenende became prime minister of a center-right coalition government. In October, Balkenende's government collapsed following disagreements within the List Pim Fortuyn Party. Elections were held on 22 January 2003, and the Christian Democrats narrowly defeated the Labor Party in the Second Chamber. After 125 days, a coalition government was formed comprising the Christian Democrats, the free-market liberal People's Party for Freedom and Democracy, and the socially liberal Democrats.

The Netherlands gave political support to the military action taken by the United States and United Kingdom against Saddam Hussein's regime in Iraq in 2003. Although the Netherlands has a history of open immigration and integration, the increased controversies in Europe surrounding Islamic fundamentalism and immigration have plagued it as well. On 2 November 2004, filmmaker and publicist Theo van Gogh was assassinated reportedly by a Dutch-Moroccan Islamic youth group.

Queen Juliana abdicated in 1980 in favor of her daughter, Beatrix. Juliana died 20 March 2004. In 1966, Beatrix had married Claus von Amsberg, a German diplomat, and his title remained that of Prince of the Netherlands when Beatrix became Queen. Their firstborn son, and Crown Prince, Willem-Alexander was born in 1967. Beatrix and Claus von Amsberg had two other sons, Johan Friso and Constantijn, before Prince Claus's death in 2002. Prince Willem-Alexander has two daughters with his wife, Princess Máxima: Princess Catharina-Amalia was born 7 June 2003, and Princess Alexia was born 26 June 2005.

13 GOVERNMENT

The Netherlands is a constitutional monarchy, under the house of Orange-Nassau. The monarch and the Council of Ministers together are called the Crown, and is the center of executive power. The prime minister is the active head of government, is a member of the Council of Ministers, the head of the cabinet, and usually the leader of the largest party within the ruling party coalition. Executive power is also shared with the cabinet, which must have the support of a majority in the parliament. Cabinet ministers may not be members of the parliament. The Council of State, instituted as an advisory body for the government in 1532, is appointed by and presided over by the monarch. It is composed of a vice president, councilors (28 maximum), and honorary members (25 maximum). The council considers all legislation proposed by the sovereign or the cabinet before it is submitted to the parliament. While functioning in an advisory capacity, the council has executive powers when it implements orders of the sovereign and it has judiciary powers when it acts in disputes and citizen appeals concerning the government.

Legislative power is exercised jointly by the crown and the States-General (Staten-Generaal), a bicameral parliament. The upper house (Eerste Kamer) consists of 75 members elected for four years by the provincial representative councils on the basis of proportional representation. The lower house (Tweede Kamer) has 150 members elected for four years directly by the people, also on the basis of proportional representation. Only the lower house has the right to introduce bills and to move amendments, but the upper house can accept or reject bills passed by the other chamber.

All Dutch citizens who have reached the age of 18 years and reside within the Netherlands have the right to vote. All citizens who have reached the age of 18 years are eligible for election to the States-General.

Every year on the third Tuesday in September, the session of the States-General is opened at the Hague by the monarch. In the speech from the throne, the government's program for the year is announced. The monarch acts as an adviser to the cabinet, may propose bills, and signs all bills approved by the legislature. Theoretically she could refuse to sign a bill, but this never occurs in practice because the cabinet is responsible for the actions of the ruler. Thus, if the queen should refuse to sign a bill, the cabinet must resign and she must then find a new cabinet acceptable to the parliament.

Immediately following elections, the monarch appoints a formateur to advise on the program and composition of the new cabinet, and form the Council of Ministers. If he fails to bring together a new ministry, a new formateur is appointed, and so on until a new cabinet has been formed.

14 POLITICAL PARTIES

Throughout the political history of the Netherlands, religion has played an important role. During World War II, strenuous efforts were made to reduce this role, but denominational parties continued to exercise considerable influence. However, since the mid-1960s the general trend has been toward the polarization of politics into conservative and progressive parties, and denominational parties have lost voter support.

The religious political party with the largest membership throughout the postwar period was the Catholic People's Party (Katholieke Volkspartij—KVP), which favored democratic government and a middle-of-the-road social policy. It began to lose votes in the 1960s and the KVP joined the Anti-Revolutionary Party (Anti-Revolutionaire Partij—ARP) and the right-wing Christian Historical Union (Christelijk-Historische Unie—CHU) to form the Christian Democratic Appeal (Christen-Democratisch Appèl—CDA) to contest the 1977 elections, and has since been a major political force. The Labor party (Partij van de Arbeid—PvdA) vied for political leadership with the KVP in the first decades of the postwar period, polling about the same number of votes in national elections until 1972, when the PvdA won a plurality of nearly 25% of the total vote and emerged as the dominant member of a centrist coalition government. The Labor Party, a social democratic party that resulted from the merger of three socialist and liberal parties, has appealed mainly to national interests rather than to socialist ones, although it does favor redistribution and solidarity. Since 1986, it has pursued de-radicalization and has moved to the political center. The conservative People's Party for Freedom and Democracy (Volkspartij voor Vrijheid en Democratie—VVD) advocates free enterprise, separation of church and state, and individual liberties.

Since 1965, discontent with the major political parties and erosion of party discipline have led to the establishment of change-oriented parties like Democrats 66 (Democraten 66—D66), which pushes for greater democratic accountability, political transparency, and involvement of the citizen in the policy process. Smaller parties include the left-wing Green Left (GroenLinks—GL), which is the product of a merger of socialist and ecology parties in 1991. Three small social conservative Calvinist parties have been at the heart of much political debate and change in the end of the 20th and beginning of the 21st century: the Political Reformed Party (Staatkundig Gereformeerde Partij—SGP) which was denied state funding in 2005 for prohibiting women from becoming full members, the Reformed Political Union (Gereformeerd Politiek Verbond—GPV) and the Reformatorian Political Federation (Reformatorische Politieke Federation—RPF) merged in 2001 to form the far-right Christian Union (ChristenUnie), the fifth-largest party in 2005, that combines fundamental religious values on abortion, gay marriage, and euthanasia, with socially democratic views on economic, immigration, and environmental issues.

As no single party commands a majority in the States-General, the governing cabinet is a coalition of various party representatives, according to their numerical strength. In 1994, for the first time in 80 years, a coalition emerged which did not include a confessional party. The Labor party won a plurality of votes in spite of an absolute loss of votes. Its closest ally, D66, absolutely refused to join a coalition government with the Christian Democrats. In 1994, the first "purple" cabinet emerged, led by Wim Kok of the Labor party, and composed of D66 and the VVD. In 1998 the government fell after D66 failed to push through parliament a bill to make more use of referendums. A month later, in June 1998, voters brought back the purple coalition and Kok led another government of VVD, D66, and PvdA.

Willem Kok initially let it be known in various interviews that he would stand again in the 2002 election, greatly increasing the likelihood of another four years of Labor Party leadership. However, in April 2002, Kok's government resigned following an official report criticizing its role in the 1995 Srebrenica massacre in the former Yugoslavia, when some 100 lightly armed Dutch peacekeepers failed to stop Bosnian Serb forces from murdering around 7,000 Muslims.

Elections were held on 15 May 2002, and resulted in a victory for the Christian Democrats. A surprise showing was made by the List Pim Fortuyn (LPF); a political party formed just a month earlier by the anti-immigrant politician Pim Fortuyn. Fortuyn was assassinated just prior to the election, but his party came in second. Labor, the VVD, and D66 all suffered losses. Christian Democratic leader Jan Peter Balkenende became prime minister; however, his government collapsed in October 2002, and new elections were held on 22 January 2003.

Following the January 2003 elections, the 150 seats in the Second Chamber of the Legislature were distributed as follows: CDA, 28.6% (44 seats); PvdA, 27.3% (42 seats); VVD, 17.9% (28 seats); SP, 6.3% (9 seats); LPF, 5.7% (8 seats); GL, 5.1% (8 seats); D66, 4.1% (6 seats); the Christian Union (CU), 2.1% (3 seats); and the conservative Calvinist party Political Reformed Party (SGP), 1.6% (2 seats). The PvdA scored an increase of 19 seats over the May 2002 elections, and the LPF suffered a loss of 18 seats. After prohibitive disagreement in the formation of a CDA-PvdA cabinet, the center-right CDA, the conservative VVD, and the center-left D66 formed a coalition with Balkenende again as prime minister.

The next general elections were scheduled for May 2007.

15 LOCAL GOVERNMENT

Through 2005, the country was divided into 12 provinces, each governed by a locally direct-elected representative provincial council (provinciale staten). The size of the council depends on the number of inhabitants in the province. Members are elected for four-year terms. From among their members, the councils elect provincial executives (gedeputeerde staten) with six to eight members. Each province has a commissioner appointed by and representing the Crown.

The smaller municipalities (496 in 2003) are administered by municipal councils, which are elected directly for four-year terms by the local inhabitants and make local bylaws. The executive powers of the municipality are entrusted to a corporate board consisting of a burgomaster and two to six aldermen; the latter are elected from and by the council, while the burgomaster (mayor) is appointed by the Crown. The important function of flood control and water management is exercised by autonomous public authorities, some of which date as far back as the 13th century.

16 JUDICIAL SYSTEM

The judiciary is independent and the judges irremovable except for malfeasance or incapacity. Roman law still is basic, but the judicial system is largely patterned on that of France. There is no jury system, and the state rather than the individual acts as initiator of legal proceedings. Administrative justice is separate from civil and criminal justice and not uniform in dispensation.

The supreme judiciary body is the Supreme Court of the Netherlands (Court of Cassation). As of 2005 it was staffed by 24 justices. Its principal task is to supervise administration of justice and to review the judgments of lower courts. There are five courts of appeal *(gerechtshoven),* which act as courts of first instance only in fiscal matters. They are divided into chambers of three justices each. The 19 district courts *(arrondissementsrechtsbanken)* deal as courts of first instance with criminal cases and civil cases not handled by the 62 subdistrict courts. Most of these courts are manned by single magistrates. In 2002, the subdistrict courts were incorporated administratively into the district courts; a subdistrict court section is now formed at these courts. There also are juvenile courts and special arbitration courts (for such institutions as the Stock Exchange Association and professional organizations).

Normally appointed for life, judges are usually retired at age 70.

17 ARMED FORCES

In 2005 there were 53,130 active personnel in the Netherlands' armed forces, with reserves numbering 54,400. The army numbered 23,150. Equipment included 283 main battle tanks, 569 armored infantry fighting vehicles, 94 armored personnel carriers, and 407 artillery pieces. The navy had 17,130 personnel including 3,100 marines. Its fleet included four tactical submarines and 14 surface combatants (six destroyers and eight frigates). The naval aviation unit of 950 was equipped with 10 maritime patrol aircraft and 21 antisubmarine/search and rescue helicopters. The air force has 11,050 active personnel plus 5,000 reservists subject to immediate recall. The air force had 108 combat capable aircraft and 30 attack helicopters. A paramilitary force known as the Royal Military Constabulary numbered 6,800 persons. The United States stationed about 303 personnel in the Netherlands. The Netherlands maintained forces abroad in Germany, Iceland, Italy and the Netherlands Antilles. The nation also participated in UN and peacekeeping missions in five other countries including Iraq and Afghanistan. The military budget in 2005 totaled $9.7 billion.

18 INTERNATIONAL COOPERATION

The Netherlands is a founding member of the United Nations, having joined on 10 December 1945. It participates in ECE, ECLAC, ESCAP, and several nonregional specialized agencies, such as the FAO, the World Bank, IAEA, ILO, UNESCO, UNHCR, UNIDO, and the WHO. In addition, the Netherlands is a member of the WTO, the Asian Development Bank, the African Development Bank, the Council of Europe, the Euro-Atlantic Partnership Council, G-10 (Paris Club), the Western European Union, the European Union, NATO, OSCE, and OECD. The Netherlands is a permanent observer at OAS. The Netherlands is the home site of the International Court of Justice, Eurojust, Europol, the Organization for the Prohibition of Chemical Weapons, and the International Criminal Court.

On 1 January 1948, Belgium, the Netherlands, and Luxembourg established a joint customs union, Benelux; since that time, the three countries have freed nearly all of their mutual imports from quantitative restrictions. On 3 February 1958, the Benelux Economic Union was established to make it possible for each participating country to apply itself more intensively to the production for which it is best suited as well as to extend the total market for the member countries.

The Netherlands is a part of the Australia Group, the Zangger Committee, the European Organization for Nuclear Research (CERN), the Nuclear Suppliers Group (London Group), the Organization for the Prohibition of Chemical Weapons, and the Nuclear Energy Agency. In environmental cooperation, the Netherlands is part of the Antarctic Treaty; the Basel Convention; Conventions on Biological Diversity, Whaling, and Air Pollution; Ramsar; CITES; the London Convention; International Tropical Timber Agreements; the Kyoto Protocol; the Montréal Protocol; MARPOL; the Nuclear Test Ban Treaty; and the UN Conventions on the Law of the Sea, Climate Change and Desertification.

19 ECONOMY

The Netherlands has an advanced economy, which combines high per capita income with a fairly even income distribution. An industrial nation with limited natural resources, the Netherlands bases its economy on the importation of raw materials for processing into finished products for export. Food processing, metallurgy, chemicals, manufacturing, and oil refining are the principal industries. Agriculture is particularly important to the economy, as about 60% of total agricultural production is exported.

Because of its geographic position on the sea, outstanding harbor facilities, and numerous internal waterways, the Netherlands became a trading, transporting, and brokerage nation. A major role in the economy has always been played by the service industries, such as banks, trading companies, shipping enterprises, and brokerage and supply firms. The economy, being involved in international trade, is sharply affected by economic developments abroad—including fluctuations in prices of primary goods—over which the Netherlands has little or no control.

Growth in GDP averaged just under 3% per year during 1988–95 with exceptionally strong growth occurring in 1989 (4.8%) and particularly slow growth in 1993 (1.8%). Inflation was low, averaging about 2% a year between 1986 and 1998. The unemployment rate fell from 10.5% in 1985 to 8.4% in 1995, and has continued to fall steadily, reaching an estimated 6% in 2004. For the four years 1997 to 2000, real GDP growth averaged 4%, well ahead of most of Europe. Growth slowed due to the global economic slowdown of 2001 to 2.8% and was brought close to a standstill in 2002, with estimated growth of 0.3%. Real GDP growth averaged 1.2% over the 2000–04 period. GDP growth was estimated at 0.5% in 2005, but was forecast to pick up to 2% in 2006 and to 2.7% in 2007. Inflation jumped from 2.2% in 1999 and 2.6% in 2000 to a yearly average of 4.5% in 2001 due mainly to a hike in the VAT rate, and increases in gasoline and food prices. The inflation rate averaged 2.7% over the 2000–04 period. The inflation rate in 2005 was estimated at 1.6%; it was forecast to remain at that rate in 2006.

20 INCOME

The US Central Intelligence Agency (CIA) reports that in 2005 the Netherlands's gross domestic product (GDP) was estimated at $500.0 billion. The CIA defines GDP as the value of all final goods and services produced within a nation in a given year and computed on the basis of purchasing power parity (PPP) rather than value as measured on the basis of the rate of exchange based on current dollars. The per capita GDP was estimated at $30,500. The annual growth rate of GDP was estimated at 0.6%. The average inflation rate in 2005 was 1.6%. It was estimated that agriculture accounted for 2.1% of GDP, industry 24.4%, and services 73.5%.

According to the World Bank, in 2003 remittances from citizens working abroad totaled $767 million or about $47 per capita and accounted for approximately 0.1% of GDP.

The World Bank reports that in 2003 household consumption in Netherlands totaled $208.63 billion or about $12,878 per capita based on a GDP of $511.5 billion, measured in current dollars rather than PPP. Household consumption includes expenditures of individuals, households, and nongovernmental organizations on goods and services, excluding purchases of dwellings. It was estimated that for the period 1990 to 2003 household consumption grew at an average annual rate of 2.8%. In 2001 it was estimated that approximately 17% of household consumption was spent on food, 7% on fuel, 2% on health care, and 13% on education.

21 LABOR

As of 2005, the Netherlands' labor force numbered an estimated 7.53 million. In 2002 (the latest year for which data was available), 74.1% were employed in services, 20.3% in manufacturing, 4% in agriculture, and the remainder in undefined occupations. The unemployed represented about 6.7% of the workforce in 2005, compared with 1.2% in 1970, and 13% in 1985.

As of 2005, workers in the Netherlands were allowed to organize and join unions, engage in collective bargaining and to exercise the right to strike. However, strikes are rare. Labor unions in 2005 accounted for about 25% of the country's workforce. However, collective bargaining agreements cover about 86% of the labor force. Antiunion discrimination is prohibited.

The law stipulates a 40-hour workweek, but in 2005 the average workweek was 30.6 hours (20 hours for part-time employees and 38.7 hours for full-time employees). The five-day workweek has been generally adopted. Workers receive workers' compensation, unemployment insurance, sick pay, payment for legal holidays, and paid vacations. The employment of women and adolescents for night work is forbidden. The minimum wage for adults in 2005 was $1,517 per month, and was capable of providing a worker and family with a decent living standard. However, most workers earn more. There is a reduced minimum wage for workers under 23, which uses a sliding scale ranging from 35% of the adult minimum wage for a 16-year-old to 85% for those 22 years of age. The minimum age for employment is 16 years. These laws are effectively enforced.

22 AGRICULTURE

More than 27% of the total land area of the Netherlands is under seasonal or permanent crop production. Grasslands account for about 54% of all agricultural lands. Most farms are effectively managed and worked intensively with mechanical equipment. The many cooperatives have added to the efficiency of production and distribution.

Although agricultural production has decreased in recent years, labor productivity in Dutch agricultural and horticultural industries has risen sharply. The number of holdings declined by over 17% from the mid-1970s to the mid-1980s; in 2002 there were 89,580 agricultural holdings, of which 45% were smaller than 10 hectares (25 acres). In 2003 there were 108,230 full-time and 153,250 part-time workers in the agricultural labor force. The

crop output in 2003 was valued at almost €10.6 billion, fifth highest in the EU after France, Italy, Spain, and Germany.

Much of the soil in the east and southeast is poor. Moreover, large regions are so moist because of their low altitude that only grass can be grown profitably, a condition that has led to the enormous development of the dairy industry. The best land is found in reclaimed polders. Principal crops and output in 2004 (in thousands of tons) were sugar beets, 6,292; potatoes, 7,488; wheat, 1,224; barley, 288; rye, 17; and triticale, 19.

The Netherlands is famous for its bulbs grown for export, principally tulip, hyacinth, daffodil, narcissus, and crocus. Flower growing is centered at Aalsmeer (near Amsterdam), and nurseries are situated mainly at Boskoop. Bulb growing, done principally at Lisse and Hillegom, between Haarlem and Leiden, has been extended in recent years to areas of North Holland. In 2002, there were 11,793 horticultural holdings and land area for growing bulbs totaled 17,139 hectares (42,350 acres).

Since the beginning of the 20th century, the government has been helping the agrarian sector through extension services, the promotion of scientific research, and the creation of specific types of agricultural education. In the 1930s, an extensive system of governmental controls of agricultural production was introduced, and after World War II (1939–45), an even more active policy was initiated, which evolved into integrated planning covering practically every aspect of rural life. In recent years, the government has actively encouraged the consolidation of small landholdings into larger, more efficient units.

23 ANIMAL HUSBANDRY

World-renowned Dutch dairy products outrank all other agricultural produce, and livestock provides two-thirds of total agricultural value. In 2005 there were 3.86 million head of cattle, 11.1 million pigs, 1.2 million sheep, and 86 million chickens. Milk production in 2005 totaled 10.5 million tons. Meat production in 2005 was 2.35 million tons (including pork, 1,299,000; beef and veal, 388,000; and poultry, 646,000). Butter production was 102,000 tons; cheese, 671,000 tons.

Friesland is the most important region for the production of milk and butter. Excellent grazing lands and a long growing season have greatly helped the Frisian dairy industry, whose main support is the famed Frisian strain of cows. The making of cheese is connected with such famous brands as those named for Edam and Gouda, towns in the province of South Holland, and Alkmaar in North Holland.

In 2003, the value of animal products was €7.61 billion. The output of animal products has gradually been falling since 1996, when production was valued at €9.37 billion. The Netherlands regularly imports calves from the United Kingdom. In 1995, the Dutch Ministry of Agriculture, in response to the possible connection of bovine spongiform encephalopathy (BSE) in cattle to Creutzfeldt-Jakob disease in humans, responded with a program to destroy all imported UK veal calves. The total slaughter amounted to 64,000 calves and led to losses of approximately $32 million to the livestock industry.

24 FISHING

Although no longer as important as it was in the 16th and 17th centuries, fishing still contributes substantially to the food supply. Annual fish consumption in the Netherlands is 21.9 kg (32.2 lb) per person. In 2003 the Dutch fishing fleet had 393 cutters, 17 trawlers, and 69 mussel dredgers; the total capacity of the fishing fleet that year was 195,307 gross tons. About half of the fish catch is landed at the ports of Scheveningen and Ijmuiden. The Dutch fishing industry faces declining fish stocks and quota cuts from the EU that make profitability difficult because of excess capacity. In 2003, Dutch imports of fish products totaled $1.7 billion and exports exceeded $2.18 billion.

The total catch in 2003 was 593,305 tons, consisting primarily of mackerel, mussels, sardines, herring, plaice, and whiting. Shrimp, oysters, sole, and other saltwater fish were also caught.

25 FORESTRY

One of the least forested countries in Europe, the Netherlands produces only about 8% of its wood requirements. Woodland, chiefly pine, covers about 375,000 hectares (927,000 acres), or only 11.1% of the total land area, of which state forest areas comprise some 37%; private owners, 31%; provincial and local governments, 14%; and nature conservation organizations, 18%. Productive woodlands total about 230,000 hectares (580,000 acres); output of timber was approximately 1,026,000 cu m (36.2 million cu ft) in 2004. The Netherlands imports about 95% of its softwood lumber needs, mostly from Sweden, Finland, and Russia. Domestic sources of temperate hardwood lumber usually meet 20–30% of annual demand; production totaled 80,000 cu m (2.8 million cu ft) in 2004.

The Dutch wood industry is focused on the furniture, construction, packing, and pulp and paper sectors. The total turnover of the Dutch furniture sector in 2004 was almost €2 billion; the turnover in the Dutch pulp and paper industry was also around €2 billion. The Netherlands is the ninth biggest European producer of pulp and paper, annually producing 3.3 million tons of paper and paperboard at 27 sites, with over 70% exported to neighboring countries.

Afforestation has not kept pace with increasing consumption. The Dutch government would like to become at least 25% self-sufficient in wood fiber by 2025. In order to meet this goal, some 3.9 million cu m (137.7 million cu ft) of fiber would need to be produced annually (assuming current consumption trends). Currently, Dutch wood fiber production is only 1.2 million cu m (42 million cu ft). During 1990–2000, only 1,000 hectares (2,500 acres) of forest were planted. The government established a goal in 1994 of increasing forested land by 3,000 hectares (7,400 acres) annually until 2020.

26 MINING

The Netherlands was an important regional producer of natural gas and petroleum and played a major role as a transshipment center for mineral materials entering and leaving Europe—Rotterdam was the world's largest container port. The only other mineral of commercial importance was salt, and the only other mining operations left in the country were involved in the extraction of limestone, peat, and sand and gravel. The production of salt from the mines at Hengelo and Delfzijl was one of the oldest industries in the country; an estimated 5.0 million tons was produced in 2003 (various types), unchanged since 1999. Akzo Nobel Salt BV was the leading producer of salt. Magnesium chloride and oxide were produced in a plant at Veendam from extracted salt brines. Also produced in 2003 were hydraulic cement, nitrogen, industrial sand, sodium compounds, and sulfur. No metals were mined, but an estimated 3 million tons of iron ore was sintered from imported ore in 2003, unchanged from 2000. Coal was mined in Limburg until 1974. Among the country's leading industries in 2003 were metal products, chemicals, petroleum, and construction, and chemicals and fuels were top export commodities.

27 ENERGY AND POWER

The Netherlands, which has little waterpower, depends mostly on natural gas and petroleum as energy sources.

Natural gas is The Netherlands' most abundant fossil fuel, with major fields located in the North Sea. As of August 2005, the North Sea region contained 169.8 trillion cu ft of natural gas, of which Norway and the Netherlands account for more than 75%. As of 1 January 2002, the Netherlands had proven natural gas reserves of 1.693 trillion cu m. In 2003, production of natural gas totaled 2.6 trillion cu ft. However, natural gas output has fallen as a result of government policy. The country's Natural Gas Law caps production at 2.68 trillion cu ft annually, between 2003 and 2007. From 2008 through 2013, production will be further limited to 2.47 trillion cu ft per year. This policy was instituted so that the country's natural gas reserves will be maintained for future use. In 2002, domestic consumption of natural gas totaled 1.764 trillion cu ft.

The Netherlands' second principal energy source is oil. As of 1 January 2002, the country's proven reserves of oil totaled 88.06 million barrels. In 2002, total oil production included 46,330 barrels per day of crude oil. Although oil output was up from 2000 at 89,000 barrels per day, the nation was still dependent on imported petroleum. In 2002, imports of crude and refined oil products averaged 2,266,990 barrels per day. Consumption of refined petroleum products in that year averaged 899,170 barrels per day. Exports of all petroleum products that year averaged 1,421,620 barrels per day. The Netherlands also re-exports two-thirds of all its imported petroleum in the form of refined oil products. Refinery output in 2002 averaged 1,723,250 barrels per day.

The Netherlands's demand for coal came to 14,803,000 short tons in 2002, all of it imported. Imports that year totaled 24,586,000 short tons; 10,210,000 short tons were re-exported.

Production of electric power in 2002 totaled 91.117 billion kWh, of which thermal power plants using oil and coal as fuel supplied 90% of the power generated. Nuclear power plants accounted for 4%, and other alternative sources 5.4%. Hydropower accounted for less than 1%. Nuclear generating capacity is provided chiefly by a 450 MW station in Borssele, Zeeland. As of 2002, the Netherlands was one of five European Union (EU) countries that had declared a moratorium on building new nuclear facilities. Consumption of electricity in 2002 was 101.138 billion kWh. Installed capacity in 2002 was 20.378 million kW.

28 INDUSTRY

Because of World War II and its consequences (the high rate of population increase and the severing of economic ties with Indonesia), drastic structural changes took place in the Dutch economy, and the further development of industry became important. Industry increased to such an extent that it produced 32% of GDP in 1990. Since then, however, industrial production has declined, accounting for 24.5% of GDP in 2004.

Since World War II, the metallurgical industry in particular has made tremendous progress. Philips, the Dutch electronics giant, has become the greatest electrical products firm in Europe as well as one of the world's major exporters of electric bulbs and appliances. Unilever, the British-Dutch consumer products company, has grown to become one of the world's largest corporations. The Heineken brewing company is one of the world's largest brewing companies in terms of sales volume and profitability. More phenomenal has been the success of Royal Dutch/Shell, which began as a small concern in 1890 and grew to become one of the world's largest income producers. Rotterdam's suburb of Pernis has the largest oil refinery in Europe. Akzo Nobel produces healthcare products, coatings, and chemicals. DSM produces nutritional and pharma ingredients, performance materials, and industrial chemicals.

Pig iron is exported, produced from imported ore at the Velsen-Ijmuiden plant, situated where the canal from Amsterdam reaches the North Sea. The chemical industry has grown increasingly important, but the once prosperous textile industry in Enschede has declined because of foreign competition.

Industrial products include petroleum, metal and engineering products, and pharmaceutical products. The Netherlands produces electrical machinery and equipment (including computers and computer parts), and microelectronics. Agroindustries are important: the Netherlands is one of the world's three largest exporters of agricultural produce. Dairy farming and market gardening are the major agricultural industries. The Netherlands also produces cigarettes, beer, canned fish, cocoa and cocoa products, coffee, tea, sugar, candies, biscuits, and potato flour.

29 SCIENCE AND TECHNOLOGY

Advanced scientific research and development (R&D) has provided the technological impetus for the Netherlands' economic recovery since World War II. Dutch universities have traditionally carried out fundamental scientific research, and the government has promoted research activities through the Netherlands Organization for Scientific Research, established in 1988, and the Netherlands Organization for Applied Scientific Research, established in 1930. It also has supported scientific organizations such as the Energy Development Corp. and Energy Research Foundation, Aerospace Development Agency, National Aerospace Laboratory, and Netherlands Maritime Institute.

The highly developed electrotechnical industry produces computers, telecommunications systems, electronic measurement and control equipment, electric switching gear and transformers, and medical and scientific instruments. Dutch firms designed and constructed the Netherlands' astronomical satellites and play a major role in the European Space Agency. The important aerospace industry is led by the world-famous firm of Fokker, which produced Europe's bestselling passenger jet aircraft, the F-27 Friendship, and has been active in the consortium that developed the European Airbus. In 2002, high-tech exports were valued at $33.667 billion and accounted for 28% of manufactured exports.

Expenditures on scientific R&D in 2001 totaled $8.6 trillion, or 1.89% of GDP. Of that amount, 51.8% came from the business sector, followed by government sources at 36.2%. Foreign sources ac-

counted for 11%, with higher education at 1.1%. In that same year, there were 2,826 scientists and engineers and 1,424 technicians per million people that were engaged in R&D.

Among the Netherlands' 39 scientific and technical learned societies, the most prominent is the Royal Netherlands Academy of Sciences, founded in 1808. The country also has 37 scientific and technical research institutes. In Leiden are located the National Museum of Natural History and the National Museum of History of Science and Medicine. The Netherlands has 16 universities offering courses in basic and applied sciences. In 1987–97, science and engineering students accounted for 39% of university enrollment. In 2002, of all bachelor's degrees awarded, 16.4% were in the sciences (natural, mathematics and computers, engineering).

30 DOMESTIC TRADE

A considerable but declining part of Dutch retail business is still conducted by small enterprises, which are usually owner operated. Some of the larger department stores in the cities have branches in small towns, and there are several nationwide supermarket chains. Cooperatives and associations are important in both purchasing and producing.

Amsterdam is the chief center for commerce and trade, with Rotterdam and The Hague next. Many companies use the Netherlands as a distribution center for European markets. Terms of sale usually call for payment within 90 days. A value-added tax of 19% applies to most goods.

Business offices are generally open from 9 AM to 5 PM on weekdays and are closed Saturdays. Retail stores usually open between 8 and 9 AM and close between 6 and 7 PM Tuesday through Friday. On Mondays, many shops are closed in the mornings. Most cities have late-night shopping (until 9 PM) on Thursdays or Fridays. In the main cities, many shops are open on Sunday from 12 to 5 PM.

The country's most important trade fair is held at Utrecht, twice each year, in the spring and fall.

31 FOREIGN TRADE

The Dutch have traditionally been a powerful force in international trade. The Netherlands is the world's eighth-largest exporting nation. As exports and imports of goods and services both ac-

Principal Trading Partners – Netherlands (2003)

(In millions of US dollars)

Country	Exports	Imports	Balance
World	227,344.0	208,995.3	18,348.7
Germany	51,891.7	38,186.2	13,705.5
Belgium	24,153.4	21,667.0	2,486.4
United Kingdom	23,243.6	14,453.5	8,790.1
France-Monaco	22,220.0	10,993.0	11,227.0
Italy-San Marino-Holy See	13,256.7	4,977.9	8,278.8
United States	12,082.0	17,743.6	-5,661.6
Spain	8,591.8	4,180.4	4,411.4
Sweden	4,356.7	4,105.3	251.4
Switzerland-Liechtenstein	3,912.3	2,823.7	1,088.6
Austria	3,410.5	...	3,410.5

(…) data not available or not significant.

SOURCE: 2003 International Trade Statistics Yearbook, New York: United Nations, 2004.

count for well over 60% of GDP, the backbone of Dutch prosperity is foreign trade. Rotterdam is Europe's largest port (and third in the world in 2005, after Shanghai and Singapore), handling twice as much cargo as its nearest European rival, Antwerp. The Netherlands' geographical position as a key hub of Europe's transportation system and the small size of its domestic market have made the Dutch economy one of the most open and outward-looking in the world.

Principal Dutch exports in the early 2000s were manufactured goods, machines, electronics, chemicals, petroleum products, natural gas, and foods. Chief imports are manufactured products, machines, crude petroleum, chemicals, and clothing. From 1981 through 2005, the Netherlands experienced trade surpluses each year.

32 BALANCE OF PAYMENTS

Dutch merchandise and services exports have grown to represent more than 60% of GDP, making the Dutch economy one of the most internationally oriented in the world. Economic expansion of the Netherlands in the period immediately after World War II paralleled a generally favorable balance of payments. After occasional and minor deficits on current accounts during the mid-1960s, a major deficit occurred in 1970. Since then, the current-accounts balance has generally registered a surplus, despite increased costs of oil imports during the 1970s and beginning in 2005. The Netherlands' reliance upon exports that are resistant to recessions (such as some food and agricultural products, and semifinished products such as chemicals) has protected the Dutch economy from weaker demand from Germany and other EU countries during recessions. In 2004, exports totaled $311.2 billion and imports $280.5 billion, resulting in a trade surplus of $30.7 billion. The current account surplus was $13.5 billion.

33 BANKING AND SECURITIES

The Netherlands Bank, nationalized in 1948, is the central bank. It issues the currency and supervises the privately owned banks. Since the 1950s, the Netherlands Bank had used reserve regulations and the central bank discount rate as instruments of monetary policy, but with the introduction of the European Central Bank, those responsibilities are now more centralized for all of the EU. The Dutch financial services industry has a long and distinguished history and has introduced many banking innovations to the world. Since the late 1980s, the sector has undergone a revolution. A common strategic desire to expand and to gain more financial strength, combined with deregulation of the financial market, prompted several bank mergers and the formation of financial conglomerates of banks and insurance groups. As a result, the number of dominant participants in the market has diminished to a handful, each providing the full range of financial services. The Netherlands Middenstands-bank (NMB) and the state-owned Postbank merged to form the NMB Postbank in 1989, which in turn merged again with the Nationale Nederlanden insurance group to form the International Nederlanden Groep (ING) in 1991. The large ABN and Amro commercial banking groups joined up to form ABN-Amro in 1990. VSB-bank, a conglomerate of savings banks, teamed up with the Ameu insurance group and Belgium's AG insurance group in 1990 to form the Dutch-Belgian Fortis group. Rabobank, a large cooperative group which

Balance of Payments – Netherlands (2003)		
(In millions of US dollars)		
Current Account		**16,405.0**
Balance on goods	26,648.0	
Imports	-225,733.0	
Exports	252,380.0	
Balance on services	-1,186.0	
Balance on income	-1,244.0	
Current transfers	-7,813.0	
Capital Account		**-2,028.0**
Financial Account		**-23,088.0**
Direct investment abroad	-35,204.0	
Direct investment in Netherlands	15,695.0	
Portfolio investment assets	-57,001.0	
Portfolio investment liabilities	82,000.0	
Financial derivatives	-468.0	
Other investment assets	-63,605.0	
Other investment liabilities	35,494.0	
Net Errors and Omissions		**7,791.0**
Reserves and Related Items		**920.0**

(…) data not available or not significant.

SOURCE: *Balance of Payment Statistics Yearbook 2004*, Washington, DC: International Monetary Fund, 2004.

specializes in the provision of agricultural credits and mortgage facilities but has been rapidly expanding its product portfolio in recent years, took a 50% share in the Robeco investment group in 1996. The robust nature of the Dutch banking industry came to the fore once again in December 1999. Although it ultimately failed, ING made headlines through its attempted takeover of the French Crédit Commercial de France (CCF). Had ING's bid succeeded, it would have been the first successful merger of a French bank with another European financial institution.

The International Monetary Fund reports that in 2001, currency and demand deposits—an aggregate commonly known as M1—were equal to $145.3 billion. In that same year, M2—an aggregate equal to M1 plus savings deposits, small time deposits, and money market mutual funds—was $409.3 billion.

The Netherlands has the oldest stock exchange in the world, the Amsterdam Stock Exchange (ASE); founded in the early 17th century, it is now one of the largest stock exchanges in operation. The issuance of new securities on the exchange is supervised by the Netherlands Bank, acting in cooperation with the commercial banks and stockbrokers.

The comparatively large share of foreign security listings and capital supply gives the ASE an international importance disproportionate to its size. Its strong international orientation is also reflected in the fact that its share of Europe's total market capitalization far outweighs the relative importance of the Dutch economy. The multinational nature of the major Dutch companies, which has led to their shares being quoted on a number of international stock markets, means that stock price levels on the ASE are heavily influenced by developments elsewhere. The three largest companies, Royal Dutch Shell, Unilever, and ING, account for around 50% of total stock market capitalization.

In order to enhance the international competitiveness of the ASE, many reform measures have been taken in the past few years, with varying degrees of success. These include the introduction of a new electronic trading system open to foreign-based brokers, a division of the market into a wholesale and a retail segment, and a revamp of the exchange's organizational structure. Moreover, in early 1996, under pressure from the government, the stock exchange introduced an arrangement that aims to reduce the influence of the wide range of anti-takeover devices quoted corporations are permitted, which has long been considered as one of the exchange's most important shortcomings. Under the new arrangement, a prospective buyer who has gained 70% of a company's shares can turn to the Amsterdam Court of Justice after a period of 12 months.

On 1 January 1997, the Amsterdam Exchanges (AEX) was formed by the merger of the Amsterdam Stock Exchange (ASE) and the city's European Options Exchange (EDE). From approximately 680 at the end of January, the AEX index of 25 leading shares rose to 700 on 11 February 1997 and sped on to almost 775 by mid-March before suffering a correction prompted by the release of disappointing financial results by a brewing company, Grolsch, and fears of interest rate increases in the United States. In 1998 the world capitalization rankings placed the equity market eighth in the world, while the volume of options contracts at the options market ranked fourth. By early 2003, however, the AEX index had dropped to 303.21, down 39% from the previous year. As of 2004, a total of 177 companies were listed on the EURON-EXT Amsterdam exchange, which had a market capitalization of $622.284 billion. In 2004, the AEX rose 3.1% from the previous year to 348.1.

³⁴INSURANCE

There are two sectors of the insurance industry in the Netherlands: the companies operating under control laws set down by the EC and supervised by the government, and the companies (mutuals, reinsurance, marine and aviation) not under official supervision. Compulsory third-party motor insurance has been in effect since 1935. In addition, insurance for workers, hunters, nuclear facilities, and pensions are compulsory. In 2003, the value of all direct insurance premiums written totaled $50.266 billion, of which life insurance premiums accounted for $25.371 billion. In 2002, the top nonlife insurer was Achmea Zorg, which had gross written nonlife premiums of $1,196.1 million, while the leading life insurer that same year was Nationale Nederlanden Leven, with gross written life insurance premiums of $4,236.9 million.

³⁵PUBLIC FINANCE

The government has gradually cut the deficit from 10% of GDP in 1983 to 2.75% in 1996, slightly below the 3% Maastricht criteria for European Economic and Monetary Union (EMU) in 1999. The deficit is largely financed by government bonds. Financing is also covered by issuing Dutch Treasury Certificates, which replaced a standing credit facility for short-term deficit financing with the Netherlands Central Bank. Under the Maastricht Treaty, the Netherlands Central Bank was abolished in 1994. Although the private sector is the cornerstone of the economy, the government plays a vital role in the Netherlands' economy. It decides microeconomic policy and tax laws, as well as working toward structural and regu-

Public Finance – Netherlands (2003)		
(In millions of euros, central government figures)		
Revenue and Grants	**184,341**	**100.0%**
Tax revenue	103,128	55.9%
Social contributions	67,918	36.8%
Grants	412	0.2%
Other revenue	12,883	7.0%
Expenditures	**197,864**	**100.0%**
General public services	43,780	22.1%
Defense	7,182	3.6%
Public order and safety	7,334	3.7%
Economic affairs	11,810	6.0%
Environmental protection	739	0.4%
Housing and community amenities	1,082	0.5%
Health	20,562	10.4%
Recreational, culture, and religion	1,745	0.9%
Education	21,443	10.8%
Social protection	82,187	41.5%

(…) data not available or not significant.

SOURCE: *Government Finance Statistics Yearbook 2004*, Washington, DC: International Monetary Fund, 2004.

latory reforms. Public spending, however, had dropped to 46% of GDP as of 2000 as privatization and deregulation continued.

The US Central Intelligence Agency (CIA) estimated that in 2005 the Netherlands's central government took in revenues of approximately $291.8 billion and had expenditures of $303.7 billion. Revenues minus expenditures totaled approximately -$11.9 billion. Public debt in 2005 amounted to 56.2% of GDP. Total external debt was $1.645 trillion.

The International Monetary Fund (IMF) reported that in 2003, the most recent year for which it had data, central government revenues were €184,341 million and expenditures were €197,864 million. The value of revenues was us$208,060 million and expenditures us$222,489 million, based on a market exchange rate for 2003 of us$1 = €.8860 as reported by the IMF. Government outlays by function were as follows: general public services, 22.1%; defense, 3.6%; public order and safety, 3.7%; economic affairs, 6.0%; environmental protection, 0.4%; housing and community amenities, 0.5%; health, 10.4%; recreation, culture, and religion, 0.9%; education, 10.8%; and social protection, 41.5%.

³⁶TAXATION

Principal taxes raised by the central government are income and profits taxes levied on individuals and companies, a value-added tax (VAT) on goods and services, and a tax on enterprises of public bodies (except agricultural enterprises). There is a wealth tax of 0.7% also levied on nonexempt taxable capital of individuals. Provinces and municipalities are not authorized to impose income taxes, and may impose other taxes only to a limited extent. The most important tax levied by municipalities is a real estate tax paid partly by owners and partly by occupants. Residents are taxed on both their local and foreign incomes, but nonresidents pay taxes only on income earned in the Netherlands.

The tax on the net profits of corporations in 2005 was 27% for annual profits up to €22,689 and 31.5% on the increment of profits above that. Depreciation and other business deductions are permitted. Capital gains were taxed at the same rates, although some capital gains were tax-exempt. Withholding taxes up to a maximum of 25% were applied to dividends, although there is no withholding if the dividends are being paid by a subsidiary to a nonresident parent company, owning more than 25% of the payer. Companies can qualify for tax exemptions and tax reductions under investment incentive regimes. Branches of foreign companies are treated the same as Dutch companies in accordance with the fiscal regime under which they qualify.

Incomes are taxed on a graduated scale, with a top rate of 52%. There are also liberal deductions for dependents. Taxes are withheld by the state on the incomes of wage earners. In the tax reforms of 2001 marginal income tax rates were set in a course of increases in the lower rates, and decreases in the higher ones. The progressive schedule consists of four brackets, not counting a tax-exempt base for each individual taxpayer. Gift and inheritance taxes range from 5–68% depending on the family relationship of the donor or deceased.

The Netherlands' main indirect tax is its VAT introduced 1 January 1969 with a standard rate of 12% and a reduced rate of 4% on basics. Effective 1 January 2001, the standard rate was increased from 17.5% to 19% with a reduced rate of 6%, the latter applied to basic foodstuffs, books, newspapers and periodicals, public ground and sea transport, water supplies, sports centers, and pharmaceuticals. Exempted from VAT are exported goods, medical, cultural, and educational services, and credit and insurance transactions. Other taxes include excise taxes, energy taxes and taxes on legal transactions and on motor vehicles.

37 CUSTOMS AND DUTIES

The Dutch government has a traditionally liberal policy on tariffs and its membership in the Benelux Economic Union, the European Union, and other international trade organizations has resulted in comparatively low import duties. Tariffs on imports from the dollar area have also been liberalized and about 90% of imports from the United States are unrestricted quantitatively. Manufactured goods from the United States are generally subject to a duty ranging from 5–8% based on the cost, insurance and freight (CIF) value of the goods. Raw materials are usually not subject to import duties.

Imports are subject to EU customs regulations and tariff rates, plus VAT and other charges levied at entry through customs.

38 FOREIGN INVESTMENT

The Netherlands has favorable tax structures for investors, which has made the country one of the top recipients of foreign direct investment in the European Union. The Netherlands has consistently been ranked as one of the most attractive destinations for FDI in the world, ranking sixth among the ten largest foreign investors in the world, as well as the sixth-largest global recipient of FDI (2004). The government has encouraged foreign corporations to set up branch plants in the Netherlands and to establish joint ventures with Dutch companies in order to benefit from the introduction of new production techniques and improved methods of management that outside firms often bring. The government does not discriminate between foreign and domestic companies; foreign entrepreneurs have the same business privileges and obligations as Dutch businessmen and women. As a result, foreign companies operate in virtually all industries, including high-technology electronics, chemicals, metals, electrical equipment, textiles, and food processing. The labor force is largely well-educated and multilingual.

The corporation tax is 34.5%, but the corporate taxation regime is expected to be reformed in 2006–07. The Corporation Tax Act provides for a participation exemption, applicable to both foreign and domestic shareholdings, thus preventing double taxation when the profits of a subsidiary are distributed to its parent company. Although income taxes were lowered in 2001, the basic rate of the value-added tax was raised from 17.5% to 19%.

Annual foreign direct investment (FDI) inflows were $11 billion in 1997, down from $16.6 billion in 1996, but then soared to $37.6 billion in 1998. The peak was reached in 2000 and 2001, when total inflows reached $52 billion and $50 billion, respectively. However, in 2002, FDI inflow fell to an estimated $30 billion, and to $19.3 billion in 2003. By 2004, the total stock of FDI had reached $387 billion, about 75% of GDP.

Overall, the United States, the United Kingdom, Germany, Belgium, and France are the primary sources of and destinations for FDI with the Netherlands.

Foreign companies established in the Netherlands account for roughly one-third of industrial production and employment in industry. At the end of 2004, an estimated 31.5% of foreign establishments in the Netherlands came from the United States, 19.5% from Germany, 14% from the United Kingdom, 7% from Scandinavia, 17% from the rest of Europe, 9% from Asia, and the remaining 2% from other non-OECD and non-EU countries.

39 ECONOMIC DEVELOPMENT

For nearly four decades after World War II Dutch governments aimed at increased industrialization. During the 1990s, however, industrial growth slowed, while the service sector continued to expand. In this regard, the Netherlands has made the transition to a more liberalized high technology economy quite successfully.

In an effort to encourage industrialization after the Second World War, the maintenance of internal monetary equilibrium was vitally important, and the government has largely succeeded in this task. Successive governments pursued a policy of easy credits and a "soft" currency, but after the Netherlands had fully recovered from the war by the mid-1950s, a harder currency and credit policy came into effect. In the social sphere, stable relationships were maintained by a deliberate governmental social policy seeking to bridge major differences between management and labor. The organized collaboration of workers and employers in the Labor Foundation has contributed in no small measure to the success of this policy, and as a result, strikes are rare.

Successive wage increases helped bring the overall wage level in the Netherlands up to that of other EC countries by 1968. The Dutch government's policy, meanwhile, was directed toward controlling inflation while seeking to maintain high employment. In 1966, the government raised indirect taxes to help finance rising expenditures, particularly in the fields of education, public transportation, and public health. Further attempts to cope with inflation and other economic problems involved increased government control over the economy. Wage and price controls were imposed in 1970–71, and the States-General approved a measure granting the government power to control wages, rents, dividends, health and insurance costs, and job layoffs during 1974.

During the mid-1980s, the nation experienced modest recovery from recession; the government's goal was to expand recovery and reduce high unemployment, while cutting down the size of the annual budget deficit. The government generally sought to foster a climate favorable to private industrial investment through such measures as preparing industrial sites, subsidizing or permitting allowances for industrial construction and equipment, assisting in the creation of new markets, granting subsidies for establishing industries in distressed areas, and establishing schools for adult training. In 1978, the government began, by means of a selective investment levy, to discourage investment in the western region (Randstad), while encouraging industrial development in the southern province of Limburg and the northern provinces of Drenthe, Friesland, and Groningen.

The Netherlands' largest economic development projects have involved the reclamation of land from the sea by construction of dikes and dams and by the drainage of lakes to create polders for additional agricultural land. The Zuider Zee project closed off the sea and created the freshwater Ijsselmeer by means of a 30 km (19 mi) barrier dam in 1932, and subsequently drained four polders enclosing about 165,000 hectares (408,000 acres). After a storm washed away dikes on islands in Zeeland and South Holland in 1953, killing some 1,800 people, the Delta project was begun. This project, designed to close estuaries between the islands with massive dams, was officially inaugurated in 1986; the cost was $2.4 billion. The Delta works include a storm-surge barrier with 62 steel gates, each weighing 500 tons that are usually left open to allow normal tidal flow in order to protect the natural environment. Another major engineering project was construction of a bridge and tunnel across the Western Schelde estuary in the south to connect Zeeland Flanders more directly with the rest of the country.

Beginning in the 1980s, Dutch governments began stressing fiscal discipline by reversing the growth of the welfare state and ending a policy of inflation-based wage indexing. The latter policy represented a spirit of consensus among labor and management. At a time when other labor unions fought losing battles with management, Dutch unions agreed to a compromise on this cherished issue in return for a business promise to emphasize job creation. By the late 1990s, these reforms had paid off as Dutch unemployment plummeted to below 5%. As of the early 2000s, the Netherlands had among the lowest unemployment rates in the industrialized world. As of 2005, the Dutch economy was being heralded around the world for its combination of strong employment growth, low inflation, falling public budget deficits, low inequality, and strong social welfare policies.

In January 2004, the government launched its Innovation Partnerships Grant Program, to promote cooperation in research and development. The program encourages businesses and public-sector knowledge institutes to study and launch national and international partnerships. Some 5,000 Dutch companies are conducting research to develop new products and to boost quality and efficiency. The country's five largest multinationals—Philips, Shell, Akzo Nobel, DSM, and Unilever—are at the forefront of industrial research and development.

The Netherlands' commitment to the project of further European integration, however, was stalled in 2005, when on 1 June Dutch voters rejected the EU constitution by a wide margin (62% to 38%). This vote followed directly upon the heels of the French rejection of the constitution. Many Dutch "no" voters, however, said they were pro-European, but feared that small countries were losing influence in an EU dominated by larger ones. The Dutch treasure their sound money and liberal social policies, and do not want to see these eroded.

40 SOCIAL DEVELOPMENT

A widespread system of social insurance and assistance is in effect. The first laws were implemented in 1901. All residents are provided with old-age and survivorship benefits. Disability pensions are available to all employees, self-employed workers, students, and those disabled since childhood. Unemployment, accidents, illness, and disability are covered by insurance, which is compulsory for most employees and voluntary for self-employed persons. Maternity grants and full insurance for the worker's family are also provided, as are family allowances for children. The government covers the total cost for family allowances. Women receive one month of maternity leave with full pay. Exceptional medical expenses are covered for all residents.

Legislation mandates equal pay for equal work and prohibits dismissal due to marriage, pregnancy, or motherhood. However, cultural factors and lack of day care discourages women from employment. Many women work in part-time positions and are underemployed, and on average women earn less than men. Sexual harassment in the workplace is an issue, and in 2004, the government funded an awareness campaign to combat the problem. Domestic violence is an issue, especially among ethnic minorities. The government provides programs to reduce and prevent violence against women.

Human rights are fully respected in the Netherlands. There were incidents of discrimination against religious minorities and some immigrant groups.

41 HEALTH

The Netherlands has a social insurance system similar to Germany's. About two-thirds of workers are covered by the social insurance program; the remainder are covered by private insurance. Under the Health Insurance Act, everyone with earned income of less than 50,900 guilders per year pays a monthly contribution in return for which they receive medical, pharmaceutical, and dental treatment and hospitalization. People who earn more than this have to take out private medical insurance. The state also pays for preventive medicine including vaccinations for children, school dental services, medical research, and the training of health workers. Preventive care emphasizes education, a clean environment, and regular exams and screenings. As of 2004, there were an estimated 329 physicians, 1,334 nurses, 47 dentists and 20 pharmacists per 100,000 people.

The general health situation has been excellent over a long period, as is shown by an estimated general mortality rate of 8.7 per 1,000 as of 2002 and an infant mortality of only 5.04 per 1,000 live births in 2005, down markedly from the 12.7 rate in 1970. The maternal mortality rate was 7 per 100,000 live births. These low rates are attributed to a rise in the standard of living; improvements in nutrition, hygiene, housing, and working conditions; and the expansion of public health measures. In 2005, average life expectancy was 78.81 years.

Most doctors and hospitals operate privately. A system of hospital budgeting, which was introduced in 1983, has helped contain costs. In 1990, a proposal to increase competition among insurers, eliminating the distinction between public and private insurers, was developed. A reference price system—to control pharmaceuticals especially—was introduced in 1991. Total health care expenditure was estimated at 8.7% of GDP.

The Ministry of Public Health and Environment is entrusted with matters relating to health care, but health services are not centrally organized. There are numerous local and regional health centers and hospitals, many of which are maintained by religious groups.

In 2002, the estimated birth rate was 11.6 per 1,000 people; 75% of married women (ages 15 to 49) used contraception. The total fertility rate was 1.7 children for each woman living throughout childbearing years. Immunization rates for children up to one year old were as follows: diphtheria, pertussis, and tetanus, 95%; polio, 97%; and measles, 96%.

Major causes of death were attributed to cardiovascular problems and cancer. The HIV/AIDS prevalence was 0.20 per 100 adults in 2003. As of 2004, there were approximately 19,000 people living with HIV/AIDS in the country. There were an estimated 100 deaths from AIDS in 2003.

42 HOUSING

During World War II, more than 25% of the nation's two million dwellings were damaged: 95,000 dwellings were completely destroyed, 55,000 were seriously damaged, and 520,000 were slightly damaged. The housing shortage remained acute until 1950, when an accelerated program of housing construction began, and in 1953 the government decided to increase the house-building program to a level of 65,000 dwellings a year. Since then, the production rate has far exceeded both the prewar rate and yearly forecasts. From 1945 to 1985, nearly four million dwellings were built. In 1985 alone, 98,131 dwellings were built, bringing the total housing stock to 5,384,100 units by the end of the year. Most of the new units were subsidized by the national government. Subsidies are granted to municipalities, building societies, and housing associations, which generally build low-income multiple dwellings. Government regulations, which are considerable, are laid down in the Housing Act of 1965 and the Rental Act of 1979.

The government determines on an annual basis the scope of the construction program. On the basis of national estimates, each municipality is allocated a permissible volume of construction. Within this allocation, the municipalities must follow certain guidelines; central government approval is required for all construction projects exceeding a specific cost. All construction must conform to technical and aesthetic requirements, as established by the government.

In 2005, the number of dwellings was at about 6,861, with an average of 2.3 residents per dwelling. The number of residents per dwelling has nearly halved since WWII. Approximately 71,609 new dwellings were constructed in 2004. About 76% of the dwellings built in 2004 were owner occupied.

43 EDUCATION

The present Dutch education system has its origins in the Batavian Republic which was constituted after the French Revolution. The role of education gained importance in the Civil and Constitutional Regulations of 1789, and the first legislation on education was passed in 1801. After 1848, the municipalities, supported by state funds, were responsible for managing the schools. Private schools were not originally supported by the government. However, after 1917, private and state schools received equal state funding.

School attendance between the ages of 5 and 18 is compulsory. Apart from play groups and crèches (which do not come under the Ministry of Education), there are no schools for children below the age of four. Children may, however, attend primary school from the age of four. Primary school covers eight years of study. Secondary school is comprised of three types: (1) general secondary school, with two options, the four-year junior general secondary school (MAVO) and the five-year senior general secondary school (HAVO); (2) preuniversity—the athenaeum or the gymnasium—both lasting for six years in preparation for university education; and (3) vocational secondary schools with four-year programs. Special education is provided to children with physical, mental, or social disabilities at special primary and secondary schools. Whenever possible, these children are later transferred into mainstream schools for continued education. The academic year runs from September to June.

Primary school enrollment in 2003 was estimated at about 99% of age-eligible students. The same year, secondary school enrollment was about 89% of age-eligible students. It is estimated that about 98.4% of all students complete their primary education. In 2003, private schools accounted for about 68.7% of primary school enrollment and 83.3% of secondary enrollment.

Facilities have been opened in various municipalities for adult education. Open schools and open universities have also been introduced. Vocational and university education is provided at the eight universities and five institutes (Hogescholen), which are equivalent to universities. These are funded entirely by the government. There are also seven theological colleges. In 2003, about 58% of the tertiary age population were enrolled in some type of higher education program. The adult literacy rate for 2000 was estimated at about 99%.

As of 2003, public expenditure on education was estimated at 5.1% of GDP, or 10.7% of total government expenditures.

44 LIBRARIES AND MUSEUMS

The largest public library is the Royal Library at The Hague, which has about 2.2 million volumes; this also serves as the national library. Outstanding libraries are found in the universities: Amsterdam, with over 2.6 million volumes; Leiden, 2.7 million volumes; Utrecht, two million volumes; Groningen, 2.7 million volumes; and Erasmus of Rotterdam, 800,000 volumes. The technical universities at Delft, Wageningen, and Tilburg also have excellent collections. Libraries of importance are found in some provincial capitals, such as Hertogenbosch, Leeuwarden, Middelburg, and Maastricht. Also noteworthy are the International Institute of Social History at Amsterdam, which houses important collections of historical letters and documents, such as the Marx-Engels Archives; and the Institute of the Netherlands Economic-Historical

Archive, which has its library in Amsterdam and its collection of old trade archives at the Hague. There are about 500 public libraries across the country. The Netherlands Public Library Association was founded in 1972.

Among Amsterdam's many museums, particularly outstanding are the Rijksmuseum (1800), the Stedelijk Museum (1895) with special collections of modern art, the Van Gogh Museum (1979), the Museum of the Royal Tropical Institute (1910), and the Jewish Historical Museum (1932). Among Amsterdam's newest museums are the Huis Marseille (1999), which has historic and modern photography exhibits, the hands-on New Metropolis Interactive Science and Technology Museum (1997), and the Tattso Museum (1996). The Boymans–Van Beuningen Museum in Rotterdam has older paintings as well as modern works and a fine collection of minor arts. The Hague's Mauritshuis and the Frans Hals Museum at Haarlem have world-renowned collections of old masters. Other collections of national interest are in the Central Museum in Utrecht, the National Museum of Natural History in Leiden, Teyler's Museum in Haarlem, and the Folklore Museum in Arnhem. In the past, the most important art museums were found mainly in the large population centers of western Holland, but there are now museums of interest in such provincial capitals as Groningen, Leeuwarden, Arnhem, and Maastricht. The government stimulates the spread of artistic culture by providing art objects on loan and by granting subsidies to a number of privately owned museums. There are dozens of museums dedicated to the work of individual Dutch artists.

45 MEDIA

The post office, telegraph, and telephone systems are operated by the government. The state's monopoly on postal services is confined to delivery of letters and postcards; about half of other deliveries are handled by private firms. Significant improvements in the phone systems began in 2001 through the introduction of the third generation of the Global System for Mobile Communications. In 2003, there were an estimated 614 mainline telephones for every 1,000 people. The same year, there were approximately 768 mobile phones in use for every 1,000 people.

There are several radio networks. The Netherlands Broadcasting Foundation, a joint foundation, maintains and makes available all studios, technical equipment, record and music libraries, orchestras, and other facilities. Broadcasting to other countries is carried on by the Netherlands World Broadcasting Service, which is managed by a board of governors appointed by the minister of cultural affairs. As of 2004 there were 4 AM and 246 FM stations. There were also about 21 television stations. Shortwave programs are transmitted in Dutch, Afrikaans, Arabic, English, French, Indonesian, Portuguese, and Spanish. Annual license fees are charged to radio and television set owners. Commercial advertising was introduced in 1967–68 and limited to fixed times before and after news broadcasts. In 2003, there were an estimated 980 radios and 648 television sets for every 1,000 people. About 401.4 of every 1,000 people were cable subscribers. Also in 2003, there were 466.6 personal computers for every 1,000 people and 522 of every 1,000 people had access to the Internet. There were 3,779 secure Internet servers in the country in 2004.

The Dutch were among the first to issue regular daily newspapers. The oldest newspaper, the *Oprechte Haarlemsche Courant*, was founded in 1656 and is published today as the *Haarlemsche Courant*. The Dutch press is largely a subscription press, depending for two-thirds of its income on advertising. Editorial boards, however, are usually completely independent of the commercial management.

In 2004, the largest national and regional newspapers, with daily circulations, were: *De Telegraaf* (Amsterdam), 776,000; *De Volkskrant* (Amsterdam), 323,000; *Algemeen Dagblad* (Amsterdan), 303,000; *NRC Handelsblad* (Rotterdam), 262,000; *De Gelderlander* (Gelderland), 193,000; *Dagblad van het Noorden* (Groningen), 173,000; *Apeldoornse Courant* (Apeldoorn), 159,000; *Noordhollands Dagblad* (Alkmaar), 155,000; *Brabants Dagblad* (North Brabant), 153,300; *De Stem* (Breda), 140,000; *Dagblad Tubantia* (Enschede), 136,000; *Haagsche Courant* (The Hague), 117,000; and *Trouw* (Amsterdam), 117,000.

Complete freedom of speech and press is guaranteed by the constitution, and the government is said to fully support free expression in practice.

46 ORGANIZATIONS

Associations established on the basis of economic interests include the Federation of Netherlands Industries, the Netherlands Society for the Promotion of Industry and Commerce, the Federation of Christian Employers in the Netherlands, the National Bankers Association, and chambers of commerce in Amsterdam, Rotterdam, The Hague, and other cities.

Learned societies include the Royal Netherlands Academy of Arts and Sciences, the Royal Antiquarian Society, the Netherlands Anthropological Society, the Historical Association, the Royal Netherlands Geographical Society, and similar bodies in the fields of botany, zoology, philology, mathematics, chemistry, and other sciences. The Royal Netherlands Association for the Advancement of Medicine, the General Netherlands Society for Social Medicine and Public Health, the Royal Dutch Medical Association, and the Netherlands Association for Psychiatry and Neurology are some of the organizations active in the field of medicine. The International Statistical Institute is based in the Netherlands. The International Esperanto Institute and the International Montessori Association are also located in the country.

In the arts, there are such groupings as the Society for the Preservation of Cultural and Natural Beauty in the Netherlands, the Society of Netherlands Literature, the St. Luke Association, the Society for the Advancement of Music, the Royal Netherlands Association of Musicians, Holland Society of Arts and Sciences, and national societies of painters, sculptors, and architects. The Netherlands Center of the International Association of Playwrights, Editors, Essayists and Novelists (PEN), the Netherlands Branch of the International Law Association, and the Netherlands Foundation for International Cooperation are among the organizations active internationally in their fields.

National youth organizations include the Evangelical Students of the Netherlands, Dutch United Nations Student Association, Junior Chamber, Youth Organization for Freedom and Democracy, The Netherlands Scouting Association, and YMCA/YWCA. There are numerous sports associations for all ages. The Netherlands is home to the International Korfball Federation. Women's organizations include Netherlands Association for Women's Interests, Women's Work and Equal Citizenship and the Netherlands Council of Women.

International organizations with national chapters include Amnesty International, Defence for Children International, Greenpeace International, Habitat for Humanity, and the Red Cross.

47 TOURISM, TRAVEL, AND RECREATION

Travel in the Netherlands by public railway, bus, and inland-waterway boat service is frequent and efficient. Principal tourist attractions include the great cities of Amsterdam, Rotterdam, and the Hague, with their famous monuments and museums, particularly the Rijksmuseum in Amsterdam; the flower gardens and bulb fields of the countryside; and North Sea beach resorts. Modern hotels and large conference halls in the large cities are the sites of numerous international congresses, trade shows, and other exhibitions.

Recreational opportunities include theaters, music halls, opera houses, cinemas, zoos, and amusement parks. Popular sports include football (soccer), swimming, cycling, sailing, and hockey. Foreign visitors need only a valid passport for stays of up to 90 days. Proof of sufficient funds, health insurance coverage, return/onward ticket, and lodging reservations may be required upon arrival. Within eight days of arrival, visitors staying long term must register with the local police

In 2003, approximately 6,930,500 tourists visited the Netherlands, of whom 22% were from the United Kingdom. There were 88,146 hotel rooms with 180,158 beds and an occupancy rate of 43%. Travelers stayed an average of two nights. Tourism expenditure receipts totaled $11.7 billion in 2002.

In 2005, the US Department of State estimated the daily cost of staying in Amsterdam at $328; the Hague, $258; and in Rotterdam, $339.

48 FAMOUS NETHERLANDERS

The Imitation of Christ, usually attributed to the German Thomas à Kempis, is sometimes credited to the Dutch Gerhard Groote (1340–84); written in Latin, it has gone through more than 6,000 editions in about 100 languages. Outstanding Dutch humanists were Wessel Gansfort (1420?–89), precursor of the Reformation; Rodolphus Agricola (Roelof Huysman, 1443–85); and the greatest of Renaissance humanists, Desiderius Erasmus (Gerhard Gerhards, 1466?–1536). Baruch (Benedict de) Spinoza (1632–77), the influential pantheistic philosopher, was born in Amsterdam.

The composers Jacob Obrecht (1453–1505) and Jan Pieterszoon Sweelinck (1562–1621) were renowned throughout Europe; later composers of more local importance were Julius Röntgen (1855–1932), Alfons Diepenbrock (1862–1921), and Cornelis Dopper (1870–1939). Bernard van Dieren (1887–1936), a composer of highly complex music of distinct individuality, settled in London. Henk Badings (b.Bandung, Java, 1907–87) was a prolific composer of international repute. Outstanding conductors of the Amsterdam Concertgebouw Orchestra include Willem Mengelberg (1871–1951), Eduard van Beinum (1901–59), and Bernard Haitink (b.1929), who also was principal conductor of the London Philharmonic from 1967 to 1979, music director of the Royal Opera House, Covent Garden, from 1987–2002, and principal conductor of the Dresden Staatskapelle from 2002.

Hieronymus Bosch van Aken (1450?–1516) was a famous painter. Dutch painting reached its greatest heights in the 17th century, when Rembrandt van Rijn (1606–69) and Jan Vermeer (1632–75) painted their masterpieces. Other great painters of the period were Frans Hals (1580–1666), Jan Steen (1626–69), Jacob van Ruisdael (1628–82), and Meindert Hobbema (1638–1709). Two more recent painters, Vincent van Gogh (1853–90) and Piet Mondrian (1872–1944), represent two widely divergent artistic styles and attitudes. Maurits C. Escher (1898–1972) was a skilled and imaginative graphic artist.

Hugo Grotius (Huig de Groot, 1583–1645), who is often regarded as the founder of international law, is famous for his great book, *On the Law of War and Peace.* The outstanding figure in Dutch literature was Joost van den Vondel (1587–1679), poet and playwright. Another noted poet and playwright was Constantijn Huygens (1596–1687), father of the scientist Christian. Popular for several centuries were the poems of Jacob Cats (1577–1660). Distinguished historians include Johan Huizinga (1872–1945) and Pieter Geyl (1887–1966). Anne Frank (b.Germany, 1929–45) became the most famous victim of the Holocaust with the publication of the diary and other material that she had written while hiding from the Nazis in Amsterdam.

Jan Pieterszoon Coen (1587–1630), greatest of Dutch empire builders, founded the city of Batavia in the Malay Archipelago (now Jakarta, the capital of Indonesia). Two Dutch naval heroes, Maarten Harpertszoon Tromp (1597–1653) and Michel Adriaanszoon de Ruyter (1607–76), led the Dutch nation in triumphs in sea wars with France, England, and Sweden. Peter Minuit (Minnewit, 1580–1638) founded the colonies of New Amsterdam (now New York City) and New Sweden (now Delaware). Peter Stuyvesant (1592–1672) took over New Sweden from the Swedish and lost New Netherland (now New York State) to the British.

Leading scientists include the mathematician Simon Stevinus (1548–1620); Christian Huygens (1629–95), mathematician, physicist, and astronomer; Anton van Leeuwenhoek (1632–1723), developer of the microscope; Jan Swammerdam (1637–80), authority on insects; and Hermann Boerhaave (1668–1738), physician, botanist, and chemist. Among more recent scientists are a group of Nobel Prize winners: Johannes Diderik van der Waals (1837–1923), authority on gases and fluids, who received the award for physics in 1910; Jacobus Hendricus van 't Hoff (1852–1911), chemistry, 1901; Hendrik Antoon Lorentz (1853–1928) and Pieter Zeeman (1865–1943), who shared the 1902 award for physics; Heike Kamerlingh Onnes (1853–1926), physics, 1913; Willem Einthoven (1860–1927), physiology, 1924; Christiaan Eijkman (1858–1930), physiology, 1929; Petrus Josephus Wilhelmus Debye (1884–1966), chemistry, 1936; Frits Zernike (1888–1966), physics, 1953; Jan Tinbergen (1903–94), economic science, 1969; Dutch-born Tjalling Koopmans (1910–85), who shared the 1975 prize for economic science; Simon van der Meer (b.1925), cowinner of the physics prize in 1984; Paul J. Crutzen (b.1933), who shared the 1995 chemistry prize; and Gerardus 't Hooft (b.1946) and Martinus J.G. Veltman (b.1931), who shared the 1999 physics prize. The 1911 Nobel Prize for peace was awarded to Tobias Michael Carel Asser (1838–1913).

The head of state since 1980 has been Queen Beatrix (b.1938).

⁴⁹DEPENDENCIES

Aruba and the Netherlands Antilles are part of the Kingdom of the Netherlands; descriptions of them are given in the volume on the *Americas* under Netherlands American Dependencies.

⁵⁰BIBLIOGRAPHY

Annesley, Claire (ed.). *A Political and Economic Dictionary of Western Europe*. Philadelphia: Routledge/Taylor and Francis, 2005.

Fuykschot, Cornelia. *Hunger in Holland: Life during the Nazi Occupation*. Amherst, N.Y.: Prometheus Books, 1995.

Gelauff, George (ed.). *Fostering Productivity: Patterns, Determinants, and Policy Implications*. Boston: Elsevier, 2004.

Houben, Marc. *International Crisis Management: The Approach of European States*. New York: Routledge, 2005.

International Smoking Statistics: A Collection of Historical Data from 30 Economically Developed Countries. New York: Oxford University Press, 2002.

Leijenaar, Monique. *Political Empowerment of Women: The Netherlands and Other Countries*. Boston: Martinus Nijhoff, 2004.

McElrath, Karen (ed.). *HIV and AIDS: A Global View*. Westport, Conn.: Greenwood Press, 2002.

Raven, G. J. A. and N. A. M. Rodgers (eds.). *Navies and Armies: the Anglo-Dutch Relationship in War and Peace, 1688–1988*. Edinburgh: J. Donald, 1990.

Wessels, Wolfgang, Andreas Maurer, and Jürgan Mittag (eds.). *Fifteen into One?: the European Union and Its Member States*. New York: Palgrave, 2003.

Wolters, Menno and Peter Coffey (eds.). *The Netherlands and EC Membership Evaluated*. New York: St. Martin's, 1990.

Zanden, J. L. van. *The Rise and Decline of Holland's Economy: Merchant Capitalism and the Labour Market*. New York: St. Martin's, 1993.

NORWAY

Kingdom of Norway
Kongeriket Norge

CAPITAL: Oslo

FLAG: The national flag has a red field on which appears a blue cross (with an extended right horizontal) outlined in white.

ANTHEM: *Ja, vi elsker dette landet (Yes, We Love This Country).*

MONETARY UNIT: The krone (Kr) of 100 øre is the national currency. There are coins of 50 øre and 1, 5, and 10 kroner, and notes of 20, 50, 100, 200, 500, and 1,000 kroner. Kr1 = $0.15798 (or $1 = Kr6.33) as of 2005.

WEIGHTS AND MEASURES: The metric system is the legal standard.

HOLIDAYS: New Year's Day, 1 January; Labor Day, 1 May; National Independence Day, 17 May; Christmas, 25 December; Boxing Day, 26 December. Movable religious holidays include Holy Thursday, Good Friday, Easter Monday, Ascension, and Whitmonday.

TIME: 1 PM = noon GMT.

¹LOCATION, SIZE, AND EXTENT

Norway occupies the western part of the Scandinavian peninsula in northern Europe, with almost one-third of the country situated N of the Arctic Circle. It has an area of 324,220 sq km (125,182 sq mi). Comparatively, the area occupied by Norway is slightly larger than the state of New Mexico. Extending 1,752 km (1,089 mi) NNE–SSW, Norway has the greatest length of any European country; its width is 430 km (267 mi) ESE–WNW. Bounded on the N by the Arctic Ocean, on the NE by Finland and Russia, on the E by Sweden, on the S by the Skagerrak, on the SW by the North Sea, and on the W by the Norwegian Sea of the Atlantic Ocean, Norway has a land boundary length of 2,544 km (1,581 mi) and a total coastline estimated at 21,925 km (13,624 mi).

Norway's capital city, Oslo, is in the southern part of the country.

²TOPOGRAPHY

Norway is formed of some of the oldest rocks in the world. It is dominated by mountain masses, with only one-fifth of its total area less than 150 m (500 ft) above sea level. The average altitude is 500 m (1,640 ft). The Glittertinden (2,472 m/8,110 ft, including a glacier at the summit) and Galdhøpiggen (2,469 m/8,100 ft), both in the Jotunheimen, are the highest points in Europe north of the Alpine-Carpathian mountain range. The principal river, the Glåma, 611 km (380 mi) long, flows through the timbered southeast. Much of Norway has been scraped by ice, and there are 1,700 glaciers totaling some 3,400 sq km (1,310 sq mi). In the Lista and Jaeren regions in the far south, extensive glacial deposits form agricultural lowlands. Excellent harbors are provided by the almost numberless fjords, deeply indented bays of scenic beauty that are never closed by ice and penetrate the mainland as far as 182 km (113 mi). Along many coastal stretches is a chain of islands known as the skjærgård.

³CLIMATE

Because of the North Atlantic Drift, Norway has a mild climate for a country so far north. With the great latitudinal range, the north is considerably cooler than the south, while the interior is cooler than the west coast, influenced by prevailing westerly winds and the Gulf Stream. Oslo's average yearly temperature ranges from about 5°C (41°F) in January to 28°C (82°F) in July. The annual range of coastal temperatures is much less than that of the continental interior. The eastern valleys have less than 30 cm (12 in) of rain yearly, whereas at Haukeland in Masfjord the average rainfall is 330 cm (130 in).

Norway is the land of the midnight sun in the North Cape area, with 24-hour daylight from the middle of May to the end of July, during which the sun does not set. Conversely, there are long winter nights from the end of November to the end of January, during which the sun does not rise above the horizon and the northern lights, or aurora borealis, can be seen.

⁴FLORA AND FAUNA

The richest vegetation is found in the southeast around Oslofjord, which is dominated by conifers (spruce, fir, and pine); at lower levels, deciduous trees such as oak, ash, elm, and maple are common. Conifers are seldom found at altitudes above 1,000 m (3,300 ft). Above the conifer zone extends a zone of birch trees; above that, a zone of dwarf willow and dwarf birch, and a zone of lichens and arctic plants. In areas exposed to salt sea winds, there is little tree growth. Of the larger wild animals, elk, roe deer, red deer, and badger survive, as do fox, lynx, and otter. Bird life is abundant and includes game birds such as capercaillie (cock of the woods) and black grouse. In the rivers are found trout, salmon, and char.

As of 2002, there were at least 54 species of mammals, 241 species of birds, and over 1,700 species of plants throughout the country.

5 ENVIRONMENT

Norway's plentiful forests, lakes, flora, and wildlife have suffered encroachment in recent years from the growing population and consequent development of urban areas, roads, and hydroelectric power. The forest floor and waterways have been polluted by Norway's own industry and by airborne industrial pollution from central Europe and the British Isles in the form of acid rain. The acid rain problem has affected the nation's water supply over an area of nearly 7,000 sq mi.

Annual particulate emissions have averaged 22 tons and hydrocarbon emissions have been about 270 tons. In 1992, Norway was among the 50 nations with the world's heaviest emissions of carbon dioxide from industrial sources, which totaled 60.2 million metric tons, a per capita level of 14.03 metric tons. In 2000, however, the total of carbon dioxide emissions was at 49.9 million metric tons. Transportation vehicle emissions are also a significant source of air pollution.

By the early 1980s, the government had enacted stringent regulations to prevent oil spills from wells and tankers operating on the Norwegian continental shelf. Coastal protection devices have since been installed, and new technologies to prevent oil damage have been developed. Industry, mining, and agriculture have polluted 16% of Norway's lake water. The nation has a total of 382 cu km of renewable water resource; 72% of the annual withdrawal is used for industrial activity and 8% is used for farming.

Pollution control laws operate on the premise that the polluter must accept legal and economic responsibility for any damage caused and for preventing any recurrence; the state makes loans and grants for the purchase of pollution control equipment. Municipal authorities supervise waste disposal.

Since its creation in 1972, the Ministry of the Environment has been Norway's principal environmental agency. Between 1962 and 1985, 15 national parks, with a total area of more than 5,000 sq km (2,000 sq mi), and more than 150 nature reserves were established. In 2003, about 6.8% of the total land area was protected. The West Norwegian Fjords—Geirangerfjord and Naerofjord—were named as a natural UNESCO World Heritage site in 2005. The country has 37 Ramsar wetland sites.

According to a 2006 report issued by the International Union for Conservation of Nature and Natural Resources (IUCN), threatened species included 9 types of mammals, 6 species of birds, 7 species of fish, 1 type of mollusk, 8 species of other invertebrates, and 2 species of plants. Threatened species include the Baltic sturgeon, marsh snail, and freshwater pearl mussel.

6 POPULATION

The population of Norway in 2005 was estimated by the United Nations (UN) at 4,620,000, which placed it at number 114 in population among the 193 nations of the world. In 2005, approximately 15% of the population was over 65 years of age, with another 20% of the population under 15 years of age. There were 99 males for every 100 females in the country. According to the UN, the annual population rate of change for 2005–10 was expected to be 0.3%, a rate the government viewed as too low. The projected population for the year 2025 was 5,114,000. The overall population density was 14 per sq km (37 per sq mi), with most inhabitants concentrated in the southern areas of the country.

The UN estimated that 78% of the population lived in urban areas in 2005, and that urban areas were growing at an annual rate of 1.18%. The capital city, Oslo, had a population of 795,000 in that year. The only other towns with populations exceeding 100,000 were Bergen (242,158) and Trondheim (156,161). Most provincial cities are small, with only Stavanger (115,157), Kristiansand (76,066), and Drammen (56,688) having more than 50,000.

7 MIGRATION

From 1866 on, North America received great waves of immigration from Norway, including an estimated 880,000 Norwegian immigrants to the United States by 1910. The United States and Canada still provide residence for many of the estimated 400,000 Norwegians living abroad. Emigration in recent years has not been significant. Norwegians moving abroad numbered 23,271 in 2004; immigrants to Norway totaled 36,482. Of the over 20,000 European immigrants, 4,308 were from Sweden; of the 3,875 Africans, 1,068 were from Somalia; of the 8,848 Asian immigrants, 1,220 were from Thailand. Migrants from the United States numbered 1,405. In 2005, Norway's immigrant population numbered 364,981. Of these 301,045 were first-generation immigrants, 361,143 were foreign-born, and 213,303 were foreign citizens. In 2004, internal migration between municipalities was 190,446 and between counties it was 89,940.

Norway is an important resettlement country; as of 2001, it had an allocation of 1,300 places in cooperation with the United Nations High Commissioner for Refugees (UNHCR). In 2004, 7,950 asylum applications were submitted. Main countries of origin included Russia, Serbia and Montenegro, Nigeria, and Afghanistan. The estimated net migration rate for 2005 was 1.73 migrants per 1,000 population.

8 ETHNIC GROUPS

The Norwegians have for centuries been a highly homogeneous people of Germanic (Nordic, Alpine, and Baltic) stock, generally tall and fair-skinned, with blue eyes. Small minority communities include some 20,000 Sami (Lapps) and 7,000 descendants of Finnish immigrants.

9 LANGUAGES

Norwegian, closely related to Danish and Swedish, is part of the Germanic language group. In addition to the letters of the English alphabet, it has the letters æ, å, and ø. Historically, Old Norse was displaced by a modified form of Danish for writing, but in the 19th century there arose a reaction against Danish usages. Many dialects are spoken. There are two language forms, Bokmål and Nynorsk; the former (spoken by a large majority of Norwegians) is based on the written, town language, the latter on country dialects. Both forms of Norwegian have absorbed many modern international words, particularly from British and American English, despite attempts to provide indigenous substitutes.

While Norwegian is the official language, English is spoken widely in Norway, especially in the urban areas. The Sami (Lapps) in northern Norway have retained their own language, which is of Finno-Ugric origin. There is also a small Finnish-speaking minority.

10 RELIGIONS

Citizens are generally considered to be members of the Evangelical Lutheran Church of Norway, which is the state church, unless they specifically indicate other affiliations. As such, reports indicate that about 86% of the population are nominally affiliated with the Evangelical Lutheran Church. About 3.4% of the population belong to other Protestant denominations; 1.6% are Muslim and 1% are Roman Catholic. Buddhists, Jews, Orthodox Christians, Sikhs, and Hindus make up less that 1% of the population. The Norwegian Humanist Association, an organization for atheists and the nonreligious, claims about 69,652 adults as registered members.

The constitution provides for religious freedom for all faiths, even though the religion of state is designated as the Evangelical Lutheran Church of Norway. The king nominates the Lutheran bishops and the Lutheran church receives an endowment from the state. The constitution states that the king and half of the cabinet must be members of this church. There are a number of interfaith groups within the country, including the Cooperation Council for Faith and Secular Society, the Oslo Coalition for Freedom of Religious Beliefs, and the Ecumenical Council of Christian Communities.

11 TRANSPORTATION

In spite of Norway's difficult terrain, the road system has been well engineered, with tunnels and zigzags, particularly in the fjordlands of the west; but there are problems of maintenance because of heavy rain in the west and freezing in the east. Road transport accounts for nearly 90% of inland passenger transport. As of 2002, the total length of highway was 91,852 km (57,074 mi), of which 71,185 km (44,232 mi) were paved, including 178 km (111 mi) of expressways. As of 2003, there were 1,932,663 passenger cars and 468,500 commercial vehicles in use. The state railway operates bus routes and has been steadily increasing its activities in this field, which is heavily subsidized by the government. In 2004, there was 4,077 km (2,533 mi) of rail line in operation, all of it standard gauge, of which 2,518 km (1,564 mi) were electrified.

With a merchant fleet of 740 vessels of 1,000 GRT or more, totaling 18,820,495 GRT, as of 2005, Norway possessed one of the world's largest fleets. The sale of Norwegian ships and their registration abroad, which increased considerably during the mid-1980s, severely reduced the size of the fleet. In 1988, the Norwegian International Ship Register program began, whereby ships could be registered offshore, thus allowing foreign vessels to operate under the Norwegian flag while reducing costs to shipowners. Oslo and Bergen have excellent harbor facilities, but several other ports are almost as fully equipped.

Norway had an estimated 101 airports in 2004. As of 2005, a total of 67 had paved runways, and there was also one heliport. Flesland at Bergen, Sola at Stavanger, and Fornebu and Gardermoen at Oslo are the main centers of air traffic. External services are operated by the Scandinavian Airlines System (SAS), which is 21% Norwegian-owned. Braathens Air Transport operates most of the domestic scheduled flights. Important internal air services include that linking Kirkenes, Tromsø, and Bodø; 2,000 km (1,240 mi) long, this air route is reputed to be the most difficult to operate in western Europe. In 2003, about 12.779 million passengers were carried on scheduled domestic and international flights.

12 HISTORY

Humans have lived in Norway for about 10,000 years, but only since the early centuries of the Christian era have the names of tribes and individuals been recorded. This was the period when small kingdoms were forming; the name Norge ("Northern Way") was in use for the coastal district from Vestfold to Hålogaland before AD 900. The Viking period (800–1050) was one of vigorous expansion, aided by consolidation of a kingdom under Olav Haraldsson.

From the death of Olav in 1030, the nation was officially Christian. During the next two centuries—a period marked by dynastic conflicts and civil wars—a landed aristocracy emerged, displacing peasant freeholders. A common legal code was adopted in 1274–76, and the right of succession to the crown was fixed. Shortly before, Iceland (1261) and Greenland (1261–64) came under Norwegian rule, but the Hebrides (Western Isles), also Norwegian possessions, were lost in 1266. Before 1300, Hanseatic merchants of the Baltic towns secured control of the essential grain imports, weakening the Norwegian economy.

Norway lost its independence at the death of Haakon V in 1319, when Magnus VII became ruler of both Norway and Sweden. The Black Death ravaged the country in the middle of the 14th century. In 1397, the three Scandinavian countries were united under Queen Margrethe of Denmark. Sweden left the union in 1523, but for nearly 300 more years Norway was ruled by Danish governors. Although the loss to Sweden of the provinces of Bohuslän (1645), Härjedalen (1658), and Jämtland (1645) was a handicap, gradual exploitation of the forest wealth improved Norwegian status. Denmark's alliance with France during the Napoleonic Wars resulted in the dissolution of the union. With the Peace of Kiel (1814), Norway was ceded to Sweden, but the Faroe Islands, Iceland, and Greenland were retained by Denmark. However, Norwegians resisted Swedish domination, adopted a new constitution on 17 May 1814, and elected the Danish Prince Christian Frederick as king of Norway. Sweden then invaded Norway, but agreed to let Norway keep its constitution in return for accepting union with Sweden under the rule of the Swedish king. During the second half of the 19th century, the *Storting* (parliament) became more powerful; an upsurge of nationalist agitation, both within the Storting and among Norway's cultural leaders, paved the way for the referendum that in 1905 gave independence to Norway. Feelings ran high on both sides, but once the results were announced, Norway and Sweden settled down to friendly relations. The Danish Prince Carl was elected king of Norway, assuming the name Haakon VII.

Although Norway remained neutral during World War I, its merchant marine suffered losses. Norway proclaimed its neutrality during the early days of World War II, but Norwegian waters were strategically too important for Norway to remain outside the war. Germany invaded on 9 April 1940; the national resistance was led by King Haakon, who in June escaped together with the government, representing the legally elected Storting, to England, where he established Norway's government-in-exile. Governmental affairs in Oslo fell to Vidkun Quisling, a Fascist leader and former Norwegian defense minister who had aided the German invasion and whose name subsequently became a synonym for collaborator; after the German surrender, he was arrested, convicted of treason, and shot. During the late 1940s, Norway abandoned its former neutrality, accepted Marshall Plan aid from the United States, and joined NATO. King Haakon died in 1957 and was succeeded by Olav V. King Harald V succeeded his father who died 17 January 1991.

The direction of economic policy has been the major issue in Norwegian postwar history, especially as related to taxation and the degree of government intervention in private industry. Economic planning was introduced, and several state-owned enterprises have been established. Prior to the mid-1970s, Labor Party-dominated governments enjoyed a broad public consensus for their foreign and military policies. A crucial development occurred in November 1972, when the Norwegian electorate voted in a referendum to reject Norway's entry into the EC despite a strong pro-EC posture adopted by the minority Labor government. After the 1973 general elections, the Labor Party's hold on government policies began to erode, and in the 1981 elections, the party lost control of the government to the Conservatives. Although the non-Socialists retained a small majority in the 1985 elections, disagreements among them permitted Labor to return to office in 1986.

Norway reconfirmed its rejection of the European Union on 28 November 1994, when the vote was cast 52% against, 47.8% for joining Europe. However, in December 2002, Prime Minister Kjell Magne Bondevik stated a new referendum would probably be held on EU membership. Public opinion polls in June 2003 registered 51.9% of the electorate in favor of joining the EU; 38.2% were opposed and 9.9% were undecided.

Norway was forthright in its support for the US-led war on terror following the 11 September 2001 terrorist attacks. It supported the NATO decision to invoke Article 5 of the alliance's constitution, pledging all members to collective security in the event of an attack on one. However, Norway did not support the US-led war in Iraq that began on 19 March 2003. Prime Minister Bondevik held that international weapons inspectors authorized by UN Security Council Resolution 1441 to inspect Iraq's weapons programs should have been given more time to do their work, and that military action should not be taken without an express Security Council resolution authorizing it. Eight out of ten Norwegian voters agreed in March 2003 that Norway should not support the US and British decision to go to war against Iraq.

On 19 January 2004, the Norwegian cargo ship *Rocknes* capsized after striking rocks in a fjord off the coast of Bergen. Eighteen crew members were killed, most of them Filipinos. Nearly 1,000 animals were oiled, a concern for environmentalists. Another concern for environmentalists was Norway's rejection of the 1986 International Whaling Commission's ban on whaling. Norway began whaling on a commercial basis in 1993.

In the general election held on 12 September 2005, the center-left led by Jens Stoltenberg's Labor Party in a "red-green alliance" with the Socialist and Center parties won more than half the seats in parliament, defeating Bondevik's center-right minority coalition. The populist far-right Progress Party increased its number of seats held in parliament by 12, to 38, and it became the nation's largest opposition party.

¹³GOVERNMENT

Norway is a constitutional monarchy. The constitution of 17 May 1814, as subsequently amended, vests executive power in the king and legislative power in the Storting. Prior to 1990, sovereignty descended to the eldest son of the monarch. A constitutional amendment in May 1990 allows females to succeed to the throne. The amendment only affects those born after 1990. The sovereign must be a member of the Evangelical Lutheran Church of Norway, which he heads. Royal power is exercised through a cabinet (the Council of State), consisting of a prime minister and at least seven other ministers of state (these numbered 18 in 2005). Since the introduction of parliamentary rule in 1884, the Storting has become the supreme authority, with sole control over finances and with power to override the king's veto under a specified procedure. While the king is theoretically free to choose his own cabinet, in practice the Storting selects the ministers, who must resign if the Storting votes no confidence.

The Storting was made up of 169 representatives in 2005 (an increase of four over the 2001 election) from 19 counties. Election for a four-year term is by direct suffrage at age 18, on the basis of proportional representation. After election, the Storting divides into two sections by choosing one-fourth of its members to form the upper chamber *Lagting*, with the rest constituting the lower chamber *Odelsting*. The Odelsting deals with certain types of bills (chiefly proposed new laws) after the committee stage and forwards them to the Lagting, which, after approval, sends them to the king for the royal assent; financial, organizational, political, and other matters are dealt with in plenary session. Where the two sections disagree, a two-thirds majority of the full Storting is required for passage. Constitutional amendments also require a two-thirds vote. The constitution provides that the Storting may not be dissolved.

A special parliamentary ombudsman supervises the observance of laws and statutes as applied by the courts and by public officials. His main responsibility is to protect citizens against unjust or arbitrary treatment by civil servants.

¹⁴POLITICAL PARTIES

The present-day Conservative Party (Høyre) was established in 1885. The Liberal Party (Venstre), founded in 1885 as a counterbalance to the civil servant class, became the rallying organization of the Agrarian Friends' Association. The party's political program stresses social reform. Industrial workers founded the Labor Party (Arbeiderparti) in 1887 and, with the assistance of the Liberals, obtained universal male suffrage in 1898 and votes for women in 1913. The Social Democrats broke away from the Labor Party in 1921–22, and the Communist Party (Kommunistparti), made up of former Laborites, was established in 1923. The moderate Socialists reunited and revived the Labor Party organization in 1927. The Agrarian (Farmers) Party was formed in 1920; it changed its name to the Center Party (Senterparti) in 1958. The Christian People's Party (Kristelig Folkeparti), founded in 1933, and also known as the Christian Democratic Party, supports the principles of Christianity in public life.

For several decades, the Liberals were either in office or held the balance of power, but in 1935, as a result of the economic depression, an alliance between the Agrarian and Labor parties led to the

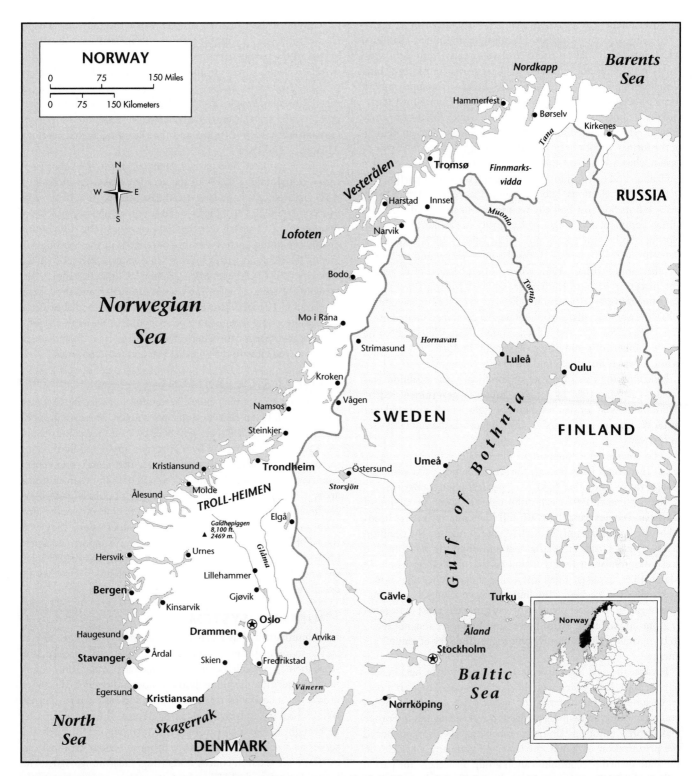

LOCATION: 57°57′31″ to 71°11′8″ N; 4°30′13″ to 31°10′4″ E. BOUNDARY LENGTHS: Finland, 729 kilometers (455 miles); Russia, 167 kilometers (104 miles); Sweden, 1,619 kilometers (1,011 miles); total coastline, 21,925 kilometers (13,703 miles). TERRITORIAL SEA LIMIT: 4 miles.

formation of a Labor government. During World War II, the main parties formed a national cabinet-in-exile. Political differences between right and left sharpened in the postwar period. Attempts to form a national coalition among the four non-Socialist parties proved unsuccessful until the 1965 elections, when they gained a combined majority of 80 seats in the Storting. Per Borten, who

was appointed in October 1965 to form a non-Socialist coalition government, retained office in the 1969 elections, although with a majority of only two seats.

In the 1973 general elections, the Labor Party received only 35.3% of the national vote; its representation in the Storting shrank to 62 seats, but with its Socialist allies, it was able to form a minority government. The Christian People's Party, meanwhile, registered gains, as did the Socialist Electoral League, a new coalition, which was able to take a number of votes away from the Labor Party. In 1975, the Socialist Electoral League was transformed into a single grouping known as the Socialist Left Party, comprising the former Socialist People's Party, the Norwegian Communist Party, and the Democratic Socialist Party (formed in 1972); the transformation, which resulted in a platform that voiced criticism neither of the former USSR nor of Leninist ideology, marked the first occasion when a Western Communist Party voted to dissolve its organization and merge into a new grouping with other parties.

In the 1977 elections, Labor expanded its representation to 76 seats, but its Socialist Left ally won only two seats, and their coalition commanded a single-seat majority in the Storting. Odvar Nordli, who became prime minister in January 1976, succeeding the retiring Trygve Bratteli, formed a new cabinet and remained in office until February 1981, when he quit because of ill health. His successor was Gro Harlem Brundtland, Norway's first woman prime minister. Her term in office lasted only until September, when the non-Socialist parties obtained a combined total of more than 56% of the vote and a Conservative, Kåre Willoch, became prime minister of a minority government. In April 1983, the government was transformed into a majority coalition.

Following the loss of a vote of confidence, the coalition was replaced in May 1986 by a Labor minority government led by Brundtland, who formed a cabinet of eight female ministers out of 18. With an average age of 47, her cabinet was the youngest ever in Norway.

Labor increased its support in the 1993 election, winning 67 seats. The Center Party became the second-largest party while the Conservatives and other right-wing parties suffered a decline.

The September 1997 election brought to power a coalition of Christian People's party, Liberals, and Center party and was headed by the Lutheran minister, Kjell Magne Bondevik. The coalition claimed only 42 seats in parliament and Bondevik was forced to seek compromises with opposition parties to pass legislation. In March 1999 his government lost a vote of confidence after Bondevik refused to weaken antipollution laws to allow the construction of gas-fired power plants. Norway generates most of its power from nonpolluting hydro power and Bondevik was not ready to compromise Norway's environment for the sake of natural gas energy.

Because the next legislative elections could only be held in September 2001, Jens Stoltenberg, the elected leader of the Labor party, became prime minister at the age of 41, becoming Norway's youngest leader. Stoltenberg pledged to seek strong ties to Europe and favored European Union membership. He also announced the privatization of Statoil, the state's oil company, and Telenor, the state-owned telecommunication group. Especially, the partial sell-off of Statoil was of huge symbolic significance because of its role as the guardian of the nation's oil and gas wealth.

In the September 2001 parliamentary elections, the Labor Party came in first, although it suffered its worst defeat since 1924, taking only 24.3% of the vote, compared with 35% in 1997. Voters were disgruntled with high tax rates—in some cases 50%—and inadequate public services, including hospitals, schools, and public transportation. The far-right Progress Party gained seats. Bondevik was returned to power as prime minister, putting together a coalition of the Christian People's Party, the Liberals, and the Conservatives, with support from the Progress Party. The distribution of the parties' electoral strength in the Storting following the 2001 elections was as follows: Labor Party, 24.3% (43 seats); Conservative Party, 21.2% (38 seats); Progress Party, 14.7% (26 seats); Christian People's Party, 12.5% (22 seats); Socialist Left Party, 12.4% (23 seats); Center Party, 5.6% (10 seats); the fisherman's Coastal Party, 3.9% (2 seats); and the extreme-left Red Electoral Alliance, 1.7% (1 seat).

In the September 2005 parliamentary elections, the Labor Party came in first, taking 32.7% of the vote (61 seats), an increase of 8.4% (18 seats) over the 2001 elections. The Progress Party came in second with 22.1% of the vote (38 seats), an increase of 7.4% of the vote (and 12 seats) over the 2001 elections. The distribution of the remaining parties' electoral strengths in the Storting following the elections was as follows: Conservative Party, 14.1% (23 seats); Socialist Left Party, 8.8% (15 seats); Christian People's Party, 6.8% (11 seats); Center Party, 6.5% (11 seats); and the Liberal Party, 5.9% (10 seats). Jens Stoltenberg, leader of the Labor Party, claimed he would devote more of the country's oil wealth to jobs, schools, and care for the elderly. Stoltenberg was to form a coalition government with the Socialist Left and Center parties.

15 LOCAL GOVERNMENT

Norway has 435 municipalities (*kommuner*) of varying size, each administered by an elected municipal council. They are grouped into 19 counties (*fylker*), each governed by an elected county council. Each county is headed by a governor appointed by the king in council. Oslo is the only urban center that alone constitutes a county; the remaining 18 counties consist of both urban and rural areas. County and municipal councils are popularly elected every four years. The municipalities have wide powers over the local economy, with the state exercising strict supervision. They have the right to tax and to use their resources to support education, libraries, social security, and public works such as streetcar lines, gas and electricity works, roads, and town planning, but they are usually aided in these activities by state funds.

16 JUDICIAL SYSTEM

Each municipality has a conciliation council (*forliksråd*), elected by the municipal council, to mediate in lesser civil cases so as to settle them, if possible, before they go to court; under some conditions the conciliation councils also render judgments. The courts of first instance are town courts (*byrett*) and rural courts (*herredsrett*), which try both civil and criminal cases. Their decisions may be brought before a court of appeals (*lagmannsrett*), which also serves as a court of first instance in more serious criminal cases. There are six such courts: Borgarting, Eidsivating, Agder, Gulating, Frostating and Hålogaland. Appeals may be taken to the Supreme Court (*Høyesterett*) at Oslo, which consists of a chief justice and 18 judges. Special courts include a Social Insurance Court and a Labor Disputes Court who mediates industrial relations disputes.

The judiciary is independent of both the legislative and the executive branches. In criminal cases, defendants are afforded free legal counsel. Indigent persons are granted free legal counsel in certain civil cases as well.

17ARMED FORCES

Norway's armed forces in 2005 had a total strength of 25,800 active personnel with reserves numbering 219,000. The Army of 14,700 was equipped with 165 main battle tanks, 157 armored infantry fighting vehicles, 189 armored personnel carriers, and 634 artillery pieces. The Navy numbered 6,100 active personnel, including 270 in the coast guard and 160 coastal defense personnel. The Navy operated 6 tactical submarines, 3 frigates, 15 coastal and patrol vessels, and 10 mine warfare ships. The Air Force consisted of 5,000 personnel operating 61 combat capable aircraft, in addition to 15 (each) transport and training aircraft, and 12 search and rescue helicopters. The Air Force also mans air defense guns and missiles.

Norway is the host nation for the NATO Allied Forces North headquarters and provides troops or observers for eight peacekeeping operations. The nation's defense budget in 2005 totaled $4.69 billion.

18INTERNATIONAL COOPERATION

Norway has been a member of the United Nations since 27 November 1945; the country participates in the ECE and several nonregional specialized agencies, such as the FAO, IAEA, the World Bank, UNSECO, UNHCR, UNIDO, and the WHO. Norwegian experts serve in many countries under the UN Technical Assistance program. Norway has participated in at least 30 UN peacekeeping operations. The Norwegian Peace Corps, launched as an experiment in 1963, was made a permanent part of Norway's program of international aid in 1965.

Norway is a member of the WTO, the African Development Bank, the Asian Development Bank, the Council of the Baltic Sea States, the Euro-Atlantic Partnership Council, the Inter-American Development Bank, the Council of Europe, EFTA, the OSCE, the Paris Club, NATO, the Nordic Council, the Nordic Investment Bank, and OECD. The country holds observer status in the OAS and is an associate member of the Western European Union. A referendum on EU membership was held in November 1994; 52% of the electorate voted against membership.

Norway is part of the Australia Group, the Zangger Committee, the Nuclear Suppliers Group (London Group), the Nuclear Energy Agency, the European Organization for Nuclear Research (CERN), and the Organization for the Prohibition of Chemical Weapons. In environmental cooperation, Norway is part of the Antarctic Treaty, the Basel Convention, the Convention on Biological Diversity, Ramsar, CITES, the London Convention, International Tropical Timber Agreements, the Kyoto Protocol, the Montréal Protocol, MARPOL, the Nuclear Test Ban Treaty, and the UN Conventions on the Law of the Sea, Climate Change and Desertification.

19ECONOMY

Norway, with its long coastline and vast forests, is traditionally a fishing and lumbering country, but since the end of World War II it has greatly increased its transport and manufacturing activities. The exploitation since the late 1970s of major oil reserves in the North Sea has had considerable impact on the Norwegian economy.

Foreign trade is a critical economic factor. Exports bring in over 40% of the GDP. As a trading nation without a large domestic market, Norway was especially vulnerable to the effects of the worldwide recession of the early 1980s and is sensitive to fluctuations in world prices, particularly those of oil, gas, and shipping. Since the early 1980s, Norway's exports have been dominated by petroleum and natural gas, which produced 56% of commodity exports in 2003.

Norway has a mixed economy with the government owning about 32% of the listed shares on the Oslo stock exchange, and holding shares in around 10–15% of Norwegian industry (as of 2005). State ownership is most dominant in the oil, hydroelectric, and mining sectors. At considerable expense, the government provides subsidies for industry, agriculture, and outlying regions. About half of the total goes to agriculture.

Norwegian competitiveness in the global economy is hampered by a small population (4.6 million), a restrictive immigration policy, and an expensive social welfare system that places high tax burdens on the population.

In the early 1980s, the nation's economy became increasingly dependent on oil revenues, which stimulated domestic consumption and, at the same time, increased costs and prices, thus hampering the competitiveness of Norway's other export industries. The drastic decline of oil prices in 1986 caused the value of Norway's exports to fall by about 20%. Recently, the service sector has grown, accounting for 61.6% of GDP (2004 est.)

From 1949 to 1989 the real GDP rose on the average by 3.9% per year. The GDP fell in 1988 for the first time in 30 years. Since 1989, however, growth resumed, averaging only 1.3% during 1989–91, but climbing by an annual average of 3.7% during 1992–94. In 1998, GDP growth was 2.4%, inflation was 2.3%, and unemployment was 2.6%. In 1999, low world oil prices helped reduce growth to 1.1%, while their recovery, in 2000 helped raise GDP growth to 2.3%. GDP growth fell to 1% by 2002 and to 0.5% in 2003, largely due to the global economic slowdown of 2001–02. The economy recovered strongly in 2004, with real GDP growing by 2.9%. Economic growth was forecast to peak in 2005 at 3%, before falling slightly to 2.5% in 2006.

Unemployment averaged about 3.3% 1999 to 2002, while annual price inflation was about 2.9%. The unemployment rate stood at 4.3% in 2004, and the annual CPI inflation rate was forecast at 1.8% in 2005. Government statistics show that government spending as a percent of GDP declined from 39% in 1999 to about 34.5% in 2001, down from the estimated 50% reported by the OECD in the mid-1990s. Government spending as a percent of GDP stood at approximately 40% in 2005.

Norwegian voters rejected European Union membership in 1994. However, Norway is a member of the European Economic Area (EEA) which consists of the EU member countries together with Norway, Iceland, and Liechtenstein. Membership gives Norway most of the rights and obligation of the EU single market but very little ability to influence EU decisions.

20INCOME

The US Central Intelligence Agency (CIA) reports that in 2005 Norway's gross domestic product (GDP) was estimated at $194.7

billion. The CIA defines GDP as the value of all final goods and services produced within a nation in a given year and computed on the basis of purchasing power parity (PPP) rather than value as measured on the basis of the rate of exchange based on current dollars. The per capita GDP was estimated at $42,400. The annual growth rate of GDP was estimated at 3.8%. The average inflation rate in 2005 was 2.1%. It was estimated that agriculture accounted for 2.2% of GDP, industry 37.2%, and services 60.6%.

According to the World Bank, in 2003 remittances from citizens working abroad totaled $322 million or about $71 per capita and accounted for approximately 0.1% of GDP.

The World Bank reports that in 2003 household consumption in Norway totaled $101.96 billion or about $22,350 per capita based on a GDP of $220.9 billion, measured in current dollars rather than PPP. Household consumption includes expenditures of individuals, households, and nongovernmental organizations on goods and services, excluding purchases of dwellings. It was estimated that for the period 1990 to 2003 household consumption grew at an average annual rate of 3.4%. In 2001 it was estimated that approximately 16% of household consumption was spent on food, 11% on fuel, 5% on health care, and 4% on education.

21 LABOR

In 2005, Norway's labor force totaled an estimated 2.4 million workers. As of 2003, services accounted for 74% of the workforce, with 22.1% in industry, and around 4% in the agricultural sector. From 1960–88, Norway's average unemployment rate was only 1.6%. Unemployment gradually increased during the 1970s, and decreased from 5.5% in 1991 to 3.9% in 2002. As of 2005, the unemployment rate was estimated at 4.2%.

As of 2005, about 55% of the labor force was unionized. Under Norwegian law, workers can organize and join unions, engage in collective bargaining, and strike. Government employees, including military personnel, can also organize unions and bargain collectively. Antiunion discrimination is prohibited by law.

In 1919, the eight-hour day was established, together with paid holiday periods. In 1986, the workweek was reduced to 37.5 hours, where as of 2005, it remained. There is also 25 days of paid leave, with 31 days for those 60 and older. There is no legal minimum wage. Wages scales are set through negotiations involving local government, employers and workers. Children between the ages of 13 and 18 years may engage in light work that will not negatively affect their health or education, but only on a part-time basis.

22 AGRICULTURE

Agricultural land in 2003 comprised 873,000 hectares (2,157,000 acres), or about 2.9% of the country's total land (excluding Svalbard and Jan Mayen). While the area under wheat and mixed grains has dropped sharply since 1949, that for rye, oats, and barley has more than doubled. The greater part of these crops is used to supplement potatoes and hay in the feeding of livestock. In 2004, the area planted with barley, oats, rye, and triticale covered 12,380 hectares (30,590 acres), while wheat covered 65,000 hectares (161,000 acres).

In 2005, Norway had 53,277 agricultural holdings, 96% held by individuals. Because of the small size of the holdings, many farm families pursue additional occupations, mainly in forestry, fishing,

and handicrafts. Yields in 2004 included 1,076,000 tons of coarse grain and 340,000 tons of potatoes. Østfold county accounts for 20% of Norway's grain production; Hedmark county for one-third of potato production. Norway imports most of its grain and large quantities of its fruits and vegetables.

With steep slopes and heavy precipitation, Norway requires substantial quantities of fertilizers to counteract soil leaching. Smallholders and those in marginal farming areas in the north and in the mountains receive considerable government assistance for the purchase of fertilizers. Mechanization of agriculture is developing rapidly. In 2003, Norwegian farmers used 130,000 tractors and 13,400 combines.

Since 1928, the state has subsidized Norwegian grain production; a state monopoly over the import of grains maintains the price of Norwegian-grown grains. The Ministry of Agriculture has divisions dealing with agricultural education, economics, and other aspects. Each county has an agricultural society headed by a government official. These societies, financed half by the district and half by the state, implement government schemes for improving agricultural practices.

23 ANIMAL HUSBANDRY

Norway is self-sufficient in farm animals and livestock products. In 2005, there were 2,417,000 sheep, 920,000 head of cattle, 515,000 hogs, 28,000 horses, and 3,300,000 fowl. Norway is well known for its working horses. By careful breeding, Norway has developed dairy cows with very good milk qualities; artificial insemination is now widely used. In 2005, production included 83,600 tons of beef and veal, 116,500 tons of pork, 25,400 tons of mutton and lamb, 1,721,000 tons of milk, 81,200 tons of cheese, 51,000 tons of eggs, and 13,000 tons of butter. Norwegian production of milk, cheese, and meat satisfies local demand.

The breeding of furbearing animals has been widely undertaken, and good results have been obtained with mink. In 2003, there were 320,000 farm-raised foxes, 440,000 mink, and 203,000 deer. Reindeer graze in the north and on the lichen-clad mountains. In 2004, wild game hunting yielded 36,770 moose, 3,895 wild reindeer, and 25,896 red deer.

24 FISHING

Seafood is Norway's third-largest export item, after petroleum products and metals. In 2004, the value of Norway's seafood exports amounted to $4.2 billion, with salmon and trout accounting for 44%. Norway's wild fish catch in 2004 amounted to 2.5 million tons, valued at $1.5 billion. The main commercial species are herring, cod, mackerel, and sardines.

Cod spawn in March and April off the Lofoten Islands. The Lofoten fisheries are coastal, permitting the use of small craft, but there has been increased use of large trawlers that fish in the waters of Greenland, the Norwegian Sea, and the Barents Sea. Cod roe and liver (yielding cod-liver oil) are valuable by-products. In recent years there has been concern about declining wild fish stocks in the sea, but for Norway the wild fish catches seem to increase almost every year. According to the Norwegian Institute of Marine Research, the most important fish stocks in northern Norwegian waters have stabilized, and will remain at a high level in the years to come. The traditional wage system is on a share-of-the-catch basis. In view of the seasonal nature of the fisheries, many men work also in agriculture or forestry, and the supplementary income from part-time fishing is important to small farmers.

Aquaculture is also important in Norway, with over 3,500 workers and 700 facilities located along the entire coast from the Swedish border in the south to Finnmark far north of the Arctic Circle. The production of farmed salmon reached 537,000 tons in 2004, accounting for 45% of the world's farmed salmon production.

In 2003, sealing expeditions hunting in the Arctic Ocean caught 12,870 seals. Norway was one of the four countries that did not agree to phase out whaling by 1986, having opposed a 1982 resolution of the International Whaling Commission to that effect. In 2003, 647 minke whales were reportedly caught.

25 FORESTRY

Norway's forestland totals 8,868,000 hectares (21,913,000 acres), of which over 80% is owned by individuals, 9% by the state, and 7% by local governments; the remainder is held by institutions, companies, and cooperatives.

The state subsidizes silviculture and the building of forest roads. In 2004, removals amounted to 8,780,000 cu m (309.9 million cu ft), of which 86% was coniferous industrial wood and 14% was fuel wood. Sawn wood production in 2004 totaled 2,230,000 cu m (78.7 million cu ft); wood pulp, 2,528,000 tons; and paper and paperboard, 2,294,000 tons. The value of forest products exported was $1.8 billion in 2004, when Norway's trade surplus in forest products amounted to $641 million. The Norwegian Forest Research Institute has centers near Oslo and Bergen.

26 MINING

Mining was Norway's oldest major export industry. Some working mines were established more than 300 years ago and, for a time, silver, iron, and copper were important exports. Iron pyrites and iron ore were still mined in considerable quantities. Petroleum and gas comprised Norway's leading industry in 2004, and metals, chemicals, and mining were among other leading industries. Among export commodities, petroleum and petroleum products ranked first, while metals and chemicals followed close behind. Known deposits of other minerals were small; they included limestone, quartz, dolomite, feldspar, and mica (flake). In 2004, production of iron ore and concentrate (metal content) was 408,000 metric tons, up from 340,000 metric tons in 2003. Titanium (metal content) production in 2004 was 387,000 metric tons. Norway also produced nickel, hydraulic cement, dolomite, feldspar, graphite, lime (hydrated, quicklime), limestone, flake mica, nepheline syenite, nitrogen, olivine sand, quartz, quartzite, soapstone, steatite, sulfur (as a by-product), and talc. No lead or zinc was mined from 1998 through 2004, and no copper or pyrite from 1999 through 2004. The largest titanium deposit in Europe was at Soknedal. A large plant at Thamshavn used half the Orkla mines' output of pyrites for sulfur production. Reserves of minerals generally have been depleted, except for olivine, which was abundant. There has been recent gold exploration, and a zinc exploration program in the Roros district confirmed the existence of extensive stratiform sulfide mineralization with dimensions of a type that could host commercial deposits.

27 ENERGY AND POWER

Norway has Western Europe's largest proven reserves of oil, which are located on the country's continental shelf. Norway is also the second-largest supplier of natural gas to continental Europe and one of the largest producers in the world. In spite of its oil and gas reserves, hydropower is the primary source of electric power for Norway.

As of 1 January 2005, Norway's proven reserves of oil amounted to 8.5 billion barrels. In 2004, Norway produced an estimated 3,183,900 barrels of oil per day, of which crude oil accounted for 88%. Domestic consumption for oil averaged 244,300,000 barrels of oil per day. In 2005, Norway's crude oil refining capacity averaged 310,000 barrels per day, according to the Oil and Gas Journal. There are two major refining facilities: the 200,000 barrel-per-day Mongstad plant, which is operated by 71% government owned Statoil; and the 110,000 barrel-per-day Slagen plant, which is operated by ExxonMobil.

Norway's natural gas reserves are mainly in the North Sea, although the Barents and Norwegian Seas are known to have significant reserves. As of 1 January 2005, Norway's proven reserves of natural gas were estimated at 73.6 trillion cu ft. In 2003, natural gas production was estimated at 2.6 trillion cu ft, with domestic consumption that year estimated at 146.2 billion cu ft.

Norway's reserves of coal, unlike its reserves of oil and natural gas, are very modest. In 2003, Norway's recoverable coal reserves were estimated at 5.5 million short tons. Output and consumption that year were estimated at 3.2 million short tons and 1.4 million short tons, respectively.

Norway's installed electric power generating capacity in 2003 was estimated at 26.6 GW. In that same year, electric power output was estimated at 1205.6 billion kWh, of which hydroelectric generated power amounted to 99% of the electricity produced. Geothermal/other and conventional thermal generated power account for the remainder. Domestic consumption in 2003 was estimated at 106.1 billion kWh.

28 INDUSTRY

Manufacturing, mining, and crude petroleum and gas production accounted for nearly 36.3% of the GDP in 2004. The most important export industries are oil and gas extraction, metalworking, pulp and paper, chemical products, and processed fish. Products traditionally classified as home market industries (electrical and nonelectrical machinery, casting and foundry products, textiles, paints, varnishes, rubber goods, and furniture) also make an important contribution. Electrochemical and electrometallurgical products—aluminum, ferroalloys, steel, nickel, copper, magnesium, and fertilizers—are based mainly on Norway's low-cost electric power. Without any bauxite reserves of its own, Norway has thus been able to become a leading producer of aluminum. Industrial output is being increasingly diversified.

About half of Norway's industries are situated in the Oslofjord area. Other industrial centers are located around major cities along the coast as far north as Trondheim. Norway has two oil refineries. Daily Norwegian offshore production in 2003 averaged

3.26 million barrels of oil. In the early 2000s, despite an improvement in world oil prices, investment in offshore oil and natural gas remained in decline, in part due to the completion of major projects, such as the Aasgard field. Norway's oil and gas reserves are declining; discovered oil reserves were projected to last 18 years in 2000, and natural gas reserves to last 95 years. The state oil company is Statoil. Norway's price support level for the oil industry is low, at around $20 per barrel of oil. Norway's oil economy employs more than 100,000 Norwegians.

Norway is also Europe's largest natural gas producer, and one of the largest natural gas exporters in the world. Natural gas reserves were measured at 1.71 trillion cu m in 2005. By 2020, natural gas production in Norway will overtake its oil output.

As Norway's economy will not be able to depend indefinitely upon oil, it must diversify. In addition to developing its knowledge-based economy (biotechnology, nanotechnology, the Internet, and knowledge-services), Norway may look to further develop its mineral resources.

²⁹SCIENCE AND TECHNOLOGY

A highly advanced industrialized nation, Norway invested $2,625.414 million or 1.6% of its GDP into research and development (R&D) in 2001. Of that amount, 51.7% came from the business sector, followed by government sources at 39.8%. Foreign sources accounted for 7.1% and higher education at 1.4%. In 2002, high-tech exports were valued at $2.863 billion and accounted for 22% of manufactured exports. Public funds come either as direct grants from the central government or as proceeds from the State Football Pool, whose net receipts are divided between research and sports. In 2001 (the latest year for which data was available), there were 1,524 technicians and 4,442 scientists and engineers engaged in R&D per million people.

The four principal research councils are the Agricultural Research Council of Norway, the Norwegian Research Council for Science and the Humanities, the Royal Norwegian Council for Scientific and Industrial Research, and the Norwegian Fisheries Research Council, each attached to separate government ministries. The councils recruit researchers by means of fellowship programs and allocate research grants to universities. They are part of the Science Policy Council of Norway, an advisory board to the government on all research matters. Principal areas of current study are arctic research, specifically studies of the northern lights; oceanography, especially ocean currents; marine biology, with special attention to fish migration; and meteorology.

The Royal Norwegian Society of Sciences and Letters, founded in 1760, has a Natural Sciences section. The country has 12 other scientific and technical learned societies and 24 scientific and technical research institutes. Located in Oslo are the Botanical Garden and Museum (founded in 1814), the Norwegian Museum of Science and Industry (founded in 1914), and other museums devoted to mineralogy-geology, paleontology, and zoology. The country has six universities and colleges offering courses in basic and applied sciences. In 1987–97, science and engineering students accounted for 26% of university enrollment. In 2002, of all bachelor's degrees awarded, 14.5% were in the sciences (natural, mathematics and computers, engineering).

³⁰DOMESTIC TRADE

Oslo, the principal merchandising center, handles the distribution of many import products; Bergen and Stavanger are other west coast distribution centers. Trondheim is the chief northern center; Tromsø and Narvik are also important. The largest number of importers, exporters, and manufacturers' agents are in Oslo and Bergen. An 11% value-added tax (VAT) applies to many food products. A 25% VAT applies to most other goods and services, effective 2005.

Cooperative societies are an important distribution factor, with local groups operating retail stores for many kinds of consumer goods, especially in the food sector. Food market chains have developed rapidly in recent years. The Norwegian Cooperative Union and Wholesale Society represents a large number of societies, with over half a million members. Agricultural cooperatives are active in produce marketing and cooperative purchasing societies (*Felleskjöp*) do much of the buying of farm equipment, fertilizer, and seed.

The Norwegian Consumer Council (established by the Storting in 1953) advances and safeguards the fundamental interests of consumers. It publishes comprehensive reports on accepted standards for key consumer goods, conducts conferences and buying courses in various parts of Norway, arranges consumer fairs, and cooperates closely with other organizations and institutions interested in consumer protection. Newspapers provide an important medium for advertisements; trade and other journals carry advertising, but the state-owned radio and television do not. However, in 1992, a national commercial television channel, TV2, was established in competition with the noncommercial Norwegian Broadcasting Corporation (NRK). TV2 currently has the sole right to broadcast advertising via Norwegian Telecom's terrestrial broadcasting network. Advertising is not permitted on NRK, but the growth of foreign-based commercial television channels broadcasting by satellite, and commercial television channels broadcasting via cable, opened the way for nationwide advertising on television. The advent of commercial television and radio advertising in Norway has led to new official control systems.

Shopping hours are usually from 9 AM to 5 PM on weekdays (often until 7 PM on Thursdays) and from 9 AM to 1 or 3 PM on Saturdays. Banks stay open from 9 AM to 3:30 PM Mondays, Tuesdays, Wednesdays, and Fridays, and until 5 PM on Thursdays. Some manufacturers and major businesses will close for three to four weeks in July and/or August for a summer vacation.

³¹FOREIGN TRADE

Foreign trade plays an exceptionally important role in the Norwegian economy, accounting, with exports of goods and services, for some 43% of the GDP in the mid-1990s and about 41% in 2004. Exports are largely based on oil, natural gas, shipbuilding, metals, forestry (including pulp and paper), fishing, and electrochemical and electrometallurgical products. Norway is the world's third-largest exporter of oil, after Saudi Arabia and Russia. The manufacture of oil rigs, drilling platforms, and associated equipment has developed into a sizable export industry. Norway im-

Principal Trading Partners – Norway (2003)

(In millions of US dollars)

Country	Exports	Imports	Balance
World	67,934.5	39,848.2	28,086.3
United Kingdom	14,438.1	2,853.5	11,584.6
Germany	8,845.6	5,281.6	3,564.0
Netherlands	6,525.4	1,783.9	4,741.5
United States	5,873.7	2,053.9	3,819.8
France-Monaco	5,575.6	1,728.5	3,847.1
Sweden	5,020.3	6,396.7	-1,376.4
Denmark	2,603.3	3,129.9	-526.6
Canada	2,483.0	806.5	1,676.5
Italy-San Marino-Holy See	2,397.0	1,577.3	819.7
Belgium	1,831.6	814.3	1,017.3

(…) data not available or not significant.

SOURCE: *2003 International Trade Statistics Yearbook,* New York: United Nations, 2004.

Balance of Payments – Norway (2003)

(In millions of US dollars)

Current Account		**28,444.0**
Balance on goods		27,910.0
Imports	-41,162.0	
Exports	69,071.0	
Balance on services		2,244.0
Balance on income		1,367.0
Current transfers		-3,076.0
Capital Account		**680.0**
Financial Account		**-20,121.0**
Direct investment abroad		-2,226.0
Direct investment in Norway		1,958.0
Portfolio investment assets		-19,290.0
Portfolio investment liabilities		12,629.0
Financial derivatives		-126.0
Other investment assets		-23,171.0
Other investment liabilities		10,106.0
Net Errors and Omissions		**-8,706.0**
Reserves and Related Items		**-297.0**

(…) data not available or not significant.

SOURCE: *Balance of Payment Statistics Yearbook 2004,* Washington, DC: International Monetary Fund, 2004.

ports considerable quantities of motor vehicles and other transport equipment, raw materials, and industrial equipment.

Exports tripled between 1974 and 1981, largely on the strength of the petroleum sector, which accounted for a negligible percentage of exports in 1974 but half the total export value in 1981. During the same period, imports advanced by 93%. Following years of trade deficits, Norway had surpluses from 1980 through 1985. However, the drastic fall in oil prices caused a decline in export value resulting in deficits between 1986 and 1988. Since 1989, Norway has once again consistently recorded trade surpluses. In 2004, the value of Norwegian exports was $76.64 billion, and the value of imports totaled $45.96 billion, for a trade surplus of $30.68 billion. The leading markets for Norway's exports in 2004 were: the United Kingdom (22.3% of all exports), Germany (12.9%), the Netherlands (9.9%), France (9.6%), and the United States (8.4%). Norway's leading suppliers in 2004 were: Sweden (15.7% of all imports), Germany (13.6%), Denmark (7.3%) the United Kingdom (6.5%), and the United States (4.9%). In total, 78.2% of all Norwegian exports are traded with the EU, and Norway receives 70.8% of its imports from the EU.

32 BALANCE OF PAYMENTS

Norway's foreign exchange reserves have been built up to meet adverse developments in the balance of payments without the necessity of a retreat from the liberalization of imports. Until the oil boom of the late 1970s, imports regularly exceeded exports, but large deficits on current account were more than offset by the capital account surplus, giving a net increase in foreign exchange reserves. As of 2005 Norway was the world's third-largest exporter of oil, behind only Saudi Arabia and Russia.

Norway's economy is less open to trade than the Western European average, with total exports and imports of goods and services equal to 41.5% and 27.3% of GDP, respectively, in 2002.

The price of oil rose sharply in 2005 (averaging $53.27 per barrel), and was forecast to remain at $50.50 per barrel in 2006. The higher oil prices were expected to boost Norway's trade surplus in both years, which means that the current account surplus will also widen, reaching 17.3% of GDP in 2005, before narrowing slightly in 2006. The current account balance was estimated at $30.52 billion in 2004.

33 BANKING AND SECURITIES

The Bank of Norway was founded as a commercial bank in 1816; in 1949, all its share capital was acquired by the state. It is the central bank and the sole note-issuing authority. The bank discounts treasury bills and some commercial paper; trades in bonds, foreign exchange, and gold and silver; and administers foreign exchange regulations. The bank also receives money for deposit on current account but generally pays no interest on deposits. The head office is in Oslo, and there are 20 branches.

In 1938 there were 105 commercial banks, but mergers brought the total down to only 31 in 1974 and 21 in 1984. As of 1993, the total was down to 20. The three largest—the Norske Creditbank, Bergen Bank, and Christiania Bank og Kreditkasse—account for more than half of the total resources of the commercial banks. In 1988, a number of small savings banks and one medium-sized commercial bank, Sunnmorsbanken, became illiquid or insolvent. Most were rescued by merging with larger banks. After a slight improvement in 1989, however, banks' positions deteriorated again in 1990 following heavy losses sustained in the securities markets. As commercial property prices continued to fall, the position of the country's second and third-largest commercial banks, Christiania and Fokus, became increasingly precarious. To prevent a loss of confidence in the banking system, the government established a Government Bank Insurance Fund in March 1991. Within months this was called upon to provide capital to support the country's three largest banks, two of which—Christiania and Fokus—were by then insolvent.

By the late 1990s, increasing pressure fell upon Norway to shed its nationalistic protection of its banking industry and allow for foreign investment, particularly from its Nordic neighbors. Throughout the fall of 1998 and into 1999, attention centered on the fate of Christiania as two attempted merger attempts fell through. In mid-October 1999, Christiania was seeking to merge with Merita-Nordbanken in order to avert a hostile takeover by either Swedish Svenska Handelbanken or Danish Den Norske Bank.

Ten state banks and other financial institutions serve particular industries or undertakings, including agriculture, fisheries, manufacturing, student loans, mortgages, and others. Although savings banks also have been merging in recent years, there were still 133 private savings banks and many credit associations in 1993.

A law of 1961 contains measures to implement the principle that banking policies are to be based on social as well as economic and financial considerations. The government appoints 25% of the representatives on the board of every commercial bank with funds of over Kr100 million. Guidelines for these banks are worked out cooperatively with public authorities.

The International Monetary Fund reports that in 2001, currency and demand deposits—an aggregate commonly known as M1—were equal to $73.4 billion. In that same year, M2—an aggregate equal to M1 plus savings deposits, small time deposits, and money market mutual funds—was $87.6 billion. The discount rate, the interest rate at which the central bank lends to financial institutions in the short term, was 8.5%.

The stock exchanges of Norway are at Oslo (the oldest, founded 1818), Trondheim, Bergen, Kristiansund, Drammen, Stavanger, Ålesund, Haugesund, and Fredrikstad. Amid the increasing consolidation among European stock exchanges in the late 1990s, calls increased for the Norwegian markets to merge. As of 2004, there were 148 companies listed on the Oslo exchange, which had a market capitalization of $141.430 billion. In 2004, the Oslo exchange rose 31.3% from the previous year to 821.6.

³⁴INSURANCE

Norwegian insurance can be undertaken only by joint-stock companies of mutual assistance associations. Foreign life insurance companies have practically ceased to operate in Norway. Life insurance policies and those for pension schemes are exempt from income tax and cannot be written by firms doing other insurance work.

The crown in 1767 initiated compulsory fire insurance in towns and this fund still exists. Workers' compensation, third-party auto liability, pharmaceutical product liability, and aircraft liability are all compulsory insurances as well.

For marine insurance, stock companies now are more important than mutual associations. While a number of foreign insurance underwriters transact business in Norway, there is considerable direct insurance of Norwegian vessels abroad, especially in London. Most other insurance, such as automobile and burglary, is underwritten by Norwegian concerns. The insurance regulatory authority is the Banking, Insurance, and Securities Commission (BISC). The insurance sector is highly regulated, deeply influenced by the failure of a nonlife insurance company, Dovre, which spurred the Insurance Activities Act of 1988, which became effective in April 1989. The Insurance Activities Act of 1988 allows the BISC to control premium rates, monitor the financial position of insurance companies, and the risks that the insurance company writes. The BISC has wide powers of intervention. Com-

panies may engage in insurance business after special permission has been granted and a license is obtained from the government. Recent liberalization throughout Europe promises to change radically the structure of the Norwegian insurance industry as foreign firms tap into the market. Direct insurance premiums written in 2003 totaled US$11.532 billion, of which US$5.501 billion of the total was nonlife insurance premiums, and US$6.031 billion was life insurance. In 2003, Norway's top nonlife insurer was If Skadeforsikring, which had gross written nonlife premiums of US$1,436.6 million. In 2004, the country's leading life insurer was Vital, with gross written life insurance premiums of $2,344.6 million.

³⁵PUBLIC FINANCE

Norway's fiscal year coincides with the calendar year. As one of the per capita richest countries in the world, Norway has a great deal of money to spend on investment, focusing especially on the offshore oil sector. The government maintains a Petroleum Fund that reached $67 billion at the end of 2001. The Fund will be used to finance government programs once oil and gas resources are depleted.

The US Central Intelligence Agency (CIA) estimated that in 2005 Norway's central government took in revenues of approximately $176.1 billion and had expenditures of $131.3 billion. Revenues minus expenditures totaled approximately $44.8 billion. Public debt in 2005 amounted to 36% of GDP. Total external debt was $281 billion.

The International Monetary Fund (IMF) reported that in 2003, the most recent year for which it had data, central government revenues were Kr746.8 billion and expenditures were Kr605.3 billion. The value of revenues was US$105 million and expenditures US$85 million, based on an exchange rate for 2003 of US$1 = Kr7.0802 as reported by the IMF. Government outlays by function were as follows: general public services, 17.5%; defense, 5.0%; public order and safety, 2.6%; economic affairs, 10.1%; environmental protection, 0.3%; housing and community amenities, 0.2%; health,

Public Finance – Norway (2003)		
(In billions of kroner, central government figures)		
Revenue and Grants	**746.8**	**100.0%**
Tax revenue	429.56	57.5%
Social contributions	155.27	20.8%
Grants	2.07	0.3%
Other revenue	159.9	21.4%
Expenditures	**605.3**	**100.0%**
General public services	105.64	17.5%
Defense	30.55	5.0%
Public order and safety	15.8	2.6%
Economic affairs	61.43	10.1%
Environmental protection	2.06	0.3%
Housing and community amenities	0.94	0.2%
Health	96.27	15.9%
Recreational, culture, and religion	7.11	1.2%
Education	39.13	6.5%
Social protection	246.39	40.7%

(...) data not available or not significant.

SOURCE: *Government Finance Statistics Yearbook 2004*, Washington, DC: International Monetary Fund, 2004.

15.9%; recreation, culture, and religion, 1.2%; education, 6.5%; and social protection, 40.7%.

36TAXATION

Both the central government and the municipal governments levy income and capital taxes. There is also a premium payable to the National Insurance Scheme. For individual taxpayers, income taxes and premiums adhere to the pay-as-you-earn system.

Taxes on corporations are paid in the year following the income year. As of 2004, corporate income taxes are levied at a flat rate of 28% of aggregate income. Companies involved in oil or gas pay a special oil tax of 50% in addition to the standard 28%. All income from capital is taxable at 28%. Although dividends received by resident shareholders from Norwegian countries are taxed at the corporate rate, a credit for the tax already paid by the distributing company on income effectively negates the tax. Dividends paid to nonresident shareholders are taxed at 25%. Interest and royalty income are not subject to a withholding tax.

Personal income taxes are levied at progressive tax rates that have a top rate of 55.3%. However, that rate is made up of: a combined 28% rate for national and municipal taxes; a national gross income tax of rate of 19.5%; and the employee's social security contribution of 7.8% (3% for pensioners, and 10.7% for the self-employed). A number of additional deductions from taxable income are available including allowance for some travel expenses, insurance payments, mortgage interest payments, living allowances, and deductions for contributions to capital investments. A withholding tax on wages can be credited against income taxes. There is also a municipal wealth tax, ranging from 0–1.1% and a land tax with rates from 0.2–0.7%. Gifts and inheritances are taxed according to progressive schedules with a maximum rate of 30%.

The main indirect tax is Norway's value-added tax (VAT), with a standard rate that has increased from 20% in 1999 to 24% in 2004. A reduced rate of 12% is applied to basic foodstuffs, and there is an extensive list of VAT-exempt goods and services, including health and social services, education, passenger transport, hotel accommodations, travel agents, government supplies, etc. Stamp duties are charged at a rate of 2.5%.

37CUSTOMS AND DUTIES

Heavily dependent on foreign trade, Norway has traditionally supported abolition of trade barriers. During the 1950s, direct control of imports was gradually abolished. Tariff rates on industrial raw materials and most manufactured goods are low. Duties on finished textile products are levied at 15–25%.

A signatory of GATT and a member of EFTA, Norway has bilateral trade agreements with many countries in every part of the world. In 1973, Norway signed a Special Relations Agreement with the European Community (now the European Union), whereby both sides abolished all tariffs on industrial goods over the 1973–77 period. Other trade goods receiving gradual tariff reductions were fish, agricultural products, and wine.

Although Norwegian voters rejected EU membership in a 1994 referendum, Norway, as a member of the European Economic Area (EEA) maintains a free trade agreement with the European Union.

38FOREIGN INVESTMENT

Norway welcomes foreign investment as a matter of policy and in general grants national treatment to foreign investors. Investment is encouraged particularly in the key offshore petroleum sector, mainland industry (including high-technology and other advanced areas), and in less developed regions such as northern Norway. Corporate taxation is levied at a flat rate of 28%, low by European standards.

Foreign capital has traditionally been largely centered in Norway's electrochemical and electrometallurgical industries, the primary iron and metal industry, and mining. The discovery of oil and natural gas in the North Sea area spurred foreign investments. The Ekofisk oil field was discovered in 1969 by an American Phillips Petroleum Co. consortium, including Petrofina of Belgium, ENI of Italy, and Norway's Petronord. A joint Norwegian-Phillips group company, Norpiepe, was formed in 1973 to construct the pipelines and to operate them for 30 years. Another US company, McDermott International, was awarded a $150-million contract in 1982 to lay pipe from the Statfjord gas field in the North Sea to the Norwegian mainland. In 1995, 11 international oil and gas companies announced plans for a $1.2–$1.35 billion gas pipeline from Norway's North Sea production area to the European continent. That same year, Fokus, Norway's third-largest commercial bank, fell under foreign control as foreign investors captured more than half the shares for sale in the bank's privatization.

Foreign direct investment (FDI) stock in Norway totaled about $21.4 billion in 1997. FDI inflow was nearly $3 billion in 1997 and more than $3.3 billion in 1998. Annual FDI inflow peaked in 1999 and 2000, at $6.7 billion and $6.3 billion, respectively, but in the global economic slowdown of 2001 fell to $2.8 billion. In 2002, FDI inflows increased to $3.4 billion. In terms of its attractiveness for foreign investment, Norway was ranked fourth in the world on UNCTAD's list of 140 countries for the period 1998 to 2000, up from fifth place for 1988 to 1990. Total FDI stock in Norway as of 2001 was $40.2 billion, equivalent to 18.7% of GDP. Norway's share in world FDI flows has been approximately equal to its share of world GDP.

Outward FDI flows from Norway averaged $5.3 billion for the four years 1999 to 2002. More than 2,000 enterprises have foreign investors holding at least 20% of the capital. Total outward FDI stock held by Norwegians totaled $40.7 billion as of 2001.

In 2003, FDI comprised 20.4% of GDP; total FDI stock in Norway was Kr327.1 billion ($46.2 billion). Leading investors were (in order) Sweden, the Netherlands, Denmark, the United States, and the United Kingdom. Most of Norway's investment abroad goes to (in order) the United States, the United Kingdom, Sweden, Denmark, the Netherlands, and Germany.

39ECONOMIC DEVELOPMENT

The government holds shares in a number of large enterprises: a minority of shares in most industrial establishments and all or controlling shares in some armaments factories, as well as in chemical and electrometallurgical companies, power stations, and mines. The government also participates in joint industrial undertakings with private capital, in enterprises too large or risky for private capital, and in establishments with shares formerly held by German interests. Government policy also aims at attracting foreign investment.

Rapid industrial development and exploitation of resources are major governmental goals, with special emphasis on northern Norway, where development has lagged behind that of the southern areas. The Development Fund for North Norway, established in 1952, together with a policy of tax concessions, resulted in progress there at a rate more rapid than that of the rest of the country. The exploitation of offshore oil and natural gas reserves has had a profound effect on Norway's economy. Increased oil revenues have expanded both domestic consumption and investment. The government has used oil revenues to ease taxes and increase public investment in regional development, environmental protection, social welfare, education, and communications. Although the expansion of innovative oil development projects continues (one of which was the $4.2 billion Heidrun oil project), Norway is looking to produce more natural gas than oil. The $5 billion Troll gas field was one such project.

A tax law permits industry and commerce to build up tax-free reserves for future investment, foreign sales promotion, and research. Designed to provide a flexible tool for influencing cyclical developments, the law's intent is to help ensure that total demand at any given time is sufficient to create full employment and strong economic growth. In the late 1970s, the government introduced combined price and wage agreements in an effort to restrain inflation and ensure real increases in buying power for consumers.

To stimulate industry, incentives are available for undertakings in the north as well as in other economically weak regions; companies may set aside up to 25% of taxable income for tax-free investment. Tariff incentives are available for essential imports. A Regional Development Fund grants low-interest, long-term loans to firms to strengthen the economy of low-income, high-unemployment areas anywhere in the country.

In 1991, the government introduced a three-year program to improve infrastructure and reduce unemployment. This plan was to spend nearly Kr10 billion, primarily for road and rail communications, with the money coming from budget cuts in other areas.

Although Norwegians rejected EU membership in a 1994 referendum, Norway's economy is largely integrated with that of the EU. Norway has a free trade agreement with the EU; its currency is generally kept on par with the euro. Yet despite these elements of association, Norway retains extensive control over its own economic development policies.

Norway has been active in aiding developing nations under the Norwegian Agency for International Development (Norad). The leading recipients have been Tanzania, Mozambique, Zambia, Bangladesh, Nicaragua, and Ethiopia. Norway is one of five countries meeting the UN international aid target for donor countries (0.7% of national income); Norway gave 0.87% of gross domestic product (GDP) in 2004, more than any other country, ahead of Luxemburg, Denmark, Sweden, and the Netherlands.

The country's Petroleum Fund reached $190 billion in 2005; the fund will be used to finance government programs once Norway's oil and gas resources run out. As of 2005, unemployment was low, wages were high, and the UN ranked Norway as the most desirable country in which to live. Non-oil business was also booming in 2005; a survey of some 114,000 non-oil companies showed an average 43.9% increase in profits. However, high taxes and a welfare system burdened by an aging population remain challenges for continued economic prosperity.

40 SOCIAL DEVELOPMENT

Norway has been a pioneer in the field of social welfare and is often called a welfare state. Accident insurance for factory workers was introduced in 1894, unemployment insurance in 1906, compulsory health insurance in 1909, and accident insurance for fishermen in 1908 and for seamen in 1911. In the 1930s, further social welfare schemes were introduced: an old-age pension scheme; aid for the blind and crippled; and unemployment insurance for all workers except fishermen, whalers, sealers, civil servants, domestic servants, self-employed persons, salesmen, and agents. In the postwar period, health insurance became compulsory for all employees and available to self-employed persons; coverage includes dependents, with medical treatment including hospital and other benefits. Sickness benefits, family allowances during hospitalization, and grants for funeral expenses are paid. Costs of this scheme are met by deductions from wages and contributions by employers and by state and local authorities. Public assistance, available in Norway since 1845, supplements the foregoing programs. Social welfare has long included maternity benefits with free prenatal clinics.

The National Insurance Act, which came into effect in 1967, provides old-age pensions, rehabilitation allowances, disability pensions, widow and widower pensions, and survivor benefits to children. Membership is obligatory for all residents of Norway, including noncitizens, and for Norwegian foreign-service employees. Pensions begin at the age of 67. As of 2004, the system of varying rates for employers was reformed to eliminate intermediate levels. The source of funds is divided between employees, employers, and the government funds any deficit.

Workers' compensation covers both accidents and occupational diseases. Compensation is paid to a widow until she remarries, and to children up to the age of 18 (or for life if they are unemployable). Dependent parents and grandparents also are eligible for life annuities. Family allowance coverage, in force since 1946, is provided for children under the age of 16.

The law mandates equal wages for equal work by men and women, although economic discrimination persists. An Equal Rights Ombudsman addresses complaints of sexual discrimination. A provision protecting against sexual harassment is outlined in the Working Environment Act. A resolution mandating that 40% of publicly held companies be directed by women by 2005, and noncompliance will result in removal from the stock exchange in 2007. Violence against women persisted but is seriously investigated and prosecuted by authorities. Victim's assistance programs and battered women's shelters are available.

Human rights are fully respected and protected in Norway. Provisions exist to protect the rights and cultural heritage of minority peoples. The Sami (Lapps) located in the northeast are entitled to schooling in their local language, and also receive radio and television broadcast subtitled in Sami. The Sami also have a constituent assembly that acts as a consultative body on issues that affect them.

41 HEALTH

Since 1971, there has been a tax-based National Insurance Scheme. The public health service and the hospitals are the responsibility of the government at the central, county, and municipal levels. There are very few private hospitals in Norway. Hospital care is free of charge, but a minor sum is charged for medicine and primary health care. As of 1984, there has been a ceiling on the total amount one must pay for medical services. There is a three-part system made up of regional hospitals serving parts of the country, central hospitals serving the various counties, and local hospitals, also run by the counties. The country is in need of more nursing homes for the elderly. Most general hospitals are public; others are owned by the Norwegian Red Cross or other health or religious organizations. As of 2004, there were an estimated 356 physicians per 100,000 people. In addition, Norway had the second most nurses per capita at an estimated 2,065 per 100,000 population, and the most dentists at 125 per 100,000 people. Total health care expenditure was estimated at 9.2% of GDP.

On the local level, health councils are responsible for public health services, including tuberculosis control and school health services, and for environmental sanitation. Only in densely populated areas are public health officers appointed on a full-time basis; otherwise they engage in private practice as well. In some areas, they are the only physicians available.

Infant mortality has been appreciably reduced and in 2005 stood at 3.70 per 1,000 live births, one of the lowest rates in the world. As of 2002, the crude birth rate and overall mortality rate were estimated at, respectively, 12.4 and 9.8 per 1,000 people. About 71% of married women (ages 15 to 49) use contraception. Low birth weight was seen in 5% of all births. The maternal mortality rate was only 6 per 100,000 live births. Average life expectancy, among the highest in the world, was 79.40 years in 2005. The HIV/AIDS prevalence was 0.10 per 100 adults in 2003. As of 2004, there were approximately 2,100 people living with HIV/AIDS in the country. There were an estimated 100 deaths from AIDS in 2003.

Children up to one year of age were vaccinated against diphtheria, pertussis, and tetanus, 92%; polio, 92%; and measles, 93%. Tuberculosis tests are given on a regular basis from infancy onward. Children go through a comprehensive vaccination program and also receive psychotherapy and dental care throughout their nine years of basic school.

The heart disease mortality rates were higher than the average for high human development countries. In the mid-1990s the likelihood of dying after age 65 of heart disease was 340 per 1,000 people for men and 374 per 1,000 for women.

42 HOUSING

Before World War II, responsibility for housing rested mainly with the municipalities, but the state has since assumed the major burden. Loans and subsidies keep rents under a certain percentage of a family's income. Cooperative housing has made great progress in such densely populated areas as Oslo, where the Oslo Housing and Savings Society pioneered the practice for Norway. With housing problems compounded by wartime destruction and postwar increases in marriages and in the birthrate, Norway built more dwellings per 1,000 inhabitants than any other European country, completing between 31,000 and 42,000 units annually from 1967 through 1981.

Home construction financing has come principally from two state loan organizations, the Norwegian Smallholdings and Housing Bank and the Norwegian State Housing Bank, but one-fourth of the nation's housing is still privately financed.

As of 2001, Norway had 1,961,548 dwelling units; 57% of them were detached houses. About 29% of the housing stock was built 1981–2001. About 19.5% of the housing stock was built in 1945 or earlier. About 77% of all dwellings were owner occupied. In 2002, at least 22,980 new dwellings were under construction and in 2003 about 22,677 units were started. According to estimates for 2004, about 52% of all households lived in single-family detached homes and 82% of all households were owner occupied. The rate of overcrowding (defined as having fewer rooms in the dwelling than the number of people in the household) was only at about 6%.

43 EDUCATION

Elementary school education has been compulsory since the middle of the 18th century. As of 1997, education is compulsory for 10 years of study, with students entering school in the year that they reach the age of six. Primary school covers seven years of study, followed by three years of lower secondary school. At this stage, students may choose to continue in a three-year general secondary school (gymnasium), which prepares students for the university. Since 1976, the upper secondary school system has also included vocational schools of various types, operated by the state, by local authorities, and by the industrial sector. A three-year trade apprenticeship program is also available for some secondary students.

Local authorities generally provide school buildings and equipment and the central government contributes funds towards teachers' salaries and covers a considerable proportion of the cost of running the schools. Although there are private schools, government authorities bear a major share of the financial responsibility for these through a system of grants.

In 2001, about 80% of children between the ages of three and five were enrolled in some type of preschool program. Primary school enrollment in 2003 was estimated at about 100% of age-eligible students. The same year, secondary school enrollment was about 96% of age-eligible students. It is estimated that about nearly all students complete their primary education. The student-to-teacher ratio for primary school was at about 10:1 in 2003; the ratio for secondary school was about 9:1.

Norway's institutions of higher education include 130 colleges and four universities. The four major universities include the University of Oslo (founded in 1811), the University of Bergen (1948), the University of Trondheim (1969), and the University of Tromsø (1969). Representing fields not covered by the universities, there are also specialized institutions, such as the Agricultural University of Norway (near Oslo); the Norwegian School of Economics and Business Administration (Bergen); and the Norwegian College of Veterinary Medicine (Oslo). Universities and colleges in Norway serve a dual function—both learning and research. At the four universities, degrees are granted at three levels: Lower degree (a four-year study program); higher degree (five to seven-year course of study); and doctorate degree. There are also courses lasting from five to seven years in law, medicine, agriculture, or engineering.

With a goal of placing adults on an equal standing with the educated youth and giving them access to knowledge and job skills, a program of adult education was introduced in August 1977. An official administrative body for adult education exists in all municipalities and counties. However, the Ministry of Education and Research has the highest administrative responsibility for adult education. Folk high schools are associated with a long Scandinavian tradition of public enlightenment. There are more than 80 folk schools in Norway geared toward providing personal growth and development rather than academic achievement. In 2003, about 81% of the tertiary age population were enrolled in some type of higher education program; 64% for men and 99% for women. The adult literacy rate has been estimated at about 99%.

As of 2003, public expenditure on education was estimated at 7.6% of GDP, or 16.2% of total government expenditures.

44 LIBRARIES AND MUSEUMS

The National Library of Norway in Oslo has over two million volumes in its central library. Since 1882, copies of all Norwegian publications have had to be deposited in the national library; since 1939, copies have been deposited at Bergen and Trondheim as well. Bergen University Library has over one million volumes, largely devoted to the natural sciences. Oslo University Library (founded in 1811), has the largest academic library system in the country, with four libraries and a central administrative unit. A special collection at the Oslo University Library includes the world's largest collection of materials on the life and works of Henrik Ibsen as part of the Centre for Ibsen Studies. The library of the Scientific Society in Trondheim, founded in 1760, is the country's oldest research library and has over one million volumes, including 330,000 pictures and UNESCO and GATT (General Agreement on Tariffs and Trade) documents. The Tromsø Museum Library has been organized to make it the research library for the north. There are technical and specialized libraries at many research institutes and higher educational centers. State archives are kept in Oslo, and there are record offices for provincial archives at Oslo, Kristiansund, Stavanger, Bergen, Hamar, Trondheim, and Tromsø.

The first municipal libraries were founded in the late 18th century. By law every municipality and every school must maintain a library; each such library receives financial support from state and municipality. Regional libraries also have been created. A special library service is provided for ships in the merchant navy, and a floating library service provides books to fishermen-farmers living in the sparsely populated regions.

There are natural history museums in Oslo, Stavanger, Bergen, Trondheim, and Tromsø. Oslo, Lillehammer, and Bergen have notable art collections. A traveling "national gallery" was established in 1952. The most important museums in Norway are those dealing with antiquities and folklore, such as the Norwegian Folk Museum in Oslo. Oslo has a unique collection of ships from the Viking period. Open-air museums in Oslo and elsewhere show old farm and other buildings, as well as objects of Norwegian historical and cultural interest. Also in Oslo are the International Museum of Children's Art; the Munch Museum, displaying the works of Edvard Munch, Norway's most famous artist; Norway's Resistance Museum, detailing the country's occupation during World War II;

and the Viking Ship Museum. Among Norway's newer museums are the Astrup Fearnley Fine Arts Museum (1993), which features modern art; the National Museum of Contemporary Art (1990); and the Stenerson Museum (1994), which exhibits paintings from the 19th and 20th centuries. All three museums are in Oslo. There are at least three museums in the country that are dedicated to Henrik Ibsen.

45 MEDIA

Most of the telecommunications network is operated by the government-owned Televerket. The state owns all telephone facilities. In 2003, there were an estimated 713 mainline telephones for every 1,000 people. The same year, there were approximately 909 mobile phones in use for every 1,000 people.

The first private broadcasting stations launched in 1981. The public Norwegian Broadcasting Corp. continues to operate two television channels and three national radio stations, as well as a number of local radio stations. As of 1998 Norway had 5 AM and at least 650 FM radio broadcasting stations. Educational broadcasts supplement school facilities in remote districts. Radio license fees have not been required since 1977. Television programming on an experimental basis was initiated in 1958 and full-scale television transmission began in July 1960. In 2003, there were an estimated 3,324 radios and 884 television sets for every 1,000 people. About 184.5 of every 1,000 people were cables subscribers. Also in 2003, there were 528.3 personal computers for every 1,000 people and 346 of every 1,000 people had access to the Internet. There were 1,130 secure Internet servers in the country in 2004.

The Norwegian press is characterized by a large number of small newspapers. Five regional dailies account for about 20% of the total press circulation in the country. *Verdens Gang* and *Dagbladet*, both national tabloids, account for another 20% of circulation totals. The largest dailies (with their affiliations and circulations in 2004 unless noted) are: *Verdens Gang* (independent, 365,000), *Aftenposten*, (independent, 398,000), *Dagbladet* (liberal, 183,000), *Daens Naeringsliv* (60,027 in 2002), and *Arbeiderbladet* (Labor Party, 51,790 in 2002). Major regional papers include: *De Fire Neste* (Drammen, 442,000 circulation in 2002), *Hedmark* (Hamar, 91,100 in 2002), *Bergens Tidende* (in Bergen, independent, 89,000 in 2004), *Adresseavisen* (Trondheim, conservative, 85,000 in 2004), *Stavanger Aftenblad* (Stavanger, independent, 69,000 in 2004), *Faedrelandsvennen* (Kristiansund, independent, 46,960 in 2002), *Akershus* (Lillestrom, 42,100 in 2002), *Haugesunds Avis* (Hauguesund, 38,490 in 2002), and *Sunnmorsposten* (Ålesund, independent, 37,900 in 2002).

The constitution provides for freedom of speech and of the press and the government generally respects these rights.

46 ORGANIZATIONS

Cooperative societies are numerous and important in Norway. About 2,500 agricultural cooperatives are active; these include purchasing, processing, and marketing organizations. Some 528 retail cooperatives are affiliated with the Norwegian Cooperative Union and Wholesale Society.

Doctors are organized in the Norwegian Medical Association and in local associations. Farming organizations and agricultural cooperatives are represented in the Federation of Agriculture. There are associations of small and large forest owners, fur breeders, and employers' organizations in most sectors of industry, as well as a central Norwegian Employers' Confederation.

The Norwegian Academy of Science and Letters, the Royal Norwegian Society of Science and Letters, the Norwegian Academy of Technological Sciences, and the Society for the Advancement of Science are leading learned society. Other learned and professional organizations include the Nobel Committee of the Storting, which awards the Nobel Peace Prize; the Norwegian Research Council for Science and the Humanities; and various legal, scientific, economic, literary, historical, musical, artistic, and research societies.

National youth organizations include the Norwegian Student Union, Christian Democratic Party Youth, En Verden Youth, European Democratic Students, European Good Templar Youth Federation, Federation of Young Conservatives, Norwegian Union of Social Democratic Youth, Norwegian YWCA/YMCA, and the Norwegian Guides and Scouts Association. There are numerous sports associations and clubs.

Health and relief organizations include the Norwegian Red Cross, the Norwegian Women's Health Organization, and societies to combat a variety of conditions and diseases. Volunteer service organizations, such as the Lions Clubs International, are also present. International organizations with national chapters include Amnesty International and CARE Norge.

47 TOURISM, TRAVEL, AND RECREATION

Norway's main tourist attractions are the cities of Oslo, Bergen, and Trondheim, which are connected by road, rail, and daily flights; the marvelous scenery of the fjord country in the west; and the arctic coast with the North Cape and "midnight sun." In 2005, UNESCO named two Norwegian fjords, the Geirangerfjord and the Naeroyfjord to its World Heritage List.

A favorite method of tourist travel is by coastal steamer, sailing from Bergen northward to Kirkenes, near the Soviet frontier. Many cruise ships ply the Norwegian fjords and coastal towns as far north as Spitsbergen. Notable outdoor recreational facilities include the Oslomarka, a 100,000 hectare (247,000 acre) area located near Oslo, with ski trails and walking paths. To compensate for the shortness of winter days, several trails are illuminated for evening skiing. Other popular sports include ice skating, freshwater fishing, mountaineering, hunting (grouse, reindeer, and elk), and football (soccer). In 1994, Norway hosted the XVII Olympic Winter Games in Lillehammer, and the women's soccer team won the World Cup in 1995.

There are major theaters in Oslo and Bergen, as well as six regional theaters; Den Norske Opera in Oslo; and four symphony orchestras. International musical events include the Bergen Festival, held annually in late May or early June; and several jazz festivals in July.

No passport is required of visitors from the Nordic area, but travelers arriving in Norway directly from non-Nordic countries are subject to passport control. A visa is not required for visits of up to 90 days.

Tourist expenditure receipts totaled $3 billion when 3,146,000 tourists visited Norway in 2003. There were 67,114 hotel rooms with 143,798 beds and an occupancy rate of 35%.

In 2005, the US Department of State estimated the daily cost of staying in Oslo at $308, and Stavanger, $304.

48 FAMOUS NORWEGIANS

Ludvig Holberg (1684–1745), the father of Danish and Norwegian literature, was a leading dramatist whose comedies are still performed. Henrik Wergeland (1808–45), Norway's greatest poet, was also a patriot and social reformer; his sister Camilla Collett (1813–95), author of the first Norwegian realistic novel, was a pioneer in the movement for women's rights. Henrik Ibsen (1827–1906), founder of modern dramas, placed Norway in the forefront of world literature. Bjørnstjerne Bjørnson (1832–1910), poet, playwright, and novelist, received the Nobel Prize for literature in 1903. Other noted novelists are Jonas Lie (1833–1908); Alexander Kielland (1849–1906); Knut Hamsun (1859–1952), Nobel Prize winner in 1920; Sigrid Undset (1882–1949), awarded the Nobel Prize in 1928; and Johan Bojer (1872–1959).

Ole Bull (1810–80) was a world-famous violinist. Edvard Grieg (1843–1907) was the first Norwegian composer to win broad popularity. His leading contemporaries and successors were Johan Svendsen (1840–1911), Christian Sinding (1856–1941), Johan Halvorsen (1864–1935), and Fartein Valen (1887–1953). Kirsten Flagstad (1895–1962), world-renowned soprano, served for a time as director of the Norwegian State Opera. In painting, Harriet Backer (1845–1932), Christian Krohg (1852–1925), and Erik Werenskiold (1855–1938) were outstanding in the traditional manner; leading the way to newer styles was Edvard Munch (1863–1944), an outstanding expressionist, as well as Axel Revold (1887–1962) and Per Krohg (1889–1965). Norway's foremost sculptor is Gustav Vigeland (1869–1943); the Frogner Park in Oslo is the site of a vast collection of his work in bronze and granite.

Outstanding scientists are Christopher Hansteen (1784–1873), famous for his work in terrestrial magnetism; Niels Henrik Abel (1802–29), noted for his work on the theory of equations; Armauer (Gerhard Henrik) Hansen (1841–1912), discoverer of the leprosy bacillus; Vilhelm Bjerknes (1862–1951), who advanced the science of meteorology; Fridtjof Nansen (1861–1930), an oceanographer and Arctic explorer who won the Nobel Peace Prize in 1922 for organizing famine relief in Russia; Otto Sverdrup (1854–1930), Roald Amundsen (1872–1928), and Bernt Balchen (1899–1973), polar explorers; Johan Hjort (1869–1948), a specialist in deep-sea fishery research; Regnar Frisch (1895–1978), who shared the first Nobel Prize in Economic Science in 1969 for developing econometrics; Odd Hassel (1897–1981), co-winner of the 1969 Nobel Prize in chemistry for his studies of molecular structure; and Thor Heyerdahl (1914–2002), explorer and anthropologist.

The first secretary-general of the UN was a Norwegian, Trygve (Halvdan) Lie (1896–1968), who served from 1946 to 1953. The historian Christian Louis Lange (1869–1938) was co-winner of the Nobel Peace Prize in 1921.

Sonja Henie (1913–69) was the leading woman figure skater of her time, and Liv Ullmann (b.1939) is an internationally known actress. Linn Ullmann (b.1966), daughter of Liv Ullman and Ingmar Bergman, is a respected novelist and journalist. Grete Waitz (b.1953) is a champion long-distance runner.

49 DEPENDENCIES

Svalbard

The Svalbard group includes all the islands between 10° and 35° E and 74° and 81° N: the archipelago of Spitsbergen, White Island

(Kvitøya), King Charles' Land (Kong Karls Land), Hope Island, and Bear Island (Bjørnøya), which have a combined area of about 62,700 sq km (24,200 sq mi). The largest islands are Spitsbergen, about 39,400 sq km (15,200 sq mi); North-East Land (Nordaust-landet), 14,530 sq km (5,610 sq mi); Edge Island (Edgeøya), 5,030 sq km (1,940 sq mi); and Barents Island (Barentsøya), 1,330 sq km (510 sq mi). Svalbard's population totaled 2,868 in 2002, down fromm 3,181 at the end of 1991. The population is 55.4% Norwegian and 44.3% Russian and Ukrainian.

Discovered by Norwegians in the 12th century and rediscovered in 1596 by the Dutch navigator Willem Barents, Svalbard served in the 17th and 18th centuries as a base for British, Dutch, Danish, Norwegian, German, and other whalers, but no permanent sovereignty was established. Russian and Norwegian trappers wintered there, and coal mining started early in the 20th century. Norway's sovereignty was recognized by the League of Nations in 1920, and the territory was taken over officially by Norway in 1925. Much of the high land is ice-covered; glaciers descend to the sea, where they calve to produce icebergs. The west and south coasts have many fjords, while the western coastal lowland is up to 10 km (6 mi) broad.

The most important mineral, coal, occurs in vast deposits in Spitsbergen. The west coast is kept clear of ice for six months of the year by the relatively warm water of the North Atlantic Drift, but an air temperature as low as -62°C (-80°F) has been recorded. In this region there are 112 days without the sun's appearance above the horizon.

The chief official, a governor, lives at Longyearbyen; his administration is controlled by the Ministry of Industry. Coal mining is the main industry, with Norwegian-worked mines at Longyearbyen, Sveagruva, and Ny Ålesund and Russian worked mines at Barentsburg, Grumantbyen, and elsewhere. Russia has extraterritorial rights in the areas where they mine. Cod fishing takes place around Bear Island, but whaling has virtually ceased. Norwegian sealers hunt seals, polar bears, and walrus in the summer. For centuries, trappers wintered in Spitsbergen to catch fox and bear while the pelts were in the best condition, but few trappers have wintered there in recent years.

Communications are maintained during the summer months by ships from Tromsø carrying goods and passengers, while colliers put in frequently at the mine piers. There are no roads and no local ship services.

Jan Mayen

Located in the Norwegian Sea at 70°30′ N and 8°30′ W, 893 km (555 mi) from Tromsø, the island of Jan Mayen has an area of about 380 sq km (150 sq mi). The island is dominated by the volcano Beerenberg, 2,277 m (7,470 ft) high, which is responsible for its existence; a major eruption occurred in September 1970. Jan Mayen was discovered by Henry Hudson in 1607 and was visited in 1614 by the Dutch navigator Jay Mayen, who used it subsequently as a whaling base. In 1929, the island was placed under Norwegian sovereignty. It is the site of a meteorological station and an airfield.

Bouvet Island

Bouvet Island (Bouvetøya), situated at 54°26′ S and 3°24′ E in the South Atlantic Ocean, was discovered in 1739, and in 1928 was placed under Norwegian sovereignty. An uninhabited volcanic island of 59 sq km (23 sq mi), Bouvet is almost entirely covered by ice and is difficult to approach.

Peter I Island

Peter I Island (Peter I Øy), an uninhabited Antarctic island of volcanic origin, is located at 68°48′ S and 90°35′ W. It has an area of 249 sq km (96 sq mi), rises to over 1,233 m (4,045 ft), and is almost entirely ice-covered. The island was discovered in 1821 by a Russian admiral. In 1931, it was placed under Norwegian sovereignty, and by a parliamentary act of 1933 became a dependency.

Queen Maud Land

Queen Maud Land (Dronning Mauds land) consists of the sector of Antarctica between 20°W and 45°E, adjoining the Falkland Islands on the W and the Australian Antarctic Dependency on the E. It was placed under Norwegian sovereignty in 1939, and has been a Norwegian dependency since 1957. The land is basically uninhabited, except for several stations operated by Japan, South Africa, and Russia.

50 BIBLIOGRAPHY

Annesley, Claire (ed.). *A Political and Economic Dictionary of Western Europe*. Philadelphia: Routledge/Taylor and Francis, 2005.

Berdal, Mats R. *The United States, Norway and the Cold War 1954-60*. New York: St. Martin's, 1997.

Charbonneau, Claudette. *The Land and People of Norway*. New York: HarperCollins, 1992.

Houben, Marc. *International Crisis Management: The Approach of European States*. New York: Routledge, 2005.

International Smoking Statistics: A Collection of Historical Data from 30 Economically Developed Countries. New York: Oxford University Press, 2002.

Jochens, Jenny. *Women in Old Norse Society*. Ithaca, N.Y.: Cornell University Press, 1995.

Kemp, Graham and Douglas P. Fry (eds.). *Keeping the Peace: Conflict Resolution and Peaceful Societies Around the World*. New York: Routledge, 2004.

Kiel, Anne Cohen. *Continuity and Change: Aspects of Contemporary Norway*. New York: Oxford University Press, 1993.

Making a Historical Culture: Historiography in Norway. Edited by William H. Hubbard et al. Boston: Scandinavian University Press, 1995.

March, Linda Davis. *Norway: A Quick Guide to Customs and Etiquette*. Portland, Ore.: Graphic Arts Books, 2005.

Nelsen, Brent F. (ed.). *Norway and the European Community: the Political Economy of Integration*. Westport, Conn.: Praeger, 1993.

Norway: A History from the Vikings to Our Own Times. Boston: Scandinavian University Press, 1995.

POLAND

Republic of Poland
Rzeczpospolita Polska

CAPITAL: Warsaw (Warszawa)

FLAG: The national flag consists of two horizontal stripes, the upper white and the lower red.

ANTHEM: *Jeszcze Polska nie zginela (Poland Is Not Yet Lost).*

MONETARY UNIT: The zloty (z) is a paper currency of 100 groszy. There are coins of 1, 2, 5, 10, 20, and 50 groszy and 1, 2, 5, 10, 20, 50, and 100 zlotys, and notes of 10, 20, 50, 100, 200, 500, 1,000, 2,000, and 5,000 zlotys. A currency reform on 1 January 1995 replaced 10,000 old zlotys with 1 new zloty. z1 = $0.31348 (or $1 = z3.19) as of 2005.

WEIGHTS AND MEASURES: The metric system is the legal standard.

HOLIDAYS: New Year's Day, 1 January; Labor Day, 1 May; National Day, 3 May; Victory Day, 9 May; All Saints' Day, 1 November; Christmas, 25–26 December. Movable holidays are Easter Monday and Corpus Christi.

TIME: 1 PM = noon GMT.

¹LOCATION, SIZE, AND EXTENT

Situated in Eastern Europe, Poland has an area of 312,680 sq km (120,726 sq mi), extending 689 km (428 mi) E–W and 649 km (403 mi) N–S. It is bounded on the N by the Baltic Sea, on the N and E by Russia, Lithuania, Belarus, and Ukraine, on the S by Slovakia and the Czech Republic, and on the W by Germany, with a total land boundary of 2,788 km (1,794 mi) and a coastline of 491 km (305 mi). Comparatively, the area occupied by Poland is slightly smaller than the state of New Mexico.

Before World War II, Poland encompassed a territory of nearly 390,000 sq km (150,600 sq mi). On 11 July 1920, an armistice mediated by Britain in a Polish-Soviet conflict established the "Curzon line" (named for George Nathaniel Curzon, the British statesman who proposed it), conferring the former Austrian territory of Galicia to the Soviet side. However, under the Treaty of Riga (1921), all of Galicia was assigned to Poland, and a boundary well to the east of the Curzon line prevailed until World War II. At the Yalta Conference in February 1945, the Allies accepted Soviet claims to eastern Poland, with a border running approximately along the Curzon line.

On 21 April 1945, a Polish-Soviet treaty of friendship and co-operation was signed, followed by a new agreement on the Polish-Soviet border. To compensate for the loss of 46% of Poland's territory to the USSR, the Potsdam Conference of July–August 1945 placed former German territories east of the Oder (Odra) and western Neisse rivers under Polish administration, pending a final determination by a German peace treaty. On 6 August 1950, an agreement was signed between Poland and the GDR according to which both parties recognized the frontier on the Oder-Neisse line. The Federal Republic of Germany (FRG) recognized this boundary under the terms of a treaty signed with Poland on 7 December 1970 and ratified by the FRG on 23 May 1972.

Poland's capital city, Warsaw, is located in the east central part of the country.

²TOPOGRAPHY

Poland's average altitude is 173 m (568 ft); 75.4% of the land is less than 200 m (656 ft) above sea level. The highest point, Mount Rysy (2,499 m/8,199 ft), is located in the Tatra Mountains on the Slovakian border. The principal topographic regions are an undulating central lowland with a crystalline platform and warped bedrock; the Baltic highland in the north, a glaciated region with many lakes and sandy soils; and the coastland, a narrow lowland with promontories, bays, and lakes. The southern uplands are marked by rich loam and mineral deposits.

Several important navigable rivers drain into the Baltic Sea, among them the Vistula (Wisla), the Oder, the Bug, and the Warta. There are over 6,000 lakes in the northern lake region. Good harbors have been developed on the Baltic Sea.

³CLIMATE

Poland has a continental climate, conditioned especially by westerly winds. Only the southern areas are humid. Summers are cool, and winters range from moderately cold to cold. The average mean temperature is about 7°C (45°F); temperatures in Warsaw range, on average, from -6° to -1°C (21–30°F) in January and from 13° to 24°C (55–75°F) in July. Precipitation is greatest during the summer months, lasting 85 to 100 days. Annual rainfall ranges from about 50 cm (20 in) in the lowlands and 135 cm (53 in) in the mountains; the overall average is about 64 cm (25 in).

⁴FLORA AND FAUNA

Coniferous trees, especially pine, account for 70% of the forests; deciduous species include birch, beech, and elm. Lynx, wildcat, European bison, moose, wild horse (tarpan), and wild goat are among the few remaining large mammals. Birds, fish, and insects are plentiful. As of 2002, there were at least 84 species of mammals, 233 species of birds, and over 2,450 species of plants throughout the country.

5 ENVIRONMENT

Poland's environmental situation has improved since the ousting of its communist regime, which has been accompanied by decreased emphasis on heavy industry and increased government awareness of environmental issues. However, Poland has yet to recover from the overexploitation of forests during World War II and the loss of about 1.6 million hectares (4 million acres) of forestland after the war. As of the mid-1990s, 75% of Poland's forests have been damaged by airborne contaminants and acid rain. In 2000, about 29.7% of the total land area was forested.

Pollution of the air, water, and land was the most significant environmental problem facing Poland in the 1990s. Air pollution results from hazardous concentrations of airborne dust and chemicals, including carbon dioxide, nitrogen compounds, fluorine, formaldehyde, ammonia, lead, and cadmium. In 1992 Poland had the world's 12th highest level of industrial carbon dioxide emissions, which totaled 341.8 million metric tons, a per capita level of 8.9 metric tons. In 1996, the total rose to 356 million metric tons. However, some measures for reduction must be working, since in 2000, the total of carbon dioxide emissions was at 301.3 million metric tons. Industry-related pollution affects particularly the Katowice region, where dust and sulfur dioxide emissions exceed acceptable levels.

Water pollution in the Baltic Sea is 10 times higher than ocean water. Poland has 54 cu km of renewable water. Eleven percent of the annual withdrawal is used to support farming and 76% is for industrial purposes.

The nation's wildlife has also suffered from degeneration of its habitats. As of 2003, 12.4% of Poland's total land area was protected. According to a 2006 report issued by the International Union for Conservation of Nature and Natural Resources (IUCN), threatened species included 12 types of mammals, 12 species of birds, 3 species of fish, 1 type of mollusk, 14 species of other invertebrates, and 4 species of plants. The cerambyx longicorn and rosalia longicorn are among the endangered species. The wild horse has become extinct.

6 POPULATION

The population of Poland in 2005 was estimated by the United Nations (UN) at 38,163,000, which placed it at number 32 in population among the 193 nations of the world. In 2005, approximately 13% of the population was over 65 years of age, with another 17% of the population under 15 years of age. There were 94 males for every 100 females in the country. According to the UN, the annual population rate of change for 2005–10 was expected to be stagnant at 0.0%, a rate the government viewed as too low. The fertility rate, at 1.6 births per woman in 2005, has been below replacement level since the mid-1990s. The projected population for the year 2025 was 36,661,000. The population density was 118 per sq km (306 per sq mi).

The UN estimated that 62% of the population lived in urban areas in 2005, and that urban areas were growing at an annual rate of 0.18%. The capital city, Warsaw (Warszawa), had a population of 2,200,000 in that year. Other large metropolitan areas and their estimated populations were Katowice, 2,914,000; Lódz, 943,000; Gdańsk, 851,000; and Kraków (Crakow), 822,000.

7 MIGRATION

Large-scale emigration from Poland took place before World War II, with the heaviest exodus in the decades before World War I. Between 1871–1915, a total of 3,510,000 Poles, Polish Jews, and Ukrainians emigrated, about half of them to the United States. Emigration diminished greatly during the interwar period, when France became the chief country of destination. From 1921–38, some 1,400,000 Poles emigrated, while 700,000 returned. Poland suffered a net population loss of nearly 11,000,000 between 1939–49 through war losses, deportations, voluntary emigrations, and population transfers arising out of territorial changes. An estimated 6,000,000 Germans left the present western territories of Poland when these territories came under Polish jurisdiction, and since the end of World War II more than 7,500,000 Poles have settled in the area. From the 1950s through the 1980s, Germans leaving for Germany constituted the bulk of emigrants; Jews also left in substantial numbers for Israel, both in the immediate postwar years and during the 1950s and 1960s. Another emigration wave occurred after the imposition of martial law in December 1981. In 2000, the total number of migrants was 2,088,000. In 2003, total remittances to Poland were $2.8 billion. In 2005, the Polish Ministry of Labor reported that 500,000 Poles were legally employed in 15 EU countries. Amongst these, Germany was the chief destination for Polish migrant labor, 350,000 legally admitted workers, including 90% employed seasonally in agriculture.

Since 1989, Poland has been open to refugees. However, while tens of thousands of people transit Poland every year, the number of recognized refugees has been rather limited. As of 2004, there were 2,507 recognized refugees. Since 1997, there has been a significant increase in the number of asylum applicants, from some 800 in 1995 to 3,743 in 2004. The main country of origin was the Russian Federation, with smaller numbers from India and Pakistan. In that same year, 340 Poles sought asylum in Canada. In 2005, the net migration rate was -0.49 migrants per 1,000 population. The government views the migration levels as satisfactory.

8 ETHNIC GROUPS

Before World War II, over 30% of the people living within the boundaries of Poland were non-Poles. As a result of World War II, and of the boundary changes and population transfers that followed, Poland today is a predominantly homogeneous state with only about 3% of the population being non-Polish. According to the most recent census (2002), Poles constitute about 98% of the total population. Germans make up 0.4%, Ukrainians account for 0.1%; and Belarussians, 0.1%. There are about 50,000 Lithuanians in the country. There is also a significant number of Roma.

9 LANGUAGES

Polish is one of the western Slavic languages using the Latin alphabet and the only major Slavic language to preserve the old Slavic nasal vowels. It is easily distinguishable from other Slavic languages by the frequent accumulation of consonants. In addition to the letters of the English alphabet, it has the following letters and diphthongs: *a, ch, ci, cz, dź, dzi, e, l, ń, ni, ó, rz, ś, si, sz, z, ż, ź*, and *zi*. It has no *q, v,* or *x*. Among the several dialects are Great Polish (spo-

POLAND

0   50   100 Miles

0   50   100 Kilometers

LOCATION: 14°7′ to 24°8′ E; 49° to 54°50′ N. BOUNDARY LENGTHS: Baltic coastline, 491 kilometers (304 miles); Russia, 432 kilometers (268 miles); Lithuania 91 kilometers (56 miles); Belarus, 605 kilometers (378 miles); and Ukraine, 428 kilometers (265 miles); Czech Republic, 658 kilometers (408 miles); Slovakia, 444 kilometers (275 miles); Germany, 456 kilometers (286 miles). TERRITORIAL SEA LIMIT: 12 miles.

ken around Poznań), Kuyavian (around Inowroclaw), Little Polish (around Cracow), Silesian (around Katowice and Wroclaw), and Mazovian (around Warsaw and extending north and east). Some philologists consider that Kashubian, spoken along the Baltic, is not a Polish dialect but a separate language.

Many Poles speak English, French, German, or Russian, and understand other Slavic languages in varying degrees. By law, ethnic minorities have the right to be taught in their own language.

10 RELIGIONS

Poland has historically been one of the world's most strongly Roman Catholic countries. During the period of Communist domination that began in 1945, that church suffered extensive repression by the state. A change in party leadership in October 1956, however, brought about a new relationship between church and state, which included voluntary religious instruction in schools and other guarantees to the Roman Catholic Church. In 1974, the Polish government established permanent working contacts with

the Holy See. The position of the Church was further enhanced when the archbishop of Cracow, Karol Cardinal Wojtyla, became Pope John Paul II in 1978. In 1989, the Roman Catholic Church was finally granted legal status and control of its schools, hospitals, and its university in Lublin. A concordat was signed with the Vatican in 1993 and ratified by parliament in 1998.

It is estimated that over 96% of Poles are nominally Roman Catholics. About 509,700 people, about 1.3% of the population, are registered members of the Eastern Orthodox Church, 82,000 are Greek Catholics, 124,294 are Jehovah's Witnesses, and 79,050 are Lutherans (Augsburg). Other established Christian denominations include Old Catholic Mariavits, Polish-Catholics, Pentecostals, Seventh-Day Adventists, Baptists, Methodists, the Church of Christ, Reformed Lutherans, Mormons, and the New Apostolic Church. About 109 people are registered members of Muslim associations; there are, however, many more Muslims in the country who are not officially registered with a group. About 895 people are registered Hare Krishnas. A 2001 poll indicated that only 58%

of the entire population were active practitioners of their chosen faith.

On the eve of World War II, an estimated 3,351,000 Jews lived in Poland, more than in any other country; they constituted about 10% of the Polish population and nearly 20% of world Jewry. During the course of the Nazi occupation (1939–45), nearly 3,000,000 Polish Jews were killed, many of them in extermination camps such as Auschwitz (Oświecim), near Cracow. Most of the survivors had fled to the USSR; at the end of the war, only about 55,000 Jews remained in Poland. Repatriation raised the total Jewish population to 250,000 in 1946. However, the establishment of the State of Israel in 1948, combined with a series of anti-Semitic outbreaks in Poland (including a government-led campaign in 1968–69), induced most Jews to emigrate. As of 2003, Poland had only about 20,000–30,000 Jews living in the country.

¹¹TRANSPORTATION

In 2004, Poland's operational rail network totaled 23,852 km (14,835 mi) of broad and standard gauge rail lines, of which 11,962 km (7,440 mi) were electrified. Of all lines in use, standard gauge accounts for nearly all at 23,223 km (14,445 mi). In terms of line length the Polish State Railways (PKP) is the third-largest railway system in Europe. However, equipment and service is far behind EU countries. In 2000 PKP began privatization of passenger, cargo and infrastructure.

There is a dense road and highway network. Improvement and repair have not kept up with the increased usage—an 80% increase in freight and a 1,800% increase in passenger transport between 1950 and 1970, and a 60% increase in freight traffic and a 70% increase in passenger transport during 1971-82. In 2001 out of a total of 364,697 km (226,842 mi) of roadways, 249,088 km (154,932 mi) were paved roads, including 399 km (248 mi) of expressways. In 2003, there were 11,243,800 passenger cars and 2,274,600 commercial vehicles.

As of 2005, Poland had seven merchant ships of 1,000 GRT or more, totaling 154,710 GRT. Before World War II, Polish merchant marine operations were mainly with the Western countries, especially the United States, but much of the current traffic is with Asian and African countries. The major ports are Szczecin, Gdynia, Gdánsk, and Swinoujáscie. The ports were badly damaged during World War II but have since been rehabilitated and enlarged. As of 2003, there were 3,812 km (2,369 mi) of navigable rivers and canals. The principal inland waterways are the Oder, with Szczecin near its mouth, the Wista, and the Warta.

In 2004, Poland had an estimated 123 airports. As of 2005, a total of 84 had paved runways, and there were also two heliports. Polish Air Transport (Polskie Linie Lotnicze-LOT), organized in 1922 and reorganized after World War II, is a state enterprise, with Warsaw's Okecie International Airport as the center. In 2003, about 3.252 million passengers were carried on scheduled domestic and international airline flights.

¹²HISTORY

The land now known as Poland was sparsely populated in prehistoric times. The oldest preserved settlements, most notably at Biskupin in northwest Poland, date back to 1000 BC. A lack of Roman conquest and settlement delayed early urbanization in relation to the territories of Western Europe such as Germany and France. Slavic tribes, from whom modern Poles are descendants in terms of language and culture, began settling Poland in the fourth and fifth centuries AD after the Hunnic invasions and mass migrations of peoples from Asia to Europe. By AD 800, the population was probably around one million and stabilized into permanent settlements. Rulers of the Piast dynasty united the Polish tribes of the Vistula and Oder basins about the middle of the 10th century. In 966, Mieszko I, a member of this dynasty, was baptized, and consequently Poland became a Christian nation. Thirty-three years later, his eldest son and successor, Boleslaw I "the Brave" (992–1025), whose military campaigns took him as far east as Kiev, secured recognition of Polish sovereignty and received a royal crown from Holy Roman Emperor Otto III, becoming the first king of Poland.

During the next three centuries, Poland was continually embroiled in conflicts with the Germans to the west and with the Eastern Slavs and Mongol invaders to the east, while developing cultural relations with Western civilizations. Foreign penetration and internal difficulties led to the division of Poland among members of the Piast dynasty. Under Casimir III "the Great" (1333–1370), the last of the Piast rulers, Poland was restored to unity and greatness. Casimir made peace with the Teutonic Knights, added Galicia to the realm, and welcomed Jewish refugees from the west; internally, law was codified, administration centralized, and a university was established in Kraków in 1364. In 1386, a Polish-Lithuanian federal union was created through a dynastic marriage, which also gave birth to the Jagiellonian dynasty, named for Jagiello, grand duke of Lithuania, who ruled Poland as Ladislas II (1386–1434). The union extended from the Baltic to the Black Sea and held control over other territories in Central Europe, notably West Prussia and Pomerania. The combined forces of the union annihilated the Teutonic Knights in 1410, in the Battle of Grunwald. The 16th century, known as Poland's Golden Age, saw the flourishing of the arts, scholarship, and architecture, most notable examples of which are the poetry of Jan Kochanowski, the revolutionary astronomical work of Nicolaus Copernicus, and the Renaissance architecture of old Kraków. During this time Poland was the largest state in Europe and a regional military power. In order to preserve the union during the reign of Sigismund II (1548–72), the last of the Jagiellonians, provisions were made for an elective monarch and a single parliament (Sejm) for Poland and Lithuania. The fact that kings were elected by the Polish/Lithuanian gentry (szlachta) and the ratification of the first constitution in Europe in 1792 are often mentioned to support the claim that Poland is a pioneer of European democracy.

Unfortunately, many of the political reforms contributed to the nation's subsequent decline. The szlachta had progressively gained influence and power at the expense of the king. Meeting in the Sejm, the gentry adopted the legislative practice whereby a single dissenting voice was sufficient to block passage. Such policies prevented any decisive action by the government with the gentry cementing their position of power in an economy based on agricultural serfdom. The nobility imposed such far-reaching limitations upon the monarchy that national unity and integrity could not be maintained. Internal disorders, including the Cossack and peasant uprising (1648–49) led by Bogdan Chmielnicki against Polish domination of the Ukraine—a revolt that struck with particular ferocity against Polish Jews, many of whom had served as agents of the nobility in administering Ukrainian lands—further weakened the nation, as did the very destructive Swedish invasion in 1655–60. In 1683, Polish troops led by John III Sobieski (1674–96) rescued Vienna from a Turkish siege, but this was perhaps the last great military victory of an increasingly weakened and war-weary state.

The decline of Poland's power was taken advantage of by its neighboring states. A Russian, Prussian, and Austrian agreement led to the first partitioning of Poland in 1772; the second (1793) and third (1795) partitions led to the demise of Poland as a sovereign state. Galicia was ruled by Austria-Hungary, northwestern Poland by Prussia, and the Ukraine and eastern and central Poland by Russia, which extended its domains to include the Duchy of Warsaw, reconstituted as the Kingdom of Poland (under Russian imperial rule) at the Congress of Vienna in 1815. The Poles rebelled in 1830 and 1863 against the tsarist rulers, but each insurrection was suppressed. However, the peasants were emancipated by Prussia in 1823, by Austria in 1849, and by Russia in 1864. Galicia, which won partial autonomy from Austria following the Habsburg monarchy's constitutional reforms, became the cultural center of the Poles.

With the Russian Revolution of 1917 and the defeat of the Central Powers in World War I, Poland regained its independence. On 18 November 1918, Jozef Pilsudski, leader of the prewar anti-Russian independence movement, formed a civilian government. Dispute over the eastern borders of the re-born state led to a military clash with the Soviet Union. The conflict, in which the Bolshevik hope of spreading socialist revolution beyond Poland to Germany and France was dashed by a fortuitous Polish counterattack near Warsaw, ended with the Treaty of Riga in 1921, under which Galicia was restored to Poland.

In the next two decades Poland was plagued by economic difficulties and political instability, and by increasingly menacing pressures from its Soviet and German neighbors. Following the Nazi-Soviet Pact in 1939, Germany invaded Poland on 1 September, occupying Warsaw four weeks later. Meanwhile, the USSR began occupation of the eastern half of the country on 17 September, despite nonaggression treaties Poland signed with both the USSR and Germany. Almost immediately Nazi forces began to brutally oppress large segments of the Polish population and loot Poland's industrial sector and major resources such as timber, coal, and wheat. Ghettos for Jews were set up in Warsaw and other cities, and numerous concentration camps were established on Polish territory, including the extermination camp at Auschwitz, where at least one million people perished between 1940 and 1944. Poland suffered tremendous losses in life and property during World War II. An estimated six million Poles were killed, half of them Jews; 2.5 million were deported for compulsory labor in Germany; more than 500,000 were permanently crippled; and the remaining population suffered virtual starvation throughout the Nazi occupation. Losses in property were evaluated at z258 billion (more than us$50 billion).

The seeds of Poland's postwar political history were sown long before the war ended. A Polish government-in-exile was set up in France and later in the United Kingdom. Units of the Polish army fought together with the Allies while in Poland underground groups, organized along political lines, maintained resistance activities. The Home Army (*Armia Krajowa*) was the major non-Communist resistance group and took its orders from the government-in-exile in London. Although formally allied to the Soviet Union, relations between Moscow and the London-based Polish government continued to deteriorate, especially after the discovery of mass graves of thousands of Polish officers murdered by the Soviets in 1940. In July 1944, the Polish National Council, a Soviet-backed resistance group, set up the Polish Committee of National Liberation as a provisional government in liberated Lublin, declaring the émigré Polish government illegal. In August 1944 the Home Army in Warsaw rose against the Nazis in hopes of liberating the capital in step with the Soviet military advance. In the events that followed and still breed controversy to this day, the Red Army halted its advance and allowed the Nazis to use their remaining forces to brutally suppress the rising and completely destroy the city. It was only on 17 January 1945 that the Red Army entered Warsaw and installed the provisional pro-Soviet government. At Yalta, the Allies agreed to accept the Curzon line, thereby awarding the USSR nearly half of former Polish territory (including Galicia) in return for a Soviet agreement to broaden the political base of the provisional government with the addition of non-Communist Polish leaders. After subsequent negotiations, the Provisional Government of National Unity was formally recognized by the United States and Britain in July 1945.

Despite Stalin's promises of free elections, a bloc of four parties dominated by the Communists emerged victorious in the elections of January 1947. The Communists and the Socialists merged in December 1948 to form the Polish United Workers' Party (PZPR). The PZPR consistently followed a pro-Soviet policy. Domestically, the party pursued a reconstruction program stressing agriculture and industrial development. It shunned the Marshall Plan and, in its first two decades, renounced all dealings with the Western powers.

The first decade of Communist rule was dominated by Stalinist repressions, tensions with the Roman Catholic Church, and a strong-handed Soviet influence, as practiced by Konstantin Rokossovsky, a Soviet general of Polish birth, who became Poland's defense minister in 1949 and served as deputy prime minister from 1952 until his resignation four years later. Rising nationalist sentiment, heightened by stagnating economic conditions, led to worker riots in Poznan on 28–29 July 1956. In response to the unrest, a new Polish Politburo, headed by Wladyslaw Gomulka (who had been purged from the PZPR in 1949 and subsequently imprisoned because of his nationalist leanings), introduced liberalizations, including the abolition of farm collectivization, and improved relations with the Church. Conditions improved from those immediately after the war, but by the late 1950s, the reform movement had been halted, and the government took a harder line against dissent. In 1968 there were student demonstrations against the government in the university centers; the Gomulka regime countered with a political offensive in which many government officials and party members accused of anti-Socialist or pro-Zionist sentiments were removed from office, and an estimated 12,000 Polish Jews left Poland.

Two years later, following a drought in 1969 and an exceptionally severe winter, demonstrations by shipyard workers in Gdańsk broke out on 16 December 1970 to protest economic conditions, the privileges of the Communist party elite, and an announced rise in food prices. The government responded with military force and after widespread violence, with soldiers firing on striking workers, at least 44 people were killed. The unrest led to the removal from power of Gomulka and the installation of Edward Gierek as the first secretary of the politburo on December 20. Under continued pressure from strikes, Gierek's government postponed the controversial incentive system and froze prices at their new levels. After receiving a substantial long-term Soviet grant (estimated at $100 million), the Polish government rolled back prices to their pre-December 1970 levels, and labor peace was restored. In a move to bolster his support, Gierek reinstated Church control over thousands of religious properties in northwestern Poland to which the government had held title since 1945.

During the 1970s, Gierek's government vigorously pursued a policy of détente with the West. Three US presidents visited Poland and Gierek himself traveled to the United States and to several West European countries. Peace agreements governing the Oder-Neisse line and formally recognizing Polish sovereignty in former German territories were concluded with West Germany, and trade pacts were signed with the United States, Britain, France, Italy, Austria, and other nations. With a bold plan of creating a "second Japan," Gierek secured huge loans (several billion dollars) from the West in hopes of building an industrial export economy and improving living conditions, which were at this point glaringly inferior to those in the capitalist world. Although many ambitious projects were undertaken, including the building of an oil refinery in Gdańsk and a new steel works plant in Katowice, mismanagement and the inefficiency of the socialist economy crippled real economic output and the prospects of repaying the foreign debts became increasingly dim. In 1976, the government announced food price increases but had to rescind them after the workers responded by striking. During the next several years, the economic situation kept deteriorating, and Polish nationalism, buoyed in 1978 by the election of the archbishop of Kraków to the papacy as John Paul II, continued to rise. In July 1980, new meat price increases were announced, and within a few weeks, well-organized workers all over Poland demanded a series of economic and political concessions, including the right to organize independent trade unions outside of the Communist party. The center of labor activity was the Lenin Shipyard in Gdańsk, where in a public ceremony on 31 August, government officials agreed to allow workers the right to organize and to strike. The independent labor movement Solidarity, headed by Lech Walesa, the leader of the Gdańsk workers, and strongly supported by the Roman Catholic clergy, soon claimed a membership of about 10 million (about a fourth of the population), with its ranks filled not only with workers but also intellectuals. That month, Stanislaw Kania replaced Gierek as first secretary.

For more than a year, the government and Solidarity leaders negotiated, with Catholic Church officials often acting as mediators. As Solidarity became more and more overtly political—demanding, for example, free parliamentary elections—Poland's Communist leaders came under increasing pressure from the USSR to stop the "anti-Socialist" and "anti-Soviet" forces. On 18 October 1981, Gen. Wojciech Jaruzelski, prime minister since February, replaced Kania as first secretary. On 13 December, after union leaders in Gdańsk called for a national referendum on forming a non-Communist government in Poland, Jaruzelski set up the Military Council for National Salvation and declared martial law. To what

extent Jaruzelski's abrupt crackdown was carried out to prevent direct Soviet military intervention is still unclear, although evidence suggests that the Kremlin had not drawn up any plans for a military intrusion into Poland. Almost the whole leadership of Solidarity, including Walesa, was arrested, and the union was suspended. Despite further strikes and rioting, which resulted in several deaths, the military had soon gained complete control. More than 10,000 people were arrested and detained for up to 12 months, and all rights and freedoms gained in the preceding year and a half were abolished. In January 1982, the United States imposed sanctions against Poland, including withdrawal of most-favored-nation status, veto of Poland's entry into the IMF, and suspension of fishing rights in US waters and of LOT flights to the United States. Protests and rioting continued sporadically into 1983, and some Solidarity leaders remained active underground, but these disturbances did not seriously threaten the military regime. On 22 July 1983, the government formally ended martial law and proclaimed an amnesty, but a series of legislative measures had meanwhile institutionalized many of the powers the government had exercised, including the power to dissolve organizations, forbid public meetings, and run the universities.

The internal political situation stabilized to such a degree that in July 1984 the government proclaimed a general amnesty, and the United States began to lift its sanctions the following month (the last sanctions were lifted in early 1987). When an outspoken priest, Father Jerzy Popieluszko, was kidnapped and subsequently murdered by two secret police officers, the government, in an unprecedented step, permitted a trial to take place in February 1985 in the result of which four security officers were convicted and sentenced. Another amnesty was proclaimed in September 1986, leading to the release of all remaining political prisoners. Economically, however, the country was spiraling out of control. Continued declines in standards of living and shortages of even basic necessities led to waves of strikes throughout Poland in spring and fall 1988, essentially paralyzing the nation. By November 1987 public antipathy had been so widespread that the government called for the first public referendum to be held in Poland in more than 40 years; this was also the first open election to be held within the Warsaw Pact. Although the ballot itself asked only for public support of an accelerated economic reform package, the people of Poland understood the referendum to be a vote of confidence in the government itself. The final tally was approximately two-thirds in support of the government, but because of a Solidarity-inspired voter boycott, only 67% of the eligible voters cast their ballots, which meant that the referendum failed to pass, a first-ever defeat for the government.

In autumn 1988, the entire government resigned and it became clear that talks with labor activists were inevitable. The negotiations leading up to the so-called "round-table talks," which finally opened in February 1989, were as delicate and prolonged as the talks themselves. However, in April 1989 agreement was reached on a number of unprecedented concessions: Solidarity was recognized as a legal entity; the post of president was created, to be filled by legislative appointment; some independent media were permitted to operate; and the Catholic Church was given full legal status. In June 1989 came perhaps the most far-reaching change, the establishment of a senate, complementing the existing Sejm, with the seats to be filled by open election. In addition, 35% of the seats in the Sejm were also made subject to direct election.

The government did all it could to make it difficult for opposition candidates to run: only two months were allowed in which candidates could gather the petitions necessary to get on the ballot, and the ballots themselves listed candidates alphabetically, with no indication of party affiliation. Despite those efforts, Solidarity won a decisive victory; 99 of the 100 seats in the Senate went to Solidarity members. Moreover, many government candidates in the *Sejm* lost seats because voters crossed out the names of unopposed government candidates, thus denying them the necessary 50% of the total votes cast.

In June 1989, the newly elected parliament named General Wojciech Jaruzelski Poland's president by the slenderest of margins. Two months later, Solidarity pressed to balance Jaruzelski's post of president with a non-Communist prime minister and at this point the discredited PZPR could do little but comply. Although it was widely expected that Lech Walesa might lead the first Solidarity government, he demurred, instead putting forward Tadeusz Mazowiecki, who took office on 24 August 1989, as the first non-Communist prime minister in the Eastern Bloc. That autumn, motivated at least in part by the events unfolding in Poland, a wave of "velvet revolutions" spread across Eastern Europe culminating in the fall of the Berlin Wall. These events further accelerated the de-Sovietization of Polish government. In September 1990, Jaruzelski resigned, opening the way for new elections.

The election of Walesa as president was the formal end to Poland's Communist rule, with Poland rejoining the community of democratic nations. In what would become known as "shock therapy," the previously Socialist economy was abruptly opened to free market forces. Although initially inflation sky-rocketed and economic output continued to fall, by 1997 Poland was attracting large amounts of foreign investment and enjoying the highest growth rates in Europe. At the same time, not everyone enjoyed economic prosperity and political discord continued to grow. The number of political parties ballooned, making it difficult to undertake such complex and contentious issues as large-scale privatization, economic rationalization of Soviet-era giant industry, and fundamental constitutional revision. The October 1991 election saw 69 parties competing, with 29 actually winning seats, none of them with more than 14% of the vote. Inevitably, this resulted in coalition governments without clear mandates, giving Poland five prime ministers and four governments in 1991–93. This proliferation of parties reflected disparities among the electorate that emerged once the Communists had been removed as a unifying focus for opposition.

In the September 1993 election, the two most popular parties, the Polish Peasant Party (PSL) and the Democratic Left Alliance (SLD) were made up largely of ex-Communists or other figures from the governments of the past. The apparent rejection of the gains of Solidarity and the return of the vanquished ex-Communists was variously interpreted as a rejection of "shock-therapy" economic transformation, the electorate's nostalgia for the more ordered life of the past, and a vote against the Catholic Church, or at least its social agenda of asserting close control on social issues such as abortion, school curriculum, and women's role in society.

Fears associated with the return of the many ex-Communists to power proved unfounded. Although differing from their predecessors on the pace of Poland's economic transformation, the government of Polish Peasant Party (PSL) leader Waldemar Pawlak, and his Democratic Left Alliance (SLD) partner, Aleksander Kwasniewski, remained generally committed to Poland's course of democratization and economic transition. The Constitution Commission proposed a new constitution that passed the National Assembly in April 1997, and was approved in a national referendum on 23 May 1997.

The parliamentary elections of 1997 saw the return to power of centrist and right of center Solidarity legacy parties, with Solidarity Electoral Action (AWS) and the Freedom Union (UW) forming a coalition with Jerzy Buzek as prime minister. The Buzek government presided over many successful reforms, including reorganization of local and regional administration, but an economic downturn and rising unemployment caused the voters to resoundingly return the reigns of power to the post-Communist SLD in 2001.

In 2005 the power pendulum swung again to the right with the scandal ridden SLD achieving less than 12% of the vote and the right of center Law and Justice (PiS) and centrist Civic Platform (PO) gaining the majority. The constant and almost predictable shift of power can be interpreted as a political maturation of the young democracy or as the failure of either side to address the main economic issue of unemployment, which reached its maximum level of 20% in December 2004. The exception to the changing political tides has been the reformed Communist Aleksander Kwasniewski of the SLD, who beat Walesa to be elected president in 1995 and won a second term in 2000.

It has been on the international scene that Poland has made its most visible strides since the end of Communist rule. In 1997, NATO invited Poland, along with the Czech Republic and Hungary, to join the alliance, and the three countries became members in March 1999. In May 2004 Poland became a member of the European Union (EU) and is now the organization's sixth most populous member. Poland asserted itself as a close American ally by being one of the few countries to participate in the 2003 invasion of Iraq and subsequently administering an Iraqi occupied zone with the initial involvement of 2,400 of its own troops. Poland has also attempted to play a leading role in the politics of eastern and central Europe and has invested its political capital in encouraging democratization in Belarus and supporting the Orange Revolution in the Ukraine in December 2004.

Since joining the EU, investment and economic growth picked up, with new manufacturing jobs coming from Western Europe. However, corruption, inefficient bureaucracy and weak infrastructure continued to be problems and slowed economic growth. Unemployment began to drop, but at 17.9% it still remained the highest in the European Union.

13 GOVERNMENT

Until 1997, the form of government in Poland was in the midst of a protracted transformation, which left a number of its important features unclear. Without a formal constitution, Poland had been functioning on a much-amended form of its Communist-era constitution. The most important modifications were the Jaruzelski government's concessions of April 1989, which created both the Senate and the office of president, and a package of amendments passed in October 1992 which are collectively called the

"Little Constitution." Another important modification was the agreement of 1990, which made the presidency a popularly elected post, rather than parliamentary appointment.

The president is directly elected, for a term of five years. The post has traditional executive obligations and powers, such as the duty to sign into law or veto legislations, but also retains substantial legislative powers, including the right to introduce bills and draft legal amendments.

During his tenure, Lech Walesa fought to widen the powers of the presidency, arguing that at least during the transition period Poland required a strong president able to resolve impasses and disputes on the basis of "practical experience," rather than on points of legal niceties.

Walesa's successor, Aleksander Kwasniewski, succeeded in putting forth a new constitution in 1997.

The parliament consists of two houses, the Sejm, or lower house, with 460 seats, and the Senate, with 100 seats. The members of both houses serve four-year terms. Seats are filled on the basis of party lists; there is a minimum national vote threshold of 5% for parties, or 8% for coalitions, with the votes for parties which fail to reach those minimums assigned to victorious parties. The prime minister proposes, the president appoints, and the Sejm approves the Council of Ministers or cabinet. The president, who is elected by popular vote for a five-year term, appoints the prime minister, who is then confirmed by the Sejm.

14 POLITICAL PARTIES

After the political poverty of its Communist past, Poland initially saw a proliferation of political parties ranging across the full political spectrum, from the rabidly xenophobic nationalism of the Polish National Front (whose leader, Janusz Bryczkowski, invited Russian extremist Vladimir Zhirinovsky to Poland in 1994) to the socialist party, Union of Labor (UP). In between were special interest and even quirky parties, of which the best example may be the Polish Beerdrinkers' Party. Overall, 69 parties participated in the 1991 parliamentary elections, of which 29 gained seats, none with more than 14% of the total vote. By 1993, however, the political scene was stabilizing. Only 35 parties participated in that election; perhaps more significantly, only five received seats.

The local elections of 1994 showed the emergence of three basic political orientations shaped by shifting coalitions of parties, with the parties themselves often dissolving and reorganizing under new names. The Polish political spectrum slightly deviates from the traditional notions of right and left in part because in contrast to most countries where labor movements are associated with the political left, the Polish right has its roots in the Solidarity labor movement.

The Polish far right was initially represented by several coalitions: the Alliance for Poland, which included the Christian National Union, the Center Alliance, the Movement for the Republic, Peasant Alliance, and the Conservative Coalition, and the 11 November Agreement, which included the Conservative Party, the Party of Christian Democrats, the Christian-Peasant Alliance, and the Real Politics Union (a radical *laissez-faire* party). These parties generally favored a major role for the Catholic Church, and tended to draw their support from Poland's rural sectors; in 1994, they did best in the eastern districts. The religious right is represented by the League of Polish Families (LPR), which has a social

platform based on traditional Catholic values and was not in favor of Polish membership in the EU. LPR won 7.97% of the vote in the October 2005 elections.

The mainstream right was represented in the years 1997-2001 by Elective Action Solidarity (AWS). AWS led the government in coalition with UW. However, after a resounding defeat in 2001 AWS dissolved and its members eventually migrated to either the centrist Civic Platform (PO) or the right of center Law and Justice (PiS). PiS supports continuous but careful economic reforms, is in favor of raising retirement benefits, and remains socially conservative, as evidenced by the prohibition of a gay pride parade in Warsaw by its leader Lech Kaczynski in 2005. Another important aspect of the PiS is a strong stand against corruption. In the recent parliamentary elections in October 2005 PiS was the most popular party with 26.99% of the vote.

The center was dominated by Freedom Union (UW), which was formed in April 1994, when the Liberal Democratic Congress merged with the Democratic Union. The centrist position derives largely from the intellectual wing of the original Solidarity, favoring radical economic transformation, while being less concerned with immediate impact upon workers. UW formed a coalition with AWS as the junior partner in 1997–2000. UW's most prominent member was Leszek Balcerowicz, the architect of the "shock therapy" economic reform and president of Poland's National Bank. After the elections of 1997 UW largely dissolved, with its members joining the newly formed Civic Platform (PO), which also absorbed politicians from AWS. Both the UW and PO draw much of their support from smaller cities and university centers, such as Kraków, and the prosperous regions of western Poland. In the last parliamentary election in October 2005, PO's platform included a proposal for a 15% flat tax. PO was the second most popular party with 24.14% and was set to rule in a coalition with PiS.

The left, which was almost entirely discredited in 1991, has shown remarkable resilience. Through the 1990s, the two major parties were the Democratic Left Alliance (SLD) and the Polish Peasant Party (PSL), both descendents of elements of the old Communist party and its affiliates. The far left (some would argue far-right) is dominated by Self-Defense (SO) headed by Andrzej Lepper. Lepper's party is in favor of protectionist agriculture and sometimes anti-western isolationist foreign policy. In 2001 the Democratic Left Alliance (SLD) in coalition with the Labor Union (UP), a minor left-wing party, won a decisive victory and formed a government under Leszek Miller. Although Miller's government presided over Poland's entry into the European Union, it became increasingly unpopular due to a series of scandals involving corruption and bribery, and failure to accelerate economic growth. With Miller himself forced to resign amid scandal in May 2005, SLD continued to rule as a minority government under Marek Belka until the elections in October 2005. Unhappy with Miller's leadership of the party, many members withdrew from SLD in 2004 and formed a new leftist party called Polish Social Democracy (SDPL). In the October 2005 elections SLD won 11.31%, SO 11.41% and PSL 6.96%. SDPL failed to make the 3% threshold to enter the parliament.

In addition to the major parties, a German Minority Party is active with most of its support from the Opole region in southwest Poland.

In the 1995 presidential elections, Aleksander Kwasniewski of SLD beat Lech Walesa by a small margin (51.7% to 48.3%) to become president for a five-year term. He was reelected in 2000 with 53.9% of the vote to nonparty candidate Andrzej Olechowski's 17.3% and AWS chairman Marian Krzaklewski's 15.6%. In a striking reversal, Walesa finished seventh with 0.8% of the vote.

Constitutionally limited to only two terms, Kwasniewski did not run again in 2005. The October presidential elections saw 14 candidates compete. In the first round the top five contenders were Donald Tusk (PO) with 36.33% of the vote, Lech Kaczynski (PiS) with 33.10%, Andrzej Lepper (SO) with 15.11%, and Marek Borowski (SDPL) with 10.33%. The SDL candidate withdrew from the election due to a scandal. In the second round, which included only the top two candidates, Tusk and Kaczynski, Kaczynski won with 54.04% of the vote to Tusk's 45.96%. Kaczynski's term as president extended to 2010.

15 LOCAL GOVERNMENT

Poland had been divided into 49 administrative districts, or *voivodships*, which were the basic administrative units under the Communists. In 1989 Solidarity government replaced that system with one in which the basic unit was the *gmina*, or local authority, which owned property and had responsibility for its own budget. The *gmina* elected a council, which appointed the executive officials actually responsible for day-to-day administration of the locality.

In 1994, there were 2,383 such local councils, with a mixed system of election. In districts containing more than 40,000 people, of which there were 110 in 1994, council representation was proportionally determined, based upon party affiliation. In the smaller districts, council representatives were elected by direct majority vote.

Originally these *gmina* councils were similar in makeup to the Solidarity Citizens Committees, from which they originated. Increasingly, however, the councils differentiated themselves, some becoming controlled by national parties, others remaining dominated by personalities who responded primarily to local issues.

Changes in local government structure were introduced in 1999, transforming Poland's 49 provinces into 16 new ones. A three-tier division of government was established: municipalities/communes, 308 counties (*powiaty*), and 16 provinces (*wojewodztwa*). Each of these divisions is governed by a council. Council members are directly elected, and appoint and dismiss the heads of the municipalities/communes (*wojt*), the town mayors, the *starosta* or head of the county, and the speaker of the provincial councils.

16 JUDICIAL SYSTEM

There is a four-tiered court system in Poland: regional, provincial, appellate divisions, and a Supreme Court. The Supreme Court, the highest judicial organ, functions primarily as a court of appeal. The Supreme Court and lower courts are divided into criminal, civil, military, labor, and family chambers. Judges are nominated by the National Judicial Council and are appointed by the president for life.

There is also a Constitutional Tribunal which offers opinions on legislation and exercises authority of judicial review. Constitutional Tribunal judges are appointed to nine-year terms by the Sejm.

Defendants enjoy a presumption of innocence and have the right to appeal. Although the judiciary is independent, it suffers from inefficiency, lack of resources and lack of public confidence.

17 ARMED FORCES

Polish armed forces numbered 141,500 active personnel in 2005, with reservists numbering 234,000. Army personnel numbered an estimated 89,000 members, equipped with 947 main battle tanks, 435 reconnaissance vehicles, 1,281 armored infantry fighting vehicles, 33 armored personnel carriers, and 1,482 artillery pieces. The army's aviation arm included 65 attack and 80 support helicopters. Naval manpower in 2005 totaled 12,300, including 2,000 naval aviation personnel. Equipment included three tactical submarines, one destroyer, three frigates, four corvettes, 19 patrol/coastal vessels, and 22 mine warfare vessels. The naval aviation wing was supplied with 18 combat capable aircraft and a total of 30 helicopters for use in search and rescue, antisubmarine warfare and for support missions. The air force had 30,000 active personnel and 142 combat capable aircraft, including 28 fighter and 53 fighter ground attack aircraft, as well as 53 transport and 220 training aircraft. Poland also had a paramilitary force of 21,400 personnel, of which 14,100 were border guards and 7,300 police. Poland provided troops and observers to 13 different nations or regions as part of UN, NATO or European Union missions. The defense budget in 2005 amounted to $5.16 billion.

18 INTERNATIONAL COOPERATION

Poland is a charter member of the United Nations, having signed on 24 October 1945; it participates in ECE and several nonregional specialized agencies, such as the FAO, IAEA, the World Bank, UNESCO, UNIDO, and the WHO. Poland was admitted to NATO on 12 March 1999. The nation is also a member of the Council of Europe, the Council of the Baltic Sea States, the Euro-Atlantic Partnership Council, the European Bank for Reconstruction and Development, the OECD, and the OSCE. Poland became a member of the European Union in 2004. The country has observer status in the OAS.

Polish troops have supported UN missions and operations in Kosovo (est. 1999), Lebanon (est. 1978), Western Sahara (est. 1991), Ethiopia and Eritrea (est. 2000), Liberia (est. 2003), Georgia (est., 1993), and the DROC (est. 1999), among others. In 2003, Poland assumed command of division of multinational forces working on peacekeeping and stabilization efforts in Iraq.

Poland is part of the Australia Group, the Zangger Committee, the European Organization for Nuclear Research (CERN), the Nuclear Suppliers Group (London Group), and the Organization for the Prohibition of Chemical Weapons. In environmental cooperation, Poland is part of the Antarctic Treaty, the Basel Convention, Conventions on Biological Diversity and Air Pollution, Ramsar, CITES, the London Convention, the Kyoto Protocol, the Montréal Protocol, MARPOL, the Nuclear Test Ban Treaty, and the UN Conventions on the Law of the Sea, Climate Change and Desertification.

19 ECONOMY

Until 1990, Poland had a centrally planned economy that was primarily state controlled. Agriculture, however, was only partly socialized, with state farms and cooperatives accounting for 23% of the country's total farmland in 1984. Since World War II, agriculture's predominance in the economy has been waning; in 1990, it accounted for 16.2% of the NMP, compared to 22.7% in 1970. In 2004, its contribution to GDP was an estimated 2.9%, although it continued to employ about 24% of the labor force. Poland, with its sizable coastline, has become a maritime nation of some note, having developed three major ports on the Baltic and a greatly expanded shipbuilding industry, which in 1991 produced 53 ships. In 2003, yearly production was reported as 50 ships, about one-tenth of the number of ships produced by South Korea and Japan, the industry leaders. However, in June 2002 the Szczecin Shipyards, considered an example of successful privatization, declared bankruptcy. Poland has rich coal deposits, but it lacks some important natural resources, such as petroleum and iron ore.

During 1971–75, Poland's NMP increased by about 12.8% annually; the growth was, to a substantial degree, the result of loans from the West. After 1975, however, Poland's economic performance deteriorated because of excessive investments, internal market problems, several bad harvests, the worldwide recession, and the political upheaval of 1980–81. An economic growth rate of 2.5% annually during 1976–78 was followed by declines of 2% in 1979, 4% in 1980, 12% in 1981, and 5.5% in 1982, while the debt to Western governments reached nearly $25 billion by 1983, rising to $33 billion in 1991, when the total hard-currency debt reached $52.5 billion. During 1980–91, the GNP grew at an annual average rate of only 1.2%. Inflation averaged 54.3% annually in the 1980s.

With Poland subjected to the "shock therapy" of a transition to a market economy, GDP fell 31.5% from 1990–92 and consumer prices shot up almost sixfold. However, the economy did not stay down long and it soon became one of the most robust in Eastern and Central Europe thanks to the government's tight fiscal and monetary policies. The economy grew by just under 7% in 1995, and by 5.5% in 1996 and 1997, for an average of over 5% a year 1994 to 1997. Most of the growth since 1991 came from the booming private sector, by 1997 accounting for about 70% of GDP (up from 50% in 1992), due in large part to the creation of new private firms. Poland's pace of growth declined after 1998, as the economy was impacted by the Russian financial crisis and then the global economic slowdown in 2001. In 1998, growth fell to 4.8%; in 1999, 4.1%; in 2000, to 4%; and in 2001, to 1%. Signs of economic recovery began to be seen in 2003. In 2002 GDP grew at 1.4%, but in 2003 at 3.8% and reached an impressive 5.3% in 2004, when Poland joined the EU. Similarly, inflation shot up to 10.1% in 2000 with the recovery of oil prices, but in 2001 moderated to 5.5%. In 2002 inflation was only 1.9%, in 2003 0.8%, in 2004 3.6% and in 2005 3.2%. The growth of the economy was accompanied by privatization. About 72% of the economy had been privatized by 2002, and the government has continued to privatize state-owned industries in recent years by successfully utilizing the Warsaw Stock Exchange to this end. The goal is to achieve the ownership structure similar to that of other EU member states, where private ownership is close to 80%.

The major problems facing the economy are unemployment and persistently high fiscal deficits. Unemployment increased to 13% in 1999, to 15% in 2000, to 16% in 2001, to 17% reaching 20% in 2002, before it started to fall again, to 19% in 2004 and 17.3% in 2005. On 7 June 2003, 75% in a vote with a 57.34% turnout (above the 50% minimum turnout required) voted "yes" to the referendum of Poland's joining the EU. Poland became a member of the EU on 1 May 2004. Economists estimate that it will take decades for per capita average income in Poland, which was about $4,800 in 2002 ($9,500 in purchasing power parity terms), to reach the EU average. In 2004 per capita average grew to $12,000.

20 INCOME

The US Central Intelligence Agency (CIA) reports that in 2005 Poland's gross domestic product (GDP) was estimated at $489.3 billion. The CIA defines GDP as the value of all final goods and services produced within a nation in a given year and computed on the basis of purchasing power parity (PPP) rather than value as measured on the basis of the rate of exchange based on current dollars. The per capita GDP was estimated at $12,700. The annual growth rate of GDP was estimated at 3.3%. The average inflation rate in 2005 was 2.1%. It was estimated that agriculture accounted for 2.8% of GDP, industry 31.7%, and services 65.5%.

According to the World Bank, in 2003 remittances from citizens working abroad totaled $2.314 billion or about $61 per capita and accounted for approximately 1.1% of GDP. Foreign aid receipts amounted to $1.2 trillion or about $31 per capita and accounted for approximately 0.6% of the gross national income (GNI).

The World Bank reports that in 2003 household consumption in Poland totaled $136.49 billion or about $3,573 per capita based on a GDP of $209.6 billion, measured in current dollars rather than PPP. Household consumption includes expenditures of individuals, households, and nongovernmental organizations on goods and services, excluding purchases of dwellings. It was estimated that for the period 1990 to 2003 household consumption grew at an average annual rate of 4.7%. In 2001 it was estimated that approximately 28% of household consumption was spent on food, 19% on fuel, 6% on health care, and 1% on education. It was estimated that in 2003 about 17% of the population had incomes below the poverty line.

21 LABOR

The labor force in 2005 totaled an estimated 17.1 million persons. As of 2003, agriculture accounted for 18.4% of the workforce, with industry at 28.6% and 53% in the services sector. In 2005, the estimated unemployment rate was 18.3%, with considerable underemployment as well.

Unions have the right to strike and bargain collectively, although union officials report that workers in the private sector are encouraged not to join unions by their employers and workers organizing unions often face discrimination. According to press reports, 17% of Poland's workforce was unionized.

The labor code prohibits employment for children under the age of 15. There are strict rules governing the work standards for those between 15 and 18 years old, however these are not regularly enforced. The minimum wage in state-owned enterprises was around $300 per month as of 1 January 2006. However, a large number of construction and seasonal agricultural workers earn less than the minimum wage. The legal standard workweek is 40 hours with 35 hours of uninterrupted rest per week. Overtime is subject to premium pay rates. The labor code defines occupational safety and health standards but they are not consistently enforced.

22 AGRICULTURE

In 2003, agriculture engaged 18.4% of the Polish labor force (as compared with 53.5% in 1948 and 39.9% in 1967). About 62% of Poland's land is agricultural; of this area, 78% is cultivated. Overall agricultural output during 1980–90 fell by nearly 0.4% annually. Between 1990 and 2000, agricultural production dropped by 0.2% annually. Crop output was valued at nearly €5.76 billion in 2003. During 2002–04, crop output was down 8.5% compared with 1999–2001. In 2005, agriculture accounted for 5% of GDP, down from 14.5% in 1985.

The transition from an agricultural economy is due partly to territorial changes resulting from World War II (1939–45); largely agricultural areas were transferred to the USSR, whereas the areas acquired in the west were predominantly industrial. During the war, approximately one-third of the Polish farms were completely or partly laid waste, and five-sixths of the hogs and two-thirds of the cattle and sheep were destroyed, leaving farmers almost without draft animals and fertilizer. At the same time, population transfers delayed cultivation in the areas of resettlement.

Land redistribution followed both world wars but was much more extensive after World War II. A 1944 decree expropriated all holdings larger than 100 hectares (247 acres); land belonging to Germans or collaborators was also expropriated. Attempts at collectivization were generally resisted; after 1956, most collective farms were disbanded and their land redistributed. During the 1990s, about 3.7 million Poles were engaged in small plot farming (with an average farm size of 6 hectares/15 acres) on 2.1 million private farms, which produced about 75% of agricultural output. In 2003, Poland had over 2,172,000 agricultural holdings and the largest number of full-time agricultural employment in the 25-nation EU, at over 1,048,000 workers, and another 3,248,000 part-time agricultural workers that year.

In 2004, principal crops and their estimated yields (in thousands of tons) were potatoes, 13,746; sugar beets, 11,471; wheat, 9,450; rye, 4,129; barley, 3,476; triticale, 3,349 (highest in the world); and oats, 1,462. Yields have been poor because of infertile soil, insufficient use of fertilizers, and inadequate mechanization, in addition to the drought. There were 1,310,500 tractors in 1997, up from 620,724 during 1979–81. Although grain production has been Poland's traditional agricultural pursuit, since World War II, Poland has become an importer—instead of an exporter—of grains, particularly wheat.

Poland grows an assortment of fruits and vegetables. Fruit and berry yields (in thousands of tons) for 2004 included: apples, 2,500; currants, 192; strawberries, 185; raspberries, 42; plums, 119; and pears, 77. Field vegetable production in 2004 (in thousands of tons) included: cabbage, 1,370; carrots, 928; onions, 866; cucumbers, 256; cauliflower, 206; and tomatoes, 213.

23 ANIMAL HUSBANDRY

Pastures covered about 10.7% of the total land area in 2003. The government has encouraged the development of livestock production through increased fodder supply and improvement in breeding stock and partial tax relief for hog raising. Emphasis has been placed on the raising of hogs and sheep. In 2005, there were 18.1 million pigs, 5,483,000 head of cattle, and 316,000 sheep. In 2005 there were an estimated 90 million chickens, 5 million ducks, 3 million geese, and 600,000 turkeys.

Estimated livestock production in 2005 included (in thousands of tons): pork, 1,923; beef and veal, 304; poultry, 984; mutton, 1.6; and milk, 11,401. Butter production in 2005 was 190,000 tons; cheese, 595,000; and honey, 12,500.

24 FISHING

Most of the fishing industry has been brought under state ownership. Sea fishing is conducted in the Baltic and North seas and in the Atlantic (Labrador, Newfoundland, and African waters), and there are inland fisheries in lakes, ponds, and rivers. The 2003 saltwater catch was 160,260 tons, predominantly sprat, herring, and cod; freshwater fishing yielded about 54,520 tons. Aquaculture in 2003 produced 54,000 tons. Exports of fish products amounted to $313.2 million in 2003, with processed and preserved fish and caviar accounting for $100 million.

25 FORESTRY

As of 2003, 28.4% of Poland's land was forested. Pine, larch, spruce, and fir are the most important varieties of trees. Polish forests are subject to difficult growing conditions such as wide temperature fluctuations in winter, hurricane strength winds, and unusually high temperatures in summer. Most Polish forests grow on highly degraded sandy soils that hold little moisture. Moreover, much of Poland suffered from drought during the 1990s. Almost 50% of forests are young trees; only 17% of the stand can be cut. The Wielkopolski National Forest, a reservation in Rogalin, is famous for its thousand-year-old oak trees.

Despite the adversity, the forest products industry was one of the most rapidly growing sectors of the Polish economy in the 1990s. Since 1992, output of value-added products has doubled, excluding sawn timber. Wood processing occurs in the Biala Podlaska region, while large areas of forest in the Zamosc region foster development in the furniture industry. In 2004, exports of furniture were valued at $3.4 billion (mainly to Germany), making it a leading export commodity. In 2004, over 80% of furniture production was exported, compared to 17% in 1989. The timber cut in 2004 was estimated at 28 million cu m (1 billion cu ft) of roundwood. The annual allowable cut is typically around 28.7 million cu m (1.01 billion cu ft), equivalent to 33% of annual growth. Poland was once an exporter of timber, but given the booming construction of private homes, domestic production does not meet local demand. In 2004, imports of forestry products exceeded exports by $233.2 million.

The government has been attempting to offset losses from territorial redistribution and wartime destruction by afforestation. During 1990–2000, the forested area increased in size by an annual average of 18,000 hectares (44,500 acres) per year. Although land is being returned to forests, industrial pollution and pests are still causing deterioration. As of 2004, 31% of commercial forests were plantation or regrowth forests.

26 MINING

Poland ranked third globally in mined zinc, sixth in silver, seventh in coal and sulfur (a major export commodity), among the top ten in mine copper (3% of world output, and second in Europe and Central Eurasia), and was a leading producer in Central Eurasia and Europe of lead, lime, nitrogen, and salt. Poland had 9% of world sulfur reserves, about 6% of world copper ore reserves, and had significant resources of bituminous coal, salt, silver, and lead and zinc ores. The mining and quarrying sector, which included mineral fuels and processing, accounted for around 2% of Poland's gross domestic product (GDP) in 2002, which grew by 2.3% in that year from 2001. Total sales by the mining and quarrying sector contracted by 3% in 2002, with sales by the coal, lignite and peat mining industries falling by 5.8% in that same year.

Mine output of metals in 2002 included: mined zinc, 171,200 metric tons, down from 172,300 in 2001; silver (refined, primary), 1,229 metric tons; copper (ore and concentrate by metal content), 1,071,000 metric tons; and lead (by total mine content), 120,400 metric tons, down from 121,600 metric tons in 2001. All copper ore was mined by KGHM S.A., in the Lubin area; the government's share in KGHM's stock was 52%. Total copper reserves were 2,300 million tons containing 44 million tons of metal. Lead and zinc resources totaled 184 million tons; limestone and marl, 17,450 million tons; and gravel aggregates, 14,600 million tons. No gold was mined in 2003. Important industrial minerals produced in 2003 included hydraulic cement (10.948 million metric tons), glass sand (1.6 million tons), and sulfur (native [Frasch]), by-product, and from gypsum), 1.195 million tons. Also produced in 2002 were palladium, platinum, selenium, anhydrite, diatomite, feldspar, fuller's earth, fire clay, kaolin, gypsum, magnesite ore (crude), nitrogen, foundry sand, filing sand, lime sand, quartz, quartz crystal, sodium compounds, dolomite, limestone, and crushed and dimension stone. Barite mining, at Boguszow, was stopped in 1997, because of large-scale flooding.

Poland's mining and mineral-processing industry was extensive and appeared well positioned to respond to the country's rising needs for all forms of raw materials, especially those consumed by the construction sector. A major trend in Poland's nonferrous metals sector was the denationalization program that encompassed the aluminum, copper, and zinc industries. The acquisition of former German territories in 1945 enriched Poland with hard coal and, to a lesser extent, zinc and lead. Iron ore was found around Czestochowa, in south-central Poland, but in deposits of low metal content. Uranium deposits occurred in Lower Silesia.

27 ENERGY AND POWER

Poland has only modest reserves of crude oil and natural gas. The country's main domestic energy sources are coal, lignite, and peat; and rivers remain a largely untapped source of power.

As of 1 January 2004, Poland had proven reserves of crude oil estimated at 96.4 million barrels and proven natural gas reserves estimated at 5.83 trillion cu ft. In 2003, oil production was estimated to average 23,500 barrels per day, while consumption in that year was tentatively placed at 424,000 barrels per day. As a result, Poland was a net importer of oil, most of which comes from Russia. Poland has the largest crude oil refining capacity in North-Central Europe, estimated at 350,000 barrels per day, as of 1 January 2004.

With natural gas reserves estimated at 5.83 trillion cu ft, as of 1 January 2004, Poland was North Central Europe's largest natural gas producer. In 2002, Poland produced an estimated 196 billion cu ft of natural gas, which accounted for 41% of domestic consumption, and came to an estimated 479 billion cu ft.

Coal, as previously noted, is Poland's most abundant energy source. Proven coal reserves at the beginning of 2003 amounted to 24.4 billion tons (of which about two-thirds are anthracite and bituminous), and are the largest in North Central Europe. In 2002, production of all types of coal was estimated at 177.8 million short tons, with demand at an estimated 149 million short tons in that year. Poland's hard coal reserves are concentrated in Upper Silesia, near the border with the Czech Republic. Other major coal basins are located in Lower Silesia and Lublin. Although the coal industry is one of the country's largest employers, a major restructuring of the industry has been initiated. From 1998 through 2002, employment in the industry went from 248,000 to 140,000 by the close of 2002. In addition, a further restructuring was planned for the period 2003 through 2006, and involves further reductions in employment and the closing of inefficient mines.

In 2002, Poland's electric power generating capacity was estimated at 29.307 million kW, of which 28.404 billion kW of capacity was dedicated to conventional thermal fuel plants. Hydroelectric capacity in 2002 was put at 0.868 billion kW, followed by geothermal/other at 0.035 billion kW. Electricity production in 2002 came to 133.980 billion kWh, of which 97.6% was from fossil fuels, 1.6% from hydropower, and less than 1% from other renewable sources. Consumption of electricity in 2002 was 117.533 billion kWh. In 2001, coal accounted for 93% of Poland's primary energy production. However, consumption had declined 23% between 1993 and 2002.

Poland has been gradually deregulating its power market since 1998. Each year an increasing number of companies are allowed to choose their own electricity provider. By 2006 the sector will be completely open.

28 INDUSTRY

Leading industries in Poland include food processing, fuel, metals and metal products, automotive parts, chemicals, coal mining, glass, shipbuilding, and textiles. Industrial production increased by 14.5% annually during 1971–75, but in the late 1970s, the growth rate began to fall. During the 1980s, it grew at an annual rate of 1.1%. With the destabilizing effects of the dissolution of the Soviet bloc and central planning, industrial production initially fell by 26% in 1990 before returning to positive growth between 1991–98. Poland produced 10 million tons of steel per year in the mid-1990s. Sulfur is another important industrial commodity; and its production totaled 1,901 tons per year. The cement industry turned out 12.3 million tons during the same period.

Light industries were long relegated to a secondary position but, since the 1970s, Poland has increased its production of durable household articles and other consumer goods. In the mid-1990s, Poland produced 401,000 automatic washing machines, 584,000 refrigerators and freezers, 841,000 television sets, 307,000 radios, and 21,000 tape recorders and dictaphones per year.

Currently Poland is among the top 10 world producers of coal, copper and sulphur, and among the top 20 producers of sulphuric acid, cement, television sets, passenger cars, buses and trucks, and power engineering. Poland is also a leading world producer of some food stuffs such as rye, sugar beets, meat, milk barley, wheat, sugar, and eggs.

Since the accession to the EU, there has been a rapid increase in exports as well as in relocation of production facilities such as car and truck assembly plants and household appliances plants from Western Europe to Polish commercial zones such as Lódz and Wroclaw. In addition, there have been many investments from non-European countries such as plans to build an LCD factory near Wroclaw by the South Korean concern LG Electronics.

29 SCIENCE AND TECHNOLOGY

Destruction of the Polish scientific community, buildings, and equipment during World War II was nearly total, requiring a tremendous rebuilding program. Attached to the various university faculties and government bodies are institutes, laboratories, and clinics devoted primarily to research, but some offering advanced instruction. In 1952, the Polish Academy of Sciences, established in Warsaw, replaced the old Polish Academy of Sciences and Letters of Cracow; it has sections of biological sciences; mathematical, physical, and chemical sciences; technical sciences; agricultural and forestry sciences; medical sciences; and earth and mining sciences. As of 1996, 54 scientific and technological research institutes were affiliated with the Academy of Sciences, and there were 101 scientific and technological research institutes attached to government ministries. In Warsaw are located a botanical garden and museums devoted to zoology, technology, and the earth. The Polish Maritime Museum is located in Gdańsk. The Nicholas Kopernik Museum in Frambork includes exhibits on the history of medicine and astronomy.

Research and development (R&D) expenditures in 2002 amounted to $2.4 trillion or 0.59% of GDP. Of that amount, 61.1% came from government sources, followed by the business sector at 31%. Higher education, private nonprofit groups and foreign sources accounted for 2.9%, 0.3% and 4.8%, respectively. Personnel engaged in R&D in that same year included 1,469 scientists and engineers and 296 technicians per million people. High technology exports in 2002 totaled $915 million, or 3% of the country's manufactured exports.

In 1996, Poland had 50 universities offering courses in basic and applied sciences. In 1987–1997, science and engineering students accounted for 28% of university enrollment. In 2002, of all bachelor's degrees awarded, 16.3% were in the sciences (natural, mathematics and computers, engineering).

30 DOMESTIC TRADE

In 1990, Poland replaced its 40-year old centrally planned economy with a free market system. Most small enterprises were privatized, bringing an end to chronic shortages of consumer goods. At the end of 1996, the share of private enterprises in retail trade exceeded 90%. The resulting increase in domestic demand was a primary factor in strengthening the business cycle. In the past few years, the trend in retail establishments, particularly in major cities, has moved from small, independent shops to international supermarket chains, hypermarkets, and large specialty stores. However, small business-owners have been forming associations aimed at promoting and preserving local, independent retailing.

Offices are open from 8 or 9 AM to 4 PM Monday through Friday. Food stores are open from 6 or 7 AM to 7 PM; other stores, from 11 AM to 7 or 8 PM; and banks, from 9 AM to 4 PM Monday through Friday, and 9 AM to 1 PM on Saturday. The most important trade exhibition is the annual Poznan International Fair, which takes place in June.

According to World Bank report published in 2004, Poland is among the top 10 countries improving their operating climate for enterprises. There were over 90 franchises in operation, with national firms as well as foreign firms represented. The number of foreign enterprises has been growing constantly. According to GUS (the Central Statistical Office), in 2002, about 10–12% of the retail market was operated by foreign firms, particularly through chain stores providing a range of goods from food and apparel to furniture and hardware supplies; in the first half of 2004, the number of foreign enterprises exceeded 50,000 an increase of 1,034 companies. The attractiveness of Poland is connected with its advantageous geographical location, EU membership, low labor costs and a high number of people with higher education. The largest inflow of foreign direct investment has been recorded by the manufacturing sector, especially by the automotive and electronic equipment and pharmaceutical branches.

31 FOREIGN TRADE

Until recently, foreign trade was a state monopoly under the control of the Ministry of Foreign Trade. After World War II, the orientation of Polish trade shifted from Western and Central European countries to Eastern Europe. This changed with the dissolution of the Soviet-bloc CMEA in 1991. In December of that year, Poland signed an association agreement with the EC (now the EU) and by 2000, 70% of its exports and 61% of its imports were going to EC members. Poland also fosters trade through its membership in the Central European Free Trade Agreement (CEFTA), which includes Hungary, the Czech Republic, and the Slovak Republic. Since gaining full membership in the EU in 2004, Polish exports to the West have continued to increase faster than imports. Trade with the countries to the east has recently recovered to the levels from before the 1998 Russian financial crisis, although it is often stifled by minor frictions with Russia and Belarus, for example the controversial restrictions on Polish meat exports to Russia in the fall of 2005.

Poland's export commodities are a mixture of manufactured goods including furniture (7.0%), garments (6.1%), motor vehicles (4.6%), iron and steel (3.9%), and ships (3.3%). Export com-

Principal Trading Partners – Poland (2003)			
(In millions of US dollars)			
Country	Exports	Imports	Balance
World	53,539.3	67,975.7	-14,436.4
Germany	17,241.5	16,543.8	697.7
France-Monaco	3,251.5	4,769.7	-1,518.2
Italy-San Marino-Holy See	3,057.7	5,752.0	-2,694.3
United Kingdom	2,676.1	2,495.8	180.3
Netherlands	2,381.8	2,267.1	114.7
Czech Republic	2,136.3	2,300.7	-164.4
Sweden	1,913.4	1,751.0	162.4
Belgium	1,711.0	1,751.7	-40.7
Ukraine	1,523.5	734.2	789.3
Russia	1,480.2	5,202.0	-3,721.8
(…) data not available or not significant.			

SOURCE: *2003 International Trade Statistics Yearbook,* New York: United Nations, 2004.

Balance of Payments – Poland (2003)

(In millions of US dollars)

Current Account		**-4,603.0**
Balance on goods	-5,725.0	
Imports	-66,732.0	
Exports	61,007.0	
Balance on services	527.0	
Balance on income	-3,639.0	
Current transfers	4,234.0	
Capital Account		**-46.0**
Financial Account		**8,734.0**
Direct investment abroad	-196.0	
Direct investment in Poland	4,123.0	
Portfolio investment assets	-1,296.0	
Portfolio investment liabilities	3,740.0	
Financial derivatives	-870.0	
Other investment assets	-1,838.0	
Other investment liabilities	5,071.0	
Net Errors and Omissions		**-2,879.0**
Reserves and Related Items		**-1,206.0**

(…) data not available or not significant.

SOURCE: *Balance of Payment Statistics Yearbook 2004,* Washington, DC: International Monetary Fund, 2004.

modities formed from natural resources include wood (2.5%); coal, lignite, and peat (2.3%); and copper (2.3%).

32 BALANCE OF PAYMENTS

Measured in terms of commodity trade figures, negative balances have been the rule in Poland in the post–World War II period. In 1991, the collapse of exports to the Soviet Union dealt a sharp blow to overall export performance. The requirement to exchange by means of hard currency for Soviet raw materials and energy prevented a repeat of the 1990 trade surplus. Poland attracted approximately $50 billion of foreign direct investment between 1990 and 2000. Net official reserves have increased in recent years, due to large capital surpluses due to foreign direct investment and portfolio inflows.

The US Central Intelligence Agency (CIA) reported that in 2002 the purchasing power parity of Poland's exports was $32.4 billion while imports totaled $43.4 billion resulting in a trade deficit of $11 billion.

According to the International Monetary Fund (IMF), in 2001 Poland had exports of goods totaling $41.7 billion and imports totaling $49.3 billion. In 2005 imports totaled €50.9 billion and exports totaled €45.0 billion.

33 BANKING AND SECURITIES

The Banking Law of 1 July 1982 substantially reformed the Polish banking system by giving banks an effective role in setting monetary and credit policy, thereby allowing them to influence economic planning. The Council of Banks, consisting of top bank officers and representatives of the Planning Commission and the Ministry of Finance, is the principal coordinating body.

The National Bank of Poland (Narodowy Bank Polski-NBP), created in 1945 to replace the former Bank of Poland, is a state institution and the bank of issue. It also controls foreign transactions and prepares financial plans for the economy. On 1 January 1970,

the National Bank merged with the Investment Bank and has since controlled funds for finance and investment transactions of state enterprises and organizations. The function of the Food Economy Bank and its associated cooperative banks is to supply short and long-term credits to rural areas. The national commercial bank, Bank Handlowy w Warszawie (BH), finances foreign trade operations. The General Savings Bank (Bank Polska Kasa Opieki-PKO), a central institution for personal savings, also handles financial transfers into Poland of persons living abroad.

In March 1985, two types of hard-currency accounts were introduced: "A" accounts, bearing interest, for currency earned in an approved way; and "B" accounts, for other currency, bearing no interest. "B" accounts can be converted into "A" accounts after one year. Major enterprises in Poland conduct their business by interaccount settlements through the National Bank rather than by check, and wages are paid in cash. Banking laws in 1989 opened the country's banking system to foreign banks.

A fundamental reorganization of the banking sector took place between 1990 and 1992. The NBP lost all its central planning functions, including holding the accounts of state enterprises, making transfers among them, crediting their operations, and exercising financial control of their activities. The NBP thus became only a central bank, and state enterprises competed with other businesses for the scarce credits available from commercial banks. Nine independent (so-called commercial), although state-owned, regional banks were created.

In 1993, the first of these, the Poznan-based Wielkopolski Bank Kredytowy (WBK), was privatized. A second highly controversial privatization took place in early 1994 with the sale of the Silesian Bank (Bank Slaski). Also, the Krakow-based Bank Przemyslowo-Handlowy (BPH) was disposed of at the start of 1995 and Bank Gdanski was sold in late 1995. With four major banks privatized, five remained to be sold off in a process that was supposed to have been completed by 1996. With no real hope of meeting this deadline, the Polish government returned in 1996 to proposals for "bank consolidation" prior to privatization. A major round of privatization was due to begin in 1998-99 beginning with the sale of Pekao, the country's largest commercial bank. This sale finally put over half of the industry's holdings in private hands. At the same time, foreign investment in Polish banks continued to increase. Citibank, ING, Commerzbank, Allied Irish Bank, and J.P. Morgan were leading foreign investors in 1998. In 2001, Bank Handlowy w Warszawie SA merged with Citibank (Poland) SA, but retained its historic name.

The International Monetary Fund reports that in 2001, currency and demand deposits—an aggregate commonly known as M1—were equal to $23.0 billion. In that same year, M2—an aggregate equal to M1 plus savings deposits, small time deposits, and money market mutual funds—was $82.8 billion. The money market rate, the rate at which financial institutions lend to one another in the short term, was 16.2%. The discount rate, the interest rate at which the central bank lends to financial institutions in the short term, was 14%.

In early 1991 important legislation was introduced to regulate securities transactions and establish a stock exchange in Warsaw. At the same time, a securities commission was formed for consumer protection. A year later, the shares of 11 Polish companies were being traded weekly on the new exchange. Restructuring the

Public Finance – Poland (2001)

(In millions of zlotys, central government figures)

Revenue and Grants	**223,659**	**100.0%**
Tax revenue	127,203	56.9%
Social contributions	69,504	31.1%
Grants	426	0.2%
Other revenue	26,526	11.9%
Expenditures	**263,580**	**100.0%**
General public services	81,294	30.8%
Defense	9,052	3.4%
Public order and safety	8,592	3.3%
Economic affairs	11,988	4.5%
Environmental protection	...	...
Housing and community amenities	5,325	2.0%
Health	2,151	0.8%
Recreational, culture, and religion	1,861	0.7%
Education	12,731	4.8%
Social protection	135,615	51.5%

(…) data not available or not significant.

SOURCE: *Government Finance Statistics Yearbook 2004*, Washington, DC: International Monetary Fund, 2004.

financial market not only was necessary for increasing the overall efficiency of the economy and accelerating privatization, but also was a precondition for the rapid influx of Western capital critical to economic development.

When the Warsaw Stock Exchange opened in April 1991, it had only five listed companies, but by September 1996 that figure had increased to 63. Into 1998, the market still suffered growing pains similar to those afflicting other emerging markets. In particular, the high liquidity of Polish stocks made Poland particularly vulnerable to panic selling. Market capitalization in 2001 was $26 billion, down 17% from the $31.3 billion level of 2000. The WIG All Share Performance Index was at 13,922.2 in 2001, down 22% from 17.847.6 in 2000. As of 2004, a total of 225 companies were listed on the Warsaw Stock Exchange, which had a market capitalization of $71.102 billion. In 2004 the WIG All Share Performance Index rose 27.9% from the previous year to 26,636.2.

34 INSURANCE

In 1948, all insurance other than social insurance was included in a centralized State Insurance Bureau, with the former reinsurance organization, Warta, continuing its activity. In 1994, Warta was privatized and was one of three major insurers who, together, controlled over 90% of Poland's insurance market. In 1999, 54 licensed insurance companies competed in the Polish market.

Insurance is dominated by a state concern, PZU, but a number of Western companies, including the United Kingdom's Commercial Union (CU), have been tempted into joint ventures in the life insurance end of this underdeveloped market. CU began its Polish operations in cooperation with the Wielkopolski Bank Kredytowy (WBK) bank. It sold around 130,000 policies in its first four years. PZU was privatized in 1999. In Poland, third-party auto liability, farmer's liability, fire insurance, workers' compensation, and nuclear liability are all compulsory. For 2003, the value of direct premiums written totaled $6.258 billion, of which nonlife premiums accounted for $3.946 billion. In 2003, Poland's top nonlife insurer

was PZU, while PZU Zycie was the nation's leading life insurer, with gross written nonlife and life insurance premiums of $1.86 billion and $1.32 billion, respectively.

35 PUBLIC FINANCE

The annual budget is presented to the Sejm in December and becomes effective for the fiscal year beginning on 1 January. A new set of economic reforms, announced in early 2002, aim to improve the country's investment climate and public finances. Privatization in the former Eastern bloc nation has been fairly successful, with approximately two-thirds of GDP now coming from the private sector. By the early 1990s, Poland was the first formerly planned economy in Eastern Europe to come out of recession and experience economic growth.

The US Central Intelligence Agency (CIA) estimated that in 2005 Poland's central government took in revenues of approximately $52.7 billion and had expenditures of $63.2 billion. Revenues minus expenditures totaled approximately -$10.4 billion. Public debt in 2005 amounted to 47.3% of GDP. Total external debt was $123.4 billion.

The International Monetary Fund (IMF) reported that in 2001, the most recent year for which it had data, central government revenues were z223.6 million and expenditures were z263.58 million. The value of revenues was us$54.6 billion and expenditures us$65.6 billion, based on a market exchange rate for 2001 of us$1 = z4.0939 as reported by the IMF. Government outlays by function were as follows: general public services, 30.8%; defense, 3.4%; public order and safety, 3.3%; economic affairs, 4.5%; housing and community amenities, 2.0%; health, 0.8%; recreation, culture, and religion, 0.7%; education, 4.8%; and social protection, 51.5%.

36 TAXATION

Personal income tax in Poland in 2005 is progressively structured with a top rate of 40%, although under certain circumstances, an individual may opt to be taxed at a flat 19% rate on business income. Individuals realizing capital gains from the sale of land, a building, or dwelling not used for business purposes is subject to a 10% rate.

Poland has a general corporate profits tax rate of 19%. Capital gains and branch operations are each taxed at the corporate rate. Dividends and interest paid to residents and nonresidents are taxed at a flat 19% rate. Income from interest, fees and royalties are subject to a 20% withholding rate, unless other rates have been agreed to in bilateral tax treaties (BITs). Poland has BITs with at least 66 countries. In the BIT with the United States, withholding rates are 0% on interest income, 10% on income from royalties, and 5% on dividend income if the receiving company owns at least 10% of voting shares.

The main indirect tax is a system of value-added taxes (VATs). There are four VAT rates: 22% on most goods and some services; 7% on processed foodstuffs and construction materials; 3% on unprocessed foodstuffs; 0% on exported goods and services; and "VAT-exempt" applied to several groups of services, including financial services, insurance and health care. Excise taxes are charged on alcohol, cars, petrol, and tobacco products. There is also a civil transactions tax.

³⁷CUSTOMS AND DUTIES

Poland uses the Harmonized System of Classification. Products are divided into three categories to determine which rate they receive: developing nations, WTO members, and countries with which Poland has a special trade relationship such as a bilateral preferential trade agreement. Under the terms of a 1992 agreement, Poland uses the EU Nomenclature System of Tariff classification and has granted duty-free status to over 1,000 line items from EU countries. Tariffs range from 0% to nearly 400%. In addition, all goods are subject to a 5% import tax, an excise tax on luxury items, and a VAT of 0%, 3%, 7%, or 22%, depending on the commodity. As a result of its efforts to join in the next round of EU expansion, Poland is bringing its trade regulations in line with EU standards.

³⁸FOREIGN INVESTMENT

Prior to World War II, considerable foreign capital was invested in the Polish economy, particularly in petroleum and mining, which were mostly foreign owned. A nationalization decree in 1946 confiscated foreign properties and nationalized Poland's industries, eliminating foreign investments completely. The decree provided for no compensation procedures and foreign governments involved negotiated directly with Poland. The first joint venture with Western counterparts (one Austrian and one US company) was formed in early 1987 to build a new airport terminal in Warsaw. In mid-1991, there were 4,100 foreign registrations, worth $506 million, and in 1993 another $2 billion in foreign investment entered Poland. Among the industrial companies sold to Western interests were Polam-Pila (lightbulbs) to Phillips, Polkolor (TV sets) to Thomson, Pollena-Bydgoszcz (detergents) to Unilever, and Wedel (confectioneries) to Pepsico Foods.

In 1996–97, Poland continued to invite foreign investors to help the government turn some of its banks and oil, arms, and telecommunications companies over to the private sector. In October 1996 President Aleksander Kwasniewski stated that the government's campaign to shed costly state-owned enterprises had been successful, with the private sector now accounting for about 70% of the goods and services produced in the economy. Total foreign direct investment (FDI) reached nearly $27.3 billion in 1998. FDI inflow in 1998 was $6.3 billion, up from nearly $5 billion in 1997, and increased to $7.2 billion in 1999, undeterred by the effects of the Russian financial crisis. Annual FDI inflow peaked at over $9.3 billion in 2000, having grown at an average rate of 44% a year since 1991 to 2000. Total FDI stock was over $42 billion in 2000. In 2001 and 2002, the economic slowdown, and, particularly, the worldwide decline in foreign investments, helped reduce annual FDI inflows into Poland to $8.3 billion in 2001 and to $6.06 billion in 2002. Cumulative FDI as of 2002 was $61.45 billion.

³⁹ECONOMIC DEVELOPMENT

After World War II, the economy of Poland was centrally planned and almost completely under state control, especially in nonagricultural sectors. The nationalized industries and businesses operated within the national economic plan and were governed by the directives issued by the pertinent ministries. After 1963, however, centralized planning and management were somewhat relaxed, and state-owned enterprises gained more freedom in the design and implementation of their programs. Private undertakings were confined to personal crafts and trades and agriculture.

Under the three-year plan for 1947–49, principal emphasis was placed on the reconstruction of war-devastated areas and industries, in order to raise production and living conditions at least to their prewar levels. Economic planning followed Soviet lines, setting production goals that determined tasks for each sector on a long-term basis. Under the six-year plan for 1950–55, the emphasis continued to be on heavy industry, and the housing, transport, agriculture, and consumer sectors lagged. The five-year plan for 1956–60, originally cast along the same lines, was modified after the 1956 disturbances. It called for a lessened rate of industrial expansion and for increases in agricultural output, housing, consumer goods, and social services. Under a long-range plan for 1961–75, which governed the three five-year plans falling within that period, emphasis was placed on a direct improvement in living standards. The first and second of these plans (1961–65 and 1966–70) were oriented toward investments intended (1) to develop the raw-material base of the country, especially the newly discovered resources of sulfur, copper, and lignite; (2) to secure employment opportunities for the rapidly growing population of working age; and (3) to improve Poland's international trade balance. The five-year plan for 1961–65 reached its industrial targets but fell short in the areas of agriculture and consumer goods. The period 1966–70 witnessed two poor agricultural years in addition to export lags, and there were shortages of basic food commodities in 1969–70.

In late 1970, violent protests erupted over the government's stepped-up efforts to increase production. After the change in political leadership from Gomulka to Gierek, government emphasis shifted from heavy industry to light, consumer-oriented production. In addition, through a concentration of investment in mechanization, fertilizers, and other farm improvements, the government sought and achieved a 50% increase in food production. Overall, the 1971–75 five-year plan achieved its main targets by a wide margin, with industrial production up about 73%. The 1976–80 plan, which aimed at a 50% increase in industrial production and a 16% increase in agricultural output, ran into difficulty almost from the beginning, and by 1979 the economy had entered a period of decline and dislocation that continued into 1982. An economic reform stressing decentralization of the economy was introduced in January 1982, but it failed to produce any significant improvements. With price rises and consumer goods shortages continuing to fuel popular discontent, the government in March 1983 announced a three-year austerity plan for 1983–85. Its aims included a general consolidation of the economy, self-sufficiency in food production, and increased emphasis on housing and the production of industrial consumer goods. By 1986, the economy had rebounded. The 1986–90 plan expected the national income to grow 3–3.5% annually, industrial output to increase by 3.2% each year, and exports to grow by 5% (in fixed prices) annually. These goals were not reached. A "second stage," proclaimed in 1986, called for more autonomy for individual enterprises and for more efficient management, with top jobs filled without regard to political affiliations.

The Economic Transformation Program adopted in January 1990 aimed to convert Poland from a planned to a market economy. Measures were aimed at drastically reducing the large budget deficit, abolishing all trade monopolies, and selling many state-owned enterprises to private interests.

The slow pace of privatization picked up somewhat in 1995, as 512 smaller state enterprises were transferred to private National Investment Funds under the Mass Privatization Program, but large-scale industry remained largely under state control. However, the government subsequently made an attempt to privatize such large-scale sectors of the economy as banks and oil, arms, and telecommunications. Poland in the early 2000s was in the process of bringing its economic policies in line with EU standards. These policies promise even further liberalization and foreign investment into the Polish economy. Poland officially joined the EU in May 2004. In 2002, the government announced a new set of economic reforms, including improving the investment climate (particularly for small- and medium-sized enterprises), and improving the country's public finances to prepare the way for the adoption of the euro. Recently, the government has focused utilizing the EU funds to improve Poland's infrastructure.

40 SOCIAL DEVELOPMENT

A social insurance institute administers social security programs through a network of branch offices, under the provision of new legislation passed in 1998 and implemented in 1999. Social security, including social insurance and medical care, covers virtually the entire population. Old age, disability, and survivors' pensions are provided, as well as family allowances, sickness benefits, maternity benefits, workers' compensation, and unemployment. The system is funded by contributions from employers and employees and government subsidies. In 2004 a revised universal system of family allowances funded by the government covers all residents.

The constitution establishes that all citizens are equal, regardless of gender, but discrimination persists. Women participate actively in the labor force, but are concentrated in low-paying professions and earn less than men on average. Also, women are more likely to be fired and less likely to be promoted than men. Violence against women and domestic abuse remain a widespread problem. The law does not provide restraining orders, and even convicted abusers generally go unpunished. As of 2004, there were not enough shelters for battered women. Sexual harassment in the workplace is slowly being addressed.

The Romani minority living in Poland faces discrimination by local authorities. Anti-Semitic harassment, vandalism, and violence persist. The judicial system is hampered by inefficiency and budget constraints, and there are marginal restrictions on freedoms of speech and press.

41 HEALTH

As of 2004, there were an estimated 220 physicians, 490 nurses, and 30 dentists per 100,000 people. The same year, the total health care expenditure was estimated at 6.2% of GDP.

Poland's birth rate was an estimated 10.3 per 1,000 people as of 2002. Approximately 75% of married women (ages 15 to 49) used contraception. Poland immunized children up to one year old against tuberculosis, 94%; diphtheria, pertussis, and tetanus, 98%; polio, 96%; and measles, 97%.

Life expectancy in 2005 averaged 74.74 years and infant mortality was 7.36 per 1,000 live births. The general mortality rate was 10 per 1,000 people.

There were many cases of tuberculosis as part of the spread of the disease throughout much of Eastern Europe. The heart disease mortality rate for Polish men and women was below average for high development countries. The likelihood of dying after 65 of heart disease was 240 in 1,000 for men and 201 in 1,000 for women. The HIV/AIDS prevalence was 0.10 per 100 adults in 2003. As of 2004, there were approximately 14,000 people living with HIV/AIDS in the country. There were an estimated 100 deaths from AIDS in 2003.

42 HOUSING

Almost 40% of all urban dwelling space was destroyed during World War II. Although investment in public housing has increased, and credits have been assigned for cooperative and private construction, the housing shortage remained critical five decades later. The average wait for an apartment ranged from 10–15 years. In 1984 there were 10,253,000 dwelling units; an additional 193,000 dwelling units were constructed in 1985. In 2002, there were about 12.5 million dwelling units registered in the census serving about 13.3 million households; about 93.9% of these were occupied dwellings. About 67.6% of all dwellings were in urban areas. About 55.2% of all dwellings were owned by private individuals. The average number of persons per dwelling was 3.25. At least 76.2% of all dwellings were built after 1944. The housing deficit in 2002 was estimated at about 1,567,000; an estimated 6.5 million people were living in substandard housing.

43 EDUCATION

Primary, secondary, and most university and other education is free. State and local expenditure on education is, therefore, substantial. Lower schools are financed by local budgets, higher and vocational schools from the state budget. As of 2003, public expenditure on education was estimated at 5.6% of GDP, or 12.8% of total government expenditures.

Since 1999, the school system, which is centralized, consists of an six-year primary school followed by a three-year lower secondary general education school. Students then have an option to enroll in a four-year technical school, a three-year upper secondary school, or a two- to three year vocational school. Vocational schools are attended by students studying technology, agriculture, forestry, economy, education, health services, and the arts. The academic year runs from October to June.

In 2001, about 49% of children between the ages of three and six were enrolled in some type of preschool program. Primary school enrollment in 2003 was estimated at about 98% of age-eligible students. The same year, secondary school enrollment was about 91% of age-eligible students. It is estimated that about 98.5% of all students complete their primary education. The student-to-teacher ratio for primary school was at about 13:1 in 2003; the ratio for secondary school was about 14:1.

Higher learning is under the jurisdiction of the Ministry of Higher Education and other ministries. A matriculation examination, which is common for all students, is required for admission to institutions of higher learning. As of 2004, there were 128 state institutions of higher learning and 304 nonstate institutions. Jagiellonian University, among the oldest in Europe, was established at Cracow in 1364. Other prominent universities are the Warsaw University; the Central School of Planning and Statistics (Warsaw); the Higher Theater School (Warsaw); the Academy of Fine Arts (Cracow); and the Adam Mickiewicz University (Poznań). During the communist era the Roman Catholic University at Lublin was the only free private university in the Socialist bloc. Evening and extramural courses are available for anyone who is interested and is not a part of the school system. Foreign students are also welcome to study in Poland, either as regular students or at their summer schools. In 2003, about 60% of the tertiary age population were enrolled in some type of higher education program; 50% for men and 71% for women. The adult literacy rate for 2003 was estimated at about 99.8%.

As of 2003, public expenditure on education was estimated at 5.6% of GDP, or 12.8% of total government expenditures.

44 LIBRARIES AND MUSEUMS

The National Library, established in Warsaw in 1928, is the second-largest in Poland, with about 2.8 million items, including periodicals, manuscripts, maps, illustrations, and music. Other important libraries are the Public University and the government departmental libraries in Warsaw; Poland's largest library, the Jagiellonian University Library in Cracow, which has 3.5 million volumes; and the Ossolineum Library in Wroclaw. There are over 9,000 public libraries in the country. Lax security at Poland's libraries poses a challenge to the preservation of rare documents: in 1998, a scientific library in Cracow reported the theft of a rare book by Nicholas Copernicus, and in 1999, the Jagiellonian University Library reported the theft of an indeterminate number of rare manuscripts.

Of the more than 500 museums in Poland, the foremost is the National Museum in Warsaw, which has an extensive and important art collection as well as a collection of Polish art from the 12th century to present day. Other important museums are the National Museum in Cracow, notable for its collection of Far Eastern Art, and the National Museum in Poznań, which has a celebrated collection of musical instruments. Cracow also has an important collection of European decorative arts at the Wawel Royal Castle, housed in a 16th century manor house, and the Czartoryski Museum, a world-class collection of antiquities and contemporary artifacts including 35,000 prints, drawings, and paintings. Warsaw has dozens of museums, including the Center for Contemporary Art, founded in 1986, in Ujazdowski Castle; the Museum of Independence, founded in 1990, chronicling Poland's pivotal role in the collapse of the Soviet Empire; the Museum of Polish Emigration to America; the Frederick Chopin Museum, chronicling the life of one of the country's best-known composers; the Marie Curie Museum, housed at her birthplace; and the Museum of the Jewish Historical Institute.

45 MEDIA

In 2003, there were an estimated 319 mainline telephones for every 1,000 people; about 500,000 people were on a waiting list for telephone service installation. The same year, there were approximately 451 mobile phones in use for every 1,000 people.

In 2004, the government-owned Polish Television (TVP) was the most widely viewed network with four channels accounting for about 54% of the broadcasting market share. The main privately held competitors were the TVN and Polsat networks. Cable television and various satellite services are available. As of 1998,

there were 14 AM and 777 FM radio stations. In 2003, there were an estimated 523 radios and 229 television sets for every 1,000 people. About 94 of every 1,000 people were cable subscribers. Also in 2003, there were 142 personal computers for every 1,000 people and 232 of every 1,000 people had access to the Internet. There were 565 secure Internet servers in the country in 2004.

The largest Polish daily newspapers, with circulation as noted, are: *Trybuna Slaska*, 800,000 in 2002; *Gazeta Wyborcza*, 558,000 in 2004; 460,000 (weekend edition in 2005); *Express Wieczorny*, 400,000 in 2002; *Zycie Warszawy, Express Illustrowany*, 370,000; *Gazeta Poznanska*, 320,000 (weekend edition); *Gazeta Robotnicza*, 315,000; *Fakt*, 300,000 in 2003; *Czas Krakowski*, 260,000 in 2002 (weekend edition); *Nasz Dziennik*, 250,000 in 2005; *Sztandar Mlodych*, 250,000 in 2002; and *Rzeczpospolita*, 244,000 in 2004.

Though the constitution provides for free speech and a free press, there are some restrictions on these rights. The Penal Code prohibits speech which publicly insults or ridicules the Polish state or its principal organs; it also prohibits advocating discord or offending religious groups. Though the media are not censored, they may be subject to prosecution under these and other penal codes.

46 ORGANIZATIONS

The Polish Chamber of Commerce and the Chamber of Foreign Trade promote foreign trade by furnishing information, establishing or extending commercial relations, and arranging for Polish participation in trade fairs, and exhibitions abroad. The most important worker's organization in Poland is Solidarity, founded in 1980 by Lech Welesa. There are a number of professional associations and trade unions representing a wide variety of occupations.

The P.E.N. Club–Poland is based in Warsaw. The Frederick Chopin Society is a multinational organization promoting the life and works of this Polish composer and pianist. Several professional associations, such as the Polish Medical Association, also serve to promote research and education in specific fields.

There are also many cultural, sports and social organizations in Poland. National youth organizations include the European Federalist Youth, Junior Chamber, Polish Students' Union, Polish Environmental Youth Movement, Union of Young Christian Democrats, The Polish Scouting and Guiding Association, and YMCA/YWCA. There are numerous sports associations promoting amateur competitions in a wide variety of sports for athletes of all ages. There are organizations affiliated with the Special Olympics and the Paralympic Committee, as well as the Olympic Committee.

National women's organizations include the Democratic Women's Union and the Polish Association of University Women. Other social action groups include the Helsinki Human Rights Foundation and Fundacja Stefana Batorego, a group which promotes a democratic and open society. There are national chapters of the Red Cross Society, Habitat for Humanity, UNICEF, and Amnesty International.

47 TOURISM, TRAVEL, AND RECREATION

The main tourist attractions include the historic city of Cracow, which suffered little war damage; the resort towns of Zakopane, in the Tatras, and Sopot, on the Baltic; and the restored Old Town in Warsaw, as well as the capital's museums and Palace of Science and Culture. Camping, hiking, and football (soccer) are among the most popular recreational activities.

Foreign visitors to Poland must have a valid passport. All visitors are required to carry a visa except citizens of over 30 nations including the United States and members of the European Union.

There were approximately 52 million visitors who arrived in Poland in 2003, about 99% of whom came from Europe. Hotel rooms numbered 68,588 with 134,323 beds and an occupancy rate of about 36%. The average length of stay was three nights. That year tourism receipts totaled $4.7 billion.

In 2005, the US Department of State estimated the cost of staying in Warsaw at $286 per day. Elsewhere in Poland, daily travel expenses were estimated to be between $139 and $221.

48 FAMOUS POLES

Figures prominent in Polish history include Mieszko I (fl.10th century), who led Poland to Christianity; his son and successor, Boleslaw I ("the Brave," d.1025), the first king of sovereign Poland; Casimir III ("the Great," 1309–70), who sponsored domestic reforms; and John III Sobieski (1624–96), who led the Polish-German army that lifted the siege of Vienna in 1683 and repelled the Turkish invaders. Tadeusz Andrzej Bonawentura Kościuszko (1746–1817), trained as a military engineer, served with colonial forces during the American Revolution and then led a Polish rebellion against Russia in 1794; he was wounded, captured, and finally exiled. Kazimierz Pulaski (1747–79) fought and died in the American Revolution, and Haym Salomon (1740–85) helped to finance it. The reconstituted Polish state after World War I was led by Józef Pilsudski (1867–1935), who ruled as a dictator from 1926 until his death. Polish public life since World War II has been dominated by Wladyslaw Gomulka (1905–82), Edward Gierek (1913–2001), and Gen. Wojciech Jaruzelski (b.1923), Communist leaders, respectively, during 1956–70, during 1970–80, and after 1981. Important roles have also been played by Stefan Cardinal Wyszynski (1901–81), Roman Catholic primate of Poland, archbishop of Gniezno and Warsaw, and frequent adversary of the postwar Communist regime; Karol Wojtyla (1920–2005), archbishop of Cracow from 1963 until his elevation to the papacy as John Paul II in 1978; and Lech Walesa (b.1943), leader of the Solidarity movement during 1980–81, Nobel Peace Prize laureate in 1983, and President of Poland from 1990 to 1995.

The father of Polish literature is Nicholas Rey (1505–69), one of the earliest Polish writers to turn from Latin to the vernacular. Poland's golden age is marked by the beginning of literature in Polish; its greatest poet was Jan Kochanowski (1530–84). Notable among 19th-century poets and dramatists was Adam Mickiewicz (1798–1855), whose *The Books of the Polish Nation and of the Polish Pilgrimage*, *Pan Tadeusz*, and other works exerted a paramount influence on all future generations. Other leading literary figures were the poets and dramatists Juliusz Slowacki (1809–49) and Zygmunt Krasiński (1812–59), whose *Dawn* breathed an inspired patriotism. Józef Kraszewski (1812–87), prolific and patriotic prose writer, is considered the father of the Polish novel. The leading late-19th-century novelists were the realists Aleksander Glowacki (1847–1912), who wrote under the pseudonym of Boleslaw Prus, and Henryk Sienkiewicz (1846–1916), Poland's first Nobel Prize winner (1905), whose *The Trilogy* described the 17th-century wars of Poland; he is internationally famous for *Quo Vadis*. Another Nobel Prize winner (1924) was the novelist Wladyslaw Reymont (1867–1925), acclaimed for *The Peasants*. A Pole who achieved stature as an English novelist was Joseph Conrad (Józef Teodor Konrad Korzeniowski, 1857–1924). Other important literary figures around the turn of the century were the playwright and painter Stanislaw Wyspiański (1869–1907), the novelist Stefan Zeromski (1864–1926), and the novelist Stanislaw Ignacy Witkiewicz (1885–1939). The best-known modern authors are novelist and short-story writer Isaac Bashevis Singer (1904–91), a Nobel Prize winner in 1978 and a US resident after 1935; the satirist Witold Gombrowicz (1904–69); science-fiction writer Stanislaw Lem (b.1921); the dissident novelist Jerzy Andrzejewski (1909–83); the poet Czeslaw Milosz (1911–2004), a Nobel Prize winner in 1980 and resident of the United States after 1960; and novelist Jerzy Kosinski (1933–91), who lived in the United States after 1957 and wrote in English.

The greatest Polish composer was Frédéric Chopin (1810–49), born in Warsaw, who lived in Paris after 1831. A popular composer was Stanislaw Moniuszko (1819–72), founder of the Polish national opera and composer of many songs; he influenced such later composers as Wladyslaw Zeleński (1837–1921), Zygmunt Noskowski (1846–1909), and Stanislaw Niewiadomski (1859–1936). Other prominent musicians include the pianist Ignacy Jan Paderewski (1860–1941), also his country's first prime minister following World War I; the great harpsichordist Wanda Landowska (1877–1959); the renowned pianist Arthur Rubinstein (1887–1982); the violinist Wanda Wilkomirska (b.1929); the conductor Stanislaw Skrowaczewski (b.1923); and the composers Mieczyslaw Karlowicz (1876–1909) and Karol Szymanowski (1883–1937). Witold Lutoslawski (1913–94) and Krzysztof Penderecki (b.1933) are internationally known contemporary composers.

The first Polish painters of European importance were Piotr Michalowski (1800–55) and Henryk Rodakowski (1823–94). In the second half of the 19th century, Polish realism reached its height in the historical paintings of Jan Matejko (1838–93), Artur Grottger (1837–67), Juliusz Kossak (1824–99), and Józef Brandt (1841–1915), as well as in genre painting and the landscapes of Wojciech Gerson (1831–1901), Józef Szermentowski (1833–76), Aleksander Kotsis (1836–77), Maksymilian Gierymski (1846–74), Aleksander Gierymski (1849–1901), and Józef Chelmoński (1849–1914). Feliks Topolski (1907–89), who lived in London after 1935, is well known for his oil paintings, watercolors, and drawings. Andrzej Wajda (b.1926), Roman Polański (b.1933), an expatriate since the mid-1960s, Krzysztof Zanussi (b.1939), and Krzysztof Kieślowski (1941–1996) are famous film directors, and Jerzy Grotowski (1933–1999) was a well-known stage director.

The outstanding scientist and scholar Nicolaus Copernicus (Mikolaj Kopernik, 1473–1543) is world renowned. Among Poland's brilliant scientists are Maria Sklodowska-Curie (1867–1934), a codiscoverer of radium and the recipient of two Nobel Prizes, and Casimir Funk (1884–1967), the discoverer of vitamins. Oskar Lange (1904–66) achieved renown as an economist.

⁴⁹DEPENDENCIES

Poland has no territories or colonies.

⁵⁰BIBLIOGRAPHY

Eckhart, Karl, et al (eds.) *Social, Economic and Cultural Aspects in the Dynamic Changing Process of Old Industrial Regions: Ruhr District (Germany), Upper Silesia (Poland), Ostrava Region (Czech Republic).* Piscataway, N.J.: Transaction Publishers, 2003.

Frucht, Richard (ed.). *Eastern Europe: An Introduction to the People, Lands, and Culture.* Santa Barbara, Calif.: ABC-CLIO, 2005.

Hoshi, Iraj, Ewa Balcerowicz, and Leszek Balcerowicz (eds.). *Barriers to Entry and Growth of New Firms in Early Transition: A Comparative Study of Poland, Hungary, Czech Republic, Albania, and Lithuania.* Boston: Kluwer Academic Publishers, 2003.

McElrath, Karen (ed.). *HIV and AIDS: A Global View.* Westport, Conn.: Greenwood Press, 2002.

Otfinoski, Steven. *Poland.* 2nd ed. New York: Facts On File, 2004.

Reuvid, Jonathan, and Marat Terterov, (eds.). *Doing Business with Poland.* Sterling, Va.: Kogan Page, 2003.

Rose-Ackerman, Susan. *From Elections to Democracy: Building Accountable Government in Hungary and Poland.* New York: Cambridge University Press, 2005.

Sanford, George. *Historical Dictionary of Poland.* Lanham, Md.: Scarecrow, 2003.

Steinlauf, Michael. *Bondage to the Dead: Poland and the Memory of the Holocaust.* Syracuse, N.Y.: Syracuse University Press, 1997.

Tworzecki, Hubert. *Parties and Politics in Post-1989 Poland.* Boulder, Colo.: Westview, 1996.

Walesa, Lech. *The Struggle and the Triumph: An Autobiography.* New York: Arcade, 1992.

Women in Polish Society. Edited by Rudolf Jaworski and Bianka Pietrow. Boulder, Colo.: East European Monographs, 1992.

World Bank. *Understanding Poverty in Poland.* Washington, D.C.: World Bank, 1995.

PORTUGAL

Portuguese Republic
República Portuguesa

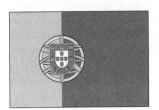

CAPITAL: Lisbon (Lisboa)

FLAG: The national flag, adopted in 1911, consists of a green field at the hoist and a larger red field. At the junction of the two, in yellow, red, blue, and white, is the national coat of arms.

ANTHEM: *A Portuguesa (The Portuguese)*.

MONETARY UNIT: The escudo (E) was replaced by the euro as official currency as of 2002. The euro is divided into 100 cents. There are coins in denominations of 1, 2, 5, 10, 20, and 50 cents and 1 euro and 2 euros. There are notes of 5, 10, 20, 50, 100, 200, and 500 euros. €1 = $1.25475 (or $1 = €0.79697) as of 2005.

WEIGHTS AND MEASURES: The metric system is the legal standard.

HOLIDAYS: New Year's Day, 1 January; Carnival Day, 15 February; Anniversary of the Revolution, 25 April; Labor Day, 1 May; National Day, 10 June; Assumption, 15 August; Republic Day, 5 October; All Saints' Day, 1 November; Independence Day, 1 December; Immaculate Conception, 8 December; Christmas, 25 December. Movable religious holidays include Carnival Day, Good Friday, and Corpus Christi.

TIME: GMT.

¹LOCATION, SIZE, AND EXTENT

The westernmost country of Europe, Portugal occupies the greater portion of the western littoral of the Iberian Peninsula. Portugal has an area of 92,391 sq km (35,672 sq mi), including the Azores (Açores) Archipelago, and Madeira and Porto Santo. Comparatively, the area occupied by Portugal is slightly smaller than the state of Indiana. The mainland of Portugal extends 561 km (349 mi) N–S and 218 km (135 mi) E–W. Bordered on the N and E by Spain and on the s and w by the Atlantic Ocean, Portugal has a total boundary length of 3,007 km (1,868 mi), of which 1,793 km (1,114 mi) is coastline.

Portugal's capital city, Lisbon, is located on Portugal's west coast.

²TOPOGRAPHY

Portugal exhibits sharp topographic contrasts. Although the north is largely lowland or land of medium altitude, the distribution of highlands is unequal north and south of the Tagus (Tejo) River. From north to south, the principal mountain ranges are the Peneda (reaching a maximum height of 1,416 m/4,646 ft), Gerêz (1,507 m/4,944 ft), Marão (1,415 m/4,642 ft), Montemuro (1,382 m/4,534 ft), the Açor (1,340 m/4,396 ft), and Lousã (1,204 m/3,950 ft), all north of the Tagus. The uplands of Beira, traversed by the Tagus on its way to the sea, contain Portugal's highest peak, Estrêla (1,991 m/6,532 ft). Westward lies the low coast of the Beira Littoral. The Tagus and Sado basins lie adjacent to the hilly area of Estremadura and rise to the hills of Alentejo on the east.

The interior lowland of lower Alentejo, farther south, is limited by the hills of Algarve. The south coast, from the mouth of the Guadiana to Cape St. Vincent, is mainly steep, but northward from Cape St. Vincent to the Tagus, including the great Bay of Setúbal and the estuary of the Tagus, the coast is low. North of the Tagus, it rises steeply toward the hills of Sintra, beyond which is a low coast of dunes interrupted by the marshes of Aveiro. Beyond the mouth of the Douro River, the coast is steep all the way to the Spanish frontier and the mouth of the Minho River. The larger rivers—the Minho, the Douro, the Tagus, and the Guadiana—all rise in Spain. The Douro has the longest course in Portugal (322 km/200 mi).

Portugal is located on the Eurasian Tectonic Plate near its southern boundary with the African plate. The region is seismically active, but fortunately, most earthquakes within the last century have been fairly moderate and were primarily centered in the northern part of the country. One of the most destructive earthquakes in history occurred in Lisbon on 1 November 1755 when an 8.7 magnitude earthquake was felt throughout the country and triggered a tsunami. The destruction from these events caused the deaths of about 70,000 people.

³CLIMATE

Marked seasonal and regional variations within temperate limits characterize the climate. In the north, an oceanic climate prevails: cool summers and rainy winters (average rainfall 125–150 cm/50–60 in annually), with occasional snowfall. Central Portugal has hot summers and cool, rainy winters, with 50–75 cm (20–30 in) average annual rainfall. The southern climate is very dry, with rainfall not exceeding 50 cm (20 in) along the coast. In Lisbon, the average temperature is about 24°C (75°F) in July and 4°C (39°F) in January. The annual mean temperature in Portugal is 16°C (61°F).

⁴FLORA AND FAUNA

Three types of vegetation can be distinguished in Portugal: the green forests of eucalyptus, pine, and chestnut in the north; the open dry grasslands, interrupted by stands of cork and other types of evergreen oak, in the central areas; and the dry, almost steppe-like grasslands and evergreen brush in the south. Few wild animals remain in Portugal. The coastal waters abound with fish, sardines and tuna being among the most common species. As of 2002, there were at least 63 species of mammals, 235 species of birds, and over 5,000 species of plants throughout the country.

5 ENVIRONMENT

Air and water pollution are significant environmental problems especially in Portugal's urban centers. Industrial pollutants include nitrous oxide, sulfur dioxides, and carbon emissions. In 1996, industrial carbon dioxide emissions totaled 47.9 million metric tons. In 2000, the total of carbon dioxide emissions was at 59.8 million metric tons.

The nation's water supply, especially in coastal areas, is threatened by pollutants from the oil and cellulose industries. Portugal has 38 cu km of renewable water, of which 48% of the annual withdrawal is used to support farming and 37% is for industrial activity. The nation's wildlife and agricultural activities are threatened by erosion and desertification of the land. The principal environmental agencies in Portugal include the Ministry of Quality of Life and the Office of the Secretary of State for the Environment. The nation's basic environmental legislation dates from 1976.

According to a 2006 report issued by the International Union for Conservation of Nature and Natural Resources (IUCN), threatened species included 15 types of mammals, 15 species of birds, 1 type of reptile, 20 species of fish, 67 types of mollusks, 15 species of other invertebrates, and 15 species of plants. Threatened species in Portugal include the Spanish Lynx, rosalia, Mediterranean monk seal, and Spanish imperial eagle. The São Miguel bullfinch and three species of turtle (green sea, hawksbill, and leatherback) were endangered in the Azores. The Mediterranean monk seal and four species of turtle (green sea, hawksbill, Kemp's ridley, and leatherback) were endangered in Madeira. The Madeiran land snail and the Canarian black oyster catcher have become extinct.

6 POPULATION

The population of Portugal in 2005 was estimated by the United Nations (UN) at 10,576,000, which placed it at number 76 in population among the 193 nations of the world. In 2005, approximately 17% of the population was over 65 years of age, with another 16% of the population under 15 years of age. There were 94 males for every 100 females in the country. According to the UN, the annual population rate of change for 2005–10 was expected to be stagnant at 0.0%, a rate the government viewed as too low. The projected population for the year 2025 was 10,356,000. The overall population density was 115 per sq km (298 per sq mi), with approximately two-thirds of the population living in coastal areas.

The UN estimated that 53% of the population lived in urban areas in 2005, and that urban areas were growing at an annual rate of 0.93%. The capital city, Lisbon (Lisboa), had a population of 1,962,000 in that year. Porto, the next largest city, had a metropolitan population of 1,551,950. These two metropolitan areas account for most of the urban dwellers in the country.

7 MIGRATION

Portuguese emigration, which decreased from an annual average of 48,000 persons during the decade 1904–13 to 37,562 in 1961,

increased sharply after 1963 as a result of acute labor shortages in other European countries, especially in France and the Federal Republic of Germany (FRG). By 1970, it was estimated that more than 100,000 Portuguese were emigrating yearly. Legal emigration to the FRG continued to increase until November 1973, when the FRG suspended non-EC immigration. Overall, more than 130,000 Portuguese emigrated in 1973. Because of the loss of Portugal's African colonies in 1975, an estimated 800,000 Portuguese settlers returned to Portugal. Since then at least 25,000 generally return from abroad each year, mostly from other European countries or America. As of 1989, some 4,000,000 Portuguese were living abroad, mainly in France, Germany, Brazil, South Africa, Canada, Venezuela, and the United States. In 2003, remittances home came to $2.8 billion.

In 2001, Portugal introduced major innovations to its immigration law, together with multiple and flexible visa arrangements, duties were clarified and the legalization process streamlined. Children born to immigrants living in the country legally for at least six years would automatically be granted citizenship. In 2003, Ukrainians displaced Brazilians as the dominant nationality. There were 466,000 legal migrants at the end of 2004, including 52,037 Africans. In 2004, there were a total of 377 refugees and no asylum applications were filed. In 1999 the net migration rate was -1.51 migrants per 1,000 population; by 2005 it was an estimated 3.49 per 1,000 population.

8 ETHNIC GROUPS

The Portuguese people represent a mixture of various ethnic strains. In the north are traces of Celtic influence; in the south, Arab and Berber influence is considerable. Other groups—Lusitanians, Phoenicians, Carthaginians, Romans, Visigoths, and Jews—also left their mark on the Portuguese people. The present-day Portuguese population is one of the most homogeneous in Europe. Minority groups are primarily made up of immigrants, both legal and illegal, from Brazil, African colonies, and Eastern Europe. Legal immigrants account for about 5% of the total population. There are about 50,000 Roma in the country.

9 LANGUAGES

Portuguese, the national language, evolved from ancient dialects of Latin; its rules of orthography were reformulated in 1911. Portuguese is also the official language of Brazil and the former African provinces. Mirandese is a second official language, but is not as widely used. Spanish, French, and English are the most common second languages.

10 RELIGIONS

According to 2004 reports, about 80% of the population aged 12 or older identified themselves as Roman Catholic; though many claimed that they are not active participants in the church. Protestants constituted about 4% of the populace; and various other groups made up about 1%. Nearly 3% claimed no religious affiliation. Christian groups include Seventh-Day Adventists, the Church of Jesus Christ of Latter-day Saints, Orthodox Christians, and Brazilian syncretic Catholic churches. There are about 35,000 Muslims, 700 Jews, and small groups of Buddhists, Taoists, and Zoroastrians. About 7,000 people are Hindus. There are also congregations of the Igreja Universal do Reino de Deus (the Universal

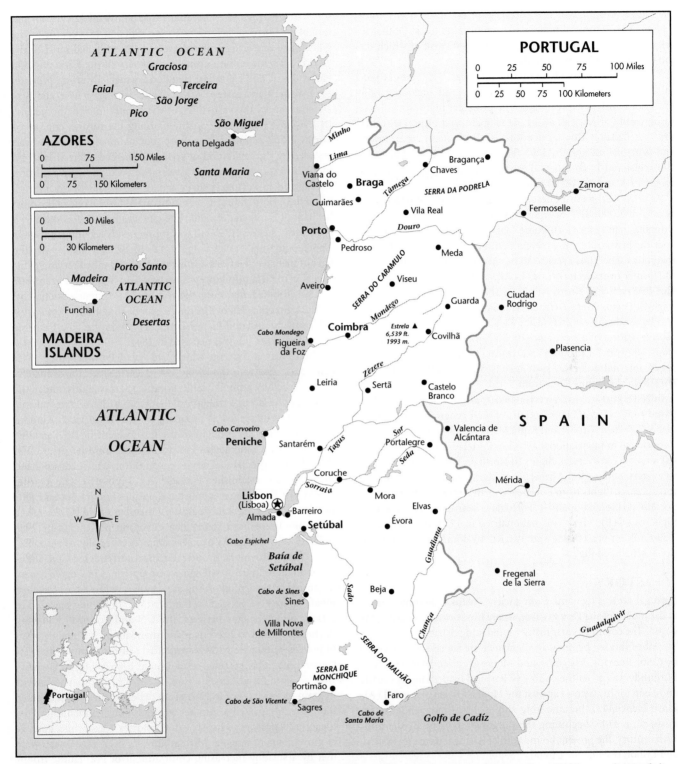

LOCATION: 36°57′39″ to 42°9′8″ N; 6°11′10″ to 9°29′45″ W. BOUNDARY LENGTHS: Spain, 1,214 kilometers (755 miles); Atlantic coastline, 1,793 kilometers (1,113 miles). TERRITORIAL SEA LIMIT: 12 miles.

Church of the Kingdom of God), which originated in Brazil. The Church of Scientology claims to have about 200 active members.

In 2001, a new law on religious freedom was passed to extend to minority religions more of the privileges previously granted only to the Roman Catholic Church. The Catholic Church has, however, maintained a special status with the government through a 1940 concordat which was amended in 2004. Certain Catholic holidays are recognized as national holidays.

¹¹TRANSPORTATION

The Portuguese railways are almost entirely owned and operated by the state-owned Portuguese Railway Company. As of 2004, the railway system, which is adequate for Portugal's needs, totals 2,850 km (1,771 mi) of broad and narrow gauge track. Of that total, broad gauge accounts for 2,576 km (1,602 mi), of which 623 km (387 mi) have been electrified.

The length of usable highways in 2002 was 17,135 km (10,657 mi), of which 14,736 km (9,165 mi) were paved, including 1,659 km (1,031 mi) of expressways. The principal highways connect Lisbon and Porto with La Coruña in Spain, and Lisbon with Madrid via Badajoz. Bus service links all Portuguese cities, towns, and principal villages. In 2003 there were 5,241,100 motor vehicles registered in continental Portugal, including 3,966,000 passenger cars, and 1,275,100 commercial vehicles.

As of 2005, the Portuguese merchant fleet had 114 oceangoing vessels of 1,000 GRT or more, totaling 872,557 GRT. The main shipping firm is the Portuguese Maritime Transport Co., created after the private shipping companies were nationalized in 1975. It maintains scheduled services to the Azores, Madeira, Macao, and the former overseas territories in Africa. There is also regular service to Brazil and North America. The chief ports—Lisbon (the largest), Porto, Ponta Delgada, and Sines—are all fully equipped and have adequate warehousing facilities. Portugal has created a captive register of convenience on Madeira for Portuguese-owned ships, allowing for taxation and crewing benefits. As of 2003, Portugal's internal waterway system consisted of a 210 km (130 mi) stretch on the Douro River from Porto.

In 2004, Portugal had an estimated 65 airports, 42 of which had paved runways as of 2005. Because of their geographical position, Lisbon's Portela Airport and Santa Maria in the Azores are of great importance in international aviation. Portela is one of the principal airports for overseas flights to North and South America and to western and central Africa; Santa Maria is a stopping point for transoceanic flights from Europe to North America. The most important aviation company in Portugal is Transportes Aereos Portugueses (TAP), which was nationalized in 1975. In 2003, about 7.590 million passengers were carried on domestic and international scheduled flights.

12 HISTORY

Portugal derives its name from ancient Portus Cale (now Porto), at the mouth of the Douro River, where the Portuguese monarchy began. The country's early history is indistinguishable from that of the other Iberian peoples. Lusitanians were successively overrun by Celts, Romans, Visigoths, and Moors (711). In 1094, Henry of Burgundy was given the county of Portugal by the king of Castile and León for his success against the Moors; his son, Alfonso I (Alfonso Henriques), became king and achieved independence for Portugal in 1143, beginning the Burgundy dynasty. By the mid-13th century, the present boundaries of Portugal were established, and Lisbon became the capital.

During the reign of King John (João) I, the founder of the powerful Aviz dynasty and husband of the English princess Philippa of Lancaster, the Portuguese defeated the Spanish in a war over the throne (1385), established a political alliance with England (by the Treaty of Windsor in 1386) that has endured to the present day, and inaugurated their most brilliant era. Prince Henry the Navigator (Henrique o Navegador), a son of John I, founded a nautical school at Sagres, where he gathered the world's best navigators, cosmographers, geographers, and astronomers and commenced a series of voyages and explorations that culminated in the formation of the Portuguese Empire. In the 15th and 16th centuries, the golden age of Portugal, Portuguese explorers sailed most of the world's seas; made the European discovery of the Cape of Good Hope, Brazil, and Labrador; founded Portugal's overseas provinces in western and eastern Africa, India, Southeast Asia, and Brazil; and poured the vast riches of the empire into the homeland. In 1580–81, Philip II of Spain, claiming the throne, conquered Portugal and acquired its empire, but national sovereignty was restored by the revolution of 1640 and the accession of John IV, founder of the Bragança dynasty, to the Portuguese throne. John IV ushered in Portugal's silver age, the 17th and 18th centuries, when the wealth of Brazil once more made Lisbon one of the most brilliant of European capitals. The city was largely destroyed by a great earthquake in 1755 but was subsequently rebuilt. During the Napoleonic wars, Portugal, faithful to its British alliance, was the base of British operations against the French in the Iberian Peninsula. The royal family, however, withdrew to Brazil, and from 1807 to 1821, Río de Janeiro was the seat of the Portuguese monarchy. In 1822, Brazil, ruled by Pedro, the son of King John VI of Portugal, formally declared its independence; Pedro became Emperor Pedro I of Brazil but was deposed in 1831.

The Bragança dynasty, which had ruled Portugal since 1640, came to an end with the revolution of 1910, when the monarchy was replaced by a republican regime. Lack of stability under the new republic led to a military dictatorship in 1926. Marshal António Carmona served as president from 1926 to 1951. António de Oliveira Salazar, brought to the government in 1928 as minister of finance, emerged as Portugal's prime minister in 1932. In 1933, Salazar proclaimed a new constitution, which consolidated his regime and established Portugal as a corporative state. During World War II, Portugal supported the Allies but did not take part in combat; it subsequently became a member of NATO.

Despite its reduced status as a European power, Portugal attempted to maintain its overseas empire, especially its resource-rich African provinces. In 1961, Portugal surrendered Goa, Daman, and Diu to India. In the same year, uprisings in Angola began, organized by the Union of Angolan Peoples in protest against Portugal's oppressive policies in the territory. These uprisings led to serious disagreements between the UN and Portugal; following Portugal's refusal to heed its recommendations for liberalization of policies with a view toward eventual self-government, the UN General Assembly passed a resolution in 1965 calling for a worldwide economic and arms boycott of Portugal in order to force it to grant independence to its African dependencies. Subsequently, the Assembly passed a number of resolutions condemning Portugal for its policies in its African territories. Meanwhile, guerrilla movements in Angola, Mozambique, and Guinea-Bissau were met by a steadily increasing commitment of Portuguese troops and supplies.

Salazar, who served as prime minister of Portugal from 1932 to 1968, died in July 1970 at the age of 81. When he was incapacitated in September 1968, he was succeeded by Marcello Caetano. The unwillingness of the Caetano regime to institute democratic and economic reforms, coupled with growing discontent over the continuance of the ever more costly colonial war in Africa, led to a military coup by the left-wing Armed Forces Movement in April 1974. Broad democratic liberties were immediately granted and opposition political parties legalized, while the corporate state apparatus was gradually dismantled. A decolonization program was also begun, resulting by November 1975 in the independence of all of Portugal's African provinces.

The first provisional coalition government came to power in May 1974, with Gen. António Sebastião Ribeiro de Spínola, whose book *Portugal and the Future* had played a key role in focusing antiwar sentiment among the military, as president. In September 1974, after a power struggle with the leftist forces, Gen. Spínola resigned and was replaced by Gen. Francisco da Costa Gomes. Following an unsuccessful right-wing coup attempt in March 1975, Gen. Spínola was forced to flee the country, along with a number of officers. The continued dissension between right and left—and between Communist and Socialist factions on the left—was evidenced by the numerous provisional governments that followed the coup. In April 1975, general elections were held for a Constituent Assembly, whose task was to draw up a new constitution. Legislative elections were held in April 1976 and presidential elections in June. Gen. António dos Santos Ramalho Eanes was elected president, and the leader of the Portuguese Socialist Party, Mário Alberto Nobre Lopes Soares, became prime minister. Mainly as a result of policy differences within the governing coalition, this administration fell in July 1978 and was replaced by a caretaker cabinet.

After a succession of different coalitions, the Socialist Party won a 35% plurality in the parliamentary elections of April 1983, and Soares was again named prime minister, forming a coalition government with the center-right Social Democratic Party (Partido Social Democratico—PSD). Political turbulence increased after the election, and in 1984, urban terrorism appeared. In the following year, Portugal entered the EC, boosting the economy. Political instability continued, however, and a general election was called in October 1985. The vote brought the PSD to power with a slim plurality; Prof. Aníbal Cavaço Silva was able to form a minority government. In 1986, four candidates ran for president; none was able to win a majority, and in the ensuing runoff election, former Prime Minister Soares won a narrow victory to become the nation's first civilian president in 60 years. In 1987, the government lost a vote of confidence, and Soares called a general election; the PSD under Silva won a majority in the Assembly, achieving the first such government since democracy was restored in 1974.

The PSD was returned to power in 1991 and Mário Soares was reelected president for a second five-year term on 13 January 1991. Economic recession, government deficits, and regional development initiatives were major concerns in the 1990s.

Following the success of the Socialist Party (Partido Socialist—PS) in the legislative elections held in October 1995, Socialist Jorge Sampaio defeated Silva to succeed Soares as president on 14 January 1996. (Sampaio won reelection for a second five-year term in January 2001.) Antonio Guterres was reappointed prime minister. The goal of the Guterres government was to prepare Portugal for entry into the European economic and monetary union. Successive austerity measures were legislated, with the support of the center-right PSD, to guarantee Portugal's participation in the euro zone (this took place in 1999). The socialist government at the same time presided over a remarkable economic recovery after 1996. Thanks to strong economic growth and a real drop in unemployment, the PS retained power after the 10 October 1999 Assembly elections. Its program for the succeeding four years was to speed up Portugal's economic and bureaucratic modernization in order to attract investment and promote export-led growth.

The Socialist government's ability to manage a slowing economy deteriorated in Guterres' second term, and the PS suffered a major defeat in local elections held in December 2001. Guterres resigned, and early elections were held in March 2002. They resulted in a change in government, with the center-right PSD forming a coalition with the conservative Popular Party. PSD leader José Manuel Durão Barroso was named prime minister. Durão Barroso experienced his own troubles with the economy, as Portugal headed into a recession at the end of 2002 and into 2003. Portugal's economy was forecast to grow by 0.4% in 2003, the worst performance in the euro currency zone. As well, Portugal's budget deficit in 2002 was far above the 3% of GDP limit established by the EU's Growth and Stability Pact, putting it in jeopardy of punitive sanctions from the EU. In 2005, GDP growth was forecast at just 0.5%, and the budget deficit was 6.8% of GDP.

Portugal's overseas possession, Macau, was turned over to Chinese administration on 20 December 1999. Portugal supported independence for its former colony of East Timor; this was achieved in May 2002. Portugal took steps to normalize relations with Indonesia following the independence of East Timor.

Barroso supported the United States in its war in Iraq which began in 2003. The prime minister faced criticism from within parliament and among the Portuguese electorate for his stance. In July 2004, Barroso resigned as prime minister to become president of the European Commission. Pedro Santana Lopes, his successor as leader of the PSD, formed a new government. Four months into Lopes's government, President Sampaio called for early elections amidst growing public dissent over the center-right government's inability to tackle the country's economic problems. The general elections were held in February 2005; the Socialists swept to victory and José Sócrates became prime minister. The Socialists secured their first absolute majority in parliament since democracy returned to Portugal in 1974. Sócrates said his primary objective would be to boost the economy by investing in training and technology. His government had to face the task of bringing the budget deficit under control and putting a stop to rising unemployment.

The government declared a national calamity in August 2003 as forest fires swept across vast areas of woodlands; an area the size of Luxembourg was lost to the fires. At least 18 people were killed, and the damages were estimated at €1 billion. Portugal was plagued by deadly wildfires once again in August 2005. They were said to be the worst in recent times. Portugal appealed to the EU for emergency financial aid to cover the costs to farmers of lost harvests in the wake of the fires.

Presidential elections were held on 22 January 2006. Social Democratic Party candidate and former Prime Minister Aníbal Cavaco Silva won with 50.54% of the vote. Independent candidate Manuel Alegre Duarte came in second with 20.74% of the vote.

13 GOVERNMENT

A constitution made public on 9 April 1975 and effective 25 April 1976 stipulated that the Armed Forces Movement would maintain governmental responsibilities as the guarantor of democracy and defined Portugal as a republic "engaged in the formation of a classless society." The document provided for a strong, popularly elected president, empowered to appoint the prime minister and cabinet. This constitution was substantially revised in 1982 and later in 1989; the most important new provisions were the elimination of the military Council of the Revolution and the limitation of presidential power. The new government system is parliamentary.

According to the constitution as amended (further amendments were added in 1992, to accommodate the Maastricht Treaty on European Union; in 1997, to allow referendums; and in 2001, to facilitate extradition), the president is elected by popular vote for a five-year term. The president appoints the prime minister and, at the prime minister's proposal, a Council of Ministers. A Council of State advises the president. The main lawmaking body is the unicameral Assembly of the Republic, the 230 members of which are directly elected to four-year terms, subject to dissolution. Suffrage is universal from age 18.

14 POLITICAL PARTIES

Under the Salazar regime, although the constitution did not prohibit political activity, the National Union (União Nacional) was the only political party represented in the legislature. Candidates of the old Center parties, which had been active prior to 1926–28, were allowed to participate in national elections starting in 1932, although none were ever elected.

After the 1974 revolution, several right-wing parties were banned, and various left-wing parties that had functioned underground or in exile were recognized. Among these was the Portuguese Communist Party (Partido Comunista Português—PCP), which was founded in 1921 and is Portugal's oldest political party. It is especially strong among industrial workers and southern farm workers. The government also recognized the Portuguese Socialist Party (Partido Socialista Português—PSP), founded in exile in 1973, and the Popular Democratic Party (Partido Popular Democrático—PPD), formed during the Caetano regime; both the PSP and the PPD favored the establishment of a Western European-style social democracy. Tied to the policies of the Caetano regime was the Social Democratic Center (Centro Democrático Social—CDS), founded in 1974, which held its first conference in January 1975 and became a target for left-wing disruptions. In June 1976, Gen. António Ramalho Eanes, the army chief of staff, who was supported by the major non-communist parties, won election as Portugal's first president.

In 1979, the right-of-center Democratic Alliance (Aliança Democrática—AD) was formed by the Social Democratic Party (Partido Social Democrático—PSD), founded in 1974; the CDS; and the People's Monarchist Party (Partido Popular Monárquico—PPM). The leftist United People's Alliance (Aliança Povo Unido), also formed in 1979, included the People's Democratic Movement (Movimento Democrático Popular—MDP), dating from 1969, and the PCP.

The Republican and Socialist Front (Frente Republicana e Socialista—FRS), formed in 1980, consists of the PSP, the Union of the Socialist and Democratic Left (União da Esquerda Socialista Democrática—UESD), founded in 1978, and Social Democratic Independent Action (Acção Social Democrata Independente—ASDI), founded in 1980. The People's Democratic Union (União Democrática Popular—UDP), dating from 1974, comprises political groups of the revolutionary left.

In October 1985, former President Eanes's centrist Democratic Renewal Party (Partido Renovador Democrático—PRD) entered the ballot for the first time, taking 18% of the vote. In 1991, the seats were distributed as follows: PSO, 135; PSP, 72; CDU, 17; Center Democrats, 5; National Solidarity, 1. The latter was formed in 1990 to address the needs of pensioners.

In the legislative elections of 10 October 1999, the seats were distributed as follows: PS, 114; PSD, 83; CDU, 17; CDS/PP, 15, and Left Bloc, 2. Antonio Manuel de Oliviera Guterres was reappointed prime minister. The first PS victory in October 1995 carried through to the presidential elections of 14 January 1996, when Jorge Sampaio was elected president, with 53.8% of the vote to Aníbal Silva's 46.2%.

Guterres ruled during a downturn in the global economy in his second term, and in December 2001 he resigned following a defeat for the PS in municipal elections. The PSD, led by José Manuel Durão Barroso, won 40.1% of the vote and took 105 seats in parliament in the 17 March 2002 elections, to the PS's 37.9% and 96 seats. The Popular Party (PP) won 8.8% of the vote and secured 14 seats; the PSD formed a coalition government with the PP. Also winning seats were the CDU (Unitarian Democratic Coalition, comprised of the Portuguese Communist Party and the Greens), 7% of the vote and 12 seats; and the Left Bloc (BE—comprised of the communist Democratic People's Union, the Revolutionary Socialist Party, and the extreme left party Politics XXI), 2.8% of the vote and 3 seats.

Sampaio called for early legislative elections in December 2004 because he lacked confidence in the governing center-right government of Pedro Santana Lopes (who became prime minister in July 2004 after Barroso stepped down to become president of the European Commission). The elections were held in February 2005. The results were as follows: PS, 45.1% of the vote (121 seats); PSD, 28.7% (75 seats); CDU, 7.6% (14 seats); PP, 7.3% (12 seats); BE, 6.4% (8 seats). The next elections were scheduled for February 2009.

15 LOCAL GOVERNMENT

Portugal is grouped into districts, including 18 on the mainland and the autonomous regions of the Azores and Madeira islands. Each district has a governor, appointed by the minister of the interior, and an assembly. There are more than 300 municipalities, subdivided into parishes.

16 JUDICIAL SYSTEM

Justice is administered by ordinary and special courts, including a Constitutional Tribunal; the Supreme Court of Justice in Lisbon, consisting of a president and some 60 judges; five courts of appeal, at Lisbon, Porto, Coimbra, Évora and Guimarães; courts of first instance in every district; and special courts. The jury system was reintroduced in 1976, but it is used only when requested by either the prosecutor or the defendant.

The judiciary is independent and impartial. Citizens enjoy a wide range of protections of fundamental civil and political rights which are outlined in the constitution with specific reference to the Universal Declaration of Human Rights. An Ombudsman, elected by the Assembly of the Republic (legislature) to a four-year term, serves as the nation's chief civil and human rights officer.

The legal system is based on the civil law system. Portugal accepts compulsory jurisdiction of the International Court of Justice with reservations.

¹⁷ARMED FORCES

As of 2005, the total armed forces of Portugal numbered 44,900 active personnel. Reservists numbered 210,930 for all services. The army had 26,700 personnel, with equipment that included 187 main battle tanks, 40 reconnaissance vehicles, 353 armored personnel carriers, and over 350 artillery pieces. The navy had 10,950 active members, including 1,980 marines. The navy operated two tactical submarines, six frigates, and 29 patrol/coastal vessels. The air force had 7,250 active personnel and was equipped with 50 combat capable aircraft, including 19 fighters, two reconnaissance and six maritime patrol aircraft. Paramilitary police and republican guards numbered 47,700. The United States maintains a military presence with 1,008 personnel. Armed forces personnel are deployed to eight different countries either in a support role or as part of UN, European Union or NATO missions. The 2005 defense budget totaled $2.43 billion.

¹⁸INTERNATIONAL COOPERATION

Portugal joined the United Nations on 14 December 1955 and participates in ECE and several nonregional specialized agencies, such as the FAO, IAEA, the World Bank, ILO, UNESCO, UNIDO, and the WHO. The nation is one of the 12 original signatories to NATO. Portugal is a member of the WTO, the OECD, the African Development Bank, the Asian Development Bank, the Council of Europe, the Euro-Atlantic Partnership Council, the European Bank for Reconstruction and Development, the OSCE, and the Western European Union. Portugal joined the European Union in 1986. It also has observer status in the OAS and the Latin American Integration Association (LAIA).

Portugal has offered support to UN missions and operations in Kosovo (est. 1999), East Timor (est. 2002), and Burundi (est. 2004).

Portugal belongs to the Australia Group, the Zangger Committee, the European Organization for Nuclear Research (CERN), the Nuclear Suppliers Group (London Group), the Nuclear Energy Agency, and the Organization for the Prohibition of Chemical Weapons. In environmental cooperation, Portugal is part of the Basel Convention, Conventions on Biological Diversity and Air Pollution, Ramsar, CITES, the London Convention, International Tropical Timber Agreements, the Kyoto Protocol, the Montréal Protocol, MARPOL, and the UN Conventions on the Law of the Sea, Climate Change and Desertification.

¹⁹ECONOMY

Manufacturing and construction together accounted for 30.2% of Portugal's GDP in 2004. The largest industries are clothing, textiles, and footwear; food processing; wood pulp, paper, and cork; metal working; oil refining; chemicals; fish canning; wine; and tourism. Agriculture, forestry, hunting and fishing employs about 12.5% of the work force (down from 26.2% in 1971) but contributed about 5.9% of the GDP in 2004. The percent of the labor force in services rose from 39% in 1971 to 52.4% in 2000, accounting for about 63.9% of GDP in 2004. Traditionally, productivity has been hampered by low investment and a lack of machinery and fertil-

izers. The economy experienced robust growth after 1993, however, primarily due to increased investment and domestic consumption, both in turn traceable to advantages Portugal gained through its entry into the European Community in 1986. In 1986, Portuguese income was about 52% of the EU average; by 2002, GDP per capita on a purchasing power parity basis had risen to over 70% of the EU average. In 2005, it was expected to be 65.1%. Economic growth, which had been above the EU average for most of the 1990s, fell back during 2001–04.

From the end of 1973 through 1983, the energy crisis and insufficient liquidity jeopardized economic growth, which dropped still further following the overthrow of the Caetano regime in April 1974. GNP growth in 1974 fell to 2.3% from 8.1% in the previous year. The decline was caused by a sharp drop in new offers of investment and credit from abroad (investors feared rising Communist influence and government takeovers of private firms), coupled with a decline in tourism and a massive increase in unemployment primarily resulting from the return of Portuguese settlers and soldiers from newly independent Angola. During the late 1970s, Portugal adopted an austerity program and succeeded in lowering inflation to 16.6% and increasing GDP growth to 5.5% in 1980. However, adverse interest and exchange rates and a severe drought during 1980–81 resulted in a resurgence of inflation (an estimated 22.5% in 1982) and sluggish economic growth (1.7% in 1981 and 2% in 1982).

In mid-1983, the Soares government implemented an IMF stabilization plan of drastic internal tightening, which brought steady economic improvement. The persistent current account deficits ended in 1985, partially as a result of the decline in world oil prices and entry into the EC. The Silva government's economic liberalization emphasized competitiveness and accountability. From 1987 to 1999 Portugal was the net recipient of financial inflow from the EU of about $27 billion, most disbursed through the European Regional Development Fund. The money was spent on infrastructural improvements, most notably the highway system. With the accession into the EU of 10 new central and east European countries in 2004, Portugal lost its historic competitive advantage in Europe due to low labor costs in the new EU members.

Through the 1990s, until the beginning of 2001, Portugal enjoyed strong economic growth generally above the EU average. The economy grew 4.2% in 1998, at 3.1% in 1999, and at 3.3% in 2000. Unemployment was at 5% in 1998, but dropped to 4.5% in 1999 and then to 4% in 2000. Even as growth slowed to 2.2% in 2001, unemployment in Portugal remained below most of its neighbors, at 4.2%. In 2002, growth slowed to 0.4% and unemployment increased to 5.05%. Inflation in Portugal has been moderate but growing, increasing from 2.4% in 1998 to 4.6% in 2000. Consumer prices rose 4.4% in 2001 and about 3.7% in 2002. The Socialist government pledged its dedication both to meeting the Maastricht monetary convergence criteria and to increasing social spending, including provision of a guaranteed minimum income. This policy bore fruit when Portugal qualified for the first round of entry into the Economic and Monetary Union (EMU) in 1999. As of January 2002, the euro became Portugal's only official currency. The government's privatization program reduced the public sector to 7.5% of GDP and 2.6% of employment by the end of 1999 from 19.7% of GDP and 5.5% of employment in 1988.

In 2003, the economy was officially in a recession, with the GDP declining by 1.1%. Unemployment shot up to 6.5%. In 2004, real GDP growth was in the positive figures once again, albeit estimated at a paltry 1.1%. Unemployment that year remained at 6.5%. After weak growth in 2005, GDP growth was expected to rise modestly in 2006, to 1%, and to 1.6% in 2007, as domestic demand picked up. Inflation was forecast to remain comparatively low in 2006–07 (the inflation rate stood at 2.4% in 2004), although increases in the rate of value-added tax (VAT) and in excise duties in mid-2005—in addition to high oil prices—was forecast to lead to a sharp increase in inflation in early 2006.

The unofficial, or underground, economy is estimated at 20% of official GDP, about the same level as that of Spain and Italy.

20 INCOME

The US Central Intelligence Agency (CIA) reports that in 2005 Portugal's gross domestic product (GDP) was estimated at $194.8 billion. The CIA defines GDP as the value of all final goods and services produced within a nation in a given year and computed on the basis of purchasing power parity (PPP) rather than value as measured on the basis of the rate of exchange based on current dollars. The per capita GDP was estimated at $18,400. The annual growth rate of GDP was estimated at 0.7%. The average inflation rate in 2005 was 2.4%. It was estimated that agriculture accounted for 5.2% of GDP, industry 28.9%, and services 65.9%.

According to the World Bank, in 2003 remittances from citizens working abroad totaled $3.024 billion or about $291 per capita and accounted for approximately 2.0% of GDP.

The World Bank reports that in 2003 household consumption in Portugal totaled $74.27 billion or about $7,141 per capita based on a GDP of $147.9 billion, measured in current dollars rather than PPP. Household consumption includes expenditures of individuals, households, and nongovernmental organizations on goods and services, excluding purchases of dwellings. It was estimated that for the period 1990 to 2003 household consumption grew at an average annual rate of 2.8%. In 2001 it was estimated that approximately 29% of household consumption was spent on food, 7% on fuel, 2% on health care, and 19% on education.

21 LABOR

The labor force in Portugal in 2005 totaled an estimated 5.52 million. As of 2003, the services sector employed 55.8% of the country's workforce, with industry at 32.6% and agriculture at 12.7%. In 2005, the estimated unemployment rate was 7.3%.

As of 2005, workers in Portugal can form and join unions, can engage in collective bargaining and strikes. About 35% of the nation's workforce was unionized as of 2005. Armed forces and police personnel are banned from striking, but they have unions and have legal mechanisms to settle grievances. The government approves all collective bargaining contracts and regulates such matters as social insurance, pensions, hours of labor, and vacation provisions. Strikes are generally resolved quickly through negotiations.

A minimum wage was established in 1975. In 2005, the minimum monthly salary was about $449, which is not sufficient to provide a decent standard of living to a worker and family. However, rent controls and subsidized food and utilities help increase the standard of living. In addition, most workers earn more than

this amount. The maximum legal workday is 10 hours, with the workweek set at 40 hours with a minimum of 12 hours between workdays. Overtime is limited to two hours per day up to 200 hours annually. Minimum standards of occupational safety and health are set by law, but they are not adequately enforced and workplace accidents do occur, particularly in the construction industry. The minimum working age is 16 years.

22 AGRICULTURE

In 2003, 25.3% of the land was considered arable. Of the 2.3 million hectares (5.7 million acres), 74% was cultivated with seasonal crops and 26% was under permanent crops. In 2003, the gross agricultural product accounted for 4% of GDP. Estimates of agriculture production in 2004 included potatoes, 1,250,000 tons; tomatoes, 1,100,000 tons; corn, 798,000 tons; wheat, 251,000 tons; olives, 270,000 tons; rice, 148,000 tons; and rye, 27,000 tons. Production of olive oil reached 30,000 tons in 2004/05. Wine, particularly port and Madeira from the Douro region and the Madeira islands, is an important agricultural export; production totaled 724 million liters in 2004. Portugal is the world's ninth-largest producer of wine, although Portugal's wines are mostly unknown internationally apart from port and rosé. Under the influence of EU policies, vineyard areas have been reduced in recent years. In 2004, the value of agricultural products imported by Portugal exceeded that of agricultural exports by $3.36 billion.

According to government estimates, about 900,000 hectares (2,200,000 acres) of agricultural land were occupied between April 1974 and December 1975 in the name of land reform; about 32% of the occupations were ruled illegal. In January 1976, the government pledged to restore the illegally occupied land to its owners, and in 1977, it promulgated the Land Reform Review Law. Restoration of illegally occupied land began in 1978.

Agriculture is the main problem area of the economy; yields per hectare are less than one-third of the European average, with a severe drought in 1991/92 only exacerbating the problem. The situation has actually been deteriorating since the mid-1970s, with many yields falling and arable and permanent crop areas declining. By 1999, crop output was only 87% of what it had been on average during 1989–91. However, during 2002–04, crop output was down 1.8% from 1999–2001. With the reform of the EU's Common Agriculture Policy (CAP), a significant reduction in the number of producers through consolidation (especially in the north) will result in the end of traditional, subsistence-like based agriculture. Between 1995 and 2003, the number of agricultural holdings decreased from 450,600 to 359,200, while the value of crop output increased from €3.7 billion to €4.33 billion during that time.

23 ANIMAL HUSBANDRY

The Alentejo region is Portugal's grazing heartland. In 2005, Portuguese livestock population estimates included 5,000,000 sheep, 2,248,000 hogs, and 1,443,000 head of cattle. There were 547,000 goats, 125,000 donkeys, 40,000 mules, 17,000 horses, 35,000,000 chickens, and 7,000,000 turkeys in 2005. Mules and donkeys, as well as horses and oxen, often provide draft power for the farms. The main districts for cattle are northern and north-central Portugal; most of the sheep, goats, and pigs are raised in the central and southern sections. In 2005, Portugal's meat production included an estimated 321,000 tons of pork, 242,000 tons of poultry meat, 119,500 tons of beef and veal, and 22,100 tons of mutton. Other production estimates for 2005 included 2,076,000 tons of milk, 132,450 tons of eggs, 75,600 tons of cheese, and 26,000 tons of butter.

24 FISHING

Three main fields of activity make up the Portuguese fishing enterprise: coastal fishing, with sardines as the most important catch; trawl fishing on the high seas; and cod fishing on the Grand Banks, off Newfoundland. In 2004, the Portuguese fishing fleet consisted of 10,089 vessels with 112,978 GRT. National fish landings totaled 210,526 tons in 2004, of which aquaculture accounted for 3.6%. Dominant species are sardines, mackerel, red fish, scabbardfish, and octopus. These species accounted for nearly half the landings. Virtually all the total catch is sold fresh, but small amounts of sardines and octopus are frozen. The total catch fell from 375,413 tons in 1973 to 247,596 tons in 1983 but increased to 325,349 tons in 1991. The average annual catch during 1990–94 was 295,007 tons, 318,600 tons during 1995–99, and 205,611 tons during 2000–04. The annual catch declined since the 1990s because Portugal was affected by internationally-set limits (Total Allowable Catches) that restrict fishing access for certain species in the international waters of the North Atlantic and by EU fishing quotas. The fishing potential has also been affected by a reduction in the national fleet in association with EU fleet reduction incentives. The Portuguese fishing fleet was reduced by 40% during 1990–2000. There was an additional 5% reduction in fleet tonnage during 2000–04.

25 FORESTRY

With about 40% of the total land area forested, Portugal is an important producer of forestry products. The country is the world's leading producer of cork, harvested exclusively from cork oak (*Quercus suber*) found predominantly in the Mediterranean region. Portugal ordinarily supplies around 175,000 tons of cork per year (about half of world output) from some 725,000 hectares (1,791,000 acres) of cork forests. Portugal is also an important producer of resin and turpentine. Roundwood production in 2004 was 9,672,000 cu m (341.4 million cu ft), with a sawn wood output of 1,383,000 cu m (48.8 million cu ft). Other commodities produced that year included wood pulp, 1,935,000 tons; paper and paperboard, 1,536,000 tons; and particleboard and other wood-based panels, 1,215,000 cu m (42.9 million cu ft). In 2004, timber and other forest product exports amounted to $1,684 million. Wine stoppers account for 55% of cork export value. Cork demand has fallen in recent years, and production is limited by the botanical fact that a single tree can only be stripped once every nine years. Eucalyptus logs (the crux of the pulp industry) are exported as well; forestation of eucalyptus is a major national controversy, with opponents charging that it displaces traditional farmers and damages the soil and water table. Pine accounts for most lumber exports.

26 MINING

Portugal's mineral wealth is significant but the deposits are scattered and are not easily exploitable on a large scale. The country's most important metallic mineral resources are copper, tin and tungsten. Portugal is a leading producer of mined copper in the European Union (EU), as well as being an important producer of dimension stone and tungsten concentrates. Minerals were one of the country's dynamic industrial sectors, mainly because of the discovery and development of the Neves-Corvo copper and tin deposits. The Panasqueira mine was one of the world's largest producers of tungsten concentrates.

In 2003, the output of mined copper (metal content) was 77,581 metric tons, up slightly from 77,227 metric tons in 2002. Output of mined tungsten (metal content) was 715 metric tons, compared to 693 metric tons in 2002. Tin mine output (metal content) in 2003 totaled 354 metric tons, down from 574 metric tons in 2002. Production of iron ore and concentrates (gross weight) in 2003 totaled was estimated at 14,000 metric tons, unchanged from 2002. Portugal also produced white arsenic, manganese, silver, uranium, anhydrite, hydraulic cement, refractory clays, diatomite, feldspar, gypsum, kaolin, hydrated lime, quicklime, lepidolite (a lithium mineral), nitrogen, pyrite and pyrrhotite (including cuprous), rock salt, sand, soda ash, sodium sulfate, stone (basalt, dolomite, diorite, gabbro, granite, both crushed and ornamental, graywacke, calcite marl limestone, marble, ophite, quartz, quartzite, schist, slate, and syenite), sulfur, and talc. Marble, mainly from the Evora District, was the most valuable of the stone products. A new deposit, at the Aljustrel mine/mill complex, encompassing five massive sulfide deposits, could be brought into production relatively quickly as a low-cost zinc producer; the most significant deposit, at Feitais, had 12 million tons of proven and probable minable zinc reserves with an average grade of 5.67% zinc, 1.7% lead, and 64 grams per ton of silver, and 1.6 million tons of proven and probable copper ore reserves with an average grade of 2.2% copper, 0.97% zinc, and 14 grams per ton of silver.

The southern Iberian Peninsula, known as the Iberian Pyrite Belt (IPB), was one of the most mineralized areas of Western Europe and was geologically very complex. The IPB's internationally well-known volcanogenic massive sulfide (VMS) deposits, in the southwestern part of the peninsula, dated to the Upper Devonian and the Lower Carboniferous ages. Clusters of deposits occurred around individual volcanic centers, and the largest individual deposit located to date may have held an original reserve of 500 million tons, out of IPB's total resource of 1,725 million tons. Sulfide deposit resources in 1999 were 1,100 million tons.

The government continued its privatization program and was proceeding with legislation to privatize many public companies, part of a broader program to make the economy more market driven. The structure of the mineral industry could change in the near future because of significant mining exploration by several foreign companies, particularly for copper, gold, kaolin, lead, lithium, pyrites, and tin. The IPB was the prime area for exploration activity, and had an above-average potential for success based on an unusually high number of large VMS deposits.

27 ENERGY AND POWER

Portugal operates two refineries, which allows the country to meet a portion of its refined petroleum product needs. However, the country must import all of the crude oil it refines, as well as additional amounts of refined petroleum products, in addition to all of the natural gas and coal the country consumes.

In 2002, Portugal's two refineries, one at Sines and the other at Porto, had a combined output of 271,740 barrels per day. However, domestic demand for refined oil in that year averaged 343,160 barrels per day. Imports of refined and crude petroleum averaged a combined 355,580 barrels per day, although the country did re-export an average of 28,790 barrels per day.

Natural gas imports and consumption for 2002 totaled 109.83 billion cu ft and 109.26 billion cu ft, respectively. Demand for coal in 2003 was met entirely by imports. Consumption of coal that year totaled 5.9 million short tons, most of which was used to generate electricity.

Portugal's electric generating capacity in 2002 totaled 10.394 million kW, of which hydroelectric capacity accounted for 3.963 million kW, and conventional thermal capacity accounting for 6.217 million kW. Geothermal/other capacity accounted for 0.214 million kW. Total output of electric power in 2002 came to 43.439 billion kWh, of which conventional thermal sources provided 33.633 billion kWh, and hydroelectric 7.722 billion kWh. Geothermal/other provided 2.084 billion kWh. Demand for electric power totaled 42.297 billion kWh.

28 INDUSTRY

Industry (including construction, energy, and water) employs about one-third of the labor force, and its contribution to the national economy has grown significantly in recent decades. It accounted for 30.2% of GDP in 2004. Industrial production in 2004 had maintained a 1.1% growth rate over 2003. Portuguese industry is mainly light; the development of heavy industry has been hampered by a shortage of electric power. Textiles—especially cottons and woolens—are the oldest and most important of Portugal's manufactures. Other principal industries are automotive assembly, electronics, glass, porcelain, and pottery, footwear, cement, cellulose and paper, rubber and chemicals, cork and cork products, and food industries (mainly canned fish). Small artisan industries, such as jewelry and homespun and hand-embroidered clothing, are of local importance.

Manufactured goods in the early 2000s included cement, wood pulp, crude steel for ingots, paper and paperboard, and radios and televisions. In 2005, footwear, textiles, wood and cork, chemicals, paper, and food and beverages (wine) were the central industries. In addition, the country has increased its role in Europe's automotive sector, and has a fine mold-making industry.

Foreign competition has cut into Portugal's textile industry. Following the expiration of the World Trade Organization's long-standing system of textile quotas at the beginning of 2005, the EU signed an agreement with China in June 2005, imposing new quotas on 10 categories of textile goods, limiting growth in those categories to between 8% and 12.5% a year. The agreement runs until 2007, and was designed to give European textile manufacturers time to adjust to a world of unfettered competition. Nevertheless, barely a month after the EU-China agreement was signed, China reached its quotas for sweaters, followed soon after by blouses, bras, T-shirts, and flax yarn. Tens of millions of garments piled up in warehouses and customs checkpoints, which affected both retailers and consumers.

29 SCIENCE AND TECHNOLOGY

In 1996, Portugal had 18 scientific and technological learning societies, and 20 scientific and technological research institutes. The leading scientific academy is the Lisbon Academy of Sciences, founded in 1779. In 1996, Portugal had 27 universities and col-

leges offering courses in basic and applied sciences. Attached to the University of Lisbon is the Museum and Laboratory of Mineralogy and Geology, founded in 1837. In 1987–97, science and engineering students accounted for 36% of university enrollment. In 2000 (the latest year for which data was available) of all bachelor's degrees awarded, 17.5% were for the sciences (natural, mathematics and computers, engineering). Total government expenditures on research and development (R&D) in 2001 totaled $1.548.302 million, or 0.84% of GDP. Of that amount, 61% came from government sources, while the business sector accounted for 31.5%. In 2002, R&D spending amounted to $1,732.108 million, or 0.93% of GDP. In that same year, there were 1,842 scientists and engineers engaged in R&D per million people. High technology exports in 2002 totaled $1.628 billion, or 7% of the country's manufactured exports.

30 DOMESTIC TRADE

Lisbon and Porto are the two leading commercial and distribution centers. Larger retail stores, shopping malls, and supermarkets have become well-established in many areas. Franchising has also gained ground, particularly in the clothing and fast-food markets. Direct marketing through television and mail order sales has grown considerably. The most common advertising media are newspapers, outdoor billboards, radio, and television; movie theaters also carry advertisements.

The usual business hours are from 9 AM to 6 PM, Monday through Friday. Banking hours are generally 8:30 AM to 2:45 PM, Monday through Friday. An increasing number of shopping centers in urban areas have more flexible hours, including hours on Sundays.

31 FOREIGN TRADE

Portugal's foreign trade balance has regularly shown a heavy deficit, which it finances through net receipts from tourism, remittances from Portuguese workers abroad, and net transfers from the EU. In 2004, merchandise exports were an estimated $37.9 billion, and imports totaled $56.2 billion, which widened the trade deficit to $18.2 billion, up from $13.4 billion in 2003, as a result of stronger domestic demand.

Principal Trading Partners – Portugal (2002)

(In millions of US dollars)

Country	Exports	Imports	Balance
World	26,485.0	39,982.6	-13,497.6
Spain	5,439.1	11,552.0	-6,112.9
Germany	4,789.2	5,962.5	-1,173.3
France-Monaco	3,535.5	4,097.8	-562.3
United Kingdom	2,778.4	2,080.4	698.0
United States	1,480.5	832.8	647.7
Italy-San Marino-Holy See	1,266.2	2,695.1	-1,428.9
Belgium	1,191.9	1,223.5	-31.6
Netherlands	1,030.2	1,826.5	-796.3
Angola	536.9	...	536.9
Sweden	390.4	465.3	-74.9

(…) data not available or not significant.

SOURCE: *2003 International Trade Statistics Yearbook*, New York: United Nations, 2004.

In 2004, Portugal's exports consisted of capital goods (34.8% of total exports), consumer goods (32.4%), raw materials and intermediate products (30.2%), and energy products (2.6%). The major imports in 2004 consisted of capital goods (33.9% of all imports), raw materials and intermediate products (30.5%), consumer goods (24.6%), and energy products (11%). Portugal's leading markets in 2004 were Spain (24.9% of all exports), France (14%), Germany (13.5%), the United Kingdom (9.6%), the United States (6.1%), and Italy (4.3%). In all, 79.4% of all exports were traded with the 25 EU member nations. Portugal's leading suppliers in 2004 were Spain (29.3% of all imports), Germany (14.3%), France (9.3%), Italy (6.1%), the United Kingdom (4.6%), and the United States (2.4%). In total, 76.6% of all imports came from the 25 EU member nations. Portugal received 5% of its imports from OPEC nations.

32 BALANCE OF PAYMENTS

Despite chronic trade deficits, Portugal until 1973 managed to achieve a balance-of-payments surplus through tourist revenues and remittances from emigrant workers. With the economic dislocations of 1974, net tourist receipts fell 30%; the trade deficit almost doubled; and emigrant remittances stagnated—thus, the 1973 payments surplus of $255.7 million became a $647.7 million deficit in 1974. Emigrant remittances grew steadily between 1976 and 1980, when they peaked at $2,946 million. Because of this, Portugal's balance of payments improved and in 1979 even showed a surplus of $761 million. Subsequently, increasing trade deficits resulted in balance-of-payments deficits that reached $3.2 billion in 1982. By 1985, however, the deficit had become a surplus of $0.4 billion, which rose to $1.1 billion in 1986; the chief reason was the weakening dollar, which boosted the value of tourism earnings and remittances. The 1990 Portuguese external payments surplus stabilized at the previous year's record level of nearly $4 billion. After a few years of surplus boom, mainly due to the enormous influx of foreign capital and transfers to Portugal following EC membership in 1986, measures were taken in July 1990 to restrict foreign credit and investment thereby helping the authorities get better control over monetary aggregates. These measures, along with the hiatus in international investment caused by the 1990–91 Persian Gulf crisis and some deterioration in the merchandise trade account contributed to halting the growth of the total nonmonetary balance.

The country's large current account deficit was 7.5% of GDP in 2002. Although foreign direct investment (FDI) in new manufacturing projects, such as the automotive and electronics sectors, increased in the 1990s, in the early 2000s FDI flowed to lower-cost manufacturing locations in central and eastern Europe, away from Portugal. In 2004, the current account deficit grew to $13.7 billion (8.1% of GDP), up from $8.4 billion in 2003. The current account deficit was expected to widen in 2005, reflecting deteriorating export competitiveness and slower external demand, but lower oil prices from the second half of 2006 were predicted to help narrow the deficit slightly in 2006–07.

33 BANKING AND SECURITIES

All 22 banks in Portugal, except for three foreign-owned ones (Banco do Brasil, Credit Franco-Portugais, and the Bank of London and South America), were nationalized in 1975. A 1983 law, however, permitted private enterprise to return to the banking industry. The Bank of Portugal, the central bank (founded in 1846), functions as a bank of issue, while the European Central Bank controls monetary policy.

During the late 1990s, Portugal's banking industry underwent significant restructuring due to foreign investment and consolidation. A major series of consolidations in 1996 left Banco Comercial Português (BCP), Banco Pinto and Sotto Mayor, and Banco Portugeuês de Investimento as the three largest private banks. Further consolidation came in 1999 when Spain's Banco Santander Central Hispano (BSCH) merged with Champalimaud. Fearing increased Spanish influence in the Portuguese banking industry, the Portuguese government sought to block the deal and the dispute appeared headed for the European Court. Ultimately, Portugal's finance minister, Joaquim Pina Moura, forged a compromise in which BSCH acquired two banks in the Champalimaud group.

The International Monetary Fund reports that in 2001, currency and demand deposits—an aggregate commonly known as M1—were equal to $47.0 billion. In that same year, M2—an aggregate equal to M1 plus savings deposits, small time deposits, and money market mutual funds—was $111.7 billion.

Portugal's two stock exchanges, located in Lisbon and Porto, were closed after the coup of April 1974. The Lisbon exchange reopened in 1976, and the Porto exchange in 1981. In January 1992 the market was split into three tiers, of which the first is the major liquid market: this included the 11 firms whose shares are traded regularly and which have a minimum market capitalization of E500 million. Trading outside the stock exchanges is still widespread. Into the late 1990s trade on the exchange continued to grow as continued privatization led to greater amounts of Initial Public Offerings (IPOs). As of 2004, there were 56 companies listed on the EURONEXT Portugal exchange, which had a market capitalization of $73.404 billion. In 2004, the PSI 20 Index rose 12.6% from the previous year to 7,600.2.

Balance of Payments – Portugal (2003)

(In millions of US dollars)

Current Account		-8,437.0
Balance on goods	-13,357.0	
Imports	-46,114.0	
Exports	32,757.0	
Balance on services	3,931.0	
Balance on income	-2,418.0	
Current transfers	3,408.0	
Capital Account		3,081.0
Financial Account		-1,141.0
Direct investment abroad	-125.0	
Direct investment in Portugal	969.0	
Portfolio investment assets	-21,045.0	
Portfolio investment liabilities	15,430.0	
Financial derivatives	74.0	
Other investment assets	-10,113.0	
Other investment liabilities	13,670.0	
Net Errors and Omissions		43.0
Reserves and Related Items		6,455.0

(…) data not available or not significant.

SOURCE: *Balance of Payment Statistics Yearbook 2004*, Washington, DC: International Monetary Fund, 2004.

³⁴INSURANCE

Portugal's domestic insurance companies were nationalized in 1975. Foreign companies were required to accept government representatives among their directors. A new law, approved in 1983, allowed the private sector to reenter the domestic insurance industry. Almost all Portuguese companies sell life and nonlife insurance, although some specialize in reinsurance only. In the wake of the reprivatization of the insurance industry, many insurance companies have sought alliances with banks. This position, in turn, serves as an impediment to new entrants into the insurance field, particularly from foreign countries. However, the market is opening up and brokers from any European Union (EU) country can operate in Portugal. Third-party auto insurance and workers' compensation are compulsory in Portugal. Contractors, travel agents, insurance brokers and other professionals are also required to carry liability insurance. In 2003, the value of direct insurance premiums written totaled $10.810 billion, of which life insurance premiums accounted for $6.122 billion. In that same year, Portugal's top nonlife insurer was Fidelidade-Mundial, which had gross written nonlife premiums of $998.9 million. The country's leading life insurer, Occidental Vida, that year, had gross written life insurance premiums of $1,039.9 million.

³⁵PUBLIC FINANCE

Portugal's budgets (accounting for the effects of loans and transfers) have been in deficit since 1974. Major factors contributing to the deficits included spending on health and education programs, funding for major public investment projects, and large state-owned enterprise payrolls. To finance the deficit, the government issued bonds in the domestic market, which also serves the monetary policy purpose of absorbing excess liquidity. The government's objective to join the Economic and Monetary Union (EMU) was achieved in 1999. Since then, monetary policy responsibilities have been absorbed by the European Central Bank. Public debt exceeded 3% of GDP in 2001, exceeding EU limits and

opening the country up to sanctions from the rest of the EU. By 2004 it continued to hover around 3%, but was expected to top 6% in 2005. In 2005 the EU ordered the country to reduce deficits, which the government planned to do by raising the value-added tax and cutting spending.

The US Central Intelligence Agency (CIA) estimated that in 2005 Portugal's central government took in revenues of approximately $78.8 billion and had expenditures of $90.2 billion. Revenues minus expenditures totaled approximately -$11.4 billion. Public debt in 2005 amounted to 69.4% of GDP. Total external debt was $298.7 billion.

³⁶TAXATION

The national corporate tax rate in Portugal as of 2005 was 25%, although rates in Madeira were 22.5% and 17.5% in the Azores. In addition, municipalities can levy a 10% surtax on the tax liability, pushing the effective rate to 27.5%. Allowable deductions in calculating taxable corporate income include depreciation, interest payments, executives' salaries, and royalties. Capital gains are taxed at 25%. Dividends paid to parent companies by subsidiaries (owned at least 25% by the payee) are excluded from taxable income to avoid double taxation. Otherwise dividends are taxed at general income tax rates.

The progressive personal income tax schedule has six bands, not including a tax-exempt base. The schedule bands as of 2003 were 15% (up to €4,100); 14% (on the next increment of income to €6.201); 24% (on the next increment to €15,375); 34% (on the next increment to €35,363): 38% (on the next increment to €51,251); and 40% (on the increment of income above €15,375). Social security taxes amount to 23.75% of nominal income. There are also taxes municipal taxes on the value of real estate.

The main indirect tax is Portugal's value-added tax (VAT) introduced 1 January 1986 with a standard rate of 16%, which was raised to 17% as of 1 January 1995 and to 19% as of 6 May 2002. There is also a reduced rate of 5% (applied to basic foodstuffs, water supplies, books, newspapers and periodicals, social housing, some medical equipment and drugs, hotel accommodations, repair and domestic services); an intermediate "parking" rate of 12% (applied to some foodstuffs, catering, and some fuels and lubricants); and exemptions from VAT (for social services, some medical and dental services, waste collection and disposal, transportation services, gold transfers to the central bank, and cremation.). For the Azores and Madeira, the standard VAT rate is 13%, the reduced rate 4% and the parking rate 8%. Other transactions taxes include stamp duties and transfer fees.

³⁷CUSTOMS AND DUTIES

Portugal uses the Harmonized Nomenclature and Classification System (HS) to organize imports into tariff categories. Almost all tariffs are levied on an ad valorem basis according to the EU Customs Code, excepting luxury goods and petroleum, which have special higher rates. Portugal adheres to all EU trade policies, including multilateral trade agreements, and conforms to WTO regulations. It also levies a value-added tax (VAT) of up to 21% on most imports, although there is a lower rate of 5%. In Madeira and

---

Public Finance – Portugal (2001)

(In millions of euros, central government figures)

Revenue and Grants	**46,890**	**100.0%**
Tax revenue	27,067	57.7%
Social contributions	14,592	31.1%
Grants	616	1.3%
Other revenue	4,615	9.8%
Expenditures	**51,823**	**100.0%**
General public services	...	...
Defense	...	...
Public order and safety	...	...
Economic affairs	...	...
Environmental protection	...	...
Housing and community amenities	...	...
Health	...	...
Recreational, culture, and religion	...	...
Education	...	...
Social protection	...	...

(...) data not available or not significant.

SOURCE: *Government Finance Statistics Yearbook 2004*, Washington, DC: International Monetary Fund, 2004.

the Azores, the lower rates of 4% and 13% apply. The VAT on imports from EU countries is not collected until the product is sold.

38 FOREIGN INVESTMENT

The government actively promotes foreign investment as an integral part of its economic development policy, and specifically through a government agency, API (Agency for Investment in Portugal). As a member of the European Union, Portugal abides by the investment rules that govern the rest of the union. New foreign investment legislation was enacted in 1986. The Institute of Foreign Investment (ICEP) is the supervising agency. Foreign investment is permitted in all sectors except ports, water management, rail services, public service telecommunications operators, and the arms industry. Portugal restricts non-EU investment in regular air transport to 49%, and restricts non-EU investment in television operations to 15%. Even in these areas, however, deregulation is under way. The foreign investment code contains liberal profit remittance regulations and tax incentives. The rate of corporation tax was reduced from 30% to 25% in 2004 as part of that year's budget, but rates in most municipalities are higher by some three percentage points due to the effects of local surcharges.

Foreign direct investment (FDI) inflows in Portugal averaged about $2 billion per year in 1992–95, or 1.6% of GDP. Main investing countries are the United Kingdom, Spain, and France. The financial sector accounted for about 60% of all new foreign investment. In 1998, FDI inflows reached $3.1 billion, up from $2.5 billion in 1997, but fell to $1.2 billion in 1999. FDI inflows soared to $6.4 billion in 2000, and were still above $6 billion in 2001, despite the global economic slowdown.

Total FDI inflows into Portugal in 2003 were €852.2 million. Portuguese FDI abroad was in the negative numbers, at -€84.6 million. Portugal invests most heavily in Brazil and Spain, followed by Germany and other EU countries. Low labor costs, combined with unrestricted access to the EU market, have attracted foreign investment in new manufacturing projects, especially in the automotive and electronics sectors. However, FDI has slowed as low-cost manufacturing locations in central and Eastern Europe have become increasingly appealing to investors, especially since the admission of 10 new EU members in 2004. Therefore, Portugal can no longer afford to rely solely upon low wage costs to attract further investment.

39 ECONOMIC DEVELOPMENT

In 1975, radical economic transformations were accomplished through a series of decrees that nationalized the domestically owned parts of major sectors of the national economy. These decrees affected the leading banks, insurance companies (representing 99% of insurance companies' capital), petroleum refineries, the transportation sector, the steel industry, and eventually Portugal's leading privately owned industrial monopoly, Companhia União Fabril. At the same time, large-scale agrarian reform measures led to expropriation of many of the country's privately owned large landholdings; other holdings were seized illegally by peasants. In an attempt to stimulate agricultural production, the government decreed a 30% reduction in the price of fertilizer to farm workers and small and medium farmers. When the nationalization and agrarian reform measures met with only limited success, partly because of liquidity problems, an emergency austerity

plan was approved by the Council of Ministers in October 1975. The program included wage and import controls and the reduction of subsidies on consumer goods.

As a result of Portugal's entry into the EC (now EU), the highly protected, unresponsive, and inefficient economy is being transformed. State intervention is being reduced, and the physical infrastructure is being modernized. Privatization began in 1989, with the share of gross domestic product (GDP) for non-financial public enterprises reduced from 17.9% in 1985 to 10.7% in 1991. In 1992, $3.6 billion was raised as banks, insurance companies, and a 25% interest in Petrogal—the state oil company—were sold. The government estimated that privatized companies would represent half of stock market capitalization by the end of 1994.

In 1996 and 1997, a series of important investments and acquisitions were made by companies such as Sonae and Jernimo Martins, Portugal's leading retail distributors; Cimpor, a cement producer; and Portugal Telecom and Electricidade de Portugal, the last of which was privatized. The big banks were developing new overseas operations as well. The best indicator of Portugal's economic progress was Portugal's acceptance into the European Economic and Monetary Union in 1999.

During the 1990s and into the 2000s, the economy grew at rates well above EU averages; however, growth slowed in 2002–03, and fell below the euro-area average for the first time in close to a decade. In 2002, the external current account deficit remained one of the largest (in relation to GDP) among industrialized countries. The unemployment rate also increased sharply. Nonetheless, an inflow of capital funds has financed infrastructure projects.

In 2001, Portugal became the first country to breach the eurozone's Stability and Growth pact budget deficit target of 3%, with a gap equal to 4.2% of GDP. Portugal's government met the 3% target in 2002 and 2003, but despite a hiring freeze and other measures, the country had a structural budget deficit in 2004 projected at 4.9%. Public spending was expected to equal 47.9% of GDP in 2004. The 2005 budget projected a structural deficit in excess of 3%, and violated the 60% limit on public debt. Due to labor reform legislation, which took effect in early 2004, and corporate and personal tax cuts in 2004 and 2005, the government expected the economy to recover strongly in 2006.

The government is attempting to change Portugal's economic development model from one based on public consumption and public investment to one focused on exports and private investment.

40 SOCIAL DEVELOPMENT

A social insurance and social assistance program has been frequently updated since 1935. The program provides old-age, disability, sickness, and unemployment benefits, family allowances, and health and medical care. The system is funded by payroll contributions from employers and employees. The government subsidizes social pensions for those persons not employed. Retirement is set at age 50 for miners, age 55 for fishermen and seamen, and age 65 for other professions. Medical benefits are provided to all residents, and cash sickness and maternity benefits are provided to employees. Maternity benefits of 100% of earnings and benefits are paid for 120 days for all employed persons. Paternity and adoption benefits are also available. There is a need based family allowance, a special education allowance, and a funeral grant.

Women have full rights and protections under both the constitution and civil code. According to law, women must receive equal pay for equal work. In practice, however, a salary gap still exists between men and women. Spousal abuse and other violence against women are widespread problems and remain underreported. The judicial system is supportive when cases are brought forward. Sexual harassment in the workplace is considered a crime, but only if committed by a superior.

Immigrants from Portugal's former African colonies face social prejudice and discrimination. There were reports of right-wing groups carrying out racially motivated attacks against immigrants and other nonethnic Portuguese. Human rights are generally respected in Portugal. Prison conditions are poor, but the government is engaging in dialogue with human rights organizations on this and other issues.

41 HEALTH

The public health care sector is by far the largest. The country planned to construct 12 new hospital districts, 84 health centers, and 5 technical schools for nurses, and to enlarge or remodel several hospital centers, hospital districts, and maternity wards. The Santa Maria Hospital in Lisbon is the largest hospital in Portugal. The number of physicians in Portugal grew steadily throughout the 1990s. As of 2004, there were an estimated 324 physicians, 374 nurses, 44 dentists, and 84 pharmacists per 100,000 people. Total health care expenditure was estimated at 7.7% of GDP.

As of 2002, the crude birth rate and overall mortality rate were estimated at, respectively, 11.5 and 10.2 per 1,000 people. Approximately 66% of married women (ages 15 to 49) were using contraception. The infant mortality rate decreased from 61 to 5.05 per 1,000 live births between 1968 and 2005. Average life expectancy in 2005 was 77.53 years.

The leading natural causes of death are circulatory disorders, cancer, and respiratory disorders. Children up to one year of age were vaccinated against diphtheria, pertussis, and tetanus, 95%, and measles, 99%. The cancer and heart disease rates in Portugal are well below the industrialized countries average.

The HIV/AIDS prevalence was 0.40 per 100 adults in 2003. As of 2004, there were approximately 22,000 people living with HIV/AIDS in the country. There were an estimated 1,000 deaths from AIDS in 2003.

42 HOUSING

According to the 2001 census, Portugal had about 5,054,922 dwelling units. However, about 65% of all families live in dilapidated structures and nearly 8.5% live in shacks. While the Government Social Housing Program has made some progress in rehousing families into more adequate structures, there are not enough programs to help the households rise above the poverty level. Traditional Portuguese houses are made of brick walls and tile roofs.

43 EDUCATION

Basic education is compulsory for nine years. This includes three cycles of four, two, and three years each. Secondary level education covers a three-year program; students choose between general secondary, professional, and specialized technical or vocational schools. The academic year runs from September to July.

In 2001, about 70% of children between the ages of three and five were enrolled in some type of preschool program. Primary school enrollment in 2003 was estimated at about 100% of age-eligible students. The same year, secondary school enrollment was about 85% of age-eligible students. It is estimated that about 98% of all students complete their primary education. The student-to-teacher ratio for primary school was at about 13:1 in 2003; the ratio for secondary school was about 8:1. In 2003, private schools accounted for about 10.5% of primary school enrollment and 14.7% of secondary enrollment.

Coimbra University, founded in 1290, is Portugal's oldest institution of higher learning, and the universities of Lisbon and Porto are two of the largest. There are also art schools, music schools, and a school of tropical medicine. The Portuguese Catholic University was instituted by decree of the Holy See. In 2003, about 56% of the tertiary age population were enrolled in some type of higher education program; 48% for men and 64% for women. The adult literacy rate for 2003 was estimated at about 93.3%.

As of 2003, public expenditure on education was estimated at 5.8% of GDP, or 12.7% of total government expenditures.

44 LIBRARIES AND MUSEUMS

The leading libraries of Portugal are the National Library, founded in 1796 (about 2.3 million volumes) and the Library of the Academy of Sciences (400,000) in Lisbon, the University Library in Coimbra (one million), and the Municipal Library in Porto (1.27 million). The Public Libraries Programme in Portugal was launched in 1987 with a goal of providing public library services in each of the country's 275 municipalities. By 1999, about 166 libraries had been established.

There are some 300 museums in Portugal. Most feature exhibits relating to Portuguese history. Lisbon has the National Museum of Ancient Art, the Museum of Decorative Arts, the Calouste Gulbenkian Museum, and the Center for Modern Art, as well as the National Museum of Natural History. The Abbey of the Friars of St. Jerome in Belém and the Battle Abbey in Batalha contain some of the finest examples of Portuguese art. There are dozens of municipal ethnographic and historic museums, as well as many finely restored castles and manors.

45 MEDIA

Direct radiotelephone service connects Portugal with its former and current overseas provinces in Africa and Asia. In 2003, there were an estimated 411 mainline telephones for every 1,000 people. The same year, there were approximately 898 mobile phones in use for every 1,000 people.

The government broadcasting network, Radiodifusão Portuguesa, and Radio Renascenca, a religious network, operate AM and FM stations. The state-owned television network, Radiotelevisão Portuguesa, offers color broadcasts on two channels. In 2005, there were an additional 300 local and regional commercial radio stations and at least two other commercial television stations. In 2003, there were an estimated 299 radios and 413 television sets for every 1,000 people. About 128.2 of every 1,000 people were cable subscribers. Also in 2003, there were 134.4 personal computers for every 1,000 people and 194 of every 1,000 people had access to the Internet. There were 458 secure Internet servers in the country in 2004.

The constitution of 1976 guaranteed freedom of the press. The principal daily newspapers (with their affiliation estimated 2002 circulations) include: *Correo da Manha* (independent, 85,000), *Diario de Noticias* (Communist, 75,560), *Publico* (75,000), *Diario Popular* (leftist, 62,000), *A Capital* (leftist, 40,000), *Jornal de Noticias* (leftist, 90,000), *Comercio do Porto* (moderate, 30,300), and *Oprimeiro de Janeiro* (conservative, 20,200). The weekly paper *Expresso* has a circulation of 160,000.

46 ORGANIZATIONS

The principal current organizations are syndicates, the majority of which are linked to the national trade union confederation; residents' commissions; workers' commissions; and popular assemblies. Many of these associations, particularly in rural areas, are involved in local community improvement projects as well as political and cultural activities. There are four chambers of commerce and three main industrial organizations, the oldest of which, the Industrial Association of Porto, dates from 1849.

The Academy of Sciences Lisbon is primarily a scholarly and research organization. Several professional associations also promote research and public education in a variety of fields, particularly in medicine and healthcare. There are organizations for hobbyists, including the multinational Federation of European Philatelic Associations.

National youth organizations include Association of Young Farmers of Portugal, Communist Youth of Portugal, International Friendship League of Portugal, Monarchist Youth of Portugal, the Scout Federation of Portugal, and YMCA/YWCA. There are several sports associations in the country, representing a variety of pastimes such as tae kwon do, badminton, tennis, and track and field. There is a national chapter of the Special Olympics.

The Kiwanis and Lion's Clubs also have active programs. Amnesty International, Habitat for Humanity, and the Red Cross have national chapters.

47 TOURISM, TRAVEL, AND RECREATION

Portugal's historic cities—Lisbon, Porto, Coimbra, and others—offer numerous museums, old churches, and castles. Most villages still celebrate market days with dances and other festivities. There are more than 800 km (500 mi) of beaches. The Portuguese bullfight (differing from the Spanish variety in that the bulls are not killed) is a popular spectator sport; the season lasts from Easter Sunday to October. Football (soccer) is popular as both a participant and a spectator sport. A valid passport is required; visas are needed for stays of more than 90 days.

Tourism has become a major contributor of foreign exchange earnings and a stimulus to employment and investment in the hotel industry and related services. The number of tourists was 11,644,231 in 2002. Hotel rooms numbered 105,986 in 2003 with 238,759 beds and an occupancy rate of 38%.

The daily cost of staying in Lisbon, according to 2005 US Department of State estimates, was $232. Other areas were between $159 and $255, with some rates varying by season.

48 FAMOUS PORTUGUESE

During Portugal's golden age, the 15th and 16th centuries, the small Portuguese nation built an overseas empire that stretched halfway around the globe. Prince Henry the Navigator (Henrique Navegador, 1394–1460) laid the foundations of the empire. Among the leaders in overseas exploration were Bartholomeu Dias (1450?–1500), the first European to round the Cape of Good Hope; Vasco da Gama (1469–1524), who reached India and founded Portuguese India in 1498; and Pedro Alvares Cabral (1460?–1526), who took possession of Brazil for Portugal in 1500. Ferdinand Magellan (Fernão de Magalhães, 1480?–1521) led a Spanish expedition, the survivors of which were the first to sail around the world, although Magellan himself was killed after reaching the Philippines. Afonso de Albuquerque (1453–1515) was foremost among the builders of Portugal's Far Eastern empire.

Famous literary figures of the golden age include the historians Diogo do Couto (1542–1616) and João de Barros (1496–1570); Portugal's greatest writer, Luis Vas de Camões (1524?–80), the author of *Os Lusiadas*, the Portuguese national epic, and of lyric and dramatic poetry; the dramatists Gil Vicente (1465?–1537?) and Francisco de Sá de Miranda (1482–1558); the poets Bernardim Ribeiro (1482?–1552) and Diogo Bernardes (1532?–96?); and the travel writer Fernão Mendes Pinto (1509–83). Portugal's leading painter was Nuno Gonçalves (fl.1450–80).

Among the noted Portuguese of more recent times are Sebastião José de Carvalho e Mello, marquis de Pombal (1699–1782), the celebrated prime minister of King Joseph Emanuel (José Manuel, 1715–77); the novelists Camilo Castelo Branco, viscount of Correia-Botelho (1825–90), and José Maria Eça de Queiróz (1843–1900); the poets João Baptista da Silva Leitão, viscount of Almeida-Garrett (1799–1854), Antero Tarquinio de Quental (1842–91), João de Deus Nogueira Ramos (1830–96), Teófilo Braga (1843–1924), and Abilio Manuel Guerra Junqueiro (1850–1923); the satirist José Duarte Ramalho Ortigão (1836–1915); and the painter Domingos António de Sequeira (1768–1837). António Caetano de Abreu Freire Egas Moniz (1874–1955) won the Nobel Prize in physiology in 1949.

António de Oliveira Salazar (1889–1970), prime minister for more than 30 years, was Portugal's best-known modern leader. Gen. (later Marshal) António Sebastião Ribeiro de Spínola (1910–96) played a key role in the revolution of April 1974. Gen. António dos Santos Ramalho Eanes (b.1935) became president in 1976 and was reelected in 1980. Other political leaders include: Mário Alberto Nobre Lopes Soares (b.1924), Francisco Sá Carneiro (1934–80), Jorge Fernando Branco de Sampaio (b.1939), Aníbal António Cavaco Silva (b.1939), António Manuel de Oliveira Guterres (b.1949)—a former prime minister who became the United Nations High Commissioner for Refugees, and José Manuel Durão Barroso (b.1956)—a former prime minister who became president of the European Commission.

49 DEPENDENCIES

Between 1974 and 1976, all of Portugal's overseas possessions in Africa—including Angola, the Cape Verde Islands, Portuguese Guinea (now Guinea-Bissau), Mozambique, and São Tomé and Príncipe—became independent countries in accordance with the Armed Forces Movement's decolonization policy. After the Portuguese withdrew from East Timor, in the Indonesian archipelago, the former colony was invaded by Indonesian forces in 1975 and became a province of Indonesia in 1976; East Timor became an independent nation in 2002. Macau, on the south coast of China, was a "Chinese territory under Portuguese administration" from 1975–99.

50 BIBLIOGRAPHY

Anderson, James M. *The History of Portugal*. Westport, Conn.: Greenwood Press, 2000.

Annesley, Claire (ed.). *A Political and Economic Dictionary of Western Europe*. Philadelphia: Routledge/Taylor and Francis, 2005.

Birmingham, David. *A Concise History of Portugal*. Cambridge: Cambridge University Press, 1993.

Graham, Lawrence F., and Harry M. Makler (eds.) *The Portuguese Military and the State: Rethinking Transitions in Europe and Latin America*. Boulder, Colo.: Westview Press, 1993.

Hilton, Ronald. *A Bibliography of Spain and Portugal*. Lanham, Md.: Scarecrow Press, 1999.

International Smoking Statistics: A Collection of Historical Data from 30 Economically Developed Countries. New York: Oxford University Press, 2002.

Magone, José M. *European Portugal: The Difficult Road to Sustainable Democracy*. Houndmills, U.K.: Macmillan, 1997.

Manuel, Paul Christopher. *The Challenges of Democratic Consolidation in Portugal*. Westport, Conn.: Praeger, 1996.

Nataf, Daniel. *Democratization and Social Settlements: The Politics of Change in Contemporary Portugal*. Albany: State University of New York Press, 1995.

Ortiz Griffin, Julia. *Spain and Portugal*. New York: Facts On File, 2006.

Wessels, Wolfgang, Andreas Maurer, and Jürgan Mittag (eds.). *Fifteen into One?: the European Union and Its Member States*. New York: Palgrave, 2003.

Wheeler, Douglas L. *Historical Dictionary of Portugal*. Lanham, Md.: Scarecrow Press, 2002.

Wiarda, Howard J. *Politics in Iberia: The Political Systems of Spain and Portugal*. New York: HarperCollins, 1993.

ROMANIA

Romania

CAPITAL: Bucharest (Bucuresti)

FLAG: The national flag, adopted in 1965, is a tricolor of blue, yellow, and red vertical stripes.

ANTHEM: *Trei culori (Three Colors).*

MONETARY UNIT: The leu (L) is a paper currency of 100 bani. There are coins of 25 bani and 1, 3, 5, 10, 20, 50, and 100 lei, and notes of 10, 25, 50, 100, 200, 500, 1,000, and 5,000 lei. L1 = $0.00003 (or $1 = L28800) as of 2005.

WEIGHTS AND MEASURES: The metric system is the legal standard.

HOLIDAYS: New Year's Day, 1 January; International Labor Day, 1–2 May; Liberation Day, 23 August; National Day, 1 December; Christmas Day, 25 December.

TIME: 2 PM = noon GMT.

¹LOCATION, SIZE, AND EXTENT

Situated in Eastern Europe, north of the Balkan Peninsula, Romania has a total area of 237,500 sq km (91,699 sq mi). Comparatively, the area occupied by Romania is slightly smaller than the state of Oregon. The dimensions of the country are 789 km (490 mi) E–W and 475 km (295 mi) N–S. It is bounded on the N and NE by Ukraine and Moldova, on the E by the Black Sea, on the S by Bulgaria, on the SW by Serbia, and on the W by Hungary, with a total boundary length of 2,733 km (1,698 mi), of which 225 km (140 mi) is coastline. Romania's capital city, Bucharest, is located in the south central part of the country.

²TOPOGRAPHY

The backbone of Romania is formed by the Carpathian Mountains, which swing southeastward and then westward through the country. The southern limb of this arc-shaped system is known as the Transylvanian Alps, whose compact, rugged peaks rise to 2,543 m (8,343 ft) in Mt. Moldoveanu, Romania's highest. The eastern Carpathians have an average elevation of 1,000 m (3,300 ft) and exceed 1,900 m (6,200 ft) only in the highest ranges.

On the eastern and southern fringes of the Carpathian arc are the low plateaus and plains of Walachia, extending to the Prut River (Moldovan border) in the east and to the Danube (Bulgarian border) in the south. On the inside of the Carpathian arc is the Transylvanian Basin, a hilly region dissected by the wide, deep valleys of the Mures and Somes rivers.

The Dobruja, located between the lower Danube and the Black Sea, is an eroded plateau with average elevations of 400 to 600 m (1,310–1,970 ft). Except for the low-lying, swampy Danube Delta in the north, the Black Sea coast of the Dobruja is steep, facing the sea with almost vertical cliffs.

Romania is susceptible to severe earthquakes. An earthquake that struck Romania on 4 March 1977 destroyed or severely damaged some 33,000 buildings and left more than 34,000 families homeless. The shock, measuring 7.2 on the open-ended Richter scale, was the most severe in Europe since a series of shocks in October–November 1940, also in Romania.

³CLIMATE

Romania's climate is of the moderate humid continental type, exposed to predominant northerly cold winds in the winter and moderate westerly winds from the Atlantic in the summer. Average January temperatures range from -4°C to 0° C (25–32°F). During the summer, the highest temperatures are recorded in the Danube Valley (24°C/75°F). Temperatures decrease toward the high elevations in the northwest and toward the southeast, where the Black Sea exerts a moderating influence. Precipitation decreases from west to east and from the mountains to the plains, with an annual average of between 100 and 125 cm (about 40 and 50 in) in the mountains and about 38 cm (15 in) in the delta.

⁴FLORA AND FAUNA

Natural vegetation consists mainly of steppe like grasslands in the Moldavian and Walachian lowlands, with tall, deep-rooted grasses in the more humid sections and short, shallow-rooted grass in the drier parts. The Carpathian system is covered with forests, with deciduous trees at lower elevations and conifers at altitudes above 1,070–1,220 m (3,500–4,000 ft). Alpine meadows occupy the highest parts of the mountains.

Wild animals, including the black chamois, Carpathian deer, wolves, hares, marten, brown bear, lynx, boar, and fox, have sought refuge in the sparsely inhabited and forested Carpathians. Water birds flourish in the Danube Delta, and sturgeon abound in the waters of the lower Danube. Carp, bream, and pike populate the lakes; dace, barbel, and trout are found in rivers and streams.

As of 2002, there were at least 84 species of mammals, 257 species of birds, and over 3,400 species of plants throughout the country.

5 ENVIRONMENT

Rapid industrialization since World War II has caused widespread water and air pollution, particularly in Prahova County, an oil-refining region. The nation has 42 cu km of renewable water sources, with about 59% of the annual withdrawal used to support farming and 33% used for industrial purposes.

Air pollution is heaviest in the nation's cities, where industry produces hazardous levels of sulphur dioxide. In 1992, Romania had the world's 28th highest level of industrial carbon dioxide emissions, which totaled 122.1 million metric tons, a per capita level of 5.24 metric tons. However, by 2000 total of carbon dioxide emissions had dropped to 86.3 million metric tons.

Damage to the nation's soils from erosion and pollution has decreased agricultural production by 50% in some areas. Acid rain originating in Hungary is another environmental problem. Some water conservation programs were initiated in the mid-1980s, but the Environmental Protection Law of 1972 has not been strictly enforced.

Romania's forests and natural steppes have been encroached on by farmers. Radioactivity from the Chernobyl nuclear site, two floods, and two earthquakes have also contributed to the nation's environmental problems. Moreover, intensive exploitation of forests before, during, and immediately after World War II necessitated a reforestation program that, between 1950 and 1964, resulted in the replanting of 1,159,600 hectares (2,865,400 acres).

As of 2003, 4.7% of Romania's total land area was protected. According to a 2006 report issued by the International Union for Conservation of Nature and Natural Resources (IUCN), threatened species included 15 types of mammals, 13 species of birds, 2 types of reptiles, 10 species of fish, 22 species of invertebrates, and 1 species of plant. The Romanian bullhead perch, Atlantic sturgeon, slender-billed curlew, and Mediterranean monk seals are among those listed as endangered.

6 POPULATION

The population of Romania in 2005 was estimated by the United Nations (UN) at 21,612,000, which placed it at number 50 in population among the 193 nations of the world. In 2005, approximately 14% of the population was over 65 years of age, with another 16% of the population under 15 years of age. There were 95 males for every 100 females in the country. According to the UN, the annual population rate of change for 2005–10 was expected to be -0.2%, a rate the government viewed as too low. To address the decline in population, the government established the Population Commission in 2004. The projected population for the year 2025 was 18,129,000. The population density was 91 per sq km (235 per sq mi).

The UN estimated that 53% of the population lived in urban areas in 2005, and that urban areas were growing at an annual rate of 0.09%. The capital city, Bucharest (Bucureşti), had a population of 1,853,000 in that year. Other major cities and their population estimates were Constanţa, 350,581; Iaşi, 348,000; Timişoara, 334,115; Cluj-Napoca, 332,00; Galati, 326,141; Braşov, 323,736; Craiova, 313,000; Ploieşti, 253,623; and Brăila, 235,763.

7 MIGRATION

Population shifts numbering in the millions occurred as a result of the two world wars—because of territorial changes, deportation and liquidation of Jews by the Nazis, flight before the Soviet military forces, deportations to the USSR, expulsion of the Volksdeutsche (ethnic Germans), and departures following the Communist takeover and before stringent security measures halted the flow. About 117,950 Jews emigrated to Israel between 1948 and 1951; another 90,000 were permitted to emigrate during 1958–64. Some 120,000 ethnic Germans left Romania between 1978–88, and some 40,000 ethnic Hungarians fled in 1987 alone. In 1990, 80,346 people left, 78% to Germany, 9% to Hungary. Some 44,160 Romanians emigrated in 1991 and 31,152 in 1992. In 1992, 103,787 Romanians were given asylum in Germany, but in September of that year Germany returned 43,000 refugees, over half of whom were Gypsies. According to *Migration News*, in 2005 the Romanian government discouraged illegal migration by preventing some 1–4 million Romanians from leaving to travel to EU countries on the grounds that they had insufficient funds, or could not prove that they were merely visiting abroad. In addition, returning Romanians who overstay 90 days abroad have their passports confiscated. Between 1990–2000, remittances to Romania increased tenfold. In 2003 remittances were $7.3 million.

During the Kosovo crisis in 1999, Romania offered to accept 6,000 Kosovar refugees from Macedonia under the UNHCR/IOM Humanitarian Evacuation Programme. It only actually hosted about 100, until the end of July 1999 when all but one returned to Kosovo. By the end of 2004, there were a total of 2,237 persons of concern to the United Nations High Commissioner for Refugees (UNHCR) in Romania, 1,627 refugees, 210 asylum seekers primarily from Iraq, and 400 stateless Roma.

From 1991–2003, some 10,000 Romanians per year were permanent emigrants. In 2004, 3,730 Romanians applied for asylum in 10 countries, predominantly to Italy. In 2005, the net migration rate was an estimated -0.13 migrants per 1,000 population.

8 ETHNIC GROUPS

According to the 2002 census, Romanians constitute about 89.5% of the total population. Hungarians make up the largest minority group with about 6.6% of the total population. Roma account for about 2.5% of the population according to census figures; however, international groups estimate that the actual number of Roma may include up to 10% of the population. Despite government efforts for improvement, the Romani community continues to face discrimination and harassment. Lesser minority groups include Ukrainians (0.3%), Germans (0.3%), and Russians (0.2%). Others include Turks, Serbs, Croats, Jews, Poles, Bulgarians, Czechs, Greeks, Armenians, Tatars, and Slovaks.

9 LANGUAGES

Romanian is the official language. As a Romance language derived from the Latin spoken in the Eastern Roman Empire, Latin word elements make up 85–90% of the modern Romanian vocabulary. In the 2,000 years of its development, the language was also influenced by contacts with Slavonic, Albanian, Hungarian, Greek, and Turkish. Of the loanwords, Slavonic elements are the most numerous. Earliest Romanian written texts still extant date from the 16th

ROMANIA

0   50   100 Miles

0   50   100 Kilometers

UKRAINE

BUKOVINA

MOLDOVA

HUNGARY

Budapest

Debrecen

Satu Mare

Marghita

Baia Mare

Chernivsti

Suceava

Botosani

Zalău

Someş

Bistriţa

Bistriţa

Iaşi

Oradea

Cluj-Napoca

Bicaz
Reservoir

Piatra Neamţ

Chişinău

Odessa

MUNTII
APUSENI

Tirgu
Mureş

Bacău

Szeged

Arad

Sighişoara

Prut

Mureş

Sfîntu
Georghe

Focsani

Siret

Timişoara

Sibiu

Hunedoara

Moldoveanu
8,343 ft.
▲ 2543 m.

Braşov

Galaţi

Reşiţa

TRANSYLVANIAN ALPS

Rîmnicu Vîlcea

Buzău

Brăila

Mouths
of the
Danube

Tulcea

Belgrade

Tîrgu Jiu

Tîrgovişte

Ploieşti

Ialomiţa

Lacul
Razelm

Jiu

Olt

Piteşti

Argeş

SERBIA

Drobeta-Turnu
Severin

Slatina

Bucharest

Cernavodă

Constanţa

Dunărea

Craiova

Dunărea (Danube)

Giurgiu

Black
Sea

(Danube)

Romania

Pleven

Varna

BULGARIA

Burgas

CARPATHIAN MOUNTAINS

LOCATION: 48°15′06″ to 43°37′07″ N; 20°15′44″ to 29°41′24″ E. BOUNDARY LENGTHS: Ukraine, 531 kilometers (329 miles); Moldova, 450 kilometers (279 miles); Black Sea coastline, 234 kilometers (145 miles); Bulgaria, 608 kilometers (377 miles); Serbia, 476 kilometers (295 miles); Hungary, 445 kilometers (277 miles).
TERRITORIAL SEA LIMIT: 12 miles.

century. In addition to letters of the English alphabet, Romanian has the letters ă, î, â, ş, and ţ. Hungarian and German are spoken by a large percentage of the inhabitants of Transylvania.

10 RELIGIONS

According to the 2002 census, about 86.8% of the population were members of the Romanian Orthodox Church, one of the autocephalous Eastern Orthodox churches. Under Bulgarian influence, the Slavonic rite was maintained in the Romanian Church until the 17th century, when Romanian became the liturgical language. The Romanian Church enjoyed a large measure of autonomy in the Middle Ages and, after Romania achieved full independence from the Turks in 1878, was formally declared independent of the Patriarchate of Constantinople; it is now headed by its own

patriarch. The Greek Catholic (Uniate) Church was formed in 1698 by the Transylvanian Orthodox, who acknowledged the jurisdiction of the Holy See. In October 1948, the new Communist regime compelled the Uniate Church to sever its ties with Rome and to merge with the Romanian Orthodox Church.

Roman Catholics account for about 4.7% of the population. The Greek Catholic Church is also represented as a recognized religion in the country. Protestant denominations make up about 7.5% of the population. Officially recognized Protestant denominations include the Reformed Church (which is the largest in the country), the Romanian Evangelical Church, the Unitarian Church (mostly Hungarian), Baptists, Seventh-Day Adventists, Pentecostals, Jehovah's Witnesses, and the Evangelical Augustinian Church. Islam and Judaism are also officially recognized religions; there are about 67,257 Muslims and 10,200 Jews. There are also small communities of Methodists, Presbyterians, Baha'is, God's Children (The Family), Hare Krishnas, Zen Buddhists, and Mormons (Church of Jesus Christ of Latter-day Saints), all of which are not officially recognized by the state.

The constitution provides for religious freedom, but the government retains a great deal of legal control over religious groups and activities. The Romanian Orthodox Church holds substantial influence in political and social venues. All religious groups must register with the government. Those that are granted official recognition are eligible for state support; the government officially recognizes 17 religions. Proselytizing is not illegal, but minority religions engaging in such activities have reported restrictions and harassment by local government officials. Some tension does exist between religious groups; particularly between the Romanian Orthodox and minority groups.

11 TRANSPORTATION

Romania is strategically located at the crossroads of Europe and Asia. As of 2004, Romania's railroad network totaled 11,385 km (7,074 mi), of standard, broad and narrow gauge lines, of which 3,888 km (2,416 mi) were electrified. Standard gauge railways predominate at 10,898 km (6,779 mi), followed by narrow gauge at 427 km (266 mi), and broad gauge railways making up the remainder.

There were 198,755 km (123,625 mi) of roads at the end of 2002, of which 100,173 km (62,307 mi) were paved, including 113 km (70 mi) of expressways. In 2003, there were 3,087,628 passenger cars and 635,342 commercial vehicles in use.

Only the Danube and, to a lesser extent, the Prut rivers are suitable for inland navigation, which accounts for only about 1% of the total freight traffic. The main Danube ports include Galati, Brăila, and Giurgiu. At Giurgiu, on the main transportation line between Romania and Bulgaria, a road-and-rail bridge was completed in 1954, replacing the former Danube ferry to Ruse, Bulgaria. A major project, the Danube-Black Sea Canal, designed to bypass the shallow, silted arms of the Danube Delta, was started in 1949 but abandoned in 1953. It was revived in the early 1980s and opened in 1984. The canal is 64 km (40 mi) long and connects Cernavoda with Constanța. Overall, Romania as of 2004, had 1,731 km (1,076 mi) of navigable inland waterways The Romanian merchant fleet consisted of 34 vessels of 1,000 GRT or more, totaling 395,350 GRT in 2005, and was based in Constanța, the nation's chief Black Sea port.

Romanian airports totaled an estimated 61 in 2004. As of 2005, a total of 25 had paved runways, and there was also one heliport. Otopeni International Airport, near Bucharest, was opened in 1970 and remains the nation's principal international air terminal. Baneasa Airport, also near Bucharest, handles local traffic. Other important airports include M. Kogalniceanu at Constanța and Giarmata at Timişoara. Romanian Air Transport (Transporturile Aeriene Române-TAROM) and Romanian Air Lines (Liniile Aeriene Române-LAR) are the primary air carriers. In 2003, about 1.251 million passengers were carried on scheduled domestic and international airline flights.

12 HISTORY

Archaeological excavations show that the land now known as Romania has been inhabited for thousands of years. Agriculture was introduced in the 6th century BC, and by the 3rd century BC the Cucuteni civilization had produced polychrome pottery. The Dacians, of Thracian stock, had become a distinct people by the end of the 1st century BC. The kingdom of Dacia reached the highest stage of its development toward the end of the 1st century AD, in the reign of Decebalus (87–106), but after four years of war, Dacia fell to the Roman Emperor Trajan in AD 106. The withdrawal of the Romans in AD 271 left the Romanians a partly Christianized Dacian-Roman people, speaking Latin and living in towns and villages built on the Roman pattern. In the following centuries, as Dacia was overrun by successive waves of invaders, the early Romanians are believed to have sought refuge in the mountains or to have migrated south of the Danube River. There the Dacian-Romanians, assimilating Slavic influences, became known by the 7th century as Vlachs (Walachians). The Vlachs apparently remained independent of their neighbors, but came under Mongol domination in the 13th century.

The establishment of the two principalities of Walachia and Moldavia in the late 13th and early 14th centuries opened one of the most important chapters in the history of Romania. Walachia came under Turkish suzerainty in 1476 and Moldavia in 1513; 13 years later, Transylvania, which had been under Hungarian control since 1003, also passed into Turkish hands. The tide of Ottoman domination began to ebb under Russian pressure in the second half of the 17th century; in 1699, under the Treaty of Karlowitz, Transylvania was taken by Austria (later Austria-Hungary), and in 1812, Russia obtained Bessarabia, a section of Moldavia, from the Turks. The Congress of Paris in 1856, which ended the Crimean War, guaranteed the autonomy of the principalities of Walachia and Moldavia and forced Russia to return the southernmost part of Bessarabia to Moldavia. The two principalities formed a union in 1859, with Alexandru Ioan Cuza as its first prince, but he was replaced in 1866 by Carol I of the house of Hohenzollern-Sigmaringen, under a new governing document that proclaimed Romania a constitutional monarchy. At the Congress of Berlin in 1878, Romania obtained full independence from Turkey but returned southern Bessarabia to Russia. Under the rule of Carol I, Romania developed into a modern political and economic unit.

As a result of the Balkan Wars in 1912–13, Romania gained southern Dobruja from Bulgaria. Carol I died in 1914 and was succeeded by Ferdinand I. In World War I, Romania joined the Allies and as a result acquired Bessarabia from Russia, Bukovina from Austria, and Transylvania from Hungary. The establishment of a greatly expanded Romania was confirmed in 1919–20 by the treaties of St. Germain, Trianon, and Neuilly. In the early postwar period, Ion Bratianu (son of a 19th-century premier) instituted agrarian and electoral reforms. Both Ferdinand and Bratianu died in 1927. A brief regency period under Iuliu Maniu, Peasant Party leader, was followed in 1930 by the return to Romania of Carol II, who, having earlier renounced his right of succession, now deposed his nine-year-old son, Michael (Mihai), and established a royal dictatorship.

As economic conditions deteriorated, Fascism and anti-Semitism became increasingly powerful, and Carol II sought to appease both Germany and the USSR, which by August 1939 had concluded their nonaggression agreement. In 1940, Romania ceded Bessarabia and northern Bukovina to the USSR, northern Transylvania to Hungary, and southern Dobruja to Bulgaria. In the same year, Carol II abdicated in favor of his son Michael, and German troops entered the country. Romania joined the Axis in war against the Allies in 1941. As Soviet forces drove into Romania in 1944, a coup overthrew the wartime regime of Gen. Ion Antonescu on 23 August, and Romania joined the Allies against Germany. A Communist-led coalition government under Premier Petru Groza was set up in March 1945. King Michael was forced to abdicate on 30 December 1947, and the Romanian People's Republic was proclaimed. The Paris Peace Treaty of 1947 fixed Romania's frontiers as of 1 January 1941, with the exception of the border with Hungary, which was restored as of 1 January 1938, so northern Transylvania was once again part of the Romanian state.

The Communist constitution of 1948 was superseded in 1952 by a constitution patterned more directly on that of the USSR. In international affairs, Romania followed a distinctly pro-Soviet line, becoming a member of CMEA and the Warsaw Pact. Internally, the regime nationalized the economy and pursued a policy of industrialization and the collectivization of agriculture. During the 1960s, however, and especially after the emergence of Nicolae Ceausescu as Communist Party and national leader, Romania followed a more independent course, increasing its trade with Western nations and avoiding a definite stand in the Sino-Soviet dispute. In 1967, Romania was the only Communist country that did not break diplomatic relations with Israel following the Six-Day War. In 1968, Romania denounced the Soviet intervention in Czechoslovakia and the USSR-Romania treaty of friendship and cooperation expired; a new accord was not signed until 1970. Further examples of Romania's independent foreign policy in the 1970s were the gradual improvement of relations with China, numerous bilateral agreements with the nations of Western Europe, and President Ceausescu's state visit in December 1973 to Washington, where he signed a joint declaration on economic, industrial, and technical cooperation with the United States. In the 1970s and early 1980s, Romania also became increasingly involved in the nonaligned movement. In 1982, Ceausescu called on the USSR to withdraw from Afghanistan.

In contrast to some other East European countries, there was relatively little political and cultural dissent in Romania during the first 30 years of Communist rule. In 1977, however, about 35,000 miners in the Jiu Valley, west of Bucharest, went on strike because of economic grievances. Afterwards, the Romanian Communist Party hierarchy was frequently reshuffled, ostensibly to improve economic management, with Ceausescu and several members of his family (particularly his wife, Elena) increasing their power.

In the early and mid-1980s, there were a number of work stoppages and strikes caused by food and energy shortages. In early 1987, Ceausescu indicated that Romania would not follow the reform trend initiated by Mikhail Gorbachev in the USSR.

The progress of *perestroika* (restructuring) in the Soviet Union, intensified by the wave of "velvet revolutions" which rolled across Eastern Europe in autumn 1989, only served to highlight the repressiveness of the Ceausescu regime, which had all but starved and frozen the country to death in its attempt to repay international indebtedness, which President Ceausescu said in April 1989 had

been US$10 billion. The regime was also single-mindedly pushing ahead with the "systemization plan" begun in March 1988, which intended to force about half the country's peasants into urbanized "agro-industrial" complexes by bulldozing their villages.

The policy was especially offensive to the 2.5 million Hungarians in Romania's western regions, who understood the policy to be an attempt to further undercut their cultural autonomy. In mid-December 1989, abysmal economic conditions and ethnic tension led to spontaneous demonstrations in the western city of Timişoara. When the Securitate, Romania's secret police, attempted to deport Laszlo Toekes, a popular clergyman who had been a leading spokesperson for the local Hungarians, thousands of people took to the streets. Troops were summoned, and two days of rioting ensued, during which several thousand citizens were killed.

News of the riot, and of the government's handling of it, fanned further demonstrations around the country. Probably unwisely, President Ceausescu went ahead with a planned three-day visit to Iran. Upon his return, he convened a mass rally at which he attempted to portray his opponents as fascists. However, the rally turned into an antigovernment demonstration, in which the army sided with the demonstrators.

Ceausescu and his wife attempted to flee the country, but were apprehended, tried, and summarily executed, on 25 December 1989. Several days of fighting raged, as the Securitate and the army battled for power. A hastily assembled Council of National Salvation took power, repealing a number of Ceausescu's most hated policies and laws. The Council's president was Ion Iliescu, a former secretary of the Communist Party, who had been one of several signatories to a letter, which had accused Ceausescu of gross mismanagement of Romania's economy, made public in March 1989. The prime minister, Peter Roman, was also a prominent Communist.

Although the Council contained some non-Communists, the majority had been prominent officials in Ceausescu's regime, which prompted almost continuous public protests. Despite a continued government monopoly on media, political opposition groups managed to rally public support to demand the banning of the Communist Party, and the widening of the government. In February 1990, Iliescu agreed, replacing the 145-member Council of National Salvation with a 241-member Council of National Unity, which included members of opposition parties, national minorities, and former political prisoners; it also contained the full membership of the former Council, and Iliescu remained president.

Parliamentary elections were held in May 1990 against a background of continued civil unrest, especially in the Hungarian west. Although international observers considered the elections to have been generally fair, the National Salvation Front—now a political party—made ruthless use of its media monopoly to take about two-thirds of the parliamentary seats from a divided, disorganized, and inexperienced opposition. Iliescu was elected president, with about 85% of the votes, in a contest in which there had been more than 94% voter turnout.

The conviction that ex-Communists had "stolen" the election brought continued demonstrations in Bucharest and elsewhere. In April 1990, in a move that was criticized internationally, the Iliescu government trucked in miners from the northern part of the country, urging them to beat up and disperse the demonstrators, ending what threatened to become a coup d'etat against Iliescu.

After the failure of those demonstrations, the opposition began to link up into parties, hoping to challenge Iliescu and his party in the next parliamentary elections, to be held in 1992. Popular discontent, however, continued to find more direct expression. Angry that the promises which had brought them to Bucharest in June had not been kept, the miners returned in September 1991, this time to link up with many of the opposition figures that they earlier had attacked, now to mount a mass attack on the government. Iliescu had no choice but to dismiss Prime Minister Roman, replacing him with Theodor Stolojan, an economist who managed to contain popular discontent until the general elections of September 1992, largely by delaying implementation of economic reforms. The parliamentary elections demonstrated a wide diffusion of political support. Iliescu's National Salvation Front won 28% of the seats, making it the largest party, but the Democratic Convention, an anti-Communist opposition coalition with a strong monarchist wing, took 20%, while former Prime Minister Roman's National Salvation Front, now opposed to Iliescu, took 10%. The remaining 42% of the seats were divided among five other parties.

The popular vote for president showed that Iliescu still had support, although it had dropped to just above 60% of the electorate. The success of his opponent, Emil Constantinescu, a former rector of Bucharest University, demonstrated the continuing hostility to Iliescu and the other ex-Communists who had managed to retain power.

Iliescu's dismissal of Stolojan, in November 1992, was widely seen as a recognition of that significant minority's opposition. Iliescu chose Nicolae Vacaroiu as prime minister, who had no earlier ties to the Ceausescu or Iliescu governments. However, the move was addressed as much to the International Monetary Fund (IMF) as the rest of the international financial community, which had emerged as Romania's chief source of support. Continued political instability and the fitful pace of privatization, combined with a strong nationalist bloc in the parliament which warned against "selling out" Romania to foreigners, all kept foreign investment quite low, a total of only about $785 million for all of 1990–94. As a consequence Romania has had to rely upon loans from Western sources, especially the IMF, piling up foreign debt at the rate of about $1 billion a year. In return for this infusion of cash the foreign donors have set stringent requirements of economic reform, which Romania is not finding easy to meet.

Romania's fitful progress toward democratization exacerbates the social pressures of its continued economic decline. Romanians began the post-Ceausescu period as among the poorest people in Europe, and their economy worsened for several years. Inflation for 1992 was 210%, and more than 300% for 1993, while unemployment was almost 10%. Most significantly, production fell for the first couple of years after the anti-Communist revolution. Beginning in 1994, however, Romania began slowly turning its economy around. In 1996, it even applied for membership in the European Union (EU)—although it knew that admission before 2000 was doubtful.

In November 1996, presidential and parliamentary elections were held as the economy, while still fairly grim, continued to improve in several sectors. Popular opposition to the ex-Communist

Iliescu had grown strong leading up to the elections, mainly due to broken promises of economic security and widespread corruption that saw the enrichment of a small clique of ex-Communist insiders amid general economic hardships across the country. Iliescu also failed to deliver on many privatization schemes, angering the middle-class merchants. In the election's first round on 3 November, the Democratic Convention Alliance of Opposition Groups, led by Emil Constantinescu, Iliescu's 1990 opponent, earned the highest percentage of votes (30%) followed by Iliescu's Party of Social Democracy (PDSR) and the Social Democratic Union (22%), and former prime minister Peter Roman's center-left party (13%). In the presidential election, neither Iliescu nor Constantinescu received a majority, so a runoff was held on 17 November, in which Constantinescu took 54% of the vote, becoming Romania's first true post-Communist leader. The West was thrilled with the victory, as Constantinescu was seen as significantly more pro-free market and pro-international investment than Iliescu. The new government immediately began imposing austerity measures, vowing to reduce the deficit significantly by the end of 1997. However, it was hobbled by disagreements among coalition members, and in March 1998, the prime minister, Victor Ciorbea, was replaced by Radu Vasile. The government's position was weakened even further in January 1999 when it backed down in the face of demands by striking coal miners in order to avert potential violence. In December 1999, in order to save face, and boost the popularity of the coalition for the upcoming elections, President Constantinescu forced Radu Vasile to resign and replaced him with Mugur Isarescu, the governor of the Romanian National Bank.

By the first half of 2000, the failure of the reformist government to bring about the promised economic recovery had led to widespread disenchantment. Inflation, unemployment, and debt remained serious problems, and Romania had also failed to achieve its major foreign policy objectives—admission to NATO and the EU. Public discontent had led to a resurgence in the popularity by Iliescu's ex-Communists, who won a decisive victory in the June local elections. At midyear it was widely expected that the November general elections would bring a change in both the government and the presidency, and it was considered possible that Iliescu himself might stage a political comeback.

Presidential and parliamentary elections were held on 26 November 2000, which were won by Iliescu's PDSR. Iliescu became president after a second round of voting was held on 10 December, defeating extreme right-wing candidate Corneliu Vadim Tudor of the xenophobic Greater Romania Party (PRM). Tudor has been compared to France's Jean-Marie Le Pen, Russia's Vladimir Zhirinovsky, Austria's Jörg Haider, and the late Pym Fortuyn of the Netherlands. Voter turnout was around 60%, 20% lower than in 1996. Iliescu won 36.4% of the vote in the first round, to Tudor's 28.3%; in the second round, Iliescu took 66.8%, and Tudor won 33.2% of the vote.

In December 2001, under pressure from the EU, Romania repealed a provision of its penal code that discriminated against homosexuals. In November 2002, NATO formally invited Romania to join the organization, one of seven Eastern European nations to join in 2004.

Although between 2000 and 2004 Romania registered some of the highest economic growth rates in Europe, endemic corruption and internal problems within the ruling PDSR led to a surprise victory by the Truth and Justice Alliance in the November 2004 elections. Traian Basescu, a former sea captain who served as the minister of transportation from 1996 to 2000, and as the mayor of Bucharest from 2000 to 2004, won the presidential elections. Basescu, who ran for the Truth and Justice Alliance, garnered 51.23% of the votes in the second round, while his opponent, Adrian Nastase, the former prime minister of Romania and a member of PDSR got 48.77%. The Alliance formed by the National Liberal Party (PNL) and the Democratic Party (PD), sustains a fragile parliamentary majority with the backing of the UDMR, the Humanist Party (PUR), and several ethnic minority groups.

Internal problems within the Alliance, the kidnapping of three Romanian journalists in Iraq, and massive floods that covered most of Romania in the spring and summer of 2005 threatened to break the coalition apart. President Basescu and the new prime minister, Calin Popescu Tariceanu, agreed to put their differences aside in order to achieve one of the most important goals for Romania—the accession to the EU.

In April 2005, the European parliament gave the green light to Romania and Bulgaria, with 497 votes in favor of the accession, 93 against, and 71 abstentions; both countries are expected to join in 2007. The EU specified however that Romania's accession could be delayed until 2008 if the reform of the judicial system failed and if the fight against corruption was not intensified.

13 GOVERNMENT

The Council for National Unity enacted a new constitution for Romania in November 1991, and the document carried many of the hallmarks of Soviet-era constitutions, granting rights in some articles and revoking them in others. In October 2003, the constitution was revised, following a national referendum. The legal system is generally based on Romania's old 1923 constitution, and on the constitution of France's Fifth Republic.

The present arrangement has a directly elected president who serves for a maximum of two five-year terms; he is head of state. The president, in consultation with the parliament, names the prime minister. The prime minister, in turn, chooses his governing body, which has to be approved by the parliament. The government, together with the president, represents the executive power in the country.

The legislature is made up of two houses, the Senate, with 137 seats (one senator for 160,000 inhabitants), and the Chamber of Deputies, with 332 seats (one deputy for 70,000 inhabitants); members of both bodies are directly elected on a proportional representation basis to serve four-year terms.

14 POLITICAL PARTIES

After the coup against Ceausescu, some 80 political parties appeared—some new; others, like the Liberals and the Peasant Party, revivals of prewar parties that the Communists had outlawed. The dominant party in the 1990 elections, however, proved to be the National Salvation Front (NSF), which took two-thirds of the seats in the National Assembly.

By 1992, the NSF had split over the issue of whether or not to support Iliescu. The main party renamed itself the Party of Social Democracy in Romania (PDSR), while a pro-Iliescu wing became the Democratic National Salvation Front, and an anti-Iliescu wing, headed by ex-Prime Minister Roman, became the Front

for National Salvation (FSN). The PDSR took 28% of the vote and the FSN, 10%.

The second-largest party in the 1992 elections was a coalition, called the Democratic Convention of Romania (DCR), which incorporated such parties as the National Peasant Party Christian Democratic (PNTCD), the Movement of Civic Alliance, the Party of Civic Alliance, Liberal Party '93, and the Social Democratic Party. There are also small ultranationalist parties, the Party of Romanian National Unity and the Greater Romania Party (PRM), and the Communists have been reborn as the Socialist Labor Party. Despite superficial political differences, all three parties are anti-Hungarian, anti-Gypsy, and anti-Semitic, as well as anti-democratic.

In the parliamentary elections held on 3 November 1996, the PDSR lost its majority standing, and the DCR won a strong majority. The DCR became the ruling party with 53 seats in the Senate and 122 in the Chamber of Deputies; the PSDR held 41 and 91, respectively; the Social Democratic Union, 23 and 53; Hungarian Democratic Union, 8 and 19; Greater Romania Party, 8 and 19; and National Union Party, 7 and 18. Victor Ciorbea, a trade union leader and former mayor of Bucharest, became prime minister, and Emil Constantinescu became president.

Parliamentary and presidential elections were held on 26 November 2000, which were won by the PDSR. The PDSR merged with the Romanian Social Democratic Party to form the Social Democratic Party (PSD), and with the Humanist Party of Romania, formed the Democratic Social Pole of Romania. This coalition won 155 of 346 seats in the Chamber of Deputies and 65 of 143 seats in the Senate. The PRM took 84 seats in the Chamber of Deputies and 37 in the Senate; the Democratic Party took 31 and 13 seats, respectively; the National Liberal Party won 30 and 13; the Hungarian Democratic Alliance (UDMR) won 27 and 12; and 19 ethnic parties were represented with 1 seat each in the Chamber of Deputies.

On 28 November 2004, the Truth and Justice Alliance, comprised of the National Liberal Party (PNL) and the Democratic Party (PD), scored a surprise victory over the ruling PSD. The Alliance formed a fragile coalition with UDMR, the Humanist Party (which recently changed its name to the Conservative Party), and several ethnic minorities. The coalition holds only 169 of 332 seats in the Chamber of Deputies, and 71 of 137 seats in the Senate, while PSD won 110 and 45 respectively, and PRM 32 and 19. At that time there were also 19 deputies with no political affiliation.

15 LOCAL GOVERNMENT

Romania is divided into 41 counties (judete), as well as the municipality of Bucharest, which has separate status. Below the counties, there are three other categories of local authority: approximately 2,800 communes (with populations up to 5,000), 280 orase (towns with populations of approximately 5,000–20,000) and 86 municipalities. In the Ceausescu era the counties were administered by appointees of the central government, whose responsibility was solely to Bucharest. The Iliescu government attempted to reshape local government, but most sources agree that the result was to further remove authority from the countryside. Much of Romania is deeply rural, with almost no contact between localities or with the central government.

While more than 40% of the Romanian population lives in the rural countryside, attending to a highly fragmented agricultural system, almost 40% of the national wealth is concentrated in Bucharest. As a result, prominent figures from all of Romania's main provinces have pleaded for a more decentralized government system. To date, all 41 counties are led by a prefect who is appointed by the government. The prefects respond directly to the Ministry of Public Administration.

16 JUDICIAL SYSTEM

The 1992 law on reorganization of the judiciary established a four-tier legal system, including the reestablishment of appellate courts, which existed prior to Communist rule in 1952. The four tiers consist of courts of first instance, intermediate appellate level courts, a Supreme Court, and a Constitutional Court. The Constitutional Court, six of whose nine members are chosen by the parliament and three by the president, has judicial responsibility for judicial review of constitutional issues. The Constitutional Court judges are appointed for nine-year terms. The Supreme Court was reorganized under a separate 1993 law; its members are appointed by the president of Romania and exercise ultimate authority over all other courts in the country. The judges of the Supreme Court are appointed for a term of six years and may serve consecutive terms.

Under the law, the courts are independent of the executive branch. The constitution vests authority for selection and promotion of judges in the Ministry of Justice. Judges are appointed for life by the president upon recommendation from a panel of judges and prosecutors selected by parliament.

Alongside this ordinary court system is a three-tiered military court system, which handles cases involving military personnel.

17 ARMED FORCES

The Romanian armed forces have been reorganized in the wake of the revolution of 1989–90, which destroyed the Communist armed forces and security establishment. In 2005, the armed forces numbered 97,200 active personnel, supported by 104,000 reservists. There were 66,000 active personnel in the Army, 7,200 in the Navy, and 14,000 in the Air Force. The Army was equipped with 1,258 main battle tanks, four reconnaissance vehicles, 177 armored infantry fighting vehicles, 1,583 armored personnel carriers, and 1,238 artillery pieces. The Navy operated one frigate, six corvettes, 38 patrol/coastal vessels, 12 mine warfare, and 11 logistics/support vessels. The Air Force was equipped with 106 combat capable aircraft, including 25 fighters and 68 fighter ground attack aircraft, as well as 8 assault helicopters. Romania also had a paramilitary force of 79,900 members that consisted of 22,900 border guards and an estimated gendarmerie of 57,000. Romania participated in Operation Enduring Freedom in Afghanistan and in peacekeeping or military missions in 10 other countries or regions. The defense budget in 2005 was $2.10 billion.

18 INTERNATIONAL COOPERATION

Romania, which became a member of the United Nations on 14 December 1955, participates in ECE and several nonregional specialized agencies, such as the World Bank, the ILO, the FAO, UNESCO, UNIDO, and the WHO. Romania served on the UN Security Council from 2004–05. The Romanian government has supported UN missions and operations in Kosovo (est. 1999), Ethiopia and Eritrea (est. 2000), Liberia (est. 2003), Burundi (est. 2004), and Côte d'Ivoire (est. 2004), among others.

Romania is also a member of the WTO, G-9, G-77, the Council of Europe, the Black Sea Economic Cooperation Zone, the Euro-Atlantic Partnership Council, the European Bank for Reconstruction and Development, and the OSCE. Romania became a member of NATO in 2004. The country has observer status in the OAS and the Latin American Integration Association (LAIA). Romania is an applicant for membership in the European Union.

Romania is part of the Australia Group, the Zangger Committee, the Organization for the Prohibition of Chemical Weapons, and the Nuclear Suppliers Group (London Group). In environmental cooperation, Romania is part of the Antarctic Treaty, the Basel Convention, Conventions on Biological Diversity and Air Pollution, Ramsar, CITES, the Kyoto Protocol, the Montréal Protocol, MARPOL, the Nuclear Test Ban Treaty, and the UN Conventions on the Law of the Sea, Climate Change and Desertification.

19 ECONOMY

Before World War II, the economy was predominantly agricultural, with agriculture and forestry contributing 38.1% of the national income in 1938, and industry (including construction) 35.2%. As a result of the industrialization program of the Communist government, this ratio has changed greatly. In 1996, agriculture and forestry contributed 19% to national income; industry, 36%; construction, 7%; and services, 38%. Within industry, structural changes reflected the government's emphasis on the development of heavy industry, particularly machine-building, as opposed to consumer goods. The relative neglect of the agricultural sector, in addition to peasants' resistance to collectivization, resulted in agricultural difficulties, including shortages.

The basic organization of economic management in Romania was highly centralized, like its original Soviet model, with few of the modifications introduced elsewhere in Eastern Europe. During the late 1970s and in the 1980s, the continued emphasis on industrial expansion and consequent neglect of agriculture led to food shortages and rationing. Romania's economic problems in the 1980s were exacerbated by the government's program to reduce foreign debt: the debt was indeed reduced, from $10.5 billion in 1981 to $6.6 billion at the end of 1987, but at the cost of reduced industrial development. In addition, two extremely harsh winters (1985 and 1987) resulted in widespread power shortages and loss of production. In the 1990s, foreign debt has once again been on the rise; after reaching a low of $3.5 billion in 1992, it had risen to $10 billion in 1998.

The transition to a market economy also proved extremely painful. By 1992, grain production was only two-thirds of the 1989 level, GDP had fallen by 30%, industrial production had fallen 47% and inflation had reached 300%. Growth returned weakly in 1993, with GDP increasing 1%, but then gained some momentum, rising 3.9% in 1994, 6.9% in 1995 and 4% in 1996. In 1997, the government entered into an arrangement with the IMF for a standby agreement (SBA) supported by a credit line of $430 million, but the agreement was suspended because of the government's slowness in implementing agricultural reform. At the end of 1997,

GDP had fallen -6.6% and inflation had soared to 151.4%. The effects of the Russian financial crisis in 1998, which came to a head in August, spread quickly to Romania, helping produce a further contraction of 7.3% of GDP for the year. Inflation, however, under new government restraints, moderated to 40.6%. Despite an austerity budget for 1999, inflation increased to 54.8% and the GDP contracted 3.2% for the year. In August 1999 the government entered into another SBA with the IMF, and in 2000 and 2001, GDP registered positive growth (1.6% and 4.1%, respectively), and decreasing inflation rates (40.7% and 37.5%, respectively). In October 2001 the government entered into its third SBA arrangement with the IMF, which was successfully completed in October 2003. In July 2004, a stand-by agreement was signed with the IMF. The agreement is to be completed in two years and is aimed at decreasing the account deficit and the inflation rate through a mix of monetary policies and structural reforms.

Romania's macroeconomic performance improved dramatically in the 21st century. Between 2001 and 2003, the GDP registered a 5% average growth; in 2004 the growth rate jumped to 8.3%—second only to Latvia in Europe. Inflation has decreased steadily over this time period, to reach single digit values (at 9.6%) in 2004, and predicted to fall to 7.5% in 2005, and 5.0% in 2006. The unemployment rate has remained fairly stable, averaging around 6% between 1997 and 2004.

This growth of the economy can be attributed to several factors. First and foremost, household consumption has expanded radically, fueled by higher real wages and remittances sent from people working abroad. Investments are another factor that contributed to this growth, peaking in 2004 with the acquiring of Petrom (the national oil company) by the Austrian OMV. Exports improved annually at double digits, although strong internal demand translated into higher imports.

Today, Romania boasts a technologically advanced market economy, a diverse and dynamic economic base, agricultural self-sufficiency, and a strong will to sustain the present economic boom.

20 INCOME

The US Central Intelligence Agency (CIA) reports that in 2005 Romania's gross domestic product (GDP) was estimated at $186.4 billion. The CIA defines GDP as the value of all final goods and services produced within a nation in a given year and computed on the basis of purchasing power parity (PPP) rather than value as measured on the basis of the rate of exchange based on current dollars. The per capita GDP was estimated at $8,300. The annual growth rate of GDP was estimated at 5.2%. The average inflation rate in 2005 was 8.9%. It was estimated that agriculture accounted for 13.1% of GDP, industry 33.7%, and services 53.2%.

According to the World Bank, in 2003 remittances from citizens working abroad totaled $124 million or about $6 per capita and accounted for approximately 0.2% of GDP. Foreign aid receipts amounted to $601 million or about $28 per capita and accounted for approximately 1.1% of the gross national income (GNI).

The World Bank reports that in 2003 household consumption in Romania totaled $40.32 billion or about $1,858 per capita based on a GDP of $57.0 billion, measured in current dollars rather than PPP. Household consumption includes expenditures of individuals, households, and nongovernmental organizations on goods and services, excluding purchases of dwellings. It was estimated that for the period 1990 to 2003 household consumption grew at an average annual rate of 2.2%. In 2001 it was estimated that approximately 36% of household consumption was spent on food, 9% on fuel, 3% on health care, and 20% on education. It was estimated that in 2002 about 28.9% of the population had incomes below the poverty line.

21 LABOR

Romania's labor force in 2005 was estimated at 9.31 million people. As of 2004, agriculture accounted for 31.6%, with 30.7% in industry, and 37.7% in the services sector. Unemployment was estimated at 6.5% in 2005. The Romanian economy is in the process of privatization. Private firms accounted for 64.5% of the workforce in 2001. However, the government was still prominent in the large industrial sector.

Labor legislation adopted in 1991 guarantees the right of private sector employees to associate freely, organize and join unions, bargain collectively, and carry out strikes. In 2005, there were about 18 nationwide trade confederations plus smaller independent unions. Unions are permitted to strike, but only after all attempts at arbitration have failed and a 48-hour advance notice is given to employers. However there have been complaints that the courts are biased towards ruling strikes illegal. Also, while the law protects the right to bargain collectively, contracts arising from collective bargaining have not been consistently enforced. However, at the branch and unit level, collective bargaining contracts covered around 80% of Romania's workforce in 2005.

Most employees work a five-day, 40-hour week with overtime pay rates for weekends, holidays and work over 40 hours. The minimum wage in 2005 was $105 per month, and while the government also subsidizes necessities such as housing and health care, this does not provide a decent standard of living for a worker and family. Children under the age of 16 years are not permitted to work, although 15-year-olds may be employed with parental consent. Minors are also banned from working under hazardous conditions. However, child labor remains a problem in Romania. Neither the government nor industry has the resources to enforce safety and health standards in the workplace.

22 AGRICULTURE

Although under Communism the emphasis had been on industrialization, Romania is still largely an agricultural country. Of the total land area, 43% was arable land in 2003. Agriculture engaged about 15% of the active population and accounted for 12% of GDP in 2003.

The government began forming collective farms in 1949 and had largely completed the collectivization process by 1962. By 1985, of a total of 15,020,178 hectares (37,115,460 acres) of agricultural land, 29.7% was in state farms, with another 60.8% in large cooperative farms. The socialized sector consisted of 3,745 collectives, 419 state farms, and 573 farming mechanization units by 1985. The Land Reform of 1991 returned 80% of agricultural land to private ownership. Of the 14.8 million acres of agricultural land in 1996, some 2.6 million private producers farmed 44.6%; 20,400 associations of private producers farmed 25%; 1,171 state farms operated 12.8%; and public land accounted for the remaining 17.6%. Average farm size for private producers that year was 2.5 hectares (6.2 acres); for associations, 180 hectares (445 acres);

and for state farms, 1,620 hectares (4,003 acres). In 2003, Romania had 4,484,890 agricultural holdings, the highest in the European Union. That year, 64% of holdings were used for crops, 35% for animal farming, and 1% for agricultural services.

Grain growing has been the traditional agricultural pursuit, but the acreage has been reduced since World War II, and more area has been assigned to industrial and fodder crops. The 2004 production totals (in thousand tons) for major crops was wheat, 7,735; barley, 1,406; corn, 4,452; oats, 447; soybeans, 298; sunflower seeds, 1,558; sugar beets, 673; vegetables and melons, 4,573; potatoes, 4,230; and grapes, 1,230. In 2004, Romania produced an estimated 57 million liters of wine. That year, exports of agricultural products totaled $765.3 million and agricultural imports amounted to $2,145 million.

23 ANIMAL HUSBANDRY

Romania has some 4.8 million hectares (11.9 million acres) of pastures. Animal production in Romania has developed somewhat more rapidly than crop production. The 1970 value of total livestock production, including the increase in herds and flocks as well as livestock products, was slightly more than double the level of 1938, and the 1974 value was 34% above that of 1970. In view of the initially low level of Romanian livestock production, development has been slow, however. The major reasons for the inadequate increases had been lack of economic incentives, insufficient fodder, and inadequate shelter. Since the overthrow of the Ceausescu regime in 1989, privatization of much of the grazing land has begun. In order to improve livestock raising, the government continues to stress agricultural modernization. Livestock productivity during 2002–04 was 10.8% higher than during 1999–2001.

The livestock numbers (in thousands) for 2005 were cattle, 2,950; hogs, 6,500; sheep, 7,430; and chickens, 87,500. After several years of livestock reduction, the hog and poultry inventories rose at the end of 1995, due to increases in the private sector. Sheep numbers have dropped because of exports. State farms were also forced to cut their flocks due to reduced grazing land and financial difficulties.

Production of livestock food products for 2005 consisted of 781,380 tons of meat, 5,720,000 tons of cow's milk, 344,000 tons of sheep's milk, 37,900 tons of cheese, 405,600 tons of eggs, and 7,154 tons of butter. In 2004, exports of meat amounted to $37.2 million.

24 FISHING

Romania lost an important fishing region and nearly all its caviar-producing lakes with the cession of Bessarabia to the USSR in 1940. But the Black Sea, the Danube and its floodlands, as well as other rivers, lakes, and ponds, are favorable to the development of the fishing industry, which expanded rapidly during the early 1970s. About 90% of the fish comes from the Danube floodlands and delta and 10% from the Black Sea. In 2003, the total catch was 19,092 tons, as compared with 95,473 tons in 1991 and 16,000 in 1960.

25 FORESTRY

In 2004, forests covered 6.5 million hectares (16 million acres), representing about 27% of the total area of Romania, with 68% of forests state-owned. The forests are found mainly in the Carpathi-

an Mountains and in Transylvania, and are 70% hardwood (mostly beech and oak) and 30% softwood (mainly spruce and pine). Commercial forests account for 98% of the total forest area. About 40% of Romania's forests are damaged, and up to 25% are defoliated. Insects, air pollution, and fires are the main causes of tree damage. The amount of timber permitted to be cut is approved annually by the Romanian parliament, and was set at 18 million cu m (643 million cu ft) for 2005 (63% from state-owned forests). Roundwood production in 2004 was estimated at 17,500,000 cu m (618 million cu ft). Domestic lumber production is estimated at 5 million cu m (175 million cu ft) with more than half coming from small factories. Romania's furniture industry consists of about 2,400 furniture producers employing about 100,000 people, with exports of around €850 million in 2004. Forestry accounts for 3.5% of GDP and 9% of exports.

Between 1976 and 1985, 580,000 hectares (1,433,200 acres) were reforested. After the collapse of the Communist regime, domestic demand, exports, and reforestation plummeted. During 1990–2000, some 15,000 hectares (37,000 acres) were annually reforested. Since trade liberalization in 1997, Romania's wood industry has expanded; there are nearly 7,000 small and medium sized firms.

26 MINING

Romania's production of metals, industrial minerals, and mineral fuels was mainly of regional importance. The country is a producer of aluminum, copper, lead, zinc, manganese, steel and ferroalloys.

Production of mined iron ore (gross weight) totaled 304,000 tons in 2003. Mined copper production (gross weight) totaled 21,317 metric tons in 2003. Bismuth (metal) output in 2003 was estimated at 40 metric tons in 2003, while gold mine output (metal content) in that year came to 400 kg. Silver mine production (metal content) totaled 18 metric tons in 2003. Among industrial minerals in 2003, Romania produced barite, bentonite, diatomite, feldspar, fluorspar, graphite, gypsum (394,000 tons), kaolin, lime (2.025 million tons), lime, nitrogen (content of ammonia), pyrites, salt, sand and gravel, caustic soda, soda ash, sulfur, and talc.

Metals and metalworking in the region were well documented by Roman times, when Romania and Bulgaria, respectively known as Dacia and Thrace, were important sources of base and precious metals. Gold and nonferrous metals mined in the region remained attractive investment opportunities.

27 ENERGY AND POWER

Although Romania is the largest producer of oil in Central and Eastern Europe, it is a net importer of oil. The country also dominates the downstream petroleum industry in Southeastern Europe.

As of 1 January 2005, Romania had proven oil reserves estimated at 956 million barrels. Although Romania's oil production averaged an estimated 114,000 barrels per day in 2004, domestic demand for that year averaged an estimated 277,000 barrels per day, making the country a net importer, that year averaging 163,000 barrels per day. Romania is also the region's largest producer of refined petroleum products. Of the 11 refineries located in Southeastern Europe, 10 are located in Romania.

Romania, as of 1 January 2005, had proven reserves of natural gas estimated at 3.6 trillion cu ft. In 2002, natural gas production totaled an estimated 470 billion cu ft, while demand that year came to an estimated 646 billion cu ft, thus requiring imports totaling an estimated 176 billion cu ft.

In 2002, Romania had recoverable coal reserves estimated at 1,606 million short tons. As with oil and natural gas, Romania's demand for coal outstripped production. In 2002, demand was estimated at 36.3 million short tons, while output in that same year came to an estimated 33.6 million short tons. Imports that year were estimated at 2.7 million short tons. Romania's coal production consists of low-quality brown coal (lignite), while imports consist of anthracite for use in thermal power plants.

Romania's electric power is mostly generated by conventional thermal fuel plants, followed by hydroelectric and a single nuclear power plant. In 2002, Romania's electric generating capacity came to 21.568 million kW, with conventional thermal fuel plants accounting for 14.741 million kW, hydroelectric plants 6.122 million kW, and nuclear power for 0.705 million kW. Production in 2002 totaled 52.367 billion kWh, of which 59.9% was from fossil fuels, 30.3% from hydropower, and the rest from the country's sole nuclear plant. Consumption of electricity in 2002 was 45.847 billion kWh.

Romania's Cernavoda nuclear plant has one operating reactor. However, a second reactor is to start generating commercial power in 2006.

28 INDUSTRY

Industrial development received about half of all investment during the 1951–80 period. As officially measured, the average annual growth rate in gross industrial production between 1950 and 1980 was 12.3%, one of the highest in Eastern Europe. In 1993, however, industrial production was at only 47% of the 1989 level. The next year, industrial production increased by 3.3%. In 1995, it increased by 9.4% in absolute volume and was 13% higher than the 1992 output. In 1996, industrial production increased by 9.9% with the largest increases coming in the processing industry (12.5%) and machine and electronics (27.3%). After the Russian collapse of 1997, however, the industrial growth rate for 1998 was -17%. Industrial production picked up after Romania began to recover from its recession in 2000, and in 2001, the industrial growth rate was 6.5%.

Although industry continues to be a large sector of the economy (38% of GDP in 2003), it is partially in need of modernization and restructuring. (Agriculture contributed 13% to the GDP in 2003, while services came in first with 49.1%.) Key industries in 2004 included textiles and footwear, light machinery and automobile assembly, construction materials, metallurgy, chemicals, food processing, and petroleum refining. While in 2001 all of Romania's car manufacturers produced 68,761 automobiles, by 2004, Dacia alone produced 94,720.

Romania has been fairly successful in privatizing its industrial base—in 2005, less than 5% of the industrial assets were still in the hands of the state. While some privatizations have been plagued by corruption accusations, and while some of the newly privatized companies are not yet economically viable, the rest have benefited from switching leadership. Some of success stories include the privatization of Dacia (Romania's main car manufacturer), and of Petrom (the national oil company), which were acquired by Renault and OMV respectively; the privatization of the bank sector has also been hailed as an important step towards a functional market economy—BCR and CEC, two of Romania's largest banks, are to be fully privatized by 2006.

29 SCIENCE AND TECHNOLOGY

The Romanian Academy, founded in 1866, has sections of mathematical sciences, physical sciences, chemical sciences, biological sciences, economical sciences, technical sciences, agricultural sciences and forestry, medical sciences, and science and technology of information. The Academy of Medical Sciences and the Academy of Agricultural and Forestry Sciences were both founded in 1969. All three organizations are located in Bucharest, and in 1996, had 67 research institutes attached to them.

In 2002, total research and development (R&D) expenditures amounted to $555.266 million or 0.38% of GDP. Of that amount, 48.4% came from the government, while the business sector accounted for 41.6%. Foreign sources provided 7.1%, while higher education accounted for 3%. In that same year, there were 286 technicians and 910 scientists and engineers engaged in R&D per one million people. High technology exports in 2002 were valued at $390 million, or 3% of the country's manufactured exports. In 1996, Romania had 22 universities offering courses in basic and applied sciences. In 1987–97, science and engineering students accounted for 21% of university enrollment.

30 DOMESTIC TRADE

Wholesale and retail trade were entirely in the socialized sector before 1990. By 1993, however, 50% of retail trade had been privatized. Since 1996, the government has worked more diligently, yet slowly, to create a market economy by eliminating consumer subsidies, liberalizing the exchange rates, and initiating tighter monetary policies. Further privatization programs are also underway and the government is considering ways to promote and encourage foreign commercial investment.

Domestic trade of consumer goods has been limited to local markets. There are only a few professional distributors and independent retailers tend to be rather small. The chief seaport is at Constanţa. Cluj-Napoca, Timişoara, Iaşi, Craiova, and Braşov serve as regional industrial centers and railroad hubs. Oradea serves as a regional marketing and shipping center for livestock and agriculture. Arad is a regional commercial and industrial center in the west while Pitesti serves as a hub for the south-central region. Turgu-Mures serves as a regional industrial and agricultural center for central Romania.

Stores are open daily, except Sunday, from 10 AM to 6 PM. Food shop and retail department store hours are 7 AM to 9 PM Monday to Saturday and 7 AM to 12 noon on Sundays. There are however shops, especially small privately owned neighborhood stores, that are open nonstop. Also, the number of retailers and products has increased dramatically in the past years. Big companies like Metro, Billa, Selgros, and Carrefour opened stores in most of Romania's big cities, offering an increasing array of products.

Offices generally open at 7 or 8 AM and close at 3 or 4 PM. Exchange counters in banks transact public business from 8 AM to 12 noon, but exchange offices at border crossings remain open 24 hours a day.

Principal Trading Partners – Romania (2003)

(In millions of US dollars)

Country	Exports	Imports	Balance
World	17,618.1	24,003.2	-6,385.1
Italy-San Marino-Holy See	4,288.3	4,697.2	-408.9
Germany	2,771.0	3,560.0	-789.0
France-Monaco	1,295.2	1,748.0	-452.8
United Kingdom	1,181.6	794.1	387.5
Turkey	902.0	923.7	-21.7
Netherlands	627.7	467.3	160.4
United States	619.1	554.1	65.0
Hungary	617.2	868.0	-250.8
Austria	567.2	847.1	-279.9
Greece	425.9	324.4	101.5

(…) data not available or not significant.

SOURCE: *2003 International Trade Statistics Yearbook,* New York: United Nations, 2004.

31 FOREIGN TRADE

Before 1990, foreign trade was a state monopoly carried out through export-import agencies under the administration of the Ministry of Foreign Trade. Since World War II, the orientation and structure of Romanian foreign trade have shifted. Before the war, cereals, oil, timber, livestock, and animal derivatives accounted for over 90% of total exports, while consumer goods (60%) and raw materials (20%) accounted for the bulk of the imports. Under the Communist industrialization program, structural changes were particularly striking in exports, with machinery and nonedible consumer goods emerging as important export items. Foreign trade was in surplus throughout the 1980s, but fell into deficit in the 1990s. Romania's increasing trade deficit after 1994 was due in large part to the depreciation of its currency, large energy imports (despite large domestic reserves), and the loss of two important export markets due to international sanctions: Iraq and the former Yugoslavia (Serbia and Montenegro). The low quality of Romania's export products has also contributed to its large trade deficits. Additionally, with 80% of all imports taking the form of raw materials—principally oil, natural gas, and minerals—the country has little foreign exchange for the importation of equipment and technology of the type needed to modernize its sluggish industrial sector.

Exports in 2000 totaled $10.4 billion and imports $13.1 billion; the major export categories were apparel (22%); machinery and electric equipment (19%); metals and their manufactures (17%); mineral fuels (7.2%); chemicals and related exports (5.8%); and food products, beverages, and tobacco (2.6%). By 2004, the exports doubled to $21 billion (FOB—Free on Board), while the imports grew to $28 billion (CIF—Cost, Freight, and Insurance). For 2005, the exports were expected to grow to $25 billion, and the imports to $31 billion. Major export groups in 2004 were manufactures (especially textiles and footwear), basic metals and articles, and mineral products; the major import groups included capital goods, food, fuel and energy.

Trade with the EU countries, especially Germany, has increased substantially in recent years, largely because of Romania's expanding need for advanced Western technology and equipment. In the first quarter of 2004, Romania's main export markets were Italy (with 22.8% of total exports), Germany (15.5%), France (8.5%), Turkey (6.8%), the United Kingdom (6.8%), Hungary (3.6%), Austria (3.3%), the Netherlands (3.2%), Greece (2.6%), and the United States (2.3%). Imports came mainly from Italy (16.9% of the total imports), Germany (13.8%), the Russian Federation (8.0%), France (7.0%), Turkey (4.3%), the United Kingdom (3.6%), Austria (3.4%), Ukraine (3.4%), China (3.2%), and Hungary (3.2%)

32 BALANCE OF PAYMENTS

Trade with Western countries has involved growing amounts of credits in recent years. As a result of a series of devaluations of the Romanian leu dating from February 1990, Western imports became increasingly costly while the quality of Romania's exports significantly declined. Romania's poor performance was additionally due to its reliance on the importation of raw materials—such as oil, natural gas and minerals—which accounted for as much as 80% of imports in 1995, leaving little exchange currency for equipment and technology.

Current account deficits have been financed in large measure by loans and grants from international financial institutions, but Romania has attempted to diversify its sources of external financing. Romania's external debt stood at $11.6 billion in 2001. The country's international risk ratings have made it difficult for Romania to borrow from the private international credit market.

The US Central Intelligence Agency (CIA) reported that in 2001 the purchasing power parity of Romania's exports was $11.5 billion while imports totaled $14.4 billion resulting in a trade deficit of $2.9 billion.

The International Monetary Fund (IMF) reported that in 2001 Romania had exports of goods totaling $11.4 billion and imports totaling $14.4 billion. The services credit totaled $1.99 billion and debit $2.20 billion. The exports of goods and services rose to $24.6 billion in 2004, while the imports grew to $29.2 billion; the trade deficit totaled $4.6 billion.

Balance of Payments – Romania (2003)

(In millions of US dollars)

Current Account		**-3,311.0**
Balance on goods	-4,537.0	
Imports	-22,155.0	
Exports	17,618.0	
Balance on services	70.0	
Balance on income	-705.0	
Current transfers	1,861.0	
Capital Account		**213.0**
Financial Account		**4,400.0**
Direct investment abroad	-39.0	
Direct investment in Romania	1,844.0	
Portfolio investment assets	9.0	
Portfolio investment liabilities	569.0	
Financial derivatives	…	
Other investment assets	72.0	
Other investment liabilities	1,945.0	
Net Errors and Omissions		**-289.0**
Reserves and Related Items		**-1,013.0**

(…) data not available or not significant.

SOURCE: *Balance of Payment Statistics Yearbook 2004,* Washington, DC: International Monetary Fund, 2004.

³³BANKING AND SECURITIES

Romanian banks were nationalized in 1948. Established in 1880, the bank of issue is the National Bank of the Socialist Republic of Romania, which also extends short-term loans to state enterprises and supervises their financial activities. The Romanian Bank for Development (1990) finances investments of state enterprises and institutions and grants long-term credit. As investments increased in volume, this bank was required to intensify its control over the use of funds allocated for investment. The Romanian Bank for Foreign Trade conducts operations with foreign countries. Savings are deposited with the Loans and Savings Bank. In 1974, New York's Manufacturers Hanover Trust opened an office in Bucharest, the first such instance for a Western commercial bank in a communist nation.

Romania has generally been very cautious in its approach to banking reform. Since 1990, the financial sector has undergone a fundamental overhaul, although the pace of change has been slower than elsewhere in the region. The number of banks rose from five in December 1990 to 41 by the end of 2000—including four branches of foreign banks, four branches of joint ventures based abroad, and 33 domestic banks. The foreign specialized banks—for development, agriculture, and foreign trade—still handle almost all of the business in these areas. The Romanian Commercial Bank is still the banker to most Romanian firms, while the Savings Bank retains a virtual monopoly on personal savings deposits. At decade's end, Romania's financial institutions, like the rest of its economy, remained in severe and protracted crisis. Despite repeated calls from the IMF to privatize, the seven state-owned banks still controlled 70% of all assets in Romania's banks. Moreover, these banks continued to be plagued by bad debt.

The International Monetary Fund reports that in 2001, currency and demand deposits—an aggregate commonly known as M1—were equal to $2.1 billion. In that same year, M2—an aggregate equal to M1 plus savings deposits, small time deposits, and money market mutual funds—was $9.3 billion. The discount rate, the interest rate at which the central bank lends to financial institutions in the short term, was 35%.

Romania set up its first postwar stock exchange in 1995, after the enabling legislation has been delayed for several years. The RASDAQ (Romanian Association of Securities Dealers Automatic Quotation), an over-the-counter securities market, opened in 1996. As of 2001, the total market capitalization of the RADAQ was $2.1 billion, up 98% from the previous year. As of 2004, a total of 4,030 companies were listed on the combined Bucharest Stock Exchange and RASDAQ exchanges, which had a combined market capitalization of $11.786 billion. In 2004, the BET Index rose 101% from the previous year to 4,364.7.

³⁴INSURANCE

During the Communist era, all commercial insurance was nationalized. Since 1991, casualty, automobile, and life insurance have been made available through private insurers with foreign partners. Private insurers are only legally permitted as joint-stock or limited liability companies. Policies available include life, automobile, maritime and transport, aircraft, fire, civil liability, credit and guarantee, and agricultural insurance, with third-party auto insurance compulsory. Foreign insurance companies and agencies

are now allowed to set up representative offices within Romania, though they must have a joint venture with a local company; a foreign company can own any percentage but 100%. In 2003, the value of all direct insurance premiums written totaled $795 million, of which nonlife premiums accounted for $608 million. Romania's top nonlife insurer that year had direct written nonlife premiums of $139.5 million, while the nation's leading life insurer had gross written life insurance premiums of $79.2 million.

³⁵PUBLIC FINANCE

The annual budget is presented to the Grand National Assembly around December and becomes effective for the fiscal year on 1 January. The state budget, prepared by the Ministry of Finance, is a central part of the financial plan for the whole economy. The reduction of the growth rate of expenditures during the early 1980s was in keeping with an economic stabilization program designed to hold down domestic investment and consumption. As a result of fiscal reforms begun since the fall of the Ceausescu regime in December 1989, adherence to IMF fiscal targets, and an unanticipated inflation-fed revenue windfall during the first half, the central government unofficially recorded a relatively modest deficit for 1991. Privatization of industry was accomplished in 1992 with the transfer of 30% of the shares of about 6,000 state-owned businesses to five private ownership funds, in which each adult citizen received certificates of ownership. As of the first decade of the 21st century, the government's priorities included reigning in of its fiscal policy, continuing to develop its relationship with the IMF, and continuing the process of privatization.

The US Central Intelligence Agency (CIA) estimated that in 2005 Romania's central government took in revenues of approximately $29.9 billion and had expenditures of $31.3 billion. Revenues minus expenditures totaled approximately -$1.4 billion. Public debt in 2005 amounted to 21.1% of GDP. Total external debt was $29.47 billion.

Public Finance – Romania (2001)

(In billions of lei, central government figures)

Revenue and Grants	312,534	100.0%
Tax revenue	137,200	43.9%
Social contributions	128,918	41.2%
Grants	1,345	0.4%
Other revenue	45,071	14.4%
Expenditures	354,837	100.0%
General public services	64,525	18.2%
Defense	18,056	5.1%
Public order and safety	25,239	7.1%
Economic affairs	49,286	13.9%
Environmental protection	...	...
Housing and community amenities	6,626	1.9%
Health	54,839	15.5%
Recreational, culture, and religion	4,007	1.1%
Education	20,862	5.9%
Social protection	111,396	31.4%

(...) data not available or not significant.

SOURCE: *Government Finance Statistics Yearbook 2004*, Washington, DC: International Monetary Fund, 2004.

The International Monetary Fund (IMF) reported that in 2001, the most recent year for which it had data, central government revenues were L312,534 billion and expenditures were L354,837 billion. The value of revenues was us$9 million and expenditures us$11 million, based on a market exchange rate for 2001 of us$1 = L33,200.1 as reported by the IMF. Government outlays by function were as follows: general public services, 18.2%; defense, 5.1%; public order and safety, 7.1%; economic affairs, 13.9%; housing and community amenities, 1.9%; health, 15.5%; recreation, culture, and religion, 1.1%; education, 5.9%; and social protection, 31.4%.

36 TAXATION

Romania's taxation system in the 1990s was notable for its erratic and confusing nature, but with reforms in late 1999 there has been movement towards uniformity and simplicity. As of 2005, the standard corporate income tax rate in Romania was 16%. Profits from nightclubs, casinos, and discotheques were taxed at the standard corporate rate, with the stipulation that total tax could not be lower than 5% of qualifying gross revenue earnings. Capital gains are taxable at the normal corporate income tax rate of 16%, although a lower rate of 10% applies to the sale of corporate shares held in Romanian companies and the sale of Romanian real estate if the seller owned the real estate or shares for more than two years, and if the buyer is not related to the seller. Dividends, paid to either residents or resident companies by Romanian firms are subject to 10% withholding. Dividends paid to nonresident companies or individuals by Romanian firms are subject to a 15% withholding tax. Interest and royalties earned through nonresident companies are subject to withholding tax rates of 5% and 15%, respectively.

As part of the tax reform; Romania's top marginal rate for personal income tax was dropped from 60% to 40%. Personal income tax in 2003 was levied according to a progressive schedule with rates ranging from 18% (for taxable income above $67/month; as of 1 January 2003 the monthly personal deduction was about $57.35 up from $51 in 2002), to 40% plus $98/month (on increments of monthly income above $370), with intermediate rates of 23% plus $12; 28% plus $35; and 34% plus $62. The tax-exempt limit for a monthly pension payment was raised from $159 in 2002 to $182 in 2003. There are also property taxes.

The main indirect tax is Romania's value-added tax (VAT), with a standard rate of 19% as of 2005. Many basic services are exempt from VAT including banking and financial services. Other taxes include excise and stamp taxes.

37 CUSTOMS AND DUTIES

Romania joined the European Free Trade Association (EFTA) in December 1992 and signed an association agreement with the European Union early in 1993, which provided for Romania to adapt to EU economic-commercial standards over a 10-year period. Under an interim collaborative agreement effective 1 May 1993, a revised Romanian import tariff schedule was introduced with preferential tariffs for imports from European Union and EFTA member nations. Generally, customs duties range from 0–30%, with a weighted average of 11.7%. For imports of ores and fuels, the duties are zero or 3–10%. Duties are higher for cigarettes (8 ECUs plus 20%), spirits (100–150%), wines (20%), beer (55–70%),

and coffee (80%). Tariff rates are on an ad valorem basis. There is also a value-added tax (VAT) of 19% levied on almost all goods.

38 FOREIGN INVESTMENT

Foreign investment was negligible before the overthrow of the Communist regime. A new 1991 foreign investment law was enacted in 1991. Incentives to foreign investors include tax holidays and reduction, full foreign ownership of an enterprise, and full conversion and repatriation of after-tax profits. However, the latter is a drawn-out process because of the central bank's shortage of hard currency.

In 1997, the inflow of foreign direct investment (FDI) reached $1.2 billion, and then rose to a record of over $2 billion in 1998. Affected by the Russian financial crisis of August 1998, FDI inflow fell to a little over $1 billion in 1999. Annual FDI inflow averaged about $1.1 billion from 2000 to 2002. The FDI inflow continued to grow, reaching $1.6 billion in 2003, and a whopping $5.1 billion in 2004.

France, Austria, the Netherlands, Germany, the United States, and Italy have been the largest sources of FDI. The largest foreign operations are in the automobile, steel, oil and banking industries.

39 ECONOMIC DEVELOPMENT

The economy of Romania before 1990 was centrally planned and, for the most part, under complete state control. The nationalized industries and other economic enterprises operated within the state economic plan and were governed by the directives issued by the pertinent ministries. Economic planning, conducted by the State Planning Commission, emulated the Soviet example.

Nationalization of industry, mining, transportation, banking, and insurance on 11 June 1948 was followed by one-year economic plans in 1949 and 1950. These were succeeded by the first five-year plan (1951–55), which laid the groundwork for rapid industrialization, with emphasis on heavy industry, primarily machine-building. The state's second five-year plan (1956–60) provided for an increase of industrialization by 60–65%. Greater attention was given to consumer goods and to agriculture. A subsequent six-year plan (1960–65) envisaged an overall industrial increase of 110%, especially in producer goods. The five-year plan for 1966–70 realized an overall industrial increase of 73%. The five-year plans for 1971–75, 1976–80, and 1981–85 called for further industrial expansion and, according to official figures, during 1966–85 industrial production grew by 9.5% annually. The eighth five-year plan, for 1986–90, projected a 13.3–14.2% annual increase in Romania's net industrial production.

In the farming sector, the government has assiduously pursued a policy of collectivization. By virtue of the 22 March 1945 land reform, most farms over 50 hectares (123 acres)—a total of about 1.5 million hectares (3.7 million acres)—were confiscated without compensation. In 1949, the remaining large private farms were seized, and their 500,000 hectares (1,236,000 acres) organized into state farms. Various pressures, including coercion, were used to force peasants into joining. In April 1962, collectivization was announced as virtually completed, although there were farms, especially in remote areas, that were left in the hands of their rightful owners. Agricultural development in following years was comparatively neglected.

As of 1 January 1979, Romania began implementing the "new economic-financial mechanism," an attempt to introduce into the Romanian economy the principle of workers' self-management as previously developed elsewhere in Eastern Europe, notably in the former Yugoslavia and Hungary. Accordingly, autonomous production units were expected to plan for their own revenues and expenditures and manpower needs. These separate plans were, however, to be harmonized with the national economic plan, so that Romania's centralized system of goal and price setting was not significantly altered.

One of the major economic targets in the 1980s was the reduction of foreign debt, which was achieved but at the cost of drastic austerity measures and reduced industrial growth. After the fall of Communism, a major objective was the privatization of 6,200 state enterprises. The economy was to be completely restructured, with the emphasis on private ownership and adherence to the market for the allocation of resources. By late 1996, nearly all the country's agricultural land had been returned to private ownership, but only 65% of all eligible recipients had been officially given title. By 2002, Romania had privatized many major state-owned enterprises, with the help of the World Bank, International Monetary Fund (IMF), and the European Union. The private sector in 2002 accounted for an estimated 65% of gross domestic product (GDP).

Economic growth declined in the late 1990s, but picked up in the early 2000s. Inflation, once a problem (it stood at 18% at the end of 2002), has been reduced to single figures in 2004, and is predicted to drop to 5% by 2006. In 2004, the foreign direct investment in Romania reached $5.1 billion (second only to the Czech Republic in Europe), while the GDP registered a whopping 8.3% increase (second only to Latvia in Europe). The economy is expected to grow at a rate of around 7% in the coming years.

Romania is seeking admission to the European Union, with accession envisaged for 2007. The accession could however be postponed until 2008 if Romania fails to implement the necessary reforms (one of the biggest problems that still needs to be addressed is corruption). The center-right government that was elected in 2004 is confident however that 2007 is a realistic target, and is working hard towards achieving that goal. In December 2004 Romania closed the pre-accession negotiation with the European Union, in October 2004 it received the "functionally market economy" status, and it is looking to continue its sustained economic growth in the years preceding the accession.

However, one of the biggest concerns that Romanian policy makers are having is the capacity of the country to respond to EU market pressures once it will be part of that organization. While some sectors have registered significant progress, others are still lagging and will probably suffer once the accession is completed. For example, Romania's main car manufacturer, Dacia—now owned by Renault, has been very successful in acquiring an important share of the internal and external market with its new model—Logan; the information technology (IT) industry is one of the most vibrant in Europe (a study recently done by Brainbench found that Romania is in fourth place globally, in terms of its IT workforce numbers). The agriculture sector, on the other hand, suffers from fragmentation, lack of economic cohesion (economies of scale are hard to achieve on small parcels of land that are owned by people with different interests), and a lack of future perspective.

In 2005, the new center-right government has introduced a 16% flat tax on both wages and firm turnover—one of Europe's most liberal taxation systems. This fiscal reform is expected to strengthen the economic boom, increase foreign investment, bring to light the gray economy, and lower corruption.

40 SOCIAL DEVELOPMENT

A social insurance system has been in place since 1912. Social security covers most wage earners, and a voluntary system is in place for persons wishing additional coverage. Old-age pensions are granted at age 65 for men and at 60 for women. Those engaged in hazardous or arduous work are eligible for retirement earlier. The program is funded by contributions from employers and employees, with deficits covered by the government. Workers who do not meet the conditions of duration of employment at retirement age are provided with social assistance. Survivors' benefits are payable to the spouse, father and mother, and brothers and sisters who are dependents of the deceased, and to children up to age 16. Workers' compensation and unemployment insurance are also provided, as well as maternity benefits and family allowances.

All residents are entitled to medical care. Families with children under age 16 receive family allowances and a birth grant for each child. In addition to state social insurance, other schemes cover members of artisans' cooperatives, the clergy, and the professions.

The constitution guarantees equal pay for equal work, but women are still concentrated in low-paying professions. Few women are in senior management positions in the private sector. Women also face considerable employment discrimination in Romania's harsh economic climate and suffer from a higher rate of unemployment than do men. Violence against women, including rape, is a serious problem. It is difficult to bring rape cases to trial because the victim's testimony is not considered sufficient evidence; medical evidence and witnesses are required. Domestic abuse is widespread.

Ethnic Hungarians are the largest minority and are subject to discrimination. The Roma population continues to be harassed, and there are reports of anti-Semitic activity. Human rights are generally respected although there were continued reports of the mistreatment of detainees. The government has improved prison conditions and instituted vocational training, but prisons are still overcrowded.

41 HEALTH

As part of a broader social and economic transition, Romania's health care system underwent major reforms in the 1990s as it was transformed from a centralized, tax-based system to a pluralistic one based on contractual relationships between health care providers and insurance funds. Until the end of the decade, primary care was provided mainly through some 6,000 public-sector dispensaries throughout the country, with each patient assigned to a facility. Patients have subsequently been allowed to choose their own dispensary and general practitioner. As of 2004, there were an estimated 189 physicians, 402 nurses, and 23 dentists per 100,000 people. Total health care expenditure was estimated at 4.6% of GDP.

Increased mother and child care lowered the infant mortality rate from 143 per 1,000 live births in 1948 to 15.39 in 2005.

The general health of the population has likewise improved, with several previously serious diseases eliminated or greatly reduced (e.g., diphtheria, tuberculosis), although proper sanitation was available to only 53% of the population and safe drinking water to 58%. Leading causes of death were cardiovascular disease, cancer, and respiratory diseases. Overall mortality was 12.3 per 1,000 people as of 2002. Average life expectancy in 2005 was 71.35 years. Romania's birth rate in 2002 was an estimated 10.8 per 1,000 people. About 48% of married women (ages 15 to 49) used contraception. The total fertility rate was 1.3 children per woman during her childbearing years. Immunization rates for children up to one year old were: tuberculosis, 100%; diphtheria, pertussis, and tetanus, 97%; polio, 97%; and measles, 97%.

The HIV/AIDS prevalence was 0.10 per 100 adults in 2003. As of 2004, there were approximately 6,500 people living with HIV/AIDS in the country. There were an estimated 350 deaths from AIDS in 2003.

42 HOUSING

Inadequate housing has been a serious problem since World War II. Romanian housing suffered from the 1940 earthquake, war damage, neglect, and inadequate repair and maintenance after the war. An increase in the urban population caused by industrialization and emphasis on capital construction exacerbated the problem. Since 1965, the government has encouraged private construction by state support in the form of credits and expertise. However, an uncertain economy means that maintenance for existing properties has been somewhat poor.

In 1999, the total housing stock was at about 7.88 million units. At the 2002 census, there were 8,107,114 dwellings serving 21.6 million people. About 56.8% of all dwellings were single-family detached houses of two or three rooms. About 97% of all units are under private ownership. About 47% of all residential buildings were built in the period 1945–70.

43 EDUCATION

Education is compulsory for students between the ages of 6 and 16. The general course of study includes four years of primary school followed by four years of lower secondary school. Students may attend art or trade schools after their primary education is complete. At the upper secondary level, students may choose between schools offering general studies, vocational programs, or technical studies. Upper secondary programs generally last from three to four years. The academic year runs from October to June.

In 2001, about 75% of children between the ages of three and six were enrolled in some type of preschool program. Primary school enrollment in 2003 was estimated at about 89% of age-eligible students. The same year, secondary school enrollment was about 81% of age-eligible students. It is estimated that about 89.4% of all students complete their primary education. The student-to-teacher ratio for primary school was at about 18:1 in 2003; the ratio for secondary school was about 14:1.

Admission to an advanced institution depends on a variety of factors, including the student's social background. Over half the students receive government assistance. Yearly quotas are established by the Ministry of Education according to manpower needs. Students in some fields must first complete six months of practical work in industry or agriculture.

In 1959, the Romanian Victor Babes University (founded 1919) and the János Bolyai University (1945) for Hungarian minority students, both in Cluj-Napoca, were merged into the Babes-Bolyai University in order to strengthen "socialist patriotism." There are six other universities—in Bucharest (founded in 1864), Braşov (1971), Craiova (1966), Galati (1948), Iaşi (1860), and Timişoara (1962).

Like the other formerly Communist countries, Romania has emphasized polytechnic education in recent years. This "link of education with life" in the early grades means studying practical subjects; however, beginning in the upper grades there are work programs, often directly in enterprises, in workshops, or on collective farms, depending on the locality.

In 2003, about 35% of the tertiary age population were enrolled in some type of higher education program. The adult literacy rate for 2004 was estimated at about 97.3%. As of 2003, public expenditure on education was estimated at 3.5% of GDP.

44 LIBRARIES AND MUSEUMS

The National Library in Bucharest holds over 8.7 million items. The Romanian Academy Library in Bucharest is also a national library. It holds about 10 million items, mainly on the history and culture of the Romanian people. The next largest public libraries are the university libraries at Bucharest (1.4 million volumes), Iaşi (3 million), and Cluj-Napoca (3.6 million).

Romania has some 400 museums. Bucharest is home to many of the most important museums, including the National History Museum of Romania, the National Museum of Art, and the newer Historical Museum of Bucharest (founded in 1984) and Cotroceni National Museum (1991), featuring Romanian fine art, architecture, and decorative art. Also in the capital are the Cecilia and Frederick Storck Museum, highlighting the works of Karl Storck, a great Romanian sculptor, and his family, also prominent artists; the Curteo Veche Museum, featuring archaeological exhibits and housed in a 15th-century palace; and the Museum of Romanian Literature.

45 MEDIA

In 2003, there were an estimated 199 mainline telephones for every 1,000 people; about 465,000 people were on a waiting list for telephone service installation. The same year, there were approximately 324 mobile phones in use for every 1,000 people.

In 2004, Romanian Public Television controlled four national stations. Radio Romania operates one domestic and one external service. There are several privately owned commercial stations in both television and radio. As of 1998, there were 40 AM and 202 FM radio broadcasting stations. A 1995 report indicated there were 48 television stations. In 2003, there were an estimated 358 radios and 697 television sets for every 1,000 people. About 172.5 of every 1,000 people are cable subscribers. Also in 2003, there were 96.6 personal computers for every 1,000 people and 184 of every 1,000 people had access to the Internet. There were 65 secure Internet servers in the country in 2004.

The leading daily newspapers (with 2002 circulation figures) are *Evenimentul Zilei* (*Events of the Day*, 200,000); *Adevarul de Cluj* (*Truth of Cluj*, 200,000); *Romania Libera* (*Free Romania*, 100,000); *Adevarul* (*Truth*, 85,000); and *Libertatea* (*Liberty*, 75,000).

Though the constitution provides for freedom of expression and prohibits censorship, it is illegal to "defame" the country. Journalists are prosecuted under this law and sentenced to prison terms.

46 ORGANIZATIONS

Economic organizations concerned with Romania's internal and external economic activities include the Romanian Chamber of Commerce and Industry. In 1992 the Council for National Minority Affairs was formed for the discussion of minority issues. The organization helps the government formulate policies favorable to the minorities of the country. The body is headed by the Secretary General of the government. Representatives from 16 officially recognized minority groups and 12 government ministries make up the organization.

There are also many cooperatives in key sectors of the economy. Many Romanian farmers belong to the private Farmers' Federation. There are about 4,000 farming cooperatives and 41 district unions. A large cooperative located in the manufacturing and consumers sectors of the economy is the Central Union of Commerce and Credit Cooperative. There are over 2,500 production and 850 credit cooperatives. Another important cooperative is the Central Union of Handicraft Cooperatives. The National Union of the Consumers' Cooperatives is based in Bucharest. There is also an active Association for the Protection of Consumers.

The Romanian Academy was founded in 1866 to promote public interest, education, and research in scientific fields. Several professional associations also promote research and public education in specific fields, such as the Romanian Medical Association.

Serving a very specific cultural niche, the Transylvania Society of Dracula, based in Bucharest, promotes the study of the Bram Stoker novel, *Dracula*, and the life of Prince Vlad Dracula, on whom the book is loosely based.

National youth organizations include the Free Youth Association of Bucharest, the League of Students, National Union of Independent Students of Romania, Junior Chamber, Romanian Council of Churches-Youth Unit, the National Scout Organization of Romania, and YMCA/YWCA. There are several sports associations representing a variety of pastimes, such as tennis, skating, track and field, baseball and softball, and badminton.

Civitas Foundation for the Civil Society, established in 1992, sponsors community development and social programs promoting an open, democratic society. Other social action groups include the League for the Defense of Human Rights in Romania and the Women's Association of Romania. There are national chapters of the Red Cross Society, UNICEF, and Habitat for Humanity.

47 TOURISM, TRAVEL, AND RECREATION

The Carpathian Mountains, the Black Sea coast, and the Danube region were developed to attract large numbers of tourists. Major attractions include many old cities and towns (Braşov, Constanţa, Sibiu, Sighisoara, Suceava, Timişoara, and others) and more than 120 health resorts and spas. The monasteries in Bukovina are famous for their exterior frescoes. Castle Dracula, the castle of Prince Vlad of Walachia, has been a tourist attraction since the 1970s.

Popular sports are football (soccer), skiing, hiking, swimming, canoeing, wrestling, handball, and gymnastics. Between 1965 and 1984, Romanian athletes won 176 Olympic medals (48 gold, 52 silver, and 76 bronze). Romania was the only Socialist country to send athletes to the 1984 games in Los Angeles; all the others, following the USSR's lead, boycotted these games.

A valid passport is required to enter Romania of all foreign nationals except those of the countries of the European Union who only need an identity card. Citizens of the United States, Canada and most European countries do not need a visa for stays of up to 90 days.

In 2003, tourist arrivals numbered 5,594,828, of whom 96% came from Europe. Tourism expenditure receipts totaled $523 million. There were 97,320 hotel rooms with 201,636 beds and an occupancy rate of 34%. The average length of stay was 3.5 nights.

In 2004, the US Department of State estimated the daily cost of staying in Bucharest at $228. Other areas were significantly lower at $152 per day.

48 FAMOUS ROMANIANS

Perhaps the most famous historical figure in what is now Romania was Vlad (1431?–76), a prince of Walachia who resisted the Turkish invasion and was called Tepes ("the impaler") and Dracula ("son of the devil") because of his practice of impaling his enemies on stakes; he was made into a vampire by Bram Stoker in his novel *Dracula*. The first leader of Communist Romania was Gheorghe Gheorghiu-Dej (1901–65), who held the office of premier from 1952 to 1955 and of president of the State Council from 1961 until his death. Nicolae Ceausescu (1918–89) was general secretary of the Communist Party between 1965 and 1989 and head of state from 1967 to 1989; his wife, Elena (1919–89), was a member of the Permanent Bureau of the Executive Committee of the Communist Party.

Ion Heliade-Radulescu (1802–72) founded the Bucharest Conservatory and the National Theater and became first president of the Romanian Academy. Mihail Kogalniceanu (1817–91), a leading statesman in the early Romanian monarchy, inaugurated modern Romanian historiography. Vasile Alecsandri (1821–90) was a leader of the traditionalist school of writers, which sought its inspiration in the Romanian past rather than in imitations of foreign writers. Mihail Eminescu (1850–89) is regarded as an outstanding poet, famous for romantic lyricism. His friend Ion Creanga (1837–87) drew from folklore and wrote with a gaiety and gusto recalling Rabelais. The nation's greatest playwright was Ion Luca Caragiale (1852–1912), who excelled in social comedy; an internationally famous Romanian-born playwright, Eugène Ionesco (1912–94), settled in Paris in 1938. Mihail Sadoveanu (1880–1961) was an important novelist in the period between the two world wars. Romanian-born Elie Wiesel (b.1928), in the United States from 1956, is a writer on Jewish subjects, especially the Holocaust, and a winner of the Nobel Peace Prize in 1986. Romanian-born Mircea Eliade (1907–86) was a scholar in comparative religion and comparative mythology, in the United States from 1948. Romanian-born Tristan Tzara (1896–1963), a literary and artistic critic who settled in Paris, was one of the founders of Dadaism. Nicolae Grigorescu (1838–1907) and Ion Andreescu (1850–82) were leading painters, as was Theodor Aman (1831–91), a modern artist and founder of the School of Fine Arts in Bucharest. Saul Steinberg (1914–1999) was a cartoonist and illustrator, best known for his work for *The New Yorker* magazine; he emigrated to the United States in 1942. Sculpture was greatly advanced by Constantin Brâncusi (1876–

1957). Perhaps the greatest names Romania has given to the musical world are those of the violinist and composer Georges Enescu (1881–1955), known for his *Romanian Rhapsodies,* and the pianist Dinu Lipatti (1917–50). A prominent tennis player is Ilie Nastase (1946–94); gymnast Nadia Comaneci (b.1961) won three gold medals at the 1976 Olympics and two gold medals at the 1980 games.

⁴⁹DEPENDENCIES

Romania has no territories or colonies.

⁵⁰BIBLIOGRAPHY

Achim, Viorel. *The Roma in Romanian History.* New York: Central European University Press, 2004.

Carey, Henry F. (ed.). *Romania since 1989: Politics, Economics, and Society.* Lanham, Md.: Lexington Books, 2004.

Frucht, Richard (ed.). *Eastern Europe: An Introduction to the People, Lands, and Culture.* Santa Barbara, Calif.: ABC-CLIO, 2005.

Gallagher, Tom. *Modern Romania: The End of Communism, the Failure of Democratic Reform, and the Theft of a Nation.* New York: New York University Press, 2005.

Gross, Peter. *Mass Media in Revolution and National Development: The Romanian Laboratory.* Ames, Iowa: Iowa State University Press, 1996.

International Smoking Statistics: A Collection of Historical Data from 30 Economically Developed Countries. New York: Oxford University Press, 2002.

Kellogg, Frederick. *The Road to Romanian Independence.* West Lafayette, Ind.: Purdue University Press, 1995.

McElrath, Karen (ed.). *HIV and AIDS: A Global View.* Westport, Conn.: Greenwood Press, 2002.

Sanborne, Mark. *Romania.* 2nd ed. New York: Facts On File, 2004.

Treptow, Kurt W. *Historical Dictionary of Romania.* Lanham, Md.: Scarecrow, 1996.

RUSSIA

Russian Federation

Rossiyskaya Federatsiya

CAPITAL: Moscow

FLAG: Equal horizontal bands of white (top), blue, and red.

ANTHEM: *Patriotic Song.*

MONETARY UNIT: The ruble (R) is a paper currency of 100 kopecks. There are coins of 1, 2, 3, 5, 10, 15, 20, and 50 kopecks and 1 ruble, and notes of 100, 200, 500, 1,000, 5,000, 10,000 and 50,000 rubles. R1 = $0.03550 (or $1 = R28.17) as of 2005.

WEIGHTS AND MEASURES: The metric system is the legal standard.

HOLIDAYS: New Year's Day, 1–2 January; Christmas, 7 January; Women's Day, 8 March; Spring and Labor Day, 1–2 May; Victory Day, 9 May; State Sovereignty Day, 12 June; Socialist Revolution Day, 7 November.

TIME: 3 PM Moscow = noon GMT.

¹LOCATION, SIZE, AND EXTENT

Russia is located in northeastern Europe and northern Asia. It is the largest country in the world—slightly less than 1.8 times the size of the United States—with a total area of 17,075,200 sq km (6,592,771 sq mi). Russia shares boundaries with the Arctic Ocean on the N; northern Pacific Ocean on the E; China, Mongolia, Kazakhstan, the Caspian Sea, Azerbaijan, Georgia on the S; and the Black Sea, Ukraine, Belarus, Latvia, Estonia, Finland on the W with a total land boundary of 19,990 km (12,421 mi) and a coastline of 37,653 km (23,396 mi). Russia's capital city, Moscow, is located in the western part of the country.

²TOPOGRAPHY

From west to east, the country can be roughly divided into five large geographic regions: the Great European Plain, the Ural Mountains, the West Siberian Plain, the Central Siberian Plateau, and the mountains of the northeast and southeast. The Great European and West Siberian Plains contain a variety of terrain, including grasslands and farmlands as well as forests, swamps, and large regions of tundra. The Caucasus Mountains, located between the Black Sea and the Caspian Sea at the southwest of the Great European Plain, are divided into two chains separated by lowlands. The Caucasus Mountains form the border with Russia, Azerbaijan, and Georgia and mark the boundary between Asia to the south and Europe to the north. The highest peak in the Caucasus Mountains is the extinct volcano Mt. Elbrus (5,642 m/18,510 ft); this is also the highest peak in Russia and Europe. The lowest point in Russia is at the Caspian Sea, 28 m (92 ft) below sea level. The Caspian Sea is the world's largest lake.

The plains are divided by the Ural Mountains, which define the boundary between Asia on the east and Europe on the west. They extend about 2,100 km (1,300 mi) from the Arctic Ocean to the northern border of Kazakhstan; the highest point in the Urals is Mt. Narodnaya at 1,894 m (6,212 ft). The Central Siberian Plateau ranges in height from 500–700 m (1,600–2,300 ft). A number of rivers and deep canyons stretch across this area. The highest mountains of the eastern region are the Altay Shan, which reach a peak of 4,619 m (15,157 ft) at Mt. Pelukha. The other eastern mountain regions average less than 3,048 m (10,000 ft) in height.

The longest river in Russia is the Ob, which stretches through the West Siberian Plain to the Arctic Ocean for a length of 5,410 km (3,362 mi). The most important river commercially is the Volga, which stretches for 3,689 km (2,293 mi) through the Great European Plain to the Caspian Sea. The Volga is the longest river in Europe. The Dnieper is another important river in this region. The Amur River flows along the southeast border of the country into the Pacific. The largest lake in Russia is Lake Baikal (Ozero Baykal—30,510 sq km/11.870 sq mi), located in the southern plateau region.

Despite its size, only a small percentage of Russia's land is arable, with much of it too far north for cultivation.

Most of western Russia is located on the Eurasian Tectonic Plate, with seismic activity occurring frequently in the Caucasus Mountains. The eastern coast lies on the North American Plate near the boundary with the Pacific Plate. This eastern coast is part of the "Ring of Fire," a seismically active band surrounding the Pacific Ocean. While many of the resulting earthquakes are moderate (below 6.0 magnitude on the Richter scale), more severe quakes are not uncommon. In 2003, a 6.8 magnitude quake occurred near Primorye in July. In September of the same year, a 7.3 magnitude quake occurred along the Xinjiang border region; in October a 6.7 magnitude quake hit in southwestern Siberia; and in December another 6.7 quake hit at Komandorskiye Ostrova. On 10 June 2004, a 6.9 magnitude quake occurred at the Kamchatka Peninsula (Poluostrov Kamchatka).

³CLIMATE

Most of the country has a continental climate, with long, cold winters and brief summers. There is a wide range of summer and winter temperatures and relatively low precipitation. January temperatures are in the range of 6°C (45°F) on the southeastern shore of the Black Sea. A record low temperature of -71°C (-96°F) was recorded in 1974 at the northeast Siberian village of Oymyakon, the lowest temperature ever recorded anywhere in the world for an inhabited region. In many areas of Siberia the soil never thaws for more than a foot.

Annual precipitation decreases from about 64–76 cm (25–30 in) in the European region to less than 5 cm (2 in) a year in parts of Central Asia. The tundra has long winters, with summers lasting one or two months, and receives 8–12 months of snow or rain. The far northern forest, like most of the country, has long severe winters, short summers, and extremely short springs and autumns. Precipitation is low but falls throughout the year, varying from 53 cm (21 in) at Moscow to 20–25 cm (8–10 in) in eastern Siberia. The steppes have very cold winters and hot, dry summers.

[4] FLORA AND FAUNA

Russia has several soil and vegetation zones, each with its characteristic flora and fauna. Northernmost is the so-called arctic desert zone, which includes most of the islands of the Arctic Ocean and the seacoast of the Taymyr Peninsula. These areas are characterized by the almost complete absence of plant cover; only mosses and lichens are to be found. Birds and mammals associated with the sea (sea calf, seal, and walrus) are typical of this zone.

The tundra, which extends along the extreme northern part of Asia, is divided into arctic, moss-lichen, and shrubby tundra subzones. Only dwarf birches, willows, lichens, and mosses grow in the thin layer of acidic soil. Indigenous fauna include the arctic fox, reindeer, white hare, lemming, and common and willow ptarmigan.

South of the tundra is the vast forest zone, or taiga, covering half of the country; the soil here is podzolic. The northern areas of this zone are characterized by the alternation of tundra landscape with sparse growth of birches, other deciduous trees, and spruce. Farther south are spruce, pine, fir, cedar, and some deciduous trees. There are subzones of mixed and broadleaf forests on the Great Russian Plain in the southern half of the forest zone. Wildlife in the taiga include moose, Russian bear, reindeer, lynx, sable, squirrel, and among the birds, capercaillie, hazel-grouse, owl, and woodpecker. In the broadleaf woods are European wild boar, deer, roe deer, red deer, mink, and marten.

Farther south is the forest-steppe zone, a narrow band with the boundaries of the Great Russian plain and the West Siberian low country. Steppes with various grasses alternate with small tracts of oak, birch, and aspen. Still farther south, the forest-steppe changes to a region of varied grasses and small plants. The black and chestnut soils of this zone produce the best agricultural land in Russia. Typical mammals are various rodents (hamsters and jerboas); birds include skylarks, cranes, eagles, and the great bustard.

In the semidesert zone, plant cover includes xerophytic grasses and shrubs. Typical animals are the wildcat and saiga antelope; lizards, snakes, and tortoises are common. The semidesert areas and the deserts of Central Asia and Kazakhstan make up a separate subregion.

As of 2002, there were at least 269 species of mammals, 528 species of birds, and over 11,400 species of plants throughout the country.

[5] ENVIRONMENT

Decades of Soviet mismanagement resulted in the catastrophic pollution of land, air, rivers, and seacoasts. Air pollution is especially a problem in the Urals and Kuznetsk (where vast populations are exposed to hazardous emissions from metal-processing plants) as well as in the Volga and Moscow regions. In 1992 Russia had the world's third-highest level of industrial carbon dioxide emissions, which totaled 2.1 billion metric tons, a per capita level of 14.11 metric tons. However, in 1996 the total dropped to 1.5 billion metric tons and in 2000 the total was about 1.4 billion metric tons.

The Volga River has been damaged through rash exploitation of hydroelectric power. Lake Baikal (Ozero Baykul) is the largest freshwater reservoir in the world, but has been heavily polluted through agricultural and industrial development.

About 7.8% of Russia's total land area was protected as of 2003, including 8 natural UNESCO World Heritage Sites and 35 Ramsar wetland sites. According to a 2006 report issued by the International Union for Conservation of Nature and Natural Resources (IUCN), threatened species included 43 types of mammals, 47 species of birds, 6 types of reptiles, 18 species of fish, 1 type of mollusk, 29 species of other invertebrates, and 7 species of plants. Threatened species included Atlantic sturgeon, beluga, crested shelduck, Amur leopard, Siberian tiger, Mediterranean monk seal, Wrangel lemming, and the Oriental stork. The great auk, Palla's cormorant, and Steller's sea cow have become extinct.

[6] POPULATION

The population of Russia in 2005 was estimated by the United Nations (UN) at 143,025,000, which placed it at number 8 in population among the 193 nations of the world. In 2005, approximately 13% of the population was over 65 years of age, with another 16% of the population under 15 years of age. There were 87 males for every 100 females in the country. According to the UN, the annual population rate of change for 2005–10 was expected to be -0.6%, a rate the government viewed as too low. Russia's fertility rate is among the lowest in the world. The projected population for the year 2025 was 130,175,000. The overall population density was 8 per sq km (22 per sq mi), but the population is distributed unequally, with rural areas being very sparsely populated.

The UN estimated that 73% of the population lived in urban areas in 2005, and that urban areas were growing at an annual rate of -0.49%. The capital city, Moscow, had a population of 10,469,000 in that year. Other large urban areas and their population estimates include St. Petersburg (formerly Leningrad), 5,315,000; Novosibirsk, 1,425,000; Nizhniy Novgorod (formerly Gorkiy), 1,288,000; Yekaterinburg (formerly Sverdlovsk), 1,420,000; Samara (formerly Kuybyshev), 1,140,000; Omsk, 1,132,000; Kazan', 1,108,000; Rostov-on-Don, 1,081,000; Chelyabinsk, 1,067,000; Ufa, 1,035,000; Volgograd, 1,016,000; Perm, 984,000; Krasnoyarsk, 912,000; Saratov, 868,000; and Voronezh, 842,000.

[7] MIGRATION

During 1979–88, Russia gained 1,747,040 people through net migration from other Soviet republics. Germany took in 156,299 former Soviet Germans in 1991. As of May, 1996, there were

RUSSIA

LOCATION: 60°0′ N; 30°0′ E. BOUNDARY LENGTHS: Total land boundary lengths, 20,139 kilometers (12,514 miles); Azerbaijan, 284 kilometers (177 miles); Belarus, 959 kilometers (596 miles); China (southeast), 3,605 kilometers (2,240 miles); China (south), 40 kilometers (25 miles); Estonia, 290 kilometers (180.2 miles); Finland, 1,313 kilometers (816 miles); Georgia, 723 kilometers (450 miles); Kazakstan, 6,846 kilometers (4,254 miles); North Korea, 19 kilometers (12 miles); Latvia, 217 kilometers (135 miles); Lithuania, 227 kilometers (141 miles); Mongolia, 3,441 kilometers (2,138 miles); Norway, 167 kilometers (104 miles); Poland 432 kilometers (268 miles); Ukraine, 1,576 kilometers (980 miles); total coastline 37,653 kilometers (23,398 miles).

still 75,000 internally displaced persons from the Chernobyl accident in 1986. Following the military conflicts in Chechnya of 1994, 220,000 people fled to the neighboring republics of Daghestan, Ingushetia, and North Ossetia. Between 1989–95, 169,000 Russians returned from Azerbaijan, and 296,000 returned from Kyrgyzstan. Between 1991–95, 50,000 Russians returned from Belarus; 614,000 returned from Kazakhstan; and 300,000 from Tajikistan. In 1991, 400,000 returned from Uzbekistan, and 100,000 returned from Turkmenistan from 1993–95. As reported in 2005 by the US Department of State, Russia is a major source of women trafficked globally for the purpose of sexual exploitation. It is also a significant destination and transit country for persons trafficked for sexual and labor exploitation from regional and neighboring countries into Russia, and on to the Gulf states, Europe, Asia, and North America. In addition, the International Labour Organization estimated that of the five million illegal immigrants in Russia, 20% are victims of forced labor. Trafficking of children and of

child sex tourism is also reported. Internal trafficking from rural to urban areas remained a problem.

As of 1999, there were 400 refugees, 10,000 asylum seekers, 173,000 internally displaced people (mainly from Chechnya and Ingushetia), and an estimated 3.5–4 million forced migrants. By the end of 2004, there were 1,852 refugees, 315 asylum seekers, 54 returned refugees, mainly from the surrounding former Soviet states. In addition, there were 334,796 internally displaced persons, which included 100,000 Afghans in a refugee-like situation, 73,004 forced migrants, 10,755 Meskhetians, and 5,177 non-CIS asylum seekers.

In 2005, the net migration rate was an estimated 1.03 migrants per 1,000 population. Remittances reported for 2003 were $300 million.

8 ETHNIC GROUPS

According to the 2002 census, about 79.8% of the population is Russian. Tatars constitute 3.8%, Ukrainians make up 2%, Bashkir account for 1.2%, and Chuvash form 1.1%. Belarussians and Moldovans each make up less than 1% of the population. The Romani population, according to the 2002 census, was reported at about 182,000 people; however, unofficial estimates place the number at about 1.2 million. Small communities of indigenous groups include the Buryats in Siberia and the Enver, Tafarli, and Chukchi in the North.

⁹LANGUAGES

About 90% of the population speaks Russian, a member of the eastern group of Slavic languages. It is highly inflected, with nouns, pronouns, and adjectives declined in six cases. There are three grammatical genders. The language, which has been written since about AD 1000, uses the Cyrillic alphabet of 33 letters. In addition, a wide variety of other Slavic, Finno–Ugric, Turkic, Mongol, Tungus, and Paleo–Asiatic languages also are spoken. In the republic of Dagestan alone, two million people share 28 languages, 14 of which are unwritten.

The breakup of the Soviet Union has produced a surge in regional autonomy and a backlash against the Russian language and the Cyrillic alphabet in many of Russia's 21 republics. Tatarstan, for example, is considering a reintroduction of the Latin script for Tatar, while Buriatia may restore Old Mongol lettering for Buriat. Stalin imposed the Cyrillic alphabet on Russia's minority groups in an effort to make Russian the national language. Russian is the official language of the country and one of the six official languages of the United Nations.

¹⁰RELIGIONS

The Russian Orthodox Church (ROC) dates back to the "Kievan Rus" period (the first organized Russian state). In 988, Prince Vladimir, in order to gain an alliance with the powerful Byzantine Empire, declared Christianity as the religion of his realm and mandated the baptism of Kiev's population and the construction of cathedrals. During the Mongol occupation (1240–1480), the head of the ROC (Metropolitan) was moved to Moscow. Throughout the reign of the tsars, Orthodoxy was synonymous with autocracy and national identity. After the Communist revolution of 1917, the Soviet government, based on Marxism, imposed a dogma of militant atheism and subordinated the ROC through fear and persecution. Other Christians, Muslims, and Jews were also oppressed (anti-Semitism was widespread before and after the 1917 revolution). Since 1985 and the subsequent dissolution of the Soviet Union, thousands of churches have been reopened; freedom of religion was incorporated into the draft constitution of 1993.

According to a 2004 report from the Ministry of Justice, there were about 21,664 registered religious groups in the country. The Russian Orthodox Church had the largest number, at about 11,525 registered groups. It is estimated that about 50% of the population describe consider themselves to be Russian Orthodox, but a much smaller percentage are actually active church members. Other Orthodox denominations include the Russian Orthodox Autonomous Church, the Russian Orthodox Church Abroad, the True Orthodox Church, the Russian Orthodox Free Church, and the Ukrainian Orthodox Church.

Islam is the largest minority religion, with about 3,537 registered groups and, perhaps over 1,000 unregistered groups. Muslims are believed to make up about 14% of the population. Protes-

tants make up the third-largest group of the country with a variety of denominations, including Pentecostals (1,467 groups), Baptists (979 groups), Lutherans, Methodists, Presbyterians, and the Church of Christ. There are also registered groups of Seventh-Day Adventists, Jehovah's Witnesses (386 groups), the Church of Jesus Christ of Latter-day Saints, Mennonites, and the Salvation Army. The Molokane (28 groups) and Dukhobor are Christian-based movements that originated in Russia. There are about 267 Jewish registered groups, with an estimated 600,000–1,000,000 Jews in the country. There are 80 groups of Hare Krishnas. Hindus, Scientologists, Taoists, Baha'is, Zoroastrians, Buddhists, Karaites, and shamanists are also represented. There are about 11 registered pagan groups.

The 1997 Law on Freedom of Conscience does not claim a state religion but recognizes Russian Orthodoxy, Judaism, Islam, and Buddhism as traditional religions. Theoretically, no special privileges are granted to these traditional religions; however, the ROC has made special agreements with the government that seem to place the church in a preferred status. Many citizens and government officials consider the acceptance or practice of Russian Orthodoxy to be a form of nationalism. Though registration is not required, many groups do so in order to enjoy certain tax and legal benefits. Some minority groups have reported incidents of discrimination and harassment on social and local political levels.

¹¹TRANSPORTATION

Russia's transportation system is extensive, but is in a state of general decay. Maintenance, modernization, and expansion are required for Russia's infrastructure, much of which operates beyond capacity.

Railroads have long been an important means of transportation in Russia. In the 1890s, a vast state-sponsored program of railway construction commenced, with the goal of nurturing private enterprise, exploiting natural resources, and expanding heavy industry (especially metallurgy and mineral fuels). The Trans-Siberian Railroad was the cornerstone of this development. From 1898–1901, more than 3,000 km (1,900 mi) of track were constructed per year. Railroad development also figured prominently during the Soviet era. Railways in 2004 extended some 87,157 km (54,160 mi), of which 86,200 km (53,616 mi) were primarily 1.52-m broad gauge track.

There were 537,289 km (334,194 mi) of highways in 2001 (the latest year for which data was available), of which 362,133 km (225,247 mi) were paved. As of 2003, there were 23,383,000 passenger cars and 5,400,000 commercial vehicles registered for use. Many imports from Europe are increasingly arriving in Russia. Russia's ratio of population per car is 6.2.

Marine access has been important to Russia ever since the construction of St. Petersburg was ordered by Peter the Great on the marshland adjoining the Gulf of Finland, in order to provide imperial Russia with a "window on the West." Other important maritime ports include Kaliningrad, on the Baltic Sea; Murmansk and Arkhangel'sk, both on the Barents Sea; Novorossiysk, on the Black Sea; Vladivostok and Nakhodka, both on the Sea of Japan; Tiksi on the Laptev Sea; and Magadan and Korsakov on the Sea of Okhotsk (the latter is on Sakhalin). As of 2004, Russia had 96,000 km (59,712 mi) of navigable inland waterways. Of that total, 72,000 km (44,784 mi) were in European Russia and linked the Black

Sea, the White Sea, the Baltic Sea, the Caspian Sea and the Sea of Azov. Major inland ports include Nizhniy Novgorod, Kazan', Khabarovsk, Krasnoyarsk, Samara, Moscow, Rostov, and Volgograd. The merchant fleet consisted in 2005 of 1,194 ships of 1,000 GRT or over, totaling 4,521,472 GRT. Early in the 21st century, a new port is scheduled to be built in the Batareynaya Harbor of the Baltic Sea about 70 km (43 mi) southwest of St. Petersburg. The new facility will handle oil shipments.

In 2004, Russia had an estimated 2,586 airports and airfields. As of 2005, a total of 640 had paved runways, and there were also 42 heliports. Principal airports include Novy at Khabarovsk, Sheremetyevo and Vnukovo at Moskva, Tolmachevo at Novosibirsk, Rostov-Na-Donu, Pulkovo at St. Petersburg, Adler at Sochi, and Yekaterinburg at Coltsovo. In 2003, about 22.723 million passengers were carried on scheduled domestic and international flights.

12 HISTORY

The history of Russia is usually dated from the 9th century AD when a loose federation of the eastern Slavic tribes was achieved under the legendary Rurik. At this time, Kiev was the political and cultural center. Vulnerable due to the flat land that surrounded them, the Kievan rulers sought security through expansion—a policy that subsequent Russian leaders frequently pursued.

By the 11th century, Kievan Rus had united all the eastern Slavs. However, over the next two centuries, Kievan dominance was eroded by other Slavic and non-Slavic centers of power. The Mongol conquest of Russia marked the eclipse of Kiev as a center of power. When Mongol power declined and collapsed in the 14th and 15th centuries, it was Moscow that emerged as the new Russian power center. The military victories of Grand Duke Ivan III (r. 1462–1505) in particular established Moscow's predominance over almost all other Russian principalities. In 1547, Grand Duke Ivan IV was crowned as the first "Tsar of All the Russians."

When the Rurik dynasty died out in 1598, Russia experienced internal political turmoil and territorial encroachment from the West. In 1618, the first of the Romanovs was crowned tsar, and Russia set about regaining the territory it had lost. In the 17th century, Russian power expanded across Siberia to the Pacific Ocean. During the reign of Peter I (r. 1682–1725), Russian power was extended to the Baltic Sea in the early 18th century. It was under Peter that the Russian capital was moved from Moscow to St. Petersburg, on the Baltic Sea.

Russian power expanded further into Europe and Asia during the 18th century. The French Emperor, Napoleon, attacked Russia in 1812. Despite the considerable advances that he made, he was forced to withdraw from Russia and back across Europe in 1814. By the end of the Napoleonic wars in 1815, Russia had acquired Bessarabia (Moldova), Finland, and eastern Poland.

Russia's European borders remained relatively stable in the 19th century. It was during this period, though, that Russia completed its conquest of the Caucasus, Central Asia, and what became its Maritime Province (Vladivostok).

From the rise of Moscow after the Mongols until the early 20th century, Russia was ruled as an autocracy. Peter I founded a senate, but this was an advisory and honorific body, not a legislative one.

Some reform was made. Alexander II (r. 1855–81) emancipated the serfs of Russia in 1861. Alexander II appeared to be embarking on a course of political reform involving elections when he was assassinated by revolutionaries in 1881. Alexander III (r. 1881–94), his son, ended political reform efforts and reverted to autocratic rule. Under him, however, economic development made considerable progress in Russia.

The autocratic nature of Tsarist rule generated growing opposition in Russia, beginning with the abortive "Decembrist" uprising of 1825. By the reign of the last tsar, Nicholas II (r. 1894–1917), many opposition groups had arisen. With the Tsarist regime's weakness evident as a result of its defeats in the 1905 Russo-Japanese War, a revolutionary movement grew up in Russia that same year. Under the leadership of the socialists, revolutionary "soviets" or councils seized power in parts of St. Petersburg and Moscow. The government was able to defuse the revolutionary impetus through promising an elected Duma (legislature). The First Duma (1906) met only briefly; its demands for land reform were unacceptable to the tsar, who dissolved it. The Second Duma (1907) was also dissolved shortly after it was convened. A Third Duma (1907–11) and Fourth Duma (1912–17) were elected on more restrictive franchises. While the Third Duma in particular made some progress in economic and social reform, the Tsar and his ministers retained firm control over the government.

It was Russia's disastrous involvement in World War I that led to the end of the monarchy. By early 1917, Russia had suffered a number of defeats in its struggle with superior German forces. The war and continued autocratic rule had grown increasingly unpopular. Riots broke out in the major cities in March 1917. The Tsar attempted to dissolve the Fourth Duma, but it refused to be dissolved. "Soviets" again rose up in Petrograd (St. Petersburg had been renamed in 1914) and Moscow. Nicholas II was forced to abdicate on 15 March 1917.

A provisional government, based on the old Fourth Duma, was declared. But its authority was challenged by the Soviets. In addition, the provisional government refused to end Russia's involvement in the war. This was seen as a major decision, which only a duly elected government could make. Over the course of 1917, the Mensheviks (socialists) increasingly gained control over the provisional government but lost control over the Soviets to the Bolsheviks, led by Vladimir Lenin. On the night of 6 November 1917, the Bolsheviks seized control of St. Petersburg.

Elections for a Constituent Assembly organized by the provisional government took place on 25 November 1917—Russia's freest elections until the 1990s. Only 168 of the 703 deputies elected were Bolsheviks. The Constituent Assembly convened on 18 January 1918, but was prevented from meeting again by Bolshevik forces.

Lenin moved quickly to end Russia's involvement in World War I. In March 1918, he agreed to a peace treaty with Germany, which deprived Russia of considerable territory (it was at this time that the Bolsheviks moved the capital back to Moscow). From 1918 to 1921, the Bolsheviks fought a civil war against a large number of opponents, whom they defeated. After the German surrender to the Western powers in November 1918, Lenin's forces moved to take back the territory it had given up. Except for Finland, Poland, the Baltic states (temporarily), and Bessarabia (Moldova), Lenin's forces succeeded in regaining what they had given up.

The Bolshevik regime was based on Marxist-Leninist ideology. It sought to overthrow the rule of economic "oppressors" (the aristocracy and the bourgeoisie) and replace it with rule by the proletariat. There were two main concepts in Lenin's political theory: the dictatorship of the proletariat and democratic centralism. In Lenin's view, the working class had to impose dictatorial rule over its class enemies to prevent them from regaining power. But within the instrument of this class dictatorship—the Communist Party—there was to be freedom of debate. Once a policy question had been resolved, however, debate was to cease.

Theoretically, power in the Communist Party was vested in an elected party congress, which then elected a smaller Central Committee, which in turn elected an even smaller Politburo to run day-to-day affairs. In fact, it was the top party leadership—Lenin and his Politburo colleagues—who established and maintained dictatorial control.

After the civil war, Lenin relented on his ambitious plans for the state to control the entire economy. He ushered in the New Economic Policy (NEP), which allowed peasants to own land and sell their produce at market, and permitted private business to operate (though the state retained control of large enterprises). Lenin died on 21 January 1924. A power struggle among the top Communist leaders broke out. By 1928, Joseph Stalin had eliminated all his rivals and achieved full power. He then ended NEP and ushered in a brutal period of forced industrialization and collectivization of agriculture. Stalin's rule was especially harsh in the non-Russian republics of the USSR. Scholars estimate that as many as 20 million Soviet citizens died during the 1928–38 period either because of state terror or famine.

In August 1939, the infamous Nazi-Soviet pact was signed dividing Eastern Europe into spheres of influence. Under this agreement, the USSR regained most of the territories that had belonged to the Russian Empire but had been lost during the Russian Revolution (Poland, the Baltic states, and Bessarabia [Moldova]). But on 22 June 1941, Hitler's forces invaded the USSR and Moscow quickly lost all the territory that it had recently gained. German forces reached the outskirts of Moscow. With the help of massive materiel shipments from the United States and other Western countries, Soviet forces were able to rally and drive the Germans back. By the end of the war in May 1945, the USSR had reconquered everything it lost. With the Red Army in Eastern Europe, Stalin was able to establish satellite Communist regimes in Poland, Czechoslovakia, Hungary, Romania, Bulgaria, and East Germany. (Communist regimes also came to power in Yugoslavia and Albania, but did not remain allied to Moscow.)

Stalin's rule was especially harsh during the last years of his life. He died in 1953 and the ensuing power struggle was eventually won by Nikita Khrushchev. Khrushchev ended the terror of the Stalin years, but the basic features of the Stalinist system (Communist Party monopoly on power, centralized economy allowing for little private initiative, limited opportunities for free expression) remained until Mikhail Gorbachev came to power in March 1985.

Realizing that the old Stalinist system had led to a stagnant economy, which would undermine the USSR's ability to remain a superpower, Gorbachev sought to reform the Communist system. But although greater freedom of expression led to an enhanced understanding of the serious economic and ethnic problems the USSR faced, Gorbachev was unwilling to implement the economic and other reforms necessary to create a free-market democracy. The intense division on how to solve the problems faced by the USSR led to the ultimate dissolution in 1991 of the country into its separate republics.

For the first time, relatively free multicandidate elections were held in Russia in March 1990. In May 1990, the new Russian Supreme Soviet selected Boris Yeltsin as its chairman. Yeltsin had been an ally of Gorbachev until they disagreed over the pace of reform and Yeltsin was pushed out of the Politburo and his other positions. On 12 June 1991, the first elections to the Russian presidency were held, and Yeltsin won. Yeltsin played the central role in foiling the August 1991 coup attempt by Soviet conservatives against Gorbachev.

On 8 December 1991, Yeltsin, together with the leaders of Ukraine and Belarus, formed the nucleus of the Commonwealth of Independent States (CIS), which spelled the end of the USSR later that month. Like the other former Soviet republics, Russia had become an independent sovereign state.

In early 1992, Yeltsin and his acting prime minister, Egor Gaidar, sought to introduce rapid economic reform. Price controls were lifted on all but a few items. Prices rose rapidly, and as time passed, public opposition to economic reform grew. The Yeltsin government's relations with the legislature grew increasingly acrimonious. Many of the deputies had close ties with the state-run economy and bureaucracy, which were threatened by economic reform.

Much of Russian politics in 1993 consisted of bitter squabbling between Yeltsin and the legislature. No progress was made on drafting a new constitution to replace the much-amended Soviet-era constitution that still governed Russia.

On 21 September 1993, Yeltsin unilaterally dissolved the Supreme Soviet and introduced rule by presidential decree until new legislative elections and a referendum on his draft constitution could be held on 12 December. Many of the anti-Yeltsin legislators refused to accept Yeltsin's suspension, and barricaded themselves inside the legislature building. On 3 October, forces loyal to the legislature briefly occupied the office of the mayor of Moscow and attempted to seize the Ostankino television center. Forces loyal to Yeltsin, backed by the military, attacked and seized the legislature building. A state of emergency and press censorship were briefly introduced. Yeltsin banned several opposition parties, purged opponents from the government, and reaffirmed his intention to serve out his full term.

The constitutional referendum and legislative elections were held as planned in December 1993. The electorate approved Russia's first post-Communist constitution, which called for a strong presidency. In the legislative elections, though, the Communist and ultra nationalist forces did well. Analysts attribute the Communist's strong showing to popular dissatisfaction with the radical economic reforms that had depressed the economy and left the Russian people at subsistence levels. Only 50% of the electorate turned out to vote. After a hard-fought campaign, Yeltsin won reelection on 3 July 1996 with 54% of the vote. Some 67% of the voters turned out for the elections.

As Yeltsin struggled to stabilize the government and reform the economy, nationalistic fervor in the "ethnic" republics tore at the fabric of the Russian Federation. War broke out in Chechnya in December 1994 after the rebellious North Caucasus region claimed its independence. The inability of the Russian military to subdue the region led to a withdrawal of Russian forces in late 1996. The bloody and unpopular conflict ultimately led Yeltsin to sign a peace treaty with Chechen leader Aslan Maskhadov on 12 May 1997. The agreement deferred a decision on the region for five years. In the meantime, Russia claimed that the region remained a part of Russia, while Chechnya (called Ichkeria by the rebels) claimed it was already independent.

Russia's position in the world was further weakened in 1997 when three of its former satellites (Hungary, Poland, and the Czech Republic) were admitted to NATO effective in 1999. Romania and Slovenia were in line to join next. Russia, initially opposed to the new admissions, ultimately signed a pact for mutual cooperation with NATO on 27 May 1997. The pact established a new NATO-Russia council for consultation on security issues and NATO assured Russia that it had no plans to deploy nuclear weapons on the territories of any new members. For its part, Russia pledged its commitment to transforming itself into a democracy. Seeking also to improve relations with Ukraine, on 31 May 1997, Yeltsin signed a treaty of "friendship, cooperation, and partnership" with Ukraine's president Leonid Kuchma. The agreement affirmed that the Russian-populated Crimean peninsula was indeed part of Ukraine. At issue was ownership of the old Soviet Black Sea Fleet and use of the naval port at Sebastopol. Under the agreement, Russia took 80% of the fleet and a 20-year lease on Sevastopol's main bays. In addition to affirmation of its territorial boarders, Ukraine was to receive US$100 million a year in rent for the bays.

Yeltsin dismissed his entire cabinet in March 1998, causing the currency to take a one-day dip. In August 1998, the Russian currency collapsed, and the country experienced the worst harvest in 45 years. The government defaulted on US$40 billion in ruble bonds, and the banking system experienced a swift decline. Losses during 1999 were estimated at two billion dollars per month. In February 1999 Prime Minister Primakov met with IMF officials to reschedule debt payment aid. Accounts of large-scale money laundering were reported in both 1998 and 1999 by Russian mobsters and offshore money-laundering operations. The Russian Central Bank had used the ruble to prop up defunct parastatals, and the banks were lending money from state coffers that were empty to begin with. The lack of active currency prompted the downward spiral of the entire economy.

The conflict with Chechnya never really ended. On 23 September 1999, following a series of Chechen terrorist attacks (which might have been a provocation by Russian intelligence), Yeltsin signed the order to begin military action in Chechnya. When Vladimir Putin became prime minister and a head of FSB (former KGB), he ordered a withdrawal of most of the military troops from Chechnya. He employed instead the use of intelligence forces and local police to fight the separatists. Presidential elections were held and Kadirov was elected president. The conflict however was not resolved. The war with Chechnya raged on through the summer of 2000, climaxing with a bomb attack in a Moscow subway that killed 11 and wounded many others. It was estimated that about one dozen Russian fighters lost their lives daily on the Russian-Chechen border during 1999. This was not the only front on which Russia showed a military presence: Yeltsin called for the

removal of NATO from Yugoslavia in early 1999, but his bark was stronger than his bite.

President Yeltsin resigned in December 1999, under allegations of financial crimes and from ailing health. Supported by the former president, Vladimir Putin was elected to the executive. Putin graduated from the Law School of the Leningrad State University and joined the KGB. In the 1980s, he was sent to East Germany where he handled issues of economic intelligence. He returned to Leningrad in 1989, and left the KGB to enter the St. Petersburg University administration. After about a year, he left the university to join the administration of the newly elected major of Leningrad: Sobchak. Putin transferred to Moscow in 1996 to work in presidential apparatus. In 1998, Putin was made a head of FSB. The Yeltsin Administration decided that Putin was the right person to deal with opposition and protect their best interests. In contrast with the gregarious and outgoing Yeltsin, Putin seemed cold and ascetic. Additionally, Putin's initial success in Chechnya brought him widespread public sympathy and support.

President Putin took office in 2000. After some time as president, Putin assembled a new team known as "The People of the St. Petersburg;" his closest confidante was Sergey Ivanov, a potential successor to Putin as president in 2008.

President Putin had certain concerns that he felt called for his immediate attention. Putin's first concern was to make Russia even more centralized, which he accomplished by limiting the power of regional leaders. Secondly, Putin was determined to bring monopolies under state control and cut the oligarch's access to the decision-making process. Finally, he was concerned about the state of the military.

Putin's policy to centralize the state was aimed at regional governors. Almost immediately upon taking the office he established seven super-regions and passed a law that enabled the president to appoint the heads of these regions himself, while governors were to be chosen by electorate. Moreover, Putin passed two other meaningful laws that transformed the legislative branch of the Russian Federation and the balance of power in the government. The first law altered the composition of the Federation Council (upper house of the parliament), to deprive governors of their seats. The second law granted the president the power to dismiss regional leaders and legislatures.

Following the 11 September 2001 terrorist attacks on the United States, Putin turned Russian foreign policy towards the West. He came out in favor of Russia joining the counterterrorism campaign announced by US president George W. Bush, despite opposition from his own advisors and from the Russian political elite. This shift in policy coincided with a move for closer relations with Europe; Russia became a member of the Council of Europe, and began to strengthen its civil society and rule of law, designed to bring it into the good graces of the EU. Russia accepted the arrival of US and coalition troops in some Central Asian republics in the US-led war in Afghanistan to oust the Taliban regime and the al-Qaeda network. Russia tacitly accepted the arrival of US Special Forces into Georgia in 2002: the United States wished to combat what it believed to be international terrorists linked to the al-Qaeda network in the Pankisi Gorge region of Georgia. However, on 11 September 2002, when Putin announced Russia would take unilateral action against Chechen fighters and international terrorists in the Pankisi Gorge; the United States stated its unequivocal opposition to any such unilateral military action.

In May 2002, Russia and the United States announced a new agreement on strategic nuclear weapons reduction: operationally deployed strategic nuclear warheads would be reduced by each side to a level of 1,700–2,200 over the next 10 years. This "Moscow Treaty" was followed by an agreement between Russia and NATO foreign ministers to establish a "NATO-Russia Council" in which Russia and the 19 NATO countries would have an equal role in decision-making on counterterrorism policy and policy on other security threats. The "Moscow Treaty" was counterbalanced by events in June, however, when the United States announced it formally withdrew from the 1972 Anti-Ballistic Missile Treaty and Russia subsequently pulled out of the START II Treaty.

Concerns about Russia's guarantee of freedom of speech were raised in January 2002, when the last major independent television network in Russia, TV-6, was forced by the government to stop broadcasting. The government claimed the sole reason for the shutdown was bankruptcy, but many were not convinced that Putin's decision was purely business-related. The Russian media are either state-owned or controlled by "oligarchs" such as Boris Berezovsky and Vladimir Gusinsky, and in bringing court cases against these men, the government effectively took control of their media outlets, curbing independent reporting and causing a setback to freedom of speech and press.

The conflict with Chechnya intensified in 2002. On 23 October, Chechen separatist rebels seized a theater in Moscow and held some 800 hostages for three days. The hostage-takers demanded that Putin withdraw Russian troops from Chechnya. On 26 October, the president ordered an early-morning raid on the theater, using the gas Fentanyl, a fast-acting opiate that was meant to incapacitate the rebels. As a result of the operation, 117 hostages died, all but one (who died of gunshot wounds) due to the effects of the gas. All 50 of the hostage-takers died. Putin claimed the operation was an unprecedented success, but many wondered about the effectiveness of the raid due to the number of hostages who died. That December, suicide bombers attacked the Grozny headquarters of the pro-Moscow Chechen administration led by Akhmed Kadyrov, and more than 50 people were killed. It was the first use of suicide bombers undertaken by Chechen separatist rebels against Russia, and Putin described the attack as "inhuman." In March 2003, a referendum on a new constitution for Chechnya was approved, stipulating that Chechnya would remain a part of the Russia; many were critical of Russia for holding the referendum before peace was established.

On 8 November 2002, the UN Security Council unanimously passed Resolution 1441, calling upon Iraq to disarm itself of chemical, biological, and nuclear weapons, to allow the immediate return of UN and International Atomic Energy Agency (IAEA) arms inspectors (they had been expelled in 1998), and to comply with all previous UN resolutions regarding the country since the end of the Gulf War in 1991. Arms inspectors began work in Iraq, but the United States and the United Kingdom were dissatisfied with the slow pace of inspections and began to prepare for war. On 19 March 2003, the United States launched air strikes against Iraq, and war began. US-Russian relations were severely tested at the end of 2002 and into 2003, as Russia sided with France and Germany in their opposition to war. In mid-April, Putin, who had

previously called the war "a big political mistake," was softening his tone toward the United States and the United Kingdom, and stressed the importance of Russia's role in a postwar Iraq. Analysts estimate that in 2003 Iraq had US$52 billion in contracts with Russia, primarily in energy and communications.

In September 2004, ongoing conflict with Chechnya took the form of a major terrorist attack on a public schools in Beslan, Northern Ossetia. The shocking actions of terrorism in Beslan gave President Putin the momentum to push through his radical administrative reforms. Investigations revealed that Beslan tragedy was a result of incompetence and corruption of regional leaders and the lack of coordination between the regional executives and police. The reorganization of the Federation Council (substituting appointed senators for elected governors) was followed by a number of actions. The system of direct vote for governors was abandoned in favor of a system whereby the president appointed the governors; State Duma elections were to be based solely on party ballots, therefore eliminating elections in one-mandate districts; and a Public Chamber—a public body on a federal level that was supposed to become an intermediary between society and the state—was created.

New constitutional amendments were not well received and caused controversy in the Duma. There was a negative reaction by the Communist Party, Liberal Democratic Party, Yabloko, and Union of Right Forces. Even Putin's own Unity Party survived a split in opinions, with some members opposing Putin's reforms. European powers and the United States do not always agree with Russia's policies toward Chechnya, considering them to violate human rights. In December 2004 President Putin met with German Chancellor Gerhard Schroeder to discuss the possibility of European involvement in the conflict. In essence, no one knew how to formulate a solution fo this conflict, since territorial disputes have existed in Chechnya for centuries.

Putin's presidency had a positive effect on Russia's long-struggling economy. In the period 1999–2004, the Russian economy experience annual growth of 7%. After inheriting a weak economy caused by financial crises of 1998, Putin passed legislature aimed at reforming the economy. As of 2006, it appeared that these reforms established solid, long-term institutional changes that were enabling high growth rates.

13 GOVERNMENT

Russia is a democratic federative state based on rule of law with a division of power among the legislative, executive, and judicial branches. It is a constitutional government, based on a post-Soviet constitution, which was approved in a referendum held 12 December 1993. The constitution establishes a bicameral legislature known as the Federal Assembly. The lower house (State Duma) consists of 450 elected deputies while the 178-member upper house (Council of the Federation) is composed of representatives of the provinces and autonomous republics that make up Russia.

The executive branch of the presidential administration consisted of three bodies: Administration of the President, generally responsible for domestic political issues, Government, usually in charge of economic development, and the Security Council of the Russian Federation, chiefly responsible for the foreign policy, security and defense of the country. The responsibilities of the three centers in the executive branch often overlap.

The president is elected by popular vote for a four-year term; elections were held 14 March 2004 (next were scheduled to be held March 2008). As of 2005 the president of the Russian Federation was Vladimir Vladimirovich Putin (acting president since 31 December 1999 and reelected president since 7 May 2000).

The president heads the Executive Branch—currently the president is the Head of State and the Supreme Commander in Chief of the Armed Forces. According to the constitution of 1993, the president drafts and issues legal regulations, settles disputes, and ensures that the constitution is observed. The president is also responsible for ensuring the state's mechanisms for protecting and respecting citizen's rights and liberties.

The president appoints the cabinet and other top government posts, but the appointments must be confirmed by the legislature. Presidential appointments of prime minister, deputy prime ministers, and chairman of the central bank are subject to confirmation by the State Duma while appointments of high court judges and the prosecutor general are subject to confirmation by the Council of the Federation. The president can refuse to accept the State Duma's rejection of an appointment to the prime ministership. If the State Duma refuses three times to confirm a new prime minister, the president may dissolve the lower house and order new elections. If the State Duma votes a no-confidence motion against the prime minister and cabinet twice within three months, the president may respond either by dismissing the cabinet or dissolving the State Duma. The president, however, cannot dissolve the State Duma due to its passing a no-confidence motion during the first year of the State Duma's term of office.

The president protects the nation's independence, sovereignty, and integrity, and prevents aggression against Russia or its allies. The president may declare war or a state of emergency on his own authority. Finally, the president must ensure the peaceful and democratic development of the country.

Impeachment of the president is provided for in the constitution, but is very difficult. Two-thirds of the State Duma must vote to initiate the impeachment process. Both the Constitutional Court, established to arbitrate any disputes between the executive and legislative branches, and the Supreme Court must review the charges. The findings of all three organizations are then submitted to the Council of the Federation, which can impeach the president by a two-thirds majority vote. This process must be completed within three months from beginning to end.

The President's Administration or Presidential Executive Office is an important governmental body that prepares the president's bills for submission to the State Duma. It prepares drafts of decrees, orders, instructions, presidential speeches, and other documents. The Presidential Executive Office coordinates all of the president's interactions with various political parties and leaders, nongovernmental organizations (NGOs), nonprofit organizations, unions, and foreign governments. Although the president oversees the work of the Executive Office, it is the Chief of Staff of the Presidential Executive Office who manages it. As of 2006, this position was held by Dmitry Medvedev (since October 2003).

The government is responsible for financial, credit, and monetary policies. It also develops uniform state policies regarding culture, science, education, health, social welfare, ecology, and all other areas of social life. The government is headed by the prime minister (Mikhail Fradkov since 5 March 2004). The president presides over government meetings and gives instructions to the government and other federal bodies.

The Security Council is responsible for national security, including but not limited to state security, public security, safety, socioeconomic security, and security in the spheres of defense, information, the military, and international affairs. The Security Council also advises the president on security issues. It interacts with the Scholarly Council made up of representatives of the Russian Academy of Science and the specialized academies of science and educational institutions and individual experts. The president is also chairman of the Security Council.

The State Council is an advisory body that deals with the issues, especially those related to economic and social reforms. The president also acts as chairman of the State Council, and the acting secretary is the Secretary of State (Alexander S. Abramov as of 2005). The State Council is composed of the leaders of the local governments.

During his presidency, Putin shifted the balance of power within the Executive Branch; during the Yeltsin era, power was distributed equally, but Putin shifted the center of power to the President's Administration.

The legislative branch, the Federal Assembly, consists of two chambers. The State Duma (Gosuderstvennaya Duma), the lower house, is made up of 450 seats; 225 seats elected by proportional representation from party lists winning at least 5% of the vote and 225 seats from single-member constituencies. Members are elected by direct popular vote to serve four-year terms. The upper house or Federation Council (Sovet Federalistov) is made up of 178 seats. Members Federation Council were appointed by the president and legislative officials in each of the 89 federal administrative units (Chechnya included).

The two chambers of the Federal Assembly have different powers and responsibilities. The State Duma is more powerful. The Federation Council has jurisdiction over issues affecting the provinces and autonomous republics, including border changes and the use of force within Russia. Its other responsibility is to confirm justices of the Constitutional court, Supreme Court, and Superior Court of Arbitration. It also handles the bills dealing with finance and treaty ratifications. The State Duma handles all other bills. Even those bills that are proposed by the Federation Council must first be considered by the Duma.

14 POLITICAL PARTIES

In the elections to the State Duma held 12 December 1993, 225 of the 450 seats were elected on the basis of proportional representation from party lists, which had to receive a minimum of 5% of the national vote to gain representation. The other 225 seats were elected from single-member districts.

The party to receive the largest number of seats (76) was the radical reformist Russia's Choice led by Boris Yeltsin's former acting prime minister, Egor Gaidar. The centrist New Regional Policy group (which was actually formed by nonaligned deputies from single member districts after the election) won 65. Vladimir Zhirinovsky's ultranationalist, antidemocratic Liberal Democratic Party won 63. The pro-Communist Agrarian Party won 55 seats, while the Communist Party of the Russian Federation won 45. Six other parties or blocs (some of which were also formed after the election) won between 12 and 30 seats each.

Deputies to the 178-seat Council of the Federation were elected in two-member districts, where they mostly ran as individuals. Of the 171 seats that were filled, only 27 identified themselves with a particular party. The ultranationalists, Communists, and their sympathizers predominated in the State Duma.

In the December 1995 elections, the Communists again dominated the Duma, taking 149 of the 450 seats. They were supported by two left-wing factions, Power to the People (37 seats) and the Agrarians (35); together they were only 5 votes shy of an outright majority. The center-right party, Our Home Is Russia, won 50 seats, as did Vladimir Zhirinovsky's far-right Liberal Democratic Party, and Yabloko, the moderate-reformist bloc led by Grigoriy Yavlinsky.

In the December 1999 Duma elections, six parties surmounted the 5% threshold on the party list vote, accounting for over 80% of the votes cast. Three of the six parties that received seats in the party list vote were created just prior to the election. (This did not include the newly formed ultranationalist Zhirinovskiy bloc, which was essentially a relabeling of his Liberal Democratic Party.) Unity ("The Bear") was created in late September 1999 by the Yeltsin government, and the Union of Right-Wing Forces and Fatherland-All Russia (OVR) in August 1999. In contrast to previous Duma races, many liberal groups (with the major exception of Yabloko) cooperated in forming the Union of Right-Wing Forces electoral bloc to enhance their chances for surmounting the 5% hurdle. The newly formed Unity and Union blocs received crucial publicity when Putin endorsed them. Results from the single-member constituency races added some seats to those gained by the six successful parties and provided a few seats for minor parties. In all, the Communist Party won 120 seats, Unity 73, OVR 70, Union 29, Yabloko 20, and the Zhirinovskiy bloc 19. Unaffiliated candidates won 95 seats, and a few seats faced runoffs. A little over one-third of the deputies elected were incumbents from the previous Duma.

In general, the election represented a major loss for Our Home (headed by presidential aspirant and former prime minister Viktor Chernomyrdin), which no longer was a faction in the legislature. Zhirinovskiy's bloc lost more than half its seats, compared to 1995, as did Yabloko. The new Duma convened in January 2000, and in a bold move, Unity and the Communist Party temporarily joined forces to grab the largest number of leadership posts and committee chairmanships.

In the first round of the June 1996 presidential election, Aleksandr I. Lebed received 15% of the vote to Yeltsin's 35% and Communist party candidate Gennadiy A. Zyuganov's 32%. Lebed, a retired general viewed by voters as a tough law-and-order strong man, dropped out of the race when Yeltsin named him national security advisor. Lebed gave his support to Yeltsin, which helped Yeltsin win 54% of the vote in the 3 July 1996 election. Two months later, however, Yeltsin forced Lebed out of the government. Yeltsin was barred from running for a third term.

Toward the end of his second term Yeltsin confronted growing unpopularity and instability in his administration. Opposition forces (including Communist party, Moscow-oriented Yuri Luzhkov and groups of local governors) did not take any drastic measures to bring Yeltsin down.

The Communist Party tried unsuccessfully to reconcile a range of leftist groups to back a common candidate, Genadiy Zuganov,

against Vladimir Putin. Another candidate, Yurii Luzhkov, won the support of Muscovites and attempted to appeal for support to the governors. Meanwhile the governors were forming coalitions that later resulted in the formation of the Fatherland-All Russia (OVR) party affiliated with Yevgeni Primakov. Primakov was a popular politician who was credited with bringing Russia out of the 1998 financial crises. As a result, OVR became a threat to Yeltsin. In response, Yeltsin organized a media campaign to discredit the OVR party and Primakov in particular, and to promote Vladimir Putin.

In 1999, six months before the end of his term, President Yeltsin resigned from power, appointing Putin as an acting president. Putin then issued a decree granting Yeltsin and his family complete immunity from persecution. Yeltsin's resignation moved the term of election to March, leaving the opponents with less time to prepare. In little time, Putin managed to organize strong support for Unity and forged cooperation between Unity and OVR. In the first round of presidential elections held on 26 March 2000, among the 11 candidates, Putin won 53% of 75.2 million votes, trumping his nearest rival by 23.7%. The runner-up, Gennadiy Zyuganov, received 29%, down from the 32% he received in the first round of the 1996 race. Putin was formally inaugurated as president on 7 May 2000.

National elections were held again 7 December 2003, with Putin's Unity party winning 37.1% of the vote. The Communist Party came in second with 12.7% of the vote, and Vladimir Zhirinovsky's ultranationalist party (the Liberal Democratic Party) took 11.6%. The pro-Western liberal parties—Union of Right Forces (SPS) and Yabloko—faired poorly. Another leftist-nationalist party, Rodina, was formed. The Organization for Security and Cooperation in Europe (OSCE) said the government used resources and control of the media to dominate the election.

In March 2004, Putin ran for a second term. He was reelected with more than 70% of the vote. His closest opponent, Communist Party candidate Nikolai Kharitonov, got 13.7%. The next presidential election was scheduled for March 2008.

15 LOCAL GOVERNMENT

Russia has a complicated patchwork of regional and local governments, including 89 federal subjects of constituencies. Those 89 units are not of equal status. Russia is divided into 6 krais, 49 oblasts, 1 autonomous oblast, 10 autonomous okrugs, and two independent cities (Moscow and St. Petersburg). There are also 21 autonomous republics where non-Russian minorities predominate (or once predominated). The Chechen republic of Ichkeria, is, de facto, a separate state, although not recognized as such by the federal authorities.

For all but the 21 autonomous republics, President Yeltsin issued decrees reorganizing the system of local government in October 1993. Each unit has an elected legislature. Most of these are unicameral, though two (Magadan Oblast and Altai Krai) opted for bicameral ones. In late 1996 and early 1997, regional popular elections of governors took place, replacing the system of appointments by the president. By contrast, the Russian president never appointed the heads of the 21 autonomous republics. These (usually called presidents) were selected in whatever manner is prescribed by their individual constitutions. The regional and republic executive and legislative heads were ex officio members of the

Russian Federal Assembly's upper chamber, the Federation Council, where they endeavor to guard local power against encroachment from Moscow.

When Putin came to power, he felt it necessary to bring the regional leaders under a more central control, reversing bottom-to-top relations from the Yeltsin-era. In 2000, Putin set out to correct regional relations by grouping the administrative units of Russia into seven regional administrative districts: Northwest, Central, Volga, North Caucasus, Ural, Siberia, and Far East. A presidential representative is appointed to each. Putin appointed seven presidential representatives to coordinate the activities of federal organs. In February 2001, the law went into effect that allowed the president to dismiss governors. Furthermore, after the September 2004 Beslan School tragedy, Putin passed a bill to abolish popular elections for Russia's regional governors and to elect all State Duma deputies according to a proportional party system, abolishing single-mandate districts.

16 JUDICIAL SYSTEM

The judicial system is divided into three branches. There are courts of general jurisdiction (including military courts), which are subordinated to the Supreme Court; the arbitration (commercial) court system, which is under the High Court of Arbitration; and the Constitutional Court, which arbitrates any disputes between the executive and legislative branches and determines questions pertaining to constitutional issues. Civil and criminal cases are tried in courts of primary jurisdiction (municipal and regional), courts of appeals, and higher courts.

Procurators are also organized at the district, regional, and federal levels. The head of the procurators, the Procurator General, is nominated by the president and confirmed by the Federation Council. The trials are inquisitorial, not adversarial, and procurators are quite influential in nonjury trial.

17 ARMED FORCES

With the collapse of the original Soviet Union in 1992, Russia established a separate Ministry of Defense and military establishment upon the wreckage of the Soviet armed forces. Still formidable in terms of weapons and equipment, the Russian armed forces reached a low state of morale and effectiveness in 1993, "hollowed" by low-manning, the failure of draft calls, diversion to survival tasks rather than training, and lack of discipline. In the following years, military reforms were undertaken. The first phase, completed by the end of 1998, involved reorganization of the military command structure, redistricting, and troop reductions. The second phase focused on equipment modernization and operational readiness. Readiness was also improved in response to the NATO bombing of Serbia following hostilities in Kosovo.

In 2005, active Russian armed forces personnel numbered 1,037,000, with the number of reservists totaling 20,000,000. The Russian Army in 2005 had an estimated 395,000 active members, which were backed by a formidable weapons inventory of over 22,800 main battle tanks, 150 light tanks, more than 2,000 reconnaissance vehicles, over 15,090 armored infantry fighting vehicles, more than 9,900 armored personnel carriers, over 30,045 artillery pieces (towed and self-propelled), and over 628 attack helicopters. Russia has assumed the responsibility of the Soviet Union to reduce by treaty its strategic arsenal and conventional forces in Europe, but remains the world's second most formidable nuclear nation. Russia's nuclear arsenal is estimated at 12,000–19,000 strategic and nonstrategic nuclear weapons.

The Russian Navy has surrendered little of its strength to the break-away republics. The Navy numbers 142,000 personnel. It controls 46 tactical submarines, including 8 nuclear-powered nonballistic missile submarines (SSGNs), and 18 nuclear-powered attack submarines (SSNs). Major surface combat units include 1 aircraft carrier, 6 cruisers, 15 destroyers, 19 frigates, 25 corvettes, 72 patrol and coastal vessels, 41 mine warfare ships, and 436 logistics/support vessels. The naval air arm has an estimated 35,000 personnel backed by 226 combat capable aircraft including 58 bombers, 49 fighters, 68 fighter ground attack aircraft, 11 attack helicopters, and 120 antisubmarine warfare helicopters. Naval infantry and coastal defense forces (designed for naval base defense) deploy 9,500 troops with ground combat artillery and missile weapons.

Russia's Air Force consists of a long-range aviation command, a tactical aviation command, military transport aviation command, training schools, and operational combat units. As of 2005, active personnel numbered an estimated 170,000. The principal tactical weapons systems remain MiG and Su fighters and fighter-attack aircraft and armed helicopters. In 2005, the Air Force had 1,852 combat capable aircraft that included 1,094 fighters and 757 fighter ground attack aircraft.

Russia's joint service Strategic Deterrent Forces had an estimated 129,000 active personnel in 2005. Of that total, the Navy accounted for 11,000 personnel and was responsible for the nation's fleet of 15 SSBNs and its submarine launched ballistic missile force. The Air Force accounted for another 38,000 personnel through its Long-Range Aviation Command, which was responsible for the country's strategic bomber force of 80 aircraft. Another estimated 40,000 personnel were assigned to three Rocket Armies and were known as Strategic Missile Force Troops. This element of the Strategic Defense Forces was responsible for the operation of the nation's land-based ICBMs, of which there were around 570 launchers carrying 2,035 nuclear warheads. In addition to the Strategic Defense Forces, another 40,000 personnel were assigned to the Space Forces, whose mission was to detect a possible missile attack on the Russian Federation and its allies, as well as to implement the nation's Ballistic Missile Defense (BMD) and the launch and control of military/dual-use spacecraft.

There are also 415,100 paramilitary forces assigned to specialized security functions for border protection, river patrols, customs duties, installation and plant protection, transportation security, riot duty, and internal security. The number of border guards are estimated at 160,000, while interior troops number 170,000.

Although Russia has scaled back the Soviet Union's defense forces, the Russian armed forces still maintain a global presence. In addition to troops remaining in Armenia, Georgia, Moldova, and Tajikistan, Russia maintains military missions or units in the Ukraine, Syria, and Africa. Russian units have also participated in peacekeeping operations in the region and supported the UN in other separate missions. The defense budget in 2005 totaled $18.8 billion.

18 INTERNATIONAL COOPERATION

Russia has essentially assumed and expanded upon the foreign relations ties established by the former Soviet Union. In one form or another, it has held a seat in the United Nations since 24 October 1945; it is a part of several nonregional specialized agencies, such as IAEA, ICAO, ILO, UNHCR, UNIDO, and the WHO. Russia is a permanent member of the UN Security Council. The nation is also member of APEC, the Commonwealth of Independent Nations, the Black Sea Economic Cooperation Zone, the Council of the Baltic Sea States, the Council of Europe, the Euro-Atlantic Partnership Council, the European Bank for Reconstruction and Development, G-8, the Paris Club (G-10), and the OSCE. In June 2001, leaders of Russia, China, Kazakhstan, Kyrgyzstan, Tajikistan and Uzbekistan met in China to launch the Shanghai Cooperation Organization (SCO) and sign an agreement to fight terrorism and ethnic and religious militancy while promoting trade. The country holds observer status in the OAS, the WTO, and the Latin American Integration Association (LAIA). Russia is a dialogue partner in ASEAN and part of the ASEAN Regional Forum.

The Russian government has supported UN operations and missions in Kosovo (est. 1999), Western Sahara (est. 1991), Ethiopia and Eritrea (est. 2000), Liberia (est. 2003), Sierra Leone (est. 1999), East Timor (est. 2002), Georgia (est. 1993), and Burundi (est. 2004), among others. Russia is a partner in the Middle East Peace Process "Quartet." The country is a guest in the Nonaligned Movement.

Russia is part of the Zangger Committee, the Organization for the Prohibition of Chemical Weapons, and the Nuclear Suppliers Group (London Group). It is an observer in the European Organization for Nuclear Research (CERN). In environmental cooperation, Russia is part of the Antarctic Treaty; the Basel Convention; Conventions on Biological Diversity, Whaling, and Air Pollution; Ramsar; CITES; the London Convention; International Tropical Timber Agreements; the Kyoto Protocol; the Montréal Protocol; MARPOL; the Nuclear Test Ban Treaty; and the UN Conventions on the Law of the Sea and Climate Change.

19 ECONOMY

Russia's economy, $1.5 trillion in purchasing power parity (PPP) terms (as of 2005), is the largest within the former Soviet bloc. It was undergoing a painful transformation from a centrally planned economy to a market-oriented one with limited public ownership. Per capita income in 2005 was only $5,165 in nominal terms, although $10,758 in PPP terms. By 2004, services comprised the largest sector of the economy (61.2%), while industrial production accounted for 33.9% of GDP. The manufacturing centers around Moscow and St. Petersburg are the most important, as they were for the entire former USSR. Russia has rich energy and mineral resources, including large deposits of iron ore, coal, phosphates, and nonferrous metals, as well as one-fifth of the world's gold deposits and substantial oil and gas reserves. There are also vast forest resources. Agricultural production accounted for 4.9% of GDP in 2004. Although the share of agriculture in total output fell from 14% in 1991 to 4.9% in 2004, the collapse has led to underemployment rather than unemployment among rural workers, and therefore agriculture still accounted for more than 12% of official

employment in 2002. There is an acute excess demand for goods, especially consumer goods.

Russia's economic situation deteriorated rapidly after the breakup of the Soviet Union, which destroyed major economic links. President Yeltsin's 1992 economic reform program slashed defense spending, eliminated the old centralized distribution system, established private financial institutions, decentralized foreign trade, and began a program of privatizing state owned enterprises. Success was not immediate, however, as the GDP declined by over 12% in 1994 and 4% in 1995. By then, 25% of the population was living in poverty, corruption was rampart, and segments of the economy had gone "underground" to escape backbreaking taxes and bureaucratic regulation. However, government policies kept unemployment at the relatively low rate of 8%, even though there was no money to pay salaries and pensions. A stabilization program enacted in 1995 tightened the budget, liberalized trade, and lowered inflation through noninflationary financing of the budget deficit. Although the economy declined by 3.6% in 1996, segments of the economy were showing signs of recovery. In 1997, overall GDP registered its first positive growth, albeit only 0.9%. Inflation moderated to 11.3% from 21.8% in 1996, and unemployment fell from 9.3% to 9%. In a major privatization program, the government turned over to the growing private sector thousands of enterprises.

However, in 1998, the effects of the 1997 Asian financial crisis swept the economy, propelling a massive outflow of foreign investment. In August 1998 it became the Russian financial crisis as the government defaulted on payments due on $40 billion in ruble bonds and allowed the ruble to depreciate. Real GDP fell 4.9% in 1998 as inflation shot up to 84.5%. However, Russia weathered the crisis well: in 1999, one year after the crisis, real GDP increased by the highest percentage since the fall of the Soviet Union, the ruble stabilized, inflation was modest, and investment began to increase again. In 1999, real GDP increased 5.4%, and in 2000, a strong 8.3% while inflation fell to 36.5% in 1999 and then to 20.2% in 2000. The global economic slowdown after 2001 served to decelerate but not reverse economic recovery as GDP growth fell to 4.9% in 2001 and then to 3.5% in 2002. Inflation fell to 18.6% in 2001, and 16.5% in 2002, above predictions of 11–13% mainly because of increased fuel costs. Official unemployment, which peaked at 11.8% and 11.7% in 1998 and 1999, moderated to an estimated 8% in 2002, down from 8.9% in 2001.

From 2001–05, real GDP growth averaged 6.1%, and inflation averaged 14.9%. From 2000 to 2005, Russia ran trade and budget surpluses. GDP growth was forecast at 5.8% in 2005; inflation hit 11.7% in 2004, and was predicted to near 13% in 2005, well above a revised target of 10%. Although real GDP growth had slowed by 2005, high oil prices were expected to limit the extent of the deceleration, especially in 2006. Even though proceeds from the sale of oil strengthen the ruble, damaging competitiveness, high oil prices have not compensated for a lack of effective governmental economic policy. Oil production began to stagnate in late 2004; oil companies must look beyond the easy-to-tap oil reserves of western Siberia for new fields. Also, a string of investigations launched against Yukos, a major oil company, culminating in the arrest of its CEO, Mikhail Khodorkovsky, in the fall of 2003, raised concerns that President Vladimir Putin was granting more influence to forces within his government that desire to reassert state control over the economy. Companies looking to invest in Russia discover a plethora of rules that are often changed and capriciously applied; the large, unwieldy, corrupt bureaucracy is impossible to avoid. The gas, electricity, and railway industries are dominated by inefficient monopolies, particularly Gazprom, the state gas monopoly. Ownership structures are opaque, not transparent, but according to some estimates, 20 large conglomerates account for up to 70% of Russian GDP. Capital flight was a net $33 billion in 2004. These problems must be addressed if full economic reform is to be achieved.

20 INCOME

The US Central Intelligence Agency (CIA) reports that in 2005 the Russian Federation's gross domestic product (GDP) was estimated at $1.5 trillion. The CIA defines GDP as the value of all final goods and services produced within a nation in a given year and computed on the basis of purchasing power parity (PPP) rather than value as measured on the basis of the rate of exchange based on current dollars. The per capita GDP was estimated at $10,700. The annual growth rate of GDP was estimated at 5.9%. The average inflation rate in 2005 was 12.9%. It was estimated that agriculture accounted for 5% of GDP, industry 35%, and services 60%.

According to the World Bank, in 2003 remittances from citizens working abroad totaled $1.453 billion or about $10 per capita and accounted for approximately 0.3% of GDP. Foreign aid receipts amounted to $1,255 million or about $9 per capita and accounted for approximately 0.3% of the gross national income (GNI).

The World Bank reports that in 2003 household consumption in Russia totaled $219.03 billion or about $1,532 per capita based on a GDP of $430.1 billion, measured in current dollars rather than PPP. Household consumption includes expenditures of individuals, households, and nongovernmental organizations on goods and services, excluding purchases of dwellings. It was estimated that for the period 1990 to 2003 household consumption grew at an average annual rate of 0.9%. In 2001 it was estimated that approximately 28% of household consumption was spent on food, 16% on fuel, 7% on health care, and 15% on education. It was estimated that in 2004 about 17.8% of the population had incomes below the poverty line.

21 LABOR

In 2005, Russia's labor force was estimated at 74.22 million. As of 2004, it was estimated that agriculture accounted for 10.3% of the country's workforce, with 68.3% in the services sector, and 21.4% in industry. Although Russia's unemployment rate in 2005 was estimated at 7.6%, a considerable number of workers were underemployed.

A legacy from the Soviet era, the Federation of Independent Trade Unions of Russia (FNPR) still dominates organized labor and claims to represent 80% of all workers. The mining and air transport industries (along with the state sector) are highly unionized. Overall, about 46% of the workforce is at least nominally organized, with around 90% of them members of the FNPR. The legal right to strike is hindered by complex requirements. Court rulings have determined that nonpayment of wages, the most prevalent labor complaint, is an individual issue and cannot be addressed by the union. The right to bargain collectively is not regularly protected.

The monthly minimum wage was $28 as of September 2005, which was not sufficient to provide a family with a decent standard of living. Most workers earn more than this amount, however it was estimated that 18% of the workforce earned less. Although the labor code provides a maximum regular workweek of 40 hours with a 24-hour rest period, many laborers put in 10- to 12-hour days. Children under the age of 16 are banned from most employment, but 14 year old minors can work under certain conditions with the approval of a parent or guardian. In such cases, the health and the welfare of the child must not be threatened. While these provisions are generally enforced through government action, prevailing social norms and a large pool of low-wage adult workers, child labor remains a problem, especially in the informal economy. The law establishes minimum standards of workplace safety and worker health, but these are not effectively enforced.

22 AGRICULTURE

In 2003, Russia had 124.4 million hectares (307.4 million acres) of arable land (8.5% of the world's total), covering 7.6% of the country's land area. In 2003, the share of agriculture in the GDP was 5%. Agricultural production dropped by an average of 6% annually during 1990–2000. However, during 2002–04, crop production was 13.1% higher than during 1999–2001. A surge in imports of food products during that period is the direct result of difficulties faced by domestic farmers and processors, and has brought with it a desire for protection from foreign competition in the name of national security. In 2004, Russia's agricultural trade deficit was over $10.1 billion, fifth highest in the world.

The 2004 harvest included (in millions of tons): wheat, 45.4; potatoes, 35.9; sugar beets, 21.8; barley, 17.2; vegetables, 15.5; oats, 5; sunflower seeds, 4.8; corn, 3.5; rye, 2.9; buckwheat, 0.6; soybeans, 0.6; and rice, 0.5. The government is promoting the expansion of small-plot farming; about 150,000 new farms have begun operating since 1991, primarily in the south.

Agricultural policy has changed several times since market reforms began. Low interest loans were initially offered to the old state farms, but the government's budget soon could not afford all the demands made by farmers. The low interest loans were replaced by in-kind loans to suppliers, which were then modified to in-kind loans from the federal government to local governments. The general agricultural policy trend is now an ongoing devolution of power from the federal government to local governments.

23 ANIMAL HUSBANDRY

Some 91.9 million hectares (227 million acres) are pastureland, representing 5.6% of the total area. In 2005, the livestock population included: cattle, 22,987,700; sheep, 15,499,700; and pigs, 13,412,800. Russia also had 1.5 million horses, 328.9 million chickens, 2.7 million geese, and 2.5 million turkeys in 2005.

The 2005 meat production amounts included (in thousands of tons): beef, 1,915; pork, 1,610; mutton, 123; and poultry, 1,130. In 1999, Russia's livestock production was only 50% of what it had been in 1990. During 2002–04, livestock production was 7.8% higher than during 1999–2001. Milk production in 2005 was estimated at 30.9 million tons (down from 55.7 million tons in 1991), and egg production amounted to 2 billion tons in 2005. Infrastructural and distributional problems have exacerbated declining production. Many Russian dairy farms have been unprofitable due to low-quality dairy cows, limited supplies of quality feed, and lack of support services. Continued decline in livestock production, especially poultry, as well as the rapid growth of imports have been a source of trade friction. In 2004, Russia imported over $2 billion in meat and meat products.

24 FISHING

Russia's fish production ranks eighth in the world, following China, Peru, USA, Indonesia, Japan, India, and Chile. In 2003, 91% of the catch was marine, while 9% came from inland waters. The total catch in 2003 was 3,429,121 tons. The main species of the commercial catch in 2003 included (in thousands of tons): whiting, 360; herring, 335; cod, 277; and salmon, 188. Russia is a leading producer of crabmeat, fish roe, whole groundfish, and salmon products. More than half of Russian fish product exports consist of frozen products. Exports of frozen fish fillets in 2003 were valued at $141.9 million; and roe, $145.6 million.

Russia is known for its sturgeon and caviar. About 70% of the world's sturgeon stocks are in the Caspian Sea. Illegal trade of sturgeon and caviar have resulted in all 11 of Russia's commercial sturgeon species to be in decline. The Russian share of the world caviar market is estimated at 23–30%.

Overfishing and pollution of territorial waters have forced fishermen farther away from traditional fishing waters. For example, pollutants like mercury have partly caused the decline of the sturgeon and pike perch catches, which fell by 50% and 90%, respectively, from 1974 to 1987 in the Caspian Sea. Similar ecological problems also have affected fishing in the Azov Sea. Russia's enormous fishing fleet has many old vessels, and fuel shortages are common. Since 1991, more than 70 vessels have been leased from Spanish, Norwegian, and German shipbuilding yards. In 2003 alone, 36 Russian fishing vessels of 100 gross tons or more were added to the fishing fleet. Russian fishing vessels account for about 24% of the world's fishing fleet capacity.

Despite problems with pollution, the Russian catch expanded during the 1980s (the marine catch by 24%, the freshwater catch by 26%) due to intensified fishing in dam reservoirs, consumption substitution toward nontraditional fish stocks, and acceptance of higher levels of contaminants. Since 1990, the production of fish and fish products has declined without interruption. Direct subsidies from the federal government ceased in 1994. As a result, the proportion of unprocessed fish products has steadily risen since 1990. Badly worn ships and equipment continue to limit production. Russia is eligible to catch up to five million tons of fish outside its territorial waters, but typically only reaches one million tons.

25 FORESTRY

Russia's forested areas are vast. In 2000 an estimated 851.4 million hectares (2,104 million acres) were classified as forested—an area larger than the total land area of Australia. Only half of this area is commercially accessible and only 7–10% is currently exploited. Russia contains 25% of the world's forested area; 20% of the world's forests are in Siberia. The forest stock in Russia is 80% coniferous, consisting mainly of spruce, fir, larch, and pine in subarctic areas; these stands account for 52% of the world's coniferous areas. De-

ciduous trees (birch, oak, beech, ash, maple, elm) grow further south and account for 13% of the world's deciduous forests.

In 2004, the timber cut yielded 182 million cu m (6.4 billion cu ft) of roundwood. Production that year included (in cubic meters): sawn timber, 21,500,000; plywood and particleboard, 7,159,000. Paper and paperboard production totaled 6,789,000 tons. In 2004, Russian exports of forest products were valued at over $5.4 billion. China, Finland, and Japan are the major export markets.

In 1992, a year after the dissolution of the USSR, the forest products industry underwent massive changes. Hundreds of inexperienced new businessmen were attracted to the business of buying logs from newly unregulated leskhozes (forest villages legally entitled to harvest and manage forests). Widespread privatization in the forest products industry began in 1993. Rocleskhoz, the federal forest service, is responsible for overseeing management of forests. The forestry industry is a multi-layered bureaucracy where wood processing companies must pay about 40 different taxes, which has prompted some to act outside the official system. During the 1990s, about 50% of all forestry firms went out of business, and about 60% of the firms remaining are believed to be on the verge of bankruptcy. The failing firms are often pressured to cut trees and sell logs for quick cash to pay off debts so they will be allowed to stay in business. Poaching, unsustainable logging, and fire damage are growing problems. Much of the forestry equipment is too old or expensive to operate, with the result that output per worker is at 1960s levels. Although the allowable forest cut is 559 million cu m (1.97 billion cu ft), an estimated 52% of logging enterprises were operating at a loss in 2005. Though the government is trying to encourage exports of higher value products, lack of investment has hindered plans to decrease the 40% export share of softwood and hardwood logs. Russia's forestry sector only contributes 3% to GDP.

26 MINING

With bountiful and diverse minerals, Russia, the world's largest country in land area, occupying 75% of the former Soviet Union, had a significant percentage of the world's mineral resources and mineral production. Russia is one of the largest producers of palladium and nickel, as well as of aluminum and platinum-group metals (PGMs), potash, gold, and mined copper. Russia also produced a large percentage of the Commonwealth of Independent States' (CIS) bauxite, coal, cobalt, diamond, lead, mica, natural gas, oil, tin, zinc, and many other metals, industrial minerals, and mineral fuels. Exports under the "Mineral Products" category accounted for around 75% or $80 billion of Russia's exports by value in 2002. Of that total, natural gas exports by value totaled over $15 billion, while crude oil and petroleum products accounted for nearly another $40 billion in 2002.

More than half of Russia's mineral resources were east of the Urals. The most significant regions for mining were Siberia, particularly East Siberia, for cobalt, columbium (niobium), copper (70% of Russia's reserves), gold, iron ore, lead (76% of the country's reserves), molybdenum, nickel (becoming depleted), PGMs, tin, tungsten, zinc, asbestos, diamond, fluorspar, mica, and talc; the Kola Peninsula, for cobalt, columbium, copper, nickel, rare-earth metals, phosphate (the majority, in the form of apatite), and tantalum; North Caucasus (copper, lead, molybdenum, tungsten, and zinc); the Russian Far East (gold, lead, silver, tin, tungsten, and zinc); the Urals, with bauxite, beryllium, cobalt, copper, iron ore, lead, magnesite, nickel, titanium, vanadium, zinc, asbestos, bismuth, potash (96% of the country's reserves), soda ash, talc, and vermiculite; and the region near the Arctic Circle (cobalt, gold, mercury, nickel, tin, phosphate, and uranium). The Kaliningrad region contained 95% of the world's amber deposits, and Russia possessed 10% of the world's copper reserves. Metallurgical enterprises in Kola, North Caucasus, and the Urals were operating on rapidly depleting resource bases, and were experiencing raw material shortages.

A large percentage of Russian reserves were in remote northern and eastern regions that lack transport, were distant from major population and industrial centers, and experience severe climates, and enterprises built there in the Soviet era had curtailed operations sharply. Efforts to develop new large deposits of nonferrous metals near the eastern Baikal-Amur railroad were not progressing. One researcher proposed the creation of small mining enterprises to develop the rich small deposits of eastern Russia. Reserves of iron ore were sufficient to last 15–20 years; those of nonferrous metals, 10–30 years. Reserves of major minerals included potash, 1.8 billion tons; magnesite, 585 million tons; bauxite, 250 million tons; phosphate rock, 240 million tons; asbestos, 100 million tons; fluorspar, 60 million tons; manganese, 15 million tons; nickel, 6.3 million tons; vanadium, 5 million tons; zinc, 4 million tons; antimony, 3 million tons; and lead, 3 million tons.

Output of iron ore (gross weight) was 84.236 million tons in 2002, up from an estimated 82.5 million metric tons in 2001. The largest producer was Kursk Magnetic Anomaly, at Zheleznogorsk and Gubkin, with a 50 million ton per year capacity.

Output of copper was 695,000 metric tons in 2002. The Noril'sk complex, in East Siberia, produced 70% of the country's copper, and planned to increase output of cuprous ore from its Oktyabr'skiy underground mine, from 100,000 tons per year to 1.6 million tons, because the cuprous ores were 40% higher in copper content than the nickel-rich ores. The Oktyabr'skiy mine supplied 70% of Noril'sk's copper output, and was planning to decrease production of the nickel-rich ores.

PGM production included 69,000 kg of palladium, and 34,000 kg of platinum. Sixty percent of PGM output came from the Oktyabr'skiy mine, Noril'sk, and a plan to expand output at the mine of cuprous ores by a factor of 16 was projected to yield more PGMs, as would two new nickel-rich mines, the Glubokiy and the Skalisty, that had a high PGM content.

The output of other metals in 2002 was: bauxite, 3.8 million metric tons (estimated); mined nickel, 310,000 metric tons (estimated); mined zinc, 130,000 metric tons; mined lead, 13,500 metric tons (estimated); magnesite, one million metric tons (estimated); mined tin, 2,900 metric tons (estimated); titanium sponge, from the Perm' region in the Urals, 23,000 metric tons (estimated); molybdenum, 2,900 metric tons (estimated); and mined cobalt, 4,600 metric tons (estimated). Gold mine output was 158,000 kg (estimated). Russia also produced the metal minerals alumina, nepheline concentrate, antimony, white arsenic, bismuth, chromium, manganese, mercury, silver, tungsten, and baddeleyite zirconium. Russia, which had the capacity to mine vanadium, stopped mining beryllium in the mid-1990s, and continued producing cobbed beryl.

Industrial mineral production in 2002 included: phosphate rock (apatite concentrate and sedimentary rock), 4.4 million metric tons (estimated); marketable potash, 4.4 million metric tons (estimated); mica, 100,000 metric tons (estimated); fluorspar concentrate, 200,000 metric tons (estimated); and gem and industrial diamonds, 11.5 million carats each. Russia also produced the industrial minerals amber, asbestos, barite, boron, hydraulic cement, kaolin clay, feldspar, graphite, gypsum, iodine, lime, lithium minerals, nitrogen, salt, sodium compounds, sulfur (including native and pyrites), sulfuric acid, talc, and vermiculite. Russia's only producer of amber, Kaliningrad Amber Works, was the world's largest producer, yielding 441.8 tons in 2000, 364.5 in 1999, and 512.2 in 1998.

Despite decreased metal output compared with the Soviet period (e.g., 20% as much tin), Russia was producing more aluminum, lead, and zinc in 2000 than during the Soviet era. Ten percent of the technology employed in the nonferrous mining and metallurgy sector was rated as world class, labor productivity was one-third below that of advanced industrialized countries, and energy expenditures were 20–30% higher. Another problem was that the resource base for metallurgical enterprises was not competitive in terms of quality, with the exception of antimony, copper, nickel, and molybdenum. More than one-half of industrial mineral output was exported, depriving the domestic sector of needed supplies, especially barite, bentonite, crystalline graphite, and kaolin. Russia has not been successful in attracting foreign investment for developing its mineral deposits, because of high and unpredictable taxes, an unreliable legal system, insecure licensing, unequal treatment between domestic and foreign partners, a weak banking system, and the inability to directly export commodities.

27 ENERGY AND POWER

Russia possesses enormous reserves of oil, natural gas, and coal. It is the largest exporter of natural gas in the world, the world's second-largest exporter of petroleum, and the third-largest consumer of energy in the world.

As of 1 January 2005, Russia's proven reserves of oil were estimated at 60 billion barrels, according to the Oil and Gas Journal. Most of that oil is located between the Central Siberian Plateau and the Ural Mountains, in Western Siberia. Of that amount, about 14 billion barrels are located just north of Japan on Sakhalin Island. Although Russian production fell from 7,819,000 barrels per day in 1992 to 6,070,000 barrels per day in 1998, output since 1999 has risen steadily to an estimated 9,300,000 barrels per day in 2004. Russia has 41 oil refineries with a combined crude oil processing capacity estimated at 5.44 million barrels per day, as of December 2004. However, many are inefficient, old and in need of being modernized. Exports are handled by pipeline, rail and barge transport. For the period January through September 2004, pipelines carried 60% or 4 million barrels of oil per day. Exports by rail accounted for 33% of oil exports, or 2.2 million barrels per day. Barges and other traffic accounted for 7% or two million barrels per day. In 2004, net oil exports were estimated at 6.7 million barrels per day.

As of 1 January 2005, Russia had the world's largest reserves of natural gas, estimated at 1,680 trillion cubic ft, more than two times those of Iran, the next largest county. Russia in 2004 was also the world's largest producer and exporter of natural gas. In that year, natural gas output totaled an estimated 22.4 trillion cu ft, with exports at an estimated 6.5 trillion cu ft. However, in spite of its vast reserves of natural gas, Russia's natural gas production and consumption have remained relatively flat since 1992. In that year natural gas production totaled 22.62 trillion cu ft, with domestic demand at 16.46 trillion cu ft. In 2004, production and consumption were estimated at 21.80 trillion cubic ft and 15.29 cu ft, respectively. The main causes for this are: aging fields; insufficient export pipeline capacity; government regulation; and Russia's state-run natural gas monopoly, Gazprom, which operates the country's network of natural gas pipelines, and produces almost 90% of the country's natural gas. In addition, three major gas fields in Western Siberia, the Urengoi, Yamburg, and Medvezh'ye Fields, which provide Gazprom with more than 70% of its production, are in decline.

Russia's proven coal reserves, estimated at 173 billion short tons as of 1 January 2004, were also the second-largest in the world. Coal production in 2003, according to the Energy Information Administration (EIA), was estimated at 294.1 million short tons, while output in 2004, was estimated by the Russian Energy Ministry at 308.6 million short tons, less than one-third of US production. Domestic demand for coal in 2003 was estimated at 254.8 million short tons.

Although electric power generation fell following the breakup of the Soviet Union, output has begun to recover since 1999. In 2003 and 2004, Russian electric power output was estimated at 850.6 billion kWh, and at 915.0 billion kWh, respectively. Consumption of electricity in 2003 and 2004 was estimated at 780.0 billion kWh and 860.0 billion kWh, respectively. Total installed capacity in 2004 was estimated at 208 million kW, of which thermal generation accounted for 68% of electrical capacity, hydro accounted for 22% of capacity, and nuclear 10% of capacity. As of February 2005, Russia had more than 440 thermal and hydroelectric generating stations and 31 nuclear reactors. In 2001, a 1,000 MW reactor began operating at the Rostov facility.

28 INDUSTRY

Major manufacturing industries include crude steel, cars and trucks, aircraft, machine equipment, chemicals (including fertilizers), plastics, cement and other building materials, medical and scientific instruments, textiles, handicrafts, paper, television sets, appliances, and foodstuffs.

Steel production remains a key industry. Once the world leader in the production of steel, that Russian industry fell on hard times in the 1980s as Soviet-made products could not keep up with the quality or output of competitors. Nonetheless, plants continue to operate although less than half use updated equipment.

Aluminum and nickel production continue, particularly in mineral-rich Siberia. The largest companies are the Noril'sk Nickel Joint-Stock Company, Bratsk Aluminum, Krasnoyarsk Aluminum, and Sayan Aluminum. European Russia and the Ural region continue to serve as the center for the production of textiles and machine industry. Chemical production is scattered throughout the country, while the center of the oil and gas industry remains the region of the Caucasus Mountains and Caspian Sea. Russia holds the world's largest natural gas reserves, the second-largest coal reserves, and the eighth-largest oil reserves. It is also the world's largest exporter of natural gas, the second-largest oil ex-

porter, and the third-largest energy consumer. The oil industry is dominated by 11 large companies which account for around 90% of production and close to 80% of refining. Russia had 41 oil refineries in 2005, with a total capacity of 5.44 million barrels per day. Russia's energy riches bring it political power. As of 2006, a proposed 1,200 km, $5 billion gas pipeline along the Baltic seabed was due to be completed in 2010; it would offer Russia's gas export monopoly, Gazprom, a direct link with its main Western European markets, bypassing Poland and the Baltic states, which had hoped for an alternate route bringing them extra transit fees.

Industrial expansion is mainly in consumer goods and food processing, often embraced by enterprises converting from military production, which dominated industry output in the former Soviet Union.

Russia's industrial base is outmoded and must be restructured or replaced in order for the country to maintain strong economic growth. Nonetheless, Russia emerged from its 1998 economic crisis with an industrial growth rate of 5.2% in 2001. That year, industry accounted for 39% of GDP and employed 28% of the work force. In 2004, the industrial production growth rate was 6.4%; industry accounted for 33.9% of GDP and some 22% of the labor force. Oil, natural gas, metals, and timber made up 80% of Russia's exports in 2004, followed by iron and steel, aluminum, and machinery and equipment. Russia's wealth of, and export of, natural resources leave it vulnerable to swings in world prices. Other industrial areas of growth in the mid-2000s included construction, automotive equipment, aircraft, and food processing.

29 SCIENCE AND TECHNOLOGY

The Russian Academy of Sciences, founded in 1725, is the chief coordinating body for scientific research in Russia through its science councils and commissions. It has sections of physical, technical, and mathematical sciences; chemical, technological, and biological sciences, and earth sciences, and controls a network of nearly 300 research institutes. The Russian Academy of Agricultural Sciences, founded in 1929, has departments of plant breeding and genetics; arable farming and the use of agricultural chemicals; feed and fodder crops production; plant protection; livestock production; veterinary science; mechanization, electrification, and automation in farming; forestry; the economics and management of agricultural production; land reform and the organization of land use; land reclamation and water resources; and the storage and processing of agricultural products. It controls a network of nearly 100 research institutes. It supervises a number of research institutes, experimental and breeding stations, dendraria and arboreta. The Russian Academy of Medical Sciences, founded in 1944, has departments of preventive medicine, clinical medicine, and medical and biological sciences, and controls a network of nearly 100 research institutes.

The Russian Federation in 2002 had 3,415 scientists and engineers, and 579 technicians engaged in research and development (R&D) per million people. In the same period, R&D expenditures totaled $14,733.916 million, or 1.24% of GDP. Of that amount, the largest portion, 58.4%, came from government sources, while business accounted for 30.8%. Higher education, private nonprofit organizations and foreign sources accounted for 0.3%, 0.1% and 8%, respectively. High technology exports in 2002 totaled $2.897 billion, or 13% of the country's manufactured exports.

Russia has nearly 250 universities and institutes offering courses in basic and applied sciences. In 1987–97, science and engineering students accounted for 50% of university enrollment.

30 DOMESTIC TRADE

A central marketplace is a common feature of urban areas in Russia. Outside of Moscow and St. Petersburg, small open markets and kiosks are the primary retail establishments. Nationwide distribution channels are still largely undefined.

Many consumer goods, which were often traded via the black market during the Soviet era, are now openly available. However, inflation and slow economic recovery severely constrain domestic purchasing power. Since the underground economy was so well-developed during the Soviet period, distribution and trade through informal channels is still common. The appearance and rapid development of organized crime in post-Soviet Russia may also be seen as a result of Russia's affinity for informal domestic economic activity; local businesses are often forced to pay protection money to organized crime. Commercial advertisement, virtually unknown during the Soviet era, is now commonly used.

As of 2006, a value-added tax of 18% (VAT) applies to most goods and services. The VAT is reduced to 10% for certain foods and children's clothing. Pharmaceuticals and certain financial services are exempt. In 2004, a regional 5% sales tax was abolished. Credit cards are being accepted at major hotels and restaurants in Moscow and St. Petersburg, but many other retail establishments still operate on a cash-only basis.

Business hours are generally 9 AM to 5 PM, Monday to Friday, but the most common times to find workers working is from 10 AM to 6 PM. In the provinces, work finishes earlier.

31 FOREIGN TRADE

Principal exports have traditionally been oil, natural gas, minerals, military equipment and weapons, gold, shipping, and transport services. Principal imports include machinery and equipment, consumer goods, medicines, meat, grain, sugar, and semifinished metal products. Mainly because of high international oil prices, export revenue soared after 2000. Import growth picked up over the same period as a result of rising real incomes and real ruble appreciation. The trade surplus increased to $87 billion in 2004.

The primary exports in 2004 were: oil, fuel, and gas (54.6% of all exports); precious metals (15.8%); machinery and transportation equipment (6.8%); and chemicals (6%). The main imports were: machinery and transportation equipment (27.6% of total imports); food, beverages, and agricultural products (12.3%); chemicals (11%); and metals (4.9%). Russia's major markets in 2004 were Germany (7.9% of all exports), the Netherlands (6.1%), China (6.1%), and the United States (5.7%). Russia's main suppliers in 2004 were Germany (13% of all imports), Ukraine (5.8%), China (5.8%), and Italy (5.1%).

32 BALANCE OF PAYMENTS

Foreign trade was largely deregulated in early 1992, and the trade balance contracted throughout the year; exports declined by 35% to $15.4 billion, while imports fell by 24% to $14.9 billion during the first half of 1992 compared with the same period of 1991. The current account deficit was estimated at $4 billion in 1992, due to the significant decrease in imports. As of the beginning of

1993, there was a dire shortage of hard currency reserves, which severely limited importation possibilities of consumer and capital goods. Since 1993, however, Russia has run a surplus on the current account.

In 2004, Russia's total exports were $182 billion and imports were $94.8 billion for a trade surplus of roughly $87 billion. The current-account surplus had been sizeable as of 2004, reaching $60.6 billion that year. The current-account balance averaged 10% of GDP over the 2001–05 period.

33 BANKING AND SECURITIES

The Central Bank of the Russian Federation was created in January 1992 from the old Soviet banking system headed by Gosbank (The Soviet State Bank). The bank heads a two-tier banking system, and implements a monetary policy and regulates the com-

Principal Trading Partners – Russia (2003)

(In millions of US dollars)

Country	Exports	Imports	Balance
World	133,716.8	57,415.2	76,301.6
Special Categories	28,046.0	447.5	27,598.5
Netherlands	8,253.0	1,255.9	6,997.1
China	7,815.1	3,300.9	4,514.2
Belarus	7,559.3	4,898.7	2,660.6
Germany	6,344.9	8,104.9	-1,760.0
Ukraine	6,265.9	4,397.8	1,868.1
Italy-San Marino-Holy See	5,787.6	2,397.7	3,389.9
Cyprus	4,242.5	...	4,242.5
United Kingdom	3,905.0	1,428.8	2,476.2
Finland	3,726.8	1,846.4	1,880.4

(…) data not available or not significant.

SOURCE: *2003 International Trade Statistics Yearbook,* New York: United Nations, 2004.

Balance of Payments – Russia (2003)

(In millions of US dollars)

Current Account		**35,845.0**
Balance on goods	60,493.0	
Imports	-75,436.0	
Exports	135,929.0	
Balance on services	-11,092.0	
Balance on income	-13,171.0	
Current transfers	-385.0	
Capital Account		**-995.0**
Financial Account		**342.0**
Direct investment abroad	-9,727.0	
Direct investment in Russia	6,725.0	
Portfolio investment assets	-2,543.0	
Portfolio investment liabilities	-2,338.0	
Financial derivatives	640.0	
Other investment assets	-16,472.0	
Other investment liabilities	24,056.0	
Net Errors and Omissions		**-7,430.0**
Reserves and Related Items		**-27,762.0**

(…) data not available or not significant.

SOURCE: *Balance of Payment Statistics Yearbook 2004,* Washington, DC: International Monetary Fund, 2004.

mercial banking sector by setting the reserve requirements and the discount rate. The currency unit of Russia is the ruble, a currency that is in the process of becoming fully convertible with world currency. Russia, along with a few other countries of the former Soviet Union, decided to keep the ruble as its currency. The other important state bank is the Rosevneshtorgbank (Bank for Foreign Trade of the Russian Federation).

Around 2,000 commercial banks operate in Russia, a third of which are former specialized state banks. The rest are new institutions. Commercial banks include the Commercial Bank Industriaservis, the Commercial Credit Bank, the Commercial Conservation Bank, the Commercial Innovation Bank, the International Moscow Bank, St. Petersburg's Investment Bank, and the Construction Bank. The International Bank is a bank whose shares are owned by western banks, such as Citibank (US) and the Barclays Groups (UK), interested in doing business in the country.

Sberbank held around 86% of the population's savings in 1994. Having around 2,000 branches, it is by far the largest banking institution in the country. Sberbank became a joint-stock company in 1991, with the Central Bank taking a 20% shareholding. In addition to Sberbank (the Savings Bank), there were four other specialized banks: the Foreign Trade Bank (Vneshtorgbank), which is now more concerned with retail and corporate banking; the Bank for Construction and Industry (Promstroibank); the Agriculture Bank (Agroprombank); and the Social Sector Bank (Zhilotsbank). Formerly these were joint-stock banks but they relied on cheap credit from Gosbank.

The International Monetary Fund reports that in 2001, currency and demand deposits—an aggregate commonly known as M1—were equal to $40.9 billion. In that same year, M2—an aggregate equal to M1 plus savings deposits, small time deposits, and money market mutual funds—was $72.8 billion. The money market rate, the rate at which financial institutions lend to one another in the short term, was 10.1%. The discount rate, the interest rate at which the central bank lends to financial institutions in the short term, was 25%.

Russia had a small stock market in 1992. The market is considered an emerging market by Western investors with the potential for significant growth in coming years. Although the first stock market opened in Moscow in 1991, over 100 were in operation by 1996. The range, as well as the volume, of securities traded has been rapidly expanding. Inadequate regulation and custody registration systems have been the main bottlenecks in development. A Commission for Securities and Stock Market was established in late 1994. The second half of 1996 witnessed a huge rally in the value of Russian equity as it became clear that economic reforms would continue following the reelection of Boris Yeltsin as president.

Nevertheless, Russia's financial woes continued. In August 1998 the government defaulted on its debt. This action, in turn, led to the collapse of Russia's financial markets as the government abandoned support for the ruble and ceased bond payments. As a result, many banks became insolvent; only Central Bank intervention allowed many depositors to rescue a portion of their funds. Since Sberbank was originally a savings bank for the Soviet people, after the financial crisis of 1998 it received individual accounts from banks liquidated by the government. As a result, it has an unmatched network of 50 branches and over 2,000 outlets handling millions of accounts, both private and commercial. Also following the 1998 crisis, a group of new banks actually grew larger because of their avoidance of speculation in the short term loans on which the government had to default, and their dedication to professional services. These banks, which have prospered despite the weak economy (or perhaps because of it), include the Bank of Moscow, Alfa-Bank, Rosbank, Mezhprombank, Mosbusinessbank, MDM Bank, Sobinbank, National Reserve Bank, and Gazprom Bank.

The subsequent adoption of a tight monetary policy prevented the onset of hyperinflation and has contributed to the ongoing recovery. In fact, 2001 saw a considerable amount of economic firming. Market capitalization in combined Russian stock markets was, at $76 billion, nearly double the 2000 level, and the RSF Russia 100 Index, at 8602.7, was up 91% from the previous year. As of January 2002, the RSF Russia 100 Index was replaced by the S&P/RUX Composite Index. As of end 2004, that index stood at 760.9, up 15% from the previous year. In 2004, there were 215 companies listed on Russia's stock exchanges, which as of that year had a combined market capitalization of $267.957 billion.

³⁴INSURANCE

In 1993, a total of 1,524 Russian companies were licensed to sell insurance and another 750 companies had applied for licenses. However, fewer than 2% of the operating firms had assets over R100 million ($80,000), and premium volume for the first nine months of 1993 amounted to only 1.3% of the GDP (as compared with volume of 2.9% for the former Soviet Union in 1990).

Property insurance is the largest segment of the market with 880 companies. There are 775 cargo insurance firms, and 600 that sell life insurance. The various companies are gradually consolidating into groups.

Regulation of the industry is low. For example, in 1994, to open a business, the minimum capital requirement was two million rubles for an insurance company and 15 million rubles for reinsurance. Rosgosstrakh held a virtual monopoly on the domestic insurance market with 90% of policies, while Ingosstrakh held about 50% of the market in export and import insurance. One of the largest newcomers is Ask, a commercial company. Foreign ownership in insurance companies in 2002 was limited to 49% in order to protect private insurers. The industry is regulated by the Russian Insurance Inspectorate. Compulsory insurance includes third-party automobile liability, medical insurance, pension, social insurance, and fire and accident insurance. Starting in January of 1996, companies were able to deduct their insurance premiums as a business expense for tax purposes.

In 2003, the value of all direct insurance premiums written totaled $14.088 billion, of which nonlife premiums accounted for $9.220 billion. For that same year, Russia's top nonlife insurer was Ingosstrakh, with gross written nonlife premiums (excluding compulsory insurance) of $416 million, while the country's leading life insurers that year, was Stolichnoe, with gross domestic life insurance premiums of $1,319.8 million.

³⁵PUBLIC FINANCE

Since the breakup of the COMECON and the Soviet Union, trade disruptions and friction between Russia and the governments of the former Soviet republics had led to an enormous expansion of

Public Finance – Russia (2003)

(In billions of rubles, central government figures)

Revenue and Grants	**3,644.5**	**100.0%**
Tax revenue	1,758.5	48.3%
Social contributions	1,107.8	30.4%
Grants	1.1	<1.0%
Other revenue	777	21.3%
Expenditures	**3,348.6**	**100.0%**
General public services	1,177.3	35.2%
Defense	381.8	11.4%
Public order and safety	273.4	8.2%
Economic affairs	163.8	4.9%
Environmental protection	11.3	0.3%
Housing and community amenities	...	...
Health	38.2	1.1%
Recreational, culture, and religion	28.7	0.9%
Education	100.4	3.0%
Social protection	1,173.8	35.1%

(…) data not available or not significant.

SOURCE: *Government Finance Statistics Yearbook 2004*, Washington, DC: International Monetary Fund, 2004.

the fiscal deficit. The deficit was financed largely through sales of domestic government securities and borrowing from international financial institutions.

The US Central Intelligence Agency (CIA) estimated that in 2005 the Russian Federation's central government took in revenues of approximately $176.7 billion and had expenditures of $125.6 billion. Revenues minus expenditures totaled approximately $51.1 billion. Public debt in 2005 amounted to 15.6% of GDP. Total external debt was $230.3 billion.

The International Monetary Fund (IMF) reported that in 2003, the most recent year for which it had data, central government revenues were R3,644.5 billion and expenditures were R3,348.6 billion. The value of revenues was us$119 million and expenditures us$109 million, based on an exchange rate for 2003 of us$1 = R30.6920 as reported by the IMF. Government outlays by function were as follows: general public services, 35.2%; defense, 11.4%; public order and safety, 8.2%; economic affairs, 4.9%; environmental protection, 0.3%; health, 1.1%; recreation, culture, and religion, 0.9%; education, 3.0%; and social protection, 35.1%.

36TAXATION

Russia's tax system has historically been confusing, inefficient, unwieldy, and overbearing. Businesses and individuals routinely fail to pay their taxes on time, if at all. The government's need for money to pay pensions and salaries fueled a proliferation of taxes, including a tax on people crossing Russia's borders, additional levies on freight, new transit fees, and a tax on yields from government securities. In 1996, 26 tax collectors were killed, six were kidnapped, and 41 had their homes burned down. In the first half of 1997, the government only collected 57% of its targeted tax revenues.

Since 1999, the tax system has been the focus of a major reform effort aimed at reducing tax loads, improving collection rates, and bringing the system in line with those of advanced, market economies. The new Tax Code cut the number of official taxes from over 200 to about 40, and sought to end many loopholes. Part One of the new Tax Code, effective 1 January 1999, set out the administrative framework for the new system. There are three levels of taxation, federal, regional, and local. The principal taxes collected at the federal level are the profit tax on organizations (with payments divided among all three levels of government), a capital gains tax, a personal income tax (13% flat tax), the Unified Social Tax (replacing payroll contributions to four separate social benefit funds), a value-added tax (VAT—with the standard rate of 18% as of 2005), excise taxes, a securities tax (0.8% on nominal value with exemptions for initial issues), customs duties and customs fees, and federal license fees. At the regional level the principal taxes are an assets tax (2.2%), a real estate tax, a transport tax, sales taxes (maximum 5% in 2003), a tax on gambling, and regional license fees. Two turnover taxes at the state level, a social infrastructure maintenance tax (Housing Fund Tax) and a road users' tax, considered to be among the most onerous under the previous tax system, have been abolished; the Housing Fund Tax in 2001, and the roads tax in 2003. At the local level there are land taxes, individual property taxes, taxes on advertising expenses (beyond allowable limits as a proportion of sales), inheritance and gift taxes, and local license fees.

As of 2005, the corporate income tax was 24%, with payments split 5% to the federal budget, 13–17% payable to the regional governments, and 2% to the local level. Because regional governments are allowed to reduce their corporate rate to as low as 13%, the total minimum rate is 20%. Foreign companies pay withholding of 20%, and dividends paid to nonresidents are charged a 15% withholding rate (down from 18%).

The most striking provision in Russia's 1999 tax reforms is the replacement of its progressive income tax schedule (set out in the tax law of December 1991 with rates from 12–30%) with a flat tax of 13% applied to almost all income categories. The rationale is that the lower, simpler tax will generate more revenue by reducing Russia's pervasive tax-evasion. Exceptions to the 13% rate include a 15% rate on dividend income and on the income of nonresidents from Russian sources. There are also taxes on gambling income, lottery prizes, deemed income from low-interest or interest-free loans, some insurance payments, and excessive bank interest. The Unified Social Tax is a regressive schedule of payroll taxes ranging from 35.6–2% and is based on the gross income received by the employee. All voluntary insurance payments are tax deductible.

Russia's VAT, its main indirect tax, had a standard rate of 18% as of January 2005 that was scheduled to 16% as of January 2006. Exemptions from VAT for pharmaceuticals and license fees have been narrowed or removed. There are also excise taxes on items such as gasoline and other oil products, natural gas, alcohol, tobacco, and cars, motorcycles, and jewelry.

37CUSTOMS AND DUTIES

In 1992, Russia eliminated many of the import restrictions imposed by the former Soviet Union. At the beginning of 2001, Russia put into effect a new and simpler tariff structure, consisting of four basic rates: 5%, 10%, 15%, and 20%. This effectively lowered the tariff ceiling from 30% to 20%. There is also an 18% value-added tax (VAT) on most imported goods, except for food products, which carry a VAT of only 10%. There are excise taxes on luxury goods, alcohol, tobacco, and autos. In total, these duties make imported goods essentially noncompetitive in the troubled Russian economy.

38 FOREIGN INVESTMENT

In September 1991, a foreign investment law promoting the transfer of capital, technology, and know-how went into effect. Nonresidents may acquire partial shareholdings or form wholly owned subsidiaries in Russia. Foreign firms may obtain licenses to exploit natural resources. Foreign investors can be exempted from import duties and export taxes, and there is limited relief from profits tax, varying by sector and region. However, foreign investors remain concerned with the overall business climate in Russia. Vague business laws, an incoherent tax system, crime and corruption in commercial transactions, and a weak commitment to reform continue to erode investor confidence.

In 1997, the annual inflow of foreign direct investment (FDI) to Russia peaked at $4.87 billion, but then fell to $2.76 billion in 1998 in the context of the Russian financial crisis. FDI recovered to $3.3 billion in 1999, and for the three years 2000, 2001, and 2002 averaged about $2.6 billion a year. Cumulative FDI in Russia from 1991 to April 2003 was $19.6 billion. Russia's share of world FDI flows has persistently been only about 30% of its share of world GDP, an indication of its lack of success in attracting foreign investment.

As of 2005, roughly three-quarters of the economy had been privatized, although many privatized enterprises continue to have significant state-held blocks of shares. Tax reforms since 2000 have aimed to rationalize the tax system, reducing the number of taxes and the corporate tax burden. The corporate tax rate was lowered from 35% to 24% at the start of 2002. FDI inflows averaged 1.6% of GDP over the 2001–05 period. Investment inflows for the first nine months of 2004 amounted to just over $29 billion (this figure includes direct investment, portfolio investment, and "other" investment—largely trade credits). The top foreign investors in Russia are Germany, the United Kingdom, Luxembourg, the Netherlands, the United States, France, and Switzerland.

39 ECONOMIC DEVELOPMENT

In 1991, Russia's parliament enacted legislation aimed at fully privatizing the commercial and service sector by 1994 and placing about half the medium and large companies in private hands by 1995. By the end of 1992, about 6,000 firms had applied to become joint-stock companies, and 1,560 had completed the process; almost one-third of Russia's approximately 250,000 small businesses had been privatized. Housing privatization began late in 1992, and over 2.6 million apartments—about 8% of the total—had been privatized by the end of 1993. In 1996, the government claimed that the nonstate sector produced approximately 70% of gross domestic product (GDP), up from 62% in 1995. Russia's Communist-dominated parliament, however, was quick to criticize the government's privatization efforts which they thought were responsible for the economic decline. In March 1997, over two million people took part in a national strike protesting the economic hardships of privatization and over 100,000 attended rallies in Moscow and St. Petersburg. The government, however, was committed to privatization and largely ignored the parliament and the protests.

During the financial crisis of 1998, Russia became the first modern country to default on its debt. The subsequent collapse of the ruble and investor flight left analysts concerned that Russia would face famine and even governmental collapse. Instead, a period of fiscal restraint restored growth to the Russian economy although it remains vulnerable to sudden fluctuations in the world market. Russia in the early 2000s remained current on its foreign debt; service of the foreign debt amounted to around $14 billion in 2002.

Russia's GDP increased by 4.3% in 2002 over 2001. Lowered inflation and high oil prices fueled that growth. Unemployment and underemployment remain problems, however. In 1998 the government passed an improved bankruptcy code, and in 2001, the Duma passed a deregulation package to improve the business and investment sector. A new corporate tax code went into effect in 2002, lowering the corporate tax rate to 24% from 35%. Cumulative foreign investment increased by 20% in 2002, but was mostly due to increases in loans and trade credits. The banking system is poorly developed, which inhibits economic development. In 2002, the US Department of Commerce designated Russia a "market economy," and the country was invited by the G-7 nations to take part in negotiations, causing the group to be named the G-8.

As of 2006, Russia's reforms had made considerable progress since Vladimir Putin became president in 2000. Progress in such sensitive areas as utilities restructuring and housing reform is slower than in those areas that were targeted by the 2000–02 reform agenda, namely tax reform and deregulation. As of 2006, roughly three-quarters of the Russian economy had been privatized, although the state still held significant blocks of shares in privatized businesses. The large, unwieldy and corrupt bureaucracy remains a problem for reform. Russia ended 2005 with its seventh straight year of economic growth, which averaged about 6.5% annually since the 1998 financial crisis. Russia also improved its international financial position over this period, with foreign debt declining from 90% of GDP in 1998 to approximately 28% of GDP in 2004. Strong oil export earnings allowed Russia to increase its foreign reserves from $12 billion to some $120 billion by yearend 2004. These achievements raised business and investor confidence in Russia's economy, but, in addition to problems already mentioned, the manufacturing base is in serious need of modernization, the banking system is weak, there is a widespread lack of trust in institutions, and underemployment is a severe problem. President Putin by 2006 had taken a number of steps to shore up presidential power, and concerns have been raised that certain forces within the government are looking to reassert further state control over the economy.

40 SOCIAL DEVELOPMENT

A social insurance system provides pensions for old-age, survivorship, and disability. The program is funded by employer payrolls, and self-employed persons and independent farmers contribute a fixed amount monthly. The government provides subsidies when needed. The first laws governing sickness benefits were implemented in 1912. All citizens and refugees are entitled to medical care; employed persons receive cash benefits for sickness. There is also a benefit provided to those caring for a sick child. Work injury is funded by the employer. Maternity benefits cover 100% of earnings from between 10 and 12 weeks before the expected date of childbirth and 10 to 16 weeks after childbirth. A universal system of family allowances provides a birth grant, a funeral grant, and a monthly benefit for each child under the age of 16.

The constitution prohibits discrimination based on race, sex, religion, language, social status or other circumstances. Despite these constitutional provisions, employment discrimination against women and minorities occurs. On average women earn significantly less than men and cluster in the lower-paid jobs and professions. The high cost of maternity care benefits leads some employers to hire men rather than women. Women suffer disproportionately in situations of worker layoffs. There is no law against sexual harassment and abuses in the workplace are common. Spousal abuse is a widespread problem and is treated as a domestic matter rather than a criminal offense. It was estimated in 2004 that 70% of wives were victims of some kind of domestic abuse. Sexual violence and other crimes against women are underreported and the government provides no support services to victims.

In general human rights are respected, but serious violations occur concerning the struggle against rebels in Chechnya. Also, ethnic minorities are subjected to harassment, searches, and arrest by police, and are sometimes denied local authority permission to reside in Moscow. Anti-Semitic rhetoric is increasing and several instances of intimidation and violence have been reported. Muslims continue to face discrimination. Prisoners are subject to mistreatment, unhealthy living conditions, and lack of medical care.

41 HEALTH

As of the mid-1990s, the overall organization of the health care system has largely been carried over from the Soviet era. Primary care has been delivered through basic units called *uchastoks*. In rural areas, these districts are served by health posts staffed by midwives or physicians' assistants, while health centers and urban polyclinics are available in larger population centers. The secondary-care network has also been retained from the Soviet era and consisted of *uchastok* hospitals and health centers, district hospitals and polyclinics, and regional hospitals and polyclinics. Medical facilities throughout the country are generally inadequate, with equipment that is both outdated and in poor condition. A survey conducted in the mid-1990s found a high level of dissatisfaction with the health care system on the part of both the general public and health care personnel, as well as widespread support for privatization. As of 2004, there were an estimated 417 physicians, 787 nurses, and 32 dentists per 100,000 people. Total health care expenditure was estimated at 4.6% of GDP.

As of 2002, the crude birth rate and overall mortality rate were estimated at, respectively, 9.7 and 13.9 per 1,000 people. Infant mortality was 15.39 per 1,000 live births in 2005 and average life expectancy was 67.10 years. The total fertility rate was 1.3 children per woman during her childbearing years. Children up to one year of age were immunized against tuberculosis, 97%; diphtheria, pertussis, and tetanus, 87%; polio, 97%; and measles, 95%.

The heart disease mortality rates for Russian men and women were higher than the average for countries of high human development. The HIV/AIDS prevalence was 1.10 per 100 adults in 2003. As of 2004, there were approximately 860,000 people living with HIV/AIDS in the country. There were an estimated 9,000 deaths from AIDS in 2003.

After the breakup of the Soviet Union diphtheria spread from Russia to its former republics in epidemic numbers. The incidence of tuberculosis was 123 per 100,000 people. The Russian Federation and countries of Central and Eastern Europe lag behind the West in injury prevention. The accidental death rate for children 5–14 in was 39.6 per 100,000 for boys and 16.4 per 100,000 for girls. Deaths by suicide are also very high in the Russian Federation at 41.7 per 100,000 people for men and 7.9 per 100,000 for women (aged 15–24).

42 HOUSING

The right to housing is guaranteed to all citizens by the constitution, but providing for adequate housing for all has become a problem in a time of major economic reforms. In the Soviet-era, most housing (state-owned) was provided free or at very low costs for many citizens. Since 2002, economic reform has called for many residents to begin paying more of the costs for rent, maintenance, and utilities. The government still allows somewhat generous subsidies for low-income families. But the main housing problem seems to be in maintenance and renovation of buildings that are in urgent need of both structural repairs and upgrades in utility systems. In 2004 it was estimated that at least two million people lived in housing that was officially classified as dilapidated. About 11% of all homes were in urgent need of repair and about 9% of all homes needed to be demolished and rebuilt. The annual need for renovation of the existing housing stock was estimated at about 4.5%. In 2004, about 70% of all housing was privately owned.

43 EDUCATION

Education, mostly free and state funded, is also compulsory for 10 years. Primary school covers four years, followed by another five years of basic school. Senior secondary schools offer two-year programs. Vocational secondary schools offer a four-year course of studies. Although Russian is the most common medium of instruction, other languages are also taught, especially at the secondary level. In the early 1990s, many privately owned institutions were opened, and the education system was modified with the introduction of a revised curriculum. The academic year runs from September to June.

In 2001, about 92% of children between the ages of four and five were enrolled in some type of preschool program. Primary school enrollment in 2003 was estimated at about 90% of age-eligible students. In 2001, secondary school enrollment was estimated at about 90% of all age-eligible students. It is estimated that about 93.5% of all students complete their primary education. The student-to-teacher ratio for primary school was at about 17:1 in 2003; the ratio for secondary school was about 11:1.

The St. Petersburg State University, which was founded in 1724, is well known for its education. In 2004, there were 685 state and 367 accredited nonstate higher education institutions in Russia. In 2003, about 69% of the tertiary age population were enrolled in some type of higher education program, 59% for men and 79% for women. The adult literacy rate for 2004 was estimated at about 99.4%.

As of 2003, public expenditure on education was estimated at 3.8% of GDP, or 10.7% of total government expenditures.

44 LIBRARIES AND MUSEUMS

The Russian State Library in Moscow serves as the national library as well as a public, with the largest collection in the country (about

45 million items). It should not be confused with Russian National Library in St. Petersburg, which is one of the oldest public libraries in eastern Europe; it holds over 34 million volumes. There are over 50,000 public libraries throughout the country. Some of the larger collections include the Gorky Moscow Institute of Literature library in Moscow (13.2 million volumes), the State University of Technology library in St. Petersburg (2.9 million volumes), the Bauman Moscow State Engineering University library (three million volumes), the Moscow M. V. Lomonosov State University (7.27 million volumes), the State University at Petersburg (6.4 million volumes), and dozens of other massive collections throughout the country. The Russian Library Association was established in 1994.

Russia has over 1,000 museums. Russian museums house some of the finest collections of European art in the world, the best known of which is the Hermitage in St. Petersburg. Also in St. Petersburg are Dostoevsky Memorial House-Museum, the Literary Museum of the Institute of Russian Literature, the State Russian Museum, and the State Museum of Sculpture, housing the country's largest collection of sculpture. Among the dozens of important museums in Moscow are the State Historical Museum, the State Literature Museum, the Tolstoy House Museum, the Pushkin Museum, the Chekhov House Museum, the Paleontological Museum of the Academy of Sciences, and the Cathedral of the Assumption, a religious arts museum housed in a 15th-century cathedral. The St. Petersburg Erotica Museum opened in 2004.

45 MEDIA

As of 1999, over 1,000 companies were licensed to offer telecommunications services. In 2003, there were an estimated 242 mainline telephones for every 1,000 people; over 5 million people were on a waiting list for telephone service installation. The same year, there were approximately 249 mobile phones in use for every 1,000 people.

In 2004, there were about 2,500 television stations in the country, with about 66% completely or partially owned by the government. The government also maintained ownership of the largest radio stations, Radio Mayak and Radio Rossiya, and the news agencies ITAR TASS and RIA Novosti. In 2000, there were 418 radios and 421 television sets for every 1,000 people. In 2003, there were about 88.7 personal computers in use for every 1,000 people. There were 6 million Internet subscribers in 2002.

In 2005, there were more than 400 daily newspapers in circulation. In 2005, Russia's major daily newspapers, all published in Moscow, were: Moskovski Komsomolets (Moscow Communist Youth, 800,000 est. circulation in 2005); Komsomolskaya Pravda (686,000 in 2005); Trud (Labor, 613,000 in 2005); Rossiiskaya Gazeta (374,000 in 2005); Izvestia (209,000 in 2004); Kommersant (94,000 in 2005); and Nezarisimaya Gazeta (27,000 in 2004). Argumenty I Fakty is a popular weekly with an estimated 2005 circulation of 2.9 million. Novaya Gazeta, published twice a week, has a 2004 estimated circulation of 106,000. Vedomosti is a business daily owned as a joint venture of the Wall Street Journal, Financial Times, and the Independent Media group (a Dutch organization); it has an estimated circulation of 42,000. In 2004, there were an estimated 45,000 registered local periodicals and newspapers.

The constitution provides for freedom of the press and mass information, and the government is said at present to respect these provisions. However, the law contains provisions which give broad interpretive authority to government at all levels for the enforcement of secrecy of sensitive information. Russians are enjoying a freer media than at any time in recent history.

46 ORGANIZATIONS

A chamber of commerce that promotes the economic and business activities of the country to the rest of the world operates in Moscow. The Russian Academy of Entrepreneurship assists business owners. There are several professional associations representing a wide variety fields, such as the Health Workers Union of the Russian Federation and the Association of Russian Automobile Dealers. Some professional associations also promote public education and research in specific technical or scientific fields, such as the Russian Medical Society.

National youth organizations include the Girl Guides and Girl Scouts of Russia, The All-Russia Scout Organizations, the Youth Agrarian Union of Russia, the Siberian Youth Initiative, and YMCA/YWCA. Sports associations are popular and represent a wide variety of pastimes. There are active chapters of the Paralympic Committee and the Special Olympics. The Gaia International Women's Center promotes the advancement of women in business and politics. Several women's groups are organized under the umbrella of the Women's Union of Russia.

Volunteer service organizations, such as the Lions Clubs and Kiwanis International, are also present. The All-Russian Society for Disabled represents the concerns of over 2.5 million people. The International Red Cross and the Red Crescent operate branches throughout the federation. There are also branches of Amnesty International, Greenpeace, United Way, UNICEF, and Habitat for Humanity.

47 TOURISM, TRAVEL, AND RECREATION

In September 1992, Russia lifted its travel restrictions on foreigners, opening the entire country to visitors and tourists. Moscow is a major tourist destination with many attractions including Red Square, the Kremlin, St. Basil's Cathedral, and many other monasteries, churches, museums and other cultural attractions. The most famous of Moscow's parks and gardens is Gorky Park. St. Petersburg is a beautifully preserved neoclassical city with palace-lined waterways. Attractions include the State Hermitage Museum, Peter and Paul Fortress, and the Nevsky Prospekt. Football (soccer), ice hockey, and tennis are popular sports in Russia. Maria Sharapova won the Wimbledon women's title in 2004.

There were 22,521,059 visitors who arrived in Russia in 2003, about 90% of the tourists came from Europe. Tourism receipts totaled $5.8 billion that year. Hotel rooms numbered 177,200 with 364,000 beds and an occupancy rate of 34%.

In 2005, the US Department of State estimated the daily expenses of staying in Moscow at $378. Other areas were less expensive averaging $279 per day.

48 FAMOUS RUSSIANS

Notable among the rulers of prerevolutionary Russia were Ivan III (the Great, 1440–1505), who established Moscow as a sovereign state; Peter I (the Great, 1672–1725), a key figure in the modernization of Russia; Alexander I (1777–1825), prominent both in the war against Napoleon and the political reaction that followed the war; and Alexander II (1818–81), a social reformer who freed the serfs. Mikhail Gorbachev (b.1931) came to power in 1985, initiated reforms of the old Communist system and won the Nobel Peace Prize in 1990.

Mikhail Lomonosov (1711–65), poet and grammarian, also was a founder of natural science in Russia. The poet Gavrila Derzhavin (1743–1816) combined elements of topical satire with intimate, lyrical themes. Aleksandar Radishchev (1749–1802) criticized both religion and government absolutism. Nikolay Karamzin (1766–1826), an early translator of Shakespeare, was the founder of Russian Sentimentalism. The fables of Ivan Krylov (1768/69?–1844) exposed human foibles and the shortcomings of court society. Russia's greatest poet, Aleksandr Pushkin (1799–1837), was also a brilliant writer of prose. Other outstanding poets were Fyodor Tyutchev (1803–73), Mikhail Lermontov (1814–41), and Afanasy Fet (Shen-shing 1820–92). Nikolay Gogol (1809–52), best known for his novel *Dead Souls* and his short stories, founded the realistic trend in Russian literature. Vissarion Belinsky (1811–48) was an influential critic. Noted radical philosophers were Aleksandr Hertzen (1812–70). Nikolay Chernyshevshy (1828–89), and Nikolay Dobrolyubov (1812–91), satirized the weakness of Russian society. Ivan Turgenev (1818–83) is noted for his sketches, short stories, and the novel *Fathers and Sons*. Fyodor Dostoyevsky (1821–81) wrote outstanding psychological novels (*Crime and Punishment, The Brothers Karamazov*). Leo (Lev) Tolstoy (1828–1910), perhaps the greatest Russian novelist (*War and Peace, Anna Karenina*), also wrote plays, essays and short stories. Aleksandr Ostrovsky (1823–86) was a prolific dramatist. The consummate playwright and short-story writer Anton Chekhov (1860–1904) was the greatest Russian writer of the late 19th century. Leonid Nikolayevich Aandreyev (1871–1919) wrote plays and short stories. The novels, stories, and playas of Maksim Gorky (Aleksey Peshkov, 1868–1936) bridged the tsarist and Soviet periods. Ivan Bunin (1870–1953) received the Nobel Prize in 1933 for his novels and short stories. Georgy Plekhanov (1856–1918), a Marxist philosopher and propagandist, also was a literary critic and art theorist, as was Anatoly Lunacharsky (1875–1933).

Russian composers of note include Mikhail Glinka (1804–57), Aleksandar Borodin (1833–87), also a distinguished chemist, Mily Balakirev (1837–1910), Modest Mussorgsky (1839–81), Pyotr Ilyich Tchaikovsky (1840–93), Nikolay Rimsky-Korsakov (1844–1908), Aleksandr Skryabin (1871–1915), Sergey Rakhmaninov (1873–1943), Igor Stravinsky (1882–1971), Sergey Prokofyev (1891–1953), Aram Ilyich Khachaturian (1903–78), Dmitry Kabalevsky (1904–87), and Dmitry Shostakovich (1906–75). Two of the greatest bassos of modern times are the Russian-born Fyodor Chaliapin (1873–1938) and Alexander Kipnis (1891–1978). Serge Koussevitzky (1874–1951), noted conductor of the Boston Symphony Orchestra, was important in Russian musical life before the Revolution.

Outstanding figures in the ballet are the impresario Sergey Diaghilev (1872–1929); the choreographers Marius Petipa (1819–1910), Lev Ivanov (1834–1901), and Mikhail Fokine (1880–1942); the ballet dancers Vaslav Nijinsky (1890–1950), Anna Pavlova (1881–1931), Tamaara Karsavina (1885–1978), Galina Ulanova (1909–1998), and Maya Plisetskaya (b.1925); and the ballet teacher Agrippina Vaganova (1879–1951).

Outstanding figures in the theater include Kostantin Stanislavsky (Alekseyev, 1863–1938), director, actor and theorectician; Vladimir Nemirovich-Danchenko (1858–1943), director, playwright, and founder, with Stanislavsky, of the Moscow Art Theater; and Vsevolod Meyerhold (1873–1942), noted for innovations in stagecraft. Important film directors were Vsevolod Pudovkin (1893–1953), Aleksandr Dovzhenko (1864–1956), Sergey Eisenstein (1898–1948), Vasily Shiksin (1929–74), and Andrei Tarkovsky (1932–87).

Varfolomey (Bartolomeo Francesco) Rastrelli (1700–1771) designed many of the most beautiful buildings in St. Petersburg. Other important Russian architects include Vasily Bazhenov (1737–99), Matvey Kazakov (1733–1812), Andreyan Zakharov (1761–1811), Ivan Starov (1806–58), Vasily Perov (1833/34–82), Vasily Vereshchagin (1842–1904), Ilya Repin (1844–1930), Mikhail Vrubel (1856–1910), Leon (Lev) Bakst (Rosenberg, 1866–1924), and Aleksansr Benois (1870–1960). Modern Russian artists whose work is internationally important include the Suprematist painters Kasimir Malevich (1878–1935) and El (Lazar) Lissitzky (1890–1941), the "Rayonist" painters Natalya Goncharova (1881–1962) and Mikhail Larionov (1881–1964), the Constructivist artist Vladimir Tatlin (1885–1953), and the Spatial sculptor Aleksandar Rodchenko (1891–1956). Famous Russian-born artists who left their native country to work abroad include the painters Alexei von Jawlensky (1864–1941), Vasily Kandinsky (1866–1944), Marc Chagall (1897–1985), and Chaim Soutine (1894–1943) and the sculptors Antoine Pevsner (1886–1962), his brother Naum Gabo (1890–1977), Alexander Archipenko (1887–1964), and Ossip Zadkine (1890–1967).

Prominent Russian scientists of the 19th and 20th centuries include the chemist Dmitry Ivanovich Mendeleyev (1834–1907), inventor of the periodic table; Aleksandr Mikhailovich Butlerov (1828–86), a creator of the theory of chemical structure; Nikolay Yegorovich Zhukovsky (1847–1921), a founder of modern hydrodynamics and aerodynamics; Pyotr Nikolayevich Lebedev (1866–1912), who discovered the existence of the pressure of light; Nikolay Ivanovich Lobachevsky (1792–1856), pioneer in non-Euclidean geometry; Ivan Petrovich Pavlov (1849–1936), creator of the theory on the higher nervous systems of animals and man, who received the Nobel Prize in 1904 for his work on digestive glands; Ilya Ilyich Mechnikov (Elie Metchnikoff, 1845–1916), who received the Nobel Prize in 1908 for his Phagocyte theory; Kliment Arkadyevich Timiryazev (1843–1920), biologist and founder of the Russian school of plant physiology; and Aleksandr Stepanovich Popov (1859–1906), pioneer in radio transmission. Among later scientists and inventors are Ivan Vladimirovich Michurin (1855–1935), biologist and plant breeder; Konstantin Eduardovich Tsiolkovsky (1857–1935), scientist and the inventor in the field of the theory and technology of rocket engines, interplanetary travel and aerodynamics; Vladimir Petrovich Filatov (1875–1956), ophthalmologist; Ivan Pavlovich Bardin (1883–1960), metallurgist; Yevgeny Nikanorovich Pavlovsky (1884–1965), parasitologist; Nikolay Ivanovich Vavilov (1887–1943), geneticist; and Leon Theremin (Lev Termen, 1896–1993), pioneer of electronic music. Cosmonaut Yuri Alekseyevich Gagarin (1934–68) was the first person to ever venture into space.

⁴⁹DEPENDENCIES

The Russian Federation has no territories or dependencies.

⁵⁰BIBLIOGRAPHY

Appel, Hilary. *A New Capitalist Order: Privatization and Ideology in Russia and Eastern Europe*. Pittsburgh, Pa.: University of Pittsburgh Press, 2004.

Aslund, Anders. *How Russia Became a Market Economy*. Washington, D.C.: Brookings Institution, 1995.

Blasi, Joseph R. *Kremlin Capitalism: The Privatization of the Russian Economy*. Ithaca, N.Y.: ILR Press, 1997.

Gooding, John. *Rulers and Subjects: Government and People in Russia, 1801–1991*. New York: St. Martin's Press, 1996.

Howe, Sonia E. (ed.). *A Thousand Years of Russian History*. New York: Nova Science, 2005.

Hunter, Robert Edwards. *Engaging Russia as Partner and Participant: The Next Stage of NATO-Russia Relations*. Santa Monica, Calif.: RAND, 2004.

International Smoking Statistics: A Collection of Historical Data from 30 Economically Developed Countries. New York: Oxford University Press, 2002.

Mandel, David. *Labour after Communism: Auto Workers and Their Unions in Russia, Ukraine, and Belarus*. New York: Black Rose Books, 2004.

Mastyugina, Tatiana. *An Ethnic History of Russia: Pre-Revolutionary Times to the Present*. Westport, Conn.: Greenwood Press, 1996.

McCann, Leo (ed.). *Russian Transformations: Challenging the Global Narrative*. New York: RoutledgeCurzon, 2004.

Miller, Steven E. and Dmitri Trenin (eds.). *The Russian Military: Power and Policy*. Cambridge, Mass.: MIT Press, 2004.

Peterson, D. J. *Russia and the Information Revolution*. Santa Monica, Calif.: RAND, 2005.

Pushkareva, N. L. *Women in Russian History: From the Tenth to the Twentieth Century*. Armonk, N.Y.: M. E. Sharpe, 1997.

Raymond, Boris, and Paul Duffy. *Historical Dictionary of Russia*. Lanham, Md.: Scarecrow, 1998.

Shleifer, Andrei. *A Normal Country: Russia after Communism*. Cambridge, Mass.: Harvard University Press, 2005.

Shoemaker, Merle Wesley. *Russia and the Commonwealth of Independent States, 2005*. 36th ed. Harpers Ferry, W.V.: Stryker-Post Publications, 2005.

Summers, Randal W., and Allan M. Hoffman (ed.). *Domestic Violence: A Global View*. Westport, Conn.: Greenwood Press, 2002.

Terterov, Marat (ed.). *Doing Business with Russia: A Guide to Investment Opportunities and Business Practice*. 4th ed. Sterling, Va.: Kogan Page, 2005.

Thurston, Robert W. *Life and Terror in Stalin's Russia, 1934–1941*. New Haven: Yale University Press, 1996.

Tuller, David. *Cracks in the Iron Closet: Travels in Gay and Lesbian Russia*. Boston: Faber and Faber, 1996.

Urban, Michael E. *The Rebirth of Politics in Russia*. Cambridge, England: Cambridge University Press, 1997.

Wyman, Matthew. *Public Opinion in Postcommunist Russia*. New York: St. Martin's Press, 1997.

Yeltsin, Boris Nikolayevich. *The Struggle for Russia*. New York: Times Books, 1994.

SAN MARINO

The Most Serene Republic of San Marino
La Serenissima Repubblica di San Marino

CAPITAL: San Marino

FLAG: The flag is divided horizontally into two equal bands, sky blue below and white above.

ANTHEM: *Onore a te, onore, o antica repubblica (Honor to You, O Ancient Republic).*

MONETARY UNIT: The Italian lira was replaced by the euro as official currency as of 2002. The euro is divided into 100 cents. There are coins in denominations of 1, 2, 5, 10, 20, and 50 cents and 1 euro and 2 euros. There are notes of 5, 10, 20, 50, 100, 200, and 500 euros. €1 = $1.25475 (or $1 = €0.79697) as of 2005. The country issues its own coins in limited numbers as well. Coins of San Marino may circulate in both the republic and in Italy.

WEIGHTS AND MEASURES: The metric system is the legal standard.

HOLIDAYS: New Year's Day, 1 January; Epiphany, 6 January; Anniversary of St. Agatha, second patron saint of the republic, and of the liberation of San Marino (1740), 5 February; Anniversary of the Arengo, 25 March; Investiture of the Captains-Regent, 1 April and 1 October; Labor Day, 1 May; Fall of Fascism, 28 July; Assumption and August Bank Holiday, 14–16 August; Anniversary of the Foundation of San Marino, 3 September; All Saint's Day, 1 November; Commemoration of the Dead, 2 November; Immaculate Conception, 8 December; Christmas, 24–26 December; New Year's Eve, 31 December. Movable religious holidays include Easter Monday and Ascension.

TIME: 1 PM = noon GMT.

¹LOCATION, SIZE, AND EXTENT

San Marino is the third-smallest country in Europe. With an area of 60 sq km (23 sq mi), it extends 13.1 km (8.1 mi) NE–SW and 9.1 km (5.7 mi) SE–NW. Comparatively, the area occupied by San Marino is about 0.3 times the size of Washington, DC. It is a landlocked state completely surrounded by Italy, with a total boundary length of 39 km (24 mi).

²TOPOGRAPHY

The town of San Marino is on the slopes and at the summit of Mt. Titano (755 m/2,477 ft), and much of the republic is coextensive with the mountain, which has major limestone pinnacles. Each of the peaks is crowned by old fortifications; on the north by a castle and the other two by towers. Level areas around the base of Mt. Titano provide land for agricultural use. The San Marino River begins in Italy and flows northward through the western portion of the country, forming part of the nation's western border. The Ausa River in the northwest and the Marano River of the east central region both drain into the Adriatic Sea.

³CLIMATE

The climate is that of northeastern Italy: rather mild in winter, but with temperatures frequently below freezing, and warm and pleasant in the summer, reaching a maximum of 26°C (79°F). Winter temperatures rarely fall below 7°C (19°F). Annual rainfall averages between 56 and 80 cm (22 to 32 in).

⁴FLORA AND FAUNA

The republic has generally the same flora and fauna as northeastern Italy. The hare, squirrel, badger, fox, and porcupine are among the more common animals seen. Most of the landscape has been cultivated with orchards, vineyards, and olive groves.

⁵ENVIRONMENT

Urbanization is the primary concern for the environment; however, the country has shown great care for environmental protection and preservation both within its own borders and in the global arena. Environmental protection is controlled by the Ministry of State for Territory, Environment, and Agriculture. San Marino has no endangered species; however, the lesser horseshoe bat and the common otter are listed as near threatened.

⁶POPULATION

The population of San Marino in 2005 was estimated by the United Nations (UN) at 30,000, which placed it at number 189 in population among the 193 nations of the world. In 2005, approximately 16% of the population was over 65 years of age, with another 15% of the population under 15 years of age. According to the UN, the annual population rate of change for 2005–10 was expected to be 0.3%, a rate the government viewed as satisfactory. The projected population for the year 2025 was 30,000. The population density was 500 per sq km (1,295 per sq mi). San Marino is one of the most densely populated countries in the world.

The UN estimated that 84% of the population lived in urban areas in 2005, and that urban areas were growing at an annual rate of 0.89%. The capital city, San Marino, had a population of 5,000 in that year.

7 MIGRATION

Immigrants come chiefly from Italy; emigration is mainly to Italy, the United States, France, and Belgium. Foreigners who have been resident in San Marino for 30 years can become naturalized citizens.

In 1999, the net migration rate was 4.23 migrants per 1,000 population. In 2005, there was an increase to an estimated 10.84 migrants per 1,000 population. In 2000 the number of migrants living in San Marino was 9,000, approximately one-third of the total population. The government views the migration levels as satisfactory.

8 ETHNIC GROUPS

The native population is predominantly of Italian origin.

9 LANGUAGES

Italian is the official language.

10 RELIGIONS

It has been estimated that over 95% of the population is Roman Catholic; however, while Roman Catholicism is dominant, it is not the state religion. The Catholic Church does receive direct benefits from the State, but so do other charities, including two religions—the Waldensian Church and Jehovah's Witnesses. There are small groups of Baha'is and Muslims. Certain Catholic holidays are recognized as national holidays.

11 TRANSPORTATION

Streets and roads within the republic totaled about 220 km (140 mi) in 2002, and there is regular bus service between San Marino and Rimini. Motor vehicle registrations in 1995 included 22,945 passenger cars and 3,546 commercial vehicles. An electric railroad, 32 km (20 mi) long, between Rimini and San Marino was inaugurated in 1932. Damaged as a result of a British air raid on 26 June 1944, it has been out of service since that time. A 1.5-km (0.9-mi) cable-car service from the city of San Marino to Borgo Maggiore is operated by the government. There is helicopter service between San Marino and Rimini in summer.

12 HISTORY

San Marino, the oldest republic in the world, is the sole survivor of the independent states that existed in Italy at various times from the downfall of the Western Roman Empire to the proclamation of the Kingdom of Italy in 1861. (The Vatican City State, which is also an independent enclave in Italy, was not constituted in its present form until the 20th century.)

According to tradition, the republic was founded in AD 301 by Marinus, a Christian stonecutter who fled from Dalmatia to avoid religious persecution; later canonized, St. Marinus is known in Italian as San Marino. If founded at the time asserted by tradition, San Marino is the oldest existing national state in Europe. There was a monastery in San Marino in existence at least as early as 885.

Because of the poverty of the region and the difficult terrain, San Marino was rarely disturbed by outside powers, and it generally avoided the factional fights of the Middle Ages. For a time, it joined the Ghibellines and was therefore interdicted by Pope Innocent IV in 1247–49. It was protected by the Montefeltro family, later dukes of Urbino, and in 1441, with Urbino, it defeated Sigismondo Malatesta and extended the size of its territory. It was briefly held by Cesare Borgia in 1503, but in 1549 its sovereignty was confirmed by Pope Paul III. In 1739, however, a military force under a papal legate, Cardinal Giulio Alberoni, occupied San Marino and unsuccessfully attempted to get the Sanmarinese to acknowledge his sovereignty over them. In the following year, Pope Clement II terminated the occupation and signed a treaty of friendship with the tiny republic. Napoleon allowed San Marino to retain its liberty; the Sanmarinese are said to have declined his offer to increase their territory on the grounds that smallness and poverty alone had kept them from falling prey to larger states.

In 1849, Giuseppe Garibaldi, the liberator of Italy, took refuge from the Austrians in San Marino; he departed voluntarily shortly before the Austrians were to invade the republic to capture him. San Marino and Italy entered into a treaty of friendship and customs union in 1862. This treaty was renewed in March 1939 and amended in September 1971.

During the period of Mussolini's rule in Italy, San Marino adopted a Fascist type of government. Despite its claim to neutrality in World War II, Allied planes bombed it on 26 June 1944. The raid caused heavy damage, especially to the railway line, and killed a number of persons. San Marino's resources were sorely taxed to provide food and shelter for the over 100,000 refugees who obtained sanctuary during the war.

The elections of 1945 put a coalition of Communists and left-wing Socialists in control of the country. In 1957, some defections from the ruling coalition were followed by a bloodless revolution, aided by Italy, against the government. The leftists surrendered, and some were imprisoned. The rightists, chiefly Christian Democrats, won the election of 1959 and remained in power until 1973, chiefly in coalition with the Social Democrats. In March 1973, after splitting with the Social Democrats, the Christian Democrats formed an unstable coalition with the Socialists. After new elections in May 1978, the Communists, the Socialists, and the Socialist Unity Party, who together commanded a one-seat majority in the legislature, formed a governing coalition; San Marino thus became the only West European country with a Communist-led government. This coalition governed until 1986, when a Communist–Christian Democratic coalition replaced it; this was the first coalition government formed by these two parties in San Marino's history.

As of 2005, the ruling coalition was composed of the Sanmarinese Christian-Democratic Party and the Sanmarinese Socialist Party. In December 2003, Fabio Berardi was named secretary of state for foreign and political affairs, the equivalent of the office of a prime minister.

San Marino's high standard of living makes Sanmarinese citizenship a valuable commodity. With the only ways for foreigners to obtain citizenship being to reside in San Marino for 30 years or marry a male citizen, the government passed a law in August 1999 prohibiting female household servants under 50 because of the potential for elderly men to fall for their young female help who may have suspicious motives.

Also in 1999, San Marino joined the European Monetary Union and adopted the euro as its currency. The Europe-wide single currency was forecast to boost tourism but simultaneously hurt Sanmarinese bank revenues as the banks would no longer be able to charge fees for currency exchange. In June 2000, the OECD accused Sanmarinese banks of making the country a "harmful" tax haven; San Marino promised to reform its banking practices.

Because San Marino has a customs union with Italy, it enjoys all of the benefits that flow from European Union membership. However, San Marino's goal ultimately is to become a full-fledged member of the EU.

13 GOVERNMENT

Legislative power is exercised by the Grand and General Council (Consiglio Grande e Generale) of 60 members, regularly elected every five years by universal suffrage at age 18. The Council elects from among its members a State Congress (Congresso di Stato) of 10 members (3 secretaries of state and 7 ministers of state), which makes most administrative decisions and carries them out. In 1960, universal male suffrage was established in place of the previous system, whereby only heads of families voted. Women also received the franchise effective in 1960 and were first permitted to run for office in 1974 (they voted in national elections for the first time in 1964). Nearly 100% of eligible voters participate in elections.

Two members of the Council are named every six months to head the executive branch of the government; one represents the town of San Marino and the other the countryside. The terms of these officials, called captains-regent (capitani reggenti), begin on 1 April and 1 October. The captains-regent, who must be native-born citizens, are eligible for reelection after three years. As of September 2005, the captains-regent were Cesare Gasperoni (PDCS) and Fausta Simona Morganti (Party of Democrats—PD). The secretary of state for foreign and political affairs serves the function of a prime minister. Fabio Berardi was chosen to fill this office in December 2003. The next election for captains-regent was scheduled for March 2006 and for secretary of state for foreign and political affairs in June 2006.

14 POLITICAL PARTIES

The political parties in San Marino have close ties with the corresponding parties in Italy. Parties represented in the Grand and General Council following the 2001 elections were as follows: Christian Democratic Party (PDCS), 25; San Marino Socialist Party (PSS), 15; the Party of Democrats (PD), 12; Popular Alliance of Sanmarinese Democrats for the Republic (APDS), 5; Communist Refounding (RCS), 2; and the Sanmarinese National Alliance (ANS), 1. The next election was scheduled to be held by June 2006.

15 LOCAL GOVERNMENT

San Marino consists of nine administrative divisions or castles (castelli): Acquaviva, Borgo Maggiore, Chiesanuova, Domagnano, Faetano, Fiorentino, Monte Giardino, San Marino, and Serravalle. Each castle has an auxiliary council, elected for a four-year term.

LOCATION: 12°27′ E and 43°56′ N.

It is headed by an official called the captain of the castle, who is elected every two years.

16 JUDICIAL SYSTEM

There is a civil court, a criminal court, and a superior court, but most criminal cases are tried before Italian magistrates because, with the exception of minor civil suits, the judges in Sanmarinese cases are not allowed to be citizens of San Marino. Appeals go, in the first instance, to an Italian judge residing in Italy. The highest appellate court is the Council of Twelve, chosen for six-year terms from members of the Grand and General Council. The rights of the accused, including the rights to a public trial, legal counsel and other procedural safeguards, are guaranteed by law and observed in practice.

17 ARMED FORCES

The San Marino militia nominally consists of all able-bodied citizens between the ages of 16 and 55, but the armed forces actually maintained are principally for purposes of ceremonial display; these include the noble guard used in various functions.

18 INTERNATIONAL COOPERATION

San Marino became a member of the United Nations on 2 March 1992; it belongs to several nonregional specialized agencies, such as the FAO, the World Bank, ILO, UNCTAD, UNESCO, and the WHO.

San Marino is also a member of the OSCE and the Council of Europe. In environmental cooperation, the nation is part of the Convention on Biological Diversity, the Nuclear Test Ban Treaty, and the UN Conventions on Climate Change and Desertification.

19 ECONOMY

Farming was formerly the principal occupation, but it has been replaced in importance by light manufacturing. However, the main sources of income are tourism, which accounted for more than 50% in 2001, and remittances from Sanmarinese living abroad. Some government revenue comes from the sale of postage stamps and coins and from Italy's subsidy to San Marino in exchange for which San Marino does not impose customs duties. The GDP growth has been impressive and consistent, averaging 7.68% from 1997 to 2001. Inflation, at 2% in 1997, increased to 3.3% in 2001, averaging 2.8% across the five-year period. Unemployment dropped steadily from 4.9% in 1997 to 2.6% in 2001. In purchasing power parity (PPP) terms, per capita income was at $34,600 in 2001.

The fact that San Marino is an enclave of Italy means that, apart from political links, it shares strong economic ties to the latter. The two countries form a customs union and share the same currency, although San Marino mints its own coins. Migrant workers from surrounding Italian regions boost the country's small labor force. The economic data available for San Marino is scattered and highly estimative.

Thus, in 2002 the GDP was $1.1 billion, and per capita income, in real terms, reached $29,000. The economy seems to be fairly dynamic as in 2004 the GDP growth rate was 2%. Natural resources include building stone and agricultural products (wheat, grapes, maize, olives, cattle, pigs, horses, meat, cheese, and hides).

20 INCOME

The US Central Intelligence Agency (CIA) reports that in 2005 San Marino's gross domestic product (GDP) was estimated at $940.0 million. The CIA defines GDP as the value of all final goods and services produced within a nation in a given year and computed on the basis of purchasing power parity (PPP) rather than value as measured on the basis of the rate of exchange based on current dollars. The per capita GDP was estimated at $34,600. The annual growth rate of GDP was estimated at 7.5%. The average inflation rate in 2001 was 3.3%.

21 LABOR

In the latest years for which data was available, the labor force in 1999 totaled about 18,500. In 2000, it was estimated that the services sector provided employment for 57% of the workforce, with industry accounting for 42% and agriculture 1%. The unemployment rate in 2001 stood at 2.6%.

Labor federations include the Democratic Federation of Sanmarinese Workers, affiliated with the International Confederation of Free Trade Unions, and the General Federation of Labor.

About 50% of the workforce is unionized. The minimum working age is 16 without any exceptions. In 2001, the minimum wage was $1,200 per month although most wages are higher than the minimum.

22 AGRICULTURE

About 17% of the land is arable. Annual crop production includes wheat and grapes, as well as other grains, vegetables, fruits, and fodder.

23 ANIMAL HUSBANDRY

Livestock raising uses some 1,400 hectares (3,500 acres), or about 23% of the total area. Cattle, hogs, sheep, and horses are raised.

24 FISHING

There is no fishing.

25 FORESTRY

Small quantities of wood are cut for local use.

26 MINING

San Marino had no commercial mineral resources.

27 ENERGY AND POWER

Electric power is imported from Italy.

28 INDUSTRY

Manufacturing is limited to light industries such as textiles, bricks and tiles, leather goods, clothing, and metalwork. Cotton textiles are woven at Serravalle; bricks and tiles are made in La Dogana, which also has a dyeing plant; and cement factories and a tannery are located in Acquaviva, as well as a paper-making plant. Synthetic rubber is also produced. The pottery of Borgo Maggiore is well known. Gold and silver souvenirs are made for the tourist trade. Other products are Moscato wine, olive oil, and baked goods. A significant source of revenue is the selling of stamps to foreign collectors.

29 SCIENCE AND TECHNOLOGY

Sanmarinese students generally pursue their scientific and technical training abroad, since science and technology resources are domestically limited. The Universita Degli Studi, founded in 1987, has a department of technology. The Institute of Cybernetics, founded in 1965, offers courses in computer science.

30 DOMESTIC TRADE

There are small general stores in the capital and the smaller towns. Billboards and newspapers are the main advertising medium. A weekly market is held at Borgo Maggiore, which also sponsors an annual fair for the sale of cattle and sheep. Most retail trade within the country is focused on goods and services that support the tourism industry.

31 FOREIGN TRADE

Records of foreign trade are not published, but it is known that imports exceed exports. Principal exports are wine, textiles, furniture, quarried stone, ceramics, and handicrafts. The chief imports are raw materials and a wide variety of consumer goods. San Marino has a customs union with Italy. In 1999, San Marino joined the European Monetary Union (EMU), further strengthening its ties to the EU.

Estimates of the US State Department show that in 2001, exports totaled around $2.0 billion, while imports amounted to $2.1 billion. More than 85% of the exports went to Italy, and included mainly manufactured goods, lime, wood, and food. Most of the imports came also from Italy and included consumer manufactures, food, and raw materials (including energy). San Marino also does trade with countries in Western and Eastern Europe, with South America, China, and Taiwan.

32 BALANCE OF PAYMENTS

Since imports and exports are not subject to customs duties, no record is kept of foreign payments transactions. Receipts from tourism, remittances from Sanmarinese working abroad, and sales of postage stamps to foreign collectors are principal sources of foreign exchange.

33 BANKING AND SECURITIES

The principal bank, the Cassa di Risparmio, was founded in 1882. Other banks include the Banca Agricola and the Cassa Rurale. There are no securities transactions in San Marino. In 1999 San Marino joined the European Monetary Union (EMU) and adopted the euro.

34 INSURANCE

Several major Italian insurance companies have agencies in San Marino.

35 PUBLIC FINANCE

The government derives its revenues mainly from the worldwide sale of postage stamps, direct and indirect taxes, and yearly sub-

sidies by the Italian government. State budgets have increased sharply in recent years.

The US Central Intelligence Agency (CIA) estimated that in 2000 San Marino's central government took in revenues of approximately $400 million and had expenditures of $400 million.

The International Monetary Fund (IMF) reported that in 2002, the most recent year for which it had data, central government revenues were €438,922 and expenditures were €426,864. The value of revenues was us$413,064 and expenditures us$388,722, based on a market exchange rate for 2002 of us$1 = €1.0626 as reported by the IMF. Government outlays by function were as follows: general public services, 14.5%; public order and safety, 2.9%; economic affairs, 14.3%; environmental protection, 3.2%; housing and community amenities, 2.3%; health, 18.1%; recreation, culture, and religion, 2.3%; education, 9.4%; and social protection, 32.8%.

36 TAXATION

Legislation introducing San Marino's first income tax was passed by the Grand and General Council in October 1984. A general income tax is applied progressively to individuals (12–50% in 1992) and a flat rate of 24% to corporations. Also levied are a stamp duty, registration tax, mortgage tax, and succession duty.

37 CUSTOMS AND DUTIES

San Marino's trade policy is governed by its customs union with Italy. There is a one-phase duty system on imported goods, which closely follows the rates of the Italian value-added tax (VAT) system. In 1992, there was a 14% tax on imports. In 1999 San Marino joined the European Monetary Union.

38 FOREIGN INVESTMENT

Information on foreign investment is not available.

39 ECONOMIC DEVELOPMENT

In addition to promoting tourism in San Marino, the government has encouraged the establishment of small-scale industries and service-oriented enterprises (40–60 employees) by offering tax exemptions for 5–10 years.

The tourist industry is the main source of revenue for the country (about 50% of total revenues), so economic development strategies are coiled around this sector. More than 3 million tourists visit the small republic every year, and they constitute the primary market for all of San Marino's other industries. Stamps are one of the country's main export goods.

40 SOCIAL DEVELOPMENT

A social insurance system provides pensions for old age and disability. Employers, employees, and the government all contribute to the system. Self-employed contributions vary. There is universal medical coverage and maternity benefits of 100% of earnings for five months. All employees and self-employed persons have work injury insurance. Unemployment is only available to salaried employees and excludes civil servants.

The law mandates that women have equal access to employment opportunities, and in practice women face little or no discrimination in employment and in pay. Women actively participate in all

---

Public Finance – San Marino (2002)

(In thousands of euros, central government figures)

Revenue and Grants	438,922	100.0%
Tax revenue	219,894	50.1%
Social contributions	94,358	21.5%
Grants	4,648	1.1%
Other revenue	120,021	27.3%
Expenditures	426,864	100.0%
General public services	61,975	14.5%
Defense	...	...
Public order and safety	12,569	2.9%
Economic affairs	61,118	14.3%
Environmental protection	13,809	3.2%
Housing and community amenities	10,008	2.3%
Health	77,424	18.1%
Recreational, culture, and religion	9,816	2.3%
Education	40,143	9.4%
Social protection	140,003	32.8%

(...) data not available or not significant.

SOURCE: *Government Finance Statistics Yearbook 2004*, Washington, DC: International Monetary Fund, 2004.

careers including high public office. Laws protect women from violence, and instances of spousal abuse are infrequent.

The government is committed to protecting human rights. Prisons meet international standards and are open for inspection by human rights monitors.

41 HEALTH

Public health institutions include the State Hospital (opened in 1975), a dispensary for the poor, and a laboratory of hygiene and prophylaxis. All citizens receive free, comprehensive medical care. As of 2004, there were an estimated 251 physicians, 506 nurses, 26 midwives, 41 dentists, and 52 pharmacists per 100,000 people.

As of 2002, the crude birth rate and overall mortality rate were estimated at, respectively, 10.6 and 7.8 per 1,000 people. In 2005, the estimated average life expectancy was 81.62 years and infant mortality was estimated at 5.73 per 1,000 live births. The estimated maternal mortality was 5 per 100,000 live births.

The immunization rates for children under one year old in San Marino were as follows: diphtheria, pertussis, and tetanus, 93%; polio, 100%; measles, 96%; and hepatitis B, 98%.

42 HOUSING

San Marino has over 7,000 dwellings, virtually all with electricity and piped-in water. Most new construction is financed privately. The housing stock for the nation is generally adequate to supply the population. Government concerns are primarily focused on preventing over-construction of rural areas.

43 EDUCATION

Primary education is compulsory for all children between the ages of 6 and 16; the adult literacy rate is about 98%. The program of instruction is patterned after the Italian curriculum, and San Marinese school certificates are recognized by Italy. Children go through five years of primary education followed by three years of secondary education at the first stage and a further three years of senior secondary school. At the secondary level, students may choose to attend technical or vocational programs instead of general (classical) studies. The academic year runs from October to July.

In 2000, there were about 1,000 students enrolled in primary school and 1,000 enrolled in secondary school. Nearly all students complete their primary education.

The University of San Marino is the primary institution of higher education. The adult literacy rate has been estimated at about 96%.

44 LIBRARIES AND MUSEUMS

In the capital city is the Biblioteca di Stato, containing a library of some 110,000 books, documents, and pamphlets. The Palazzo del Valloni also houses the state archives, as well as a collection of rare coins and medals. The State University has a small collection of 23,000 volumes.

The Palazzo del Governo (built in 1894) and most other large buildings in the capital are of comparatively recent date, but many monuments have been rebuilt in an earlier style. In 2001, there were 10 museums in the country. One of them is devoted to the postage stamps of San Marino and other countries. The National Gallery of Modern Art is also in San Marino. The 14th-century church of San Francesco has paintings by several minor masters. The three old fortresses of Guaita, Fratta, and Montale are situated on the three pinnacles of Mt. Titano. There is also a museum in Borgia Maggiore devoted to objects connected with Garibaldi's stay in the republic.

45 MEDIA

An automatic telephone system, integrated into Italy's system, served 20,600 mainline telephones in 2002. The same year, there were an additional 16,800 mobile cellular phones in use throughout the country. In 1998, there were 3 FM radio stations and one television station receiving mostly foreign broadcasts. San Marino RTV was the state-owned national TV and radio broadcaster. There were 595 radios and 357 television sets per 1,000 population in 1997. In 2002, there were 14,300 Internet users in the country. In 2004, there were 1,763 Internet hosts.

In 2002, there were five major daily newspapers: *Il Nuovo Titano* (circulation 1,300), *Riscossa Socialista, Notiziario, San Marino,* and *La Scintilia.* There are also a number of government bulletins. The law provides for freedom of speech and of the press and the government generally respects these rights in practice.

46 ORGANIZATIONS

Business and labor organizations include the National Association for Industry of San Marino, National Small Enterprise Association of San Marino, Autonomous Workers Association of San Marino, Labour Confederation of San Marino, and the Democratic Workers Confederation of San Marino.

National youth organizations include the Young Christian Democrats and The Catholic Guide and Scout Association of San Marino. There are sports associations representing athletes in a variety of pastimes, such as weightlifting, tennis, football (soccer), and track and field. Many sports clubs are affiliated with the national Olympic Committee and other international organizations.

Volunteer service organizations, such as the Lions Clubs and Kiwanis International, are also present. The Red Cross and UNICEF have national chapters.

47 TOURISM, TRAVEL, AND RECREATION

The government has promoted tourism so successfully that in the summer during the 1980s the number of San Marino residents was often exceeded by the number of visitors (20,000–30,000 daily). Growth in the tourist industry has increased the demand for San Marino's stamps and coins, gold and silver souvenirs, handicrafts, and pottery.

Principal attractions are the three medieval fortresses at the summit of Mt. Titano and the magnificent view from there of Rimini and the Adriatic Sea. The State Tourism, Sports, and Entertainment Board maintains various recreational facilities.

There were 683 hotel rooms in 2003, with 1,549 beds. The average length of stay was 1.5 nights that year.

In 2005, the US Department of State estimated the daily cost of travel in San Marino at $227.

48 FAMOUS SANMARINESE

Giambattista Belluzzi, a 16th-century military engineer in the service of Florence, was born in San Marino. Well-known Italians who were associated with San Marino include Cardinal Giulio Alberoni (1664–1752), who attempted to subject the republic to papal domination in 1739–40; Count Alessandro Cagliostro (Giuseppe Balsamo, 1743–95), a Sicilian adventurer, imposter, and alchemist; Bartolommeo Borghesi (1781–1860), an antiquarian, epigrapher, and numismatist, who resided in San Marino from 1821 to 1860; and Giuseppe Garibaldi (1807–82), the great Italian patriot, who obtained refuge from the Austrians in San Marino in 1849.

49 DEPENDENCIES

San Marino has no territories or colonies.

50 BIBLIOGRAPHY

Catling, Christopher. *Umbria, the Marches, and San Marino*. Lincolnwood, Ill.: Passport, 1994.

Duursma, Jorri. *Self-Determination, Statehood, and International Relations of Micro-states: the Cases of Liechtenstein, San Marino, Monaco, Andorra, and the Vatican City*. New York: Cambridge University Press, 1996.

Johnson, Virginia Wales. *Two Quaint Republics: Andorra and San Marino*. Boston: Estes, 1913.

Kochwasser, Friedrich. *San Marino: die Älteste und Kleinste Republik der Welt*. Herrenalb: Horst Erdmann, 1961.

SERBIA

Republic of Serbia

CAPITAL: Belgrade

FLAG: The flag has three equal horizontal stripes of red (top), blue, and white, with the coat of arms set slightly to the hoist side.

ANTHEM: *Boze Pravde (God of Justice)*

MONETARY UNIT: The new dinar (JD) replaced the dinar on 24 January 1994. JD1 = $0.01499 (or $1 = JD66.68973; as of 2 June 2006).

WEIGHTS AND MEASURES: The metric system is in force.

HOLIDAYS: New Year's Day, 1 and 2 January; Orthodox Christmas, 7 January; Orthodox New Year, 13 January; Unification of Serbia, 28 March; FR Yugoslavia Day, 27 April; Labor Day, 1 May; Victory Day, 9 May; St. Vitus Day, 28 June; Serbian Uprising, 7 July.

TIME: 1 PM = noon GMT.

¹LOCATION, SIZE, AND EXTENT

Serbia is situated on the central part of the Balkan Peninsula. The total area was approximately 88,412 sq km (34,135 sq mi). The entire country is about the size of Maine. Serbia is bordered on the N by Hungary, on the NE by Romania, on the E by Bulgaria, on the S by Macedonia and Albania, on the SW by Montenegro, on the W by Bosnia and Herzegovina, and on the NW by Croatia; total land boundary length is 2,114.2 km (1,313.76 mi). There are territorial disputes with Bosnia and Herzegovina over Serbian-populated areas.

Serbia's capital is Belgrade, situated in north central Serbia.

²TOPOGRAPHY

Rich fertile plains are found in the Serbian north, while in the east there are limestone ranges and basins. Nearly half of Serbia is mountainous, with the Dinaric Alps on the western border, the North Albanian Alps (Prokletija) and the Sar Mountains in the south, and the Balkan Mountains along the southeast border. The highest point is Daravica, in the North Albanian Alps, at 2,656 m (8,714 ft). Of its mountains, 15 reach heights of over 2,000 m (6,600 ft).

The Danube is the longest river. With a total length of 2,783 km (1,729 mi), about 588 km (365 mi) flows from west to east through the northern region of Serbia. The Tisa, Sava and Morava rivers are major tributaries of the Danube.

Located on the Eurasian Tectonic Plate, there are several fault lines running through the country which seismically active. Earth tremors are fairly common and destructive earthquakes have occurred.

³CLIMATE

In the north, winters are cold and summers are hot and humid. In the central and southern regions, the climate is more continental. Annual precipitation in most of the country is 56 to 190 cm (22 to 75 in).

⁴FLORA AND FAUNA

The forests of Serbia contain about 170 broadleaf species of trees and shrubs, along with about 35 coniferous species. The animals found in Serbia include types of hare, pheasant, deer, stag, wild boar, fox, chamois, mouflon, crane, duck, and goose. As of 2002, in the union of Serbia and Montenegro, there were at least 96 species of mammals, 238 species of birds, and over 4,000 species of plants throughout the country.

⁵ENVIRONMENT

Industrial wastes are dumped into the Sava, which flows into the Danube. Air pollution is a problem around Belgrade and other industrial cities. Thermal energy plants utilize technology from the 1950s and mostly burn lignite; since combustion is inefficient, air pollution is a major problem in Kosovo. Destructive earthquakes are a natural hazard.

In 2001, the union of Serbia and Montenegro had 104 protected areas, covering about 3.3% of the nation's total land area. There are four Wetlands of International Importance in Serbia and three World Heritage Sites. According to a 2006 report issued by the International Union for Conservation of Nature and Natural Resources (IUCN), the number of threatened species in the union of Serbia and Montenegro included 10 types of mammals, 10 species of birds, 1 type of reptile, 1 species of amphibian, 20 species of fish, 19 species of invertebrates, and 1 species of plants. Threatened species include Atlantic sturgeon, slender-billed curlew, black vultures, asps, bald ibis, Danube salmon, several species of shark, the red wood ant, and beluga. At least one type of mollusk has become extinct.

⁶POPULATION

The population of Serbia in 2002 was 7,498,001 (excluding Kosovo). In 2005, in the union of Serbia and Montenegro, approximately 14% of the population was over 65 years of age, with another 19% of the population under 15 years of age. There were 99 males for every 100 females in the country. According to the UN, the annual population rate of change for 2005–10 was expected to be 0.2%, due to a low fertility rate and high emigration rate. The government of Serbia and Montenegro viewed the population decline as a major concern. The population density of the union of Serbia and Montenegro was 105 per sq km (272 per sq mi).

The UN estimated that 52% of the population of the union of Serbia and Montenegro lived in urban areas in 2005, and that urban areas were growing at an annual rate of 0.47%. The capital city, Belgrade, had a population of 1,576,124 in 2002.

⁷MIGRATION

The following information on migration pertains to the union of Serbia and Montenegro based on statistics gathered prior to Montenegro's independence in 2006. During the 1960s and 1970s, many Serbs fled from the Yugoslav Socialist Federal Republic, seeking political and economic freedom. The breakup of the Yugoslav SFR in the early 1990s and the ethnic hostilities that came in its aftermath resulted in enormous migrations to and from its various former republics. During the first half of 1999, the situation of refugees and internally displaced people deteriorated even further. As of 30 June 1999, the United Nations High Commissioner for Refugees (UNHCR) reported 508,000 refugees from Bosnia and Herzegovina and Croatia; 770,000 returnees to Kosovo, and 500,000 other refugees remained; 220,000 Serb, Montenegrin, and Roma internally displaced persons from Kosovo were living in other parts of the former Yugoslavia. The total number of migrants in 2000 was 626,000. By the end of 2004, these numbers were still rising; UNHCR reported a total of 627,476 persons of concern. There were 276,683 refugees, 180,117 Croatians and over 95,000 from Bosnia and Herzegovina. In addition, in that same year there were 248,154 internally displaced persons, 85,000 local residents at risk, 8,143 refugees who returned primarily to Croatia), and another 9,456 refugees returning to other places of origin during the year. In 2004, over 204,000 Serbs and Montenegrins were refugees in Germany, the United Kingdom, Sweden, Switzerland, Canada, France, and Australia. Also, in that same year over 29,000 Serbs and Montenegrins sought asylum in 18 countries primarily in Europe, in the United Kingdom and the United States.

In 2005 the net migration rate was an estimated -1.3 migrants per 1,000 population, down from 3.9 migrants per 1,000 in 1990. The government views the migration levels as too high. Worker remittances in 2003 amounted to $2.7 billion.

⁸ETHNIC GROUPS

Ethnic Serbs constitute a majority in Serbia, at about 82.86% (excluding Kosovo). There are 37 different ethnicities in Serbia. Ethnic Albanians are concentrated in the Kosovo region of southwest Serbia. Ethnic Hungarians make up about 3.91% of the population and live in northern Serbia near the Hungarian border. The remaining population consists primarily of Slavic Muslims, Bulgarians, Slovaks, Macedonians, Croats, Roma, Montenegrins, Ruthenians, Romanians, Vlachs, Bunjevci, and Turks.

⁹LANGUAGES

Serbian is the official language; more than 95% of the population speak it; Albanian accounts for the remaining 5%. The script in official use is Cyrillic, while the Latin script is also used. In the areas inhabited by ethnic minorities, the languages and scripts of the minorities are in official use, as provided by law.

¹⁰RELIGIONS

The ancestors of the Serbs converted to Christianity in the 9th century and sided with Eastern Orthodoxy after the Great Schism of 1054 that split Christendom between the Eastern and Roman Churches. The Serbian Orthodox Church has been autonomous since 1219. Islam came to the area from the Ottoman Turks in the 15th century. Though there is no state religion, the Serbian Orthodox Church does receive some preferential treatment from the state.

About 78% of the total population of the union of Serbia and Montenegro prior to Montenegro's independence in 2006 were Serbian Orthodox. Muslims accounted for 5% of the total population, Roman Catholics for 4%, and Protestants 1%. Protestant denominations include Baptists, Adventists, Reformed Christians, Evangelical Christians, Evangelical Methodists, Jehovah's Witnesses, the Church of Christ, Mormons, and Pentecostals. There is a small Jewish community in the country. In Kosovo, Islam is the dominant religion, but Serbs in Kosovo are generally Serbian Orthodox.

¹¹TRANSPORTATION

In 2002, Serbia had 3,619 km (2,248.8 mi) of railroads, all of it standard gauge. Railways connect Belgrade with Budapest and Zagreb. The Belgrade-Bar line links Serbia to Montenegro and terminates at the Adriatic Sea. Rail service is provided by locomotives manufactured in the 1950s and 1960s.

Asphalt road length totaled 42,692 km (26,528.8 mi) in 2002 in Serbia, and there were 24,860 km (15,448 mi) of concrete roads. While the freeway between Belgrade and Zagreb is officially open, the lack of normal relations between Serbia and Croatia has kept commercial traffic on the highway to a minimum. In 2003, there were 1,650,000 passenger cars and 155,000 commercial vehicles in the union of Serbia and Montenegro.

The Danube, Sava, and Tisa are important commercial rivers, with ports at Belgrade, Novi Sad, Sabac, Pancevo, Smederevo, and Prahovo. Serbia's river fleet has a large transport capacity in Europe. As of 2004, the union of Serbia and Montenegro's navigable inland waterway system totaled 587 km (365 mi).

There were an estimated 43 airports in Serbia in 2004. As of 2005, half of them had paved runways, and there were also four heliports. Yugoslav Aero Transport (YAT) operates from Belgrade. YAT is considering upgrading its aging fleet for European destinations. Passengers carried on scheduled domestic and international flights in 2003 in the union of Serbia and Montenegro were about 1.298 million.

¹²HISTORY

The Serbs, one of the large family of Slavic nations, first began settling in the Balkans around the 7th century in the areas now known as Bosnia, Kosovo, and Montenegro, straddling the line that since AD 395 had divided the Eastern and Western halves of the Roman Empire.

Tracing the origins of the Serbs (and Croats) has fueled many debates among historians, but there seems to be a consensus on

LOCATION: Approximately 41°50′ to 46°10′ N; 19°5′ to 23° E. BOUNDARY LENGTHS: Romania, 476 kilometers (296 miles); Bulgaria, 318 kilometers (198 miles); Macedonia, 221 kilometers, (137 miles); Albania, 115 kilometers (70 miles); Montenegro, 203 kilometers (126 miles); Bosnia and Herzegovina, 302 kilometers (187 miles); Croatia (north), 241 kilometers (150 miles); Hungary, 151 kilometers (94 miles).

their Sarmatian (Iranian) origin. Having assimilated into the Slavic tribes, the Serbs migrated with them west into central Europe (White Serbia) in the Saxony area and from there moved to the Balkans around AD 626 upon an invitation by the Byzantine emperor Heraclius to assist him in repelling the Avar and Persian attack on Constantinople. Having settled in the Balkan area the

Serbs organized several principalities of their own, made up of a number of clans headed by leaders known as *zupans*. Both the Byzantine Empire and the Bulgars tried to conquer them, but the Serbs were too decentralized to be conquered.

Between the 9th and 12th centuries, several Serbian principalities evolved, among them Raška in the mountainous north of Montenegro and southern Serbia, and Zeta (south Montenegro along the Adriatic coast), whose ruler Mihajlo (Michael) was anointed king by Pope Gregory VII in 1077.

In the late 10th century the Bulgarian khan (leader) Samuilo extended his control over Bosnia, Raška, and Zeta, north to the Sava River, and south over Macedonia. Raška became the area from where the medieval Serbian empire developed. Stephen Nemanja, grand zupan of Raška, fought against the Byzantines in AD 1169, and added Zeta to his domain in 1186. He built several Serbian monasteries, including Hilandar on Mount Athos. His son, Rastko, became a monk (Sava) and the first Serbian archbishop of the new Serbian Autocephalous Church in 1219. The second son, Stephen, received his crown from Pope Innocent IV in 1202. Stephen developed political alliances that, following his death in 1227, allowed Serbia to resist the pressure from Bulgaria and, internally, keep control over subordinate zupans. Archbishop Sava (later Saint Sava) preferred the Byzantine Church and utilized the Orthodox religion in his nation-building effort. He began by establishing numerous Serbian-Orthodox monasteries around Serbia. He also succeeded in turning Zeta from Catholicism to Serbian Orthodoxy.

The medieval Serbian empire, under Stephen Dušan the Mighty (1331–55) extended from the Aegean Sea to the Danube (Belgrade), along the Adriatic and Ionian coasts from the Neretva River to the Gulf of Corinth and controlled, aside from the central Serbian lands, Macedonia, Thessaly, the Epirus, and Albania. The Serbian Church obtained its own patriarchate, with its center in Peć. Serbia became an exporting land with abundant crops and minerals. Dušan, who was crowned tsar of "the Serbs and Greeks" in 1346, gave Serbia its first code of laws based on a combination of Serbian customs and Byzantine law. His attempt to conquer the throne of Byzantium failed, however, when the Byzantines called on the advancing Ottoman Turks for help in 1345. Even though Dušan withstood the attacks from the Turks twice (in 1345 and 1349), the gates to Europe had been opened, and the Ottoman Turks had initiated their campaign to subjugate the Balkans.

Under Ottoman Rule

Dušan's heirs could not hold his empire together against the Turks and the Nemanja dynasty ended with the death of his son Stephen Uroš in 1371, the same year his brothers Vukašin and Ivan Ugleš were killed at the battle of Marica. The defeat of the Serbs at Kosovo Polje in 1389 in an epochal battle that took the lives of both Sultan Murad I and Serbian prince Lazar left Serbia open to further Turkish conquest. Following a series of wars, the Turks succeeded in overtaking Constantinople in 1453 and all of Serbia by 1459. For the next three-and-a-half centuries, Serbs and others had to learn how to survive under Ottoman rule.

The Turks did not make any distinctions based on ethnicity, but only on religion. Turkish Muslims were the dominant class while Christians and Jews were subordinated. While maintaining their religious and cultural autonomy, the non-Turks developed most of the nonmilitary administrative professions and carried on most of the economic activities, including internal trade and trade with other countries of the Christian world. There was no regular conscription of non-Turks into the sultan's armies, but non-Turks were taxed to pay for defense. Christian boys between the age of eight and twenty were forcibly taken from their families to be converted to Islam and trained as "Janissaries" or government administrators. Some these former Christians became administrators and even became grand viziers (advisers) to sultans.

Urban dwellers under Ottoman rule, involved in crafts, trade, and the professions, fared much better than the Christian peasantry, who were forced into serfdom. Heavy regular taxes were levied on the peasants, with corruption making the load so unbearable that the peasants rebelled.

Two distinct cultures lived side by side—Turkish Muslim in cities and towns as administrative centers and Christian Orthodox in the countryside of Serbia. The numerous Serbian monasteries built around the country since the Nemanja dynasty became the supportive network for Serbian survival. The Serbian Church was subjected after 1459 to the Greek patriarchate for about a century until a Serbian patriarchate emerged again. The Serbian patriarchate covered a large area from north of Ohrid to the Hungarian lands north of the Danube and west through Bosnia.

The Serbian Diaspora

Over the two centuries 1459–1659 many Serbs left their lands and settled north of the Sava and Danube Rivers where Hungary had promised their leader ("Vojvoda") an autonomous arrangement in exchange for military service against the Turks. The region is called "Vojvodina" by Serbs, even though the Hungarians had reneged on their promise of autonomy. Fleeing the Turkish conquest many Serbs and Croats settled in Venetian- occupied Dalmatia and continued fighting against the Turks from fortified areas. The wars between Austria and the Turks in the late 17th through the mid-18th centuries caused both mass migrations from Serbia and the hardening of Ottoman treatment of their Christian subjects. Following the defeat of the Turks in 1683 at the gates of Vienna by a coalition led by Poland's king Jan Sobieski, the Christian armies pursued the Turks all the way to Macedonia and had a good chance to drive the Turks off the European continent. Turk reprisals were violent and many Serbs fled, leaving Serbian lands, particularly Kosovo, unpopulated. Albanians, whom the Turks favored because they were mostly Muslims, moved in. Conversion to Islam increased considerably.

A second large-scale migration took place 50 years later, after the 1736–39 Austrian defeat by the Turks. All these movements of population resulted in the loss of the Kosovo area—the cradle of Serbian nationhood—to Albanians. As a result, the Serbs were unable to give up control over an area to which they feel a tremendously deep emotional attachment, even though they represent only about 10% of its population. This situation persisted and remained unresolved as of the early 21st century.

Serbian Revolts and Independence

Meanwhile, two areas of active Serbian national activity developed, one under the Turks in the northern Šumadija region and the other in Hungary. Šumadija, a forested region, became the refuge for many *hajduks* (Serbian "Robin Hoods") that raided Turkish establishments. These hajduks were legendary heroes among the Serbian people.

In 1805, the Serbs defeated the Turks and gained control of the Belgrade region. The sultan agreed to Serbian terms for political autonomy in September 1806. A partially elected government structure was established, and by 1811 the Serbian assembly confirmed Karadjordje as supreme leader with hereditary rights. The drive of Serbia for complete independence was thwarted, however, because Serbia was still under Ottoman rule. The Turks reoccupied Serbia by 1813, retaliating against the Serbs by pillaging, looting, enslaving women and children, while killing all males over age 15, and torturing any captured leader.

A second uprising by the Serbs occurred in 1815 and spread all over Šumadija. It was led by Miloš Obrenović, who had participated in the first revolt. Successful in repelling Turkish forces, Obrenović gained the support of the Russian tsar, and after some six months he negotiated an agreement giving Serbia a *de facto* autonomy in its internal administration. By 1830, Serbia had gained its full autonomy and Miloš was recognized as an hereditary prince of Serbia. Serbia was internationally accepted as a virtually independent state.

Miloš Obrenović was an authoritarian ruler who had to be forced to promulgate a constitution for Serbia, establishing a council of chiefs sharing power with him. In 1838 a council was appointed to pass laws and taxes, a council of ministers was created, and provisions were formulated for an eventual assembly. A succession of rulers were installed and deposed over the next decade until, in 1848, the Serbian assembly demanded the incorporation of Vojvodina into Serbia.

The 1858 assembly restored Miloš Obrenović to power, but he died in 1860 and was succeeded, again, by his son Mihajlo. Mihajlo built up the Serbian army to fight a war of liberation against the Turks as a first step towards the goal of a Greater Serbia. Mihajlo developed a highly centralized state organization, a functioning parliament, two political parties, a judicial system, and urban educational institutions prior to his murder in 1868. Mihajlo's cousin, Milan, succeeded him, and accomplished total independence from the Ottomans in 1882. Despite this success, during the same period Austria conquered Bosnia and Herzegovina, badly wanted by Serbia. Milan became dependent on Austria when that country saved Serbia from an invasion by Bulgaria.

Milan Obrenović abdicated in 1889 in favor of his son Alexander, who abolished the constitution, led a corrupt and scandalous life, and was murdered along with his wife, the premier, and other court members by a group of young officers in June 1903. The assembly then called on Peter, Alexander Karadjordjević's son, to take the crown. Under Peter Karadjordjević, a period of stable political and economic development ensued, interrupted by the 1908 Austrian annexation of Bosnia and Herzegovina, the 1912 and 1913 Balkan wars, and World War I (1913–18).

The Balkan Wars

Austria's annexation of Bosnia and Herzegovina was carried out in 1908 with the full backing of Germany. The Serbs saw Austria's move as a serious blow to their goal of a Greater Serbia with an outlet to the Adriatic Sea through Bosnia and Herzegovina. They turned to the only other possible access routes to the sea—Macedonia, with its port city of Salonika, and the northern coast of Albania. The Balkan countries (Serbia, Bulgaria, Montenegro, and Greece) formed the Balkan League and attacked Turkey in 1912, quickly defeated them and driving them to the gates of Constantinople. Austria and Italy opposed a Serbian outlet to the Adriatic in Albania, supporting instead an independent Albanian state and assisted its establishment in 1913. Serbia, deprived of access to the sea, requested it from Bulgaria. Bulgaria responded by attacking Serbia and Greece, hoping to obtain all of Macedonia. The resulting second Balkan War ended with the defeat of Bulgaria by Serbia, Montenegro, Greece, Romania, and Turkey, which gained back Adrianople and Thrace. Romania gained northern Dobrudja, Serbia kept central and northern Macedonia, and Greece was given control over the southern part with Salonika and Kavalla in addition to southern Epirus.

Austria viewed Serbian expansion with great alarm, and the "Greater Serbia" plans became a serious threat to the Austro-Hungarian empire. The Austro-Hungarians felt Serbia had to be restrained by whatever means, including war. They needed only a spark to ignite a conflagration against the Serbs.

World War I and Royal Yugoslavia

The spark was provided by the 28 June 1914 assassination in Sarajevo of Austria's Archduke Ferdinand and his wife. The archduke's visit to Sarajevo during large-scale maneuvers was viewed as a provocation by Bosnian Serbs, and they conspired to assassinate him with the assistance of the Serbian secret organization, Black Hand, which had also been behind the murder of Serbian king Miloš and his wife in 1903.

Austria presented an ultimatum to Serbia on 23 July with 10 requests, all of which were accepted by Serbia in a desperate effort to avoid a war. Austria, however, declared war on Serbia on 28 July 1914. They began bombing Belgrade the same day and sent armies across the Danube and Sava rivers to invade Serbia on 11 August 1914, taking the Serbs by surprise. The Serbian army twice repelled the Austrian forces in 1914, with tremendous losses in men and materials and civilian refugees. In addition, a typhus epidemic exacted some 150,000 victims among Serbian soldiers and civilians throughout Serbia, where there were almost no doctors or medical supplies. Still, an army of some 120,000 men joined the Allied forces holding the Salonika front in the fall of 1916. From there, after two years, they were successful in driving the Austrian forces out of Serbia in October 1918.

The Serbian elite's political goal for the main outcome of World War I was the same—a greater Serbia, with the liberation of their South Slavic brethren, particularly Serbs, from the Austro-Hungarian yoke. The dissolution of the Austro-Hungarian empire was not yet an operational concept. On 20 July 1916 the Corfu Declaration delineated the future joint state of Serbs, Croats, and Slovenes while treating both Macedonians and Montenegrins as Serbs.

But Austro-Hungary was losing the war and disintegrating from the inside. In May 1917, the "Yugoslav Club" in the Vienna parliament, consisting of deputies from Slovenia, Istria, and Dalmatia issued a declaration demanding the independence of all Slovenes, Croats, and Serbs united in one national state. (The phrase "under the scepter of the Hapsburgs" was added to their declaration for safety reasons, to avoid prosecution for treason.) Poles, Czechs, and Slovaks were also agitating for their independence, and they all had received support from their communities in the United States. On 20 October 1918, US President Woodrow Wilson declared his support for the independence of all the nation subjects of the Austro-Hungarian monarchy.

Under the leadership of Monsignor Anton Korošec, a council of Slovenes, Croats, and Serbs was formed in Zagreb, Croatia, to negotiate a union with the Kingdom of Serbia. The Serbian army entered Belgrade on 1 November 1918 and proceeded to take over the Vojvodina region. The armistice ending World War I was signed on 3 November 1918, and on 6–9 November a conference was held in Geneva by Serbia's prime minister Nikola Pašić, Monsignor Korošec, and the Yugoslav Committee.

The conference was empowered by the Zagreb Council to negotiate for it with the Allies. Prime Minister Pašić could not ignore the provisional government set up by elected representatives of the Slovenes, Croats, and Serbs. Thus, Pašić signed a declaration setting up a joint provisional government with the right of the National Council in Zagreb to administer its territories until a constitutional assembly could be elected to agree on the form of government for the new state. However, the Serbian government reneged on Pašić's commitment. The National Council delegation with Monsignor Korošec was detained abroad and, given the pressures from the ongoing Italian occupation of Slovene and Croat territories and the urgent need for international recognition, the National Council sent a delegation to Belgrade on 27 November 1918 to negotiate terms for unification with Serbia. But time was running out and the unification was proclaimed on 1 December 1918 without any details on the nature of the new state, since Bosnia and Herzegovina, Vojvodina, and Montenegro had already voted for their union with Serbia.

The Corfu declaration of 1917 had left open the issue of the unitarist or federalist structure of the new state by providing for a constitutional assembly to decide the issue on the basis of a "numerically qualified majority." Serbs interpreted this to mean a simple majority whereas others advocated a two-thirds majority. Following the 28 November 1920 elections, the simple majority prevailed, and a constitution (mirroring the 1903 constitution of Serbia) for a unitary state was approved on 28 June 1921 by a vote of 223 to 35, with 111 abstentions out of a total of 419 members. The 50 members of the Croatian Peasant Party refused to participate in the work of the assembly, advocating instead an independent Croatian Republic.

After 10 years of a contentious parliamentary system that ended in the murder of Croatian deputies and their leader Stjepan Radić, King Alexander abrogated the 1921 constitution, dissolved the parliament and political parties, took over power directly, renamed the country "Yugoslavia," and abolished the 33 administrative departments.

A new policy was initiated with the goal of creating a single "Yugoslav" nation out of the three "tribes" of Serbs, Croats, and Slovenes. In practice, this meant the Serbian king's hegemony over the rest of the nation. The reaction was intense, and King Alexander himself was assassinated in Marseille in 1934. Alexander's cousin, Prince Paul, assumed power and managed to reach an agreement in 1939 with the Croats. An autonomous Croatian *banovina* (territory headed by a leader called a *ban*) headed by Ivan Subašić was established, including most Croatian lands outside of the Bosnia and Herzegovina area. Strong opposition developed among Serbs and there was no time for further negotiations, since Prince Paul's government was deposed on 27 March 1941 and Germany's Adolph Hitler and his allies (Italy, Hungary, Bulgaria) attacked Yugoslavia on 6 April 1941.

World War II

Yugoslavia was divided up and occupied by Germany and its allies. Serbia was put under the administration of General Milan Nedić who was allowed to organize his own military force for internal peacekeeping purposes. In Serbia the resistance was led by the "Cetniks," the "Yugoslav army in the homeland." The Cetniks recognized the authority of the Yugoslav government-in-exile, which, in fact, promoted Draža Mihajlović to general and appointed him its Minister of War. In the fall of 1941 Mihajlović and Josip Broz Tito, who led the Communist partisan movement, met to seek agreement on a common front against the Nazis. However, Mihajlović saw that Tito's goal was to conquer Yugoslavia for Communism. Mihajlović could not go along with this, nor could he accept Tito's request that he subordinate his command to Tito. A civil war between the two movements (under foreign occupation) followed. Meanwhile, large numbers of Serbs fled Croatia, either to join the partisans or to seek refuge in the Dalmatian areas under Italian control. British leader Winston Churchill, convinced by reports that Mihajlović was collaborating with the Germans while Marshal Tito's partisans were against the Germans, decided to recognize Tito as the legitimate Yugoslav resistance. Though aware of Tito's Communist allegiance to Stalin, Churchill threw his support to Tito.

When Soviet armies, accompanied by Tito, entered Yugoslavia from Romania and Bulgaria in the fall of 1944, military units and civilians that had opposed the partisans had no choice but to retreat to Austria or Italy. After the end of the war, the Communist-led forces took control of Serbia and Yugoslavia and instituted a violent dictatorship that committed systematic crimes and human rights violations. Thousands upon thousands of their former opponents who were returned from Austria by British military authorities were tortured and massacred by partisan executioners. General Mihajlović was captured in Bosnia in March 1946 and publicly tried and executed on 17 July 1946.

Communist Yugoslavia

Such was the background for the formation of the second Yugoslavia as a Federative People's Republic of five nations (Slovenes, Croats, Serbs, Macedonians, Montenegrins) with their individual republics and Bosnia and Herzegovina as a buffer area with its mix of Serb, Muslim, and Croat populations. The problem of large Hungarian and Muslim Albanian populations in Serbia was solved by creating for them the autonomous region of Vojvodina (Hungarian minority) and Kosovo (Muslim Albanian majority) that assured their political and cultural development.

Tito attempted a balancing act to satisfy most of the nationality issues that were carried over, unresolved, from the first Yugoslavia. However, he failed to satisfy anyone. The numerically stronger Serbs had lost the Macedonian area they considered Southern Serbia; lost the opportunity to incorporate Montenegro into Serbia; lost direct control over the Hungarian minority in Vojvodina and Muslim Albanians of Kosovo (viewed as the cradle of the Serbian nation since the Middle Ages); were not able to incorporate into Serbia the large Serbian-populated areas of Bosnia; and had not obtained an autonomous region for the large minority Serbian population within the Croatian Republic. The official position of the Marxist Yugoslav regime was that national rivalries and conflicting interests would gradually diminish through their sublimation into a new Socialist order. Without capitalism, nationalism was supposed to wither away. Therefore, in the name of their unity and brotherhood motto, any nationalistic expression of concern was prohibited.

After a short post-war coalition government, the elections of 11 November 1945—boycotted by the non-Communist coalition parties—gave the Communist-led People's Front 90% of the vote. A Constituent Assembly met on 29 November, abolished the monarchy and established the Federative People's Republic of Yugoslavia. In January 1946, a new constitution was adopted based on the 1936 Soviet constitution.

Yugoslavia was expelled from the Soviet-dominated Cominform Group in 1948, and was forced to find its own road to Socialism, balancing its position between the North Atlantic Treaty Organization (NATO) alliance and the Soviet bloc. Tito quickly nationalized the economy through a policy of forced industrialization, supported by the collectivization of the agriculture.

The agricultural reform of 1945–46 included limited private ownership of a maximum of 35 hectares (85 acres) and a limited free market (after the initial forced delivery of quotas to the state at very low prices) but had to be abandoned because of resistance by the peasants. Collectivization was initiated in 1949 but had to be abandoned by 1958 because its inefficiency and low productivity could not support the concentrated effort of industrial development.

By the 1950s, Yugoslavia had initiated the development of its internal trademark: self-management of enterprises through workers councils and local decision-making. Following the failure of the first five-year plan (1947–51), the second five-year plan (1957–61) was completed in four years by relying on the well-established self-management system. Economic targets were set from the local to the republic level and then coordinated by a federal planning institute to meet an overall national economic strategy. This system supported a period of very rapid industrial growth in the 1950s. But public subsidies, cheap credit, and other artificial measures led to a serious crisis by 1961, leading to the introduction of market socialism in 1965. Laws abolished most price controls and halved import duties while withdrawing export subsidies. Councils were given more decision-making power on investing their earnings, and they also tended to vote for higher salaries to meet steep increases in the cost of living. Unemployment grew rapidly even though political factories were still subsidized. The government responded by relaxing restrictions on labor migration particularly to West Germany, encouraging up to 49% foreign investment in joint enterprises, and removing barriers to the exchange of ideas.

Yugoslavia began to develop a foreign policy independent of the Soviet Union. In October 1949, Yugoslavia was elected to one of the nonpermanent seats on the United Nations (UN) Security Council and openly condemned North Korea's aggression in South Korea. Tito intensified his commitment to the movement of nonaligned "third world" nations in cooperation with Jawaharlal Nehru of India, Gamal Abdel-Nasser of Egypt, and others.

With the September 1961 Belgrade summit conference of nonaligned nations, Tito became the recognized leader of the movement. The nonaligned position served Tito's Yugoslavia well by allowing Tito to draw on economic and political support from the Western powers while neutralizing any aggression from the Soviet bloc. Tito condemned all Soviet aggression. Just before his death on 4 May 1980, Tito condemned the Soviet invasion of Afghanistan. In the 1970s and 1980s, Yugoslavia maintained fairly good relations with its neighboring states by playing down or solving pending disputes and developing cooperative projects and increased trade.

As an integral part of the Yugoslav federation, Serbia naturally was impacted by Yugoslavia's internal and external political developments. The main problem facing communist Yugoslavia was the force of nationalism.

As nationalism was on the rise in Yugoslavia, particularly in Croatia and Slovenia, Serbs were facing a real dilemma with the rising of Albanian nationalism in Kosovo. After World War II, Tito had set up Kosovo as an autonomous province and the Albanians were able to develop their own political and cultural autonomy, including a university with instructors and textbooks from Albania. Immigration from Albania also increased and after Tito's death in 1980, Albanians became more assertive and began agitating for a republic of their own, since by then they comprised about 80% of Kosovo's population.

The reverberations of the Kosovo events were very serious throughout Yugoslavia since most non-Serbs viewed the repression of the Albanians as a possible precedent for the use of force elsewhere. Serbs were accused of using a double standard—one for themselves in the defense of Serbs in Kosovo by denying the Albanians' political autonomy and violating their human rights, and a different standard for themselves by demanding political autonomy and human rights for Serbs in Croatia.

In 1986, the Serbian Academy of Arts and Sciences issued a draft manifesto that called for the creation of a unified Serbia whereby all lands inhabited by Serbs would be united with Serbia while bringing Kosovo under control to be eventually repopulated by Serbs. To accomplish this goal, the 1974 constitution would need to be amended into an instrument for a recentralizing effort of both the government and the economy.

Recentralization vs. Confederation

In 1986, work was begun on amendments to the 1974 constitution that, when submitted in 1987, created a furor, particularly in Slovenia and Croatia. The main points of contention were the creation of a unified legal system, the establishment of central control over the means of transportation and communication, the centralization of the economy into a unified market, and the granting of more control to Serbia over its autonomous provinces of Kosovo and Vojvodina. These moves were all viewed as coming at the expense of the individual republics. Serbia also proposed replacing the bicameral federal Skupština (assembly) with a tricameral one where deputies would no longer be elected by their republican assemblies but through a "one person, one vote" nationwide system. Slovenia, Croatia, and Bosnia and Herzegovina strongly opposed the change, just as they opposed the additional Chamber of Associated Labor that would have increased the federal role in the economy.

Meanwhile, Slobodan Milošević had become the head of the Communist Party in Serbia in early 1987. An ardent advocate of the Serbs in Kosovo (and elsewhere) and a vocal proponent of the recentralizing constitutional amendments, he was able to take control of the leadership in Montenegro and Vojvodina and impose Serbian control over Kosovo.

The Slovenian Communist Party had taken the leadership in opposing the recentralizing initiatives and in advocating a confederate reorganization of Yugoslavia. Thus a political dueling took place between Slovenia and Serbia. Slobodan Milošević directed the organization of mass demonstrations by Serbs in Ljubljana, the capital city of Slovenia. Serbs began a boycott of Slovenian products, withdrew savings from Slovenian banks, and terminated economic cooperation and trade with Slovenia. The tensions with Serbia convinced the Slovenian leadership of the need to undertake protective measures and, in September 1989, draft amendments to the constitution of Slovenia were published that included the right to secession, the sole right of the Slovenian legislature to introduce martial law, and the right to control deployment of armed forces in Slovenia. The latter seemed particularly necessary since the Yugoslav Army was largely controlled by a Serbian and Montenegrin officer corps.

A last attempt at salvaging Yugoslavia was made when the League of Communists of Yugoslavia convened in January 1990 to review proposed reforms. The Slovenian delegation walked out on 23 January 1990 when their attempts to broaden the reforms was rebuffed.

Yugoslavia's Dissolution

In October 1990, Slovenia and Croatia published a joint proposal for a confederation of Yugoslavia as a last attempt at a negotiated solution, but to no avail. The Slovenian legislature also adopted a draft constitution proclaiming that "Slovenia will become an independent state. . . ." On 23 December, a plebiscite was held on Slovenia's secession from Yugoslavia if a confederate solution could not be negotiated within a six-month period. An overwhelming majority of 88.5% of voters approved the secession provision, and on 26 December 1990 a Declaration of Sovereignty was also adopted. All federal laws were declared void in Slovenia as of 20 February 1991 and, since no negotiated agreement was possible, Slovenia declared its independence on 25 June 1991.

On 27 June, the Yugoslav army tried to seize control of Slovenia under the pretext that it was its constitutional duty to assure the integrity of Socialist Yugoslavia. The Slovenian "territorial guards" surrounded Yugoslav army tank units, isolated them, and engaged in close combat along border checkpoints, and the Yugoslav units often surrendered. Over 3,200 Yugoslav army soldiers surrendered, and the Slovenes scored an international public relations coup by having the prisoners call their parents all over Yugoslavia to come to Slovenia and take their sons back home. The European Community negotiated a cease-fire after ten days, with a three-month moratorium of Slovenia's implementation of independence.

The collapse of Communist regimes in Eastern Europe in 1989 had a deep impact in Yugoslavia. Communist leaders there realized that, in order to stay in power, they needed to embrace the goals of nationalistic movements. In Serbia and Montenegro, the Communists won on 9 December 1990 on the basis of their strong Serbian nationalism. In its last years, Yugoslavia became a house divided, prompting the parliament of Slovenia to pass a resolution on 20 February 1991 proposing the division of Yugoslavia into two separate states.

Suppression of Kosovo and Revolt in Croatia

On 2 July 1990, Albanian members of the Yugoslav legislature declared Kosovo a separate territory within the Yugoslav federation. Three days later, on 5 July 1990, the Serbian parliament countered the Albanian move by suspending the autonomous government of Kosovo. The next month (August 1990), an open Serb insurrection against the Croatian government was initiated apparently with the support of Slobodan Milošević. On 17 March 1991, Milošević declared that Krajina, a region in Croatia, was a Serbian autonomous region. Clashes between the Serbian militia and Croatian police required the use of Yugoslav army units to keep the peace.

The Serbian determination to maintain a united Yugoslavia hardened, while the determination of the Slovenes and Croats to gain their independence grew stronger. This caused the closing of ranks by the Yugoslav army command in support of the Serbian leadership and Slobodan Milošević. Since there was no substantial Serbian population in Slovenia, its secession did not present a real problem to Milošević, but secession by Croatia and Bosnia and Herzegovina would necessitate border revisions to allow land with Serbian populations to be joined to Serbia.

The new constitution promulgated by Serbia in September 1990 provided for a unicameral legislature of 250 seats and the elimination of autonomy for Vojvodina and Kosovo. The first elections were held on 9 December 1990. More than 50 parties and 32 presidential candidates participated. Slobodan Milošević's Socialist Party of Serbia received two-thirds of the votes and 194 out of the 250 seats. The Movement for Renewal, headed by Vuk Drašković, received 19 seats while the Democratic Party won 7 seats. With the mandate from two-thirds of the electorate, Slobodan Milošević had complete control of Serbia. Having gained control of Serbia, Montenegro, Kosovo, and Vojvodina, Milošević controlled four of the eight votes in the collective presidency of Yugoslavia. With the collective presidency stalemated, the top army leadership became more independent of the normal civilian controls and was able to make its own political decisions on rendering support to the Serbs in Croatia and their armed rebellion.

On 3 June 1991 Bosnia and Herzegovina and Macedonia proposed the formation of a Community of Yugoslav Republics as a compromise. In this community, national defense, foreign policy, and a common market would be centrally administered while all other areas would fall to the jurisdiction of the member states (except for the armed forces and diplomatic representation). But it was already too late. Serbia disliked the confederate nature of the proposal and objected to leaving an opening for the establishment of separate armed forces. In addition, Milošević and the army had already committed to the support of the revolt of the Serbs in Croatia. At their meeting in Split on 12 June 1991, Milošević and Croatia's president Tudjman were past the stage of salvaging Yugoslavia when discussing how to divide Bosnia and Herzegovina into ethnic cantons.

The international community stood firmly in support of the preservation of Yugoslavia, of the economic reforms initiated by the Marković government, and of the peaceful solution to the centralist vs. confederate conflict. The United States and the European Community had indicated that they would not recognize the independence of Slovenia and Croatia if they unilaterally seceded from the Yugoslav Federation. With the then-Soviet Union also supporting Socialist Federal Yugoslavia, Milošević was assured of strong international backing. Slovenia and Croatia proceeded with their declarations of independence on 25 June 1991.

As a shrewd politician, Slobodan Milošević knew that a military attack on a member republic would deal a mortal blow to both the idea and the reality of a Yugoslavia in any form. Thus, following the Yugoslav army's attack on Slovenia on 27 June 1991, Milošević and the Serbian leadership concentrated on the goal of uniting all Serbian lands to Serbia.

This position led to the direct use of the Yugoslav army and its superior capabilities in establishing the Serbian autonomous region of Krajina in Croatia. Increased fighting from July 1991 caused tremendous destruction of entire cities (Vukovar), and large scale damage to the medieval city of Dubrovnik. Croatia, which was poorly armed and caught by surprise, fought over a seven-month period. It suffered some 10,000 dead, 30,000 wounded, over 14,000 missing, and lost to the Krajina Serbs (and to the Yugoslav Army) about one-third of its territory, from Slavonia to the west and around the border with Bosnia and south to northern Dalmatia.

The intervention of the European Community (as earlier in the case of Slovenia) and the United Nations (UN) brought about a cease-fire on 3 January 1992. UN peacekeepers were stationed by March 1991 to separate the Serb-controlled areas from Croatian army and paramilitary forces. Milošević had very good reasons to press the Krajina Serbs and the Yugoslav army to accept the cease-fire because the Serb forces had already achieved control of about one-third of Croatian territory. He was confident that the UN forces would actually protect the Serb-occupied territories from the Croats.

Aggression in Bosnia and Herzegovina

In the meantime, a far worse situation was developing in Bosnia and Herzegovina. Following the deployment in Croatia of UN peacekeepers, the Yugoslav army moved into Bosnia and Herzegovina. Bosnia and Herzegovina held a referendum on independence in February 1992 in accordance with the European Community's conditions for eventual international recognition. In 1991, Bosnia and Herzegovina was about 44% Muslim, 31% Serbian, 17% Croatian, and 6% Yugoslav. Milošević's goal of unifying all Serbian lands would become impossible with an independent Bosnia and Herzegovina. Therefore, Bosnian Serbs abstained from voting, while 64% of eligible voters approved of an independent Bosnia and Herzegovina by an almost unanimous 99.7%.

At the same time, a provisional agreement had been reached at a conference in Lisbon in late February 1992 on dividing Bosnia and Herzegovina into three ethnic units, with related central power sharing. This agreement was rejected by the Muslim side, and the Bosnian Serbs, who had earlier organized their territory into the Serbian Republic of Bosnia and Herzegovina, prepared for hostilities with the support of the Yugoslav army and volunteers from Serbia and Montenegro.

International recognition of Bosnia and Herzegovina came on 6 April 1992, the anniversary of the 1941 Nazi invasion of Yugoslavia. The fear of another genocidal orgy against Serbs steeled the Serbs' determination to fight for their own survival. On 1 March 1992 a Serbian wedding party was attacked in the Muslim section of Sarajevo. This was the spark that ignited the fighting in Bosnia and Herzegovina. Serbs pounded Sarajevo for two years, reducing it to rubble. They took control of two-thirds of the territory, and carried out ferocious "ethnic cleansing" of Muslims in areas they intended to add to their own. Under international pressure, the Yugoslav army moved to Serbia, leaving to the Bosnian Serbs an abundance of weaponry and supplies.

Serbia and Montenegro formed their own Federal Republic of Yugoslavia on 27 April 1992. Despite the lack of international support, Milošević was elected president in December with 56% versus 34% for his opponent, Milan Panić. Inflation, unemployment, and savage corruption convinced Milošević to support the various plans for bringing about peace to Bosnia and Herzegovina. Even with the eventual settlement of hostilities in Bosnia and Herzegovina, Yugoslavia faced serious internal political problems in addition to its ruined economy: the tradition of independence in Montenegro, the Albanian majority in Kosovo, the Muslims of the Sandžak area, the Hungarians in Vojvodina, and independent Macedonia.

Kosovo

Kosovo was the center of the Serbian kingdom in the Middle Ages. Firmly attached to their Christian faith and opposed to conversion into Islam, large numbers of Serbs were forced to leave the Kosovo region because of Turkish persecutions. In their place Muslim Albanians were settled in increasing numbers so that liberation of Serbian Kosovo in 1912 actually liberated an almost entirely Albanian area. By the end of World War II, the Kosovo area was already about 70% Albanian. Tito granted Kosovo a special autonomous status, keeping Serbian hopes alive that eventually Serbs could repopulate Kosovo.

The Albanians clamored for their right to self-determination and a republic of their own (still within Yugoslavia). Albanians increased their pressure on the remaining Serbian population, which had dwindled to some 10% of the total by 1991. Cries of genocide were raised by Serbian media, and a series of bloody clashes justified Slobodan Milošević's administration to develop a new Serbian constitution of September 1990, drastically limiting Kosovo's autonomy. Albanians then organized their own political parties, the strongest of which became the Kosovo Democratic Alliance led by Ibrahim Rugova.

In a street meeting on 2 July 1990, the adjourned Kosovo Assembly adopted a declaration proclaiming Kosovo a separate republican entity. Serbs reacted by suspending the Kosovo Assembly on 5 July 1990. Most of the Albanian delegates had to flee the country to avoid imprisonment.

Serbia found itself in a very peculiar and dangerous situation. Through several past centuries the Serbian people expanded their reach by forced mass migrations and wars that have contributed to the depopulation of its own cradle area—Kosovo. The Serbian claims to these lands were being contested by neighboring states or other older populations. Serbia and Montenegro became isolated and were facing adversary states.

The Ongoing Conflict

The quest to create a "Greater Serbia"—that is, to unite the Serbs under a single Serbian government—resulted in continued fighting, particularly in Bosnia and Herzegovina. Over 8,000 Bosnian Muslim men and boys were summarily executed at Srebrenica in July 1995. On 8 September 1995, the leaders of Serbia, Croatia, and Bosnia and Herzegovina agreed on a new governmental structure for Bosnia and Herzegovina; the three parties soon afterwards refined their agreement to include a group presidency, a parliament, and a constitutional court in which Bosnia and Herzegovina and Croatia would share power with the Serbian republic.

In October 1995, Bosnia and Herzegovina accused the Bosnian Serbs of war crimes, leading to international suspicion that Serbian soldiers had massacred thousands of Muslims. Pressured by air strikes and diplomacy, Serb authorities joined leaders from Bosnia and Herzegovina and Croatia on 31 October 1995 in Dayton, Ohio, for a round of peace talks sponsored by the United States. On 21 November 1995, the three presidents of Bosnia and Herzegovina, Croatia, and Serbia finally agreed to terms that would end the fighting in Bosnia and Herzegovina after four years and an estimated 250,000 casualties. The agreement, formally signed in Paris in mid-December, called for 60,000 UN peacekeepers. The United States then ended its economic sanctions against Serbia.

Enforcement of the peace was difficult and problems arose over the exchange of prisoners. The United States ordered the leaders of the former warring parties to meet in Rome in February 1996 to recommit themselves to the Dayton agreement. Meanwhile, the International Criminal Tribunal for the former Yugoslavia at The Hague set out to find and prosecute Serbian soldiers accused of atrocities. In March 1996, the UN Tribunal filed its first charges. Among those cited were Serb generals Djordje Djukic and Ratko Mladic, and Bosnian Serb leader Radovan Karadzic. The latter two remained at large, spurring accusations by the United States and Europe that the Serbian government was protecting the international outlaws. In May 1996, Serbian President Milošević pledged that Karadzic would be removed from power. The presidents of Serbia, Croatia, and Bosnia and Herzegovina agreed to hold Bosnian elections in mid-September 1996.

While international suspicion swirled about him for his role in the Bosnian conflict, Serbian President Milošević was not very successful in delivering promised reforms for Serbia. In March 1996, a demonstration in Belgrade brought out 20,000 protestors against the Milošević regime, which opponents charged with starting the Bosnian conflict and devastating the Serbian economy.

Mass demonstrations against Milošević flared later in 1996 when he voided local elections won by the opposition. In December, the Milošević administration shut down Belgrade's independent radio station, which further alienated Serb citizens. Thousands of protesters met in the streets of Belgrade, hoping to topple the Milošević administration. In February 1997, Milošević relented and agreed to recognize the results of the previous local elections, in which opposition parties won majorities in 14 of Serbia's 19 largest cities. In July 1997, Milošević was appointed to the presidency of Yugoslavia by the federal parliament, allowing him to maintain control for another four years.

During early March of 1999, Albanian moderates led by Ibrahim Rugova (president of the self-proclaimed Republic of Kosovo) and representatives of the Yugoslav government held talks in Ramboullet, France; they came up with a plan to give Kosovo back its autonomy under a three-year NATO occupational guarantee. The Serbs refused to sign the accord, and Yugoslav forces grew to 40,000 in Kosovo, continuing hostilities. Beginning 24 March 1999 NATO forces bombed Serbia and Kosovo, in an attempt to check human rights violations and end fighting. NATO bombs and cruise missiles fell on military targets in Belgrade and Pristina. Fears ran high that other European nations would get involved in the conflict and take sides, resulting in a third world war. Rus-

sia disagreed with the NATO bombing runs, attempting its own peace process. After 11 weeks of bombing, casualties reported by the Yugoslav government amounted to 462 soldiers and 114 police officers, but NATO estimates claimed 5,000 had died including 2,000 civilians. On 3 June, the Yugoslav government accepted a peace plan that involved removing Yugoslav troops from Kosovo, and giving some autonomy to the province. NATO troops entered Kosovo on 12 June to enforce the peace plan. Some 170,000 Kosovar Serbs were thrown out of Kosovo by the ethnic Albanian majority during the conflict, adding to an already large refugee population.

On 29 June 1999, 10,000 Serbian protestors gathered in Čačak, in northern Serbia, to demand the resignation of Milošević. In August, more than 100,000 Serbians called for an end to his rule in a march on Belgrade. The UN began the unwieldy task of reconciliation in the region during the fall of 1999. Kosovo was to remain under the sovereignty of Yugoslavia as a Serbian province, but with some future determination of further self-government (scheduled to follow the fall of the Milošević regime). The next regular presidential elections were set for 2001. Sweeping constitutional changes in July 2000 changed the presidential term so that Milošević could run for two additional four-year terms. They also made the weight of the Montenegran vote in the Yugoslav parliament equal to its population, or only 7%. Milošević called presidential elections early, for 24 September 2000; most believed that they would be rigged in his favor, and were planning to boycott the elections.

Milošević banned international observers from the process of monitoring the 24 September elections. The opposition to Milošević was strong, and a crowd of 150,000 turned out for the final pre-election rally against him. The opposition claimed victory in the election, with Vojislav Kostunica proclaiming himself the "people's president." The Federal Election Commission called for a second vote, stating that neither candidate had won an outright majority; this plan was met with worldwide opposition.

On 27 September, 250,000 people took to the streets to demand that Milošević step down. On 28 September, the Electoral Commission announced that while the Democratic Opposition group had won the largest single block of seats, the Socialists and their coalition partners had won an absolute majority. By 2 October, protesters had called a general strike, were blocking Belgrade's main streets and had caused a halt to economic activity in other Yugoslav cities. On 4 October 2000, the Constitutional Court annulled the election results and ruled that Milošević should serve out his last term in office. Tens of thousands of opposition supporters stormed and burned the parliament building on 5 October and captured the state television service; police joined the crowds. Kostunica told approximately 500,000 supporters at a rally in Belgrade that Serbia had been liberated. On 6 October, Milošević conceded defeat, and Kostunica was sworn in as president on 7 October. He stated his first objective as president would be to right the economy and lead reconstruction efforts. Milošević was indicted for atrocities in Kosovo by the UN war crimes tribunal in The Hague. A bounty of us$5 million was offered by the US government to find the war criminal, but he remained in power even after losing the war.

The European Union (EU) and United States lifted their economic sanctions against Yugoslavia, and in November the country rejoined the UN; Kostunica indicated the country wanted to join the EU as soon as possible. In January 2001, Yugoslavia and Albania reestablished diplomatic relations after they had been broken off during the crisis in Kosovo in 1999.

On 1 April 2001, Milošević was arrested at his home in Belgrade after a tense standoff in which shots were fired; he had been charged with corruption and abuse of power within Yugoslavia. Kostunica had originally ruled out extraditing Milošević to the war crimes tribunal at The Hague. Milošević was formerly indicted by the tribunal in May 1999 for alleged war crimes in Kosovo; other indictments later included war crimes carried out in Bosnia and Herzegovina and Croatia, including charges of genocide carried out in Bosnia and Herzegovina from 1992–95. This was the first time a sitting head of state had been charged with war crimes. In June, then-Serbian prime minister Zoran Djindjic authorized the extradition of Milošević to the tribunal, exacerbating a rift between him and Kostunica, who favored a trial for Milošević in Belgrade. Milošević's trial at The Hague began in February 2002; Milošević died of a heart attack in prison in The Hague on 11 March 2006 with just 50 hours of testimony left before the conclusion of the trial.

Serbia and Montenegro

On 14 March 2002, in an agreement mediated by the EU, Serbia and Montenegro agreed to consign the Yugoslav Republic to history and create a loose federation called "Serbia and Montenegro." Both republics would share defense and foreign policies, but would maintain separate economies, currencies (the dinar for Serbia and the euro for Montenegro), and customs services for the immediate future. Each republic would have its own parliament with a central 126-member parliament located in Belgrade. Montenegrin president Milo Djukanovic reluctantly agreed to the union, commiting Montenegro to a three-year moratorium on an independence referedum, but in April, the Montenegrin government collapsed over differences on the new union. Kosovo, which remained under UN administration, remained part of Serbia. This angered many Kosovo activists, although the agreement looked to some as possibly accelerating the process of independence for the province. The parliament of the Federal Republic of Yugoslavia voted to disband itself on 4 February 2003, dissolving the country and introducing the new state of Serbia and Montenegro. Both republics agreed they would be able to hold referendums on full independence in 2006.

Serbian presidential elections were held on 29 September 2002, with 55.5% of registered voters casting ballots. Kostunica won 30.9% of the vote, and his opponent Miroljub Labus finished second with 27.4%. The second round of voting was held two weeks later, with Kostunica winning 66.8% of the votes, to 30.9% for Labus. However, voter turnout failed to reach a mandated 50% (it was 45.5%), and the elections were declared to be invalid. Natasa Micic, formerly the speaker of parliament, became acting president. She stated Serbian presidential elections would be held after the adoption of the new Serbian constitution, after it was harmonized with the constitution of Serbia and Montenegro. Montenegrin general elections were held in October 2002, and in November, Djukanovic resigned as president to take on the job of prime minister. Presidential elections held in Montenegro in December 2002 and February 2003 were invalidated due to low voter turn-

out. Filip Vujanovich was finally elected president of Montenegro in the third round of voting.

On 7 March 2003, Svetozar Marovic, deputy leader of the Montenegrin Democratic Party of Socialists, was elected the first president of Serbia and Montenegro after Kostunica stepped down as president of the former Yugoslavia. Marovic was the only candidate to run; the next presidential elections were to be held in 2007.

On 12 March 2003, Serbian prime minister Zoran Djindjic was assassinated outside the main government building in Belgrade. Members of criminal organizations were suspected of carrying out the assassination; Djindjic had declared war on organized crime in Serbia, which was said to flourish under Milošević. After the assassination, Serbia was placed under a state of emergency and police arrested some 1,000 people, including members of Serbia's secret service and policemen. Zoran Zivkovic, a leading official of the ruling Democratic Party, was elected prime minister to replace Djindjic.

While the Montenegrins managed to elect a president for their small republic, the Serbs failed to do so, even after the third voting round (in November 2003), due to low voter turnout. In addition, the indecisive parliamentary elections results from December 2003 led to a crisis within the Serbian parliament. The crisis was ended on March 2004 when former Yugoslav president, Vojislav Kostunica, was appointed the new prime minister of Serbia. In June 2004, the Serbs also got a new president, Boris Tadic. Tadic, the leader of the Democratic Party, managed to defeat his main contender—the nationalist Tomislav Nikolic, taking 52.34% of the tally in the second voting round.

In February 2005, officials from Montenegro asked their Serbian counterparts for an early vote on independence, claiming the union was inefficient and that it squandered money. Vojislav Kostunica refused the proposal and indicated that European integration and economic development should be the main focus of Serbia and Montenegro. A referendum on full independence for Montenegro was held on 21 May 2006; to be accepted internationally, a 55% majority was required for a "yes" vote. The vote on independence was 55.5% in favor. Voter turnout was 86.3%. A demand by pro-Serbian unionist parties for a recount was rejected. Serb politicians, Orthodox church leaders, and Montenegrins from the mountainous inland regions bordering Serbia opposed secession. However, ethnic Montenegrins and Albanians from the coastal area favored indpendence. Serbian President Boris Tadic recognized the independence of Montenegro. Serbia became the successor state to the union of Serbia and Montenegro, inheriting its UN seat and seats in other international institutions: the newly independent Montenegro would have to apply for UN and EU membership on its own, once it had been granted recognition by other states. Serbia's ambition to join the EU was hampered by its failure to arrest key war crimes suspects, including Ratko Mladic. Serbia inherited legal claim to the UN-administered province of Kosovo.

13 GOVERNMENT

Prior to Montenegro's independence in 2006, the union of Serbia and Montenegro was a confederal parliamentary democratic republic, with two constituent states—the Republic of Serbia and the Republic of Montenegro. As of June 2006, the Serbian province of Kosovo remained governed by the UN Interim Administration Mission in Kosovo (UNMIK), and had self-government. The Serbian province of Vojvodina is nominally autonomous. A constitutional charter for the state of Serbia and Montenegro was ratified by both the Serbian and Montenegrin parliaments in January 2003, and the constitution for the unified state was approved on 4 February 2003. The constitution allowed the member republics to hold independence referendums in 2006, which Montenegro did on 21 May of that year.

Following the dissolution of the union of Serbia and Montenegro on 5 June 2006, the Republic of Serbia was faced with drafting a new constitution. As of June 2006, Serbia had a legislature (National Assembly) of 250 deputies chosen in direct general elections for a period of four years. The deputies in the National Assembly elect the government of the Republic of Serbia, which, together with the president, represents the country's executive authority. The Serbian government was formed on 3 March 2004 with the appointment of Vojislav Kostunica as the prime minister. Boris Tadić was serving as president in June 2006. The judiciary is independent.

[14] POLITICAL PARTIES

The Republic of Serbia held parliamentary elections on 28 December 2003. The following political parties won seats in the National Assembly: Serbian Radical Party, 82 seats; Democratic Party of Serbia, 53 (includes candidates of the People's Democratic Party, the Serbian Liberal Party, and the Serbian Democratic Party); the Democratic Party, 37 (includes candidates from the Civic Alliance of Serbia, Democratic Center, Social Democratic Union, Bosniak Democratic Party of Sandzak, and the Social Liberal Party of Sandzak); the G17 Plus, 34 (including candidates from the Social Democratic Party); the Serbian Renewal Movement, 22; and the Socialist Party of Serbia, 22.

Other minor parties and coalitions which were not represented in the National Assembly include: Together for Tolerance; Democratic Alternative; For National Unity; Otpor; and Independent Serbia.

[15] LOCAL GOVERNMENT

The Republic of Serbia is made up of 29 districts and the city of Belgrade. Each district is, in turn, divided into several municipalities.

Serbia's ethnic diversity often makes local governance a burdensome task. Besides Serbs and Albanians, there are considerable populations of Romanians, Hungarians, Roma, Bulgarians, Bosnians, Croats, Slovaks, and Montenegrins.

[16] JUDICIAL SYSTEM

The Serbian Constitutional Court determines whether Serbian laws, regulations and other enactments are in conformity with the Serbian constitution. Any citizen may begin an initiative in the Court. The Supreme Court is the highest appellate court. It also has an administrative law department with jurisdiction over all appeals of final decisions by administrative organs. As of 2002, a new intermediate appellate body became effective, the Court of Appeals. It has jurisdiction over appeals from the municipal and district courts. Its decisions may be appealed to the Supreme Court. The Administrative Court provides first instance review of all final administrative organ decisions. The decisions of the Administrative Court may be appealed to the Supreme Court.

The district courts' jurisdiction is limited to first instance matters. The courts have jurisdiction to try criminal offenses punishable by ten years' imprisonment or more, and other specified offenses, juvenile offenses, civil disputes of substantial value and in other specified areas, labor disputes, and certain other matters. There are 30 district courts in Serbia. The 143 municipal courts are the principal first instance courts. The courts have first instance jurisdiction over all criminal and civil cases that do not fall within the first instance jurisdiction of the district courts.

Commercial courts have jurisdiction over a wide range of commercial disputes, including copyright, privatization, foreign investment, unfair competition, maritime and other matters. These courts also are responsible for the registration of commercial enterprises. There are 16 commercial courts, and their decisions may be appealed to the High Commercial Court, located in Belgrade. Decisions of the latter court may be appealed to the Supreme Court.

[17] ARMED FORCES

The following information on armed forces pertains to the union of Serbia and Montenegro prior to Montenegro's independence in 2006. Active armed forces numbered approximately 65,300 in 2005, supported by 250,000 reservists. The Army had 55,000 active personnel and was equipped with 962 main battle tanks, 525 armored infantry fighting vehicles, 288 armored personnel carriers and 2,729 artillery pieces. The Navy had 3,800 active personnel, including 900 Marines. Major naval units included eight tactical submarines, three frigates, 31 patrol/coastal vessels, 10 mine warfare ships, 23 amphibious landing craft, and seven logistical/support vessels. The Air Force had 6,500 active members, along with 101 combat capable aircraft, including 39 fighters, 51 fighter ground attack aircraft and 17 armed helicopters. There was also a paramilitary force that consisted of 45,100 personnel, of which an estimated 4,100 made up special police units, 35,000 were Ministry of Interior personnel and an estimated 6,000 were Montenegrin Ministry of Interior Personnel. Sixteen military personnel were stationed in four African countries under UN command. In addition, military contingents from 45 countries were stationed in Serbia and Montenegro as part of the Kosovo Peace Implementation Force. The defense budget in 2005 totaled $706 million.

[18] INTERNATIONAL COOPERATION

The Socialist Federal Republic of Yugoslavia was an original member of the United Nations (1945) until its dissolution and the establishment of Bosnia and Herzegovina, Croatia, Slovenia, the Former Yugoslav Republic of Macedonia, and the Federal Republic of Yugoslavia as new states. The Federal Republic of Yugoslavia was admitted to the United Nations on 1 November 2000. Following the adoption and promulgation of the Constitutional Charter of Serbia and Montenegro on 4 February 2003, the name of the Federal Republic of Yugoslavia was changed to Serbia and Montenegro. Following Montenegro's referendum on independence, Serbia became the sucessor state to the union of Serbia and Montenegro on 5 June 2006, and thus retained its membership in international bodies, including the UN and the specialized UN agencies, such as the FAO, UNESCO, UNHCR, UNIDO, the World Bank, IAEA, and the WHO.

Serbia is a member of the Council of Europe, the Black Sea Economic Cooperation Zone, the European Bank for Reconstruction and Development, and the OSCE. It has observer status in the OAS and the WTO. In environmental cooperation, the country is part of Basel Convention, Ramsar, the London Convention, the Montréal Protocol, and the UN Conventions on the Law of the Sea and Climate Change.

[19]ECONOMY

During the UN economic sanctions that lasted from 1992 to 1995, economic activity was extremely limited. By 1994, hyperinflation had brought formal economic activity to a virtual halt. By 1996, GDP had fallen to only 50.8% of 1990s total. Industry declined to just 46.6% of 1990s output; agriculture, 94.4%; construction, 37.5%; transportation, 29.3%; trade, 60.6%; and services, 81.1%. Formal lifting of these sanctions occurred in October 1996. However, the United States sponsored an "Outer Wall" of sanctions, which prevented Yugoslavia from joining international organizations and financial institutions. Taken together, the "Outer Wall," the Kosovo war, and continuing corruption continued to stifle economic development. In October 2000, the coalition government began implementation of stabilization and market-reform measures. Real growth in 2000 was reported as 5%. A donors' conference in June 2001 raised $1.3 billion in pledges for help in infrastructural rebuilding. Real GDP in 2001 was 5.5% and an estimated 4% in 2002. The average lending rate, at 79.6% in 2000 dropped to 33.2% in 2001, reflecting some improvement in economic security.

Economic output was positive but volatile after 2002, dropping 2.1% in 2003 and jumping to 8% in 2004; in 2005 it was estimated at 5.5%. Inflation was on a downward spiral, reaching 9.8%, but grew again in 2005 (to 15.5%) as a result of the increase of service and oil derivatives prices. Unemployment remained unusually high, hovering around 30%, but a large chunk of the unemployed are considered to work in the informal economy. One of Serbia's main tasks was to bring about fiscal and monetary stability, and create a legal framework that will allow the market economy to flourish.

[20]INCOME

The CIA defines GDP as the value of all final goods and services produced within a nation in a given year and computed on the basis of purchasing power parity (PPP) rather than value as measured on the basis of the rate of exchange based on current dollars. The per capita GDP was estimated at $5,000 in 2005. The annual growth rate of GDP was estimated at 5.5%. The average inflation rate in 2005 was 15.5%. It was estimated that agriculture accounted for 16.6% of GDP, industry 25.5%, and services 57.9%.

According to the World Bank, in 2003 remittances from citizens working abroad totaled $1.397 billion or about $172 per capita and accounted for approximately 6.8% of GDP. Foreign aid receipts amounted to $1,317 million or about $163 per capita and accounted for approximately 6.4% of the gross national income (GNI).

The World Bank reported that in 2003 household consumption in Serbia and Montenegro totaled $18.27 billion or about $2,246 per capita based on a GDP of $20.7 billion, measured in current dollars rather than PPP. Household consumption includes expenditures of individuals, households, and nongovernmental organizations on goods and services, excluding purchases of dwellings. It was estimated that in 1999 about 30% of the population had incomes below the poverty line.

[21]LABOR

The labor force in the union of Serbia and Montenegro was estimated at 3.22 million in 2005. The unemployment rate in 2005 was estimated at 31.6%, with Kosovo's unemployment at around 50%. There was no data available as to the ocupational breakdown of the country's workforce.

With the exception of the military, all workers are entitled to form unions. However, the majority of unions are government-sponsored or affiliated: independent unions are rare. Therefore, unions have not been effective in improving work conditions or wage structure increases. Virtually all of the workers in the formal economy are union members. Strikes are permitted and are utilized especially to collect unpaid wages. Collective bargaining is still at rudimentary level.

The minimum employment age is 16 although younger children frequently work on family farms. As of 2005, there was no national minimum wage rate. On average, the full-time monthly wage in the public sector that year was $181, while the average wage in the private sector was $250. Niether wage rate offered a decent living wage for a family. The official workweek is set at 40 hours, with required rest periods and overtime limited to 20 hours per week or 40 hours per month. Health and safety standards are not a priority due to harsh economic circumstances.

[22]AGRICULTURE

The union of Serbia and Montenegro had 3,717,000 hectares (9,160,000 acres) of arable land in 2003. Serbia historically accounted for 60% of agricultural production. Vojvodina is the major agricultural region. In 2000, 20% of the labor force was engaged in agriculture.

Between 1991 and 1996, total agricultural production declined by 10%. During that time, production of farm crops fell by 9%; cereals by 12%. Viticultural production, however, increased by 51%. However, by 1999, total agricultural output was at 92% of the average during 1989–91. During 2002–04, crop production was 10% higher than during 1999–2001.

Agriculture contributed an estimated 17% to GDP in 2002. Major crops produced in 2004 included (in thousands of tons): corn, 6,287; wheat, 2,746; sugar beets, 2,643; potatoes, 1,098; and grapes, 490.

Serbia has a network of agrarian organizations in the form of chambers, farmers' cooperatives, and unions.

[23]ANIMAL HUSBANDRY

In 2005, the livestock population in the union of Serbia and Montenegro included 3,550,000 pigs and hogs, 1,796,600 sheep, 1,230,000 head of cattle, 182,000 goats, 40,000 horses, and 17,464,000 poultry. Total meat production that year was 848,240 tons; milk, 1,852,000 tons. Between 1990 and 1999, total livestock production increased by 1.8%, but during 2002–04 it fell by 5.4% from 1999–2001.

²⁴FISHING

The total catch in 2003 was 3,665 tons in the union of Serbia and Montenegro, 86% from inland waters. Common carp accounts for much of the inland catch.

²⁵FORESTRY

In 2000, estimated forest coverage was 2,887,000 hectares (7,134,000 acres) in the former Yugoslavia. Total roundwood production in the union of Serbia and Montenegro in 2004 was 3,520,000 cu m (124.3 billion cu ft), of which about 75% came from public forests. Sawnwood production amounted to 575,000 cu m (20.3 million cu ft); plywood and particle board, 59,000 cu m (2.1 million cu ft). In 2004, exports of forest products amounted to nearly $139.1 million; imports, $352.9 million.

²⁶MINING

In 2003 industrial production in the union of Serbia and Montenegro fell by 3% compared to 2002, although mining and quarrying operations reported a 1% increase from 2002. Aggregated production from the metals mining sector in 2003 fell by 33% from the previous year, although the output of basic metals increased by 2%. The country also confronted continuing economic sanctions and the loss of control of Kosovo, with its ores and production facilities for nickel, lead, zinc, coal, lignite, ferronickel, and tin-plate. In light of this, Serbia and Montenegro's gross domestic product (GDP) was officially reported to have increased by 3% in 2003. The country had significant capacities to produce refined aluminum, lead, silver, and zinc. In 2003, the output of bauxite fell by about 12% from 2002, although aluminum output remained at around 2002 levels. Although exports of primary aluminum and aluminum alloys grew by 18% in 2002, from 2001, eight-month data (January through August) for 2003 appeared to indicate a steep drop in those exports. Mining in Serbia dates back to the Middle Ages, when silver, gold, and lead were extracted.

Mine output of metals in 2003 were: lead ore (gross weight), 183,000 metric tons, down from 733,000 metric tons in 2000 and 284,000 metric tons in 2002; bauxite (gross weight), 540,000 metric tons, down from 612,000 metric tons in 2002 and from 630,000 metric tons in 2000; agglomerate iron ore and concentrate saw no recorded production from 2001 through 2003; and copper ore (gross weight), 5,710,000 tons, down from 12,896,000 tons in 2000 and from 7,968,000 tons in 2002. Production of silver in 2003 totaled 2,028 kg, down from 6,838 kg in 2002. Output of refined gold in 2003 was estimated at 600 kg, down from 900 kg in 2002. In 2003, the country also produced alumina, magnesium, palladium, platinum, and selenium. Among the industrial minerals produced were asbestos, bentonite, ceramic clay, fire clay, feldspar, pumice, lime, magnesite, mica, kaolin, gypsum, quartz sand, salt, nitrogen, caustic soda, sodium sulfate, sand and gravel, and stone.

²⁷ENERGY AND POWER

The Electric Utility Company of Serbia (EPS) has control over coal mines, electric power sources (hydroelectric power plants, thermal power plants, heating plants) and grid distribution systems. Serbia has abundant hydroelectric potential, but there are fre-

quent electrical blackouts and brownouts during the peak winter months. Since 1992 energy supplies have been interrupted by UN and US sanctions. Hydroelectric projects are located on the Danube, Drina, Vlasina, and Lim rivers. Thermal plants are located at Kostolac and in Kosovo. Total electrical generating capacity in 2002 was 9.6 million kW. Electric power production in that year amounted to 31.696 billion kWh, of which 67% was thermal and 33% hydroelectric. Consumption of electricity in 2002 was 33.090 billion kWh.

Serbia is the only Balkan country with substantial coal deposits. Proven reserves as of 1999 totaled 18.2 billion tons, 95% of which was lignite. The country's largest lignite mine has an annual capacity of 14,000 tons. Total coal output in 2002 was 39,568,000 short tons, of which lignite accounted for 39,445,000 short tons. Coal imports totaled 310,000 short tons in 2002, of which 171,000 short tons was hard coal.

Serbia has limited proven reserves of oil and natural gas. As of 1 January 2002, these reserves totaled 38.75 million barrels and 24.07 billion cu m, respectively. Production of crude oil in the union of Serbia and Montenegro in 2002 averaged 14,000 barrels per day. Refined petroleum product output in that year averaged 53,000 barrels per day. Imports of petroleum products in 2002 averaged 68,98 barrels per day, which included an average of 37,460 barrels per day of crude oil. Demand for refined oil products in 2002 averaged 83,82 barrels per day.

Natural gas production totaled 22.95 billion cu ft in 2002. Dry consumption totaled 80.87 billion cu ft. Dry gas imports totaled 59.68 billion cu ft in 2002.

²⁸INDUSTRY

Serbia contributed 35% to the total industrial production of the former Yugoslav SFR. Between 1989 and 1996, total industrial output fell by 60%. Production declines by sector during that time were as follows: metals and electrical products, 85%; textiles, leather, and rubber products, 75%; wood products, 63%; nonmetals, 56%; and chemicals and paper, 54%. In the mid-1990s, industry accounted for approximately 50% of the country's GDP.

The industrial production growth rate in 2000 was 11%, and industry accounted for 36% of GDP in 2001. Principal industries in Serbia include machine building (aircraft, trucks, automobiles, tanks and weapons, electrical equipment, agricultural machinery), metallurgy, textiles, footwear, foodstuffs, appliances, electronics, petroleum products, chemicals, and pharmaceuticals. The country produced 8,978 automobiles in 2001, a 30% decline from 2000; it also produced 555 heavy trucks in 2000, a 33% increase over 1999.

The industrial production growth rate in 2002 was only 1.2%, way under the real GDP growth rate—an indication that industry plays an increasing marginal role in the economy. In 2005, the industry of Serbia and Montenegro made up only 25.5% of the GDP. Agriculture contributed with 16.6%, and services came in first with 57.9%.

In 2000, there were 696,540 workers employed in industrial and mining companies in the Republic of Serbia, comprising 52% of the total active labor force. Small enterprises employed 82,273 workers, with 146,972 in medium-size and 457,286 in large enterprises. The Law on Privatization established conditions for reform of the industrial sector. Large industrial enterprises with financial difficulties are obliged to undertake a program of restructuring, which, it is hoped, will further attract foreign investment.

29 SCIENCE AND TECHNOLOGY

A large communications satellite station was made operational in Ivanica during the 1970s. Scientific and technological policies are developed and implemented by the Ministry of Science and Technology of the Republic of Serbia. As of 2002, there were a combined 1,330 scientists and 568 technicians engaged in research and development (R&D) per million people in the union of Serbia and Montenegro. There were 98 registered research institutions in Serbia and six public universities.

A nationwide scientific and technological development policy formulated in 1994 created 250 five-year basic research projects in all scientific disciplines.

30 DOMESTIC TRADE

Belgrade serves as the economic and commercial center of the country. Pristina and Subotica serve as regional market centers. The domestic economy has been held back for the past few years due the lack of major privatization reforms and trouble in the general European economy. Hours of business are usually between 8 AM and 4 PM.

31 FOREIGN TRADE

The United Nations imposed sanctions on international trade with Yugoslavia in May 1992 and lifted them in December 1995. During the war, when sanctions were in force, dozens of Cypriot companies, set up by senior Serbian officials and businessmen, trafficked millions of dollars in illegal trade.

Trade started to catch up in subsequent years, and in 2004 exports in the union of Serbia and Montenegro reached $3.2 billion (FOB—Free on Board). In the same year, imports were almost triple that amount, at $9.5 billion (FOB), indicating that the economy in the two republics was in disarray, but that the union was trying to renew its industrial base. Most of the import commodities included machinery and transport equipment, fuels and lubricants, manufactured goods, chemicals, food and live animals, and raw materials. The imports mainly came from Germany (18.5%), Italy (16.5%), Austria (8.3%), Slovenia (6.7%), Bulgaria (4.7%), and France (4.5%). Exports included manufactured goods, food and live animals, and raw materials, and largely went to Italy (which receive 29% of total exports), Germany (16.6%), Austria (7%), Greece (6.7%), France (4.9%), and Slovenia (4.1%).

Imports were expected to be constrained by tight fiscal and monetary policies, while exports will be encouraged through targeted policy measures, and as a result of a restructured and more competitive economic base.

32 BALANCE OF PAYMENTS

The US Central Intelligence Agency (CIA) reported that in 2005 the purchasing power parity of Serbia and Montenegro's exports was $5.485 billion while imports totaled $11.94 billion.

Exports of goods and services totaled $5.9 billion in 2004, up from $4.2 billion in 2003. Imports grew from $8.7 billion in 2003, to $12.8 billion in 2004. Consequently, the resource balance was on a negative upsurge, growing from -$4.5 billion in 2003, to -$7.1 billion in 2004. A similar trend was registered for the current ac-

count balance, which deteriorated from -$2.0 billion in 2003, to -$3.1 billion in 2004. The national reserves (including gold) were $3.6 billion in 2003, covering less than 6 months of imports; by 2004, they increased to $4.3 billion.

33 BANKING AND SECURITIES

Serbia's banking system was still hampered by the history of international sanctions. Banks are severely hampered by a lack of liquidity, a result of the tight monetary policy prevalent in the country.

34 INSURANCE

Insurance of public transport passengers, motor vehicle insurance, aircraft insurance, and insurance on bank deposits are compulsory. Only domestic insurance companies may provide insurance. In 2003, the value of all direct insurance premiums written in the union of Serbia and Montenegro totaled $436 million, of which nonlife premiums accounted for $420 million. In that same year, the top nonlife insurer was Dunav, which had gross written nonlife premiums of $138.6 million, while the country's leading life insurer was Zepter, which had gross written life insurance premiums of $7.1 million.

35 PUBLIC FINANCE

The US Central Intelligence Agency (CIA) estimated that in 2005 the union of Serbia and Montenegro's central government took in revenues of approximately $11.4 billion and had expenditures of $11.1 billion. Revenues minus expenditures totaled approximately $330 million. Public debt in 2005 amounted to 53.1% of GDP. Total external debt was $15.43 billion.

36 TAXATION

The republic of Serbia has a standard corporate tax rate of 10%. Capital gains derived from the sale of industrial property rights, real estate, shares and other securities, and capital participations are considered taxable income, and are taxed at the corporate rate. However, gains arising from certain government bonds or from bonds issued by the national bank are excluded from the tax. Dividends, interest and royalties are subject to a 20% withholding tax. Other taxes includes a value-added tax (VAT), with a standard rate of 18% and a lower rate of 8%, property taxes, transfer taxes, a tax on financial transactions, payroll taxes, and social security contributions. In Serbia, the republic government, rather than the city governments, collects local taxes and then disperses part of the funds to city officials. Local factories pay no city taxes in Serbia.

37 CUSTOMS AND DUTIES

Serbia's has six tariff rates that range from 1–30%, with a weighted duty average of 9.37%. Serbia applies a VAT of 18%, with an 8% reduced rate for basic foodstuffs, medicines, published materials, public utilities and certain services. Serbia imposes excise taxes on certain luxury goods.

Serbia has established free trade zones (FTZ) in Smederrevo, Kovin, Nis, Belgrade, Novi Sad, Šabac, Pahovo, Sombor, Sremska Mitrovica, Subotica, and Zrenjanin.

38 FOREIGN INVESTMENT

Foreign investment was severely restricted during the years of the economic embargo. Since the sanctions have been lifted, foreign investors from neighboring countries, Russia, and Asia have expressed an interest in capital investment. The main sectors attracting the interest of foreign investors are metal manufacturing and machinery, infrastructure improvement, agriculture and food processing, and chemicals and pharmaceuticals. Foreign investors may hold majority shares in companies.

In 1997, foreign direct investment (FDI) inflows into the former Yugoslavia reached $740 million, but dried up with the onset of the conflict in Kosovo. FDI inflows averaged $122.5 million in 1998 and 1999, then fell to $25 million in 2000. In 2001, FDI inflow reached $125 million.

In the following years, Serbia and Montenegro undertook an aggressive program of reforms aimed at both re-establishing the area as a major transportation hub, and at attracting foreign investment. These policies seem to have paid off as in 2004, capital inflows jumped to $3.4 billion. While Serbia is still considered to be a risky place for doing business, the political and economic climate is steadily improving.

39 ECONOMIC DEVELOPMENT

Officials in general see revitalization of the infrastructure (roads, rail and air transport, telecommunications, and power production) as one step toward economic recovery. Another important aspect of economic reconstruction will be the revival of former export industry, such as agriculture, textiles, furniture, pharmaceuticals, and nonferrous metallic ores.

The Kosovo war in 1999 left much of Serbia's infrastructure in ruins, but reconstruction efforts were proceeding slowly in the early 2000s. The new government that came to power in 2000 faced numerous economic challenges. Nevertheless, inflation decreased sharply from 113% at the end of 2000 to 23% in April 2002. In 2002, the International Monetary Fund (IMF) approved a three-year $829 million Extended Arrangement to support Serbia and Montenegro's (then Yugoslavia's) 2002–05 economic program. In 2002, the dinar became convertible. Privatization has been slow, and foreign direct investment lagged in the early 2000s.

While politically, and economically, Serbia is much more stable than in previous years, the economy is still in a quasi-state of disarray, with rampant unemployment, with a large grey market, and a relapsing industrial base. Foreign investors, as well as several international financial institutions (EBRD, IMF, and the World Bank), have recognized economic reforms as being ositive, and in 2004 increased their capital transfers to the region.

In 2005 there was a boom in several sectors: trade, financial services and transport and communications. The growth is to be sustained by continued investment in newly privatized companies, by strong local demand, and by an expansion of the services sector.

40 SOCIAL DEVELOPMENT

A social insurance system, updated in 2003, provides old age, disability, and survivorship benefits. The pension plan is funded by contributions from both employers and employees. The retirement varies depending on years of insurance; retirement from insured employment is necessary. Each Republic provides its own system for sickness and maternity benefits. Medical services are provided directly to patients through government facilities. Workers' compensation, unemployment benefits, and family allowances are also available. Family allowances vary according to the number of children in the family are adjusted periodically for cost of living changes.

Traditional gender roles keep women from enjoying equal status with men and few occupy positions of leadership in the private sector. However, women are active in human rights and political organizations. High levels of domestic abuse persist and social pressures prevent women from obtaining protection against abusers.

The government's human rights record remains poor and is additionally marred by the crisis in Kosovo, where police are responsible for beatings, rape, torture, and killings, committed with impunity. In May 1999, the International Criminal Tribunal for the former Yugoslavia in The Hague indicted Yugoslavian president Slobodan Milosevic for war crimes against the citizens of Kosovo. Milosevic was brought to trial at The Hague in 2002 for war crimes and crimes against humanity in Kosovo and Croatia, and for war crimes, crimes against humanity, and genocide in Bosnia and Herzegovina; in March 2006 Milosevic died in prison before a verdict could be decided.

41 HEALTH

The government provides obligatory health care to citizens for preventive, diagnostic, therapeutic, and rehabilitative services. There were 228 health institutions and about 3,000 other clinics, mostly private in Serbia and Montenegro in the mid-2000s. As of 2004, there were an estimated 20 physicians per 100,000 people. The University Clinical Center in Belgrade conducts about nine million examinations and 46,000 emergency operations per year and functions as one of the World Health Organization's largest diagnostic and referral centers.

In 2005 infant mortality in the union of Serbia and Montenegro was reported at 15.53 per 1,000 live births. Overall mortality was 9.7 per 1,000 people in the Republic of Serbia. Average life expectancy in 2005 in the union was 74.73 years.

The HIV/AIDS prevalence was 0.20 per 100 adults in 2003 in the union of Serbia and Montenegro. As of 2004, there were approximately 10,000 people living with HIV/AIDS in the country. There were an estimated 100 deaths from AIDS in 2003.

42 HOUSING

At the beginning of 1996, the former Yugoslavia had 3,124,000 dwellings, with an average of 3.4 persons per dwelling. Housing area at that time averaged 20 sq m (215 sq ft) per person. New housing completions during 1995 totaled 14,337 units, of which 11,847 were in the public sector, and 2,490 were in the private sector. According to a 1999 assessment, it was estimated that about 120,000 dwellings were damaged or destroyed in Kosovo due to internal conflicts. About 50,000 homes had been damaged in Serbia. Overcrowding, particularly in urban areas, has become more of a problem as Serbian refugees have returned from Croatia and Bosnia and Herzegovina. In 2002, the nation counted about 2,790,411 households with an average of 2.89 people per household.

43 EDUCATION

As of 2005/2006, education was compulsory for nine years of primary school. This may be followed by three years of secondary school, with students having the option to attend general, vocational, or art schools. The academic year runs from October to July. In 2001, about 43% of children between the ages of three and six in the union of Serbia and Montenegro were enrolled in some type of preschool program. Primary school enrollment in 2001 was estimated at about 96% of age-eligible students. The same year, secondary school enrollment was about 82% of age-eligible students. It is estimated that about 96% of all students complete their primary education. The student-to-teacher ratio for primary school was at about 20:1 in 2000; the ratio for secondary school was about 14:1.

Serbia has six universities (at Belgrade, Novi Sad, Pristina, Nis, and Kragujevac) with 76 academic departments. In 2001, it was estimated that about 36% of the tertiary age population in the union of Serbia and Montenegro were enrolled in tertiary education programs. The adult literacy rate for 2004 was estimated at about 96.4%.

As of 2003, public expenditure on education was estimated at 3.3% of GDP.

44 LIBRARIES AND MUSEUMS

The National Library of Serbia (1.6 million volumes) is in Belgrade. The Matica Srpska Library has over 3 million volumes in holdings. The Serbian Academy of Arts and Sciences in Belgrade has about one million volumes and the library system at the University of Belgrade has 1.45 million volumes. The Belgrade City Library is the largest public lending library system in the country; the network contains 14 branches and over 1.7 million items in collection.

Serbia has over 2,500 cultural monuments, including about 100 museums and 37 historical archives libraries. The Belgrade National Museum, founded in 1844, includes exhibits featuring national history, archaeology, medieval frescoes, and works by Yugoslavian and other European artists. Belgrade also has the Museum of Modern Art, the Museum of the Serbian Orthodox Church, the Museum of Natural History, and the Museum of Science and Technology, which opened in 1989.

45 MEDIA

In 2003, there were an estimated 243 mainline telephones for every 1,000 people in the union of Serbia and Montenegro; about 313,500 people were on a waiting list for telephone service installation. The same year, there were approximately 338 mobile phones in use for every 1,000 people. PTT Serbia is the monopoly owner/operator of Serbia's telecom network. There are 2.2 million installed fixed lines (700,000 are duplex shared lines) in the republic.

In Serbia and Montenegro, only the RTS television network was owned by the state; the other six (BK, TV Studio Spectrum Čačak, Kanal 9 Kragujevac, Pink, Palma, and Art Kanal) are privately owned. The ownership and editorial positions of television and radio stations usually reflects regional politics. Government control over independent broadcasts and the print media has discouraged political opposition parties that have called for greater democracy

and a more open economy. In 2004, Serbia and Montenegro had about 297 radios and 282 television sets for every 1,000 people. The same year, there were 27.1 personal computers for every 1,000 people and 79 of every 1,000 people had access to the Internet. There were nine secure Internet servers in the country in 2004.

In 1791, the first Serbian-language newspaper was published in Vienna, Austria. Privately owned newspapers are sometimes critical of the government. The dailies with the largest circulation (as of 2002) are *Politika* (*Politics*, 300,000) and *Vecernje Novosti* (*Evening News*, 169,000). Other newspapers that are essentially controlled by the government, include (with 2002 circulation) *Borba* (85,000), *Jedinstvo* (6,090), *Dnevnik* (61,000), and *Pobjeda* (19,400). There are several minority language newspapers.

While the government provides for freedom of speech and of the press, libel suits have been fairly prevalent and some media sources have practiced self-censorship in order to avoid problems with government officials.

46 ORGANIZATIONS

The Chamber of Commerce and Economy of Serbia is located in Belgrade.

The Matica Srpska was founded in Novi Sad in 1824 as a literary and cultural society. The Serbian Academy of Science and Art was founded in Belgrade in 1886. There are several organizations for professional journalists, including the Journalists' Federation of Yugoslavia, the Journalists' Association of Serbia, Independent Journalists' Association, and the Association of Private Owners of the Media.

National youth organizations include the Bureau of International Cooperation of Youth of Serbia, Union of Socialist Youth of Yugoslavia, and the Junior Chamber. Scouting organizations are also active. The Child Rights Centre and Child to Child are national groups working to promote the rights of children and youth. Creative Youth of Novi Sad offers a variety of educational, volunteer, and development programs for youth as well. There are a variety of sports associations available promoting amateur competition among athletes of all ages. There are active chapters of the Paralympic Committee, as well as a national Olympic Committee. There is a national chapter of the Red Cross Society.

47 TOURISM, TRAVEL, AND RECREATION

Rich architecture, museums, galleries, cathedrals, parks, and rivers, are just some of the attractions that bring visitors to Serbia. The largest two of Serbia's five national parks are Djerdap (64,000 ha/158,000 acres) and Sar planina (39,000 ha/96,000 acres). Serbia has dozens of spa resorts such as Vrnjacka Banja, Mataruska Banja, and Niska Banja. Serbia has three UNESCO heritage sites. Popular sports in Serbia are rafting, hunting, fishing, skiing, and cycling.

All visitors need a valid passport to enter Serbia. Serbia requires an onward/return ticket, sufficient funds for the stay, and a certificate showing funds for health care. Visas are required for all nationals except those of 41 countries including the United States, Australia, and Canada.

In 2003, about 1.4 million tourists arrived in Serbia and Montenegro, of whom 93% came from Europe. Hotel rooms numbered 2,435 with 4,926 beds and an occupancy rate of 46%

According to 2005 US Department of State estimates, the cost of staying in Belgrade was $340 per day. The daily costs elsewhere in the country averaged $157.

48 FAMOUS SERBS

Sava Rastko Nemanjic (c.1174–1235) was the first Serbian archbishop and a writer who became one of Serbia's most prominent figures of the Middle Ages. Vuk Stefanovic Karadzic (1787–1864) reformed the Serbian language by clarifying grammar, standardizing the spelling, and compiling a dictionary. Dositej Obradovic (1742–1811) was a famous writer, philosopher, and teacher.

Djordje Petrovic Karadjordje (1768–1817) led a rebellion against the Turks in 1804. Zivojin Misic (1855–1921) was a distinguished military leader during World War I. Prince Miloš Obrenović (r.1815–1839) founded the Obrenović dynasty and ruled Serbia as an absolute monarch. King Alexander of Yugoslavia (1888–1934) was assassinated in Marseille, France. Prince Paul of Yugoslavia (1893–1976) ruled as a regent for Peter II (1923–70) from 1934 to 1941 and was forced into exile after signing a secret pact with the Nazi government.

Slobodan Milošević (1941–2006) was elected president of Serbia in 1990 and 1992 before being elected president of Yugoslavia in July 1997. He came before the UN's International Criminal Tribunal for the Former Yugoslavia in 2002 for genocide, crimes against humanity, and war crimes, and died of a heart attack in his cell just months before the trial was due to end.

Ibrahim Rugova (1944–2006) was president of Kosovo and its leading political party, the Democratic League of Kosovo (LDK). During the many conflicts in Kosovo, Rugova was regarded as a moderate ethnic Albanian leader, and later by some as "Father of the Nation."

Ivo Andrić (1892–1975) received the Nobel Prize for Literature in 1961. Danilo Kiš (1935–89) established his reputation with his work A Tomb for Boris Davidovich (1976). Other notable Serbian authors include Meša Selimović, Miloš Crnjanski, Milorad Pavić, Dobrica Ćosić and David Albahari. Anastas Jovanović (1817–99) was a pioneering photographer. Kirilo Kutlik set up the first school of art in Serbia in 1895. Nadežda Petrović (1873–1915) was influenced by Fauvism while Suva Šumanović worked in Cubism. Other Serbian artists include Milan Konjović, Marko Čelebonović, Petar Lubarda, Milo Milunović, and Vladimir Veličković.

49 DEPENDENCIES

Serbia has no dependencies or territories.

50 BIBLIOGRAPHY

Bennett, Christopher. *Yugoslavia's Bloody Collapse: Causes, Course and Consequences*. London: Hurst and Company, 1995.

Bokovoy, Melissa, Jill A. Irvine, and Carol S. Lilly, (ed.). *State-Society Relations in Yugoslavia, 1945-1992*. New York: St. Martin's, 1997.

Brankovic, Srbobran. *Serbia at War with Itself: Political Choice in Serbia 1990-1994*. Belgrade: Sociological Society of Serbia, 1995.

Cevallos, Albert. *Whither the Bulldozer? Nonviolent Revolution and the Transition to Democracy in Serbia*. Washington, D.C.: U.S. Institute of Peace, 2001.

Cohen, Lenard J. *Broken Bonds: Yugoslavia's Disintegration and Balkan Politics in Transition*. Boulder, Colo.: Westview, 1995.

Denitch, Bogdan Denis. *Ethnic Nationalism: The Tragic Death of Yugoslavia*. Minneapolis: University of Minnesota Press, 1996.

Dyker, David A., and Ivan Vejvoda, (ed.). *Yugoslavia and After: A Study in Fragmentation, Despair and Rebirth*. New York: Longman, 1996.

Frucht, Richard (ed.). *Eastern Europe: An Introduction to the People, Lands, and Culture*. Santa Barbara, Calif.: ABC-CLIO, 2005.

International Smoking Statistics: A Collection of Historical Data from 30 Economically Developed Countries. New York: Oxford University Press, 2002.

Judah, Tim. *The Serbs: History, Myth, and the Destruction of Yugoslavia*. New Haven, Conn.: Yale University Press, 1997.

Klemencic, Matjaz. *The Former Yugoslavia's Diverse Peoples: A Reference Sourcebook*. Oxford, Eng.: ABC-Clio, 2003.

Lampe, John R. *Yugoslavia as History: Twice There Was a Country*. New York: Cambridge University Press, 1996.

Malešević, Siniša. *Ideology, Legitimacy, and the New State: Yugoslavia, Serbia, and Croatia*. Portland, Ore.: Frank Cass, 2002.

Pavkovic, Aleksandar. *The Fragmentation of Yugoslavia: Nationalism in a Multinational State*. New York: St. Martin's, 1997.

Ramet, Sabrina P. *Balkan Babel: The Disintegration of Yugoslavia from the Death of Tito to Ethnic War*. Boulder, Colo.: Westview, 1996.

Schuman, Michael. *Serbia and Montenegro*. 2nd ed. New York: Facts On File, 2004.

Sell, Louis. *Slobodan Milosevic and the Destruction of Yugoslavia*. Durham, N.C.: Duke University Press, 2002.

Terterov, Marat (ed.). *Doing Business with Serbia and Montenegro*. Sterling, Va.: Kogan Page, 2004.

West, Richard. *Tito: And the Rise and Fall of Yugoslavia*. New York: Carroll and Graf, 1995.

SLOVAKIA

Slovak Republic
Slovenska Republika

CAPITAL: Bratislava

FLAG: Horizontal bands of white (top), blue, and red superimposed with a crest of a white double cross on three blue mountains.

ANTHEM: *Nad Tatru sa blyska (Over Tatra it lightens).*

MONETARY UNIT: The currency of the Slovak Republic is the Slovak koruna (sk) consisting of 100 hellers, which replaced the Czechoslovak Koruna (kcs) on 8 February 1993. There are coins of 10, 20, and 50 hellers and 1, 2, 5, and 10 korun, and notes of 20, 50, 100, 500, 1,000, and 5,000 korun. sk1 = $0.03333 (or $1 = sk30) as of 2005.

WEIGHTS AND MEASURES: The metric system is the legal standard.

HOLIDAYS: New Year's Day, 1 January; May Day, 1 May; Anniversary of Liberation, 8 May; Day of the Slav Apostles, 5 July; Anniversary of the Slovak National Uprising, 29 August; Reconciliation Day, 1 November; Christmas, 24–26 December. Movable holiday is Easter Monday.

TIME: 1 PM = noon GMT.

¹LOCATION, SIZE, AND EXTENT

Slovakia is a landlocked country located in Eastern Europe. Comparatively, it is about twice the size of the state of New Hampshire with a total area of 48,845 sq km (18,859 sq mi). Slovakia shares boundaries with Poland on the N, Ukraine on the E, Hungary on the s, and Austria and the Czech Republic on the w, and has a total boundary length of 1,355 km (842 mi). Slovakia's capital city, Bratislava, is located on the southwestern border of the country.

²TOPOGRAPHY

The topography of Slovakia features rugged mountains in the central and northern part of the country, and lowlands in the south. The High Tatras (Tatry) mountains along the Polish border are interspersed between many lakes and deep valleys. The highest peak in the country, Gerlachovsy, is found in the High Tatras with an elevation of 2,655 m (8,711 ft). Bratislava is situated in Slovakia's only substantial region of plains, where the Danube River forms part of the border with Hungary.

³CLIMATE

Slovakia's climate is continental, with hot summers and cold winters. In July the mean temperature is 21°C (70°F). January's mean temperature is -1°C (30°F). Rainfall averages roughly 49 cm (19.3 in) a year and can exceed 200 cm (80 in) annually in the High Tatras.

⁴FLORA AND FAUNA

Some original steppe grassland areas can be found in the southwestern lowland region, where marsh grasses and reeds are also abundant. While oak is a primary tree found in the lowlands, beech, spruce, pine, and mountain maple are found on mountain slopes. Alpine meadows include carnations, glacial gentians, and edelweiss. The High Tatras support the growth of many types of moss, lichens, and fungi. Mammals found in the country include fox, rabbits, and wild pig. A wide variety of birds inhabit the valleys of Slovakia. Carp, pike, and trout are found in the country's rivers, lakes, and streams. As of 2002, there were at least 85 species of mammals, 199 species of birds, and over 3,100 species of plants throughout the country.

⁵ENVIRONMENT

Like the Czech Republic, Slovakia has had its air contaminated by sulfur dioxide emissions resulting from the use of lignite as an energy source by the former Czechoslovakia, which once had the highest levels of sulfur dioxide emissions in Europe. Slovakia instituted a program to reduce pollution in the late 1980s. Air pollution by metallurgical plants endangers human health as well as the environment, and lung cancer is prevalent in areas with the highest pollution levels. Airborne emissions in the form of acid rain, combined with air pollution from Poland and the former German Democratic Republic, have damaged Slovakia's forests. Land erosion caused by agricultural and mining practices is also a significant problem.

There are 13 Ramsar wetland sites in the country and 2 natural UNESCO World Heritage sites. According to a 2006 report issued by the International Union for Conservation of Nature and Natural Resources (IUCN), threatened species included 7 types of mammals, 11 species of birds, 1 type of reptiles, 8 species of fish, 6 types of mollusks, 13 species of other invertebrates, and 2 species of plants. Threatened species include the Danube salmon, marsh snail, and false ringlet butterfly.

⁶POPULATION

The population of Slovakia in 2005 was estimated by the United Nations (UN) at 5,382,000, which placed it at number 109 in population among the 193 nations of the world. In 2005, approximately 12% of the population was over 65 years of age, with another 18% of the population under 15 years of age. There were 94 males for every 100 females in the country. According to the UN, the annual population rate of change for 2005–10 was expected to be stagnant at 0.0%, a rate the government viewed as too low. The projected population for the year 2025 was 5,237,000. The overall population density was 110 per sq km (284 per sq mi), with the highest density concentrated in the river valleys.

The UN estimated that 56% of the population lived in urban areas in 2005, and that urban areas were growing at an annual rate of 0.57%. The capital city, Bratislava, had a population of 425,000 in that year. Košice had a population of 242,066.

⁷MIGRATION

Slovakia receives about 400 refugees every year. In April 1999 Slovakia granted temporary protection to 90 refugees from Kosovo. Of these, 70 left Slovakia in July 1999 and returned home. In 2004, Slovakia had 409 refugees, and maintained higher numbers of asylum seekers, including 2,916 from India, China, Russia, and Armenia. In 2005, the net migration rate was an estimated 0.3 migrants per 1,000 population.

⁸ETHNIC GROUPS

The population is about 85.8% Slovak according to the latest census (2001). Hungarians, heavily concentrated in southern border areas, total 10.6%. While the census reported that Roma make up about 1.6% of the populace, unofficial estimates place the number at about 7%. Czechs, Ruthenians, Ukrainians, Germans, Poles, and various other groups account for the remainder.

⁹LANGUAGES

Slovak is the official language, spoken by about 83.8% of the population. It belongs to the western Slavic group and is written in the Roman alphabet. There are only slight differences between Slovak and Czech, and the two are mutually intelligible. Slovak lacks the ě, ů, and ř in Czech but adds ä, ľ, ô, and ŕ. As in Czech, q, w, and x are found only in foreign words. A minority language like Hungarian may be used for official business if its speakers make up at least 20% of the population on the local level.

¹⁰RELIGIONS

The Slovak Republic has been a strongly Catholic region, even during the period of communist repression of religion from 1944–89. According to the 2001 census, about 69% of the population were Roman Catholics. About 7% of the population were Augsburg Lutheran, 4% were Byzantine Catholics, 2% were members of the Reformed Christian Church, and 1% were Orthodox. Other registered groups include Jehovah's Witnesses, Baptists, Brethren Church members, Seventh-Day Adventists, Apostolic Church members, Evangelical Methodists, and members of the Christian Corps in Slovakia and the Czechoslovak Hussite Church. There are small communities of Muslims and Jews. About 12% of the population claimed no religious affiliation.

There are about 30 unregistered groups in the country, including: Hare Krishnas, Shambaola Slovakia, Shri Chinmoy, Zazen International Slovakia, Zen Centermyo Sahn Sah, the Church of Scientology, the Baha'i Faith, the Society of Friends of Jesus Christ (Quaker), Nazarenes, and the Church of Jesus Christ of Latter-day Saints (Mormon).

The constitution provides for freedom of religion and this right is generally respected in practice. While there is no specific state religion, the government signed an international treaty with the Vatican in 2001 which creates a special relationship between the state and the Roman Catholic Church. Though the government has signed special agreements with at least 11 other religious groups within the country, these agreements are subject to national law, while the Vatican agreement is governed by international law, making the latter more difficult to amend. The government offers subsidies to registered religious groups based on the number of clergy within the organization. Since the Catholic Church is the predominant religion, this church receives the largest amount of money.

¹¹TRANSPORTATION

There were some 3,662 km (2,277 mi) of broad, standard and narrow gauge railroads in 2004, primarily consisting of the Bratislava-Koice route. Of that total, standard gauge railways predominated at 3,512 km (2,184 mi), followed by 100 km (62 mi) of broad gauge.

The road system totaled 42,970 km (26,727 mi) in 2002, of which 37,698 km (23,448 mi) were paved, including 302 km (188 mi) of expressways. In 2003, there were 1,356,185 passenger cars and 161,559 commercial vehicles registered for use.

As an inland country, Slovakia relies on the Danube, 172 km (45 mi), for transportation of goods. Bratislava and Komárno are the major ports on the Danube, which connects with the European waterway system to Rotterdam and the Black Sea. In 2005, Slovakia's merchant fleet was comprised of 24 ships of 1,000 GRT or more, totaling 41,891 GRT.

Slovakia had an estimated 34 airports in 2004. As of 2005 a total of 17 had paved runways, and there was also a single heliport. Air service in Slovakia is conducted primarily through M.R. Stefanik Airport at Bratislava. In 2003, about 208,000 passengers were carried on scheduled domestic and international airline flights.

¹²HISTORY

The first known peoples of the territory of present-day Slovakia were Celts, who lived in the region about 50 BC. The Celts were pushed out by Slavs, who moved in from the east at the beginning of the modern era. A Frankish merchant named Samo formed the first unified state in the region in the mid-7th century. The Moravia Empire appeared in the 9th century, incorporating parts of present-day Slovakia. Although the first Christian missionaries active in the area were Orthodox (including the monks Cyril and Methodius, who introduced an alphabet of their own invention—still called Cyrillic—in which to write the Slavic languages), it was the Roman church that eventually established dominance. At the end of the 9th century the Magyars (Hungarians) began to move into Slovakia, incorporating the territory into their own.

LOCATION: 47°44′ to 49°37′ N; 16°51′ to 22°34′ E. BOUNDARY LENGTHS: Total boundary lengths, 1,355 kilometers (842 miles); Austria, 91 kilometers (57 miles); Czech Republic, 215 kilometers (134 miles); Hungary, 515 kilometers (320 miles); Poland, 444 kilometers (275 miles); Ukraine, 90 kilometers (56 miles).

For many centuries the Hungarians treated the Slovaks as subject people, so it was not until the 13th century, when Hungary had been ravished by Tatar invasions, that the territory began to develop. Some contact with the Czechs, who speak a closely related language, began in the early 15th century, as refugees from the Hussite religious wars in Bohemia moved east.

After the Turkish victory at Mohacs in 1526 the Kingdom of Hungary was divided into three parts; so-called "Royal Hungary," which included Slovakia, was passed to the rule of the Hapsburg dynasty. Bratislava became the Hapsburg capital until the end of the 17th century, when the Turks were driven from Hungarian territory, and the Hungarian capital moved to Budapest. Although there was some religious spillover of Protestantism from the west, Slovakia was solidly in control of the Catholic Counter-Reformation, establishing the long tradition of strong church influence in the region.

In the late 18th century the attempt of the Hapsburg rulers, especially Josef II (1765–1790), to germanify the empire led to a rise in Hungarian nationalism, which in turn stimulated a rise in Slovak national self-consciousness. During the 1848 Revolution a program, "Demands of the Slovak Nation," was formulated, which called for the use of Slovak in schools, courts, and other settings, and demanded creation of a Slovak assembly. These demands were rejected, and the Hungarians continued their efforts to suppress Slovak nationalism. When the Austro-Hungarian Empire was

formed in 1867, the Hungarians began a program of intense Magyarification. In the absence of a Slovak intellectual elite, nationalistic ideals were largely maintained by the local clergy.

When World War I began the Slovaks joined with the Czechs and other suppressed nationalities of the Austro-Hungarian Empire in pushing for their own state. Czech and Slovak immigrants in America were united in their efforts to prod the United States to recognize a postwar combined Czech and Slovak state. The Czechs declared independence on 28 October 1918, and the Slovaks seceded from Hungary two days later, to create the Czecho-Slovak Republic.

The relationship between the two parts of the new state was never firmly fixed. The Czech lands were more developed economically, and Czech politicians dominated the political debate. Although they were supported by a portion of Slovak society, there remained a large constituency of Slovak nationalists, most of them in Jozef Tiso's People's Party, who wanted complete independence.

Attempts to deal with Slovak separatist sentiments occupied a good deal of legislative time during the first Czechoslovak Republic, particularly since economic development continued to favor the Czech lands over the Slovak.

In 1938 Adolph Hitler demanded that the Sudeten German area, in the Czech part of the country, be ceded to Germany. Representatives of Germany, Italy, France, and the United Kingdom met in Munich, without participation by Czechoslovakia, and decided that in order to achieve "peace in our time" Germany could occupy the Sudetenland, which it did in October 1938. Slovak nationalists argued that once the dismemberment of Czechoslovakia had begun, they too should secede, particularly because both Poland and Hungary also took advantage of the situation to seize parts of Slovakia. When Hitler's forces seized Prague in March 1939, a separate Slovak state was declared, which immediately fell under Nazi domination. Although nominally independent, the Slovakia of President Tiso was never more than a Nazi puppet.

During the war Slovak leaders like Stefan Osusky and Juraj Slavik cooperated with E. Benes' Czechoslovak government-in-exile, headquartered in London. There was also a small group of Slovak communists who took refuge in Moscow. In December 1943 a Slovak National Council was formed in opposition to the Tiso government, with both democratic and communist members. They began an uprising in Banska Bystrica in August 1944, which failed because of lack of support by both the West and the Soviet Union. When the war ended, the Slovak National Council took control of the country. Soviet attempts to use Slovak nationalism as a tool of control failed in the 1946 elections, when noncommunist parties received 63% of the vote. The communists switched their tactics to encouraging civil disorder and arresting people accused of participation in the wartime Slovak government. Tiso himself was executed in 1947.

Elsewhere in Czechoslovakia, the communists had been the largest vote getters in the 1946 elections, but in 1948 it seemed that they might lose. Rather than risk the election, they organized a Soviet-backed coup, forcing President Benes to accept a government headed by Klement Gottwald, a communist. Benes resigned in June 1948, leaving the presidency open for Gottwald, while A. Zapotocky became prime minister.

Once Czechoslovakia became a People's Republic, and a faithful ally of the Soviet Union, a wave of purges and arrests rolled over the country, from 1949 to 1954. In 1952 a number of high officials, including Foreign Minister V. Clementis and R. Slansky, head of the Czech Communist Party, were hanged for "Tito-ism" and "national deviation."

Gottwald died in March 1953, a few days after Stalin, setting off the slow erosion of communist control. Zapotocky succeeded to the presidency, while A. Novotny became head of the party; neither had Gottwald's authority, and so clung even more tightly to the Stalinist methods, which, after Nikita Khrushchev's secret denunciation of Stalin in 1956, had begun to be discredited even in the USSR. Novotny became president upon Zapotocky's death in 1957, holding Czechoslovakia in a tight grip until well into the 1960s.

Khrushchev's liberalization in the USSR encouraged liberals within the Czechoslovak party to try to emulate Moscow. Past abuses of the party, including the hanging of Slansky and Clementis, were repudiated, and Novotny was eventually forced to fire many of his most conservative allies, including Karol Bacilek, head of the Slovak Communist Party, and Viliam Siroky, premier for more than a decade. Slovaks detested both men because of their submission to Prague's continued policies of centralization, which in practice subordinated Slovak interests to those of the Czechs.

Alexander Dubček, the new head of the Slovak Communist Party, attacked Novotny at a meeting in late 1967, accusing him

of undermining economic reform and ignoring Slovak demands for greater self-government. Two months later, in January 1968, the presidency was separated from the party chairmanship, and Dubček was named head of the Czechoslovak Communist Party, the first Slovak ever to hold the post.

Novotny resigned in March 1968, and Czechoslovakia embarked on a radical liberalization, which Dubček termed "socialism with a human face." The leaders of the other eastern bloc nations and the Soviet leaders viewed these developments with alarm. Delegations went back and forth from Moscow during the "Prague Spring" of 1968, warning of "counter-revolution." By July the neighbors' alarm had grown; at a meeting in Warsaw they issued a warning to Czechoslovakia against leaving the socialist camp. Although Dubček himself traveled to Moscow twice, in July and early August, to reassure Soviet party leader Brezhnev, the Soviets remained unconvinced.

Finally, on the night of 20–21 August 1968, military units from all the Warsaw Pact nations except Romania invaded Czechoslovakia, to "save it from counter-revolution." Dubček and other officials were arrested, and the country was placed under Soviet control. Difficulties in finding local officials willing to act as Soviet puppets caused the Soviets to play on Czech and Slovak antagonisms. On 31 December 1968 the country was made into a federative state, comprised of the Czech Socialist Republic and the Slovak Socialist Republic, each with its own legislature and government. In April Gustav Husak, once a reformer, but now viewing harmony with the USSR as the highest priority, was named head of the Czech Communist Party. A purge of liberals followed, and in May 1970 a new Soviet-Czechoslovak friendship treaty was signed; in June Dubček was expelled from the party.

Between 1970 and 1975 nearly one-third of the party was dismissed, as Husak consolidated power, re-establishing the priority of the federal government over its constituent parts and, in May 1975, reuniting the titles of party head and republic president.

Once again it was liberalization in the USSR which set off political change in Czechoslovakia. Husak ignored Soviet leader Mikhail Gorbachev's calls for perestroika and glasnost until 1987, when he reluctantly endorsed the general concept of Party reform, but delayed implementation until 1991. Aging and in ill health, Husak announced his retirement in December 1987, declaring that Milos Jakes would take his post; Jakes had been a life-long compromiser and accommodator who was unable to control dissenting factions within his party, which were now using the radical changes in the Soviet Union as weapons against one another.

Enthusiasm for political change was not as great in Slovakia as it was in the Czech west, where in November 1989 people had begun to gather on Prague's Wenceslas Square, demanding free elections. The so-called "velvet revolution" ended on 24 November, when Jakes and all his government resigned. Novotny resigned his presidency soon after.

Alexander Dubček was brought out of exile and put forward as a potential replacement, but the hostility of Czech intellectuals and activists, who felt that they had to drag unwilling Slovaks into the new era, made it impossible to choose a Slovak as president. The choice fell instead on Vaclav Havel, a Czech playwright and dissident, who was named president by acclamation on 29 December 1989, while Dubček was named leader of the National Assembly.

Dismantling the apparatus of a Soviet-style state began immediately, but economic change came more slowly, in part because elections were not scheduled until June 1990. The old struggle between Czechs and Slovaks intensified, as Slovaks grew increasingly to resist the programs of economic and political change being proposed in Prague. Slovak demands led to an almost immediate renaming of the country, as the Czech and Slovak Federal Republic.

In the June elections the Slovaks voted overwhelmingly for Public Against Violence, the Slovak partner of the Czech Civic Forum, which meant that economic transformation was begun. Again there was much greater enthusiasm for returning to private ownership in the west than there was in the east, intensifying Slovak separatism. In December 1990 the country's Federal Assembly attempted to defuse the problem by increasing the roles of the Czech and Slovak regional governments, but it also gave President Havel extraordinary powers, to head off attempts at Slovak secession. The nationalists found an articulate and persuasive voice for growing separatist sentiments in Vladimir Meciar, the Slovak premier.

During a visit to Bratislava in March 1991, President Havel was jeered by thousands of Slovaks, making obvious the degree of Slovak discontent. Meciar was replaced in April 1991, by Jan Carnogursky, but the easing of tensions was only temporary, since Carnogursky, too, favored an independent Slovakia.

By June 1992 matters had reached a legislative impasse, so new federal elections were called. Slovakia chose to hold elections for its National Council at the same time. In July the new Slovak legislature issued a declaration of sovereignty and adopted a new constitution as an independent state, to take effect 1 January 1993. Throughout 1991 and 1992 a struggle followed, with the Federal Assembly and president on one side, trying to devise ways of increasing the strength of the federal state, and the Czech and Slovak National Councils, or legislatures, on the other, seeking to shore up their own autonomy at the expense of the central authorities. Although polls indicated that most Slovaks continued to favor some form of union with the Czechs, the absence of any national figure able or willing to articulate what form that union might take, left the field to the separatists and the charismatic Meciar.

In the federal election the vote split along national and regional lines, with the Czechs voting for right-of-center, reformist candidates, especially Vaclav Klaus's Civic Democratic Party, while the Slovaks voted for leftist and nationalist parties, especially Vladimir Meciar's Movement for a Democratic Slovakia (MDS). Although the federal government and President Havel continued to try to hold the state together, Czech Prime Minister Klaus made it clear that the Czechs would offer no financial incentives or assistance to induce the Slovaks to remain in the union. Increasingly the republics began to behave as though they were already separate so that, for example, by the end of 1992, 25.2% of Czech industry had been privatized, while only 5.3% of Slovak industry had. By the end of 1992 it was obvious that separation was inevitable. The two prime ministers, Klaus and Meciar, agreed to the so-called "velvet divorce," which took effect 1 January 1993. Czechs and Slovaks alike have objected that this move was never put to a popular referendum.

The new constitution created a 150-seat National Assembly, which elects the head of state, the president. Despite the strong showing of his party, Prime Minister Meciar was unable to get his first candidate through, and so put up Michal Kovac, a Dubček supporter and former finance minister in Slovakia, who had served as the last chairman of Czechoslovakia's federal parliament.

The Meciar government rejected the moves toward political and economic liberalization which the Czechs were pursuing, attempting instead to retain a socialist-style government, with strong central control. Swift economic decline, especially relative to the Czech's obviously growing prosperity, combined with Meciar's own erratic and autocratic manner, caused him to lose a vote of no-confidence in March 1994.

Kovac was elected for a five-year term by the National Parliament on 8 February 1993; on 12 December 1994 he appointed Meciar prime minister. Meciar's party (MDS), which won 35% of the vote in the 1994 elections, formed a ruling government with the Slovak National Party and the Association of Slovak Workers. However, Meciar again was slow to implement economic reforms, and his attempts to consolidate his power via undemocratic legislation were rebuffed in 1996 by President Kovac. The MDS-led coalition government managed to remain in power until the September 1998 elections. During the MDS era, opportunities to privatize state-owned property were used to reward political loyalty, and election laws were changed in a way that favored the MDS. Much of the legislation introduced by the Meciar government was found to be unconstitutional.

Under the new election laws, the Slovak Democratic Coalition (SDC) was formed by five small political groups in 1997. Mikulas Dzurinda was its leader. Elections held in September 1998 saw the SDC gain 26.33% of the vote. On 30 October 1998, SDC formed a coalition government with Dzurinda as prime minister.

In January 1999, parliament passed a new law allowing for the direct election of the president. Presidential elections were held on 15 and 29 May, and in the second round, Rudolf Schuster of the small centrist Party of Civic Understanding (SOP) was elected with 57.2% of the vote over Meciar (42.8%). The Organization for Security and Cooperation in Europe (OSCE) found the elections to be free and fair. In July 1999, a law was passed improving the status of minority languages. In February 2001, parliament amended the constitution as a step toward gaining membership in the EU and NATO. Among the 85 amendments bringing the 1992 constitution in line with EU judiciary and financial standards were the creation of an ombudsman as a public protector of human rights, and an initiative to have the government support the aspirations of ethnic Slovaks living abroad to preserve their national identity and culture.

Parliamentary elections were held on 20 and 21 September 2002, and although Meciar's HZDS party won the most seats in the 150-member National Council (36), three core center-right parties formed a coalition without left-wing parties that had previously hampered it. Dzurinda continued in office as prime minister.

At a NATO summit in Prague held in November 2002, Slovakia was formally invited to join the organization, and in December, it was one of 10 new countries invited to join the EU. In the spring of 2004, it became member of both these organizations. Also, in April 2004, a new president was elected, Ivan Gasparovic. Although in the first voting round Gasparovic received less votes than his main contestant—Meciar—he managed to rally the support of the other presidential candidates in the second round, taking 59.9% of the vote. In May 2005, Slovakia ratified the EU constitution.

13 GOVERNMENT

The constitution that the Slovak National Assembly adopted in July 1992 calls for a unicameral legislature of 150 members (the National Council of the Slovak Republic). Voting is by party slate, with proportional seat allotment affecting the gains of the winner. Thus, in the 1994 election, Meciar's party gained 61 of the 150 seats, with only 35% of the popular vote. In the 2002 election, Meciar's party gained 36 seats in the National Council, with 19.5% of the vote. The government is formed by the leading party, or coalition of parties, and the prime minister is head of the government. A coalition of center-right parties formed the government in 2002. Head of state is the president, who, after 1999, was directly elected by popular vote for a five-year term. A cabinet is appointed by the president on the recommendation of the prime minister. Rudolf Schuster was Slovakia's first directly elected president; Ivan Gasparovic was elected president in 2004, defeating Meciar in the second round of voting. The next presidential election was to be held April 2009.

14 POLITICAL PARTIES

There were 18 parties contesting the 150 seats of the National Council in the 1994 election, but only 7 or 8 were considered to be serious contenders, because of the necessity of receiving 5% of the total vote in order to take a seat. In 2002, there were 7 parties that won seats in the National Council. The single most popular party in 1994 was the Movement for a Democratic Slovakia (HZDS), which won 35% of the vote. By 2002, HZDS won just 19.5% of the vote and 36 seats; although it won the most votes it was unable to form a government. Prime Minister Mikulas Dzurinda headed a coalition consisting of the Slovak Democratic and Christian Union (SDKU) with 15.1% of the vote and 28 seats; the Party of the Hungarian Coalition (SMK) with 11.2% of the vote and 20 seats; the Christian Democratic Movement (KDH) with 8.3% of the vote and 15 seats; and the Alliance of a New Citizen (ANO) with 8% of the vote and 15 seats. Also winning seats in parliament were the populist Smer Party (Party Direction—Third Way) with 13.5% of the vote and 25 seats, and the Slovak Communist Party with 6.3% of the vote and 11 seats. The next legislative elections were to be held September 2006.

15 LOCAL GOVERNMENT

Slovakia is currently divided into 79 districts and 8 regions (kraje), and each region has a parliament and governor. In February 2001, in an effort to speed up Slovakia's EU accession process, the parliament implemented a series of constitutional changes aimed at decentralizing the country's power structure. Thus, the state audit office, the judiciary, and the minorities gain in independence and authority. In January 2002, Slovakia was divided into eight Upper-Tier Territorial Units—self-governing entities, named after their principal city. These changes responded to one of EU's key requirements for increased decentralization and flexibility of the administrative apparatus.

16 JUDICIAL SYSTEM

The judicial system consists of a republic-level Supreme Court as the highest court of appeal; 8 regional courts seated in regional capitals; and 55 local courts seated in some district capitals. The courts have begun to form specialized sections, including commercial, civil, and criminal branches.

The 13-member Constitutional Court reviews the constitutionality of laws as well as the constitutional questions of lower level courts and national and local government bodies. Until 2002, parliament nominated and the president appointed the Constitutional Court and Supreme Court judges, and parliament chose all other judges based on the recommendations from the Ministry of Justice. In 2002, however, parliament passed legislation creating a Judicial Council, composed of judges, law professors, and other legal experts, to nominate judges. All judges except those of the Constitutional Court are now appointed by the president from a list proposed by the 18-member Council. The president still appoints the Constitutional Court judges from a slate of candidates nominated by parliament.

The constitution declares the independence of the judiciary from the other branches of government. Judges are appointed for life, but Constitutional Court judges serve seven-year terms. There is also a military court system, and appeals may be taken to the Supreme Court and the Constitutional Court. Defendants in criminal cases have the right to free legal counsel and are guaranteed a fair and open public trial.

17 ARMED FORCES

In 2005 the total active armed forces of Slovakia numbered 20,195, with estimated reserves numbering 20,000. The Army had 12,860 active personnel, armed with 271 main battle tanks, 291 reconnaissance vehicles, 404 armored infantry fighting vehicles, 120 armored personnel carriers, and 374 artillery pieces. Air Force personnel totaled 5,160, equipped with 71 combat capable aircraft and 19 attack helicopters. As of 2005, there were 4,700 members in paramilitary units, including border police, guard troops, civil defense troops, and railway defense troops. Slovak armed forces in 2005 were deployed to eight countries or regions as part of NATO, European Union or UN missions. The defense budget for 2005 was $828 million.

18 INTERNATIONAL COOPERATION

Slovakia is a member of the United Nations, which it joined in 1993 when Czechoslovakia agreed to split into two parts. Slovakia serves on several nonregional specialized agencies, such as the FAO, UNESCO, UNIDO, the World Bank, ILO, and the WHO. The country is also a member of the Council of Europe, the European Bank for Reconstruction and Development, the OECD, OSCE, the Euro-Atlantic Partnership Council, and the WTO. Slovakia became an official member of NATO and the European Union in 2004. The country has observer status in the OAS and is an affiliate member of the Western European Union.

The government has actively participated in US- and NATO-led military actions in Iraq and Afghanistan. The country also participates in a joint Czech-Slovak peacekeeping force in Kosovo and supports UN missions and operations in Sierra Leone (est. 1999) and Cyprus (est. 1964).

Slovakia serves on the Australia Group, the Zangger Committee, the European Organization for Nuclear Research (CERN), the Nuclear Energy Agency, the Nuclear Suppliers Group (London Group), and the Organization for the Prohibition of Chemical Weapons. In environmental cooperation, is part of the Antarctic Treaty, the Basel Convention, Conventions on Biological Diversity and Air Pollution, Ramsar, CITES, the Kyoto Protocol, the Montréal Protocol, MARPOL, the Nuclear Test Ban Treaty, and the UN Conventions on the Law of the Sea, Climate Change, and Desertification

19 ECONOMY

Slovakia is continuing the difficult transformation from a centrally controlled economy to a market-oriented economy with some measure of success. Sustained GDP growth, although slowed after 1998, has been achieved, and inflation has moderated to single digits. While privatization has been carried out at an uneven pace, macroeconomic performance has improved steadily with 4.8% growth in 1994 and an average annual GDP growth rate of 6.66% 1995 to 1997. In 1998, however, the effects of the Russian financial crisis slowed investment and demand, reducing annual GDP growth to 4.4% in 1998, and to 1.9% in 1999. The pace of growth accelerated slowly from 2000 to 2002, from 2.2% to 3.3% to 4.4%, respectively. Average annual inflation after independence fell from 13.4% to 5.8% in 1996, but then hit double digits again in 2000, at 12%. In 2000 the government implemented austerity measures that helped to bring inflation down to 7.3% in 2001 and 3.1% in 2002. Unemployment remains a serious concern, at 19.8% in 2001 and 17.2% in 2002. The per capita GDP in purchasing power parity (PPP) terms, at $8,300 in 1998, had reached $11,500 (CIA est.) in 2001.

The progress made by the Dzurinda government between 2001 and 2004 has been remarkable. In 2004, Slovakia joined NATO and the EU, most of the major privatizations have been completed, massive foreign investment has been attracted to the country, and the economic expansion has been significant (despite the general European slowdown). In 2004, the GDP growth rate was 5.5%, up from 4.5% in 2003; for 2005, it was expected to stabilize at 5.3%. Inflation was on the upsurge in 2003, reaching 8.6%, but by 2004 it decreased to 7.5%, and was expected to decrease even further in 2005, to 2.9%. Unemployment was reduced steadily since 2001, but at 14.3% in 2004 it was still very high, and negatively influenced the economic performance of Slovakia. Other factors that affect the healthiness of the economy are corruption and poor living conditions for the population.

20 INCOME

The US Central Intelligence Agency (CIA) reports that in 2005 Slovakia's gross domestic product (GDP) was estimated at $85.1 billion. The CIA defines GDP as the value of all final goods and services produced within a nation in a given year and computed on the basis of purchasing power parity (PPP) rather than value as measured on the basis of the rate of exchange based on current dollars. The per capita GDP was estimated at $15,700. The annual growth rate of GDP was estimated at 5.1%. The average inflation rate in 2005 was 2.8%. It was estimated that agriculture accounted for 3.6% of GDP, industry 29.7%, and services 66.7%.

According to the World Bank, in 2003 remittances from citizens working abroad totaled $425 million or about $79 per capita and accounted for approximately 1.3% of GDP. Foreign aid receipts amounted to $160 million or about $30 per capita and accounted for approximately 0.5% of the gross national income (GNI).

The World Bank reports that in 2003 household consumption in Slovakia totaled $18.15 billion or about $3,368 per capita based on a GDP of $32.7 billion, measured in current dollars rather than PPP. Household consumption includes expenditures of individuals, households, and nongovernmental organizations on goods and services, excluding purchases of dwellings. It was estimated that for the period 1990 to 2003 household consumption grew at an average annual rate of 4.1%. In 2001 it was estimated that approximately 26% of household consumption was spent on food, 16% on fuel, 5% on health care, and 12% on education.

21 LABOR

As of 2005, there was an estimated 2.62 million people in Slovakia's workforce. As of 2003, agriculture accounted for 5.8%, with 29.3% in industry, 9% in construction, and 55.9% in the services sector. Unemployment was estimated at 11.5% in 2005.

Unions are freely allowed to organize in Slovakia as well as engage in collective bargaining. Strikes are legal only if they meet certain stringent requirements. About 45% of the workforce was unionized in 2002.

Children may not work until the age of 15. After age 16, minors may work without restrictions as to hours or condition of work. These provisions are effectively enforced by the government. The minimum wage was $105 per month in 2002. The standard workweek was 42.5 hours, although under collective bargaining agreements, many workweeks are 40 hours. The government sets minimum occupational health and safety standards and it effectively monitors them.

22 AGRICULTURE

Agriculture engaged 9% of the economically active population in 2000. The total cultivated area in 2003 was 1,564,000 hectares (3,865,000 acres), or 33% of the land area. Agriculture accounted for about 4% of GDP in 2003.

Barley and hops are important agricultural exports; fruit, wine, and seed oil are also produced for export. Important crops in Slovakia in 2004 (in thousands of tons) included: wheat, 1,764; barley, 916; corn, 862; potatoes, 382; rye, 124; and sugar beets, 1,599. In 2003, 22,615 tractors and 3,748 combines were in use.

During 1980–90, agricultural production grew by an average of 1.6% annually. During 1990–2000, agriculture increased by an annual average of 1.2%. Cereal production in 1999 was only 71% of the average during 1989–91. In 2004, cereal production was 6.9% higher than during 1999–2001.

23 ANIMAL HUSBANDRY

Some 874,000 hectares (2,160,000 acres) of land are meadows and pastures, representing 18.2% of the total land area. In 2005, there were some 1,300,000 pigs, 580,000 head of cattle, 316,000 sheep, 9,000 horses, and 5,600,000 chickens. Meat production was estimated at 314,000 tons in 2005, with pork accounting for 44%; beef,

14%; turkey, 23%; chicken, 14%; and others, 5%. Milk production was 1,153,000 tons in 2005. Due to the concern over bovine spongiform encephalopathy (mad cow disease), in July 1996 Slovakia banned selected imports and transit of cattle and sheep, and beef and mutton imports and transits coming from the United Kingdom, Ireland, Portugal, France, and Switzerland.

24 FISHING

Fishing is only a minor source of the domestic food supply. Production comes mostly from mountain streams and stocked ponds. Some of the rivers and ponds near Bratislava are polluted with chemicals and petrochemical seepings, impairing the growth of fish stocks regionally. The total catch in 2003 was 2,527 tons, with common carp and rainbow trout the dominant species.

25 FORESTRY

About 45% of Slovakia is under forest cover. Forests have been severely damaged by acid rain from coal-fired power stations. Roundwood production in 2004 was 7,240,000 cu m (255.6 million cu ft). Slovakian forest product exports include paper, wood, and furniture. In 2004, wood pulp production amounted to 520,000 tons; paper and paperboard, 798,000 tons; and wood-based panels, 508,000 cu m (17.9 million cu ft). Slovakia's trade surplus in forestry products was nearly $331.8 million in 2004.

26 MINING

Metal and metal products, particularly aluminum and steel, comprised Slovakia's leading industries in 2002, each of which was heavily dependent upon imports of raw materials. Gas, coke, oil, nuclear fuel, and chemicals were other top industries. Industrial mineral production in 2002 included: dolomite, 1.357 million tons, down from 1.471 million tons in 2001; lime (hydrated and quicklime), 911,000 tons; magnesite concentrate, 930,000 metric tons, down from 961,000 metric tons in 2001; crude gypsum and anhydrite, 121,700 metric tons; salt, 97,400 metric tons; barite concentrate, 25,820 metric tons, up from 14,450 metric tons in 2001; bentonite, 66,128 metric tons; kaolin, 24,600 metric tons; perlite, 18,630 metric tons, up from 14,910 metric tons in 2001; and zeolites, 15,000 metric tons. The Košice magnesite mines were put on care-and-maintenance. Also produced in 2002 were arsenic, diatomite, feldspar, illite, iron ore, refractory clays, nitrogen, sand and gravel, sodium compounds, limestone and other calcareous stones, crushed stone, sulfur, sulfuric acid, and talc. No zinc, lead, gold, silver, or copper was mined in 2002. Other mineral resources included antimony ore, mercury, brick soils, ceramic materials, and stonesalt. All mining companies were government owned.

27 ENERGY AND POWER

Total electric power production in 2002 amounted to 30.486 billion kWh, of which 26.9% was from fossil fuels, 17.1% from hydropower, and 55.9% from nuclear power. By 2001 nuclear power accounted for 54% of production, thanks to two new reactors that had come on line between 1998 and 2000, reducing Slovakia's dependence on fossil fuels and allowing it to become a net exporter of electricity. Consumption of electricity in 2002 was 24.196 billion kWh. As of 2002, total installed capacity was 7,417,000 kW.

Slovenske elektrarne (SE) is Slovakia's main power producer, accounting for 91% of the country's generating capacity.

Coal mining produced some 3,752,000 short tons of lignite in 2002, from reserves estimated at 190 million tons in 2001. In 2002, Slovakia imported 6,076,000 short tons of coal, of which 5,103,000 short tons consisted of hard coal.

As of 1 January 2004, Slovakia had crude oil reserves of 9 million barrels, natural gas reserves of 0.53 trillion cu ft., and a crude oil refining capacity of 115,000 barrels per day. Production of oil in 2003 was estimated at 3,500 barrels per day. Natural gas output in 2002 was estimated at 7.5 billion cu ft. Domestic demand for oil averaged 81,000 barrels per day in 2003. Natural gas consumption in 2002, was estimated at 270 billion cu ft. In 2002, natural gas was used by 80% of all Slovak households.

28 INDUSTRY

Major industries include heavy engineering, armaments, iron and steel production, nonferrous metals, and chemicals. In 2000, industry accounted for 34% of Slovakia's GDP, and the industrial growth rate was estimated at 4% in 2001. Foreign firms such as Volkswagen, US Steel, and Whirlpool are major investors in Slovak industry. Although privatization was ongoing in 2002 (including the Slovak Gas Company and oil-pipeline operator Transpetrol), and the country was attracting more foreign investment, many firms untouched by foreign investment were in trouble. Nonetheless, many Slovakian enterprises were restructuring and modernizing their equipment and methods. Slovakia produced 182,003 automobiles in 2001, and 264 heavy trucks in 2000. The country had one oil refinery in 2002, with a capacity of 115,000 barrels per day.

By 2004, the industrial sector had suffered a series of setbacks. Its representation in the total economic output had decreased to 30.1%, it employed only 29.3% of the labor force, and the industrial production growth rate was only 5.1%—as opposed to the 5.5% GDP growth rate. Agriculture made up 3.5% of the GDP and employed 5.8% of the working population; services came in first with 66.4% and 55.9% respectively; 9% of the workforce was employed by the construction sector. Major industries in 2004 were: metal and metal products; food and beverages; electricity, gas, coke, oil, nuclear fuel; chemicals and manmade fibers; machinery; paper and printing; earthenware and ceramics; transport vehicles; textiles; electrical and optical apparatus; and, rubber products.

29 SCIENCE AND TECHNOLOGY

The Slovak Academy of Sciences, founded in 1953, has departments of exact and technical sciences and of natural sciences and chemistry, and 36 affiliated research institutes. The Council of Scientific Societies, headquartered in Bratislava, coordinates the activities of 16 societies concerned with specific scientific and technical fields. Natural history exhibits are displayed in the Slovak National Museum in Bratislava, the Central Slovak Museum in Banská Bstrica, and the Museum of Eastern Slovakia in Košice. The Slovak Mining Museum, founded in 1900, is located in Banská Stiavnica. Eight universities offer scientific and technical degrees. In 1987–97, science and engineering students accounted for 40% of university enrollment.

In 2002, research and development (R&D) expenditures totaled $407.279 million, or 0.59% of GDP. Of that amount, 53.6%

came from the business sector, followed by government sources at 44.1%. Foreign sources accounted for 2.1% and higher education 0.1%. In that same year, there were 1,707 scientists and engineers, and 564 technicians per one million people that were engaged in R&D. High technology exports in 2002 totaled $386 million, or 3% of the country's manufactured exports.

30 DOMESTIC TRADE

Bratislav is the primary commercial center of the country. Other major centers include Košice, Trencin, Zilina, and Poprad. Nitra is a primary distribution center for agricultural products.

Retail trade is currently undergoing rapid privatization along with other sectors of the economy. As of 2002, about 98% of all retail establishments were privatized. Most establishments are small, family-owned shops specializing in one type of product, such as groceries, flowers, books, clothing, music, etc. However, the trend is slowly moving towards larger Western-style stores and hypermarkets that offer a wider variety of products under one roof. Wholesalers tend to be directly involved in the retailing of their products as well. A few franchise firms have recently made their way into the country.

Retail shops are generally open from 9 AM to 6 PM, Monday through Friday. New chain stores are open seven days a week from about 7 AM to 8 PM. Grocery stores often operate from 6 AM to 7 PM. Many stores will open for half a day on Saturdays, but most businesses and shops are closed on Sundays.

31 FOREIGN TRADE

The Czech Republic, which used to account for as much as one-third of Slovakia's foreign trade, has dropped behind Germany as Slovakia's leading trade partner. Trade with the former Soviet Union has declined in importance and has increasingly been replaced by trade with the OECD, whose members buy over 90% of all Slovak exports.

In the Far East, China has emerged as the top trading partner, with imports and exports between the two nations increasing by almost 300% in 1995.

In 2004, exports totaled $29.2 billion (FOB—Free on Board), and were only slightly surpassed by imports at $29.7 billion (FOB).

Vehicles (25.9%), machinery and electrical equipment (21.3%), base metals (14.6%), chemicals and minerals (10.1%), and plastics (5.4%) topped the list for Slovakia's export commodities. Slovakia's main export partners were Germany (which received 34.4% of total exports), the Czech Republic (14.7%), Austria (8.2%), Italy (5.8%), Poland (5.3%), the United States (4.5%), and Hungary (4.3%). The imports were distributed among the following categories: machinery and transport equipment (41.1%), intermediate manufactured goods (19.3%), fuels (12.3%), chemicals (9.8%), and miscellaneous manufactured goods (10.2%). Most of the imports came from Germany (26.1%), the Czech Republic (21.3%), Russia (9.1%), Austria (6.6%), Poland (4.9%), and Italy (4.9%).

32 BALANCE OF PAYMENTS

A decline in foreign trade in 2001 caused the central bank to revise its forecast of the current account deficit up from 4% to 5.7% of GDP.

The US Central Intelligence Agency (CIA) reported that in 2001 the purchasing power parity of Slovakia's exports was $12.9 billion while imports totaled $15.4 billion resulting in a trade deficit of $2.5 billion.

The International Monetary Fund (IMF) reported that in 2000 Slovakia had exports of goods totaling $11.9 billion and imports totaling $12.8 billion. The services credit totaled $2.2 billion and debit $1.81 billion.

Exports of goods and services totaled $31.5 billion in 2004, up from $25.1 billion in 2003. Imports grew from $25.5 billion in 2003, to $32.6 billion in 2004. Although Slovakia has managed to keep a fine balance between imports and exports, the resource balance was on a negative upsurge, growing from -$407 million in 2003, to -$1.2 billion in 2004. A similar trend was registered for the current account balance, which deteriorated from -$278 million in 2003, to -$1.4 billion in 2004. The national reserves (including gold) were $12.1 billion in 2003, covering approximately

---

Principal Trading Partners – Slovakia (2003)

(In millions of US dollars)

Country	Exports	Imports	Balance
World	21,958.4	22,603.1	-644.7
Germany	6,769.9	5,758.3	1,011.6
Czech Republic	2,834.0	3,234.3	-400.3
Italy-San Marino-Holy See	1,650.0	1,395.8	254.2
Austria	1,632.3	990.1	642.2
United States	1,154.3	440.5	713.8
Hungary	1,070.1	776.0	294.1
Poland	1,049.5	797.1	252.4
France-Monaco	771.0	958.9	-187.9
Netherlands	593.0	372.6	220.4
United Kingdom	463.8	482.1	-18.3

(...) data not available or not significant.

SOURCE: *2003 International Trade Statistics Yearbook,* New York: United Nations, 2004.

Balance of Payments – Slovakia (2003)

(In millions of US dollars)

Current Account		**-282.0**
Balance on goods		-649.0
Imports	-22,593.0	
Exports	21,944.0	
Balance on services		241.0
Balance on income		-119.0
Current transfers		245.0
Capital Account		**102.0**
Financial Account		**1,661.0**
Direct investment abroad		-24.0
Direct investment in Slovakia		559.0
Portfolio investment assets		-742.0
Portfolio investment liabilities		168.0
Financial derivatives		17.0
Other investment assets		-20.0
Other investment liabilities		1,703.0
Net Errors and Omissions		**27.0**
Reserves and Related Items		**-1,508.0**

(...) data not available or not significant.

SOURCE: *Balance of Payment Statistics Yearbook 2004,* Washington, DC: International Monetary Fund, 2004.

six months of imports; by 2004, they decreased to $11.7 billion, covering only four months of imports.

33 BANKING AND SECURITIES

Four years after the Soviet system relinquished control over the eastern bloc, Slovakia formed a National Bank. In January 1992 the banking system of Czechoslovakia was split. From that point on the National Bank of Slovakia was charged with the responsibility of circulating currency and regulating the banking sector. At the end of 2002, there were 23 commercial banks operating in the Slovak Republic, including the Investment and Development Bank (1992); People's Bank (1992); Postal Bank Inc. (1991); Industrial Bank, Inc. (1992); First Commercial Bank Inc. (1993); Slovak Credit Bank (1993); Slovak Agricultural Bank (1991); and the General Credit Bank (1990). Twelve of the 23 commercial banks were partly or wholly foreign-owned. In addition, two branches and 10 representative offices of foreign banks had been established. In 2000, plans called for the privatization of the three largest banks, Vseobecna Uverova Banka (VUB), Slovenska Sporitelna, and Investicna a Rozvoyova Banka (IRB) by the end of the year. The International Monetary Fund reports that in 2001, currency and demand deposits—an aggregate commonly known as M1—were equal to $4.7 billion. In that same year, M2—an aggregate equal to M1 plus savings deposits, small time deposits, and money market mutual funds—was $13.9 billion. The money market rate, the rate at which financial institutions lend to one another in the short term, was 7.76%.

The Bratislava Stock Exchange (BSE) opened on 8 July 1990 and acts as a share holding company formed by all Slovakian financial institutions, banks and savings banks, and companies authorized to trade securities. Brokers and other mediators are not permitted in the trading system. The volume of stocks traded on the BSE, however, remained low until 1996. In 2001, there were 844 companies listed on the BSE, with a trading value of $966 million (up 141% from 2000) and total market capitalization of $665 million (down 10.3% from 2000). As of 2004, a total of 258 companies were listed on the BSE, which had a market capitalization of $4.410 Billion. The Bratislava Option and Futures Exchange opened in 1994.

34 INSURANCE

The pre-World War II insurance companies and institutions of the former Czechoslovakia after 1945 were reorganized, merged, nationalized and centralized. Since 1952, the insurance industry has been administered by the State Insurance Office, under the jurisdiction of the Ministry of Finance, and two enterprises conducted insurance activities, the Czech and the Slovak Insurance Enterprises of the State. In 1997, at least 20 insurance companies were doing business in Slovakia. Nonetheless, the Slovak Insurance Company remains the only company authorized to write the compulsory third-party automobile liability insurance. Lawyers, architects and dentists are also required to carry liability insurance. There are no restrictions on foreign ownership of companies. In 2003, the value of all direct insurance premiums written totaled $1.140 billion, of which nonlife premiums accounted for $676 million. In that same year, the top nonlife and life insurer was Allianz Poistovna, which had gross written nonlife premiums

Public Finance – Slovakia (2003)		
(In billions of koruny, central government figures)		
Revenue and Grants	**422.55**	**100.0%**
Tax revenue	200.79	47.5%
Social contributions	168.64	39.9%
Grants	0.19	<1.0%
Other revenue	52.93	12.5%
Expenditures	**461.99**	**100.0%**
General public services	95.37	20.6%
Defense	21.71	4.7%
Public order and safety	23.11	5.0%
Economic affairs	47	10.2%
Environmental protection	3.46	0.7%
Housing and community amenities	3.9	0.8%
Health	93.72	20.3%
Recreational, culture, and religion	5.49	1.2%
Education	15.7	3.4%
Social protection	153.23	33.2%

(…) data not available or not significant.

SOURCE: *Government Finance Statistics Yearbook 2004,* Washington, DC: International Monetary Fund, 2004.

totaling $369.8 million, and gross written life insurance premiums of $141.9 million.

35 PUBLIC FINANCE

Since the dissolution of Czechoslovakia, the Slovak government has implemented several measures to compensate for the large loss of fiscal transfers it received from the Federation, which were equivalent to between Sk20–25 billion in 1992. The Slovak government's initial budget was balanced at the beginning of 1992, with revenues and expenditures equivalent to Sk159 billion. Since that time, however, Slovakia's budget has fallen into deficit. Privatization efforts have been successful, attracting a large amount of foreign direct investment (FDI).

The US Central Intelligence Agency (CIA) estimated that in 2005 Slovakia's central government took in revenues of approximately $21.4 billion and had expenditures of $23.1 billion. Revenues minus expenditures totaled approximately -$1.6 billion. Public debt in 2005 amounted to 16.9% of GDP. Total external debt was $25.81 billion.

The International Monetary Fund (IMF) reported that in 2003, the most recent year for which it had data, central government revenues were SK422.55 billion and expenditures were SK461.99 billion. The value of revenues was US$11 million and expenditures US$12 million, based on an exchange rate for 2003 of US$1 = SK36.773 as reported by the IMF. Government outlays by function were as follows: general public services, 20.6%; defense, 4.7%; public order and safety, 5.0%; economic affairs, 10.2%; environmental protection, 0.7%; housing and community amenities, 0.8%; health, 20.3%; recreation, culture, and religion, 1.2%; education, 3.4%; and social protection, 33.2%.

36 TAXATION

The principal taxes are corporate income tax, personal income tax, and value-added tax. Individuals are liable for tax on all sources of worldwide income. Corporate income tax is levied on joint stock companies, limited liability companies, and limited partnerships. In 2005, the corporate tax rate for resident companies was 19%. Capital gains were also taxed at 19%. Dividends paid out of after-tax profits are not taxed. Interest income from loans or bands are taxed at the corporate rate, as is income from royalties. Other taxes include a road tax, excise duties, import duties, and taxes on property.

As of 2005, individual income was taxed according at a flat 19% rate. Dividends paid to individuals is not taxed. Income from interest and capital are included in total income.

The principle indirect tax is Slovakia's value-added tax (VAT). As of 2005, the standard rate was 19% and was applied to most transactions. However, exports are zero-rated, and financial, broadcasting, insurance and educational services are exempt.

37 CUSTOMS AND DUTIES

As a WTO member, Slovakia uses the Brussels Tariff Nomenclature. Goods imported into Slovakia are liable to three kinds of charges: customs duties, value-added tax (VAT) of 10% or 19%, and an excise tax. A 3% import surcharge was eliminated on 1 January 2001. However, Slovakia imposes surcharges on approximately 80% of its imports. Slovakia is also a member of the Central European Free Trade Area (CEFTA) along with Bulgaria, the Czech Republic, Hungary, Poland, Romania, and Slovenia.

38 FOREIGN INVESTMENT

Prior to the defeat of Prime Minister Vladimir Meciar, Slovakia experienced difficulty attracting foreign investment due to perceived political uncertainty and vacillations in its privatization policy. The government has introduced tax incentives to attract more capital from abroad.

Annual foreign direct investment (FDI) inflow was $220 million in 1997 and rose to $648 million in 1998. Affected by the Russian financial crisis, FDI inflow fell to $390 million in 1999, but then recovered sharply in 2000 to reach a peak of over $2 billion. FDI inflow to Slovakia in 2001 was $1.5 billion. The Netherlands has been the single largest investor.

At the end of the first three quarters in 2004, cumulative foreign investment had risen to $11.4 billion. Most of the capital inflow was generated through privatization sales, but since 2003 significant greenfield investments have been made. In 2004, Hyundai invested $1.5 billion in its first European assembly plant; Ford constructed a $400 million gearbox production plant in the same year. Most of the investments went to industrial manufacturing (38.2%), the banking sector (22.7%), retail and wholesale (11.7%), and to the production and distribution of gas and electricity (11.0%). The biggest investing countries were Germany (with 22.7% of total investments), the Netherlands (16%), and Austria (14.3%).

39 ECONOMIC DEVELOPMENT

The government in the early 1990s slowed economic reforms due to the social burden imposed by the transformation to a market economy. Measures included stimulation of demand through price subsidies and public spending. Slovakia's most successful structural reform has been privatization. The first stage of large-scale privatization included 751 companies, and a second stage, which involved 650 medium- and large-scale enterprises, was implemented in late 1993.

However, the Meciar government was slow to implement the $1.5 billion privatization program after he regained power in 1994 and the country continued to rely heavily on foreign aid. Western investors cheered his defeat and replacement by reformer Mikulas Dzurinda in 1998. The Dzurinda government quickly earned praise for its implementation of reforms. The renewed liberalization measures, combined with a new attitude toward Slovakia's Roma (Gypsy) population, caused the EU to place Slovakia back on its list of candidate members. In December 2002, Slovakia was officially invited to join the EU, and accession took place in May 2004.

Slovakia's foreign debt at the beginning of 2002 was about $11 billion, approximately 55% of gross domestic product (GDP). The current account deficit was high, largely due to a shortfall in foreign trade. Foreign direct investment (FDI) has been relatively small in recent years, although FDI in 2000 alone was greater than cumulative investment received by Slovakia in the preceding 10 years. Although growth was strong and inflation relatively low in the early 2000s, the unemployment rate remained high. By 2002, the main banks and utilities had been privatized; but further corporate restructuring and labor market reform, improved banking supervision, and strengthening state administration and the judicial system remained structural reforms to be implemented.

A strong economic expansion followed in 2003 and 2004, with GDP growth rates of 4.5% and 5.5% respectively. In 2004, Slovakia joined NATO and the EU, which greatly improved the stability of the political and economic climate. In addition, an investment friendly environment was created, which led to a dramatic increase in the inflow of foreign capital. In 2005, Slovakia was considered by the World Bank the world's top performer in improving its business climate over the last year; in the same year it was deemed one of the top 20 countries in the world for ease of doing business. As of 2006, Slovakia was able to boast a highly skilled and relatively low-cost labor force, an attractive tax system (19% flat tax), a liberal labor code, and a favorable geographic location.

40 SOCIAL DEVELOPMENT

Slovakia's social security system was first introduced in 1906. The current program was implemented in 2004. Old age, disability and survivor's pensions are funded by employee and employer contributions as well as government subsidies. Retirement is set at age 62 for both men and women. The first laws covering sickness benefits were instituted in 1888. A family allowance system provides benefits for all residents funded totally by the government. There are also sickness and maternity benefits, a workers' compensation program, and unemployment benefits.

Women and men are equal under the law, enjoying the same property, inheritance, and other rights, however discrimination persists. Women on the average earn 30% less than men. Despite legal safeguards, the small number of women in private and public leadership roles is evidence of continuing cultural barriers to full equality. The Coordinating Committee for Women's Affairs has not been successful at protecting women against violence, health risks, or economic disadvantages. Domestic abuse and sexual violence against women remains an extensive and underreported problem.

Roma minorities suffer from high levels of unemployment and housing discrimination. Attacks against Roma and other minorities by skinhead extremists were reported. Human rights were generally well respected, but some democratic freedoms were not respected. These include the intimidation of political opponents and interference with the media. There were also reports of police abuse of Roma.

41HEALTH

Since 1995 general public health services have been organized into a system of state health institutes. However, primary health care services, formerly operated by the state, are now separate from the public health sector and reimbursed through a compulsory insurance program. As of 2004 there were 77 polyclinics in the country; Slovakia had 84 hospitals, 23 specialized institutes, and 1 maternity facility. As of 2004, there were an estimated 325 physicians, 731 nurses, 44 dentists, 48 pharmacists, and 7 midwives per 100,000 people. Total health care expenditure was estimated at 6.5% of GDP.

Life expectancy in 2005 was 74.50 years and infant mortality was 7.41 per 1,000 live births. As of 2002, the crude birth rate and overall mortality rate were estimated at, respectively, 10.1 and 9.2 per 1,000 people. A Slovakian woman living through her childbearing years had an average of 1.3 children. A large proportion of Slovakian women (74%) used some form of contraception. Immunization rates for children up to one year old were impressively high: tuberculosis, 90%; diphtheria, pertussis, and tetanus, 98%; polio, 98%; and measles, 98%.

The HIV/AIDS prevalence was 0.10 per 100 adults in 2003. As of 2004, there were approximately 200 people living with HIV/AIDS in the country. There were an estimated 100 deaths from AIDS in 2003.

42HOUSING

In 1992, the Slovak Association of Towns and Villages, comprised of some 2,000 towns, was engaged in recovering all housing units from former state administration authorities. As of 2001, there were about 1,884,846 dwelling units nationwide. Most of these were detached houses. About 88% of all dwellings were permanently occupied. About 11% of all dwellings were unoccupied. Of the permanently occupied units, the average number of rooms per unit was 3.2; nearly 73% of all dwellings had 3 rooms or more. The average number of people per dwelling was also 3.21. About 76.3% of all dwellings had central heating and 92.8% had a separate bathroom or shower facility. About 28,507 units were considered unsuitable for habitation.

43EDUCATION

Slovakia has an estimated adult literacy rate of 99%. Education is compulsory for nine years, approximately up to the age of 15. This basic schooling is accomplished in two stages of four years and five years. At the secondary level, there are a variety of general, vocational, professional, and art school programs to choose from. Most secondary programs last about four years.

In 2001, about 82% of children between the ages of three and five were enrolled in some type of preschool program. Primary school enrollment in 2003 was estimated at about 86% of age-eligible students. The same year, secondary school enrollment was about 88% of age-eligible students. It is estimated that about 99% of all students complete their primary education. The student-to-teacher ratio for primary school was at about 18:1 in 2003; the ratio for secondary school was about 13:1.

Slovakia has 13 universities, with the oldest being Cornenius (Komensky) University in Bratislava—founded in 1919. The Pavel Josef Afarík University, founded in 1959, is in Košice. In 2003, it was estimated that about 34% of the tertiary age population were enrolled in tertiary education programs. The adult literacy rate for 2004 was estimated at about 99%.

As of 2003, public expenditure on education was estimated at 4.4% of GDP, or 13.8% of total government expenditures.

44LIBRARIES AND MUSEUMS

The most important library in Slovakia is the Slovak National Library (4.4 million volumes), founded in 1863 and located at Martin. The State Scientific Library in Banská Bstrica (1926) holds almost two million volumes, and the Comenius University in Bratislava has the country's largest university collection of 2.2 million volumes. In total there are over 450 libraries in universities and other higher-educational institutions and about 2,600 public library branches nationwide.

The Slovak National Gallery (1948), the Slovak National Museum (1924), the Natural History Museum (1948), and the History Museum (1924), are all in Bratislava. The administrators of the Slovak National Museum also sponsor the branch museums of the Museum of Archaeology, the Museum of Ethnography, the Museum of Music, the Museum of Puppetry and Toys, and the Museum of Jewish Culture. The State Gallery of Art is in Banská Bstrica. There are dozens of regional museums throughout the country.

45MEDIA

In 2003, there were an estimated 241 mainline telephones for every 1,000 people; about 7,000 people were on a waiting list for telephone service installation. The same year, there were approximately 684 mobile phones in use for every 1,000 people.

There are three government boards appointed by a majority vote of parliament to supervise radio and television broadcasting: The Slovak Television Council and the Slovak Radio Council establish broadcasting policy for state-owned television and radio. The Slovak Council for Radio and Television Broadcasting issues broadcast licenses for nongovernment groups and administers advertising laws and other regulations. The privately owned TV Markiza has the widest broadcast audience. In 2005, there were at two other commercial television stations and at least four commercial radios stations. The public broadcaster, Slovak TV and Radio, sponsored two national television networks and five national radio networks. In 2003, there were an estimated 965 radios and 409 television sets for every 1,000 people. About 127.3 of every 1,000 people were cable subscribers. Also in 2003, there were 180.4 personal computers for every 1,000 people and 256 of every 1,000 people had access to the Internet. There were 63 secure Internet servers in the country in 2004.

In 2002, there were 14 major daily newspapers, including (with average circulation figures): *Novy Cas* (*New Time*, 230,000), *Pravda* (*Truth*, 165,000), *Praca* (*Labor*, 80,000), and *SMENA* (a youth journal, 80,000). The daily sports newspaper *Sport* had a circulation of 85,000 in 2002. The two major Hungarian newspapers are the daily *Uj Szo* (*New Word*, 42,000) and the weekly *Szabad Ujsag* (*Free Journal*, 40,000). There are also a number of government bulletins and small circulation publications printed by and for minority language groups.

46 ORGANIZATIONS

The Slovak Chamber of Commerce and Industry is located in Bratislava. There are professional associations for a number of occupations, including teaching and a number of medical professions.

The Slovak Academy of Sciences promotes public interest, education, and research in various scientific fields. Cultural and educational associations include the Organization of Slovak Writers. The Slovak Medical Association promotes research and education on health issues and works to establish common policies and standards in healthcare. There are several other associations dedicated to research and education for specific fields of medicine and particular diseases and conditions.

National youth organizations include the Association of Slovak Students, Civic Democratic Youth, YMCA/YWCA, and Slovak Scouting. There are several sports associations promoting amateur competition in a variety of pastimes, such as Frisbee, aikido, badminton, baseball, figure skating, floorball, and track and field; many sports associations are affiliated with international groups as well. There are national chapters of the Paralympic Committee and the Special Olympics, as well as a national Olympic Committee.

Kiwanis and Lion's Clubs have programs in the country. Women's organizations include the Alliance of Women in Slovakia. Greenpeace, Habitat for Humanity, and the Red Cross have national chapters.

47 TOURISM, TRAVEL, AND RECREATION

Slovakia's outdoor tourist attractions include mountains (the most famous being the High and Low Tatras), forests, cave formations, and over 1,000 mineral and hot springs. In addition, tourists can visit ancient castles, monuments, chateaux, museums, and galleries. Slovakia is also home to many health spas. Horse racing is a national pastime. Golf, skiing, mountaineering, and rafting are popular sports among tourists. All visitors are required to have valid passports, onward/return tickets and sufficient funds for their stay. Visas are required for nationals of 154 countries including China, Australia, and India.

In 2003, about 1.4 million tourists arrived in Slovakia. There were 35,853 hotel rooms that year with 90,773 beds and an occupancy rate of 38%. The average length of stay was three nights.

According to 2005 US Department of State estimates, the cost of staying in Bratislava was $272 per day. Estimated daily travel costs elsewhere in the country averaged $157.

48 FAMOUS SLOVAKS

Ján Kollár (1793–1852), writer, poet, Slavist, and archaeologist, was a Slovak patriot who championed the Slav struggle against foreign oppression. Ludovít Stúr (1815–56) is the founder of the Slovak literary language and modern Slovak literature. Founder of scientific Slavic studies was Pavel Josef Safačrík (1795–1861), whose *Slavonic Antiquities* had great scholarly influence. Andrej Hlinka (1864–1938) led the Slovak Catholic autonomist movement. The greatest Slovak poet, Pavel Hviezdoslav (1849–1921), translated foreign poetry, refined the language, and contributed to Slovak awakening. The Robin Hood of the Slovaks, Juraj Jánošík (1688–1713), fought the Hungarians. Milan Rastislav Stefánik (1880–1919), military leader, astronomer, and ally of Tomáš Masaryk, represented the Slovaks in their struggle for liberty. Alexander Dubček (1921–92) was first secretary of the Czechoslovak Communist Party (1968–69). His attempt to increase civil liberties led to the invasion of Czechoslovakia by the Warsaw Pact in 1968. In 1989 he was elected the Federal Assembly's first speaker.

49 DEPENDENCIES

Slovakia has no territories or colonies.

50 BIBLIOGRAPHY

Frucht, Richard (ed.). *Eastern Europe: An Introduction to the People, Lands, and Culture*. Santa Barbara, Calif.: ABC-CLIO, 2005.

Kirschbaum, Stanislav J. *Historical Dictionary of Slovakia*. Lanham, Md.: Scarecrow, 1998.

———. *A History of Slovakia: The Struggle for Survival*. 2nd ed. New York: St. Martin's Press, 2005.

Labour Market and Social Policies in the Slovak Republic. Paris: Organisation for Economic Cooperation and Development, 1996.

McElrath, Karen (ed.). *HIV and AIDS: A Global View*. Westport, Conn.: Greenwood Press, 2002.

Mikus, Joseph A. *Slovakia: A Political and Constitutional History: With Documents*. Bratislava: Slovak Academy Press, 1995.

Reuvid, Jonathan. *Doing Business with Slovakia*. Sterling, Va.: Kogan Page, 2004.

Slovakia and the Slovaks: A Concise Encyclopedia. Edited by Milan Strhan and David P. Daniel. Bratislava: Encyclopedical Institute of the Slovak Academy of Science, Goldpress Publishers, 1994.

SLOVENIA

Republic of Slovenia
Republika Slovenije

CAPITAL: Ljubljana

FLAG: Equal horizontal bands of white (top), blue, and red with seal superimposed on upper hoist side.

ANTHEM: *Zive naj vsi narodi.* (The national anthem begins, "Let all nations live . . .")

MONETARY UNIT: The currency of Slovenia is the tolar (SLT), which consists of 100 stotinov. There are coins of 50 stotinov and 1, 2, and 5 tolars, and notes of 10, 20, 50, and 200 tolars. SLT1 = $0.00534 (or $1 = SLT187.42) as of 2005.

WEIGHTS AND MEASURES: The metric system is in force.

HOLIDAYS: New Year, 1–2 January; Prešeren Day, Day of Culture, 8 February; Resistance Day, 27 April; Labor Days, 1–2 May; National Statehood Day, 25 June; Assumption, 15 August; Reformation Day, 31 October; All Saints' Day, 1 November; Christmas Day, 25 December; Independence Day, 26 December. Movable holidays are Easter Sunday and Monday.

TIME: 1 PM = noon GMT.

¹LOCATION, SIZE, AND EXTENT

Slovenia is located in central Europe. Slovenia is slightly larger than the state of New Jersey with a total area of 20,273 sq km (7,827 sq mi). Slovenia shares boundaries with Austria on the N, Hungary on the E, Croatia on the S, and the Adriatic Sea and Italy on the W, and has a total land boundary of 1,334 km (829 mi) and a coastline of 46.6 km (29 mi). Slovenia's capital city, Ljubljana, is located near the center of the country.

²TOPOGRAPHY

The topography of Slovenia features a small coastal strip on the Adriatic, the Julian Alps adjacent to Italy, the Karawanken Mountains of the northern border with Austria, and mixed mountains and valleys with numerous rivers in the central and eastern regions. The highest point of Mt. Triglav is found in the Julian Alps with an elevation of 2,864 m (9,396 ft). The longest river is the Sava, which flows through the center of the country for 221 km (137 mi). A unique feature of Slovenia is the presence of over 6,500 karst formed caves, the most well-known being the Skocjan caves in the southwest, which are designated as a natural UNESCO World Heritage Site.

³CLIMATE

Slovenia's coastal climate is influenced by the Mediterranean Sea. Its interior climate ranges from mild to hot summers, with cold winters in the plateaus and valleys to the east. In Ljubljana, July's mean temperature is 20°C (68°F). The mean temperature in January is -1°C (30°F). Rainfall in the capital averages 139 cm (59 in) a year.

⁴FLORA AND FAUNA

The region's climate has given Slovenia a wealth of diverse flora and fauna. Ferns, flowers, mosses, and common trees populate the landscape. There are subtropical plants along the Adriatic Sea. Wild animals include deer, brown bear, rabbit, fox, and wild boar. Farmers plant vineyards on the hillsides and raise livestock in the fertile lowlands of the country. As of 2002, there were at least 75 species of mammals, 201 species of birds, and over 3,200 species of plants throughout the country.

⁵ENVIRONMENT

Slovenia's natural environment suffers from damage to forests by industrial pollutants, especially chemical and metallurgical plant emissions and the resulting acid rain. Water pollution is also a problem. The Sava River is polluted with domestic and industrial waste; heavy metals and toxic chemicals can be found in the coastal waters. The country is subject to flooding and earthquakes.

As of 2003, 6% of Slovenia's total land area was protected. One of the largest protected areas is Triglav National Park. According to a 2006 report issued by the International Union for Conservation of Nature and Natural Resources (IUCN), threatened species included 7 types of mammals, 7 species of birds, 2 species of amphibians, 16 species of fish, and 42 species of invertebrates. Threatened species include the Italian agile frog, slender-billed curlew, beluga, Danube salmon, the garden dormouse, and the great snipe.

⁶POPULATION

The population of Slovenia in 2005 was estimated by the United Nations (UN) at 1,998,000, which placed it at number 141 in population among the 193 nations of the world. In 2005, approximately 15% of the population was over 65 years of age, with another 14% of the population under 15 years of age. There were 95 males for every 100 females in the country. According to the UN, the annual population rate of change for 2005–10 was expected to be -0.1%, a rate the government viewed as satisfactory. The fertility rate, at 1.4 births per woman, has been below replacement levels since the mid-1990s. The projected population for the year 2025 was 2,014,000. The population density was 99 per sq km (256 per sq mi).

The UN estimated that 51% of the population lived in urban areas in 2005, and that urban areas were growing at an annual rate of 0.03%. The capital city, Ljubljana, had a population of 256,000 in that year. Maribor had a population of 110,668.

⁷MIGRATION

In 1995, Slovenia was harboring 29,000 refugees from the former Yugoslav SFR. Of the 5,000–10,000 that remained in 1999, most had opted not to take Slovene citizenship during a six-month window of opportunity in 1991–92 and had been living in the country as stateless persons ever since. In 1999, parliament passed legislation that offered these persons permanent resident status; a six-week window for applications closed at the end of the year. The number of migrants living in Slovenia in 2000 was 51,000. By the end of 2004, there were 304 refugees in Slovenia and 323 asylum seekers. In addition, there were 584 citizens of the former Yugoslavia who remained of concern to the United Nations High Commissioner for Refugees (UNHCR). The net migration rate in 2005 was an estimated 1 migrant per 1,000 population. The government views the migration levels as satisfactory.

⁸ETHNIC GROUPS

According to the 2002 census, the total population is about 83.1% Slovene. Minority groups include Serbs (2%), Croats (1.8%), and Bosniaks (1.1%). There are about 10,467 Muslims, 6,243 Hungarians, 6,186 Albanians, 3,246 Roma and 2,254 Italians.

⁹LANGUAGES

Like Serbo-Croatian, Macedonian, and Bulgarian, Slovene is a language of the southern Slavic group. It is closest to Serbo-Croatian, but the two are not mutually intelligible. Slovene is written in the Roman alphabet and has the special letters č, š, and ž. The letters q, w, x, and y are missing. As of 2002, 91% of the populace spoke Slovene; 6% spoke Serbo-Croatian; and 3% used various other languages.

¹⁰RELIGIONS

According to the 2002 census, the largest denominational group in the country was the Roman Catholic Church, representing about 57.8% of the population. There is also a Slovenian Old Catholic Church and some Eastern Orthodox that made up about 2% of the population. Although Calvinism played an important role during the Reformation, the only well-established Protestant group is the Evangelical Lutheran Church of Slovenia, which has about 14,736 members. Muslims make up about 2.4% of the population. The census reported only 99 Jews. About 199,264 people responded as atheists. Freedom of religion is guaranteed in the constitution. Religious organizations register with the Office of Religious Communities in order to secure legal status and conduct business.

¹¹TRANSPORTATION

Rail lines, emanating from Ljubljana, connect the capital to Kranj and Jesenice, Postojna and Novo Gorica, Celje and Maribor, and Nova Mesto before continuing to Austria, Italy, and Croatia. As of 2004, there were some 1,201 km (747 mi) of railway, all of it standard gauge. Of that total, 499 km (310 mi) are electrified. With over 150 passenger stations and 140 freight stations, almost every town in Slovenia can be reached by train. Slovenian Railways uses high-speed trains and container transports.

In 2002, Slovenia had 20,250 km (12,596 mi) of roads, all of which were paved, and included 456 km (284 mi) of expressways. Slovenia has two expressways: one connecting Ljubljana, Postojna, and Razdrto with the coastal region; the other linking Ljubljana with Kranj and the Gorenjska region in the northwest and with the Karawanken tunnel to Austria. In 2003, there were 889,600 passenger cars and 69,300 commercial vehicles registered for use.

The principal marine port is Koper. Technically there is no merchant fleet, but Slovenian owners have registered their respective vessels in 23 countries as of 2005.

Slovenia had an estimated 14 airports in 2004, 6 of which had paved runways as of 2005. In 2003, about 758,000 passengers were carried on scheduled domestic and international flights.

¹²HISTORY

Origins and Middle Ages

Slovenia is located in the central European area where Latin, Germanic, Slavic, and Magyar people have come into contact with one another. The historical dynamics of these four groups have impacted the development of this small nation.

Until the 8th–9th centuries AD, Slavs used the same common Slavic language that was codified by St. Cyril and Methodius in their AD 863 translations of Holy Scriptures into the Slavic tongue. Essentially an agricultural people, the Slovenes settled from around AD 550 in the eastern Alps and in the western Pannonian Plains. The ancestors of today's Slovenes developed their own form of political organization in which power was delegated to their rulers through an "electors" group of peasant leaders/soldiers (the "Kosezi"). Allies of the Bavarians against the Avars, whom they defeated in AD 743, the Carantania Slovenes came under control of the numerically stronger Bavarians and both were overtaken by the Franks in AD 745.

In 863, the Greek scholars Constantine (Cyril) and Methodius were sent to Moravia, having first developed an original alphabet (called "Glagolitic") and translated the necessary Holy Scriptures into the Slavic tongue of the time. The work of the two "Apostles of the Slavs" was opposed by the Frankish Bishops who accused them of teaching heresy and using a nonsacred language and script. Invited by Pope Nicholas I to Rome to explain their work, the brothers visited with the Slovene Prince Kocelj in 867 and took along some 50 young men to be instructed in the Slavic scriptures and liturgy that were competing with the traditionally "sacred" liturgical languages of Latin and Greek. Political events prevented the utilization of the Slavic language in Central European Churches with the exception of Croatia and Bosnia. However, the liturgy in Slavic spread among Balkan and Eastern Slavs.

Slovenes view the installation of the Dukes of Carinthia with great pride as the expression of a nonfeudal, bottom-up delegation of authority—by the people's "electors" through a ceremony inspired by old Slavic egalitarian customs. All the people assembled would intone a Slovene hymn of praise—"Glory and praise to God Almighty, who created heaven and earth, for giving us and our land the Duke and master according to our will."

LOCATION: 46°15′ N; 15°10′ E. BOUNDARY LENGTHS: Total boundary lengths, 999 kilometers (621 miles); Austria 262 kilometers (163 miles); Croatia, 455 kilometers (283 miles); Italy, 199 kilometers (124 miles); Hungary, 83 kilometers (52 miles).

This ceremony lasted for 700 years with some feudal accretions and was conducted in the Slovenian language until the last one in 1414. The uniqueness of the Carinthian installation ceremony is confirmed by several sources, including medieval reports, the writing of Pope Pius II in 1509, and its recounting in Jean Bodin's *Treatise on Republican Government* (1576) as "unrivaled in the entire world." In fact, Thomas Jefferson's copy of Bodin's *Republic* contains Jefferson's own initials calling attention to the description of the Carinthian installation and, therefore, to its conceptual impact on the writer of the American Declaration of Independence.

The eastward expansion of the Franks in the 9th century brought all Slovene lands under Frankish control. Carantania then lost its autonomy and, following the 955 victory of the Franks over the Hungarians, the Slovene lands were organized into separate frontier regions. This facilitated their colonization by German elements while inhibiting any effort at unifying the shrinking Slovene territories. Under the feudal system, various families of mostly Germanic nobility were granted fiefdoms over Slovene lands and competed among themselves bent on increasing their holdings.

The Bohemian King Premysl Otokar II was an exception and attempted to unite the Czech, Slovak, and Slovene lands in the second half of the 13th century. Otokar II acquired the Duchy of

Austria in 1251, Styria in 1260, and Carinthia, Carniola, and Istria in 1269, thus laying the foundation for the future Austrian empire. However, Otokar II was defeated in 1278 by a Hapsburg-led coalition that conquered Styria and Austria by 1282. The Hapsburgs, of Swiss origin, grew steadily in power and by the 15th century became the leading Austrian feudal family in control of most Slovene lands.

Christianization and the feudal system supported the Germanization process and created a society divided into "haves" (German) and "have nots" (Slovene), which were further separated into the nobility/urban dwellers versus the Slovene peasants/serfs. The Slovenes were deprived of their original, egalitarian "Freemen" rights and subjected to harsh oppression of economic, social, and political nature. The increasing demands imposed on the serfs due to the feudal lords' commitment in support of the fighting against the Turks and the suffering caused by Turkish invasions led to a series of insurrections by Slovene and Croat peasants in the 15th to 18th centuries, cruelly repressed by the feudal system.

Reformation

The Reformation gave an impetus to the national identity process through the efforts of Protestant Slovenes to provide printed materials in the Slovenian language in support of the Reformation movement itself. Martin Luther's translation of the New Testament into German in 1521 encouraged translations into other vernaculars, including the Slovenian. Thus Primož Trubar, a Slovenian Protestant preacher and scholar, published the first *Catechism* in Slovenian in 1551 and, among other works, a smaller elementary grammar (*Abecedarium*) of the Slovenian language in 1552. These works were followed by the complete Slovenian translation of the Bible by Jurij Dalmatin in 1578, printed in 1584. The same year Adam Bohorič published, in Latin, the first comprehensive grammar of the Slovenian language which was also the first published grammar of any Slavic language. The first Slovenian publishing house (1575) and a Jesuit College (1595) were established in Ljubljana, the central Slovenian city, and between 1550 and 1600 over 50 books in Slovenian were published. In addition, Primož Trubar and his co-workers encouraged the opening of Slovenian elementary and high schools. This sudden explosion of literary activity built the foundation for the further development of literature in Slovenian and its use by the educated classes of Slovenes. The Catholic Counter-Reformation reacted to the spread of Protestantism very strongly within Catholic Austria, and slowed down the entire process until the Napoleonic period. Despite these efforts, important cultural institutions were established, such as an Academy of Arts and Sciences (1673) and the Philharmonic Society in 1701 (perhaps the oldest in Europe).

The Jesuits, heavily involved in the Counter-Reformation, had to use religious literature and songs in the Slovene language, but generally Latin was used as the main language in Jesuit schools. However, the first Catholic books in Slovenian were issued in 1615 to assist priests in the reading of Gospel passages and delivery of sermons. The Protestant books in Slovenian were used for such purposes, and they thus assisted in the further development of a standard literary Slovenian. Since Primož Trubar used his dialect from the Carniola region, it heavily influenced the literary standard. From the late 17th and through the 18th century the Slovenes continued their divided existence under Austrian control.

Standing over trade routes connecting the German/Austrian hinterland to the Adriatic Sea and the Italian plains eastward into the Balkan region, the Slovenes partook of the benefits from such trade in terms of both economic and cultural enrichment. Thus by the end of the 18th century, a significant change occurred in the urban centers where an educated Slovene middle class came into existence. Deeply rooted in the Slovene peasantry, this element ceased to assimilate into the Germanized mainstream and began to assert its own cultural/national identity. Many of their sons were educated in German, French, and Italian universities and thus exposed to the influence of the Enlightenment. Such a person was, for instance, Baron Ziga Zois (1749–1819), an industrialist, landowner, and linguist who became the patron of the Slovene literary movement. When the ideas of the French Revolution spread through Europe and the Napoleonic conquest reached the Slovenes, they were ready to embrace them.

During the reign of Maria Teresa (1740–80) and Joseph II (1780–90), the influence of Jansenism—the emancipation of serfs, the introduction of public schools (in German), equality of religions, closing of monasteries not involved in education or tending to the sick—weakened the hold of the nobility. On the other hand, the stronger Germanization emphasis generated resistance to it from an awakening Slovene national consciousness and the publication of Slovene nonreligious works, such as Marko Pohlin's

Abecedika (1765), a *Carniolan Grammar* (1783) with explanations in German, and other educational works in Slovenian, which include a Slovenian-German-Latin dictionary (1781). Pohlin's theory of metrics and poetics became the foundation of secular poetry in Slovenian, which reached its zenith only 50 years later with France Prešeren (1800–49), still considered the greatest Slovene poet. Just prior to the short Napoleonic occupation of Slovenia, the first Slovenian newspaper was published in 1797 by Valentin Vodnik (1758–1819), a very popular poet and grammarian. The first drama in Slovenian appeared in 1789 by Anton Tomaž Linhart (1756–95), playwright and historian of Slovenes and South Slavs. Both authors were members of Baron Zois' circle.

Napoleon and the Spring of Nations

When Napoleon defeated Austria and established his Illyrian Provinces (1809–13), comprising the southern half of the Slovenian lands, parts of Croatia, and Dalmatia all the way to Dubrovnik with Ljubljana as the capital, the Slovene language was encouraged in the schools and also used, along with French, as an official language in order to communicate with the Slovene population. The four-year French occupation served to reinforce the national awakening of the Slovenes and other nations that had been submerged through the long feudal era of the Austrian Empire. Austria, however, regained the Illyrian Provinces in 1813 and reestablished its direct control over the Slovene lands.

The 1848 "spring of nations" brought about various demands for national freedom of Slovenes and other Slavic nations of Austria. An important role was played by Jernej Kopitar with his influence as librarian/censor in the Imperial Library in Vienna, as the developer of Slavic studies in Austria, as the mentor to Vuk Karadžić (one of the founders of the contemporary Serbo-Croatian language standard), as the advocate of Austro-Slavism (a state for all Slavs of Austria), and as author of the first modern Slovenian grammar in 1808. In mid-May 1848, the "United Slovenia" manifesto demanded that the Austrian Emperor establish a Kingdom of Slovenia with its own parliament, consisting of the then-separate historical regions of Carniola, Carinthia, Styria, and the Littoral, with Slovenian as its official language. This kingdom would remain a part of Austria, but not of the German Empire. While other nations based their demands on the "historical statehood" principle, the Slovenian demands were based on the principle of national self-determination some 70 years before American President Woodrow Wilson would embrace the principle in his "Fourteen Points."

Matija Kavčič, one of 14 Slovenian deputies elected to the 1848–49 Austrian parliament, proposed a plan of turning the Austrian Empire into a federation of 14 national states that would completely do away with the system of historic regions based on the old feudal system. At the 1848 Slavic Congress in Prague, the Slovenian delegates also demanded the establishment of the Slovenian University in Ljubljana. A map of a United Slovenia was designed by Peter Kozler based on then available ethnic data. It was confiscated by Austrian authorities, and Kozler was accused of treason in 1852 but was later released for insufficient evidence. The revolts of 1848 were repressed after a few years, and absolutistic regimes kept control on any movements in support of national rights. However, recognition was given to equal rights of the Slovenian language in principle, while denied in practice by the German/Hungarian element that considered Slovenian the language of servants and peasants. Even the "minimalist" Maribor program of 1865 (a common assembly of deputies from the historical provinces to discuss mutual problems) was fiercely opposed by most Austrians that supported the Pan-German plan of a unified German nation from the Baltic to the Adriatic seas. The Slovenian nation was blocking the Pan-German plan simply by being located between the Adriatic Sea (Trieste) and the German/Austrian Alpine areas; therefore, any concessions had to be refused in order to speed up its total assimilation. Hitler's World War II plan to "cleanse" the Slovenians was an accelerated approach to the same end by use of extreme violence.

Toward "Yugoslavism"

In 1867, the German and Hungarian majorities agreed to the reorganization of the state into a "Dualistic" Austro-Hungarian Monarchy in order to be better able to control the minority elements in each half of the empire. The same year, in view of such intransigence, the Slovenes reverted back to their "maximalist" demand of a "United Slovenia" (1867 Ljubljana Manifesto) and initiated a series of mass political meetings, called "Tabori," after the Czech model. Their motto became "Umreti nočemo!" ("We refuse to die!"), and a movement was initiated to bring about a cultural/political coalition of Slovenes, Croats, and Serbs of Austro-Hungary in order to more successfully defend themselves from the increasing efforts of Germanization/Magyarization. At the same time, Slovenes, Croats, and Serbs followed with great interest several movements of national liberation and unification, such as those in Italy, Germany, Greece, and Serbia, and drew from them much inspiration. While Austria lost its northern Italian provinces to the Italian "Risorgimento," it gained, on the other hand, Bosnia and Herzegovina through occupation (1878) and annexation (1908). These actions increased the interest of Slovenes, Croats, and Serbs of Austro-Hungary in a "Trialistic" arrangement that would allow the South Slavic groups ("Yugoslavs") to form their own joint (and "Third") unit within Austro-Hungary. A federalist solution, they believed, would make possible the survival of a country to which they had been loyal subjects for many centuries. Crown Prince Ferdinand supported this approach, called "The United States of greater Austria" by his advisers, also because it would remove the attraction of a Greater Serbia. But the German leadership's sense of its own superiority and consequent expansionist goals prevented any compromise and led to two world wars.

World War I and Royal Yugoslavia

Unable to achieve their maximalist goals, the Slovenes concentrated their effort at the micro-level and made tremendous strides prior to World War I in introducing education in Slovenian, organizing literary and reading rooms in every town, participating in economic development, upgrading their agriculture, organizing cultural societies and political parties, such as the Catholic People's Party in 1892 and the Liberal Party in 1894, and participating in the Socialist movement of the 1890s. World War I brought about the dissolution of centuries-old ties between the Slovenes and the Austrian Monarchy and the Croats/Serbs with the Hungarian Crown. Toward the end of the war, on 12 August 1918, the National Council for Slovenian Lands was formed in Ljubljana. On 12 October 1918, the National Council for all Slavs of former Austro-Hungary was founded in Zagreb, Croatia, and was chaired by Msgr. Anton Korošec, head of the Slovenian People's Party. This Council proclaimed on 29 October 1918 the separation of the South Slavs from Austro-Hungary and the formation of a new state of Slovenes, Croats, and Serbs.

A National Government for Slovenia was established in Ljubljana. The Zagreb Council intended to negotiate a Federal Union with the Kingdom of Serbia that would preserve the respective national autonomies of the Slovenes, Croats, and Serbs. Msgr. Korošec had negotiated a similar agreement in Geneva with Nikola Pašić, his Serbian counterpart, but a new Serbian government reneged on it. There was no time for further negotiations due to the Italian occupation of much Slovenian and Croatian territory and only Serbia, a victor state, could resist Italy. Thus, a delegation of the Zagreb Council submitted to Serbia a declaration expressing the will to unite with The Kingdom of Serbia. At that time, there were no conditions presented or demand made regarding the type of union, and Serbia immediately accepted the proposed unification under its strongly centralized government; a unitary "Kingdom of Serbs, Croats, and Slovenes" was declared on 1 December 1918. Because of the absence of an initial compromise between the Unitarists and Federalists, what became Yugoslavia never gained a solid consensual foundation. Serbs were winners and viewed their expansion as liberation of their Slavic brethren from Austria-Hungary, as compensation for their tremendous war sacrifices, and as the realization of their "Greater Serbia" goal. Slovenes and Croats, while freed from the Austro-Hungarian domination, were nevertheless the losers in terms of their desired political/cultural autonomy. In addition, they suffered painful territorial losses to Italy (some 700,000 Slovenes and Croats were denied any national rights by Fascist Italy and subjected to all kinds of persecutions) and to Austria (a similar fate for some 100,000 Slovenes left within Austria in the Carinthia region).

After 10 years of a contentious parliamentary system that ended in the murder of Croatian deputies and their leader Stjepan Radić, King Alexander abrogated the 1921 constitution, dissolved the parliament and political parties, took over power directly, and renamed the country "Yugoslavia." He abolished the 33 administrative departments that had replaced the historic political/national regions in favor of administrative areas named mostly after rivers. A new policy was initiated with the goal of creating a single "Yugoslav" nation out of the three "Tribes" of Serbs, Croats, and Slovenes. But in practice this policy meant the King's Serbian hegemony over the rest of the nations. The reaction was intense, and King Alexander himself fell victim of Croat-Ustaša and Macedonian terrorists and died in Marseille in 1934. A regency ruled Yugoslavia, headed by Alexander's cousin, Prince Paul, who managed to reach an agreement in 1939 with the Croats. An autonomous Croatian "Banovina" headed by "Ban" Ivan Subašić was established, including most Croatian lands outside of the Bosnia and Herzegovina area. Strong opposition developed among Serbs because they viewed the Croatian Banovina as a privilege for Croats while Serbs were split among six old administrative units with a large Serbian population left inside the Croatian Banovina itself. Still, there might have been a chance for further similar agreements that would have satisfied the Serbs and Slovenes. But there was no time left—Hitler and his allies (Italy, Hungary, Bulgaria) attacked Yugoslavia on 6 April 1941, after a coup on 27 March 1941 had deposed Prince Paul's government, which had yielded to

Hitler's pressures on 25 March. Thus the first Yugoslavia, born out of the distress of World War I, had not had time to consolidate and work out its problems in a mere 23 years and was then dismembered by its aggressors. Still, the first Yugoslavia allowed the Slovenes a chance for fuller development of their cultural, economic, and political life, in greater freedom and relative independence for the first time in modern times.

World War II

Slovenia was divided in 1941 among Germany, Italy, and Hungary. Germany annexed northern Slovenia, mobilized its men into the German army, interned, expelled, or killed most of the Slovenian leaders, and removed to labor camps the populations of entire areas, repopulating them with Germans. Italy annexed southern Slovenia but did not mobilize its men. In both areas, particularly the Italian, resistance movements were initiated by both nationalist groups and by Communist-dominated Partisans, the latter particularly after Hitler's attack on the Soviet Union on 22 June 1941. The Partisans claimed monopoly of the resistance leadership and dealt cruelly with anyone that dared to oppose their intended power grab. Spontaneous resistance to the Partisans by the non-Communist Slovenian peasantry led to a bloody civil war in Slovenia under foreign occupiers, who encouraged the bloodshed. The resistance movement led by General Draža Mihajlović, appointed minister of war of the Yugoslav government-in-exile, was handicapped by the exile government's lack of unity and clear purpose (mostly due to the fact that the Serbian side had reneged on the 1939 agreement on Croatia). On the other hand, Winston Churchill, convinced by rather one-sided reports that Mihajlović was "collaborating" with the Germans while the Partisans under Marshal Tito were the ones "who killed more Germans," decided to recognize Tito as the only legitimate Yugoslav resistance. Though aware of Tito's communist allegiance to Stalin, Churchill threw his support to Tito, and forced the Yugoslav government-in-exile into a coalition government with Tito, who had no intention of keeping the agreement and, in fact, would have fought against an Allied landing in Yugoslavia along with the Germans.

When Soviet armies, accompanied by Tito, entered Yugoslavia from Romania and Bulgaria in the fall of 1944, military units and civilians that had opposed the Partisans retreated to Austria or Italy. Among them were the Cetnik units of Draža Mihajlović and "homeguards" from Serbia, Croatia, and Slovenia that had been under German control but were pro-Allies in their convictions and hopes. Also in retreat were the units of the Croatian Ustaša that had collaborated with Italy and Germany in order to achieve (and control) an "independent" greater Croatia and, in the process, had committed terrible and large-scale massacres of Serbs, Jews, Gypsies, and others who opposed them. Serbs and Partisans counteracted, and a fratricidal civil war raged over Yugoslavia. After the end of the war, the Communist-led forces took control of Slovenia and Yugoslavia and instituted a violent dictatorship that committed systematic crimes and human rights violations on an unexpectedly large scale. Thousands upon thousands of their former opponents that were returned, unaware, from Austria by British military authorities were tortured and massacred by Partisan executioners.

Communist Yugoslavia

Such was the background for the formation of the second Yugoslavia as a Federative People's Republic of five nations (Slovenes, Croats, Serbs, Macedonians, Montenegrins) with their individual republics and Bosnia and Herzegovina as a buffer area with its mix of Serb, Muslim, and Croat populations. The problem of large Hungarian and Muslim Albanian populations in Serbia was solved by creating for them the autonomous region of Vojvodina (Hungarian minority) and Kosovo (Muslim Albanian majority) that assured their political and cultural development. Tito attempted a balancing act to satisfy most of the nationality issues that were carried over unresolved from the first Yugoslavia, but failed to satisfy anyone.

Compared to pre-1941 Yugoslavia where Serbs enjoyed a controlling role, the numerically stronger Serbs had lost both the Macedonian area they considered "Southern Serbia" and the opportunity to incorporate Montenegro into Serbia, as well as losing direct control over the Hungarian minority in Vojvodina and the Muslim Albanians of Kosovo, viewed as the cradle of the Serbian nation since the Middle Ages. They further were not able to incorporate into Serbia the large Serbian populated areas of Bosnia and had not obtained an autonomous region for the large minority of Serbian population within the Croatian Republic. The Croats, while gaining back the Medjumurje area from Hungary, and from Italy, the cities of Rijeka (Fiume), Zadar (Zara), some Dalmatian islands, and the Istrian Peninsula had, on the other hand, lost other areas. These included the Srem area to Serbia, and also Bosnia and Herzegovina, which had been part of the World War II "independent" Croatian state under the Ustaša leadership.

In addition, the Croats were confronted with a deeply resentful Serbian minority that became ever more pervasive in public administrative and security positions. The Slovenes had regained the Prekmurje enclave from Hungary and most of the Slovenian lands that had been taken over by Italy following World War I (Julian region and Northern Istria), except for the "Venetian Slovenia" area, the Gorizia area, and the port city of Trieste. The latter was initially part of the UN protected "Free Territory of Trieste," split in 1954 between Italy and Yugoslavia with Trieste itself given to Italy. Nor were the Slovenian claims to the southern Carinthia area of Austria satisfied. The loss of Trieste was a bitter pill for the Slovenes and many blamed it on the fact that Tito's Yugoslavia was, initially, Stalin's advance threat to Western Europe, thus making the Allies more supportive of Italy.

The official position of the Marxist Yugoslav regime was that national rivalries and conflicting interests would gradually diminish through their sublimation into a new Socialist order. Without capitalism, nationalism was supposed to wither away. Therefore, in the name of their "unity and brotherhood" motto, any nationalistic expression of concern was prohibited and repressed by the dictatorial and centralized regime of the "League of Yugoslav Communists" acting through the "Socialist Alliance" as its mass front organization.

After a short postwar "coalition" government period, the elections of 11 November 1945, boycotted by the non-communist "coalition" parties, gave the Communist-led People's Front 90% of the vote. A Constituent Assembly met on 29 November, abolishing the monarchy and establishing the Federative People's Republic of Yugoslavia. In January 1946 a new constitution was adopted, based on the 1936 Soviet constitution. The Stalin-engineered expulsion of Yugoslavia from the Soviet-dominated Cominform Group in 1948 was actually a blessing for Yugoslavia after its leadership was able to survive Stalin's pressures. Survival had to be justified, both practically and in theory, by developing a "Road to Socialism" based on Yugoslavia's own circumstances. This new "road map" evolved rather quickly in response to some of Stalin's accusations and Yugoslavia's need to perform a balancing act between the North Atlantic Treaty Organization (NATO) alliance and the Soviet bloc. Tito quickly nationalized the economy through a policy of forced industrialization, to be supported by the collectivization of the agriculture.

The agricultural reform of 1945–46 (limited private ownership of a maximum of 35 hectares/85 acres, and a limited free market after the initial forced delivery of quotas to the state at very low prices) had to be abandoned because of the strong resistance by the peasants. The actual collectivization efforts were initiated in 1949 using welfare benefits and lower taxes as incentives along with direct coercion. But collectivization had to be abandoned by 1958 simply because its inefficiency and low productivity could not support the concentrated effort of industrial development.

By the 1950s Yugoslavia had initiated the development of its internal trademark: self-management of enterprises through workers councils and local decision-making as the road to Marx's "withering away of the state." The second five-year plan (1957–61), as opposed to the failed first one (1947–51), was completed in four years by relying on the well-established self-management system. Economic targets were set from the local to the republic level and then coordinated by a Federal Planning Institute to meet an overall national economic strategy. This system supported a period of very rapid industrial growth in the 1950s from a very low base. But a high consumption rate encouraged a volume of imports far in excess of exports, largely financed by foreign loans. In addition, inefficient and low productivity industries were kept in place through public subsidies, cheap credit, and other artificial measures that led to a serious crisis by 1961.

Reforms were necessary and, by 1965, "market socialism" was introduced with laws that abolished most price controls and halved import duties while withdrawing export subsidies. After necessary amounts were left with the earning enterprise, the rest of the earned foreign currencies were deposited with the national bank and used by the state, other enterprises, or were used to assist less-developed areas. Councils were given more decision-making power in investing their earnings, and they also tended to vote for higher salaries in order to meet steep increases in the cost of living. Unemployment grew rapidly even though "political factories" were still subsidized. The government thus relaxed its restrictions to allow labor migration, particularly to West Germany where workers were needed for its thriving economy. Foreign investment was encouraged up to 49% in joint enterprises, and barriers to the movement of people and exchange of ideas were largely removed.

The role of trade unions continued to be one of transmission of instructions from government to workers, allocation of perks along with the education/training of workers, monitoring legislation, and overall protection of the self-management system. Strikes were legally neither allowed nor forbidden, but until the 1958 miners strike in Trbovlje, Slovenia, were not publicly acknowledged and were suppressed. After 1958 strikes were tolerated as an indication of problems to be resolved. Unions, however, did not initiate strikes but were expected to convince workers to go back to work.

Having survived its expulsion from the Cominform in 1948 and Stalin's attempts to take control, Yugoslavia began to develop a foreign policy independent of the Soviet Union. By mid-1949 Yugoslavia withdrew its support from the Greek Communists in their civil war against the then-Royalist government. In October 1949, Yugoslavia was elected to one of the nonpermanent seats on the UN Security Council and openly condemned North Korea's aggression towards South Korea. Following the "rapprochement" opening with the Soviet Union, initiated by Nikita Khrushchev and his 1956 denunciation of Stalin, Tito intensified his work on developing the movement of nonaligned "third world" nations as Yugoslavia's external trademark in cooperation with Nehru of India, Nasser of Egypt, and others. With the September 1961 Belgrade summit conference of nonaligned nations, Tito became the recognized leader of the movement. The nonaligned position served Tito's Yugoslavia well by allowing Tito to draw on economic and political support from the Western powers while neutralizing any aggression from the Soviet bloc. While Tito had acquiesced, reluctantly, to the 1956 Soviet invasion of Hungary for fear of chaos and any liberalizing impact on Yugoslavia, he condemned the Soviet invasion of Dubček's Czechoslovakia in 1968, as did Romania's Ceausescu, both fearing their countries might be the next in line for "corrective" action by the Red Army and the Warsaw Pact. Just before his death on 4 May 1980, Tito also condemned the Soviet invasion of Afghanistan. Yugoslavia actively participated in the 1975 Helsinki Conference and agreements and the first 1977–78 review conference that took place in Belgrade, even though Yugoslavia's one-party Communist regime perpetrated and condoned numerous human rights violations. Overall, in the 1970s–80s Yugoslavia maintained fairly good relations with its neighboring states by playing down or solving pending disputes such as the Trieste issue with Italy in 1975, and developing cooperative projects and increased trade.

Compared to the other republics of the Federative People's Republic of Yugoslavia, the Republic of Slovenia had several advantages. It was 95% homogeneous. The Slovenes had the highest level of literacy. Their prewar economy was the most advanced and so was their agriculture, which was based on an extensive network of peasant cooperatives and savings and loans institutions developed as a primary initiative of the Slovenian People's Party ("clerical"). Though ravaged by the war, occupation, resistance and civil war losses, and preoccupied with carrying out the elimination of all actual and potential opposition, the Communist government faced the double task of building its Socialist economy while rebuilding the country. As an integral part of the Yugoslav federation, Slovenia was, naturally, affected by Yugoslavia's internal and external political developments. The main problems facing communist Yugoslavia/Slovenia were essentially the same as the unresolved ones under Royalist Yugoslavia. As the "Royal Yugoslavism" had failed in its assimilative efforts, so did the "Socialist Yugoslavism" fail to overcome the forces of nationalism. In the case of Slovenia there were several key factors in the continued attraction to its national identity: more than a thousand years of historical development; a location within Central Europe (not part of the Balkan area) and related identification with Western European civilization; the Catholic religion with the traditional role of Catholic priests (even under the persecutions by the Communist regime); the most developed and productive economy with a standard of living far superior to most other areas of the Yugoslav Federation; and finally, the increased political and economic autonomy enjoyed by the Republic after the 1974 constitution, particularly following Tito's death in 1980. Tito's motto of "unity and brotherhood" was replaced by "freedom and democracy" to be achieved through either a confederate rearrangement of Yugoslavia or by complete independence.

In December 1964, the eighth Congress of the League of Communists of Yugoslavia (LCY) acknowledged that ethnic prejudice and antagonisms existed in socialist Yugoslavia and went on record against the position that Yugoslavia's nations had become obsolete and were disintegrating into a socialist "Yugoslavism." Thus the republics, based on individual nations, became bastions of a strong Federalism that advocated the devolution and decentralization of authority from the federal to the republic level. "Yugoslav Socialist Patriotism" was at times defined as a deep feeling for both one's own national identity and for the socialist self-management of Yugoslavia. Economic reforms were the other focus of the Eighth LCY Congress, led by Croatia and Slovenia with emphasis on efficiencies and local economic development decisions with profit criteria as their basis. The "liberal" bloc (Slovenia, Croatia, Macedonia, Vojvodina) prevailed over the "conservative" group and the reforms of 1965 did away with central investment planning and "political factories." The positions of the two blocs hardened into a national-liberal coalition that viewed the conservative, centralist group led by Serbia as the "Greater Serbian" attempt at majority domination. The devolution of power in economic decision-making spearheaded by the Slovenes assisted in the "federalization" of the League of Communists of Yugoslavia as a league of "quasi-sovereign" republican parties. Under strong prodding from the Croats, the party agreed in 1970 to the principle of unanimity for decision-making that, in practice, meant a veto power for each republic. However, the concentration of economic resources in Serbian hands continued with Belgrade banks controlling half of total credits and some 80% of foreign credits. This was also combined with the fear of Serbian political and cultural domination, particularly with respect to Croatian language sensitivities, which had been aroused by the use of the Serbian version of Serbo-Croatian as the norm, with the Croatian version as a deviation. The debates over the reforms of the 1960s led to a closer scrutiny, not only of the economic system, but also of the decision-making process at the republic and federal levels, particularly the investment of funds to less developed areas that Slovenia and Croatia felt were very poorly managed, if not squandered. Other issues fueled acrimony between individual nations, such as the 1967 Declaration in Zagreb claiming a Croatian linguistic and literary tradition separate from the Serbian one, thus undermining the validity of the Serbo-Croatian language. Also, Kosovo Albanians and Montenegrins, along with Slovenes and Croats, began to assert their national rights as superior to the Federation ones.

The language controversy exacerbated the economic and political tensions between Serbs and Croats, which spilled into the easily inflamed area of ethnic confrontations. To the conservative centralists the devolution of power to the republic level meant the subordination of the broad "Yugoslav" and "Socialist" interests to the narrow "nationalist" interest of republic national majorities. With the Croat League of Communists taking the liberal position in 1970, nationalism was rehabilitated. Thus the "Croatian Spring" bloomed and impacted all the other republics of Yugoslavia. Meanwhile, through a series of 1967–68 constitutional amendments that had limited federal power in favor of the republics and autonomous provinces, the federal government came to be seen by liberals more as an inter-republican problem-solving mechanism bordering on a confederate arrangement. A network of inter-republican committees established by mid-1971 proved to be very efficient at resolving a large number of difficult issues in a short time. The coalition of liberals and nationalists in Croatia also generated sharp condemnation in Serbia whose own brand of nationalism grew stronger, but as part of a conservative/centralist alliance. Thus the liberal/federalist versus conservative/centralist opposition became entangled in the rising nationalism within each opposing bloc. The situation in Croatia and Serbia was particularly difficult because of their minorities issues—Serbian in Croatia and Hungarian/Albanian in Serbia.

Serbs in Croatia sided with the Croat conservatives and sought a constitutional amendment guaranteeing their own national identity and rights and, in the process, challenged the sovereignty of the Croatian nation and state as well as the right to self-determination, including the right to secession. The conservatives won and the amendment declared that "the Socialist Republic of Croatia (was) the national state of the Croatian nation, the state of the Serbian nation in Croatia, and the state of the nationalities inhabiting it."

Slovenian "Spring"

Meanwhile, Slovenia, not burdened by large minorities, developed a similar liberal and nationalist direction along with Croatia. This fostered an incipient separatist sentiment opposed by both the liberal and conservative party wings. Led by Stane Kavčič, head of the Slovenian government, the liberal wing gained as much local political latitude as possible from the federal level during the early 1970s "Slovenian Spring." By the summer of 1971, the Serbian party leadership was pressuring President Tito to put an end to the "dangerous" development of Croatian nationalism. While Tito wavered because of his support for the balancing system of autonomous republic units, the situation quickly reached critical proportions.

Croat nationalists, complaining about discrimination against Croats in Bosnia and Herzegovina, demanded the incorporation of Western Herzegovina into Croatia. Serbia countered by claiming Southeastern Herzegovina for itself. Croats also advanced claims to a larger share of their foreign currency earnings, to the issuance of their own currency, the creation of their own national bank that would directly negotiate foreign loans, the printing of Croatian postage stamps, the creation of a Croatian army, and recognition of the Croatian Sabor (assembly) as the highest Croatian political body, and, finally, to Croatian secession and complete independence. Confronted with such intensive agitation, the liberal Croatian party leadership could not back down and did not try to restrain the maximalist public demands nor the widespread university students' strike of November 1971. This situation caused a loss of support from the liberal party wings of Slovenia and even Macedonia. At this point Tito intervened, condemned the Croatian liberal leadership on 1 December 1971, and supported the conservative wing. The liberal leadership group resigned on 12 December 1971. When Croatian students demonstrated and demanded an independent Croatia, the Yugoslav army was ready to move in if necessary. A wholesale purge of the party liberals followed with tens of thousands expelled, key functionaries lost their positions, several thousand were imprisoned (including Franjo Tudjman who later became president in independent Croatia), and leading Croatian nationalist organizations and their publications were closed.

On 8 May 1972, the Croatian party also expelled its liberal wing leaders and the purge of nationalists continued through 1973 in Croatia, as well as in Slovenia and Macedonia. However, the issues and sentiments raised during the "Slovene and Croat Springs" of 1969–71 did not disappear. Tito and the conservatives were forced to satisfy nominally some demands. The 1974 constitution was an attempt to resolve the strained inter-republican relations as each republic pursued its own interests over and above an overall "Yugoslav" interest. The repression of liberal-nationalist Croats was accompanied by the growing influence of the Serbian element in the Croatian Party (24% in 1980) and police force (majority) that contributed to the continued persecution and imprisonments of Croatian nationalists into the 1980s.

Yugoslavia—House Divided

In Slovenia, developments took a direction of their own. The purge of the nationalists took place as in Croatia but on a lesser scale, and after a decade or so, nationalism was revived through the development of grassroots movements in the arts, music, peace, and environmental concerns. Activism was particularly strong among young people, who shrewdly used the regime-supported youth organizations, youth periodicals—such as *Mladina* (in Ljubljana) and *Katedra* (in Maribor)—and an independent student radio station. The journal *Nova Revija* published a series of articles focusing on problems confronting the Slovenian nation in February 1987; these included such varied topics as the status of the Slovenian language, the role of the Communist Party, the multiparty system, and independence. The *Nova Revija* was in reality a Slovenian national manifesto that, along with yearly public opinion polls showing ever higher support for Slovenian independence, indicated a definite mood toward secession. In this charged atmosphere, the Yugoslav army committed two actions that led the Slovenes to the path of actual separation from Yugoslavia. In March 1988, the army's Military Council submitted a confidential report to the federal presidency claiming that Slovenia was planning a counter revolution and calling for repressive measures against liberals and a *coup d'etat*. An army document delineating such actions was delivered by an army sergeant to the journal *Mladina*. But, before it could be published, *Mladina's* editor and two journalists were arrested by the army on 31 March 1988. Meanwhile, the strong intervention of the Slovenian political leadership succeeded in stopping any army action. But the four men involved in the affair were put on trial by the Yugoslav army.

The second army *faux pas* was to hold the trial in Ljubljana, capital of Slovenia, and to conduct it in the Serbo-Croatian language, an action declared constitutional by the Yugoslav presidency, claiming that Slovenian law could not be applied to the Yugoslav army. This trial brought about complete unity among Slovenians in opposition to the Yugoslav army and what it represented, and the four individuals on trial became overnight heroes. One of them was Janez Janša who had written articles in *Mladina* critical of the Yugoslav army and was the head of the Slovenian pacifist movement and president of the Slovenian Youth Organization. (Ironically, three years later Janša led the successful defense of Slo-

venia against the Yugoslav army and became the first minister of defense of independent Slovenia.) The four men were found guilty and sentenced to jail terms from four years (Janša) to five months. The total mobilization of Slovenia against the military trials led to the formation of the first non-Communist political organizations and political parties. In a time of perceived national crisis, both the Communist and non-Communist leadership found it possible to work closely together. But from that time on the liberal/nationalist vs. conservative/centralist positions hardened in Yugoslavia and no amount of negotiation at the federal presidency level regarding a possible confederal solution could hold Yugoslavia together any longer.

Since 1986, work had been done on amendments to the 1974 constitution that, when submitted in 1987, created a furor, particularly in Slovenia, due to the proposed creation of a unified legal system, the establishment of central control over the means of transportation and communication, centralization of the economy into a unified market, and the granting of more control to Serbia over its autonomous provinces of Kosovo and Vojvodina. This all came at the expense of the individual republics. A recentralization of the League of Communists was also recommended but opposed by liberal/nationalist groups. Serbia's President Slobodan Milošević also proposed changes to the bicameral Federal Skupština (Assembly) by replacing it with a tricameral one where deputies would no longer be elected by their republican assemblies but through a "one person, one vote" national system. Slovenia, Croatia, and Bosnia and Herzegovina strongly opposed the change as they opposed the additional Chamber of Associated Labor that would have increased the federal role in the economy. The debates over the recentralizing amendments caused an even greater focus in Slovenia and Croatia on the concept of a confederative structure based on self-determination by "sovereign" states and a multiparty democratic system as the only one that could maintain some semblance of a "Yugoslav" state.

By 1989 and the period following the Serbian assertion of control in the Kosovo and Vojvodina provinces, as well as in the republic of Montenegro, relations between Slovenia and Serbia reached a crisis point: Serbian President Milošević attempted to orchestrate mass demonstrations by Serbs in Ljubljana, the capital city of Slovenia, and the Slovenian leadership vetoed it. Then Serbs started to boycott Slovenian products, to withdraw their savings from Slovenian banks, and to terminate economic cooperation and trade with Slovenia. Serbian President Milošević's tactics were extremely distasteful to the Slovenians and the use of force against the Albanian population of the Kosovo province worried the Slovenes (and Croats) about the possible use of force by Serbia against Slovenia itself. The tensions with Serbia convinced the Slovenian leadership of the need to take necessary protective measures. In September 1989, draft amendments to the constitution of Slovenia were published that included the right to secession, and the sole right of the Slovenian legislature to introduce martial law. The Yugoslav army particularly needed the amendment granting control over deployment of armed forces in Slovenia, since the Yugoslav army, controlled by a mostly Serbian/Montenegrin officer corps dedicated to the preservation of a Communist system, had a self-interest in preserving the source of their own budgetary allocations of some 51% of the Yugoslav federal budget.

A last attempt at salvaging Yugoslavia was to be made at the extraordinary Congress of the League of Communists of Yugoslavia convened in January 1990 to review proposed reforms such as free multiparty elections, and freedom of speech. The Slovenian delegation attempted to broaden the spectrum of reforms but was rebuffed and walked out on 23 January 1990, pulling out of the Yugoslav League. The Slovenian Communists then renamed their party the Party for Democratic Renewal. The political debate in Slovenia intensified and some 19 parties were formed by early 1990. On 10 April 1990 the first free elections since before World War II were held in Slovenia, where there still was a three-chamber Assembly: political affairs, associated labor, and territorial communities. A coalition of six newly formed democratic parties, called *Demos,* won 55% of the votes, with the remainder going to the Party for Democratic Renewal, the former Communists (17%), the Socialist Party (5%), and the Liberal Democratic Party—heir to the Slovenia Youth Organization (15%). The *Demos* coalition organized the first freely elected Slovenian government of the post-Communist era with Dr. Lojze Peterle as the prime minister.

Milan Kucan, former head of the League of Communists of Slovenia, was elected president with 54% of the vote in recognition of his efforts to effect a bloodless transfer of power from a monopoly by the Communist party to a free multiparty system and his standing up to the recentralizing attempts by Serbia.

Toward Independence

In October 1990, Slovenia and Croatia published a joint proposal for a Yugoslavian confederation as a last attempt at a negotiated solution, but to no avail. The Slovenian legislature also adopted in October a draft constitution proclaiming that "Slovenia will become an independent state." On 23 December 1990, a plebiscite was held on Slovenia's disassociation from Yugoslavia if a confederate solution could not be negotiated within a six-month period. An overwhelming majority of 89% of voters approved the secession provision and a declaration of sovereignty was adopted on 26 December 1990. All federal laws were declared void in Slovenia as of 20 February 1991, and since no negotiated agreement was possible, Slovenia declared its independence on 25 June 1991. On 27 June 1991, the Yugoslav army tried to seize control of Slovenia and its common borders with Italy, Austria, and Hungary under the pretext that it was the army's constitutional duty to assure the integrity of Socialist Yugoslavia. The Yugoslav army units were surprised and shocked by the resistance they encountered from the Slovenian "territorial guards," who surrounded Yugoslav army tank units, isolated them, and engaged in close combat, mostly along border checkpoints that ended in most cases with Yugoslav units surrendering to the Slovenian forces. Fortunately, casualties were limited on both sides. Over 3,200 Yugoslav army soldiers surrendered and were well treated by the Slovenes, who scored a public relations coup by having the prisoners call their parents all over Yugoslavia to come to Slovenia and take their sons back home.

The war in Slovenia ended in 10 days due to the intervention of the European Community, who negotiated a cease-fire and a three-month moratorium on Slovenia's implementation of independence, giving the Yugoslav army time to retreat from Slovenia by the end of October 1991. Thus Slovenia was able to "disassociate" itself from Yugoslavia with a minimum of casualties, although the military operations caused considerable physical damages estimated at almost US$3 billion. On 23 December 1991, one year following the independence plebiscite, a new constitution was adopted by Slovenia establishing a parliamentary democracy with a bicameral legislature. Even though US Secretary of State James Baker, in his visit to Belgrade on 21 June 1991, had declared that the United States opposed unilateral secessions by Slovenia and Croatia and that the United States would therefore not recognize them as independent countries, such recognition came first from Germany on 18 December 1991, from the European Community on 15 January 1992, and finally from the United States on 7 April 1992. Slovenia was accepted as a member of the UN on 23 April 1992 and has since become a member of many other international organizations, including the Council of Europe in 1993 and the NATO related Partnership for Peace in 1994.

On 6 December 1992, general elections were held in accordance with the new constitution, with 22 parties participating and eight receiving sufficient votes to assure representation. A coalition government was formed by the Liberal Democrats, Christian Democrats, and the United List Group of Leftist Parties. Dr. Milan Kucan was elected president, and Dr. Janez Drnovšek became prime minister. In 1997 a compromise was struck which allowed Poland, the Czech Republic, and Hungary to join the NATO alliance in 1999 while Romania and Slovenia were identified as prime candidates for future nomination into the alliance. Also in 1997, Slovenia signed an association agreement with the European Union (EU) and was invited to talks on EU membership.

In the 1970s, Slovenia had reached a standard of living close to the one in neighboring Austria and Italy. However, the burdens imposed by the excessive cost of maintaining a large Yugoslav army, heavy contributions to the Fund for Less Developed Areas, and the repayments on a US$20 billion international debt, caused a lowering of its living standard over the 1980s. The situation worsened with the trauma of secession from Yugoslavia, the war damages suffered, and the loss of the former Yugoslav markets. In spite of all these problems Slovenia has made progress since independence by improving its productivity, controlling inflation, and reorienting its exports to Western Europe. The Slovenian economy has been quite strong since 1994, growing at an annual rate of about 4% during the late 1990s. Based on past experience, its industriousness, and good relationship with its trading partners, Slovenia has a very good chance of becoming a successful example of the transition from authoritarian socialism to a free democratic system and a market economy capable of sustaining a comfortable standard and quality of life.

Although governed from independence by centrist coalitions headed by Prime Minister Janez Drnovšek, the coalition collapsed in April 2000. Economist and center-right Social Democrat Party leader Andrej Bajuk became prime minister, until elections on 15 October 2000 saw Drnovšek return to power at the head of a four-party coalition. Drnovšek ran for president in elections held on 1 December 2002, and emerged with 56.5% of the vote in the second round, defeating Barbara Brezigar, who took 43.5%. Both supported EU and NATO membership for Slovenia. Liberal Democrat Anton Rop took over as prime minister when Drnovšek was elected president. The next presidential election was to be held fall 2007.

In the spring of 2004, Slovenia became a member of NATO and the EU. Later that year it held parliamentary elections, which were won by the center-right Slovenian Democratic Party—the first time in 13 years that a party other than the Liberal Democrats took power. In December 2004, Janez Jansa, who served as defense minister in previous governments, became, with the support of the parliament, prime minister. Jansa promised to reduce state administrative costs and to speed up the euro adoption process. The next National Assembly elections were scheduled for October 2008. In February 2005, Slovenia ratified the EU constitution.

13 GOVERNMENT

Slovenia is a republic based on a constitution adopted on 23 December 1991, one year following the plebiscite that supported its independence. As of early 2006, the president was Janez Drnovšek, elected in November 2002. The prime minister was Janez Jansa, elected in October 2004.

The constitution provides for a National Assembly as the highest legislative authority with 90 seats. Deputies are elected to four-year terms of office. The National Council, with 40 seats, has an advisory role, and councilors represent social, economic, professional, and local interests. They are elected to five-year terms of office and may propose laws to the National Assembly, request the latter to review its decisions, and may demand the calling of a constitutional referendum.

The executive branch consists of a president of the republic who is also Supreme Commander of the Armed Forces, and is elected to a five-year term of office, limited to two consecutive terms. The president calls for elections to the National Assembly, proclaims the adopted laws, and proposes candidates for prime minister to the National Assembly. A Council of Ministers to advise the president is nominated by the prime minister and elected by the National Assembly.

14 POLITICAL PARTIES

Parliamentary elections were held on 3 October 2004, with the Slovene Democratic Party (SDS) garnering the highest number of seats—29; the Liberal Democratic Party (which dominated the political scene since Slovenia's independence, in 1991) got 23; the United List of Social Democrats (ZLSD), 10 seats; New Slovenia (Nsi), 9 seats; Slovene People's Party (SLS), 7 seats; Slovenian National Party (SNS), 6 seats; Democratic Party of Retired People of Slovenia (DeSUS), 4 seats; Italian Minority, 1 seat; and the Hungarian Minority, 1 seat. The SDS forged a coalition with two center-right parties—Nsi and SLS—and a center-left party—DeSUS. In November 2004, the National Assembly elected Janez Jansa prime minister, with 57 votes in favor. The next parliamentary elections were scheduled for October 2008.

Party candidates are elected by each district. A candidate is only elected when votes for each party reach a given threshold. A new electoral code was passed in 2000, raising the threshold for securing seats from 3.2% to 4% and ending the use of preferential party lists for allocating seats to candidates who did not win direct mandates.

15 LOCAL GOVERNMENT

The commune or municipality (obccina) is the basic self-managed sociopolitical community. There are 193 municipalities and 11 urban municipalities in Slovenia, which have directly elected councils as their representative bodies. A municipality must have at least 5,000 inhabitants. An urban municipality must have at least 20,000 inhabitants, be the place of employment for at least 15,000 people, and be the geographic, economic, and cultural center of the area. There are 58 state administrative units in Slovenia, which have jurisdiction over one or several municipalities. Advisory committees are formed to ensure cooperation between municipal bodies and administrative units. Members of these committees are appointed by the municipal councils. There are also local, village, and ward communities in Slovenia.

In May 2005, the country was divided into 12 statistical regions, and the government plans another partition into 10 to 12 administrative regions. This new divide might follow the borders of the statistical regions, but parliamentary debates, and constitutional changes, had to precede this process.

16 JUDICIAL SYSTEM

The judicial system consists of local and district courts and a Supreme Court, which hears appeals from these courts. A nine-member Constitutional Court resolves jurisdictional disputes and rules on the constitutionality of legislation and regulations. The Constitutional Court also acts as a final court of appeal in cases requiring constitutional interpretation.

Judges are elected by parliament after nomination by a Judicial Council composed of 11 members—six judges selected by their peers and five persons elected by the National Assembly on nomination of the president. The constitution guarantees the independence of judges. Judges are appointed to permanent positions subject to an age limit.

The constitution affords criminal defendants a presumption of innocence, open court proceedings, the right to an appeal, a prohibition against double jeopardy, and a number of other procedural due process protections.

17 ARMED FORCES

The Slovenian armed forces numbered 6,550 active personnel in 2005, with 20,000 reservists. The Slovene Army was equipped with 70 main battle tanks, eight reconnaissance vehicles, 26 armored infantry fighting vehicles, 64 armored personnel carriers, and 140 artillery pieces. The Army's air wing of 530 personnel operated three transport and 12 training fixed wing aircraft, as well as 13 helicopters. There was also a small maritime element with 47 active personnel, operating a single patrol boat. Paramilitary personnel consisted of a 4,500-member police force, with 5,000 reservists. Slovenia participated in UN, NATO, and European Union peacekeeping or military missions in four regions or countries. The defense budget in 2005 totaled $580 million.

18 INTERNATIONAL COOPERATION

Slovenia was admitted to the United Nations in 1992; it is part of several nonregional specialized agencies, such as the FAO, IAEA, UNCTAD, UNESCO, UNIDO, ILO, the World Bank and the WHO. Slovenia is also a member of the Council of Europe, OSCE, the WTO, the European Bank for Reconstruction and Development, the Inter-American Development Bank, NATO, the Euro-Atlantic Partnership Council, and the European Union. The country holds observer status in the OAS and is a member affiliate of the Western European Union.

Slovenia is part of the Australia Group, the Zangger Committee, and the Nuclear Suppliers Group (London Group). In environmental cooperation, the nation is part of the Basel Convention, Conventions on Biological Diversity and Air Pollution, Ramsar, CITES, the London Convention, the Kyoto Protocol, the Montréal Protocol, MARPOL, the Nuclear Test Ban Treaty, and the UN Conventions on the Law of the Sea, Climate Change, and Desertification.

19 ECONOMY

Before its independence, Slovenia was the most highly developed and wealthiest republic of the former Yugoslav SFR, with a per capita income more than double that of the Yugoslav average, and nearly comparable to levels in neighboring Austria and Italy. The painful transition to a market-based economy was exacerbated by the disruption of intra-Yugoslav trade. However, Slovenia's economy has not suffered as much as was predicted during the break-up of the Yugoslav SFR, due to strong ties with Western Europe. Whereas GDP fell by 9% in 1991 and 6% in 1992, the 1993 GDP grew by 1.3%. Since then real GDP growth has averaged 4% a year. In 2001 and 2002, a weak external environment slowed growth to 3% and 2.9% (est.). Until 1991 to 1999, Slovenia's budget deficit rarely exceeded 1% of GDP. In 2000 and 2001, the general government debt increased to 1.4% of GDP, and was projected to reach 2.9% in 2002. The unemployment rate (ILO definition) has fallen from 7.6% in 1999 to 6.4% in 2001 and an estimated 6.3% in 2002. Inflation as measured by consumer prices (end of period) rose from 8% in 1998 and 1999 to 8.9% in 2000, but then fell to 7% in 2001 and 7.2%(est.) in 2002.

Under the Communists, large parts of the economy were nationalized, with most restructuring involving the infrastructure, electricity, telecommunications, utilities, major banks, insurers, and the steel industry. Subsequent reforms enabled managers and workers to purchase up to 60% of their companies. As a result, nearly 70% of manufacturing firms in Slovenia are owned by their employees.

Slovenia freed prices and implemented a privatization law in November 1992, which has enabled private businesses to expand. The Slovene privatization program began in 1993 and involved 1,500 companies, 1,000 of which had completed privatization by mid-1997, including most small and medium-sized enterprises. In 2001, an estimated 55% of the economy had been privatized.

The outlook for Slovenia's economy is good, as both inflation and unemployment are expected to continue edging down. By 2002 the country's real GDP per capita had risen to about 70% the EU average, and in May 2004 Slovenia was accepted as a full member of the latter.

Moderate growth rates were registered in 2003 and 2004 (2.5% and 3.9% respectively), and the trend was expected to continue in 2005, with a predicted GDP growth rate of 3.6%. Inflation continued on its downward spiral, reaching 5.6% in 2003, and 3.3% in 2004; predictions show it to continue to decrease in 2005, at 2.6%. Unemployment has remained fairly stable (although on a slight decrease path), hovering around 10.5%. Slovenia remains one of the most developed Central and Eastern European countries and

was the first to make the transition from a borrower status to a partner at the World Bank. Privatizations, structural reforms, and policy implementations have happened at an accelerated pace, and Slovenia is expected to adopt the euro by 2007.

20 INCOME

The US Central Intelligence Agency (CIA) reports that in 2005 Slovenia's gross domestic product (GDP) was estimated at $42.1 billion. The CIA defines GDP as the value of all final goods and services produced within a nation in a given year and computed on the basis of purchasing power parity (PPP) rather than value as measured on the basis of the rate of exchange based on current dollars. The per capita GDP was estimated at $20,900. The annual growth rate of GDP was estimated at 3.8%. The average inflation rate in 2005 was 2.4%. It was estimated that agriculture accounted for 2.8% of GDP, industry 36.9%, and services 60.3%.

According to the World Bank, in 2003 remittances from citizens working abroad totaled $255 million or about $128 per capita and accounted for approximately 0.9% of GDP. Foreign aid receipts amounted to $66 million or about $33 per capita and accounted for approximately 0.2% of the gross national income (GNI).

The World Bank reports that in 2003 household consumption in Slovenia totaled $15.10 billion or about $7,570 per capita based on a GDP of $27.7 billion, measured in current dollars rather than PPP. Household consumption includes expenditures of individuals, households, and nongovernmental organizations on goods and services, excluding purchases of dwellings. It was estimated that for the period 1990 to 2003 household consumption grew at an average annual rate of 3.4%. In 2001 it was estimated that approximately 27% of household consumption was spent on food, 14% on fuel, 4% on health care, and 16% on education.

21 LABOR

As of 2005, Slovenia's labor force totaled an estimated 920,000 persons. As of 2002, agriculture accounted for 6% of the workforce, with industry at 40% and 55% in the services sector. Unemployment was estimated at 9.8% in 2005.

The constitution provides that the establishment, activities, and recruitment of members of labor unions shall be unrestricted. There are two main labor federations, with constituent branches throughout the society, as well as a smaller regional union. Virtually all workers except for police and military personnel are eligible to form and join unions. The right to strike is also guaranteed by the constitution. Collective bargaining is still undergoing development, and the government still has the principal role in setting labor conditions.

The minimum wage was $373 monthly in 2002, although increasingly, private businesses are setting pay scales directly with their employees' unions or representatives. The workweek is 42 hours, and the minimum working age is 16. Occupational health and safety standards are set by the government and regularly enforced.

22 AGRICULTURE

Some 202,000 hectares (499,000 acres), or 10% of the total land area, were in use as cropland in 2003. Agriculture contributed about 3% to GDP in 2003; Slovenia was the least agriculturally active of all the republics of the former Yugoslav SFR. Major crops produced in 2004 included: wheat, 147,000 tons; corn, 357,000 tons; potatoes, 171,000 tons; sugar beets, 213,000 tons; olives, 2,100 tons; and fruit, 411,000 tons (of which grapes accounted for 33%).

23 ANIMAL HUSBANDRY

Permanent pasture land covers about 15% of the total land area. Sheep and cattle breeding, as well as dairy farming, dominate the agricultural sector of the economy. In 2005, the livestock population included: pigs, 534,000; cattle, 451,000; sheep, 94,000; goats, 22,000; horses, 20,000; and chickens, 4.8 million. Meat production in 2005 included 45,500 tons of beef, 70,000 tons of pork, and 64,000 tons of poultry. Productivity rates for livestock and dairy farming are comparable to much of Western Europe. In 2005, 654,000 tons of milk and 20,000 tons of eggs were produced. Poultry and eggs are some of the few agricultural products where Slovenia's domestic production still exceeds domestic demand.

24 FISHING

The total catch in 2003 was 2,635 tons, 49% from marine fishing. The freshwater catch is dominated by rainbow trout and common carp. Exports of fish products amounted to $7.3 million in 2003, up from $5.1 million in 1997. The fishing sector accounts for less than 1% of foreign investment.

25 FORESTRY

Forests cover 55% of the total area; they are Slovenia's most significant natural resource. Roundwood production was 2,551,000 cu m (90 million cu ft) in 2004. Production included wood pulp, 153,000 tons; paper and paperboard, 557,600 tons; and wood-based panels, 474,000 cu m (16.7 million cu ft). Exports of forest product in 2004 totaled $624 million. The furniture-making industry is also a prominent consumer of forest products.

26 MINING

Slovenia's output of metals in 2003 included refined and secondary lead, aluminum ingot, and crude steel. The country's mining and quarrying sector accounted for around 0.9% of Slovenia's gross domestic product (GDP) in 2003. Slovenia's industrial output grew by about 1.4% in 2003 from 2002. Apart from being a substantial producer of quartz, quartzite and glass sand (200,000 metric tons in 2003), Slovenia was also a modest producer of common clay, coke and petroleum products. In 2003 output of: aluminum ingot (primary and secondary) totaled 109,800 metric tons; crude steel, 543,000 metric tons; and lead (refined and secondary), 15,000 metric tons. Industrial mineral production in 2003 included: cement, 1.3 million tons; bentonite, 4,000 metric tons; lime, 150,000 tons; salt (all sources) 125,000 metric tons; and di-

mension stone, 12,603 metric tons. Also produced was pumice, and sand and gravel.

27 ENERGY AND POWER

Slovenia, with miniscule reserves of oil and no natural gas reserves, is heavily reliant upon imports to meet its petroleum and natural gas needs.

In 2002, Slovenia's imports of all petroleum products averaged 53,640 barrels per day, of which crude oil imports averaged 100 barrels per day. Distillates and gasoline were the top two refined oil products imported that year, averaging 28,140 barrels per day and 18,180 barrels per day, respectively. Crude oil production in 2002 averaged 100 barrels per day. Domestic demand for refined oil products averaged 51,040 barrels per day. Domestic output of refined oil products averaged 100 barrels per day.

Slovenia imported all of the natural gas it consumed in 2002. Imports and demand for dry natural gas totaled 34.26 billion cu ft.

Coal was Slovenia's most abundant fossil fuel. Domestic output of all coal products totaled 5,166,000 short tons in 2002, of which lignite or brown coal accounted for 4,462,000 short tons. Coal product imports in 2002 totaled 694,000 short tons, of which 631,000 short tons was hard coal, and 63,000 short tons were coke. Demand for coal products in 2002 totaled 6,212,000 short tons.

Slovenia's electric power generation sector relies upon fossil fuels, hydropower and nuclear power. In 2002, total installed electrical capacity was 2.735 million kW, of which conventional thermal capacity was the largest at 1.220 million kW. Hydroelectric capacity that year stood at 0.839 million kW, followed by nuclear at 0.676 million kW. Electric power production in 2002 amounted to 13.882 billion kWh, with nuclear energy providing the largest portion of electric power generated at 5.310 billion kWh, followed by conventional thermal sources at 5.120 billion kWh and hydropower at 3.355 billion kWh. Domestic consumption of electricity totaled 11.780 billion kWh in 2002.

Slovenia imports oil from the former republics of the USSR and the developing world to supply a refinery at Lendava. Coal is mined at Velenje. Natural gas is used extensively for industry and is supplied by the former USSR and Algeria via 305 km (190 mi) of natural gas pipelines.

28 INDUSTRY

Manufacturing is widely diversified. Important manufacturing sectors include: electrical and nonelectrical machinery, metal processing, chemicals, textiles and clothing, wood processing and furniture, transport equipment, and food processing. In the composition of total value-added by economic activity, the share from industry declined from 50% in 1989 to 43% in 1991. Industry declined still further to 36% of GDP by 2001. Industrial production, which fell by about 25% in the early 1990s due in part to the international sanctions against Serbia, grew by an estimated 1% in 1996 and increased by 3.3% in 2001. The recovery of industrial production has been slower than expected, as the shift from parastatal to private ownership continues. Only in the late 1990s were steps taken to privatize key industrial sectors such as telecommunications, utilities, and steel. Slovenia produced 116,082 automobiles in 2001, a 6% decline from 2000.

The industry seemed to have stabilized by 2004, contributing 36% to the total GDP, and with an industrial production growth rate that equaled the GDP growth rate, at 3.9%; industry employed 40% of the labor force. Agriculture made up 3% of the total economy, and employed 6% of the working people; services came in first, with 60% and 55% respectively. Main industries included ferrous metallurgy and aluminum products, lead and zinc smelting, electronics (including military electronics), trucks, electric power equipment, wood products, textiles, chemicals, machine tools.

²⁹SCIENCE AND TECHNOLOGY

The Slovenian Academy of Sciences and Arts, founded in 1938, has institutes conducting research in biology, paleontology, and medicine. Headquartered in Ljubljana are the Association of Engineers and Technicians of Slovenia; the Association of Mathematicians, Physicists, and Astronomers of Slovenia, and the Society for Natural Sciences of Slovenia. The Ljubljana Geological Institute was founded in 1946, and the Institute for Karst Research a year later in Postojna. The University of Ljubljana has faculties of arts and sciences; natural sciences and technology; architecture, civil engineering, and geodesy; electrical and computer engineering; mechanical engineering; medicine; and veterinary medicine. The University of Maribor has a college of agriculture, a faculty of technical sciences, and a center for applied mathematics and theoretical physics. In 1987–97, science and engineering students accounted for 26% of university enrollment.

In 2002 research and development (R&D) expenditures totaled $562.019 million, or 1.54% of GDP. Of that amount, the largest portion came from the business sector at 60%, followed by government sources at 35.6%. Foreign sources accounted for 3.7% and higher education 0.6%. In that same year, there were 2,364 scientists and engineers engaged in R&D per one million people. High technology exports in 2002 were valued at $488 million, or 5% of the country's manufactured exports.

³⁰DOMESTIC TRADE

Slovenia's domestic economy has historically been small, thus necessitating an emphasis on exports. New legislation in 1994 regarding tax exemptions on imported inputs was expected to help domestic companies compete with foreign firms. More recent reforms are aimed at encouraging and increasing both local and foreign investment.

There are a number of wholesalers and retailers throughout the country. American and European franchises have been established within the country. Installment financing, even for small ticket items, is common. Consumer prices are generally high due to the high cost of labor and transportation. The government maintains price controls on certain goods and services, such as gasoline, railway travel, telecommunications, and milk.

Retail hours are generally between 8 AM and 8 PM on weekdays. Stores may be open for a half-day on Saturdays.

³¹FOREIGN TRADE

Slovenia has reoriented much of its trade away from its former Yugoslav neighbors toward Western Europe. Sanctions imposed by the UN on trade with Serbia severed Slovenia from its largest

Principal Trading Partners – Slovenia (2003)

(In millions of US dollars)

Country	Exports	Imports	Balance
World	12,766.7	13,849.7	-1,083.0
Germany	2,947.7	2,668.9	278.8
Italy-San Marino-Holy See	1,674.0	2,533.6	-859.6
Croatia	1,141.4	503.5	637.9
Austria	935.0	1,164.0	-229.0
France-Monaco	721.5	1,390.0	-668.5
Bosnia-Herzegovina	532.9	88.7	444.2
United States	464.8	334.9	129.9
Russia	394.4	352.8	41.6
Serbia and Montenegro	392.6	76.3	316.3
Poland	351.8	214.5	137.3

(…) data not available or not significant.

SOURCE: *2003 International Trade Statistics Yearbook,* New York: United Nations, 2004.

foreign market. In 1992, 55% of Slovenia's exports were sent to the European Union (EU), and only 30% to Croatia and the other former Yugoslav republics. By 2000, the EU was buying 64% of Slovenia's exports.

Slovenia manufactures and exports mostly motor vehicles (8.5%), furniture (6.8%), and household electrical equipment (5.7%). Other exports include medicinal and pharmaceutical products (4.5%), clothes (4.4%), paper (3.4%), and iron and steel (3.3%).

In 2004, exports totaled $15 billion (FOB—Free on Board), with imports slightly higher at $16 billion (FOB). Slovenia's main export partners were Germany (which received 18.3% of total exports), Italy (11.6%), Austria (11.5%), France (7.4%), Croatia (7.4%), and Bosnia and Herzegovina (4.8%). Imports included machinery and transport equipment, manufactured goods, chemicals, fuels and lubricants, food, and mainly came from Germany (19.9%), Italy (17%), Austria (14.9%), France (10.2%), and Hungary (3.8%).

³²BALANCE OF PAYMENTS

Slovenia's public finances are among the strongest and most stable of the emerging nations in Eastern and Central Europe.

The US Central Intelligence Agency (CIA) reported that in 2002 the purchasing power parity of Slovenia's exports was $10.3 billion while imports totaled $11.1 billion resulting in a trade deficit of $800 million.

The International Monetary Fund (IMF) reported that in 2001 Slovenia had exports of goods totaling $9.34 billion and imports totaling $9.96 billion. The services credit totaled $1.96 billion and debit $1.46 million.

Exports of goods and services totaled $19.3 billion in 2004, up from $15.7 billion in 2003. Imports grew from $15.7 billion in 2003, to $19.5 billion in 2004. Although Slovenia has managed to keep a fine balance between imports and exports, the resource balance was on a negative upsurge, growing from -$19 million in 2003, to -$212 million in 2004. A similar trend was registered for the current account balance, which deteriorated from -$99 million in 2003, to -$275 million in 2004. The national reserves (including gold) were $8.6 billion in 2003, covering more than six months of imports; by 2004, they grew to $8.9 billion.

Balance of Payments – Slovenia (2003)

(In millions of US dollars)

Current Account		**-98.9**
Balance on goods		-625.4
Imports	-13,538.4	
Exports	12,913.0	
Balance on services		606.6
Balance on income		-187.8
Current transfers		107.8
Capital Account		**-190.9**
Financial Account		**545.2**
Direct investment abroad		-466.0
Direct investment in Slovenia		337.0
Portfolio investment assets		-220.0
Portfolio investment liabilities		-30.3
Financial derivatives		...
Other investment assets		-922.6
Other investment liabilities		1,847.0
Net Errors and Omissions		**54.8**
Reserves and Related Items		**-310.2**

(…) data not available or not significant.

SOURCE: *Balance of Payment Statistics Yearbook 2004*, Washington, DC: International Monetary Fund, 2004.

Public Finance – Slovenia (2003)

(In billions of tolars, central government figures)

Revenue and Grants	**2,529.8**	**100.0%**
Tax revenue	1,242	49.1%
Social contributions	918.8	36.3%
Grants	36.2	1.4%
Other revenue	332.9	13.2%
Expenditures	**2,609.3**	**100.0%**
General public services	279.6	10.7%
Defense	72.5	2.8%
Public order and safety	105.4	4.0%
Economic affairs	219.8	8.4%
Environmental protection	23.2	0.9%
Housing and community amenities	22.7	0.9%
Health	389.1	14.9%
Recreational, culture, and religion	67.9	2.6%
Education	361.8	13.9%
Social protection	1,067.3	40.9%

(…) data not available or not significant.

SOURCE: *Government Finance Statistics Yearbook 2004*, Washington, DC: International Monetary Fund, 2004.

33 BANKING AND SECURITIES

The Bank of Slovenia is the country's central bank, and it is independent of the government. It has pursued a tight monetary and credit policy, aimed at the gradual reduction of inflation, since the introduction of the tolar in October 1991. The bank ended some of the worst abuses of the banking system under the Yugoslavian federation, such as enterprises setting up their own banks from which they borrowed freely.

At the end of 1996, the Bank of Slovenia changed its method of calculating the revalorization rate for other banks. From January 1997, the rate is derived from price increases over the preceding six months, instead of four months as before.

Yet not until 1999 did Slovenia move to reform its banking sector by privatizing some of its largest banks and permitting foreign investment. Two of the largest state-owned banks, Nova Ljubljanska Banka and Nova Kreditna banka Maribor, were prime candidates for privatization. Analysts also expected large-scale consolidation to follow in the wake of the banking divestment.

The International Monetary Fund reports that in 2001, currency and demand deposits—an aggregate commonly known as M1—were equal to $1.9 billion. In that same year, M2—an aggregate equal to M1 plus savings deposits, small time deposits, and money market mutual funds—was $10.8 billion. The money market rate, the rate at which financial institutions lend to one another in the short term, was 6.9%.

Commercial banks in the country include the Albania Joint-Stock Company. The currency unit is the tolar (Slt).

The Ljubljana Stock Exchange, abolished in 1953, was reopened in December 1989. As of 2001, it listed 38 securities and had 60 members. Total market capitalization was $2.8 billion that year, and trading value was $794 million, an increase of 30.5% from the previous year. As of 2004, a total of 140 companies were listed on the Ljubljana Stock Exchange, which had a market capitalization of $9.677 billion. Trading value that year was $1.170 billion, up 14.7% from the previous year. The Ljubljana International Futures and Options Exchange, Ltd. opened in 1998.

34 INSURANCE

In 1996, the company Zavarovaluica Triglav wrote all classes of insurance. There were at least 13 companies operating in Slovenia in 1997. In 2003, the value of all direct insurance premiums written totaled $1.440 billion, of which nonlife premiums accounted for $1.095 billion. In that same year, Triglev was Slovenia's top nonlife and life insurer, with gross written premiums of $346.3 million and $145.1 million, respectively.

35 PUBLIC FINANCE

Economic management is fairly good in Slovenia. Public finances showed modest deficits of about 1.4% of GDP through 2001. The debt to GDP ratio was 37% in 2001. Privatization has been relatively successful, although some of the business practices of the Yugoslav brand of communism have carried over to the newly private enterprises.

The US Central Intelligence Agency (CIA) estimated that in 2005 Slovenia's central government took in revenues of approximately $16 billion and had expenditures of $16.7 billion. Revenues minus expenditures totaled approximately -$710 million. Public debt in 2005 amounted to 29.9% of GDP. Total external debt was $20.57 billion.

The International Monetary Fund (IMF) reported that in 2003, the most recent year for which it had data, central government revenues were SLT2,529.8 billion and expenditures were SLT2,609.3 billion. The value of revenues was us$12 million and expenditures us$12 million, based on an exchange rate for 2003 of us$1 = SLT207.11 as reported by the IMF. Government outlays by function were as follows: general public services, 10.7%; defense, 2.8%; public order and safety, 4.0%; economic affairs, 8.4%; environmental protection, 0.9%; housing and community amenities,

0.9%; health, 14.9%; recreation, culture, and religion, 2.6%; education, 13.9%; and social protection, 40.9%.

³⁶TAXATION

As of 2005, Slovenia had a flat 25% tax rate on corporate income. Capital gains are included as business income and taxed at the same corporate rate. Generally, the withholding tax on dividends distributed to residents and nonresidents is 25%, as it is with interest and royalties. The resident branches of foreign companies are taxed at the same 25% rate as Slovenian companies.

Personal income is taxed according to a progressive schedule up to 50%. All taxpayers can subtract 11% of their annual income from their taxable base. In addition, families with children can deduct 10% of their income for the first child and 5% for each additional child. There is a standard 3% deduction for investment in real estate, plus allowances for other living expenses, medical expenses, etc. Payroll taxes are assessed for health insurance and employment. There are gift and inheritance, and land taxes.

A sales tax of 20% on consumer products and 10% on services was replaced as of 1 July 1999 with Slovenia's value-added tax (VAT) introduced at a standard rate of 19% and a reduced rate of 7.5%. As of 1 January 2002 the standard rate was increased to 20% and the reduced rate upped to 8.5%, where it stood as of 2005. The reduced rate applies to food, medicines and agricultural products. Exports, insurance, banking and financial services are exempt. There are also excise taxes on alcohol, tobacco, and fuel.

³⁷CUSTOMS AND DUTIES

Imports to Slovenia are generally unrestricted, except for certain agricultural, textile, and wood products. Customs duties on raw materials are 0–5%, semifinished products are assessed 5–10%, and equipment is charged 8–15%, while finished products or consumer goods are levied 15–27%. Many import taxes have been abolished, and further liberalization is planned. However, a sales tax and a customs clearance fee still exist.

The European Union (EU) signed a cooperation agreement with Slovenia in April 1993, which provided for greater access to the EU market. Slovenia also entered into trade agreements with Hungary, the Czech Republic, and Slovakia in 1993 that will gradually eliminate most trade barriers. By 1997, countries enjoying most-favored nation (MFN) status with Slovenia were assessed a 10.7% weighted average tariff. In 1999, following a reduction in its bilateral tariff with the European Union, Slovenia also lowered its MFN tariff.

³⁸FOREIGN INVESTMENT

Since independence, the foreign investment climate has steadily improved in Slovenia, despite constraints that have inhibited investment. The small domestic economy has been viewed by many prospective investors as the least risky of the former Yugoslav republics, but to date Slovenia's share of world foreign direct investment (FDI) flows have been well below its share of world GDP. From 1988 to 1990, its share of world FDI was 60% of its share of world GDP, and from 1998 to 2000, it was only 30% of its share of world GDP.

Until the late 1990s Slovenia retained several barriers to foreign investment. Any company incorporated in Slovenia was required to have a majority of Slovenes on its board of directors, or a managing director or proxy of Slovene nationality. Foreign companies and individuals of foreign nationality were prohibited from owning land in Slovenia. However, any company incorporated in Slovenia was permitted to purchase real estate, regardless of the origin of its founding capital. Liberalization laws enacted in 1999 lowered the threshold of foreign direct investment from 50% to 10%. This allowed more foreign investors to avert the custody account regime.

FDI inflow amounted to $375.2 million in 1997, but fell to about $250 million in 1998. In 1999 and 2000, FDI inflows averaged close to $180 million. In 2001, contrary to the trend toward the decline of foreign investment worldwide, FDI inflow into Slovenia rose to a record $442 million.

Despite its overall attractiveness, Slovenia has not managed to attract significant levels of FDI, as compared to some other Central and Eastern European Countries (like Hungary or the Czech Republic). At the end of 2003 the total stock of FDI in the country was roughly $5.1 billion, with the majority of capital inflows coming from the European Union. A major reason for the recent poor performance in this sector can be attributed to the shelving of proposed privatizations in the energy, telecommunication, and financial sectors by the government of Slovenia.

³⁹ECONOMIC DEVELOPMENT

The most productive of the former Yugoslav republics, Slovenia enjoys a high degree of prosperity and stability, and has made a successful transition to a market economy. It has become a member of the International Monetary Fund (IMF) as well as the World Bank; it obtained an $80 million loan for financial rehabilitation from the latter. The EBRD loaned Slovenia $50 million for the improvement of the railway sector. The country is a founding member of the WTO. Unlike the rest of the former communist states of Eastern Europe, Slovenia never received assistance from the International Monetary Fund. Its per capita gross domestic product (GDP) is comparable to EU members Portugal and Greece.

Slovenia's economy is heavily dependent upon foreign trade, with trade equaling around 120% of GDP. The budgets for 2003 and 2004 restricted the public deficit to 1% of GDP. Inflation fell from 200% in 1992 to 7.5% in 2002. Further privatizations—especially in the telecommunications, financial, and energy sectors—were planned as of 2003 but were put on hold indefinitely. Foreign direct investment has been high since 2000, almost tripling from 2001 to 2002 (accounting for 6.5% of GDP), but returned to lower levels in 2003 and 2004.

On 1 May 2004 Slovenia joined the European Union, which further strengthened the aura of political and economic stability it already had. It is one of the first 10 newly accepted countries, expected to introduce the euro by 2007. Slovenia registered steady growth rates since 1993 and is now behaving like a fully developed economy, boasting a modern and extensive infrastructure, a highly educated work force, and a prime geographic location. However, the levels of foreign investment remained under the capacity of the Slovenian economy, due in part to protectionist measures by the government. Corruption, although lower than in other Central and Eastern European countries, remains an issue that has to be addressed.

40 SOCIAL DEVELOPMENT

Slovenia's first social insurance programs were established in 1922, and were updated in 2003. The system provides old age, disability, survivor's pensions, sickness, work injury, and unemployment benefits. The pension system covers most employed persons. Funds are provided by employee and employer contributions, with any unforeseen deficit covered by the government. The government funds the total cost for some groups of insured including veterans. The age of retirement is variable, depending upon the numbers of years worked. A universal system of family allowances provides benefits to families with children with incomes below a specified monthly amount. There is a maternity grant available to all permanent residents in Slovakia to purchase clothing and other necessities for a newborn child.

Women and men have equal status under the law. Discrimination against women or minorities in housing, jobs, or other areas is illegal. Officially, both spouses are equal in marriage, and the constitution asserts the state's responsibility to protect the family. Women are well represented in business, academia, and government, although they still hold a disproportionate share of lower-paying jobs. On average, women earn less than men. Violence against women is underreported, but awareness has been increasing. There have been improved efforts to assist victims. The constitution provides for special protection for children.

The constitution ensures minority participation in government by mandating that Italian and Hungarian minorities each receive at least one representative in the National Assembly. The Roma population continues to experience discrimination. Human rights are generally respected by the government and upheld by the legal and judicial systems.

41 HEALTH

In 1992, health care reforms were adopted to modify the health care system in place when Slovenia was part of the former Communist country of Yugoslavia. Direct health care funding by the government was replaced by a mostly employer-funded system run in conjunction with a new system of compulsory public health insurance. However, Slovenia still provides universal, comprehensive health care to all its citizens and its health cares system remains fairly centralized. As of 2004, there were an estimated 219 physicians, 717 nurses, 59 dentists and 39 pharmacists per 100,000 people. In the same year, total health care expenditure was estimated at 7.6% of GDP. In 2002 Slovenia had 26 hospitals, which included nine regional facilities, three local general hospitals, and the country's main teaching hospital and tertiary care center, the Clinical Center in Ljubljana.

In 2000, each Slovenian woman had an average of 1.2 children during her childbearing years. An estimated 11 mothers died during childbirth or pregnancy for each 100,000 live births. The infant mortality rate, which was 15 deaths per 1,000 in 1980, dropped significantly by 2005 to only 4.45 infant deaths per 1,000 live births. The immunization rates for a child under one were as follows: diphtheria, pertussis, and tetanus, 91%, and measles, 82%. The life expectancy at birth was 76.14 years by 2005.

The leading cause of death was cardiovascular disease, to which nearly half of all deaths were attributed. The other major causes of mortality, in order of prevalence, were cancer, injuries, poisoning, respiratory diseases, and diseases of the digestive system. The

HIV/AIDS prevalence was 0.10 per 100 adults in 2003. As of 2004, there were approximately 9,000 people living with HIV/AIDS in the country. There were an estimated 500 deaths from AIDS in 2003.

42 HOUSING

According to the 2002 census, there were 777,772 dwelling units. About 92% of all dwellings were privately owned by a citizen and 82% of all dwellings were owner occupied. About 44% of all households were living in single-family detached homes and 52% of all dwellings were in urban areas. About 94,635 dwellings, or 12% of the housing stock, had been built since 1991. The average household had 2.8 people.

Since the 1991 Housing Act, the State is no longer directly responsible for housing provisions. Municipalities have responsibility for social housing projects. The State does, however, offer subsidized loans for the construction of individual private homes and nonprofit rental housing.

43 EDUCATION

Between 1999 and 2009, Slovenia will be gradually replacing an eight-year basic schooling program with a nine-year program, which will contain three-cycles of three years each and cover primary and lower secondary studies. Upper secondary studies generally cover an additional three to four years with students given the options of attending general, technical, or vocational schools. The academic year runs from October to June.

In 2001, about 73% of children between the ages of three and six were enrolled in some type of preschool program. Primary school enrollment in 2003 was estimated at about 93% of age-eligible students. The same year, secondary school enrollment was about 93% of age-eligible students. It is estimated that about 95% of all students complete their primary education. The student-to-teacher ratio for primary school was at about 13:1 in 2003; the ratio for secondary school was about 14:1.

Higher education at public institutions is free for native, full-time students and students from other European Union countries. Slovenia has 3 universities, 3 art academies or professional colleges, and 10 private higher education institutions. The University of Ljubljana, founded in 1919, has 25 faculties. The University of Maribor has a faculty for teaching, a faculty for economics and business, and a faculty for technology. There are also two colleges attached to it. In 2003, it was estimated that about 68% of the tertiary age population were enrolled in tertiary education programs; 58% for men and 79% for women. The adult literacy rate for 2004 was estimated at about 99.7%.

As of 2003, public expenditure on education was estimated at 6.1% of GDP.

44 LIBRARIES AND MUSEUMS

The National and University Library of Slovenia is located in Ljubljana and holds 2.3 million items. The University of Ljubljana maintains 39 faculty libraries. The University of Maribor Library maintains eight faculty libraries and serves as a legal depository for all Slovenica materials printed in the Slovene language. The Slovenian Academy of Sciences and Arts, also in the capital, holds 450,000 volumes. There are about 60 public library systems, with over 280 branch locations and nine mobile library services. One of the largest, the Oton Župančič Public Library in Ljubljana, maintains six locations and a mobile service. There are about 138 special libraries in the country, including the Slovene National Museum Library that holds about 200,000 printed materials.

Ljubljana hosts the National Gallery, Museum of Modern Art, Museum of Architecture, National Museum of Slovenia, Slovene Sports Museum, and the Slovene Ethnographic Museum, among others. The Technology Museum of Slovenia is in Vrhnika. The National Liberation Museum is in Maribor, a city which also hosts several smaller art and history museums. The Slovene Religious Museum is in Gorica. There are dozens of other regional museums throughout the country, including several in restored historical houses and castles.

45 MEDIA

In 2003, there were an estimated 407 mainline telephones for every 1,000 people. The same year, there were approximately 871 mobile phones in use for every 1,000 people.

In 2004, three of the six national television channels were operated by the government-subsidized RTV Slovenia network. Pop TV and Kanal A are the two main private network operators. Every major town has a radio station. RTV Slovenia operates three national radio stations and several regional ones. Radio Hit and Radio City are the two main private network operators. Minority language television and radio broadcasts were available. As of 2005, about two-thirds of all households were connected to satellite or cable television services. In 2003, there were an estimated 405 radios and 366 television sets for every 1,000 people. About 160.3 of every 1,000 people were cable subscribers. Also in 2003, there were 300.6 personal computers for every 1,000 people and 376 of every 1,000 people had access to the Internet. There were 130 secure Internet servers in the country in 2004.

As of 2002, there were four major independent daily and several weekly newspapers published. The dailies are *Delo* (2002 circulation of 90,000), *Slovenske Novice* (80,000), *Dnevnik* (62,000), and *Vecer* (70,000).

The constitution provides for free expression, including freedom of speech and the press; however, it is said that lingering self-censorship and some indirect political pressures do continue to influence the media.

46 ORGANIZATIONS

The Slovenia Chamber of Commerce (Chamber of Economy of Slovenia) coordinates all economic activities within and outside the country. In the 1990s, two large associations of trade unions were formed: the Confederation of New Trade Unions of Slovenia and the Association of Independent Trade Unions. There are professional associations for the advancement of research and education in a variety of medical fields.

The Slovenian Academy of Sciences and the Arts was founded in 1938.

National youth organizations include the UN Student Club of Slovenia, the Catholic Student Movement of Slovenia, the Students Union of Slovenia, Girl Guides, and the Scout Association of Slovenia. There are sports associations promoting amateur competition among athletes of all ages; many of these groups are affiliated with international counterparts as well. Women's organizations include The Center for Gender and Politics at the Peace Institute and Soroptimist International.

International organizations with national chapters include Amnesty International, the Society of St. Vincent de Paul, UNICEF, and the Red Cross.

47 TOURISM, TRAVEL, AND RECREATION

The rich architecture, museums, caves, and springs are some of Slovenia's main tourist attractions. Health resorts are popular, many in the north where there are mineral and thermal springs. The 10 casinos also attract visitors each year, making entertainment a major part of the tourism industry. Slovenia has convention centers in Ljubljana and three other cities and international airports in Ljubljana, Maribor, and Portoroz. Popular recreational activities include skiing, snowboarding, tennis, golf, mountain climbing, canoeing, and fishing. Visitors from Europe and most other countries can enter Slovenia without visas.

In 2003, there were 1,052,847 tourist arrivals in Slovenia. Hotel rooms numbered 15,534 with 31,997 beds and a 47% occupancy rate. Tourism expenditure receipts totaled $1.4 billion.

According to 2005 US Department of State estimates, the daily cost of staying in Ljubljana was estimated at $217.

48 FAMOUS SLOVENIANS

Milan Kučan (b.1941) was president from 1991–2002, when he was succeeded by Janez Drnovšek (b.1950), who had previously served as prime minister. In 1551, Primož Trubar translated the New Bible into Slovene. The poet, Valentin Vodnik (1754–1819), wrote poems in praise of Napoleon; literature in praise of the French flourished during the French occupation of Slovenia in 1813. Slovenian tennis star Mima Jausovec (b.1956) won the Italian Open in 1976 and the French Open in 1977.

49 DEPENDENCIES

Slovenia has no territories or colonies.

50 BIBLIOGRAPHY

Benderly, Jill, and Evan Kraft, (eds.). *Independent Slovenia: Origins, Movements, Prospects.* New York: St. Martin's Press, 1994.

Carmichael, Cathie. *Slovenia.* Santa Barbara, Calif.: Clio Press, 1996.

Fink-Hafner, Danica, and John R. Robbins, (eds.). *Making a New Nation: The Formation of Slovenia.* Brookfield, Vt.: Dartmouth Publishing Company, 1997.

Frucht, Richard (ed.). *Eastern Europe: An Introduction to the People, Lands, and Culture.* Santa Barbara, Calif.: ABC-CLIO, 2005.

Gottfried, Ted. *Slovenia.* New York: Benchmark Books, 2005.

McElrath, Karen, (ed.). *HIV and AIDS: A Global View.* Westport, Conn.: Greenwood Press, 2002.

Pavlovic, Vukasin, and Jim Seroka, (eds.). *The Tragedy of Yugoslavia: The Failure of Democratic Transformation.* Armonk, N.Y.: M. E. Sharpe, 1992.

Plut-Pregelj, Leopoldina. *Historical Dictionary of Slovenia.* Lanham, Md.: Scarecrow Press, 1996.

Summers, Randal W., and Allan M. Hoffman, (eds.). *Domestic Violence: A Global View.* Westport, Conn.: Greenwood Press, 2002.

Svetlik, Ivan, (ed.). *Social Policy in Slovenia: Between Tradition and Innovation.* Brookfield, Vt.: Ashgate, 1992.

SPAIN

Kingdom of Spain
España

CAPITAL: Madrid

FLAG: The national flag, adopted in 1785, consists of three horizontal stripes: a yellow one—equal in size to the other two combined—between two red ones, with the coat of arms on the yellow stripe.

ANTHEM: *Marcha Real Granadera (March of the Royal Grenadier).*

MONETARY UNIT: The peseta was replaced by the euro as official currency as of 2002. The euro is divided into 100 cents. There are coins in denominations of 1, 2, 5, 10, 20, and 50 cents and 1 euro and 2 euros. There are notes of 5, 10, 20, 50, 100, 200, and 500 euros. €1 = $1.25475 (or $1 = €0.79697) as of 2005.

WEIGHTS AND MEASURES: The metric system is the legal standard.

HOLIDAYS: New Year's Day, 1 January; St. Joseph's Day, 19 March; Epiphany, 31 March; Day of St. Joseph the Artisan, 1 May; St. James's Day, 25 July; Assumption, 15 August; National Day and Hispanic Day, 12 October; All Saints' Day, 1 November; Immaculate Conception, 8 December; Christmas, 25 December. Movable religious holidays include Holy Thursday, Good Friday, Easter Monday, and Corpus Christi.

TIME: 1 PM = noon GMT.

¹LOCATION, SIZE, AND EXTENT

Occupying the greater part of the Iberian Peninsula, Spain is the third-largest country in Europe, with an area of 504,782 sq km (194,897 sq mi). Comparatively, the area occupied by Spain is slightly more than twice the size of the state of Oregon. This total includes the Balearic Islands (Islas Baleares) in the western Mediterranean Sea and the Canary Islands (Islas Canarias) in the Atlantic Ocean west of Morocco; both island groups are regarded as integral parts of metropolitan Spain. The Spanish mainland extends 1,085 km (674 mi) E–W and 950 km (590 mi) N–S. Bordered by the Bay of Biscay, France, and Andorra on the N, by the Mediterranean on the E and S, by Gibraltar and the Strait of Gibraltar on the S, by the Gulf of Cádiz on the SW, and by Portugal and the Atlantic on the W, Spain has a total land boundary of 1,918 km (1,192 mi) and a coastline of 4,964 km (3,084 mi). Spain also holds Ceuta, Melilla, and other "places of sovereignty" in the north of Morocco.

Spain has long claimed Gibraltar, a narrow peninsula on the south coast, which was taken by a British-Dutch fleet in 1704 and became a British colony under the Treaty of Utrecht (1713). In 2003, Gibraltar residents voted to remain a British colony and demanded greater participation in talks between the United Kingdom and Spain concerning the future of Gibraltar. The United Kingdom plans to grant Gibraltar greater autonomy, but Spain does not agree with this plan.

Spain's capital city, Madrid, is located in the center of the country.

²TOPOGRAPHY

Continental Spain is divided into five general topographic regions: (1) The northern coastal belt is a mountainous region with fertile valleys and large areas under pasture and covered with forests. (2) The central plateau, or Meseta, with an average altitude of about 670 m (2,200 ft), comprises most of Castilla y León, Castilla–La Mancha, and the city of Madrid. (3) Andalucía, with Sevilla its largest city, covers the whole of southern and southwestern Spain and, except for the flat fertile plain of the Guadalquivir River, is a mountainous region with deep fertile valleys. (4) The Levante is on the Mediterranean coastal belt, with Valencia its chief city. (5) Catalonia (Cataluña) and the Ebro Valley comprise the northeastern region.

Spain has six principal mountain ranges—the Pyrenees, the Cordillera Cantábrica, the Montes de Toledo, the Sierra Morena, the Serranías Penibéticas, and the Sistema Ibérico. The principal peaks are Pico de Aneto (3,404 m/11,168 ft) in the Pyrenees and Mulhacén (3,478 m/11,411 ft) in the Penibéticas. The main rivers are the Tagus (Tajo), Duero, Guadiana, and Guadalquivir, which flow to the Atlantic, and the Ebro, which flows to the Mediterranean. The Duero and the Guadalquivir form broad valleys and alluvial plains and at their mouths deposit saline soils, creating deltas and salt marshes. The coastline has few natural harbors except the estuaries (rías) in the northwest, formed by glaciers, and those in the Levante and the south, created by sandbars during the Quaternary period.

The Canary Islands are a group of 13 volcanic islands, of which 6 are barren. They have a ruggedly mountainous terrain interspersed with some fertile valleys. Spain's highest mountain, Pico de Teide (3,718 m/12,198 ft), is on Tenerife. The Balearic Islands are a picturesque group with sharply indented coastlines; they combine steep mountains with rolling, fertile ranges.

³CLIMATE

The climate of Spain is extremely varied. The northern coastal regions are cool and humid, with an average annual temperature of

14°c (57°F); temperatures at Bilbao range from an average of 10°c (50°F) in January–March to 19°c (66°F) during July–September. The central plateau is cold in the winter and hot in the summer; Madrid has a winter average of about 8°c (46°F) and a summer average of 23°c (73°F). In Andalucía and the Levante, the climate is temperate except in summer, when temperatures sometimes reach above 40°c (104°F) in the shade. The northern coastal regions have an average annual rainfall of 99 cm (39 in); the southern coastal belt has 41–79 cm (16–31 in); and the interior central plain averages no more than 50 cm (20 in) annually.

4 FLORA AND FAUNA

Because of its wide variety of climate, Spain has a greater variety of natural vegetation than any other European country; some 8,000 species are cataloged. Nevertheless, vegetation is generally sparse. In the humid areas of the north there are deciduous trees (including oak, chestnut, elm, beech, and poplar), as well as varieties of pine. Pine, juniper, and other evergreens, particularly the ilex and cork oak, and drought-resistant shrubs predominate in the dry southern region. Much of the Meseta and of Andalucía has steppe vegetation. The Canaries, named for the wild dogs (Canariae insulae) once found there, support both Mediterranean and African flora. A small, yellow-tinged finch on the islands has given the name "canary" to a variety of yellow songbirds widely bred as house pets. Animal life in Spain is limited by the pressure of population and few wild species remain. As of 2002, there were at least 82 species of mammals, 281 species of birds, and over 5,000 species of plants throughout the country.

5 ENVIRONMENT

Extensive forests are now limited to the Pyrenees and the Asturias-Galicia area in the north because centuries of unplanned cutting have depleted stands. Fire eliminates 700,000 to 1,000,000 hectares of forestland each year. Government reforestation schemes meet with difficulties where sheep and goats graze freely over large areas. During the 1980s, an average of 92,000 hectares (227,000 acres) were reforested annually. Erosion affects about 18% of the total land mass of Spain.

Air pollution is also a problem in Spain. In 1995 industrial carbon dioxide emissions totaled 223.2 million metric tons (a per capita level of 5.72 metric tons), ranking Spain 20th compared to the other nations of the world. In 2000, the total of carbon dioxide emissions was at 282.9 million metric tons. Industrial and agricultural sources contribute to the nation's water pollution problem. Spain is also vulnerable to oil pollution from tankers which travel the shipping routes near the nation's shores. Spain's cities produce about 13.8 million tons of solid waste per year.

Principal environmental responsibility is vested in the Directorate General of the Environment, within the Ministry of Public Works and Urban Affairs. As of 2003, 8.5% of the country's total land area is protected, including 4 natural UNESCO World Heritage sites and 49 Ramsar wetland sites. According to a 2006 report issued by the International Union for Conservation of Nature and Natural Resources (IUCN), threatened species included 20 types of mammals, 20 species of birds, 8 types of reptiles, 4 species of amphibians, 24 species of fish, 27 types of mollusks, 36 species of other invertebrates, and 14 species of plants. Threatened species included the Spanish lynx, Pyrenean ibex, Mediterranean monk seal, northern bald ibis, Spanish imperial eagle, Cantabrian capercaillie, dusky large blue and Nevada blue butterflies, and on the Canary Islands, the green sea turtle and Hierro giant lizard. The Canarian black oystercatcher and the Canary mouse have become extinct.

6 POPULATION

The population of Spain in 2005 was estimated by the United Nations (UN) at 43,484,000, which placed it at number 29 in population among the 193 nations of the world. In 2005, approximately 17% of the population was over 65 years of age, with another 15% of the population under 15 years of age. There were 96 males for every 100 females in the country. According to the UN, the annual population rate of change for 2005–10 was expected to be 0.1%, a rate the government viewed as too low. The projected population for the year 2025 was 46,164,000. The population density was 86 per sq km (223 per sq mi).

The UN estimated that 76% of the population lived in urban areas in 2005, and that urban areas were growing at an annual rate of 0.21%. The capital city, Madrid, had a population of 5,103,000 in that year. Other large urban areas and their estimated populations include Barcelona (4,424,000), Valencia (796,549), Sevilla (704,154), Zaragoza (647,373), and Málaga (558,287).

7 MIGRATION

Emigration of Spanish workers to the more industrialized countries of Western Europe, notably to the Federal Republic of Germany (FRG), France, Switzerland, and Belgium, increased markedly during the 1960s, but since 1973 the number of Spaniards returning to Spain has been greater than the number of those leaving. Nevertheless, more than 1.7 million Spanish citizens were residing outside the country in 1987. In 2001 there were 1,109,060 foreign residents in Spain, 2.5% of total population. There were 234,937 Moroccans, 84,699 Ecuadorians, 80,183 British, 62,506 Germans, 48,710 Colombians, 44,798 French, and 42,634 Portuguese.

Internal migration was 685,966 in 1990. In the past it has been directed toward the more industrialized zones and the great urban centers, and away from the rural areas. Rural-to-urban and urban-to-rural migration is now roughly in balance.

Placed into practice in 2001, Plan Greco was a scheme to regularize the immigration process; it was paralleled by a labor quota system aimed at responding to short and long-term labor shortages. However, both employers and labor unions agreed that the 2002 labor quota was a failure, falling short of the necessary workers. Between 1995–2004 Spain's legal foreign-born population quadrupled from 500,000 to 2,000,000. All the same, Spain still had an estimated 1.2 million unauthorized migrants at the end of 2004. In 2005, Spain had its fifth and largest legalization program with 690,679 unauthorized foreign workers applying.

A gateway into Europe, Spain receives large numbers of non-European migrants through Ceuta and Melilla. Between 1984–98, an estimated 8,000 people were granted refugee status. In 2004, 15,675 illegal migrants traveled on 740 boats that were intercepted, and in 2005 a boat with 300 Moroccans attempting to enter southern Spain was seized. In 1998, 6,654 people applied for asylum in Spain, up from 4,730 in 1996, however by 2004 none applied. Also in 2004, 5,635 people were recognized as refugees and there were 14 others of concern to the United Nations High Com-

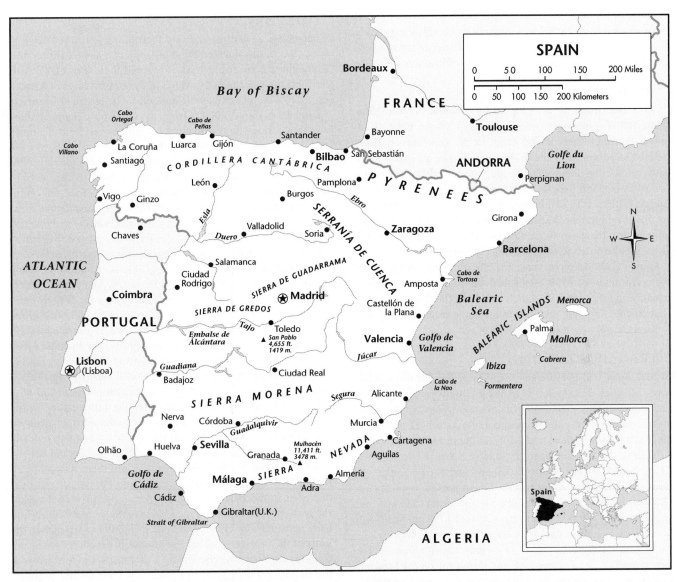

LOCATION: 36° to 43°47′ N; 3°19′ E to 9°30′ W. BOUNDARY LENGTHS: France, 623 kilometers (387 miles); Andorra, 65 kilometers (40 miles); Mediterranean coastline, 1,670 kilometers (1,038 miles); Gibraltar, 1 kilometer (0.6 miles); Portugal, 1,214 kilometers (754 miles); Atlantic and Bay of Biscay coastlines, 2,234 kilometers (1,388 miles). The Balearic Islands extend from 1°12′ to 4°19′ E and 38°38′ to 40°5′ N; coastline, 910 kilometers (565 miles). The Canary Islands, 1,400 kilometers (900 miles) to the southwest, extend from 13°20′ to 18°19′ W and 27°38′ to 29°25′ N; coastline, 1,126 kilometers (700 miles). territorial sea limit: 12 miles.

missioner for Refugees (UNHCR). In 2005, the net migration rate was an estimated 0.99 migrants per 1,000 population. In 2003 worker remittances were $4.7 billion.

8ETHNIC GROUPS

Ethnological studies reveal a homogeneous Latin stock in three-fourths of the country. The greatest contrasts are found between those of Celtic, Iberic, and Gothic antecedents in the north and those of southern lineage. The great mobility of the population toward the urban centers, the coast, and the islands has contributed to the diffusion of ethnic characteristics.

Cultural groups, but not properly distinct ethnic groups, include the Castilians of central Spain, the Asturians and the Basques of Vizcaya, Álava, Guipúzcoa, and (in part) Navarra provinces in the north, the Catalans of Catalonia, the Galicians of the far northwest, and the Andalusians of the south. The Basques, Galicians, and Catalans consider themselves separate nations within Spain;

they enjoy considerable cultural, economic, and political autonomy. Estimates of the Roma population are usually given as several hundred thousand.

9LANGUAGES

According to the 1978 constitution, Spanish is the national language. Castilian, the dialect of the central and southern regions, is spoken by most Spaniards (74%) and is used in the schools and courts. Regional languages—Catalan (spoken by 17% of the population), Galician (7%), Basque (2%), Bable, and Valencian—are also official in the respective autonomous communities, where education is bilingual.

Regional languages are spoken by over 16 million persons in Spain. A majority of those who live in the northeastern provinces and the Balearic Islands spoke Catalan, a neo-Latin tongue. Galician, close to Portuguese, was used in Galicia, in the northwest corner of Spain. The Basques in northern Spain spoke Basque, a pre-Roman language unrelated to any other known tongue and using an ancient script. Bable, a form of Old Castilian was spoken in Asturias (northwest), and Valencian, a dialect of Catalan, was used by inhabitants of the eastern province of Valencia.

10 RELIGIONS

In 2003, the Center for Sociological Investigations reported that about 81% of respondents were nominally Catholic, but 42% admitted that they never attend Mass. In the same survey, 11.6% claimed to be agnostics and 4.1% claimed to be atheists. Protestants, numbering about 350,000, are represented by the Federation of Evangelical Religious Entities. The Federation of Spanish Islamic Entities (FEERI), located in Córdoba, reports that there are about one million Muslims, including both legal and illegal immigrants. There are about 40,000–50,000 Jews in the country. There are also about 9,000 practicing Buddhists.

Roman Catholicism was once the official religion of Spain, but the constitution of 1978 established the principles of religious freedom and separation of church and state. The Roman Catholic Church does, however, continue to maintain certain privileges, as well as monetary support, from the state.

11 TRANSPORTATION

In 2002, Spain had an estimated 346,858 km (215,538 mi) of roadways, of which 343,389 km (213,382 mi) were paved highways, including 9,063 km (5,632 mi) of expressways. The Mediterranean and Cantábrico routes are the most important. In 2003, there were 19,293,263 passenger cars and 4,255,275 commercial vehicles.

In 2004, the National Spanish Railway Network encompassed 14,781 km (9,194 mi) of broad, standard and narrow gauge railways, of which broad gauge was the largest portion at 11,829 km (7,358 mi), followed by narrow gauge at 1,954 km (1,215 mi), and standard gauge at 998 km (621 mi). A total of 7,718 km (4,801 mi) of railway (broad, standard and narrow gauge) were electrified.

Of Spain's 200 ports, 26 are of commercial significance. The largest are Barcelona, Tarragona, and Cartagena on the Mediterranean, Algeciras on the Strait of Gibraltar, La Coruña on the Atlantic, and Las Palmas and Santa Cruz de Tenerife in the Canaries. The port of Bilbao, on the Bay of Biscay, can accommodate tankers of up to 500,000 tons. Substantial improvements were made during the 1970s at Gijón, Huelva, and Valencia. Scheduled ferry services connect Spain with neighboring countries and North Africa. In 2005, the merchant fleet was comprised of 182 vessels of 1,000 GRT or more, totaling 1,740,974 GRT. As of 2003, Spain had 1,045 km (650 mi) of navigable inland waterways.

Spain had an estimated 156 airports and airfields in 2004. As of 2005, a total of 95 had paved runways, and there were also eight heliports. Principal airports include Alicante, Prat at Barcelona, Ibiza, Lanzarote, Gran Canaria at Las Palmas, Barajas at Madrid, Málaga, Menorca, Son San Juan at Palma Mallorca, and Valencia. The state-owned Iberia Air Lines has regular connections with 50 countries and 89 cities in Europe, Africa, Asia (including the Middle East), and the Western Hemisphere. Other Spanish airlines are Aviaco, Air Europa, Viva Air, Binter Canarias, and Spanair. In 2003, about 42.507 million passengers were carried on domestic and international flights, and 879 million ton-km (546 million ton-mi) of freight.

12 HISTORY

Archaeological findings indicate that the region now known as Spain has been inhabited for thousands of years. A shrine near Santander, discovered in 1981, is believed to be over 14,000 years old, and the paintings discovered in the nearby caves of Altamira in 1879 are of comparable antiquity. The recorded history of Spain begins about 1000 BC, when the prehistoric Iberian culture was transformed by the invasion of Celtic tribes from the north and the coming of Phoenician and Greek colonists to the Spanish coast. From the 6th to the 2nd century BC, Carthage controlled the Iberian Peninsula up to the Ebro River; from 133 BC, with the fall of Numantia, until the barbarian invasions of the 5th century AD, Rome held Hispania, from which the name Spain is derived. During the Roman period, cities and roads were built, and Christianity and Latin, the language from which Spanish originated, were introduced. In the 5th century, the Visigoths, or western Goths, settled in Spain, dominating the country until 711, when the invading Moors defeated King Roderick. All of Spain, except for a few northern districts, knew Muslim rule for periods ranging from 300 to 800 years. Under Islam, a rich civilization arose, characterized by prosperous cities, industries, and agriculture and by brilliant writers, philosophers, and physicians, including Jews as well as Muslims. Throughout this period (711–1492), however, Christian Spain waged intermittent and local war against the Moors. The most prominent figure in this battle was El Cid, who fought for both Christians and Moors in the 11th century. By the 13th century, Muslim rule was restricted to the south of Spain. In 1492, Granada, the last Moorish stronghold on Spanish soil, fell, and Spain was unified under Ferdinand II of Aragón and Isabella I of Castile, the "Catholic Sovereigns." Until then, Aragón (consisting of Aragón, Catalonia, Valencia, and the Balearic Islands) had been an independent kingdom, which had expanded toward the eastern Mediterranean, incorporating Sicily and Naples, and had competed with Genoa and Venice. In order to strengthen the unity of the new state, Moors and Jews were expelled from Spain; Catholic converts who chose to stay were subject to the terrors of the Inquisition if suspected of practicing their former religions. The year 1492 also witnessed the official European discovery of the Americas by Christopher Columbus, sailing under the Castilian flag. In 1519, Ferdinand Magellan, a Portuguese in the service of Spain, began the first circumnavigation of the world, completed in 1522 by Juan Sebastián Elcano.

The 16th century, particularly under Charles I, who was also Holy Roman Emperor Charles V, was the golden age of Spain: its empire in the Americas produced vast wealth; its arts flourished; its fleet ruled the high seas; and its armies were the strongest in Europe. By the latter part of the 16th century, however, under Philip II, the toll of religious wars in Europe and the flow of people and resources to the New World had drained the strength of the Spanish nation; in 1588, the "invincible" Spanish Armada was defeated by England. Spain's continental power was ended by wars with England, the Netherlands, and France in the 17th century and by the War of the Spanish Succession (1701–14), which also established the Bourbon (Borbón) dynasty in Spain. In 1808, the enfeebled Spanish monarchy was temporarily ended, and Napoleon Bonaparte's brother Joseph was proclaimed king of Spain. On 2 May 1808, however, the Spanish people revolted and, later assisted by the British, drove the French from Spain. In the post-Napoleonic period, the Bourbons were restored to the Spanish throne, but a spirit of liberalism, symbolized by the 1812 Constitution of Cádiz, remained strong.

Much of the 19th and early 20th centuries were consumed in passionate struggles between radical republicanism and absolute monarchy. Abroad, imperial Spain lost most of its dominions in the Western Hemisphere as a result of colonial rebellions in the first half of the 19th century; Cuba, Puerto Rico, and the Philippines were lost as a result of the Spanish-American War in 1898. Spain remained neutral in World War I but in the postwar period engaged in extensive military action to maintain its colonial possessions in Morocco. Early defeats in the Moroccan campaign paved the way in 1923 for the benevolent dictatorship of Primo de Rivera, who successfully ended the war in 1927 and remained in power under the monarchy until 1930. In 1931, after municipal elections indicated a large urban vote in favor of a republic, Alfonso XIII left Spain and a republic was established.

The constitution of December 1931 defined Spain as a "democratic republic of workers," with "no official religion," respecting the "rules of international law . . . renouncing war as an instrument of national policy and recognizing the principle of regional autonomy." Neither right nor left had a parliamentary majority, and on the whole the coalition governments were ineffective. On 17 July 1936, an army revolt against the republic took place in Spanish Morocco. On the following day, Gen. Francisco Franco landed in Spain, and for the next two and a half years, until 31 March 1939, Spain was ravaged by civil war. The two contending parties were the Republicans, made up partly of democrats and partly of antidemocratic left-wing groups, and the rebels (Nationalists), who favored the establishment of a right-wing dictatorship. Almost from the beginning, a number of foreign countries intervened. Germany and Italy furnished manpower and armaments to the Nationalists, while the USSR, Czechoslovakia, and Mexico supported the Republicans. Finally the Republicans were defeated, and General Franco formed a corporative state. Under the Franco regime, Spain gave aid to the Axis powers in World War II but was itself a nonbelligerent.

The Postwar Years

Diplomatically isolated following the end of World War II, Spain in succeeding decades improved its international standing, in part by signing economic and military agreements with the United States in 1953 and 1963. Spain was admitted to the UN in 1955. While relations with its European neighbors approached normality, the repressive nature of the Franco regime kept Spain apart from the main social, political, and economic currents of postwar Western Europe.

On 22 July 1969, Juan Carlos de Borbón y Borbón was officially designated by Franco as his successor, to rule with the title of king; formally, Franco had been ruling as regent for the prince since 1947. On 20 November 1975, Gen. Franco died at the age of 82, thus ending a career that had dominated nearly four decades of Spanish history. Two days later, Juan Carlos I was sworn in as king. He reconfirmed Carlos Arias Navarro as prime minister on 5 December. Despite Juan Carlos I's announcement, in early 1976, of a program of moderate political and social reform, the new government was received with widespread demonstrations by labor groups and Catalan and Basque separatists. Continued political

unrest, coupled with a sharp rise in living costs, led ultimately to the king's dismissal of Arias Navarro, who was replaced, on 7 July, by Adolfo Suárez González.

On 15 June 1977, the first democratic elections in Spain in 40 years took place, with the Union of the Democratic Center (Unión de Centro Democrático—UCD), headed by Suárez, winning a majority in the new Cortes. The Cortes prepared a new constitution (in many respects similar to that of 1931), which was approved by popular referendum and sanctioned by the king in December 1978. In the elections of March 1979, the UCD was again the victor, and in the April local elections it captured more than 75% of the municipalities.

When Suárez announced his resignation in January 1981, the king named Leopoldo Calvo Sotelo y Bustelo to the premiership. As the Cortes wavered over the appointment, a group of armed civil guards stormed parliament on 23 February and held more than 300 deputies hostage for 17 hours. The attempted coup was swiftly neutralized by the king, who secured the loyalty of other military commanders. The plotters were arrested, and Sotelo was swiftly confirmed. A year of political wrangling followed; by mid-1982 the UCD was in disarray, and Sotelo called new elections. In October 1982, the Spanish Socialist Worker's Party (Partido Socialista Obrero Español—PSOE), headed by Felipe González Márquez, won absolute majorities in both houses of parliament. The new government was characterized by its relative youthfulness—the average age of cabinet ministers was 41—and by the fact that its members had no links with the Franco dictatorship. In the 1986 and 1989 elections, the PSOE again won majorities in both houses of parliament. The PSOE failed to win a majority in 1993 but governed with the support of the Basque and Catalan nationalist parties.

A continuing problem since the late 1960s has been political violence, especially in the Basque region. Political murders and kidnappings, mainly perpetrated by the separatist Basque Nation and Liberty (Euzkadi ta Askatasuna), commonly known as ETA, by the Antifascist Resistance Groups (GRAPO), and by several right-wing groups, abated only slightly in recent years. Another uncertainty in Spain's political future was the role of the military. Several army officers were arrested in October 1982 on charges of plotting a preelection coup, which reportedly had the backing of those involved in the February 1981 attempt. Spain joined NATO in 1982, but the membership question became so controversial that a referendum on it was held in March 1986; about two-thirds of the electorate voted, and 53% chose continued NATO membership. On 1 January of that year, Spain became a full member of the EC (now EU). In January 1988, the United States, acceding to Spain's demands, agreed to withdraw 72 jet fighters based near Madrid.

Spain received considerable recognition with the holding of the 1992 Summer Olympics in Barcelona, and Expo 92, a world's fair, in Sevilla. Other notable events included the designation of Madrid as the culture capital of Europe in 1992.

Throughout 1995–2000 Basque terrorists continued their attacks on civilian, police, and military targets and began to target more visible political targets. In August of 1995, the terrorists came close to assassinating King Juan Carlos while he was vacationing on the island of Majorca, off the southeastern coast of Spain. In 1997 Basque terrorists killed an important Socialist official of one of the Basque regions. In 2000, Jose Luis Lopez de la Calle, a Madrid newspaper columnist who was outspoken in his criticism of the Basque group, ETA, was shot to death outside his home. Thousands marched in the streets to protest his killing.

In 1995 information came to light that revealed that from 1983 to 1987 government officials in cooperation with the Civil Guard (Spain's national police force) formed death squads to hunt down and kill Basque terrorists living in France. The squads were disbanded after France agreed to greater cooperation with Spanish authorities, but not before 27 suspected Basque terrorists had been killed. The existence of the death squads may have remained a secret, but two death squad members were caught in the course of an attack and prosecuted for murder. At first government officials secured the silence of these two men by agreeing to make yearly payments to their wives, but by 1994 they felt that the story should no longer be hidden and revealed it to the world from their jail cells. Initially, Prime Minister Gonzalez had been charged with having knowledge of the attacks but an official inquiry into the charges concluded that they were groundless and he was completely exonerated.

Although French and Spanish security officials worked together to combat terrorism, violence attributed to the Basque terrorists continued into the 2000s. However, public support for Basque terrorists had waned nearly completely. A 1996 Basque execution of a kidnapped university professor brought out almost a half-million protesters in Madrid alone denouncing the Basque terrorists. A year later and again in 2000, assassinations allegedly carried out by Basque terrorists triggered large protests as well. The ETA was suspected of being behind bombings in several tourist resorts in June 2002 as an EU summit was held in Seville. In February 2003, Basque Socialist Party activist Joseba Pagazaurtundua was assassinated; the shooting was attributed to the ETA. Batasuna, the separatist Basque political party believed to be the political arm of the ETA, was banned by the Supreme Court in 2003. This ban prevented Batasuna candidates from running in municipal elections that year. In February 2005, a car bomb exploded in Madrid, injuring about 40 people: ETA was suspected of being responsible for the attack. In May 2005, the government offered to hold peace talks with the ETA if the group disarmed.

As Spain attempts to hold itself together against regional separatism, it joined with seven other nations in 1995 to create a passport-free zone that allowed much greater mobility between them. Spain also rejoined the NATO Military Command in the mid-1990s, making it once again a full member of the alliance. The adjustments to Spain's economy carried out in the mid- and late-1990s were successful. As a result, Spain was one of the 11 countries that joined together in launching the euro, the European Union's single currency, on 1 January 1999. (Greece joined shortly thereafter, bringing the number of countries in the euro zone to 12.)

On 11 July 2002, 12 Moroccan frontier guards landed on the island of Perejil, which is claimed by Spain, and claimed it as Moroccan territory. Spain's Prime Minister José María Aznar opposed the occupation, and sent troops to evacuate the Moroccan guards. Diplomatic relations between Spain and Morocco improved in December 2002, when plans were made for the return of each state's ambassadors.

During 2002 and into 2003, Aznar affirmed Spain's support for the United States and British position on the use of military force to force Iraq to disarm itself of weapons of mass destruction. Over 90% of Spain's citizens were against a war in Iraq, which began on 19 March 2003. Spain's pro-US stance alienated France and Germany, among other nations opposing the use of military force. Spain did not commit combat troops to fight alongside US and British forces, but it sent 900 troops trained in medical support and anti-mine specialties to assist the coalition forces.

On 11 March 2004, Madrid suffered a major terrorist attack as four rush-hour trains were bombed simultaneously in 10 explosions, killing 191 people and wounding more than 1,400. An Islamic group with links to the al-Qaeda organization was later blamed for the attacks. The attacks took place three days prior to general elections. On 12 March, massive demonstrations in many Spanish cities were held (some 11.4 million people took part, more than a fourth of the Spanish population), which denounced terrorism, and in part the Aznar administration for its support of the war in Iraq and the presence of Spanish troops there. In the general elections held on 14 March, the Socialists, led by José Luis Rodríguez Zapatero, defied earlier public opinion polls and won nearly 43% of the vote for a gain of 39 seats in the Congress of Deputies. When Zapatero was sworn in as president of the government and prime minister in April, he ordered the withdrawal of all Spanish troops from Iraq. The next presidential elections were scheduled for March 2008.

In February 2005, Spanish voters approved the EU constitution in a referendum by 77%. However, the French and Dutch rejections of the constitution in May and June 2005 indefinitely shelved plans for the EU to adopt such a document for itself.

In June 2005, the Spanish parliament defied the Roman Catholic Church by legalizing gay marriage and granting homosexual couples the same adoption and inheritance rights as heterosexual couples. As of late 2005, four countries in the world—Spain, the Netherlands, Belgium, and Canada—had legalized same-sex marriages.

¹³GOVERNMENT

Between 1966 and 1978, Spain was governed under the Organic Law of the Spanish State. A new constitution, approved by the Cortes on 31 October 1978 and by the electorate in a national referendum on 6 December, and ratified by King Juan Carlos I on 27 December 1978, repealed all the laws of the Franco regime and confirmed Spain as a parliamentary monarchy. It also guaranteed the democratic functioning of all political parties, disestablished the Roman Catholic Church, and recognized the right to autonomy of distinct nationalities and regions.

According to the constitution, the king is the head of state, symbolizing its unity. Legislative power is vested in the Cortes Generales (General Courts), consisting of two chambers: the Congreso de los Diputados (Congress of Deputies) with 350 members (deputies); and the Senado (Senate) with 259 members (senators). All deputies and 208 of the senators are popularly elected to four-year terms under universal adult suffrage. The remaining senators (51) are chosen by the assemblies in the 17 autonomous regions. The government, which is answerable to the congress, consists of the president (prime minister), vice president, and ministers, all appointed by the king. The supreme consultative organ of government is the Council of State. Also established by the constitution is the function of "defender of the people," inspired by medieval tradition and by the Scandinavian ombudsman. Suffrage is universal at age 18.

14 POLITICAL PARTIES

The Falange, known officially as the Nationalist Movement, was the only legally functioning party in Spain during the Franco regime. Founded in 1933 by José Antonio Primo de Rivera, it dated in its later form from 1937, when various right-wing groups were united under Gen. Franco. Nationalists, monarchists, and national syndicalists (Fascists) were the leading groups within the Falange. It lost some of its former power and much of its prestige during the last decades of Franco's regime. On 21 December 1974, the Franco government passed a law conferring a limited right of political association. On 9 June 1976, after Franco's death, the Cortes voted to legalize political parties; by the 1977 parliamentary elections, no fewer than 156 political parties were organized into 10 national coalitions and 12 regional alliances.

The Spanish political scene is characterized by changing parties and shifting alliances. The Union of the Democratic Center (Unión de Centro Democrático—UCD) was formed as an electoral coalition of smaller moderate parties. From 1977 to 1982, the UCD was the governing political body, headed first by Adolfo Suárez González and then by Leopoldo Calvo Sotelo y Bustelo. In late 1981, the UCD began to disintegrate; it won only 8% of the vote in the 1982 elections and was dissolved in February 1983. A new centrist party, the Democratic and Social Center (Centro Democrático y Social—CDS), was created in 1982. The Spanish Socialist Worker's Party (Partido Socialista Obrero Español—PSOE), which traces its lineage to the late 19th century, won absolute majorities in both chambers of the Cortes in October 1982 and June 1986.

The right is represented by the Popular Party or PP, embracing the Alianza Popular, the Christian Democratic Partido Demócrata Popular, and the Partido Liberal; the coalition took 26% of the 1986 vote. An extreme rightist party, New Force (Fuerza Nueva), lost its only seat in parliament in 1982 and thereupon dissolved. The Communist Party (Partido Comunista—PC), legalized in 1977, was one of the most outspoken "Eurocommunist" parties in the late 1970s, harshly criticizing the former USSR for human rights abuses. In the 1986 election, the PC formed part of the United Left coalition (Izquierda Unida—IU), which included a rival Communist faction and several socialist parties; the IU's share of the vote was 4.6%. Nationalist parties function in Catalonia, Andalucía, the Basque Provinces, and other areas. The most powerful are the Catalan Convergence and Union (CIU), the Basque Nationalists (PNV), and the Canaries Coalition (CC).

Despite charges of corruption and economic mismanagement, the PSOE secured electoral victories in 1989 and 1993; however, the party finished 17 seats short of a parliamentary majority in 1993. A noticeable shift toward the conservative PP was evident with a 34-seat gain between 1989 and 1993. PSOE secretary-general Felipe Gonzalez Marquez received endorsement for a fourth term as prime minister, receiving support from the small Basque and Catalan nationalist parties.

In 1996, however, Gonzalez was turned out of power by José María Aznar, a young conservative leader with little international visibility. Aznar, as leader of PP, won reelection as prime minister in the March 2000 election, the first in which a center-right party won majority control of the government outright. In the March 2004 election, which was held three days after the 11 March Madrid train bombings, Aznar's PP lost 39 seats in the Congress of Deputies and the PSOE gained 35 seats to hold 164 seats in the chamber. The PSOE victory was seen to have been a reaction to the train bombings, which were blamed in part on the Aznar administration for its support of the US-led war in Iraq. José Luis Rodríguez Zapatero of the PSOE became prime minister.

The distribution of seats in the Congress of Deputies following the March 2004 election was as follows: PSOE, 164; PP, 148; CIU, 10; ERC (a Catalan party), 8; PNV, 7; CC, 3; IU, 2; and others, 8. Election results for the Senate were as follows: PP, 102; PSOE, 81; Entesa Catalona de Progress, 12; PNV, 6; CIU, 4; and CC, 3. The next elections for the Congress of Deputies and the Senate were scheduled for March 2008.

15 LOCAL GOVERNMENT

Spain is divided into 17 autonomous regions, each of which has an elected assembly and a governor appointed by the central government. Municipalities are gradually becoming consolidated; their number had declined to about 8,000 by the early 2000s. Each municipality has a mayor (*alcalde*) and councilmen (*concejales*); the councilmen, directly elected by the people, elect the mayors. Fifty-one of the 259 members of the Senate are chosen by the regional assemblies.

The statutes governing the Basque and Catalan autonomous communities, providing for regional high courts and legislative assemblies, were approved by referendum in October 1979; the statutes for Galicia in December 1980; and those for Andalucía in October 1981. Autonomy statutes for the other 11 historic regions of continental Spain and the Balearic and Canary Islands were subsequently approved and a regular electoral process begun.

16 JUDICIAL SYSTEM

According to the 1978 constitution, the judiciary is independent and subject only to the rule of law. The highest judicial body is the Supreme Court (*Tribunal Supremo*), the president of which is nominated by the 20 judges of the General Council of the Judiciary and appointed by the king.

Territorial high courts (*audiencias*) are the courts of last appeal in the 17 regions of the country; provincial audiencias serve as appellate courts in civil matters and as courts of first instance in criminal cases. On the lowest level are the judges of the first instance and instruction, district judges, and justices of the peace.

The National High Court (*Audiencia Nacional*), created in 1977, has jurisdiction over criminal cases that transgress regional boundaries and over civil cases involving the central state administration. The constitution of 1978 also established the 12-member Constitutional Court (*Tribunal Constitucional*), with competence to judge the constitutionality of laws and decide disputes between the central government and the autonomous regions. The European Court of Human Rights is the final arbiter in cases concerning human rights.

Defendants in criminal cases have the right to counsel at state expense if indigent. The constitution prohibits arbitrary arrest and detention. Suspects may be held for no more than three days without a judicial hearing.

A jury system was established in 1995, and a new penal code was enacted in 1996.

The constitution provides for the right to a fair public trial and the government respects this provision in practice.

17 ARMED FORCES

In 2005, Spain's active armed forces totaled 147,255 active personnel. Reservists numbered 319,000 for all three services. The 95,600-member Army was armed with 323 main battle tanks, 270 reconnaissance vehicles, 144 armored infantry fighting vehicles, 2,022 armored personnel carriers, and 2,013 artillery pieces. The Navy had 19,455 active personnel, including 814 naval aviation personnel and 5,300 Marines. Major naval units included one aircraft carrier, 12 frigates, 5 tactical submarines, 36 coastal and patrol vessels, in addition to various mine warfare, amphibious and transport vessels. The Spanish Air Force had 22,750 personnel and 177 combat capable aircraft, including 75 fighters and 91 fighter ground attack aircraft. Spain in 2005 had a paramilitary force of 73,360 personnel, of which 72,600 were members of the Guardia Civil. Another 760 comprised the Guardia Civil del Mar. Spain provided troops to UN peacekeeping and other European Union and NATO military missions in eight regions or countries. In 2005 Spain's defense budget totaled spent $8.8 billion.

18 INTERNATIONAL COOPERATION

Spain joined the United Nations on 14 December 1955; it participates in ECE, ECLAC, and several nonregional specialized agencies, such as the FAO, UNESCO, UNHCR, UNIDO, ILO, the World Bank, and the WHO. Spain is also a member of the Council of Europe, the African Development Bank, the Asian Development Bank, the European Bank for Reconstruction and Development, the Inter-American Development Bank, NATO, OECD, the WTO, OSCE, the Paris Club, the Western European Union, and the European Union. The nation holds observer status in the OAS and the Latin American Integration Association (LAIA).

Spain has supported UN missions and operations in Kosovo (est. 1999), Ethiopia and Eritrea (est. 2000), Burundi (est. 2004), Haiti (est. 2004), and the DROC (est. 1999). The nation is part of the Australia Group, the Zangger Committee, the Nuclear Suppliers Group (London Group), and the Nuclear Energy Agency. In environmental cooperation, Spain is part of the Antarctic Treaty; the Basel Convention; Conventions on Biological Diversity, Whaling, and Air Pollution; Ramsar; CITES; the London Convention; International Tropical Timber Agreements; the Kyoto Protocol; the Montréal Protocol; MARPOL; the Nuclear Test Ban Treaty; and the UN Conventions on the Law of the Sea, Climate Change, and Desertification.

19 ECONOMY

Agriculture, livestock, and mining—the traditional economic mainstays—no longer occupy the greater part of the labor force or provide most of the exports. In order to offset the damage suffered by the industrial sector during the Civil War and to cope with the problems created by Spain's post-World War II isolation, the Franco regime concentrated its efforts on industrial expansion. Especially after 1953, the industrial sector expanded rapidly. In terms of per capita income, Spain's economy stands at 80% of the four largest West European economies, with an estimated GDP (purchasing power parity) of $23,300 per person in 2004.

From 1974 through the early 1980s, the Spanish economy was adversely affected by international factors, especially oil price increases. Tourism is a major source of foreign exchange, and in 2000 was generating 10% of GDP (up from 3.3% in 1995) and employing, directly or indirectly, one eighth of the labor force. Spain is the world's second most popular tourist destination, after France. Spain had 53.6 million tourists in 2004, a 3.4% increase over 2003, despite the terrorist attacks on Spain's commuter trains on 11 March 2004, which killed 191 people and injured 1,500. The annual GDP growth rate during 1974–77 was 3%, higher than that in other OECD countries, but the inflation rate reached 24% in 1977. Real GDP growth slowed to about 1.6% during 1980–85, averaged 3.5% between 1985 and 1992, but slowed to a yearly average of 1.3% between 1993–95. By 1998, however, it had increased to 3.5%, and in 1999 and 2000, averaged over 4%. The global economic slowdown after 2001 helped reduce GDP growth to 2.5% in 2001 and to 2.3% in 2002. Real GDP growth averaged 3.3% over the period 2000–04. Spanish economic growth was expected to be 3.1% in 2005, due to strong momentum in the domestic economy, and then was forecast to gradually slow to 2.4% by 2007. This slowdown was forecast to stabilize the large current account deficit, which was estimated at 5.9% of GDP in 2005.

Consumer prices rose 37% between 1989 and 1995, and unemployment rose from 17.3% to 21.3%, the highest in the EU. Macroeconomic improvements from 1995 to 1998, however, were sufficient for Spain to be included in the first group of EU members to enter the Economic and Monetary Union (EMU) in 1999. By 1998 inflation had been reduced to 1.8%. From 1999 to 2002, inflation was held to between 2% and 4%. Unemployment fell to 18.7% in 1998 and then to 15.7% in 1999. Although still quite high, unemployment continued to fall—to 13.9% in 2000 and 10.5% in 2001—before registering an increase to 11.2% in 2002. The inflation rate averaged 3.3% from 2000–04. Inflation was predicted to fall from the rate of 3.4% in 2005, as was unemployment; the unemployment rate in 2004 stood at 10.4%. The Rodriguez Zapatero government pursued job creation upon coming into power in April 2004; joblessness is among the highest in the EU, and profound changes to labor market regulations have been called for to reduce unemployment further.

20 INCOME

The US Central Intelligence Agency (CIA) reports that in 2005 Spain's gross domestic product (GDP) was estimated at $1.0 trillion. The CIA defines GDP as the value of all final goods and services produced within a nation in a given year and computed on the basis of purchasing power parity (PPP) rather than value as measured on the basis of the rate of exchange based on current dollars. The per capita GDP was estimated at $25,100. The annual growth rate of GDP was estimated at 3.3%. The average inflation rate in 2005 was 3.4%. It was estimated that agriculture accounted for 3.4% of GDP, industry 28.7%, and services 67.9%.

According to the World Bank, in 2003 remittances from citizens working abroad totaled $6.068 billion or about $148 per capita and accounted for approximately 0.7% of GDP. Foreign aid receipts amounted to $672 million and accounted for approximately 3.7% of the gross national income (GNI).

The World Bank reports that in 2003 household consumption in Spain totaled $485.78 billion or about $11,819 per capita based on a GDP of $838.7 billion, measured in current dollars rather than PPP. Household consumption includes expenditures of individuals, households, and nongovernmental organizations on goods and services, excluding purchases of dwellings. It was estimated that for the period 1990 to 2003 household consumption grew at an average annual rate of 2.6%. In 2001 it was estimated that approximately 33% of household consumption was spent on food, 11% on fuel, 3% on health care, and 5% on education.

21 LABOR

In 2005, Spain's labor force totaled an estimated 20.67 million. As of 2004, the workforce was distributed as follows: services 64.6%; manufacturing, mining and construction 30.1%; and agriculture 5.3%. Employment in agriculture has been in steady decline; many farm workers have been absorbed by construction and industry. Unemployment averaged about 22% during 1997, but had fallen to 11% by 2002. As of 2005, Spain's unemployment rate was estimated at 10.1%.

The constitution of 1978 guarantees the freedom to form unions and the right to strike. The law provides for the right to bargain collectively, and unions exercise this right in practice. In the private sector, as of 2005, 85–90% of workers were covered by a collective bargaining agreement. Discrimination against union activity is illegal. In 2005, approximately 15% of the workforce was unionized.

The monthly minimum wage was $620 in 2005. This wage provides a decent standard of living for a family. The regular workweek was 40 hours, with a mandated 36-hour rest period. In addition, workers receive 12 paid holidays per year and one month's paid vacation. The legal minimum age for employment was 16 years, and this is enforced by the Ministry of Labor and Social Affairs.

22 AGRICULTURE

During 1970–2003, the proportion of the GDP from agriculture fell from 11.3% to 3%, and the proportion of workers employed in agriculture decreased from 26% to about 7%. Arable cropland in 2003 covered 18,715,000 hectares (46,245,000 acres), of which 67% was used for field crops, and 33% planted with olive trees, vineyards, and orchards.

In 2003, Spain's crop output was valued third highest among the EU nations, at over €27.1 billion. Agricultural commodities harvested in 2004 (in thousands of tons) included wheat, 7,108; barley, 10,609; corn, 4,748; rice, 900; beans, 19; sugar beets, 6,997; sunflower seeds, 785; grapes, 7,148; peaches, 1,107; potatoes, 2,570; and tomatoes, 4,367. Grapes are cultivated in every region; the most important olive groves are in Andalucía. After France and Italy, Spain is the world's leading wine producer, with an estimated 421 million liters produced in 2004. Within the domestic market, the use of sunflower oil and soybean oil has grown considerably.

Agricultural mechanization has been increasing steadily. In 2003 there were 943,653 tractors and 50,454 harvester-threshers. The use of fertilizers has also increased. The Institute for Agrarian Development and Reform directly or indirectly regulates some 10 million hectares (25 million acres) of land, promoting intensive cultivation and irrigation to improve productivity.

23 ANIMAL HUSBANDRY

Spain's pastures cover about 23% of the total area. Because much of Spain is arid or semiarid, sheep are by far the most important domestic animals. In 2005, Spain's livestock population (in millions) included sheep, 22.5; hogs, 25.2; and cattle, 6.7. There also were 2.8 million goats, 240,000 horses, 142,000 asses, and 110,000 mules in 2005. Meat production that year included (in thousands of tons): pork, 3,310; poultry, 1,341; beef and veal, 715; and lamb and mutton, 235. In 2005, milk production was 7.4 million tons (12% from sheep and goats); 725,000 tons of eggs were also produced.

24 FISHING

Fishing is important, especially along the northern coastline. The Spanish fishing fleet is the largest within the European Union (EU). As of 2004, the fleet had a capacity of 491,246 gross tons, 26% of EU total and about 6% of the world's fishing fleet capacity.

In 2004, the total quantity of fish caught by Spanish vessels and landed in Spanish ports amounted to 875,000 tons (including nonedible fish). The main species landed in 2003 were (in thousands of tons): sardines, 55.8; yellowfin tuna, 108.7; skipjack tuna, 155.4; and Atlantic mackerel, 23.6.

The most common species processed by the Spanish canning industry are: tuna, mussels, sardines, white tuna, cephalopod, mackerel, and anchovy. In 2003, Spain exported 95.9 million tons of canned fish, valued at $385 million. Exports of seafood that year amounted to 529.6 million tons, worth $1,105 million.

The main aquacultural commodities are mussels, trout, oysters, clams, and gilthead bream. Mussel production began in 1940 in northwestern Spain, and today there are thousands of floating mollusk beds found in many Spanish bays. Trout farming began in 1960, and is located in the north and northwest. In 2003, aquacultural production included 248,827 tons of mussels and 33,113 tons of trout. Spain is the world's second leading producer of mussels after China.

25 FORESTRY

Spain's forested area in 2004 was estimated at 15 million hectares (37 million acres), of which 7.5 million hectares (18.5 million acres) was commercial forest (73% softwood, 27% temperate hardwood). The northern Cantabrian range accounts for about one-third of the timberland. In addition, Spain has 2.5 million hectares (6.2 million acres) of woodlots typically comprised of oaks and cork trees, located mostly in the west (especially in Estremadura and Salamanca). During 1999–2003, the annual average area reforested was 75,000 hectares (185,000 acres).

Roundwood production in 2004 was 16.3 million cu m (575 million cu ft), with about 13% used as fuel wood. Spain is one of the largest producers of cork, its most important commercial forest product. Spain's annual production of cork amounts to about 110,000 tons, or 32% of world production. Scotch and maritime pine, as well as radiata pine, are the main softwood lumber species produced in Spain; eucalyptus and poplar are the principal hardwood species. In 2004, Spain imported $4.9 billion in forest products, primarily lumber ($989.4 million) and wood-based panels ($699 million).

26 MINING

Spain had some of the most mineralized territory in Western Europe, including the volcanic-hosted massive sulfide (VMS) deposits of the Iberian Pyrite Belt (IPB) of southern Spain. The IPB alone was estimated to have yielded 1.7 billion tons of sulfides, and more than 80 VMS deposits have been recorded in which individual tonnages were in excess of one million tons. Spain had the largest known reserves of celestite (Europe's sole producer, ranking second in world production, behind Mexico); was home to the richest mercury deposit in the world and one of the biggest open-pit zinc mines in Europe; and remained the leading producer of sepiolite, with 70% of world reserves (around Madrid). Spain was the largest EU producer of mine lead and zinc, and a major producer of pyrites, among other nonferrous and precious metals. Production far exceeded domestic consumption for most nonmetallic minerals, and Spain was a net exporter to other EU countries of lead, mercury, nonmetallic-mineral manufactured products, slate, other crude industrial minerals, and zinc. In terms of value, Spain was one of the leading EU countries, with one of its highest levels of self-sufficiency in mineral raw materials. Almost all known minerals were found in Spain, and mining was still a notable, though much diminished, factor in the economy. Of the 100 minerals mined, 18 were produced in large quantities—bentonite, copper, fluorspar, glauberite, gold, iron, lead, magnetite, mercury, potash, pyrites, quartz, refractory argillite, sea and rock salt, sepiolitic salts, tin, tungsten, and zinc. Metals and chemicals were leading industries in 2002. The output of lead, zinc, and copper ores, all once important to the Spanish economy, has been declining. The number of active operations has halved in recent years, with copper production a notable casualty. Quarried mineral products, particularly quarried stone, accounted for a significant share of the value of all minerals produced.

Lead mine output was 1,765 metric tons in 2003, down from 6,171 metric tons in 2002 and 36,000 metric tons in 2001. Zinc mine output totaled 44,600 metric tons in 2003, down from 69,926 metric tons in 2002 and from 164,900 metric tons in 2001. Copper mine production in 2003 was estimated at 643 metric tons, down from 1,248 metric tons in 2002 and from 9,748 metric tons in 2001. Gold mine output in 2003 totaled 5,362 kg, up from 5,158 kg in 2002 and from 3,720 kg in 2001. Silver mine output in 2003 totaled 2,246 kg in 2003, down from 3,409 kg in 2002, and from 54,836 kg in 2001. Germanium oxide, tin, titanium dioxide, and uranium also were mined. Because of market conditions, iron mining was halted in 1997, after 588,000 tons (metal content) was produced in 1996. Iron ore was one of Spain's principal mineral assets, with 6 million tons of total reserves in the north (Basque provinces, Asturias, León) and in Andalucía; the Alquife mine, in Granada, which was closed for maintenance, had a capacity of 4 million tons per year.

Among industrial minerals, Spain in 2003 produced an estimated: 10 million tons of marl; 12 million tons of dolomite; 5 million tons of ornamental marble; 2.48 million tons of limestone; 690,395 metric tons (reported) of meerschaum sepiolite; 594,355 metric tons of potash (reported); and 150,000 metric tons of calcined magnesite (from deposits in Navarra and Lugo), unchanged from 2002. Spain also produced barite, bromine, calcium carbonate, hydraulic cement, clays (including attapulgite, bentonite, and washed kaolin), diatomite, tripoli, feldspar, fluorspar (acid-grade

and metallurgical grade), gypsum, anhydrite, andalusite kyanite, hydrated lime and quicklime, mica, nitrogen, mineral pigments (ocher and red iron oxide), pumice, salt (including rock, marine, and by-product from potash), silica sand (including as by-product of feldspar and kaolin production), soda ash, natural sulfate (including glauberite and thenardite), large quantities of all stone (including basalt, chalk, ornamental granite, ophite, phonolite, porphyry, quartz, quartzite, sandstone, serpentine, slate), strontium minerals, sulfur, talc, and steatite.

Historically, minerals belonged to the state, with the industry comprising a mix of state-owned, state-and-privately owned, and privately owned companies. However, the Spanish government has been moving rapidly toward privatization and continued to do so in 2003. In mid-2002, legislation was passed that would abolish state and private monopolies. The economic development of certain areas, such as the Asturias and the Basque regions, was based on their mineral wealth, and mining continued to be an important current and potential source of income in these and other mineral-rich areas. The independent government of Andalucía completed its first mining development plan (1996–2000). Several old and new prospects were being evaluated, and exploration activity was high, particularly for feldspar (in Badajoz, Toledo, and Salamanca), garnet (Galicia), pyrites (Badajoz), and rutile and zircon (Cuidad Real). The main polymetallic deposits included Tharsis, Scotiel, Rio Tinto, and Aznalcollar.

27 ENERGY AND POWER

Spain has only small reserves of oil and natural gas, with coal being the country's most abundant energy source.

As of 1 January 2002, Spain's proven reserves of oil and natural gas came to 10.5 million barrels and 254.9 million cu m, respectively. In 2004, Spain's production of oil averaged 5,980 barrels per day in 2004 (7,099 barrels per day in 2001), while consumption in that year averaged 1.5687 million barrels per day. As a result, Spain had to rely heavily on imports to meet its petroleum needs. Spain has seven active oil fields all of them operated by Repsol-YPF. Spain's refining sector has a combined capacity of 1.27 million barrels and is spread among seven refineries, of which the largest is the Cadiz plant operated by Cepsa, with a capacity of 240,000 barrels per day. However, Repsol-YPF has the largest total capacity at 520,000 barrels per day.

As with oil, Spain relies heavily on imports to meet its natural gas needs. In 2003, Spain produced 7.3 billion cu ft of natural gas, but demand that year totaled 822 billion cu ft. Spanish demand for natural gas rose sharply between 1993 and 2003, increasing by 266%, and was driven in large part by the introduction of gas-fired power plants. In 2002, of the 1,073.7 billion cu ft of natural gas imported by Spain, Algeria was the main source, providing 627.7 billion cu ft, followed by Norway at 116.0 cu ft and Qatar at 107.2 billion cu ft. Nigeria, Oman and other countries accounted for the remainder.

Spain's most abundant energy source is coal. In 2003, Spain had reserves of 584 million short tons, with production in that year at 22.7 million short tons. However, as with oil and natural gas, demand for coal in 2003 outstripped supply, with consumption at 45.6 million short tons, thus necessitating imports to fill the gap.

Spain is the European Union's fifth-largest electricity market. Production of electricity in 2002 reached 230.082 billion kWh, of which fossil fuels accounted for 134.834 billion kWh, hydropower at nuclear at 59.865 billion kWh, hydropower at 22.807 billion kWh and geothermal/other sources at 12.576 billion kWh. Demand for electric power in 2002 totaled 219.305 billion kWh. Electric power capacity in 2002 totaled 50.591 million kW, of which conventional thermal capacity accounted for 26.359 million kW, hydroelectric at 12.744 million kW, nuclear at 7.519 million kW, and geothermal/other at 3.969 million kW. Spain, as of July 2005, had nine nuclear reactors in operation. However, the Jose Cabrera nuclear plant is slated for closure in April 2006.

28 INDUSTRY

Industrial production grew by 3% in 2004, and industry accounted for 28.5% of GDP. The chief industrial sectors are food and beverages, textiles and footwear, energy, and transport materials. Chemical production, particularly of superphosphates, sulfuric acid, dyestuffs, and pharmaceutical products, is also significant. Of the heavy industries, iron and steel, centered mainly in Bilbao and Avilés, is the most important. Petroleum refinery production capacity at Spain's nine refineries was 1.27 million barrels per day in 2004. Approximately three million automobiles were produced in Spain in 2004; automobiles are Spain's leading manufacturing industry, accounting for about 5% of GDP and exporting more than 80% of output.

Prior to the 1990s wave of privatization, government participation in industry was through the National Industrial Institute (INI), which owned mining enterprises, oil refineries, steel and chemical plants, shipbuilding yards, and artificial fiber factories, or through Patrimonio. As of 2005, Telefónica, Gas Natural, and the petrochemical company Repsol had been privatized. A wave of consolidations was taking place in the energy industry, as Gas Natural launched a $28.1 billion unsolicited bid for Endesa, a Spanish electricity company, mirroring a series of energy deals taking place across Europe in 2005. In the Spanish mobile-phone market, which was growing strongly in 2005, France Télécom bought an 80% stake in Amena, Spain's third-largest mobile phone operator, behind Telefónica and Britain's Vodafone.

Industries demonstrating significant growth in the early 2000s were metalworking industries, due to increased production in shipbuilding, data-processing equipment, and other transportation equipment. Other growth sectors included food processing, medical products and services, chemicals, computer equipment, electronics, footwear, construction and security equipment, cosmetics and jewelry, and industrial machinery. In the early 2000s, the construction industry was aided by such public works projects as a high-speed train link between Madrid and Barcelona, and an increase in property development on the Mediterranean coast.

Foreign competition has cut into the Spanish textile industry. Following the expiration of the World Trade Organization's long-standing system of textile quotas at the beginning of 2005, the EU signed an agreement with China in June 2005, imposing new quotas on 10 categories of textile goods, limiting growth in those categories to between 8% and 12.5% a year. The agreement runs until 2007, and was designed to give European textile manufacturers time to adjust to a world of unfettered competition. Nevertheless, barely a month after the EU-China agreement was signed, China reached its quotas for sweaters, followed soon after by blouses, bras, T-shirts, and flax yarn. Tens of millions of garments piled up in warehouses and customs checkpoints, which affected both retailers and consumers.

29 SCIENCE AND TECHNOLOGY

The Council for Scientific Research, founded in 1940, coordinates research in science and technology and operates numerous constituent research institutes in a wide variety of disciplines. The Royal Academy of Exact, Physical, and Natural Sciences, founded in 1916, is the nation's chief scientific academy. The National Science Museum and the National Railway Museum are located in Madrid, and two geology museums are located in Barcelona. Spain has 32 universities, colleges, and polytechnics offering courses in basic and applied sciences.

In 1987–97, science and engineering students accounted for 31% of university enrollment. In 2002, of all bachelor's degrees awarded, 23.8% were for the sciences (natural, mathematics and computers, engineering). In 2002, total expenditures on research and development (R&D) amounted to $9,101.393 million, or 1.04% if GDP. Of that amount, the business sector accounted for the largest portion at 48.9%, followed by the government at 39.1%. Higher education and foreign sources accounted for 5.2% and 6.8%, respectively. In that same year, there were 742 technicians and 2,036 scientists and engineers engaged in R&D per one million people. High technology exports in 2002 were valued at $6.777 billion, or 7% of the country's manufactured exports.

30 DOMESTIC TRADE

Madrid and Barcelona are the primary commercial hubs for distribution of goods throughout the country. Spain has no free ports, but free-zone privileges are granted at Barcelona, Bilbao, Cádiz, Vigo, and the Canary Islands. There are bonded warehouses at the larger ports. The government has established a market distribution program to regulate the flow of goods to and from the producing and consuming areas. Since 1972, wholesale market networks have been established in cities with more than 150,000 inhabitants. The National Consumption Institute promotes consumer cooperatives and credit unions.

A wide variety of shops are available in Spain, from small specialty boutiques to large department stores, shopping centers, and outlet stores. Franchises are becoming more popular throughout the country. As of 2003, there were about 960 franchise firms with over 48,000 franchised units represented in the country, with national companies holding ownership of 82% of them. Direct marketing and sales, particularly through mail order and television sales, are also gaining in popularity. A 16% value-added tax applies to most goods and services. This rate is reduced for some products, such as food, books, and medical supplies. Advertising is largely through newspapers, magazines, radio, and motion picture theaters.

Usual business hours are from 9 AM to 6 PM, Monday through Friday. Banks are open from 8:30 AM to 2:30 PM, Monday through Friday, and to 1 PM on Saturday. Department stores are often open from 10 AM to 8 PM, Monday through Saturday. Many small shops and businesses are often closed in the afternoons, from 2 PM to 4 or 5 PM.

[31] FOREIGN TRADE

Traditionally, exports consisted mainly of agricultural products (chiefly wine, citrus fruits, olives and olive oil, and cork) and minerals. While agricultural products and minerals remain important, they have, since the 1960s, been overtaken by industrial exports. Imports habitually exceed exports by a large margin.

Of Spain's export commodities, transport-related items make up more than 20% of the total. Fruits, nuts, and vegetables are also exported in sizable amounts. Spain is the world's largest producer of olive oil; the country supplies about one-third of the olive oil in the world. Footwear and chemicals (chiefly pharmaceuticals) are other important exports.

The liberalization of product markets and more effective antitrust mechanisms have been called for as ways to boost Spain's economic growth potential. Merchandise exports rose to $184.1 billion in 2004. Strong domestic demand resulted in a larger increase in imports, causing the trade deficit to widen from $45.1 billion in 2003 to $65.8 billion in 2004. Spain's leading markets in 2004 were France (19.4% of all exports), Germany (11.7%), and Portugal and Italy (each with 9% of Spain's total exports). In all, the EU accounted for 73.9% of Spain's total exports. Leading suppliers in 2004 were Germany (16.1% of Spanish imports), France (15.2%), Italy (9.1%), and the United Kingdom (6.1%). The EU made up 65.6% of all imports that year.

[32] BALANCE OF PAYMENTS

Tourism, remittances from Spaniards living abroad, investment income, and loans to the private sector have been the principal factors that help to offset recurrent trade deficits, especially deficits in merchandise trade and net investment income. Between 1992 and 1995 exports grew by 70% and imports grew by approximately the same amount. In 2000, Spain experienced a large increase in its trade deficit due in large measure to increased petroleum prices, the weakness of the euro, and decreased competitiveness. The current account deficit widened considerably in 2004 to 5.3% of GDP, up from 3.6% in 2003, largely due to the large trade deficit of $65.8 billion, which was caused by strong domestic demand and an increase in imports. In 2004, the current account balance stood at -$30.89 billion.

[33] BANKING AND SECURITIES

The banking and credit structure centers on the Bank of Spain, the government's national bank of issue since 1874. The bank acts as the government depository as well as a banker's bank for discount and other operations. The European Central Bank determines monetary policy for the EU. Other "official" but privately owned banks are the Mortgage Bank of Spain, the Local Credit Bank of Spain, the Industrial Credit Bank, the Agricultural Credit Bank, and the External Credit Bank.

In 2002, the private banking system consisted of 146 banks, comprising national banks, industrial banks, regional banks, local banks, and foreign banks. The liberalization of the banking system and Spain's entry into the EC raised the number and presence of foreign banks. During the process of financial liberalization required by the EU, the government tried to promote a series of mergers within the banking industry, which it hoped could enable the banks to compete more effectively. As a result, there were two major mergers: Banco de Vizcaya and Banco de Bilbao formed Banco Bilbao Vizcaya (BBV), and Banco Central and Banco Hispanoamericano merged to form Banco Central Hispanoamercano (BCH). The government also brought together all the state-owned banking institutions to form Corporación Bancaria de España, better known by its trade name Argentaria, whose most important component is Banco Exterior (BEX). The government subsequently privatized a 50% stake in Argentaria in 1993 and a further 25% in early 1996. Ultimately, the state sold its remaining 25% share in Argentaria, thereby leaving the banking sector entirely in private hands. In October 1999, BBV took over Argentaria to create Spain's largest banking group. The International Monetary Fund reports that in 2001, currency and demand deposits—an aggregate commonly known as M1—were equal to $193.7 billion. In that same year, M2—an aggregate equal to M1 plus savings depos-

Principal Trading Partners – Spain (2003)

(In millions of US dollars)

Country	Exports	Imports	Balance
World	158,213.2	210,860.5	-52,647.3
France-Monaco	30,394.1	34,079.9	-3,685.8
Germany	19,008.0	34,551.5	-15,543.5
Italy-San Marino-Holy See	15,486.4	19,348.6	-3,862.2
Portugal	15,262.4	6,778.4	8,484.0
United States	6,478.9	7,639.6	-1,160.7
Netherlands	5,318.6	8,525.6	-3,207.0
Belgium	4,756.3	6,423.4	-1,667.1
Mexico	2,508.1	1,646.0	862.1
Morocco	2,133.4	1,812.7	320.7
Turkey	1,989.8	2,029.4	-39.6

(…) data not available or not significant.

SOURCE: *2003 International Trade Statistics Yearbook*, New York: United Nations, 2004.

Balance of Payments – Spain (2003)

(In millions of US dollars)

Current Account		**-23,676.0**
Balance on goods		-42,923.0
Imports	-202,468.0	
Exports	159,545.0	
Balance on services		30,922.0
Balance on income		-11,919.0
Current transfers		-56.0
Capital Account		**9,982.0**
Financial Account		**4,444.0**
Direct investment abroad		-23,350.0
Direct investment in Spain		25,513.0
Portfolio investment assets		-91,061.0
Portfolio investment liabilities		40,908.0
Financial derivatives		-369,947.0
Other investment assets		-14,437.0
Other investment liabilities		70,570.0
Net Errors and Omissions		**-6,237.0**
Reserves and Related Items		**15,487.0**

(…) data not available or not significant.

SOURCE: *Balance of Payment Statistics Yearbook 2004*, Washington, DC: International Monetary Fund, 2004.

its, small time deposits, and money market mutual funds—was $548.2 billion. The money market rate, the rate at which financial institutions lend to one another in the short term, was 4.36%.

Spain has major stock exchanges in Madrid, Barcelona, Bilbao, and Valencia. These exchanges are open for a few hours a day, Tuesday through Friday. Since 1961, foreign investment in these exchanges has increased rapidly. The major commercial banks invest in the equity and debt securities of private firms and carry on brokerage businesses as well. Latibex, a Madrid-based stock exchange providing a market for the trading (in euros) of Latin American stocks, opened in late 1999. The exchange lists companies based in Latin American nations such as Argentina, Brazil, Chile, Columbia, and Venezuela. As of 2004, there were 3,272 companies listed on the BME Spanish Exchanges, which had a market capitalization of $940.673 billion.

34 INSURANCE

Insurance companies are supervised by the government through the Direccion General de Seguros. The Spanish insurance market is characterized by a relatively large number of insurers with one organization dominating the industry. Latest information available indicates an insurance market in Spain with moderate penetration when compared to North America and Europe, especially for life products. Recently, however, Spanish insurance firms such as Euroseguros are taking advantage of linguistic, cultural, and historical ties and are expanding operations to Latin America. Compulsory insurance includes third-party automobile liability, workers' compensation, hunters', nuclear and professional liability, and personal injury insurance. Workers' compensation and property insurance can only be obtained through the government. Spain's insurance market is made up of both local and foreign insurers, with the local insurers often owned by Spanish banks. In 2003, the value of all direct insurance premiums written totaled $47.014 billion, of which nonlife premiums accounted for $26.972 billion. In that same year, the top nonlife insurer was MAPFRE Mutualidad, which had gross written nonlife premiums of $2,088.2 million, while the country's leading life insurer was Mapfre Vida, which had gross written life insurance premiums of $1,808.6 million.

35 PUBLIC FINANCE

The public sector deficit in 1996 was equivalent to 4.3% of GDP (compared to 3.8% in 1993 and 4.4% in 1992). Because of Spain's desire to enter the European Monetary Union, it had to meet stringent limits on its public debt and finances, including a 3% debt-to-GDP ratio. The government trimmed the budget by reducing the civil service payroll and limiting transfers to government-owned companies.

The US Central Intelligence Agency (CIA) estimated that in 2005 Spain's central government took in revenues of approximately $440.9 billion and had expenditures of $448.4 billion. Revenues minus expenditures totaled approximately -$7.5 billion. Public debt in 2005 amounted to 48.5% of GDP. Total external debt was $1.249 trillion.

Government outlays by function were as follows: general public services, 28.6%; defense, 3.7%; public order and safety, 3.8%; economic affairs, 6.2%; environmental protection, 0.2%; housing and community amenities, 0.1%; health, 15.3%; recreation, culture, and religion, 1.2%; education, 1.6%; and social protection, 39.3%.

Public Finance – Spain (2001)

(In millions of euros, central government figures)

Revenue and Grants	**212,571**	**100.0%**
Tax revenue	105,530	49.6%
Social contributions	87,146	41.0%
Grants	8,088	3.8%
Other revenue	11,807	5.6%
Expenditures	**211,539**	**100.0%**
General public services	60,492	28.6%
Defense	7,821	3.7%
Public order and safety	8,104	3.8%
Economic affairs	13,011	6.2%
Environmental protection	516	0.2%
Housing and community amenities	263	0.1%
Health	32,308	15.3%
Recreational, culture, and religion	2,530	1.2%
Education	3,442	1.6%
Social protection	83,052	39.3%

(…) data not available or not significant.

SOURCE: *Government Finance Statistics Yearbook 2004*, Washington, DC: International Monetary Fund, 2004.

36 TAXATION

As of 2005, Spain had a basic corporation tax rate of 35%. A reduced rate of 30% is applied to companies with annual turnover of less than €6 million in the preceding tax year on initial profits of €90,151. Generally, capital gains are taxed at the corporate rate, while dividends, interest and royalties are subject to withholding taxes of 15%, 15% and 25%, respectively.

Spain, as of 2005, had a progressive individual income tax with a top rate of 45%. The tax is imposed on aggregate income and includes dividends, interest and royalties received. However, dividends received from a resident company may be subject to an imputation credit. There is also a wealth tax with a maximum rate of 2.5%.

The main indirect tax is Spain's value-added tax (VAT), introduced 1 January 1986 as a condition for membership in the European Union (EU). As of 2005, the VAT had a standard rate of 16%, with two reduced rates: 4% on basic necessities; and 7% on food, dwellings, tourism and certain transport services. Indirect taxes include levies on inheritances, documents, sales, special products (alcohol, petroleum, and others), luxury items, and fiscal monopolies.

37 CUSTOMS AND DUTIES

Spain, a member of the European Union and the World Trade Organization, adheres to EU and GATT trading rules. Spain determines customs duties based on cost, insurance, and freight (CIF), and applies the EU Common External Tariff to non-EU imports. Most customs costs amount to 20–30% of CIF (cost, insurance, freight), including the duty, the VAT, and customs agent and handling fees.

38 FOREIGN INVESTMENT

In keeping with the rest of the European Union, in recent years the Spanish government has instituted a wholesale revision of its previously restrictive foreign investment laws. With the exception of strategic sectors, up to 100% foreign investment is permitted in all sectors of the Spanish economy. The corporation tax is levied at a standard rate of 35% and at 30% on the first €90,151 for companies with a turnover of less than €5 million.

In 1998, foreign direct investment (FDI) inflow was nearly $12 billion, up from $7.7 billion in 1997, and peaking at $37.5 billion in 2000. In 2001, FDI inflow fell to $21.8 billion. From 1998 to 2001 FDI inflow averaged about $19 billion a year, and in 2001 cumulative FDI stock totaled approximately $157 billion. Outward FDI from Spain from 1998 to 2001 averaged about $31.1 billion, and in 2001 cumulative foreign stock held by Spaniards totaled about $184 billion.

In 2004, new investment in Spain totaled $18.4 billion. Spanish FDI outflows totaled $54.5 billion. In 2004, cumulative FDI stock in Spain totaled $346.7 billion. Cumulative outward FDI stock totaled $332.6 billion. In 2003, most new FDI in Spain came from (in order): the United States, the Netherlands, the United Kingdom, Canada, Luxembourg, Italy, Germany, France, and Sweden. From 2000–04, FDI inflows as a percentage of GDP averaged 4%. In 2004, Spain was the 11th most attractive country in the world for US investors, up from 17th place, according to the FDI Confidence Index. In 2004, Spain was the largest net EU-25 investor, while the United Kingdom was the largest net recipient of FDI.

39 ECONOMIC DEVELOPMENT

After 1939, Spanish economic policy was characterized by the attempt to achieve economic self-sufficiency. This policy, largely imposed by Spain's position during World War II and the isolation to which Spain was subjected in the decade following 1945, was also favored by many Spanish political and business leaders. In 1959, following two decades of little or no overall growth, the Spanish government acceded to reforms suggested by the International Monetary Fund (IMF), OECD, and IBRD, and encouraged by the promise of foreign financial assistance, announced its acceptance of the so-called Stabilization Plan, intended to curb domestic inflation and adverse foreign payment balances.

Long-range planning began with Spain's first four-year development plan (1964–67), providing a total investment of ₧355 billion. The second four-year plan (1968–71) called for an investment of ₧553 billion, with an average annual growth of 5.5% in GNP. The third plan (1972–75) called for investments of ₧871 billion; drastic readjustments had to be made in 1975 to compensate for an economic slump brought on by increased petroleum costs, a tourist slowdown, and a surge in imports. A fifth plan (1976–79) focused on development of energy resources, with investments to increase annually by 9% increments. A stabilization program introduced in 1977 included devaluation of the peseta and tightening of monetary policy. The economic plan of 1979–82 committed Spain to a market economy and rejected protectionism.

Accession to the EU generated increased foreign investment but also turned Spain's former trade surplus with the EU into a growing deficit: the lowering of tariffs boosted imports, but exports did not keep pace. The government responded by pursuing market liberalization and deregulation, in hopes of boosting productivity and efficiency to respond to EU competition. A number of projects, such as the construction of airports, highways, and a high-speed rail line between Madrid and Seville, received EU funding.

To prepare Spain for European economic and monetary union, the government in 1992 planned to cut public spending. The currency was devalued three times in 1992–93. Additionally, Spain was a principal beneficiary of the EU's "harmonization fund." This fund provides financial support to poorer EU nations to attempt to reduce the disparities in economic development.

After an economic downturn in the early and mid-1990s, the Spanish economy turned around to register a new dynamism characterized by strong growth rates and a rise in foreign investment sparked by increased liberalization. Moreover, unemployment dropped and inflation remained in check. Spain capped its success by entering the Economic and Monetary Union (EMU) in 1999. Reducing the public sector deficit, decreasing unemployment, reforming labor laws, lowering inflation, and raising per capita gross domestic product (GDP) were all goals in the early 2000s. Economic growth was forecast at 3.1% in 2005. The construction sector was thriving, driven by higher levels of investment and public infrastructure projects.

Spain cushioned the effects of the 2001–03 global economic slowdown on its economy through effective management of fiscal policy, but the constraints of the European Stability and Growth Pact—which requires EU members to keep their budget deficits within 3% of GDP—continues to limit freedom to maneuver. After coming to power in April 2004, the Socialist government made little change in economic policy. Despite a decline in unemployment in the early 2000s, the jobless rate remains one of the highest in the EU. Expansion of the services sector, including retailing, tourism, banking, and telecommunications, has led to recent economic growth. Spain has developed a greenhouse industry in the southeast region of the country, which has become one of the most competitive suppliers of fresh produce to the main European markets. Fishing remains a growth industry as well.

40 SOCIAL DEVELOPMENT

The social insurance system provides pensions for employees in industry and services, with a special system for the self-employed, farmers, domestic workers, seamen and coal miners. The system is funded through employee and employer contributions, and an annual government subsidy. The fund provides for health and maternity benefits, old age and incapacity insurance, a widow and widower pension, orphan pension's, a family subsidy, workers' compensation, job-related disability payments, unemployment insurance and a funeral grant. Retirement is set at age 65, but is allowed at age 64 under certain conditions. Maternity benefits are payable for 16 weeks, and is applicable to adoption as well. Fathers may also take parental leave. Work injury legislation was first instituted in 1900 and covers all employed persons. It is funded solely by the employer.

Discrimination against women in the workplace persists although it is prohibited by law. The female rate of unemployment is about twice that for men, and the median salary for women was lower than that of men. There are a growing number of women entering the medical and legal professions. Women take an active role in politics. The law prohibits sexual harassment in the workplace but it is not effectively enforced. The government takes steps to address the problems of domestic abuse and violence against women. The Integral Law Against Gender Violence enacted in 2005 provides harsher penalties to those convicted of domestic violence. The government is strongly committed to children's welfare and rights.

Roma minorities suffer from housing, education, and employment discrimination. The government provides mechanisms for legal redress for discrimination and harassment for Roma and other minorities. In addition, a growing number of right-wing extremist attacks against minorities have been reported in recent years. Human rights abuses have been committed by both the government and Basque (ETA) separatist groups. The ETA has carried out killings and kidnapping, while the government has failed to prevent the mistreatment of prisoners.

41HEALTH

Following the adoption of the country's constitution, Spain's health care system underwent major reforms in the 1980s and 1990s. Instead of being organized directly as part of the social security system, it was transformed to the more decentralized National Health System. Coverage was extended further than before and the primary care network was reorganized. Spanish officials say that public contributions to the cost of health care must be limited in the face of potentially unlimited demand. Total health care expenditure was estimated at 7% of GDP.

The public sector in health care is the largest and continues to grow. There are 354 public hospitals, 149 private hospitals, and 312 private business hospitals. The public health sector contracts a significant number of beds from both types of private hospitals. As of 2004, there were an estimated 320 physicians, 362 nurses, 43 dentists, 77 pharmacists per 100,000 people. Recent programs have created special residences for elderly and retired people, eye clinics, a network of government health centers in the principal cities, and more than a dozen human tissue and organ banks for transplantation and research.

As of 2002, the crude birth rate and overall mortality rate were estimated at, respectively, 9.3 and 9.2 per 1,000 people. About 59% of married women (ages 15 to 49) were using contraception. Average life expectancy in 2005 was 78 years. That year the infant mortality rate was 4.42 per 1,000 live births, down from 38 in 1965. Immunization rates for children up to one year old were: diphtheria, pertussis, and tetanus, 88%; polio, 88%; and measles, 90%.

Leading causes of death were communicable diseases and maternal/perinatal causes, noncommunicable diseases, and injuries. The HIV/AIDS prevalence was 0.70 per 100 adults in 2003. As of 2004, there were approximately 140,000 people living with HIV/AIDS in the country. There were an estimated 1,000 deaths from AIDS in 2003.

The smoking rates for both men and women in Spain are above the average of "high human development" countries as defined by the World Bank. Approximately 58% of men and 27% of women were smokers. However, the likelihood of dying after the age of 65 of heart disease was below the highly industrialized country average at 235 (male) and 277 (female) per 1,000 people.

42HOUSING

A housing boom beginning around 1998-2001 saw the creation of over two million new houses with about 600,000 new houses built in 2000. In 2000, about 20–25% of the housing market was attributed to those building second homes/vacation homes. At the 2001 census, there were about 20,946,554 dwellings nationwide.

About 31.9% were single-family dwellings; 35% were dwellings in multi-family buildings. About 16% of the existing stock was built in the period 1991–2001; with an average of about 307,000 units per year. Some 52% of all dwellings were owned by private individuals; 46% were owned by communities. Nearly 90% of all dwellings were listed in good condition; 195,910 dwellings were listed as in ruin.

43EDUCATION

Since 1990, schooling has been compulsory for ten years, including six years of primary school and four years of secondary school. Many students continue on for an additional two years of higher secondary school. Vocational programs are available at the secondary level. The academic year runs from October to July.

Most children between the ages of three and five are enrolled in some type of preschool program. Primary school enrollment in 2003 was estimated at about 100% of age-eligible students. The same year, secondary school enrollment was about 96% of age-eligible students. It is estimated that nearly all students complete their primary education. The student-to-teacher ratio for primary school was at about 14:1 in 2003; the ratio for secondary school was about 11:1. In 2003, private schools accounted for about 33% of primary school enrollment and 29% of secondary enrollment.

The Pontifical University of Salamanca, founded in 1254, is the oldest university, while the University of Madrid has the largest student body. In 2003, it was estimated that about 62% of the tertiary age population were enrolled in tertiary education programs; 57% for men and 67% for women. The adult literacy rate for 2003 was estimated at about 97.9%.

As of 2003, public expenditure on education was estimated at 4.5% of GDP, or 11.3% of total government expenditures.

44LIBRARIES AND MUSEUMS

The National Library in Madrid (four million volumes), the Library of Catalonia in Barcelona (one million volumes), the university libraries of Santiago de Compostela (one million volumes), Salamanca (906,000 volumes), Barcelona (two million volumes), and Sevilla (777,000 volumes), Valladolid (500,000 volumes), and the public library in Toledo (with many imprints from the 15th to the 18th centuries) are among the most important collections. Spain also has 61 historical archives, among them the Archivo General de Indias in Sevilla, with 60,000 volumes and files, and the archives of Simancas, with 86,000 volumes and files. In total, Spain's public library collection holds more than 32.8 million volumes. There are over 2,500 public libraries nationwide. In the province of Barcelona there are about 143 public libraries and 8 mobile services.

The Prado, in Madrid, with its extensive collection of Spanish art, is the most famous museum of Spain and one of the best in the world, featuring Picasso's world-famous *Guernica*. The National Archaeological Museum, also in Madrid, contains the prehistoric cave paintings of Altamira. The Museum of Modern Art, in Barcelona, houses excellent cubist and surrealist collections. There are also important art collections in the Escorial and Aranjuez palaces, near Madrid. Also in Madrid are the Museum of America, with artifacts from Spain's colonial holdings; the African Museum, with exhibits of many African cultures, especially Makonde art from Mozambique; and the Antiquities Collection of the Academy of

History, founded in 1738, which houses Iberian and Visigoth artifacts, Islamic art, 4th century relics, including the Silver Dish of Theodosius, general European art, and 11th century documents. Barcelona also has the Museum of Ceramics, the Museum of Decorative Arts, a Picasso museum, the National Museum of Catalonian Art, and the Museum of Perfume. The Guggenheim Museum Bilbao, designed by American architect Frank Gehry, opened in 1997 as a joint project of the Guggenheim Foundation and the Basque regional government. The innovative design of the 24,000-sq-m (257,000 sq-ft) metal-and-stone structure has won worldwide attention and acclaim.

45 MEDIA

The government owns, operates, or supervises all internal telephone, telegraph, and radio and television service. Postal and telegraph facilities are provided by the Mail and Telecommunications Service. The National Telephone Co. is an autonomous enterprise. In 2003, there were an estimated 434 mainline telephones for every 1,000 people. The same year, there were approximately 909 mobile phones in use for every 1,000 people.

RadioTelevision Espanola operates public radio and television broadcasts. There are hundreds of privately owned stations as well. In 2003, there were an estimated 330 radios and 564 television sets for every 1,000 people. About 24.3 of every 1,000 people were cable subscribers. Also in 2003, there were 196 personal computers for every 1,000 people and 239 of every 1,000 people had access to the Internet. There were 2,837 secure Internet servers in the country in 2004.

There are about 100 daily papers published in Spain, but very few have a circulation exceeding 100,000. Sunday newspaper editions have become increasingly common, with circulations often double the weekday runs. English-language papers are now printed in Madrid and Palma de Mallorca. There are also over 3,000 magazines, bulletins, and journals. Formerly, the Falange published the newspapers in all provincial capitals and controlled some 35% of the total national circulation; censorship was obligatory. In 1966, a new press law abolished censorship but established stiff penalties for editors who published news "contrary to the principles of the national interest"; offending newspapers could be seized.

The leading Spanish dailies, with 2005 weekday circulations, include: *El País* (Madrid), 458,000; *El Mundo* (Madrid), 310,000; *ABC* (Madrid and Sevilla), 277,000; *La Vanguardia* (Barcelona), 202,000; *El Periódico de Cataluña* (Barcelona, published in both Spanish and Catalan), 172,000; *El Correo* (Bilbao), 126,000; and *El Diario Vasco* (San Sebastian), 90,000. *Marca*, a sports daily, was believed to be the most widely read paper in the country.

The 1978 constitution guarantees freedom of the press and the government is said to uphold this freedom in practice.

46 ORGANIZATIONS

Under the Falangist system of corporate organization, all branches of society were required to participate in business and in agricultural or professional syndicates. Despite this system, cooperatives emerged in various sectors of Spanish society, among them agricultural, consumer, credit, industrial, maritime, fishing, rural, housing, and educational organizations. Chambers of commerce function in all provincial capitals, and there are numerous industrial and trade associations. The Association of Mediterra-

nean Chambers of Commerce and Industry is based in Barcelona. Trade and professional associations exist representing a broad range of occupations.

Cultural and educational organizations include the Royal Academy of Belles Lettres, the Scientific and Literary and Art Society, the Association of Spanish Artists and Sculptors, The Royal Society of Physics, Institute of Catalan Studies, and the Society of Natural Sciences.

National youth organizations include Christian Democratic Youth of Spain, Socialist Youth, Junior Chamber, a national students' union, the Counting Federation of Spain, Girl Guides, and chapters of YMCA/YWCA. There are sports associations representing a wide variety of pastimes.

National women's organizations include University Women of Spain and the National Council of Women in Spain. International organizations with national chapters include Save the Children, Amnesty International, Greenpeace, and the Red Cross.

47 TOURISM, TRAVEL, AND RECREATION

Many are attracted to the country by its accessibility, warm climate, beaches, and relatively low costs. Among the principal tourist attractions are Madrid, with its museums, the Escorial Palace, and the nearby Valley of the Fallen (dead in the civil war); Toledo, with its churches and its paintings by El Greco; the Emerald Coast around San Sebastián; the Costa Brava on the coast of Catalonia, north of Barcelona; Granada, with the Alhambra and the Generalife; Sevilla, with its cathedral and religious processions; and the Canary and Balearic islands.

Football (soccer) is the most popular sport in Spain, and many cities have large soccer stadiums; Spain was host to the World Cup competition in 1982. Barcelona was the site of the 1992 Summer Olympics, and in the same year, an International Exposition was held in Sevilla. Among traditional attractions are the bullfights, held in Madrid from April through October, and pelota, an indoor ball game in which spectators bet on the outcome.

Passports are required to enter Spain. Citizens of many countries, including the United States, may stay up to 90 days without a visa.

In 2003, tourist arrivals numbered 51,829,596 with tourist expenditure receipts of $46 billion. There were 740,747 hotel rooms, with 1,451,883 beds and an occupancy rate of 54%. Visitors stayed an average of four nights on their trips to Spain.

In 2005, the US Department of State estimated the daily cost of staying in Madrid at $330; in Barcelona, $367; and other areas, $262.

48 FAMOUS SPANIARDS

The Hispanic-Roman epoch produced the philosopher and dramatist Marcus (or Lucius) Annaeus Seneca (54 BC–AD 39), while the Gothic period was marked by the encyclopedist Isidore of Seville (560?–636), author of the *Etymologies*. Important Spanish thinkers of the Middle Ages included Averroës (Ibn Rushd, or Abu al-Walid Muhammad ibn Ahmad ibn Rushd, 1126–98), philosopher; Maimonides (Moses ben Maimon, also known as the Rambam, 1135–1204), the great Jewish physician and philosopher; Benjamin de Tudela (d.1173), geographer and historian; King Alfonso X (the Wise, 1226?–84), jurist, historian, musician, and astronomer; Juan Ruiz (1283?–1351?), archpriest of Hita, the greatest Spanish medieval poet; and Fernando de Rojas (1475?–1538?), a dramatic poet. El Cid (Rodrigo Díaz de Vivar, 1043?–99) has become the national hero of Spain for his fight against the Moors, although he also fought for them at times.

The golden age of Spanish exploration and conquest began with the Catholic Sovereigns, Ferdinand (1452–1516) and Isabella (1451–1504), in the late 15th century. The first great explorer for Spain was Christopher Columbus (Cristoforo Colombo or Cristóbal Colón, 1451–1506), a seaman of Genoese birth but possibly of Judeo-Catalán origin, who made four voyages of discovery to the Americas, the first landing occurring on 12 October 1492 on the island of Guanahaní (probably on the island now called San Salvador) in the Bahamas. Among the later explorers, Alvar Núñez Cabeza de Vaca (1490?–1557?), Hernando de Soto (d.1542), and Francisco Vázquez de Coronado (1510–54) became famous for their explorations in the southern and southwestern parts of the present US; Juan Ponce de León (1460?–1521), for his travels in Florida; Vasco Núñez de Balboa (1475–1517), for his European discovery of the Pacific Ocean and claim of it for Spain; Francisco Pizarro (1470?–1541), for his conquest of Peru; and Hernán Cortés (1485–1547) for his conquest of Mexico. Juan de la Costa (1460?–1510) was a great cartographer of the period. Spanish power was at its greatest under Charles I (1500–1558), who was also Holy Roman Emperor Charles V. It began to decline under Philip II (1527–98).

In Spanish art, architecture, and literature, the great age was the 16th century and the early part of the 17th. Among the painters, El Greco (Domenikos Theotokopoulos, b.Crete, 1541–1614), Lo Spagnoletto (Jusepe de Ribera, 1589?–1652?), Francisco de Zurbarán (1598?–1660), Diego Rodriguez de Silva y Velázquez (1599–1660), and Bartolomé Esteban Murillo (1617–82) were the leading figures. In architecture, Juan de Herrera (1530–97), the designer of the royal palace, monastery, and tomb of the Escorial, and the baroque architect José Churriguera (1650–1723) are among the most important names. In literature, the dramatists Lope Félix de Vega Carpio (1562–1635) and Pedro Calderón de la Barca (1600–1681) and the novelist Miguel de Cervantes y Saavedra (1547–1616), author of *Don Quixote,* are immortal names. Other leading literary figures include the great poet Luis de Góngora y Argote (1561–1627), the satirist Francisco Gómez de Quevedo y Villegas (1580–1645), and the playwrights Tirso de Molina (Gabriel Téllez, 1571?–1648) and Mexican-born Juan Ruiz de Alarcón y Mendoza (1580?–1639). Outstanding personalities in the annals of the Roman Catholic Church are St. Ignatius de Loyola (Iñigo de Oñez y Loyola, 1491–1556), founder of the Jesuit order; St. Francis Xavier (Francisco Javier, 1506–52), Jesuit "apostle to the Indies"; and the great mystics St. Teresa of Ávila (Teresa de Cepeda y Ahumada, 1515–82) and St. John of the Cross (Juan de Yepes y Álvarez, 1542–91). The phenomenon of pulmonary blood circulation was discovered by Michael Servetus (Miguel Servet, 1511–53), a heretical theologian, while he was still a medical student.

The 16th century was also the golden age of Spanish music. Cristóbal de Morales (1500?–53) and Tomás Luis de Vittoria (1549?–1611) were the greatest Spanish masters of sacred vocal polyphony. Important composers include Luis Milán (1500?–1565?), Antonio de Cabezón (1510–66), Alonso Mudarra (1510–80), and Miguel de Fuenllana. Juan Bermudo (1510?–55?), Francisco de Salinas (1513–90), and Diego Ortiz (c.1525–c.1570) were theo-

rists of note. Two leading 18th-century composers in Spain were the Italians Domenico Scarlatti (1685–1757) and Luigi Boccherini (1743–1805). Padre Antonio Soler (1729–83) was strongly influenced by Scarlatti. Leading modern composers are Isaac Albéniz (1860–1909), Enrique Granados y Campina (1867–1916), Manuel du Falla (1876–1946), and Joaquín Turina (1882–1949). World-famous performers include the cellist and conductor Pablo Casals (1876–1973), the guitarist Andrés Segovia (1894–1987), operatic singers Victoria de los Angeles (Victoria Gómez Cima, 1923–2005), José Carreras (b.1946), and Placido Domingo (b.1941), and the pianist Alicia de Larrocha (b.1923).

Francisco Goya y Lucientes (1746–1828) was the outstanding Spanish painter and etcher of his time. Pablo Ruiz y Picasso (1881–1973) was perhaps the most powerful single influence on contemporary art; other major figures include Juan Gris (1887–1927), Joan Miró (1893–1983), and Salvador Dali (1904–89), who, like Picasso, spent most of his creative life outside Spain. The sculptor Julio González (1876–1942) was noted for his work in iron. A leading architect was Antonio Gaudí (1852–1926); an influential modern architect was José Luis Sert (1902–83), dean of the Graduate School of Design at Harvard University for 16 years.

Miguel de Unamuno y Jugo (1864–1936) and José Ortega y Gasset (1883–1955) are highly regarded Spanish philosophers. Benito Pérez Galdos (1843–1920) was one of the greatest 19th-century novelists. Other Spanish novelists include Pedro Antonio de Alarcón (1833–91), Emilia Pardo Bazán (1852–1921), Vicente Blasco Ibáñez (1867–1928), Pío Baroja y Nessi (1872–1956), Ramón Pérez de Ayala (1880–1962), and Ramón José Sender (1902–82). Prominent dramatists include José Zorrilla y Moral (1817–93), José de Echegaray y Eizaguirre (1832–1916), and Jacinto Benavente y Martínez (1886–1954). The poets Juan Ramón Jiménez (1881–1958) and Vicente Aleixandre (1900–84) were winners of the Nobel Prize for literature in 1956 and 1977, respectively. Other outstanding poets are Gustavo Adolfo Bécquer (1836–70), Antonio Machado Ruiz (1875–1939), Pedro Salinas (1891–1951), Jorge Guillén (1893–1984), Dámaso Alonso (1898–1990), Federico García Lorca (1899–1936), Luis Cernuda (1902–63), and José Angel Valente (1929–2000). Ramón María del Valle-Inclán (1866–1936) was a novelist, dramatist, poet, and essayist. A noted novelist, essayist, and critic was Azorín (José Martínez Ruiz, 1876–1967). Salvador de Madariaga y Rojo (1886–1978) was an important cultural historian and former diplomat. Luis Buñuel (1900–83), who also lived in Mexico, was one of the world's leading film directors. Pedro Almodóvar (b.1951) is a contemporary film director, and Antonio Banderas (b.1960) is a Spanish film actor who has had success in Hollywood.

Santiago Ramón y Cajal (1852–1934), histologist, was awarded the first Nobel Prize for medicine in 1906. The physicians Gregorio Marañón (1887–1960) and Pedro Laín Entralgo (1908–2001) were scholars and humanists of distinction. Juan de la Cierva y Codorniu (1896–1937) invented the autogyro. Severo Ochoa (1905–93), who lived in the United States, won the Nobel Prize for medicine in 1959.

Francisco Franco (1892–1975), the leader of the right-wing insurgency that led to the Spanish Civil War (1936–39), was chief of state during 1939–47 and lifetime regent of the Spanish monarchy after 1947. After Franco's death, King Juan Carlos I (b.1938) guided Spain through the transitional period between dictatorship and democracy.

⁴⁹DEPENDENCIES

Spanish "places of sovereignty" on the North African shore, which are part of metropolitan Spain subject to special statutes owing to their location, include Alborán Island (at 35°56′ N and 3°2′ w), Islas de Alhucemas (at 35°13′ N and 3°52′ w), Islas Chafarinas (at 35°10′ N and 2°26′ w), and Perejil (at 35°54′ N and 5°25′ w). The two major places of sovereignty are Ceuta and Melilla. Ceuta (19 sq km/7.3 sq mi; population 71,403 in 1993) is a fortified port on the Moroccan coast opposite Gibraltar. Melilla (12.3 sq km/4.7 sq mi; resident population 55,613 in 1993), on a rocky promontory on the Rif coast, is connected with the African mainland by a narrow isthmus. Melilla has been Spanish since 1496; Ceuta since 1580. Since 1956, Morocco has repeatedly advanced claims to these areas. Under the 1978 constitution, Ceuta and Melilla are represented in the Cortes by one deputy and two senators each.

⁵⁰BIBLIOGRAPHY

Alexander, Yonah (ed.). *Combating Terrorism: Strategies of Ten Countries*. Ann Arbor, Mich.: University of Michigan Press, 2002.

Annesley, Claire (ed.). *A Political and Economic Dictionary of Western Europe*. Philadelphia: Routledge/Taylor and Francis, 2005.

Douglass, Carrie B. *Bulls, Bullfighting, and Spanish Identities*. Tucson: University of Arizona Press, 1997.

Gagnon, Alain G. and James Tully, (ed.). *Multinational Democracies*. New York: Cambridge University Press, 2001.

Grabowski, John F. *Spain*. San Diego: Lucent Books, 2000.

Gunther, Richard. *Politics, Society, and Democracy: The Case of Spain*. Boulder, Colo.: Westview Press, 1993.

McElrath, Karen, (ed.). *HIV and AIDS: A Global View*. Westport, Conn.: Greenwood Press, 2002.

Newton, Michael T. *Institutions of Modern Spain: A Political and Economic Guide*. Updated and expanded ed. New York: Cambridge University Press, 1997.

Olson, James S., (ed.). *Historical Dictionary of the Spanish Empire, 1402–1975*. New York: Greenwood Press, 1992.

Ortiz Griffin, Julia. *Spain and Portugal*. New York: Facts On File, 2006.

Orwell, George. *Homage to Catalonia*. New York: Harcourt Brace Jovanovich, 1969.

Pritchett, V. S. *The Spanish Temper*. New York: Knopf, 1954.

Smith, Angel. *Historical Dictionary of Spain*. Lanham, Md.: Scarecrow, 1996.

Spanish Women in the Golden Age: Images and Realities. Edited by Magdalena S. Sanchez and Alain Saint-Saens. Westport, Conn.: Greenwood, 1996.

Summers, Randal W., and Allan M. Hoffman, (ed.). *Domestic Violence: A Global View*. Westport, Conn.: Greenwood Press, 2002.

Wessels, Wolfgang, Andreas Maurer, and Jürgan Mittag (eds.). *Fifteen into One?: the European Union and Its Member States*. New York: Palgrave, 2003.

SWEDEN

Kingdom of Sweden
Konungariket Sverige

CAPITAL: Stockholm

FLAG: The national flag, dating from 1569 and employing a blue and gold motif used as early as the mid-14th century, consists of a yellow cross with extended right horizontal on a blue field.

ANTHEM: *Du gamla, du fria, du fjallhöga nord (O Glorious Old Mountain-Crowned Land of the North).*

MONETARY UNIT: The krona (Kr) is a paper currency of 100 öre. There are coins of 50 öre and 1, 2, 5, and 10 kronor, and notes of 5, 10, 20, 50, 100, 500, and 1,000 kronor. Kr1 = $0.13661 (or $1 = Kr7.32) as of 2005.

WEIGHTS AND MEASURES: The metric system is the legal standard, but some old local measures are still in use, notably the Swedish mile (10 kilometers).

HOLIDAYS: New Year's Day, 1 January; Epiphany, 6 January; Labor Day, 1 May; Midsummer Day, Saturday nearest 24 June; All Saints' Day, 5 November; Christmas, 25–26 December. Movable religious holidays include Good Friday, Easter Monday, Ascension, and Whitmonday.

TIME: 1 PM = noon GMT.

¹LOCATION, SIZE, AND EXTENT

Fourth in size among the countries of Europe, Sweden is the largest of the Scandinavian countries, with about 15% of its total area situated north of the Arctic Circle. Extreme length N–S is 1,574 km (978 mi) and greatest breadth E–W is 499 km (310 mi). Sweden has a total area of 449,964 sq km (173,732 sq mi): land area, 410,934 sq km (158,663 sq mi); water area, 39,030 sq km (15,070 sq mi), including some 96,000 lakes. Comparatively, the area occupied by Sweden is slightly larger than the state of California. Sweden is bounded on the N and NE by Finland, on the E by the Gulf of Bothnia, on the SE by the Baltic Sea, on the SW by the Öresund, the Kattegat, and the Skagarrak, and on the W by Norway, with a total boundary length of 5,423 km (3,370 mi), of which 3,218 km (2000 mi) is coastline. The two largest Swedish islands in the Baltic Sea are Gotland and Öland. Sweden's capital city, Stockholm, is located on the southeast Baltic Sea coast.

²TOPOGRAPHY

Northern Sweden (Norrland) slopes from the Kjölen Mountains along the Norwegian frontier (with the high point at Kebnekaise, 2,111 m/6,926 ft) to the coast of the Gulf of Bothnia. The many rivers—notably the Göta, the Dal, the Ångerman, the Ume, and the Lule—flow generally toward the southeast and have incised the plateau surface; waterfalls abound. Central Sweden, consisting of a down-faulted lowland, has several large lakes, of which Vänern (5,584 sq km/2,156 sq mi) is the largest in Europe outside the former USSR. To the south of the lake belt rises the upland of Smaland and its small but fertile appendage, Skane. The lowlands were once submerged and so acquired a cover of fertile, silty soils. Much of Sweden is composed of ancient rock; most ice erosion has resulted in generally poor sandy or stony soils. The best, most lime-rich soils are found in Skane, and this southernmost district is the leading agricultural region; it resembles Denmark in its physical endowments and development.

³CLIMATE

Because of maritime influences, particularly the warm North Atlantic Drift and the prevailing westerly airstreams, Sweden has higher temperatures than its northerly latitude would suggest. Stockholm averages -3°C (26°F) in February and 18°C (64°F) in July. As would be expected from its latitudinal extent, there is a wide divergence of climate between northern and southern Sweden: the north has a winter of more than seven months and a summer of less than three, while Skane in the south has a winter of about two months and a summer of more than four. The increasing shortness of summer northward is partly compensated for by comparatively high summer temperatures, the greater length of day, and the infrequency of summer cloud; the considerable cloud cover in winter reduces heat loss by radiation.

Annual rainfall averages 61 cm (24 in) and is heaviest in the southwest and along the frontier between Norrland and Norway; the average rainfall for Lapland is about 30 cm (12 in) a year. The maximum rainfall occurs in late summer, and the minimum in early spring. There is considerable snowfall, and in the north snow remains on the ground for about half the year. Ice conditions in the surrounding seas, especially the Gulf of Bothnia, often are severe in winter and seriously interfere with navigation.

⁴FLORA AND FAUNA

Vegetation ranges from Alpine-Arctic types in the north and upland areas to coniferous forests in the central regions and deciduous trees in the south. Common trees include birch, aspen, beech elm, oak, and Norway spruce. Black cock, woodcock, duck, partridge, swan, and many other varieties of birds are abundant. Fish and insects are plentiful. As of 2002, there were at least 60 species of mammals, 259 species of birds, and over 1,750 species of plants throughout the country.

5 ENVIRONMENT

Sweden's relatively slow population growth and an effective conservation movement have helped preserve the nation's extensive forest resources. By the end of 1985 there were 19 national parks covering 618,070 hectares (1,527,276 acres), 1,215 nature reserves of 870,748 hectares (2,151,653 acres), and 2,016 other protected landscape areas of 540,064 hectares (1,334,520 acres). As of 2003, protected areas accounted for 9.1% of Sweden's total land area, including 51 Ramsar wetland sites. Principal responsibility for the environment is vested in the National Environmental Protection Agency.

In 2000, the total of carbon dioxide emissions was at 46.9 million metric tons. Other pollutants include sulphur air, nitrogen compounds, oil, VOCs (volatile organic compounds), radon, and methane. The pollution of the nation's water supply is also a significant problem. Factory effluents represent a threat to water quality, and airborne sulfur pollutants have so acidified more than 16,000 lakes that fish can no longer breed in them. Sweden has 171 cu km of renewable water resources with 9% of annual withdrawals used for farming and 55% used for industrial purposes.

One of the most controversial environmental questions was put to rest by a March 1980 referendum in which a small plurality of the electorate (39.3%) supported expansion of nuclear power to no more than 12 reactors by the mid-1980s, but with provisions for the nationalization of nuclear energy, for energy conservation, and for the phaseout of nuclear power within an estimated 20–25 years. As of 2005, there were still 10 nuclear power reactors providing nearly half of the nation's electricity.

According to a 2006 report issued by the International Union for Conservation of Nature and Natural Resources (IUCN), threatened species included 5 types of mammals, 9 species of birds, 6 species of fish, 1 type of mollusk, 12 species of other invertebrates, and 3 species of plants. Threatened species include the blue ground beetle and cerambyx longhorn. Protected fauna include the wild reindeer, golden eagle, and crane.

6 POPULATION

The population of Sweden in 2005 was estimated by the United Nations (UN) at 9,029,000, which placed it at number 84 in population among the 193 nations of the world. In 2005, approximately 17% of the population was over 65 years of age, with another 18% of the population under 15 years of age. There were 98 males for every 100 females in the country. According to the UN, the annual population rate of change for 2005–10 was expected to be 0.1%, a rate the government viewed as satisfactory. The projected population for the year 2025 was 9,936,000. The overall population density was 20 per sq km (52 per sq mi), but the southern two-fifths of the country are more densely populated, with approximately 80% of the population living there.

The UN estimated that 84% of the population lived in urban areas in 2005, and that urban areas were growing at an annual rate of 0.18%. The capital city, Stockholm, had a population of 1,697,000 in that year. Göteborg had a metropolitan population of 829,000. Other large cities (and their estimated populations) include Malmö (267,171), Uppsala (130,000), Västerås (129,987), Örebro (95,354), and Norrköping (83,000).

7 MIGRATION

In the period 1865–1930, nearly 1,400,000 Swedes, or about one-fifth of the country's population, emigrated; over 80% went to the United States, and about 15% to other Nordic countries. The exodus ended by the 1930s, when resource development in Sweden started to keep pace with the population growth. In the 1960s there was a flood of immigration—especially by Finns—that increased the number of aliens in Sweden from 190,621 to 411,280. The number remained steady in the 1970s but increased, though at a slower rate, in the 1980s.

As of 1999, 3,729 people had been evacuated from Macedonia to Sweden under the UNHCR/IOM Humanitarian Evacuation Programme. Evacuees, as well as Kosovars who had already sought asylum but whose cases were still pending, were granted temporary protection for an 11-month period, renewable for a maximum of four years. During 2004, 73,408 refugees were hosted in Sweden. Main countries of origin for refugees included Iraq (23,918), Bosnia and Herzegovina (25,836), Serbia and Montenegro (20,890), and Iran (5,181). Asylum applications came from 25 countries of origin, the largest numbers from Serbia and Montenegro, and Iraq. The net migration rate in 2005 was an estimated 1.67 migrants per 1,000 population. Worker remittances in 2002 were $190 million.

8 ETHNIC GROUPS

The Swedes are primarily Scandinavians of Germanic origin. There are about 17,000 to 20,000 Sami (Lapps) within the country. The remaining 12% of the population is comprised of foreign-born or first-generation immigrants, including Finns in the north, Danes, Iraqis, Iranians, Norwegians, Greeks, and Turks.

9 LANGUAGES

Swedish is a national language. In addition to the letters of the English language, it has å, ä, and ö. Swedish is closely related to Norwegian and Danish. Many Swedes speak English and German, and many more understand these languages. The Sami speak their own language. There is also a spread of Finnish-speaking people from across the frontier.

10 RELIGIONS

For hundreds of years, the Church of Sweden, an Evangelical Lutheran church, represented the religion of state. However, in 2000, the Church and government placed into effect a formal separation of church and state, with a stipulation that the Church of Sweden will continue to receive a certain degree of state support. This new agreement triggered a decline in membership for this church. According to recent estimates, about 79.6% of the population belong to the Church of Sweden, down from over 85% in 2000. Protestant groups other than the Church of Sweden have about 400,000 people. Roman Catholics constitute less than 1% of the populace, with about 140,000 members. About 100,000 people are members of Christian Orthodox churches, including Greek, Serbian, Syrian, Romanian, and Macedonian. The number of Muslims is at about 350,000, with about 100,000 active practitioners primarily of the Sunni and Shia branches. There are also about 20,000 Jews

(Orthodox, Conservative, and Reform), with about half being active. Buddhists and Hindus number around 3,000 to 4,000 each. It is estimated that about 15–20% of the adult population are atheists. Small numbers of people are represented by groups such as the Church of Scientology, Hare Krishnas, Opus Dei, and the Unification Church.

The constitution provides for freedom of religion. Since the separation of church and state, all religions are eligible for financial support from the government through the "church tax." Individuals may now designate which organization they wish to receive their contribution, or they may receive a tax reduction. The Commission for State Grants to Religious Communities is the government body that oversees religious funding, in cooperation with the Swedish Free Church Council.

The Muslim and Jewish communities have protested government laws which they believe interfere with religious practice. For instance, a 1930 law requires the use of anesthesia before slaughter of animals in order to minimize suffering. This practice interferes with kosher. A 2001 law requires that mohels (who perform circumcisions according to Jewish customs) must be certified by the National Board of Health and the procedure must be completed in the presence of a medical doctor or an anesthesia nurse. Some Jews (and Muslims) claim that this interferes with their religious ceremony; as of 2005, the law was scheduled for review.

11 TRANSPORTATION

As of 2002, the total length of highways was 213,237 km (132,633 mi), of which about 167,604 km (104,250 mi) were paved, including 1,514 km (942 mi) of expressways. As of 2003, there were 4,078,000 passenger cars and 435,561 commercial vehicles. In 1967, Sweden changed from left- to right-hand traffic. As of 2004, Sweden's 11,481 km (7,141 mi) railroad system was operated by the state-owned Statens Järnvagar. Of that total, 9,400 km (5,847 mi) of the track was electrified. All tracks are standard gauge.

Since the 1960s, the number of ships in the merchant navy has decreased because of competition from low-cost shipping nations and, more recently, the slump in world trade. Sweden has an increasing number of special-purpose vessels, such as fruit tramps, ore carriers, and oil tankers. Most of the larger vessels, representing the majority of Sweden's commercial tonnage, are engaged in traffic that never touches home ports, and less than half of Swedish foreign trade is carried in Swedish ships. Göteborg, Stockholm, and Malmö, the three largest ports, and a number of smaller ports are well-equipped to handle large oceangoing vessels. In 2005, the Swedish merchant fleet consisted of 205 ships of 1,000 GRT or more, with a combined capacity of 2,702,763 GRT. Canals in central Sweden have opened the lakes to seagoing craft; inland waterways add up to 2,052 km (1,275 mi), navigable by small steamers and barges.

In 2004 there were an estimated 254 airports. As of 2005, a total of 155 had paved runways, and there were also two heliports. Arlanda international airport at Stockholm received its first jet aircraft in 1960; other principal airports are Sturup at Malmö and Landvetter at Göteborg. The Scandinavian Airlines System (SAS) is operated jointly by Sweden, Denmark, and Norway, each of which owns a 50% share of the company operating in its own territory; the other half in Sweden is owned by private investors. Linjeflyg, a subsidiary of SAS, operates a domestic service to most of the larger cities and resorts. In 2003, about 11.586 million passengers were carried on scheduled domestic and international flights.

12 HISTORY

Sweden and the Swedes are first referred to in written records by the Roman historian Tacitus, who, in his Germania (AD 98), mentions the Suiones, a people "mighty in ships and arms." These people, also referred to as Svear, conquered their southern neighbors, the Gotar, merged with them, and extended their dominion over most of what is now central and southern Sweden. In the 9th and 10th centuries when Vikings from the Norwegian homeland traveled west to Iceland, Greenland and farther afield to Newfoundland, Vikings from eastern Sweden raided areas southeastward across Russia to Constantinople. Archeologists and historians hold that the descendants of one of their chieftains, Rurik, founded the Kievan Russian state. Some other settled regions and place-names in various parts of Europe also show Swedish influence through rune-stones found across Eastern Europe.

In the Viking era, the Swedish kingdom took shape but was not very centralized. Political power became more centralized with the advent of Christianity, which came gradually between the 9th and 11th centuries. During the 12th century, the Swedish kingdom consolidated internally and under the guise of the crusades began to expand into the Baltic, incorporating Finland, between 1150 and 1300. Among the institutions established in Sweden during the 12th and 13th centuries were Latin education, new modes and styles of architecture and literature, town life, and a more centralized monarchy with new standards in royal administration—all with significant economic, legal, and social implications.

Norway and Sweden were united in 1319 under the infant king Magnus VII, but Waldemar IV, King of Denmark, regained Skåne, the southern part of Sweden, and all the Scandinavian countries were united in the Kalmar Union under his daughter Margaret (Margrethe) in 1397. For over a century, Sweden resisted Danish rule, and the union was marked by internal tensions.

In 1523, following a war with Denmark whose notable feature was the Stortorget (Great Square) massacre in Stockholm where hundreds of Swedish nobles were executed, the Swedes elected Gustavus Vasa (Gustaf I) to the Swedish throne. A great king and the founder of modern Sweden, Gustavus made Lutheranism the state religion, established a hereditary monarchy, and organized a national army and navy. His successors incorporated Estonia and other areas in Eastern Europe. The growth of nationalism, the decline of the Hanseatic League's control of Baltic trade, and Protestantism contributed to the rise of Sweden in the following century.

Another great king and one of the world's outstanding military geniuses, Gustavus Adolphus (Gustaf II Adolf, r.1611–32), is generally regarded as the creator of the first modern army. He defeated Poland and conquered the rest of Livonia, and by winning a war with Russia acquired Ingermanland and Karelia. In the period of the Thirty Years' War (1618–48), Sweden was the foremost Protestant power on the Continent, and for the following half century the Baltic Sea became a Swedish lake. Although the king was killed at Lützen in 1632, his policies were carried on during the reign of his daughter Christina by the prime minister, Axel Oxenstierna. By terms of the Peace of Westphalia (1648) Sweden gained

Pomerania and the archbishopric of Bremen, part of the Holy Roman Empire. Swedish expansionism resulted, in 1658, in the recapture of the southern Swedish provinces that Denmark had retained since the early 16th century. Renewed wars extended the Swedish frontier to the west coast while reducing Danish control over trade by taking away the eastern shore of the Öresund.

Under young Charles XII (r.1697–1718), Sweden fought the Great Northern War (1700–1721) against a coalition of Denmark, Poland, Saxony, and Russia. Sweden at first was militarily successful, but after a crushing defeat by Russian forces under Peter the Great (Peter I) in 1709 at the Battle of Poltava, the nation lost territories to Russia, Prussia, and Hannover. Thereafter Sweden was a second-rate power. Throughout the 18th century there was internal dissension between those that favored increased political liberties and constitutionally shared political power and those who favored monarchical absolutism. In 1770, a power struggle between the nobility and the commoner estates, including the clergy, burghers and farmers, ended when Gustav III carried out a bloodless coup and restored absolutism. Gustavus III (r.1771–92), a poet, playwright, and patron of the arts and sciences, and founder of the Swedish Academy, was eventually assassinated by a group of disgruntled nobles.

Sweden entered the Napoleonic Wars in 1805, allying itself with Great Britain, Austria, and Russia against France. Russia switched sides in 1807, however, and the ensuing Russo-Swedish conflict (1808–9) resulted in the loss of Finland. King Gustavus IV was then overthrown by the army, and a more democratic constitution was adopted. In 1810, one of Napoleon's marshals, a Frenchman from Pau named Jean Baptiste Jules Bernadotte, was invited to become the heir to the Swedish throne. Three years later, he brought his adopted country once again over to the side of the allies against Napoleon in the last full-scale war fought by Sweden. His reward for being on the winning side of the Napoleonic wars was to wrest a reluctant Norway from Danish control. After a show of Swedish force, Norway was forced into political union with Sweden that lasted until 1905 when the union was largely peacefully dissolved.

Bernadotte assumed the name Charles John (Carl Johan) and succeeded to the Swedish throne in 1818 as Charles XIV John. The Bernadotte dynasty, which has reigned successively since 1818, gradually relinquished virtually all of its powers, which were assumed by the Riksdag, Sweden's parliament. Sweden has become one of the most progressive countries in the world. Industry was developed, the cooperative movement began to play an important part in the economy, and the Social Democratic Labor Party gained a dominant position in political life.

Carl XVI Gustaf has been king since the death of his grandfather, Gustav VI Adolf, in 1973. In September 1976, a coalition of three non-Socialist parties won a majority in parliamentary elections, ending 44 years of almost uninterrupted Social Democratic rule that had established a modern welfare state. The country's economic situation worsened, however, and the Social Democrats were returned to power in the elections of September 1982. Prime Minister Olof Palme, leader of the Social Democratic Party since 1969, was assassinated in February 1986. In the ensuing years, investigators have been unable to establish a motive for the killing or to find the assassin.

Sweden and Neutrality

Sweden remained neutral in both world wars; during World War II, however, Sweden had difficulty maintaining neutrality as its Nordic neighbors were drawn into the conflict. Sweden served as a haven for refugees from the Nazis, allowed the Danish resistance movement to operate on its soil, and sent volunteers to assist Finland's fight against the Russians. On the other hand, Sweden was compelled to comply with German demands to transport its troops through Sweden to and from Nazi-occupied Norway. After the war, Sweden did not join NATO, as did its Scandinavian neighbors Norway and Denmark, but it did become a member of the UN in 1946 and participated in some of the European Recovery Program benefits. In 1953, Sweden joined with Denmark, Norway, Iceland, and, later, Finland to form the Nordic Council, and was instrumental in creating EFTA in 1960. Subsequently Sweden declined an invitation to join the EEC with Denmark, Ireland, and the United Kingdom; a free-trade agreement with the EEC was signed 22 July 1972. Sweden's post-WWII foreign policy has been termed "active neutrality." Neutral Sweden tried to mediate in the Cold War confrontation between the Western and Soviet blocs and sought a major role in development assistance toward newly independent countries in the Third World.

Sweden's traditional policy of neutrality was strained in late October 1981 when a Soviet submarine ran aground inside a restricted military zone near the Swedish naval base at Karlskrona. The Swedish government protested this "flagrant violation of territorial rights" and produced reasons for believing that the submarine had been carrying nuclear weapons. Swedish naval vessels raised the damaged submarine and permitted it to return to the Soviet fleet in early November. In 1984, a Swedish military report stated that at least 10 "alien" submarines had been detected in Swedish waters.

The environment and nuclear energy were major political issues in the 1980s. In the 1990s and into the new century, the major concerns have been conflicts over immigration policies, the economy, and Sweden's relationship to the European Communities. Sweden's economic crisis led to large-scale public spending cuts by a center-right government. In 1991, Sweden applied for membership in the EC against a background of considerable opposition. In May 1993, the Riksdag altered Sweden's long-standing foreign policy of neutrality. In the future, neutrality would only be followed in time of war. The Riksdag also opened up the possibility of Sweden's participation in defense alliances, which remains a hotly debated issue in Sweden.

In 1994, Swedes voted to join the EU and the country officially became a member on 1 January 1995. Sweden did not join the 11 EU countries participating in the launch of the new European currency, the euro, on 1 January 1999. Public opinion over the succeeding years softened on the issue of euro membership, however, and a referendum on joining the monetary union was held on 14 September 2003. The ruling Social Democratic Party supported euro membership, but its coalition partners in 2003, the ex-communist Left Party and the Greens, were strongly opposed, as those parties feared Sweden would lose not only its currency, but its status as an advanced welfare state. On 10 September, Swedish Foreign Minister Anna Lindh was stabbed in a Stockholm department store by an assailant unknown to her; she died the next day. Lindh was one of the primary spokespersons for the "yes" campaign for the euro, and was one of the country's best-loved politicians; many thought she could have become prime minister. The referendum was defeated by a margin of 56.1% to 41.8% with a turnout of 81.2%.

Following the 11 September 2001 terrorist attacks on the United States, Sweden pledged support for US-led retaliation against terrorists. At the same time, Sweden relaxed further its policy of neutrality, and some have speculated that it will eventually join NATO. Sweden since 1992 has been a member of NATO's "Partnership for Peace" program, and in 1999, the first Swedish troops were sent to Kosovo in the Balkans. In February 2002, Prime Minister Göran Persson's government made the decision for Sweden to enter into military alliances and defensive pacts with other nations. As of 2005, Swedish troops were also serving in Liberia, the Democratic Republic of the Congo, and Afghanistan. Sweden at the turn of the 21st century was concerned with issues of international terrorism and organized transnational crime, such as drug smuggling and trafficking in human beings.

Sweden pledged itself to give 1% of its GNP to development assistance for poor countries, effective 2006. Sweden will give priority to four areas: conflict prevention measures, the fight against drugs, efforts to combat HIV/AIDS, and sexual and reproductive health and rights.

13 GOVERNMENT

Sweden developed as a constitutional monarchy under the constitution of 1809, which remained in effect until 1 January 1975, when a new instrument of government replaced it. Legislative authority is vested in the parliament (Riksdag). The monarch ceded involvement in power-brokering among the parties as early as 1917 when the Liberals and Social Democrats entered into a coalition. Today, the monarch performs only ceremonial duties as the official head of state; the monarch's last political duty, regular participation in cabinet meetings, was taken away under the most recent constitution. The king must belong to the Lutheran Church; the throne was hereditary only for male descendants until 1980, when female descendants were granted the right to the throne.

The Riksdag was bicameral until 1971, when a unicameral body of 350 members serving three-year terms was established; the 1975 constitution provided for 349 members, and the parliamentary term was lengthened to four years in 1994. All members of the Riksdag are directly elected by universal suffrage at age 18. Voter turnout has traditionally been very high in Sweden, though in the 2002 election turnout dipped to 80.1% compared with turnout over 86% for the previous two elections. Foreign nationals may vote in regional and municipal elections. Elections at all levels are simultaneous and are held on the third Sunday of September every fourth year. The parties' share of the national vote is directly translated into seats in Riksdag. Interim national elections may be called by the government between regular elections, but the mandate of the interim election is valid only for the remaining portion of the regular four-year parliamentary term of office.

In Sweden's parliamentary system, executive power lies with the government, or cabinet, that is formed by the majority party in parliament or by a coalition of parties. Sweden has also functioned with a minority government in which the largest party does not enjoy a majority in parliament and must form ad-hoc coalitions with other parties in the Riksdag. The cabinet as a whole is

LOCATION: 55°20′ to 69°4′N; 10°58′ to 24°10′ E. BOUNDARY LENGTHS: Finland, 586 kilometers (364 miles); coastline, 2,746 kilometers (1,706 miles); Norway, 1,619 kilometers (1,006 miles); Gotland Island coastline, 400 kilometers (249 miles); Öland Island coastline, 72 kilometers (45 miles). TERRITORIAL SEA LIMIT: 12 miles.

responsible for all government decisions and must defend their legislative agenda in the plenary sessions of the Riksdag. A vote of no confidence by an absolute majority of the Riksdag allows for the forced resignation of individual ministers or of the entire cabinet. A vote of no confidence becomes moot if within one week of the vote the government calls for new elections for the entire Riksdag.

Chief executive power is wielded by the prime minister, who is formally proposed by the speaker of the Riksdag and confirmed by vote of the parliamentary parties. The prime minister appoints a cabinet usually consisting of 18–20 members reflecting the party or coalition of parties in power. Once a week the government takes decisions in a formal meeting presided over by the prime minister. The cabinet as a whole discusses all-important decisions prior to taking a decision. After a decision has been taken by the cabinet, the ministers practice collective responsibility in which all support the decision taken by the government. Ministers may issue directives but administrative decisions are taken by central boards, which have their respective spheres of activity delimited by the Riksdag.

National referenda on policy questions of national importance are permitted by the constitution. Sweden's parliament has the highest level of political representation of women in the world; 11 of the 20 ministers in the 2005 government were women, and 45% of the Riksdag members are women.

14 POLITICAL PARTIES

The unicameral system and the electoral system of proportional representation have allowed almost exact equality in proportional representation among the constituencies on the national level and has produced a multiparty system. The constitution requires, however, that a party must gain at least 4% of the national popular vote or 12% in a constituency to be represented in the Riksdag. Sweden has for many years utilized the party list system in which the candidates for office from any given party are listed in order of party preference. If a party won 10 seats in the Riksdag, the top 10 candidates from that party would be represented in parliament. In 1998, voters for the first time had the option of indicating which candidates on the party list whom they preferred to see elected to parliament and to local councils. A given candidate must receive at least 8% of his or her party's ballots in any electoral district to be moved to the top of the party's nomination list. If no candidate attains the 8% threshold, the party's nomination list remains in force.

Sweden had a stable party system until the end of the 1980s. The parties of the political right include the Moderate (formerly Conservative) Party (Moderata Samlingspartiet, M), which favors tax reform and trimming the welfare state; the Liberal Party (Folkpartiet Liberalerna, FP), which is a traditional European liberal party; and the Center (formerly Agrarian) Party (Centerpartiet, C), which has in the past represented rural interests and has tried to refashion itself as an "alternative" centrist party favoring environmental issues. The left side of the Swedish political spectrum includes the dominant Social Democratic Party (Socialdemokratiska Arbetarepartiet, S), which is responsible for creating the welfare state and which gets considerable support from organized labor in Sweden; and the Left (formerly Communist Left) Party (Vänsterpartiet, V), which has distanced itself from its communist past and now advocates positions that champion gender equality and attracts voters that are wary of the Social Democrats' move toward the center. In 1988, the environmentalist Green Party (Miljöpartiet de Gröna, MP) joined the long-standing par-

ties on the left represented in the Riksdag. In the 1991 election, two new parties emerged on the right, the Christian Democrats (Kristdemokraterna, KD) and the New Democracy Party (Ny Demokratiska, NyD).

Except for a brief period in 1936, the Social Democratic Labor Party was in power almost uninterruptedly from 1932 to 1976, either alone or in coalition. In 1945, the Social Democrats dissolved the wartime Grand Coalition Cabinet representing every party except the Left Party Communists and launched a program of social reform. Although inflation and other difficulties slowed the Social Democratic program, steadily mounting production encouraged the government to push through its huge social welfare program, which was sanctioned in principle by all major parties.

The Social Democrats held or controlled all parliamentary majorities until the elections of September 1976 when a non-Socialist coalition including the Center Party, the Moderates, and the Liberals won 180 of the 349 seats at stake. The center-right coalition retained control in the 1979 election with a reduced majority of 175 seats and a stronger showing for the Moderates. In the election on 19 September 1982, however, the Social Democrats returned to power. Olof Palme, who had been the Social Democratic prime minister from 1969 to 1976, was able to put together a new coalition cabinet on 8 October 1982. His party remained in power, though with a reduction of seats, following the 1985 election. Palme was assassinated in February 1986; he was succeeded by Ingvar Carlsson.

The 1988 election was a watershed that registered political discontentment. The Social Democrats lost seats as the Moderates' and Liberals' share of the vote continued to increase. More remarkably, for the first time in 70 years, a new party gained representation in the Riksdag—the Green Party (MP), which obtained 20 seats. The Social Democrats were narrowly defeated in September 1991, and the government of Ingvar Carlsson gave way to that of Carl Bildt (Moderate Party), who headed a minority four-party, center-right coalition composed of the Moderates, the Liberals, the Center Party, and the Christian Democratic party, which together controlled 170 seats.

The 1991 election represented a gain for two previously unrepresented parties—Christian Democrats (26 seats) and New Democracy (25 seats)—who managed to exceed the 4% threshold while the Greens fell below the threshold and lost representation in the Riksdag. New Democracy emerged prior to the 1991 general election as a party of discontent urging tax cuts and reduced immigration. The Left Party-Communists were renamed the Left Party (VP) in 1990.

The Moderate Coalition, which promised to end Sweden's deepening recession, found itself unable to address the country's problems, largely because of Social Democrat and popular opposition to its cost-cutting measures. In 1994, the Social Democrats were returned to office by a population reluctantly willing to bear austerity if initiated and directed by the party that created the welfare state. The Social Democratic Coalition government under Prime Minister Ingvar Carlsson navigated Sweden through the referendum on Swedish membership into the EU in late 1994. Carlsson was replaced as prime minister by the former finance minister, Göran Persson.

The September 1998 election represented a protest vote against the mainstream parties and perhaps greater voter polarization in

Sweden. The mainstream party of the left, the Social Democrats, had their worst election showing in over 70 years but maintained power in a minority government dependent upon support from a formal alliance from the Left and Green parties. The Social Democrats slipped from 45.3% of the vote in 1994 to 36.4% in 1998, while the Left Party advanced from 6.2% in 1994 to 12% in 1998 and the Greens returned to the Riksdag with 4.5% of the national vote. Similarly on the right, the Christian Democrats advanced from 4.1% of vote in 1994 to 11.8% in 1998 at the expense of the more centrist Center and Liberal parties, which narrowly passed the 4% threshold. The Moderates' share of the vote held basically steady.

Much of this discontent in the 1998 election was attributed to the budget tightening process that resulted in major cutbacks in social welfare benefits. A growing level of public distrust of politicians was fueled by prominent scandals of misuse of public funds. The reform to allow voters to select individual candidates did not seem to have diminished the distance between voters and elected representatives as only 29.9% took advantage of the opportunity to do so at the national level.

The 2002 general election campaign focused largely on the issues of immigration and membership in the euro zone. The Liberals and Moderates supported a plan to import large numbers of guest workers, who would be classed as noncitizens. The Social Democrats and the Left Party denounced this plan. The Social Democrats registered a strong showing in the elections, winning 39.8% of the vote (up from 36.4% in 1998) and taking 144 of 349 seats in the Riksdag. The Social Democrats under Göran Persson formed a government with the Left Party (8.3% of the vote and 30 seats) and the Greens (4.6% and 17 seats). However, the Liberal Party, with its immigration plan, increased its strength in parliament, with 13.3% of the vote (up from 4.7% in 1998) and 48 seats. The Christian Democrats fell from 11.8% in 1998 to 9.1% of the vote in 2002 (33 seats). The Moderates took 15.2% of the vote and 55 seats. The next general elections were to be held September 2006.

15 LOCAL GOVERNMENT

Local self-government has a long tradition in Sweden as the civil role of the Lutheran Church has been gradually reduced. The first legislation establishing municipal governance is the Local Government Ordinances of 1862 that separated religious tasks from civil tasks which were given to cities and rural municipal districts. On 1 January 2000, the Church of Sweden separated from the central government, and local parishes lost their local government status.

Decentralization is markedly characteristic of Sweden's governmental structure. With the most recent reforms there are two types of local governance in Sweden: the municipality, or *kommun*, as the local unit and the county council as the regional unit. The country is divided into 21 counties, 2 regions, 289 municipalities, and one "county council-free municipality" on the island of Gotland, each with an elected council. Local government is administered by county councils and municipalities consisting of at least 20 members popularly elected, on a proportional basis, for four years. Under each council is an executive board with various committees. In addition, there is a governor (prefect), the government-appointed head of the administrative board in each of Swe-

den's counties, who holds supreme police and other supervisory authority. Local authorities are responsible for most social welfare services, including hospitals, elementary education, certain utilities, and the police force. It is up to the Swedish cabinet and parliament to decide on the overall framework of public sector activities, but within these wide parameters, local governments have a large measure of freedom to implement public programs.

16 JUDICIAL SYSTEM

Ordinary criminal and civil cases are tried in a local court (*tingsrätt*), consisting of a judge and a panel of lay assessors appointed by the municipal council. Above these local courts are six courts of appeal (*hovrätter*). The highest tribunal is the Supreme Court (*Högsta Domstolen*), made up of at least 16 justices. Special cases are heard by the Supreme Administrative Court and other courts. The Swedish judicial procedure uses a jury of the Anglo-US type only in press libel suits. Capital punishment, last employed in 1910, is expressly forbidden by the constitution.

The judiciary is independent of executive control or political influence. The right to counsel of criminal defendants is restricted to cases in which the maximum penalty possible is six-month imprisonment or greater.

Sweden originated the judicial practice of the ombudsman when its first ombudsman was designated in 1766. The office has been in continuous existence since 1809. The institution has also been enshrined by the constitution and provides parliamentary control over the executive. The Riksdag elects four ombudsmen representing various interests such as consumers, gender equality, the press, children, the disabled, those experiencing ethnic and/ or sexual orientation discrimination. The ombudsman is charged with supervising the observance of laws and statutes as applied by the courts and by public officials, excluding cabinet ministers, members of the Riksdag, or directly elected local government officials. The ombudsmen are concerned especially with protecting the civil rights of individual citizens and of religious and other groups. There are some 5,000 complaints lodged with the office of the ombudsman annually, though about 40% are dismissed immediately for a variety of reasons. Only about 20–25% of these complaints are investigated fully and usually reflect an individual caught on a bureaucratic "merry-go-round." Ombudsmen may admonish or prosecute offenders, although prosecutions are relatively rare.

17 ARMED FORCES

Sweden's policy of neutrality and nonalignment requires a strong, modern, and independent defense establishment. The budget allocated $5.6 billion for defense in 2005. Active armed forces that year totaled 27,600 with reservists numbering 262,000. The Army in 2005 had 13,800 active personnel, with 280 main battle tanks, 705 armored infantry fighting vehicles, 1,521 armored personnel carriers, and 820 artillery pieces. The Swedish Navy had 7,900 active personnel including a 1,300-member coastal defense force, and a 320-member naval aviation wing. There are naval stations at Stockholm, Karlskrona, and Göteborg. Major naval units include seven tactical submarines, 36 patrol and coastal vessels, and 21 mine warfare vessels. The Air Force in 2005 totaled 5,900 active personnel, operating 170 combat capable aircraft, including 13 fighter ground attack aircraft and 151 JAS-39 Gripen multi-role aircraft. A 600-person paramilitary force acts as the nation's coast guard and there are more than 35,000 people that belong to voluntary auxiliary organizations. Sweden participates in UN and peacekeeping missions in 11 countries or regions.

18 INTERNATIONAL COOPERATION

Sweden joined the United Nations on 19 November 1946; it takes part in ECE and several nonregional specialized agencies, such as UNESCO, UNCTAD, UNHCR, the FAO, the World Bank, IAEA, ILO, and the WHO. The country served on the UN Security Council from 1997–98. The first UN Conference on the Human Environment was held in Stockholm in June 1972. Together with Denmark, Finland, Iceland, and Norway, Sweden has been a member of the advisory Nordic Council since 1953 and cooperates with these other Scandinavian countries in social welfare and health insurance and in freeing frontiers of passport control. The nation is also a member of the Asian Development Bank, the African Development Bank, the Council of the Baltic Sea States, G-6, G-9, the Paris Club (G-10), the Inter-American Development Bank, the Nordic Investment Bank, OECD, OSCE, the NATO Partnership for Peace, and the Council of Europe. In 1995, Sweden became a member of the European Union. It has observer status in the OAS and the Western European Union.

Sweden has offered support to UN missions and operations in Kosovo (est. 1999), India and Pakistan (est. 1949), Ethiopia and Eritrea (est. 2000), Liberia (est. 2003), Sierra Leone (est. 1999), East Timor (est. 2002), Georgia (est. 1993), and the DROC (est. 1999), among others. Sweden is part of the Australia Group, the Zangger Committee, the European Organization for Nuclear Research (CERN), the Nuclear Suppliers Group (London Group), Organization for the Prohibition of Chemical Weapons, and the Nuclear Energy Agency.

In environmental cooperation, Sweden is part of the Antarctic Treaty; the Basel Convention; Conventions on Biological Diversity, Whaling, and Air Pollution; Ramsar; CITES; the London Convention; International Tropical Timber Agreements; the Kyoto Protocol; the Montréal Protocol; MARPOL; the Nuclear Test Ban Treaty; and the UN Conventions on the Law of the Sea, Climate Change, and Desertification.

19 ECONOMY

Sweden is a highly industrialized country. The shift from agriculture to industry began in the 1930s and developed rapidly during the postwar period. Average annual growth of the GDP declined from 4.3% in the 1960s to 2% in the 1970s and to 1.6% in the 1980s. It grew by 1.4% in 1990 but fell 1.4% in 1991, 1.9% in 1992, and 2.1% in 1993, the longest period of decline in the 20th century. In 1994, the economy grew by 2.2%, ending the deeply troubling reversals of past years. From 1998 to 2000 GDP growth averaged 3.77%, but the global economic slowdown from 2001 helped reduce GDP growth to 1.6% in 2001 and 1.9% in 2002. Growth remained sluggish in 2003, but picked up in 2004. Real GDP growth was expected to accelerate from 2.4% in 2005 to 3% in 2006, before a modest slowdown in 2007. Over the 2001–05 period, real GDP growth averaged 2%.

Swedish living standards and purchasing power are among the highest in the world. However, inflation was a problem for several years after the international oil shocks of the 1970s, the annual rise

in consumer prices peaking at 13.7% in 1980 after the second oil shock. The rate of price increases declined thereafter, but was still 10.4% in 1990 and 9.4% in 1991 before falling to 2.2% in 1992. By 1998 and 1999, inflation had all but disappeared, with annual rates of 0.4% and 0.3% respectively. In 2000, inflation rose to 1.3%, and during 2001 and 2002, the annual inflation rate averaged 2.5%. By 2005, the annual inflation rate averaged 0.7%, but inflationary pressures were expected to rise gradually over the period 2006–07. Over the 2001–05 period, inflation averaged 1.5%.

After hitting 14% in 1994, unemployment began to gradually recede. By 1998, unemployment was down to 6.5%, and by 2001, 3.9%. The unemployment rate stood at 4% in 2002, and was estimated at 5.6% in 2004. However, by 2005, the unemployment rate remained well above the government's 4% target: an unadjusted figure of 7.1% was registered in June 2005. While not high by European standards, many economists believed the true number of the unemployed is even larger.

Swedish industry is outstanding in supplying quality goods and specialized products—ball bearings, high-grade steel, machine tools, and glassware—that are in world demand. Intimate contact between trade, industry, and finance is a feature of the economy, as is the spread of factories to rural districts. Some natural resources are ample, the foremost being lumber, iron ore, and waterpower. Sweden's lack of oil and coal resources makes it dependent on imports for energy production, despite abundant waterpower.

20 INCOME

The US Central Intelligence Agency (CIA) reports that in 2005 Sweden's gross domestic product (GDP) was estimated at $266.5 billion. The CIA defines GDP as the value of all final goods and services produced within a nation in a given year and computed on the basis of purchasing power parity (PPP) rather than value as measured on the basis of the rate of exchange based on current dollars. The per capita GDP was estimated at $29,600. The annual growth rate of GDP was estimated at 2.4%. The average inflation rate in 2005 was 0.5%. It was estimated that agriculture accounted for 1.8% of GDP, industry 28.6%, and services 69.7%.

According to the World Bank, in 2003 remittances from citizens working abroad totaled $578 million or about $65 per capita and accounted for approximately 0.2% of GDP.

The World Bank reports that in 2003 household consumption in Sweden totaled $147.76 billion or about $16,499 per capita based on a GDP of $301.6 billion, measured in current dollars rather than PPP. Household consumption includes expenditures of individuals, households, and nongovernmental organizations on goods and services, excluding purchases of dwellings. It was estimated that for the period 1990 to 2003 household consumption grew at an average annual rate of 1.7%. In 2001 it was estimated that approximately 17% of household consumption was spent on food, 12% on fuel, 4% on health care, and 14% on education.

21 LABOR

In 2005, Sweden's labor force was estimated at 4.49 million persons. As of 2003, the services sector accounted for 75.1% of the workforce, with 22.6% engaged in industry, 2.1% in agriculture, and the remainder in undefined occupations. The unemployment rate in 2005 was estimated at 6%.

In 2005, about 80% of Swedish wage earners are members of trade unions, and within certain industrial branches the percentage is even higher. The trade union movement is based on voluntary membership, and there is neither a closed shop nor a union shop. Although workers have the right to strike, employers also have the right to use the lockout.

Agreements between employers and trade unions are generally worked out by negotiation. Public mediators or mediation commissions intervene if necessary. A labor court, made up of three impartial members and five representing employers, workers, and salaried employees, has jurisdiction over the application and interpretation of collective agreements already signed and may impose damages on employers, trade unions, or trade union members violating a contract. For many years, an overwhelming majority of the court's decisions have been unanimous, and since the end of the 1930s industrial peace has generally prevailed. In 1997, management and labor agreed to a new negotiating framework that has decreased strikes and increased wages. Swedish law requires employee representation on company boards of directors. A law passed in 1983 introduced employee funds, partly funded by contributions from profits of all Swedish companies, which give unions and employees equity in companies, while providing the companies with investment capital.

The legal minimum age for full-time employment is 16 years old, but only under the supervision of local authorities. In addition, minors under 18 can only work in the daytime and must be supervised. The regular workweek cannot exceed 40 hours, and overtime is limited to 48 hours over a four-week period and a total of 200 hours a year. However, these regulations may be modified by collective bargaining agreement. A minimum of five weeks of holiday with pay is stipulated by law. There is no national minimum wage: wages are negotiated in collective bargaining agreements. Workers, even at the lowest end of the pay scale, are able to provide a decent standard of living for their families. Health and safety standards are very high and are stringently enforced.

22 AGRICULTURE

Only about 3% of Sweden's labor force earned their living in agriculture in 2000, compared with more than 50% at the beginning of the 20th century and about 20% in 1950. Production exceeds domestic consumption; however, a considerable amount of food is imported. About 6.5% of the land area of Sweden, or 2,672,000 hectares (6,603,000 acres), is classed as land cultivated with permanent or temporary crops. In 2003 there were 66,780 holdings with more than two hectares (five acres) of arable land. Farm holdings are intensively tilled; fertilizers are used heavily and mechanization is increasing. During 1980–90, the agricultural sector grew by an annual average of 1.5%. However, during 1990–2000, it remained essentially unchanged. During 2002–04, crop production was 3% higher than during 1999–2001.

Most farmers are elderly, and few small farms have a successor waiting to replace the present farmer. Government policy in recent years has been to merge small unprofitable farms into larger units of 10–20 hectares (25–50 acres) of arable land with some woodland, the size estimated able to support a family in the same living standard as an industrial worker. Most Swedish farmers are small landowners who also support themselves through forestry and fishing, and in 2003, 51% of farms were less than 20 hectares (50 acres) in extent. Farmer participation in the government's set-aside program resulted in about 300,000 hectares (741,300 acres) of cropland being retired from production in 1990, and again in 1991. The full-time farm labor force has fallen from 45,000 in 1995 to 32,000 in 2003.

Grains (particularly oats, wheat, barley, and rye), potatoes and other root crops, vegetables, and fruits are the chief agricultural products. Sugar beet cultivation in Skåne is important and produces almost enough sugar to make Sweden self-sufficient. In 2004, Sweden produced 1,691,900 tons of barley; 925,300 tons of oats; 2,412,300 tons of wheat; 979,100 tons of potatoes; and 133,400 tons of rye.

In the last 50 years, Swedish agricultural policy for major commodities has developed under an official system of import levies, export support, and market intervention. This policy was in response to the economic depression of the 1930s, and for the country's need for food security in times of risk or war. The Warfare Preparedness Program, developed after World War II (1939–45), protected Swedish agriculture, resulting in high costs and overproduction. In 1991, a five-year agricultural reform program came into effect, whereby most subsidies and price regulations were eliminated, allowing consumer demand to determine production volumes. By 1995, Sweden's agricultural policy was fully in line with EU rules. Sweden also enacted a plan to convert 10% of the country's arable land to ecological, or organic, agriculture by increasing taxes on energy, fertilizers, and biocides. The government has also introduced incentives to promote the production of biomass for energy production. Due to a relatively short growing season, Sweden relies heavily on imported food and agricultural products. In 2003, agricultural and food products accounted for 8% of Sweden's imports.

23 ANIMAL HUSBANDRY

Although the long winters necessitate indoor feeding from October to May, pastoral farming is important, and about 80% of farm income derives from animal products, especially dairy products. In 2005, there were 1.6 million head of cattle. Beef production totaled 142,100 tons in 2005. Liquid milk production totaled 3.32 million tons in 2005. Other dairy products made that year were cheese, 121,800 tons, and butter, 50,000 tons. Because the oversufficiency of butter before 1970 weakened Sweden's position in world markets, the government encouraged farmers to shift to meat production. An agricultural reform program in the early 1990s dismantled many of the price regulations and subsidies for products like milk and meat in favor of market-oriented pricing. As these adjustments were made, the number of dairy producers fell from 24,786 in 1990 to 12,168 by 2000. Sweden's beef industry is now supported by direct EU subsidies and in programs connected with less favored area and environment supports.

The sheep population was 479,400 in 2005, and pigs numbered 1,823,000. There were 6,600,000 chickens during the same year. Fur farms breed large numbers of mink and a declining number of fox. Reindeer are raised by 51 Sami (Lapp) communities in the north, and between 1970 and 2003 the reindeer population in Lapp villages increased from 166,200 to 238,800.

24 FISHING

Fish is an important item in the Swedish diet, and Sweden is both a major importer of fish products and a principal supplier to other countries. Göteborg, Bohus, and Halland are the principal fishing districts, but large quantities of fish are caught all along the coasts. At the beginning of 2004, there were 1,597 vessels in the Swedish fishing fleet, with 1,731 professional fishermen. Herring, cod, plaice, flounder, salmon, eel, mackerel, and shellfish are the most important saltwater varieties. Freshwater fish include trout, salmon, and crayfish, a national delicacy. In 2003, there were 360 aquacultural enterprises, yielding 4,585 tons of fish. The saltwater fish catch increased from 228,000 tons in 1971 to 259,000 tons in 1984, overcoming a significant drop in the 1974–79 period because of government conservation measures and the declining number of fishermen. The total catch amounted to 293,209 tons in 2003. By tradition, a large part of the annual catch is landed in Denmark. Fish for feed is the largest single commodity, accounting for 65% of the 2003 catch. Total landings were valued at $107.5 million in 2003. Herring and cod accounted for 19% and 6%, respectively, of total landings.

25 FORESTRY

Sweden is one of the world's most heavily forested countries, with forests covering some 70% of the land area. Around 55% of the land area consists of productive forestry land, for a total of 22.7 million hectares (56.1 million acres). The percentage has only varied between 55.5% and 58.1 since the first National Forestry Inventory of 1923–29. Virtually all of Sweden's forests are regrowth; virgin forests cover 788,000 hectares (1,947,000 acres) and are almost exclusively found in national parks and nature reserves. The growing stock is estimated at 3 billion cu m (106 billion cu ft). The annual growth amounts to about 101 million cu m (3.5 billion cu ft). Annual removals decreased from an average of 70.8 million cu m (2.5 billion cu ft) during 1970/71–1974/75 to an average of 55.5 million cu m (1.96 billion cu ft) during 1976/77–1980/81 but increased to roughly 83 million cu m (2.93 billion cu ft) during recent years. Important varieties include spruce (46% of commercial stands), pine (38%), birch (11%), and oak, beech, alder, and aspen (5% combined). About half of the total forest area is owned by private persons and 30% by private corporations and rural communes. The government owns most of the remaining 20% of forests, but they are located, for the most part, in the north, where climatic conditions slow the trees' growth.

Forestry and farming are interdependent everywhere except in the most fertile plains; in northern Sweden, almost one of every two men works in the woods for at least part of the winter. Both the number of workers and the productivity of those who stayed on declined in the late 1970s. Since the early 1970s, the number of employees in the forestry sector has fallen by over 40%.

The exploitation of forest wealth ranks second in importance in the economy (after metal-based industry). Sweden competes with Canada for world leadership in the export of wood pulp and is the world's leading exporter of cellulose. In 2004, net exports of wood and wood products came to $14.9 billion and made up 12% of exports. The total timber felled in 2004 amounted to an estimated 63.3 million cu m (2.38 billion cu ft), of which coniferous sawlogs accounted for 53% of production; pulpwood, 38%; and fuel wood,

9%. Mostly roads and trains are used to transport timber; only a few of the biggest rivers are used. About 70% of timber harvested comes from clear-cutting, and 30% from thinning. About 60% of Sweden's annual forestry production is exported every year. Sweden is the third-largest exporter of paper and board, supplying 10% of the export market, with production amounting to 3% of the world's total. In 2004, Sweden's production of sawn timber reached its highest level ever. That year, Sweden's 180 major saw mills processed 16.9 million cu m (597 million cu ft) of lumber, 44 mills produced 12.8 million tons of pulp, and 46 paper facilities manufactured 11.9 million tons of paper.

A forest policy introduced in 1980 coordinates forestry measures more closely with industrial needs and places increased emphasis on clear-cutting and more complete use of the forest biomass, including stumps and small trees. The government, through the Forest Commission, enforces pest control, the prevention of premature cutting, and the use of proper methods of preserving permanent forest cover. The government decided in the early 1990s to eliminate subsidies to commercial forestry because such subsidies had been counterproductive in a strongly competitive international market. Nature conservation agreements between forest owners and the government have been established to protect and develop natural areas. Between 1994 and 2003, 1,750 agreements were negotiated, with landowners' compensation totaling $11.2 million.

In January 2005 a severe storm raged through southern Sweden and caused major damage to forests. About 75 million cu m (2.6 billion cu ft) of timber, nearly the total annual cut for all of Sweden, was damaged by the storm, 80% Norway spruce.

26 MINING

Since ancient days, mining and the iron industry have been of great importance in the economic life of Sweden, which was among the most active mining countries in Europe. In addition to iron ore, Sweden also is a producer of primary metals such as zinc, copper and lead, as well as industrial minerals such as dolomite, feldspar, granite, kaolin, quartz and limestone. Sweden accounted for a large percentage of Western Europe's iron output, and was home to the region's largest gold mine.

Iron-ore production in 2004 (concentrate and pellets) was estimated at 22,300,000 metric tons, up from an estimated 21,500,000 metric tons in 2003. The Bergslagen region, in central Sweden, yielded high-grade ores for quality steel. Gold mine output in 2004 totaled 5,300 kg, up from 4,300 kg in 2003, while silver mine output in 2004 totaled 292,600 kg, down from 306,800 kg in 2003. Lead mine output in 2004 totaled 33,900 metric tons, while copper mine output, in that year, totaled 85,500 metric tons. Zinc mine output in 2004 totaled 160,600 metric tons. Lead, copper, zinc, gold, and silver were produced in the rich Skellefte (Boliden) region, where bismuth, cobalt, and huge quantities of arsenic were also found. The open-pit Björgal gold mine upgraded its facility, to increase production capacity to 3,000 kg per year, from 2,600 kg per year in 1996. Further south, phosphate, tungsten, kyanite, and pyrite were found. Sweden also produced hydraulic cement, kaolin clay, feldspar, fertilizer, graphite, lime, quartz, quartzite, dimension and crushed stone (including dolomite, granite (for domestic use and for export), limestone, sandstone, and slate), sulfur, and soapstone talc. Marble (in Askersund) and ilmenite were also found in Sweden.

27 ENERGY AND POWER

Sweden has no proven reserves of oil or natural gas, and only small reserves of coal. However, the country does possess the ability to refine crude oil, and with many rivers, waterfalls, and lakes, the country has favorable conditions for waterpower.

As of 1 January 2005, Sweden had no proven reserves of natural gas or crude oil, but did have a crude oil refining capacity of 434,000 barrels per day. Sweden's limited coal reserves, as of 2001, were placed at one million short tons. Since the 1970s, Sweden has been reducing its petroleum imports. The share of oil in the primary energy supply declined from nearly 70% in 1979 to 31.6% in 2002. In the same year, nuclear energy accounted for another 29.6% of primary energy, hydroelectricity 30%, coal 4.1%, natural gas 1.5%, and renewable sources for the rest. In 2002, Sweden's imports of all petroleum products, including crude oil, averaged 510,990 barrels per day. Of that amount, crude oil accounted for 370,430 barrels per day. Refined oil output in 2002 averaged 381,640 barrels per day, while demand that year for refined products averaged 337,340 barrels per day.

In 2002, Sweden's demand for dry natural gas totaled 34.47 billion cu ft, all of which was met by imports, which came to 34.75 billion cu ft. There was no domestic production of coal in 2002. All of Sweden's coal needs were met by imports. In that year, imports of coal totaled 3,666,000 short tons, of which 3,042,000 short tons consisted of hard coal, and 624,000 tons of coke.

Sweden's electric generating sector is marked by a high dependence upon hydroelectric power, and to a lesser extent on nuclear power. Total electric power generating capacity in 2002 was 33.793 million kW, of which hydroelectric generating capacity came to 16.523 million kW and nuclear power at 9.436 million kW. Conventional thermal fuel generating capacity in 2002 stood at 7.536 million kW, with geothermal/other sources at 0.298 million kW. For that same year, electric power output totaled 140.662 billion kWh, of which 4.4% was from fossil fuels, 46.8% from hydropower, 45.6% from nuclear power, and 3.2% from other sources. Consumption of electricity in 2002 was 136.172 billion kWh.

Sweden's heavy use of nuclear energy stems from an ambitious nuclear energy program, under which seven nuclear reactors came into operation between 1972 and 1980. By 1986, 12 units offered a capacity of 9.4 million kWh. However, by 2010, all 12 will be shut down. Plants fired by natural gas will replace nuclear energy's role. Energy conservation, development of alternative energy sources, and increased use of imported coal are also planned.

More than half of Sweden's hydroelectric output is produced underground. Because of environmental considerations, high production costs, and low world market prices, Sweden's substantial uranium reserves—some 250,000–300,000 tons (or about 20% of the known world reserves)—have not been exploited.

28 INDUSTRY

The basic resources for industrial development are forests, iron ore, and waterpower. Forest products, machinery, and motor vehicles are primary exports. Industrial production accounted for 29% of GDP in 2001. From 1990 to 1992, Swedish industry suffered as a result of the deep national recession as well as an overpriced labor pool. In those years, manufacturing output fell by 10%. Between 1989 and 1992, 260,000 Swedes lost their jobs in the manufacturing sector. As the economy rebounded in subsequent years, however, especially the growth turnaround in 1994–96, industrial output has grown. In 1996, it was up 17% from 1990. Between 1993 and 1996, industrial investments more than doubled. Industrial growth remained a solid 4.5% in 2001 and 5.5% in 2004.

Since the end of World War II, emphasis has shifted from production of consumer goods to the manufacture of export items. Swedish-made ships, airplanes, and automobiles are considered outstanding in quality. Sweden's motor vehicle producers are Volvo and SAAB-Scania. As evidence of the growing consolidation of the world automotive industry, however, in 1990 the US's General Motors Corp. made a successful offer for half of Saab's automotive operations, and in 2000 it bought the remaining 50%. In 1999, the US's Ford Motor Co. purchased Sweden's Volvo car operations (excluding its heavy truck operations). In 2005, General Motors indicated it would begin to make the first truly non-Swedish Saab, by building the automobiles in Germany to save costs.

Before World War II, virtually the entire tonnage of iron and steel products consisted of high-grade steels, but in recent years exports have included considerable quantities of commercial grades. Transport equipment and iron and steel are of declining importance, however, while exports of machinery, precision equipment, chemicals, and paper have been growing in value.

Sweden is a world leader in telecommunications, computers, electronics, robotics, pharmaceutical and medical products, and biotechnology. Sweden's Ericsson is the world's largest telecommunications service provider, with 18,000 service professionals in over 140 countries in 2005. Ericsson supports networks that handle more than 550 million subscribers. Sweden has the largest number of biotechnology companies per capita in the world.

29 SCIENCE AND TECHNOLOGY

Sweden's high-quality scientific and technological development is renowned throughout the world. Technological products invented or developed by Swedish firms include the self-aligning ball bearing, the cream separator, the three-phase electric motor, and a refrigerator without moving parts. Sweden's more recent applications of sophisticated technology range from powder metallurgy to the Hasselblad camera and the Viggen jet fighter. Six of Sweden's largest industrial corporations are engineering companies: Volvo, SAAB-Scania, ASEA, Electrolux, SKF, and L. M. Ericsson. In 2002, high-tech exports were valued at $10.76 billion and accounted for 16% of manufactured exports.

State-financed research, centering on the universities, is directed by the Council for Planning and Coordination of Research. Long-term industrial research and development is the responsibility of the government through the National Board for Technological Development. In 1987–97, Swedish students graduating with science and engineering degrees account for 38% of all university students. In 2002, of all bachelor's degrees awarded, 30.3% were for the sciences (natural, mathematics and computers, engineering). In 2001, expenditures for research and development (R&D) totaled $9.6 billion, or 4.27% of GDP. Of that amount, the business sector accounted for 71.9%, followed by the government at 21%, higher education at 3.8% and foreign sources at 3.4%. As of 2001, there were 5,171 scientists and engineers engaged in R&D per million people.

Institutions that have played an important role in the advancement of science, both in Sweden and throughout the world, are the Nobel Foundation, which sponsors annual awards in chemistry, physics, and physiology or medicine, as well as for peace, literature, and economic science; the Royal Academy of Sciences, founded in 1739 in Stockholm; the Royal Swedish Academy of Engineering Sciences, founded in 1919 at Stockholm; and the Karolinska Institute, founded in 1810 in Stockholm, specializing in medical research. Sweden has 18 universities that offer courses in basic and applied sciences.

³⁰ DOMESTIC TRADE

Stockholm, Gothenburg, and Malmö are the nation's primary distribution centers. Of the country's retail business, most is in private hands, but the consumer cooperative movement has long been one of the strongest in Europe. The local organizations belong to the Cooperative Union and Wholesale Society, a central buying and manufacturing organization, which operates factories, department stores, supermarkets, and specialized shops. The Swedish Federation of Trade is another important organization for importers and traders in the private sector. Competition between the cooperatives and private enterprise has improved selling methods, so that Sweden's self-service shops are among the most modern in Europe.

Department stores are located in the major cities. Franchising has become popular in the fast-food, apparel, home improvement, and business services sectors. Wholesale and retail outlets, as well as supermarkets, are plentiful. Value-added taxes apply to all goods and services. The general VAT tax is 25%, with reduced rates of 12% on food and 6% on items including books, magazines, and personal transportation.

The nation's three major trade fair/exhibition sites are the Stockholm International Fair, the Swedish Exhibition and Congress Center, and the Sollentuna Fair.

Offices and stores are open on weekdays from 9 AM to 5 or 6 PM (in summer, sometimes to 3 or 4 PM) and close early on Saturdays. However, many stores stay open one night a week, and some department stores are open on Sundays. Many businesses are closed, or management is unavailable, for extended vacations in the summer and around the Christmas holidays.

³¹ FOREIGN TRADE

Sweden is one of the world's leading free-trading nations, with about half the economy dependent upon trade, and business operating largely free of political influence. The volume of Sweden's foreign trade has increased very rapidly since World War II, mainly as a result of the gradual liberalization of trade restrictions within the framework of the OECD, EFTA, and the EU. Telecommunications equipment, automobile manufacturing, and logging dominate export commodities from Sweden. Sweden has one of the most open and competitive markets in the world, as of 2005 ranking behind only Finland and the United States in the International Competitiveness Ranking. Sweden is home to more multinational corporations per capita than any other nation in the world. It is at the economic center of the Nordic and Baltic world, a market of over 27 million consumers. The United States is the number one

export market for Swedish products (followed by Germany, Norway, the United Kingdom, and Denmark), while imports from the United States rank 8th, behind Germany, Denmark, the United Kingdom, Norway, the Netherlands, France, and Finland. In 2004, with exports of $123.1 billion and imports of $99.6 billion, Sweden had a trade surplus of $23.5 billion. The major exports in 2004 were machinery and transportation equipment (51.4% of total exports), wood and paper products (12.2%), chemicals and rubber products (12.1%), and miscellaneous manufactures (11%). The major imports in 2004 were machinery and transportation equipment (45.8% of all imports), miscellaneous manufactures (19.7%), chemicals and rubber products (12.1%), and mineral fuels and lubricants (9.7%).

Principal Trading Partners – Sweden (2003)

(In millions of US dollars)

Country	Exports	Imports	Balance
World	101,572.6	83,380.7	18,191.9
United States	11,659.2	3,259.4	8,399.8
Germany	10,256.0	15,600.0	-5,344.0
Norway	8,574.4	6,646.1	1,928.3
United Kingdom	7,942.4	6,698.9	1,243.5
Denmark	6,550.5	7,519.8	-969.3
Finland	5,853.3	4,660.7	1,192.6
Netherlands	5,046.8	5,671.7	-624.9
France-Monaco	4,962.6	4,605.5	357.1
Belgium	4,598.9	3,496.3	1,102.6
Italy-San Marino-Holy See	3,646.1	2,882.1	764.0

(…) data not available or not significant.

SOURCE: *2003 International Trade Statistics Yearbook,* New York: United Nations, 2004.

Balance of Payments – Sweden (2003)

(In millions of US dollars)

Current Account		**22,844.0**
Balance on goods		18,933.0
Imports	-83,147.0	
Exports	102,080.0	
Balance on services		1,883.0
Balance on income		297.0
Current transfers		1,732.0
Capital Account		**-46.0**
Financial Account		**-20,163.0**
Direct investment abroad		-17,341.0
Direct investment in Sweden		3,268.0
Portfolio investment assets		-13,701.0
Portfolio investment liabilities		4,134.0
Financial derivatives		1,081.0
Other investment assets		-8,349.0
Other investment liabilities		10,744.0
Net Errors and Omissions		**-558.0**
Reserves and Related Items		**-2,076.0**

(…) data not available or not significant.

SOURCE: *Balance of Payment Statistics Yearbook 2004,* Washington, DC: International Monetary Fund, 2004.

32 BALANCE OF PAYMENTS

From 1974 through 1985, Sweden ran annual current-account deficits (except in 1984) because of increases in world oil prices and a decline in the competitiveness of Swedish export products on the world market. Until 1977, deficits were financed mainly through long-term foreign private borrowing by the private sector. Thereafter, however, central government borrowing expanded rapidly. Current account deficits increased through much of the 1990s, but a turnaround began in 1996 when the deficit comprised 2% of GDP after a high of 12% in 1993. A rebounding trade balance surplus and a turnaround in direct investment aided in the improvement. The lifting of controls on foreign direct investment, combined with improved competitiveness accruing from greater wage restraint and rising productivity, are expected to bring continued interest in investing in Sweden. Also attractive is Sweden's liberal international investment policy, allowing 100% foreign ownership of virtually any sector, other than certain types of transportation and arms manufacture. The current account surplus was $28.7 billion in 2004 (equivalent to 8.3% of GDP).

33 BANKING AND SECURITIES

The Central Bank of Sweden (Sveriges Riksbank), founded in 1656, is the oldest bank in the world. It is the bank of issue and regulates domestic banking operations. The European Central Bank is responsible for determining monetary policy and setting interest rates. The largest commercial bank is the Skandinaviska Enskilda Banken. In the early 1990s, Swedish banks suffered severe losses; the government was forced to intervene and support two of the five largest commercial banks, Nordbanken and Gota Bank, by taking them over and eventually merging them, and the savings bank Forsta Sparbanken. By the end of 1996, Swedish banks showed improved results, with reduced credit losses and a stricter control of costs since the banking crises set in at the beginning of the 1990s. The smaller banks serve provincial interests. Deposit accounts at various lengths of call are used for short-term credit by industry and trade. The deregulation of financial markets has paved the way for foreign banks to open offices in Sweden. In 1997, Sweden's banking sector saw a series of mergers and acquisitions as Svenska Handelsbanken, the nation's largest bank, acquired the country's largest mortgage lender, Stadshypotek. Swedbank and Föreningsbanken merged, creating the second-largest bank. ForeningsSparbanken is now trying to merge with Skandinaviska Enskilda Banken (SEB) to compete with Nordea for dominance of the Nordic banking market. However, this deal must still garner the approval of the EU. Den Donske Bank, based in Denmark, made the first incursion by a foreign bank into the Swedish retail sector when it purchased Ostgöta Enskilda Bank. By December 2000, 41 commercial banks remained in Sweden.

Mortgage banks of various types meet the needs of property owners, home builders, farmers, and shipbuilders. Credit also is extended by some 500 local rural credit societies and by about an equal number of agricultural cooperatives. There are four semi-governmental credit concerns, organized as business companies and created in cooperation with private commercial banks to facilitate long-term lending to agriculture, industry, small industry, and exports. Although the Riksbank's note issue is not tied to its gold reserves, there is an adjustable legal limit.

The International Monetary Fund reports that in 2001, M2—an aggregate equal to currency and demand deposits plus savings deposits, small time deposits, and money market mutual funds—was $88.1 billion. The money market rate, the rate at which financial institutions lend to one another in the short term, was 4.08%. The discount rate, the interest rate at which the central bank lends to financial institutions in the short term, was 2%.

The Riksbank lends money to the commercial banks and other credit associations against securities. Traditionally, the Swedish people have preferred to save by placing money in these banks rather than by direct investment, although this seemed likely to change if the Swedish pension reforms of 1997 were fully enacted, allowing workers to decide how to invest a portion of their retirement reserves. In 1992, 118 Swedish companies and 10 foreign companies were listed on the Stockholm Stock Exchange (Stockholms Fondbörs), which was computerized that year. In 1997, the Stockholm Stock Exchange entered into a joint equity trading union with the Danish bourse, creating the first trans-national link of its kind in Europe. The joint equities market became Europe's sixth-largest.

Profits from the sale of securities are taxable provided they have been owned for less than five years. The capital gain is wholly taxable for securities held less than two years, but only 40% of the gain is taxable if the shares have been held more than two years. For machinery and equipment a minimum write-off period of three years is prescribed. The 1985 deregulation of the credit market included the removal of ceilings on lending banks, finance houses, and housing credit institutions and had the effect of diminishing part of Sweden's "gray market": direct contact between companies and private individuals with money for loans. Stockbroking is authorized by the Bank Inspection Board. As of 2004, a total of 256 companies were listed on the Stockholmsborsen, which had a market capitalization of $376.781 billion.

34 INSURANCE

The Swedish people are very life-insurance conscious. In 1985, there were at least 560 Swedish insurance companies. Most companies are very small, however, and only 65 firms operated on a nationwide scale in 1995. The five largest companies held almost 80% of total insurance assets. Automobile liability insurance is compulsory in Sweden, as are nuclear liability and workers' compensation.

Since the deregulation of financial markets in the late 1980s, new credit institutions have appeared which target niche sectors in banking and other financial services. Insurance companies, such as Skandia, have created their own banks. The National Insurance Pension Fund and private insurance funds are among the largest single domestic investors on the Stockholm Stock Exchange. The insurance regulatory authority is the Financial Supervisory Authority which is an independent state agency. In 2003, the value of all direct insurance premiums written totaled $21.040 billion, of which life insurance premiums accounted for $14.297 billion. In that same year, Sweden's top nonlife insurer was IF Skade, which had gross written nonlife premiums of $1.1 billion, while the country's leading life insurer was Alecta, with gross written life insurance premiums of $2.3 billion.

35 PUBLIC FINANCE

The financial year extends from 1 July to 30 June. Estimates are prepared in the autumn by the Ministry of the Budget and examined by the Riksdag early the following year. The budget contains two sections: an operating budget and a capital budget, the latter generally representing investments in state enterprises. The policy of running a surplus on the budget in boom years and a deficit in depression was used in the period between the two world wars and has been continued as a way of combating inflation. From 1982 to 1989, the budget balance improved from a deficit equivalent to about 13% of GDP to a surplus of nearly 2% of GDP. In 1990, however, a deficit reappeared that was equivalent to 1.2% of GDP. In 1991 and 1992, the budget deficits widened to 4.3% and 9.6% of GDP, respectively. The deficit increased to 12.3% of GDP in 1993, before beginning a sharp decline due to austerity measures, put in place by the Social Democrats; although smaller, deficits remained the norm through the late 1990s. Surpluses were projected for the early 2000s.

The US Central Intelligence Agency (CIA) estimated that in 2005 Sweden's central government took in revenues of approximately $210.5 billion and had expenditures of $205.9 billion. Revenues minus expenditures totaled approximately $4.6 billion. Public debt in 2005 amounted to 50.3% of GDP. Total external debt was $516.1 billion.

The International Monetary Fund (IMF) reported that in 2002, the most recent year for which it had data, central government revenues were Kr890.5 billion and expenditures were Kr883.2 billion. The value of revenues was us$91 million and expenditures us$90 million, based on an exchange rate for 2002 of us$1 = Kr9.7371 as reported by the IMF. Government outlays by function were as follows: general public services, 23.5%; defense, 5.7%; public order and safety, 3.2%; economic affairs, 9.4%; environmental protection, 0.5%; housing and community amenities, 0.6%; health, 2.9%; recreation, culture, and religion, 0.8%; education, 6.4%; and social protection, 47.2%.

36 TAXATION

With so many social services in effect, and a virtual absence of poverty, Sweden's personal income taxes are the highest in the world. As of 2005, Sweden's top personal income tax rates effectively stood at 53% to 58%. Depending upon the locality, this included municipal income taxes on employment income averaging 31%, in addition to national income tax rates of 20–25%. In addition, capital income is taxed at a flat rate of 30%. Income of non-residents is subject to a flat rate of 25%. Personal deductions vary between 8,600 and 18,100 krona ($6,364 and $13,400). A health tax is levied at 1.5%. There is also a real estate tax.

In contrast, corporations are taxed relatively lightly in comparison with those in many other countries. The national income tax rate on corporations was 28% in 2005 (separate municipal income tax on corporations was abolished as of 1985), with no distinction between distributed and undistributed profits. Capital gains are taxed like other corporate income at 28%, although capital gains on shares held for business purposes are tax exempt. The withholding tax on dividends is 30%, which is applied to nonresidents. Royalties paid to residents are not taxed, but those paid to nonresidents are subject to the corporate rate. These rates are often reduced or eliminated in bilateral tax treaties. Interest income is not subject to withholding.

Tax liability is determined according to a firm's books so long as these are properly kept. Companies are allowed considerable discretion in determining their net income for any particular year; they can take advantage of the flexible rules governing the valuation of stocks and the depreciation of equipment and machinery. Swedish companies may set aside an investment reserve in boom years and use this reserve in years of slack production.

For decades, the Swedish ratio of indirect taxes to total tax revenue was one of the lowest in the world. During World War II and the early postwar years, however, a national sales tax was in effect. The national sales tax was replaced by a value-added tax (VAT) with a standard rate of 10% on 1 January 1969. The standard rate was increased to 17.65% in 1971, to 20.63% in 1977, to 46% in 1980, to 21.51% in 1981, to 23.46% in 1983, to 25% in 1992, where it has since remained, as of 2005. Almost all goods and most services are subject to this tax. There are two reduced rates: 12%, applied to food, and 6%, applied to domestic passenger transport, newspapers, and, as of 1 January 2002, books and magazines. A zero VAT rate applies to printing services, ship and airplane building and repair, sea rescue services, prescription medicine, aircraft fuel, and gold supplied to the Central Bank.

37 CUSTOMS AND DUTIES

Tariffs were established in the 19th century to allow for the development of Swedish industry, but the rates have traditionally been among the lowest in the world. Sweden subscribes to the OECD trade liberalization program and imports, with few exceptions, are not subject to controls. As a member of EFTA, Sweden abolished customs duties against other EFTA countries by the end of 1966. In 1991, Sweden formally began the process of joining the European Union and officially became a member on 1 January 1995. Some 90% of imports from developing countries are duty-free.

In general, the importation of raw materials is duty-free. Import duties are based on freight, insurance and handling costs, broker fees, package costs, royalties or license fees, and the seller's yield if sale will be to a third party. Import restrictions apply mainly to protected agricultural products, automobiles, and trade with Eastern Europe and the Far East. Sweden applies common external European Union tariffs to imports from the United States at rates ranging from 2–14% for industrial products. Other import taxes include a 25% value-added tax (VAT). A lower 12% VAT applies for food and selected services, and a 6% rate for periodicals and books.

38 FOREIGN INVESTMENT

Sweden has some of the most liberal foreign investment laws in the world. Sweden's corporate income tax rate of 28%, one of the lowest in Europe, makes Sweden an attractive target of foreign investors. It is open to nearly all foreign investment and allows 100% foreign ownership, except in certain transportation sectors (air and maritime) and in arms manufacture. For the period 1988–1990, Sweden was ranked third of 140 countries on UNCTAD's Inward FDI Potential Index, after the United States and Canada. For the period 1988–2000, Sweden was number two, behind only the United States. Investing in Sweden is also attractive due to its competent employees, excellent infrastructure, and good access to capital. On the negative side are high labor costs, rigid labor legislation, and overall high costs in Sweden.

Sweden's outward FDI rose steadily during the 1990s, from $1.4 billion in 1993 to a peak of $41.7 billion in 2000, ahead of inward FDI for the year by $18.3 billion. Outward FDI dropped to $6.2 billion in 2001 but rose to $11.3 billion in 2002. Inward FDI flow was only $3.7 billion in 1993, but had reached $19.5 billion by 1998. FDI inflows peaked in 1999 at $60.8 billion, then moderated to $23.4 billion in 2000. The world economic slowdown reduced FDI inflows to $12.7 billion in 2001, and an estimated $11.5 billion in 2002. These figures must be considered in light of FDI flows worldwide during that period, which dropped 50%. Another dramatic decline of FDI inflows took place in 2003, with a net outflow from Sweden amounting to $15.7 billion. The rate of net outflow slowed somewhat in 2004. Over the 2001–05 period, FDI inflows amounted to 2.5% of GDP.

By 2001, cumulative FDI in Sweden totaled $155 billion, the 10th-highest total in the world. The countries with the largest Swedish investments in 2005 were, in order: the United States, Finland, the United Kingdom, the Netherlands, Belgium/Luxembourg, Norway, Germany, Switzerland, Denmark, and France.

39 ECONOMIC DEVELOPMENT

Between 1946 and 1953, the Swedish economy was dominated by expansion. Thereafter, although production continued to increase (at a lessened rate), inflation was a matter of concern. Expansion of output slowed down during the international oil crisis and recession of 1974–75, largely as a result of a weakening of foreign demand for Swedish products, but employment remained high. Thus far, the economy has managed to contain inflationary trends within reasonable limits. Although some industries (the railways, iron-ore mines, etc.) have been nationalized for a long time, private concerns carry on most of Sweden's industry, in terms of both number of workers and value of output.

During periods of unemployment such as the world recession of 1980–81, the central government and the municipalities have expended funds to provide additional employment and to keep the unemployment rate relatively low. The jobless have been put to work building dwellings and highways, extending reforestation work, and constructing water and sewer installations, harbors, lighthouses, railroads, defense projects, and telecommunications facilities. Although the government resorted to stockpiling industrial goods to combat the economic slowdown in the mid-1970s, the cost was considered too high, and the policy was not repeated during the recession of the early 1980s. More recently, the emphasis has been on cutting costs and restraining inflation to make Swedish goods more competitive in the international marketplace.

Regional development has been fostered by the use of investment funds (a tax device permitting enterprises to set aside tax-free reserves during boom years to be used for investment during recessions), relief works, and government lending to small-scale industry. A national program for regional development was introduced in 1972 to develop services and job opportunities in provinces that have lagged behind in industrial development. Projects in northern Sweden benefited most from this program.

In 1991, the government announced a plan to privatize 35 wholly or partially state-owned firms with annual turnovers totaling KR150 billion. This program was delayed by the economic recession, however. A 10-year, KR110 billion program of infrastructure investment was announced in 1994. More than 90% of the money would be spent on the road and rail networks, and a bridge that would link Malmö with Copenhagen. The Øresund Bridge opened in 2000, covering 10.5 miles (17 km). It physically links Sweden with the rest of Western Europe.

Sweden's entry into the EU in 1995 dominated the second half of the 1990s. As a result of EU membership, Sweden harmonized its trade laws with those its fellow members and continued privatization and liberalization of its economy. Sweden also qualified for membership in the Economic and Monetary Union (EMU) but decided to opt out. Future membership was contingent upon passage of a referendum, which was held in September 2003. Swedes decided not to join the euro zone by a vote of 56% to 42%. Along with the United Kingdom and Denmark, Sweden continues to stand aside from the EU's 12 other countries that, by 2005, had abandoned their old currencies.

As of 2002, around 34% of the labor force was employed in the public sector, and general government expenditure accounted for around 55% of GDP. Economic growth in the late 1990s and in the early 2000s was relatively strong, employment rates were high, there were large surpluses in both the general government and the external current accounts, and the public debt was declining. Despite the global economic slowdown of 2001–02, with the Swedish labor market situation weakening, by 2004 signs of a cyclical recovery had become clear. The strongest signs of recovery could be seen in the export industry. Sweden has made large investments in education and entrepreneurship, and is at the forefront of the global telecommunications and IT industry. These factors have contributed to a well-performing economy.

The key challenge for the Swedish economy will be to maintain the core of the social-welfare system as the population ages. Because Sweden has a budget surplus, it is better placed than most other OECD nations to do this. By 2015, the number of people 65 years of age and older is expected to be 25% larger than in 2005, while the total population in other age categories will remain largely unchanged. Although this trend is not unique to Sweden, it will need to respond to the higher demand for medical care and related social services. In this light, high labor force participation and high employment are desirable.

40 SOCIAL DEVELOPMENT

Sweden has been called the model welfare state; every citizen is guaranteed a minimum subsistence income and medical care. Social welfare legislation was introduced relatively early and was greatly expanded after World War II. The system is financed partly by insurance premium payments and partly by state and local taxation. Basic benefits are often increased by cost-of-living supplements. Employers and employees contribute to the program, with government funding certain aspects of the system. All residents are covered by sickness and maternity benefits. There is also a universal system for family allowances completely funded by the government.

Old-age pensions are paid to all residents 65 years of age or older, but an earlier retirement is possible, with a reduction in pension benefits. Under the new system, there is a flexible retirement age, starting from 61, and is funded by 6.95% of employee earnings and 6.4% of employer payroll. Unemployment insurance is administered by the trade unions and provides benefits according to salary to those who voluntarily enroll. Unemployment relief, through monetary assistance or public works, is provided by the central government or by state-subsidized municipalities.

Compulsory health service was introduced in 1955. Hospital care is free for up to two years. Medical services and medicines are provided at substantially reduced rates or, in some cases, without charge. In the event of illness, employed persons and women staying at home to raise children receive cash payments and get further benefits according to income. Costs of confinement and maternity allowances for women are covered by health insurance. There is also a national program of dental insurance.

Workers' compensation is coordinated with the national health service scheme. This type of insurance, financed entirely by employers, covers work time as well as travel to and from work for all employees. Benefits include free medical treatment, medicines, and appliances. Annuities are paid to persons permanently disabled, and funeral benefits and pensions to dependents are provided in case of death. Public assistance is provided for blind or infirm persons confined to their homes and to people who are in sanitariums, special hospitals, or charitable institutions.

The law requires women to have equal opportunities and equal pay. Despite these legal protections, women are underrepresented in higher-paying jobs, and often receive less pay for equal work. The Equal Opportunity Ombudsman, a government official, reviews equality plans required by employers and investigates allegations of gender discrimination. Violence against women, primarily spousal abuse, persists, although the government has many programs to deal with these issues. The laws protect women, and shelters and other assistance to victims is available. Strict laws protecting children from abuse are also in effect.

There is general tolerance for religious and ethnic minorities, although right-wing and neo-nazi activities are reported. The government protects and supports minority languages. Human rights are deeply respected in Sweden.

41 HEALTH

The national health insurance system, financed by the state and employer contributions, was established in January 1955 and covers all Swedish citizens and alien residents. Total expenditure for health care insurance was 7.9% of the gross domestic product. Principal health care reform issues in the 1990s include universal and equal access to services and equitable funding of health care. For rural medical attention, doctors are supplemented by district nurses. Only about 5% of all physicians are in full-time private practice. The corresponding figure for private dentists, however, is more than 50%. Swedish hospitals are well known for their high standards.

Cardiovascular disease accounted for about half of all deaths; cancer was the next leading cause of death. Many health problems are related to environment and lifestyle (including tobacco smoking, alcohol consumption, and overeating). The smoking rates were similar between men (22%) and women (24%) over the age of 15. Periodic campaigns are conducted to reduce tuberculosis (with a nationwide X-ray survey), cancer, rheumatism, and venereal diseases.

Immunization rates for children under age one were as follows: diphtheria, pertussis, and tetanus, 99% and measles, 96%. There is a well-developed prenatal service. Children receive free dental care until the age of 20.

Sweden's population is the world's oldest; nearly one in five people is 64 years of age or older. In 2005, average life expectancy in Sweden was 80.40 years. As of 2002, the crude birth rate and overall mortality rate were estimated at, respectively, 9.8 and 10.6 per 1,000 people. Infant mortality has been sharply reduced, from 60 per 1,000 live births in 1920 to 2.77 per 1,000 in 2000, one of the lowest rates in the world.

The HIV/AIDS prevalence was 0.10 per 100 adults in 2003. As of 2004, there were approximately 3,600 people living with HIV/AIDS in the country. There were an estimated 100 deaths from AIDS in 2003.

42 HOUSING

In 1998, there were 4.3 million dwellings nationwide. Of these, about 2.3 million were multi-family dwellings and the remainder were one- or two-family homes. In 1998, about 20% of all dwellings were tenant owned, 40% were rental units, and 20% were owner occupied. There were about 4.2 million households that year, with an average of 2.1 people per household. In 1999, 15,000 new dwellings were started. The projected number of dwellings in 2004 was 4,379,541.

Nearly all of Sweden's housing stock was modernized during a mass housing improvement program in the 1980s. Most houses are built by private contractors, but more than half of new housing is designed, planned, and financed by nonprofit organizations and cooperatives. NPOs and cooperatives provide dwellings for members who are designated as tenant-owners of their dwellings.

The government subsidizes new construction and reconditioning, helps various groups to obtain better housing, and extends credit at interest rates lower than those obtainable in the open market. A system of rent controls, introduced in 1942 and designed to freeze rents at the existing rate, was abolished in 1975. It has been replaced by a policy known as a utility-value provision, through which the rent of a flat may not be higher than that of a similar flat in the same area which is of the same general value to the occupant. Many tenant organizations negotiate rental agreements with landlords and rent increases can be reviewed by a tribunal. The National Board of Housing, Building, and Planning estimates that 250,000 new dwellings will be built from 2000–10. About 30,000 dwellings per year will be renovated or rebuilt during the same period.

43 EDUCATION

Education is free and compulsory between ages 7 and 15. A nine-year comprehensive course was introduced in 1962. All pupils receive the same course of instruction for six years; beginning in the seventh year the curriculum is differentiated, and students may choose between a classical and a vocational course. About 80% of all students then enter gymnasium (senior high school) or continuation schools. The gymnasium specializes in classical or modern languages or science; after the three-year course, students may take a final graduating examination. The continuation schools offer a two-year curriculum that is more practical and specialized than that of the gymnasium and leads more quickly to the practice of a trade. Both comprehensive schools and secondary schools are administered by local authorities, while the central government provides grants-in-aid to cover the greater part of the costs.

In 2001, about 75% of children between the ages of three and six were enrolled in some type of preschool program. Primary school enrollment in 2003 was estimated at about 100% of age-eligible students. The same year, secondary school enrollment was about 99% of age-eligible students. It is estimated that nearly all students complete their primary education. The student-to-teacher ratio for primary school was at about 11:1 in 2003; the ratio for secondary school was about 13:1. In 2003, private schools accounted for about 5% of primary school enrollment and 3.9% of secondary enrollment.

Sweden's six universities, all largely financed by the state, are at Uppsala (founded in 1477), Lund (1666), Stockholm (1877), Göteborg (1891), and Umea and Linköping (both completed in 1963). Uppsala and Lund have four faculties each—law, theology, medicine, and philosophy (arts and sciences). Stockholm has faculties of humanities, law, mathematics, and science; Göteborg, medicine and humanities. There are also more than two dozen specialized schools and institutions of university rank for such subjects as medicine, dentistry, pharmacology, veterinary science, music, economics, commerce, technology, agriculture, and forestry. Tuition is free, except for some special courses; most university students receive government loans to help them meet their living expenses.

Sweden has an active adult general education movement in which some three million persons participate each year. People's schools and other educational institutions give courses for all those who want to study. All the universities have extension divisions for general studies. There are 130 state-subsidized folk high schools for working adults that provide courses ranging in length from a few days to 80 weeks. In 2003, it was estimated that about 83% of the tertiary age population were enrolled in tertiary education programs. The adult literacy rate has been estimated at about 99%.

As of 2003, public expenditure on education was estimated at 7.7% of GDP, or 12.8% of total government expenditures.

44 LIBRARIES AND MUSEUMS

The four major libraries, the Royal Library at Stockholm (three million volumes) and the university libraries of Uppsala (5.4 million), Lunds (3.2 million), and Göteborg (2.7 million), receive free copies of all Swedish publications. There are technical and other special libraries, all of which have an interlibrary loan scheme with the university libraries, the state-aided municipal libraries, and the 24 county libraries. The largest public library is the Stockholm Public Library which holds over 2.1 million books and over 150,000 materials of other media. The Stockholm Public Library supports 44 city branches, 60 hospital branches, 90 lending points in workplaces and correctional facilities, and bookmobile services. The Göteborg Public Library holds 1.6 million volumes. Altogether, the public library systems had a combined total of about 46.3 million volumes. The Swedish Library of Talking Books and Braille is a government program that works through local public libraries; founded in 1955, the library has over 86,500 talking book titles (in 50 languages) and over 12,000 books in Braille. The Swedish Authors' Fund administers a library loan compensation system that pays an author royalties each time a book is borrowed.

Most of the outstanding museums are in Stockholm. Especially renowned are the rich art collections of the Swedish National Art Museum and the sculptures of Carl Milles in the artist's former home at Millesgarden in Lidingö. In Stockholm are located the Swedish Museum of Natural History (founded 1739) and the National Museum of Science and Technology (founded 1924). The Aquaria Vatten Museum, opened in 1991, is a natural history museum that includes a shark aquarium, salmon ladder, and living rain forest. The Nobel Museum celebrates the life and work of Alfred Nobel and many of the Nobel Prize laureates; the Nobel Museum also houses the 15,000-volume private library of Alfred Nobel. Göteborg has a number of museums including the Göteborg Art Gallery and a maritime museum reflecting the interests of that city. The finest Swedish folk museum is in Skansen, near Stockholm. Göteborg also has a public affairs museum including an exhibit of the history of the East India Tea Company of Sweden. Lund has the Museum of Cultural History and the Museum of Zoology. The Victoria Museum for Egyptian Antiquities is in Uppsala.

45 MEDIA

In 2003, there were an estimated 736 mainline telephones for every 1,000 people. The same year, there were approximately 980 mobile phones in use for every 1,000 people.

Sveriges Radio and Television operates several public broadcasting channels. There are several private commercial stations, including satellite and cable networks. As of 1999, there were a total of 5 AM and 360 FM radio stations and 163 television stations. In 2003, there were an estimated 2,811 radios and 965 television sets for every 1,000 people. About 246 of every 1,000 people were cable subscribers. Also in 2003, there were 621.3 personal computers for every 1,000 people and 573 of every 1,000 people had access to the Internet. There were 2,354 secure Internet servers in the country in 2004.

The Swedish press is said to be the oldest in which censorship is legally forbidden. The first regular newspaper, *Post-och Inrikes Tidningar,* appeared in 1645 and is still published. The first daily was *Norrköpings Tidningen* (1758). In 2001, there were 169 daily newspapers and 455 weeklies.

News is drawn largely from the Swedish News Agency (Tidningarnas Telegrambyra—TT), an agency owned by the Swedish press. The leading newspapers in Stockholm (with affiliation and circulation rates in 2005) were: *Aftonbladet* (Labor, 441,000), *Expressen* (liberal, 342,000), *Dagens Nyheter* (independent, 363,000), and *Svenska Dagbladet* (conservative, 179,000). In other regions, the leading papers in 2002 were: *Göteborgs-Posten* in Göteborg, (liberal, circulation 246,000), *Idag Vast* in Göteborg (172,800 in 2002), *Sydsvenskan* in Malmö (155,600 in 2002), *Sydsvenska Dagbladet* in Malmö (independent liberal, 136,000), *GT* in Göteborg (68,500 in 2002), *Nerikes Allehanda* in Örebro (68,000 in 2002), *Upsala Nya Tidning* in Uppsala (64,400 in 2002), *Kvallsposten* in Malmö (62,900 in 2002) and *Nya Wermlands-Tidningen* in Karlstad (conservative, 59,500 in 2002).

⁴⁶ORGANIZATIONS

Almost all farmers are members of agricultural cooperatives, which buy supplies and sell products for the farmers and represent farmers' interests to state agencies. Over 300,000 farmers belong to a member body of the Federation of Swedish Farmers, a powerful organization that provides farmers with legal and tax advice as well as educational services on agricultural matters. There are two farm credit institutions, a dairies association, a meat marketing association, and an egg marketing association. The National Union of Swedish Farmers (formed in 1905) supplies its members with fertilizer, seeds, feeds, and other supplies and buys their crops.

The Federation of Swedish Industries (founded 1910) is active in promoting trade. Chambers of commerce operate in all the principal cities and towns. There are specialist industrial and trade associations such as those of the glass exporters and wood exporters. There are professional organizations in agriculture, archaeology, art, education, engineering, ethnology, geography, geology, law, literature, mathematics, medicine, music, science, and other fields. The Swedish Medical Association is a major physicians union.

The three most distinguished scholarly organizations are the Swedish Academy (founded 1786), the Royal Academy of Letters, History, and Antiquities (founded 1753), and the Royal Academy of Arts and Sciences (founded 1776). The Nobel Foundation administers the trust fund established by Swedish scientist and inventor Alfred Nobel (1833-96) and presents the annual Nobel Prizes. The Royal Swedish Academy of Sciences assists in awarding the annual Nobel Prizes for physics, chemistry, and economic sciences. The Swedish National Council for Cultural Affairs helps promote study in arts and culture, in part by serving as an advisory council for the national cultural budget. The Swedish P.E.N. Centre is based in Stockholm. There are several clubs and associations available for hobbyists and amateur participants in a variety of fields, such as the Gothenburg Ornithological Society.

Numerous national youth organizations include the Association of Young Catholics in Sweden, Center Party University Students Federation, Christian Democratic Youth Union, Good Templar Youth of Sweden, Liberal Student Federation, Swedish 4-H Youth, Junior Chamber. Swedish National Union of Students, Young Left of Sweden, YMCA/YWCA, and the Swedish Guide and Scout Council. Some youth councils are organized under the National Council of Swedish Youth Organizations. There are numerous sports associations promoting amateur competitions for athletes of all ages.

The Women's Front serves as an umbrella organization for groups campaigning for equal rights. There are strong women's groups within political parties. International organizations with national chapters include Greenpeace, Save the Children, Amnesty International, and the Red Cross.

⁴⁷TOURISM, TRAVEL, AND RECREATION

Tourism, a major industry in Sweden, was stagnant in the 1990s due to a value-added tax on hotels, restaurants, and travel services. Since 2000, however, the industry has steadily grown.

Principal tourist sites include the Royal Palace in Stockholm, the "garden city" of Göteborg, the resort island of Öland off the Baltic coast, and the lake and mountain country in the north. Cultural centers in Stockholm are the Royal Opera, Royal Dramatic Theater, and Berwald Concert Hall. Popular recreational activities include football (soccer), polo, skiing, ice skating, swimming, mountain climbing, and gymnastics.

The number of foreign tourists to Sweden cannot be reliably ascertained because of uncontrolled tourist movements across borders within Scandinavia; statistics of Scandinavian visitors to Sweden have not been kept since 1951. However, tourist arrivals totaled 7,627,000 in 2003, when tourism receipts reached $6.5 billion. That year Sweden had 96,372 hotel rooms and 184,771 beds with a 34% occupancy rate. All visitors must have a valid passport as well as sufficient funds for their stay and an onward/return ticket. Citizens of 133 countries including the United Kingdom, Russia, and China are required to carry an entry visa. Citizens of Canada, the United States, Western European countries, and some other nations may enter Sweden with a valid passport and do not require a visa.

In 2005, the US Department of State estimated the cost of staying in Stockholm at $419 per day.

⁴⁸FAMOUS SWEDES

Esaias Tegnér (1782–1846), considered the national poet of Sweden, and Erik Gustaf Geijer (1783–1847), historian and poet, are the best-known Swedish writers of the early 19th century. A new impulse was given to literature by August Strindberg (1849–1912), a major literary figure whose powerful, socially oriented plays and stories reflected the advanced thought of the age. Selma Lagerlöf (1858–1940), who won the Nobel Prize for literature in 1909, showed in her novels a depth of narrative genius reminiscent of the Norse sagas. Other Swedish winners of the Nobel Prize for literature were the novelist and poet Karl Gustav Verner von Heidenstam (1859–1940), in 1916; the novelist and short-story writer Pär Lagerkvist (1891–1974), in 1951; and the novelists Eyvind Johnson (1900–1976) and Harry Edmund Martinson (1904–78), who shared the 1974 award. A noted contemporary novelist is Vilhelm Moberg (1889–1974).

The painter, etcher, and sculptor Anders Leonhard Zorn (1860–1920) and the sculptor Carl Milles (1875–1955) are the greatest figures in Swedish art. The outstanding Swedish musician of the 19th century was Franz Adolf Berwald (1796–1868), composer of symphonies, operas, and chamber music. August Johan Söderman (1832–76) is considered the leading Swedish operatic composer. Two famous sopranos were Jenny Lind (1820–87), the "Swedish nightingale," and Christine (Kristina) Nilsson (1843–1921). Outstanding 20th-century musicians are the composers Wilhelm Stenhammar (1871–1927), Hugo Alfvén (1872–1960), Ture Rangström (1884–1947), Kurt Atterberg (1887–1974), Hilding Constantin Rosenberg (1892–1985), and the singers Jussi Björling (1910–60) and Birgit Nilsson (1918–2006).

Famous 18th-century scientists were the astronomer and physicist Anders Celsius (1705–44), who devised the temperature scale named after him; the chemist Karl Wilhelm Scheele (1742–86); and the botanist Carolus Linnaeus (Carl von Linné, 1707–78), who established the classification schemes of plants and animals named after him. Emanuel Swedenborg (1688–1772) was a scientist, philosopher, and religious writer whose followers founded a religious sect in his name.

Svante August Arrhenius (1859–1927), a great pioneer in physical chemistry, is renowned for his theory of electrolytic dissociation and his speculations in the field of cosmic physics; in 1903, he was awarded the Nobel Prize for chemistry. Other Swedish Nobel Prize winners in science or medicine are Gustaf Dalén (1869–1957), for his work in automatic beacons for coast lighting (1912); Allvar Gullstrand (1862–1930), for work on dioptics of the eye (1911); Karl Manne Georg Siegbahn (1886–1978), for work on X-ray spectroscopy (1924); The (Theodor) Svedberg (1884–1971), for work in colloidal chemistry (1926); Hans Karl August Simon von Euler-Chelpin (b.Augsburg, 1873–1964), for work in enzyme chemistry (1929); George Karl de Hevesy (b.Budapest, 1885–1966), for work on isotopes (1943); Arne Wilhelm Kaurin Tiselius (1902–71), for investigations in electrophoresis (1948); Axel Hugo Theodor Theorell (1903–82), for work on enzymes (1955); Ragnar Arthur Granit (Finland, 1900–91), for "discoveries in primary physiological and chemical visual processes in the eye" (1967); Hannes Olof Gösta Alfvén (1908–95), for work in magnetohydrodynamics (1970); and Ulf von Euler-Chelpin (1905–83), for work on the treatment of nervous and mental disorders (1970). In addition, Kai M. Siegbahn (b.1918) shared the 1981 Nobel Prize in physics for developing spectroscopy; and Sune Karl Bergström (1916–2004) and Bengt Ingemar Samuelsson (b.1934) shared the 1982 prize in medicine for their research on prostaglandins. Bergström also served as chairman of the Nobel Foundation.

Three distinguished political economists are Karl Gunnar Myrdal (1898–1987), who was awarded the 1974 Nobel Prize in economic science for work in the theory of money and economic fluctuations and whose 1944 book *An American Dilemma* contributed to the overthrowing of legally sanctioned racial segregation in the United States; Bertil Gotthard Ohlin (1899–1979), who shared the 1977 prize for his contribution to international trade theory; and Dag Hammarskjöld (1905–61), who was secretary-general of the UN from 1953 until his death and was posthumously awarded the 1961 Nobel Prize for peace. Other Swedish winners of the Nobel Peace Prize were Klas Pontus Arnoldson (1844–1916), in 1908; Karl Hjalmar Branting (1860–1925), in 1921; Nathan Söderblom (Lars Olof Jonathan, 1866–1931), in 1930; and Alva Reimer Myrdal (1902–86), the wife of Gunnar Myrdal, in 1982.Swedish inventors who have done much to promote manufacturing and technical advances include the Swedish-American John Ericsson (1803–89), who pioneered the screw propeller and designed the first Western armored-turret warship, the *Monitor;* Alfred Nobel (1833–96), inventor of dynamite and progenitor of the Nobel Prizes; Lars Magnus Ericsson (1846–1926), who contributed much to the development of telephones; and Gustaf de Laval (1845–1913), who developed steam turbines and invented a centrifugal cream separator.

One of the most noted film directors of our times is Ingmar Bergman (b.1918); other noted directors were Victor Seastrom (Sjöström, 1879–1960) and Mauritz (Moshe) Stiller (b.Finland, 1883–1928). Famous screen personalities have included Greta Garbo (Greta Louisa Gustafsson, 1905–90) and Ingrid Bergman (1917–82). More recent stars of Swedish theater and films include Erland Josephson (b.1923), Max Von Sydow (b.1929), Ingrid Thulin (1929–2004), Harriet Andersson (b.1932), and Bibi Andersson (b.1935). Sweden's sports stars include five-time Wimbledon tennis champion Björn Borg (b.1956); Alpine skiing champion Ingemar Stenmark (b.1956); and eight-time Rolex Player of the Year (as of 2005) golfer Annika Sörenstam (b.1970).

49 DEPENDENCIES

Sweden has no territories or colonies.

50 BIBLIOGRAPHY

Annesley, Claire (ed.). *A Political and Economic Dictionary of Western Europe*. Philadelphia: Routledge/Taylor and Francis, 2005.

Esaiasson, Peter. *Representation from Above: Members of Parliament and Representative Democracy in Sweden*. Aldershot, England: Dartmouth, 1996.

Fant, Kenne. *Alfred Nobel: A Biography*. New York: Arcade, 1993.

International Smoking Statistics: A Collection of Historical Data from 30 Economically Developed Countries. New York: Oxford University Press, 2002.

Micheletti, Michele. *Civil Society and State Relations in Sweden*. Brookfield, Vt.: Avebury, 1995.

Remaking the Welfare State: Swedish Urban Planning and Policy-Making in the 1990s. Edited by Ingemar Elander, Abdul Khakee, and Sune Sunesson. Brookfield, Vt.: Avebury, 1995.

Roberts, Michael. *Gustavus Adolphus*. 2nd ed. New York: Longman, 1992.

Sandelin, Bo (ed.). *The History of Swedish Economic Thought*. London; New York: Routledge, 1991.

Scobbie, Irene. *Historical Dictionary of Sweden*. Metuchen, N.J.: Scarecrow, 1995.

Streissguth, Thomas. *Raoul Wallenberg: Swedish Diplomat and Humanitarian*. New York: Rosen, 2001.

Wessels, Wolfgang, Andreas Maurer, and Jürgan Mittag (eds.). *Fifteen into One?: the European Union and Its Member States*. New York: Palgrave, 2003.

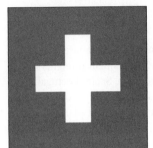

SWITZERLAND

Swiss Confederation

[French] *Suisse; (Confédération Suisse);* [German] *Schweiz; (Schweizerische Eidgenossenschaft);* [Italian] *Svizzera; (Confederazione Svizzera);* [Romansch] *Svizra (Confederaziun Helvetica)*

CAPITAL: Bern

FLAG: The national flag consists of an equilateral white cross on a red background, each arm of the cross being one-sixth longer than its width.

ANTHEM: The Swiss Hymn begins "Trittst in Morgenrot daher, Seh' ich dich in Strahlenmeer" ("Radiant in the morning sky, Lord, I see that Thou art nigh").

MONETARY UNIT: The Swiss franc (SwFr) of 100 centimes, or rappen, is the national currency. There are coins of 1, 5, 10, 20, and 50 centimes and 1, 2, and 5 francs, and notes of 10, 20, 50, 100, 500, and 1,000 francs. SwFr 1 = $0.81301 (or $1 = SwFr 1.23) as of 2005.

WEIGHTS AND MEASURES: The metric system is the legal standard.

HOLIDAYS: New Year, 1–2 January; Labor Day, 1 May; Christmas, 25–26 December. Movable religious holidays include Good Friday, Easter Monday, Ascension, and Whitmonday.

TIME: 1 PM = noon GMT.

¹LOCATION, SIZE, AND EXTENT

A landlocked country in central Europe, Switzerland has an area of 41,290 sq km (15,942 sq mi), extending 348 km (216 mi) E–W and 220 km (137 mi) N–S. Comparatively, the area occupied by Switzerland is slightly less than twice the size of New Jersey. Bounded on the N by Germany, on the E by Liechtenstein and Austria, on the SE and S by Italy, and on the W and NW by France, Switzerland has a total boundary length of 1,852 km (1,151 mi).

Switzerland's capital city, Bern, is located in the western part of the country.

²TOPOGRAPHY

Switzerland is divided into three natural topographical regions: (1) the Jura Mountains in the northwest, rising between Switzerland and eastern France; (2) the Alps in the south, covering three-fifths of the country's total area; and (3) the central Swiss plateau, or Mittelland, consisting of fertile plains and rolling hills that run between the Jura and the Alps. The Mittelland, with a mean altitude of 580 m (1,900 ft), covers about 30% of Switzerland and is the heartland of Swiss farming and industry; Zürich, Bern, Lausanne, and Geneva (Genève) are on the plateau. The central portion of the Alps, around the St. Gotthard Pass, is a major watershed and the source of the Rhine, which drains into the North Sea; of the Aare, a tributary of the Rhine; of the Rhône, which flows into the Mediterranean; and of the Ticino, a tributary of the Po, and of the Inn, a tributary of the Danube, which flow into the Adriatic and the Black seas, respectively.

The highest point in Switzerland is the Dufourspitze of Monte Rosa at 4,634 m (15,203 ft); the lowest is the shore of Lake Maggiore at less than 195 m (640 ft). The second-highest and most celebrated of the Swiss Alps is the Matterhorn (4,478 m/14,692 ft), long a challenge to mountaineers and first scaled in 1865.

Switzerland has 1,484 lakes, more than 12,900 smaller bodies of water, and many waterfalls. Lake Geneva (Léman), with an area of 581 sq km (224 sq mi), is considered the largest Swiss lake, though its southern shore is in France. Lake Neuchâtel, the largest lake totally within Switzerland, has an area of 218 sq km (84 sq mi). Switzerland also contains more than 1,000 glaciers, many the relics of Pleistocene glaciation. The largest area of permanent ice is in the Valais.

³CLIMATE

The climate of Switzerland north of the Alps is temperate but varies with altitude, wind exposure, and other factors; the average annual temperature is 9°C (48°F). The average rainfall varies from 53 cm (21 in) in the Rhône Valley to 170 cm (67 in) in Lugano. Generally, the areas to the west and north of the Alps have a cool, rainy climate, with winter averages near or below freezing and summer temperatures seldom above 21°C (70°F). South of the Alps, the canton of Ticino has a warm, moist, Mediterranean climate, and frost is almost unknown. The climate of the Alps and of the Jura uplands is mostly raw, rainy, or snowy, with frost occurring above 1,830 m (6,000 ft).

⁴FLORA AND FAUNA

Variation in climate and altitude produces a varied flora and fauna. In the lowest zone (below 550 m/1,800 ft), chestnut, walnut, cypress, and palm trees grow, as well as figs, oranges, and almonds; up to 1,200 m (3,940 ft), forests of beech, maple, and oak; around 1,680 m (5,500 ft), fir and pine; around 2,130 m (7,000 ft), rhododendron, larches, dwarf and cembra pine, and whortleberries; and above the snow line, more than 100 species of flowering plants, including the edelweiss. Wild animals include the chamois, boar, deer, otter, and fox. There are large birds of prey, as well as snipe, heath cock, and cuckoo. Lakes and rivers teem with fish. As of 2002, there were at least 75 species of mammals, 199 species of birds, and over 3,000 species of plants throughout the country.

5 ENVIRONMENT

The Swiss have long been aware of the need to protect their natural resources. Switzerland's federal forestry law of 1876 is among the world's earliest pieces of environmental legislation. Since 1953, provisions for environmental protection have been incorporated in the federal constitution. A measure creating a federal role in town and rural planning by allowing the central government to set the ground rules for the cantonal master plans took effect in January 1980.

Air pollution is a major environmental concern in Switzerland; automobiles and other transportation vehicles are the main contributors. In 2000, the total of carbon dioxide emissions was at 39.1 million metric tons. Strict standards for exhaust emissions were imposed on new passenger cars manufactured after October 1987. Water pollution is also a problem due to the presence of phosphates, fertilizers, and pesticides in the water supply. The nation has 40 cu km of renewable water resources, of which 73% of the annual withdrawal is used for industrial purposes. The country's cities have produced about 3.1 million tons of solid waste annually. On 1 November 1986, as a result of a fire in a chemical warehouse near Basel, in northern Switzerland, some 30 tons of toxic waste flowed into the Rhine River, killing an estimated 500,000 fish and eels. Despite a Swiss report in January 1987 that damage to the river had not been so great as was first thought, most environmentalists considered the chemical spill a major disaster.

Chemical contaminants and erosion damage the nation's soil and limit productivity. In 1986, the Swiss Federal Office of Forestry issued a report stating that 36% of the country's forests had been killed or damaged by acid rain and other types of air pollution.

Important environmental groups include the Swiss League for the Protection of Nature, founded in 1909; the Swiss Foundation for the Protection and Care of the Landscape, 1970; and the Swiss Society for the Protection of the Environment. The principal federal agency is the Department of Environment.

According to a 2006 report issued by the International Union for Conservation of Nature and Natural Resources (IUCN), threatened species included 4 types of mammals, 8 species of birds, 1 species of amphibian, 4 species of fish, 30 species of invertebrate, and 2 species of plants. The northern bald ibis and the Italian spadefoot toad are extinct; the false ringlet butterfly, Italian agile frog, and marsh snail are threatened. The bear and wolf were exterminated by the end of the 19th century, but the lynx, once extinct in Switzerland, has been reestablished.

6 POPULATION

The population of Switzerland in 2005 was estimated by the United Nations (UN) at 7,446,000, which placed it at number 95 in population among the 193 nations of the world. In 2005, approximately 16% of the population was over 65 years of age, with another 16% of the population under 15 years of age. There were 94 males for every 100 females in the country. According to the UN, the annual population rate of change for 2005–10 was expected to be 0.2%, a rate the government viewed as too low. The projected

population for the year 2025 was 7,401,000. The population density was 180 per sq km (467 per sq mi).

The UN estimated that 68% of the population lived in urban areas in 2005, and that population in urban areas was declining at an annual rate of -0.06%. The capital city, Bern, had a population of 320,000 in that year. The largest metropolitan area is Zürich, with 984,000 residents in 2000. Other large cities and their estimated populations include Basel, 186,871; Geneva, 185,526; and Lausanne, 126,766.

7 MIGRATION

Foreign residents in Switzerland comprised about 20% of the total population in 1998. Nearly a third of all resident foreigners were of Italian nationality; the former Yugoslavia, Spain, Portugal, Germany and Turkey were the next-leading countries of origin. In April 1987, Swiss voters approved a government plan to tighten rules on immigration and political asylum.

From the beginning of the civil war in Bosnia, Switzerland took in some 27,000 Bosnian refugees by 1997, granting most only temporary protection. In 1997, 8,000 singles and couples without children returned to Bosnia; another 2,800 returned voluntarily. Nonetheless, as a result of the drastic increase in the number of asylum seekers, Switzerland suspended its resettlement policy in mid-1998.

As a result of the Kosovo conflict, Switzerland again faced a major increase in asylum seekers in 1999. The Swiss government offered temporary protection to about 65,000 Kosovars living in the country. In 2004, Switzerland hosted 47,678 refugees, 18,633 asylum seekers, and 25 stateless persons. Main countries of origin for refugees included Bosnia and Herzegovina, Serbia and Montenegro, and Turkey. Asylum applications came from 19 countries of origin, the largest numbers from Bulgaria and Belarus. The net migration rate in 2005 was an estimated 3.58 migrants per 1,000 population. Worker remittances in 2002 were $146 million.

8 ETHNIC GROUPS

The four ethnolinguistic groups (Germanic, French, Italian, and Rhaeto-Romansch) that make up the native Swiss population have retained their specific characteristics. Originally, the country was inhabited by Celtic tribes in the west and south and by Rhaetians in the east. With the collapse of Roman rule, Germanic tribes poured in, among them the Alemanni and Burgundians. The Alemanni ultimately became the dominant group, and the present Alemannic vernacular (Schwyzertütsch, or Schweizerdeutsch) is spoken by nearly two-thirds of the total population as their principal language. About 65% of the population is German, 18% is French, 10% is Italian, 1% is Romansch, and 6% are of various other groups.

9 LANGUAGES

Switzerland is a multilingual state with four national languages—German, French, Italian, and Rhaeto-Romansch. About 63.7% of the resident population speaks German as their principal language, predominantly in northern, central, and western Switzerland; 19.2% speak French, mainly in the west and southwest; 7.6% Italian, primarily in the southern region closest to Italy; and 0.6% Rhaeto-Romansch, used widely only in the southeastern canton of

SWITZERLAND

0   25   50 Miles

0   25   50 Kilometers

LOCATION: 5°57′24″ to 10°29′36″ E; 45°49′8″ to 47°48′35″ N. BOUNDARY LENGTHS: Germany, 334 kilometers (208 miles); Liechtenstein, 41 kilometers (25 miles); Austria, 164 kilometers (103 miles); Italy, 740 kilometers (460 miles); France, 573 kilometers (355 miles).

Graubünden (Grisons). The remaining 8.9% speak various other languages. There are numerous local dialects.

10 RELIGIONS

Religious denominations as of a 2002 report stood at about 44% Roman Catholic, 47% Protestant, 4.5% Muslim, and about 1% Orthodox Christian. There are about 17,577 members of the Jewish community and about 11,748 Old Catholics. About 12% of the population claimed no religious affiliation.

There is no official state church and religious freedom is guaranteed. However, all of the cantons financially support at least one of three traditional denominations—Roman Catholic, Old Catholic, or Protestant—with money collected through taxes. In all cantons, individuals may also choose not to contribute to church taxes if they do not formally belong to a church. As a result, since the 1970s there has been a trend of individuals formally resigning their church membership in order to avoid church taxation. According to the latest statistics, about 41.8% of the population are Roman Catholic, 33% are Protestant, 4.3% are Muslim, and 1.8% are Orthodox Christians. Jews, Buddhists, Hindis, and other Christian churches each report membership of less than 1% of the population. About 11% have no church affiliation.

11 TRANSPORTATION

As of 2004, Switzerland's railway system consisted of 4,527 km (2,816 mi) of standard and narrow gauge track. Of that total, 3,232 km were standard gauge. Nearly all of the railway system (4,494 km/2,795 mi) was electrified. Because of its geographical position, Switzerland is an international railway center, with traffic moving from France, Germany, Austria, and northern Europe through the

Simplon, Lötschberg, and St. Gotthard tunnels to Italy and southern Europe.

The Swiss road network covered 71,212 km (44,293 mi) in 2002, all of which was paved, and included 1,706 km (1,061 mi) of expressways. In 2003, there were 3,753,890 passenger cars, and 335,958 commercial vehicles. The longest road tunnel in the world, the 17-km (10.6-mi) St. Gotthard, in the Ticino, opened in September 1980.

Inland waterway (65 km/40 mi) traffic is an important component of Swiss transportation. Basel, the only river port, has direct connections to Strasbourg, the German Rhineland, the Ruhr, Rotterdam, and Antwerp. The Rhine-Rhône canal provides an alternative link between Basel and Strasbourg. There are 12 navigable lakes. During World War II, the Swiss organized a merchant marine to carry Swiss imports and exports on the high seas. In 2005, it consisted of 23 ships of 1,000 GRT or more, totaling 604,843 GRT. Switzerland's merchant fleet is larger than that of any other landlocked nation.

There were an estimated 65 airports in 2004. As of 2005, a total of 42 had paved runways and there were also two heliports. Swissair, partially owned by the federal and local governments, is the flag line of Switzerland. It has flights from the principal international airports at Zürich, Geneva (Cointrin), and Basel to major European cities, North and South America, the Middle East, Asia, and West Africa. In 2003, about 10.589 million passengers were carried on scheduled domestic and international flights, and 1,248 million freight ton-km of service.

12 HISTORY

The Helvetii, a Celtic tribe conquered by Julius Caesar in 58 BC, were the first inhabitants of Switzerland (Helvetia) known by name. A Roman province for 200 years, Switzerland was a prosperous land with large cities (Avenches was the capital) and a flourishing trade. In AD 250, however, Switzerland was occupied by the Alemanni, a Germanic tribe, and in 433 by the Burgundians. The Franks, who defeated the Alemanni in 496 and the Burgundians about 534, incorporated the country into the Frankish Empire. Under Frankish rule, new cities were founded; others, such as Zürich and Lausanne, were rebuilt; and Christianity was introduced.

In 1032, some 200 years after the death of Charlemagne, king of the Franks, and the defeat of his weak successors, Switzerland became part of the Holy Roman Empire. In the 13th century, it was placed under the House of Habsburg. Harsh domination resulted in the rebellion of several cities and the formation on 1 August 1291 of the "eternal alliance" between the three forest cantons of Schwyz, Uri, and Unterwalden, the first step toward the Swiss Confederation. The Habsburgs invaded the three provinces, but with their defeat at Morgarten Pass on 15 November 1315, the Swiss secured their independence. By 1353, five other cantons, Luzern (1332), Zürich (1351), Glarus and Zug (1352), and Bern (1353), had joined the confederacy. All these allies were called Swiss (Schwyzer), after the largest canton. Four victories over Austria (1386, 1388, 1476, and 1499) confirmed the confederation. The Swiss also defeated Charles of Burgundy, whose ambitions threatened their independence until his death in 1477. Complete independence was secured by the Treaty of Basel (1499) with the Holy Roman Empire. Switzerland thereafter remained unmo-

lested by foreign troops until the French Revolution of 1789. Such legendary or real heroes as William Tell, Arnold von Winkelried, and Nikolaus von der Flüe symbolized Swiss bravery and love of freedom. The Helvetian Confederation (Eidgenossenschaft) continued to grow with the inclusion of Aargau (1415), Thurgau (1460), Fribourg and Solothurn (1481), Basel and Schaffhausen (1501), and Appenzell (1513). As of 1513, there were 13 cantons and several affiliated cities and regions. Swiss sovereignty reached south of the crest of the Alps into the Ticino. The Swiss also controlled many of the vital mountain passes linking southern and northern Europe.

The power of the Confederation was, however, undermined by conflicts stemming from the Reformation, led by Ulrich Zwingli in Zürich and John Calvin in Geneva. Seven cantons resisted the Reformation, and a prolonged conflict resulted. In its first round, Zwingli was killed in action (1531). The Catholic cantons later allied with Savoy and Spain. The struggle with the Protestant cantons centered during the Thirty Years' War (1618–48) on control of the Valtelline pass. The Treaty of Westphalia ending that war granted the Swiss Confederation formal recognition of independence by all European powers.

In the following centuries, the Catholic-Protestant conflict continued with varying success for each side. Apart from this struggle, a number of abortive uprisings against oligarchic control occurred in such places as Geneva and the canton of Vaud. The oligarchs were still in power in most cantons when the French Revolution broke out. With the progress of the revolution, radical groups gained the upper hand in several cities. In 1798, the Helvetic Republic was proclaimed, under French tutelage, and during the Napoleonic imperial era Switzerland was governed as an appendage of France. Boundaries were partly redrawn, and six new cantons were added to the original 13.

In 1815, the Congress of Vienna reconstituted the independent Swiss Confederation with three additional cantons (for a total of 22) and recognized its perpetual neutrality. Switzerland, however, did not remain untouched by the great conflict between liberalism and conservatism that affected all of Europe in the first half of the 19th century. Many revolutionaries found temporary refuge in Switzerland and influenced some of its citizens. Under their goading, several cantons introduced more progressive governments and liberalized their old constitutions.

In 1848, a new federal constitution, quite similar to that of the United States, was promulgated. Meanwhile, the struggle between Protestants and Catholics had culminated in the Secession (Sonderbund) War of 1847, in which the Protestant cantons quickly overcame the secessionist movement of the seven Catholic cantons. As a result of the war, federal authority was greatly strengthened.

In 1874, the constitution was again revised to enlarge federal authority, especially in fiscal and military affairs. Since the last quarter of the 19th century, Switzerland has been concerned primarily with domestic matters, such as social legislation, communications, and industrialization. In foreign affairs, it remained rigidly neutral through both world wars, resolutely determined to protect its independence with its highly reputed militia. In 1978, Switzerland's 23rd sovereign canton, Jura, was established by nationwide vote. In 1991, Switzerland celebrated the 700th anniversary of Confederation.

Despite its neutrality, Switzerland has cooperated wholeheartedly in various international organizations, offering home and hospitality to such diverse bodies as the League of Nations, the Red Cross, and the UPU. Switzerland has long resisted joining the UN, however, partly on the grounds that imposition of sanctions, as entailed in various UN resolutions, is contrary to a policy of strict neutrality. In a March 1986 referendum, a proposal for UN membership, approved by the Federal Assembly, was rejected by Swiss voters. Switzerland is a member of most specialized UN agencies and is a party to the Statute of the International Court of Justice. Swiss attitudes toward UN membership changed at the beginning of the 21st century, as citizens decreasingly saw participation in the UN as jeopardizing the country's neutrality. In a referendum held on 3 March 2002, nearly 55% of Swiss voters approved of joining the UN, but approval by the country's 23 cantons received a narrower 12 to 11 vote. On 10 September 2002 Switzerland became a full member of the UN.

Foreign governments have targeted Switzerland's tight bank secrecy laws as providing a haven for tax evasion and money laundering. The EU maintains that if Switzerland were to join the body, such laws would have to be reformed. Switzerland suffered from the global economic downturn that began in 2001; it employs 220,000 people (out of a total population of some seven million) in financial services, of which more than half work in banking. The Swiss have also expressed ambivalence toward Europe. In December 1992, the Swiss rejected participation in the two major European organizations—the European Economic Area (EEA) of the European Union (EU). Fearing adverse effects from nonparticipation, the Swiss government has taken steps to bring the country's laws and economy into harmony with the EEA. Because of the fact that all legislation can be subjected to referenda, however, the government is finding it difficult to alter certain protectionist policies and to lower certain barriers. Officially, the government is committed to eventually joining the EU, although in order to do so it will have to convince a majority of voters it is the correct path.

In a blow to Euro skeptics, in June 2005 voters, in a referendum endorsed by a 55–45% majority, planned to join the other European Union members then in the Schengen passport-free travel zone. Voters also approved joining the EU's Dublin agreement on handling asylum seekers, and of participating in further coordination of policing and crime-fighting. In September 2005, a bilateral accord on the free movement of labor to the 10 newest EU member states was approved in a referendum.

In October 2003, the right-wing Swiss People's Party (SVP) became the largest force in the National Council after winning 26.6% of the vote in general elections. That December, parliament decided to grant the SVP the second post in the seven-seat government at the expense of the Christian Democrats, altering the "magic formula" which had brought stability to Swiss politics since 1959.

13 GOVERNMENT

The Swiss Confederation is a federal union governed, until 2000, under the constitution of 1874, which vested supreme authority in the Federal Assembly, the legislative body, and executive power in the Federal Council. On 1 January 2000, a new federal constitution entered into force, replacing the 1874 constitution. The new constitution formally separates and codifies four pillars of Swiss constitutional law: democracy; the rule of law; social welfare; and federalism. Fundamental rights, such as freedom of speech and assembly, which had not been explicitly mentioned in the 1874 constitution, now received their formal expression.

The Federal Assembly consists of two chambers: the National Council (*Nationalrat*) of 200 members, elected by direct ballot for four-year terms by citizens 18 years of age or older, and the Council of States (*Ständerat*) of 46 members, two appointed by each of the 20 cantons, and one from each of the six half-cantons, and paid by the cantons; deputies are elected according to the laws of the cantons. Legislation must be approved by both houses.

The Federal Council of seven members is elected for four-year terms by joint session of the Federal Assembly. The president and vice president of the Federal Council and of the Confederation are elected by the assembly for one-year terms and cannot be reelected to the same office until after the expiration of another year. The seven members of the Federal Council, which has no veto power, are the respective heads of the main departments of the federal government. After general elections held in October 2003, the four-party power-sharing agreement known as the "magic formula"—whereby the Free Democrats, Social Democrats, and Christian Democrats each held two seats, and the Swiss People's Party held one seat—was disturbed, as the SVP, which had campaigned on an antiforeigner and anti-EU platform, became the largest party in parliament. The Christian Democrats forfeited one seat to the SVP. After the 2004 election for president, the Federal Council elected Samuel Schmid. The Federal Council meets in secret and tries to appear congenial at all times. Moritz Luenberger won the 2005 election and took office 8 January 2006.

The cantons are sovereign in all matters not delegated to the federal government by the constitution and may force federal law to a plebiscite by the right of referendum. In addition, by popular initiative, 50,000 citizens may demand a direct popular vote on any legislation or regulation proposed by the federal government, and 100,000 citizens may demand a referendum on a constitutional revision. Any proposed amendments to the constitution must be submitted for public approval.

In 1971, Swiss women were granted the right to vote in federal elections. In November 1990, the Federal Court ruled in favor of female suffrage in the half-canton of Appenzell-Inner Rhoden, the last area with male-only suffrage.

14 POLITICAL PARTIES

Swiss politics are generally stable, and until 2003, the strengths of the chief political parties varied little over the past several decades. The conduct of national-level politics is generally calm and is marked by mutual esteem and cooperation. On the cantonal and municipal levels, however, the give-and-take of political life is more lively and unrestrained, as well as more partisan. The ruling Federal Council is made up of what the Swiss refer to as the "magic formula" coalition, an informal, but strictly adhered to, arrangement whereby the four largest political parties fill the seven positions on the Federal Council. The four strongest parties are now the Swiss People's Party, a right-wing, xenophobic and anti-EU party; the Social Democratic Party, similar to the Scandinavian Social Democrats, which advocates wider state participation in industry and strong social legislation; the Radical Free Democratic Party, a progressive middle-class party, which favors increased social welfare, strengthening of national defense, and a democratic federally structured government; and the Christian Democrats (formerly the Christian Social-Conservatives), a clerical federalist party, which opposes centralization of power. The Swiss People's Party was formed in 1971 by a union of the Farmers, Traders, and Citizens Party, which favored agrarian reform, protective tariffs, and a stronger national defense, and the Democratic Party, a leftist middle-class group. Other parties include the League of Independents, a progressive, middle-class consumers' group; the Communist-inclined Workers Party, with some strength in Zürich, Basel, and Geneva; the Liberal Party; and the Independent and Evangelical Party, which is Protestant, federalist, and conservative. In 1985, two small right-wing parties were formed: the National Socialist Party and the Conservative and Liberal Movement.

After the October 1991 elections the Radical Democratic Party held 44 seats, Social Democrats 42 seats, Christian Democrats 37 seats, Swiss People's Party 25 seats, Greens 14 seats, Liberals 10 seats, and minor parties, 28 seats.

In the Council of States, the 46 seats were distributed as follows in 1991: Radical Democratic Party 18 seats, Christian Democrats 16 seats, Social Democrats 4 seats, Liberals 3 seats, Independents 1 seat, and Ticino League 1 seat.

The 1995 elections for the National Council saw the Radical Democratic Party take 45 seats; the Social Democratic Party, 54; the Christian Democratic People's Party, 34; the Swiss People's Party, 30; the Greens, 8; the Liberal Party, 7; the Alliance of Independents Party, 6; the Swiss Democratic Party, 3; the Evangelical People's Party, 3; the Workers' Party, 2; and the Ticino League, 2.

In the Council of States, the 46 seats were distributed as follows: Radical Democrats, 17; Christian Democrats, 17; Swiss People's Party, 4; Social Democrats, 3; Liberals, 3; Independents, 1; Ticino League, 1.

Following the October 1999 elections, the Social Democratic Party took 51 seats; the Swiss People's Party took 44; the Radical Democratic Party, 43; Christian Democrats, 35; Greens, 9; Liberals, 6; Evangelical People's Party, 3; the xenophobic Swiss Democratic Party, 1; the conservative Federal Democratic Union, 1; the Workers' Party, 2; the Ticino League, 2; Independents, 1; the socialist party Solidarities, 1; and the progressive Christian Social Party, 1.

In the Council of States after the 1999 elections, the Radical Democratic Party held 18 seats; the Christian Democrats held 15; the Swiss People's Party had 7; and the Social Democrats held 6.

Following the 2003 elections, in the National Council the Swiss People's Party took 55 seats; the Social Democratic Party took 54; the Radical Free Democratic Party took 36; the Christian Democrats took 28; the Greens took 13; and other small parties held 14 seats. In the Council of States the Christian Democrats took 15 seats; the Radical Free Democrats took 14; the Swiss People's Party took 8; the Social Democrats took 6; and others held three seats. The next elections were scheduled to take place October 2007.

15 LOCAL GOVERNMENT

The Swiss Confederation consists of 23 sovereign cantons, three of which are divided into half-cantons (i.e., 20 cantons and six half-cantons). The most recent of these, Jura, was formed from six French-speaking districts in the German-speaking area of Bern Canton in 1978. In 1993, the German-speaking Laufental district

of Beru joined the canton of Basel-Land. This was the first time a political unit in Switzerland left one canton to join another. Swiss cantons are highly autonomous and exercise wide administrative control, with the weak federal government controlling only foreign affairs, national security, customs, communications, and monetary policy. The cantons have their own constitutions and laws, and are responsible for their own public works, education, care of the poor, justice, and police forces. Local forms of government vary, but each canton has a legislative council (called Grand Conseil, Grosser Rat, Kantonsrat, or Gran Consiglio), which appoints a chief executive. In a few of the small cantons, the general assembly of all voting citizens, or Landesgemeinde, decides on major matters by voice vote; in the majority of the cantons, this ancient institution has been replaced by referendum. Communes, numbering over 3,000, are the basic units of local government. For the most part, Swiss districts (Bezirke), constituting a middle level of organization between the cantons and communes, are little more than judicial circuits.

16 JUDICIAL SYSTEM

The Federal Court of Justice in Lausanne is composed of 30 permanent members appointed for six-year terms by the Federal Assembly. Until 2000, the court had both original and final jurisdiction in the majority of cases where a canton or the federal government was involved, and was the highest appeals court for many types of cases. Judicial reforms carried out in 2000 reduced the caseload of the Federal Court, by creating a federal criminal court and federal administrative bodies with judicial competence. Now, the Federal Court exists as a pure appellate court.

Each canton has its own cantonal courts. District courts have three to five members and try lesser criminal and civil cases. Each canton has an appeals court and a court of cassation, the jurisdiction of which is limited to reviewing judicial procedures. Capital punishment was abolished in 1942. Minor cases are tried by a single judge, difficult cases by a panel of judges, and murder and other serious crimes by a public jury.

The judiciary is independent and free from interference by other branches of government. The trials are fair and the judicial process is efficient. The judicial system is based on civil law influenced by customary law. Switzerland accepts compulsory jurisdiction of the International Court of Justice.

17 ARMED FORCES

Switzerland's armed forces in 2005 were built around a core of 4,300 active military personnel and a well-trained force of 210,000 citizen-soldier reservists that can be mobilized within 48 hours. The country has universal compulsory military service for males at age 19–20, followed by varied annual training requirements until age 42 (55 for officers), with exemption only for physical disability. Initial basic training of 15 weeks is followed by regular short training periods. In addition, there is also a paramilitary civil defense force of 105,000 members. When fully mobilized, Switzerland's land forces (Army) would have an estimated manpower of 153,200, with 355 main battle tanks, 446 reconnaissance vehicles, 127 armored infantry fighting vehicles, 1049 armored personnel carriers, and 1,008 artillery pieces. The land forces also have a marine arm that is outfitted with 10 patrol/coastal boats. The air force, when fully mobilized, had an estimated 32,900 personnel and has 90 combat capable aircraft, including 57 fighters and 33 fighter ground attack aircraft.

Swiss fighting men are world famous, and from the 16th to the 19th century some two million Swiss served as mercenaries in foreign armies. The modern Swiss citizen-soldier is trained only for territorial defense in prepared mountain positions, which is his only mission. A continuing legacy of Swiss mercenary service is the ceremonial Vatican Swiss Guard. Switzerland has military personnel deployed to eight countries or regions under UN, NATO, European Union or other auspices. The military budget in 2005 totaled $3.82 billion.

18 INTERNATIONAL COOPERATION

Although it was a member of and served as the site for the League of Nations, Switzerland was not a member of the United Nations until 10 September 2002, partly from a fear of compromising traditional Swiss neutrality. The country participates in ECE and in several nonregional specialized agencies, such as the FAO, UNESCO, UNHCR, UNIDO, the World Bank, ILO, IAEA, and the WHO. Switzerland has actively participated in the OSCE. The nation is also a member of the Asian Development Bank, the African Development Bank, the Euro-Atlantic Partnership Council, the European Bank for Reconstruction and Development, the Council of Europe, the Paris Club, the Inter-American Development Bank, OSCE, EFTA, the WTO, and the OECD. Switzerland holds observer status in the OAS and the Latin American Integration Association (LAIA). The headquarters of the International Committee of the Red Cross is located in Geneva. Switzerland is also the repository of the Geneva Convention, governing treatment of civilians, prisoners, and the wounded in wartime.

Switzerland is part of the NATO Partnership for Peace and a guest of the Nonaligned Movement. The nation has supported UN missions and operations in Kosovo (est. 1999), Ethiopia and Eritrea (est. 2000), and the DROC (est. 1999). Switzerland is part of the Australia Group, the Zangger Committee, the European Organization for Nuclear Research (CERN), the Nuclear Suppliers Group (London Group), the Organization for the Prohibition of Chemical Weapons, and the Nuclear Energy Agency.

In environmental cooperation, Switzerland is part of the Antarctic Treaty; the Basel Convention; Conventions on Biological Diversity, Whaling, and Air Pollution; Ramsar; CITES; the London Convention; International Tropical Timber Agreements; the Kyoto Protocol; the Montréal Protocol; MARPOL; the Nuclear Test Ban Treaty; and the UN Conventions on Climate Change and Desertification.

19 ECONOMY

Because of the paucity of its minerals and other raw materials and its limited agricultural production, Switzerland depends upon imports of food and fodder and industrial raw materials, which it finances with exports of manufactured goods. Agriculture is important (in agriculture, Switzerland is about 60% self-sufficient) though limited by a scarcity of level and fertile land, but manufacturing engages more than five times as many workers as farming. Swiss manufacturers excel in quality of workmanship rather than quantity of output. Other important branches of the economy include international banking, insurance, tourism, and transportation. Switzerland ranks among leading countries in research and

development (R&D), and is among the world's top five countries for R&D for biotech and nanotechnology.

Switzerland was less affected than most other nations by the worldwide recession of the early 1980s and experienced a strong recovery beginning in 1983. However, between 1986 and 1992, GNP grew by an annual average of only 0.7% and it fell in 1991, 1992, and 1993. From 1993–95, growth averaged barely 1% a year and decreased once again in 1996. In 1998, however, the economy grew by 2% and by 1.9% in 1999, before soaring, relatively speaking, to 3.4% in 2000. Switzerland's economy was in recession in 2002: the global international slowdown in 2001 and the appreciation of the Swiss franc brought small contractions in 2001 (-0.9%) and 2002 (-0.2%). The financial sector was particularly affected by the slowdown in the economy. However, by 2004, the economy was growing by 1.7%, thanks to eastern and Asian export markets. The GDP growth rate was forecast for 1.5% in 2006 and 2% in 2007.

From 1990 to 1992, the annual inflation rate averaged 5.1%. By 1994 inflation had plummeted to 0.9%; it was 1.8% in 1995, 0.8% in 1996, and 0% in 1998. From 1999 to 2002, average annual inflation was about 1%. In 2004, the inflation rate stood at 0.9% and at 1.1% in 2005. Despite high oil prices forecast for 2006, inflation was expected to remain low. Swiss unemployment has remained consistently low in comparison with other countries, although it reached an unusually high 4.5% in 1993. In 1994 unemployment was 3.8%, and 3.6% in 1998—rates a fraction of France and Germany. Unemployment fell further, to an average annual rate of 2.3%, 1999 to 2002. The unemployment rate in 2004 had risen to 3.4%, and young workers (ages 15–25) were particularly hard hit, as were restaurant and hotel industry workers. Meanwhile, the Swiss GDP per capita—in 2004, $48,596 in market exchange rate terms and $34,160 in purchasing power parity (PPP) terms—continued to be among the highest in the world.

20 INCOME

The US Central Intelligence Agency (CIA) reports that in 2005 Switzerland's gross domestic product (GDP) was estimated at $262.1 billion. The CIA defines GDP as the value of all final goods and services produced within a nation in a given year and computed on the basis of purchasing power parity (PPP) rather than value as measured on the basis of the rate of exchange based on current dollars. The per capita GDP was estimated at $35,000. The annual growth rate of GDP was estimated at 1.2%. The average inflation rate in 2005 was 1.2%. It was estimated that agriculture accounted for 1.5% of GDP, industry 34%, and services 64.5%.

According to the World Bank, in 2003 remittances from citizens working abroad totaled $1.709 billion or about $233 per capita and accounted for approximately 0.5% of GDP.

The World Bank reports that in 2003 household consumption in Switzerland totaled $167.22 billion or about $22,751 per capita based on a GDP of $320.1 billion, measured in current dollars rather than PPP. Household consumption includes expenditures of individuals, households, and nongovernmental organizations on goods and services, excluding purchases of dwellings. It was estimated that for the period 1990 to 2003 household consumption grew at an average annual rate of 1.3%. In 2001 it was estimated that approximately 19% of household consumption was spent on food, 9% on fuel, 3% on health care, and 18% on education.

21 LABOR

In 2005, the Swiss workforce numbered an estimated 3.8 million. As of 2003, the service sector employed 72% of the labor force, with 23.9% engaged in industry, and 4.1% in agriculture. Foreign workers account for about 30% of the country's workforce. In 2005, Switzerland's unemployment rate was estimated at 3.8%.

About 25% of the labor force was unionized in 2005. Swiss law provides for and regulates union organization and collective bargaining. Most labor disputes are settled on the basis of a so-called peace agreement existing since 1937 between the head organizations of employers and employees. Other collective disputes are dealt with by the various cantonal courts of conciliation. Strikes are rare and Switzerland generally records the lowest number of days lost to strikes in the OECD. Approximately 50% of the country's labor force in 2005 was covered by collective bargaining agreements.

The legally mandated maximum workweek is set at 45 hours for blue- and white-collar workers in the services, industrial and retail sectors. A 50-hour workweek covers the rest. Minors as young as 13 may perform light work for up to nine hours per week during the school year and 15 hours otherwise. There are severe restrictions on the hours and conditions of employment of workers until the age of 20. There is no government mandated minimum wage. The Federal Labor Act and the Code of Obligations mandate various other workplace requirements.

22 AGRICULTURE

Some 443,000 hectares (1,095,000 acres), or about 10.8% of the country's total land area, is under seasonal or permanent crops. Most of the cultivable land is in the Mittelland, or central plateau, and the cantons regularly producing the largest quantities of wheat are Bern, Vaud, Fribourg, Zürich, and Aargau. Soil quality is often poor, but yields have been increasing as a result of modern technology. In 2003, agriculture contributed 2% to GDP.

Agricultural production provides only about 60% of the nation's food needs. Although productivity per worker has been increasing steadily, the proportion of the total labor force engaged in agriculture has fallen from 30% in 1900 to about 4.2% in 2000. Between 1955 and 2003, the number of farm holdings fell from 205,997 to 65,866. Some principal crops, with their production figures for 2004, were as follows: potatoes, 484,000 tons; sugar beets, 1,340,000 tons; wheat, 456,000 tons; barley, 230,000 tons; maize, 220,000 tons; oats, 35,000 tons; and rye, 20,000 tons. In the same year, an estimated 11.6 million liters of wine were produced, and there were 15,000 hectares (37,000 acres) of vineyards.

Swiss agricultural policy is highly regulated, with fixed prices and quota restrictions maintained on several products. Domestic production is encouraged by the imposition of protective customs and duties on imported goods, and by restrictions on imports. The Federal Council has the authority to fix prices of bread grains, flour, milk, and other foodstuffs. Production costs in Switzerland, as well as international exchange rates favorable to the Swiss franc, make competition with foreign products difficult. This highly protectionist system has led to excess production and mounting costs associated with the management of surpluses. The Uruguay Round and subsequent Swiss implementation of its provisions in July 1995 (along with rising costs in the agricultural sec-

tor) has forced the government to begin reforming its agricultural support system.

23 ANIMAL HUSBANDRY

More than half of Switzerland's productive area is grassland exploited for hay production and/or grazing. Livestock production contributes about 2% to GDP. Dairying and cattle breeding are practiced, more or less intensively, in all but the barren parts of the country and, during the summer months, even at altitudes of more than 1,200 m (4,000 ft). In 2005 there were 1,540,000 head of cattle and 1,594,000 pigs, 443,000 sheep and 74,000 goats. Meat production in 2005 included (in tons): pork, 233,000; beef, 134,000; poultry, 58,000; mutton/lamb, 6,000; and horse meat, 1,000. Swiss cheeses are world famous; production was 178,000 tons in 2005. That year, 34,000 tons of eggs were produced.

While home production almost covers or exceeds the domestic requirements for milk and dairy products, substantial quantities of eggs and meat must be imported. New agricultural reforms for 2004–07 entail the progressive abolition of the milk quota system, and changes in import tariffs for meat. Selective cattle breeding, research, and improvement of production standards are promoted by the federal government and by farmers' cooperatives. Exports of milk, dairy products, and eggs amounted to $467.6 million in 2004.

24 FISHING

Fishing is relatively unimportant but is carried on in many Swiss rivers and on lakes Constance, Neuchâtel, and Geneva. The total catch was 2,950 tons in 2003. Rainbow trout, whitefish, and perch are the main species. Local fish supply about 12% of domestic needs.

25 FORESTRY

Forests occupied 1,199,000 hectares (2,962,000 acres) in 2000. About two-thirds of the forested land is owned by communes; most of the remainder is owned privately. Federal and cantonal governments account for about 8%. About 80% of the wood in Swiss forests is coniferous, primarily spruce; the remaining 20% is deciduous, predominantly red beech.

The timber cut yielded 4,713,000 cu m (166 million cu ft) of roundwood in 2004, with 21% used as fuel wood. The government estimates that the annual cut represents only two-thirds of potential. Forestry production in 2004 amounted to about 1,505,000 cu m (53 million cu ft) of sawnwood, 1,777,000 tons of paper and paperboard, and 271,000 tons of wood pulp. The trade deficit in forestry products amounted to $169 million in 2004.

26 MINING

Mining, exclusively of industrial minerals for construction, played a minor role in Switzerland's economy. Metal mining has ceased, reserves of the small deposits of iron, nickel-cobalt, gold, and silver were mostly depleted, and new mining activities were discouraged for environmental reasons. Industrial minerals produced in 2004 included hydraulic cement, common clay, gravel, gypsum, lime, nitrogen, salt, sand, stone, and sulfur (from petroleum refining). Metal processing, restricted to primary and secondary aluminum, secondary lead, and steel, depended on imported raw materials or scrap. Environmental concerns have led to a policy to curtail or gradually cease smelting activities. The production and export of chemicals were among the nation's leading industries. Steel was another leading export commodity. A large diamond center, Switzerland was actively involved in cutting and polishing diamonds, and played a big role in international trade activities.

27 ENERGY AND POWER

Switzerland is heavily dependent on imported oil, natural gas and coal to meet its hydrocarbon needs, although it does have the refining capacity to permit a modest amount of refined petroleum products to be exported.

In 2002, Switzerland's imports of all petroleum products averaged 277,350 barrels per day, of which 99,860 barrels per day were crude oil. Total refinery output in 2002 averaged 104,280 barrels per day. Demand for refined oil products in 2002 averaged 267,230 barrels per day, allowing Switzerland to export an average of 11,550 barrels per day of refined oil products.

In 2002, Switzerland's imports and consumption of natural gas each totaled 107.18 billion cu ft. Coal imports that year totaled 169,000 short tons, with demand at 221,000 short tons.

Switzerland's electric power plants had an installed capacity of 17.268 million kW in 2002, of which hydroelectric plants accounted for 13.240 million kW of capacity, followed by nuclear plants at 3.200 million kW, conventional thermal plants at 0.453 million kW and geothermal/other plants at 0.375 million kW. Electricity production in 2002 totaled 63.240 billion kWh, of which 1.6% was from fossil fuels, 55.1% from hydropower, 40.9% from nuclear power, and 2.3% from renewable sources.

28 INDUSTRY

Manufacturing industries contributed 34% of GDP in 2003. The industrial growth rate in 2004 was 4.7%. Swiss industries are chiefly engaged in the manufacture, from imported raw materials, of highly finished goods for domestic consumption and for export. Most of the industrial enterprises are located in the plains and the Swiss plateau, especially in the cantons of Zürich, Bern, Aargau, St. Gallen, Solothurn, Vaud, Basel (Baselstadt and Baselland), and Thurgau. Some industries are concentrated in certain regions: the watch and jewelry industry in the Jura Mountains; machinery in Zürich, Geneva, and Basel; chemical industries (dyes and pharmaceuticals) in Basel; and the textile industry in northeastern Switzerland. In 1993, the industrial sector was targeted for assistance by a government-initiated revitalization program; in 1995, the sector again benefited from government policy when the turnover tax was replaced by a value-added tax system, expected to relieve industry of SwFr1–2 billion per year in taxes. Switzerland, along with Germany and Japan, is at the forefront of the emerging industry of environmental technology.

The textile industry, using wool, cotton, silk, and synthetics, is the oldest Swiss industry and, despite foreign competition resulting from the elimination of textile quotas by the World Trade Organization in 2005, remains important. The machine industry, first among Swiss industries today, produces goods ranging from heavy arms and ammunition to fine precision and optical instruments. Switzerland is the world's largest exporter of watches and watch products (followed by Hong Kong and China), with exports worth $9 billion in 2004. For the first half of 2005, Swiss watch exports were up 11% over the same period in 2004 and exceeding

forecasts. Chemicals, especially dyes and pharmaceuticals, also are important. As of 2003, Switzerland had a 4.3% share of the world export of chemical and pharmaceutical products, and ranked 9th among the largest export nations. Pharmaceutical exports as a percentage of total chemical industry exports increased from 40% in 1980 to 70.3% in 2003. Switzerland has also developed a major food industry, relying in part on the country's capacity for milk production. Condensed milk was first developed in Switzerland, as were two other important processed food products: chocolate and baby food. The Swiss company Nestlé S. A., headquartered in Vevey, is one of the world's largest food companies. In addition to Switzerland's major industries, such as textiles, nonmetallic minerals, and watchmaking and clockmaking, others, such as chemicals, plastics, and paper, have grown rapidly.

29 SCIENCE AND TECHNOLOGY

The major scientific learned societies, headquartered in Bern, are the Swiss Academy of Sciences, founded in 1815, and the Swiss Academy of Engineering Sciences, founded in 1981. About two-thirds of the funds for Swiss research and development (R&D), a high proportion by world standards, are supplied by industry and the rest by federal and cantonal governments. In 2000 (the latest year for which data was available), expenditures for R&D totaled $5,316.302 million, or 2.63% of GDP. Of that amount, the business sector accounted for 69.1%, followed by the government at 23.2%, foreign sources at 4.3%, higher education at 2.1% and private nonprofit organizations at 1.4%. For that same year, there were 3,594 scientists and 2,315 technicians per million people, that were engaged in R&D. The Swiss National Science Foundation was established in 1952 to finance noncommercial research for which funds would not otherwise be available. Most such spending is in the important chemicals sector. The Ministry of Public Economy, the center for federal agricultural research, has six research stations. In 2002, high-tech exports were valued at $17.077 billion and accounted for 21% of manufactured exports. In that same year, of all bachelor's degrees awarded, 25.7% were for the sciences (natural, mathematics and computers, engineering).

30 DOMESTIC TRADE

Zürich, the largest city, is the commercial, financial, and industrial center of Switzerland. Basel is the second most important commercial city, followed by Geneva and Lausanne. Most Swiss wholesale firms are importers as well, specializing in one commodity or a group of related commodities.

The trend in retail trade is moving from independent establishments to larger supermarkets, department stores, and discount chains. As such, many small retailers have joined together to form purchasing cooperatives. However, Switzerland is a challenging market for franchising, due to Switzerland's limited market size, high salaries, and high costs of services; also, consumer preference for high quality and authentic products or a new innovative idea over already existing products is another challenge facing potential franchisees. Companies sponsoring home shopping parties (Tupperware, Mary Kay, Body Shop, etc.) have become very popular. Some agricultural products, such as butter, grains, and edible fats and oils, are subject to import controls and price controls apply to many goods and services. The use of electronic debit cards for purchases is growing rapidly.

Advertising, mostly entrusted to firms of specialists, uses as media billboards, movie theaters, television, local transportation facilities, railroads, newspapers, and magazines.

Usual business hours are from 8 or 9 AM to 5 or 6 PM. Shops are normally open from 9 AM to 6:30 PM on weekdays but only to 5 PM on Saturdays; some shops close from 12 PM to 2 PM at lunchtime. In larger cities, shops generally extend their hours until 8 PM on one evening of the week, usually Thursday. Banks are open to the public from 8:30 AM to 4:30 PM Monday–Friday.

31 FOREIGN TRADE

Switzerland's export commodities are split into two categories: machinery sold to other manufacturers, and commodities used by consumers. The country exports a large number of the world's watches and clocks.

While Switzerland is not a member of the EU, it has been seeking ways to adopt some of the advantages of membership without relinquishing sovereignty. As of 2005, 62% of Swiss exports were destined for the EU market. As of 2004, Switzerland's main export partners, in order of importance, were Germany, the United States, France, Italy, the United Kingdom, and Spain. By that date, Switzerland's primary import partners were Germany, Italy, France, the United States, the Netherlands, and Austria.

32 BALANCE OF PAYMENTS

In the past, Switzerland typically had a foreign trade deficit. More recently, however, this imbalance was more than compensated for by income from services, investments, insurance, and tourism. Restructuring of enterprises in the 1990s, due to the strength of the Swiss franc, caused the export-oriented manufacturing sector to become highly successful. Exports of goods and services amounted to some 46% of GDP in 2000.

In 2004, merchandise exports totaled $138.2 billion, and merchandise imports $122.6 billion, for a trade surplus of $15.6 billion. The current account surplus amounted to $50.6 billion, equivalent to 14.2% of GDP, making Switzerland a net creditor nation.

33 BANKING AND SECURITIES

In 2000, Switzerland had two major banks, 24 cantonal banks, and numerous foreign-owned banks, savings banks, and other banks and finance companies. There were a total of 375 banks in the country in that year. The bank balance-sheet total per capita in Switzerland is higher than that of any other nation in the world. Total assets of the Swiss banking system amounted to $1.3 trillion at the end of 2000, while total securities deposits were $3.4 trillion. Moreover, registered banks and bank-like finance companies numbered 494 in 1995, offering the Swiss, on average, the greatest access to banking services of all the world's nations.

The government-supervised Swiss National Bank, incorporated in 1905 and the sole bank of issue, is a semiprivate institution owned by the cantons, by former banks of issue, and by the public. The National Bank acts as a central clearinghouse and participates in many foreign and domestic banking operations. The two big banks, (United Bank of Switzerland (UBS) and Credit Suisse Group) dominate the Swiss banking scene and are expanding aggressively overseas. They are universal banks, providing a full range of services to all types of customers.

Regional banks specialize in mortgage lending and credits for small businesses. Since 1994, most of the country's regional banks have been linked in a common holding company providing back-office operations and other services to members in a bid to cut costs.

Foreign banks make up about a third of banks active in Switzerland. In contrast to domestic banks, their numbers have risen over the last decade but their business is increasingly focused on asset management, mostly of funds from abroad. On 1 January 1995 a new banking law came into effect allowing for foreign banks to open subsidiaries, branches, or representative offices in the country without first getting approval of the Federal Banking Commission.

The transactions of private and foreign banks doing business in Switzerland traditionally play a significant role in both Swiss and

Principal Trading Partners – Switzerland (2003)

(In millions of US dollars)

Country	Exports	Imports	Balance
World	100,693.3	96,447.6	4,245.7
Germany	20,983.7	31,144.1	-10,160.4
United States	11,375.2	5,325.0	6,050.2
France-Monaco	8,806.4	10,395.6	-1,589.2
Italy-San Marino-Holy See	8,323.9	10,299.0	-1,975.1
United Kingdom	4,894.8	3,910.3	984.5
Japan	4,019.9	2,028.3	1,991.6
Spain	3,536.1	2,262.4	1,273.7
Austria	3,323.7	4,079.2	-755.5
Netherlands	3,273.6	4,813.4	-1,539.8
China, Hong Kong SAR	2,976.2	482.2	2,494.0

(…) data not available or not significant.

SOURCE: *2003 International Trade Statistics Yearbook*, New York: United Nations, 2004.

Balance of Payments – Switzerland (2003)

(In millions of US dollars)

Current Account		43,292.0
Balance on goods		6,961.0
Imports	-108,482.0	
Exports	115,443.0	
Balance on services		15,066.0
Balance on income		26,429.0
Current transfers		-5,166.0
Capital Account		-763.0
Financial Account		-30,136.0
Direct investment abroad		-15,926.0
Direct investment in Switzerland		12,603.0
Portfolio investment assets		-32,902.0
Portfolio investment liabilities		-1,662.0
Financial derivatives		…
Other investment assets		-4,631.0
Other investment liabilities		12,383.0
Net Errors and Omissions		-8,988.0
Reserves and Related Items		-3,405.0

(…) data not available or not significant.

SOURCE: *Balance of Payment Statistics Yearbook 2004*, Washington, DC: International Monetary Fund, 2004.

foreign capital markets; however, precise accounting of assets and liabilities in this sector are not usually made available as public information. Switzerland's strong financial position and its tradition (protected by the penal code since 1934) of preserving the secrecy of individual bank depositors have made it a favorite depository with persons throughout the world. (However, Swiss secrecy provisions are not absolute and have been lifted to provide information in criminal investigations.) The Swiss Office for Compensation executes clearing traffic with foreign countries.

In 1997, Swiss banks came under heavy criticism for losing track of money, gold, and other valuables belonging to Jewish Holocaust victims and held by the banks during World War II. Records also showed the banks had closed thousands of victims' accounts without notice after the war. The banks claimed they had lost the old records, but a group of journalists found the records archived in Lausanne in April of that year.

Also in 1997, an embarrassed Swiss government selected four members to a panel empowered to run a fund for Holocaust victims. Nobel laureate, Elie Weisel, a concentration camp survivor, turned down an invitation to serve as one of the three foreign members on the board. The fund, intended to help impoverished Holocaust victims and their families, is supported by funds appropriated by Nazis from Jews sent to concentration camps. Much of the gold, jewels, bonds, and currency taken by the Nazis had been placed in Swiss banks. In March 1998, Switzerland's banks agreed to create a $1.25 billion fund designed to compensate Holocaust survivors and their families.

Swiss banks were also under fire in 1997 for possibly facilitating money laundering of drug money accrued by a former Mexican president's brother and for failing to adequately recover the billions of dollars supposedly plundered by former Zairian dictator Mobuto Sese Seko, who was overthrown that year. All the negative publicity has caused some to question the usefulness of Swiss banks' much-lauded secrecy.

The International Monetary Fund reports that in 2001, currency and demand deposits—an aggregate commonly known as M1—were equal to $102.9 billion. In that same year, M2—an aggregate equal to M1 plus savings deposits, small time deposits, and money market mutual funds—was $326.3 billion. The money market rate, the rate at which financial institutions lend to one another in the short term, was 1.65%. The discount rate, the interest rate at which the central bank lends to financial institutions in the short term, was 1.59%.

Stock exchanges operate in Geneva (founded 1850), Basel (1875), and Zürich (1876). The Zürich exchange is the most important in the country. In terms of market capitalization, the Swiss stock exchanges rank seventh in the world, behind New York, Tokyo, Osaka, London, Frankfurt, and Paris, as of 1997. Overall, turnover, including shares, bonds, and options, amounted to SwFr1.2 trillion in 2002, a drop of 2.3% from the prior year. The open outcry stock exchanges in Zürich, Geneva, and Basel closed in 1994 when a national electronic stock exchange for all securities trading began operations in August. In 2004, a total of 282 companies were listed on the SWX Swiss Exchange, which had a market capitalization of $825.849 billion.

34 INSURANCE

The Swiss people are the most heavily insured in the world, although this reflects social insurance such as health insurance, as well as more commercial types of business. Nevertheless, Swiss insurers now rely on foreign business for two-thirds of their premium income. The insurance sector has been steadily deregulated during the 1990s. One of the last set of controls was scrapped in 1996 when the fixed tariff regime for third-party vehicle insurance was abolished. As of 1999, Swiss insurance companies numbered over 100.

Switzerland controls an estimated one-third of the world's reinsurance, and insurance income represents a major item in the Swiss balance of payments. Insurance investments are represented heavily in the Swiss capital market, and Swiss insurance firms have invested widely in foreign real estate. About half the domestic insurance business is in the hands of the state. The Swiss Reinsurance Co. in Zürich is the largest of its kind in the world. As of 1999, about 10% of all Swiss insurance companies dealt solely with reinsurance. There are several types of compulsory insurance in Switzerland, including workers' compensation, third-party automobile liability, fire, pension, hunters', aircraft, nuclear power station, old age, unemployment, and disability insurance. In 1999, the total income of the Swiss domestic insurance market was 48 million, making it the 12th largest insurance market globally. In 2003, the value of all direct insurance premiums written totaled $40.760 billion, of which life insurance premiums accounted for $24.713 billion. In that same year, Switzerland's top nonlife insurer was Winterthur, which had gross written nonlife premiums of $2.21 billion, while Winterthur Leben was the country's leading life insurer, with gross written life insurance premiums of $6.09 billion.

35 PUBLIC FINANCE

The Swiss government has been known historically for maintaining a relatively high degree of austerity in comparison to its European neighbors. In 1991, the federal government incurred a budget deficit of over SwFr1.5 billion, the first budget discrepancy in seven years. Cantonal budgets also were in deficit. These deficits continued throughout the 1990s and into the 2000s, prompting governments at all levels to take further cost-cutting steps. As an international creditor, debt management policies are not relevant to Switzerland, which participates in the Paris Club debt reschedulings and is an active member of the OECD.

The US Central Intelligence Agency (CIA) estimated that in 2005 Switzerland's central government took in revenues of approximately $138.1 billion and had expenditures of $143.6 billion. Revenues minus expenditures totaled approximately -$5.5 billion. Public debt in 2005 amounted to 53.3% of GDP. Total external debt was $856 billion.

The International Monetary Fund (IMF) reported that in 2001, the most recent year for which it had data, central government revenues were SwFr81,727 million and expenditures were SwFr80,498 million. The value of revenues was us$48,428 million and expenditures us$47,700 million, based on a market exchange rate for 2001 of us$1 = SwFr1.6876 as reported by the IMF. Government outlays by function were as follows: general public services, 18.1%; defense, 6.2%; public order and safety, 0.8%; economic

Public Finance – Switzerland (2001)

(In millions of Swiss francs, central government figures)

Revenue and Grants	**81,727**	**100.0%**
Tax revenue	43,200	52.9%
Social contributions	32,391	39.6%
Grants	2,307	2.8%
Other revenue	3,829	4.7%
Expenditures	**80,498**	**100.0%**
General public services	14,566	18.1%
Defense	4,956	6.2%
Public order and safety	620	0.8%
Economic affairs	11,749	14.6%
Environmental protection	...	...
Housing and community amenities	781	1.0%
Health	215	0.3%
Recreational, culture, and religion	482	0.6%
Education	2,650	3.3%
Social protection	44,479	55.3%

(…) data not available or not significant.

SOURCE: *Government Finance Statistics Yearbook 2004,* Washington, DC: International Monetary Fund, 2004.

affairs, 14.6%; housing and community amenities, 1.0%; health, 0.3%; recreation, culture, and religion, 0.6%; education, 3.3%; and social protection, 55.3%.

36 TAXATION

The Swiss Confederation, the cantons, and the communes all levy taxes on income or profits. Periodic federal, cantonal, and communal taxes also are charged against capital values belonging to corporations and other corporate entities. The cantons all levy wealth taxes based on individual net assets, stamp duties, taxes on entertainment or admissions, and special charges for educational, social, and sanitary services. Most cantons also levy a tax surcharge on members of certain major churches for the support of those religions. Localities may impose taxes on land, rents, and entertainment, as well as a head tax and a dog tax.

Although corporate income taxes are taxed at a flat rate of 8.5%, the effective rate is actually between 8% and 25% when federal and cantonal taxes are taken into account. Generally, capital gains received by a company are taxed as ordinary business income at regular business rates. However, different rules may apply to gains received from real estate or to real estate companies at the cantonal/communal level. Generally, dividends distributed by Swiss companies are taxed as ordinary income, to which a withholding rate of 35% is applied. However, applicable participation exemption rules may lower the federal tax liability for the recipient. Interest income from banks, and publicly offered debentures, bonds and other debt instruments issued by a Swiss borrower are subject to a withholding rate of 35%. However, loans from a foreign parent company to Swiss subsidiaries and commercial loans, generally are exempt.

Federal tax is levied on personal income at rates up to 11.5%. However, cantonal rates can range from 10% to around 30%. Various deductions and personal allowances are granted according to circumstances. Those between the ages of 20 and 50 who do not fulfill their military obligation are liable for an additional tax.

Cantonal and communal taxes are generally imposed at progressive rates.

In 1995 Switzerland replaced its old system of taxing turnover with a value-added tax (VAT) similar to those of its European neighbors. As of 2005, the VAT was 7.6% and was levied on all deliveries of goods and services, including investments, consumer goods, animals and plants, consulting and entertainment services, license fees, and the sale of rights. The VAT is also levied on imported goods and services. However, hotel and lodging services are subject to a lower rate of 3.6%, while items such as foodstuffs, medicines, newspapers, farming supplies and agricultural products were subject to a 2.4% rate. Exports were zero-rated. There are also miscellaneous federal taxes, such as stamp duties, payroll and excise taxes.

37 CUSTOMS AND DUTIES

Switzerland joined EFTA in 1960 and became a full member of the GATT group in 1966. In 1973, Switzerland entered into an industrial free trade agreement with the European Community (now the European Union). Duties on industrial imports from the European Community were eliminated by 1977. Although it generally favors free trade, Switzerland protects domestic agriculture for national defense reasons and its customs tariff, established in 1921, is primarily a revenue-raising instrument. Specific duties, low for raw materials, moderate for semifinished goods, and high for manufactured goods, are levied by weight of import. Import duties average 3.2% on industrial goods. Switzerland gives preferential treatment to imports from developing nations. Other import taxes include a 3% statistical tax, a standard 7.6% VAT, and an environmental tax. Specific luxuries like cigarettes and spirits are subject to an excise tax. Quotas regulate the importation of certain agricultural items such as white wine.

38 FOREIGN INVESTMENT

Switzerland is generally open to foreign investment and grants foreign investors national treatment. However, the government restricts investment in vacation real estate, utilities, and other sectors considered essential to national security (such as hydroelectric and nuclear power plants, operation of oil pipelines, operation of airlines and marine navigation, and the transportation of explosive materials). There are no restrictions on repatriation of profits. Federal grants are offered for investments in depressed areas. The cantonal governments offer tax and nontax incentives for new investments or extensions of existing investments on a case-by-case basis.

In 1997, total foreign direct investment (FDI) stock in Switzerland exceeded $56.58 billion (22% of GDP). US companies accounted for 23% of that total. By 1999, FDI stock had risen to over $83 billion (32% of GDP), and the United States share to 26.6%. FDI inflows were $6.6 billion in 1997, climbing to a peak of $16.3 billion in 2000, before falling back to about $10 billion in 2001. In 2003, FDI inflows amounted to $12.2 billion.

Stocks of Swiss FDI abroad totaled $170 billion (62.3% of GDP) in 1997 rising to $205.2 billion (79% of GDP) in 1999. In 1999, the largest holders of Swiss outward FDI were the United States (with $45 billion, 23%); the United Kingdom ($23.7 billion, 11.5%); Germany ($17.4 billion, 8.5%); the Netherlands ($12.5 billion, 6.1%);

and France ($10.4 billion, 5%). FDI outflows in 2003 amounted to $10.9 billion.

39 ECONOMIC DEVELOPMENT

Private enterprise is the basis of Swiss economic policy. Although government intervention has traditionally been kept to a minimum, the international monetary crises from late 1974 to mid-1975 led to imposition of various interim control measures; in 1982, with inflation rising, a constitutional amendment mandating permanent government price controls was approved by popular referendum. The Swiss National Bank has followed a general policy of limiting monetary growth. To further raise the standard of living, the government also grants subsidies for educational and research purposes, promotes professional training, and encourages exports. Although certain foreign transactions are regulated, there is free currency exchange and a guarantee to repatriate earnings of foreign corporations.

The cause of the remarkable stability of Switzerland's economy lies in the adaptability of its industries; in the soundness of its convertible currency, which is backed by gold to an extent unmatched in any other country; and in the fact that the particular pattern of Swiss democracy, where every law may be submitted to the popular vote, entails taking into account the wishes of all parties whose interests would be affected by a change in legislation.

Switzerland's development assistance program takes the form of technical cooperation, preferential customs treatment for certain third-world products, and a limited number of bilateral aid arrangements.

The question of future European Union (EU) membership remains a point of contention among the Swiss. The French-speaking minority overwhelmingly favors EU membership, while the German-speaking majority strongly opposes it. In a 2000 referendum, Swiss voters approved closer ties to the EU. Some of the key provisions of the deal included agreement to allow EU trucks transit rights through Switzerland, as well as granting Swiss freedom of movement in the EU. Full access to the Swiss market by the original 15 EU member countries was achieved in a June 2004 agreement, ending as a result the "national preference." Switzerland approved another pact, the Schengen-Dublin agreement with the EU, in June 2005, which allows for the free movement of peoples, although fears of cheap labor coming from new EU member nations remained. However, voters approved by a referendum held on 25 September 2005 a measure to extend the provision of free movement of peoples to the 10 predominantly eastern European nations which joined the EU in 2004.

A new ordinance covering the banking sector was enacted in 2002, to combat money laundering and the financing of terrorism. Switzerland joined the UN in 2002.

40 SOCIAL DEVELOPMENT

There is a social insurance system and mandatory occupational pension system financed by employer and employee contributions as well as governmental subsidies. Old-age pensions are paid at age 65 for men and 63 for women. Disability and survivorship pensions are also available to qualified recipients. Sickness and Maternity benefits were first implemented in 1911. Medical care is available to all persons living in Switzerland, and there is a voluntary insurance plan for all employees to provide cash benefits. Maternity benefits are payable up to 16 weeks. Work injury insurance is compulsory, with contribution rates varying according to risk. Unemployment and disability is also covered. Family allowances are provided by the cantons, but there is a federal program covering agricultural workers. Some cantons provide birth grants.

The law provides for equal pay and prohibits gender discrimination, but there is significant bias against women in the workplace. Women earn less than men, and are less likely to receive training. There are few women in managerial positions, and they are also promoted less than men. Sexual harassment in the workplace continues, although laws and advocacy groups work to eradicate the problem. The Federal Office for Equality Between Women and Men and the Federal Commission on Women are charged with eliminating all types of gender discrimination. Physical and sexual violence against women and domestic abuse persist.

Extremist organizations continue physical and verbal attacks on religious, racial, and ethnic minorities. The government is taking some action to curtail the activities of these groups. Human rights are generally respected in Switzerland.

41 HEALTH

Health standards and medical care are excellent. The pharmaceuticals industry ranks as one of the major producers of specialized pharmaceutical products. Managed-care systems are widely used, especially with a "gatekeeper" component to control costs. As of 2004, there were an estimated 352 physicians, 834 nurses, 48 dentists, and 62 pharmacists per 1,000 people. The ratio of doctors per population varies by region, with the highest proportions in Basle and Geneva and the lowest in Appenzell. Total health care expenditure was estimated at 10.4% of GDP.

As of 2002, the crude birth rate and overall mortality rate were estimated at, respectively, 9.8 and 8.8 per 1,000 people. About 71% of married women (ages 15 to 49) were using contraception. The fertility rate was 1.5 children per woman surviving her childbearing years in 2000. The infant mortality rate, which had been 70.3 per 1,000 live births in 1924, was 4.39 in 2005. The vaccination rates for DPT and measles were, respectively, 94% and 81%. In 2005, life expectancy was averaged at 80.39 years.

There were about nine cases of tuberculosis per 100,000 people reported in 1999. Cardiovascular disease-related deaths numbered nearly 30,000 in the mid-1990s. Tobacco consumption has dramatically decreased from 3.1 kg (6.8 lbs) per year per adult in 1984–86 to 2.4 kg (5.3 lbs) in 1995. In 1996, voters in Zurich approved a government plan to supply heroin addicts with free access to their drug.

The HIV/AIDS prevalence was 0.40 per 100 adults in 2003. As of 2004, there were approximately 13,000 people living with HIV/AIDS in the country. There were an estimated 100 deaths from AIDS in 2003.

42 HOUSING

Although housing standards are comparatively high, there are shortages in certain areas. In the mid-1990s, less than 40,000 new dwellings per year were constructed in communities of 2,000 or more inhabitants, down from 44,228 in 1985. In 2000, there were about 3,115,399 private households and about 1,377,552 residential buildings. About 30% of all residential buildings were designed for two or more households. The total housing stock in 2001 was about 3,604,340 dwellings.

43 EDUCATION

Education at all levels is first and foremost the responsibility of the cantons. Thus, Switzerland has 26 different systems based on differing education laws and varied cultural and linguistic needs. The cantons decide on the types of schools, length of study, teaching materials, and teachers' salaries. Education is compulsory in most cantons for nine years, and in a few for eight. An optional 10th year has been introduced in several cantons. Church schools in some cantons are tax supported. After primary school, students complete the compulsory portion of their education in various types of secondary Grade I schools, which emphasize vocational or academic subjects to varying degrees. Secondary Grade II schools, which are not compulsory, include trade and vocational preparatory schools and gymnasiums, which prepare students for the university and lead to the *matura*, or higher school-leaving certificate.

Switzerland has a large number of private schools attracting primarily foreign students. These schools, most of them located in the French-speaking cantons, are known for their high-quality education, of either the academic or "finishing school" variety.

In 2001, about 97% of children between the ages of five and six were enrolled in some type of preschool program. Primary school enrollment in 2003 was estimated at about 99% of age-eligible students. The same year, secondary school enrollment was about 87% of age-eligible students. It is estimated that about 98.6% of all students complete their primary education. The student-to-teacher ratio for primary school was at about 13:1 in 2000; the ratio for secondary school was about 10:1. In 2003, private schools accounted for about 3.7% of primary school enrollment and 7% of secondary enrollment.

Switzerland has 10 cantonal universities, including four in French-speaking areas and four in German-speaking ones. The universities' expenditures are largely financed by the cantons, with a 53% contribution from the Confederation. Approximately one-third of all higher-level educational funding goes to research and development. The largest universities are those of Zürich, Geneva, and Basel; others include those of Lausanne, Bern, Fribourg, and Neuchâtel. The Federal Institute of Technology in Zürich, the Economics College at St. Gallen, and the Federal Institute of Technology in Lausanne are also important. In 2003, it was estimated that about 49% of the tertiary age population were enrolled in tertiary education programs; 53% for men and 44% for women. The adult literacy rate has been estimated at about 99%.

As of 2003, public expenditure on education was estimated at 5.8% of GDP, or 15.1% of total government expenditures.

44 LIBRARIES AND MUSEUMS

The library of Basel University (3 million volumes) and the Swiss National Library in Bern (3.6 million volumes) are the largest in Switzerland. The University of Geneva has 1.8 million volumes; the University of Lausanne has about 1.7 million; and the University of Fribourg has two million. Switzerland has an extensive public library system with about 2,344 service points holding over 28 million volumes in total. The Library and Archives of the Unit-

ed Nations is located in Geneva, as is the library of the International Labor Organization (over 580,000 items).

The National Museum, a federal institution in Zürich, houses historic objects; other historical museums are located in Basel, Bern, and Geneva. Basel houses both the Museum of Ancient Art and the Basel Museum of Fine Arts, which has a fine collection of 15th- and 16th-century German masterworks, paintings by Dutch artists of the 17th and 18th centuries, and a survey from Corot to Picasso. The Museum of Fine Arts in Bern contains paintings by old masters and impressionists (Klee Foundation). The Zürich Art Museum houses modern Swiss paintings, as well as works by Dutch and Flemish masters of the 17th century. Geneva houses the Museum of the Voltaire Institute, the Museum of the Institute of Henri Dunant, founder of the International Red Cross, the Jean-Jacques Rousseau Museum, and the Museum of Modern and Contemporary Art, which opened in 1994. The League of Nations (United Nations) Museum is in Geneva. There are arts and crafts museums in most of the larger cities, and Neuchâtel has an ethnographic museum. Many fine examples of Romanesque, Gothic, and Baroque architecture are found in Switzerland.

45 MEDIA

The postal system and the telephone, telegraph, radio, and television systems are government owned and operated. The telephone system is completely automatic. International communications, air navigation services, and the new electronic media, including data transmission and electronic mail, are the province of Radio Suisse, a public corporation. In 2003, there were an estimated 744 mainline telephones for every 1,000 people. The same year, there were approximately 843 mobile phones in use for every 1,000 people.

Broadcasting is controlled by the Swiss Broadcasting Corp. (SBC), an autonomous corporation under federal supervision. A number of independent local radio stations have been operating since 1983. Radio programs are broadcast in German, French, Italian, and Romansch. As of 1999, Switzerland had seven AM and 50 FM radio stations and 108 television stations. In 2003, there were an estimated 1,002 radios and 552 television sets for every 1,000 people. About 376.2 of every 1,000 people were cable subscribers. Also in 2003, there were 708.7 personal computers for every 1,000 people and 351 of every 1,000 people had access to the Internet. There were 2,821 secure Internet servers in the country in 2004.

A few papers, such as the *Neue Zürcher Zeitung* and the *Tribune de Genève,* are widely read even beyond the borders of Switzerland and have excellent international coverage. The Agence Télégraphique Suisse (Schweizerische Depeschenagentur), co-owned by some 40 newspaper publishers, is Switzerland's most important national news agency.

Among the largest dailies in 2005 were *Blick* (in Zürich, circulation 362,000), *Tages-Anzeiger* (Zürich, 231,000), and *Neue Zürcher Zeitung* (Zürich, 151,000). *Tribune de Genève* was the best-selling French daily in 2005 with a circulation of about 71,000. *Corriere del Ticino* is a best-selling Italian paper with a 2005 circulation of about 39,000. The *Schweizer Illustrierte* (circulation 195,894) is the most popular illustrated weekly, and the *Nebelspalter* (38,630) is the best-known satirical periodical.

The constitution provides for freedom of speech and a free press, and the government is said to uphold these freedoms in practice.

46 ORGANIZATIONS

Both agricultural and consumer cooperatives are numerous. The Swiss Office for Commercial Expansion is an important foreign trade promotion organization. The Swiss Federation of Commerce and Industry also promotes commerce, trade and industry. The Swiss Confederation of Trade Unions serves the interests of workers/employees. The International Labour Organization has a base office in Geneva. There are chambers of commerce in all the major cities. Trade unions and professional associations exist for most occupations.

Geneva serves as home to a variety of international organizations including the International Red Cross and Red Crescent Society, the World Council of Churches, the Lutheran World Federation, the World Alliance of Reformed Churches, The World Health Organization, and the World Scout Foundation. Several United Nation's committee offices are based here as well, the UN Economic Commission for Europe, UN Environment Programme, UN High Commission for Refugees, the UN Institute for Training and Research, and the UN Research Institute for Social Development. Other international organizations with national chapters include Amnesty International, Defence for Children International, Caritas, and Greenpeace.

There are numerous cultural and educational organizations. A few with national interest include the Swiss Academy of Humanities and Social Sciences, the Swiss Academy of Medical Sciences, and the Swiss Academy of Sciences. The European Center for Culture is a multinational organization promoting understanding and cooperation between cultures.

Active youth groups within the country include Junior Chamber, YMCA/YWCA, and the Swiss Guide and Scout Movement. There are a large number of sports associations nationwide, including several international organizations such as the International Baseball Federation, the International Basketball Federation, and the International Gymnastic Federation. The International Olympic Committee is based in Lausanne.

Several human rights, social justice, and social action organizations exist, including the Association of International Consultants on Human Rights, the Berne Declaration, Green Cross, The National Council of Women of Switzerland, and the Women's International League for Peace and Freedom. The International Alliance Women and the Women's World Summit Foundation both focus on health and equal rights for women. Soroptimist International of Europe is a multinational organization of business-women working toward the causes of peace, justice, health, and equal rights.

47 TOURISM, TRAVEL, AND RECREATION

Switzerland has long been one of the most famous tourist areas in the world, and Swiss hospitality and the Swiss hotel industry are justly renowned. Scenic attractions are manifold, and in the Swiss Alps and on the shores of the Swiss lakes there are features of interest for the skier, the swimmer, the hiker, the mountain climber, and the high alpinist. There are approximately 50,000 km (31,000 mi) of marked footpaths and 500 ski lifts. The hotels are among the best in the world; Switzerland pioneered in modern hotel management and in specialized training for hotel personnel. Central Switzerland and the Geneva region attract the largest number of foreign tourists. Passports and visas are required of all visitors except citizens of the Americas, Europe, Japan, Australia, and New Zealand who do not need visas for stays of up to 90 days.

In 2003, there were 6,530,108 visitors who arrived in Switzerland, almost 28% of whom were German. Tourism receipts totaled $11.3 billion, and hotel rooms numbered 139,969 with 258,726 beds and an occupancy rate of 38%. Visitors stayed an average of three nights.

In 2005, the US Department of State estimated the daily cost of staying in Geneva at $380; in Zürich, $295; in Basel, $379; and in Montreux at $394.

48 FAMOUS SWISS

World-famous Swiss scientists include the physician and alchemist Philippus Aureolus Paracelsus (Theophrastus Bombastus von Hohenheim, 1493?–1541); the outstanding mathematicians Johann Bernoulli (1667–1748) and Leonhard Euler (1707–83); the geologist Louis Agassiz (Jean Louis Rodolphe Agassiz, 1807–73), who was active in the United States; the physiologist, pathologist, and surgeon Emil Theodor Kocher (1841–1917), who received the Nobel Prize for medicine in 1909; Charles Édouard Guillaume (1861–1938) and the German-born Albert Einstein (1879–1955, a naturalized Swiss citizen), Nobel Prize winners in physics in 1920 and 1921, respectively; and Paul Karrer (b.Russia, 1889–1971), authority on vitamins, who shared the 1937 Nobel Prize in chemistry. Other Nobel Prize winners in the sciences include Alfred Werner (1866–1919; chemistry, 1913); Yugoslav-born Leopold Ruzicka (1887–1976; chemistry, 1939); Yugoslav-born Vladimir Prelog (1906–1998; chemistry, 1975); Austrian-born Wolfgang Pauli (1900–1958; physics, 1945); Paul Hermann Müller (1899–1965), Walter Rudolf Hess (1881–1973), and Polish-born Tadeus Reichstein (1897–1996), Nobel laureates for medicine in 1948, 1949, and 1950, respectively; Werner Arber (b.1929; medicine, 1978); Heinrich Rohrer (b.1933; physics, 1986); and K. Alex Müller (b.1927) and German-born J. Georg Bednorz (b.1950), for physics in 1987.

Jean-Jacques Rousseau (1712–78), a Geneva-born philosopher, musician, novelist, and diarist in France, was a great figure of the 18th century whose writings exerted a profound influence on education and political thought. Swiss-born Mme. Germaine de Staël (Anne Louise Germaine Necker, 1766–1817) was acclaimed the world over as defender of liberty against Napoleon. Other noted Swiss writers include Albrecht von Haller (1708–77), also an anatomist and physiologist; the novelists and short-story writers Johann Heinrich David Zschokke (1771–1848) and Jeremias Gotthelf (Albert Bitzius, 1797–1854), also a clergyman and poet; and the poets and novelists Gottfried Keller (1819–90), Conrad Ferdinand Meyer (1825–98), and Carl Spitteler (1845–1924), the last of whom won the Nobel Prize for literature in 1919. The diaries of the philosopher, poet, and essayist Henri-Frédéric Amiel (1821–81) are famous as the stirring confessions of a sensitive man's aspirations and failures. Charles Ferdinand Ramuz (1878–1947) is often regarded as the most powerful Swiss writer since Rousseau. The German-born novelist and poet Hermann Hesse (1877–1962) was awarded the Nobel Prize for literature in 1946. Other recent and contemporary Swiss writers include Robert Walser (1878–1956), a highly individualistic author, and the novelists and playwrights Max Rudolf Frisch (1911–91) and Friedrich Dürrenmatt (1921–

90), whose psychological dramas have been performed throughout Europe and the United States.

Ludwig Senfl (1490–1543) was an outstanding Renaissance composer. The *Dodecachordon* (1547) of Henricus Glareanus (Heinrich Loris, 1488–1563) was one of the most important music treatises of the Renaissance period. Swiss-born composers of more recent times include Ernest Bloch (1880–1959), Othmar Schoeck (1886–1957), Arthur Honegger (1892–1955), Frank Martin (1890–1974), Ernst Lévy (1895-1981), Conrad Beck (1901-89), and Paul Burkhard (1911–77). Ernest Ansermet (1883–1969) was a noted conductor. Renowned Swiss painters include Konrad Witz (1400–1447), Henry Fuseli (Johann Heinrich Füssli, 1741–1825), Arnold Böcklin (1827–1901), Ferdinand Hodler (1853–1918), and Paul Klee (1879–1940). In sculpture and painting, artist Alberto Giacometti (1901–66) won world acclaim for his hauntingly elongated figures. Le Corbusier (Charles Édouard Jeanneret, 1887–1965) was a leading 20th-century architect.

Swiss religious leaders include Ulrich Zwingli (1484–1531), French-born John Calvin (Jean Chauvin, 1509–64), and Karl Barth (1886–1968). Other famous Swiss are Johann Heinrich Pestalozzi (1746–1827), an educational reformer who introduced new teaching methods; Ferdinand de Saussure (1857–1913), the founder of modern linguistics; Auguste Henri Forel (1848–1931), psychologist and entomologist; the noted art historians Jakob Burckhardt (1818–97) and Heinrich Wölfflin (1864–1945); the psychiatrists Eugen Bleuler (1857–1939), Carl Gustav Jung (1875–1961), and Hermann Rorschach (1884–1922); Jean Piaget (1896–1980), authority on child psychology; and the philosopher Karl Jaspers (1883–1969). Swiss winners of the Nobel Prize for peace are Henri Dunant (1828–1910) in 1901, founder of the Red Cross, and Elie Ducommun (1833–1906) and Charles Albert Gobat (1843–1914), both in 1902.

⁴⁹DEPENDENCIES

Switzerland has no territories or colonies.

⁵⁰BIBLIOGRAPHY

Annesley, Claire (ed.). *A Political and Economic Dictionary of Western Europe*. Philadelphia: Routledge/Taylor and Francis, 2005.

Diem, Aubrey. *Switzerland: Land, People, Economy*. Kitchener, Ont.: Media International, 1994.

Hilowitz, Janet Eve (ed.). *Switzerland in Perspective*. New York: Greenwood Press, 1990.

International Smoking Statistics: A Collection of Historical Data from 30 Economically Developed Countries. New York: Oxford University Press, 2002.

Linder, Wolf. *Swiss Democracy: Possible Solutions to Conflict in Multicultural Societies*. Houndsmills, U.K.: Macmillan, 1994.

McElrath, Karen (ed.). *HIV and AIDS: A Global View*. Westport, Conn.: Greenwood Press, 2002.

Meier, Heinz K. *Switzerland*. Santa Barbara, Calif.: Clio Press, 1990.

Sectoral Trends in the Swiss Economy. Zürich: Union Bank of Switzerland, Dept. of Economic Research. 1995.

Steinberg, Jonathan. *Why Switzerland?* 2nd ed. Cambridge: Cambridge University Press, 1996.

Switzerland: An Inside View: Politics, Economy, Culture, Society, Nature. Zürich: Der Alltag/Scalo Verlag, 1992.

UKRAINE

Ukraina

CAPITAL: Kiev (Kyyiv)

FLAG: Equal horizontal bands of azure blue (top) and yellow.

ANTHEM: *The National Anthem of Ukraine.*

MONETARY UNIT: The official currency, introduced in early 1993, is the hryvnia (HRN), which consists of 100 shahy. $1 = HRN0.19493 (or $1 = HRN5.13) as of 2005.

WEIGHTS AND MEASURES: The metric system is used.

HOLIDAYS: New Year's Day, 1–2 January; Christmas, 7 January; Women's Day, 8 March; Spring and Labor Day, 1–2 May; Victory Day, 9 May; Ukrainian Independence Day, 24 August.

TIME: 2 PM = noon GMT.

¹LOCATION, SIZE, AND EXTENT

Ukraine, the second-largest country in Europe, is located in Eastern Europe, bordering the Black Sea, between Poland and Russia. Comparatively, Ukraine is slightly smaller than the state of Texas with a total area of 603,700 sq km (233,090 sq mi). Ukraine shares boundaries with Belarus on the N, Russia on the E, the Black Sea on the s, Romania, Moldova, Hungary, and Slovakia on the w, and Poland on the NW. Ukraine's location is one of strategic importance at the crossroads between Europe and Asia. Its land boundary totals 4,663 km (2,897 mi) and its coastline is 2,782 km (1,729 mi). Ukraine's capital city, Kiev, is located in the north central part of the country.

²TOPOGRAPHY

The topography of Ukraine consists mainly of fertile plains (steppes) and plateaus. True mountains (the Carpathians) are found only in the west and in the Crimean Peninsula in the extreme south. The Dnieper Uplands run through a central region of the country. The Donets Hills and Azov Uplands are located along the eastern border.

The coastal region of the Black Sea is a lowland area. The indent of Karkint Bay nearly separates the Crimean Peninsula from the mainland. The Kerch Strait connects the Black Sea to the Sea of Azov, which lies between Ukraine and Russia covering an area of 37,599 sq km (14,517 sq mi). An area of wetlands, the Polesye Marshes, is located near the northwest border.

The most important river in Ukraine is the Dnipro (Dnieper), the third longest river in Europe. It serves as a major source of hydro-electric power. Other major rivers include the Danube, Western Buh, the Tisza, the Pripyat, and the Desna. There are over 20,000 small lakes throughout the country, but the largest lakes are artificial, created by dams along the Dnipro.

³CLIMATE

The climate is subtropical on the Crimean Peninsula. Precipitation is disproportionately distributed, highest in the west and north,

least in the east and southeast. Winters vary from cool along the Black Sea to cold farther inland. Summers are warm across the greater part of the country, except for the south where it becomes hot.

The rest of the country's climate is temperate. The mean temperature in July is about 10°C (66°F). In January, however, the mean temperature drops to -6°C (21°F). Average rainfall is 50 cm (20 in) a year, with variations in different regions.

⁴FLORA AND FAUNA

The land's soil, chernozem (black soil), is very fertile. When the Ukraine was part of the former Soviet Union it was called the country's "bread basket." A steppe zone covers about a third of the southern region of the country. Mixed shrubs, grasses, and evergreens can be found along the Mediterranean-like zone of the Crimean coast. Forest regions include such tree species as beech, linden, oak, and spruce. European bison, fox, and rabbits can be found living on the vast steppes of the country. As of 2002, there were at least 108 species of mammals, 245 species of birds, and over 5,100 species of plants throughout the country.

⁵ENVIRONMENT

Ukraine's environmental problems include the nuclear contamination which resulted from the 1986 Chernobyl accident. One-tenth of Ukraine's land area was affected by the radiation. According to UN reports, approximately one million people were exposed to unsafe levels of radiation through the consumption of food. Approximately 3.5 million hectare (8.6 million acre) of agricultural land and 1.5 million hectare (3.7 million acre) of forest were also contaminated.

Pollution from other sources also poses a threat to the environment. Ukraine releases polluted water, heavy metal, organic compounds, and oil-related pollutants into the Black Sea. The water supply in some areas of the country contains toxic industrial chemicals up to 10 times the concentration considered to be within safety limits.

Air pollution is also a significant environmental problem in the Ukraine. In 1992, Ukraine had the world's seventh-highest level of industrial carbon dioxide emissions, which totaled 611.3 million metric tons, a per capita level of 11.72. However, in 2000, the total of carbon dioxide emissions was at 342.8 million metric tons. The pollution of the nation's water has resulted in large-scale elimination of the fish population, particularly in the Sea of Azov.

As of 2003, only 3.9% of Ukraine's total land area was protected, including 33 Wetlands of International Importance. According to a 2006 report issued by the International Union for Conservation of Nature and Natural Resources (IUCN), threatened species included 14 types of mammals, 13 species of birds, 2 types of reptiles, 11 species of fish, 14 species of invertebrates, and 1 species of plant. Threatened species include the European bison, the Russian desman, and the Dalmatian pelican. The wild horse has become extinct.

6 POPULATION

The population of Ukraine in 2005 was estimated by the United Nations (UN) at 47,110,000, which placed it at number 26 in population among the 193 nations of the world. In 2005, approximately 16% of the population was over 65 years of age, with another 15% of the population under 15 years of age. There were 85 males for every 100 females in the country. According to the UN, the annual population rate of change for 2005–10 was expected to be -0.7%, a rate the government viewed as too low. The projected population for the year 2025 was 41,650,000. The population density was 78 per sq km (202 per sq mi), with the Dnieper Lowlands and the Donets Basin being the most densely populated regions.

The UN estimated that 68% of the population lived in urban areas in 2005, and that population in urban areas was declining at an annual rate of -0.57%. The capital city, Kiev (Kyyiv), had a population of 2,618,000 in that year. Other cities and their estimated populations were Kharkiv, 1,436,000; Dnipropetrovs'k, 1,036,000; Odesa, 1,010,000; Donetsk, 992,000; Lvov, 876,000; and Zaporizhzhya, 798,000.

7 MIGRATION

Since the breakup of the former Soviet Union, tens of thousands of Ukrainians have returned to the Ukraine. Between 1989–95, 15,000 returned from Azerbaijan, and 39,000 returned from Kyrgyzstan. Between 1991–95, 15,000 returned from Belarus; 82,000 returned from Kazakhstan; and 30,000 returned from Tajikistan. There were still 150,000 ecological migrants internally displaced from the 1986 Chernobyl accident. As of February 1996, 250,000 Tatars had returned from Central Asia, mostly from Uzbekistan. These Tatars belong to the 500,000 Tatars that were forcibly deported from the Crimean peninsula under the Stalin regime. The signature of an agreement between Ukraine and Uzbekistan in 1998 on the simultaneous release from Uzbek citizenship and acquisition of Ukrainian citizenship enabled more than 38,000 Crimean Tatars to obtain Ukrainian citizenship. Many of the rest of the Crimean Tatars in Central Asia wish to return to the Crimea.

Due to a series of amendments to the Law of Citizenship and a naturalization campaign, all formerly deported stateless persons residing in Ukraine had acquired Ukrainian citizenship as of 1999. The total number of migrants living in the Ukraine in 2000 was 6,947,000. In 2004, there were 2,459 refugees and 1,838 asylum seekers in the Ukraine. In addition, in that same year there were 80,569 others of concern to the United Nations High Commissioner for Refugees (UNHCR), made up of 2,809 Abkhazia, 6,500 Crimean Tartars (formerly deported persons), and 71,260 stateless persons. Also in 2004, 50,693 Ukrainians were refugees in Germany, and 28,484 in the United States, and over 5,000 Ukrainians sought asylum in 10 countries, in Europe, the United Kingdom, and the United States.

The net migration rate was estimated as -0.63 migrants per 1,000 population in 2005. The government views the immigration level as too low, and the emigration level as too high. Worker remittances in 2003 were $185 million.

8 ETHNIC GROUPS

According to the latest census (2001), 77.8% of the total population is Ukrainian. Russians form 17.3%, mainly in eastern Ukraine. Belarussians, Moldovans, Crimean Tatars, Bulgarians, Hungarians, Romanians, Poles, and Jews each account for less than 1% of the population. About 700,000 Rusyns (Ruthenians) live within the country, but they are not an officially recognized ethnic group.

9 LANGUAGES

Like Russian, Ukrainian is an eastern Slavic language. It has several distinctive vowel and consonant sounds, however. It is written in the Cyrillic alphabet but has three extra letters. Ukrainian began to emerge as a separate language from Russian in the late 12th century. Ukrainian is the official language and is spoken by about 67% of the population. Russian is spoken by about 24% of the population. Other languages include Romanian, Polish, and Hungarian.

10 RELIGIONS

Ukraine was Christianized by St. Volodymyr in 988. Under Soviet rule, churches and religion were subject to suppression and political manipulation, a situation that ended with the declaration of independence in 1991. Based on a 2003 survey, over 90% of the population claim to be Christians, primarily from one of three denominations: the Ukrainian Orthodox Church—Moscow Patriarchate (10.7%), the Ukrainian Orthodox Church—Kiev Patriarchate (14.8%), and the Ukrainian Autocephalous Orthodox Church (1%).

About 6.4% of the religiously active population are members of the Ukrainian Greek Catholic Church, also known as the Uniate, Byzantine, or Eastern Rite church. Roman Catholics claim about 2% of the population and are largely concentrated in the formerly Austro-Hungarian and Polish western territories. Other Christian groups represented include Baptists, Pentecostals, Jehovah's Witnesses, Mormons, Anglicans, Lutherans, Methodists, Calvinists, Pentecostals and Evangelicals. The head of the Spiritual Directorate of the Muslims of Ukraine estimates that there are as many as two million members of the nation's Muslim community. Islam is practiced mainly by the Tatar population of the autonomous republic of the Crimea. There are an estimated 300,000 Jews in the country. Small communities of Buddhists, Baha'is, and Hare Krishnas are also present.

The constitution provides for freedom of religion and this right is generally respected. However, some smaller and nontraditional religious groups have reported problems in meeting government

UKRAINE

0   100   200 Miles

0   100   200 Kilometers

LOCATION: 49°0' N; 32°0' E. BOUNDARY LENGTHS: Total boundary lengths, 4,558 kilometers (2,834 miles); Belarus, 891 kilometers (554 miles); Hungary, 103 kilometers (64 miles); Moldova, 939 kilometers (584 miles); Poland, 428 kilometers (266 miles); Romania (southeast), 169 kilometers (105 miles); Romania (west), 362 kilometers (225 miles); Russia 1,576 kilometers (980 miles); Slovakia, 90 kilometers (56 miles).

registration requirements. An All-Ukrainian Council, composed of members from various religions, meets regularly with the State Committee of Religious Affairs to discuss potential problems between religions.

11TRANSPORTATION

As of 2004, there were 22,473 km (13,988 mi) of railway in the Ukraine, all of it 1.5 m (broad) gauge. Highways in 2002 totaled 169,679 km (105,540 mi), of which 164,249 km (102,162 mi) are hard-surfaced, including 1,770 km (1,100 mi) of expressways. In 2003, there were 5,603,800 passengers cars and 985,700 commercial vehicles registered for use.

The main marine ports are Berdyans'k, Illichivs'k, Kerch, Kherson, Mariupol', Mykolayiv, Odesa, and Sevastopol'. The merchant marine fleet had 201 ships of 1,000 GRT or over, for a total capacity of 675,904 GRT in 2005. There are 1,672 km (1,040 mi) of navigable inland waterways as of 2004. The Dnipro River is the primary inland waterway, but the Danube, western Pivd Buh, Pryp'yat', and Desna are also used for import-export traffic.

Ukraine had an estimated 656 airports in 2004. As of 2005 a total of 199 had paved runways, and there were also 10 heliports. The largest airports are in Kiev, Kharkiv, Donetsk, Odesa, and Simferopol'. In 2003, 1.477 million passengers were carried on scheduled domestic and international airline flights.

12HISTORY

Ukrainians, Russians, and Belarussians belong to the eastern branch of the Slavic peoples, all of which trace their origins to medieval Kievan Rus. Kievan Rus was established in the 9th century AD. St. Volodymyr the Great, one of the most celebrated rulers of Kievan Rus, adopted Christianity as the national faith in 988. Internal strife in the 12th century and the Mongol invasion in the 13th led to the ultimate destruction of Kievan Rus as a major power. Halych-Volhynia in Western Ukraine, however, became the new political center until it fell to Polish-Lithuanian rule in the 14th century. During the following centuries Ukraine found itself the object of power struggles among its more powerful neighbors.

In a protracted struggle against Poland, Ukrainian Cossacks were able to establish an independent state in the 16th and 17th centuries. To safeguard Ukrainian independence from the Poles, Ukraine concluded the Treaty of Pereyaslav in 1654 with Moscow. The nature of this agreement has generated much historical controversy: Russian historians claim that, as part of the agreement, Ukraine accepted Moscow's rule, while Ukrainians claim that Ukraine was to retain its autonomy. The ensuing war between Russia and Poland resulted in the partition of Ukraine. Most of the rest of Ukraine's territory was incorporated into the Russian Empire with the partition of Poland in 1795. Small parts of Ukrainian territory to the west were absorbed by the Hapsburg Empire.

A Ukrainian national movement arose in the 19th century. Later, the collapse of the Tsarist regime and the chaos of the Russian revolution in 1917 allowed Ukraine to assert its independence. In April 1917, the National Ukrainian Assembly met in Kiev and in November proclaimed the creation of the Ukrainian People's Republic. When the Bolsheviks formed a rival Ukrainian Communist government, the National Assembly proclaimed the independence for Ukraine on 22 January 1918.

On 1 November 1918, an independent Republic of Western Ukraine was declared after the disintegration of the Austro-Hungarian Empire. On 22 January 1919, the Ukrainian People's Republic and the Republic of Western Ukraine united and established an independent Ukrainian state, recognized by over 40 other nations.

The new government, however, could not maintain its authority in the face of civil strife and the threat of the approaching Bolshevik, pro-Tsarist, and Polish forces. By 1920, eastern Ukraine fell to the Bolsheviks and became the Ukrainian Soviet Socialist Republic while Poland occupied most of western Ukraine. Small areas of the west went to Romania, Hungary, and Czechoslovakia.

Early Soviet policy allowed for cultural autonomy and local administration by Ukrainian Communists. But Stalin changed this liberal policy in the 1930s when he initiated strict Russification and persecution of Ukrainian nationalists. This policy culminated in the Soviet-engineered famine of 1932–33 that resulted in the death of 7 to 10 million Ukrainians.

The 1939 Nazi-Soviet pact assigned Poland's Ukrainian territory to the Soviet sphere of influence. When Germany invaded the Soviet Union in 1941, Ukrainian nationalists in L'vin proclaimed the restoration of the Ukrainian state. The Germans arrested these nationalists and turned Ukraine into a German colony. When it became clear that the Nazis wanted to enslave them and not liberate them, a resistance movement led by nationalists fought both the Soviet and German armies. During World War II, Ukraine lost six million people through death or deportation and a total of 18,000 villages were destroyed.

The Ukrainian resistance movement continued to fight in Soviet Ukraine (the western Ukraine which had been part of Poland had been incorporated into the Ukrainian S.S.R.). It was not until the 1950s that they were completely defeated by the better-equipped Soviet Red Army.

In March 1990, semi-free elections for parliament were held. The Communist-dominated parliament declared Ukraine a sovereign state on 16 July 1990. On 24 August 1991, following the failed coup in Moscow, the parliament proclaimed the independence of Ukraine and declared that only the constitution and laws of Ukraine were valid on its territory. On 1 December 1991 the citizens of Ukraine confirmed this proclamation with a 90.3% vote

in favor of independence. At the time of this referendum, Leonid Kravchuk was elected as the first president.

Ukraine joined Russia and Belarus in creating the Commonwealth of Independent States (CIS) in December 1991. This agreement was meant to facilitate coordination of policy in various fields. But despite their efforts, Ukrainian-Russian differences arose in several areas, including the command and control of nuclear weapons, the formation of a unified military command, and the character and pace of economic reform.

In light of the 1986 Chernobyl nuclear power plant accident, Ukraine declared its intention to become a nuclear-free state. However, this process progressed much more slowly than expected. The lack of fuel resources and disagreements with Russia over pricing had induced the government to keep the Chernobyl plant running. The START I agreement received the Ukrainian parliament's conditional ratification in November 1993 and unconditional ratification in February 1994, but the transfer of nuclear weapons to Russia did not occur as smoothly as planned. On 6 May 1992 it was announced that all Ukrainian tactical nuclear weapons had been shipped to Russia for dismantling. However, Ukraine cited Russia's failure to dismantle these weapons, inadequate compensation, and security concerns as the reasons for not turning over its entire strategic arsenal.

The CIS countries agreed to a unified nuclear command, but Ukraine declared its intent to create its own national conventional military and opposed any efforts to create a unified CIS conventional force. President Kravchuk declared all conventional forces on Ukrainian territory to be the property of Ukraine. This has given rise to disputes and disagreements about the Black Sea fleet, to which Russia has also laid claim.

Since its independence, Ukraine has experienced unrest in some of the predominantly Russian areas in the east and southeast. Crimea is the most notable example, declaring independence on 6 May 1992. At the same time the Russian parliament approved a resolution that declared the 1954 Soviet grant of the Crimea to Ukraine unconstitutional and void. This resolution, however, was rejected by Russian president Boris Yeltsin. Demands for secession in Crimea have continued to complicate Ukrainian-Russian relations.

Ukraine adopted a new constitution in June 1996 establishing a presidency (elected for a five-year term) and a one-chamber parliament called the Supreme Council (elected for a four-year term). Under transitional provisions, President Leonid Kuchma, elected over incumbent Leonid Kravchuk in 1994, was to serve until elections in 1999. The Supreme Council adopted a new civil code in June 1997. In the same year, Ukraine signed a 10-year friendship treaty with Russia and an agreement with Western nations on shutting down the Chernobyl nuclear plant by 2005. It was shut down in 2000. Public discontent with the slow pace of economic reforms was evident in the strong showing by the Communist Party in the 1998 legislative elections, in which it won 25% of the vote (116 of 450 seats). However, support for the party did not translate into support for union with Russia, proposed by Petro Symonenko, the party's candidate in the 1999 presidential elections. Leonid Kuchma was reelected in a November 1999 runoff election with 56% of the vote and nominated central bank chairman Victor Yushchenko to be prime minister. Soon after taking office, Yushchenko reached a restructuring agreement with foreign bond holders to avoid default on the nation's $2.6 billion foreign debt. As the new century began, Ukraine's much-needed economic reforms remained stalled by the long-standing problems of corruption and political stalemate between reformists and their parliamentary opponents.

In November 2000, the body of Ukrainian journalist Georgiy Gongadze was found decapitated: opposition demonstrators alleged Kuchma was involved in the murder of the journalist who was critical of the administration, and there were calls for Kuchma's impeachment. Kuchma denied the allegations, but in February 2001, the EU called for an inquiry into the journalist's murder. In September 2002, an ad hoc commission set up by parliament to investigate Gongadze's murder recommended that criminal charges be brought against the president and other top officials, based on tape recordings of a meeting at which Kuchma allegedly asked security officials to "take care" of the journalist. Anti-Kuchma protests were held throughout the country to call for the president's resignation. All six national television stations were off the air on the morning of the 16 September demonstrations, purportedly for "maintenance." Many protesters were beaten and arrested. In October, the Kiev Court of Appeals opened a criminal case against Kuchma, based upon the allegations of his involvement in the murder.

In parliamentary elections held on 30 March 2002, Ukrainians voted for many opposition parties, although parties opposed to Kuchma alleged widespread fraud. In April, Yushchenko's government was dismissed following a no-confidence vote in parliament; he was replaced with Viktor Yanukovych—the governor of the eastern province of Donetsk Oblast.

Although Yushchenko is respected in the West for fighting corruption and furthering economic reforms, he is unpopular with many Ukrainian businessmen, who are seen to be corrupt. Presidential elections were scheduled for 2004, and Kuchma was constitutionally barred from running for a third term. In 2002, he announced plans to amend the constitution and weaken his executive powers. This was seen as a move to transfer power to parliament, in the event that a reformer such as Yushchenko would be elected president. Kuchma's plans also included splitting parliament into two chambers. In March 2003, Yushchenko stated he feared the new amendments would postpone presidential elections for two years, and extend Kuchma's rule until 2006. Tens of thousands of protesters nationwide took to the streets in March, calling once again on Kuchma to resign for abuse of office, arms dealing, vote-rigging, corruption, the involvement in Gongadze's murder, and for impoverishing the country.

For the 2004 presidential elections Yushchenko announced that he would be running as an independent. His main contender was the current prime minister Viktor Yanukovych. Since the latter was backed by Kuchma, and by most of the Ukrainian TV channels, Yushchenko relied heavily on direct interaction with the people for bringing his message across.

The initial vote was held on the 31 October 2004 and neither of the two candidates obtained a comfortable lead—Yushchenko won 39.87% of the votes, while Yanukovych won 39.32%. A second voting round was therefore staged on 21 November, with the final vote tally showing Yanukovych as the winner. However, observers noted several cases where the voting process was rigged to Yanukovych's favor. The suspicion that loomed over the Oc-

tober elections was strengthened by the major discrepancies between the exit poll results conducted by the observers, and the official vote count. As a result, Yushchenko called for the people from Kiev, and from all over the country, to take to the streets and protest. After 13 days, the so-called Orange Revolution (named so after the orange ribbons worn by Yushchenko's supporters) determined the Supreme Court to nullify the election results and order a re-run, to be held on 26 December 2004. This time, Yushchenko emerged victorious, by an 8% margin. Yanukovych contested the results but eventually stepped down from his post.

In January 2005, Yushchenko was sworn in as president, and in February 2005 he nominated Yulia Tymoshenko—one of his former deputies, and an ardent supporter of the Orange Revolution—as prime minister. Although there had been some controversy regarding her "oligarch status" (she is one of the wealthiest people in Ukraine), her nomination was accepted by the parliament with 373 out of 450 possible votes. On 8 September 2005, after only a couple of months as prime minister, and following several resignations and accusations of corruption, Tymoshenko and her government were ousted by Yushchenko. Yuriy Yekhanurov, head of the Dnipropetrovsk Oblast state administration, was appointed as the new prime minister.

Drawing on the political capital he garnered in the West after winning the troubled 2004 elections (he was allegedly poisoned with dioxins that lead to severe facial disfigurements), Yushchenko pressed for EU and NATO integration. Both organizations cautioned, however, that the pace of political, economic and military reforms would have to be increased before Ukraine's candidacy could be seriously considered. Constitutional reforms went into effect on 1 January 2006.

13 GOVERNMENT

Ukraine is governed by a constitution adopted in June 1996, which allows for an elected parliament and president. The constitution was amended on December 2004 as a response to the presidential election crisis.

The Ukrainian parliament consists of a single chamber with 450 seats called the Rada (Supreme Council). Seats are allocated proportionally to the parties that acquire more than 3% of the electoral votes. Members of parliament currently serve four-year terms, while the president serves a five-year term. (Following the 2006 elections members of parliament will serve five-year terms.) The prime minister and cabinet are nominated by the president and confirmed by the Supreme Council. Although many parties participate in the elections, many candidates run as independents as well.

Ukraine's first postindependence presidential elections were held in two rounds on 26 June and 10 July 1994. In this election, the incumbent Leonid Kravchuk was defeated by his former prime minister, Leonid Kuchma, who was reelected in November 1999. In December 2004, following massive popular protests and after the Supreme Court ordered a re-run of the allegedly rigged November 2004 elections, Kuchma's former prime minister—Viktor Yushchenko—was elected president.

14 POLITICAL PARTIES

There are some 120 political parties active in Ukraine. They fall roughly into four different categories: radical nationalist, democratic nationalist, liberal-centrist, and Communist-socialist.

The radical nationalist parties are fearful of Russia and advocate a strong presidency. Their commitment to democracy—particularly if regions of Ukraine seek to secede—is not firm. The democratic nationalist parties are also fearful of Russia, but also appear strongly committed to democracy, individual rights, and the protection of private property. The influential Rukh Party (Ukrainian Popular Movement), which won 43 seats in the 1998 elections, belongs to this group. The liberal-centrist parties are particularly concerned with promoting free market economic reform. They are also committed to democracy and individual rights. The communist-socialist parties oppose privatization and seek continued state control of the economy. They generally favor close relations with Russia. The most important party in this group, the Communist Party of Ukraine, won 116 seats in 1998.

In the March 2002 parliamentary elections, many parties grouped together into voting blocs. Winning the most seats in the Rada was the "Our Ukraine" coalition, led by Viktor Yushchenko, which took 23.6% of the vote and 112 of 450 seats. The coalition was registered in January 2002, and then included the Ukrainian People's Rukh Party (registered in 2003 as the Ukrainian People's Party), the People's Rukh of Ukraine, the Congress of Ukrainian Nationalists, the Reforms and Order Party, Solidarity, the Liberal Party, the Youth Party of Ukraine, the Christian People's Union, the Go Forward, Ukraine! Party, and the Republican Christian Party. In March 2003, Yushchenko announced a "new political force" would be created that would form the basis for a European-style political party. Yushchenko was elected president in December 2004.

Also gaining seats in parliament in the 2002 elections were: the "For a United Ukraine" bloc, 101; the Communist Party, 67; the United Social-Democratic Party of Ukraine, 24; the Socialist Party of Ukraine, 23; the Yuliya Tymoshenko bloc, 21; the Democratic Party of Ukraine/Democratic Union liberal bloc, 4; the "Unity" bloc, 3; and independents and others held 95 seats.

On 8 September 2005, the government led by Yuliya Tymoshenko was ousted by Yushchenko after allegations of corruption made their way into the media.

Parliamentary elections were held on 26 March 2006. Yanukovych's Party of Regions won the most seats, taking 186 of 450 (32.1%). Tymoshenko's Bloc won 129 seats (22.3%); Our Ukraine, 81 seats (13.9%); the Socialist Party of Ukraine 33 seats (5.7%); and the Communist Party of Ukraine 21 seats (3.7%). The next parliamentary elections were scheduled for March 2011.

15 LOCAL GOVERNMENT

Ukraine is divided into 24 administrative regions (oblasts) plus the autonomous Republic of Crimea. In addition, the cities of Kiev, the capital of Ukraine, and Sevastopol, capital of Crimea, enjoy oblast status. The oblast is divided into districts, each of which has a representative in the Rada (Supreme Council).

A strong secessionist movement has risen up in Crimea. In a nonbinding referendum held in 1994, over 78% of the 1.3 million people who voted supported greater autonomy from Ukraine. In 1995 Ukraine's parliament and President Leonid Kuchma moved to contain secessionist elements in the region. Kuchma temporarily took direct control over the area and afterward decreed that he must approve all candidates for premier of the region. The Crimea adopted a new constitution in 1999 providing for additional budgetary autonomy from the rest of Ukraine.

In spite of the election of the reform-oriented Yushchenko in 2004, Ukrainian local government officials complained that budget expenditures were still done in a centralized and inefficient fashion. On 13 September 2005 the Constitutional Court of Ukraine enforced a series of constitutional amendments that shift most of the presidential clout to the parliament. The new laws came in effect on 1 January 2006 and were expected to give more power to local governments.

16 JUDICIAL SYSTEM

The court system, until 2001, remained similar to that which existed under the former Soviet regime. In July 2001, a series of laws were passed designed to bring existing legislation regarding the judiciary and the administration of justice more in line with the requirements for an independent judiciary. The three levels of courts are rayon (also known as regional or people's courts), oblast (provincial) courts, and the Supreme Court. All three levels serve as courts of first instance, the choice of level varying with the severity of the crime. A case heard in first instance at the rayon level can be appealed through the next two higher stages. A case heard in first instance in the Supreme Court is not subject to appeal or review. A 1992 law added a Constitutional Court to the existing system. The Constitutional Court consists of 19 members appointed for nine-year terms. It is the final interpreter of legislation and the constitution, and it determines the constitutionality of legislation, presidential edicts, cabinet acts, and acts of the Crimean autonomous republic.

The Rada (Supreme Council) selects judges on recommendation from the Ministry of Justice based partly upon government test results. Oblast and Supreme Court judges must have five years of experience in order to be appointed and may not be members of political parties.

A new constitution, adopted in 1996, and amended in 2004, provides that the judiciary is funded separately from the Ministry of Justice to ensure an independent judiciary. Because the courts are funded by the Ministry of Justice, however, they have been subject to executive influence, and have suffered from corruption and inefficiency.

17 ARMED FORCES

Ukraine was able to quickly organize an impressive national army, in part because it had always been an important contributor to the Soviet armed forces. In 2005 Ukranian armed forces numbered 187,600 active personnel with 1,000,000 reservists. Ground forces (Army) numbered 125,000 and was organized into three commands and a number of specialized brigades and regiments of artillery, special forces, air defense, rocket and missile, and attack helicopter units. It was equipped with 3,784 main battle tanks, 600 reconnaissance vehicles, 3,043 armored infantry fighting vehicles, 8,492 armored personnel carriers, and 3,705 artillery pieces. The Air Force and Air Defense Force had a combined total of 49,100 active personnel, that operated 444 combat capable aircraft, including 26 bombers, 280 fighters, and 187 fighter ground attack aircraft. The Air Defense force was outfitted with 825 surface-to-air missile batteries. The Navy numbered 13,500 personnel. Major naval units included one tactical submarine, one frigate, three corvettes, and five patrol/coastal vessels. A cruiser and another frigate are listed as nonoperational. The Navy's aviation arm had up to 2,500 active personnel. Equipment included 11 fixed wing and 72 rotary wing antisubmarine warfare aircraft. The Navy also had a single brigade of 3,000 naval infantry personnel.

Of greatest international concern has been the fate of the ICBMs and strategic bombers on Ukrainian soil, which are supposed to return to Russia for dismantling. As of 2000, the number of ICBMs had been reduced from 174 to 44. As of 2005 the number of strategic bombers had been cut to 26.

Paramilitary forces included an estimated 39,900 internal security troops, 45,000 border guards, 14,000 coast guard personnel, and more than 9,500 civil defense troops. The Ukraine participated in missions in eight foreign countries or regions. The defense budget for 2005 was $1.09 billion.

18 INTERNATIONAL COOPERATION

Ukraine became a member of the United Nations on 24 October 1945; the country is part of the ECE and several nonregional specialized agencies, such as the IAEA, the FAO, the World Bank, UNCTAD, UNESCO, UNIDO, and the WHO. It is a member of the Commonwealth of Independent States (CIS), the Council of Europe, the Black Sea Economic Cooperation Zone, the Euro-Atlantic Partnership Council, the European Bank for Reconstruction and Development, and the OSCE. The nation has observer status in the WTO, the OAS, and the Nonaligned Movement. In 2001, Georgia, Uzbekistan, Ukraine, Azerbaijan, and Moldova formed a social and economic development union known as GUAAM. Uzbekistan withdrew from the partnership in 2005.

Ukraine is an active member of the NATO Partnership for Peace. The government has supported UN missions and operations in Kosovo (est. 1999), Lebanon (est. 1978), Ethiopia and Eritrea (est. 2000), Liberia (est. 2003), Sierra Leone (est. 1999), Georgia (est. 1993), and the DROC (est. 1999). Ukraine is a member of the Zangger Committee and the Nuclear Suppliers Group (London Group).

In environmental cooperation, Ukraine is part of the Basel Convention, the Conventions on Biological Diversity and Air Pollution, Ramsar, CITES, the London Convention, the Kyoto Protocol, the Montréal Protocol, MARPOL, and the UN Conventions on the Law of the Sea and Climate Change.

19 ECONOMY

Ukraine was central to the Soviet agricultural and industrial system. The rich agricultural land of this region (commonly called the "breadbasket" of the former Soviet Union) provided 46% of Soviet agricultural output in the 1980s, and also accounted for 25% of the USSR's coal production. Ukraine's economic base is dominated by industry, which accounts for over 45% of GDP (2005 est.). However, agriculture continues to play a major role in the economy, representing about 18% of GDP.

Real GDP declined 3% in 1990, 11% in 1991, and an estimated 15% in 1992. Recovery in 1997 was cut short by the effects of the Russian financial crisis of 1998. Real GDP fell -1.7% in 1998

and -0.2% in 1999. However, the economy has registered strong positive growth since 2000—5.9% in 2000; 9.1% in 2001, and a projected 5% in 2002—despite the global slowdown beginning in 2001. Official unemployment since 1999 has averaged about 4.2%. Inflation, averaging 21.67% 1998 to 2000, was reduced to a single-digit rate (6%) in 2001, and reached 0.8% in 2002. Although still high, this is a marked improvement over the 400% hyperinflation that plagued the country in 1994. In response to the hyperinflation, the government introduced a new currency and instituted mass privatization in 1995. Yet the country remained plagued by a slow economic decline. A new civil code adopted by parliament in 1997 was expected to stabilize the country's business climate. Economic recovery beginning in 2000 is attributable to a number of factors: double-digit growth in industrial output in 2001; a good grain harvest resulting from good weather and reduced governmental controls; improved export competitiveness from the depreciation of the currency in 1998–99; the clearance of many wage and pension arrears; increased domestic demand as a result of wage and pension increases granted in 2000 and 2001; considerable idle capacity; and the expansion of export markets.

This economic expansion continued in the following years, with GDP growth rates of 5.2% in 2002, 9.6% in 2003, and an astonishing 12.1% in 2004; the economy was expected to grow by 6.0% in 2005. Inflation started growing again after 2002, reaching 12% in 2004, and being expected to reach 14.0% in 2005. The unemployment rate remained fairly stable, hovering around 3.5%.

Ukraine's economic dynamism was driven mainly by exports. The most effective growth engines in 2003–04 were manufactured goods, construction, oil and gas transport, services, private consumption, and government spending. The end of 2004 saw a hampering of this trend as three rounds of presidential elections and weeks of protesting throughout the country (the Orange Revolution), took their toll on the Ukrainian economy. The newly elected president has openly stated that Ukraine will take a clear course towards an open market economy, and that the mid-term goal is EU integration. His reign, although plagued by corruption and government inefficiency, promises great potential for the future.

20 INCOME

The US Central Intelligence Agency (CIA) reports that in 2005 Ukraine's gross domestic product (GDP) was estimated at $340.4 billion. The CIA defines GDP as the value of all final goods and services produced within a nation in a given year and computed on the basis of purchasing power parity (PPP) rather than value as measured on the basis of the rate of exchange based on current dollars. The per capita GDP was estimated at $7,200. The annual growth rate of GDP was estimated at 4.4%. The average inflation rate in 2005 was 13.9%. It was estimated that agriculture accounted for 18.5% of GDP, industry 45.2%, and services 36.1%.

According to the World Bank, in 2003 remittances from citizens working abroad totaled $330 million or about $7 per capita and accounted for approximately 0.7% of GDP. Foreign aid receipts amounted to $323 million or about $7 per capita and accounted for approximately 0.7% of the gross national income (GNI).

The World Bank reports that in 2003 household consumption in Ukraine totaled $28.07 billion or about $580 per capita based on a GDP of $50.1 billion, measured in current dollars rather than PPP. Household consumption includes expenditures of individuals, households, and nongovernmental organizations on goods and services, excluding purchases of dwellings. It was estimated that for the period 1990 to 2003 household consumption fell at an average annual rate of -3.6%. In 2001 it was estimated that approximately 34% of household consumption was spent on food, 16% on fuel, 6% on health care, and 4% on education. It was estimated that in 2003 about 29% of the population had incomes below the poverty line.

21 LABOR

As of 2005, the Ukraine's labor force totaled an estimated 20.46 million persons. In 2003, the services sector accounted for 51.2% of the workforce, with 29.9% in industry and 18.9% in agriculture. For the year 2005, Ukraine's official unemployment rate was 3.8%. However, the International Labor Organization had calculated that the country's actual unemployment rate was around 9–10%, due to the large number of workers that were either underemployed or not registered as unemployed.

In November 1992, the official Soviet-era unions were renamed the Federation of Trade Unions (FPU), which began then to operate independently from the government. Since 1992, many independent unions have been formed, providing an alternative to the official unions in most sectors of the economy. As of 2002, estimates of independent union membership was estimated to be three million. Membership in the FPU was thought to be 14 million. The right to strike is protected, except for the military, police, and continuing process plants.

The minimum employment age is 17, although children aged 15 to 17 can be employed by businesses with governmental permission. However, child labor remains a problem. In 2002, the minimum wage was $22 per month, which was significantly below the cost of living. The maximum workweek is set at 40 hours; the law also provides for a minimum of 24 days of vacation per year. Ukraine's laws set forth occupational health and safety standards but these are frequently ignored in practice and are not sufficiently enforced by the government.

22 AGRICULTURE

About 57% of the total land area is arable, with another 14% utilized as permanent pasture land. Agriculture accounted for 14% of GDP in 2003. As in other former Soviet republics, total agricultural production dramatically declined after 1990. The average annual decline during 1990–2000 was 5.8%. By 1999, the agricultural sector was only producing 47% as much as it had during 1989–91. However, during 2002–04, crop production was 12.8% higher than during 1999–2001. Production amounts in 2004 included (in 1,000 tons): sugar beets, 16,502; potatoes, 20,755; wheat, 17,517; fruit, 2,131; sunflower seeds, 3,050; cabbage, 1,559; grapes, 500; raspberries, 20; rapeseed, 148; soybeans, 363; and tobacco, 4.

Ukraine's steppe region in the south is possibly the most fertile region in the world. Ukraine's famous humus-rich black soil accounts for one-third of the world's black soil and holds great potential for agricultural production. However, the soil is rapidly losing its fertility due to improper land and crop management. Ukraine typically produced over half of the sugar beets and one-fifth of all grains grown for the former USSR. In addition, two of the largest vegetable-oil research centers in the world are at Odessa and Zaporizhzhya. Agroindustry accounts for one-third of agricultural employment. To some extent, however, agroindustrial development has been hampered by the deteriorating environment as well as a shortage of investment funds due to the aftermath of the nuclear power plant disaster at Chernobyl. According to estimates, nearly 60,000 hectares (148,250 acres) of arable land in the Chernobyl vicinity are now unavailable for cultivation. Out of 33 million hectares (81.5 million acres) of total arable land, more than 17 million hectares (42 million acres) are depleted, 10 million hectares (24.7 million acres) are eroded, and another 10 million have excessive acidity. Furthermore, 17% of arable land is located in areas where there is risk of drought.

23 ANIMAL HUSBANDRY

Just under 14% of Ukraine's total land area is composed of permanent pasture land. As of 2005, there were 6.9 million head of cattle, 6.5 million pigs, 875,000 sheep, 894,000 goats, 120 million chickens, and 20 million ducks. Horses, turkeys, goats, ducks, and rabbits are also bred and raised. Between 1990 and 2000, livestock production declined by 50%. Lack of finances for buying fuel pushed farmers in the public sector to sell their cattle abroad, mostly to Asian buyers. During 2002–04, livestock production was up 7.2% from 1999–2001. In 2005, meat production included: beef, 556,000 tons (down from 1,986,000 tons in 1990); pork, 510,000 tons (1,576,000 tons in 1990); and poultry, 470,000 tons (708,000 tons in 1990). There are several factors involved with Ukraine's declining meat production: decentralization of meat processing, with greater use of processing facilities at the farms; lack of cheap credits to buy animals; and antiquated meat processing equipment. Milk and egg production in 2005 amounted to 14.3 million tons and 726,000 tons, respectively. In 2004, exports of meat and meat products were valued at $191.8 million; milk, dairy, and eggs, $438.5 million. In 2005, Ukraine produced 60,500 tons of honey, fifth highest in the world.

24 FISHING

Fishing occurs mainly on the Black Sea. In 2003, the total catch came to 248,198 tons, reflecting diminished landings since the 1990 catch of 1,048,360 tons. Mackerel and sardines together accounted for 22% of the 2003 catch. Exports of fish and fish products amounted to $17.6 million in 2003. Ukrainian fish consumption per capita amounts to 12.8 kg (28.2 lb) per year—less than half that of western Europe (24.2 kg/53.2 lb).

25 FORESTRY

About 16.5% of the total area was forest in 2000. While the radioactive contamination of forestland from the 1986 Chernobyl disaster is well-known, there is also widespread land, water, and air pollution from toxic wastes, which has also adversely affected timberlands. Forestry production in 2004 included: roundwood, 4.8 million cu m (169 million cu ft); wood-based panels, 1,308,000 cu m (46.2 million cu ft); wood pulp, 27,000 tons; and paper and paperboard, 701,000 tons.

26 MINING

Ukraine is one of the world's leading producers of iron ore, as well as a major world producer of ferroalloys, ilmenite, steel, and manganese ore (with 75% of the former Soviet Union's reserves). The mining and metallurgical industry employed 500,000 persons;

270,000 worked in ironmaking, steelmaking, and ferroalloys enterprises. In 2002, over 60% by value of Ukraine's $18 billion in exports came from the "mineral products" category. Ferrous and nonferrous metals were Ukraine's top export commodities in 2002. Fuel and petroleum products were the country's second-leading export commodities.

Production outputs for 2002 included: marketable iron ore (gross weight), 58.9 million metric tons; manganese, mined in the Nikopol' and Bol'shoy Tokmak basins (metal content), 940,000 metric tons; rock salt, 2.3 million metric tons (estimated); and potash (at the Stebnik and Kalush mines), 60,000 metric tons. In addition, Ukraine produced alumina, mercury, titanium (ilmenite and rutile concentrates), zirconium (the FSU's only ore producer), cement, clays (bentonite and kaolin), graphite, nitrogen, and sulfur (from the Rozdol and Yavoriv deposits). Iron ore production, concentrated at seven mining and beneficiation complexes in the Krivyy Rih (Krivoy Rog) Basin, and at the Poltavskiy complex, fell by 50% from 1990 through 1995. Explored iron ore reserves totaled 33 billion tons, including 28 billion tons of industrial reserves; total capacity was 108.5 million tons per year. Manganese reserves totaled 2.2 billion tons, and annual capacity was 6 million tons. No antimony, cadmium lead, nickel, tin, zinc, zircon, dolomite, limestone fluxes, quartz, soda ash, talc, or uranium was mined in the past several years, the Ukraine having sharply reduced or ceased producing a number of these commodities as a result of the large reduction in demand following the breakup of the Soviet Union.

At the end of the 1980s, Ukraine mined 5% of the world's output of mineral products. After the breakup of the Soviet Union, production fell precipitously, and recovery of the mining sector was considered critical for the country's economic recovery. A 1999 law provided tax benefits for mining and metal industry firms for two and a half years. By 2000, the privatization of small-scale enterprises was virtually completed. The mining industry was a major source of waste, having accumulated 30 billion tons of mineral wastes.

27 ENERGY AND POWER

Ukraine has only modest reserves of oil and natural gas, but more robust reserves of coal.

As of 1 January 2004, Ukraine had proven oil reserves estimated at 395 million barrels, according to the Oil and Gas Journal. In 2003 and 2004, oil production was estimated at 86,800 barrels per day and 86,000 barrels per day, respectively. However, consumption outstripped output for both years. In 2003, demand for oil averaged an estimated 415,000 barrels per day, and at an estimated 422,000 barrels per day in 2004. Net imports of oil in 2003 were estimated at 328,200 barrels per day, and at an estimated 336,000 barrels per day in 2004. Imports in 2003 accounted for around 80% of demand, most of which came from Russia. Most of Ukraine's oil reserves are located in the eastern Dnieper-Donetsk basin.

Ukraine's six oil refineries have a combined crude oil refining capacity estimated as of 1 January 2004 at 1.05 million barrels per day. However, domestic consumption of refined oil products is just over 30% of capacity, and have even had problems securing enough crude oil to supply the country's needs.

Ukraine, as of 1 January 2004, had proven natural gas reserves estimated at 39.6 trillion cu ft, according to the Oil and Gas Jour-

nal. In 2003, natural gas production was estimated at 0.69 trillion cu ft, with consumption that year estimated at 3.03 trillion cu ft. As a result, Ukraine has had to resort to imports to make up the difference. In 2003, net imports of natural gas were estimated at 2.34 trillion cu ft. Turkmenistan has become its primary source for natural gas imports, following an agreement signed in 2001 that calls for 8.8 trillion cu ft per year to be provided from 2002 to 2006.

In 2004, Ukraine had coal reserves estimated at 37.6 billion short tons, of which 17.9 billion short tons consisted of anthracite and bituminous coal, and 19.7 billion short tons consisted of sub-bituminous coal and lignite. In 2003, coal production was estimated at 63.5 million short tons. However, demand for coal that year totaled 67 billion short tons, making Ukraine a net importer of coal. Most of the country's coal comes from the eastern region in the Donetsk/Donbas basin.

Ukraine's electric power generating capacity in 2002 totaled 52.811 million kW, of which conventional thermal plants accounted for 36.241 million kW of capacity, and nuclear power 11.835 million kW. Hydroelectric capacity in that year accounted for 4.731 million kW of capacity and geothermal/other 0.004 million kW. Electric power output in 2002 totaled 163.870 billion kWh, of which conventional thermal fueled plants provided 80.777 billion kWh, followed by nuclear plants with 73.380 billion kWh, hydroelectric with 9.691 billion kWh, and geothermal/other with 0.022 billion kWh. In 2003, electric power output rose to an estimated 177 billion kWh. Demand for electricity in 2002 totaled 149.284 billion kWh. In 2003, consumption rose to an estimated 156 billion kWh. As of January 2005, Ukraine had four nuclear power plants in operation, providing 40% of the country's electric power.

28 INDUSTRY

Ukraine, with strong scientific and technological sectors, is a major producer of heavy machinery and industrial equipment for sectors including mining, steelmaking, and chemicals. Significant products also include nonnumerically controlled machine tools, large electrical transformers, and agricultural machinery. Ukraine's industries are important suppliers of products—including automobiles, clothing, foodstuffs, timber, and paper—to other former Soviet republics. Ukraine also retains much of the industry associated with the space program of the former USSR. Industry accounted for 40% of GDP in 2000, and the industrial production growth rate for 2001 was 14.2%. Industrial sectors slated for growth in the early 2000s were food processing and packing, textiles, woodworking, furniture and building materials, automotive parts, pharmaceuticals, medical equipment, and aerospace. The construction sector experienced growth during that period; construction spending grew by 9% in the first quarter of 2001. Ukraine produced 31,824 automobiles in 2001, and 1,417 heavy trucks in 2000, a 74% increase over 1999.

In 2004, the representation of industry in the GDP grew to 45.1%, while its representation in the labor force was 32%; agriculture made up 18% of the economy and 24% of the labor force, while services came in second with a 36.9% representation in the GDP and 44% in the labor force. The industrial production growth rate was 16.5% in 2004, with the fastest growing industries being: machine building (which registered a 30.7% growth as opposed to the previous year), construction (23.8%), wood processing, paper and printing (26%), processing industry (15.5%), and light industry (14%).

29 SCIENCE AND TECHNOLOGY

The Ukrainian Academy of Sciences, founded in 1919, has sections of physical engineering and mathematical sciences, and chemical engineering and biological sciences; it has 66 scientific and technical research institutes attached to it. The Ukrainian Academy of Agrarian Sciences has 13 research institutes, and the Ukrainian Academy of Medical Sciences has six research institutes. All three academies are headquartered in Kiev. A botanical museum is located in Kiev. Ukraine has 92 universities, polytechnics, and institutes that offer courses in basic and applied sciences. In 1987–97, science and engineering students accounted for 42% of university enrollment. In 2002, research and development (R&D) expenditures totaled $2,805.687 million, or 1.18% of GDP. Of that amount, government provided the largest portion at 37.4%, followed by the business sector at 33.4%, foreign sources at 26.2%, higher education and private nonprofit organizations at 0.4% each, with 2.3% listed as undistributed. In that same year, there were 1,749 scientists and engineers, and 456 technicians engaged in R&D per million people. High technology exports in 2002 were valued at $572 million, accounting for 5% of the country's manufactured exports.

30 DOMESTIC TRADE

As of 2002, nearly all of the previously state-owned retail establishments have been privatized. Chain stores, supermarkets, and brand-name specialty stores, many of which are owned by Ukrainians, have become more common in major cities. Department stores, smaller grocery and specialty stores, and bazaars are more common since prices at these establishments are more in line with lower and middle-class spending capabilities. About 40–60% of consumer goods are domestically produced. There are some successful foreign franchises, but the practice of franchising has not become widespread. A value-added tax of 20% applies to most goods and services.

31 FOREIGN TRADE

Ukraine exports products to 140 countries of the world. Its main export products are ferrous metals and metal products, engines, transport and mechanical equipment, chemicals, and vehicles. Top import items include mineral products, automobiles, transportation equipment, chemicals, and textiles. Ukraine relies heavily on trade, particularly with the other former Soviet republics, although not nearly as much as it had before the breakup. Inter-republic trade accounted for 73% of its total imports in 1988 and 85% of its total exports. In 1991, imports from the other republics equaled 26% of GDP and exports to them amounted to 25% of GDP. However, trade with former USSR states has since rebounded, with Ukraine taking in 59% of its imports from them and selling 33% of its exports to them in 2000.

In 1991/92, inter-republic trade contracted severely, partly due to a breakdown in payment mechanisms, and trade with other countries dropped as well. Much of Ukraine's foreign trade has been carried out in the context of intergovernmental agreements. However, the government has since stabilized its foreign trade. In 2000, total imports were valued at $14 billion, and total exports at $14.6 billion. Ukraine trades heavily with the other former Soviet republics, and since 1993 has had extensive trade ties with China.

In 2004, exports totaled $32.9 billion and imports $31.4 billion, making Ukraine one of the few countries in the region with a positive trade balance. Export commodities include ferrous and non-ferrous metals, fuel and petroleum products, chemicals, machinery and transport equipment, and food products. The main export partners were Russia (where 18% of all exports went), Germany (5.8%), Turkey (5.7%), Italy (5%), and the United States (4.6%). Imports included energy, chemicals, machinery and equipment, and they mainly came from Russia (41.8%), Germany (9.6%), and Turkmenistan (6.7%). The current account balance in 2004 was $4.6 billion.

Principal Trading Partners – Ukraine (2002)

(In millions of US dollars)

Country	Exports	Imports	Balance
World	17,927.4	16,975.9	951.5
Russia	3,148.7	6,299.1	-3,150.4
Turkey	1,235.1	195.3	1,039.8
Italy-San Marino-Holy See	839.3	460.4	378.9
Germany	735.7	1,627.0	-891.3
China	667.1	258.8	408.3
United Kingdom	531.8	259.0	272.8
Hungary	525.1	188.8	336.3
United States	505.0	464.0	41.0
Poland	505.0	536.7	-31.7
Spain	373.0	101.8	271.2

(…) data not available or not significant.

SOURCE: *2003 International Trade Statistics Yearbook,* New York: United Nations, 2004.

Balance of Payments – Ukraine (2003)

(In millions of US dollars)

Current Account		**2,891.0**
Balance on goods		-269.0
Imports	-24,008.0	
Exports	23,739.0	
Balance on services		1,557.0
Balance on income		-581.0
Current transfers		2,184.0
Capital Account		**-17.0**
Financial Account		**264.0**
Direct investment abroad		-13.0
Direct investment in Ukraine		1,424.0
Portfolio investment assets		1.0
Portfolio investment liabilities		-923.0
Financial derivatives		…
Other investment assets		-940.0
Other investment liabilities		715.0
Net Errors and Omissions		**-965.0**
Reserves and Related Items		**-2,173.0**

(…) data not available or not significant.

SOURCE: *Balance of Payment Statistics Yearbook 2004,* Washington, DC: International Monetary Fund, 2004.

32 BALANCE OF PAYMENTS

The financial crisis of 1998 caused a large outflow of capital, and reserves fell to less than a third of their level in 1997. Due to a major exchange rate adjustment that made Ukrainian products more competitive in both external and internal markets, reserves recovered somewhat in 1999. From June 2000 to July 2001, reserves increased dramatically, back to pre-1998 levels. This growth is surprising in light of the fact that the country has received almost no external funding since 1998, when foreign investors began avoiding Ukraine. Following the 1998 devaluation of the hryvnia, trade surpluses drove the growth in reserves, and the balance of payments situation improved. Reserve growth also improved due to Ukraine's default on its sovereign debt. As of the early 2000s, Ukraine's balance of payments position was expected to be heavily influenced by its trade with Russia.

The US Central Intelligence Agency (CIA) reported that in 2001 the purchasing power parity of Ukraine's exports was $17.3 billion while imports totaled $17.1 billion resulting in a trade surplus of $200 million. The International Monetary Fund (IMF) reported that in 2001 Ukraine had exports of goods totaling $17.1 billion and imports totaling $16.9 billion. The services credit totaled $4 billion and debit $3.58 billion.

The exports of good and services increased steadily, growing from $28.9 billion in 2003, to 39.7 billion in 2004. At the same time, exports managed to stay above the level of imports, establishing Ukraine as one of the few export driven economies in the region. Imports of goods and services totaled 27.6 billion in 2003, and 34.8 billion in 2004, giving Ukraine a positive resource balance in both years: 1.3 billion and 4.9 billion respectively. Its reserves (including gold) grew from 6.9 billion in 2003 to 9.5 billion in 2004, covering almost four months of imports.

33 BANKING AND SECURITIES

The National Bank of Ukraine (NBU) is the country's national bank and was established in June 1991. It has since assumed the function of a central bank. The commercial banking sector is dominated by the big five banks of Prominvest Bank, Ukrania, Ukreximbank, Eximbank and Oshadbank. Of these, Ukreximbank and Oshchadbank remain state controlled. As of 2001, Ukraine had 195 banks, but of these, only 153 remained in operation. Of these banks, approximately a quarter have foreign exchange licenses, and one-third are members of the Ukrainian Interbank Currency Exchange. It is generally acknowledged that Ukraine has too many banks and that there will be numerous mergers and failures in the coming years. In 1995 alone more than 20 banks went out of business, almost 80 changed ownership, and only eight new banks entered the market. Foreign banks, however, have been slow to enter the market.

The NBU implements monetary control through reserve requirements and the interest rates it charges banks on funds transferred from the state savings bank. Before November 1992, the NBU was able to obtain additional rubles by running a surplus on transactions with other republics in the ruble zone. However, with inflation accelerating since early 1991, the supply of rubles proved insufficient to meet the economy's needs, and Ukraine consequently resorted to the use of coupons. The resulting rise in inflation was the main factor behind Ukraine's enforced departure from the ruble zone in November 1992.

The International Monetary Fund reports that in 2001, currency and demand deposits—an aggregate commonly known as M1—were equal to $5.5 billion. In that same year, M2—an aggregate equal to M1 plus savings deposits, small time deposits, and money market mutual funds—was $8.4 billion. The money market rate, the rate at which financial institutions lend to one another in the short term, was 16.57%. The discount rate, the interest rate at which the central bank lends to financial institutions in the short term, was 12.5%.

The Law on Securities and the Stock Exchange came into effect in January 1992. There are seven stock exchanges and seven commodities exchanges, although these are more like the auction houses that sprang up after the collapse of the Soviet Union in 1991 as conduits for goods rather than the securities exchanges found in the West. Capital markets are undeveloped even by the standards of countries such as Russia. The Ukrainian Stock Exchange (USE), established in 1992, acts to coordinate primary and secondary market trading of Ukrainian securities. In 2001, the exchange had 131 companies listed and total market capitalization of $1.4 billion. Trading value was $226 million, with a turnover ratio of 13.9%. As of 2004, there were 155 companies listed with the country's First Securities Trading System (PFTS), which had a market capitalization of $11.778 billion. Trading value in that year totaled $201 million, with a turnover ratio of 2.5%.

34 INSURANCE

Among the insurance companies operating in Ukraine in 1997 were: Asko-Kiev Central Insurance Co.; Factotum Joint-Stock Insurance Co., First International Insurance Group; Ometa-Inster Joint-Stock Insurance Co.; Skide Insurance Co.; and Slavia. Beginning in August 1998, the Ukrainian government required that foreign visitors purchase mandatory "emergency medical insurance" from the Ukrainian State Insurance Company. In addition, personal accident insurance is required for all passengers on public transportation. Foreign shareholders in insurance companies may not exceed 49%. In 2003, the value of all direct insurance premiums written totaled $1.712 billion, of which nonlife premiums accounted for $1.699 billion. In that same year, Lemma was the top nonlife insurer, with gross written nonlife premiums for direct business only of $124.8 million, while Grawe Ukraina was the country's leading life insurer, with gross written life insurance premiums of $4.8 million.

35 PUBLIC FINANCE

Ukraine has displayed positive growth in recent years, but long term growth will require certain market reforms. The economy is burdened by excessive government regulation, and major sectors such as energy and telecommunications remain to be privatized. Corporate governance is weak, and corruption is rampant. In the early 2000s, the government sought ways to reform the tax code to eliminate corruption and legitimize economic activity. Ukraine receives aid from the IMF, although the relationship between those two entities has not always been successful; Ukraine has had problems adhering to IMF monetary conditions.

The US Central Intelligence Agency (CIA) estimated that in 2005 Ukraine's central government took in revenues of approxi-

Public Finance – Ukraine (2002)

(In millions of hryvnias, central government figures)

Revenue and Grants	**69,252**	**100.0%**
Tax revenue	31,646	45.7%
Social contributions	24,083	34.8%
Grants	3,269	4.7%
Other revenue	10,254	14.8%
Expenditures	**69,028**	**100.0%**
General public services	15,704	22.8%
Defense	3,536	5.1%
Public order and safety	4,677	6.8%
Economic affairs	6,671	9.7%
Environmental protection	...	...
Housing and community amenities	36	0.1%
Health	2,158	3.1%
Recreational, culture, and religion	433	0.6%
Education	4,981	7.2%
Social protection	30,832	44.7%

(…) data not available or not significant.

SOURCE: *Government Finance Statistics Yearbook 2004*, Washington, DC: International Monetary Fund, 2004.

mately $22.9 billion and had expenditures of $24.4 billion. Revenues minus expenditures totaled approximately -$1.5 billion. Public debt in 2005 amounted to 20.5% of GDP. Total external debt was $33.93 billion.

The International Monetary Fund (IMF) reported that in 2002, the most recent year for which it had data, central government revenues were HRN69,252 million and expenditures were HRN69,028 million. The value of revenues was US$13,001 million and expenditures US$12,959 million, based on an exchange rate for 2002 of US$1 = HRN5.3266 as reported by the IMF. Government outlays by function were as follows: general public services, 22.8%; defense, 5.1%; public order and safety, 6.8%; economic affairs, 9.7%; housing and community amenities, 0.1%; health, 3.1%; recreation, culture, and religion, 0.6%; education, 7.2%; and social protection, 44.7%.

36 TAXATION

In 1997/98 Ukraine reformed its tax system. As of 2005, the standard corporate tax rate was 25%, although preferential regimes are available for special economic zones. Capital gains for companies are taxed at the corporate rate. Withholding taxes on income from royalties and interest is 15%. Companies distributing dividends to residents and nonresidents are required to pay a 25% advance tax on the dividends. The tax can then be credited against the company's profits.

Personal income is taxed at a flat 13% rate. Capital gains received by individuals are subject to a 13% withholding tax. Dividends received by resident and nonresident individuals are subject to a 15% withholding tax.

The Ukraine's main indirect tax is its value-added tax (VAT), with a standard rate of 20%. A 0% VAT rate applies to exports and international transportation services. Some medicines, baby food, educational, medical and insurance services, and the sale of land are also exempt.

37 CUSTOMS AND DUTIES

Import licenses are required for all foreign trade activities in Ukraine. Ukraine has signed trade agreements with the United States, Russia, Iran, Turkmenistan, the United Arab Emirates, and several other former Soviet republics. As of 2002, tariffs on imports range from 0–20%, with the tariff on automobiles being the highest. Preferential tariffs are given to developing countries and privileged tariffs are given to countries that have trade agreements with Ukraine. Other duties include a 20% VAT and excise taxes (up to 300%). In 2000, the number of categories of goods eligible for excise tax was reduced from 20 to five: alcohol, automobiles, jewelry, oil products, and tobacco.

38 FOREIGN INVESTMENT

Among the transitional economies of Eastern Europe, nowhere has the gap between economic potential and economic performance been wider than in the Ukraine, and nowhere has the gap been more glaring than in the foreign investment statistics. By 2000, total foreign direct investment (FDI) in the Ukraine was still less than $4 billion, compared with $40 billion that had flowed into Poland and $20 billion into Hungary during the same period.

Independence was first greeted by a rush of inward investment. In 1991, the number of joint ventures operating in Ukraine rose from 76 in October 1990 to 189 in October 1991. Following the enactment in March 1992 of a more favorable foreign investment law, joint ventures jumped to 1,400 early in 1993. Most of these ventures were in industry, with a few engaged in foreign trade. The government's 1993 economic plan included tax incentives and other benefits for investors in specific areas including agro-industrial enterprises, energy, and production of consumer goods. However, by 1996 and 1997, rampant official graft and corruption were crippling foreign investment. Several significant multinational corporations withdrew from Ukraine after government decrees were issued that steered business to state-owned firms in which government officials were stakeholders. This action occurred despite the Foreign Investment Law of 1996, which purported to put foreign investors on an equal footing with Ukrainian nationals, and President Kuchma's pledge to battle corruption. The government had declared a need for $40 billion in foreign investment, but only $2.8 billion was invested between 1992 and 1998.

In 1997 the law "On Special (Free) Economic Zones" was adopted, establishing three types of special investment zones: free economic zones (FEZs), territories with a special investment regime (SEZs), and territories of priority development (TPDs). As of 2002, there were nine TPDs and eleven FEZs and SEZs. In 2002, the special zones attracted investment totaling $909 million, both domestic and foreign, but pressure has been brought by the IMF to either eliminate the special zones or curb their tax and regulatory exemptions.

Annual foreign direct investment (FDI) inflow peaked at $747 billion in 1998, up from $623 billion in 1997, before falling to $471 billion in 1999 in the wake of the Russian financial crisis. FDI inflow recovered to $593 billion in 2000, but then fell back to $531 million in the global economic slowdown of 2001. Contrary to the worldwide trend of reduced FDI flow after the 11 September 2001 terrorist attacks, the Ukraine had its best year since independence, with inflow increasing over 15% to an estimated $738.7 million in

2002. As of October 2002, total FDI since 1992 amounted to almost $5 billion.

As of 1 October 2002, according the Ukraine State Statistics Committee, FDI had come from 112 countries. The United States remained the largest source of FDI, with $843 million or 17% of the total. US-based sources were also probably involved in some of the FDI flows from Cyprus (11% of the total) and the British Virgin Islands (6.4%). The United Kingdom accounted for 9.5% of total FDI in the Ukraine since 1992; the Netherlands, 7.8%; the Russian Federation, 6.5%; Germany, 5%; Switzerland, 4.2%; Austria, 3.9%; and Korea, 3.5%. The remaining 24.2% came from 102 other countries. Per capita FDI stock increased from $78 at the end of 2000 to $102 at the beginning of October 2002.

In 2004, Ukraine was a much more attractive market for foreign investments, receiving $1.4 billion of direct FDI—an increase of 22% from the previous year. Most of this investment went to production machinery and equipment, with food processing, agricultural processing, machine building, coal, oil and gas, and light industry being other important recipients of foreign funds. This growth however was well under the potential of the Ukrainian market, especially if one considers that in the same year, its neighbor, Romania, received over 5 billion in direct FDI. At the end of 2004, the level of foreign investment since 1992 rose to 7.7 billion—ten times as low as the same figure in Poland. Major investors in 2004 included: Cyprus (14.1%), the United States (13.6%), the United Kingdom (10.4%), Germany (7.1%), the Netherlands (6.8%), Virgin Islands (6.1%), Russia (5.5%), Switzerland (4.9%), and Austria (4%).

39 ECONOMIC DEVELOPMENT

In 1993, Ukraine's parliament tentatively approved a new economic reform plan to stabilize the republic's economy, attract more capital from abroad, and lay the groundwork for a market economy. Measures proposed included stricter monetary and banking regulation, and the elimination of monopolies in industries. A privatization program was underway in sectors including retail trade, services, the food industry, agriculture, and housing.

Since the election of President Kuchma in 1994, the government has implemented a far-reaching economic reform program. Almost all price and trade controls have been abolished in an effort to stabilize the new market economy. Privatization began in earnest in 1995, and a new convertible currency was adopted in 1996. In the 1990s, Ukraine continued to register negative growth. By the end of the 1990s, real gross domestic product (GDP) declined to 40% of its pre-independence level. In late 1998, the International Monetary Fund (IMF) loaned Ukraine another $2.2 billion after Ukraine promised to introduce more fiscal discipline.

The economy started to grow in 2000; GDP growth in 2002 was over 4.5%. Small- and medium-sized enterprises were privatized by 2002, but the energy and telecommunications sectors had yet to be privatized. The government passed a foreign investment law, but bureaucratic hurdles, poor corporate governance, corruption, and the weak enforcement of contract law by courts all hamper investment. At the end of October 2002, total foreign direct investment into the country amounted to around $4.9 billion, which was one of the lowest figures in the region. In 2002, land reforms were ongoing, supporting growth in the agricultural sector.

The economy took off in 2003 and 2004, and was deemed one of the most dynamic in Europe (the GDP growth rate in 2004 was 12.1%). The election of Viktor Yushchenko at the end of 2004, and the political turmoil that preceded it, hampered this expansive pulse. The new president stated however that the country is on the right path and that the economy will start booming again. Ukraine boasts a highly qualified work force, cheap labor and competitive costs, a relatively well-developed transportation and communications infrastructure, and a strategic geographic location. In addition, the large market—47 million people—makes it a prime location for foreign investment.

40 SOCIAL DEVELOPMENT

The social security system provides all employees with old age, disability, and survivor's pensions. The program is funded primarily from employer contributions, with a small contribution from employees and government subsidies as needed. Retirement is normally at age 60 for men and 55 for women, although this is reduced by five years for those engaged in arduous work and mothers with five or more children. There is a dual system of medical benefits. Cash benefits for sickness are provided for employed persons, while a universal medical care system exists for all residents. Maternity benefits of 100% of wages for 70 days before and 56 days after the expected date of childbirth are payable to all employed women. Workers' compensation and unemployment benefits are also provided. Special provisions exist for Chernobyl victims. Family allowances are provided to families with large numbers of children.

The law provides women with the same employment rights as men, although they rarely attain high-level managerial or political positions. Women who are employed mostly work in low-paying jobs or in industries that have trouble paying their employees on time. Help wanted ads often specify gender. Violence against women, domestic abuse, and sexual harassment in the workplace are pervasive.

Human rights violations continue. Harassment of racial minorities and religious intolerance are increasing problems. Anti-Semitic incidents and societal discrimination of ethnic minorities are commonplace. The Roma population is subject to abuse by police and general intolerance by the public. Prisoners are mistreated by authorities and live in substandard conditions. The government interferes with freedom of the press and with the electoral process.

41 HEALTH

Deterioration of the economy and declining living standards have had a negative impact on birth and mortality rates and women's and children's health standards need much improvement. Although safe water was available to 96.5%, proper sanitation was available to only 70% of the urban population and 8% of the rural population in the mid-1990s. Poor nutrition is another major problem in the Ukraine, and a shortage of basic supplies exacerbates the health care situation.

The country has established 156 independent children's hospitals. Altogether there were a total of 700,000 hospital beds. In addition, there were 6,500 outpatient polyclinical institutions. As of 2004, there were an estimated 297 physicians, 766 nurses, and 39 dentists per 100,000 people.

Infant mortality was reported at 10.11 per 1,000 live births in 2005. Life expectancy was 69.68 years in 2005. As of 2002, the crude birth rate and overall mortality rate were estimated at, respectively, 10 and 16 per 1,000 people. Immunization rates for children up to one year old were: tuberculosis, 95%; diphtheria, pertussis, and tetanus, 96%; polio, 97%; and measles, 97%.

The leading causes of death were cardiovascular and respiratory diseases, cancer, traumas, and accidents. The HIV/AIDS prevalence was 1.40 per 100 adults in 2003. As of 2004, there were approximately 360,000 people living with HIV/AIDS in the country. There were an estimated 20,000 deaths from AIDS in 2003.

The likelihood of dying after age 65 of heart disease in Ukraine was below the average for medium human development as defined by the World Bank. In the mid-1990s, that rate exceeded 300 per 1,000 for men and 295 per 1,000 for women. On the other hand, cancer rates for men were higher. Death after age 65 from cancer was 133 per 1,000 people in the mid-1990s.

42 HOUSING

Before 1994, most housing and utility costs were covered by the government through a policy which was causing major federal debt. Through an IMF approved program of economic reforms put in place in October 1994, residents were asked to contribute a much greater amount toward there own rent and utilities. Unfortunately, many households were unable to do so. An average three-person household, living in a three-room flat of about 500 sq m (5,381.96 sq ft) was charged expenses of about $30 per month. The average monthly income of such a family was $50. In 1995, the government put in place a subsidy program to assist low-income families in meeting rising housing costs, but funding for housing continues to be a problem.

At the 2001 census, there were 18,200,567 households counted representing 47,726,518 people. About 44% of all households lived in individual houses; another 44.6% lived in a separate apartment unit. The average amount of living space was 14 sq m (150.69 sq ft) per person.

43 EDUCATION

Most schools are state run. Education is compulsory for nine years, with students starting at age six or seven. These first nine years are completed through four years of elementary school and five years of lower secondary school. Students may continue in general secondary schools offering two- or three-year courses of study, or a specialized education secondary program of about three years. Vocational programs of four or five years are also available at the secondary level. While Ukrainian is the most commonly taught language and medium of instruction, other languages, such as Russian, Hungarian, Polish, Moldovan, or Crimean-Tatar, are offered based on the ethnic composition of the particular school district. The academic year runs from September to June.

In 2001, about 52% of children between the ages of three and six were enrolled in some type of preschool program. Primary school enrollment in 2003 was estimated at about 84% of age-eligible students. The same year, secondary school enrollment was about 85% of age-eligible students. It is estimated that about 97.6% of all students complete their primary education. The student-to-teacher ratio for primary school was at about 19:1 in 2003; the ratio for secondary school was about 13:1.

There are over 900 colleges, technical schools, vocational schools, universities, and other institutes of higher education. The Kyiv-Mohyla Academy was founded in 1632. Other universities are: Lviv University (1795), Kharkiv University (1804), Taras Shevchenko National University (1834), Odessa University (1868). In 2003, it was estimated that about 62% of the tertiary age population were enrolled in tertiary education programs. The adult literacy rate for 2004 was estimated at about 99.4%.

As of 2003, public expenditure on education was estimated at 5.4% of GDP, or 20.3% of total government expenditures.

44 LIBRARIES AND MUSEUMS

The largest library in the country is the Vernadsky National Library of Ukraine in Kiev, which holds over 15 million items, including the collection of the Presidents of Ukraine, archive copies of Ukrainian printed documents from 1917, and the archives of the National Academy of Sciences of Ukraine. The National Parliamentary Library of Ukraine in Kiev holds 65,000 volumes. Also in Kiev, the National Library of Ukraine for Children has a collection of over 440,000 volumes. Other large collections include the V.G. Korolenko State Scientific Library with 6.7 million volumes and the libraries at Lviv Polytechnic University (3 million), Franko State University in Lviv (2.5 million), Shevchenko Kiev University (2.7 million), and Kiev Polytechnic Institute (2.5 million). There are reported to be about 21,857 public libraries operating in Ukraine with an overall stock of about 336.7 million books.

Kiev has the Kiev State Museum of Russian Art, the Kiev State Museum of Ukrainian Art, the State Historical Museum, the Museum of Cultural Heritage, the National Museum of Medicine, the State Museum of Ukrainian Decorative Folk Art, and the Soros Center for Contemporary Art. There are also several small house museums in Kiev. There is a Museum of Fine Arts in Lugansk. Lviv houses the State Museum of Ethnography and Arts and Crafts and the Literary Museum of Ivan Franko. Odessa is home to the Odessa Museum of Fine Arts, the Museum of Literature, the Naval Museum, the Odessa Museum of Western and Oriental Art, the Odessa Archaeological Museum, and the Pushkin Museum.

45 MEDIA

In 2003, there were an estimated 216 mainline telephones for every 1,000 people; over 2 million people were on a waiting list for telephone service installation. The same year, there were approximately 136 mobile phones in use for every 1,000 people.

Most broadcast media is state-owned or controlled by political parties or other powerful business interests. In 2004, there were six national television stations. While there are many privately-owned radio and television stations, they are generally heavily influenced by the government and political parties. In 2000, there were 456 television sets for every 1,000 people. In 2003, there were an estimated 889 radios for every 1,000 people. The same year, there were 19 personal computers for every 1,000 people and 19 of every 1,000 people had access to the Internet. There were 53 secure Internet servers in the country in 2004.

Among the leading newspapers (with 2005 daily circulation) are: *Segodnya* (published in Russian, 849,000 circulation), *Fakty I Commentarii* (published in Russian, 761,000 circulation), *Silski Visti* (Ukrainian, 537,000), *Vecherniye Vesti* (Russian, 500,000),

Ukrayina Moloda (Ukrainian, 163,000), and *Den* (Russian and Ukrainian, 62,500).

The constitution and a 1991 law provide for free speech and a free press. Criticism of the government is said to be tolerated, though some journalists practice self-censorship because of occasional pressures from the government.

46 ORGANIZATIONS

The Ukraine Chamber of Commerce and the Congress of Business Circles of Ukraine promotes the commercial and business activities of the country to the rest of the world. Many of Ukraine's trade unions belong to the umbrella organization called the Federation of Independent Trade Unions. Professional associations are active in several different fields. There is an active Ukrainian Consumers' Association.

National cultural organizations include the Ukrainian Cultural Educational Organization and Flamenko, which promotes cultural exchange programs. National youth organizations include the Council of Ukrainian Students, the Ukrainian Fund of International Youth Cooperation, Junior Chamber, Ukrainian Girl Guides and Girls Scouts Association, the Compass Club, and YMCA/YWCA. There are several sports associations promoting amateur competition for athletes of all ages.

National social action organizations include the Ukrainian Center for Human Rights, the Ukrainian Environmental Association, the Ukrainian Legal Foundation, Freedom House (advocating the development of democratic institutions), The Children's Fund, and Zhinocha Hromada, an organization focused on encouraging women to be active in economic and community development. International organizations with national chapters include Caritas, UNICEF, Amnesty International, and the Red Cross.

47 TOURISM, TRAVEL, AND RECREATION

Kiev, Ukraine's major cultural center, is known for its beautiful churches and golden-domed cathedrals, although much of its classic architecture was destroyed or obscured by Communist planners in the 1930s. The cathedral of St. Sophia, built in the 11th century, is one of the finest examples of Russo-Byzantine architecture. Another major tourist attraction is the Golden Gate, an 11th-century fortification restored in 1982. Lviv (formerly Lvov) offers architectural sights ranging from late-13th-century Russian to 16th-century Gothic structures.

In 2003, about 12.5 million visitors arrived in Ukraine, over 5 million of whom came from Russia. There were 32,572 hotel rooms with 86,243 beds and an occupancy rate of 30%. Travelers stayed in Ukraine an average of three nights per trip. Tourism expenditure receipts totaled $1.2 billion. A valid passport is required for all travelers to enter Ukraine. Visas are not required for citizens of Japan, Canada, Switzerland, Liechtenstein, the United States, and the European Union countries, for stays of up to 90 days. To visit the nation, all other travelers need a visa. Medical insurance which covers Ukraine is required for all US citizens.

According to 2005 estimates from the US Department of State, the cost of staying in Kiev was $271 per day, other areas were less at $177 per day.

48 FAMOUS UKRAINIANS

Leonid M. Kravchuk and Vitold P. Fokin were respectively the first president and prime minister of Ukraine. Leonid Brezhnev (Dneprodzershinsk, Ukraine, 1906–82) led the Soviet Union from 1966–82. Outstanding representatives of the culture and literature of Ukraine include poet Taras Shevchenko (1814–61) and the Jewish writer Sholom Aleichem (Solomon Rabinowitz, 1859–1916).

49 DEPENDENCIES

Ukraine has no territories or colonies.

50 BIBLIOGRAPHY

Aslund, Anders (ed.). *Economic Transformation in Russia*. New York: St. Martin's, 1994.

Buckley, Mary. *Redefining Russian Society and Polity*. Boulder, Colo.: Westview Press, 1993.

Dean, Martin. *Collaboration in the Holocaust: Crimes of the Local Police in Belorussia and Ukraine, 1941–44*. New York: St. Martin's Press, 2000.

Goncharenko, Alexander. *Ukrainian-Russian Relations: an Unequal Partnership*. London: Royal United Services Institute for Defense Studies, 1995.

Kohut, Zenon E., Bohdan Y. Nebesio, and Myroslav Yurkevich. *Historical Dictionary of Ukraine*. Lanham, Md.: Scarecrow, 2005.

Koropeckyj, I. S., (ed.). *The Ukrainian Economy: Achievements, Problems, Challenges*. Cambridge, Mass.: Harvard University Press, 1992.

Mandel, David. *Labour after Communism: Auto Workers and Their Unions in Russia, Ukraine, and Belarus*. New York: Black Rose Books, 2004.

McElrath, Karen (ed.). *HIV and AIDS: A Global View*. Westport, Conn.: Greenwood Press, 2002.

The Modern Encyclopedia of Russian, Soviet and Eurasian History. Gulf Breeze, Fla.: Academic International Press, 1994.

Otfinoski, Steven. *Ukraine*. 2nd ed. New York: Facts On File, 2004.

Schulz-Torge, Ulrich-Joachim (ed.). *Who's Who in Russia Today: A Biographical Dictionary of More than 2,100 Individuals from the Russian Federation Including the Other Fourteen USSR Republics*. New Providence: K.G. Saur, 1994.

Shen, Raphael. *Ukraine's Economic Reform: Obstacles, Errors, Lessons*. Westport, Con.: Praeger, 1996.

Solovev, Vladimir. *Boris Yeltsin: A Political Biography*. New York: Putnam, 1992.

Terterov, Marat (ed.). *Doing Business with Ukraine*. Sterling, Va.: Kogan Page, 2005.

Yeltsin, Boris Nikolayevich. *The Struggle for Russia*. New York: Times Books, 1994.

Zeilig, Leo and David Seddon. *A Political and Economic Dictionary of Africa*. Philadelphia: Routledge/Taylor and Francis, 2005.

UNITED KINGDOM

United Kingdom of Great Britain and Northern Ireland

CAPITAL: London

FLAG: The Union Jack, adopted in 1800, is a combination of the banners of England (St. George's flag: a red cross with extended horizontals on a white field), Scotland (St. Andrew's flag: a white saltire cross on a blue field), and Ireland (St. Patrick's flag: a red saltire cross on a white field). The arms of the saltire crosses do not meet at the center.

ANTHEM: *God Save the Queen.*

MONETARY UNIT: The pound sterling (£) is a paper currency of 100 pence. Before decimal coinage was introduced on 15 February 1971, the pound had been divided into 20 shillings, each shilling representing 12 pennies (p) or pence; some old-style coins are still in circulation. Under the new system, there are coins of 1, 2, 5, 10, 20, and 50 pence and 1 and 2 pounds, and notes of 5, 10, 20, and 50 pounds. £1 = $1.85185 (or $1 = £0.54) as of 2005.

WEIGHTS AND MEASURES: Although the traditional imperial system of weights and measures is still in use (sample units: of weight, the stone of 14 pounds equivalent to 6.35 kilograms; of length, the yard equivalent to 0.914 meter; of capacity, a bushel equivalent to 36.37 liters), a changeover to the metric system is in progress.

HOLIDAYS: New Year's Day, 1 January; Good Friday; Easter Monday (except Scotland); Late Summer Holiday, last Monday in August or 1st in September (except Scotland); Christmas, 25 December; and Boxing Day, 1st weekday after Christmas. Also observed in Scotland are bank holidays on 2 January and on the 1st Monday in August. Northern Ireland observes St. Patrick's Day, 17 March; and Orangeman's Day, 12 July, commemorating the Battle of the Boyne in 1690.

TIME: GMT.

¹LOCATION, SIZE, AND EXTENT

The United Kingdom is situated off the northwest coast of Europe between the Atlantic Ocean on the N and NW and the North Sea on the E, separated from the Continent by the Strait of Dover and the English Channel, 34 km (21 mi) wide at its narrowest point, and from the Irish Republic by the Irish Sea and St. George's Channel. Its total area of 244,820 sq km (94,526 sq mi) consists of the island of Great Britain—formed by England, 130,439 sq km (50,363 sq mi); Wales, 20,768 sq km (8,018 sq mi); and Scotland, 78,783 sq km (30,418 sq mi)—and Northern Ireland, 14,120 sq km (5,452 sq mi), on the island of Ireland, separated from Great Britain by the North Channel. Comparatively, the area occupied by the United Kingdom is slightly smaller than the state of Oregon.

There are also several island groups and hundreds of small single islands, most of them administratively part of the mainland units. The United Kingdom extends about 965 km (600 mi) N–S and about 485 km (300 mi) E–W. Its total boundary length is 12,789 km (7,947 mi), of which 12,429 km (7,723 mi) is coastline. The Isle of Man, 588 sq km (227 sq mi), and the Channel Islands, comprising Jersey, Guernsey, Alderney, and Sark, with a combined area of 194 sq km (75 sq mi), are not part of the United Kingdom but are dependencies of the crown. The 0° meridian of longitude passes through the old Royal Observatory, located at Greenwich in Greater London. The United Kingdom's capital city, London, is located in the southeast part of Great Britain.

²TOPOGRAPHY

England is divided into the hill regions of the north, west, and southwest and the rolling downs and low plains of the east and southeast. Running from east to west on the extreme north Scottish border are the Cheviot Hills. The Pennine Range runs north and south from the Scottish border to Derbyshire in central England. The rest of the countryside consists mainly of rich agricultural lands, occasional moors, and plains. South of the Pennines lie the Midlands (East and West), a plains region with low, rolling hills and fertile valleys. The eastern coast is low-lying, much of it less than 5 m (15 ft) above sea level; for centuries parts of it have been protected by embankments against inundation from gales and unusually high tides. Little of the south and east rises to higher than 300 m (1,000 ft).

The highest point in England is Scafell Pike (978 m/3,210 ft) in the famed Lake District of the northwest. The longest of the rivers flowing from the central highlands to the sea are the Severn (about 340 km/210 mi) in the west and the Thames (about 320 km/200 mi) in the southeast. Other rivers include the Humber, the Tees, the Tyne, and the Tweed in the east, the Avon and Exe in the south, and the Mersey in the west.

Scotland has three distinct topographical regions: the Northern Highlands, occupying almost the entire northern half of the country and containing the highest point in the British Isles, Ben Nevis (1,343 m/4,406 ft), as well as Loch Ness, site of a fabled "monster"; the Central Lowlands, with an average elevation of about 150 m

(500 ft) and containing the valleys of the Tay, Forth, and Clyde rivers, as well as Loch Lomond, Scotland's largest lake; and the Southern Uplands, rising to their peak at Merrick (843 m/2,766 ft), with moorland cut by many valleys and rivers.

Wales is largely mountainous and bleak, with much of the land suitable only for pasture. The Cambrian Mountains occupy almost the entire area and include Wales's highest point, Mt. Snowdon (1,086 m/3,563 ft). There are narrow coastal plains in the south and west and small lowland areas in the north, including the valley of the Dee.

Northern Ireland consists mainly of low-lying plateaus and hills, generally about 150 to 180 m (500–600 ft) high. The Mourne Mountains in the southeast include Slieve Donard (852 m/2,796 ft), the highest point in Northern Ireland. In a central depression lies Lough Neagh, the largest lake in the United Kingdom.

The United Kingdom's long and rugged coastline, heavily indented, has towering cliffs and headlands and numerous bays and inlets, among them the deep and narrow lochs and the wide firths of Scotland. Many river estuaries serve as fine harbors.

³CLIMATE

Despite its northern latitude, the United Kingdom generally enjoys a temperate climate, warmed by the North Atlantic Drift, a continuation of the Gulf Stream, and by southwest winds. Mean monthly temperatures range (north to south) from 3°C to 5°C (37–41°F) in winter and from 12°C to 16°C (54–61°F) in summer. The mean annual temperature in the west near sea level ranges from 8°C (46°F) in the Hebrides to 11°C (52°F) in the far southwest of England. Rarely do temperatures rise in summer to over 32°C (90°F) or drop in winter below -10°C (14°F).

Rainfall, averaging more than 100 cm (40 in) throughout the United Kingdom, is heaviest on the western and northern heights (over 380 cm/150 in), lowest along the eastern and southeastern coasts. Fairly even distribution of rain throughout the year, together with the prevalence of mists and fogs, results in scanty sunshine—averaging from half an hour to two hours a day in winter and from five to eight hours in summer.

In the spring of 1997 there was an intense drought in southern and western England; the previous two years were the driest in England and Wales since reliable record-keeping began in 1767.

⁴FLORA AND FAUNA

With its mild climate and varied soils, the United Kingdom has a diverse pattern of natural vegetation. Originally, oak forests probably covered the lowland, except for the fens and marsh areas, while pine forests and patches of moorland covered the higher or sandy ground. Over the centuries, much of the forest area, especially on the lowlands, was cleared for cultivation. Fairly extensive forests remain in east and north Scotland and in southeast England. Oak, elm, ash, and beech are the most common trees in England. Pine and birch are most common in Scotland. Almost all the lowland outside the industrial centers is farmland, with a varied seminatural vegetation of grasses and flowering plants. Wild vegetation consists of the natural flora of woods, fens and marshes, cliffs, chalk downs, and mountain slopes, the most widespread

being the heather, grasses, gorse, and bracken of the moorlands. There are over 1,600 plant species in the country.

The fauna is similar to that of northwestern continental Europe, although there are fewer species. Some of the larger mammals—wolf, bear, boar, and reindeer—are extinct, but red and roe deer are protected for sport. Common smaller mammals are foxes, hares, hedgehogs, rabbits, weasels, stoats, shrews, rats, and mice; otters are found in many rivers, and seals frequently appear along the coast. There are at least 50 species of mammal native to the region. There are few reptiles and amphibians. Roughly 230 species of birds reside in the United Kingdom, and another 200 are migratory. Most numerous are the chaffinch, blackbird, sparrow, and starling. The number of large birds is declining, however, except for game birds—pheasant, partridge, and red grouse—which are protected. With the reclamation of the marshlands, waterfowl are moving to the many bird sanctuaries. The rivers and lakes abound in salmon, trout, perch, pike, roach, dace, and grayling. There are more than 21,000 species of insects.

⁵ENVIRONMENT

Government officials and agencies with principal responsibility for environmental protection are the Department of the Environment, the Department of the Environment for Northern Ireland, and the secretaries of state for Scotland and Wales. The National Trust (for Places of Historic Interest or Natural Beauty), an organization of more than 1.3 million members, has acquired some 750 km (466 mi) of coastline in England, Northern Ireland, and Wales. In addition, 127 km (79 mi) of coastline in Scotland are protected under agreement with the National Trust of Scotland. Two countryside commissions, one for England and Wales and one for Scotland, are charged with conserving the beauty and amenities of rural areas. By 1982, the former had designated 10 national parks, covering 13,600 sq km (5,250 sq mi), or 9% of the area of England and Wales. An additional 36 areas of outstanding beauty have been designated, covering 17,000 sq km (6,600 sq mi). Scotland has 40 national scenic areas, with more than 98% of all Scottish lands under the commission's jurisdiction. Northern Ireland has eight designated areas of outstanding natural beauty, seven country parks, and one regional park. There are also seven forest parks in Great Britain and nine in Northern Ireland. England and Wales have 600,000 hectares (1,500,000 acres) of common land, much of which is open to the public. The Nature Conservancy Council manages 214 national nature reserves in Great Britain and 41 in Northern Ireland.

Air pollution is a significant environmental concern for the United Kingdom. In 1992 the nation had the world's eighth-highest level of industrial carbon dioxide emissions, which totaled 566.2 million metric tons, a per capita level of 9.78 metric tons. In 2000, the total of carbon dioxide emissions was at 567.8 million metric tons. In addition, its sulphur contributes to the formation of acid rain in the surrounding countries of Western Europe. Air quality abatement has improved greatly in the United Kingdom as a result of the Control of Pollution Act of 1974 and other legislation. London is no longer densely smog-ridden, and winter sunlight has been increasing in various industrial cities.

Water pollution from agricultural sources is also a problem. The nation has 145 cubic km of water of which 3% of annual withdrawals is used for farming activity and 77% for industrial pur-

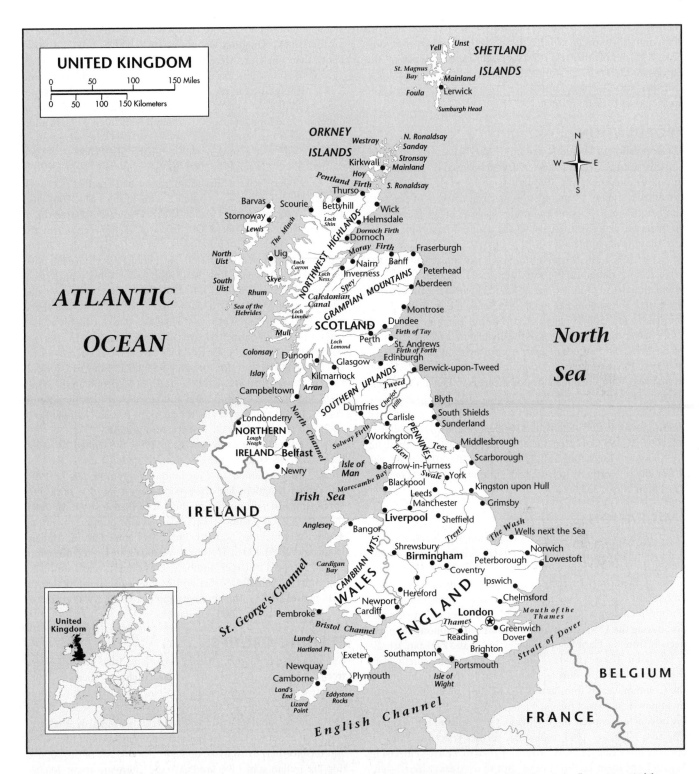

UNITED KINGDOM

0   50   100   150 Miles
0 50 100 150 Kilometers

LOCATION: 49°56′ to 60°50′N; 1°45′E to 8°10′W. BOUNDARY LENGTHS: Total coastline, 12,429 kilometers (7,722 miles), of which Northern Ireland's comprises 375 kilometers (233 miles); Irish Republic, 360 kilometers (225 miles). TERRITORIAL SEA LIMIT: 3 miles.

poses. The United Kingdom's cities produce an average of 22 million tons of solid waste per year. Pollution of the Thames has been reduced to one-quarter of its level in the 1950s, and more than 80% of the population is served by sewage treatment plants.

The Food and Environment Protection Act of 1985 introduced special controls over dumping and marine incineration in re-

sponse to the problems of regulation of oil and gas development and of large-scale dumping at sea.

As of 2003, 20.9% of the United Kingdom's total land area is protected, including 163 Ramsar wetland sites and 5 natural UNESCO World Heritage Sites. According to a 2006 report issued by the International Union for Conservation of Nature and

Natural Resources (IUCN), threatened species included 10 types of mammals, 10 species of birds, 12 species of fish, 2 types of mollusks, 8 species of other invertebrates, and 13 species of plants. The European otter, Atlantic sturgeon, Atlantic ridley, Eskimo curlew, and Spengler's freshwater mussel are classified as endangered. The great auk has become extinct.

6 POPULATION

The population of United Kingdom in 2005 was estimated by the United Nations (UN) at 60,068,000, which placed it at number 22 in population among the 193 nations of the world. In 2005, approximately 16% of the population was over 65 years of age, with another 18% of the population under 15 years of age. There were 96 males for every 100 females in the country. According to the UN, the annual population rate of change for 2005–10 was expected to be 0.2%, a rate the government viewed as satisfactory. The projected population for the year 2025 was 64,687,000. The overall population density was 245 per sq km (635 per sq mi); in England there were 371 persons per sq km (961 per sq mi), with 4,233 persons per sq km (10,968 per sq mi) in Greater London.

The UN estimated that 89% of the population lived in urban areas in 2005, and that urban areas were growing at an annual rate of 0.36%. The capital city, London, had a population of 7,619,000 in that year. Other major metropolitan areas in England, with estimated populations, were Birmingham, 2,215,000; Manchester, 2,193,000; Leeds, 1,402,000; and Liverpool, 975,000. Other large English towns include Sheffield, 516,000; Bradford, 478,800; Bristol, 406,500; and Coventry, 300,844. The major cities in Scotland are Glasgow (1,099,400) and Edinburgh (460,000). Belfast, the major city in Northern Ireland, had a population of 287,500; and Cardiff, in Wales, 305,000.

7 MIGRATION

From 1815–1930, the balance of migration was markedly outward, and well over 20 million persons left Britain, settling mainly within the British Empire and in the United States. Since 1931, however, the flow has largely been inward. From 1931–40, when emigration was very low, there was extensive immigration from Europe, including a quarter of a million refugees seeking sanctuary; during the 1950s, immigration from the Commonwealth, especially from the Caribbean countries, India, and Pakistan, steadily increased. The net influx of some 388,000 people (chiefly from the Commonwealth) during 1960–62 led to the introduction of the Commonwealth Immigrants Act of 1962, giving the government power to restrict the entry of Commonwealth citizens lacking adequate prospects of employment or means of self-support. Effective 1 January 1983, a new law further restricted entry by creating three categories of citizenship, two of which—citizens of British Dependent Territories and "British overseas citizens"—entail no right to live in the United Kingdom. Those in the last category, consisting of an estimated 1.5 million members of Asian minorities who chose to retain British passports when Malaysia and Britain's East African lands became independent, may not pass their British citizenship to their children without UK government approval.

Immigration is now on a quota basis. From 1986–91, 1,334,000 persons left the United Kingdom to live abroad, and 1,461,000 came from overseas to live in the United Kingdom, resulting in a net in-migration of 127,000. The total number of foreign residents in the United Kingdom was about 1,875,000 in 1990. Of these, more than one-third were Irish (638,000). Indians were second (155,000) and Americans third (102,000). Between the 1990s and 2002, net migration in the United Kingdom rose from 50,000 per year to 172,000. In spite of guest worker programs, the number of unauthorized foreigners grew to around 500,000 in 2003. In addition to these increases, "failed" asylum seekers who were subject to "removal" were a burden, with estimates at 155,000 to 283,000 in the United Kingdom in 2004. In that same year, Prime Minister Tony Blair declared that immigration had reached a "crunch point." Migration became a political issue of the 5 May 2005 elections. Conservative Party leader Michael Howard declared that if he were elected the United Kingdom would stop recognizing the 1951 UN Conventions on Refugees and an annual limit of 20,000 would be placed on immigration. The Labour Party stayed in power and Prime Minister Tony Blair proposed a tiered point system to control immigration. In July 2005 the Home Office estimated that there were 570,000 unauthorized foreigners. A five-tiered guest worker system was introduced: tier one, for highly skilled migrants and investors; tier two, for skilled workers in shortage occupations; tier three, for unskilled workers via accredited recruiters, and tier four, for foreign students, and tier five, for cultural exchange workers. After the death of 52 people in the 2 July 2005 bombings in London tubes and buses by British-born South Asians, tension increased and the far-right British National Party called for revamped laws to restrict immigration.

In response to the Kosovo crisis in 1999, the United Kingdom received 4,346 Kosovar refugees from Macedonia under the UNHCR/IOM Humanitarian Evacuation Programme. As of 1999, the United Kingdom had the second-largest number of asylum applications in Europe, but by 2004 it ranked seventh. In 2004, there were 9,800 asylum seekers. Main countries of origin among 47 countries included Somalia, India, Sri Lanka, Eritrea, Afghanistan, and the DROC. However, in 2004 the United Kingdom hosted refugees in larger numbers, 289,059 refugees from, Iraq, Afghanistan, Somalia, Serbia and Montenegro, Iran, Sri Lanka, Turkey, and DROC. The net migration rate in 2005 was estimated as 2.18 migrants per 1,000 population.

8 ETHNIC GROUPS

The present-day English, Welsh, Scots, and Irish are descended from a long succession of early peoples, including Iberians, Celts, Romans, Anglo-Saxons, Danes, and Normans, the last of whom invaded and conquered England in 1066–70. According to the 2001 census, about 83.6% of UK residents are English. The Scottish form about 8.6% of the population, Welsh account for 4.9%, and the Northern Irish make up 2.9%. About 1.8% of the population are Indian, and 1.3% are Pakistani. There are about 300,000 persons who belong to a group known as Travellers, a blend of Roma, Irish, and other ethnic groups who maintain an itinerant lifestyle.

9 LANGUAGES

Spoken throughout the United Kingdom and by over 456 million people throughout the world, English is second only to Mandarin Chinese in the number of speakers in the world. It is taught extensively as a second language and is used worldwide as a language of commerce, diplomacy, and scientific discourse. In northwestern Wales, Welsh, a form of Brythonic Celtic, is the first language of most of the inhabitants.

Approximately 26% of those living in Wales speak Welsh (up from 19% in 1991). Some 60,000 or so persons in western Scotland speak the Scottish form of Gaelic (down from 80,000 in 1991), and a few families in Northern Ireland speak Irish Gaelic. On the Isle of Man, the Manx variety of Celtic is used in official pronouncements; in the Channel Islands some persons still speak a Norman-French dialect. French remains the language of Jersey for official ceremonies.

10 RELIGIONS

There is complete religious freedom in the United Kingdom. All churches and religious societies may own property and conduct schools. Established churches are the Church of England (Anglican) and the Church of Scotland (Presbyterian). The former is uniquely related to the crown in that the sovereign must be a member and, on accession, promise to uphold the faith; it is also linked with the state through the House of Lords, where the archbishops of Canterbury and York have seats. The archbishop of Canterbury is primate of all England. The monarch appoints all officials of the Church of England. The established Church of Scotland has a Presbyterian form of government: all ministers are of equal status and each of the congregations is locally governed by its minister and elected elders.

About 71.6% of the population belong to one of the four largest Christian denominations in the country: the Church of England, the Roman Catholic Church, the Church of Scotland, and the Methodist Church in Britain (originally established as a type of revival movement by the Church of England minister John Wesley, 1703–91). Many immigrants have established community religious centers in the United Kingdom. Such Christian groups include Greek, Russian, Polish, Serb-Orthodox, Estonian and Latvian Orthodox, and the Armenian Church; Lutheran churches from various parts of Europe are also represented. A total of about 2% of the population are Jehovah's Witnesses, Mormons, Christian Scientists, or Unitarians. The Anglo-Jewish community, with an estimated 300,000 members, is the second-largest group of Jews in Western Europe. There are also sizable communities of Muslims, Sikhs, Hindus, and Buddhists.

In Northern Ireland, about 53% of the population are nominally Protestants and 44% are nominally Catholics; only about 30–35% of all Northern Irish are active participants in religious services. The Protestants and Catholics in Northern Ireland tend to live in self-segregated communities.

11 TRANSPORTATION

In Great Britain, railways, railway-owned steamships, docks, hotels, road transport, canals, and the entire London passenger transport system—the largest urban transport system in the world—were nationalized on 1 January 1948 under the control of the British Transport Commission (BTC). In 1962, the BTC was replaced by the British Railways Board, the London Transport Board, the British Transport Docks Board, and the British Waterways Board. Under the 1968 Transport Act, national transport operations were reorganized, with the creation of the National Freight Corp., the Freight Integration Council, and the National

Bus Co. Organization of public transport in Northern Ireland is autonomous.

In 2003, Great Britain had 392,931 km (244,403 mi) roadway, all of it paved, including 3,431 km (2,134 mi) of express motorways. Licensed motor vehicles in Great Britain numbered 32,576,891 as of 2003, including 29,007,820 passenger cars and 3,569,071 commercial vehicles. The Humber Bridge, the world's longest single-span suspension bridge, with a center span of 1,410 m (4,626 ft), links the city of Hull with a less developed region to the south. Eurotunnel, a British-French consortium, recently built two high-speed 50-km (31-mi) rail tunnels beneath the seabed of the English Channel. The project, referred to as the "Chunnel," links points near Folkestone, England (near Dover), and Calais, France. The Channel Tunnel is the largest privately financed construction project to date, with an estimated cost (in 1991) of $15 billion; it also has the longest tunnel system (38 km/24 mi) ever built under water. In November 1996, a truck aboard a freighter entering the tunnel caught fire, causing serious damage to the tunnel but no loss of life. Partial operations were resumed within a few weeks, and all repairs were completed by May 1997.

There were 17,274 km (10,727 mi) of standard and narrow gauge railway in Great Britain in 2004, including 5,296 km (3,289 mi) of electrified track. Standard gauge accounts for nearly all of the nation's railway system at 16,814 km (10,441 mi). Underground railway systems operate in London, Glasgow, and Liverpool. In London, the Underground consists of some 3,875 cars that operate over about 408 km (254 mi) of track, 167 km (104 mi) of which is underground. The Underground, the oldest part of which dates to 1863, operates 20 hours per day and is comprised of 248 stations on 11 lines that provide 2.7 million rides per day. In early 1997 the government proposed privatizing London's subway system because of lack of funds needed to restore the aging network. Capital investment has been diminished since the 1960s, resulting in increasing failures of signals and rolling stock and the deterioration of stations and track.

Great Britain has about 3,200 km (1,988 mi) of navigable inland waterways, mainly canals dating back to the pre-railroad age, of which as of 2004, some 620 km (386 mi) are still in commercial use. Great Britain has some 300 ports, including the Port of London, one of the largest in the world. Other major ports are Liverpool, Southampton, Hull, Clydeport (near Glasgow), the inland port of Manchester, and Bristol. The British merchant fleet, privately owned and operated, consists of 429 ships of 1,000 GRT or more, totaled 9,181,284 GRT in 2005. In an effort to curb the flagging of British merchant ships to less regulatory foreign nations, a British offshore registry program was initiated in the late 1980s. Under this program, merchant ships registered to the Isle of Man, Gibraltar, the Cayman Islands, and the Turks and Caicos Islands are entitled to fly the Red Ensign as if under the administration of the United Kingdom.

The Civil Aviation Authority was created in 1971 as an independent body responsible for national airline operations, traffic control, and air safety. In 2004, there were an estimated 471 airports. As of 2005 a total of 334 had paved runways, and there were also 11 heliports. International flights operate from London's Heathrow; Gatwick, London's second airport; Glasgow, in Scotland; Ringway (for Manchester); Aldergrove (for Belfast); and Elmdon (for Birmingham). The two government-owned airlines, British European Airways and British Overseas Airways Corp., were amalgamated in 1974 to form British Airways (BA). In 1984, BA was reestablished as British Airways PLC, a public limited company under government ownership, soon thereafter to be sold wholly to the public. There are a number of privately operated airlines, some of which operate air taxi services. British Caledonian, which maintained scheduled flights on both domestic and international routes, merged with British Airways in 1988. The Concorde, a supersonic jetliner developed jointly in the 1960s by the United Kingdom and France at a cost exceeding £1 billion, entered service between Heathrow and the United States in 1976. In 2003, the United Kingdom's airlines performed 5,251 million freight ton-km of freight service, and carried 76.377 million passengers on domestic and international flights.

12 HISTORY

The earliest people to occupy Britain are of unknown origin. Remains of these early inhabitants include the stone circles of Avebury and Stonehenge in Wiltshire. Celtic tribes from the Continent, the first known settlers in historical times, invaded before the 6th century BC. The islands were visited in ancient times by Mediterranean traders seeking jet, gold, pearls, and tin, which were being mined in Cornwall. Julius Caesar invaded in 55 BC but soon withdrew. In the 1st century AD, the Romans occupied most of the present-day area of England, remaining until the 5th century.

With the decline of the Roman Empire and the withdrawal of Roman troops (although many Romans had become Britonized and remained on the islands), Celtic tribes fought among themselves, and Scots and Picts raided from the north and from Ireland. Early raids by Angles, Saxons, and Jutes from the Continent soon swelled into invasions, and the leaders established kingdoms in the conquered territory while the native Celts retreated into the mountains of Wales and Cornwall. Although the Welsh were split into a northern and a southern group, they were not permanently subdued. In the 10th century, a Welsh king, Howel the Good (Hywel Dda), united Wales, codified the laws, and encouraged the Welsh bards.

Among the new English kingdoms, that of the West Saxons (Wessex) became predominant, chiefly through the leadership of Alfred the Great, who also had to fight a new wave of invasions by the Danes and other Norsemen. Alfred's successors were able to unify the country, but eventually the Danes completed their conquest, and King Canute (II) of Denmark became ruler of England by 1017. In 1042, with the expiration of the Scandinavian line, Edward the Confessor of Wessex became king. At his death in 1066, both Harold the Saxon and William, duke of Normandy, claimed the throne. William invaded England and defeated Harold in the Battle of Hastings, beginning the Norman Conquest (1066–70).

William I instituted a strong government, which lasted through the reigns of his sons William II and Henry I. The latter's death in 1135 brought a period of civil war and anarchy, which ended with the accession of Henry II (1154), who instituted notable constitutional and legal reforms. He and succeeding English kings expanded their holdings in France, touching off a long series of struggles between the two countries.

The Magna Carta

Long-standing conflict between the nobles and the kings reached a climax in the reign of King John with the victory of the barons, who at Runnymede in 1215 compelled the king to grant the Magna Carta. This marked a major advance toward the parliamentary system. Just half a century later, in 1265, Simon de Montfort, earl of Leicester, leader of the barons in their opposition to Henry III, summoned the first Parliament, with representatives not only of the rural nobility but also of the boroughs and towns. In the late 13th century, Edward I expanded the royal courts and reformed the legal system; he also began the first systematic attempts to conquer Wales and Scotland. In 1282, the last Welsh king, Llewellyn ap Gruffydd, was killed in battle, and Edward I completed the conquest of Wales. Two years later, the Statute of Rhuddlan established English rule. The spirit of resistance survived, however, and a last great uprising against England came in the early 15th century, when Owen Glendower (Owain ap Gruffydd) led a briefly successful revolt.

Scotland was inhabited in early historic times by the Picts and by roaming bands of Gaels, or Celts, from Ireland. Before the Romans left Britain in the 5th century, Scotland had been converted to Christianity by St. Ninian and his disciples. By the end of the following century, four separate kingdoms had been established in Scotland. Norsemen raided Scotland from the 8th to the 12th century, and some settled there. Most of the country was unified under Duncan I (r.1034–40). His son, Malcolm III (r.1059–93), who gained the throne after defeating Macbeth, the murderer of his father, married an English princess, Margaret (later sainted), and began to anglicize and modernize the lowlands.

Scotland United

Under David I (r.1124–53), Scotland was united, responsible government was established, walled towns (known as burghs) were developed, and foreign trade was encouraged. William the Lion (r.1165–1214) was captured by Henry II of England in 1174 and forced to accept the Treaty of Falaise, by which Scotland became an English fief. Although Scotland purchased its freedom from Richard I, the ambiguous wording of the agreement allowed later English kings to revive their claim.

When Alexander III died in 1286, Edward I of England, who claimed overlordship of Scotland, supported the claims of John Baliol, who was crowned in 1293. Edward began a war with Philip of France and demanded Scottish troops, but the Scots allied themselves with Philip, beginning the long relationship with France that distinguishes Scottish history. Edward subdued the Scots, put down an uprising led by William Wallace, executed Wallace in 1305, and established English rule. Baliol's heir was killed by Robert the Bruce, another claimant, who had himself crowned (1309), captured Edinburgh, and defeated Edward II of England decisively at Bannockburn in 1314. In 1328, Edward III signed a treaty acknowledging Scotland's freedom.

Under Edward III, the Hundred Years' War (1337–1453) with France was begun. Notable victories by Edward the Black Prince (son of Edward III), Henry IV, and Henry V led to no permanent gains for England, and ultimately the English were driven out of France. The plague, known as the Black Death, broke out in England in 1348, wiping out a third of the population; it hastened the breakdown of the feudal system and the rise of towns. The 14th century was for England a time of confusion and change. John Wycliffe led a movement of reform in religion, spreading radical ideas about the need for churchly poverty and criticizing many established doctrines and practices. A peasant rebellion led by Wat Tyler in 1381 demanded the abolition of serfdom, monopolies, and the many restrictions on buying and selling.

In 1399, after 22 years of rule, Richard II was deposed and was succeeded by Henry IV, the first king of the house of Lancaster. The war with France continued, commerce flourished, and the wool trade became important. The Wars of the Roses (1455–85), in which the houses of Lancaster and York fought for the throne, ended with the accession of Henry VII, a member of the Tudor family, marking the beginning of the modern history of England.

The Tudors

Under the Tudors, commerce was expanded, English seamen ranged far and wide, and clashes with Spain (accelerated by religious differences) intensified. Earlier English dominance had not had much effect on Wales, but the Tudors followed a policy of assimilation, anglicizing Welsh laws and practices. Finally, under Henry VIII, the Act of Union (1536) made English the legal language and abolished all Welsh laws "at variance with those of England." In 1531, Henry separated the Anglican Church from Rome and proclaimed himself its head. After his death (1547), the succession to the throne became a major issue during the reigns of Edward VI (1547–53), Mary I (1553–58), and Elizabeth I (1558–1603).

In Scotland, James I (r.1406–37) had done much to regulate Scottish law and improve foreign relations. His murder in 1437 began a century of civil conflict. James IV (r.1488–1513) married Margaret Tudor, sister of Henry VII of England, a marriage that was ultimately to unite the crowns of England and Scotland.

French influence in Scotland grew under James V (r.1513–42), who married Mary of Guise, but the Scottish people and nobility became favorably inclined toward the Reformation, championed by John Knox. After James's death, Mary ruled as regent for her daughter, Mary, Queen of Scots, who had married the dauphin of France, where she lived as dauphiness and later as queen. By the time Mary returned to Scotland (1561), after the death of her husband, most of the Scots were Protestants. A pro-English faction had the support of Queen Elizabeth I against the pro-French faction, and Mary, who claimed the throne of England, was imprisoned and executed (1587) by Elizabeth. Under Elizabeth, England in 1583 acquired its first colony, Newfoundland, and in 1588 defeated the Spanish Armada; it also experienced the beginning of a golden age of drama, literature, and music, among whose towering achievements are the plays of William Shakespeare.

Oliver Cromwell and the Commonwealth

Elizabeth was succeeded by Mary's son, James VI of Scotland, who became James I of England (r.1603–25), establishing the Stuart line. Under James and his son, Charles I (r.1625–49), the rising middle classes (mainly Puritan in religion) sought to make Parliament superior to the king. In the English Civil War, which broke out in 1642, Charles was supported by the Welsh, who had remained overwhelmingly Catholic in feeling, but most Scots opposed him. Charles was tried and executed in 1649, and Oliver

Cromwell as Protector ruled the new Commonwealth until his death in 1658. Cromwell ruthlessly crushed uprisings in Ireland and suppressed the Welsh. In 1660, Charles II, eldest son of the executed king, regained the throne. The Restoration was marked by a reaction against Puritanism, by persecution of the Scottish Covenanters (Presbyterians), by increased prosperity, and by intensified political activity; during this period, Parliament managed to maintain many of its gains. Charles II's younger brother, James II (r.1685–88), who vainly attempted to restore Roman Catholicism, was overthrown in 1688 and was succeeded by his daughter, Mary II, and her Dutch husband, William III, who were invited to rule by Parliament. By this transfer of power, known to English history as the Glorious Revolution, the final supremacy of Parliament was established. Supporters of James II (Jacobites) in Scotland and Ireland, aided by France, sought to restore the deposed Stuart line, but their insurrection was suppressed in 1690 at the Battle of the Boyne, fought on the banks of the Irish river of that name.

In Wales, after Cromwell and the Commonwealth, the people began to turn to Calvinism; dissent grew, and such ministers as Griffith Jones, a pioneer in popular education, became national leaders. Most Welsh were won to the Calvinistic Methodist Church, which played a large part in fostering a nonpolitical Welsh nationalism. A long struggle to disestablish the Church of England in Wales culminated successfully in a 1914 act of Parliament.

Colonial Expansion

English colonial expansion developed further in the 17th and 18th centuries, in competition with France and the Netherlands, while at the same time the English merchant marine gained commercial supremacy over the Dutch. The wars of the Grand Alliance (1688–97) and of the Spanish Succession (1701–14) consolidated Britain's overseas possessions. At home, to ensure Scottish allegiance to England and prevent possible alliances with inimical countries, the Act of Union of Scotland and England was voted by the two parliaments in 1707, thereby formally creating the kingdom of Great Britain under one crown and with a single Parliament composed of representatives of both countries. This union held, despite Jacobite uprisings in 1715 and 1745–46, the latter under Prince Charles (Bonnie Prince Charlie, or the Young Pretender, grandson of James II); his defeat at Culloden Moor was the last land battle fought in Great Britain. Scottish affairs eventually became the province of the secretary of state for Scotland, a member of the British cabinet. Nevertheless, a nationalist movement demanding independence for Scotland persists to this day.

The accession of George I of the House of Hanover in 1714 (a great-grandson of James I) saw the beginning of the modern cabinet system, with the king leaving much of the governing to his ministers. The 18th century was a time of rapid colonial and mercantile expansion abroad and internal stability and literary and artistic achievement at home. Britain won control of North America and India in the Seven Years' War (ended in 1763 by the Treaty of Paris), which also established British supremacy over the seas; however, the American Revolution (1775–83) cost Britain its most important group of colonies. A few years later, British settlement of Australia and then of New Zealand became key elements in the spreading British Empire. Britain increased its power further by its leading role in the French Revolutionary Wars and in the defeat of Napoleon and French expansionist aims.

Birth of the United Kingdom

In 1800, with the Act of Union of Great Britain and Ireland, the United Kingdom formally came into being. The conquest of Ireland had never been consolidated; the Act of Union followed an Irish rebellion in 1798 after the failure of a demand for parliamentary reform. But although the act established Irish representation in Parliament, the Irish question continued to cause trouble throughout the 19th century. Absentee landlordism, particularly in the 26 southern counties, fostered poverty and hatred of the English. Moreover, there was a growing division of interest between these counties and the six counties of the north, popularly called Ulster, where, early in the 17th century, Protestant Scots and English had settled on land confiscated by the British crown after a rebellion. While the north gradually became Protestant and industrial, the rest of Ireland remained Catholic and rural. With the introduction of the first Home Rule Bill in 1886, the northern Irish, fearing domination by the southern Catholic majority, began a campaign that ended in the 1920 Government of Ireland Act, which established separate domestic legislatures for the north and south, as well as continued representation in the UK Parliament. The six northern counties accepted the act and became Northern Ireland. The 26 southern counties, however, did not accept it; in 1921, the Anglo-Irish Treaty was signed, by which these counties left the United Kingdom to become the Irish Free State (now the Irish Republic, or Éire), which was officially established in 1922.

Queen Victoria's Reign

The Industrial Revolution, beginning in the second half of the 18th century, provided the economic underpinning for British colonial and military expansion throughout the 1800s. However, the growth of the factory system and of urbanization also brought grave new social problems. The enclosure of grazing land in the Scottish highlands and the industrialization of southern Wales were accompanied by extensive population shifts and led to large-scale emigration to the United States, Canada, and Australia. Reform legislation came slowly, although the spirit of reform and social justice was in the air. Slavery was abolished throughout the British Empire in 1834. The great Reform Acts of 1832, 1867, and 1884 enfranchised the new middle class and the working class. Factory acts, poor laws, and other humanitarian legislation did away with some of the worst abuses, and pressure mounted for eliminating others. The long reign of Queen Victoria (1837–1901) saw an unprecedented commercial and industrial prosperity. This was a period of great imperial expansion, especially in Africa, where at the end of the century Britain fought settlers of predominantly Dutch origin in the South African (or Boer) War. Toward the end of the century, also, the labor movement grew strong, education was developed along national lines, and a regular civil service was finally established.

The 20th Century

The vast economic and human losses of World War I, in which nearly 800,000 Britons were killed, brought on serious disturbances in the United Kingdom as elsewhere, and the economic depression of the 1930s resulted in the unemployment of millions of workers. In 1931, the Statute of Westminster granted the status of equality to the self-governing British dominions and created the concept of a British Commonwealth of Nations. During the late 1930s, the government of Prime Minister Neville Chamberlain sought to avoid war by appeasing Nazi Germany, but after Hitler invaded Poland, the United Kingdom declared war on Germany on 3 September 1939. Prime Minister Winston Churchill led the United Kingdom during World War II in a full mobilization of the population in the armed services, in home defense, and in war production. Although victorious, the United Kingdom suffered much destruction from massive German air attacks, and the military and civilian death toll exceeded 900,000. At war's end, a Labour government was elected; it pledged to carry out a full program of social welfare "from the cradle to the grave," coupled with the nationalization of industry. Medicine was socialized, other social services were expanded, and several industries were put under public ownership. Complete nationalization of industry, however, was halted with the return to power of the Conservatives in 1951. During Labour's subsequent terms in office, from 1964 to 1970 and from 1974 to 1979, little further nationalization was attempted.

Post-World War II Era

To a large extent, the United Kingdom's postwar history can be characterized as a prolonged effort to put the faltering economy on its feet and to cope with the economic, social, and political consequences of the disbandment of its empire. By early 1988, all that remained of what had been the largest empire in the world were 14 dependencies, many of them small islands with tiny populations and few economic resources. The United Kingdom has remained firmly within the Atlantic alliance since World War II. A founding member of the North Atlantic Treaty Organization (NATO) and European Free Trade Association (EFTA), the United Kingdom overcame years of domestic qualms and French opposition when it entered the European Community (EC) on 1 January 1973. After a Labour government replaced the Conservatives in March 1974, the membership terms were renegotiated, and United Kingdom voters approved continued British participation by a 67.2% majority in an unprecedented national referendum.

The principal domestic problems in the 1970s were rapid inflation, labor disputes, and the protracted conflict in Northern Ireland. Long-smoldering tensions between Protestants and Catholics erupted into open warfare after civil rights protests in 1969 by Catholics claiming discrimination and insufficient representation in the government. The Protestant reaction was violent, and the Irish Republican Army (IRA), seeking the union of Ulster with the Irish Republic, escalated the conflict by committing terrorist acts in both Northern Ireland and England. British troops, first dispatched to Belfast and Londonderry in August 1969, have remained there since.

On 30 March 1972, Northern Ireland's parliament (Stormont) was prorogued, and direct rule was imposed from London. Numerous attempts to devise a new constitution failed, as did other proposals for power sharing. In 1982, legislation establishing a new 78-member Northern Ireland Assembly was enacted. Elections were held that October, but the 19 Catholic members chosen refused to claim their seats. Meanwhile, the violence continued, one of the victims being the British war hero Earl Mountbatten of Burma, who was murdered while vacationing in Ireland on 27 August 1979. In October 1980, IRA members imprisoned in Ulster began a series of hunger strikes; by the time the strikes ended the following October 10 men had died. In November 1985, the United Kingdom and the Irish Republic signed an agreement committing both governments to recognition of Northern Ireland as part of the United Kingdom and to cooperation between the two governments by establishing an intergovernmental conference concerned with Northern Ireland and with relations between the two parts of Ireland.

The "Downing Street Declaration" of December 1993 between British Prime Minister John Major and Irish Prime Minister Albert Reynolds over the future of Northern Ireland suggested that undisclosed contacts had been maintained for some time between the Irish Republican Army (IRA), Sinn Feìn (the political wing of the IRA), and the British government. Tony Blair, who became prime minister in May 1997, also invested in normalization of relations between Ireland and the United Kingdom and in a long-term solution to the sectarian strife in Northern Ireland. In 1998, Ireland and the United Kingdom signed a peace agreement (Good Friday agreement) in which Ireland pledged to amend Articles 2 and 3 of the Irish constitution, which lay claim to the territory in the North. In return, the United Kingdom promised to amend the Government of Ireland Act.

In 1979, a Conservative government, headed by Margaret Thatcher, came to power with a program of income tax cuts and reduced government spending. Thatcher, who won reelection in 1983 and 1987, embarked on a policy of "privatizing"—selling to the private sector—many of the UK's nationalized businesses. In foreign policy, the government's most dramatic action was sending a naval task force to the Falkland Islands following Argentina's occupation of the islands on 2 April 1982. After intense fighting, British administration was restored to the Falklands on 14 June.

Thatcher's leadership was challenged by Conservative MPs in November 1990, and she failed to win the necessary absolute majority. Thatcher withdrew and was replaced by John Major. The Conservatives were returned to power in April 1992 with a reduced majority. Major's government sought to redefine Conservative values with a renewed emphasis on law and order.

Labour Party leader Tony Blair was elected prime minister on 2 May 1997, ending 18 years of Conservative Party rule and signaling a major shift in British domestic policy (he was reelected in 2001 and 2005). Blair, who moved his party to the center of the political spectrum during the campaign, pledged initiatives to modernize Britain's political structures. To that effect, he organized the creation of regional assemblies for Scotland and Wales and a municipal government for London. The regional parliaments were ratified by a referendum in late 1997 and began their first session in 1998. The city council for greater London came into being in mid-2000 and London's first mayor in 15 years was Ken Livingstone (reelected 2004), a left-wing Labourite not much liked by the middle-of-the-road Blairites.

As promised, Blair's government also restructured the House of Lords to do away with the large number of hereditary peers. Only 75 of the 650 hereditary peers now sit in the House of Lords alongside 500 life peers, several senior judges, 26 bishops of the Church of England, and 15 deputy speakers.

The Blair government has also spent much time in tackling the Northern Ireland problem. The Good Friday Accord of 1998 en-visioned a Catholic-Protestant administration and the gradual decommissioning of the IRA. The power-sharing government came into being in December 1999, but was suspended 11 weeks later because the IRA refused to make any disarmament commitments. A breakthrough occurred in May 2000 when the IRA agreed to allow leading international figures to inspect arms dumps and to begin the process of complete and verifiable disarmament. The Protestant party voted to revive the power-sharing arrangements on 27 May 2000 and the UK government promised to restore substantial authority to the new Northern Irish cabinet (this was accomplished on 29 May). However, decommissioning of the IRA did not progress in early 2001. In October 2002, Sinn Feìn's offices at Stormont (the Northern Ireland Assembly) were raided due to a large police investigation into intelligence-gathering operations on behalf of Irish republicans. On 14 October, devolution was suspended due to the spying allegations and direct rule from London was reimposed on Northern Ireland. Blair announced in May 2003 elections for the National Assembly would be postponed, due to the lack of evidence of peaceful intentions on behalf of the IRA. Elections were held on 26 November 2003, however, with the pro-British Democratic Unionist Party (DUP) and Sinn Feìn forming the two largest parties. On 28 July 2005, the IRA announced it would halt its armed campaign to oust British rule. The statement was received with skepticism by the DUP.

Prime Minister Blair offered strong support for the US-led war on terrorism begun after the 11 September 2001 attacks on the United States; British forces took part in the campaign in Afghanistan to oust the Taliban regime. The United Kingdom in 2002–03 also stood with the United States in its diplomatic and military efforts to force Saddam Hussein's regime in Iraq to disarm itself of any weapons of mass destruction it might possess. The war in Iraq began on 19 March 2003. British forces fought side-by-side with US forces, especially in southern Iraq. In the aftermath of the war, Blair indicated a central role must be played by the UN in the reconstruction of Iraq; in this he stood with other European leaders. In October 2004, the Iraq Survey Group (ISG) concluded there had been no weapons of mass destruction in Iraq for some time before the war. British intelligence withdrew a controversial claim that Saddam Hussein could have used WMD with 45 minutes' notice. Blair acknowledged that the intelligence had been flawed, but denied having misrepresented it in making the case for war. Another controversy related to the Iraq War was the publication by *The London Times* on 1 May 2005 of a memo (subsequently labeled the "Downing Street memo") containing an overview of a secret 23 July 2002 meeting among British intelligence, government, and defense leaders discussing the build-up to the Iraq War. The memo included direct reference to classified US policy of the time and indicated that "intelligence and facts were being fixed" around the policy of removing Saddam Hussein from power. This was taken to show that US intelligence prior to the war had been deliberately falsified, and not just mistaken. The memo suggested that the UN weapons inspections that began after 8 November 2002 were manipulated to provide a legal pretext for the war, and that the removal by force of the Iraq regime had been planned prior to the date of the secret British meeting. In the United States, demands for an explanation of the revelations contained in the memo and calls for a formal Congressional inquiry were ignored by the Bush administration.

In mid-2005 the United Kingdom was wracked by terrorist violence. On 7 July 2005 four suicide bombers struck London's transit system, killing 52 people and injuring more than 700. Three underground trains were bombed, as was one double-decker bus. Two weeks later, on 21 July, bombings of three underground trains and one bus were attempted, but the suicide bombers' bombs failed to fully detonate. On 22 July, a Brazilian man, Jean Charles de Menezes, was shot to death at the Stockwell underground station by British police who believed him to be implicated in the bombing attempts. He was found not to have played any role in the 21 July attacks.

The United Kingdom remains one of three European Union (EU) members not adopting European economic and monetary union and embracing the euro as its currency. The other two nations are Denmark and Sweden.

13 GOVERNMENT

The United Kingdom is a monarchy in form but a parliamentary democracy in substance. The sovereign—Elizabeth II since 1952—is head of state and as such is head of the legislature, the executive, and the judiciary, commander-in-chief of the armed forces, and temporal head of the established Church of England. In practice, however, gradually evolving restrictions have transmuted the sovereign's legal powers into instruments for affecting the popular will as expressed through Parliament. In the British formulation, the sovereign reigns but does not rule, for the sovereign is under the law and not above it, ruling only by approval of Parliament and acting only on the advice of her ministers.

The United Kingdom is governed, in the name of the sovereign, by Her Majesty's Government—a body of ministers who are the leading members of whichever political party the electorate has voted into office and who are responsible to Parliament. Parliament itself, the supreme legislative authority in the realm, consists of the sovereign, the House of Lords, and the House of Commons. Northern Ireland had its own parliament (Stormont) subordinate to Westminster; however, because of civil strife in Ulster, the Stormont was prorogued on 30 March 1972, and direct rule was imposed from Westminster. After several abortive attempts over the next decade to devise a system of home-rule government acceptable to both Protestant and Catholic leaders, the 78-member Northern Ireland Assembly was established in 1982, but it was dissolved in 1986. As a result of the 1998 "Good Friday Agreement," a Catholic-Protestant power-sharing government came into being in 1999. It was suspended in October 2002, and direct rule from London returned.

In 1979, proposals for the establishment of elected legislatures in Wales and Scotland failed in the former and, though winning a bare plurality, fell short of the required margin for approval (40% of all eligible voters) in the latter. Regional parliaments for Scotland and Wales were ratified by referendum in 1997, however, and they began their first sessions in 1998.

The sovereign formally summons and dissolves Parliament. The House of Lords, whose size has been greatly reduced, used to count about 1,200 peers, including hereditary peers, spiritual peers (archbishops and bishops of the Church of England), and life peers (eminent persons unwilling to accept a hereditary peerage). Over the centuries, its powers have gradually been reduced; today, its main function is to bring the wide experience of its members into the process of lawmaking. As of 2005, the House of Commons had 646 members. A general election must be held every five years but is often held sooner. All British subjects 18 years old and over may vote in national elections; women won equal franchise with men in 1922. Citizens of Ireland resident in Britain may also vote, as may British subjects abroad for a period of five years after leaving the United Kingdom.

Each Parliament may during its lifetime make or unmake any law. Parliamentary bills may be introduced by either house, unless they deal with finance or representation; these are always introduced in the Commons, which has ultimate authority for lawmaking. The House of Lords may not alter a financial measure or delay for longer than a year any bill passed by the Commons in two successive sessions. Bills passed by both houses receive the traditional royal assent and become law as acts of Parliament; no bill has received a royal veto for more than 200 years. The Speaker of the Parliament is the chief officer of the House of Commons. The Speaker is nonpartisan and functions impartially. The first female Speaker was elected in 1992.

Executive power is vested in the prime minister, who, though nominally appointed by the sovereign, is traditionally the leader of the majority party in Parliament. The prime minister is assisted by ministers, also nominally appointed by the sovereign, who are chosen from the majority party and mostly from the Commons, which must approve the government's general policy and the more important of its specific measures. The most senior ministers, about 20, compose the cabinet, which meets regularly to decide policy on major issues. Ministers are responsible collectively to Parliament for all cabinet decisions; individual ministers are responsible to Parliament for the work of their departments. There are around 30 major central government departments, each staffed by members of the permanent civil service.

The British constitution is made up of parliamentary statutes, common law, and traditional precepts and practices known as conventions, all evolved through the centuries. Largely unwritten, it has never been codified and is constantly evolving.

14 POLITICAL PARTIES

UK parliamentary government based on the party system has evolved only during the past 100 years. Although the 18th-century terms "Whig" and "Tory" indicated certain political leanings, there was no clear-cut division in Parliament and no comprehensive party organization. Not until the 19th-century Reform Acts enfranchised millions of new voters did the modern party system develop. The British party system is based on the assumption that there are at least two parties in the Commons, each with a sufficiently united following to be able to form an alternative government at any time. This assumption is recognized in the fact that the largest minority party is officially designated as Her Majesty's Opposition; its leader, who designates a "shadow government," is paid a salary from public funds.

The main political parties represented in Parliament today are the Labour Party, the Conservative Party, and the Liberal Democrats (a coalition of the Liberal and Social Democratic parties, which voted in favor of a formal merger in 1988). From time to time during the past 50 years, other parties have arisen or have splintered off from the main groups, only to disappear or to become reabsorbed. Thus, the Fascists, who were of some significance before World War II, no longer put up candidates for elections. The British Communist Party has not elected a candidate to Parliament since 1950.

Since World War I, the Labour Party has replaced the Liberal Party, a major force during the late 19th century, as the official opposition to a Conservative government. Founded in 1900 as the political arm of the already powerful trade union movement, the Labour Party was until 1918 a federation of trade unions and socialist groups and had no individual members. Today, its constituent associations consist of affiliated organizations (such as trade unions, cooperative societies, branches of socialist societies, and trade councils), as well as individual members organized into wards. Its program calls for public ownership of the means of production, improvement of the social and economic conditions of the people, defense of human rights, cooperation with labor and socialist organizations of other countries, and peaceful adjustment of international disputes. Between the world wars, it established two short-lived Labour governments while still a minority party, and then joined Churchill's coalition government in World War II. Returned to power with a huge majority in 1945, Labour instituted a program of full employment through planned production; established social services to provide adequate medical care, old age care, nutrition, and educational opportunities for all; began the nationalization of basic industries; and started to disband the empire by granting independence to India, Pakistan, Ceylon (now Sri Lanka), and Burma (Myanmar).

If the rapid rise of the Labour Party has been an outstanding feature of 20th-century British politics, the continuing vitality and adaptability of the Conservative Party, successor of the 18th-century Tories, has been no less remarkable. In foreign affairs, there has been little difference between the parties since World War II. Both have generally been firm allies of the United States, and both are pledged to the maintenance of NATO. The two parties have also been in general agreement about the country's social and economic needs. They differ mainly on the degree of state control to be applied to industry and commerce and on practical methods of application. Conservative emphasis is on free enterprise, individual initiative, and restraining the power of the unions. Even on these matters, however, pragmatism is the norm. In office, the Conservatives have let stand much of Labour's social program, and Labour, during Britain's economic difficulties in the late 1970s, imposed its own policy of wage restraints.

After World War II, Labour was in power during 1945–51, 1964–70, 1974–79, and since 1997; the Conservatives have held office during 1951–64, 1970–74, and 1979–97. Scottish National Party members were decisive in the fall of the Labour government in March 1979, after Labour was unable to enact its program for limited home rule (including elected legislatures) in Scotland and Wales. In elections of 3 May 1979, after a campaign fought mainly on economic grounds, Conservatives won 339 seats, with 43.9% of the vote, to Labour's 268 seats, with 36.9%, and Margaret Thatcher replaced James Callaghan as prime minister. Amid growing dissension, the Labour Party moved leftward in the early 1980s and broke with the Conservatives over defense policy, committing itself to the removal of all nuclear weapons from the United Kingdom and, in 1986, to the removal of US nuclear bases. The Social Democratic Party, founded in 1981 by moderate former Labour ministers, had by 30 September 1982 obtained 30 seats in Parlia-

ment, 27 of whose occupants were breakaway Labour members. In the elections of 9 June 1983, the Conservatives increased their parliamentary majority, winning 397 seats and about 42% of the vote. The Labour Party captured 209 seats and 28% of the vote, its poorest showing in more than five decades. The Alliance of Liberals and Social Democrats won 25% of the vote but only 23 seats (Liberals 17, Social Democrats 6). Minor parties took 5% of the vote and 21 seats.

In the elections of 11 June 1987, the Conservatives won 376 seats and about 42% of the vote. The Labour Party won 229 seats and 31% of the vote. The Liberal-Social Democratic Alliance won nearly 23% of the vote but only 22 seats (Liberals 17, Social Democrats 5). Minor parties took about 4% of the vote and 23 seats: Ulster Unionist (Northern Ireland), 9; Democratic Unionist (Northern Ireland), 3; Scottish National Party, 3; Plaid Cymru (Welsh Nationalist), 3; Social Democratic and Labour Party (Northern Ireland), 3; Sinn Feìn (Northern Ireland), 1; and Popular Unionist (Northern Ireland), 1.

The general election of 9 April 1992 resulted in a continuation of Conservative government under John Major with 42% of the vote and 336 seats. Labour followed with 34% of the vote and 271 seats. The Liberal Democrats took almost 18% of the vote, which netted 20 seats. Minor parties received 3% of the vote and 17 seats.

The Labour Party, under the leadership of Tony Blair, won a landslide victory in the general election of 1 May 1997, restoring it to power for the first time in 18 years. Of 659 possible seats, the Labour Party won 418 (43.1%), gaining 146 seats; the Conservative Party won only 165 seats (30.6%), losing 178 seats. The Liberal Democrats won 46 seats (16.7%), a gain of 26 seats since 1992 and the most seats held by the party since the 1920s. Other parties received 9.6% of vote, with the following representation after the 1997 elections: Ulster Unionist, 10; Scottish National, 6; Plaid Cymru, 4; Social Democrat and Labour, 3; Democratic Unionist, 2; Sinn Feìn, 2; Independent, 2; and United Kingdom Unionist, 1.

The June 2001 election was called "the quiet landslide" following the major victory of the Labour Party in the 1997 election. Labour won 40.7% of the vote and secured 413 seats; the Conservative Party gained only one seat (166) and registered 31.7% of the vote. The Liberal Democrats gained six seats (52; 18.3% of the vote) from their historic high in 1997. Other parties received 9.3% of the vote, with the following representation after the 2001 election: Ulster Unionist, 6; Scottish National, 5; Democratic Unionist, 5; Plaid Cymru, 4; Sinn Feìn, 4; Social Democrat and Labour, 3; and Independent, 1.

In the general election held on 5 May 2005, Labour lost 47 seats but retained its majority with 356 seats in Parliament (35.3% of the vote); the Conservatives gained 33 seats to end up with 198 (32.3% of the vote). The Liberal Democrats held 62 seats after gaining 11 (22.1% of the vote). Other parties garnered 10.3% of the vote, with the following representation in Parliament after the election: Democratic Unionist Party, 9; Scottish National Party, 6; Sinn Feìn, 5; Plaid Cymru, 3; Social Democrat and Labour Party, 3; Ulster Unionist Party, 1; Independent Kidderminster Hospital and Health Concern, 1; and others, 2. The next parliamentary election was to be held in May 2010.

¹⁵LOCAL GOVERNMENT

The scope of local governing bodies is defined and limited by acts of Parliament, which also makes certain ministers responsible for the efficient functioning of local services. In England, local government is supervised by the Department of the Environment; the regional parliaments supervise local governments in Wales and Scotland; and Northern Ireland, which was supposed to also have devolved powers, was placed back under the supervision of the Department of the Environment for Northern Ireland.

From 1965 to 1985, Greater London, the nation's largest metropolitan area, was subdivided into 32 London boroughs; the Greater London Council was the chief administrative authority. Under the Local Government Act of 1985, however, the Greater London Council was abolished and its functions were transferred to London borough and metropolitan district councils, excepting certain services (such as police and fire services and public transport) now administered by joint borough and council authorities. The Labour Party government returned local government to London. However, the mayor's office has a limited budget and few policy powers. The mayor's office coordinates relationship among the different boroughs and controls local transport (Underground).

Under the Local Government Act of 1972, the county system that had prevailed throughout the rest of England and Wales was replaced by a two-tier structure of counties and districts. In the 1990s, local governmental structures were reorganized, and single-tier administrations with responsibility for all areas of local government were reestablished. There are currently 46 unitary authorities in England, and 34 shire counties split into 238 non-metropolitan districts. These in turn are subdivided into electoral wards and districts. In 2000, a two-tier structure was reestablished for London; it has 32 boroughs and the City of London. Scotland is subject to the administration of both the UK government in Westminster and the Scottish executive in Edinburgh, and Wales is subject to the administration of Westminster and the National Assembly for Wales in Cardiff. Scotland is divided into 32 council areas, which in turn are divided into electoral wards and communities. Wales is subdivided into 22 unitary authorities, which in turn are divided into electoral divisions and communities. Northern Ireland is subject to the administration of both the UK government and the Northern Ireland Executive in Belfast. It is divided into 26 districts, which in turn are divided into electoral wards. The United Kingdom has more than 10,000 electoral wards/divisions. The minimum voting age in local elections is 18.

¹⁶JUDICIAL SYSTEM

The United Kingdom does not have a single body of law applicable throughout the realm. Scotland has its own distinctive system and courts; in Northern Ireland, certain spheres of law differ in substance from those operating in England and Wales. A feature common to all UK legal systems, however—and one that distinguishes them from many continental systems—is the absence of a complete code, since legislation and unwritten or common law are all part of the "constitution."

The main civil courts in England and Wales are 218 county courts for small cases and the High Court, which is divided into the chancery division, the family division, and the Queen's Bench division (including the maritime and commercial courts), for the more important cases. Appeals from the county courts may also be heard in the High Court, though the more important ones come before the Court of Appeal; a few appeals are heard before the House of Lords, which is the ultimate court of appeal for civil cases throughout the United Kingdom. In Scotland, civil cases are heard at the sheriff courts (corresponding roughly to the English county courts) and in the Outer House of the Court of Session, which is the supreme civil court in Scotland; appeals are heard by the Inner House of the Court of Session. Trial by jury in civil cases is common in Scotland but rare in the rest of the United Kingdom.

Criminal courts in England and Wales include magistrates' courts, which try less serious offenses (some 96% of all criminal cases) and consist most often of three unpaid magistrates known as justices of the peace, and 78 centers of the Crown Court, presided over by a bench of justices or, in the most serious cases, by a High Court judge sitting alone. All contested cases receive a jury trial. Cases involving persons under 17 years of age are heard by justices of the peace in specially constituted juvenile courts. Appeals may be heard successively by the Crown Court, the High Court, the Court of Criminal Appeal, and in certain cases by the House of Lords. In Scotland, minor criminal cases are tried without jury in the sheriff courts and district courts, and more serious cases with a jury in the sheriff courts. The supreme criminal court is the High Court of the Justiciary, where cases are heard by a judge sitting with a jury; this is also the ultimate appeals court.

All criminal trials are held in open court. In England, Wales, and Northern Ireland, 12-citizen juries must unanimously decide the verdict unless, with no more than two jurors dissenting, the judge directs them to return a majority verdict. Scottish juries of 15 persons are permitted to reach a majority decision and, if warranted, a verdict of "not proven." Among temporary emergency measures passed with the aim of controlling terrorism in Northern Ireland are those empowering ministers to order the search, arrest, and detention of suspected terrorists and permitting juryless trials for terrorist acts in Northern Ireland.

Central responsibility for the administration of the judicial system lies with the lord chancellor (who heads the judiciary and also serves as a cabinet minister and as speaker of the House of Lords) and the home secretary (and the secretaries of state for Scotland and for Northern Ireland). Judges are appointed by the crown, on the advice of the prime minister, lord chancellor, or the appropriate cabinet ministries.

In 2005 Parliament passed the Constitutional Reform Act of 2005, which provides for a Supreme Court of the United Kingdom to abolish the appellate jurisdiction of the House of Lords and to reduce the role of the lord chancellor, among other changes.

The United Kingdom accepts the compulsory jurisdiction of the International Court of Justice with reservations.

¹⁷ARMED FORCES

After the general demobilization that followed World War II, compulsory national service for all eligible males over 19 years of age was introduced. Call-ups of national servicemen ceased in 1960, but those who had been trained formed part of the general reserve until June 1974, when the national service legislation expired. Reserves now form part of the long-term reserve established in 1964, composed of all men under 45 years of age who have served in the regular army since 28 February 1964, plus the highly trained units of the territorial army volunteer reserve. Home service forces are stationed in Northern Ireland, Gibraltar, and the Falkland Islands.

Total active army strength in 2005 was 116,760. Equipment included 543 main battle tanks, 475 reconnaissance vehicles, 575 armored infantry fighting vehicles, 2,503 armored personnel carriers, and 877 artillery pieces. The navy had 26,430 personnel including 7,000 Royal Marines and 6,200 naval aviation personnel. Major units of the British fleet included 15 nuclear submarines (four SSBNs; 11 SSNs), three aircraft carriers, 11 destroyers, 20 frigates, 24 coastal/patrol, 22 mine warfare, and three amphibious and 26 logistical/support ships. The Royal Air Force had a strength of 48,140 active personnel, with 339 combat capable aircraft, including 128 fighters, 117 strike/fighter ground attack, and 74 pure fighter ground attack aircraft. As of 2005, the United Kingdom's strategic missile force was based on 58 submarine launched ballistic missiles (SLBMs) with fewer than 200 operational warheads.

Basing its defense policy on NATO, the British government in the 1970s reduced its overseas commitments. The defense budget for 2005 was $51.1 billion. British troops participate in a number of peacekeeping missions. The United States has 9,800 military personnel stationed in the United Kingdom.

18 INTERNATIONAL COOPERATION

The United Kingdom became a charter member of the United Nations on 24 October 1945; it participates in the ECE, ECLAC, and ESCAP, as well as in all the nonregional specialized agencies. The United Kingdom is a permanent member of the UN Security Council. The United Kingdom is also a member of the Council of Europe, the European Union, NATO, OECD, OSCE, the African Development Bank, the Asian Development Bank, the Caribbean Development Bank, G-5. G-7, G-8, the Paris Club (G-10), and the WTO. The headquarters of the IMO is in London. The country holds observer status in the OAS.

The Commonwealth of Nations, an organization of 49 states, provides a means for consultation and cooperation, especially on economic matters, between the United Kingdom and its former colonies. Its main coordinating organ is the Commonwealth Secretariat, which was established in London in 1965 and is headed by a secretary-general appointed by the heads of the member governments. The heads of governments hold biennial meetings; meetings also are held by diplomatic representatives known as high commissioners and among other ministers, officials, and experts.

Despite controversy within the nation itself, the United Kingdom has been a strong supporter of the US-led international war on terrorism. The country has support UN missions and operations in Kosovo (est. 1999), Liberia (est. 2003), Sierra Leone (est. 1999), Georgia (est. 1993), the DROC (est. 1999), and Cyprus (est. 1964), among others. The United Kingdom is part of the Australia Group, the Zangger Committee, the European Organization for Nuclear Research (CERN), the Nuclear Suppliers Group (London Group), the Nuclear Energy Agency, and the Organization for the Prohibition of Chemical Weapons. The nation holds guest status in the Nonaligned Movement.

In environmental cooperation, the United Kingdom is part of the Antarctic Treaty; the Basel Convention; Conventions on Biological Diversity, Whaling, and Air Pollution; Ramsar; CITES; the London Convention; International Tropical Timber Agreements; the Kyoto Protocol; the Montréal Protocol; MARPOL; the Nuclear Test Ban Treaty; and the UN Conventions on the Law of the Sea, Climate Change and Desertification.

19 ECONOMY

The United Kingdom—one of the most highly industrialized countries in the world, with the world's fourth-largest economy, and one of four countries in Western Europe with a trillion dollar economy (the others are Germany, France, and Italy)—lives by manufacture, trade, and financial and commercial services. Apart from coal and low-grade iron ore, some timber, building materials, and natural gas and North Sea oil, it has few natural resources. Agriculture provides 60% of the food needed with only about 2% of the labor force. The remainder of the United Kingdom's food supply and most raw materials for its industries have to be imported and paid for largely through exports of manufactures and services. The United Kingdom is in fact one of the world's largest markets for food and agricultural products and the fifth-largest trading nation. Vast quantities of imported wheat, meat, butter, livestock feeds, tea, tobacco, wool, and timber have been balanced by exports of machinery, ships, locomotives, aircraft, and motor vehicles. The pattern of exports is gradually changing, however. Post World War II reduction in output of textiles—once a leading British export—due to competition from Asia, and in coal output, because of competition from oil and mines in Europe, has been offset by industries such as electronics and chemicals. A major source of earnings is the variety of commercial services that stem from the United Kingdom's role as central banker of the sterling area. Shipping, income from overseas investment, insurance, and tourism also make up an important part of the economy.

The British economy is one of the strongest in Europe: as of the early 2000s, inflation, interest rates, and unemployment remained low. Since the 1979–81 recession, the British economy has posted steady gains. Between 1983 and 1990, real GDP increased by nearly 25%. Individual productivity increased by 14% during the 1980–85 period and another 25% during 1985–90. In less than a decade, the United Kingdom went from heavy dependence on imported oil to energy self-sufficiency, but this ended in 1989, although the United Kingdom's dependence on energy imports in the 1990s was far lower than in the past. Inflation fell from 18% in 1980 to an annual rate of 1.9% by July 1987. However, it averaged 6.3% a year during 1988–92 before falling to 1.6% in 1993. From 1994 to 1997, annual growth was over 3% (3.125%), but fell an average 2.5% from 1998 to 1999. An increase to 3.1% in 2000 was slowed to 2% and 1.6% in the global economic slowdown of 2001–03, exacerbated by the high value of the pound and the bursting of the "new economy" bubble, which hurt manufacturing and exports. Inflation, which stood at 2.7% in 1998, had fallen to 2.2% in 2002. After falling to 5.8% in 1990, the unemployment rate crept up to 10.4% in 1993 but declined to 8% in 1995, and 7.5% in 1998. In 2002, recorded unemployment was 5.1%. The estimated unemployment rate in 2004 was 4.8%. Real GDP growth stood at an average 2.3% from 2001–05. Inflation during that period averaged 1.5%. Real GDP grew by 1.8% in 2005, and was forecast to expand by just 1.6% in 2006, before rebounding to 2.1% in 2007.

In the 1980s and 1990s, the government privatized many major companies, as well as a number of subsidiaries of nationalized industries and other businesses. Among the major companies privatized were British Telecom, British Gas, British Steel, British Airways, British Aerospace, Rolls-Royce, Austin Rover, Cable and Wireless, ICL, British water utilities, British Coal, and British Rail.

20 INCOME

The US Central Intelligence Agency (CIA) reports that in 2005 the United Kingdom's gross domestic product (GDP) was estimated at $1.9 trillion. The CIA defines GDP as the value of all final goods and services produced within a nation in a given year and computed on the basis of purchasing power parity (PPP) rather than value as measured on the basis of the rate of exchange based on current dollars. The per capita GDP was estimated at $30,900. The annual growth rate of GDP was estimated at 1.8%. The average inflation rate in 2005 was 3.2%. It was estimated that agriculture accounted for 1.1% of GDP, industry 26%, and services 72.9%.

According to the World Bank, in 2003 remittances from citizens working abroad totaled $5.029 billion or about $85 per capita and accounted for approximately 0.3% of GDP.

The World Bank reports that in 2003 household consumption in United Kingdom totaled $1.174 trillion or about $19,814 per capita based on a GDP of $1.8 trillion, measured in current dollars rather than PPP. Household consumption includes expenditures of individuals, households, and nongovernmental organizations on goods and services, excluding purchases of dwellings. It was estimated that for the period 1990 to 2003 household consumption grew at an average annual rate of 3.1%. In 2001 it was estimated that approximately 14% of household consumption was spent on food, 9% on fuel, 3% on health care, and 3% on education. It was estimated that in 2002 about 17% of the population had incomes below the poverty line.

21 LABOR

The total workforce of the United Kingdom in 2005 was estimated at 30.07 million. As of 2004, the services sector accounted for 79.5% of the labor force, with industry at 19.1% and agriculture only 1.5%. Between 1983 and 1992 there was a substantial shift in employment from previously dominant manufacturing to service industries. Employment in industry, which had been 7,788,000 in 1983, was down to 4,986,000 in 1998. The unemployment rate in 2005 was estimated at 4.7%.

The Employment Relations Act protects union organization, the statutory right to strike, and minimum employment standards. Nearly all trade unions of any size are affiliated with the Trades Union Congress (TUC), the national center of the trade union movement. There is also a separate Scottish Trades Union Congress. The legal status of the trade unions is defined by the Trade Union and Labor Relations Act of 1974. Restrictions on the power of the trade unions are embodied in the Employment Acts of 1980 and 1982 and in the Trade Union Act of 1984. As of 2005, about 29% of Britain's workforce was unionized. In the public sector, 57% of the labor force belongs to a union, while in the private sector only 17% are union members.

The standard workweek is limited to 48 hours, which is averaged over a period of 17 to 26 weeks. Besides the statutory public holidays, most employees have at least four weeks' annual vacation with pay. Children under the age of 16 are not permitted

to work unless it is part of an educational experience. Children under age 13 are prohibited from working in any capacity. As of 2005, the national minimum wage rate varied from $7.45 per hour to $8.82 per hour depending upon the employee's age. Although these rates are insufficient to provide a decent living standard, the gap is filled by a range of government benefits, which includes free medical care under the National Health Service.

22 AGRICULTURE

Agriculture is intensive and highly mechanized, producing about 60% of the United Kingdom's food needs. Agriculture's importance has declined in recent years; including forestry and fishing, it contributed about 1% to the GDP in 2003, down from 2.3% in 1971. In 2003, agricultural products accounted for 4.9% of exports and there was an agricultural trade deficit of almost $20.2 billion (second after Japan). Agriculture engages 1% of the labor force.

Nearly 24% of Great Britain's land area was devoted to crops in 2003. There were about 280,600 holdings, down from 422,000 in the late 1960s. In Great Britain roughly 70% of the farms are primarily or entirely owner-occupied, but in Northern Ireland nearly all are.

Most British farms produce a variety of products. The type of farming varies with the soil and climate. The better farming land is generally in the lowlands. The eastern areas are predominantly arable, and the western predominantly for grazing. Chief crops (with estimated 2004 production in tons) were barley, 5,860,000; wheat, 15,706,000; potatoes, 6,000,000; sugar beets, 7,600,000; oats, 652,000; and oilseed rape, 1,600,000. Mechanization and research have greatly increased agricultural productivity; between 1989 and 1999, for example, production of wheat per hectare rose 12%; of barley, 7%; and of sugar beets, 32%. The yield of cereal crops increased by almost 10% between 1992–94 and 2002–04. Consequently, the United Kingdom now produces about 60% of its total food needs, whereas prior to World War II (1939–45), it produced only about 33%, and in 1960, less than half. The estimated number of tractors in the United Kingdom in 2003 was 500,000, as against 55,000 in 1939; some 47,000 combines were also in use.

23 ANIMAL HUSBANDRY

Livestock continues to be the largest sector of the farming industry. The United Kingdom raises some of the world's finest pedigreed livestock and is the leading exporter of pedigreed breeding animals. Most of the internationally famous breeds of cattle, sheep, hogs, and farm horses originated in the United Kingdom. In England and Wales, fattening of animals for food is the predominant activity in the southeast, the east, and the Midlands, while stock rearing is widespread in northern England and in Wales. In Scotland, dairying predominates in the southwest, cropping and fattening in the east, and sheep raising in the hilly regions. Northern Ireland's livestock industry provides 90% of its agricultural income.

In 2005, there were about 10,378,000 head of cattle (including two million dairy cows), 35,253,000 sheep and goats, and 4,851,000 hogs. There are also an estimated 157 million chickens. Output of livestock products for 2005 included 747,000 tons of beef and veal, 310,000 tons of mutton and lamb, 704,000 tons of pork, 1,573,000 tons of poultry, 14,577,000 tons of milk, 133,000 tons of butter, and 399,000 tons of cheese.

The most highly reputed beef breeds are Hereford and Aberdeen Angus; distinguished dairy breeds are Guernsey, Jersey, and Ayrshire. To ensure sound breeding, there is compulsory licensing of bulls. On 20 March 1996 the British government reported concern over a possible link between bovine spongiform encephalopathy (BSE, or the so-called "Mad Cow" disease) in cattle and a new variant of Creutzfeldt-Jakob disease in humans. BSE was first identified in the United Kingdom in 1986. Transmission of BSE to cattle occurs from contaminated meat and bone meal in concentrate feed, with sheep or cattle as the original source. The United Kingdom is the only country with a high incidence of the disease, and the epidemic was mainly due to recycling affected bovine material back to cattle before a ban on ruminant feed began in July 1988. As a result, consumption of beef dropped and many countries banned imports of British cattle and beef.

24 FISHING

Lying on the continental shelf, the British Isles are surrounded by waters mainly less than 90 m (300 ft) deep, which serve as excellent fishing grounds and breeding grounds for fish. Small fishing villages are found all along the coast, but the modern large-scale industry is concentrated at Hull, Grimsby, Fleetwood, Yarmouth, and Lowestoft in England. The major herring landings are made at numerous east coast ports of Scotland, notably Aberdeen. The fishing industry has been declining, but it remains important to Scotland, which accounts for 67% by weight of all fish landings in the United Kingdom; England and Wales account for 30% and Northern Ireland for 3%.

The deep-sea fleet has declined in recent years, primarily because the adoption by most nations, including the United Kingdom, of a 200-mi fishery limit decreased the opportunity to fish in distant waters. Some of the larger vessels have, instead, turned to fishing for mackerel and herring off the west coast. The British fishing fleet had a capacity of 223,039 gross tons in 2004, about 12% of EU capacity. Landings of all types of fish by UK fishing vessels totaled 457,712 tons in 2004 (27% shellfish). Leading species caught that year were mackerel (115,299 tons), herring (56,214 tons), and haddock (45,384 tons). The United Kingdom exported $1,669 million in fishery products in 2003, while imports were valued at $2,507 million.

Salmon farming takes place primarily in Scotland; total UK production of farmed salmon in 2003 was around 145,600 tons. Domestic demand for seafood grew during the late 1990s due to public concerns over beef tainted by bovine spongiform encephalopathy (BSE, or Mad Cow disease).

25 FORESTRY

The estimated total area of woodland in 2002 was 2.8 million hectares (6.89 million acres), or over 10% of Great Britain's land area. Roughly 40% of the area is in England, 49% in Scotland, and 11% in Wales. State-owned forests cover 33% of the forest area, and 67% are in the private sector. The principal species in the forest area are spruces (34%), pines (22%), oak (9%) and larch (8%), with smaller amounts of beech, ash, birch, and fir. The lumber industry employs about 55,000, and supplies the United Kingdom with 13% of its timber demand. Because of the high proportion of unproduc-

tive woodland, largely a legacy of overfelling during the two world wars, major efforts have been directed toward rehabilitation.

The timber cut in 2004 yielded an estimated 8.1 million cu m (286 million cu ft) of roundwood. In 2004, UK sawmills cut 4.93 million cu m (174 million cu ft) of logs to produce 2.76 million cu m (97.4 million cu ft) of sawn lumber. Except for the two wartime periods, home woodlands have made only a limited contribution in this century to the national requirements in wood and wood products, almost 90% of which are met by imports. The United Kingdom imports softwood lumber from Canada, hardwood lumber and softwood plywood from the United States, hardwood veneer from Germany, hardwood plywood from Russia, and particleboard from Belgium.

The Forestry Commission promotes development of afforestation and increased timber production. Clearance of forests for agriculture began in the Neolithic and Bronze Ages, so that by the time of the Domesday survey in 1086, only 15% of England was forested. There was a considerable degree of reforestation in the second half of the 20th century. During 1990–2000, the total forest area increased by 0.6%.

26 MINING

Although the United Kingdom had comparatively few mineral resources (except for North Sea oil), it was a significant player in the world mining and mineral-processing industries, because of the extensive range of UK companies that had interests in the international mineral industry. An organized coal-mining industry has been in existence for over 300 years, 200 years longer than in any other country, and has traditionally been by far the most important mineral industry. Mine production of ferrous and nonferrous metals has been declining for more than 30 years, as reserves became depleted, necessitating imports for the large and important metal processing industry. Metals, chemicals, coal, and petroleum were among the country's leading industries in 2003, and fuels and chemicals ranked second and third, respectively, among export commodities. The industrial minerals sector has provided a significant base for expanding the extractive industries, and companies had a substantial interest in the production of domestic and foreign aggregates, ball clay, kaolin (china clay), and gypsum. The United Kingdom was a leading world producer and exporter of ball clay and kaolin; operations were mainly in Dorsetshire and Devonshire.

Other minerals extracted in 2003 included: common sand and gravel, 91 million tons (estimated); crushed limestone, 82 million tons (estimated); crushed dolomite, 12.950 million tons (reported); crushed igneous rock, 50.4 million tons (estimated); china clay kaolin (dry weight sales), 2.097 million tons (reported); ball and pottery clay (dry weight sales), 885,000 tons (reported); potash, 621,000 tons (reported); dimension sandstone, 250,000 tons (estimated); gypsum and anhydrite, 1.7 million tons (estimated); fluorspar (all grades), 56,000 tons (estimated); and crushed chalk, 8.5 million tons (estimated). Lead and hematite iron ore were worked on a small scale. The output of iron ore (gross weight) dropped from an estimated 1,000 metric tons in 1999, to 500 metric tons in 2003. Alumina was produced from imported bauxite. Zinc and tungsten are no longer mined. In 2003, the United Kingdom also produced barite and witherite, bromine, hydraulic cement, clays (including fire clay, fuller's earth, and shale), feldspar (china stone), quicklime and hydrated lime, nitrogen, rock and brine salt, sodium compounds, slate, sulfur, pyrophyllite and soapstone talc, and titania. Most slate mining was in northern Wales, and the Penrhyn quarry, at Bethesda, was considered the world's largest, and has been in operation for more than 400 years. Small amounts of calcite stone were produced from 1999 through 2003.

Most nonfuel mineral rights in the United Kingdom were privately owned, except gold and silver, the rights to which were vested in the royal family and were known as Crown Rights. Onshore exploration activities were to be directed mainly toward precious metals, mainly gold. In Northern Ireland, the rights to license and to work minerals were vested in the state.

27 ENERGY AND POWER

The United Kingdom (UK) is the European Union's (EU) largest petroleum and natural gas producer, thanks to its offshore oil reserves in the North Sea. It is also one of Europe's largest consumers of energy.

The United Kingdom, as of 1 January 2005 had proven oil reserves estimated at 4.49 billion barrels, according to the Oil and Gas Journal. The bulk of these reserves are located in the North Sea, on the UK Continental Shelf. Sizable reserves also are located north of the Shetland Islands, with smaller amounts located in the North Atlantic. The United Kingdom also has Europe's largest onshore oil field, the Wytch Farm field. In 2004, oil production averaged an estimated 2.08 million barrels per day, with domestic consumption that year estimated at 1.86 million barrels per day. Net exports that same year averaged an estimated 0.22 million barrels per day. The United Kingdom's crude oil refining capacity, as of 1 January 2003 totaled an estimated 1.8 million barrels per day. British Petroleum (BP) has the most refining capacity in the United Kingdom, operating a 196,000 barrel-per-day facility in Grangemouth, Scotland, and a 163,000-barrel-per-day facility in Coryton, England. The largest refinery in the United Kingdom is the 321,000 barrel per day Fawley facility, operated by ExxonMobil. The United Kingdom is simultaneously a major importer and exporter of oil. Since North Sea oil is a light, high-quality oil, the United Kingdom exports this oil and imports crude oils of various qualities. In 2002, imports of petroleum, including crude oil, averaged 1,439,900 barrels per day, of which crude oil accounted for 1,060,110 barrels per day. In 2002, imports of dry natural gas totaled 180.11 billion cu ft.

As of 1 January 2005, the United Kingdom's proven natural gas reserves were estimated at 20.8 trillion cu ft. In 2002, natural gas production totaled an estimated 3.6 trillion cu ft, of which an estimated 3.3 trillion cu ft was consumed domestically. Net exports of natural gas that year were estimated at 0.3 trillion cu ft.

The United Kingdom is the fifth-largest producer of coal in the EU. In 2001, the country had recoverable coal reserves estimated at 1.65 billion short tons. According to the UK Department of Trade and Industry (DTI), a total of 31.1 million short tons were produced in 2003. However, this figure is down by 82% from the early 1970s. In addition, demand for coal has also dwindled. In 1970, according to the DTI, consumption fell from 175.9 million short tons to 68.7 million short tons in 2003. Falling domestic demand and a surge in cheap imported coal put coal imports at 35.7 million short tons in 2003. Of that total, 38% came from South Africa, 18% from Australia, and 16% from Russia. Also in

that year, electric power generation accounted for 86% of all coal consumption.

In 2003, according to the DTI, installed electric power generating capacity totaled 78.5 GW, of which conventional thermal plants accounted for 77% of capacity, followed by nuclear at 15%, hydropower at 5%, and 2% from other renewable sources. Electric power output in 2003 totaled 376.8 billion kWh, with consumption that same year at 399.8 billion kWh. Imports that year totaled 5.1 billion kWh, most of which came from France, according to the DTI. The UK electric power sector is privatized and competitive. Distributors and generators of electricity trade power on a wholesale market.

28 INDUSTRY

The United Kingdom is one of the most highly industrialized countries in the world. The industrial sector of the economy declined in relative importance after 1973, because of the worldwide economic slowdown; however, output rose in 1983 and 1984 and in 1985 was growing at an annual rate of 3%. Manufacturing accounted for 25.1% of GDP in 1985, 22.3% in 1992, and 26.3% in 2004. Since World War II, some traditional industries have markedly declined—e.g., cotton textiles, steel, shipbuilding, locomotives—and their place has been taken by newer industries, such as electronics, offshore oil and gas products, and synthetic fibers. The United Kingdom had a total oil refining capacity of 1.8 million barrels per day in 2005. In the chemicals industry, plastics and pharmaceuticals have registered the most significant growth.

The pattern of ownership, organization, and control of industry is varied: public, private, and cooperative enterprises are all important. The public sector plays a significant role; however, since 1979 the government has sold off a number of companies and most manufacturing is conducted by private enterprise. Although the average firm is still fairly small, there has been a trend in recent years toward the creation of larger enterprises.

Metals, engineering, and allied industries—including steel, nonferrous metals, vehicles, and machinery—employ nearly half of all workers in manufacturing. The United Kingdom's automotive industry produced 1.75 million automobiles in 2002. It also produced 14,682 heavy trucks in 2000. Britain's aerospace industry is among the world's foremost. Rolls-Royce, which was privatized in 1987, is one of the principal aero-engine manufacturers in the world. British Aerospace, nationalized during 1978–80 but now privately owned again, manufactures civil aircraft, such military aircraft as the Harrier and the Hawk advanced trainer, and guided weapons, including the Rapier ground-to-air missile.

While the relative importance of the textile and clothing industries has declined considerably since World War II, the United Kingdom continues to produce high-quality woolen textiles. Nevertheless, foreign competition has significantly cut into the textile industry. Following the expiration of the World Trade Organization's longstanding system of textile quotas at the beginning of 2005, the EU signed an agreement with China in June 2005, imposing new quotas on 10 categories of textile goods, limiting growth in those categories to between 8% and 12.5% a year. The agreement runs until 2007, and was designed to give European textile manufacturers time to adjust to a world of unfettered competition. However, barely a month after the EU-China agreement was signed, China reached its quotas for sweaters, followed soon after by blouses, bras, T-shirts, and flax yarn. Tens of millions of garments piled up in warehouses and customs checkpoints, which affected both retailers and consumers.

Certain smaller industries in the United Kingdom are noted for the quality of their craftsmanship—e.g., pottery, jewelry, goldware, and silverware. Other sectors are the cement industry (which focuses on the manufacture of Portland cement, a British invention); the rubber industry, the world's oldest; paper industries; and leather and footwear. The industrial sector's 26.3% share of GDP in 2004 continues to demonstrate the importance of industry to the development of the British economy. The industrial production growth rate declined in 2004, however, to 0.9%. Industrial production was forecast to contract by 1.3% in 2005.

29 SCIENCE AND TECHNOLOGY

Great Britain, preeminent in the Industrial Revolution from the mid-18th to the mid-19th century, has a long tradition of technological ingenuity and scientific achievement. It was in the United Kingdom that the steam engine, spinning jenny, and power loom were developed and the first steam-powered passenger railway entered service. To British inventors also belongs credit for the miner's safety lamp, the friction match, the cathode ray tube, stainless steel, and the first calculating machine. One of the most famous scientific discoveries of the 20th century, the determination of the double-helix structure of the deoxyribonucleic acid (DNA) molecule, took place at the Laboratory of Molecular Biology at Cambridge University. In February 1997 the first successful cloning of an animal from an adult (resulting in "Dolly" the lamb) was performed at the Roslin Institute near Edinburgh, Scotland's leading animal research laboratory. The United Kingdom is also in the forefront of research in radio astronomy, laser holography, and superconductivity.

The total national expenditure for research and development (R&D) in 2002 was $29.06 billion, or 1.88% of GDP. Of that amount, the business sector provided the largest portion at 46.7%, followed by the government at 26.9%. Foreign sources accounted for 20.5%, with higher education and private nonprofit organizations providing 1% and 4.9%, respectively. In 1998 (the latest year for which data was available) there were 2,691 scientists and engineers that were engaged in research and development per one million people. In 2002, of all bachelor's degrees awarded, 31.4% were in the sciences (natural, mathematics and computers, engineering).

The leading government agency for supporting science and technology is the Ministry of Defense, which plays an important role in both the United Kingdom's national security and its role in NATO. In addition, government-industry cooperation in aerospace, biotechnology and electronics have opened new frontiers in science. In 2002, high-tech exports were valued at $71.481 billion and accounted for 31% of manufactured exports.

The largest issue facing British scientists, engineers and technicians is the challenge of providing new technological innovations in the global economy. In 1993, a government white paper, *Realizing our Potential*, called for the most sweeping changes in British science and technology since World War II. Among the changes called for in this white paper is the creation of a "technology forecasting program" which will allow scientists and engineers from all over Great Britain to have a more direct say in setting national

science and technology priorities. It is likely that many of the recommendations from the white paper will be incorporated into national science and technology priorities, including the technology forecasting program, over time.

The most prestigious scientific institution in the United Kingdom is the Royal Society, founded in 1660 in London. The British Association for the Advancement of Science, headquartered in London, promotes public understanding of science and technology.

30 DOMESTIC TRADE

London is the leading wholesale and importing center, accounting for more than half the total wholesale turnover. Other important distribution centers are Liverpool, Manchester, Bristol, Glasgow, and Hull.

Supermarkets have hurried to diversify into other businesses recently because of competition, falling prices, and a mature domestic market. As of 2005, the franchise industry was worth over £9 billion per year in the United Kingdom alone: the industry employs some 330,000 people, with more than 31,000 franchisees operating their own franchised business. Direct marketing is common. A value-added tax of 17.5% applies to most goods and services.

Normal banking hours are 9 AM to 5 PM, Monday through Friday, but this may vary in country areas. Business hours in London are 9 AM to 5:30 PM, Monday through Friday; shops in certain areas may be open to 7:30 one night a week, usually Wednesday or Thursday. Outside of London, the shops of each town or village may close for a half or full day at midweek. Saturday shopping hours are 9 AM to 5:30 PM. Sunday shopping is becoming increasingly available, from 10 AM to 4 PM.

31 FOREIGN TRADE

The United Kingdom—the world's fifth-largest trading nation, the fifth-largest exporter of goods, and the second-largest exporter of services—is highly dependent on foreign trade. It must import almost all its copper, ferrous metals, lead, zinc, rubber, and raw cot-

Principal Trading Partners – United Kingdom (2003)

(In millions of US dollars)

Country	Exports	Imports	Balance
World	320,057.2	399,478.3	-79,421.1
United States	48,080.4	39,360.3	8,720.1
Germany	33,292.7	54,046.1	-20,753.4
France-Monaco	30,209.0	33,060.0	-2,851.0
Netherlands	21,692.1	25,615.2	-3,923.1
Ireland	20,815.4	16,433.1	4,382.3
Belgium	17,610.3	19,945.6	-2,335.3
Spain	14,330.7	13,844.3	486.4
Italy-San Marino-Holy See	13,836.1	19,357.9	-5,521.8
Special Categories	12,414.2	13,329.6	-915.4
Sweden	6,210.9	7,511.5	-1,300.6

(…) data not available or not significant.

SOURCE: *2003 International Trade Statistics Yearbook,* New York: United Nations, 2004.

ton; most of its tin, raw wool, hides and skins, and many other raw materials; and about one-third of its food.

The United Kingdom's major export commodities are manufactured items, crude petroleum, chemicals, food, beverages, and tobacco. As of 2005, the top 14 best prospect sectors for trade and investment in the United Kingdom were aircraft and parts, apparel, automotive parts and service equipment, computers and peripherals, cosmetics and toiletries, drugs and pharmaceuticals, education and training, furniture, medical equipment, pollution control, renewable energy equipment, safety and security equipment, telecommunications equipment, and travel and tourism.

In 2004, the United Kingdom's major exports were finished manufactures (53% of total exports), semi-manufactures (29.6%), and oils and other fuels (9.4%). Major imports were finished manufactures (56.9% of all imports), semi-manufactures (24.2%), and food, beverages, and tobacco (8.9%). The United Kingdom's leading markets in 2004 were the United States (15% of all exports), Germany (11.5%), France (9.8%), and Ireland (7%). Leading suppliers were Germany (13.9% of all imports), the United States (8.8%), France (8%), and the Netherlands (7.2%). Exports of goods totaled $349.6 billion in 2004, and imports totaled $456.9 billion, resulting in a trade deficit of $107.3 billion.

32 BALANCE OF PAYMENTS

Throughout the 1960s, revaluations of other currencies adversely affected the pound sterling. Large deficits in the balance of payments appeared in 1964 and 1967, leading to devaluation in November 1967. Another run on sterling prompted a decision to let the pound float on 23 June 1972. The pound then declined steadily, dropping below a value of $2.00 for the first time on 9 March 1976. The oil crisis and the rise in commodity prices in 1974 were even harsher blows to the UK economy. Increasing unemployment, the worldwide recession, and a large budgetary deficit placed the government in an extremely difficult position, since replenishment

of currency reserves cost more in terms of sterling, and the need to curb inflation prevented expansion in the economy. Borrowing from the oil-producing states and the EU helped finance the deficits, but a further approach to the IMF became necessary. During the late 1970s, the United Kingdom's visible trade balance was generally negative, although surpluses on invisibles sometimes were sufficient to produce a surplus in the current account.

Increased North Sea oil exports helped produce substantial trade surpluses in 1980–82. The United Kingdom has run a deficit in visible trade since 1983, reaching a peak of $47 billion in 1989, as consumer demand for imported goods ballooned. As recession took hold, imports fell, reducing the visible trade deficit dramatically in 1991. The devaluation of the pound, following the United Kingdom's late 1992 withdrawal from the EU's Exchange Rate Mechanism, increased the cost of imports at the end of 1992. However, the sterling's trade-weighted exchange rate index stabilized by 1995. In recent years, the export-oriented manufacturing sector has been challenged by an overvalued exchange rate. The United Kingdom is a major overseas investor (especially in the United States) and has an extremely important service sector, dominated by banking and insurance, which consistently generates invisible trade credits.

In 2002, the United Kingdom's current account balance was -$13 billion, or -0.8% of GDP. The current account balance in 2003 was -1.6% of GDP. Exports of goods totaled $349.6 billion in 2004, and imports totaled $456.9 billion, resulting in a trade deficit of $107.3 billion. The current account balance in 2004 was -$33.46 billion.

33 BANKING AND SECURITIES

The United Kingdom is known throughout the world for its expertise in the field of banking, ranking third in the world after New York and Tokyo. Most activity takes place in the City of London, which has the greatest concentration of banks and the largest insurance market in the world. Until the Labour government of Tony Blair disengaged it from the Treasury, the Bank of England, established in 1694 as a corporate body and nationalized in 1946, held the main government accounts, acted as government agent for the issue and registration of government loans and other financial operations, and was the central note-issuing authority, with the sole right to issue bank notes in England and Wales (some banks in Scotland and Northern Ireland have limited note-issuing rights). It administered exchange control for the Treasury and is responsible for the application of the government's monetary policy to other banks and financial institutions. After its separation from the Treasury, the Bank of England retained the power to establish interest rates, while the Treasury continued to reign in public spending.

The banks handling most domestic business are mainly limited liability companies. The four major clearing commercial banking groups are Barclays, Lloyds, Midland, and National Westminster. These banks carry out most of the commercial banking in England and Wales. In Scotland, which has its own clearing system, there are three clearing banks: the Bank of Scotland, the Clydesdale Bank, and the Royal Bank of Scotland. Other institutions, notably the building societies, have begun to compete with the clearing banks by providing current and deposit account facilities.

Balance of Payments – United Kingdom (2003)		
(In billions of US dollars)		
Current Account		**-33.5**
Balance on goods		-77.3
Imports	-384.3	
Exports	307.0	
Balance on services		-269.1
Balance on income		36.0
Current transfers		-16.0
Capital Account		**2.1**
Financial Account		**27.1**
Direct investment abroad		-51.2
Direct investment in United Kingdom		15.5
Portfolio investment assets		-56.3
Portfolio investment liabilities		149.3
Financial derivatives		-8.5
Other investment assets		-432.3
Other investment liabilities		410.5
Net Errors and Omissions		**1.8**
Reserves and Related Items		**2.6**
(…) data not available or not significant.		

SOURCE: *Balance of Payment Statistics Yearbook 2004*, Washington, DC: International Monetary Fund, 2004.

There are concerns that Frankfurt, Germany, will develop as the major financial center in the EU. The City of London's role in this context is under threat mainly because Frankfurt is the site of the European Central Bank, which controls monetary policy for the euro-area EU states.

The National Savings Movement, started in 1916, encourages widespread savings investment by small depositors in trustee savings banks and the National Savings Bank (formerly known as the Post Office Savings Bank), the largest organization of its kind in the world, with about 20,000 in post offices. Merchant banks are of great importance in the financing of trade, both domestic and overseas. In addition, about 275 overseas banks are directly represented in London.

After the "Big Bang"—the deregulation of the United Kingdom's financial markets—the Financial Services Act, which became law in November 1986, set out a system of self-regulating organizations (SROs) to oversee operations in different markets under the overall control of an umbrella body, the Securities and Investment Board (SIB). In 1996 there were five SROs covering the main financial activities, and since April 1988 any firm conducting investment business must have authorization to do so from the appropriate SRO. The International Monetary Fund reports that in 2001, M2—an aggregate equal to currency and demand deposits plus savings deposits, small time deposits, and money market mutual funds—was $1.63 trillion. The money market rate, the rate at which financial institutions lend to one another in the short term, was 5.08%.

In 1762, a club of securities dealers was formed in London to fix rules for market transactions, and in 1773 the first stock exchange was opened in London. In 1801, the London Stock Exchange was constructed on part of its present site. Since that time, it has provided a market for the purchase and sale of securities and has played an important part in providing new capital for industry. The Stock Exchange opened to international competition in October 1986, permitting wider ownership of member firms. Minimum rates of commission on stock sales were abolished. In April 1982, the London Gold Futures Market began operations; it is the only market in Europe making possible worldwide, round-the-clock futures dealings in the metal. As of 2004, a total of 2,486 companies were listed on the London Stock Exchange, which had a market capitalization of £1.47 trillion.

34 INSURANCE

London is the leading international insurance center. Lloyd's, the world-famous society of private insurers, was originally established in the 17th century as a center for marine insurance but has since built up a worldwide market for other types of insurance.

The Central Statistical Office (CSO) recently compiled information on institutions whose primary business is the long-term investment of funds in the securities markets. It covers pension funds, insurance companies, investment trusts, unit trusts, and property trusts. Total net investment by institutions in 1994 was £45.4 billion ($69.6 billion), down from the record £51.6 billion in 1993. The biggest net investment by an institutional group was that of the long-term insurance companies, with £24.2 billion of this total.

In the mid-1990s, total life insurance in force came to £1.04 trillion. In the United Kingdom, third-party automobile liability, em-

ployers' liability, nuclear facility liability, oil pollution liability, aircraft operators' liability and professional liability is compulsory, with the government having a monopoly on workers' compensation. In 2003, the value of all direct insurance premiums written totaled $246.733 billion, of which life insurance premiums accounted for $154.842 billion. For that same year, the top nonlife insurer was Norwich Union, with net written nonlife premiums of £5 billion, while the nations leading life insurer had gross written life insurance premiums of £8.148 billion.

35 PUBLIC FINANCE

The onset of recession in 1990 led to an increased level of public borrowing—about £14 billion in 1991–92, or 2.25% of GDP. By 1993–94, the public sector borrowing requirement had risen to £50 billion, or 8.1% of GDP. In 1994 the government initiated a series of stringent fiscal measures designed to curb the spiraling public sector borrowing requirement (PSBR). Since 1998, the United Kingdom has taken aggressive steps to reform its public spending activities. Reforms included limits on expenditures, higher governmental accountability regarding spending, better resource budgeting, and improved spending flexibility.

The US Central Intelligence Agency (CIA) estimated that in 2005 the United Kingdom's central government took in revenues of approximately $881.4 billion and had expenditures of $951 billion. Revenues minus expenditures totaled approximately -$69.6 billion. Public debt in 2005 amounted to 42.2% of GDP. Total external debt was $7.107 trillion.

The International Monetary Fund (IMF) reported that in 2003, the most recent year for which it had data, general government revenues were £441,048 million and expenditures were £478,748 million. The value of revenues was us$720,078 million and expenditures us$771,339 million, based on a market exchange rate for 2003 of us$1 = £.6125 as reported by the IMF. Government outlays by function were as follows: general public services, 6.3%; defense,

Public Finance – United Kingdom (2003)

(In millions of British pounds, general government figures)

Revenue and Grants	**441,048**	**100.0%**
Tax revenue	316,610	71.8%
Social contributions	85,689	19.4%
Grants	3,881	0.9%
Other revenue	34,868	7.9%
Expenditures	**478,748**	**100.0%**
General public services	29,970	6.3%
Defense	32,980	6.9%
Public order and safety	24,963	5.2%
Economic affairs	37,626	7.9%
Environmental protection	6,303	1.3%
Housing and community amenities	8,920	1.9%
Health	81,356	17.0%
Recreational, culture, and religion	6,251	1.3%
Education	60,060	12.5%
Social protection	190,319	39.8%

(…) data not available or not significant.

SOURCE: *Government Finance Statistics Yearbook 2004*, Washington, DC: International Monetary Fund, 2004.

6.9%; public order and safety, 5.2%; economic affairs, 7.9%; environmental protection, 1.3%; housing and community amenities, 1.9%; health, 17.0%; recreation, culture, and religion, 1.3%; education, 12.5%; and social protection, 39.8%.

36 TAXATION

Taxes on income include a graduated individual income tax and a corporation tax. Although personal income taxes are still high, they have been reduced several times since 1980.

As of 1 April 2004 the United Kingdom (UK) imposed a standard 30% corporate profits income tax rate. However, for companies with profits under £300,000, the rate was 19%. For companies with profits under £10,000, the rate was 0%. In addition, companies having profits up to £1.5 million, marginal relief was available. There is a 50% petroleum tax assessed on profits from all exploration and production which is deductible from other corporate tax. Capital gains are taxed at the standard corporate rate, but nonresidents companies are generally not taxed on capital gains derived from the sale of shares in a resident subsidiary company. However, companies that derive capital gains from the sale of assets that are located in and are used to carry on business activity in the United Kingdom are subject to the capital gains tax. Dividends are not taxed. Income from interest and royalties are subject to withholding taxes of 20% and 22%, respectively.

Income tax is charged on all income that has its origin in Britain and on all income arising abroad of persons resident in Britain. However, the United Kingdom has entered into agreements with many countries to provide relief from double taxation. Generally, the United Kingdom has a progressive personal income tax structure with a top rate of 40%. For the 2005/2006 fiscal year, a 10% rate was applied to taxable income up to £2,090. A 22% rate was applied on income up to £32,400, with a 40% rate on income above that amount. Inheritance taxes are 40%. Each taxpayer's marginal rate applies to capital gains in excess of £8,500. The main local taxes are land assessments, or "rates."

In January 1973, a value-added tax (VAT) was introduced with a standard rate of 10%, replacing the purchase tax, and bringing the UK's tax policy into harmony with the EU. In 1991, the standard rate was increased to 17.5% and in 1997, the reduced rate, applied to some medicines, medical equipment, heating oil, gas, electricity, small service businesses and some transportation services, was lowered from 8% to 5%. A zero rate applies to most foods, books, newspapers and periodicals, and certain other goods. Services such as insurance, health, education, and land and rents are also exempt. Other taxes are levied on petroleum products, tobacco, and alcoholic drinks. There are also various stamp duties.

37 CUSTOMS AND DUTIES

Import licensing and quotas were the general rule in the United Kingdom between 1939 and 1959. For specified items from specified countries or groups of countries, an individual license was required for each import. In June 1959, however, the United Kingdom began to remove important controls on virtually all raw materials and basic foodstuffs and on some machinery imported from the United States. With UK entry into the free trade area of the EU, a tariff-free area has been created. In addition, the United Kingdom uses the EU's common external tariff for non-EU imports. Rates range from 2–14% on most goods. The four principal types of import charges are customs duties, agricultural levies, value-added taxes, and excise duties on goods such as alcohol, tobacco, and tobacco products. The United Kingdom also levies a VAT on imports with a standard rate of 17.5%, with reduced rates ranging from 0–5%.

38 FOREIGN INVESTMENT

London is considered to be Europe's top financial and business center. London is the headquarters for some 130 of the top 500 global companies. With few exceptions, the United Kingdom does not discriminate between nationals and foreign individuals, and imposes few impediments to foreign ownership. Public-sector procurement policies seek best value and best practice regardless of national origin. The privatization of state-owned utilities is ongoing, and offers additional opportunities for foreign investment. The tax rate on the profits of large companies is 30%, but the effective tax burden is higher; it rose markedly after the Labour government assumed office in 1997.

Over the 10-year period 1992 to 2002, foreign direct investment (FDI) inflow totaled $484.5 billion, the second highest in the world (after the United States by some distance: the United States' 10-year total was $1.3 trillion). In 1997, FDI inflow rose 60% over 1996 to $33.3 billion, placing the United Kingdom third in the world, behind the United States and China. FDI inflow peaked in 2000 at $116.6 billion (a fourth-place finish, behind the United States, Belgium-Luxembourg, and Germany), and then fell to $62 billion in the economic slowdown of 2001. The stock of inward FDI by yearend 2003 was $672 billion. Direct investment inflows in 2003 were $14.5 billion, down from $27.8 billion in 2002. From 2001–05, FDI inflows averaged 2.9% of GDP.

The United Kingdom's outward FDI has normally exceeded its inward flow. Before World War I, British overseas investments were valued at more than $30 billion (adjusted into 1960 dollars). Even in the period between the two world wars, British foreign investments remained remarkably high. After World War II, the United Kingdom, having given up many of its overseas dependencies and having incurred enormous foreign debts to wage the war, had to liquidate a large part of its overseas holdings. As its economy recovered, the United Kingdom again began to invest overseas. From 1955 to 1964, gross total private capital outflow was at an annual average of £300 million. The abolition of exchange controls in 1979 also encouraged overseas investment. By 1985, private British investment overseas (direct and portfolio) had risen to £76.7 billion ($101 billion). In 1994, outward FDI amounted to £100 billion ($154 billion). In 1997, the outflow was $43.7 billion. By yearend 2003, the stock of outward UK FDI investment totaled $1.129 billion. FDI outflows in 2003 totaled $55.1 billion, up from $35.2 billion in 2002.

The United States and the United Kingdom are the largest foreign investors in each other's country. By the end of 2003, the United States had invested $273 billion (historical cost) in the United Kingdom. After the United States, the most popular destinations for outward UK FDI in 2003 were France and Canada. For inward FDI, the Netherlands was the largest overall investor in the United Kingdom in 2003, followed by the United States and Germany.

The United Kingdom is the most favored inward investment location in Europe, attracting over 40% of all direct investment in the EU.

39 ECONOMIC DEVELOPMENT

Like many other industrialized nations of the West, the United Kingdom has sought to combine steady economic growth with a high level of employment, increased productivity, and continuing improvement in living standards. Attainment of these basic objectives, however, had been hindered after World War II by recurrent deficits in the balance of payments and by severe inflationary pressures. As a result, economic policy has chiefly had to be directed toward correcting these two underlying weaknesses in the economy. When crises have arisen, emergency measures have often conflicted with long-term objectives. In 1967, for example, the government devalued the pound by 14% in order to improve the balance-of-payments position, but simultaneously increased taxes and reduced the growth rate of public expenditures in order to restrain home demand in both public and private sectors. Since the almost uninterrupted upward trend in prices resulted principally from the tendency for money income to rise faster than the volume of production, the government sought to institute a policy designed to align the rise in money income with increases in productivity.

Various bodies have been set up to foster economic development and improve industrial efficiency, notably the National Economic Development Council, established in 1962 but abolished in 1992, was responsible for the coordination of industry. Another important body, created in 1974, the National Enterprise Board, was set up to help plan industrial investment, particularly in manufacturing and export industries; the NEB was combined with the National Research and Development Corp. in 1981 to form the British Technology Group, which was privatized in 1991. The Labour government in the 1970s began to de-emphasize increased social services and government participation in the economy and to stress increased incentives for private investment. (A notable exception was in the exploitation of North Sea oil resources.) General investment incentives included tax allowances on new buildings, plants, and machinery. The Conservative government elected in 1979 sought to reduce the role of government in the economy by improving incentives, removing controls, reducing taxes, moderating the money supply, and privatizing several large state-owned companies. This policy was continued by succeeding Conservative governments into the 1990s. The election of a Labour government in 1997 did not reverse this trend. Indeed, privatization is now widely accepted by most of the Labour Party (with the exception of the dwindling numbers of the wing of the party with strong ties to trade unions).

The United Kingdom has long been a major source of both bilateral aid (direct loans and grants) and multilateral aid (contributions to international agencies) to developing countries. To coordinate the overall aid program and its proportions of bilateral and multilateral aid, capital aid, and technical assistance, the Ministry of Overseas Development was set up in 1962. Its functions were subsequently taken over by the Overseas Development Administration (ODA) and are now administered by the Department for International Development (DFID). Since 1958, the terms for development loans have progressively softened, and a policy of interest-free loans for the poorest developing countries was introduced in 1965. Unlike other donors, the United Kingdom provides funds to the recipient governments, rather than funding individual projects. The United Kingdom made a commitment to increase its official development assistance (ODA) from 0.26% of GNP in 1997 to 0.33% in 2003–04 (the UN's target for donor countries' development aid is 0.7% of GNP). In 2004, the United Kingdom actually donated 0.34% of its GNP for development aid, or $7.836 billion. The United Kingdom's aid budget was set to increase to over $8.2 billion for 2005–06, and to $10.6 billion by 2008.

The most important issue facing Britain in the early 2000s was membership in the Economic and Monetary Union (EMU). Labour Prime Minister Tony Blair decided to opt out of EMU at its inception in 1998 and promised a referendum on British membership. By 2005, however, there was little or no prospect of the United Kingdom holding a referendum on joining the EMU over the succeeding five years. The opposition Conservatives oppose abandoning the pound and have the support of a majority of the British population on the issue. The government in 2005 devoted its attention on the domestic front to improving such public services as health, education, and transportation. Large increases in public spending have been set aside for this purpose, but public finances have deteriorated to an extent due to lowered tax receipts. An additional long-term priority for the Labour government in 2005 was to implement reforms to raise the country's productivity performance, which remains below the OECD average.

Another long-term economic problem facing the United Kingdom is the aging of its population and the pressures this phenomenon will place on its pension system. By 2035 the number of pensioners in the United Kingdom will rise by 45% as the postwar baby boomer generation retires; by 2050 the increase will reach 55%. If these people are to maintain their standards of living in relation to the rest of society, the share of GDP transferred to them will have to rise sharply, from 9.4% in 2005 to 14.5% in 2050. One option is to raise the state pension age, which was 65 for men and 60 for women in 2005; the government's Pensions Commission proposes a yearly rise in the retirement age per decade, so that it would reach 68 by 2050. Higher public spending on pensions is another option, but that will mean workers will have to pay more taxes to support the aging population.

40 SOCIAL DEVELOPMENT

A gradually evolved system of social security, placed in full operation in 1948, provides national insurance, industrial injuries insurance, family allowances, and national assistance throughout the United Kingdom. The National Insurance scheme provides benefits for sickness, unemployment, maternity, and widowhood, as well as guardian's allowances, retirement pensions, and death grants. The program is financed by contributions from employees, employers, and the government. A percentage of these contributions are allocated to the National Health Service which provides extensive benefits to workers and their families. Retirement pensions cover men at 65 and women at 60, and benefits increase annually to adjust for cost of living. The first work injury law was instituted in 1897, and currently covers all employees with the exception of the self-employed. There is a universal child benefit and tax credit to residents with one or more children, funded by the government.

Financial assistance for the poor is provided through a system of benefits in the form of a supplementary pension for those over statutory retirement age and a supplementary allowance for others. It also provides temporary accommodation for the homeless in specially designated reception centers. For poverty-stricken families in which the head of the household is in full-time employment, a family income supplement is paid. Maternity benefits cover women who have been employed for 26 weeks.

Equal opportunity between the sexes is provided for by law, although some discrimination against women continues. Sexual harassment is a problem in the workplace and women on average earn 18% less than men. Violence against women persists, however there are many laws providing protection and the substantial penalties are strictly enforced. In 2004 domestic violence accounted for one-fourth of all violent crime. The government is committed to children's rights and welfare.

Although racial discrimination is prohibited by law, people of Asian and African origin are subject to discrimination and harassment. Ethnic minorities are also more likely to be stopped and searched by police. The government at all levels fully respects the legal right to freedom of religion. Human rights organizations have criticized legislation in Northern Ireland which denies suspects the right to immediate legal counsel and the right to silence. There are also some security-related restrictions on the freedoms of assembly and association in Northern Ireland.

⁴¹HEALTH

Life expectancy has increased from 50 years at birth in 1900 to 78.38 years in 2005. Rising living standards, medical advances, the growth of medical facilities and their general availability, and the smaller size of the family are some factors in the improved health of the British people. Deaths from infectious diseases have been greatly reduced, although the proportion of deaths from circulatory diseases—including heart attacks and strokes—and cancer has risen. Infant mortality has decreased from 142 per 1,000 live births in 1900–02 to 5.16 in 2005. As of 2002, the crude birth rate and overall mortality rate were estimated at, respectively, 11.3 and 10 per 1,000 people. A high portion of women aged 15–44 used birth control in the mid-1990s (82%).

A comprehensive National Health Service (NHS), established in 1948, provides full medical care to all residents of the United Kingdom. NHS delivers health care through 129 health authorities, each of which receives money from the government and then purchases a preset amount of treatment each year from hospitals. Included are general medical, dental, pharmaceutical, and optical services; hospital and specialist services (in patients' homes when necessary) for physical and mental illnesses; and local health authority services (maternity and child welfare, vaccination, prevention of illness, health visiting, home nursing, and other services). The patient is free to choose a family doctor from any in the service, subject to the physician's acceptance. General tax revenues meet most of the cost of the NHS; the remainder is paid through National Health Insurance contributions and charges for certain items, including eyeglasses and prescription drugs. Compared with other OECD countries, the United Kingdom's per capita expenditure on health care is low. In the United Kingdom, 6.9% of the GDP went to health expenditures.

All specialist and auxiliary health services in England are the direct responsibility of the secretary of state for social services. In Wales, Scotland, and Northern Ireland the corresponding services and administrative bodies are under the respective secretaries of state. All hospitals, except a few run mostly by religious orders, are also in the NHS. In 1991, the United Kingdom implemented major reforms in its health care services, including improvements in virtually all facets of the program. Areas of concern included incidence of coronary/stroke, cancer, accidents, mental illness, and HIV/AIDS. Smoking prevalence was similar between men (28%) and women (26%) over 15 years old. Half the British population is currently overweight. These high rates have been attributed to a sedentary lifestyle during leisure time.

The NHS is has been undergoing restructuring; increased numbers of NHS hospitals are being decentralized by conversion to NHS Trust, established in 1991. NHS costs Britain's taxpayers more than $73 billion per year. An aging population, costlier treatments, and a budget crisis have forced the cancellation of nonemergency treatment at some centers. The number of beds available is below the level of demand, causing long waits for treatment.

As of 2004, there were an estimated 166 physicians, 497 nurses, 40 dentists, 59 pharmacists and 43 midwives per 100,000 people. The immunization rates for children under one year of age were as follows: diphtheria, pertussis, and tetanus, 92%; polio, 94%; measles, 92%; and tuberculosis, 75%. The rates for DPT and measles were, respectively, 93% and 91%. Since 1982, to help control the spread of AIDS, the government has funded and implemented measures for blood testing, research, public education, and other social services relating to the disease. The HIV/AIDS prevalence was 0.20 per 100 adults in 2003. As of 2004, there were approximately 51,000 people living with HIV/AIDS in the country. There were an estimated 500 deaths from AIDS in 2003.

⁴²HOUSING

At the 2001 census, there were about 25,456,00 dwellings in the United Kingdom. Of these, 21,207,000 were in England, 2,345,000 in Scotland, 1,274,000 in Wales, and 649,000 in Northern Ireland.

In England, 79.9% of all households lived in detached houses or bungalows and 19.7% lived in flats, maisonettes, or apartments. About 68% of all homes were owner occupied; 19% of households were renting from a social landlord (defined as a Council, Housing Association, or registered Social Landlord), and 12% were renting from a private owner. The average number of rooms per household was 5.33. In 2003, the estimated dwelling stock was at 21,464,000.

In Wales at the 2001 census, 88.2% of all households lived in houses or bungalows and 11.4% lived in flats, maisonettes, or apartments. About 71% of all homes were owner occupied; 18% were rented from social landlords and 11% were rented from private owners. The average number of rooms per household was 5.59. It was estimated that about 1.5 million households in England and Wales were overcrowded. The highest percentage was found in London, with about 17% of households overcrowded. In Wales, only about 4% of all households were overcrowded. Even so, the degree of overcrowding in the United Kingdom is lower than in most European countries.

In Scotland in 2001, 20% of all housing was in the form of detached homes, 20% were semidetached, 22% were terraced homes, and 8% were flats or maisonettes, and 4% other. The same year in Northern Ireland, 34% of dwellings were detached homes, 23% were semidetached homes, 35% were terraced homes, and 7% were flats or maisonettes, and 2% other. The 2003 estimate of dwelling stock for Northern Ireland was 669,000 dwellings.

Over 50% of families now live in a post-1945 dwelling, usually a two-story house with a garden. Most homeowners finance their purchase through a home mortgage loan from a building society, bank, insurance company, or other financial institution. New houses are built by both the public and private sectors, but most are built by the private sector for sale to owner-occupiers. The main providers of new subsidized housing are housing associations, which own, manage, and maintain over 600,000 homes in England alone and completed over nearly 30,000 new homes for rent or shared ownership per year in the mid-1990s. Local housing authorities were in the past primarily concerned with slum clearance; however, large-scale clearance virtually ended in the mid-1980s, with emphasis shifting to modernization of substandard homes and community improvement.

43 EDUCATION

Although responsibility for education in the United Kingdom rests with the central government, schools are mainly administered by local education authorities. The majority of primary students attend state schools that are owned and maintained by local education authorities. A small minority attend voluntary schools mostly run by the churches and also financed by the local authorities.

Education is compulsory for all children between the ages of 5 and 16. Since 1989, the government has introduced a "National School Curriculum" in England and Wales comprised of four key stages: five to seven (infants); 7 to 11 (juniors); 11 to 14 (pre-GCSE); and 14 to 16 (GCSE). Similar reforms are being introduced in Scotland and Northern Ireland. The main school examination, the General Certificate of Secondary Education (GCSE) is taken in England, Wales, and Northern Ireland at around the age of 16. A separate exam system exists in Scotland. Of the 2,500 registered independent schools, the largest and most important (Winchester, Eton, Harrow, and others) are known in England as "public schools." Many have centuries of tradition behind them and are world famous. The academic year runs from September to July.

In 2001, about 83% of children between the ages of three and four were enrolled in some type of preschool program. Primary school enrollment in 2003 was estimated at about 100% of age-eligible students. The same year, secondary school enrollment was about 95% of age-eligible students. Most students complete their primary education. The student-to-teacher ratio for primary school was at about 17:1 in 2003; the ratio for secondary school was about 19:1. In 2003, private schools accounted for about 4.9% of primary school enrollment and 55.8% of secondary enrollment.

Including the Open University, a nonresidential institution whose courses are conducted by television and radio broadcasts and correspondence texts, Britain had 47 universities in the 1990s (compared with 17 in 1945). As a result of legislation, nearly all polytechnics have become universities and started awarding their own degrees in 1993. The Universities of Oxford and Cambridge date from the 12th and 13th centuries, respectively; the Scottish universities of St. Andrews, Glasgow, Aberdeen, and Edinburgh from the 15th and 16th centuries. Besides the universities, there are more than 800 other institutions of higher education, including technical, art, and commercial colleges run by local authorities.

National policy stipulates that no person should be excluded from higher education by lack of means. More than 90% of stu-dents in higher education hold awards from public or private funds. In 1997, the government began to reconsider its policy of cost-free tuition by announcing that students would become responsible for some of the expense. In 2003, it was estimated that about 64% of the tertiary age population were enrolled in tertiary education programs. The adult literacy rate has been estimated at about 99%.

As of 2003, public expenditure on education was estimated at 5.3% of GDP, or 11.5% of total government expenditures.

44 LIBRARIES AND MUSEUMS

London has more than 500 libraries, among them the British Library, which is the national library and the largest library in the United Kingdom, with about 150 million items in 2005 and an average acquisition rate of about 3 million items per year. Special collections and treasures include the Magna Carta, a notebook of Leonardo da Vinci, original manuscripts of Jane Austen and James Joyce (among others), and musical manuscripts of G.F. Handel and the Beatles (among others). There is a branch location of the British Library at Boston Spa, West Yorkshire. The National Library of Scotland, with about seven million volumes, is in Edinburgh, and the National Library of Wales, with some four million volumes, in Aberystwyth. Each of these is a copyright library, entitled to receive a copy of every new book published in the United Kingdom. The Bodleian Library at Oxford University is also a copyright library with about 6.7 million volumes; there are nine branch locations of the Bodleian in Oxford. Oxford University sponsors over 100 departmental libraries. The Cambridge University Library, also a copyright library, has 5.9 million volumes throughout five locations.

Other major libraries in London include the University of London Central Library (two million), the London Library (the largest public subscription library), the Science Museum Library (600,000), the Victoria and Albert Museum Art Library, the Public Record Office (containing such national historical treasures as the Domesday Book), and the libraries of such institutions as the Royal Institute of International Affairs (140,000), the Royal Commonwealth Society (150,000), the Royal Geographical Society (150,000), the Royal Academy of Arts (22,000), and the National Library for the Blind. In 2002 a Women's Library opened in London giving a home to publications documenting women's lives in Britain.

There are major libraries at the Universities of Edinburgh (2.4 million), Glasgow (1.4 million), Queen's University in Belfast (1.1 million), and St. Andrew's (920,000). Manchester Metropolitan University has one million volumes.

London has about 395 public libraries. The South Western Regional Library System links the public libraries of Bristol, Devon, Foursite (Somerset, South Gloucestershire, North Somerset, Bath and North East Somerset), Gloucestershire, Swindon, and Wiltshire. The Edinburgh City Libraries maintain a central library and 25 branch libraries, as well as a mobile unit and two lending locations, plus several hospitals. Over 50 public libraries in Scotland were established through the assistance of the industrialist Andrew Carnegie. Nearly all of the public libraries in Scotland are linked via the Internet. Public libraries in Northern Ireland are managed by five regional Education and Library Boards. The Belfast Education and Library Board maintains the Belfast Central

Library and 20 community public libraries, as well as two mobile libraries.

The United Kingdom is a museum-lover's dream. Almost every city and large town has museums of art, archaeology, and natural history. There are more than 1,000 museums and art galleries, ranging from nearly two dozen great national institutions to small collections housed in a few rooms. London has the British Museum (founded 1759), with its vast collections of archaeological and ethnographic material from all over the world, and the Victoria and Albert Museum, including extensive collections of works of fine and applied arts. In the late 1990s, the British Museum was struggling financially; trustees rejected admission fees, and a multimillion-dollar deficit was projected when the government, which had funded most of the $84.5 million budget through the National Lottery, began reducing contributions. The National Gallery, the Tate Gallery, and the National Portrait Gallery are among other prestigious London art museums. Other museums located in London include the London Transport Museum (founded 1978), the National Maritime Museum (1934), the Natural History Museum (1963), and the Science Museum (1857). There is also a collection of royal ceremonial dress at Kensington Palace, and the Sherlock Holmes Museum, featuring Victorian memorabilia, opened in 1990. The Tate Gallery of Modern Art, featuring rotating exhibits arranged by theme, opened in May 2000. There are important museums and art galleries in Liverpool, Manchester, Leicester, Birmingham, Bristol, Norwich, Southampton, York, Glasgow, Leeds, and other cities. Oxford and Cambridge each have many museums, and several other universities also have important collections. Private art collections in historic family mansions are open to the public at specified times.

The National Museum and Gallery of Wales and the Museum of Welsh Life are in Cardiff. There is also a Welsh State Museum in Llanberis. The national museums of Scotland include the Royal Museum, the Museum of Scotland, and the National War Museum of Scotland, all in Edinburgh. The Museum of Scottish Country Life is in East Kilbride. There are at least three museums in Scotland that celebrate the life and work of native poet Robert Burns. The Ulster Museums and the Northern Irish Folk Museum are in Belfast.

45 MEDIA

The Post Office, founded in 1635, was the first in the world to institute adhesive stamps as proof of payment for mail. It now operates nearly all postal services. As authorized by 1981 legislation, the Thatcher government relaxed postal and telecommunications monopolies in some areas. The Telecommunications Act of 1984 further promoted competition and denationalized British Telecommunications (Telecom). In 2003, there were an estimated 591 mainline telephones for every 1,000 people. The same year, there were approximately 841 mobile phones in use for every 1,000 people.

Radio and television broadcasting services are provided by the British Broadcasting Corp. (BBC), which was established as a public corporation in 1927, and by the Independent Television Commission (ITC) and the Radio Authority, commercial concerns whose powers are defined in the Independent Broadcasting Authority Act of 1973. The BBC broadcasts on two television channels and the Independent Television Commission broadcasts

on ITV and Channel Four, which began operating in 1982. BBC Radio offers five national radio networks in the medium- and long-wave bands, as well as FM programming and an overseas service in 37 languages. Both the BBC and IBA operate local radio services; the BBC has 39 local stations (including 2 for the Channel Islands). In September of 1992, the first national commercial radio station, Classic FM, was inaugurated. Since then, several commercial stations have entered the market. As of 1999, there were 225 AM and 525 (mostly repeater) FM radio stations and 78 television stations. In 2003, there were an estimated 1,445 radios and 950 television sets for every 1,000 people. About 57.2 of every 1,000 people were cable subscribers. Also in 2003, there were 405.7 personal computers for every 1,000 people and 423 of every 1,000 people had access to the Internet. There were 21,034 secure Internet servers in the country in 2004.

There are over 100 daily and Sunday newspapers, some 2,000 weekly papers, numerous specialized papers, and about 7,000 periodicals in circulation throughout the United Kingdom. Nine Sunday papers and 12 daily morning papers are "national" in the sense of circulating throughout Britain. National dailies, with their political tendencies and their average daily circulations in 2004 (as available), are: *The Sun*, left of center, 3,301,223; *Daily Mail*, independent conservative, 2,403,528; *Daily Mirror*, independent left-wing, 1,777,408; *Daily Telegraph*, independent conservative, 907,048; *Daily Express*, independent conservative, 929,323; *Daily Star*, independent, 882,709; *The Times*, independent, 658;182; *The Observer*, 433,934; *Financial Times*, independent, 426,369; *The Guardian*, independent, 371,494; and *Evening Standard*, independent, 361,340. Of these, *The Times* was the only paper that showed an increase (of 4.3%) in sales from 2003, all others saw a decline in circulation.

In 2004, the newspaper with the highest circulation was the tabloid *News of the World*, which distributes over 3.7 million papers per week. Six other Sunday papers have circulations in the millions. The provincial press included more than 100 daily and Sunday newspapers and some 1,600 weeklies in 2004.

In 2004, major papers outside of London included: *The Express and Star*, Wolverhampton (162,509); *Manchester Evening News*, Manchester (148,094); *Liverpool Echo*, Liverpool (135,273); *Evening Mail*, Birmingham (104,219); *Evening Chronicle*, Newcastle-Upon-Tyne (91,523); the *Yorkshire Evening Post*, Leeds (81,804); and *Sunday Mercury*, Birmingham (79,527). The weekly *Berrow's Worcester Journal*, founded in 1690, claims to be the world's oldest continuously circulating newspaper.

Wales has five daily newspapers: *South Wales Echo* (in Cardiff, 59,200 circulation in 2004), *South Wales Evening Post* (West Glamorgan, 58,269), *Western Mail* (Cardiff, 44,470), *South Wales Argus* (Gwent, 31,803), and *Evening Leader* (Clwyd, 26,968).

Scotland has six morning, five evening, and four Sunday papers, plus the Scottish editions of the *Daily Mail* and the *Sunday Express*. The *Glasgow Herald* (2004 circulation 78,746) and *The Scotsman* (68,408), an Edinburgh paper, are the most influential. Others include: *Sunday Mail* (in Glasgow, 584,671 circulation in 2004), *Daily Record* (Glasgow, 478,980), *Evening Times* (Glasgow, 95,126), *The Press and Journal* (Aberdeen, 88,599), *Courier and Advertiser* (Dundee, 83,186), and *Evening News* (Edinburgh, 68,479). About 120 weekly papers are published in Scottish towns.

Northern Ireland has two morning papers, one evening paper, and one Sunday paper, all published in Belfast, plus a number of weeklies. The largest is the evening paper, *Belfast Telegraph* (circulation 94,602).

Britain's ethnic minorities publish over 60 newspapers and magazines, most of them weekly, fortnightly or monthly. These include the Chinese *Sing Tao* and *Wen Wei Po*, the Urdu *Daily Jang*, and the Arabic *Al-Arab* (the foregoing are all dailies), as well as newspapers in Gujarati, Bengali, Hindi and Punjabi. The *Weekly Journal*, aimed at Britain's black community, was begun in 1992.

The over 7,000 periodicals published weekly, monthly, or quarterly cover a huge range of special interests. Leading opinion journals are *New Statesman, The Economist,* and *Spectator*. The *Times Literary Supplement* is highly influential in cultural affairs. The chief news agency is Reuters, a worldwide organization servicing British papers with foreign and Commonwealth news and the world press with British and foreign news.

Although there is no government censorship of news or opinion, the Official Secrets Act, stringent libel and slander laws, and restrictions governing the disclosure of court proceedings do impose limitations on press freedom. In addition, the press regulates itself through the Press Council, which adjudicates complaints about newspaper practices from local officials and the public. Views critical of the government are well established.

46 ORGANIZATIONS

The national body representing British industry is the Confederation of British Industry, incorporated in 1965 and directly or indirectly representing about 250,000 companies. The Association of British Chambers of Commerce (founded in 1860) has 240 affiliated UK chambers. Agricultural organizations include the National Farmers' Union, agricultural cooperative societies, and other specialized associations. There are numerous professional associations for nearly every occupation. While some of these include members from all of the United Kingdom, there are also several associations particularly for Scottish businesses and professionals.

A vast number of organizations in the United Kingdom carry on programs in every phase of human activity. Voluntary social service organizations number in the thousands. Social work on a national scale is carried out largely under religious sponsorship. Cooperation between Protestant churches is fostered by the British Council of Churches. The Council of Christians and Jews works for cooperation between these faiths. The principal coordinating body in general social service is the National Council of Social Service. There are national chapters of the Red Cross Society, Amnesty International, Greenpeace, Habitat for Humanity, and other major international organizations.

The British Council promotes a wider knowledge of the United Kingdom and its people abroad and develops cultural relations with other countries. There are more than 300 learned societies. The Arts Council of Great Britain (founded in 1946) promotes the fine arts and higher artistic standards, and advises government bodies on artistic matters. The Royal Academy and the Royal Scottish Academy are other leading bodies in the arts. The National Book League, the Royal Society of Literature, the British Academy, the English Association, the Bibliographical Society, and other groups foster interest in literature, language, and scholarship. There are also numerous clubs for hobbyists, enthusiasts, and fans with a wide variety of interests.

The Arts Council of Wales was established in 1967. Arts and Cultural organizations in Scotland include the Royal Scottish Academy of Music and Drama; the Royal Celtic Society; the Royal Scottish Academy of Painting, Sculpture and Architecture; the Royal Scottish Country Dance Society; the Scottish Arts Council; and the Scottish Games Association. Clan associations are also popular in Scotland, with many providing genealogical research and social events and contact. The Ulster Historical Foundation in Belfast is a prominent genealogical research group.

The National Council for Voluntary Youth Services includes most of the largest youth groups. The leading political parties, major religious denominations, and some adult voluntary organizations, such as the Red Cross, maintain youth organizations. There are also a Scouts Association and a Girl Guides Association. There are numerous sports associations for participants of all ages. The Scottish Games Association specifically promotes traditional Highland games.

47 TOURISM, TRAVEL, AND RECREATION

The United Kingdom is a popular tourist destination, rich in natural as well as cultural attractions. Landscapes range from farmlands and gardens to sandy beaches, moors, and rocky coasts. Architectural sights include stone and thatched cottages, stately country houses, mansions, and castles. Among the many historic dwellings open to the public are the Welsh castles Cilgerran (11th century), Dolbadarn (12th century), and Conway and Caernarvon (both 13th century); the 10-century-old Traquair House near Peebles, the oldest continuously inhabited house in Scotland, and the Palace of Holyroodhouse in Edinburgh; and Warwick Castle, near Stratford-upon-Avon, the birthplace of William Shakespeare. Distinguished cathedrals include St. Paul's in London and those in Canterbury, Exeter, Norwich, Winchester, and York. At Bushmills, in Northern Ireland, the oldest distillery in the world may be visited, and some of Scotland's 100 malt whiskey distilleries also offer tours.

Among London's extraordinary attractions are Buckingham Palace, the Tower of London, and Westminster Abbey. Of the wide range of entertainment available, London is particularly noted for its theater, including the Royal Shakespeare Company. Folk music may be heard throughout the United Kingdom; traditional community gatherings for music and dancing, called ceilidhs, are held in Scotland, often in pubs, and Edinburgh is the site of one of the world's largest folk festivals, as well as an annual festival of classical music and other performing arts.

Scotland, where golf developed in the 15th century, has many superb golf courses, as does the rest of the United Kingdom; some 70 Highland Games and Gatherings take place in Scotland from May to September. Other popular sports include fishing, riding, sailing, rugby, cricket, and football (soccer). Wimbledon is the site of perhaps the world's most prestigious tennis competition. London hosted the summer Olympics in 1908 and 1948, and is scheduled to host again in 2012. England hosted and won the World Cup soccer championship in 1966.

In principle, foreigners entering the United Kingdom must have a valid passport and a visa issued by British consular authorities abroad. However, citizens of Ireland do not need a passport, and citizens of OECD, Commonwealth, and Latin American countries, among others, need no visa. There were 24,715,000 visitors who arrived in the United Kingdom in 2003. Tourism receipts totaled $30.6 billion that year.

In 2005, the US Department of State estimated the daily cost of staying in London at $410. Other areas averaged $342 per day.

48 FAMOUS BRITONS

Rulers and Statesmen

English rulers of renown include Alfred the Great (849–99), king of the West Saxons, who defeated and held off the Danish invaders; William I (the Conqueror, 1027–87), duke of Normandy, who conquered England (1066–70) and instituted many changes in the structure of English government and society; Henry II (1133–89), who centralized the power of the royal government, and his sons Richard I (the Lion-Hearted, 1157–99), leader of the Third Crusade, and John (1167?–1216), from whom the barons wrested the Magna Carta; Edward I (1239–1307), who subdued Wales and established the parliamentary system; Edward III (1312–77), who for a time conquered part of France, and did much to promote English commerce; Henry VIII (1491–1547), who separated the Anglican Church from the Roman Catholic Church and centralized administrative power; Elizabeth I (1533–1603), during whose reign, begun in 1558, England achieved great commercial, industrial, and political power, and the arts flourished; and Victoria (1819–1901), under whom Britain attained unprecedented prosperity and empire.

Among the statesmen distinguished in English history are Thomas à Becket (1118?–70), archbishop of Canterbury, who defended the rights of the church against the crown; Simon de Montfort, earl of Leicester (1208?–65), who in 1265 summoned the first Parliament; and Thomas Wolsey (1475?–1530), cardinal, archbishop of York, and Henry VIII's brilliant lord chancellor. Oliver Cromwell (1599–1658) established a republican and Puritan Commonwealth. Sir Robert Walpole, first earl of Oxford (1676–1745), unified cabinet government in the person of the prime minister and laid the foundations for free trade and a modern colonial policy. As England moved increasingly toward democratic government, important progress was achieved under the liberal statesmen William Pitt, first earl of Chatham (1708–78); his son William Pitt (1759–1806); and Charles James Fox (1749–1806). Outstanding statesmen of the 19th century were William Wilberforce (1759–1833); Henry John Temple, third Viscount Palmerston (1784–1865); Sir Robert Peel (1788–1850); Benjamin Disraeli, earl of Beaconsfield (1804–81); and William Ewart Gladstone (1809–98). Twentieth-century leaders include David Lloyd George, first earl of Dwyfor (1863–1945), prime minister during World War I; and Sir Winston Leonard Spencer Churchill (1874–1965), prime minister during World War II, historian, and winner of the Nobel Prize for literature in 1953. In 1979, Margaret (Hilda Roberts) Thatcher (b.1925) became the nation's first woman prime minister. The reigning monarch since 1952 has been Queen Elizabeth II (b.1926). The heir to the throne is Charles, prince of Wales (b.1948), whose marriage on 29 July 1981 to Lady Diana Frances Spencer (1961–1997; at marriage, Diana, princess of Wales) was seen by a worldwide television audience of 750 million people.

Explorers and Navigators

British explorers and navigators played an important part in charting the course of empire. Sir Martin Frobisher (1535?–94), who set sail from England in search of the Northwest Passage, reached Canada in 1576. Sir Francis Drake (1545?–96) was the first Englishman to sail around the world. John Davis (1550?–1605) explored the Arctic and Antarctic, sailed to the South Seas, and discovered the Falkland Islands. Henry Hudson (d.1611) explored the Arctic regions and North America. Sir Walter Raleigh (1552?–1618) was a historian and poet, as well as a navigator and colonizer of the New World. James Cook (1728–79) charted the coasts of Australia and New Zealand. Scottish-born David Livingstone (1813–73) explored central Africa while doing missionary work. Welsh-born Henry Morton Stanley (John Rowlands, 1841–1904) was sent by a US newspaper to find Livingstone in 1871 and, having done so, returned for further exploration of Africa. Sir Richard Francis Burton (1821–90), an Orientalist known for his translation of the *Arabian Nights,* and John Hanning Speke (1827–64) explored central Africa while searching for the source of the Nile.

Great British military figures include John Churchill, first duke of Marlborough (1650–1722), who attained many victories in the War of the Spanish Succession and in later campaigns against the French; Horatio, Viscount Nelson (1758–1805), the foremost British naval hero, whose career was climaxed by victory and death at Trafalgar; the Irish-born soldier-statesman Arthur Wellesley, first Duke of Wellington (1769–1852), whose brilliant campaigns culminated in the defeat of Napoleon at Waterloo; General Charles George Gordon (1833–85), who gained victories in China, acquiring the nickname "Chinese," and died while fighting against the Mahdi in Khartoum; Field Marshal Viscount Montgomery (Bernard Law Montgomery, 1887–1976), British military leader during World War II; Welsh-born Thomas Edward Lawrence (1888–1935), known as "Lawrence of Arabia," who led the Arabs in uprisings against the Turks during World War I; and Lord Mountbatten of Burma (Louis Battenberg, 1900–1979), supreme Allied commander in Southeast Asia (1943–46) and last viceroy and first governor-general of India (1946–48).

Philosophers and Legal Scholars

Sir Thomas Littleton (1407?–81) wrote *Tenures,* a comprehensive work on English land law that was used as a textbook for over three centuries. Sir Edward Coke (1552–1634), a champion of the common law, wrote the *Institutes of the Laws of England,* popularly known as *Coke on Littleton.* Sir William Blackstone (1723–80) wrote *Commentaries on the Laws of England,* which became a basic text in modern legal education and strongly influenced the evolution of jurisprudence in the United States as well as in Britain. The jurist-philosopher Jeremy Bentham (1748–1832) championed liberal law reform.

Roger Bacon (1214?–92), philosopher and scientist, wrote treatises ranging over the whole field of human knowledge. John Duns Scotus (1265?–1308) was a Scottish-born dialectician and theologian. William of Ockham (1300?–1349) laid the foundation of the modern theory of the separation of church and state. John Wesley (1703–91) was the founder of Methodism. Chief among modern philosophers are Thomas Hobbes (1588–1679), John Locke (1632–1704), the Irish-born bishop and idealist thinker George Berkeley (1685–1753), John Stuart Mill (1806–73), Alfred North Whitehead (1861–1947), George Edward Moore (1873–1958),

Ludwig Joseph Johann Wittgenstein (b.Austria, 1889–1951), and Sir Alfred Jules Ayer (b.1910-1989). A philosopher and mathematician who widely influenced contemporary social thought was Bertrand Arthur William Russell, third Earl Russell (1872–1970).

Historians and Economists

Noted historians include Raphael Holinshed (d.1580?), Edward Gibbon (1737–94), John Emerich Edward Dalberg-Acton, first Baron Acton (1834–92), William Edward Hartpole Lecky (1836–1903), John Richard Green (1837–83), Frederic William Maitland (1850–1906), George Macaulay Trevelyan (1876–1962), Giles Lytton Strachey (1880–1932), Sir Lewis Bernstein Namier (1880–1960), Arnold Joseph Toynbee (1889–1975), and Edward Hallett Carr (1892–1982).

Thomas Robert Malthus (1766–1834) and David Ricardo (1772–1823) were among the first modern economists. Robert Owen (1771–1858) was an influential Welsh-born socialist, industrial reformer, and philanthropist. Walter Bagehot (1826–77) was a distinguished critic and social scientist. The theories of John Maynard Keynes (Baron Keynes, 1883–1946) have strongly influenced the economic practices of many governments in recent years. Sir James George Frazer (1854–1941), a Scottish-born anthropologist and author of *The Golden Bough,* was a pioneer in the fields of comparative religion and comparative mythology. Herbert Spencer (1820–1903) was an influential economic and social philosopher. Sir Arthur John Evans (1851–1941) was an archaeologist who explored the ruins of ancient Crete. Anna Freud (b.Austria, 1895–1982), daughter of Sigmund Freud, and Melanie Klein (b.Austria, 1882–1960) were psychoanalysts influential in the study of child development. Noted anthropologists include Sir Edward Burnett Tylor (1832–1917); Polish-born Bronislaw Kasper Malinowski (1884–1942); Louis Seymour Bazett Leakey (1903–72) and his wife, Mary Leakey (1913–96), who discovered important fossil remains of early hominids in Tanzania; and Ashley Montagu (1905–1999).

Scientists

Present-day concepts of the universe largely derive from the theories of the astronomer and physicist Sir James Hopwood Jeans (1877–1946), the astronomers Sir Arthur Stanley Eddington (1882–1946) and Sir Fred Hoyle (1915–2001), and the radio astronomers Sir Martin Ryle (1918–84) and Anthony Hewish (b.1924), who shared the Nobel Prize for physics in 1974. Other British scientists and inventors who won fame for major contributions to knowledge include William Harvey (1578–1657), physician and anatomist, who discovered the circulation of the blood; Irish-born Robert Boyle (1627–91), physicist and chemist, who investigated the properties of gases; Sir Isaac Newton (1642–1727), natural philosopher and mathematician, who discovered gravity and made important advances in calculus and optics; German-born physicist Gabriel Daniel Fahrenheit (1686–1736), who introduced the temperature scale named after him; James Watt (1736–1819), the Scottish-born engineer who invented the modern condensing steam engine; Edward Jenner (1749–1823), who discovered the principle of vaccination; the great chemists John Dalton (1766–1844), who advanced the atomic theory, and Sir Humphry Davy (1778–1829); George Stephenson (1781–1848), inventor of the locomotive steam engine; Michael Faraday (1791–1867), a chemist and physicist noted for his experiments in electricity; Scottish-born geologist Sir Charles Lyell (1797–1875), the

father of modern geology; Charles Darwin (1809–82), the great naturalist who advanced the theory of evolution; James Prescott Joule (1818–89), a physicist who studied heat and electrical energy; Thomas Henry Huxley (1825–95), a biologist who championed Darwin's theory; James Clerk Maxwell (1831–79), the Scottish-born physicist who developed the hypothesis that light and electromagnetism are fundamentally of the same nature; Sir Alexander Fleming (1881–1955), bacteriologist, who received the 1945 Nobel Prize for medicine for the discovery of penicillin in 1928; and Francis Harry Compton Crick (1916–2004) and Maurice Hugh Frederick Wilkins (New Zealand, 1916–2004), two of the three winners of the 1962 Nobel Prize in physiology or medicine for their research into the structure of the DNA molecule.

Literature and the Arts

Geoffrey Chaucer (1340?–1400) wrote the *Canterbury Tales* and other works that marked the height of medieval English poetry. Other major medieval poets were John Gower (1325?–1408) and William Langland (1332?–1400?). William Caxton (1422–91) was the first English printer. Sir Thomas Malory (fl.1470) derived from French and earlier English sources the English prose epic traditionally known as *Morte d'Arthur.* Two religious reformers who translated the Bible into English, making it accessible to the common people, were John Wycliffe (1320?–84), who made the first complete translation, and William Tyndale (1492?–1536), who made the first translation from the original languages instead of Latin.

During the reign of Elizabeth I, England's golden age, emerged the dramatist and poet William Shakespeare (1564–1616), a giant of English and world literature, and a galaxy of other fine poets and playwrights. Among them were Edmund Spenser (1552?–99), Irish-born author of the *Faerie Queene;* the poet and soldier Sir Philip Sidney (1554–86); and the dramatists Christopher Marlowe (1564–93) and Ben Jonson (1572–1637). Outstanding writers of the Stuart period include the philosopher, scientist, and essayist Francis Bacon (1561–1626), first Baron Verulam Viscount St. Albans; John Donne (1572–1631), the greatest of the metaphysical poets; the lyric poet Robert Herrick (1591–1674); John Milton (1608–74), author of *Paradise Lost* and other poems and political essays; John Bunyan (1628–88), who created the classic allegory *Pilgrim's Progress;* and the poet, playwright, and critic John Dryden (1631–1700). The greatest Restoration dramatists were William Wycherley (1640–1716) and William Congreve (1670–1729). Two authors of famous diaries mirroring the society of their time were John Evelyn (1620–1706) and Samuel Pepys (1633–1703).

Distinguished writers of the 18th century include the Irish-born satirist Jonathan Swift (1667–1745), author of *Gulliver's Travels;* the essayists Joseph Addison (1672–1719) and Sir Richard Steele (1672–1729), whose journals were the prototypes of modern magazines; the poets Alexander Pope (1688–1744) and Thomas Gray (1716–71); the critic, biographer, and lexicographer Samuel Johnson (1709–84); and the Irish-born playwrights Oliver Goldsmith (1730?–74), also a poet and novelist, and Richard Brinsley Sheridan (1751–1816). The poet and artist William Blake (1757–1827) worked in a unique mystical vein.

The English Romantic movement produced a group of major poets, including William Wordsworth (1770–1850); Samuel Taylor Coleridge (1772–1834); George Noel Gordon Byron, sixth Lord Byron (1788–1824); Percy Bysshe Shelley (1792–1822); and

John Keats (1795–1821). Victorian poets of note included Alfred, Lord Tennyson (1809–92); Elizabeth Barrett Browning (1806–61); her husband, Robert Browning (1812–89); Dante Gabriel Rossetti (1822–82); his sister, Christina Georgina Rossetti (1830–94); Algernon Charles Swinburne (1837–1909); and Gerard Manley Hopkins (1844–89). Edward FitzGerald (1809–83) is famous for his free translations of Omar Khayyam's *Rubáiyát*. Matthew Arnold (1822–88) was a noted poet and critic. Other prominent critics and essayists include Charles Lamb (1775–1834), William Hazlitt (1778–1830), Thomas De Quincey (1785–1859), John Ruskin (1819–1900), Leslie Stephen (1832–1904), and William Morris (1834–96). Thomas Babington Macaulay (1800–1859) was a distinguished statesman, essayist, and historian. John Henry Cardinal Newman (1801–90) was an outstanding Roman Catholic theologian. Irish-born Oscar Fingal O'Flahertie Wills Wilde (1854–1900) was famous as a playwright, novelist, poet, and wit.

Major poets of the 20th century include Alfred Edward Housman (1859–1936); Walter John de la Mare (1873–1956); Dame Edith Sitwell (1887–1964); US-born Thomas Stearns Eliot (1888–1965), winner of the Nobel Prize in 1949; Wystan Hugh Auden (1907–73); Welsh-born Dylan Thomas (1914–53); Philip Larkin (1922–85); and Ted Hughes (1930–98). Prominent critics include Frank Raymond Leavis (1895–1978) and Sir William Empson (1906–84).

The English novel's distinguished history began with Daniel Defoe (1660–1731), Samuel Richardson (1689–1761), Henry Fielding (1707–54), and Laurence Sterne (1713–68). It was carried forward in the 19th century by Jane Austen (1775–1817), William Makepeace Thackeray (1811–63), Charles Dickens (1812–70), Charles Reade (1814–84), Anthony Trollope (1815–82), the Brontë Sisters—Charlotte (1816–55) and Emily (1818–48)—George Eliot (Mary Ann Evans, 1819–80), George Meredith (1828–1909), Samuel Butler (1835–1902), and Thomas Hardy (1840–1928), who was also a poet. The mathematician Lewis Carroll (Charles Lutwidge Dodgson, 1832–98) became world-famous for two children's books, *Alice in Wonderland* and *Through the Looking Glass.* Rudyard Kipling (1865–1936), author of novels, stories, and poems, received the Nobel Prize for literature in 1907. Sir Arthur Conan Doyle (1859–1930) is known throughout the world as the creator of Sherlock Holmes.

Twentieth-century fiction writers of note include the Polish-born Joseph Conrad (Teodor Józef Konrad Korzeniowski, 1857–1924); Herbert George Wells (1866–1946), who was also a popular historian and a social reformer; Arnold Bennett (1867–1931); John Galsworthy (1867–1933), also a playwright, who received the Nobel Prize in 1932; William Somerset Maugham (1874–1965), also a playwright; Edward Morgan Forster (1879–1970); Virginia Woolf (1882–1941); David Herbert Lawrence (1885–1930); Joyce Cary (1888–1957); Katherine Mansfield (b.New Zealand, 1888–1923); Dame Agatha Christie (1881–1976), also a playwright; Dame Ivy Compton-Burnett (1892–1969); Dame Rebecca West (b.Ireland, 1892–1983), also known for her political writings and as an active feminist; Aldous Huxley (1894–1963); John Boynton Priestley (1894–1984), also a playwright; Irish-born Robert Ranke Graves (1895–1985), also a poet, novelist, scholar, and critic; George Orwell (Eric Blair, 1903–50), also a journalist and essayist; Evelyn Waugh (1903–66); Graham Greene (1904–91); Anthony Dymoke Powell (1905–2000); Henry Green (Henry Vincent Yorke, 1905–74); Charles Percy Snow (Baron Snow, 1905–80), also an essayist

and a physicist; William Golding (1911–93), Nobel Prize winner in 1983; Lawrence George Durrell (b.India, 1912–90); Anthony Burgess (1917–93); Doris Lessing (b.Iran, 1919); John Le Carré (David John Moore Cornwell, b.1931), and Ian McEwan (b.1948). The dominant literary figure of the 20th century was George Bernard Shaw (1856–1950), Dublin-born playwright, essayist, critic, and wit. Sir Kingsley William Amis (1922–1995) was a novelist, poet, critic, and teacher; his son Martin Amis (b.1949) became a novelist as well. Dame Antonia Susan "A.S." Byatt (b.1936) has been hailed by some as one of the great postmodern novelists in England. Byatt's younger sister Margaret Drabble (b.1939) is a novelist as well. Fay Weldon (b.1931) is a novelist, short story writer, playwright and essayist whose work has been associated with feminism. Hanif Kureishi (b.1954) is a Pakistani-British playwright, author, and director. Kazuo Ishiguro (b.1954) is a British author of Japanese origin. Joanne "J.K." Rowling (b.1965) is most famous as author of the Harry Potter fantasy series. Zadie Smith (b.1975) has been celebrated as one of Britain's most talented young authors. The playwright-composer-lyricist Sir Noel Coward (1899–1973) directed and starred in many of his sophisticated comedies. Harold Pinter (b.1930) has been a highly influential playwright; he was awarded the Nobel Prize for literature in 2005.

Actors and Actresses

The British stage tradition dates back to Richard Burbage (d.1619), the greatest actor of Shakespeare's time, and Edmund Kean (1787–1833), the greatest tragedian of the Romantic era. Luminaries of the modern theater are Dame Ellen Alicia Terry (1848–1928), Dame Sybil Thorndike (1882–1976), Dame Edith Evans (1888–1976), Sir Ralph Richardson (1902–83), Sir John Gielgud (1904–2000), Laurence Olivier (Baron Olivier of Brighton, 1907–1989), Sir Michael Redgrave (1908–85), and Derek George Jacobi (b.1938). Prominent stage directors are Peter Stephen Paul Brook (b.1925) and Sir Peter Reginald Frederick Hall (b.1930). Major contributors to the cinema have included the comic actor and director Charlie (Sir Charles Spencer) Chaplin (1889–1977); the directors Sir Alexander Korda (Sandor Corda, b.Hungary, 1893–1956), Sir Alfred Hitchcock (1899–1980), Sir Carol Reed (1906–76), Sir David Lean (1908–91), Sir Richard Attenborough (b.1923), and Stephen Frears (b.1941); and actors Cary Grant (Archibald Alexander Leach, 1904–86), Sir Alec Guinness (1914–2000), Deborah Kerr (b.1921), Welsh-born Richard Burton (1925–84), Belgian-born Audrey Hepburn (1929–1993), Irish-born Peter O'Toole (b.1932), Dame Elizabeth Taylor (b.1932), Dame Maggie Natalie Smith (b.1934), Dame Judi Dench (b.1934), Vanessa Redgrave (b.1937), Glenda Jackson (b.1936), Jacqueline Bisset (b.1944), Sir Michael Caine (b.1933), Albert Finney (b.1936), Ralph Fiennes (b.1962), Miranda Richardson (b.1958), Rachel Weisz (b.1971), Tilda Swinton (b.1960), and Kate Winslet (b.1975).

Architects

Great English architects were Inigo Jones (1573–1652) and Sir Christopher Wren (1632–1723). Famous artists include William Hogarth (1697–1764), Sir Joshua Reynolds (1723–92), Thomas Gainsborough (1727–88), Joseph Mallord William Turner (1775–1851), John Constable (1776–1837), the illustrator Aubrey Beardsley (1872–98), Graham Sutherland (1903–80), Francis Bacon (b.Ireland, 1910–92), and David Hockney (b.1937). Roger Eliot Fry (1866–1934) and Kenneth Mackenzie Clark (Lord Clark, 1903–83) were influential art critics. Sir Jacob Epstein (b.US,

1880–1959), Henry Moore (1898–1986), and Dame Barbara Hepworth (1903–75) are world-famous British sculptors. The most famous British potter was Josiah Wedgwood (1730–95).

Composers

English composers of note include John Dunstable (1370?–1453), whose works exerted a profound influence on continental musicians; William Byrd (1543–1623) and Orlando Gibbons (1583–1625), who were proficient in both sacred and secular music; the great lutenist and songwriter John Dowland (1563–1626); the madrigalists John Wilbye (1574–1638) and Thomas Weelkes (1575?–1623); Henry Purcell (1659?–95), a brilliant creator of vocal and chamber works; German-born George Frederick Handel (Georg Friedrich Händel, 1685–1759), a master of baroque operas, oratorios, and concerti; and Sir Arthur Seymour Sullivan (1842–1900), whose musical settings of the librettos of Sir William Schwenk Gilbert (1836–1911) are among the most popular comic operas of all time. Significant 20th-century figures include Sir Edward Elgar (1857–1934), Frederick Delius (1862–1934), Ralph Vaughan Williams (1872–1958), Sir William Walton (1902–83), Sir Michael Kemp Tippett (1905–98), Edward Benjamin Britten (Baron Britten, 1913–76), Peter Maxwell Davies (b.1934), and, in popular music, John Winston Lennon (1940–80) and James Paul McCartney (b.1942) of the Beatles. Notable performers include pianists Dame Myra Hess (1890–1965) and Sir Clifford Curzon (1907–82), violinist Sir Yehudi Menuhin (1916–1999), guitarist-lutenist Julian Bream (b.1933), singers Sir Peter Pears (1910–86) and Dame Janet Baker (b.1933), and conductors Sir Thomas Beecham (1879–1961), Sir Adrian Boult (1889–1983), Sir John Barbirolli (1899–1970), Sir Georg Solti (b.Hungary, 1912–1997), and Sir Colin Davis (b.1927).

Athletes

Notable British athletes include Sir Roger Bannister (b.1929), who on 6 May 1954 became the first person to run a mile in under four minutes; golfer Tony Jacklin (b.1944), winner of the British Open in 1969 and the US Open in 1970; three-time world champion John Young "Jackie" Stewart (b.1939), a Scottish race-car driver; and the yachtsman Sir Francis Chichester (1901–72), winner of the first single-handed transatlantic race (1970) and the first sailor to make a solo circumnavigation of the globe (1966–67). Tennis player Sarah Virginia Wade (b.1945) won three Grand Slam singles titles and five Grand Slam doubles titles; she is particularly remembered for winning the women's singles title at Wimbledon in the championship's centenary year in 1977.

Natives of Scotland and Wales

Duncan I (r.1034–40) was the first ruler of the historical kingdom of Scotland. Macbeth (r.1040–57), who killed Duncan and seized the throne, furnished the subject of one of Shakespeare's greatest plays. Margaret (d.1093), Duncan's daughter-in-law, reformed the Church, won fame for piety and charity, and was made a saint. William Wallace (1272?–1306) led a rebellion against the English occupation. Robert the Bruce (1274–1329), ruler of Scotland (1306–29), won its independence from England. Mary, Queen of Scots (Mary Stuart, 1542–87), a romantic historical figure, is the subject of many plays and novels. Her son James VI (1566–1625) became England's King James I.

Before the union with England, outstanding poets writing in Scottish include Robert Henryson (1425?–1500?), William Dunbar (1460?–1520?), Gavin Douglas (1474–1522), and Sir David Lindsay (1490?–1555). One of the finest Scottish poets was William Drummond (1585–1649). Sir Thomas Urquhart (1611–60) produced a noted translation of Rabelais. John Knox (1514?–72) was the founder of Presbyterianism. David Hume (1711–76) was an outstanding philosopher and historian. Economist and philosopher Adam Smith (1723–90) influenced the development of world economy and politics. James Boswell (1740–95) wrote the brilliant *Life of Samuel Johnson*. The 18th century produced several important poets, notably Allan Ramsay (1686–1758), James Thomson (1700–48), James Macpherson (1736–96), and the national poet of Scotland, Robert Burns (1759–96). A major 19th-century essayist and social critic was Thomas Carlyle (1795–1881). Scottish novelists of prominence include Tobias George Smollett (1721–71); Sir Walter Scott (1771–1832); Robert Louis Stevenson (1850–94), also a poet; John Buchan, first Lord Tweedsmuir (1875–1940); and Sir James Matthew Barrie (1860–1937), who also wrote popular plays.

Distinguished figures who were active primarily in Wales include the 6th-century monk Dewi (d.588?), who became St. David, the patron saint of Wales; Rhodri the Great (844–77), who attained rule over most of Wales and founded two great ruling houses; Howel the Good (Hywel Dda, 910–50), whose reformed legal code became the standard of Welsh law for centuries; the Lord Rhys ap Gruffydd (1155–97), ruler of southern Wales, who founded the national Eisteddfod; Dafydd ap Gwilym (fl.1340–70), a remarkable poet; and Owen Glendower (Owain ap Gruffydd, 1359?–1416), the national hero of Wales, who led a rebellion against English rule. Bishop William Morgan (1541?–1604) made a Welsh translation of the Bible which, with revisions, is still in use. Among literary figures are Ellis Wynne (1671–1734), Daniel Owen (1836–95), and Sir Owen Morgan Edwards (1858–1920).

Two natives of Northern Ireland—Betty Williams (b.1943), a Protestant, and Mairead Corrigan (b.1944), a Roman Catholic—received the Nobel Peace Prize (awarded in 1977) for their leadership of a peace movement in Ulster.

49 DEPENDENCIES

British overseas dependencies include the British Indian Ocean Territory and St. Helena (described in the *Africa* volume under UK African Dependencies); and Bermuda, the British Antarctic Territory, the British Virgin Islands, the Cayman Islands, the Falkland Islands, The Turks and Caicos Islands, Anguilla and Montserrat (described in the *Americas* volume under UK American Dependencies).

Gibraltar

The colony of Gibraltar (5.83 sq km/2.25 sq mi in area), the smallest UK dependency, is a narrow peninsula connected to the southwest coast of Spain. From a low, sandy plain in the north, it rises sharply in the 430-m (1,400-ft) Rock of Gibraltar, a shrub-covered mass of limestone, with huge caves. Gibraltar has a pleasantly temperate climate, except for occasional hot summers. Average annual rainfall is 89 cm (35 in). There is a rainy season from December to May. The resident civilian population, almost entirely of European origin, was estimated at 27,714 in mid-2002. Gibraltar is an important port of call for cargo and passenger ships. There is a naval base at the northeast gate of the Strait of Gibraltar and a military airfield that is used by private companies. Telegraph, radio, and television are privately operated. The telephone system is government owned.

Known as Calpe in ancient times, Gibraltar was successively occupied by Phoenicians, Carthaginians, Romans, and Visigoths. Its strategic value was recognized early. In AD 711, it was captured by Moors under Tariq, and since then it has been known as Jabal Tariq or Gibraltar. It remained in Moor hands, except for short periods, until Spain took it in 1462. In 1704, a combined English-Dutch fleet captured Gibraltar, and it was officially transferred to Britain by the Treaty of Utrecht in 1713. Since 1964, Spain has tried to negotiate the return of Gibraltar to Spanish control. However, in a referendum held in 1967, Gibraltarians voted overwhelmingly (12,138 to 44) to retain their link with Britain. Since then, Spain has continued to raise the issue at the UN and put direct pressure on the Gibraltarians by closing the land frontier between the peninsula and the Spanish mainland and suspending the ferry service between Gibraltar and Algeciras; the border was reopened to limited pedestrian traffic in December 1982 and fully reopened in February 1985.

Under the 1969 constitution, Gibraltar is governed by a House of Assembly with 18 members, 15 of whom are elected by popular vote. The governor (who is also commander of the fortress) retains direct responsibility for defense and external affairs and can intervene in domestic affairs.

Gibraltar was once largely dependent on British subsidies, but in the late 1990s had made the transition to private sector industry. Tourism (with about six million visitors annually), reexports (largely fuel for shipping), shipping services, and duties on consumer goods contribute to the economy. Local industries are tobacco and coffee processing. The Gibraltar pound is at par with the British pound. The financial sector accounts for about 15% of GDP. Exports in 1998 (mainly reexports of petroleum and petroleum products) totaled an estimated US$81.1 million, and imports US$492 million. There is an income tax and an estate duty.

Illiteracy is negligible. Education is compulsory between the ages of 5 and 15. There are 12 primary schools, two single-sex comprehensive secondary schools, and the College of Further Education. The armed forces have their own schools; attendance by civilian children is available. Language spoken at home include Spanish, Italian, and Portuguese, but the language of business and schools is English. The colony has a serious housing shortage.

Pitcairn Island

Pitcairn is a mountainous island of volcanic origin about 4.5 sq km (1.75 sq mi) in area, in the South Pacific at 25°4′ s and 130°6′w. Three smaller islands (Henderson, Ducie, and Oeno) associated with Pitcairn are uninhabited. Pitcairn Island was discovered in 1767 by the British and settled in 1790 by H.M.S. *Bounty* mutineers and the Polynesian women who accompanied them from Tahiti. The population, mainly descendants of the *Bounty* mutineers, after reaching a peak of 233 in 1937, decreased to 120 in 1962 and to about 52 in 1992 to 47 in 2002. Most of the younger members of the community have migrated to New Zealand. The climate is warm, with very little change throughout the year.

There is one village, Adamstown. Pitcairn is administered, together with the three other small islands, as a UK colony by the UK high commissioner in New Zealand. The local government consists of an island magistrate and a 10-member Island Coun-

cil. Six of the Council's members are elected. New Zealand dollars (NZ$) are used locally; NZ$1 = US$0.5132 (or US$1 = NZ$1.9486). There is no port or harbor; goods from ships are conveyed ashore in longboats. Cargo ships plying the route between Panama and New Zealand call periodically.

The main occupation is subsistence agriculture. A small surplus of fresh fruit and vegetables is sold to passing ships. Fish are abundant. Imports, mainly food, come from New Zealand. Fruit, woven baskets, carved curios, and stamps are sold to ships' passengers.

⁵⁰ BIBLIOGRAPHY

20th Century British History. Oxford: Oxford University Press, 1990.

Alexander, Yonah (ed.). *Combating Terrorism: Strategies of Ten Countries.* Ann Arbor, Mich.: University of Michigan Press, 2002.

Bruce, Duncan. *The Mark of the Scots: Their Astonishing Contributions to History, Science, Democracy, Literature and the Arts.* Secaucus, N.J.: Carol, 1997.

The Cambridge History of English Literature. 15 vols. Cambridge: Cambridge University Press, 1964-1968.

Childs, Peter and Mike Storry (eds.). *British Cultural Identities.* New York: Routledge, 1997.

The Columbia Companion to British History. Edited by Juliet Gardiner and Neil Wenborn. New York: Columbia University Press, 1997.

Cook, Chris. *The Longman Handbook of Modern British History, 1714–1995.* 3rd ed. New York: Longman, 1996.

Cox, Andrew W. *The Political Economy of Modern Britain.* Cheltenham, U.K.: E. Elgar, 1997.

Delderfield, Eric R. *Kings and Queens of England and Great Britain.* New York: Facts on File, 1990.

Foster, R. F. (ed.). *The Oxford History of Ireland.* New York: Oxford University Press, 1992.

Gagnon, Alain G. and James Tully, (eds.). *Multinational Democracies.* New York: Cambridge University Press, 2001.

Glynn, Sean. *Modern Britain: An Economic and Social History.* New York: Routledge, 1996.

Human Rights in the United Kingdom. Edited by R. J. F. Gordon and Richard Wilmot-Emith. New York: Oxford University Press, 1996.

Lee, C. H. *Scotland and the United Kingdom: The Economy and the Union in the Twentieth Century.* Manchester, England: Manchester University Press, 1995.

McElrath, Karen (ed.). *HIV and AIDS: A Global View.* Westport, Conn.: Greenwood Press, 2002.

Norton, Philip. *The British Polity.* 3rd ed. New York: Longman, 1994.

O'Neill, Michael (ed.). *Devolution and British Politics.* New York: Pearson/Longman, 2004.

Sampanis, Maria. *Preserving Power through Coalitions: Comparing the Grand Strategy of Great Britain and the United States.* Westport, Conn.: Praeger, 2003.

Summers, Randal W., and Allan M. Hoffman (ed.). *Domestic Violence: A Global View.* Westport, Conn.: Greenwood Press, 2002.

VATICAN

The Holy See (State of the Vatican City)
Santa Sede (Stato della Cittá del Vaticano)

CAPITAL: Vatican City

FLAG: The flag consists of two vertical stripes, yellow at the hoist and white at the fly. On the white field, in yellow, are the crossed keys of St. Peter, the first pope, surmounted by the papal tiara (triple crown).

ANTHEM: *Pontifical March* (no words).

MONETARY UNIT: In 1930, after a lapse of 60 years, the Vatican resumed issuance of its own coinage—the lira (L)—but it agreed to issue no more than 300 million lire in any year. There are coins of 10, 20, 50, 100, and 500 lire. Both Italy and the Vatican adopted the euro as official currency in 2002. The euro is divided into 100 cents. There are coins in denominations of 1, 2, 5, 10, 20, and 50 cents and 1 euro and 2 euros. There are notes of 5, 10, 20, 50, 100, 200, and 500 euros. The Vatican lira is fixed at 1,936.17 lire per euro. €1 = $1.25475 (or $1 = €0.79697) as of 2005.

WEIGHTS AND MEASURES: The metric system is in use.

HOLIDAYS: Roman Catholic religious holidays; the coronation day of the reigning pope; days when public consistory is held.

TIME: 1 PM = noon GMT.

¹LOCATION, SIZE, AND EXTENT

Located within Rome, Vatican City is the smallest state in Europe and in the world. It is a roughly triangular area of 0.44 sq km (0.17 sq mi) lying near the west bank of the Tiber River and to the west of the Castel Sant'Angelo. On the w and s it is bounded by the Leonine Wall. The Vatican area comprises the following: St. Peter's Square, enclosed by Giovanni Lorenzo Bernini's quadruple colonnade; St. Peter's Basilica, the largest Christian church in the world, to which the square serves as an entrance; a quadrangular area north of the square in which there are administrative buildings and Belvedere Park; the pontifical palaces, or the Vatican proper, lying west of Belvedere Park; and the Vatican Gardens, which occupy about half the acreage.

Outside Vatican City itself, extraterritoriality is exercised over a number of churches and palaces in Rome, notably the Lateran Basilica and Palace in the Piazza San Giovanni, the Palace of San Callisto at the foot of the Janiculum hill, and the basilicas of Santa Maria Maggiore and San Paolo fuori le Mura. Extraterritoriality outside the city of Rome extends to the papal villa and its environs (almost 40 hectares/100 acres) at Castel Gandolfo, 24 km (15 mi) SE of Rome, and to the area (about 420 hectares/1,040 acres) at Santa Maria di Galeria, some 19 km (12 mi) N of Rome, where a Vatican radio station was established in 1957.

²TOPOGRAPHY

Vatican City lies on a slight hill not far from the Tiber River.

³CLIMATE

Winters are mild, and although summer temperatures are high during the day, the evenings are cold. Temperatures in January av-erage 7°C (45°F); in July, 24°C (75°F). There is little rain from May to September; October and November are the wettest months.

⁴FLORA AND FAUNA

The gardens are famous for their fine collection of orchids and other exotic flora. Vatican City, being entirely urban, does not have a distinctive fauna.

⁵ENVIRONMENT

The environment of Vatican City is similar to that of Rome (see Italy). Though there are no specific endangered species, according to a 2006 report issued by the International Union for Conservation of Nature and Natural Resources (IUCN) there are five species with minimal or least concern. These are the long-tailed field mouse, the European water vole, the Crucian carp, the bank vole, and the red fox.

⁶POPULATION

The population of Holy See in 2005 was estimated by the United Nations (UN) at 798, which placed it at number 193 in population among the 193 nations of the world. According to the UN, the annual population rate of change for 2005–10 was expected to be -0.9%, a rate the government viewed as satisfactory. The projected population for the year 2025 was 1,000. The population density was 2273 per sq km (5887 per sq mi).

⁷MIGRATION

Does not apply.

⁸ETHNIC GROUPS

Although the citizenry of the Vatican includes cardinals and other clergymen from all parts of the world, most of the inhabitants are

Italian. The members of the Swiss Guard are a notable exception. Pope Benedict XVI is German.

9 LANGUAGES

Italian is the official language of Vatican City, but Latin is the official language of the Holy See (the seat of jurisdiction of the pope as spiritual leader) and is employed for most papal encyclicals and other formal pronouncements. As the ordinary working language, Italian is in greater use. French, German, and other languages are used.

10 RELIGIONS

Vatican City is the center of the worldwide organization of the Roman Catholic Church and the seat of the pope. Roman Catholicism is the official religion and the primary business of the state itself.

11 TRANSPORTATION

Vatican City is easily reached by the public transportation system of Rome. It has its own railroad station, with 862 m (2,828 ft) of track, which connect to Italy's network at Rome's Saint Peter's station. Vatican City also has a helicopter landing pad.

12 HISTORY

Since the time of St. Peter, regarded by the Church as the first pope, Rome has been the seat of the popes, except in periods of great turbulence, when the pontiffs were forced to take refuge elsewhere, most notably in Avignon, France, from 1309 to 1377. The Roman papal residence before modern times was usually in the Lateran or Quirinal rather than in the Vatican Palace.

The Vatican City State and the places over which the Vatican now exercises jurisdiction are the sole remnants of the States of the Church, or Papal States, which at various times, beginning in 755, included large areas in Italy and, until the French Revolution, even parts of southern France. Most of the papal domain fell into the hands of King Victor Emmanuel II in 1860 in the course of the unification of Italy. By 1870, Pope Pius IX, supported by a garrison of French troops, retained rule over only the besieged city of Rome and a small territory surrounding it. Upon the withdrawal of the French garrison to take part in the Franco-Prussian War, the walls of Rome were breached by the besieging forces on 20 September, and the city fell. On 2 October, following a plebiscite, the city was annexed to the kingdom of Italy and made the national capital.

In May 1871, the Italian government promulgated a Law of Guarantees, which purported to establish the relations between the Italian kingdom and the papacy. The enactment declared the person of the pope to be inviolate, guaranteed him full liberty in his religious functions and in the conduct of diplomatic relations, awarded an annual indemnity in lieu of the income lost when the Papal States were annexed, and provided the right of extraterritoriality over the Vatican and the papal palaces. Pius IX refused to accept the law or the money allowance; he and his successors chose to become "prisoners of the Vatican." Until 1919, Roman Catholics were prohibited by the papacy from participating in the Italian government.

The so-called Roman Question was brought to an end by the conclusion on 11 February 1929 of three Lateran treaties between the Vatican and Italy. One treaty recognized the full sovereignty of the Vatican and established its territorial extent. Another treaty was a concordat establishing the Roman Catholic Church as the state church of Italy. The remaining treaty awarded the Vatican 750 million old lire in cash and one billion old lire in interest-bearing state bonds in lieu of all financial claims against Italy for annexing the Papal States. The constitution of the Italian Republic, adopted in 1947, substantially embodies the terms of the Lateran treaties. In 1962–65, the Vatican was the site of the Second Vatican Council, the first worldwide council in almost a century. Convened by Pope John XXIII and continued under Paul VI, the Council resulted in modernization of the Church's role in spiritual and social matters.

Ecumenism was the hallmark of the reign (1963–78) of Pope Paul VI. In a move to further Christian unity, he met with Athenagoras, the ecumenical patriarch of the Eastern Orthodox Church, in Jerusalem in 1964. In 1973, Paul VI conferred with the Coptic Orthodox patriarch of Alexandria; later in that same year, he met the exiled Dalai Lama, the first such meeting between a pope and a Buddhist leader. Steps were also taken to improve Roman Catholic-Jewish relations, including a 1965 declaration that Jews are not to be held collectively guilty of the death of Jesus. On doctrinal questions Pope Paul VI was generally conservative, reaffirming papal infallibility, disciplining dissident priests, and reiterating traditional Church opposition to all "artificial" methods of contraception, including abortion and sterilization. In September 1972, the concept of an all-male celibate priesthood was upheld.

Pope Paul VI was succeeded by Pope John Paul I, who reigned for only 34 days. John Paul I's sudden death, on 28 September 1978, brought about the election of Polish Cardinal Karol Wojtyla as John Paul II, the first non-Italian pontiff elected in over 450 years. On 13 May 1981, John Paul II was wounded in Vatican Square by a Turkish gunman, who is serving a life sentence. The alleged accomplices, three Bulgarians and three Turks, were acquitted of conspiracy in the assassination attempt on 29 March 1986 because of lack of evidence.

During his reign (1978–2005), John Paul II traveled widely, a practice begun by Paul VI. He also established himself as a conservative in doctrinal matters, as indicated in 1982 by his elevation to the status of personal prelature of Opus Dei, an international organization of 72,000 laity and priests known for its doctrinal fidelity. He spent much of his papacy railing against materialism and moral laxity. During John Paul II's papacy, the Lateran treaties of 1929 were superseded in 1984 by a new concordat under which the pope retained temporal authority over Vatican City but Roman Catholicism was no longer Italy's state religion.

Throughout the 1990s, John Paul tried to build bridges to the Islamic world. Iran's president visited the Vatican in 1999 and a controversial trip to Iraq to talk to Saddam Hussein was cancelled that same year. He also traveled to Israel in March 2000 where he visited different Holocaust memorials during this trip and went to Bethlehem to reaffirm the Holy See's support for an independent Palestinian homeland.

John Paul II came out against embryonic or stem-cell research in 2001, stating it would lead to other evils such as "euthanasia and infanticide." Following the 11 September 2001 terrorist attacks on the United States, John Paul II urged harmony between Christians and Muslims. He initially stated that conflicts must

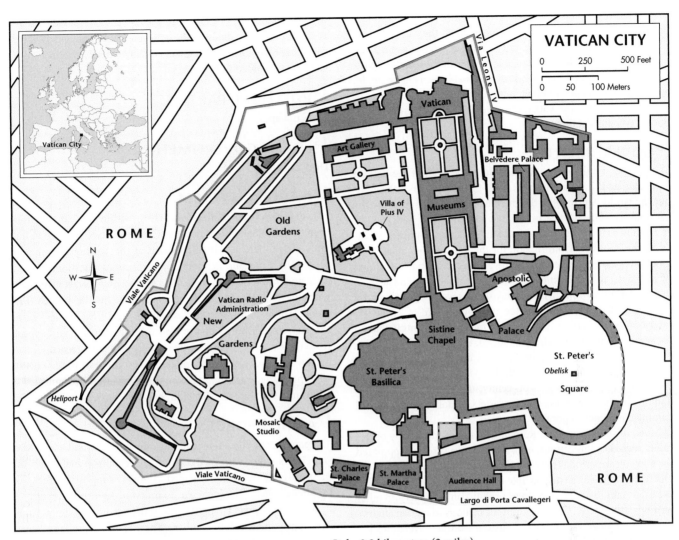

BOUNDARY LENGTHS: Italy, 3.2 kilometers (2 miles).

not be resolved by force, but by peaceful negotiation; however, he subsequently indicated the United States might need to use force against terrorists in the name of self-defense. When the Al Aqsa intifada—begun in September 2000 in Israel and the West Bank and Gaza Strip—intensified in the spring of 2002, John Paul II appealed for peace in the region, saying "nothing is resolved by war." He also reasserted his firm belief in peace over the use of force during the 2002–03 diplomatic and military crisis in Iraq. Nevertheless, his criticism of the conflict did not prevent war. Following the defeat of the Saddam Hussein regime in April 2003, John Paul II stated the Iraqi people should be responsible for the rebuilding of Iraq, while working closely with the international community, meaning the UN.

The Vatican announced in December 2002 it would open its archives relating to interactions with Nazi Germany from 1922–39 to scholars. The Catholic Church has been criticized for not doing enough to stop the persecution of Jews during the Holocaust.

Following the eruption of sex scandals in the United States regarding pedophile priests, John Paul II called for an emergency meeting with US cardinals in April 2002. US bishops had approved a "zero tolerance" policy on priests accused of sexual abuse, which would have priests suspended immediately following an accusation of abuse, but the Vatican demanded certain protections for the rights of priests.

In May 2003, the Vatican officially confirmed the pope suffered from Parkinson's disease. Despite his illness and his suffering from severe arthritis, John Paul II continued to travel exhaustively until his death on 2 April 2005.

Cardinal Joseph Ratzinger, a close confidante of John Paul II, was chosen on 19 April 2005 as the next pope, and was given the name Pope Benedict XVI. Ratzinger, originally from Cologne, Germany, was 78 years old at the time of his election; this made him the oldest pope ever elected. He predicted that his tenure would be short and that his primary purpose would be to complete John Paul II's work. He was formally installed as pope on 24 April 2005. As a cardinal, Ratzinger was known as a hard-line advocate of Vatican orthodoxy. He strongly opposed abortion, homosexuality, and religious pluralism. A long-time friend and ally of John Paul II, Ratzinger's selection as pope was greeted with dismay by more liberal factions within the Catholic Church. Many feared that he would divide, rather than unite, Catholics worldwide. In the early months of his papacy, Pope Benedict XVI supported the conservative stance of his predecessor. In May 2005, Benedict XVI called on voters in Italy to boycott a referendum that would repeal restrictions on artificial insemination and embryonic research. However, in October 2005, the Vatican completed a document that appeared to relax its stance against homosexuality somewhat. A change in policy on those entering the priesthood suggested that gay men who had lived a chaste life for at least three years prior to their admission to a seminary would be eligible. Previously, the Vatican banned homosexuals from priesthood, regardless of their status.

13 GOVERNMENT

The pope is simultaneously the absolute sovereign of the Vatican City State and the head of the Roman Catholic Church throughout the world. Since 1984, the pope has been represented by the cardinal secretary of state in the civil governance of Vatican City. In administering the government of the Vatican, the pope is assisted by the Pontifical Commission for the Vatican City State. Religious affairs are governed under the pope's direction by a number of ecclesiastical bodies known collectively as the Roman Curia.

The Pontifical Commission consists of seven cardinals and a lay special delegate, assisted since 1968 by a board of 21 lay advisers. Under the commission are the following: a central council (heading various administrative offices); the directorships of museums, technical services, economic services (including the postal and telegraph systems), and medical services; the guard; the Vatican radio system and television center; the Vatican observatory; and the directorship of the villa at Castel Gandolfo, the traditional summer residence of popes.

Much of the work of the Roman Curia is conducted by offices called sacred congregations, each headed by a cardinal appointed for a five-year period. These are the Sacred Congregation for the Doctrine of the Faith (responsible for faith and morals, including the examination and and, if necessary, prohibition of books and other writings), the Sacred Congregation for Bishops (diocesan affairs), the Sacred Congregation for the Eastern Churches (relations between Eastern and Latin Rites), the Sacred Congregation for the Sacraments, the Sacred Congregation for Divine Worship, the Sacred Congregation for the Clergy, the Sacred Congregation for Religious Orders and Secular Institutes (monastic and lay communities), the Sacred Congregation for the Evangelization of Peoples (missions), the Sacred Congregation for the Causes of Saints (beatification and canonization), and the Sacred Congregation for Catholic Education (seminaries and religious schools). There are also secretariats for Christian unity, non-Christians, and non-believers, and there are permanent and temporary councils and commissions for various other functions.

A pope serves from his election until death. On his decease, the College of Cardinals is called into conclave to choose a successor from their number. The usual method is to vote on the succession; in this case, the cardinal who receives two-thirds plus one of the votes of those present is declared elected. Pending the election, most Vatican business is held in abeyance.

Before the reign of Pope John XXIII, the size of the College of Cardinals was limited to 70. Pope John raised the membership to 88, and his successor, Pope Paul VI, increased the number to 136. Paul VI also decreed that as of 1 January 1971, cardinals would cease to be members of departments of the Curia upon reaching the age of 80 and would lose the right to participate in the election of a pope. In 2001, Pope John Paul II created 44 new cardinals, and the number of cardinals in the college at that time was 184, representing 68 countries. The 2005 conclave to select John Paul II's successor included 117 cardinals.

14 POLITICAL PARTIES

Does not apply.

15 LOCAL GOVERNMENT

Does not apply.

16 JUDICIAL SYSTEM

For ordinary legal matters occurring within Vatican territory, there is a tribunal of first instance. Criminal cases are tried in Italian courts. There are three tribunals at the Vatican for religious cases. The Apostolic Penitentiary determines questions of penance and absolution from sin. The Roman Rota deals principally with marital issues but is also competent to handle appeals from any decisions of lower ecclesiastical courts. In exceptional cases, the Supreme Tribunal of the Apostolic Signature hears appeals from the Rota, which ordinarily is the court of last resort.

New codes of canon law for the government of the Latin Rite churches and the administration of the Curia were promulgated in 1918 and 1983. Eastern Rite churches have their own canon law.

17 ARMED FORCES

The papal patrol force now consists only of the Swiss Guard, who, sometimes armed with such ceremonial weapons as halberds, walk their posts in picturesque striped uniforms supposedly designed by Michelangelo. The force was founded in 1506 and is recruited from several Roman Catholic cantons of Switzerland. It now numbers approximately 100 members. There is also a civilian security force, responsible to the Central Office of Security, which protects Vatican personnel and property, and the art treasures owned by the Church. The Vatican maintains its own jail.

18 INTERNATIONAL COOPERATION

Vatican City's diplomatic relations are conducted by its secretariat of state and the Council for Public Affairs of the Church. The Vatican holds permanent observer status in the United Nations and several specialized agencies, such as UNESCO, IAEA, UNEP, WHO, the World Food Program (WFP), United Nations Center for Human Settlements (UNCHS), and the FAO. The Vatican is also an observer with the African Union and the WTO. It is a member of the OSCE, holds a guest seat in the Nonaligned Movement, and participates in the Organization for the Prohibition of Chemical Weapons (OPCW).

19 ECONOMY

The Vatican, being essentially an administrative center, is dependent for its support on the receipt of charitable contributions, the fees charged those able to pay for the services of the congregations and other ecclesiastical bodies, and interest on investments. Funds are also raised from the sale of stamps, religious literature, and mementos and from museum admissions. Vatican City's economy is not commercial in the usual sense.

The labor force is small and is primarily employed in services and small industry. Most of the people working in the Vatican (dignitaries, priests, nuns, guards, and 3,000 lay workers) live outside the city.

In 2002, the city budget totaled $245.2 million, while expenditures reached $260.4 million.

20 INCOME

Does not apply.

21 LABOR

The labor force consists mainly of priests and other ecclesiastics, who serve as consultants or councilors; about 3,000 laborers, who live outside the Vatican; the guards; the nuns, who do the cooking, cleaning, laundering, and tapestry repair; and the cardinals, archbishops, bishops, and other higher dignitaries. Some ecclesiastical officials live outside Vatican City and commute from the secular city. The Association of Vatican Lay Workers, a trade union, has 1,800 members.

Lay employees of the Vatican have always had to be Roman Catholics and swear loyalty to the Pope. Under a new set of rules of conduct implemented in October 1995, new employees have to sign a statement binding them to observe the moral doctrines of the Roman Catholic Church.

22 AGRICULTURE

Does not apply.

23 ANIMAL HUSBANDRY

Does not apply.

24 FISHING

Does not apply.

25 FORESTRY

Does not apply.

26 MINING

Does not apply.

27 ENERGY AND POWER

As of 1 November 2005, all electric power was supplied by Italy, but the Vatican's generating plant had a capacity of 5,000 kW in 1990.

28 INDUSTRY

A studio in the Vatican produces mosaic work, and a sewing establishment produces uniforms. There is a large printing plant, the Vatican Polyglot Press, which produces coins, medals, and postage stamps.

29 SCIENCE AND TECHNOLOGY

The Vatican promotes the study of science and mathematics through the Pontifical Academy of Sciences, which dates from 1603. The Vatican Observatory was begun by Pope Gregory XIII. It has modern instruments, an astrophysics laboratory, and a 33,000-volume library.

30 DOMESTIC TRADE

The Vatican is basically a noncommercial economy, with no major imports or exports. Primary domestic industries include printing, mosaics, and staff uniforms. Products for retail sale are primarily postage stamps, tourist souvenirs, and publications.

31 FOREIGN TRADE

Does not apply, as the Vatican does not really have foreign trade. Its entire economy is based on tourism and donations (known as Peter's Pence) from Catholics around the world. However, the Vatican remains extremely wealthy despite its complete lack of natural resources because of the priceless artwork it possesses.

32 BALANCE OF PAYMENTS

Does not apply.

33 BANKING AND SECURITIES

The Vatican bank, known as the Institute for Religious Works (Istituto per le Opere di Religione—IOR), was founded in 1942. It carries out fiscal operations and invests and transfers the funds of the Vatican and of Roman Catholic religious communities throughout the world. The Administration of the Patrimony of the Holy See manages the Vatican's capital assets.

34 INSURANCE

Does not apply.

35 PUBLIC FINANCE

State income is derived from fees paid by the public for visiting the art galleries and from the sale of Vatican City postage stamps, tourist mementos, and publications. The Vatican also receives income in the form of voluntary contributions (Peter's pence) from all over the world and from interest on investments. The Prefecture for Economic Affairs coordinates Vatican finances.

The US Central Intelligence Agency (CIA) estimated that in 2002 the Holy See's central government took in revenues of approximately $245.2 million and had expenditures of $260.4 million. Revenues minus expenditures totaled approximately -$15.2 million.

36 TAXATION

Residents of Vatican City pay no taxes.

37 CUSTOMS AND DUTIES

Vatican City imposes no customs tariffs.

38 FOREIGN INVESTMENT

No recent figures are available.

39 ECONOMIC DEVELOPMENT

The Vatican administers industrial, real estate, and artistic holdings valued in the hundreds of millions of dollars. Investments have been in a wide range of enterprises, with makers of contraceptives and munitions specifically excepted.

⁴⁰SOCIAL DEVELOPMENT

Celibacy is required of all Roman Catholic clergy, except permanent deacons. The Church upholds the concept of family planning through such traditional methods as rhythm and abstinence but resolutely opposes such "artificial methods" as contraceptive pills and devices, as well as abortion and sterilization. Five important papal encyclicals—*Rerum Novarum* (1870), *Quadragesimo Anno* (1931), *Mater et Magistra* (1961), *Pacem in Terris* (1963), and *Laborem Exercens* (1981)—have enunciated the Church position on matters of workers' rights and social and international justice.

⁴¹HEALTH

The health services directorate, under the Pontifical Commission for the Vatican City State, is responsible for health matters.

⁴²HOUSING

A small portion of the Vatican Palace (about 200 out of 1,000 rooms) serve as the residence for the pope, the secretary of state, high court officials, high officials in close attendance to the pope, and some administrative and scientific officials. Quarters for the Swiss Guard and the gendarmes are also located in the palace. Some officials and visitors find housing in Italy just outside of the Vatican borders. There is no information available on other housing within the state itself.

⁴³EDUCATION

The Vatican is a major center for higher education for Roman Catholic clergy, particularly those being trained for upper level church positions. Adult literacy is 100%. About 65 papal educational institutions are scattered throughout Rome; some of the more important (all prefixed by the word "Pontifical") are the Gregorian University, the Biblical Institute, the Institute of Oriental Studies, the Lateran Athenaeum, the Institute of Christian Archaeology, and the Institute of Sacred Music. There were a total of 14,403 students in 1996 with 1,872 teaching staff in all higher-level institutions.

⁴⁴LIBRARIES AND MUSEUMS

The Apostolic Library of the Vatican is one of the most famous in the world. Founded in 1450 by Pope Nicholas V, the collection includes more than 1.1 million books, 72,000 manuscripts, 8,300 incunabula, 80,000 archival files, and 100,000 engravings. The Vatican Secret Archives, so called because originally they were strictly private records of the Vatican affairs, were opened to students in 1880. Literary scholars come from all over the world to study the collection of manuscripts. In 1994, librarians began entering the entire card catalogue of printed books into a computerized file accessible via the Internet.

Besides over a dozen museums, some of which figure among the greatest in the world, Vatican City includes as part of its decoration frescoes painted by Raphael (in the Stanze), Michelangelo (in the Sistine and Pauline Chapels), and other great Renaissance artists. In April 1994, after more than 14 years of careful cleaning, Michelangelo's frescoes became fully visible again. Among the museums in the Vatican are the Pius Clementine, the Chiaramon-

ti, and New Wing (exhibiting antique sculpture); the Gregorian Etruscan and the Gregorian Egyptian museums; the Pinacoteca (paintings); the Collection of Modern Religious Art; the frescoed chapels, rooms, and galleries; and the Sacred and the Profane museums, which are administered by the Vatican Library.

⁴⁵MEDIA

The state maintains its own telegraph and postal facilities and has a 2,000-line automatic telephone exchange tied into the Italian system. Radio Vatican, founded in 1931, comprises two facilities, one in Vatican City proper and the other outside Rome at Santa Maria di Galeria. There are 3 AM and 4 FM stations; in addition, shortwave broadcasts can reach the entire world. Programs in 34 languages are broadcast regularly. There is also one television station. The Vatican Television Center, founded in 1983, produces and distributes religious programs. Agenzia Fides and Missionary Service News Agency are the primary news agencies.

Vatican City is an important center for publishing. A semiofficial newspaper of wide fame, *L'Osservatore Romano,* founded in 1861, is published daily, with an estimated 2002 circulation of 70,000 copies. Since 1934, the Vatican has also published *L'Osservatore della Domenica,* an illustrated weekly. The *Acta Apostolicae Sedis* (Record of the Apostolic See) appears regularly on a monthly basis and occasionally at other times; it publishes papal encyclicals and other official papers. An annual, the *Annuario Pontificio,* is issued as a record of the Vatican and the Roman Catholic hierarchy. The International Religious Press Service (Agenzia Internazionale Fides—AIF), founded in 1927, distributes news of missionary activity and publishes *Information* (weekly, in various languages, including English), *Documentation* (irregular), and *Photographic Service* (weekly).

In the mid-1990s, nearly 50 periodicals were published, with a total circulation of almost 60,000. The book publishers for the Vatican are the Vatican Editions (Libreria Editrice Vaticana), the Vatican Apostolic Library (Biblioteca Apostolica Vaticana), and the Vatican Polyglot Press (Tipografia Poliglotta Vaticana).

⁴⁶ORGANIZATIONS

The organizations at the Vatican are chiefly learned societies devoted to theology, science, archaeology, liturgy, and martyrdom. The Pontifical Academy of Sciences promotes study in mathematics and the physical and natural sciences. The Pontifical Council for Culture, founded in 1982, focuses on the study of unbelief and religious indifference, particularly concerning the cause and effect of nonreligious or antireligious attitudes in various cultures. The Apostleship of the Sea, based in the Vatican, is an organization of ship, port, and nautical school chaplains (and other sailors) who offer a wide variety of support to maritime workers and their families. Caritas International, representing social service organizations in 200 countries, is based in the Vatican. The World Federation of Catholic Medical Associations is also based in the Vatican.

⁴⁷TOURISM, TRAVEL, AND RECREATION

The Vatican is regularly visited by tourists in Rome, by pilgrims attracted by the jubilees proclaimed by the pope every 25 years, and by other special occasions. While there are no public accommodations in the Vatican, special inexpensive facilities are often arranged in Rome for pilgrims. No passport or identification is usually needed for admission to the public parts of the Vatican.

In 2005, the US Department of State estimated the average daily spending in the Vatican at $490.

⁴⁸ FAMOUS POPES

By virtue of their position of world importance, many popes are persons of fame. Among those who greatly increased the secular power of the papacy were St. Gregory I (the Great, 540?–604), pope from 590 to 604, who also was influential in matters of doctrine, liturgy, and missionary work; St. Gregory VII (Hildebrand, 1020?–1085), pope from 1073 to 1085, who engaged in conflict with Holy Roman Emperor Henry IV, forcing him to do public penance at the village of Canossa, and later was driven from Rome by him; and Alexander VI (Rodrigo Lanzol y Borja, b. Spain, 1431?–1503), pope from 1492 to 1503, who also divided colonial territories in the New World between Spain and Portugal.

The most significant 19th-century pope was Pius IX (Giovanni Maria Mastai-Ferretti, 1792–1878), pope from 1846 to 1878, who lost the Papal States to the kingdom of Italy and convened the First Vatican Council (1869–70), which established the doctrine of papal infallibility in matters of faith and morals. The first popes who reigned since the establishment of the Vatican City State in 1929 were Pius XI (Achille Damiano Ratti, 1857–1939), from 1922 to 1939, and Pius XII (Eugenio Pacelli, 1876–1958), from 1939 to 1958.

John XXIII (Angelo Giuseppe Roncalli, 1881–1963), pope from 1958 to 1963, made history by convening the Second Vatican Council (1962–65), by altering the text of the canon of the mass for the first time since the 7th century, and by strongly defining the position of the Church on problems of labor and social progress (in his encyclical *Mater et Magistra* of June 1961). His greatest achievement was generally considered to be his eighth encyclical, *Pacem in Terris* (issued on 10 April 1963), a profound plea for peace, in which he hailed the UN as a defender of human rights.

Paul VI (Giovanni Battista Montini, 1897–1978), pope from 1963 to 1978, continued Pope John's effort to attain unity of the Christian world. On 4 October 1965, he addressed the UN General Assembly, appealing for world peace and international cooperation. He presided over the concluding sessions of the Second Vatican Council and traveled to many places, including the Holy Land.

Albino Luciani (1912–78), patriarch of Venice, was elected pope on 26 August 1978 and took the name John Paul I. He died on 28 September after a reign of only 34 days. His successor, John Paul II (Karol Wojtyla, 1920–2005), was elevated to the papacy on 16 October 1978. This former archbishop of Cracow was not only the first Polish pope but also the first non-Italian pope since the Renaissance. Despite suffering severe wounds in a 1981 assassination attempt, John Paul II continued to travel widely. To the dismay of Jewish and other leaders, John Paul II granted Austrian President Kurt Waldheim (b.1918) an audience in June 1987, despite accusations that Waldheim had taken part in war crimes during World War II when he was an officer in the German army. John Paul opposed abortion, contraception, homosexuality, divorce, the ordination of women, capital punishment, embryonic stem cell research, euthanasia, and war. He died on 2 April 2005.

A German pope, Pope Benedict XVI (Joseph Alois Ratzinger, b.1927) succeeded John Paul II in 2005, and continued the traditional Catholic doctrines mapped out by his predecessor.

⁴⁹ DEPENDENCIES

The Vatican has no territories or colonies.

⁵⁰ BIBLIOGRAPHY

Duursma, Jorri. *Self-Determination, Statehood, and International Relations of Micro-States: The Cases of Liechtenstein, San Marino, Monaco, Andorra, and the Vatican City*. New York: Cambridge University Press, 1996.

Hartt, Frederick. *Michelangelo Buonarroti*. New York: H.N. Abrams, 2004.

McDowell, Bart. *Inside the Vatican*. Washington, D.C.: National Geographic Society, 2005.

Reese, Thomas J. *Inside the Vatican: The Politics and Organization of the Catholic Church*. Cambridge, Mass.: Harvard University Press, 1996.

Rhodes, Anthony Richard Ewart. *The Vatican in the Age of the Cold War, 1945–1980*. Norwich: Michael Russell, 1992.

Tronzo, William (ed.). *St. Peter's in the Vatican*. New York: Cambridge University Press, 2005.

INDEX TO COUNTRIES AND TERRITORIES

This alphabetical list includes countries and dependencies (colonies, protectorates, and other territories) described in the encyclopedia. Countries and territories described in their own articles are followed by the continental volume (printed in *italics*) in which each appears. Country articles are arranged alphabetically in each volume. For example, Argentina, which appears in *Americas*, is listed this way: Argentina—*Americas*. Dependencies are listed here with the title of the volume in which they are treated, followed by the name of the article in which they are dealt with. In a few cases, an alternative name for the same place is given in parentheses at the end of the entry. The name of the volume *Asia and Oceania* is abbreviated in this list to *Asia*.

Adélie Land—*Asia:* French Pacific Dependencies: French Southern and Antarctic Territories
Afars and the Issas, Territory of the—*Africa:* Djibouti
Afghanistan—*Asia*
Albania—*Europe*
Algeria—*Africa*
American Samoa—*Asia:* US Pacific Dependencies
Andaman Islands—*Asia:* India
Andorra—*Europe*
Angola—*Africa*
Anguilla—*Americas:* UK American Dependencies: Leeward Islands
Antarctica—*United Nations:* Polar Regions
Antigua and Barbuda—*Americas*
Arctic—*United Nations:* Polar Regions
Argentina—*Americas*
Armenia—*Europe*
Aruba—*Americas:* Netherlands American Dependencies: Aruba
Ashmore and Cartier Islands—*Asia:* Australia
Australia—*Asia*
Austria—*Europe*
Azerbaijan—*Asia*
Azores—*Europe:* Portugal

Bahamas—*Americas*
Bahrain—*Asia*
Bangladesh—*Asia*
Barbados—*Americas*
Basutoland—*Africa:* Lesotho
Bechuanaland—*Africa:* Botswana
Belarus—*Europe*
Belau—*Asia:* Palau
Belgium—*Europe*
Belize—*Americas*
Benin—*Africa*
Bermuda—*Americas:* UK American Dependencies
Bhutan—*Asia*
Bolivia—*Americas*
Bonin Islands—*Asia:* Japan (Ogasawara Islands)
Borneo, North—*Asia:* Malaysia
Bosnia and Herzegovina—*Europe*
Botswana—*Africa*

Bouvet Island—*Europe:* Norway
Brazil—*Americas*
British Antarctic Territory—*Americas:* UK American Dependencies
British Guiana—*Americas:* Guyana
British Honduras—*Americas:* Belize
British Indian Ocean Territory—*Africa:* UK African Dependencies
British Virgin Islands—*Americas:* UK American Dependencies
Brunei Darussalam—*Asia*
Bulgaria—*Europe*
Burkina Faso—*Africa*
Burma—*Asia:* Myanmar
Burundi—*Africa*

Caicos Islands—*Americas:* UK American Dependencies
Cambodia—*Asia*
Cameroon—*Africa*
Canada—*Americas*
Canary Islands—*Europe:* Spain
Cape Verde—*Africa*
Caroline Islands—*Asia:* Federated States of Micronesia; Palau
Carriacou—*Americas:* Grenada
Cayman Islands—*Americas:* UK American Dependencies
Central African Republic—*Africa*
Ceuta—*Europe:* Spain
Ceylon—*Asia:* Sri Lanka
Chad—*Africa*
Chile—*Americas*
Chilean Antarctic Territory—*Americas:* Chile
China—*Asia*
Christmas Island (Indian Ocean)—*Asia:* Australia
Christmas Island (Pacific Ocean)—*Asia:* Kiribati
Cocos Islands—*Americas:* Costa Rica
Cocos (Keeling) Islands—*Asia:* Australia
Colombia—*Americas*
Columbus, Archipelago of—*Americas:* Ecuador (Galapagos Islands)
Comoros—*Africa*
Congo—*Africa*
Congo, Democratic Republic of (former Zaire)—*Africa*
Cook Islands—*Asia:* New Zealand

ISBN 13: 978-1-4144-1094-4
ISBN 10: 1-4144-1094-5

ISBN-13: 978-1-4144-1094-4
ISBN-10: 1-4144-1094-8

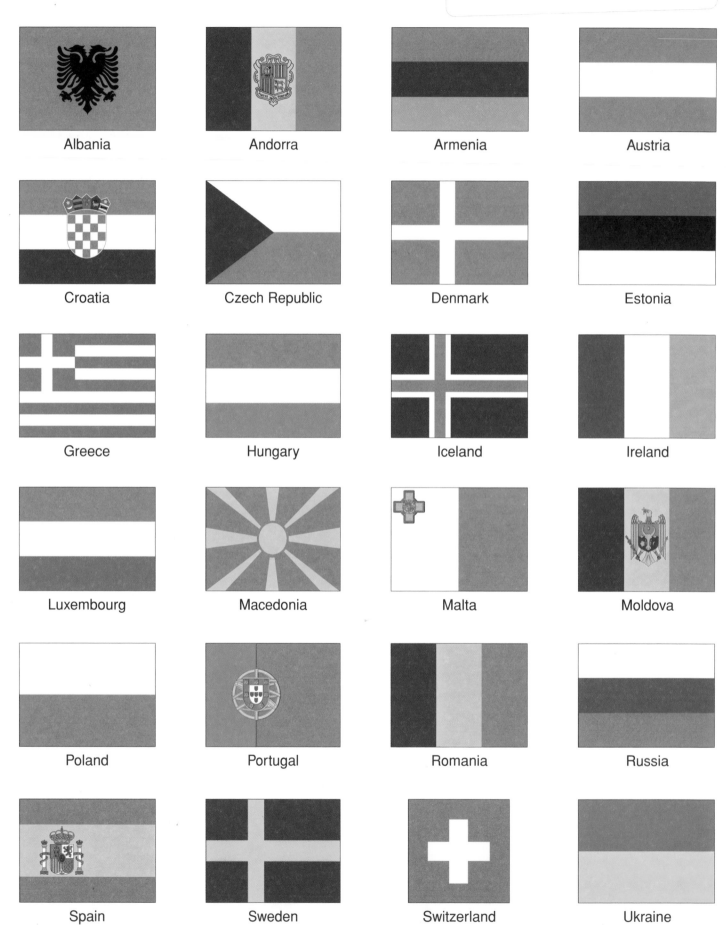

Albania	Andorra	Armenia	Austria
Croatia	Czech Republic	Denmark	Estonia
Greece	Hungary	Iceland	Ireland
Luxembourg	Macedonia	Malta	Moldova
Poland	Portugal	Romania	Russia
Spain	Sweden	Switzerland	Ukraine